Literary Theory:
An Anthology

For *Gabriel* and *Nathaniel*

LITERARY THEORY:
AN ANTHOLOGY

SECOND EDITION

Edited by Julie Rivkin and Michael Ryan

Blackwell
Publishing

© 1998, 2004 by Blackwell Publishing Ltd
Apparatus, selection, and arrangement © 1998, 2004 by Julie Rivkin and Michael Ryan

BLACKWELL PUBLISHING
350 Main Street, Malden, MA 02148-5020, USA
9600 Garsington Road, Oxford OX4 2DQ, UK
550 Swanston Street, Carlton, Victoria 3053, Australia

The right of Julie Rivkin and Michael Ryan to be identified as the Authors of the Editorial
Material in this Work has been asserted in accordance with the UK Copyright, Designs, and
Patents Act 1988.

First published 1998
Second edition published 2004 by Blackwell Publishing Ltd

11 2012

Library of Congress Cataloging-in-Publication Data

Literary theory, an anthology / edited by Julie Rivkin and Michael Ryan. – 2nd ed.
       p.   cm.
     Includes bibliographical references and index.
     ISBN 978-1-4051-0695-5 (alk. paper)— ISBN 978-1-4051-0696-2 (pb : alk. paper)
        1. Literature—Philosophy. 2. Literature—History and criticism—
     Theory, etc. I. Rivkin, Julie. II. Ryan, Michael, 1951–

     PN45.L512   2004
     801—dc22

                                                    2003060354

A catalogue record for this title is available from the British Library.

Set in 10.5 on 12.5 pt Ehrhardt
by Kolam Information Services Pvt. Ltd, Pondicherry, India
Printed and bound in Singapore
by Fabulous Printers Pte Ltd

The publisher's policy is to use permanent paper from mills that operate a sustainable
forestry policy, and which has been manufactured from pulp processed using acid-free and
elementary chlorine-free practices. Furthermore, the publisher ensures that the text paper
and cover board used have met acceptable environmental accreditation standards.

For further information on
Blackwell Publishing, visit our website:
www.blackwellpublishing.com

Contents

Part Four   Post-structuralism, Deconstruction, Post-modernism

Part Five   Psychoanalysis and Psychology

Part Six   Historicisms

Part Seven   Political Criticism: From Marxism to Cultural Materialism

Part Eight   Feminism

Part Nine   Gender Studies

Part Ten   Ethnic Literary and Cultural Studies, Critical Race Theory

Preface

This book began, as one might guess, in the classroom. We have been teaching courses in contemporary literary theory for the past two decades, and we have each had the familiar experience of not being able to match the design of our courses to any anthology currently available. The move from awkwardly assembled xerox packets to an actual anthology has been both a natural outgrowth of our teaching and an astonishingly complex process of research, selection, and projection. For although the germ of the book was our own classroom(s), its destination has always been many classrooms, courses no doubt much different than any we ourselves might teach, and yet ones that our selections would ideally work both to accommodate and to enrich.

The scale of the volume is one expression of its projected flexibility; we felt that an anthology of literary theory needed not only to cover the range of theoretical perspectives or approaches that characterize the era "after the New Criticism," the era that we take to be that of contemporary literary theory, but also to represent those perspectives with reasonable depth and range. The effect of such a decision, we hope, is that many kinds of courses will find a home in these selections, that a course that takes as its focus Structuralism, Post-structuralism, Post-colonialism, or Psychoanalysis and Gender Studies will find this anthology as useful as one that makes a more extensive survey of theoretical perspectives.

The anthology opens with formalisms – both Russian and American – in a gesture that marks its organization as partly chronological and partly heuristic. That is, we take formalism – at least in its American avatar of New Criticism – to mark the condition of students' theoretical awareness before beginning the journey into "theory." To the degree that they have been taught a form of "close reading" as the basic task of literary analysis, they are practicing formalists, though the practice may be, like that of the prose-speaking M. Jourdain in Molière's *Bourgeois Gentilhomme*, an unself-conscious one. Exploring the theoretical premises of a New Critical practice, placing those in conjunction with a historically unrelated yet theoretically cognate predecessor, Russian Formalism, seems like an appropriate way to initiate an exposure to "theory" in its less familiar guises.

The parts themselves have undergone many evolutions; the issue of where to draw the lines, what denomination to use, and where to locate certain selections has been as theoretically complex as it has been practically consequential. While "Deconstruction," for example, enjoyed a separate life in literary critical history in the US in the 1970s and 1980s, we felt it more appropriate to place it within its historical and intellectual French context, and so you will find Derrida amongst Deleuze and Guattari, and Baudrillard under "Post-structuralism, Deconstruction, and Post-modernism." The question of how to categorize some of the more recent kinds of theory, regarding gender and post-coloniality especially, was also difficult, and we opted for big tents in both instances: "Gender Studies," "Ethnic Literary and Cultural Studies," and "Post-colonial and Trans-national Studies." A separate section could easily have been devoted to any of these theoretical projects, each of which has already produced its own "classic" texts, and while attending to these developments has been one goal of the anthology, we wished as well to embrace both the heterodox and the newly canonical. Some of the names in our table of contents may not be readily recognizable for this reason, and our inclusion of these texts is less a sign of presumption regarding future canonicity than it is an indicator of our desire to locate the anthology as much in the contemporary realm as possible. That has meant guessing, and we based our guesses on what we felt would be exciting or helpful in the classroom.

In a desire both to be as inclusive as possible and to represent works not commonly anthologized, we have done a certain amount of excerpting. Our principle has been to represent the core of a given work, and if, to that end, we have sacrificed portions of texts that readers will deem necessary, we can only suggest that our selections constitute a useful beginning to a more extensive acquaintance. We apologize in advance for any such textual editing deemed brutal.

One anomaly of this anthology – though we feel a motivated one – comes in the form of introductions to the parts. Recognizing the pedagogical importance of introductions, we initially selected works that could serve this purpose from the wide range of what has been published. But in certain cases, we found that no one framed the theoretical project in quite the way that our own selections required, and thus found it necessary to write out, in a sense, the logic of our own selection. Thus, while our initial plan was always to let the editorial task be one of selection, to let the theorists speak for themselves, we found that in certain cases our work of selection would not be well served unless accompanied by an appropriate introduction. In some cases we were able to perform this task with relative brevity; in other cases we found a longer exposition required. So although the parts are variously introduced, our hope is that in each case the job is done in such a way that the selections that follow make sense to students encountering the material for the first time.

In making an anthology of this kind, one cannot help but be aware of one's location in the "canon wars," those struggles in recent years over who or what shall be taught in general literature or cultural history courses on the undergraduate level. To the degree that it at all self-consciously engages with those debates, this book is an effort to bring together from a variety of heterogeneous origins some of the literary theories that have helped inspire those debates, in as much as they are about new methods of literary, cultural, and social analysis.

A final word about our cover illustration. The words "No Radio" refer to a sign people put in their cars in New York City. It means "don't bother breaking into the body of this car; the radio has already been either stolen or else removed by the owner." We asked Blackwell to use this image because it speaks to the reservations many still feel about "theory" and about its association with the ideology of mastery through critical analysis that murders to dissect. It also speaks, of course, to our hesitations as editors engaged in the compilation and dissemination of such theories. We would not summon the image (and we would not engage in the work) if we did not feel that "theory" is itself filled with doubt regarding the objectivist ideal the image so carefully mocks. Some theories do indeed fulfill the aspirations of the man with the heart in his hand, but we hope you will feel that there are many others in this book that adopt the perspective of the woman on the table.

Preface to the Second Edition

This second edition of *Literary Theory: An Anthology* records in its arrangement changes that have occurred since we did the first edition. Post-Colonial Studies has emerged as a distinct enough area from Ethnic Studies to merit a section of its own. And Ethnic Studies has been deepened and broadened by the emergence of new scholarly voices in Native American, Asian American, and Hispanic American literary studies. We have added a new section entitled "Rhetoric, Phenomenology, Reader Response" to make up for an absence in the first edition. We have also extended the reach of the sections on Psychoanalysis, History, Structuralism, Marxism, and Cultural Studies by including new selections. Our aim, as in the first edition, has been to combine a sense of the intellectual background of a critical or theoretical approach with a representative sampling of voices in the contemporary critical scene. We have designed this edition to be used on its own, but it can also be used in tandem with *Literary Theory: A Practical Introduction*, which conducts readings of a small selection of literary works from the theoretical perspectives represented in this anthology.

Acknowledgments

We have occasionally modified translations.

Without Asha Nadkarny and Chi Chan, this book would not exist. We thank them, and we thank all the students in our introductory criticism courses over the years who helped shape our perceptions of what literary theory is and of what *Literary Theory* would have to be.

And thank you, Gabriel and Nathaniel, for being so patient.

The editors and publisher gratefully acknowledge the permission granted to reproduce the copyright material in this book:

Louis Althusser: Extracts from *Lenin and Philosophy* by Louis Althusser, translated by B. Brewster (London: New Left Books, 1971). Copyright © François Maspero, La Découverte, Paris, 1968. Reprinted by permission of Éditions La Découverte and the publishers, Verso.

Gloria Anzaldua: Extracts from *Borderlands/ La Frontera: The New Mestiza* by Gloria Anzaldua (San Francisco: Aunt Lute Books, 1987). Copyright © 1987 by Gloria Anzaldua and Aunt Lute Books, reprinted by permission of the author and publishers.

Nancy Armstrong: Extract from *Feminisms*, edited by R. Warhol (New Brunswick: Rutgers University Press, 1996, pp. 913–30). Originally published in *The Other Perspective in Gender & Culture*, edited by Maccanell (Columbia University Press). Reprinted by permission of Columbia University Press.

J. L. Austin: Extract from *How to do Things with Words* by John L. Austin, edited by J. O. Urmson and Marina Sbisa (Cambridge, Mass.: Harvard University Press, 1975, pp. 4–38). Copyright © 1962, 1975 by the President and Fellows of Harvard College. Reprinted with permission of Harvard University Press and Oxford University Press.

Mikhail Bakhtin: Extract from *The Dialogic Imagination: Four Essays* by M. M. Bakhtin, edited by Michael Holquist, translated by Caryl Emerson and Michael Holquist (Austin: University of Texas Press, 1981). Copyright © 1981, reprinted by permission of the University of Texas Press. Extracts from *Rabelais and His World* by M. M. Bakhtin, translated by Helene Iswolsky (Cambridge, MA: The MIT Press, 1968), reprinted by permission of The MIT Press.

Roland Barthes: Extracts from *Mythologies* by Roland Barthes, translated by Annette Lavers (New York: Hill & Wang, 1972). Translation copyright © 1972 by Jonathan Cape Ltd. Reprinted by permission of Hill & Wang, a division of Farrar, Straus and Giroux, LLC, and the Random House Group Ltd.

Georges Bataille: Extracts from *Visions of Excess* by Georges Bataille (Minneapolis: University of Minnesota Press, 1985). Original French language edition copyright © 1970 by Éditions Galimard, English translation copyright © 1985 by The University of Minnesota, reprinted by permission of University of Minnesota Press.

Jean Baudrillard: Extract from *Simulations* by Jean Baudrillard, (New York: Semiotext(e), 1982, pp. 166–84). Reprinted by permission of The MIT Press, Cambridge, Mass.

Walter Benjamin: Extracts from *Illuminations* by Walter Benjamin (New York: Harcourt, Brace & World, 1968, pp. 166–75, 176–84). Copyright © 1955 by Suhrkamp Verlag, Frankfurt, a.M., English translation by Harry Zohn © 1968 and renewed 1996 by Harcourt, Inc., reprinted by permission of Harcourt, Inc. and Suhrkamp Verlag.

Homi K. Bhabha: Extracts from *Race, Writing and Difference*, edited by Henry Louis Gates, (Chicago: University of Chicago Press, 1985, pp. 163–84). Reprinted by permission of University of Chicago Press and Homi K. Bhabha.

Pierre Bourdieu: Extracts from *Distinction: A Social Critique of the Judgement of Taste* by Pierre Bourdieu, translated by Richard Nice (Cambridge, Mass.: Harvard University Press, 1984, pp. 466–84, 596–97). Copyright © 1984 by the President and Fellows of Harvard College and Routledge & Kegan Paul, Ltd. Reprinted by permission of Harvard University Press and Taylor & Francis Books Ltd.

Edward Kamau Brathwaite: Extracts from *English Literature: Opening Up the Canon. Selected Papers from the English Institute*, edited by Leslie A. Fiedler and Houston A. Baker, Jr. (Baltimore: Johns Hopkins University Press, 1979, pp. 15–33, 46–51). Copyright © 1981 The Johns Hopkins University Press. Reprinted with permission of The Johns Hopkins University Press.

Cleanth Brooks: "The Formalist Critics" by Cleanth Brooks. First published in *The Kenyon Review* Winter 1951, OS Vol. XIII, No. 1. Copyright © The Kenyon Review. "The Language of Paradox" from *The Well Wrought Urn*, copyright 1947 and renewed 1975 by Cleanth Brooks. Reprinted by permission of Harcourt, Inc.

Judith Butler: "Performative Acts and Gender Constitution: An Essay in Phenomenology and Feminist Theory" from *Theatre Journal* 40:4 (1988), pp. 519–31. Copyright © 1988 The Johns Hopkins University Press. Reprinted with permission of The Johns Hopkins University Press.

Michel de Certeau: Extract from *The Practice of Everyday Life* by Michel de Certeau, translated by Steven Rendall (Berkeley: University of California Press, 1984, pp. 29–42, 212–13). © Éditions Gallimard, Paris 1990. Reprinted by permission of University of California Press and Éditions Gallimard.

Seymour Chatman: Extract from *Style and Structure in Literature: Essays in the New Stylistics*, edited by Roger Fowler (Oxford: Blackwell Publishers, 1975, pp. 213–57). Reprinted by permission of Blackwell Publishing Ltd.

Nancy Chodorow: Extract from *The Reproduction of Mothering* by Nancy Chodorow (Berkeley: University of California Press, 1978, pp. 92–110). Reprinted by permission of University of California Press.

Hélène Cixous and Catherine Clément: Extracts from *The Newly Born Woman* by Hélène Cixous and Catherine Clément (Minneapolis: University of Minnesota Press/I.B. Tauris & Co., 1986). Original French language edition copyright © 1975 by Union Generale d'Éditions, Paris. English translation copyright © 1986 by The University of Minnesota, reprinted by permission of the publishers.

Jonathan Culler: Extract from *Structuralist Poetics: Structuralism, Linguistics and the Study of Literature* by Jonathan Culler (Ithaca, NY: Cornell University Press and New York: Routledge, 1975, pp. 4–5, 6–7, 8–9). Copyright © 1975 by Jonathan Culler. Used by permission of the publisher, Cornell University Press and Routledge/Taylor & Francis Books, Inc.

Gilles Deleuze and Felix Guattari: Extracts from *A Thousand Plateaus* by Gilles Deleuze and Felix Guattari (Minneapolis: University of Minnesota Press, 1987). English translation copyright © 1987 by the University of Minnesota Press. Originally published as *Mille Plateaux*, volume 2 of *Capitalisme et Schizophrenie* © 1980 by Les Éditions de Minuit, Paris. Reprinted by permission of the University of Minnesota Press and the Continuum International Publishing Group.

Jacques Derrida: Extract from *Speech and Phenomena and Other Essays on Husserl's Theory of Signs*, by Jacques Derrida, translated by David B. Allison (Evanston: Northwestern University Press, 1973, pp. 142–9). Reprinted by permission of the publisher. Extract from *Of Grammatology*, translated by Gayatri Chakrovorty Spivak, (Baltimore: Johns Hopkins University Press, 1977, pp. 6–26, 302–16). Copyright © 1977 Jacques Derrida. Reprinted with permission of The Johns Hopkins University Press and Georges Borchardt, Inc. Extract from *Positions* by Jacques Derrida (London: Continuum International Publishing Group, 1981 pp. 17–29). Reprinted by permission of the Continuum International Publishing Group and University of Chicago Press.

Boris Eichenbaum: Extracts from "The Theory of Formal Method" by Boris Eichenbaum in *Readings in Russian Poetics*, edited by Ladislav Matejka and Krystyna Pomoroska, translated by I. R. Titunk (Ann Arbor: Michigan Slavic Publications, 1978). Reprinted by permission of the publishers, Department of Slavic Languages and Literatures, The University of Michigan.

C. C. Eldridge: Extract from *The Imperial Experience* by C. C. Eldridge (Basingstoke: Palgrave/Macmillan, 1996, pp. 20–34). Reproduced with permission of Palgrave Macmillan.

Frantz Fanon: Extract from *Black Skin, White Masks* by Frantz Fanon, translated by Charles Lam Markmann, (New York: Grove Press, 1967, pp. 141–54). Copyright © 1967 by Grove Press Inc. and copyright © 1997 Éditions du Seuil. Reprinted by permission of Grove/Atlantic Inc and Éditions du Seuil.

Stanley Fish: Extract from *Surprised by Sin: The Reader in Paradise Lost* by Stanley Fish (Basingstoke: Palgrave Macmillan, 1967, pp. 1–15, 20–46). Reproduced with permission of Palgrave Macmillan. Extract from "Interpretive Communities" from "Interpreting the Variorum," by Stanley Fish in *Critical Inquiry* 2:3 (Chicago: University of Chicago Press, 1976, pp. 465–86). Reprinted by permission of University of Chicago Press and the author.

Shelley Fisher Fishkin: Extract from *Criticism and the Color Line: Desegregating American Literary Studies*, edited by Henry B. Wonham (New Brunswick: Rutgers University Press, 1996, pp. 251–90).

John Fiske: Extract from *Channels of Discourse, Reassembled: Television and Contemporary Criticism* edited by Robert C. Allen (Chapel Hill: University of North Carolina Press and New York: Routledge, 1992). Copyright © 1992 by the University of North Carolina Press. Used by permission of the publisher. Extract from *Television Culture* (London: Methuen, 1987) by John Fiske, reprinted by permission of the author and Methuen/Taylor & Francis Books, Inc.

Michel Foucault: Extract from *The Archaeology of Knowledge* by Michel Foucault (London: Tavistock Publications, 1972). English Translation copyright © 1972 by Tavistock Publications Limited. Originally published in French as *L'Archeologie du Savoir*, copyright © 1969 by Éditions Gallimard. Reprinted by permission of Georges Borchardt, Inc., for Éditions Gallimard, and the Random House Group Ltd. Extract from *Discipline and Punish* by Michel Foucault (New York: Pantheon, 1977). English translation copyright © 1977 by Alan Sheridan. Originally published in French as *Surveiller et Punir*, copyright © 1975 by Éditions Gallimard. Reprinted by permission of Georges Borchardt, Inc., for Éditions Gallimard, and The Penguin Group (UK). Extract from *The History of Sexuality* by Michel Foucault (New York: Random House, 1978). Copyright

© Random House 1978. Originally published in French as *La Volanté du Savoir*, copyright © Éditions Gallimard 1976. Reprinted by permission of Georges Borchardt, Inc., for Éditions Gallimard, and The Penguin Group (UK).

Sigmund Freud: Extract from *The Interpretation of Dreams* by Sigmund Freud, translated by James Strachey, published in the United States by Basic Books, Inc., 1956 by arrangement with George Allen & Unwin Ltd and The Hogarth Press Ltd. Extract from "On Narcissism" by Sigmund Freud from *The Collected Papers, Volume 4*, authorized translation under the supervision of Joan Riviere, published in the United States by Basic Books, Inc. by arrangement with The Hogarth Press Ltd and the Institute of Psycho-Analysis, London. Extract from *The Uncanny* by Sigmund Freud, translated by James Strachey, by permission of A. W. Freud et al., by arrangement with Sigmund Freud Copyrights, represented by Mark Paterson & Associates. Extract from *Beyond the Pleasure Principle* by Sigmund Freud, translated by James Strachey. Copyright © 1961 by James Strachey. Sigmund Freud Copyrights, The Institute of Psycho-Analysis and The Hogarth Press Ltd for permission to quote from *The Standard Edition of the Complete Psychological Works of Sigmund Freud*, translated and edited by James Strachey. Reprinted by permission of The Random House Group Ltd and Liveright Publishing Corporation. Extract from *Group Psychology and the Analysis of the Ego* by Sigmund Freud, translated by James Strachey. Copyright © 1959, 1922 by the Institute of Psycho-Analysis and Angela Richards. Copyright © 1959 by Sigmund Freud Copyrights Ltd. Copyright © 1959 by James Strachey. Sigmund Freud Copyrights, The Institute of Psycho-Analysis and The Hogarth Press Ltd for permission to quote from *The Standard Edition of the Complete Psychological Works of Sigmund Freud*, translated and edited by James Strachey. Reprinted by permission of The Random House Group Ltd and W. W. Norton & Company, Inc.

John Frow: Extract from *Marxism and Literary History* by John Frow (Cambridge, Mass.: Harvard University Press, 1986, pp. 170–87, 259–61).

Sandra Gilbert and Susan Gubar: Extracts from *The Mad Woman in the Attic: 19th Century Literature* by Sandra M. Gilbert and Susan Gubar (New Haven: Yale University Press, 1980). Copyright © 1980 by S. M. Gilbert and S. Gubar. Reprinted by permission of Yale University Press.

Antonio Gramsci: "Hegemony" from *Antonio Gramsci The Prison Notebooks*, edited and translated by Quintin Hoare and Geoffrey Nowell-Smith (London: Lawrence and Wishart, 1971). Reprinted by permission of the publisher.

Stephen Greenblatt: Extract from *Shakespearean Negotiations: The Circulation of Social Energy in Renaissance England* by Stephen Greenblatt (Berkeley: University of California Press, 1988, pp. 94–128). Reprinted by permission of University of California Press.

Judith Halberstam: Extract from *Female Masculinity* by Judith Halberstam (Durham: Duke University Press, 1998, pp. 1–29, 279–81). Copyright © 1998, all rights reserved. Used by permission of the publisher.

Dick Hebdige: Extacts from *Subculture: The Meaning of Style* by Dick Hebdige (London: Methuen, 1979). Reprinted by permission of the author and Methuen/Taylor & Francis Books, Inc.

G. W. F. Hegel: Extract from *Hegel's Science of Logic* by G. W. F. Hegel, translated by A. V. Miller (New York: Humanities Press, 1969). Reprinted by permission of Humanities Press International, Inc., all rights reserved.

Martin Heidegger: Extracts from *Essays in Metaphysics: Identity and Difference* by Martin Heidegger (New York: Philosophical Library Inc, 1960). Reprinted by permission of Regeen R. Najar, Philosophical Library.

Geraldine Heng: "'A Great Way to Fly': Nationalism, the State, and the Varieties of Third-World Feminism" by Geraldine Heng, from *Feminist Genealogies, Colonial Legacies, Global Movements* by Jacqui Alexander and C. T. Mohanty, (New York: Routledge, 1997, pp. 30–45). Reprinted by permission of Routledge/Taylor & Francis Books, Inc.

Max Horkheimer and Theodor Adorno: Extract from *Dialectic of Enlightenment* by Max Horkheimer and Theodor Adorno (New York: Herder & Herder, 1972) Copyright © 1944, Social Sciences Association. Reprinted by permission of the Continuum International Publishing Group, Inc.

Edmund Husserl: Extract from *Ideas* by Edmund Husserl (New York: Collier Books, 1967).

Luce Irigaray: Extracts from *This Sex Which is Not One* by Luce Irigaray, translated by Catherine Porter and Carolyn Burke (Ithaca, NY: Cornell University Press, 1985, pp. 74–80, 170–91). Translation copyright © 1985 Cornell University. Reprinted by permission of the publisher.

Roman Jakobson: Extract from *On Language* by Roman Jakobson, edited by Linda R. Waugh and Monique Monville-Burston (Cambridge, Mass.: Harvard University Press, 1990, pp. 115–33). Copyright © 1990 by the Roman Jakobson Trust and Krystyna Pomorska, Jakobson Trust, Inc. All rights reserved. Reprinted by permission of the publisher and the Jakobson Trust.

Barbara Johnson: "Writing" by Barbara Johnson in *Critical Terms for Literary Study*, edited by Frank Lentricchia and Thomas McLaughlin (Chicago: University of Chicago Press, 1990, pp. 39–47). Reprinted by permission of University of Chicago Press and Barbara Johnson.

Coppélia Kahn: Extract from "The Hand That Rocks the Cradle: Recent Gender Theories and Their Implications" by Coppélia Kahn, in *The (M)other Tongue: Essays in Psychoanalytic Interpretation* edited by Shirley Nelson Garner, Claire Kahane, and Madelon Sprengnether (Ithaca, NY: Cornell University Press, 1985). Copyright © 1985 Cornell University. Used by permission of the publisher.

Immanuel Kant: Extract from *Kant's Critique of Pure Reason* by Immanuel Kant (Basingstoke: Macmillan, 1929, pp. 82–91).

Jamaica Kincaid: Extract from *A Small Place* by Jamaica Kincaid (New York: Farrar, Straus & Giroux, 1988). Copyright © 1988 by Jamaica Kincaid, reprinted by permission of Farrar, Straus & Giroux, LLC.

Adam Krims: Extract from *Rap Music and the Poetics of Identity* by Adam Krims (Cambridge: CUP, 2000, pp. 93–122). Reprinted by permission of the author and Cambridge University Press.

Jacques Lacan: "The Mirror Stage as Formative of the I" by Jacques Lacan, translated by Alan Sheridan, "The Agency of the Letter in the Unconscious or Reason Since Freud" by Jacques Lacan, translated by Alan Sheridan from *Ecrits: A Selection* by Jacques Lacan, translated by Alan Sheridan (New York: Norton, 1977). Copyright © 1966 by Éditions du Seuil. English translation copyright © 1977 by Tavistock Publications. Used by permission of W. W. Norton & Company, Inc and Routledge/Taylor & Francis Books, Inc.

Richard Lanham: Extracts from *Analyzing Prose* by Richard Lanham (New York: Scribner, 1983, pp. 119–36, 251–5).

Ania Loomba: Extract from *Colonialism-Postcolonialism* by Ania Loomba (New York: Routledge, 1998, p. 1–19). Reprinted by permission of Routledge/Taylor & Francis Books, Inc, and the author.

Ian F. Haney Lopez: "The Social Construction of Race" by Ian F. Haney Lopez from *Critical Race Theory: The Cutting Edge*, edited by R. Delgado (Philadelphia: Temple

University Press, 2000, pp. 163–75). Reprinted by permission of Temple University Press and Ian F. Haney Lopez.

Audre Lorde: Extract from *Sister Outsider* by Audre Lorde (Trumansburg, NY: Crossing Press, 1984). Copyright © 1984 by Audre Lorde, The Crossing Press, a division of Ten Speed Press, Berkeley, CA 94707, www.tenspeed.com. Reprinted with permission.

Lisa Lowe: "Heterogeneity, Hybridity, Multiplicity: Marking Asian-American Differences" by Lisa Lowe in *Diaspora*, Vol. 1, No. 1, 1991, pp. 24–44, University of Toronto Press. Reprinted by permission of University of Toronto Press Incorporated.

Jean-François Lyotard: Extracts from *The Postmodern Condition: A Report on Knowledge* by Jean-François Lyotard, translated by Geoff Bennington and Brian Massumi (Minneapolis: University of Minnesota Press and Manchester: Manchester University Press, 1984, pp. xxiii–xxv, 31–47, 64–7). English translation and Foreword copyright 1984 by the University of Minnesota. Original French language edition copyright 1979 by Les Éditions de Minuit. Reprinted by permission of University of Minnesota Press and Manchester University Press.

Pierre Macherey: Extracts from *Theory of Literary Production* by Pierre Macherey (New York: Routledge, 1978, pp. 82–4, 85–9, 90–5). Reprinted by permission of Éditions la Découverte and Routledge/Taylor & Francis Books, Inc.

Karl Marx: "Grundrisse" and "Capital" from *Karl Marx: Selected Writings* edited by David McLellan (Oxford: OUP, 1977). Copyright © David McLellan 1977. Reprinted by permission of David McLellan. "The German Ideology: Part 1," translated by Robert C. Tucker, "Wage, Labor and Capital" translated by Robert C. Tucker from *The Marx-Engels Reader, second edition* (New York: Norton, 1978). Copyright © 1978, 1972 by W. W. Norton & Company, Inc. Used by permission of W. W. Norton & Company, Inc.

Anne McClintock: "The Angel of Progress: Pitfalls of the Term 'Post-Colonialism'," in *Social Text*, Vol. 10, No. 2, pp. 84–98. Copyright © 1992, Duke University Press. All rights reserved. Used by permission of the publisher.

Louis Montrose: Extract from *Professing the Renaissance: The Poetics and Politics of Culture*. Copyright © Louis Montrose 1989. Reproduced by kind permission of the author.

Toni Morrison: Extract from *Playing in the Dark* by Toni Morrison (Cambridge, Mass.: Harvard University Press, 1992). Reprinted by permission of International Creative Management, Inc. Copyright © 1992 by Toni Morrison.

Michael Moon: "A Small Boy and Others" from *Comparative American Identities* edited by Hortense Spillers (New York: Routledge, 1991). Reprinted by permission of Hortense Spillers.

Antonio Negri: Extract from *The Savage Anomaly: The Power of Spinoza's Metaphysics and Politics* by Antonio Negri (Minneapolis: University of Minnesota Press, 1991, pp. 211–29). Originally published as *L'anomalia selvaggia. Salvaggio su potere e potenza in Baruch Spinoza*. Copyright 1981 by Giangiacomo Feltrinelli Editore. English translation copyright 1991 by the Regents of the University of Minnesota. Reprinted by permission of University of Minnesota Press.

Friedrich Nietzsche: Extract from *The Will to Power*, translated by Walter Kaufmann (New York: Random House, 1967). Copyright © 1967 by Random House, reprinted by permission of Random House, Inc.

Chidi Okonkwo: Extracts from *Decolonization Agnostics in Postcolonial Fiction* by Chidi Okonkwo (Basingstoke: Macmillan, 1999, pp. 155–66, 170–6). Reproduced with permission of Palgrave Macmillan.

Robert Dale Parker: Extract from *The Invention of Native American Literature* by Robert Dale Parker (Ithaca, NY: Cornell University Press, 2003, pp. 1–18). Copyright © 2003 by Cornell University. Used by permission of the publisher.

Vladimir Propp: Extract from *Morphology of the Folktale*, Second Edition, by Vladimir Propp, translated by Laurence Scott, revised and edited with a preface by Louis A. Wagner (Austin: University of Texas Press, 1968). Copyright © 1968, reprinted by permission of the University of Texas Press.

Gayle Rubin: Extracts from "The Traffic in Women" by Gayle Rubin, first published in *Toward an Anthropology of Women* edited by Rayna Reiter (New York: Monthly Review Press, 1975), Copyright © by Gayle Rubin, reprinted by permission of the author. "Sexual Transformations" from *The Lesbian and Gay Studies Reader* edited by Henry Abelove et al. (New York: Routledge, 1993), extracted from "Thinking Sex," first published in *Pleasure and Danger* edited by Carol Vance (New York: Routledge & Kegan Paul, 1984). Copyright © Gayle Rubin 1984, reprinted by permission of the author.

Edward Said: Extract from *Culture and Imperialism* by Edward W. Said (New York: Knopf, 1993, pp. 80–97). Copyright © 1993 by Edward W. Said. Reprinted by permission of Alfred A. Knopf, a division of Random House, Inc., and The Wylie Agency, London.

Ferdinand de Saussure: Extracts from *Course in General Linguistics* by Ferdinand de Saussure, edited by Charles Bally and Albert Sechehage, translated by Wade Baskin (New York: Philosophical Library, 1959). Reprinted by permission of Regeen R. Najar, The Philosophical Library, New York.

Eve Kosofsky Sedgwick: Extract from "Introduction: Axiomatic" pp. 8–13, 27–35 from *Epistemology of the Closet* by Eve Kosofsky Sedgwick, University of California Press (1990). Reprinted by permission of University of California Press.

Viktor Shklovsky: Extract from *Russian Formalist Criticism: Four Essays* translated and with an introduction by Lee T. Lemon and Marion J. Reis (Lincoln, University of Nebraska Press, 1965). Copyright © 1965 by the University of Nebraska Press. Copyright renewed 1993 by the University of Nebraska Press. Reprinted by permission of the University of Nebraska Press.

Alan Sinfield: "Cultural Materialism and the Politics of Dissident Reading" from *Faultlines* (Berkeley: University of California Press, 1992). Copyright © Alan Sinfield 1992. Copyright © 1992 The Regents of the University of California, reprinted by permission of Oxford University Press and the University of California Press.

Gayatri Chakravorty Spivak: "Three Women's Texts and a Critique of Imperialism" by Gayatri Chakravorty Spivak from *Race, Writing and Difference*, edited by H. L. Gates (Chicago: University of Chicago Press, 1987, pp. 262–80). Reprinted by permission of Gayatri Chakravorty Spivak.

Eric Sundquist: Extract from *To Wake the Nations: Race in the Making of American Literature* by Eric J. Sundquist (Cambridge, Mass.: Harvard University Press, 1993, pp. 135–49, 152, 154, 175–82). Copyright © 1993 by the President and Fellows of Harvard College. Reprinted by permission of the publisher

Ngugi wa Thiong'o: Extract from *Decolonising the Mind: The Politics of Language in African Literature* by Ngugi wa Thiong'o (London: James Currey Ltd, 1986, pp. 4–20, 87–102).

E. P. Thompson: Extract from *Witness Against the Beast: William Blake and the Moral Law* by E. P. Thompson (New York: New Press, 1993, pp. 174–94). Copyright © 1993. Reprinted by permission of The New Press (800) 233–4830 and Cambridge University Press.

Bessel A. van der Kolk and Alexander C. McFarlane: Extract from *Traumatic Stress* by Bessel A. van der Kolk and Alexander C. McFarlane (New York: The Guilford Press, 1996, pp. 3–17). Reprinted by permission of The Guilford Press.

Dennis Walder: Extract from *Post-Colonial Literatures in English: History, Language Theory* by Dennis Walder (Oxford: Blackwell Publishers, 1998, pp. 23–41). Reprinted by permission of Blackwell Publishing.

Raymond Williams: Extract from *The Country and the City* by Raymond Williams (Oxford: OUP, 1973, pp. 60–7, 96–119). Copyright © 1973 by Raymond Williams. Reprinted by permission of Oxford University Press, Inc.

W. K. Wimsatt, Jr.: Extract from *The Verbal Icon* by W. K. Wimsatt, Jr. (Lexington, Ky.: University of Kentucky Press, 1954, pp. 69–83). Copyright © 1954 by the University of Kentucky Press, University of Kentucky Press (1974). Reprinted by permission of the publisher.

Slavoj Žižek: Extracts from *The Sublime Object of Ideology* by Slavoj Žižek (London, New York: Verso, 1989). Reprinted by permission of the publishers.

Every effort has been made to trace copyright holders and to obtain their permission for the use of copyright material. The publisher apologizes for any errors or omissions in the above list and would be grateful if notified of any corrections that should be incorporated in future reprints or editions of this book.

PART ONE

Formalisms: Russian Formalism
and New Criticism

CHAPTER 1

Introduction: Formalisms

Julie Rivkin and Michael Ryan

It has become a commonplace of literary study that to study literature is to study language, yet prior to the formalist movements of the early twentieth century – Russian Formalism and American New Criticism – the study of literature was concerned with everything about literature except language, from the historical context of a literary work to the biography of its author. How literary language worked was of less importance than what a literary work was about. Two movements in early twentieth-century thought helped move literary study away from this orientation. The first movement was the attempt on the part of philosophers of science like Edmund Husserl to isolate objects of knowledge in their unmixed purity. The Russian Formalists, a group of young scholars (Viktor Shklovsky, Roman Jakobson, Boris Tomashevsky, Boris Eichenbaum) who wrote in the teens and twenties, were influenced by this approach. For them, literature would be considered not as a window on the world but as something with specifically literary characteristics that make it literature as opposed to philosophy or sociology or biography. Literature is not a window for looking at sociological themes or philosophic ideas or biographical information; rather, it is a mural or wall painting, something with a palpability of its own which arrests the eye and merits study. The manipulation of representational devices may create a semblance of reality and allow one to have the impression of gazing through glass, but it is the devices alone that produce that impression, and they alone are what makes literature literary.

The second movement was the attempt on the part of idealist philosophers like Benedetto Croce to develop a new aesthetics, or philosophy of art, which would rebut the claim of science that all truth is grounded in empirical facts knowable through scientific methods. Art provides access to a different kind of truth than is available to science, a truth that is immune to scientific investigation because it is accessible only through connotative language (allusion, metaphor, symbolism, etc.) and cannot be rendered in the direct, denotative, fact-naming language of the sciences. The American New Critics (Cleanth Brooks, William K. Wimsett, John Crowe Ransom, Allen Tate) were influenced by the new aesthetic philosophies. For them, literature should be studied for the way literary language differs from ordinary practical language and for the unique truths conveyed only through such literary language.

The Russian Formalists were interested both in describing the general characteristics of literary language and in analyzing the specific devices or modes of operation of such language. Perhaps their most famous general claim is that literary language consists of an act of defamiliarization, by which they mean that such literature presents objects or experiences from such an unusual perspective or in such unconventional and self-conscious language that our habitual, ordinary, rote perceptions of those things are disturbed. We are forced to see things that had become automatic and overly familiar in new ways. Shklovsky cites the example of Tolstoy, who presents a meditation on property from the point of view of a horse, or who recounts the story of a flogging in such a blank manner that the then accepted practice seems strange and novel to the otherwise inured reader.

More specifically, the Formalists were interested in analyzing literature into its component parts and in describing its principal devices and modes of operation. This analysis took two main forms in the two major genres of prose narrative and poetry, concentrating in the first on the operations of narrative and in the second on sound in verse. The Formalists noticed that narrative literature consisted of two major components: the plot, by which they meant the story as narrated within the pages of the book (with all the attendant arrangements of chronological sequence, point of view, etc.), and the story, by which they meant the sequence of events in the order and the actual duration in which they ostensibly occurred. Once this simple distinction is made, one can begin to analyze all of the features of story-telling, the many devices such as point of view, delayed disclosure, narrative voice, and the like that go into the creation of the imaginary story through the manipulation of plot or story-telling devices. One can, for example, begin to study a novel like *The Scarlet Letter* for its narrative strategies instead of for the ways in which it depicts Puritanism.

In the analysis of poetry, the Formalist focus was on the qualities of poetic language that distinguish it from ordinary practical language, the distinction between the literary and the non-literary being more pronounced in this genre. Whereas ordinary language must subordinate its rules of operation (grammar) to the practical goal of communicating information, poetic language is distinguished by the foregrounding of such devices or motifs as euphony, rhythm, alliteration, consonance, repetition, and rhyme which obey a very different logic from that required to communicate information. A meteorologist might say that "precipitation in the Iberian peninsula is concentrated in the central plateau," and in light of that practical use of language, the internal rhyming of "the rain in Spain falls mainly on the plain" will seem impractical and unnecessary, but it is such devices that make poetry a distinct linguistic undertaking, a mode of language use with autonomous rules of operation which, unlike grammar, are not subordinated to a practical function. While practical speech facilitates access to information by making language as transparent as possible, poetic speech contorts and roughens up ordinary language and submits it to what Roman Jakobson called "organized violence," and it is this roughening up of ordinary language into tortuous "formed speech" that makes poetry poetry rather than a weather report.

While literature for the Formalists is characterized by invariant patterns, recurring devices, and law-like relations, it also changes over time and varies from one historical epoch to another. The Formalists account for such change in two ways. They claim that literary evolution is the result of the constant attempt to disrupt existing literary conventions and to generate new ones. And they argue that literary change is the result of the autonomous evolution of literary devices.

A more traditional concept of the content/form distinction might lead one to conclude that literature changes when the world changes because literature merely gives form to ideas and realities that lie outside the literary realm and constitute its cause or motivation. But for the Formalists, literary devices owe no debt to such motivations; they evolve autonomously of them and are motivated entirely by literary origins. For literature to be literature, it must constantly defamiliarize the familiar, constantly evolve new procedures for story-telling or poetry-making. And such change is entirely autonomous of the social and historical world from which the materials of literature are taken. Cervantes' satiric novel *Don Quixote*, for example, makes fun of the popular romantic novels about knights and quests which constituted the dominant form of story-telling in his day. It emerged not because of changes in the world or in Cervantes' life but rather as a result of a specifically literary evolution. The new device of the problematic hero was made possible and necessary by the development of the novel form itself.

You will find a major Russian Formalist, Roman Jakobson, placed under Structuralism in this anthology because there is a strong historical as well as methodological link between the two intellectual movements. Many of the original Formalists were linguists, with Jakobson being the most influential. He left Russia in 1920 and traveled to Czechoslovakia, where he was part of the linguistic circles that inspired French Structuralism in the 1940s and 1950s. The Structuralists, whose work was particularly influential in France through the 1960s, share a methodological interest with Formalist linguistics in that they saw culture in general as constituted by the same rules of operation that one finds in language. Although the Russian Formalists were suppressed by the Stalinist government in Russia in the 1920s, news of their work was borne West by East European émigrés such as René Wellek, Julia Kristeva, and Tzvetan Todorov, where it helped shape French Structuralism as well as such literary critical schools as poetics, stylistics, and narratology.

The impulse toward formal analysis was not limited in Russia to the group of thinkers usually clustered under the rubric Russian Formalists. Vladimir Propp was a scholar of folktales who wrote at the same time as the Formalists and who analyzed the component features of folktale narratives. A wide range of tales could be shown to share the same sequence of narrative motifs, from "the hero leaves home" to "the hero receives a magic token" to "the hero is tested in battle." The work of Mikhail Bakhtin, while it is historically at odds with the Formalists in its emphasis on the social and ideological features of literature, shares their concern with describing those formal elements that make a literary genre such as the novel distinct from other literary forms. His work also represents an expansion of the original Formalist undertaking to include not only genres but also extra-literary uses of language such as that of the carnival, which Bakhtin saw influencing the work of certain writers such as François Rabelais.

While the Russian Formalist movement was scientific and rational, the other major formalist school – American New Criticism – was anti-scientific and interested in the nonrational dimension of art. Both critical movements nevertheless shared an interest in what it is about literary language that makes it different from the ordinary use of language, and both considered the proper object of literary study to be literary texts and how they worked rather than authors' lives or the social and historical worlds to which literature refers. Two well-known terms that are part of a New Critical legacy – the intentional fallacy and the affective fallacy – name this act of delimiting the object of literary study and separating it from biography or sociology. According to the intentional fallacy, meaning resides in the verbal design of a literary work, not in

statements regarding his or her intention that the author might make. According to
the affective fallacy, the subjective effects or emotional reactions a work provokes in
readers are irrelevant to the study of the verbal object itself, since its objective
structure alone contains the meaning of the work.

While the Russian Formalists were concerned with elucidating the modes of operation of entire genres such as the novel, the New Critics concentrated their energies
on individual literary works, especially poems. "Close reading" is the term most
often used to describe their method. The purpose of such close reading was not,
however, the analysis of literary devices or motifs considered as an end in itself. It
was instead the elucidation of the way literature embodies or concretely enacts universal truth, what the New Critics called "concrete universals."

Poetry, they argued, differs from ordinary practical speech, which uses language
denotatively (one word for one thing), in that poetry uses language connotatively or
in a way that evokes secondary meanings. Such language use allows poetry to be both
concrete and specific as well as universal and general. An urn can be both an ordinary object *and* a metaphor for the eternal durability of art. Poetic language thus
reconciles the ordinarily opposed elements of the concrete and the universal, the
specific word and general meaning, body and spirit. Such reconciliation is possible in
connotative poetic tropes such as paradox, irony, and metaphor, tropes which either
join ordinary objects to universal meanings (metaphor, symbol) or reconcile seemingly opposed elements (irony, paradox). Cleanth Brooks, for example, notices in a
famous close reading that Keats' poem "Ode on a Grecian Urn" is full of paradoxes
such as "Cold pastoral" and "unheard melodies" which imply both life and death at
once, the paradoxical cohabitation of what is vivid and moving with what is frozen
and still. This is so, Brooks argues, because the poem is about how art, figured in the
urn, is more vivid than life itself, even though it seems lifeless. Although dead, it
possesses eternal life.

The practical denotative language of science cannot name such truth because such
language is limited to the naming of positive empirical facts that can be grasped by
the senses. The realm of universal meaning, however, is beyond sensory experience
and cannot be analyzed using scientific methods. It can only be alluded to indirectly
in poetic language and cannot be paraphrased in literal, denotative speech. For the
American New Critics, therefore, the description of literary devices such as metaphor, irony, and paradox was inseparable from a theory of universal meaning that
was a polemical response to modern positivist science. While the Russian Formalists
sought a value-free mode of critical description, one that would scientifically specify
what it is about literature that is literary, the New Critics informed the study of
literature with a concern for traditional religious and aesthetic values of a kind being
displaced by science, in this case, the values of Christian theology and idealist aesthetics (that is, an aesthetics rooted in the idea that universal truth is available
through art of a kind that is not determined by material social and historical circumstances). Those values have receded in importance with time, and the legacy of
the New Criticism that has remained most abiding is the concern with the close
reading of texts and with the analysis of the operation of literary language in all its
complexity.

CHAPTER 2

The Formal Method

Boris Eichenbaum

In this recapitulation of the early work of the Russian Formalist critics, first published in 1926, Eichenbaum, an original member of the Society for the Study of Poetic Language (or *Opoyaz*), which was founded in 1916, sums up the group's major achievements. Polemicizing against the Symbolists, who believed literary form was the clothing of spiritual meaning, the formal critics countered that the primary motivating factor in literature is form itself, the techniques and devices an artist uses.

The organization of the Formal method was governed by the principle that the study of literature should be made specific and concrete ...

[The Formalists'] basic point was, and still is, that the object of literary science, as literary science, ought to be the investigation of the specific properties of literary material, of the properties that distinguish such material from material of any other kind, notwithstanding the fact that its secondary and oblique features make that material properly and legitimately exploitable, as auxiliary material, by other disciplines. The point was consummately formulated by Roman Jakobson:

> The object of study in literary science is not literature but "literariness," that is, what makes a given work a literary work. Meanwhile, the situation has been that historians of literature act like nothing so much as policemen, who, out to arrest a certain culprit, take into custody (just in case) everything and everyone they find at the scene as well as any passers-by for good measure. The historians of literature have helped themselves to everything – environment, psychology, politics, philosophy. Instead of a science of literature they have worked up a concoction of homemade disciplines. They seem to have forgotten that those subjects pertain to their own fields of study – to the history of philosophy, the history of culture, psychology, and so on, and that those fields of study certainly may utilize literary monuments as documents of a defective and second-class variety among other materials.[1]

To establish this principle of specificity without resorting to speculative aesthetics required the juxtaposing of the literary order of facts with another such order. For this purpose one order had to be selected from among existent orders, which, while contiguous with the literary order, would contrast with it in terms of functions. It was just such a methodological procedure that produced the opposition between "poetic" language and "practical" language. This opposition was set forth in the first *Opojaz* publications (L. Jakubinskij articles), and it served as the activating principle for the Formalists' treatment of the fundamental problems of poetics. Thus, instead of an orientation toward a history of culture or of social life, toward psychology, or aesthetics, and so on, as had been customary for literary scholars, the Formalists came up with their own characteristic orientation toward linguistics, a discipline contiguous with poetics in regard to the material under investigation, but one approaching that material from a different angle and with different kinds of problems to solve. ...

The comparison of poetic language with practical language was made in general terms by Lev Jakubinskij in his first article, "On Sounds in Verse Language."[2] The formulation of the difference between the two language systems ran as follows:

> The phenomena of language ought to be classified according to the purpose for which the speaker uses his language resources in any given instance. If the speaker uses them for the purely practical purpose of communication, then we are dealing with the system of *practical language* (discursive thought), in which language resources (sounds, morphological segments, and so forth) have no autonomous value and are merely a *means* of communication. But it is possible to conceive and in fact to find language systems in which the practical aim retreats to the background (it does not necessarily disappear altogether), and language resources acquire autonomous value.

It was important to establish this difference as a foundation for building a poetics.

The natural conclusion from all these observations and principles was that poetic language is not just a language of "images," and that sounds in verse are not at all mere elements of external euphony serving only to "accompany" meaning, but that they do have autonomous value. The stage was set for a reexamination of Potebnja's general theory with its basic assertion that poetry is "thinking in images." This conception, which was the one accepted by the theorists of Symbolism, made it requisite to regard the sounds of verse as the "expression" of something standing behind a poem and to interpret them either as onomatopoeia or as "painting with sounds." Andrej Belyj's studies are especially illustrative of this. Belyj found in two lines of Pushkin the complete "picture in sounds" of champagne being poured from a bottle into a glass and in Blok's repetition of cluster *rdt* the "tragedy of turning sober."[3] Such attempts, verging on parody, to "explain" alliterations were bound to provoke on our part energetic opposition in terms of basic theory and our endeavors to demonstrate concretely that sounds in verse exist outside any connection with imagery and have an independent speech function.

L. Jakubinskij's articles linguistically substantiated the autonomous value of sounds in verse. Osip Brik's article "Sound Repetitions"[4] brought actual material to the fore (excerpts from Pushkin and Lermontov) and arranged it in various typological classes. After disputing the popular notion of poetic language as the language of "images," Brik came to the following conclusion:

> However the interrelationship of sound and image may be regarded, one thing is certain: sounds and sound harmonies are not merely a euphonic extra but are the result of an autonomous poetic endeavor. The orchestration of poetic speech is not fully accounted for by a repertoire of overt euphonic devices, but represents in its entirety the complex production of the interaction of the general laws of euphony. Rhythm, alliteration, and so forth are only the obvious manifestation of particular instances of basic euphonic laws.

In contrast to Belyj's works, Brik's article contained no interpretations of what particular cases of alliteration were supposed to mean; the article limited itself to the supposition that repetition in verse is analogous to tautology in folklore, that is, that repetition in these instances plays some aesthetic role in its own right. "It is likely that we are dealing here with various manifestations of the same general poetic principle – the principle of simple combination, the material being either the sounds of the words, or their meaning, or both." This sort of predication of one device applied to a wide range of material was very characteristic of the early period of the Formalists' work. . . .

The Formalists simultaneously freed themselves from the traditional correlation of "form-content" and from the conception of form as an outer cover or as a vessel into which a liquid (the content) is poured. The facts testified that the specificity of art is expressed not in the elements that go to make up a work but in *the special way they are used*. By the same token, the concept of "form" took on a different meaning; it no longer had to be paired with any other concept, it no longer needed correlation.

In 1914, before the *Opojaz* alliance and during the days of the Futurists' public demonstrations, Sklovskij published a pamphlet, *The Resurrection of the Word*.[5] Relying in part on Potebnja and Veselovskij (the question of imagery had then not yet acquired crucial meaning), he advanced the principle of the palpableness (*oscutimost*) of form as the specific criterion of perception in art:

> We do not experience the familiar, we do not see it, we recognize it. We do not see the walls of our rooms. We find it very difficult to catch mistakes when reading proof (especially if it is in a language we are very used to), the reason being that we cannot force ourselves to see, to read, and not just "recognize," a familiar word. If it is a definition of "poetic" perception or of "artistic" perception in general we are after, then we must surely hit upon this definition: "artistic" perception is a perception that entails awareness of form (perhaps not only form, but invariably form).

It should be evident that *perception* figures here not as a simple psychological concept (the perception of the individual human beings) but as an element of art in itself, since it is impossible for art to exist without being perceived. A concept of form in a new meaning had now come into play – not just the outer covering but the whole entity, something concrete and dynamic, substantive in itself, and unqualified by any correlation. This signalized a decisive departure from the principles of Symbolism, which had held that something already "substantive" was supposed to emanate "through form." It also meant that "aestheticism" – a delectation with certain elements of form consciously divorced from "content" – had likewise been overcome.

This, however, did not yet constitute an adequate basis for concrete work: To supplement the points established by the recognition of a difference between poetic language and practical language and by the recognition that the specificity of art is expressed in a special usage of material, the principle of the palpableness of form had to be made concrete enough to foster the analysis of form itself – form understood as content. It had to be shown that the palpableness of form results from special artistic procedures[6] acting on perceivers so as to force them to experience form. Sklovskij's "Art as Procedure,"[7] a kind of manifesto of the Formal method, set the stage for the concrete analysis of form. Here the removal from Potebnja and Potebnjaism and by the same token from the principles of Symbolism was made perfectly explicit. The article opens with objections to Potebnja's basic stand on imagery and on the relationship of the image with what it is meant to explain. Sklovskij points out among other things that images are almost always static.

The more light you shed on a literary period, the more you become convinced that the images you had considered to be the creation of a certain particular poet had been borrowed by him from other poets, virtually unchanged. All that the work of poetic schools amounts to is the acquisition and demonstration of new procedures for deploying and elaborating verbal materials; in particular, it amounts much more to deploying images than creating them. Images are handed down; and poetry involves far more reminiscence of images than thinking in them. In any case, imagistic thinking is not that factor whose change constitutes the essence of the momentum of poetry.

Further on, the difference between the poetic and the prosaic image is pointed out. The poetic image is defined as one of the means of poetic language – a procedure equal in the task it fulfills to other procedures of poetic language: parallelism (simple and negative), comparison, repetition, symmetry, hyperbole, etc. The concept of the image was relegated to a position within the general system of poetic procedures, and so it had lost its overriding importance for theory. Concomitantly, the principle of artistic economy, a principle deeply embedded in the theory of art, had been refuted. Sklovskij countered by advancing the procedure of "making it strange" (*ostranenie*) and the procedure of impeded form, "which augments the difficulty and the duration of perception, since the process of perception in art is an end in itself and is supposed to be prolonged." Art is conceived as a way of breaking down automatism in perception, and the aim of the image is held to be, not making a meaning more accessible for our comprehension, but bringing about a special perception of a thing, bringing about the "seeing," and not just the "recognizing," of it. Hence the usual connection between the image and the procedure of "making strange."

The break with Potebnjaism was definitely formulated in Sklovskij's "Potebnja."[8] He repeats once again that the use of images and symbols does not constitute the distinguishing feature of poetic language as against prosaic (practical) language.

> Poetic language is distinguished from prosaic language by the palpableness of its construction. The palpableness may be brought about by the acoustical aspect or the articulatory aspect or the semiological aspect. Sometimes what is palpable is not the structure of the words but the use of words in a construction, their arrangement. One of the means of creating a palpable construction, the very fabric of which is experienced, is the poetic image, but it is only one of the means . . . If scientific poetics is to be brought about, it must start with the factual assertion, founded on massive evidence, that there are such things as "poetic" and "prosaic" languages, each with their different laws, and it must proceed from an analysis of those differences.

These articles may be considered the summation of the initial period in the Formalists' work. The main accomplishment of that period consisted in establishing a number of theoretical principles to serve as working hypotheses for a further concrete investigation of facts; it also surmounted popularly held theories derived from Potebnjaism. As is evident from the articles cited, the basic efforts of the Formalists were directed neither toward the study of so-called "form" nor toward the construction of a special "method," but toward substantiating the claim that verbal art must be studied in its specific features, that it is essential for that purpose to take the different functions of poetic and practical languages as the starting point. As for "form," all that concerned the Formalists was to shift the meaning of that badly confused term in such a way as to obviate its persistent association with the concept of "content," a term even more badly confused than form and totally unscientific. It was important to do away with the traditional correlation and by so doing to enrich the concept of form with new meanings. As matters further evolved, it was the concept of "procedure" that had a far greater significance, because it stemmed directly from the recognition of the difference between poetic and practical languages.

Before I turn to the Formalists' endeavors in literary history, I want to bring to a conclusion my survey of the theoretical principles and problems contained in the *Opojaz* works of the earliest period. In that article by Sklovskij already discussed, there is another concept that played a major role in the subsequent study of the novel: the concept of "motivation" (*motivirovka*). The determination of various procedures of plot formation (serial construction, parallelism, framing, concatenation, and others) established the distinction between the elements of a work's construction and the elements comprising the material it uses (the story stuff, the choice of motifs, of protagonists, of themes, etc.). This distinction was then stressed especially heavily, because the main task was to establish the unity of any chosen structural procedure within the greatest possible diversity of material. Older scholarship had operated exclusively with material conceived as the "content" and had relegated everything else to "outer form," which it regarded as a matter of interest only to fanciers of form, or even as a matter of no interest at all. That is the derivation of the naive and touching "aestheticisms" by which our older critics and historians of literature discovered the "neglect of form" in Tjutcov's poetry and simply "poor form" in writers like Nekrasov or Dostoevskij.

What saved the situation was the fact that form was forgiven these writers out of deference to the profundity of their ideas or attitudes. It was only natural that the Formalists, during their years of struggle and polemics against traditions of that sort, should have directed all their efforts toward promoting the significance of structural procedures and subordinating everything else as *motivation*.

The concept of motivation enabled the Formalists to approach literary works (in particular, novels and short stories) at even closer range and to observe the details of their construction. And that is just what Sklovskij did in his next two studies, *Plot Unfolding* and *Sterne's Tristram Shandy and the Theory of the Novel.*[9] In both of these works he scrutinized the relationship between procedure and motivation, using Cervantes's *Don Quixote* and Sterne's *Tristram Shandy* as material for a study of the construction of story and novel outside the context of literary historical problems. *Don Quixote* is viewed as a point of transition from story collections (like the *Decameron*) to the single-hero novel, structured on the procedure of concatenation, with a journey serving as motivation.

That *Don Quixote* was the novel singled out for special attention had to do with the fact that procedure and motivation are not so integrated in it as to produce a fully motivated novel with all parts fused together. The material is often merely interpolated and not infused; the procedures of plot formation and the techniques of manipulating material to further the plot stand out sharply, whereas the later development of novel construction goes "the way of ever more tightly wedging fragments of material into the very body of the novel." In the course of analyzing "how *Don Quixote* is made," Sklovskij, among other things, points out the hero's pliability and infers that this very "type" of hero came about "under the impact of devising the construction of the novel." Thus, the predominance of the construction, of the plot over material, was stressed.

The most suitable material for illustrating theoretical problems of this sort is, understandably enough, art which is not fully motivated or which deliberately tears away motivation and bares its construction. The very existence of works with an intentionally bared construction necessarily stands these problems in good stead as confirmation of the importance of their treatment and the real fact of their pertinence. Moreover, it is precisely the light shed by these problems and principles that elucidates the works themselves. And that was exactly the case with Sterne's *Tristram Shandy*. Thanks to Sklovskij's study, this novel not only contributed illustrations for theoretical postulations but also acquired a new meaning of its own so that it attracted fresh attention. Against the background of a new-found interest in its construction, Sterne's novel became a piece of contemporary writing, and Sterne became a topic of discussion for people who, until then, had seen nothing in his novel except tedious chatter or curios, or who had viewed it from the angle of its much-made-of "sentimentalism," a "sentimentalism" for which Sterne was as little responsible as Gogol was for "realism."

Observing in Sterne a deliberate baring of constructional procedures, Sklovskij argues that the very design of construction is emphasized in Sterne's novel: Sterne's awareness of form, brought out by way of his violation of form, is what in fact constitutes the content of the novel. At the end of his study, Sklovskij formulates the distinction between plot (*sjuzet*) and story-stuff (*fabula*):

> The concept of *plot* is too often confused with the depiction of events – with what I tentatively propose terming "story-stuff." The story-stuff actually is only material for filling in the plot. Therefore, the plot of *Evgenij Onegin* is not the hero's romance with Tat'jana but the plot-processing of this story-stuff worked out by introducing intermittent digressions .... The forms of art are to be explained by their artistic immanence, not by real-life motivation. When an artist holds back the action of a novel, not by employing intruders, for example, but simply by transposing the order of the parts, he makes us aware of the aesthetic laws underlying both procedures of composition.

It was in connection with the construction of the short story that my article "How Gogol's 'Overcoat' Is Made"[10] was written. The article couples the problem of plot with the problem of *skaz*, that is, the problem of a construction based on a narrator's manner of narrating. I tried to show that Gogol's text "is composed of animated locutions and verbalized emotions," that "words and sentences were chosen and linked together in Gogol on the principle of expressive *skaz*, in which a special role belongs to articulation, miming, sound gestures, etc." From that point of view the composition of *The Overcoat* proved on analysis to be built on a successive alternation of comic *skaz* (with its anecdotes, play on words, etc.) and sentimental-melodramatic declamation, thus imparting to the story the character of a grotesque. In this connection, the ending of *The Overcoat* was interpreted as an apotheosis of the grotesque – something like the mute scene in *The Inspector General*. Traditional arguments about Gogol's "romanticism" or "realism" proved to be unnecessary and irrelevant.

The problem of the study of prose fiction was therefore moved off dead center. A distinction had been established between the concept of plot, as that of construction, and the concept of story-stuff, as that of material; the typical procedures of plot formation had been clarified thanks to which the stage was now set for work on the history and theory of the novel; concomitantly, *skaz* had been advanced as the constructional principle of the plotless story. These studies exercised an influence detectable in a whole series of investigations produced in later years by persons not directly connected with *Opojaz* ...

Things were somewhat different in the case of poetry. Vast numbers of works by Western and Russian theorists, the Symbolists' practical and theoretical experiments, debates over the concepts of rhythm and meter, and the whole corpus of specialized literature to which those debates gave rise between 1910 and 1917, and finally, the appearance of the Futurists' new verse forms – all this did not so much facilitate as complicate the study of verse and even the formulation of the problems involved. Instead of addressing themselves to the basic issues, many investigators devoted their efforts to special problems in metrics or to the task of sorting out the systems and views already amassed. Meanwhile, no theory of verse, in the broad sense of the word, was to be had; there was no theoretical illumination of the problem of verse rhythm or of the connection between rhythm and syntax or of sounds in verse (the Formalists had only identified a certain linguistic groundwork), or of verse vocabulary and semantics, and so on. In other words, the problem of verse, as such, remained essentially up in the air. An approach was needed which would steer away from particular problems of metrics and would engage verse from some more fundamental point of view. What was needed, first of all, was a restatement of the problem of rhythm in such a way that the problem would not hinge on metrics and would encompass the more substantive aspects of verse language ...

The start was made by Osip Brik's "On Rhythmic-Syntactic Figures."[11] Brik's report demonstrated the actual existence in verse of constant syntactic formations inseparably bound with rhythm. Therefore the concept of rhythm relinquished its abstract character and touched on the very fabric of verse – *the phrase unit*. Metrics retreated to the background, retaining a significance as the rudiments, the alphabet, of verse. This step was as important for the study of verse as the coupling of plot with construction had been for the study of prose fiction. The discovery of rhythmic-syntactic figures conclusively discredited the notion that rhythm is an external increment, something confined to the surface of speech. The theory of verse was led down a line of inquiry which treated rhythm as the structural base from which all elements of verse – nonacoustical as well as acoustical – derived definition....

According to Tomatsevskij,

> Verse speech is speech *organized* in its sound aspect. But inasmuch as sound aspect is a complex phenomenon, only some one particular element of sound is canonized. Thus in classical metrics the canonized element is the word stress, which classical metrics proceeded to subject to codification as a norm under its rules ... But once the authority of traditional forms is even slightly shaken, the compelling thought arises that these primary features do not exhaust the nature of verse, that verse is viable also in its secondary features of sound, that there is such a thing as a recognizable rhythm along with meter, that verse can be written with only its secondary features observed, that *speech can sound like verse even without its observing a meter.*

The importance of "rhythmic impulse," a concept which had already figured in Brik's work, is affirmed by Tomatsevskij as the general rhythmic operational mode:

> Rhythmic procedures can participate in various degrees in the creation of a rhythmic impression of artistic value: in individual works some one procedure or another may predominate; some one procedure or another may be the *dominant*. Focus on one rhythmic procedure or another determines the character of the work's concrete rhythm, and, with this in mind, verse may be classified as tonic-metrical verse (e.g., the

description of the battle in *Poltava*), intonational-melodic verse (Zukovskij's poetry), and harmonic verse (typical of Russian Symbolism in its later years).

Verse form, so understood, is not in opposition to any "content" extrinsic to it; it is not forced to fit inside this "form" but is conceived of as the genuine content of verse speech. Thus the very concept of form, as in our previous works, emerges with a new sense of sufficiency.

Notes

1 *Novejsaja russkaja poezija. Nabrosok pervyj* [Recent Russian Poetry, Sketch 1] (Prague, 1921), p. 11.
2 "O zvukax stixotvornogo jazyka" in *Sborniki po teorii poeticeskogo jazyka, Vypusk pervyj* (Petrograd, 1916).
3 See Andrej Belyj's articles in the collection of essays, *Skify* (1917), and in *Vetv* (1917), and in my article, "O zvukax v stixe" [On Sound in Verse] (1920), reprinted in the collection of my essays, *Skvoz literaturu* (1924).
4 "Zvukovye povtory," in *Sborniki po teorii poeticeskogo jazyka, Vypusk II* (Petrograd, 1917).
5 *Voskresenie slova*.
6 The Russian word "*priëm*" has usually been translated as "device" or "technique." We follow Striedter's suggestion that the word be translated as "procedure." See "Zur formalistischen Theorie der Prosa und der literarischen Evolution," in *Texte der Russischen Formalisten* (Munich, 1969) (cited by Jan Broekman, *Structuralism: Moscow, Prague, Paris* (Boston, 1974)).
7 "Iskusstvo kak priëm," in *Sborniki po teorii poeticeskogo jazyka, Vypusk II* (Petrograd, 1917).
8 "Potebnja," in *Poetika: Sborniki po teorii poeticeskogo jazyka* (Petrograd, 1919).
9 *Razvertyvanie sjuzeta* and *Tristam Sendi Sterna i teorija romana* (published separately by *Opojaz* in 1921).
10 "Kak sdelana 'Sinel' Gogolja," in *Poetika* (1919).
11 "O ritmiko-sintakticeskix figurax" (a report delivered to *Opojaz* in 1920 and not only never published but even, I believe, never fully completed).

CHAPTER 3

Art as Technique

Viktor Shklovsky

One of the founders of the Formalist study group in Petrograd in the early twentieth century, Shklovsky was also one of its most innovative thinkers. In seeking to move literary study out of the realm of religion and into that of science, Shklovsky and his colleagues argued against the Symbolists who conceived of poetry in spiritualist terms. In continuing the effort to exactly delineate the "literary" quality of those devices and techniques that separates them from ordinary prose, Shklovsky argues in this essay (1916) that such devices impede normal perceptions. This essay demonstrates the similarity between the formal scholarly undertaking and the innovations in poetry that were occurring at the same time in Europe, such as Dada. Concerned with writing that would be brutally honest and shockingly new, these writers rejected traditional culture and traditional artistic forms that had for them become both boring and overly conventional. Shklovsky, thinking along similar lines, saw all poetry as producing a shock effect that disrupted habitual ways of seeing and thinking.

If we start to examine the general laws of perception, we see that as perception becomes habitual, it becomes automatic. Thus, for example, all of our habits retreat into the area of the unconsciously automatic; if one remembers the sensations of holding a pen or of speaking in a foreign language for the first time and compares that with his feeling at performing the action for the ten thousandth time, he will agree with us. Such habituation explains the principles by which, in ordinary speech, we leave phrases unfinished and words half expressed. In this process, ideally realized in algebra, things are replaced by symbols. Complete words are not expressed in rapid speech; their initial sounds are barely perceived. Alexander Pogodin offers the example of a boy considering the sentence "The Swiss mountains are beautiful" in the form of a series of letters: *T, S, m, a, b*.[1]

This characteristic of thought not only suggests the method of algebra, but even prompts the choice of symbols (letters, especially initial letters). By this "algebraic" method of thought we apprehend objects only as shapes with imprecise extensions; we do not see them in their entirety but rather recognize them by their main characteristics. We see the object as though it were enveloped in a sack. We know what it is by its configuration, but we see only its silhouette. The object, perceived thus in the manner of prose perception, fades and does not leave even a first impression; ultimately even the essence of what it was is forgotten. Such perception explains why we fail to hear the prose word in its entirety (see Leo Jakubinsky's article[2]) and, hence, why (along with other slips of the tongue) we fail to pronounce it. The process of "algebrization," the over-automatization of an object, permits the greatest economy of perceptive effort. Either objects are assigned only one proper feature – a number, for example – or else they function as though by formula and do not even appear in cognition:

> I was cleaning and, meandering about, approached the divan and couldn't remember whether or not I had dusted it. Since these movements are habitual and unconscious I could not remember and felt that it was impossible to remember – so that if I had dusted it and forgot – that is, had acted unconsciously, then it was the same as if I had not. If some conscious person had been watching, then the fact could be established. If, however, no one was looking, or looking on unconsciously, if the whole complex lives of many people go on unconsciously, then such lives are as if they had never been.[3]

And so life is reckoned as nothing. Habitualization devours work, clothes, furniture, one's wife, and the fear of war. "If the whole complex lives of many people go on unconsciously, then such lives are as if they had never been." And art exists that one may recover the sensation of life; it exists to make one feel things, to make the stone *stony*. The purpose of art is to impart the sensation of things as they are perceived and not as they are known. The technique of art is to make objects "unfamiliar," to make forms difficult, to increase the difficulty and length of perception because the process of perception is an aesthetic end in itself and must be prolonged. *Art is a way of experiencing the artfulness of an object: the object is not important* . . .

After we see an object several times, we begin to recognize it. The object is in front of us and we know about it, but we do not see it[4] – hence we cannot say anything significant about it. Art removes objects from the automatism of perception in several ways. Here I want to illustrate a way used repeatedly by Leo Tolstoy, that writer who, for Merezhkovsky at least, seems to present things as if he himself saw them, saw them in their entirety, and did not alter them.

Tolstoy makes the familiar seem strange by not naming the familiar object. He describes an object as if he were seeing it for the first time, an event as if it were happening for the first time. In describing something he avoids the accepted names of its parts and instead names corresponding parts of other objects. For example, in "Shame" Tolstoy "defamiliarizes" the idea of flogging in this way: "to strip people who have broken the law, to hurl them to the floor, and to rap on their bottoms with switches," and, after a few lines, "to lash about on the naked buttocks." Then he remarks:

> Just why precisely this stupid, savage means of causing pain and not any other – why not prick the shoulders or any part of the body with needles, squeeze the hands or the feet in a vise, or anything like that?

I apologize for this harsh example, but it is typical of Tolstoy's way of pricking the conscience. The familiar act of flogging is made unfamiliar both by the description and by the proposal to change its form without changing its nature. Tolstoy uses this technique of "defamiliarization" constantly. The narrator of "Kholstomer," for example, is a horse, and it is the horse's point of view (rather than a person's) that makes the content of the story seem unfamiliar. Here is how the horse regards the institution of private property:

> I understood well what they said about whipping and Christianity. But then I was absolutely in the dark. What's the meaning of "his own," "his colt"? From these

phrases I saw that people thought there was some sort of connection between me and the stable. At the time I simply could not understand the connection. Only much later, when they separated me from the other horses, did I begin to understand. But even then I simply could not see what it meant when they called me "man's property." The words "my horse" referred to me, a living horse, and seemed as strange to me as the words "my land," "my air," "my water."

But the words made a strong impression on me. I thought about them constantly, and only after the most diverse experiences with people did I understand, finally, what they meant. They meant this: In life people are guided by words, not by deeds. It's not so much that they love the possibility of doing or not doing something as it is the possibility of speaking with words, agreed on among themselves, about various topics. Such are the words "my" and "mine," which they apply to different things, creatures, objects, and even to land, people, and horses. They agree that only one may say "mine" about this, that or the other thing. And the one who says "mine" about the greatest number of things is, according to the game which they've agreed to among themselves, the one they consider the most happy. I don't know the point of all this, but it's true. For a long time I tried to explain it to myself in terms of some kind of real gain, but I had to reject that explanation because it was wrong.

Many of those, for instance, who called me their own never rode on me – although others did. And so with those who fed me. Then again, the coachman, the veterinarians, and the outsiders in general treated me kindly, yet those who called me their own did not. In due time, having widened the scope of my observations, I satisfied myself that the notion "my," not only has relation to us horses, has no other basis than a narrow human instinct which is called a sense of or right to private property. A man says "this house is mine" and never lives in it; he only worries about its construction and upkeep. A merchant says "my shop," or "my dry goods shop," for instance, and does not even wear clothes made from the better cloth he keeps in his own shop.

There are people who call a tract of land their own, but they never set eyes on it and never take a stroll on it. There are people who call others their own, yet never see them. And the whole relationship between them is that the so-called "owners" treat the others unjustly.

There are people who call women their own, or their "wives," but their women live with other men. And people strive not for the good in life, but for goods they can call their own.

I am now convinced that this is the essential difference between people and ourselves. And therefore, not even considering the other ways in which we are superior, but considering just this one virtue, we can bravely claim to stand higher than men on the ladder of living creatures. The actions of men, at least those with whom I have had dealings, are guided by *words* – ours by deeds.

The horse is killed before the end of the story, but the manner of the narrative, its technique, does not change:

Much later they put Serpukhovsky's body, which had experienced the world, which had eaten and drunk, into the ground. They could profitably send neither his hide, nor his flesh, nor his bones anywhere.

But since his dead body, which had gone about in the world for twenty years, was a great burden to everyone, its burial was only a superfluous embarrassment for the people. For a long time no one had needed him; for a long time he had been a burden on all. But nevertheless, the dead who buried the dead found it necessary to dress this bloated body, which immediately began to rot, in a good uniform and good boots; to lay it in a good new coffin with new tassels at the four corners, then to place this new coffin in another of lead and ship it to Moscow; there to exhume ancient bones and at just that spot, to hide this putrefying body, swarming with maggots, in its new uniform and clean boots, and to cover it over completely with dirt.

Thus we see that at the end of the story Tolstoy continues to use the technique even though the motivation for it (the reason for its use) is gone.

In *War and Peace* Tolstoy uses the same technique in describing whole battles as if battles were something new. These descriptions are too long to quote; it would be necessary to extract a considerable part of the four-volume novel. But Tolstoy uses the same method in describing the drawing room and the theater:

The middle of the stage consisted of flat boards; by the sides stood painted pictures representing trees, and at the back a linen cloth was stretched down to the floor boards. Maidens in red bodices and white skirts sat on the middle of the stage. One, very fat, in a white silk dress, sat apart on a narrow bench to which a green pasteboard box was glued from behind. They were all singing something. When they had finished, the maiden in white approached the prompter's box. A man in silk with tight-fitting pants on his fat legs approached her with a plume and began to sing and spread his arms in dismay. The man in the tight pants finished his song alone; then the girl sang. After that both remained silent as the music resounded; and the man, obviously waiting to begin singing his part with her again, began to run his fingers over the hand of the girl in the white dress. They finished their song together, and everyone in the theater began to clap and shout. But the men and women on stage, who represented lovers, started to bow, smiling and raising their hands.

In the second act were pictures representing monuments and openings in the linen cloth representing the moonlight, and they raised lamp shades on a frame. As the musicians started to play the bass horn and counter-bass, a large number of people in black mantels poured onto the stage from right and left. The people, with something like daggers in their hands, started to wave their arms. Then still more people came running out and began to drag away the maiden who had been wearing a white dress but who now wore one of sky blue. They did not drag her off immediately, but sang with her for a long time before dragging her away. Three times they struck on something metallic behind the side scenes, and everyone got down on his knees and began to chant a prayer. Several times all of this activity was interrupted by enthusiastic shouts from the spectators . . .

Anyone who knows Tolstoy can find several hundred such passages in his work. His method of seeing things out of their normal context is also apparent in his last works. Tolstoy described the dogmas and rituals he attacked as if they were unfamiliar, substituting everyday meanings for the customarily religious meanings of the words common in church ritual. Many persons were painfully wounded; they considered it blasphemy to present as strange and monstrous what they accepted as sacred. Their reaction was due chiefly to the technique through which Tolstoy perceived and reported his environment. And after turning to what he had long avoided, Tolstoy found that his perceptions had unsettled his faith.

The technique of defamiliarization is not Tolstoy's alone. I cited Tolstoy because his work is generally known.

Now, having explained the nature of this technique, let us try to determine the approximate limits of its application. I personally feel that defamiliarization is found almost everywhere form is found . . . An image is not a permanent referent for those mutable complexities of life which are revealed through it, its purpose is not to make

us perceive meaning, but to create a special perception of the object – *it creates a vision of the object instead of serving as a means for knowing it* ...

Such constructions as "the pestle and the mortar," or "Old Nick and the infernal regions" (*Decameron*) are also examples of the technique of defamiliarization. And in my article on plot construction I write about defamiliarization in psychological parallelism. Here, then, I repeat that the perception of disharmony in a harmonious context is important in parallelism. The purpose of parallelism, like the general purpose of imagery, is to transfer the usual perception of an object into the sphere of new perception – that is, to make a unique semantic modification.

In studying poetic speech in its phonetic and lexical structure as well as in its characteristic distribution of words and in the characteristic thought structures compounded from the words, we find everywhere the artistic trademark – that is, we find material obviously created to remove the automatism or perception; the author's purpose is to create the vision which results from that deautomatized perception. A work is created "artistically" so that its perception is impeded and the greatest possible effect is produced through the slowness of the perception. As a result of this lingering, the object is perceived not in its extension in space, but, so to speak, in its continuity. Thus "poetic language" gives satisfaction. According to Aristotle, poetic language must appear strange and wonderful; and, in fact, it is often actually foreign: the Sumerian used by the Assyrians, the Latin of Europe during the Middle Ages, the Arabisms of the Persians, the Old Bulgarian of Russian literature, or the elevated, almost literary language of folk songs. The common archaisms of poetic language, the intricacy of the sweet new style [*dolce stil nuovo*],[5] the obscure style of the language of Arnaut Daniel with the "roughened" [*harte*] forms *which make pronunciation difficult* – these are used in much the same way. Leo Jakubinsky has demonstrated the principle of phonetic "roughening" of poetic language in the particular case of the repetition of identical sounds. The language of poetry is, then, a difficult, roughened, impeded language. In a few special instances the language of poetry approximates the language of prose, but this does not violate the principle of "roughened" form.

> Her sister was called Tatyana
> For the first time we shall
> Willfully brighten the delicate
> Pages of a novel with such a name

wrote Pushkin. The usual poetic language for Pushkin's contemporaries was the elegant style of Derzhavin; but Pushkin's style, because it seemed trivial then, was unexpectedly difficult for them. We should remember the consternation of Pushkin's contemporaries over the vulgarity of his expressions. He used the popular language as a special device for prolonging attention, just as his contemporaries generally used Russian words in their usually French speech (see Tolstoy's examples in *War and Peace*).

Just now a still more characteristic phenomenon is under way. Russian literary language, which was originally foreign to Russia, has so permeated the language of the people that it has blended with their conversation. On the other hand, literature has now begun to show a tendency towards the use of dialects (Remizov, Klyuyev, Essenin, and others,[6] so unequal in talent and so alike in language, are intentionally provincial) and/or barbarisms (which gave rise to the Severyanin group[7]). And

currently Maxim Gorky is changing his diction from the old literary language to the new literary colloquialism of Leskov.[8] Ordinary speech and literary language have thereby changed places (see the work of Vyacheslav Ivanov and many others). And finally, a strong tendency, led by Khlebnikov, to create a new and properly poetic language has emerged. In the light of these developments we can define poetry as *attenuated, tortuous* speech. Poetic speech is *formed speech*. Prose is ordinary speech – economical, easy, proper, the goddess of prose [*dea prosae*] is a goddess of the accurate, facile type, of the "direct" expression of a child. I shall discuss roughened form and retardation as the general *law* of art at greater length in an article on plot construction.[9]

Nevertheless, the position of those who urge the idea of the economy of artistic energy as something which exists in and even distinguishes poetic language seems, at first glance, tenable for the problem rhythm. Spencer's description of rhythm would seem to be absolutely incontestable:

> Just as the body in receiving a series of varying concussions, must keep the muscles ready to meet the most violent of them, as not knowing when such may come: so, the mind in receiving unarranged articulations, must keep its perspectives active enough to recognize the least easily caught sounds. And as, if the concussions recur in definite order, the body may husband its forces by adjusting the resistance needful for each concussion; so, if the syllables be rhythmically arranged, the mind may economize its energies by anticipating the attention required for each syllable.[10]

This apparent observation suffers from the common fallacy, the confusion of the laws of poetic and prosaic language. In *The Philosophy of Style* Spencer failed utterly to distinguish between them. But rhythm may have two functions. The rhythm of prose, or a work song like "Dubinushka," permits the members of the work crew to do their necessary "groaning together" and also eases the work by making it automatic. And, in fact, it is easier to march with music than without it, and to march during an animated conversation is even easier, for the walking is done unconsciously. Thus the rhythm of prose is an important automatizing element; the rhythm of poetry is not. There is "order" in art, yet not a single column of a Greek temple stands exactly in its proper order; poetic rhythm is similarly disordered rhythm. Attempts to systematize the irregularities have been made, and such attempts are part of the current problem in the theory of rhythm. It is obvious that the systematization will not work, for in reality the problem is not one of complicating the rhythm but of disordering the rhythm – a disordering which cannot be predicted. Should the disordering of rhythm become a convention, it would be ineffective as a procedure for the roughening of language. But I will not discuss rhythm in more detail since I intend to write a book about it.

Notes

1   Alexander Pogodin, *Yazyk, kak tvorchestvo* [*Language as Art*] (Kharkov, 1913), p. 42. [The original sentence was in French, "*Les montagnes de la Suisse sont belles*," with the appropriate initials.]

2   Leo Jakubinsky, *Sborniki*, I (1916).

3   Leo Tolstoy's *Diary*, entry dated February 29, 1897. [The date is transcribed incorrectly; it should read March 1, 1897.]

4   Viktor Shklovsky, *Voskresheniye slova* [*The Resurrection of the Word*] (Petersburg, 1914).

5   Dante, *Purgatorio*, 24:56. Dante refers to the new lyric style of his contemporaries. [Trans.]

6   Alexy Remizov (1877–1957) is best known as a novelist and satirist; Nicholas Klyuyev (1885–1937) and Sergey Essenin (1895–1925) were "peasant poets." All three were noted for their faithful reproduction of Russian dialects and colloquial language. [Trans.]

7   A group noted for its opulent and sensuous verse style. [Trans.]

8   Nicholas Leskov (1831–95), novelist and short story writer, helped popularize the *skaz*, or yarn, and hence, because of the part dialect peculiarities play in the *skaz*, also altered Russian literary language. [Trans.]

9   Shklovsky is probably referring to his *Razvyortyvaniye syuzheta* [*Plot Development*] (Petrograd, 1921). [Trans.]

10 Herbert Spencer, *The Philosophy of Style* [(Humboldt Library, vol. XXXIV; New York, 1882), p. 169. The Russian text is slightly shortened from the original].

CHAPTER 4

The Formalist Critics

Cleanth Brooks

Published (1951) in *The Raritan Review*, this polemic in favor of the New Criticism was written by one of the major practitioners and promoters of the new approach to literature – Cleanth Brooks. Brooks had studied in Cambridge with I. A. Richards, who first laid the foundation for the New Criticism in his *Principles of Literary Criticism* (1924). Upon his return to the United States, Brooks began writing a series of books, from *An Approach to Literature* (1936) to *The Well-Wrought Urn: Studies in the Structure of Poetry* (1947), that helped establish "close reading" as the dominant form of literary study in the American academy from the 1940s through the late 1960s.

Here are some articles of faith I could subscribe to:

That literary criticism is a description and an evaluation of its object.

That the primary concern of criticism is with the problem of unity – the kind of whole which the literary work forms or fails to form, and the relation of the various parts to each other in building up this whole.

That the formal relations in a work of literature may include, but certainly exceed, those of logic.

That in a successful work, form and content cannot be separated.

That form is meaning.

That literature is ultimately metaphorical and symbolic.

That the general and the universal are not seized upon by abstraction, but got at through the concrete and the particular.

That literature is not a surrogate for religion.

That, as Allen Tate says, "specific moral problems" are the subject matter of literature, but that the purpose of literature is not to point a moral.

That the principles of criticism define the area relevant to literary criticism; they do not constitute a method for carrying out the criticism.

Such statements as these would not, however, even though greatly elaborated, serve any useful purpose here. The interested reader already knows the general nature of the critical position adumbrated – or, if he does not, he can find it set forth in writings of mine or of other critics of like sympathy. Moreover, a condensed restatement of the position here would probably beget as many misunderstandings as have past attempts to set it forth. It seems much more profitable to use the present occasion for dealing with some persistent misunderstandings and objections.

In the first place, to make the poem or the novel the central concern of criticism has appeared to mean cutting it loose from its author and from his life as a man, with his own particular hopes, fears, interests, conflicts, etc. A criticism so limited may seem bloodless and hollow. It will seem so to the typical professor of literature in the graduate school, where the study of literature is still primarily a study of the ideas and personality of the author as revealed in his letters, his diaries, and the recorded conversations of his friends. It will certainly seem so to literary gossip columnists who purvey literary chitchat. It may also seem so to the young poet or novelist, beset with his own problems of composition and with his struggles to find a subject and a style and to get a hearing for himself.

In the second place, to emphasize the work seems to involve severing it from those who actually read it, and this severance may seem drastic and therefore disastrous. After all, literature is written to be read. Wordsworth's poet was a man speaking to men. In each *Sunday Times*, Mr J. Donald Adams points out that the hungry sheep look up and are not fed; and less strenuous moralists than Mr Adams are bound to feel a proper revulsion against "mere aestheticism." Moreover, if we neglect the audience which reads the work, including that for which it was presumably written, the literary historian is prompt to point out that the kind of audience that Pope had did condition the kind of poetry that he wrote. The poem has its roots in history, past or present. Its place in the historical context simply cannot be ignored.

I have stated these objections as sharply as I can because I am sympathetic with the state of mind which is prone to voice them. Man's experience is indeed a seamless garment, no part of which can be separated from the rest. Yet if we urge this fact, of inseparability against the drawing of distinctions, then there is no point in talking about criticism at all. I am assuming that distinctions are necessary and useful and indeed inevitable.

The formalist critic knows as well as anyone that poems and plays and novels are written by men – that they do not somehow happen – and that they are written as expressions of particular personalities and are written from all sorts of motives – for money, from a desire to express oneself, for the sake of a cause, etc. Moreover, the formalist critic knows as well as anyone that literary works are mere potential until they are read – that is, that they are recreated in the minds of actual readers, who vary enormously in their capabilities, their interests, their prejudices, their ideas. But the formalist critic is concerned primarily with the work itself. Speculation on the mental processes of the author takes the critic away from the work into biography and psychology. There is no reason, of course, why he should not turn away into biography and psychology. Such explorations are very much worth making. But they should not be confused with an account of the work. Such studies describe the process of composition, not the structure of the thing composed, and they may be performed quite as validly for the poor work as for the good one. They may be validly performed for any kind of expression – nonliterary as well as literary.

On the other hand, exploration of the various readings which the work has received also takes the critic away from the work into psychology and the history of taste. The various imports of a given work may well be worth studying. I. A. Richards has put us all in his debt by demonstrating what different experiences may be derived from the same poem by an apparently homogeneous group of readers; and the scholars have pointed out, all along, how different Shakespeare appeared to an eighteenth-century as compared with a nineteenth-century audience; or how sharply divergent are the estimates of John Donne's lyrics from historical period to historical period. But such work, valuable and necessary as it may be, is to be distinguished from a criticism of the work itself. The formalist critic, because he wants to criticize the work itself, makes two assumptions: (1) he assumes that the relevant part of the author's intention is what he got actually into his work; that is, he assumes that the author's intention as realized is the "intention" that counts, not necessarily what he was conscious of trying to do, or what he now remembers he was then trying to do. And (2) the formalist critic assumes an ideal reader: that is, instead of focusing on the varying spectrum of possible readings, he attempts to find a central point of reference from which he can focus upon the structure of the poem or novel.

But there *is* no ideal reader, someone is prompt to point out, and he will probably add that it is sheer arrogance that allows the critic, with his own blindsides and prejudice, to put himself in the position of that ideal reader. There is no ideal reader, of course, and I suppose that the practicing critic can never be too often reminded of the gap between his reading and the "true" reading of the poem. But for the purpose of focusing upon the poem rather than upon his own reactions, it is a defensible strategy. Finally, of course, it is the strategy that all critics of whatever persuasion are forced to adopt. (The alternatives are desperate: either we say that one person's reading is as good as another's and equate those readings on a basis of absolute equality and thus deny the possibility of any standard reading. Or else we take a lowest common denominator of the various readings that have been made; that is, we frankly move from literary criticism into socio-psychology. To propose taking a consensus of the opinions of "qualified" readers is simply to split the ideal reader into a group of ideal readers.) As consequences of the distinction just referred to, the formalist critic rejects two popular tests for literary value. The first proves the value of the work from the author's "sincerity" (or the intensity of the author's feelings as he composed it). If we heard that Mr Guest testified that he put his heart and soul into his poems, we would not be very much impressed, though I should see no reason to doubt such a statement from Mr Guest. It would simply be critically irrelevant. Ernest Hemingway's statement in a recent issue of *Time* magazine that he counts his last novel his best is of interest for Hemingway's biography, but most readers of *Across the River and Into the Trees* would agree that it proves nothing at all about the value of the novel – that in this case the judgment is simply pathetically inept. We discount also such tests for poetry as that proposed by A. E. Housman – the bristling of his beard at the reading of a good poem. The intensity of his reaction has critical significance only in proportion as we have already learned to trust him as a reader. Even so, what it tells us is something about Housman – nothing decisive about the poem.

It is unfortunate if this playing down of such responses seems to deny humanity to either writer or reader. The critic may enjoy certain works very much and may be indeed intensely moved by them. I am, and I have no embarrassment in admitting the fact; but a detailed description of my emotional state on reading certain works has little to do with indicating to an interested reader what the work is and how the parts of it are related.

Should all criticism, then, be self-effacing and analytic? I hope that the answer is implicit in what I have already written, but I shall go on to spell it out. Of course not. That will depend upon the occasion and the audience. In practice, the critic's job is rarely a purely critical one. He is much more likely to be involved in dozens of more or less related tasks, some of them trivial, some of them important. He may be trying to get a hearing for a new author, or to get the attention of the freshman sitting in the back row. He may be comparing two authors, or editing a text; writing a brief newspaper review or reading a paper before the Modern Language Association. He may even be simply talking with a friend, talking about literature for the hell of it. Parable, anecdote, epigram, metaphor – these and a hundred other devices may be thoroughly legitimate for his varying purposes. He is certainly not to be asked to suppress his personal enthusiasms or his interest in social history or in politics. Least of all is he being asked to *present* his criticisms as the close reading of a text. Tact, common sense, and uncommon sense if he has it, are all requisite if the practicing critic is to do his various jobs well.

But it will do the critic no harm to have a clear idea of what his specific job as a critic is. I can sympathize with writers who are tired of reading rather drab "critical analyses," and who recommend brighter, more amateur, and more "human" criticism. As ideals, these are excellent; as recipes for improving criticism, I have my doubts. Appropriate vulgarizations of these ideals are already flourishing, and have long flourished – in the class room presided over by the college lecturer of infectious enthusiasm, in the gossipy Book-of-the-Month Club bulletins, and in the columns of the *Saturday Review of Literature*.

I have assigned the critic a modest, though I think an important, role. With reference to the help which the critic can give to the practicing artist, the role is even more modest. As critic, he can give only negative help. Literature is not written by formula: he can have no formula to offer. Perhaps he can do little more than indicate whether in his opinion the work has succeeded or failed. Healthy criticism and healthy creation do tend to go hand in hand. Everything else being equal, the creative artist is better off for being in touch with a vigorous criticism. But the other considerations are never equal, the case is always special, and in a given case the proper advice could be: quit reading criticism altogether, or read political science or history or philosophy – or join the army, or join the church.

There is certainly no doubt that the kind of specific and positive help that someone like Ezra Pound was able to give to several writers of our time is in one sense the most important kind of criticism that there can be. I think that it is not unrelated to the kind of criticism that I have described: there is the same intense concern with the text which is being built up, the same concern with "technical problems." But many other things are involved – matters which lie outside the specific ambit of criticism altogether; among them a knowledge of the personality of the particular writer, the ability to stimulate, to make positive suggestions.

A literary work is a document and as a document can be analyzed in terms of the forces that have produced it, or it may be manipulated as a force in its own right. It mirrors the past, it may influence the future. These facts it would be futile to deny, and I know of no critic who does deny them. But the reduction of a work of literature to its causes does not constitute literary criticism; nor does an estimate of its effects. Good literature is more than effective rhetoric applied to true ideas – even if we could agree upon a philosophical yardstick for measuring the truth of ideas and even if we could find some way that transcended nose-counting for determining the effectiveness of the rhetoric.

A recent essay by Lionel Trilling bears very emphatically upon this point. (I refer to him the more readily because Trilling has registered some of his objections to the critical position that I maintain.) In the essay entitled "The Meaning of a Literary Idea," Trilling discusses the debt to Freud and Spengler of four American writers, O'Neill, Dos Passos, Wolfe, and Faulkner. Very justly, as it seems to me, he chooses Faulkner as the contemporary writer who, along with Ernest Hemingway, best illustrates the power and importance of ideas in literature. Trilling is thoroughly aware that his choice will seem shocking and perhaps perverse, "because," as he writes, "Hemingway and Faulkner have insisted on their indifference to the conscious intellectual tradition of our time and have acquired the reputation of achieving their effects by means that have the least possible connection with any sort of intellectuality or even with intelligence."

Here Trilling shows not only acute discernment but an admirable honesty in electing to deal with the hard cases – with the writers who do not clearly and easily make the case for the importance of ideas. I applaud the discernment and the honesty, but I wonder whether the whole discussion in his essay does not indicate that Trilling is really much closer to the so-called "new critics" than perhaps he is aware. For Trilling, one notices, rejects any simple one-to-one relation between the truth of the idea and the value of the literary work in which it is embodied. Moreover, he does not claim that "recognizable ideas of a force or weight are 'used' in the work," or "new ideas of a certain force and weight are 'produced' by the work." He praises rather the fact that we feel that Hemingway and Faulkner are "intensely at work upon the recalcitrant stuff of life." The last point is made the matter of real importance. Whereas Dos Passos, O'Neill, and Wolfe make us "feel that they feel that they have said the last word," "we seldom have the sense that [Hemingway and Faulkner]...have misrepresented to themselves the nature and the difficulty of the matter they work on."

Trilling has chosen to state the situation in terms of the writer's activity (Faulkner is intensely at work, etc.). But this judgment is plainly an inference from the quality of Faulkner's novels – Trilling has not simply heard Faulkner say that he has had to struggle with his work. (I take it Mr Hemingway's declaration about the effort he put into the last novel impresses Trilling as little as it impresses the rest of us.)

Suppose, then, that we tried to state Mr Trilling's point, not in terms of the effort of the artist, but in terms of the structure of the work itself. Should we not get something very like the terms used by the formalist critics? A description in terms of "tensions," of symbolic development, of ironies and their resolution? In short, is not the formalist critic trying to describe in terms of the dynamic form of the work itself how the recalcitrancy of the material is acknowledged and dealt with?

Trilling's definition of "ideas" makes it still easier to accommodate my position to his. I have already quoted a passage in which he repudiates the notion that one has to show how recognizable ideas are "used" in the work, or new ideas are "produced" by the work. He goes on to write: "All that we need to do is account for a certain aesthetic effect as being in some important part achieved by a mental process which is not different from the process by which discursive ideas are conceived, and which is to be judged by some of the criteria by which an idea is judged." One would have to look far to find a critic "formal" enough to object to this. What some of us have been at pains to insist upon is that literature does not simply "exemplify" ideas or "produce" ideas – as Trilling acknowledges. But no one claims that the writer is an inspired idiot. He uses his mind and his reader ought to use his, in processes "not different from the process by which discursive ideas are conceived." Literature is not inimical to ideas. It thrives upon ideas but it does not present ideas patly and neatly. It involves them with the "recalcitrant stuff of life." The literary critic's job is to deal with that involvement.

The mention of Faulkner invites a closing comment upon the critic's specific job. As I have described it, it may seem so modest that one could take its performance for granted. But consider the misreadings of Faulkner now current, some of them the work of the most brilliant critics that we have, some of them quite wrong-headed, and demonstrably so. What is true of Faulkner is only less true of many another author, including many writers of the past. Literature has many "uses" – and critics propose new uses, some of them exciting and spectacular. But all the multiform uses to which literature can be put rest finally upon our knowing what a given work "means." That knowledge is basic.

CHAPTER 5

The Language of Paradox

Cleanth Brooks

In this essay from *The Well-Wrought Urn* (1947), Brooks defines the New Critical conception of poetry. Brooks' essay makes clear the debt the New Critics owed to Romanticism and especially to the idealist poetic theories of Wordsworth and Coleridge. Romanticism, in their work, represented an attempt to reassert the claims of religion in the face of the rationalist skeptical critique of religion that emerged in the eighteenth century. The New Criticism is in some respects a latter-day Romantic school of thought that also seeks to reintroduce religious meaning into literary study.

Few of us are prepared to accept the statement that the language of poetry is the language of paradox. Paradox is the language of sophistry, hard, bright, witty; it is hardly the language of the soul. We are willing to allow that paradox is a permissible weapon which a Chesterton may on occasion exploit. We may permit it in epigram, a special subvariety of poetry; and in satire, which though useful, we are hardly willing to allow to be poetry at all. Our prejudices force us to regard paradox as intellectual rather than emotional, clever rather than profound, rational rather than divinely irrational.

Yet there is a sense in which paradox is the language appropriate and inevitable to poetry. It is the scientist whose truth requires a language purged of every trace of paradox; apparently the truth which the poet utters can be approached only in terms of paradox. I overstate the case, to be sure; it is possible that the title of this chapter is itself to be treated as merely a paradox. But there are reasons for thinking that the overstatement which I propose may light up some elements in the nature of poetry which tend to be overlooked.

The case of William Wordsworth, for instance, is instructive on this point. His poetry would not appear to promise many examples of the language of paradox. He usually prefers the direct attack. He insists on simplicity; he distrusts whatever seems sophistical. And yet the typical Wordsworth poem is based upon a paradoxical situation. Consider his celebrated

> It is a beauteous evening, calm and free,
> The holy time is quiet as a Nun,
> Breathless with adoration. ...

The poet is filled with worship, but the girl who walks beside him is not worshiping. The implication is that she should respond to the holy time, and become like the evening itself, nunlike; but she seems less worshipful than inanimate nature itself. Yet

> If thou appear untouched by solemn thought,
> Thy nature is not therefore less divine:
> Thou liest in Abraham's bosom all the year;
> And worship'st at the Temple's inner shrine,
> God being with thee when we know it not

The underlying paradox (of which the enthusiastic reader may well be unconscious) is nevertheless thoroughly necessary, even for that reader. Why does the innocent girl worship more deeply than the self-conscious poet who walks beside her? Because she is filled with an unconscious sympathy for all of nature, not merely the grandiose and solemn. One remembers the lines from Wordsworth's friend, Coleridge:

> He prayeth best, who loveth best
> All things both great and small.

Her unconscious sympathy is the unconscious worship. She is in communion with nature "all the year," and her devotion is continual whereas that of the poet is sporadic and momentary. But we have not done with the paradox yet. It not only underlies the poem, but something of the paradox informs the poem, though, since this is Wordsworth, rather timidly. The comparison of the evening to the nun actually has more than one dimension. The calm of the evening obviously means "worship," even to the dull-witted and insensitive. It corresponds to the trappings of the nun, visible to everyone. Thus, it suggests not merely holiness, but, in the total poem, even a hint of Pharisaical holiness, with which the girl's careless innocence, itself a symbol of her continual secret worship, stands in contrast.

Or consider Wordsworth's sonnet, "Composed upon Westminster Bridge." I believe that most readers will agree that it is one of Wordsworth's most successful poems; yet most students have the greatest difficulty in accounting for its goodness. The attempt to account for it on the grounds of nobility of sentiment soon breaks down. On this level, the poem merely says: that the city in the morning light presents a picture which is majestic and touching to all but the most dull of soul; but the poem says very little more about the sight: the city is beautiful in the morning light and it is awfully still. The attempt to make a case for the poem in terms of the brilliance of its images also quickly breaks down: the student searches for graphic details in vain; there are next to no realistic touches. In fact, the poet simply huddles the details together:

> silent, bare,
> Ships, towers, domes, theatres, and temples lie
> Open unto the fields...

We get a blurred impression – points of roofs and pinnacles along the skyline, all twinkling in the morning light. More than that, the sonnet as a whole contains some very flat writing and some well-worn comparisons.

The reader may ask: Where, then, does the poem get its power? It gets it, it seems to me, from the paradoxical situation out of which the poem arises. The speaker is honestly surprised, and he manages some sense of awed surprise into the poem. It is odd to the poet that the city should be able to "wear the beauty of the morning" at all. Mount Snowdon, Skiddaw, Mont Blanc – these wear it by natural right, but surely not grimy, feverish London. This is the point of the almost shocked exclamation:

> Never did sun more beautifully steep
> In his first splendour, valley, rock, or hill...

The "smokeless air" reveals a city which the poet did not know existed: man-made London is a part of nature too, is lighted by the sun of nature, and lighted to as beautiful effect.

> The river glideth at his own sweet will ...

A river is the most "natural" thing that one can imagine; it has the elasticity, the curved line of nature itself. The poet had never been able to regard this one as a real river – now, uncluttered by barges, the river reveals itself as a natural thing, not at all disciplined into a rigid and mechanical pattern: it is like the daffodils, or the mountain brooks, artless, and whimsical, and "natural" as they. The poem closes, you will remember, as follows:

> Dear God! the very houses seem asleep;
> And all that mighty heart is lying still!

The city, in the poet's insight of the morning, has earned its right to be considered organic, not merely mechanical. That is why the stale metaphor of the sleeping houses is strangely renewed. The most exciting thing that the poet can say about the houses is that they are *asleep*. He has been in the habit of counting them dead – as just mechanical and inanimate; to say they are "asleep" is to say that they are alive, that they participate in the life of nature. In the same way, the tired old metaphor which sees a great city as a pulsating heart of empire becomes revivified. It is only when the poet sees the city under the semblance of death that he can see it as actually alive – quick with the only life which he can accept, the organic life of "nature."

It is not my intention to exaggerate Wordsworth's own consciousness of the paradox involved. In this poem, he prefers, as is usual with him, the frontal attack. But the situation is paradoxical here as in so many of his poems. In his preface to the second edition of the *Lyrical Ballads* Wordsworth stated that his general purpose was "to choose incidents and situations from common life" but so to treat them that "ordinary things should be presented to the mind in an unusual aspect." Coleridge was to state the purpose for him later, in terms which make even more evident Wordsworth's exploitation of the paradoxical: "Mr Wordsworth ... was to propose to himself as his object, to give the charm of novelty to things of every day, and to excite a feeling analogous to the supernatural, by awakening the mind's attention from the lethargy of custom, and directing it to the loveliness and the wonders of the world before us ..." Wordsworth, in short, was consciously attempting to show his audience that the common was really uncommon, the prosaic was really poetic.

Coleridge's terms, "the charm of novelty to things of every day," "awakening the mind," suggest the Romantic preoccupation with wonder – the surprise, the revelation which puts the tarnished familiar world in a new light. This may well be the *raison d'être* of most Romantic paradoxes; and yet the neo-classic poets use paradox for much the same reason. Consider Pope's lines from "The Essay on Man":

> In doubt his Mind or Body to prefer;
> Born but to die, and reas'ning but to err;
> Alike in ignorance, his Reason such,
> Whether he thinks too little, or too much ...
>
> Created half to rise, and half to fall;
> Great Lord of all things, yet a Prey to all;
> Sole Judge of Truth, in endless Error hurl'd;
> The Glory, Jest, and Riddle of the world!

Here, it is true, the paradoxes insist on the irony, rather than the wonder. But Pope too might have claimed that he was treating the things of everyday, man himself, and awakening his mind so that he would view himself in a new and blinding light. Thus, there is a certain awed wonder in Pope just as there is a certain trace of irony implicit in the Wordsworth sonnets. There is, of course, no reason why they should not occur together, and they do. Wonder and irony merge in many of the lyrics of Blake; they merge in Coleridge's Ancient Mariner. The variations in emphasis are numerous. Gray's "Elegy" uses a typical Wordsworth "situation" with the rural scene and with peasants contemplated in the light of their "betters." But in the "Elegy" the balance is heavily tilted in the direction of irony, the revelation an ironic rather than a startling one:

> Can storied urn or animated bust
> Back to its mansion call the fleeting breath?
> Can Honour's voice provoke the silent dust?
> Or Flatt'ry sooth the dull cold ear of Death?

But I am not here interested in enumerating the possible variations; I am interested rather in our seeing that the paradoxes spring from the very nature of the poet's language: it is a language in which the connotations play as great a part as the denotations. And I do not mean that the connotations are important as supplying some sort of frill or trimming, something external to the real matter in hand. I mean that the poet does not use a notation at all – as the scientist may properly be said to do so. The poet, within limits, has to make up his language as he goes.

T. S. Eliot has commented upon "that perpetual slight alteration of language, words perpetually juxtaposed in new and sudden combinations," which occurs in poetry. It is perpetual; it cannot be kept out of the poem; it can only be directed and controlled. The tendency of science is necessarily to stabilize terms, to freeze them into strict denotations; the poet's tendency is by contrast disruptive. The terms are continually modifying each other, and thus violating their dictionary meanings. To take a very simple example, consider the adjectives in the first lines of Wordsworth's evening sonnet: *beauteous, calm, free, holy, quiet, breathless*. The juxtapositions are hardly startling; and yet notice this: the evening is like a nun breathless with adoration. The adjective "breathless" suggests tremendous excitement; and yet the evening is not only quiet but *calm*. There is no final contradiction, to be sure: it is *that* kind of calm and *that* kind of excitement, and the two states may well occur together. But the poet has no one term. Even if he had a polysyllabic technical term,

the term would not provide the solution for his problem. He must work by contradiction and qualification.

We may approach the problem in this way: the poet has to work by analogies. All
of the subtler states of emotion, as I. A. Richards has pointed out, necessarily
demand metaphor for their expression. The poet must work by analogies, but the
metaphors do not lie in the same plane or fit neatly edge to edge. There is a continual tilting of the planes; necessary overlappings, discrepancies, contradictions. Even
the most direct and simple poet is forced into paradoxes far more often than we
think, if we are sufficiently alive to what he is doing.

But in dilating on the difficulties of the poet's task, I do not want to leave the
impression that it is a task which necessarily defeats him, or even that with his
method he may not win to a fine precision. To use Shakespeare's figure, he can

> with assays of bias
> By indirections find directions out.

Shakespeare had in mind the game of lawn bowls in which the bowl is distorted, a
distortion which allows the skillful player to bowl a curve. To elaborate the figure,
science makes use of the perfect sphere and its attack can be direct. The method of
art can, I believe, never be direct – is always indirect. But that does not mean that
the master of the game cannot place the bowl where he wants it. The serious
difficulties will only occur when he confuses his game with that of science and
mistakes the nature of his appropriate instrument. Mr Stuart Chase a few years ago,
with a touching naïveté, urged us to take the distortion out of the bowl – to treat
language like notation.

I have said that even the apparently simple and straightforward poet is forced into
paradoxes by the nature of his instrument. Seeing this, we should not be surprised to
find poets who consciously employ it to gain a compression and precision otherwise
unobtainable. Such a method, like any other, carries with it its own perils. But the
dangers are not overpowering; the poem is not predetermined to a shallow and
glittering sophistry. The method is an extension of the normal language of poetry,
not a perversion of it.

I should like to refer the reader to a concrete case.

Donne's "Canonization" ought to provide a sufficiently extreme instance. The
basic metaphor which underlies the poem (and which is reflected in the title) involves a sort of paradox. For the poet daringly treats profane love as if it were divine
love. The canonization is not that of a pair of holy anchorites who have renounced
the world and the flesh. The hermitage of each is the other's body; but they do
renounce the world, and so their title to sainthood is cunningly argued. The poem
then is a parody of Christian sainthood; but it is an intensely serious parody of a sort
that modern man, habituated as he is to an easy yes or no, can hardly understand. He
refuses to accept the paradox as a serious rhetorical device; and since he is able to
accept it only as a cheap trick, he is forced into this dilemma. Either: Donne does not
take love seriously; here he is merely sharpening his wit as a sort of mechanical
exercise. Or: Donne does not take sainthood seriously; here he is merely indulging in
a cynical and bawdy parody.

Neither account is true; a reading of the poem will show that Donne takes both
love and religion seriously; it will show, further, that the paradox is here his inevit-

able instrument. But to see this plainly will require a closer reading than most of us give to poetry.

The poem opens dramatically on a note of exasperation. The "you" whom the speaker addresses is not identified. We can imagine that it is a person, perhaps a friend, who is objecting to the speaker's love affair. At any rate, the person represents the practical world which regards love as a silly affectation. To use the metaphor on which the poem is built, the friend represents the secular world which the lovers have renounced.

Donne begins to suggest this metaphor in the first stanza by the contemptuous alternatives which he suggests to the friend:

> ... chide my palsie, or my gout,
> My five gray haires, or ruin'd fortune flout ...

The implications are: (1) All right, consider my love as an infirmity, as a disease, if you will, but confine yourself to my other infirmities, my palsy, my approaching old age, my ruined fortune. You stand a better chance of curing those; in chiding me for this one, you are simply wasting your time as well as mine. (2) Why don't you pay attention to your own welfare – go on and get wealth and honor for yourself. What should you care if I do give these up in pursuing my love?

The two main categories of secular success are neatly, and contemptuously epitomized in the line

> Or the Kings reall, or his stamped face ...

Cultivate the court and gaze at the king's face there, or, if you prefer, get into business and look at his face stamped on coins. But let me alone.

This conflict between the "real" world and the lover absorbed in the world of love runs through the poem; it dominates the second stanza in which the torments of love, so vivid to the lover, affect the real world not at all –

> What merchants ships have my sighs drown'd?

It is touched on in the fourth stanza in the contrast between the word "Chronicle" which suggests secular history with its pomp and magnificence, the history of kings and princes, and the word "sonnets" with its suggestions of trivial and precious intricacy. The conflict appears again in the last stanza, only to be resolved when the unworldly lovers, love's saints who have given up the world, paradoxically achieve a more intense world. But here the paradox is still contained in, and supported by, the dominant metaphor: so does the holy anchorite win a better world by giving up this one.

But before going on to discuss this development of the theme, it is important to see what else the second stanza does. For it is in this second stanza and the third, that the poet shifts the tone of the poem, modulating from the note of irritation with which the poem opens into the quite different tone with which it closes.

Donne accomplishes the modulation of tone by what may be called an analysis of love-metaphor. Here, as in many of his poems, he shows that he is thoroughly self-conscious about what he is doing. This second stanza, he fills with the conventionalized figures of the Petrarchan tradition: the wind of lovers' sighs, the floods of lovers' tears, etc. – extravagant figures with which the contemptuous secular friend might be expected to tease the lover. The implication is that the poet himself recognizes the absurdity of the Petrarchan love-metaphors. But what of it? The very absurdity of the jargon which lovers are expected to talk makes for his argument: their love, however absurd it may appear to the world, does no harm to the world. The practical friend need have no fears: there will still be wars to fight and lawsuits to argue.

The opening of the third stanza suggests that this vein of irony is to be maintained. The poet points out to his friend the infinite fund of such absurdities which can be applied to lovers:

> Call her one, mee another flye,
> We'are Tapers too, and at our owne cost die . . .

For that matter, the lovers can conjure up for themselves plenty of such fantastic comparisons: they know what the world thinks of them. But these figures of the third stanza are no longer the threadbare Petrarchan conventionalities; they have sharpness and bite. The last one, the likening of the lovers to the phoenix, is fully serious, and with it, the tone has shifted from ironic banter into a defiant but controlled tenderness.

The effect of the poet's implied awareness of the lovers' apparent madness is to cleanse and revivify metaphor; to indicate the sense in which the poet accepts it, and thus to prepare us for accepting seriously the fine and seriously intended metaphors which dominate the last two stanzas of the poem.

The opening line of the fourth stanza,

> Wee can dye by it, if not live by love,

achieves an effect of tenderness and deliberate resolution. The lovers are ready to die to the world; they are committed; they are not callow but confident. (The basic metaphor of the saint, one notices, is being carried on; the lovers in their renunciation of the world have something of the confident resolution of the saint. By the bye, the word "legend"

> . . . if unfit for tombes and hearse
> Our legend bee –

in Donne's time meant "the life of a saint.") The lovers are willing to forego the ponderous and stately chronicle and to accept the trifling and insubstantial "sonnet" instead; but then if the urn be well wrought it provides a finer memorial for one's ashes than does the pompous and grotesque monument. With the finely contemptuous, yet quiet phrase, "halfe-acre tombes," the world which the lovers reject expands into something gross and vulgar. But the figure works further; the pretty sonnets will not merely hold their ashes as a decent earthly memorial. Their legend, their story, will gain them canonization; and approved as love's saints, other lovers will invoke them.

In this last stanza, the theme receives a final complication. The lovers in rejecting life actually win to the most intense life. This paradox has been hinted at earlier in the phoenix metaphor. Here it receives a powerful dramatization. The lovers in becoming hermits, find that they have not lost the world, but have gained the world in each other, now a more intense, more meaningful world. Donne is not content to treat the lovers' discovery as something which comes to them passively, but rather as something which they actively achieve. They are like the saint, God's athlete:

> Who did the whole worlds soule contract, and drove
> Into the glasses of your eyes. ...

The image is that of a violent squeezing as of a powerful hand. And what do the lovers "drive" into each other's eyes? The "Countries, Townes," and "Courts," which they renounced in the first stanza of the poem. The unworldly lovers thus become the most "worldly" of all.

The tone with which the poem closes is one of triumphant achievement, but the tone is a development contributed to by various earlier elements. One of the more important elements which works toward our acceptance of the final paradox is the figure of the phoenix, which will bear a little further analysis.

The comparison of the lovers to the phoenix is very skillfully related to the two earlier comparisons, that in which the lovers are like burning tapers, and that in which they are like the eagle and the dove. The phoenix comparison gathers up both: the phoenix is a bird, and like the tapers, it burns. We have a selected series of items: the phoenix figure seems to come in a natural stream of association. "Call us what you will," the lover says, and rattles off in his desperation the first comparisons that occur to him. The comparison to the phoenix seems thus merely another outlandish one, the most outrageous of all. But it is this most fantastic one, stumbled over apparently in his haste, that the poet goes on to develop. It really describes the lovers best and justifies their renunciation. For the phoenix is not two but one, "we two being one, are it"; and it burns, not like the taper at its own cost, but to live again. Its death is life: "Wee dye and rise the same ..." The poet literally justifies the fantastic assertion. In the sixteenth and seventeenth centuries to "die" means to experience the consummation of the act of love. The lovers after the act are the same. Their love is not exhausted in mere lust. This is their title to canonization. Their love is like the phoenix.

I hope that I do not seem to juggle the meaning of die. The meaning that I have cited can be abundantly justified in the literature of the period; Shakespeare uses "die" in this sense; so does Dryden. Moreover, I do not think that I give it undue emphasis. The word is in a crucial position. On it is pivoted the transition to the next stanza,

> Wee can dye by it, if not live by love,
> And if unfit for tombes ...

Most important of all, the sexual submeaning of "die" does not contradict the other meanings: the poet is saying: "Our death is really a more intense life"; "We can afford to trade life (the world) for death (love), for that death is the consummation of life"; "After all, one does not expect to live by love, one expects, and wants, to die by it." But in the total passage he is also saying: "Because our love is not mundane, we can give up the world"; "Because our love is not merely lust, we can give up the other lusts, the lust for wealth and power"; "because," and this is said with an inflection of irony as by one who knows the world too well, "because our love can outlast its consummation, we are a minor miracle, we are love's saints." This passage

with its ironical tenderness and its realism feeds and supports the brilliant paradox
with which the poem closes.

There is one more factor in developing and sustaining the final effect. The poem
is an instance of the doctrine which it asserts; it is both the assertion and the realization of the assertion. The poet has actually before our eyes built within the song the
"pretty room" with which he says the lovers can be content. The poem itself is the
well-wrought urn which can hold the lovers' ashes and which will not suffer in
comparison with the prince's "halfe-acre tomb."

And how necessary are the paradoxes? Donne might have said directly, "Love in a
cottage is enough." "The Canonization" contains this admirable thesis, but it contains
a great deal more. He might have been as forthright as a later lyricist who wrote,
"We'll build a sweet little nest, / Somewhere out in the West, / And let the rest of the
world go by." He might even have imitated that more metaphysical lyric, which
maintains, "You're the cream in my coffee." "The Canonization" touches on all these
observations, but it goes beyond them, not merely in dignity, but in precision.

I submit that the only way by which the poet could say what "The Canonization"
says is by paradox. More direct methods may be tempting, but all of them enfeeble
and distort what is to be said. This statement may seem the less surprising when we
reflect on how many of the important things which the poet has to say have to be
said by means of paradox: most of the language of lovers is such – "The Canonization" is a good example; so is most of the language of religion – "He who would save
his life, must lose it"; "The last shall be first." Indeed, almost any insight important
enough to warrant a great poem apparently has to be stated in such terms. Deprived
of the character of paradox with its twin concomitants of irony and wonder, the
matter of Donne's poem unravels into "facts," biological, sociological, and economic.
What happens to Donne's lovers if we consider them "scientifically," without benefit
of the supernaturalism which the poet confers upon them? Well, what happens to
Shakespeare's lovers, for Shakespeare uses the basic metaphor of "The Canonization" in his *Romeo and Juliet*? In their first conversation, the lovers play with the
analogy between the lover and the pilgrim to the Holy Land. Juliet says:

> For saints have hands that pilgrims' hands do touch and palm to palm is holy palmers' kiss.

Considered scientifically, the lovers become Mr Aldous Huxley's animals, "quietly
sweating, palm to palm."

For us today, Donne's imagination seems obsessed with the problem of unity; the
sense in which the soul is united with God. Frequently, as we have seen, one type of
union becomes a metaphor for the other. It may not be too far-fetched to see both as
instances of, and metaphors for, the union which the creative imagination itself effects.
Coleridge has of course given us the classic description of its nature and power. It
"reveals itself in the balance or reconcilement of opposite or discordant qualities: of
sameness, with difference; of the general, with the concrete; the idea, with the image;
the individual, with the representative; the sense of novelty and freshness, with old
and familiar objects; a more than usual state of emotion, with more than usual order
…" It is a great and illuminating statement, but is a series of paradoxes. Apparently
Coleridge could describe the effect of the imagination in no other way.

Shakespeare, in one of his poems, has given a description that oddly parallels that
of Coleridge.

> Reason in it selfe confounded,
> Saw Division grow together,
> To themselves yet either neither,
> Simple were so well compounded.

I do not know what his "The Phoenix and the Turtle" celebrates. Perhaps it *was* written to honor the marriage of Sir John Salisbury and Ursula Stanley; or perhaps the Phoenix is Lucy, Countess of Bedford; or perhaps the poem is merely an essay on Platonic love. But the scholars themselves are so uncertain, that I think we will do little violence to established habits of thinking, if we boldly pre-empt the poem for our own purposes. Certainly the poem is an instance of that magic power which Coleridge sought to describe. I propose that we take it for a moment as a poem about that power;

> So they loved as love in twaine,
> Had the essence but in one,
> Two distincts, Division none,
> Number there in love was slaine.

> Hearts remote, yet not asunder;
> Distance and no space was seene,
> Twixt this Turtle and his Queene;
> But in them it were a wonder ...

> Propertie was thus appalled,
> That was the selfe was not the same;
> Single Natures double name,
> Neither two no one was called.

Precisely! The nature is single, one, unified. But the name is double, and today with our multiplication of sciences, it is multiple. If the poet is to be true to his poetry, he must call it neither two nor one: the paradox is his only solution. The difficulty has intensified since Shakespeare's day: the timid poet, when confronted with the problem of "Single Natures double name," has too often flunked it. A history of poetry from Dryden's time to our own might bear as its subtitle "The Half-Hearted Phoenix."

In Shakespeare's poem, Reason is "in it selfe confounded" at the union of the Phoenix and the Turtle; but it recovers to admit its own bankruptcy:

> Love hath Reason, Reason none,
> If what parts, can so remaine...

and it is Reason which goes on to utter the beautiful threnos with which the poem concludes:

> Beautie, Truth, and Raritie,
> Grace in all simplicitie,
> Here enclosed, in cinders lie.

> Death is now the Phoenix nest,
> And the Turtles loyall brest,
> To eternitie doth rest...

Truth may seeme, but cannot be,
Beautie bragge, but tis not she,
Truth and Beautie buried be.

To this urne let those repaire,
That are either true or faire,
For these dead Birds, sigh a prayer.

Having pre-empted the poem for our own purposes, it may not be too outrageous to go on to make one further observation. The urn to which we are summoned, the urn which holds the ashes of the phoenix, is like the well-wrought urn of Donne's "Canonization" which holds the phoenix-lovers' ashes: it is the poem itself. One is reminded of still another urn, Keats's Grecian urn, which contained for Keats, Truth and Beauty, as Shakespeare's urn encloses "Beautie, Truth, and Raritie." But there is a sense in which all such well-wrought urns contain the ashes of a Phoenix. The urns are not meant for memorial purposes only, though that often seems to be their chief significance to the professors of literature. The phoenix rises from its ashes; or ought to rise; but it will not arise for all our mere sifting and measuring the ashes, or testing them for their chemical content. We must be prepared to accept the paradox of the imagination itself; else "Beautie, Truth, and Raritie" remain enclosed in their cinders and we shall end with essential cinders, for all our pains.

Appendix

"THE CANONIZATION"
John Donne

For Godsake hold your tongue, and let me love,
    Or chide my palsie, or my gout,
My five gray haires, or ruin'd fortune flout,
    With wealth your state, your minde with Arts improve,
        Take you a course, get you a place,
        Observe his honour, or his grace,
Or the Kings reall, or his stamped face,
    Contemplate, what you will, approve,
    So you will let me love.

Alas, alas, who's injur'd by my love?
    What merchants ships have my sighs drown'd?
Who saies my teares have overflow'd his ground?
    When did my colds a forward spring remove?
        When did the heats which my veines fill
        Adde one more to the plaguie Bill?
Soldiers finde warres, and Lawyers finde out still
    Litigious men, which quarrels move,
    Though she and I do love.

Call us what you will, wee are made such by love;
    Call her one, mee another flye,

We'are Tapers too, and at our owne cost die,
    And wee in us finde the'Eagle and the Dove.
      The Phoenix ridle hath more wit
      By us, we two being one, are it.
So to one neutrall thing both sexes fit,
    Wee dye and rise the same, and prove
    Mysterious by this love.

Wee can dye by it, if not live by love,
    And if unfit for tombes and hearse
Our legend bee, it will be fit for verse;
    And if no peece of Chronicle wee prove,
      We'll build in sonnets pretty roomes;
      As well a well wrought urne becomes
The greatest ashes, as halfe-acre tombes,
    And by these hymnes, all shall approve
    Us *Canoniz'd* for Love:

And thus invoke us; You whom reverend love
    Made one anothers hermitage;
You, to whom love was peace, that now is rage;
    Who did the whole worlds soule contract, and drove
      Into the glasses of your eyes
      (So made such mirrors, and such spies,
That they did all to you epitomize,)
    Countries, Townes, Courts: Beg from above
    A patterne of your love!

CHAPTER 6

The Structure of the Concrete Universal

W. K. Wimsatt, Jr.

In this selection from *The Verbal Icon* (1954), a major statement of New Critical theory, W. K. Wimsatt argues that great literature embodies universals in concrete form. All great literature, therefore, is essentially metaphoric. It makes the general concrete and lends specific form to disembodied ideas. He concludes polemically that criticism should aim for the objective description of form – perhaps the central tenet of the New Criticism.

The central argument of this essay, concerning what I shall call the "concrete universal," proceeds from the observation that literary theorists have from early times to the present persisted in making statements which in their contexts seem to mean that a work of literary art is in some peculiar sense a very individual thing or a very universal thing or both. What that paradox can mean, or what important fact behind the paradox has been discerned by such various critics as Aristotle, Plotinus, Hegel, and Ransom, it will be the purpose of the essay to inquire, and by the inquiry to discuss not only a significant feature of metaphysical poetics from Aristotle to the present day but the relation between metaphysical poetics and more practical and specific rhetorical analysis. In the brief historical survey which forms one part of this essay it will not be my purpose to suggest that any of these writers meant exactly what I shall mean in later parts where I describe the structure of poetry. Yet throughout the essay I shall proceed on the theory not only that men have at different times used the same terms and have meant differently, but that they have sometimes used different terms and have meant the same or somewhat the same. In other words, I assume that there is continuity in the problems of criticism, and that a person who studies poetry today has a legitimate interest in what Plato said about poetry.

The view of common terms and their relations to classes of things from which I shall start is roughly that which one may read in the logic of J. S. Mill, a view which is not much different from the semantic view of today and for most purposes not much different from the Aristotelian and scholastic view. Mill speaks of the word and its denotation and connotation (the term, referent and reference, the sign, denotatum and designatum[1] of more recent terminologies). The denotation is the *it*, the individual thing or the aggregate of things to which the term may refer; the connotation is the *what*, the quality or classification inferred for the it, or implicitly predi-

cated by the application of the term or the giving of the name.* One main difference between all modern positivistic, nominalistic, and semantic systems and the scholastic and classical systems is that the older ones stress the similarity of the individuals denoted by the common term and hence the real universality of meaning, while the modern systems stress the differences in the individuals, the constant flux even of each individual in time and space and its kinetic structure, and hence infer only an approximate or nominal universality of meaning and a convenience rather than a truth in the use of general terms. A further difference lies in the view of how the individual is related to the various connotations of terms which may be applied to it. That is, to the question: What is it? the older writers seem to hold there is but one (essentially right) answer, while the moderns accept as many answers as there are classes to which the individual may be assigned (an indefinite number). The older writers speak of a proper essence or whatness of the individual, a quality which in some cases at least is that designated by the class name most commonly applied to the individual: a bench is a bench, essentially a bench, accidentally a heavy wooden object or something covered with green paint. "When we say *what* it is," observes Aristotle, "we do not say 'white,' or 'hot,' or 'three cubits long,' but 'a man' or 'a god.' "[2] And this view is also a habit scarcely avoidable in our own daily thinking, especially when we think of living things or of artifacts, things made by us or our fellows for a purpose. What is it? Bench, we think, is an adequate answer. An assemblage of sticks painted green, we consider freakish.

II

Whether or not one believes in universals, one may see the persistence in literary criticism of a theory that poetry presents the concrete and the universal, or the individual and the universal, or an object which in a mysterious and special way is both highly general and highly particular. The doctrine is implicit in Aristotle's two statements that poetry imitates action and that poetry tends to express the universal. It is implicit again at the end of the classic period in the mystic doctrine of Plotinus, who in his later writing on beauty reverses the Platonic objection that art does not know the ultimate reality of the forms. Plotinus arrives at the view that the artist by a kind of bypass of the inferior natural productions of the world soul reaches straight to the forms that lie behind in the divine intelligence.[3] Another version of the classic theory, with affinities for Plotinus, lies in the scholastic phrase *resplendentia formae*.

Cicero's account of how Zeuxis painted an ideal Helen from the five most beautiful virgins of Crotona is a typical development of Aristotelian theory, in effect the familiar neoclassic theory found in Du Fresnoy's *Art of Painting*, in the writings of Johnson, especially in the tulip passage in *Rasselas*, and in the *Discourses* and *Idlers* of Reynolds. The business of the poet is not to number the streaks of the tulip; it is to give us not the individual, but the species. The same thing is stated in a more complicated way by Kant in telling how the imagination constructs the "aesthetical normal Idea":

---

* The terms "denotation" and "connotation" are commonly and loosely used by literary critics to distinguish the dictionary meaning of a term (denotation) from the vaguer aura of suggestion (connotation). Both these are parts of the connotation in the logical sense.

> It is the image for the whole race, which floats among all the variously different
> intuitions of individuals, which nature takes as archetype in her productions of the
> same species, but which seems not to be fully reached in any individual case.[4]

And Hegel's account is as follows:

> The work of art is not only for the sensuous apprehension as sensuous object, but its
> position is of such a kind that as sensuous it is at the same time essentially addressed to
> the *mind*.[5]

> In comparison with the show or semblance of immediate sensuous existence or of
> historical narrative, the artistic semblance has the advantage that in itself it points
> beyond self, and refers us away from itself to something spiritual which it is meant to
> bring before the mind's eye.... The hard rind of nature and the common world give the
> mind more trouble in breaking through to the idea than do the products of art.[6]

The excellence of Shakespeare, says Coleridge, consists in a "union and interpenetration of the universal and particular." In one terminology or another this idea of a
concrete universal is found in most metaphysical aesthetic of the eighteenth and
nineteenth centuries.

A modern literary critic, John Crowe Ransom, speaks of the argument of a poem
(the universal) and a local texture or tissue of concrete irrelevance. Another literary
critic, Allen Tate, manipulating the logical terms "extension" and "intension," has
arrived at the concept of "tension" in poetry. "Extension," as logicians use the word,
is the range of individuals denoted by a term (denotation); "intension" is the total of
qualities connoted (connotation). In the ordinary or logical use of the terms, extension and intension are of inverse relationship – the wider the one, the shallower the
other. A poem, says Tate, as I interpret him, is a verbal structure which in some
peculiar way has both a wide extension and a deep intension.

Not all these theories of the concrete universal lay equal stress on the two sides of
the paradox, and it seems indicative of the vitality of the theory and of the truth
implicit in it that the two sides have been capable of exaggeration into antithetic
schools and theories of poetry. For Du Fresnoy, Johnson, and Reynolds poetry and
painting give the universal; the less said about the particulars the better. This is the
neoclassic theory, the illustrations of which we seek in Pope's *Essay on Man* or in
Johnson's *Ramblers*, where the ideas are moral and general and concerned with
"nature," "one clear, unchanged, and universal light." The opposite theory had
notable expression in England, a few years before Johnson wrote *Rasselas*, in Joseph
Warton's *Essay on Pope:*

> A minute and particular enumeration of circumstances judiciously selected, is what
> chiefly discriminates poetry from history, and renders the former, for that reason, a
> more close and faithful representation of nature than the latter.

And Blake's marginal criticism of Reynolds was: "THIS Man was Hired to Depress
art." "To Generalize is to be an Idiot. To Particularize is the Alone Distinction of
Merit. General Knowledges are those Knowledges that Idiots possess." "Sacrifice
the Parts: What becomes of the whole?" The line from Warton's *Essay* to Croce's
Aesthetic seems a straight and obvious one, from Thomson's specific descriptions of

flowers to the individual act of intuition-expression which is art – its opposite and enemy being the concept or generality.[7] The two views of art (two that can be held by different theorists about the same works of art) may be startlingly contrasted in the following passages about fictitious character – one a well known statement by Johnson, the other by the philosopher of the *élan vital*.

> [Shakespeare's] characters are not modified by the customs of particular places, unprac-tised by the rest of the world; by the peculiarities of studies or professions, which can operate but upon small numbers; or by the accidents of transient fashions or temporary opinions: they are the genuine progeny of common humanity, such as the world will always supply, and observation will always find. His persons act and speak by the influ-ence of those general passions and principles by which all minds are agitated, and the whole system of life is continued in motion. In the writings of other poets a character is too often an individual; in those of Shakespeare it is commonly a species.
>
> Hence it follows that art always aims at what is *individual*. What the artist fixes on his canvas is something he has seen at a certain spot, on a certain day, at a certain hour, with a colouring that will never be seen again. What the poet sings of is a certain mood which was his, and his alone, and which will never return. . . . Nothing could be more unique than the character of Hamlet. Though he may resemble other men in some respects, it is clearly not on that account that he interests us most.[8]

Other critics, notably the most ancient and the most modern, have tried to hold the extremes together. Neither of the extremes gives a good account of art and each leads out of art. The theory of particularity leads to individuality and originality (Edward Young was another eighteenth century Crocean), then to the idiosyncratic and the unintelligible and to the psychology of the author, which is not in the work of art and is not a standard for judgment. The theory of universality as it appears in Johnson and Reynolds leads to platitude and to a standard of material objectivity, the average tulip, the average human form, some sort of average.[9]

III

"Just representations of general nature," said Johnson, and it ought to be noted, though it perhaps rarely is, that two kinds of generality are involved, as indeed they are in the whole neoclassic theory of generality. There is the generality of logic or classification, of the more general as opposed to the more specific, "essential" gener-ality, one might say. And there is the generality of literal truth to nature, "existen-tial" generality. The assumption of neoclassic theory seems to be that these two must coincide. As a matter of fact they may and often do, but need not. Thus: "purple cow" is a more general (less specific) term and concept than "tan cow with a broken horn," yet the latter is more general or true to nature. We have, in short, realism or fantasy, and in either there may be various degrees of the specific or the general. We have *A Journal of the Plague Year* and *The Rambler, Gulliver's Travels* and *Rasselas*. The fact that there are a greater number of "vicissitudes" and "miscarriages" (favor-ite *Rambler* events) in human experience than plagues at London, that there are more tan cows than tan cows with broken horns, makes it true in a sense that a greater degree of essential generality involves a greater degree of existential. But in this sense the most generally reliable concept is simply that of "being."

The question is how a work of literature can be either more individual (unique) or more universal than other kinds of writing, or how it can combine the individual and the universal more than other kinds. Every description in words, so far as it is a direct description ("The barn is red and square") is a generalization. That is the nature of words. There are no individuals conveyed in words but only more or less specific generalizations, so that Johnson is right, though we have to ask him what degree of verbal generality makes art, and whether "tulip" is a better or more important generality than "tulip with ten streaks," or whether "beauty" is not in fact a much more impressive generality than "tulip." On the other hand, one cannot deny that in some sense there are more tulips in poetry than pure abstracted beauty. So that Bergson is right too; only we shall have to ask him what degree of specificity in verbal description makes art. And he can never claim complete verbal specificity or individuality, even for Hamlet.

If he could, if a work of literary art could be looked on as an artifact or concrete physical work, the paradox for the student of universals would return from the opposite direction even more forcibly – as it does in fact for theorists of graphic art. If Reynolds' picture "The Age of Innocence" presents a species or universal, what species does it present? Not an Aristotelian essence – "a man," or "humanity," nor even a more specific kind of being such as "womanhood." For then the picture would present the same universal as Reynolds' portrait of Mrs. Siddons as "The Tragic Muse," and all differences between "The Age of Innocence" and "The Tragic Muse" would be aesthetically irrelevant. Does the picture then present girl-hood, or barefoot girlhood, or barefoot girlhood in a white dress against a gloomy background? All three are equally valid universals (despite the fact that makeshift phrases are required to express two of them), and all three are presented by the picture. Or is it the title which tells us what universal is presented, "The Age of Innocence," and without the title should we not know the universal? The question will be: What in the individual work of art demands that we attribute to it one universal rather than another?

We may answer that for poetry it is the generalizing power of words already mentioned, and go on to decide that what distinguishes poetry from scientific or logical discourse is a degree of irrelevant concreteness in descriptive details. This is in effect what Ransom says in his doctrine of argument and local irrelevance, but it seems doubtful if the doctrine is not a version of the theory of ornamental metaphor. The argument, says Ransom, is the prose or scientific meaning, what the poem has in common with other kinds of writing. The irrelevance is a texture of concreteness which does not contribute anything to the argument but is somehow enjoyable or valuable for its own sake, the vehicle of a metaphor which one boards heedless of where it runs, whether crosstown or downtown – just for the ride. So Ransom nurses and refines the argument, and on one page he makes the remark that the poet searches for "suitability" in his particular phrases, and by suitability Ransom means "the propriety which consists in their denoting the particularity which really belongs to the logical object."[10] But the difference between "propriety" and relevance in such a context is not easy to see. And relevance is logic. The fact is that all concrete illustration has about it something of the irrelevant. An apple falling from a tree illustrates gravity, but apple and tree are irrelevant to the pure theory of gravity. It may be that what happens in a poem is that the apple and the tree are somehow made more than usually relevant.

Such a theory, not that of Johnson and Reynolds, not that of Warton and Bergson, not quite that of Ransom, is what I would suggest – yet less as a novelty than as something already widely implicit in recent poetical analyses and exegeses, in those of Empson, for instance, Tate, Blackmur, or Brooks. If a work of literature is not in a simple sense either more individual or more universal than other kinds of writing, it may yet be such an individual or such a complex of meaning that it has a special relation to the world of universals. Some acute remarks on this subject were made by Ruskin in a chapter of *Modern Painters* neglected today perhaps because of its distasteful ingredient of "noble emotion." Poetry, says Ruskin in criticizing Reynolds' *Idlers*, is not distinguished from history by the omission of details, nor for that matter by the mere addition of details. "There must be something either in the nature of the details themselves, or the method of using them, which invests them with poetical power." Their nature, one may add, as assumed through their relation to one another, a relation which may also be called the method of using them. The poetic character of details consists not in what they say directly and explicitly (as if roses and moonlight were poetic) but in what by their arrangement they *show* implicitly.

IV

"One," observes Ben Jonson, thinking of literature, "is considerable two waies: either, as it is only separate, and by it self: or as being compos'd of many parts it beginnes to be one as those parts grow or are wrought together."[11] A literary work of art is a complex of detail (an artifact, if we may be allowed that metaphor for what is only a verbal object), a composition so complicated of human values that its interpretation is dictated by the understanding of it, and so complicated as to seem in the highest degree individual – a concrete universal. We are accustomed to being told, for example, that what makes a character in fiction or drama vital is a certain fullness or rotundity: that the character has many sides. Thus E. M. Forster:

> We may divide characters into flat and round. Flat characters were called "humours" in the seventeenth century, and are sometimes called types, and sometimes caricatures. In their purest form, they are constructed round a single idea or quality: when there is more than one factor in them, we get the beginning of the curve towards the round. The really flat character can be expressed in one sentence such as "I never will desert Mr. Micawber."

It remains to be said, however, that the many traits of the round character (if indeed it is one character and not a hodgepodge) are harmonized or unified, and that if this is so, then all the traits are chosen by a principle, just as are the traits of the flat character. Yet it cannot be that the difference between the round and flat character is simply numerical; the difference cannot be merely that the presiding principle is illustrated by more examples in the round character. Something further must be supposed – a special interrelation in the traits of the round character. Bobadil is an example of the *miles gloriosus*, a flat humour. He swears by "The foot of Pharaoh," takes tobacco, borrows money from his landlady, is found lying on a bench fully dressed with a hangover, brags about his feats at the siege of Strigonium, beats Cob, a poor water carrier, and so on. It is possible that he has numerically as many traits as Falstaff, one of the most vital of all characters. But one of the differences between Falstaff and Bobadil is that the things Falstaff says are funny; the things Bobadil says are not. Compared to Falstaff, Bobadil is unconscious, an opaque butt. There is the vitality of consciousness in Falstaff. And further there is the crowning complexity of self-consciousness. The fact that Morgann could devote a book to arguing that Falstaff is not a coward, that lately Professor Wilson has argued that at Gadshill Falstaff may exhibit, " 'all the common symptoms of the malady' of cowardice" and at the same time persuade the audience that he has " 'never once lost his self-possession,' " the fact that one can conceive that Falstaff in the Gadshill running-away scene really knows that his assailants are the Prince and Poins – all this shows that in Falstaff there is a kind of interrelation among his attributes, his cowardice, his wit, his debauchery, his presumption, that makes them in a special way an organic harmony. He is a rounded character not only in the sense that he is gross (a fact which may have tempted critics to speak of a rounded character) or in the sense that he is a bigger bundle of attributes, stuffed more full, than Bobadil or Ralph Roister Doister; but in the sense that his attributes make a circuit and connection. A kind of awareness of self (a high and human characteristic), with a pleasure in the fact, is perhaps the central principle which instead of simplifying the attributes gives each one a special function in the whole, a double or reflex value. Falstaff or such a character of self-conscious "infinite variety"[*] as Cleopatra are concrete universals because they have no class names, only their own proper ones, yet are structures of such precise variety and centrality that each demands a special interpretation in the realm of human values.

Character is one type of concrete universal; there are other types, as many perhaps as the central terms of criticism; but most can be learned I believe by examination of metaphor – the structure most characteristic of concentrated poetry. The language of poets, said Shelley, "is vitally metaphorical: that is, it marks the before unapprehended relations of things and perpetuates their apprehension." Wordsworth spoke of the abstracting and modifying powers of the imagination. Aristotle said that the greatest thing was the use of metaphor, because it meant an eye for resemblances. Even the simplest form of metaphor or simile ("My love is like a red, red rose") presents us with a special and creative, in fact a concrete, kind of abstraction different from that of science. For behind a metaphor lies a resemblance between two classes, and hence a more general third class. This class is unnamed and most likely remains unnamed and is apprehended only through the metaphor. It is a new conception for which there is no other expression. Keats discovering Homer is like a traveler in the realms of gold, like an astronomer who discovers a planet, like Cortez gazing at the Pacific. The title of the sonnet, "On First Looking into Chapman's Homer," seems to furnish not so much the subject of the poem as a fourth member of a central metaphor, the real subject of the poem being an abstraction, a certain kind of thrill in discovering, for which there is no name and no other description, only the four members of the metaphor pointing, as to the center of their pattern. The point of the poem seems to lie outside both vehicle and tenor.

To take a more complicated instance, Wordsworth's "Solitary Reaper" has the same basic metaphorical structure, the girl alone reaping and singing, and the two bird images, the nightingale in Arabian sands and the cuckoo among the Hebrides,

---

[*] I do not mean that self-consciousness is the only principle of complexity in character, yet a considerable degree of it would appear to be a requisite for poetic interest.

the three figures serving the parallel or metaphorical function of bringing out the abstraction of loneliness, remoteness, mysterious charm in the singing. But there is also a kind of third-dimensional significance, in the fact that one bird is far out in the northern sea, the other far off in southern sands, a fact which is not part of the comparison between the birds and the girl. By an implication cutting across the plane of logic of the metaphor, the girl and the two birds suggest extension in space, universality, and world communication – an effect supported by other details of the poem such as the overflowing of the vale profound, the mystery of the Erse song, the bearing of the song away in the witness' heart, the past and future themes which the girl may be singing. Thus a central abstraction is created, of communication, telepathy in solitude, the prophetic soul of the wide world dreaming on things to come – an abstraction which is the effect not wholly of the metaphor elaborated logically (in a metaphysical way) but of a working on two axes, by association rather than by logic, by a three-dimensional complexity of structure.

To take yet a third instance, metaphoric structure may appear where we are less likely to realize it explicitly – in poetic narratives, for example, elliptically concealed in the more obvious narrative outlines. "I can bring you," writes Max Eastman, "examples of diction that is metrical but not metaphoric – a great part of the popular ballads, for example – and you can hardly deny that they too are poetic." But the best story poems may be analyzed, I believe, as metaphors without expressed tenors, as symbols which speak for themselves. "La Belle Dame Sans Merci," for example (if a literary ballad may be taken), is about a knight, by profession a man of action, but sensitive, like the lily and the rose, and about a faery lady with wild, wild eyes. At a more abstract level, it is about the loss of self in the mysterious lure of beauty – whether woman, poetry, or poppy. It sings the irretrievable departure from practical normality (the squirrel's granary is full), the wan isolation after ecstasy. Each reader will experience the poem at his own level of experience or at several. A good story poem is like a stone thrown into a pond, into our minds, where ever widening concentric circles of meaning go out – and this because of the structure of the story.

"A poem should not mean but be." It is an epigram worth quoting in every essay on poetry. And the poet "nothing affirmeth, and therefore never lieth." "Sit quidvis," said Horace, "simplex dumtaxat et unum." It seems almost the reverse of the truth. "Complex dumtaxat et unum" would be better: Every real poem is a complex poem, and only in virtue of its complexity does it have artistic unity. A newspaper poem by Edgar Guest* does not have this kind of unity, but only the unity of an abstractly stated sentiment.

The principle is expressed by Aristotle when he says that beauty is based on unity in variety, and by Coleridge when he says that "The Beautiful, contemplated in its

---

* A reader whose judgment I esteem tells me that such a name appears in a serious discussion of poetics anomalously and in bad taste. I have allowed it to remain (in preference to some more dignified name of mediocrity) precisely because I wish to insist on the existence of badness in poetry and so to establish an antithetic point of reference for the discussion of goodness. Relativistic argument often creates an illusion in its own favor by moving steadily in a realm of great and nearly great art. See, for example, George Boas, *A Primer for Critics* (Baltimore, 1937), where a cartoon by Daumier appears toward the end as a startling approach to the vulgar. The purpose of my essay is not judicial but theoretical, that is, not to exhibit original discoveries in taste, but to show the relationship between examples acknowledged to lie in the realms of the good and the bad.

essentials, that is, in *kind* and not in *degree*, is that in which the *many*, still seen as many becomes one," and that a work of art is "rich in proportion to the variety of parts which it holds in unity."

V

It is usually easier to show how poetry works than to show why anyone should want it to work in a given way. Rhetorical analysis of poetry has always tended to separate from evaluation, technique from worth. The structure of poems as concrete and universal is the principle by which the critic can try to keep the two together. If it be granted that the "subject matter" of poetry is in a broad sense the moral realm, human actions as good or bad, with all their associated feelings, all the thought and imagination that goes with happiness and suffering (if poetry submits "the shews of things to the desires of the Mind"), then the rhetorical structure of the concrete universal, the complexity and unity of the poem, is also its maturity or sophistication or richness or depth, and hence its value. Complexity of form is sophistication of content. The unity and maturity of good poems are two sides of the same thing. The kind of unity which we look for and find in poetry is attained only through a degree of complexity in design which itself involves maturity and richness. For a visual diagram of the metaphysics of poetry one might write vertically the word complexity, a column, and give it a head with Janus faces, one looking in the rhetorical direction, unity, and the other in the axiological, maturity.

A final point to be made is that a criticism of structure and of value is an objective criticism. It rests on facts of human psychology (as that a man may love a woman so well as to give up empires), facts, which though psychological, yet are so well acknowledged as to lie in the realm of what may be called public psychology – a realm which one should distinguish from the private realm of the author's psychology and from the equally private realm of the individual reader's psychology (the vivid pictures which poetry or stories are supposed to create in the imagination, or the venerable action of catharsis – all that poetry is said to *do* rather than to *be*). Such a criticism, again, is objective and absolute, as distinguished from the relative criticism of idiom and period. I mean that this criticism will notice that Pope is different from Shakespeare, but will notice even more attentively that Shakespeare is different from Taylor the Water Poet and Pope different from Sir Richard Blackmore. Such a criticism will be interested to analyze the latter two differences and see what these differences have in common and what Shakespeare and Pope have in common, and it will not despair of describing that similarity (that formula or character of great poetry) even though the terms be abstract and difficult. Or, if we are told that there is no universal agreement about what is good – that Pope has not been steadily held in esteem, that Shakespeare has been considered a barbarian, the objective analyst of structures can at least say (and it seems much to say) that he is describing a class of poems, those which through a peculiar complexity possess unity and maturity and in a special way can be called both individual and universal. Among all recorded "poems," this class is of a relative rarity, and further this class will be found in an impressive way to coincide with those poems which have by some body of critics, some age of educated readers, been called great.

The function of the objective critic is by approximate descriptions of poems, or multiple restatements of their meaning, to aid other readers to come to an intuitive and full realization of poems themselves and hence to know good poems and distinguish them from bad ones. It is of course impossible to tell all about a poem in other words. Croce tells us, as we should expect him to, of the "impossibility of ever rendering in logical terms the full effect of any poetry or of other artistic work." "Criticism, nevertheless," he tells us, "performs its own office, which is to discern and to point out exactly where lies the poetical motive and to formulate the divisions which aid in distinguishing what is proper to every work."[12] The situation is something like this: In each poem there is something (an individual intuition – or a concept) which can never be expressed in other terms. It is like the square root of two or like pi, which cannot be expressed by rational numbers, but only as their *limit*. Criticism of poetry is like 1.414... or 3.1416 ..., not all it would be, yet all that can be had and very useful.

Notes

1 Charles W. Morris, "Esthetics and the Theory of Signs," in *Journal of Unified Science*, VIII (1939), 131–50.

2 *Metaphysics*, VII (Z), 1 (1028). Cp. Mortimer J. Adler, *The Problem of Species* (New York, 1940), 24–5.

3 "The arts are not to be slighted on the ground that they create by imitation of natural objects; for, to begin with, these natural objects are themselves imitations; then, we must recognize that they give no bare reproduction of the thing seen but go back to the ideas from which Nature itself derives." *Enneads*, V, viii, 1, *Plotinus – The Fifth Ennead*, trans. Stephen MacKenna (London, 1926), 74.

4 *Kant's Critique of Judgment*, trans. J. H. Bernard (London, 1931), 88–9.

5 *The Introduction to Hegel's Philosophy of Fine Art*, trans. Bernard Bosanquet (London, 1886), 67. Cf. Walter T. Stace, *The Meaning of Beauty* (London, 1929), 41.

6 *The Introduction to Hegel's Philosophy of Fine Art*, 16. Cf. pp. 72–8, 133–7.

7 It is true that Croce has protested: "Ce qu'on démontre comme inconciliable avec le principe de la pure intuition, ce n'est pas l'universalité, mais la valeur intellectualiste et transcendante donnée dans l'art à l'universalité, sous la forme de l'allégorie ou du symbole." "Le Caractère de Totalité de l'Expression Artistique," in *Bréviaire d'Esthétique*, trans. Georges Bourgin (Paris, 1923), 170. But the main drift of Croce's aesthetic, in being against conceptualization, is radically against the universal.

8 Henri Bergson, *Laughter, An Essay on the Meaning of the Comic* (New York, 1928), 161–2.

9 Roger Fry in his Introduction to Reynolds' *Third Discourse* argues that the species presented in painting are not those of the natural, but those of the social world, as king, knight, beggar. *Discourses*, ed. Roger Fry (London, 1905), 46. And a modern critic of sculpture, R. H. Wilenski, offers what is perhaps the last retreat of the doctrine of universals in visual art: not man, flower, or animal but the forms of life analogous in (that is, common to) man, flower, and animal are abstracted and presented pure in sculptural art. R. H. Wilenski, *The Meaning of Modern Sculpture* (London, 1939), 159–60.

10 *The New Criticism* (Norfolk, 1941), 315. Maritain, coming from a different direction, arrives at somewhat the same poser. "If it pleases a futurist to paint a lady with only one eye, or a quarter of an eye, nobody denies him such a right: all one is entitled to require – and here is the whole problem – is that the quarter eye is all the lady needs *in the given case*." *Art and Scholasticism* (New York, 1937), 28. Here indeed is the whole problem. Aristotle said, "Not to know that a hind has no horns is a less serious matter than to paint it inartistically." *Poetics*, XXV, 5.

11 *Discoveries*, ed. Maurice Castelain (Paris, 1906), 139. Jonson translates from Heinsius.

12 *Ariosto, Shakespeare and Corneille* (London, 1920), 146–7.

PART TWO

Structuralism, Linguistics, Narratology

CHAPTER 1

Introduction: The Implied Order: Structuralism

Julie Rivkin and Michael Ryan

Structuralism begins with the work of Ferdinand de Saussure, an early twentieth-century Swiss linguist who argued that language should be studied as if it were frozen in time and cut transversely like a leaf. What results is a vision of the entire language system as it exists in implied or unconscious fashion in any spoken utterance. Utterances are merely the manifestation of the rules of the system that lend order to the heterogeneity of language. This notion of an implied order is central to the Structuralist undertaking, as it spreads out from linguistics to anthropology and philosophy and to literary criticism through the course of the twentieth century.

Structuralism derives both historically and logically from Formalism. Roman Jakobson, one of the original Formalists, was also, by virtue of emigration, one of the first major influences on French Structuralism, which flourished from the 1950s through the 1960s. The scientific impulse evident in Formalism also finds its fulfillment in the Structuralist emphasis on the task of adducing the internal system or order of linguistic, cultural, and literary phenomena.

From Jakobson, early Structuralists such as anthropologist Claude Lévi-Strauss learned of Saussure's ideas about language. Lévi-Strauss began to see that culture, like language, is a system characterized by an internal order of interconnected parts that obey certain rules of operation. A structure is both like a skeleton and like a genetic code in that it is the principle of stability and coherence in any cultural system, while also being the principle of action that allows the culture to exist in time as a living thing. After meeting Jakobson in New York during their mutual exile during World War II, Lévi-Strauss began to think about culture as a form of communication like language. What was communicated between cultural participants were tokens, like words, that enacted and reproduced the basic assumptions and rules of the culture. In his analysis of kinship systems, *Elementary Structures of Kinship* (1949), Lévi-Strauss argued that primitive cultures maintain peace between social groups by using women as tokens in marriage. Such inter-familial and inter-tribal marriages function as a form of communication and create personal or family relations that work to diminish the possibility of conflict. Lévi-Strauss went on to conduct famous studies of myths that noticed, in the same manner as Russian critic Vladimir Propp's path-breaking work on folk tales, that such myths, despite their heterogeneity and multiplicity, told the same kernel narratives. Those narratives tended to work to resolve contradictions in the culture, such as that between a conception of humans as plant-growing and peaceful and humans as hunters and warriors. The many versions of the Oedipus myth, for example, all tell a story about the conflict between the idea that humans emerge from the earth ("Oedipus" means lame in the foot) and the idea that they are born from other humans (hence the sanctity of the incest taboo). The tale's function is to provide a mediation to the contradiction between nature (sexuality) and culture (rule against incest) by forbidding natural sex between family members.

The second major contribution that Saussure made to Structuralism was his conception of the linguistic sign. Words, he noted, are signs, and linguistics rightly belongs to another discipline called semiology, which would study the way signs, including words, operate. Words are signs in that they consist of two faces or sides – the signifier, which is the phonic component, and the signified, which is the ideational component. A word is both a sound and an idea or image of its referent. Alongside and often in conjunction with the Structural anthropology of Lévi-Strauss, there developed in France in the 1950s, especially in the work of Roland Barthes, a concern with the study of the semiological dimension of literature and culture. A work of literature, Barthes noted, is, after all, nothing but an assemblage of signs that function in certain ways to create meaning. In studying culture, Barthes noticed that films, commodities, events, and images are lent meaning by their association with certain signs. Barthes went on in the 1960s to become one of the major practitioners of semiological analysis in literature. His most important books are *Writing Degree Zero* (1953), *Mythologies* (1957), *On Racine* (1963), *Critical Essays* (1964), *Elements of Semiology* (1965), and *S/Z* (1970).

A direct link between French Structuralism and Russian Formalism was established in 1965 with the publication of Tzvetan Todorov's collected translations of the Formalists' *Theory of Literature*. Todorov's work is associated most often with the study of narrative, and he helped formulate the Structuralist conception of narrative as the common element of organization among diverse examples. In his study of Henry James's tales, for example ("The Structural Analysis of Narrative" in *Poetics of Prose* [1971]), he contends that they all revolve around a missing center, a point of desire that is sought but that never appears. The study of narrative (or narratology, as it is also called) is one of the most abiding strands of Structuralist thinking.

By the mid-1960s, Structuralism was the dominant school of thought in French intellectual life, and its influence is evident in the work of historian Michel Foucault, psychoanalyst Jacques Lacan, literary critic Julia Kristeva, and philosopher Louis Althusser. Foucault's work at that time included *The Order of Things: An Archeology of the Human Sciences* (*Les Mots et les choses*, 1966), *The Archeology of Knowledge* (1969), and *The Order of Discourse* (1970). Foucault is important for drawing attention to the role of language in the conceptual frameworks or "epistemes" that are used in different epochs for understanding the world. Words provide us with maps for assigning order to nature and to society. Foucault notices that what counts as knowledge changes with time, and with each change, the place of language in knowledge is also modified. In one era, the world is considered to be a site of analogies between levels, but in a later epoch, the world is broken down into discrete parts that are then organized into taxonomies.

Foucault is important as well for developing the idea of discourse and of discourse formation. A discursive formation is a coherent group of assumptions and language practices that applies to one region of knowledge, or expresses the beliefs of a social group, or articulates rules and ideals regarding kinds of behavior. Modern science is a discursive formation in that it is characterized both by a list of discoveries and a body of knowledge, but also by recognized and widely accepted linguistic forms for describing the methods and findings of science. When we get to feminism, you will encounter feminists who speak of the "discourse of patriarchy," the set of ways of thinking and of practicing language that lend coherence to male rule in society. They also describe the discourse of advice books that educated women prior to the modern era in how to behave "properly" as women, that is, in how to be "chaste, silent, and obedient."

Foucault's work draws attention to the fact that many assumptions in a culture are maintained by language practices that comprise a common tool both for knowing the world and for constructing it. By construction here, we mean the translation of physical realities into discursive realities. The "dominant discourse" of the US, for example, is one that lends great privilege to the "freedom" of the individual. The physical reality of modern life is hemmed in and constrained in many complex ways, from laws that allow police to search automobiles without cause to an economic system that requires enormous amounts of time spent at the workplace under some-one else's control. Nevertheless, this physical and institutional reality is rendered discursively in the American lexicon as "freedom." Just as all women were far from being chaste, silent, and obedient, despite what the dominant discourse of the advice or courtesy books mandated, so also most Americans have limited access to the kind of pure freedom the dominant term seems to imply. What Foucault noted was that the world we live in is shaped as much by language as by knowledge or perception. Indeed, according to him, knowledge and perception always occur through the medi-ation of language. We would not be able to know anything if we were not able to order the world linguistically in certain ways.

In his later work, Foucault explores the way sexuality is characterized over history in different discourses of the body (*History of Sexuality* [1976]). And he examines the change in regimes of social discipline from medieval times to modern times (*Discipline and Punish* [1975]).

CHAPTER 2

The Linguistic Foundation

Jonathan Culler

Jonathan Culler's *Structuralist Poetics* (1975) was one of the first complete introductions in English to the French structuralist movement in literary criticism. In this selection, he proposes an analogy between the structuralist description of how language operates and the rules and conventions that make up human culture.

The notion that linguistics might be useful in studying other cultural phenomena is based on two fundamental insights: first, that social and cultural phenomena are not simply material objects or events but objects or events with meaning, and hence signs; and second, that they do not have essences but are defined by a network of relations, both internal and external. Stress may fall on one or the other of these propositions – it would be in these terms, for example, that one might try to distinguish semiology and structuralism – but in fact the two are inseparable, for in studying signs one must investigate the system of relations that enables meaning to be produced and, reciprocally, one can only determine what are the pertinent relations among items by considering them as signs.

Structuralism is thus based, in the first instance, on the realization that if human actions or productions have a meaning there must be an underlying system of distinctions and conventions which makes this meaning possible. Confronted with a marriage ceremony or a game of football, for example, an observer from a culture where these did not exist could present an objective description of the actions which took place, but he would be unable to grasp their meaning and so would not be treating them as social or cultural phenomena. The actions are meaningful only with respect to a set of institutional conventions. Wherever there are two posts one can kick a ball between them but one can score a goal only within a certain institutionalized framework. As Lévi-Strauss says in his "Introduction à l'œuvre de Marcel Mauss," "particular actions of individuals are never symbolic in themselves; they are the elements out of which is constructed a symbolic system, which must be collective" (p. xvi). The cultural meaning of any particular act or object is determined by a whole system of constitutive rules: rules which do not regulate behavior so much as create the possibility of particular forms of behavior. The rules of English enable sequences of sound to have meaning; they make it possible to utter grammatical or ungrammatical sentences. And analogously, various social rules make it possible to marry, to score a goal, to write a poem, to be impolite. It is in this sense that a culture is composed of a set of symbolic systems. . . .

To claim that cultural systems may with profit be treated as "languages" is to suggest that one will understand them better if one discusses them in terms provided by linguistics and analyzes them according to procedures used by linguists. In fact, the range of concepts and methods which structuralists have found useful is fairly restricted and only some half-dozen linguists could qualify as seminal influences. The first, of course, is Ferdinand de Saussure, who waded into the heterogeneous mass of linguistic phenomena and, recognizing that progress would be possible only if one isolated a suitable object for study, distinguished between speech acts (*la parole*) and the system of a language (*la langue*). The latter is the proper object of linguistics. Following Saussure's example and concentrating on the system which underlies speech sounds, members of the Prague linguistic circle – particularly Jakobson and Trubetzkoy – effected what Lévi-Strauss called the "phonological revolution" and provided what was to later structuralists the clearest model of linguistic method. Distinguishing between the study of actual speech sounds (phonetics) and the investigation of those aspects of sound that are functional in a particular language (phonology), Trubetzkoy argued that "phonology should investigate which phonic differences are linked, in the language under consideration, with differences of meaning, how these differentiating elements or marks are related to one another, and according to what rules they combine to form words and phrases" (*Principes de phonologie*, pp. 11–12). Phonology was important for structuralists because it showed the systematic nature of the most familiar phenomena, distinguished between the system and its realization and concentrated not on the substantive characteristics of individual phenomena but on abstract differential features which could be defined in relational terms....

The basic distinction on which modern linguistics rests, and which is equally crucial to the structuralist enterprise in other fields, is Saussure's isolation of *langue* from *parole*. The former is a system, an institution, a set of interpersonal rules and norms, while the latter comprises the actual manifestations of the system in speech and writing. It is, of course, easy to confuse the system with its manifestations, to think of English as the set of English utterances. But to learn English is not to memorize a set of utterances; it is to master a system of rules and norms which make it possible to produce and understand utterances. To know English is to have assimilated the system of the language. And the linguist's task is not to study utterances for their own sake; they are of interest to him only in so far as they provide evidence about the nature of the underlying system, the English language.

Within linguistics itself there are disagreements about what precisely belongs to *langue* and what to *parole*: whether, for example, an account of the linguistic system should specify the acoustic and articulatory features that distinguish one phoneme from another (/p/ is "voiceless" and /b/ "voiced"), or whether such features as "voiced" and "voiceless" should be thought of as the manifestations in *parole* of what, in *la langue* itself, is a purely formal and abstract distinction. Such debates need not concern the structuralist, except in so far as they indicate that structure can be defined at various levels of abstraction.[1] What does concern him is a pair of distinctions which the differentiation of *langue* from *parole* is designed to cover between rule and behavior and between the functional and the nonfunctional.

The distinction between rule and behavior is crucial to any study concerned with the production or communication of meaning. In investigating physical events one may formulate laws which are nothing other than direct summaries of behavior, but in the case of social and cultural phenomena the rule is always at some distance from actual behavior and that gap is a space of potential meaning. The instituting of the simplest rule, such as "members of this club will not step on cracks in the pavement," may in some cases determine behavior but indubitably determines meaning: the placing of one's feet on the pavement, which formerly had no meaning, now signifies either compliance with or deviation from the rule and hence an attitude towards the club and its authority. In social and cultural systems behavior may deviate frequently and considerably from the norm without impugning the existence of the norm. Many promises are in fact broken, but there still exists a rule in the system of moral concepts that promises should be kept; though of course if one never kept any promises doubts might arise as to whether one understood the institution of promising and had assimilated its rules.

Note

1   Cf. N. C. Spence, "A Hardy Perennial: The Problem of *la langue* and *la parole*," *Archivum linguisticum* 9 (1957), pp. 1–27.

CHAPTER 3

Course in General Linguistics

Ferdinand de Saussure

Assembled by students from class notes and published in 1916, Ferdinand de Saussure's *Course in General Linguistics* quickly became one of the most influential books of the twentieth century. It inspired a wide range of work in anthropology, sociology, philosophy, and literary criticism that is usually referred to as Structuralism.

In separating language from speaking we are at the same time separating: (1) what is social from what is individual; and (2) what is essential from what is accessory and more or less accidental.

Language is not a function of the speaker; it is a product that is passively assimilated by the individual. It never requires premeditation, and reflection enters in only for the purpose of classification, which we shall take up later.

Speaking, on the contrary, is an individual act. It is willful and intellectual. Within the act, we should distinguish between: (1) the combinations by which the speaker uses the language code for expressing his own thought; and (2) the psychophysical mechanism that allows him to exeriorize those combinations.

To summarize, these are the characteristics of language:

(1) Language is a well-defined object in the heterogeneous mass of speech facts. It can be localized in the limited segment of the speaking-circuit where an auditory image becomes associated with a concept. It is the social side of speech, outside the individual who can never create nor modify it by himself; it exists only by virtue of a sort of contract signed by the members of a community. Moreover, the individual must always serve an apprenticeship in order to learn the functioning of language; a child assimilates it only gradually. It is such a distinct thing that a man deprived of the use of speaking retains it provided that he understands the vocal signs that he hears.

(2) Language, unlike speaking, is something that we can study separately. Although dead languages are no longer spoken, we can easily assimilate their linguistic organisms. We can dispense with the other elements of speech; indeed, the science of language is possible only if the other elements are excluded.

(3) Whereas speech is heterogeneous, language, as defined, is homogeneous. It is a system of signs in which the only essential thing is the union of meanings and sound-images, and in which both parts of the sign are psychological.

(4) Language is concrete, no less so than speaking; and this is a help in our study of it. Linguistic signs, though basically psychological, are not abstractions; associations which bear the stamp of collective approval – and which added together constitute language – are realities that have their seat in the brain.

We have just seen that language is a social institution; but several features set it apart from other political, legal, etc. institutions.

We must call in a new type of facts in order to illuminate the special nature of language.

Language is a system of signs that express ideas, and is therefore comparable to a system of writing, the alphabet of deaf-mutes, symbolic rites, polite formulas, military signals, etc. But it is the most important of all these systems.

A science that studies the life of signs within society is conceivable; it would be a part of social psychology and consequently of general psychology; I shall call it *semiology* (from Greek *semeion*, "sign"). Semiology would show what constitutes signs, what laws govern them. Since the science does not yet exist, no one can say what it would be; but it has a right to existence, a place started out in advance. Linguistics is only a part of the general science of semiology; the laws discovered by semiology will be applicable to linguistics, and the latter will circumscribe a well-defined area within the mass of anthropological facts . . .

Sign, Signified, Signifier

Some people regard language, when reduced to its elements, as a naming-process only – a list of words, each corresponding to the thing that it names. For example:

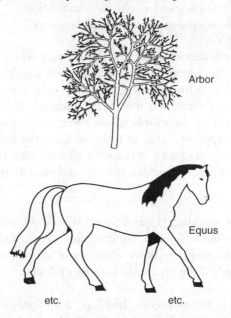

Arbor

Equus

etc.   etc.

This conception is open to criticism at several points. It assumes that ready-made ideas exist before words . . . ; it does not tell us whether a name is vocal or psychological in nature (*arbor*, for instance, can be considered from either viewpoint); finally, it lets us assume that the linking of a name and a thing is a very simple operation – an assumption that is anything but true. But this rather naive approach can bring us near the truth by showing us that the linguistic unit is a double entity, one formed by the associating of two terms.

We have seen in considering the speaking-circuit that both terms involved in the linguistic sign are psychological and are united in the brain by an associative bond. This point must be emphasized. The linguistic sign unites, not a thing and a name, but a concept and a sound-image.[1] The latter is not the material sound, a purely physical thing, but the psychological imprint of the sound, the impression that it makes on our senses. The sound-image is sensory, and if I happen to call it "material," it is only in that sense, and by way of opposing it to the other term of the association, the concept, which is generally more abstract.

The psychological character of our sound-images becomes apparent when we observe our own speech. Without moving our lips or tongue, we can talk to ourselves or recite mentally a selection of verse. Because we regard the words of our language as sound-images, we must avoid speaking of the "phonemes" that make up the words. This term, which suggests vocal activity, is applicable to the spoken word only, to the realization of the inner image in discourse. We can avoid that misunderstanding by speaking of the *sounds* and *syllables* of a word provided we remember that the names refer to the sound-image.

The linguistic sign is then a two-sided psychological entity that can be represented by the drawing:

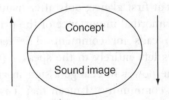

The two elements are intimately united, and each recalls the other. Whether we try to find the meaning of the Latin word *arbor* or the word that Latin uses to designate the concept "tree," it is clear that only the associations sanctioned by that language appear to us to conform to reality, and we disregard whatever others might be imagined.

Our definition of the linguistic sign poses an important question of terminology. I call the combination of a concept and a sound-image a *sign*, but in current usage the term generally designates only a sound-image, a word, for example (*arbor*, etc.). One tends to forget that *arbor* is called a sign only because it carries the concept "tree," with the result that the idea of the sensory part implies the idea of the whole.

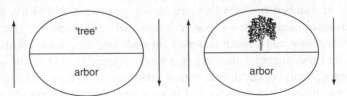

Ambiguity would disappear if the three notions involved here were designated by three names, each suggesting and opposing the others. I propose to retain the word *sign* [*signe*] to designate the whole and to replace *concept* and *sound-image* respectively by *signified* [*signifié*] and *signifier* [*signifiant*]; the last two terms have the advantage of indicating the opposition that separates them from each other and from the whole of which they are parts. As regards *sign*, if I am satisfied with it, this is simply because I do not know of any word to replace it, the ordinary language suggesting no other.

The linguistic sign, as defined, has two primordial characteristics. In enunciating them I am also positing the basic principles of any study of this type.

Principle I: The Arbitrary Nature of the Sign

The bond between the signifier and the signified is arbitrary. Since I mean by sign the whole that results from the associating of the signifier with the signified, I can simply say: *the linguistic sign is arbitrary*.

The idea of "sister" is not linked by any inner relationship to the succession of sounds *s-ö-r* which serves as its signifier in French; that it could be represented equally by just any other sequence is proved by differences among languages and by the very existence of different languages: the signified "ox" has as its signifier *b-ö-f* on one side of the border and *o-k-s* (*Ochs*) on the other.

No one disputes the principle of the arbitrary nature of the sign, but it is often easier to discover a truth than to assign to it its proper place. Principle I dominates all the linguistics of language; its consequences are numberless. It is true that not all of them are equally obvious at first glance; only after many detours does one discover them, and with them the primordial importance of the principle...

The word *arbitrary* also calls for comment. The term should not imply that the choice of the signifier is left entirely to the speaker (we shall see below that the individual does not have the power to change a sign in any way once it has become established in the linguistic community); I mean that it is unmotivated, i.e. arbitrary in that it actually has no natural connection with the signified.

In concluding let us consider two objections that might be raised to the establishment of Principle I:

1 *Onomatopoeia* might be used to prove that the choice of the signifier is not always arbitrary. But onomatopoeic formations are never organic elements of a linguistic system. Besides, their number is much smaller than is generally supposed. Words like French *fouet* "whip" or *glas* "knell" may strike certain ears with suggestive sonority, but to see that they have not always had this priority we need only examine their Latin forms (*fouet* is derived from *fagus* "beech-tree," *glas* from *classicum* "sound of a trumpet"). The quality of their present sounds, or rather the quality that is attributed to them, is a fortuitous result of phonetic evolution.

As for authentic onomatopoeic words (e.g. *glug-glug*, *tick-tock*, etc.), not only are they limited in number, but also they are chosen somewhat arbitrarily, for they are only approximate and more or less conventional imitations of certain sounds (cf. English *bow-wow* and French *oua-oua*). In addition, once these words have been introduced into the language, they are to a certain extent subject to the same evolution – phonetic, morphological, etc. – that other words undergo (cf. *pigeon*, ultimately from the vulgar Latin *pipio* derived in turn from an onomatopoeic formulation):

obvious proof that they lose something of their original character in order to assume that of the linguistic sign in general, which is unmotivated.

2 *Interjections*, closely related to onomatopoeia, can be attacked on the same grounds and come no closer to refuting our thesis. One is tempted to see in them spontaneous expressions of reality dictated, so to speak, by natural forces. But for most interjections we can show that there is no fixed bond between their signified and their signifier. We need only compare two languages on this point to see how much such expressions differ from one language to the next (e.g. the English equivalent of French *aïe!* is *ouch!*). We know, moreover, that many interjections were once words with specific meanings (cf. French *diable!* "darn!" *mordieu!* "golly!" from *mort Dieu* "God's death," etc.).[2]

Onomatopoeic formations and interjections are of secondary importance, and their symbolic origin is in part open to dispute.

Principle II: The Linear Nature of the Signifier

The signifier, being auditory, is unfolded solely in time from which it gets the following characteristics: (a) it represents a span, and (b) the span is measurable in a single dimension; it is a line.

While Principle II is obvious, apparently linguists have always neglected to state it, doubtless because they found it too simple; nevertheless, it is fundamental, and its consequences are incalculable. Its importance equals that of Principle I; the whole mechanism of language depends upon it. In contrast to visual signifiers (nautical signals, etc.) which can offer simultaneous groupings in several dimensions, auditory signifiers have at their command only the dimension of time. Their elements are presented in succession; they form a chain. This feature becomes readily apparent when they are represented in writing and the spatial line of graphic marks is substituted for succession in time.

Sometimes the linear nature of the signifier is not obvious. When I accent a syllable, for instance, it seems that I am concentrating more than one significant element on the same point. But this is an illusion; the syllable and its accent constitute only one phonational act. There is no duality within the act but only different oppositions to what precedes and what follows ...

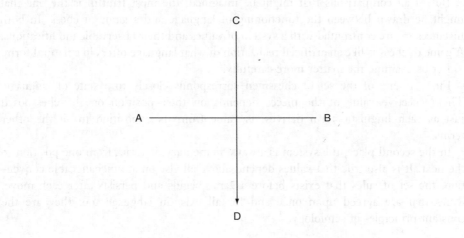

Certainly all sciences would profit by indicating more precisely the coordinates along which their subject matter is aligned. Everywhere distinctions should be made, according to the following illustration, between (1) *the axis of simultaneities* (AB), which stands for the relations of coexisting things and from which the intervention of time is excluded; and (2) *the axis of successions* (CD), on which only one thing can be considered at a time but upon which are located all the things on the first axis together with their changes.

... [T]o indicate more clearly the opposition and crossing of two orders of phenomena that relate to the same object, I prefer to speak of *synchronic* and *diachronic* linguistics. Everything that relates to the static side of our science is synchronic; everything that has to do with evolution is diachronic. Similarly, *synchrony* and *diachrony* designate respectively a language-state and an evolutionary phase ....

The Difference between the Two Classes Illustrated by Comparisons

To show both the autonomy and the interdependence of synchrony we can compare the first to the projection of an object on a plane surface. Any projection depends directly on the nature of the object projected, yet differs from it – the object itself is a thing apart. Otherwise there would not be a whole science of projections; considering the bodies themselves would suffice. In linguistics there is the same relationship between the historical facts and a language-state, which is like a projection of the facts at a particular moment. We do not learn about synchronic states by studying bodies, i.e. diachronic events, any more than we can learn about geometric projections by studying, even carefully, the different types of bodies.

Similarly if the stem of a plant is cut transversely, a rather complicated design is formed by the cut surface; the design is simply one perspective of the longitudinal fibers, and we would be able to see them on making a second cut perpendicular to the first. Here again one perspective depends on the other; the longitudinal cut shows the fibers that constitute the plant, and the transversal cut shows their arrangement on a particular plane; but the second is distinct from the first because it brings out certain relations between the fibers – relations that we could never grasp by viewing the longitudinal plane.

But of all comparisons that might be imagined, the most fruitful is the one that might be drawn between the functioning of language and a game of chess. In both instances we are confronted with a system of values and their observable modifications. A game of chess is like an artificial realization of what language offers in a natural form.

Let us examine the matter more carefully.

First, a state of the set of chessmen corresponds closely to a state of language. The respective value of the pieces depends on their position on the chessboard just as each linguistic term derives its value from its opposition to all the other terms.

In the second place, the system is always momentary; it varies from one position to the next. It is also true that values depend above all else on an unchangeable convention, the set of rules that exists before a game begins and persists after each move. Rules that are agreed upon once and for all exist in language too; they are the constant principles of semiology.

Finally, to pass from one state of equilibrium to the next, or – according to our terminology – from one synchrony to the next, only one chesspiece has to be moved; there is no general rummage. Here we have the counterpart of the diachronic phenomenon with all its peculiarities. In fact:

(a) In each play only one chesspiece is moved; in the same way in language, changes affect only isolated elements.
(b) In spite of that, the move has a repercussion on the whole system; it is impossible for the player to foresee exactly the extent of the effect. Resulting changes of value will be, according to the circumstances, either nil, very serious, or of average importance.
(c) In chess, each move is absolutely distinct from the preceding and the subsequent equilibrium. The change effected belongs to neither state: only states matter.

In a game of chess any particular position has the unique characteristic of being freed from all antecedent positions; the route used in arriving there makes absolutely no difference; one who has followed the entire match has no advantage over the curious party who comes up at a critical moment to inspect the state of the game; to describe this arrangement, it is perfectly useless to recall what had just happened ten seconds previously. All this is equally applicable to language and sharpens the radical distinction between diachrony and synchrony. Speaking operates only on a language-state, and the changes that intervene between states have no place in either state.

At only one point is the comparison weak: the chessplayer *intends* to bring about a shift and thereby to exert an action on the system, whereas language premeditates nothing. The pieces of language are shifted – or rather modified – spontaneously and fortuitously. The umlaut of *Hände* for *hanti* and *Gäste* for *gasti* produced a new system for forming the plural but also gave rise to verbal forms like *trägt* from *tragit*, etc. In order to make the game of chess seem at every point like the functioning of language, we would have to imagine an unconscious or unintelligent player. This sole difference, however, makes the comparison even more instructive by showing the absolute necessity of making a distinction between the two classes of phenomena in linguistics. For if diachronic facts cannot be reduced to the synchronic system which they condition when the change is unintentional, all the more will they resist when they set a blind force against the organization of a system of signs....

Linguistic Value from a Conceptual Viewpoint

When we speak of the value of a word, we generally think first of its property of standing for an idea, and this is in fact one side of linguistic value. But if this is true, how does *value* differ from *signification*? Might the two words be synonyms? I think not, although it is easy to confuse them, since the confusion results not so much from their similarity as from the subtlety of the distinction that they mark.

From a conceptual viewpoint, value is doubtless one element in signification, and it is difficult to see how signification can be dependent upon value and still be distinct from it. But we must clear up the issue or risk reducing language to a simple naming-process.

Let us first take signification as it is generally understood and as it was pictured on page 61. As the arrows in the drawing show, it is only the counterpart of the sound-image. Everything that occurs concerns only the sound-image and the concept when we look upon the word as independent and self-contained.

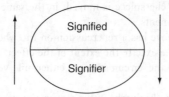

But here is the paradox: on the one hand the concept seems to be the counterpart of the sound-image, and on the other hand the sign itself is in turn the counterpart of the other signs of language.

Language is a system of interdependent terms in which the value of each term results solely from the simultaneous presence of the others, as in the diagram:

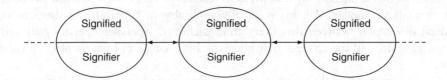

How, then, can value be confused with signification, i.e. the counterpart of the sound-image? It seems impossible to liken the relations represented here by horizontal arrows to those represented above by vertical arrows. Putting it another way and again taking up the example of the sheet of paper that is cut in two, it is clear that the observable relation between the different pieces A, B, C, D, etc. is distinct from the relation between the front and back of the same piece as in A/A', B/B', etc.

To resolve the issue, let us observe from the outset that even outside language all values are apparently governed by the same paradoxical principle. They are always composed:

(1)   of a *dissimilar* thing that can be *exchanged* for the thing of which the value is to be determined; and

(2)   of *similar* things that can be *compared* with the thing of which the value is to be determined.

Both factors are necessary for the existence of a value. To determine what a five-franc piece is worth one must therefore know: (1) that it can be exchanged for a fixed quantity of a different thing, e.g. bread; and (2) that it can be compared with a similar value of the same system, e.g. a one-franc piece, or with coins of another system (a dollar, etc.). In the same way a word can be exchanged for something dissimilar, an idea; besides, it can be compared with something of the same nature, another word. Its value is therefore not fixed so long as one simply states that it can be "exchanged" for a given concept, i.e. that it has this or that signification: one must also compare it with similar values, with other words that stand in opposition to it. Its content is really fixed only by the concurrence of everything that exists outside it. Being part of a system, it is endowed not only with a signification but also and especially with a value, and this is something quite different.

A few examples will show clearly that this is true. Modern French *mouton* can have the same signification as English *sheep* but not the same value, and this for several reasons, particularly because in speaking of a piece of meat ready to be served on the table, English uses *mutton* and not *sheep*. The difference in value between *sheep* and *mouton* is due to the fact that *sheep* has beside it a second term while the French word does not.

Within the same language, all words used to express related ideas limit each other reciprocally; synonyms like French *redouter* "dread," *craindre* "fear," and *avoir peur* "be afraid" have value only through their opposition: if *redouter* did not exist, all its content would go to its competitors. Conversely, some words are enriched through contact with others: e.g. the new element introduced in *décrépit* (un vieillard *décrépit*) results from the coexistence of *décrépi* (un mur *décrépi*). The value of just any term is accordingly determined by its environment; it is impossible to fix even the value of the word signifying "sun" without first considering its surroundings: in some languages it is not possible to say "sit in the *sun*."

Everything said about words applies to any term of language, e.g. to grammatical entities. The value of a French plural does not coincide with that of a Sanskrit plural even though their signification is usually identical; Sanskrit has three numbers instead of two (*my eyes, my ears, my arms, my legs*, etc. are dual);[3] it would be wrong to attribute the same value to the plural in Sanskrit and in French; its value clearly depends on what is outside and around it.

If words stood for pre-existing concepts, they would all have exact equivalents in meaning from one language to the next; but this is not true. French uses *louer* (*une maison*) "let (a house)" indifferently to mean both "pay for" and "receive payment for," whereas German uses two words, *mieten* and *vermieten*; there is obviously no exact correspondence of values. The German verbs *schatzen* and *urteilen* share a number of significations, but that correspondence does not hold at several points.

Inflection offers some particularly striking examples. Distinctions of time, which are so familiar to us, are unknown in certain languages. Hebrew does not recognize even the fundamental distinctions between the past, present, and future. Proto-Germanic has no special form for the future; to say that the future is expressed by the present is wrong, for the value of the present is not the same in Germanic as in languages that have a future along with the present. The Slavic languages regularly single out two aspects of the verb: the perfective represents action as a point, complete in its totality; the imperfective represents it as taking place, and on the line of time. The categories are difficult for a Frenchman to understand, for they are unknown in French; if they were predetermined, this would not be true. Instead of pre-existing ideas then, we find in all the foregoing examples *values* emanating from the system. When they are said to correspond to concepts, it is understood that the concepts are purely differential and defined not by their positive content but negatively by their relations with the other terms of the system. Their most precise characteristic is in being what the others are not.

Now the real interpretation of the diagram of the signal becomes apparent. Thus means that in French the concept "to judge" is linked to the sound-image *juger*; in

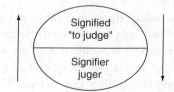

short, it symbolizes signification. But it is quite clear that initially the concept is nothing, that is only a value determined by its relations with other similar values, and that without them the signification would not exist. If I state simply that a word signifies something when I have in mind the associating of a sound-image with a concept, I am making a statement that may suggest what actually happens, but by no means am I expressing the linguistic fact in its essence and fullness.

Linguistic Value from a Material Viewpoint

The conceptual side of value is made up solely of relations and differences with respect to the other terms of language, and the same can be said of its material side. The important thing in the word is not the sound alone but the phonic differences that make it possible to distinguish this word from all others, for differences carry signification.

This may seem surprising, but how indeed could the reverse be possible? Since one vocal image is no better suited than the next for what it is commissioned to express, it is evident, even *a priori* that a segment of language can never in the final analysis be based on anything except its noncoincidence with the rest. *Arbitrary* and *differential* are two correlative qualities.

The alteration of linguistic signs clearly illustrates this. It is precisely because the terms *a* and *b*, as such, are radically incapable of reaching the level of consciousness – one is always conscious of only the *a/b* difference – that each term is free to change according to laws that are unrelated to its signifying function. No positive sign characterizes the genitive plural in Czech *zen*; still the two forms *zena: zen* function as well as the earlier forms *zena: zenb; zen* has value only because it is different.

Here is another example that shows even more clearly the systematic role of phonic differences: in Greek, *ephen* is an imperfect and *esten* an aorist although both words are formed in the same way; the first belongs to the system of the present indicative of *phemi* "I say," whereas there is no present *stemi*; now it is precisely the relation *phemi: ephen* that corresponds to the relation between the present and the imperfect (cf. *deiknumi: edeiknun*, etc.). Signs function, then, not through their intrinsic value but through their relative position.

In addition, it is impossible for sound alone, a material element, to belong to language. It is only a secondary thing, substance to be put to use. All our conventional values have the characteristic of not being confused with the tangible element which supports them. For instance, it is not the metal in a piece of money that fixes its value. A coin nominally worth five francs may contain less than half its worth of silver. Its value will vary according to the amount stamped upon it and according to its use inside or outside a political boundary. This is even more true of the linguistic signifier, which is not phonic but incorporeal – constituted not by its material substance but by the differences that separate its sound-image from all others.

The foregoing principle is so basic that it applies to all the material elements of language, including phonemes. Every language forms its words on the basis of a system of sonorous elements, each element being a clearly delimited unit and one of a fixed number of units. Phonemes are characterized not, as one might think, by their own positive quality but simply by the fact that they are distinct. Phonemes are above all else opposing, relative, and negative entities.

Proof of this is the latitude that speakers have between points of convergence in the pronunciation of distinct sounds. In French, for instance, general use of a dorsal *r* does not prevent many speakers from using a tongue-tip trill; language is not in the least disturbed by it; language requires only that the sound be different and not, as one might imagine, that it have an invariable quality. I can even pronounce the French *r* like German *ch* in *Bach*, *doch*, etc., but in German I could not use *r* instead of *ch*, for German gives recognition to both elements and must keep them apart. Similarly, in Russian there is no latitude for *t* in the direction of *t'* (palatalized *t*), for the result would be the confusing of two sounds differentiated by the language (cf. *govorit'* "speak" and *goverit* "he speaks"), but more freedom may be taken with respect to *th* (aspirated *t*) since this sound does not figure in the Russian system of phonemes.

Since an identical state of affairs is observable in writing, another system of signs, we shall use writing to draw some comparisons that will clarify the whole issue. In fact:

1 The signs used in writing are arbitrary; there is no connection, for example, between the letter *t* and the sound that it designates.
2 The value of letters is purely negative and differential. The same person can write *t* for instance, in different ways:

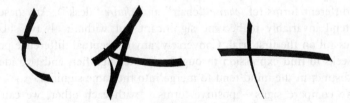

    The only requirement is that the sign for *t* not be confused in his script with the signs used for *l*, *d*, etc.

3 Values in writing function only through reciprocal opposition within a fixed system that consists of a set number of letters. This third characteristic, though not identical to the second, is closely related to it, for both depend on the first. Since the graphic sign is arbitrary, its form matters little or rather matters only within the limitations imposed by the system.

4 The means by which the sign is produced is completely unimportant, for it does not affect the system (this also follows from characteristic 1). Whether I make the letters in white or black, raised or engraved, with pen or chisel – all this is of no importance with respect to their signification.

The Sign Considered in Its Totality

Everything that has been said up to this point boils down to this: in language there are only differences. Even more important: a difference generally implies positive terms between which the difference is set up; but in language there are only differences *without positive terms.* Whether we take the signified or the signifier, language has neither ideas nor sounds that existed before the linguistic system, but only conceptual and phonic differences that have issued from the system. The idea or phonic substance that a sign contains is of less importance than the other signs that surround it. Proof of this is that the value of a term may be modified without either its meaning or its sound being affected, solely because a neighboring term has been modified.

But the statement that everything in language is negative is true only if the signified and the signifier are considered separately; when we consider the sign in its totality, we have something that is positive in its own class. A linguistic system is a series of differences of sound combined with a series of differences of ideas; but the pairing of a certain number of acoustical signs with as many cuts made from the mass of thought engenders a system of values; and this system serves as the effective link between the phonic and psychological elements within each sign. Although both the signified and the signifier are purely differential and negative when considered separately, their combination is a positive fact; it is even the sole type of facts that language has, for maintaining the parallelism between the two classes of differences is the distinctive function of the linguistic institution.

Certain diachronic facts are typical in this respect. Take the countless instances where alteration of the signifier occasions a conceptual change and where it is obvious that the sum of the ideas distinguished corresponds in principle to the sum of the distinctive signs. When two words are confused through phonetic alteration (e.g. French *décrépit* from *decrepitus* and *décrépi* from *crispus*), the ideas they express will also tend to become confused if only they have something in common. Or a word may have different forms (cf. *chaise* "chair" and *chaire* "desk"). Any nascent difference will tend invariably to become significant but without always succeeding or being successful on the first trial. Conversely, any conceptual difference perceived by the mind seeks to find expression through a distinct signifier, and two ideas that are no longer distinct in the mind tend to merge into the same signifier.

When we compare signs – positive terms – with each other, we can no longer speak of difference; the expression would not be fitting, for it applies only to the comparing of two sound-images, e.g. *father* and *mother*, or two ideas, e.g. the idea "father" and the idea "mother"; two signs, each having a signified and signifier, are not different but only distinct. Between them there is only *opposition.* The entire mechanism of language, with which we shall be concerned later, is based on oppositions of this kind and on the phonic and conceptual differences that they imply.

What is true of value is true also of the unit. A unit is a segment of the spoken chain that corresponds to a certain concept; both are by nature purely differential.

Applied to units, the principle of differentiation can be stated in this way: *the characteristics of the unit blend with the unit itself.* In language, as in any semiological system, whatever distinguishes one sign from the others constitutes it. Difference makes character just as it makes value and the unit.

Another rather paradoxical consequence of the same principle is this: in the last analysis what is commonly referred to as a "grammatical fact" fits the definition of the unit, for it always expresses an opposition of terms; it differs only in that the opposition is particularly significant (e.g. the formation of German plurals of the type *Nacht: Nächte*). Each term present in the grammatical fact (the singular without umlaut or final *-e* in opposition to the plural with umlaut and *-e*) consists of the interplay of a number of oppositions within the system. When isolated, neither *Nacht* nor *Nächte* is anything: thus everything is opposition. Putting it another way, the *Nacht: Nächte* relation can be expressed by an algebraic formula a/b in which a and b are not simple terms but result from a set of relations. Language, in a manner of speaking, is a type of algebra consisting solely of complex terms. Some of its oppositions are more significant than others; but units and grammatical facts are only different names for designating diverse aspects of the same general fact: the functioning of linguistic oppositions. This statement is so true that we might very well approach the problem of units by starting from grammatical facts. Taking an opposition like *Nacht: Nächte*, we might ask what are the units involved in it. Are they only the two words, the whole series of similar words, *a* and *ä*, or all singulars and plurals, etc.?

Units and grammatical facts would not be confused if linguistic signs were made up of something besides differences. But language being what it is, we shall find nothing simple in it regardless of our approach; everywhere and always there is the same complex equilibrium of terms that mutually condition each other. Putting it another way, *language is form and not a substance*. This truth could not be over-stressed, for all the mistakes in our terminology, all our incorrect ways of naming things that pertain to language, stem from the involuntary supposition that the linguistic phenomenon must have substance.

Notes

1   The term sound-image may seem to be too restricted inasmuch as beside the representation of the sounds of a word there is also that of its articulation, the muscular image of the phonational act. But for F. de Saussure, language is essentially a depository, a thing received from without. The sound-image is par excellence the natural representation of the word as a fact of potential language, outside any actual use of it in speaking. The motor side is thus implied or, in any event, occupies only a subordinate role with respect to the sound-image. [Ed.]

2   Cf. English *goodness!* and *zounds!* (from *God's wounds*). [Trans.]

3   The use of the comparative form for two and the superlative for more than two in English (e.g. may the *better* boxer win: the *best* boxer in the world) is probably a remnant of the old distinction between the dual and the plural number. [Trans.]

CHAPTER 4

Morphology of the Folk-tale

Vladimir Propp

Though not a member of either Russian Formalist group, Vladimir Propp wrote within the same intellectual current that sought to make literary study more scientific. His *Morphology of the Folk-Tale* (1927) in its very title suggests the scientific character of his undertaking. Propp is one of the first Structuralists in that he sought to delineate the innate order that existed in a disparate body of texts. Like a scientist searching for the one law that binds a number of different, physically distinct phenomena together and accounts for their similarities, Propp studied hundreds of Russian folk-tales or oral stories and came to the conclusion that they all followed the same pattern. This inner structure of the various tales constitutes its morphology.

Let us first of all attempt to formulate our task. As already stated in the foreword, this work is dedicated to the study of *fairy* tales. The existence of fairy tales as a special class is assumed as an essential working hypothesis. By "fairy tales" are meant at present those tales classified by Aarne under numbers 300 to 749. This definition is artificial, but the occasion will subsequently arise to give a more precise determination on the basis of resultant conclusions. We are undertaking a comparison of the themes of these tales. For the sake of comparison we shall separate the component parts of fairy tales by special methods; and then, we shall make a comparison of tales according to their components. The result will be a morphology (i.e., a description of the tale according to its component parts and the relationship of these components to each other and to the whole).

What methods can achieve an accurate description of the tale? Let us compare the following events:

1 A tsar gives an eagle to a hero. The eagle carries the hero away to another kingdom.
2 An old man gives Sucenko a horse. The horse carries Sucenko away to another kingdom.
3 A sorcerer gives Ivan a little boat. The boat takes Ivan to another kingdom.
4 A princess gives Ivan a ring. Young men appearing from out of the ring carry Ivan away into another kingdom, and so forth.[1]

Both constants and variables are present in the preceding instances. The names of the dramatis personae change (as well as the attributes of each), but neither their actions nor functions change. From this we can draw the inference that a tale often attributes identical actions to various personages. This makes possible the study of the tale *according to the functions of its dramatis personae.*

We shall have to determine to what extent these functions actually represent recurrent constants of the tale. The formulation of all other questions will depend upon the solution of this primary question: how many functions are known to the tale?

Investigation will reveal that the recurrence of functions is astounding. Thus Baba Jaga, Morozko, the bear, the forest spirit, and the mare's head test and reward the stepdaughter. Going further, it is possible to establish that characters of a tale, however varied they may be, often perform the same actions. The actual means of the realization of functions can vary, and as such, it is a variable. Morozko behaves differently than Baba Jaga. But the function, as such, is a constant. The question of *what* a tale's dramatis personae do is an important one for the study of the tale, but the questions of *who* does it and *how* it is done already fall within the province of accessory study. The functions of characters are those components which could replace Veselovskij's "motifs," or Bedier's "elements." We are aware of the fact that the repetition of functions by various characters was long ago observed in myths and beliefs by historians of religion, but it was not observed by historians of the tale (cf. Wundt and Negelein[2]). Just as the characteristics and functions of deities are transferred from one to another, and, finally, are even carried over to Christian saints, the functions of certain tale personages are likewise transferred to other personages. Running ahead, one may say that the number of functions is extremely small, whereas the number of personages is extremely large. This explains the twofold quality of a tale: its amazing multiformity, picturesqueness, and color, and on the other hand, its no less striking uniformity, its repetition.

Thus the functions of the dramatis personae are basic components of the tale, and we must first of all extract them. In order to extract the functions we must define them. Definition must proceed from two points of view. First of all, definition should in no case depend on the personage who carries out the function. Definition of a function will most often be given in the form of a noun expressing an action (interdiction, interrogation, flight, etc.). Secondly, an action cannot be defined apart from its place in the course of narration. The meaning which a given function has in the course of action must be considered. For example, if Ivan marries a tsar's daughter, this is something entirely different than the marriage of a father to a widow with two daughters. A second example: if, in one instance, a hero receives money from his father in the form of 100 rubles and subsequently buys a wise cat with this money, whereas in a second case, the hero is rewarded with a sum of money for an accomplished act of bravery (at which point the tale ends), we have before us two morphologically different elements – in spite of the identical action (the transference of money) in both cases. Thus, identical acts can have different meanings, and vice versa. *Function is understood as an act of a character, defined from the point of view of its significance for the course of the action.*

The observations cited may be briefly formulated in the following manner:

1 *Functions of characters serve as stable, constant elements in a tale, independent of how and by whom they are fulfilled. They constitute the fundamental components of a tale.*
2 *The number of functions known to the fairy tale is limited.*

If functions are delineated, a second question arises: in what classification and in what sequence are these functions encountered?

A word, first, about sequence. The opinion exists that this sequence is accidental. Veselovskij writes, "The selection and *order* of tasks and encounters (examples of motifs) already presupposes a certain *freedom*." Sklovskij stated this idea in even sharper terms: "It is quite impossible to understand why, in the act of adoption, the *accidental* sequence [Sklovskij's italics] of motifs must be retained. In the testimony of witnesses, it is precisely the sequence of events which is distorted most of all." This reference to the evidence of witnesses is unconvincing. If witnesses distort the sequence of events, their narration is meaningless. The sequence of events has its own laws. The short story too has similar laws, as do organic formations. Theft cannot take place before the door is forced. Insofar as the tale is concerned, it has its own entirely particular and specific laws. The sequence of elements, as we shall see later on, is strictly *uniform*. Freedom within this sequence is restricted by very narrow limits which can be exactly formulated. We thus obtain the third basic thesis of this work, subject to further development and verification:

3   *The sequence of functions is always identical . . .*
4   *All fairy tales are of one type in regard to their structure . . .*

The Functions of Dramatis Personae

[W]e shall enumerate the functions of the dramatis personae in the order dictated by the tale itself . . .

A tale usually begins with some sort of initial situation . . .

After the initial situation there follow functions:

I   ONE OF THE MEMBERS OF A FAMILY ABSENTS HIMSELF FROM HOME. (Definition: *absentation*. Designation: B.)

Usual forms of absentation: going to work, to the forest, to trade, to war, "on business."

II   AN INTERDICTION IS ADDRESSED TO THE HERO. (Definition: *interdiction*. Designation: y.)

1 (yl) "You dare not look into this closet" (159). "Take care of your little brother, do not venture forth from the courtyard" (113). "If Baba Jaga comes, don't you say anything, be silent" (106). "Often did the prince try to persuade her and command her not to leave the lofty tower," etc. (265) . . .

III   THE INTERDICTION IS VIOLATED. (Definition: *violation*. Designation: a.)

The forms of violation correspond to the forms of interdiction . . . (the tsar's daughters go into the garden [B3]; they are *late* in returning home) . . .

At this point a new personage, who can be termed the *villain*, enters the tale. His role is to disturb the peace of a happy family, to cause some form of misfortune, damage, or harm. The villain(s) may be a dragon, a devil, bandits, a witch, or a stepmother, etc. . . .

IV   THE VILLAIN MAKES AN ATTEMPT AT RECONNAISSANCE. (Definition: *reconnaissance*. Designation: E.)

1 *The reconnaissance has the aim of finding out the location of children, or sometimes of precious objects, etc.* (E1). A bear says: "Who will tell me what has become of the tsar's children? Where did they disappear to?" (201); a clerk: "Where do you get these precious stones?" ...

V THE VILLAIN RECEIVES INFORMATION ABOUT HIS VICTIM. (Definition: *delivery*. Designation: t.)

1 *The villain directly receives an answer to his question* (41). The chisel answers the bear: "Take me out into the courtyard and throw me to the ground; where I stick, there's the hive." To the clerk's question about the precious stones, the merchant's wife replies: "Oh, the hen lays them for us," etc. ...

VI THE VILLAIN ATTEMPTS TO DECEIVE HIS VICTIM IN ORDER TO TAKE POSSESSION OF HIM OR OF HIS BELONGINGS. (Definition: *trickery*. Designation: n.)

The villain, first of all, assumes a disguise. A dragon turns into a golden goat (n1) or a handsome youth (204); a witch pretends to be a "sweet old lady" (2G5) and imitates a mother's voice (108); a priest dresses himself in a goat's hide (258); a thief pretends to be a beggarwoman (189); then follows the function itself.

1 *The villain uses persuasion* (n1). A witch tries to have a ring accepted (114); a godmother suggests the taking of a steam bath (187); a witch suggests the removal of clothes (264) and bathing in a pond (265); a beggar seeks alms (189).[3]

Notes

1 See Afanas'ev, Nos 171, 139, 138, 156.
2 W. Wundt, "Mythus und Religion," *Volkerpsychologie* 11, Section 1; Negelein, *Germanische Mythologie*. Negelein creates an exceptionally apt term, *Depossedierte Gottheiten*.
3 The rest of Propp's functions are: (7) The victim unknowingly helps the villain by being deceived or influenced by the villain. (8) The villain harms a member of the family or a member of the family lacks or desires something. (9) This lack or misfortune is made known; the hero is given a request or a command, and he goes or is sent on a mission/quest. (10) The seeker (often the hero) plans action against the villain. (11) The hero leaves home. (12) The hero is tested, attacked, interrogated, and receives either a magical agent or a helper. (13) The hero reacts to the actions of the future donor. (14) The hero uses the magical agent. (15) The hero is transferred to the general location of the object of his mission/quest. (16) The hero and villain join in direct combat. (17) The hero is branded. (18) The villain is defeated. (19) The initial misfortune or lack is set right. (20) The hero returns home. (21) The hero is pursued. (22) The hero is rescued from pursuit. (23) The hero arrives home or elsewhere and is not recognized. (24) A false hero makes false claims. (25) A difficult task is set for the hero. (26) The task is accomplished. (27) The hero is recognized. (28) The false hero/villain is exposed. (29) The false hero is transformed. (30) The villain is punished. (31) The hero is married and crowned. (Thanks to John Fiske for this summary.)

CHAPTER 5

Two Aspects of Language

Roman Jakobson

Roman Jakobson helped found the Moscow Linguistic Circle, and he worked with Viktor Shklovsky at the Society for the Study of Poetic Language. After emigrating from Russia in 1920, he worked in Prague with the Prague Linguistic Circle. Eventually, he made his way to the US, where he helped inspire Claude Lévi-Strauss, another European exile driven from home by the Nazis, to invent Structuralist Anthropology, an attempt to merge linguistic theory and anthropological analysis. Jakobson, along with N. S. Troubetzkoy, contributed to the "phonological revolution," the insight that words are generated from differences between distinctive features such as voiced and unvoiced or aspirated and non-aspirated sounds. This selection was first published in 1956.

The varieties of aphasia are numerous and diverse, but all of them oscillate between the two polar types just described. Every form of aphasic disturbance consists in some impairment, more or less severe, either of the faculty for selection and substitution or for combination and contexture. The former affliction involves a deterioration of metalinguistic operations, while the latter damages the capacity for maintaining the hierarchy of linguistic units. The relation of similarity is suppressed in the former, the relation of contiguity in the latter type of aphasia. Metaphor is alien to the similarity disorder, and metonymy to the contiguity disorder.

The development of a discourse may take place along two different semantic lines: one topic may lead to another either through their similarity or through their contiguity. The metaphoric way would be the most appropriate term for the first case and the metonymic way for the second, since they find their most condensed expression in metaphor and metonymy respectively. In aphasia one or the other of these two processes is restricted or totally blocked – an effect which makes the study of aphasia particularly illuminating for the linguist. In normal verbal behavior both processes are continually operative, but careful observation will reveal that under the influence of a cultural pattern, personality, and verbal style, preference is given to one of the two processes over the other.

In a well-known psychological test, children are confronted with some noun and told to utter the first verbal response that comes into their heads. In this experiment two opposite linguistic predilections are invariably exhibited: the response is intended either as a substitute for, or as a complement to the stimulus. In the latter case the stimulus and the response together form a proper syntactic construction, most usually a sentence. These two types of reaction have been labeled substitutive and predicative.

To the stimulus *hut* one response was *burnt out*; another is *a poor little house*. Both reactions are predicative; but the first creates a purely narrative context, while in the second there is a double connection with the subject *hut*; on the one hand, a positional (namely, syntactic) contiguity, and on the other a semantic similarity.

The same stimulus produced the following substitutive reactions: the tautology *hut*; the synonyms *cabin* and *hovel*; the antonym *palace*, and the metaphors *den* and *burrow*. The capacity of two words to replace one another is an instance of positional similarity, and, in addition, all these responses are linked to the stimulus by semantic similarity (or contrast). Metonymical responses to the same stimulus, such as *thatch*, *litter*, or *poverty*, combine and contrast the positional similarity with semantic contiguity.

In manipulating these two kinds of connection (similarity and contiguity) in both their aspects (positional and semantic) – selecting, combining, and ranking them – an individual exhibits his personal style, his verbal predilections and preferences.

In verbal art the interaction of these two elements is especially pronounced. Rich material for the study of this relationship is to be found in verse patterns which require a compulsory parallelism between adjacent lines, for example in Biblical poetry or in the West Finnic and, to some extent, the Russian oral traditions. This provides an objective criterion of what in the given speech community acts as a correspondence. Since on any verbal level – morphemic, lexical, syntactic, and phraseological – either of these two relations (similarity and contiguity) can appear – and each in either of two aspects – an impressive range of possible configurations is created. Either of the two gravitational poles may prevail. In Russian lyrical songs, for example, metaphoric constructions predominate, while in the heroic epics the metonymic way is preponderant.

In poetry there are various motives which determine the choice between these alternants. The primacy of the metaphoric process in the literary schools of romanticism and symbolism has been repeatedly acknowledged, but it is still insufficiently realized that it is the predominance of metonymy which underlies and actually predetermines the so-called "realistic" trend, which belongs to an intermediary stage between the decline of romanticism and the rise of symbolism and is opposed to both. Following the path of contiguous relationships, the realistic author metonymically digresses from the plot to the atmosphere and from the characters to the setting in space and time. He is fond of synecdochic details. In the scene of Anna Karenina's suicide Tolstoy's artistic attention is focused on the heroine's handbag; and in *War and Peace* the synecdoches "hair on the upper lip" or "bare shoulders" are used by the same writer to stand for the female characters to whom these features belong.

The alternative predominance of one or the other of these two processes is by no means confined to verbal art. The same oscillation occurs in sign systems other than language.[1] A salient example from the history of painting is the manifestly metonymical orientation of cubism, where the object is transformed into a set of synecdoches; the surrealist painters responded with a patently metaphorical attitude. Ever since the productions of D. W. Griffith, the art of the cinema, with its highly developed capacity for changing the angle, perspective, and focus of "shots," has broken with the tradition of the theater and ranged an unprecedented variety of synecdochic "close-ups" and metonymic "set-ups" in general. In such pictures as those of Charlie Chaplin, these devices in turn were superseded by a novel, metaphoric "montage" with its "lap dissolves" – the filmic similes.[2]

The bipolar structure of language (or other semiotic systems), and, in aphasia, the fixation on one of these poles to the exclusion of the other require systematic comparative study. The retention of either of these alternatives in the two types of aphasia must be confronted with the predominance of the same pole in certain styles, personal habits, current fashions, etc. A careful analysis and comparison of these phenomena with the whole syndrome of the corresponding type of aphasia is an imperative task for joint research by experts in psychopathology, psychology, linguistics, poetics, and semiotics, the general science of signs. The dichotomy here discussed appears to be of primal significance and consequence for all verbal behavior and for human behavior in general.[3]

To indicate the possibilities of the projected comparative research, we choose an example from a Russian folk tale which employs parallelism as a comic device: "Thomas is a bachelor; Jeremiah is unmarried" (*Foma xolost; Erjoma nezenat*). Here the predicates in the two parallel clauses are associated by similarity: they are in fact synonymous. The subjects of both clauses are masculine proper names and hence morphologically similar, while on the other hand they denote two contiguous heroes of the same tale, created to perform identical actions and thus to justify the use of synonymous pairs of predicates. A somewhat modified version of the same construction occurs in a familiar wedding song in which each of the wedding guests is addressed in turn by his first name and patronymic: "Gleb is a bachelor; Ivanovic is unmarried." While both predicates here are again synonyms, the relationship between the two subjects is changed: both are proper names denoting the same man and are normally used contiguously as a mode of polite address.

In the quotation from the folk tale the two parallel clauses refer to two separate facts, the marital status of Thomas and the similar status of Jeremiah. In the verse from the wedding song, however, the two clauses are synonymous: they redundantly reiterate the celibacy of the same hero, splitting him into two verbal hypostases.

The Russian novelist Gleb Ivanovic Uspenskij (1840–1902) in the last years of his life suffered from a mental illness involving a speech disorder. His first name and patronymic, *Gleb Ivanovic*, traditionally combined in polite intercourse, for him split into two distinct names designating two separate beings: Gleb was endowed with all his virtues, while Ivanovic, the name relating the son to the father, became the incarnation of all Uspenskij's vices. The linguistic aspect of this split personality is the patient's inability to use two symbols for the same thing, and it is thus a similarity disorder. Since the similarity disorder is bound up with the metonymical bent, an examination of the literary manner Uspenskij had employed as a young writer takes on particular interest. And the study of Anatolij Kamegulov, who analyzed Uspenskij's style, bears out our theoretical expectations. He shows that Uspenskij had a particular penchant for metonymy, and especially for synecdoche, and that he carried it so far that "the reader is crushed by the multiplicity of detail unloaded on him in a limited verbal space, and is physically unable to grasp the whole, so that the portrait is often lost."[4]

To be sure, the metonymical style in Uspenskij is obviously prompted by the prevailing literary canon of his time, late nineteenth-century "realism"; but the personal stamp of Gleb Ivanovic made his pen particularly suitable for this artistic trend in its extreme manifestations and finally left its mark upon the verbal aspect of his mental illness.

A competition between both devices, metonymic and metaphoric, is manifest in any symbolic process, either intrapersonal or social. Thus in an inquiry into the structure of dreams, the decisive question is whether the symbols and the temporal sequences used are based on contiguity (Freud's metonymic "displacement" and synecdochic "condensation") or on similarity (Freud's "identification and symbolism").[5] The principles underlying magic rites have been resolved by Frazer into two types: charms based on the law of similarity and those founded on association by contiguity. The first of these two great branches of sympathetic magic has been called "homoeopathic" or "imitative," and the second, "contagious magic."[6] This bipartition is indeed illuminating. Nonetheless, for the most part, the question of the two poles is still neglected, despite its wide scope and importance for the study of any symbolic behavior, especially verbal, and of its impairments. What is the main reason for this neglect?

Similarity in meaning connects the symbols of a metalanguage with the symbols of the language referred to. Similarity connects a metaphorical term with the term for which it is substituted. Consequently, when constructing a metalanguage to interpret tropes, the researcher possesses more homogeneous means to handle metaphor, whereas metonymy, based on a different principle, easily defies interpretation. Therefore nothing comparable to the rich literature on metaphor[7] can be cited for the theory of metonymy. For the same reason, it is generally realized that romanticism is closely linked with metaphor, whereas the equally intimate ties of realism with metonymy usually remain unnoticed. Not only the tool of the observer but also the object of observation is responsible for the preponderance of metaphor over metonymy in scholarship. Since poetry is focused upon sign, and pragmatical prose primarily upon referent, tropes and figures were studied mainly as poetical devices. The principle of similarity underlies poetry; the metrical parallelism of lines or the phonic equivalence of rhyming words prompts the question of semantic similarity and contrast; there exist, for instance, grammatical and anti-grammatical but never agrammatical rhymes. Prose, on the contrary, is forwarded essentially by contiguity. Thus, for poetry, metaphor, and for prose, metonymy is the line of least resistance and, consequently, the study of poetical tropes is directed chiefly toward metaphor. The actual bipolarity has been artificially replaced in these studies by an amputated, unipolar scheme which, strikingly enough, coincides with one of the two aphasic patterns, namely with the contiguity disorder.[8]

Notes

1 I ventured a few sketchy remarks on the metonymical turn in verbal art ("Pro relizm u mystectvi," *Vaplite*, Kharkov, 1927, No. 2).

2 Cf. B. Balazs, *Theory of the Film* (London, 1952).

3 For the psychological and sociological aspects of this dichotomy see Bateson's views on "progressional" and "selective integration" and Parsons's on the "conjunction–disjunction dichotomy" in children's development: J. Ruesch and G. Bateson, *Communication, the Social Matrix of Psychiatry* (New York, 1951), pp. 183 ff.; T. Parsons and R. F. Bales, *Family, Socialization and Interaction Process* (Glencoe, 1955), pp. 119 f.

4 A. Kamelgulov, *Stil' Gleba Uspenskogo* (Leningrad, 1930), pp. 65, 145. One of such disintegrated portraits cited by the monograph: "From underneath an ancient straw cap with a black spot on its shield, there peeked two braids resembling the tusks of a wild boar; a chin grown fat and pendulous and definitively spread over the greasy collars of the calico dicky and in thick layer lay on the coarse collar of the canvas coat, firmly buttoned on the neck. From below this coat to the eyes of the observer there protruded massive hands with a ring, which had eaten

into the fat finger, a cane with a copper top, a significant bulge of the stomach and the presence of very broad pants, almost of muslin quality, in the broad ends of which hid the toes of the boots."

5 S. Freud, *Die Traumdeutung*, 9th edn (Vienna, 1950).
6 J. G. Frazer, *The Golden Bough: A Study in Magic and Religion*, Part 1, 3rd edn (Vienna, 1950), ch. III.
7 C. F. P. Stutterheim, *Het begrip metaphoor* (Amsterdam, 1941).
8 Thanks are due to Hugh McLean for his valuable assistance and to Justinia Besharov for her original observations on tropes and figures.

CHAPTER 6

Mythologies

Roland Barthes

Roland Barthes played a major role in the development of Structuralist and Post-Structuralist literary criticism in France from the 1950s to the 1970s. In his early work, *Elements of Semiology* (1965), he introduced the ideas of Saussure to the French intellectual community, and he offered a wide range of exemplary applications of "semiology," or the science of signs, to everything from literature to fashion and cuisine. He went on to write numerous works of Structuralist literary criticism. After 1968, influenced by the work of Jacques Derrida, Barthes turned away from classic Structuralism's concern with the orders of signs and worked instead on the disordering potential of literary semiosis, its tendency to transgress the identities and boundaries (such as the idea of the "author") that define traditional literary study. His essay "Death of the Author" (1968) is something of a Post-Structuralist manifesto, and this stage of Barthes's work achieves its most mature manifestation in his famous *S/Z* (1970), a lengthy reading of a short story by Balzac. These selections from *Mythologies* date from 1957.

In myth, we find again the tri-dimensional pattern which I have just described: the signifier, the signified and the sign. But myth is a peculiar system, in that it is constructed from a semiological chain which existed before it: it *is a second-order semiological system*. That which is a sign (namely the associative total of a concept and an image) in the first system, becomes a mere signifier in the second. We must here recall that the materials of mythical speech (the language itself, photography, painting, posters, rituals, objects, etc.), however different at the start, are reduced to a pure signifying function as soon as they are caught by myth. Myth sees in them only the same raw material; their unity is that they all come down to the status of a mere language. Whether it deals with alphabetical or pictorial writing, myth wants to see in them only a sum of signs, a global sign, the final term of a first semiological chain. And it is precisely this final term which will become the first term of the greater system which it builds and of which it is only a part. Everything happens as if myth shifted the formal system of the first significations sideways. As this lateral shift is essential for the analysis of myth, I shall represent it in the following way, it being understood, of course, that the spatialization of the pattern is here only a metaphor:

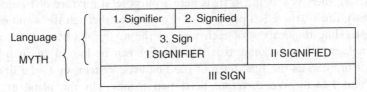

It can be seen that in myth there are two semiological systems, one of which is staggered in relation to the other: a linguistic system, the language (or the modes of representation which are assimilated to it), which I shall call the *language-object*, because it is the language which myth gets hold of in order to build its own system; and myth itself, which I shall call *metalanguage*, because it is a second language, *in which* one speaks about the first. When he reflects on a metalanguage, the semiologist no longer needs to ask himself questions about the composition of the language-object, he no longer has to take into account the details of the linguistic schema; he will only need to know its total term, or global sign, and only inasmuch as this term lends itself to myth. This is why the semiologist is entitled to treat in the same way writing and pictures: what he retains from them is the fact that they are both *signs*, that they both reach the threshold of myth endowed with the same signifying function, that they constitute, one just as much as the other, a language-object.

It is now time to give one or two examples of mythical speech. I shall borrow the first from an observation by Valéry.[1] I am a pupil in the second form in a French *lycée*. I open my Latin grammar, and I read a sentence, borrowed from Aesop or Phaedrus: *quia ego nominor leo*. I stop and think. There is something ambiguous about this statement: on the one hand, the words in it do have a simple meaning: *because my name is lion*. And on the other hand, the sentence is evidently there in order to signify something else to me. Inasmuch as it is addressed to me, a pupil in the second form, it tells me clearly: I am a grammatical example meant to illustrate the rule about the agreement of the predicate. I am even forced to realize that the sentence in no way *signifies* its meaning to me, that it tries very little to tell me something about the lion and what sort of name he has; its true and fundamental signification is to impose itself on me as the presence of a certain agreement of the predicate. I conclude that I am faced with a particular, greater, semiological system, since it is co-extensive with the language: there is, indeed, a signifier, but this signifier is itself formed by a sum of signs, it is in itself a first semiological system (*my name is lion*). Thereafter, the formal pattern is correctly unfolded: there is a signified (*I am a grammatical example*) and there is a global signification, which is none other than the correlation of the signifier and the signified; for neither the naming of the lion nor the grammatical example are given separately.

And here is now another example: I am at the barber's, and a copy of *Paris-Match* is offered to me. On the cover, a young Negro in a French uniform is saluting, with his eyes uplifted, probably fixed on a fold of the tricolour. All this is the *meaning* of the picture. But, whether naively or not, I see very well what it signifies to me: that France is a great Empire, that all her sons, without any colour discrimination, faithfully serve under her flag, and that there is no better answer to the detractors of an alleged colonialism than the zeal shown by this Negro in serving his so-called oppressors. I am therefore again faced with a greater semiological system: there is a signifier, itself already formed with a previous system (*a black soldier is giving the French salute*); there is a signified (it is here a purposeful mixture of Frenchness and militariness); finally, there is a presence of the signified through the signifier.

Before tackling the analysis of each term of the mythical system, one must agree on terminology. We now know that the signifier can be looked at, in myth, from two points of view: as the final term of the linguistic system, or as the first term of the mythical system. We therefore need two names. On the plane of language, that is, as the final term of the first system, I shall call the signifier: *meaning* (*my name is lion, a Negro is giving the French salute*); on the plane of myth, I shall call it: *form*. In the case of the signified, no ambiguity is possible: we shall retain the name *concept*. The third term is the correlation of the first two: in the linguistic system, it is the *sign*; but it is not possible to use this word again without ambiguity, since in myth (and this is the chief peculiarity of the latter), the signifier is already formed by the *signs* of the language. I shall call the third term of myth the *signification*. This word is here all the better justified since myth has in fact a double function: it points out and it notifies, it makes us understand something and it imposes it on us. . . .

The Romans in Films

In Mankiewicz's *Julius Caesar*, all the characters are wearing fringes. Some have them curly, some straggly, some tufted, some oily, all have them well combed, and the bald are not admitted, although there are plenty to be found in Roman history. Those who have little hair have not been let off for all that, and the hairdresser – the king-pin of the film – has still managed to produce one last lock which duly reaches the top of the forehead, one of those Roman foreheads, whose smallness has at all times indicated a specific mixture of self-righteousness, virtue and conquest.

What then is associated with these insistent fringes? Quite simply the label of Roman-ness. We therefore see here the mainspring of the Spectacle – the *sign* – operating in the open. The frontal lock overwhelms one with evidence, no one can doubt that he is in Ancient Rome. And this certainty is permanent: the actors speak, act, torment themselves, debate 'questions of universal import', without losing, thanks to this little flag displayed on their foreheads, any of their historical plausibility. Their general representativeness can even expand in complete safety, cross the ocean and the centuries, and merge into the Yankee mugs of Hollywood extras: no matter, everyone is reassured, installed in the quiet certainty of a universe without duplicity, where Romans are Romans thanks to the most legible of signs: hair on the forehead.

A Frenchman, to whose eyes American faces still have something exotic, finds comical the combination of the morphologies of these gangster-sheriffs with the little Roman fringe: it rather looks like an excellent music-hall gag. This is because for the French the sign in this case overshoots the target and discredits itself by letting its aim appear clearly. But this very fringe, when combed on the only naturally Latin forehead in the film, that of Marlon Brando, impresses us and does not make us laugh; and it is not impossible that part of the success of this actor in Europe is due to the perfect integration of Roman capillary habits with the general morphology of the characters he usually portrays. Conversely, one cannot believe in Julius Caesar, whose physiognomy is that of an Anglo-Saxon lawyer – a face with which one is already acquainted through a thousand bit parts in thrillers or comedies, and a compliant skull on which the hairdresser has raked, with great effort, a lock of hair.

In the category of capillary meanings, here is a sub-sign, that of nocturnal surprises: Portia and Calpurnia, woken up at dead of night, have conspicuously uncombed hair. The former, who is young, expresses disorder by flowing locks: her unreadiness is, so to speak, of the first degree. The latter, who is middle-aged, exhibits a more painstaking vulnerability: a plait winds round her neck and comes to rest on her right shoulder so as to impose the traditional sign of disorder, asymmetry. But these signs are at the same time excessive and ineffectual: they postulate a 'nature' which they have not even the courage to acknowledge fully: they are not 'fair and square'.

Yet another sign in this *Julius Caesar*: all the faces sweat constantly. Labourers, soldiers, conspirators, all have their austere and tense features streaming (with Vaseline). And close-ups are so frequent that evidently sweat here is an attribute with a purpose. Like the Roman fringe or the nocturnal plait, sweat is a sign. Of what? Of moral feeling. Everyone is sweating because everyone is debating something within himself; we are here supposed to be in the locus of a horribly tormented virtue, that is, in the very locus of tragedy, and it is sweat which has the function of conveying this. The populace, upset by the death of Caesar, then by the arguments of Mark Antony, is sweating, and combining economically, in this single sign, the intensity of its emotion and the simplicity of its condition. And the virtuous men, Brutus, Cassius, Casca, are ceaselessly perspiring too, testifying thereby to the enormous physiological labour produced in them by a virtue just about to give birth to a crime. To sweat is to think – which evidently rests on the postulate, appropriate to a nation of businessmen, that thought is a violent, cataclysmic operation, of which sweat is only the most benign symptom. In the whole film, there is but one man who does not sweat and who remains smooth-faced, unperturbed and watertight: Caesar. Of course Caesar, the *object* of the crime, remains dry since *he* does not know, *he does not think*, and so must keep the firm and polished texture of an exhibit standing isolated in the courtroom.

Here again, the sign is ambiguous: it remains on the surface, yet does not for all that give up the attempt to pass itself off as depth. It aims at making people understand (which is laudable) but at the same time suggests that it is spontaneous (which is cheating); it presents itself at once as intentional and irrepressible, artificial and natural, manufactured and discovered. This can lead us to an ethic of signs. Signs ought to present themselves only in two extreme forms: either openly intellectual and so remote that they are reduced to an algebra, as in the Chinese theatre, where a flag on its own signifies a regiment; or deeply rooted, invented, so to speak, on each occasion, revealing an internal, a hidden facet, and indicative of a moment in time, no longer of a concept (as in the art of Stanislavsky, for instance). But the intermediate sign, the fringe of Roman-ness or the sweating of thought, reveals a degraded spectacle, which is equally afraid of simple reality and of total artifice. For although it is a good thing if a spectacle is created to make the world more explicit, it is both reprehensible and deceitful to confuse the sign with what is signified. And it is a duplicity which is peculiar to bourgeois art: between the intellectual and the visceral sign is hypocritically inserted a hybrid, at once elliptical and pretentious, which is pompously christened '*nature*'.

Soap-powders and Detergents

The first World Detergent Congress (Paris, September 1954) had the effect of authorizing the world to yield to *Omo* euphoria: not only do detergents have no harmful effect on the skin, but they can even perhaps save miners from silicosis. These products have been in the last few years the object of such massive advertising that they now belong to a region of French daily life which the various types of psycho-analysis would do well to pay some attention to if they wish to keep up to date. One could then usefully contrast the psycho-analysis of purifying fluids (chlorinated, for example) with that of soap-powders (*Lux*, *Persil*) or that of detergents (*Omo*). The relations between the evil and the cure, between dirt and a given product, are very different in each case.

Chlorinated fluids, for instance, have always been experienced as a sort of liquid fire, the action of which must be carefully estimated, otherwise the object itself would be affected, 'burnt'. The implicit legend of this type of product rests on the idea of a violent, abrasive modification of matter: the connotations are of a chemical or mutilating type: the product 'kills' the dirt. Powders, on the contrary, are separating agents: their ideal role is to liberate the object from its circumstantial imperfection: dirt is 'forced out' and no longer killed; in the *Omo* imagery, dirt is a diminutive enemy, stunted and black, which takes to its heels from the fine immaculate linen at the sole threat of the judgment of *Omo*. Products based on chlorine and ammonia are without doubt the representatives of a kind of absolute fire, a saviour but a blind one. Powders, on the contrary, are selective, they push, they drive dirt through the texture of the object, their function is keeping public order not making war. This distinction has ethnographic correlatives: the chemical fluid is an extension of the washerwoman's movements when she beats the clothes, while powders rather replace those of the housewife pressing and rolling the washing against a sloping board.

But even in the category of powders, one must in addition oppose against advertisements based on psychology those based on psycho-analysis (I use this word without reference to any specific school). '*Persil* Whiteness' for instance, bases its prestige on the evidence of a result; it calls into play vanity, a social concern with appearances, by offering for comparison two objects, one of which is *whiter than* the other. Advertisements for *Omo* also indicate the effect of the product (and in superlative fashion, incidentally), but they chiefly reveal its mode of action; in doing so, they involve the consumer in a kind of direct experience of the substance, make him the accomplice of a liberation rather than the mere beneficiary of a result; matter here is endowed with value-bearing states.

Omo uses two of these, which are rather novel in the category of detergents: the deep and the foamy. To say that *Omo* cleans in depth (see the Cinéma-Publicité advertisement) is to assume that linen is deep, which no one had previously thought, and this unquestionably results in exalting it, by establishing it as an object favourable to those obscure tendencies to enfold and caress which are found in every human body. As for foam, it is well known that it signifies luxury. To begin with, it appears to lack any usefulness; then, its abundant, easy, almost infinite proliferation allows one to suppose there is in the substance from which it issues a vigorous germ, a healthy and powerful essence, a great wealth of active elements in a small original volume. Finally, it gratifies in the consumer a tendency to imagine matter as something airy, with which contact is effected in a mode both light and vertical, which is sought after like that of happiness either in the gustatory category (foie gras, entremets, wines), in that of clothing (muslin, tulle), or that of soaps (film-star in her bath). Foam can even be the sign of a certain spirituality, inasmuch as the spirit has the reputation of being able to make something out of nothing, a large surface of effects out of a small volume of causes (creams have a very different 'psychoanalytical' meaning, of a soothing kind: they suppress wrinkles, pain, smarting, etc.). What matters is the art of having disguised the abrasive function of the detergent under the delicious image of a substance at once deep and airy which can govern the molecular order of the material without damaging it. A euphoria, incidentally, which must not make us forget that there is one plane on which *Persil* and *Omo* are one and the same: the plane of the Anglo-Dutch trust *Unilever*.

The *Blue Guide*

The *Blue Guide*[2] hardly knows the existence of scenery except under the guise of the picturesque. The picturesque is found any time the ground is uneven. We find again here this bourgeois promoting of the mountains, this old Alpine myth (since it dates back to the nineteenth century) which Gide rightly associated with Helvetico-Protestant morality and which has always functioned as a hybrid compound of the cult of nature and of puritanism (regeneration through clean air, moral ideas at the sight of mountain-tops, summit-climbing as civic virtue, etc.). Among the views elevated by the *Blue Guide* to aesthetic existence, we rarely find plains (redeemed only when they can be described as fertile), never plateaux. Only mountains, gorges, defiles and torrents can have access to the pantheon of travel, inasmuch, probably, as they seem to encourage a morality of effort and solitude. Travel according to the *Blue Guide* is thus revealed as a labour-saving adjustment, the easy substitute for the morally uplifting walk. This in itself means that the mythology of the *Blue Guide* dates back to the last century, to that phase in history when the bourgeoisie was enjoying a kind of new-born euphoria in *buying* effort, in keeping its image and essence without feeling any of its ill-effects. It is therefore in the last analysis, quite logically and quite stupidly, the gracelessness of a landscape, its lack of spaciousness or human appeal, its verticality, so contrary to the bliss of travel, which account for its interest. Ultimately, the *Guide* will coolly write: '*The road becomes very picturesque (tunnels)*': it matters little that one no longer sees anything, since the tunnel here has become the sufficient sign of the mountain; it is a financial security stable enough for one to have no further worry about its value over the counter.

Just as hilliness is overstressed to such an extent as to eliminate all other types of scenery, the human life of a country disappears to the exclusive benefit of its monuments. For the *Blue Guide*, men exist only as 'types'. In Spain, for instance, the Basque is an adventurous sailor, the Levantine a light-hearted gardener, the Catalan a clever tradesman and the Cantabrian a sentimental highlander. We find again here this disease of thinking in essences, which is at the bottom of every bourgeois mythology of man (which is why we come across it so often). The ethnic reality of Spain is thus reduced to a vast classical ballet, a nice neat commedia dell'arte, whose improbable typology serves to mask the real spectacle of conditions, classes and professions. For the *Blue Guide*, men exist as social entities only in trains, where they fill a 'very mixed' Third Class. Apart from that, they are a mere introduction, they constitute a charming and fanciful decor, meant to surround the essential part of the country: its collection of monuments.

If one excepts its wild defiles, fit for moral ejaculations, Spain according to the *Blue Guide* knows only one type of space, that which weaves, across a few nondescript lacunae, a close web of churches, vestries, reredoses, crosses, altar-curtains, spires (always octagonal), sculpted groups (Family and Labour), Romanesque porches, naves and life-size crucifixes. It can be seen that all these monuments are religious, for from a bourgeois point of view it is almost impossible to conceive a History of Art which is not Christian and Roman Catholic. Christianity is the chief purveyor of tourism, and one travels only to visit churches. In the case of Spain, this imperialism is ludicrous, for Catholicism often appears there as a barbaric force which has stupidly defaced the earlier achievements of Muslim civilization: the mosque at Cordoba, whose wonderful forest of columns is at every turn obstructed by massive blocks of altars, or a colossal Virgin (set up by Franco) denaturing the site which it aggressively dominates – all this should help the French bourgeois to glimpse at least once in his life that historically there is also a reverse side to Christianity.

Generally speaking, the *Blue Guide* testifies to the futility of all analytical descriptions, those which reject both explanations and phenomenology: it answers in fact none of the questions which a modern traveller can ask himself while crossing a countryside which is real *and which exists in time*. To select only monuments suppresses at one stroke the reality of the land and that of its people, it accounts for nothing of the present, that is, nothing historical, and as a consequence, the monuments themselves become undecipherable, therefore senseless. What is to be seen is thus constantly in the process of vanishing, and the *Guide* becomes, through an operation common to all mystifications, the very opposite of what it advertises, an agent of blindness. By reducing geography to the description of an uninhabited world of monuments, the *Blue Guide* expresses a mythology which is obsolete for a part of the bourgeoisie itself. It is unquestionable that travel has become (or become again) a method of approach based on human realities rather than 'culture': once again (as in the eighteenth century, perhaps) it is everyday life which is the main object of travel, and it is social geography, town-planning, sociology, economics which outline the framework of the actual questions asked today even by the merest layman. But as for the *Blue Guide*, it still abides by a partly superseded bourgeois mythology, that which postulated (religious) Art as the fundamental value of culture, but saw its 'riches' and 'treasures' only as a reassuring accumulation of goods (cf. the creation of museums). This behaviour expressed a double urge: to have at one's disposal a cultural alibi as ethereal as possible, and to maintain this alibi in the toils of a computable and acquisitive system, so that one could at any moment do the accounts of the ineffable. It goes without saying that this myth of travel is becoming quite anachronistic, even among the bourgeoisie, and I suppose that if one entrusted the preparation of a new guide-book to, say, the lady-editors at *L'Express* or the editors of *Match*, we would see appearing, questionable as they would still probably be, quite different countries: after the Spain of Anquetil or Larousse, would follow the Spain of Siegfried, then that of Fourastié. Notice how already, in the *Michelin Guide*, the number of bathrooms and forks indicating good restaurants is vying with that of 'artistic curiosities': even bourgeois myths have their differential geology.

It is true that in the case of Spain, the blinkered and old-fashioned character of the description is what is best suited to the latent support given by the *Guide* to Franco. Beside the historical accounts proper (which are rare and meagre, incidentally, for it is well known that History is not a good bourgeois), those accounts in which the Republicans are always '*extremists*' looting churches – but nothing on Guernica – while the good 'Nationalists', on the contrary, spend their time '*liberating*', solely by '*skilful strategic manoeuvres*' and '*heroic feats of resistance*', let me mention the flowering of a splendid myth-alibi: that of the *prosperity* of the country. Needless to say, this prosperity is 'statistical' and 'global', or to be more accurate: 'commercial'. The *Guide* does not tell us, of course, how this fine prosperity is shared out: *hierarchically*, probably, since they think it fit to tell us that '*the serious and patient effort of this people has also included the reform of its political system, in order to achieve regeneration through the loyal application of sound principles of order and hierarchy.*'[3]

The Great Family of Man

A big exhibition of photographs has been held in Paris, the aim of which was to show the universality of human actions in the daily life of all the countries of the world: birth, death, work, knowledge, play, always impose the same types of behaviour; there is a family of Man.

The Family of Man, such at any rate was the original title of the exhibition which came here from the United States. The French have translated it as: *The Great Family of Man*. So what could originally pass for a phrase belonging to zoology, keeping only the similarity in behaviour, the unity of a species, is here amply moralized and sentimentalized. We are at the outset directed to this ambiguous myth of the human 'community', which serves as an alibi to a large part of our humanism.

This myth functions in two stages: first the difference between human morphologies is asserted, exoticism is insistently stressed, the infinite variations of the species, the diversity in skins, skulls and customs are made manifest, the image of Babel is complacently projected over that of the world. Then, from this pluralism, a type of unity is magically produced: man is born, works, laughs and dies everywhere in the same way; and if there still remains in these actions some ethnic peculiarity, at least one hints that there is underlying each one an identical 'nature', that their diversity is only formal and does not belie the existence of a common mould. Of course this means postulating a human essence, and here is God re-introduced into our Exhibition: the diversity of men proclaims his power, his richness; the unity of their gestures demonstrates his will. This is what the introductory leaflet confides to us when it states, by the pen of M. André Chamson, that '*this look over the human condition must somewhat resemble the benevolent gaze of God on our absurd and sublime ant-hill*'. The pietistic intention is underlined by the quotations which accompany each chapter of the Exhibition: these quotations often are 'primitive' proverbs or verses from the Old Testament. They all define an eternal wisdom, a class of assertions which escape History: '*The Earth is a Mother who never dies, Eat bread and salt and speak the truth*, etc.' This is the reign of gnomic truths, the meeting of all the ages of humanity at the most neutral point of their nature, the point where the obviousness of the truism has no longer any value except in the realm of a purely 'poetic' language. Everything here, the content and appeal of the pictures, the discourse which justifies them, aims to suppress the determining weight of History: we are held back at the surface of an identity, prevented precisely by sentimentality from penetrating into this ulterior zone of human behaviour where historical alienation introduces some 'differences' which we shall here quite simply call 'injustices'.

This myth of the human 'condition' rests on a very old mystification, which always consists in placing Nature at the bottom of History. Any classic humanism postulates that in scratching the history of men a little, the relativity of their institutions or the superficial diversity of their skins (but why not ask the parents of

Emmet Till, the young Negro assassinated by the Whites what *they* think of *The Great Family of Man*?), one very quickly reaches the solid rock of a universal human nature. Progressive humanism, on the contrary, must always remember to reverse the terms of this very old imposture, constantly to scour nature, its 'laws' and its 'limits' in order to discover History there, and at last to establish Nature itself as historical.

Examples? Here they are: those of our Exhibition. Birth, death? Yes, these are facts of nature, universal facts. But if one removes History from them, there is nothing more to be said about them; any comment about them becomes purely tautological. The failure of photography seems to me to be flagrant in this connection: to reproduce death or birth tells us, literally, nothing. For these natural facts to gain access to a true language, they must be inserted into a category of knowledge which means postulating that one can transform them, and precisely subject their naturalness to our human criticism. For however universal, they are the signs of an historical writing. True, children are *always* born: but in the whole mass of the human problem, what does the 'essence' of this process matter to us, compared to its modes which, as for them, are perfectly historical? Whether or not the child is born with ease or difficulty, whether or not his birth causes suffering to his mother, whether or not he is threatened by a high mortality rate, whether or not such and such a type of future is open to him: this is what your Exhibitions should be telling people, instead of an eternal lyricism of birth. The same goes for death: must we really celebrate its essence once more, and thus risk forgetting that there is still so much we can do to fight it? It is this very young, far too young power that we must exalt, and not the sterile identity of 'natural' death.

And what can be said about work, which the Exhibition places among great universal facts, putting it on the same plane as birth and death, as if it was quite evident that it belongs to the same order of fate? That work is an age-old fact does not in the least prevent it from remaining a perfectly historical fact. Firstly, and evidently, because of its modes, its motivations, its ends and its benefits, which matter to such an extent that it will never be fair to confuse in a purely gestural identity the colonial and the Western worker (let us also ask the North African workers of the Goutte d'Or district in Paris what they think of *The Great Family of Man*). Secondly, because of the very differences in its inevitability: we know very well that work is 'natural' just as long as it is 'profitable', and that in modifying the inevitability of the profit, we shall perhaps one day modify the inevitability of labour. It is this entirely historified work which we should be told about, instead of an eternal aesthetics of laborious gestures.

So that I rather fear that the final justification of all this Adamism is to give to the immobility of the world the alibi of a 'wisdom' and a 'lyricism' which only make the gestures of man look eternal the better to defuse them.

Notes

1 *Tel Quel*, II, p. 191.
2 Hachette World Guides, dubbed 'Guide Bleu' in French.
3 [Franciso Franco, head of the Nationalists, led a fascist coup against the Republican government of Spain in 1936–8. He ruled Spain until his death in 1975. Eds.]

CHAPTER 7

The Archaeology of Knowledge

Michel Foucault

First published in 1969, *The Archaeology of Knowledge* describes discourses as transpersonal systems of language that embody the ideas, values, and shared vocabularies of communities of knowledge. Foucault's book was Structuralist to the degree that it displaced from center stage the traditional human subject of knowledge. Discourses are characterized by rules and conventions that exceed the control of any one author, and indeed, they regulate what authors say and know. Foucault's work along these lines was especially influential for scholars interested in such things as advice and etiquette books for women and important, though minor, texts adjacent to famous literary works that might have been ignored in the past because they were not "great works" or by "major figures."

The Unities of Discourse

The use of concepts of discontinuity, rupture, threshold, limit, series, and transformation present all historical analysis not only with questions of procedure, but with theoretical problems. It is these problems that will be studied here (the questions of procedure will be examined in later empirical studies – if the opportunity, the desire, and the courage to undertake them do not desert me). These theoretical problems too will be examined only in a particular field: in those disciplines – so unsure of their frontiers, and so vague in content – that we call the history of ideas, or of thought, or of science, or of knowledge.

But there is a negative work to be carried out first: we must rid ourselves of a whole mass of notions, each of which, in its own way, diversifies the theme of continuity. They may not have a very rigorous conceptual structure, but they have a very precise function. Take the notion of tradition: it is intended to give a special temporal status to a group of phenomena that are both successive and identical (or at least similar); it makes it possible to rethink the dispersion of history in the form of the same; it allows a reduction of the difference proper to every beginning, in order to pursue without discontinuity the endless search for the origin; tradition enables us to isolate the new against a background of permanence, and to transfer its merit to originality, to genius, to the decisions proper to individuals. Then there is the notion of influence, which provides a support – of too magical a kind to be very amenable to analysis – for the facts of transmission and communication; which refers to an apparently causal process (but with neither rigorous delimitation nor theoretical definition) the phenomena of resemblance or repetition; which links, at a distance and through time – as if through the mediation of a medium of propagation such defined unities as individuals, *œuvres,* notions, or theories. There are the notions of development and evolution: they make it possible to group a succession of dispersed events, to link them to one and the same organizing principle, to subject them to the exemplary power of life (with its adaptations, its capacity for innovation, the incessant correlation of its different elements, its systems of assimilation and exchange), to discover, already at work in each beginning, a principle of coherence and the outline of a future unity, to master time through a perpetually reversible relation between an origin and an end that are never given, but are always at work. There is the notion of "spirit," which enables us to establish between the simultaneous or successive phenomena of a given period a community of meanings, symbolic links, an interplay of resemblance and reflexion, or which allows the sovereignty of collective consciousness to emerge as the principle of unity and explanation. We must question those ready-made syntheses, those groupings that we normally accept before any examination, those links whose validity is recognized from the outset. We must oust those forms and obscure forces by which we usually link the discourse of one man with that of another; they must be driven out from the darkness in which they reign. And instead of according them unqualified, spontaneous value, we must accept, in the name of methodological rigor, that, in the first instance, they concern only a population of dispersed events.

We must also question those divisions or groupings with which we have become so familiar. Can one accept, as such, the distinction between the major types of discourse, or that between such forms or genres as science, literature, philosophy, religion, history, fiction, etc., and which tend to create certain great historical individualities? We are not even sure of ourselves when we use these distinctions in our own world of discourse, let alone when we are analyzing groups of statements which, when first formulated, were distributed, divided, and characterized in a quite different way: after all, "literature" and "politics" are recent categories, which can be applied to medieval culture, or even classical culture, only by a retrospective hypothesis, and by an interplay of formal analogies or semantic resemblances; but neither literature, nor politics, nor philosophy and the sciences articulated the field of discourse, in the seventeenth or eighteenth century, as they did in the nineteenth century. In any case, these divisions – whether our own, or those contemporary with the discourse under examination – are always themselves reflexive categories, principles of classification, normative rules, institutionalized types: they, in turn, are facts of discourse that deserve to be analyzed beside others; of course, they also have complex relations with each other, but they are not intrinsic, autochthonous, and universally recognizable characteristics.

But the unities that must be suspended above all are those that emerge in the most immediate way: those of the book and the *œuvre*. At first sight, it would seem that one could not abandon these unities without extreme artificiality. Are they not given in the most definite way? There is the material individualization of the book, which occupies a determined space, which has an economic value, and which itself indicates, by a number of signs, the limits of its beginning and its end; and there is the establishment of an *œuvre*, which we recognize and delimit by attributing a certain number of texts to an author. And yet as soon as one looks at the matter a little more closely the difficulties begin. The material unity of the book? Is this the same in the case of an anthology of poems, a collection of posthumous fragments, Desargues' *Traité des Coniques*, or a volume of Michelet's *Histoire de France*? Is it the same in the case of Mallarmé's *Un Coup de dés*, the trial of Gilles de Rais, Butor's *San Marco*, or a Catholic missal? In other words, is not the material unity of the volume a weak, accessory unity in relation to the discursive unity of which it is the support? But is this discursive unity itself homogeneous and uniformly applicable? A novel by Stendhal and a novel by Dostoevsky do not have the same relation of individuality as that between two novels belonging to Balzac's cycle *La Comédie humaine*; and the relation between Balzac's novels is not the same as that existing between Joyce's *Ulysses* and the *Odyssey*. The frontiers of a book are never clear-cut: beyond the title, the first lines, and the last full stop, beyond its internal configuration and its autonomous form, it is caught up in a system of references to other books, other texts, other sentences: it is a node within a network. And this network of references is not the same in the case of a mathematical treatise, a textual commentary, a historical account, and an episode in a novel cycle; the unity of the book, even in the sense of a group of relations, cannot be regarded as identical in each case. The book is not simply the object that one holds in one's hands; and it cannot remain within the little parallelepiped that contains it: its unity is variable and relative. As soon as one questions that unity, it loses its self-evidence; it indicates itself, constructs itself, only on the basis of a complex field of discourse...

Once these immediate forms of continuity are suspended, an entire field is set free. A vast field, but one that can be defined nonetheless: this field is made up of the totality of all effective statements (whether spoken or written), in their dispersion as events and in the occurrence that is proper to them. Before approaching, with any degree of certainty, a science, or novels, or political speeches, or the *œuvre* of an author, or even a single book, the material with which one is dealing is, in its raw, neutral state, a population of events in the space of discourse in general. One is led therefore to the project of a *pure description of discursive events* as the horizon for the search for the unities that form within it. This description is easily distinguishable from an analysis of the language. Of course, a linguistic system can be established (unless it is constructed artificially) only by using a corpus of statements, or a collection of discursive facts; but we must then define, on the basis of this grouping, which has value as a sample, rules that may make it possible to construct other statements than these: even if it has long since disappeared, even if it is no longer spoken, and can be reconstructed only on the basis of rare fragments, a language (*langue*) is still a system for possible statements, a finite body of rules that authorizes an infinite number of performances. The field of discursive events, on the other hand, is a grouping that is always finite and limited at any moment to the linguistic sequences that have been formulated; they may be innumerable, they may, in sheer size, exceed the capacities of recording, memory, or reading: nevertheless they form a finite grouping. The question posed by language analysis of some discursive fact or other is always: according to what rules has a particular statement been made, and consequently according to what rules could other similar statements be made? The description of the events of discourse poses a quite different question: how is it that one particular statement appeared rather than another?

It is also clear that this description of discourses is in opposition to the history of thought. There too a system of thought can be reconstituted only on the basis of a definite discursive totality. But this totality is treated in such a way that one tries to rediscover beyond the statements themselves the intention of the speaking subject, his conscious activity, what he meant, or, again, the unconscious activity that took place, despite himself, in what he said or in the almost imperceptible fracture of his actual words; in any case, we must reconstitute another discourse, rediscover the silent murmuring, the inexhaustible speech that animates from within the voice that one hears, re-establish the tiny, invisible text that runs between and sometimes collides with them. The analysis of thought is always allegorical in relation to the discourse that it employs. Its question is unfailingly: what was being said in what was said? The analysis of the discursive field is orientated in a quite different way; we must grasp the statement in the exact specificity of its occurrence; determine its conditions of existence, fix at least its limits, establish its correlations with other statements that may be connected with it, and show what other forms of statement it excludes. We do not seek below what is manifest the half silent murmur of another discourse; we must show why it could not be other than it was, in what respect it is exclusive of any other, how it assumes, in the midst of others and in relation to them, a place that no other could occupy. The question proper to such an analysis might be formulated in this way: what is this specific existence that emerges from what is said and nowhere else?

We must ask ourselves what purpose is ultimately served by this suspension of all the accepted unities, if, in the end, we return to the unities that we pretended to question at the outset. In fact, the systematic erasure of all given unities enables us first of all to restore to the statement the specificity of its occurrence, and to show that discontinuity is one of those great accidents that create cracks not only in the geology of history but also in the simple fact of the statement; it emerges in its historical irruption; what we try to examine is the incision that it makes, that irreducible – and very often tiny – emergence. However banal it may be, however unimportant its consequences may appear to be, however quickly it may be forgotten after its appearance, however little heard or however badly deciphered we may suppose it to be, a statement is always an event that neither the language (*langue*) nor the meaning can quite exhaust. It is certainly a strange event: first, because on the one hand it is linked to the gesture of writing or to the articulation of speech, and also on the other hand it opens up to itself a residual existence in the field of a memory, or in the materiality of manuscripts, books, or any other form of recording; secondly, because, like every event, it is unique, yet subject to repetition, transformation, and reactivation; thirdly, because it is linked not only to the situations that provoke it, and to the consequences that it gives rise to, but at the same time, and in accordance with a quite different modality, to the statements that precede and follow it.

But if we isolate, in relation to the language and to thought, the occurrence of the statement/event, it is not in order to spread over everything a dust of facts. It is in order to be sure that this occurrence is not linked with synthesizing operations of a purely psychological kind (the intention of the author, the form of his mind, the rigor of his thought, the themes that obsess him, the project that traverses his existence and gives it meaning) and to be able to grasp other forms of regularity, other types of relations. Relations between statements (even if the author is unaware of them; even if the statements do not have the same author; even if the authors were unaware of each other's existence); relations between groups of statements thus established (even if these groups do not concern the same, or even adjacent, fields; even if they do not possess the same formal level; even if they are not the locus of assignable exchanges); relations between statements and groups of statements and events of a quite different kind (technical, economic, social, political). To reveal in all its purity the space in which discursive events are deployed is not to undertake to re-establish it in an isolation that nothing could overcome; it is not to close it upon itself; it is to leave oneself free to describe the interplay of relations within it and outside it.

The third purpose of such a description of the facts of discourse is that by freeing them of all the groupings that purport to be natural, immediate, universal unities, one is able to describe other unities, but this time by means of a group of controlled decisions. Providing one defines the conditions clearly, it might be legitimate to constitute, on the basis of correctly described relations, discursive groups that are not arbitrary, and yet remain invisible. Of course, these relations would never be formulated for themselves in the statements in question (unlike, for example, those explicit relations that are posed and spoken in discourse itself, as in the form of the novel, or a series of mathematical theorems). But in no way would they constitute a sort of secret discourse, animating the manifest discourse from within; it is not therefore an interpretation of the facts of the statement that might reveal them, but the analysis of their coexistence, their succession, their mutual functioning, their reciprocal determination, and their independent or correlative transformation . . .

Discursive Formations

Whenever one can describe, between a number of statements, such a system of dispersion, whenever, between objects, types of statement, concepts, or thematic choices, one can define a regularity (an order, correlations, positions and functionings, transformations), we will say, for the sake of convenience, that we are dealing with a *discursive formation* – thus avoiding words that are already overladen with conditions and consequences, and in any case inadequate to the task of designating such a dispersion, such as "science," "ideology," "theory," or "domain of objectivity." The conditions to which the elements of this division (objects, mode of statement, concepts, thematic choices) are subjected we shall call the *rules of formation*. The rules of formation are conditions of existence (but also of coexistence, maintenance, modification, and disappearance) in a given discursive division.

We can now complete the analysis and see to what extent it fulfills, and to what extent it modifies, the initial project.

Taking those group figures which, in an insistent but confused way, presented themselves as *psychology, economics, grammar, medicine*, we asked on what kind of unity they could be based: were they simply a reconstruction after the event, based on particular works, successive theories, notions and themes some of which had been abandoned, others maintained by tradition, and again others fated to fall into oblivion only to be revived at a later date? Were they simply a series of linked enterprises?

We sought the unity of discourse in the objects themselves, in their distribution, in the interplay of their differences, in their proximity or distance – in short, in what is given to the speaking subject; and, in the end, we are sent back to a setting-up of relations that characterizes discursive practice itself; and what we discover is neither a configuration, nor a form, but a group of *rules* that are immanent in a practice, and define it in its specificity. We also used, as a point of reference, a unity like *psychopathology*: if we had wanted to provide it with a date of birth and precise limits, it would no doubt have been necessary to discover when the word was first used, to what kind of analysis it could be applied, and how it achieved its separation from neurology on the one hand and psychology on the other. What has emerged is a

unity of another type, which does not appear to have the same dates, or the same surface, or the same articulations, but which may take account of a group of objects for which the term psychopathology was merely a reflexive, secondary, classificatory rubric. Psychopathology finally emerged as a discipline in a constant state of renewal, subject to constant discoveries, criticisms, and corrected errors; the system of formation that we have defined remains stable. But let there be no misunderstanding: it is not the objects that remain constant, nor the domain that they form; it is not even their point of emergence or their mode of characterization; but the relation between the surfaces on which they appear, on which they can be delimited, on which they can be analyzed and specified.

In the descriptions for which I have attempted to provide a theory, there can be no question of interpreting discourse with a view to writing a history of the referent. In the example chosen, we are not trying to find out who was mad at a particular period, or in what his madness consisted, or whether his disturbances were identical with those known to us today. We are not asking ourselves whether witches were unrecognized and persecuted madmen and madwomen, or whether, at a different period, a mystical or aesthetic experience was not unduly medicalized. We are not trying to reconstitute what madness itself might be, in the form in which it first presented itself to some primitive, fundamental, deaf, scarcely articulated[1] experience, and in the form in which it was later organized (translated, deformed, travestied, perhaps even repressed) by discourses, and the oblique, often twisted play of their operations. Such a history of the referent is no doubt possible; and I have no wish at the outset to exclude any effort to uncover and free these "prediscursive" experiences from the tyranny of the text. But what we are concerned with here is not to neutralize discourse, to make it the sign of something else, and to pierce through its density in order to reach what remains silently anterior to it, but on the contrary to maintain it in its consistency, to make it emerge in its own complexity. What, in short, we wish to do is to dispense with "things." To "depresentify" them. To conjure up their rich, heavy, immediate plenitude; which we usually regard as the primitive law of a discourse that has become divorced from it through error, oblivion, illusion, ignorance, or the inertia of beliefs and traditions, or even the perhaps unconscious desire not to see and not to speak. To substitute for the enigmatic treasure of "things" anterior to discourse, the regular formation of objects that emerge only in discourse. To define these *objects* without reference to the *ground*, the foundation *of things*, but by relating them to the body of rules that enable them to form as objects of a discourse and thus constitute the conditions of their historical appearance. To write a history of discursive objects that does not plunge them into the common depth of a primal soil, but deploys the nexus of regularities that govern their dispersion.

However, to suppress the stage of "things themselves" is not necessarily to return to the linguistic analysis of meaning. When one describes the formation of the objects of a discourse, one tries to locate the relations that characterize a discursive practice, one determines neither a lexical organization, nor the scansions of a semantic field: one does not question the meaning given at a particular period to such words as "melancholia" or "madness without delirium," nor the opposition of content between "psychosis" and "neurosis." Not, I repeat, that such analyses are regarded as illegitimate or impossible; but they are not relevant when we are trying to discover, for example, how criminality could become an object of medical expertise, or sexual

deviation a possible object of psychiatric discourse. The analysis of lexical contents defines either the elements of meaning at the disposal of speaking subjects in a given period, or the semantic structure that appears on the surface of a discourse that has already been spoken; it does not concern discursive practice as a place in which a tangled plurality – at once superposed and incomplete – of objects is formed and deformed, appears and disappears.

The sagacity of the commentators is not mistaken: from the kind of analysis that I have undertaken, *words* are as deliberately absent as *things* themselves; any description of a vocabulary is as lacking as any reference to the living plenitude of experience. We shall not return to the state anterior to discourse – in which nothing has yet been said, and in which things are only just beginning to emerge out of the grey light; and we shall not pass beyond discourse in order to rediscover the forms that it has created and left behind it; we shall remain, or try to remain, at the level of discourse itself. Since it is sometimes necessary to dot the "i'"s of even the most obvious absences, I will say that in all these searches, in which I have still progressed so little, I would like to show that "discourses," in the form in which they can be heard or read, are not, as one might expect, a mere intersection of things and words: an obscure web of things, and a manifest, visible, colored chain of words; I would like to show that discourse is not a slender surface of contact, or confrontation, between a reality and a language (*langue*), the intrication of a lexicon and an experience; I would like to show with precise examples that in analyzing discourses themselves, one sees the loosening of the embrace, apparently so tight, of words and things, and the emergence of a group of rules proper to discursive practice. These rules define not the dumb existence of a reality, nor the canonical use of a vocabulary, but the ordering of objects. "Words and things" is the entirely serious title of a problem, it is the ironic title of a work that modifies its own form, displaces its own data, and reveals, at the end of the day, a quite different task. A task that consists of not – of no longer – treating discourses as groups of signs (signifying elements referring to, contents or representations) but as practices that systematically form the objects of which they speak. Of course, discourses are composed of signs; but what they do is more than use these signs to designate things. It is this *more* that renders them irreducible to the language (*langue*) and to speech. It is this "more" that we must reveal and describe.

Note

1   This is written against an explicit theme of my book *Madness and Civilization*, and one that recurs particularly in the Preface.

CHAPTER 8

The Structure of Narrative Transmission

Seymour Chatman

Seymour Chatman's *Story and Discourse: Narrative Structure in Fiction and Film* (1978) played an important role in the development of modern "narratology." In this earlier essay (1972), he begins to develop the idea that narrative is a discourse that follows conventions and rules.

It is popular nowadays to assume that narrative is a semiological or quasi-semiological structure quite separate from the language or other medium which communicates it. As such it consists of an expression plane (called 'narrative discourse', or simply 'discourse') and a content plane (called 'story').[1] The expression plane contains the set of narrative *statements*, where 'statement' is independent of and more abstract than any particular manifestation. A certain posture in the ballet, a series of film shots, a whole paragraph in a novel, or only a single word – any of these might be the actualizations of a single narrative statement, since *narrative* as such is independent of medium. The fundamental narrative verb is DO, or where the subject is patient, rather than agent, HAPPEN. As Aristotle maintains, *action* is the fundamental narrative element. Of course, actions are only performed by (or happen to) actors, upon or in reference to objects. So we must recognize not only narrative statements of actions – I will call them PROCESS statements – but also narrative statements of existence which I will call EXISTENCE statements (these include descriptions).

Crosscutting this dichotomy is another which is based on whether the statement is directly presented to the audience or mediated by someone – the someone we call the narrator. Direct presentation presumes a kind of 'overhearing' or 'spying' on the audience's part; in mediated narration, on the other hand, the audience is directly addressed by a narrator. This is essentially the ancient distinction between *mimesis* and *diegesis*, or in modern terms between *showing* and *telling*. Insofar as there is telling, there must be a teller, a narrating voice. To specify the four consequent possibilities, I propose the terms ENACTS (the operation of an unmediated or 'shown' process statement), RECOUNTS (that of a 'told' process statement), PRESENTS (that of a 'shown' stasis statement) and DESCRIBES (that of a 'told' stasis statement). It is essential to understand that 'statement' is used here in an abstract sense, independent of any particular medium. We can still agree with Aristotle that mimesis is the mode of the drama and diegesis that of the dithyramb or pure lyric expression, and that epic or narrative is a mixed mode, combining elements both of direct and imitated speech. Cinema of course can also contain diegetic elements – for instance, captions and legends which help to set the scene or which recount interven-

ing events. And Brecht has brought such devices into the theatre. But the medium of drama is more typically presentational; there do not need to be existence statements, since the existents are simply *there*, on the stage or screen – characters, props, stage-settings. Of course, mixed modes are possible: for instance, a character may narrate a story on stage, or the like. The cinema regularly uses a disembodied narrative voice (technically marked in scripts as 'Voice Over'). It sometimes happens that there is a virtual redundancy – the narrative voice telling exactly what the camera shows; good examples occur in Robert Bresson's film version of Bernanos' *Journal d'un Curé de Campagne*. For this, as for other reasons, the narrative film has affinities with literary narrative that it does not share with plays. Indeed, the term 'narrative film' is often used to distinguish this genre from the 'documentary'. Ballet, too, is radically mimetic; but comic-strips are generally mixed (although a fad for the pantomimic style has recently developed). Literary narrative can be more or less purely mimetic: stories can be written consisting solely of dialogue, for example.

So a central consideration for the theory of narrative is the transmitting source which is postulated. By 'transmission' I simply mean the class of kinds of narrative presentation which includes as its two subclasses showing and telling (always remembering that *narrative* showing is different from, say, theatrical showing). We can distinguish two broad categories, according to whether or not there is an explicit narrator, and if there is, whether his existence is obvious, that is overt, or covert. This distinction is often subsumed under the term 'point of view', but it is clear that that term can be seriously misleading and so will be avoided in the present work.[2]

The initial question, then, is whether a narrator is present, and if he is, how his presence is recognized and how strongly it is felt by the audience. The narrator comes into existence when the story itself is made to seem a demonstrable act of communication. If an audience feels that it is in some sense spoken *to* (regardless of the medium), then the existence of a teller must be presumed. In other cases, the audience feels that it is directly witnessing the action. Naturally, in all but the scenic arts – like drama and the ballet – pure mimesis, that is, direct witnessing, is an illusion. The question, then, is how this illusion is achieved, by what convention does a reader, for example, accept the idea that it is 'as if' he were personally on the scene, though the fact is that he comes to it by turning pages and reading words. It is clear that the author must make special efforts to preserve the illusion that the events are literally happening before the reader's eyes. And it is only very recently – within the last hundred years – that attempts at a purely 'dramatic' narrative have been made.

That it is essential not to confuse author and narrator is now a commonplace of modern criticism. As Monroe C. Beardsley argues, '. . . the speaker of a literary work cannot be identified with the author – and therefore the character and condition of the speaker can be known by internal evidence alone – unless the author has provided a pragmatic context, or a claim of one, that connects the speaker with himself.'[3] And even in such a context, it is preferable to speak not of the author, but of the 'author', or even better, '"author"-narrator', for he is simply one of the possible kinds of narrators. The 'author'-narrator is never equivalent to the flesh-and-blood Dickens or Hemingway or Fielding. If he were, we could not account for the inevitable discrepancies between the values and ideas and experiences of authors as we know them from biographies, and the values, ideas and experiences implicit in their works. Or between two works by the same author, between the 'Fielding' of *Tom*

Jones and the 'Fielding' of *Jonathan Wild*, or *Amelia*.[4] These considerations have suggested the utility of a term like Wayne Booth's 'implied author':

> As he writes (the real author), creates not simply an ideal, impersonal 'man in general' but an implied version of 'himself' that is different from the implied authors we meet in other men's works. . . . Whether we call this implied author an 'official scribe', or adopt the term recently revived by Kathleen Tillotson – the author's 'second self' – it is clear that the picture the reader gets of this presence is one of the author's most important effects. However impersonal he may try to be, his reader will inevitably construct a picture of the official scribe who writes in this manner – and of course that official scribe will never be neutral toward all values.[5]

He is 'implied', i.e., he is a construction or reconstruction by the reader, and he is not the narrator, but rather the man who invented the narrator (if there is one), in short, the man who stacked the cards in this particular way, who had *these* things happen to *these* people. The distinction is particularly evident in the case of the 'unreliable narrator' (another of Booth's happy coinages). What makes a narrator unreliable is that his values diverge strikingly from that of the implied author's; that is, 'the norms of the work' conflict with the view of the events and existents that the narrator is presenting, and we become suspicious of his sincerity or competence to tell the 'truth'. The implied author can be at virtual odds with his 'author'-narrator. There is always an implied author, though there might not be a single real author in the ordinary sense (i.e., the narrative may have been composed by committee, by a disparate group of people over a long period of time, as were many folk ballads, by random-number generation by a computer, or whatever).[6] And what establishes the character of the implied author is the moral and other norms of the work taken as a whole.

> Our sense of the implied author includes not only the extractable meanings but also the moral and emotional content of each bit of action and suffering of all of the characters. It includes, in short, the intuitive apprehension of a completed whole; the chief values to which this implied author is committed, regardless of what party his creator belongs to in real life, is that which is expressed by the total form.[7]

Preliminary to any discussion of the structure of discourse in literary narratives is an understanding of the linguistic and linguistic-philosophical basis for reports of speech, thought, physical action and so on, since it is at least partly on these grounds that the reader makes his decision about who is speaking, thinking or whatever, and in particular whether there is an express narrator or not.

The clearest evocations of a narrator are, of course, direct intrusions, the use of the personal pronoun 'I' or epithets like 'the author', or 'your narrator' and so on. Others (to be discussed below) are, rather, inferential: statements interpreting a character's behaviour or action presuppose an interpreter, hence a narrator. (To say that it is the 'author' – i.e. the implied author – is simply to say that he elects to appear as a narrator.) General commentaries on fate, the nature of the world or whatever presume a commentator, hence, again, a narrator. And so on. Somewhat less obvious are simple descriptions of a character's action or state of being. 'John sat in a chair' might in some sense be taken as the issue of a narrator's voice since John would not ordinarily be thought of as *saying* those words to himself. In this instance he would hardly verbalize to himself what he was doing. The ordinary convention is that a character is not verbally conscious of his location, or if he is, the consciousness would not take the bald form of mentally speaking the words 'I sat in the chair.'

There is then a set of sentences which by their form as well as content may be identified as utterances of a narrator. Clearly distinct from these are sentences attributable to the voices (external or internal) of characters, whose forms are more numerous and complex than is usually assumed. It is essential to be clear about them, since they are the elements of any discussion of the structure of literary narrative that pretends to exactness.

A convenient basis for such distinctions is provided by a recent movement in philosophy called 'speech act' theory. This is not linguistics in the strict sense: it is not concerned with the grammatical composition of sentences in a language, but rather with their role in the communication situation, particularly in their function as actual acts by speaker. We owe the theory to the English philosopher John Austin.[8] According to Austin, the intention of sentences – what he calls their 'illocutionary' aspect – is to be sharply distinguished from their grammatical, or 'locutionary' aspect, and from the effect which they achieve on the hearer, or 'perlocutionary' aspect. Thus, when a speaker utters a sentence in English (or any natural language), he is seen as doing at least two, and possibly three things: (1) he is making that sentence, that is, forming it according to the rules of English grammar, and (2) he is performing a quite separate act *in* saying it, an act which might equally be performed by non-linguistic means. For example, if he says 'Jump into the water', he is performing (1) the locution 'Jump into the water' according to the standard English rules for imperative constructions. At the same time, he is performing (2) the illocution of *commanding*, an act corresponding in some way to non-linguistic acts like pushing his interlocutor toward the water. If he accomplishes the intention of the illocution, in this case if he succeeds in getting his interlocutor to jump into the pool, he has performed (3) the perlocution of *persuading*. Note that perlocution, if it occurs, is the same whether the communicative act is verbal, that is illocutionary, or not.

Perhaps the best way to distinguish between these categories and to show that they are not cross-determined is to set up an illustrative table. Take, for example the illocutionary act of 'predicting':[9]

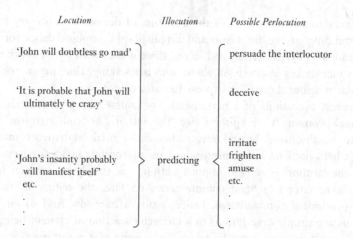

Locution	Illocution	Possible Perlocution
'John will doubtless go mad'		persuade the interlocutor
'It is probable that John will ultimately be crazy'		deceive
'John's insanity probably will manifest itself' etc.	predicting	irritate frighten amuse etc.

That is, any given illocution, say, prediction, can be couched in any one of a number of locutions, using different syntactic and lexical elements. At the same

'Owing to his gloomy and tragic death', on the other hand, however much it may relate syntactically to structures like 'His death was gloomy and tragic' does not have a primarily descriptive function. Rather, it states an event, the manner of which is, in the unfolding of the plot, secondary to the event itself; thus a narrative-statement paraphrase might be something like *He died gloomily and tragically*. (I am not, of course, presuming to rewrite Dostoevsky, but simply to highlight the purely narrative aspect of these sentences.)

There occurs in this passage still another category of speech acts that asserts neither actions nor description but does something that might be called 'generalizes' or 'opines'. This turns up in segments like 'yet one pretty frequently to be met with' and 'he was one of those senseless persons who...' The second may seem to take of the form of assertion, say 'There exists a class of senseless persons who...' But it differs in an important way from a clear-cut narrative assertion like 'There was a man named Fyodor Pavlovitch Karamazov'. A true narrative assertion is always integral to the story, and cannot be questioned by a reader, since to do so is to prevent the narrative from proceeding, to deny its very fabric. The author must be granted, by convention, the right to posit all those entities and actions necessary to his narrative. But assertions which are opinions do not have this warranty: they refer to the narrator's view of the world at large, not to the infraworld of the story, and the reader can immediately recognize this departure from the necessities of that infraworld. When the narrator says that there are persons who are senseless and yet capable of looking after their affairs, and that such fellows are frequently met with, he is presumably referring to the real world, the world outside the fiction; such fellows could be met on the streets of Moscow. Since it bears on the outside world, an 'opinion' in the strict speech-act sense makes an apparent truth-claim; one can reasonably ask whether the narrator is right or wrong on independent grounds. But it would not be meaningful to ask whether there was or was not such a person named Fyodor Pavlovitch Karamazov. The same point can be made about the difference between descriptive opinions, like 'Such a class is frequently met with...' and genuine descriptions like 'He was vicious', and so on. A statistical survey of personality types of the nineteenth century is a logical possibility; but since no claims that Fyodor ever existed can be made, it is impossible to judge whether or not he was vicious.[12] The speech-acts of *characters*, on the other hand, tend to be different. Although a character can, of course, tell a story within the main story, most of his speech acts will be appropriate to that actual framing scene and those will have all the variety in the (imagined) world: that is, his speech acts, like his other acts, will be addressed to the other characters and objects around him. So he enters into a wider set of relationships than do the narrator and the (implied) reader. To give just two brief examples: When Clarissa Harlowe in Richardson's novel writes 'I beg your excuse for not writing sooner,' the purported illocution is *apologizing*. When her mother writes 'I cannot but renew my cautions on your master's kindness,' there is a *warning*. And so on. Now of course a narrator can – and Fielding's narrators often do – apologize and warn. But they can only perform these acts in relation to the present situation, namely the narrative relationship which they have with their reader – they can only apologize or warn about the narrative itself, if they are to remain merely narrators. In Book II of *Tom Jones*, Fielding performs the speech act of *stating an intention*, but the intention is clearly in reference to the narrative:

> Though we have properly enough entitled this our work, a history, and not a life; nor
> an apology for a life, as is more in fashion; yet we intend in it rather to pursue the
> method of those writers, who profess to disclose the revolutions of countries, than to
> imitate the painful and voluminous historian... Now it is our purpose, in the ensuing
> pages, to pursue a contrary method. When any extraordinary scene presents itself (as we
> trust will often be the case), we shall spare no pains nor paper to open it at large to our
> reader; but if whole years should pass without producing anything worthy his notice,
> we shall not be afraid of a chasm in our history; but shall hasten on to matters of
> consequence, and leave such periods of time totally unobserved.

And it is clear that such passages must always be ancillary to the central speech-act
function of a narrator, namely to narrate. That cannot be a character's central function, for then he would become a narrator (a 'character-narrator' to be sure). Rather,
characters use language to argue, to make love, carry on business, rhapsodize, cogi-
tate, promise, make commitments, lie, and so on, always within the boundaries of the
fictive world of the story.

Of course, it is possible to introduce illocutionary anomalies; consider the
following passage from Samuel Beckett's *Watt*:

> And then to pass on to the next generation there was Tom's boy young Simon aged
> twenty, whose it is painful to relate
>
>   ?
>
> and his young cousin wife his uncle Sam's girl Ann, aged nineteen, whose it will be
> learnt with regret beauty and utility were greatly diminished by two withered arms and
> a lame leg of unsuspected tubercular origin, and Sam's two surviving boys Bill and Mat
> aged eighteen and seventeen respectively, who having come into this world respectively
> blind and maim were known as Blind Bill and Maim Mat respectively, and Sam's other
> married daughter Kate aged twenty-one years, a fine girl but a bleeder (1), and her
> young cousin husband her uncle Jack's son Sean aged twenty-one years, a sterling
> fellow but a bleeder too...

To the word 'bleeder' Beckett has appended the following footnote: '(1) Haemophilia
is, like enlargement of the prostate, an exclusively male disorder. But not in
this work.' Richard Ohmann's interpretation of the anomaly is worth quoting *in
extenso*:

> Since our narrator has just told us that Kate is a bleeder, it is at best quixotic for him to
> inform us now that such a condition is medically impossible, and then to step out of his
> role *within* the novel altogether. What shall we say of the text? It is not exactly contra-
> dictory, since the statement about poor Kate is made within the fictive world of the
> novel, while that about haemophilia is outside it. (In this respect, the passage is akin to
> G. E. Moore's paradox – that one cannot say 'It's snowing, but I don't believe it's
> snowing.') Nor is it pertinent to say that the narrator has violated truth conditions: we
> don't *expect* a novel to tell truth in this sense. And certainly there is nothing syntactic-
> ally wrong with the anomalous sequence. Yet I imagine many would share my feeling
> that what Beckett has written here is not simply unusual, or bizarre, or irregular, but
> un-English. That is to say, the passage violates some tacit rule for conducting discourse
> in English, some common understanding about how we will talk with one another. This
> understanding is perhaps roughly analogous to the rule violated by 'whose it will be
> learnt with regret beauty,' rather than to the expectations that make 'a sterling fellow
> but a bleeder' surprising.[13]

He analyses the anomaly by reference to the concept of that kind of speech act which Austin calls 'performative', a particularly pure speech act since it asserts nothing true or false, but simply performs the act in question. Where the performative is a 'statement', its requirements are something like the following:

> To make a *statement* felicitously, I must, among other things, utter a declarative sentence (criterion 1). I must be the right person to make the *statement* (2). I will not get away with *stating* that a memory of your grandfather just crossed your mind. I must not mumble (3) or break off in the middle (4). I must believe what I say (5), and I must not ground my future conduct or speech in a contrary understanding of the state of the world (6).

Ohmann goes on to show that Beckett's footnote does not in fact satisfy these requirements:

> It is here that the Beckett passage goes awry. Either it fails on rule 5, in that the narrator holds an improper set of beliefs for the act of stating that Kate was a bleeder, or it fails on rule 6, in that he comforts himself inappropriately afterward – namely, in writing the footnote. So one or the other of his statements is infelicitous – breaks the contract that exists between writer and reader. The second sentence of the footnote compounds the breach. For behind the act of stating is the all-encompassing illocutionary act of telling a story, and, by rule 5, the teller always endorses the fictive world of the story for its duration, and, again by convention, does not acknowledge that it *is* a fiction. When Beckett's narrator admits a discrepancy between his fictive world and the real world, he violates both rules. Hence he sets the reader at odds with the text, in a way that produces disorientation and amusement, but which, on a deeper plane, calls into question the very possibility, or at least the reasonableness, of building narratives or trying to make sense of human conduct, or indeed, maintaining a society.

This strikes me as an illuminating analysis, acceptable in every detail except the argument that the discrepancy is linguistic, that the anomaly is 'un-English'. I don't dispute it in the trivial sense that the anomaly could equally occur in German or Swahili, since I take Ohmann's 'un-English' to mean something like 'unlinguistic', but I would argue that it is not only unlinguistic, but 'unnarrative', since such an anomaly could be communicated even in another discursive medium. Consider, for example, trick photography in the cinema. Now it is perfectly conceivable that a trick-shot should occur – say a man flying unaided through the air – which is denied by the rest of the film (it never happens again, or no character sees it, or if one does, he simply shakes his head and dismisses it as 'seeing things'); yet the act may be perfectly 'true' in some deeper sense of the film's meaning. Wouldn't that be a parallel to Kate's being a bleeder in this fiction, even though that is not possible in the real world? Since there have been films made without words, without even captions, we must conclude that the anomaly is not in the language but in the discourse. To say that something is 'unnarrative' is simply to say that the discourse has introduced elements which are contradicted by reference to the ordinary laws of nature, and moreover that these have been called attention to within the work itself. As Ohmann points out, the narrator is here expressly withdrawing his 'endorsement' of the fictive world. However, it is not enough to say that he has violated rules and leave it at that. What has happened is that he has expanded into another kind of discourse, a kind of ironic narrative or narrative *manqué*, a narrative 'calling into question the building of narratives' which creates its own discursive form.

Fundamental to any analysis of the complex relations between speech acts of the narrator (if any) and of characters is a purely linguistic description of the basic ways of communicating speech (external voice) or thought (internal voice). A basic distinction is that between quotation and report, or in the more traditional terms, 'direct' and 'indirect' style. The distinction between *oratio recta* and *oratio obliqua* has been a grammatical commonplace for centuries. It is usually formulated in terms of speech – the difference between ' "I have to go," she said' and 'She said that she had to go'. But obviously the same applies to quotations and reports of thinking: ' "I have to go," she thought' and 'She thought that she had to go'. It seems worthwhile to maintain this dichotomy, since, in narrative, speech and thought are significantly different actions.

The grammatical differences between direct and indirect styles are quite clearcut. In both cases there are two clauses: for clarity's sake I shall call the introductory clause the 'tag',[14] and the second clause the 'report'. The tag is the clause doing the reporting or quoting (in the above case 'She said') and the report clause contains that which is reported or quoted ('I have to go' or 'She had to go'). The differences between the two involve (1) the tense of the predicate of the report clause ('have' becomes 'had'), and (2) the person of the subject of the report clause ('I' becomes 'she').

But there has grown up within the last century another distinction which crosscuts that between direct and indirect style, namely that between normal, or, as I call them, 'tagged', and 'free' style (*erlebte Rede, style indirect libre*).[15] Free sentences are simply those with the tag clauses deleted: thus 'I have to go' is the direct free counterpart of both the direct tagged speech 'She said, "I have to go"' and of the direct tagged thought 'She thought, "I have to go"'; while 'She had to go' is the indirect free counterpart of indirect tagged 'She said that she had to go' and 'She thought that she had to go'. Or in tabular form:

	Free	*Tagged*
Direct		
Speech	I have to go	'I have to go,' she said
Thought	I have to go	'I have to go,' she thought
Indirect		
Speech	She had to go	She said that she had to go
Thought	She had to go	She thought that she had to go

(Or better 'It occurred to her that she had to go,' since 'She thought that she had to go' might be itself a free reduction of '[She said] that she thought that she had to go'.) It is clear that direct free speech and direct free thought are expressed identically and thus ambiguously, as are indirect free speech and thought. Further, there is an additional ambiguity implicit in such indirect free constructions as 'She had to go', which might equally issue from the voice of the narrator.

Though narrative discourse is ultimately couched in words, it is not identical or coterminous with the linguistic manifestation. For example, we must recognize that the choice between indirect and direct discourse – between 'John said that he was fine' and 'John said "I am fine" ' – is essentially discursive though its actualization happens to entail certain actual linguistic choices, for example 'that' vs. zero and 'he' vs. 'I'. But other, nonlinguistic features are also part of discourse. For example, the presence or absence of quotation marks (punctuation systems are not part of the 'natural language' but a separate superimposed system). 'Dots of ellipsis' . . . showing change of time and place is another example of a non-linguistic signal in literary narrative. Such dots are not part of the language, not even of the written language, in the sense that a punctuation mark is, for example, the question mark, '?', which correlates with syntactic divisions and may also be a sign for a phonological feature like rising intonation. The fact that 'dots of ellipsis' may be used for other purposes – to show suspension of a structure, or to connect a title with a page number in the table of contents – is beside the point. In some narratives it is a signal of 'abrupt transition in time and place'; in others it may be used in quite another literary discursive function, for example, Virginia Woolf's short story 'The Mark on the Wall', where it signals the breaking in of reality on the free associative fantasy of the protagonist-narrator.[16] Another example of non-linguistic but discursive elements are the 'tears' to be found on several of the letters in *Les Liaisons dangereuses*, or of *Pamela*. They are part of the larger semiotic context, the communication situation. The essential thing is not to confuse narrative discourse and linguistic manifestation, between which there is no necessary correlation.[17] Say that the author needs to express a certain action by John, for example, that John stole some money. Here the discourse is necessarily in the Process or Does mode. But the linguistic manifestation of such a narrative statement need not use a transitive verb at all. For example, the copula would work equally well: 'John's theft was in the headlines'. The discursive predication *Do* exists nonetheless; it is implicit in the noun phrase 'John's theft', and the mere surface manifestation, the actual choice of an English verb, is not significant at the narrative level.

So the expression 'process statements in the *Does* or *Happens* mode' must not be understood to mean any particular class of sentences in English or another language; it refers, rather, more abstractly, to a *narrative statement*, in the technical sense in which that term is being used. Narrative discourse may make use of the grammar of the language in ways that would be anomalous in other kinds of discourse. A short story by Truman Capote called 'A Christmas Memory'[18] is narrated by the protagonist, who was a child during the story time but who recounts the events retrospectively as an adult. Thus the first sentences are 'Imagine a morning in late November. A coming of winter morning more than twenty years ago': the illocution is *invitation* or the like. But in the third paragraph, after a description of an old woman, the boy's distant cousin, who is the other main character, we read: 'The person to whom she is speaking is myself. I am seven . . .' Other kinds of discourse could not allow the juxtaposition of 'I am seven' and 'This happened to me over twenty years ago'. But the logic here is perfectly clear: the simple present tense is used as a 'dramatic present', in other words we are to read it as if we had been transported backward in time and were witnessing the events with our very eyes. Or as if we were at a theatre (the next best thing), the narrator first appearing before the curtain and saying 'Imagine – so-and-so', and then stepping back as the curtain opened to reveal the very scene (though he will come back on-stage and continue to talk to the audience, standing immediately 'behind' the small boy).

A similar phenomenon is the use of the preterite with adverbs of present time: 'of course, she *was coming* to the party *tonight*'.

Much more could be said about the linguistic basis of literary narrative structure. But my ultimate goal is a description of the variety of narrative transmission. A logical way to proceed, I think, is from structures with the least presumption of a narrator's presence – that is, 'transcripts', through those where the narrator is indirectly present – to those in which he is not only present but highly vocal in his own person. I have space here for only the first end of the spectrum; I shall take up the question of more obvious intervention by narrators in a later paper.

First, an important theoretical presumption. Throughout, my discussion is based on the notion of the freedom of discourse *features* to combine in various ways, rather than that of homogeneous and fixed genres (although a rough generic classification will serve as a basis of organization). By discourse feature I mean a single property of the narrative discourse, for example, the use of the first person singular, or the use or non-use of time summary. Variety among narratives is thus accounted for in terms of various mixtures of independent features, not by an endless proliferation of categories or a Procrustean reduction of instances into normative types. Literary theory in general and narrative theories in particular have suffered from too powerful reduction into a small number of genres, with the consequence that the full discursive complexities of individual cases are missed because they don't 'fit' or get interpreted somehow as exceptional, or even worse, aberrant. The problem can be illustrated by reference to a recent book of F. Stanzel.[19] Stanzel reduces narrative discursive structure – what he calls the 'narrative situation' (*Erzählsituationen*) – to three types, 'authorial', 'first person' and 'figural':

> If the author emerges by addressing the reader, by commenting on the action, by reflections, etc., the reader will bridge the gap between his own world and fictional reality under the guidance, so to speak, of the author. This is *authorial* narration. If the reader has the illusion of being present on the scene in one of the figures (characters), then *figural* narration is taking place. If the point of observation does not lie in any of the novel's figures, although the perspective gives the reader the feeling of being present as an imaginary witness of the events then the presentation can be called *neutral*.[20]

Examples are *Tom Jones*, *Moby Dick*, and *The Ambassadors*. He tries to account for non-canonic cases (of which there are an 'endless number', a 'continuous, ever-changing series',[21]) by means of the following model:

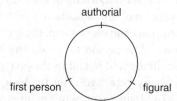

Mixed forms are explained as occupying midway positions on the circumference of the circle: '...the narrative situation of *Henry Esmond* (combining authorial and first-person forms) serves to prove that it is possible to realize intermediary forms which unite characteristic aspects of the surrounding novel types.[22] But when we consider these intermediary forms in detail, we begin to run into difficulty, a difficulty that derives from two related problems: (1) the categories are not genuinely parallel; and (2) the model seems to insist that a form must be transitional between two poles only. Obviously a narrative might contain features characteristic of all three classes (if there are only three).

Let us consider Stanzel's categories as if they were composites of distinctive features of the kind used in linguistic notation – use of the third (or first) person pronoun, existence of a narrator, and presence of the narrator in the fictional or experiencing world, the world of the characters.

	Third person	There is a Narrator[23]	Narrator is present in the fictional world
authorial	+	+	−
figural	+	−	−
first person	−	+	+

We are immediately struck by the fact that these features are not as clearly formulated nor as independent as this sort of display implies. The 'third-person' column and 'first-person' row betray a basic equivoque in the theory, an indication that the analysis hasn't gone far enough to uncover the really basic elements. In saying that the use of the first or third person is criterial, he is implying that the choice is made by each of the three narrative situations in the same way, for example, that the first person novel is narrated by a narrator who refers to himself in the first person, while 'The authorial novel is narrated in the third person'.[24] But 'narrated in the third person' cannot be parallel to 'narrated in the first person'. In a first-person narrative, it is the *narrator* who is referred to by the first person. In an 'authorial' narrative it is the *characters* (including the hero) who are referred to by the third person. The narrator of *Tom Jones*, refers to himself in the first person and to Tom in the third; on the first page,

> The provision, then, which we have here made is no other than *Human Nature*. Nor do I fear that my sensible reader, though most luxurious in his taste, will start, cavil, or be offended, because I have named but one article.

Even where Fielding introduces a third-person expression like 'the author', it is clearly a euphemism of no structural importance, a mere stylistic variant of 'I'.

A similar point must be made about the figural form. Like other critics, Stanzel seems to be confused about who is actually speaking in a 'central consciousness' novel like *The Ambassadors*. He writes

> The past perfect of the second verb can already be viewed from the experiential present of Strether: 'The Sunday of the next week was a wonderful day, and Chad Newsome had let his friend know in advance that he had provided for it. There had already been a question of his taking him to see the great Gloriani...(p. 133).' It subsequently becomes clear that this flashback represents a retrospection on the part of Strether. It takes place at the moment of his arrival at the home of the artist...[25]

But 'on the part of Strether' is surely incorrect if Stanzel means that Strether is *saying* this to himself; this is *not* a free reduction of the indirect thought form 'And Strether remembered that Chad had let him know...' or the like. On the contrary, a narrator and only a narrator could utter this particular sentence; it is precisely a narrator's epitome of what was understood between Chad and Strether.

The mere use of the first or third person is not a particularly powerful feature for distinguishing discursive types. Both Molly Bloom and Ishmael refer to themselves as 'I', but that hardly justifies placing *Ulysses* and *Moby Dick* in the same structural category – precisely because Molly is not a narrator. Indeed there *is* no narrator at this point in *Ulysses*, a situation which Stanzel's tripartite categorization does not easily allow for. For if we put interior monologue in the figural category, 'figural' cannot be equated with 'third-person narration'. In short, 'Third-' and 'First-person' are useless as features in themselves, without specification of the precise narrative element to which they refer.

The point of this critique of Stanzel is not to castigate the book, which I consider to be a useful contribution to our knowledge of narrative structure, but rather to demonstrate the difficulties of any system that reduces narratives to a limited number of set categories, in a taxonomic, rather than a feature kind of analysis. It is clearly preferable to consider the features separately, always allowing for a wide spectrum of possibilities of combination, and to think of the form of *any* narrative as built up out of its own congeries of features.

Since the narrator is a feature like any other and thus subject to dosage in any given narrative, a natural basis of discussion is the degree to which a narrative statement or a whole work presupposes his existence. The negative pole – the pole of pure mimesis – is that occupied by statements purporting to be direct transcripts of a character's behaviour. Properly speaking, in literature pure mimesis is only possible where that behaviour is only linguistic. The positive pole – the pole of pure diegesis – is where the narrator speaks in his proper voice, using the pronoun 'I' or the like and expresses views which are not so much the story as his *view* of the story (interpretations, general or moral observations and the like).

The negative pole, the absolutely unmediated story or pure transcript or record, consists of nothing beyond the speech or verbalized thoughts of characters, omitting even such minimal marks of narrative presence as 'he thought' or 'he said'. The use of such tags, however, is not a strong indicator of narrative mediation, for the convention of 'he said' is not much more conspicuous than that of the use of separate paragraphs to indicate a change of speaker in dialogue or of the character's name followed by a colon in printed forms of plays. (As such it is a feature of *discourse*, rather than of the medium.) Mediation does begin to appear when the tag employs certain 'interpretative' verbs – 'he surmised' or 'he insinuated', or the like. The minimal phrases 'he said' or 'he felt' present a kind of norm; they add nothing – they represent a minimal representation in the process mode.

Theoretically, quoted dialogue is the minimal case; the only necessary assumption is that the author has copied the speech of the character. What we have is something like the transcript of a sound recording. We cannot avoid the implication that *somebody* has done the copying, but convention has it that we forget the act of transcription and assume that the expression is a pure act of mimesis. Even this form entails a transformation, from the modality of oral to that of written speech; the 'purest' instance of unmediated witnessing would have to be that in which the quoted text purported to be itself written – a letter, diary or whatever – in which a character's sentiments were depicted. The 'implied author' then is only a compiler.

Somewhat more distant from the pure mimetic pole is the depiction of actions other than overt speech, involving internal processes – thoughts, feelings, sense impressions, and so on – as well as external but non-verbal movement. In the first, the convention is that the author can read and copy out into words what is going on in the mind of a character. This obviously presupposes a machine somewhat more complex than a sound recorder – a machine for reading thoughts (including perceptions, sensations, unarticulated feelings), and putting them into linguistic form. It is not only the impregnability of the skull that makes this transcription difficult, but also the fact that a certain amount of mental activity is non-verbal and therefore verbal depiction entails the same minimal necessity for interpretation as does the depiction of more overtly visible non-verbal behaviour.[26]

Obviously, written narrative cannot directly imitate physical actions – like sitting down – the way drama does. When an actor sits down he imitates with the movements of his body the character's movements as he interprets them – it is he, not the playwright, who embodies the character. He performs the more immediate mimesis. And, as I have suggested, mediation always opens the possibility for interpretation: when we read in a narrative 'John fell into the chair' or 'John lounged about', there is obviously more than a mere imitation in words of John's action – there is a hint at least of a comment on that action. This is *logically* true to a certain degree even if the term is as neutral as can be – 'sat' rather than 'lounged'. Even 'sat' implies something, if nothing more than the fact that more loaded terms have been avoided: perhaps something like 'John (*simply*) sat down'. The convention has it that there is a scale of interpretation: more neutral words suggest an avoidance of intervention. The bare description of physical action is felt to be essentially non-mediated. We make such assumptions as long as we feel that the implied author has done his best to avoid judging or commenting upon, interpreting (or whatever) the action. What these verbs precisely entail may not always be possible to specify, but, clearly, certain words and grammatical structures imply such judgement and others do not: for example, 'lounged' instead of 'sat'. Or syntactically, the whole class of sentence adverbs, which necessarily entail a speaker's judgement on the content of the sentence they modify: for example, 'Obviously, John was tired,' which is possibly a transformation of 'It is obvious *to me, the narrator*, that John was tired', that is, 'I have judged the matter and found it to be thus and so'.

I cannot attempt here a detailed account of the various forms of mediated narrative transmission, and must content myself with a schema. The organization may be simple, proceeding from narratives involving *least* in the way of presuppositions about how the material reaches the audience to those presupposing the most. I am not presenting an air-tight taxonomy of narrative types but simply (hopefully) logical characterization of *one* feature of the narrative, namely the narrator.

Written Records

Of all the forms of literary narrative, those imitating already written documents – like letters and journals – are most directly transcriptional. They reduce the implied author to a mere collector of documents; the only power he has is the narratively trivial one of collating the letters or editing the journal so that the typesetter could set the book. He is not even faced with the problem of transforming speech into writing, since he has before him the literal artifacts written by the characters; the only purported change is that of handwriting into print. He is not even a stenographer (with the stenographer's options about punctuation and so on), but merely a compiler. He may or may not make his presence known; if he does it is usually in the guise of 'editor' or the like.

The journal novel differs from the epistolary novel in respect to whom it implies to be the reader. The implied reader of a letter is the addressee and correspondent; the implied reader of a private journal is usually the writer himself. Its purpose is not informational but rather in the way of *aide-mémoire* or assessment and analysis of his developing situation. Like the letter-writer, and unlike the retrospective first-person narrator, the journal-writer does not know what will happen next, what will be the ultimate outcome of the plot.

Again, as in the epistolary narrative, the journal-writer may be a narrator, keeping track of events for his own edification and memory. But a simple transcription of things that have happened to him may not be his primary interest. Consider these passages from Sartre's *Nausea*; on the narrator's (Roquentin's) profession:

> I don't think the historian's trade is much given to psychological analysis. In our work we have to do only with sentiments in the whole, to which we give generic titles such as Ambition and Interest.

On his own habits, seen at a neutral distance:

> ...there is something new about my hands, a certain way of picking up my pipe or fork. Or else it's the fork which now has a certain way of having itself picked up, I don't know....

In such contexts, when narrative does appear, it often serves the function of example:

> ...a little while ago, just as I was coming into my room, I stopped short because I felt in my hand a cold object which held my attention through a sort of personality. I opened my hand, looked: I was simply holding the door-knob.

It is interesting to consider some of the possibilities of the journal convention in other narrative media, for instance, the film. Robert Bresson's *Diary of a Country Priest* (1950), after Bernanos' novel, illustrates some of the possibilities. Especially at the beginning, brief shots illustrating the quality of the curé's daily life in his tiny vicarage are interlaced with shots of his hand writing the journal (his physical and mental distress frequently being reflected in the blottings or erratic handwriting). At the same time his own voice – rather a voice-over, since his lips do not move – reads what he is writing in the journal. The peculiar narrative flexibility of the cinema is illustrated by the fact that the journal can continue to be *read aloud* by the 'voice-over' effect, even when the visual image is not of the journal but of the action depicted by the journal at that moment. Thus the action that we see, in the present tense, so to speak, is the visual counterpart of what we hear, in the past tense, from the curé's lips. This leads to certain interesting effects. At one point, for example, his voice breaks off and says that he must write down immediately what is happening; then there is a cut immediately to an action, as the voice-over ceases. This leaves the audience a bit disoriented. Are we to assume that the action has suddenly gone ahead of the journal, that what was only future and incipient in the journal has become present and actual in the image: that is, is it that the narrative convention is suddenly broken? Or is this simply a flashback without journal specification (as elsewhere: the voice-over says 'I arrived home', then stops speaking and the action continues purely visually)? Only the context helps us to figure out that the former is the case.

Another interesting effect is utilized several times to show that the mind of the curé is unable to grasp what is being said to him (not only illness but naïveté plagues him – he says plaintively at one point that he will never understand human beings).

What happens is this: the action is completely in the dramatic rather than the narrative mode, that is, the narrative voice-over is still. He is conversing with another character, the countess, for example; the camera is focussed on him as he listens to her speak, though it is her voice we hear. Then her voice suddenly becomes weaker, though still audible, and the *journal*-voice-over starts speaking conjointly with her voice, though louder, as it explains why he cannot understand what she's saying. The multi-channel capacity of the cinema has only begun to make use of these interesting special effects.

Speech Records

In the transcription of speech, the implied author is presumed to be nothing more than a stenographer. The unmediated record of speech can be that of a single character, the classic 'dramatic' monologue, or of two or more, that is, unmediated dialogue. In 'dramatic monologues' one character speaks to another, a silent listener (not to the 'reader', since there is no relationship established upon which this could be based).[27] The essential characteristic of the dramatic monologue as of dialogue in general is that the speaker is *not* principally involved in recounting, since in that case, he would become a narrator, and the scene only the frame for a secondary narrative.

An example of rather pure dramatic monologue is Dorothy Parker's story 'Lady with a Lamp', the record of the speech of an unnamed character to her friend Mona, who is suffering a nervous breakdown and whom she is ostensibly trying to comfort but whom she only manages to make worse. The story begins and continues in the discursive technique of direct free speech:

Well, Mona! Well, you poor sick thing, you! Ah, you look so little and white and *little*, you do, lying there in that great big bed. That's what you do – go and look so childlike and pitiful nobody'd have the heart to scold you. And I ought to scold you, Mona. Oh, yes, I should so too. Never letting me know you were ill.

The expression 'I should so too' implies that at this point Mona has protested that she should not be scolded. Her verbal reaction never actually appears in print; but always is inferable from what her friend says.

I was mistaken, that's all. I simply thought that after – Oh, now, you don't have to do that. You never have to say you're sorry, to *me*. I understand.

(Mona's apology presumably interrupts the speaker at 'after'.)

You stay right the way you're lying, and I'll – Because you shouldn't move around, I'm sure. It must be terribly bad for you. All right, dear, you can move around all you want to. All right, I must be crazy. I'm crazy, then. We'll leave it like that.

(Mona presumably asks why she shouldn't move around, interrupting the speaker at 'I'll', to which the speaker responds 'Because . . .' Then, presumably, Mona disagrees, so the speaker acquiesces, saying 'all right'.)

At the end the speaker has so upset Mona that she becomes alarmed herself at the reaction:

Mona, don't! Mona, stop it! Please, Mona! You mustn't talk like that, you mustn't say such things.

(Mona has perhaps threatened to do herself in.)

Finally, in desperation, the speaker calls to Mona's maid, Edie, the change of interlocutor being visually indicated by putting the paragraph in italics:

Edie, Oh, Edie! Edie, I think you'd better get Dr. Britton on the telephone, and tell him to come down and give Miss Morrison something to quiet her. I'm afraid she's got herself a bit upset.

Obviously, the dramatic monologue is so special an effect that there must be some overwhelming reason for its employment. It is clear that in 'Lady with a Lamp' the notion of a character's moral and psychological obtuseness and even unconscious malice is supported by the technique of keeping her interlocutor – her victim – unheard. Thus content finds a direct formal counterpart in technique.

Dialogue is so commonplace and well-understood that little comment need be made. Practically every novel or story contains narratives made up in smaller or greater part or quoted speeches of one character to another. What does need to be recognized is that narratives that rely totally or predominantly on records of characters' speeches – whether monologues or dialogues – entail more inference than other kinds of narrative, or if not more, at least a special kind of inference. To a greater degree than normal, the reader is required to interpret the illocutionary force of the sentences that are spoken by the characters; that is, he is supposed to infer what they 'mean' in the context of the action, even if there are no direct reports of that action, indeed even if the whole action can only be constructed through such inferences. It's as if he were supposed to supply, metatextually, the correct verb tag – 'complained', 'argued', 'pleaded' or whatever – to characterize the speech act. Consider for example the following sentences from Hemingway's 'Hills Like White Elephants':

The girl was looking off at the line of hills. They were white in the sun and the country was brown and dry.
    'They look like white elephants,' she said.
    'I've never seen one.' The man drank his beer.
    'No, you wouldn't have.'
    'I might have,' the man said. 'Just because you say I wouldn't have doesn't prove anything.'

The girl first *poeticizes* or the like (italics for illocutions). The man may seem to be *admitting ignorance*, that is, at least, if the locution had occurred in another context; in this context, however, in response to the poeticism, the remark sounds more like a *rejection* of her flight of fancy, and is done with a hint of self-satisfaction. She then *criticizes* or *belittles* him. He in turn *defends* himself and *challenges her authority* to make judgements about him.

We make these inferences about speech-acts as we make all our inferences in reading – in terms of our ordinary knowledge of the world, our ordinary expectations of human behaviour in the society we know. That is perhaps why pure speech-report narratives are harder to understand across profound cultural borders.

Several narrative theorists[28] have used the word 'soliloquy' to describe another sort of unmediated narration of speech, citing as examples such works as Virginia Woolf's

The Waves and Faulkner's *As I Lay Dying*. Is the transfer of the term to narrative structure useful? Is this a separate narrative category? Let us recall its meaning in the drama. The standard examples – Hamlet's and Macbeth's soliloquies – contain at least the following features:

(*a*)   the character does in fact speak (in the cinematic version, by a technical trick, his lips remain closed but we hear his voice);

(*b*)   either he is alone, on stage, or if there are others they show by their demeanour and actions that they do not hear him;

(*c*)   he traditionally faces the audience;

(*d*)   but he does not necessarily name the audience; the second person pronoun or the imperative, if used, are addressed either to himself or, in formal apostrophe, to someone not present ('Oh ye Gods,' or the like);

(*e*)   thus the audience is not being addressed, but rather overhears the character's address to himself or to someone not present;

(*f*)   the style and diction of the soliloquy tend to be very much of a piece with the character's ordinary dialogue; thus if he speaks in a formal and poetic manner to the other characters, that is the style of the soliloquy, too; there is no attempt to modify his language to show that it is an *inner* phenomenon;

(*g*)   the content often constitutes an explanation of or comment on the character's situation.

Features (*a*) and (*b*) are obligatory, the rest optional but usual.

Now in what sense can passages in narrative be called soliloquies? *The Waves* and *As I Lay Dying* do in fact exhibit some of these features.[29] In *The Waves* characters are said to *speak*: the tag 'he (she) said' is usually present, and passages attributed to each character are always in quotation marks:

> 'Susan has passed us,' said Bernard. 'She has passed the tool-house door with her handkerchief screwed into a ball. She was not crying, but her eyes, which are so beautiful, were narrow as cats' eyes before they spring. I shall follow her, Neville. I shall go gently behind her, to be at hand, with my curiosity, to comfort her when she bursts out in a rage and thinks, "I am alone".'

As I Lay Dying does not use tags, but name-captions are used to identify each speaker, as in a playscript.

DARL

> Jewel and I come up from the field, following the path in single file. Although I am fifteen feet ahead of him, anyone watching us from the cotton-house can see Jewel's frayed and broken straw hat a full head above my own.

In neither novel do other characters respond directly to the statements of the speaker; thus we infer that the others have not 'heard' them. Thus the form cannot be 'dramatic monologue' or the like. Though Bernard seems to be addressing Neville directly, there is nothing in Neville's next speech (which occurs no less than four pages and ten speakers later) to suggest an acknowledgement of what Bernard has said; indeed, there is no way of knowing whether Bernard is even present at the moment he speaks (the scenic sense is very weak in *The Waves* in any case):

'Where is Bernard?' said Neville. 'He has my knife. We were in the tool-shed making boats, and Susan came past the door....'

The same thing is true of *As I Lay Dying*; the only time there is an interchange between characters is when their conversation is reported by the soliloquizer, in which case the soliloquy itself has become a narrative within a narrative:

CORA

...'She ought to taken those cakes anyway,' Kate says.
'Well,' I say, 'reckon she never had no use for them now'. 'She ought to taken them,' Kate says...

As for the optional features of soliloquy, discussed above, I cannot recall an instance where the reader is named or addressed in either *The Waves* or *As I Lay Dying*. In the rare cases that 'you' occurs in the former, it serves very much the apostrophe effect, as in Louis' speech upon finishing school;

'I am most grateful to you men in black gowns, and you, dead, for your leading, for your guardianship...'

It would seem then that soliloquies can only occur in a tagged, never a free format, for the simple reason that they must be recognized unambiguously as speech, not thought, or rather as a stylized, expressionistic form beyond mere thinking or speaking. As we have seen there is no way of telling, if the tags are removed, which is operative. In this sense, *As I Lay Dying* is more ambiguous than *The Waves*, since only the name-captions are given, but no specification as to whether the named character thinks or speaks the words that follow. My own feeling is that we are to assume that these words are neither spoken nor thought naturalistically by the characters, but rather are attributed to them in some extra-naturalistic way. And it may be that the form of *As I Lay Dying* warrants the establishment of a catergory separate from speech records.

Records of Thought and Feeling

The representation of a character's consciousness may also be unmediated (although the very fact that it is revealed may imply a shade more mediation than in the strict speech record). But 'consciousness' as a concept in narrative needs careful examination. I can only present a brief sketch, and attempt to account for a few cases which are often lumped together, under terms like 'stream of consciousness'.

Without plunging into psychology, one can distinguish on the basis of simple introspection, for the purposes of narrative analysis, two kinds of mental activity: that which entails language and that which does not.[30] I am sometimes conscious of *saying* to myself words like 'I must get milk and bread', but I am not ordinarily conscious of saying to myself as I pass a garden 'The rose is red' or 'See that red rose' or 'The redness of the rose'. It is the first kind of thinking, the kind that apparently is already present in the mind in verbalized form, that appears in narrative as unmediated thought in the strict sense. A visual medium like the cinema can imitate a red rose directly, non-verbally, and it can show that it is the object of a character's perception by simple conventions, like first showing the character look offscreen, and then 'cutting' to the rose itself. The effect is equivalent to 'The character sees the red rose' or even, with contextual support, 'The character sees that the rose is red'. But literature is a verbal art, and even non-verbal sensations must be transformed into words; this inevitably raises the question of who is performing this transformation. But let us take these problems one at a time.

The most obvious and direct means of handling verbalized thoughts is to treat them as 'unspoken speech', placing them in quotation marks, accompanied by tags like 'he thought'. From *Pride and Prejudice*,

> Elizabeth almost stared at her. – 'Can this be Mr. Darcy!' thought she.

According to the schema presented above, this is direct tagged thought: the tense of the report clause is present, not past as it would be in the case of indirect style. The implied author has become mind-reader, in addition to stenographer. But he is no more than that; he does not interpret; he takes down only the words – and the exact words, diction and syntax – as they are 'spoken' in the character's mind. As such the tense remains present, and self-reference to the character is expressed in the first person.

But it is very easy – and has long been commonplace in European fiction – to drop quotation marks, and more recently to drop the tag. The result is direct free thought. This is a form of presentation or enactment which in extended form has often gone under the name of 'interior monologue' or 'stream of consciounsess'. The features which characterize this kind of presentation are:

1 The character's self-reference, if any, is in the first person pronoun.
2 Verb predicates, if any, are in the present tense.

There are three additional logical implications:

3 The language – idiom, diction, word- and syntactic-choice – are appropriate to the character, whether or not a narrator is also present.
4 Allusions to anything in the character's experience are made with no more explanation than would be needed in his own thinking, that is,
5 There is no presumptive audience other than the thinker himself, no deference to the ignorance or expository needs of a reader or another character.

Conditions one, two, and four are not, of course, unique to direct free thought; they apply equally to any form of unmediated speech – dramatic monologue, dialogue, and soliloquy (but not to indirect free thought and speech, which are mediated, albeit minimally and sometimes ambiguously so).

For an example of free direct thought it is appropriate to turn to Joyce's *Ulysses*, say the first chapter of Section II, where we first meet Leopold Bloom:

> (1) Mr. Leopold Bloom ate with relish the inner organs of beasts and fowls. (2) He liked thick giblet soup, nutty gizzards, a stuffed roast heart, liver slices fried with crustcrumbs, fried hencod's roes. (3) Most of all he liked grilled mutton kidneys which gave to his palate a fine tang of faintly scented urine.

(4)   Kidneys were in his mind as he moved about the kitchen softly, righting her breakfast things on the humpy tray.

(5)   Gelid light and air were in the kitchen but out of doors gentle summer morning everywhere. (6) Made him feel a bit peckish.

(7)   The coals were reddening.

(8)   Another slice of bread and butter: three, four: right.

(9)   She didn't like her plate full. (10) Right. (1) He turned from the tray, lifted the kettle off the hob and set it sideways on the fire. (12) It sat there, dull and squat, its spout stuck out. (13) Cup of tea soon. (14) Good. (15) Mouth dry. (16) The cat walked stiffly round a leg of the table with tail on high.

(17)   – Mkgnao!

(18)   – O, there you are, Mr. Bloom said, turning from the fire. (19) The cat mewed in answer and stalked again stiffly round a leg of the table, mewing. (20) Just how she stalks over my writing-table. (21) Prr. (22) Scratch my head. (23) Prr.

(24)   Mr. Bloom watched curiously, kindly, the lithe black form. (25) Clean to see: the gloss of her sleek hide, the white button under the butt of her tail, the green flashing eyes. (26) He bent down to her, his hands on his knees.

(27)   – Milk for the pussens, he said.

(28)   Mrkgnao! the cat cried.

(29)   They call them stupid. (30) They understand what we say better than we understand them. (31) She understands all she wants to. (32) Vindictive too. (33) Wonder what I look like to her. (34) Height of a tower? (35) No, she can jump me.

(36)   – Afraid of the chickens she is, he said mockingly. (37) Afraid of the chook-chooks. (38) I never saw such a stupid pussens as the pussens.

(39)   Cruel. (40) Her nature. (41) Curious mice never squeal.

(42)   Seem to like it.

(43)   Mrkrgnao! the cat said loudly.

(44)   She blinked up out of her avid shameclosing eyes, mewing plaintively and long, showing him her milkwhite teeth. (45) He watched the dark eyeslits narrowing with greed till her eyes were green stones. (46) Then he went to the dresser, took the jug Hanlon's milkman had just filled for him, poured warm-bubbled milk on a saucer and set it slowly on the floor.

It is important to recognize that this passage, which is often cited as a standard example of 'stream of consciousness', only approaches free direct thought gradually. The first four sentences are straightforwardly narrated in conventional fashion, by an effaced narrator, whose existence is only known by the fact that the character is referred to in the third person and his actions represented in the past tense. Further, that such actions are summarized ('ate', 'liked') in the first paragraph posits a narrator who assumes somewhat more than the barest powers of observation – more than, say, the charge of the Hemingwayesque narrator. Joyce's narrator tells us what the character habitually did, and also verbalizes what we assume was only an unverbalized feeling in Bloom's own consciousness ('which gave to his palate a fine tang of faintly scented urine').

Joyce brings the narration into the present scene in the fourth sentence, preserving the narrator's right to pronounce upon the contents of the character's mind. The narrator continues to do so in the fifth, sixth and seventh sentences, although the truncated syntax (deletion of 'was' between 'morning' and 'everywhere' and of 'it' before 'made') hints at a move toward another kind of transmission.

That happens in sentence eight: 'Another slice of bread and butter: three, four: right'. Here the shift is to free thought; it is *not* the truncated syntax *per se* which makes it such, since we've already had that without a shift in transmissional mode, but rather the fact that, in context, any way we fill the syntax out will necessitate the recognition of ellipsis of the tag 'He thought'. In other words, it is not so much a question of whether this is short for 'I'd (or he'd) better prepare another slice of bread and butter' or 'It would be a good idea to have another slice of bread or butter' or whatever, but rather that regardless of the actual original content of that sentence, it is one that Bloom *thinks*. How do we know that? Simply because the word 'right' cannot be attributed to the narrator; it is Bloom's and not the narrator's word. In this context, the narrator could not possibly be imagined to be weighing the 'rightness' of Bloom's action; only Bloom can do so.

However, since so much is deleted, and in particular, the verb-tense, we cannot know if the mode is indirect or direct free thought. (The indirect form would be '(He thought) that was right', and the direct would be 'That's right (he thought)'.) The verb tense, however, is kept in sentence nine, which establishes it clearly as indirect free thought. Ten is ambiguous again, but on the principle of inertia, we assume that it is indirect. Eleven and twelve resume the direct narration.

'Soon', however, brings us back to Bloom's mind: it is a word actually reverberating in his mind or *could be* so reverberating (which is the most we can ever assume in the style of indirect free thought), but again for lack of verb tense we can't tell whether it is direct free or indirect free – 'I'll have a cup of tea soon', or 'He'd have a cup of tea soon'. Similarly with fourteen and fifteen – 'That's good' or 'That was good', 'My mouth's dry' or 'His mouth was dry'. Fifteen resumes the direct narration, and seventeen and eighteen, of course, are dialogue, that is direct tagged speech. Nineteen is narration.

But twenty resumes the quotation of Bloom's mind: it is the first unequivocal instance of his free *direct* thought, since the verb is in the present tense ('stalks'). Twenty-one through twenty-three, of course, are Bloom's 'quotations' of what the cat says: the full form would be ' "'Purr. Scratch my head,' she's saying," he thought.' Twenty-four resumes the narration, while twenty-five goes back to the earlier ambiguous free style, without a verb. Twenty-six is narrative and twenty-seven and twenty-eight are direct tagged speech.

The next paragraph, sentences twenty-nine through thirty-five, is entirely in the direct free thought mode, with present tense verbs and first-person self-reference ('we', 'I'). Thirty-six is direct tagged speech, continued in thirty-seven and thirty-eight by direct free speech.

The next paragraph, thirty-nine through forty-two, is again indeterminately free thought. The rest of the passage is narrated.

So we can see that it takes relatively little in the way of direct free thought (in this case slightly less than half of the sentences) to suggest strongly the effect of 'stream of consciousness'. And further that though fragmentary syntax, free association and the like may accompany this style, the only *necessary* condition is the technique of free direct thought, meaning the use of self-reference by first person pronoun and present tense verbs; for even where these have been deleted, they must be presumed.

The use of direct free thought in mixed passages of 'stream of consciousness' permits the same sort of irony between character and narrator as does the sustained limited third person, 'central consciousness' manner of *The Ambassadors* or *Madame Bovary*.

This is quite different from sustained indirect free style, where the effect is more often (though not necessarily) one of sympathy or identity of view between character and narrator. An example from the first page of Virginia Woolf's *Mrs. Dalloway*:

> Mrs. Dalloway said she would buy the flowers herself. For Lucy had her work cut out for her. The doors would be taken off their hinges; Rumplemayer's men were coming.

The communal or sympathetic mode is established immediately in *Mrs. Dalloway* by means of indirect tagged leading to indirect free forms. The first sentence of the novel is indirect tagged speech: 'Mrs. Dalloway said she would buy the flowers herself.' (Speech is hardly ever communicated this way in the 'stream of consciousness' chapters in *Ulysses*. When it occurs, it is almost always in the direct form, set off by Joyce's own peculiar punctuation – an initial dash instead of quotation marks). The difference is fundamental; it is not that the words *are* the character's words: only that they *might* be. By establishing the indirect report, Virginia Woolf prepares the way for indirect free statements which are indifferently attributable to either narrator or character; and this is what I mean by calling it a 'sympathetic' mode – narrator and character are so close, in such sympathy, that it doesn't matter to whom the statement is attributed; either could have made it:

> For Lucy had her work cut out for her.

Either 'For you see, dear reader, Lucy had her work cut out for her,' (i.e. 'I, the narrator observe that'), or 'Mrs. Dalloway remembered that Lucy had her work cut out for her.' Indeed the ambiguity goes even further, since in respect to Mrs. Dalloway the form is indifferently speech or thought; it could just as well mean 'Mrs. Dalloway *said* that Lucy had her work cut out for her.'[31] Since none of these is excluded, they all hover in suspension within the sentence, and there is established a sense that the narrator has not only access to but unusual affinity with the character's mind. She is part of an 'in'-group; we infer a communal form: 'It was understood by all parties (including the narrator) that Lucy had her work cut out for her.' And if we look back to the first sentence, we discover an interesting thing which prepares us for this consensus: Mrs. Dalloway is reported simply as saying she would buy the flowers, not as saying that to any particular person. It is a pronouncement, not a bit of dialogue. The implication again is communal, ridden with a sense of broader social context: Mrs. Dalloway is accustomed to having an audience, consisting of at least servants, attendants; the fact that it is not necessary, even in the first sentence, to specify her audience implies immediately that she regularly has one.

(The same kind of consensus operates at the beginning of Katherine Mansfield's 'The Garden Party': 'And after all the weather was ideal. They could not have had a more perfect day for a garden party if they had ordered it.' Indistinguishably the thought of one or all the family, or what one of them said to the others, or a report of the consensus of their attitudes, or the narrator's judgement – but which differs in no way from theirs.)

Thus the very narrative structure corroborates at the outset a fundamental distinction between *Mrs. Dalloway* and *Ulysses*: Mrs. Dalloway, the brilliant socialite, tied in so many ways to her society, always surrounded by people – husbands, friends, daughters, ex-lovers, servants, and even a sympathetic narrator – as opposed to those loners, Stephen Dedalus and Leopold Bloom, living on the margins of their society (for different reasons, of course), in conflict with it, unable to communicate with it – except obliquely, at odd moments. And their narrator distant, objective, even at times ironic:

> Mr. Leopold Bloom ate with relish the inner organs of beasts and fowls. He liked thick giblet soup, nutty gizzards, a stuffed roast heart, liver slices fried with crustcrumbs, fried hencod's roes. Most of all he liked grilled mutton kidneys which gave to his palate a fine tang of faintly scented urine.

The second sentence of *Mrs. Dalloway*:

> The doors would be taken off their hinges; Rumplemayer's men were coming.

Again the effect is communal: it is the common understanding that Rumplemayer's men were coming. The future is conveyed by the past tense of 'will' and the past progressive 'were coming'. In *Ulysses*, on the other hand, the future only exists in the character's musings, and so is always in the present tense form (or in an elliptical non-finite verb form):

> He heard then a warm heavy sigh, softer, as she turned over and the loose brass quoits of the bedstead jingled. Must get those settled really.
>
> He pulled the halldoor to after him very quietly, more till the footleaf dropped gently over the threshold, a limp lid. Looked shut. All right till I come anyhow. He walked on, waiting to be spoken to, trailing his ashplant by his side. Its ferrule followed lightly on the path, squealing at his heels. My familiar, after me, calling Steeeeeeeeeephen. A wavering line along the path. They will walk on it tonight.

The detachment of interior monologue vs. the sympathy of the indirect free style: Professor Dorrit Cohn has well expressed the sense of intimacy between narrator and character in the latter:

> By allowing the same tense to describe the individual's view of reality and that reality itself, inner and outer world become one, eliminating explicit distance between the narrator and his creature. Two linguistic levels, inner speech with its idiosyncrasy and author's report with its quasi-objectivity, become fused into one, so that the same current seems to pass through narrating and figural consciousness.[32]

At the same time, however, she shows that this is only one of the possibilities: the

> narrator is, in a sense, the imitator of his character's silent utterances. This mimetic quality of the narrated monologue was repeatedly emphasized by its early theorists. Now imitation implies two basic possibilities: fusion with the subject, in which the actor identifies with, 'becomes' the person he imitates; or distance from the subject, a mock-identification that leads to caricature. Accordingly, there are two divergent directions open to the narrated monologue, depending on which imitative tendency prevails: the lyric and the ironic.[33]

So consensus or sympathy and intimacy between narrator and character is not the only aesthetic artifact of indirect free style. Consider the ironies in this passage from

Madame Bovary which starts out as straight narrative and goes into indirect free style (ending up as direct tagged speech):

> ... Charles ... attendit patiemment le retour de sa femme pour avoir des explications. Si elle n'avait point instruit de ce billet, c'était afin de lui épargner des tracas domestiques; elle s'assit sur ses genoux, le caresse ... (etc.) – Enfin, tu conviendras que, vu la quantité, ce n'est pas trop cher.

Here the indirect free style supports rather the notion of the commonplaceness of Emma's action, how frequent an occurrence it was, how often she pulled the wool over Charles' eyes; and more generally the implication 'You know how it is done in petit-bourgeois circles.'

Indirect free style is one of the chief devices for indicating the speech and thinking of characters in partially unmediated narratives; it provides the structure for a middle ground of consciousness between total submersion in that consciousness, as in the 'stream of consciousness', and the Jamesian effect of relatively distanced observation by a narrator of a mediated 'central consciousness' or 'post of observation' – a topic for a later stage of this inquiry.

Notes

1   This article is a development of work on the narrative, begun in 'New Ways of Analyzing Narrative Structure', *Language and Style*, 2 (1969), pp. 3–36, and continued in 'The Structure of Fiction', *University Review*, 37 (1971), pp. 190–214.

2   The disabling ambiguity is discussed in an article by Sister Kristin Morrison called 'James's and Lubbock's Differing Points of View', *Nineteenth Century Fiction*, 16 (1961), 245–56. Sister Morrison shows that Lubbock and his followers used the term in the sense of the narrative perspective of the speaker (the narrator), that is, the inner workings of his mind; while James usually used it in the sense of the perspective of the knower or reader. Even more confusingly, the term often bears the non-literary sense of 'mental attitude or opinion' or 'interest' (as in 'From China's point of view, President Nixon's visit was very important'). To say that *The Ambassadors* everywhere presents Strether's 'point of view' is valid only if the latter sense is meant, for the speaker is clearly an outside narrator, and along with his *interpretation* of Strether's consciousness, he also gives us, sometimes ironically, his own view of Strether's situation.

3   Monroe C. Beardsley, *Aesthetics* (New York: Harcourt, Brace and World, 1958), p. 240. Compare Kathleen Tillotson, *The Tale and the Teller* (London: Rupert Hart-Davis, 1959), p. 22: 'The "narrator" ... is a method rather than a person; indeed the "narrator" never is the author as man; much confusion has arisen from the identification, and much conscious art has been overlooked. Writing on George Eliot in 1877, Dowden said that the form that most persists in the mind after reading her novels is not any of the characters, but "one who, if not the real George Eliot, is that second self who writes her books and lives and speaks through them." The "second self", he goes on, is "more substantial than any mere human personality", and has "fewer reserves"; while "behind it, lurks well pleased the veritable historical self secure from impertinent observation and criticism".'

4   Wayne C. Booth, *The Rhetoric of Fiction* (Chicago: University of Chicago Press, 1961), p. 72 makes an excellent observation: 'the author of *Jonathan Wild* is by implication very much concerned with public affairs and with the effects of unchecked ambition on the "great men" who attain to power in the world,' while 'the author who greets us on page one of *Amelia* has none of that air of facetiousness combined with general insouciance that we meet ... in *Joseph Andrews*,' but rather imparts an 'air of sententious solemnity'.

5   Booth, pp. 70–1. Booth discuss the problem of finding a good term for this entity on p. 73.

6   These possibilities are suggested by Christian Metz, *Essais sur la signification au cinéma* (Paris: Klincksieck, 1968), p. 29.

7   Booth, pp. 73–4. At another point (p. 151) Booth states: 'Even the novel in which no narrator is dramatized creates an implicit picture of an author who stands behind the scenes, whether as stage manager, as puppeteer, or as an indifferent God, silently paring his fingernails ... Insofar as a novel does not refer directly to this author, there will be no distinction between him and the implied, undramatized narrator; in Hemingway's "The Killers", for example, there is no narrator other than the implicit second self that Hemingway creates as he writes.' Here I must disagree: surely – if the terms are to mean anything at all – we must recognize the presence of the implied author, but not that of the narrator. Booth's term 'implied undramatized narrator' seems unnecessarily complex to describe what is nothing but the mere absence of a narrative voice. Why is it a 'mistake' typical of the 'unexperienced reader', as Booth claims, to assume that stories like 'The Killers' 'come to him unmediated' (p. 152)? Whatever mediation appears is surely that of the 'implied author', not that of a narrator: I assume that an example would be the fact that Nick and George and Henry are named from the outset (the reader 'knows' them even at the very first appearance) whereas the gangsters Al and Max are first 'the men', and the reader only learns their names as Nick, George, and Henry learn them, suggesting that the story occurs from the perspective of the latter. But the device of naming is surely that of the implied author, not that of the narrator. (I owe this example to Thomas O. Sloan.)

8   John Austin, *How to Do Things with Words* (New York: Oxford University Press, 1962). See also John Searle, *Speech Acts* (London: Cambridge University Press, 1969).

9   William Alston, in *Philosophy of Language* (Englewood Cliffs, NJ: Prentice-Hall, 1964), p. 35, proposes this as one of a number of other illocutionary acts, including reporting, announcing, admitting, opining, asking, reprimanding, requesting, suggesting, ordering, proposing, expressing, congratulating, promising, thanking, and exhorting.

10 Richard Ohmann, 'Speech Acts and the Definition of Literature', *Philosophy of Rhetoric*, 1 (1968).

11 For an interesting account of how literary information is communicated in sentences see Richard Ohmann: 'Literature as Sentences', *Essays on the Language of Literature*, ed. Seymour B. Chatman and Samuel R. Levin (Boston: Houghton-Mifflin, 1962), pp. 231–8. Ohmann analyses several sentences from literary texts in terms of their syntactic structures.

12 'Opining' is like the narrative function called 'referential' (or 'cultural' or 'gnomic') which Roland Barthes (*S/Z*, Paris: Seuil, 1970, p. 25) applies to passages like the following (from Balzac's 'Sarrasine'): 'J'étais plongé dans une de ces rêveries profondes qui saisissent tout le monde, même un homme frivole, au sein des fêtes les plus tumultueuses'. ('Referential' in the sense that it permits the discourse to *refer outward* into the real world, to some kind of scientific or moral authority.) Note, again, the use of a certain kind of vocabulary that reveals the function, i.e. *'one of those* profound reveries that seizes *everybody* ...'. And so on.

13 In *Literary Style: A Symposium*, ed. Seymour Chatman (New York: Oxford University Press, 1971), pp. 244–5.

14 Sometimes referred to as the 'verbum dicendi'; see, for example, Dorrit Cohn, 'Narrated Monologue: Definition of a Fictional Style', *Comparative Literature*, 18 (1966), 105.

15 See the bibliography in footnotes to Dorrit Cohn's article and that in Stephen Ullmann's 'Reported Speech and Internal Monologue in Flaubert', *Style in the French Novel* (London: Cambridge University Press, 1957).

16 Its generalized, non-specific semantic import is, thus, like the various transitions between shots in the cinema: the simple cut, the dissolve, the fade-out and -in, the wipe, and so on. These clearly 'mean', but they do not have specific meanings, i.e. in some contexts the dissolve may mean 'at a place and time considerably different from that represented in the previous scene (as opposed to the cut which usually signals a briefer span)' or 'in the mind of the character', or 'a new motif in the action', and so on.

17 Though it contains many excellences, David Lodge's *Language of Fiction* (London: Routledge and Kegan Paul, 1966) makes too much of the role of language in the narrative composite. There are other kinds of structures in narrative than linguistic, even though it is obvious, as Lodge urges, that 'the critic of the novel has no special dispensation from that close and sensitive engagement with language which we naturally expect from the critic of poetry' (p. 47). But language is no more basic than anything else that goes into the narrative. It is simply one of several systems, or codes, and there is no need to *rank* these, Aristotle to the contrary notwithstanding. Each code has its value, and different narrative styles highlight one system or the other. In James, language means a great deal, in Dreiser, relatively little.

18   In *Breakfast at Tiffany's and Three Stories* (New York: Signet, 1959).

19   Stanzel, *Narrative Situations in the Novel* (Bloomington: Indiana University Press, 1969).

20   Stanzel, p. 23.

21   Stanzel, p. 59.

22   Stanzel, p. 62.

23   The distribution in this column is identical for certain other features mentioned by Stanzel, like temporal posteriority of the narrator to the events of the fictional world, and power to compress or summarize those events.

24   Stanzel, p. 38. And later he speaks of 'the authorial narrator's characteristic reluctance to speak in the first person' (p. 69).

25   Stanzel, p. 107.

26   By the same token a purely physical act of this sort does not ordinarily presume consciousness on the part of the character, so that from the narrative-discursive point of view it is unlike a thought. Of course, 'John sat down' *may* mean that he not only sat down but that he was conscious of sitting down. But we assume that it doesn't, unless we have strong contextual evidence to the contrary, for example, where the mode is indirect free, so that every sentence bears a bit of the character's consciousness about it. However, many verbs imply in themselves an element of consciousness along with their physical aspects: verbs like 'wait', 'hand (something to)', and so on.

27   There is no point, I think, in limiting 'dramatic monologue' to poetry and excluding it from prose, merely because its earliest and most famous exponent was Robert Browning (as Melvin Friedman does in *Stream of Consciousness* (New Haven: Yale University Press, 1955), p. 26). A simple but useful definition appears in Joseph Shipley's *Dictionary of World Literature* (Paterson, NJ: Littlefield, Adams and Co., 1960), p. 273: 'The dramatic monologue is a character sketch, or a drama condensed into a single episode, presented in a one-sided conversation by one person to another or to a group.'

28   For example, Robert Humphrey, *Stream of Consciousness in the Modern Novel* (Berkeley and Los Angeles: University of California Press, 1959), pp. 35–8. For Humphrey, soliloquy is 'defined as the technique of representing the psychic content and processes of a character directly from character to reader without the presence of an author, but with an audience tacitly assumed' (whereas interior monologue does not acknowledge the presence of an audience). As I argue below, 'tacit assumption' should not be taken to mean that the character directly *names* the audience; rather, because he seems to be explaining or commenting upon what is happening or has happened and need not do so for his own sake, our presumption is that he is doing it for the reading audience.

29   Thus L. E. Bowling is incorrect in referring to *The Waves* as an 'interior monologue' novel: see 'What is the Stream of Consciousness Technique?', *PMLA*, 65 (1950), p. 339.

30   The distinction is well emphasized in Bowling, p. 342. Edouard Dujardin, *Le Monologue intérieur* (Paris: Messein, 1931) uses the term 'monologue traditionnel' to refer to this form, but this draws too close a parallel with theatrical monologue.

31   This 'triguity' among the possibilities – character's speaking voice or character's mental voice or narrator's voice – explains a line from Jane Austen's *Persuasion* that troubled David Lodge (*Language of Fiction*, p. 15): 'He had always been lucky; he knew that he should be still.' Lodge writes 'We seem to be hearing him speaking to Anne, or to himself... This is not obvious, but is, I think, indicated by the word *knew*. If the narrator's voice were speaking with full authority here, some more guarded word like *thought, supposed, believed* would have been used.' But the triguity would persist there too; the real source of it is the deletion (if there is such) of a possible *earlier* tag 'say': Is it 'He *said* that he knew that he should be still' or simply 'He knew that he should be still' (and if the latter, does it mean 'He knew: "I shall be still"',' or 'I, the narrator, report that he knew he should be still (whether, perhaps, he was conscious of *saying* that to himself or not)')?

32   Cohn, p. 99. Others have also noted this effect: see, for example W. J. M. Bronzwaer, *Tense in the Novel* (Groningen: Wolters-Noordhoff Publishing, 1970), ch. III, who uses the term 'emphatic'.

33   Cohn, pp. 110–11.

PART THREE

Rhetoric, Phenomenology,
Reader Response

CHAPTER 1

Introduction: Language and Action

Julie Rivkin and Michael Ryan

In this section, we bring together two sides of the equation of reading – the production of language acts known as rhetoric and the reception of such acts in reading and interpretation. The dialogic structure of the literary text requires that both sides be taken into account. Rhetoric, the formulation of language for readers, invites and solicits a response from readers.

In ancient Greece and Rome, language was recognized as an important feature of social and political life. Training in how to think properly took the form of training in how to use language effectively. Logic, the right use of such mental processes as induction and deduction, was studied in conjunction with rhetoric, the use of forms to give shape to language and the use of language to make argumentative points and attain emotional effects. In the modern period, the rise of a positivist model of science and the development of more refined forms of abstract mathematical logic eroded the link between philosophy and rhetoric. A study of the forms, tropes, topics, and genres of discourse was no longer considered sufficient for gaining an understanding of how thinking worked or of how far logic could be extended and elaborated. Rhetoric receded in importance in the humanities. Some literary scholars, like Kenneth Burke in the 1930s, still spoke of the importance of rhetoric for an understanding of social action and literary form, but they were few in number. The intellectual movement called Positivism, which favored scientific method and the study of positive facts, displaced rhetoric from its central place in the humanities in education.

One of the major intellectual revolutions of the twentieth century consisted of restoring importance to the study of language. It began in linguistics and carried over into anthropology, philosophy, and the literary criticism of the Russian Formalists and the French Structuralists. Continental philosophers, such as Ernst Cassirer and Martin Heidegger, were among the first to argue for the centrality of language to human experience and to social institutions. Language philosophers in England, such as Ludwig Wittgenstein and J. L. Austin, noted that human knowledge takes place in language and that language is central to human social activity. In conjunction with these intellectual movements there arose a new interest in rhetoric on the part of literary scholars in the mid to late twentieth century.

The work of J. L. Austin, especially his seminal *How To Do Things With Words* (1962), provoked an interest in the way language acts to create institutions, social bonds, emotional effects, and modified realities. He described a class of what he called "performative utterances," statements such as "I pronounce you man and wife" or "I sentence you to death" that make things happen in the world. The

American philosopher John Searle, in his books *Speech Acts* (1970) and *The Social Construction of Language* (1995), played an especially important role in furthering Austin's "speech act" theory. Literary critics have used the theory to study how literary language takes the form of lies, promises, excuses, etc.

Austin's work and speech-act theory in general more rightly belong to the field of pragmatics, the study of the active work of language to achieve certain effects in particular situations. Language is both a means of representing things and thoughts and a means of acting in the world. In the contemporary era, the study of the language of literature, which is usually called "stylistics," blends with the study of language in many other arenas of use. Modern rhetoricians examine, for example, the use of language in the discourse of medicine or of economics. They are concerned particularly with the way language contains embedded within it schemas for understanding the world in a particular way. An important assumption of such discourse analysis is that language shapes people's perceptions of the world. Further developments in speech-act theory contend that language also actively constructs social reality. Institutions such as money depend on language acts that create them and guarantee their credibility.

Like such social institutions, literature depends on being read in a certain way in order to be effective and successful. It is written for an audience, and that audience is implied in the text. Reception, response, and interpretation are in a sense preordained by the rhetoric of the literary work, but the audience also plays a role in shaping how the work will be understood and what meanings it will have. Each new generation and each new group of readers in a new setting brings to a work different codes for understanding it.

One of the first literary critics, the Greek philosopher Aristotle, noticed that a work of literature is as remarkable for its effects as for its causes. Tragedy, he famously remarked, succeeds not so much for reasons of formal perfection as for reasons of the emotional transformation that it works on audiences. The turn in the tragic plot is also a turn of emotion in the audience as, with the tragic hero, the audience moves from blindness to recognition. Such recognition is both a moment of cognitive turning or revelation and a moment of affective response and fellow-feeling. Identified with the hero, we also identify with his feelings of horror or pain or despair. His sense of revolt at the mockery Fate works on human delusions is our own.

A sense of the importance of the contact between literary work and its audiences was shunted aside by later aesthetic theories, especially those developed under the auspices of Romanticism. They emphasized the genius of the writer or creator in bringing the ideal and the real, the universal and the concrete, together in a work of art. Attention shifted from the psychological and emotional link between work and audience to the inner harmony or organic unity of the work itself. These aesthetic theories were Platonic rather than Aristotelian, more indebted to the idealism of Plato than to the realism of Aristotle. If a work of literature had an effect on its audience worth noting, it was to inspire awe at the way it provided a sublime glimpse into Eternity.

Two schools of thought worked to resuscitate interest in the role of the audience in literature. One was the historical school that in the eighteenth century argued that to know the meaning of older texts, one had to reconstruct the context in which they were originally written. Who a work was addressed to in part determined how it should retroactively be interpreted. The other school was the philosophy of Immanuel Kant, who argued that knowledge is shaped by inner mental categories that operate prior to any sense experience. They determine how we know the world. Knowledge that was made up of sensory experience alone would have no unity or coherence. Such ideational unity could be provided only by logical operations that the mind could produce. One implication of this argument was to shift attention toward the work of the observer in constructing knowledge both of the world and of art.

The important point for literary criticism is that the mind comes to literature or to reading already prepared to follow the logic of the narrative or the verse form, to formulate judgments, and to ascribe or deduce meaning. While there may be an object called *King Lear* that exists independently in the world, its very construction as an orderly narrative assumes certain capacities on the part of its audience. They must be capable of recognizing the temporal structure of the play as a unity. As a play in which certain kinds of speech are practiced, certain conclusions are reached, and certain kinds of character delineated, it presupposes that the audience is capable of perceiving this display of literary signs as a coherent order. Each person's reading will be shaped by mental operations that are idiosyncratic and determined by that person's life history and sociocultural context, but some are universal in character (and thus pretty much the same for everyone). The universal mental operations have to do with the ability to follow the logic of temporal narrative and to recognize the different placements of characters in space from scene to scene. The more socially and historically specific (and therefore variable) *a priori* judgments vary according to gender (some women might read the play differently from some men and find Goneril more attractive, for example, than Cordelia) or geography (someone in a country suffering from tyrannical rulers might find the demise of Lear a pleasing, rather than a tragic, resolution).

The Kantian investigation of the role of the mind in shaping knowledge of the world and, by implication, shaping the perception of the work of art was continued by Edmund Husserl at the beginning of the twentieth century. His work on the phenomenology of knowledge deepened an understanding of the operations of consciousness in bringing to sensory experience an ideational and presensory component that was a feature of the mind itself. Husserl was interested in delimiting the pure ideas that were possible only in consciousness. Other philosophers in the same tradition, especially Martin Heidegger and Hans-Georg Gadamer, worked out a compromise between the historicist position and the Kantian one. Knowledge, they argued, occurs in time and history; it cannot achieve the kind of transcendence Husserl especially desired for it. Instead, all knowledge is interpretation, a transfer of meaning from one moment of history into another that always inflects what is known with the categories and assumptions of the later moment. Gadamer, in *Truth and Method* (1972), went so far as to argue that as a result all knowledge will be tinged with error.

The leap from these conclusions to an understanding of the role of the reader's cognition in the work of art was executed by Georges Poulet and Roman Ingarden. The phenomenological literary criticism of Poulet, especially his book *Metamorphoses of the Circle* (1961), transferred to American criticism a sense of the importance of the reader's experience of a literary work. Ingarden's *Cognition of the Work of Art* (1968) argued for an essential link between the work of the audience and the work itself.

The US critic most responsible for disseminating the idea that the reader's experience is as important as those qualities inherent to the work itself was Stanley Fish. Fish argued, famously, that "there is no text in this class," by which he meant that the reader's experience takes precedence over a description of the formal features of the work and, in fact, constitutes those formal features. (See *Is there a Text in this Class?* [1980].) Those features cannot be described except insofar as the mind grasps them. Hence, they have no independent existence apart from the reader's response to them.

More recent thinkers along these lines have explored such things as the psychological workings of reader response to a work of literature. Such work takes two forms. One is an analysis of the way a work manipulates such feeling states as desire, anxiety, and fear. A work of art evokes and directs libidinal urges in its audience. Another strand of work studies actual audiences and asks how they respond to a particular writer. Finally, researchers have also taken to noticing how a single work can be remade by different moments of history or interpreted differently by differently located social agents. *King Lear*, for example, was produced for many years with a happy ending that the culture of the nineteenth century found more appealing than its original tragic conclusion. John Frow has noted that Homer's *Iliad* changes remarkably from one epoch to another, as translators give shape to the original that is usually inflected with their own culture's concerns and preoccupations. French sociologist Pierre Bourdieu argues in his book, *Distinction* (1979), that audiences have different tastes that are largely determined by class location and educational level. We classify literary works according to schemes that we have inherited from our culture and from our social class situation.

CHAPTER 2

Transcendental Aesthetic

Immanuel Kant

First published in 1781, Kant's *Critique of Pure Reason* argued that the mind is an active constructor of our knowledge of the world. While earlier philosophers had noted that experience (the empirical sensation of objects by the mind) played a role in building mental concepts, according to Kant they failed to account for the mind's own *a priori* operations. Such operations occur before experience and make it possible.

General Observations on Transcendental Aesthetic

I.   To avoid all misapprehension, it is necessary to explain, as clearly as possible, what our view is regarding the fundamental constitution of sensible knowledge in general.

What we have meant to say is that all our intuition is nothing but the representation of appearance; that the things which we intuit are not in themselves what we intuit them as being, nor their relations so constituted in themselves as they appear to us, and that if the subject, or even only the subjective constitution of the senses in general, be removed, the whole constitution and all the relations of objects in space and time, nay space and time themselves, would vanish. As appearances, they cannot exist in themselves, but only in us. What objects may be in themselves, and apart from all this receptivity of our sensibility, remains completely unknown to us. We know nothing but our mode of perceiving them – a mode which is peculiar to us, and not necessarily shared in by every being, though, certainly, by every human being. With this alone have we any concern. Space and time are its pure forms, and sensation in general its matter. The former alone can we know *a priori*, that is, prior to all actual perception; and such knowledge is therefore called pure intuition. The latter is that in our knowledge which leads to its being called *a posteriori* knowledge, that is, empirical intuition. The former inhere in our sensibility with absolute necessity, no matter of what kind our sensations may be; the latter can exist in varying modes. Even if we could bring our intuition to the highest degree of clearness, we should not thereby come any nearer to the constitution of objects in themselves. We should still know only our mode of intuition, that is, our sensibility. We should, indeed, know it completely, but always only under the conditions of space and time – conditions which are originally inherent in the subject. What the objects may be in themselves would never become known to us even through the most enlightened knowledge of that which is alone given us, namely, their appearance.

The concept of sensibility and of appearance would be falsified, and our whole teaching in regard to them would be rendered empty and useless, if we were to accept the view that our entire sensibility is nothing but a confused representation of things, containing only what belongs to them in themselves, but doing so under an aggregation of characters and partial representations that we do not consciously distinguish. For the difference between a confused and a clear representation is merely logical, and does not concern the content. No doubt the concept of 'right', in its common-sense usage, contains all that the subtlest speculation can develop out of it, though in its ordinary and practical use we are not conscious of the manifold representations comprised in this thought. But we cannot say that the common concept is therefore sensible, containing a mere appearance. For 'right' can never be an appearance; it is a concept in the understanding, and represents a property (the moral property) of actions, which belongs to them in themselves. The representation of a body in intuition, on the other hand, contains nothing that can belong to an object in itself, but merely the appearance of something, and the mode in which we are affected by that something; and this receptivity of our faculty of knowledge is termed sensibility. Even if that appearance could become completely transparent to us, such knowledge would remain *toto coelo* different from knowledge of the object in itself.

The philosophy of Leibniz and Wolff, in thus treating the difference between the sensible and the intelligible as merely logical, has given a completely wrong direction to all investigations into the nature and origin of our knowledge. This difference is quite evidently transcendental. It does not merely concern their [logical] form, as being either clear or confused. It concerns their origin and content. It is not that by our sensibility we cannot know the nature of things in themselves in any save a confused fashion; we do not apprehend them in any fashion whatsoever. If our subjective constitution be removed, the represented object, with the qualities which sensible intuition bestows upon it, is nowhere to be found, and cannot possibly be found. For it is this subjective constitution which determines its form as appearance.

We commonly distinguish in appearances that which is essentially inherent in their intuition and holds for sense in all human beings, from that which belongs to their intuition accidentally only, and is valid not in relation to sensibility in general but only in relation to a particular standpoint or to a peculiarity of structure in this or that sense. The former kind of knowledge is then declared to represent the object in itself, the latter its appearance only. But this distinction is merely empirical. If, as generally happens, we stop short at this point, and do not proceed, as we ought, to treat the empirical intuition as itself mere appearance, in which nothing that belongs to a thing in itself can be found, our transcendental distinction is lost. We then believe that we know things in themselves, and this in spite of the fact that in the world of sense, however deeply we enquire into its objects, we have to do with nothing but appearances. The rainbow in a sunny shower may be called a mere appearance, and the rain the thing in itself. This is correct, if the latter concept be taken in a merely physical sense. Rain will then be viewed only as that which, in all experience and in all its various positions relative to the senses, is determined thus, and not otherwise, in our intuition. But if we take this empirical object in its general character, and ask, without considering whether or not it is the same for all human sense, whether it represents an object in itself (and by that we cannot mean the drops of rain, for these are already, as appearances, empirical objects), the question as to the relation of the representation to the object at once becomes transcendental. We then realise that not only are the drops of rain mere appearances, but that even their round shape, nay even the space in which they fall, are nothing in themselves, but merely modifications or fundamental forms of our sensible intuition, and that the transcendental object remains unknown to us.

The second important concern of our Transcendental Aesthetic is that it should not obtain favour merely as a plausible hypothesis, but should have that certainty and freedom from doubt which is required of any theory that is to serve as an organon. To make this certainty completely convincing, we shall select a case by which the validity of the position adopted will be rendered obvious . . .

Let us suppose that space and time are in themselves objective, and are conditions of the possibility of things in themselves. In the first place, it is evident that in regard to both there is a large number of *a priori* apodeictic and synthetic propositions. This is especially true of space, to which our chief attention will therefore be directed in this enquiry. Since the propositions of geometry are synthetic *a priori*, and are known with apodeictic certainty, I raise the question, whence do you obtain such propositions, and upon what does the understanding rely in its endeavour to achieve such absolutely necessary and universally valid truths? There is no other way than through concepts or through intuitions; and these are given either *a priori* or *a posteriori*. In their latter form, namely, as *empirical* concepts, and also as that upon which these are grounded, the *empirical* intuition, neither the concepts nor the intuitions can yield any synthetic proposition except such as is itself also merely empirical (that is, a proposition of experience), and which for that very reason can never possess the necessity and absolute universality which are characteristic of all geometrical propositions. As regards the first and sole means of arriving at such knowledge, namely, in *a priori* fashion through mere concepts or through intuitions, it is evident that from mere concepts only analytic knowledge, not synthetic knowledge, is to be obtained. Take, for instance, the proposition, "Two straight lines cannot enclose a space, and with them alone no figure is possible," and try to derive it from the concept of straight lines and of the number two. Or take the proposition, "Given three straight lines, a figure is possible," and try, in like manner, to derive it from the concepts involved. All your labour is vain; and you find that you are constrained to have recourse to intuition, as is always done in geometry. You therefore give yourself an object in intuition. But of what kind is this intuition? Is it a pure *a priori* intuition or an empirical intuition? Were it the latter, no universally valid proposition could ever arise out of it – still less an apodeictic proposition – for experience can never yield such. You must therefore give yourself an object *a priori* in intuition, and ground upon this your synthetic proposition. If there did not exist in you a power of *a priori* intuition; and if that subjective condition were not also at the same time, as regards its form, the universal *a priori* condition under which alone the object of this outer intuition is itself possible; if the object (the triangle) were something in itself, apart from any relation to you, the subject, how could you say that what necessarily exist in you as subjective conditions for the construction of a triangle, must of necessity belong to the triangle itself? You could not then add anything new (the figure) to your concepts (of three lines) as something which must necessarily be met with in the object, since this object is [on that view] given antecedently to your knowledge, and not by means of it. If, therefore, space (and the same is true of time) were not merely a form of your intuition, containing conditions *a priori*, under which alone things can be outer objects to you, and without which subjective conditions outer objects are in themselves nothing, you could not in regard to outer objects determine anything whatsoever in an *a priori* and synthetic manner. It is, therefore, not merely possible or probable, but indubitably certain, that space and time, as the necessary conditions of all outer and inner experience, are merely subjective conditions of all our intuition, and that in relation to these conditions all objects are therefore mere appearances, and not given us as things in themselves which exist in this manner. For this reason also, while much can be said *a priori* as regards the form of appearances, nothing whatsoever can be asserted of the thing in itself, which may underlie these appearances.

II.   In confirmation of this theory of the ideality of both outer and inner sense, and therefore of all objects of the senses, as mere appearances, it is especially relevant to observe that everything in our knowledge which belongs to intuition – feeling of pleasure and pain, and the will, not being knowledge, are excluded – contains nothing but mere relations; namely, of locations in an intuition (extension), of change of location (motion), and of laws according to which this change is determined (moving forces). What it is that is present in this or that location, or what it is that is operative in the things themselves apart from change of location, is not given through intuition. Now a thing in itself cannot be known through mere relations; and we may therefore conclude that since outer sense gives us nothing but mere relations, this sense can contain in its representation only the relation of an object to the subject, and not the inner properties of the object in itself. This also holds true of inner sense, not only because the representations of the *outer senses* constitute the proper material with which we occupy our mind, but because the time in which we set these representations, which is itself antecedent to the consciousness of them in experience, and which underlies them as the formal condition of the mode in which we posit them in the mind, itself contains [only] relations of succession, coexistence, and of that which is coexistent with succession, the enduring. Now that which, as representation, can be antecedent to any and every act of thinking anything, is intuition; and if it contains nothing but relations, it is the form of intuition. Since this form does not represent anything save in so far as something is posited in the mind, it can be nothing but the mode in which the mind is affected through its own activity (namely, through this positing of its representation), and so is affected by itself; in other words, it is nothing but an inner sense in respect of the form of that sense. Everything that is represented through a sense is so far always appearance, and consequently we must either refuse to admit that there is an inner sense, or we must recognise that the subject, which is the object of the sense, can be represented through it only as appearance, not as that subject would judge of itself if its intuition were self-activity only, that is, were intellectual. The whole difficulty is as to how a subject can inwardly intuit itself; and this is a difficulty common to every theory. The consciousness of self (apperception) is the simple representation of the 'I', and if all that is manifold in the subject were given by the *activity of the self*, the inner intuition would be intellectual. In man this consciousness demands inner perception of the manifold which is antecedently given in the subject, and the mode in which this manifold is given in the mind must, as non-spontaneous, be entitled sensibility. If the faculty of coming to consciousness of oneself is to seek out (to apprehend) that which lies in the mind, it must affect the mind, and only in this way can it give rise to an intuition of itself. But the form of this intuition, which exists antecedently in the mind, determines, in the representation of time, the mode in which the manifold is together in the mind, since it then intuits itself not as it would represent itself if immediately self-active, but as it is affected by itself, and therefore as it appears to itself, not as it is.

III. When I say that the intuition of outer objects and the self-intuition of the mind alike represent the objects and the mind, in space and in time, as they affect our senses, that is, as they appear, I do not mean to say that these objects are a mere *illusion*. For in an appearance the objects, nay even the properties that we ascribe to them, are always regarded as something actually given. Since, however, in the relation of the given object to the subject, such properties depend upon the mode of intuition of the subject, this object as *appearance* is to be distinguished from itself as object *in itself*. Thus when I maintain that the quality of space and of time, in conformity with which, as a condition of their existence, I posit both bodies and my own soul, lies in my mode of intuition and not in those objects in themselves, I am not saying that bodies merely *seem* to be outside me, or that my soul only *seems* to be given in my self-consciousness. It would be my own fault, if out of that which I ought to reckon as appearance, I made mere illusion.[1] That does not follow as a consequence of our principle of the ideality of all our sensible intuitions – quite the contrary. It is only if we ascribe *objective reality* to these forms of representation, that it becomes impossible for us to prevent everything being thereby transformed into mere *illusion*. For if we regard space and time as properties which, if they are to be possible at all, must be found in things in themselves, and if we reflect on the absurdities in which we are then involved, in that two infinite things, which are not substances, nor anything actually inhering in substances, must yet have existence, nay, must be the necessary condition of the existence of all things, and moreover must continue to exist, even although all existing things be removed, – we cannot blame the good Berkeley for degrading bodies to mere illusion. Nay, even our own existence, in being made thus dependent upon the self-subsistent reality of a non-entity, such as time, would necessarily be changed with it into sheer illusion – an absurdity of which no one has yet been guilty.

IV. In natural theology, in thinking an object [God], who not only can never be an object of intuition to us but cannot be an object of sensible intuition even to himself, we are careful to remove the conditions of time and space from his intuition – for all his knowledge must be intuition, and not *thought*, which always involves limitations. But with what right can we do this if we have previously made time and space forms of things in themselves, and such as would remain, as *a priori* conditions of the existence of things, even though the things themselves were removed? As conditions of all existence in general, they must also be conditions of the existence of God. If we do not thus treat them as objective forms of all things, the only alternative is to view them as subjective forms of our inner and outer intuition, which is termed sensible, for the very reason that it is *not original*, that is, is not such as can itself give us the existence of its object – a mode of intuition which, so far as we can judge, can belong only to the primordial being. Our mode of intuition is dependent upon the existence of the object, and is therefore possible only if the subject's faculty of representation is affected by that object.

This mode of intuiting in space and time need not be limited to human sensibility. It may be that all finite, thinking beings necessarily agree with man in this respect, although we are not in a position to judge whether this is actually so. But however universal this mode of sensibility may be, it does not therefore cease to be sensibility. It is derivative (*intuitus derivativus*), not original (*intuitus originarius*), and therefore not an intellectual intuition. For the reason stated above, such intellectual intuition seems to belong solely to the primordial being, and can never be ascribed to a dependent being, dependent in its existence as well as in its intuition, and which through that intuition determines its existence solely in relation to given objects.[2] This latter remark, however, must be taken only as an illustration of our aesthetic theory, not as forming part of the proof.

Conclusion of the Transcendental Aesthetic

Here, then, in pure *a priori* intuitions, space and time, we have one of the factors required for solution of the general problem of transcendental philosophy: *how are synthetic a priori judgments possible?* When in *a priori* judgment we seek to go out beyond the given concept, we come in the *a priori* intuitions upon that which cannot be discovered in the concept but which is certainly found *a priori* in the intuition corresponding to the concept, and can be connected with it synthetically. Such judgments, however, thus based on intuition, can never extend beyond objects of the senses; they are valid only for objects of possible experience.

Notes

1   The predicates of the appearance can be ascribed to the object itself, in relation to our sense, for instance, the red colour or the scent to the rose. [But what is illusory can never be ascribed as predicate to an object (for the sufficient reason that we then attribute to the object, taken by itself, what belongs to it only in relation to the senses, or in general to the subject), for instance, the two handles which were formerly ascribed to Saturn.] That which, while inseparable from the representation of the object, is not to be met with in the object in itself, but always in its relation to the subject, is appearance. Accordingly the predicates of space and time are rightly ascribed to the objects of the senses, as such; and in this there is no illusion. On the other hand, if I ascribe redness to the rose *in itself* [handles to Saturn], or extension to all outer objects *in themselves*, without paying regard to the determinate relation of these objects to the subject, and without limiting my judgment to that relation, illusion then first arises. [The passage enclosed in brackets conflicts with the main argument, and is probably a later addition carelessly inserted.]

2   [May be more freely translated as: "through that intuition is conscious of its own existence only in relation to given objects".]

CHAPTER 3

Ideas

Edmund Husserl

First published in 1913, Edmund Husserl's *Ideas: General Introduction to Pure Phenomenology* played a crucial role in the development of twentieth-century European philosophy. Husserl's focus on consciousness and its operations lay at the origin of mid-century phenomenological literary criticism, which studied the movement of consciousness in the literary text.

The Thesis of the Natural Standpoint and its Suspension

The world of the natural standpoint: I and my world about me

Our first outlook upon life is that of natural human beings, imaging, judging, feeling, willing, "*from the natural standpoint.*" Let us make clear to ourselves what this means in the form of simple meditations which we can best carry on in the first person.

I am aware of a world, spread out in space endlessly, and in time becoming and become, without end. I am aware of it, that means, first of all, I discover it immediately, intuitively, I experience it. Through sight, touch, hearing, etc., in the different ways of sensory perception, corporeal things somehow spatially distributed are *for me simply there*, in verbal or figurative sense "present," whether or not I pay them special attention by busying myself with them, considering, thinking, feeling, willing. Animal beings also, perhaps men, are immediately there for me; I look up, I see them, I hear them coming towards me, I grasp them by the hand; speaking with them, I understand immediately what they are sensing and thinking, the feelings that stir them, what they wish or will. They too are present as realities in my field of intuition, even when I pay them no attention. But it is not necessary that they and other objects likewise should be present precisely in my *field of perception*. For me real objects are there, definite, more or less familiar, agreeing with what is actually perceived without being themselves perceived or even intuitively present. I can let my attention wander from the writing-table I have just seen and observed, through the unseen portions of the room behind my back to the verandah, into the garden, to the children in the summer-house, and so forth, to all the objects concerning which I precisely "know" that they are there and yonder in my immediate co-perceived surroundings – a knowledge which has nothing of conceptual thinking in it, and first changes into clear intuiting with the bestowing of attention, and even then only partially and for the most part very imperfectly.

But not even with the added reach of this intuitively clear or dark, distinct or indistinct *co-present* margin, which forms a continuous ring around the actual field of perception, does that world exhaust itself which in every waking moment is in some conscious measure "present" before me. It reaches rather in a fixed order of being the limitless beyond. What is actually perceived, and what is more or less clearly co-present and determinate (to some extent at least), is partly pervaded, partly girt about with a *dimly apprehended depth or fringe of indeterminate reality*. I can pierce it with rays from the illuminating focus of attention with varying success. Determining representations, dim at first, then livelier, fetch me something out, a chain of such recollections takes shape, the circle of determinacy extends ever farther, and eventually so far that the connexion with the actual field of perception as the *immediate* environment is established. But in general the issue is a different one: an empty mist of dim indeterminacy gets studded over with intuitive possibilities or presumptions, and only the "form" of the world as "world" is foretokened. Moreover, the zone of indeterminacy is infinite. The misty horizon that can never be completely outlined remains necessarily there.

As it is with the world in its ordered being as a spatial present – the aspect I have so far been considering – so likewise is it with the world in respect to its *ordered being in the succession of time*. This word now present to me, and in every waking "now" obviously so, has its temporal horizon, infinite in both direction, its known and unknown, its intimately alive and its unalive past and future. Moving freely within the moment of experience which brings what is present into my intuitional grasp, I can follow up these connexions of the reality which immediately surrounds me. I can shift my standpoint in space and time, look this way and that, turn temporally forwards and backwards; I can provide for myself constantly new and more or less clear and meaningful perceptions and representations, and images also more or less clear, in which I make intuitable to myself whatever can possibly exist really or supposedly in the steadfast order of space and time.

In this way, when consciously awake, I find myself at all times, and without my ever being able to change this, set in relation to a world which, through its constant changes, remains one and ever the same. It is continually "present" for me, and I myself am a member of it. Therefore this world is not there for me as a mere *world of facts and affairs*, but, with the same immediacy, as a *world of values*, a *world of goods*, a *practical world*. Without further effort on my part I find the things before me furnished not only with the qualities that befit their positive nature, but with value-characters such as beautiful or ugly, agreeable or disagreeable, pleasant or unpleasant, and so forth. Things in their immediacy stand there as objects to be used, the "table" with its "books," the "glass to drink from," the "vase," the "piano," and so forth. These values and practicalities, they too belong to *the constitution of the "actually present" objects as such*, irrespective of my turning or not turning to consider them or indeed any other objects. The same considerations apply of course just as well to the men and beasts in my surroundings as to "mere things." They are my "friends" or my "foes," my "servants" or "superiors," "strangers" or "relatives," and so forth.

The "Cogito." My natural world-about-me and the ideal worlds-about-me

It is then to this world, *the world in which I find myself and which is also my world-about-me*, that the complex forms of my manifold and shifting *spontaneities* of consciousness stand related: observing in the interests of research the bringing of meaning into conceptual form through description; comparing and distinguishing, collecting and counting, presupposing and inferring, the theorizing activity of consciousness, in short, in its different forms and stages. Related to it likewise are the diverse acts and states of sentiment and disapproval, joy and sorrow, desire and aversion, hope and fear, decision and action. All these, together with the sheer acts of the Ego, in which I become acquainted with the world as *immediately* given me, through spontaneous tendencies to turn towards it and to grasp it, are included under the one Cartesian expression: *Cogito*. In the natural urge of life I live continually in *this fundamental form of all "wakeful" living*, whether in addition I do or do not assert the *cogito*, and whether I am or am not "reflectively" concerned with the Ego and the *cogitare*. If I am so concerned, a new *cogito* has become livingly active, which for its part is not reflected upon, and so not objective for me.

I am present to myself continually as someone who perceives, represents, thinks, feels, desires, and so forth; and *for the most part* herein I find myself related in present experience to the fact-world which is constantly about me. But I am not always so related, not every *cogito* in which I live has for its *cogitatum* things, men, objects or contents of one kind or another. Perhaps I am busied with pure numbers and the laws they symbolize: nothing of this sort is present in the world about me, this world of "real fact." And yet the world of numbers also is there for me, as the field of objects with which I am arithmetically busied; while I am thus occupied some numbers or constructions of a numerical kind will be at the focus of vision, girt by an arithmetical horizon partly defined, partly not; but obviously this being-there-for-me, like the being there at all, is something very different from this. *The arithmetical world is there for me only when and so long as I occupy the arithmetical standpoint.* But the *natural* world, the world in the ordinary sense of the word, is *constantly there for me*, so long as I live naturally and look in its direction. I am then at the *"natural standpoint,"* which is just another way of stating the same thing. And there is no need to modify these conclusions when I proceed to appropriate to myself the arithmetical world, and other similar "worlds," by adopting the corresponding standpoint. The natural world *still remains "present,"* I am at the natural standpoint after as well as before, and in this respect *undisturbed by the adoption of new standpoints*. If my *cogito* is active *only* in the worlds proper to the new standpoints, the natural world remains unconsidered; it is now the background for my consciousness as act, but it is *not the encircling sphere within which an arithmetical world finds its true and proper place*. The two worlds are present together but *disconnected*, apart, that is, from their relation to the Ego, in virtue of which I can freely direct my glance or my acts to the one or to the other.

The "other" Ego-subject and the intersubjective natural world-about-me

Whatever holds good for me personally, also holds good, as I know, for all other men whom I find present in my world-about-me. Experiencing them as men, I understand and take them as Ego-subjects, units like myself, and related to their natural surroundings. But this in such wise that I apprehend the world-about-them and the world-about-me objectively as one and the same world, which differs in each case only through affecting consciousness differently. Each has his place whence he sees the things that are present, and each enjoys accordingly different appearances of the things. For each, again, the fields of perception and memory actually present are different, quite apart from the fact that even that which is here intersubjectively known in common is known in different ways, is differently apprehended, shows different grades of clearness, and so forth. Despite all this, we come to understandings with our neighbours, and set up in common an objective spatio-temporal fact-world as *the world about us that is there for us all, and to which we ourselves none the less belong.*

The General Thesis of the Natural Standpoint

That which we have submitted towards the characterization of what is given to us from the natural standpoint, and thereby of the natural standpoint itself, was a piece of pure description *prior to all "theory."* In these studies we stand bodily aloof from all theories, and by "theories" we here mean anticipatory ideas of every kind. Only as facts of our environment, not as agencies for uniting facts validly together, do theories concern us at all. But we do not set ourselves the task of continuing the pure description and raising it to a systematically inclusive and exhaustive characterization of the data, in their full length and breadth, discoverable from the natural standpoint (or from any standpoint, we might add, that can be knit up with the same in a common consent). A task such as this can and must – as scientific – be undertaken, and it is one of extraordinary importance, although so far scarcely noticed. Here it is not ours to attempt. For us who are striving towards the entrance-gate of phenomenology all the necessary work in this direction has already been carried out; the few features pertaining to the natural standpoint which we need are of a quite general character, and have already figured in our descriptions, and been sufficiently *and fully clarified.* We even made a special point of securing this full measure of clearness.

We emphasize a most important point once again in the sentences that follow: I find continually present and standing over against me the one spatio-temporal fact-world to which I myself belong, as do all other men found in it and related in the same way to it. This "fact-world," as the world already tells us, I find to *be out there,* and also *take it just as it gives itself to me as something that exists out there.* All doubting and rejecting of the data of the natural world leaves standing the *general thesis of the natural standpoint.* "The" world is as fact-world always there; at the most it is at odd points "other" than I supposed, this or that under such names as "illusion," "hallucination," and the like, must be struck *out of it,* so to speak; but the "it" remains ever, in the sense of the general thesis, a world that has its being out there. To know it more comprehensively, more trustworthily, more perfectly than the naïve lore of experience is able to do, and to solve all the problems of scientific knowledge which offer themselves upon its ground, that is the goal of the *sciences of the natural standpoint....*

We limit still further the theme of our inquiry. Its title ran: Consciousness, or more distinctly *Conscious experience (Erlebnis) in general,* to be taken in an extremely wide sense about whose exact definition we are fortunately not concerned. Exact definitions do not lie at the threshold of analysis of the kind we are here making, but are a later result involving great labour. As starting-point we take consciousness in a pregnant sense which suggests itself at once, most simply indicated through the Cartesian *cogito,* "I think." As is known Descartes understood this in a sense so wide as to include every case of "I perceive, I remember, I fancy, I judge, feel, desire, will," and all experiences of the Ego that in any way resemble the foregoing, in all the countless fluctuations of their special patterns. The Ego itself to which they are all related, spontaneous, in receptive or any other "attitude," and indeed the Ego in any and every sense, we leave at first out of consideration. We shall be concerned with it later, and fundamentally. For the present there is sufficient other material to serve as support for our analysis and grasp of the essential. And we shall find ourselves forthwith referred thereby to enveloping connexions of experience which compel us to widen our conception of a conscious experience beyond this circle of specific *cogitationes*.

We shall consider conscious experiences *in the concrete fullness and entirety* with which they figure in their concrete context – the *stream of experience* – and to which they are closely attached through their own proper essence. It then becomes evident that every experience in the stream which our reflexion can lay hold on has *its own essence open to intuition*, a "content" which can be considered in its *singularity in and for itself*. We shall be concerned to grasp this individual content of the *cogitatio* in its *pure* singularity, and to describe it in its general features, excluding everything which is not to be found in the *cogitatio* as it is in itself. We must likewise describe the *unity of consciousness* which is demanded *by the intrinsic nature of the cogitationes*, and so necessarily demanded that they could not be without this unity.

CHAPTER 4

Classical Rhetoric

Edward P. J. Corbett

The publication of Edward Corbett's book on classical rhetoric in 1965 was indicative of the revival of interest in rhetoric that took place in the latter half of the twentieth century. In his book, Corbett reviews the major components of classical rhetoric, from the "topics" or kinds of discourse to the figures of speech.

Figures of Speech

We come now to a consideration of figures of speech. It is fair enough to regard figures of speech as the "graces of language," as the "dressing of thought," as "embellishments," for indeed they do "decorate" our prose and give it "style," in the couturier's sense. But it would be a mistake to regard embellishment as the chief or sole function of figures. The classical rhetoricians certainly did not look upon them as decorative devices primarily. Metaphor, according to Aristotle, did give "charm and distinction" to our expression; but even more than that, metaphor was another way to *give* "clearness" and "liveliness" to the expression of our thoughts. Figures, in his view, provided one of the best ways to strike that happy balance between "the obvious and the obscure," so that our audience could grasp our ideas promptly and thereby be disposed to accept our arguments.

"What, then, can oratorical imagery effect?" Longinus asked. He was even more explicit than Aristotle in pointing out the rhetorical function of figures: "Well, it is able in many ways to infuse vehemence and passion into spoken words, while more particularly when it is combined with the argumentative passages it not only persuades the hearer but actually makes him its slave." – *On the Sublime*, XV, 9.

It was Quintilian who most explicitly related the figures to the *logos*, *pathos*, and *ēthos* of argument. Quintilian looked upon the figures as another means of lending "credibility to our arguments," of "exciting the emotions," and of winning "approval for our characters as pleaders" (*Instit. Orat.*, IX, i). This view of the function of figures of speech is perhaps the most reliable attitude to adopt toward these devices of style. Because figures can render our thoughts vividly concrete, they help us to communicate with our audience clearly and effectively; because they stir emotional responses, they can carry truth, in Wordsworth's phrase, "alive into the heart by passion"; and because they elicit admiration for the eloquence of the speaker or writer, they can exert a powerful ethical appeal.

Sister Miriam Joseph in her book *Shakespeare's Use of the Arts of Language* reclassified the more than two hundred figures distinguished by the Tudor rhetoricians according to the four categories: grammar, logos, pathos, and ethos. In doing this, she was able to demonstrate, quite convincingly, that the three "schools" of rhetoric during the Renaissance (the Ramists, the traditionalists, and the figurists) saw the figures as being intimately connected with the topics of invention. Metaphor, for instance, involving comparison of like things, is tied up with the topic of similarity; antithesis, involving the juxtaposition of opposites, is tied up with the topic of dissimilarity or of contraries. Then there were figures, like apostrophe, that were calculated to work directly on the emotions, and figures, like comprobatio, that were calculated to establish the ethical image of the speaker or writer. In our exposition we shall frequently point out the relationship of the figures either with grammar or with the three modes of persuasive appeal.

The mention of two hundred figures of speech in the previous paragraph may have appalled the student. If pressed, most students could name – even if they could not define or illustrate – a half dozen figures of speech. But where did those *other* figures come from? and what are they? In their passion for anatomizing and categorizing knowledge, the Humanists of the Renaissance delighted in classifying and subclassifying the figures. Admittedly, they were being overly subtle in distinguishing such a multitude of figures. The most widely used classical handbook in the Renaissance schools, *Rhetorica ad Herennium*, required the students to learn only 65 figures. Susenbrotus, in his popular *Epitome troporum ac schematum* (1540), distinguished 132 figures. But Henry Peacham, in his 1577 edition of *The Garden of Eloquence*, pushed the number up to 184. Pity the poor Tudor schoolboy who was expected to define and illustrate and to use in his own compositions a goodly number of these figures.

We are not going to plague the student with a long catalogue of figures, but we are going to introduce more figures than he has met with in his previous study of style. If nothing else, the student should become aware, through this exposure, that his language has more figurative resources than he was conscious of. And he may discover that he has been using many of the figures of speech all his life. For men did not begin to use figures of speech only after academicians had classified and defined them; rather, the figures were classified and defined after men had been using them for centuries. Like the principles of grammar, poetics, and rhetoric, the doctrine of the figures was arrived at inductively. Rhetoricians merely gave "names" to the verbal practices of their fellow men.

What do we mean by the term "figures of speech"? We mean the same thing that Quintilian meant when he used the term *figura*: "any deviation, either in thought or expression, from the ordinary and simple method of speaking, a change analogous to the different positions our bodies assume when we sit down, lie down, or look back.... Let the definition of a figure, therefore, be *a form of speech artfully varied from common usage* (Ergo figura sit arte aliqua novata forma dicendi)" – *Instit. Orat.*, IX, i, 11.

We will use "figures of speech" as the generic term for any artful deviations from the ordinary mode of speaking or writing. But we will divide the figures of speech into two main groups – the *schemes* and the *tropes*. A scheme (Greek *schēma*, form, shape) involves a deviation from the ordinary pattern or arrangement of words. A trope (Greek *tropein*, to turn) involves a deviation from the ordinary and principal signification of a word.

Both types of figures involve a *transference* of some kind: a trope, a transference of meaning; a scheme, a transference of order. When Shakespeare's Mark Antony said,

"Brutus is an honorable man," he was using the trope called irony, because he was "transferring" the ordinary meaning of the word *honorable* to convey a different meaning to his audience. If Mark Antony had said, "Honorable is the man who gives his life for his country," he would have been using a species of the scheme hyperbaton, because he would be "transferring" the usual order of words. In a sense, of course, both schemes and tropes involve a change of "meaning," since both result in effects that are different from the ordinary mode of expression. But for all practical purposes, our distinction is clear enough to enable the student to distinguish between a scheme and a trope.

The terms used to label the various figures appear formidable – strange, polysyllabic words, most of them merely transliterated from the Greek. But technical terms, in any discipline, are always difficult at first sight; they are difficult, however, mainly because they are unfamiliar. Whenever we study a new discipline we have to learn the "names" of things peculiar to that discipline. Inevitably these specialized terms will be puzzling, but they will remain puzzling only until we learn to connect the *sign* with the concept or thing for which it stands. The word *tree* is difficult for the child only until he learns to associate the sound or the graphic mark of this word with the thing that it designates. The term *prosopopeia* will frighten the student at first, but once he gets to the point where he can immediately associate the term with its significance, *prosopopeia* will be no more frightening to the student than the familiar terms *metaphor* and *simile*. We could, as the Renaissance rhetorician George Puttenham tried to do, invent English terms for the various figures, but since they would have to be coined terms, they would not necessarily be any easier to learn than the classical terms. However, wherever a familiar Anglicized term exists for a figure, we will use that term instead of the classical one.

In any case, we must not look upon terminology as an end in itself. Just as we can speak and write our native language without knowing the names of the parts of speech, so we can use and respond to figurative language without knowing the names of the figures. Nomenclature, in any study, is a convenience for purposes of classification and discussion. But an awareness of the various figures of speech can increase our verbal resources, and if we make a conscious effort to learn the figures of speech, it is likely that we will resort to them more often.

The Schemes

Schemes of words

We shall not dwell very long on schemes of words because while they occur frequently in poetry – especially in the poetry of earlier centuries – they rarely occur in prose. The schemes of words (sometimes called *orthographical schemes*, because they involve changes in the spelling or sound of words) are formed (1) by adding or subtracting a letter or a syllable at the beginning, middle, or end of a word, or (2) by exchanging sounds. Terms like the following are of more concern to the grammarian and the prosodist than to the rhetorician:

> *prosthesis* – adding a syllable in front of word – e.g. *beloved* for *loved*
> *epenthesis* – adding a syllable in the middle of word – e.g. *visitating* for *visiting*
> *proparalepsis* – adding a syllable at the end of word – e.g. *climature* for *climate*

aphaeresis – subtracting a syllable from the beginning of word – e.g. *'neath* for *beneath*
syncope – subtracting a syllable from the middle of word – e.g. *prosprous* for *prosperous*
apocope – subtracting a syllable from the end of word – e.g. *even* for *evening*
metathesis – transposition of letters in a word – e.g. *clapse* for *clasp*
antisthecon – change of sound – e.g. *wrang* for *wrong*

One can easily see that all of these involve a change in the shape or configuration of words. Poets used to employ such schemes to accommodate the rhyme or the rhythm of a line of verse. And because such changes are associated primarily with poetry, it is customary to regard such altered words as "poetic diction." Perhaps the situation in modern prose where we are most likely to use schemes of words would be the dialogue in a story. If a character in a story habitually clipped syllables from his words or mispronounced certain words, we might try to indicate those speech habits with spelling changes. Readers of *Finnegans Wake* could supply numerous examples of other uses that James Joyce made of orthographical schemes in his remarkably ingenious prose.

Schemes of Construction

1   Schemes of Balance

PARALLELISM – similarity of structure in a pair or series of related words, phrases, or clauses.

Examples: He tried to make the law equitable, precise, and comprehensive.

To contain the enemy forces, to reinforce his own depleted resources, to inspirit the sagging morale of his troops, and to re-assess the general strategy of the campaign – these were his objectives when he took command.

It is rather for us to be here dedicated to the great task remaining before us – that from those honored dead we take increased devotion to that cause for which they gave the last full measure of devotion; that we here highly resolve that these dead shall not have died in vain; that this nation, under God, shall have a new birth of freedom; and that government of the people, by the people, for the people, shall not perish from the earth. – Abraham Lincoln

Parallelism is one of the basic principles of grammar and rhetoric. The principle demands that equivalent things be set forth in co-ordinate grammatical structures. So nouns must be yoked with nouns, prepositional phrases with prepositional phrases, adverb clauses with adverb clauses. When this principle is ignored, not only is the grammar of co-ordination violated, but the rhetoric of coherence is wrenched. Students must be made to realize that violations of parallelism are serious, not only because they impair communication but because they reflect disorderly thinking. Whenever the student sees a co-ordinating conjunction in one of his sentences, he should check to make sure that the elements joined by the conjunction are of the same grammatical kind. Such a check would prevent him from writing sentences like this: "He was jolly, a good talker, and even better as a drinker."

When the parallel elements are similar not only in structure but in length (that is, the same number of words, even the same number of syllables), the scheme is called *isocolon.* For example: His purpose was *to impress the ignorant, to perplex the dubious,* and *to confound the scrupulous.* The addition of symmetry of length to similarity of structure contributes greatly to the rhythm of sentences. Obviously, the student should not strive for isocolon every time he produces parallel structure. Such regularity of rhythm would approach the recurrent beat of verse.

Since parallelism is a device that we resort to when we are specifying or enumerating pairs or series of like things, it is easy to see the intimate relationship between this device of form and the topic of similarity. See the analysis of the rhetorical effect of parallelism in Clark Kerr's sentence in the previous section.

ANTITHESIS – the juxtaposition of contrasting ideas, often in parallel structure.

Examples: Contempt is the proper punishment of affectation, and detestation the just consequence of hypocrisy.

Many things difficult to design prove easy to perform.

If you are pleased with prognostics of good, you will be terrified likewise with tokens of evil.

If of Dryden's fire the blaze is brighter, of Pope's the heat is more regular and constant.

All of these examples are quoted from Dr. Johnson, in whose prose, antithesis is such a pronounced feature that we have come to associate this structural device with his name. But antithesis was a scheme greatly admired by all the rhetoricians.

It was the unknown author of *Rhetorica ad Alexandrum* who most clearly pointed up the fact that the opposition in an antithesis can reside either in the words or in the ideas or in both:

An antithesis occurs when both the wording and the sense, or one or other of them, are opposed in a contrast. The following would be an antithesis both of wording and sense: "It is not fair that my opponent should become rich by possessing what belongs to me, while I sacrifice my property and become a mere beggar." In the following sentence we have a merely verbal antithesis: "Let the rich and prosperous give to the poor and needy"; and an antithesis of sense only in the following: "I tended him when he was sick, but he has been the cause of very great misfortune to me." Here there is no verbal antithesis, but the two actions are contrasted. The double antithesis (that is, both of sense and of wording) would be the best to use; but the other two kinds are also true antitheses. (From *Rhetorica ad Alexandrum,* Ch. 26, trans. E. S. Forster)

Nicely managed, antithesis can produce the effect of aphoristic neatness and can win for the author a reputation for wit. Antithesis is obviously related to the topic of dissimilarity and the topic of contraries. (See the analysis of antithesis in Clark Kerr's sentence.)

2   Schemes of unusual or inverted word order (hyperbaton)

ANASTROPHE – inversion of the natural or usual word order.

Examples: Backward run the sentences, till reels the mind. (From a parody of the style of *Time* Magazine.)

With folly no man is willing to confess himself very intimately acquainted. – Dr. Johnson

People that he had known all his life he didn't really know. – student theme

Perfectly does anastrophe conform to our definition of a scheme as "an artful deviation from the ordinary pattern or arrangement of words." Because such deviation surprises expectation, anastrophe can be an effective device for gaining attention. But its chief function is to secure emphasis. It is a commonplace that the beginning and end of a clause are the positions of greatest emphasis. Words placed in those positions draw special attention, and when those initial or terminal words are not normally found in those positions, they receive extraordinary emphasis.

PARENTHESIS – insertion of some verbal unit in a position that interrupts the normal syntactical flow of the sentence.

Examples: But wherein any man is bold – I am speaking foolishly – I also am bold. . . . Are they ministers of Christ? I – to speak as a fool – am more. – St. Paul, 2 Cor. 11, 21 and 23

He tried – who could do more? – to restrain the fury of the mob.

The extraordinary number of bills passed during that session (312 of them) did not speak well of the Congressmen's capacity for deliberation.

The distinguishing mark of parenthesis is that the interpolated member is "cut off" from the syntax of the rest of the sentence. A parenthesis abruptly – and usually briefly – sends the thought off on a tangent. Although the parenthetical matter is not necessary for the grammatical completeness of the sentence, it does have a pronounced rhetorical effect. For a brief moment, we hear the author's voice, commenting, editorializing, and, for that reason, the sentence gets an emotional charge that it would otherwise not have. Note, for instance, the difference in effect if the parenthetical element in St. Paul's first sentence is syntactically integrated with the rest of the sentence: "But I am speaking foolishly if I claim that wherein any man is bold, I also am bold."

APPOSITION – placing side by side two co-ordinate elements, the second of which serves as an explanation or modification of the first.

Examples: John Morgan, the president of the Sons of the Republic, could not be reached by phone.

A great many second-rate poets, in fact, are second-rate just for this reason, that they have not the sensitiveness and consciousness to perceive that they feel differently from the preceding generation and therefore must use words differently. – T. S. Eliot

Men of this kind – soldiers of fortune, pool-hall habitués, gigolos, beachcombers – expend their talents on trivialities.

Apposition is such a common method of expansion in modern prose that it hardly seems to conform to our definition of a scheme as "an artful deviation from the

ordinary patterns of speech." But if one reflects upon his own experience, he will have to acknowledge that appositional structures seldom occur in impromptu speech. Apposition may not be the exclusive property of written prose, but it certainly occurs most frequently in written prose – in a situation, in other words, where we have time to make a conscious choice of our arrangement of words. So there is something *artful* about the use of the appositive. And there is something out-of-the-ordinary about the appositive, too. Although the appositive does not disturb the natural flow of the sentence as violently as parenthetical expressions do (mainly because the appositive is grammatically co-ordinate with the unit that it follows), it does interrupt the flow of the sentence, interrupts the flow to supply some gratuitous information or explanation.

3   Schemes of omission

ELLIPSIS – deliberate omission of a word or of words which are readily implied by the context.

Examples: And he to England shall along with you. – *Hamlet*, III, iii, 4

As with religion, so with education. In colonial New England, education was broad-based, but nevertheless elitist; and in its basic assumptions, intellectualist. – David Marquand, *Encounter* (March 1964)

When in doubt, play trumps.

Ellipsis can be an artful and arresting means of securing economy of expression. We must see to it, however, that the understood words are grammatically compatible. If we wrote, "The ringleader was hanged, and his accomplices imprisoned," we would be guilty of a solecism, because the understood *was* is not grammatically compatible with the plural subject (*accomplices*) of the second clause. And we produce a "howler" if we say, "While in the fourth grade, my father took me to the zoo."

ASYNDETON – deliberate omission of conjunctions between a series of related clauses.

Examples: I came, I saw, I conquered.

They may have it in well-doing, they may have it in learning, they may have it even in criticism. – Matthew Arnold

The infantry plodded forward, the tanks rattled into position, the big guns swung their snouts toward the rim of the hills, the planes raked the underbrush with gunfire.

The Tudor rhetoricians had a special name for the omission of conjunctions between single words or phrases. They would have labelled the following as instances of brachylogia:

...and that government of the people, by the people, for the people, shall not perish from the earth. – Abraham Lincoln

...that we shall pay any price, bear any burden, meet any hardship, support any friend, oppose any foe to assure the survival and the success of liberty. – John F. Kennedy

But there seems to be no good reason why we cannot use the single term *asyndeton* for all these instances of omission of conjunctions. The principal effect of asyndeton is to produce a hurried rhythm in the sentence. Aristotle observed that asyndeton was especially appropriate for the conclusion of a discourse, because there, perhaps more than in any other place in the discourse, we may want to produce the emotional reaction that can be stirred by, among other means, rhythm. And Aristotle concluded his *Rhetoric* with an instance of asyndeton that is noticeable even in translation: "I have done. You have heard me. The facts are before you. I ask for your judgment."

The opposite scheme is polysyndeton (deliberate use of many conjunctions). Note how the proliferation of conjunctions in the following quotation slows up the rhythm of the prose and produces an impressively solemn note:

> And God said, "Let the earth bring forth living creatures according to their kinds: cattle and creeping things and beasts of the earth according to their kinds." And it was so. And God made the beasts of the earth according to their kinds and the cattle according to their kinds and everything that creeps upon the ground according to its kind. And God saw that it was good. – Genesis, 1:24–25

Ernest Hemingway uses polysyndeton to create another effect. Note how the repeated *and*'s in the following passage suggest the flow and continuity of experience:

> I said, "Who killed him?" and he said, "I don't know who killed him but he's dead all right," and it was dark and there was water standing in the street and no lights and windows broke and boats all up in the town and trees blown down and everything all blown and I got a skiff and went out and found my boat where I had her inside Mango Key and she was all right only she was full of water. – Hemingway, "After the Storm"

Polysyndeton can also be used to produce special emphasis. Note the difference in effect of these two sentences:

> This semester I am taking English, history, biology, mathematics, sociology, and physical education.

> This semester I am taking English and history and biology and mathematics and sociology and physical education.

4 Schemes of repetition
ALLITERATION – repetition of initial or medial consonants in two or more adjacent words.

> *Examples:* The moan of doves in immemorial elms
> And murmuring of innumerable bees, – Tennyson, *The Princess*

> After life's fitful fever he sleeps well. – *Macbeth*, III, ii, 22

> It is lawful to picket premises for the purpose of peacefully persuading persons to refrain from trespassing.

In Anglo-Saxon poetry, *alliteration* rather than rhyme was the device to bind verses together. Because it contributes to the euphony of verse or prose, alliteration became a conspicuous feature of Euphuistic prose and Romantic poetry. Because it is such an obvious mannerism, alliteration is rarely used in modern prose. It is sometimes used today, however, for special effects – as a mnemonic device for slogans (Better Business Builds Bigger Bankrolls) and advertising catch-lines (Spark*l*ing...F*l*avorful... Mi*ll*er High *L*ife...The Champagne of *Bottle Beer*...Brewed on*l*y in Mi*l*waukee. Sometimes alliteration is deliberately used for humorous effect: He was a preposterously pompous proponent of precious pedantry.

> ASSONANCE – the repetition of similar vowel sounds, preceded and followed by different consonants, in the stressed syllables of adjacent words.

> *Example:* An old, mad, bl*i*nd, desp*i*sed, and d*y*ing king –
>   Princes, the dregs of their d*u*ll race, who flow
>   Through p*u*blic scorn – m*u*d from a m*u*ddy spring –
>   – Shelley, "Sonnet: England in 1819"

Assonance, a device of sound, like alliteration, is used mainly in poetry. A prose writer might deliberately use assonance to produce certain onomatopoeic or humorous effects. The danger for the prose writer, however, lies in the careless repetition of similar vowel-sounds, producing awkward jingles like this: "He tries to revise the evidence supplied by his eyes."

> ANAPHORA – repetition of the same word or group of words at the beginnings of successive clauses.

> *Examples:* The Lord sitteth above the water floods. The Lord remaineth a King forever. The Lord shall give strength unto his people. The Lord shall give his people the blessing of peace. – Psalm 29

> We shall fight on the beaches, we shall fight on the landing-grounds, we shall fight in the fields and in the streets, we shall fight in the hills. – Winston Churchill

> This is the essence – this is the heart – this is the day-to-day stuff of our duty in this Assembly as we see it: to build mightier mansions, to keep strengthening the United Nations. – Adlai E. Stevenson

Whenever anaphora occurs, we can be sure that the author has used it deliberately. Since the repetition of the words helps to establish a marked rhythm in the sequence of clauses, this scheme is usually reserved for those passages where the author wants to produce a strong emotional effect. Note how Reinhold Niebuhr combines anaphora with plays on words to produce this neat aphorism: "Man's capacity for justice makes democracy possible; but man's inclination to injustice makes democracy necessary."

> EPISTROPHE – repetition of the same word or group of words at the ends of successive clauses.

> *Examples:* Shylock: I'll have my bond! Speak not against my bond!
>   I have sworn an oath that I will have my bond!
>   – *Merchant of Venice*, III, iii, 3–4

When I was a child, I spoke like a child, I thought like a child, I reasoned like a child. –
  St. Paul, 1 Cor. 13, 11

After a war that everyone was proud of, we concluded a peace that nobody was proud
  of. – Walter Bagehot

He's learning fast. Are you earning fast? – Advertisement for Aetna Life Insurance

Epistrophe not only sets up a pronounced rhythm but secures a special emphasis, both by repeating the word and by putting the word in the final position in the sentence.

EPANALEPSIS – repetition at the end of a clause of the word that occurred at the beginning of the clause.

Example: Blood hath bought blood, and blows have answer'd blows:
    Strength match'd with strength, and power confronted power.
        – Shakespeare, *King John*, II, i, 329–30

Epanalepsis is rare in prose, probably because when the emotional situation arises that can make such a scheme appropriate, poetry seems to be the only form that can adequately express the emotion. It would seem perfectly natural for a father to express his grief over the death of a beloved son in this fashion: "He was flesh of my flesh, bone of my bone, blood of my blood." But would the father be speaking prose or poetry? Perhaps the only answer we could give is that it is heightened language of some sort, the kind of language which, despite its appearance of contrivance, springs spontaneously from intense emotion. Repetition, we know, is one of the characteristics of highly emotional language. And in this instance what better way for the father to express the intimacy of the relationship with his son than by the repetition of words at the beginning and end of successive groups of words?
    Perhaps the best general advice about the use of epanalepsis – in fact of all those schemes that are appropriate only to extraordinary circumstances – would be, "If you find yourself consciously deciding to use epanalepsis, don't use it." When the time is appropriate, the scheme will present itself unbidden.

ANADIPLOSIS – repetition of the last word of one clause at the beginning of the following clause.

Examples: Labor and care are rewarded with success, success produces confidence, confidence relaxes industry, and negligence ruins the reputation which diligence had raised. – Dr. Johnson, *Rambler*, No. 21

They point out what is perfectly obvious, yet seldom realized: That if you have a lot of things you cannot move about a lot, that furniture requires dusting, dusters require servants, servants require insurance stamps. . . . It [property] produces men of weight. Men of weight cannot, by definition, move like the lightning from the East unto the West. – E. M. Forster, "My Wood," *Abinger Harvest*

CLIMAX – arrangement of words, phrases, or clauses in an order of increasing importance.

Examples: More than that, we rejoice in our sufferings, knowing that suffering produces endurance, endurance produces character, and character produces hope, and hope does not disappoint us, because God's love has been poured into our hearts through the Holy Spirit which has been given to us. – St. Paul, Romans, 5, 3–5

Let a man acknowledge obligations to his family, his country, and his God.

In our institutions of higher learning one finds with the passing years more and more departmentalized pedants hiding in the holes of research, seeking to run away from embarrassing questions, afraid of philosophy and scared to death of religion. – Bernard Iddings Bell, "Perennial Adolescence"

Climax can be considered a scheme of repetition only when, as in the first example quoted above, it is a continued anadiplosis involving three or more members. Otherwise, as in the second and third examples, it is simply a scheme which arranges a series in an order of gradually rising importance. This latter variety of climax can be looked upon as a scheme related to the topic of degree, and it is the kind of climax that the student will most often find in modern prose and that he will probably find occasion to use in his own prose.

ANTIMETABOLE – repetition of words, in successive clauses, in reverse grammatical order.

Examples: One should eat to live, not live to eat. – Molière, *L'Avare*

You like it, it likes you. – Advertising slogan for Seven-Up

Mankind must put an end to war – or war will put an end to mankind. – John F. Kennedy, United Nations Speech, 1961

Ask not what America can do for you – ask what you can do for your country. – John F. Kennedy, Inaugural Address

All of these examples have the air of the "neatly turned phrase" – the kind of phrasing that figures in most memorable aphorisms. Would the sentence from President Kennedy's Inaugural Address be so often quoted if it had read something like this: "Do not ask what America can do for you. You would do better to ask whether your country stands in need of *your* services"? The "magic" has now gone out of the appeal. It would be a profitable exercise for the student to take several of the schemes presented in this section and convert them into ordinary prose. Such an exercise would undoubtedly reveal what the schemes add to the expression of the thought.

Similar to antimetabole is the scheme called chiasmus ("the criss-cross"). Chiasmus reverses the grammatical structures in successive clauses, but unlike antimetabole, does not repeat the words. Example: "I am indisposed to work, but to beg I am ashamed." Both antimetabole and chiasmus can be used to reinforce antithesis.

POLYPTOTON – repetition of words derived from the same root.

Examples: The Greeks are *strong*, and *skilful* to their *strength*,
  Fierce to their *skill*, and to their *fierceness* valiant;
                                    – Shakespeare, *Troilus and Cressida*, I, i, 7–8

No man is *just* who deals *unjustly* with another man.

He is a man to *know* because he's *known*.

In the midst of all this dark, this void, this emptiness, I, more *ghostly* than a *ghost*, cry, "Who? Who?" to no answer. – Loren Eiseley, "The Uncompleted Man," *Harper's* (March 1964)

Their *blood bleeds* the nation of its sanguine assurance.

Not as a call to *battle*, though *embattled* we are. – John F. Kennedy, Inaugural Address

Polyptoton is very much akin to those plays on words that we will investigate in the next section on tropes.

The Tropes

Metaphor and simile

METAPHOR – an implied comparison between two things of unlike nature that yet have something in common.
SIMILE – an explicit comparison between two things of unlike nature that yet have something in common.
Examples (all from student themes):

He had a posture like a question-mark. (simile)

On the final examination, several students went down in flames. (metaphor)

Like an arrow, the prosecutor went directly to the point. (simile)

The question of federal aid to parochial schools is a bramble patch. (metaphor)

Silence settled down over the audience like a block of granite. (simile)

Birmingham lighted a runaway fuse, and as fast as the headlines could record them, demonstrations exploded all over the country. (metaphor)

We shall treat of metaphor and simile together because they are so much alike. The difference between metaphor and simile lies mainly in the manner of expressing the comparison. Whereas metaphor says, "David was a lion in battle," simile says, "David was *like* a lion in battle." Both of these tropes are related to the topic of similarity, for although the comparison is made between two things of unlike nature (*David* and *lion*), there is some respect in which they are similar (e.g., they are courageous, or they fight ferociously, or they are unconquerable in a fight). The thing with which the first thing is compared is to be understood in some "transferred sense": *David* is not literally a *lion*, but he is a lion in some "other sense."

An extended or continued metaphor is known as an allegory. We see one of these sustained metaphors in *The Battle of the Books*, where Jonathan Swift compares the classical writers, not to the spider, which spins its web out of its own entrails, but to the far-ranging bee:

> As for us the ancients, we are content with the bee to pretend to nothing of our own, beyond our wings and our voices, that is to say, our flights and our language. For the rest, whatever we have got has been by infinite labor and search, and ranging through every corner of nature; the difference is that instead of dirt and poison, we have chosen to fill our hives with honey and wax, thus furnishing mankind with the two noblest of things, which are sweetness and light.

Closely allied to this form of extended metaphor is parable, an anecdotal narrative designed to teach a moral lesson. The most famous examples of parable are those found in the New Testament. In the parable of the sower of seeds, for instance, our interest is not so much in the tale of a man who went out to sow some seeds as in what each detail of the anecdote "stands for," in what the details "mean." Whenever the disciples were puzzled about what a particular parable meant, they asked Christ to interpret it for them.

And while we are talking about these analogical tropes, we should warn the student to be on his guard against the "mixed metaphor," which results when he loses sight of the terms of his comparison. When Joseph Addison said, "There is not a single view of human nature which is not sufficient to extinguish the seeds of pride," it is obvious that he is mixing two different metaphors. We could say "to extinguish the *flames* of pride" or "to *water* the seeds of pride," but we cannot mix the notion of extinguishing with that of seeds. The rhetoricians sometimes called such "wrenching of words" *catachresis*.

SYNECDOCHE – a figure of speech in which a part stands for the whole.

Examples:

genus substituted for the species:
  vessel for *ship, weapon* for *sword, creature* for *man, arms* for *rifles, vehicle* for *bicycle*

species substituted for the genus:
  bread for *food, cutthroat* for *assassin*

part substituted for the whole:
  sail for *ship, hands* for *helpers, roofs* for *houses*

matter for what is made from it:
  silver for *money, canvas* for *sail, steel* for *sword*

In general, we have an instance of synecdoche when the part or genus or adjunct that is mentioned suggests something else. It is an *oblique* manner of speaking. All of the following illustrate this trope: "Give us this day our daily *bread*." "All *hands* were summoned to the quarter-deck." "Not *marble*, nor the gilded monuments of princes, shall outlive this powerful *rhyme*." "They braved the *waves* to protect their father-land." "Brandish your *steel*, men." "Are there no *roofs* in this town that will harbor an honorable man?" "It is pleasing to contemplate a *manufacture* rising gradually from its first mean state by the successive *labors* of innumerable *minds*." – Johnson, *Rambler* No. 9. "The door closed upon the extempore surgeon and midwife, and *Roaring Camp* sat down outside, smoked its pipe, and awaited the issue." – Bret Harte, "The Luck of Roaring Camp."

METONYMY – substitution of some attributive or suggestive word for what is actually meant.

Examples: crown for *royalty*, *mitre* for *bishop*, *wealth* for *rich people*, *brass* for *military officers*, *bottle* for *wine*, *pen* for *writers*

Metonymy and synecdoche are so close to being the same trope that George Campbell, the eighteenth-century rhetorician, wondered whether we should make any great effort to distinguish them. Those rhetoricians who did make the effort to discriminate these tropes would label the following as examples of metonymy:

He slinks out of the way of the humblest *petticoat*. – G. B. Shaw

As if the *kitchen* and the *nursery* were less important than the *office* in the city. – G. B. Shaw

"Who is this Son of Man?" Jesus said to them, "The *light* is with you for a little longer. Walk while you have the *light* lest the *darkness* overtake you." – John 13, 34–5

He addressed his remarks to the *chair*.

He was addicted to the *bottle*.

Yesterday I sold a *Rembrandt*.

If the nearness of our last necessity brought a nearer conformity into it, there were happiness in *hoary hairs* and no calamity in *half senses*. – Sir Thomas Browne

In Europe, we gave the *cold shoulder* to De Gaulle, and now he gives the *warm hand* to Mao Tse-tung. – Richard Nixon

PUNS – generic name for those figures which make a play on words.

(1) Antanaclasis – repetition of a word in two different senses.

Learn a *craft* so that when you grow older you will not have to earn your living by *craft*.

Never serve the coffee without the *cream* – Harvey's Bristol *Cream* (advertising slogan)

(2) Paronomasia – use of words alike in sound but different in meaning.

It was a *foul* act to steal my *fowl*.

RCA – A *sound* tradition (advertisement for a stereo set).

(3) Syllepsis – use of a word understood differently in relation to two or more other words, which it modifies or governs.

He *lost* his hat and his temper.

Here thou, great Anna! whom three realms obey
Dost sometimes counsel *take* – and sometimes tea. – Alexander Pope

The figure of zeugma is somewhat like syllepsis, but whereas in syllepsis the single word is grammatically and idiomatically compatible with both of the other words that it governs, in a zeugma the single word does not fit grammatically or idiomatically with one member of the pair. If we say, "Jane *has murdered* her father, and may you too" or "He maintained a *flourishing* business and racehorse," we would be producing an instance of zeugma, because in both sentences the underlined word is either grammatically or idiomatically incongruous with one member (in these examples, the second member) of the pair it governs. Those two lines from Pope's *Rape of the Lock* which are often classified as zeugma – "Or stain her honour, or her new brocade" and "Or lose her heart, or necklace, at a ball" – would, according to our definition, be examples of syllepsis. Syllepsis is the only one of these two figures which can be considered a form of pun. Zeugma, if skillfully managed, could be impressive as a display of wit, but often enough, zeugma is nothing more than a faulty use of the scheme of ellipsis.

ANTHIMERIA – the substitution of one part of speech for another.

Examples: I'll *unhair* thy head. – Shakespeare, *Antony and Cleopatra*, II, v, 64

A mile before his tent fall down, and *knee*
The way into her mercy. – Shakespeare, *Coriolanus*, V, i, 5

The thunder would not *peace* at my bidding. – Shakespeare, *King Lear*, IV, vi, 103

Dozens of other examples of anthimeria could be quoted from Shakespeare's plays. If a word was not available for what he wanted to express, Shakespeare either coined a word or used an old word in a new way. Today's writer must use *anthimeria* seldom and with great discretion unless he is truly a master of the existing English language. On the other hand, an apt creation can be pungent, evocative, witty, or memorable. English today is a rich, flexible language, because words have been borrowed, changed, and created. Think of all the ways in which a word like *smoke* has been used since it first came into the language:

The smoke rose from the chimney.
The chimney smokes.

He smoked the ham.

He smokes.

He asked for a smoke.

He objected to the smoke nuisance.

He noticed the smoky atmosphere.

He tried smoking on the sly.

He smoked out the thief.

His dreams went up in smoke.

The Ferrari smoked along the wet track.

Someday someone will say, if it hasn't been said already, "He looked at her smokily."

PERIPHRASIS (antonomasia) – substitution of a descriptive word or phrase for a proper name or of a proper name for a quality associated with the name.

Examples: The *Splendid Splinter* hit two more *round-trippers* today.

The Negro does not escape *Jim Crow* when he moves into a higher-income bracket.

She may not have been a *Penelope*, but she was not as unfaithful as the gossips made her out to be.

When his swagger is exhausted, he drivels into erotic poetry or sentimental uxoriousness. And the *Tennysonian King Arthur* posing at *Guinevere* becomes *Don Quixote* grovelling before *Dulcinea*. – G. B. Shaw

The frequency with which we meet this trope, even in modern prose, is evidence of the urge in man to express familiar ideas in uncommon ways. Circumlocutions and tags can become tiresome clichés (as they often do on the sports page), but when they display a fresh, decorous inventiveness, they can add grace to our writing. It is the trite or overly ingenious oblique expression that wearies the reader.

PERSONIFICATION (prosopoeia) – investing abstractions or inanimate objects with human qualities or abilities.

Examples: The ground thirsts for rain.

The very stones cry out for revenge.

Can Honor's voice provoke the silent dust,
Or Flatt'ry sooth the dull cold ear of Death? – Thomas Gray

Personification is such a familiar figure that there is no need to multiply examples of it. This is one of the figures that should be reserved for passages designed to stir the emotions. Another emotional figure, closely allied to personification, is apostrophe (addressing an absent person or a personified abstraction). Here is an example of apostrophe from Sir Walter Raleigh's *History of the World*:

O eloquent, just, and mighty Death! whom none could advise, thou hast persuaded; what none hath dared, thou hast done; and whom all the world has flattered, thou only hast cast out of the world and despised. Thou hast drawn together all the far-stretched greatness, all the pride, cruelty, and ambition of man, and covered it all with these two narrow words, *Hic jacet.*

HYPERBOLE – the use of exaggerated terms for the purpose of emphasis or heightened effect.

Examples: His eloquence would split rocks.

It's really ironical...I have gray hair. I really do. The one side of my head – the right side – is full of millions of gray hairs. – Holden Caulfield in *Catcher in the Rye*

My left leg weighs three tons. It is embalmed in spices like a mummy. I can't move. I haven't moved for five thousand years. I'm of the time of Pharaoh. – Thomas Bailey Aldrich, "Marjorie Daw"

Hyperbole is so steadily droned into our ears that most of us have ceased to think of it as a figure of speech. Advertisers and teenagers can hardly talk without using superlatives. Perhaps we would not be so much amused by the Oriental greeting, "We welcome you, most honorable sir, to our miserable abode," if we stopped to consider how exaggerated many of our forms of greeting, address, and compliment are.

Hyperbole can be a serviceable figure of speech if we learn to use it with restraint and for a calculated effect. Under the stress of emotion, it will slip out naturally and will then seem appropriate. If we can learn to invent fresh hyperboles, we will be able to produce the right note of emphasis (as in the first example above) or humor (as in the quotation from Aldrich).

Being related to the topic of degree, hyperbole is like the figure called auxesis (magnifying the importance or gravity of something by referring to it with a disproportionate name). So a lawyer will try to impress a jury by referring to a scratch on the arm as "a wound" or to pilfering from the petty-cash box as "embezzlement." We can accept Mark Antony's reference to the wound that Brutus inflicted on Caesar as "the most unkindest cut of all," but the occasion seemed not to warrant Senator Joseph McCarthy's classic remark, "That's the most unheard of thing I ever heard of."

LITOTES – deliberate use of understatement, not to deceive someone but to enhance the impressiveness of what we say.

Examples: It was a not unhappy crowd that greeted the team at the airport.

Scaliger's influence in France was not inconsiderable during the sixteenth century. – Joel E. Spingarn, *Literary Criticism in the Renaissance*

Last week I saw a woman flayed, and you will hardly believe how much it altered her appearance for the worse. – Jonathan Swift, *A Tale of a Tub*

I am a citizen of no mean city. – St. Paul

Litotes is a form of meiosis (a lessening). The same lawyer whom we saw in the previous section using auxesis might represent another of his clients by referring to a case of vandalism as "boyish highjinks." A rose by any other name will smell as sweet, but a crime, if referred to by a name that is not too patently disproportionate, may lose some of its heinousness.

RHETORICAL QUESTION (erotema) – asking a question, not for the purpose of eliciting an answer but for the purpose of asserting or denying something obliquely.

Examples: What! Gentlemen, was I not to foresee, or foreseeing was I not to endeavor to save you from all these multiplied mischiefs and disgraces?...Was I an Irishman on that day that I boldly withstood our pride? or on the day that I hung down my head and wept in shame and silence over the humiliation of Great Britain? I became unpopular in England for the one, and in Ireland for the other. What then? What obligation lay on me to be popular? – Edmund Burke, *Speech to the Electors of Bristol*

Wasn't the cult of James a revealing symbol and symbol of an age and society which wanted to dwell like him in some false world of false art and false culture? – Maxwell Geismar, *Henry James and His Cult*

The rhetorical question is a common device in impassioned speeches, but it can be used too in written prose. It can be an effective persuasive device, subtly influencing the kind of response one wants to get from an audience. The manner in which the question is phrased can determine either a negative or an affirmative response. If we say, "Was this an act of heroism?" the audience will respond, in the proper context, with a negative answer. By inducing the audience to make the appropriate response, the rhetorical question can often be more effective as a persuasive device than a direct assertion would be.

IRONY – use of a word in such a way as to convey a meaning opposite to the literal meaning of the word.

Examples: For Brutus is an *honourable* man;
So are they all, all *honourable* men. – Shakespeare, *Julius Caesar*, III, ii, 88–9

It is again objected, as a very absurd, ridiculous custom that a set of men should be suffered, much less employed and hired, to bawl one day in seven against the *lawfulness* of those methods most in use toward the pursuit of greatness, riches, and pleasure, which are the constant practice of all men alive on the other six. But this objection is, I think, a little unworthy of *so refined* an age as ours. – Swift, *Argument Against the Abolishing of Christianity*

As a trope which quite definitely conveys a "transferred meaning," irony is related to the topic of contraries or the topic of contradiction. A highly sophisticated device, irony must be used with great caution. If one misjudges the intelligence of his audience, he may find that his audience is taking his words in their ostensible sense rather than in the intended opposite sense.

The Tudor rhetoricians had a special name for the kind of irony in which one proposed to pass over some matter, yet managed subtly to reveal the matter anyway. They called this kind of irony *paralipsis*. A notable example of paralipsis is found in Mark Antony's famous "Friends, Romans, countrymen" speech in *Julius Caesar:*

> Let but the commons hear this testament,
> Which (pardon me) I do not mean to read,
> And they would go and kiss dead Caesar's wounds...
> Have patience, gentle friends; I must not read it.
> It is not meet you know how Caesar lov'd you....
> 'Tis good you know not that you are his heirs.
>
> (III, ii, 136–51)

A look at the entire speech will show how Antony, despite his disclaimers, managed to let the mob know what was in Caesar's last will.

ONOMATOPOEIA – use of words whose sound echoes the sense.

> *Examples:* 'Tis not enough no harshness gives offense,
> The sound must seem an echo to the sense:
> Soft is the strain when Zephyr gently blows,
> And the smooth stream in smoother numbers flows;
> But when loud surges lash the sounding shore,
> The hoarse, rough verse should like the torrent roar:
> When Ajax strives some rock's vast weight to throw,
> The line too labors, and the words move slow;
> Not so, when swift Camilla scours the plain,
> Flies o'er the unbending corn, and skims along the main.
>
> – Pope, *Essay on Criticism*, II, 364–73

Over the cobbles he clattered and clashed in the dark innyard. – Alfred Noyes, "The Highwayman"

The spray was hissing hot, and a huge jet of water burst up from its midst.

In the passage quoted above from Pope, some of the onomatopoeic effects are produced by the rhythm of the lines as well as by the sounds of words. Since onomatopoeia seeks to match sound with sense, it is easy to see why this figure was commonly associated with the topic of similarity. Onomatopoeia will be used much less frequently in prose than in poetry, yet it still has its appropriate uses in prose. Wherever sound-effects can be used to set the emotional or ethical tone of a passage, onomatopoeia can make a contribution. In seeking to discredit a person or an act, we could reinforce the effect of pejorative diction with cacophony. In a phrase like "a dastardly episode," we reveal our attitude toward the event not only by the unpleasant connotations of the word *dastardly* but also by the harsh sound of the word.

OXYMORON – the yoking of two terms which are ordinarily contradictory.

> *Examples:* expressions like *sweet pain, cheerful pessimist, conspicuous by his absence, cruel kindness, thunderous silence, luxurious poverty, abject arrogance, make haste slowly.*

By thus combining contradictories, the writer produces a startling effect, and he may, if his oxymorons are fresh and apt, win for himself a reputation for wit. There is displayed in this figure, as in most metaphorical language, what Aristotle considered a special mark of genius: the ability to see similarities. Here are some examples of oxymoron:

> Thou, silent form, dost tease us out of thought
> As doth eternity: Cold Pastoral!

> Keats, "Ode on a Grecian Urn"

But that he may not be thought to conceive nothing but things inconceivable, he has at last thought on a way by which human sufferings may produce good effect. – Dr. Johnson, Review of a treatise by Soame Jenyns

Much as he had accomplished, she could not but observe that his most splendid successes were almost invariably failures, if compared with the ideal at which he aimed. – Nathaniel Hawthorne, "The Birthmark"

As an evolutionist, I never cease to be astounded by the past. – Loren Eiseley, "The Uncompleted Man," *Harper's* (March 1964)

CHAPTER 5

How To Do Things With Words

J. L. Austin

J. L. Austin's *How To Do Things With Words* (1962) is one of those books that at first seem unremarkable but become increasingly more remarkable with time. Austin describes a class of utterances, which he calls "performatives," that effect actions in the world. John Searle popularized and deepened Austin's work in his book *Speech Acts* (1969). Austin's work has been important for Post-Structuralists and for gender theorists.

Lecture I

Preliminary isolation of the performative[1]

The type of utterance we are to consider here is not, of course, in general a type of nonsense; though misuse of it can, as we shall see, engender rather special varieties of 'nonsense'. Rather, it is one of our second class – the masqueraders. But it does not by any means necessarily masquerade as a statement of fact, descriptive or constative. Yet it does quite commonly do so, and that, oddly enough, when it assumes its most explicit form. Grammarians have not, I believe, seen through this 'disguise', and philosophers only at best incidentally.[2] It will be convenient, therefore, to study it first in this misleading form, in order to bring out its characteristics by contrasting them with those of the statement of fact which it apes.

We shall take, then, for our first examples some utterances which can fall into no hitherto recognized *grammatical* category save that of 'statement', which are not non-sense, and which contain none of those verbal danger-signals which philosophers have by now detected or think they have detected (curious words like 'good' or 'all', suspect auxiliaries like 'ought' or 'can', and dubious constructions like the hypothetical): all will have, as it happens, humdrum verbs in the first person singular present indicative active.[3] Utterances can be found, satisfying these conditions, yet such that

A they do not 'describe' or 'report' or constate anything at all, are not 'true or false'; and

B the uttering of the sentence is, or is a part of, the doing of an action, which again would not *normally* be described as saying something.

This is far from being as paradoxical as it may sound or as I have meanly been trying to make it sound: indeed, the examples now to be given will be disappointing.

Examples:

(E. *a*) 'I do (sc. take this woman to be my lawful wedded wife)' – as uttered in the course of the marriage ceremony.[4]

(E. *b*) 'I name this ship the *Queen Elizabeth*' – as uttered when smashing the bottle against the stem.

(E. *c*) 'I give and bequeath my watch to my brother' – as occurring in a will.

(E. *d*) 'I bet you sixpence it will rain tomorrow.'

In these examples it seems clear that to utter the sentence (in, of course, the appropriate circumstances) is not to *describe* my doing of what I should be said in so uttering to be doing[5] or to state that I am doing it: it is to do it. None of the utterances cited is either true or false: I assert this as obvious and do not argue it. It needs argument no more than that 'damn' is not true or false: it may be that the utterance 'serves to inform you' – but that is quite different. To name the ship *is* to say (in the appropriate circumstances) the words 'I name, &c.'. When I say, before the registrar or altar, &c., 'I do', I am not reporting on a marriage: I am indulging in it.

What are we to call a sentence or an utterance of this type?[6] I propose to call it a *performative sentence* or a performative utterance, or, for short, 'a performative'. The term 'performative' will be used in a variety of cognate ways and constructions, much as the term 'imperative' is.[7] The name is derived, of course, from 'perform', the usual verb with the noun 'action': it indicates that the issuing of the utterance is the performing of an action – it is not normally thought of as just saying something.

A number of other terms may suggest themselves, each of which would suitably cover this or that wider or narrower class of performatives: for example, many performatives are *contractual* ('I bet') or *declaratory* ('I declare war') utterances. But no term in current use that I know of is nearly wide enough to cover them all. One technical term that comes nearest to what we need is perhaps 'operative', as it is used strictly by lawyers in referring to that part, i.e. those clauses, of an instrument which serves to effect the transaction (conveyance or what not) which is its main object, whereas the rest of the document merely 'recites' the circumstances in which the transaction is to be effected.[8] But 'operative' has other meanings, and indeed is often used nowadays to mean little more than 'important'. I have preferred a new word, to which, though its etymology is not irrelevant, we shall perhaps not be so ready to attach some preconceived meaning.

Can saying make it so?

Are we then to say things like this:

'To marry is to say a few words', or

'Betting is simply saying something'?

Such a doctrine sounds odd or even flippant at first, but with sufficient safeguards it may become not odd at all.

A sound initial objection to them may be this; and it is not without some importance. In very many cases it is possible to perform an act of exactly the same kind *not* by uttering words, whether written or spoken, but in some other way. For example, I may in some places effect marriage by cohabiting, or I may bet with a totalisator machine by putting a coin in a slot. We should then, perhaps, convert the propositions above, and put it that 'to say a few certain words is to marry' or 'to marry is, in some cases, simply to say a few words' or 'simply to say a certain something is to bet'.

But probably the real reason why such remarks sound dangerous lies in another obvious fact, to which we shall have to revert in detail later, which is this. The uttering of the words is, indeed, usually a, or even *the*, leading incident in the performance of the act (of betting or what not), the performance of which is also the object of the utterance, but it is far from being usually, even if it is ever, the *sole* thing necessary if the act is to be deemed to have been performed. Speaking generally, it is always necessary that the *circumstances* in which the words are uttered should be in some way, or ways, *appropriate*, and it is very commonly necessary that either the speaker himself or other persons should *also* perform certain *other* actions, whether 'physical' or 'mental' actions or even acts of uttering further words. Thus, for naming the ship, it is essential that I should be the person appointed to name her, for (Christian) marrying, it is essential that I should not be already married with a wife living, sane and undivorced, and so on: for a bet to have been made, it is generally necessary for the offer of the bet to have been accepted by a taker (who must have done something, such as to say 'Done'), and it is hardly a gift if I *say* 'I give it you' but never hand it over.

So far, well and good. The action may be performed in ways other than by a performative utterance, and in any case the circumstances, including other actions, must be appropriate. But we may, in objecting, have something totally different, and this time quite mistaken, in mind, especially when we think of some of the more awe-inspiring performatives such as 'I promise to...' Surely the words must be spoken 'seriously' and so as to be taken 'seriously'? This is, though vague, true enough in general – it is an important commonplace in discussing the purport of any utterance whatsoever. I must not be joking, for example, nor writing a poem. But we are apt to have a feeling that their being serious consists in their being uttered as (merely) the outward and visible sign, for convenience or other record or for information, of an inward and spiritual act: from which it is but a short step to go on to believe or to assume without realizing that for many purposes the outward utterance is a description, *true or false*, of the occurrence of the inward performance. The classic expression of this idea is to be found in the *Hippolytus* (1. 612), where Hippolytus says

$$\text{ἡ γλῶσσ ὀμώμοχ', ἡ δὲ φρὴν ἀνώμοτος,}$$

i.e. 'my tongue swore to, but my heart (or mind or other backstage artiste) did not.'[9] Thus 'I promise to...' obliges me – puts on record my spiritual assumption of a spiritual shackle.

It is gratifying to observe in this very example how excess of profundity, or rather solemnity, at once paves the way for immodality. For one who says 'promising is not merely a matter of uttering words! It is an inward and spiritual act!' is apt to appear as a solid moralist standing out against a generation of superficial theorizers: we see him as he sees himself, surveying the invisible depths of ethical space, with all the distinction of a specialist in the *sui generis*. Yet he provides Hippolytus with a let-out, the bigamist with an excuse for his 'I do' and the welsher with a defence for his

'I bet'. Accuracy and morality alike are on the side of the plain saying that *our word is our bond*.

If we exclude such fictitious inward acts as this, can we suppose that any of the other things which certainly are normally required to accompany an utterance such as 'I promise that . . .' or 'I do (take this woman . . .)' are in fact described by it, and consequently do by their presence make it true or by their absence make it false? Well, taking the latter first, we shall next consider what we actually do say about the utterance concerned when one or another of its normal concomitants is *absent*. In no case do we say that the utterance was false but rather that the utterance – or rather the *act*,[10] e.g. the promise – was void, or given in bad faith, or not implemented, or the like. In the particular case of promising, as with many other performatives, it is appropriate that the person uttering the promise should have a certain intention, viz. here to keep his word: and perhaps of all concomitants this looks the most suitable to be that which 'I promise' does describe or record. Do we not actually, when such intention is absent, speak of a 'false' promise? Yet so to speak is *not* to say that the utterance 'I promise that . . .' is false, in the sense that though he states that he does, he doesn't, or that though he describes he misdescribes – misreports. For he *does* promise: the promise here is not even *void*, though it is given *in bad faith*. His utterance is perhaps misleading, probably deceitful and doubtless wrong, but it is not a lie or a misstatement. At most we might make out a case for saying that it implies or insinuates a falsehood or a misstatement (to the effect that he does intend to do something): but that is a very different matter. Moreover, we do not speak of a false bet or a false christening; and that we *do* speak of a false promise need commit us no more than the fact that we speak of a false move. 'False' is not necessarily used of statements only.

Lecture II

We were to consider, you will remember, some cases and senses (only some, Heaven help us!) in which to *say* something is to *do* something; or in which *by* saying or *in* saying something we are doing something. This topic is one development – there are many others – in the recent movement towards questioning an age-old assumption in philosophy – the assumption that to say something, at least in all cases worth considering, i.e. all cases considered, is always and simply to *state* something. This assumption is no doubt unconscious, no doubt is wrong, but it is wholly natural in philosophy apparently. We must learn to run before we can walk. If we never made mistakes how should we correct them?

I began by drawing your attention, by way of example, to a few simple utterances of the kind known as performatories or performatives. These have on the face of them the look – or at least the grammatical make-up – of 'statements'; but nevertheless they are seen, when more closely inspected, to be, quite plainly, *not* utterances which could be 'true' or 'false'. Yet to be 'true' or 'false' is traditionally the characteristic mark of a statement. One of our examples was, for instance, the utterance 'I do' (take this woman to be my lawful wedded wife), as uttered in the course of a marriage ceremony. Here we should say that in saying these words we are *doing* something – namely, marrying, rather than *reporting* something, namely *that* we are marrying. And the act of marrying, like, say, the act of betting, is at least *preferably* (though still not *accurately*) to be described as *saying certain words*, rather than as performing a different, inward and spiritual, action of which these words are merely the outward and audible sign. That this is so can perhaps hardly be *proved*, but it is, I should claim, a fact.

It is worthy of note that, as I am told, in the American law of evidence, a report of what someone else said is admitted as evidence if what he said is an utterance of our performative kind: because this is regarded as a report not so much of something he *said*, as which it would be hear-say and not admissible as evidence, but rather as something he *did*, an action of his. This coincides very well with our initial feelings about performatives.

So far then we have merely felt the firm ground of prejudice slide away beneath our feet. But now how, as philosophers, are we to proceed? One thing we might go on to do, of course, is to take it all back: another would be to bog, by logical stages, down. But all this must take time. Let us first at least concentrate attention on the little matter already mentioned in passing – this matter of 'the appropriate circumstances'. To bet is not, as I pointed out in passing, merely to utter the words 'I bet, &c.': someone might do that all right, and yet we might still not agree that he had in fact, or at least entirely, succeeded in betting. To satisfy ourselves of this, we have only, for example, to announce our bet after the race is over. Besides the uttering of the words of the so-called performative, a good many other things have as a general rule to be right and to go right if we are to be said to have happily brought off our action. What these are we may hope to discover by looking at and classifying types of case in which something *goes wrong* and the act – marrying, betting, bequeathing, christening, or what not – is therefore at least to some extent a failure: the utterance is then, we may say, not indeed false but in general *unhappy*. And for this reason we call the doctrine of *the things that can be and go wrong* on the occasion of such utterances, the doctrine of the *Infelicities*.

Suppose we try first to state schematically – and I do not wish to claim any sort of finality for this scheme – some at least of the things which are necessary for the smooth or 'happy' functioning of a performative (or at least of a highly developed explicit performative, such as we have hitherto been alone concerned with), and then give examples of infelicities and their effects. I fear, but at the same time of course hope, that these necessary conditions to be satisfied will strike you as obvious.

(A. 1)   There must exist an accepted conventional procedure having a certain conventional effect, that procedure to include the uttering of certain words by certain persons in certain circumstances, and further,

(A. 2)   the particular persons and circumstances in a given case must be appropriate for the invocation of the particular procedure invoked.

(B. 1)   The procedure must be executed by all participants both correctly and

(B. 2)   completely.

(Γ. 1)   Where, as often, the procedure is designed for use by persons having certain thoughts or feelings, or for the inauguration of certain consequential conduct on the part of any participant, then a person participating in and so invoking the procedure must in fact have those thoughts or feelings, and the participants must intend so to conduct themselves,[11] and further

(Γ. 2)   must actually so conduct themselves subsequently.

Now if we sin against any one (or more) of these six rules, our performative utterance will be (in one way or another) unhappy. But, of course, there are considerable differences between these 'ways' of being unhappy – ways which are intended to be brought out by the letter-numerals selected for each heading.

The first big distinction is between all the four rules A and B taken together, as opposed to the two rules Γ (hence the use of Roman as opposed to Greek letters). If we offend against any of the former rules (A's or B's) – that is if we, say, utter the formula incorrectly, or if, say, we are not in a position to do the act because we are, say, married already, or it is the purser and not the captain who is conducting the ceremony, then the act in question, e.g. marrying, is not successfully performed at all, does not come off, is not achieved. Whereas in the two Γ cases the act *is* achieved, although to achieve it in such circumstances, as when we are, say, insincere, is an abuse of the procedure. Thus, when I say 'I promise' and have no intention of keeping it, I have promised but. . . . We need names for referring to this general distinction, so we shall call in general those infelicities A. 1–B. 2 which are such that the act for the performing of which, and in the performing of which, the verbal formula in question is designed, is not achieved, by the name MISFIRES: and on the other hand we may christen those infelicities where the act *is* achieved ABUSES (do not stress the normal connotations of these names!). When the utterance is a misfire, the procedure which we purport to invoke is disallowed or is botched: and our act (marrying, &c.) is void or without effect, &c. We speak of our act as a purported act, or perhaps an attempt – or we use such an expression as 'went through a form of marriage' by contrast with 'married'. On the other hand, in the Γ cases, we speak of our infelicitous act as 'professed' or 'hollow' rather than 'purported' or 'empty', and as not implemented, or not consummated, rather than as void or without effect. But let me hasten to add that these distinctions are not hard and fast, and more especially that such words as 'purported' and 'professed' will not bear very much stressing. Two final words about being void or without effect. This does not mean, of course, to say that we won't have done anything: lots of things will have been done – we shall most interestingly have committed the act of bigamy – but we shall *not* have done the purported act, viz. marrying. Because despite the name, you do not when bigamous marry twice. (In short, the algebra of marriage is BOOLEAN.) Further, 'without effect' does not here mean 'without consequences, results, effects'.

Next, we must try to make clear the general distinction between the A cases and the B cases, among the misfires. In both of the cases labelled A there is *misinvocation* of a procedure – either because there *is*, speaking vaguely, no such procedure, or because the procedure in question cannot be made to apply in the way attempted. Hence infelicities of this kind A may be called *Misinvocations*. Among them, we may reasonably christen the second sort – where the procedure does exist all right but can't be applied as purported – *Misapplications*. But I have not succeeded in finding a good name for the other, former, class. By contrast with the A cases, the notion of the B cases is rather that the procedure is all right, and it does apply all right, but we muff the execution of the ritual with more or less dire consequences: so B cases as opposed to A cases will be called *Misexecutions* as opposed to Misinvocations: the purported act is *vitiated* by a flaw or hitch in the conduct of the ceremony. The Class B. 1 is that of Flaws, the Class B. 2 that of Hitches.

We get then the following scheme:[12]

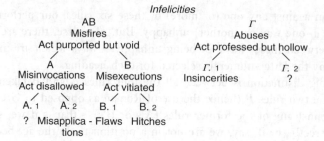

I expect some doubts will be entertained about A. 1 and Γ. 2; but we will postpone them for detailed consideration shortly.

But before going on to details, let me make some general remarks about these infelicities. We may ask:

(1)   To what variety of 'act' does the notion of infelicity apply?
(2)   How complete is this classification of infelicity?
(3)   Are these classes of infelicity mutually exclusive?

Let us take these questions in (that) order.

(1)   How widespread is infelicity?

Well, it seems clear in the first place that, although it has excited us (or failed to excite us) in connexion with certain acts which are or are in part acts of *uttering words*, infelicity is an ill to which *all* acts are heir which have the general character of ritual or ceremonial, all *conventional* acts: not indeed that *every* ritual is liable to every form of infelicity (but then nor is every performative utterance). This is clear if only from the mere fact that many conventional acts, such as betting or conveyance of property, can be performed in non-verbal ways. The same sorts of rule must be observed in all such conventional procedures – we have only to omit the special reference to verbal utterance in our A. This much is obvious.

But, furthermore, it is worth pointing out – reminding you – how many of the 'acts' which concern the jurist are or include the utterance of performatives, or at any rate are or include the performance of some conventional procedures. And of course you will appreciate that in this way and that writers on jurisprudence have constantly shown themselves aware of the varieties of infelicity and even at times of the peculiarities of the performative utterance. Only the still widespread obsession that the utterances of the law, and utterances used in, say, 'acts in the law', *must* somehow be statements true or false, has prevented many lawyers from getting this whole matter much straighter than we are likely to – and I would not even claim to know whether some of them have not already done so. Of more direct concern to us, however, is to realize that, by the same token, a great many of the acts which fall within the province of Ethics are *not*, as philosophers are too prone to assume, simply in the last resort *physical movements*: very many of them have the general character, in whole or part, of conventional or ritual acts, and are therefore, among other things, exposed to infelicity.

Lastly we may ask – and here I must let some of my cats on the table – does the notion of infelicity apply to utterances *which are statements*? So far we have produced the infelicity as characteristic of the *performative* utterance, which was 'defined' (if we can call it so much) mainly by contrast with the supposedly familiar 'statement'. Yet I will content myself here with pointing out that one of the things that has been happening lately in philosophy is that close attention has been given even to 'statements' which, though not false exactly nor yet 'contradictory', are yet outrageous. For instance, statements which refer to something which does not exist as, for example, 'The present King of France is bald.' There might be a temptation to assimilate this to purporting to bequeath something which you do not own. Is there not a presupposition of existence in each? Is not a statement which refers to something which does not exist not so much false as void? And the more we consider a statement not as a sentence (or proposition) but as an act of speech (out of which the others are logical constructions) the more we are studying the whole thing as an act. Or again, there are obvious similarities between a lie and a false promise. We shall have to return to this matter later.

(2)   Our second question was: How complete is this classification?

   (i)   Well, the first thing to remember is that, since in uttering our performatives we are undoubtedly in a sound enough sense 'performing actions', then, as actions, these will be subject to certain whole dimensions of unsatisfactoriness to which all actions are subject but which are distinct – or distinguishable – from what we have chosen to discuss as infelicities. I mean that actions in general (not all) are liable, for example, to be done under duress, or by accident, or owing to this or that variety of mistake, say, or otherwise unintentionally. In many such cases we are certainly unwilling to say of some such act simply that it was done or that he did it. I am not going into the general doctrine here: in many such cases we may even say the act was 'void' (or voidable for duress or undue influence) and so forth. Now I suppose some very general high-level doctrine might embrace both what we have called infelicities *and* these other 'unhappy' features of the doing of actions – in our case actions containing a performative utterance – in a single doctrine: but we are not including this kind of unhappiness – we must just remember, though, that features of this sort can and do constantly obtrude into any case we are discussing. Features of this sort would normally come under the heading of 'extenuating circumstances' or of 'factors reducing or abrogating the agent's responsibility', and so on.

   (ii)   Secondly, as *utterances* our performatives are *also* heir to certain other kinds of ill which infect *all* utterances. And these likewise, though again they might be brought into a more general account, we are deliberately at present excluding. I mean, for example, the following: a performative utterance will, for example, be *in a peculiar way* hollow or void if said by an actor on the stage, or if introduced in a poem, or spoken in soliloquy. This applies in a similar manner to any and every utterance – a sea-change in special circumstances. Language in such circumstances is in special ways – intelligibly – used not seriously, but in ways *parasitic* upon its normal use – ways which fall under the doctrine of the *etiolations* of language. All this we are *excluding* from consideration. Our performative utterances, felicitous or not, are to be understood as issued in ordinary circumstances.

   (iii)   It is partly in order to keep this sort of consideration at least for the present out of it, that I have not here introduced a sort of 'infelicity' – it might

really be called such – arising out of 'misunderstanding'. It is obviously necessary that to have promised I must normally

(A)   have been *heard* by someone, perhaps the promisee;
(B)   have been understood by him as promising.

If one or another of these conditions is not satisfied, doubts arise as to whether I
have really promised, and it might be held that my act was only attempted or was
void. Special precautions are taken in law to avoid this and other infelicities, e.g. in
the serving of writs or summonses. This particular very important consideration we
shall have to return to later in another connexion.

(3)   Are these cases of infelicity mutually exclusive? The answer to this is obvious.
    (*a*)   No, in the sense that we can go wrong in two ways at once (we can
    insincerely promise a donkey to give it a carrot).
    (*b*)   No, more importantly, in the sense that the ways of going wrong 'shade
    into one another' and 'overlap', and the decision between them is 'arbitrary' in
    various ways.
    Suppose, for example, I see a vessel on the stocks, walk up and smash the bottle
hung at the stem, proclaim 'I name this ship the *Mr. Stalin*' and for good measure
kick away the chocks: but the trouble is, I was not the person chosen to name it
(whether or not – an additional complication – *Mr. Stalin* was the destined name;
perhaps in a way it is even more of a shame if it was). We can all agree

(1)   that the ship was not thereby named;[13]
(2)   that it is an infernal shame.

One could say that I 'went through a form of' naming the vessel but that my 'action'
was 'void' or 'without effect', because I was not a proper person, had not the
'capacity', to perform it: but one might also and alternatively say that, where there is
not even a pretence of capacity or a colourable claim to it, then there is no accepted
conventional procedure; it is a mockery, like a marriage with a monkey. Or again one
could say that part of the procedure is getting oneself appointed. When the saint
baptized the penguins, was this void because the procedure of baptizing is inappropriate to be applied to penguins, or because there is no accepted procedure of baptizing anything except humans? I do not think that these uncertainties matter in theory,
though it is pleasant to investigate them and in practice convenient to be ready, as
jurists are, with a terminology to cope with them.

Lecture III

In our first lecture we isolated in a preliminary way the performative utterance as not,
or not merely, saying something but doing something, as not a true or false report of
something. In the second, we pointed out that though it was not ever true or false it
still was subject to criticism – could be unhappy, and we listed six of these types of
Infelicity. Of these, four were such as to make the utterance Misfire, and the act
purported to be done null and void, so that it does not take effect; while two, on the

contrary, only made the professed act an abuse of the procedure. So then we may seem to have armed ourselves with two shiny new concepts with which to crack the crib of Reality, or as it may be, of Confusion – two new keys in our hands, *and* of course, simultaneously two new skids under our feet. In philosophy, forearmed *should* be forewarned. I then stalled around for some time by discussing some general questions about the concept of the Infelicity, and set it in its general place in a new map of the field. I claimed (1) that it applied to *all* ceremonial acts, not merely verbal ones, and that these are more common than is appreciated; I admitted (2) that our list was *not* complete, and that there are indeed other whole dimensions of what might be reasonably called 'unhappiness' affecting ceremonial performances in general and utterances in general, dimensions which are certainly the concern of philosophers; and (3) that, of course, different infelicities can be combined or can overlap and that it can be more or less an optional matter how we classify some given particular example.

We were next to take some examples of infelicities – of the infringement of our six rules. Let me first remind you of rule A. 1, that there must exist an accepted conventional procedure having a certain conventional effect, that procedure to include the uttering of certain words by certain persons in certain circumstances; and rule A. 2 of course, completing it, was that the particular persons and circumstances in a given case must be appropriate for the invocation of the particular procedure invoked.

There must exist an accepted conventional procedure having a certain conventional effect, the procedure to include the uttering of certain words by certain persons in certain circumstances.

A. 1
The latter part, of course, is simply designed to restrict the rule to cases of utterances, and is not important in principle.

Our formulation of this rule contains the two words 'exist' and 'accepted' but we may reasonably ask whether there can be any sense to 'exist' except 'to be accepted', and whether 'be in (general) use' should not be preferred to both. Hence we must not say '(1) exist, (2) be accepted' at any rate. Well, in deference to this reasonable query, let us take just 'accepted' *first*.

If somebody issues a performative utterance, and the utterance is classed as a misfire because the procedure invoked is *not accepted*, it is presumably persons other than the speaker who do not accept it (at least if the speaker is speaking *seriously*). What would be an example? Consider 'I divorce you', said to a wife by her husband in a Christian country, and both being Christians rather than Mohammedans. In this case it might be said, 'nevertheless he has not (successfully) divorced her: we admit only some other verbal or non-verbal procedure'; or even possibly 'we (*we*) do not admit any procedure at all for effecting divorce – marriage is indissoluble.' This may be carried so far that we reject what may be called a *whole code* of procedure, e.g. the code of honour involving duelling: for example, a challenge may be issued by 'my seconds will call on you', which is equivalent to 'I challenge you', and we merely shrug it off. The general position is exploited in the unhappy story of Don Quixote.

Of course, it will be evident that it is comparatively simple if we *never* admit any 'such' procedure at all – that is, any procedure at all for doing that sort of thing, or that procedure *anyway* for doing that particular thing. But equally possible are the cases where we do sometimes – in certain circumstances or at certain hands – accept a procedure, but *not* in any other circumstances or at other hands. And here we may often be in doubt (as in the naming example above) whether an infelicity should be brought into our present class A. 1 or rather into A. 2 (or even B. 1 or B. 2). For example, at a party, you say, when picking sides, 'I pick George': George grunts 'I'm not playing.' Has George been picked? Undoubtedly, the situation is an unhappy one. Well, we may say, you have not picked George, whether because there is no convention that you can pick people who aren't playing or because George in the circumstances is an inappropriate object for the procedure of picking. Or on a desert island you may say to me 'Go and pick up wood'; and I may say 'I don't take orders from you' or 'you're not entitled to give me orders' – I do not take orders from you when you try to 'assert your authority' (which I might fall in with but may not) on a desert island, as opposed to the case when you are the captain on a ship and therefore genuinely have authority.

Now we could say, bringing the case under A. 2 (Misapplication): the procedure – uttering certain words, &c. – was O.K. and accepted, but the circumstances in which it was invoked or the persons who invoked it were wrong: 'I pick' is only in order when the object of the verb is 'a player', and a command is in order only when the subject of the verb is 'a commander' or 'an authority'.

Or again we could say, bringing the case under rule B. 2 (and perhaps we should reduce the former suggestion to this): the procedure has not been completely executed; because it is a necessary *part* of it that, say, the person to be the object of the verb 'I order to…' must, by some previous procedure, tacit or verbal, have first constituted the person who is to do the ordering an authority, e.g. by saying 'I promise to do what you order me to do.' This is, of course, *one* of the uncertainties – and a purely general one really – which underlie the debate when we discuss in political theory whether there is or is not or should be a social contract.

It appears to me that it does not matter in principle at all how we decide in particular cases – though we may agree, either on the facts or by introducing further definitions, to prefer one solution rather than another – but that it is important in principle to be clear:

(1) as against B. 2 that however much we take into the procedure it would still be possible for someone to reject it *all*;

(2) that for a procedure to be *accepted* involves more than for it merely to be the case that it is *in fact generally used*, even actually by the persons now concerned; and that it must remain in principle open for anyone to reject any procedure – or code of procedures – even one that he has already hitherto accepted – as may happen with, for example, the code of honour. One who does so is, of course, liable to sanctions; others refuse to play with him or say that he is not a man of honour. *Above all* all must not be put into flat factual circumstances; for this is subject to the old objection to deriving an 'ought' from an 'is'. (Being accepted is *not* a circumstance in the right sense.) With many procedures, for example playing games, however appropriate the circumstances may be I may still not be playing, and, further, we should contend that in the last resort it is doubtful if 'being accepted' is definable as being 'usually' employed. But this is a more difficult matter.

Now secondly, what could be meant by the suggestion that sometimes a procedure may not even exist – as distinct from the question whether it is accepted, and by this or that group, or not?[14]

(i) We have the case of procedures which 'no longer exist' merely in the sense that though once generally accepted, they are no longer generally accepted, or even accepted by anybody; for example the case of challenging; and

(ii) we have even the case of procedures which someone is initiating. Sometimes he may 'get away with it' like, in football, the man who first picked up the ball and ran. Getting away with things is essential, despite the suspicious terminology. Consider a possible case: to say 'you were cowardly' may be to reprimand you or to insult you: and I can make my performance explicit by saying 'I reprimand you', but I cannot do so by saying 'I insult you' – the reasons for this do not matter here.[15] All that does matter is that a special variety of non-play[16] can arise if someone *does* say 'I insult you': for while insulting is a conventional procedure, and indeed primarily a verbal one, so that in a way we cannot help understanding the procedure that someone who says 'I insult you' is purporting to invoke, yet we are bound to non-play him, not merely because the convention is not accepted, but because we vaguely feel the presence of some bar, the nature of which is not immediately clear, against its ever being accepted.

Much more common, however, will be cases where it is uncertain how far a procedure extends – which cases it covers or which varieties it could be made to cover. It is inherent in the nature of any procedure that the limits of its applicability, and therewith, of course, the 'precise' definition of the procedure, will remain vague. There will always occur difficult or marginal cases where nothing in the previous history of a conventional procedure will decide conclusively whether such a procedure is or is not correctly applied to such a case. Can I baptize a dog, if it is admittedly rational? Or should I be non-played? The law abounds in such difficult decisions – in which, of course, it becomes more or less arbitrary whether we regard ourselves as deciding (A. 1) that a convention does not exist or as deciding (A. 2) that the circumstances are not appropriate for the invocation of a convention which undoubtedly does exist: either way, we shall tend to be bound by the 'precedent' we set. Lawyers usually prefer the latter course, as being to apply rather than to make law.

There is, however, a further type of case which may arise, which might be classified in many ways, but which deserves a special mention.

The performative utterances I have taken as examples are all of them highly developed affairs, of the kind that we shall later call *explicit* performatives, by contrast with merely *implicit* performatives. That is to say, they (all) begin with or include some highly significant and unambiguous expression such as 'I bet', 'I promise', 'I bequeath' – an expression very commonly also used in naming the act which, in making such an utterance, I am performing – for example betting, promising, bequeathing, &c. But, of course, it is both obvious and important that we can on occasion use the utterance 'go' to achieve practically the same as we achieve by the utterance 'I order you to go': and we should say cheerfully in either case, describing subsequently what someone did, that he ordered me to go. It may, however, be uncertain in fact, and, so far as the mere utterance is concerned, is always left uncertain when we use so inexplicit a formula as the mere imperative 'go', whether the utterer is ordering (or is purporting to order) me to go or merely advising, entreating, or what not me to go. Similarly 'There is a bull in the field' may or may not be a warning, for I *might* just be describing the scenery and 'I shall be there' may or may not be a promise. Here we have primitive as distinct from explicit performatives; and there may be nothing in the circumstances by which we can decide whether or not the utterance is performative at all. Anyway, in a given situation it can be open to me to take it as *either* one or the other. It was a performative formula – *perhaps* – but the procedure in question was not sufficiently explicitly invoked. Perhaps I did not *take it as* an order or was not anyway *bound* to take it as an order. The person did not *take it as* a promise: i.e. in the particular circumstance he did not accept the procedure, on the ground that the ritual was incompletely carried out by the original speaker.

We could assimilate this to a faulty or incomplete performance (B. 1 or B. 2): except that it is complete really, though not unambiguous. (In the law, of course, this kind of inexplicit performative *will* normally be brought under B. 1 or B. 2 – it is made a rule that to bequeath inexplicitly, for instance, is either an incorrect or an incomplete performance; but in ordinary life there is no such rigidity.) We could also assimilate it to Misunderstandings (which we are not yet considering): but it would be a special kind, concerning the force of the utterance as opposed to its meaning. And the point is not here just that the audience *did not* understand but that it did not *have* to understand, e.g. to *take it as* an order.

We might indeed even assimilate it to A. 2 by saying that the procedure is not designed for use where it is not clear that it is being used – which use makes it altogether void. We might claim that it is only to be used in circumstances which make it unambiguously clear that it is being used. But this is a counsel of perfection.

A. 2.   *The particular persons and circumstances in a given case must be appropriate for the invocation of the particular procedure invoked.*

We turn next to infringements of A. 2, the type of infelicity which we have called Misapplications. Examples here are legion. 'I appoint you', said when you have already been appointed, or when someone else has been appointed, or when I am not entitled to appoint, or when you are a horse: 'I do', said when you are in the prohibited degrees of relationship, or before a ship's captain not at sea: 'I give', said when it is not mine to give or when it is a pound of my living and non-detached flesh. We have various special terms for use in different types of case – '*ultra vires*', 'incapacity', 'not a fit or proper object (or person, &c.)', 'not entitled', and so on.

The boundary between 'inappropriate persons' and 'inappropriate circumstances' will necessarily not be a very hard and fast one. Indeed 'circumstances' can clearly be extended to cover in general 'the natures' of all persons participating. But we must distinguish between cases where the inappropriateness of persons, objects, names, &c., is a matter of 'incapacity' and simpler cases where the object or 'performer' is of the wrong kind or type. This again is a roughish and vanishing distinction, yet not without importance (in, say, the law). Thus we must distinguish the cases of a clergyman baptizing the wrong baby with the right name or baptizing a baby 'Albert' instead of 'Alfred', from those of saying 'I baptize this infant 2704' or 'I promise I will bash your face in' or appointing a horse as Consul. In the latter cases there is something of the wrong kind or type included, whereas in the others the inappropriateness is only a matter of incapacity.

Some overlaps of A. 2 with A. 1 and B. 1 have already been mentioned: perhaps we are more likely to call it a misinvocation (A. 1) if the person *as such* is inappropriate than if it is just because it is not the duly appointed one – if *nothing* – no antecedent procedure or appointment, &c. – could have put the matter in order. On the other hand, if we take the question of *appointment* literally (position as opposed to status) we might class the infelicity as a matter of wrongly executed rather than as misapplied procedure – for example, if we vote for a candidate before he has been nominated. The question here is how far we are to go back in the 'procedure'.

Next we have examples of B (already, of course, trenched upon) called Misexecutions.

B. 1. *The procedure must be executed by all participants correctly.*

These are flaws. They consist in the use of, for example, wrong formulas – there is a procedure which is appropriate to the persons and the circumstances, but it is not gone through correctly. Examples are more easily seen in the law; they are naturally not so definite in ordinary life, where allowances are made. The use of inexplicit formulas might be put under this heading. Also under this heading falls the use of vague formulas and uncertain references, for example if I say 'my house' when I have two, or if I say 'I bet you the race won't be run today' when more than one race was arranged.

This is a different question from that of misunderstanding or slow up-take by the audience; a flaw in the ritual is involved, however the audience took it. One of the things that cause particular difficulty is the question whether when two parties are involved '*consensus ad idem*' is necessary. Is it essential for me to secure *correct understanding* as well as everything else? In any case this is clearly a matter falling under the B rules and not under the Γ rules.

B. 2. *The procedure must be executed by all participants completely.*

These are hitches; we attempt to carry out the procedure but the act is abortive. For example: my attempt to make a bet by saying 'I bet you sixpence' is abortive unless you say 'I take you on' or words to that effect; my attempt to marry by saying 'I will' is abortive if the woman says 'I will not'; my attempt to challenge you is abortive if I say 'I challenge you' but I fail to send round my seconds; my attempt ceremonially to open a library is abortive if I say 'I open this library' but the key snaps in the lock; conversely the christening of a ship is abortive if I kick away the chocks before I have said 'I launch this ship.' Here again, in ordinary life, a certain laxness in procedure is permitted – otherwise no university business would ever get done!

Naturally sometimes uncertainties about whether anything further is required or not will arise. For example, are you required to accept the gift if I am to give you something? Certainly in formal business acceptance is required, but is this ordinarily so? Similar uncertainty arises if an appointment is made without the consent of the person appointed. The question here is how far can acts be unilateral? Similarly the question arises as to when the act is at an end, what counts as its completion?[17]

In all this I would remind you that we were *not* invoking such further dimensions of unhappiness as may arise from, say, the performer making a simple mistake of fact or from disagreements over matters of fact, let alone disagreements of opinion; for example, there is no convention that I can promise you to do something to your detriment, thus putting myself under an obligation to you to do it; but suppose I say 'I promise to send you to a nunnery' – when I think, but you do not, that this will be for your good, or again when you think it will but I do not, or even when we both think it will, but in fact, as may transpire, it will not? Have I invoked a non-existent convention in inappropriate circumstances? Needless to say, and as a matter of general principle, there can be no satisfactory choice between these alternatives, which are too unsubtle to fit subtle cases. There is no short cut to expounding simply the full complexity of the situation which does not exactly fit any common classification.

It may appear in all this that we have merely been taking back our rules. But this is not the case. Clearly there are these six possibilities of infelicity even if it is sometimes uncertain which is involved in a particular case: and we *might* define them, at least for given cases, if we wished. And we must at all costs avoid over-simplification, which one might be tempted to call the occupational disease of philosophers if it were not their occupation.

Notes

1 Everything said in these sections is provisional, and subject to revision in the light of later sections.

2 Of all people, jurists should be best aware of the true state of affairs. Perhaps some now are. Yet they will succumb to their own timorous fiction, that a statement of 'the law' is a statement of fact.

3 Not without design: they are all 'explicit' performatives, and of that prepotent class later called 'exercitives'.

4 [Austin realized that the expression 'I do' is not used in the marriage ceremony too late to correct his mistake. We have let it remain in the text as it is philosophically unimportant that it is a mistake. J. O. Urmson.]

5 Still less anything that I have already done or have yet to do.

6 'Sentences' form a class of 'utterances', which class is to be defined, so far as I am concerned, grammatically, though I doubt if the definition has yet been given satisfactorily. With performative utterances are contrasted, for example and essentially, 'constative' utterances: to issue a constative utterance (i.e. to utter it with a historical reference) is to make a statement. To issue a performative utterance is, for example, to make a bet. See further below on 'illocutions'.

7 Formerly I used 'performatory': but 'performative' is to be preferred as shorter, less ugly, more tractable, and more traditional in formation.

8 I owe this observation to Professor H. L. A. Hart.

9 But I do not mean to rule out all the offstage performers – the lights men, the stage manager, even the prompter; I am objecting only to certain officious understudies.

10 We shall avoid distinguishing these precisely because the distinction is not in point.

11 It will be explained later why the having of these thoughts, feelings, and intentions is not included as just one among the other 'circumstances' already dealt with in (A).

12 [Austin from time to time used other names for the different infelicities. For interest some are here given: A. 1, Non-plays; A. 2, Misplays; B, Miscarriages; B. 1, Misexecutions; B. 2, Non-executions; Γ, Disrespects; Γ. 1, Dissimulations; Γ. 2, Non-fulfilments, Disloyalties, Infractions, Indisciplines, Breaches. J. O. Urmson.]

13 Naming babies is even more difficult; we might have the wrong name and the wrong cleric – that is, someone entitled to name babies but not intended to name *this* one.

14 If we object here to saying that there is doubt whether it 'exists' – as well we may, for the word gives us currently fashionable creeps which are in general undoubtedly legitimate, we might say that the doubt is rather as to the precise nature or definition or comprehension of the procedure which undoubtedly does exist and *is* accepted.

15 Many such possible procedures and formulas would be disadvantageous if recognized; for example, perhaps we ought not to allow the formula 'I promise you that I'll thrash you.' But I am told that in the hey-day of student duelling in Germany it was the custom for members of one club to march past members of a rival club, each drawn up in file, and then for each to say to his chosen opponent as he passed, quite politely, 'Beleidigung', which means 'I insult you.'

16 ['Non-play' was at one time Austin's name for the category A. 1 of infelicities. He later rejected it but it remains in his notes at this point. J. O. Urmson.]

17 It might thus be doubted whether failure to hand a gift over is a failure to complete the gift or an infelicity of type Γ.

CHAPTER 6

Tacit Persuasion Patterns

Richard Lanham

In this enlightening chapter from his book, *Analyzing Prose* (1983, 2003), Richard Lanham examines the implied rhetorical patterns of persuasive style. He asks why it is that repetition and linguistic crossing are so conducive to persuasion. And he demonstrates through many examples that writing often assumes shapes that carry with them an implicit tendency to harmonize with our own expectations as readers and therefore to more easily persuade. The glossary of rhetorical terms that follows is also from the same book.

Some social situations seem to carry within themselves a kind of natural persuasiveness, suggest by their very shape a "logical" or "just" outcome. The game theorists who have studied these shapes have christened them "tacit bargaining" patterns, patterns which tacitly suggest a certain outcome. Assume, for example, that you and I are paratroopers dropped behind enemy lines. We become separated during the descent and, since we carelessly failed to plan for such an eventuality, we don't know where to meet. We do, though, have the same map:

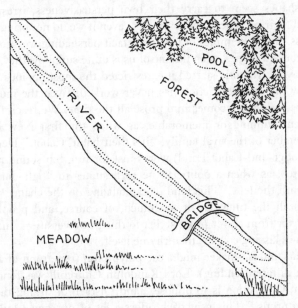

I land in the meadow. You – though I don't know it – come down in the forest. Where would you guess I would guess you might guess that we might "logically" meet? Most people say the bridge. Why? It is not in the center of the map. And if it were, would that make a difference? Obviously it would, because the center provides a natural focus. And so, though off-center, does the bridge. It comes as close to a crossroads, a natural meeting point, as this map affords. If we had both grown up in this area, and spent many a long summer's afternoon at the forest pool, it would be a different story. Or suppose, instead, that a red army entered the mapped area from the wooded side and a white army from the meadow. Each had orders to occupy as much territory as possible without actively engaging the enemy. Chances are they'd both stop at the river. These tacit bargaining situations occur all the time. Their "logic," though, often seems hidden and seldom really logical. If you are the boss and I ask for a raise from $20 to $25 per hour you might say you'll "meet me halfway" at $22.50 per hour. It somehow "seems fair." Actually my going rate may be $25 and so $22.50 will not be "logical," that is to say commonly thought fair, at all: If so, I ought to have asked for a raise from $20 to $30 per hour so that the tacit bargaining logic would operate with real "logic" – at least from my point of view – to suggest $25 per hour.

Something analogous to these tacit bargaining patterns occurs in verbal style. Shapes, either sound patterns or sight patterns, often seem to bring with them their own kind of illogical persuasion. We might call them "tacit persuasion" patterns. For the most part, we simply don't know why they affect us as they do. It must come from how the brain processes information but that doesn't really tell us anything. To answer the question properly, we would need to ask how the visual cortex processes visual patterns and then apply that information to chiasmus, say, or isocolon or, why does the axial symmetry of the human body incline us to relish the same kind of symmetry in the outside world? (Think of all those symmetrical patterns we've come across in prose style.) I'm not competent to do this kind of analysis, even if we had time for it here. We don't. We can offer only a general caution: shape makes a lot of difference in prose. A great deal of persuasion occurs in this way and most of it remains tacit, unacknowledged. Some shapes seem to carry their own persuasiveness, irrespective of their content. We feel their presence subconsciously, even if we do not bring that knowledge to self-awareness. A few examples of how such tacit persuading works may alert you to these subcutaneous strategies, even if none of us is quite sure how they work.

We have always – Aristotle started it – restricted the most obvious tacit bargaining shapes to poetry, but the restriction has never worked. Even the most obvious tacit bargaining shape – rhyme – comes into prose all the time. We reach for it every time we want to seem cunning or memorable, as when the first New England Lodge rejoined to a member of the rival family, "It's their habit, Cabot." Here the rhyme (it *is* a rhyme in Lodge-and-Cabot Land) works just for fun, but sound resemblance can yoke meaning, too, as when a politician never hesitates to "fight for the right" but remains "deft with the left." This kind of capitalizing on the chance resemblances of language occurs all the time. Do it too much, of course, and people get annoyed. You've moved over from clever prose stylist to third-rate versifier. And so prose more often uses rhyme's kissing cousins than rhyme itself.

Thus a lapidary phrase-maker might use polyptoton (repetition of a word with the same root but a different ending). Lord Randolph Churchill was fond of saying that "The duty of an Opposition is to oppose," and Disraeli of urging that "Adventures are to the adventurous." This neat trick offers a lot of put-down mileage, especially in the "[Law] is too important to leave to the [lawyers]" form, filling in for "Law" and "lawyer"whatever profession you want to disparage. Or you vary the form by using a synonym instead of the same root word, as when George Bernard Shaw sighed "How wonderful is youth: why must it be wasted on children?" Such a pattern becomes a kind of mold for thought, or machinery for generating it.

Or we can use a homonymic pun *(paronomasia)*, as in "If life is a gamble, make it also a gambol." No *etymological* logic galvanizes this capitalization on linguistic chance. "Gambol" comes from the Italian word *gamba* (leg) and "gamble" from the Anglo-Saxon word for game, *gamen*. But the near-rhyme invites us to a tacit bargain: yes, gamble and gambol ought to be equivalent in something besides sound. Chance should lead to pleasure.

Even the most dedicated opponents of pleasure and language play have been tempted by the near-rhyme polyptotonic habit. The very hammer of the rhetors, Socrates, says (albeit ironically) when he is accused of dressing up to go to Agathon's house: χαλὸς παρὰ χαλόν – "One must be beautiful when going to visit the beautiful." Proverbs, in the European languages at least, use polyptotonic techniques all the time. "*Homo proponit sed Deus disponit* – Man proposes but God disposes." Why does it work so well? What itch does it scratch? If I say of a now-faded classical beauty, "She is but a shadow of her faded middle-aged self," ho-hum. But, "She has faded long since to the shadow of a shade," seems to echo time itself. Why do we want to become Rabelaisian word-spinners, take a word and conjugate or decline its essence out? The tacit power here seems to flow from conjugatability itself, from the transforming power exercised when we use one part of speech for another (the rhetorical term for this is *anthimeria*) or change form or case. The root word exudes a power the whole range of tacit persuasion patterns can draw upon.

Polyptoton is often reinforced by another tacit persuasion pattern – alliteration. Churchill writes "We shall not flag or fail." An Elizabethan storyteller calls Helen of Troy "a piece of price." The liberated puritan calls a misfortune "sad as Sunday." Clichés pickle themselves in a similar alliterative form: "cool, calm, and collected," "fast and furious," "flight of fancy," "forbidden fruit," "top to toe," "enough to make your blood boil." Why do we find this alliterative, "following the letter" form of tacit persuasion so attractive? No one knows for sure. Clearly the pleasure is childlike and, as Freud argued, harks back to babbling, to the fun we had with sounds before they were disciplined by meaning. But this doesn't go far in explaining how alliteration works in mature prose. Alliteration, after all only a kind of front rhyme, poses the same fundamental question. Why do we like it?

The simpler question – how does it work? – involves tacit persuasion at its most obvious. In the map illustration we began with, there just happened to be a bridge across the river. We met there by capitalizing on that chance. Alliteration, or front rhyme, has been traditionally more acceptable in prose than end-rhyme but both do the same thing – capitalize on chance. These patterns can do it just for fun, as in the clichés I've just listed. Or they can underscore other tacit persuasion patterns – chiasmus, isocolon, or climax, for example. This powerful glue can connect elements without logical relationship. Because alliteration does work so well, because we acknowledge the "rightness" of "fate's fickle finger" with a part of our mind not under logical control, people have always resented alliteration and tried to outlaw it. It has no right to work as well as it does.

Language is full of these chance resemblances of sound and spelling and prose stylists have always capitalized on them, used them to suggest a natural affinity between objects or concepts which logically possessed none. Such plays on words, because they please us so, persuade us more than their logical content merits. Certain shapes of phrasing do the same thing. Antithesis provides perhaps the best example of this second kind of tacit persuasion magic. As a habit of mind, antithesis may well be intrinsic to how we think, part of the brain's now-familiar right and left hemi-sphericality. And, beginning with Darwin (in *The Expression of the Emotions in Man and Animals*), it has been argued that human gesture, too, seems to operate on antithetical principles. If a dog stands erect and bristles its hair as an evolutionary gesture of defiance, then flat hair and a lowly, cringing posture may develop by antithesis – as a formal rather than an evolutionary posture. However persuasive these long-range explanations, clearly antithesis taps a deep power somewhere; its use as a tacit bargaining pattern occurs far too often to be caused by chance. And again, not only powerful but dead easy to work. The root pattern is called "chiasmus" because, diagrammed, it forms an "X" and the Greek word for X is *chi*. When John Kennedy constructed his famous bromide "Ask not what your country can do for you but what you can do for your country," he went to the Well of Antithesis for his active ingredient. Where does the "X" power come from?

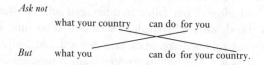

Obviously a verbal judo is at work here. By keeping the phrase but inverting its meaning we use our opponent's own power to overcome him, just as a judo expert does. So a scholar remarked of another's theory, "Cannon entertains that theory because that theory entertains Cannon." The pun on "entertain" complicates the chiasmus here, but the judo still prevails – Cannon is playing with the power of his own mind rather than figuring out the secrets of the universe.

The New Testament uses chiasmus repeatedly to suggest the fundamental reci-procity of human ethics, the tacit bargain that we ignore at our peril. Just think about how much New Testament wisdom comes in this form. Not only "Do unto others as you would have them do unto you," but:

The first shall be last and
the last shall be first.

Judge not, that ye be not judged.

For with what judgment ye judge,
ye shall be judged.

And with what measure ye mete
it shall be measured to you again.

He that findeth his life shall lose it; and
he that loseth his life for my sake shall find it.

For judgment I am come into this world,
that they which see not might see,
and that they which see might be blind.

Such a persistent pattern can suggest balance and inversion of all kinds. Here it points insistently to the absolute inversion of worldly values which Christian ethics implies, a 180-degree reversal which literally makes the last into the first.

The X-pattern sometimes almost *defines* words. Professional football players, for example, use a chiasmus proverb to think about injuries:

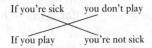

What's going on here? The X seems to establish two different, mutually exclusive roles. It excludes, *by its form*, the temptation to stand in the middle – play, but if you don't play well, blame it on being sick. The X-form provides precisely the diagrammatic force a player needs, the force to separate experience into two mutually exclusive camps. The player makes a tacit bargain with himself. Pattern supplies reassurance.

Winston Churchill used the X-form differently, but still for reassurance, in his famous Mansion House speech in November of 1942. He said, of the African campaign, "This is not the end. It is not even the beginning of the end. But it is perhaps, the end of the beginning." Not *cheap* reassurance. Don't get your hopes up. Don't mistake the first chapter for the last. But, still, yes, get your *long-term* hopes up, because I've imposed a pattern on the war: beginning-end of beginning-beginning of end-end. The AB–BA flip-flop suggests a reversal of fortune by its very shape. You know where you are, and the "logic of the pattern" will ultimately carry you to victory, because the end of the beginning leads – by the X-form logic – to the beginning of the end. As always, Churchill takes pleasure in verbal pattern for its own sake, and this too consoles us. Only strong men can enjoy word games while in grave danger. Ultimate cool.

George Bernard Shaw varies this form in an exchange about sexual chastity in *Man and Superman*.

Doña Ana: Don Juan: a word against chastity is an insult to me.
Don Juan: I say nothing against your chastity, Señora, since it took the form of a husband and twelve children. What more could you have done had you been the most abandoned of women?
Doña Ana: I could have had twelve husbands and no children, that's what I could have done.

Don Juan's strong serve right on the line is slammed directly back in his face.

We might, as a last instance of this most obvious tacit bargaining pattern, instance former Attorney General John Mitchell's stirring words about the Watergate disaster: "When the going gets tough, the tough get going." Sounds great, huh? Hard times bring out the greatness in the great. Alas, as John Dean saw when he passed this apothegm on from Mitchell to posterity, the reversal-logic here suggests another and opposite meaning: "When the going gets tough, sensible people take the first train out." Dean's suggested redefinition was cleverly turned but it only reemphasizes the tacit-persuasion logic chiasmus always invokes: the second half of the assertion seems to follow inevitably from the first because the shape of the phrasing says so. The two senses of Mitchell's epigram are diametrically opposed, but both depend on the same tacit-persuasion power that chiasmus, by the nature of its symmetrical geometry, seems to create.

Repetition works almost as strongly as X inversion. Instead of ABBA, we get ABAB. I open the *Viking Book of Aphorisms* at random and find:

To be engaged	in opposing wrong
affords but slender guarantee	for being right.

Let not thy will		roar	
when thy power	can but	whisper.	

Antithesis still works here, but in the words alone. The pattern is ABAB, the sense ABBA. The ABAB parallelism draws the opposing poles of meaning so close together that magnetic force can flow between them. This magnetic pattern is often the basic form for aphorism. So here. The aphorist piles "opposing wrong" on top of "being right" and "be engaged" on top of "affords slender guarantee." Often, as here, one of the pairs, A or B, generates more electricity than the other. But not always.

Let not	*thy will*		*roar*
when	*thy power*	can but	*whisper.*

Here A and B work with equal strength. Sometimes this equal kind of pattern seems too pat, a little cute. Unequal pairs seem to work better as in this proverb from the great UCLA basketball coach, John Wooden:

Don't let what you can't do
Interfere with what you can do.

As someone addicted to just this folly, I draw daily consolation from Wooden's exhortation. But why does it work so well? Where does the tacit persuasion come from? Well, somehow from those horizontal and vertical visual coordinates considered earlier. From the way "can't do" and "can do" are visually insulated from one another by "interfere."

The isocolon in these aphorisms operates with brute simplicity: equal length = equal entity. Then put two of them in parallel but make the sense an X-pattern, and the paradoxical electricity which galvanizes aphorism begins to flow. The terms may not really be so antithetical as the pattern implies, but the energetic quickness of the play hides this.

Patterns like these become templates for thinking; they both frame thinking and, by their formal "logic," urge certain thoughts upon us. To take a trivial instance, I just now got up from my desk to get a drink of water. I've been writing all morning and my hand has fallen asleep from cramp. As I was drinking the water my subconscious mind must have been thinking "I have written too much. I should stop for lunch." But this thought came *as an aphorism*:

Your hand can go to sleep	from writing too much
as well as	from writing too little.

The pattern somehow had prompted as well as formed the thought. This formal back-pressure works on several levels. Every argument has two sides, we like to say, but it may have seven or eight. It "has two sides" because for many reasons it proves convenient to give it two sides. The formal pressure manifest in tacit persuasion never lets up.

Two basic tacit persuasion patterns have now emerged, inversion and repetition, ABBA and ABAB. In this kind of visual geometry, there can be only one more, climax/anticlimax, an extension of the ABAB pattern either up or down. Since the aphorism reveals this geometry so clearly (since that clear geometry is what defines an aphorism!) let's stay with this form. Churchill said about the Battle of Britain pilots: "Never in the field of human conflict was so much owed by so many to so few." First, a simple root expansion,

$$A \ B \qquad A' \ B' \qquad A'' \ B''$$
$$ABABAB - \text{so much/so many/so few/}.$$

But with complications. "Much" and "many" are alike (and so yoked by alliteration) but "few" stands opposite to them. A′ repeats A but A″ stands as an antithetical climax to it. "So much" and "so many" lead us to expect a third repetition instead of the antithesis. Climax, but based on an antithetical pattern.

We've seen *anaphora* (similar opening patterns) at work before. In the next example, Churchill uses it to build a straightforward climax, a repetition that grows but does not reverse itself:

> We shall not flag or fail. We shall fight in France, we shall fight on the seas and oceans, we shall fight with growing confidence and growing strength in the air, we shall defend our island, whatever the cost may be, we shall fight on the beaches, we shall fight on the landing grounds, we shall fight in the fields and in the streets, we shall fight in the hills; we shall never surrender. (*Blood, Toil, Tears and Sweat: The Speeches of Winston Churchill*, edited by David Cannadine, Boston: Houghton Mifflin, (1989)

The climactic progression stands out.

> We shall not flag or fail.
> We shall fight in France,
> we shall fight on the seas and oceans,
> we shall fight with growing confidence and growing strength in the air,
> we shall defend our island, whatever the cost may be,
> we shall fight on the beaches,
> we shall fight on the landing grounds,
> we shall fight in the fields and in the streets,
> we shall fight in the hills;
> we shall never surrender.

Nice symmetry, for a start. The "f" alliteration set up with "*f*lag or *f*ail" continues through "fight" to the climactic "we shall never surrender" with only one slight break in the middle, where "we shall de*f*end" defers the alliteration to the second syllable. This break states the general theme whose particulars are itemized before and after. *Before*, a survey of offensive fighting – in France, at sea, in the air; *after*, a survey of where the fighting will occur if the enemy does invade – on the beaches and on the landing grounds (stage one), then fields and streets (stage two), then in the hills (stage three), and finally the climax – "we shall never surrender."

The whole pattern equalizes two kinds of statements: 1) where Britain will fight; 2) that she will defend the island, whatever the cost, will never surrender. The equalizing is done by the list and the list is paced by the summary comment ("we shall defend our island") halfway through and climaxed by "we shall never surrender." The form welds both processes into a chain of certainties. By our tacit agreement, Churchill's assertion becomes a proleptic fact. And, oddly enough, a kind of reversal occurs here too, for we are so sure the "no surrender" spirit prevails that we refuse to believe the invasion will succeed, the backward steps from landing ground to field to street to hills will be taken.

The *locus classicus* for the tacit persuasion patterns we have been discussing is a linguistically lunatic Elizabethan short novel, John Lyly's *Euphues*. Lyly came down to London from Oxford in the 1570s determined to make a splash. This otherwise commendable resolve issued in the publication of *Euphues, The Anatomy of Wit* (1578). *Euphues* is a prodigal-son type who goes to Naples, steals his best friend's girl, and after she jilts him, comes home to repent. Not much happens in the silly and sketchy plot, and if we read *Euphues* for the plot we really will hang ourselves. (Dr Johnson commented on the detailed psychological portraiture in Samuel Richardson's long novels: "Why, Sir, if you were to read Richardson for the story, your impatience would be so much fretted that you would hang yourself."). But when we read it for the style we're tempted to do the same thing. The book consists mostly of moralizing speeches, couched in a style so full of antithesis, isocolon, climax, and alliteration that it comes to be *about* tacit persuasion patterns. A typical sentence-paragraph:

> When parents have more care how to leave their children wealthy than wise, and are more desirous to have them maintain the name than the nature of a gentleman; when they put gold into the hands of youth where they should put a rod under their girdle; when instead of awe they make them past grace and leave them rich executors of goods and poor executors of godliness – then it is no marvel that the son, being left rich by his father's will, becomes retchless by his own will.

Maybe a chart will help

When parents have more care how   to leave their   children
                                        *w*ealthy than *w*ise
    and are more desirous   to have   them maintain
                               the *n*ame than the *n*ature
                                      of a gentleman;
when they put *g*old into the hands of youth
where they should put a *r*od under their *g*irdle
when instead of awe
    they make them past *g*race   and leave them   rich executors of   goods and
                                        poor executors of   godliness
    then it is no marvel that the son   *b*eing left   *r*ich by his father's *will*
                                      *b*ecomes   *r*etchless by his own *will*.

The italicized alliteration only begins the game. It is intensified by word repetition ("executors . . . executors"/"will . . . will" – this repetition is called *diacope*). The isocolon, stacking up phrases equal in length and structure, jumps off the chart. And there is hidden rhyme like the m*a*intain/n*a*me/n*a*ture patterns. Antithetical words are pulled closer together by the alliteration: "wealthy/wise; name/nature; goods/godliness." The goods/godliness pairing creates a kind of sight-and-sound slant pun. Good and God both sound and look somewhat alike, *as if* they might be different forms of the same root word. The ABAB isocolons sometimes omit the second A:

leave their children	wealthy than
(leave their children)	wise

leave them	rich executors of goods and
(leave them)	poor executors of godliness.

But even here sometimes a smaller full ABAB pattern lurks:

A	B
rich executors	of goods

A	B
poor executors	of godliness

And the last pair of parallel phrases generates a Chinese box effect:

A	B
being left rich	by his father's will
becomes retchless	by his own will

Fair enough, but look at the chiasmus hidden in the A side:

	A	B
	left	rich
	retch-	less
	B	A

A self-generating dynamic operates between chiasmus and the double-isocolon (ABAB), each threatening to turn into, or overlay, the other. It begins to work in the goods/godliness contrast:

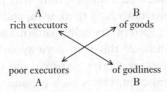

	A	B
	rich executors	of goods
	poor executors	of godliness
	A	B

Straightforward double-isocolon, but a reader of Lyly is so conditioned to antitheses that he starts to make them at the least suggestion. Chiasmus as well as double-isocolon has become a *way of perceiving*. So we start to cross them here:

rich executors	*goods*
poor executors	*god*liness

And out pops the central moral of this relentless moralizing: people poor in goods are rich in godliness and vice versa. Not always true? The proverbial wisdom disagrees and the tacit persuasion patterns have been enlisted to help convince us.

The sentence, with its "when . . . when . . . where . . . when . . . THEN" periodic suspension, constitutes a climactic syllogism which expresses the central theme of Lyly's prodigal son tale – prodigal sons are made, not born. They are the sons of prodigal fathers. A sensible point but stale. But look at it from Lyly's point of view. He didn't have anything new to say. In his moral world, nothing new was left to say. How make a splash, then? You let the tacit persuasion patterns generate the meaning for you. Finding yourself with nothing to say, you deliver yourself methodically into the arms of chance. Since you make a splash by being extreme, he does this extremely. And so *Euphues*, whatever help it may provide for prodigal sons, comes to be a tacit persuasion pattern-book of Lyly's method of composition which, in this respect, resembles John Cage's practice of composing using patterns from *I Ching*.

We see better illustrated here than in any other prose style I know the back-pressure form exerts on thought. Vernon Lee, an acute student of English style, once called syntax "the cast left by long repeated acts of thought." Lyly turned this observation on its head, thought becoming the cast left by infinitely repeated tacit persuasion patterns.

Prose like this stands at the typographical interface between prose and poetry. Lyly maximizes the tension between horizontal and vertical coordinates which verse typography allows but prose typography does not. Lyly's prose wants to be diagrammed. Its pronounced visual coordinates allegorize a search for moral ones, form a geometrical analogue for the proverbial wisdom it heaps upon us.

Compulsively patterned prose like this is hard for us to take. The Elizabethans, on the other hand, loved it. It started a fad for such elaborate patterning, a fad which, unlike most fads, left a permanent trace after it faded away. It offered written English a new set of patterns, a hypotactic periodicity that contrasted sharply with the paratactic running style which had constituted the main road of prose up to that time. It made patterns that were tacit in Greek and Latin overt in English.

We don't like the compulsive repetition. But even more, we don't like the direction in which the intellectual current flows – from pattern to thought, rather than vice versa. We have thought, ever since this patterning was repudiated by the plain styles which followed upon the scientific revolution, that *thought came first*. Words only dress it up. Western educational history, until that time, mostly thought otherwise. Verbal patterns were instruments to think with, and they were taught as part of the training in how to think. Pattern/thought, pattern/thought, pattern/thought – a continuing oscillation. We shall see this pair of viewpoints return when we come to consider electronic text. Patterning there is dynamic and three-dimensional but, even more than with print or manuscript, exerts back-pressure on how we think, and how we learn to think.

One more tacit persuasion pattern – the list. It creates a world of equal integers which permits systematic search and arrangement. Metaphor generalizes experience. The list *iterates* it, describes the universe by describing each particular in it. It underlies more prose than we usually realize. Here's an egregious example, again from Shaw's *Man and Superman*. A born-again moralizing Don Juan meets the Devil in Hell, and proceeds to badmouth the beautiful people he meets there. The Devil replies: "Señor Don Juan: you are uncivil to my friends." I'll render Don Juan's reply to this civil rejoinder directly in schematic form:

Pooh! why should I be civil to them or to you? In this Palace of Lies a truth or two will not hurt you. Your friends are all the dullest dogs I know.

> They are not beautiful: **they are only** decorated.
> They are not clean: **they are only** shaved and starched.
> They are not dignified: **they are only** fashionably dressed.
> They are not educated: **they are only** college passmen.
> They are not religious: **they are only** pewrenters.
> They are not moral: **they are only** conventional.
> They are not virtuous: **they are only** cowardly.
>
> They are not even vicious: they are only "frail."
>
> They are not artistic: **they are only** lascivious.
> They are not prosperous: **they are only** rich.
> They are not loyal: **they are only** servile;
>
> not dutiful, **only sheepish;**
> not public spirited, **only patriotic;**
> not courageous, **only quarrelsome;**
> not determined, **only obstinate;**
> not masterful, **only domineering;**
> not self-controlled, **only obtuse;**
> not self-respecting, **only vain;**
> not kind, **only sentimental;**
> not social, **only gregarious;**
> not considerate, **only polite;**
> not intelligent, **only opinionated;**
> not progressive, **only factious;**
> not imaginative, **only superstitious;**
> not just, **only vindictive;**
> not generous, **only propitiatory;**
> not disciplined, **only cowed;**
>
> and not truthful at all:
> liars every one of them,
> to the very backbone of their souls.

Don Juan is in harrowing hell, enumerating all its falsities, one by one. He uses the classic strategy of *epitheton*, here a string of paired epithets, one representing the truth, the other its hellish similacrum. Once the list gets going, we accept its tacit logic, that experience can be adequately described by contrasting epithets. An introduction precedes the list; a ringing generalization ("liars every one of them") concludes it. The rocking rhythm is slightly varied midway by the variation I have emphasized: They are not *even* vicious: they are only "frail." The list builds, pair by pair, into a terrific rant. But, somewhere towards the end, we begin to wonder if Don Juan does not become imprisoned by his formula. The game of pairing, the formal pleasure, takes over from the thought. We begin, that is, to look *at* the list rather than through it. I've encouraged this process, of course, by my reformatting and color coding. In regular consecutive prose on the page, and especially when spoken aloud, they carry us along in the rush.

Shaw meant us, though, to think about this list as a list, to notice the argumentative power of the tacit bargaining formula he employs. We can tell by the comment which immediately follows the list. Don Juan's listeners include not only the Devil but The Statue, the illustrious Commander of the Calatrava, the father of Doña Ana, whom Don Juan, in life, had slain in a swordfight. They are all friends now – that already-mentioned devilish civility of Hell – and the Commander's response is enthusiastic.

> Your flow of words is simply amazing, Juan. How I wish I could have talked like that to my soldiers.

The Commander is admiring the list *as a list*, looking *at* it rather than *through* it, he praises it as a rhetorical effect. There is no better way to deflate an opponent's argument than to praise the manner of its delivery. It is an old Hollywood putdown: "Wow! Terrific! Who writes your stuff?" Shaw uses Don Juan both to advance an argument and to illustrate the power of tacit-bargaining verbal patterns.

A list creates a world of equal integers which permits systematic search and arrangement. It underlies more prose than we usually realize. Lyly uses it all the time:

If I be	in Crete	I can lie
if	in Greece	I can shift
if	in Italy	I can court it.

I can carouse	with Alexander
abstain	with Romulus
eat	with the epicure
fast	with the Stoic
sleep	with Endymion
watch	with Chrysippus

The list aims to exhaust the riches of the universe, to have been everywhere and to have done everything. The list is based on fraudulent conversion from numerical extension to infinity, from quantity to quality. List enough items and you'll have grasped the essence, generalized, grasped intuitively. It's not true, but it seems so.

The basic tacit persuasion patterns – the antithesis and balance of the "X" and "double-isocolon" patterns, the climax often built upon them, and the iterative listing as alternate to climax – often develop into one another.

Taken together, they seem to represent all the basic patterns available. Not many styles are so compulsive as to be *about* these patterns but many use them. For example, from the *Declaration of Independence*:

> When in the Course of human events, it becomes necessary for one people to dissolve the political bands which have connected them with another, and to assume among the Powers of the earth, the separate and equal station to which the Laws of Nature and of

Nature's God entitle them, a decent respect to the opinions of mankind requires that they should declare the causes which impel them to the separation.

Our old friend the "when-then" syllogism, the "then" being understood ("entitle them, *then* a decent..."). Then the lists start:

> We hold these truths to be self-evident:
>> that all men are created equal
>> that they are endowed by their Creator with certain unalienable Rights
>> That among these are Life, Liberty and the Pursuit of Happiness
>> that to secure these rights...
>> that whenever any form of Government...

The list form is stressed by the repeated "that"s. Take them out and the tacit-persuasion list pattern submerges:

> We hold several truths to be self-evident. All men have been created equal and endowed with certain unalienable Rights, by their Creator. These rights include Life, Liberty and the Pursuit of Happiness. To secure these rights Men institute governments which derive their just powers from the consent of the governed. Whenever any form of Government...

Notice how the climax ("Life, Liberty and the Pursuit of Happiness") loses power without the listing to play off against? You can deflate the whole document simply by subtracting the anaphora. Try it:

> He has refused his Assent to Laws, the most wholesome and necessary for the public good.
> He has forbidden his Governors to pass Laws of immediate and pressing importance, unless suspended in their operation till his Assent should be obtained...
> He has refused to pass other Laws for the accommodation of large districts of people, unless those people would relinquish the right of Representation in the Legislature...
> He has called together legislative bodies at places unusual, uncomfortable and distant from the depository of their Public Records...
> He has dissolved Representative Houses repeatedly, for opposing with manly firmness his invasions on the rights of the people.
> He has refused for a long time, after such dissolutions, to cause others to be elected...
> He has endeavoured to prevent the population of these States; for that purpose obstructing the Laws of Naturalization of Foreigners; refusing to pass others to encourage their migration hither, and raising the conditions of new Appropriations of Lands...
> For protecting them, by a mock Trial, from Punishment for any Murders which they should commit on the Inhabitants of these States:
> For cutting off our Trade with all parts of the world:
> For imposing taxes on us without our Consent:
> For depriving us in many cases, of the benefits of Trial by Jury:
> For transporting us beyond Seas to be tried for pretended offences...

And so on, through several more repetitions. Exhausting but exhaustive, a damning list as reductively egalitarian as the political philosophy it argues for – all these sins equal, all equally sinful.

Such repetitive patterning makes *Euphues* look like a model of restraint. Why doesn't it vex us as much? Familiarity makes us look through it rather than at it, of course. But mostly, we feel that its august subject – a political revolution – *deserves* the pomp of such ceremonial repetition. Feeling the list *as a list* intensifies the egalitarian argument. The double-isocolon patterns emerge here as a direct formal implication of the anaphora–list-making.

	A		B
	He has refused his Assent to Laws,		the most wholesome and necessary
	A′		B′
	He has forbidden his Governors		
	to pass laws		of immediate and pressing importance
	A		B
	He has dissolved Representative		
	Houses		for opposing
	A′		B′
	He has refused		after such dissolutions

A suggestion of chiasmus:

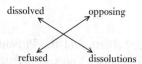

The two lines of the X differ in kind: polyptoton creates the "dissolved" axis synonym but not the "opposing-refused" one. A double-I pattern lurks below the surface in other places, too. For example:

	A		B
	unless suspended in their operation		till his Assent
	A′		B′
	when so suspended he has utterly neglected		to attend to them.

And *tricolon*, three-element climax, occurs as well, here reinforced by *anaphora* through *homoioteleuton* (similar endings):

He has endeavored to prevent the population of these States;
for that purpose
    obstructing the Laws of Naturalization of Foreigners:
    refusing to pass others to encourage their migration hither and
    raising the conditions of new Appropriations of Lands.

The chiasmus here more often than not hesitates on the brink of self-consciousness:

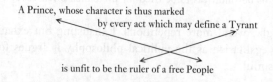

Or happening on a scale too large to notice:

A	B
He has combined with others to subject us	and unacknowledged
to a jurisdiction foreign to our constitution,	by our Laws
A′	B′
giving his assent to their acts	of pretended legislation

A and A′ are yoked by his *combining* and his *assenting;* B and B′ by "laws" and "legislation." And isn't there an X-pattern suggested too?

The whole document moves from list-making through the parallelism, balance, and antithesis that come from chiasmus and isocolon to the resolution of tricolon climax. The balance and antithesis patterns don't declare themselves; the list pattern blows a trumpet. And so, at the end, does the resonating *tricolon:*

> we mutually pledge to each other
> > our Lives
> > our Fortunes and
> > our sacred Honor.

How could anyone resist this? And that is what the tacit persuasion patterns are all about, forming the path of least resistance. In their ideal form they have the nice symmetry we have seen: list ⟷ X and double-I ⟷ climax. They constitute, in fact, as we can now see, the basic beginning ⟷ middle ⟷ ending strategies for sentences. Put them to work in actual prose and they grow so complex that, like the other exploratory patterns we've been examining in these chapters, they become less a component of style than style itself, the inevitability that revolutions seek in events themselves and find so often only in the words used to describe them.

A Brief Glossary of Rhetorical Terms[*]

Classical rhetoric was divided into five parts:
1   Invention
2   Arrangement
3   Style
4   Memory
5   Delivery

And into three areas of use:
1   Deliberative (to debate in political bodies)
2   Judicial (to plead in law courts)
3   Epideictic or Panegyric (to praise, blame, or show off)

alloiósis.   Breaking down a subject into alternatives:
> Your tax accountant, on the pros and cons of taking a chancy deduction: "You can either eat well or sleep well."

---

[*] For a fuller listing, see Richard A. Lanham, *A Handlist of Rhetorical Terms* (Berkeley: University of California Press, 1969).

amplificátio. A generic term for all the ways an argument can be expanded and enriched.

anadiplósis. Repetition of the last word of one line or clause to begin the next.

anacolúthon. Ending a sentence with a different construction from that with which it began.

anáphora. Repetition of the same word at the beginning of successive clauses or verses:

> It is the most grievous consequence of what we have done and of what we have left undone in the last five years – five years of futile good intentions, five years of eager search for the line of least resistance, five years of uninterrupted retreat of British power, five years of neglect of our air defences.

anthiméria. Using one part of speech for another:

> Who *authored* this tripe, anyway?

antístrophe. See *epiphora*.

aporía. True or feigned doubt or deliberation about an issue:

> "Dora is rather difficult to – I would not, for the world, say, to rely upon, because she is the soul of purity and truth – but rather difficult to – I hardly know how to express it, really, Agnes."

apóstrophe. Breaking off a speech or conversation to address a person or thing absent:

> "Mother, dear, you should have lived to see this!"

catachrésis. A wildly unlikely metaphor:

> "Mom will have kittens when she hears this."

chiásmus. The order in the second half of an expression reverses that of the first:

> "When the going gets tough, the tough get going."

Or, as in the old Mark Cross slogan:

> "Everything for the horse but the rider and everything for the rider but the horse."

The term is derived from the Greek letter X (chi), whose shape, if the two halves of the construction are diagrammed, it resembles.

climax. Mounting by degrees through words or sentences of increasing weight and in parallel construction:

> So a Victorian schoolmaster rebuked a dilatory student who wouldn't learn Latin vowel quantities: "If you do not take more pains, how can you ever expect to write good longs and shorts? If you do not write good longs and shorts, how can you ever be a man of taste? If you are not a man of taste, how can you ever be of use in the world?"

conduplicátio. Repetition of a word or words in succeeding clauses.

corréctio. Correction or revision of a word or phrase used previously.

diácope. Repetition of a word or phrase with one or more words in between:

> "Give me strength, O Lord, give me strength!"

effíctio.	The head-to-toe inventory of a person's charms once so common in English poetry: "My Lady's hair is threads of beaten gold, Her front the purest Chrystal eye hath seen, Her eyes the brightest stars the heavens hold . . ." and so on.
enárgia.	A general term for vivid, vigorous description.
enumerátio.	Division of subject into adjuncts, cause into effects, antecedent into consequents: "How do I love thee? Let me count the ways. I love thee to the depth and breadth and height. . . ."
épanaphora.	Intensive *anaphora.*
epímone.	Frequent repetition of phrase or question, dwelling on a point.
epíphora.	Opposite of *anaphora*, repetition of a word or phrase at the end of several clauses or sentences: "When I was a child, I spake as a child, I understood as a child, I thought as a child."
epithéton.	Repeated or regular qualification of a noun by an appropriate adjective; an adjective that regularly accompanies a noun, as in "heartfelt thanks."
epizeúxis.	Emphatic repetition of a word with no words in between: "O Horror! Horror! Horror!"
ethopoeía.	Putting oneself into the character of another so as to express that person's thoughts and feelings more vividly.
éthos.	The character or set of emotions which a speaker reenacts in order to affect an audience.
homoioteleúton.	Use of a series of words with similar endings: "The expres*sion* of the func*tion* of the facilita*tion* of the condemna*tion* of the amputa*tion*," as a licensed bureaucrat might put it.
hypóphora.	Raising questions and answering them.
hypozeúxis.	Every clause in a sentence has its own subject and verb: "Madame, the guests are come, supper served up, you called, my young lady asked for, the nurse cursed in the pantry, and everything in extremity."
isócolon.	A succession of phrases of equal length and corresponding structure: "Never in the history of mankind have so many owed so much to so few."
lítotes.	Denial of the contrary, understatement in order to intensify: "I am not unacquainted with the pleasures of money, for I love the stuff!"
meiósis.	Belittling comparison: "Banker's hot rod" for a Ferrari coupe
metónymy.	Substitution of cause for effect (or vice versa) or proper name for quality (or vice versa): So Winston Churchill wrote to his wife during WW II, "I can't tell you how we are coming but we're coming by puff-puff."

occupátio.	Emphasizing a point by pointedly seeming to pass it over: "I will not discuss his criminal record, his several jail terms, the daring escape and bloody recapture – bygones are bygones."
oxymóron.	A condensed paradox: "Icy hot," "darkness visible," "act naturally"
paramológia.	Conceding a point to seem fair; giving away a weaker point to make a stronger: "Of course I stole; what mother with starving children would do otherwise?"
parechésis.	Repeating the same sound in words close together: "Gaunt as the ghastliest of glimpses that gleam through the gloom of the gloaming when ghosts go aghast."
paromoiósis.	Use of similar sounds to reinforce isocolon: "Seeing the sincere affection of the mind cannot be expressed by the mouth and that no art can unfold the entire love of the heart, I am earnestly to beseech you not to measure the firmness of my faith by the fewness of my words."
páthos.	A general term for any kind of rhetorical figure which appeals directly to the emotions of an audience. *Ethos*, then, is the emotional set of the speaker; *pathos*, the emotional set the speaker wants to evoke in the audience.
plóce.	Repetition of a word with a different meaning after the interval of another word or words: "On the walls were pictured groups of early Americans signing things and still earlier Americans shooting arrows at things. But all over the immaculate mushroom-coloured carpet, and in what could be seen of a sort of Empire-style room opening off on the left, stood groups of present-day Americans drinking things."
polýptoton.	Repetition of words from the same root but in different forms or with different endings: "Society is no comfort to one not sociable."
synécdoche.	Substitution of part for whole, genus for species, or vice versa: "All hands on deck."
tapinósis.	Debasing language or epithet: "Rhymester" for "poet" Often synonymous with *meiosis*.
trícolon.	The pattern of three phrases in parallel, so common in Western writing after Cicero: "Clear leadership, violent action, rigid decisions, one way or the other, form the only path not only of victory, but of safety and even of mercy."
trópe.	A rhetorical figure (metaphor, for example) which changes the meaning of a phrase. A *trope* is usually contrasted with a *scheme* (*isocolon*, for example), which only changes the shape of a phrase.
zéugma.	One verb is made to govern several objects, each in a different way: "Here thou, great *Anna!* whom three realms obey Dost sometimes counsel take – and sometimes Tea."

CHAPTER 7

Not so much a Teaching as an Intangling

Stanley Fish

With the publication of *Surprised by Sin* in 1967, Stanley Fish launched a long, successful career as the most passionate defender of reader response criticism in the United States, a career that culminated with the publication of his humorously entitled *Is there a Text in this Class?* in 1980. In this selection from *Surprised by Sin*, Fish notices how John Milton manipulates his readers in order to advance his moral argument.

> *The right thing in speaking really is that we should be satisfied not to annoy our hearers, without trying to delight them: we ought in fairness to fight our case with no help beyond the bare facts: nothing, therefore, should matter except the proof of those facts. Still, as has been said, other things affect the result considerably, owing to the defects of our hearers.*
>
> ARISTOTLE, *Rhetoric*

(i) The Defects of our Hearers

I would like to suggest something about *Paradise Lost* that is not new except for the literalness with which the point will be made: (1) the poem's centre of reference is its reader who is also its subject; (2) Milton's purpose is to educate the reader to an awareness of his position and responsibilities as a fallen man, and to a sense of the distance which separates him from the innocence once his; (3) Milton's method is to re-create in the mind of the reader (which is, finally, the poem's scene) the drama of the Fall, to make him fall again exactly as Adam did and with Adam's troubled clarity, that is to say, 'not deceived'. In a limited sense few would deny the truth of my first two statements; Milton's concern with the ethical imperatives of political and social behaviour would hardly allow him to write an epic which did not attempt to give his audience a basis for moral action; but I do not think the third has been accepted in the way that I intend it.

A. J. A. Waldock, one of many sensitive readers who have confronted the poem since 1940, writes: '*Paradise Lost* is an epic poem of singularly hard and definite outline, expressing itself (or so at least would be our first impressions) with unmistakable clarity and point.'[1] In the course of his book Waldock expands the reservation indicated by his parenthesis into a reading which predicates a disparity between Milton's intention and his performance:

> In a sense Milton's central theme denied him the full expression of his deepest interests. It was likely, then, that as his really deep interests could not find outlet in his poem in the right way they might find outlet in the wrong way. And to a certain extent they do; they find vents and safety-valves often in inopportune places. Adam cannot give Milton much scope to express what he really feels about life; but Satan is there, Satan gives him scope. And the result is that the balance is somewhat disturbed; pressures are set up that are at times disquieting, that seem to threaten more than once, indeed, the equilibrium of the poem.[2]

The 'unconscious meaning' portion of Waldock's thesis is, I think, as wrong as his description of the reading experience as 'disquieting' is right. If we transfer the emphasis from Milton's interests and intentions which are available to us only from a distance, to our responses which are available directly, the disparity between intention and execution becomes a disparity between reader expectation and reading experience; and the resulting 'pressures' can be seen as part of an intelligible pattern. In this way we are led to consider our own experience as a part of the poem's subject.

By 'hard and definite outline' I take Waldock to mean the sense of continuity and direction evoked by the simultaneous introduction of the epic tradition and Christian myth. The 'definiteness' of a genre classification leads the reader to expect a series of formal stimuli – martial encounters, complex similes, an epic voice – to which his response is more or less automatic; the hardness of the Christian myth predetermines his sympathies; the union of the two allows the assumption of a comfortable reading experience in which conveniently labelled protagonists act out rather simple roles in a succession of familiar situations. The reader is prepared to hiss the devil off the stage and applaud the pronouncements of a partisan and somewhat human deity who is not unlike Tasso's 'il Padre eterno'. But of course this is not the case; no sensitive reading of *Paradise Lost* tallies with these expectations, and it is my contention that Milton ostentatiously calls them up in order to provide his reader with the shock of their disappointment. This is not to say merely that Milton communicates a part of his meaning by a calculated departure from convention; every poet does that; but that Milton consciously wants to worry his reader, to force him to doubt the correctness of his responses, and to bring him to the realization that his inability to read the poem with any confidence in his own perception is its focus.

Milton's programme of reader harassment begins in the opening lines; the reader, however, may not be aware of it until line 84 when Satan speaks for the first time. The speech is a powerful one, moving smoothly from the *exclamatio* of 'But O how fall'n' (84) to the regret and apparent logic of 'till then who knew / The force of those dire Arms' (93–4), the determination of 'courage never to submit or yield' (108) and the grand defiance of 'Irreconcilable to our grand Foe, / Who now triumphs, and in th' excess of joy / Sole reigning holds the Tyranny of Heav'n' (122–4). This is our first view of Satan and the impression given, reinforced by a succession of speeches in Book I, is described by Waldock: 'fortitude in adversity, enormous endurance, a certain splendid recklessness, remarkable powers of rising to an occasion, extraordinary qualities of leadership (shown not least in his salutary taunts)'.[3] But in each case Milton follows the voice of Satan with a comment which complicates, and according to some, falsifies, our reaction to it:

> So spake th' Apostate Angel, though in pain,
> Vaunting aloud, but rackt with deep despair.
> (125–6)

Waldock's indignation at this authorial intrusion is instructive:

> If one observes what is happening one sees that there is hardly a great speech of Satan's that Milton is not at pains to correct, to damp down and neutralize. He will put some glorious thing in Satan's mouth, then, anxious about the effect of it, will pull us gently by the sleeve, saying (for this is what it amounts to): 'Do not be carried away by this fellow: he *sounds* splendid, but take my word for it. . . . ' Has there been much despair in what we have just been listening to? The speech would almost seem to be incompatible with that. To accept Milton's comment here . . . as if it had a validity equal to that of the speech itself is surely very naïve critical procedure . . . in any work of imaginative literature at all it is the demonstration, by the very nature of the case, that has the higher validity; an allegation can possess no comparable authority. Of course they should agree; but if they do not then the demonstration must carry the day. (pp. 77–8)

There are several assumptions here:

(1)   There is a disparity between our response to the speech and the epic voice's evaluation of it.
(2)   Ideally, there should be no disparity.
(3)   Milton's intention is to correct *his* error.
(4)   He wants us to discount the effect of the speech through a kind of mathematical cancellation.
(5)   The question of relative authority is purely an aesthetic one. That is, the reader is obliged to hearken to the most dramatically persuasive of any conflicting voices.

Of these I can assent only to the first. The comment of the epic voice unsettles the reader, who sees in it at least a partial challenge to his own assessment of the speech. The implication is that there is more (or less) here than has met the ear; and since the only ear available is the reader's, the further implication is that he has failed in some way to evaluate properly what he has heard. One must begin by admitting with Waldock the impressiveness of the speech, if only as a *performance* that commands attention as would any forensic *tour de force*; and attention on that level involves a corresponding inattention on others. It is not enough to analyse, as Lewis and others have, the speciousness of Satan's rhetoric. It is the nature of sophistry to lull the reasoning process; logic is a safeguard against a rhetorical effect only after the effect has been noted. The deep distrust, even fear, of verbal manipulation in the seventeenth century is a recognition of the fact that there is no adequate defence against eloquence at the moment of impact. (The appeal of rhetoric was traditionally associated with the weakness of the fallen intellect – the defect of our hearers; its fine phrases flatter the desires of the cupidinous self and perpetuate the disorder which has reigned in the soul since the Fall.)[4] In other words one can analyse the process of deception only after it is successful. The reader who is stopped short by Milton's rebuke (for so it is) will, perhaps, retrace his steps and note more carefully the inconsistency of a Tyranny that involves an excess of joy, the perversity of 'study of revenge, immortal hate' (a line that had slipped past him sandwiched respectably between will and courage), the sophistry of the transfer of power from the 'Potent

Victor' of 95 to the 'Fate' of 116, and the irony, in the larger picture, of 'that were *low* indeed' and 'in *foresight* much advanc't'. The fit reader Milton has in mind would go further and recognize in Satan's finest moment – 'And courage never to submit or yield' – an almost literal translation of *Georgic* IV. 84, 'usque adeo obnixi non cedere'. Virgil's 'praise' is for his bees whose heroic posturing is presented in terms that are at least ambiguous:

> ipsi per medias acies insignibus alis
> ingentes animos angusto in pectore versant,
> usque adeo obnixi non cedere, dum gravis aut hos
> aut hos versa fuga victor dare terga subegit.
> hi motus animorum atque haec certamina tanta
> pulveris exigui iactu compressa quiescunt.
>
> (82–7)[5]

If we apply these verses to Satan, the line in question mocks him and in the unique time scheme of *Paradise Lost* looks both backward (the Victor has already driven the rebel host to flight) and forward (in terms of the reading experience, the event is yet to come). I believe that all this and more is there, but that the complexities of the passage will be apparent only when the reader has been led to them by the necessity of accounting for the distance between his initial response and the *obiter dictum* of the epic voice. When he is so led, the reader is made aware that Milton is correcting not a mistake of composition, but the weakness all men evince in the face of eloquence. The error is his, not Milton's; and when Waldock invokes some unidentified critical principle ('they should agree') he objects to an effect Milton anticipates and desires.

But this is more than a stylistic trick to ensure the perception of irony. For, as Waldock points out, this first epic interjection introduces a pattern that is operative throughout. In Books I and II these 'correctives' are particularly numerous and, if the word can be used here, tactless. Waldock falsifies his experience of the poem, I think, when he characterizes Milton's countermands as gentle; we are not warned ('Do not be carried away by this fellow'), but accused, taunted by an imperious voice which says with no consideration of our feelings, 'I know that you *have been* carried away by what you have just heard; you should not have been; you have made a mistake, just as I knew you would'; and we resent this rebuke, not, as Waldock suggests, because our aesthetic sense balks at a clumsy attempt to neutralize an unintentional effect, but because a failing has been exposed in a context that forces us to acknowledge it. We are angry at the epic voice, not for fudging, but for being right, for insisting that we become our own critics. There is little in the human situation more humiliating in both senses of the word, than the public acceptance of a deserved rebuke.

Not that the reader falls and becomes one of Satan's party. His involvement in the speech does not *directly* compromise his position in a God-centred universe, since his response (somewhat unconscious) is to a performance rather than to a point of view that he might be led to adopt as his own. As Michael Krouse notes, 'the readers for whom Milton wrote . . . were prepared for a Devil equipped with what appear on the surface to be the best of arguments' (*Milton's Samson and the Christian Tradition*, p. 102). As a Christian who has been taught every day to steel himself against diabolical wiles, the reader is more than prepared to admit the justness of the epic voice's *judgment* on Satan. It is the phrase 'vaunting aloud' that troubles, since it seems to deny even the academic admiration one might have for Satan's art as apart from his morality and to suggest that such admiration can never really be detached from the possibility of involvement (if only passive) in that morality. The sneer in 'vaunting' is aimed equally at the performance and anyone who lingers to appreciate it. (Satan himself delivers the final judgment on this and on all his speeches at IV. 83: 'Whom I seduc'd/With other promises and other *vaunts*'.) The danger is not so much that Satan's argument will persuade (one does not accord the father of lies an impartial hearing), but that its intricacy will engage the reader's attention and lead him into an error of omission. That is to say, in the attempt to follow and analyse Satan's soliloquy, the larger contexts in which it exists will be forgotten. The immediate experience of the poetry will not be qualified by the perspective of the poem's doctrinal assumptions. Arnold Stein writes, 'the formal perspective does not force itself upon Satan's speech, does not label and editorialize the impressive wilfulness out of existence; but rather sets up a dramatic conflict between the local context of the immediate utterance and the larger context of which the formal perspective is expression. This conflict marks . . . the tormented relationship between the external boast and the internal despair.'[6] Stein's comment is valuable, but it ignores the way the reader is drawn into the poem, not as an observer who coolly notes the inter- action of patterns (this is the mode of Jonsonian comedy and masque), but as a participant whose mind is the *locus* of that interaction. Milton insists on this since his concern with the reader is necessarily more direct than it might be in any other poem; and to grant the reader the status of the slightly arrogant perceiver-of-ironies Stein invents would be to deny him the full *benefit* (I use the word deliberately, confident that Milton would approve) of the reading experience. Stein's 'dramatic conflict' is there, as are his various perspectives, but they are actualized, that is translated into felt meaning, only through the more pervasive drama (between reader and poem) I hope to describe.

A Christian failure need not be dramatic; if the reader loses himself in the work- ings of the speech even for a moment, he places himself in a compromising position. He has taken his eye from its proper object – the glory of God, and the state of his own soul – and is at least in danger. Sin is a matter of degrees. To think 'how fine this all sounds, even though it is Satan's', is to be but a few steps from thinking, 'how fine this all sounds' – and no conscious qualification. One begins by simultan- eously admitting the effectiveness of Satan's rhetoric and discounting it because it *is* Satan's, but at some point a reader trained to analyse as he reads will allow admir- ation for a technical skill to push aside the imperative of Christian watchfulness. To be sure, this is not sin. But from a disinterested appreciation of technique one moves easily to a grudging admiration for the technician and then to a guarded sympathy and finally, perhaps, to assent. In this case, the failure (if we can call it that) involves the momentary relaxation of a vigilance that must indeed be eternal. Richard Baxter (*The Saints Everlasting Rest, c.* 1650) warns: 'Not only the open profane, the swearer, the drunkard, and the enemies of godliness, will prove hurtful companions to us, though these indeed are chiefly to be avoided: but too frequent society with persons merely civil and moral, whose conversation is empty and unedifying, may much divert our thoughts from heaven.' In Book IX, Eve is 'yet sinless' when she talks with Satan and follows him to the forbidden tree; but Milton indicates the danger and its vehicle at line 550:

> Into the heart of Eve his words made way,
> Though at the voice much marvelling.

Eve (innocently) surrenders her mind to wonderment ('much marvelling') at the technical problem of the seeming-serpent's voice ('What may this mean? Language of Man pronounc't / By Tongue of Brute') and forgets Adam's injunction to 'strictest watch' (363). There is at least one assertion of Satan's that Eve should challenge, since it contradicts something she herself has said earlier. The proper response to Satan's salutatory 'Fairest resemblance of thy Maker fair' (538) has been given, in effect, by Eve when she recognizes Adam's superior 'fairness' at IV. 490 ('I . . . see / How beauty is excell'd by manly grace / And wisdom, which alone is truly fair'). Her failure to give that response again is hardly fatal, but it does involve a deviation (innocent but dangerous) from the strictness of her watch. Of course to rebuke the serpent for an excess in courtesy might seem rude; tact, however, is a social virtue and one which Milton's heroes are rarely guilty of. Eve is correct when she declares that the talking serpent's voice 'claims attention due' (566), but attention *due* should not mean *complete* attention. Satan is the arch-conjurer here, calling his audience's attention to one hand (the mechanics of his articulation), doing his real work with the other ('Into the heart of Eve his words made way'). In Book I, Milton is the conjurer: by naming Satan he disarms us, and allows us to feel secure in the identification of an enemy who traditionally succeeds through disguise (serpent, cherub). But as William Haller notes, in *The Rise of Puritanism*, nothing is more indicative of a graceless state than a sense of security: 'Thus we live in danger, our greatest danger being that we should feel no danger, and our safety lying in the very dread of feeling safe' (New York/London, 1957, p. 156). Protected from one error (the possibility of listening sympathetically to a disguised enemy) we fall easily into another (spiritual inattentiveness) and fail to read Satan's speech with the critical acumen it demands. In the opening lines of Book X, Milton comments brusquely on Adam's and Eve's fall:

> For still they knew, and ought to have still remember'd. (12)

Paradise Lost is full of little moments of forgetfulness – for Satan, for Adam and Eve, and, most important, for the reader. At I. 125–6, the epic voice enters to point out to us the first of these moments and to say in effect, ' "For still you knew and ought to have still remembered," remembered who you are (Paradise has already been lost), where you are ("So spake th'Apostate Angel")', and what the issues are (salvation, justification). In this poem the isolation of an immediate poetic effect involves a surrender to that effect, and is a prelude to error, and possibly to sin. Milton challenges his reader in order to protect him from a mistake he must make before the challenge can be discerned. If this seems circular and even unfair, it is also, as I shall argue later, necessary and inevitable.

The result of such encounters is the adoption of a new way of reading. After I. 125–6 the reader proceeds determined not to be caught out again; but invariably he is. If Satanic pronouncements are now met with a certain caution, if there is a new willingness to search for complexities and ironies beneath simple surfaces, this mental armour is never quite strong enough to resist the insidious attack of verbal power; and always the irritatingly omniscient epic voice is there to point out a deception even as it succeeds. As the poem proceeds and this little drama is repeated, the reader's only gain is an awareness of what is happening to him; he understands that his responses are being controlled and mocked by the same authority, and realizes that while his efforts to extricate himself from this sequence are futile, that very futility becomes a way to self-knowledge. *Control* is the important concept here, for my claim is not merely that this pattern is in the poem (it would be difficult to find one that is not), but that Milton (*a*) consciously put it there and (*b*) expected his reader to notice it. . . .

The lesson in both poems is that the only defence against verbal manipulation (or appearances) is a commitment that stands above the evidence of things that are seen, and the method of both poems is to lead us beyond our perspective by making us feel its inadequacies and the necessity of accepting something which baldly contradicts it. The result is instruction, and instruction is possible only because the reader is asked to observe, analyse, and *place* his experience, that is, to think about it.

In the divorce tracts Milton reveals the source of this poetic technique when he analyses the teaching of Christ, 'not so much a teaching, as an intangling'.[7] Christ is found 'not so much interpreting the Law with his words, as referring his owne words to be interpreted by the Law'.[8] Those who would understand him must themselves decipher the obscurities of his sayings, 'for Christ gives no full comments or continu'd discourses . . . scattering the heavenly grain of his doctrin like pearle heer and there, which requires a skilfull and laborious gatherer.'[9] In order better to instruct his disciples, who 'yet retain'd the infection of loving old licentious customs', he does not scruple to mislead them, temporarily: 'But why did not Christ seeing their error informe them? for good cause; it was his profest method not to teach them all things at all times, but each thing in due place and season . . . the Disciples took it [one of his gnomic utterances] in a manifest wrong sense, yet our Saviour did not there informe them better. . . . Yet did he not omitt to sow within them the seeds of sufficient determining, agen the time that his promis'd spirit should bring all things to their memory.'[10] 'Due season' means when they are ready for it, and they will be ready for it when the seeds he has sown obliquely have brought them to the point where a more direct revelation of the truth will be efficacious; until then they are allowed to linger in error or at least in partial ignorance. Recently H. R. MacCallum has shown how Michael uses just this strategy of indirection and misdirection to lead Adam from the sickness of despair to faith and spiritual health.[11] Michael's strategy in Book XI is Milton's strategy in the entire poem, whereby his reader becomes his pupil, taught according to his present capacities in the hope that he can be educated, in tract of time, to enlarge them. By first 'intangling' us in the folds of Satan's rhetoric, and then 'informing us better' in 'due season', Milton forces us to acknowledge the *personal* relevance of the Arch-fiend's existence; and, in the process, he validates dramatically one of western man's most durable commonplaces, the equation of the rhetorical appeal (representative of the world of appearances) with the weakness of the 'natural man', that is, with the 'defects of our hearers'.

(ii)   Yet Never Saw

The wariness these encounters with demonic attraction make us feel is part of a larger pattern in which we are taught the hardest of all lessons, distrust of our own

abilities and perceptions. This distrust extends to all the conventional ways of knowing that might enable a reader to locate himself in the world of any poem. The
questions we ask of our reading experience are in large part the questions we ask of
our day-to-day experience. Where are we, what are the physical components of our
surroundings, what time is it? And while the hard and clear outline of *Paradise Lost*
suggests that the answers to these questions are readily available to us, immediate
contexts repeatedly tell us that they are not. Consider, for example, the case of
Satan's spear. I have seen responsible critics affirm, casually, that Satan's spear is as
large as the mast of a ship; the poem of course affirms nothing of the kind, but more
important, it deliberately encourages such an affirmation, at least temporarily:

> His spear, to equal which the tallest Pine
> Hewn on *Norwegian* Hills to be the Mast
> Of some great Ammiral, were but a wand.
> (I. 292–4)

Throughout *Paradise Lost*, Milton relies on the operation of three truths so obvious
that many critics fail to take them into account: (1) the reading experience takes place
in time, that is, we necessarily read one word after another; (2) the childish habit of
moving the eyes along a page and back again is never really abandoned although in
maturity the movement is more mental than physical, and defies measurement; therefore the line as a unit is a resting place even when rhyme is absent; (3) a mind asked to
order a succession of rapidly given bits of detail (mental or physical) seizes on the
simplest scheme of organization which offers itself. In this simile, the first line supplies
that scheme in the overt comparison between the spear and the tallest pine, and
the impression given is one of equality. This is not necessarily so, since logically the
following lines could assert any number of things about the relationship between
the two objects; but because they are objects, offering the mind the convenience of
focal points that are concrete, and because they are linked in the reading sequence by
an abstract term of relationship (equal), the reader is encouraged to take from the line
an image, however faint and wavering, of the two side by side. As he proceeds that
image will be reinforced, since Milton demands that he attach to it the information
given in 293 and the first half of 294; that is, in order to maintain the control over the
text that a long syntactical unit tends to diminish, the reader will accept 'hewn on
Norwegian hills' as an adjunct of the tallest pine in a very real way. By providing a
scene or background (*memoria*) the phrase allows him to strengthen his hold on what
now promises to be an increasingly complex statement of relationships. And in the
construction of that background the pine frees itself from the hypothetical blur of the
first line; it is now real, and through an unavoidable process of association the spear
which stood in an undefined relationship to an undefined pine is seen (and I mean the
word literally) in a kind of apposition to a conveniently visual pine. (This all happens
very quickly in the mind of the reader who does not have time to analyse the cerebral
adjustments forced upon him by the simile.) In short, the equation (in size) of the two
objects, in 292 only a possibility, is posited by the reader in 292–4 because it simplifies
his task; and this movement towards simplification will be encouraged, for Milton's fit
reader, by the obvious reference in 'to be the Mast / Of some great Ammiral' to the
staff of the Cyclops Polyphemus, identified in the *Aeneid* as a lopped pine[12] and
likened in the *Odyssey* to 'the mast of some black ship of twenty oars'.[13]

The construction of the image and the formulation of the relationship between its components are blocked by the second half of line 294, 'were but a wand'. This does several things, and I must resort to the mechanical aid of enumeration:

(1) In the confusion that follows this rupture of the reading sequence, the reader loses his hold on the visual focal points, and is unable to associate firmly the wand with either of them. The result is the momentary diminution of Satan's spear as well as the pine, although a second, and more wary reading, will correct this; but corrected, the impression remains (in line 295 a miniature Satan supports himself on a wand-like spear) and in the larger perspective, this aspect of the simile is one of many instances in the poem where Milton's praise of Satan is qualified even as it is bestowed.

(2) The simile illustrates Milton's solution of an apparently insoluble problem. How does a poet provide for his audience a perspective that is beyond the field of its perception? To put the case in terms of *Paradise Lost*, the simile as it functions in other poems will not do here. A simile, especially an epic simile, is an attempt to place persons and/or things, perceived in *a* time and *a* space, in the larger perspective from which their significance must finally be determined. This is possible because the components of the simile have a point of contact – their existence in the larger perspective – which allows the poem to yoke them together without identifying them. Often, part of the statement a simile makes concerns the relationship between the components and the larger perspective in addition to the more obvious relationship between the components themselves; poets suggest this perspective with words like smaller and greater. Thus a trapped hero is at once like and unlike a trapped wolf, and the difference involves their respective positions in a hierarchy that includes more than the physical comparison. A complex and 'tight' simile then can be an almost scientific description of a bit of the world in which for 'the immediate relations of the crude data of experience' are substituted 'more refined logical entities, such as relations between relations, or classes of relations, or classes of classes of relations'.[14] In Milton's poem, however, the components of a simile often do not have a point of contact that makes their comparison possible in a meaningful (relatable or comprehensible) way. A man exists and a wolf exists and if categories are enlarged sufficiently it can be said without distortion that they exist on a comparable level; a man exists and Satan (or God) exists, but any statement that considers their respective existences from a human perspective, however inclusive, is necessarily reductive, and is liable to falsify rather than clarify; and of course the human perspective is the only one available. To return to Book I, had Milton asserted the identity of Satan's spear and the tallest pine, he would not only have sacrificed the awe that attends incomprehensibility; he would also have lied, since clearly the *personae* of his extra-terrestrial drama are not confined within the limitations of our time and space. On the other hand, had he said that the spear is larger than one can imagine, he would have sacrificed the concreteness so necessary to the formulation of an effective image. What he does instead is grant the reader the convenience of concreteness (indeed fill his mind with it) and then tell him that what he sees is not what is there ('there' is never located). The result is almost a feat of prestidigitation: for the rhetorical negation of the scene so painstakingly constructed does not erase it; we are relieved of the necessity of believing the image true, but permitted to retain the solidity it offers our straining imaginations. Paradoxically, our awareness of the inadequacy of what is described and what we can apprehend

provides, if only negatively, a sense of what cannot be described and what we cannot apprehend. Thus Milton is able to suggest a reality beyond this one by forcing us to feel, dramatically, its unavailability.

(3) Finally, the experience of reading the simile tells us a great deal about ourselves. How large is Satan's spear? The answer is, we don't know, although it is important that for a moment we think we do. Of course, one can construct, as James Whaler does, a statement of relative magnitudes (Spear is to pine as pine is to wand)[15] but while this may be logical, it is not encouraged by the logic of the reading experience which says to us: If one were to compare Satan's spear with the tallest pine the comparison would be inadequate. I submit that any attempt either to search out masts of Norwegian ships or to determine the mean length of wands is irrelevant.

Another instance may make the case clearer. In Book III, Satan lands on the Sun:

> There lands the Fiend, a spot like which perhaps
> Astronomer in the Sun's lucent Orb
> Through his glaz'd optic Tube yet never saw.
>
> (588–90)

Again in the first line two focal points (spot and fiend) are offered the reader who sets them side by side in his mind; again the detail of the next one and one half lines is attached to the image, and a scene is formed, strengthening the implied equality of spot and fiend; indeed the physicality of the impression is so persuasive that the reader is led to join the astronomer and looks with him through a reassuringly specific telescope ('glaz'd optic Tube') to see – nothing at all ('yet never saw'). In both similes the reader is encouraged to assume that his perceptions extend to the object the poet would present, only to be informed that he is in error; and both similes are constructed in such a way that the error must be made before it can be acknowledged by a surprised reader. (The parallel to the rhetorical drama between demonic attraction and authorial rebuke should be obvious.) For, however many times the simile is re-read, the 'yet never saw' is unexpected. The mind cannot perform two operations at the same time, and one can either cling to the imminence of the disclaimer and repeat, silently, ' "yet never saw" is coming, "yet never saw" is coming', or yield to the demands of the image and attend to its construction; and since the choice is really no choice at all – after each reading the negative is only a memory and cannot compete with the immediacy of the sensory evocation – the tail-like half line always surprises.

Of course Milton wants the reader to pull himself up and re-read, for this provides a controlled framework within which he is able to realize the extent and implication of his difficulty, much like the framework provided by the before and after warnings surrounding Belial's speech. The implication is personal; the similes and many other effects say to the reader: 'I know that you rely upon your senses for your apprehension of reality, but they are unreliable and hopelessly limited.' Significantly, Galileo is introduced in both similes; the Tuscan artist's glass represents the furthest extension of human perception, and that is not enough. The entire pattern, of which the instances I analyse here are the smallest part, is, among other things, a preparation for the moment in Book VIII when Adam responds to Raphael's astronomical dissertation: 'To whom thus Adam clear'd of doubt'. Reader reaction is involuntary: cleared of doubt? by that impossibly tortuous and equivocal description of two all too probable universes?[16] By this point, however, we are able to place our reaction, since

Adam's experience here parallels ours in so many places (and a large part of the poem's meaning is communicated by our awareness of the relationship between Adam and ourselves). He *is* cleared of doubt, not because he now knows how the universe is constructed, but because he knows that he cannot know; what clears him of doubt is the certainty of self-doubt, and as with us this certainty is the result of a superior's willingness to grant him, momentarily, the security of his perspective. Milton's lesson is one that twentieth-century science is just now beginning to learn:

> Finally, I come to what it seems to me may well be from the long-range point of view the most revolutionary of the insights to be derived from our recent experiences in physics, more revolutionary than the insights afforded by the discoveries of Galileo and Newton, or of Darwin. This is the insight that it is impossible to transcend the human reference point.... The new insight comes from a realization that the structure of nature may eventually be such that our processes of thought do not correspond to it sufficiently to permit us to think about it at all.[17]

In *Paradise Lost*, our sense of time proves as illusory as our sense of space and physicality. Jackson Cope quotes with approval Sigfried Giedion and Joseph Frank, who find in modern literature a new way of thinking about time:

> The flow of time which has its literary reflection in the Aristotelian development of an action having beginning, middle and end is...frozen into the labyrinthine planes of a spatial block which...can only be perceived by travelling both temporally and physically from point to point, but whose form has neither beginning, middle, end nor center, and must be effectively conceived as a simultaneity of multiple views.[18]

And Mrs. Isabel MacCaffrey identifies the 'simultaneity of multiple views' with the eternal moment of God, a moment, she argues, that Milton makes ours:

> The long view of time as illusory, telescoped into a single vision, had been often adopted in fancy by Christian writers.... Writing of Heaven and the little heaven of Paradise, Milton by a powerful releasing act of the imagination transposed the intuitive single glance of God into the poem's mythical structure. Our vision of history becomes for the time being that of the Creator 'whose eye Views all things at one view' (ii. 189– 90); like him, we are stationed on a 'prospect high Wherin past, present, future he beholds.'
>
> (iii. 77–8)[19]

The experience of every reader, I think, affirms the truth of these statements; Milton does convince us that the world of his poem is a static one which 'slights chronology in favor of a folded structure which continually returns upon itself, or a spiral that circles about a single center'.[20] The question I would ask is how does he so convince us? His insistence on simultaneity is easily documented. How many times do we see Christ ascend, after the war in Heaven, after the passion, after Harrowing Hell, after giving Satan his death wound, after the creation, after the final conflagration, at the day of final judgment? How many times do our first parents fall, and how many times are they accorded grace? The answer to all these questions is, 'many times' or is it all the time (at each point of time) or perhaps at one, and the same, time. My difficulty with the preceding sentence is a part of my point: I cannot let go of the word 'time' and the idea of sequence; timelessness (I am forced to resort to a question-begging negative) is an interesting concept, but we are all of us trapped in the necessity of experiencing in time, and the attempt even to conceive of a state where words like day and evening measure space rather than duration is a difficult one; Chaucer's Troilus, among others, is defeated by it. Mrs. MacCaffrey asserts that 'spatial imagining' is part of Milton's 'mental climate' and the researches of Walter Ong, among others, support her; but if Milton has implanted the eternal moment 'into the poem's mythical structure', how does the reader, who, in Cope's words, must travel 'temporally and physically from point to point', root it out? Obviously many readers do not; witness the critics who are troubled by contradictory or 'impossible' sequences and inartistic repetitions. Again the reactions of these anti-Miltonists are the surest guide to the poet's method; for it is only by encouraging and then 'breaking' conventional responses and expectations that Milton can point his reader beyond them. To return to Waldock, part of the poem's apparently 'hard and definite' outline is the easy chronology it seems to offer; but the pressures of innumerable local contexts demand adjustments that give the lie to the illusion of sequence and reveal in still another way the inability of the reader to consider this poem as he would any other.

In the opening lines of Book I, chronology and sequence are suggested at once in what is almost a plot line: man disobeys, eats fruit, suffers woe and awaits rescue. It is a very old and simple story, one that promises a comfortable correlation of plot station and emotional response: horror and fear at the act, sorrow at the result, joy at the happy ending, the whole bound up in the certain knowledge of cause and effect. As Milton crowds more history into his invocation the reader, who likes to know what time it is, will attempt to locate each detail on the continuum of his story line. The inspiration of the shepherd, Moses, is easily placed between the Fall and the restoration; at this point many readers will feel the first twinge of complication, for Moses is a type of Christ who as the second Adam restores the first by persevering when he could not; as one begins to construct statements of relationship between the three, the clarity of lines 1–3 fades. Of course there is nothing to force the construction of such statements, and Milton thoughtfully provides in the very next line the sequence-establishing phrase, 'In the Beginning'. Reassured both by the ordering power of 'beginning' and by the allusion to Genesis (which is, after all, the original of all once-upon-a-times), the reader proceeds with the invocation, noting, no doubt, all the riches unearthed by generations of critical exegesis, but still firmly in control of chronology; and that sense of control is reinforced by the two-word introduction to the story proper: 'Say first', for with the first we automatically posit a second and then a third, and in sum, a neat row of causal statements leading all the way to an end already known.

The security of sequence, however, is soon taken away. I have for some time conducted a private poll with a single question: 'What is your reaction when the second half of line 54 – "for *now* the thought" – tells you that you are *now* with Satan, in Hell?' The unanimous reply is, 'surprise', and an involuntary question: how did I come to be here? Upon re-reading, the descent to Hell is again easy and again unchartable. At line 26 the time scheme is still manageable: there is (*a*) poem time, the *now* in which the reader sits in his chair and listens, with Milton, to the muse, and (*b*) the named point in the past when the story ('our Grand Parents . . . so highly to fall off') and our understanding of it ('say first what cause') is assumed to begin. At 33, the 'first' is set back to the act of Satan, now suggested but not firmly identified as the 'cause' of 27, and a third time (*c*) is introduced, further from (*a*) than (*b*), yet still manageable; but Satan's act also has its antecedent: 'what time his Pride / Had cast him out from Heav'n' (36–7); by this point, 'what time' is both an assertion and a question as the reader struggles to maintain an awkward, backward-moving perspective. There is now a time (*d*) and after (that is, before) that an (*e*) 'aspiring...He trusted to have equall'd the most High' (38, 40). Time (*f*) breaks the pattern, returning to (*d*) and providing, in the extended description of 44–53, a respite from sudden shifts. To summarize: the reader has been asked repeatedly to readjust his idea of 'in the beginning' while holding in suspension two plot lines (Adam's and Eve's and Satan's) that are eventually, he knows, to be connected. The effort strains the mind to its capacity, and the relief offered by the vivid and easy picture of Satan falling is more than welcome.[21] It is at this time, when the reader's attention has relaxed, that Milton slips by him the 'now' of 54 and the present tense of 'torments', the first present in the passage. The effect is to alert the reader both to his location (Hell) and to his inability to retrace the journey that brought him there. Re-reading leads him only to repeat the mental occupations the passage demands, and while the arrival in Hell is anticipated, it is always a surprise. The technique is of course the technique of the spot and spear similes, and of the clash between involuntary response and authorial rebuke, and again Milton's intention is to strip from us another of the natural aids we bring to the task of reading. The passage itself tells us this in lines 50–1, although the message may pass unnoted at first: 'Nine times the Space that measures Day and Night'. Does space measure day and night? Are day and night space? The line raises these questions, and the half-line that follows answers them, not 'to mortal men' who think in terms of duration and sequence, not to us. In this poem we must, we will, learn a new time.

The learning process is slow at first; the reader does not necessarily draw the inferences I do from this early passage; but again it is the frequency of such instances that makes my case. In Book II, when the fallen Angels disperse, some of them explore 'on bold adventure' their new home. One of the landmarks they pass is 'Lethe the River of Oblivion', and Milton pauses to describe its part in God's future plans: 'At certain revolutions all the damn'd / ...They ferry over this *Lethean* Sound / Both to and fro, their sorrow to augment, / And wish and struggle, as they pass to reach / The tempting stream, with one small drop to lose / In sweet forgetfulness all pain and woe, / All in one moment and so near the brink; / But Fate withstands' (597–8, 604–10). At 614 the poet continues with 'Thus roving on / In confus'd march forlorn', and only the phrase 'advent'rous bands' in 615 tells the reader that the poet has returned to the fallen angels. The mistake is a natural one: 'forlorn' describes perfectly the state of the damned, as does 'Confus'd march' their movements 'to and fro': indeed a second reflection suggests no mistake at all; the fallen angels *are* the damned, and one drop of Lethe *would* allow them to lose their woe in the oblivion Moloch would welcome. Fate *does* withstand. What Milton has done by allowing this momentary confusion is to point to the identity of these damned and all damned. As they fly past Lethe the fallen angels are all those who will become them; they do not stand for their successors (the word defeats me), they *state* them. In *Paradise Lost*, history and the historical sense are denied and the reader is forced to see events he necessarily perceives in sequence as time-identities. Milton cannot recreate the eternal moment, but by encouraging and then blocking the construction of sequential relationships he can lead the reader to accept the necessity of, and perhaps even apprehend, negatively, a time that is ultimately unavailable to him because of his limitations.

This translation of felt ambiguities, confusions, and tautologies into a conviction of timelessness in the narrative is assured partially by the uniqueness of Milton's 'fable'. 'For the Renaissance', notes Mrs. MacCaffrey, 'all myths are reflections, distorted or mutilated though they may be, of the one true myth.'[22] For Milton all history is a replay of the history he is telling, all rebellions one rebellion, all falls one fall, all heroism the heroism of Christ. And his readers who share this Christian view of history will be prepared to make the connection that exists potentially in the detail of the narrative. The similes are particularly relevant here. The first of these compares Satan to Leviathan, but the comparison, to the informed reader, is a tautology; Satan *is* Leviathan and the simile presents two aspects of one, rather than the juxtaposition of two, components. This implies that Satan is, at the moment of the simile, already deceiving 'The Pilot of some small night-founder'd Skiff'; and if the reader has attended to the lesson of his recent encounter with the epic voice he recognizes himself as that pilot, moored during the speech of I. 84–126 by the side of Leviathan. The contests between Satan and Adam, Leviathan and the pilot, rhetoric and the reader – the simile compresses them, and all deceptions, into a single instant, forever recurring. The celebrated falling-leaves simile moves from angel-form to leaves to sedge to Busiris and his Memphian Chivalry, or in typological terms (Pharaoh and Herod are the most common types of Satan) from fallen angels to fallen angels. The compression here is so complex that it defies analysis: the fallen angels as they *lie* on the burning lake (the Red Sea) are already *pursuing* the Sojourners of Goshen (Adam and Eve, the Israelites, the reader) who are for the moment *standing* on the safe shore (Paradise, the reader's chair). In Book XII. 191, Pharaoh becomes the River-Dragon or Leviathan (Isaiah xxvii. 1), pointing to the ultimate unity of the Leviathan and falling leaves similes themselves. As similes they are uninformative; how numberless are the falling angels? they are as numberless as Pharaoh's host, that is, as fallen angels, and Pharaoh's host encompasses all the damned who have been, are, and will be, all the damned who will fly longingly above Lethe. As vehicles of perception, however, they tell us a great deal, about the cosmos as it is in a reality we necessarily distort, about the ultimate subjectivity of sequential time, about ourselves.

There are many such instances in the early books and together they create a sensitivity to the difficulties of writing and reading this particular poem. When Milton's epic voice remarks that pagan fablers err relating the story of Mulciber's ejection from Heaven (I. 747), he does not mean to say that the story is not true, but that it is a distorted version of the story he is telling, and that any attempt to apprehend the nature of the angels' fall by comparing it to the fall of Mulciber or of Hesiod's giants involves another distortion that cannot be allowed if *Paradise Lost* is to be read correctly. On the other hand the attempt is hazarded (the reader cannot help it), the distortion is acknowledged along with the unavailability of the correct reading, and Milton's point is made despite, or rather because of, the intractability of his material. When Satan's flight from the judgment of God's scales (IV. 1015) is presented in a line that paraphrases the last line of the *Aeneid*, the first impulse is to translate the allusion into a comparison that might begin, 'Satan is like Turnus in that . . .'; but of course, the relationship as it exists in a reality beyond that formed by our sense of literary history, is quite the opposite. Turnus's defiance of the fates and his inevitable defeat are significant and comprehensible only in the light of what

Satan did in a past that our time signatures cannot name and is about to do in a present (poem time) that is increasingly difficult to identify. Whatever the allusion adds to the richness of the poem's texture or to Milton's case for superiority in the epic genre, it is also one more assault on the confidence of a reader who is met at every turn with demands his intellect cannot even consider.

(iii) The Good Temptation

Most poets write for an audience assumed fit. Why is the fitness of Milton's audience a concern of the poem itself? One answer to this question has been given in the preceding pages: only by forcing upon his reader an awareness of his limited perspective can Milton provide even a negative intuition of what another would be like; it is a brilliant solution to the impossible demands of his subject, enabling him to avoid the falsification of anthropomorphism and the ineffectiveness of abstraction. Another answer follows from this one: the reader who fails repeatedly before the pressures of the poem soon realizes that his difficulty proves its major assertions – the fact of the Fall, and his own (that is Adam's) responsibility for it, and the subsequent woes of the human situation. The reasoning is circular, but the circularity is appropriate to the uniqueness of the poem's subject matter; for while in most poems effects are achieved through the manipulation of reader response, this poet is telling the story that *created* and still creates the responses of its reader and of all readers. The reader who falls before the lures of Satanic rhetoric displays again the weakness of Adam, and his inability to avoid repeating that fall throughout indicates the extent to which Adam's lapse has made the reassertion of right reason impossible. Rhetoric is thus simultaneously the sign of the reader's infirmity and the means by which he is brought first to self-knowledge, and then to contrition, and finally, perhaps, to grace and everlasting bliss.

St. Paul articulates the dilemma of fallen man when he cries, 'For the good that I would I do not: but the evil which I would not, that I do' (Romans vii. 19). The true horror of the Fall is to be found here, in the loss of that happy state in which man's faculties worked in perfect harmony, allowing him accurately to assess his responsibilities and to meet them. Fallen man is hopelessly corrupt and his corruption resists even the grace freely offered to him through the intercession of Jesus Christ. Man's soul becomes the scene of a battle between the carnality of the first Adam (the old, unregenerate, man) and the righteousness of the second (the new, regenerate, man); and in the seventeenth century the image of an intestine warfare that is simultaneously the sign of the Fall and an indication of the possibility of redemption is to be seen everywhere:

> There is in Man, by reason of his general *Corruption*, such a distemper wrought, as that there is not onely *crookednesse* in, but *dissension* also, and fighting betweene his parts: And, though the Light of our *Reason* be by Man's Fall much dimmed and decayed; yet the remainders thereof are so adverse to our unruly *Appetite*, as that it laboureth against us.
> (Edward Reynolds, *A Treatise of the Passions and Faculties of the Soul of Man*, London, 1640)

> Reason therefore may rightly discern the thing which is good, and yet the will of man not incline itself thereunto, as often the prejudice of sensible experience doth oversway.
> (Hooker, *Ecclesiastical Polity*, i, vii. 6)

Our erected wit maketh us know what perfection is, and yet our infected will keepeth us from reaching unto it.

(Sidney, *Apology*)

Milton transforms this commonplace into a poetic technique; he leads us to feel again and again the conflict between the poem's assumed morality and our responses, and to locate the seat of that conflict in our fallen nature and not in any failure in composition. In short, the reader's difficulty is the result of the act that is the poem's subject. The reading experience becomes the felt measure of man's loss and since Milton always supplies a corrective to the reader's errors and distortions, what other critics have seen as the 'disquieting' aspect of that experience can be placed in a context that makes sense of it.

When, in the second part of *Pilgrim's Progress*, Christiana wonders why she and her companion Mercy were not forewarned of the danger lurking 'so near the Kings Palace' or, better still, provided with a 'Conductor', Reliever answers: 'Had my Lord granted you a Conductor, you would not neither, so have bewailed that oversight of yours in not asking for one, as now you have occasion to do. So all things work for good, and tend to make you more wary';[23] and Mercy adds, 'by this neglect, we have an occasion ministred unto us to behold our own imperfections'.[24] With the same compassionate and deliberate neglect, Milton makes the whole of *Paradise Lost* just such an occasion, the poet's version of what the theologian calls a 'good temptation':

A good temptation is that whereby God tempts even the righteous for the purpose of proving them, not as though he were ignorant of the disposition of their hearts, but for the purpose of exercising or manifesting their faith or patience...or of lessening their self confidence, and reproving their weakness, that...they themselves may become wiser by experience.[25]

The temptation is good because by means of it the secret corruption within is exposed, and consequently we are better able to resist the blandishments of less benevolent tempters. In the struggle against sin, no weapon is more effective than a knowledge of the areas likely to be under attack:

Thou must be carefull and diligent to finde out the subtilty, devices, and sleights of the devill, by which he doth assault thee very cunningly; for he hath a neere conjecture unto what sinnes thou art most inclined...and accordingly he fits his temptations.

(*A Garden of Spirituall Flowers*, 1638, p. 285)

There is secret corruption within, which will never be found out but by searching...the benefit is great which waysoever things turn. If upon examination we find that we have not grace in truth, then the mistake is discovered, and the danger prevented. If we find that we have grace, we may take the comfort of it.

(Thomas Watson, *Christian Soldier; Or, Heaven Taken By Storm*, 1669, p. 52)

I feelingly know the weakness of my own heart, and I am not ignorant of the Devil's malice and subtilty, and how he will make the fiercest assaults where I am weakest.

(John Corbet, *Self-Imployment in Secret*, 1681, pp. 41–2)

The deceitfulness of man's heart is such, writes Daniel Dyke, that we should welcome 'fit occasions' of trial which 'give a vent to corruption'; for 'many are inwardly
full of corruption; but they shew it not, onely for want of occasion' (*The Mystery of
Selfe-Deceiving*, 1615, p. 329). It is our duty, insists John Shower, to 'bring [our]
Hearts and Ways to a Trial, but 'most...are unwilling [because] they are stupidly
secure and see not the necessity of this duty' (*Serious Reflections On Time And
Eternity*, Glasgow, 1828, 1st edn., 1689, p. 175). Milton compels this duty by fitting
temptations to our inclinations and then confronting us immediately with the evidence of our fallibility. And in the process, he fosters the intense self-consciousness
which is the goal of spiritual self-examination:

> When on the Sudden, and by Incogitancy I have spoken a Word, which upon Second
> Thoughts is doubtful to me, though I had not such doubt in the speaking of it, I have
> been much perplexed about it, and have engaged myself to a greater watchfulness.
>
> (Corbet, *Self-Imployment*, p. 32)

> And when upon this inquiry, we find we have contracted any sullages or pollutions,
> then we must cleanse them from that filth, and *take heed to them*, that is, keep a
> continual watch over them, and be still upon our guard, that we be not surpriz'd by
> any new Temptation.
>
> (Edmund Arwaker, *Thoughts well Employ'd*, 1697, p. 21)

Note the similarity between the sequence of mental actions described by Corbet –
mistake, correction, instruction – and my description of the reader's experience in
Books I and II.

The long-range result of this technique is the creation of a 'split reader', one who is
continually responding to two distinct sets of stimuli – the experience of individual
poetic moments and the ever present pressure of the Christian doctrine – and who
attaches these responses to warring forces within him, and is thus simultaneously the
location and the observer of their struggle. This division in the reader is nowhere more
apparent or more central to Milton's intention than in Book IX when Adam chooses to
disobey. Waldock raised a very real question (which he then answered too quickly)
when he argued that at its most crucial point, 'the poem asks from us, at one and the
same time, two incompatible responses...that Adam did right, and...that he did
wrong. The dilemma is as critical as that, and there is no way of escape.'[26] Almost
immediately Paul Turner replied by pointing out that the poet does not want us to
escape: 'What would happen if...the reader did *not* feel inside himself a strong, almost
overwhelming impulse to do what Adam did. What sort of significance...would
remain?'[27] The ambivalence of the response is meaningful because the reader is able to
identify its components with different parts of his being: one part, faithful to what he
has been taught to believe (his 'erected wit') and responsive to the unmistakable sentiments of the poem's official voice, recoils in the presence of what he *knows* to be wrong;
but another part, subversive and unbidden (his 'infected will') surprises and overcomes
him and Adam is secretly applauded. It would be a mistake to deny either of these
impulses; they must be accepted and noted because the self must be accepted before it
can be transformed. The value of the experience depends on the reader's willingness to
participate in it fully while at the same time standing apart from it. He must pass
judgment on it, at least on that portion of it which is a reflection of his weakness. So
that if we retain Waldock's formula, a description of the total response would be, Adam

is wrong, no, he's right, but, then, of course he is wrong, and so am I. This last is not so much a product of the scene itself as of the moral conditioning the poem has exposed us to and of the self-consciousness it encourages. In effect the reader imposes this final certainty on the ambiguity of the poetic moment (this is the way of escape), but, in doing so, he does not deny its richness; indeed he adds to it by *ordering* it, by providing another perspective which gives the ambiguity meaning and renders it edifying; *he* now supplies the correcting perspective supplied earlier by the epic voice. Moreover, the uneasiness he feels at his own reaction to the fact of sin is a sign that he is not yet lost. The saint is known not by the absence of sin, but by his hatred of it:

> First, before hee come to doe the sinne, he hath no purpose to doe it, but his purpose and desire is to doe the will of God, contrary to that sinne. Secondly, in the act of doing of the sinne, his heart riseth against it, yet by the force of temptation, and by the mighty violence of the flesh hee is haled on and pulled to do wickednesse. Thirdly, after hee hath sinned, he is sore displeased with himself for it and truly repenteth.[28]

In the pattern I discern in the poem, the reader is continually surprised by sin and in shame, 'sore displeased with himself,' his heart 'riseth against it'.

One might ask at this point, why read a poem that treats its reader so badly? Why continue to suffer an experience that is unpleasant? The answer is simply that for the seventeenth-century Puritan and indeed for any Christian in what we might call the Augustinian tradition, the kind of discomfort I have been describing would be para-doxically a source of comfort and the unpleasantness a source of pleasure. Milton did not write for the atheist, but for the 'cold' Christian (neither saint nor apostate) who cannot help but allow the press of ordinary life to 'divert his thoughts from Heav'n'. In the same way, the sense of sin so necessary to a properly disposed Christian soul, is blunted rather than reinforced by the familiar recitation of scriptural common-places in sermons. One may hear every day of the depravity of natural man and of the inefficacy of unaided human efforts, but, inevitably, the incantational repetition of a truth lessens its immediate and personal force, and the sinner becomes compla-cent in a verbal and abstract contrition. *Paradise Lost* is immediate and forceful in the communication of these unflattering truths, again following the example of Christ who administers to the Pharisees 'not by the middling temper... but by the other extreme of *antidote*... a sharp & corrosive sentence against a foul and putrid licence; not to eate into the flesh, but into the sore'.[29] In the manner of the Old Law, the poem is designed to 'call forth and develop our natural depravity;... that it might impress us with a slavish fear... that it might be a schoolmaster to bring us to the righteousness of Christ'.[30] And since perpetual vexation and self-doubt are signs that the spirit of the Lord is at work, the reader welcomes an experience he knows to be salutary to his spiritual health; a 'good temptation' Milton points out 'is therefore rather to be desired'.[31] 'They whose hearts are pierced by the Ministry of the word, they are carryed with love and respect to the Ministers of it' (Thomas Hooker).

It should be noted, in addition, that the reading offered here is a partial one. I have isolated this pattern in order to make a precise and rather narrow point about the way the poem works on one level. In Milton's larger scheme the conviction that man can do nothing is accompanied by the conviction that Christ has taken it upon himself to do it all. As Joseph Summers writes, in another context, 'The essential "act" is that the individual should abandon the pretence that he *can* act in any way pertaining to salvation: he must experience the full realization that salvation belongs to God, that nothing he can do either by faith or works can help. The doctrine is moreover, "comforting", for "all things" are "more ours by being his" ' (*George Herbert*, p. 61). We are told this at the first – 'till one greater Man / Restore us and regain the blissfull Seat' – but in the course of our struggles with Books I and II, we *forget*, as Milton intends us to, so that we can be reminded dramatically by the glorious sacrifice of Book III. Milton impresses us with the negativity and despair of one aspect of Christian doctrine so that he can send us joyfully to the promise of another.

Notes

1   *Paradise Lost and its Critics* (Cambridge, 1947), p. 15. I consider Waldock's book to be the most forthright statement of an anti-Miltonism that can be found in the criticism of Leavis and Eliot, and, more recently, of Empson, R. J. Zwi Werblowsky, H. R. Swardson and John Peter. Bernard Bergonzi concludes his analysis of Waldock by saying, 'no attempt has been made to defend the poem in the same detailed and specific manner in which it has been attacked' (*The Living Milton*, ed. Frank Kermode, London, 1960, p. 171). This essay is such an attempt. Bergonzi goes on to assert that 'a successful answer to Waldock would have to show that narrative structure of *Paradise Lost does* possess the kind of coherence and psychological plausibility that we have come to expect from the novel. Again there can be no doubt that it does not' (p. 174). I shall argue that the coherence and psychological plausibility of the poem are to be found in the relationship between its effects and the mind of its reader. To some extent my reading has been anticipated by Joseph Summers in his brilliant study, *The Muse's Method* (Harvard, 1962). See especially pp. 30–1: 'Milton anticipated ... the technique of the "guilty reader". . . . The readers as well as the characters have been involved in the evil and have been forced to recognize and to judge their involvement.' See also Anne Ferry's *Milton's Epic Voice: The Narrator in Paradise Lost* (Harvard, 1963), pp. 44–66: 'We are meant to remember that the events of the poem have already occurred ... and that it is because of what happens in the poem, because we and all men were corrupted by the Fall, that we stand in need of a guide to correct our reading of it. The narrative voice is our guide' (p. 47). Finally I refer the reader to Douglas Knight's excellent article, 'The Dramatic Center of *Paradise Lost*', *South Atlantic Quarterly* (1964), pp. 44–59, which reached me only after this manuscript was substantially completed. Mr. Knight argues, as I do, for the analytic nature of the reading experience. Our emphases are different (he focuses mainly on the similes) but our general conclusions accord perfectly: 'The poem's material and structure fuse as they put pressure on the reader to assess and estimate the place where he is to stand; Adam and Eve can almost be said to dramatize for him a mode of action which is his own if he reads the poem properly. For *Paradise Lost* is a work of art whose full achievement is one of mediation and interactivity among three things: a way of reading the poem, an estimate of it as a whole work, and a reader's proper conduct of his life' (pp. 56–7).

2   *Paradise Lost and its Critics*, p. 24.

3   Ibid., p. 77.

4   The tradition begins with Plato's opposition of rhetoric to dialectic. Socrates' interlocutors *discover* the truth for themselves, when, in response to his searching questions, they are led to examine their opinions and, perhaps, to refute them. The rhetorician, on the other hand, creates a situation in which his auditors have no choice but to accept the beliefs he urges on them. In *The Testimony of the President, Professors, Tutors, and Hebrew Instructor of Harvard College in Cambridge, Against the Reverend Mr. George Whitefield, And his Conduct* (Boston, 1744), Whitefield is censured because of 'his power to raise the People to any Degree of Warmth he pleases, whereby they stand ready to receive almost any Doctrine he is pleased to broach ...' (p. 13). The danger lies in the weakness of the fallen intellect which is more likely

to be swayed by appearances than by the naked presentation of the truth. In recognition of this danger, the Puritan preacher first sets out the points of doctrine in the form of a Ramist 'proof' before turning in the 'uses' to the figures of exhortation. 'For a minister to lure men to an emotional reception of the creed before their imaginations had conceived it, before their intellects were convinced of it and their wills had deliberately chosen to live by it, was fully as immoral as openly to persuade them to wrong doing' (Perry Miller, *The New England Mind: The Seventeenth Century*, Beacon Press Edition, Boston, 1961, p. 308). A similar distrust of rhetoric manifests itself in the writings of the Baconian empiricists. Figurative language is said to be useless for the description of experiments or the formulation of conclusions, and rhetorical appeals are disdained because they dull intellects which should be alertly analytic. Bacon protests against the delivery (presentation) of knowledge 'in such form as may be best believed, and not as may be best examined' and advises instead 'the method of the mathematiques' (*Selected Writings*, ed. H. G. Dick, New York, 1955, p. 304). To Hobbes geometry is 'the only science that it has pleased God hitherto to bestow on mankind', a science which, as Aristotle said, no one uses fine language in teaching (*Leviathan*, ed. H. W. Schneider, New York, 1958, p. 41). Sprat believes that eloquence, 'this vicious volubility of *Tongue*' should be 'banish'd out of all *civil Societies*' because the ornaments of speaking 'are in open defiance against *Reason*' and hold too much correspondence with the passions, giving the mind 'a motion too changeable, and bewitching, to consist with *right practice*' (*The History of the Royal Society of London*, 1667, p. 111). . . . Complementing the fear of rhetoric is a faith in the safeguards provided by the use of analytical method. Where one short-circuits the rational and panders to the emotions, the other speaks directly to the reason. Where one compels assent without allowing due deliberation, the other encourages the auditor or reader to examine the progress of a composition at every point, whether it be a poem, a sermon, or the report of an experiment. 'Now my plan', announces Bacon, 'is to proceed regularly and gradually from one axiom to another.' However complex the experiment, he proposes to 'subjoin a clear account of the manner in which I made it; that men knowing exactly how each point was made out, may see whether there be any error connected with it' (*Preface to the Great Instauration*, in *The English Philosophers From Bacon to Mill*, ed. E. A. Burtt, New York, 1939, p. 21). Puritan preachers dispose their texts with the same care so that their auditors can receive the discourse according to the manner of its composition. The focus is always on the mind, which must be led, step by step, and with a consciousness of an answering obligation, to a clear understanding of conceptual content. (Again we see the similarity to Platonic dialectic.) In writing *Paradise Lost*, then, Milton is able to draw upon a tradition of didacticism which finds its expression in a distrust of the affective and an insistence on the intellectual involvement of the listener-pupil; in addition he could rely on his readers to associate logic and the capacity for logical reasoning with the godly instinct in man, and the passions, to which rhetoric appeals, with his carnal instincts.

5   As Davis Harding points out (*The Club of Hercules*, Urbana, Ill., 1962, pp. 103–8), this passage is also the basis of the bee simile at line 768. The reader who catches the allusion here at line 108 will carry it with him to the end of the book and to the simile. One should also note the parallel between the epic voice's comment at 126 and Virgil's comment on Aeneas' first speech (as Milton's early editors noted it): 'Talia voce refert, curisque ingentibus aeger/spem voltu simulat, premit altum corde dolorem'. But as is always the case in such comparisons, Satan suffers by it, since his deception is self-deception and involves an attempt to deny (to himself) the reality of an authority greater than his, while Aeneas' deception is, in context, an evidence of his faith in the promise of a higher authority. The hope he feigns is only partially a pretence; if it were all pretence, he would not bother.

6   *Answerable Style: Essays on Paradise Lost* (Minneapolis, 1953), p. 124. Frank Kermode's analysis in *The Living Milton* (p. 106) supports my position: 'He uses the epic poet's privilege of intervening in his own voice, and he does this to regulate the reader's reaction; but some of the effects he gets from this device are far more complicated than is sometimes supposed. The corrective comments inserted after Satan has been making out a good case for himself are not to be lightly attributed to a crude didacticism; naturally they are meant to keep the reader on the right track, but they also allow Milton to preserve the energy of the myth. While we are

hearing Satan we are not hearing the comment; for the benefit of a fallen audience the moral correction is then applied, but its force is calculatedly lower; and the long-established custom of claiming that one understands Satan better than Milton did is strong testimony to the tact with which it is done.' Anne Ferry (*Milton's Epic Voice*) is closer to Stein: 'The speech is meant to belie the inner experience and the comment to point out the power of the contradiction. Satan's words do not sound despairing precisely because the division within him is so serious. Only the inspired narrator can penetrate the appearance to discover the reality' (p. 120). Mrs. Ferry's discussion of this pattern focuses on her conception of the narrator as a divided being: 'These didactic comments remind us of the narrator's presence and his special vision in order that we may accept his moral interpretation of the story. . . . They are not *opposed* to the action of the poem, but are part of the total pattern of that action, not checks upon our immediate responses to drama, but a means of expressing the speaker's double point of view, his fallen knowledge and his inspired vision' (p. 56). It seems to me that the didactic comments *are* checks upon our immediate responses; nor do I believe it an oversimplification 'to make the speaker' a judge 'who lectures us like a prig just when we are most involved in the story'. I agree whole-heartedly, however, with Mrs. Ferry's arranging of interpretative hierarchies: 'So that when we find complexity in our response to the behavior or speech of a character and to the statement of the narrator which interprets it, we must judge the character by the interpretation, not the interpretation by the character's words or acts' (p. 16). I would add (and this is the heart of my thesis) that we must judge ourselves in the same way.

7 *Complete Prose Works of John Milton*, vol. ii, ed. Ernest Sirluck (New Haven, 1959), p. 642.

8 Ibid., p. 301.

9 Ibid., p. 338.

10 Ibid., pp. 678–9.

11 'Milton and Sacred History: Books XI and XII of *Paradise Lost*', in *Essays in English Literature from the Renaissance to the Victorian Age, Presented to A. S. P. Woodhouse*, ed. Millar MacLure and F. W. Watt (Toronto, 1964), pp. 149–68.

12 iii. 659. Harding insists that 'if this passage does not conjure up a mental picture of Polyphemus on the mountaintop, steadying his footsteps with a lopped pine . . . it has not communicated its full meaning to us' (*The Club of Hercules*, p. 63). In my reading a 'full reading' of the passage involves the recognition of the inadequacy of the mental picture so conjured up.

13 The translation is E. V. Rieu's in the Penguin Classic Edition (Baltimore, 1946), p. 148.

14 A. N. Whitehead in *The Limits of Language*, ed. Walker Gibson (New York, 1962), pp. 13–14. In classical theory, metaphor is the figure of speech whose operation bears the closest resemblance to the operations of dialectic and logic. Aristotle defines it in the *Poetics* as 'a transference either from genus to species or from species to genus, or from species to species'.

15 'The Miltonic Simile', *PMLA*, xlvi (1931), 1064.

16 Milton clearly anticipates this reaction when he describes the dialogue in the 'argument'; 'Adam inquires concerning celestial Motions, is *doubtfully* answer'd' (emphasis mine). See also v. 261–6: 'As when by night the Glass / of *Galileo*, less assur'd, observes / Imagin'd Lands and Regions in the Moon: / Or Pilot from amidst the *Cyclades* / *Delos* or *Samos* first appearing kens / A cloudy spot.' It should be noted that in all these passages certain details form a consistent pattern: Galileo, the moon, spots (representing an unclear vision), etc. The pattern is fulfilled in Raphael's disquisition on the possible arrangement of the heavens. See Greene's excellent reading of Raphael's descent (*The Descent from Heaven*, p. 387): 'The fallen reader's imperfect reason must strain to make out relations as the pilot strains with his physical eyes, as Galileo strains with his telescope, as the fowls gaze with mistaken recognition on the angel, as Adam and Eve will fail to strain and so blur our vision.' See also Northrop Frye, *The Return of Eden* (Toronto, 1965), p. 58: 'Galileo thus appears to symbolize, for Milton, the gaze outward on physical nature, as opposed to the concentration inward on human nature, the speculative reason that searches for new places, rather than the moral reason that tries to create a new state of mind.'

17 P. W. Bridgman, quoted in *The Limits of Language*, p. 21.

18 *The Metaphoric Structure of Paradise Lost* (Baltimore, 1962), pp. 14–15.

19 *Paradise Lost as 'Myth'* (Cambridge, Mass., 1959), p. 53.

20 Ibid., p. 45.

21 The technique is reminiscent of Virgil's 'historical present', which is used to bring the action of the epic before the reader's eyes. Recently Helen Gardner has reached conclusions similar to those offered here concerning the operation of time and space in the poem. See her *A Reading of Paradise Lost* (Oxford, 1965), pp. 39–51: 'Milton's poem must move in time, yet he continually suggests that the time of the poem is an illusion' (39); 'Milton, as he plays us into his poem, is using our human measurement to convey vastness sensuously' (40); 'He continually satisfies and then defeats our powers of visualization' (41). See also Roy Daniells, *Milton, Mannerism and Baroque* (Toronto, 1963), p. 98; W. B. C. Watkins, *An Anatomy of Milton's Verse* (Baton Rouge, La., 1955), p. 44; Anne Ferry, *Milton's Epic Voice*, pp. 46–7.

22 *Paradise Lost as 'Myth'*, p. 14.

23 p. 196.

24 Loc. cit.

25 *The Works of John Milton*, ed. F. A. Patterson et al. (New York, 1933), xv. 87–9. Cf. David Pareus, quoted in Arnold Williams's *The Common Expositor* (Chapel Hill, NC, 1948), p. 113: 'God is said to try man not that he may discover what he does not know (he knows even our inmost thoughts), but that we may discover our weakness, which *we* do not know' (emphasis mine). In his 'Apology for his Book' Bunyan defends a method similar to Milton's: 'You see the ways the Fisher-man doth take / To catch the Fish; what Engins doth he make? / . . . . Yet Fish there be, that neither Hook, nor Line, / Nor Snare nor Net, nor Engine can make thine; / They must be grop'd for, and be tickled too, / Or they will not be catcht, what e're you do' (p. 3); 'This Book will make a Travailer of thee, / If by its Counsel thou wilt ruled be; / It will direct thee to the Holy Land, / If thou wilt its Directions understand; / Yea, it will make the sloathful active be; / The Blind also, delightful things to see' (pp. 6–7).

26 *Paradise Lost and its Critics*, p. 56. See also Peter, *Critique*, pp. 130–1.

27 'Woman and the Fall of Man', *English Studies*, xxix (1948), 16.

28 *A Garden of Spirituall Flowers* (1638), p. 212. See also John Preston, *Sins Overthrow or A Godly and Learned Treatise of Mortification* (London, 1633), p. 60: 'But there is great difference betwixt the slacknesse of the Saints, and the wicked backsliding: the godly [61] they may slacke, but it is for a time; he is cold and remisse in the duties of holinesse, but it lasts not, it vanisheth away: on the other side, the wicked lye and continue in Apostacy unto the end; in these it is naturall, but unto the other it is but the instigation of the divell working by some lust upon one of the faculties.' These are of course commonplace statements, and examples could be multiplied *ad infinitum*.

29 *Complete Prose Works*, ii. 668.

30 *The Works of John Milton*, xvi. 131.

31 See note 25.

CHAPTER 8

Interpretive Communities

Stanley Fish

This selection from Fish's most anthologized essay, "Interpreting the Variorum" (1976), contains his argument for a concept of interpretive communities, groups of readers who share a set of conventions for understanding literary works in certain ways. According to Fish, the formal properties of literary works exist only as they are activated by such communities of readers. Literature, in other words, is both production and consumption at once.

It seems then that the price one pays for denying the priority of either forms or intentions is an inability to say how it is that one ever begins. Yet we do begin, and we continue, and because we do there arises an immediate counterobjection to the preceding pages. If interpretive acts are the source of forms rather than the other way around, why isn't it the case that readers are always performing the same acts or a sequence of random acts, and therefore creating the same forms or a random succession of forms? How, in short, does one explain these two "facts" of reading? (1) The same reader will perform differently when reading two "different" (the word is in quotation marks because its status is precisely what is at issue) texts; and (2) different readers will perform similarly when reading the "same" (in quotes for the same reason) text. That is to say, both the stability of interpretation among readers and the variety of interpretation in the career of a single reader would seem to argue for the existence of something independent of and prior to interpretive acts, something which produces them. I will answer this challenge by asserting that both the stability and the variety are functions of interpretive strategies rather than of texts.

Let us suppose that I am reading *Lycidas*. What is it that I am doing? First of all, what I am not doing is "simply reading," an activity in which I do not believe because it implies the possibility of pure (that is, disinterested) perception. Rather, I am proceeding on the basis of (at least) two interpretive decisions: (1) that *Lycidas* is a pastoral and (2) that it was written by Milton. (I should add that the notions "pastoral" and "Milton" are also interpretations; that is, they do not stand for a set of indisputable, objective facts; if they did, a great many books would not now be getting written.) Once these decisions have been made (and if I had not made these I would have made others, and they would be consequential in the same way), I am immediately predisposed to perform certain acts, to "find," by looking for, themes (the relationship between natural processes and the careers of men, the efficacy of poetry or of any other action), to confer significances (on flowers, streams, shepherds, pagan deities), to mark out "formal" units (the lament, the consolation, the turn, the affirmation of faith, and so on). My disposition to perform these acts (and others; the list is not meant to be exhaustive) constitutes a set of interpretive strategies, which, when they are put into execution, become the large act of reading. That is to say, interpretive strategies are not put into execution after reading (the pure act of perception in which I do not believe); they are the shape of reading, and because they are the shape of reading, they give texts their shape, making them rather than, as it is usually assumed, arising from them. Several important things follow from this account:

(1) I did not have to execute this particular set of interpretive strategies because I did not have to make those particular interpretive (pre-reading) decisions. I could have decided, for example, that *Lycidas* was a text in which a set of fantasies and defenses find expression. These decisions would have entailed the assumption of another set of interpretive strategies (perhaps like that put forward by Norman Holland[1] in *The Dynamics of Literary Response*) and the execution of that set would have made another text.

(2) I could execute this same set of strategies when presented with texts that did not bear the title (again a notion which is itself an interpretation) *Lycidas, a Pastoral Monody*. I could decide (it is a decision some have made) that *Adam Bede*[2] is a pastoral written by an author who consciously modeled herself on Milton (still remembering that "pastoral" and "Milton" are interpretations, not facts in the public domain); or I could decide, as Empson[3] did, that a great many things not usually considered pastoral were in fact to be so read; and either decision would give rise to a set of interpretive strategies, which, when put into action, would *write* the text I write when reading *Lycidas*. (Are you with me?)

(3) A reader other than myself who, when presented with *Lycidas*, proceeds to put into execution a set of interpretive strategies similar to mine (how he could do so is a question I will take up later), will perform the same (or at least a similar) succession of interpretive acts. He and I then might be tempted to say that we agree about the poem (thereby assuming that the poem exists independently of the acts either of us performs); but what we really would agree about is the way to write it.

(4) A reader other than myself who, when presented with *Lycidas* (please keep in mind that the status of *Lycidas* is what is at issue), puts into execution a different set of interpretive strategies will perform a different succession of interpretive acts. (I am assuming, it is the article of my faith, that a reader will always execute some set of interpretive strategies and therefore perform some succession of interpretive acts.) One of us might then be tempted to complain to the other that we could not possibly be reading the same poem (literary criticism is full of such complaints) and he would be right; for each of us would be reading the poem he had made.

The large conclusion that follows from these four smaller ones is that the notions of the "same" or "different" texts are fictions. If I read *Lycidas* and *The Waste Land*[4] differently (in fact I do not), it will not be because the formal structures of the two poems (to term them such is also an interpretive decision) call forth different interpretive strategies but because my predisposition to execute different interpretive strategies will *produce* different formal structures. That is, the two poems are different because I have decided that they will be. The proof of this is the possibility of doing the reverse (that is why point 2 is so important). That is to say, the answer to the question "why do different texts give rise to different sequences of interpretive acts?" is that *they don't have to*, an answer which implies strongly that "they" don't exist. Indeed, it has always been possible to put into action interpretive strategies designed to make all texts one, or to put it more accurately, to be forever making the same text. Augustine urges just such a strategy, for example, in *On Christian Doctrine* where he delivers the "rule of faith" which is of course a rule of interpretation.[5] It is dazzlingly simple: everything in the Scriptures, and indeed in the world when it is properly read, points to (bears the meaning of) God's love for us and our answering responsibility to love our fellow creatures for His sake. If only you should come upon something which does not at first seem to bear this meaning, that "does not literally pertain to virtuous behavior or to the truth of faith," you are then to take it "to be figurative" and proceed to scrutinize it "until an interpretation contributing to the reign of charity is produced." This then is both a stipulation of what meaning there is and a set of directions for finding it, which is of course a set of directions – of interpretive strategies – for making it, that is, for the endless reproduction of the same text. Whatever one may think of this interpretive program, its success and ease of execution are attested to by centuries of Christian exegesis. It is my contention that any interpretive program, any set of interpretive strategies, can have a similar success, although few have been as spectacularly successful as this one. (For some time now, for at least three hundred years, the most successful interpretive program has gone under the name "ordinary language.")[6] In our own discipline programs with the same characteristic of always reproducing one text include psychoanalytic criticism, Robertsonianism[7] (always threatening to extend its sway into later and later periods), numerology (a sameness based on the assumption of innumerable fixed differences).

The other challenging question – "why will different readers execute the same interpretive strategy when faced with the 'same' text?" – can be handled in the same way. The answer is again that *they don't have to*, and my evidence is the entire history of literary criticism. And again this answer implies that the notion "same text" is the product of the possession by two or more readers of similar interpretive strategies.

But why should this ever happen? Why should two or more readers ever agree, and why should regular, that is, habitual, differences in the career of a single reader ever occur? What is the explanation on the one hand of the stability of interpretation (at least among certain groups at certain times) and on the other of the orderly variety of interpretation if it is not the stability and variety of texts? The answer to all of these questions is to be found in a notion that has been implicit in my argument, the notion of *interpretive communities*. Interpretive communities are made up of those who share interpretive strategies not for reading (in the conventional sense) but for writing texts, for constituting their properties and assigning their intentions. In other words, these strategies exist prior to the act of reading and therefore determine the shape of what is read rather than, as is usually assumed, the other way around. If it is an article of faith in a particular community that there are a variety of texts, its members will boast a repertoire of strategies for making them. And if a community believes in the existence of only one text, then the single strategy its members employ will be forever writing it. The first community will accuse the members of the second of being reductive, and they in turn will call their accusers superficial. The assumption in each community will be that the other is not correctly perceiving the "true text," but the truth will be that each perceives the text (or texts) its interpretive strategies demand and call into being. This, then, is the explanation both for the stability of interpretation among different readers (they belong to the same community) and for the regularity with which a single reader will employ different interpretive strategies and thus make different texts (he belongs to different communities). It also explains why there are disagreements and why they can be debated in a principled way: not because of a stability in texts, but because of a stability in the makeup of interpretive communities and therefore in the opposing positions they make possible. Of course this stability is always temporary (unlike the longed for and timeless stability of the text). Interpretive communities grow larger and decline, and individuals move from one to another; thus, while the alignments are not permanent, they are always there, providing just enough stability for the interpretive battles to go on, and just enough shift and slippage to assure that they will never be settled. The notion of interpretive communities thus stands between an impossible ideal and the fear which leads so many to maintain it. The ideal is of perfect agreement and it would require texts to have a status independent of interpretation. The fear is of interpretive anarchy, but it would only be realized if interpretation (text making) were completely random. It is the fragile but real consolidation of interpretive communities that allows us to talk to one another, but with no hope or fear of ever being able to stop.

In other words interpretive communities are no more stable than texts because interpretive strategies are not natural or universal, but learned. This does not mean that there is a point at which an individual has not yet learned any. The ability to interpret is not acquired; it is constitutive of being human. What is acquired are the ways of interpreting and those same ways can also be forgotten or supplanted, or complicated or dropped from favor ("no one reads that way anymore"). When any of these things happens, there is a corresponding change in texts, not because they are being read differently, but because they are being written differently.

The only stability, then, inheres in the fact (at least in my model) that interpretive strategies are always being deployed, and this means that communication is a much more chancy affair than we are accustomed to think it. For if there are no fixed texts, but only interpretive strategies making them, and if interpretive strategies are not natural, but learned (and are therefore unavailable to a finite description), what is it that utterers (speakers, authors, critics, me, you) do? In the old model utterers are in the business of handing over ready-made or prefabricated meanings. These meanings are said to be encoded, and the code is assumed to be in the world independently of the individuals who are obliged to attach themselves to it (if they do not they run the danger of being declared deviant). In my model, however, meanings are not extracted but made and made not by encoded forms but by interpretive strategies that call forms into being. It follows then that what utterers do is give hearers and readers the opportunity to make meanings (and texts) by inviting them to put into execution a set of strategies. It is presumed that the invitation will be recognized, and that presumption rests on a projection on the part of a speaker or author of the moves *he* would make if confronted by the sounds or marks he is uttering or setting down.

It would seem at first that this account of things simply reintroduces the old objection; for isn't this an admission that there is after all a formal encoding, not perhaps of meanings, but of the directions for making them, for executing interpretive strategies? The answer is that they will only *be* directions to those who already have the interpretive strategies in the first place. Rather than producing interpretive acts, they are the product of one. An author hazards his projection, not because of something "in" the marks, but because of something he assumes to be in his reader. The very existence of the "marks" is a function of an interpretive community, for they will be recognized (that is, made) only by its members. Those outside that community will be deploying a different set of interpretive strategies (interpretation cannot be withheld) and will therefore be making different marks.

So once again I have made the text disappear, but unfortunately the problems do not disappear with it. If everyone is continually executing interpretive strategies and in that act constituting texts, intentions, speakers, and authors, how can any one of us know whether or nor he is a member of the same interpretive community as any other of us? The answer is that he can't, since any evidence brought forward to support the claim would itself be an interpretation (especially if the "other" were an author long dead). The only "proof" of membership is fellowship, the nod of recognition from someone in the same community, someone who says to you what neither of us could ever prove to a third party: "we know." I say it to you now, knowing full well that you will agree with me (that is, understand) only if you already agree with me.

Notes

1 American reader-response critic (b. 1927), who employs psychoanalyis: *Dynamics* was published in 1968.
2 An 1859 novel by the English writer George Eliot.
3 William Empson (1906–1984), English critic and poet, whose works include *Some Versions of Pastoral* (1935).
4 A 1922 poem by the American-born poet and critic T. S. Eliot.
5 *On Christian Doctrine* (ca. 395 C.E.).
6 The study of how everyday language is used. Strictly speaking, this is a 20th-century movement started by the Austrian-born philosopher Ludwig Wittgenstein (1889–1941), though it is rooted in the work of the English empiricist John Locke (1632–1704).
7 That is, the scripturally based criticism inspired by D. W. Robertson Jr. (1914–92), a critic of medieval literature.

CHAPTER 9

Text and System

John Frow

Along with Tony Bennett, John Frow is one of the most important contemporary Formalist theorists. In this selection from his book *Marxism and Literary History* (1986), he cunningly demonstrates how readers (and translators) make substantive changes in the meaning of a text over time. The same text from Homer's *The Iliad* is translated with great variability from one generation to another. Frow uses this evidence of interpretive variability to argue that texts are more like complicated assemblages of writing and interpretation within contexts than they are independent entities with firm boundaries.

Borges's "Pierre Menard, Author of *Don Quixote*" is a perfectly serious joke that we are still learning how to take seriously.[1] This story of an obscure provincial "novelist" who by an immense labor (the traces of which are lost) managed to produce a fragmentary text coinciding completely, at the verbal level, with several chapters of *Don Quixote* has usually been read as a meditation on the nature of reading and the nature of authorship. Macherey and Mike Gane both stress that Menard's enterprise "poses the question of reading in the most active possible manner: writing."[2] Alicia Borinsky notes that it "puts into play the question of authorship as the production of voice and, in doing so... questions the kind of continuity that exists between that hypothetical voice and its discourse" (although she herself then restores the onto-logical link between author and text by reconstructing the voice of "Borges" as that of "the aristocracy of intelligence in Argentine political history").[3] But in another sense the question of authorship is quite secondary. It is true that the narrator locates the difference between the two texts within a biographical framework; but his explanation of why it is that "the text of Cervantes and that of Menard are verbally identical, but the second is almost infinitely richer" (Borges, 49) is made in terms of the different systems of intertextuality within which the second is inscribed. Thus its disdainful avoidance of the Hispanicizing exoticism popularized by Mérimée "indicates a new approach to the historical novel. This disdain condemns *Salammbô*, without appeal" (48). The apparent anachronism of the discourse on arms and letters is explained by reference to "the influence of Nietzsche" (48). And the address to "truth, whose mother is history," which in the seventeenth-century text is "a mere rhetorical eulogy of history," becomes in the twentieth-century text, written by "a contemporary of William James," a radical epistemological proposition (49).

The point is surely that, once we have disposed of the red herring of authorship, what is at stake is the historicity of a single, verbally self-identical text; what the parable suggests is that "textual 'identity' under changing conditions becomes 'difference.'"[4] The question I deliberately begged..., which dealt with "internally" constructed intertextual structures, was that of those intertextual relations not constructed or controlled by the text. This is the question of the instability of the "internal," the fact that intrinsic structures are not given but are variably constructed in accordance with changing intertextual relations. Let me propose, schematically, that every text is marked by a multiple temporality: the time of its production (the "internal" time of its rewriting or repetition of prevailing literary and ideological norms), and the times of its reception (in which this textual process is transformed by its entry into new intertextual relationships). The serial or lateral movement of a text between systems produces new texts, and new kinds of text. Such a formulation should in principle preclude an ontological definition of literary function.... The value and function of texts should "be viewed differently according to the different places they occupied within the received cultures of different societies and different historical periods," and "literariness" would depend primarily "not on the formal properties of a text in themselves but on the position which those properties establish for the text within the matrices of the prevailing ideological field. Literariness resides, not in the text, but in the relations of inter-textuality inscribed within and between texts."[5] ...

It is not a question of denying the specific difference of literary texts from other language types but rather of constructing this difference as an object of historical understanding and of accounting for its effect in each case on the selection and semantic transformation of the literary corpus. And it is because the literariness of a text, its very existence *as* a "literary" text, is not an innate property that methodological priority must be given to the literary system or systems in which it is assigned its function. The mode of operation of a text cannot be pregiven by the structure of the genre since relations of signification, and hence the status of genre conventions themselves, are prescribed within a specific social articulation of discursive functions.

Thus the following texts[6] are all realizations of the "same" genre conventions and even of the "same" initial production:

> ...so full of bloud, of dust, of darts, lay smit
> Divine Sarpedon that a man must have an excellent wit
> That could but know him; and might fail — so from his utmost head
> Even to the low plants of his feet his forme was altered.
> All thrusting neare it every way, as thick as flies in spring   5
> That in a sheepe-cote (when new milke assembles them) make wing
> And buzze about the top-full pailes. Nor ever was the eye
> Of Jove averted from the fight; he viewd, thought ceaselessly
> And diversly upon the death of great Achilles' friend —
> If Hector there (to wreake his sonne) should with his javelin end   10
> His life and force away his armes, or still augment the field.
> He then concluded that the flight of much more soule should yeeld
> Achilles' good friend more renowne, and that even to their gates
> He should drive Hector and his host; and so disanimates
> The mind of Hector that he mounts his chariot and takes Flight   15
> Up with him.
>
>   (Chapman, *Homer's Iliad*, Book 16)

> Now great *Sarpedon*, on the sandy Shore,
> His heav'nly Form defac'd with Dust and Gore,
> And stuck with Darts by warring Heroes shed;
> Lies undistinguish'd from the vulgar dead.

His long-disputed Corpse the Chiefs inclose.   5
On ev'ry side the busy Combate grows;
Thick, as beneath some Shepherd's thatch'd Abode,
The Pails high-foaming with a milky Flood,
The buzzing Flies, a persevering Train,
Incessant swarm, and chas'd, return again.   10
  Jove view'd the Combate with a stern Survey,
And Eyes that flash'd intolerable Day;
Fix'd on the Field his Sight, his Breast debates
The Vengeance due, and meditates the Fates;
Whether to urge their prompt Effect, and call   15
The Force of *Hector* to *Patroclus*' Fall,
This Instant see his short-liv'd Trophies won,
And stretch him breathless on his slaughter'd Son;
Or yet, with many a Soul's untimely flight,
Augment the Fame and Horror of the Fight?   20
To crown *Achilles*' valiant Friend with Praise
At length he dooms; and that his last of Days
Shall set in Glory; bids him drive the Foe;
Nor unattended, see the Shades below.
Then *Hector's* Mind he fills with dire dismay;   25
He mounts his Car, and calls his Hosts away.
              (Pope, *The Iliad of Homer*, Book 16)

And now not even a clear-sighted man could any longer have known noble Sarpedon, for with darts and blood and dust was he covered wholly from head to foot. And ever men thronged about the dead, as in a steading flies buzz around the full milk-pails, in the season of spring when the milk drenches the bowls, even so thronged they about the dead. Nor ever did Zeus turn from the strong fight his shining eyes, but ever looked down on them, and much in his heart he debated of the slaying of Patroklos, whether there and then above divine Sarpedon glorious Hector should slay him likewise in strong battle with the sword, and strip his harness from his shoulders, or whether to more men yet he should deal sheer labour of war. And thus to him as he pondered it seemed the better way, that the gallant squire of Achilles, Peleus' son, should straight-way drive the Trojans and Hector of the helm of bronze towards the city and should rob many of their life. And in Hector first he put a weakling heart, and leaping into his car Hector turned in flight.

                                        (Lang, Leaf, and Myers, *Iliad*, Book 16)

          No longer
could a man, even a knowing one, have made out the godlike
Sarpedon, since he was piled from head to ends of feet under
a mass of weapons, the blood and the dust, while others about him
kept forever swarming over his dead body, as flies   5
through a sheepfold thunder about the pails overspilling
milk, in the season of spring when the milk splashes in the buckets.
So they swarmed over the dead man, nor did Zeus ever
turn the glaring of his eyes from the strong encounter,
but kept gazing forever upon them, in spirit reflective,   10
and pondered hard over many ways for the death of Patroklos;
whether this was now the time, in this strong encounter
when there over godlike Sarpedon glorious Hektor

should kill him with the bronze, and strip the armour away from his shoulders,
or whether to increase the steep work of fighting for more men.   15
In the division of his heart this way seemed best to him,
for the strong henchman of Achilleus, the son of Peleus,
once again to push the Trojans and bronze-helmed Hektor
back on their city, and tear the life from many. In Hektor
first of all he put a temper that was without strength.   20
He climbed to his chariot and turned to flight, and called to the other
Trojans to run.

> (Lattimore, *The Iliad of Homer*, Book 16)

And nobody, including those who saw him lie,
A waxen god asleep on his outstretched hand,
Could know him now.

> But if you can imagine how
> Each evening when the dairy pails come in   5
> Innumerable flies throng around
> The white ruff of the milk,
> You will have some idea of how the Greeks and Trojans
> Clouded about Sarpedon's body.

And all this time God watched his favourite enemies: 10
Considering. Minute Patroclus, a fleck
Of spinning radium on his right hand –
Should he die now? Or push the Trojans back still more?
And on his left, Prince Hector, like a golden mote –
Should he become a coward for an hour   15
And run for Troy while Patroclus steals Sarpedon's gear
That glistens like the sea at early morning?

> The left goes down.
> In the half-light Hector's blood turned milky
> And he ran for Troy.   20

> (Logue, *Patrocleia of Homer*)

To these I might have added Maginn's 1850 translation of passages of the *Odyssey* into an archaicizing ballad form; Worsley's translation of the *Odyssey* into Spenserian stanzas (1861); Mackail's Pre-Raphaelite version of the *Odyssey* (1903); and Rouse's (1938) and Rieu's (1950) renditions of the Homeric epics as novels of action. But these few examples will suffice to demonstrate the ways in which the "same" text is a radically different piece of poetry in the context of different systems. The question of the relationship of these texts to an "original" text is not irrelevant, but this original is not the notional Homer of the eighth or ninth century B.C., not an author or a text situated at a fixed (and unreconstructable) point of origin; it is a sixteenth- or an eighteenth- or a twentieth-century "Homer," a particular mode of authority of the classical.

The texts demonstrate too the extent to which this mode of authority is fused with the major ideological categories of particular social formations; as this authority decays, the fusion becomes less intrinsic, and translation becomes an active recuperation of social content, until in the final text the diminished authority of the classical allows it to be used in direct contradiction to other modes of social authority, including its own vestigial academic prestige.

Chapman's text is imbued with a metaphysical conception of human agency: this concern is realized through the use of key ambiguities ("plants," a lexeme which is now obsolete but which must, even in the early seventeenth century, have functioned as a latent organic pun; "forme," which is ambivalently a material and a spiritual concept; and "disanimates / The mind of Hector," in which the strong presence of the Latin root tends to override the literal sense and foreground the tension between human agency and divine intervention); through a syntax which depends heavily on the use of nontransactive verbs ("lay smit," "was altered"), which replaces the main verb of the second sentence with a present participle, and which elides the warriors in the indeterminate "all"; and through the allegorization of "Flight."

Pope's text works through a categorical framework which opposes and relates glory to death and then overlays this opposition with the dichotomized categories of social class: Sarpedon's "heav'nly Form" loses all rank and distinction to become one with the "vulgar dead." Patroclus, by contrast, balances the categories: "Trophies," "Fame," "Praise," and "Glory" are played against "short-liv'd," "Horror," and "his last of Days / Shall set"; this balancing means both the triumph of social hierarchy over death ("Nor unattended, see the Shades below") and yet also, in the dialectical perspective of a second reading, the opposite of this: death destroys social status, *and* social status survives death. This effect, or this *expectation*, of detached equivocality is achieved in part through the exploitation of syntactic ambiguity, especially in the use of participles ("high-foaming," "Fix'd") and causal sequencing ("To crown...he dooms," "and that...bids him"). "Thick" in line 7 refers both backward to "Combate" and forward to "Flies," and in this transition the individual warriors are subsumed within the two moments of the metaphor: the hypostatized action, which "grows" and is "busy," and the train of flies, a thoroughly Popean image of the disaffected mob. The vantage point here is that of Jove, an absolute monarch who is nevertheless subject to the ultimate constitutional check of the Fates.

The Lang, Leaf, and Myers translation is much less confident about its own social relevance; it is an ornamental text insofar as it uses Anglo-Saxon heroic models which certainly "translate" Homer but do so into categories which are dead. Zeus dealing "sheer labour of war," for example, is dubious because it is imitating an archaic concept of fate. Archaism both of vocabulary ("darts," "steading," "helm") and syntax ("was he covered," "even so thronged they") is the predominant stylistic feature, and its effect is to increase radically the redundancy of the text. In the extended simile there is a double stylistic tautology: "ever men thronged about the dead" / "even so thronged they about the dead"; "the full milk-pails, in the season of spring" / "when the milk drenches the bowls." The chiasmic geometry of the simile is autonomized and frozen by its lack of any function except self-reference. Surface elegance screens an underlying incoherence. Where the previous texts had drawn up a balance sheet of honor and death, here it simply "seemed" to Zeus "the better way." Similarly the nominalized form "the slaying of Patroklos" blurs considerations of tense and causality.

Lattimore's text relies much less on surface archaism, but it is equally academic and in fact it follows closely the syntax of Lang, Leaf, and Myers. In the extended simile, "steading" is replaced by "sheepfold," which is modern English; "bowls" by "buckets," which is comprehensible; and "buzz" by "thunder," which is stronger but less appropriate. But the structure of chiasmic repetition remains unchanged. Lattimore's hexameter attempts a partial recuperation of an oral mode – through the use of feminine endings, spondaic feet ("more men," "steep work"), repetition ("forever ... ever ... forever," "strong encounter"), and formulaic epithet ("the strong henchman of Achilleus, the son of Peleus"); but these devices serve only to underline the distance between the two texts and the subordination of the later piece of writing to an alien text.

Logue's *Patrocleia*, by contrast, actively insists on its difference from this alien text, and uses anachronism as a way of identifying the authority of the classical with the ideologies of militarism and patriarchy. The text is a countertext, a deconstruction (but also an explication) of the social force of a literary norm. The fragmentation of epic homogeneity is achieved through a juxtaposition of lyrical discourse with politicized techniques of disruption. On the one hand lyrical cohesion is established through the binding together of chains of imagery which integrate the extended simile into its context: "clouded" not only refers to the mass of flies/warriors (this perspective is extended and defined in the wanton God's consideration of the "fleck" and "mote") but also picks up the opacity of "milk," which then goes forward to "Hector's blood turned milky," and perhaps also to the "half-light." Yet the simile is detached from its context, not only graphically but also by the stress on its rhetorical function ("if you can imagine how"). The play of perspectives, corresponding partly to the paragraphing, is of a novelistic complexity: line 1 particularizes point of view to participants in the action, and so subjectivizes the metaphor of the (syntactically ambiguous) second line. Line 4 reasserts narratorial objectivity. The third paragraph switches to the vantage point of a detached God, but also sets up a tension with the irony of "favourite enemies" and the intrusively figurative language of "spinning radium," "like a golden mote," and "that glistens like the sea at early morning." The lineation of the last paragraph then switches the perspective to that of a detached commentator undermining heroic rhetoric.

Five different Homers, then: five modes of collusion and conflict between social categories and an economy of literary conventions which works these categories and which also, especially in the later texts, works their refraction and their consolidation in previous literary economies. Translation makes the point neatly; but the same is true of a single linguistically constant text in its passage through time. *Don Quixote* is a component of every subsequent Spanish literary system, and to a lesser degree of most subsequent European systems, but it is a slightly different text in each case. This productive power of the literary system (the system is of course also partly produced by the tradition it incorporates) means that it cannot simply be defined empirically as a collection of texts. The system is rather a normative regime, a semantic code which governs the nature and the limits of literariness and the relations of signification which are socially possible and legitimate for the genres it recognizes. It produces new texts, and new texts from old texts, and new ways of reading and writing and framing texts; but since the invention of Literature some time in the eighteenth century, it has also produced the appearance of the universality and autonomy of the literary text.

Let me recall the three levels at which Tynjanov defines the concept of system. It refers in the first instance to the literary text as a hierarchically ordered structure of elements. But the text is constituted as such only in its intertextual relation to the codes of the literary system, and in particular in its integration to the subsystem of the codes of genre. At a third level the text and the literary system are defined, given a determinate shape and function, through their relation to the "system of systems" – let us say their interdiscursive relation to other signifying formations and to the institutions and practices in which these are articulated. At each of these levels the concept of system works dynamically: time is a structural component of the system in the form of a play of actual or potential discontinuity between the levels of code and message.

I have suggested that the concept of literary system is equivalent to that of a discursive formation. But it should be clear that the mode of existence of the formation is not "merely" discursive, or rather that discourse is defined in such a way as to include its particular conditions of possibility: it constitutes a complex unity of semantic material, rhetorical modes, forms of subjectivity and agency, rules of availability, specific discursive practices, and specific institutional sites. All of these may overlap with the constituents of other discursive formations, and any formation will tend to be internally contradictory: the space of a discursive system is not unitary or homogeneous. What binds it together, more or less, is the normative authority it wields as an institution, an authority which is more or less strictly exercised and which is always the attempted imposition of a centralizing unity rather than the achieved fact of such a unity. Institutional authority, which by definition is asymmetrically distributed between "central" and "marginal" members of the institution, is deployed in particular to maintain the purity and the solidity of boundaries, and this involves both defining appropriate and inappropriate practices of language and restricting access to these practices to certified or qualified agents. The converse of this is the establishment of the "internal" categories of the institution as a particular range of possible functions. In the case of the literary system this means defining the functions of author, reader, and text and the possible relations between them; and delimiting the specificity of literary discourse, as though it were ontologically grounded. In terms of this normative regulation (and despite the diversity of the literary genres) the "literary" is reified as a distinct and unitary language game, and the logics of its forms (its genres, its rhetorical strategies and densities, its degrees of "keying")[7] are coded as being appropriate to the institution.

Peter Bürger has described in similar terms the conditions of constitution of the aesthetic:

> Works of art are not received as single entities, but within institutional frameworks and conditions that largely determine the function of the works. When one refers to the function of an individual work, one generally speaks figuratively; for the consequences that one may observe and infer are not primarily a function of its special qualities but rather of the manner which regulates the commerce with works of this kind in a given society or in certain strata or classes of a society. I have chosen the term "institution of art" to characterize such framing conditions.[8]

But rather than describing the full set of social practices and conditions which govern the commerce with and constitution of the work of art, Bürger tends to equate the institution with a particular set of discourses about art (manifestos, for example) which, as aesthetic ideologies, are only a part of the total aesthetic apparatus. As a counterexample it might be worthwhile to consider briefly the systemic conditions of constitution of the Homeric texts.

Marthe Robert gives an incisive account, in *The Old and the New*, of their contradictory activations in antiquity. The primary function of the epics is pedagogic: they are thought to incorporate a code of morality, a summary of wisdom, a compendium of the most varied forms of knowledge, and information about the smallest details of life. Even Plato, in the *Protagoras*, recommends that the teacher have his students learn by heart the "works of good poets" in which "they meet with many admonitions, many descriptions and praises and eulogies of good men in times past, that the boy in envy may imitate them and yearn to become even as they."[9] In daily life the Homeric texts have almost the force of law. At the same time, however, this pedagogic authority is contested by the existence in antiquity of a tradition of logical and moral criticism of the texts. It is in order to close off this contradiction that the texts are reconstituted within a new institution of reading: that of allegorical exegesis. Here "Homer" is construed as the author of scientific, philosophical, mystical, or political treatises *disguised* as works of fiction. The distinction between the letter (the textual surface) and the inner meaning, corresponding to a further distinction between the ordinary (naive) and the initiated reader, makes possible a sacralization of the texts which endows them with the highest conceivable spiritual authority (they are constituted as Scriptures) (83). This exegetical activity is the basis for a succession of later exegetical practices: the great Alexandrine commentaries, for example; the syntheses of neo-Platonism and Christianity in the allegorizing recuperations of Homer for the Renaissance; or the contemporary research of philologists, archaeologists, and anthropologists. One of the most important changes of direction was that brought about by the radical historicism of nineteenth-century philology. This new paradigm of reading constructed the Homeric epics as the manifestation of the spirit of a folk, which entailed redefining the author function in such a way that it could be filled by a group ("the people") rather than an individual. In addition, the Romantic revolution stressed the Aryan origins of the epic (which it read through the model of folklore) and established strict concordances between all the European epic cycles (86): hence the Victorian translators' use of Anglo-Saxon heroic models, and the dispute between Newman and Arnold as to whether the ballad form is the appropriate vehicle for capturing the primitive purity of the Greek epics.[10] The dominant metaphor here is that of the "childhood of humanity," the organic historicism of which has plagued Marxist literary theory ever since Marx used the phrase (it is drawn directly from Hegel's *Ästhetik*) in a famous passage of the *Grundrisse*.[11]

Moral and exegetical pedagogy have been the most important supports of the different regimes of reading through which the Homeric texts have been variously constituted; but other institutional bases have at different times provided their conditions of possibility. One of the most recently excavated is that of the tradition of bardic recitation. As a result of the work of Milman Parry and Albert Lord (originally on twentieth-century Yugoslavian epic recitation), we now have a very different understanding both of the mode of composition (cumulative, formulaic, dependent on particular mnemonic trainings, and fusing the functions of author and performer) and of the conditions of enunciation of the Greek epic cycles (ritual recitations in an oral, preliterate culture, with a mix of functions including the repetition/commemoration of a stable world order, the filiation of the present with this past order, together with various profane informative functions).[12] A complementary account (for example Charles Autran, *Homère et les origines sacerdotales de l'épopée*, summarized in Robert, 89–91) stresses the cultic function of the epics and their close link with the caste of priests. The poems are written (composed) in a language which was *always* archaic and archaicizing, an artificial composite of different dialects drawn from the ritual language of the cults. In this perspective, the epics combine the functions of religious propaganda and legitimation of the nobility; they appear as "a collection of pious legends, designed to perpetuate the continuity of the great heroic families, which take pains to establish their divine ancestry" (91). Hence the structural importance of genealogies and nomenclatures, "which prove by continuity of lineage the theocratic origins of the aristocracy and royalty." In short: "Composed on command and according to absolutely fixed rules, the epic contains only the truth of the priestly caste on which it depended. This caste exploited the prestige and the influence of poetry, and expressed in turn its solidarity with a political and social system – the aristocracy – identified with the order of the world" (91).

But it must be stressed that this function of class legitimation is a recurrent function of the Homeric epics, not necessarily in terms of any inherent formal or thematic properties but purely and simply through their fetishized value as the Classic. Pope's translation appropriates their prestige for the culture of a restored aristocracy. At the height of the British Empire the classics continue to form the basis of the civil service entry examinations,[13] and in both England and France constitute the major point of distinction between the "elaborated" and "restricted" training offered by the secondary and primary schooling systems.[14] Rather than having a continuous value (or manifesting a "transcendence of historical conditions"), the Homeric epics are one of the means by which claims to cultural and hence political continuity are validated. Two contradictory moments of this process of constant retotalization and reintegration of the past into a qualitatively different present are, on the one hand, the cultural renaissances in which new class ideologies seek a legitimation and an expressive "mask" in material from a different period, and on the other hand, the ideological mechanisms of eternalization – the museum, the school text, the reference book, the television adaptation – which strip the "masterpieces" of their specific historical differences. It is the clarification of these mechanisms that becomes relevant, since, in Macherey's words: "Homer's *Iliad*, the 'work' of an 'author' exists only for us, and in relation to new material conditions into which it has been reinscribed and reinvested with a new significance: however odd it may seem, it did not exist for the Greeks and the problem of its conservation is thus not a relevant one. To go further: it is as if we ourselves had written it (or at least composed it anew)."[15]

The forms of rewriting of the Homeric texts differ radically with the historically different forms of literary system in which they occur, but in all cases the rewriting is the result of a complex articulation of the literary system with other institutions (the school, religion), institutionalized practices (moral or religious training, commemoration, or else a relatively autonomous aesthetic function), and other discursive formations (religious, scientific, ethical). The ties between the literary system and its institutional bases may be close or they may be relatively loose, and the functions of the system are not necessarily homogeneous. But the system is always a network of norms and of processes and sites for the implementation (or contestation) of these norms.

What the literary system crucially governs are ways of reading, the interpretive grids through which texts are constituted. The concept of reading and of the reading subject has been the focus of intensive theorization in recent years, but it is also the site of an extraordinary lack of clarity. The status of "the reader" has been especially murky. The commonsense assumption that the reader is an empirical individual quickly leads both to an atomistic relativism and to an inability to theorize the modes of textual inscription of reading. Conversely, a concentration on this inscription can hypostatize it as an immanent textual structure and so lead both to a disregard of the differences between the uses made of texts and to a disqualification of "deviant" readings. Empirical readers, inscribed readers, and ideal or informed or normal readers all have an uncanny ability to duplicate the readings preferred by the critic.

Similarly intensive theorization of reading has taken place in communication studies, where it assumes the more general (and perhaps more urgent) form of a debate about conflicting models of the communication process. David Morley gives a useful summary of two opposed traditions. On the one hand there is that of the Frankfurt School's account of the effects of "mass culture," in which manipulative signifying practices are seen as having a relatively ineluctable and unmediated impact; and with it that of the journal *Screen* (the unification is unfair but convenient), which describes the positioning of viewers such that they are shaped as unitary subjects in the apprehension of the imaginary unity of a discourse. On the other hand there is a tradition of research into the behavioral effects of the media or into the selective use of cultural messages ("uses and gratifications" analysis); in this tradition the emphasis is on the diversity of appropriations of texts. Morley himself attempts to reconstruct a heterogeneous range of readings of a single text across a number of social groups (ambivalently classified in terms of "subculture" or of "class") and so to explore the effects of the television text at the level of "the structuring of discourses and the provision of frameworks of interpretation and meaning."[16] Part of the power of his analysis lies simply in the radical incompatibility of the twenty-eight reconstructed readings of the television program *Nationwide*. But the analysis is also theoretically provocative in its elaboration of Paul Willemen's argument for a lack of smooth fit between the subject position constructed for a viewer/reader in a particular text and the range of subject positions constructed in other discourses and practices.[17] If analysis is expanded from the "abstract signifying mechanisms" of a text toward "the field of interdiscourse in which it is situated,"[18] then it becomes clear that the text produces no *necessary* effects, since the historical "subject" exceeds the subject positions of a text:

> The "subject" exists only as the articulation of the multiplicity of particular subjectivities borne by an individual (as legal subject, familial subject, etc.), and it is the nature of this differential and contradictory positioning within the field of ideological discourse which provides the theoretical basis for the differential reading of texts and the existence of differential positions in respect to the position preferred by the text.[19]

Or more concisely, in Claire Johnston's words, "Real readers are subjects in history rather than mere subjects of a single text."[20] The problem with any such formulation, however, is that it tends easily to slip back into talk of a *non*contradictory subject, a subject unified as "real," "historical," or (for Morley) "empirical."[21] Any such realism of the subject then restores precisely that opposition of subject and object, reader and text, which, in its assumption of entities fully constituted prior to the textual process, is the major weakness of traditional theories of reading.

One of the most cogent cases against this polarity is that argued by Stanley Fish in the process of redefining his early commitment to a reader-centered aesthetic. This aesthetic had relied upon a strong demarcation between text and reader, conceived as independently constituted entities; even the relatively greater emphasis he laid upon "the structure of the reader's experience" still left intact the text/reader dichotomy. (In any case this reader was only ever *derived* from the text: at times from some "objective" structure such as an interpretive crux, at times from the absence of such a structure, as when Fish postulates "a reading that is fleetingly available, although no one has acknowledged it because it is a function not of the words on the page but of the experience of the reader.")[22] But, as Fish comes to argue, the problem with any such opposition of subject to object is that it takes for granted "the distinction between interpreters and the objects they interpret. That distinction in turn assumes that interpreters and their objects are two different kinds of *a*contextual entities, and within these twin assumptions the issue can only be one of control: will texts be allowed to constrain their own interpretation or will irresponsible interpreters be allowed to obscure and overwhelm texts?" (336). The way out of this bind is to recognize that text and reader are categories given by particular interpretive strategies, and that the criteria of interpretation are therefore internal to discourse rather than given by the reality of texts or readers (238).

Once the interpretive process is understood in this conventionalist manner, a number of interesting consequences ensue. One is that it becomes necessary to dispense with an ontologically grounded differentiation between language varieties:

> When we communicate, it is because we are parties to a set of discourse agreements which are in effect decisions as to what can be stipulated as a fact. It is these decisions and the agreement to abide by them, rather than the availability of substance, that makes it possible to refer, whether we are novelists or reporters for the *New York Times*. One might object that this has the consequence of making all discourse fictional; but it would be just as accurate to say that it makes all discourse serious, and it would be better still to say that it puts all discourse on a par. (242)

A second consequence is that language is seen always to be determinate in relation to a particular context; it is not limitlessly plural, but it is also not *inherently* determinate. And this means that there may be a plurality of determinate and stable meanings for a plurality of contexts. Underpinning this understanding of the constitutive status of discourse is the premise that linguistic and interpretive norms "are not embedded in the language (where they may be read out by anyone with sufficiently clear, that is, unbiased, eyes) but inhere in an institutional structure within which one hears utterances as already organized with reference to certain assumed purposes and goals" (306). Reading is thus relativized to the semiotic and situational constraints of a discursive formation, the institutional dimension of which Fish calls the "interpretive community." It is this dimension which makes possible agreement and disagreement – not as relations of truth and error but as a coincidence or conflict of interpretive frames.

Fish's attempt to theorize the institutional determinants of reading through the concept of the interpretive community is seriously flawed, however, by its inability to account in any sort of political terms for contradiction within or between communities and by its disregard of the relations of power which sustain communities. A complementary theorization of reading as a semiotic institution is that of Mircea Marghescou. Noting the plurality of possible valid readings of a text, Marghescou concludes that none of them therefore has a formal necessity. What they all have in common, however, is that they insert the signifier into a new semantic field in which it tends to the realization of all its semantic possibilities. This functional constant is not an effect of the particular speech situation or of the formal structure of the message; nor is it the product of a subjective intention, because it is a shared semantic code which gives information about the operability of a text. Marghescou designates as the *regime* of a text this supralinguistic semantic code which assigns the message to its type and labels it with directions for use without specifying a particular content. In itself, he argues, the text is a purely virtual entity, and "only a regime designating the textual function through opposition to its linguistic function and above all to other possible semantic functions could give form to this virtuality, transform the linguistic form into information."[23] Unlike the phenomenological concept of an "aesthetic attitude," the regime is conceived not as a fact of consciousness, nor even as an intersubjective consensus, but as a semiotic constraint.

These formulations make it possible to consider the interpretive process in systemic terms. The regime, the semiotic institution, determines the historically specific mode of existence of texts, as well as the point at which the line between the literary and the nonliterary is drawn. Further, the categories of text, author, and reader have the status not of entities but of variable *functions*; they are products of determinate practices of reading, produced by, not given for, interpretation. These functions in turn mediate the textual transactions of real readers and writers, circumscribing both the actual operations each can perform and their representation of each other as textual functions.[24] Writer and reader are not the fixed and isolated origin and conclusion of the textual process, nor is their relationship that of a constant factor to an uncontrolled variable (as is the case with Wolfgang Iser's oscillation between and, in practice, ultimate conflation of an "implied reader," understood as an *overt* – "intended" – textual function, and a real reader external to the textual process).[25] Both "writer" and "reader" are the categories of a particular literary system and of particular regimes within it, and only as such are they amenable to theorization. But these categories are therefore unstable, and they shift in value as texts are translated from one literary system to another. Finally, interpretation, and a limited and definite range of contradictory interpretive strategies, are themselves constituted as determinate social practices within a specific historical regime. In short, the regime of reading is what allows readers to do work upon texts, to accept or transform readings offered as normative, to mesh reading with other social practices and other semiotic domains, and indeed to formulate and reformulate the categories of the regime itself.

From this theoretical basis it becomes possible to move to a meta-interpretive level where our concern is not with the rightness or wrongness of a particular reading but with the formal and social conditions and preconditions of interpretation: that is, with an analysis of the politics of reading and the historicity of readings – the synchronic and diachronic heterogeneity of interpretation. This shift of level has been characteristic, I think, of much recent literary theory, under the double influence of structuralism's construction of its theoretical goal as a poetics rather than a practice of reading, and the demand made by reception theory that our own reading be relativized to the chain of prior interpretations. The move seems to me a positive one for two reasons: first, because of its generosity toward disparate readings, its insistence not on disqualifying invalid readings but on recognizing the politically and historically relative validity of different interpretations;[26] and second, because it opens the way to an inscription of our own situation (political, methodological, historical) in the object of analysis as a component of that object....

Such a shift of level entails paying particular attention to the institutions within which literary criticism adopts the form of a practice: that is, above all, to the educational apparatuses, which promote specific forms of circulation of writing and specific valorizations of certain kinds of writing,[27] and which seek to impose a hegemonic "consensus" while making available certain possibilities of resistance. What is crucial here is that the literary system not be thought of as a monolithic unity. It is systematic only in the sense of providing a space of dispersion, but not in terms of any underlying epistemic coherence; certainly there is no necessary structural or functional homology between discursive formations.

Tony Bennett has used the concept of a reading formation to theorize the construction of text-reader relations within contradictory interpretive frames (and in particular to theorize "the necessary disparity which exists between the discourses of criticism and the reading formations, circulating outside the academy, through which popular reading is organized").[28] His argument is directed against that sleight of hand by which particular class-specific discourses of value elevate their criteria of judgment into universally normative principles which can be appealed to against the criteria of other, contradictory discourses of value. Bennett's interest is in the rim of social and institutional conditions governing interpretation, and in the political possibility of choice between one socioepistemological frame and another. But a possible consequence of this stress is that the details of any particular interpretation will be seen as relatively unimportant to the extent that they will be derivable from the hermeneutic protocols given as the preconditions of reading. The question of what happens within an interpretive frame once it is chosen or imposed is left open: it is a technical question, a question of application or realization.

Against any such objectification of the conditions of reading and valuation one must stress that aesthetic judgment is always a judgment about the determinate ideological force to be attached to an utterance in a particular historical conjuncture. Value and meaning can be read off neither from the "text itself" nor from the rules of a reading formation, because the act of judgment involved is situational, political, and itself helps to construct "the text," the interpretive frame, and an overlapping but contradictory relation to competing interpretive positions. Clearly this varies historically: some frames are more rigid than others, and different kinds of text tend to demand more or less work of the reader. But in all cases the interpretive frame is not simply *prior* to particular readings, inexorably governing them, but is inferred, guessed at, constituted by a reading. Interpretive frames are fuzzy and continuously negotiable; and any account of the literary system needs to be accompanied by a continuous deconstruction of the concept of system.

Notes

1   Jorge Luis Borges, "Pierre Menard, Author of Don Quixote," in *Fictions*, ed. Anthony Kerrigan (London: John Calder, 1965); hereafter cited in the text.
2   Mike Gane, "Borges/Menard/Spinoza," *Economy and Society*, 9, no. 4 (November 1980), 411; cf. Pierre Macherey, *A Theory of Literary Production*, trans. Geoffrey Wall (London: Routledge and Kegan Paul, 1978), p. 250.
3   Alicia Borinsky, "Repetition, Museums, Libraries: Jorge Luis Borges," *Glyph*, 2 (1977), 92, 97.
4   Gane, "Borges/Menard/Spinoza," p. 416.
5   Tony Bennett, *Formalism and Marxism* (London: Methuen, 1979), p. 59.

6 George Chapman, *Homer's Iliad* (London: George Routledge and Sons, 1903), p. 218; Alexander Pope, *The Iliad of Homer*, ed. Maynard Mack, Twickenham Edition of the Poems of Alexander Pope, vol. 8 (London and New Haven: Methuen and Yale University Press, 1967), pp. 273–4; Andrew Lang, Walter Leaf, and Ernest Myers, *The Iliad of Homer* (London: Macmillan, 1883), p. 334; *The Iliad of Homer*, trans. Richmond Lattimore (Chicago: University of Chicago Press, 1951), pp. 347–8; Christopher Logue, *Patrocleia of Homer* (Ann Arbor: University of Michigan Press, 1963), pp. 41–2 – a slightly different version is published in Logue's *War Music* (1981; reprint, Harmondsworth: Penguin, 1984), pp. 32–3.

7 The concept of keying is taken from Erving Goffman, *Frame Analysis: An Essay on the Organization of Experience* (New York: Harper and Row, 1974), p. 44, where it is defined as a modulation to a secondary ontological framework.

8 Peter Bürger, *Theory of the Avant-Garde*, trans. Michael Shaw, Theory and History of Literature, vol. 4 (Minneapolis: University of Minnesota Press, 1984), p. 12.

9 Marthe Robert, *The Old and the New*, trans. Carol Cosman (Berkeley: University of California Press, 1977), p. 75; hereafter cited in the text.

10 Matthew Arnold, "On Translating Homer," lectures 1–3 (1861–2), and Francis W. Newman, "Homeric Translation in Theory and Practice" (1861), in *Essays by Matthew Arnold* (London: Oxford University Press, 1914).

11 Karl Marx, "Introduction," *Grundrisse: Foundations of the Critique of Political Economy*, trans. Martin Nicolaus (Harmondsworth: Penguin, 1973), p. 111. On this passage cf. particularly O. K. Werckmeister, "Marx on Literature and Art," *New Literary History*, 4, no. 3 (Spring 1973), 518.

12 Milman Parry, *The Making of Homeric Verse: The Collected Papers of Milman Parry*, ed. Adam Parry (Oxford: Oxford University Press, 1971); Albert Lord, *The Singer of Tales* (Cambridge, Mass.: Harvard University Press, 1960); Walter J. Ong, *Orality and Literacy: The Technologizing of the Word* (London: Methuen, 1982), pp. 17–30.

13 E. C. Mack, *Public Schools and British Opinion Since 1860*, cited in Jacqueline Rose, *The Case of Peter Pan, or The Impossibility of Children's Fiction* (London: Macmillan, 1984), p. 152.

14 Cf. Renée Balibar et al., *Les Français fictifs* (Paris: Hachette, 1974).

15 Pierre Macherey, "Problems of Reflection," trans. John Coombes, *Literature, Society and the Sociology of Literature: Proceedings of the Conference Held at the University of Essex, July 1976* (Colchester: University of Essex, 1977), p. 45.

16 David Morley, *The "Nationwide" Audience: Structure and Decoding*, BFI Television Monograph 11 (London: BFI, 1980), p. 31.

17 Paul Willemen, "Notes on Subjectivity," *Screen*, 19, no. 1 (Spring 1978).

18 Morley, *The "Nationwide" Audience*, p. 158.

19 Ibid., p. 161.

20 Claire Johnston, "The Subject of Feminist Film Theory/Practice," *Screen*, 21, no. 2 (Summer 1980), 30.

21 Morley, *The "Nationwide" Audience*, p. 162. The other major theoretical problems with Morley's analysis are the assumption that the reconstructed readings are the transparent representation of an experience rather than the conventional discursive construction of an interview answer; the fact that as a result of the distinction between an "ideological problematic" and an enunciative "mode of address" (p. 139) the latter is implicitly excluded from the former and so marginalized; and that this marginalization is then used to render less problematical the "oppositional" stance of some socially conservative groups.

22 Stanley Fish, *Is there a Text in this Class?: The Authority of Interpretive Communities* (Cambridge, Mass.: Harvard University Press, 1980), pp. 153–4; hereafter cited in the text.

23 Mircea Marghescou, *Le Concept de littérarité* (The Hague: Mouton, 1974), p. 47.

24 Didier Coste, "Trois conceptions du lecteur et leur contribution à une théorie du texte littéraire," *Poétique*, 43 (1980), 357.

25 Wolfgang Iser, *The Implied Reader* (Baltimore: Johns Hopkins University Press, 1974); *The Act of Reading: A Theory of Aesthetic Response* (Baltimore: Johns Hopkins University Press, 1978), esp. pp. 34–5 and 167.

26 Marx describes the categories of bourgeois economics as being "forms of thought which are socially valid (*gültig*), and therefore objective, for the relations of production belonging to this historically determinate mode of social production." Karl Marx, *Capital: A Critique of Political Economy, I*, trans. Ben Fowkes (Harmondsworth: Penguin, 1976), p. 169.

27 Cf. Keith Tribe, "Literary Methodology," *Economy and Society*, 9, no. 2 (May 1980), 248.

28 Tony Bennett, "Text, Readers, Reading Formations," *Literature and History*, 9, no. 2 (Autumn 1983), 218.

CHAPTER 10

Distinction

Pierre Bourdieu

In this selection from *Distinction* (1979), French sociologist Pierre Bourdieu argues that all taste in literature is an effect of prior determinants. One's class position, one's training in culture, one's education – all of these factors classify us as readers and sort us into groups who favor one kind of literature over another.

Classes and Classifications

If I have to choose the lesser of two evils, I choose neither.
Karl Kraus

Taste is an acquired disposition to 'differentiate' and 'appreciate',[1] as Kant says – in other words, to establish and mark differences by a process of distinction which is not (or not necessarily) a distinct knowledge, in Leibniz's sense, since it ensures recognition (in the ordinary sense) of the object without implying knowledge of the distinctive features which define it.[2] The schemes of the habitus, the primary forms of classification, owe their specific efficacy to the fact that they function below the level of consciousness and language, beyond the reach of introspective scrutiny or control by the will. Orienting practices practically, they embed what some would mistakenly call *values* in the most automatic gestures or the apparently most insignificant techniques of the body – ways of walking or blowing one's nose, ways of eating or talking – and engage the most fundamental principles of construction and evaluation of the social world, those which most directly express the division of labour (between the classes, the age groups and the sexes) or the division of the work of domination, in divisions between bodies and between relations to the body which borrow more features than one, as if to give them the appearances of naturalness, from the sexual division of labour and the division of sexual labour. Taste is a practical mastery of distributions which makes it possible to sense or intuit what is likely (or unlikely) to befall – and therefore to befit – an individual occupying a given position in social space. It functions as a sort of social orientation, a 'sense of one's place', guiding the occupants of a given place in social space towards the social positions adjusted to their properties, and towards the practices or goods which befit the occupants of that position. It implies a practical anticipation of what the social meaning and value of the chosen practice or thing will probably be, given their distribution in social space and the practical knowledge the other agents have of the correspondence between goods and groups.

Thus, the social agents whom the sociologist classifies are producers not only of classifiable acts but also of acts of classification which are themselves classified. Knowledge of the social world has to take into account a practical knowledge of this world which pre-exists it and which it must not fail to include in its object, although, as a first stage, this knowledge has to be constituted *against* the partial and interested representations provided by practical knowledge. To speak of habitus is to include in the object the knowledge which the agents, who are part of the object, have of the object, and the contribution this knowledge makes to the reality of the object. But it is not only a matter of putting back into the real world that one is endeavouring to know, a knowledge of the real world that contributes to its reality (and also to the force it exerts). It means conferring on this knowledge a genuinely constitutive power, the very power it is denied when, in the name of an objectivist conception of objectivity, one makes common knowledge or theoretical knowledge a mere reflection of the real world.

Those who suppose they are producing a materialist theory of knowledge when they make knowledge a passive recording and abandon the 'active aspect' of know-ledge to idealism, as Marx complains in the *Theses on Feuerbach*, forget that all knowledge, and in particular all knowledge of the social world, is an act of construc-tion implementing schemes of thought and expression, and that between conditions of existence and practices or representations there intervenes the structuring activity of the agents, who, far from reacting mechanically to mechanical stimulations, re-spond to the invitations or threats of a world whose meaning they have helped to produce. However, the principle of this structuring activity is not, as an intellectual-ist and anti-genetic idealism would have it, a system of universal forms and categories but a system of internalized, embodied schemes which, having been constituted in the course of collective history, are acquired in the course of individual history and function in their *practical* state, *for practice* (and not for the sake of pure knowledge).

Embodied Social Structures

This means, in the first place, that social science, in constructing the social world, takes note of the fact that agents are, in their ordinary practice, the subjects of acts of construction of the social world; but also that it aims, among other things, to describe the social genesis of the principles of construction and seeks the basis of these principles in the social world.[3] Breaking with the anti-genetic prejudice which often accompanies recognition of the active aspect of knowledge, it seeks in the objective distributions of properties, especially material ones (brought to light by censuses and surveys which all presuppose selection and classification), the basis of the systems of classification which agents apply to every sort of thing, not least to the distributions themselves. In contrast to what is sometimes called the 'cognitive' approach, which, both in its ethnological form (structural anthropology, ethnoscience, ethnosemantics, ethnobotany etc.) and in its sociological form (interactionism, ethnomethodology etc.), ignores the question of the genesis of mental structures and classifications, social science enquires into the relationship between the principles of division and the social divisions (between the generations, the sexes etc.) on which they are based, and into the variations of the use made of these principles according to the position occupied in the distributions (questions which all require the use of statistics).

The cognitive structures which social agents implement in their practical knowledge of the social world are internalized, 'embodied' social structures. The practical knowledge of the social world that is presupposed by 'reasonable' behaviour within it implements classificatory schemes (or 'forms of classification', 'mental structures' or 'symbolic forms' – apart from their connotations, these expressions are virtually interchangeable), historical schemes of perception and appreciation which are the product of the objective division into classes (age groups, genders, social classes) and which function below the level of consciousness and discourse. Being the product of the incorporation of the fundamental structures of a society, these principles of division are common to all the agents of the society and make possible the production of a common, meaningful world, a common-sense world.

All the agents in a given social formation share a set of basic perceptual schemes, which receive the beginnings of objectification in the pairs of antagonistic adjectives commonly used to classify and qualify persons or objects in the most varied areas of practice. The network of oppositions between high (sublime, elevated, pure) and low (vulgar, low, modest), spiritual and material, fine (refined, elegant) and coarse (heavy, fat, crude, brutal), light (subtle, lively, sharp, adroit) and heavy (slow, thick, blunt, laborious, clumsy), free and forced, broad and narrow, or, in another dimension, between unique (rare, different, distinguished, exclusive, exceptional, singular, novel) and common (ordinary, banal, commonplace, trivial, routine), brilliant (intelligent) and dull (obscure, grey, mediocre), is the matrix of all the commonplaces which find such ready acceptance because behind them lies the whole social order. The network has its ultimate source in the opposition between the 'élite' of the dominant and the 'mass' of the dominated, a contingent, disorganized multiplicity, interchangeable and innumerable, existing only statistically. These mythic roots only have to be allowed to take their course in order to generate, at will, one or another of the tirelessly repeated themes of the eternal sociodicy, such as apocalyptic denunciations of all forms of 'levelling', 'trivialization' or 'massification', which identify the decline of societies with the decadence of bourgeois houses, i.e., a fall into the homogeneous, the undifferentiated, and betray an obsessive fear of number, of undifferentiated hordes indifferent to difference and constantly threatening to submerge the private spaces of bourgeois exclusiveness.[4]

The seemingly most formal oppositions within this social mythology always derive their ideological strength from the fact that they refer back, more or less discreetly, to the most fundamental oppositions within the social order: the opposition between the dominant and the dominated, which is inscribed in the division of labour, and the opposition, rooted in the division of the labour of domination, between two principles of domination, two powers, dominant and dominated, temporal and spiritual, material and intellectual etc. It follows that the map of social space previously put forward can also be read as a strict table of the historically constituted and acquired categories which organize the idea of the social world in the minds of all the subjects belonging to that world and shaped by it. The same classificatory schemes (and the oppositions in which they are expressed) can function, by being specified, in fields organized around polar positions, whether in the field of the dominant class, organized around an opposition homologous to the opposition constituting the field of the social classes, or in the field of cultural production, which is itself organized around oppositions which reproduce the structure of the dominant class and are homologous to it (e.g., the opposition between bourgeois and avant-garde theatre). So the fundamental opposition constantly supports second, third or n^{th} rank oppositions (those which underlie the 'purest' ethical or aesthetic judgements, with their high or low sentiments, their facile or difficult notions of beauty, their light or heavy styles etc.), while euphemizing itself to the point of misrecognizability.

Thus, the opposition between the heavy and the light, which, in a number of its uses, especially scholastic ones, serves to distinguish popular or petit-bourgeois tastes from bourgeois tastes, can be used by theatre criticism aimed at the dominant fraction of the dominant class to express the relationship between 'intellectual' theatre, which is condemned for its 'laborious' pretensions and 'oppressive' didacticism, and 'bourgeois' theatre, which is praised for its tact and its art of skimming over surfaces. By contrast, 'intellectual' criticism, by a simple inversion of values, expresses the relationship in a scarcely modified form of the same opposition, with lightness, identified with frivolity, being opposed to profundity. Similarly, it can be shown that the opposition between right and left, which, in its basic form, concerns the relationship between the dominant and the dominated, can also, by means of a first transformation, designate the relations between dominated fractions and dominant fractions within the dominant class; the words right and left then take on a meaning close to the meaning they have in expressions like 'right-bank' theatre or 'left-bank' theatre. With a further degree of 'de-realization', it can even serve to distinguish two rival tendencies within an avant-garde artistic or literary group, and so on.

It follows that, when considered in each of their uses, the pairs of qualifiers, the system of which constitutes the conceptual equipment of the judgement of taste, are extremely poor, almost indefinite, but, precisely for this reason, capable of eliciting or expressing the sense of the indefinable. Each particular use of one of these pairs only takes on its full meaning in relation to a universe of discourse that is different each time and usually implicit – since it is a question of the system of self-evidences and presuppositions that are taken for granted in the field in relation to which the speakers' strategies are defined. But each of the couples specified by usage has for undertones all the other uses it might have – because of the homologies between the fields which allow transfers from one field to another – and also all the other couples which are interchangeable with it, within a nuance or two (e.g., fine/crude for light/heavy), that is, in slightly different contexts.

The fact that the semi-codified oppositions contained in ordinary language reappear, with very similar values, as the basis of the dominant vision of the social world, in all class-divided social formations (consider the tendency to see the 'people' as the site of totally uncontrolled appetites and sexuality) can be understood once one knows that, reduced to their formal structure, the same fundamental relationships, precisely those which express the major relations of order (high/low, strong/weak etc.) reappear in all class-divided societies. And the recurrence of the triadic structure studied by Georges Dumézil, which Georges Duby shows in the case of feudal society to be rooted in the social structures it legitimates, may well be, like the invariant oppositions in which the relationship of domination is expressed, simply a necessary outcome of the intersection of the two principles of division which are at work in all class-divided societies – the division between the dominant and the dominated, and the division between the different fractions competing for dominance in the name of different principles, *bellatores* (warriors) and *oratores* (scholars) in feudal society, businessmen and intellectuals now.[5]

Knowledge without Concepts

Thus, through the differentiated and differentiating conditionings associated with the different conditions of existence, through the exclusions and inclusions, unions (marriages, affairs, alliances etc.) and divisions (incompatibilities, separations, struggles etc.) which govern the social structure and the structuring force it exerts, through all the hierarchies and classifications inscribed in objects (especially cultural products), in institutions (for example, the educational system) or simply in language, and through all the judgements, verdicts, gradings and warnings imposed by the institutions specially designed for this purpose, such as the family or the educational system, or constantly arising from the meetings and interactions of everyday life, the social order is progressively inscribed in people's minds. Social divisions become principles of division, organizing the image of the social world. Objective limits become a sense of limits, a practical anticipation of objective limits acquired by experience of objective limits, a 'sense of one's place' which leads one to exclude oneself from the goods, persons, places and so forth from which one is excluded.

The *sense* of limits implies *forgetting* the limits. One of the most important effects of the correspondence between real divisions and practical principles of division, between social structures and mental structures, is undoubtedly the fact that primary experience of the social world is that of doxa, an adherence to relations of order which, because they structure inseparably both the real world and the thought world, are accepted as self-evident. Primary perception of the social world, far from being a simple mechanical reflection, is always an act of cognition involving principles of construction that are external to the constructed object grasped in its immediacy; but at the same time it is an act of miscognition, implying the most absolute form of recognition of the social order. Dominated agents, who assess the value of their position and their characteristics by applying a system of schemes of perception and appreciation which is the embodiment of the objective laws whereby their value is objectively constituted, tend to attribute to themselves what the distribution attributes to them, refusing what they are refused ('That's not for the likes of us'), adjusting their expectations to their chances, defining themselves as the established order defines them, reproducing in their verdict on themselves the verdict the economy pronounces on them, in a word, condemning themselves to what is in any case their lot, *ta beautou*, as Plato put it, consenting to be what they have to be, 'modest', 'humble' and 'obscure'. Thus the conservation of the social order is decisively reinforced by what Durkheim called 'logical conformity',[6] i.e., the orchestration of categories of perception of the social world, which, being adjusted to the divisions of the established order (and thereby to the interests of those who dominate it) and common to all minds structured in accordance with those structures, present every appearance of objective necessity.[7]

The system of classificatory schemes is opposed to a taxonomy based on explicit and explicitly concerted principles in the same way that the dispositions constituting taste or ethos (which are dimensions of it) are opposed to aesthetics or ethics. The sense of social realities that is acquired in the confrontation with a particular form of social necessity is what makes it possible to act *as if* one knew the structure of the social world, one's place within it and the distances that need to be kept.

The ideology of the utopian thinker, rootless and unattached, 'free-floating', without interests or profits, together with the correlative refusal of that supreme form of materialistic vulgarity, the reduction of the unique to the class, the explanation of the higher by the lower, the application to the would-be unclassifiable of explanatory models fit only for the 'bourgeois', the petit-bourgeois, the limited and common, scarcely inclines intellectuals to conceptualize the sense of social position, still less their own position and the perverse relation to the social world it forces on them. (The perfect example is Sartre, whose whole work and whole existence revolve around this affirmation of the intellectual's subversive point of honour. This is seen particularly clearly in the passage in *Being and Nothingness* on the psychology of Flaubert, which can be read as a desperate effort to save the person, in the person of the intellectual, an uncreated creator, begotten by his own works, haunted by 'the project of being God', from every sort of reduction to the general, the type, the class, and to affirm the transcendence of the ego against 'what Comte called *materialism*, that is, explaining the higher by the lower.')[8]

The practical mastery of classification has nothing in common with the reflexive mastery that is required in order to construct a taxonomy that is simultaneously coherent and adequate to social reality. The practical 'science' of positions in social space is the competence presupposed by the art of behaving *comme il faut* with persons and things that have and give 'class' ('smart' or 'unsmart'), finding the right distance, by a sort of practical calculation, neither too close ('getting familiar') nor too far ('being distant'), playing with objective distance by emphasizing it (being 'aloof', 'stand-offish') or symbolically denying it (being 'approachable', 'hobnobbing'). It is no way implies the capacity to situate oneself explicitly in the classification (as so many surveys on social class ask people to do), still less to describe this classification in any systematic way and state its principles.

There is no better opportunity to observe the functioning of this sense of the place one occupies than in condescension strategies, which presuppose both in the author of the strategy and in the victims a practical knowledge of the gap between the place really occupied and the place fictitiously indicated by the behaviour adopted (e.g., in French, use of the familiar *tu*). When the person 'naturally' identified with a Rolls Royce, a top hat or golf (see appendix 4) takes the metro, sports a flat cap (or a polo neck) or plays football, his practices take on their meaning in relation to this attribution by status, which continues to colour the real practices, as if by superimposition. But one could also point to the variations that Charles Bally observed in the style of speech according to the social gap between the interlocutors, or the variations in pronunciation according to the addressee: the speaker may, as appropriate, move closer to the 'accent' of an addressee of (presumed) higher status or move away from it by 'accentuating' his ordinary accent.[9]

The practical 'attributive judgement' whereby one puts someone in a class by speaking to him in a certain way (thereby putting oneself in a class at the same time) has nothing to do with an intellectual operation implying conscious reference to explicit indices and the implementation of classes produced by and for the concept. The same classificatory opposition (rich/poor, young/old etc.) can be applied at any point in the distribution and reproduce its whole range within any of its segments (common sense tells us that one is always richer or poorer than someone, superior or inferior to someone, more right-wing or left-wing than someone – but this does not entail an elementary relativism).

In a series of interviews (n = 30) on the social classes, based on a test which involved classifying thirty occupations (written on cards), the respondents often first asked how many classes the set should be divided into, and then several times modified the number of classes and the criteria of classification, so as to take account of the different dimensions of each occupation and therefore the different respects in which it could be evaluated; or they spontaneously suggested that they could carry on sub-dividing indefinitely. (They thereby exposed the artificiality of the situation created by a theoretical inquiry which called for the adoption of a theoretical attitude to which, as their initial uncertainty indicated, the respondents were quite unaccustomed.) And yet they almost always agreed on the ranks of the different occupations when taken two by two. (Lenski made similar observations in an experiment in which the respondents were asked to rank the families in a small town in New England.)[10]

It is not surprising that it is possible to fault the practical sense of social space which lies behind class-attributive judgement; the sociologists who use their respondents' self-contradictions as an argument for denying the existence of classes simply reveal that they understand nothing of how this 'sense' works or of the artificial situation in which they are making it work. In fact, whether it is used to situate oneself in social space or to place others, the sense of social space, like every practical sense, always refers to the particular situation in which it has to orient practices. This explains, for example, the divergences between surveys of the representation of the classes in a small town ('community studies') and surveys of class on a nation-wide scale.[11] But if, as has often been observed, respondents do not agree either on the number of divisions they make within the group in question, or on the limits of the 'strata' and the criteria used to define them, this is not simply due to the fuzziness inherent in all practical logics. It is also because people's image of the classification is a function of their position within it.

So nothing is further removed from an act of cognition, as conceived by the intellectualist tradition, than this sense of the social structure, which, as is so well put by the word *taste* – simultaneously 'the faculty of perceiving flavours' and 'the capacity to discern aesthetic values' – is social necessity made second nature, turned into muscular patterns and bodily automatisms. Everything takes place as if the social conditionings linked to a social condition tended to inscribe the relation to the social world in a lasting, generalized relation to one's own body, a way of bearing one's body, presenting it to others, moving it, making space for it, which gives the body its social physiognomy. Bodily hexis, a basic dimension of the sense of social orientation, is a practical way of experiencing and expressing one's own sense of social value. One's relationship to the social world and to one's proper place in it is never more clearly expressed than in the space and time one feels entitled to take from others; more precisely, in the space one claims with one's body in physical space, through a bearing and gestures that are self-assured or reserved, expansive or constricted ('presence' or 'insignificance') and with one's speech in time, through the interaction time one appropriates and the self-assured or aggressive, careless or unconscious way one appropriates it.[12]

There is no better image of the logic of socialization, which treats the body as a 'memory-jogger', than those complexes of gestures, postures and words – simple interjections or favourite clichés – which only have to be slipped into, like a theatrical costume, to awaken, by the evocative power of bodily mimesis, a universe of ready-made feelings and experiences. The elementary actions of bodily gymnastics, especially the specifically sexual, biologically pre-constructed aspect of it, charged with social meanings and values, function as the most basic of metaphors, capable of evoking a whole relationship to the world, 'lofty' or 'submissive', 'expansive' or 'narrow', and through it a whole world. The practical 'choices' of the sense of social orientation no more presuppose a representation of the range of possibilities than does the choice of phonemes; these enacted choices imply no acts of choosing. The logocentrism and intellectualism of intellectuals, combined with the prejudice inherent in the science which takes as its object the psyche, the soul, the mind, consciousness, representations, not to mention the petit-bourgeois pretension to the status of 'person', have prevented us from seeing that, as Leibniz put it, 'we are automatons in three-quarters of what we do', and that the ultimate values, as they are called, are never anything other than the primary, primitive dispositions of the body, 'visceral' tastes and distastes, in which the group's most vital interests are embedded, the things on which one is prepared to stake one's own and other people's bodies. The sense of distinction, the *discretio* (discrimination) which demands that certain things be brought together and others kept apart, which excludes all misalliances and all unnatural unions – i.e., all unions contrary to the common classification, to the *diacrisis* (separation) which is the basis of collective and individual identity – responds with visceral, murderous horror, absolute disgust, metaphysical fury, to everything which lies in Plato's 'hybrid zone', everything which passes understanding, that is, the embodied taxonomy, which, by challenging the principles of the incarnate social order, especially the socially constituted principles of the sexual division of labour and the division of sexual labour, violates the mental order, scandalously flouting common sense.

> It can be shown that socialization tends to constitute the body as an analogical operator establishing all sorts of practical equivalences between the different divisions of the social world – divisions between the sexes, between the age groups and between the social classes – or, more precisely, between the meanings and values associated with the individuals occupying practically equivalent positions in the spaces defined by these divisions. And it can be shown that it does so by integrating the symbolism of social domination and submission and the symbolism of sexual domination and submission into the same body language – as is seen in etiquette, which uses the opposition between the straight and the curved or, which amounts to the same thing, between raising (oneself) and lowering (oneself), as one of the generative principles of the marks (of respect, contempt etc.) used to symbolize hierarchical relations.

Advantageous Attributions

The basis of the pertinence principle which is implemented in perceiving the social world and which defines all the characteristics of persons or things which can be perceived, and perceived as positively or negatively interesting, by all those who apply these schemes (another definition of common sense), is based on nothing other than the interest the individuals or groups in question have in recognizing a feature and in identifying the individual in question as a member of the set defined by that feature; interest in the aspect observed is never completely independent of the advantage of observing it. This can be clearly seen in all the classifications built around a stigmatized feature which, like the everyday opposition between homosexuals and heterosexuals, isolate the interesting trait from all the rest (i.e., all other forms of sexuality), which remain indifferent and undifferentiated. It is even clearer in all 'labelling judgements', which are in fact accusations, *categoremes* in the original Aristotelian sense, and which, like insults, only wish to know one of the properties constituting the social identity of an individual or group ('You're just a...'), regarding, for example, the married homosexual or converted Jew as a 'closet queen' or covert Jew, and thereby in a sense doubly Jewish or homosexual. The logic of the stigma reminds us that social identity is the stake in a struggle in which the stigmatized individual or group, and, more generally, any individual or group insofar as he or it is a potential object of categorization, can only retaliate against the partial perception which limits it to one of its characteristics by highlighting, in its self-definition, the best of its characteristics, and, more generally, by struggling to impose the taxonomy most favourable to its characteristics, or at least to give to the dominant taxonomy the content most flattering to what it has and what it is.

Those who are surprised by the paradoxes that ordinary logic and language engender when they apply their divisions to continuous magnitudes forget the paradoxes inherent in treating language as a purely logical instrument and also forget the social situation in which such a relationship to language is possible. The contradictions or paradoxes to which ordinary language classifications lead do not derive, as all forms of positivism suppose, from some essential inadequacy of ordinary language, but from the fact that these socio-logical acts are not directed towards the pursuit of logical coherence and that, unlike philological, logical or linguistic uses of language – which ought really to be called scholastic, since they all presuppose *schole*, i.e., leisure, distance from urgency and necessity, the absence of vital stakes, and the scholastic institution which in most social universes is the only institution capable of providing all these – they obey the logic of the parti pris, which, as in a court-room, juxtaposes not logical judgements, subject to the sole criterion of coherence, but charges and defences. Quite apart from all that is implied in the oppositions, which logicians and even linguists manage to forget, between the art of convincing and the art of persuading, it is clear that scholastic usage of language is to the orator's, advocate's or politician's usage what the classificatory systems devised by the logician or statistician concerned with coherence and empirical adequacy are to the categorizations and categoremes of daily life. As the etymology suggests, the latter belong to the logic of the trial.[13] Every real inquiry into the divisions of the social world has to analyse the interests associated with membership or non-membership. As is shown by the attention devoted to strategic, 'frontier' groups such as the 'labour aristocracy', which hesitates between class struggle and class collaboration, or the 'cadres', a category of bureaucratic statistics, whose nominal, doubly negative unity conceals its real dispersion both from the 'interested parties' and from their opponents and most observers, the laying down of boundaries between the classes is inspired by the strategic aim of 'counting in' or 'being counted in', 'cataloguing' or 'annexing', when it is not the simple recording of a legally guaranteed state of the power relation between the classified groups.

Leaving aside all cases in which the statutory imposition of an arbitrary boundary (such as a 30-kilo limit on baggage or the rule that a vehicle over two tons is a van) suffices to eliminate the difficulties that arise from the sophism of the heap of grain,[14] boundaries – even the most formal-looking ones, such as those between age-groups – do indeed freeze a particular state of social struggles, i.e., a given state of the distribution of advantages and obligations, such as the right to pensions or cheap fares, compulsory schooling or military service. And if we are amused by Alphonse Allais's story of the father who pulls the communication cord to stop the train at the very moment his child becomes three years old (and so needs a ticket to travel), it is because we immediately see the sociological absurdity of an imaginary variation which is as impeccably logical as those on which logicians base their beloved paradoxes. Here the limits are frontiers to be attacked or defended with all one's strength, and the classificatory systems which fix them are not so much means of knowledge as means of power, harnessed to social functions and overtly or covertly aimed at satisfying the interests of a group.

> A number of ethical, aesthetic, psychiatric or forensic classifications that are produced by the 'institutional sciences', not to mention those produced and inculcated by the educational system, are similarly subordinated to social functions, although they derive their specific efficacy from their apparent neutrality. They are produced in accordance with the specific logic, and in the specific language, of relatively autonomous fields, and they combine a real dependence on the classificatory schemes of the dominant habitus (and ultimately on the social structures of which these are the product) with an apparent independence. The latter enables them to help to legitimate a particular state of the classification struggle and the class struggle. Perhaps the most typical example of these semi-autonomous systems of classification is the system of adjectives which underpins scholastic 'appreciations'.[15]

Commonplaces and classificatory systems are thus the stake of struggles between the groups they characterize and counterpose, who fight over them while striving to turn them to their own advantage. Georges Duby shows how the model of the three orders, which fixed a state of the social structure and aimed to make it permanent by codifying it, was able to be used simultaneously and successively by antagonistic groups: first by the bishops, who had devised it, against the heretics, the monks and the knights; then by the aristocracy, against the bishops and the king; and finally by the king, who, by setting himself up as the absolute subject of the classifying operation, as a principle external and superior to the classes it generated (unlike the three orders, who were subjects but also objects, judges but also parties), assigned each group its place in the social order, and established himself as an unassailable vantage-point.[16] In the same way it can be shown that the schemes and commonplaces which provide images of the different forms of domination, the opposition between the sexes and age-groups as well as the opposition between the generations, are similarly manipulated. The 'young' can accept the definition that their elders offer them, take advantage of the temporary licence they are allowed in many societies ('Youth must have its fling'), do what is assigned to them, revel in the 'specific virtues' of youth, *virtù*, virility, enthusiasm, and get on with their own business – knight-errantry for the scions of the mediaeval aristocracy,[17] love and violence for the youth of Renaissance Florence, and every form of regulated, ludic wildness (sport, rock etc.) for contemporary adolescents – in short, allow themselves to be kept in the state of 'youth', that is, irresponsibility, enjoying the freedom of irresponsible behaviour in return for renouncing responsibility.[18] In situations of specific crisis, when the order of successions is threatened, 'young people', refusing to remain consigned to 'youth', tend to consign the 'old' to 'old age'. Wanting to take the responsibilities which define adults (in the sense of socially complete persons), they must push the holders of responsibilities into that form of irresponsibility which defines old age, or rather retirement. The wisdom and prudence claimed by the elders then collapse into conservatism, archaism or, quite simply, senile irresponsibility. The newcomers, who are likely to be also the biologically youngest, but who bring with them many other distinctive properties, stemming from changes in the social conditions of production of the producers (i.e., principally the family and the educational system), escape the more rapidly from 'youth' (irresponsibility) the readier they are to break with the irresponsible behaviour assigned to them and, freeing themselves from the internalized limits (those which may make a 50-year-old feel 'too young reasonably to aspire' to a position or an honour), do not hesitate to push forward, 'leap-frog' and 'take the escalator' to precipitate their predecessors' fall into the past, the outdated, in short, social death. But they have no chance of winning the struggles over the limits which break out between the age-groups when the sense of the limits is lost, unless they manage to impose a new definition of the socially complete person, including in it characteristics normally (i.e., in terms of the prevailing classificatory principle) associated with youth (enthusiasm, energy and so on) or characteristics that can supplant the virtues normally associated with adulthood.

In short, what individuals and groups invest in the particular meaning they give to common classificatory systems by the use they make of them is infinitely more than their 'interest' in the usual sense of the term; it is their whole social being, everything which defines their own idea of themselves, the primordial, tacit contract whereby they define 'us' as opposed to 'them', 'other people', and which is the basis of the exclusions ('not for the likes of us') and inclusions they perform among the characteristics produced by the common classificatory system.

Social psychologists have observed that any division of a population into two groups, however arbitrary, induces discriminatory behaviour favourable to members of the agents' own group and hostile to members of the other group, even if it has adverse effects for the former group.[19] More generally, they describe under the term 'category differentiation' the operations whereby agents construct their perception of reality, in particular the process of accentuating differences vis-à-vis 'outsiders' (dissimilation) and reinforcing similarities with insiders (assimilation).[20] Similarly, studies of racism have shown that whenever different groups are juxtaposed, a definition of the approved, valorized behaviour tends to be contrasted with the despised, rejected behaviour of the other group.[21] Social identity lies in difference, and difference is asserted against what is closest, which represents the greatest threat. Analysis of stereotyping, the propensity to assume a correspondence between membership of a category (e.g., Nordic or Mediterranean, Western or Oriental) and possession of a particular property, so that knowledge of a person's category strongly influences judgements of him, is in line with analysis of that sort of social stereotyping in which all the members of a social formation tend to concur in attributing certain properties to members of the different social classes.

The fact that, in their relationship to the dominant classes, the dominated classes attribute to themselves strength in the sense of labour power and fighting strength – physical strength and also strength of character, courage, manliness – does not prevent the dominant groups from similarly conceiving the relationship in terms of the scheme strong/weak; but they reduce the strength which the dominated (or the young, or women) ascribe to themselves to brute strength, passion and instinct, a blind, unpredictable force of nature, the unreasoning violence of desire, and they attribute to themselves spiritual and intellectual strength, a self-control that predisposes them to control others, a strength of soul or spirit which allows them to conceive their relationship to the dominated – the 'masses', women, the young – as that of the soul to the body, understanding to sensibility, culture to nature.

The Classification Struggle

Principles of division, inextricably logical and sociological, function within and for the purposes of the struggle between social groups; in producing concepts, they produce groups, the very groups which produce the principles and the groups against which they are produced. What is at stake in the struggles about the meaning of the social world is power over the classificatory schemes and systems which are the basis of the representations of the groups and therefore of their mobilization and demobilization: the evocative power of an utterance which puts things in a different light (as happens, for example, when a single word, such as 'paternalism', changes the whole experience of a social relationship) or which modifies the schemes of perception, shows something else, other properties, previously unnoticed or relegated to the background (such as common interests hitherto masked by ethnic or national differences); a separative power, a distinction, *diacrisis, discretio*, drawing discrete units out of indivisible continuity, difference out of the undifferentiated.

Only in and through the struggle do the internalized limits become boundaries, barriers that have to be moved. And indeed, the system of classificatory schemes is constituted as an objectified, institutionalized system of classification only when it has ceased to function as a sense of limits so that the guardians of the established order must enunciate, systematize and codify the principles of production of that order, both real and represented, so as to defend them against heresy; in short, they must constitute the doxa as orthodoxy. Official systems of classification, such as the theory of the three orders, do explicitly and systematically what the classificatory schemes did tacitly and practically. Attributes, in the sense of predicates, thereby become *attributions*, powers, capacities, privileges, prerogatives, attributed to the holder of a post, so that war is no longer what the warrior does, but the *officium*, the specific function, the raison d'être, of the *bellator*. Classificatory *discretio*, like law, freezes a certain state of the power relations which it aims to fix forever by enunciating and codifying it. The classificatory system as a principle of logical and political division only exists and functions because it reproduces, in a transfigured form, in the symbolic logic of differential gaps, i.e., of discontinuity, the generally gradual and continuous differences which structure the established order; but it makes its own, that is, specifically symbolic, contribution to the maintenance of that order only because it has the specifically symbolic power to make people see and believe which is given by the imposition of mental structures.

Systems of classification would not be such a decisive object of struggle if they did not contribute to the existence of classes by enhancing the efficacy of the objective mechanisms with the reinforcement supplied by representations structured in accordance with the classification. The imposition of a recognized name is an act of recognition of full social existence which transmutes the thing named. It no longer exists merely de facto, as a tolerated, illegal or illegitimate practice, but becomes a *social* function, i.e., a mandate, a mission (*Beruf*), a task, a role – all words which express the difference between authorized activity, which is assigned to an individual or group by tacit or explicit delegation, and mere usurpation, which creates a 'state of affairs' awaiting institutionalization. But the specific effect of 'collective representations', which, contrary to what the Durkheimian connotations might suggest, may be the product of the application of the same scheme of perception or a common system of classification while still being subject to antagonistic social uses, is most clearly seen when the word precedes the thing, as with voluntary associations that turn into recognized professions or corporate defence groups (such as the trade union of the 'cadres'), which progressively impose the representation of their existence and their unity, both on their own members and on other groups.

A group's presence or absence in the official classification depends on its capacity to get itself recognized, to get itself noticed and admitted, and so to win a place in the social order. It thus escapes from the shadowy existence of the 'nameless crafts' of which Emile Benveniste speaks: business in antiquity and the Middle Ages, or illegitimate activities, such as those of the modern healer (formerly called an 'empiric'), bone-setter or prostitute. The fate of groups is bound up with the words that designate them: the power to impose recognition depends on the capacity to mobilize around a name, 'proletariat', 'working class', 'cadres' etc., to appropriate a common name and to commune in a proper name, and so to mobilize the union that makes them strong, around the unifying power of a word.[22]

In fact, the order of words never exactly reproduces the order of things. It is the relative independence of the structure of the system of classifying, classified words (within which the distinct value of each particular label is defined) in relation to the structure of the distribution of capital, and more precisely, it is the time-lag (partly resulting from the inertia inherent in classification systems as quasi-legal institutions sanctioning a state of a power relation) between changes in jobs, linked to changes in the productive apparatus, and changes in titles, which creates the space for symbolic strategies aimed at exploiting the discrepancies between the nominal and the real, appropriating words so as to get the things they designate, or appropriating things while waiting to get the words that sanction them; exercising responsibilities without having entitlement to do so, in order to acquire the right to claim the legitimate titles, or, conversely, declining the material advantages associated with devalued titles so as to avoid losing the symbolic advantages bestowed by more prestigious labels or, at least, vaguer and more manipulable ones; donning the most flattering of the available insignia, verging on imposture if need be – like the potters who call themselves 'art craftsmen', or technicians who claim to be engineers – or inventing new labels, like physiotherapists (*kinésithérapeutes*) who count on this new title to separate them from mere masseurs and bring them closer to doctors. All these strategies, like all processes of competition, a paper-chase aimed at ensuring constant distinctive gaps, tend to produce a steady inflation of titles – restrained by the inertia of the institutionalized taxonomies (collective agreements, salary scales etc.) – to which legal guarantees are attached. The negotiations between antagonistic interest groups, which arise from the establishment of collective agreements and which concern, inseparably, the tasks entailed by a given job, the properties required of its occupants (e.g., diplomas) and the corresponding advantages, both material and symbolic (the name), are an institutionalized, theatrical version of the incessant struggles over the classifications which help to produce the classes, although these classifications are the product of the struggles between the classes and depend on the power relations between them.

The Reality of Representation and the Representation of Reality

The classifying subjects who classify the properties and practices of others, or their own, are also classifiable objects which classify themselves (in the eyes of others) by appropriating practices and properties that are already classified (as vulgar or distinguished, high or low, heavy or light etc. – in other words, in the last analysis, as popular or bourgeois) according to their probable distribution between groups that are themselves classified. The most classifying and best classified of these properties are, of course, those which are overtly designated to function as signs of distinction or marks of infamy, stigmata, especially the names and titles expressing class membership whose intersection defines social identity at any given time – the name of a nation, a region, an ethnic group, a family name, the name of an occupation, an educational qualification, honorific titles and so on. Those who classify themselves or others, by appropriating or classifying practices or properties that are classified and classifying, cannot be unaware that, through distinctive objects or practices in which their 'powers' are expressed and which, being appropriated by and appropriate to classes, classify those who appropriate them, they classify themselves in the eyes of other classifying (but also classifiable) subjects, endowed with classificatory schemes analogous to those which enable them more or less adequately to anticipate their own classification.

Social subjects comprehend the social world which comprehends them. This means that they cannot be characterized simply in terms of material properties, starting with the body, which can be counted and measured like any other object in the physical world. In fact, each of these properties, be it the height or volume of the body or the extent of landed property, when perceived and appreciated in relation to other properties of the same class by agents equipped with socially constituted schemes of perception and appreciation, functions as a symbolic property. It is therefore necessary to move beyond the opposition between a 'social physics' – which uses statistics in objectivist fashion to establish distributions (in both the statistical and economic senses), quantified expressions of the differential appropriation of a finite quantity of social energy by a large number of competing individuals, identified through 'objective indicators' – and a 'social semiology' which seeks to decipher meanings and bring to light the cognitive operations whereby agents produce and decipher them. We have to refuse the dichotomy between, on the one hand, the aim of arriving at an objective 'reality', 'independent of individual consciousnesses and wills', by breaking with common representations of the social world (Durkheim's 'pre-notions'), and of uncovering 'laws' – that is, significant (in the sense of non-random) relationships between distributions – and, on the other hand, the aim of grasping, not 'reality', but agents' representations of it, which are the whole 'reality' of a social world conceived 'as will and representation'.

In short, social science does not have to choose between that form of social physics, represented by Durkheim – who agrees with social semiology in acknowledging that one can only know 'reality' by applying logical instruments of classification[23] – and the idealist semiology which, undertaking to construct 'an account of accounts', as Harold Garfinkel puts it, can do no more than record the recordings of a social world which is ultimately no more than the product of mental, i.e., linguistic, structures. What we have to do is to bring into the science of scarcity, and of competition for scarce goods, the practical knowledge which the agents obtain for themselves by producing – on the basis of their experience of the distributions, itself dependent on their position in the distributions – divisions and classifications which are no less objective than those of the balance-sheets of social physics. In other words, we have to move beyond the opposition between objectivist theories which identify the social classes (but also the sex or age classes) with discrete groups, simple countable populations separated by boundaries objectively drawn in reality, and subjectivist (or marginalist) theories which reduce the 'social order' to a sort of collective classification obtained by aggregating the individual classifications or, more precisely, the individual strategies, classified and classifying, through which agents class themselves and others.[24]

One only has to bear in mind that goods are converted into distinctive signs, which may be signs of distinction but also of vulgarity, as soon as they are perceived relationally, to see that the representation which individuals and groups inevitably project through their practices and properties is an integral part of social reality. A class is defined as much by its *being-perceived* as by its *being*, by its consumption – which need not be conspicuous in order to be symbolic – as much as by its position in the relations of production (even if it is true that the latter governs the former). The Berkeleian – i.e., petit-bourgeois – vision which reduces social being to perceived being, to seeming, and which, forgetting that there is no need to give theatrical performances (*représentations*) in order to be the object of mental representations, reduces the social world to the sum of the (mental) representations which the various groups have of the theatrical performances put on by the other groups, has the virtue of insisting on the relative autonomy of the logic of symbolic representations with respect to the material determinants of socio-economic condition. The individual or collective classification struggles aimed at transforming the categories of perception and appreciation of the social world and, through this, the social world itself, are indeed a forgotten dimension of the class struggle. But one only has to realize that the classificatory schemes which underlie agents' practical relationship to their condition and the representation they have of it are themselves the product of that condition, in order to see the limits of this autonomy. Position in the classification struggle depends on position in the class structure; and social subjects – including intellectuals, who are not those best placed to grasp that which defines the limits of their thought of the social world, that is, the illusion of the absence of limits – are perhaps never less likely to transcend 'the limits of their minds' than in the representation they have and give of their position, which defines those limits.

Notes

1 I. Kant, *Anthropology from a Pragmatic Point of View* (Carbondale and Edwardsville: Southern Illinois University Press, 1978), p. 141.

2   G. W. Leibniz, 'Meditationes de cognitione, veritate et ideis' in *Opuscula Philosophica Selecta* (Paris: Boivin, 1939), pp. 1–2 (see also *Discours de Métaphysique*, par. 24). It is remarkable that to illustrate the idea of 'clear but confused' knowledge, Leibniz evokes, in addition to the example of colours, tastes and smells which we can distinguish 'by the simple evidence of the senses and not by statable marks', the example of painters and artists who can recognize a good or bad work but cannot justify their judgement except by invoking the presence or absence of a 'je ne sais quoi.'

3   It would be the task of a genetic sociology to establish how this sense of possibilities and impossibilities, proximities and distances is constituted.

4   Just as the opposition between the unique and the multiple lies at the heart of the dominant philosophy of history, so the opposition, which is a transfigured form of it, between the brilliant, the visible, the distinct, the distinguished, the 'outstanding', and the obscure, the dull, the greyness of the undifferentiated, indistinct, inglorious mass is one of the fundamental categories of the dominant perception of the social world.

5   See G. Duby, *Les trois ordres ou l'imaginaire du féodalisme* (Paris: Gallimard, 1978).

6   E. Durkheim, *Elementary Forms of the Religious Life* (London: Allen and Unwin, 1915), p. 17.

7   A more detailed account of the theoretical context of these analyses will be found in P. Bourdieu, "Symbolic Power" in *Identity and Structure*, ed. D. Gleeson (Driffield: Nafferton Books, 1977), pp. 112–19; also in *Critique of Anthropology*, 4 (Summer 1979), 77–85.

8   Cf. J.-P. Sartre, *Being and Nothingness* (London: Methuen, 1969), pp. 557–65, esp. 562.

9   See H. Giles, 'Accent Mobility: A Model and Some Data', *Anthropological Linguistics*, 15 (1973), 87–105.

10 See G. Lenski, 'American Social Classes: Statistical Strata or Social Groups?', *American Journal of Sociology*, 8 (September 1952), 139–44.

11 These divergences also emerge, in the same survey, when the respondents are first asked to define social classes at the level of their town and then at the level of the whole country; the rate of non-response rises strongly in the latter case, as does the number of classes perceived.

12 Ordinary perception, which applies to practices the scheme of the broad and the narrow, or the expansive and the constrained, anticipates the discoveries of the most refined social psychology, which establishes the existence of a correlation between the room one gives oneself in physical space and the place one occupies in social space. On this point, see S. Fisher and C. E. Cleveland, *Body Image and Personality* (New York: Van Nostrand, 1958).

13 This is true in the ordinary sense but also in the sense of Kafka [*procès* = 'process' but also 'trial' – cf. Kafka's *Die Prozess, The Trial, Le Procès* in French – translator], who offers an exemplary image of this desperate striving to regain a social identity that is by definition ungraspable, being the infinite limit of all categoremes, all imputations.

14 The sophism of the heap of wheat and all the paradoxes of physical continua mean, as Poincaré observed, that one has simultaneously $A = B$, $B = C$ and $A < C$, or again, $A_1 = A_2$, $A_2 = A_3$, … $A_{99} = A_{100}$ and $A_1 < A_{100}$. In other words, though it is clear that one grain does not make a heap, nor do two grains, or three, it is not easy to say whether the heap begins at 264 grains or 265; in other words, whether 265 grains make a heap, but not 264.

15 See P. Bourdieu and M. de Saint Martin, 'Les catégories de l'entendement professoral', *Actes*, 3 (1975), 68–93.

16 See Duby, *Les trois ordres*, esp. pp. 422–3.

17 Ibid., pp. 63–4, and 'Les "jeunes" dans la société aristocratique dans la France du Nord-Ouest au XIIème siècle', *Annales*, 19 (September–October 1964), 835–46.

18 Much the same could be said of women, were they not denied most of the advantages of renouncing responsibility, at least outside the bourgeoisie.

19 M. Billing and H. Tajfel, 'Social Categorization and Similarity in Inter-group Behaviour', *European Journal of Social Psychology*, 3 (1973), 27–52.

20 See, for example, H. Tajfel, 'Quantitative Judgement in Social Perception', *British Journal of Psychology*, 50 (1959), 16–21, and H. Tajfel and A. L. Wilkes, 'Classification and Quantitative Judgement', ibid., 54 (1963), 101–4; and for an overview of research in this area, W. Doise,

L'articulation psychosociologique et les relations entre groupes (Brussels: A. de Boeck, 1976), pp. 178–200.

21 'Wherever the groups and classes are set in sharp juxtaposition, the values and mores of each are juxtaposed. Out of group opposition there arises an intense opposition of values, which comes to be projected through the social order and serves to solidify social stratification.' L. Copeland, 'The Negro as a Contrast Conception' in E. Thompson (ed.), *Race Relations and the Race Problem* (Durham, NC: Duke University Press, 1959), pp. 152–79.

22 '. . . le pouvoir unificateur du nom, du mot d'ordre' – the unifying power of the name/noun, the rallying cry ('order word'). (Translator's note.)

23 One scarcely needs to point out the affinity between social physics and the positivist inclination to see classifications either as arbitrary, 'operational' divisions (such as age groups or income brackets) or as 'objective' cleavages (discontinuities in distributions or bends in curves) which only need to be recorded.

24 Here is a particularly revealing expression (even in its metaphor) of this social marginalism: 'Each individual is responsible for the demeanour image of himself and the deference image of others, so that for a complete man to be expressed, individuals must hold hands in a chain of ceremony, each giving deferentially with proper demeanour to the one on the right what will be received deferentially from the one on the left.' E. Goffmann, 'The Nature of Deference and Demeanour', *American Anthropologist*, 58 (June 1956), 473–502. '. . . routinely the question is that of whose opinion is voiced most frequently and most forcibly, who makes the minor ongoing decisions apparently required for the coordination of any joint activity, and whose passing concerns have been given the most weight. And however trivial some of these *little gains and losses* may appear to be, *by summing them all up* across all the social situations in which they occur, we can see that their total effect is enormous. The expression of subordination and domination through this swarm of situational means is more than a mere tracing or symbol or ritualistic affirmation of the social hierarchy. These expressions *considerably constitute* the hierarchy.' E. Goffmann, 'Gender Display'. (Paper presented at the Third International Symposium, 'Female Hierarchies', Harry Frank Guggenheim Foundation, April 3–5, 1974); italics mine.

PART FOUR

Post-structuralism, Deconstruction, Post-modernism

CHAPTER 1

Introduction: Introductory Deconstruction

Julie Rivkin and Michael Ryan

Around 1967 in Paris, Structuralism, which had dominated French intellectual life for much of the 1960s, was displaced by a new intellectual movement. The new thinking in philosophy, sociology, and literature that began to emerge around 1967 in the work of such French thinkers as Jacques Derrida, Julia Kristeva, Gilles Deleuze, Luce Irigaray, Hélène Cixous, Jean-François Lyotard, and Jean Baudrillard is usually referred to as Post-structuralism because it departed so radically from the core assumptions of Structuralism. In 1979, Lyotard wrote a book called *The Post-Modern Condition* that described the contemporary era as one in which the old "grand narratives" of the world, from Humanism to Marxism, had lost their validity and been replaced by a proliferation of "micro" stories. Lyotard borrowed the term "Post-Modernism" from US culture, where it had been used to describe a self-reflexive style of writing that broke with standard literary conventions. Almost immediately, "Post-modernism" began to be applied to both the contemporary era and to Post-structuralism.

Another term widely associated with Post-structuralism is "deconstruction." Deconstruction is the name of a method of critique developed by Jacques Derrida, a philosopher whose writing is central to the emergence of Post-structuralism. In 1967, he published three books that effectively put an end to Structuralism and launched a new era in French intellectual life. The books were *Writing and Difference, Of Grammatology*, and *Speech and Phenomenon*. The first was a collection of essays on philosophy and literature; the second a long critical reading of Lévi-Strauss, Saussure, and Rousseau; the third a "deconstruction" of the *Logical Investigations* of Edmund Husserl.

What did Derrida do that was so revolutionary? He began with the concept of difference that he found in the work of Friedrich Nietzsche, Martin Heidegger, and Ferdinand de Saussure. It recalled for him the work of Greek philosophers who stood outside the dominant Greek tradition of Aristotle and Plato. For Aristotle, knowledge consists of the analysis of objects in terms of their essences; Plato invented the "metaphysical" notion of an ideal realm of ideas that transcended or existed outside and apart from physical reality. The so-called "pre-Socratic" philosophers, on the other hand, were interested in the process of space and time that wove together all material objects in a "sumploke," or confluence, of being. They emphasized change over stasis and the blending together of things over their discreteness or separable identities.

Derrida brought these related strains of thought together. He began by focusing on Saussure's concept of the diacritical nature of the linguistic sign, according to which the identity of a sign is constituted by its differences from other signs. For this to be the case, according to Derrida, there had to be a more primordial process of differentiation at work that affected everything having to do with language, thought, and reality. His name for this more primordial process was *"différance,"* by which he meant a simultaneous process of deferment in time and difference in space. One present moment assumes past present moments as well as future present moments; to be "present," a present moment presupposes its difference from other presents. Similarly, the presence of an object of conscious perception or of a thought in the mind is shaped by its difference from other objects or thoughts. This simultaneous movement of temporal deferment and spatial difference, both ongoing processes that constitute being, are what Derrida means by *"différance."* Ideas and things are like signs in language; there are no identities, only differences.

This idea challenged the central assumptions of metaphysics. According to that tradition, the most fundamental or foundational components of knowledge and the criteria of truth were presence, substance, essence, and identity – not difference. True ideas were present to consciousness, and the essence of a thing consisted of its being fully present to itself. But such presence, according to Derrida, is produced by spatial differences and temporal delays, in short, by *différance*. When you point to a presence (of a thing or of an idea), you are referred to some other from which it differs. Each presence bears the "trace" of its others. When you see the world, what you see is not identities but a network of relations between things whose difference from one another allows them to appear to be separate and identifiable. What is present to the mind in conscious experience is a kind of ghost effect, a flickering of passing moments that are differentially constituted by their relations and their interconnectedness. They have no full, substantial presence (much as a flicking of cards of slightly different pictures of the same thing creates the effect of seeing the actual thing in motion).

The same is true of ideas in the mind. When philosophers think of a concept like "nature" that is distinct from "culture," they are in fact using concepts that could not exist as identities apart from their difference from one another. The difference between the two concepts must preexist the concepts. The concept of nature is simply the concept of culture differed and deferred. It is the *différance* of culture. One important implication of this insight is that if all things (all objects, ideas, and words) are produced as identities by their differences from other things, then a complete determination of identity (a statement of what something "is" fully and completely "in itself") would require an endless inventory of relations to other terms in a potentially infinite network of differences. Truth, as a result, will always be incomplete.

To say that reality and thought are differential is to say that they are like signs. Derrida noted that the structure of signification is a structure of difference. Signs refer to something else – an idea or an object – from which they differ. Either they represent an idea which they signify in order to mean something, or, they must substitute for the presence of an object in the world that they designate. In either case, the ideas and the objects are of a different order of being from signs. The identity, presence, and substance of the sign are constituted by or as difference. Moreover, all signifiers relate to an other – the signified – that makes their identity relational and differential. And all signifieds are in turn themselves differential; they too are signifiers. They consist of the reference from one thing to another. Reference inhabits reality and makes it possible.

If every object derives its identity from its difference from other objects, then every thing or object and every idea or concept refers to something else to be what it "is." Like signifiers, all things bear the "trace" of something to which they refer in an ongoing network of relays and references. The structure of signification is internal to reality and to thought. Yet signification is normally thought of as something added on to reality that stands outside its substantive presence. Reality is matter, and signification is a network of differences.

Yet, if all things are produced by difference, then the very criterion that separates signification in language from thought and reality – that it operates through the substitution of one thing for another and that the sign refers to something other in order to be what it "is" – no longer holds. Because the presence of a thing or of an idea depends on something other than itself, it too is a sign. To determine what an idea in the mind "is," one must shuttle from it to the others whose difference shapes it. Each one substitutes or stands in for the first, much as a sign stands in for the thing it designates.

What this suggests is that no presence or substance of an object or of an idea is complete in itself. Each presence requires supplementation by something else to which it refers or relates and from which it differs. This accounts for one of Derrida's more controversial ideas – that of the "supplement at the origin." By this, he meant that if one tries to grasp the presence of something, one encounters a difference, not something substantial. One term, an other, slips in through a differential relation and takes the place of the first. As a result, one must say that there is no "first." The second term takes its place immediately because the "first" depends on its difference from the second to "be" anything. Instead of an original presence, what one encounters is a supplementary relationship between terms.

Another way of putting this is to say that the movement of signification, whereby one thing refers to another in a relationship of difference, allows the presence of ideas and objects to come into being in the first place. Signification is therefore not something standing outside presence (the presence of ideas or of objects) that is added on later to an already intact and constituted presence. Presence cannot exist without being from the very outset caught up in the movement of difference and signification. In his early work, Derrida used the word "text" to refer to the way the structure of difference in reality resembles signification, and this accounts for his conclusion that all reality is "textual." That is, it is made possible by difference, the inter-supplementation of terms, the trace structure whereby one thing depends on others to be what it "is," and the referential character of identity.

That insight poses a threat to the metaphysical tradition in philosophy that Plato initiated. Metaphysical philosophy founded itself on the assumption that signification was an external contrivance added on to the substance of reality and to the ideality of thought. Metaphysics assumed especially that ideas exist apart from signs and that the presence that guarantees truth in the mind exists prior to all signification. It is this kind of belief that allowed, for example, the New Critics to claim that poetry embodies ideas that are universal. The New Criticism assumes that ideas are of a different ideal order than the physical and technical mechanisms of signification.

This kind of assumption, according to Derrida, is an inflection of the metaphysical tradition of philosophy that posited the possibility of a "transcendental signified," the possibility that ideas somehow exist apart from signification. Such ideas are not themselves signifiers; they exist outside the differential network that makes signification possible. Once this standard of transcendent truth is established, it becomes normative, a measure of value. In relation to its supposed truthfulness, a host of other terms associated with signification and connoting difference could be declared to be secondary and derivative, a falling away from the standard and a depletion of substance. They are often associated with immorality in the metaphysical tradition as well as with writing, that purely external, empty technique that bears no immediate relationship to the living voice of consciousness, that other criterion of truthfulness in the metaphysical tradition.

In criticizing this tradition, Derrida noticed that metaphysical philosophy's metaphors, the way it described its fundamental values, were supposed to be added on to that philosophy's truth, yet truth was created by using metaphors that were never accounted for. The most powerful of these metaphors was the spatial distinction between an inside and an outside. Derrida noted that the metaphysical system of thought simply took for granted that one could differentiate between an inside and an outside without recourse to a technique such as differentiation that had not been accounted for. The inside of thought and of reality was described as being present to itself, full, immediate, natural, true, substantive, and prior to all signifying substitution. The outside was described as the realm of signification that was added on to thought and to reality. The living voice of consciousness for this reason was declared superior to mere writing, an external artificial contrivance that was a dead letter, not a living, breathing presence. The substance of objects was conceived as an internal essence that owed nothing to external relations. But, Derrida noted, it is the act of spatial differentiation that allows one to think of inside and outside, truth and falsity, substance and representation, etc. in the first place. This act of spatial differentiation precedes and makes possible the foundations of metaphysics, its most basic values and ideals, ideals that supposedly sanctified the superiority and priority of identity to difference and of the interiority of mental ideas to the spatialization associated with external writing. It is not so much that the outside is declared to be inside in a simple inversion of premises; rather, a more primordial process of differentiation is shown to encompass both inside and outside so that the distinction between the two becomes untenable.

As a result of this argument, all the values of the metaphysical tradition had to be put in question because they all assumed the primacy and the priority of presence, substance, and identity as foundations while nonetheless describing the fact that difference, something insubstantial and nonpresent, made them possible. All of the categories and hierarchies that placed presence over difference, immediacy over mediation, identity over substitution, nature over culture, speech in the mind over external writing, essence over accident, substance over technology, etc., have to be rethought. It is no longer possible to characterize difference, substitution, repetition, and the like as nontruth if the truthfulness of true ideas, their presence in the mind as something palpable, present, and immediate, itself depends on difference and is produced by *différance*.

If one could not rigorously distinguish between the realm of signification and the realms of thought and reality because thought and reality are also differential, then the criterion for distinguishing signification from reality no longer holds, and the metaphysical value system collapses. The basis for a number of metaphysical prejudices was thereby discredited. The authentic, the original, the natural, the living, the immediate, and the present could no longer be declared normal, standard, and more true than terms connoting artifice, derivation, substitution, difference, and representational repetition. All of our notions of authenticity, originality, and the like that were sustained by the fiction of a truth completely separate from the structure of signification have to be rethought. In literature especially, it becomes important to reexamine all of those moments where virtue is described as what is authentic, present to itself, self-identical, aloof from signs, true, and real, while vice is described as what is artificial, changeable, infected by the ruses of signification, false, and unreal. According to Derrida, what one will find is that the authentic will itself prove to be an artifact, the original derivative, the self-identical a double, the natural itself contrived and conventional, substance itself form, etc.

Moreover, one can no longer assume, as New Critics did, for example, that signs are physical, while thought is spiritual or ideal, that one is a realm of artifice and representation, the other of universal truth. Literary texts do not harbor "transcendental signifieds," points where truth appears in a realm separated entirely from signifiers. Such apparent moments of meaning or truth also pertain to the order of signification and difference. They too are signifiers. To point to the presence of an idea, a truth, or a meaning in a work of literature is to point to something whose identity depends on its difference from other terms in an endless chain of supplements.

If the old metaphysical ideas regarding a transcendental signified that stands outside signifying substitution are disabled in this way, what results is a world in which the grounding of truth in some authority becomes much more difficult. If behind or within the old model of truth as a ground outside signification is merely more signification, then in essence, we have arrived at a conventionalist theory of truth. The notion that truth is a presence or essence in consciousness that is a ground of authority is no longer feasible. If such presence is inseparable from representation, then like representation, it is shaped by conventions regarding how those acts of representation work. It must be haggled over and settled on through agreements. It is not a natural substance that is self-identical and aloof from differences that shape it; rather it is a formal arrangement that is contingent on other things than "itself." What it is "in itself" is a performance or rehearsal of those conventions, codes, and agreements, which means, of course, that it is not really something "in itself."

We have spent so much time on Derrida's ideas because those ideas are central to what happened afterwards in the work of such thinkers as Irigaray, Cixous, Deleuze, and Lyotard. Their work reflects the shift Derrida engineered away from the centrality of consciousness in philosophical discussion and toward a sense that the world is a field of contingency, not natural order, that the identities of truth that philosophy takes for granted are unstable, that the truthful orders of value we live by may be rhetorical acts of linguistic meaning-making, rather than representations of preexisting truth, that the substance of thought and of reality conceals insubstantial processes that constitute them, etc. Deleuze's move from the arboresque to the rhizomatic, Kristeva's move from the symbolic to the semiotic, Lyotard's move from grand narratives to micro-narratives, Cixous and Irigaray's move from the phallocentric to the feminine – all bear the imprint of Derrida's move from substance, presence, and identity to *différance*.

CHAPTER 2

On Truth and Lying in an Extra-moral Sense

Friedrich Nietzsche

Doubts regarding the ability of the human mind to attain certain knowledge of the kind Positivism promised began to arise in the late nineteenth century. Positivism had so dominated the early nineteenth century that few questioned the ability of the mind to achieve a purely factual, scientific knowledge of the world. Using the very observations regarding perception that science itself produced, Friedrich Nietzsche (1844–1900), a German philosopher best known for his writings about early Greek philosophy, began to question in this early essay (1873) the assumptions regarding the certainty of knowledge that dominated his culture.

The intellect, as a means for the preservation of the individual, develops its chief power in dissimulation. . . . What indeed does man know about himself? Oh! that he could but once see himself complete, placed as it were in an illuminated glass-case! Does not nature keep secret from him most things, even about his body, e.g., the convolutions of the intestines, the quick flow of the blood-currents, the intricate vibrations of the fibers, so as to banish and lock him up in proud, delusive knowledge? Nature threw away the key; and woe to the fateful curiosity which might be able for a moment to look out and down through a crevice in the chamber of consciousness, and discover that man, indifferent to his own ignorance, is resting on the pitiless, the greedy, the insatiable, the murderous and, as it were, hanging in dreams on the back of a tiger? . . .

[W]hat after all are those conventions of language? Are they possibly products of knowledge, of the love of truth; do the designations and the things coincide? Is language the adequate expression of all realities?

Only by means of forgetfulness can man ever arrive at imagining that he possesses "truth" in that degree just indicated. If he does not mean to content himself with truth in the shape of tautology, that is, with empty husks, he will always obtain illusions instead of truth. What is a word? The expression of a nerve-stimulus in sounds. But to infer a cause outside us from the nerve-stimulus is already the result of a wrong and unjustifiable application of the proposition of causality. How should we dare, if truth with the genesis of language, if the point of view of certainty with the designations had alone been decisive; how indeed should we dare to say: the stone is hard; as if "hard" was known to us otherwise; and not merely as an entirely subjective stimulus. We divide things according to genders; we designate the tree as masculine [*der Baum* in German], the plant as feminine [*die Pflanze* in German]:

what arbitrary metaphors! How far flown beyond the canon of certainty! We speak of a "serpent"; the designation fits nothing but the sinuosity, and could therefore also appertain to the worm. What arbitrary demarcations! what one-sided preferences given sometimes to this, sometimes to that quality of a thing! The different languages placed side by side show that with words truth or adequate expression matters little: for otherwise there would not be so many languages. . . . A nerve-stimulus, first transformed into a percept! First metaphor! The percept again copied into a sound! Second metaphor! And each time he leaps completely out of one sphere right into the midst of an entirely different one. . . .

Let us especially think about the formation of ideas. Every word becomes at once an idea not by having, as one might presume, to serve as a reminder for the original experience happening but once and absolutely individualized, to which experience such word owes its origin, no, but by having simultaneously to fit innumerable, more or less similar (which really means never equal, therefore altogether unequal) cases. Every idea originates through equating the unequal. As certainly as no one leaf is exactly similar to any other, so certain is it that the idea "leaf" has been formed through an arbitrary omission of these individual differences, through a forgetting of the differentiating qualities, and this idea now awakens the notion that in nature there is, besides the leaves, a something called "the leaf," perhaps a primal form according to which all leaves were woven, drawn, accurately measured, colored, crinkled, painted, but by unskilled hands, so that no copy had turned out correct and trustworthy as a true copy of the primal form. . . .

What therefore is truth? A mobile army of metaphors, metonymies, anthropomorphisms: in short a sum of human relations which became poetically and rhetorically intensified, metamorphosed, adorned, and after long usage seem to a notion fixed, canonic, and binding; truths are illusions of which one has forgotten that they *are* illusions; worn-out metaphors which have become powerless to affect the senses; coins which have their obverse effaced and now are no longer of account as coins but merely as metal.

Still we do not yet know whence the impulse to truth comes, for up to now we have heard only about the obligation which society imposes in order to exist: to be truthful, that is, to use the usual metaphors, therefore expressed morally: we have heard only about the obligation to lie according to a fixed convention, to lie gregariously in a style binding for all. Now man of course forgets that matters are going thus with him; he therefore lies in that fashion pointed out unconsciously and according to habits of centuries' standing – and by *this very unconsciousness*, by this very forgetting, he arrives at a sense for truth. Through this feeling of being obliged to designate one thing as "red," another as "cold," a third one as "dumb," awakes a moral emotion relating to truth. Out of the antithesis "liar" whom nobody trusts, whom all exclude, man demonstrates to himself the venerableness, reliability, usefulness of truth. Now as a "*rational*" being he submits his actions to the sway of abstractions; he no longer suffers himself to be carried away by sudden impressions, by sensations, he first generalizes all these impressions into paler, cooler ideas, in order to attach to them the ship of his life and actions. Everything which makes man stand out in bold relief against the animal depends on this faculty of volatilizing the concrete metaphors into a schema, and therefore resolving a perception into an idea. For within the range of those schemata a something becomes possible that never could succeed under the first perceptual impressions: to build up a pyramidal order with castes and grades, to create a new world of laws, privileges, sub-orders, delimitations, which now stands opposite the other perceptual world of first impressions and assumes the appearance of being the more fixed, general, known, human of the two and therefore the regulating and imperative one. Whereas every metaphor of perception is individual and without its equal and therefore knows how to escape all attempts to classify it, the great edifice of ideas shows the rigid regularity of a Roman Columbarium and in logic breathes forth the sternness and coolness which we find in mathematics. He who has been breathed upon by this coolness will scarcely believe that the idea too, bony and hexahedral, and permutable as a die, remains however only as the *residuum of a metaphor*, and that the illusion of the artistic metamorphosis of a nerve-stimulus into percepts is, if not the mother, then the grandmother of every idea. Now in this game of dice, "Truth" means to use every die as it is designated, to count its points carefully, to form exact classifications, and never to violate the order of castes and the sequences of rank. . . .

One may here well admire man, who succeeded in piling up an infinitely complex dome of ideas on a movable foundation and as it were on running water, as a powerful genius of architecture. Of course in order to obtain hold on such a foundation it must be as an edifice piled up out of cobwebs, so fragile, as to be carried away by the waves: so firm, as not to be blown asunder by every wind. In this way man as an architectural genius rises high above the bee; she builds with wax, which she brings together out of nature; he with the much more delicate material of ideas, which he must first manufacture within himself. He is very much to be admired here – but not on account of his impulse for truth, his bent for pure cognition of things. If somebody hides a thing behind a bush, seeks it again and finds it in the self-same place, then there is not much to boast of, respecting this seeking and finding; thus, however, matters stand with the seeking and finding of "truth" within the realm of reason. If I make the definition of the mammal and then declare after inspecting a camel, "Behold a mammal," then no doubt a truth is brought to light thereby, but it is of very limited value, I mean it is anthropomorphic through and through, and does not contain one single point which is "true-in-itself," real and universally valid, apart from man. The seeker after such truths seeks at the bottom only the metamorphosis of the world in man, he strives for an understanding of the world as a human-like thing and by his battling gains at best the feeling of an assimilation. Similarly, as the astrologer contemplated the stars in the service of man and in connection with their happiness and unhappiness, such a seeker contemplates the whole world as related to man, as the infinitely protracted echo of an original sound: man; as the multiplied copy of the one arch-type: man. His procedure is to apply man as the measure of all things, whereby he starts from the error of believing that he has these things immediately before him as pure objects. He therefore forgets that the original metaphors of perception are metaphors, and takes them for the things themselves.

Only by forgetting that primitive world of metaphors, only by the congelation and coagulation of an original mass of similes and percepts pouring forth as a fiery liquid out of the primal faculty of human fancy, only by the invincible faith, that *this* sun, *this* window, *this* table is a truth in itself: in short, only by the fact that man forgets himself as subject, and what is more as an *artistically creating* subject: only by all this does he live with some repose, safety, and consequence. If he were able to get out of the prison walls of this faith, even for an instant only, his "self-consciousness" would be destroyed at once. Already it costs him some trouble to admit to himself that the insect and the bird perceive a world different from his own, and that the question, which of the two world-perceptions is more accurate, is quite a senseless one, since to decide this question it would be necessary to apply the standard of *right perception*, i.e. to apply a standard which *does not exist*. On the whole it seems to me that the "right perception" – which would mean the adequate expression of an object in the subject – is a nonentity full of contradictions: for between two utterly different spheres, as between subject and object, there is no causality, no accuracy, no expression, but at the utmost an aesthetical relation, I mean a suggestive metamorphosis, a stammering translation into quite a distinct foreign language, for which purpose however there is needed at any rate an intermediate sphere, an intermediate force, freely composing and freely inventing.

CHAPTER 3

The Will to Power

Friedrich Nietzsche

Nietzsche died before being able to complete what was to be his major work, *The Will to Power* (1885–6). In it, he argues that the essential drive in all life is a yearning for mastery. Nietzsche links this yearning to knowledge. When we know the world, we master its temporally fluid and spatially diverse reality by fixing identities with words. For Nietzsche, philosophical courage consists of being able to tolerate the nonidentical and meaningless character of existence without having to resort to words that posit identities or meanings in things. The world merely exists (what he calls the "eternal return" of the same), and there is no theological origin or conclusion to history. This skepticism regarding the likelihood of a separate spiritual realm in existence carries over into Post-Structuralism, which also questions the more secular versions of this ideal of transcendence, especially the notion that the realm of meaning is essentially distinct from the realm of signification. When the Post-Structuralists declare that there is no "transcendental signified," they are echoing Nietzsche's claim that there is teleology, no theological origin or goal to the world.

499

"Thinking" in primitive conditions (pre-organic) is the crystallization of forms, as in the case of crystal. – In *our* thought, the essential feature is fitting new material into old schemas ("Procrustes" = bed), *making* equal what is new.

500

... The same equalizing and ordering force that rules in the idioplasm, rules also in the incorporation of the outer world: our sense perceptions are already the result of this assimilation and equalization in regard to *all* the past in us; they do not follow directly upon the "impression" –

501

All thought, judgment, perception, considered as comparison, has as its precondition a "*positing* of equality," and earlier still a "*making* equal." The process of making equal is the same as the process of incorporation of appropriated material in the amoeba.

511

Equality and similarity.

1 The coarser organ sees much apparent equality;
2 the mind *wants* equality, i.e., to subsume a sense impression into an existing series: in the same way as the body *assimilates* inorganic matter.

Toward an understanding of logic: *the will to equality is the will to power* – the belief that something is thus and thus (the essence of *judgment*) is the consequence of a will that things as much as possible *shall be* equal.

512

Logic is bound to the condition: assume there are identical cases. In fact, to make possible logical thinking and inferences, this condition must first be treated fictitiously as fulfilled. That is: the will to logical truth can be carried through only after a fundamental *falsification* of all events is assumed. From which it follows that a drive rules here that is capable of employing both means, firstly falsification, then the implementation of its own point of view: logic does *not* spring from the will to truth.

513

The inventive force that invented categories labored in the service of our needs, namely of our need for security, for quick understanding on the basis of signs and sounds, for means of abbreviation: "substance," "subject," "object," "being," "becoming" have nothing to do with metaphysical truths. –

It is the powerful who made the names of things into law, and among the powerful it is the greatest artists in abstraction who created the categories.

514

A morality, a mode of living tried and *proved* by long experience and testing, at length enters consciousness as a law, as *dominating* – And therewith the entire group of related values and states enters into it: it becomes venerable, unassailable, holy, true; it is part of its development that its origin should be forgotten – That is a sign it has become master –

Exactly the same thing could have happened with the categories of reason: they could have prevailed, after much groping and fumbling, through their relative utility – There came a point when one collected them together, raised them to consciousness as a whole – and when one commanded them, i.e., when they had the effect of a command – From then on, they counted as a priori, as beyond experience, as irrefutable. And yet perhaps they represent nothing more than the expediency of a certain race and species – their utility alone is their "truth" –

515

Not "to know" but to schematize – to impose upon chaos as much regularity and form as our practical needs require. . . .

516

We are unable to affirm and to deny one and the same thing: this is a subjective empirical law, not the expression of any "necessity" but only of an inability.

If, according to Aristotle, the law of contradiction is the most certain of all principles, if it is the ultimate and most basic, upon which every demonstrative proof rests, if the principle of every axiom lies in it; then one should consider all the more rigorously what *presuppositions* already lie at the bottom of it. Either it asserts something about actuality, about being, as if one already knew this from another source; that is, as if opposite attributes *could* not be ascribed to it. Or the proposition means: opposite attributes *should* not be ascribed to it. In that case, logic would be an imperative, not to know the true, but to posit and arrange a world that shall be called true by us.

In short, the question remains open: are the axioms of logic adequate to reality or are they a means and measure for us to *create* reality, the concept "reality," for ourselves? – To affirm the former one would, as already said, have to have a previous knowledge of being – which is certainly not the case. The proposition therefore contains no *criterion of truth*, but an *imperative* concerning that which *should* count as true. . . .

517

In order to think and infer it is necessary to assume beings: logic handles only formulas for what remains the same. That is why this assumption would not be proof of reality: "beings" are part of our perspective. The "ego" as a being (– not affected by becoming and development).

The fictitious world of subject, substance, "reason," etc., is needed – : there is in us a power to order, simplify, falsify, artificially distinguish. "Truth" is the will to be master over the multiplicity of sensations: – to classify phenomena into definite categories. In this we start from a belief in the "in-itself" of things (we take phenomena as *real*).

The character of the world in a state of becoming as incapable of formulation, as "false," as "self-contradictory." Knowledge and becoming exclude one another. Consequently, "knowledge" must be something else: there must first of all be a will to make knowable, a kind of becoming must itself create the deception of beings . . .

542

If the character of existence should be false – which would be possible – what would truth, all our truth, be then? – An unconscionable falsification of the false? The false raised to a higher power? –

543

In a world that is essentially false, truthfulness would be an antinatural tendency: such a tendency could have meaning only as a means to a higher power of falsehood. In order for a world of the true, of being, to be invented, the truthful man would first have to be created (including the fact that such a man believes himself "truthful").

Simple, transparent, not in contradiction with himself, durable, remaining always the same, without wrinkle, fold, concealment, form: a man of this kind conceives a world of being as "God" in his own image.

For truthfulness to be possible, the whole sphere of man must be very clean, small, and respectable; advantage in every sense must be with the truthful man. – Lies, deception, dissimulation must arouse astonishment – . . .

552

When one has grasped that the "subject" is not something that creates effects, but only a fiction, much follows.

It is only after the model of the subject that we have invented the reality of things and projected them into the medley of sensations. If we no longer believe in the effective subject, then belief also disappears in effective things, in reciprocation, cause and effect between those phenomena that we call things.

There also disappears, of course, the world of effective atoms: the assumption of which always depended on the supposition that one needed subjects.

At last, the "thing-in-itself" also disappears, because this is fundamentally the conception of a "subject-in-itself." But we have grasped that the subject is a fiction. The antithesis "thing-in-itself" and "appearance" is untenable; with that, however, the concept "appearance" also disappears.

If we give up the effective subject, we also give up the object upon which effects are produced. Duration, identity with itself, being are inherent neither in that which is called subject nor in that which is called object: they are complexes of events apparently durable in comparison with other complexes – e.g., through the difference in tempo of the event (rest–motion, firm–loose: opposites that do not exist in themselves and that actually express only variations in degree that from a certain perspective appear to be opposites. There are no opposites: only from those of logic do we derive the concept of opposites – and falsely transfer it to things).

If we give up the concept "subject" and "object," then also the concept "substance" – and as a consequence also the various modifications of it, e.g., "matter," "spirit," and other hypothetical entities, "the eternity and immutability of matter," etc. We have got rid of *materiality*.

From the standpoint of morality, the world is false. But to the extent that morality itself is a part of this world, morality is false.

Will to truth is a making firm, a making true and durable, an abolition of the false character of things, a reinterpretation of it into beings. "Truth" is therefore not something there, that might be found or discovered – but something that must be created and that gives a name to a process, or rather to a will to overcome that has in itself no end – introducing truth, as a *processus in infinitum*, an active determining – not a becoming conscious of something that is in itself firm and determined. It is a word for the "will to power."

Life is founded upon the premise of a belief in enduring and regularly recurring things; the more powerful life is, the wider must be the knowable world to which we, as it were, attribute being. Logicizing, rationalizing, systematizing as expedients of life.

Man projects his drive to truth, his "goal" in a certain sense, outside himself as a world that has being, as a metaphysical world, as a "thing-in-itself," as a world already in existence. His needs as creator to invent the world upon which he works, anticipate it; this anticipation (this "belief" in truth) is his support...

Man seeks "the truth": a world that is not self-contradictory, not deceptive, does not change, a *true* world – a world in which one does not suffer; contradiction, deception, change – causes of suffering! He does not doubt that a world as it ought to be exists; he would like to seek out the road to it. (Indian critique: even the "ego" as apparent, as not real.)

Whence does man here derive the concept reality? – Why is it that he derives *suffering* from change, deception, contradiction? and why not rather his happiness? –

Contempt, hatred for all that perishes, changes, varies – whence comes this valuation of that which remains constant? Obviously, the will to truth is here merely the desire for a world of the constant.

The senses deceive, reason corrects the errors; consequently, one concluded, reason is the road to the constant; the least sensual ideas must be closest to the "true world." – It is from the senses that most misfortunes come – they are deceivers, deluders, destroyers. –

Happiness can be guaranteed only by being; change and happiness exclude one another. The highest desire therefore contemplates unity with what has being. This is the formula for: the road to the highest happiness.

In summa: the world as it ought to be exists; this world, in which we live, is an error – this world of ours ought not to exist.

Belief in what has being is only a consequence: the real *primum mobile* is disbelief in becoming, mistrust of becoming, the low valuation of all that becomes –

What kind of man reflects in this way? An unproductive, suffering kind, a kind weary of life. If we imagine the opposite kind of man, he would not need to believe in what has being; more, he would despise it as dead, tedious, indifferent –

The belief that the world as it ought to be is, really exists, is a belief of the unproductive who do *not desire to create a world* as it ought to be. They posit it as already available, they seek ways and means of reaching it. "Will to truth" – *as the failure of the will to create....*

Whoever is incapable of laying his will into things, lacking will and strength, at least lays some *meaning* into them, i.e., the faith that there is a will in them already.

It is a measure of the degree of strength of will to what extent one can do without meaning in things, to what extent one can endure to live in a meaningless world *because one organizes a small portion of it oneself....*

Overthrowing of philosophers through the destruction of the world of being: intermediary period of nihilism: before there is yet present the strength to reverse values and to deify becoming and the apparent world as the only world, and to call them good...

CHAPTER 4

Identity and Difference

Martin Heidegger

With Friedrich Nietzsche, Martin Heidegger (1889–1976) played a crucial role in the development of Derrida's deconstructive philosophy. Heidegger in *Being and Time* (1937) situated philosophy in the world of existence and displaced the purely rationalist focus that had preoccupied philosophy for several centuries. In this selection from his essay "Identity and Difference" (1957), he elaborates on the necessity of difference to any determination of identity.

Metaphysics thinks Existence as such, in general. Metaphysics thinks Existence as such, that is, in the Whole. Metaphysics thinks the Being of Existence in the fathoming unity of the greatest generality, that is, the universal equi-valence, as well as in the understanding unity of totality, which is highest above all else. Thus, we presuppose the Being of Existence as authenticating reason. Hence, all metaphysics is, basically, the fathoming from the very bottom, reasoning which renders account of the ground, replies, and finally calls it to account....

[A]lways and everywhere Being means the Being of Existence...

[I]n the case of the Being of Existence and the Existence of Being we are concerned every time with a difference.

We think of Being, therefore, as object only when we think it as different from Existence and think Existence as different from Being. Thus difference proper emerges. If we attempt to form an image of it, we shall discover that we are immediately tempted to comprehend difference as a relation which our thinking has added to Being and to Existence. As a result, difference is reduced to a distinction, to a product of human intelligence.

However, let us assume for once that difference is an addition resulting from our forming of a mental image, then the problem arises: An addition to what? And the answer we get is: to Existence. Well and good. But what do we mean by this "Existence"? What else do we mean by it than such as it is? Thus we accommodate the alleged addition, the idea of a difference, under Being. Yet, "Being" itself proclaims: Being which is *Existence*. Wherever we would introduce difference as an alleged addition, we always meet Existence and Being in their difference.... Existence and Being, each in its own way, are to be discovered through and in difference... What we call difference we find everywhere and at all times in the object of thought, in Existence as such, and we come up against it in a manner so free of doubt that we do not pay any particular attention to it.... What is the meaning of this oft-mentioned Being? If under these conditions Being exhibits itself as a being of…, in the genitive of difference, then the question just asked would be more to the point if rephrased: What in your opinion is difference if both Being as well as Existence each in their own way appear *through difference*? …

What is at stake is really the object of thought more objectively considered…In other words, it is Being thought of as emerging from difference.…

What we are now primarily concerned with in our undertaking is gaining an insight into the possibility of thinking of difference as an issue which is to clarify in how far the onto-theological constitution of metaphysics derives its original essence from the issue which we meet at the beginning of the history of metaphysics, runs through its periods and yet remains everywhere hidden, and hence forgotten, as the issue in an oblivion which escapes even us.

CHAPTER 5

Heterology

Georges Bataille

Georges Bataille, an independent scholar who never held an academic position, played an important role in the development of Post-Structuralist thinking. His interest in anthropology, especially in the seminal work of Marcel Mauss, *The Gift* (1925), inspired him to develop the concept of an economy based on "expenditure without reserve" (without holding back or return). Post-Structuralists like Derrida found in this concept a prefiguration of their own notions of an excess of differential relations that overruns the bounds of meaning and truth. Bataille was also interested in liminal experiences where a culture's homogeneous interior met, was repelled by, and expelled an exterior that was heterogeneous. Usually, that outside was conceived as being a realm of madness, sexual excess, and non-utilitarian and wasteful behavior. Bataille noticed a curious affinity between the "waste" of a culture and the "sacred," since both are considered to be purely exterior to normal life. The following selection was written in 1930, but much of Bataille's important work, such as *The Cursed Share* (1949) and *Eroticism* (1957), was written later.

Appropriation and Excretion

1   The division of social facts into religious facts (prohibitions, obligations, and the realization of sacred action) on the one hand and profane facts (civil, political, juridical, industrial, and commercial organization) on the other, even though it is not easily applied to primitive societies and lends itself in general to a certain number of confusions, can nevertheless serve as the basis for the determination of two polarized human impulses: EXCRETION and APPROPRIATION....

   The process of appropriation is characterized by a homogeneity (static equilibrium) of the author of the appropriation, and of objects as final result, whereas excretion presents itself as the result of a heterogeneity, and can move in the direction of an ever greater heterogeneity, liberating impulses whose ambivalence is more and more pronounced. The latter case is represented by, for example, sacrificial consumption in the elementary form of the orgy, which has no other goal than the incorporation in the person of irreducibly heterogeneous elements, insofar as such elements risk provoking an increase of force (or more exactly an increase of *mana*)....

4   Man does not only appropriate his food, but also the different products of his activity: clothes, furniture, dwellings, and instruments of production. Finally, he appropriates land divided into parcels. Such appropriations take place by means of a more or less conventional homogeneity (identity) established between the possessor

and the object possessed. It involves sometimes a personal homogeneity that in primitive times could only be solemnly destroyed with the aid of an excretory rite, and sometimes a general homogeneity, such as that established by the architect between a city and its inhabitants.

In this respect, production can be seen as the excretory phase of a process of appropriation, and the same is true of selling.

5   The homogeneity of the kind realized in cities between men and that which surrounds them is only a subsidiary form of a much more consistent homogeneity, which man has established throughout the external world by everywhere replacing *a priori* inconceivable objects with classified series of conceptions or ideas. The identification of all the elements of which the world is composed has been pursued with a constant obstinacy, so that scientific conceptions, as well as the popular conceptions of the world, seem to have voluntarily led to a representation as different from what could have been imagined *a priori* as the public square of a capital is from a region of high mountains.

This last appropriation – the work of philosophy as well as of science or common sense – has included phases of revolt and scandal, but it has always had as its goal the establishment of the homogeneity of the world, and it will only be able to lead to a terminal phase in the sense of excretion when the irreducible waste products of the operation are determined.

Philosophy, Religion, and Poetry in Relation to Heterology

6   The interest of philosophy resides in the fact that, in opposition to science or common sense, it must positively envisage the waste products of intellectual appropriation. Nevertheless, it most often envisages these waste products only in abstract forms of totality (nothingness, infinity, the absolute), to which it itself cannot give a positive content; it can thus freely proceed in speculations that more or less have as a goal, all things considered, the *sufficient* identification of an endless world with a finite world, an unknowable (noumenal) world with the known world.

Only an intellectual elaboration in a religious form can, in its periods of autonomous development, put forward the waste products of appropriative thought as the definitively heterogeneous (sacred) object of speculation....

Religion thus differs from a practical and theoretical *heterology*[1] (even though both are equally concerned with sacred or excremental facts), not only in that the former excludes the scientific rigor proper to the latter (which generally appears as different from religion as chemistry is from alchemy), but also in that, under normal conditions, it betrays the needs that it was not only supposed to regulate, but satisfy....

The Heterological Theory of Knowledge

9   When one says that heterology scientifically considers questions of heterogeneity, one does not mean that heterology is, in the usual sense of such a formula, the science of the heterogeneous. The heterogeneous is even resolutely placed outside the reach of scientific knowledge, which by definition is only applicable to homogeneous elements. Above all, heterology is opposed to any homogeneous representation of the world, in other words, to any philosophical system. The goal of such represen-

tations is always the deprivation of our universe's sources of excitation and the development of a servile human species, fit only for the fabrication, rational consumption, and conservation of products. But the intellectual process automatically limits itself by producing of its own accord its own waste products, thus liberating in a disordered way the heterogeneous excremental element. Heterology is restricted to taking up again, consciously and resolutely, this terminal process which up until now has been seen as the abortion and the shame of human thought.

In that way it [heterology] leads to the complete reversal of the philosophical process, which ceases to be the instrument of appropriation, and now serves excretion; it introduces the demand for the violent gratifications implied by social life.

10   Only, on the one hand, the process of limitation and, on the other, the study of the violently alternating reactions of antagonism (expulsion) and love (reabsorption) obtained by positing the heterogeneous element, lie within the province of heterology as science. This element itself remains indefinable and can only be determined through negation. The specific character of fecal matter or of the specter, as well as of unlimited time or space, can only be the object of a series of negations, such as the absence of any possible common denominator, irrationality, etc. It must even be added that there is no way of placing such elements in the immediate objective human domain, in the sense that the pure and simple objectification of their specific character would lead to their incorporation in a homogeneous intellectual system, in other words, to a hypocritical cancellation of the excremental character. . . .

As soon as the effort at rational comprehension ends in contradiction, the practice of intellectual scatology requires the excretion of unassimilable elements, which is another way of stating vulgarly that a burst of laughter is the only imaginable and definitively terminal result – and not the means – of philosophical speculation. And then one must indicate that a reaction as *insignificant* as a burst of laughter derives from the extremely vague and distant character of the intellectual domain, and that it suffices to go from a speculation resting on abstract facts to a practice whose mechanism is not different, but which immediately reaches concrete heterogeneity, in order to arrive at ecstatic trances and orgasm.

Principles of Practical Heterology

13   Excretion is not simply a middle term between two appropriations, just as decay is not simply a middle term between the grain and the ear of wheat. The inability to consider in this latter case decay as an end in itself is the result not precisely of the human viewpoint but of the specifically intellectual viewpoint (to the extent that this viewpoint is in practice subordinate to a process of appropriation). . . .

[I]t is necessary to posit the limits of science's inherent tendencies and to constitute a knowledge of the *non-explainable, difference*, which supposes the immediate access of the intellect to a body of material prior to any intellectual reduction. Tentatively, it is enough to present the facts according to their nature and, with a view to defining the term *heterogeneous*, to introduce the following considerations:

1   Just as, in religious sociology, *mana* and *taboo* designate forms restricted to the particular applications of a more general form, the *sacred*, so may the *sacred* itself be considered as a restricted form of the *heterogeneous* . . .

2 Beyond the properly sacred things that constitute the common realm of religion or magic, the *heterogeneous* world includes everything resulting from *unproductive* expenditure[2] (sacred things themselves form part of this whole). This consists of everything rejected by *homogeneous* society as waste or as superior transcendent value. Included are the waste products of the human body and certain analogous matter (trash, vermin, etc.); the parts of the body; persons, words, or acts having a suggestive erotic value; the various unconscious processes such as dreams or neuroses; the numerous elements or social forms that *homogeneous* society is powerless to assimilate: mobs, the warrior, aristocratic and impoverished classes, different types of violent individuals or at least those who refuse the rule (madmen, leaders, poets, etc.);

3 Depending upon the person *heterogeneous* elements will provoke affective reactions of varying intensity, and it is possible to assume that the object of any affective reaction is necessarily *heterogeneous* (if not generally, at least with regard to the subject). There is sometimes attraction, sometimes repulsion, and in certain circumstances, any object of repulsion can become an object of attraction and vice versa;

4 *Violence, excess, delirium, madness* characterize heterogeneous elements to varying degrees: active, as persons or mobs, they result from breaking the laws of social *homogeneity*. This characteristic does not appropriately apply to inert objects, yet the latter do present a certain conformity with extreme emotions (if it is possible to speak of the violent and excessive nature of a decomposing body);

5 The reality of *heterogeneous* elements is not of the same order as that of *homogeneous* elements. *Homogeneous* reality presents itself with the abstract and neutral aspect of strictly defined and identified objects (basically, it is the specific reality of solid objects). *Heterogeneous* reality is that of a force or shock. It presents itself as a charge, as a value, passing from one object to another in a more or less abstract fashion, almost as if the change were taking place not in the world of objects but only in the judgments of the subject. The preceding aspect nevertheless does not signify that the observed facts are to be considered as subjective: thus, the action of the objects of erotic activity is manifestly rooted in their objective nature. Nonetheless, in a disconcerting way, the subject does have the capacity to displace the exciting value of one element onto an analogous or neighboring one.[3] In heterogeneous reality, the symbols charged with affective value thus have the same importance as the fundamental elements, and the part can have the same value as the whole. It is easy to note that, since the structure of knowledge for a *homogeneous* reality is that of science, the knowledge of a *heterogeneous* reality as such is to be found in the mystical thinking of primitives and in dreams: it is identical to the structure of the *unconscious*.[4]

6 In summary, compared to everyday life, *heterogeneous* existence can be represented as something *other*, as *incommensurate*, by charging these words with the *positive* value they have in *affective* experience.

Notes

1 The science of what is completely other. The term *agiology* would perhaps be more precise, but one would have to catch the double meaning of *agio* (analogous to the double meaning of *sacer*, *soiled* as well as *holy*). But it is above all the term *scatology* (the science of excrement) that retains in the present circumstances (the specialization of the sacred) an incontestable expressive value as the doublet of an abstract term such as *heterology*.

2 Cf. G. Bataille, "La notion de dépense," in *La Critique sociale* 7 (January 1933), p. 302.

3   It appears that the displacements are produced under the same conditions as are Pavlov's
    conditioned reflexes.
4   On the primitive mind, cf. Lévy-Bruhl, *La Mentalité primitive*; Cassirer, *Das mythische Denken*;
    on the unconscious, cf. Freud, *The Interpretation of Dreams*.

CHAPTER 6

Différance[1]

Jacques Derrida

In his 1968 essay, "Différance," Derrida describes the process of spatial and temporal movement that he claims makes all thought and all reality possible. To justify it, he draws on the work of Saussure, Heidegger, and Nietzsche. He also alludes to the work of the pre-Socratic philosophers such as Anaximander.

Saussure argued that there is no substance in language. All language consists of differences. In language there are only forms, not substances, and by that he meant that all apparently substantive units of language are generated by other things that lie outside them, but these external characteristics are actually internal to their make-up. A "form" is something external that shapes material into a particular identity or substance. All elements of language have identity only in so much as they are produced by a network of differences, and each element will itself consist of further differentiations, endlessly.

Derrida contends that thought and our perception of reality are governed by similar processes. Traditional philosophy held that we see actual presences and substances in the world and that our ideas have presence and substance that guarantees their truthfulness. Derrida set about demonstrating that ideas especially are like units of language; they are generated by difference; they have no substance apart from the networks of differences (each bearing the traces of other elements and other differences) that generate them as effects. But of course, as in language, those processes that generate them do not have a palpable or graspable presence of their own. Like forms, they are empty, nonpresent, and nonsubstantive.

In this essay, he uses two axes to talk about the work of difference that produces presence as an effect that the mind then mistakenly assumes is a substance that guarantees truthfulness. The first is time. When we think of anything, we cannot grasp it in the "present moment," because that present moment is always passing away. Presence is shadowed by the death of presence, its shuttling past the mind into the oblivion of the past. Similarly, any current present moment bears in it the future present moments toward which it is moving. The differences between these "presents" constitute the "present" we attempt to grasp as something substantive before our minds. The second axis is space, and the same process of difference haunts the idea of a spatially determinate identity of presence. Any spatially locatable object of thought or idea has an identity or presence of its own only by differing from other things.

Another term for this operation of difference that shadows presence is "trace." All ideas and all objects of thought and perception bear the trace of other things, other moments, other "presences." To bear the trace of other things is to be shadowed by "alterity," which literally means "otherness."

Derrida concludes this essay by evoking the pre-Socratic notion of the "sumploke" or "confluence of being." What the concept of differance leads to is a sense that everything in existence is relationally connected. We can sort it out into parts, but we should not assume those parts are pure and original or that they are pure identities. They are the effects of other processes of relation and differentiation. Derrida will elsewhere argue that what this means is that all things are signs and that all reality is "textual," in that all parts refer to or signify other parts, which are themselves signifiers of other parts. If we bear in mind the traditional definition of writing as the sign of a sign (the written sign of mental speech), then all reality is in a sense *graphic*, a form of writing. At the origin of thought is not a purely present idea but rather what Derrida calls "archi-writing," and by that he means the process he here describes as the spatio-temporal movement of "differance."

Derrida brings Saussure's notion of difference to bear on philosophical concepts. Like signs in language, he argues, they too are given identity by their differences from one another. He famously notes that philosophical oppositions such as the intelligible and the sensible, nature and culture, the ideal and physical, etc. can be shown to be produced by differance. Many literary critics have mistakenly limited deconstruction to this "undoing of binary opposition," but the questioning of oppositions is only one part of Derrida's undertaking, which aims to put in question the values and assumptions of the metaphysical philosophical tradition.

The verb "to differ" [*différer*] seems to differ from itself. On the one hand, it indicates difference as distinction, inequality, or discernibility; on the other, it expresses the interposition of delay, the interval of a *spacing* and *temporalizing* that puts off until "later" what is presently denied, the possible that is presently impossible. Sometimes the *different* and sometimes the *deferred* correspond [in French] to the verb "to differ." This correlation, however, is not simply one between act and object, cause and effect, or primordial and derived.

In the one case "to differ" signifies nonidentity; in the other case it signifies the order of the *same*. Yet there must be a common, although entirely differant[2] [*différante*], root within the sphere that relates the two movements of differing to one another. We provisionally give the name *differance* to this *sameness* which is not *identical*: by the silent writing of its *a*, it has the desired advantage of referring to differing, *both* as spacing/temporalizing and as the movement that structures every dissociation.

As distinct from difference, differance thus points out the irreducibility of temporalizing (which is also temporalization – in transcendental language which is no longer adequate here, this would be called the constitution of primordial temporality – just as the term "spacing" also includes the constitution of primordial spatiality). Differance is not simply active (any more than it is a subjective accomplishment); it rather indicates the middle voice, it precedes and sets up the opposition between passivity and activity. With its *a*, differance more properly refers to what in classical language would be called the origin or production of differences and the differences between differences, the *play* [*jeu*] of differences. Its locus and operation will therefore be seen wherever speech appeals to difference.

Différance is neither a *word* nor a *concept*. In it, however, we shall see the juncture rather than the summation – of what has been most decisively inscribed in the thought of what is conveniently called our "epoch": the difference of forces in Nietzsche, Saussure's principle of semiological difference, differing as the possibility of [neurone] facilitation,[3] impression and delayed effect in Freud, difference as the irreducibility of the trace of the other in Levinas, and the ontic-entological difference in Heidegger. Reflection on this last determination of difference will lead us to consider differance as the *strategic* note or connection – relatively or provisionally *privileged* – which indicates the closure of presence, together with the closure of the conceptual order and denomination, a closure that is effected in the functioning of traces.

I SHALL SPEAK, THEN, OF A LETTER – the first one, if we are to believe the alphabet and most of the speculations that have concerned themselves with it.

I shall speak then of the letter *a*, this first letter which it seemed necessary to introduce now and then in writing the word "difference." This seemed necessary in the course of writing about writing, and of writing within a writing whose different strokes all pass, in certain respects, through a gross spelling mistake, through a violation of the rules governing writing, violating the law that governs writing and regulates its conventions of propriety. In fact or theory we can always erase or lessen this spelling mistake, and, in each case, while these are analytically different from one another but for practical purposes the same, find it grave, unseemly, or, indeed, supposing the greatest ingenuousness, amusing. Whether or not we care to quietly overlook this infraction, the attention we give it beforehand will allow us to recognize, as though prescribed by some mute irony, the inaudible but displaced character of this literal permutation. We can always act as though this makes no difference. I must say from the start that my account serves less to justify this silent spelling mistake, or still less to excuse it, than to aggravate its obtrusive character.

On the other hand, I must be excused if I refer, at least implicitly, to one or another of the texts that I have ventured to publish. Precisely what I would like to attempt to some extent (although this is in principle and in its highest degree impossible, due to essential *de jure* reasons) is to bring together an *assemblage* of the different ways I have been able to utilize – or, rather, have allowed to be imposed on me – what I will provisionally call the word or concept of differance in its new spelling. It is literally neither a word nor a concept, as we shall see. I insist on the word "assemblage" here for two reasons: on the one hand, it is not a matter of describing a history, of recounting the steps, text by text, context by context, each time showing which scheme has been able to impose this graphic disorder, although this could have been done as well; rather, we are concerned with the *general system of all these schemata*. On the other hand, the word "assemblage" seems more apt for suggesting that the kind of bringing together proposed here has the structure of an interlacing, a weaving, or a web, which would allow the different threads and different lines of sense or force to separate again, as well as being ready to bind others together.

In a quite preliminary way, we now recall that this particular graphic intervention was conceived in the writing-up of a question about writing; it was not made simply to shock the reader or grammarian. Now, in point of fact, it happens that this graphic difference (the *a* instead of the *e*), this marked difference between two apparently vocalic notations, between vowels, remains purely graphic: it is written or read, but it is not heard. It cannot be heard, and we shall see in what respects it is also beyond the order of understanding. It is put forward by a silent mark, by a tacit monument, or, one might even say, by a pyramid – keeping in mind not only the capital form of the printed letter but also that passage from Hegel's *Encyclopaedia* where he compares the body of the sign to an Egyptian pyramid. The *a* of differance, therefore, is not heard; it remains silent, secret, and discreet, like a tomb.[4]

It is a tomb that (provided one knows how to decipher its legend) is not far from signaling the death of the king.

It is a tomb that cannot even be made to resonate. For I cannot even let you know, by my talk, now being spoken before the Société Française de Philosophie, which difference I am talking about at the very moment I speak of it. I can only talk about this graphic difference by keeping to a very indirect speech about writing, and on the condition that I specify each time that I am referring to difference with an *e* or differance with an *a*. All of which is not going to simplify matters today, and will give us all a great deal of trouble when we want to understand one another. In any event, when I do specify which difference I mean – when I say "with an *e*" or "with an *a*" – this will refer irreducibly to a *written text*, a text governing my talk, a text that I keep in front of me, that I will read, and toward which I shall have to try to lead your hands and eyes. We cannot refrain here from going by way of a written text, from ordering ourselves by the disorder that is produced therein – and this is what matters to me first of all.

Doubtless this pyramidal silence of the graphic difference between the *e* and the *a* can function only within the system of phonetic writing and within a language or grammar historically tied to phonetic writing and to the whole culture which is inseparable from it. But I will say that it is just this – this silence that functions only within what is called phonetic writing – that points out or reminds us in a very opportune way that, contrary to an enormous prejudice, there is no phonetic writing. There is no purely and strictly phonetic writing. What is called phonetic writing can only function – in principle and *de jure*, and not due to some factual and technical inadequacy – by incorporating nonphonetic "signs" (punctuation, spacing, etc.); but when we examine their structure and necessity, we will quickly see that they are ill described by the concept of signs. Saussure had only to remind us that the play of difference was the functional condition, the condition of possibility, for every sign; and it is itself silent. The difference between two phonemes, which enables them to exist and to operate, is inaudible. The inaudible opens the two present phonemes to hearing, as they present themselves. If, then, there is no purely phonetic writing, it is because there is no purely phonetic phone. The difference that brings out phonemes and lets them be heard and understood [*entendre*] itself remains inaudible.

It will perhaps be objected that, for the same reasons, the graphic difference itself sinks into darkness, that it never constitutes the fullness of a sensible term, but draws out an invisible connection, the mark of an inapparent relation between two spectacles. That is no doubt true. Indeed, since from this point of view the difference between the *e* and the *a* marked in "differance" eludes vision and hearing, this happily suggests that we must here let ourselves be referred to an order that no longer refers to sensibility. But we are not referred to intelligibility either, to an ideality not fortuitously associated with the objectivity of *theorein* or understanding. We must be referred to an order, then, that resists philosophy's founding opposition between the sensible and the intelligible. The order that resists this opposition, that resists it because it sustains it, is designated in a movement of differance (with an *a*) between two differences or between two letters. This differance belongs neither to the voice nor to writing in the ordinary sense, and it takes place, like the strange space that will assemble us here for the course of an hour, *between* speech and writing and beyond the tranquil familiarity that binds us to one and to the other, reassuring us sometimes in the illusion that they are two separate things.

Now, HOW AM I TO SPEAK OF the *a* of differance? It is clear that it cannot be *exposed*. We can expose only what, at a certain moment, can become *present*, manifest; what can be shown, presented as a present, a being-present in its truth, the truth of a present or the presence of a present. However, if differance is (I also cross out the "is") what makes the presentation of being-present possible, it never presents itself as such. It is never given in the present or to anyone. Holding back and not exposing itself, it goes beyond the order of truth on this specific point and in this determined way, yet is not itself concealed, as if it were something, a mysterious being, in the occult zone of a nonknowing. Any exposition would expose it to disappearing as a disappearance. It would risk appearing, thus disappearing.

Thus, the detours, phrases, and syntax that I shall often have to resort to will resemble – will sometimes be practically indiscernible from – those of negative theology. Already we had to note that differance is *not*, does not exist, and is not any sort of being-present (*on*). And we will have to point out everything that it *is not*, and, consequently, that it has neither existence nor essence. It belongs to no category of being, present or absent. And yet what is thus denoted as differance is not theological, not even in the most negative order of negative theology. The latter, as we know, is always occupied with letting a supraessential reality go beyond the finite categories of essence and existence, that is, of presence, and always hastens to remind us that, if we deny the predicate of existence to God, it is in order to recognize him as a superior, inconceivable, and ineffable mode of being. Here there is no question of such a move, as will be confirmed as we go along. Not only is differance irreducible to every ontological or theological – onto-theological – reappropriation, but it opens up the very space in which onto-theology – philosophy – produces its system and its history. It thus encompasses and irrevocably surpasses onto-theology or philosophy.

For the same reason, I do not know where to begin to mark out this assemblage, this graph, of differance. Precisely what is in question here is the requirement that there be a *de jure* commencement, an absolute point of departure, a responsibility arising from a principle. The problem of writing opens by questioning the *arche*. Thus what I put forth here will not be developed simply as a philosophical discourse that operates on the basis of a principle, of postulates, axioms, and definitions and that moves according to the discursive line of a rational order. In marking out differance, everything is a matter of strategy and risk. It is a question of strategy because no transcendent truth present outside the sphere of writing can theologically command the totality of this field. It is hazardous because this strategy is not simply one in the sense that we say that strategy orients the tactics according to a final aim, a *telos* or the theme of a domination, a mastery or an ultimate reappropriation of movement and field. In the end, it is a strategy without finality. We might call it blind tactics or empirical errance, if the value of empiricism did not itself derive all its meaning from its opposition to philosophical responsibility. If there is a certain errance in the tracing-out of differance, it no longer follows the line of logico-philosophical speech or that of its integral and symmetrical opposite, logico-empirical speech. The concept of *play* [*jeu*] remains beyond this opposition; on the eve and aftermath of philosophy, it designates the unity of chance and necessity in an endless calculus.

By decision and, as it were, by the rules of the game, then, turning this thought around, let us introduce ourselves to the thought of differance by way of the theme of strategy or stratagem. By this merely strategic justification, I want to emphasize that the efficacy of this thematics of differance very well may, and even one day must, be sublated, i.e., lend itself, if not to its own replacement, at least to its involvement in a series of events which in fact it never commanded. This also means that it is not a theological thematics.

I will say, first of all, that differance, which is neither a word nor a concept, seemed to me to be strategically the theme most proper to think out, if not master (thought being here, perhaps, held in a certain necessary relation with the structional limits of mastery), in what is most characteristic of our "epoch." I start off, then, strategically, from the place and time in which "we" are, even though my opening is not justifiable in the final account, and though it is always on the basis of differance and its "history" that we can claim to know who and where "we" are and what the limits of an "epoch" can be.

Although "difference" is neither a word nor a concept, let us nonetheless attempt a simple and approximative semantic analysis which will bring us in view of what is at stake [*en vue de l'enjeu*]. We do know that the verb "to differ" [*différer*] (the Latin verb *differre*) has two seemingly quite distinct meanings; in the *Littré* dictionary, for example, they are the subject of two separate articles. In this sense, the Latin *differre is* not the simple translation of the Greek *diapherein*; this fact will not be without consequence for us in tying our discussion to a particular language, one that passes for being less philosophical, less primordially philosophical, than the other. For the distribution of sense in the Greek *diapherein* does not carry one of the two themes of the Latin *differre*, namely, the action of postponing until later, of taking into account, the taking-account of time and forces in an operation that implies an economic reckoning, a detour, a respite, a delay, a reserve, a representation – all the concepts that I will sum up here in a word I have never used but which could be added to this series: *temporalizing*. "To differ" in this sense is to temporalize, to resort, consciously or unconsciously, to the temporal and temporalizing mediation of a detour that suspends the accomplishment or fulfillment of "desire" or "will," or carries desire or will out in a way that annuls or tempers their effect. We shall see, later, in what respects this temporalizing is also a temporalization and spacing, is space's becoming-temporal and time's becoming-spatial, is "primordial constitution" of space and time, as metaphysics or transcendental phenomenology would call it in the language that is here criticized and displaced.

The other sense of "to differ" [*différer*] is the most common and most identifiable, the sense of not being identical, of being other, of being discernible, etc. And in "differents," whether referring to the alterity of dissimilarity or the alterity of allergy or of polemics, it is necessary that interval, distance, *spacing* occur among the different elements and occur actively, dynamically, and with a certain perseverance in repetition.

But the word "difference" (with an *e*) could never refer to differing as temporalizing or to difference as *polemos*. It is this loss of sense that the word differance (with an *a*) will have to schematically compensate for. Differance can refer to the whole complex of its meanings at once, for it is immediately and irreducibly multivalent, something which will be important for the discourse I am trying to develop. It refers to this whole complex of meanings not only when it is supported by a language or interpretive context (like any signification), but it already does so somehow of itself. Or at least it does so more easily by itself than does any other word: here the *a* comes more immediately from the present participle [*différant*] and brings us closer to the action of "differing" that is in progress, even before it has produced the effect that is constituted as different or resulted in difference (with an *e*). Within a conceptual system and in terms of classical requirements, differance could be said to designate the productive and primordial constituting causality, the process of scission and division whose differings and differences would be the constituted products or effects. But while bringing us closer to the infinitive and active core of differing, "differance" with an *a* neutralizes what the infinitive denotes as simply active, in the same way that "parlance" does not signify the simple fact of speaking, of speaking to or being spoken to. Nor is resonance the act of resonating. Here in the usage of our language we must consider that the ending -*ance* is undecided between active and passive. And we shall see why what is designated by "differance" is neither simply active nor simply passive, that it announces or rather recalls something like the middle voice, that it speaks of an operation which is not an operation, which cannot be thought of either as a passion or as an action of a subject upon an object, as starting from an agent or from a patient, or on the basis of, or in view of, any of these *terms*. But philosophy has perhaps commenced by distributing the middle voice, expressing a certain intransitiveness, into the active and the passive voice, and has itself been constituted in this repression.

How are differance as temporalizing and differance as spacing conjoined?

Let us begin with the problem of signs and writing – since we are already in the midst of it. We ordinarily say that a sign is put in place of the thing itself, the present thing – "thing" holding here for the sense as well as the referent. Signs represent the present in its absence; they take the place of the present. When we cannot take hold of or show the thing, let us say the present, the being-present, when the present does not present itself, then we signify, we go through the detour of signs. We take up or give signs; we make signs. The sign would thus be a deferred presence. Whether it is a question of verbal or written signs, monetary signs, elect-oral delegates, or political representatives, the movement of signs defers the moment of encountering the thing itself, the moment at which we could lay hold of it, consume or expend it, touch it, see it, have a present intuition of it. What I am describing here is the structure of signs as classically determined, in order to define – through a commonplace characterization of its traits – signification as the differance of temporalizing. Now this classical determination presupposes that the sign (which defers presence) is conceivable only *on the basis of* the presence that it defers and *in view of* the deferred presence one intends to reappropriate. Following this classical semiology, the substitution of the sign for the thing itself is both *secondary* and *provisional*: it is second in order after an original and lost presence, a presence from which the sign would be derived. It is provisional with respect to this final and missing presence, in view of which the sign would serve as a movement of mediation.

In attempting to examine these secondary and provisional aspects of the substitute, we shall no doubt catch sight of something like a primordial differance. Yet we could no longer even call it primordial or final, inasmuch as the characteristics of origin, beginning, *telos*, *eschaton*, etc., have always denoted presence – *ousia*, *parousia*, etc. To question the secondary and provisional character of the sign, to oppose it to a "primordial" differance, would thus have the following consequences:

1   Differance can no longer be understood according to the concept of "sign," which has always been taken to mean the representation of a presence and has been

constituted in a system (of thought or language) determined on the basis of and in view of presence.

2   In this way we question the authority of presence or its simple symmetrical contrary, absence or lack. We thus interrogate the limit that has always constrained us, that always constrains us – we who inhabit a language and a system of thought – to form the meaning of being in general as presence or absence, in the categories of being or beingness (*ousia*). It already appears that the kind of questioning we are thus led back to is, let us say, the Heideggerian kind, and that differance *seems* to lead us back to the ontic-ontological difference. But permit me to postpone this reference. I shall only note that between differance as temporalizing-temporalization (which we can no longer conceive within the horizon of the present) and what Heidegger says about temporalization in *Sein und Zeit* (namely, that as the transcendental horizon of the question of being it must be freed from the traditional and metaphysical domination by the present or the now) – between these two there is a close, if not exhaustive and irreducibly necessary, interconnection.

But first of all, let us remain with the semiological aspects of the problem to see how differance as temporalizing is conjoined with differance as spacing. Most of the semiological or linguistic research currently dominating the field of thought (whether due to the results of its own investigations or due to its role as a generally recognized regulative model) traces its genealogy, rightly or wrongly, to Saussure as its common founder. It was Saussure who first of all set forth the *arbitrariness of signs* and the *differential character* of signs as principles of general semiology and particularly of linguistics. And, as we know, these two themes – the arbitrary and the differential – are in his view inseparable. Arbitrariness can occur only because the system of signs is constituted by the differences between the terms, and not by their fullness. The elements of signification function not by virtue of the compact force of their cores but by the network of oppositions that distinguish them and relate them to one another. "Arbitrary and differential" says Saussure "are two correlative qualities."

As the condition for signification, this principle of difference affects the *whole sign*, that is, both the signified and the signifying aspects. The signified aspect is the concept, the ideal sense. The signifying aspect is what Saussure calls the material or physical (e.g., acoustical) "image." We do not here have to enter into all the problems these definitions pose. Let us only cite Saussure where it interests us:

> The conceptual side of value is made up solely of relations and differences with respect to the other terms of language, and the same can be said of its material side. . . . Everything that has been said up to this point boils down to this: in language there are only differences. Even more important: a difference generally implies positive terms between which the difference is set up; but in language there are only differences *without positive terms*. Whether we take the signified or the signifier, language has neither ideas nor sounds that existed before the linguistic system, but only conceptual and phonic differences that have issued from the system. The idea or phonic substance that a sign contains is of less importance than the other signs that surround it.[5]

The first consequence to be drawn from this is that the signified concept is never present in itself, in an adequate presence that would refer only to itself. Every concept is necessarily and essentially inscribed in a chain or a system, within which it refers to another and to other concepts, by the systematic play of differences. Such a play, then – differance – is no longer simply a concept, but the possibility of conceptuality, of the conceptual system and process in general. For the same reason, differance, which is not a concept, is not a mere word; that is, it is not what we represent to ourselves as the calm and present self-referential unity of a concept and sound [*phonie*]. We shall later discuss the consequences of this for the notion of a word.

The difference that Saussure speaks about, therefore, is neither itself a concept nor one word among others. We can say this *a fortiori* for differance. Thus we are brought to make the relation between the one and the other explicit.

Within a language, within the *system* of language, there are only differences. A taxonomic operation can accordingly undertake its systematic, statistical, and classificatory inventory. But, on the one hand, these differences *play a role* in language, in speech as well, and in the exchange between language and speech. On the other hand, these differences are themselves *effects*. They have not fallen from the sky ready made; they are no more inscribed in a *topos noētos* than they are prescribed in the wax of the brain. If the word "History" did not carry with it the theme of a final repression of differance, we could say that differences alone could be "historical" through and through and from the start.

What we note as *differance* will thus be the movement of play that "produces" (and not by something that is simply an activity) these differences, these effects of difference. This does not mean that the differance which produces differences is before them in a simple and in itself unmodified and indifferent present. Differance is the nonfull, nonsimple "origin"; it is the structured and differing origin of differences.

Since language (which Saussure says is a classification) has not fallen from the sky, it is clear that the differences have been produced; they are the effects produced, but effects that do not have as their cause a subject or substance, a thing in general, or a being that is somewhere present and itself escapes the play of difference. If such a presence were implied (quite classically) in the general concept of cause, we would therefore have to talk about an effect without a cause, something that would very quickly lead to no longer talking about effects. I have tried to indicate a way out of the closure imposed by this system, namely, by means of the "trace." No more an effect than a cause, the "trace" cannot of itself, taken outside its context, suffice to bring about the required transgression.

As there is no presence before the semiological difference or outside it, we can extend what Saussure writes about language to signs in general: "Language is necessary in order for speech to be intelligible and to produce all of its effects; but the latter is necessary in order for language to be established; historically, the fact of speech always comes first."[6]

Retaining at least the schema, if not the content, of the demand formulated by Saussure, we shall designate by the term *differance* the movement by which language, or any code, any system of reference in general, becomes "historically" constituted as a fabric of differences. Here, the terms "constituted," "produced," "created," "movement," "historically," etc., with all they imply, are not to be understood only in terms of the language of metaphysics, from which they are taken. It would have to be shown why the concepts of production, like those of constitution and history, remain accessories in this respect to what is here being questioned; this, however, would draw us too far away today, toward the theory of the representation of the "circle" in which we seem to be enclosed. I only use these terms here, like many other concepts, out of strategic convenience and in order to prepare the deconstruction of the system they form at the point which is now most decisive. In any event, we will have understood, by virtue of the very circle we appear to be caught up in, that differance, as it is written here, is no more static than genetic, no more structural than historical. Nor is it any less so. And it is completely to miss the point of this orthographical impropriety to want to object to it on the basis of the oldest of metaphysical oppositions – for example, by opposing some generative point of view to a structuralist-taxonomic point of view, or conversely. These oppositions do not pertain in the least to differance; and this, no doubt, is what makes thinking about it difficult and uncomfortable.

If we now consider the chain to which "differance" gets subjected, according to the context, to a certain number of nonsynonymic substitutions, one will ask why we resorted to such concepts as "reserve," "protowriting," "prototrace," "spacing," indeed to "supplement" or "*pharmakon*," and, before long, to "hymen," etc.[7]

Let us begin again. Differance is what makes the movement of signification possible only if each element that is said to be "present," appearing on the stage of presence, is related to something other than itself but retains the mark of a past element and already lets itself be hollowed out by the mark of its relation to a future element. This trace relates no less to what is called the future than to what is called the past, and it constitutes what is called the present by this very relation to what it is not, to what it absolutely is not; that is, not even to a past or future considered as a modified present. In order for it to be, an interval must separate it from what it is not; but the interval that constitutes it in the present must also, and by the same token, divide the present in itself, thus dividing, along with the present, everything that can be conceived on its basis, that is, every being – in particular, for our metaphysical language, the substance or subject. Constituting itself, dynamically dividing itself, this interval is what could be called *spacing*; time's becoming-spatial or space's becoming-temporal (*temporalizing*). And it is this constitution of the present as a "primordial" and irreducibly nonsimple, and, therefore, in the strict sense nonprimordial, synthesis of traces, retentions, and protentions (to reproduce here, analogically and provisionally, a phenomenological and transcendental language that will presently be revealed as inadequate) that I propose to call protowriting, prototrace, or differance. The latter (is) (both) spacing (and) temporalizing.[8]

Given this (active) movement of the (production of) difference without origin, could we not, quite simply and without any neographism, call it *differentiation?* Among other confusions, such a word would suggest some organic unity, some primordial and homogeneous unity, that would eventually come to be divided up and take on difference as an event. Above all, formed on the verb "to differentiate," this word would annul the economic signification of detour, temporalizing delay, "deferring." I owe a remark in passing to a recent reading of one of Koyré's texts entitled "Hegel at Jena."[9] In that text, Koyré cites long passages from the Jena *Logic* in German and gives his own translation. On two occasions in Hegel's text he encounters the expression "*differente Beziehung.*" This word (*different*), whose root is Latin, is extremely rare in German and also, I believe, in Hegel, who instead uses *verschieden* or *ungleich*, calling difference *Unterschied* and qualitative variety *Verschiedenheit*. In the Jena *Logic*, he uses the word *different* precisely at the point where he deals with time and the present. Before coming to Koyré's valuable remark, here are some passages from Hegel, as rendered by Koyré:

The infinite, in this simplicity is – as a moment opposed to the self-identical – the negative. In its moments, while the infinite presents the totality to (itself) and in itself, (it is) excluding in general, the point or limit; but in this, its own (action of) negating, it relates itself immediately to the other and negates itself. The limit or moment of the present (*der Gegenwart*), the absolute "this" of time or the now, is an absolutely negative simplicity absolutely excluding all multiplicity from itself, and by this very fact is absolutely determined; it is not an extended whole or *quantum* within itself (and) which would in itself also have an undetermined aspect or qualitative variety, which of itself would be related, indifferently (*gleichguldig*) or externally to another but on the contrary, this is an absolutely different relation of the simple.[10]

And Koyré specifies in a striking note: "Different relation *differente Beziehung*. We could say: differentiating relation." And on the following page, from another text of Hegel, we can read: "*Diese Beziehung ist Gegenwart, als eine differente Beziehung*" (This relation is [the] present, as a different relation). There is another note by Koyré: "The term '*different*' is taken here in an active sense."

Writing "differing" or "differance" (with an *a*) would have had the utility of making it possible to translate Hegel on precisely this point with no further qualifications – and it is a quite decisive point in his text. The translation would be, as it always should be, the transformation of one language by another. Naturally, I maintain that the word "differance" can be used in other ways, too; first of all, because it denotes not only the activity of primordial difference but also the temporalizing detour of deferring. It has, however, an even more important usage. Despite the very profound affinities that differance thus written has with Hegelian speech (as it should be read), it can, at a certain point, not exactly break with it, but rather work a sort of displacement with regard to it. A definite rupture with Hegelian language would make no sense, nor would it be at all likely; but this displacement is both infinitesimal and radical. I have tried to indicate the extent of this displacement elsewhere; it would be difficult to talk about it with any brevity at this point.

Differences are thus "produced" – differed – by differance. But *what* differs, or *who* differs? In other words, *what is* differance? With this question we attain another stage and another source of the problem.

What differs? Who differs? What is differance?

If we answered these questions even before examining them as questions, even before going back over them and questioning their form (even what seems to be most natural and necessary about them), we would fall below the level we have now reached. For if we accepted the form of the question in its own sense and syntax ("What?," "What is?," "Who is?"), we would have to admit that differance is derived, supervenient, controlled, and ordered from the starting point of a being-present, one capable of being something, a force, a state, or power in the world, to which we could give all kinds of names: a *what*, or being-present as a *subject*, a *who*. In the latter case, notably, we would implicitly admit that the being-present (for example, as a self-present being or consciousness) would eventually result in differing: in delaying or in diverting the fulfillment of a "need" or "desire," or in differing from itself. But in none of these cases would such a being-present be "constituted" by this differance.

Now if we once again refer to the semiological difference, what was it that Saussure in particular reminded us of? That "language [which consists only of differences] is not a function of the speaking subject." This implies that the subject (self-identical or even conscious of self-identity, self-conscious) is inscribed in the language, that he is a "function" of the language. He becomes a *speaking* subject only by conforming his speech – even in the aforesaid "creation," even in the aforesaid "transgression" – to the system of linguistic prescriptions taken as the system of differences, or at least to the general law of differance, by conforming to that law of language which Saussure calls "language without speech." "Language is necessary for the spoken word to be intelligible and so that it can produce all of its effects."[11]

If, by hypothesis, we maintain the strict opposition between speech and language, then differance will be not only the play of differences within the language but the relation of speech to language, the detour by which I must also pass in order to speak, the silent token I must give, which holds just as well for linguistics in the strict sense as it does for general semiology; it dictates all the relations between usage and the formal schema, between the message and the particular code, etc. Elsewhere I have tried to suggest that this differance within language, and in the relation between speech and language, forbids the essential dissociation between speech and writing that Saussure, in keeping with tradition, wanted to draw at another level of his presentation. The use of language or the employment of any code which implies a play of forms – with no determined or invariable substratum – also presupposes a retention and protention of differences, a spacing and temporalizing, a play of traces. This play must be a sort of inscription prior to writing, a protowriting without a present origin, without an *arche*. From this comes the systematic crossing-out of the *arche* and the transformation of general semiology into a grammatology, the latter performing a critical work upon everything within semiology – right down to its matrical concept of signs – that retains any metaphysical presuppositions incompatible with the theme of differance.

We might be tempted by an objection: to be sure, the subject becomes a *speaking* subject only by dealing with the system of linguistic differences; or again, he becomes a *signifying* subject (generally by speech or other signs) only by entering into the system of differences. In this sense, certainly, the speaking or signifying subject would not be self-present, insofar as he speaks or signifies, except for the play of linguistic or semiological differance. But can we not conceive of a presence and self-presence of the subject before speech or its signs, a subject's self-presence in a silent and intuitive consciousness?

Such a question therefore supposes that prior to signs and outside them, and excluding every trace and differance, something such as consciousness is possible. It supposes, moreover, that, even before the distribution of its signs in space and in the world, consciousness can gather itself up in its own presence. What then is consciousness? What does "consciousness" mean? Most often in the very form of "meaning" ["*vouloir dire*"], consciousness in all its modifications is conceivable only as self-presence, a self-perception of presence. And what holds for consciousness also holds here for what is called subjective existence in general. Just as the category of subject is not and never has been conceivable without reference to presence as *hypokeimenon* or *ousia*, etc., so the subject as consciousness has never been able to be evinced otherwise than as self-presence. The privilege accorded to consciousness thus means a privilege accorded to the present; and even if the transcendental temporality of consciousness is described in depth, as Husserl described it, the power of synthesis and of the incessant gathering-up of traces is always accorded to the "living present."

This privilege is the ether of metaphysics, the very element of our thought insofar as it is caught up in the language of metaphysics. We can only de-limit such a closure today by evoking this import of presence, which Heidegger has shown to be the onto-theological determination of being. Therefore, in evoking this import of presence, by an examination which would have to be of a quite peculiar nature, we question the absolute privilege of this form or epoch of presence in general, that is, consciousness as meaning [*vouloir dire*] in self-presence.

We thus come to posit presence – and, in particular, consciousness, the being-next-to-itself consciousness – no longer as the absolutely matrical form of being but as a "determination" and an "effect." Presence is a determination and effect within a system which is no longer that of presence but that of differance; it no more allows the opposition between activity and passivity than that between cause and effect or in-determination and determination, etc. This system is of such a kind that even to designate consciousness as an effect or determination – for strategic reasons, reasons that can be more or less clearly considered and systematically ascertained – is to continue to operate according to the vocabulary of that very thing to be delimited.

Before being so radically and expressly Heideggerian, this was also Nietzsche's and Freud's move, both of whom, as we know, and often in a very similar way, questioned the self-assured certitude of consciousness. And is it not remarkable that both of them did this by starting out with the theme of differance?

This theme appears almost literally in their work, at the most crucial places. I shall not expand on this here; I shall only recall that for Nietzsche "the important main activity is unconscious" and that consciousness is the effect of forces whose essence, ways, and modalities are not peculiar to it. Now force itself is never present; it is only a play of differences and quantities. There would be no force in general without the difference between forces; and here the difference in quantity counts more than the content of quantity, more than the absolute magnitude itself.

> Quantity itself therefore is not separable from the difference in quantity. The difference in quantity is the essence of force, the relation of force with force. To fancy two equal forces, even if we grant them opposing directions, is an approximate and crude illusion, a statistical dream in which life is immersed, but which chemistry dispels.[12]

Is not the whole thought of Nietzsche a critique of philosophy as active indifference to difference, as a system of reduction or adiaphoristic repression? Following the same logic – logic itself – this does not exclude the fact that philosophy lives *in* and *from* differance, that it thereby blinds itself to the *same*, which is not the identical. The same is precisely differance (with an *a*), as the diverted and equivocal passage from one difference to another, from one term of the opposition to the other. We could thus take up all the coupled oppositions on which philosophy is constructed, and from which our language lives, not in order to see opposition vanish but to see the emergence of a necessity such that one of the terms appears as the differance of the other, the other as "differed" within the systematic ordering of the same (e.g., the intelligible as differing from the sensible, as sensible differed; the concept as differed-differing intuition, life as differing-differed matter; mind as differed-differing life; culture as differed-differing nature; and all the terms designating what is other than *physis* – *technē*, *nōmos*, society, freedom, history, spirit, etc. – as *physis* differed or *physis* differing: *physis in differance*). It is out of the unfolding of this "same" as differance that the sameness of difference and of repetition is presented in the eternal return.

In Nietzsche, these are so many themes that can be related with the kind of symptomatology that always serves to diagnose the evasions and ruses of anything disguised in its differance. Or again, these terms can be related with the entire thematics of active interpretation, which substitutes an incessant deciphering for the disclosure of truth as a presentation of the thing itself in its presence, etc. What results is a cipher without truth, or at least a system of ciphers that is not dominated by truth value, which only then becomes a function that is understood, inscribed, and circumscribed.

We shall therefore call differance this "active" (in movement) discord of the different forces and of the differences between forces which Nietzsche opposes to the entire system of metaphysical grammar, wherever that system controls culture, philosophy, and science.

It is historically significant that this diaphoristics, understood as an energetics or an economy of forces, set up to question the primacy of presence qua consciousness, is also the major theme of Freud's thought; in his work we find another diaphoristics, both in the form of a theory of ciphers or traces and an energetics. The questioning of the authority of consciousness is first and always differential.

The two apparently different meanings of differance are tied together in Freudian theory: differing [*le différer*] as discernibility, distinction, deviation, diastem, *spacing*; and deferring [*le différer*] as detour, delay, relay, reserve, *temporalizing*. I shall recall only that:

1   The concept of trace (*Spur*), of facilitation (*Bahnung*), of forces of facilitation are, as early as the composition of the *Entwurf*, inseparable from the concept of difference. The origin of memory and of the psyche as a memory in general (conscious or unconscious) can only be described by taking into account the difference between the facilitation thresholds, as Freud says explicitly. There is no facilitation [*Bahnung*] without difference and no difference without a trace.

2   All the differences involved in the production of unconscious traces and in the process of inscription (*Niederschrift*) can also be interpreted as moments of differance, in the sense of "placing on reserve." Following a schema that continually guides Freud's thinking, the movement of the trace is described as an effort of life to protect itself by *deferring* the dangerous investment, by constituting a reserve (*Vorrat*). And all the conceptual oppositions that furrow Freudian thought relate each concept to the other like movements of a detour, within the economy of differance. The one is only the other deferred, the one differing from the other. The one is the other in differance, the one is the differance from the other. Every apparently rigorous and irreducible opposition (for example that between the secondary and primary) is thus said to be, at one time or another, a "theoretical fiction." In this way again, for example (but such an example covers everything or communicates with everything), the difference between the pleasure principle and the reality principle is only difference as detour (*Aufschieben*, *Aufschub*). In *Beyond the Pleasure Principle*, Freud writes

> Under the influence of the ego's instincts of self-preservation, the pleasure principle is replaced by the reality principle. This latter principle does not abandon the intention of ultimately obtaining pleasure, but it nevertheless demands and carries into effect the postponement of satisfaction, the abandonment of a number of possibilities of gaining satisfaction and the temporary toleration of unpleasure as a step on the long indirect road (*Aufschub*) to pleasure.[13]

Here we touch on the point of greatest obscurity, on the very enigma of differance, on how the concept we have of it is divided by a strange separation. We must not hasten to make a decision too quickly. How can we conceive of differance as a systematic detour which, within the element of the same, always aims at either finding again the pleasure or the presence that had been deferred by (conscious or unconscious) calculation, and, *at the same time*, how can we, on the other hand, conceive of differance as the relation to an impossible presence as an expenditure without reserve, as an irreparable loss of presence, an irreversible wearing-down of energy, or indeed as a death instinct and a relation to the absolutely other that apparently breaks up any economy? It is evident – it is evidence itself – that system and nonsystem, the same and the absolutely other, etc., cannot be conceived *together*.

If differance is this inconceivable factor, must we not perhaps hasten to make it evident, to bring it into the philosophical element of evidence, and thus quickly dissipate its mirage character and illogicality, dissipate it with the infallibility of the calculus we know well – since we have recognized its place, necessity, and function within the structure of differance? What would be accounted for philosophically here has already been taken into account in the system of differance as it is here being calculated. I have tried elsewhere, in a reading of Bataille,[14] to indicate what might be the establishment of a rigorous, and in a new sense "scientific," *relating* of a "restricted economy" – one having nothing to do with an unreserved expenditure, with death, with being exposed to nonsense, etc. – to a "general economy" or system that, so to speak, *takes account of* what is unreserved. It is a relation between a differance that is accounted for and a differance that fails to be accounted for, where the establishment of a pure presence, without loss, is one with the occurrence of absolute loss, with death. By establishing this relation between a restricted and a general system, we shift and recommence the very project of philosophy under the privileged heading of Hegelianism.

The economic character of differance in no way implies that the deferred presence can always be recovered, that it simply amounts to an investment that only temporarily and without loss delays the presentation of presence, that is, the perception of gain or the gain of perception. Contrary to the metaphysical, dialectical, and "Hegelian" interpretation of the economic movement of differance, we must admit a game where whoever loses wins and where one wins and loses each time. If the diverted presentation continues to be somehow definitively and irreducibly withheld, this is not because a particular present remains hidden or absent, but because differance holds us in a relation with what exceeds (though we necessarily fail to recognize this) the alternative of presence or absence. A certain alterity – Freud gives it a metaphysical name, the unconscious – is definitively taken away from every process of presentation in which we would demand for it to be shown forth in person. In this context and under this heading, the unconscious is not, as we know, a hidden, virtual, and potential self-presence. It is differed – which no doubt means that it is woven out of differences, but also that it sends out, that it delegates, representatives or proxies; but there is no chance that the mandating subject "exists" somewhere, that it is present or is "itself," and still less chance that it will become conscious. In this sense, contrary to the terms of an old debate, strongly symptomatic of the metaphysical investments it has always assumed, the "unconscious" can no more be classed as a "thing" than as anything else; it is no more of a thing than an implicit or masked consciousness. This radical alterity, removed from every possible mode of presence, is characterized by irreducible after-effects, by delayed effects. In order to describe them, in order to read the traces of the "unconscious" traces (there are no "conscious" traces), the language of presence or absence, the metaphysical speech of phenomenology, is in principle inadequate.

The structure of delay (*retardement: Nachträglichkeit*) that Freud talks about indeed prohibits our taking temporalization (temporalizing) to be a simple dialectical complication of the present; rather, this is the style of transcendental phenomenology. It describes the living present as a primordial and incessant synthesis that is constantly led back upon itself, back upon its assembled and assembling self, by retentional traces and protentional openings. With the alterity of the "unconscious," we have to deal not with the horizons of modified presents – past or future – but with a "past" that has never been nor will ever be present, whose "future" will never be produced or reproduced in the form of presence. The concept of trace is therefore incommensurate with that of retention, that of the becoming-past of what had been present. The trace cannot be conceived – nor, therefore, can differance – on the basis of either the present or the presence of the present.

A past that has never been present: with this formula Emmanuel Levinas designates (in ways that are, to be sure, not those of psychoanalysis) the trace and the enigma of absolute alterity, that is, the Other [*autrui*]. At least within these limits, and from this point of view, the thought of differance implies the whole critique of classical ontology undertaken by Levinas. And the concept of trace, like that of differance, forms – across these different traces and through these differences between traces, as understood by Nietzsche, Freud, and Levinas (these "authors' names" serve only as indications) – the network that sums up and permeates our "epoch" as the de-limitation of ontology (of presence).

The ontology of presence is the ontology of beings and beingness. Everywhere, the dominance of beings is solicited by differance – in the sense that *sollicitare* means, in old Latin, to shake all over, to make the whole tremble. What is questioned by the thought of differance, therefore, is the determination of being in presence, or in beingness. Such a question could not arise and be understood without the difference between Being and beings opening up somewhere. The first consequence of this is that differance is not. It is not a being-present, however excellent, unique, principal, or transcendent one makes it. It commands nothing, rules over nothing, and nowhere does it exercise any authority. It is not marked by a capital letter. Not only is there no realm of differance, but differance is even the subversion of every realm. This is obviously what makes it threatening and necessarily dreaded by everything in us that desires a realm, the past or future presence of a realm. And it is always in the name of a realm that, believing one sees it ascend to the capital letter, one can reproach it for wanting to rule.

Does this mean, then, that differance finds its place within the spread of the ontic-ontological difference, as it is conceived, as the "epoch" conceives itself within it, and particularly "across" the Heideggerian meditation, which cannot be gotten around?

There is no simple answer to such a question.

In one particular respect, differance is, to be sure, but the historical and epochal *deployment* of Being or of the ontological difference. The *a* of difference marks the *movement* of this deployment.

And yet, is not the thought that conceives the *meaning* or *truth* of Being, the determination of difference as ontic-ontological difference – difference conceived within the horizon of the question of *Being* – still an intrametaphysical effect of differance? Perhaps the deployment of differance is not only the truth or the epoch-ality of Being. Perhaps we must try to think this *unheard-of* thought, this silent tracing, namely, that the history of Being (the thought of which is committed to the Greco-Western logos), as it is itself produced across the ontological difference, is only one epoch of the *diapherein*. Then we could no longer even call it an "epoch," for the concept of epochality belongs within history understood as the history of Being. Being has always made "sense," has always been conceived or spoken of as such, only by dissimulating itself in beings; thus, in a particular and very strange way, differance (is) "older" than the ontological difference or the truth of Being. In this age it can be called the play of traces. It is a trace that no longer belongs to the horizon of Being but one whose sense of Being is borne and bound by this play; it is a play of traces or differance that has no meaning and is not, a play that does not belong. There is no support to be found and no depth to be had for this bottomless chessboard where being is set in play.

It is perhaps in this way that the Heraclitean play of the *hen diapheron heautōi*, of the one differing from itself, of what is in difference with itself, already becomes lost as a trace in determining the *diapherein* as ontological difference.

To think through the ontological difference doubtless remains a difficult task, a task whose statement has remained nearly inaudible. And to prepare ourselves for venturing beyond our own logos, that is, for a differance so violent that it refuses to be stopped and examined as the epochality of Being and ontological difference, is neither to give up this passage through the truth of Being, nor is it in any way to "criticize," "contest," or fail to recognize the incessant necessity for it. On the contrary, we must stay within the difficulty of this passage; we must repeat this passage in a rigorous reading of metaphysics, wherever metaphysics serves as the norm of Western speech, and not only in the texts of "the history of philosophy." Here we must allow the trace of whatever goes beyond the truth of Being to appear/ disappear in its fully rigorous way. It is a trace of something that can never present itself; it is itself a trace that can never be presented, that is, can never appear and manifest itself as such in its phenomenon. It is a trace that lies beyond what pro-foundly ties fundamental ontology to phenomenology. Like differance, the trace is never presented as such. In presenting itself it becomes effaced; in being sounded it dies away, like the writing of the *a*, inscribing its pyramid in differance.

We can always reveal the precursive and secretive traces of this movement in metaphysical speech, especially in the contemporary talk about the closure of ontol-ogy, i.e., through the various attempts we have looked at (Nietzsche, Freud, Levinas) – and particularly in Heidegger's work.

The latter provokes us to question the essence of the present, the presence of the present.

What is the present? What is it to conceive the present in its presence?

Let us consider, for example, the 1946 text entitled "Der Spruch des Anaximan-der." Heidegger there recalls that the forgetting of Being forgets about the difference between Being and beings:

> But the point of Being (*die Sache des Seins*) is to be the Being *of* beings. The linguistic form of this enigmatic and multivalent genitive designates a genesis (*Genesis*), a proven-ance (*Herkunft*) of the *present* from presence (*des Anwesenden aus dem Anwesen*). But with

the unfolding of these two, the essence (*Wesen*) of this provenance remains hidden (*verborgen*). Not only is the essence of this provenance not thought out, but neither is the simple relation between presence and present (*Anwesen und Anwesenden*).

Since the dawn, it seems that presence and being-present are each separately something. Imperceptibly, presence becomes itself a present.... The essence of presence (*Das Wesen des Anwesens*), and thus the difference between presence and present, is forgotten. *The forgetting of Being is the forgetting of the difference between Being and beings.*[15]

In recalling the difference between Being and beings (the ontological difference) as the difference between presence and present, Heidegger puts forward a proposition, indeed, a group of propositions; it is not our intention here to idly or hastily "criticize" them but rather to convey them with all their provocative force.

Let us then proceed slowly. What Heidegger wants to point out is that the difference between Being and beings, forgotten by metaphysics, has disappeared without leaving a trace. The very trace of difference has sunk from sight. If we admit that differance (is) (itself) something other than presence and absence, if it *traces*, then we are dealing with the forgetting of the difference (between Being and beings), and we now have to talk about a disappearance of the trace's trace. This is certainly what this passage from "Der Spruch des Anaximander" seems to imply:

The forgetting of Being is a part of the very essence of Being, and is concealed by it. The forgetting belongs so essentially to the destination of Being that the dawn of this destination begins precisely as an unconcealment of the *present* in its *presence*. This means: the history of Being begins by the forgetting of Being, in that Being retains its essence, its difference from beings. Difference is wanting; it remains forgotten. Only what is differentiated – the present and presence (*das Anwesende und das Anwesen*) – becomes uncovered, but not *insofar as* it is differentiated. On the contrary, the matinal trace (*die frühe Spur*) of difference effaces itself from the moment that presence appears as a being-present (*das Anwesen und ein Anwesendes erscheint*) and finds its provenance in a supreme (being)-present (*in einem höchsten Anwesenden*).[16]

The trace is not a presence but is rather the simulacrum of a presence that dislocates, displaces, and refers beyond itself. The trace has, properly speaking, no place, for effacement belongs to the very structure of the trace. Effacement must always be able to overtake the trace; otherwise it would not be a trace but an indestructible and monumental substance. In addition, and from the start, effacement constitutes it as a trace – effacement establishes the trace in a change of place and makes it disappear in its appearing, makes it issue forth from itself in its very position. The effacing of this early trace (*die frühe Spur*) of difference is therefore "the same" as its tracing within the text of metaphysics. This metaphysical text must have retained a mark of what it lost or put in reserve, set aside. In the language of metaphysics the paradox of such a structure is the inversion of the metaphysical concept which produces the following effect: the present becomes the sign of signs, the trace of traces. It is no longer what every reference refers to in the last instance; it becomes a function in a generalized referential structure. It is a trace, and a trace of the effacement of a trace.

In this way the metaphysical text is *understood*; it is still readable, and remains to be read. It proposes both the monument and the mirage of the trace, the trace as simultaneously traced and effaced, simultaneously alive and dead, alive as always to simulate even life in its preserved inscription; it is a pyramid.

Thus we think through, without contradiction, or at least without granting any pertinence to such contradiction, what is perceptible and imperceptible about the trace. The "matinal trace" of difference is lost in an irretrievable invisibility, and yet even its loss is covered, preserved, regarded, and retarded. This happens in a text, in the form of presence.

Having spoken about the effacement of the matinal trace, Heidegger can thus, in this contradiction without contradiction, consign or countersign the sealing of the trace. We read on a little further:

> The difference between Being and beings, however, can in turn be experienced as something forgotten only if it is already discovered with the presence of the present (*mit dem Anwesen des Anwesenden*) and if it is thus sealed in a trace (*so eine Spur geprägt hat*) that remains preserved (*gewahrt bleibt*) in the language which Being appropriates.[17]

Further on still, while meditating upon Anaximander's τὸ χρεών, translated as *Brauch* (sustaining use), Heidegger writes the following:

> Dispensing accord and deference (*Fug und Ruch verfügend*), our sustaining use frees the present (*das Anwesende*) in its sojourn and sets it free every time for its sojourn. But by the same token the present is equally seen to be exposed to the constant danger of hardening in the insistence (*in das blosse Beharren verhärtet*) out of its sojourning duration. In this way sustaining use (*Brauch*) remains itself and at the same time an abandonment (*Aushändigung*: handing-over) of presence (*des Anwesens*) *in den Un-fug*, to discord (dis-jointedness). Sustaining use joins together the dis- (*Der Brauch fügt das Un-*).[18]

And it is at the point where Heidegger determines *sustaining use* as *trace* that the question must be asked: can we, and how far can we, think of this trace and the *dis-* of differance as *Wesen des Seins*? Doesn't the *dis* of differance refer us beyond the history of Being, beyond our language as well, and beyond everything that can be named by it? Doesn't it call for – in the language of being – the necessarily violent transformation of this language by an entirely different language?

Let us be more precise here. In order to dislodge the "trace" from its cover (and whoever believes that one tracks down some *thing*; one tracks down tracks), let us continue reading this passage:

> The translation of τὸ χρεών, "sustaining use" (*Brauch*) does not derive from cogitations of an etymologico-lexical nature. The choice of the word "sustaining use" derives from an antecedent translation (*Übersetzen*) of the thought that attempts to conceive difference in the deployment of Being (*im Wesen des Seins*) toward the historical beginning of the forgetting of Being. The word "sustaining use" is dictated to thought in the apprehension (*Erfahrung*) of the forgetting of Being. τὸ χρεών, properly names a trace (*Spur*) of what remains to be conceived in the word "sustaining use," a trace that quickly disappears (*alsbald verschwindet*) into the history of Being, in its world-historical unfolding as Western metaphysics.[19]

How do we conceive of the outside of a text? How, for example, do we conceive of what stands opposed to the text of Western metaphysics? To be sure, the "trace that quickly disappears into the history of Being,…as Western metaphysics," escapes all the determinations, all the names it might receive in the metaphysical text. The trace is sheltered and thus dissimulated in these names; it does not appear in the text as the trace "itself." But this is because the trace itself could never itself appear as such. Heidegger also says that difference can never appear *as such*: "Lichtung des Unterschiedes kann deshalb auch nicht bedeuten, dass der Unterschied als der Unterschied erscheint." There is no essence of differance; not only can it not allow itself to be taken up into the *as such* of its name or its appearing, but it threatens the authority of the *as such* in general, the thing's presence in its essence. That there is no essence of differance at this point also implies that there is neither Being nor truth to the play of writing, *insofar as* it involves differance.

For us, differance remains a metaphysical name; and all the names that it receives from our language are still, so far as they are names, metaphysical. This is particularly so when they speak of determining differance as the difference between presence and present (*Anwesen/Anwesend*), but already and especially so when, in the most general way, they speak of determining differance as the difference between Being and beings. "Older" than Being itself, our language has no name for such a differance. But we "already know" that if it is unnameable, this is not simply provisional; it is not because our language has still not found or received this *name*, or because we would have to look for it in another language, outside the finite system of our language. It is because there is no *name* for this, not even essence or Being – not even the name "differance," which is not a name, which is not a pure nominal unity, and continually breaks up in a chain of different substitutions.

"There is no name for this": we read this as a truism. What is unnameable here is not some ineffable being that cannot be approached by a name; like God, for example. What is unnameable is the play that brings about the nominal effects, the relatively unitary or atomic structures we call names, or chains of substitutions for names. In these, for example, the nominal effect of "differance" is itself involved, carried off, and reinscribed, just as the false beginning or end of a game is still part of the game, a function of the system.

What we do know, what we could know if it were simply a question of knowing, is that there never has been and never will be a unique word, a master name. This is why thinking about the letter *a* of differance is not the primary prescription, nor is it the prophetic announcement of some imminent and still unheard-of designation. There is nothing kerygmatic about this "word" so long as we can perceive its reduction to a lower-case letter.

There will be no unique name, not even the name of Being. It must be conceived without *nostalgia*; that is, it must be conceived outside the myth of the purely maternal or paternal language belonging to the lost fatherland of thought. On the contrary, we must *affirm* it – in the sense that Nietzsche brings affirmation into play – with a certain laughter and with a certain dance.

After this laughter and dance, after this affirmation that is foreign to any dialectic, the question arises as to the other side of nostalgia, which I will call Heideggerian *hope*. I am not unaware that this term may be somewhat shocking. I venture it all the same, without excluding any of its implications, and shall relate it to what seems to me to be retained of metaphysics in "Der Spruch des Anaximander," namely, the quest for the proper word and the unique name. In talking about the "first word of Being" (*das frühe Wort des Seins*: τὸ χρεών), Heidegger writes,

The relation to the present, unfolding its order in the very essence of *presence*, is unique (*ist eine einzige*). It is pre-eminently incomparable to any other relation; it belongs to the uniqueness of Being itself (*Sie gehört zur Einzigkeit des Seins selbst*). Thus, in order to name what is deployed in Being (*das Wesende des Seins*), language will have to find a single word, the unique word (*ein einziges, das einzige Wort*). There we see how hazardous is every word of thought (every thoughtful word: *denkende Wort*) that addresses itself to Being (*das dem Sein zugesprochen wird*). What is hazarded here, however, is something impossible, because Being speaks through every language; everywhere and always.[20]

Such is the question: the marriage between speech and Being in the unique word, in the finally proper name. Such is the question that enters into the affirmation put into play by differance. The question bears (upon) each of the words in this sentence: "Being / speaks / through every language; / everywhere and always /."

Notes

1 This essay appeared originally in the *Bulletin de la Société française de philosophie*, LXII, No. 3 (July–September, 1968), pp. 73–101. Derrida's remarks were delivered as a lecture at a meeting of the Société at the Sorbonne, in the Amphithéâtre Michelet, on January 27, 1968, with Jean Wahl presiding. Professor Wahl's introductory and closing remarks have not been translated. The essay was reprinted in *Théorie d'ensemble*, a collection of essays by Derrida and others, published by Editions Seuil in 1968. It is reproduced here by permission of Editions Seuil.

2 [The reader should bear in mind that "differance," or difference with an *a*, incorporates two significations: "to differ" and "to defer." – Trans.]

3 [For the term "facilitation" (*frayage*) in Freud, cf. "Project for a Scientific Psychology" in *The Complete Psychological Works of Sigmund Freud*, 24 vols (New York and London: Macmillan, 1964) I, p. 300, n. 4 by the translator, James Strachey: "The word 'facilitation' as a rendering of the German '*Bahnung*' seems to have been introduced by Sherrington a few years after the *Project* was written. The German word, however, was already in use." The sense that Derrida draws upon here is stronger in the French or German, that is, the opening-up or clearing-out of a pathway. In the context of the "Project for a Scientific Psychology I," facilitation denotes the conduction capability that results from a difference in resistance levels in the memory and perception circuits of the nervous system. Thus, lowering the resistance threshold of a contact barrier serves to "open up" a nerve pathway and "facilitates" the excitatory process for the circuit. Cf. also J. Derrida, *L'Ecriture et la différence*, ch. VII, "Freud et la scène de l'écriture" (Paris: Seuil, 1967), esp. pp. 29–305. – Trans.]

4 [On "pyramid" and "tomb" see J. Derrida, "Le Puits et la pyramide," in *Hegel et la pensée moderne* (Paris: Presses Universitaires de France, 1970), esp. pp. 44–5. – Trans.]

5 Ferdinand de Saussure, *Cours de linguistique générale*, ed. C. Bally and A. Sechehaye (Paris: Payot, 1916); English translation by Wade Baskin, *Course in General Linguistics* (New York: Philosophical Library, 1959), pp. 117–18, 120.

6 Saussure, *Course in General Linguistics*, p. 18.

7 [On "supplement" see *Speech and Phenomena*, ch. 7, pp. 88–104. Cf. also Derrida, *De la grammatologie* (Paris: Editions de Minuit, 1967). On "*pharmakon*" see Derrida, "La Pharmacie de Platon," *Tel Quel*, No. 32 (Winter 1967), pp. 17–59; No. 33 (Spring 1968), pp. 4–48. On "hymen" see Derrida, "La Double séance," *Tel Quel*, No. 41 (Spring 1970), pp. 3–43; No. 42 (Summer 1970), pp. 3–45. "La Pharmacie de Platon" and "La Double séance" have been reprinted in a recent text of Derrida, *La Dissémination* (Paris: Editions du Seuil, 1972). – Trans.]

8 [Derrida often brackets or "crosses out" certain key terms taken from metaphysics and logic, and in doing this, he follows Heidegger's usage in *Zur Seinsfrage*. The terms in question no longer have their full meaning, they no longer have the status of a purely signified content of expression – no longer, that is, after the deconstruction of metaphysics. Generated out of the

play of differance, they still retain a vestigial trace of sense, however, a trace that cannot simply be gotten around (*incontourable*). An extensive discussion of all this is to be found in *De la grammatologie*, pp. 31–40. – Trans.]

9   Alexandre Koyré, "Hegel à Iena," *Revue d'histoire et de philosophie religieuse*, XIV (1934), pp. 420–58; reprinted in Koyré, *Etudes d'histoire de la pensée philosophique* (Paris: Armand Colin, 1961), pp. 135–73.

10 Koyré, *Etudes d'histoire*, pp. 153–4. [The quotation from Hegel (my translation) comes from "Jenenser Logik, Metaphysik, und Naturphilosophie," *Sämtliche Werke* (Leipzig: F. Meiner, 1925), XVIII, p. 202. Koyré reproduces the original German text on pp. 153–4, n. 2. – Trans.]

11 Saussure, *Course in General Linguistics*, p. 37.

12 G. Deleuze, *Nietzsche et la philosophie* (Paris: Presses Universitaires de France, 1970), p. 49.

13 Freud, *Complete Psychological Works*, XVIII, p. 10.

14 Derrida, *L'Ecriture et la différence*, pp. 369–407.

15 Martin Heidegger, *Holzwege* (Frankfurt: V. Klostermann, 1957), pp. 335–6. [All translations of quotations from *Holzwege* are mine. – Trans.]

16 Ibid., p. 336.

17 Ibid.

18 Ibid., pp. 339–40.

19 Ibid., p. 340.

20 Ibid., pp. 337–8.

CHAPTER 7

Of Grammatology

Jacques Derrida

Of Grammatology (1967) is a polemic against the metaphysical tradition in philosophy from Plato to Husserl. That tradition sought a basis for determining truth in the operations of the mind or *logos*. The mind's ability to grasp the presence of an object or of an idea was the gold standard of truthfulness. In this "logocentric" conception of truth, objects and ideas were conceived as being substances and presences that could exist apart from differance and supplementarity. The techniques of signification especially were considered alien to the presence of ideas. Mere "re-presentation" in language was an artificial supplement to and a substitute for ideas but was not itself a bearer of authentic presence or ideational substance. Derrida notices that this assumption is necessarily phonological and phonocentric. It associates the ability of the mind to grasp pure ideas with mental speech and the voice of consciousness. The mind's ability to hear itself speak and think is closely associated with the metaphysical notion that ideas transcend the ordinary empirical world of language and signification. In this tradition, the external contrivances and techniques of signification in language, writing especially, have to be added onto mental speech and to ideal meaning if it is to be communicated. But according to metaphysics such supplementary addition is alien to the purely ideal quality of thought and of mental speech, which is purely expressive of the living immediacy of presence.

Derrida's critique of this tradition notices that writing in the metaphysical tradition is a recurring delinquent. It more than any other form of signification is associated with the loss of presence and with untruth. Writing is a signifier of a signifier, the graphic sign of mental speech, itself a sign of ideas. As such, it is doubly removed from true ideas in consciousness. It represents the twin dangers of difference and alterity (or otherness) because it depends on something else or "other" to be "itself." As such, it is the perfect embodiment of the concept of the differential constitution of identity. Derrida examines those texts in the metaphysical tradition that discuss the origin of language and notices that the origin of language is described as a moment of presence that is prior to all signification. Writing, especially, is characterized as alien to presence because it is merely "supplementary," an addition to presence in the mind as rendered in mental speech. Derrida finds that when writers like Rousseau describe an origin of language that is supposedly a pure natural presence prior to signification and to writing, what they describe instead is differance. Derrida calls this version of differance "proto-" or "archi-writing" because differance and writing are two names for the same structure of supplementation whereby the identity of one term requires reference to and supplementation by an-other to be itself. One cannot isolate presence from difference or the identity of presence from differential relations that necessarily and in an essential way contaminate it with the characteristics of writing. If everything is differential, then everything is, like writing, a signifier of a signifier. To be "itself," it must refer to "others" which are themselves referential or differential.

Logocentric metaphysics consistently banishes writing as a defective addition to presence, but when one reads metaphysical texts in a deconstructive manner, what one finds is that writing (as a metaphor for differance) is the precondition of presence. Presence cannot exist outside of a structure of supplementarity and signification, a network of differential relations between terms that permit identities to form. Yet, as Derrida notes, ideas cannot elude spatialization. If they are to be expressed in language, they must contain the potential to be re-presented within them. They must be capable of differing from themselves and assuming another form that doubles them and re-presents their presence. Derrida contends this is the case because they are already doubled within themselves. The process of differance, the network of signification which makes meaning possible by differentially linking signifying elements, allows ideas to come into being in the first place, but what this means is that each single element is in its very constitution doubled. It is both "itself" and its "others," a double rather than a singular thing. Rather than be an external feature added on to the identity of individual ideas, the doubling of difference produces and makes possible ideation in the first place. Ideas could not assume the form of external representation if the doubling that re-presentation represents did not inhabit ideas from the get go. And what this means is that a certain spatial relation – between a thing and its other(s) – inhabits all presence. Each presence is re-presented (by its others) in its essence, in its origin, and in "itself."

In this book, Derrida's method is most explicitly deconstructive in that he seems to use writers' texts against themselves. Whenever one examines how writers in the metaphysical tradition designate a moment of pure presence, he finds, they invariably have recourse to differentiations that situate presence within a network of relations between terms. They declare the priority of presence but describe the priority of differance. Saussure, for example, is loyal to the metaphysical tradition when he makes speech prior to and more central than writing. Yet his argument works in a way that undermines his own premises. He declares writing secondary, but in order to do so, he must begin by differentiating an inside from an outside, an inside of language that is speech from an outside that is the realm of writing and graphic notation. Yet this initial act of differentiation is never accounted for by Saussure. It begins his argument but, like writing, it remains outside his thinking, like an empty supplement, both a danger to his thought and the remedy that makes his thought possible. In later works, Derrida will draw attention to the problematic nature of this "his" in "his thought." He will note that our thinking is made possible by processes of signification and by movements of differance that lie outside our subjective control. In so doing, he will shift focus away from the "logos" and from the idea that consciousness is central in the determination of truth. "To deconstruct" in some sense means to notice the a-logical, a-human processes that make our thinking possible while also making it other than what we think.

Some vocabulary:

"Phenomenon, phenomenology." The philosophy of Edmund Husserl was called phenomenology. A phenomenon is the idea of an object, its mental representation. Husserl was concerned with describing the operations of consciousness that would allow true ideas to be grasped by the mind.

"Epoch, epoche, epochal." Epoch (from the Greek word *epoche*) refers to Husserl's phenomenological reduction, whereby all contingent, worldly, empirical features of an object are separated out from the idea of that object so that the mind can grasp it as a pure idea. Another term for this operation is "bracketing" or putting out of play.

Derrida plays with "epoch" by using it to mean both the reduction of worldly contingency (eliminating signification from ideation, most notably) and the historical era in which metaphysics reigned from Plato down to Husserl.

"Logos" is the Greek word for mind or reason as well as language. Many philosophers in the metaphysical tradition tried to locate a basis for truth in the mind. Derrida suggests that such ideal truth is conceived by these philosophers as a substance or presence that the mind grasps in some pure way aloof from signification and especially from that secondary form of signification called writing. In the logos, the authority and reality of ideal truth is guaranteed by its link both to consciousness's ability to be aware of itself or present to itself and by its ability to hear itself speak. The "phonic" element of thought is thus linked to the ability of the logos to guarantee truth as presence in the mind. For this reason, Derrida here identifies "logocentrism" with "phonocentrism."

"Onto-theology" literally means "religion of being." "Ontos" is the Greek word for being, and being in this sense means the existence of things or the underlying fact of existence (i.e., that things exist at all instead of not existing). Such theology, according to Derrida, is characterized by the belief that being is a presence or a substance, rather than something which more resembles a computer screen in that it is generated as an effect by relations between different things each of whose identity is also differential, part of a network of relations. If Derrida's claim that "differance" underlies reality is the case, then reality as it appears in our minds, the "being" of things, is produced as an effect of spatial differences between things or between different moments in time. The presence of being is a "ghost effect" created by the fluttering past the screen of our minds of things with no identity of their own apart from their differences or relations. To believe that being is pure presence is therefore theological, an act of faith rather than an accurate perception. A related term is "ontico-ontological difference," a phrase from Martin Heidegger that refers to his idea that one must distinguish between the field of existing things (the ontic) and the basic fact of being (ontology).

"Aufhebung" and "Erinnerung." These two words from the German philosopher G. W. F. Hegel, a major metaphysical thinker, refer to the metaphysical belief that language gives expression to ideas that prior to that expression lead a purely spiritual existence in the mind. Ideation is not physical, according to the metaphysical philosophers; it exists in another realm from physical matter. Ideas that are expressed in signs in language merely bear spirit out of itself, but it then always returns to itself. That return is captured by the word "Erinnerung" which means "memory." Signs remember the spirit they bear in them, the ideal meaning they carry, according to Hegel.

"Aufhebung" means "sublimation," and it refers to the way ideas supposedly enter the exterior realm of signification and are then resurrected into spirit in the act of interpretation that finds meaning in the signs that bear ideas. According to this theory, when we communicate, ideas leave the realm of pure ideality in the mind, enter the external mechanisms of signification, and are then converted back into spirit when someone understands or interprets what is being communicated. Derrida points out that writing or signification has always had a dual meaning in the idealist tradition: on the one hand, it is a secondary addition to ideas that remembers them. It has meaning only in so much as it recalls the meaning or idea that animated it. On the other hand, writing represents the forgetting of the truth of mental speech or of ideas. It threatens ideas and mental speech with loss of meaning. He chooses "writing" as his primary metaphor for "differance" in *Of Grammatology* for this reason. It indicates the way all ideality and all ideal notions of truth are plagued by a necessity they cannot expel. Writing (differance) makes them possible yet at the same time is the instrument for assuring the impossibility of the claim that ideas are purely ideal or are pure presences or substances in the mind.

"Trace" refers to the fact that all things (ideas, objects) that seem to have an identity are in fact constituted by their relations to or difference from other ideas and objects. They bear the "trace" of the other. Another name for such "otherness" is "alterity."

The End of the Book and the Beginning of Writing

*Socrates, he who does not write** – Nietzsche

However the topic is considered, the *problem of language* has never been simply one problem among others. But never as much as at present has it invaded, *as such*, the global horizon of the most diverse researches and the most heterogeneous discourses, diverse and heterogeneous in their intention, method, and ideology. The devaluation of the word "language" itself, and how, in the very hold it has upon us, it betrays a loose vocabulary, the temptation of a cheap seduction, the passive yielding to fashion, the consciousness of the avant-garde, in other words – ignorance – are evidences of this effect. This inflation of the sign "language" is the inflation of the sign itself, absolute inflation, inflation itself. Yet, by one of its aspects or shadows, it is itself still a sign: this crisis is also a symptom. It indicates, as if in spite of itself, that a historico-metaphysical epoch *must* finally determine as language the totality of its problematic horizon. It must do so not only because all that desire had wished to wrest from the play of language finds itself recaptured within that play but also because, for the same reason, language itself is menaced in its very life, helpless, adrift in the threat of limitlessness, brought back to its own finitude at the very moment when its limits seem to disappear, when it ceases to be self-assured, contained, and *guaranteed* by the infinite signified which seemed to exceed it.

The program

By a slow movement whose necessity is hardly perceptible, everything that for at least some twenty centuries tended toward and finally succeeded in being gathered under the name of language is beginning to let itself be transferred to, or at least summarized under, the name of writing. By a hardly perceptible necessity, it seems as though the concept of writing – no longer indicating a particular, derivative, auxiliary form of language in general (whether understood as communication, relation, expression, signification, constitution of meaning or thought, etc.), no longer designating the exterior surface, the insubstantial double of a major signifier, *the signifier of the signifier* – is beginning to go beyond the extension of language. In all senses of the word, writing thus *comprehends* language. Not that the word "writing" has ceased to designate the signifier of the signifier, but it appears, strange as it may

---

* "Aus dem Gedankenkreise der Geburt der Tragödie," I. 3. *Nietzsche Werke* (Leipzig, 1903), vol. 9, part 2 i, p. 66.

seem, that "signifier of the signifier" no longer defines accidental doubling and fallen secondarity. "Signifier of the signifier" describes on the contrary the movement of language: in its origin, to be sure, but one can already suspect that an origin whose structure can be expressed as "signifier of the signifier" conceals and erases itself in its own production. There the signified always already functions as a signifier. The secondarity that it seemed possible to ascribe to writing alone affects all signifieds in general, affects them always already, the moment they *enter the game*. There is not a single signified that escapes, even if recaptured, the play of signifying references that constitute language. The advent of writing is the advent of this play; today such a play is coming into its own, effacing the limit starting from which one had thought to regulate the circulation of signs, drawing along with it all the reassuring signifieds, reducing all the strongholds, all the out-of-bounds shelters that watched over the field of language. This, strictly speaking, amounts to destroying the concept of "sign" and its entire logic. Undoubtedly it is not by chance that this *overwhelming* supervenes at the moment when the extension of the concept of language effaces all its limits. We shall see that this overwhelming and this effacement have the same meaning, are one and the same phenomenon. It is as if the Western concept of language (in terms of what, beyond its plurivocity and beyond the strict and problematic opposition of speech [*parole*] and language [*langue*], attaches it *in general* to phonematic or glossematic production, to language, to voice, to hearing, to sound and breath, to speech) were revealed today as the guise or disguise of a primary writing:[1] more fundamental than that which, before this conversion, passed for the simple "supplement to the spoken word" (Rousseau). Either writing was never a simple "supplement," or it is urgently necessary to construct a new logic of the "supplement." It is this urgency which will guide us further in reading Rousseau.

These disguises are not historical contingencies that one might admire or regret. Their movement was absolutely necessary, with a necessity which cannot be judged by any other tribunal. The privilege of the *phonè* does not depend upon a choice that could have been avoided. It responds to a moment of *economy* (let us say of the "life" of "history," or of "being as self-relationship"). The system of "hearing (understanding)-oneself-speak" through the phonic substance – which *presents itself* as the non-exterior, nonmundane, therefore nonempirical or noncontingent signifier – has necessarily dominated the history of the world during an entire epoch, and has even produced the idea of the world, the idea of world-origin, that arises from the difference between the worldly and the non-worldly, the outside and the inside, ideality and nonideality, universal and nonuniversal, transcendental and empirical, etc.[2]

With an irregular and essentially precarious success, this movement would apparently have tended, as toward its *telos*, to confine writing to a secondary and instrumental function: translator of a full speech that was fully *present* (present to itself, to its signified, to the other, the very condition of the theme of presence in general), technics in the service of language, *spokesman*, interpreter of an originary speech itself shielded from interpretation.

Technics in the service of language: I am not invoking a general essence of technics which would be already familiar to us and would help us in *understanding* the narrow and historically determined concept of writing as an example. I believe on the contrary that a certain sort of question about the meaning and origin of writing precedes, or at least merges with, a certain type of question about the meaning and origin of technics. That is why the notion of technique can never simply clarify the notion of writing.

It is therefore as if what we call language could have been in its origin and in its end only a moment, an essential but determined mode, a phenomenon, an aspect, a species of writing. And as if it had succeeded in making us forget this, and *in wilfully misleading us*, only in the course of an adventure: as that adventure itself. All in all a short enough adventure. It merges with the history that has associated technics and logocentric metaphysics for nearly three millennia. And it now seems to be approaching what is really its own *exhaustion*: under the circumstances – and this is no more than one example among others – of this death of the civilization of the book, of which so much is said and which manifests itself particularly through a convulsive proliferation of libraries. All appearances to the contrary, this death of the book undoubtedly announces (and in a certain sense always has announced) nothing but a death of speech (of a *so-called* full speech) and a new mutation in the history of writing, in history as writing. Announces it at a distance of a few centuries. It is on that scale that we must reckon it here, being careful not to neglect the quality of a very heterogeneous historical duration: the acceleration is such, and such its qualitative meaning, that one would be equally wrong in making a careful evaluation according to past rhythms. "Death of speech" is of course a metaphor here: before we speak of disappearance, we must think of a new situation for speech, of its subordination within a structure of which it will no longer be the archon.

To affirm in this way that the concept of writing exceeds and comprehends that of language, presupposes of course a certain definition of language and of writing. If we do not attempt to justify it, we shall be giving in to the movement of inflation that we have just mentioned, which has also taken over the word "writing," and that not fortuitously. For some time now, as a matter of fact, here and there, by a gesture and for motives that are profoundly necessary, whose degradation is easier to denounce than it is to disclose their origin, one says "language" for action, movement, thought, reflection, consciousness, unconsciousness, experience, affectivity, etc. Now we tend to say "writing" for all that and more: to designate not only the physical gestures of literal pictographic or ideographic inscription, but also the totality of what makes it possible; and also, beyond the signifying side, the signified side itself. And thus we say "writing" for all that gives rise to an inscription in general, whether it is literal or not and even if what it distributes in space is alien to the order of the voice: cinematography, choreography, of course, but also pictorial, musical, sculptural "writing." One might also speak of athletic writing, and with even greater certainty of military or political writing in view of the techniques that govern those domains today. All this to describe not only the system of notation secondarily connected with these activities but the essence and the content of these activities themselves. It is also in this sense that the contemporary biologist speaks of writing and *pro-gram* in relation to the most elementary processes of information within the living cell. And, finally, whether it has essential limits or not, the entire field covered by the cybernetic *program* will be the field of writing. If the theory of cybernetics is by itself to oust all metaphysical concepts – including the concepts of soul, of life, of value, of choice, of memory – which until recently served to separate the machine from man,[3] it must conserve the notion of writing, trace, grammè [written mark], or grapheme, until its own historico-metaphysical character is also exposed. Even before being determined as human (with all the distinctive characteristics that have always been attributed to man and the entire system of significations that they imply) or nonhuman, the *grammè* – or the *grapheme* – would thus name the element. An element without simplicity. An element, whether it is understood as the medium or as the irreducible atom, of the arche-synthesis in general, of what one must forbid oneself to define within the system of oppositions of metaphysics, of what consequently one should not even call *experience* in general, that is to say the origin of *meaning* in general.

This situation has always already been announced. Why is it today in the process of making itself known *as such* and *after the fact*? This question would call forth an interminable analysis. Let us simply choose some points of departure in order to introduce the limited remarks to which I shall confine myself. I have already alluded to *theoretical* mathematics; its writing – whether understood as a sensible *graphie* [manner of writing] (and that already presupposes an identity, therefore an ideality, of its form, which in principle renders absurd the so easily admitted notion of the "sensible signifier"), or understood as the ideal synthesis of signifieds or a trace operative on another level, or whether it is understood, more profoundly, as the *passage* of the one to the other – has never been absolutely linked with a phonetic production. Within cultures practicing so-called phonetic writing, mathematics is not just an enclave. That is mentioned by all historians of writing; they recall at the same time the imperfections of alphabetic writing, which passed for so long as the most convenient and "the most intelligent"[4] writing. This enclave is also the place where the practice of scientific language challenges intrinsically and with increasing profundity the ideal of phonetic writing and all its implicit metaphysics (metaphysics *itself*), particularly, that is, the philosophical idea of the *epistémè*; also of *istoria*, a concept profoundly related to it in spite of the dissociation or opposition which has distinguished one from the other during one phase of their common progress. History and knowledge, *istoria* and *epistémè* have always been determined (and not only etymologically or philosophically) as detours for the purpose of the reappropriation of presence.

But beyond theoretical mathematics, the development of the *practical methods* of information retrieval extends the possibilities of the "message" vastly, to the point where it is no longer the "written" translation of a language, the transporting of a signified which could remain spoken in its integrity. It goes hand in hand with an extension of phonography and of all the means of conserving the spoken language, of making it function without the presence of the speaking subject. This development, coupled with that of anthropology and of the history of writing, teaches us that phonetic writing, the medium of the great metaphysical, scientific, technical, and economic adventure of the West, is limited in space and time and limits itself even as it is in the process of imposing its laws upon the cultural areas that had escaped it. But this nonfortuitous conjunction of cybernetics and the "human sciences" of writing leads to a more profound reversal.

The signifier and truth

The "rationality" – but perhaps that word should be abandoned for reasons that will appear at the end of this sentence – which governs a writing thus enlarged and radicalized, no longer issues from a logos. Further, it inaugurates the destruction, not the demolition but the de-sedimentation, the de-construction, of all the significations that have their source in that of the logos. Particularly the signification of *truth*. All the metaphysical determinations of truth, and even the one beyond metaphysical onto-theology that Heidegger reminds us of, are more or less immediately inseparable from the instance of the logos, or of a reason thought within the lineage of the logos, in whatever sense it is understood: in the pre-Socratic or the philosophical sense, in the sense of God's infinite understanding or in the anthropological sense, in the pre-Hegelian or the post-Hegelian sense. Within this logos, the original and essential link to the *phonè* has never been broken. It would be easy to demonstrate this and I shall attempt such a demonstration later. As has been more or less implicitly determined, the essence of the *phonè* would be immediately proximate to that which within "thought" as logos relates to "meaning," produces it, receives it, speaks it, "composes" it. If, for Aristotle, for example, "spoken words (ta en tē phonē) are the symbols of mental experience (pathēmata tes psychēs) and written words are the symbols of spoken words" (*De interpretatione*, 1, 16a 3) it is because the voice, producer of *the first symbols*, has a relationship of essential and immediate proximity with the mind. Producer of the first signifier, it is not just a simple signifier among others. It signifies "mental experiences" which themselves reflect or mirror things by natural resemblance. Between being and mind, things and feelings, there would be a relationship of translation or natural signification; between mind and logos, a relationship of conventional symbolization. And the *first* convention, which would relate immediately to the order of natural and universal signification, would be produced as spoken language. Written language would establish the conventions, interlinking other conventions with them.

> Just as all men have not the same writing so all men have not the same speech sounds, but mental experiences, of which these are the *primary symbols* (semeīa prótos), are the same for all, as also are those things of which our experiences are the images (*De interpretatione*, 1, 16a. Italics added).

The feelings of the mind, expressing things naturally, constitute a sort of universal language which can then efface itself. It is the stage of transparence. Aristotle can sometimes omit it without risk.[5] In every case, the voice is closest to the signified, whether it is determined strictly as sense (thought or lived) or more loosely as thing. All signifiers, and first and foremost the written signifier, are derivative with regard to what would wed the voice indissolubly to the mind or to the thought of the signified sense, indeed to the thing itself (whether it is done in the Aristotelian manner that we have just indicated or in the manner of medieval theology, determining the *res* as a thing created from its *eidos*, from its sense thought in the logos or in the infinite understanding of God). The written signifier is always technical and representative. It has no constitutive meaning. This derivation is the very origin of the notion of the "signifier." The notion of the sign always implies within itself the distinction between signifier and signified, even if, as Saussure argues, they are distinguished simply as the two sides of one and the same leaf. This notion remains therefore within the heritage of that logocentrism which is also a phonocentrism: absolute proximity of voice and being, of voice and the meaning of being, of voice and the ideality of meaning. Hegel demonstrates very clearly the strange privilege of sound in idealization, the production of the concept and the self-presence of the subject.

> This ideal motion, in which through the sound what is as it were the simple subjectivity [*Subjektivität*], the soul of the material thing expresses itself, the ear receives also in a theoretical [*theoretisch*] way, just as the eye shape and colour, thus allowing the inter-

iority of the object to become interiority itself [*läßt dadurch das Innere der Gegenstände für das Innere selbst werden*] (*Esthétique*, III. I tr. fr. p. 16).[*] ... The ear, on the contrary, perceives [*vernimmt*] the result of that interior vibration of material substance without placing itself in a practical relation toward the objects, a result by means of which it is no longer the material form [*Gestalt*] in its repose, but the first, more ideal activity of the soul itself which is manifested [*zum Vorschein kommt*] (p. 296).[†]

What is said of sound in general is a fortiori valid for the *phonè* by which, by virtue of hearing (understanding)-oneself-speak – an indissociable system – the subject affects itself and is related to itself in the element of ideality.

We already have an indication that phonocentrism merges with the historical determination of the meaning of being in general as *presence*, with all the subdetermi-nations which depend on this general form and which organize within it their system and their historical sequence (presence of the thing to the sight as *eidos*, presence as substance/essence/existence [*ousia*], temporal presence as point [*stigmè*] of the now or of the moment [*nun*], the self-presence of the cogito, consciousness, subjectivity, the co-presence of the other and of the self, intersubjectivity as the intentional phenomenon of the ego, and so forth). Logocentrism would thus support the deter-mination of the being of the entity as presence. To the extent that such a logocent-rism is not totally absent from Heidegger's thought, perhaps it still holds that thought within the epoch of onto-theology, within the philosophy of presence, that is to say within philosophy *itself*. This would perhaps mean that one does not leave the epoch whose closure one can outline. The movements of belonging or not belonging to the epoch are too subtle, the illusions in that regard are too easy, for us to make a definite judgement.

The epoch of the logos thus debases writing considered as mediation of mediation and as a fall into the exteriority of meaning. To this epoch belongs the difference between signified and signifier, or at least the strange separation of their "parallel-ism," and the exteriority, however extenuated, of the one to the other. This appur-tenance is organized and hierarchized in a history. The difference between signified and signifier belongs in a profound and implicit way to the totality of the great epoch covered by the history of metaphysics, and in a more explicit and more systematically articulated way to the narrower epoch of Christian creationism and infinitism when these appropriate the resources of Greek conceptuality. This appurtenance is essen-tial and irreducible; one cannot retain the convenience or the "scientific truth" of the Stoic and later medieval opposition between *signans* and *signatum* without also bringing with it all its metaphysico-theological roots. To these roots adheres not only the distinc-tion between the sensible and the intelligible – already a great deal – with all that it controls, namely, metaphysics in its totality. And this distinction is generally accepted as self-evident by the most careful linguists and semiologists, even by those who believe that the scientificity of their work begins where metaphysics ends. Thus, for example:

> As modern structural thought has clearly realized, language is a system of signs and linguistics is part and parcel of the science of signs, or *semiotics* (Saussure's *sémiologie*). The medieval definition of sign – "*aliquid stat pro aliquo*" – has been resurrected and

---

[*]   Georg Wilhelm Friedrich Hegel, *Werke*, Suhrkamp edition (Frankfurt am Main, 1970), vol. 14, p. 256; translated as *The Philosophy of Fine Art* by F. P. Osmaston (London, 1920), vol. 3, pp. 15–16.
[†]   Hegel, p. 134; Osmaston, p. 341.

put forward as still valid and productive. Thus the constitutive mark of any sign in general and of any linguistic sign in particular is its twofold character: every linguistic unit is bipartite and involves both aspects – one sensible and the other intelligible, or in other words, both the *signans* "signifier" (Saussure's *signifiant*) and the *signatum* "signified" (*signifié*). These two constituents of a linguistic sign (and of sign in general) necessarily suppose and require each other.[6]

But to these metaphysico-theological roots many other hidden sediments cling. The semiological or, more specifically, linguistic "science" cannot therefore hold on to the difference between signifier and signified – the very idea of the sign – without the difference between sensible and intelligible, certainly, but also not without retaining, more profoundly and more implicitly, and by the same token the reference to a signified able to "take place" in its intelligibility, before its "fall," before any expulsion into the exteriority of the sensible here below. As the face of pure intelligibility, it refers to an absolute logos to which it is immediately united. This absolute logos was an infinite creative subjectivity in medieval theology: the intelligible side of the sign remains turned toward the word and the face of God.

Of course, it is not a question of "rejecting" these notions; they are necessary and, at least at present, nothing is conceivable for us without them. It is a question at first of demonstrating the systematic and historical solidarity of the concepts and gestures of thought that one often believes can be innocently separated. The sign and divinity have the same place and time of birth. The age of the sign is essentially theological. Perhaps it will never *end*. Its historical *closure* is, however, outlined.

Since these concepts are indispensable for unsettling the heritage to which they belong, we should be even less prone to renounce them. Within the closure, by an oblique and always perilous movement, constantly risking falling back within what is being deconstructed, it is necessary to surround the critical concepts with a careful and thorough discourse – to mark the conditions, the medium, and the limits of their effectiveness and to designate rigorously their intimate relationship to the machine whose deconstruction they permit; and, in the same process, designate the crevice through which the yet unnameable glimmer beyond the closure can be glimpsed. The concept of the sign is here exemplary. We have just marked its metaphysical appurtenance. We know, however, that the thematics of the sign have been for about a century the agonized labor of a tradition that professed to withdraw meaning, truth, presence, being, etc., from the movement of signification. Treating as suspect, as I just have, the difference between signified and signifier, or the idea of the sign in general, I must state explicitly that it is not a question of doing so in terms of the instance of the present truth, anterior, exterior or superior to the sign, or in terms of the place of the effaced difference. Quite the contrary. We are disturbed by that which, in the concept of the sign – which has never existed or functioned outside the history of (the) philosophy (of presence) – remains systematically and genealogically determined by that history. It is there that the concept and above all the work of deconstruction, its "style," remain by nature exposed to misunderstanding and nonrecognition.

The exteriority of the signifier is the exteriority of writing in general, and I shall try to show later that there is no linguistic sign before writing. Without that exteriority, the very idea of the sign falls into decay. Since our entire world and language would collapse with it, and since its evidence and its value keep, to a certain point of derivation, an indestructible solidity, it would be silly to conclude from its placement within an epoch that it is necessary to "move on to something else," to dispose of the sign, of the term and the notion. For a proper understanding of the gesture that we are sketching here, one must understand the expressions "epoch," "closure of an epoch," "historical genealogy" in a new way; and must first remove them from all relativism.

Thus, within this epoch, reading and writing, the production or interpretation of signs, the text in general as fabric of signs, allow themselves to be confined within secondariness. They are preceded by a truth, or a meaning already constituted by and within the element of the logos. Even when the thing, the "referent," is not immediately related to the logos of a creator God where it began by being the spoken/ thought sense, the signified has at any rate an immediate relationship with the logos in general (finite or infinite), and a mediated one with the signifier, that is to say with the exteriority of writing. When it seems to go otherwise, it is because a metaphoric mediation has insinuated itself into the relationship and has simulated immediacy; the writing of truth in the soul, opposed by *Phaedrus* (278a) to bad writing (writing in the "literal" [*propre*] and ordinary sense, "sensible" writing, "in space"), the book of Nature and God's writing, especially in the Middle Ages; all that functions as *metaphor* in these discourses confirms the privilege of the logos and founds the "literal" meaning then given to writing: a sign signifying a signifier itself signifying an eternal truth, eternally thought and spoken in the proximity of a present logos. The paradox to which attention must be paid is this: natural and universal writing, intelligible and nontemporal writing, is thus named by metaphor. A writing that is sensible, finite, and so on, is designated as writing in the literal sense; it is thus thought on the side of culture, technique, and artifice; a human procedure, the ruse of a being accidentally incarnated or of a finite creature. Of course, this metaphor remains enigmatic and refers to a "literal" meaning of writing as the first metaphor. This "literal" meaning is yet unthought by the adherents of this discourse. It is not, therefore, a matter of inverting the literal meaning and the figurative meaning but of determining the "literal" meaning of writing as metaphoricity itself.

In "The Symbolism of the Book," that excellent chapter of *European Literature and the Latin Middle Ages*, E. R. Curtius describes with great wealth of examples the evolution that led from the *Phaedrus* to Calderon, until it seemed to be "precisely the reverse" (tr. fr. p. 372)[*] by the "newly attained position of the book" (p. 374) [p. 306]. But it seems that this modification, however important in fact it might be, conceals a fundamental continuity. As was the case with the Platonic writing of the truth in the soul, in the Middle Ages too it is a writing understood in the metaphoric sense, that is to say a *natural*, eternal, and universal writing, the system of signified truth, which is recognized in its dignity. As in the *Phaedrus*, a certain fallen writing continues to be opposed to it. There remains to be written a history of this metaphor, a metaphor that systematically contrasts divine or natural writing and the human and laborious, finite and artificial inscription. It remains to articulate rigorously the stages of that history, as marked by the quotations below, and to follow the theme of God's book (nature or law, indeed natural law) through all its modifications.

---

[*] Ernst Robert Curtius, "Das Buch als Symbol." *Europäische Literatur und lateinisches Mittelalter* (Bern, 1948), p. 307. French translation by Jean Bréjoux (Paris, 1956): translated as *European Literature and the Latin Middle Ages*, by Willard R. Trask, Harper Torchbooks edition (New York, 1963), pp. 305, 306.

Rabbi Eliezer said: "If all the seas were of ink, and all ponds planted with reeds, if the sky and the earth were parchments and if all human beings practised the art of writing – they would not exhaust the Torah I have learned, just as the Torah itself would not be diminished any more than is the sea by the water removed by a paint brush dipped in it."[7]

Galileo: "It [the book of Nature] is written in a mathematical language."[*]

Descartes: "... to read in the great book of Nature..."[†]

Demea, in the name of natural religion, in the *Dialogues*, ... of Hume: "And this volume of nature contains a great and inexplicable riddle, more than any intelligible discourse or reasoning."[††]

Bonnet: "It would seem more philosophical to me to presume that our earth is a book that God has given to intelligences far superior to ours to read, and where they study in depth the infinitely multiplied and varied characters of His adorable wisdom."

G. H. von Schubert: "This language made of images and hieroglyphs, which supreme Wisdom uses in all its revelations to humanity – which is found in the inferior [*nieder*] language of poetry – and which, in the most inferior and imperfect way [*auf der allerniedrigsten und unvolkommensten*], is more like the metaphorical expression of the dream than the prose of wakefulness, ... we may wonder if this language is not the true and wakeful language of the superior regions. If, when we consider ourselves awakened, we are not plunged in a millennial slumber, or at least in the echo of its dreams, where we only perceive a few isolated and obscure words of God's language, as a sleeper perceives the conversation of the people around him."[§]

Jaspers: "The world is the manuscript of an other, inaccessible to a universal reading, which only existence deciphers."[‖]

Above all, the profound differences distinguishing all these treatments of the same metaphor must not be ignored. In the history of this treatment, the most decisive separation appears at the moment when, at the same time as the science of nature, the determination of absolute presence is constituted as self-presence, as subjectivity. It is the moment of the great rationalisms of the seventeenth century. From then on, the condemnation of fallen and finite writing will take another form, within which we still live: it is non-self-presence that will be denounced. Thus the exemplariness of the "Rousseauist" moment, which we shall deal with later, begins to be explained. Rousseau repeats the Platonic gesture by referring to another model of presence: self-presence in the senses, in the sensible cogito, which simultaneously carries in itself the inscription of divine law. On the one hand, *representative*, fallen, secondary, instituted writing, writing in the literal and strict sense, is condemned in *The Essay*

[*] Quoted in Curtius, op. cit. (German), p. 326, (English), p. 324; Galileo's word is "philosophy" rather than "nature."
[†] Ibid. (German) p. 324, (English) p. 322.
[††] David Hume, *Dialogues Concerning Natural Religion*, ed. Norman Kemp Smith (Oxford, 1935), p. 193.
[§] Gotthilf Heinrich von Schubert, *Die Symbolik des Traumes* (Leipzig, 1862), pp. 23–4.
[‖] Quoted in P. Ricoeur, *Gabriel Marcel et Karl Jaspers* (Paris, 1947), p. 45.

on the Origin of Languages (it "enervates" speech; to "judge genius" from books is like "painting a man's portrait from his corpse," etc.). Writing in the common sense is the dead letter, it is the carrier of death. It exhausts life. On the other hand, on the other side of the same proposition, writing in the metaphoric sense, natural, divine, and living writing, is venerated; it is equal in dignity to the origin of value, to the voice of conscience as divine law, to the heart, to sentiment, and so forth.

> The Bible is the most sublime of all books,... but it is after all a book.... It is not at all in a few sparse pages that one should look for God's law, but in the human heart where His hand deigned to write (*Lettre à Vernes*).[*]

> If the natural law had been written only in the human reason, it would be little capable of directing most of our actions. But it is also engraved in the heart of man in ineffaceable characters.... There it cries to him (*L'état de guerre*.)[†]

Natural writing is immediately united to the voice and to breath. Its nature is not grammatological but pneumatological. It is hieratic, very close to the interior holy voice of the *Profession of Faith*, to the voice one hears upon retreating into oneself: full and truthful presence of the divine voice to our inner sense: "The more I retreat into myself, the more I consult myself, the more plainly do I read these words written in my soul: be just and you will be happy.... I do not derive these rules from the principles of the higher philosophy. I find them in the depths of my heart written by nature in characters which nothing can efface."[††]

There is much to say about the fact that the native unity of the voice and writing is *prescriptive*. Arche-speech is writing because it is a law. A natural law. The beginning word is understood, in the intimacy of self-presence, as the voice of the other and as commandment.

There is therefore a good and a bad writing: the good and natural is the divine inscription in the heart and the soul; the perverse and artful is technique, exiled in the exteriority of the body. A modification well within the Platonic diagram: writing of the soul and of the body, writing of the interior and of the exterior, writing of conscience and of the passions, as there is a voice of the soul and a voice of the body. "Conscience is the voice of the soul, the passions are the voice of the body" [p. 249]. One must constantly go back toward the "voice of nature," the "holy voice of nature," that merges with the divine inscription and prescription; one must encounter oneself within it, enter into a dialogue within its signs, speak and respond to oneself in its pages.

> It was as if nature had spread out all her magnificence in front of our eyes to offer its text for our consideration.... I have therefore closed all the books. Only one is open to all eyes. It is the book of Nature. In this great and sublime book I learn to serve and adore its author.

The good writing has therefore always been *comprehended*. Comprehended as that which had to be comprehended: within a nature or a natural law, created or not, but first

---

[*]   *Correspondance complète de Jean Jacques Rousseau*, ed. R. A. Leigh (Geneva, 1967), vol. V, pp. 65–6. The original reads "l'évangile" rather than "la Bible."

[†]   Rousseau, *Oeuvres complètes*, Pléiade edition, vol. III, p. 602.

[††]   Derrida's reference is *Emile*, Pléiade edition, vol. 4, pp. 589, 594. My reference is *Emile*, tr. Barbara Foxley (London, 1911), pp. 245, 249. Subsequent references to this translation are placed within brackets.

thought within an eternal presence. Comprehended, therefore, within a totality, and enveloped in a volume or a book. The idea of the book is the idea of a totality, finite or infinite, of the signifier; this totality of the signifier cannot be a totality, unless a totality constituted by the signified preexists it, supervises its inscriptions and its signs, and is independent of it in its ideality. The idea of the book, which always refers to a natural totality, is profoundly alien to the meaning of writing. It is the encyclopedic protection of theology and of logocentrism against the disruption of writing, against its aphoristic energy, and, as I shall specify later, against difference in general. If I distinguish the text from the book, I shall say that the destruction of the book, as it is now under way in all domains, denudes the surface of the text. That necessary violence responds to a violence that was no less necessary.

The written being/the being written

The reassuring evidence within which Western tradition had to organize itself and must continue to live would therefore be as follows: the order of the signified is never contemporary, is at best the subtly discrepant inverse or parallel – discrepant by the time of a breath – from the order of the signifier. And the sign must be the unity of a heterogeneity, since the signified (sense or thing, noeme or reality) is not in itself a signifier, a *trace*: in any case is not constituted in its sense by its relationship with a possible trace. The formal essence of the signified is *presence*, and the privilege of its proximity to the logos as *phonè* is the privilege of presence. This is the inevitable response as soon as one asks: "what is the sign?," that is to say, when one submits the sign to the question of essence, to the "ti esti." The "formal essence" of the sign can only be determined in terms of presence. One cannot get around that response, except by challenging the very form of the question and beginning to think that the sign ɪs that ill-named ᴛʜɪɴɢ, the only one, that escapes the instituting question of philosophy: "what is . . . ?"[8]

Radicalizing the concepts of *interpretation, perspective, evaluation, difference*, and all the "empiricist" or nonphilosophical motifs that have constantly tormented philosophy throughout the history of the West, and besides, have had nothing but the inevitable weakness of being produced in the field of philosophy, Nietzsche, far from remaining *simply* (with Hegel and as Heidegger wished) *within* metaphysics, contributed a great deal to the liberation of the signifier from its dependence or derivation with respect to the logos and the related concept of truth or the primary signified, in whatever sense that is understood. Reading, and therefore writing, the text were for Nietzsche "originary"[9] operations (I put that word within quotation marks for reasons to appear later) with regard to a sense that they do not first have to transcribe or discover, which would not therefore be a truth signified in the original element and presence of the logos, as *topos noetos*, divine understanding, or the structure of a priori necessity. To save Nietzsche from a reading of the Heideggerian type, it seems that we must above all not attempt to restore or make explicit a less naive "ontology," composed of profound ontological intuitions acceding to some originary truth, an entire foundationality hidden under the appearance of an empiricist or metaphysical text. The virulence of Nietzschean thought could not be more competely misunderstood. On the contrary, one must *accentuate* the "naiveté" of a breakthrough which cannot attempt a step outside of metaphysics, which cannot *criticize* metaphysics radically without still utilizing in a certain way, in a certain type or a certain style of *text*, propositions that, read within the philosophic corpus, that is to say according to Nietzsche ill-read or unread, have always been and will always be "naivetés," incoherent signs of an absolute appurtenance. Therefore, rather than protect Nietzsche from the Heideggerian reading, we should perhaps offer him up to it completely, underwriting that interpretation without reserve; in a *certain way* and up to the point where, the content of the Nietzschean discourse being almost lost for the question of being, its form regains its absolute strangeness, where his text finally invokes a different type of reading, more faithful to his type of writing: Nietzsche has *written what* he has written. He has written that writing – and first of all his own – is not originarily subordinate to the logos and to truth. And that this subordination has *come into being* during an epoch whose meaning we must deconstruct. Now in this direction (but only in this direction, for read otherwise, the Nietzschean demolition remains dogmatic and, like all reversals, a captive of that metaphysical edifice which it professes to overthrow. On that point and in that *order of reading*, the conclusions of Heidegger and Fink are irrefutable), Heideggerian thought would reinstate rather than destroy the instance of the logos and of the truth of being as "primum signatum": the "transcendental" signified ("transcendental" in a certain sense, as in the Middle Ages the transcendental – *ens, unum, verum, bonum* – was said to be the "primum cognitum") implied by all categories or all determined significations, by all lexicons and all syntax, and therefore by all linguistic signifiers, though not to be identified simply with any one of those signifiers, allowing itself to be precomprehended through each of them, remaining irreducible to all the epochal determinations that it nonetheless makes possible, thus opening the history of the logos, yet itself being only through the logos; that is, *being nothing* before the logos and outside of it. The logos of being, "Thought obeying the Voice of Being,"[10] is the first and the last resource of the sign, of the difference between *signans* and *signatum*. There has to be a transcendental signified for the difference between signifier and signified to be somewhere absolute and irreducible. It is not by chance that the thought of being, as the thought of this transcendental signified, is manifested above all in the voice: in a language of words [*mots*]. The voice *is heard* (understood) – that undoubtedly is what is called conscience – closest to the self as the absolute effacement of the signifier: pure auto-affection that necessarily has the form of time and which does not borrow from outside of itself, in the world or in "reality," any accessory signifier, any substance of expression foreign to its own spontaneity. It is the unique experience of the signified producing itself spontaneously, from within the self, and nevertheless, as signified concept, in the element of ideality or universality. The unworldly character of this substance of expression is constitutive of this ideality. This experience of the effacement of the signifier in the voice is not merely one illusion among many – since it is the condition of the very idea of truth – but I shall elsewhere show in what it does delude itself. This illusion is the history of truth and it cannot be dissipated so quickly. Within the closure of this experience, the word [*mot*] is lived as the elementary and undecomposable unity of the signified and the voice, of the concept and a transparent substance of expression. This experience is considered in its greatest purity – and at the same time in the condition of its possibility – as the experience of "being." The word "being," or at any rate the words designating the sense of being in different languages, is, with some others, an "originary word" ("*Urwort*"),[11] the transcendental word assuring the possibility of being-word to all other words. As such, it is precomprehended in all language and –

this is the opening of *Being and Time* – only this precomprehension would permit the opening of the question of the meaning of being in general, beyond all regional ontologies and all metaphysics: a question that broaches philosophy (for example, in the *Sophist*) and lets itself be taken over by philosophy, a question that Heidegger repeats by submitting the history of metaphysics to it. Heidegger reminds us constantly that the meaning of being is neither the word "being" nor the concept of being. But as that meaning is nothing outside of language and the language of words, it is tied, if not to a particular word or to a particular system of language (concesso non dato), at least to the possibility of the word in general. And to the possibility of its irreducible simplicity. One could thus think that it remains only to choose between two possibilities. (1) Does a modern linguistics, a science of signification breaking the unity of the word and breaking with its alleged irreducibility, still have anything to do with "language?" Heidegger would probably doubt it. (2) Conversely, is not all that is profoundly meditated as the thought or the question of being enclosed within an old linguistics of the word which one practices here unknowingly? Unknowingly because such a linguistics, whether spontaneous or systematic, has always had to share the presuppositions of metaphysics. The two operate on the same grounds.

It goes without saying that the alternatives cannot be so simple.

On the one hand, if modern linguistics remains completely enclosed within a classical conceptuality, if especially it naively uses the word *being* and all that it presupposes, that which, within this linguistics, deconstructs the unity of the word in general can no longer, according to the model of the Heideggerian question, as it functions powerfully from the very opening of *Being and Time*, be circumscribed as ontic science or regional ontology. In as much as the question of being unites indissolubly with the precomprehension of the *word being*, without being reduced to it, the linguistics that works for the deconstruction of the constituted unity of that word has only, in fact or in principle, to have the question of being posed in order to define its field and the order of its dependence.

Not only is its field no longer simply ontic, but the limits of ontology that correspond to it no longer have anything regional about them. And can what I say here of linguistics, or at least of a certain work that may be undertaken within it and thanks to it, not be said of all research *in as much as and to the strict extent that* it would finally deconstitute the founding concept-words of ontology, of being in its privilege? Outside of linguistics, it is in psychoanalytic research that this breakthrough seems at present to have the greatest likelihood of being expanded.

Within the strictly limited space of this breakthrough, these "sciences" are no longer *dominated* by the questions of a transcendental phenomenology or a fundamental ontology. One may perhaps say, following the order of questions inaugurated by *Being and Time* and radicalizing the questions of Husserlian phenomenology, that this breakthrough does not belong to science itself, that what thus seems to be produced within an ontic field or within a regional ontology, does not belong to them by rights and leads back to the question of being itself.

Because it is indeed the *question* of being that Heidegger asks metaphysics. And with it the question of truth, of meaning, of the logos. The incessant meditation upon that question does not restore confidence. On the contrary, it dislodges the confidence at its own depth, which, being a matter of the meaning of being, is more difficult than is often believed. In examining the state just before all determinations of being, destroying the securities of onto-theology, such a meditation contributes, quite as much as the most contemporary linguistics, to the dislocation of the unity of the meaning of being, that is, in the last instance, the unity of the word.

It is thus that, after evoking the "voice of being," Heidegger recalls that it is silent, mute, insonorous, wordless, originarily *a-phonic* (*die Gewähr der lautlosen Stimme verborgener Quellen . . .*). The voice of the sources is not heard. A rupture between the originary meaning of being and the word, between meaning and the voice, between "the voice of being" and the *"phonè,"* between "the call of being," and articulated sound; such a rupture, which at once confirms a fundamental metaphor, and renders it suspect by accentuating its metaphoric discrepancy, translates the ambiguity of the Heideggerian situation with respect to the metaphysics of presence and logocentrism. It is at once contained within it and transgresses it. But it is impossible to separate the two. The very movement of transgression sometimes holds it back short of the limit. In opposition to what we suggested above, it must be remembered that, for Heidegger, the meaning of being is never simply and rigorously a "signified." It is not by chance that that word is not used; that means that being escapes the movement of the sign, a proposition that can equally well be understood as a repetition of the classical tradition and as a caution with respect to a technical or metaphysical theory of signification. On the other hand, the sense of being is literally neither "primary," nor "fundamental," nor "transcendental," whether understood in the scholastic, Kantian, or Husserlian sense. The restoration of being as "transcending" the categories of the entity, the opening of the fundamental ontology, are nothing but necessary yet provisional moments. From *The Introduction to Metaphysics* onward, Heidegger renounces the project of and the word ontology.[12] The necessary, originary, and irreducible dissimulation of the meaning of being, its occultation within the very blossoming forth of presence, that retreat without which there would be no history of being which was completely *history* and history of *being*, Heidegger's insistence on noting that being is produced as history only through the logos, and is nothing outside of it, the difference between being and the entity – all this clearly indicates that fundamentally nothing escapes the movement of the signifier and that, in the last instance, the difference between signified and signifier *is nothing*. This proposition of transgression, not yet integrated into a careful discourse, runs the risk of formulating regression itself. One must therefore *go by way of* the question of being as it is directed by Heidegger and by him alone, at and beyond onto-theology, in order to reach the rigorous thought of that strange nondifference and in order to determine it correctly. Heidegger occasionally reminds us that "being," as it is fixed in its general syntactic and lexicological forms within linguistics and Western philosophy, is not a primary and absolutely irreducible signified, that it is still rooted in a system of languages and an historically determined "significance," although strangely privileged as the virtue of disclosure and dissimulation; particularly when he invites us to meditate on the "privilege" of the "third person singular of the present indicative" and the "infinitive." Western metaphysics, as the limitation of the sense of being within the field of presence, is produced as the domination of a linguistic form.[13] To question the origin of that domination does not amount to hypostatizing a transcendental signified, but to a questioning of what constitutes our history and what produced transcendentality itself. Heidegger brings it up also when in *Zur Seinsfrage*, for the same reason, he lets the word "being" be read only if it is crossed out (*kreuzweise Durchstreichung*). That mark of deletion is not, however, a "merely negative symbol" (p. 31) [p. 83]. That deletion is the final writing of an epoch. Under its strokes the presence of a transcendental signified is effaced while still remaining legible, is destroyed while making visible the very idea of the sign. In as much as it de-limits onto-theology, the metaphysics of presence and logocentrism, this last writing is also the first writing.

To come to recognize, not within but on the horizon of the Heideggerian paths, and yet in them, that the meaning of being is not a transcendental or trans-epochal signified (even if it was always dissimulated within the epoch) but already, in a truly *unheard* of sense, a determined signifying trace, is to affirm that within the decisive concept of ontico-ontological difference, *all is not to be thought at one go*; entity and being, ontic and ontological, "ontico-ontological," are, in an original style, *derivative* with regard to difference; and with respect to what I shall later call *differance*, an economic concept designating the production of differing/deferring. The ontico-ontological difference and its ground (*Grund*) in the "transcendence of Dasein" (*Vom Wesen des Grundes* [Frankfurt am Main, 1955], p. 16 [p. 29]) are not absolutely originary. Differance by itself would be more "originary," but one would no longer be able to call it "origin" or "ground," those notions belonging essentially to the history of onto-theology, to the system functioning as the effacing of difference. It can, however, be thought of in the closest proximity to itself only on one condition: that one begins by determining it as the ontico-ontological difference before erasing that determination. The necessity of passing through that erased determination, the necessity of that *trick of writing* is irreducible. An unemphatic and difficult thought that, through much unperceived mediation, must carry the entire burden of our question, a question that I shall provisionally call *historial* [*historiale*]. It is with its help that I shall later be able to attempt to relate differance and writing.

The hesitation of these thoughts (here Nietzsche's and Heidegger's) is not an "incoherence": it is a trembling proper to all post-Hegelian attempts and to this passage between two epochs. The movements of deconstruction do not destroy structures from the outside. They are not possible and effective, nor can they take accurate aim, except by inhabiting those structures. Inhabiting them *in a certain way*, because one always inhabits, and all the more when one does not suspect it. Operating necessarily from the inside, borrowing all the strategic and economic resources of subversion from the old structure, borrowing them structurally, that is to say without being able to isolate their elements and atoms, the enterprise of deconstruction always in a certain way falls prey to its own work. This is what the person who has begun the same work in another area of the same habitation does not fail to point out with zeal. No exercise is more widespread today and one should be able to formalize its rules.

Hegel was already caught up in this game. *On the one hand*, he undoubtedly *summed up* the entire philosophy of the logos. He determined ontology as absolute logic; he assembled all the delimitations of philosophy as presence; he assigned to presence the eschatology of parousia, of the self-proximity of infinite subjectivity. And for the same reason he had to debase or subordinate writing. When he criticizes the Leibnizian characteristic, the formalism of the understanding, and mathematical symbolism, he makes the same gesture: denouncing the being-outside-of-itself of the logos in the sensible or the intellectual abstraction. Writing is that forgetting of the self, that exteriorization, the contrary of the interiorizing memory, of the *Erinnerung* that opens the history of the spirit. It is this that the *Phaedrus* said: writing is at once mnemotechnique and the power of forgetting. Naturally, the Hegelian critique of writing stops at the alphabet. As phonetic writing, the alphabet is at the same time more servile, more contemptible, more secondary ("alphabetic writing expresses *sounds* which are themselves signs. It consists therefore of the signs of signs ['*aus Zeichen der Zeichen*'," *Enzyklopädie*, § 459)* but it is also the best writing, the mind's writing; its effacement before the voice, that in it which respects the ideal interiority of phonic signifiers, all that by which it sublimates space and sight, all that makes of it the writing of history, the writing, that is, of the infinite spirit relating to itself in its discourse and its culture:

> It follows that to learn to read and write an alphabetic writing should be regarded as a means to infinite culture (*unendliches Bildungsmittel*) that is not enough appreciated; because thus the mind, distancing itself from the concrete sense-perceptible, directs its attention on the more formal moment, the sonorous word and its abstract elements, and contributes essentially to the founding and purifying of the ground of interiority within the subject.

In that sense it is the *Aufhebung* of other writings, particularly of hieroglyphic script and of the Leibnizian characteristic that had been criticized previously through one and the same gesture. (*Aufhebung* is, more or less implicitly, the dominant concept of nearly all histories of writing, even today. It is *the* concept of history and of teleology.) In fact, Hegel continues: "Acquired habit later also suppresses the specificity of alphabetic writing, which consists in seeming to be, in the interest of sight, a detour [*Umweg*] through hearing to arrive at representations, and makes it into a hieroglyphic script for us, such that in using it, we do not need to have present to our consciousness the mediation of sounds."

It is on this condition that Hegel subscribes to the Leibnizian praise of nonphonetic writing. It can be produced by deaf mutes, Leibniz had said. Hegel:

> Beside the fact that, by the practice which transforms this alphabetic script into hieroglyphics, the aptitude for abstraction acquired through such an exercise *is conserved* [italics added], the reading of hieroglyphs is for itself a deaf reading and a mute writing (*ein taubes Lesen und ein stummes Schreiben*). What is audible or temporal, visible or spatial, has each its proper basis and in the first place they are of equal value; but in alphabetic script there is only *one* basis and that following a specific relation, namely, that the visible language is related only as a sign to the audible language; intelligence expresses itself immediately and unconditionally through speech (ibid.).

What writing itself, in its nonphonetic moment, betrays, is life. It menaces at once the breath, the spirit, and history as the spirit's relationship with itself. It is their end, their finitude, their paralysis. Cutting breath short, sterilizing or immobilizing spiritual creation in the repetition of the letter, in the commentary or the *exegesis*, confined in a narrow space reserved for a minority, it is the principle of death and of difference in the becoming of being. It is to speech what China is to Europe: "It is only to the exegeticism[14] of Chinese spiritual culture that their hieroglyphic writing is suited. This type of writing is, besides, the part reserved for a very small section of a people, the section that possesses the exclusive domain of spiritual culture. . . . A hieroglyphic script would require a philosophy as exegetical as Chinese culture generally is" (ibid.).

---

* *Enzyklopädie der philosophischen Wissenschaften in Grundrisse*, Suhrkamp edition (Frankfurt am Main, 1970), pp. 273–6).

If the nonphonetic moment menaces the history and the life of the spirit as self-presence in the breath, it is because it menaces substantiality, that other metaphysical name of presence and of *ousia*. First in the form of the substantive. Nonphonetic writing breaks the noun apart. It describes relations and not appellations. The noun and the word, those unities of breath and concept, are effaced within pure writing. In that regard, Leibniz is as disturbing as the Chinese in Europe: "This situation, the analytic notation of representations in hieroglyphic script, which seduced Leibniz to the point of wrongly preferring this script to the alphabetic, rather contradicts the fundamental exigency of language in general, namely the noun.... All difference [*Abweichung*] in analysis would produce another formation of the written substantive."

The horizon of absolute knowledge is the effacement of writing in the logos, the retrieval of the trace in parousia, the reappropriation of difference, the accomplishment of what I have elsewhere called[15] the *metaphysics of the proper* [*le propre* – self-possession, propriety, property, cleanliness].

Yet, all that Hegel thought within this horizon, all, that is, except eschatology, may be reread as a meditation on writing. Hegel is *also* the thinker of irreducible difference. He rehabilitated thought as the *memory productive* of signs. And he re-introduced, as I shall try to show elsewhere, the essential necessity of the written trace in a philosophical – that is to say Socratic – discourse that had always believed it possible to do without it; the last philosopher of the book and the first thinker of writing....

The theorem and the theater

[In Rousseau's *Essay on the Origin of Languages*] the history of the voice and its writing is comprehended between two mute writings, between two poles of universality relating to each other as the natural and the artificial: the pictogram and algebra. The relationship of natural to artificial or arbitrary is itself subject to the law of "extremes" which "touch one another." And if Rousseau suspects alphabetic writing without condemning it absolutely, it is because there are worse. It is structurally but the next to the last step of that history. Its artifice has a limit. Unbound to any particular language, it yet refers to the *phonè* or language in general. As phonetic writing, it keeps an essential relationship to the presence of a speaking subject *in general*, to a transcendental locutor, to the voice as the self-presence of a life which hears itself speak. In that sense, phonetic writing is not absolute evil. It is not the letter of death. Nevertheless, it announces death. To the extent that that writing progresses with consonantic chilling, it allows the anticipation of the ice, speech degree zero: the disappearance of the vowel, the writing of a dead language. The consonant, which is easier to write than the vowel, initiates this end of speech in the universal writing, in algebra:

> It would be easy to construct a language consisting solely of consonants, which could be written clearly but not spoken. Algebra has something of such a language. When the orthography of a language is clearer than its pronunciation, this is a sign that it is written more than it is spoken. This may have been true of the scholarly language of the Egyptians; as is the case for us with the dead languages. In those burdened with useless consonants, writing seems to have preceded speech: and who would doubt that such is the case with Polish? [*Essay*], Chap. 7 [p. 28].

The universal characteristic, writing become purely conventional through having broken all links with the spoken language – such then would be absolute evil. With the *Logic of Port-Royal*, Locke's *Essay*, Malebranche, and Descartes, Leibniz was one of Rousseau's primary philosophic readings.[16] He is not cited in the *Essay* but in the fragment on *Pronunciation*. With as much suspicion as the "art of Raymond Lully" in *Emile* (p. 575) [p. 425].

> Languages are made to be spoken, writing serves only as supplement to speech; if there
> are some languages that are only written, and that one cannot speak, belonging only to
> the sciences, it would be of no use in civil life. Such is algebra, such was no doubt the
> universal language that Leibniz looked for. It would probably have been more useful to
> a Metaphysician than to an Artisan (p. 1249).

The universal writing of science would thus be absolute alienation. The autonomy of the representer becomes absurd: it has attained its limit and broken with all represented, with all living origin, with all living present. In it supplementarity is accomplished, that is to say emptied. The supplement, which is neither simply the signifier nor simply the representer, does not take the place of a signified or a represented, as is prescribed by the concepts of signification or representation or by the syntax of the words "signifier" or "representer." The supplement comes in the place of a lapse, a nonsignified or a nonrepresented, a nonpresence. There is no present before it, it is not preceded by anything but itself, that is to say by another supplement. The supplement is always the supplement of a supplement. One wishes to go back *from the supplement to the source*: one must recognize that there is *a supplement at the source*.

Thus it is always already algebraic. In its writing, the visible signifier, has always already begun to separate itself from speech and to supplant it. The nonphonetic and universal writing of science is also in that sense a *theorem*. It is enough to look in order to calculate. As Leibniz said, "*ad vocem referri non est necesse* ["it is not necessary to return to the voice"]."

Through that silent and mortal glance the complicities of science and politics are exchanged: more precisely of modern political science. "The letter killeth" (*Emile*, p. 226) [p. 159].

Where should one search, in the city, for that lost unity of glance and speech? In what *space* can one again *listen to himself*? Can the theater, which unites spectacle and discourse, not take up where the unanimous assembly left off? "For a long time now one speaks in public only through books, and if one says something in person to the public that interests it, it is in the theater" (*Pronunciation*, p. 1250).

But the theater itself is shaped and undermined by the profound evil of representation. It is that corruption itself. For the stage is not threatened by anything but itself. Theatrical representation, in the sense of exposition, of production, of that which is placed out there (that which the German *Darstellung* translates) is contaminated by supplementary re-presentation. The latter is inscribed in the structure of representation, in the space of the stage. Let us not be mistaken, what Rousseau criticizes in the last analysis is not the content of the spectacle, the sense *represented* by it, although that *too* he criticizes: it is re-presentation itself. Exactly as within the political order, the menace has the shape of the representative.

In fact, after having evoked the misdeeds of the theater considered in the content of what it stages, in its *represented*, the *Letter to d'Alembert* incriminates representation and the *representer*: "Beyond these effects of the theatre, which are relative to what is *performed* [*representées*], there are others *no less necessary* which relate directly to the *stage* and to the *persons who perform* [*représentants*]; and it is to them that the previously mentioned Genevans attribute the taste for luxury, adornment, and dissipation, whose introduction among us they rightly fear."[17] Immorality, then, attaches, to the very status of the representer (performer). Vice is his natural bent. It is normal that he who has taken up representation as a profession should have a taste for external and artificial signifiers, and for the perverse use of signs. Luxury, fine clothes, and dissipation are not signifiers incidentally coming about here and there, they are the crimes of the signifier or the representer itself.

Double consequence:

1. There are two sorts of public persons, two men of spectacle: on the one hand the orator or preacher, on the other the actor. The former represents himself, in him the representer and the represented are one. But the actor is born out of the rift between the representer and the represented. Like the alphabetic signifier, like the letter, the actor himself is not inspired or animated by any particular language. He signifies nothing. He hardly lives, he lends his voice. It is a mouthpiece. Of course the difference between the orator or preacher and the actor presupposes that the former does his duty, says what he has to say. If they do not assume ethical responsibility for their word, they become actors, hardly even actors, for the latter make a duty of saying what they do not think:

> The orator and the preacher, it could be said, make use of their persons as does the actor. The difference is, however, very great. When the orator appears in public, it is to speak and not to show himself off; he *represents only himself*: he fills only his own proper role, speaks only in his own name, says, or ought to say, only what he thinks; *the man and the role being the same* [being] [*étant le même être*], he is *in his place*; he is in the situation of any citizen who fulfils the functions of his estate. But an actor on the stage, displaying other sentiments than his own, saying only what he is made to say, *often representing a chimerical being*, annihilates himself, as it were, and is lost in his hero. And, in this forgetting of the man, if something remains of him, it is used as the plaything of the spectators (p. 187; italics added) [pp. 80–1].

It is the best possible situation: the actor accepts the role and loves what he incarnates. The situation may be still worse. "What shall I say of those who seem to be afraid of having too much merit as they are and who degrade themselves to the point of playing characters whom they would be quite distressed to resemble?" [p. 81].

The identity of the representer and the represented may be accomplished in two ways. The better way: by the effacement of the representer and the personal presence of the represented (the orator, the preacher); or the worse way: it is not illustrated by the actor alone (representer emptied of what he represents) but by a certain society, that of the worldly Parisians who have, in order to find themselves there, alienated themselves in a certain theater, theater of a theater, play representing the comedy of that society. "It is nevertheless solely for these people that theatrical entertainments are made. They are represented by fictitious characters in the middle of the theater, and show themselves in real ones on each side; they are at once persons of the drama on the stage, and comedians in the boxes" (*La Nouvelle Héloïse*, p. 252).* This total

---

* *Eloisa*: or, *A Series of Original Letters*, collected and published by Mr. J. J. Rousseau, Citizen of Geneva, translated from the French, 2d edition (London, 1761), 2: 60.

alienation of the represented within the representer is the negative aspect of the social pact. In both cases, the represented is reappropriated when he is lost without reserve in his representation. In what terms should the elusive difference which separates the positive from the negative aspect, the authentic social pact from a forever-perverted theater, from a *theatrical* society, be defined?

2. The signifier is the death of the festival. The innocence of the public spectacle, the good festival, the dance around the water hole, would open a theater without representation. Or rather a stage without a show: without *theater*, with nothing to see. Visibility – a moment ago the theorem, here the theater – is always that which, separating it from itself, breaches [*entame*] the living voice.

But what is a stage which presents nothing to the sight? It is the place where the spectator, presenting himself as spectacle, will no longer be either seer [*voyant*] or voyeur, will efface within himself the difference between the actor and the spectator, the represented and the representer, the object seen and the seeing subject. With that difference, an entire series of oppositions will deconstitute themselves one by one. Presence will be full, not as an object which is *present* to be seen, to give itself to intuition as an empirical unit or as an *eidos* holding itself *in front of* or *up against*; it will be full as the intimacy of a self-presence, as the consciousness or the sentiment of self-proximity, of self-sameness [*propriété*]. That public festival will therefore have a form analogous to the electoral meetings of a free and legiferant assembled people: the representative differance will be effaced in the self-presence of sovereignty. "The exaltation of the collective festival has the same structure as the general will of *The Social Contract*. The description of *public joy* gives us the lyrical aspect of the general will: it is the aspect that it assumes in its Sunday best."[18] The text is well known. It recalls the evocation of the festival in the *Essay*. Let us reread it in order to recognize the desire of making *representation* disappear, with all the meanings that converge in that word: delay and delegation, repetition of a present in its sign or its concept, the proposition or opposition of a show, an object to be seen:

> What! Ought there to be no entertainments in a republic? On the contrary, there ought to be many. It is in republics that they were born, it is in their bosom that they are seen to flourish with a truly festive air. [*Letter to d'Alembert*, p. 125]

These innocent spectacles will take place outdoors and they will have nothing "effeminate" or "mercenary" about them. The sign, money, ruse, passivity, and servility will be excluded from them. No one will use anyone, no one will be an object for anyone. There will no longer be, after a certain fashion, anything to see:

> But what then will be the objects of these entertainments? What will be shown in them? Nothing, if you please. With liberty, wherever abundance reigns, well-being also reigns. Plant a stake crowned with flowers in the middle of a square; gather the people together there, and you will have a festival. Do better yet; let the spectators become an entertainment to themselves; make them actors themselves; do it so that each sees and loves himself in the others so that all will be better united. *Letter to M. d'Alembert*, pp. 224–5 [p. 126]

We must note that this festival without object is also a festival without sacrifice, without expense, and without play. Above all without masks.[19] It has no outside although it takes place out of doors. It maintains itself in a purely interior relation to itself. "So that each sees and loves himself in the others." In a certain way, it is confined and sheltered, whereas the hall of the theater, wrenched away from itself by the games and detours of representation, diverted from itself and torn by differance, multiplies the outside in itself. There are many *games* [*jeux*] within the public festival but no *play* [*jeu*] at all, if one understands by that singular term the substitution of contents, the exchange of presences and absences, chance and absolute risk. That festival represses the relationship with death; what was not necessarily implied in the description of the enclosed theatre. These analyses can turn in both directions.

At any rate, play is so much absent from the festival that the dance is admitted as the initiation into marriage and is contained within the closure of the ball. Such is at least the interpretation to which Rousseau submits, to fix it carefully, the meaning of his text on the festival. One could make him say quite a different thing. And Rousseau's text must constantly be considered as a complex and many-leveled structure; in it, certain propositions may be read as interpretations of other propositions that we are, up to a certain point and with certain precautions, free to read otherwise. Rousseau says A, then for reasons that we must determine, he interprets A into B. A, which was already an interpretation, is reinterpreted into B. After taking cognizance of it, we may, without leaving Rousseau's text, isolate A from its interpretation into B, and discover possibilities and resources there that indeed belong to Rousseau's text, but were not produced or exploited by him, which, for equally legible motives, he *preferred to cut short* by a gesture neither witting nor unwitting. In his description of the festival, for example, there are propositions which could very well have been interpreted in the sense of Antonin Artaud's[20] theater of cruelty or of the festival and sovereignty of which Georges Bataille has proposed the concepts. But these propositions are interpreted otherwise by Rousseau himself, who transforms play into games and the dance into a ball, expense into presence.

What ball are we speaking of here? To understand that, one must first understand the praise of the open air. The open air is undoubtedly Nature and in that respect it must lead Rousseau's thoughts in a thousand ways, through all the themes of pedagogy, promenade, botany, and so on. But more precisely, the open air is the element of the voice, the liberty of a breath that nothing breaks into pieces. A voice that can make itself heard in the open air is a free voice, a clear voice that the northern principle has not yet muzzled with consonants, not yet broken, articulated, compartmentalized, and which can reach the interlocutor immediately. The open air is frankness, the absence of evasions, of representative mediations among living spoken words. It is the element of the Greek city, "the great concern" of which was "its liberty." The north limits the possibilities of the open air: "Your severer climates add to your needs; for half the year your public squares are uninhabitable; *the flatness of your languages unfits them for being heard in the open air*; you sacrifice more for profit than for liberty, and fear slavery less than poverty" (*The Social Contract*, p. 431) [p. 79; italics added]. Once again the northern influence is pernicious. But a northern man must live like a northerner. To adopt or adapt southern customs in the North is pure folly and worse servitude (ibid.). One must therefore find substitutes in the North or in winter. The winter substitute of the festival is our dance for young brides-to-be. Rousseau recommends the practice: unequivocally and as he himself says, without scruple; and what he says of winter illuminates after a fashion what he might have said of summer.

> Winter, a time consecrated to the private association of friends, is less appropriate to public festivals. There is, however, one sort concerning which I wish there were not so many scrupulous doubts raised, that is, the balls for young marriageable persons. I have never understood why people are so worried about dancing and the gatherings it occasions, as if there were something worse about dancing than singing, as if these amusements were not both equally an inspiration of nature, as if it were a crime for those who are destined to be united to be merry together in a decent recreation. Man and woman were formed for one another. God wants them to fulfill their destiny, and certainly the first and holiest of all the bonds of society is marriage.[21]

One should comment word by word on the long and edifying discourse that follows. A hinge articulates the entire argument: the full daylight of presence avoids the dangerous supplement. One must allow pleasures to "a lively and frolicsome youth" to avoid their "substituting more dangerous ones" and to prevent "private meetings adroitly concerted [from] tak[ing] the place of public gatherings." "Innocent joy is likely to evaporate in the full light of day; but vice is a friend of shadows" (*Letter to M. d'Alembert*, p. 227) [p. 129]. Furthermore, the nudity that presents the body itself is less dangerous than the recourse to sartorial signifiers, to the northern supplement, to "artful dress": the latter is not "less dangerous than an absolute nudity the habit of which would soon turn the first effects into indifference and perhaps distaste." "Is it not known that statues and paintings only offend the eyes when a mixture of clothing renders the nudity obscene? The immediate power of the senses is weak and limited; it is through the intermediary of the imagination that they make their greatest ravages; it is the business of the imagination to irritate the desires" (p. 232) [p. 134]. It will have been noticed that representation – the picture – rather than perception, is chosen to illustrate the danger of the supplement whose efficiency is the imagination. And it will then be noticed that, in a note inserted into the heart of this praise of marriage, anticipating the errors of posterity, Rousseau makes only one exception to his denials:

> It is something amusing for me to imagine the judgments that many will make of my tastes on the basis of my writings. On the basis of this one they will not fail to say: "that man is crazy about dancing"; it bores me to watch dancing; "he cannot bear the drama"; I love the drama passionately; "he has an aversion to women"; on that score I shall be only too easily vindicated (p. 229) [p. 131 n].

Thus the North, winter, death, imagination, representation, the irritation of desires – this entire series of supplementary significations – does not designate a natural place or fixed terms: rather a periodicity. Seasons. In the order of time, or rather like time itself, they speak the movement by which the presence of the present separates from itself, supplants itself, replaces itself by absenting itself, produces itself in self-substitution. It is this that the metaphysics of presence as self-proximity wishes to efface by giving a privileged position to a sort of absolute now, the *life* of the present, the living present. The coldness of representation not only breaks self-presence but also the originarity of the present as the absolute form of temporality.

This metaphysics of presence constantly reappears and is resumed in Rousseau's text whenever the fatality of the supplement seems to limit it. It is always necessary to add a supplement of presence to the presence that is concealed. "The great remedy to the miseries of this world" is "absorption into the present moment," says

Rousseau in *The Solitaries*. The present is originary, that is to say the determination of origin always has the form of presence. Birth is the birth (of) presence. Before it there is no presence; and from the moment that presence, holding or announcing itself to itself, breaches its plenitude and starts the chain of its history, death's work has begun. Birth in general is written as Rousseau describes his own: "I cost my mother her life; and my birth was the first of my misfortunes" (*Confessions*, p. 7) [p. 5]. Every time that Rousseau tries to recapture an essence (in the form of an origin, a right, an ideal limit), he always leads us back to a point of full presence. He is less interested in the present, in the being-present, than in the presence of the present, in its essence as it appears to itself and is retained in itself. Essence is presence. As life, that is as self-presence, it is birth. And just as the present goes out of itself only to return to itself, a rebirth is possible which, furthermore, is the only thing that permits all the repetitions of origin. Rousseau's discourse and questions are possible only in the anticipation of a rebirth or a reactivation of the origin. Rebirth, resurrection, or reawakening always appropriate to themselves, in their fugitive immediacy, the plenitude of presence returning to itself.

That return to the presence of the origin is produced after each catastrophe, at least in so far as it *reverses* the order of life without destroying it. After a divine finger had *turned* the order of the world *over* [*renversé*] by inclining the axis of the globe on the axis of the universe and had thus willed that "men [be] sociable," the festival around the water hole was possible and pleasure was immediately present to desire. After a "great Danish dog" had *knocked* Jean-Jacques *over* [*renversé*] in the second *Promenade*; when after "the fall" which had *precipitated* him ("my head was thrown down lower than my feet") it was first necessary to *recount* to him the "accident" that he had not been able to experience; when he explains to us what happened at the moment when, he says twice, "I came to myself," "I came back to consciousness," – it is indeed awakening as re-awakening to pure presence that he describes, always according to the same model: not anticipation, not memory, not comparison, not distinction, not articulation, not situation. Imagination, memory, and signs are effaced. All landmarks on the physical or psychical landscape are natural.

> The state in which I found myself in that instant was too singular not to make a description of it here.
> The night was coming on. I perceived the sky, some stars, and a little grass. This first sensation was a delicious moment. I did not feel anything except through them. I was born in that instant to life, and it seemed to me that I filled with my light existence all the objects which I perceived. Entirely given up to the present moment, I did not remember anything; I had no distinct notion of my individuality, not the least idea of what had happened to me; I did not know who I was nor where I was; I felt neither evil nor fear, nor trouble.

And, as around the water hole, and on the Isle of St. Pierre, the enjoyment [*jouissance*] of pure presence is that of a certain flow. Presence being born. Origin of life, blood's resemblance to water. Rousseau continues:

> I saw my blood flowing as I might have looked at a brooklet, without dreaming even that this blood in any way belonged to me. I felt in the whole of my being a ravishing calm, to which, each time that I think of it, I find nothing comparable in the whole action of known pleasures (p. 1005) [p. 49].

Are there other or more archetypal pleasures? This pleasure, which is the only pleasure, is at the same time properly *unimaginable*. Such is the paradox of the imagination: it alone arouses or irritates desire but also it alone, and for the same reason, in the same movement, extends beyond or divides presence. Rousseau would like to separate the awakening to presence from the operation of imagination; he always presses on toward that impossible limit. For the awakening of presence projects or rejects us immediately outside of presence where we are "led...by that living interest, foresightful and all-providing [*prévoyant et pourvoyant*], which...always throws us far from the present, and which does not exist for natural man" (*Dialogues*).[22] Function of representation, imagination is also the temporalizing function, the excess of the present and the economy of what exceeds presence. There is no unique and full present (but is there presence then?) except in the imagination's sleep: "The sleeping imagination does not know at all how to extend its being into two different times" (*Emile*, p. 69). When it appears, signs, fiduciary values [legal tender and trusts], and letters emerge, and they are worse than death.

> How many merchants lament in Paris over some misfortune in India!... There is a healthy, cheerful, strong, and vigorous man; it does me good to see him....A letter comes by post....[He] falls into a swoon. When he comes to himself he weeps, laments, and groans, he tears his hair, and his shrieks re-echo through the air. You would say he was in convulsions. Fool, what harm has this bit of paper done you? What limb has it torn away?...We no longer live in our own place, we live outside it. What does it profit me to live in such fear of death, when all that makes life worth living remains? (*Emile*, pp. 67–8) [p. 47]

Rousseau himself articulates this chain of significations (essence, origin, presence, birth, rebirth) on the classical metaphysics of the entity as *energy*, encompassing the relationships between being and time in terms of the now as being in action (*energeia*):

> Delivered from the disquietude of hope, and *sure of thus gradually losing that one desire*, seeing that the past was no longer anything to me, I undertook to put myself completely in the situation of a man who begins to live. I told myself that in fact *we were always beginning, and that there was no other link in our existence but a succession of present moments of which the first is always that which is in action*. We are born and die every moment of our life.

It follows – but it is a *liaison* that Rousseau works very hard to elide – that the very essence of presence, if it must always be repeated within any other presence, opens originarily, within presence itself, the structure of representation. And if essence *is* presence, there is no essence of presence nor presence of essence. There is a play of representation and eliding that liaison or that consequence, Rousseau places play out of play: he eludes, which is another way of playing, or rather, as the dictionaries say, of playing (with). What is thus eluded is the fact that representation does not suddenly encroach upon presence; it inhabits it as the very condition of its experience, of desire, and of enjoyment [*jouissance*]. The interior doubling of presence, its halving, makes it appear as such, that is to say, concealing enjoyment in frustration, makes it disappear as such. Placing representation outside, which means placing the outside outside, Rousseau would like to make of the supplement of presence a pure and simple addition, a contingence: thus wishing to elude what, in the interior of presence, calls forth the substitute, and is constituted only in that appeal, and in its trace.

Thence the letter. Writing is the evil of representative repetition, the double that opens desire and contemplates and binds [*re-garde*] enjoyment. Literary writing, the traces of the *Confessions*, speak that doubling of presence. Rousseau condemns the evil of writing and looks for a haven within writing. It repeats enjoyment symbolically. And just as enjoyment has never been present except in a certain repetition, so writing, recalling enjoyment, gives it as well. Rousseau eludes its admission but not the pleasure. We recall those texts ("Saying to myself I have rejoiced, I rejoice again. . . ." "I rejoice again in a pleasure that no longer is." . . . "Incessantly occupied with the thought of my past happiness, I recall it, so to speak, chew the cud of it to such an extent that, when I desire it, I am able to enjoy it over again") [p. 607]. Writing *represents* (in every sense of the word) enjoyment. It plays enjoyment, renders it present and absent. It is play. And it is because it is also the good fortune of enjoyment repeated that Rousseau practices it while condemning it: "I shall set down in writing those ['delightful contemplations'] which may still come to me: each time that I reread them will give me new pleasure" (*Reveries*, p. 999) [p. 38].

This entire digression was necessary in order to mark well that, unless some extrinsic desire is invested in it, Leibniz's universal characteristic represents the very death of enjoyment. It leads the representer to the limit of its excess. Phonetic writing, however abstract and arbitrary, retained some relationship with the presence of the represented voice, to its possible presence in general and therefore to that of a certain passion. A writing that breaks with the *phonè* radically is perhaps the most rational and effective of scientific machines; it no longer responds to any desire or rather *it signifies its death to desire*. It was what already operated within speech as writing and machine. It is the representer in its pure state, without the represented, or without the order of the represented naturally linked to it. That is why this pure conventionality ceases, being pure, to be of any use within "civil life," which always mingles nature and convention. The perfection of convention here touches its opposite extreme, it is death and the perfect alienation of the instrument of civil order. The telos of the alienation of writing has in Rousseau's eyes the form of scientific technical writing, wherever it can act, that is to say even outside of areas reserved for "science" or "technology." It is not by chance that in mythology, the Egyptian in particular, the god of sciences and technology is also the god of writing; and that it is he (Thoth, Theuth, Teuthus or his Greek homologue Hermes, god of the ruse, of trade, and of thieves) whom Rousseau incriminates in the *Discourse on the Arts and Sciences*. (Plato had already denounced his invention of writing at the end of the *Phaedrus*.)

> An ancient tradition passed out of Egypt into Greece, that some god, who was an enemy to the repose of mankind, was the inventor of the sciences.* . . . In fact, whether we turn to the annals of the world, or supplement with philosophical investigations the uncertain chronicles of history, we shall not find for human knowledge an origin answering to the idea we are pleased to entertain of it at present. . . . Their evil origin is indeed, but too plainly reproduced in their objects. [Cole, op. cit., p. 131.]

---

* It is easy to see the allegory in the fable of Prometheus: and it does not appear that the Greeks, who chained him to the Caucasus, had a better opinion of him than the Egyptians had of their god Teuthus (p. 12).

The supplement of (at) the origin

In the last pages of the chapter "On Script," the critique, the appreciative presentation, and the history of writing, *declares* the absolute exteriority of writing but *describe* the interiority of the principle of writing to language. The sickness of the outside (which comes from the outside but also draws outside, thus equally, or inversely, the sickness of the homeland, a homesickness, so to speak) is in the heart of the living word, as its principle of effacement and its relationship to its own death. In other words, it does not suffice to show, it is in fact not a question of showing, the interiority of what Rousseau would have believed exterior; rather to speculate upon the power of exteriority as constitutive of interiority: of speech, of signified meaning, of the present as such; in the sense in which I said, a moment ago, that the representative mortal doubling-halving constituted the living present, without adding itself to presence; or rather constituted it, paradoxically, by being added to it. The question is of an originary supplement, if this absurd expression may be risked, totally unacceptable as it is within classical logic. Rather the supplement of origin: which supplements the failing origin and which is yet not derived; this supplement is, as one says of a spare part [*une pièce*], of the original make [*d'origine*] [or a document, establishing the origin.]

Thus one takes into account that the absolute *alterity* of writing might nevertheless affect living speech, from the outside, within its inside: *alter it* [for the worse]. Even as it has an independent history, as we have seen, and in spite of the inequalities of development, the play of structural correlations, writing marks the history of speech. Although it is born out of "needs of a different kind" and "according to circumstances entirely independent of the duration of the people," although these needs might "never have occurred," the irruption of this absolute contingency determined the interior of an essential history and affected the interior unity of a life, *literally infected* it. It is the strange essence of the supplement not to have essentiality: it may always not have taken place. Moreover, literally, it has never taken place: it is never present, here and now. If it were, it would not be what it is, a supplement, taking and keeping the place of the other. What alters for the worse the living nerve of language ("Writing, which would seem to crystallize language, is precisely what alters it; it changes not the words but the spirit of language . . . ") has therefore above all not taken place. Less than nothing and yet, to judge by its effects, much more than nothing. The supplement is neither a presence nor an absence. No ontology can think its operation.

As Saussure will do, so does Rousseau wish at once to maintain the exteriority of the system of writing and the maleficent efficiency with which one singles out its symptoms on the body of the language. But am I saying anything else? Yes, in as much as I show the interiority of exteriority, which amounts to annulling the ethical qualification and to thinking of writing beyond good and evil; yes above all, in as much as we designate the impossibility of formulating the movement of supplementarity within the classical logos, within the logic of identity, within ontology, within the opposition of presence and absence, positive and negative, and even within dialectics, if at least one determines it, as spiritualistic or materialistic metaphysics has always done, within the horizon of presence and reappropriation. Of course the *designation* of that impossibility escapes the language of metaphysics only by a hairsbreadth. For the rest, it must borrow its resources from the logic it deconstructs. And by doing so, find its very foothold there.

One can no longer see disease in substitution when one sees that the substitute is substituted for a substitute. Is that not what the *Essay describes*? "[Writing substitutes] exactitude for expressiveness." Expression is the expression of affect, of the passion at the origin of language, of a speech that was first substituted for song, marked by *tone* and *force*. Tone and force signify the *present voice*: they are anterior to the concept, they are singular, they are, moreover, attached to vowels, the vocalic and not the consonantic element of language. The force of expression amounts only to vocalic sounds, when the subject is there in person to utter his passion. When the subject is no longer there, force, intonation, and accent are lost in the concept. Then one writes, one "substitutes" in vain "accentual marks" for "accent," one bows to the generality of the law: "In writing, one is forced to use all the words according to their conventional meaning. But in speaking, one varies the meanings by varying one's tone of voice, determining them as one pleases. Being less constrained to clarity one can be more forceful. And it is not possible for a language that is written to retain its vitality as long as one that is only spoken" [*Essay*, pp. 21–2].

Thus writing is always atonal. The place of the subject is there taken by another, it is concealed. The spoken sentence, which is valuable only once and remains "proper only to the place where it is," loses its place and its proper meaning as soon as it is written down. "The means used to overcome [*suppléer*] this weakness tend to stretch out written language and make it elaborately prolix; and many books written in discourse will enervate speech itself."

But if Rousseau could say that "words [*voix*], not sounds [*sons*], are written," it is because words are distinguished from sounds exactly by what permits writing – consonants and articulation. The latter replace only themselves. Articulation, which replaces accent, is the origin of languages. Altering [for the worse] through writing is an originary exteriority. It is the origin of language. Rousseau describes it without declaring it. Clandestinely.

A speech without consonantic principle, what for Rousseau would be a speech sheltered from all writing, would not be speech;[23] it would hold itself at the fictive limit of the inarticulate and purely natural cry. Conversely, a speech of pure consonants and pure articulation would become pure writing, algebra, or dead language. The death of speech is therefore the horizon and origin of language. But an origin and a horizon which do not hold themselves at its exterior borders. As always, death, which is neither a present to come nor a present past, shapes the interior of speech, as its trace, its reserve, its interior and exterior difference: as its supplement.

But Rousseau could not think this writing, that takes place *before* and *within* speech. To the extent that he belonged to the metaphysics of presence, he *dreamed* of the simple exteriority of death to life, evil to good, representation to presence, signifier to signified, representer to represented, mask to face, writing to speech. But all such oppositions are irreducibly rooted in that metaphysics. Using them, one can only operate by reversal, that is to say by confirmations. The supplement is none of these terms. It is especially not more a signifier than a signified, a representer than a presence, a writing than a speech. None of the terms of this series can, being comprehended within it, dominate the economy of difference or supplementarity. Rousseau's *dream* consisted of making the supplement enter metaphysics by force.

But what does that mean? The opposition of dream to wakefulness, is not that a representation of metaphysics as well? And what should dream or writing be if, as we know now, one may dream while writing? And if the scene of dream is always a scene of writing? At the bottom of a page of *Emile*, after having once more cautioned us against books, writing, signs ("What is the use of inscribing on their brains a list of symbols which mean nothing for them?"), after having opposed the "tracing" of these artificial signs to the "indelible characters" of the Book of Nature, Rousseau adds a note: "... the dreams of a bad night are given to us as philosophy. You will say I too am a dreamer; I admit it, but I do what others fail to do, I give my dreams as dreams, and leave the reader to discover whether there is anything in them which may prove useful to those who are awake" [p. 76].

Notes

1 To speak of a primary writing here does not amount to affirming a chronological priority of fact. That debate is well-known; is writing, as affirmed, for example, by Metchaninov and Marr, then Loukotka, "anterior to phonetic language?" (A conclusion assumed by the first edition of the Great Soviet Encyclopedia, later contradicted by Stalin. On this debate, cf. V. Istrine, "Langue et écriture," *Linguistique*, pp. 35, 60. This debate also forms around the theses advanced by P. van Ginneken. On the discussion of these propositions, cf. James Février, *Histoire de l'écriture* [Payot, 1948–59], pp. 5 f.). I shall try to show below why the terms and premises of such a debate are suspicious.

2 I shall deal with this problem more directly in *La voix et le phénomène* (Paris, 1967) [*Speech and Phenomena*].

3 Wiener, for example, while abandoning "semantics," and the opposition, judged by him as too crude and too general, between animate and inanimate etc., nevertheless continues to use expressions like "organs of sense," "motor organs," etc. to qualify the parts of the machine.

4 Cf., e.g., EP, pp. 126, 148, 355, etc. From another point of view, cf. Roman Jakobson, *Essais de linguistique générale* (tr. fr. [Nicolas Ruwet, Paris, 1963], p. 116) [Jakobson and Morris Halle, *Fundamentals of Language* (The Hague, 1956), p. 16].

5 This is shown by Pierre Aubenque (*Le problème de l'être chez Aristotle* [Paris, 1966], pp. 106 f.). In the course of a provocative analysis, to which I am here indebted, Aubenque remarks: "In other texts, to be sure, Aristotle designates as symbol the relationship between language and things: 'It is not possible to bring the things themselves to the discussion, but, instead of things, we can use their names as symbols.' The intermediary constituted by the mental experience is here suppressed or at least neglected, but this suppression is legitimate, since, mental experiences behaving like things, things can be substitued for them immediately. On the other hand, one cannot by any means substitute names for things" (pp. 107–8).

6 Roman Jakobson, *Essais de linguistique générale*, tr. fr., p. 162 ["The Phonemic and Grammatical Aspects of Language in their Interrelations," *Proceedings of the Sixth International Congress of Linguistics* (Paris, 1949), p. 6]. On this problem, on the tradition of the concept of the sign, and on the originality of Saussure's contribution within this continuity, cf. Ortigues, pp. 54 f.

7 Cited by Emmanuel Levinas, in *Difficile liberté* [Paris, 1963], p. 44.

8 I attempt to develop this theme elsewhere (*Speech and Phenomena*).

9 This does not, by simple inversion, mean that the signifier is fundamental or primary. The "primacy" or "priority" of the signifier would be an expression untenable and absurd to formulate illogically within the very logic that it would legitimately destroy. The signifier will never by rights precede the signified, in which case it would no longer be a signifier and the "signifying" signifier would no longer have a possible signified. The thought that is announced in this impossible formula without being successfully contained therein should therefore be stated in another way; it will clearly be impossible to do so without putting the very idea of the sign into suspicion, the "sign-of" which will always remain attached to what is here put in question. At the limit therefore, that thought would destroy the entire conceptuality organized around the concept of the sign (signifier and signified, expression and content, and so on).

10   Postface to *Was ist Metaphysik?* [Frankfurt am Main, 1960], p. 46. The insistence of the voice also dominates the analysis of *Gewissen* [conscience] in *Sein und Zeit* (pp. 267 f.) [pp. 312 f.].

11   Cf. *Das Wesen der Sprache* ["The Nature of Language"], and *Das Wort* ["Words"], in *Unterwegs zur Sprache* [Pfüllingen], 1959 [*On the Way to Language*, tr. Peter D. Hertz (New York, 1971)].

12   [Martin Heidegger, *Einführung in die Metaphysik* (Tübingen, 1953) translated as *An Introduction to Metaphysics* by Ralph Manheim (New Haven, 1959).] Tr. French Gilbert Kahn [Paris, 1967], p. 50.

13   *Introduction à la métaphysique*, tr. fr. p. 103 [*Einführung* p. 70; *Introduction*, p. 92]. "All this points in the direction of what we encountered when we characterized the Greek experience and interpretation of being. If we retain the usual interpretation of being, the word 'being' takes its meaning from the unity and determinateness of the horizon which guided our understanding. In short: we understand the verbal substantive 'Sein' through the infinitive, which in turn is related to the 'is' and its diversity that I have described. The definite and particular verb form 'is,' the *third person singular of the present indicative*, has here a pre-eminent rank. We understand 'being' not in regard to the 'thou art,' 'you are,' 'I am,' or 'they would be,' though all of these, just as much as 'is,' represent verbal inflections of 'to be.'... And involuntarily, almost as though nothing else were possible, we explain the infinitive 'to be' to ourselves through the 'is.'
      "Accordingly, 'being' has the meaning indicated above, recalling the Greek view of the essence of being, hence a determinateness which has not just dropped on us accidentally from somewhere but has dominated our historical being-there since antiquity. At one stroke our search for the definition of the meaning of the word 'being' becomes explicitly what it is, namely a reflection on the source of our hidden history." I should, of course, cite the entire analysis that concludes with these words.

14   *dem Statarischen*, an old German word that one has hitherto been tempted to translate as "immobile" or "static" (see [Jean] Gibelin [tr. *Leçons sur la philosophie de la religion* (Paris, 1959)], pp. 255–7.

15   "La parole soufflée," ED.

16   *Confessions*, p. 237 [p. 245].

17   Garnier edition, p. 168 [p. 57]. Italics added.

18   Starobinski, *La transparence*, p. 119. I refer also to the entire chapter devoted to the fête (p. 114), which Starobinski opposes to the theater as a *"world of transparence"* to a *"world of opacity."*

19   It is well-known that Rousseau ruthlessly denounced the mask, from the *Letter to M. d'Alembert* to the *Nouvelle Héloise*. One of the tasks of pedagogy consists precisely in neutralizing the effects of masks upon children. For let us not forget, "all children are afraid of masks" (*Emile*, p. 43) [p. 30]. The condemnation of writing is also, as if self-evidently, an ambiguous condemnation of the mask.

20   Among other analogies, by this distrust, with regard to the spoken text, of Corneille and Racine who were nothing but "talkers" even though, "imitating the English," they must sometimes "place the stage itself within representation" (*La Nouvelle Héloise*, p. 253) [*Eloisa* II, p. 62]. But surely these reconciliations must be effected with the greatest caution. The context sometimes places an infinite distance between two identical propositions.

21   Page 226 [pp. 127–8]. One will relate to this the following passage from *Emile*: "but when spring returns, the snow will melt and the marriage will remain; you must reckon for all seasons" (p. 570) [p. 411].

22   Cf. also *Emile*, pp. 66–9 [pp. 46–8].

23   Rousseau dreams of an unarticulated language, but he describes the origin of languages as the passage from the cry to articualtion. The consonant which for him goes hand in hand with articulation, is the becoming-language of sound, the becoming-phonetic of natural sonority. It is the consonant that gives the possibility of a linguistic pertinence to sound, by inscribing it within an opposition. Jakobson has shown, against current prejudices, that "in the acquisition of language, the first vocalic opposition is posterior to the first consonantal oppositions; there is thus a stage when the consonants already fulfill a distinctive function, whereas the unique vowel yet serves only as stress to the consonant and as material for expressive variations. Thus we see the consonants acquiring phonemic value before vowels" ("Les lois phoniques du langage enfantin et leur place dans la phonologie générale," *Selected Writings* [The Hague, 1962], I: 325).

CHAPTER 8

Semiology and Grammatology

Jacques Derrida

In this interview from 1968, Derrida discusses two texts – his reading of Saussure in *Of Grammatology* (1967) and his reading of Husserl in *Speech and Phenomenon* (1967). In this selection, he provides a very succinct account of the significance of "differance."

Interview with Julia Kristeva

Kristeva: Semiology today is constructed on the model of the sign and its correlates: *communication* and *structure*. What are the "logocentric" and ethnocentric limits of these models, and how are they incapable of serving as the basis for a notation attempting to escape metaphysics?

Derrida: All gestures here are necessarily equivocal. And supposing, which I do not believe, that someday it will be possible *simply* to escape metaphysics, the concept of the sign will have marked, in this sense, a simultaneous impediment and progress. For if the sign, by its root and its implications, is in all its aspects metaphysical, if it is in systematic solidarity with stoic and medieval theology, the work and the displacement to which it has been submitted – and of which it also, curiously, is the instrument – have had *delimiting* effects. For this work and displacement have permitted the critique of how the concept of the sign belongs to metaphysics, which represents a simultaneous *marking* and *loosening* of the limits of the system in which this concept was born and began to serve, and thereby also represents, to a certain extent, an uprooting of the sign from its own soil. This work must be conducted as far as possible, but at a certain point one inevitably encounters "the logocentric and ethnocentric limits" of such a model. At this point, perhaps, the concept is to be abandoned. But this point is very difficult to determine, and is never pure. All the heuristic and critical resources of the concept of the sign have to be exhausted, and exhausted equally in all domains and contexts. Now, it is inevitable that not only inequalities of development (which will always occur), but also the necessity of certain contexts, will render strategically indispensable the recourse to a model known elsewhere, and even at the most novel points of investigation, to function as an obstacle.

To take only one example, one could show that a semiology of the Saussurian type has had a double role. *On the one hand*, an absolutely decisive critical role:

1 It has marked, against the tradition, that the signified is inseparable from the signifier, that the signified and signifier are the two sides of one and the same production. Saussure even purposely refused to have this opposition or this "two-sided unity" conform to the relationship between soul and body, as had always been

done. "This two-sided unity has often been compared to the unity of the human person, composed of a body and a soul. The comparison is hardly satisfactory." (*Cours de linguistique générale*, p. 145)

2 By emphasizing the *differential* and *formal* characteristics of semiological functioning, by showing that it "is impossible for sound, the material element, itself to belong to language" and that "in its essence it [the linguistic signifier] is not at all phonic" (p. 164); by desubstantializing both the signified content and the "expressive substance" – which therefore is no longer in a privileged or exclusive way phonic – by making linguistics a division of general semiology (p. 33), Saussure powerfully contributed to turning against the metaphysical tradition the concept of the sign that he borrowed from it.

And yet Saussure could not not confirm this tradition in the extent to which he continued to use the concept of the sign. No more than any other, this concept cannot be employed in both an absolutely novel and an absolutely conventional way. One necessarily assumes, in a non-critical way, at least some of the implications inscribed in its system. There is at least one moment at which Saussure must renounce drawing all the conclusions from the critical work he has undertaken, and that is the not fortuitous moment when he resigns himself to using the word "sign," lacking anything better. After having justified the introduction of the words "signified" and "signifier," Saussure writes: "As for *sign*, if we retain it, it is because we find nothing else to replace it, everyday language suggesting no other" (pp. 99–100). And, in effect, it is difficult to see how one could evacuate the *sign* when one has begun by proposing the opposition signified/signifier.

Now, "everyday language" is not innocent or neutral. It is the language of Western metaphysics, and it carries with it not only a considerable number of presuppositions of all types, but also presuppositions inseparable from metaphysics, which, although little attended to, are knotted into a system. This is why *on the other hand:*

1 The maintenance of the rigorous distinction – an essential and juridical distinction – between the *signans* and the *signatum*, the equation of the *signatum* and the concept (p. 99),[1] inherently leaves open the possibility of thinking a *concept signified in and of itself,* a concept simply present for thought, independent of a relationship to language, that is of a relationship to a system of signifiers. By leaving open this possibility – and it is inherent even in the opposition signifier/signified, that is in the sign – Saussure contradicts the critical acquisitions of which we were just speaking. He accedes to the classical exigency of what I have proposed to call a "transcendental signified," which in and of itself, in its essence, would refer to no signifier, would exceed the chain of signs, and would no longer itself function as a signifier. On the contrary, though, from the moment that one questions the possibility of such a transcendental signified, and that one recognizes that every signified is also in the position of a signifier,[2] the distinction between signified and signifier becomes problematical at its root. Of course this is an operation that must be undertaken with prudence for: (a) it must pass through the difficult deconstruction of the entire history of metaphysics which imposed, and never will cease to impose upon semiological science in its entirety this fundamental quest for a "transcendental signified" and a concept independent of language; this quest not being imposed from without by something like "philosophy," but rather by everything that links our language, our culture, our "system of thought" to the history and system of metaphysics; (b) nor is it a question of confusing at every level, and in all simplicity, the signifier

and the signified. That this opposition or difference cannot be radical or absolute does not prevent it from functioning, and even from being indispensable within certain limits – very wide limits. For example, no translation would be possible without it. In effect, the theme of a transcendental signified took shape within the horizon of an absolutely pure, transparent, and unequivocal translatability. In the limits to which it is possible, or at least *appears* possible, translation practices the difference between signified and signifier. But if this difference is never pure, no more so is translation, and for the notion of translation we would have to substitute a notion of *transformation:* a regulated transformation of one language by another, of one text by another. We will never have, and in fact have never had, to do with some "transport" of pure signifieds from one language to another, or within one and the same language, that the signifying instrument would leave virgin and untouched.

2 Although he recognized the necessity of putting the phonic substance between brackets ("What is essential in language, we shall see, is foreign to the phonic character of the linguistic sign" [p. 21]. "In its essence it [the linguistic signifier] is not at all phonic" [p. 164]), Saussure, for essential, and essentially metaphysical, reasons had to privilege speech, everything that links the sign to *phonē*. He also speaks of the "natural link" between thought and voice, meaning and sound (p. 46). He even speaks of "thought-sound" (p. 156). I have attempted elsewhere to show what is traditional in such a gesture, and to what necessities it submits. In any event, it winds up contradicting the most interesting critical motive of the *Course*, making of linguistics the regulatory model, the "pattern" for a general semiology of which it was to be, by all rights and theoretically, only a part. The theme of the arbitrary, thus, is turned away from its most fruitful paths (formalization) toward a hierarchizing teleology: "Thus it can be said that entirely arbitrary signs realize better than any others the ideal of the semiological process; this is why language, the most complex and most widespread of the systems of expression, is also the most characteristic one of them all; in this sense linguistics can become the *general pattern for all semiology*, even though language is only a particular system" (p. 101). One finds exactly the same gesture and the same concepts in Hegel. The contradiction between these two moments of the *Course* is also marked by Saussure's recognizing elsewhere that "it is not spoken language that is natural to man, but the faculty of constituting a language, that is, a system of distinct signs...," that is, the possibility of the *code* and of *articulation*, independent of any substance, for example, phonic substance.

3 The concept of the sign (signifier/signified) carries within itself the necessity of privileging the phonic substance and of setting up linguistics as the "pattern" for semiology. *Phonē*, in effect, is the signifying substance *given to consciousness* as that which is most intimately tied to the thought of the signified concept. From this point of view, the voice is consciousness itself. When I speak, not only am I conscious of being present for what I think, but I am conscious also of keeping as close as possible to my thought, or to the "concept," a signifier that does not fall into the world, a signifier that I hear as soon as I emit it, that seems to depend upon my pure and free spontaneity, requiring the use of no instrument, no accessory, no force taken from the world. Not only do the signifier and the signified seem to unite, but also, in this confusion, the signifier seems to erase itself or to become transparent, in order to allow the concept to present itself as what it is, referring to nothing other than its presence. The exteriority of the signifier seems reduced. Naturally this experience is a lure, but a lure whose necessity has organized an entire structure, or an entire

epoch; and on the grounds of this epoch a semiology has been constituted whose concepts and fundamental presuppositions are quite precisely discernible from Plato to Husserl, passing through Aristotle, Rousseau, Hegel, etc.

4 To reduce the exteriority of the signifier is to exclude everything in semiotic practice that is not psychic. Now, only the privilege accorded to the phonetic and linguistic sign can authorize Saussure's proposition according to which the "linguistic sign is therefore a two-sided *psychic* entity" (p. 99). Supposing that this proposition has a rigorous sense in and of itself, it is difficult to see how it could be extended to every sign, be it phonetic-linguistic or not. It is difficult to see therefore, except, precisely, by making of the phonetic sign the "pattern" for all signs, how general semiology can be inscribed in a psychology. However, this is what Saussure does: "One can thus conceive of a science that would study the life of signs at the heart of social life; it would form a part of social psychology, and consequently of general psychology; we will name it semiology (from the Greek *sēmeion*, 'sign'). It would teach what signs consist of, what laws regulate them. Since it does not yet exist, one cannot say what it will be; but it has a right to exist, its place is determined in advance. Linguistics is only a part of this general science, the laws that semiology will discover will be applicable to linguistics, and the latter will find itself attached to a well defined domain in the set of human facts. It is for the psychologist to determine the exact place of semiology" (p. 33).

Of course modern linguists and semioticians have not remained with Saussure, or at least with this Saussurean "psychologism." The Copenhagen School and all of American linguistics have explicitly criticized it. But if I have insisted on Saussure, it is not only because even those who criticize him recognize him as the founder of general semiology and borrow most of their concepts from him; but above all because one cannot simply criticize the "psychologistic" usage of the concept of the sign. Psychologism is not the poor usage of a good concept, but is inscribed and prescribed within the concept of the sign itself, in the equivocal manner of which I spoke at the beginning. This equivocality, which weighs upon the model of the sign, marks the "semiological" project itself and the organic totality of its concepts, in particular that of *communication*, which in effect implies a *transmission charged with making pass, from one subject to another, the identity* of a *signified* object, of a *meaning* or of a *concept* rightfully separable from the process of passage and from the signifying operation. Communication presupposes subjects (whose identity and presence are constituted before the signifying operation) and objects (signified concepts, a thought meaning that the passage of communication will have neither to constitute, nor, by all rights, to transform). *A* communicates *B* to *C*. Through the sign the emitter communicates something to a receptor, etc.

The case of the concept of *structure*, that you also bring up, is certainly more ambiguous. Everything depends upon how one sets it to work. Like the concept of the sign – and therefore of semiology – it can simultaneously confirm and shake logocentric and ethnocentric assuredness. It is not a question of junking these concepts, nor do we have the means to do so. Doubtless it is more necessary, from within semiology, to transform concepts, to displace them, to turn them against their presuppositions, to reinscribe them in other chains, and little by little to modify the terrain of our work and thereby produce new configurations; I do not believe in decisive ruptures, in an unequivocal "epistemological break," as it is called today. Breaks are always, and fatally, reinscribed in an old cloth that must continually, interminably be undone. This interminability is not an accident or contingency; it is essential, systematic, and theoretical. And this in no way minimizes the necessity and relative importance of certain breaks, of the appearance and definition of new structures . . .

Kristeva: What is the *gram* as a "new structure of nonpresence"? What is *writing* as *différance*? What rupture do these concepts introduce in relation to the key concepts of semiology – the (phonetic) *sign* and *structure*? How does the notion of *text* replace, in grammatology, the linguistic and semiological notion of what is *enounced*?

Derrida: The reduction of writing – as the reduction of the exteriority of the signifier – was part and parcel of phonologism and logocentrism. We know how Saussure, according to the traditional operation that was also Plato's, Aristotle's, Rousseau's, Hegel's, Husserl's, etc., excludes writing from the field of linguistics – from language and speech – as a phenomenon of exterior representation, both useless and danger-ous: "The linguistic object is not defined by the combination of the written word and the spoken word, the latter alone constituting this object" (p. 45); "writing is foreign to the internal system [of language]" (p. 44); "writing veils our view of language: it does not clothe language, but travesties it" (p. 51). The tie of writing to language is "superficial," "factitious." It is "bizarre" that writing, which should only be an "image," "usurps the principal role" and that "the natural relationship is inversed" (p. 47). Writing is a "trap," its action is "vicious" and "tyrannical," its misdeeds are monstrosities, "teratological cases," "linguistics should put them under observation in a special compartment" (p. 54), etc. Naturally, this representativist conception of writing ("Language and writing are two distinct sign systems; the unique *raison d'être* of the second is to *represent* the first" [p. 45]) is linked to the practice of phonetic-alphabetic writing, to which Saussure realizes his study is "limited" (p. 48). In effect, alphabetical writing seems to present speech, and at the same time to erase itself before speech. Actually, it could be shown, as I have attempted to do, that there is no purely phonetic writing, and that phonologism is less a consequence of the practice of the alphabet in a given culture than a certain ethical or axiological *experience* of this practice. Writing *should* erase itself before the plenitude of living speech, perfectly represented in the transparence of its notation, immediately present for the subject who speaks it, and for the subject who receives its meaning, content, value.

Now, if one ceases to limit oneself to the model of phonetic writing, which we privilege only by ethnocentrism, and if we draw all the consequences from the fact that there is no purely phonetic writing (by reason of the necessary spacing of signs, punctuation, intervals, the differences indispensable for the functioning of graph-emes, etc.), then the entire phonologist or logocentrist logic becomes problematical. Its range of legitimacy becomes narrow and superficial. This delimitation, however, is indispensable if one wants to be able to account, with some coherence, for the principle of difference, such as Saussure himself recalls it. This principle compels us not only not to privilege one substance – here the phonic, so called temporal, sub-stance – while excluding another – for example, the graphic, so called spatial, substance – but even to consider every process of signification as a formal play of differences. That is, of traces.

Why traces? And by what right do we reintroduce grammatics at the moment when we seem to have neutralized every substance, be it phonic, graphic, or other-wise? Of course it is not a question of resorting to the same concept of writing and of simply inverting the dissymmetry that now has become problematical. It is a question, rather, of producing a new concept of writing. This concept can be called *gram* or *différance*. The play of differences supposes, in effect, syntheses and referrals which forbid at any moment, or in any sense, that a simple element be *present* in and of itself, referring only to itself. Whether in the order of spoken or written discourse, no element can function as a sign without referring to another element which itself is not simply present. This interweaving results in each "element" – phoneme or grapheme – being constituted on the basis of the trace within it of the other elements of the chain or system. This interweaving, this textile, is the *text* produced only in the transformation of another text. Nothing, neither among the elements nor within the system, is anywhere ever simply present or absent. There are only, everywhere, differences and traces of traces. The gram, then, is the most general concept of semiology – which thus becomes grammatology – and it covers not only the field of writing in the restricted sense, but also the field of linguistics. The advantage of this concept – provided that it be surrounded by a certain interpretive context, for no more than any other conceptual element it does not signify, or suffice, by itself – is that in principle it neutralizes the phonologistic propensity of the "sign," and *in fact counterbalances* it by liberating the entire scientific field of the "graphic substance" (history and systems of writing beyond the bounds of the West) whose interest is not minimal, but which so far has been left in the shadows of neglect.

The gram as *différance*, then, is a structure and a movement no longer conceivable on the basis of the opposition presence/absence. *Différance* is the systematic play of differences, of the traces of differences, of the *spacing* by means of which elements are related to each other. This spacing is the simultaneously active and passive (the *a* of *différance* indicates this indecision as concerns activity and passivity, that which cannot be governed by or distributed between the terms of this opposition)[3] production of the intervals without which the "full" terms would not signify, would not function. It is also the becoming-space of the spoken chain – which has been called temporal or linear; a becoming-space which makes possible both writing and every correspondence between speech and writing, every passage from one to the other.

The activity or productivity connoted by the *a* of *différance* refers to the generative movement in the play of differences. The latter are neither fallen from the sky nor inscribed once and for all in a closed system, a static structure that a synchronic and taxonomic operation could exhaust. Differences are the effects of transformations, and from this vantage the theme of *différance* is incompatible with the static, synchronic, taxonomic, ahistoric motifs in the concept of *structure*. But it goes without saying that this motif is not the only one that defines structure, and that the production of differences, *différance*, is not astructural: it produces systematic and regulated transformations which are able, at a certain point, to leave room for a structural science. The concept of *différance* even develops the most legitimate principled exigencies of "structuralism."

Language, and in general every semiotic code – which Saussure defines as "classifications" – are therefore effects, but their cause is not a subject, a substance, or a being somewhere present and outside the movement of *différance*. Since there is no presence before and outside semiological *différance*, one can extend to the system of signs in general what Saussure says of language: "Language is necessary for speech to be intelligible and to produce all its effects; but speech is necessary for language to be established; historically, the fact of speech always comes first." There is a circle here, for if one rigorously distinguishes language and speech, code and message, schema and usage, etc., and if one wishes to do justice to the two postulates thus enunciated, one does not know where to begin, nor how something can begin in general, be it language or speech. Therefore, one has to admit, before any dissociation of language and speech, code and message, etc. (and everything that goes along with such a dissociation), a systematic production of differences, the *production* of a system of differences – a *différance* – within whose effects one eventually, by abstraction and according to determined motivations, will be able to demarcate a linguistics of language and a linguistics of speech, etc.

Nothing – no present and in-*different* being – thus precedes *différance* and spacing. There is no subject who is agent, author, and master of *différance*, who eventually and empirically would be overtaken by *différance*. Subjectivity – like objectivity – is an effect of *différance*, an effect inscribed in a system of *différance*. This is why the *a* of *différance* also recalls that spacing is temporization, the detour and postponement by means of which intuition, perception, consummation – in a word, the relationship to the present, the reference to a present reality, to a *being* – are always *deferred*. Deferred by virtue of the very principle of difference which holds that an element functions and signifies, takes on or conveys meaning, only by referring to another past or future element in an economy of traces. This economic aspect of *différance*, which brings into play a certain not conscious calculation in a field of forces, is inseparable from the more narrowly semiotic aspect of *différance*. It confirms that the subject, and first of all the conscious and speaking subject, depends upon the system of differences and the movement of *différance*, that the subject is constituted only in being divided from itself, in becoming space, in temporizing, in deferral; and it confirms that, as Saussure said, "language [which consists only of differences] is not a function of the speaking subject." At the point at which the concept of *différance*, and the chain attached to it, intervenes, all the conceptual oppositions of metaphysics (signifier/signified; sensible/intelligible; writing/speech; passivity/activity; etc.) – to the extent that they ultimately refer to the presence of something present (for example, in the form of the identity of the subject who is present for all his operations, present beneath every accident or event, self-present in its "living speech," in its enunciations, in the present objects and acts of its language, etc.) – become nonpertinent. They all amount, at one moment or another, to a subordination of the movement of *différance* in favor of the presence of a value or a *meaning* supposedly antecedent to *différance*, more original than it, exceeding and governing it in the last analysis. This is still the presence of what we called above the "transcendental signified."

Notes

1   J. D. That is, the intelligible. The difference between the signifier and the signified has always
    reproduced the difference between the sensible and the intelligible. And it does so no less in the
    twentieth century than in its stoic origins. "Modern structuralist thought has clearly established
    this: language is a system of signs, and linguistics is an integral part of the science of signs,
    semiotics (or to use Saussure's terms, *semiology*). The medieval definition – *aliquid stat pro aliquo*
    – resuscitated by our epoch has shown itself to be still valid and fruitful. Thereby, the consti-
    tutive mark of every sign in general, of the linguistic sign in particular, resides in its double
    character: every linguistic unity is bipartite, and comports two aspects: one sensible and the

other intelligible – on the one hand, the *signans* (Saussure's *signifier*), and on the other, the *signatur* (*the signified*)." (Roman Jakobson, *Essais de linguistique générale* [Paris: Editions de Minuit, 1963], p. 162.)

2   Ed. N. See *De la grammatologie*, pp. 196–8.

3   T. N. In other words, *différance* combines and confuses "differing" and "deferring" in both their active and passive senses.

CHAPTER 9

Writing

Barbara Johnson

An American school of deconstructive criticism developed out of Jacques Derrida's work. Its leading proponents were Paul de Man and J. Hillis Miller. While Derrida sought to dislocate the assumptions of metaphysics in philosophy, these critics were concerned with the dislocation of naïve assumptions about meaning in literary texts. Texts are figural or rhetorical, and they refer endlessly to other texts, not to a knowable presence of truth or to determinable meanings that might, as the New Critics assumed, be said to constitute "universals." In this selection, Barbara Johnson, a student of de Man and herself a leading practitioner of American deconstruction, explains how the French concern with "writing" is linked to the deconstructive project.

How is it that the word "writing" has come to be considered a critical term? Isn't "writing" simply one of those aspects of literature that can be taken for granted? Isn't it merely the medium through which a reader encounters words on a page – for example, these?

Every essay in this volume communicates to some extent *by means of* the very thing it is talking *about*. Nowhere is this more obvious than in the case of writing. An essay about writing, therefore, is an unclosable loop: it is an attempt to comprehend that which it is comprehended by. The non-Euclidean logic of such reciprocal inclusion has often itself been an object of attention in recent theoretical discussions of writing. That is only one of the consequences that the study of writing has entailed.

Writing about writing is hardly a new phenomenon, however. From Omar Khayyám's moving finger to Rousseau's trembling hand, from the broken tables of Moses to the purloined letters of Poe and Alice Walker, from Borges's encyclopedia to Wordsworth's lines left upon a seat in a yew tree, images of writing in writing testify to an enduring fascination with the mechanics and materiality of the written word. A comprehensive treatment of the question of writing is obviously beyond the scope of the present essay. I will therefore concentrate on a particular recent moment of reflection about writing – the theoretical "revolution" in France in 1967 – which has had a decisive impact upon the shape of literary studies today.

Writing (*l'écriture*) came to philosophical, psychoanalytic, and literary prominence in France in the 1960s, primarily through the work of Jacques Derrida, Roland Barthes, and other writers who were at that time associated with the journal *Tel Quel*. Philippe Sollers, in a "Program" that heads the group's collective theoretical volume, proclaimed in 1967: "A comprehensive theory arising out of a thought about the practice of writing cries out for elaboration." Writing, it seemed, was to become the key to all mythologies. The sudden spectacular interest in writing sprang from many different sources, some of which I will outline quickly here.

As early as 1953, in *Writing Degree Zero*, Roland Barthes had investigated the paradoxical relationship that existed in the nineteenth century in France between the development of a concept of Literature (with a capital *L*) and the growing sense of a breakdown in the representational capacities of language. Literature was in some ways being exalted as a substitute religion, but it was a religion whose high priests seemed only to proclaim the obscurity, imperfection, or unreliability of their own medium. The proper names associated with the elaboration of *both* sides of this phenomenon are Flaubert and Mallarmé. These writers, says Barthes, *constructed* the object Literature in the very act of announcing its death. In later essays, Barthes lays out a theory of literature based on a split between the classic notion of a *work* (*œuvre*) – considered as a closed, finished, reliable representational *object* – and the modern notion of a *text* – considered as an open, infinite *process* that is both meaning-generating and meaning-subverting. "Work" and "text" are thus not two different kinds of object but two different ways of viewing the written word. What interests Barthes is the *tension* between the concept of Literature and the concept of textuality. While Literature is seen as a series of discrete and highly meaningful Great Works, textuality is the manifestation of an open-ended, heterogeneous, disruptive force of signification and erasure that transgresses all closure – a force that is operative even within the Great Works themselves.

Closure versus subversion, product versus practice, meaning-containing object versus significance-scattering process: Barthes' theory of writing owes a great deal, as we shall see, both to Marxism and to psychoanalysis. But the *Tel Quel* writers' involvement with Marxism and psychoanalysis takes on its particular coloring, strangely enough, through the mediation of Saussurian linguistics. How does this happen?

In his *Course in General Linguistics* (first published by his students in 1916, with new editions in 1948 and 1966), Ferdinand de Saussure mapped out a science of linguistics based not on the historical ("diachronic") development of families of languages but on the structural ("synchronic") properties of language "as such," frozen in time as a *system*. This "structuralist" perspective, also developed in the 1950s in anthropology by Claude Lévi-Strauss, involves viewing the system as a set of relations among elements governed by rules. The favorite analogy for such systems is chess: whatever the particular properties of an individual "man" (ivory, wood, plastic), the "man" is involved in a system of moves and relations that can be known and manipulated in themselves. From the structural point of view, there is no difference between ivory and plastic. There is difference between king, queen, and knight, or between white and black.

Saussure's most enduring contribution has been his description of the *sign* as the unit of the language system. The sign is composed of two parts: a mental image or concept (the "signified"), and a phonic or graphic vehicle (the "signifier"). The sign is thus both conceptual and material, sense and sound, spirit and letter at once. The existence of numerous languages indicates that the relation between the signifier and the signified in any given sign is arbitrary (there is no natural resemblance between sound and idea), but once fixed, that relation becomes a convention that cannot be modified at will by any individual speaker. By thus deciding that what is relevant to a structural study of language is neither history ("diachrony") nor reality (the "refer-ent") but rather the system of differential relations among signs, Saussure set up a tremendously enabling, as well as limiting, heuristic perspective for analysis. And by asserting that signs signify not as independently meaningful units corresponding to external objects but as elements whose value is generated by their difference from neighboring elements in the system, Saussure put forth a notion of *difference* (not identity) as the origin of meaning.

Saussure's suspension of interest in history and the external world would seem to place him at the farthest remove from Marxism. But theorists of writing saw a connection between the signifier/signified relation and the materialism/idealism rela-tion: If the signifier was the material condition of the existence of ideas, then the privileging of the signified resembled the fetishization of commodities resulting from bourgeois idealism's blindness to labor and to the material conditions of economic existence. The liberation of the signifier, the rebellion against idealist repressions, and the unleashing of the forces of difference and desire against the law and order of identity were all part of the program for change that developed in France in the 1960s. Whether linguistic materiality and economic materiality are linked *only* by analogy, or whether there is some profound interimplication between them, is still a subject for debate today. But whatever the case, the repressive return to order that followed the strikes and demonstrations in France in May 1968 squelched the opti-mism of those who might have believed in any simple connection between liberating the signifier and changing the class structure of society.

The understanding of what it might mean to liberate the signifier also had roots in the psychoanalytic theory of Jacques Lacan. For many years prior to the 1966 publi-cation of his *Ecrits* (*Writings*), Lacan had been conducting a seminar in which he attempted to work out a radically new way of reading Freud. What he emphasized in Freud's writing was the discovery that "the unconscious is structured like a lan-guage." The unconscious is *structured*. It is not a reservoir of amorphous drives and energies but a system of articulations through which repressed ideas return in dis-placed form. Freud's comparison of a dream to a rebus is extended as an analogy for all effects of the unconscious: just as each element in a rebus must be translated separately in order to decipher the total message, so each element in a dream is a knot of associations that must be explored without regard for the dream's surface coherence. Dreams, slips of the tongue, parapraxes, hysterical symptoms, and other expressions of the unconscious are for Lacan manifestations of a "signifying chain," a structure of associations that resembles an unconscious foreign language. Conscious-ness attempts to disregard this language in order to control and define the identity of the self, but the psychoanalyst's task is to attempt to hear that language despite the ego's efforts to scramble it. Using the terminology of Saussure, Lacan calls the units of unconscious expression "signifiers," linked to repressed "signifieds." But the search for the signified can only take the form of a sliding along the chain of signifiers. In other words, there is no one-to-one link between signifier and signified but rather an "effect of signified" generated by the movement from one signifier to another. Freud never comes to the end of his dream analyses, never "solves" their enigma, but it feels as though something like insight is achieved by following out the dreamer's chains of associations.

Lacan's troubling of Saussure's one-to-one link between signifiers and signifieds actually turns out to have its counterpart in Saussure's own work. Beginning in 1964,

Jean Starobinski began publishing strange notebooks in which Saussure attempted to prove that certain late Latin poems contained hidden proper names anagrammatically dispersed throughout their texts. The poems, in other words, contained extra signifiers, readable only to those in the know. Whether or not these anagrams were a secret key to late Latin poetics, the notion that the signifier could take the lead in creating poetic effects appealed to students of poetry. Saussure's anagrams prompted Julia Kristeva, among others, to theorize an anagrammatic (or paragrammatic) functioning in poetic language as such.

The claim that signifiers can generate effects even when the signified is unknown serves as the basis for Lacan's famous reading of Poe's story "The Purloined Letter." In that story, an unscrupulous minister steals a compromising letter from the queen under the unsuspecting eyes of the king. An amateur detective, Dupin, is commissioned by the stymied prefect of police to get the letter back. Dupin suspects that the minister has hidden the letter in plain sight, just as it had been when he stole it. Dupin then repeats the minister's act and steals the letter back for the queen. Lacan emphasizes the way in which the characters' actions are determined by the position of the letter among them. Neither the letter's contents (the never-revealed "signified") nor the individual identities of the people (the psychological equivalent of Saussure's ivory and wood chessmen) determine the course of the plot. It is the movement of the letter that dictates the characters' actions.

The rebus, the anagram, and the letter are clearly all manifestations of *writing*. They are graphic, articulated, material instantiations of systems of marks that simultaneously obscure and convey meaning. They are also something other than mere transcriptions of the spoken word. In other words, they are not examples of *phonetic* writing. It is this "something other" that must be kept in mind as we now turn to the work of the most important French theorist of writing, Jacques Derrida.

It was in 1967 that Derrida published three major books devoted to the question of writing: *Writing and Difference, Of Grammatology*, and *Speech and Phenomena*. Derrida's project in these writings is to reevaluate the structuring principles of Western metaphysics. Western philosophy, writes Derrida, has analyzed the world in terms of binary oppositions: mind vs. body, good vs. evil, man vs. woman, presence vs. absence. Each of these pairs is organized hierarchically: the first term is seen as higher or better than the second. According to Derrida, the opposition between speech and writing has been structured similarly: speech is seen as immediacy, presence, life, and identity, whereas writing is seen as deferment, absence, death, and difference. Speech is primary; writing secondary. Derrida calls this privileging of speech as self-present meaning "logocentrism."

In his three volumes of 1967, Derrida gives rigorous attention to the paradox that the Western tradition (the "Great Books") is filled with *writings* that privilege *speech*. By closely analyzing those writings, Derrida attempts to uncover the ways in which the Great Books rebel against their own stated intention to say that speech is better than writing. What his analyses reveal is that even when a text *tries* to privilege speech as immediacy, it cannot completely eliminate the fact that speech, like writing, is based on a *différance* (a Derridean neologism meaning both "deferment" and "difference") between signifier and signified inherent in the sign. Speakers do not beam meanings directly from one mind to another. Immediacy is an illusion. Properties normally associated with writing inevitably creep into a discussion designed to privilege speech. Thus, for example, although Saussure wishes to treat speech as primary and writing as secondary for an understanding of language, he describes language as a "dictionary in the head" or as "linear" – a spatial term more applicable to writing than to speech. Or, to take another example, when Socrates tells Phaedrus that proper teaching must take place orally rather than in writing, he nevertheless ends up describing the truths such teaching is supposed to reach as being "*inscribed* in the soul." Because a gap of heterogeneity and distance is fundamental to the structure of language, Derrida sees "speech" as being ultimately structured like "writing." This emphasis on writing as the more originary category is designed to counter the history of logocentrism and to track the functioning of *différance* in structures of signification.

Many literary texts seem in fact to stage some version of this encounter between the search for spoken immediacy or identity and the recourse to writing and difference. The following poem by Edward Taylor (ca. 1642–1729), for example, does not seem to expect to end up talking about writing:

Meditation 6

Am I thy gold? Or purse, Lord, for thy wealth,
    Whether in mine or mint refined for thee?
I'm counted so, but count me o'er thyself,
    Lest gold washed face, and brass in heart I be.
    I fear my touchstone touches when I try
    Me and my counted gold too overly.

Am I new minted by thy stamp indeed?
    Mine eyes are dim; I cannot clearly see.
Be thou my spectacles that I may read
    Thine image and inscription stamped on me.
    If thy bright image do upon me stand,
    I am a golden angel in thy hand.

Lord, make my soul thy plate, thine image bright
    Within the circle of the same enfile
And on its brims in golden letters write
    Thy superscription in an holy style.
    Then I shall be thy money, thou my horde:
    Let me thy angel be, be thou my Lord.

Written in a style of extended metaphor known as the metaphysical conceit, this poem sets out to express spiritual value in terms of material value (gold). The most obvious figure for the conjunction between the spiritual and the material is the word "angel," which means both a heavenly being and an old English coin. Through this spiritual/material alloy, the poem attempts to make human value both derive from and coincide with divine value, to eliminate the space of difference or distance between the human and the divine.

The poem is composed of a series of questions and imperatives addressed to God. While these aim to alleviate doubt, difference, and distance, they seem only to widen the gap they attempt to close. Am I gold or purse? value-object or container? the poet asks. He then pursues the first possibility, only to stumble upon a new inside/outside opposition: "Lest gold washed face, and brass in heart I be." The gold begins to resemble a sign, with no guaranteed correlation between face (signifier) and heart (signified). The becoming-sign process continues in the second stanza, where the speaker is "stamped" with an image and an inscription. The speaker is now a reader, and what he reads is himself. God has become an image, and a corrective lens. In the final stanza, the text ("inscription") that was dimly decipherable in the second stanza turns out not yet to have been written. While the poem still yearns for a perfectly reciprocal container/contained relation ("I shall be thy money, thou my horde"), this relation now requires the active intervention of writing ("in golden letters write/Thy superscription"). In his increasingly aggressive submissiveness, the speaker tries to order God to take his place as the writer.

From metal to image to letters, from touching to reading to writing, from counted to almost-read to not-yet-written, the speaker seems to be farther away from coincidence with God at the end than he was at the beginning. The mediating elements only increase the *différance*. Yet this *différance* is also the space of the poem's existence. The speaker cannot *write* his way into an immediacy that would eliminate writing. Nor can he write himself into a submissiveness great enough to overtake the fact that it is he, not God, who writes. His conceit will never succeed in erasing the "conceit" of writing itself.

The logic of writing is thus a double logic: writing is called upon as a necessary remedy for *différance*, but at the same time it *is* the very *différance* for which a remedy must be sought. In Derrida's analyses of writing, this logic is called the logic of the *supplément*. In French, the word *supplément* means both an "addition" and a "substitute." To say that "A is a *supplément* to B" is thus to say something ambiguous. Addition and substitution are not exactly contradictory, but neither can they be combined in the traditional logic of identity. In the poem, the inscriptions, images, and even spectacles function as *suppléments:* they are at once additions and substitutes simultaneously bridging and widening the gap between God and the speaker. Some sense of the way in which supplementary logic differs from the binary logic of identity (A = A) and noncontradiction (A ≠ not A) may be derived from the following list. In this list, all statements are to be taken as *simultaneously* equivalent to the statement "A is a *supplément* to B." (In terms of the Taylor poem, say B = the presence of, or coincidence with, God; and A = writing).

> A is added to B.
> A substitutes for B.
> A is a superfluous addition to B.
> A makes up for the absence of B.
> A usurps the place of B.
> A makes up for B's deficiency.
> A corrupts the purity of B.
> A is necessary so that B can be restored.
> A is an accident alienating B from itself.
> A is that without which B would be lost.
> A is that through which B is lost.
> A is a danger to B.
> A is a remedy to B.
> A's fallacious charm seduces one away from B.
> A can never satisfy the desire for B.
> A protects against direct encounter with B.

Supplementary logic is not only the logic *of* writing – it is also a logic that can only really exist *in* writing. That is, it is a nonintuitive logic that inheres (Lacan would say, "in-sists") in a text as a system of traces. Like an algebraic equation with more than one unknown, supplementary logic cannot be held in the head but must be worked out in external form. It is no accident that the word "differential" is central both to calculus and to Derrida's theory of writing.

Derrida's theory of writing turns out to have been, in fact, a theory of reading. The epigraph to his *Writing and Difference* is a quotation from Mallarmé: "Le tout sans nouveauté qu'un espacement de la lecture" ("All without innovation except for a certain spacing-out of reading"). What does it mean to introduce "space" into reading? For Mallarmé, it means two things. It means giving a signifying function to the materiality – the blanks, the typefaces, the placement on the page, the punctuation – of writing. And it also means tracking syntactic and semantic ambiguities in such a way as to generate multiple, often conflicting, meanings out of a single utterance. The "meaning" of a Mallarmé text, like that of a dream, cannot be grasped intuitively as a whole but must be worked out rigorously by following each strand in a network of relations. What Derrida generalizes and analyzes in other writings is this "spacing" that Mallarmé attempts to maximize. In his reading of Plato's *Phaedrus*, for instance, Derrida follows the ambiguity of the word *pharmakon*, which Plato uses to describe writing itself. If *pharmakon* can mean both "poison" and "remedy," what does it mean to call writing a *pharmakon*? As Derrida points out, translators of Plato have rendered this word by choosing to favor one side or the other of the ambiguity according to the context. They have subordinated its ambiguity to their notion of what makes the most sense. They have thus subordinated "writing" as spacing and ambiguity to "speech" as single intention. The ambiguity of the poison / remedy relation is tamed thereby into something far less unsettling. "Sense" is achieved, however, at a cost. To know the difference between poison and remedy may be reassuring, but that reassurance may well make it difficult to come to grips with the meaning of Socrates' death.

Thus "reading," for Derrida, involves following the "other" logics of structures of signification inscribed in writing that may or may not be in conformity with traditional logics of meaning, identity, consciousness, or intention. It involves taking seriously the elements that a standard reading disregards, overlooks, or edits out. Just as Freud rendered dreams and slips of the tongue *readable* rather than dismissing them as mere nonsense or error, so Derrida sees signifying force in the gaps, margins, figures, echoes, digressions, discontinuities, contradictions, and ambiguities of a text. When one writes, one writes more than (or less than, or other than) one thinks. The reader's task is to read what is written rather than simply attempt to intuit what might have been meant.

The possibility of reading materiality, silence, space, and conflict within texts has opened up extremely productive ways of studying the politics of language. If each text is seen as presenting a major claim that attempts to dominate, erase, or distort various "other" claims (whose traces nevertheless remain detectable to a reader who goes against the grain of the dominant claim), then "reading" in its extended sense is deeply involved in questions of authority and power. One field of conflict and domination in discourse that has been fruitfully studied in this sense is the field of sexual politics. Alice Jardine, in *Gynesis* (1985), points out that since logocentric logic has been coded as "male," the "other" logics of spacing, ambiguity, figuration, and indirection are often coded as "female," and that a critique of logocentrism can enable a critique of "phallocentrism" as well. A theory and practice of female writing (*écriture féminine*) has been developed in France by such writers as Hélène Cixous and Luce Irigaray, who have attempted to write the specificity of female biological and ideological difference. While Cixous, Irigaray, and others work on the relations between writing and the body, many feminists on both sides of the Atlantic have been interested in the gender implications of the relations between writing and silence. In *The Madwoman in the Attic* (1979), Sandra Gilbert and Susan Gubar show how nineteenth-century women writers struggle for authorship against the silence that has already been prescribed for them by the patriarchal language they must both use and transform. Adrienne Rich also explores the traces of women's silence in a collection of essays entitled *On Lies, Secrets, and Silence* (1979). These and other works have as their project the attempt to read the suppressed, distorted, or disguised messages that women's writing has encoded. They require a reading strategy that goes beyond apparent intentions or surface meanings, a reading that takes full advantage of writing's capacity to preserve that which cannot yet, perhaps, be deciphered.

The writings of Western male authorities have often encoded the silence, denigration, or idealization not only of women but also of other "others." Edward Said, in *Orientalism* (1978), analyzes the discursive fields of scholarship, art, and politics in which the "Oriental" is projected as the "other" of the European. By reading against the grain of the writers' intentions, he shows how European men of reason and benevolence could inscribe a rationale for oppression and exploitation within their very discourse of Enlightenment. . . .

Suggested Readings

Abel, Elizabeth, ed. 1982. *Writing and Sexual Difference.*
Barthes, Roland. [1953] 1967. *Writing Degree Zero.*
Derrida, Jacques. [1967a] 1978. *Of Grammatology.*
——[1967b] 1973. *Speech and Phenomena.*
——[1967c] 1973. *Writing and Difference.*
Gates, Henry Louis, Jr., ed. 1986. *"Race," Writing, and Difference.*
Ong, Walter, 1982. *Orality and Literacy.*

CHAPTER 10

The Newly Born Woman

Hélène Cixous

Hélène Cixous in *The Newly Born Woman* (1975), from which this selection is taken, helped to define "French feminism" for a generation of anglophone feminists. She is famous for advocating "feminine writing," a new paratactic style of expression that would give voice to all that Western rationalism has repressed. Drawing on Derrida's critique of metaphysics, Cixous describes the tradition of gender representation as an oppositional one in which all that connotes women is portrayed as being secondary to male rationalist principles. Interestingly, she argues that feminine writing is a practice that both men and women can engage in, and one of her most famous analyses is of Joyce's *Ulysses*.

Sorties: Out and Out: Attacks/Ways Out/Forays

Where is she?
Activity/passivity
Sun/Moon
Culture/Nature
Day/Night
Father/Mother
Head/Heart
Intelligible/Palpable
Logos/Pathos
Form, convex, step, advance, semen, progress
Matter, concave, ground – where steps are taken, holding- and dumping-ground
Man
Woman

Always the same metaphor: we follow it, it carries us, beneath all its figures, wherever discourse is organized. If we read or speak, the same thread or double braid is leading us throughout literature, philosophy, criticism, centuries of representation and reflection. Thought has always worked through opposition, Speaking/Writing, Parole/Ecriture, High/Low.

Through dual, hierarchical oppositions. Superior/Inferior. Myths, legends, books. Philosophical systems. Everywhere (where) ordering intervenes, where a law organizes what is thinkable by oppositions (dual, irreconcilable; or sublatable, dialectical). And all these pairs of oppositions are *couples*. Does that mean something? Is the fact that Logocentrism subjects thought – all concepts, codes and values – to a binary system, related to "the" couple, man/woman?

> Nature/History
> Nature/Art
> Nature/Mind
> Passion/Action

Theory of culture, theory of society, symbolic systems in general – art, religion, family, language – it is all developed while bringing the same schemes to light. And the movement whereby each opposition is set up to make sense is the movement through which the couple is destroyed. A universal battlefield. Each time, a war is let loose. Death is always at work.

> Father/son
> Relations of authority, privilege, force.
> The Word/Writing Relations: opposition, conflict, sublation, return.
> Master/slave
> Violence
> Repression.

We see that "victory" always comes down to the same thing: things get hierarchical. Organization by hierarchy makes all conceptual organization subject to man. Male privilege, shown in the opposition between *activity* and *passivity*, which he uses to sustain himself. Traditionally, the question of sexual difference is treated by coupling it with the opposition: activity/passivity.

There are repercussions. Consulting the history of philosophy – since philosophical discourse both orders and reproduces all thought – one notices[1] that it is marked by an absolute *constant* which orders values and which is precisely this opposition, activity/passivity.

Moreover, woman is always associated with passivity in philosophy. Whenever it is a question of woman, when one examines kinship structures, when a family model is brought into play. In fact, as soon as the question of ontology raises its head, as soon as one asks oneself "what is it?", as soon as there is intended meaning. Intention: desire, authority – examine them and you are led right back ... to the father. It is even possible not to notice that there is no place whatsoever for woman in the calculations. Ultimately the world of being can function while precluding the mother. No need for a mother, as long as there is some motherliness: and it is the father, then, who acts the part, who is the mother. Either woman is passive or she does not exist. What is left of her is unthinkable, unthought. Which certainly means that she is not thought, that she does not enter into the oppositions, that she does not make a couple with the father (who makes a couple with the son).

There is Mallarmé's tragic dream,[2] that father's lamentation on the mystery of paternity, that wrenches from the poet the mourning, the mourning of mournings, the death of the cherished son: this dream of marriage between father and son. – And there's no mother then. A man's dream when faced with death. Which always threatens him differently than it threatens a woman.

"a union
a marriage, splendid   And dreams of filiation
– and with life   that is masculine, dreams
still in me   of God the father
I shall use it   issuing from himself
for . . .   in his son – and
so not mother then?"   no mother then

She does not exist, she can not be; but there has to be something of her. He keeps, then, of the woman on whom he is no longer dependent, only this space, always virginal, as matter to be subjected to the desire he wishes to impart.

And if we consult literary history, it is the same story. It all comes back to man – to *his* torment, his desire to be (at) the origin. Back to the father. There is an intrinsic connection between the philosophical and the literary (to the extent that it conveys meaning, literature is under the command of the philosophical) and the phallocentric. Philosophy is constructed on the premise of woman's abasement. Subordination of the feminine to the masculine order, which gives the appearance of being the condition for the machinery's functioning.

Now it has become rather urgent to question this solidarity between logocentrism and phallocentrism – bringing to light the fate dealt to woman, her burial – to threaten the stability of the masculine structure that passed itself off as eternal-natural, by conjuring up from femininity the reflections and hypotheses that are necessarily ruinous for the stronghold still in possession of authority. What would happen to logocentrism, to the great philosophical systems, to the order of the world in general if the rock upon which they founded this church should crumble?

If some fine day it suddenly came out that the logocentric plan had always, inadmissibly, been to create a foundation for (to found and fund) phallocentrism, to guarantee the masculine order a rationale equal to history itself.

So all the history, all the stories would be there to retell differently; the future would be incalculable; the historic forces would and will change hands and change body – another thought which is yet unthinkable – will transform the functioning of all society. We are living in an age where the conceptual foundation of an ancient culture is in the process of being undermined by millions of a species of mole (Topoi, ground mines) never known before.

When they wake up from among the dead, from among words, from among laws
Once upon a time . . . [. . .]

It is impossible to predict what will become of sexual difference – in another time (in two or three hundred years?). But we must make no mistake: men and women are caught up in a web of age-old cultural determinations that are almost unanalyzable in their complexity. One can no more speak of "woman" than of "man" without being trapped within an ideological theater where the proliferation of representations, images, reflections, myths, identifications, transform, deform, constantly change everyone's Imaginary and invalidate in advance any conceptualization.[3]

Nothing allows us to rule out the possibility of radical transformation of behaviors, mentalities, roles, political economy – whose effects on libidinal economy are unthinkable – today. Let us simultaneously imagine a general change in all the structures of training, education, supervision – hence in the structures of reproduction of ideological results. And let us imagine a real liberation of sexuality, that is to say, a transformation of each one's relationship to his or her body (and to the other body), an approximation to the vast, material, organic, sensuous universe that we are. This cannot be accomplished, of course, without political transformations that are equally radical. (Imagine!) Then "femininity" and "masculinity" would inscribe quite differently their effects of difference, their economy, their relationship to expenditure, to lack, to the gift. What today appears to be "feminine" or "masculine" would no longer amount to the same thing. No longer would the common logic of difference be organized with the opposition that remains dominant. Difference would be a bunch of new differences.

But we are still floundering – with few exceptions – in Ancient History.

The Masculine Future

There are some exceptions. There have always been those uncertain, poetic persons who have not let themselves be reduced to dummies programmed by pitiless repression of the homosexual element. Men or women: beings who are complex, mobile, open. Accepting the other sex as a component makes them much richer, more various, stronger, and – to the extent that they are mobile – very fragile. It is only in this condition that we invent. Thinkers, artists, those who create new values, "philosophers" in the mad Nietzschean manner, inventors and wreckers of concepts and forms, those who change life cannot help but be stirred by anomalies – complementary or contradictory. That doesn't mean that you have to be homosexual to create. But it does mean that there is no *invention* possible, whether it be philosophical or poetic, without there being in the inventing subject an abundance of the other, of variety: separate-people, thought-/people, whole populations issuing from the unconscious, and in each suddenly animated desert, the springing up of selves one didn't know – our women, our monsters, our jackals, our Arabs, our aliases, our frights. That there is no invention of any other I, no poetry, no fiction without a certain homosexuality (the I/play of bisexuality) acting as a crystallization of my ultrasubjectivities.[4] I is this exuberant, gay, personal matter, masculine, feminine or other where I enchants, I agonizes me. And in the concert of personalizations called I, at the same time that a certain homosexuality is repressed, symbolically, substitutively, it comes through by various signs, conduct-character, behavior-acts. And it is even more clearly seen in writing.

Thus, what is inscribed under Jean Genêt's name, in the movement of a text that divides itself, pulls itself to pieces, dismembers itself, regroups, remembers itself, is a proliferating, maternal femininity. A phantasmic meld of men, males, gentlemen, monarchs, princes, orphans, flowers, mothers, breasts gravitates about a wonderful "sun of energy" – love, – that bombards and disintegrates these ephemeral amorous anomalies so that they can be recomposed in other bodies for new passions.

She is bisexual:

What I propose here leads directly to a reconsideration of *bisexuality*. To reassert the value of bisexuality;[5] hence to snatch it from the fate classically reserved for it in which it is conceptualized as "neuter" because, as such, it would aim at warding off castration. Therefore, I shall distinguish between two bisexualities, two opposite ways of imagining the possibility and practice of bisexuality.

1 Bisexuality as a fantasy of a complete being, which replaces the fear of castration and veils sexual difference insofar as this is perceived as the mark of a mythical

separation – the trace, therefore, of a dangerous and painful ability to be cut. Ovid's Hermaphrodite, less bisexual than asexual, not made up of two genders but of two halves. Hence, a fantasy of unity. Two within one, and not even two wholes.

2 To this bisexuality that melts together and effaces, wishing to avert castration I oppose the *other bisexuality*, the one with which every subject, who is not shut up inside the spurious Phallocentric Performing Theater, sets up his or her erotic universe. Bisexuality – that is to say the location within oneself of the presence of both sexes, evident and insistent in different ways according to the individual, the nonexclusion of difference or of a sex, and starting with this "permission" one gives oneself, the multiplication of the effects of desire's inscription on every part of the body and the other body.

For historical reasons, at the present time it is woman who benefits from and opens up within this bisexuality beside itself, which does not annihilate differences but cheers them on, pursues them, adds more: in a certain way *woman is bisexual* – man having been trained to aim for glorious phallic monosexuality. By insisting on the primacy of the phallus and implementing it, phallocratic ideology has produced more than one victim. As a woman, I could be obsessed by the scepter's great shadow, and they told me: adore it, that thing you don't wield.

But at the same time, man has been given the grotesque and unenviable fate of being reduced to a single idol with clay balls. And terrified of homosexuality, as Freud and his followers remark. Why does man fear *being* a woman? Why this refusal (*Ablehnung*) of femininity? The question that stumps Freud. The "bare rock" of castration. For Freud, the repressed is not the other sex defeated by the dominant sex, as his friend Fliess (to whom Freud owes the theory of bisexuality) believed; what is repressed is leaning toward one's own sex.[5]

Psychoanalysis is formed on the basis of woman and has repressed (not all that successfully) the femininity of masculine sexuality, and now the account it gives is hard to disprove.

We women, the derangers, know it only too well. But nothing compels us to deposit our lives in these lack-banks; to think that the subject is constituted as the last stage in a drama of bruising rehearsals; to endlessly bail out the father's religion. Because we don't desire it. We don't go round and round the supreme hole. We have no *woman's* reason to pay allegiance to the negative. What is feminine (the poets suspected it) affirms: . . . and yes I said yes I will Yes, says Molly (in her rapture); carrying *Ulysses* with her in the direction of a new writing; I said yes, I will. Yes.

To say that woman is somehow bisexual is an apparently paradoxical way of displacing and reviving the question of difference. And therefore of writing as "feminine" or "masculine."

I will say: today writing is woman's. That is not a provocation, it means that woman admits there is an other. In her becoming-woman she has not erased the bisexuality latent in the girl as in the boy. Femininity and bisexuality go together in a combination that varies according to the individual, spreading the intensity of its force differently and (depending on the moments of their history) privileging one component or another. It is much harder for man to let the other come through him. Writing is the passageway, the entrance, the exit, the dwelling place of the other in me – the other that I am and am not, that I don't know how to be, but that I feel passing, that makes me live – that tears me apart, disturbs me, changes me, who? – a feminine one, a masculine one, some? – several, some unknown, which is indeed what gives me the desire to know and from which all life soars. This peopling gives neither rest nor security, always disturbs the relationship to "reality," produces an uncertainty that gets in the way of the subject's socialization. It is distressing, it wears you out; and for men this permeability, this nonexclusion is a threat, something intolerable.

In the past, when carried to a rather spectacular degree, it was called "possession." Being possessed is not desirable for a masculine Imaginary, which would interpret it as passivity – a dangerous feminine position. It is true that a certain receptivity is "feminine." One can, of course, as History has always done, exploit feminine reception through alienation. A woman, by her opening up, is open to being "possessed," which is to say, dispossessed of herself.

But I am speaking here of femininity as keeping alive the other that is confided to her, that visits her, that she can love as other. The loving to be other, another, without its necessarily going the route of abasing what is same, herself.

As for passivity, in excess, it is partly bound up with death. But there is a nonclosure that is not submission but confidence and comprehension; that is not an opportunity for destruction but for wonderful expansion.

Through the same opening that is her danger, she comes out of herself to go to the other, a traveler in unexplored places; she does not refuse, she approaches, not to do away with the space between, but to see it, to experience what she is not, what she is, what she can be.

Writing is working; being worked; questioning (in) the between (letting oneself be questioned) of same *and of* other without which nothing lives; undoing death's work by willing the togetherness of one-another, infinitely charged with a ceaseless exchange of one with another – not knowing one another and beginning again only from what is most distant, from self, from other, from the other within. A course that multiplies transformations by the thousands...

If there is a self proper to woman, paradoxically it is her capacity to depropriate herself without self-interest: endless body, without "end," without principal "parts"; if she is a whole, it is a whole made up of parts that are wholes, not simple, partial objects but varied entirety, moving and boundless change, a cosmos where eros never stops traveling, vast astral space. She doesn't revolve around a sun that is more star than the stars.

That doesn't mean that she is undifferentiated magma; it means that she doesn't create a monarchy of her body or her desire. Let masculine sexuality gravitate around the penis, engendering this centralized body (political anatomy) under the party dictatorship. Woman does not perform on herself this regionalization that profits the couple head-sex, that only inscribes itself within frontiers. Her libido is cosmic, just as her unconscious is worldwide: her writing also can only go on and on, without ever inscribing or distinguishing contours, daring these dizzying passages in other, fleeting and passionate dwellings within him, within the hims and hers whom she inhabits just long enough to watch them, as close as possible to the unconscious from the moment they arise; to love them, as close as possible to instinctual drives, and then, further, all filled with these brief identifying hugs and kisses, she goes and goes on infinitely. She alone dares and wants to know from within where she, the one excluded, has never ceased to hear what-comes-before-language reverberating. She lets the other tongue of a thousand tongues speak – the tongue, sound without barrier or death. She refuses life nothing. Her tongue doesn't hold back but holds forth, doesn't keep in but keeps on enabling. Where the wonder of being several and turmoil is expressed, she does not protect herself against these unknown feminines; she surprises herself at seeing, being, pleasuring in her gift of changeability. I am spacious singing Flesh: onto which is grafted no one knows which I – which masculine or feminine, more or less human but above all living, because changing I.

Notes

1   All Derrida's work traversing-detecting the history of philosophy is devoted to bringing this to light. In Plato, Hegel, and Nietzsche, the same process continues: repression, repudiation, distancing of woman, a murder that is mixed up with history as the manifestation and representation of masculine power.

2   "For Anatole's Tomb" (Seuil, p. 138). This is the tomb in which Mallarmé keeps his son from death and watches over him as his mother.

3   There are encoded paradigms projecting the robot couple man/woman, as seen by contemporary societies that are symptomatic of a consensus of repetition. See the UNESCO issue of 1974, which is devoted to the International Woman's Year.

4   *Prénoms de Personne* [*Nobody's First Names*]. Cixous, Editions du Seuil: "Les Contes de Hoffman" ["Tales of Hoffman"], pp. 112ff.

5   See *Nouvelle Revue de Psychoanalyse* no. 7, *Bisexualité et différence des sexes* (Spring 1973).

CHAPTER 11

The Postmodern Condition

Jean-François Lyotard

Jean-François Lyotard's *The Post-Modern Condition* (1979) announced a new moment in cultural history called "Post-Modernism." Post-Modernism is skeptical regarding reason, sees technology as an instrument as much of destruction as of progress, and rejects the premises of industrial society. Lyotard also characterizes Post-Modernism as a skepticism toward what he calls "metanarratives." By that, he means stories about the world that strive to sum it all up in one account. The Post-Modern temperament finds such conclusive stories unsuited to the world. Instead, according to Lyotard, Post-Modernism favors seeing the world in more rhetorical terms as a field of contending smaller narratives, where people strive to make their point of view and their interests paramount by making their narratives more convincing.

Post-Modernism is faulted for not taking a stand on issues of value. All values are topics of debate, and the debate should, according to Lyotard, continue endlessly. The only wrong consists of closing off debate. Values, its detractors contend, must be decided. And while all issues or problems facing society can be endlessly debated, at some point decisions need to be made regarding what values shall prevail. According to Lyotard, many such decisions are indeed made, but they usually consist of an assertion of non-rhetorical power by those in a dominant position materially in society. And such decisions always close off debate and preclude further story-telling, further rhetorical contest.

The object of this study is the condition of knowledge in the most highly developed societies. I have decided to use the word *postmodern* to describe that condition. The word is in current use on the American continent among sociologists and critics; it designates the state of our culture following the transformations which, since the end of the nineteenth century, have altered the game rules for science, literature, and the arts. The present study will place these transformations in the context of the crisis of narratives.

Science has always been in conflict with narratives. Judged by the yardstick of science, the majority of them prove to be fables. But to the extent that science does not restrict itself to stating useful regularities and seeks the truth, it is obliged to legitimate the rules of its own game. It then produces a discourse of legitimation with respect to its own status, a discourse called philosophy. I will use the term modern to designate any science that legitimates itself with reference to a metadiscourse of this kind making an explicit appeal to some grand narrative, such as the dialectics of Spirit, the hermeneutics of meaning, the emancipation of the rational or working subject, or the creation of wealth.[1] For example, the rule of consensus between the sender and addressee of a statement with truth-value is deemed acceptable if it is cast in terms of a possible unanimity between rational minds: this is the Enlightenment narrative, in which the hero of knowledge works toward a good ethico-political end – universal peace. As can be seen from this example, if a metanarrative implying a philosophy of history is used to legitimate knowledge, questions are raised concerning the validity of the institutions governing the social bond: these must be legitimated as well. Thus justice is consigned to the grand narrative in the same way as truth.

Simplifying to the extreme, I define *postmodern* as incredulity toward metanarratives. This incredulity is undoubtedly a product of progress in the sciences: but that progress in turn presupposes it. To the obsolescence of the metanarrative apparatus of legitimation corresponds, most notably, the crisis of metaphysical philosophy and of the university institution which in the past relied on it. The narrative function is losing its functors, its great hero, its great dangers, its great voyages, its great goal. It is being dispersed in clouds of narrative language elements – narrative, but also denotative, prescriptive, descriptive, and so on. Conveyed within each cloud are pragmatic valencies specific to its kind. Each of us lives at the intersection of many of these. However, we do not necessarily establish stable language combinations, and the properties of the ones we do establish are not necessarily communicable.

Thus the society of the future falls less within the province of a Newtonian anthropology (such as stucturalism or systems theory) than a pragmatics of language particles. There are many different language games – a heterogeneity of elements. They only give rise to institutions in patches – local determinism.

The decision makers, however, attempt to manage these clouds of sociality according to input/output matrices, following a logic which implies that their elements are commensurable and that the whole is determinable. They allocate our lives for the growth of power. In matters of social justice and of scientific truth alike, the legitimation of that power is based on its optimizing the system's performance – efficiency. The application of this criterion to all of our games necessarily entails a certain level of terror, whether soft or hard: be operational (that is, commensurable) or disappear.

The logic of maximum performance is no doubt inconsistent in many ways, particularly with respect to contradiction in the socio-economic field: it demands both less work (to lower production costs) and more (to lessen the social burden of the idle population). But our incredulity is now such that we no longer expect salvation to rise from these inconsistencies, as did Marx.

Still, the postmodern condition is as much a stranger to disenchantment as it is to the blind positivity of delegitimation. Where, after the metanarratives, can legitimacy reside? The operativity criterion is technological; it has no relevance for judging what is true or just. Is legitimacy to be found in consensus obtained through discussion, as Jürgen Habermas thinks? Such consensus does violence to the heterogeneity of language games. And invention is always born of dissension. Postmodern knowledge is not simply a tool of the authorities; it refines our sensitivity to differences and reinforces our ability to tolerate the incommensurable. Its principle is not the expert's homology, but the inventor's paralogy.

Here is the question: is a legitimation of the social bond, a just society, feasible in terms of a paradox analogous to that of scientific activity? What would such a paradox be? . . .

Narratives of the Legitimation of Knowledge

We shall examine two major versions of the narrative of legitimation. One is more political, the other more philosophical; both are of great importance in modern history, in particular in the history of knowledge and its institutions.

The subject of the first of these versions is humanity as the hero of liberty. All peoples have a right to science. If the social subject is not already the subject of scientific knowledge, it is because that has been forbidden by priests and tyrants. The right to science must be reconquered. It is understandable that this narrative would be directed more toward a politics of primary education, rather than of universities and high schools.[2] The educational policy of the French Third Republic (1871–1940) powerfully illustrates these presuppositions.

It seems that this narrative finds it necessary to de-emphasize higher education. Accordingly, the measures adopted by Napoleon regarding higher education are generally considered to have been motivated by the desire to produce the administrative and professional skills necessary for the stability of the State.[3] This overlooks the fact that in the context of the narrative of freedom, the State receives its legitimacy not from itself but from the people. So even if imperial politics designated the institutions of higher education as a breeding ground for the officers of the State and secondarily, for the managers of civil society, it did so because the nation as a whole was supposed to win its freedom through the spread of new domains of knowledge to the population, a process to be effected through agencies and professions within which those cadres would fulfill their functions. The same reasoning is a fortiori valid for the foundation of properly scientific institutions. The State resorts to the narrative of freedom every time it assumes direct control over the training of the "people," under the name of the "nation," in order to point them down the path of progress.[4] . . .

But, as I have said, the problem of legitimacy can be solved using the other procedures as well. The difference between them should be kept in mind: today, with the status of knowledge unbalanced and its speculative unity broken, the first version of legitimacy is gaining new vigor.

According to this version, knowledge finds its validity not within itself, not in a subject that develops by actualizing its learning possibilities, but in a practical subject – humanity. The principle of the movement animating the people is not the self-legitimation of knowledge, but the self-grounding of freedom or, if preferred, its self-management. The subject is concrete, or supposedly so, and its epic is the story of its emancipation from everything that prevents it from governing itself. It is assumed that the laws it makes for itself are just, not because they conform to some outside nature, but because the legislators are, constitutionally, the very citizens who are subject to the laws. As a result, the legislator's will – the desire that the laws be just – will always coincide with the will of the citizen, who desires the law and will therefore obey it.

Clearly, this mode of legitimation through the autonomy of the will[5] gives priority to a totally different language game, which Kant called imperative and is known today as prescriptive. The important thing is not, or not only, to legitimate denotative utterances pertaining to the truth, such as "The earth revolves around the sun," but rather to legitimate prescriptive utterances pertaining to justice, such as "Carthage must be destroyed" or "The minimum wage must be set at x dollars." In this context, the only role positive knowledge can play is to inform the practical subject about the reality within which the execution of the prescription is to be inscribed. It allows the subject to circumscribe the executable, or what it is possible to do. But the executory, what should be done, is not within the purview of positive knowledge. It is one thing for an undertaking to be possible and another for it to be just. Knowledge is no longer the subject, but in the service of the subject: its only legitimacy (though it is formidable) is the fact that it allows morality to become reality.

This introduces a relation of knowledge to society and the State which is in principle a relation of the means to the end. But scientists must cooperate only if they judge that the politics of the State, in other words the sum of its prescriptions, is just. If they feel that the civil society of which they are members is badly represented by the State, they may reject its prescriptions. This type of legitimation grants them the authority, as practical human beings, to refuse their scholarly support to a political power they judge to be unjust, in other words, not grounded in a real autonomy. They can even go so far as to use their expertise to demonstrate that such autonomy is not in fact realized in society and the State. This reintroduces the critical function of knowledge. But the fact remains that knowledge has no final legitimacy outside of serving the goals envisioned by the practical subject, the autonomous collectivity.[6]

This distribution of roles in the enterprise of legitimation is interesting from our point of view because it assumes, as against the system-subject theory, that there is no possibility that language games can be unified or totalized in any metadiscourse. Quite to the contrary, here the priority accorded prescriptive statements – uttered by the practical subject – renders them independent in principle from the statements of science, whose only remaining function is to supply this subject with information.

Two remarks:

1 It would be easy to show that Marxism has wavered between the two models of narrative legitimation I have just described. The Party takes the place of the University, the proletariat that of the people or of humanity, dialectical materialism that of speculative idealism, etc. Stalinism may be the result, with its specific relationship with the sciences: in Stalinism, the sciences only figure as citations from the metanarrative of the march towards socialism, which is the equivalent, of the life of the spirit. But on the other hand Marxism can, in conformity to the second version, develop into a form of critical knowledge by declaring that socialism is nothing other than the constitution of the autonomous subject and that the only justification for the sciences is if they give the empirical subject (the proletariat) the means to emancipate itself from alienation and repression: this was, briefly, the position of the Frankfurt School.

2 The speech Heidegger gave on May 27, 1933, on becoming rector of the university of Freiburg-in-Breisgau,[7] can be read as an unfortunate episode in the history of legitimation. (Heidegger became rector after joining the Nazi Party, as was required by law. He openly supported National Socialism.) Here, speculative science has become the questioning of being. This questioning is the "destiny" of the German people, dubbed an "historico-spiritual people." To this subject are owed the three services of labor, defense, and knowledge. The University guarantees a metaknowledge of the three services, that is to say, science. Here, as in idealism, legitimation is achieved through a metadiscourse called science, with ontological pretensions. But here the metadiscourse is questioning, not totalizing. And the University, the home of this metadiscourse, owes its knowledge to a people whose "historic mission" is to

bring that metadiscourse to fruition by working, fighting, and knowing. The calling of this people-subject is not to emancipate humanity, but to realize its "true world of the spirit," which is "the most profound power of conservation to be found within its forces of earth and blood." This insertion of the narrative of race and work into that of the spirit as a way of legitimating knowledge and its institutions is doubly unfortunate: theoretically inconsistent, it was compelling enough to find disastrous echoes in the realm of politics.

Delegitimation

In contemporary society and culture – postindustrial society, postmodern culture[8] – the question of the legitimation of knowledge is formulated in different terms. The grand narrative has lost its credibility, regardless of what mode of unification it uses, regardless of whether it is a speculative narrative or a narrative of emancipation.

The decline of narrative can be seen as an effect of the blossoming of techniques and technologies since the Second World War, which has shifted emphasis from the ends of action to its means; it can also be seen as an effect of the redeployment of advanced liberal capitalism after its retreat under the protection of Keynesianism during the period 1930–60, a renewal that has eliminated the communist alternative and valorized the individual enjoyment of goods and services.

Anytime we go searching for causes in this way we are bound to be disappointed. Even if we adopted one or the other of these hypotheses, we would still have to detail the correlation between the tendencies mentioned and the decline of the unifying and legitimating power of the grand narratives of speculation and emancipation.

It is, of course, understandable that both capitalist renewal and prosperity and the disorienting upsurge of technology would have an impact on the status of knowledge. But in order to understand how contemporary science could have been susceptible to those effects long before they took place, we must first locate the seeds of "delegitimation"[9] and nihilism that were inherent in the grand narratives of the nineteenth century....

The potential for erosion intrinsic to the other legitimation procedure, the emancipation apparatus flowing from the *Aufklärung* (Enlightenment), is no less extensive than the one at work within speculative discourse. But it touches a different aspect. Its distinguishing characteristic is that it grounds the legitimation of science and truth in the autonomy of interlocutors involved in ethical, social, and political praxis. As we have seen, there are immediate problems with this form of legitimation: the difference between a denotative statement with cognitive value and a prescriptive statement with practical value is one of relevance therefore of competence. There is nothing to prove that if a statement describing a real situation is true, it follows that a prescriptive statement based upon it (the effect of which will necessarily be a modification of that reality) will be just.

Take, for example, a closed door. Between "The door is closed" and "Open the door" there is no relation of consequence as defined in propositional logic. The two statements belong to two autonomous sets of rules defining different kinds of relevance, and therefore of competence. Here, the effect of dividing reason into cognitive or theoretical reason on the one hand, and practical reason on the other, is to attack the legitimacy of the discourse of science. Not directly, but indirectly, by revealing that it is a language game with its own rules (of which the a priori conditions of knowledge in Kant provide a first glimpse) and that it has no special calling to supervise the game of praxis (nor the game of aesthetics, for that matter). The game of science is thus put on a par with the others.

If this "delegitimation" is pursued in the slightest and if its scope is widened (as Wittgenstein does in his own way, and thinkers such as Martin Buber and Emmanuel Levinas in theirs)[10] the road is then open for an important current of postmodernity: science plays its own game; it is incapable of legitimating the other language games. The game of prescription, for example, escapes it. But above all, it is incapable of legitimating itself, as speculation assumed it could.

The social subject itself seems to dissolve in this dissemination of language games. The social bond is linguistic, but is not woven with a single thread. It is a fabric formed by the intersection of at least two (and in reality an indeterminate number) of language games, obeying different rules. Wittgenstein writes: "Our language can be seen as an ancient city: a maze of little streets and squares, of old and new houses, and of houses with additions from various periods; and this surrounded by a multitude of new boroughs with straight regular streets and uniform houses."[11] And to drive home that the principle of unitotality – or synthesis under the authority of a metadiscourse of knowledge – is inapplicable, he subjects the "town" of language to the old sorites paradox by asking: "how many houses or streets does it take before a town begins to be a town?"[12]

New languages are added to the old ones, forming suburbs of the old town: "the symbolism of chemistry and the notation of the infinitesimal calculus."[13] Thirty-five years later we can add to the list: machine languages, the matrices of game theory, new systems of musical notation, systems of notation for nondenotative forms of logic (temporal logics, denotic logics, modal logics), the language of the genetic code, graphs of phonological structures, and so on.

We may form a pessimistic impression of this splintering: nobody speaks all of those languages, they have no universal metalanguage, the project of the system-subject is a failure, the goal of emancipation has nothing to do with science, we are all stuck in the positivism of this or that discipline of learning, the learned scholars have turned into scientists, the diminished tasks of research have become compart-mentalized and no one can master them all.[14] Speculative or humanistic philosophy is forced to relinquish its legitimation duties,[15] which explains why philosophy is facing a crisis wherever it persists in arrogating such functions and is reduced to the study of systems of logic or the history of ideas where it has been realistic enough to surrender them.[16]

Turn-of-the-century Vienna was weaned on this pessimism: not just artists such as Musil, Kraus, Hofmannsthal, Loos, Schönberg, and Broch, but also the philosophers Mach and Wittgenstein.[17] They carried awareness of and theoretical and artistic responsibility for delegitimation as far as it could be taken. We can say today that the mourning process has been completed. There is no need to start all over again. Wittgenstein's strength is that he did not opt for the positivism that was being developed by the Vienna Circle,[18] but outlined in his investigation of language games a kind of legitimation not based on performativity. That is what the postmodern world is all about. Most people have lost the nostalgia for the lost narrative. It in no way follows that they are reduced to barbarity. What saves them from it is their knowledge that legitimation can only spring from their own linguistic practice and communicational interaction. Science "smiling into its beard" at every other belief has taught them the harsh austerity of realism.[19] . . .

Capitalism solves the scientific problem of research funding in its own way: directly by financing research departments in private companies, in which demands for performativity and recommercialization orient research first and foremost toward technological "applications"; and indirectly by creating private, state, or mixed-sector research foundations that grant program subsidies to university departments, research laboratories, and independent research groups with no expectation of an immediate return on the results of the work – this is done on the theory that research must be financed at a loss for a certain length of time in order to increase the probability of its yielding a decisive, and therefore highly profitable, innovation.[20] Nation-states, especially in their Keynesian period,[21] follow the same rule: applied research on the one hand, basic research on the other. They collaborate with corporations through an array of agencies.[22] The prevailing corporate norms of work management spread to the applied science laboratories: hierarchy, centralized decision making, teamwork, calculation of individual and collective returns, the development of saleable programs, market research, and so on.[23] Centers dedicated to "pure" research suffer from this less, but also receive less funding.

The production of proof, which is in principle only part of an argumentation process designed to win agreement from the addressees of scientific messages, thus falls under the control of another language game, in which the goal is no longer truth, but performativity – that is, the best possible input/output equation. The State and/or company must abandon the idealist and humanist narratives of legitimation in order to justify the new goal: in the discourse of today's financial backers of research, the only credible goal is power. Scientists, technicians, and instruments are purchased not to find truth, but to augment power.

The question is to determine what the discourse of power consists of and if it can constitute a legitimation. At first glance, it is prevented from doing so by the traditional distinction between force and right, between force and wisdom – in other words, between what is strong, what is just, and what is true. I referred to this incommensurability earlier in terms of the theory of language games, when I distinguished the denotative game (in which what is relevant is the true/false distinction) from the prescriptive game (in which the just/unjust distinction pertains) from the technical game (in which the criterion is the efficient/inefficient distinction). "Force" appears to belong exclusively to the last game, the game of technology. I am excluding the case in which force operates by means of terror. This lies outside the realm of language games, because the efficacy of such force is based entirely on the threat to eliminate the opposing player, not on making a better "move" than he. Whenever efficiency (that is, obtaining the desired effect) is derived from a "Say or do this, or else you'll never speak again," then we are in the realm of terror, and the social bond is destroyed.

But the fact remains that since performativity increases the ability to produce proof, it also increases the ability to be right: the technical criterion, introduced on a massive scale into scientific knowledge, cannot fail to influence the truth criterion. The same has been said of the relationship between justice and performance: the probability that an order would be pronounced just was said to increase with its chances of being implemented, which would in turn increase with the performance capability of the prescriber. This led Luhmann to hypothesize that in postindustrial societies the normativity of laws is replaced by the performativity of procedures.[24]

"Context control," in other words, performance improvement won at the expense of the partner or partners constituting that context (be they "nature" or men), can pass for a kind of legitimation.[25] De facto legitimation.

This procedure operates within the following framework: since "reality" is what provides the evidence used as proof in scientific argumentation, and also provides prescriptions and promises of a juridical, ethical, and political nature with results, one can master all of these games by mastering "reality." That is precisely what technology can do. By reinforcing technology, one "reinforces" reality, and one's chances of being just and right increase accordingly. Reciprocally, technology is reinforced all the more effectively if one has access to scientific knowledge and decision-making authority.

This is how legitimation by power takes shape. Power is not only good performativity, but also effective verification and good verdicts. It legitimates science and the law on the basis of their efficiency, and legitimates this efficiency on the basis of science and law. It is self-legitimating, in the same way a system organized around performance maximization seems to be.[26] Now it is precisely this kind of context control that a generalized computerization of society may bring. The performativity of an utterance, be it denotative or prescriptive, increases proportionally to the amount of information about its referent one has at one's disposal. Thus the growth of power, and its self-legitimation, are now taking the route of data storage and accessibility, and the operativity of information.

The relationship between science and technology is reversed. The complexity of the argumentation becomes relevant here, especially because it necessitates greater sophistication in the means of obtaining proof, and that in turn benefits performativity. Research funds are allocated by States, corporations, and nationalized companies in accordance with this logic of power growth. Research sectors that are unable to argue that they contribute even indirectly to the optimization of the system's performance are abandoned by the flow of capital and doomed to senescence. The criterion of performance is explicitly invoked by the authorities to justify their refusal to subsidize certain research centers.[27]

Notes

1 These grand narratives are what Lyotard calls "metanarratives," philosophical stories which legitimate all other discourse.
2 A trace of this politics is to be found in the French institution of a philosophy class at the end of secondary studies, and in the proposal by the Groupe de recherches sur l'enseignement de la philosophie (GREPH) to teach "some" philosophy starting at the beginning of secondary studies: see their *Qui a peur de la philosophie?* (Paris: Flammarion, 1977), sec. 2, "La Philosophie déclassée." This also seems to be the orientation of the curriculum of the CEGEP's in Quebec, especially of the philosophy courses (see for example the *Cahiers de l'enseignement collégial* (1975–76) for philosophy).
3 See H. Janne, "L'Université et les besoins de la société contemporaine," *Cahiers de l'Association internationale des Universités*, 10 (1970): 5; quoted by the Commission d'étude sur les universités, *Document de consultation* (Montréal, 1978).
4 A "hard," almost mystico-military expression of this can be found in Julio de Mesquita Filho, *Discorso de Paraninfo da primeiro turma de licenciados pela Faculdade de Filosofia, Ciêncas e Letras da Universidade de São Paulo* (25 January 1937), and an expression of it adapted to the modern

problems of Brazilian development in the *Relatorio do Grupo de Rabalho, Reforma Universitaria* (Brasilia: Ministries of Education and Culture, etc., 1968). These documents are part of a dossier on the university in Brazil, kindly sent to me by Helena C. Chamlian and Martha Ramos de Carvalho of the University of São Paulo.

5   Its principle is Kantian, at least in matters of transcendental ethics – see the *Critique of Practical Reason*. When it comes to politics and empirical ethics, Kant is prudent: since no one can identify himself with the transcendental normative subject, it is theoretically more exact to compromise with the existing authorities. See for example, "Antwort an der Frage: 'Was ist "Aufklärung"?'" (1784) [English trans. Lewis White Beck, in *Critique of Practical Reason and Other Writings in Moral Philosophy* (Chicago: Chicago University Press, 1949)].

6   See Kant, "Antwort"; Jürgen Habermas, *Strukturwandel der Öffentlichkeit* (Frankfurt: Luchterhand, 1962) [*The Structural Transformation of the Public Sphere: An Inquiry into a Category of Bourgeois Society*, trans. Thomas Burger and Frederick Lawrence (Cambridge, Mass.: MIT, 1989)]. The principle of Öffentlichkeit ("public" or "publicity" in the sense of "making public a private correspondence" or "public debate") guided the action of many groups of scientists at the end of the 1960s, especially the group "Survivre" (France), the group "Scientists and Engineers for Social and Political Action" (USA), and the group "British Society for Social Responsibility in Science."

7   A French translation of this text by G. Granel can be found in *Phi*, supplement to the *Annales de l'université de Toulouse – Le Mirail* (Toulouse: January 1977).

8   Certain scientific aspects of postmodernism are inventoried by Ihab Hassan in "Culture, Indeterminacy, and Immanence: Margins of the (Postmodern) Age," *Humanities in Society*, 1 (1978): 51–85.

9   Claus Mueller uses the expression "a process of delegitimation" in *The Politics of Communication* (New York: Oxford University Press, 1973), p. 164.

10 Martin Buber, *Ich und Du* (Berlin: Schocken Verlag, 1922) [Eng. trans. Ronald G. Smith, *I and Thou* (New York: Charles Scribner's Sons, 1937)]. and *Dialogisches Leben* (Zürich: Müller, 1947); Emmanuel Levinas, *Totalité et Infinité* (La Haye: Nijhoff, 1961) [Eng. trans. Alphonso Lingis, *Totality and Infinity: An Essay on Exteriority* (Pittsburgh: Duquesne University Press, 1969)], and "Martin Buber und die Erkenntnistheorie" (1958), in *Philosophen des 20 Jahrhunderts* (Stuttgart: Kohlhammer, 1963).

11 *Philosophical Investigations*, sec. 18, p. 8 [by Ludwig Wittgenstein, trans. G. E. M. Anscombe (New York: Macmillan, 1958)].

12 Ibid.

13 Ibid.

14 See for example, "La taylorisation de la recherche," in *(Auto) critique de la science*, pp. 291–3, And especially D. J. de Solla Price, *Little Science, Big Science* (New York: Columbia University Press, 1963), who emphasizes the split between a small number of highly productive researches (evaluated in terms of publication) and a large mass of researchers with low productivity. The number of the latter grows as the square of the former, so that the number of high productivity researchers only really increases every twenty years. Price concludes that science considered as a social entity is "undemocratic" (p. 59) and that "the eminent scientist" is a hundred years ahead of "the minimal one" (p. 56).

15 See J. T. Desanti, "Sur le rapport traditionnel des sciences et de la philosophie" in *La Philosophie silencieuse, ou critique des philosophies de la science* (Paris: Seuil, 1975).

16 The reclassification of academic philosophy as one of the human sciences in this respect has a significance far beyond simply professional concerns. I do not think that philosophy as legitimation is condemned to disappear, but it is possible that it will not be able to carry out this work, or at least advance it, without revising its ties to the university institution. See on this matter the preamble to the *Projet d'un institut polytechnique de philosophie* (typescript Département de philosophie, Université de Paris VIII, 1979).

17 See Allan Janik and Stephan Toulmin, *Wittgenstein's Vienna* (New York: Simon & Schuster, 1973), and J. Piel (ed.), "Vienne début d'un siècle," *Critique*, 339–40 (1975).

18 See Jürgen Habermas, "Dogmatismus, Vernunft unt Entscheidung – Zu Theorie und Praxis in der verwissenschaftlichen Zivilisation" (1963), in *Theorie und Praxis [Theory and Practice*, abr. edn of 4th German edn, trans. John Viert (Boston: Beacon Press, 1971)].

19 "Science Smiling into its Beard" is the title of chap. 72, vol. 1 of Musil's *The Man Without Qualities*. Cited and discussed by J. Bouveresse, "La Problématique du sujet".

20 This was one of Lazarsfeld's conditions for agreeing to found what was to become the Mass Communication Research Center at Princeton in 1937. This produced some tension: the radio industries refused to invest in the project; people said that Lazarsfeld started things going but finished nothing. Lazarsfeld himself said to Morrison, "I usually put things together and hoped they worked." Quoted by D. Morrison, "The Beginning of Modern Mass Communication Research," *Archives européennes de sociologie*, 19, no. 2 (1978): 347–59.

21 John Maynard Keynes (1883–1946), English economist, proposed increased government spending to stimulate economic activity.

22 In the United States, the funds allocated to research and development by the federal government were, in 1956, equal to the funds coming from private capital; they have been higher since that time (OCDE, 1956).

23 Robert Nisbet, *Degradation*, ch. 5, provides a bitter description of the penetration of "higher capitalism" into the university in the form of research centers independent of departments. The social relations in such centers disturb the academic tradition. See too in *(Auto)critique de la science*, the chapters "Le prolétariat scientifique," "Les chercheurs," "La Crise des mandarins."

24 Niklas Luhmann (a contemporary German sociologist), *Legitimation durch Verfahren* (Neuweid: Luchterhand, 1969).

25 Commenting on Luhmann, Mueller writes, "In advanced industrial society legal-rational legitimation is replaced by a technocratic legitimation that does not accord any significance to the beliefs of the citizen or to morality per se" (*Politics of Communication*, p. 135). There is a bibliography of German material on the technocratic question in Habermas, *Theory and Practice*.

26 Gilles Fauconnier gives a linguistic analysis of the control of truth in "Comment contrôler la vérité? Remarques illustrées par des assertions dangereuses et pernicieuses en tout genre," *Actes de la recherche en sciences sociales*, 25 (1979): 1–22.

27 Thus in 1970 the British University Grants Committee was "persuaded to take a much more positive role in productivity, specialization, concentration of subjects, and control of building through cost limits" [*The Politics of Education: Edward Boyle and Anthony Crosland in Conversation with Maurice Kogan* (Harmondsworth, Eng.: Penguin, 1971), p. 196]. This may appear to contradict declarations such as that of Brooks, quoted above (note 52). But (1) the "strategy" may be liberal and the "tactics" authoritarian, as Edwards says elsewhere; (2) responsibility within the hierarchy of public authorities is often taken in its narrowest sense, namely the capacity to answer for the calculable performance of a project; (3) public authorities are not always free from pressures from private groups whose performance criterion is immediately binding. If the chances of innovation in research cannot be calculated, then public interest seems to lie in aiding all research, under conditions other than that of efficiency assessment after a fixed period.

CHAPTER 12

Simulacra and Simulations

Jean Baudrillard

Sociologist Jean Baudrillard began his work on culture by studying the semiotics of advertising and consumption. He noted that reality was being increasingly replaced by sign systems that recodified and replaced the real. Instead of real cars or refrigerators, we come instead, under a regime of controlled consumption shaped by marketing and advertising, to consume signs of status or of self-identity. In his 1976 book, *Symbolic Exchange and Death*, for example, he argues that cultural history since the Renaissance can be reconceived as a successive series of simulacral regimes, ways of replacing the world with increasingly powerful regimes of signification. In a deconstructive mode, Baudrillard argues that eventually in contemporary times, the referent disappears altogether and people come to live in pure simulations, replications of reality that resemble it in all respects save they are representations through and through. In Baudrillard's perhaps most famous assertion regarding such simulations, he maintained that events like the Gulf War of 1990 "did not happen." In those events, reality was so shaped by the media and so replaced by representations that the events might as well have not happened. All that people "knew" or "experienced" of them came to them through carefully controlled images. The following selection, "Simulacra and Simulations," was published in 1981.

> The simulacrum is never that which conceals the truth – it is the truth which conceals that there is none.
> The simulacrum is true.
>
> Ecclesiastes

If we were able to take as the finest allegory of simulation the Borges tale where the cartographers of the Empire draw up a map so detailed that it ends up exactly covering the territory (but where, with the decline of the Empire this map becomes frayed and finally ruined, a few shreds still discernible in the deserts – the metaphysical beauty of this ruined abstraction, bearing witness to an imperial pride and rotting like a carcass, returning to the substance of the soil, rather as an aging double ends up being confused with the real thing), this fable would then have come full circle for us, and now has nothing but the discrete charm of second-order simulacra.[1]

Abstraction today is no longer that of the map, the double, the mirror or the concept. Simulation is no longer that of a territory, a referential being or a substance. It is the generation by models of a real without origin or reality: a hyperreal. The territory no longer precedes the map, nor survives it. Henceforth, it is the map that precedes the territory – *precession of simulacra* – it is the map that engenders the territory and if we were to revive the fable today, it would be the territory whose shreds are slowly rotting across the map. It is the real, and not the map, whose vestiges subsist here and there, in the deserts which are no longer those of the Empire, but our own. *The desert of the real itself.*

In fact, even inverted, the fable is useless. Perhaps only the allegory of the Empire remains. For it is with the same imperialism that present-day simulators try to make the real, all the real, coincide with their simulation models. But it is no longer a question of either maps or territory. Something has disappeared: the sovereign difference between them that was the abstraction's charm. For it is the difference which forms the poetry of the map and the charm of the territory, the magic of the concept and the charm of the real. This representational imaginary, which both culminates in and is engulfed by the cartographer's mad project of an ideal coextensivity between the map and the territory, disappears with simulation, whose operation is nuclear and genetic, and no longer specular and discursive. With it goes all of metaphysics. No more mirror of being and appearances, of the real and its concept; no more imaginary coextensivity: rather, genetic miniaturization is the dimension of simulation. The real is produced from miniaturized units, from matrices, memory banks and command models – and with these it can be reproduced an indefinite number of times. It no longer has to be rational, since it is no longer measured against some ideal or negative instance. It is nothing more than operational. In fact, since it is no longer enveloped by an imaginary, it is no longer real at all. It is a hyperreal: the product of an irradiating synthesis of combinatory models in a hyperspace without atmosphere.

In this passage to a space whose curvature is no longer that of the real, nor of truth, the age of simulation thus begins with a liquidation of all referentials – worse: by their artificial resurrection in systems of signs, which are a more ductile material than meaning, in that they lend themselves to all systems of equivalence, all binary oppositions and all combinatory algebra. It is no longer a question of imitation, nor of reduplication, nor even of parody. It is rather a question of substituting signs of the real for the real itself; that is, an operation to deter every real process by its operational double, a metastable, programmatic, perfect descriptive machine which provides all the signs of the real and short-circuits all its vicissitudes. Never again will the real have to be produced: this is the vital function of the model in a system of death, or rather of anticipated resurrection which no longer leaves any chance even in the event of death. A hyperreal henceforth sheltered from the imaginary, and from any distinction between the real and the imaginary, leaving room only for the orbital recurrence of models and the simulated generation of difference.

The Divine Irreference of Images

To dissimulate is to feign not to have what one has. To simulate is to feign to have what one hasn't. One implies a presence, the other an absence. But the matter is more complicated, since to simulate is not simply to feign: "Someone who feigns an illness can simply go to bed and pretend he is ill. Someone who simulates an illness produces in himself some of the symptoms" (Littré). Thus, feigning or dissimulating leaves the reality principle intact: the difference is always clear, it is only masked; whereas simulation threatens the difference between "true" and "false", between "real" and "imaginary". Since the simulator produces "true" symptoms, is he or she ill or not? The simulator cannot be treated objectively either as ill, or as not ill. Psychology and medicine stop at this point, before a thereafter undiscoverable truth of the illness. For if any symptom can be "produced," and can no longer be accepted as a fact of nature, then every illness may be considered as simulatable and simulated, and medicine loses its meaning since it only knows how to treat "true" illnesses by their objective causes. Psychosomatics evolves in a dubious way on the edge of the illness principle. As for psychoanalysis, it transfers the symptom from the organic to the unconscious order: once again, the latter is held to be real, more real than the former; but why should simulation stop at the portals of the unconscious? Why couldn't the "work" of the unconscious be "produced" in the same way as any other symptom in classical medicine? Dreams already are.

The alienist, of course, claims that "for each form of the mental alienation there is a particular order in the succession of symptoms, of which the simulator is unaware and in the absence of which the alienist is unlikely to be deceived." This (which dates from 1865) in order to save at all cost the truth principle, and to escape the specter raised by simulation: namely that truth, reference and objective causes have ceased to exist. What can medicine do with something which floats on either side of illness, on either side of health, or with the reduplication of illness in a discourse that is no longer true or false? What can psychoanalysis do with the reduplication of the discourse of the unconscious in a discourse of simulation that can never be unmasked, since it isn't false either?[2]

What can the army do with simulators? Traditionally, following a direct principle of identification, it unmasks and punishes them. Today, it can reform an excellent simulator as though he were equivalent to a "real" homosexual, heart-case or lunatic. Even military psychology retreats from the Cartesian clarities and hesitates to draw the distinction between true and false, between the "produced" symptom and the authentic symptom. "If he acts crazy so well, then he must be mad." Nor is it mistaken: in the sense that all lunatics are simulators, and this lack of distinction is the worst form of subversion. Against it, classical reason armed itself with all its categories. But it is this today which again outflanks them, submerging the truth principle.

Outside of medicine and the army, favored terrains of simulation, the affair goes back to religion and the simulacrum of divinity: "I forbade any simulacrum in the temples because the divinity that breathes life into nature cannot be represented." Indeed it can. But what becomes of the divinity when it reveals itself in icons, when it is multiplied in simulacra? Does it remain the supreme authority, simply incarnated in images as a visible theology? Or is it volatilized into simulacra which alone deploy their pomp and power of fascination – the visible machinery of icons being substituted for the pure and intelligible Idea of God? This is precisely what was feared by the Iconoclasts, whose millennial quarrel is still with us today.[3] Their rage to destroy images rose precisely because they sensed this omnipotence of simulacra, this facility they have of erasing God from the consciousnesses of people, and the overwhelming, destructive truth which they suggest: that ultimately there has never been any God; that only simulacra exist; indeed that God himself has only ever been his own simulacrum. Had they been able to believe that images only occulted or masked the Platonic idea of God, there would have been no reason to destroy them. One can live with the idea of a distorted truth. But their metaphysical despair came from the idea that the images concealed nothing at all, and that in fact they were not images, such as the original model would have made them, but actually perfect simulacra forever radiant with their own fascination. But this death of the divine referential has to be exorcised at all cost.

It can be seen that the iconoclasts, who are often accused of despising and denying images, were in fact the ones who accorded them their actual worth, unlike the iconolaters, who saw in them only reflections and were content to venerate God at one remove. But the converse can also be said, namely that the iconolaters possessed the most modern and adventurous minds, since, underneath the idea of the apparition of God in the mirror of images, they already enacted his death and his disappearance in the epiphany of his representations (which they perhaps knew no longer represented anything, and that they were purely a game, but that this was precisely the greatest game – knowing also that it is dangerous to unmask images, since they dissimulate the fact that there is nothing behind them).

This was the approach of the Jesuits, who based their politics on the virtual disappearance of God and on the worldly and spectacular manipulation of consciences – the evanescence of God in the epiphany of power – the end of transcendence, which no longer serves as alibi for a strategy completely free of influences and signs. Behind the baroque of images hides the grey eminence of politics.

Thus perhaps at stake has always been the murderous capacity of images: murderers of the real; murderers of their own model as the Byzantine icons could murder the divine identity. To this murderous capacity is opposed the dialectical capacity of representations as a visible and intelligible mediation of the real. All of Western faith and good faith was engaged in this wager on representation: that a sign could refer to the depth of meaning, that a sign could *exchange* for meaning and that something could guarantee this exchange – God, of course. But what if God himself can be simulated, that is to say, reduced to the signs which attest his existence? Then the whole system becomes weightless; it is no longer anything but a gigantic simulacrum: not unreal, but a simulacrum, never again exchanging for what is real, but exchanging in itself, in an uninterrupted circuit without reference or circumference.

So it is with simulation, insofar as it is opposed to representation. Representation starts from the principle that the sign and the real are equivalent (even if this equivalence is Utopian, it is a fundamental axiom). Conversely, simulation starts from the Utopia of this principle of equivalence, *from the radical negation of the sign as value*, from the sign as reversion and death sentence of every reference. Whereas representation tries to absorb simulation by interpreting it as false representation, simulation envelops the whole edifice of representation as itself a simulacrum.

These would be the successive phases of the image:

1   It is the reflection of a basic reality.
2   It masks and perverts a basic reality.
3   It masks the *absence* of a basic reality.
4   It bears no relation to any reality whatever: it is its own pure simulacrum.

In the first case, the image is a *good* appearance: the representation is of the order of sacrament. In the second, it is an *evil* appearance: of the order of malefice. In the third, it *plays at being* an appearance: it is of the order of sorcery. In the fourth, it is no longer in the order of appearance at all, but of simulation.

The transition from signs which dissimulate something to signs which dissimulate that there is nothing, marks the decisive turning point. The first implies a theology of truth and secrecy (to which the notion of ideology still belongs). The second inaugurates an age of simulacra and simulation, in which there is no longer any God to recognize his own, nor any last judgement to separate truth from false, the real from its artificial resurrection, since everything is already dead and risen in advance.

When the real is no longer what it used to be, nostalgia assumes its full meaning. There is a proliferation of myths of origin and signs of reality; of second-hand truth, objectivity and authenticity. There is an escalation of the true, of the lived experience; a resurrection of the figurative where the object and substance have disappeared. And there is a panic-stricken production of the real and the referential, above and parallel to the panic of material production. This is how simulation appears in the phase that concerns us: a strategy of the real, neo-real and hyperreal, whose universal double is a strategy of deterrence.

Hyperreal and Imaginary

Disneyland is a perfect model of all the entangled orders of simulation. To begin with it is a play of illusions and phantasms: pirates, the frontier, future world, etc. This imaginary world is supposed to be what makes the operation successful. But, what draws the crowds is undoubtedly much more the social microcosm, the miniaturized and *religious* revelling in real America, in its delights and drawbacks. You park outside, queue up inside, and are totally abandoned at the exit. In this imaginary world the only phantasmagoria is in the inherent warmth and affection of the crowd, and in that sufficiently excessive number of gadgets used there to specifically maintain the multitudinous affect. The contrast with the absolute solitude of the parking lot – a veritable concentration camp – is total. Or rather: inside, a whole range of gadgets magnetize the crowd into direct flows; outside, solitude is directed onto a single gadget: the automobile. By an extraordinary coincidence (one that undoubtedly belongs to the peculiar enchantment of this universe), this deep-frozen infantile world happens to have been conceived and realized by a man who is himself now cryogenized; Walt Disney, who awaits his resurrection at minus 180 degrees Centigrade.

The objective profile of the United States, then, may be traced throughout Disneyland, even down to the morphology of individuals and the crowd. All its values are exalted here, in miniature and comic-strip form. Embalmed and pacified. Whence the possibility of an ideological analysis of Disneyland (L. Marin does it well in *Utopies, jeux d'espaces*): digest of the American way of life, panegyric to American values, idealized transposition of a contradictory reality. To be sure. But this conceals something else, and that "ideological" blanket exactly serves to cover over a *third-order simulation*: Disneyland is there to conceal the fact that it is the "real" country, all of "real" America, which *is* Disneyland (just as prisons are there to conceal the fact that it is the social in its entirety, in its banal omnipresence, which is carceral). Disneyland is presented as imaginary in order to make us believe that the rest is real, when in fact all of Los Angeles and the America surrounding it are no longer real, but of the order of the hyperreal and of simulation. It is no longer a question of a false representation of reality (ideology), but of concealing the fact that the real is no longer real, and thus of saving the reality principle.

The Disneyland imaginary is neither true nor false: it is a deterrence machine set up in order to rejuvenate in reverse the fiction of the real. Whence the debility, the infantile degeneration of this imaginary. It is meant to be an infantile world, in order to make us believe that the adults are elsewhere, in the "real" world, and to conceal the fact that real childishness is everywhere, particularly among those adults who go there to act the child in order to foster illusions of their real childishness.

Moreover, Disneyland is not the only one. Enchanted Village, Magic Mountain, Marine World: Los Angeles is encircled by these "imaginary stations" which feed reality, reality-energy, to a town whose mystery is precisely that it is nothing more than a network of endless, unreal circulation: a town of fabulous proportions, but without space or dimensions. As much as electrical and nuclear power stations, as much as film studios, this town, which is nothing more than an immense script and a perpetual motion picture, needs this old imaginary made up of childhood signals and faked phantasms for its sympathetic nervous system.

Political Incantation

Watergate. Same scenario as Disneyland (an imaginary effect concealing that reality no more exists outside than inside the bounds of the artificial perimeter): though here it is a scandal-effect concealing that there is no difference between the facts and their denunciation (identical methods are employed by the CIA and the *Washington Post* journalists). Same operation, though this time tending towards scandal as a means to regenerate a moral and political principle, towards the imaginary as a means to regenerate a reality principle in distress.

The denunciation of scandal always pays homage to the law. And Watergate above all succeeded in imposing the idea that Watergate *was* a scandal – in this sense it was an extraordinary operation of intoxication: the reinjection of a large dose of political morality on a global scale. It could be said along with Bourdieu that: "The specific character of every relation of force is to dissimulate itself as such, and to acquire all its force only because it is so dissimulated"; understood as follows: capital, which is immoral and unscrupulous, can only function behind a moral superstructure, and whoever regenerates this public morality (by indignation, denunciation, etc.) spontaneously furthers the order of capital, as did the *Washington Post* journalists.

But this is still only the formula of ideology, and when Bourdieu enunciates it, he takes "relation of force" to mean the *truth* of capitalist domination, and he *denounces* this relation of force as itself a *scandal*: he therefore occupies the same deterministic and moralistic position as the *Washington Post* journalists. He does the same job of purging and reviving moral order, an order of truth wherein the genuine symbolic violence of the social order is engendered, well beyond all relations of force, which are only elements of its indifferent and shifting configuration in the moral and political consciousnesses of people.

All that capital asks of us is to receive it as rational or to combat it in the name of rationality, to receive it as moral or to combat it in the name of morality. For they are *identical*, meaning *they can be read another way*: before, the task was to dissimulate scandal; today, the task is to conceal the fact that there is none.

Watergate is not a scandal: this is what must be said at all cost, for this is what everyone is concerned to conceal, this dissimulation masking a strengthening of morality, a moral panic as we approach the primal (mise-en-)scene of capital: its instantaneous cruelty; its incomprehensible ferocity; its fundamental immorality – these are what are scandalous, unaccountable for in that system of moral and economic equivalence which remains the axiom of leftist thought, from Enlightenment theory to communism. Capital doesn't give a damn about the idea of the contract which is imputed to it: it is a monstrous unprincipled undertaking, nothing more. Rather, it is "enlightened" thought which seeks to control capital by imposing rules on it. And all that recrimination which replaced revolutionary thought today comes down to reproaching capital for not following the rules of the game. "Power is unjust; its justice is a class justice; capital exploits us; etc." – as if capital were linked by a contract to the society it rules. It is the left which holds out the mirror of equivalence, hoping that capital will fall for this phantasmagoria of the social contract and fulfill its obligation towards the whole of society (at the same time, no need for revolution: it is enough that capital accept the rational formula of exchange).

Capital in fact has never been linked by a contract to the society it dominates. It is a sorcery of the social relation, it is *a challenge to society* and should be responded to as such. It is not a scandal to be denounced according to moral and economic rationality, but a challenge to take up according to symbolic law.

Moebius: Spiralling Negativity

Hence Watergate was only a trap set by the system to catch its adversaries – a simulation of scandal to regenerative ends. This is embodied by the character called "Deep Throat," who was said to be a Republican grey eminence manipulating the leftist journalists in order to get rid of Nixon – and why not? All hypotheses are possible, although this one is superfluous: the work of the Right is done very well, and spontaneously, by the Left on its own. Besides, it would be naive to see an embittered good conscience at work here. For the Right itself also spontaneously does the work of the Left. All the hypotheses of manipulation are reversible in an endless whirligig. For manipulation is a floating causality where positivity and negativity engender and overlap with one another; where there is no longer any active or passive. It is by putting an *arbitrary* stop to this revolving causality that a principle of political reality can be saved. It is by the *simulation* of a conventional, restricted perspective field, where the premises and consequences of any act or event are calculable, that a political credibility can be maintained (including, of course, "objective" analysis, struggle, etc.). But if the entire cycle of any act or event is envisaged in a system where linear continuity and dialectical polarity no longer exist, in a field *unhinged by simulation*, then all determination evaporates, every act terminates at the end of the cycle having benefited everyone and been scattered in all directions.

Is any given bombing in Italy the work of leftist extremists; or of extreme right-wing provocation; or staged by centrists to bring every terrorist extreme into disrepute and to shore up its own failing power; or again, is it a police-inspired scenario in order to appeal to calls for public security? All this is equally true, and the search for proof – indeed the objectivity of the fact – does not check this vertigo of interpretation. We are in a logic of simulation which has nothing to do with a logic of facts and an order of reasons. Simulation is characterized by a *precession of the model*, of all models around the merest fact – the models come first, and their orbital (like the bomb) circulation constitutes the genuine magnetic field of events. Facts no longer have any trajectory of their own, they arise at the intersection of the models; a single fact may even be engendered by all the models at once. This anticipation, this precession, this short-circuit, this confusion of the fact with its model (no more divergence of meaning, no more dialectical polarity, no more negative electricity or implosion of poles) is what each time allows for all the possible interpretations, even the most contradictory – all are true, in the sense that their truth is exchangeable, in the image of the models from which they proceed, in a generalized cycle. . . .

It would take too long to run through the whole range of operational negativity, of all those scenarios of deterrence which, like Watergate, try to revive a moribund principle by simulated scandal, phantasm, murder – a sort of hormonal treatment by negativity and crisis. It is always a question of proving the real by the imaginary; proving truth by scandal; proving the law by transgression; proving work by the strike; proving the system by crisis and capital by revolution; and for that matter proving ethnology by the dispossession of its object (the Tasaday). Without counting: proving theater by anti-theater; proving art by anti-art; proving pedagogy by anti-pedagogy; proving psychiatry by anti-psychiatry, etc., etc.

Everything is metamorphosed into its inverse in order to be perpetuated in its purged form. Every form of power, every situation speaks of itself by denial, in order to attempt to escape, by simulation of death, its real agony. Power can stage its own murder to rediscover a glimmer of existence and legitimacy. Thus with the American presidents: the Kennedys are murdered because they still have a political dimension. Others – Johnson, Nixon, Ford – only had a right to puppet attempts, to simulated murders. But they nevertheless needed that aura of an artificial menace to conceal that they were nothing other than mannequins of power. In olden days the king (also the god) had to die – that was his strength. Today he does his miserable utmost to pretend to die, so as to preserve the *blessing* of power. But even this is gone.

To seek new blood in its own death, to renew the cycle by the mirror of crisis, negativity and anti-power: this is the only alibi of every power, of every institution attempting to break the vicious circle of its irresponsibility and its fundamental nonexistence, of its déjà-vu and its déjà-mort.

Strategy of the Real

Of the same order as the impossibility of rediscovering an absolute level of the real, is the impossibility of staging an illusion. Illusion is no longer possible, because the real is no longer possible. It is the whole *political* problem of the parody, of hypersimulation or offensive simulation, which is posed here.

For example: it would be interesting to see whether the repressive apparatus would not react more violently to a simulated hold-up than to a real one? For a real hold-up only upsets the order of things, the right of property, whereas a simulated hold-up interferes with the very principle of reality. Transgression and violence are less serious, for they only contest the *distribution* of the real. Simulation is infinitely more dangerous since it always suggests, over and above its object, that *law and order themselves might really be nothing more than a simulation.*

But the difficulty is in proportion to the peril. How to feign a violation and put it to the test? Go and simulate a theft in a large department store: how do you convince the security guards that it is a simulated theft? There is no "objective" difference: the same gestures and the same signs exist as for a real theft; in fact the signs incline neither to one side nor the other. As far as the established order is concerned, they are always of the order of the real.

Go and organize a fake hold-up. Be sure to check that your weapons are harmless, and take the most trustworthy hostage, so that no life is in danger (otherwise you risk committing an offence). Demand ransom, and arrange it so that the operation creates the greatest commotion possible. In brief, stay close to the "truth", so as to test the reaction of the apparatus to a perfect simulation. But you won't succeed: the web of artificial signs will be inextricably mixed up with real elements (a police officer will really shoot on sight; a bank customer will faint and die of a heart attack; they will really turn the phoney ransom over to you). In brief, you will unwittingly find yourself immediately in the real, one of whose functions is precisely to devour every attempt at simulation, to reduce everything to some reality: that's exactly how the established order is, well before institutions and justice come into play.

In this impossibility of isolating the process of simulation must be seen the whole thrust of an order that can only see and understand in terms of some reality, because it can function nowhere else. The simulation of an offence, if it is patent, will either be punished more lightly (because it has no "consequences") or be punished as an offence to public office (for example, if one triggered off a police operation "for nothing") – but *never as simulation*, since it is precisely as such that no equivalence with the real is possible, and hence no repression either. The challenge of simulation is irreceivable by power. How can you punish the simulation of virtue? Yet as such it is as serious as the simulation of crime. Parody makes obedience and transgression equivalent, and that is the most serious crime, since it *cancels out the difference upon which the law is based*. The established order can do nothing against it, for the law is a second-order simulacrum whereas simulation is a third-order simulacrum, beyond true and false, beyond equivalences, beyond the rational distinctions upon which function all power and the entire social stratum. Hence, *failing the real*, it is here that we must aim at order.

This is why order always opts for the real. In a state of uncertainty, it always prefers this assumption (thus in the army they would rather take the simulator as a true madman). But this becomes more and more difficult, for it is practically impossible to isolate the process of simulation; through the force of inertia of the real which surrounds us, the inverse is also true (and this very reversibility forms part of the apparatus of simulation and of power's impotency): namely, *it is now impossible to isolate the process of the real*, or to prove the real.

Thus all hold-ups, hijacks and the like are now as it were simulation hold-ups, in the sense that they are inscribed in advance in the decoding and orchestration rituals of the media, anticipated in their mode of presentation and possible consequences. In brief, where they function as a set of signs dedicated exclusively to their recurrence as signs, and no longer to their "real" goal at all. But this does not make them inoffensive. On the contrary, it is as hyperreal events, no longer having any particular contents or aims, but indefinitely refracted by each other (for that matter like so-called historical events: strikes, demonstrations, crises, etc.[4]), that they are precisely unverifiable by an order which can only exert itself on the real and the rational, on ends and means: a referential order which can only dominate referentials, a determinate power which can only dominate a determined world, but which can do nothing about that indefinite recurrence of simulation, about that weightless nebula no longer obeying the law of gravitation of the real – power itself eventually breaking apart in this space and becoming a simulation of power (disconnected from its aims and objectives, and dedicated to *power effects* and mass simulation).

The only weapon of power, its only strategy against this defection, is to reinject realness and referentiality everywhere, in order to convince us of the reality of the social, of the gravity of the economy and the finalities of production. For that purpose it prefers the discourse of crisis, but also – why not? – the discourse of desire. "Take your desires for reality!" can be understood as the ultimate slogan of power, for in a nonreferential world even the confusion of the reality principle with the desire principle is less dangerous than contagious hyperreality. One remains among principles, and there power is always right.

Hyperreality and simulation are deterrents of every principle and of every object-ive; they turn against power this deterrence which is so well utilized for a long time itself. For, finally, it was capital which was the first to feed throughout its history on the destruction of every referential, of every human goal, which shattered every ideal distinction between true and false, good and evil, in order to establish a radical law of equivalence and exchange, the iron law of its power. It was the first to practice deterrence, abstraction, disconnection, deterritorialization, etc.; and if it was capital which fostered reality, the reality principle, it was also the first to liquidate it in the extermination of every use value, of every real equivalence, of production and wealth, in the very sensation we have of the unreality of the stakes and the omnipotence of manipulation. Now, it is this very logic which is today hardened even more *against* it. And when it wants to fight this catastrophic spiral by secreting one last glimmer of reality, on which to found one last glimmer of power, it only multiplies the *signs* and accelerates the play of simulation.

As long as it was historically threatened by the real, power risked deterrence and simulation, disintegrating every contradiction by means of the production of equiva-lent signs. When it is threatened today by simulation (the threat of vanishing in the play of signs), power risks the real, risks crisis, it gambles on remanufacturing artifi-cial, social, economic, political stakes. This is a question of life or death for it. But it is too late.

Whence the characteristic hysteria of our time: the hysteria of production and reproduction of the real. The other production, that of goods and commodities, that of *la belle époque* of political economy, no longer makes any sense of its own, and has not for some time. What society seeks through production, and overproduction, is the restoration of the real which escapes it. That is why *contemporary "material" production is itself hyperreal*. It retains all the features, the whole discourse of trad-itional production, but it is nothing more than its scaled-down refraction (thus the hyperrealists fasten in a striking resemblance a real from which has fled all meaning and charm, all the profundity and energy of representation). Thus the hyperrealism of simulation is expressed everywhere by the real's striking resemblance to itself.

Power, too, for some time now produces nothing but signs of its resemblance. And at the same time, another figure of power comes into play: that of a collective demand for *signs* of power – a holy union which forms around the disappearance of power. Everybody belongs to it more or less in fear of the collapse of the political. And in the end the game of power comes down to nothing more than the *critical* obsession with power: an obsession with its death; an obsession with its survival which becomes greater the more it disappears. When it has totally disappeared, logically we will be under the total spell of power – a haunting memory already foreshadowed everywhere, manifesting at one and the same time the satisfaction of having got rid of it (nobody wants it any more, everybody unloads it on others) and grieving its loss. Melancholy for societies without power: this has already given rise to fascism, that overdose of a powerful referential in a society which cannot terminate its mourning.

But we are still in the same boat: none of our societies know how to manage their mourning for the real, for power, for the *social itself*, which is implicated in this same breakdown. And it is by an artificial revitalization of all this that we try to escape it. *Undoubtedly this will even end up in socialism*. By an unforeseen twist of events and an irony which no longer belongs to history, it is through the death of the social that socialism will emerge – as it is through the death of God that religions emerge. A twisted coming, a perverse event, an unintelligible reversion to the logic of reason. As is the fact that power is no longer present except to conceal that there is none. A simulation which can go on indefinitely, since – unlike "true" power which is, or was, a structure, a strategy, a relation of force, a stake – this is nothing but the object of a social *demand*, and hence subject to the law of supply and demand, rather than to violence and death. Completely expunged from the *political* dimension, it is dependent, like any other commodity, on production and mass consumption. Its spark has disappeared; only the fiction of a political universe is saved.

Likewise with work. The spark of production, the violence of its stake no longer exists. Everybody still produces, and more and more, but work has subtly become something else: a need (as Marx ideally envisaged it, but not at all in the same sense), the object of a social "demand," like leisure, to which it is equivalent in the general run of life's options. A demand exactly proportional to the loss of stake in the work process.[5] The same change in fortune as for power: the *scenario* of work is there to conceal the fact that the work-real, the production-real, has disappeared. And for that matter so has the strike-real too, which is no longer a stoppage of work, but its alternative pole in the ritual scansion of the social calendar. It is as if everyone has "occupied" their work place or work post, after declaring the strike, and resumed production, as is the custom in a "self-managed" job, in exactly the same terms as before, by declaring themselves (and virtually being) in a state of permanent strike.

This isn't a science-fiction dream: everywhere it is a question of a doubling of the work process. And of a double or locum for the strike process – strikes which are incorporated like obsolescence in objects, like crises in production. Then there are no longer any strikes or work, but both simultaneously, that is to say something else entirely: a wizardry of work, a *trompe l'oeil*, a scenodrama (not to say melodrama) of production, collective dramaturgy upon the empty stage of the social.

It is no longer a question of the *ideology* of work – of the traditional ethic that obscures the "real" labour process and the "objective" process of exploitation – but of the scenario of work. Likewise, it is no longer a question of the ideology of power, but of the *scenario* of power. Ideology only corresponds to a betrayal of reality by signs; simulation corresponds to a short-circuit of reality and to its reduplication by signs. It is always the aim of ideological analysis to restore the objective process; it is always a false problem to want to restore the truth beneath the simulacrum.

This is ultimately why power is so in accord with ideological discourses and discourses on ideology, for these are all discourses of *truth* – always good, even and especially if they are revolutionary, to counter the mortal blows of simulation.

Notes

1 Counterfeit and reproduction imply always an anguish, a disquieting foreignness: the uneasiness before the photograph, considered like a witch's trick – and more generally before any technical apparatus, which is always an apparatus of reproduction, is related by Benjamin to the uneasiness before the mirror-image. There is already sorcery at work in the mirror. But how much more so when this image can be detached from the mirror and be transported, stocked, reproduced at will (cf. *The Student of Prague*, where the devil detaches the image of the student from the mirror and harasses him to death by the intermediary of this image). All reproduction implies therefore a kind of black magic, from the fact of being seduced by one's own image in the water, like Narcissus, to being haunted by the double and, who knows, to the mortal turning back of this vast technical apparatus secreted today by man as his own image (the narcissistic mirage of technique, McLuhan) and that returns to him, cancelled and distorted – endless reproduction of himself and his power to the limits of the world. Reproduction is diabolical in its very essence; it makes something fundamental vacillate. This has hardly changed for us: simulation (that we describe here as the operation of the code) is still and always the place of a gigantic enterprise of manipulation, of control and of death, just like the imitative object (primitive statuette, image of photo) always had as objective an operation of black image.

2 There is furthermore in Monod's book a flagrant contradiction, which reflects the ambiguity of all current science. His discourse concerns the code, that is the third-order simulacra, but it does so still according to "scientific" schemes of the second-order – objectiveness, "scientific" ethic of knowledge, science's principle of truth and transcendence. All things incompatible with the indeterminable models of the third-order.

3 "It's the feeble 'definition' of TV which condemns its spectator to rearranging the few points retained into a kind of *abstract work*. He participates suddenly in the creation of a reality that was only just presented to him in dots: the television watcher is in the position of an individual who is asked to project his own fantasies on inkblots that are not supposed to represent anything." TV as perpetual Rorschach test. And furthermore: "The TV image requires each instant that we 'close' the spaces in the mesh by a convulsive sensuous participation that is profoundly kinetic and tactile."

4 The entire current "psychological" situation is characterized by this short circuit.

Doesn't emancipation of children and teenagers, once the initial phase of revolt is passed and once there has been established the *principle* of the *right* to emancipation, seem like the *real* emancipation of parents. And the young (students, high-schoolers, adolescents) seem to sense it in their always more insistent demand (though still as paradoxical) for the presence and advice of parents or of teachers. Alone at last, free and responsible, it seemed to them suddenly that other people possibly have absconded with their true liberty. Therefore, there is no question of "leaving them be." They're going to hassle them, not with any emotional or material spontaneous demand, but with an exigency that has been premeditated and corrected by an implicit oedipal knowledge. Hyperdependence (much greater than before) distorted by irony and refusal, *parody of libidinous original mechanisms*. Demand without content, without referent, unjustified, but for all that all the more severe – naked demand with no possible answer. The contents of knowledge (teaching) or of affective relations, the pedagogical or familial referent having been eliminated in the act of emancipation, there remains only a demand linked to the empty form of the institution – perverse demand, and for that reason all the more obstinate. "Transferable" desire (that is to say non-referential, un-referential), desire that has been fed by lack, by the place left vacant, "liberated," desire captured in its own vertiginous image, desire of desire, as pure form, hyperreal. Deprived of symbolic substance, it doubles back upon itself, draws its energy from its own reflection and its disappointment with itself. This is literally today the "demand," and it is obvious that unlike the "classical" objective or transferable relations this one here is insoluble and interminable.

Simulated Oedipus.

François Richard: "Students asked to be seduced either bodily or verbally. But also they are aware of this and they play the game, ironically. 'Give us your knowledge, your presence, you have the word, speak, you are there for that.' Contestation certainly, but not only: the more authority is contested, vilified, the greater the need for authority as such. They play at Oedipus also, to deny it all the more vehemently. The 'teach', he's Daddy, they say; it's fun, you play at incest, malaise, the untouchable, at being a tease – in order to de-sexualize finally." Like one under analysis who asks for Oedipus back again, who tells the "oedipal" stories, who has the "analytical" dreams to satisfy the supposed request of the analyst, or to resist him? In the same way the student goes through his oedipal number, his seduction number, gets chummy, close, approaches, dominates – but this isn't desire, it's simulation. Oedipal psychodrama of simulation (neither less real nor less dramatic for all that). Very different from the real libidinal stakes of knowledge and power or even of a real mourning for the absence of same (as could have happened after 1968 in the universities). Now we've reached the phase of desperate reproduction, and where the stakes are nil, the simulacrum is maximal – exacerbated and parodied simulation at one and the same time – as interminable as psychoanalysis and for the same reasons.

The interminable psychoanalysis.

There is a whole chapter to add to the history of transference and countertransference: that of their liquidation by simulation, of the impossible psychoanalysis because it is itself, from now on, that produces and reproduces the unconscious as its institutional substance. Psychoanalysis dies also of the exchange of the *signs* of the unconscious. Just as revolution dies of the exchange of the critical signs of political economy. This short circuit was well known to Freud in the form of the gift of the analytic dream, or with the "uninformed" patients, in the form of the gift of their analytic knowledge. But this was still interpreted as resistance, as detour, and did not put fundamentally into question either the process of analysis or the principle of transference. It is another thing entirely when the unconscious itself, the discourse of the unconscious becomes unfindable – according to the same scenario of simulative anticipation that we have seen at work on all levels with the machines of the third order. The analysis then can no longer end, it becomes logically and historically interminable, since it stabilizes on a puppet-substance of reproduction, an unconscious programmed on demand – an impossible-to-break-through point around which the whole analysis is rearranged. The messages of the unconscious have been short-circuited by the psychoanalysis "medium." This is libidinal hyperrealism. To the famous categories of the real, the symbolic and the imaginary, it is going to be necessary to add the hyperreal, which captures and obstructs the functioning of the three orders.

5   Athenian democracy, much more advanced than our own, had reached the point where the vote was considered as payment for a service, after all other repressive solutions had been tried and found wanting in order to insure a quorum.

CHAPTER 13

A Thousand Plateaus

Gilles Deleuze and Felix Guattari

Philosopher Gilles Deleuze's book on Nietzsche, *Nietzsche and Philosophy* (1961), helped inaugurate the interest in Nietzsche's work that would culminate later in the decade in the emergence of Post-Structuralism. Other books by Deleuze, such as *The Logic of Meaning* (1969), explored the underside of Structuralism, the realm of nonsense that sustained the order-making rules of language. His collaboration with Felix Guattari resulted in two important Post-Structuralist books – *The Anti-Oedipus* (1972), a critique of Freudian psychoanalysis, and *A Thousand Plateaus: Capitalism and Schizophrenia* (1980) – an ambitious model of history and of the world. Deleuze and Guattari in that latter work describe a conflict between two modes of social organization that coincide with two models of reality. One is arboresque and favors order and hierarchy. The other is rhizomatic and favors an undoing of all such orders and hierarchies. A rhizome is the root of a plant that travels laterally underground and proliferates unpredictably. History, the writers argue, alternates between moments of fixity and power that they called "territorialization" and moments of "deterritorialization" or undoing, when fixed orders fall apart and are transformed.

The two of us wrote *Anti-Oedipus* together. Since each of us was several, there was already quite a crowd. Here we have made use of everything that came within range, what was closest as well as farthest away. We have assigned clever pseudonyms to prevent recognition. Why have we kept our own names? Out of habit, purely out of habit. To make ourselves unrecognizable in turn. To render imperceptible, not ourselves, but what makes us act, feel, and think. Also because it's nice to talk like everybody else, to say the sun rises, when everybody knows it's only a manner of speaking. To reach, not the point where one no longer says I, but the point where it is no longer of any importance whether one says I. We are no longer ourselves. Each will know his own. We have been aided, inspired, multiplied.

A book has neither object nor subject; it is made of variously formed matters, and very different dates and speeds. To attribute the book to a subject is to overlook this working of matters, and the exteriority of their relations. It is to fabricate a beneficent God to explain geological movements. In a book, as in all things, there are lines of articulation or segmentarity, strata and territories; but also lines of flight, movements of deterritorialization and destratification. Comparative rates of flow on these lines produce phenomena of relative slowness and viscosity, or, on the contrary, of acceleration and rupture. All this, lines and measurable speeds, constitutes an *assemblage*. A book is an assemblage of this kind, and as such is unattributable. It is a multiplicity – but we don't know yet what the multiple entails when it is no longer attributed, that is, after it has been elevated to the status of a substantive. One side of a machinic assemblage faces the strata, which doubtless make it a kind of organism, or signifying totality, or determination attributable to a subject; it also has a side facing a *body without organs* [BwO], which is continually dismantling the organism, causing asignifying particles or pure intensities to pass or circulate and attributing to itself subjects that it leaves with nothing more than a name as the trace of an intensity. What is the body without organs of a book? There are several, depending on the nature of the lines considered, their particular grade or density, and the possibility of their converging on a "plane of consistency" assuring their selection. Here, as elsewhere, the units of measure are what is essential: *quantify writing*. There is no difference between what a book talks about and how it is made. Therefore a book also has no object. As an assemblage, a book has only itself, in connection with other assemblages and in relation to other bodies without organs. We will never ask what a book means, as signified or signifier, we will not look for anything to understand in it. We will ask what it functions with, in connection with what other things it does or does not transmit intensities, in which other multiplicities its own are inserted and metamorphosed, and with what bodies without organs it makes its own converge. A book exists only through the outside and on the outside. A book itself is a little machine; what is the relation (also measurable) of this literary machine to a war machine, love machine, revolutionary machine, etc. – and an *abstract machine* that sweeps them along? We have been criticized for overquoting literary authors. But when one writes, the only question is which other machine the literary machine can be plugged into, must be plugged into in order to work. Kleist and a mad war machine, Kafka and a most extraordinary bureaucratic machine . . . (What if one became animal or plant *through* literature, which certainly does not mean literarily? Is it not first through the voice that one becomes animal?) Literature is an assemblage. It has nothing to do with ideology. There is no ideology and never has been.

All we talk about are multiplicities, lines, strata and segmentarities, lines of flight and intensities, machinic assemblages and their various types, bodies without organs and their construction and selection, the plane of consistency, and in each case the units of measure. *Stratometers, deleometers, BwO units of density BwO units of convergence*: Not only do these constitute a quantification of writing, but they define writing as always the measure of something else. Writing has nothing to do with signifying. It has to do with surveying, mapping, even realms that are yet to come.

A first type of book is the root-book. The tree is already the image of the world, or the root the image of the world-tree. This is the classical book, as noble, signifying, and subjective organic interiority (the strata of the book). The book imitates the world, as art imitates nature: by procedures specific to it that accomplish what nature cannot or can no longer do. The law of the book is the law of reflection, the One that becomes two. How could the law of the book reside in nature, when it is what presides over the very division between world and book, nature and art? One that becomes two: whenever we encounter this formula, even stated strategically by Mao or understood in the most "dialectical" way possible, what we have before us is the most classical and well reflected, oldest, and weariest kind of thought. Nature doesn't work that way: in nature, roots are taproots with a more multiple, lateral, and circular system of ramification, rather than a dichotomous one. . . .

The radicle-system, or fascicular root, is the second figure of the book, to which our modernity pays willing allegiance. This time, the principal root has aborted, or its tip has been destroyed; an immediate, indefinite multiplicity of secondary roots grafts onto it and undergoes a flourishing development. This time, natural reality is what aborts the principal root, but the root's unity subsists, as past or yet to come, as possible. We must ask if reflexive, intellectual reality does not compensate for this state of things by demanding an even more comprehensive secret unity, or a more extensive totality. Take William Burroughs's cut-up method: the folding of one text onto another, which constitutes multiple and even adventitious roots (like a cutting), implies a supplementary dimension to that of the texts under consideration. In this supplementary dimension of folding, unity continues its intellectual labor. That is why the most resolutely fragmented work can also be presented as the Total Work or Magnum Opus. Most modern methods for making series proliferate or a multiplicity grow are perfectly valid in one direction, for example, a linear direction, whereas a unity of totalization asserts itself even more firmly in another, circular or cyclic, dimension. Whenever a multiplicity is taken up in a structure, its growth is offset by a reduction in its laws of combination. The abortionists of unity are indeed angel makers, *doctores angelici*, because they affirm a properly angelic and superior unity. Joyce's words, accurately described as having "multiple roots," shatter the linear unity of the word, even of language, only to posit a cyclic unity of the sentence, text, or knowledge. Nietzsche's aphorisms shatter the linear unity of knowledge, only to invoke the cyclic unity of the eternal return, present as the nonknown in thought. This is as much as to say that the fascicular system does not really break with dualism, with the complementarity between a subject and an object, a natural reality and a mental reality: unity is consistently thwarted and obstructed in the object, while a new type of unity triumphs in the subject. The world has lost its pivot; the subject can no longer even dichotomize, but accedes to a higher unity, of ambivalence or overdetermination, in an always supplementary dimension to that of its object. The world has become chaos, but the book remains the image of the world: radicle-chaosmos rather than root-cosmos. A strange mystification: a book all the more total for being fragmented. At any rate, what a vapid idea, the book as the image of the world. In truth, it is not enough to say, "Long live the multiple," difficult as it is to raise that cry. No typographical, lexical, or even syntactical cleverness is enough to make it heard. The multiple must *be made*,...A system of this kind could be called a rhizome. A rhizome as subterranean stem is absolutely different from roots and radicles. Bulbs and tubers are rhizomes. Plants with roots or radicles may be rhizomorphic in other respects altogether: the question is whether plant life in its specificity is not entirely rhizomatic. Even some animals are, in their pack form. Rats are rhizomes. Burrows are too, in all of their functions of shelter, supply, movement, evasion, and breakout. The rhizome itself assumes very diverse forms, from ramified surface extension in all directions to concretion into bulbs and tubers. When rats swarm over each other. The rhizome includes the best and the worst: potato and couchgrass, or the weed. Animal and plant, couchgrass is crabgrass. We get the distinct feeling that we will convince no one unless we enumerate certain approximate characteristics of the rhizome.

   1 and 2   Principles of connection and heterogeneity: any point of a rhizome can be connected to anything other, and must be. This is very different from the tree or root, which plots a point, fixes an order. The linguistic tree on the Chomsky model still begins at a point S and proceeds by dichotomy. On the contrary, not every trait in a rhizome is necessarily linked to a linguistic feature: semiotic chains of every

nature are connected to very diverse modes of coding (biological, political, economic, etc.) that bring into play not only different regimes of signs but also states of things of differing status. *Collective assemblages of enunciation* function directly within *machinic assemblages*; it is not impossible to make a radical break between regimes of signs and their objects. Even when linguistics claims to confine itself to what is explicit and to make no presuppositions about language, it is still in the sphere of a discourse implying particular modes of assemblage and types of social power. Chomsky's grammaticality, the categorical S symbol that dominates every sentence, is more fundamentally a marker of power than a syntactic marker: you will construct grammatically correct sentences, you will divide each statement into a noun phrase and a verb phrase (first dichotomy...). Our criticism of these linguistic models is not that they are too abstract but, on the contrary, that they are not abstract enough, that they do not reach the *abstract machine* that connects a language to the semantic and pragmatic contents of statements, to collective assemblages of enunciation, to a whole micropolitics of the social field. A rhizome ceaselessly establishes connections between semiotic chains, organizations of power, and circumstances relative to the arts, sciences, and social struggles. A semiotic chain is like a tuber agglomerating very diverse acts, not only linguistic, but also perceptive, mimetic, gestural, and cognitive: there is no language in itself, nor are there any linguistic universals, only a throng of dialects, patois, slangs, and specialized languages. There is no ideal speaker-listener, any more than there is a homogeneous linguistic community. Language is, in Weinreich's words, "an essentially heterogeneous reality."[1] There is no mother tongue, only a power takeover by a dominant language within a political multiplicity. Language stabilizes around a parish, a bishopric, a capital. It forms a bulb. It evolves by subterranean stems and flows, along river valleys or train tracks; it spreads like a patch of oil.[2] It is always possible to break a language down into internal structural elements, an undertaking not fundamentally different from a search for roots. There is always something genealogical about a tree. It is not a method for the people. A method of the rhizome type, on the contrary, can analyze language only by decentering it onto other dimensions and other registers. A language is never closed upon itself, except as a function of impotence.

3   Principle of multiplicity: it is only when the multiple is effectively treated as a substantive, "multiplicity," that it ceases to have any relation to the One as subject or object, natural or spiritual reality, image and world. Multiplicities are rhizomatic, and expose arborescent pseudomultiplicities for what they are. There is no unity to serve as a pivot in the object or to divide in the subject. There is not even the unity to abort in the object or "return" in the subject. A multiplicity has neither subject nor object, only determinations, magnitudes, and dimensions that cannot increase in number without the multiplicity changing in nature (the laws of combination therefore increase in number as the multiplicity grows). Puppet strings, as a rhizome or multiplicity, are tied not to the supposed will of an artist or puppeteer but to a multiplicity of nerve fibers, which form another puppet in other dimensions connected to the first: "Call the strings or rods that move the puppet the weave. It might be objected that its *multiplicity* resides in the person of the actor; who projects it into the text. Granted; but the actor's nerve fibers in turn form a weave. And they fall through the gray matter, the grid, into the undifferentiated... The interlay approximates the pure activity of weavers attributed in myth to the Fates or Norns."[3] An assemblage is precisely this increase in the dimensions of a multiplicity that

necessarily changes in nature as it expands its connections. There are no points or positions in a rhizome, such as those found in a structure, tree, or root. There are only lines. When Glenn Gould leads up the performance of a piece, he is not just displaying virtuosity, he is transforming the musical points into lines, he is making the whole piece proliferate. The number is no longer a universal concept measuring elements according to their emplacement in a given dimension, but has itself become a multiplicity that varies according to the dimensions considered the primacy of the domain over a complex of numbers attached to that domain. We do not have units (*unités*) of measure, only multiplicities or varieties of measurement. The notion of unity (*unité*) appears only when there is a power takeover in the multiplicity by the signifier or a corresponding subjectification proceeding: This is the case for a pivot-unity forming the basis for a set of biunivocal relationships between objective arguments or points, or for the One that divides following the law of a binary of differentiation in the subject. Unity always operates in an empty tension supplementary to that of the system considered (overcoding). The point is that a rhizome or multiplicity never allows itself to be overcoded, never has available a supplementary dimension over and above its number of lines, that is, over and above the multiplicity of numbers attached to those lines. All multiplicities are flat, in the sense that they fill or occupy all of their dimensions: we will therefore speak of a *plane of consistency* of multiplicities, even though the dimensions of this "plane" increase with the number of connections that are made on it. Multiplicities are defined by the outside: by the abstract line, the line of flight or deterritorialization according to which they change in nature and connect with other multiplicities. The plane of consistency (grid) is the outside of all multiplicities. The line of flight marks: the reality of a finite number of dimensions that the multiplicity effectively fills; the impossibility of a supplementary dimension, unless the multiplicity is transformed by the line of flight; the possibility and necessity of flattening all of the multiplicities on a single plane of consistency or exteriority, regardless of their number of dimensions. The ideal for a book would be to lay everything out on a plane of exteriority of this kind, on a single page, the same sheet: lived events, historical determinations, concepts, individuals, groups, social formations. Kleist invented a writing of this type, a broken chain of affects and variable speeds, with accelerations and transformations, always in a relation with the outside. Open rings. His texts, therefore, are opposed in every way to the classical or romantic book constituted by the interiority of a substance or subject. The war machine-book against the State apparatus-book. *Flat multiplicities of n dimensions* are asignifying and asubjective. They are designated by indefinite articles, or rather by partitives (*some* couchgrass, *some* of a rhizome . . .).

4   Principle of asignifying rupture: against the oversignifying breaks separating structures or cutting across a single structure. A rhizome may be broken, shattered at a given spot, but it will start up again on one of its old lines, or on new lines. You can never get rid of ants because they form an animal rhizome that can rebound time and again after most of it has been destroyed. Every rhizome contains lines of segmentarity according to which it is stratified, territorialized, organized, signified, attributed, etc., as well as lines of deterritorialization down which it constantly flees. There is a rupture in the rhizome whenever segmentary lines explode into a line of flight, but the line of flight is part of the rhizome. These lines always tie back to one another. That is why one can never posit a dualism or a dichotomy, even in the rudimentary form of the good and the bad. You may make a rupture, draw a line of

flight, yet there is still a danger that you will reencounter organizations that restratify everything, formations that restore power to a signifier, attributions that reconstitute a subject – anything you like, from Oedipal resurgences to fascist concretions. Groups and individuals contain microfascisms just waiting to crystallize. Yes, couch-grass is also a rhizome. Good and bad are only the products of an active and temporary selection, which must be renewed.

How could movements of deterritorialization and processes of reterritorialization not be relative, always connected, caught up in one another? The orchid deterritorializes by forming an image, a tracing of a wasp; but the wasp reterritorializes on that image. The wasp is nevertheless deterritorialized, becoming a piece in the orchid's reproductive apparatus. But it reterritorializes the orchid by transporting its pollen. Wasp and orchid, as heterogeneous elements, form a rhizome. It could be said that the orchid imitates the wasp, reproducing its image in a signifying fashion (mimesis, mimicry, lure, etc.). But this is true only on the level of the strata – a parallelism between two strata such that a plant organization on one imitates an animal organization on the other. At the same time, something else entirely is going on: not imitation at all but a capture of code, surplus value of code, an increase in valence, a veritable becoming, a becoming-wasp of the orchid and a becoming-orchid of the wasp. Each of these becomings brings about the deterritorialization of one term and the reterritorialization of the other; the two becomings interlink and form relays in a circulation of intensities pushing the deterritorialization ever further. There is neither imitation nor resemblance, only an exploding of two heterogeneous series on the line of flight composed by a common rhizome that can no longer be attributed to or subjugated by anything signifying. . . . Transversal communications between different lines scramble the genealogical trees. Always look for the molecular, or even submolecular, particle with which we are allied. We evolve and die more from our polymorphous and rhizomatic flus than from hereditary diseases, or diseases that have their own line of descent. The rhizome is an antigenealogy.

The same applies to the book and the world: contrary to a deeply rooted belief, the book is not an image of the world. It forms a rhizome with the world, there is an aparallel evolution of the book and the world; the book assures the deterritorialization of the world, but the world effects a reterritorialization of the book, which in turn deterritorializes itself in the world (if it is capable, if it can). Mimesis is a very bad concept, since it relies on binary logic to describe phenomena of an entirely different nature. The crocodile does not reproduce a tree trunk, any more than the chameleon reproduces the colors of its surroundings. The Pink Panther imitates nothing, it reproduces nothing, it paints the world its color, pink on pink; this is its becoming-world, carried out in such a way that it becomes imperceptible itself, asignifying, makes its rupture, its own line of flight, follows its "aparallel evolution" through to the end. The wisdom of the plants: even when they have roots, there is always an outside where they form a rhizome with something else – with the wind, an animal, human beings (and there is also an aspect under which animals themselves form rhizomes, as do people, etc.). "Drunkenness as a triumphant irruption of the plant in us." Always follow the rhizome by rupture; lengthen, prolong, and relay the line of flight; make it vary, until you have produced the most abstract and tortuous of lines of n dimensions and broken directions. Conjugate deterritorialized flows. Follow the plants: you start by delimiting a first line consisting of circles of convergence around successive singularities; then you see whether inside that line new circles of convergence establish themselves, with new points located outside the limits and in other directions. Write, form a rhizome, increase your territory by deterritorialization, extend the line of flight to the point where it becomes an abstract machine covering the entire plane of consistency. "Go first to your old plant and watch carefully the watercourse made by the rain. By now the rain must have carried the seeds far away. Watch the crevices made by the runoff, and from them determine the direction of the flow. Then find the plant that is growing at the farthest point from your plant. All the devil's weed plants that are growing in between are yours. Later...you can extend the size of your territory by following the watercourse from each point along the way."[4] Music has always sent out lines of flight, like so many "transformational multiplicities," even overturning the very codes that structure or arborify it; that is why musical form, right down to its ruptures and proliferations, is comparable to a weed, a rhizome.[5]...

In contrast to centered (even polycentric) systems with hierarchical modes of communication and preestablished paths, the rhizome is an acentered, nonhierarchical, nonsignifying system without a General and without an organizing memory or central automaton, defined solely by a circulation of states. What is at question in the rhizome is a relation to sexuality – but also to the animal, the vegetal, the world, politics, the book, things natural and artificial – that is totally different from the arborescent relation: all manner of "becomings."

A plateau is always in the middle, not at the beginning or the end. A rhizome is made of plateaus. Gregory Bateson uses the word "plateau" to designate something very special: a continuous, self-vibrating region of intensities whose development avoids any orientation toward a culmination point or external end. Bateson cites Balinese culture as an example: mother–child sexual games, and even quarrels among men, undergo this bizarre intensive stabilization. "Some sort of continuing plateau of intensity is substituted for [sexual] climax, war, or a culmination point. It is a regrettable characteristic of the Western mind to relate expressions and actions to exterior or transcendent ends, instead of evaluating them on a plane of consistency on the basis of their intrinsic value."[6] For example, a book composed of chapters has culmination and termination points. What takes place in a book composed instead of plateaus that communicate with one another across microfissures, as in a brain? We call a "plateau" any multiplicity connected to other multiplicities by superficial underground stems in such a way as to form or extend a rhizome. We are writing this book as a rhizome. It is composed of plateaus. We have given it a circular form, but only for laughs. Each morning we would wake up, and each of us would ask himself what plateau he was going to tackle, writing five lines here, ten there. We had hallucinatory experiences, we watched lines leave one plateau and proceed to another like columns of tiny ants. We made circles of convergence. Each plateau can be read starting anywhere and can be related to any other plateau. To attain the multiple, one must have a method that effectively constructs it; no typographical cleverness, no lexical agility, no blending or creation of words, no syntactical boldness, can substitute for it. In fact, these are more often than not merely mimetic procedures used to disseminate or disperse a unity that is retained in a different dimension for an image-book. Technonarcissism. Typographical, lexical, or syntactic creations are necessary only when they no longer belong to the form of expression of a hidden unity, becoming themselves dimensions of the multiplicity under consideration; we only know of rare successes in this.[7] We ourselves were unable to do it. We just used words that in turn function for us as plateaus. RHIZOMATICS = SCHIZO-ANALYSIS = STRATOANALYSIS = PRAGMATICS = MICROPOLITICS. These words are concepts, but concepts are lines, which is to say, number systems attached to a particular dimension of the multiplicities (strata, molecular chains, lines of flight or rupture, circles of convergence, etc.). Nowhere do we claim for our concepts the title of a science. We are no more familiar with scientificity than we are with ideology; all we know are assemblages. And the only assemblages are machinic assemblages of desire and collective assemblages of enunciation. No *signifiance*, no subjectification: writing to the *n*th power (all individuated enunciation remains trapped within the dominant significations, all signifying desire is associated with dominated subjects). An assemblage, in its multiplicity, necessarily acts on semiotic flows, material flows, and social flows simultaneously (independently of any recapitulation that may be made of it in a scientific or theoretical corpus). There is no longer a tripartite division between a field of reality (the world) and a field of representation (the book) and a field of subjectivity (the author). Rather, an assemblage establishes connections between certain multiplicities drawn from each of these orders, so that a book has no sequel nor the world as its object nor one or several authors as its subject. In short, we think that one cannot write sufficiently in the name of an outside. The outside has no image, no signification, no subjectivity. The book as assemblage with the outside, against the book as image of the world. A rhizome-book, not a dichotomous, pivotal, or fascicular book. Never send down roots, or plant them, however difficult it may be to avoid reverting to the old procedures. "Those things which occur to me, occur to me not from the root up but rather only from somewhere about their middle. Let someone then attempt to seize them, let someone attempt to seize a blade of grass and hold fast to it when it begins to grow only from the middle."[8] Why is this so difficult? The question is directly one of perceptual semiotics. It's not easy to see things in the middle, rather than looking down on them from above or up at them from below, or from left to right or right to left: try it, you'll see that everything changes. It's not easy to see the grass in things and in words (similarly, Nietzsche said that an aphorism had to be "ruminated"; never is a plateau separable from the cows that populate it, which are also the clouds in the sky).

History is always written from the sedentary point of view and in the name of a unitary State apparatus, at least a possible one, even when the topic is nomads. What is lacking is a Nomadology, the opposite of a history....Even in the realm of theory, especially in the realm of theory, any precarious and pragmatic framework is better than tracing concepts, with their breaks and progress changing nothing. Impercept-ible rupture, not signifying break....The nomads invented a war machine in oppos-ition to the State apparatus. History has never comprehended nomadism, the book has never comprehended the outside. The State as the model for the book and for thought has a long history: logos, the philosopher-king, the transcendence of the Idea, the interiority of the concept, the republic of minds, the court of reason, the functionaries of thought, man as legislator and subject. The State's pretension to be a world order, and to root man. The war machine's relation to an outside is not another "model"; it is an assemblage that makes thought itself nomadic, and the book a working part in every mobile machine, a stem for a rhizome (Kleist and Kafka against Goethe)....

A rhizome has no beginning or end; it is always in the middle, between things, interbeing, *intermezzo*. The tree is filiation, but the rhizome is alliance, uniquely alliance. The tree imposes the verb "to be," but the fabric of the rhizome is the conjunction, "and . . . and . . . and . . ." This conjunction carries enough force to shake and uproot the verb "to be." Where are you going? Where are you coming from? What are you heading for? These are totally useless questions. Making a clean slate, starting or beginning again from ground zero, seeking a beginning or a foundation – all imply a false conception of voyage and movement (a conception that is methodical, pedagogical, initiatory, symbolic . . .). But Kleist, Lenz, and Büchner have another way of traveling and moving: proceeding from the middle, through the middle, coming and going rather than starting and finishing.[9] American literature, and already English literature, manifest this rhizomatic direction to an even greater extent; they know how to move between things, establish a logic of the AND, overthrow ontology, do away with foundations, nullify endings and beginnings. They know how to practice pragmatics. The middle is by no means an average; on the contrary, it is where things pick up speed. *Between* things does not designate a localizable relation going from one thing to the other and back again, but a perpendicular direction, a transversal movement that sweeps one *and* the other away, a stream without beginning or end that undermines its banks and picks up speed in the middle . . .

Notes

1 U. Weinreich, W. Labov, and M. Herzog, "Empirical Foundations for a Theory of Language," in W. Lehmann and Y. Malkeiel (eds.), *Directions for Historical Linguistics* (1968), p. 125; cited by Françoise Robert, "Aspects sociaux du changement dans une grammaire générative," *Langages*, no. 32 (December 1973), p. 90. [Trans.]

2 Bertil Malmberg, *New Trends in Linguistics*, trans. Edward Carners (Stockholm: Lund 1964), pp. 65–7 (the example of the Castilian dialect).

3 Ernst Jünger, *Approches; drogues et ivresse* (Paris: Table Ronde, 1974), p. 304, sec. 218.

4 Carlos Castaneda, *The Teachings of Don Juan* (Berkeley: University of California Press, 1971), p. 88.

5 Pierre Boulez, *Conversations with Célestin Deliège* (London: Eulenberg Books, 1976): "a seed which you plant in compost, and suddenly it begins to proliferate like a weed" (p. 15) and on musical proliferation: "a music that floats, and in which the writing itself makes it impossible for the performer to keep in with a pulsed time" (p. 69 [translation modified]).

6 Gregory Bateson, *Steps to an Ecology of Mind* (New York: Ballantine Books, 1972), p. 113. It will be noted that the word "plateau" is used in classical studies of bulbs, tubers, and rhizomes; see the entry for "bulb" in M. H. Baillon, *Dictionnaire de botanique* (Paris: Hachette, 1876–92).

7 For example, Joëlle de La Casinière, *Absolument nécessaire. The Emergency Book* (Paris: Minuit, 1973), a truly nomadic book. In the same vein, see the research in progress at the Montfaucon Research Center.

8 *The Diaries of Franz Kafka*, ed. Max Brod, trans. Joseph Kresh (New York: Schocken, 1948), p. 12.

9 See Jean-Cristophe Bailly's description of movement in German Romanticism, in his introduction to *La Légende dispersée: la description du mouvement dans le romantisme allemand* (Paris: Union Générale d'Editions, 1976), pp. 18 ff.

PART FIVE

Psychoanalysis and Psychology

CHAPTER 1

Introduction: Strangers to Ourselves: Psychoanalysis

Julie Rivkin and Michael Ryan

A picture of the human mind as a unified whole that can achieve full awareness of itself has been central to western thought since the seventeenth century. The "cogito" or thinking self defines our humanity and our civility, our difference from animals chained to blind nature and uncontrollable instincts. In the early part of the twentieth century, the assurance of that self-description was disturbed by Sigmund Freud's book, *The Interpretation of Dreams* (1900), which described a discovery that would become the centerpiece of a new discipline called psychoanalysis. His discovery was that the human mind contains a dimension that is only partially accessible to consciousness and then only through indirect means such as dreams or neurotic symptoms. The "unconscious," as he called it, is a repository of repressed desires, feelings, memories, and instinctual drives, many of which, according to Freud, have to do with sexuality and violence. In subsequent books and studies such as *Beyond the Pleasure Principle*, "A Case of Infantile Neurosis," *Three Essays on Sexuality, The Ego and the Id*, and *The Psychopathology of Everyday Life*, Freud argued that our mental lives derive largely from biological drives, that the highest achievements and ideals of civilization are inseparable from instinctual urges toward pleasure, constancy, and the release of excitation and energy. As each child grows and enters first the family then society, he or she learns to repress those instinctual drives and the conscious desires they instigate and to mold aggressive and sexual impulses as well as an initially grandiose sense of self to the demands of life with others. Repression is essential to civilization, the conversion of animal instinct into civil behavior, but such repression creates what might be called a second self, a stranger within, a place where all that cannot for one reason or another be expressed or realized in civil life takes up residence. This, for Freud, explains why people experience what he calls "uncanny" feelings of doubleness that consist of a sense that something strange coexists with what is most familiar inside ourselves. It also explains why we compulsively repeat certain gestures, desires, experiences, and self-induced situations that might be quite distressing but also compellingly unavoidable. We cannot help but do so because they are brought about by forces and drives within ourselves over which we exercise very little conscious control because they arise from something or somewhere that is beyond our control – the unconscious.

Freud discovered the unconscious by studying patients with neurotic symptoms which pointed towards unresolved conflicts between unconscious inclinations or feelings and the repressive demands of the ego or conscious self. He noticed that such patients engaged in behavior that frequently embodied desires or fears (persistent phobic anxiety about animals, for example) whose repetitiveness suggested that the patient was in the grip of something outside his awareness or her control. Freud borrowed from his teacher Josef Breuer a method of analysis whereby patients would say whatever came to their minds regardless of how seemingly meaningless or unpertinent. In this way, he found that patients divulged thoughts and feelings that had been kept repressed in the unconscious and hidden from the patient's own conscious view. One patient, for example, experienced a recurring fear of animals that turned out, through his free associations or thoughts, to refer to his childhood fear of his father, something he had repressed and forgotten.

In studying his patients, Freud realized that the unconscious often expresses itself in the form of dreams, since at night during sleep, the vigilance of the repressive ego in regard to unconscious desire is stilled. Dreams, Freud found, express wishes or desires that cannot find expression in waking life precisely because they are at odds with the requirements of the ego, which itself merely registers the requirements of the larger society. Unconscious wishes can find expression in dreams because dreams distort the unconscious material and make it appear different from itself and more acceptable to consciousness. The "dream work" displaces unacceptable material onto acceptable images, condenses several different though related unconscious elements into a single image, and turns drives into their opposites, so that they can elude censorship. A dream about not being able to serve a smoked salmon dinner to a friend might turn out to have nothing to do with dining but instead might refer to a wish not to help the friend gain weight and become more attractive to one's husband, who that very day, before the dream, mentioned how attractive he found the friend to be precisely because of her plumpness.

A similar process is at work, Freud discovered, in neurotic symptoms. They frequently displace desires, or anxieties, or drive energies that are unconscious onto expressive activities or compulsive thoughts. Such symptoms perform a variety of translative procedures on unconscious material, from compromise formation (the construction of an indirect expression that allows release of unacceptable drive energy while nonetheless honoring the imperatives of repression) to inversion (the conversion into its opposite of a desire or impulse). For example, someone raised in a strongly religious way that proscribes sexual activity may perform forbidden sexual acts ritualistically so as to seem to be respecting the norm while nonetheless attaining satisfaction. Or someone who feels great animosity toward a cold and distant mother may convert that feeling into its opposite, a fantasy that all women are themselves hostile and therefore unworthy of his love.

Other important terms in the study of symptom formation are fixation, splitting, introjection, and projection. Anxiety about entry into an adult world perceived as threatening of a too fragile sense of self or anxiety that awakens either troubling memories or drive energies will propel some people to fixate at an early state of development. They will remain attached to early forms of emotional life and sexual activity that are usually surpassed in the transition to adulthood. In some instances, for example, people who fear the passage to genital sexuality will continue to find gratification from other parts of their bodies or other activities than genital sex. Splitting is a way of dealing with anxiety by dividing the object of anxiety in two, one bearing all the negative feeling while the other embodies all the positive feelings one wishes to substitute for the anxieties the object or situation provokes. Children may, for example, direct all of their aggression or hostility toward one parent while idealizing the other, and such splitting may be as much a response to the trajectory of their own drive energies as to external parental behavior. Finally, introjection and projection are terms used to describe how the self shapes itself by adapting models from outside itself and externalizes its own feelings by assigning them to others. If introjection brings in something from someone else, creating an ideal of that person within oneself, projection throws out something from within oneself and makes it seem as if it is a trait of someone else.

Freud spent most of his life studying the boundary and the dynamic movements between the conscious self or ego and the unconscious, which he later came to call the id. The id is the site of the energy of the mind, energy that Freud characterized as a combination of sexual libido and other instincts, such as aggression, that propel the human organism through life, moving it to grow, develop, and eventually to die. That primary process of life is entirely irrational, and it cannot distinguish images and things, reasonable objects and unreasonable or socially unacceptable ones. It is the secondary processes of the mind, lodged in the ego and superego or conscience, that bring reason, order, logic, and social acceptability to the otherwise uncontrolled and potentially harmful realm of the biological drives. But, according to Freud, the drives of the unconscious, though repressed, can never be quelled entirely. They emerge in dreams, and, when the rational part of the mind fails to handle them successfully, in the seemingly irrational behavior that is neurotic symptomatology (the fears, unjustified anxieties, and compulsive behaviors that indicate something out of joint in a personality). When conscious control breaks down altogether and drives and unconscious content are expressed directly, without any mediation by consciousness, one is in the realm of psychosis or schizophrenia, which Freud distinguished from neurosis by saying that neurosis maintains the relationship to an external reality while in psychosis that relationship breaks down altogether.

Freud insisted that sexuality was evident throughout life, from childhood on. The energy of sexuality is far from exclusively genital; it can also be anal or oral, Freud noted, and it can also be displaced onto fetish objects or substitutes that replace early desired objects with ones that avoid anxiety or are responses to trauma. In one famous case study, Freud analyzed an obsessional neurotic (known as the "Wolf Man" because of a dream he had about wolves in a tree staring at him) who developed a sexually invested fondness for military dress and regimen in response to early traumatic experiences regarding his sexual identity. His anxiety provoked him to displace his sexual drive away from human objects and onto fetish substitutes.

At the core of Freud's sexual theory is the so-called "Oedipus Complex," something Freud believed all children experience as a rite of passage to adult gender identity. As befitted his time, Freud was primarily concerned with the Oedipal trajectory of the male child (hence Oedipus rather than, say, Clytemnestra or Medea). All male children, Freud argued, experience an early attachment to the mother that is sexual in nature. Only the father's intervention, separating mother from child, prevents incest. All civilization is founded on the prohibition expressed in the father's intervention. The male child learns to give up his initial "pre-Oedipal" desire for and attachment to the mother; instead, he identifies with the father (instead of longing to be the father with his mother) and learns to desire other women than the mother. He becomes an adult male heterosexual (Freud's implicit norm).

Similarly, the female child experiences an early desire for the father which takes the form of a simultaneous desire to *be* her mother, to take her place as the father's sexual object, but she too learns to relinquish that desire and to identify with her mother and to seek other objects outside the family. The crucial process in gender formation is identification, the molding of a self from equations made between one-self and external objects through the internalization of images or models of those objects.

Psychoanalytic theory after Freud divides into two strands, one called object relations, the other neo-Freudianism. While object relations theory favors a model that does without instincts almost altogether and concentrates instead on the way the self interacts with its social world, especially the initial world of primary caretakers such as the mother, neo-Freudian theory in the work of Jacques Lacan especially argues that the instinctual drives and the unconscious are more essential to psychoanalytic work than the ego, which Lacan sees as a mirage that can never fully know and master the unconscious.

The theory of identification, which places greater emphasis on social relations at the expense of the instinctual drives, was especially appealing to the object relations school of psychoanalysis that came into being after World War II in Britain and America and is associated with such names as Melanie Klein, D. W. Winnicott, and Margaret Mahler. It is concerned less with the battle between the ego and the instinctual drives, a notion that some of the theorists reject outright, than it is with the way the relations between the child and its objects, especially the mother, during the pre-Oedipal period, shape its personality. The contours of self-identity are given or shaped by that primary relationship, by whether or not it is distant, cold, and frustrating, for example, or overwhelming and engulfing. The child's ability to separate successfully from its primary unity with the mother by building self-boundaries and appropriate mental representations of an external object world will determine what kind of personality he or she will possess – be it one yearning for fusion with objects that never fully satisfy its yearning or one dominated by a feeling of being compelled to flee from relationships that threaten to overwhelm its fragile self-boundaries.

Unlike Freud, object relations theorists consider the ego to be a major part of (if not the entire) personality. How it manages to construct an internal world for itself made up of introjected fantasy objects or projections of destructive feelings onto the world during the "pre-Oedipal" stage of development is more important for such theorists than the later Oedipal stage of passage into adult gender identity. Some consider the original separation from the mother to be a primary frustration that can never be assuaged; life's longings are defined by its schema. Others like Margaret Mahler see the relation to the mother more positively as providing a "beacon" that allows the child to emerge into the world from a primary symbiotic state. And others like Melanie Klein see the child constructing a world for itself through fantasies that allow it to distinguish its destructive from its affectionate feelings through introjection/projection and the splitting between good and bad internal objects. For a child, the mother consists of "part objects" like the breast or the face. Ultimately, the child learns to engage in "reparation," the restoration of whole objects and good relations that its own destructive impulses sundered during the process of separation, individuation, and growth. While object relations theory has been criticized for at times advancing an overly optimistic picture of "adaptation" of a debatably coherent "self" to an unproblematic "environment," it has also inspired such pathbreaking work as Klaus Theweleit's *Male Fantasies*, a study of pre-Nazi literature that locates the origins of Nazism in a particular psychological formation that perceived women, communists, and Jews as external equivalents of internal boundary-threatening urges that had to be either violently expelled or regimented.

Neo-Freudianism enjoyed great popularity in France in the 1960s and 1970s and continues to be a viable school of literary criticism. In the 1950s and 1960s, Lacan developed a structuralist theory of psychoanalysis based on the linguistic theory of Saussure. Against object relations theory, Lacan argues that the ego is constructed through imaginary percepts and narcissistic fantasies, and it remains blind to its determination by the drives, the unconscious, and its placement and construction in/ by language. Before language assigns us an "I," we possess no sense of self. It is language that gives us identity (while simultaneously taking it away in the sense of something pre-given or internal). The unified self posited by object relations theory is an illusion. The child begins as fragmented drives, percepts, and attachments that eventually congeal into an imaginary identity at the "mirror stage" of development. It is through the child's original symbiotic relationship with the mother that he/she develops a false narcissistic sense of unity. The child assumes the mother is himself, and his primary desire is for her desire (of him). Desire and its realization only appear immediate, however, and what Lacan calls the Real, an impossible wholeness of self, plenitude of desire satisfaction (*jouissance*), and continuity of signifier and signified or word and object, is never possible. The mother is a congeries of part objects (*l'objet petit a*) and partial fulfillments like the breast, and the whole we imaginarily seek and imagine we have when we construct egos for ourselves is merely a way of concealing from ourselves the initial fissure or *béance* that separation from her installs permanently within our being. Indeed, our being is not founded on the mythic identity of the ego; rather it is founded on what Lacan calls our initial lack-of-being (*manque-à-être*), the initial experience of being ripped out of an original imaginary fullness of being and separated from the object – the mother – that provided us with it. More real is our overdetermination by the drives, the unconscious, and the Symbolic Order of our culture, the social languages that identify us and lend us identities, all of which exceed consciousness and never assume the form of knowable or conscious identity (which, for Lacan, is always fantasmatic). Our identity is given to us from outside, and we are constitutively alienated. The imaginary or narcissistic character of all desire merely conceals this basic fault, this radical alterity or otherness, in human existence.

The mirror stage of dyadic symbiosis with the mother must be left behind as the child develops and enters that social world. The shattering of it occurs when the child is confronted with the father's "no," which is to say, with the incest taboo that declares the mother an inappropriate object. The child then learns to accept his/her place in the Symbolic Order, that symbolic language which assigns social roles and dictates proper behavior in society. That order is like a language, since it is defined as relations between terms (mother/father, mother/son, etc.) and by a lexicon that assigns meaning or identity according to the binary opposition of presence or absence (of terms). With the initiation of the Symbolic, the original desire for the mother is repressed, and Lacan compares this to the way the signified is made absent by the signifier, and is always beneath the bar in Saussure's algorithm: S/s. The acceptance of repression and the entry into the Symbolic is itself comparable to language in that once one learns to name something, one accepts separation from it; by naming, one sacrifices the object, since the presence of the sign/word is the absence of the signified thing. The naming of objects separates one from them. The arrival of the Symbolic and the shattering of the Imaginary thus consists of the installation of a combined linguistic/psychological separation of the child both from its initial object, the mother, and from the undifferentiated matter of natural existence. We learn to be social, to have social identities, by learning to say no, to sacrifice or give up both the initial contact one has with the natural world and with one's first human objects. The mother's body is barred, and the desire for it is placed under the bar of the signifier and enters the unconscious. The small "o" other or initial object becomes the large "O" Other of the symbolic unconscious; it acquires meaning as what one cannot have and as that whose absence dictates the form of all subsequent desires, all the signifiers we pursue as hoped-for fillers for an initial unfillable absence. That bar can never be crossed, and all our desires throughout life will consist of attempts to come to terms with this separation, our "lack-of-being." The other side of the bar can enter our consciousness only in the form of substitutes, as metaphors that can indicate it only as/in its absence because the unconscious can never be present to the mind (except through substitute signifiers). Similarly, all desire is inherently metaphoric, inherently a matter of a substitute object that stands in for the initially absent mother object, and because no metaphor can embody what we ultimately desire when we desire anything, we are condemned to slide along a chain of signifiers each of which is a metonymy, a part standing in for the whole we (always) miss. Thus, unlike object relations theory, which assumes a whole self is possible that would be transparent to itself and would be defined by a healthy ego, Lacan thinks that we are constitutively split from ourselves and that we can never possibly attain wholeness in the world of objects. That is a delusion of the ego (and of ego psychology, he would add, somewhat polemically). What we can learn is to accept frustration and to come to acknowledge the lack that defines our being. We exist in a chain of signifiers of desires that never arrive at the Real, the ever absent cause of desire which is the undifferentiatedness of nature, something we can never have access to from within society except through signifiers that distance it (substitute for it) as they name it.

Psychoanalytic literary criticism begins with Freud himself, whose "The Uncanny," in part a reading of Hoffman's horror story "The Sandman," can be said to inaugurate the critical genre. Freud notices that literary texts are like dreams; they embody or express unconscious material in the form of complex displacements and condensations. The same rule that he prescribes for dream interpretation, however, also applies to literature: it is not a direct translation of the unconscious into symbols that "stand for" unconscious meanings. Rather, literature displaces unconscious desires, drives, and motives into imagery that might bear no resemblance to its origin but that nonetheless permits it to achieve release or expression. Literature, as fiction, might even be said to demonstrate these very processes of representation-through-indirection at work. For Freud in "The Uncanny," fear of castration takes the form not of a literal image, but of a metaphoric substitute that displaces the protagonist's anxiety onto a fear of losing his eyes, a fear that is available for interpretation only because language displays the latent connection.

Freud and many later psychoanalytic critics were concerned with what they thought was the primary anxiety of patriarchal culture, the male child's fears as he moves from presexual childhood to sexual adulthood, a trajectory that necessarily crosses the sexual relationship between his mother and his father. All of Nathaniel Hawthorne's fiction, for example, might be read in this light as embodying the Oedipal conflict between a son and a threatening father (as between Reverend Dimmesdale and Chillingsworth in *The Scarlet Letter*). As object relations theory shifts attention toward the pre-Oedipal realm, however, so also does later psychoanalytic criticism focus more on the relational dynamics of psychosexual development and on children's relations to their mothers in patrocentric cultures that assign child-rearing work to women. Klaus Theweleit in *Male Fantasies*, for example, studies the representations of violence against women in literature by German ex-soldiers from World War I who would eventually become major supporters of Nazism and interprets them as expressions of hostility against mothers. The literary works are characterized by images of fear in regard to women perceived as being too powerful, fear that is displaced onto anxieties about having one's self-boundaries overwhelmed by a "red flood" of Bolshevism. Nazism would be the German response to that political threat of communist revolution, an erection of a rigid social order that was the equivalent of the psychological defense these males constructed to guard themselves against personal dissolution, what Theweleit calls "body armor." Theweleit sees the relation to the mother as more determining of these men's psychological identities than that to the father, who tends to be a peripheral figure in the literature. At stake in the literature is not an ego that does battle with a paternal superego or with unconscious urges for pleasure that meet repression; rather the literature depicts a self that never fully formed, never acquired a healthy relation to the world, because of abusive child-rearing practices in German society at the time. It is this that accounts for the enormous representational violence against women who might be construed as similarly maternal and similarly abusive of self-identity.

Lacanian criticism shifts attention to language and sees it and the unconscious as almost identical. Human desire is carried by signifiers which stand in for a lack that can never be filled in. It is in the signifiers then, in language itself, that the unconscious, what of the unconscious one can know, resides. Processes of signification of the kind that are frozen temporarily in works of literature constitute the human subject and determine the shape of its life – whether one neurotically and repetitively pursues the same signifier of a possibly completely fulfilled desire (a particular kind of sexual partner) or whether one renounces such pursuits and accommodates oneself to a more mundane destiny, for example. Such fulfillment is, of course, for Lacan, an impossibility; so literature always enacts the way the chain of signifiers simply eternally displaces an end to signification, the arrival of a real referent that would be the fulfillment of desire and the end of its displacement along a chain.

For example, Hemingway's novel *A Farewell to Arms* hinges on a play on words in the title. About a wounded soldier who has an affair with a nurse who dies in the end while giving birth to their child (itself stillborn), *Arms* is about both bodily "arms" (as in the sexual embrace) and military "arms" (as in the guns that wound Jake, the hero). He wishes to escape from the military into the arms of the maternal Catherine, but he is obliged to say farewell to her arms in the end. The novel maps out the trajectory of development as Lacan describes it: the male child must learn to renounce the imaginary moment of fulfilled desire with the mother in order to accept separation and to enter the Symbolic Order. The bifurcating meanings of "arms" indicate a split in the narrative subject (the narrator shifts from "we" to "I" throughout) that testifies to the split within all human subjectivity between the conscious self and the unconscious that determines that self and between the desiring self and the ultimately impossible fulfillment of that desire (in a return to the mother's arms). The imaginary identity (of self/(m)other) must be given up, and separation (the duality of meaning implied by the fact that one can only have metaphors and not real things or complete fulfillment) accepted.[1]

Note

1   See Ben Stoltzfus, *Lacan and Literature: Purloined Pretexts* (Albany: SUNY Press, 1996), from whom we purloined this reading of the novel.

CHAPTER 2

The Interpretation of Dreams

Sigmund Freud

When it was published in 1900, Freud's *Interpretation of Dreams* launched an entirely new idea and a new discipline of human knowledge. The idea was that the mind harbors wishes or desires that lie outside awareness but that nevertheless manifest themselves at night in dreams. Dreams, when read or interpreted as a rebus or puzzle, instead of being taken literally, turn out to be translations into semi-conscious form of unconscious material. Such material is generally in the unconscious because it has been repressed, or driven from consciousness by a mental censor that judges what is fit for expression. Things unfit for expression (at the time of Freud's work) were ideas or desires having to do, for example, with sexuality. But not all dreams were of a sexual character. In the central dream analyzed in this selection, Freud, for example, has a dream that expresses an egotistical wish that his work be properly recognized.

The Dream of the Botanical Monograph

I had written a monograph on a certain plant. The book lay before me and I was at the moment turning over a folded colored plate. Bound up in each copy there was a dried specimen of the plant, as though it had been taken from a herbarium.

Analysis

That morning I had seen a new book in the window of a book-shop, bearing the title *The Genus Cyclamen* – evidently a *monograph* on that plant.

Cyclamens, I reflected, were my *wife's favorite flowers* and I reproached myself for so rarely remembering to *bring her flowers*, which was what *she* liked. – The subject of "*bringing flowers*" recalled an anecdote which I had recently repeated to a circle of friends and which I had used as evidence in favor of my theory that forgetting is very often determined by an unconscious purpose and that it always enables one to deduce the secret intentions of the person who forgets. A young woman was accustomed to receiving a bouquet of flowers from her husband on her birthday. One year this token of his affection failed to appear, and she burst into tears. Her husband came in and had no idea why she was crying till she told him that to-day was her birthday. He clasped his hand to his head and exclaimed: "I'm so sorry, but I'd quite forgotten. I'll go out at once and fetch *your flowers*." But she was not to be consoled; for she recognized that her husband's forgetfulness was a proof that she no longer had the same place in his thoughts as she had formerly. – This lady, Frau L., had met my wife two days before I had the dream, had told her that she was feeling quite well and enquired after me. Some years ago she had come to me for treatment.

I now made a fresh start. Once, I recalled, I really *had* written something in the nature of a *monograph on a plant*, namely a dissertation on the *coca-plant*, which had drawn Karl Koller's attention to the anaesthetic properties of cocaine. I had myself indicated this application of the alkaloid in my published paper, but I had not been thorough enough to pursue the matter further. This reminded me that on the morning of the day after the dream – I had not found time to interpret it till the evening – I had thought about cocaine in a kind of daydream. If ever I got glaucoma, I had thought, I should travel to Berlin and get myself operated on, incognito, in my friend's [Fliess's] house, by a surgeon recommended by him. The operating surgeon, who would have no idea of my identity, would boast once again of how easily such operations could be performed since the introduction of cocaine; and I should not give the slightest hint that I myself had had a share in the discovery. This phantasy had led on to reflections of how awkward it is, when all is said and done, for a physician to ask for medical treatment for himself from his professional colleagues. The Berlin eye-surgeon would not know me, and I should be able to pay his fees like anyone else. It was not until I had recalled this daydream that I realized that the recollection of a specific event lay behind it. Shortly after Koller's discovery, my father had in fact been attacked by glaucoma; my friend Dr Königstein, the ophthalmic surgeon, had operated on him; while Dr Koller had been in charge of the cocaine anaesthesia and had commented on the fact that this case had brought together all of the three men who had had a share in the introduction of cocaine.

My thoughts then went on to the occasion when I had last been reminded of this business of the cocaine. It had been a few days earlier, when I had been looking at a copy of a *Festschrift* in which grateful pupils had celebrated the jubilee of their teacher and laboratory director. Among the laboratory's claims to distinction which were enumerated in this book I had seen a mention of the fact that Koller had made his discovery there of the anaesthetic properties of cocaine. I then suddenly perceived that my dream was connected with an event of the previous evening. I had walked home precisely with Dr Königstein and had got into conversation with him about a matter which never fails to excite my feelings whenever it is raised. While I was talking to him in the entrance-hall, Professor *Gärtner* [Gardener] and his wife had joined us; and I could not help congratulating them both on their *blooming* looks. But Professor Gärtner was one of the authors of the *Festschrift* I have just mentioned, and may well have reminded me of it. Moreover, the Frau L., whose disappointment on her birthday I described earlier, was mentioned – though only, it is true, in another connection – in my conversation with Dr Königstein.

I will make an attempt at interpreting the other determinants of the content of the dream as well. There was *a dried specimen of the plant* included in the monograph, as though it had been a *herbarium*. This led me to a memory from my secondary school. Our headmaster once called together the boys from the higher forms and handed over the school's herbarium to them to be looked through and cleaned. Some small worms – book-worms – had found their way into it. He does not seem to have had much confidence in my helpfulness, for he handed me only a few sheets. These, as I could still recall, included some Crucifers. I never had a specially intimate contact with botany. In my preliminary examination in botany I was also given a Crucifer to identify – and failed to do so. My prospects would not have been too bright, if I had not been helped out by my theoretical knowledge. I went on from the Cruciferae to the Compositae. It occurred to me that artichokes were Compositae, and indeed I might fairly have called them *my favorite flowers*. Being more generous than I am, my wife often brought me back these favorite flowers of mine from the market.

I saw the monograph which I had written *lying before me*. This again led me back to something. I had had a letter from my friend [Fliess] in Berlin the day before in which he had shown his power of visualization; "I am very much occupied with your dream-book. *I see it lying finished before me and I see myself turning over its pages*." How much I envied him his gift as a seer! If only I could have seen it lying finished before me!

The folded colored plate. While I was a medical student I was the constant victim of an impulse only to learn things out of *monographs*. In spite of my limited means, I succeeded in getting hold of a number of volumes of the proceedings of medical societies and was enthralled by their *colored plates*. I was proud of my hankering for thoroughness. When I myself had begun to publish papers, I had been obliged to make my own drawings to illustrate them and I remembered that one of them had been so wretched that a friendly colleague had jeered at me over it. There followed, I could not quite make out how, a recollection from very early youth. It had once amused my father to hand over a book with *colored plates* (an account of a journey through Persia) for me and my eldest sister to destroy. Not easy to justify from the educational point of view! I had been five years old at the time and my sister not yet three; and the picture of the two of us blissfully pulling the book to pieces (leaf by leaf, like an *artichoke*, I found myself saying) was almost the only plastic memory that I retained from that period of my life. Then, when I became a student, I had developed a passion for collecting and owning books, which was analogous to my liking for learning out of monographs: *a favorite hobby*. (The idea of "*favorite*" had already appeared in connection with cyclamens and artichokes.) I had become a *book-worm*. I had always, from the time I first began to think about myself, referred this first passion of mine back to the childhood memory I have mentioned. Or rather, I had recognized that the childhood scene was a "screen memory" for my later bibliophile propensities.

And I had early discovered, of course, that passions often lead to sorrow. When I was seventeen I had run up a largish account at the bookseller's and had nothing to meet it with; and my father had scarcely taken it as an excuse that my inclinations might have chosen a worse outlet. The recollection of this experience from the later years of my youth at once brought back to my mind the conversation with my friend Dr Königstein. For in the course of it we had discussed the same question of my being blamed for being too much absorbed in my *favorite hobbies*.

For reasons with which we are not concerned, I shall not pursue the interpretation of this dream any further, but will merely indicate the direction in which it lay. In the course of the work of analysis I was reminded of my conversation with Dr Königstein, and I was brought to it from more than one direction. When I take into account the topics touched upon in that conversation, the meaning of the dream becomes intelligible to me. All the trains of thought starting from the dream – the thoughts about my wife's and my own favorite flowers, about cocaine, about the awkwardness of medical treatment among colleagues, about my preference for study-ing monographs and about my neglect of certain branches of science such as botany – all of these trains of thought, when they were further pursued, led ultimately to one or other of the many ramifications of my conversation with Dr Königstein. Once again the dream, like the one we first analyzed – the dream of Irma's injection – turns out to have been in the nature of a self-justification, a plea on behalf of my own rights. Indeed, it carried the subject that was raised in the earlier dream a stage further and discussed it with reference to fresh material that had arisen in the interval between the two dreams. Even the apparently indifferent form in which the dream was couched turns out to have had significance. What it meant was: "After all, I'm the man who wrote the valuable and memorable paper (on cocaine)," just as in the earlier dream I had said on my behalf: "I'm a conscientious and hard-working student." In both cases what I was insisting was: "I may allow myself to do this." . . .

The Dream-work

Every attempt that has hitherto been made to solve the problem of dreams has dealt directly with their *manifest* content as it is presented in our memory. All such attempts have endeavored to arrive at an interpretation of dreams from their manifest content or (if no interpretation was attempted) to form a judgement as to their nature on the basis of that same manifest content. We are alone in taking something else into account. We have introduced a new class of psychical material between the manifest content of dreams and the conclusions of our enquiry: namely, their *latent* content, or (as we say) the "dream-thoughts," arrived at by means of our procedure. It is from these dream-thoughts and not from a dream's manifest content that we disentangle its meaning. We are thus presented with a new task which had no previous existence: the task, that is, of investigating the relations between the manifest content of dreams and the latent dream-thoughts, and of tracing out the processes by which the latter have been changed into the former.

The dream-thoughts and the dream-content are presented to us like two versions of the same subject-matter in two different languages. Or, more properly, the dream-content seems like a transcript of the dream-thoughts into another mode of expression, whose characters and syntactic laws it is our business to discover by comparing the original and the translation. The dream-thoughts are immediately comprehensible, as soon as we have learnt them. The dream-content, on the other hand, is expressed as it were in a pictographic script, the characters of which have to be transposed individually into the language of the dream-thoughts. If we attempted to read these characters according to their pictorial value instead of according to their symbolic relation, we should clearly be led into error. Suppose I have a picture-puzzle, a rebus, in front of me. It depicts a house with a boat on its roof, a single letter of the alphabet, the figure of a running man whose head has been conjured away, and so on. Now I might be misled into raising objections and declaring that the picture as a whole and its component parts are nonsensical. A boat has no business to be on the roof of a house, and a headless man cannot run. Moreover, the man is bigger than the house; and if the whole picture is intended to represent a landscape, letters of the alphabet are out of place in it since such objects do not occur in nature. But obviously we can only form a proper judgement of the rebus if we put aside criticisms such as these of the whole composition and its parts and if, instead, we try to replace each separate element by a syllable or word that can be represented by that element in some way or other. The words which are put together in this way are no longer nonsensical but may form a poetical phrase of the greatest beauty and significance. A dream is a picture-puzzle of this sort and our predecessors in the field of dream-interpretation have made the mistake of treating the rebus as a pictorial composition: and as such it has seemed to them nonsensical and worthless.

The work of condensation

The first thing that becomes clear to anyone who compares the dream-content with the dream-thoughts is that a work of *condensation* on a large scale has been carried out. Dreams are brief, meagre and laconic in comparison with the range and wealth of the dream-thoughts. If a dream is written out it may perhaps fill half a page. The analysis setting out the dream-thoughts underlying it may occupy six, eight or a dozen times as much space. This relation varies with different dreams; but so far as my experience goes its direction never varies. As a rule one underestimates the amount of compression that has taken place, since one is inclined to regard the dream-thoughts that have been brought to light as the complete material, whereas if the work of interpretation is carried further it may reveal still more thoughts concealed behind the dream. I have already had occasion to point out that it is in fact never possible to be sure that a dream has been completely interpreted. Even if the solution seems satisfactory and without gaps, the possibility always remains that the dream may have yet another meaning. Strictly speaking, then, it is impossible to determine the amount of condensation.

There is an answer, which at first sight seems most plausible, to the argument that the great lack of proportion between the dream-content and the dream-thoughts implies that the psychical material has undergone an extensive process of condensation in the course of the formation of the dream. We very often have an impression that we have dreamt a great deal all through the night and have since forgotten most of what we dreamt. On this view, the dream which we remember when we wake up would only be a fragmentary remnant of the total dream-work; and this, if we could recollect it in its entirety, might well be as extensive as the dream-thoughts. There is undoubtedly some truth in this: there can be no question that dreams can be reproduced most accurately if we try to recall them as soon as we wake up and that our memory of them becomes more and more incomplete towards evening. But on the other hand it can be shown that the impression that we have dreamt a great deal more than we can reproduce is very often based on an illusion, the origin of which I shall discuss later. Moreover the hypothesis that condensation occurs during the dream-work is not affected by the possibility of dreams being forgotten, since this hypothesis is proved to be correct by the quantities of ideas which are related to each individual piece of the dream which has been retained. Even supposing that a large piece of the dream has escaped recollection, this may merely have prevented our having access to another group of dream-thoughts. There is no justification for supposing that the lost pieces of the dream would have related to the same thoughts which we have already reached from the pieces of the dream that have survived.[1]

In view of the very great number of associations produced in analysis to each individual element of the content of a dream, some readers may be led to doubt whether, as a matter of principle, we are justified in regarding as part of the dream-thoughts all the associations that occur to us during the subsequent analysis – whether we are justified, that is, in supposing that all these thoughts were already active during the state of sleep and played a part in the formation of the dream. Is it not more probable that new trains of thought have arisen in the course of the analysis which had no share in forming the dream? I can only give limited assent to this argument. It is no doubt true that some trains of thought arise for the first time during the analysis. But one can convince oneself in all such cases that these new connections are only set up between thoughts which were already linked in some other way in the dream-thoughts. The new connections are, as it were, loop-lines or short-circuits, made possible by the existence of other and deeper-lying connecting paths. It must be allowed that the great bulk of the thoughts which are revealed in analysis were already active during the process of forming the dream; for, after working through a string of thoughts which seem to have no connection with the formation of a dream, one suddenly comes upon one which is represented in its content and is indispensable for its interpretation, but which could not have been reached except by this particular line of approach. I may here recall the dream of the botanical monograph, which strikes one as the product of an astonishing amount of condensation, even though I have not reported its analysis in full.

How, then, are we to picture psychical conditions during the period of sleep which precedes dreams? Are all the dream-thoughts present alongside one another? or do they occur in sequence? or do a number of trains of thought start out simultaneously from different centers and afterwards unite? There is no need for the present, in my opinion, to form any plastic idea of psychical conditions during the formation of dreams. It must not be forgotten, however, that we are dealing with an *unconscious* process of thought, which may easily be different from what we perceive during purposive reflection accompanied by consciousness.

The unquestionable fact remains, however, that the formation of dreams is based on a process of condensation. How is that condensation brought about?

When we reflect that only a small minority of all the dream-thoughts revealed are represented in the dream by one of their ideational elements, we might conclude that condensation is brought about by *omission*: that is, that the dream is not a faithful translation or a point-for-point projection of the dream-thoughts, but a highly in-complete and fragmentary version of them. This view, as we shall soon discover, is a most inadequate one. But we may take it as a provisional starting-point and go on to a further question. If only a few elements from the dream-thoughts find their way into the dream-content, what are the conditions which determine their selection?

In order to get some light on this question we must turn our attention to those elements of the dream-content which must have fulfilled these conditions. And the most favorable material for such an investigation will be a dream to the construction of which a particularly intense process of condensation has contributed. I shall accord-ingly begin by choosing for the purpose the dream which I have already recorded.

The dream of the botanical monograph

Content of the Dream. – *I had written a monograph on an (unspecified) genus of plants. The book lay before me and I was at the moment turning over a folded colored plate. Bound up in the copy there was a dried specimen of the plant.*

The element in this dream which stood out most was the *botanical monograph*. This arose from the impressions of the dream-day: I had in fact seen a monograph on the genus Cyclamen in the window of a book-shop. There was no mention of this genus in the content of the dream; all that was left in it was the monograph and its relation to botany. The "botanical monograph" immediately revealed its connection with the *work upon cocaine* which I had once written. From "cocaine" the chains of thought led on the one hand to the *Festschrift* and to certain events in a University laboratory, and on the other hand to my friend Dr Königstein, the eye-surgeon, who had had a share in the introduction of cocaine. The figure of Dr Königstein further reminded me of the interrupted conversation which I had had with him the evening before and of my various reflections upon the payment for medical services among colleagues. This conversation was the actual currently active instigator of the dream; the monograph on the cyclamen was also a currently active impression, but one of an indifferent nature. As I perceived, the "botanical monograph" in the dream turned out to be an "intermediate common entity" between the two experiences of the previous day: it was taken over unaltered from the indifferent impression and was linked with the psychically significant event by copious associative connections.

Not only the compound idea, "botanical monograph," however, but each of its components, "botanical" and "monograph" separately, led by numerous connecting paths deeper and deeper into the tangle of dream-thoughts. "Botanical" was related to the figure of Professor *Gärtner* [Gardener], the *blooming* looks of his wife, to my patient *Flora* and to the lady [Frau L.] of whom I had told the story of the forgotten flowers. Gärtner led in turn to the laboratory and to my conversation with Königstein. My two patients [Flora and Frau L.] had been mentioned in the course of this conversation. A train of thought joined the lady with the flowers to my wife's *favorite flowers* and thence to the title of the monograph which I had seen for a moment during the day. In addition to these, "botanical" recalled an episode at my secondary school and an examination while I was at the University. A fresh topic touched upon in my conversation with Dr Königstein – my favorite hobbies – was joined, through the intermediate link of what I jokingly called *my favorite flower*, the artichoke, with the train of thought proceeding from the forgotten flowers. Behind "artichokes" lay, on the one hand, my thoughts about Italy and, on the other hand, a scene from my childhood which was the opening of what have since become my intimate relations with books. Thus "botanical" was a regular nodal point in the dream. Numerous trains of thought converged upon it, which, as I can guarantee, had appropriately entered into the context of the conversation with Dr Königstein. Here we find ourselves in a factory of thoughts where, as in the "weaver's masterpiece," –

> Ein Tritt tausend Fäden regt,
> Die Schifflein herüber hinüber schiessen,
> Die Fäden ungesehen fliessen,
> Ein Schlag tausend Verbindungen schlägt.[2]

So, too, "monograph" in the dream touches upon two subjects: the one-sidedness of my studies and the costliness of my favorite hobbies.

This first investigation leads us to conclude that the elements "botanical" and "monograph" found their way into the content of the dream because they possessed copious contacts with the majority of the dream-thoughts, because, that is to say, they constituted "nodal points" upon which a great number of the dream-thoughts converged, and because they had several meanings in connection with the interpretation of the dream. The explanation of this fundamental fact can also be put in another way:

each of the elements of the dream's content turns out to have been "overdetermined" – to have been represented in the dream-thoughts many times over.

We discover still more when we come to examine the remaining constituents of the dream in relation to their appearance in the dream-thoughts. The *colored plate* which I was unfolding led to a new topic, my colleagues' criticisms of my activities, and to one which was already represented in the dream, my favorite hobbies; and it led, in addition, to the childhood memory in which I was pulling to pieces a book with colored plates. The *dried specimen of the plant* touched upon the episode of the herbarium at my secondary school and specially stressed that memory.

The nature of the relation between dream-content and dream-thoughts thus becomes visible. Not only are the elements of a dream determined by the dream-thoughts many times over, but the individual dream-thoughts are represented in the dream by several elements. Associative paths lead from one element of the dream to several dream-thoughts, and from one dream-thought to several elements of the dream. Thus a dream is not constructed by each individual dream-thought, or group of dream-thoughts, finding (in abbreviated form) separate representation in the content of the dream – in the kind of way in which an electorate chooses parliamentary representatives; a dream is constructed, rather, by the whole mass of dream-thoughts being submitted to a sort of manipulative process in which those elements which have the most numerous and strongest supports acquire the right of entry into the dream-content – in a manner analogous to election by *scrutin de liste*. In the case of every dream which I have submitted to an analysis of this kind I have invariably found these same fundamental principles confirmed: the elements of the dream are constructed out of the whole mass of dream-thoughts and each one of those elements is shown to have been determined many times over in relation to the dream-thoughts.

It will certainly not be out of place to illustrate the connection between dream-content and dream-thoughts by a further example, which is distinguished by the specially ingenious interweaving of their reciprocal relations. It is a dream produced by one of my patients – a man whom I was treating for claustrophobia. It will soon become clear why I have chosen to give this exceptionally clever dream-production the title of

A lovely dream

He was driving with a large party to X Street, in which there was an unpretentious inn. (This is not the case.) *There was a play being acted inside it. At one moment he was audience, at another actor. When it was over they had to change their clothes so as to get back to town. Some of the company were shown into rooms on the ground floor and others into rooms on the first floor. Then a dispute broke out. The ones up above were angry because the ones down below were not ready, and they could not come downstairs. His brother was up above and he was down below and he was angry with his brother because they were so much pressed.* (This part was obscure.) *Moreover, it had been decided and arranged even when they first arrived who was to be up above and who was to be down below. Then he was walking by himself up the rise made by X Street in the direction of town. He walked with such difficulty and so laboriously that he seemed glued to the spot. An elderly gentleman came up to him and began abusing the King of Italy. At the top of the rise he was able to walk much more easily.*

His difficulty in walking up the rise was so distinct that after waking up he was for some time in doubt whether it was a dream or reality.

We should not think very highly of this dream, judging by its manifest content. In defiance of the rules, I shall begin its interpretation with the portion which the dreamer described as being the most distinct.

The difficulty which he dreamt of and probably actually experienced during the dream – the laborious climbing up the rise accompanied by dyspnoea – was one of the symptoms which the patient had in fact exhibited years before and which had at that time been attributed, along with certain other symptoms, to tuberculosis. (The probability is that this was hysterically simulated.) The peculiar sensation of inhibited movement that occurs in this dream is already familiar to us from dreams of exhibiting and we see once more that it is material available at any time for any other representational purpose. The piece of the dream-content which described how the climb began by being difficult and became easy at the end of the rise reminded me, when I heard it, of the masterly introduction to Alphonse Daudet's *Sappho*. That well-known passage describes how a young man carries his mistress upstairs in his arms; at first she is as light as a feather, but the higher he climbs the heavier grows her weight. The whole scene foreshadows the course of their love-affair, which was intended by Daudet as a warning to young men not to allow their affections to be seriously engaged by girls of humble origin and a dubious past.[3] Though I knew that my patient had been involved in a love-affair which he had recently broken off with a lady on the stage, I did not expect to find my guess at an interpretation justified. Moreover the situation in *Sappho* was the *reverse* of what it had been in the dream. In the dream the climbing had been difficult to begin with and had afterwards become easy; whereas the symbolism in the novel only made sense if something that had been begun lightly ended by becoming a heavy burden. But to my astonishment my patient replied that my interpretation fitted in very well with a piece he had seen at the theater the evening before. It was called *Rund um Wien* [*Round Vienna*] and gave a picture of the career of a girl who began by being respectable, who then became a *demi-mondaine* and had *liaisons* with men in high positions and so "*went up in the world*," but who ended by "*coming down in the world*." The piece had moreover reminded him of another, which he had seen some years earlier, called *Von Stufe zu Stufe* [*Step by Step*], and which had been advertised by a poster showing a staircase with a flight of *steps*.

To continue with the interpretation. The actress with whom he had had this latest, eventful *liaison* had lived in X Street. There is nothing in the nature of an inn in that street. But when he was spending part of the summer in Vienna on the lady's account he had put up [German "*abgestiegen*," literally "*stepped down*"] at a small hotel in the neighborhood. When he left the hotel he had said to his cab-driver: "Anyhow I'm lucky not to have picked up any vermin." (This, incidentally, was another of his phobias.) To this the driver had replied: "How could anyone put up at such a place! It's not a hotel, it's only an *inn*."

The idea of an inn at once recalled a quotation to his mind:

> Bei einem *Wirte* wundermild,
> Da war ich jüngst zu Gaste.[4]

The host in Uhland's poem was an *apple-tree*; and a second quotation now carried on his train of thought:

FAUST (*mit der Jüngen tanzend*):
Einst hatt' ich *einen schönen Traum*;
Da sah ich einen *Apfelbaum*,
Zwei schöne Äpfel glanzten dran,
Sie reizten mich, *ich stieg hinan*.

DIE SCHÖNE:
Der Äpfelchen begehrt ihr sehr,
Und schon vom Paradiese her.
Von Freuden fühl' ich mich bewegt,
Dass auch mein Garten solche trägt.[5]

There cannot be the faintest doubt what the apple-tree and the apples stood for. Moreover, lovely breasts had been among the charms which had attracted the dreamer to his actress.

The context of the analysis gave us every ground for supposing that the dream went back to an impression in childhood. If so, it must have referred to the wet-nurse of the dreamer, who was by then a man almost thirty years old. For an infant the breasts of his wet-nurse are nothing more nor less than an inn. The wet-nurse, as well as Daudet's Sappho, seem to have been allusions to the mistress whom the patient had recently dropped.

The patient's (elder) brother also appeared in the content of the dream, the brother being up *above* and the patient himself *down below*. This was once again the *reverse* of the actual situation; for, as I knew, the brother had lost his social position while the patient had maintained his. In repeating the content of the dream to me, the dreamer had avoided saying that his brother was up above and he himself "on the ground floor." That would have put the position too clearly, since here in Vienna if we say someone is "*on the ground floor*" we mean that he has lost his money and his position – in other words, that he has "*come down in the world.*" Now there must have been a reason for some of this part of the dream being represented by its *reverse*. Further, the reversal must hold good of some other relation between dream-thoughts and dream-content as well; and we have a hint of where to look for this reversal. It must evidently be at the end of the dream, where once again there was a *reversal* of the difficulty in going upstairs as described in *Sappho*. We can then easily see what reversal is intended. In *Sappho* the man carried a woman who was in a sexual relation to him; in the dream-thoughts the position was *reversed*, and a woman was carrying a man. And since this can only happen in childhood, the reference was once more to the wet-nurse bearing the weight of the infant in her arms. Thus the end of the dream made a simultaneous reference to *Sappho* and to the wet-nurse.

Just as the author of the novel, in choosing the name "Sappho," had in mind an allusion to Lesbian practices, so too the pieces of the dream that spoke of people "*up above*" and "*down below*" alluded to phantasies of a sexual nature which occupied the patient's mind and, as suppressed desires, were not without a bearing on his neurosis. (The interpretation of the dream did not itself show us that what were thus represented in the dream were phantasies and not recollections of real events; an analysis only gives us the *content* of a thought and leaves it to us to determine its reality. Real and imaginary events appear in dreams at first sight as of equal validity; and that is so not only in dreams but in the production of more important psychical structures.)

A "large party" meant, as we already know, a secret. His brother was simply the representative (introduced into the childhood scene by a "retrospective phantasy") of all his later rivals for a woman's affection. The episode of the gentleman who abused the King of Italy related once again, via the medium of a recent and in itself indifferent experience, to people of lower rank pushing their way into higher society. It was just as though the child at the breast was being given a warning parallel to the one which Daudet had given to young men.[6]

To provide a third opportunity for studying condensation in the formation of dreams, I will give part of the analysis of another dream, which I owe to an elderly lady undergoing psycho-analytic treatment. As was to be expected from the severe anxiety-states from which the patient suffered, her dreams contained a very large number of sexual thoughts, the first realization of which both surprised and alarmed her. Since I shall not be able to pursue the interpretation of the dream to the end, its material will appear to fall into several groups without any visible connection.

The May-beetle[7] dream

Content of the Dream. – *She called to mind that she had two may-beetles in a box and that she must set them free or they would suffocate. She opened the box and the may-beetles were in an exhausted state. One of them flew out of the open window; but the other was crushed by the casement while she was shutting it at someone's request. (Signs of disgust.)*

Analysis. – Her husband was temporarily away from home, and her fourteen-year-old daughter was sleeping in the bed beside her. The evening before, the girl had drawn her attention to a moth which had fallen into her tumbler of water; but she had not taken it out and felt sorry for the poor creature next morning. The book she had been reading during the evening had told how some boys had thrown a cat into boiling water, and had described the animal's convulsions. These were the two precipitating causes of the dream – in themselves indifferent.

She then pursued the subject of *cruelty to animals* further. Some years before, while they were spending the summer at a particular place, her daughter had been very cruel to animals. She was collecting butterflies and asked the patient for some *arsenic* to kill them with. On one occasion a moth with a pin through its body had gone on flying about the room for a long time; another time some caterpillars which the child was keeping to turn into chrysalises starved to death. At a still more tender age the same child used to tear the wings off *beetles* and butterflies. But to-day she would be horrified at all these cruel actions – she had grown so kind-hearted.

The patient reflected over this contradiction. It reminded her of another contradiction, between appearance and character, as George Eliot displays it in *Adam Bede*: one girl who was pretty, but vain and stupid, and another who was ugly, but of high character; a nobleman who seduced the silly girl, and a working man who felt and acted with true nobility. How impossible it was, she remarked, to recognize that sort of thing in people! Who would have guessed, to look at *her*, that she was tormented by sensual desires?

In the same year in which the little girl had begun collecting butterflies, the district they were in had suffered from a serious plague of *may-beetles*. The children were furious with the beetles and *crushed* them unmercifully. At that time my patient had seen a man who tore the wings off may-beetles and then ate their bodies. She herself had been born in *May* and had been married in *May*. Three days after her marriage she had written to her parents at home saying how happy she was. But it had been far from true.

The evening before the dream she had been rummaging among some old letters and had read some of them – some serious and some comic – aloud to her children. There had been a most amusing letter from a piano-teacher who had courted her when she was a girl, and another from an admirer *of noble birth*.[8]

She blamed herself because one of her daughters had got hold of a "bad" book by Maupassant.[9] The *arsenic* that the girl had asked for reminded her of the *arsenic pills* which restored the Duc de Mora's youthful strength in [Daudet's] *Le Nabab*.

"Set them free" made her think of a passage in the *Magic Flute*:

> Zur Liebe kann ich dich nicht zwingen,
> Doch geb ich dir *die Freiheit* nicht.[10]

"May-beetles" also made her think of Kätchen's words:

> Verliebt ja wie ein *Käfer* bist du mir.[11]

And in the middle of all this came a quotation from *Tannhäuser*:

> Weil du von *böser Lust* beseelt . . .[12]

She was living in a perpetual worry about her absent husband. Her fear that something might happen to him on his journey was expressed in numerous waking phantasies. A short time before, in the course of her analysis, she had lighted among her unconscious thoughts upon a complaint about her husband "growing senile." The wishful thought concealed by her present dream will perhaps best be conjectured if I mention that, some days before she dreamt it, she was horrified, in the middle of her daily affairs, by a phrase in the imperative mood which came into her head and was aimed at her husband: "Go and hang yourself!" It turned out that a few hours earlier she had read somewhere or other that when a man is hanged he gets a powerful erection. The wish for an erection was what had emerged from repression in this horrifying disguise. "Go and hang yourself!" was equivalent to: "Get yourself an erection at any price!" Dr Jenkins's arsenic pills in *Le Nabab* fitted in here. But my patient was also aware that the most powerful aphrodisiac, cantharides (commonly known as "Spanish flies"), was prepared from *crushed beetles*. This was the drift of the principal part of the dream's content.

The opening and shutting of *windows* was one of the main subjects of dispute between her and her husband. She herself was aerophilic in her sleeping habits; her husband was aerophobic. *Exhaustion* was the chief symptom which she complained of at the time of the dream. . . .

The work of condensation in dreams is seen at its clearest when it handles words and names. It is true in general that words are treated in dreams as though they were concrete things, and for that reason they are apt to be combined in just the same way as presentations of concrete things. Dreams of this sort offer the most amusing and curious neologisms.

On one occasion a medical colleague had sent me a paper he had written, in which the importance of a recent physiological discovery was, in my opinion, overestimated, and in which, above all, the subject was treated in too emotional a manner. The next night I dreamt a sentence which clearly referred to this paper: "*It's written in a positively norekdal style.*" The analysis of the word caused me some difficulty at first. There could be no doubt that it was a parody of the [German] superlatives "*kolossal*" and "*pyramidal*"; but its origin was not so easy to guess. At last I saw that the monstrosity was composed of the two names "Nora" and "Ekdal" – characters in two well-known plays of Ibsen's. [*A Doll's House* and *The Wild Duck*.] Some time before, I had read a newspaper article on Ibsen by the same author whose latest work I was criticizing in the dream. . . .

VI

Early this morning, between dreaming and waking, I experienced a very nice example of verbal condensation. In the course of a mass of dream-fragments that I could scarcely remember, I was brought up short, as it were, by a word which I saw before me as though it were half written and half printed. The word was "*erzefilisch*," and it formed part of a sentence which slipped into my conscious memory apart from any context and in complete isolation: "That has an *erzefilisch* influence on the sexual emotions." I knew at once that the word ought really to have been "*erzieherisch*" ["educational"]. And I was in doubt for some time whether the second "*e*" in "*erzefilisch*" should not have been an "*i*."[13] In that connection the word "syphilis" occurred to me and, starting to analyze the dream while I was still half asleep, I racked my brains in an effort to make out how that word could have got into my dream, since I had nothing to do with the disease either personally or professionally. I then thought of "*erzehlerisch*" [another nonsense word], and this explained the "*e*" of the second syllable of "*erzefilisch*" by reminding me that the evening before I had been asked by our governess [*Erzieherin*] to say something to her on the problem of prostitution, and had given her Hesse's book on prostitution in order to influence her emotional life – for this had not developed quite normally; after which I had talked [*erzählt*] a lot to her on the problem. I then saw all at once that the word "syphilis" was not to be taken literally, but stood for "poison" – of course in relation to sexual life. When translated, therefore, the sentence in the dream ran quite logically: "My talk [*Erzählung*] was intended to have an educational [*erzieherisch*] influence on the emotional life of our governess [*Erzieherin*]; but I fear it may at the same time have had a poisonous effect." "*Erzefilisch*" was compounded from "*erzäh-*" and "*erzieh-*."

The verbal malformations in dreams greatly resemble those which are familiar in paranoia but which are also present in hysteria and obsessions. The linguistic tricks performed by children, who sometimes actually treat words as though they were objects and moreover invent new languages and artificial syntactic forms, are the common source of these things in dreams and psycho-neuroses alike.

The analysis of the nonsensical verbal forms that occur in dreams is particularly well calculated to exhibit the dream-work's achievements in the way of condensation. The reader should not conclude from the paucity of the instances which I have given that material of this kind is rare or observed at all exceptionally. On the contrary, it is very common. But as a result of the fact that dream-interpretation is dependent upon psycho-analytic treatment, only a very small number of instances are observed and recorded and the analyses of such instances are as a rule only intelligible to experts in the pathology of the neuroses. Thus a dream of this kind was reported by Dr von Karpinska (1914) containing the nonsensical verbal form: "*Svingnum elvi.*" It is also worth mentioning those cases in which a word appears in a dream which is not in itself meaningless but which has lost its proper meaning and combines a number of other meanings to which it is related in just the same way as a "meaningless" word would be. This is what occurred, for instance, in the ten-year-old boy's dream of a "category" which was recorded by Tausk (1913). "Category" in that case meant "female genitals" and to "categorate" meant the same as "to micturate."

Where spoken sentences occur in dreams and are expressly distinguished as such from thoughts, it is an invariable rule that the words spoken in the dream are derived from spoken words remembered in the dream-material. The text of the speech is either retained unaltered or expressed with some slight displacement. A speech in a dream is often put together from various recollected speeches, the text remaining the same but being given, if possible, several meanings, or one different from the original one. A spoken remark in a dream is not infrequently no more than an allusion to an occasion on which the remark in question was made.[14]

The work of displacement

In making our collection of instances of condensation in dreams, the existence of another relation, probably of no less importance, had already become evident. It could be seen that the elements which stand out as the principal components of the manifest content of the dream are far from playing the same part in the dream-thoughts. And, as a corollary, the converse of this assertion can be affirmed: what is clearly the essence of the dream-thoughts need not be represented in the dream at all. The dream is, as it were, differently centered from the dream-thoughts – its content has different elements as its central point. Thus in the dream of the botanical monograph, for instance, the central point of the dream-content was obviously the element "botanical"; whereas the dream-thoughts were concerned with the complications and conflicts arising between colleagues from their professional obligations, and further with the charge that I was in the habit of sacrificing too much for the sake of my hobbies. The element "botanical" had no place whatever in this core of the dream-thoughts, unless it was loosely connected with it by an antithesis – the fact that botany never had a place among my favorite studies. In my patient's *Sappho* dream the central position was occupied by climbing up and down and being up above and down below; the dream-thoughts, however, dealt with the dangers of sexual relations with people of an inferior social class. So that only a single element of the dream-thoughts seems to have found its way into the dream-content, though that element was expanded to a disproportionate extent. Similarly, in the dream of the may-beetles, the topic of which was the relations of sexuality to cruelty, it is true that the factor of cruelty emerged in the dream-content; but it did so in another connection and without any mention of sexuality, that is to say, divorced from its context and consequently transformed into something extraneous. Once again, in my dream about my uncle, the fair beard which formed its center-point seems to have had no connection in its meaning with my ambitious wishes which, as we saw, were the core of the dream-thoughts. Dreams such as these give a justifiable impression of "displacement." In complete contrast to these examples, we can see that in the dream of Irma's injection the different elements were able to retain, during the process of constructing the dream, the approximate place which they occupied in the dream-thoughts. This further relation between the dream-thoughts and the dream-content, wholly variable as it is in its sense or direction, is calculated at first to create astonishment. If we are considering a psychical process in normal life and find that one out of its several component ideas has been picked out and has acquired a special degree of vividness in consciousness, we usually regard this effect as evidence that a specially high amount of psychical value – some particular degree of interest – attaches to this predominant idea. But we now discover that, in the case of the different elements of the dream-thoughts, a value of this kind does not persist or is disregarded in the process of dream-formation. There is never any doubt as to which of the elements of the dream-thoughts have the highest psychical value; we learn that by direct judgement. In the course of the formation of a dream these essential elements, charged, as they are, with intense interest, may be treated as though they were of small value, and their place may be taken in the dream by other elements, of whose small value in the dream-thoughts there can be no question. At first sight it looks as though no attention whatever is paid to the psychical intensity[15] of the various ideas in making the choice among them for the dream, and as though the only thing considered is the greater or less degree of multiplicity of their determination. What appears in dreams, we might suppose, is not what is *important* in the dream-thoughts but what occurs in them several times over. But this hypothesis does not greatly assist our understanding of dream-formation, since from the nature of things it seems clear that the two factors of multiple determination and inherent psychical value must necessarily operate in the same sense. The ideas which are most important among the dream-thoughts will almost certainly be those which occur most often in them, since the different dream-thoughts will, as it were, radiate out from them. Nevertheless a dream can reject elements which are thus both highly stressed in themselves and reinforced from many directions, and can select for its content other elements which possess only the second of these attributes.

In order to solve this difficulty we shall make use of another impression derived from our enquiry [in the previous section] into the overdetermination of the dream-content. Perhaps some of those who have read that enquiry may already have formed an independent conclusion that the overdetermination of the elements of dreams is no very important discovery, since it is a self-evident one. For in analysis we start out from the dream-elements and note down all the associations which lead off from them; so that there is nothing surprising in the fact that in the thought-material arrived at in this way we come across these same elements with peculiar frequency. I cannot accept this objection; but I will myself put into words something that sounds not unlike it. Among the thoughts that analysis brings to light are many which are relatively remote from the kernel of the dream and which look like artificial interpolations made for some particular purpose. That purpose is easy to divine. It is precisely *they* that constitute a connection, often a forced and far-fetched one, between the dream-content and the dream-thoughts; and if these elements were weeded out of the analysis the result would often be that the component parts of the dream-content would be left not only without overdetermination but without any satisfactory determination at all. We shall be led to conclude that the multiple determination which decides what shall be included in a dream is not always a primary factor in dream-construction but is often the secondary product of a psychical force which is still unknown to us. Nevertheless multiple determination must be of importance in choosing what particular elements shall enter a dream, since we can see that a considerable expenditure of effort is used to bring it about in cases where it does not arise from the dream-material unassisted.

It thus seems plausible to suppose that in the dream-work a psychical force is operating which on the one hand strips the elements which have a high psychical value of their intensity, and on the other hand, by *means of overdetermination*, creates from elements of low psychical value new values, which afterwards find their way into the dream-content. If that is so, *a transference and displacement of psychical intensities* occurs in the process of dream-formation, and it is as a result of these that the difference between the text of the dream-content and that of the dream-thoughts comes about. The process which we are here presuming is nothing less than the essential portion of the dream-work; and it deserves to be described as "dream-displacement." Dream-displacement and dream-condensation are the two governing factors to whose activity we may in essence ascribe the form assumed by dreams.

Nor do I think we shall have any difficulty in recognizing the psychical force which manifests itself in the facts of dream-displacement. The consequence of the displacement is that the dream-content no longer resembles the core of the dream-thoughts and that the dream gives no more than a distortion of the dream-wish which exists in the unconscious. But we are already familiar with dream-distortion. We traced it back to the censorship which is exercised by one psychical agency in the mind over another. Dream-displacement is one of the chief methods by which that distortion is achieved. *Is fecit cui profuit*.[16] We may assume, then, that dream-displacement comes about through the influence of the same censorship – that is, the censorship of endopsychic defence.[17]

The question of the interplay of these factors – of displacement, condensation and overdetermination – in the construction of dreams, and the question which is a dominant factor and which a subordinate one – all of this we shall leave aside for later investigation. But we can state provisionally a second condition which must be satisfied by those elements of the dream-thoughts which make their way into the dream: *they must escape the censorship imposed by resistance*. And henceforward in interpreting dreams we shall take dream-displacement into account as an undeniable fact.

Notes

1 The occurrence of condensation in dreams has been hinted at by many writers. Du Prel has a passage in which he says it is absolutely certain that there has been a process of condensation of the groups of ideas in dreams. (C. Du Prel, *Die Philosophie der Mystik* (Leipzig, 1885), p. 85.)

2 ["...a thousand threads one treadle throws, / Where fly the shuttles hither and thither, / Unseen the threads are knit together, / And an infinite combination grows." Goethe, *Faust*, Part I [Scene 4] (Bayard Taylor's translation).]

3 [*Footnote added* 1911:] What I have written below in the section on symbolism about the significance of dreams of climbing throws light upon the imagery chosen by the novelist.

4 [Literally: "I was lately a guest at an *inn* with a most gentle host." (Uhland, *Wanderlieder*, 8, "Einkehr.")]

5 ["FAUST (*dancing with the Young Witch*): *A lovely dream* once came to me, / And I beheld an *apple-tree*, / On which two lovely apples shone; / They charmed me so, I *climbed thereon*.

THE LOVELY WITCH: Apples have been desired by you, / Since first in Paradise they grew; / And I am moved with joy to know / That such within my garden grow." Goethe, *Faust*, Part I [Scene 21, Walpurgisnacht] (Bayard Taylor's translation, slightly modified).]

6 The imaginary nature of the situation relating to the dreamer's wet-nurse was proved by the objectively established fact that in his case the wet-nurse had been his mother. I may recall in this connection the anecdote of the young man who regretted that he had not made better use of his opportunities with his wet-nurse. A regret of the same kind was no doubt the source of the present dream.

7 [The commoner English equivalent for the German "*Maikäfer*" is "cockchafer." For the purposes of this dream, however, a literal translation is to be preferred.]

8 This had been the true instigator of the dream.

9 An interpolation is required at this point: "books of that kind are *poison* to a girl." The patient herself had dipped into forbidden books a great deal when she was young.

10 [Fear not, to love I'll ne'er compel thee; Yet 'tis too soon to *set thee free*. (Sarastro to Pamina in the *Finale* to Act I. – E. J. Dent's translation.)]

11 ["You are madly in love with me." Literally: "You are in love with me like a *beetle*." From Kleist's *Kätchen von Heilbronn*, IV, 2.] – A further train of thought led to the same poet's *Penthesilea*, and to the idea of *cruelty* to a lover.

12 [Literally: "Because thou wast inspired by such *evil pleasure*." This is presumably a recollection of the opening phrase of the Pope's condemnation reported by Tannhäuser in the last scene of the opera. The actual words are: "Hast du so böse Lust getheilt" – "Since thou hast shared such evil pleasure."]

13 [This ingenious example of condensation turns upon the pronunciation of the second syllable – the stressed syllable – of the nonsense word. If it is "*ze*," it is pronounced roughly like the English "say," thus resembling the second syllable of "*erzählen*" and of the invented "*erzeh-lerisch*." If it is "*zi*," it is pronounced roughly like the English "tsee," thus resembling the second syllable of "*erzieherisch*," as well as (less closely) the first syllable of "syphilis."]

14 [*Footnote added* 1909:] Not long ago I found a single exception to this rule in the case of a young man who suffered from obsessions while retaining intact his highly developed intellectual powers. The spoken words which occurred in his dreams were not derived from remarks which he had heard or made himself. They contained the undistorted text of his obsessional thoughts, which in his waking life only reached his consciousness in a modified form.

15 *Psychical* intensity or value or the degree of interest of an idea is of course to be distinguished from *sensory* intensity or the intensity of the image presented.

16 [The old legal tag: "He did the deed who gained by it."]

17 [*Footnote added* 1909:] Since I may say that the kernel of my theory of dreams lies in my derivation of dream-distortion from the censorship, I will here insert the last part of a story from *Phantasien eines Realisten* [*Phantasies of a Realist*] by "Lynkeus" (Vienna, 2nd edition, 1900 [1st edition, 1899]), in which I have found this principal feature of my theory once more expounded. The title of the story is "Träumen wie Wachen" ["Dreaming like Waking"]:

> "About a man who has the remarkable attribute of never dreaming nonsense. . . .
>
> "This splendid gift of yours, for dreaming as though you were waking, is a consequence of your virtues, of your kindness, your sense of justice, and your love of truth; it is the moral serenity of your nature which makes me understand all about you."
>
> "But when I think the matter over properly," replied the other, "I almost believe that everyone is made like me, and that no one at all ever dreams nonsense. Any dream which one can remember clearly enough to describe it afterwards – any dream, that is to say, which is not a fever-dream – must *always* make sense, and it cannot possibly be otherwise. For things that were mutually contradictory could not group themselves into a single whole. The fact that time and space are often thrown into confusion does not affect the true content of the dream, since no doubt neither of them are of significance for its real essence. We often do the same thing in waking life. Only think of fairy tales and of the many daring products of the imagination, which are full of meaning and of which only a man without intelligence could say: 'This is nonsense, for it's impossible.' "

"If only one always knew how to interpret dreams in the right way, as you have just done with mine!" said his friend.

"That is certainly no easy task; but with a little attention on the part of the dreamer himself it should no doubt always succeed. – You ask why it is that for the most part it does *not* succeed? In you other people there seems always to be something that lies concealed in your dreams, something unchaste in a special and higher sense, a certain secret quality in your being which it is hard to follow. And that is why your dreams so often seem to be without meaning or even to be nonsense. But in the deepest sense this is not in the least so; indeed, it cannot be so at all – for it is always the same man, whether he is awake or dreaming."

CHAPTER 3

On Narcissism

Sigmund Freud

Moments in Freud's work prefigure later, post-Freudian developments in psychoanalysis. This 1914 essay, for example, discusses the "ego ideal," a mental representation that gives expression, according to Freud, to repressed narcissistic libido. Later theorists will describe similar constructs as "internalizations" or as "introjections" that are modeled on external objects such as parents. Rather than give expression to libido or instinctual drives, they will come to be seen as representations built up in the self as a way of securing for itself the benefit of relations with others that have become unstable or insecure.

Observation of normal adults shows that their former megalomania has been damped down and that the psychical characteristics from which we inferred their infantile narcissism have been effaced. What has become of their ego-libido? Are we to suppose that the whole amount of it has passed into object-cathexes? Such a possibility is plainly contrary to the whole trend of our argument; but we may find a hint at another answer to the question in the psychology of repression.

We have learnt that libidinal instinctual impulses undergo the vicissitude of pathogenic repression if they come into conflict with the subject's cultural and ethical ideas. By this we never mean that the individual in question has a merely intellectual knowledge of the existence of such ideas; we always mean that he recognizes them as a standard for himself and submits to the claims they make on him. Repression, we have said, proceeds from the ego; we might say with greater precision that it proceeds from the self-respect of the ego. The same impressions, experiences, impulses and desires that one man indulges or at least works over consciously will be rejected with the utmost indignation by another, or even stifled before they enter consciousness. The difference between the two, which contains the conditioning factor of repression, can easily be expressed in terms which enable it to be explained by the libido theory. We can say that the one man has set up an *ideal* in himself by which he measures his actual ego, while the other has formed no such ideal. For the ego the formation of an ideal would be the conditioning factor of repression.

This ideal ego is now the target of the self-love which was enjoyed in childhood by the actual ego. The subject's narcissism makes its appearance displaced on to this new ideal ego, which, like the infantile ego, finds itself possessed of every perfection that is of value. As always where the libido is concerned, man has here again shown himself incapable of giving up a satisfaction he had once enjoyed. He is not willing to forgo the narcissistic perfection of his childhood; and when, as he grows up, he is disturbed by the admonitions of others and by the awakening of his own critical judgement, so that he can no longer retain that perfection, he seeks to recover it in the new form of an ego ideal. What he projects before him as his ideal is the substitute for the lost narcissism of his childhood in which he was his own ideal.

We are naturally led to examine the relation between this forming of an ideal and sublimation. Sublimation is a process that concerns object-libido and consists in the instinct's directing itself towards an aim other than, and remote from, that of sexual satisfaction; in this process the accent falls upon deflection from sexuality. Idealization is a process that concerns the *object*; by it that object, without any alteration in its nature, is aggrandized and exalted in the subject's mind. Idealization is possible in the sphere of ego-libido as well as in that of object-libido. For example, the sexual overvaluation of an object is an idealization of it. In so far as sublimation describes something that has to do with the instinct and idealization something to do with the object, the two concepts are to be distinguished from each other.

The formation of an ego ideal is often confused with the sublimation of instinct, to the detriment of our understanding of the facts. A man who has exchanged his narcissism for homage to a high ego ideal has not necessarily on that account succeeded in sublimating his libidinal instincts. It is true that the ego ideal demands such sublimation, but it cannot enforce it; sublimation remains a special process which may be prompted by the ideal but the execution of which is entirely independent of any such prompting. It is precisely in neurotics that we find the highest differences of potential between the development of their ego ideal and the amount of sublimation of their primitive libidinal instincts; and in general it is far harder to convince an idealist of the inexpedient location of his libido than a plain man whose pretensions have remained more moderate. Further, the formation of an ego ideal and sublimation are quite differently related to the causation of neurosis. As we have learnt, the formation of an ideal heightens the demands of the ego and is the most powerful factor favoring repression; sublimation is a way out, a way by which those demands can be met without involving repression.

It would not surprise us if we were to find a special psychical agency which performs the task of seeing that narcissistic satisfaction from the ego ideal is ensured and which, with this end in view, constantly watches the actual ego and measures it by that ideal. If such an agency does exist, we cannot possibly come upon it as a discovery, we can only recognize it; for we may reflect that what we call our "conscience" has the required characteristics. Recognition of this agency enables us to understand the so-called "delusions of being noticed" or more correctly, of being watched, which are such striking symptoms in the paranoid diseases and which may also occur as an isolated form of illness, or intercalated in a transference neurosis. Patients of this sort complain that all their thoughts are known and their actions watched and supervised; they are informed of the functioning of this agency by voices which characteristically speak to them in the third person ("Now she's thinking of that again," "now he's going out"). This complaint is justified; it describes the truth. A power of this kind, watching, discovering and criticizing all our intentions, does really exist. Indeed, it exists in every one of us in normal life.

Delusions of being watched present this power in a regressive form, thus revealing its genesis and the reason why the patient is in revolt against it. For what prompted the subject to form an ego ideal, on whose behalf his conscience acts as watchman, arose from the critical influence of his parents (conveyed to him by the medium of the voice), to whom were added, as time went on, those who trained and taught him and the innumerable and indefinable host of all the other people in his environment – his fellow-men – and public opinion.

In this way large amounts of libido of an essentially homosexual kind are drawn into the formation of the narcissistic ego ideal and find outlet and satisfaction in maintaining it. The institution of conscience was at bottom an embodiment, first of parental criticism, and subsequently of that of society – a process which is repeated in what takes place when a tendency towards repression develops out of a prohibition or obstacle that came in the first instance from without. The voices, as well as the undefined multitude, are brought into the foreground again by the disease, and so the evolution of conscience is reproduced regressively. But the revolt against this "censoring agency" arises out of the subject's desire (in accordance with the fundamental character of his illness) to liberate himself from all these influences, beginning with the parental one, and out of his withdrawal of homosexual libido from them. His conscience then confronts him in a regressive form as a hostile influence from without.

The complaints made by paranoics also show that at bottom the self-criticism of conscience coincides with the self-observation on which it is based. Thus the activity of the mind which has taken over the function of conscience has also placed itself at the service of internal research, which furnishes philosophy with the material for its intellectual operations. This may have some bearing on the characteristic tendency of paranoics to construct speculative systems.

CHAPTER 4

The Uncanny

Sigmund Freud

"The Uncanny" (1919) is one of Freud's most famous essays on literature. Critics often use the term "uncanny" in discussing things that appear to slip outside of normal perceptions or normal assumptions. For Freud, it named the effects of the unconscious that surprise us and create an effect of "uncanniness" because we are unaware of the operation of the unconscious.

The German word *unheimlich*[1] is obviously the opposite of *heimlich, heimisch*, meaning "familiar," "native," "belonging to the home"; and we are tempted to conclude that what is "uncanny" is frightening precisely because it is *not* known and familiar. Naturally not everything which is new and unfamiliar is frightening, however; the relation cannot be inverted. We can only say that what is novel can easily become frightening and uncanny; some new things are frightening but not by any means all. Something has to be added to what is novel and unfamiliar to make it uncanny.

On the whole, Jentsch did not get beyond this relation of the uncanny to the novel and unfamiliar. He ascribes the essential factor in the production of the feeling of uncanniness to intellectual uncertainty; so that the uncanny would always be that in which one does not know where one is, as it were. The better orientated in his environment a person is, the less readily will he get the impression of something uncanny in regard to the objects and events in it.

It is not difficult to see that this definition is incomplete, and we will therefore try to proceed beyond the equation of *unheimlich* with unfamiliar. We will first turn to other languages. But foreign dictionaries tell us nothing new, perhaps only because we speak a different language. Indeed, we get the impression that many languages are without a word for this particular variety of what is fearful.

I wish to express my indebtedness to Dr Th. Reik for the following excerpts:

LATIN: (K. E. Georges, *Deutschlateinisches Wörterbuch*, 1898). Ein *unheimlicher* Ort [an uncanny place] – locus suspectus; in unheimlicher Nachtzeit [in the dismal night hours] – intempesta nocte.

GREEK: (Rost's and Schenkl's Lexikons). Evos – strange, foreign.

ENGLISH: (from dictionaries by Lucas, Bellow, Flugel, Muret: Sanders). Uncomfortable, uneasy, gloomy, dismal, uncanny, ghastly; (of a house) haunted; (of a man) a repulsive fellow.

FRENCH: (Sachs–Villatte). Inquiétant, sinistre, lugubre, mal à son aise.

SPANISH: (Tollhausen, 1889). Sospechoso, de mal agüero, lúgubre, siniestro.

The Italian and the Portuguese seem to content themselves with words which we should describe as circumlocutions. In Arabic and Hebrew "uncanny" means the same as "daemonic," "gruesome."

Let us therefore return to the German language. In Daniel Sanders' *Wörterbuch der deutschen Sprache* (1860), the following remarks [abstracted in translation] are found upon the word *heimlich*; I have laid stress on certain passages by italicizing them.

Heimlich adj.: 1. Also *heimelich, heimelig*, belonging to the house, not strange, familiar, tame, intimate, comfortable, homely, etc.

(*a*) (Obsolete) belonging to the house or the family, or regarded as so belonging (cf. Latin *familiaris*): *Die Heimlichen*, the members of the household; *Der heimliche Rat* [him to whom secrets are revealed] Gen. xli. 45; 2 Sam. xxiii. 23; now more usually *Geheimer Rat* [Privy Councillor], cf. *Heimlicher*.

(*b*) Of animals: tame, companionable to man. As opposed to wild, *e.g.* "Wild animals ...that are trained to be *heimlich* and accustomed to men." "If these young creatures are brought up from early days among men they become quite *heimlich*, friendly," etc.

(*c*) Friendly, intimate, homelike; the enjoyment of quiet content, etc., arousing a sense of peaceful pleasure and security as in one within the four walls of his house. "Is it still *heimlich* to you in your country where strangers are felling your woods?" "She did not feel all too *heimlich* with him." "To destroy the *Heimlichkeit* of the home." "I could not readily find another spot so intimate and *heimlich* as this." "In quiet *Heimlichkeit*, surrounded by close walls." "A careful housewife, who knows how to make a pleasing *Heimlichkeit (Häuslichkeit)*[2] out of the smallest means." "The protestant rulers do not feel...*heimlich* among their catholic subjects." "When it grows *heimlich* and still, and the evening quiet alone watches over your cell." "Quiet, lovely and *heimlich*, no place more fitted for her rest." "The in and outflowing waves of the current, dreamy and *heimlich* as a cradle-song." Cf. in especial *Unheimlich*. Among Swabian and Swiss authors in especial, often as a trisyllable: "How *heimelich* it seemed again of an evening, back at home." "The warm room and the *heimelig* afternoon." "Little by little they grew at ease and *heimelig* among themselves." "That which comes from afar...assuredly does not live quite *heimelig (heimatlich* [at home], *freundnachbarlich* [in a neighborly way]) among the people." "The sentinel's horn sounds so *heimelig* from the tower, and his voice invites so hospitably." *This form of the word ought to become general in order to protect the word from becoming obsolete in its good sense through an easy confusion with II. [see below].* "'*The Zecks* [a family name] *are all 'heimlich'.*" "'*Heimlich'? What do you understand by 'heimlich'?*" "*Well,...they are like a buried spring or a dried-up pond. One cannot walk over it without always having the feeling that water might come up there again.*" "*Oh, we call it 'unheimlich'; you call it 'heimlich.' Well, what makes you think that there is something secret and untrustworthy about this family?*" Gutzkow.

II. Concealed, kept from sight, so that others do not get to know about it, withheld from others, cf. *geheim* [secret]; so also *Heimlichkeit* for *Geheimnis* [secret]. To do something *heimlich, i.e.* behind someone's back; to steal away *heimlich; heimlich* meetings and appointments; to look on with *heimlich* pleasure at someone's discomfiture; to sigh or weep *heimlich*; to behave *heimlich*, as though there was something to conceal; *heimlich* love, love-affair, sin; *heimlich* places (which good manners oblige us to conceal). I. Sam. v. 6; "The *heimlich* chamber" [privy]. 2. Kings x. 27 etc.; "To throw into pits or *Heimlichkeit*." Led the steeds *heimlich* before Laomedon." "As secretive, *heimlich*, deceitful and malicious towards cruel masters...as frank, open, sympathetic and helpful towards a friend in misfortune." "The *heimlich* art" (magic). "Where public ventilation has to stop, there *heimlich* machinations begin." "Freedom is the whispered watchword of *heimlich* conspirators and the loud battle-cry of professed revolutionaries." "A holy, *heimlich* effect." "I have roots that are most *heimlich*, I am grown in the deep earth." "My *heimlich* pranks." (Cf. *Heimtücke* [mischief]). To discover, disclose, betray someone's *Heimlichkeiten*; to concoct *Heimlichkeiten* behind my back." Cf. *Geheimnis*.

Compounds and especially also the opposite follow meaning I. (above): *Unheimlich*, uneasy, eerie, blood-curdling; "Seeming almost *unheimlich* and ghostly to him." "I had already long since felt an *unheimlich*, even gruesome feeling." "Feels an *unheimlich* horror." "*Unheimlich* and motionless like a stone-image." "The *unheimlich* mist called hill-fog." "These pale youths are *unheimlich* and are brewing heaven knows what mischief." "'*Unheimlich is the name for everything that ought to have remained . . . hidden and secret and has become visible.*'" Schelling. "To veil the divine to surround it with a certain *Unheimlichkeit*." – *Unheimlich* is not often used as opposite to meaning II. (above).

What interests us most in this long extract is to find that among its different shades of meaning the word *heimlich* exhibits one which is identical with its opposite, *unheimlich*. What is *heimlich* thus comes to be *unheimlich*. (Cf. the quotation from Gutzkow: "We call it *unheimlich*; you call it *heimlich*.") In general we are reminded that the word *heimlich* is not unambiguous, but belongs to two sets of ideas, which without being contradictory are yet very different: on the one hand, it means that which is familiar and congenial, and on the other, that which is concealed and kept out of sight. "*Unheimlich*" is customarily used, we are told, as the contrary only of the first signification of "*heimlich*," and not of the second. Sanders tells us nothing concerning a possible genetic connection between these two meanings of *heimlich*. On the other hand, we notice that Schelling says something which throws quite a new light on the concept of the *Unheimlich*, for which we were certainly not prepared. According to him, everything is *unheimlich* that ought to have remained secret and hidden but has come to light.

Some of the doubts that have thus arisen are removed if we consult Grimm's dictionary (1877, 4, Part 2, pp. 873 ff.)

We read:

Heimlich; adj. and adv. *vernaculus, occultus*; MHG. heîmelich, heîmlich.

(p. 874.) In a slightly different sense: "I feel *heimlich*, well, free from fear." . . .

[3] *(b)* Heimlich is also used of a place free from ghostly influences . . . familiar, friendly, intimate.

(p. 875: p) Familiar, amicable, unreserved.

4. From the idea of "homelike," "belonging to the house," the further idea is developed of something withdrawn from the eyes of strangers, something concealed, secret; and this idea is expanded in many ways . . .

(p. 876.) "On the left bank of the lake there lies a meadow *heimlich* in the wood." (Schiller, *Wilhelm Tell*, I, 4.) . . . Poetic licence, rarely so used in modern speech . . . *Heimlich* is used in conjunction with a verb expressing the act of concealing: "In the secret of his tabernacle he shall hide me *heimlich*." (Ps. xxvii. 5.) . . . *Heimlich* parts of the human body, *pudenda* . . . "the men that died not were smitten on their *heimlich* parts." (1 Samuel v. 12.) . . .

(c) Officials who give important advice which has to be kept secret in matters of state are called *heimlich* councillors; the adjective, according to modern usage, has been replaced by *geheim* [secret] . . . "Pharaoh called Joseph's name 'him to whom secrets are revealed'" (*heimlich* councillor). (Gen. xli. 45.)

(p. 878.) *6. Heimlich,* as used of knowledge – mystic, allegorical: a *heimlich* meaning, *mysticus, divinus, occultus, figuratus.* (p. 878.) *Heimlich* in a different sense, as withdrawn from knowledge, unconscious . . . *Heimlich* also has the meaning of that which is obscure, inaccessible to knowledge . . . "Do you not see? They do not trust us; they fear the *heimlich* face of the Duke of Friedland." (Schiller, *Wallensteins Lager*, Scene 2.)

9. The notion of something hidden and dangerous, which is expressed in the last paragraph, is still further developed, so that "heimlich" comes to have the meaning usually ascribed to "unheimlich." Thus: "At times I feel like a man who walks in the night and believes in ghosts; every corner is *heimlich* and full of terrors for him." (Klinger, *Theater*, 3. 298.)

Thus *heimlich is* a word the meaning of which develops in the direction of ambivalence, until it finally coincides with its opposite, *unheimlich. Unheimlich* is in some way or other a sub-species of *heimlich.* Let us bear this discovery in mind, though we cannot yet rightly understand it, alongside of Schelling's definition of the *Unheimlich.* If we go on to examine individual instances of uncanniness, these hints will become intelligible to us.

II

When we proceed to review the things, persons, impressions, events and situations which are able to arouse in us a feeling of the uncanny in a particularly forcible and definite form, the first requirement is obviously to select a suitable example to start on. Jentsch has taken as a very good instance "doubts whether an apparently animate being is really alive; or conversely, whether a lifeless object might not be in fact animate"; and he refers in this connection to the impression made by waxwork figures, ingeniously constructed dolls and automata. To these he adds the uncanny effect of epileptic fits, and of manifestations of insanity, because these excite in the spectator the impression of automatic, mechanical processes at work behind the ordinary appearance of mental activity. Without entirely accepting this author's view, we will take it as a starting-point for our own investigation because in what follows he reminds us of a writer who has succeeded in producing uncanny effects better than anyone else.

Jentsch writes: "In telling a story, one of the most successful devices for easily creating uncanny effects is to leave the reader in uncertainty whether a particular figure in the story is a human being or an automaton, and to do it in such a way that his attention is not focused directly upon his uncertainty, so that he may not be led to go into the matter and clear it up immediately. That, as we have said, would quickly dissipate the peculiar emotional effect of the thing. E. T. A. Hoffmann has repeatedly employed this psychological artifice with success in his fantastic narratives."

This observation, undoubtedly a correct one, refers primarily to the story of "The Sand-Man" in Hoffmann's *Nachtstücken*,[3] which contains the original of Olympia, the doll that appears in the first act of Offenbach's opera, *Tales of Hoffmann.* But I cannot think – and I hope most readers of the story will agree with me – that the theme of the doll Olympia, who is to all appearances a living being, is by any means the only, or indeed the most important, element that must be held responsible for the quite unparalleled atmosphere of uncanniness evoked by the story. Nor is this atmosphere heightened by the fact that the author himself treats the episode of Olympia with a faint touch of satire and uses it to poke fun at the young man's idealization of his mistress. The main theme of the story is, on the contrary, some-thing different, something which gives it its name, and which is always re-introduced at critical moments: it is the theme of the "Sand-Man" who tears out children's eyes.

This fantastic tale opens with the childhood recollections of the student Nathaniel. In spite of his present happiness, he cannot banish the memories associated with the mysterious and terrifying death of his beloved father. On certain evenings his mother used to send the children to bed early, warning them that "the Sand-Man was coming"; and, sure enough, Nathaniel would not fail to hear the heavy tread of a visitor, with whom his father would then be occupied for the evening. When ques-tioned about the Sand-Man, his mother, it is true, denied that such a person existed except as a figure of speech; but his nurse could give him more definite information: "He's a wicked man who comes when children won't go to bed, and throws handfuls of sand in their eyes so that they jump out of their heads all bleeding. Then he puts the eyes in a sack and carries them off to the half-moon to feed his children. They sit up there in their nest, and their beaks are hooked like owls' beaks, and they use them to peck up naughty boys' and girls' eyes with."

Although little Nathaniel was sensible and old enough not to credit the figure of the Sand-Man with such gruesome attributes, yet the dread of him became fixed in his heart. He determined to find out what the Sand-Man looked like; and one evening, when the Sand-Man was expected again, he hid in his father's study. He recognized the visitor as the lawyer Coppelius, a repulsive person whom the children were frightened of when he occasionally came to a meal; and he now identified this Coppelius with the dreaded Sand-Man. As regards the rest of the scene, Hoffmann already leaves us in doubt whether what we are witnessing is the first delirium of the panic-stricken boy, or a succession of events which are to be regarded in the story as being real. His father and the guest are at work at a brazier with glowing flames. The little eavesdropper hears Coppelius call out: "Eyes here! Eyes here!" and betrays himself by screaming aloud. Coppelius seizes him and is on the point of dropping bits of red-hot coal from the fire into his eyes, and then of throwing them into the brazier, but his father begs him off and saves his eyes. After this the boy falls into a deep swoon; and a long illness brings his experience to an end. Those who decide in favour of the rationalistic interpretation of the Sand-Man will not fail to recognize in the child's phantasy the persisting influence of his nurse's story. The bits of sand that are to be thrown into the child's eyes turn into bits of red-hot coal from the flames; and in both cases they are intended to make his eyes jump out. In the course of another visit of the Sand-Man's, a year later, his father is killed in his study by an explosion. The lawyer Coppelius disappears from the place without leaving a trace behind.

Nathaniel, now a student, believes that he has recognized this phantom of horror from his childhood in an itinerant optician, an Italian called Giuseppe Coppola, who at his university town, offers him weather-glasses for sale. When Nathaniel refuses, the man goes on: "Not weather-glasses? not weather-glasses? also got fine eyes, fine eyes!" The student's terror is allayed when he finds that the proffered eyes are only harmless spectacles, and he buys a pocket spy-glass from Coppola. With its aid he looks across into Professor Spalanzani's house opposite and there spies Spalanzani's beautiful, but strangely silent and motionless daughter, Olympia. He soon falls in love with her so violently that, because of her, he quite forgets the clever and sensible girl to whom he is betrothed. But Olympia is an automaton whose clockwork has been made by Spalanzani, and whose eyes have been put in by Coppola, the Sand-Man. The student surprises the two Masters quarrelling over their handiwork. The optician carries off the wooden eyeless doll; and the mechanician, Spalanzani, picks up Olympia's bleeding eyes from the ground and throws them at Nathaniel's breast, saying that Coppola had stolen them from the student. Nathaniel succumbs to a fresh attack of madness, and in his delirium his recollection of his father's death is mingled with this new experience. "Hurry up! hurry up! ring of fire!" he cries. "Spin about, ring of fire – Hurrah! Hurry up, wooden doll! lovely wooden doll, spin about –." He then falls upon the professor, Olympia's "father," and tries to strangle him.

Rallying from a long and serious illness, Nathaniel seems at last to have recovered. He intends to marry his betrothed, with whom he has become reconciled. One day he and she are walking through the city market-place, over which the high tower of the Town Hall throws its huge shadow. On the girl's suggestion, they climb the tower, leaving her brother, who is walking with them, down below. From the top, Clara's attention is drawn to a curious object moving along the street. Nathaniel looks at this thing through Coppola's spy-glass, which he finds in his pocket, and falls into a new attack of madness. Shouting "spin about, wooden doll!" he tries to throw the girl into the gulf below. Her brother, brought to her side by her cries, rescues her and hastens down with her to safety. On the tower above, the madman rushes round, shrieking "Ring of fire, spin about!" – and we know the origin of the words. Among the people who begin to gather below there comes forward the figure of the lawyer Coppelius, who has suddenly returned. We may suppose that it was his approach, seen through the spy-glass, which threw Nathaniel into his fit of madness. As the onlookers prepare to go up and overpower the madman, Coppelius laughs and says: "Wait a bit; he'll come down of himself." Nathaniel suddenly stands still, catches sight of Coppelius, and with a wild shriek "Yes! 'Fine eyes – fine eyes!'" flings himself over the parapet. While he lies on the paving-stones with a shattered skull the Sand-Man vanishes in the throng.

This short summary leaves no doubt, I think, that the feeling of something uncanny is directly attached to the figure of the Sand-Man, that is, to the idea of being robbed of one's eyes, and that Jentsch's point of an intellectual uncertainty has nothing to do with the effect. Uncertainty whether an object is living or inanimate, which admittedly applied to the doll Olympia, is quite irrelevant in connection with this other, more striking instance of uncanniness. It is true that the writer creates a kind of uncertainty in us in the beginning by not letting us know, no doubt purposely, whether he is taking us into the real world or into a purely fantastic one of his own creation. He has, of course, a right to do either; and if he chooses to stage his action in a world peopled with spirits, demons and ghosts, as Shakespeare does in *Hamlet*, in *Macbeth* and, in a different sense, in *The Tempest* and *A Midsummer Night's Dream*, we must bow to his decision and treat his setting as though it were real for as long as we put ourselves into his hands. But this uncertainty disappears in the course of Hoffmann's story, and we perceive that he intends to make us, too, look through the demon optician's spectacles or spy-glass – perhaps, indeed, that the author in his very own person once peered through such an instrument. For the conclusion of the story makes it quite clear that Coppola the optician really *is* the lawyer Coppelius[4] and also, therefore, the Sand-Man.

There is no question therefore, of any intellectual uncertainty here: we know now that we are not supposed to be looking on at the products of a madman's imagination, behind which we, with the superiority of rational minds, are able to detect the sober truth; and yet this knowledge does not lessen the impression of uncanniness in the least degree. The theory of intellectual uncertainty is thus incapable of explaining that impression.

We know from psycho-analytic experience, however, that the fear of damaging or losing one's eyes is a terrible one in children. Many adults retain their apprehensiveness in this respect, and no physical injury is so much dreaded by them as an injury to the eye. We are accustomed to say, too, that we will treasure a thing as the apple of our eye. A study of dreams, phantasies and myths has taught us that anxiety about one's eyes, the fear of going blind, is often enough a substitute for the dread of being castrated. The self-blinding of the mythical criminal, Oedipus, was simply a mitigated form of the punishment of castration – the only punishment that was adequate for him by the *lex talionis*. We may try on rationalistic grounds to deny that fears about the eye are derived from the fear of castration, and may argue that it is very natural that so precious an organ as the eye should be guarded by a proportionate dread. Indeed, we might go further and say that the fear of castration itself contains no other significance and no deeper secret than a justifiable dread of this rational kind. But this view does not account adequately for the substitutive relation between the eye and the male organ which is seen to exist in dreams and myths and phantasies; nor can it dispel the impression that the threat of being castrated in especial excites a peculiarly violent and obscure emotion, and that this emotion is what first gives the idea of losing other organs its intense colouring. All further doubts are removed when we learn the details of their "castration complex" from the analysis of neurotic patients, and realize its immense importance in their mental life.

Moreover, I would not recommend any opponent of the psycho-analytic view to select this particular story of the Sand-Man with which to support his argument that anxiety about the eyes has nothing to do with the castration complex. For why does Hoffmann bring the anxiety about eyes into such intimate connection with the father's death? And why does the Sand-Man always appear as a disturber of love? He separates the unfortunate Nathaniel from his betrothed and from her brother, his best friend; he destroys the second object of his love, Olympia, the lovely doll; and he drives him into suicide at the moment when he has won back his Clara and is about to be happily united to her. Elements in the story like these, and many others, seem arbitrary and meaningless so long as we deny all connection between fears about the eye and castration; but they become intelligible as soon as we replace the Sand-Man by the dreaded father at whose hands castration is expected.[5]

We shall venture, therefore, to refer the uncanny effect of the Sand-Man to the anxiety belonging to the castration complex of childhood. But having reached the idea that we can make an infantile factor such as this responsible for feelings of uncanniness, we are encouraged to see whether we can apply it to other instances of the uncanny. We find in the story of the Sand-Man the other theme on which Jentsch lays stress, of a doll which appears to be alive. Jentsch believes that a particularly favourable condition for awakening uncanny feelings is created when there is intellectual uncertainty whether an object is alive or not, and when an inanimate object becomes too much like an animate one. Now, dolls are of course rather closely connected with childhood life. We remember that in their early games children do not distinguish at all sharply between living and inanimate objects, and that they are especially fond of treating their dolls like live people. In fact, I have occasionally heard a woman patient declare that even at the age of eight she had still been convinced that her dolls would be certain to come to life if she were to look at them in a particular, extremely concentrated, way. So that here, too, it is not difficult to discover a factor from childhood. But, curiously enough, while the Sand-Man story deals with the arousing of an early childhood fear, the idea of a "living doll" excites no fear at all; children have no fear of their dolls coming to life, they may even desire it. The source of uncanny feelings would not, therefore, be an infantile fear in this case, but rather an infantile wish or even merely an infantile belief. There seems to be a contradiction here; but perhaps it is only a complication, which may be helpful to us later on.

Hoffmann is in literature the unrivalled master of conjuring up the uncanny. His *Elixire des Teufels* [The Devil's Elixir] contains a mass of themes to which one is tempted to ascribe the uncanny effect of the narrative; but it is too obscure and intricate a story to venture to summarize. Towards the end of the book the reader is told the facts, hitherto concealed from him, from which the action springs; with the result, not that he is at last enlightened, but that he falls into a state of complete bewilderment. The author has piled up too much of a kind; one's comprehension of the whole suffers as a result, though not the impression it makes. We must content ourselves with selecting those themes of uncanniness which are most prominent, and seeing whether we can fairly trace them also back to infantile sources. These themes are all concerned with the idea of a "double" in every shape and degree, with persons, therefore, who are to be considered identical by reason of looking alike; Hoffmann accentuates this relation by transferring mental processes from the one person to the other – what we should call telepathy – so that the one possesses knowledge, feeling and experience in common with the other, identifies himself with another person, so that his self becomes confounded, or the foreign self is substituted for his own – in other words, by doubling, dividing and interchanging the self. And finally there is the constant recurrence of similar situations, a same face, or character-trait, or twist of fortune, or a same crime, or even a same name recurring throughout several consecutive generations.

The theme of the "double" has been very thoroughly treated by Otto Rank.[6] He has gone into the connections the "double" has with reflections in mirrors, with shadows, guardian spirits, with the belief in the soul and the fear of death; but he also lets in a flood of light on the astonishing evolution of this idea. For the "double" was originally an insurance against destruction to the ego, an "energetic denial of the power of death," as Rank says; and probably the "Immortal" soul was the first "double" of the body. This invention of doubling as a preservation against extinction has its counterpart in the language of dreams, which is fond of representing castration by a doubling or multiplication of the genital symbol; the same desire spurred on the ancient Egyptians to the art of making images of the dead in some lasting material. Such ideas, however, have sprung from the soil of unbounded self-love, from the primary narcissism which holds sway in the mind of the child as in that of primitive man; and when this stage has been left behind the double takes on a different aspect. From having been an assurance of immortality, he becomes the ghastly harbinger of death.

The idea of the "double" does not necessarily disappear with the passing of the primary narcissism, for it can receive fresh meaning from the later stages of development of the ego. A special faculty is slowly formed there, able to oppose the rest of the ego, with the function of observing and criticizing the self and exercising a censorship within the mind, and this we become aware of as our "conscience." In the pathological case of delusions of being watched this mental institution becomes isolated, dissociated from the ego, and discernible to a physician's eye. The fact that a faculty of this kind exists, which is able to treat the rest of the ego like an object – the fact, that is, that man is capable of self-observation – renders it possible to invest the old idea of a "double" with a new meaning and to ascribe many things to it, above all, those things which seem to the new faculty of self-criticism to belong to the old surmounted narcissism of the earliest period of all.[7]

But it is not only this narcissism, offensive to the ego-criticizing faculty, which may be incorporated in the idea of a double. There are also all those unfulfilled but possible futures to which we still like to cling in phantasy, all those strivings of the ego which adverse external circumstances have crushed, and all our suppressed acts of volition which nourish in us the illusion of Free Will.[8]

But, after having thus considered the manifest motivation of the figure of a "double," we have to admit that none of it helps us to understand the extraordinarily strong feeling of something uncanny that pervades the conception; and our knowledge of pathological mental processes enables us to add that nothing in the content arrived at could account for that impulse towards self-protection which has caused the ego to project such a content outward as something foreign to itself. The quality of uncanniness can only come from the circumstance of the "double" being a creation dating back to a very early mental stage – long since left behind, and one, no doubt, in which it wore a more friendly aspect. The "double" has become a vision of terror, just as after the fall of their religion the gods took on daemonic shapes.[9]

It is not difficult to judge, on the same lines as his theme of the "double," the other forms of disturbance in the ego made use of by Hoffmann. They are a harking-back to particular phases in the evolution of the self-regarding feeling, a regression to a time when the ego was not yet sharply differentiated from the external world and from other persons. I believe that these factors are partly responsible for the impression of the uncanny, although it is not easy to isolate and determine exactly their share of it.

That factor which consists in a recurrence of the same situations, things and events, will perhaps not appeal to everyone as a source of uncanny feeling. From what I have observed, this phenomenon does undoubtedly, subject to certain conditions and combined with certain circumstances, awaken an uncanny feeling, which recalls that sense of helplessness sometimes experienced in dreams. Once, as I was walking through the deserted streets of a provincial town in Italy which was strange to me, on a hot summer afternoon, I found myself in a quarter the character of which could not long remain in doubt. Nothing but painted women were to be seen at the windows of the small houses, and I hastened to leave the narrow street at the next turning. But after having wandered about for a while without being directed, I suddenly found myself back in the same street, where my presence was now beginning to excite attention. I hurried away once more, but only to arrive yet a third time by devious paths in the same place. Now, however, a feeling overcame me which I can only describe as uncanny, and I was glad enough to abandon my exploratory walk and get straight back to the piazza I had left a short while before. Other situations having in common with my adventure an involuntary return to the same situation, but which differ radically from it in other respects, also result in the same feeling of helplessness and of something uncanny. As, for instance, when one is lost in a forest in high altitudes, caught, we will suppose, by the mountain mist, and when every endeavour to find the marked or familiar path ends again and again in a return to one and the same spot, recognizable by some particular landmark. Or when one wanders about in a dark, strange room looking for the door or the electric switch, and collides for the hundredth time with the same piece of furniture – a situation which, indeed, has been made irresistibly comic by Mark Twain, through the wild extravagance of his narration.

Taking another class of things, it is easy to see that here, too, it is only this factor of involuntary repetition which surrounds with an uncanny atmosphere what would otherwise be innocent enough, and forces upon us the idea of something fateful and unescapable where otherwise we should have spoken of "chance" only. For instance, we of course attach no importance to the event when we give up a coat and get a cloakroom ticket with the number, say, 62; or when we find that our cabin on board ship is numbered 62. But the impression is altered if two such events, each in itself indifferent, happen close together, if we come across the number 62 several times in a single day, or if we begin to notice that everything which has a number – addresses, hotel-rooms, compartments in railway-trains – always has the same one, or one which at least contains the same figures.

We do feel this to be "uncanny," and unless a man is utterly hardened and proof against the lure of superstition he will be tempted to ascribe a secret meaning to this obstinate recurrence of a number, taking it, perhaps, as an indication of the span of life allotted to him. Or take the case that one is engaged at the time in reading the works of Hering, the famous physiologist, and then receives within the space of a few days two letters from two different countries, each from a person called Hering; whereas one has never before had any dealings with anyone of that name. Not long ago an ingenious scientist attempted to reduce coincidences of this kind to certain laws, and so deprive them of their uncanny effect.[10] I will not venture to decide whether he has succeeded or not.

How exactly we can trace back the uncanny effect of such recurrent similarities to infantile psychology is a question I can only lightly touch upon in these pages; and I must refer the reader instead to another pamphlet[11] now ready for publication, in which this has been gone into in detail, but in a different connection. It must be explained that we are able to postulate the principle of a repetition-compulsion in the unconscious mind, based upon instinctual activity and probably inherent in the very nature of the instincts – a principle powerful enough to overrule the pleasure principle, lending to certain aspects of the mind their daemonic character, and still very clearly expressed in the tendencies of small children; a principle, too, which is responsible for a part of the course taken by the analyses of neurotic patients. Taken in all, the foregoing prepares us for the discovery that whatever reminds us of this inner *repetition-compulsion* is perceived as uncanny.

Now, however, it is time to turn from these aspects of the matter, which are in any case difficult to decide upon, and look for undeniable instances of the uncanny, in the hope that analysis of them will settle whether our hypothesis is a valid one.

In the story of "The Ring of Polycrates," the guest turns away from his friend with horror because he sees that his every wish is at once fulfilled, his every care immediately removed by kindly fate. His host has become "uncanny" to him. His own explanation, that the too fortunate man has to fear the envy of the gods, seems still rather obscure to us; its meaning is veiled in mythological language. We will therefore turn to another example in a less grandiose setting. In the case history of an obsessional neurotic,[12] I have described how the patient once stayed in a hydropathic establishment and benefited greatly by it. He had the good sense, however, to attribute his improvement not to the therapeutic properties of the water, but to the situation of his room, which immediately adjoined that of a very amiable nurse. So on his second visit to the establishment he asked for the same room but was told that it was already occupied by an old gentleman, whereupon he gave vent to his annoyance in the words, "Well, I hope he'll have a stroke and die." A fortnight later the old gentleman really did have a stroke. My patient thought this an "uncanny" experience. And that impression of uncanniness would have been stronger still if less time had elapsed between his exclamation and the untoward event, or if he had been able to produce innumerable similar coincidences. As a matter of fact, he had no difficulty in producing coincidences of this sort, but then not only he but all obsessional neurotics I have observed are able to relate analogous experiences. They are never surprised when they invariably run up against the person they have just been thinking of, perhaps for the first time for many months. If they say one day "I haven't had news of so-and-so for a long time," they will be sure to get a letter from him the next morning. And an accident or a death will rarely take place without having cast its shadow before on their minds. They are in the habit of mentioning this state of affairs in the most modest manner, saying that they have "presentiments" which "usually" come true.

One of the most uncanny and wide-spread forms of superstition is the dread of the evil eye.[13] There never seems to have been any doubt about the source of this dread. Whoever possesses something at once valuable and fragile is afraid of the envy of others, in that he projects on to them the envy he would have felt in their place. A feeling like this betrays itself in a look even though it is not put into words; and when a man attracts the attention of others by noticeable, and particularly by unattractive, attributes, they are ready to believe that his envy is rising to more than usual heights and that this intensity in it will convert it into effective action. What is feared is thus a secret intention of harming someone, and certain signs are taken to mean that such an intention is capable of becoming an act.

These last examples of the uncanny are to be referred to that principle in the mind which I have called "omnipotence of thoughts," taking the name from an expression used by one of my patients. And now we find ourselves on well-known ground. Our analysis of instances of the uncanny has led us back to the old, animistic conception of the universe which was characterized by the idea that the world was peopled with the spirits of humane narcissistic overestimation of subjective mental processes (such as the belief in the omnipotence of thoughts, the magical practices based upon this belief, the carefully proportioned distribution of magical powers or "mana" among various outside persons and things), as well as by all those other figments of the imagination with which man, in the unrestricted narcissism of that stage of development, strove to withstand the inexorable laws of reality. It would seem as though each one of us has been through a phase of individual development corresponding to that animistic stage in primitive men, that none of us has traversed it without preserving certain traces of it which can be reactivated and that everything which now strikes us as "uncanny" fulfills the condition of stirring these vestiges of animistic mental activity within us and bringing them to expression.[14]

At this point I will put forward two considerations which, I think, contain the gist of this short study. In the first place, if psycho-analytic theory is correct in maintaining that every emotional affect, whatever its quality, is transformed by repression into morbid anxiety, then among such cases of anxiety there must be a class in which the anxiety can be shown to come from something repressed which *recurs*. This class of morbid anxiety would then be no other than what is uncanny, irrespective of whether it originally aroused dread or some other affect. In the second place, if this is indeed the secret nature of the uncanny, we can understand why the usage of speech has extended *das Heimliche* into its opposite *das Unheimliche*;[15] for this uncanny is in reality nothing new or foreign, but something familiar and old – established in the mind that has been estranged only by the process of repression. This reference to the factor of repression enables us, furthermore, to understand Schelling's definition of the uncanny as something which ought to have been kept concealed but which has nevertheless come to light.

Notes

1   [Throughout this paper "uncanny" is used as the English translation of "*unheimlich*," literally "unhomely." – Trans.]
2   [From *Haus* = house; *Haüslichkeit* = domestic life. – Trans.]
3   Hoffmann's *Sämtliche Werke*, Grisebach Edition, 3. [A translation of "The Sand-Man" is included in *Eight Tales of Hoffmann*, translated by J. M. Cohen (London: Pan Books, 1952).]
4   Frau Dr Rank has pointed out the association of the name with "*coppella*" = crucible, connecting it with the chemical operations that caused the father's death; and also with "*coppo*" = eye-socket. [Except in the first (1919) edition this footnote was attached, it seems erroneously, to the first occurrence of the name Coppelius on this page.]
5   In fact, Hoffmann's imaginative treatment of his material has not made such wild confusion of its elements that we cannot reconstruct their original arrangement. In the story of Nathaniel's childhood, the figures of his father and Coppelius represent the two opposites into which the father-imago is split by his ambivalence; whereas the one threatens to blind him – that is, to castrate him – the other, the "good" father, intercedes for his sight. The part of the complex which is most strongly repressed, the death-wish against the "bad" father, finds expression in the death of the "good" father, and Coppelius is made answerable for it. This pair of fathers is represented later, in his student days, by Professor Spalanzani and Coppola the optician. The Professor is in himself a member of the father-series, and Coppola is recognized as identical with Coppelius the lawyer. Just as they used before to work together over the secret brazier, so now they have jointly created the doll Olympia; the Professor is even called the father of Olympia. This double occurrence of activity in common betrays them as divisions of the father-imago: both the mechanician and the optician were the father of Nathaniel (and of Olympia as well). In the frightening scene in childhood, Coppelius, after sparing Nathaniel's eyes, had screwed off his arms and legs as an experiment; that is, he had worked on him as a mechanician would on a doll. This singular feature, which seems quite outside the picture of the Sand-Man, introduces a new castration equivalent; but it also points to the inner identity of Coppelius with his later counterpart, Spalanzani the mechanician, and prepares us for the interpretation of Olympia. This automatic doll can be nothing else than a materialization of Nathaniel's feminine

attitude towards his father in his infancy. Her fathers, Spalanzani and Coppola, are, after all, nothing but new editions, reincarnations of Nathaniel's pair of fathers. Spalanzani's otherwise incomprehensible statement that the optician has stolen Nathaniel's eyes...so as to set them in the doll, now becomes significant as supplying evidence of the identity of Olympia and Nathaniel. Olympia is, as it were, a dissociated complex of Nathaniel's which confronts him as a person, and Nathaniel's enslavement to this complex is expressed in his senseless obsessive love for Olympia. We may with justice call love of this kind narcissistic, and we can understand why someone who has fallen victim to it should relinquish the real, external object of his love. The psychological truth of the situation in which the young man, fixated upon his father by his castration complex, becomes incapable of loving a woman, is amply proved by numerous analyses of patients whose story, though less fantastic, is hardly less tragic than that of the student Nathaniel.

Hoffmann was the child of an unhappy marriage. When he was three years old, his father left his small family, and was never united to them again. According to Grisebach, in his biographical introduction to Hoffmann's works, the writer's relation to his father was always a most sensitive subject with him.

6   "Der Doppelgänger."

7   I cannot help thinking that when poets complain that two souls dwell within the human breast, and when popular psychologists talk of the splitting of the ego in an individual, they have some notion of this division (which relates to the sphere of ego-psychology) between the critical faculty and the rest of the ego, and not of the antithesis discovered by psycho-analysis between the ego and what is unconscious and repressed. It is true that the distinction is to some extent effaced by the circumstance that derivatives of what is repressed are foremost among the things reprehended by the ego-criticizing.

8   In Ewers' *Der Student von Prag*, which furnishes the starting-point of Rank's study on the "double," the hero has promised his beloved not to kill his antagonist in a duel. But on his way to the dueling-ground he meets his "double," who has already killed his rival.

9   Heine, *Die Götter im Evil*.

10 P. Kammere, *Das Gesetz der Serie*.

11 [*Beyond the Pleasure Principle*. – Trans.]

12 Freud, "Notes upon a Case of Obsessional Neurosis," *Collected Papers*, vol. iii.

13 Seligmann, the Hamburg ophthalmologist, has made a thorough study of this superstition in his *Der böse Blick und Verwandtes*.

14 Cf. my book *Totem and Tabu*, part iii, "Animismus Magie und Allmacht der Gedanken"; also the footnote on p. 7 of the same book. "It would appear that we invest with a feeling of uncanniness those impressions which lend support to a belief in the omnipotence of thoughts and to the animistic attitude of mind at a time when our judgement has already rejected these same beliefs."

15 Cf. abstract on pp. 419–20.

CHAPTER 5

Beyond the Pleasure Principle

Sigmund Freud

Written in 1920, Freud's *Beyond the Pleasure Principle* was his attempt to come to terms with his realization that more seemed at work in the mind and in human life than a drive for pleasure. In this book he describes two major drives, one toward the building up of libidinal cathexes or attachments and the raising of excitation, the other toward their diminution and ultimate extinction. In this less speculative section, he discusses an example of an important principle he felt he had discovered in human life, and that is the tendency to repeat experiences or to engage in repetitive behavior. The "death drive," as he called it, seeks to repeat the earliest, pre-life experience of quiescence. But in a more mundane way, we all repeat things or seek to repeat them. In the example Freud elucidates here, he explains one kind of repetitive behavior as an attempt to deal with traumatic experiences of loss.

The different theories of children's play have only recently been summarized and discussed from the psycho-analytic point of view by Pfeifer (1919), to whose paper I would refer my readers. These theories attempt to discover the motives which lead children to play, but they fail to bring into the foreground the *economic motive*, the consideration of the yield of pleasure involved. Without wishing to include the whole field covered by these phenomena, I have been able, through a chance opportunity which presented itself, to throw some light upon the first game played by a little boy of one and a half and invented by himself. It was more than a mere fleeting observation, for I lived under the same roof as the child and his parents for some weeks, and it was some time before I discovered the meaning of the puzzling activity which he constantly repeated.

The child was not at all precocious in his intellectual development. At the age of one and a half he could say only a few comprehensible words; he could also make use of a number of sounds which expressed a meaning intelligible to those around him. He was, however, on good terms with his parents and their one servant-girl, and tributes were paid to his being a "good boy." He did not disturb his parents at night, he conscientiously obeyed orders not to touch certain things or go into certain rooms, and above all he never cried when his mother left him for a few hours. At the same time, he was greatly attached to his mother, who had not only fed him herself but had also looked after him without any outside help. This good little boy, however, had an occasional disturbing habit of taking any small objects he could get hold of and throwing them away from him into a corner, under the bed, and so on, so that hunting for his toys and picking them up was often quite a business. As he did this he gave vent to a loud, long-drawn-out "o-o-o-o," accompanied by an expression of interest and satisfaction. His mother and the writer of the present account were agreed in thinking that this was not a mere interjection but represented the German word *"fort"* ["gone"]. I eventually realized that it was a game and that the only use he made of any of his toys was to play "gone" with them. One day I made an observation which confirmed my view. The child had a wooden reel with a piece of string tied round it. It never occurred to him to pull it along the floor behind him, for instance, and play at its being a carriage. What he did was to hold the reel by the string and very skillfully throw it over the edge of his curtained cot, so that it disappeared into it, at the same time uttering his expressive "o-o-o-o." He then pulled the reel out of the cot again by the string and hailed its reappearance with a joyful *"da"* ["there"]. This, then, was the complete game – disappearance and return. As a rule one only witnessed its first act, which was repeated untiringly as a game in itself, though there is no doubt that the greater pleasure was attached to the second act.[1]

The interpretation of the game then became obvious. It was related to the child's great cultural achievement – the instinctual renunciation (that is, the renunciation of instinctual satisfaction) which he had made in allowing his mother to go away without protesting. He compensated himself for this, as it were, by himself staging the disappearance and return of the objects within his reach. It is of course a matter of indifference from the point of view of judging the effective nature of the game whether the child invented it himself or took it over on some outside suggestion. Our interest is directed to another point. The child cannot possibly have felt his mother's departure as something agreeable or even indifferent. How then does his repetition of this distressing experience as a game fit in with the pleasure principle? It may perhaps be said in reply that her departure had to be enacted as a necessary preliminary to her joyful return, and that it was in the latter that lay the true purpose of the game. But against this must be counted the observed fact that the first act, that of departure, was staged as a game in itself and far more frequently than the episode in its entirety, with its pleasurable ending.

No certain decision can be reached from the analysis of a single case like this. On an unprejudiced view one gets an impression that the child turned his experience into a game from another motive. At the outset he was in a passive situation – he was overpowered by the experience; but, by repeating it, unpleasurable though it was, as a game, he took on an active part. These efforts might be put down to an instinct for mastery that was acting independently of whether the memory was in itself pleasurable or not. But still another interpretation may be attempted. Throwing away the object so that it was "gone" might satisfy an impulse of the child's, which was suppressed in his actual life, to revenge himself on his mother for going away from him. In that case it would have a defiant meaning: "All right, then, go away! I don't need you. I'm sending you away myself." A year later, the same boy whom I had observed at his first game used to take a toy, if he was angry with it, and throw it on the floor, exclaiming: "Go to the front!" He had heard at that time that his absent father was "at the front," and was far from regretting his absence; on the contrary he made it quite clear that he had no desire to be disturbed in his sole possession of his mother.[2] We know of other children who liked to express similar hostile impulses by throwing away objects instead of persons.[3] We are therefore left in doubt as to whether the impulse to work over in the mind some overpowering experience so as to make oneself master of it can find expression as a primary event, and independently of the pleasure principle. For, in the case we have been discussing, the child may, after all, only have been able to repeat his unpleasant experience in play because the repetition carried along with it a yield of pleasure of another sort but none the less a direct one.

Nor shall we be helped in our hesitation between these two views by further considering children's play. It is clear that in their play children repeat everything that has made a great impression on them in real life, and that in doing so they abreact the strength of the impression and, as one might put it, make themselves master of the situation. But on the other hand it is obvious that all their play is influenced by a wish that dominates them the whole time – the wish to be grown-up and to be able to do what grown-up people do. It can also be observed that the unpleasurable nature of an experience does not always unsuit it for play. If the doctor looks down a child's throat or carries out some small operation on him, we may be quite sure that these frightening experiences will be the subject of the next game; but we must not in that connection overlook the fact that there is a yield of pleasure from another source. As the child passes over from the passivity of the experience to the activity of the game, he hands on the disagreeable experience to one of his playmates and in this way revenges himself on a substitute.

Nevertheless, it emerges from this discussion that there is no need to assume the existence of a special imitative instinct in order to provide a motive for play. Finally, a reminder may be added that the artistic play and artistic imitation carried out by adults, which, unlike children's, are aimed at an audience, do not spare the spectators (for instance, in tragedy) the most painful experiences and can yet be felt by them as highly enjoyable. This is convincing proof that, even under the dominance of the pleasure principle, there are ways and means enough of making what is in itself unpleasurable into a subject to be recollected and worked over in the mind. The consideration of these cases and situations, which have a yield of pleasure as their final outcome, should be undertaken by some system of aesthetics with an economic approach to its subject-matter. They are of no use for our purposes, since they presuppose the existence and dominance of the pleasure principle; they give no evidence of the operation of tendencies beyond the pleasure principle, that is, of tendencies more primitive than it and independent of it.

III

Twenty-five years of intense work have had as their result that the immediate aims of psycho-analytic technique are quite other to-day than they were at the outset. At first the analyzing physician could do no more than discover the unconscious material that was concealed from the patient, put it together, and, at the right moment, communicate it to him. Psychoanalysis was then first and foremost an art of interpreting. Since this did not solve the therapeutic problem, a further aim quickly came in view: to oblige the patient to confirm the analyst's construction from his own memory. In that endeavor the chief emphasis lay upon the patient's resistances: the art consisted now in uncovering these as quickly as possible, in pointing them out to the patient and in inducing him by human influence – this was where suggestion operating as "transference" played its part – to abandon his resistances.

But it became ever clearer that the aim which had been set up – the aim that what was unconscious should become conscious – is not completely attainable by that method. The patient cannot remember the whole of what is repressed in him, and what he cannot remember may be precisely the essential part of it. Thus he acquires no sense of conviction of the correctness of the construction that has been communicated to him. He is obliged to repeat the repressed material as a contemporary experience instead of, as the physician would prefer to see, remembering it as something belonging to the past.[4] These reproductions, which emerge with such unwished-for exactitude, always have as their subject some portion of infantile sexual life – of the Oedipus complex, that is, and its derivatives; and they are invariably acted out in the sphere of the transference, of the patient's relation to the physician. When things have reached this stage, it may be said that the earlier neurosis has now been replaced by a fresh, "transference neurosis." It has been the physician's endeavor to keep this transference neurosis within the narrowest limits: to force as much as possible into the channel of memory and to allow as little as possible to emerge as repetition. The ratio between what is remembered and what is reproduced varies from case to case. The physician cannot as a rule spare his patient this phase of the treatment. He must get him to re-experience some portion of his forgotten life, but must see to it, on the other hand, that the patient retains some degree of aloofness, which will enable him, in spite of everything, to recognize that what appears to be reality is in fact only a reflection of a forgotten past. If this can be successfully achieved, the patient's sense of conviction is won, together with the therapeutic success that is dependent on it.

In order to make it easier to understand this "compulsion to repeat," which emerges during the psycho-analytic treatment of neurotics, we must above all get rid of the mistaken notion that what we are dealing with in our struggle against resistances is resistance on the part of the unconscious. The unconscious – that is to say, the "repressed" – offers no resistance whatever to the efforts of the treatment. Indeed, it itself has no other endeavor than to break through the pressure weighing down on it and force its way either to consciousness or to a discharge through some real action. Resistance during treatment arises from the same higher strata and systems of the mind which originally carried out repression. But the fact that, as we know from experience, the motives of the resistances, and indeed the resistances themselves, are unconscious at first during the treatment, is a hint to us that we should correct a shortcoming in our terminology. We shall avoid a lack of clarity if we make our contrast not between the conscious and the unconscious but between the coherent ego I and the repressed. It is certain that much of the ego is itself unconscious, and notably what we may describe as its nucleus; only a small part of it is covered by the term "preconscious." Having replaced a purely descriptive terminology by one which is systematic or dynamic, we can say that the patient's resistance arises from his "ego," and we then at once perceive that the compulsion to repeat must be ascribed to the unconscious repressed. It seems probable that the compulsion can only express itself after the work of treatment has gone half-way to meet it and has loosened the repression.[5]

There is no doubt that the resistance of the conscious and unconscious ego operates under the sway of the pleasure principle: it seeks to avoid the unpleasure which would be produced by the liberation of the repressed. Our efforts, on the other hand, are directed towards procuring the toleration of that unpleasure by an appeal to the reality principle. But how is the compulsion to repeat – the manifestation of the power of the repressed – related to the pleasure principle? It is clear that the greater part of what is re-experienced under the compulsion to repeat must cause the ego unpleasure, since it brings to light activities of repressed instinctual impulses. That, however, is unpleasure of a kind we have already considered and does not contradict the pleasure principle: unpleasure for one system and simultaneously satisfaction for the other. But we come now to a new and remarkable fact, namely that the compulsion to repeat also recalls from the past experiences which include no possibility of pleasure, and which can never, even long ago, have brought satisfaction even to instinctual impulses which have since been repressed.

The early efflorescence of infantile sexual life is doomed to extinction because its wishes are incompatible with reality and with the inadequate stage of development which the child has reached. That efflorescence comes to an end in the most distressing circumstances and to the accompaniment of the most painful feelings. Loss of love and failure leave behind them a permanent injury to self-regard in the form of a narcissistic scar, which in my opinion...contributes more than anything to the "sense of inferiority" which is so common in neurotics. The child's sexual researches, on which limits are imposed by his physical development, lead to no satisfactory conclusion; hence such later complaints as "I can't accomplish anything; I can't succeed in anything." The tie of affection, which binds the child as a rule to the parent of the opposite sex, succumbs to disappointment, to a vain expectation of satisfaction or to jealousy over the birth of a new baby – unmistakable proof of the infidelity of the object of the child's affections. His own attempt to make a baby himself, carried out with tragic seriousness, fails shamefully. The lessening amount of affection he receives, the increasing demands of education, hard words and an occasional punishment – these show him at last the full extent to which he has been scorned. These are a few typical and constantly recurring instances of the ways in which the love characteristic of the age of childhood is brought to a conclusion.

Patients repeat all of these unwanted situations and painful emotions in the transference and revive them with the greatest ingenuity. They seek to bring about the interruption of the treatment while it is still incomplete; they contrive once more to feel themselves scorned, to oblige the physician to speak severely to them and treat them coldly; they discover appropriate objects for their jealousy; instead of the passionately desired baby of their childhood, they produce a plan or a promise of some grand present – which turns out as a rule to be no less unreal. None of these things can have produced pleasure in the past, and it might be supposed that they would cause less unpleasure to-day if they emerged as memories or dreams instead of taking the form of fresh experiences. They are of course the activities of instincts intended to lead to satisfaction; but no lesson has been learnt from the old experience of these activities having led instead only to unpleasure. In spite of that, they are repeated, under pressure of a compulsion.

What psycho-analysis reveals in the transference phenomena of neurotics can also be observed in the lives of some normal people. The impression they give is of being pursued by a malignant fate or possessed by some "daemonic" power; but psycho-analysis has always taken the view that their fate is for the most part arranged by themselves and determined by early infantile influences. The compulsion which is here in evidence differs in no way from the compulsion to repeat which we have found in neurotics, even though the people we are now considering have never shown any signs of dealing with a neurotic conflict by producing symptoms. Thus we have come across people all of whose human relationships have the same outcome:

such as the benefactor who is abandoned in anger after a time by each of his protégés, however much they may otherwise differ from one another, and who thus seems doomed to taste all the bitterness of ingratitude; or the man whose friendships all end in betrayal by his friend; or the man who time after time in the course of his life raises someone else into a position of great private or public authority and then, after a certain interval, himself upsets that authority and replaces him by a new one; or, again, the lover each of whose love affairs with a woman passes through the same phases and reaches the same conclusion. This "perpetual recurrence of the same thing" causes us no astonishment when it relates to active behavior on the part of the person concerned and when we can discern in him an essential character-trait which always remains the same and which is compelled to find expression in a repetition of the same experiences. We are much more impressed by cases where the subject appears to have a passive experience, over which he has no influence, but in which he meets with a repetition of the same fatality. There is the case, for instance, of the woman who married three successive husbands each of whom fell ill soon afterwards and had to be nursed by her on their death-beds.[6] The most moving poetic picture of a fate such as this is given by Tasso in his romantic epic *Gerusalemme Liberata*. Its hero, Tancred, unwittingly kills his beloved Clorinda in a duel while she is disguised in the armor of an enemy knight. After her burial he makes his way into a strange magic forest which strikes the Crusaders' army with terror. He slashes with his sword at a tall tree; but blood streams from the cut and the voice of Clorinda, whose soul is imprisoned in the tree, is heard complaining that he has wounded his beloved once again.

If we take into account observations such as these, based upon behavior in the transference and upon the life-histories of men and women, we shall find courage to assume that there really does exist in the mind a compulsion to repeat which overrides the pleasure principle. Now too we shall be inclined to relate to this compulsion the dreams which occur in traumatic neuroses and the impulse which leads children to play.

But it is to be noted that only in rare instances can we observe the pure effects of the compulsion to repeat, unsupported by other motives. In the case of children's play we have already laid stress on the other ways in which the emergence of the compulsion may be interpreted; the compulsion to repeat and instinctual satisfaction which is immediately pleasurable seem to converge here into an intimate partnership. The phenomena of transference are obviously exploited by the resistance which the ego maintains in its pertinacious insistence upon repression; the compulsion to repeat, which the treatment tries to bring into its service is, as it were, drawn over by the ego to its side (clinging as the ego does to the pleasure principle). A great deal of what might be described as the compulsion of destiny seems intelligible on a rational basis; so that we are under no necessity to call in a new and mysterious motive force to explain it.

Notes

1   A further observation subsequently confirmed this interpretation fully. One day the child's mother had been away for several hours and on her return was met with the words "Baby o-o-o-o!" which was at first incomprehensible. It soon turned out, however, that during

this long period of solitude the child had found a method of making *himself* disappear. He had discovered his reflection in a full-length mirror which did not quite reach to the ground, so that by crouching down he could make his mirror-image "gone." [A further reference to this story will be found in *The Interpretation of Dreams, Standard Edition*, 5, p. 461n.]

2   When this child was five and three-quarters, his mother died. Now that she was really "gone" ("o-o-o"), the little boy showed no signs of grief. It is true that in the interval a second child had been born and had roused him to violent jealousy.

3   Cf. my note on a childhood memory of Goethe's (1917b).

4   See my paper on "Recollecting, Repeating and Working Through" (*Standard Edition*, 12). [An early reference will be found in this same paper to the "compulsion to repeat," which is one of the principal topics discussed in the present work. The term "transference neurosis" in the special sense in which it is used a few lines lower down also appears in that paper.]

5   [*Footnote added* 1923:] I have argued elsewhere that what thus comes to the help of the compulsion to repeat is the factor of "suggestion" in the treatment – that is, the patient's submissiveness to the physician, which has its roots deep in his unconscious parental complex.

6   Cf. the apt remarks on this subject by C. G. Jung, "The Significance of the Father in the Destiny of the Individual," *Collected Papers on Analytic Psychology* (London, 1916), p. 156.

CHAPTER 6

Group Psychology and the Analysis of the Ego

Sigmund Freud

In this essay from 1921, Freud put forth an important concept for later psychoanalysis – identification. The child's ability to internalize representations of caregivers and others in its immediate social environment lies at the heart of later object relations theory. It seeks to account for the social character of the self, the way it is built up from relations with others. Freud here also hints at a more sociological version of the very dubious ideas of "castration" and of "castration complex," ideas that mistakenly turn historically specific and local cultural anecdotes about threats issued to children into psychological and anthropological principles. In that sociological account, what Freud calls "castration anxiety" would be seen as a misinterpretation or misnaming of an anxiety any young person feels as he or she undergoes the passage into sexual adulthood. The anxiety over loss has to do more with an anxiety over being able to fulfill the demands of the social ideal of adult sexual identity. One way of achieving an adult identity is to identify with the father or mother and to attempt to emulate them.

Identification is known to psycho-analysis as the earliest expression of an emotional tie with another person. It plays a part in the early history of the Oedipus complex. A little boy will exhibit a special interest in his father; he would like to grow like him and be like him, and take his place everywhere. We may say simply that he takes his father as his ideal. This behavior has nothing to do with a passive or feminine attitude towards his father (and towards males in general); it is on the contrary typically masculine. It fits in very well with the Oedipus complex, for which it helps to prepare the way.

At the same time as this identification with his father, or a little later, the boy has begun to develop a true object-cathexis towards his mother according to the attachment [anaclitic] type. He then exhibits, therefore, two psychologically distinct ties: a straightforward sexual object-cathexis towards his mother and an identification with his father which takes him as his model. The two subsist side by side for a time without any mutual influence or interference. In consequence of the irresistible advance towards a unification of mental life, they come together at last; and the normal Oedipus complex originates from their confluence. The little boy notices that his father stands in his way with his mother. His identification with his father then takes on a hostile coloring and becomes identical with the wish to replace his father in regard to his mother as well. Identification, in fact, is ambivalent from the very first; it can turn into an expression of tenderness as easily as into a wish for someone's removal. It behaves like a derivative of the first, *oral* phase of the organization of the libido, in which the object that we long for and prize is assimilated by eating and is in that way annihilated as such. The cannibal, as we know, has remained at this standpoint; he has a devouring affection for his enemies and only devours people of whom he is fond.[1]

The subsequent history of this identification with the father may easily be lost sight of. It may happen that the Oedipus complex becomes inverted, and that the father is taken as the object of a feminine attitude, an object from which the directly sexual instincts look for satisfaction; in that event the identification with the father has become the precursor of an object-tie with the father. The same holds good, with the necessary substitutions, of the baby daughter as well.

It is easy to state in a formula the distinction between an identification with the father and the choice of the father as an object. In the first case one's father is what one would like to *be*, and in the second he is what one would like to *have*. The distinction, that is, depends upon whether the tie attaches to the subject or to the object of the ego. The former kind of tie is therefore already possible before any sexual object-choice has been made. It is much more difficult to give a clear meta-psychological representation of the distinction. We can only see that identification endeavors to mold a person's own ego after the fashion of the one that has been taken as a model.

Let us disentangle identification as it occurs in the structure of a neurotic symptom from its rather complicated connections. Supposing that a little girl (and we will keep to her for the present) develops the same painful symptom as her mother – for instance, the same tormenting cough. This may come about in various ways. The identification may come from the Oedipus complex; in that case it signifies a hostile desire on the girl's part to take her mother's place, and the symptom expresses her object-love towards her father, and brings about a realization, under the influence of a sense of guilt, of her desire to take her mother's place: "You wanted to be your mother, and now you *are* – anyhow so far as your sufferings are concerned." This is the complete mechanism of the structure of a hysterical symptom. Or, on the other hand, the symptom may be the same as that of the person who is loved; so, for instance, Dora[2] imitated her father's cough. In that case we can only describe the state of things by saying *that identification has appeared instead of object-choice, and that object-choice has regressed to identification.* We have heard that identification is the earliest and original form of emotional tie; it often happens that under the conditions in which symptoms are constructed, that is, where there is repression and where the mechanisms of the unconscious are dominant, object-choice is turned back into identification – the ego assumes the characteristics of the object. It is noticeable that in these identifications the ego sometimes copies the person who is not loved and sometimes the one who is loved. It must also strike us that in both cases the identification is a partial and extremely limited one and only borrows a single trait from the person who is its object.

There is a third particularly frequent and important case of symptom formation, in which the identification leaves entirely out of account any object-relation to the person who is being copied. Supposing, for instance, that one of the girls in a boarding school has had a letter from someone with whom she is secretly in love which arouses her jealousy, and that she reacts to it with a fit of hysterics; then some of her friends who know about it will catch the fit, as we say, by mental infection.

The mechanism is that of identification based upon the possibility or desire of putting oneself in the same situation. The other girls would like to have a secret love affair too, and under the influence of a sense of guilt they also accept the suffering involved in it. It would be wrong to suppose that they take on the symptom out of sympathy. On the contrary, the sympathy only arises out of the identification, and this is proved by the fact that infection or imitation of this kind takes place in circumstances where even less pre-existing sympathy is to be assumed than usually exists between friends in a girls' school. One ego has perceived a significant analogy with another upon one point – in our example upon openness to a similar emotion; an identification is thereupon constructed on this point, and, under the influence of the pathogenic situation, is displaced on to the symptom which the one ego has produced. The identification by means of the symptom has thus become the mark of a point of coincidence between the two egos which has to be kept repressed.

What we have learned from these three sources may be summarized as follows. First, identification is the original form of emotional tie with an object; secondly, in a regressive way it becomes a substitute for a libidinal object-tie, as it were by means of introjection of the object into the ego; and thirdly, it may arise with any new perception of a common quality shared with some other person who is not an object of the sexual instinct. The more important this common quality is, the more success-ful may this partial identification become, and it may thus represent the beginning of a new tie.

Notes

1 See my *Three Essays* [*Standard Edition*, 7 (1905), p. 198] and Abraham, "The First Pregenital Stage of the Libido," *Selected Papers on Psycho-Analysis* (London, 1927), ch. XII.
2 In my "Fragment of an Analysis of a Case of Hysteria," *Standard Edition*, 7 (1905), pp. 82–3.

CHAPTER 7

The Mirror Stage as Formative of the Function of the I as Revealed in Psychoanalytic Experience

Jacques Lacan

Jacques Lacan's *Ecrits* (1966) was the most influential work of structuralist psychoanalysis. Lacan's work constitutes a rebuke to ego or self psychology and a return to Freud's belief in the power of the unconscious in human life. Yet his work also rewrites Freud in important ways. He inserts the self into culture. We are all shaped by the Symbolic order into which we are born, an order that determines our gender identity and our place in our families. When we learn to make symbols, we also learn to separate from our ambient childhood world of objects and achieve an independent selfhood that is experienced as loss. That lack can never be filled, and all human desire circulates around it, yearning to hark back to the lost unity. Lacan calls such yearning and the kind of consciousness it provokes the Imaginary. It is the narcissistic part of the mind that defines ego activity. Lacan placed great emphasis on Freud's contention that the ego deludes itself into thinking it controls the mind. What the ego cannot reach or know is the Real, the realm of the drives, the instincts, and the unconscious processes that shape our selves but that cannot be known by a mind that constitutes itself as the effacement of such determination. In this famous essay from 1949, Lacan describes his concept of the self as a delusory construct plagued in its very constitution by imaginary identifications with a spurious sense of wholeness or unity. Lacan's polemic is directed against those ego psychologists who were just beginning in England and America to explore the possibility that psychoanalysis should focus on the whole complex of the self in its social setting rather than on the dynamic interrelations between consciousness and the unconscious.

The conception of the mirror stage that I introduced at our last congress, thirteen years ago, has since become more or less established in the practice of the French group. However, I think it worthwhile to bring it again to your attention, especially today, for the light it sheds on the formation of the I as we experience it in psychoanalysis. It is an experience that leads us to oppose any philosophy directly issuing from the *Cogito*.

Some of you may recall that this conception originated in a feature of human behavior illuminated by a fact of comparative psychology. The child, at an age when he is for a time, however short, outdone by the chimpanzee in instrumental intelligence, can nevertheless already recognize as such his own image in a mirror. This recognition is indicated in the illuminative mimicry of the *Aha-Erlebnis*, which

Kohler sees as the expression of situational apperception, an essential stage of the act of intelligence.

This act, far from exhausting itself, as in the case of the monkey, once the image has been mastered and found empty, immediately rebounds in the case of the child in a series of gestures in which he experiences in play the relation between the movements assumed in the image and the reflected environment, and between this virtual complex and the reality it reduplicates – the child's own body, and the persons and things, around him.

This event can take place, as we have known since Baldwin, from the age of six months, and its repetition has often made me reflect upon the startling spectacle of the infant in front of the mirror. Unable as yet to walk, or even to stand up, and held tightly as he is by some support, human or artificial (what, in France, we call a "*trotte-bébé*"), he nevertheless overcomes, in a flutter of jubilant activity, the obstructions of his support and, fixing his attitude in a slightly leaning-forward position, in order to hold it in his gaze, brings back an instantaneous aspect of the image.

For me, this activity retains the meaning I have given it up to the age of eighteen months. This meaning discloses a libidinal dynamism, which has hitherto remained problematic, as well as an ontological structure of the human world that accords with my reflections on paranoiac knowledge.

We have only to understand the mirror stage as an *identification*, in the full sense that analysis gives to the term: namely, the transformation that takes place in the subject when he assumes an image – whose predestination to this phase-effect is sufficiently indicated by the use, in analytic theory, of the ancient term *imago*.

This jubilant assumption of his specular image by the child at the *infans* stage, still sunk in his motor incapacity and nursling dependence, would seem to exhibit in an exemplary situation the symbolic matrix in which the I is precipitated in a primordial form, before it is objectified in the dialectic of identification with the other, and before language restores to it, in the universal, its function as subject.

This form would have to be called the Ideal-I,[1] if we wished to incorporate it into our usual register, in the sense that it will also be the source of secondary identifications, under which term I would place the functions of libidinal normalization. But the important point is that this form situates the agency of the ego, before its social determination, in a fictional direction, which will always remain irreducible for the individual alone, or rather, which will only rejoin the coming-into-being (*le devenir*) of the subject asymptotically, whatever the success of the dialectical syntheses by which he must resolve as I his discordance with his own reality.

The fact is that the total form of the body by which the subject anticipates in a mirage the maturation of his power is given to him only as *Gestalt*, that is to say, in an exteriority in which this form is certainly more constituent than constituted, but in which it appears to him above all in a contrasting size (*un relief de stature*) that fixes it and in a symmetry that inverts it, in contrast with the turbulent movements that the subject feels are animating him. Thus, this *Gestalt* – whose pregnancy should be regarded as bound up with the species, though its motor style remains scarcely recognizable – by these two aspects of its appearance, symbolizes the mental permanence of the I, at the same time as it prefigures its alienating destination; it is still pregnant with the correspondences that unite the I with the statue in which man projects himself, with the phantoms that dominate him, or with the automaton in which, in an ambiguous relation, the world of his own making tends to find completion.

Indeed, for the *imagos* – whose veiled faces it is our privilege to see in outline in our daily experience and in the penumbra of symbolic efficacity[2] – the mirror-image would seem to be the threshold of the visible world, if we go by the mirror dispos-ition that the *imago of one's own body* presents in hallucinations or dreams, whether it concerns its individual features, or even its infirmities, or its object-projections; or if we observe the role of the mirror apparatus in the appearances of the *double*, in which psychical realities, however heterogeneous, are manifested.

That a *Gestalt* should be capable of formative effects in the organism is attested by a piece of biological experimentation that is itself so alien to the idea of psychical causality that it cannot bring itself to formulate its results in these terms. It neverthe-less recognizes that it is a necessary condition for the maturation of the gonad of the female pigeon that it should see another member of its species, of either sex; so sufficient in itself is this condition that the desired effect may be obtained merely by placing the individual within reach of the field of reflection of a mirror. Similarly, in the case of the migratory locust, the transition within a generation from the solitary to the gregarious form can be obtained by exposing the individual, at a certain stage, to the exclusively visual action of a similar image, provided it is animated by move-ments of a style sufficiently close to that characteristic of the species. Such facts are inscribed in an order of homeomorphic identification that would itself fall within the larger question of the meaning of beauty as both formative and erogenic.

But the facts of mimicry are no less instructive when conceived as cases of hetero-morphic identification, in as much as they raise the problem of the signification of space for the living organism – psychological concepts hardly seem less appropriate for shed-ding light on these matters than ridiculous attempts to reduce them to the supposedly supreme law of adaptation. We have only to recall how Roger Caillois (who was then very young, and still fresh from his breach with the sociological school in which he was trained) illuminated the subject by using the term *"legendary psychasthenia"* to classify morphological mimicry as an obsession with space in its derealizing effect.

I have myself shown in the social dialectic that structures human knowledge as paranoiac[3] why human knowledge has greater autonomy than animal knowledge in relation to the field of force of desire, but also why human knowledge is determined in that "little reality" (*ce peu de réalité*), which the Surrealists, in their restless way, saw as its limitation. These reflections lead me to recognize in the spatial captation manifested in the mirror stage, even before the social dialectic, the effect in man of an organic insufficiency in his natural reality – in so far as any meaning can be given to the word "nature."

I am led, therefore, to regard the function of the mirror stage as a particular case of the function of the *imago*, which is to establish a relation between the organism and its reality – or, as they say, between the *Innenwelt* and the *Umwelt*.

In man, however, this relation to nature is altered by a certain dehiscence at the heart of the organism, a primordial discord betrayed by the signs of uneasiness and motor uncoordination of the neonatal months. The objective notion of the anatomical incompleteness of the pyramidal system and likewise the presence of certain humoral residues of the maternal organism confirm the view I have formulated as the fact of a real *specific prematurity of birth* in man.

It is worth noting, incidentally, that this is a fact recognized as such by embryologists, by the term *foetalization*, which determines the prevalence of the so-called superior apparatus of the neurax, and especially of the cortex, which psycho-surgical operations lead us to regard as the intraorganic mirror.

This development is experienced as a temporal dialectic that decisively projects the formation of the individual into history. The *mirror stage* is a drama whose internal thrust is precipitated from insufficiency to anticipation and which manufactures for the subject, caught up in the lure of spatial identification, the succession of phantasies that extends from a fragmented body-image to a form of its totality that I shall call orthopaedic – and, lastly, to the assumption of the armor of an alienating identity which will mark with its rigid structure the subject's entire mental development. Thus, to break out of the circle of the *Innenwelt* into the *Umwelt* generates the inexhaustible quadrature of the ego's verifications.

This fragmented body – which term I have also introduced into our system of theoretical references – usually manifests itself in dreams when the movement of the analysis encounters a certain level of aggressive disintegration in the individual. It then appears in the form of disjointed limbs, or of those organs represented in exoscopy, growing wings and taking up arms for intestinal persecutions – the very same that the visionary Hieronymus Bosch has fixed, for all time, in painting, in their ascent from the fifteenth century to the imaginary zenith of modern man. But this form is even tangibly revealed at the organic level, in the lines of "fragilization" that define the anatomy of phantasy, as exhibited in the schizoid and spasmodic symptoms of hysteria.

Correlatively, the formation of the I is symbolized in dreams by a fortress, or a stadium – its inner arena and enclosure, surrounded by marshes and rubbish-tips, dividing it into two opposed fields of contest where the subject flounders in quest of the lofty, remote inner castle whose form (sometimes juxtaposed in the same scenario) symbolizes the id in a quite startling way. Similarly, on the mental plane, we find realized the structures of fortified works, the metaphor of which arises spontaneously, as if issuing from the symptoms themselves, to designate the mechanisms of obsessional neurosis – inversion, isolation, splitting, negation and displacement.

But if we were to build on these subjective givens alone – however little we free them from the condition of experience that makes us see them as partaking of the nature of a linguistic technique – our theoretical attempts would remain exposed to the charge of projecting themselves into the unthinkable of an absolute subject. This is why I have sought in the present hypothesis, grounded in a conjunction of objective data, the guiding grid for a *method of symbolic reduction*.

It establishes in the *defenses of the ego* a genetic order, in accordance with the wish formulated by Miss Anna Freud, in the first part of her great work, and situates (as against a frequently expressed prejudice) hysterical repression and its returns at a more archaic stage than obsessional inversion and its isolating processes, and the latter in turn as preliminary to paranoia alienation, which dates from the deflection of the specular I into the social I.

This moment in which the mirror stage comes to an end inaugurates, by the identification with the *imago* of the counterpart and the drama of primordial jealousy (so well brought out by the school of Charlotte Buhler in the phenomenon of infantile *transitivism*), the dialectic that will henceforth link the I to socially elaborated situations.

It is this moment that decisively tips the whole of human knowledge into media-tization through the desire of the other, constitutes its objects in an "abstract" equivalence by the cooperation of others, and turns the I into that apparatus for which every instinctual thrust constitutes a danger, even though it should correspond to a natural maturation – the very normalization of this maturation being henceforth dependent, in man, on a cultural mediation as exemplified, in the case of the sexual object, by the Oedipus complex.

In the light of this conception, the term primary narcissism, by which analytic doctrine designates the libidinal investment characteristic of that moment, reveals in those who invented it the most profound awareness of semantic latencies. But it also throws light on the dynamic opposition between this libido and the sexual libido, which the first analysts tried to define when they invoked destructive and, indeed, death instincts, in order to explain the evident connection between the narcissistic libido and the alienating function of the I, the aggressivity it releases in any relation to the other, even in a relation involving the most Samaritan of aid.

In fact, they were encountering that existential negativity whose reality is so vigor-ously proclaimed by the contemporary philosophy of being and nothingness.

But unfortunately that philosophy grasps negativity only within the limits of a self-sufficiency of consciousness, which, as one of its premises, links to the *mécon-naissances* [misrecognitions] that constitute the ego, the illusion of autonomy to which it entrusts itself. This flight of fancy, for all that it draws, to an unusual extent, on borrowings from psychoanalytic experience, culminates in the pretention of provid-ing an existential psychoanalysis.

At the culmination of the historical effort of a society to refuse to recognize that it has any function other than the utilitarian one, and in the anxiety of the individual confronting the "concentrational"[4] form of the social bond that seems to arise to crown this effort, existentialism must be judged by the explanations it gives of the subjective impasses that have indeed resulted from it; a freedom that is never more authentic than when it is within the walls of a prison; a demand for commitment, expressing the impotence of a pure consciousness to master any situation; a voyeuris-tic-sadistic idealization of the sexual relation; a personality that realizes itself only in suicide; a consciousness of the other that can be satisfied only by Hegelian murder.

These propositions are opposed by all our experience, in so far as it teaches us not to regard the ego as centered on the *perception-consciousness system* or as organized by the "reality principle" – a principle that is the expression of a scientific prejudice most hostile to the dialectic of knowledge. Our experience shows that we should start instead from the *function of méconnaissance* that characterizes the ego in all its struc-tures so markedly articulated by Miss Anna Freud. For, if the *Verneinung* [denial] represents the patent form of that function, its effects will, for the most part, remain latent, so long as they are not illuminated by some light reflected on to the level of fatality, which is where the id manifests itself.

We can thus understand the inertia characteristic of the formations of the I, and find there the most extensive definition of neurosis – just as the captation of the subject by the situation gives us the most general formula for madness, not only the madness that lies behind the walls of asylums, but also the madness that deafens the world with its sound and fury.

The sufferings of neurosis and psychosis are for us a schooling in the passions of the soul, just as the beam of the psychoanalytic scales, when we calculate the tilt of its threat to entire communities, provides us with an indication of the deadening of the passions in society.

At this junction of nature and culture, so persistently examined by modern anthropology, psychoanalysis alone recognizes this knot of imaginary servitude that love must always undo again, or sever.

For such a task, we place no trust in altruistic feeling, we who lay bare the aggressivity that underlies the activity of the philanthropist, the idealist, the pedagogue, and even the reformer.

In the recourse of subject to subject that we preserve, psychoanalysts may accompany the patient to the ecstatic limit of the *"Thou art that,"* in which is revealed to him the cipher of his mortal destiny, but it is not in our mere power as practitioners to bring him to that point where the real journey begins.

Notes

1   Throughout this article I leave in its peculiarity the translation I have adopted for Freud's *Ideal-Ich* [i.e., "je-idéal"], without further comment, other than to say that I have not maintained it since.

2   Cf. Claude Lévi-Strauss, *Structural Anthropology*, ch. X.

3   Cf. "Aggressivity in Psychoanalysis", p. 8 and *Ecrits*, p. 180.

4   *"Concentrationnaire,"* an adjective coined after World War II (this article was written in 1949) to describe the life of the concentration-camp. In the hands of certain writers it became, by extension, applicable to many aspects of "modern" life. [Trans.]

CHAPTER 8

The Instance of the Letter in the
Unconscious or Reason since Freud

Jacques Lacan

In this 1957 essay, Lacan incorporates Saussure's structural linguistics into his account of how desire works in humans. He notes that, for Saussure, signifiers move along a chain and never reach a signified. Signifiers are determined by their relations of difference to other signifiers, and their relationship to real referents is arbitrary. The move away from any signifier toward a signified merely takes one to other signifiers. The road to the signified is blocked by the essential difference between the realm of interconnected signifiers and the realm of meanings or referents that are of a completely different order and that can be signified in their absence from language only through conventional agreements. Lacan describes this difference of realms as a bar separating the signifier from the signified, and he compares it to the bar separating consciousness from the unconscious. Like the signified or referent, the content of the unconscious can be signified obliquely but never revealed as such.

Desire operates in a similar way. First, what we desire is always a signifier of something else. What we desire is desirable because it satisfies urges that hark back to our primordial experience of unity with our mother's body. All desire is shaped by that first experience, and all desired objects signify it. But that lost unity is unattainable; it is the condition of our being to be in a state of lack in relation to it. Something like a bar, then, separates our conscious yearnings from the unconscious. Our desire is motivated by the unconscious and by unconscious residues, but desire must remain in the realm of consciousness. It latches on to objects that can signify the unconscious but only as something inaccessible.

Lacan also uses rhetorical terms to account for the structure of desire. Metaphor, whereby one term substitutes for another, is his name for the relation between desire and its unconscious source. The desired object is a substitute for the real unattainable object (the mother's body; the original lost unity) whose residue in the unconscious provokes desire. Such desire can only move from one desired object to another; it can never attain its goal of restoring that lost unity of the self. It therefore resembles metonymy, which consists of reference from part to whole or between one adjacent object to another. Desire is thus a movement along a chain of desired objects, all contiguously connected, that can never convert themselves into the object of desire.

As my title suggests, beyond this "speech," what the psychoanalytic experience discovers in the unconscious is the whole structure of language. Thus from the outset I have alerted informed minds to the extent to which the notion that the unconscious is merely the seat of the instincts will have to be rethought.

But how are we to take this "letter" here? Quite simply, literally.[1]

By "letter" I designate that material support that concrete discourse borrows from language.

This simple definition assumes that language is not to be confused with the various psychical and somatic functions that serve it in the speaking subject – primarily because language and its structure exist prior to the moment at which each subject at a certain point in his mental development makes his entry into it.

Let us note then that aphasias, although caused by purely anatomical lesions in the cerebral apparatus that supplies the mental center for these functions, prove, on the whole, to distribute their deficits between the two sides of the signifying effect of what we call here "the letter" in the creation of signification. A point that will be clarified later.

Thus the subject, too, if he can appear to be the slave of language, is all the more so of a discourse in the universal movement in which his place is already inscribed at birth, if only by virtue of his proper name.

Reference to the experience of the community, or to the substance of this discourse, settles nothing. For this experience assumes its essential dimension in the tradition that this discourse itself establishes. This tradition, long before the drama of history is inscribed in it, lays down the elementary structures of culture. And these very structures reveal an ordering of possible exchanges which, even if unconscious, is inconceivable outside the permutations authorized by language.

With the result that the ethnographic duality of nature and culture is giving way to a ternary conception of the human condition – nature, society, and culture – the last term of which could well be reduced to language, or that which essentially distinguishes human society from natural societies. . . .

To pinpoint the emergence of linguistic science we may say that, as in the case of all sciences in the modern sense, it is contained in the constitutive moment of an algorithm that is its foundation. This algorithm is the following:

$$\frac{S}{s}$$

which is read as: the signifier over the signified, "over" corresponding to the bar separating the two stages. . . .

The thematics of this science is henceforth suspended, in effect, at the primordial position of the signifier and the signified as being distinct orders separated initially by a barrier resisting signification. And that is what was to make possible an exact study of the connections proper to the signifier, and of the extent of their function in the genesis of the signified.

For this primordial distinction goes well beyond the discussion concerning the arbitrariness of the sign, as it has been elaborated since the earliest reflections of the ancients, and even beyond the impasse which, through the same period, has been encountered in every discussion of the bi-univocal correspondence between the word and the thing, if only in the mere act of naming. All this, of course, is quite contrary to the appearances suggested by the importance often imputed to the role of the index finger pointing to an object in the learning process of the *infans* subject learning his mother tongue, of the use in foreign language teaching of so-called "concrete" methods.

One cannot go further along this line of thought than to demonstrate that no signification can be sustained other than by reference to another signification: in its extreme form this amounts to the proposition that there is no language (*langue*) in existence for which there is any question of its inability to cover the whole field of the signified, it being an effect of its existence as a language (*langue*) that it necessarily answers all needs. If we try to grasp in language the constitution of the object, we cannot fail to notice that this constitution is to be found only at the level of concept, a very different thing from a simple nominative, and that the *thing*, when reduced to the noun, breaks up into the double, divergent beam of the "cause" (*causa*) in which it has taken shelter in the French word *chose*, and the nothing (*rien*) to which it has abandoned its Latin dress (*rem*).

These considerations, important as their existence is for the philosopher, turn us away from the locus in which language questions us as to its very nature. And we will fail to pursue the question further as long as we cling to the illusion that the signifier answers to the function of representing the signified, or better, that the signifier has to answer for its existence in the name of any signification whatever.

For even reduced to this latter formulation, the heresy is the same – the heresy that leads logical positivism in search of the "meaning of meaning," as its objective is called in the language of the devotees. As a result, we can observe that even a text highly charged with meaning can be reduced, through this sort of analysis, to insignificant bagatelles, all that survives being mathematical algorithms that are, of course, without any meaning.

To return to our formula S/s: if we could infer nothing from it but the notion of the parallelism of its upper and lower terms, each one taken in its globality, it would remain the enigmatic sign of a total mystery. Which of course is not the case.

In order to grasp its function I shall begin by reproducing the classic yet faulty illustration . . . by which its usage is normally introduced, and one can see how it opens the way to the kind of error referred to above.

Tree

In my lecture, I replaced this illustration with another, which has no greater claim to correctness than that it has been transplanted into that incongruous dimension that the psychoanalyst has not yet altogether renounced because of his quite justified feeling that his conformism takes its value entirely from it. Here is the other diagram:

LADIES   GENTLEMEN

where we see that, without greatly extending the scope of the signifier concerned in the experiment, that is, by doubling a noun through the mere juxtaposition of two terms whose complementary meanings ought apparently to reinforce each other, a surprise is produced by an unexpected precipitation of an unexpected meaning: the image of twin doors symbolizing, through the solitary confinement offered Western Man for the satisfaction of his natural needs away from home, the imperative that he seems to share with the great majority of primitive communities by which his public life is subjected to the laws of urinary segregation.

It is not only with the idea of silencing the nominalist debate with a low blow that I use this example, but rather to show how in fact the signifier enters the signified, namely, in a form which, not being immaterial, raises the question of its place in reality. For the blinking gaze of a short-sighted person might be justified in wondering whether this was indeed the signifier as he peered closely at the little enamel signs that bore it, a signifier whose signified would in this call receive its final honors from the double and solemn procession from the upper nave.

But no contrived example can be as telling as the actual experience of truth. So I am happy to have invented the above, since it awoke in the person whose word I most trust a memory of childhood, which having thus happily come to my attention is best placed here.

A train arrives at a station. A little boy and a little girl, brother and sister, are seated in a compartment face to face next to the window through which the buildings along the station platform can be seen passing as the train pulls to a stop. "Look," says the brother, "we're at Ladies!"; "Idiot!" replies his sister, "Can't you see we're at Gentlemen."

Besides the fact that the rails in this story materialize the bar in the Saussurian algorithm (and in a form designed to suggest that its resistance may be other than dialectical), we should add that only someone who didn't have his eyes in front of the holes (it's the appropriate image here) could possibly confuse the place of the signifier and the signified in this story, or not see from what radiating center the signifier sends forth its light into the shadow of incomplete significations. . . .

One thing is certain: if the algorithm S/s with its bar is appropriate, access from one to the other cannot in any case have a signification. For in so far as it is itself only pure function of the signifier, the algorithm can reveal only the structure of a signifier in this transfer.

Now the structure of the signifier is, as it is commonly said of language itself, that it should be articulated.

This means that no matter where one starts to designate their reciprocal encroachments and increasing inclusions, these units are subjected to the double condition of being reducible to ultimate differential elements and of combining them according to the laws of a closed order.

These elements, one of the decisive discoveries of linguistics, are *phonemes*; but we must not expect to find any *phonetic* constancy in the modulatory variability to which this term applies, but rather the synchronic system of differential couplings necessary for the discernment of sounds in a given language. Through this, one sees that an essential element of the spoken word itself was predestined to flow into the mobile characters which, in a jumble of lower-case Didots or Garamonds, render validly present what we call the "letter," namely, the essentially localized structure of the signifier.

With the second property of the signifier, that of combining according to the laws of a closed order, is affirmed the necessity of the topological substratum of which the term I ordinarily use, namely, the signifying chain, gives an approximate idea: rings of a necklace that is a ring in another necklace made of rings.

Such are the structural conditions that define grammar as the order of constitutive encroachments of the signifier up to the level of the unit immediately superior to the sentence, and lexicology as the order of institutive inclusions of the signifier to the level of the verbal locution.

In examining the limits by which these two exercises in the understanding of linguistic usage are determined, it is easy to see that only the correlations between signifier and signified provide the standard for all research into signification, as is indicated by the notion of "usage" of a taxeme or semanteme which in fact refers to the context just above that of the units concerned.

But it is not because the undertakings of grammar and lexicology are exhausted within certain limits that we must think that beyond those limits signification reigns supreme. That would be an error.

For the signifier, by its very nature, always anticipates meaning by unfolding its dimension before it. As is seen at the level of the sentence when it is interrupted before the significant term: "I shall never...," "All the same it is...," "And yet there may be...." Such sentences are not without meaning, a meaning all the more oppressive in that it is content to make us wait for it.[2]

But the phenomenon is no different which by the mere recoil of a "but" brings to the light, comely as the Shulamite, honest as the dew, the negress adorned for the wedding and poor woman ready for the auction-block.

From which we can say that it is in the chain of the signifier that the meaning "insists" but that none of its elements "consists" in the signification of which it is at the moment capable.

We are forced, then, to accept the notion of an incessant sliding of the signified under the signifier – which Ferdinand de Saussure illustrates with an image resembling the wavy lines of the upper and lower Waters in miniatures from manuscripts of Genesis; a double flux marked by fine streaks of rain, vertical dotted lines supposedly confining segments of correspondence.

All our experience runs counter to this linearity, which made me speak once, in one of my seminars on psychosis, of something more like "anchoring points" ("*points de capiton*") as a schema for taking into account the dominance of the letter in the dramatic transformation that dialogue can effect in the subject.[3]

The linearity that Saussure holds to be constitutive of the chain of discourse, in conformity with its emission by a single voice and with its horizontal position in our writing – if this linearity is necessary, in fact, it is not sufficient. It applies to the chain of discourse only in the direction in which it is orientated in time, being taken as a signifying factor in all languages in which "Peter hits Paul" reverses its time when the terms are inverted.

But one has only to listen to poetry, which Saussure was no doubt in the habit of doing,[4] for a polyphony to be heard, for it to become clear that all discourse is aligned along the several staves of a score.

There is in effect no signifying chain that does not have, as if attached to the punctuation of each of its units, a whole articulation of relevant contexts suspended "vertically," as it were, from that point.

Let us take our word "tree" again, this time not as an isolated noun but at the point of one of these punctuations, and see how it crosses the bar of the Saussurian algorithm. (The anagram of "*arbre*" and "*barre*" should be noted.)

For even broken down into the double specter of its vowels and consonants, it can still call up with the robur and the plane tree the significations it takes on, in the context of our flora, of strength and majesty. Drawing on all the symbolic contexts suggested in the Hebrew of the Bible, it erects on a barren hill the shadow of the cross. Then reduces to the capital Y, the sign of dichotomy which, except for the illustration used by heraldry, would owe nothing to the tree however genealogical we may think it. Circulatory tree, tree of life of the cerebellum, tree of Saturn, tree of Diana, crystals formed in a tree struck by lightning, is it your figure that traces our destiny for us in the tortoise-shell cracked by the fire, or your lightning that causes that slow shift in the axis of being to surge up from an unnameable night into the *Enpanta* of language:

> No! says the Tree, it says No! in the shower of sparks
> Of its superb head

lines that require the harmonics of the tree just as much as their continuation:

> Which the storm treats as universally
> As it does a blade of grass.[5]

For this modern verse is ordered according to the same law of the parallelism of the signifier that creates the harmony governing the primitive Slavic epic or the most refined Chinese poetry.

As is seen in the fact that the tree and the blade of grass are chosen from the same mode of the existent in order for the signs of contradiction – saying "No!" and "treat as" – to affect them, and also so as to bring about, through the categorical contrast of the particularity of "superb" with the "universally" that reduces it, in the condensation of the "head" (*tête*) and the "storm" (*tempête*), the indiscernible shower of sparks of the eternal instant.

But this whole signifier can only operate, it may be said, if it is present in the subject. It is this objection that I answer by supposing that it has passed over to the level of the signified.

For what is important is not that the subject know anything whatsoever. (If LADIES and GENTLEMEN were written in a language unknown to the little boy and girl, their quarrel would simply be the more exclusively a quarrel over words, but no less ready to take on signification.)

What this structure of the signifying chain discloses is the possibility I have, precisely in so far as I have this language in common with other subjects, that is to say, in so far as it exists as a language, to use it in order to signify *something quite other* than what it says. This function of speech is more worth pointing out than that of "disguising the thought" (more often than not indefinable) of the subject; it is no less than the function of indicating the place of this subject in the search for the true.

I have only to plant my tree in a locution; climb the tree, even project on to it the cunning illumination a descriptive context gives to a word; raise it (*arborer*) so as not to let myself be imprisoned in some sort of *communiqué* of the facts, however official, and if I know the truth, make it heard, in spite of all the *between-the-lines* censures by the only signifier my acrobatics through the branches of the tree can constitute, provocative to the point of burlesque, or perceptible only to the practiced eye, according to whether I wish to be heard by the mob or by the few.

The properly signifying function thus depicted in language has a name. We learned this name in some grammar of our childhood, on the last page, where the shade of Quintilian, relegated to some phantom chapter concerning "final considerations on style," seemed suddenly to speed up his voice in an attempt to get in all he had to say before the end.

It is among the figures of style, or tropes – from which the verb "to find" (*trouver*) comes to us – that this name is found. This name is *metonymy*.

I shall refer only to the example given there: "thirty sails." For the disquietude I felt over the fact that the word "ship," concealed in this expression, seemed, by taking on its figurative sense, through the endless repetition of the same old example, only to increase its presence, obscured (*voilait*) not so much those illustrious sails (*voiles*) as the definition they were supposed to illustrate.

The part taken for the whole, we said to ourselves, and if the thing is to be taken seriously, we are left with very little idea of the importance of this fleet, which "thirty sails" is precisely supposed to give us: for each ship to have just one sail is in fact the least likely possibility.

By which we see that the connexion between ship and sail is nowhere but in the signifier, and that it is in the *word-to-word* connexion that metonymy is based.[6]

I shall designate as metonymy, then, the one side (*versant*) of the effective field constituted by the signifier, so that meaning can emerge there.

The other side is *metaphor*. Let us immediately find an illustration; Quillet's dictionary seemed an appropriate place to find a sample that would not seem to be chosen for my own purposes, and I didn't have to go any further than the well-known line of Victor Hugo:

> His sheaf was neither miserly nor spiteful...[7]

under which aspect I presented metaphor in my seminar on the psychoses.

It should be said that modern poetry and especially the Surrealist school have taken us a long way in this direction by showing that any conjunction of two signifiers would be equally sufficient to constitute a metaphor, except for the additional requirement of the greatest possible disparity of the images signified, needed for the production of the poetic spark, or in other words for metaphoric creation to take place. ...

The creative spark of the metaphor does not spring from the presentation of two images, that is, of two signifiers equally actualized, it flashes between two signifiers one of which has taken the place of the other in the signifying chain, the occulted signifier remaining present through its (metonymic) connexion with the rest of the chain.

One word for another: that is the formula for the metaphor. ...

It is obvious that in the line of Hugo cited above, not the slightest spark of light springs from the proposition that the sheaf was neither miserly nor spiteful, for the reason that there is no question of the sheaf's having either the merit or demerit of these attributes, since the attributes, like the sheaf, belong to Booz, who exercises the former in disposing of the latter and without informing the latter of his sentiments in the case.

If, however, his sheaf does refer us to Booz, and this is indeed the case, it is because it has replaced him in the signifying chain at the very place where he was to be exalted by the sweeping away of greed and spite. But now Booz himself has been swept away by the sheaf, and hurled into the outer darkness where greed and spite harbor him in the hollow of their negation.

But once *his* sheaf has thus usurped his place, Booz can no longer return there; the slender thread of the little word *his* that binds him to it is only one more obstacle to his return in that it links him to the notion of possession that retains him at the heart of greed and spite. So *his* generosity, affirmed in the passage, is yet reduced to *less than nothing* by the munificence of the sheaf which, coming from nature, knows neither our reserve nor our rejections, and even in its accumulation remains prodigal by our standards.

But if in this profusion the giver has disappeared along with his gift, it is only in order to rise again in what surrounds the figure of speech in which he was annihilated. For it is the figure of the burgeoning of fecundity, and it is this that announces the surprise that the poem celebrates, namely, the promise that the old man will receive in the sacred context of his accession to paternity.

So, it is between the signifier in the form of the proper name of a man and the signifier that metaphorically abolishes him that the poetic spark is produced, and it is in this case all the more effective in realizing the signification of paternity in that it reproduces the mythical event in terms of which Freud reconstructed the progress, in the unconscious of all men, of the paternal mystery.

Modern metaphor has the same structure. So the line *Love is a pebble laughing in the sunlight*, recreates love in a dimension that seems to me most tenable in the face of its imminent lapse into the mirage of narcissistic altruism.

We see, then, that metaphor occurs at the precise point at which sense emerges from non-sense, that is, at that frontier which, as Freud discovered, when crossed the other way produces the word that in French is *the* word *par excellence*, the word that is simply the signifier *"esprit"*;[8] it is at this frontier that we realize that man defies his very destiny when he derides the signifier.

But to come back to our subject, what does man find in metonymy if not the power to circumvent the obstacles of social censure? Does not this form, which gives its field to truth in its very oppression, manifest a certain servitude inherent in its presentation? . . .

Of course, as it is said, the letter killeth while the spirit giveth life. We can't help but agree, having had to pay homage elsewhere to a noble victim of the error of seeking the spirit in the letter; but we should also like to know how the spirit could live without the letter. Even so, the pretensions of the spirit would remain unassailable if the letter had not shown us that it produces all the effects of truth in man without involving the spirit at all.

It is none other than Freud who had this revelation, and he called his discovery the unconscious.

The Letter in the Unconscious

In the complete works of Freud, one out of every three pages is devoted to philological references, one out of every two pages to logical inferences, everywhere a dialectical apprehension of experience, the proportion of analysis of language increasing to the extent that the unconscious is directly concerned.

Thus in "The Interpretation of Dreams" every page deals with what I call the letter of the discourse, in its texture, its usage, its immanence in the matter in question....

The first sentence of the opening chapter announces what for the sake of the exposition could not be postponed: that the dream is a rebus. And Freud goes on to stipulate what I have said from the start, that it must be understood quite literally. This derives from the agency in the dream of that same literal (or phonematic) structure in which the signifier is articulated and analyzed in discourse. So the unnatural images of the boat on the roof, or the man with a comma for a head, which are specifically mentioned by Freud, are examples of dream-images that are to be taken *only* for their value as signifiers, that is to say, in so far as they allow us to spell out the "proverb" presented by the rebus of the dream. The linguistic structure that enables us to read dreams is the very principle of the "significance of the dream," the *Traumdeutung*.

Freud shows us in every possible way that the value of the image as signifier has nothing whatever to do with its signification, giving as an example Egyptian hieroglyphics in which it would be sheer buffoonery to pretend that in a given text the frequency of a vulture, which is an *aleph*, or of a chick, which is a *vau*, indicating a form of the verb "to be" or a plural, prove that the text has anything at all to do with these ornithological specimens. Freud finds in this writing certain uses of the signifier that are lost in ours, such as the use of determinatives, where a categorical figure is added to the literal figuration of a verbal term; but this is only to show us that even in this writing, the so-called "ideogram" is a letter.

But it does not require the current confusion on this last term for there to prevail in the minds of psychoanalysts lacking linguistic training the prejudice in favor of a symbolism deriving from natural analogy, or even of the image as appropriate to the instinct. And to such an extent that, outside the French school, which has been alerted, a distinction must be drawn between reading coffee grounds and reading hieroglyphics, by recalling to its own principles a technique that could not be justified were it not directed towards the unconscious.

It must be said that this is admitted only with difficulty and that the mental vice denounced above enjoys such favor that today's psychoanalyst can be expected to say that he decodes before he will come around to taking the necessary tour with Freud (turn as the statue of Champollion, says the guide) that will make him understand that what he does is decipher; the distinction is that a cryptogram takes on its full dimension only when it is in a lost language.

Taking the tour is simply continuing in the *Traumdeutung*.

Entstellung, translated as "distortion" or "transposition," is what Freud shows to be the general precondition for the functioning of the dream, and it is what I designated above, following Saussure, as the sliding of the signified under the signifier, which is always active in discourse (its action, let us note, is unconscious).

But what we call the two "sides" of the effect of the signifier on the signified are also found here.

Verdichtung, or "condensation," is the structure of the superimposition of the signified which metaphor takes as its field, and whose name, condensing in itself the word *Dichtung*, shows how the mechanism is connatural with poetry to the point that it envelops the traditional function proper to poetry.

In the case of *Verschiebung*, "displacement," the German term is closer to the idea of that veering off of signification that we see in metonymy and which from its first appearance in Freud is represented as the most appropriate means used by the unconscious to foil censorship.

What distinguishes these two mechanisms, which play such a privileged role in the dream-work (*Traumarbeit*), from their homologous function in discourse? Nothing, except a condition imposed upon the signifying material, called *Rücksicht auf Darstell-barkeit*, which must be translated by "consideration of the means of representation." (The translation by "role of the possibility of figurative expression" being too approximative here.) But this condition constitutes a limitation operating *within* the system of writing; this is a long way from dissolving the system into a figurative semiology on a level with phenomena of natural expression. This fact could perhaps shed light on the problems involved in certain modes of pictography which, simply because they have been abandoned in writing as imperfect, are not therefore to be regarded as mere evolutionary stages. Let us say, then, that the dream is like the parlor-game in which one is supposed to get the spectators to guess some well-known saying or variant of it solely by dumb-show. That the dream uses speech makes no difference since for the unconscious it is only one among several elements of the representation. It is precisely the fact that both the game and the dream run up against a lack of taxematic material for the representation of such logical articulations as causality, contradiction, hypothesis, etc., that proves they are a form of writing rather than of mine. The subtle processes that the dream is seen to use to represent these logical articulations, in a much less artificial way than games usually employ, are the object of a special study in Freud in which we see once more confirmed that the dream-work follows the laws of the signifier. . . .

That is why any rectification of psychoanalysis must inevitably involve a return to the truth of that discovery, which, taken in its original moment, is impossible to obscure.

For in the analysis of dreams, Freud intends only to give us the laws of the unconscious in their most general extension. One of the reasons why dreams were most propitious for this demonstration is exactly, Freud tells us, that they reveal the same laws whether in the normal person or in the neurotic.

But, in either case, the efficacy of the unconscious does not cease in the waking state. The psychoanalytic experience does nothing other than establish that the un-conscious leaves none of our actions outside its field. . . .

It is a matter, therefore, of defining the topography of this unconscious. I say that it is the very topography defined by the algorithm:

$$\frac{S}{s}$$

Is the place that I occupy as the subject of a signifier concentric or excentric, in relation to the place I occupy as subject of the signified? – that is the question.

It is not a question of knowing whether I speak of myself in a way that conforms to what I am, but rather of knowing whether I am the same as that of which I speak. And it is not at all inappropriate to use the word "thought" here. For Freud uses the term to designate the elements involved in the unconscious, that it is the signifying mechanisms that we now recognize as being there.

It is nonetheless true that the philosophical *cogito* is at the center of the mirage that renders modern man so sure of being himself even in his uncertainties about himself, and even in the mistrust he has learned to practice against the traps of self-love.

Furthermore, if, turning the weapon of metonymy against the nostalgia that it serves, I refuse to seek any meaning beyond tautology, if in the name of "war is war" and "a penny is a penny" I decide to be only what I am, how even here can I elude the obvious fact that I am in that very act?

And it is no less true if I take myself to the other, metaphoric pole of the signifying process, and if I dedicate myself to becoming what I am, to coming into being, I cannot doubt that even if I lose myself in the process I am in that process.

Now it is on these very points, where evidence will be subverted by the empirical, that the trick of the Freudian conversion lies.

This signifying game between metonymy and metaphor, up to and including the active edge that splits my desire between a refusal of the signifier and a lack of being, and links my fate to the question of my destiny, this game, in all its inexorable subtlety, is played until the match is called, there where I am not, because I cannot situate myself there.

That is to say, what is needed is more than these words with which, for a brief moment I disconcerted my audience: I think where I am not, therefore I am where I do not think. Words that render sensible to an ear properly attuned with what elusive ambiguity the ring of meaning flees from our grasp along the verbal thread.

What one ought to say is: I am not wherever I am the plaything of my thought, I think of what I am where I do not think to think.

This two-sided mystery is linked to the fact that the truth can be evoked only in that dimension of alibi in which all "realism" in creative works takes its virtue from metonymy; it is likewise linked to this other fact that we acceded to meaning only through the double twist of metaphor when we have the one and only key: the S and the s of the Saussurian algorithm are not only the same level, and man only deludes himself when he believes his true place is at their axis, which is nowhere.

Was nowhere, that is, until Freud discovered it; for if what Freud discovered isn't that, it isn't anything.

The contents of the unconscious with all their disappointing ambiguities give us no reality in the subject more consistent than the immediate; their virtue derives from the truth and in the dimension of being: *Kern unseres Wesen* are Freud's own terms.

The double-triggered mechanism of metaphor is the very mechanism by which the symptom, in the analytic sense, is determined. Between the enigmatic signifier of the sexual trauma and the term that is substituted for it in an actual signifying chain there passes the spark that fixes in a symptom the signification inaccessible to the conscious subject in which that symptom may be resolved – a symptom being a metaphor in which flesh or function is taken as a signifying element.

And the enigmas that desire seems to pose for a "natural philosophy," its frenzy mocking the abyss of the infinite, the secret collusion with which it envelops the pleasure of knowing and of dominating with *jouissance* [sexual pleasure], these amount to no other derangement of instinct than that of being caught in the rails – eternally stretching forth towards the *desire for something else* – metonymy. Hence its "perverse" fixation at the very suspension-point of the signifying chain where the memory-screen is immobilized and the fascinating image of the fetish is petrified.

There is no other way of conceiving the indestructibility of unconscious desire – in the absence of a need which, when forbidden satisfaction, does not sicken and die, even if it means the destruction of the organism itself. It is in a memory, comparable to what is called by that name in our modern thinking-machines (which are in turn based on an electronic realization of the composition of signification), it is in this sort of memory that is found the chain that *insists* on reproducing itself in the transference, and which is the chain of dead desire.

It is the truth of what this desire has been in his history that the patient cries out through his symptom, as Christ said that the stones themselves would have cried out if the children of Israel had not lent them their voice. . . .

Thus, to speak of the precise point we are treating in my seminars on Freud, little Hans, left in the lurch at the age of five by his symbolic environment, and suddenly forced to face the enigma of his sex and his existence, developed, under the direction of Freud and of his father, Freud's disciple, in mythic form, around the signifying crystal of his phobia, all the permutations possible on a limited number of signifiers.

The operation shows that even on the individual level the solution of the impossible is brought within man's reach by the exhaustion of all possible forms of the impossibilities encountered in solution by recourse to the signifying equation. It is a striking demonstration that illuminates the labyrinth of a case which so far has only been used as a source of demolished fragments. We should be struck too, by the fact that it is in the coextensivity of the development of the symptom and of its curative resolution that the nature of the neurosis is revealed: whether phobic, hysterical, or obsessive, the neurosis is a question that being poses for the subject "from where it was before the subject came into the world" (Freud's phrase, which he used in explaining the Oedipal complex to little Hans).

The "being" referred to is that which appears in a lightning moment in the void of the verb "to be" and I said that it poses its question for the subject. What does that mean? It does not pose it *in front of* the subject, since the subject cannot come to the place where it is posed, but it poses it *in place* of the subject, that is to say, in that place it poses the question *with* the subject, as one poses a problem *with* a pen, or as Aristotle's man thought *with* his soul.

Thus Freud introduced the ego into his doctrine,[9] by defining it according to the resistances that are proper to it. What I have tried to convey is that these resistances are of an imaginary nature much in the same sense as those coaptative lures that the ethology of animal behavior shows us in display or combat, and that these lures are reduced in man to the narcissistic relation introduced by Freud, which I have elaborated in my essay on the mirror stage. I have tried to show that by situating in this ego the synthesis of the perceptual functions in which the sensori-motor selections are integrated, Freud seems to abound in that delegation that is traditionally supposed to represent reality for the ego, and that this reality is all the more included in the suspension of the ego.

For this ego, which is notable in the first instance for the imaginary inertias that it concentrates against the message of the unconscious, operates solely with a view to covering the displacement constituted by the subject with a resistance that is essential to the discourse as such.

That is why an exhaustion of the mechanisms of defense, which Fenichel the practitioner shows us so well in his studies of analytic technique (while his whole reduction on the theoretical level of neuroses and psychoses to genetic anomalies in

libidinal development is pure platitude), manifests itself, without Fenichel's accounting for it or realizing it himself, as simply the reverse side of the mechanisms of the
unconscious. Periphrasis, hyperbaton, ellipsis, suspension, anticipation, retraction,
negation, digression, irony, these are the figures of style (Quintilian's *figurae senten-*
tiarum); as catachresis, litotes, antonomasia, hypotyposis are the tropes, whose terms
suggest themselves as the most proper for the labeling of these mechanisms. Can
one really see these as mere figures of speech when it is the figures themselves that
are the active principle of the rhetoric of the discourse that the analysand in fact
utters?

By persisting in describing the nature of resistance as a permanent emotional state,
thus making it alien to the discourse, today's psychoanalysts have simply shown that
they have fallen under the blow of one of the fundamental truths that Freud rediscovered through psychoanalysis. One is never happy making way for a new truth, for
it always means making our way into it: the truth is always disturbing. We cannot
even manage to get used to it. We are used to the real. The truth we repress.

Now it is quite specially necessary to the scientist, to the seer, even to the quack,
that he should be the only one to *know*. The idea that deep in the simplest (and even
sickest) of souls there is something ready to blossom is bad enough! But if someone
seems to know as much as they about what we ought to make of it... then the
categories of primitive, prelogical, archaic, or even magic thought, so easy to impute
to others, rush to our aid! It is not right that these nonentities keep us breathless
with enigmas that prove to be only too unrealizable.

To interpret the unconscious as Freud did, one would have to be as he was, an
encyclopedia of the arts and muses, as well as an assiduous reader of the *Fliegende*
Blätter. And the task is made no easier by the fact that we are at the mercy of a
thread woven with allusions, quotations, puns, and equivocations. And is that our
profession, to be antidotes to trifles?

Yet that is what we must resign ourselves to. The unconscious is neither primordial nor instinctual; what it knows about the elementary is no more than the elements
of the signifier.

The three books that one might call canonical with regard to the unconscious – *The*
Interpretation of Dreams, The Psychopathology of Everyday Life, and *Jokes and their*
Relation to the Unconscious – are simply a web of examples whose development is
inscribed in the formulas of connexion and substitution (though carried to the tenth
degree by their particular complexity – diagrams of them are sometimes provided by
Freud by way of illustration); these are the formulas we give to the signifier in its
transference-function. For in *The Interpretation of Dreams* it is in the sense of such a
function that the term *Übertragung*, or transference, is introduced, which later gave its
name to the mainspring of the intersubjective link between analyst and analysand.

Such diagrams are not only constitutive of each of the symptoms in a neurosis, but
they alone make possible the understanding of the thematic of its course and resolution. The great case-histories provided by Freud demonstrate this admirably.

To fall back on a more limited incident, but one more likely to provide us with the
final seal on our proposition, let me cite the article on fetishism of 1927,[10] and the
case Freud reports there of a patient who, to achieve sexual satisfaction, needed a
certain shine on the nose (*Glanz auf der Nase*); analysis showed that his early,
English-speaking years had seen the displacement of the burning curiosity that he
felt for the phallus of his mother, that is to say, for that eminent *manque-à-être*, for

that lack-of-being, whose privileged signifier Freud revealed to us, into a *glance at the nose*[11] in the forgotten language of his childhood, rather than a *shine on the nose.*[12]

It is the abyss opened up at the thought that a thought should make itself heard in the abyss that provoked resistance to psychoanalysis from the outset. And not, as is commonly said, the emphasis on man's sexuality. This latter has after all been the dominant object in literature throughout the ages. And in fact the more recent evolution of psychoanalysis has succeeded by a bit of comical legerdemain in turning it into a quite moral affair, the cradle and trysting-place of oblativity and attraction. The Platonic setting of the soul, blessed and illuminated, rises straight to paradise.

The intolerable scandal in the time before Freudian sexuality was sanctified was that it was so "intellectual." It was precisely in that that it showed itself to be the worthy ally of all those terrorists whose plottings were going to ruin society.

At a time when psychoanalysts are busy remodeling psychoanalysis into a right-thinking movement whose crowning expression is the sociological poem of the *autonomous ego*, I would like to say, to all those who are listening to me, how they can recognize bad psychoanalysis; this is by the word they use to deprecate all technical or theoretical research that carried forward the Freudian experience along its authentic lines. That word is *"intellectualization"* – execrable to all those who, living in fear of being tried and found wanting by the wine of truth, spit on the bread of men, although their slaver can no longer have any effect other than that leavening. . . .

The end that Freud's discovery proposes for man was defined by him at the apex of his thought in these moving terms: *Wo es war, soll Ich werden. Es* refers to the id or the unconscious, so this means "where the unconscious was, consciousness shall go." I must come to the place where that was.

This is one of reintegration and harmony, I could even say of reconciliation (*Versohnung*).

But if we ignore the self's radical excentricity to itself with which man is confronted, in other words, the truth discovered by Freud, we shall falsify both the order and methods of psychoanalytic mediation.

Notes

1   *"A la lettre."* [Trans.]
2   To which verbal hallucination, when it takes this form, opens a communicating door with the Freudian structure of psychosis – a door until now unnoticed.
3   I spoke in my seminar of June 6, 1956 of the first scene of *Athalie*, incited by an allusion – tossed off by a highbrow critic in the *New Statesman and Nation* – to the "high whoredom" of Racine's heroines, to renounce reference to the savage dramas of Shakespeare, which have become compulsional in analytic circles where they play the role of status-symbol for the Philistines.
4   The publication by Jean Starobinski, in *Le Mercure de France* (February 1964) of Saussure's notes on anagrams and their hypogrammatical use, from the Saturnine verses to the writings of Cicero, provide the corroboration that I then lacked (note 1966).
5   *"Non! dit l'Arbre, il dit: Non! dans l'étincellement / De sa tête superbe / Que la tempête traite universellement / Comme elle fait une herbe."* (Paul Valéry, "Au Platane," *Les Charmes*).
6   I pay homage here to the works of Roman Jakobson – to which I owe much of this formulation; works to which a psychoanalyst can constantly refer in order to structure his own experience, and which render superfluous the "personal communications" of which I could boast as much as the next fellow.

Indeed, one recognizes in this oblique form of allegiance the style of that immortal couple, Rosencrantz and Guildenstern, who are virtually indistinguishable, even in the imperfection of their destiny, for it survives by the same method as Jeannot's knife, and for the same reason for which Goethe praised Shakespeare for presenting the character in double form: they represent, in themselves alone, the whole *Gesellschaft*, the Association itself (*Wilhelm Meisters Lehrjahre*, ed. Trunz, Christian Wegner Verlag, Hamburg, v (5): 299) – I mean the International Psychoanalytical Association.

We should savor the passage from Goethe as a whole: "*Dieses leise Aufreten dieses Schmiegen und Biegen, dies Jasagen, Streicheln und Schmeicheln, dieses Behendigkeit, dies Schwänzein, diese Allheit und Leerheit, diese rechtliche Schurkerei, diese Unfähigkeit, wie kann sie durch einen Menschen ausgedruckt werden? Es sollten ihrer wenigstens ein Dutzend sein, wenn man sie haben könnte, denn sie bloss in Gesellschaft etwas, sie sind die Gesellschaft . . .*"

Let us thank also, in this context, the author R. M. Loewenstein of "Some Remarks on the Role of Speech in Psychoanalytic Technique" (*I. J. P.*, Nov.–Dec., 1956, XXXVII (6): 467) for taking the trouble to point out that his remarks are "based on" work dating from 1952. This is no doubt the explanation for the fact that he has learned nothing from work done since then, yet which he is not ignorant of, as he cites me as their "editor" (*sic*).

7 "Sa gerbe n'était pas avare ni haineuse," a line from "Booz endormi." [Trans.]

8 "*Mot*," in the broad sense, means "word." In the narrower sense, however, it means "a witticism." The French "*esprit*" is translated, in this context, as "wit," the equivalent of Freud's *Witz*. [Trans.]

"*Esprit*" is certainly the equivalent of the German *Witz* with which Freud marked the approach of his third fundamental work on the unconscious. The much greater difficulty of finding this equivalent in English is instructive: "wit," burdened with all the discussion of which it was the object from Davenant and Abbes to Pope and Addison, abandoned its essential virtues to "humor," which is something else. There only remains the "pun," but this word is too narrow in its connotation.

9 This and the next paragraph were rewritten solely with a view to greater clarity of expression (note 1968).

10 *Fetischismus*, G. W. XIV, p. 311; "Fetishism," *Collected Papers*, V, p. 198; *Standard Edition* XXI, p. 149.

11 English in the original. [Trans.]

12 English in the original. [Trans.]

CHAPTER 9

The Negro and Psychopathology

Frantz Fanon

Frantz Fanon's brief but remarkable life was marked by the publication of several important books, including *The Wretched of the Earth* (1961) and *Black Skin White Masks* (1952), from which this selection is taken. Trained in medicine and psychiatry, he devoted himself to the cause of the Algerian revolution against French colonialism. His thinking brings together insights into psychology and a concern for the effects of domination on subjugated peoples.

Psychoanalytic schools have studied the neurotic reactions that arise among certain groups, in certain areas of civilization. In response to the requirements of dialectic, one should investigate the extent to which the conclusions of Freud or of Adler can be applied to the effort to understand the man of color's view of the world.

It can never be sufficiently emphasized that psychoanalysis sets as its task the understanding of given behavior patterns – within the specific group represented by the family. When the problem is a neurosis experienced by an adult, the analyst's task is to uncover in the new psychic structure an analogy with certain infantile elements, a repetition, a duplication of conflicts that owe their origin to the essence of the family constellation. In every case the analyst clings to the concept of the family as a "psychic circumstance and object."[1]

Here, however, the evidence is going to be particularly complicated. In Europe the family represents in effect a certain fashion in which the world presents itself to the child. There are close connections between the structure of the family and the structure of the nation. Militarization and the centralization of authority in a country automatically entail a resurgence of the authority of the father. In Europe and in every country characterized as civilized or civilizing, the family is a miniature of the nation. As the child emerges from the shadow of his parents, he finds himself once more among the same laws, the same principles, the same values. A normal child that has grown up in a normal family will be a normal man.[2] There is no disproportion between the life of the family and the life of the nation. Conversely, when one examines a closed society – that is, a society that has been protected from the flood of civilization – one encounters the same structures as those just described. Father Trilles' *L'âme du Pygmée d'Afrique*, for instance, convinces us of that; although with every word one is aware of the need to Christianize the savage Negro soul, the book's description of the whole culture – the conditions of worship, the persistence of rites, the survival of myths – has nothing of the artificial impression given by *La philosophie bantoue*.

In both cases the characteristics of the family are projected onto the social environment. It is true that the children of pickpockets or burglars, accustomed to a certain system of clan law, would be surprised to find that the rest of the world behaved differently, but a new kind of training – except in instances of perversion or arrested development (Heuyer)[3] – should be able to direct them into a moralization, a socialization of outlook.

It is apparent in all such cases that the sickness lies in the family environment.

> For the individual the authority of the state is a reproduction of the authority of the family by which he was shaped in his childhood. Ultimately the individual assimilates all the authorities that he meets to the authority of the parents: He perceives the present in terms of the past. Like all other human conduct, behavior toward authority is something learned. And it is learned in the heart of a family that can be described, from the psychological point of view, by the form of organization peculiar to it – that is, by the way in which its authority is distributed and exercised.[4]

But – and this is a most important point – we observe the opposite in the man of color. A normal Negro child, having grown up within a normal family, will become abnormal on the slightest contact with the white world. This statement may not be immediately understandable. Therefore let us proceed by going backward. Paying tribute to Dr. Breuer, Freud wrote:

> In almost every case, we could see that the symptoms were, so to speak, like residues of emotional experiences, to which for this reason we later gave the name of psychic traumas. Their individual characters were linked to the traumatic scenes that had provoked them. According to the classic terminology, the symptoms were determined by "scenes" of which they were the mnemic residues, and it was no longer necessary to regard them as arbitrary and enigmatic effects of the neurosis. In contrast, however, to what was expected, it was not always a single event that was the cause of the symptom; most often, on the contrary, it arose out of multiple traumas, frequently analogous and repeated. As a result, it became necessary to reproduce chronologically this whole series of pathogenic memories, but in reverse order: the latest at the beginning and the earliest at the end; it was impossible to make one's way back to the first trauma, which is often the most forceful, if one skipped any of its successors.

It could not be stated more positively; every neurosis has its origins in specific *Erlebnisse* [experiences]. Later Freud added:

> This trauma, it is true, has been quite expelled from the consciousness and the memory of the patient and as a result he has apparently been saved from a great mass of suffering, but the repressed desire continues to exist in the unconscious; it is on watch constantly for an opportunity to make itself known and it soon comes back into consciousness, but in a disguise that makes it impossible to recognize; in other words, the repressed thought is replaced in consciousness by another that acts as its surrogate, its *Ersatz*, and that soon surrounds itself with all those feelings of morbidity that had been supposedly averted by the repression.

These *Erlebnisse* are repressed in the unconscious.

What do we see in the case of the black man? Unless we make use of that frightening postulate – which so destroys our balance – offered by Jung, the *collective unconscious*, we can understand absolutely nothing. A drama is enacted every day in colonized countries. How is one to explain, for example, that a Negro who has passed his baccalaureate and has gone to the Sorbonne to study to become a teacher of philosophy is already on guard before any conflictual elements have coalesced round him? René Ménil accounted for this reaction in Hegelian terms. In his view it was "the consequence of the replacement of the repressed [African] spirit in the consciousness of the slave by an authority symbol representing the Master, a symbol implanted in the subsoil of the collective group and charged with maintaining order in it as a garrison controls a conquered city."[5]

We shall see in our section on Hegel that René Ménil has made no misjudgment. Meanwhile we have the right to put a question to ourselves: How is the persistence of this reaction in the twentieth century to be explained when in other ways there is complete identification with the white man? Very often the Negro who becomes abnormal has never had any relations with whites. Has some remote experience been repressed in his unconscious? Did the little black child see his father beaten or lynched by a white man? Has there been a real traumatism? To all of this we have to answer *no*. Well, then?

If we want to answer correctly, we have to fall back on the idea of *collective catharsis*. In every society, in every collectivity, exists – must exist – a channel, an outlet through which the forces accumulated in the form of aggression can be released. This is the purpose of games in children's institutions, of psychodramas in group therapy, and, in a more general way, of illustrated magazines for children – each type of society, of course, requiring its own specific kind of catharsis. The Tarzan stories, the sagas of twelve-year-old explorers, the adventures of Mickey Mouse, and all those "comic books" serve actually as a release for collective aggression. The magazines are put together by white men for little white men. This is the heart of the problem. In the Antilles – and there is every reason to think that the situation is the same in the other colonies – these same magazines are devoured by the local children. In the magazines the Wolf, the Devil, the Evil Spirit, the Bad Man, the Savage are always symbolized by Negroes or Indians; since there is always identification with the victor, the little Negro, quite as easily as the little white boy, becomes an explorer, an adventurer, a missionary "who faces the danger of being eaten by the wicked Negroes." I shall be told that this is hardly important; but only because those who say it have not given much thought to the role of such magazines. Here is what G. Legman thinks of them:

> With very rare exceptions, every American child who was six years old in 1938 had therefore assimilated at the very least 18,000 scenes of ferocious tortures and bloody violence. . . . Except the Boers, the Americans are the only modern nation that within living memory has completely driven the autochthonous population off the soil that it had occupied.[6] America alone, then, could have had an uneasy national conscience to lull by creating the myth of the "Bad Injun,"[7] in order later to be able to bring back the historic figure of the Noble Redskin vainly defending his lands against invaders armed with rifles and Bibles; the punishment that we deserve can be averted only by denying responsibility for the wrong and throwing the blame on the victim; by proving – at least to our own satisfaction – that by striking the first and only blow we were acting solely on the legitimate ground of defense. . . . [Anticipating the repercussions of these magazines on American culture, Legman went on:] There is still no answer to the question whether this maniacal fixation on violence and death is the substitute for a forbidden sexuality or whether it does not rather serve the purpose of channeling, along a line left open by sexual censorship, both the child's and the adult's desire for aggression against

the economic and social structure which, though with their entire consent, perverts them. In both cases the root of the perversion, whether it be of a sexual or of an economic character, is of the essence; that is why, as long as we remain incapable of attacking these fundamental repressions, every attack aimed at such simple escape devices as comic books will remain futile.[8]

The black schoolboy in the Antilles, who in his lessons is forever talking about "our ancestors, the Gauls,"[9] identifies himself with the explorer, the bringer of civilization, the white man who carries truth to savages – an all-white truth. There is identification – that is, the young Negro subjectively adopts a white man's attitude. He invests the hero, who is white, with all his own aggression – at that age closely linked to sacrificial dedication, a sacrificial dedication permeated with sadism. An eight-year-old child who offers a gift, even to an adult, cannot endure a refusal. Little by little, one can observe in the young Antillean the formation and crystallization of an attitude and a way of thinking and seeing that are essentially white. When in school he has to read stories of savages told by white men, he always thinks of the Senegalese. As a schoolboy, I had many occasions to spend whole hours talking about the supposed customs of the savage Senegalese. In what was said there was a lack of awareness that was at the very least paradoxical. Because the Antillean does not think of himself as a black man; he thinks of himself as an Antillean. The Negro lives in Africa. Subjectively, intellectually, the Antillean conducts himself like a white man. But he is a Negro. That he will learn once he goes to Europe; and when he hears Negroes mentioned he will recognize that the word includes himself as well as the Senegalese. What are we to conclude on this matter?

To impose the same "Evil Spirits" on the white man and on the black man is a major error in education. If one is willing to understand the "Evil Spirit" in the sense of an attempt to personify the *id*, the point of view will be understood. If we are utterly honest, we must say that children's counting-out rhymes are subject to the same criticism. It will have already been noticed that I should like nothing more nor less than the establishment of children's magazines especially for Negroes, the creation of songs for Negro children, and, ultimately, the publication of history texts especially for them, at least through the grammar-school grades. For, until there is evidence to the contrary, I believe that if there is a traumatism it occurs during those years. The young Antillean is a Frenchman called on at all times to live with white compatriots. One forgets this rather too often.

The white family is the agent of a certain system. The society is indeed the sum of all the families in it. The family is an institution that prefigures a broader institution: the social or the national group. Both turn on the same axes. The white family is the workshop in which one is shaped and trained for life in society. "The family structure is internalized in the superego," Marcus says, "and projected into political [though I would say social] behavior."

As long as he remains among his own people, the little black follows very nearly the same course as the little white. But if he goes to Europe, he will have to reappraise his lot. For the Negro in France, which is his country, will feel different from other people. One can hear the glib remark: The Negro makes himself inferior. But the truth is that he is made inferior. The young Antillean is a Frenchman called upon constantly to live with white compatriots. Now, the Antillean family has for all practical purposes no connection with the national – that is, the French, or European – structure. The Antillean has therefore to choose between his family and European society; in other words, the individual who *climbs up* into society – white and civilized – tends to reject his family – black and savage – on the plane of imagination, in accord with the childhood *Erlebnisse* that we discussed earlier. In this case the schema of Marcus becomes

Family ← Individual → Society

and the family structure is cast back into the *id*.

The Negro recognizes the unreality of many of the beliefs that he has adopted with reference to the subjective attitude of the white man. When he does, his real apprenticeship begins. And reality proves to be extremely resistant. But, it will be objected, you are merely describing a universal phenomenon, the criterion of maturity being in fact adaptation to society. My answer is that such a criticism goes off in the wrong direction, for I have just shown that for the Negro there is a myth to be faced. A solidly established myth. The Negro is unaware of it as long as his existence is limited to his own environment; but the first encounter with a white man oppresses him with the whole weight of his blackness.[10]

Then there is the unconscious. Since the racial drama is played out in the open, the black man has no time to "make it unconscious." The white man, on the other hand, succeeds in doing so to a certain extent, because a new element appears: guilt. The Negro's inferiority or superiority complex or his feeling of equality is *conscious*. These feelings forever chill him. They make his drama. In him there is none of the affective amnesia characteristic of the typical neurotic.

Whenever I have read a psychoanalytic work, discussed problems with my professors, or talked with European patients, I have been struck by the disparity between the corresponding schemas and the reality that the Negro presents. It has led me progressively to the conclusion that there is a dialectical substitution when one goes from the psychology of the white man to that of the black.

The earliest values, which Charles Odier describes,[11] are different in the white man and in the black man. The drive toward socialization does not stem from the same motivations. In cold actuality, we change worlds. A close study should be divided into two parts:

1   a psychoanalytic interpretation of the life experience of the black man;
2   a psychoanalytic interpretation of the Negro myth.

But reality, which is our only recourse, prevents such procedures. The facts are much more complicated. What are they?

The Negro is a phobogenic object, a stimulus to anxiety. From the patient treated by Sérieux and Capgras[12] to the girl who confides to me that to go to bed with a Negro would be terrifying to her, one discovers all the stages of what I shall call the Negro-phobogenesis. There has been much talk of psychoanalysis in connection with the Negro. Distrusting the ways in which it might be applied,[13] I have preferred to call this chapter "The Negro and Psychopathology," well aware that Freud and Adler and even the cosmic Jung did not think of the Negro in all their investigations.

And they were quite right not to have. It is too often forgotten that neurosis is not a basic element of human reality. Like it or not, the Oedipus complex is far from coming into being among Negroes. It might be argued, as Malinowski contends, that the matriarchal structure is the only reason for its absence. But, putting aside the question whether the ethnologists are not so imbued with the complexes of their own civilization that they are compelled to try to find them duplicated in the peoples they study, it would be relatively easy for me to show that in the French Antilles 97 percent of the families cannot produce one Oedipal neurosis. This incapacity is one on which we heartily congratulate ourselves.[14]

With the exception of a few misfits within the closed environment, we can say that every neurosis, every abnormal manifestation, every affective erethism in an Antillean is the product of his cultural situation. In other words, there is a constellation of postulates, a series of propositions that slowly and subtly – with the help of books, newspapers, schools and their texts, advertisements, films, radio – work their way into one's mind and shape one's view of the world of the group to which one belongs.[15] In the Antilles that view of the world is white because no black voice exists. The folklore of Martinique is meager, and few children in Fort-de-France know the stories of "Compè Lapin," twin brother of the Br'er Rabbit of Louisiana's Uncle Remus. A European familiar with the current trends of Negro poetry, for example, would be amazed to learn that as late as 1940 no Antillean found it possible to think of himself as a Negro. It was only with the appearance of Aimé Césaire that the acceptance of negritude and the statement of its claims began to be perceptible. The most concrete proof of this, furthermore, is that feeling which pervades each new generation of students arriving in Paris: It takes them several weeks to recognize that contact with Europe compels them to face a certain number of problems that until their arrival had never touched them. And yet these problems were by no means invisible.[16]

Whenever I had a discussion with my professors or talked with European patients, I became aware of the differences that might prevail between the two worlds. Talking recently to a physician who had always practiced in Fort-de-France, I told him what conclusions I had arrived at; he went farther, saying that they were valid not only in psychopathology but also in general medicine. "In the same way," he added, "you never encounter a case of pure typhoid such as you studied in the textbooks; there is always a more or less manifest complication of malaria." It would be interesting to study, for example, a case of schizophrenia as experienced by a Negro – if indeed that kind of malady were to be found there.

What am I getting at? Quite simply this: When the Negro makes contact with the white world, a certain sensitizing action takes place. If his psychic structure is weak, one observes a collapse of the ego. The black man stops behaving as an *actional* person. The goal of his behavior will be The Other (in the guise of the white man), for The Other alone can give him worth. That is on the ethical level: self-esteem.

Notes

1 Jacques Lacan, "Le complèxe, facteur concret de la psychologie familiale," *Encyclopédie fran-çaise*, 8–40, 5.

2   I should like to think that I am not going to be brought to trial for this sentence. Skeptics always have a fine time asking, "What do you mean by *normal?*" For the moment, it is beyond the scope of this book to answer the question. In order to pacify the more insistent, let me refer them to the extremely instructive work by Georges Canguilhem, *Essai sur quelques problèmes concernant le normal et le pathologique* (Paris: Société d'Editions, 1950), even though its sole orientation is biological. And let me add only that in the psychological sphere the abnormal man is he who demands, who appeals, who begs.

3   Although even this reservation is open to argument. See for example the question put by Mlle. Juliette Boutonnier: "Might not perversion be an extreme arrest in affect development, furthered, if not produced, by the conditions under which the child has lived, at least as much as by the congenital tendencies that are obviously factors in it but that probably are not alone responsible?" (*Revue Française de Psychanalyse*, no. 3, 1949, pp. 403–4.)

4   Joachim Marcus, "Structure familiale et comportements politiques," L'autorité dans la famille et dans l'État, *Revue Française de Psychanalyse*, April–June, 1949.

5   A quotation borrowed from Michel Leiris, "Martinique, Guadeloupe, Haiti," *Les Temps Modernes*, February, 1950, p. 1346.

6   In this connection, it is worth noting that the Caribs experienced the same fate at the hands of French and Spanish explorers.

7   In English in the original. (Translator's note.)

8   G. Legman, "Psychopathologie des Comics," French translation by H. Robillot, *Les Temps Modernes*, May, 1949, pp. 919 ff.

9   One always sees a smile when one reports this aspect of education in Martinique. The smile comes because the comicality of the thing is obvious, but no one pursues it to its later consequences. Yet these are the important aspects, because three or four such phrases are the basis on which the young Antillean works out his view of the world.

10 In this connection it is worth remembering what Sartre said:

> Some children, at the age of five or six, have already had fights with schoolmates who call them "Yids." Others may remain in ignorance for a long time. A young Jewish girl in a family I am acquainted with did not even know the meaning of the word *Jew* until she was fifteen. During the Occupation there was a Jewish doctor who lived shut up in his home at Fontainebleau and raised his children without saying a word to them of their origin. But however it comes about, some day they must learn the truth: sometimes from the smiles of those around them, sometimes from rumor or insult. The later the discovery, the more violent the shock. Suddenly they perceive that others know something about them that they do not know, that people apply to them an ugly and upsetting term that is not used in their own families. (*Anti-Semite and Jew*, p. 75)

11 *Les deux sources consciente et inconsciente de la vie morale* (Neuchâtel: La Baconnière, 1943).

12 *Les folies raisonnantes*, cited by A. Hesnard, *L'univers morbide de la faute* (Paris: Presses Universitaires de France, 1949), p. 97.

13 I am thinking here particularly of the United States. See, for example, *Home of the Brave*.

14 On this point psychoanalysts will be reluctant to share my view. Dr. Lacan, for instance, talks of the "abundance" of the Oedipus complex. But even if the young boy has to kill his father, it is still necessary for the father to accept being killed. I am reminded of what Hegel said: "The cradle of the child is the tomb of the parents"; and of Nicolas Calas' *Foyer d'incendie* and of Jean Lacroix' *Force et faiblesses de la famille*. The collapse of moral values in France after the war was perhaps the result of the defeat of that moral being which the nation represented. We know what such traumatisms on the family level may produce.

15 I recommend the following experiment to those who are unconvinced: Attend showings of a Tarzan film in the Antilles and in Europe. In the Antilles, the young Negro identifies himself *de facto* with Tarzan against the Negroes. This is much more difficult for him in a European theater, for the rest of the audience, which is white, automatically identifies him with the savages on the screen. It is a conclusive experience. The Negro learns that one is not black without problems. A documentary film on Africa produces similar reactions when it is shown in a French city and in Fort-de-France. I will go farther and say that Bushmen and Zulus

arouse even more laughter among the young Antilleans. It would be interesting to show how in this instance the reactional exaggeration betrays a hint of recognition. In France a Negro who sees this documentary is virtually petrified. There he has no more hope of flight: He is at once Antillean, Bushman, and Zulu.

16   More especially, they become aware that the line of self-esteem that they had chosen should be inverted. We have seen in fact that the Antillean who goes to France pictures this journey as the final stage of his personality. Quite literally I can say without any risk of error that the Antillean who goes to France in order to convince himself that he is white will find his real face there.

CHAPTER 10

Pre-Oedipal Gender Configurations

Nancy Chodorow

Nancy Chodorow's *The Reproduction of Mothering* (1978) was an influential work of feminist psychoanalysis. In it, Chodorow examines the differing ways that boys and girls grow up and respond to the traditional family situation. Chodorow argues for the importance of the "pre-Oedipal" stage of development when children are more likely to be under a mother's care.

> *We knew, of course, that there had been a preliminary stage of attachment to the mother, but we did not know that it could be so rich in content and so long-lasting, and could leave behind so many opportunities or fixations and dispositions. During this time the girl's father is only a troublesome rival; in some cases the attachment to her mother lasts beyond the fourth year of life. Almost everything that we find later in her relation to her father was already present in this earlier attachment and has been transferred subsequently on to her father. In short, we get an impression that we cannot understand women unless we appreciate this phase of their pre-Oedipus attachment to their mother.*
>
> FREUD, "Femininity"

> *Our insight into this early pre-Oedipus phase in girls comes to us as a surprise, like the discovery, in another field, of the Minoan-Mycenaean civilization behind the civilization of Greece.*
>
> FREUD, "Female Sexuality"

Family structure produces crucial differentiating experiences between the sexes in oedipal object-relations and in the way these are psychologically appropriated, internalized, and transformed. Mothers are and have been the child's primary caretaker, socializer, and inner object; fathers are secondary objects for boys and girls. My interpretation of the Oedipus complex, from a perspective centered on object-relations, shows that these basic features of family structure entail varied modes of differentiation for the ego and its internalized object-relations and lead to the development of different relational capacities for girls and boys.

The feminine Oedipus complex is not simply a transfer of affection from mother to father and a giving up of mother. Rather, psychoanalytic research demonstrates the continued importance of a girl's external and internal relation to her mother, and the way her relation to her father is added to this. This process entails a relational complexity in feminine self-definition and personality which is not characteristic of masculine self-definition or personality. Relational capacities that are curtailed in boys as a result of the masculine Oedipus complex are sustained in girls.

Because of their mothering by women, girls come to experience themselves as less separate than boys, as having more permeable ego boundaries. Girls come to define themselves more in relation to others. Their internalized object-relational structure becomes more complex, with more ongoing issues. These personality features are reflected in superego development.

My investigation, then, does not focus on issues at the center of the traditional psychoanalytic account of the Oedipus complex – superego formation, gender identity, the attainment of gender role expectations, differential valuations of the sexes, and the genesis of sexual orientation. It takes other issues as equally central. I will be concerned with traditional issues only insofar as my analysis of Oedipal object-relations of boys and girls sheds new insight on the different nature of male and female heterosexual object-relations.

My interpretation of the feminine Oedipus complex relies for the most part on the early psychoanalytic account of female development. Aspects of this account of female psychology, sexuality, and development have been criticized and shown to be inaccurate or limited.[1] However, those elements of it which I emphasize – the clinically derived description and interpretation of experienced female object-relations in a nuclear family in which women mother and fathers are more remote figures to the children – have not been subjected to substantial revision within the psychoanalytic tradition nor criticism from without, and remain valid.[*]

Early Psychoanalytic Formulations

Freud's account of the boy's Oedipus complex is relatively simple and straightforward.[2] In response to, or in collaboration with, his heterosexual mother, a boy's pre-oedipal attachment to her becomes charged with phallic/sexual overtones. He comes to see his father as a rival for his mother's love and wishes to replace him. He fantasizes taking his father's penis, murdering or castrating him. He fears retaliation, and specifically castration, by his father for these wishes; thus he experiences a conflict between his self-love (narcissistic interest in his penis and body integrity) and his love for his mother (libidinal cathexis). As a result, he gives up his heterosexual attachment to his mother, radically repressing and denying his feelings toward her. (These feelings are not only repressed, but also are partly expressed in "aim-inhibited" modes, in affectionate feelings and sublimated activities.) At the same time, a "successful" resolution of his Oedipus complex requires that he remain heterosexual. Therefore, he is supposed to detach his heterosexual orientation from his mother, so that when he grows up he can reattach it to some other woman.

He receives a reward for his self-sacrifice, in addition to his avoidance of punishment. The carrot of the masculine Oedipus complex is identification with his father,

---

[*] My reading of this account, however, as a description and interpretation of family structure and its effects in male-dominant industrial capitalist society would not be accepted by all psychoanalysts.

and the superiority of masculine identification and prerogatives over feminine (if the threat of castration is the stick). A new psychic integration appears in place of the Oedipus complex, as the boy's ego is modified and transformed through the incorporation of paternal prohibitions to form his superego, and as he substitutes a general sexual orientation for the specific attachment to his mother (this attachment is composed of both the remainders of his infantile love and his newer sexualized and genitalized attachment).

Freud originally believed that the object-relational configurations of the feminine and masculine Oedipus complexes were completely symmetrical. According to this view, little girls at around age three, and as genital component drives become important, discover that they do not have a penis.[3] They automatically think they are castrated and inferior, and experience their lack as a wound to their self-esteem (a narcissistic wound). As Freud says, they "fall a victim to envy for the penis."[4] They also develop contempt for others, like their mother, who do not have penises and at the same time blame her for their own atrophied state. This contempt, plus their anger at her, leads them to turn away in anger and hostility from their mother, who has been their first love object. They turn to their father, who has a penis and might provide them with this much desired appendage. They give up a previously active sexuality for passive sexuality in relation to him. Finally, they change from wanting a penis from their father to wanting a child from him, through an unconscious symbolic equation of penis and child.

At the same time, their mother becomes a rival because she has sexual access to and possession of their father. The female Oedipus complex appears only when the mother has become a rival and the father a desired object. It consists in love for the father and rivalry with the mother, and is symmetrically opposed to the male Oedipus complex. Heterosexual orientation is thus an Oedipal outcome for girls as well as for boys. (Freud also speaks to differences in Oedipal outcome – the girl does not need to give up her Oedipus stance in the same manner as the boy, since she no longer has castration to fear.[*])

The Discovery of the Pre-Oedipal Mother–Daughter Relationship

Jeanne Lampl-de Groot described two clinical examples of a "negative Oedipus complex" in girls, in which they cathected their mothers and saw their fathers as rivals.[5] This fundamentally disrupted Freud's original postulation of Oedipal symmetry. Analysts continued to hold to much of Freud's original account, but Lampl-de Groot's discovery also substantially modified views of feminine Oedipal object-relations, and turned attention to the unique qualities of the pre-Oedipal mother–daughter relationship.

In Freud's original view, a daughter sees her mother only as someone who deprives her first of milk, then of sexual gratification, finally of a penis. A mother is seen as initiating only rivalry and hostility. In the light of Lampl-de Groot's finding, Freud reviewed his own clinical experience. He came to agree with her that the pre-

---

[*]   Freud is especially interested in the implication of this difference for feminine superego formation, but his account is not directly relevant here. Further on I examine the biases inherent in his formulation and some of its logical and clinical contradictions.

Oedipal phase was central in feminine development, that daughters, just as sons, begin life attached exclusively to their mothers.[6] Children were not originally bisexual, though they were potentially so. They were, rather, gynesexual, or matrisexual.

The discovery of the pre-Oedipal mother–daughter relationship required a general reformulation of psychoanalytic theory and its understanding of the development of object-relations. Freud had claimed that the Oedipus complex was the nucleus of neurosis and the basis of personality formation, and he was now led to revise radically this claim.[**] Freud compares his new insight into the pre-Oedipal phase of feminine development to a similarly layered historical discovery. Just as the Minoan-Mycenaean civilization underlies and explains the origins and form of classical Greece, so the pre-Oedipal phase in girls underlies and explains the origins and form of the feminine Oedipus complex.

Freud points to three major features of a girl's pre-Oedipal phase and her relationship to her mother during this phase. First, her pre-Oedipal attachment to her mother lasts through all three periods of infantile sexuality, often well into her fourth or fifth year. Second, this attachment is dramatically intense and ambivalent. Finally, Freud reports a surprising finding from his analysis of women with a strong attachment to their father: This strong attachment has been preceded by an equally strong and passionate attachment to their mother. More generally, he finds that a woman's pre-Oedipal attachment to her mother largely determines both her subsequent Oedipal attachment to her father and her later relationship to men in general.

A girl's pre-Oedipal relationship to her mother and her entrance into the Oedipus situation contrast to those of a boy. Freud and Brunswick claim that a boy's phase of pre-Oedipal mother-attachment is much shorter than a girl's, that he moves earlier into an Oedipal attachment.[7] What this means is not immediately apparent. If a girl retains a long pre-Oedipal attachment to her mother, and if a boy's Oedipal attachment is to his mother, then both boy and girl remain attached to their mother throughout the period of childhood sexuality. Brunswick suggests further that both boy and girl pass from a period of "passive" attachment to their mother to one of "active" attachment to her. On one level, then, it looks as though both boy and girl maintain similar attachments to their mother, their first love object, throughout most of their early years.

On another level, however, these attachments to the mother are very different – the retention of dichotomous formulations is necessary. On the basis of Freud's account and a later more extended discussion by Helene Deutsch in the *Psychology of Women*,[8] one can argue that the *nature* of the attachment is different. A boy's relation to his mother soon becomes focused on competitive issues of possession and phallic-sexual oppositeness (or complementarity) to her. The relation becomes embedded in triangular conflict as a boy becomes preoccupied with his father as a rival. A girl, by contrast, remains preoccupied for a long time with her mother alone. She experiences a continuation of the two-person relationship of infancy. Playing with dolls during this period, for instance, not only expresses "the *active* side of [the girl's] femininity"

[**] Since that time, major contributions to the theory of development have been concerned much more with the pre-Oedipal years – the early mother–infant relationship and early infantile development. Few analysts now hold that the Oedipus complex is the *nucleus* of neurosis, though they might say it contributes to its final *form*.

but also "is probably evidence of the exclusiveness of her attachment to her mother, with complete neglect of her father-object."[9]

The issue here is the father as an internal object, or object of conflict and ambivalence.... Fathers often become external attachment figures for children of both genders during their pre-Oedipal years. But the intensity and exclusivity of the relationship is much less than with a mother, and fathers are from the outset separate people and "special." As a result, representations of the father relationship do not become so internalized and subject to ambivalence, repression, and splitting of good and bad aspects, nor so determining of the person's identity and sense of self, as do representations of the relationship to a mother. As a boy moves into Oedipal attachment and phallic-possessive competition, and as he tries to consolidate his masculine identity, his father does become an object of his ambivalence. At this time, the girl's intense ambivalent attachment remains with her mother.

The content of a girl's attachment to her mother differs from a boy's precisely in that it is not at this time Oedipal (sexualized, focused on possession, which means focused on someone clearly different and opposite). The pre-Oedipal attachment of daughter to mother continues to be concerned with early mother–infant relational issues. It sustains the mother–infant exclusivity and the intensity, ambivalence, and boundary confusion of the child still preoccupied with issues of dependence and individuation. By contrast, the boy's "active attachment" to his mother expresses his sense of difference from and masculine oppositeness to her, in addition to being embedded in the Oedipal triangle. It helps him to differentiate himself from his mother, and his mother from his father.

The use of two different concepts for the early relationship between mother and daughter (mother–infant relationship, with reference to issues of development; pre-Oedipal, with reference to the girl's relation to her mother) obscures the convergence of the two processes. The terminological distinction is an artifact of the emergence of different aspects of psychoanalytic theory at different times ("pre-Oedipal" emerged early in investigating the feminine Oedipus complex; "mother–infant relationship" emerged later, as research focused on the early developmental stage as a distinct period).

There is analytic agreement that the pre-Oedipal period is of different length in girls and boys. There is also an agreed on, if undeveloped, formulation concerning those gender differences in the nature and quality of the pre-Oedipal mother–child relationship I have been discussing. This claim stands as an empirical finding with substantial descriptive and interpretive clinical support. The implications of these early developmental tendencies for psychological gender differences also stand on their own (Freud's claim that the early attachment to her mother affects a girl's attachment to her father and men, for instance). But Freud and his colleagues do not explain how such differences come about.

The different length and quality of the pre-Oedipal period in boys and girls are rooted in women's mothering, specifically in the fact that a mother is of the same gender as her daughter and of a different gender from her son. This leads to her experiencing and treating them differently. I do not mean this as a biological claim. I am using *gender* here to stand for the mother's particular psychic structure and relational sense, for her (probable) heterosexuality, and for her conscious and unconscious acceptance of the ideology, meanings, and expectations that go into being a gendered member of our society and understanding what gender means. Being a grown woman and mother also means having been the daughter of a mother, which affects the nature of her motherliness and quality of her mothering.

It is not easy to prove that mothers treat and experience differently pre-Oedipal boys and girls. Maccoby and Jacklin, in the currently definitive review of the observational and experimental literature of psychology on sex differences, claim that the behavioral evidence – based on interviews of parents and observations of social science researchers – indicates little differential treatment.[*][10] They report that most studies of children in the first four or five years concerning parent–child interaction, parental warmth, reaction to dependence or independence, and amount of praise and positive feedback show no difference according to the gender of the child.[**] They also report no gender difference in proximity-seeking, touching, and resistance to separation from parents or caretakers in young children.[†] These studies measure observable behaviors, which can be coded, counted and replicated, and they take for proof of gender difference only statistically significant findings.

Yet a report summarizing the proceedings of a panel on the psychology of women at the annual meeting of the American Psychoanalytic Association in 1976 claims that "there is increasing evidence of distinction between the mother's basic attitudes and handling of her boy and girl children starting from the earliest days and continuing thereafter."[11] This surprising contradiction suggests that academic psychologists and psychoanalysts must be looking at quite different things. The kinds of differences I am postulating (and that psychoanalysts are beginning to find) are differences of nuance, tone, quality. These differences are revealed in a small range of analytic clinical case material as well as in some cultural research. These cases give us insight into the subtleties of mothers' differential treatment and experiencing of sons and daughters and of the differential development that results.[††]

Pre-Oedipal Mother–Daughter Relationships: The Clinical Picture

Many psychoanalysts report cases of particular kinds of mother–infant relationships which throw light on differences in the pre-Oedipal mother–daughter and mother–son

[*] Rather, the studies they report produce such inconsistent findings that one could support almost any hypothesis about gender differences in treatment by selective references.

[**] On many measures, however, they find that where studies do report a gender difference, it tends to be in the same direction. For instance, where mothers do talk more to children of one gender, it turns out to be to girls; where they touch, hold, or spend more time feeding, it tends to be boys.

[†] The arousal of gross motor behavior, punishment, and pressure against what is thought to be gender-inappropriate behavior all tend to happen more to boys. I am wary of this seemingly scientific investigation. The message of Maccoby and Jacklin's book is that one cannot find any consistent gender differences anywhere if one looks at the "hard scientific facts." As support against biological arguments for gender differences, these findings may do the trick. But I was left feeling a little as if a magic disappearing trick had been performed. All the experiences of being manipulated, channeled, and restricted which women and men have been commenting on, and which they have felt deeply and continuously, were suddenly figments of our imagination.

[††] Not to give up on the academic psychology findings completely, we know that some forms of similar maternal behavior may produce different effects on sons and daughters. For instance, Kagan and Freeman and Crandall report that maternal criticism and lack of nurturance correlate with intellectual achievement in girls but the opposite behavior does in boys. Maternal overprotection and affection predict later conformity in boys, whereas conformity in girls is predicted by excessive severity of discipline and restrictiveness.[12] Therefore, the similarity in maternal behavior which Maccoby and Jacklin report may not have similar effects on feminine and masculine development.

relationship.[*][13] Fliess presents the psychopathological extreme and also the most numerous examples, unintentionally showing the way a certain sort of psychotic mother inflicts her pathology predominantly on daughters.[14] The mothers of his patients carried to an extreme that which is considered to be, or is described as, "normal" in the pre-Oedipal mother–infant relationship. His account is significant because, having chosen to focus on a certain kind of neurotic patient and accompanying early patient–mother relationship, it turns out that an overwhelmingly large percentage (almost eight times as many) of his case illustrations are women. His explanation for this disproportion is that "the picture is more easily recognized in the female because of the naturally longer duration of the pre-Oedipal phase."[15] This explanation is tautological, because he is talking about precisely those features of maternal behavior which in a less extreme but similar form create and maintain a pre-Oedipal relationship in the normal case.

The mothers that Fliess describes were "asymbiotic" during the period when their child needed symbiosis and experienced oneness with them. They were unable to participate empathetically in a relationship to their child. However, from the time that these daughters began to differentiate themselves mentally from their mothers and to practice physical separation, these mothers became "hypersymbiotic." Having denied their daughters the stability and security of a confident early symbiosis, they turned around and refused to allow them any leeway for separateness or individuation. Instead, they now treated their daughters and cathected them as narcissistic physical and mental extensions of themselves, attributing their own body feelings to them. The mothers took control over their daughters' sexuality and used their daughters for their own autoerotic gratification. As Fliess puts it, "The mother employs the 'transitivism' of the psychotic" – "I am you and you are me"[16] – in her experiencing and treatment of her daughter. The result, in Fliess's patients, was that these daughters, as neurotics, duplicated many features of their mothers' psychotic symptoms, and retained severe ego and body-ego distortions. Their ego and body-ego retained an undifferentiated connection to their mother. Their relation to reality was, like an infant's, mediated by their mother as external ego.

Thus, these mothers maintained their daughters in a nonindividuated state through behavior which grew out of their own ego and body-ego boundary blurring and their perception of their daughters as one with, and interchangeable with, themselves. If we are to believe Fliess's account, this particular pathology – the psychotic distortion and prolongation of the normal pre-Oedipal relationship – is predominantly a mother–daughter phenomenon.[17]

Olden, Enid Balint, and Angel provide further examples of the tendencies Fliess describes. Balint describes a state she calls "being empty of oneself" – a feeling of lack of self, or emptiness.[18] This happens especially when a person who has this feeling is with others who read the social and emotional setting differently but do not recognize this, nor recognize that the person herself is in a different world.

Balint claims that women are more likely to experience themselves this way. Women who feel empty of themselves feel that they are not being accorded a separate reality nor the agency to interpret the world in their own way. This feeling has its origins in

---

[*] In what follows, I rely on extensive accounting and quoting. This is necessary because a simple assertion of the distinctions that I wish to demonstrate would not be persuasive without the clinical illustrations.

the early mother–daughter relationship. Balint provides a case example to illustrate. She claims that the "empathy" of the patient's mother was a false empathy, that from the outset it was probably a distorted projection of what the mother thought her infant daughter's needs should be. As her daughter grew, and was able to express wants and needs, the mother systematically ignored these expressions and gave feedback not to her actual behavior but rather to what she had in the first place projected onto her child. Balint describes the results of this false empathy: "Because of this lack of feedback, Sarah felt that she was unrecognized, that she was empty of herself, that she had to live in a void."[19] This mother–infant interaction began in earliest infancy, but certainly continued throughout the patient's childhood. It is useful to quote Balint at length to indicate the quality of this mother–daughter interaction:

(*i*) [Although she] on the surface developed satisfactorily, there was apparently a vitally important area where there was no reliable understanding between mother and daughter.

(*ii*) Although the mother tried her best, she responded more to her own preconceived ideas as to what a baby ought to feel than to what her baby actually felt.... Probably Sarah's mother could not bear unhappiness or violence or fear in her child, did not respond to it, and tried to manipulate her so that everything wrong was either put right at once or denied.

(*iii*) What was missing, therefore, was the acceptance that there might be bad things, or even good ones, which must be recognized; that it is not sufficient merely to put things right; moreover, that the child was neither identical with her mother, nor with what the mother wanted her to be. . . .

Sarah's mother was impervious to any communication which was different from the picture she had of her daughter, and, in consequence, Sarah could not understand her mother's communications and felt that her mother never saw her as she was; neither found an echo in the other; and consequently only a spurious interaction between the growing child and the environment could develop.[20]

Olden describes a disruption in mother–child empathy that occurs when mothers who had originally formed (or seem to have formed) an appropriate unity with their infant were then unable to give it up.[21] She is describing "a specific psychic immaturity that will keep a mother from sensing her child's needs, from following his pace and understanding his infantile world; and in turn keep the child from developing ego capacities."[22] Olden does not note that both cases she recounts are mother–daughter cases (one in which the daughter – a child – was in analysis, the other from an analysis of the mother). Both mothers felt unreal and were depressed. Olden described characteristics that both Balint and Fliess describe. The mothers lacked real empathy but had pseudo-empathy which kept the daughters from forming their own identity, either through identifying and feeling like someone or through contrasting themselves to someone (this was more true for the daughter who had less relationship to her father). The mothers attained instinctual gratification through their daughters, not through directly using their daughters for autoerotic gratification, but by identifying vicariously with their sexuality and sex lives.

The Olden cases move even further from pathology than Balint, and further toward the norm that the direction of pathology implies. These mothers felt real closeness to their daughters, unlike the Balint and Fliess examples.[*] Olden describes

---

[*] The mothers were, in Fliess's terms, hypersymbiotic but not asymbiotic.

two very immature mothers who shared and, as it were, acted out the children's wishes yet were unable to perceive their children's real needs. These mothers and their children were extremely attached to each other; some of their friends characterized the relationship as "overidentification." Despite this emotional closeness, or perhaps on account of it, the mothers were unable to empathize with their children; the goal and function of this "closeness" was exclusively narcissistic.[23]

These mothers had maintained the primitive narcissistic mother–infant fusion with their children. This enabled them vicariously to gratify their own frustrated instinctual needs by virtue of projecting themselves onto the child.[24]

Angel provides further examples, this time by contrasting adult patients rather than by discussing the mother–infant relationship itself.[25] He is contrasting "symbiosis and pseudosymbiosis" – two versions of fantasies and wishes of merging in adult patients.

In (real) symbiosis, according to Angel, there is an extreme fear of merging as well as a wish to merge, because there is no firm sense of individuation in the first place. In pseudosymbiosis, there need not be and is not such fear, because the distinction between self and object is firm, and the wish to (re)merge is only a defensive one, usually against feelings of aggression toward the object:

1   In symbiosis, merging fantasies are a true reflection of the state of the ego; the self and object representations are merged.
2   In pseudosymbiosis, merging fantasies are defensive formations, and the self and object representations are more or less distinct.
3   In adults with true symbiotic object relations, the scale is weighted heavily on the side of fixation to the infantile symbiotic phase. In pseudosymbiosis, the element of fixation is minimal or absent, and the scale is weighted heavily on the side of defensive regression.[26]

Between symbiosis and pseudosymbiosis is a middle syndrome, which arises through fixation to the period when separateness is being established but still fluctuates and is in doubt. Like Olden, Angel does not tie his distinction to gender differences. His case examples of true symbiosis and in-between syndrome are women, however, and his case example of pseudosymbiosis is a man. This points again to gender differences in issues of separateness and sense of self.

The choices of examples by Fliess, Olden, Angel, and Balint are not accidental. The patterns of fusion, projection, narcissistic extension, and denial of separateness they describe are more likely to happen in early mother–daughter relationships than in those of mothers and sons. The same personality characteristics in mothers certainly produce problematic mother–son relationships, but of a different kind. In all these cases, the mother does not recognize or denies the existence of the daughter as a separate person, and the daughter herself then comes not to recognize, or to have difficulty recognizing, herself as a separate person. She experiences herself, rather, as a continuation or extension of (or, in the Balint case, a subsumption within) her mother in particular, and later of the world in general.

In the next two examples, my interpretation is less secure. Both authors give examples of mothers and daughters and mothers and sons to demonstrate a larger issue – as Burlingham phrases it, "empathy between infant and mother,"[27] and as

Sperling puts it, "children's interpretations and reaction to the unconscious of their mother."[28] It is my impression that although there was certainly understanding or empathy between mothers and children of both genders, and ways in which children of both genders lived out their mother's preoccupations or fantasies, the quality of the child's empathy and its reaction to the mother's unconscious differed according to gender.[*] With one possible exception,[**] Burlingham and Sperling describe girls who act *as extensions of* their mothers, who act out the aggression which their mothers feel but do not allow themselves to recognize or act on. They describe boys, by contrast, who equally intuitively *react to* their mothers' feelings and wishes as if they were the *objects* of their mothers' fantasies rather than the subjects.[†] Girls, then, seem to become and experience themselves as the self of the mother's fantasy, whereas boys become the other.

Neither Burlingham nor Sperling links her insights to gender differences. However, Burlingham mentions that when she and her children were in analysis at the same time, and an issue preoccupying her would arise in the analysis of her children, appearing "out of context . . . as if it were a foreign body,"[29] these links were more obvious with sons than daughters. Burlingham does not have an explanation. If my interpretation is right, then the explanation is that her daughter's preoccupations, as continuations of her, might appear more ego-syntonic – seeming to emerge out of her daughter's ego – and thus be less identifiable than issues which emphasized her sons as acted-on objects.

These accounts indicate the significance of gender differences, despite the lack of attention paid to these differences. With the exception of Balint, who says that being empty of oneself is found more often in women, the authors claim simply to focus on a certain kind of person and certain kind of early mother–infant relationship, and then either use predominantly mother–*daughter* examples or mother–daughter and mother–son examples which reflect gender-linked variations in the processes they discuss, as in the cases of Angel, Burlingham, and Sperling. All these accounts indicate, in different ways, that prolonged symbiosis and narcissistic over-identification are particularly characteristic of early relationships between mothers and daughters.

Pre-Oedipal Mother–Son Relationships: The Clinical Picture

Both the absence of mother–son examples in some discussions, and their character in others, indicate how early mother–daughter relationships contrast to those between a mother and son. In Burlingham and Sperling, sons are objects for their mothers, even while they maintain symbiotic bonds of empathy and oneness of identification. In the Angel case, a man pretends symbiosis when boundaries are in fact established.

---

[*] It is hard to substantiate this impression without repeating all of the cases involved. I report them, however, because there are few such cases in the literature. I encourage the most committed (or skeptical) to read them.

[**] Ann, described by Sperling.

[†] In one case, for instance, a son (Paul, described by Sperling) has become a substitute for the mother's brother, toward whom she had and continues to have very complicated feelings.

Psychoanalytic and anthropological clinical accounts further illuminate specific tendencies in early mother–son relationships.[30] Bibring argues that the decline of the husband's presence in the home has resulted in a wife "as much in need of a husband as the son is of a father."[31] This wife is likely to turn her affection and interest to the next obvious male – her son – and to become particularly seductive toward him. Just as the father is often not enough present to prevent or break up the mother–daughter boundary confusion, he is also not available to prevent either his wife's seductiveness or his son's growing reciprocated incestuous impulses. A mother, here, is again experiencing her son as a definite other – an opposite-gendered and -sexed other. Her emotional investments and conflicts, given her socialization around issues of gender and sex and membership in a sexist society, make this experience of him particularly strong. The son's solution, moreover, emphasizes differentiation buttressed by heavy emotional investment. He projects his own fears and desires onto his mother, whose behavior he then gives that much more significance and weight.

Slater's account of Greek mother–son relationships in the Classical period, read into his later work on contemporary American society, gives us further insight into the dynamics Bibring discusses.[*32] Greek marriages, Slater suggests, were characterized by a weak marital bond, and the society was ridden with sex antagonism and masculine fear and devaluation of mature women. Wives were isolated in their marital homes with children. In reaction, mothers reproduced in their own sons the same masculine fears and behaviors that their husbands and the men in their society had. They produced in these sons a precarious and vulnerable masculinity and sense of differentiation by alternating sexual praise and seductive behavior with hostile deflation, ridicule, and intrusive definitions of their sons' intrapsychic situation. Like the maternal treatment Bibring discusses, this treatment kept sons dependent on their mothers for a sense of self-sufficiency and self-esteem. At the same time, it emphasized these sons' sexuality and sexual difference, and encouraged participation in a heavily sexualized relationship in boys who had not resolved early issues of individuation and the establishment of ego boundaries.[**]

Bibring's and Slater's work implies that in societies like ours, which are male-dominated but have relatively father-absent families and little paternal participation in family life and child care, masculinity and sexual difference ("Oedipal" issues)

---

*   Slater discusses the psychic outcome of structural features of the family and the organization and ideology of gender not unique to Greek society but very much present in our own. His later works do not present his analysis in such full detail, though they assume that it is very much applicable to American society. Therefore, I rely in what follows on the analysis of Greece to shed light on our contemporary situation.

**   This combination of the blurring of generational boundaries between mother and son, and the elevation of the son to a role as masculine partner, or opposite, to the mother, replicates Lidz's description of schizophrenogenic family structure and practice for boys.[33] Slater in fact suggests that maternal treatment of sons in Greece was schizophrenogenic. He points out that we have no record of the actual incidence of madness in ancient Greek society, but that Greek culture was dominated by maternally caused madness: "No other mythology with which I am familiar contains so many explicitly designated instances of madness. . . . The most striking fact is that of all the clear instances of madness deliberately produced in one being by another, none can be said to be caused by a truly masculine or paternal agent. Most are afflicted by goddesses, and the remainder by the effeminate Dionysus, himself a previous victim at the hands of Hera. . . . Nor is the relationship between the sex of an agent and the sex of a victim a random one: in the overwhelming majority of cases madness is induced in persons of the opposite sex."[34]

become intertwined with separation-individuation ("pre-Oedipal") issues almost from the beginning of a boy's life.[*] This conclusion receives confirmation from Whiting's cross-cultural analyses of patrilocal societies with sleeping arrangements in which children sleep exclusively with their mothers during their first two years (and husband/fathers sleep elsewhere) and postpartum sex taboos.[35] Such societies are usually characterized by a general pattern of sex segregation and sex antagonism – again, a (perhaps) extreme form of the sex-gender arrangements in modern society.

Such arrangements create difficulties for the development of a sense of masculinity in boys. Although their account is allegedly about feminine role identification, Whiting and his colleagues are in fact talking about the period of early infancy. In some formulations of the problem, it is clear that they are concerned with fundamental feelings of dependence, overwhelming attachment, and merging with the mother, developed by a son during the intense and exclusive early years, that he feels he must overcome in order to attain independence and a masculine self-identification.[36] They suggest further that an explicitly sexual relationship between mother and son may exist. Citing "clinical evidence from women in our own society suggesting that nursing is sexually gratifying to some women at least,"[37] and informant reports in one society with postpartum sex taboo and mother–infant sleeping arrangements that mothers had no desire for sex as long as they were nursing, they suggest that "it is possible that the mother obtains some substitute sexual gratification from nursing and caring for her infant."[38]

Cross-cultural accounts of father-absence and mother–infant sleeping arrangements do not mention the effects of extreme father-absence and antagonism between the sexes on mother–daughter relationships or on female development.[**] It may well be that the kind of mother–daughter boundary confusion and overidentification I have discussed here is the answer. Slater suggests that it is not simply sleeping arrangements but maternal ambivalence and inconsistent behavior toward sons which lead to the results Whiting describes. Without this ambivalence and seductiveness, mother–infant sleeping arrangements may not produce conflict and dependency. Alternatively, it may be that dependency in girls is not, in the patriarchal cultural case, an obstacle to the successful attainment of femininity.

I conclude, from the evidence in Bibring's, Slater's and Whiting's accounts, that a mother, of a different gender from her son and deprived of adult emotional, social, and physical contact with men (and often without any supportive adult contact at all), may push her son out of his pre-Oedipal relationship to her into an Oedipally toned relationship defined by its sexuality and gender distinction. Her son's maleness and oppositeness as a sexual other become important, even while his being an infant remains important as well. Because of this, sons (men) come to have different kinds of pre-Oedipally engendered problems than daughters (women). Greenacre points to these in her discussion of the genesis of "perversions" and especially of fetishism, which, according to psychoanalysts, are predominantly masculine phenomena.[39]

---

[*] Slater does not restrict his discussion to the period of the early mother–son relationship. But all the relational and ego problems he discusses, and his use of the label "oral-narcissistic dilemma" to summarize these, point to early mother–infant issues: myths concerned with birth, with maternal attacks on the infant in the womb or on the neonate, with oral reincorporation by the mother; or with the maternal lack of reality principle vis-à-vis her son.

[**] In fact, their omission provided the original impetus for my study here.

Greenacre suggests that fetishes, and other perversions as well, serve to deny (on an unconscious level usually) that women do not have penises: "The phallic woman [is a] ubiquitous fantasy in perversions."[*40] The reason the fetishist needs to deny the existence of different genitalia than his own is that his sense of his own genital body identity is not firm. Being presented with different genitalia, therefore, he feels threatened and potentially castrated himself. Greenacre argues that fetishism is a result of conflict centering on issues of separation and individuation in the early years. It results from boundary confusion and a lack of sense of self firmly distinguished from his mother, leading him to experience (again, all this is probably not conscious) as his own what he takes to be the castration of first his mother and then women in general.

Greenacre's account points to gender differences surrounding early issues of differentiation and individuation. Even while primary separateness is being established in boys, issues of masculinity and conflicts around genital differences are important. Her account also leads me to conclude that the early period is sexualized for boys in a way that it is not for girls, that phallic-masculine issues become intertwined with supposedly nongender-differentiated object-relational and ego issues concerning the creation of a sense of separate self.

According to Greenacre and Herman Roiphe, children of both genders go through a phase during their second year when their genitals become important as part of their developing body self and their developing gender identity.[41] Conflictual object-relations concerning these issues can lead a child to focus anxiety and emotion on genital difference – to develop castration anxiety or penis envy. Greenacre's account indicates, however, that this aspect of individuation is more important and conflictual for men. That the early mother–son relationship is likely to emphasize phallic Oedipal issues along with pre-Oedipal individuation issues explains this difference. It is another instance in which a supposedly nongender-differentiated process has different meanings for boys and girls.[**]

In a society like ours, in which mothers have exclusive care for infants and are isolated from other adults, in which there is physical and social separation of men/fathers from women/mothers and children, and institutionalized male dominance, a mother may impose her reactions to this situation on her son, and confuse her relationship to him as an infant with a sexualized relationship to him as a male.[***] It is precisely such a situation which accounts for the early entrance into the Oedipus situation on the part of boys in our society.

---

[*] I realize that this kind of claim verges on the incredible to those unpersuaded by psychoanalytic theory. It is certainly the area in psychoanalytic theory in which I feel least comfortable, but in this case Greenacre's account is persuasive and illuminating.

[**] As noted previously, children of both genders go through a symbiotic phase of unity, primary identification, and mutual empathy with their mother, and then go through a period of differentiation from her – but these issues remain more central for women.

[***] Barbara Deck (personal communication) suggests that whether the boy is a child or an adult makes a big difference to his mother. As a little man with a penis, he excites her; however, in order for her fondling and sexualized treatment not to produce conscious guilt, he must remain a neuter baby. This ambivalence does not arise in the case of a girl baby, who is "just a baby" or at most a "baby mother/self." She is not an *other*, like a "baby husband" or a "baby father."

Conclusions

The clinical and cultural examples I have discussed all point to the conclusion that pre-Oedipal experiences of girls and boys differ. The girl's pre-Oedipal mother-love and preoccupation with pre-Oedipal issues are prolonged in a way that they are not for the boy. With the exception of Whiting's cross-cultural analysis, all the examples I cite are cases which their authors have taken to be noteworthy for their "abnormality" or "pathology." However, the extent of such pathology varies (from preoccupation to mild neurosis to psychosis). More important, there is systematic variation in the form it takes depending on whether a person is female or male – on whether we are talking about mother–daughter or mother–son relationships. In all cases the pathology reflects, in exaggerated form, differences in what are in fact normal tendencies. The cases give us, as Freud suggests about neurosis in general, insight into what we would otherwise miss just because it is subtle, typical, and familiar. These cases, then, point to typical gender differences in the pre-Oedipal period, differences that are a product of the asymmetrical organization of parenting which founds our family structure.

Because they are the same gender as their daughters and have been girls, mothers of daughters tend not to experience these infant daughters as separate from them in the same way as do mothers of infant sons. In both cases, a mother is likely to experience a sense of oneness and continuity with her infant. However, this sense is stronger, and lasts longer, vis-à-vis daughters. Primary identification and symbiosis with daughters tend to be stronger and cathexis of daughters is more likely to retain and emphasize narcissistic elements, that is, to be based on experiencing a daughter as an extension or double of a mother herself, with cathexis of the daughter as a sexual other usually remaining a weaker, less significant theme.

Other accounts also suggest that mothers normally identify more with daughters and experience them as less separate. Signe Hammer's book, *Daughters and Mothers: Mothers and Daughters*, based on interviews with over seventy-five mothers, daughters, and grandmothers, describes how issues of primary identification, oneness, and separateness follow mother–daughter pairs from a daughter's earliest infancy until she is well into being a mother or even grandmother herself:

> Most of the daughters in this book have received enough support from their mothers to emerge from the stage of complete symbiosis in early infancy. But for the vast majority of mothers and daughters, this emergence remains only partial. At some level mothers and daughters tend to remain emotionally bound up with each other in what might be called a semisymbiotic relationship, in which neither ever quite sees herself or the other as a separate person.[42]

Hammer's study is certainly confirmed by my own discussions with a number of mothers of daughters and sons, first in a women's group devoted to the discussion and analysis of mother–daughter relationships in particular and family relationships in general, and later with individual acquaintances. Finally, the resurfacing and prevalence of pre-Oedipal mother–daughter issues in adolescence (anxiety, intense and exclusive attachment, orality and food, maternal control of a daughter's body, primary identification) provide clinical verification of the claim that elements of the pre-Oedipal mother–daughter relationship are maintained and prolonged in both maternal and filial psyche.[43]

Because they are of different gender than their sons, by contrast, mothers experience their sons as a male opposite. Their cathexis of sons is more likely to consist from early on in an object cathexis of a sexual other, perhaps in addition to narcissistic components. Sons tend to be experienced as differentiated from their mothers, and mothers push this differentiation (even while retaining, in some cases, a kind of intrusive controlling power over their sons). Maternal behavior, at the same time, tends to help propel sons into a sexualized, genitally toned relationship, which in its turn draws the son into triangular conflicts.

Early psychoanalytic findings about the special importance of the pre-Oedipal mother–daughter relationship describe the first stage of a general process in which separation and individuation remain particularly female developmental issues. The cases I describe suggest that there is a tendency in women toward boundary confusion and a lack of sense of separateness from the world. Most women do develop ego boundaries and a sense of separate self. However, women's ego and object-relational issues are concerned with this tendency on one level (of potential conflict, of experience of object-relations), even as on another level (in the formation of ego boundaries and the development of a separate identity) the issues are resolved.

That these issues become more important for girls than for boys is a product of children of both genders growing up in families where women, who have a greater sense of sameness with daughters than sons, perform primary parenting functions.[*] As long as women mother, we can expect that a girl's pre-Oedipal period will be longer than that of a boy and that women, more than men, will be more open to and preoccupied with those very relational issues that go into mothering – feelings of primary identification, lack of separateness or differentiation, ego and body-ego boundary issues and primary love not under the sway of the reality principle. A girl does not simply identify with her mother or want to be like her mother. Rather, mother and daughter maintain elements of their primary relationship which means they will feel alike in fundamental ways. Object-relations and conflicts in the Oedipal period build upon this pre-Oedipal base.

Notes

1 See, for example, Roy Schafer, 1974, "Problems in Freud's Psychology of Women," *Journal of the American Psychoanalytic Association*, 22, #3, pp. 459–85; William H. Masters and Virginia E. Johnson, 1966, *Human Sexual Response*; Mary Jane Sherfey, 1966, "The Evolution and Nature of Female Sexuality in Relation to Psychoanalytic Theory," *Journal of the American Psychoanalytic Association*, 14, #1, pp. 28–128.
2 Freud, 1924, "The Dissolution of the Oedipus Complex," *SE*, vol. 19, pp. 172–9; Freud, 1933, *New Introductory Lectures on Psychoanalysis*.
3 Freud, 1925, "Some Psychical Consequences."
4 Ibid., p. 252.
5 Jeanne Lampl-de Groot, 1927, "The Evolution of the Oedipus Complex in Women," in Fliess, ed., *The Psychoanalytic Reader*, pp. 180–94.

[*] I must admit to fudging here about the contributory effect in all of this of a mother's sexual orientation – whether she is heterosexual or lesbian. Given a female gender identity, she is "the same as" her daughter and "different from" her son, but part of what I am talking about also presumes a different kind of cathexis of daughter and son deriving from her heterosexuality.

6 Freud, 1931, "Female Sexuality," *SE*, vol. 21, pp. 223–43; see also Freud, 1933, *New Intro-ductory Lectures*.

7 Freud, 1933, *New Introductory Lectures*, and Brunswick, 1940, "The Preoedipal Phase."

8 Helene Deutsch, 1944, *Psychology of Women*.

9 Freud, 1933, *New Introductory Lectures*, p. 237.

10 Maccoby and Jacklin, 1974, *The Psychology of Sex Differences*.

11 Eleanor Galenson, 1976, "Scientific Proceedings – Panel Reports," Panels on the Psychology of Women, Annual Meeting of the American Psychoanalytic Association, 1974. *Journal of the American Psychoanalytic Association*, 24, #1, p. 159.

12 Jerome Kagan and Marion Freeman, 1963, "Relation of Childhood Intelligence, Maternal Behaviors and Social Class to Behavior During Adolescence," *Child Development*, 36, pp. 899–911, and Virginia C. Crandall, 1972, "The Fels Study; Some Contributions to Per-sonality Development and Achievement in Childhood and Adulthood," *Seminars in Psychiatry*, 4, #4, pp. 383–97.

13 Robert Fliess, 1961, *Ego and Body Ego*; Klaus Angel, 1967, "On Symbiosis and Pseudosym-biosis," *Journal of the American Psychoanalytic Association*, 15, #2, pp. 294–316; Enid Balint, 1963, "On Being Empty of Oneself," *International Journal of Psycho-Analysis*, 44, #4, pp. 470–80; Melitta Sperling, 1950, "Children's Interpretation and Reaction to the Uncon-scious of Their Mothers," *International Journal of Psycho-Analysis*, 31, pp. 36–41; C. Olden, 1958, "Notes on Empathy"; and Dorothy Burlingham, 1967, "Empathy Between Infant and Mother," *Journal of the American Psychoanalytic Association*, 15, pp. 764–80.

14 Robert Fliess, 1961, *Ego and Body Ego*.

15 Ibid., p. 49.

16 Ibid., p. 48.

17 For a more accessible example of what Fliess describes – again, a mother–daughter case – see Flora Schreiber, 1973, *Sybil*.

18 Enid Balint, 1963, "On Being Empty."

19 Ibid., p. 478.

20 Ibid., p. 476.

21 Christine Olden, 1958, "Notes on Empathy."

22 Ibid., p. 505.

23 Ibid.

24 Ibid., p. 512.

25 Klaus Angel, 1967, "On Symbiosis."

26 Ibid., p. 315.

27 Dorothy Burlingham, 1967, "Empathy Between Infant."

28 Melitta Sperling, 1950, "Children's Interpretation."

29 Dorothy Burlingham, 1967, "Empathy Between Infant," p. 779.

30 Grete Bibring, 1953, "On the 'Passing of the Oedipus Complex' in a Matriarchal Family Setting," in R. M. Loewenstein, ed., *Drives, Affects, and Behavior: Essays in Honor of Marie Bonaparte*, pp. 278–84; Philip E. Slater, 1968, *The Glory of Hera*; John W. M. Whiting, 1959, "Sorcery, Sin and the Superego: A Cross-Cultural Study of Some Mechanisms of Social Control," in Clellan S. Ford (ed.), *Cross-Cultural Approaches: Readings in Comparative Re-search*, pp. 147–68; 1960, "Totem and Taboo – A Re-evaluation," in Jules H. Masserman (ed.), *Psychoanalysis and Human Values*; Whiting et al., 1958, "The Function of Male Initi-ation"; Roger V. Burton and Whiting, 1961, "The Absent Father"; and Phyllis Greenacre, 1968, "Perversions: General Considerations Regarding Their Genetic and Dynamic Back-ground," *Psychoanalytic Study of the Child*, 23, pp. 47–62.

31 Grete Bibring, 1953, "On the 'Passing of the Oedipus Complex,'" p. 281.

32 Philip E. Slater, 1968, *The Glory of Hera*, 1970, *The Pursuit of Loneliness*, 1974, *Earthwalk*.

33 Theodore Lidz, Stephen Fleck, and Alice R. Cornelison, 1965, *Schizophrenia and the Family*.

34 Philip E. Slater, 1968, *The Glory of Hera*.

35 See John Whiting, 1959, "Sorcery, Sin," and 1960, "Totem and Taboo"; Whiting et al., 1958, "The Function of Male Initiation"; and Burton and Whiting, 1961, "The Absent Father."

36 For example, Whiting et al., 1958, "The Function of Male Initiation."
37 Ibid., p. 362.
38 John Whiting, 1959, "Sorcery, Sin," p. 150.
39 Phyllis Greenacre, 1968, "Perversions."
40 Ibid., p. 47.
41 Ibid., and Herman Roiphe, 1968, "On an Early Genital Phase: With an Addendum on Genesis," *Psychoanalytic Study of the Child*, 23, pp. 348–65.
42 Signe Hammer, 1975, *Daughters and Mothers: Mothers and Daughters*.
43 See Peter Blos, 1957, *On Adolescence: A Psychoanalytic Interpretation*; Deutsch, 1944, *Psychology of Women*; Kata Levy, 1960, "Simultaneous Analysis of a Mother and Her Adolescent Daughter: The Mother's Contribution to the Loosening of the Infantile Object Tie," *Psychoanalytic Study of the Child*, 15, pp. 378–391; Marjorie P. Sprince, 1962, "The Development of a Pre-Oedipal Partnership Between an Adolescent Girl and Her Mother," *Psychoanalytic Study of the Child*, 17, pp. 418–50.

CHAPTER 11

The Black Hole of Trauma

Bessel A. van der Kolk and Alexander C. McFarlane

Attention has turned in literary criticism in recent decades to the issue of trauma. In this selection from their book *Psychological Stress: the Effects of Overwhelming Experience on Mind, Body, and Society* (1996), van der Kolk and McFarlane provide an account of how traumatic experiences can damage the psyche and leave indelible marks on it.

> *A stimulus impinging on the mind can be conceived as behaving like a "...raindrop land[ing] on a terrain of hills and valleys. The drop moves generally downhill until it ends up at the bottom of a nearby valley. The deeper the memory basin and the steeper the walls, the more likely the train of associations is likely to end up in it. In PTSD [Post Traumatic Stress Disorder] the traumatic event may be conceptualized as occupying...a Dead Sea of memory, into which all too many of the patient's associations inexorably flow" (Tank and Hopfield, 1987, p.106).*
> —As quoted in Pitman and Orr (1990, p. 469)

Experiencing trauma is an essential part of being human; history is written in blood. Although art and literature have always been preoccupied with how people cope with the inevitable tragedies of life, the large-scale scientific study of the effects of trauma on body and mind has had to wait till the latter part of this century – when the average life expectancy in the industrialized world is well above the Biblical three score and ten; when almost all children can be expected to outlive their parents; and when famine and epidemics no longer wipe out large sections of the population with the regularity that they once did.

Humans owe their ascendance in the animal kingdom to their extraordinary capacity to adapt. Throughout evolution humans have been exposed to terrible events; yet most people who are exposed to dreadful experiences survive without developing psychiatric disorders. Throughout history, some people have adapted to terrible life events with flexibility and creativity, while others have become fixated on the trauma and gone on to lead traumatized and traumatizing existences. Societies that have been massively traumatized have followed roughly similar patterns of adaptation and disintegration (e.g., Tuchman, 1978; Buruma, 1994). Many survivors seem to be able to transcend their trauma temporarily and harness their pain in acts of sublimated creation; for example, the writers and Holocaust survivors Jerzy Kosinski and Primo Levi seem to have done this, only to succumb to the despair of their memories in the end.

Despite the human capacity to survive and adapt, traumatic experiences can alter people's psychological, biological, and social equilibrium to such a degree that the memory of one particular event comes to taint all other experiences, spoiling appreciation of the present. This tyranny of the past interferes with the ability to pay attention to both new and familiar situations. When people come to concentrate selectively on reminders of their past, life tends to become colorless, and contemporary experience ceases to be a teacher. In much of the remainder of this book, we discuss what makes people vulnerable to developing such a fixation on trauma, and what can help them overcome it.

The Systematic Study of Trauma

Since psychiatry has started to organize psychological problems in a diagnostic system that is based purely on their surface manifestations, it has, as a profession, increasingly lost interest in the workings of the mind and the mystery of medicine (Nemiah, 1995). Paradoxically, this has meant that the study of trauma has become the soul of psychiatry: The development of posttraumatic stress disorder (PTSD) as a diagnosis has created an organized framework for understanding how people's biology, conceptions of the world, and personalities are inextricably intertwined and shaped by experience. The PTSD diagnosis has reintroduced the notion that many "neurotic" symptoms are not the results of some mysterious, well-nigh inexplicable, genetically based irrationality, but of people's inability to come to terms with real experiences that have overwhelmed their capacity to cope.

In important ways, an experience does not really exist until it can be named and placed into larger categories. In Biblical mythology, Adam's first and main task in Paradise was to give names to the animals; the act of naming made him master over creation. The acceptance of the formal category of PTSD was a critical first step in making it possible to name the effects of overwhelming experiences on soma and psyche, and thus to open up the systematic investigation of how people come to be overwhelmed, how different people organize tragic experiences over time, and how their suffering can be alleviated. The recognition of PTSD as a legitimate psychiatric diagnosis has led to an explosion of scientific studies that have systematically examined many notions and popular prejudices about the effects of trauma.

Although there has been and continues to be concern about stigmatizing people with psychiatric labels in general, the diagnosis of PTSD seems to have been received by victims as a legitimization and validation of their psychic distress. Having a recognizable psychiatric disorder can help people make sense of what they are going through, instead of feeling "crazy" and forsaken. A diagnosis also bestows a sense of communality with other victims.

Essentially, the introduction of the PTSD diagnosis has opened a door to the scientific investigation of the nature of human suffering. Although much of human art and religion has always focused on expressing and understanding man's afflictions, science has paid scant attention to suffering as an object of study. Hitherto, science has generally categorized people's problems as discrete psychological or biological disorders – diseases without context, largely independent of the personal histories of the patients, their temperaments, or their environments. PTSD, then, serves as a model for correcting the decontextualized aspects of today's psychiatric nomenclature. It refocuses attention back on the living person instead of our overly concrete definitions of mental "disorders" as "things" in and of themselves, bringing us back to people's own experiences and the meaning which they assign to it (Nemiah, 1989).

PTSD has turned out to be a very common disorder. Exposure to extreme stress is widespread, and a substantial proportion of exposed individuals become symptomatic. A random survey of 1,245 American adolescents showed that 23% had been the victims of physical or sexual assaults, as well as witnesses of violence against others. One out of five of the exposed adolescents developed PTSD. This suggests that approximately 1.07 million US teenagers currently suffer from PTSD (Kilpatrick, Saunders, Resnick, and Smith, 1995). Another survey (Elliot and Briere, 1995) found that 76% of American adults reported having been exposed to extreme stress. Nine percent of an urban population in a large North American city suffered from PTSD (Breslau and Davis, 1992), and approximately 20 years after the end of the Vietnam War, 15.2% of US Vietnam theater veterans continued to suffer from PTSD (Kulka et al., 1990). The majority of psychiatric inpatients have consistently been found to have histories of severe (usually intrafamilial) trauma, and at least 15% meet diagnostic criteria for PTSD itself (Saxe et al., 1993). The available figures for the rest of the industrialized world are compatible with those of the United States. Outside of that world, no data are currently available.

Most people who have been exposed to traumatic stressors are somehow able to go on with their lives without becoming haunted by the memories of what has happened to them. That does not mean that the traumatic events go unnoticed. After exposure to a trauma, most people become preoccupied with the event; having involuntary intrusive memories is a normal way of responding to dreadful experiences. This repeated replaying of upsetting memories serves the function of modifying the emotions associated with the trauma, and in most cases creates a tolerance for the content of the memories (Horowitz, 1978). However, with the passage of time, some people are unable to integrate the awful experience and start developing the specific patterns of avoidance and hyperarousal that are associated with PTSD. What distinguishes people who develop PTSD from people who are merely temporarily stressed is that they start organizing their lives around the trauma. Thus, it is the persistence of intrusive and distressing recollections, and not the direct experience of the traumatic event itself, that actually drives the biological and psychological dimensions of PTSD (McFarlane, 1992; Creamer, Burgess, and Pattison, 1992). Although most people who suffer from PTSD have considerable interpersonal and occupational problems, the degree to which the symptoms of PTSD come to affect overall functioning varies a great deal from person to person.

The scientific study of suffering inevitably raises questions of causation, and with these, issues of blame and responsibility. Historically, doctors have highlighted predisposing vulnerability factors for developing PTSD, at the expense of recognizing the reality of their patients' experiences. This search for predisposing factors probably had its origins in the need to deny that all people can be stressed beyond endurance, rather than in solid scientific data; until very recently, such data were simply not available. When the issue of causation becomes a legitimate area of investigation, one is inevitably confronted with issues of man's inhumanity to man, with carelessness and callousness, with abrogation of responsibility, with manipulation, and with failures to protect. In short, the study of trauma confronts one with the best and the worst in human nature, and is bound to provoke a range of intense personal reactions in the people involved (Herman, 1992; Wilson and Lindy, 1994; Pearlman and Saakvitne, 1995).

Reality versus Neurosis

Unlike other forms of psychological disorders, the core issue in trauma is reality: "It is indeed the truth of the traumatic experience that forms the center of its psychopathology; it is not a pathology of falsehood or displacement of meaning, but of history itself" (Caruth, 1995, p. 5). However, the critical element that makes an event traumatic is the subjective assessment by victims of how threatened and helpless they feel. So, although the reality of extraordinary events is at the core of PTSD, the meaning that victims attach to these events is as fundamental as the trauma itself. People's interpretations of the meaning of the trauma continue to evolve well after the trauma itself has ceased. This is well illustrated by a case of delayed PTSD reported by Kilpatrick et al. (1989): A woman who was raped did not develop PTSD symptoms until some months later, when she learned that her attacker had killed another rape victim. It was only when she received this information that she reinterpreted her rape as a life-threatening attack and developed full-blown PTSD.

This raises the question of how PTSD compares with the old notion of neurosis. Psychoanalysis held that the essence of neurosis is the pathological persistence of defense mechanisms employed to ward off unacceptable unconscious wishes and impulses. Over time, the ego is "hardened," defenses are consolidated, and "earlier conflict is transformed into chronic automatic modes of functioning . . . detached from the content of infantile conflict" (Shapiro, 1965, p. 7). "Once hardened, character continues to have a protective function. It 'binds' impulses in stable ways, limits flexibility, and constitutes an armor against the external world" (p. 8). Thus, the meaning that individuals cull out of the present depends on their prior experience and on the many subtle and indirect ways that their personal past has been incorporated into their current attitudes and beliefs. This can lead to a range of maladaptive responses in their current lives, to which "neurotics" keep responding as if they were reliving the past.

These notions about the nature of neurotic defense mechanisms are quite relevant in understanding how people adapt to trauma. All traumatized people develop their own peculiar defenses to cope with intrusive recollections and increased physiological arousal. Prior to the acceptance of the concepts of psychopathology that underpin PTSD, clinical thinking was dominated by the exclusive attention to secondary psychic elaborations, at the expense of paying attention to the realities that continue to drive these repetitions. The exploration of the fantasized elaborations of intrapsychic conflicts was seen as the sole purpose of the treatment of neuroses.

When people are traumatized, the choice of defenses is influenced by developmental stage, temperamental and contextual factors. Hence, the diagnosis of PTSD alone never fully captures the totality of people's suffering and the spectrum of adaptations that they engage in. However, even though psychodynamic psychiatry is invaluable in helping us understand the characterological adaptations to the memories of the trauma, the core issue in PTSD is that the primary symptoms are not symbolic, defensive, or driven by secondary gain. The core issue is the inability to integrate the reality of particular experiences, and the resulting repetitive replaying of the trauma in images, behaviors, feelings, physiological states, and interpersonal relationships. Thus, in dealing with traumatized people, it is critical to examine where they have become "stuck" and around which specific traumatic event(s) they have built their secondary psychic elaborations.

Fixation on the Trauma

The posttraumatic syndrome is the result of a failure of time to heal all wounds. The memory of the trauma is not integrated and accepted as a part of one's personal past; instead, it comes to exist independently of previous schemata (i.e., it is dissociated). Some cognitive formulations of PTSD have proposed that a traumatic experience confronts an individual with experiences completely different from what he or she has been able to imagine before, and that this confrontation with the trauma radically shakes the individual's attitudes and beliefs (Janoff-Bulman, 1992). This may be true in some cases in which people encounter totally unexpected events or are confronted with aspects of the human capacity for evil that they had never before imagined. However, often trauma does not present a radically new experience, but rather confirms some belief that an individual has tried to evade. For many patients, what is most destructive about a traumatic event is that it confirms some long-feared belief, rather than presenting them with a novel incongruity.

Immediately after a traumatic event, almost all people suffer from intrusive thoughts about what has happened (McFarlane, 1992; Creamer et al., 1992; Joseph, Yule, and Williams, 1995). These intrusions help them either to learn from the experience and plan for restorative actions (accommodation), or to gradually accept what has happened and readjust their expectations (assimilation) (cf. Lindemann, 1944; Horowitz, 1978). One way or another, the passage of time modifies the ways in which the brain processes the trauma-related information. Either it is integrated in memory and stored as an unfortunate event belonging to the past, or the sensations and emotions belonging to the event start leading a life of their own. When people develop PTSD, the replaying of the trauma leads to sensitization; with every replay of the trauma, there is an increasing level of distress. In those individuals, the traumatic event, which started out as a social and interpersonal process, comes to have secondary biological consequences that are hard to reverse once they become entrenched. This new organization of experience is thought to be the result of iterative learning patterns, in which trauma-related memories become kindled; that is, repetitive exposure etches them more and more powerfully into the brain (van der Kolk and Greenberg, 1987; Post, 1992; McFarlane, Yehuda, and Clark, in press). These biological (mal)adaptations ultimately form the underpinnings of the remaining PTSD symptoms: problems with arousal, attention, and stimulus discrimination, and a host of psychological elaborations and defenses.

Ordinarily, memories of particular events are remembered as stories that change over time and that do not evoke intense emotions and sensations. In contrast, in PTSD the past is relived with an immediate sensory and emotional intensity that makes victims feel as if the event were occurring all over again. The "Grant Study," a longitudinal study of the psychological and physical health of 200 Harvard undergraduates who participated in World War II, is a good illustration of how people process traumatic events (Lee, Vaillant, Torrey, and Elder, 1995). When these men were reinterviewed about their experiences 45 years later, those who did not have PTSD had considerably altered their original accounts; the most intense horror of the events had been diluted. In contrast, time had not modified the memories of the minority of subjects who had developed PTSD. Thus, paradoxically, the ability to transform memory is the norm, whereas in PTSD the full brunt of an experience does not fade with time.

Information Processing in PTSD

There are six critical issues that affect how people with PTSD process information: (1) They experience persistent intrusions of memories related to the trauma, which interfere with attending to other incoming information; (2) they sometimes compulsively expose themselves to situations reminiscent of the trauma; (3) they actively attempt to avoid specific triggers of trauma-related emotions, and experience a generalized numbing of responsiveness; (4) they lose the ability to modulate their physiological responses to stress in general, which leads to a decreased capacity to utilize bodily signals as guides for action; (5) they suffer from generalized problems with attention, distractibility, and stimulus discrimination; and (6) they have alterations in their psychological defense mechanisms and in personal identity. This changes what new information is selected as relevant.

Intrusions

When Charcot (1887) first described traumatic memories over a century ago, he called them "parasites of the mind." Because people with PTSD have a fundamental impairment in the capacity to integrate traumatic experiences with other life events, their traumatic memories are often not coherent stories; they tend to consist of intense emotions or somatosensory impressions, which occur when the victims are aroused or exposed to reminders of the trauma. These intrusions of traumatic memories can take many different shapes: flashbacks; intense emotions, such as panic or rage; somatic sensations; nightmares; interpersonal reenactments; character styles; and pervasive life themes (Laub and Auerhahn, 1993). Years and even decades after the original trauma, victims claim that their reliving experiences are as vivid as when the trauma first occurred (van der Kolk and Fisler, 1995). Because of this timeless and unintegrated nature of traumatic memories, victims remain embedded in the trauma as a contemporary experience, instead of being able to accept it as something belonging to the past.

The personal meaning of the traumatic experience evolves over time, and often includes feelings of irretrievable loss, anger, betrayal, and helplessness. One of the serious complications that interferes with healing is that one particular event can activate other, long-forgotten memories of previous traumas, and create a "domino effect": A person who was not previously bothered by intrusive and distressing memories may, after exposure to yet another traumatic event, develop such memories of earlier experiences. For example, in an emergency medical technician who has witnessed many gruesome and horrifying events in the course of his or her career, one more dreadful event may trigger recollections of a host of previous experiences. Similarly, a sexual assault in adulthood may provoke long-forgotten memories of childhood abuse, and medical procedures in elderly concentration camp survivors may bring back memories to which the individuals may not have had access for decades.

Paradoxically, even though vivid elements of the trauma intrude insistently in the form of flashbacks and nightmares, many traumatized people have a great deal of difficulty relating precisely what has happened. People may experience sensory elements of the trauma without being able to make sense out of what they are feeling or seeing (van der Kolk and Fisler, 1995). One of the gravest symptoms of having been overwhelmed by a traumatic experience can be total amnesia. For example, describing the reactions to trauma in some Holocaust survivors, Henry Krystal noted that "no trace of registration of any kind is left in the psyche; instead, a void, a hole, is found" (Krystal, 1968).

Over time, the initial intrusive thoughts of the trauma may come to contaminate the individual's responses to a range of other cues and reinforce the selective dominance of the traumatic memory networks (Pitman and Orr, 1990; Pitman, Orr, and Shalev, 1993). Triggers for intrusive traumatic memories may become increasingly more subtle and generalized; what should be irrelevant stimuli may become reminders of the trauma. For example, a firefighter may not be able to wear a watch because this acts as a reminder of having to get to respond to sudden emergencies, or a combat veteran may become upset by the sound of rain because it suggests the monsoon season in Vietnam. This contrasts with more typical triggers that have an obvious connection to a traumatic memory, such as sexual situations for rape victims, or the sound of a firecracker (misinterpreted as the sound of gunfire) for war veterans.

We and our colleagues (van der Kolk and Ducey, 1989; McFarlane, Weber, and Clark, 1993), using two entirely different methodologies, were able to show that people who suffer from PTSD develop biased perception, so that they respond preferentially to trauma-related triggers at the expense of being able to attend to other perceptions. As a consequence, they have smaller repertoires of neutral or pleasurable internal and environmental sensations that could be restitutive and gratifying. This decreased attention to non-trauma-related stimuli adds further to the centrality of the trauma.

Compulsive reexposure to the trauma

One set of behaviors that is not mentioned in the diagnostic criteria for PTSD is the compulsive reexposure of some traumatized individuals to situations reminiscent of the trauma. This phenomenon can be seen in a wide range of traumatized populations. For example, combat soldiers may become mercenaries or join police SWAT teams; abused women may be attracted to men who mistreat them; sexually molested children may grow up to become prostitutes. Understanding this seemingly paradoxical phenomenon is of critical importance, because it could help to clarify many forms of social deviance and interpersonal misery. Freud (1920/1955) thought that the aim of such repetition is to gain mastery, but clinical experience shows that this rarely happens; instead, repetition causes further suffering for the victims and for the people around them (van der Kolk, 1989). In this reenactment of the trauma, an individual may play the role of either victimizer or victim.

1 Harm to others.

Reenactment of victimization is a major cause of violence in society. Numerous studies have documented that many violent criminals were physically or sexually abused as children (e.g., Groth, 1979; Seghorn, Boucher, and Prentky, 1987). In a prospective study of 34 sexually molested boys, Burgess, Hartman, and McCormick (1987) found a link with drug abuse, juvenile delinquency, and criminal behavior within a few years after the abuse was first noticed. Dorothy Lewis and her colleagues (Lewis and Balla, 1976; Lewis et al., 1979) have also extensively documented the association between childhood abuse and subsequent victimization of others.

2 Self-destructiveness.

Self-destructive acts are common in abused children. Studies consistently find a highly significant relationship between childhood sexual abuse and various forms of self-harm later in life, particularly suicide attempts, cutting, and self-starving (e.g., van der Kolk, Perry, and Herman, 1991). Clinical reports consistently show that most self-mutilators have childhood histories of physical or sexual abuse or repeated surgery (Graff and Mallin, 1967; Pattison and Kahan, 1983; Briere, 1988). Simpson and Porter (1981) sum up the consensus conclusion in stating that "self-destructive activities were not primarily related to conflict, guilt, and superego pressure, but to more primitive behavior patterns originating in painful encounters with hostile caretakers during the first years of life."

3 Revictimization.

Many traumatized individuals continue to be revictimized. Rape victims are more likely to be raped again, and women who were physically or sexually abused as children are more likely to be abused as adults (van der Kolk, 1989). Victims of child sexual abuse are at high risk of becoming prostitutes (Finkelhor and Browne, 1984; Silbert and Pines, 1981). Diane Russell (1986), in her well-known study of incest's effects on the lives of women, found that few women made a conscious connection between their childhood victimization and their later drug abuse, prostitution, and suicide attempts.

These phenomena are seldom understood by either victims or clinicians as repetitive reenactments of real events from the past. Understanding and remedying the fact that traumatized people tend to lead traumatizing and traumatized lives remain among the great challenges of psychiatry.

Avoiding and numbing

Once traumatized individuals become haunted by intrusive reexperiences of their trauma, they generally start organizing their lives around avoiding having the emotions that these intrusions evoke (van der Kolk and Ducey, 1989). Avoidance may take many different forms, such as keeping away from reminders, ingesting drugs or alcohol in order to numb awareness of distressing emotional states, or utilizing dissociation to keep unpleasant experiences from conscious awareness. This avoidance of specific triggers is aggravated by a generalized numbing of responsiveness to a whole range of emotional aspects of life. Despite the fact that numbing and avoidance are lumped together in the *Diagnostic and Statistical Manual of Mental Disorders*, fourth edition (DSM-IV; American Psychiatric Association, 1994), numbing probably has a very different underlying pathophysiology from avoidance (e.g., van der Kolk et al., 1994). Studies of combat veterans (e.g., Kardiner, 1941), concentration camp survivors (Krystal, 1968), and other victim populations (Titchener, 1986) have described a gradual withdrawal and detachment from everyday activities. Krystal (1968) called this reaction "dead to the world," Kardiner (1941, p. 249) "a deterioration that is not dissimilar to that in schizophrenia," and Titchener (1986) "post-traumatic decline." Thus, many people with PTSD not only actively avoid emotional arousal, but experience a progressive decline and withdrawal, in which *any* stimulation (whether it is potentially pleasurable or aversive) provokes further detachment. To feel nothing seems to be better than feeling irritable and upset.

It would be an error to think of this detachment and withdrawal in PTSD either merely as a psychodynamic phenomenon, or as a deficit of certain neurotransmitters that can be "fixed" with the administration of neurotransmitter supplements (i.e., antidepressants or other psychopharmacological agents that stimulate the release of neurohormones). Roughly speaking, it seems that the chronic hyperarousal of PTSD depletes both the biological and the psychological resources needed to experience a wide variety of emotions (van der Kolk et al., 1985; Litz, 1992). McFarlane et al. (in press) have proposed that as intrusive memories come to dominate their thinking, people with PTSD become more and more sensitized to environmental stimuli that remind them of the trauma. Thus, over time, they become less and less responsive to various stimuli that are necessary for involvement in the present. They have proposed that this underresponsiveness leads to a series of changes in the central nervous system that are similar to the effects of prolonged sensory deprivation.

Litz et al. (1995) have proposed that the resulting failure to process emotional events fully leads to further physiological hyperarousal and to psychosomatic problems. Indeed, psychosomatic problems and emotional numbing in PTSD are intimately related (van der Kolk et al., in press). This line of investigation is further supported by the work of Pennebaker (1993) and others (e.g., Spiegel, 1992), which has shown that low levels of emotional expression lead to impairment of immune function and to an increase in physical illness.

Inability to modulate arousal

Although people with PTSD tend to deal with their environment through emotional constriction, their bodies continue to react to certain physical and emotional stimuli as if there were a continuing threat of annihilation; they suffer from hypervigilance, exaggerated startle response, and restlessness. Research has clearly established that people with PTSD suffer from conditioned autonomic arousal to trauma–related stimuli; however, evidence in recent years also suggests that many traumatized individuals suffer from extreme physiological arousal in response to a wide variety of stimuli.

People with PTSD tend to move immediately from stimulus to response without often realizing what makes them so upset. They tend to experience intense negative emotions (fear, anxiety, anger, and panic) in response to even minor stimuli; as a result, they either overreact and threaten others, or shut down and freeze. These hyperarousal phenomena represent complex psychological and biological processes, in which the continued anticipation of overwhelming threat seems to cause difficulties with attention and concentration. In turn, these difficulties give rise to distortions in information processing, including narrowing of attention onto sources of potential challenge or threat. Children and adults with such hyperarousal tend to experience sleep problems, both because they are unable to quiet themselves sufficiently to go to sleep, and because they deliberately wake themselves up in order to avoid having traumatic nightmares.

Perhaps the most distressing aspect of this hyperarousal is the generalization of threat. The world increasingly becomes an unsafe place: Innocuous sounds provoke an alerting startle response; trivial cues are perceived as indicators of danger. Ordinarily, autonomic arousal serves the very important function of alerting people to pay attention to potentially important situations. However, for persons who are chronically hyperaroused, the autonomic nervous system loses that function; the easy triggering of somatic stress reactions makes them unable to rely on their bodily sensations as an efficient warning system against impending threat. The persistent, irrelevant firing of warning signals causes physical sensations to lose their functions as signals of emotional states and, as a consequence, they stop serving as guides for action. Thus, like neutral environmental stimuli, normal physical sensations may take on a new and threatening significance. The person's own physiology becomes a source of fear.

The PTSD sufferers' inability to decipher messages from the autonomic nervous system interferes with their capacity to articulate how they are feeling (alexithymia) and makes them tend to react to their environment with either exaggerated or inhibited behaviors. After a traumatic experience, many people regress to earlier levels of coping with stress. In children, this may manifest itself as an inability to take care of themselves in such areas as feeding and toilet training; in adults, it is expressed in impulsive behavior, excessive dependence, and a loss of the capacity to make thoughtful, autonomous decisions.

Attention, distractibility, and stimulus discrimination

Freud (1911/1959) described how, in order to function properly, people need to be able to define their needs, anticipate how to meet them, and plan for appropriate action. In order to do this, they first need to be able to consider a range of options without resorting to action – a capacity Freud called "thought as experimental action." People with PTSD seem to lose this capacity; they have problems fantasizing and playing with options. Studies both of traumatized children (e.g., Rieder and Cicchetti, 1989) and of traumatized adults (e.g., van der Kolk and Ducey, 1989) indicate that when traumatized people allow themselves to fantasize, this creates the danger of breaking down their barriers against being reminded of the trauma. In order to prevent this from happening, they become constricted and seem to organize their lives around *not* feeling and *not* considering options for the best ways of responding to emotionally arousing problems. Their problems with keeping thoughts in their minds without becoming aroused contribute greatly to their impulsivity.

People with PTSD have difficulty in sorting out relevant from irrelevant stimuli; they have problems ignoring what is unimportant and selecting only what is most relevant. Easily overstimulated, they compensate by shutting down. In a study using event-related potentials, McFarlane et al. (1993) were able to demonstrate these difficulties in stimulus discrimination. The price of these problems is loss of involvement in ordinary, everyday life. This makes it even harder for these patients to get their minds off the trauma, and thus only increases the strength of their fixation on the trauma. As a result, the individuals lose the capacity to respond flexibly to their environment. This loss of flexibility may explain current findings of deficits in preservative learning and interference with the acquisition of new information (Bremner et al., 1993; Yehuda et al., 1995), as well as an inability to apply working memory to salient environmental stimuli (van der Kolk and Ducey, 1989; McFarlane et al., 1993).

Alterations in defense mechanisms and changes in personal identity

In recent years, much has been written about trauma's effects on people's sense of themselves and their relationship to their environment (Cole and Putnam, 1992; Herman, 1992; Pearlman and Saakvitne, 1995). Reiker and Carmen (1986) have pointed out that "confrontations with violence challenge one's most basic assumptions about the self as invulnerable and intrinsically worthy, and about the world as orderly and just. After abuse, the victim's view of self and world can never be the same again: it must be reconstructed to incorporate the abuse experience" (p. 362). Of course, how old a person is when the trauma happens, and what the person's previous life experiences have been like, will profoundly affect his or her interpretation of the meaning of the trauma (van der Kolk and Fisler, 1994).

Many traumatized individuals, particularly children, tend to blame themselves for having been traumatized. Assuming responsibility for the trauma allows feelings of helplessness and vulnerability to be replaced with an illusion of potential control. Ironically, rape victims who blame themselves have a better prognosis than those who do not assume this false responsibility; it allows their locus of control to remain internal and prevents helplessness (Burgess and Holstrom, 1979). Traumatized children are even more likely to blame themselves: "The child needs to hold on to an image of the parent as good in order to deal with the intensity of fear and rage which is the effect of the tormenting experiences" (Reiker and Carmen, 1986, p. 368). In the context of these sorts of conflicts, defense mechanisms are activated that are designed to provide an accommodation with an intolerable reality.

The question of shame is critical to understanding the lack of self-regulation in trauma victims and the capacity of abused persons to become abusers. Trauma is usually accompanied by intense feelings of humiliation; to feel threatened, helpless, and out of control is a vital attack on the capacity to be able to count on oneself. Shame is the emotion related to having let oneself down. The shame that accompanies such personal violations as rape, torture, and abuse is so painful that it is frequently dissociated: Victims may be unaware of its presence, and yet it comes to dominate their interactions with the environment. Denial of one's own feelings of shame, as well as those of other people, opens the door for further abuse. Being sensitive to the shame in others is an essential protection against abusing one's fellow human beings, and it requires being in touch with one's own sense of shame. Similarly, not being in touch with one's own shame leaves one vulnerable to further abuse from others. The resulting disorganized patterns of engagement are commonly seen in traumatized people who suffer from borderline personality disorder, who need to be helped to understand how this perpetuates their getting hurt and their hurting others.

Fixation on the Diagnosis

Despite efforts to capture the essence of people's response to trauma, the PTSD diagnosis does not begin to describe the complexity of how people react to overwhelming experiences. The DSM's emphasis on phenomenological diagnoses has resulted in a loss of interest in the way symptoms are interrelated and reflect subtle interactions between psychological and biological processes (Nemiah, 1995). Yet the same underlying psychopathology can have a range of symptomatic expressions. For example, when "hysteria" was first diagnosed and related to prior histories of trauma by Briquet in 1859, and subsequently by the school of the Salpêtrière under Charcot, posttraumatic symptoms were primarily expressed as conversion reactions and as psychosomatic conditions. Those patterns seem to have persisted as the primary expressions of traumatic stress during World War I. Even though the same symptoms were described in combat soldiers during World War II, descriptions of soldiers at that time focused primarily on psychophysiological reactions and loss of impulse control. Descriptions of Vietnam veterans have focused on intrusive recollections and on characterological adaptations. Does this mean that the symptomatic expression of traumatic stress has changed in Western culture over time, or have clinicians focused on different aspects of the same syndrome during the past century and a half? Given the rather marked differences in vulnerability and symptoms among Vietnam combat soldiers belonging to different ethnic groups (Kulka et al., 1990), it is likely that the prevailing culture has a marked effect on the symptomatic expression of traumatic stress.

The complexity of people's responses to trauma, and the comparative simplicity of the PTSD conceptualization, are illustrated by the recent rediscovery of the intimate association among trauma, dissociation, and somatization (van der Kolk et al., in press). Trauma can affect victims on every level of functioning: biological, psychological, social, and spiritual. Conceptualized in terms of psychiatric diagnosis, this means that PTSD has a high rate of psychiatric comorbidity with mood, dissociative, and anxiety disorders; substance abuse; and character pathology (Green, Lindy, Grace, and Leonard, 1992; Davidson, Hughes, Blazer, and George, 1991; Kulka et al., 1990). The National Comorbidity Survey (Kessler, Bromet, and Nelson, in press) and the DSM-IV field trials for PTSD (van der Kolk, Roth, Pelcovitz, and Mandel, 1993) showed that people with simple diagnoses of PTSD were less likely to seek treatment than people who suffered from associated problems, such as depression, uncontrolled anger, and dissociation. As long as they can make meaning out of the trauma, victims often experience the symptoms of PTSD as natural reactions that do not require professional help. For example, a study of Pearl Harbor survivors found they viewed their recurrent nightmares of the bombing as perfectly understandable reactions to the terrible events they had witnessed on December 7, 1941. In their case, there never was a question about the validation of their experience (Harel, Kahana, and Wilson, 1993).

Focusing solely on PTSD to describe what victims suffer from does not do justice to the complexity of what actually ails them. Excessive attention to the intrusion/numbing/arousal phenomena of PTSD may severely limit observations of how people react to trauma, and may thus interfere with appropriate treatment. The recognition of the profound personality changes that can follow childhood trauma or prolonged exposure in adults has been an important development, because these changes are major sources of distress and disability. This issue is beginning to be recognized by the inclusion of complex adaptations to trauma in the form of disturbed affect regulation, aggression against self and others, dissociative problems, somatization, and altered relationships with self and others in the "Associated Features and Disorders" section of the DSM-IV's entry on PTSD (American Psychiatric Association, 1994, p. 425).

References

American Psychiatric Association (1994). *Diagnostic and Statistical Manual of Mental Disorders*. 4th edn. Washington, DC: Author.

Bremner, D. J., Scott, T. M., Delaney, R. C., Southwick, S. M., Mason, J. W., Johnson, D. R., Innis, J. R., McCarthy, G., and Charney, D. S. (1993). Deficits in short-term memory in posttraumatic stress disorder. *American Journal of Psychiatry*, 170, 1015–19.

Breslau, N., and Davis, G. C. (1992). Posttraumatic stress disorder in an urban population of young adults: Risk factors for chronicity. *American Journal of Psychiatry*, 149, 671–5.

Briere, J. (1988). Long-term clinical correlates of childhood sexual victimization. *Annals of the New York Academy of Science*, 528, 327–34.

Briquet, P. (1859). *Traité clinique et thérapeutique de l'hystérie*. Paris: Ballière.

Buruma, I. (1994). *The Wages of Guilt: Memories of War in Germany and Japan*. New York: Farrar, Strauss, and Giroux.

Burgess, A. W., Hartman, C. R., and McCormick, A. (1987). Abused to abuser: antecedents of socially deviant behavior. *American Journal of Psychiatry*, 144, 1431–6.

Burgess, A. W., and Holstrom, E. (1979). Adaptive strategies in recovery from rape. *American Journal of Psychiatry*, 136, 1278–82.

Caruth, C. (ed.). (1995). *Trauma and Memory*. Baltimore: Johns Hopkins University Press.

Charcot, J. M. (1887). *Leçons sur les maladies du système nerveux faites à la Salpêtrière [Lessons on the illnesses of the nervous system held at the Salpêtrière]* (Vol. 3). Paris: Progrès Médical en A. Delahaye & E. Lecrosnie.

Cole, P., and Putnam, F. W. (1992). Effect of incest on self and social functioning: a developmental psychopathology perspective. *Journal of Consulting and Clinical Psychology*, 174–84.

Creamer, M., Burgess, P., and Pattison, P. (1992). Reactions to trauma: a cognitive processing model. *Journal of Abnormal Psychology*, 101, 452–9.

Davidson, J. R. T., Hughes, D., Blazer, D. G., and George, L. K. (1991). Post-traumatic stress disorder in the community: an epidemiological study. *Psychological Medicine*, 21, 713–21.

Elliot, D. M., and Briere, J. (1995). Posttraumatic stress associated with delayed recall of sexual abuse: a general population study. *Journal of Traumatic Stress*, 8(4), 629–48.

Finkelhor, D., and Browne, A. (1984). The traumatic impact of child sexual abuse: a conceptualization. *American Journal of Orthopsychiatry*, 55, 530–41.

Freud, S. (1955). Beyond the pleasure principle. In J. Strachey (ed. and trans.), *The Standard Edition of the Complete Psychological Works of Sigmund Freud* (vol. 18, pp. 3–64). London: Hogarth Press. (Original work published 1920.)

Freud, S. (1958). Formulations on the two principles of mental functioning. In J. Strachey (ed. and trans.), *The Standard Edition of the Complete Psychological Works of Sigmund Freud* (vol. 12, pp. 23–226). London: Hogarth Press. (Original work published 1911.)

Graff, H., and Mallin, R. (1967). The syndrome of wrist cutter. *American Journal of Psychiatry*, 124, 36–42.

Green, B. L., Lindy, J. D., Grace, M. C., and Leonard, A. C. (1992). Chronic posttraumatic stress disorder and diagnostic comorbidity in a disaster sample. *Journal of Nervous and Mental Disease*, 180, 70–6.

Groth, A. N. (1979). Sexual trauma in the life histories of sex offenders. *Victimology*, 4, 6–10.

Harel, A., Kahana, B., and Wilson, J. P. (1993). War and remembrance: the legacy of Pearl Harbor. In J. P. Wilson and B. Raphael (eds.), *International Handbook of Traumatic Stress Syndromes* (pp. 263–74). New York: Plenum Press.

Herman, J. L. (1992). *Trauma and Recovery*. New York: Basic Books.

Horowitz, M. (1978). *Stress Response Syndromes*. New York: Jason Aronson.

Janoff-Bulman, R. (1992). *Shattered Assumptions: Towards a New Psychology of Trauma*. New York: Free Press.

Joseph, S., Yule, W., and Williams, R. (1995). Emotional processing in survivors of the *Jupiter* cruise ship disaster. *Behaviour Research and Therapy*, 33, 187–92.

Kardiner, A. (1941). *The Traumatic Neuroses of War*. New York: Hoeber.

Kessler, R. C., Bromet, E., and Nelson, C. B. (in press). *Posttraumatic Stress Disorder in the National Comorbidity Survey*.

Kilpatrick, D. G., Saunders, B. E., Amick-McMullan, A., Best, C. L., Veronen, L. J., and Resnick, H. S. (1989). Victim and crime factors associated with the development of crime-related post-traumatic stress disorder. *Behavior Therapy*, 20, 199–214.

Kilpatrick, D. G., Saunders, B. E., Resnick, H. S., and Smith, D. W. (1995). *The National Survey of Adolescents: Preliminary Findings on Lifetime Prevalence of Traumatic Events and Mental Health Correlates*.

Krystal, H. (ed.). (1968). *Massive Psychic Trauma*. New York: International Universities Press.

Krystal, H. (1978). Trauma and affects. *Psychoanalytic Study of the Child*, 33, 81–116.

Kulka, R. A., Schlenger, W. E., Fairbank, J. A., Hough, R. L., Jordan, B. K., and Marmar, C. R. (1990). *Trauma and the Vietnam War Generation: Report of Findings from the National Vietnam Veterans Readjustment Study*. New York: Brunner/Mazel.

Langer, L. L. (1990). *Holocaust Testimonies: The Ruins of Memory*. New Haven: Yale University Press.

Laub, D., and Auerhahn, N. C. (1993). Knowing and not knowing massive psychic trauma: forms of traumatic memory. *International Journal of Psycho-Analysis*, 74, 287–301.

Lee, K. A., Vaillant, G. E., Torrey, W. C., and Elder, G. H. (1995). A 50-year prospective study of the psychological sequelae of World War II combat. *American Journal of Psychiatry*, 152(4), 516–22.

Lewis, D. O., and Balla, D. (1976). *Delinquency and Psychopathology*. New York: Grune & Stratton.

Lewis, D. O., Shanok, S. S., Pincus, J. H., and Glaser, G. H. (1979). Violent juvenile delinquency: psychiatric, neurological, psychological and abuse factors. *Journal of the American Academy of Child Psychiatry*, 18, 307–19.

Lindemann, E. (1944). Symptomatology and management of acute grief. *American Journal of Psychiatry*, 101, 141–8.

Litz, B. T. (1992). Emotional numbing in combat-related post-traumatic stress disorder: a critical review and reformulation. *Clinical Psychology Review*, 12, 417–32.

Litz, B. T., Schlenger, W. E., Weathers, F. W., Fairbank, J. A., Caddell, J. M., and LaVange, L. M. (1995). *Predictors of Emotional Numbing in Post-traumatic Stress Disorder*. Manuscript submitted for publication.

McFarlane, A. C. (1992). Avoidance and intrusion in posttraumatic stress disorder. *Journal of Nervous and Mental Disease*, 180, 258–62.

McFarlane, A. C., Weber, D. L., and Clark, C. R. (1993). Abnormal stimulus processing in posttraumatic stress disorder. *Biological Psychiatry*, 34, 311–20.

McFarlane, A. C., Yehuda, R., and Clark, C. R. (in press). The neural network theory of post-traumatic stress disorder. *Biological Psychiatry*.

Nemiah, J. C. (1989). Janet redivivus [editorial]. *American Journal of Psychiatry*, 146, 1527–9.

Nemiah, J. C. (1991). Dissociation, conversion, and somatization. In A. Tasman and A. Goldfinger (eds.), *American Psychiatric Press Review of Psychiatry* (vol. 10, pp. 248–60). Washington, DC: American Psychiatric Press.

Nemiah, J. C. (1995). Early concepts of trauma, dissociation and the unconscious: their history and current implications. In D. Bremner and C. Marmar (eds.), *Trauma, Memory and Dissociation*. Washington, DC: American Psychiatric Press.

Pattison, E. M., and Kahan, J. (1983). The deliberate self-harm syndrome. *American Journal of Psychiatry*, 140, 867–72.

Pearlman, L. A., and Saakvitne, K. W. (1995). *Trauma and the Therapist*. New York: Norton.

Pennebaker, J. W. (1993). Putting stress into words: health, linguistic, and therapeutic implications. *Behaviour Research and Therapy*, 31(6), 539–48.

Pitman, R. K., and Orr, S. (1990). The black hole of trauma. *Biological Psychiatry*, 26, 469–71.

Pitman, R. K., Orr, S., and Shalev, A. (1993). Once bitten, twice shy: beyond the conditioning model of PTSD. *Biological Psychiatry*, 33, 145–6.

Post, R. M. (1992). Transduction of psychosocial stress into the neurobiology of recurrent affective disorder. *American Journal of Psychiatry*, 149, 999–1010.

Reiker, P. P., and Carmen, E. H. (1986). The victim-to-patient process: the disconfirmation and transformation of abuse. *American Journal of Orthopsychiatry*, 56, 360–70.

Rieder, C., and Cicchetti, D. (1989). An organizational perspective on cognitive control functioning and cognitive–affective balance in maltreated children. *Developmental Psychology*, 25, 482–93.

Russell, D. (1986). *The Secret Trauma*. New York: Basic Books.

Saxe, G. N., van der Kolk, B. A., Berkowitz, R., Chinman, G., Hall, K., Lieberg, G., and Schwartz, J. (1993). Dissociative disorders in psychiatric inpatients. *American Journal of Psychiatry*, 150, 1037–42.

Seghorn, T. K., Boucher, R. J., and Prentky, R. A. (1987). Childhood sexual abuse in the lives of sexually aggressive offenders. *Journal of the American Academy of Child and Adolescent Psychiatry*, 26, 262–7.

Shapiro, D. (1965). *Neurotic Styles*. New York: Basic Books.

Silbert, M. H., and Pines, A. M. (1981). Sexual child abuse as an antecedent to prostitution. *Child Abuse and Neglect*, 5, 407–11.

Simpson, C. A., and Porter, G. L. (1981). Self-mutilation in children and adolescents. *Bulletin of the Menninger Clinic*, 45, 428–38.

Spiegel, D. (1992). Effects of psychosocial support on patients with metastatic breast cancer. *Journal of Psychosocial Oncology*, 10, 113–20.

Tank, D. W., and Hopfield, J. J. (1987). Collective computation in neuronlike circuits. *Scientific American*, 257, 104–14.

Titchener, J. L. (1986). Post-traumatic decline: a consequence of unresolved destructive drives. In C. Figley (ed.), *Trauma and its Wake* (vol. 2, pp. 5–19). New York: Brunner/Mazel.

Tuchman, B. (1978). *A Distant Mirror*. New York: Knopf.

van der Hart, O., Steele, K., Boon, S., and Brown, P. (1993). The treatment of traumatic memories: synthesis, realization, and integration. *Dissociation*, 6, 162–80.

van der Kolk, B. A. (1989). The compulsion to repeat trauma: revictimization, attachment and masochism. *Psychiatric Clinics of North America*, 12, 389–411.

van der Kolk, B. A., Dreyfuss, D., Michaels, M., Shera, D., Berkowitz, R., Fisler, R., and Saxe, G. (1994). Fluoxetine in posttraumatic stress disorder. *Journal of Clinical Psychiatry*, 55(12), 517–22.

van der Kolk, B. A., and Ducey, C. (1989). The psychological processing of traumatic experience: Rorschach patterns in PTSD. *Journal of Traumatic Stress*, 2(3), 259–274.

van der Kolk, B. A., and Fisler, R. (1994). Childhood abuse and neglect and loss of self-regulation. *Bulletin of the Menninger Clinic*, 58, 145–68.

van der Kolk, B. A., and Fisler, R. (1995). Dissociation and the fragmentary nature of traumatic memories: overview and exploratory study. *Journal of Traumatic Stress*, 9, 505–25.

van der Kolk, B. A., Greenberg, M., Boyd, H., and Krystal, J. (1985). Inescapable shock, neurotransmitters, and addiction to trauma: toward a psychobiology of posttraumatic stress. *Biological Psychiatry*, 20, 314–25.

van der Kolk, B. A., Pelcovitz, D., Roth, S., Mandel, F. S., McFarlane, A. C., and Herman, J. L. (in press). Dissociation, affect dysregulation and somatization. *American Journal of Psychiatry*.

van der Kolk, B. A., Perry, C., and Herman, J. L. (1991). Childhood origins of self-destructive behavior. *American Journal of Psychiatry*, 148, 1665–71.

van der Kolk, B. A., Roth, S., Pelcovitz, D., and Mandel, F. (1993). *Disorders of Extreme Stress: Results of the DSM-IV Field Trials for PTSD*. Washington, DC: American Psychiatric Association.

Wilson, J. P., and Lindy, J. D. (eds.). (1994). *Countertransference in the Treatment of PTSD*. New York: Guilford Press.

Yehuda, R., Keefe, R. S. E., Harvey, P. D., Levengood, R. A., Gerber, D. K., Geni, J., and Siever, L. J. (1995). Learning and memory in combat veterans with posttraumatic stress disorder. *American Journal of Psychiatry*, 152, 137–9.

PART SIX

Historicisms

CHAPTER 1

Introduction: Writing the Past

Julie Rivkin and Michael Ryan

In the early 1980s a critic named Stephen Greenblatt coined a term for the kind of criticism he was doing – he called it New Historicism – and the name stuck. Greenblatt himself went on to question the term, and to rename his own practice Cultural Poetics, but New Historicism was launched. The name is useful, however much questioned by its founder, as much because it acknowledges an older form of historicism as for its enunciation of something new. We use the term Historicisms here to indicate the range of theoretical practices that are historical, and we might well begin with a more traditional kind of historicism.

Back when New Criticism was getting itself named new, one kind of traditional criticism that it was replacing was historical. This historical work might or might not be governed by a specific theory of history – such as, for example, Marxism – but it would invariably see the historical as a context for the study of the literary work. Historical background, historical context: the language of a traditional historicism saw the literary work in the foreground and history in the background, with the task of the critic being to connect the two. The literary work might represent or refer to the historical context; the critic would make sense of the literary work by researching the history to which it referred. Without such background information, how could the reader understand anything from the wars fought in a Shakespeare play to the property laws that governed the plot of an Austen novel? One notable consequence was that a literary critic needed to read a good deal of nonliterary work, and the critic's enterprise led to the historical archive. Biographical, social, cultural, political – there were as many possibilities as there were schools of historical study, and the literary critic might share with his colleague in history a knowledge of certain eras or institutions that could make him look like an early advocate of interdisciplinarity. Indeed, such was the accusation of the New Critics, who were interested in distinguishing and clarifying the uniquely literary nature of their enterprise, and in sending the historians, sociologists, and biographers of literary study off to their separate fields of study. But history has returned to literary study, and like any repressed entity, it has done so with a vengeance. Literary study today is pervasively historical.

The first return of history falls under the denomination of New Historicism. New Historicism distinguished itself from its antecedents largely because of the way in which the concept of history it assumed had passed through a Post-Structuralist critique. What such a critique makes explicit is the textuality of history, the way in which history is only available as a collection of discourses. Foucault is the Post-Structuralist historian who most influenced this critical approach, and his histories of everything from madness to sexuality are histories of the discourses that have constructed the past. New Historians, in the wake of Foucualt, see the historical as textual, and one effect is to create a new relationship between the historical and the literary text. Because both are representations, a term very important to the New Historians (so much so that it is the title of a New Historical journal), neither one is closer to the "truth" of history. History is not some unmediated reality out there, some stable background that the literary text reflects or refers to; it is not a context. Rather, it is like the literary text itself – of a different genre, granted, but no less a discourse. Such a view might seem to undo the privilege of the literary text or of "history" – depending on whether someone valorizes an aesthetic distinction or an ontological one – but it does make it possible to study relations between texts both literary and historical and discover how they trace certain patterns and negotiate various kinds of cultural meaning.

What kinds of patterns interest the New Historian? Influenced at once by Fou-cauldian and Marxist theories of history, the New Historian focuses on issues of power – with a particular interest in the ways in which power is maintained by unofficial means such as the theatricality of royal display in the Court. This New Historicist view was most clearly articulated in response to a critique from a more Marxist school of historiography called cultural materialism. The cultural materialists argued that all power is fragile, subject to undermining by dissident elements within a society, and they believed that literature inadvertently displays the fissures in power, the moments of subversion where the precariousness of power is most palp-able. Responding to their critique, Greenblatt argued that subversion itself was a ruse of power. His essay, entitled "Invisible Bullets," referred to a ploy of English colon-ists, who characterized the diseases ravaging Native populations as God-sent punish-ment for disobedience to their colonial masters; in Greenblatt's argument, the containment of subversion was like the "invisible bullets" of germ warfare used to contain native resistance. A playwright like Shakespeare might evoke the undermin-ing of royal power in his *Henry* plays, but in the end, such undermining merely serves the ends of reinforcing that power all the more forcefully. At a certain point, subversion and containment were almost the catch phrases of New Historicism.

Another preoccupation of New Historicism is with the circulation of discourses both within and through various texts. Any text itself will have a mode of circulation – it will have a place within an economic system – but it will also serve to circulate certain discourses. To see the discourses circulating in a particular era, one needs to see not only their literary manifestation but also their presence in other kinds of cultural representations. The New Historian is selective in an approach to the arch-ive; the historical text that illuminates a pattern might be a single manifesto or conduct book, a broadside or a periodical. All texts might be called interventions in such patterns, in that they do not merely reflect but have effects on the cultural situation they represent. A New Historicist essay will often put the same reading practices into play for all the texts it studies, with the nonliterary subject to the same close reading as the literary.

At present, the exemplary New Historicist practice typified by the Greenblatt essay included here has given way to more wide-ranging kinds of historicist work. The turn to history is a crucial part of the current scene in literary study and is one conducted under the aegis of many critical approaches. Feminism and gender stud-ies, post-colonialism and ethnic studies: the categories of analysis are themselves historical, and in the anti-essentialism of the moment few would be willing to adopt a vocabulary without historicizing it. Who, for example, can speak the terms of gender or race without recognizing that they are historically constituted? Historicism in literary study received a highly visible revival with the creation of New Historicism, but in some sense the wider success of historicism is evidenced in the ways historicism has entered almost every other critical approach. Thus, the explicitly historicist selections we have included here might be extended to include everything from C. L. R. James's study of the revolution in Haiti, *The Black Jacobins*, to Gerald Vizenor's work on nostalgic imagery of the "vanishing" Native Americans, *Native Poses* to Paul Gilroy's account of a circum-Atlantic African cultural diaspora in "Black Atlantic."

A historian recently characterized his discipline as one in which knowledge is presumed to be diachronic, across time, to use the vocabulary introduced by Saussure. Saussure himself focused on a synchronic mode of analysis, we might note. Historicism today is, in fact, both diachronic and synchronic. That is, many contemporary historicist critics draw on the synchronic analysis of Saussure and his structuralist heirs, who show "reality" to be constituted of systems of signs, realms of discourse that work to construct a version of the real. Understanding "history" as discursively produced allows one to consider the source of a given discourse, its genealogy, to use a term important to Foucault, and along with its source the perspective it might serve. In a recent film entitled *The Official Story*, an Argentinian woman who teaches history in a high school is brought face to face with the discrepancy between history as she is teaching it, as her government wants her to teach it, with all of its occlusions, and history as she is living it. Reading between the lines of "the official story," she discovers an alternative discourse being produced by the mothers of the disappeared (victims of Argentina's right-wing military dictatorship), a discourse that inhabits her own family, however much the official story denies its existence. Or to cite a different example, in a preface to Frederick Douglass's *Narrative*, Wendell Phillips recounts the fable of "The Man and the Lion" in which the Lion complains that he would not be so misrepresented "when the lions write history." Frederick Douglass, a fugitive slave for whom literacy itself was against the law, was Wendell Phillips's lion, and he was writing history. Presumably the disappeared can tell no stories. No more can lions. But the metaphor of their missing stories is another way to mark the place of alternative discourses, alternative histories, of all the historical work yet to be done in the ever-expanding processes of writing the past.

CHAPTER 2

The Country and the City

Raymond Williams

Raymond Williams was the leading cultural historian in England from the 1950s to the 1980s. His work is the basis for the contemporary school of criticism known as Cultural Materialism. In his 1973 book, *The Country and the City*, he examined the changing significance of the two sites in English literature from the Renaissance down to the twentieth century.

The Morality of Improvement

(i)

The true history of the English countryside has been centred throughout in the problems of property in land, and in the consequent social and working relationships. By the eighteenth century, nearly half of the cultivated land was owned by some five thousand families. As a central form of this predominance, four hundred families, in a population of some seven or eight million people, owned nearly a quarter of the cultivated land. Beneath this domination, there was no longer, in any classical sense, a peasantry, but an increasingly regular structure of tenant farmers and wage-labourers: the social relationships that we can properly call those of agrarian capitalism. The regulation of production was increasingly in terms of an organised market.

The transition from feudal and immediately post-feudal arrangements to this developing agrarian capitalism is of course immensely complicated. But its social implications are clear enough. It is true that the predominant landowning class was also, in political terms, an aristocracy, whose ancient or ancient-seeming titles and houses offered the illusion of a society determined by obligations and traditional relations between social orders. But the main activity of this class was of a radically different kind. They lived by a calculation of rents and returns on investments of capital, and it was the process of rack-renting, engrossing and enclosure which increased their hold on the land.

Yet there was never any simple confrontation between the four hundred families and a rural proletariat. On the contrary, between these poles of the economic process there was an increasingly stratified hierarchy of smaller landowners, large tenants, surviving small freeholders and copyholders, middle and small tenants, and cottagers and craftsmen with residual common rights. A process begun in the sixteenth century was still powerfully under way, with many of the smaller farms being suppressed, especially on improved arable land, while at the same time the area of cultivated land was itself steadily and at times dramatically increased. Even within the social relations of landowner, tenant, and labourer, there was a continual evolution of new attitudes. An estate passed from being regarded as an inheritance, carrying such and such income, to being calculated as an opportunity for investment, carrying greatly increased returns. In this development, an ideology of improvement – of a transformed and regulated land – became significant and directive. Social relations which stood in the way of this kind of modernisation were then steadily and at times ruthlessly broken down.

The crisis of values which resulted from these changes is enacted in varying ways in eighteenth-century literature. In poetry, as we shall see, the idealisation of the happy tenant, and of the rural retreat, gave way to a deep and melancholy consciousness of change and loss, which eventually established, in a new way, a conventional structure of retrospect.

But before this development, there was a lively engagement with the human consequences of the new institutions and emphases. Indeed it was in just this interest that the novel emerged as the most creative form of the time. The problems of love and marriage, in a society dominated by issues of property in land, were extended from the later Jacobean comedy and the Restoration comedy of manners, and from the moral epistles of Pope, to the novels of Richardson and Fielding, and in the mode of their extension were transformed. Allworthy and Squire Western, the neighbouring landowners in Fielding's *Tom Jones*, or Lovelace in Richardson's *Clarissa*, are in some ways lineal descendants of the world of Wellborn and Overreach, and then of Tunbelly Clumsey and Young Fashion. The plot of *Tom Jones* is based on the desire to link by marriage the two largest estates in Somersetshire: the proposed marriage of Sophia Western to Blifil is conceived for this end; her marriage to Tom Jones, when he is eventually revealed as Allworthy's true heir, achieves what had formerly, for personal reasons, been rejected. Similarly, Clarissa Harlowe's proposed marriage to Solmes is part of her family's calculation in concentrating their estates and increasing their rank; it is from this that she recoils to the destructive and cynical world of the established landowning aristocrat, Lovelace.

What is dramatised, under increasing pressure, in the actions of these novels, is the long process of choice between economic advantage and other ideas of value. Yet whereas, in the plays, we saw this from one particular standpoint – the social world of London in which the contracts were made and in which, by isolation and concentration, the tone of the protesting and then the cynical observer could be established and maintained – in the novels we move out to the families themselves, and see the action in its homes and in its private character. For all the differences between Richardson and Fielding, this change is something they have in common. Instead of the formal confrontation between representatives of different groups – the wellborn and the overreachers – and the amused observation of a distanced way of the world, the action becomes internal, and is experienced and dramatised as a problem of character.

The open ideology of improvement is in fact most apparent in Defoe, but in an abstraction which marks an essential difference from Richardson and Fielding. There is some irony in this fact, in that in his *Tour of England and Wales*, in the 1720s, Defoe was an incomparable observer of the detailed realities of country life, with his notes on methods of production, marketing and rents. It is from him that we learn the degree of specialisation and market-production in early eighteenth-century agriculture, and its intricate involvement with the cities, the ports, and the early coal, iron and cloth industrial areas. It is a frankly commercial world, with hardly any pastoral tinge, and Defoe's combination of intense interest and matter-of-fact reporting is the true predecessor of the major eighteenth-century tradition of rural inquiry, which runs on through William Marshall, the *County Reports*, Arthur Young and the Annals of Agriculture, to Cobbett and the nineteenth century. This emphasis is the real line of development of a working agriculture, and is in itself a major index of change. Yet, with rare exceptions, this emphasis was in its own way an abstraction from the social relationships and the human world through which the new methods of production worked. It is only at the end of this line, in the crisis at the turn of the century, that the social and economic inquiries are adequately brought together. It is then not surprising that Defoe, for all his close and specialised observation of what was happening in the fields and markets, did not, in his novels, consider their underlying social reality. Rather he projected, into other histories, the abstracted spirit of improvement and simple economic advantage – as most notably in *Robinson Crusoe* – and created a fictional world of isolated individuals to whom other people are basically transitory and functional – as again in *Crusoe* and in *Moll Flanders*. Consciously and unconsciously, this emphasis of a condition and of an ethic was prophetic and powerful; but it is an indication of its character that what Crusoe improves is a remote island, and that what Moll Flanders trades in is her own person. The important improvement and trading were at once nearer home and more general, but the simple practice and ethic of improvement could be more readily and more singlemindedly apprehended in deliberately isolated histories.

In the real life of the country, the commercial spirit had to interlock with, and be tested by, other institutions, considerations and modes. Neither Richardson nor Fielding knew as much as Defoe about what was happening in rural England, but their emphasis, in very different ways, was on human relationships in their more detailed course: not the spirit of the time, but its more immediate experience.

Yet we cannot, in turn, make an abstraction of these human relationships. When the marriage of Sophia and Blifil is proposed, as a way of uniting the neighbouring estates, the character of Blifil is shown in the true contemporary commercial spirit:

> as to that entire and absolute possession of the heart of his mistress which romantic lovers require, the very idea of it never entered his head. Her fortune and her person were the sole objects of his wishes, of which he made no doubt soon to obtain the absolute property....[1]

Squire Western, of course, uses his daughter to unite the estates, as if it were the most natural thing in the world. And Allworthy–

> not one of those men whose hearts flutter at any unexpected and sudden tidings of worldly profit[2]

– is nevertheless recommended to us by his more sober and philosophical calculations:

> Wisdom...only teaches us to extend a simple maxim universally known and followed even in the lowest life, a little farther than that life carries it. And this is, not to buy at too dear a price. Now, whoever takes this maxim abroad with him into the grand

market of the world, and constantly applies it to honours, to riches, to pleasures, and to every other commodity which that market affords, is, I will venture to affirm, a wise man, and must be so acknowledged in the worldly sense of the word; for he makes the best of bargains, since in reality he purchases everything at the price only of a little trouble, and carries home all the good things I have mentioned, while he keeps his health, his innocence and his reputation, the common prices which are paid for them by others, entire and to himself.[3]

This, indeed, is very much the position from which *Tom Jones* is written. It is the morality of a relatively consolidated, a more maturely calculating society. From such a position, the cold greed of a Blifil, the open coarseness of a Squire Western, can be noted and criticised; but calculation, and cost, are given a wider scheme of reference. Love, honour, physical pleasure, loyalty: these, too, have to be brought into the reckoning with incomes and acres. The humanity is of a resigned and settled kind: firm and open when faced by the meaner calculators, but still itself concerned to find the balance – the true market price – of happiness. Tom Jones learns from his apparent disregard of advantage, but it is not only that his more immediate satisfactions are tolerantly underwritten; it is also that Fielding's management of the action is directed towards restoring the balance in which personal satisfaction and material advantage are reconciled, compatible, and even identical. The novel continually raises questions about the relations between material fortune and human need and impulse, but it resolves them by an adaptation in which, by an act of will, by a planned and fortunate disclosure, they come loosely and easily together. The famous irony is then the literary means by which this trick can be played, noticed, and still win. The tone of the settlement, when Jones is discovered as the rightful heir, and the estates can be united in what is also a love match, is of a deliberate – one might say a calculating – geniality –

in which, to our great pleasure, though contrary, perhaps, to thy expectation, Mr Jones appears to be the happiest of all humankind.[4]

The settlements, the adjustments, the pensions are then neatly worked; and the 'condescension, indulgence and beneficence', of this finally happy pair is such as to make those below them, the tenants and servants, bless the marriage.

There was need, certainly, for this consolidated morality. The openly cynical scramble for land and for heiresses, which had been the predominant tone of an earlier period, was succeeded, in the more settled process of the first half of the eighteenth century, by just this wider, longer-sighted building of position. Humanity, family interest, personal need, must now, if at all possible, be included in any rational and improving settlement. If it was not possible, the main current of advantage took its way, leaving its human casualties.

It is significant that this darker view comes to us, in literature, through a particular fanaticism: the isolation, by Richardson, of virginity, as a single response to the whole struggle for human value. It is true that, in *Pamela*, virginity is treated as the term of a bargain: not a value in itself, but an asset which must not be surrendered without the necessary security of marriage. But in *Clarissa* the virginity is not negotiable, at any level or by any means; it is no longer simply a physical but a spiritual virginity: an integrity of the person and the soul. When the marriage to Solmes is proposed, as part of 'the darling view of *raising a family*' (that is, of consolidating and improving the family estates), Clarissa's answer –

> 'For the sake of this plan of my brother's, am I, Madam, to be given in marriage to a man I never can endure?'[5]

– is, though quieter, in the same world as Sophia's, on the proposed marriage to Blifil –

> 'Oh! sir, such a marriage is worse than death. He is not even indifferent; I hate and detest him.'[6]

But the emphasis, in *Clarissa*, is taken right through. The exposure to Lovelace has nothing to do with the lucky chances of the market, or with raising the price of the human person. It is a total exposure, to a cynically calculating world – significantly that of an earlier kind of landowner, the unmediated because established cavalier, the 'wellborn'. No marriage contract can ratify that exposure; even rape cannot destroy Clarissa's virginity. This is the reverse of consolidation, of the necessary settlement, the striking of a bargain between advantage and value. The integrity of the human person is fanatically preserved, by its refusal to compromise and then its accepted destruction.

In his single emphasis, Richardson moved away from any negotiable world, and of course succeeded in specialising a general crisis to a personal and (in its context) fashionable issue. *Clarissa* is an important sign of that separation of virtue from any practically available world which is a feature of the later phases of Puritanism and still later of Romanticism. Though it engages with the current acquisitiveness and ambition of the landowning families, it is in the end not a criticism of a period or structure of society, but of what can be abstracted as 'the world'. This degree of retreat must be noted, but it is in its own way an answer to the problems being raised by an increasingly confident capitalist society. The specialisation of virginity, and the paradoxical isolation and even destruction of the individual as a means of survival, are connected with that specialisation of pity and charity, and the retreat from society into a nature which teaches humanity, which we shall later trace as responses to the continuing crises of a basically ruthless order, to which there was not, as yet, any available and adequate social response.

(ii)

It must then seem a world away, from the desperate and private emphases of *Clarissa*, to the calmly practical, the inquiring everyday tone of the actual agents of improvement. The social crisis can only be seen, in any connected way, when it is worked through in this everyday and general mode. As we read the agricultural writers, it is easy to accept their emphasis on a better use of the land, even when this is so often explicitly connected with the calculation of rents (Lovelace, interestingly, would never rack-rent old tenants; his income, like his sexual liberty, was inherited rather than speculative). We learn so much from these improving writers, and their achievement (together with that of the experimenting farmers and the better-known experimenting landowners), in providing more food is so impressive that it is easy for anybody who loves the land to place himself on their side. What is hardest to understand, for them as for us, is the ultimate consequence of just these improvements which in immediate terms were so readily justifiable.

To read the life of Arthur Young is to catch at once the spirit of improvement and its real complications. He grew up on an estate which had been in his father's family for generations, but which was set into order only by capital from his mother's side: a Jewish family which had come from Holland in the late seventeenth century. The old house was rebuilt into a mansion, as so often in this period. This social ambition overreached the family's income. Arthur Young was apprenticed as a merchant; he had wanted, like his father, to be a clergyman. When his father died, he had little money, and began to support himself by writing pamphlets. Then he returned to farm a copyhold of twenty acres, on his mother's small estate. Chronically short of capital, he never succeeded in becoming a successful farmer himself, but as an agricultural writer, collecting and publicising the techniques and spirit of improved production, he made a new kind of life. More than any other man, he made the case for the second great period of enclosures, in the late eighteenth and early nineteenth centuries. He travelled constantly, and in the forty-six volumes of his *Annals of Agriculture* provided the essential means of communication for the new experimental agriculture. The changes came from use of the land itself: in new crops (especially roots), in drainage and reclamation, in planned soil fertility, and in stock breeding. But Young emphasised the connections of the agricultural interest with the other new social forces of the time: with mercantile capital (as he had good reason, from his personal history, to know); with early industrial techniques (as in earth-moving, which was mechanised for harbour-building and quarrying before it was applied to farming-land); with the physical sciences (as in his collaboration with Priestley in soil-chemistry); and with political power and organisation (as in his propaganda to the King and Parliament, and in his eventual appointment as Secretary of the new Board of Agriculture).

Young touched, at every point, what we now see as the modernisation of the land in his century; but what he continually stressed was the backwardness of agriculture, its insufficient rate of progress, its neglect of great areas of waste land, its lack of investment by comparison with overseas trade. And increasingly, towards the end of his life, he admitted his own social experience and the result of his social observations. Thus improvement of land required considerable capital, and therefore the leadership of the landowners. But this not only increased the predominance of the landed interest; it created, by enclosure and engrossing to make large and profitable units, a greater number of the landless and the disinherited, who could not survive or compete in the new conditions. The slowness of many farmers to adopt the new methods was itself related to the land-holding system: since improvement often led to an increase of rent, there was a built-in deterrent at the very point of production. It was only a rare landowner, like Coke, who kept a reasonable relation between the profits of the new production and the rents of his tenants. Thus the economic process, which could be so easily justified in its own limited terms, had social results which at times contradicted it, and at other times led to the disaster of families and communities. When Young saw the full social results of the changes he had fought for, he was not alone in second thoughts and in new kinds of questioning:

> I had rather that all the commons of England were sunk in the sea, than that the poor should in future be treated on enclosing as they have been hitherto.[7] ...

Enclosures, Commons and Communities

We have considered several instances of the melancholy of eighteenth-century poems of country life, and we have seen, in Crabbe, their culmination in distress. It is worth emphasising these predominant feelings of loss and pain as we move to that common outline of the history of rural England, in which the campaign of parliamentary enclosures is seen as the destroyer of a traditional and settled rural community.

We have already seen, in Arthur Young, a first estimate of what enclosure amounted to, in its contradictory social and economic consequences. Nobody who follows these through in detail would wish to underestimate them. Yet there is a sense in which the idea of the enclosures, localised to just that period in which the Industrial Revolution was beginning, can shift our attention from the real history and become an element of that very powerful myth of modern England in which the transition from a rural to an industrial society is seen as a kind of fall, the true cause and origin of our social suffering and disorder. It is difficult to overestimate the importance of this myth, in modern social thought. It is a main source for the structure of feeling which we began by examining: the perpetual retrospect to an 'organic' or 'natural' society. But it is also a main source for that last protecting illusion in the crisis of our own time: that it is not capitalism which is injuring us, but the more isolable, more evident system of urban industrialism. The questions involved are indeed very difficult, but for just this reason they require analysis, at each point and in each period in which an element of this structure can be seen in formation.

There is no reason to deny the critical importance of the period of parliamentary enclosures, from the second quarter of the eighteenth century to the first quarter of the nineteenth century. By nearly four thousand Acts, more than six million acres of land were appropriated, mainly by the politically dominant landowners: about a quarter of all cultivated acreage. But it is then necessary to see the essential continuity of this appropriation, both with earlier and with later phases. It is necessary to stress, for example, how much of the country had already been enclosed, before this change of method in the mid-eighteenth century to a parliamentary act. The process had been going on since at least the thirteenth century, and had reached a first peak in the fifteenth and sixteenth centuries. Indeed in history it is continuous from the long process of conquest and seizure: the land gained by killing, by repression, by political bargains.

Again, as the economy develops, enclosure can never really be isolated from the mainstream of land improvements, of changes in methods of production, of price-movements, and of those more general changes in property relationships which were all flowing in the same direction: an extension of cultivated land but also a concentration of ownership into the hands of a minority.

The parliamentary procedure for enclosure made this process at once more public and more recorded. In this sense it was directly related to the quickening pace of agricultural improvement in the late eighteenth and early nineteenth centuries. In this period the area mainly affected was a belt from Yorkshire to Dorset, across the midland counties, and extending eastwards to Norfolk. The same process occurred, a little later, in the Scottish Lowlands. But large tracts elsewhere were already effectively enclosed: Kent, parts of Surrey and Sussex, parts of Essex and Suffolk; Devon,

Cornwall, Somerset and western Dorset; much of Wales and the border counties of Hereford, Shropshire, Staffordshire and Cheshire; the important cultivated areas of Lancashire, Cumberland, Westmorland, Northumberland and Durham. The social importance of enclosures is then not that they introduced a wholly new element in the social structure, but that in getting rid of the surviving open-field villages and common rights, in some of the most populous and prosperous parts of the country, they complemented and were indeed often caused by the general economic pressure on small owners and especially small tenants. No reliable figures are now available, but it can be reasonably argued that as many people were driven from the land, and from some independent status in relation to it, by the continuing processes of rack-renting and short-lease policies, and by the associated need for greater capital to survive in an increasingly competitive market, as by explicit enclosure.

The number of landless, before this period of enclosure, was in any event high: in 1690, five landless labourers to every three occupiers, as compared with a proportion of five to two in 1831. Most of the peasantry, in another sense – the classical sense of the small owner-occupiers under social and political obligations – had been bought and forced out in the period of the building of large estates in the late seventeenth and early eighteenth centuries. G. E. Mingay has concluded that those who survived this process hung on till the fall in product prices in the 1820s, and declined steadily through the nineteenth century, under general pressures:

> on the whole it seems that the level of prices and the prosperity of farming had more impact on owner-occupiers than had enclosures.[8]

The peasantry in yet another and very tenuous sense, the small tenant farmers, were of course already part of the system of agrarian capitalism. Their numbers were affected by the economics of scale, and by the aggregation of estates, but enclosure as such did not greatly affect them: in 1831 nearly half of all farms were small, by any ordinary standard. Thus there is no simple case, in the late eighteenth century, of the expropriation of a peasantry. What really happened was that in the economically dynamic areas a capitalist social system was pushed through to a position of dominance, by a form of legalised seizure enacted by representatives of the beneficiary class. This is crucially important, and in the acreage it affected – a quarter of all cultivated land – it can be said to be decisive. But it cannot be isolated from the long development of concentration of landholding, from the related stratification of owners and tenants, and from the increasing number of the landless, which were the general consequences of agrarian capitalism.

The links with the Industrial Revolution are again important, but not as the replacement of one 'order' by another. It is true that many of the landless became, often with little choice, the working class of the new industrial towns, thus continuing that movement of wage labourers to the towns which had long been evident. But the growth of the industrial working-class must be related also, and perhaps primarily, to the growth of population, itself spectacular, which though primarily related to changes in the birth and death rates in the general modernisation of the society, is related also to the increase in agricultural production which was so marked in the eighteenth century: especially in corn, but also in meat; changes themselves related to enclosure and more efficient production. The crisis of poverty, which was so marked in towns and villages alike in the late eighteenth and early nineteenth centuries, was a result of this social and economic process as a whole, and cannot be explained as the fall of one order and the institution of another. The essential connections between town and country, which had been evident throughout, reached a new, more explicit and finally critical stage. It was characteristic of rural England, before and during the Industrial Revolution, that it was exposed to increasing penetration by capitalist social relations and the dominance of the market, just because these had been power-fully evolving within its own structures. By the late eighteenth century we can properly speak of an organised capitalist society, in which what happened to the market, anywhere, whether in industrial or agricultural production, worked its way through to town and country alike, as parts of a single crisis.

Within these developments, violent alterations of condition occurred, to many thousands of tenants and labourers, and to hundreds of village communities. The new tone we have seen in eighteenth-century country writing is then related to these changes of condition, but also, as we have again seen, to ways of interpreting them. We can find the sense of collapse in Langhorne, from a part of the country where enclosure was not a main issue but where the whole economic and social process was exerting its pressures, as much as in Goldsmith, Crabbe, Cowper, and later Clare and Cobbett, from counties where enclosure was the most visible social fact.

At a certain stage, though, enclosure came to be isolated as a main cause. Young's change of mind, his recognition of social realities, came in the early years of the nineteenth century: by most acts of enclosure the poor had been injured, often grossly, and he imagined the poor man saying:

> All I know is, I had a cow and Parliament took it from me.

Cobbett, by the 1820s, was speaking of the 'madness of enclosures' and even deny-ing, with many argued instances, that they had increased production. He pointed out, what was undeniable, that the increased investment and concentration of money in the land had

> worked detriment to the labourer. It was out of his bones that the means came. It was the *deduction made from him by the rise of prices* and by the *not-rise of his wages* (Cobbett's italics).[9]

Cobbett argued in solid terms of the economics of farming, but inevitably from observation of single instances, as when he calculated that the value of bees on a particular Hampshire common was alone greater than the value of that same common enclosed, to say nothing of the cows, pigs and poultry, the apples and cherries, also raised there. But this is the familiar case of a local contrast between a mixed farming economy and the economics of specialisation and scale; in the long run, in trading terms, the latter of course prevailed.

An interesting element was then added to the argument by social observation of life on the old commons. For example Thomas Bewick the engraver, in his *Memoir* written in the 1820s, remembers a Northumberland common of the 1780s, and comments:

> On this common – the poor man's heritage for ages past, where he kept a few sheep, or a Kyloe cow, perhaps a flock of geese, and mostly a stock of bee-hives – it was with

infinite pleasure that I long beheld the beautiful wild scenery that was there exhibited, and it is with the opposite feeling that I now find all swept away. Here and there on this common were to be seen the cottage, or rather hovel, of some labouring man, built at his own expense, and mostly with his own hands; and to this he always added a garth and a garden, upon which great pains and labour were bestowed to make product- ive.... These various concerns excited the attention and industry of the hardy occu- pants, which enabled them to prosper, and made them despise being ever numbered with the parish poor. These men ... might truly be called –
    'A bold peasantry, their country's pride'.[10]

It is an attractive and wholly credible account, and we can learn from Bewick as he goes on to describe the independence and originality of mind of many of these men:

I think I see him yet, sitting on a mound, or seat, by the hedge of his garden, regardless of the cold, and intent upon viewing the heavenly bodies; pointing to them with his large hands, and eagerly imparting his knowledge;

or his description of Anthony Liddell –

The whole cast of his character was formed by the Bible, which he had read with attention, through and through. Acts of Parliament which appeared to him to clash with the laws laid down in it, as the Word of God, he treated with contempt. He maintained that the fowls of the air and the fish of the sea were free for all men; consequently, game-laws, or laws to protect the fisheries, had no weight with him;[11]

or of Thomas Forster the beekeeper, who hid many of his hives in the whin, to keep away 'the over-inquisitive'.

From recollections like these, and from more conscious and extended accounts of pre-enclosure villages, a picture was built up which has still great emotional force: of independent and honourable men, living in a working rural democracy, who were coldly and 'legally' destroyed by the new enclosing order.

It is this picture as a whole that we have, even reluctantly, to question. The character given by independence needs little argument, though the character of Thomas Forster the beekeeper, who sold the honey of his home-hives to his neigh- bours and of his whin-hives at a distance, seems already well on the way to inde- pendence in another sense: that of the private entrepreneur who has at best an ambiguous relation to his community. The other kind of character, in which a man has time and spirit to observe, to think and to read, obviously flourished in the relative independence of the cottager, but is also part of the whole history – the glory and the tragedy – of working men everywhere. I do not know any social condition in which, against all the apparent odds, such characters have not emerged: whether it is that of Bewick's commoners, or of the field labourers like Stephen Duck, or of the Sussex shepherd-diarists, or of the amateur geologists and botanists of the Lancashire mill-towns, or of the working-men scholars of our own century, the etymologists, the economists, the local historians. It is part of the insult offered to intelligence by a class-society that this history of ordinary thought is ever found surprising. There were, of course, in all these conditions, men of great capacity who gave a shape to their lives by long effort and wisdom. The values which these men lived and repre- sented are opposed, always and everywhere, by the greed and pride of money, power and, too often, established learning. In that general sense, the growth of a system which rationalised greed and pride destroyed and has continued to destroy. But what we have also to notice is how much on the defensive, in how small a space of cleared life, the independence of the cottagers was maintained. The question we have to put to this version of social history is not whether some men emerged and survived – they will always do so, under any pressures – but whether, taken as a whole, the way of life could sustain a general independence. That, after all, is the test of community, as opposed to occasional private independence. And then at once we notice, even in Bewick, that the 'parish poor' are already there, as a distinguishable class. We have to notice, what Bewick also tells us, that the independent cottagers:

> held the neighbouring gentry in the greatest estimation and respect; and these again, in
> return, did not overlook them, but were interested in knowing that they were happy
> and well.[12]

What they have is then a relative and fortunate independence, in an interval of settlement which we can be glad lasted many men's lifetimes. But it is not necessarily an order that we can oppose to what succeeded it, when the same neighbouring gentry showed their interest in a different way and enclosed the commons. The rural class-system was already there, and men were living as they could, sometimes well, in its edges, its margins, its as yet ungrasped and undeveloped areas.

Most records of loss come from these marginal lands: the commons and heaths. But parliamentary enclosure did not only operate on them. Indeed we cannot understand the social consequences of enclosure unless we distinguish between two fundamentally different processes: the enclosure of 'wastes', which in the eighteenth and nineteenth centuries accounted for some two million acres, and the enclosure of open arable fields, already under cultivation, which accounted for some four million acres. It is obvious that the social effects of these two processes must be radically different. What was being suppressed on the wastes was a marginal independence, of cottagers, squatters, isolated settlers in mainly uncultivated land. What was being suppressed in the open-field villages must have been a very different kind of community: the close nucleated villages of an old arable economy. It is remarkable, as W. G. Hoskins has observed, that there is hardly anything in literature to record the passing of such villages, though the complaints of the loss of commons are very numerous. It is possible to read Goldsmith's *Deserted Village* as such a record, but characteristically it is indirect. Yet it is the alteration of the social and economic character of the open-field arable villages that ought most to engage us, if we are thinking of any pre-enclosure 'rural democracy'. Certainly it was the changes here which contributed most substantially to the newly prosperous and consolidated agrarian capitalism. But what kind of social order really existed, in the old open-field village? We must be careful not to confuse the techniques of production – the open-field strips – with what can easily be projected from it, an 'open' and relatively equal society. It is worth looking at the description by a modern rural historian, Fussell, of 'a typical open-field village' of the early eighteenth century. There are three hundred souls. Of these, nearly two hundred are cottagers and labourers and their families, indoor servants, and the unattached poor – widows, orphans, the aged. Some seventy are the copyhold tenant farmers and their families. Some twenty are the freehold farmers and their families. The ten or twelve others are the squire and his family and the parson and his family. It is an interesting distribution, but it is not, at first sight, so dissimilar from the ordinary social structure of mature rural capitalism as to suggest a radically different social order. There are, in effect, three classes: the gentry; the small entrepreneurs; the unpropertied poor. The inequalities of condition which the village contains and supports are profound, and nobody, by any exercise of sentiment, can convert it into a 'rural democracy' or, absurdly, a commune. The social structure that will be completed after enclosure is already basically outlined.[13]

Yet there are qualifications, and it is these we must try to weigh. Among the cottagers and labourers, for example, some are craftsmen and tradesmen (blacksmith, carpenter, cobbler, carrier, publican), and these and others (though not all the others) have small rights of grazing and fuel on nearby common pastures and wastes. It is easy, in retrospect, for these rights to seem petty, but for at least some men they were an important protection against the exposure of total hire. Again and again, down to our own day, men living in villages have tried to create just this kind of margin: a rented patch or strip, an extended garden, a few hives or fruit trees. When I was a child my father had not only the garden that went with his cottage, but a strip for potatoes on a farm where he helped in the harvest, and two gardens which he rented from the railway company from which he drew his wages. Such marginal possibilities are important not only for their produce, but for their direct and immediate satisfactions and for the felt reality of an area of control of one's own immediate labour. Under the long pressures of a dominating wage-economy, these exceptional areas have been critically important: they still occur, even in towns, in some subsidiary small trade or employment. And there can be little doubt that the pre-enclosure village made such opportunities available for more men than any immediately alternative community. In that sense, a degree of loss is real. But only a degree: for by these methods, while they remained marginal, no whole community could be economically sustained, and stratification within it was still inevitable.

To what extent, then, was there ever a genuine community, in such villages, in spite of the economic and social inequalities? It is very difficult to say, for there were major factual variations (we still need many more local studies and examples), and an estimate of 'community', at this distance in time, will be always to some extent subjective. We can of course look at institutions. The manorial courts, in which the business of the village was transacted according to customary rights, are often cited as 'communal'. These were, though, steadily decaying before enclosure, and retained only a declining importance until they were superseded by the completed system of propertied rule. The processes of local law and government show the same evolution: a steady concentration of power in the hands of the landowners, and a more evident (if not a more severe) arbitrariness as these came increasingly to represent a conscious national system and interest, in the constitution of the landowners as a political class. The reality of community must then have varied enormously. The detailed record of the Warwickshire village of Tysoe, which we can study in M. K. Ashby's remarkable biography of her father (*Joseph Ashby of Tysoe*, 1961), is a relevant example.

> Until the end of the eighteenth century, Tysoe, the registers showed, had been a village of yeomen, craftsmen, tradesmen and a few labourers – not separate classes, but intermarrying, interapprenticed sections of the community, unified by farming in cooperation and by as great mutual dependence in other ways.... In earlier years the division between classes in Tysoe had been no more than function or custom called for or

worldly perspicacity earned.... After the years of wretchedness it was so deep a ditch
that every foolish mind fell into it.[14]

But what is then interesting is that this change, in 'the years of wretchedness', is not
the result of enclosure, but had preceded it. The increasing poverty in the village
became a system of pauperism, and for this enclosure could not be blamed in Tysoe.

The scarlet letters for paupers were sewn in the 1740s. The entry of 'Pauper' in
the burial register became more regular through the eighteenth century, and was
eventually shortened to a crude 'P'. Unemployment was registered from the 1780s.
The roundsman system was active from the 1760s. The smallpox came recurrently,
and the consequences of its heavy toll of lives led to peaks of poor relief in the 1770s.
This community, it is clear, was so involved in and exposed to the crises of a general
system that its neighbourliness was, at best, relative. The friendly and comparatively
informal relief of an earlier period gave way, under just this pressure, to the cold and
harsh treatment of a separate class of 'the poor'. At the same time, again before
enclosure though increasing after it, there was the more evident class-consciousness
of the parsons, as in the new style of vicarage, hedged from 'their' parishioners, and
of the more prosperous farmers, now called 'gentlemen-farmers'. Enclosure is then a
factor within this complex of change, but not a single isolated cause.

Another thing we can learn is that community must not always be seen in retrospect. In Tysoe there was a revival of community, as the village came together in the
nineteenth century, to fight for its rights of allotment in the Town Lands. In many
parts of rural Britain, a new kind of community developed as an aspect of struggle,
against the dominant landowners or, as in the labourers' revolts in the time of the
Swing machine-smashing and rick-burning or in the labourers' unions from Tolpud-
dle to Joseph Arch, against the whole class-system of rural capitalism. In many
villages, community only became a reality when economic and political rights were
fought for and partially gained, in the recognition of unions, in the extension of the
franchise, and in the possibility of entry into new representative and democratic
institutions. In many thousands of cases, there is more community in the modern
village, as a result of this process of new legal and democratic rights, than at any
point in the recorded or imagined past.

That is active community, and it must be distinguished from another version,
which is sometimes the mutuality of the oppressed, at other times the mutuality of
people living at the edges or in the margins of a generally oppressive system. This
comes out in many ways, overlapping with the community of struggle or persisting
as local and traditional habit. One way of considering the survival of this traditional
mutuality would be according to the distance of a village from its principal landowner. We have heard so much of the civilising effect of this landowning class, from
its own mouth and from the mouths it has hired, that it is worth recording the
coming of a more extreme class-consciousness – a systematic shaming of the labourers and the poor – from what were now so often the rebuilt country-houses, and
often by way of their attendant and employed clergy. The break of so many poor
families from the Church of England into the nonconformist sects is directly related
to this experience of landlord-and-parson religion. The barn-chapels of remote rural
Britain are still moving witnesses of this radical community response. But the remoteness itself is very often a factor, whether regional or local. It has always seemed
to me, from some relevant family experience, that the distance or absence of one of

those 'great houses' of the landlords can be a critical factor in the survival of a
traditional kind of community: that of tolerant neighbourliness. Matthew Arnold
gave a clue to this when he wrote, in *Culture and Anarchy*:

> When I go through the country, and see this and that beautiful and imposing seat of
> theirs crowning the landscape, 'There,' I say to myself, 'is a great fortified post of the
> Barbarians.'[15]

They had been there, indeed, from periods of direct military rule and occupation;
but they had settled into a more social order. And it was in the eighteenth century,
most visibly, that these strong points of a class spread in a close network over so
much of Britain, with subsidiary effects, on attitudes to landscape and to nature, that
we shall come to notice.

But consider, directly, their social effect. Some of them had been there for centuries, visible triumphs over the ruin and labour of others. But the extraordinary phase
of extension, rebuilding and enlarging, which occurred in the eighteenth century,
represents a spectacular increase in the rate of exploitation: a good deal of it, of
course, the profit of trade and of colonial exploitation; much of it, however, the
higher surplus value of a new and more efficient mode of production. It is fashionable to admire these extraordinarily numerous houses: the extended manors, the neo-
classical mansions, that lie so close in rural Britain. People still pass from village to
village, guidebook in hand, to see the next and yet the next example, to look at the
stones and the furniture. But stand at any point and look at that land. Look at what
those fields, those streams, those woods even today produce. Think it through as
labour and see how long and systematic the exploitation and seizure must have been,
to rear that many houses, on that scale. See by contrast what any ancient isolated
farm, in uncounted generations of labour, has managed to become, by the efforts of
any single real family, however prolonged. And then turn and look at what these
other 'families', these systematic owners, have accumulated and arrogantly declared.
It isn't only that you know, looking at the land and then at the house, how much
robbery and fraud there must have been, for so long, to produce that degree of
disparity, that barbarous disproportion of scale. The working farms and cottages are
so small beside them: what men really raise, by their own efforts or by such portion
as is left to them, in the ordinary scale of human achievement. What these 'great'
houses do is to break the scale, by an act of will corresponding to their real and
systematic exploitation of others. For look at the sites, the façades, the defining
avenues and walls, the great iron gates and the guardian lodges. These were chosen
for more than the effect from the inside out; where so many admirers, too many of
them writers, have stood and shared the view, finding its prospect delightful. They
were chosen, also, you now see, for the other effect, from the outside looking in: a
visible stamping of power, of displayed wealth and command: a social disproportion
which was meant to impress and overawe. Much of the real profit of a more modern
agriculture went not into productive investment but into that explicit social declaration: a mutually competitive but still uniform exposition, at every turn, of an established and commanding class power.

To stand in that shadow, even today, is to know what many generations of countrymen bitterly learned and were consciously taught: that these were the families,
this the shape of the society. And will you then think of community? You will see

modern community only in the welcome signs of some partial reclamation: the houses returned to some general use, as a hospital or agricultural college. But you are just as likely to see the old kinds of power still declared: in the surviving exploiters and in their modern relations – the corporation country-house, the industrial seat, the ruling-class school. Physically they are there: the explicit forms of the long class-society.

But turn for a moment elsewhere: to the villages that escaped their immediate presence; to the edges, the old commons still preserved in place-names; to the hamlets where control was remote. It can make some difference, as you go about every day, to be out of sight of that explicit command. And this is so, I do not doubt, in many surviving, precarious communities, the dispersed settlements of the west or some of the close villages of the east and midlands, where no immediate house has so outgrown its neighbours that it has visibly altered the scale. It makes a real difference that in day-to-day relations those other people and their commanding statements in stone are absent or at least some welcome distance away.

In some places still, an effective community, of a local kind, can survive in older terms, where small freeholders, tenants, craftsmen and labourers can succeed in being neighbours first and social classes only second. This must never be idealised, for at the points of decision, now as then, the class realities usually show through. But in many intervals, many periods of settlement, there is a kindness, a mutuality, that still manages to flow. It is a matter of degree, as it was in the villages before and after enclosure. When the pressure of a system is great and is increasing, it matters to find a breathing-space, a fortunate distance, from the immediate and visible controls. What was drastically reduced, by enclosures, was just such a breathing-space, a marginal day-to-day independence, for many thousands of people. It is right to mourn that loss but we must also look at it plainly. What happened was not so much 'enclosure' – the method – but the more visible establishment of a long-developing system, which had taken, and was to take, several other forms. The many miles of new fences and walls, the new paper rights, were the formal declaration of where the power now lay. The economic system of landlord, tenant and labourer, which had been extending its hold since the sixteenth century, was now in explicit and assertive control. Community, to survive, had then to change its terms.

Three Around Farnham

In this period of change, it mattered very much where you were looking from. Points of view, interpretations, selections of realities, can now be directly contrasted. In history it is a period of rural society. In literature it is a complex of different ways of seeing even the same local life.

Imagine a journey, for example, round a thirty-mile triangle of roads, in the turning years of the late eighteenth and early nineteenth centuries. It is on the borders of Hampshire and Surrey: six miles from Selborne to Chawton; ten miles from Chawton to Farnham; fourteen miles from Farnham back to Selborne. In 1793, in Selborne, Gilbert White died. In 1777, when White had been keeping his famous journal for nine years, a boy of fourteen, William Cobbett, ran away from his father's small farm at Farnham. Cobbett was to ride back through these villages, many times, and in the 1820s to write his *Rural Rides*. When Gilbert White died, Jane Austen, not far away, in another parsonage, was beginning to write her novels of country society. From 1809, in Chawton, she was beginning to publish and to write her mature works. In this small locality, overlapping within a generation, there were these three people, three writers, who could hardly be more different. Both the country seen and the idea of the country vary so much in their work that we are forced, as we read them, into a new kind of consciousness.

What Cobbett gives us is detailed social observation, from the point of view of the condition of the majority of men. He combined Arthur Young's attention to the detailed practice of a working agriculture with a more persistent social questioning and observation. Thus in 1821:

> (West of Uphusband):
> ...a group of women labourers, who were attending the measurers to measure their reaping work, presented such an assemblage of rags as I never before saw even amongst the hoppers at Farnham, many of whom are common beggars. I never before saw *country* people, and reapers too, observe, so miserable in appearance as these. There were some very pretty girls, but ragged as colts and as pale as ashes.

> (Near Cricklade):
> ...The labourers seem miserably poor. Their dwellings are little better than pig-beds, and their looks indicate that their food is not nearly equal to that of a pig. Their wretched hovels are stuck upon little bits of ground *on the road side*, where the space has been wider than the road demanded. In many places they have not two rods to a hovel. It seems as if they had been swept off the fields by a hurricane, and had found shelter under the banks on the road side! Yesterday morning was a sharp frost; and this had set the poor creatures to digging up their little plots of potatoes.... And this is '*prosperity*', is it?[16]

The great merit of Cobbett's observation is its detail. This included the facts of local variation:

> (Near Gloucester):
> ...The labourers' dwellings, as I came along, looked good, and the labourers themselves pretty well as to dress and healthiness. The girls at work in the fields (always my standard) are not in rags, with bits of shoes tied on their feet and rags tied round their ankles, as they had in Wiltshire.

This is a new voice, in a radical shift of social viewpoint:

> The landlords and the farmers can tell their own tale. They tell their own tale in remonstrances and prayers, addressed to the House. Nobody tells the tale of the labourer.[17]

This consciousness of viewpoint, of a class viewpoint, marks the distance from most previous accounts; and where Cobbett had been preceded, as in part by Crabbe, the range of detail brings in a world that marks the essential preparation for transition from the sympathetic poem to the realistic novel.

We remember Crabbe as we see Cobbett considering the relations between poverty and the quality of land:

(In Kent):
What a difference between the wife of a labouring man here, and the wife of a labouring
man in the forests and woodlands of Hampshire and Sussex! Invariably have I observed
that the richer the soil, and the more destitute of woods; that is to say, the more purely
a corn country, the more miserable the labourers.

It was in the cornlands that capitalist farming was most developed. It is on this
contrast of social conditions that Cobbett insists:

The labouring people look pretty well. They have pigs. They invariably do best in the
woodland and *forest* and *wild* countries. Where the mighty grasper has *all under his eye*,
they can get but little.

This was the social basis of his opposition to enclosures: not what happened to
production, as a total figure, but what happened, in detail, to the people and the
land. It was in this sense that he observed:

This place presents another proof of the truth of my old observation: *rich land* and *poor
labourers*.[18]

Or again, comparing the disadvantage of wage-labour with the old system of feeding
and lodging (the farmers 'cannot keep their work-people *upon so little* as they give
them in wages'), he insisted:

The land produces, on an average, what it always produced, but there is a new distribution of the produce.

What was happening meanwhile to the landowners, and to their social structure, as
rural capitalism extended? Cobbett looked very carefully at this, and made a familiar
distinction between

a resident *native* gentry, attached to the soil, known to every farmer and labourer from
his childhood, frequently mixing with them in those pursuits where all artificial distinctions are lost, practising hospitality without ceremony, from habit and not on calculation; and a gentry, only now-and-then residing at all, having no relish for country-
delights, foreign in their manners, distant and haughty in their behaviour, looking to
the soil only for its rents, viewing it as a mere object of speculation, unacquainted with
its cultivators, despising them and their pursuits, and relying, for influence, not upon
the good will of the vicinage, but upon the dread of their power. The war and paper-
system has brought in nabobs, negro-drivers, generals, admirals, governors, commissar-
ies, contractors, pensioners, sinecurists, commissioners, loan-jobbers, lottery-dealers,
bankers, stock-jobbers; not to mention the long and *black list* in gowns and three-tailed
wigs. You can see but few good houses not in possession of one or the other of these.
These, with the parsons, are now the magistrates.

It is an impressive list and Cobbett gives several names as examples. The fact that
there had been the same kind of invasion, from at least the sixteenth century, must
qualify the account. What Cobbett does not ask is where the 'invaders' came from.
Many of them, in fact, were the younger sons of that same 'resident native gentry',
who had gone out to these new ways to wealth, and were now coming back. Yet,

'native' or 'invader', the pressure on rents, and so through the tenant-farmer on the labourer, was visibly and dramatically increasing. Cobbett shortens the real time-scale, but then sees what is happening, as agrarian capitalism extends. He identifies money – first silver and gold, and then paper – as the agent of change. At first:

> its consequences came on by slow *degrees*; it made a transfer of property, but it made that transfer in so small a degree, and it left the property quiet in the hands of the new possessor for so long a time, that the effect was not violent, and was not, at any rate, such as to uproot possessors by whole districts, as the hurricane uproots the forests.[19]

This is an under-estimate of change from the sixteenth to eighteenth centuries, but what Cobbett is intent to record is the visible disturbance of his own time:

> the *small gentry*, to about the *third* rank upwards (considering there to be five ranks from the smallest gentry up to the greatest nobility) are *all gone*, nearly to a man, and the small farmers along with them. The Barings alone have, I should think, swallowed up thirty or forty of these small gentry without perceiving it. They, indeed, swallow up the biggest race of all; but innumerable small fry slip down unperceived, like caplins down the throats of the sharks, while these latter *feel* only the cod-fish.

As clearly as anyone in the whole record Cobbett raises the familiar complaint about the reduction of intermediate classes in the rural economy. But while he sees this happening, he simultaneously introduces a new criterion of judgement. Identifying with the labourer, making 'always my standard' the girls at work in the fields, Cobbett sees the ruin of the small owners and some tenant farmers, but then says of the small gentry, with a new harshness:

> So that, while they have been the active, the zealous, the efficient instruments, in compelling the working classes to submit to half-starvation, they have at any rate been brought to the most abject ruin themselves: for which I most heartily thank God.

Or again, of the farmers:

> Here is much more than enough to make me rejoice in the ruin of the farmers; and I do, with all my heart, thank God for it; seeing that it appears absolutely necessary, that the present race of them should be totally broken up, in Sussex at any rate, in order to put an end to this cruelty and insolence towards the labourers, who are by far the greater number.[20]

This is the hard anger which Cobbett shared with many of the labourers of his time, against the nearest targets to hand. It is the mood of the Bread or Blood riots of East Anglia in 1816, or of the widespread revolt of the labourers – the campaigns of 'Captain Swing' – in 1830. Cobbett noticed, in this, that he might have 'laid on the lash without a due regard to many', and he reflected:

> Born in a farm-house, bred up at the plough-tail, with a smock-frock on my back, taking great delight in all the pursuits of farmers, liking their society, and having amongst them my most esteemed friends, it is natural that I should feel, and I do feel, uncommonly anxious to prevent, as far as I am able, that total ruin which now menaces

them. But the labourer, was I to have no feeling for him? Was he not my *countryman* too? And was I not to feel indignation against those farmers, who had had the hard-heartedness to put the bell round his neck, and thus wantonly insult and degrade the class to whose toils they owed their own ease?[21]

This conflict of loyalties, and yet the final determination, marks a crucial stage. It was often the case in the forced food-levies, the riots for a minimum wage, the rick-burnings, that the immediate targets, the farmers, had little enough to give, under the pressure for rents of the more safely removed and protected landowners. It is significant indeed that, in these disturbances, dispossessed and ruined and hard-pressed farmers often joined the rioting labourers. But this was the characteristic of a developing capitalist order in the land. The riots indeed mark the last stage of the *local* confrontation, in immediate and personal terms. Such disturbances had neces-sarily to be succeeded by the organisation of class against class, in trade unionism and in its associated political movements. The structure of feeling that had held in direct appeal and in internal moral discrimination – the moral case, the moral warning, of such verse as Goldsmith's or Crabbe's – was now necessarily transformed into a different order of thinking and feeling. The maturity of capitalism as a system was forcing systematic organisation against it.

This development, so crucial in the social history of rural England, has its conse-quence in a new kind of country writing, of which Cobbett is the outrider: a change of convention, so that the interaction of classes, now the decisive history, can begin to be described: no longer in reflection, but in a newly typical action. This is the crucial bearing of the transformation of fiction into a new kind of novel, which was to become, from the 1830s, the dominant literary form. Cobbett described and cam-paigned, as a reporter and finally as a tribune. His change of viewpoint, and the changes to which he so vividly responded, are the first important signs of a new method in literature.

But this change in the novel did not happen in Cobbett's time. Through his middle years, while the social changes were happening, Jane Austen was writing from a very different point of view, from inside the houses that Cobbett was passing on the road. When he was writing about the disappearance of the small gentry he was riding through Hampshire, not far from Chawton. It was also in Hampshire that he made his list of the new owners of country-houses and estates, from nabobs to stock-jobbers. We can find ourselves thinking of Jane Austen's fictional world, as he goes on to observe:

> The big, in order to save themselves from being '*swallowed up quick*' ... make use of their *voices* to get, through place, pension, or sinecure, something back from the taxes. Others of them *fall in love* with the *daughters* and *widows* of paper-money people, big brewers, and the like; and sometimes their daughters *fall in love* with the paper-money people's sons, or the fathers of those sons; and whether they be Jews, or not, seems to be little matter with this all-subduing passion of love. But the *small gentry* have no resource.

This is a very different tone from anything that Jane Austen wrote, but it forces us to ask, as it were from the other side of the park wall: what were the conditions and the pressures within which she brought to bear her no less sharp observation; what was the social substance of her precise and inquiring personal and moral emphases?

It is a truth universally acknowledged, that Jane Austen chose to ignore the decisive historical events of her time. Where, it is still asked, are the Napoleonic wars: the real current of history? But history has many currents, and the social history of the landed families, at that time in England, was among the most important. As we sense its real processes, we find that they are quite central and structural in Jane Austen's novels. All that prevents us from realising this is that familiar kind of retrospect, taking in Penshurst and Saxham and Buck's Head and Mansfield Park and Norland and even Poynton, in which all country houses and their families are seen as belonging, effectively, to a single tradition: that of the cultivated rural gentry. The continual making and remaking of these houses and their families is suppressed, in this view, for an idealising abstraction, and Jane Austen's world can then be taken for granted, even sometimes patronised as a rural backwater, as if it were a simple 'traditional' setting. And then if the social 'background' is in this sense 'settled', we can move to an emphasis on a fiction of purely personal relationships.

But such an emphasis is false, for it is not personal relationships, in the abstracted sense of an observed psychological process, that preoccupy Jane Austen. It is, rather, personal *conduct*: a testing and discovery of the standards which govern human behaviour in certain real situations. To the social considerations already implicit in the examination of conduct, with its strong sense and exploration of the adequacy of social norms, we must add, from the evidence of the novels, a direct preoccupation with estates, incomes and social position, which are seen as indispensable elements of all the relationships that are projected and formed. Nor is this a preoccupation within a settled 'traditional' world; indeed much of the interest, and many of the sources of the action, in Jane Austen's novels, lie in the changes of fortune—the facts of general change and of a certain mobility—which were affecting the landed families at this time.

Thus it would be easy to take Sir Thomas Bertram, in *Mansfield Park*, as an example of the old settled landed gentry, to be contrasted with the new 'London' ways of the Crawfords (this is a common reading), were it not for the fact that Bertram is explicitly presented as what Goldsmith would have called 'a great West Indian': a colonial proprietor in the sugar island of Antigua. The Crawfords may have London ways, but the income to support them is landed property in Norfolk, and they have been brought up by an uncle who is an admiral. Sir Walter Elliott, in *Persuasion*, belongs to a landed family which had moved from Cheshire to Somerset, and which had been raised to a baronetcy in the Restoration, but his income, at this time, will not support his position; his heir-presumptive has 'purchased independence by uniting himself to a rich woman of inferior birth'; and the baronet is forced to let Kellynch Hall to an admiral, since, as his lawyer observes:

> This peace will be turning all our rich naval officers ashore. They will be all wanting a home. . . . Many a noble fortune has been made during the war.

The neighbouring Musgroves, the second landowning family, are, by contrast,

> in a state of alteration, perhaps of improvement. The father and mother were in the old English style, and the young people in the new.[22]

Darcy, in *Pride and Prejudice*, is a landowner established for 'many generations', but his friend Bingley has inherited £100,000 and is looking for an estate to purchase. Sir

William Lucas has risen from trade to a knighthood; Mr Bennett has £2000 a year, but an entailed estate, and has married the daughter of an attorney, whose brother is in trade. Knightley, in *Emma*, owns Donwell Abbey, and Martin, one of the new gentlemen farmers, is his tenant. The Woodhouses have little land but Emma will inherit £30,000, 'from other sources'. Elton, the vicar, has some independent property, but must make his way as he could, 'without any alliances but in trade'. Mr Weston belongs to a 'respectable family which for the last two or three generations had been rising into gentility and property'; he marries, through the militia, the daughter of 'a great Yorkshire family', and when she dies enters trade and purchases 'a little estate'. Harriet, finally revealed as the daughter of 'a tradesman, rich enough' marries her gentleman-farmer with the reasonable 'hope of more, of security, stability, and improvement'. The Coles live quietly, on an income from trade, but when this improves become 'in fortune and style of living, second only to the Woodhouses, in the immediate neighbourhood'. In *Sense and Sensibility*, the Dashwoods are a settled landowning family, increasing their income by marriages, and enlarging the settlements of their daughters; they are also enclosing Norland Common, and buying up neighbouring farms; the necessary cashing of stocks for enclosure and engrossing affect the rate of the family's immediate improvement. In *Northanger Abbey*, Catherine Morland, the daughter of a clergyman with two good livings and a considerable independence, goes with a local landowning family, the Allens, to Bath, and in that sharply observed social exchange meets the son of the family which has owned the Abbey estates since the dissolution of the monasteries; his sister has married on the 'unexpected accession' of her lover 'to title and fortune'.

To abstract this social history is of course to describe only the world of the novels within which the more particular actions begin and end. Yet it must be clear that it is no single, settled society, it is an active, complicated, sharply speculative process. It is indeed that most difficult world to describe, in English social history: an acquisitive, high bourgeois society at the point of its most evident interlocking with an agrarian capitalism that is itself mediated by inherited titles and by the making of family names. Into the long and complicated interaction of landed and trading capital, the process that Cobbett observed – the arrival of 'the nabobs, negro-drivers, admirals, generals' and so on – is directly inserted, and is even taken for granted. The social confusions and contradictions of this complicated process are then the true source of many of the problems of human conduct and valuation, which the personal actions dramatise. An openly acquisitive society, which is concerned also with the transmission of wealth, is trying to judge itself at once by an inherited code and by the morality of improvement.

The paradox of Jane Austen is then the achievement of a unity of tone, of a settled and remarkably confident way of seeing and judging, in the chronicle of confusion and change. She is precise and candid, but in very particular ways. She is, for example, more exact about income, which is disposable, than about acres, which have to be worked. Yet at the same time she sees land in a way that she does not see 'other sources' of income. Her eye for a house, for timber, for the details of improvement, is quick, accurate, monetary. Yet money of other kinds, from the trading houses, from the colonial plantations, has no visual equivalent; it has to be converted to these signs of order to be recognised at all. This way of seeing is especially representative. The land is seen primarily as an index of revenue and position; its visible order and control are a valued product, while the process of working it is hardly seen at all. Jane Austen then reminds us, yet again, of the two meanings of improvement, which were historically linked but in practice so often contradictory. There is the improvement of soil, stock, yields, in a working agriculture. And there is the improvement of houses, parks, artificial landscapes, which absorbed so much of the actually increasing wealth. Professor Habakkuk has observed that

> English landowners as a whole were a class of consumers, and the greater parts of their borrowings were contracted for non-productive purposes, to provide dowries, to fund short-term debts contracted as a result of extravagant living, to build mansions; the borrowings for enclosures, for example, were usually a small part of total indebtedness.[23]

This is not to deny the function of many landowners in agricultural improvement, but to set it in its actual social context. It is the essential commentary on what can be abstracted, technically, as the agricultural revolution: that it was no revolution, but the consolidation, the improvement, the expansion of an existing social class.

Cultivation has the same ambiguity as improvement: there is increased growth, and this is converted into rents; and then the rents are converted into what is seen as a cultivated society. What the 'revolution' is for, then, is this: this apparently attainable quality of life. Jane Austen could achieve her remarkable unity of tone – that cool and controlled observation which is the basis of her narrative method; that lightly distanced management of event and description and character which need not become either open manipulation or direct participation – because of an effective underlying and yet unseen formula: improvement is or ought to be improvement. The working improvement, which is not seen at all, is the means to social improvement, which is then so isolated that it is seen very clearly indeed.

It is not seen flatteringly. The conversion of good income into good conduct was no automatic process. Some of the conscious improvers are seen as they were: greedy and calculating materialists. But what is crucial is that the moral pretension is taken so seriously that it becomes a critique: never of the basis of the formula, but coolly and determinedly of its results, in character and action. She guides her heroines, steadily, to the right marriages. She makes settlements, alone, against all the odds, like some supernatural lawyer, in terms of that exact proportion to moral worth which could assure the continuity of the general formula. But within this conventional bearing, which is the source of her confidence, the moral discrimination is so insistent that it can be taken, in effect, as an independent value. It is often said, by literary historians, that she derives from Fielding and from Richardson, but Fielding's genial manipulative bluff and Richardson's isolating fanaticism are in fact far back, in another world. What happens in *Emma*, in *Persuasion*, in *Mansfield Park*, is the development of an everyday, uncompromising morality which is in the end separable from its social basis and which, in other hands, can be turned against it. It is in this sense that Jane Austen relates to the Victorian moralists, who had to learn to assume, with increasing unease from Coleridge to George Eliot and Matthew Arnold, that there was no necessary correspondence between class and morality; that the survival of discrimination depended on another kind of independence; that the two meanings of improvement had to be not merely distinguished but contrasted; or, as first in Coleridge, that cultivation, in its human sense, had to be brought to bear as a standard *against* the social process of civilisation. In these hands, decisively, the formula broke down: improvement was not improvement; not only not necessarily, but at times in definite contradiction. Jane Austen, it is clear, never went so far; her novels would have been very different, involving new problems of structure and language, if she had. But she provided the emphasis which had only to be taken outside the park walls, into a different social experience, to become not a moral but a social criticism. It is this transformation, and its difficulties, that we shall meet in George Eliot.

We must here emphasise again the importance of Cobbett. What he names, riding past on the road, are classes. Jane Austen, from inside the houses, can never see that, for all the intricacy of her social description. All her discrimination is, understandably, internal and exclusive. She is concerned with the conduct of people who, in the complications of improvement, are repeatedly trying to make themselves into a class. But where only one class is seen, no classes are seen. Her people are selected though typical individuals, living well or badly within a close social dimension. Cobbett never, of course, saw them as closely or as finely; but what he saw was what they had in common: the underlying economic process. A moral view of that kind had to come from outside, and of course when it came the language was rougher and harder. The precise confidence of an established world gave way to disturbing, aggressive and conflicting voices.

It was not a new experience; it had been there all the time, but only rarely recorded:

We are men formed in Christ's likeness, and we are kept like beasts.

> For Toils scarce ever ceasing press us now;
> Rest never does, but on the Sabbath, show;
> And barely that our Masters will allow.

Here I am, between Earth and Sky – so help me God. I would sooner lose my life than go home as I am. Bread I want and Bread I will have.

What we have done now is Soar against our Will but your harts is so hard as the hart of Pharo.... So now as for this fire you must not take it as a front, for if you hadent been Deserving it wee should not have dont.[24]

The first voice is from the fourteenth century; the second from the early eighteenth; the third and fourth from the early nineteenth century, in a new general crisis. It is a radically different morality from that of Jane Austen, but it is insistently moral, in its own general language. It is the voice of men who have seen their children starving, and now within sight of the stately homes and the improved parks and the self-absorbed social patterns at the ends of the drives.

Cobbett and Jane Austen mark two ways of seeing, two contrasted viewpoints, within the same country. Each kind of observation, however, is social, in the widest sense. But as we make our imaginary journey, on that triangle of roads, we discover, in Gilbert White, a different kind of observation, yet one of no less significance in the development of country writing. Anyone who lives in the country can experience at times, or seem to experience, an unmediated nature: in a direct and physical awareness of trees, birds, the moving shapes of land. What is new in Gilbert White, or at least feels new in its sustained intensity, is a development from this;

a single and dedicated observation, as if the only relationships of country living were to its physical facts. It is a new kind of record, not only of the facts, but of a way of looking at the facts: a way of looking that will come to be called scientific:

> The next bird that I procured (on the 21st of May) was a male red-backed butcher-bird, *lanius collurio*. My neighbour, who shot it, says that it might easily have escaped his notice, had not the outcries and chattering of the white-throats and other small birds drawn his attention to the bush where it was: its craw was filled with the legs and wings of beetles ...

> ... The ousel is larger than a blackbird, and feeds on haws; but last autumn (when there were no haws) it fed on yew-berries: in the spring it feeds on ivy-berries, which ripen only at that season, in March and April.[25]

These descriptions are from the formal letters published in *The Natural History of Selborne*. In tone and attention, over a lifetime, they compose a new kind of writing. It is not that White lacked what can be called 'powers of description'. When a natural event included an emotional response, as in the fearful summer of 1783, he could write to its level:

> The sun, at noon, looked as blank as a clouded moon, and shed a rust-coloured ferruginous light on the ground, and floors of rooms; but was particularly lurid and blood-coloured at rising and setting. All the time the heat was so intense that butchers' meat could hardly be eaten on the day after it was killed; and the flies swarmed so in the lanes and hedges that they rendered the horses half frantic, and riding irksome.[26]

It is simply, as the reading of his *Journal* over twenty-five years from 1768 to 1793 will confirm, that his customary mode of attention was outward: observing, inquiring, annotating, classifying. The quality of his feeling for the life around him is unquestionable; it is the devoted and delighted attention of a lifetime, from which anybody living in the country can still learn. But it is not what can easily be confused with it from many earlier and some later observations, the working of particular social or personal experience into the intricacies of things seen. White may remind us at times of Arthur Young and the other contributors to the *Annals of Agriculture*, in the close and detailed precision of his notes and observations. But what he is observing is not a working agriculture, except incidentally; it is a natural order, in a new sense: a physical world of creatures and conditions. While Cobbett and Jane Austen, in their different ways, were absorbed in a human world, Gilbert White was watching the turn of the year and the myriad physical lives inside it: nature in a sense that could now be separated from man.

It is a complicated change, and we must try to see its relation to a whole set of other changes which, through the eighteenth century, and then again in the generation of Cobbett and Jane Austen but in quite different ways, were bringing about a transformation of attitudes and feelings towards observed nature: new kinds of interest in landscape, a new self-consciousness of the picturesque, and beyond these and interacting with the more social observations, the new language, the new poetry, of Wordsworth and Clare.

Notes

1 *Tom Jones*; Bk. VI, ch. vii.
2 Ibid., Bk. VI, ch. iii.
3 Ibid.
4 Ibid., Bk. XVIII, ch. xiii.
5 *Clarissa*, Vol. I, Letters 13 and 17.
6 *Tom Jones*, Bk. VI, ch. vii.
7 *Annals of Agriculture*, XXVI, 214.
8 'The Agricultural Revolution in English History: a reconsideration', in *Essays in Agrarian History*, ed. Minchinton; Vol. 2; Newton Abbot, 1968.
9 *Opinions of William Cobbett*; ed. G. D. H. Cole; London, 1944; 86.
10 *Memoir of Thomas Bewick*; London, 1961; 27–8.
11 Ibid., 28 and 29.
12 Ibid., 32.
13 Cf. *Village Life in the 18th Century*, G. E. Fussell; Worcester, 1948; ch. ii.
14 *Joseph Ashby of Tysoe*; M. K. Ashby; Cambridge, 1961; ch. xix.
15 *Culture and Anarchy*, ch. iii.
16 *Rural Rides, op. cit.*, 13 and 15.
17 Ibid., 17 and 233.
18 Ibid., 207, 221, 34.
19 Ibid., 311, 313, 313–14.
20 Ibid., 65–6, 67.
21 Ibid., 313.
22 *Persuasion*, chs. i, iii, and v.
23 'Economic Functions of English Landowners in the 17th and 18th Centuries', in *Essays in Agrarian History*, ed. Minchinton; Vol. 1; Newton Abbot, 1968.
24 The Great Society, cit. Morton, *op. cit.*, 119; Stephen Duck; and cit. *The Making of the English Working Class*; E. P. Thompson; London, 1963; ch. vii.
25 In *Writings of Gilbert White of Selborne*; ed. H. J. Massingham; London, 1938; 63–4.
26 Ibid., 300–1.

CHAPTER 3

Witness Against the Beast

E. P. Thompson

E. P. Thompson was one of the major figures in English history writing during the last half of the twentieth century. His work, especially *The Making of the English Working Class* (1966), was notable for its engagement with the culture that shaped people's actions in the social and political arena. In this selection from his book *Witness Against the Beast* (1993), he brings his thorough knowledge of the social movements in English history in the seventeenth and eighteenth centuries to bear in a reading of William Blake's "London." He traces out philosophical roots for the words in the poem.

'London'

'London' is among the most lucid and instantly available of the *Songs of Experience*. 'The poem', John Beer writes, 'is perhaps the least controversial of all Blake's works', and 'no knowledge of his personal vision is necessary to assist the understanding'.[1] I agree with this: the poem does not require an interpreter since the images are self-sufficient within the terms of the poem's own development. Every reader can, without the help of a critic, see London simultaneously as Blake's own city, as an image of the state of English society and as an image of the human condition. So far from requiring a knowledge of Blake's personal vision it is one of those foundation poems upon which our knowledge of that vision can be built. A close reading may confirm, but is likely to add very little to, what a responsive reader had already experienced.

But since the poem is found in draft in Blake's notebook we are unusually well placed to examine it not only as product but in its process of creation. Here is the finished poem:

> I wander thro' each charter'd street,
> Near where the charter'd Thames does flow.
> And mark in every face I meet
> Marks of weakness, marks of woe.
>
> In every cry of every Man,
> In every Infants cry of fear,
> In every voice: in every ban,
> The mind-forg'd manacles I hear
>
> How the Chimney-sweepers cry
> Every blackning Church appalls,

> And the hapless Soldiers sigh,
> Runs in blood down Palace walls
>
> But most thro' midnight streets I hear
> How the youthful Harlots curse
> Blasts the new-born Infants tear
> And blights with plagues the Marriage hearse
>   (E 26–7)

In Blake's draft the first verse was originally thus:

> I wander thro each dirty street
> Near where the dirty Thames does flow
> And see in every face I meet
> Marks of weakness marks of woe[2]

The first important change is from 'dirty' to 'charter'd'. Another fragment in the notebook helps to define this alteration:

> Why should I care for the men of thames
> Or the cheating waves of charter'd streams
> Or shrink at the little blasts of fear
> That the hireling blows into my ear
>
> Tho born on the cheating banks of Thames
> Tho his waters bathed my infant limbs
> The Ohio shall wash his stains from me
> I was born a slave but I go to be free[3]

Thus 'charter'd' arose in Blake's mind in association with 'cheating' and with the 'little blasts of fear' of the 'hireling'. The second association is an obvious political allusion. To reformers the corrupt political system was a refuge for hirelings: indeed, Dr Johnson had defined in his dictionary a 'pension' as 'In England it is generally understood to mean pay given to a state hireling for treason to his country.' David Erdman is undoubtedly right that the 'little blasts of fear' suggest the proclamations, the Paine-burnings and the political repressions of the State and of Reeves' Association for Preserving Liberty and Property against Republicans and Levellers which dominated the year in which these poems were written.[4] In the revised version of 'Thames' Blake introduces the paradox which was continually to be in the mouths of radicals and factory reformers in the next fifty years: the slavery of the English poor. And he points also ('I was born a slave but I go to be free') to the first wave of emigration of reformers from the attention of Church-and-King mobs or hirelings.

But 'charter'd' is more particularly associated with 'cheating'. It is clearly a word to be associated with commerce: one might think of the Chartered Companies which, increasingly drained of function, were bastions of privilege within the government of the city. Or, again, one might think of the monopolistic privileges of the East India Company, whose ships were so prominent in the commerce of the Thames, which applied in 1793 for twenty-years' renewal of its charter, and which was under bitter attack in the reformers' press.[5]

But 'charter'd' is, for Blake, a stronger and more complex word than that, which he endows with more generalised symbolic power. It has the feel of a word which Blake has recently discovered, as, years later, he was to 'discover' the word 'golden' (which, nevertheless, he had been using for years). He is savouring it, weighing its poetic possibilities in his hand. It is in no sense a 'new' word, but he has found a way to use it with a new ironic inversion. For the word is standing at an intellectual and political crossroads. On the one hand, it was a stale counter of the customary libertarian rhetoric of the polite culture. Blake himself had used it in much this way in his early 'King Edward the Third':

> Let Liberty, the charter'd right of Englishmen,
> Won by our fathers in many a glorious field,
> Enerve my soldiers; let Liberty
> Blaze in each countenance, and fire the battle.
> The enemy fight in chains, invisible chains, but heavy;
> Their minds are fetter'd; then how can they be free?[6]

It would be only boring to accumulate endless examples from eighteenth-century constitutional rhetoric or poetry of the use of chartered rights, chartered liberties, magna carta: the word is at the centre of Whig ideology.

There is, however, an obvious point to be made about this tedious usage of 'charter'. A charter of liberty is, simultaneously, a denial of these liberties to others. A charter is something given or ceded; it is bestowed upon some group by some authority; it is not claimed as of right. And the liberties (or privileges) granted to this guild, company, corporation or even nation *exclude* others from the enjoyment of these liberties. A charter is, in its nature, exclusive.

We are at a crossroads because it is exactly this exclusive and granted quality of liberties which was under challenge; and it was under challenge from the claim to universal rights. The point becomes clear when we contrast Burke's *Reflections* and Paine's *Rights of Man*. Although Burke was every inch a rhetorician he had no taste for stale rhetoric, and he used the word 'charter' lightly in the *Reflections*. 'Our oldest reformation', he wrote, 'is that of Magna Charta':

> From Magna Charta to the Declaration of Right it has been the uniform policy of our constitution to claim and assert our liberties as an *entailed inheritance* derived to us from our forefathers, and to be transmitted to our posterity . . .
>
> We have an inheritable crown, an inheritable peerage, and a House of Commons and a people inheriting privileges, franchises, and liberties from a long line of ancestors.

Burke was concerned explicitly to define this chartered, heritable set of liberties and privileges (exclusive in the sense that it is 'an estate specially belonging to the people of this kingdom') as against any general uncircumscribed notion of 'the rights of man'. It is in vain, he wrote, to talk to these democratists:

> of the practice of their ancestors, the fundamental laws of their country . . . They have wrought underground a mine that will blow up, at one grand explosion, all examples of antiquity, all precedents, charters, and acts of parliament. They have 'the rights of men'. Against these there can be no prescription . . .

Liberty, for Burke, must have its 'gallery of portraits, its monumental inscriptions, its records, evidences, and titles'. The imagery, as so often, is that of the great house of the landed gentry, with its walks and statuary, its galleries and muniments' room.

For Burke, then, 'charter' and 'charter'd', while not over-laboured, remain among the best of good words. But not for Paine: 'I am contending for the rights of the *living*, and against their being willed away, and controuled and contracted for, by the manuscript assumed authority of the dead.' A charter implied not a freedom but monopoly: 'Every chartered town is an aristocratical monopoly in itself, and the qualifications of electors proceeds out of those chartered monopolies. Is this freedom? Is this what Mr Burke means by a constitution?' It was in the incorporated towns, with their charters, that the Test and Corporation Acts against Dissenters operated with most effect. Hence (Paine argued – and economic historians have often agreed with him) the vitality of the commerce of un-incorporated towns like Manchester, Birmingham and Sheffield. The Dissenters (he wrote), 'withdrew from the persecution of the chartered towns, where test laws more particularly operate, and established a sort of asylum for themselves in those places ... But the case is now changing. France and America bid all comers welcome, and initiate them into all the rights of citizenship.'

This is (for Paine) the first offence of 'chartered': it implies exclusion and limitation. Its second offence was in its imputation that anyone had the right to *grant* freedoms or privileges to other men: 'If we begin with William of Normandy, we find that the government of England was originally a tyranny, founded on an invasion and conquest of the country ... Magna Carta ... was no more than compelling the government to renounce a part of its assumptions.' Both these offences were criticised in a central passage which I argue lay somewhere in Blake's mind when he selected the word:

> It is a perversion of terms to say that a charter gives rights. It operates by a contrary effect – that of taking rights away. Rights are inherently in all the inhabitants; but charters, by annulling those rights in the majority, leave the right, by exclusion, in the hands of a few ... The only persons on whom they operate are the persons whom they exclude ... Therefore, all charters have no other than an indirect negative operation.

Charters, he continued, 'are sources of endless contentions in the places where they exist, and they lessen the common rights of national society'. The charters of corporate towns might, he suggested, have arisen because of garrison service: 'Their refusing or granting admission to strangers, which has produced the custom of *giving, selling and buying freedom*, has more of the nature of garrison authority than civil government' (my emphasis).

Blake by now had come to share much of Paine's political outlook, although he did not share his faith in the beneficence of commerce. He thus chose 'charter'd' out of the biggest political argument that was agitating Britain in 1791–3, and he chose it with that irony which inverted the rhetoric of Burke and asserted the definitions of 'exclusion', the annulling of rights, 'negative operation' and 'giving, selling and buying freedom'. The adjectival form – charter'd – enforces the direct commercial allusion: 'the organisation of a city in terms of trade'.[7]

The other emendation to the first verse is trivial: in the third line 'And see in every face I meet' is altered to 'And mark ... ' And yet, is it as trivial as it seems? For we already have, in the fourth line, 'Marks of weakness marks of woe'. Thus Blake has chosen, with deliberation, the triple beat of 'mark'. And we respond to this, whether we are conscious of the nature of the response or whether the words beat upon us in subliminal ways: even in these biblically illiterate days we have all heard of 'the mark of the Beast'. Some of Blake's central images – his trees, and clouds, and caves, and serpents, and roots – have such a universal presence in mythology and literature that one may spend half a lifetime in the game of hunt-the-source. And sometimes the hunting is fruitful, provided that we remember always that the source (or its echo in Blake's mind) is not the same thing as what he makes of it in his own art. Miss Kathleen Raine, a Diana among hunters, has found this:

The opening lines of *London* suggest very strongly Vergil's account of the damned in Hades:

> Nor Death itself can wholly wash their Stains;
> But long-contracted Filth ev'n in the Soul remains.
> The Reliques of inveterate Vice they wear;
> And spots of Sin obscene in ev'ry Face appear.[8]

The suggestion need not be excluded; this echo, with others, could have been in Blake's mind. But if so, *what does Blake do with it?* For Blake's poem evokes pity and forgiveness – the cries, the 'hapless Soldiers sigh', 'weakness' and 'woe' – and not the self-righteous eviction to Hades of 'long-contracted Filth', 'inveterate Vice' and 'spots of Sin obscene'. Moreover, in the amendment from 'And see' to 'And mark', Blake (or the speaker of his poem) closes the gap between the censorious observer and the faces which are observed, assimilating both within a common predicament: the marker himself appears to be marked or even to be mark*ing*.[9]

But 'mark' undoubtedly came through to the reader with a much stronger, biblical resonance. The immediate allusion called to mind will most probably have been 'the mark of the Beast', as in Revelation xiii.16–17:

> And he causeth all, both small and great, rich and poor, free and bond, to receive a mark in their right hand, or in their foreheads:
> And that no man might buy or sell, save he that had the mark, or the name of the Beast, or the number of his name.

The mark of the Beast would seem, like 'charter'd', to have something to do with the buying and selling of human values.

This question is incapable of any final proof. The suggestion has been made[10] that Blake's allusion is not to Revelation but to Ezekiel ix.4: 'And the Lord said unto him, Go through the midst of the city, through the midst of Jerusalem, and set a mark upon the foreheads of the men that sigh and that cry for all the abominations that be done in the midst thereof.' The man who is ordered to go through the city has 'a writer's inkhorn by his side'. This seems at first to fit the poem closely: in 'London' a writer goes through the city of abominations and listens to 'sighs' and 'cries'. But even a literal reading does not fit the poem's meaning. For Blake – or the 'I' of his poem – is not setting marks on foreheads, he is observing them; and the marks are those of weakness and of woe, not of lamentations over abominations. Moreover, in Ezekiel's vision the Lord then orders armed men to go through the city and to 'slay utterly old and young, both maids and little children, and women: but come not near any man upon whom is the mark...' Thus those who are marked are set apart and saved. Neither the intention nor the tone of Blake's poem coincides with Ezekiel's unedifying vision. Nor are we entitled to conflate the allusions to Revelation and to Ezekiel with some gesture towards an ulterior 'ambivalence' in which Blake has assimilated the damned to the elect. For if one point is incontestable about this poem it is that *every* man is marked: *all* share this human condition: whereas with Ezekiel it is the great *un*marked majority who are to be put to the sword. Such a conflation offers temptations to a critic but it would destroy the poem by introducing into its heart a direct contradiction of intention and of feeling. Ambiguities of this dimension are not fruitful multipliers of meaning.

There is, further, the question of what response the word 'mark' is most likely to have called up among Blake's contemporaries. I must assert that the allusions called first to mind will have been either to the 'mark of Cain' (Genesis iv.15)[11] or to the 'mark of the Beast' in Revelation. And the more radical the audience, the more preoccupied it will have been with the second. For generations radical Dissent had sermonised and pamphleteered against the Beast (Antichrist) who has had servitors 'which worshipped his image' (Revelation xvi.2): social radicalism equated these with usurers, with the rich, with those successful in buying and selling. And interpreters of Revelation always fastened with fascination upon the enigmatic verse (xiii.18): 'Let him that hath understanding count the number of the Beast: for it is the number of a man.' Such interest in millennial interpretation became rife once more in the 1790s;[12] it turned above all on these chapters of Revelation with their recurrent images of the Beast and of the destruction of Babylon, and the humble were able to turn to their own account the imprecations against kings, false prophets and the rich with which these chapters are rife. We hardly need to argue that Blake, like most radical Dissenters of his time, had saturated his imagination with the imagery of Revelation: chapter xiv (the Son of Man with the sickle, and the Last Vintage) is implanted in the structure of *Vala* and of *Jerusalem*.

These considerations, which are ones of cultural context rather than of superficial verbal similarities, lead me to reject the suggested allusion to Ezekiel. What Blake's contemporaries were arguing about in the 1790s was the rule of Antichrist and the hope of the millennium: the mark seen in 'every face' is the mark of the Beast, a mark explicitly associated with commercialism. And if we require conclusive evidence that Blake was thinking, in 'London', of Revelation, he has given us this evidence himself, with unusual explicitness. For the illumination to the poem appears to be an independent, but complementary, conception; and for this reason I feel entitled to discuss the poem also as an independent conception and within its own terms. The illumination (if I am pressed to confess my own view) adds nothing essential to the poem, but comments upon the same theme in different terms. Nor are we even certain how the poem and the illumination are united, nor why they complement each other, until we turn to *Jerusalem*, Book 4 (E 241):

> I see London blind & age-bent begging thro the Streets
> Of Babylon, led by child, his tears run down his beard

In both the poem and the illumination, London's streets appear as those of Babylon of Revelation; but in the illumination it is London himself who is wandering through them.[13]

  In the second verse the important change is from 'german forg'd links' to 'mind-forg'd manacles'. The reference was, of course, to the Hanoverian monarchy, and perhaps to the expectation that Hanoverian troops would be used against British reformers.[14] The change to 'mind-forg'd' both generalises and also places us again in that universe of Blakean symbolism in which we must turn from one poem to another for cumulative elucidation. In this case we have already noted that the image of the mind as 'fettered' by the invisible chains of its own unfreedom had appealed to Blake in his youthful 'King Edward the Third'. The development of the image is shown in another fragment in the notebook, 'How to know Love from Deceit':

> Love to faults is always blind
> Always is to joy inclind
> Lawless wingd & unconfind
> And breaks all chains from every mind
> Deceit to secresy confind
> Lawful cautious & refind
> To every thing but interest blind
> And forges fetters for the mind

The 'mind-forg'd manacles', then, are those of deceit, self-interest, absence of love, of law, repression and hypocrisy.[15] They are stronger and harder to break than the manacles of the German king and his mercenaries, since they bind the minds not only of the oppressors but also of the oppressed; moreover, they are self-forged. How then are we to read 'ban'? F. W. Bateson, a confident critic, tells us 'in every execration or curse (*not* in every prohibition)'.[16] I can't share his confidence: one must be prepared for seventeen types of ambiguity in Blake, and, in any case, the distinction between a curse and a prohibition is not a large one. The 'bans' may be execrations, but the mind may be encouraged to move through further associations, from the banns before marriage, the prohibitive and possessive ethic constraining 'lawless' love ('"Thou Shalt Not" writ over the door'), to the bans of Church and State against the publications and activities of the followers of Tom Paine.[17] All these associations are gathered into the central one of a code of morality which constricts, denies, prohibits and punishes.

  The third verse commenced in the notebook as:

> But most the chimney sweepers cry
> Blackens oer the churches walls

This second line was then changed to:

> Every blackning church appalls

The effect is one of concentration. Pertinacious critics have been able to invert most of Blake's meanings, and readers have even been found to suppose that these two lines (in their final form) are a comment upon the awakening social conscience of the churches under the influence of the evangelical revival: the churches are appalled by the plight of the chimney-sweeping boys.[18] The meaning, of course, is the opposite; and on this point the notebook entitles us to have confidence. In the first version the churches are clearly shown as passive, while the cry of the chimney-sweepers attaches itself, with the smoke of commerce, to their walls. By revising the line Blake has simply tightened up the strings of his indignation by another notch. He has packed the meaning of 'The Chimney Sweeper' of the *Songs of Experience* (whose father and mother 'are both gone up to the church' to 'praise God & his Priest & King,/ Who make up a heaven of our misery') into a single line, the adjective 'blackning' visually attaching to the Church complicity in the brutal exploitation of young childhood along with the wider consequences of the smoke of expanding commerce. 'Appalls' is used in a transitive sense familiar in Blake's time – not as 'is appalled by' but as puts to shame, puts in fear, challenges, indicts, in the same way as the dying sigh of the soldier indicts (and also threatens, with an apocalyptic image)[19] the Palace.[20] 'An ancient Proverb' in the notebook gives the three elements of a curse upon England:

> Remove away that blackning church
> Remove away that marriage hearse
> Remove away that [place: *del.*] man of blood
> You'll quite remove the ancient curse.[21]

Church, marriage and monarchy: but if he had left it at 'place', then it could have been Tyburn (or Newgate), the place of public execution – the altar of the 'Moral & Self-Righteous Law' of Babylon and Cruel Og, in the centre of London, whose public rituals Blake may have witnessed.

The poem, in its first version, was to end at this point, at 'Runs in blood down Palace walls'. But Blake was not yet satisfied: he returned, and worked through three versions of a fourth, concluding verse, squeezing it in between other drafts already on the page. One attempt reads:

> But most thro wintry streets I hear
> How the midnight harlots curse
> Blasts the new born infants tear
> And smites with plagues the marriage hearse.

Bateson tells us that 'the images are sometimes interpreted as a reference to venereal disease. But this is to read Blake too literally. The diseases that descend upon the infant and the newly married couple are apocalyptic horrors similar to the blood that runs down the palace walls.'[22]

It may be nice to think so. But the blood of the soldier is for real, as well as apocalyptic, and so is the venereal disease that blinds the new-born infant and which plagues the marriage hearse. We need not go outside the poem to document the increased discussion of such disease in the early 1790s,[23] nor, to turn the coin over, the indictment by Mary Wollstonecraft and her circle of marriage without love as prostitution. The poem makes the point very literally. Blake was often a very literal-minded man.

Another fragment in the notebook is closely related to this conclusion: a verse intended as the conclusion to 'The Human Abstract' (or so it would seem) but not used in its final version. It does not, in fact, relate directly to the imagery of 'The Human Abstract' and we may suppose that Blake, when he realised this, saw also how he could transpose the concept to make a conclusion to 'London':

> There souls of men are bought & sold
> And milk fed infancy for gold

> And youth to slaughter houses led
> And [maidens: *del.*] beauty for a bit of bread.[24]

This enables us to see, once more, that 'London' is a literal poem and it is also an apocalyptic one; or we may say that it is a poem whose moral realism is so searching that it is raised to the intensity of apocalyptic vision. For the poem is not, of course, a terrible cumulative *catalogue* of unrelated abuses and suffering. It is organised in two ways. First, and most simply, it is organised about the street-cries of London. In the first verse, we are placed with Blake (if we are entitled – as I think we are – to take him as the wandering observer) and we 'see' with his eyes. But in the second, third and fourth verses we are *hearing*, and the passage from sight to sound has an effect of reducing the sense of distance or of the alienation of the observer from his object of the first verse, and of immersing us within the human condition through which he walks. We *see* one thing at a time, as distinct moments of perception, although, by the end of the first verse, these perceptions become cumulative and repetitive ('in every face...marks...marks'). We *hear* many things simultaneously. Literally, we hear the eerie, almost animal cadence of the street-cries (and although we may now be forgetting them, if we were to be transported somehow to eight-eenth-century London, these cries would be our first and most astonishing impres-sion), the cries of the children, the 'weep', 'weep' of the chimney-sweeps, and, led on by these, we hear the more symbolic sounds of 'bans', 'manacles' and the soldier's 'sigh'. This second verse is all sounds and it moves through an acceleration of generalisation towards the third. If 'charter'd' is repeated, and if 'marks' falls with a triple beat, 'every' falls upon us no less than seven times: a single incidence in the first verse prepares for five uses in the second and a single incidence in the third ties it into the developing structure. 'Cry' also falls three times, carrying us from the second verse to the first line of the third. But in the third verse there is a thickening of sensual perception. Until this point we have seen and heard, but now we 'sense', through the sounds (the 'cry' and the 'sigh'), the activities that these indicate: the efforts of the chimney-sweep, the blackening walls of the churches, the blood of the soldier. We are not detached from this predicament; if anything, this impression of 'hearing' giving way to 'sensing' immerses us even more deeply within it.

We have been wandering, with Blake, into an ever more dense immersion. But the opening of the fourth verse ('But most thro' midnight streets I hear') appears to set us a little apart from this once more. 'I hear' takes us back from ourselves to Blake who is a little apart from the scene and listening. Nothing in the earlier verses had prepared us for the darkness of 'midnight streets', unless perhaps the 'blackning Church': what had been suggested before was the activity of the day-time streets, the street-cries, the occasions of commerce. The verse is not knitted in tidily to the rest at the level of literal organisation: the 'Marriage hearse' is a conceit more abstract than any other in the poem, apart from 'mind-forg'd manacles'. Since we know that he had intended at first to end the poem with three verses,[25] should we say that the final verse was an afterthought tacked on after the original images had ceased to beat in his mind – imperfectly soldered to the main body and still betraying signs of a separate origin?

It is a fair question. Blake, like other poets, had afterthoughts and made revisions which were unwise. And if we were to stop short at this literal or technical organisa-tion of the poem we could make a case against its final verse. But we must attend also to a second, symbolic, level of organisation. The immersion in sights and sounds is of a kind which forces one to generalise from London to 'the human condition'. The point is self-evident ('In every cry of every Man'). But this kind of statement, of which a certain school of commentators on Blake is over-fond, takes us only a little way, and a great deal less far than is sometimes knowingly implied. For 'the human condition', unless further qualified or disclosed, is nothing but a kind of metaphysical full stop. Or, worse than that, it is a bundle of solecisms about mortality and defeated aspiration. But 'the human condition' is what poets make poetry *out of*, not what they end up with. This poem is about a *particular* human condition, which acquires, through the selection of the simplest and most archetypal examples (man, infant, soldier, palace, harlot), a generalised resonance; it expresses an attitude *towards* that condition; and it offers a unitary analysis as to its character.

Two comments may be made on the attitude disclosed by Blake towards his own material. First, it is often noted that 'London' is one of the *Songs of Experience* which carries 'the voice of honest indignation'. This is true. The voice can be heard from the first 'charter'd'; it rises to full strength in the third and final verses (appalls, runs in blood, blasts, blights). But it is equally true that this voice is held in equilibrium with the voice of compassion. This is clear from the first introduction of 'mark'. If we have here (and the triple insistence enforces conviction) the 'mark of the Beast', Blake would have been entitled to pour down upon these worshippers at the shrine of false gods the full vials of his wrath:

> And there followed another angel, saying, Babylon is fallen, is fallen, that great city, because she made all nations drink of the wine of the wrath of her fornication.
> And the third angel followed them, saying with a loud voice, If any man worship the beast and his image, and receive his mark in his forehead, or in his hand,
> The same shall drink of the wine of the wrath of God, which is poured out without mixture into the cup of his indignation; and he shall be tormented with fire and brimstone in the presence of the holy angels, and in the presence of the Lamb:
> And the smoke of their torment ascendeth up for ever and ever: and they have no rest day nor night, who worship the Beast and his image, and whosoever receiveth the mark of his name.[26]

But Blake indicates 'weakness' and 'woe', and the slow rhythm of the line, checked at mid-point, suggests contemplation and pity rather than wrath. Nor is this note of grave compassion ever lost: it continues in the cries, the fear, the tear: even the soldier is 'hapless'. If 'London' is that part of that human condition which may be equally described as 'Hell', it is not a hell to which only the damned are confined, while the saved may contemplate their torments; nor is this Vergil's 'Hades'. This is a city of Everyman; nor do we feel, in our increasing immersion, that we – or Blake himself – are observers from without. These are not so much our fellow-damned as our fellow-sufferers.

The second comment upon Blake's attitude is this: his treatment of the city departs from a strong literary convention. To establish this point fully would take us further outside the poem than I mean to go. But one way of handling the city, both in itself and as an exemplar of the human condition, derived from classical (especially Juvenalian) satire; and in this it is the city's turbulence, its theatre of changing human passions, its fractured, accidental and episodic life, its swift succession of discrete images of human vice, guile or helplessness, which provided the staple of the convention. Samuel Johnson's 'London' was the place where at one corner a 'fell attorney prowls for prey' and at the next a 'female atheist talks you dead'. And the convention was, in some part, a countryman's convention, in some part a class convention – generally both: a country gentleman's convention. From whichever aspect, plebeian London was seen from outside as a spectacle. Wordsworth was still able to draw upon this convention – although with significant shifts of emphasis – in *The Prelude*.[27]

Blake's 'London' is not seen from without as spectacle. It is seen, or suffered, from within, by a Londoner. And what is unusual about *this* image of the-human-condition-as-hell is that it offers the city as a unitary experience and not as a theatre of discrete episodes. For this to be so, there must be an ulterior symbolic organisation behind the literal organisation of this street-cry following upon that. And this symbolic organisation should now, after this lengthy discussion, have become fully disclosed. The tone of compassion falls upon those who are in hell, the sufferers; but the tone of indignation falls upon the institutions of repression – mind-forg'd manacles, blackning Church, Palace, Marriage hearse. And the symbolic organisation is within the clearly conceived and developing logic of market relations. Blake does not only list symptoms: within the developing imagery which unites the poem he also discloses their cause. From the first introduction of 'charter'd' he never loses hold of the image of buying and selling although these words themselves are never used. 'Charter'd' both grants from on high and licenses and it limits and excludes; if we recall Paine it is a 'selling and buying' of freedom. What are bought and sold in 'London' are not only goods and services but human values, affections and vitalities. From freedom we move (with 'mark') to a race marked by buying and selling, the worshippers of the Beast and his image. Then we move through these values in ascendant scale: goods are bought and sold (street-cries), childhood (the chimney-sweep), human life (the soldier) and, in the final verse, youth, beauty and love, the source of life, is bought and sold in the figure of the diseased harlot who, herself, is only the other side of the 'Marriage hearse'.[28] In a series of literal, unified images of great power Blake compresses an indictment of the acquisitive ethic, endorsed by the institutions of State, which divides man from man, brings him into mental and moral bondage, destroys the sources of joy and brings, as its consequence, blindness and death.

It is now evident why the final verse is no afterthought but appeared to Blake as the necessary conclusion to the poem. The fragment left over from 'The Human Abstract'

> There souls of men are bought & sold
> And milk fed infancy for gold
> And youth to slaughter houses led
> And beauty for a bit of bread

is a synopsis of the argument in 'London'. As it stands it remains as an argument, a series of assertions which would only persuade those already persuaded. But it provided, in its last line, the image of the harlot, whose love is bought and sold, which was necessary to complete 'London' and make that poem 'shut like a box'. And the harlot not only provides a culminating symbol of the reification of values, she is also a point of junction with the parallel imagery of religious mystification and oppression: for if this is Babylon, then the harlot is Babylon's whore who brought about the city's fall 'because she made all nations drink of the wine of the wrath of her fornication'. For English radical Dissent in the eighteenth century, the whore of Babylon was not only the 'scarlet woman' of Rome, but also *all* Erastianism, all compromise between things spiritual and the temporal powers of the State, and hence, very specifically, that extraordinary Erastian formation, the Church of England. One recalls Blake's annotations to Bishop Watson (throughout), and his polemic against 'The Abomination that maketh desolate. i.e. State Religion which is the Source of all Cruelty' (E607). Hence the harlot is able to unite in a single nexus the imagery of market relations and the imagery of ideological domination by the agency of a State Church, prostituted to the occasions of temporal power.

To tie the poem up in this way was, perhaps, to add to its pessimism. To end with the blood on the Palace walls might suggest an apocalyptic consummation, a revolutionary overthrow. To end with the diseased infant is to implant life within a cycle of defeat. And yet the poem doesn't *sound* defeated, in part because the tone of compassion or of indignation offers a challenge to the logic of its 'argument',[29] in part because the logic of the symbolic analysis of market relations proposes, at the same time, if not an alternative, at least the challenge that (in compassion and in indignation) this alternative could be found.

In any case, these pages of mine have been teasing out meanings from one poem of sixteen lines. And Blake's larger meanings lie in groupings of poems, in contraries and in cumulative insights into differing states. 'London' is not about the human condition but about a particular condition or state, and a way of seeing this. This state must be set against other states, both of experience and of innocence. Thus we must place 'London' alongside 'The Human Abstract', which shows the generation of the prohibitive Tree of Mystery, whose fruit continually regenerates man's Fall: and in this conjunction 'London' (when seen as hell) shows the condition of the Fallen who lie within the empire of property, self-interest, State religion and Mystery. And when the poem is replaced within the context of the *Songs* it is easier to see the fraternal but transformed relationship which Blake's thought at this time bears to Painite radicalism and to the deist and rationalist critique of orthodox religion. 'London' is informed throughout by the antinomian contempt for the Moral Law and the institutions of State, including monarchy and marriage, just as are 'The Garden of Love' and 'The Chimney Sweeper'. With great emphasis it is coming to conclusions very close to those of Paine and his circle. A conjunction between the old antinomian tradition and Jacobinism is taking place.

But while Blake is accepting a part of the Painite argument he is also turning it to a new account. For while 'London' is a poem which a Jacobinical Londoner might have responded to and accepted, it is scarcely one which he could have written. The average supporter of the London Corresponding Society would not have written 'mind-forg'd' (since the manacles would have been seen as wholly exterior, imposed by oppressive priestcraft and kingcraft); and the voice of indignation would probably have drowned the voice of compassion, since most Painites would have found it difficult to accept Blake's vision of humankind as being simultaneously oppressed (although by very much the same forces as those described by Paine) and in a self-victimised or Fallen state. One might seem to contradict the other. And behind this would lie ulterior differences both as to the 'cause' of this human condition and also as to its 'remedy'.

For Blake had always been decisively alienated from the mechanical materialist epistemology and psychology which he saw as derived from Newton and Locke. And he did not for a moment shed his suspicion of radicalism's indebtedness to this materialism, with its prime explanatory principle of self-love. We shall return to this. So that if Blake found congenial the Painite denunciation of the repressive institutions of State and Church, it did not follow that humanity's redemption from this state could be effected by a political reorganisation of these institutions alone. There must be some utopian leap, some human rebirth, from Mystery to renewed imaginative life. 'London' must still be made over anew as the New Jerusalem. And we can't take a full view of even this poem without recalling that Blake did not always see London in this way; it was not always to be seen as Babylon or as the city of destruction in the Apocalypse. There were other times when he saw it as the city of lost innocence:

> The fields from Islington to Marybone,
> To Primrose Hill and Saint Johns Wood:
> Were builded over with pillars of gold,
> And there Jerusalems pillars stood.

> The Jews-harp-house & the Green Man;
> The Ponds where Boys to bathe delight;
> The Fields of Cows by Willans farm:
> Shine in Jerusalems pleasant sight.

And it could also be the millennial city, of that time when the moral and self-righteous law should be overthrown, and the Multitude return to Unity:

> In my Exchanges every Land
> Shall walk, & mine in every Land,
> Mutual shall build Jerusalem:
> Both heart in heart & hand in hand.

> (E 170, 172)

Notes

1 John Beer, *Blake's Humanism* (Manchester, 1968), p. 75.
2 *The Notebook of William Blake*, ed. David V. Erdman (Oxford, 1973), p. 109; hereafter cited as N.
3 N113. The obliterated title of this fragment has been recovered by David Erdman as 'Thames'.
4 See David Erdman, *Blake: Prophet against Empire*, which fully argues these points on pp. 272–9. These poems were 'forged in the heat of the Year One of Equality (September 1792 to 1793) and tempered in the "grey-brow'd snows" of Antijacobin alarms and proclamations'. See also A. Mitchell, 'The Association Movement of 1792–3', *Historical Journal*, 4: 1 (1961), 56–77; E. P. Thompson, *The Making of the English Working Class* (Harmondsworth, 1968), pp. 115–26; D. E. Ginter, 'The Loyalist Association Movement. 1792–3', *Historical Journal*, 4: 2 (1966), 179–90.
5 'The cheating waves of charter'd streams' and 'the cheating banks of Thames' should prompt one to think carefully of this as the source which first gave to Blake this use of 'charter'd'. The fullest attack from a Painite source on the East India Company did not appear until 1794: see the editorial articles in four successive numbers of Daniel Isaac Eaton's *Politics for the People*, 2: 8–11: 'The East India Charter Considered'. These constituted a full-blooded attack on the Company's commercial and military imperialism ('if it be deemed expedient to *murder* half the inhabitants of India, and *rob* the remainder, surely it is not requisite to call it *governing* them?') which carried to their furthest point criticisms of the Company to be found in the reforming and Foxite press of 1792–3. No social historian can be surprised to find the banks of the

Thames described as 'cheating' in the eighteenth century: every kind of fraud and racket, big, small and indifferent, flourished around the docks. The association of the banks of Thames with commerce was already traditional when Samuel Johnson renewed it in his 'London' (1738), especially lines 20–30. Johnson's attitude is already ambiguous: 'Britannia's glories' ('The guard of commerce, and the dread of Spain') are invoked retrospectively in conventional terms: but on Thames-side already 'all are slaves to gold, / Where looks are merchandise, and smiles are sold'. Erdman argues that the 'golden London' and 'silver Thames' of Blake's 'King Edward the Third' have already assimilated this conventional contrast in the form of irony: see Erdman, pp. 80–1.

6   E415. If we take the intention of this fragment to be ironic, then Blake was already regarding the word as suspect rhetoric.

7   Raymond Williams, *The Country and the City* (1973), p. 148.

8   Kathleen Raine, vol. 1, pp. 24–5 (citing Dryden's *Aeneid* VI. 998–1001).

9   Heather Glen has noted that 'the sense of an inevitable and imprisoning relationship between the "facts" he sees and the way in which he sees is reinforced by the use of "mark" as both verb and object'. See 'The Poet in Society: Blake and Wordsworth on London', *Literature and History* 3 (March 1976).

10 Among others, by Harold Bloom and David Erdman, and, with a different emphasis, by Heather Glen.

11 This suggestion has been pressed by Stan Smith, 'Some Responses to Heather Glen's "The Poet in Society"', *Literature and History* 4 (Autumn 1976). The 'mark of Cain' in Genesis was sometimes assimilated in theological exegesis to the mark of the Beast. The Lord curses Cain and condemns him to be a fugitive and a vagabond. Cain complains that he will be killed as an outlaw, and the Lord replies: 'Whosoever slayeth Cain, vengeance shall be taken on him seven-fold. And the Lord set a mark upon Cain, lest any finding him should kill him.' Whether the Lord did this as an act of forgiveness or as a protraction of the punishment of ostracism and outlawry (as anthropologists would argue) is a matter of interpretation. Stan Smith certainly carries the Lord's intentions very much too far when he takes the mark as a sign of 'election'. But he is surely right to argue that the poem can carry *this* ambivalence (men are 'both agents and patients, culprits and victims'), since in Blake's Christian dialectic the mark of Cain could stand simultaneously as a sign of sin and as a sign of its forgiveness. See Blake's chapter title to the 'Genesis' fragment: 'Chapter IV How Generation & Death took possession of the Natural Man & of the Forgiveness of Sins written upon the Murderers Forehead' (E667).

12 See, e.g., Thompson, pp. 127–9, 420–6, and sources cited there; and Morton D. Paley, 'William Blake, the Prince of the Hebrews, and the Women Clothed with the Sun', in Morton D. Paley and Michael Phillips (eds.), *William Blake: Essays in Honour of Sir Geoffrey Keynes* (Oxford, 1973). Swedenborgians were much concerned with interpretation of Revelation; and the verses which I have cited ('no man might buy or sell, save he that had the mark . . . of the beast') were discussed in the *New Magazine of Knowledge Concerning Heaven and Hell*, 1 (July 1790), 209–11. When Blake's acquaintance Stedman heard the news, on 6 April 1792, that Gustavus III, the King of Sweden, had been assassinated, his mind turned in the same direction: 'despotism dies away. Witness France, whose King may be compared to the beast in Revelation, whose number is 666, and LUDOVICUS added together makes the same. One, Sutherland, lately shot himself before King George . . . Such are the times': *The Journal of John Gabriel Stedman 1744–1797*, ed. Stanbury Thompson (1962), pp. 340–1; I am indebted to Michael Phillips for this reference.

13 One further suggestion may be offered about the mark of the Beast. The Muggletonians afford yet one more possible resonance of 'mark'. In Swedenborgian exegesis the 'mark of the Beast' was sometimes taken to signify the solifidian doctrine of justification by faith without works. But Blake can scarcely have been using 'mark' in this way, since this was precisely his own, antinomian, 'heresy'. The Muggletonians, however, offer a very different interpretation. In their meetings prayer was rejected, as a 'mark of weakness', and Muggleton wrote:

The mark of the beast is this, when a head magistrate or chief council in a nation or kingdom, shall set up . . . a set form of worship, he or they having no commission from God so to do, and shall cause the people by their power and authority...to worship after this manner of worship that is set up by authority, as this beast did...

Hence to receive the mark of the Beast signifies 'to worship the image set up' by established authority. L. Muggleton, *A True Interpretation of...the Whole Book of the Revelation of St John* (1808), pp. 174–5. This appears to take us very much closer to the universe of Blakean symbolism than do the Swedenborgian glosses.

14 See Erdman, pp. 277–8.

15 Blake was also thinking of priestcraft, as we know from 'The Human Abstract'. Nancy Bogen suggests (*Notes and Queries*, new series, 15: 1 (January 1968)) that he may have been reading Gilbert Imlay's *Topographical Description* (London, 1792): on the Ohio (where the Thames-born slave will go to be free) Imlay found freedom from priestcraft which elsewhere 'seems to have forged fetters for the human mind'. But the poem itself carries this suggestion only in so far as the manacles immediately precede the 'blackning Church'. Fetters and manacles were anyway part of a very general currency of imagery: see, e.g., Erdman, p. 129, n. 35.

16 F. W. Bateson, *Selected Poems of William Blake* (1957), p. 126.

17 See E. D. Hirsch, *Innocence and Experience* (New Haven, 1964), p. 264.

18 For an example of this confusion, see D. G. Gillham, *Blake's Contrary States* (Cambridge, 1966), p. 12: 'The Church is horrified at the evil of the sweeper's condition, but it is helpless to do much about it...'

19 On this point, see Erdman, pp. 278–9. The British reformers of the 1790s were, of course, at pains to stress the identity of interests of the soldiers and the people: and also to expose military injustices, flogging, forcible recruitment ('crimping'), etc.

20 Many examples could be given of this transitive use of 'appal': see also the *OED* and the last line of 'Holy Thursday' in *Experience*. Thus William Frend, who shared something of Blake's ultra-radical Christian values, wrote: 'Oh! that I had the warning voice of an ancient prophet, that I might penetrate into the innermost recesses of palaces, and appal the haranguers of senates!' Frend's 'appal' means 'throw into consternation', 'warn', 'shock'. The phrase was used in the appendix to William Frend, *Peace and Union Recommended* (St Ives, 1792): this pamphlet occasioned the celebrated case of Frend's trial before the Vice-Chancellor and his expulsion from Cambridge: see Frida Knight, *University Rebel* (1971), esp. chapter 8. The pamphlet was on sale by mid-February 1793 (William Frend, *Account of the Proceedings*...(Cambridge, 1793), p. 72), and the appendix caused especial outrage among loyalists, and by the first week in May the University had opened its proceedings against Frend. From the juxtaposition of ancient prophet, palaces and appal, and from the fact that Blake and Frend shared friends and sympathies (see Erdman, pp. 158–9), one could argue that Blake's line could carry an echo of this celebrated case. But this is highly unlikely: Erdman gives a terminal date for inscribing the *Experience* drafts in the notebook as October 1792 (N7) – although 'appalls' was introduced as a revision, perhaps subsequently. But it is unnecessary to argue for such direct influence. What we are really finding is a vocabulary and stock of images common to a particular group or a particular intellectual tradition, in this case that of radical Dissent. It is helpful to identify these groups and traditions, since they both place Blake and help us to unlock his meanings: but as to the actual 'source' we must maintain a steady scepticism.

21 N107.

22 Bateson, *Selected Poems*, p. 126. See also the more elaborate (and unhelpful) argument of Harold Bloom, *Blake's Apocalypse: A Study in Poetic Argument* (Ithaca, NY, 1963), pp. 141–2, which also discounts the clear meaning of the third line.

23 As, for example, the long review of Jesse Foot, *A Complete Treatise on the Origin, Theory, and Cure of the Lues Venerea etc.* (1792 – but based on lectures read in Dean Street, Soho, in 1790 and 1791) in *Analytical Review*, 12 (April 1792), 399, and 13 (July 1792), 261. See also the discussion in Grant C. Roti and Donald L. Kent, 'The Last Stanza of Blake's London', *Blake: An Illustrated Quarterly*, 11: 1 (Summer 1977).

24 N107.

25 This is emphasised by the fact that it was the first line of verse 3 which (in the notebook draft) was to begin with 'But most...'; 'But most the chimney sweepers cry'.

26   Revelation xiv. 8–11. These verses immediately precede those in which the Son of Man appears with 'in his hand a sharp sickle', and which lead on to 'the great winepress of the wrath of God' (xiv. 14–20) – that vision of the last vintage which worked in Blake's imagination.

27   See Williams, *Country and City*, chapter 14, and Glen, 'The Poet in Society'.

28   With 'Marriage hearse' we are at the point of junction with another universe of imagery which critics of the 'neo-Platonist' persuasion emphasise to the exclusion of all other aspects of Blake's thought. In this universe, for the spirit to assume mortal dress is a form of death or sleep: hence sexual generation generates death: hence (these would argue) 'Marriage hearse'. There are times when Blake uses images in this way, although often with more equivocation, inversion or idiosyncrasy than this kind of criticism suggests. This is not, however, one of these times. The poem is not concerned with lamenting the constrictions of the spirit within its material 'coffin' but with the 'plagues' which 'blight' sexual love and generation.

29   See F. R. Leavis, 'Justifying One's Valuation of Blake', in Paley and Phillips, *Essays*, p. 80: 'the effect of the poetry [of the *Songs*] is very far from inducing an acceptance of human defeat. One can testify that the poet himself is not frightened, and, further, that there is no malevolence, no anti-human animus, no reductive bent, in his realism . . .'

CHAPTER 4

Discipline and Punish

Michel Foucault

Michel Foucault's major work on the history of power, published in 1975, portrays power as something dispersed throughout society. In his famous example of the Panopticon, a circular prison that allows for permanent surveillance of prisoners, Foucault suggests that the citizens of Western democracies act as their own jail-keepers. They internalize the social control that monitors society and maintains the disciplined efficiency of the social system. In this work as well, Foucault began to draw attention to the role of the body in social discipline.

Historians long ago began to write the history of the body. They have studied the body in the field of historical demography or pathology; they have considered it as the seat of needs and appetites, as the locus of physiological processes and metabolisms, as a target for the attacks of germs or viruses; they have shown to what extent historical processes were involved in what might seem to be the purely biological base of existence; and what place should be given in the history of society to biological "events" such as the circulation of bacilli, or the extension of the life-span.[1] But the body is also directly involved in a political field; power relations have an immediate hold upon it; they invest it, mark it, train it, torture it, force it to carry out tasks, to perform ceremonies, to emit signs. This political investment of the body is bound up, in accordance with complex reciprocal relations, with its economic use: it is largely as a force of production that the body is invested with relations of power and domination; but, on the other hand, its constitution as labor power is possible only if it is caught up in a system of subjection (in which need is also a political instrument meticulously prepared, calculated, and used); the body becomes a useful force only if it is both a productive body and a subjected body. This subjection is not only obtained by the instruments of violence or ideology; it can also be direct, physical, pitting force against force, bearing on material elements, and yet without involving violence; it may be calculated, organized, technically thought out; it may be subtle, make use neither of weapons nor of terror and yet remain of a physical order. That is to say, there may be a "knowledge" of the body that is not exactly the science of its functioning, and a mastery of its forces that is more than the ability to conquer them: this knowledge and this mastery constitute what might be called the political technology of the body. Of course, this technology is diffuse, rarely formulated in continuous, systematic discourse; it is often made up of bits and pieces; it implements a disparate set of tools or methods. In spite of the coherence of its results, it is generally no more than a multiform instrumentation. Moreover, it cannot be localized in a particular type of institution or state apparatus.

For they have recourse to it; they use, select, or impose certain of its methods. But, in its mechanisms and its effects, it is situated at a quite different level. What the apparatuses and institutions operate is, in a sense, a micro-physics of power, whose field of validity is situated in a sense between these great functionings and the bodies themselves with their materiality and their forces.

Now, the study of this micro-physics presupposes that the power exercised on the body is conceived not as a property, but as a strategy, that its effects of domination are attributed not to "appropriation," but to dispositions, maneuvers, tactics, techniques, functionings; that one should decipher in it a network of relations, constantly in tension, in activity, rather than a privilege that one might possess; that one should take as its model a perpetual battle rather than a contract regulating a transaction or the conquest of a territory. In short this power is exercised rather than possessed; it is not the "privilege," acquired or preserved, of the dominant class, but the overall effect of its strategic positions – an effect that is manifested and sometimes extended by the position of those who are dominated. Furthermore, this power is not exercised simply as an obligation or a prohibition on those who "do not have it"; it invests them, is transmitted by them and through them; it exerts pressure upon them, just as they themselves, in their struggle against it, resist the grip it has on them. This means that these relations go right down into the depths of society, that they are not localized in the relations between the state and its citizens or on the frontier between classes and that they do not merely reproduce, at the level of individuals, bodies, gestures, and behavior, the general form of the law or government; that, although there is continuity (they are indeed articulated on this form through a whole series of complex mechanisms), there is neither analogy nor homology, but a specificity of mechanism and modality. Lastly, they are not univocal; they define innumerable points of confrontation, focuses of instability, each of which has its own risks of conflict, of struggles, and of an at least temporary inversion of the power relations. The overthrow of these "micro-powers" does not, then, obey the law of all or nothing; it is not acquired once and for all by a new control of the apparatuses nor by a new functioning or a destruction of the institutions; on the other hand, none of its localized episodes may be inscribed in history except by the effects that it induces on the entire network in which it is caught up.

Perhaps, too, we should abandon a whole tradition that allows us to imagine that knowledge can exist only where the power relations are suspended and that knowledge can develop only outside its injunctions, its demands, and its interests. Perhaps we should abandon the belief that power makes mad and that, by the same token, the renunciation of power is one of the conditions of knowledge. We should admit rather that power produces knowledge (and not simply by encouraging it because it serves power or by applying it because it is useful); that power and knowledge directly imply one another; that there is no power relation without the correlative constitution of a field of knowledge, nor any knowledge that does not presuppose and constitute at the same time power relations. These "power–knowledge relations" are to be analyzed, therefore, not on the basis of a subject of knowledge who is or is not free in relation to the power system, but, on the contrary, the subject who knows, the objects to be known and the modalities of knowledge must be regarded as so many effects of these fundamental implications of power–knowledge and their historical transformations. In short, it is not the activity of the subject of knowledge that produces a corpus of knowledge, useful or resistant to power, but power–knowledge, the processes and struggles that traverse it and of which it is made up, that determines the forms and possible domains of knowledge. . . .

Panopticism

The following, according to an order published at the end of the seventeenth century, were the measures to be taken when the plague appeared in a town.[2]

First, a strict spatial partitioning: the closing of the town and its outlying districts, a prohibition to leave the town on pain of death, the killing of all stray animals; the division of the town into distinct quarters, each governed by an intendant. Each street is placed under the authority of a syndic, who keeps it under surveillance; if he leaves the street, he will be condemned to death. On the appointed day, everyone is ordered to stay indoors: it is forbidden to leave on pain of death. The syndic himself comes to lock the door of each house from the outside; he takes the key with him and hands it over to the intendant of the quarter; the intendant keeps it until the end of the quarantine. Each family will have made its own provisions; but, for bread and wine, small wooden canals are set up between the street and the interior of the houses, thus allowing each person to receive his ration without communicating with the suppliers and other residents; meat, fish, and herbs will be hoisted up into the houses with pulleys and baskets. If it is absolutely necessary to leave the house, it will be done in turn, avoiding any meeting. Only the intendants, syndics, and guards will move about the streets and also, between the infected houses, from one corpse to another, the "crows," who can be left to die: these are "people of little substance who carry the sick, bury the dead, clean and do many vile and abject offices." It is a segmented, immobile, frozen space. Each individual is fixed in his place. And, if he moves, he does so at the risk of his life, contagion, or punishment.

Inspection functions ceaselessly. The gaze is alert everywhere: "A considerable body of militia, commanded by good officers and men of substance," guards at the gates, at the town hall and in every quarter to ensure the prompt obedience of the people and the most absolute authority of the magistrates "as also to observe all disorder, theft, and extortion." At each of the town gates there will be an observation post; at the end of each street sentinels. Every day, the intendant visits the quarter in his charge, inquires whether the syndics have carried out their tasks, whether the inhabitants have anything to complain of; they "observe their actions." Every day, too, the syndic goes into the street for which he is responsible; stops before each house: gets all the inhabitants to appear at the windows (those who live overlooking the courtyard will be allocated a window looking onto the street at which no one but they may show themselves); he calls each of them by name; informs himself as to the state of each and every one of them – "in which respect the inhabitants will be compelled to speak the truth under pain of death"; if someone does not appear at the window, the syndic must ask why: "In this way he will find out easily enough whether dead or sick are being concealed." Everyone locked up in his cage, everyone at his window, answering to his name and showing himself when asked – it is the great review of the living and the dead.

This surveillance is based on a system of permanent registration: reports from the syndics to the intendants, from the intendants to the magistrates or mayor. At the beginning of the "lock up," the role of each of the inhabitants present in the town is laid down, one by one; this document bears "the name, age, sex of everyone, notwithstanding his condition": a copy is sent to the intendant of the quarter, another to the office of the town hall, another to enable the syndic to make his daily roll call. Everything that may be observed during the course of the visits – deaths, illnesses, complaints, irregularities – is noted down and transmitted to the intendants and magistrates. The magistrates have complete control over medical treatment; they have appointed a physician in charge; no other practitioner may treat, no apothecary prepare medicine, no confessor visit a sick person without having received from him a written note "to prevent anyone from concealing and dealing with those sick of the contagion, unknown to the magistrates." The registration of the pathological must be constantly centralized. The relation of each individual to his disease and to his death passes through the representatives of power, the registration they make of it, the decisions they take on it.

Five or six days after the beginning of the quarantine, the process of purifying the houses one by one is begun. All the inhabitants are made to leave; in each room "the furniture and goods" are raised from the ground or suspended from the air; perfume is poured around the room; after carefully sealing the windows, doors, and even the keyholes with wax, the perfume is set alight. Finally, the entire house is closed while the perfume is consumed; those who have carried out the work are searched, as they were on entry, "in the presence of the residents of the house, to see that they did not have something on their persons as they left that they did not have on entering." Four hours later, the residents are allowed to re-enter their homes.

This enclosed, segmented space, observed at every point, in which the individuals are inserted in a fixed place, in which the slightest movements are supervised, in which all events are recorded, in which an uninterrupted work of writing links the center and periphery, in which power is exercised without division, according to a continuous hierarchical figure, in which each individual is constantly located, examined, and distributed among the living beings, the sick, and the dead – all this constitutes a compact model of the disciplinary mechanism. The plague is met by order; its function is to sort out every possible confusion: that of the disease, which is transmitted when bodies are mixed together; that of the evil, which is increased when fear and death overcome prohibitions. It lays down for each individual his place, his body, his disease, and his death, his well-being, by means of an omnipresent and omniscient power that subdivides itself in a regular, uninterrupted way even to the ultimate determination of the individual, of what characterizes him, of what belongs to him, of what happens to him. Against the plague, which is a mixture, discipline brings into play its power, which is one of analysis. A whole literary fiction grew up around the plague: suspended laws, lifted prohibitions, the frenzy of passing time, bodies mingling together without respect, individuals unmasked, abandoning their statutory identity and the figure under which they had been recognized, allowing a quite different truth to appear. But there was also a political dream of the plague, which was exactly its reverse: not the collective festival, but strict divisions; not laws transgressed, but the penetration of regulation into even the smallest details of everyday life through the mediation of the complete hierarchy that assured the capillary functioning of power; not masks that were put on and taken off, but the assignment to each individual of his "true" name, his "true" place, his "true" body, his "true" disease. The plague as a form, at once real and imaginary, of disorder had as its medical and political correlative discipline. Behind the disciplinary mechanisms can be read the haunting memory of "contagions," of the plague, of rebellions, crimes, vagabondage, desertions, people who appear and disappear, live and die in disorder.

If it is true that the leper gave rise to rituals of exclusion, which to a certain extent provided the model for and general form of the great Confinement, then the plague gave rise to disciplinary projects. Rather than the massive, binary division between one set of people and another, it called for multiple separations, individualizing distributions, an organization in depth of surveillance and control, an intensification and a ramification of power. The leper was caught up in a practice of rejection, of exile-enclosure; he was left to his doom in a mass among which it was useless to differentiate; those sick of the plague were caught up in a meticulous tactical partitioning in which individual differentiations were the constricting effects of a power that multiplied, articulated, and subdivided itself; the great confinement on the one hand; the correct training on the other. The leper and his separation: the plague and its segmentations. The first is marked; the second analyzed and distributed. The exile of the leper and the arrest of the plague do not bring with them the same political dream. The first is that of a pure community, the second that of a disciplined society. Two ways of exercising power over men, of controlling their relations, of separating out their dangerous mixtures. The plague-stricken town, traversed throughout with hierarchy, surveillance, observation, writing; the town immobilized by the functioning of an extensive power that bears in a distinct way over all individual bodies – this is the utopia of the perfectly governed city. The plague (envisaged as a possibility at least) is the trial in the course of which one may define ideally the exercise of disciplinary power. In order to make rights and laws function according to pure theory, the jurists place themselves in imagination in the state of nature; in order to see perfect disciplines functioning, rulers dreamt of the state of plague. Underlying disciplinary projects the image of the plague stands for all forms of confusion and disorder; just as the image of the leper, cut off from all human contact, underlies projects of exclusion.

They are different projects, then, but not incompatible ones. We see them coming slowly together, and it is the peculiarity of the nineteenth century that it applied to the space of exclusion of which the leper was the symbolic inhabitant (beggars, vagabonds, madmen and the disorderly formed the real population) the technique of power proper to disciplinary partitioning. Treat "lepers" as "plague victims," project the subtle segmentations of discipline onto the confused space of internment, combine it with the methods of analytical distribution proper to power, individualize the excluded, but use procedures of individualization to mark exclusion – this is what was operated regularly by disciplinary power from the beginning of the nineteenth century in the psychiatric asylum, the penitentiary, the reformatory, the approved school and, to some extent, the hospital. Generally speaking, all the authorities exercising individual control function according to a double mode; that of binary division and branding (mad/sane; dangerous/harmless; normal/abnormal); and that of coercive assignment, of differential distribution (who he is; where he must be; how he is to be characterized; how he is to be recognized; how a constant surveillance is to be exercised over him in an individual way, etc.). On the one hand, the lepers are treated as plague victims; the tactics of individualizing disciplines are imposed on the excluded; and, on the other hand, the universality of disciplinary controls makes it possible to brand the "leper" and to bring into play against him the dualistic mechanisms of exclusion. The constant division between the normal and the abnormal, to which every individual is subjected, brings us back to our own time, by applying the binary branding and exile of the leper to quite different objects; the existence of a whole set of techniques and institutions for measuring, supervising and correcting the abnormal brings into play the disciplinary mechanisms to which the fear of the plague gave rise. All the mechanisms of power which, even today, are disposed around the abnormal individual, to brand him and to alter him, are composed of those two forms from which they distantly derive.

Bentham's *Panopticon* is the architectural figure of this composition. We know the principle on which it was based: at the periphery, an annular building; at the center, a tower; this tower is pierced with wide windows that open onto the inner side of the ring; the peripheric building is divided into cells, each of which extends the whole width of the building; they have two windows, one on the inside, corresponding to the windows of the tower; the other, on the outside, allows the light to cross the cell from one end to the other. All that is needed, then, is to place a supervisor in a central tower and to shut up in each cell a madman, a patient, a condemned man, a worker, or a schoolboy. By the effect of backlighting, one can observe from the tower, standing out precisely against the light, the small captive shadows in the cells of the periphery. They are like so many cages, so many small theaters, in which each actor is alone, perfectly individualized and constantly visible. The panoptic mechanism arranges spatial unities that make it possible to see constantly and to recognize immediately. In short, it reverses the principle of the dungeon; or rather of its three functions – to enclose, to deprive of light, and to hide – it preserves only the first and eliminates the other two. Full lighting and the eye of a supervisor capture better than darkness, which ultimately protected. Visibility is a trap.

To begin with, this made it possible – as a negative effect – to avoid those compact, swarming, howling masses that were to be found in places of confinement, those painted by Goya or described by Howard. Each individual, in his place, is securely confined to a cell from which he is seen from the front by the supervisor; but the side walls prevent him from coming into contact with his companions. He is seen, but he does not see; he is the object of information, never a subject in communication. The arrangement of his room, opposite the central tower, imposes on him an axial visibility; but the divisions of the ring, those separated cells, imply a lateral invisibility. and this invisibility is a guarantee of order. If the inmates are convicts, there is no danger of a plot, an attempt at collective escape, the planning of new crimes for the future, bad reciprocal influences; if they are patients, there is no danger of contagion; if they are madmen there is no risk of their committing violence upon one another; if they are schoolchildren, there is no copying, no noise, no chatter, no waste of time; if they are workers, there are no disorders, no theft, no coalitions, none of those distractions that slow down the rate of work, make it less perfect or cause accidents. The crowd, a compact mass, a locus of multiple exchanges, individualities merging together, a collective effect, is abolished and replaced by a collection of separated individualities. From the point of view of the guardian, it is replaced by a multiplicity that can be numbered and supervised; from the point of view of the inmates, by a sequestered and observed solitude.[3]

Hence the major effect of the Panopticon: to induce in the inmate a state of conscious and permanent visibility that assures the automatic functioning of power. So to arrange things that the surveillance is permanent in its effects, even if it is discontinuous in its action; that the perfection of power should tend to render its actual exercise unnecessary: that this architectural apparatus should be a machine for creating and sustaining a power relation independent of the person who exercises it; in short, that the inmates should be caught up in a power situation of which they are themselves the bearers. To achieve this, it is at once too much and too little that the prisoner should be constantly observed by an inspector: too little, for what matters is that he knows himself to be observed; too much, because he has no need in fact of being so. In view of this, Bentham laid down the principle that power should be visible and unverifiable. Visible: the inmate will constantly have before his eyes the tall outline of the central tower from which he is spied upon. Unverifiable: the inmate must never know whether he is being looked at at any one moment; but he must be sure that he may always be so. In order to make the presence or absence of the inspector unverifiable, so that the prisoners, in their cells, cannot even see a shadow, Bentham envisaged not only venetian blinds on the windows of the central observation hall, but, on the inside, partitions that intersected the hall at right angles and, in order to pass from one quarter to the other, not doors but zig-zag openings; for the slightest noise, a gleam of light, a brightness in a half-opened door would betray the presence of the guardian.[4] The Panopticon is a machine for dissociating the see/being seen dyad: in the peripheric ring, one is totally seen, without ever seeing; in the central tower, one sees everything without ever being seen.[5]

It is an important mechanism, for it automatizes and disindividualizes power. Power has its principle not so much in a person as in a certain concerted distribution of bodies, surfaces, lights, gazes; in an arrangement whose internal mechanisms produce the relation in which individuals are caught up. The ceremonies, the rituals, the marks by which the sovereign's surplus power was manifested are useless. There is a machinery that assures dissymmetry, disequilibrium, difference. Consequently, it does not matter who exercises power. Any individual, taken almost at random, can operate the machine: in the absence of the director, his family, his friends, his visitors, even his servants.[6] Similarly, it does not matter what motive animates him: the curiosity of the indiscreet, the malice of a child, the thirst for knowledge of a philosopher who wishes to visit this museum of human nature, or the perversity of those who take pleasure in spying and punishing. The more numerous those anonymous and temporary observers are, the greater the risk for the inmate of being surprised and the greater his anxious awareness of being observed. The Panopticon is a marvelous machine which, whatever use one may wish to put it to, produces homogeneous effects of power.

A real subjection is born mechanically from a fictitious relation. So it is not necessary to use force to constrain the convict to good behavior, the madman to calm, the worker to work, the schoolboy to application, the patient to the observation of the regulations. Bentham was surprised that panoptic institutions could be so light: there were no more bars, no more chains, no more heavy locks; all that was needed was that the separations should be clear and the openings well arranged. The heaviness of the old "houses of security," with their fortress-like architecture, could be replaced by the simple, economic geometry of a "house of certainty." The efficiency of power, its constraining force have, in a sense, passed over to the other side – to the side of its surface of application. He who is subjected to a field of visibility, and who knows it, assumes responsibility for the constraints of power; he makes them play spontaneously upon himself; he inscribes in himself the power relation in which he simultaneously plays both roles; he becomes the principle of his own subjection.

[T]he Panopticon . . . makes it possible to draw up differences: among patients, to observe the symptoms of each individual, without the proximity of beds, the circulation of miasmas, the effects of contagion confusing the clinical tables; among schoolchildren, it makes it possible to observe performances (without there being any imitation or copying), to map aptitudes, to assess characters, to draw up rigorous classifications and, in relation to normal development, to distinguish "laziness and stubbornness" from "incurable imbecility"; among workers, it makes it possible to note the aptitudes of each worker, compare the time he takes to perform a task, and if they are paid by the day, to calculate their wages. . . .

In short, it arranges things in such a way that the exercise of power is not added on from the outside, like a rigid, heavy constraint, to the functions it invests, but is so subtly present in them as to increase their efficiency by itself increasing its own points of contact. . . .

The panoptic schema, without disappearing as such or losing any of its properties, was destined to spread throughout the social body; its vocation was to become a generalized function. The plague-stricken town provided an exceptional disciplinary model: perfect, but absolutely violent; to the disease that brought death, power opposed its perpetual threat of death; life inside it was reduced to its simplest expression; it was, against the power of death, the meticulous exercise of the right of the sword. The Panopticon, on the other hand, has a role of amplification; although it arranges power, although it is intended to make it more economic and more effective, it does so not for power itself, nor for the immediate salvation of a threatened society: its aim is to strengthen the social forces – to increase production, to develop the economy, spread education, raise the level of public morality; to increase and multiply.

How is power to be strengthened in such a way that, far from impeding progress, far from weighing upon it with its rules and regulations, it actually facilitates such progress? What intensificator of power will be able at the same time to be a multiplicator of production? How will power, by increasing its forces, be able to increase those of society instead of confiscating them or impeding them? The Panopticon's solution to this problem is that the productive increase of power can be assured only if, on the one hand, it can be exercised continuously in the very foundations of society, in the subtlest possible way, and if, on the other hand, it functions outside these sudden, violent, discontinuous forms that are bound up with the exercise of sovereignty. The body of the king, with its strange material and physical presence, with the force that he himself deploys or transmits to some few others, is at the opposite extreme of this new physics of power represented by panopticism; the domain of panopticism is, on the contrary, that whole lower region, that region of irregular bodies, with their details, their multiple movements, their heterogeneous forces, their spatial relations; what are required are mechanisms that analyze distributions, gaps, series, combinations, and which use instruments that render visible, record, differentiate, and compare: a physics of a relational and multiple power, which has its maximum intensity not in the person of the king, but in the bodies that can be individualized by these relations. At the theoretical level, Bentham defines another way of analyzing the social body and the power relations that traverse it; in terms of practice, he defines a procedure of subordination of bodies and forces that must increase the utility of power while practicing the economy of the prince. Panopticism is the general principle of a new "political anatomy" whose object and end are not the relations of sovereignty but the relations of discipline.

The celebrated, transparent, circular cage, with its high tower powerful and knowing, may have been for Bentham a project of a perfect disciplinary institution; but he also set out to show how one may "unlock" the disciplines and get them to function in a diffused, multiple, polyvalent way throughout the whole social body. These disciplines, which the classical age had elaborated in specific, relatively enclosed places – barracks, schools, workshops – and whose total implementation had been imagined only at the limited and temporary scale of a plague-stricken town, Bentham dreamt of transforming into a network of mechanisms that would be everywhere and always alert, running through society without interruption in space or in time. The panoptic arrangement provides the formula for this generalization. It programs, at the level of an elementary and easily transferable mechanism, the basic functioning of a society penetrated through and through with disciplinary mechanisms.

There are two images, then, of discipline. At one extreme, the discipline-blockade, the enclosed institution, established on the edges of society, turned inwards towards negative functions: arresting evil, breaking communications, suspending time. At the other extreme, with panopticism, is the discipline-mechanism: a functional mechanism that must improve the exercise of power by making it lighter, more rapid, more effective, a design of subtle coercion for a society to come. The movement from one project to the other, from a schema of exceptional discipline to one of a generalized surveillance, rests on a historical transformation: the gradual extension of the mechanisms of discipline throughout the seventeenth and eighteenth centuries, their spread throughout the whole social body, the formation of what might be called in general the disciplinary society.

A whole disciplinary generalization – the Benthamite physics of power represents an acknowledgement of this – had operated throughout the classical age [roughly the eighteenth century]. The spread of disciplinary institutions, whose network was beginning to cover an ever larger surface and occupying above all a less and less marginal position, testifies to this: what was an islet, a privileged place, a circumstantial measure, or a singular model, became a general formula; the regulations characteristic of the Protestant and pious armies of William of Orange or of Gustavus Adolphus were transformed into regulations for all the armies of Europe; the model colleges of the Jesuits, or the schools of Batencour or Demias following the example set by Sturm, provided the outlines for the general forms of educational discipline; the ordering of the naval and military hospitals provided the model for the entire reorganization of hospitals in the eighteenth century.

But this extension of the disciplinary institutions was no doubt only the most visible aspect of various, more profound processes.

1   *The functional inversion of the disciplines.* At first, they were expected to neutralize dangers, to fix useless or disturbed populations, to avoid the inconveniences of over-large assemblies; now they were being asked to play a positive role, for they were becoming able to do so, to increase the possible utility of individuals. Military discipline is no longer a mere means of preventing looting, desertion, or failure to obey orders among the troops; it has become a basic technique to enable the army to exist, not as an assembled crowd, but as a unity that derives from this very unity an increase in its forces; discipline increases the skill of each individual, coordinates

these skills, accelerates movements, increases fire power, broadens the fronts of attack without reducing their vigor, increases the capacity for resistance, etc. The discipline of the workshop, while remaining a way of enforcing respect for the regulations and authorities, of preventing thefts or losses, tends to increase aptitudes, speeds, output, and therefore profits; it still exerts a moral influence over behavior, but more and more it treats actions in terms of their results, introduces bodies into a machinery, forces into an economy. When, in the seventeenth century, the provincial schools or the Christian elementary schools were founded, the justifications given for them were above all negative: those poor who were unable to bring up their children left them "in ignorance of their obligations: given the difficulties they have in earning a living, and themselves having been badly brought up, they are unable to communicate a sound upbringing that they themselves never had"; this involves three major inconveniences: ignorance of God; idleness (with its consequent drunkenness, impurity, larceny, brigandage); and the formation of those gangs of beggars, always ready to stir up public disorder and "virtually to exhaust the funds of the Hôtel-Dieu."[7] Now, at the beginning of the Revolution, the end laid down for primary education was to be, among other things, to "fortify," to "develop the body," to prepare the child "for a future in some mechanical work," to give him "an observant eye, a sure hand and prompt habits."[8] The disciplines function increasingly as techniques for making useful individuals. Hence their emergence from a marginal position on the confines of society, and detachment from the forms of exclusion or expiation, confinement or retreat. Hence the slow loosening of their kinship with religious regularities and enclosures. Hence also their rooting in the most important, most central, and most productive sectors of society. They become attached to some of the great essential functions: factory production, the transmission of knowledge, the diffusion of aptitudes and skills, the war-machine. Hence, too, the double tendency one sees developing throughout the eighteenth century to increase the number of disciplinary institutions and to discipline the existing apparatuses.

2   *The swarming of disciplinary mechanisms.* While, on the one hand, the disciplinary establishments increase, their mechanisms have a certain tendency to become "de-institutionalized," to emerge from the closed fortresses in which they once functioned and to circulate in a "free" state; the massive, compact disciplines are broken down into flexible methods of control, which may be transferred and adapted. Sometimes the closed apparatuses add to their internal and specific function a role of external surveillance, developing around themselves a whole margin of lateral controls. Thus the Christian School must not simply train docile children; it must also make it possible to supervise the parents, to gain information as to their way of life, their resources, their piety, their morals. The school tends to constitute minute social observatories that penetrate even to the adults and exercise regular supervision over them: the bad behavior of the child, or his absence, is a legitimate pretext, according to Demia, for one to go and question the neighbors, especially if there is any reason to believe that the family will not tell the truth, one can then go and question the parents themselves, to find out whether they know their catechism and the prayers, whether they are determined to root out the vices of their children, how many beds there are in the house and what the sleeping arrangements are; the visit may end with the giving of alms, the present of a religious picture, or the provision of additional beds.[9]

Similarly, the hospital is increasingly conceived of as a base for the medical observation of the population outside; after the burning down of the Hôtel-Dieu in 1772, there were several demands that the large buildings, so heavy and so disordered, should be replaced by a series of smaller hospitals; their function would be to take in the sick of the quarter, but also to gather information, to be alert to any endemic or epidemic phenomena, to open dispensaries, to give advice to the inhabitants and to keep the authorities informed of the sanitary state of the region.

One also sees the spread of disciplinary procedures, not in the form of enclosed institutions, but as centers of observation disseminated throughout society. Religious groups and charity organizations had long played this role of "disciplining" the population. From the Counter-Reformation to the philanthropy of the July monarchy, initiatives of this type continued to increase; their aims were religious (conversion and moralization), economic (aid and encouragement to work), or political (the struggle against discontent or agitation). One has only to cite by way of example the regulations for the charity associations in the Paris parishes. The territory to be covered was divided into quarters and cantons and the members of the associations divided themselves up along the same lines. These members had to visit their respective areas regularly; "they will strive to eradicate places of ill-repute, tobacco shops, life-classes, gaming houses, public scandals, blasphemy, impiety, and any other disorders that may come to their knowledge." They will also have to make individual visits to the poor; and the information to be obtained is laid down in regulations: the stability of the lodging, knowledge of prayers, attendance at the sacraments, knowledge of a trade, morality (and "whether they have not fallen into poverty through their own fault"); lastly, "one must learn by skillful questioning in what way they behave at home. Whether there is peace between them and their neighbors, whether they are careful to bring up their children in the fear of God... whether they do not have their older children of different sexes sleeping together and with them, whether they do not allow licentiousness and cajolery in their families, especially in their older daughters. If one has any doubts as to whether they are married, one must ask to see their marriage certificate."[10]

3 *The state-control of the mechanisms of discipline.* In England, it was private religious groups that carried out, for a long time, the functions of social discipline;[11] in France, although a part of this role remained in the hands of parish guilds or charity associations, another – and no doubt the most important part – was very soon taken over by the police apparatus.

The organization of a centralized police had long been regarded, even by contemporaries, as the most direct expression of royal absolutism; the sovereign had wished to have "his own magistrate to whom he might directly entrust his orders, his commissions, intentions, and who was entrusted with the execution of orders and orders under the King's private seal."[12] In effect, in taking over a number of pre-existing functions – the search for criminals, urban surveillance, economic and political supervision – the police magistratures and the magistrature-general that presided over them in Paris transposed them into a single, strict, administrative machine: "All the radiations of force and information that spread from the circumference culminate in the magistrate-general.... It is he who operates all the wheels that together produce order and harmony. The effects of his administration cannot be better compared than to the movement of the celestial bodies."[13]

But, although the police as an institution were certainly organized in the form of a state apparatus, and although this was certainly linked directly to the center of political sovereignty, the type of power that it exercises, the mechanisms it operates and the elements to which it applies them are specific. It is an apparatus that must be coextensive with the entire social body and not only by the extreme limits that it embraces, but by the minuteness of the details it is concerned with. Police power must bear "over everything": it is not, however, the totality of the state nor of the kingdom as visible and invisible body of the monarch; it is the dust of events, actions, behavior, opinions – "everything that happens";[14] the police are concerned with "those things of every moment," those "unimportant things," of which Catherine II spoke in her *Great Instruction* (*Supplement to the Instruction for the drawing up of a new code*, 1769, article 535). With the police, one is in the indefinite world of a supervision that seeks ideally to reach the most elementary particle, the most passing phenomenon of the social body: "the ministry of the magistrates and police officers is of the greatest importance; the objects that it embraces are in a sense definite, one may perceive them only by a sufficiently detailed examination":[15] the infinitely small of political power.

And, in order to be exercised, this power had to be given the instrument of permanent, exhaustive, omnipresent surveillance, capable of making all visible, as long as it could itself remain invisible. It had to be like a faceless gaze that transformed the whole social body into a field of perception: thousands of eyes posted everywhere, mobile attentions ever on the alert, a long, hierarchized network which, according to Le Maire, comprised for Paris the forty-eight *commissaires*, the twenty *inspecteurs*, then the "observers," who were paid regularly, the "*basses mouches*," or secret agents, who were paid by the day, then the informers, paid according to the job done, and finally the prostitutes. And this unceasing observation had to be accumulated in a series of reports and registers; throughout the eighteenth century, an immense police text increasingly covered society by means of a complex documentary organization.[16] And, unlike the methods of judicial or administrative writing, what was registered in this way were forms of behavior, attitudes, possibilities, suspicions – a permanent account of individuals' behavior.

Now, it should be noted that, although this police supervision was entirely "in the hands of the king," it did not function in a single direction. It was in fact a double-entry system: it had to correspond by manipulating the machinery of justice, to the immediate wishes of the king, but it was also capable of responding to solicitations from below; the celebrated *lettres de cachet*, or orders under the king's private seal, which were long the symbol of arbitrary royal rule and which brought detention into disrepute on political grounds, were in fact demanded by families, masters, local notables, neighbors, parish priests; and their function was to punish by confinement a whole infra-penality, that of disorder, agitation, disobedience, bad conduct; those things that Ledoux wanted to exclude from his architecturally perfect city and which he called "offences of non-surveillance." In short, the eighteenth-century police added a disciplinary function to its role as the auxiliary of justice in the pursuit of criminals and as an instrument for the political supervision of plots, opposition movements, or revolts. It was a complex function since it linked the absolute power of the monarch to the lowest levels of power disseminated in society; since, between these different, enclosed institutions of discipline (workshops, armies, schools), it extended an intermediary network, acting where they could not intervene, disciplining the non-disciplinary spaces; but it filled in the gaps, linked them together, guaranteed with its armed force an interstitial discipline and a meta-discipline. "By means of a wise police, the sovereign accustoms the people to order and obedience."[17]

The organization of the police apparatus in the eighteenth century sanctioned a generalization of the disciplines that became coextensive with the state itself. Although it was linked in the most explicit way with everything in the royal power that exceeded the exercise of regular justice, it is understandable why the police offered such slight resistance to the rearrangement of the judicial power; and why it has not ceased to impose its prerogatives upon it, with ever-increasing weight, right up to the present day; this is no doubt because it is the secular arm of the judiciary; but it is also because, to a far greater degree than the judicial institution, it is identified, by reason of its extent and mechanisms, with a society of the disciplinary type. Yet it would be wrong to believe that the disciplinary functions were confiscated and absorbed once and for all by a state apparatus.

"Discipline" may be identified neither with an institution nor with an apparatus; it is a type of power, a modality for its exercise, comprising a whole set of instruments, techniques, procedures, levels of application, targets; it is a "physics" or an "anatomy" of power, a technology. And it may be taken over either by "specialized" institutions (the penitentiaries or "houses of correction" of the nineteenth century), or by institutions that use it as an essential instrument for a particular end (schools, hospitals), or by pre-existing authorities that find in it a means of reinforcing or reorganizing their internal mechanisms of power (one day we should show how intra-familial relations, essentially in the parents–children cell, have become "disciplined," absorbing since the classical age external schemata, first educational and military, then medical, psychiatric, psychological, which have made the family the privileged locus of emergence for the disciplinary question of the normal and the abnormal); or by apparatuses that have made discipline their principle of internal functioning (the disciplinarization of the administrative apparatus from the Napoleonic period), or finally by state apparatuses whose major, if not exclusive, function is to assure that discipline reigns over society as a whole (the police).

On the whole, therefore, one can speak of the formation of a disciplinary society in this movement that stretches from the enclosed disciplines, a sort of social "quarantine," to an indefinitely generalizable mechanism of "panopticism." Not because the disciplinary modality of power has replaced all the others; but because it has infiltrated the others, sometimes undermining them, but serving as an intermediary between them, linking them together, extending them and above all making it possible to bring the effects of power to the most minute and distant elements. It assures an infinitesimal distribution of the power relations.

A few years after Bentham, Julius gave this society its birth certificate.[18] Speaking of the panoptic principle, he said that there was much more there than architectural ingenuity: it was an event in the "history of the human mind." In appearance, it is merely the solution of a technical problem; but, through it, a whole type of society emerges. Antiquity had been a civilization of spectacle; "to render accessible to a multitude of men the inspection of a small number of objects": this was the problem to which the architecture of temples, theaters, and circuses responded. With spectacle, there was a predominance of public life, the intensity of festivals, sensual proximity. In these rituals in which blood flowed, society found new vigor and formed for a moment a single great body. The modern age poses the opposite problem: "to procure for a small number, or even for a single individual, the instantaneous view of a great multitude." In a society in which the principal elements are no longer the community and public life, but, on the one hand, private individuals and, on the other, the state, relations can be regulated only in a form that is the exact reverse of the spectacle: "It was to the modern age, to the ever-growing influence of the state, to its ever more profound intervention in all the details and all the relations of social life, that was reserved the task of increasing and perfecting its guarantees, by using and directing towards that great aim the building and distribution of buildings intended to observe a great multitude of men at the same time."

Julius saw as a fulfilled historical process that which Bentham had described as a technical program. Our society is one not of spectacle, but of surveillance; under the surface of images, one invests bodies in depth; behind the great abstraction of exchange, there continues the meticulous, concrete training of useful forces; the circuits of communication are the supports of an accumulation and a centralization of knowledge; the play of signs defines the anchorages of power; it is not that the beautiful totality of the individual is amputated, repressed, altered by our social order, it is rather that the individual is carefully fabricated in it, according to a whole technique of forces and bodies. We are much less Greeks than we believe. We are neither in the amphitheater, nor on the stage, but in the panoptic machine, invested by its effects of power, which we bring to ourselves since we are part of its mechanism. The importance, in historical mythology, of the Napoleonic character probably derives from the fact that it is at the point of junction of the monarchical, ritual exercise of sovereignty and the hierarchical, permanent exercise of indefinite discipline. He is the individual who looms over everything with a single gaze which no detail, however minute, can escape: "You may consider that no part of the Empire is without surveillance, no crime, no offense, no contravention that remains unpunished, and that the eye of the genius who can enlighten all embraces the whole of this vast machine, without, however, the slightest detail escaping his attention."[19] At the moment of its full blossoming, the disciplinary society still assumes with the Emperor the old aspect of the power of spectacle. As a monarch who is at one and the same time a usurper of the ancient throne and the organizer of the new state, he combined into a single symbolic, ultimate figure the whole of the long process by which the pomp of sovereignty, the necessarily spectacular manifestations of power, were extinguished one by one in the daily exercise of surveillance, in a panopticism in which the vigilance of intersecting gazes was soon to render useless both the eagle and the sun.

The formation of the disciplinary society is connected with a number of broad historical processes – economic, juridico-political, and, lastly, scientific – of which it forms part.

1   Generally speaking, it might be said that the disciplines are techniques for assuring the ordering of human multiplicities. It is true that there is nothing exceptional or even characteristic in this; every system of power is presented with the same problem. But the peculiarity of the disciplines is that they try to define in relation to the multiplicities a tactics of power that fulfills three criteria: firstly, to obtain the exercise of power at the lowest possible cost (economically, by the low expenditure it involves; politically, by its discretion, its low exteriorization, its relative invisibility, the little resistance it arouses); secondly, to bring the effects of this social power to their maximum intensity and to extend them as far as possible, without either failure or interval; thirdly, to link this "economic" growth of power with the output of the apparatuses (educational, military, industrial, or medical) within which it is exercised; in short, to increase both the docility and the utility of all the elements of the system. This triple objective of the disciplines corresponds to a well-known historical con-

juncture. One aspect of this conjuncture was the large demographic thrust of the eighteenth century; an increase in the floating population (one of the primary objects of discipline is to fix; it is an anti-nomadic technique); a change of quantitative scale in the groups to be supervised or manipulated (from the beginning of the seventeenth century to the eve of the French Revolution, the school population had been increasing rapidly, as had no doubt the hospital population; by the end of the eighteenth century, the peace-time army exceeded 200,000 men). The other aspect of the conjuncture was the growth in the apparatus of production, which was becoming more and more extended and complex; it was also becoming more costly and its profitability had to be increased. The development of the disciplinary methods corresponded to these two processes, or rather, no doubt, to the new need to adjust their correlation. Neither the residual forms of feudal power nor the structures of the administrative monarchy, nor the local mechanisms of supervision, nor the unstable, tangled mass they all formed together could carry out this role: they were hindered from doing so by the irregular and inadequate extension of their network, by their often conflicting functioning, but above all by the "costly" nature of the power that was exercised in them. It was costly in several senses: because directly it cost a great deal to the Treasury; because the system of corrupt offices and farmed-out taxes weighed indirectly, but very heavily, on the population; because the resistance it encountered forced it into a cycle of perpetual reinforcement; because it proceeded essentially by levying (levying on money or products by royal, seigniorial, ecclesiastical taxation; levying on men or time by *corvées* of press-ganging, by locking up or banishing vagabonds). The development of the disciplines marks the appearance of elementary techniques belonging to a quite different economy: mechanisms of power which, instead of proceeding by deduction, are integrated into the productive efficiency of the apparatuses from within, into the growth of this efficiency and into the use of what it produces. For the old principle of "levying-violence," which governed the economy of power, the disciplines substitute the principle of "mildness-production-profit." These are the techniques that make it possible to adjust the multiplicity of men and the multiplication of the apparatuses of production (and this means not only "production" in the strict sense, but also the production of knowledge and skills in the school, the production of health in the hospitals, the production of destructive force in the army).

In this task of adjustment, discipline had to solve a number of problems for which the old economy of power was not sufficiently equipped. It could reduce the inefficiency of mass phenomena: reduce what, in a multiplicity, makes it much less manageable than a unity; reduce what is opposed to the use of each of its elements and of their sum; reduce everything that may counter the advantages of number. That is why discipline fixes; it arrests or regulates movements; it clears up confusion; it dissipates compact groupings of individuals wandering about the country in unpredictable ways; it establishes calculated distributions. It must also master all the forces that are formed from the very constitution of an organized multiplicity; it must neutralize the effects of counter-power that spring from them and which form a resistance to the power that wishes to dominate it: agitations, revolts, spontaneous organizations, coalitions – anything that may establish horizontal conjunctions.

Hence the fact that the disciplines use procedures of partitioning and verticality, that they introduce, between the different elements at the same level, as solid separations as possible, that they define compact hierarchical networks, in short, that they oppose to the intrinsic, adverse force of multiplicity the technique of the continuous, individualizing pyramid. They must also increase the particular utility of each element of the multiplicity, but by means that are the most rapid and the least costly, that is to say, by using the multiplicity itself as an instrument of this growth. Hence, in order to extract from bodies the maximum time and force, the use of those overall methods known as time-tables, collective training, exercises, total and detailed surveillance. Furthermore, the disciplines must increase the effect of utility proper to the multiplicities, so that each is made more useful than the simple sum of its elements: it is in order to increase the utilizable effects of the multiple that the disciplines define tactics of distribution, reciprocal adjustment of bodies, gestures and rhythms, differentiation of capacities, reciprocal coordination in relation to apparatuses or tasks. Lastly, the disciplines have to bring into play the power relations, not above but inside the very texture of the multiplicity, as discreetly as possible, as well articulated on the other functions of these multiplicities and also in the least expensive way possible: to this correspond anonymous instruments of power, coextensive with the multiplicity that they regiment, such as hierarchical surveillance, continuous registration, perpetual assessment and classification. In short, to substitute for a power that is manifested through the brilliance of those who exercise it, a power that insidiously objectifies those on whom it is applied; to form a body of knowledge about these individuals, rather than to deploy the ostentatious signs of sovereignty. In a word, the disciplines are the ensemble of minute technical inventions that made it possible to increase the useful size of multiplicities by decreasing the inconveniences of the power which, in order to make them useful, must control them. A multiplicity, whether in a workshop or a nation, an army or a school, reaches the threshold of a discipline when the relation of the one to the other becomes favorable.

If the economic take-off of the West began with the techniques that made possible the accumulation of capital, it might perhaps be said that the methods for administering the accumulation of men made possible a political take-off in relation to the traditional, ritual, costly, violent forms of power, which soon fell into disuse and were superseded by a subtle, calculated technology of subjection. In fact, the two processes – the accumulation of men and the accumulation of capital – cannot be separated; it would not have been possible to solve the problem of the accumulation of men without the growth of an apparatus of production capable of both sustaining them and using them; conversely, the techniques that made the cumulative multiplicity of men useful accelerated the accumulation of capital. At a less general level, the technological mutations of the apparatus of production, the division of labor and the elaboration of the disciplinary techniques sustained an ensemble of very close relations.[20] Each makes the other possible and necessary; each provides a model for the other. The disciplinary pyramid constituted the small cell of power within which the separation, coordination, and supervision of tasks was imposed and made efficient; and analytical partitioning of time, gestures, and bodily forces constituted an operational schema that could easily be transferred from the groups to be subjected to the mechanisms of production; the massive projection of military methods onto industrial organization was an example of this modeling of the division of labor following the model laid down by the schemata of power. But, on the other hand, the technical analysis of the process of production, its "mechanical" breaking-down, were projected onto the labor force whose task it was to implement it: the constitution of those disciplinary machines in which the individual forces that they bring together are composed into a whole and therefore increased is the effect of this projection. Let us say that discipline is the unitary technique by which the body is reduced as a "political" force at the least cost and maximized as a useful force. The growth of a capitalist economy gave rise to the specific modality of disciplinary power, whose general formulas, techniques of submitting forces and bodies, in short, "political anatomy," could be operated in the most diverse political regimes, apparatuses, or institutions.

2   The panoptic modality of power – at the elementary, technical, merely physical level at which it is situated – is not under the immediate dependence or a direct extension of the great juridico-political structures of a society; it is nonetheless not absolutely independent. Historically, the process by which the bourgeoisie became in the course of the eighteenth century the politically dominant class was masked by the establishment of an explicit, coded, and formally egalitarian juridical framework, made possible by the organization of a parliamentary, representative regime. But the development and generalization of disciplinary mechanisms constituted the other, dark side of these processes. The general juridical form that guaranteed a system of rights that were egalitarian in principle was supported by these tiny, everyday, physical mechanisms, by all those systems of micro-power that are essentially non-egalitarian and asymmetrical that we call the disciplines. And although, in a formal way, the representative regime makes it possible, directly or indirectly, with or without relays, for the will of all to form the fundamental authority of sovereignty, the disciplines provide, at the base, a guarantee of the submission of forces and bodies. The real, corporal disciplines constituted the foundation of the formal, juridical liberties. The contract may have been regarded as the ideal foundation of law and political power; panopticism constituted the technique, universally widespread, of coercion. It continued to work in depth on the juridical structures of society, in order to make the effective mechanisms of power function in opposition to the formal framework that it had acquired. The "Enlightenment," which discovered the liberties, also invented the disciplines.

Notes

1   Le Roy Ladurie, *Contrepoint* (1973).
2   *Archives militaires de Vincennes*, A1, 516, 91 sc. This regulation is broadly similar to a whole series of others that date from the same period and earlier.
3   J. Bentham, *Works*, ed. Bowring (London, 1843), IV, pp. 60–4.
4   In the *Postscript to the Panopticon* (1791), Bentham adds dark inspection galleries painted in black around the inspector's lodge, each making it possible to observe two stories of cells.
5   In his first version of the *Panopticon*, Bentham had also imagined an acoustic surveillance, operated by means of pipes leading from the cells to the central tower. In the *Postscript* he abandoned the idea, perhaps because he could not introduce into it the principle of dissymmetry and prevent the prisoners from hearing the inspector as well as the inspector hearing them. Julius tried to develop a system of dissymmetrical listening (N. H. Julius, *Leçon sur les prisons* (1831), I, p. 8).
6   Bentham, *Works*, p. 45.
7   C. Demia, *Règlement pour les écoles de la ville de Lyon* (1716), pp. 60–1.

8   Talleyrand's Report to the Constituent Assembly, September 10, 1791, quoted by A. Léon, *La Révolution française et l'éducation technique* (1968), p. 106.

9   Demia, *Règlement pour les écoles de la ville de Lyon*, pp. 39–40.

10 In the second half of the eighteenth century, it was often suggested that the army should be used for the surveillance and general partitioning of the population. The army, as yet to undergo discipline in the seventeenth century, was regarded as a force capable of instilling it. Cf., for example, Servan, *Le Soldat citoyen* (1780).

11 Cf. L. Radzinovitz, *The English Criminal Law* (1956), II, pp. 203–14.

12 A note by Duval, first secretary at the police magistrature, quoted in F. Funck-Brentano, *Catalogue des manuscrits de la bibliothèque de l'Arsenal*, IX, p. 1.

13 T. N. Des Essarts, *Dictionnaire universel de la police* (1787), pp. 344, 528.

14 Le Maire, in a memorandum written at the request of Sartine, in answer to sixteen questions posed by Joseph II on the Parisian police. This memorandum was published by Gazier in 1879.

15 N. Delamare, *Traité de la police* (1705), unnumbered preface.

16 On the police registers in the eighteenth century cf. M. Chassaigne, *La Lieutenance générale de police* (1906).

17 E. Vattel, *Le Droit des gens* (1768), p. 162.

18 Julius, *Leçon sur les prisons*, I, p. 384–G.

19 J. B. Treilhard, *Motifs du code d'instruction criminelle* (1808), p. 14.

20 Cf. Marx, *Capital*, vol. 1, ch. XIII and the very interesting analysis in F. Guerry and D. Deleule, *Le Corps productif* (1973).

CHAPTER 5

Some Call it Fiction: On the Politics of Domesticity

Nancy Armstrong

Drawing on Foucault's description of the historical evolution of discipline in Western societies, Nancy Armstrong makes links between Victorian novels about the domestic realm and the historical context of nineteenth-century England in this 1990 essay. She is especially interested in the way gender is defined during this period when a new sense of division between a male public sphere and a female domestic sphere was being reinvented and promoted to a position of cultural legitimacy.

> *It is queer how out of touch with truth women are. They live in a world of their own, and there has never been anything like it, and never can be.*
>
> Joseph Conrad, *Heart of Darkness*

For some years now, American scholars have been puzzling out the relationship between literature and history. Apparently the right connections were not made when literary histories were first compiled. Yet in turning to the question of how some of the most famous British novelists were linked to their moment in time, I have found I must begin at step one, with extremely powerful conventions of representation. Though old and utterly familiar, nothing new has taken their place. Their potency has not diminished in this country despite the theory revolution and the calls for a new literary history that came in its wake. The conventions to which I refer are many and various indeed, but all reinforce the assumption that history consists of economic or political events, as if these were essentially different from other cultural events. Some of us – a distinct minority, to be sure – feel that to proceed on this assumption is to brush aside most of the activities composing everyday life and so shrink the category of "the political" down to a very limited set of cultural practices. And then, having classified most of our symbolic activities as "personal," "social," or "cultural" (it is all much the same), traditional histories would have us place them in a secondary relationship either to the economy or to the official institutions of state. This essay is written in opposition to models of history that confine political practices to activities directly concerned with the marketplace, the official institutions of the state, or else resistance to these. I write as one who feels that such models have not provided an adequate basis for understanding the formation of a modern bureaucratic culture or for our place, as intellectuals, within it. More than that, I regard any model that places personal life in a separate sphere and that grants literature a secondary and passive role in political history as unconsciously sexist. I believe such models necessarily fail to account for the formation of a modern bureaucratic culture because they fail to account for the place of women within it.

Some of our best theorizers of fiction's relationship to history – Raymond Williams in England and Edward Said in the United States – have done much to tear down the barrier between culture and state. They demonstrate that the middle-class hegemony succeeded in part because it constructed separate historical narratives for self and society, family and factory, literature and history. They suggest that by maintaining these divisions within culture, liberal intellectuals continue to sanitize certain areas of culture – namely, the personal, domestic, and literary. The practices that go by these names consequently appear to be benignly progressive, in their analyses, to provide a place of escape from the political world, and even to offer forms of resistance. Still, I would argue, such efforts as those of Williams and Said will be only partially successful so long as they continue to ignore *the sexual division of labor* that underwrites and naturalizes the difference between culture and politics.

The Limits of Political History

To put some life into all these abstractions, let me now turn to domestic fiction and the difficulties that scholars encounter when they try to place writing of this kind in history. Ian Watt convincingly describes the socioeconomic character of the new readership for whom Defoe, Richardson, and Fielding wrote, a readership whose rise in turn gave rise to the novel. But Watt has no similar explanation for Austen. Her popularity he ascribes to her talent, and her talent, to nature. And so he concludes that nature must have given Austen a good eye for details.[1] Although Williams moves well beyond such reflection theories in his groundbreaking account of the information revolution, his model of history ultimately serves us no better than Watt's when it comes to explaining domestic fiction. His *Long Revolution* regards intellectual labor as a political force in its own right without which capitalism could not have unfolded as smoothly and completely as it appears to have done. But however much power Williams grants this domain, it belongs to culture and, as such, exists in a secondary relationship with political history. To historicize writing, he feels compelled to give it a source in events outside of and prior to writing. He does not entertain the possibility that the classic unfolding of capitalism was predicated on writing, much less on writing by women or writing that appealed to the interests of a female readership.[2] For Williams as for Watt, historical events take place in the official institutions of state or else through resistance to these institutions, and both forms of power are exercised primarily through men.

I have found Watt and Williams especially helpful for establishing links between the history of fiction and the rise of the new middle classes in England. At the same time, I am perplexed to find that, in establishing a relationship between writing and political history, these otherwise conscientious scholars completely neglect to account for the most obvious fact of all, namely, that sometime during the eighteenth century, in the words of Virginia Woolf, "the middle class woman began to write."[3] If, as Watt and Williams say, the rise of the novel was directly related to the rise of the new middle classes, then some of our best literary evidence suggests that the rise of the novel was related to the emergence of women's writing as well. In drawing this equation, of course, I have doubled the difficulties entailed in historicizing fiction, for I have suggested that to historicize fiction we must politicize not only intellectual labor but female labor as well. Much of British fiction exists at the intersection of these two definitively modern subsets of culture and is thereby twice removed from the mainstream of political history.

The writing I call domestic fiction is gender-inflected writing. Unlike the work of earlier women of letters, it comes to us as women's writing. In designating certain forms of writing as feminine, it designates other writing as masculine. The enclosure that marks a Jane Austen novel does not simply distinguish her "world" from that of a Shakespeare, a Blake, a Dickens, or a Yeats. The boundaries it constructs between inside and outside are personal in a far more wide-reaching and historically significant way. They mark the difference between the world over which women novelists have authority – the domain of the personal – and that which is ruled by men and their politics. In doing this, Austen makes Richardson the father of the novel, for, like him, she identifies the work of the novelist with the writing of women as well as with other forms of labor that are suitably feminine.[4] To move beyond the impasse that prevents us from situating this work in history, we have it seems to me, to toss out the idea that the gendering of vast areas of culture was a consequence of political events over which men had control. To consider gender itself as a political formation over which modern cultures gave women authority, we will have to invert these priorities. Having done so, one comes face to face with the possibility that a revolution in the home preceded the spread of the factory system and all that hinged upon its becoming the means of distributing the wealth of the nation.[5]

To deal with this possibility, I begin with the proposition Marx put forth in *The German Ideology* and Gramsci later developed into the concept of "hegemony" in his essays on the formation of intellectuals and the organization of culture and education: no political revolution is complete without a cultural revolution. To dominate, the dominant group must offer to one and all a view that makes their form of domination seem true and necessary if not desirable and right. Gramsci developed the contradiction inherent in Marx's notion of labor – that labor was not only a commodity, but also a social practice – into a theory that stressed the double-sidedness of middle-class power: it controlled not only the physical dimension of production but also the social dimension. During the twentieth century, moreover, Gramsci could see that a form of power that worked through spatial location, supervision, and individuals' relationship with machines was giving way to something more ubiquitous – bureaucratic control that divided and hierarchized individuals so as to place their labor on separate social planes. And indeed, as the wage was generalized to include members of this and other bureaucracies, those who performed productive labor shrank in number and importance.

More recently, therefore, a number of us who work in the humanities and social sciences have begun to feel theories of resistance which depend upon an essentialized class or, for that matter, any other essentialized group will no longer do. Once taken up by theory, such essentialisms quickly cease to represent the possibility of power coalescing outside a pluralistic society. Rather, they identify contradictory positions within that system and, in so doing, only supply more differences in a differential system that exists on an abstract plane of ideas. The system to which I refer is no system in the abstract, however, but the disciplinary institution itself. Slouching by way of homology from one cultural site to another, it has achieved the status of a paradigm. In its atomizing structure, political issues get lost. Everything matters. All truths are equivalent – only some are more complex and, in this respect alone, more satisfying than others. In the maze of differences, the difference between positive and negative has all but disappeared, and the paradise of liberalism seems near at hand.[6]

So perceiving *her* historical moment, one can consider in a radically materialist light the Foucauldian propositions that the modern state was called into being in writing, exists mainly as a state of mind, and perpetuates itself through the well-orchestrated collection, regulation, and dissemination of information. The idea of order that Foucault sometimes calls "discourse" or "power" and at other times names "sexuality" or "discipline" is indeed a ruling idea. But in a world that is ruled more surely by ideas than by physical or economic means, one has to be especially careful not to hypothesize some corresponding "reality" as their source. We cannot grant these ideas the autonomy, universality, and mystic interconnection that they have achieved, but neither can we seek out some more primary truth behind or below them. Rather, we must understand them, as Foucault suggests, as the self-conception of a class that has achieved hegemony. And hegemony, in the case of modern post-industrial societies, depends on self-conceptions capable of swallowing up all opposition in a single system of micro-differences.

The power of the system depends upon the production of a particular form of consciousness that is at once unique and standardizing. In place of what he calls the "repressive hypothesis," the assumption that culture either "suppresses" or "imposes itself on" the individual's desire, Foucault offers a productive hypothesis that turns this commonplace on its ear. The first volume of *The History of Sexuality* argues that the very forms of subjectivity we consider most essential to ourselves as selves had no existence prior to their symbolization, that the deepest and most private recesses of our being are culturally produced.[7] His *Discipline and Punish* mounts a detailed historical argument to show that the truth of the modern individual existed first as writing, before she or he was transformed successively into speech, thought, and unconscious desire.[8] Thus Foucault enables us to see the European Enlightenment as a revolution in words, which gave writing a new and awesome power over the world of objects as it shaped the individuals who established a relationship with that world through reading. In England, I would like to suggest, this cultural revolution was the only kind of revolution to occur during the eighteenth century, because in England the revolution in words took a form that prevented popular revolution.[9]

Having torn down the conceptual barrier between writing and political history, we have cleared the way to see the intellectual labor of women as part of the mainstream of political events. Foucault will not help us achieve this particular step, however. His *History of Sexuality* is not concerned with the history of gender. Nor does it deal with the role that writing for, by, and about women played in the history of sexuality. For this reason, his procedures cannot identify the decisive events that detached family life from politics, and these are the very events that tie the formation of a domestic domain to the development of an institutional culture in England. Foucault's *Discipline and Punish* overlooks the fact that the modern household served as the groundbreaking prototype of modern institutions. His *History of Sexuality* neglects to theorize the power of that prototype as it spills over from this account of modern personal life into his account of institutional power to saturate and make intelligible the theory of discipline. Despite the anti-Cartesian thrust of his work, Foucault does not finally break through the barrier that separates his position as theorizer of the sexual subject in *The History of Sexuality* from the one he takes up in order to theorize the political subject in *Discipline and Punish*. Yet not only does he use the same figure to think out the two; he also gives the strategies producing the sexual subject (those organizing the home) priority in his thinking over the strategies that subject the individual to the state (those of disciplinary institutions).

Central to the central chapter on "Panopticism" in *Discipline and Punish* is Foucault's figure of the city under plague. In contrast with leprosy, which calls for exclusionary strategies more consistent with the aristocratic imagination of power, the plague, as he plays with the figure, seems to require inclusion and enclosure as preconditions for a modern system of surveillance. The division of the population into progressively smaller subdivisions of which the household is the basic module, is followed by the ritual purification of each and every household:

> Five or six days after the beginning of the quarantine, the process of purifying the houses one by one is begun. All the inhabitants are made to leave; in each room "the furniture and goods" are raised from the ground or suspended from the air; perfume is poured around the room; after carefully sealing the windows, doors and even the keyholes with wax, the perfume is set alight. Finally, the entire house is closed while the perfume is consumed; those who have carried out the work are searched, as they were on entry, "in the presence of the residents of the house, to see that they did not have something on their persons as they left that they did not have on entering." Four hours later, the residents are allowed to re-enter their homes. (p. 197)

Such enclosure and purification of the house produces a new household free from the taint of any unregulated intercourse with the world, its membrane permeable only to certain kinds of information. Reading this account of the plague, I am struck by the difference between its place in the modern imagination and its use by Boccaccio, who imagined a small aristocratic community safely ensconced in the country to pass the time free from the infection of the city. In this early modern world, those who remain in the city are to be regarded as a different social body altogether, behaving much like the riotous and grotesquely permeable body celebrated by Bakhtin. How significant, then, that Foucault, in contrast with Bakhtin, imagines a city purified from the inside out by the production of hygenically pure domestic spaces within the body politic! In this attempt to fantasize the present from the position of the past, households serve as magical spaces where people go to die in order that they may be reborn as modern individuals – enclosed and self-regulating.

Having pursued the internal logic of his figure thus far, Foucault extends it outward from the newly enclosed domestic world – as from a new source of power – into the cultural and political domains, and from there into history. First, he notes how a "whole literary fiction of the festival grew up around the plague: suspended laws, lifted prohibitions, the frenzy of passing time, bodies mingling together without respect, individuals unmasked, abandoning their statutory identity and the figure under which they had been recognized, allowing a quite different truth to appear. But," he continues, "there was also a political dream of the plague, which was exactly its reverse: not the collective festival, but strict divisions; not laws transgressed, but the penetration of regulation into even the smallest details of everyday life...; not masks that were put on and taken off, but the assignment to each individual of his 'true' name, his 'true' place, his 'true' disease" (pp. 197–8). On the metaphor of the city under plague thus rests Foucault's entire theory of the development of modern institutions: "If it is true that the leper gave rise to rituals of exclusion, which to a certain extent provided the model for and general form of the Great Confinement, then the plague gave rise to disciplinary projects" (p. 198). Metaphorical use of disease allows him to declare the eighteenth-century hospital with its anatomy theater as the historical prototype for the modern prison.

And to be sure, I *like* Foucault for transgressing the boundary between the therapeutic and the punitive to demonstrate how much they have in common. But this, to my mind, is also a way of avoiding the full implications of his chosen metaphor, the city under plague, implications that would destroy the differences between sexual subject and political subject, and between these and the subject's material body, all of which rest upon preserving the line that divvies up cultural information according to gender. This is the line between inside and outside that is implanted in his metaphor from the beginning to distinguish personal from political life. This is the first division of the conceptual zygote, the line without which the fantasy of an entire political world cannot develop its inexorable symmetry, a symmetry that cuts beneath and through particular features that culture manifests at one site rather than another. While he opens the category of political power considerably by including institutions other than those officially charged to distribute wealth and power, Foucault extends the cultural scope of discipline only so far as institutions that, in becoming institutions, came to be dominated by men. Thus if power does not originate in the minds of individual men or in the bodies of men collectively, it arises from the cultural patterns that make men think of themselves as certain kinds of men and exercise power accordingly.

But if one pursues the implications of Foucault's chosen metaphor for modern power, his city under plague, in contrast with a Boccaccian remedy, contains a certain form of household that is the perfect and obvious answer to the indiscriminate mingling of bodies spreading the infection. When we expand our concept of the political further even than Foucault's, we discover grounds on which to argue that the modern household rather than the clinic provided the proto-institutional setting where government through relentless supervision first appeared, and appeared in its most benevolent guise. Foucault never takes note of these continuities between home and state even though they are as plain as the words on his page. More curious still is his failure to acknowledge the fact that a home espoused by various subgroups aspiring for the status of "respectability," a home overseen by a woman, actually preceded the formation of other social institutions by at least fifty years. There is little to suggest this household took root in practice much before the beginning of the nineteenth century, even though it frequently appeared in the literature and political argumentation of the previous century. From writing, it can be argued, the new family passed into the realm of common sense, where it came to justify the distribution of national wealth through wages paid to men. Indeed, it remains extremely powerful to this day as both metaphor and metonymy, the unacknowledged model and source of middle-class power.[10]

The Power of Domesticity

It is at this point in my argument that a feminist perspective must be invoked, but it cannot be a feminism that sinks comfortably into the rhetoric of victimization. It has to be thoroughly politicized. By this I mean we must be willing to accept the idea that, as middle-class women, we are empowered, although we are not empowered in traditionally masculine ways. We have to acknowledge that as middle-class intellectuals we are not critical mirrors of a separate and more primary process orchestrated by others – be they politicians, bureaucrats, captains of industry, or simply men. As women intellectuals we are doubly implicated in the process of reproducing the state of mind upon which other openly and avowedly political institutions depend. It is on this basis that I reject the notion that women's writing exists in a domain of experience outside of political history. I can no longer accept what conventional histories assume – that such writing occupies the secondary status of a "reflection" or "consequence" of changes within more primary social institutions – the army, hospital, prison, or factory. To the contrary, my evidence reveals domestic fiction actively disentangled the language of sexual relations from that of political economy. The rhetoric of this fiction (in Wayne Booth's sense of the term) laid out a new cultural logic that would eventually become common sense, sensibility, and public opinion. In this way, female knowledge successfully combatted one kind of power, based on title, wealth, and physical force, with another, based on the control of literacy. By equating good reading with what was good for women readers, a new standard for reading laid down the semantic ground for common sense and established the narrative conventions structuring public opinion. The new standard of literacy helped to bring a new class of people into existence. This class laid claim to the right to privacy on behalf of each individual. Yet this class set in motion the systematic invasion of private life by surveillance, observation, evaluation, and remediation. In a word, it ruled, still rules, through countless microtechniques of socialization, all of which may be lumped together under the heading of education.[11] During the second half of the nineteenth century, institutions were created to perform these operations upon masses of people in much the same way as domestic fiction did upon characters.

Those of us who have grown up within an institutional culture consequently carry around a voice much like that of a fictional narrator in his or her head. Sensitive to the least sign of disorder – a foul word, a piece of clothing undone, some food sliding off one's fork, or, worse still, some loss of control over bodily functions – the presence of this voice, now nearly two hundred years old, more surely keeps us in line than fear of the police or the military. For the unofficial forms of power have a terrible advantage over those which are openly and avowedly regulatory. They make us afraid of ourselves. They operate on the supposition that we harbor desires dangerous to the general good. Believing in the presence of a self that is essentially subversive, we keep watch over ourselves – in mirrors, on clocks, on scales, through medical exams, and by means of any number of other such practices. Thus we internalize a state that is founded on the conflict between self and state interests, and we feel perfectly justified in enacting its power – which is, after all, only good for oneself – upon others.

Convinced that power exerted in and through the female domain is at least as powerful as the more conventional forms of power associated with the male, I want to sketch out the relationship between the two during the modern period. I will suggest that modern institutional cultures depend upon the separation of "the political" from "the personal" and that they produce and maintain this separation on the basis of gender – the formation of masculine and feminine domains of culture. For, I will argue, even as certain forms of cultural information were separated into these two opposing fields, they were brought together as an intricate set of pressures that operated on the subject's body and mind to induce self-regulation. We can observe this peculiarly effective collaboration of the official and unofficial forms of power perhaps most clearly in the formation of a national education system during the Victorian period and in the whole constellation of efforts that went on simultaneously to appropriate leisure time.[12] British fiction participates in both efforts and therefore demonstrates the modes of collaboration between them.

To introduce their highly influential *Practical Education* in 1801, Maria Edgeworth and her father announce their break with the curriculum that reinforced traditional political distinctions: "On religion and politics we have been silent because we have no ambition to gain partisans, or to make proselytes, and because we do not address ourselves to any sect or party."[13] In virtually the same breath, they assure readers, "With respect to what is commonly called the education of the heart, we have endeavored to suggest the easiest means of inducing useful and agreeable habits, well regulated sympathy and benevolent affections" (p. viii). Their program substitutes abstract terms of emotion and behavior for those of one's specific socioeconomic identity. Rooting identity in the very subjective qualities that earlier curricula had sought to inculcate in young women alone, the Edgeworths' program gives priority to the schoolroom and parlor over the church and courts for purposes of regulating human behavior. In doing this, their educational program promises to suppress the political signs of human identity (which is of course a powerful political gesture in its own right). Perfectly aware of the power to be exercised through education, the Edgeworths justify their curriculum for cultivating the heart on grounds that it offered a new and more effective method of policing. In their words, "It is the business of education to prevent crimes, and to prevent all those habitual propensities which necessarily lead to their commission" (p. 354).

To accomplish their ambitious political goal, the Edgeworths invoke an economy of pleasure which cannot in fact be understood apart from the novel and the criticism that was produced both to censor and to foster it. First, the Edgeworths accept the view prevailing during the eighteenth century which said that fiction was sure to mislead female desire:

> With respect to sentimental stories, and books of mere entertainment, we must remark, that they should be sparingly used, especially in the education of girls. This species of reading cultivates what is called the heart prematurely, lowers the tone of the mind, and induces indifference for those common pleasures and occupations which...constitute by far the greatest portion of our daily happiness. (p. 105)

But the same turn of mind could as easily recognize the practical value of pleasure when it is harnessed and aimed at the right goals. Convinced that "the pleasures of literature" acted upon the reader in much the same way as a child's "taste for sugarplums" (p. 80), forward-thinking educators began to endorse the reading of fiction, so long as it was governed by principles that made conformity seem desirable.

In formulating a theory of mass education in which fiction had a deceptively marginal role to play, the Edgeworths and their colleagues were adopting a rhetoric which earlier reformers had used to level charges of violence and corruption against the old aristocracy. They placed themselves in the tradition of radical Protestant dissent going back to the sixteenth century, a tradition which had always argued that political authority should be based on moral superiority. Sexual relations so often provided the terms for making this claim that no representation of the household could be considered politically neutral. To contest that notion of the state which depended upon inherited power, puritan treatises on marriage and household govern-ance represented the family as a self-enclosed social unit into whose affairs the state had no right to intervene. Against genealogy they posited domesticity. But in claiming sovereignty for the natural father over his household, these treatises were not proposing a new distribution of political power. They were simply trying to limit the monarch's power. To understand the social transformation that was achieved by the English Revolution (according to Christopher Hill, not achieved until more than a century later), we have to turn away from what we consider to be the political themes of the puritan argument and consider instead what happens to gender.[14]

According to Kathleen M. Davis, the puritan doctrine of equality insisted upon the difference of sexual roles, in which the female was certainly subordinate to the male, and not upon the equality of the woman in kind. "The result of this partner-ship," she explains, "was a definition of mutual and complementary duties and characteristics." Gender was so clearly understood in these oppositional terms that it could be graphically represented:[15]

HUSBAND	WIFE
Get goods	Gather them together and save them
Travel, seek a living	Keep the house
Get money and provisions	Do not vainly spend it
Deal with many men	Talk with few
Be "entertaining"	Be solitary and withdrawn
Be skillful in talk	Boast of silence
Be a giver	Be a saver
Apparel yourself as you may	Apparel yourself as it becomes you
Dispatch all things outdoors	Oversee and give order within

In so representing the household as the opposition of complementary genders, the authors of countless puritan tracts asked readers to imagine the household as a self-enclosed social unit. But if these authors wanted to define the family as an independent source of authority, their moment did not arrive. The puritan household consisted of a male and a female who were structurally identical, positive and nega-tive versions of the same thing. The authority of the housewife described above could not yet be imagined as a positive thing in its own right. Until she took up her vigil and began to order personal life, a single understanding of power reigned, and men fought to determine the balance among its various parts.

Unlike the authors of seventeenth-century marriage manuals and domestic econ-omies, the educational reformers of nineteenth-century England could look back on a substantial body of writing whose main purpose was to produce a historically new woman. During the centuries between the English Revolution and the present day, this woman was inscribed with values which appealed to a whole range of competing interest groups, and, through her, these groups seized authority over domestic rela-tions and personal life. In this way, I believe, they created a need for the kind of surveillance which modern institutions provide. Indeed, the last two decades of the seventeenth century saw an explosion of writing aimed at educating the daughters of the numerous aspiring social groups. The new curriculum promised to educate these women in such a way as to make them more desirable than women who had only their own rank and fortune to recommend them. This curriculum exalted a woman whose value resided chiefly in her femaleness rather than in the traditional signs of status, a woman who possessed emotional depth rather than a physically stimulating surface, one who, in other words, excelled in the very qualities that differentiated her from the male. As gender was redefined in these terms, the woman exalted by an aristocratic tradition of letters ceased to appear so desirable. In becoming the other side of this new sexual coin, she represented surface rather than depth, embodied material as opposed to moral value, and displayed idle sensuality instead of unflagging concern for the well-being of others. So conceived, the aristocratic woman no longer defined what was truly and most desirably female.

But it was not until the mid-nineteenth century that the project of defining people on the basis of gender began to acquire some of the immense political influence it still exercises today. Around the 1830s, one can see the discourse of sexuality relax its critical gaze on the aristocracy as the newly forming working classes became a more obvious target of moral reform. Authors suddenly took notice of social elements who had hardly mattered before. These reformers and men of letters discovered that rebellious artisans and urban laborers, for example, lacked the kind of motivation that supposedly characterized normal individuals. Numerous writers sought out the source of poverty, illiteracy, and demographic change in these underdeveloped individuals, whose behavior was generally found to be not only promiscuous but also ambiguously gendered. Once they succeeded in translating an overwhelming economic problem into a sexual scandal, middle-class intellectuals could step forward and offer themselves, their technology, their supervisory skills, and their institutions of education and social welfare as the appropriate remedy for growing political resistance.

In all fairness, as Foucault notes, the middle classes rarely applied institutional procedures to others without first trying them out on themselves. When putting together a national curriculum, the government officials and educators in charge adopted one modeled on the educational theory that grew up around the Edgeworths and their intellectual circle, the heirs of the dissenting tradition.[16] This was basically the same as the curriculum proposed by eighteenth-century pedagogues and reformers as the best way of producing a marriageable daughter. By the end of the eighteenth century, the Edgeworths were among those who had already determined that the program aimed at producing the ideal woman could be applied to boys just as well as to girls. And by the mid-nineteenth century, one can see the government figuring out how to administer much the same program on a mass basis. In providing the conceptual foundation for a national curriculum, a particular idea of the self thus became commonplace, and as gendered forms of identity determined how people thought of themselves as well as others, that self became the dominant social reality.

Such an abbreviated history cannot do justice to the fierce controversies punctuating the institution of a national education system in England. I simply call attention to this material as a site where political history obviously converged with the history of sexuality as well as with that of the novel to produce a specific kind of individual. I do this to suggest the political implications of representing these as separate narratives. As it began to deny its political and religious bias and to present itself instead as a moral and psychological truth, the rhetoric of reform obviously severed its ties with an aristocratic past and took up a new role in history. It no longer constituted a form of resistance but enclosed a specialized domain of culture apart from political relations where apolitical truths could be told. The novel's literary status hinged upon this event. Henceforth fiction would deny the political basis for its meaning and refer instead to the private regions of the self or to the specialized world of art but never to the use of words that created and still maintains these distinctions so basic to our culture. Favored among kinds of fiction were novels that best performed the rhetorical operations of division and self-containment and thus turned existing political information into the discourse of sexuality. These works of fiction gave novels a good name, a name free of politics, and often the name of a woman such as *Pamela*, *Evelina*, *Emma*, or *Jane Eyre*. Then, with the translation of human identity into sexual identity came widespread repression of the political literacy characterizing an earlier culture, and with it, too, mass forgetting that there was a history of sexuality to tell.

The Politics of Domestic Fiction

Let me offer a detailed example of the exchange between reader and literary text to provide a sense of how the power of domesticity works through such an exchange. Charlotte Brontë flaunted this very power in writing her novel *Shirley*. The novel contains an otherwise gratuitous scene where Shakespeare's *Coriolanus* is read aloud and critiqued, as if to give the reader precise rules for reading, rules that should fascinate literary historians. They are not Brontë's own but rules developed during the preceding century by countless authors of ladies' conduct books and educational treatises. These authors proposed the first curriculum to include native British literature. Around the time Brontë sat down to write *Shirley*, a new generation of writers had taken up the question of how to distinguish good reading from bad. Their efforts swelled the growing number of Victorian magazines. Whether or not girls should read novels was the concern that shaped the debates over a curriculum for women during the eighteenth century, then nineteenth-century pedagogical theory developed around the question of how to make fiction useful for teaching foreigners and working-class people as well as women and children. Rules for reading developed along with the national standard curriculum that extended a curriculum originally meant only for girls of the literate classes to young Englishmen and women at various levels and their counterparts throughout the colonies. It is much the same theory of education that informs our educational system today. By using this example from *Shirley* to illustrate the rationale and procedures by which Victorian intellectuals extended what had been regarded as a female form of literacy to male education, I also want to mark an important difference between Charlotte Brontë's understanding of this process and our own. She was, I believe, far more aware of the politics of literary interpretation than we are.

One of her least colorful heroines, Caroline Helstone, uses Shakespeare to while away an evening of leisure with her beloved cousin and future husband, Robert Moore, a surly manufacturer, whose authoritarian way of dealing with factory hands is earning him threats of Luddite reprisals. During this, their one intimate moment together until the end of the novel, they reject all the pastimes available to lovers in an Austen novel in favor of reading Shakespeare's *Coriolanus*. Far more detailed than any such exchange in earlier fiction, this act of reading spells out the procedures by which reading literature was thought to produce a form of knowledge that was also a form of social control. Robert Moore is half Belgian, half English. It is through reading Shakespeare that, according to Caroline, he "shall be entirely English."[17] For, as she patiently explains to him, "Your French forefathers don't speak so sweetly, nor so solemnly, nor so impressively as your English ancestors, Robert." But being English does not identify a set of political affiliations – as it would in Shakespeare's time. It refers instead to essential qualities of human mind. Caroline has selected a part for Robert to read aloud that, in her words, "is toned with something in you. It shall waken your nature, fill your mind with music, it shall pass like a skillful hand over your heart.... Let glorious William come near and touch it; you will see how he will draw the English power and melody out of its chords."

I have called this relationship between reader and text an exchange in order to stress the fact that writing cannot be turned to the task of constituting readers without giving up old features and acquiring new ones of its own; to dwell on the reader is to explain but one half of the transformational logic of this exchange. Just as Robert, the rude Belgian, becomes a gentle Englishman by reading Shakespeare, so, too, the Jacobean playwright is transformed by the domestic setting in which he is read. Caroline urges Robert to receive the English of another historical moment as the voice of an ancestor speaking to him across time and cultural boundaries. To no one's surprise, the written Shakespeare, thus resurrected, has acquired the yearnings and anxieties of an early nineteenth-century factory owner. And as we observe the Bard becoming the nineteenth-century man, we also witness an early version of our own literary training. Here, extending through the educated middle-class female to the male and, through him, acquiring universal application, we can see how voices that speak from positions vastly different in social space and time quickly translate into aspects of modern consciousness.

Thus Shakespeare becomes the means of reproducing specifically modern states of mind within the reader. Reading Shakespeare is supposed "to stir you," Caroline explains, "to give you new sensations. It is to make you feel your life strongly, not only your virtues, but your vicious, perverse points. Discover by the feeling the reading will give you at once how high and how low you are" (p. 115). If Shakespeare loses the very turns of mind that would identify him with his moment in history, then Robert loses features of a similar kind in Brontë's representation of the scene of reading. And this, of course, is the point. Reading Shakespeare translates Robert's political attitudes into essential features of mind. It simultaneously objectifies those features and subjects them to evaluation. The "English power" that Robert acquires by reading literature is simply the power of observing himself through the lens of liberal humanism – as a self flushed with the grandiosity of an ordinariness that has been totally liberated from historical bias and political commitment. For it is through this lens that the novel has us perceive the transformations that come over Robert as he reads *Coriolanus* under the gentle tutelage of Caroline Helstone: "stepping out of the narrow line of private prejudices, he began to revel in the large picture of human nature, to feel the reality stamped upon the characters who were speaking from that page before him" (p. 116).

Her tutoring induces Robert to renounce one mode of power – which Caroline associates with the imperiously patriarchal nature of Coriolanus – and to adopt another – which she identifies as a benevolent form of paternalism. As it is administered by a woman and used to mediate a sexual exchange, *Coriolanus* becomes the means for effecting historical change: *Coriolanus* becomes Caroline. Performed as writing and reading, that is, the play becomes the means of internalizing a form of authority identified with the female. The political implications of feminizing the reader are clear as Caroline gives Robert a moral to "tack to the play:... you must not be proud to your workpeople; you must not neglect chances of soothing them, and you must not be of an inflexible nature, uttering a request as austerely as if it were a command" (p. 114). Brontë is less than subtle in dramatizing the process by which reading rids Robert of the foreign devil. She seems to know exactly what political objective is fulfilled as he fills the mold of the Englishman and benevolent father. Brontë also puts the woman in charge of this process even though she gives her heroine the less imperious passages to read. Retiring, feminine, and thoroughly benign, Caroline's power is hardly visible as such. Yet she is clearly the one who declares that reading has the power "to stir you; to give you new sensations. It is to make you feel your life strongly, not only your virtues, but your vicious, perverse points" (p. 115). And when Robert has finished reading, she is the one to ask, "Now, have you felt Shakespeare?" (p. 117). She suppresses all that belongs to the past as so much noise in her effort to bring under examination the grand currents of emotion that run straight from Shakespeare to the modern day reader, a reader who is thoroughly English. In thus guiding his reading with her smiles and admonitions, Caroline executes a set of delicate procedures capable of translating any and all cultural information into shades of modern middle-class consciousness and the substance of a literary text. Although its setting – during the Luddite rebellions – makes *Shirley* anachronistic by about thirty years, the solution it proposes for the problem of political resistance, through the production of a new ruling-class mentality, marks this novel as utterly Victorian – perhaps even ahead of its time.

As similar textualizing strategies were deployed here and elsewhere throughout Victorian culture, an intricate system of psychological differences completely triumphed over a long-standing tradition of overtly political signs to usher in a new form of state power. This power – the power of representation over the thing represented – wrested authority from the old aristocracy on grounds that a government was morally obliged to rehabilitate deviant individuals rather than subdue them by force. The Peterloo Massacre of 1819 made it clear that the state's capacity for violence had become a source of embarrassment to the state. Overt displays of force worked against legitimate authority just as they did against subversive factions.[18] If acts of open rebellion had justified intervention in areas of society that government had not had to deal with before, then the government's use of force gave credence to the workers' charges of government oppression. The power of surveillance came into dominance at precisely this moment in English history, displacing traditional displays of violence. Remarkably like the form of vigilance that insured an orderly household, this power did not create equality so much as trivialize the material signs of difference by translating all such signs into differences in the quality, intensity, direction, and self-regulatory capability of an individual's desire.

In saying this, I am not suggesting that we should use British fiction to identify forms of repression or to perform acts of liberation, although my project has a definite political goal. I simply want to represent the discourse of sexuality as deeply implicated in – if not directly responsible for – the shape of the novel, and to show the novel's implication, at the same time, in producing a subject who knew herself and saw that self in relation to others according to the same feminizing strategies that had shaped fiction. I regard fiction, in other words, both as a document and as an agency of cultural history. I believe it helped to formulate the ordered space we now recognize as the household, that it made that space totally functional and used it as the context for representing normal behavior. In doing all this, fiction contested alternative bases for human relationships. As the history of this female domain is figured into political history, then, it will outline boldly the telling cultural move upon which, I believe, the supremacy of middle-class culture ultimately hinged. That is, it will reenact the moment when writing invaded, revised, and contained the household according to strategies that distinguished private from social life and thus detached sexuality from political history.

Where others have isolated rhetorical strategies that naturalize the subordination of female to male, no one has thoroughly examined the figure that differentiates the sexes as it links them together by sexual desire. And if no one asks why, how, and when gender differentiation became the root of human identity, no degree of theoretical sophistication can help us understand the totalizing power of this figure and the very real interests such power inevitably serves. So basic are the terms "male" and "female" to the semiotics of modern life that no one can use them without to some degree performing the very reifying gesture whose operations we need to understand and whose power we want to historicize. Whenever we cast our political lot in the dyadic formation of gender, we place ourselves in a classic double bind, which confines us to alternatives that are not really alternatives at all. That is to say, any political position founded primarily on sexual identity ultimately confirms the limited choices offered by such a dyadic model. Once one thinks within such a structure, sexual relationships appear as the model for all power relationships. This makes it possible to see the female as representative of all subjection and to use her subjectivity as if it were a form of resistance. Having inscribed social conflict within a domestic configuration, however, one loses sight of all the various and contrary political affiliations for which any given individual provides the site. This power of sexuality to appropriate the voice of the victim works as surely through inversion, of course, as by strict adherence to the internal organization of the model.

Still, there is a way in which I owe everything to the very academic feminism I seem to critique, for unless it were now acceptable to read women's texts as women's texts, there would be no call to historicize this area of culture. In view of the fact that women writers have been taken up by the Norton Anthology as part of the standard survey of British literature and also as a collection all of their own, and in view of the fact that we now have male feminists straining to hop on the bandwagon, I feel it is simply time to take stock. It is time to consider why literary criticism presently feels so comfortable with a kind of criticism that began as a critique both of the traditional canon and of the interpretive procedures the canon called forth. This should tell us that by carving out a separate domain for women within literary criticism, feminist criticism has yet to destabilize the reigning metaphysics of sexuality. Literary historians continue to remain aloof from but still firmly anchored in a narrow masculinist notion of politics as more and more areas within literary studies have given ground to the thematics of sexuality promoted by academic feminism. Indeed, a sexual division of labor threatens to reproduce itself within the academy whereby women scholars interpret literature as the expression of the sexual subject while male scholars attend to matters of history and politics. To subvert this process, I believe we must read fiction not as literature but as the history of gender differences and a means by which we have reproduced a class and culture specific form of consciousness.

Notes

1 Ian Watt, *The Rise of the Novel* (Berkeley: University of California Press, 1957), p. 57.

2 In *The Long Revolution* (New York: Columbia University Press, 1961), Williams sets out to show how the "creative" or cultural dimension of social experience opposed existing forms of political authority during the seventeenth and eighteenth centuries and won. Part one of his book indeed gives culture priority over the official institutions of state (as it must during the eighteenth century), claiming that cultural history "is more than a department, a special area of change. In this creative area the changes and conflicts of the whole way of life are necessarily involved" (p. 122). But latent in this promise to extend the category of "the political" broadly to include "the whole way of life" is the contradictory suggestion that political practices are also a special category of "the whole." The second notion of politics emerges in part two, where Williams describes such historical processes as the growth of the reading public, of the popular press, and of standard English through which the new middle classes converted the power of language into economic power. Here the narrow definition of political events, as those which take place in the houses of government, the courts, and the marketplace, assumes control over the "creative" cultural dimension of social experience. For example, Williams writes, "as 1688 is a significant political date, so 1695 is significant in the history of the press. For in that year Parliament declined to renew the 1662 Licensing Act, and the stage for expansion was now fully set" (p. 180). Had Williams actually gathered data that would compose the record of "the whole" of life, he might have broken out of this circle. But, in producing cultural histories, he invariably bows to tradition and stops before entering into the female domain.

3 Virginia Woolf, *A Room of One's Own* (New York: Harcourt, Brace and World, 1975), p. 69.

4 For an account of the early eighteenth-century tradition that links the novel to criminal culture, see Lennard Davis, *Factual Fictions: The Origins of the English Novel* (New York: Columbia University Press, 1983), pp. 123–37. For the objection to novels because of their quasi-erotic appeal, see John Richetti, *Popular Fiction Before Richardson's Narrative Patterns 1700–1734* (Oxford: Clarendon, 1969). In an issue of Addison's *Spectator*, for example, Mr. Spectator warns readers about the perils of May, advising that women "be in a particular Manner how they meddle with Romances, Chocolates, Novels, and the like inflamers, which I look upon to be very dangerous to be made use of during this great Carnival of Nature," quoted in *Four Before Richardson: Selected English Novels 1720–1727*, ed. William H. McBurney (Lincoln: University of Nebraska Press, 1963), p. ix. Toward the end of the eighteenth century, however, one discovers a good number of pedagogical treatises echo Austen's *Northanger Abbey* in advocating certain works of fiction as the fitting way to occupy leisure time. The fiction that was supposed to have a salutory effect on young women was either produced by lady novelists that gained currency during the age of Burney and the other lady novelists or else by earlier novelists who celebrated the same domestic virtues and saw the same form of domestic happiness as the ultimate reward for demonstrating these virtues. It was during this time, as Homer O. Brown explains, that certain novels were published under the editorship of Scott and Barbauld and marked as polite reading, and on the basis of this limited and anomalous body of works, a history of the novel was constructed backward in time (from his book, *Institutions of the English Novel in the Eighteenth Century*).

5 A number of social historians have suggested that the factory system, and with it the economic domination of the new middle classes, was stalled until the beginning of the nineteenth century. In *The Making of the English Working Class* (New York: Random House, 1966) p. 198, E. P. Thompson suggests that fear of Jacobinism produced a new alignment between landowners and industrialists that divided the traditional resistance to industrustrialization. In *The Machinery*

Question and the Making of Political Economy (Cambridge: Cambridge University Press, 1980), Maxine Berg explains how the development of political economy as a problem-solving logic at the end of the eighteenth century helped to make industrialization seem like an answer rather than a problem to be avoided at all costs. It was under such conditions that various authors first saw how many people had economic interests in common with the industrialists and described them as a class. In *Desire and Domestic Fiction: A Political History of the Novel* (New York: Oxford University Press, 1987), I carry this argument further by suggesting that well before they felt they had economic interests in common, numerous social groups ranging between the lower gentry and skilled workers were persuaded, in large part by authors un-known to us today, to buy into a single notion of personal life that centered around the kind of woman one desired to marry and the sort of happiness she would provide (pp. 59–95).

6 In discussing Feuerbach, Marx not only stresses that the "ruling ideas" of an epoch are the ideas of a ruling class who "regulate the production and distribution of ideas of their age" (p. 64). He also speculates that during the modern epoch, the production and distribution of ideas (i.e., the production of consciousness) will become increasingly important to the preserva-tion of the bourgeois "state" and to its eventual disintegration or overthrow, *The German Ideology*, Part One, ed. C. J. Arthur (New York: International Publishers, 1985). Without sliding back into the idealist philosophy from which Marx sought to rescue "the production of ideas," Gramsci applies the contradiction inherent in Marx's notion of labor to intellectual labor. The intellectual does not necessarily identify with the ruling class by reproducing the ideas inherited from the past but at certain moments may expand their political horizon by lending unity and coherence to the view of an emergent group, *The Modern Prince and Other Writings* (New York: International Publishers, 1957). In *Hegemony and Socialist Strategy*, trans. Winston Moore and Paul Cammack (London: Verso, 1985), Ernesto Laclau and Chantal Mouffe update this principle for a postmodern society by broadening Gramsci's notions of both power and resist-ance. Where the difference between production in the traditional sense and the production of information has virtually disappeared, the antagonism between worker and owner is likewise dispersed. Where such polarities could once be taken for granted, then, it becomes extremely difficult to create polarities along political lines. Laclau and Mouffe find it necessary to depart from Gramsci's reliance on the emergence of labor in conflict with capital and to turn instead to the intellectual labor of negativities and positivities out of the contemporary swamp of equiva-lences. For another important analysis of power in postmodern society, see Bonaventura de Sousa Santos, "Law and Community: The Changing Nature of State Power in Late Capital-ism," *International Journal of the Sociology of the Law* (1980), 8: 379–97.

7 Michel Foucault, *The History of Sexuality*, vol. 1, *An Introduction*, trans. Robert Hurley (New York: Pantheon, 1978).

8 *Discipline and Punish: The Birth of the Prison*, trans. Alan Sheridan (New York: Vintage, 1979). All citations are to this edition.

9 In *The Imaginary Puritan: Literature and the Origins of Personal Life* (Berkeley: University of California Press, 1992), Leonard Tennenhouse and I explain at length how the English Revo-lution failed to produce the base transformations that mark political revolution. We argue for a more adequate definition of the political, showing that while political change, in the narrow sense of the term, failed to occur, cultural change was profound and lasting. Before the modern middle classes gained economic control, and well before they gained control of the Houses of Parliament, a new class of intellectuals gained hegemony over aristocratic culture as it translated puritanism into the secular practices composing modern domesticity and personal life.

10 I have argued this at length in *Desire and Domestic Fiction*. This essay began as an early version of the introduction and later developed into a theoretical investigation of my argument with literature, history, and academic feminism. I refer readers to the book for evidence supporting the necessarily brief outline of the events in the history of modern sexuality which composes part of this essay.

11 In " 'The Mother Made Conscious': The Historical Development of a Primary School Peda-gogy," *History Workshop* (1985), vol. 20, Carolyn Steedman has researched the rationale and

analyzed the process by which the techniques of mothering were extended beyond the household and, through the establishment of a national educational system, became the gentle but unyielding girders of a new institutional culture.

12 See, for example, Peter Stallybrass and Allon White, *The Politics and Poetics of Transgression* (London: Methuen, 1986); Peter Clark, *The English Alehouse: A Social History 1200–1830* (London: Longman, 1983); Thomas Walter Laqueur, *Religion and Respectability: Sunday Schools and Working Class Culture 1780–1850* (New Haven: Yale University Press, 1976).

13 Maria Edgeworth and Robert L. Edgeworth, *Practical Education* (London, 1801), 2: ix. Citations in the text are to this edition.

14 For a discussion of the paternalism that emerged in opposition to patriarchy in seventeenth-century puritan writing, see Leonard Tennenhouse, *Power on Display: The Politics of Shakespeare's Genres* (New York: Methuen, 1986), especially the chapter entitled "Family Rites." In describing the alternative to patriarchy that arose at the end of the seventeenth and beginning of the eighteenth century in aristocratic families, Randolph Trumbach opposes the term "patriarchal" to the term "domesticity," by which he refers to the modern household. This social formation is authorized by internal relations of gender and generation rather than by way of analogy to external power relations between monarch and subject or between God and man, *The Rise of the Egalitarian Family* (New York: Academic Press, 1978), pp. 119–63.

15 Kathleen M. Davis, "The Sacred Condition of Equality – How Original were Puritan Doctrines of Marriage?" *Social History* (1977), 5: 570. Davis quotes this list from John Dod and Robert Cleaver, *A Godly Forme of Householde Gouernment* (London, 1614).

16 See Brian Simon, *Studies in the History of Education 1780–1870* (London: Lawrence and Wishart, 1960), pp. 1–62.

17 Charlotte Brontë, *Shirley*, ed. Andrew and Judith Hock (Harmondsworth: Penguin, 1974), p. 114. Citations of the text are to this edition.

18 E. P. Thompson, pp. 680–5.

CHAPTER 6

Professing the Renaissance: The Poetics and Politics of Culture

Louis Montrose

In this key essay of the "New Historicism," published in 1989, Louis Montrose outlines some of the important assumptions of this body of work. He emphasizes the role of Post-Structuralism, especially deconstruction, in influencing the New Historicist concern with what Montrose calls the "textuality of history."

There has recently emerged within Renaissance studies, as in Anglo-American literary studies generally, a renewed concern with the historical, social, and political conditions and consequences of literary production and reproduction: The writing and reading of texts, as well as the processes by which they are circulated and categorized, analyzed and taught, are being reconstrued as historically determined and determining modes of cultural work; apparently autonomous aesthetic and academic issues are being reunderstood as inextricably though complexly linked to other discourses and practices – such linkages constituting the social networks within which individual subjectivities and collective structures are mutually and continuously shaped. This general reorientation is the unhappy subject of J. Hillis Miller's 1986 Presidential Address to the Modern Language Association. In that address, Miller noted with some dismay – and with some hyperbole – that "literary study in the past few years has undergone a sudden, almost universal turn away from theory in the sense of an orientation toward language as such and has made a corresponding turn toward history, culture, society, politics, institutions, class and gender conditions, the social context, the material base."[1] By such a formulation, Miller polarizes the linguistic and the social. However, the prevailing tendency across cultural studies is to emphasize their reciprocity and mutual constitution: On the one hand, the social is understood to be discursively constructed; and on the other, language-use is understood to be always and necessarily dialogical, to be socially and materially determined and constrained.

Miller's categorical opposition of "reading" to cultural critique, of "theory" to the discourses of "history, culture, society, politics, institutions, class and gender" seems to me not only to oversimplify both sets of terms but also to suppress their points of contact and compatibility. The propositions and operations of deconstructive reading may be employed as powerful tools of ideological analysis. Derrida himself has recently suggested that, at least in his own work and in the context of European cultural politics, they have always been so: He writes that "deconstructive readings and writings are concerned not only with . . . discourses, with conceptual and seman-

tic contents....Deconstructive practices are also and first of all political and institutional practices."[2] The notorious Derridean aphorism, "*il n'y a pas de hors-texte,*"
["there is no outside of textuality"] may be invoked to abet an escape from the
determinate necessities of history, a self-abandonment to the indeterminate pleasures
of the text; however, it may also be construed as an insistence upon the ideological
force of discourse in general and of those discourses in particular which reduce the
work of discourse to the mere reflection of an ontologically prior, essential or empirical reality.

The multiplicity of unstable, variously conjoined and conflicting discourses that
may be said to inhabit the field of post-structuralist theory have in common the
problematization of those processes by which meaning is produced and grounded,
and a heightened (though, of course, necessarily limited) reflexivity concerning their
own assumptions and constraints, their methods and their motives. Miller wholly
identifies "theory" with domesticated, politically eviscerated varieties of Deconstruction, which he privileges ethically and epistemologically in relation to what he scorns
as "ideology" – that impassioned and delusional condition which "the critics and
antagonists of deconstruction on the so-called left and so-called right" (p. 289) are
said to share. Although his polemic indiscriminately though not unintentionally
lumps them with the academy's intellectually and politically reactionary forces, the
various modes of sociopolitical and historical criticism have not only been challenged
and influenced by the theoretical developments of the past two decades but have also
been vitally engaged in their definition and direction. And one such direction is the
understanding that "theory" does not reside serenely above "ideology" but rather is
mired within it. Representations of the world in written discourse are engaged in
constructing the world, in shaping the modalities of social reality, and in accommodating their writers, performers, readers, and audiences to multiple and shifting
subject positions within the world they both constitute and inhabit. Traditionally,
"ideology" has referred to the system of ideas, values, and beliefs common to any
social group; in recent years, this vexed but indispensable term has in its most general
sense come to be associated with the processes by which social subjects are formed,
re-formed and enabled to perform as conscious agents in an apparently meaningful
world.[3] In such terms, our professional practice, like our subject matter, is a production of ideology: By this I mean not merely that it bears the traces of the professor's
values, beliefs, and experiences – his or her socially constructed subjectivity – but also
that it actively instantiates those values, beliefs, and experiences. From this perspective, any claim for what Miller calls an "orientation to language as such" is itself –
always already – an orientation to language that is being produced from a position
within "history, culture, society, politics, institutions, class and gender conditions."

As if to reinforce Miller's sense of a general crisis in literary studies with the
arraignment of an egregious example, the issue of PMLA which opens with his
Presidential Address immediately continues with an article on the "politicizing" of
Renaissance Drama. The latter begins with the ominous warning that "A specter is
haunting criticism – the specter of a new historicism."[4] Edward Pechter's parody of
The Communist Manifesto points toward his claim that, although the label "New
Historicism" embraces a variety of critical practices, at its core this project is "a kind
of 'Marxist criticism'" – the latter, larger project being characterized in all its forms
and variants as a view of "history and contemporary political life as determined,
wholly or in essence, by struggle, contestation, power relations, *libido dominandi*"

(p. 292). It seems to me that, on this essentialist definition, such a project might be better labeled as Machiavellian or Hobbesian than as Marxist. In any event, Pechter's specter is indeed spectral, in the sense that it is largely the (mis)construction of the critic who is engaged in attacking it, and thus also in the sense that it has become an object of fascination and dread.

A couple of years ago, I attempted briefly to articulate and scrutinize some of the theoretical, methodological, and political assumptions and implications of the kind of work produced since the late 1970s by those (including myself) who were then coming to be labeled as "New Historicists."[5] The focus of such work has been upon a refiguring of the socio-cultural field within which canonical Renaissance literary and dramatic works were originally produced; upon resituating them not only in relationship to other genres and modes of discourse but also in relationship to contemporaneous social institutions and non-discursive practices. Stephen Greenblatt, who is most closely identified with the label "New Historicism" in Renaissance literary studies, has himself now abandoned it in favor of "Cultural Poetics," a term he had used earlier and one which perhaps more accurately represents the critical project I have described.[6] In effect, this project reorients the axis of inter-textuality, substituting for the diachronic text of an autonomous literary history the synchronic text of a cultural system. As the conjunction of terms in its title suggests, the interests and analytical techniques of "Cultural Poetics" are at once historicist and formalist; implicit in its project, though perhaps not yet adequately articulated or theorized, is a conviction that formal and historical concerns are not opposed but rather are inseparable.

Until very recently – and perhaps even now – the dominant mode of interpretation in English Renaissance literary studies has been to combine formalist techniques of close rhetorical analysis with the elaboration of relatively self-contained histories of "ideas," or of literary genres and topoi – histories that have been abstracted from their social matrices. In addition to such literary we may note two other traditional practices of "history" in Renaissance literary studies: one comprises those commentaries on political commonplaces in which the dominant ideology of Tudor–Stuart society – the unreliable machinery of socio-political legitimation – is misrecognized as a stable, coherent, and collective Elizabethan world picture, a picture discovered to be lucidly reproduced in the canonical literary works of the age; and the other, the erudite but sometimes eccentric scholarly detective work which, by treating texts as elaborate ciphers, seeks to fix the meaning of fictional characters and actions in their reference to specific historical persons and events. Though sometimes reproducing the methodological shortcomings of such older idealist and empiricist modes of historical criticism, but also often appropriating their prodigious scholarly labors to good effect, the newer historical criticism is new in its refusal of unproblematized distinctions between "literature" and "history," between "text" and "context," new in resisting a prevalent tendency to posit and privilege a unified and autonomous individual – whether an Author or a Work – to be set against a social or literary background.

In the essay of mine to which I have already referred, I wrote merely of a new historical orientation in Renaissance literary studies, because it seemed to me that those identified with it by themselves or by others were actually quite heterogeneous in their critical practices and, for the most part, reluctant to theorize those practices. The very lack of such explicit articulations was itself symptomatic of certain eclectic and empiricist tendencies that threatened to undermine any attempt to distinguish a new historicism from an old one. It may well be that these very ambiguities rendered

New Historicism less a critique of dominant critical ideology than a subject for ideological appropriation, thus contributing to its almost sudden installation as the newest academic orthodoxy, to its rapid assimilation by the "interpretive community" of Renaissance literary studies. Certainly, some who have been identified as exemplary New Historicists now enjoy the material and symbolic tokens of academic success; and any number of New Historicist dissertations, conferences, and publications testify to a significant degree of disciplinary influence and prestige. However, it remains unclear whether or not this latest "ism," with its appeal to our commodifying cult of the "new," will have been more than another passing intellectual fancy in what Fredric Jameson would call the academic marketplace under late capitalism. "The New Historicism" has not yet begun to fade from the academic scene, not is it quietly taking its place in the assortment of critical approaches on the interpreters' shelf. But neither has it become any clearer that "the New Historicism" designates any agreed-upon intellectual and institutional program. There has been no coalescence of the various identifiably New Historicist practices into a systematic and authoritative paradigm for the interpretation of Renaissance texts; nor does the emergence of such a paradigm seem either likely or desirable. What we are currently witnessing is the convergence of a variety of special interests upon "New Historicism," now constituted as a terminological site of intense debate and critique, of multiple appropriations and contestations within the ideological field of Renaissance studies itself, and to some extent in other areas of the discipline.

If Edward Pechter dubiously assimilates New Historicism to Marxism on the grounds that it insists upon the omnipresence of struggle as the motor of history, some self-identified Marxist critics are actively indicting New Historicism for its evasion of both political commitment and diachronic analysis – in effect, for its failure to be genuinely historical; while some female and male Renaissance scholars are fruitfully combining New Historicist and Feminist concerns, others are representing these projects (and/or their practitioners) as deeply antagonistic in gender-specific terms; while some see New Historicism as one of several modes of socio-criticism engaged in constructing a theoretically informed, post-structuralist problematic of historical study, others see it as aligned with a neo-pragmatist reaction against all forms of High Theory; if some see New Historicist preoccupations with ideology and social context as threatening to traditional critical concerns and literary values, others see a New Historicist delight in anecdote, narrative and what Clifford Geertz calls "thick description" as a will to construe all of culture as the domain of literary criticism – a text to be perpetually interpreted, an inexhaustible collection of stories from which curiosities may be culled and cleverly retold.[7]

Inhabiting the discursive spaces traversed by the term "New Historicism" are some of the most complex, persistent, and unsealing of the problems that professors of literature attempt variously to confront or to evade: Among them, the essential or historical bases upon which "literature" is to be distinguished from other discourses; the possible configurations of relationship between cultural practices and social, political, and economic processes; the consequences of post-structuralist theories of textuality for the practice of an historical or materialist criticism; the means by which subjectivity is socially constituted and constrained; the processes by which ideologies are produced and sustained, and by which they may be contested; the patterns of consonance and contradiction among the values and interests of a given individual, as these are actualized in the shifting conjunctures of various subject positions – as, for example, intellectual worker, academic professional, and gendered domestic, social, political and economic agent. My point is not that "the New Historicism" as a definable project, or the work of specific individuals identified by themselves or by others as New Historicists, can necessarily provide even provisional answers to such questions, but rather that the term "New Historicism" is currently being invoked in order to bring such issues into play and to stake out – or to hunt down – specific positions within the discursive spaces mapped by these issues.

The post-structuralist orientation to history now emerging in literary studies may be characterized chiastically, as a reciprocal concern with the historicity of texts and the textuality of history. By the historicity of texts, I mean to suggest the cultural specificity, the social embedment, of all modes of writing – not only the texts that critics study but also the texts in which we study them. By the textuality of history, I mean to suggest, firstly, that we can have no access to a full and authentic past, a lived material existence, unmediated by the surviving textual traces of the society in question – traces whose survival we cannot assume to be merely contingent but must rather presume to be at least partially consequent upon complex and subtle social processes of preservation and effacement; and secondly, that those textual traces are themselves subject to subsequent textual mediations when they are construed as the "documents" upon which historians ground their own texts, called "histories." As Hayden White has forcefully reminded us, such textual histories necessarily but always incompletely constitute in their narrative and rhetorical forms the "History" to which they offer access.[8] ...

"The Historicity of Texts and the Textuality of History": If such chiastic formulations are in fashion now, when the concept of referentiality has become so vexed, it may be because they figure forth from within discourse itself the model of a dynamic, unstable, and reciprocal relationship between the discursive and material domains.[9] This refiguring of the relationship between the verbal and the social, between the text and the world, involves a re-problematization or wholesale rejection of some prevalent alternative conceptions of literature: As an autonomous aesthetic order that transcends the shifting pressure and particularity of material needs and interests; as a collection of inert discursive records of "real events"; as a superstructural reflexion of an economic base. Current practices emphasize both the relative autonomy of specific discourses and their capacity to impact upon the social formation, to make things happen by shaping the subjectivities of social beings. Thus, to speak of the social production of "literature" or of any particular text is to signify not only that it is socially produced but also that it is socially productive – that it is the product of work and that it performs work in the process of being written, enacted, or read. Recent theories of textuality have argued persuasively that the referent of a linguistic sign cannot be fixed; that the meaning of a text cannot be stabilized. At the same time, writing and reading are always historically and socially determinate events, performed in the world and upon the world by gendered individual and collective human agents. We may simultaneously acknowledge the theoretical indeterminacy of the signifying process and the historical specificity of discursive practices – acts of speaking, writing, and interpreting. The project of a new socio-historical criticism is, then, to analyze the interplay of culture-specific discursive practices – mindful that it, too, is such a practice and so participates in the interplay it seeks to analyze. By such means, versions of the Real, of History, are instantiated, deployed, reproduced; and by such means, they may also be appropriated, contested, transformed.

Notes

1 J. Hillis Miller, "Presidential Address 1986. The Triumph of Theory, the Resistance to Reading, and the Question of the Material Base," *PMLA* 102 (1987), pp. 281–91; p. 283.

2 Jacques Derrida, "But, beyond...(Open Letter to Anne McClintock and Rob Nixon)," trans. Peggy Kamuf, *Critical Inquiry* 13 (1986), pp. 155–70; p. 168.

3 For a concise history of the term "ideology," see Raymond Williams, *Marxism and Literature* (Oxford: Oxford University Press, 1977), pp. 55–71. Of central importance for the sense of "ideology" I am using here is the essay on "Ideology and Ideological State Apparatuses" in Louis Althusser, *Lenin and Philosophy and Other Essays*, trans. Ben Brewster (New York and London: Monthly Review Press, 1971), pp. 127–86. According to Althusser's well-known formulation, "Ideology is a 'Representation' of the Imaginary Relationship of Individuals to their Real Conditions of Existence," which "Interpellates Individuals as Subjects" (pp. 162, 170). Althusser's theories of Ideology and the Subject have provoked considerable commentary and criticism, notably for appearing to disallow human agency in the making of history. On this debate, with special reference to the anti-Althusserian polemic of E. P. Thompson, see Perry Anderson, *Arguments Within English Marxism* (London: Verso, 1980), pp. 15–58.

A concise clarification of relevant terms is provided in Paul Smith, *Discerning the Subject* (Minneapolis: University of Minnesota Press, 1988) – which was published too late for me to have made more use of it here:

> "The individual" will be understood here as simply the illusion of whole and coherent personal organization, or as the misleading description of the imaginary ground on which different subject-positions are colligated.
>
> And thence the commonly used term "subject" will be broken down and will be understood as the term inaccurately used to describe what is actually the series of the conglomeration of *positions*, subject-positions, provisional and not necessarily indefeasible, into which a person is called momentarily by the discourses and the world that he/she inhabits.
>
> The term "agent," by contrast, will be used to mark the idea of a form of subjectivity where, by virtue of the contradictions and disturbances in and among subject-positions, the possibility (indeed, the actuality) of resistance to ideological pressure is allowed for (even though that resistance too must be produced in an ideological context). (p. xxxv)

4 Edward Pechter, "The New Historicism and Its Discontents: Politicizing Renaissance Drama," *PMLA* 102 (1987), pp. 292–303; p. 292.

5 Louis Montrose, "Renaissance Literary Studies and the Subject of History," *English Literary Renaissance* 16 (1986), pp. 5–12. Much of that essay is subsumed and reworked in the present one. My thanks to Arthur Kinney, Editor of *ELR*, for permission to reprint previously published material; and to Roxanne Klein for her continuing encouragement and advice.

6 The term "New Historicism" seems to have been introduced into Renaissance studies (with reference to cultural semiotics) in Michael McCanles, "The Authentic Discourse of the Renaissance," *Diacritics* 10: 1 (Spring 1980), 77–87. However, it seems to have gained currency from its use by Stephen Greenblatt in his brief, programmatic introduction to "The Forms of Power and the Power of Forms in the Renaissance," a special issue of *Genre* (15, 1–2 [1982], pp. 1–4). Earlier, in the Introduction to *Renaissance Self-Fashioning* (Chicago: University of Chicago Press, 1980), Greenblatt had called his project a "cultural poetics." He has returned to this term in the introductory chapter of his recent book, *Shakespearean Negotiations: The Circulation of Social Energy in Renaissance England* (Berkeley and Los Angeles: University of California Press, 1988). Here he defines the enterprise of cultural poetics as the "study of the collective making of distinct cultural practices and inquiry into the relations among these practices"; the relevant concerns are "how collective beliefs and experiences were shaped, moved from one medium to another, concentrated in manageable aesthetic form, offered for consumption [and] how the boundaries were marked between cultural practices understood to be art forms and

other, contiguous, forms of expression" (p. 5). I discuss the relevance of anthropological theory and ethnographic practice – specifically, the work of Clifford Geertz – to the study of early modern English culture in my review essay on *Renaissance Self-Fashioning*: "A Poetics of Renaissance Culture," *Criticism* 23 (1981), pp. 349–59.

7   Two influential and generally sympathetic early surveys/critiques of New Historicist work are: Jonathan Goldberg, "The Politics of Renaissance Literature: A Review Essay," *ELH* 49 (1982), pp. 514–42; and Jean E. Howard, "The New Historicism in Renaissance Studies," *English Literary Renaissance* 16 (1986), pp. 13–43. A number of critiques of New Historicism from various ideological positions have subsequently been published, and more are on the way. In addition to Pechter's hostile neo-conservative essay, within English Renaissance studies these critiques include the following: from a generally neo-Marxist perspective, Walter Cohen, "Political Criticism of Shakespeare," in Jean E. Howard and Marion F. O'Connor, eds, *Shakespeare Reproduced: The Text in History and Ideology* (New York and London: Methuen, 1987), pp. 18–46, and Don E. Wayne, "Power, Politics, and the Shakespearean Text: Recent Criticism in England and the United States," in Howard and O'Connor, eds, *Shakespeare Reproduced*, pp. 47–67; from a liberal American feminist perspective, Peter Erickson, "Rewriting the Renaissance, Rewriting Ourselves," *Shakespeare Quarterly* 38 (1987), pp. 327–37, Lynda E. Boose, "The Family in Shakespeare Studies; or – Studies in the Family of Shakespeareans; or – The Politics of Politics," *Renaissance Quarterly* 40 (1987), pp. 707–42, and Carol Thomas Neely, "Constructing the Subject: Feminist Practice and New Renaissance Discourses," *English Literary Renaissance* 18 (1988), pp. 5–18; from a deconstructionist perspective, A. Leigh DeNeef, "Of Dialogues and Historicisms," *South Atlantic Quarterly* 86 (1987), pp. 497–517. I want to record here my thanks to Alan Liu and Carolyn Porter for sharing with me their as yet unpublished studies of Renaissance New Historicism from the perspectives of English Romanticism and American studies, respectively.

In a recent essay, "Towards a Poetics of Culture," *Southern Review* (Australia) 20 (1987), pp. 3–15, Stephen Greenblatt remarks that "one of the peculiar characteristics of the 'new historicism' in literary studies is precisely how unresolved and in some ways disinguous it has been – I have been – about the relation to literary theory." Accordingly, the essay does not set out an explicit theoretical position but rather a demonstration of his resistance to theory: "I want to speculate on why this should be so by trying to situate myself in relation to Marxism on the one hand, and poststructuralism on the other" (p. 3). Greenblatt goes on to situate himself as a neo-pragmatist in relation to two totalizing discourses in each of which, "history functions . . . as a convenient anecdotal ornament upon a theoretical structure." What he seems to offer in opposition to such theoretical discourses, which collapse "the contradictions of history into a moral imperative" (p. 7), is essentially an empirical historical analysis that has not been fettered by ideology. By means of a striking personal anecdote, Greenblatt suggests that the practice of cultural poetics involves a repudiation of cultural politics. My own conviction is that their separation is no more desirable than it is possible.

8   On the constitutive discourse of the historian and the genres of history writing, see Hayden White, *Tropics of Discourse* (Baltimore: Johns Hopkins University Press, 1978).

9   Comparing Fredric Jameson's counter-Deconstructionist formulation of this relationship in terms of Marxism that is itself necessarily post-structuralist:

> The type of interpretation here proposed is more satisfactorily grasped as the rewriting of the literary text in such a way that the latter may itself be seen as the rewriting or restructuration of a prior historical or ideological *subtext*, it being always understood that that "subtext" is not immediately present as such, not some common-sense external reality, nor even the conventional narratives of history manuals, but rather must itself always be (re)constructed after the fact. . . . The whole paradox of what we have here called the subtext may be summed up in this, that the literary work or cultural object, as though for the first time, brings into being that very situation of which it is also, at one and the same time, a reaction. . . . History is inaccessible to us except in textual form. . . . It can be approached only by way of prior (re)textualization. . . . To overemphasize the active way in which the text reorganizes its subtext (in order, presumably, to reach the triumphant conclusion that the "referent" does not exist); or

on the other hand to stress the imaginary status of the symbolic act so completely as to reify its social ground, now no longer understood as a subtext but merely as some inert given that the text passively or fantasmatically "reflects" – to overstress either of these functions of the symbolic act at the expense of the other is surely to produce sheer ideology, whether it be, as in the first alternative, the ideology of structuralism, or, in the second, that of vulgar materialism. (*The Political Unconscious*, pp. 80–1)

For another Marxist consideration of and response to recent theoretical challenges to historical criticism, see "Text and History: Epilogue 1984" in Robert Weimann, *Structure and Society in Literary History*, expanded edn (Baltimore: Johns Hopkins University Press, 1984), pp. 267–323.

Introductions to materialist cultural theory include Raymond Williams's *Marxism and Literature*; Raymond Williams, *Culture* (London: Fontana, 1981); Janet Wolff, *The Social Production of Art* (London: Macmillan, 1981).

CHAPTER 7

Shakespeare and the Exorcists

Stephen Greenblatt

Stephen Greenblatt's *Shakespearean Negotiations* (1988) is rightly considered a central text of the New Historicism. In this selection on *King Lear*, Greenblatt connects the play to one of its sources, Samuel Harsnett's *A Declaration of Egregious Popish Impostures*. He notes that Shakespeare not only borrowed a vocabulary of demonic possession from the text. He also reiterated Harsnett's concern with the sacred and the question of Christian redemption.

Between the spring of 1585 and the summer of 1586, a group of English Catholic priests led by the Jesuit William Weston, alias Father Edmunds, conducted a series of spectacular exorcisms, principally in the house of a recusant gentleman, Sir George Peckham of Denham, Buckinghamshire. The priests were outlaws – by an act of 1585 the mere presence in England of a Jesuit or seminary priest constituted high treason – and those who sheltered them were guilty of a felony, punishable by death. Yet the exorcisms, though clandestine, drew large crowds, almost certainly in the hundreds, and must have been common knowledge to hundreds more. In 1603, long after the arrest and punishment of those involved, Samuel Harsnett, then chaplain to the bishop of London, wrote a detailed account of the cases, based on sworn statements taken from four of the demoniacs and one of the priests. It has been recognized since the eighteenth century that Shakespeare was reading Harsnett's book, *A Declaration of Egregious Popish Impostures*, as he was writing *King Lear*.[1]

The relation between these two texts enables us to glimpse with unusual clarity and precision the institutional negotiation and exchange of social energy. The link between *King Lear* and *A Declaration of Egregious Popish Impostures* has been known for centuries, but the knowledge has remained almost entirely inert, locked in the conventional pieties of source study. From Harsnett, we are told, Shakespeare borrowed the names of the foul fiends by whom Edgar, in his disguise as the bedlam beggar Poor Tom, claims to be possessed. From Harsnett too the playwright derived some of the language of madness, several of the attributes of hell, and a number of colorful adjectives. These and other possible borrowings have been carefully cataloged, but the question of their significance has been not only unanswered but, until recently, unasked.[2] For a long time the prevailing model for the study of literary sources, a model in effect parceled out between the old historicism and the new criticism, blocked such a question. As a freestanding, self-sufficient, disinterested art work produced by a solitary genius, *King Lear* has only an accidental relation to its sources: they provide a glimpse of the "raw material" that the artist fashioned. Insofar as this "material" is taken seriously at all, it is as part of the work's "historical background," a phrase that reduces history to a decorative setting or a convenient, well-lighted pigeonhole. But once the differentiations on which this model is based begin to crumble, then source study is compelled to change its character: history cannot simply be set against literary texts as either stable antithesis or stable background, and the protective isolation of those texts gives way to a sense of their interaction with other texts and hence of the permeability of their boundaries. "When I play with my cat," writes Montaigne, "who knows if I am not a pastime to her more than she is to me?"[3] When Shakespeare borrows from Harsnett, who knows if Harsnett has not already, in a deep sense, borrowed from Shakespeare's theater what Shakespeare borrows back? Whose interests are served by the borrowing? And is there a larger cultural text produced by the exchange?

Such questions do not lead, for me at least, to the *O altitudo!* of radical indeterminacy. They lead rather to an exploration of the institutional strategies in which both *King Lear* and Harsnett's *Declaration* are embedded. These strategies, I suggest, are part of an intense and sustained struggle in late sixteenth- and early seventeenth-century England to redefine the central values of society. Such a redefinition entailed transforming the prevailing standards of judgment and action, rethinking the conceptual categories by which the ruling elites constructed their world and which they attempted to impose on the majority of the population. At the heart of this struggle, which eventuated in a murderous civil war, was the definition of the sacred, a definition that directly involved secular as well as religious institutions, since the legitimacy of the state rested explicitly on its claim to a measure of sacredness. What is the sacred? Who defines and polices its boundaries? How can society distinguish between legitimate and illegitimate claims to sacred authority? In early modern England rivalry among elites competing for the major share of authority was characteristically expressed not only in parliamentary factions but also in bitter struggles over religious doctrine and practice.

Harsnett's *Declaration* is a weapon in one such struggle, the attempt by the established and state-supported Church of England to eliminate competing religious authorities by wiping out pockets of rivalrous charisma. Charisma, in Edward Shils's phrase, is "awe-arousing centrality,"[4] the sense of breaking through the routine into the realm of the "extraordinary" to make direct contact with the ultimate, vital sources of legitimacy, authority, and sacredness. Exorcism was for centuries one of the supreme manifestations in Latin Christianity of this charisma: "In the healing of the possessed," Peter Brown writes, "the *praesentia* of the saints was held to be registered with unfailing accuracy, and their ideal power, their *potentia*, shown most fully and in the most reassuring manner."[5] Reassuring, that is, not only or even primarily to the demoniac but to the community of believers who bore witness to the ritual and, indeed, through their tears and prayers and thanksgiving, participated in it. For unlike the sorcerer who practiced his art most frequently in the dark corners of the land, in remote rural hamlets and isolated cottages, the charismatic healer depended upon an audience: the great exorcisms of the late Middle Ages and early Renaissance took place at the heart of cities, in churches packed with spectators.

"Great troupes did daily flock thither," writes the Dominican exorcist Sebastian Michaelis about a series of exorcisms he conducted in Aix-en-Provence in the early seventeenth century, and they were, he argues, deeply moved by what they witnessed. Thus, for example, from the body of the young nun Louise, the demon Verrine cried out "with great and ghastly exclamations" that heretics and sinners would be deprived of the vision of God "for ever, for ever, for ever, for ever, for ever." The spectators were so "affrighted" with these words "that there gushed from their eyes abundance of tears, when they called to remembrance their offences which they had committed."[6]

As voluminous contemporary accounts declare, then, exorcisms were moving testimonials to the power of the true faith. But by the late sixteenth century in Protestant England neither the *praesentia* nor the *potentia* of the exorcist was reassuring to religious authorities, and the Anglican church had no desire to treat the urban masses to a spectacle whose edifying value had been called into question. Moving testimonials extorted from the devil himself – praise of the Virgin, awe in the presence of the Eucharist, acknowledgment of the authority of the pope – now seemed both fraudulent and treasonous, and the danger was as great when it came not from a Catholic healer but from a stubbornly nonconforming Protestant. Although the latter did not celebrate the power of the Virgin – when someone tried to invoke Mary's name at a Protestant exorcism, the presiding exorcist sternly rebuked him, "for there is no other name under Heaven, whereby we may challenge Salvation, but th'only name of Jesus Christ"[7] – he exalted the power of fasting and prayer and made it clear that this power did not depend upon a state-sponsored ecclesiastical hierarchy. The authorities could easily close the cathedrals to such sedition, but even relatively small assemblies in obscure private houses far from the cities had come to represent a threat.

In the *Declaration* Harsnett specifically attacks exorcism as practiced by Jesuits, but he had earlier leveled the same charges at a Puritan exorcist. And he does so not, as we might expect, to claim a monopoly on the practice for the Anglican church but to expose exorcism itself as a fraud. On behalf of established religious and secular authority, Harsnett wishes to cap permanently the great rushing geysers of charisma released in rituals of exorcism. Spiritual *potentia* will henceforth be distributed with greater moderation and control through the whole of the Anglican hierarchy, at whose pinnacle sits the sole legitimate possessor of absolute charismatic authority, the monarch, Supreme Head of the Church in England.

The arguments that Harsnett marshals against exorcism have a rationalistic cast that may mislead us, for despite appearances we are not dealing with the proto–Enlightenment attempt to construct a rational faith. Harsnett denies the presence of the demonic in those whom Father Edmunds claimed to exorcise but finds it in the exorcists themselves: "And who was the devil, the broacher, herald, and persuader of these unutterable treasons, but *Weston* [alias Edmunds] the Jesuit, the chief plotter, and...all the holy Covey of the twelve devilish comedians in their several turns: for there was neither devil, nor urchin, nor Elf, but themselves" (154–5). Hence, writes Harsnett, the "Dialogue between *Edmunds*, & the devil" was in reality a dialogue between "the devil *Edmunds*, and *Edmunds* the devil, for he played both parts himself" (86).

This strategy – the reinscription of evil onto the professed enemies of evil – is one of the characteristic operations of religious authority in the early modern period and has its secular analogues in more recent history when famous revolutionaries are paraded forth to be tried as counter-revolutionaries. The paradigmatic Renaissance instance is the case of the *benandanti*, analyzed brilliantly by the historian Carlo Ginzburg.[8] The *benandanti* were members of a northern Italian folk cult who believed that they went forth seasonally to battle with fennel stalks against their enemies, the witches. If the *benandanti* triumphed, their victory assured the peasants of good harvests; if they lost, the witches would be free to work their mischief. The Inquisition first became interested in the practice in the late sixteenth century; after conducting a series of lengthy inquiries, the Holy Office determined that the cult was demonic and in subsequent interrogations attempted, with some success, to persuade the witch-fighting *benandanti* that they were themselves witches.

Harsnett does not hope to persuade exorcists that they are devils; he wishes to expose their fraudulence and relies on the state to punish them. But he is not willing to abandon the demonic altogether, and it hovers in his work, half accusation, half metaphor, whenever he refers to Father Edmunds or the pope. Satan's function was too important for him to be cast off lightly by the early seventeenth-century clerical establishment. The same state church that sponsored the attacks on superstition in *A Declaration of Egregious Popish Impostures* continued to cooperate, if less enthusiastically than before, in the ferocious prosecutions of witches. These prosecutions, significantly, were handled by the secular judicial apparatus – witchcraft was a criminal offense like aggravated assault or murder – and hence reinforced rather than rivaled the bureaucratic control of authority. The eruption of the demonic into the human world was not denied altogether, but the problem would be processed through the proper secular channels. In cases of witchcraft, the devil was defeated in the courts through the simple expedient of hanging his human agents, not, as in cases of possession, compelled by a spectacular spiritual counterforce to speak out and depart.

Witchcraft then was distinct from possession, and though Harsnett himself is skeptical about accusations of witchcraft, his principal purpose is to expose a nexus of chicanery and delusion in the practice of exorcism.[9] By doing so he hopes to drive the practice out of society's central zone, to deprive it of its prestige, and to discredit its apparent efficacy.[10] In late antiquity, as Peter Brown has demonstrated, exorcism was based on the model of the Roman judicial system: the exorcist conducted a formal *quaestio* in which the demon, under torture, was forced to confess the truth.[11] Now, after more than a millennium, this power would once again be vested solely in the state.

Harsnett's efforts, backed by his powerful superiors, did seriously restrict the practice of exorcism. Canon 72 of the new Church Canons of 1604 ruled that henceforth no minister, unless he had the special permission of his bishop, was to attempt "upon any pretense whatsoever, whether of possession or obsession, by fasting and prayer, to cast out any devil or devils, under pain of the imputation of imposture or cozenage and deposition from the ministry."[12] Since special permission was rarely, if ever, granted, in effect exorcism had been officially halted. But it proved easier to drive exorcism from the center to the periphery than to strip it entirely of its power. Exorcism had been a process of reintegration as well as a manifestation of authority; as the ethnographer Shirokogorov observed of the shamans of Siberia, exorcists could "master" harmful spirits and restore "psychic equilibrium" to whole communities as well as to individuals.[13] The pronouncements of English bishops could not suddenly banish from the land inner demons who stood, as Peter Brown puts it, "for the intangible emotional undertones of ambiguous situations and for the uncertain motives of refractory individuals."[14] The possessed gave voice to the rage, anxiety, and sexual frustration that built up easily in the authoritarian, patriarchal, impoverished, and plague-ridden world of early modern England. The Anglicans attempted to dismantle a corrupt and inadequate therapy without effecting a new and successful cure. In the absence of exorcism Harsnett could offer the possessed only the slender reed of Jacobean medicine; if the recently deciphered journal of the Buckinghamshire physician Richard Napier is at all representative, doctors in the period struggled to treat a significant number of cases of possession.[15]

But for Harsnett the problem does not really exist, for he argues that the great majority of cases of possession are either fraudulent or subtly called into existence by the ritual designed to treat them. Eliminate the cure and you eliminate the disease. He is forced to concede that at some distant time possession and exorcism were authentic, for Christ himself had driven a legion of unclean spirits out of a possessed man and into the Gadarene swine (Mark 5:1–19); but the age of miracles has passed, and corporeal possession by demons is no longer possible. The spirit abroad is "the spirit of illusion" (*Discovery*, p. A3). Whether they profess to be Catholics or Calvinists does not matter; all modern exorcists practice the same time-honored trade: "the feat of juggling and deluding the people by counterfeit miracles" (*Discovery*, p. A2). Exorcists sometimes contend, Harsnett acknowledges, that the casting out of devils is not a miracle but a wonder – "*mirandum & non miraculum*" – but "both terms spring from one root of wonder or marvel: an effect which a thing strangely done doth procure in the minds of the beholders, as being above the reach of nature and reason" (*Discovery*, p. A4[r–v]).

The significance of exorcism, then, lies not in any intrinsic quality of the ritual or in the character of the marks of possession but in the impression made upon the minds of the spectators. In *The Discovery of Witchcraft* (1584), a remarkable book that greatly influenced Harsnett, Reginald Scot detailed some of the means used to shape this impression: the cunning manipulation of popular superstitions; the exploitation of grief, fear, and credulity; the skillful handling of illusionistic devices developed for the stage; the blending of spectacle and commentary; the deliberate arousal of anxiety coupled with the promise to allay it. Puritan exorcists throw themselves into histrionic paroxysms of prayer; Catholic exorcists deploy holy water, smoldering brimstone, and sacred relics. They seem utterly absorbed in the plight of the wretches who writhe in spectacular contortions, vomit pins, display uncanny strength, foam at the mouth, cry out in weird voices. But all of this apparent absorption in the supernatural crisis is an illusion; there is nothing real out there on the bed, in the chair, on the pulpit. The only serious action is transpiring in the minds of the audience.

Hence the exorcists take care, notes Harsnett, to practice their craft only when there is "a great assembly gathered together," and the ritual is then explicitly presented to this assembly with a formal prologue: "The company met, the *Exorcists* do tell them, *what a work of God they have in hand*, and after a long discourse, *how Sathan doth afflict the parties*, and *what strange things they shall see:* the said parties are brought forth, as it were a Bear to the stake, and being either bound in a chair, or otherwise held fast, they fall to their fits, and play their pranks point by point exactly, according as they have been instructed" (*Discovery*, p. 62).

What seems spontaneous is in fact carefully scripted, from the shaping of audience expectations to the rehearsal of the performers. Harsnett grants that to those who suspect no fraud the effect is extraordinarily powerful: "They are cast thereby into a wonderful astonishment" (*Discovery*, p. 70). Aroused by wonder to a heightened state of both attention and suggestibility, the beholders are led to see significance in the smallest gestures of the possessed and to apply that significance to their own lives. But the whole moving process is a dangerous fraud that should be exposed and punished in the courts.

To substantiate these charges the English church needed, in the language of spy stories, to "turn" one of the participants in the spectacle of possession and exorcism. In the mid-1590s the authorities were alerted to the activities of a charismatic Puritan healer named John Darrel. Through fasting and prayer he had helped to exorcise one Thomas Darling, popularly known as the Boy of Burton, and had then gone on to a still greater success in a case of mass possession, known as the Seven in Lancashire. Alarmed by this success, the authorities in 1598 found what they were looking for: William Sommers, aged twenty-one, an unstable musician's apprentice in Nottingham who was being exorcized by Darrel in a series of spectacular spiritual encounters. Under great pressure Sommers confessed to imposture and exposed – or claimed to expose – Darrel's secret methods: "As I did use any of the said gestures," testified Sommers, recalling his first manifestation in Nottingham of the symptoms of possession,

> Oh would M. Darrell say, to the standers by: see you not how he doth thus, and thus? These things signify that such and such sins do reign in this town. They also that were present having heard M. Darrell, would as I tossed with my hands, and tumbled up and down upon my bed presently collect and say: oh, he doth so for this sin, and so for that sin, whereby it came to pass, that I could do nothing in any of my fits, either that night or the day after, either stir my head, or any part of my body: look merrily, or sadly, sit or lie, speak or be silent, open or shut mine eyes, but some would still make an interpretation of it: as to be done by the Devil in me, to declare such sins in Nottingham, as they themselves imagined. (*Discovery*, p. 117).

Darrel denied ever offering an interpretation of Sommers's gestures, but he confirmed the nature of the performance:

> This evening, he acted many sins by signs & gestures, most lively representing & shadowing, them out unto us: as namely brawling, quarreling, fighting, swearing, robbing by the highways, picking and cutting of purses, burglary, whoredom, pride in men and women, hypocrisy, sluggishness in hearing of the word, drunkenness, gluttony, also dancing with the toys thereunto belonging, the manner of Antic dancers, the games of dicing and carding, the abuse of the Viol, with other instruments. At the end of sundry of these, he laughed exceedingly, diverse times clapping his hands on his thighs for joy: percase to shadow out the delight, that both himself, and sinners take in their sins. And at the end of some of them, as killing and stealing, he showed how he brought them to the Gallows, making a sign thereof. (*Discovery*, pp. 118–19)

According to Harsnett, on the Sunday following this display one of Darrel's colleagues delivered from the pulpit an "authentical reading" of the "dumb show," and this reading was in turn followed by a popular ballad: a campaign, in short, to extend the exorcist's influence beyond the immediate circle of beholders to both the elite and the masses. Harsnett, in response, participates in a massive counter-campaign to destroy this influence. Hounding or imprisoning Darrel was not enough, for persecution could easily heighten his popular appeal, and even were he conveniently to disappear, he would be succeeded by others. The exorcist had to be attacked where he had his power: in the minds of beholders or potential beholders.

Accounts of exorcism in the late sixteenth and early seventeenth centuries make it clear that the spectacle of the symptoms of demonic possession had a profoundly disturbing effect on those who witnessed them. The spectacle was evidently more than that of physical or psychic anguish; after all, the men and women of this period would have been accustomed and perhaps hardened to the sight of abject misery. Quite apart from the spectacle of public maimings and executions, an Elizabethan who survived to adolescence must have already been an aficionado of human wretchedness.

Demonic possession was something more: it was utterly strange – a fearful visitation of the perverted spiritual presences of the other world – and at the same time uncannily intimate, for if the demons were exotic tormenters with weird names, the victims were neighbors enduring their trials in altogether familiar surroundings. Hence the testimony taken from those who witnessed the sufferings combines the homely and the bizarre: an evil spirit that appeared in Suffolk became "a thick dark substance about a foot high, like to a sugar loaf, white on the top";[16] young Mary Glover's voice sounded to one witness like "the hissing of a violent *Squib*," to another like a "*Hen* that hath the *squack*," to a third like "the loathsome noise that a *Cat* maketh forcing to cast her gorge";[17] William Sommers's "entrails shot up & down like a weavers shuttle."[18] Sommers's cries seemed unutterably strange – he shrieked "with 3 several voices so hideously, and so terribly," a surgeon reports, "as they were not like any human creature" – but each of the witnesses seems to have tried immediately to place the extraordinary events in the context of the familiar. William Aldred, a preacher, reports that he stood in a crowd of about one hundred fifty persons and watched Sommers having his fits. What he noticed was Darrel praying and preaching; "then the whole congregation breaking their hitherto continued silence cried out all at once as it were with one voice unto the Lord, to relieve the distressed person: and within a quarter of an hour, or thereabouts it pleased God to hear their prayers." Joan Pie, the wife of Nottingham baker Robert Pie, also saw the fits; what she noticed was that suddenly Sommers "was plucked round upon a heap, as though his body had lain like a great brown loaf." Richard Mee, butcher, remarked that Sommers suddenly screeched "like a swine when he is in sticking."[19]

The domestication of the demonic (a zany Elizabethan version of *What Do People Do All Day?*) only serves to intensify for most of the witnesses the wonder of the supernatural visitation. Harsnett's task is to demolish this experience of wonder; he seeks to shine the sharp, clear light of ridicule on the exorcist's mysteries and thus to expose them as shabby tricks. Among the demoniac's most frightening symptoms was a running lump – variously described as resembling a kitten, a mouse, a halfpenny white loaf, a goose egg, a French walnut, and a hazelnut – that could be seen under the coverlet, moving across his body as he lay in a trance. One of the bystanders, apparently less awestruck than the rest, impulsively pounced on the lump and found that he had seized Sommers's hand. In his confession Sommers confirmed that he achieved his effect by no more complicated means than moving his fingers and toes under the coverlet. It seems impossible for this miserable expedient to produce so much as a frisson, but a skeptical witness, quoted by Harsnett, tried it out at home: "And it fell out to be so agreeable with that which the boy did, as my wife being in bed with me, was on the sudden in great fear, that *Somers* spirit had followed me" (*Discovery*, p. 240).

Held up to the light, the devil's coin is a pathetic counterfeit, fit only to frighten women and boys. Yet Harsnett is not content simply to publish Sommers's confession of fraud, in part, perhaps, because there was reason to believe that the confession was forced, in part because even if Sommers were proven to be a mere actor, other demoniacs clearly believed in all sincerity that they were possessed by devils. Moreover, the polemic had to be conducted with an odd blend of rhetorical violence and doctrinal caution. "If neither possession, nor witchcraft (contrary to that hath been so long generally & confidently affirmed)," wrote Darrel in his own defense, "why should we think that there are Devils? If no Devils, no God."[20]

No one in the Anglican church was prepared to deny the existence of Satan, any more than they were prepared to deny the existence of God. What role did Satan play then in the fraudulent dramas in which his name figured so prominently? In the case of Catholic exorcists, Harsnett is prepared to locate the demonic in the very figures who profess themselves to be the agents of God:

> Dissemblers, jugglers, impostors, players with God, his son, his angels, his saints: devisers of new devils, feigned tormentors of spirits, usurpers of the key of the bottomless pit, whippers, scourgers, batfoulers of fiends, Pandars, Ganimedeans, enhancers of lust, deflowerers of virgins, defilers of houses, uncivil, unmanly, unnatural venereans, offerers of their own mass to supposed devils, depravers of their own relics, applying them to unspeakable, detestable, monstrous deformities: prostituters of all the rites, ornaments, and ceremonies of their Church to impure villainies: profaners of all parts of the service, worship, and honour of God: violators of tombs, sacrilegious, blasphemers of God, the blessed Trinity, and the virgin *Mary*, in the person of a counterfeit devil: seducers of subjects, plotters, conspirators, contrivers of bloody & detestable treasons, against their anointed Sovereign: it would pose all hell to sample them with such another dozen. (*Declaration*, pp. 160–1)

In short, they were Jesuits. But Darrel was a Protestant and, by all accounts, a man of austere and upright life. If he could not be portrayed as the devil incarnate, where was the devil to be found? One answer, proposed by Harsnett's allies John Deacon and John Walker, was that Satan could produce the *illusion* of demonic possession. "The *Devil* (being always desirous to work among the dear children of *God* the greatest *disturbance* that may be, and finding withal some such lewd disposed *person* as is naturally inclined to all manner of *knaveries*) he taketh the opportunity of so fit a *subject*, and worketh so cunningly upon the *corruption* of *that lewd persons nature*, as the *party* himself is easily brought to believe, and to bear others also in hand, that he is (in deed and in truth) *essentially possessed of Satan*."[21]

The problem with this argument is that it undermines the clarity and force of the confession of fraudulence the authorities had worked so hard to obtain. That confession was intended to establish a fixed, stable opposition between counterfeit – the false claim of demonic agency – and reality: the unblinking, disenchanted grasp of the mechanics of illusion mongering. Now after all the devil is discovered hovering behind the demoniac's performance. And if the Prince of Darkness is actually present, then the alleged evidence of fraudulence need not trouble the exorcist. For as Satan in possessing someone has sought to hide himself under the cover of human agency, so when detected he may wish to convince observers that the signs of possession are counterfeits. "Sathan in his subtlety," argued Darrel, "hath done in the boy some sleight and trifling things, at divers times, of purpose to deceive the beholders, and to bear them in hand, that he did never greater things in him: thereby to induce them to think, that he was a counterfeit" (*Discovery*, p. 231).[22]

If Satan can counterfeit counterfeiting, there can be no definitive confession, and the prospect opens of an infinite regress of disclosure and uncertainty. "How shall I know that this is thou *William Somers?*" asked Darrel, after the boy confessed to fraud. At first Sommers had been possessed only in body; now, said the exorcist, he is "also possessed in soul" (*Discovery*, p. 186). As Harsnett perceives, this "circular folly" at the heart of the practice of exorcism prevents a decisive judicial falsification. What Harsnett needs is not further evidence of fraud in particular cases – for such evidence can always be subverted by the same strategy of demonic doubt – but a counter-strategy to disclose fraudulence *always and everywhere*: in every gesture of the demoniac, in every word and deed of the exorcist. To demystify exorcism definitively, Harsnett must demonstrate not only why the ritual was so empty but why it was so effective, why beholders could be induced to believe that they were witnessing the ultimate confrontation between good and evil, why a few miserable shifts could produce the experience of horror and wonder. He must identify not merely the specific institutional motives behind exorcism – the treasonous designs of the Catholic church or the seditious mischief of self-styled Protestant saints – but the source of the extraordinary power in exorcism itself, a power that seems to transcend the specific and contradictory ideological designs of its practitioners. He needs an explanatory model, at once metaphor and analytical tool, by which all beholders will see fraud where once they saw God. Harsnett finds that explanatory model in *theater*.[23]

Exorcisms, Harsnett argues, are stage plays, most often tragicomedies, that cunningly conceal their theatrical inauthenticity and hence deprive the spectators of the rational disenchantment that frames the experience of a play. The audience in a theater knows that its misrecognition of reality is temporary, deliberate, and playful; the exorcist seeks to make the misrecognition permanent and invisible. Harsnett is determined to make the spectators see the theater around them, to make them understand that what seems spontaneous is rehearsed, what seems involuntary carefully crafted, what seems unpredictable scripted.

Not all of the participants themselves may fully realize that they are in a stage play. The account in *A Declaration of Egregious Popish Impostures* presents the exorcists, Father Edmunds and his cohorts, as self-conscious professionals and the demoniacs (mostly impressionable young servingwomen and unstable, down-at-heels young gentlemen) as amateurs subtly drawn into the demonic stage business. Those selected to play the possessed in effect learn their roles without realizing at first that they are roles.

The priests begin by talking conspicuously about successful exorcisms abroad and describing in lurid detail the precise symptoms of the possessed. They then await occasions on which to improvise: a servingman "being pinched with penury, & hunger, did lie but a night, or two, abroad in the fields, and being a melancholic person, was scared with lightning, and thunder, that happened in the night, & lo, an evident sign, that the man was possessed" (24); a dissolute young gentleman "had a spice of the *Hysterica passio*" or, as it is popularly called, "the Mother" (25),[24] and that too is a sign of possession. An inflamed toe, a pain in the side, a fright taken from the sudden leaping of a cat, a fall in the kitchen, an intense depression following the loss of a beloved child – all are occasions for the priests to step forward and detect the awful presence of the demonic, whereupon the young "scholars," as Harsnett wryly terms the naive performers, "*frame* themselves jump and fit unto the Priests humors, to mop, mow, jest, rail, rave, roar, commend & discommend, and as the priests would have them, upon fitting occasions (according to the difference of times, places, and comers in) in all things to play the devils accordingly" (38).

To glimpse the designing clerical playwright behind the performance is to transform terrifying supernatural events into a human strategy. One may then glimpse the specific material and symbolic interests served by this particular strategy, above all by its clever disguising of the fact that it is a strategy.

The most obvious means by which the authorities of the English church and state could make manifest the theatricality of exorcism was the command performance: the ability to mime the symptoms at will would, it was argued, decisively prove the possession a counterfeit. Hence we find the performance test frequently applied in investigations of alleged supernatural visitations. In the 1590s, for example, Ann Kerke was accused of bewitching a child to death and casting the child's sister into a fit that closely resembled that of a demoniac: "her mouth being drawn aside like a purse, her teeth gnashing together, her mouth foaming, and her eyes staring."[25] The judge, Lord Anderson, ordered the sister to "show how she was tormented: she said she could not shew it, but when the fit was on her" (100). The reply was taken to be strong corroboration of the authenticity of the charge, and Anne Kerke was hanged.

A similar, if subtler, use of the performance test occurs in the early 1620s. Thomas Perry, known as the Boy of Bilson, would fall into fits upon hearing the opening verse from the gospel of John; other verses from Scriptures did not have the same effect. Three Catholic priests were called in to exorcise the evil spirit that possessed him. During the boy's fit – watched by a large crowd – one of the priests commanded the devil "to show by the sheet before him, how he would use one dying out of the Roman Catholic Church? who very unwillingly, yet at length obeyed, tossing, plucking, haling, and biting the sheet, that it did make many to weep and cry forth."[26] A similar but still fiercer demonstration was evoked in response to the names Luther, Calvin, and Fox. Then, predictably, the priest commanded the devil "to show what power he had on a good Catholic that died out of mortal sin? he thrust down his arms, trembled, holding down his head, and did no more" (51).[27] The Catholics triumphantly published an account of the case, *A Faithful Relation*.

English officials, understandably annoyed by such propaganda, remanded Perry to the custody of the bishop of Coventry and Lichfield. To test if the boy was authentically possessed or "an execrable wretch, who playest the devils part," the Bishop read aloud the verse that set off the symptoms; the boy fell into fits. When the boy recovered, the bishop told him that he would read the same verse in Greek; once again the boy fell into fits. But in fact the Bishop had not read the correct verse, and the boy had been tricked into performance. Since the Devil was "so ancient a scholar as of almost 6000 years standing" (59), he should have known Greek. The possession was proved to be a counterfeit, and the boy, it is said, confessed that he had been instructed by an old man who promised that he would no longer have to go to school.

The Protestants now produced their own account of the case, *The Boy of Bilson; or, A True Discovery of the Late Notorious Impostures of Certain Romish Priests in Their Pretended Exorcism*. "Although these and the like pranks have been often hissed of[f] the Stage, for stale and gross forgeries," the author declares, since the Catholics have ventured to publish their version, it is necessary to set the record straight. A reader of the Catholic account should understand "that he hath seen a *Comedy*, wherein the Actors, which present themselves, are these, A crafty *old man*, teaching the feats and pranks of counterfeiting a person *Demoniacal* and possessed of the *Devil*; the next, a most docible, subtle, and expert young *Boy*, far more dextrous in the Practique part, than his Master was in the Theory; after him appear three Romish *Priests*, the Authors of seducement, conjuring their only imaginary *Devils*, which they brought with them; and lastly, a *Chorus* of credulous people easily seduced, not so much by the subtlety of those *Priests*, as by their own sottishness" (9).

Performance kills belief; or rather acknowledging theatricality kills the credibility of the supernatural. Hence in the case of William Sommers the authorities not only took the demoniac's confession of fraud but also insisted that he perform his simulated convulsions before the mayor and three aldermen of Nottingham. If he could act his symptoms, then the possession would be decisively falsified. Darrel countered that "if he can act them all in such manner and form as is deposed, then he is, either still possessed, or more than a man: for no humans power can do the like."[28] But the officials denied that the original performances themselves, stripped of the awe that the spectators brought to them, were particularly impressive. Sommers's possession, Harsnett had said, was a "dumb show" that depended upon an interpretive supplement, a commentary designed at once to intensify and control the response of the audience by explicating both the significance and the relevance of each gesture. Now the state would in effect seize control of the commentary and thereby alter the spectators' perceptions. Sommers's audience would no longer see a demoniac; they would see someone playing a demoniac. Demonic possession would become theater.

After the civic officials had satisfied themselves that Sommers's possession was a theatrical imposture, an ecclesiastical commission was convened to view a repeat performance. In a bizarre twist, however, Sommers unexpectedly withdrew his confession before the startled commissioners, and he signaled this withdrawal by falling into spectacular fits before the moment appointed for the performance. The commissioners, unprepared to view these convulsions as a deliberate or self-conscious exhibition, declared that they were evidently of supernatural origin. But in less than two weeks, before the mayor and two justices, the wretched Sommers, under renewed state pressure, reaffirmed his confession of fraud, and a few days later he once again "proved" his claim by simulating fits, this time before the assize judge. The next step might have been to ask a court of law to determine whether Sommers's expressly simulated fits were identical to those he underwent when he was not confessing imposture. But the authorities evidently regarded this step, which Darrel himself demanded,[29] as too risky; instead, without calling Sommers to appear, they first obtained a conviction of the exorcist on charges of imposture and then launched a national campaign to persuade the public that possession and exorcism were illicit forms of theater.

Sommers's oscillation between the poles of authenticity and illusion are for Harsnett an emblem of the maddening doubleness implicit in the theatricality of exorcism: its power to impose itself on beholders and its half-terrifying, half-comic emptiness. Exorcists could, of course, react by demonizing the theater: Puritans like Darrel argued at length that the playhouse was Satan's temple, while the Jesuit exorcists operating clandestinely in England implied that theatrical representations of the devil in mystery plays were not mere imitations of reality but lively images based on a deep bond of resemblance. When in the 1580s a devil possessing Sara Williams refused to tell his name, the exorcist, according to the Catholic *Book of Miracles*, "caused to be drawn upon a piece of paper, the picture of a vice in a play, and the same to be burned with hallowed brimstone, whereat the devil cried out as being grievously tormented."[30] Harsnett remarks in response that "it was a pretty part in the old Church-plays, when the nimble Vice would skip up nimbly like Jacke an Apes into the devils neck, and ride the devil a course, and belabour him with his wooden dagger, til he made him roar, whereat the people would laugh to see the devil so vice-haunted" (114–15). Sara's devils, he concludes contemptuously, "be surely some of those old vice-haunted cashiered wooden-beaten devils, that were wont to frequent the stages... who are so scared with the *Idea* of a vice, & a dagger, as they durst never since look a paper-vice in the face" (115). For Harsnett the attempt to demonize the theater merely exposes the theatricality of the demonic; once we acknowledge this theatricality, he suggests, we can correctly perceive the actual genre of the performance: not tragedy but farce.

The theatricality of exorcism, to which the *Declaration* insistently calls attention, has been noted repeatedly by modern ethnographers who do not share Harsnett's reforming zeal or his sense of outrage.[31] In an illuminating study of possession among the Ethiopians of Gondar, Michel Leiris notes that the healer carefully instructs the *zâr*, or spirit, who has seized on someone how to behave: the types of cries appropriate to the occasion, the expected violent contortions, the "decorum," as Harsnett would put it, of the trance state.[32] The treatment is in effect an initiation into the performance of the symptoms, which are then cured precisely because they conform to the stereotype of the healing process. One must not conclude, writes Leiris, that there are no "real" – that is, sincerely experienced – cases of possession, for many of the patients (principally young women and slaves) seem genuinely ill, but at the same time no cases are exempt from artifice (27–8). Between authentic possession, spontaneous and involuntary, and inauthentic possession, simulated to provide a show or to extract some material or moral benefit, there are so many subtle shadings that it is impossible to draw a firm boundary (94–5). Possession in Gondar *is* theater, but theater that cannot confess its own theatrical nature, for this is not "theater played" (*théâtre joué*) but "theater lived" (*théâtre vécu*), lived not only by the spirit-haunted actor but by the audience. Those who witness a possession may at any moment be themselves possessed, and even if they are untouched by the *zâr*, they remain participants rather than passive spectators. For the theatrical performance is not shielded from them by an impermeable membrane; possession is extraordinary but not marginal, a heightened but not separate state. In possession, writes Leiris, the collective life itself takes the form of theater (96).

Precisely those qualities that fascinate and charm the ethnographer disgust the embattled clergyman: where Leiris can write of "authentic" possession in the unspoken assurance that none of his readers actually believe in the existence of "zârs," Harsnett, granted no such assurance and culturally threatened by the alternative vision of reality, struggles to prove that possession is by definition inauthentic; where the former sees a complex ritual integrated into the social process, the latter sees "a *Stygian* comedy to make silly people afraid" (69); where the former sees the theatrical expression of collective life, the latter sees the theatrical promotion of specific and malevolent institutional interests. And where Leiris's central point is that possession is a theater that does not confess its own theatricality, Harsnett's concern is to enforce precisely such a confession: the last 112 pages of *A Declaration of Egregious Popish Impostures* reprint the "several Examinations, and confessions of the parties pretended to be possessed, and dispossessed by *Weston* the Jesuit, and his adherents: set down word for word as they were taken upon oath before her Majesty's Commissioners for causes Ecclesiastical" (172). These transcripts prove, according to Harsnett, that the solemn ceremony of exorcism is a "play of sacred miracles," a "wonderful pageant" (2), a "devil Theater" (106).

The confession of theatricality, for Harsnett, demolishes exorcism. Theater is not the disinterested expression of the popular spirit but the indelible mark of falsity, tawdriness, and rhetorical manipulation. And these sinister qualities are rendered diabolical by the very concealment of theatricality that so appeals to Leiris. The spectators do not know that they are responding to a powerful, if sleazy, tragicomedy; their tears and joy, their transports of "commiseration and compassion" (74), are rendered up not to a troupe of acknowledged players but to seditious Puritans or to the supremely dangerous Catholic church. For Harsnett the theatrical seduction is not merely a Jesuitical strategy; it is the essence of the church itself: Catholicism is a "Mimic superstition" (20).[33]

Harsnett's response is to try to drive the Catholic church into the theater, just as during the Reformation Catholic clerical garments – the copes and albs and amices and stoles that were the glories of medieval textile crafts – were sold to the players. An actor in a history play taking the part of an English bishop could conceivably have worn the actual robes of the character he was representing. Far more than thrift is involved here. The transmigration of a single ecclesiastical cloak from the vestry to the wardrobe may stand as an emblem of the more complex and elusive institutional exchanges that are my subject: a sacred sign, designed to be displayed before a crowd of men and women, is emptied, made negotiable, traded from one institution to another. Such exchanges are rarely so tangible; they are not usually registered in inventories, not often sealed with a cash payment. Nonetheless they occur constantly, for through institutional negotiation and exchange differentiated expressive systems, distinct cultural discourses, are fashioned.

What happens when the piece of cloth is passed from the church to the playhouse? A consecrated object is reclassified, assigned a cash value, transferred from a sacred to a profane setting, deemed suitable for the stage. The theater company is willing to pay for the object not because it contributes to naturalistic representation but because it still bears a symbolic value, however attenuated. On the bare Elizabethan stage costumes were particularly important – companies were willing to pay more for a good costume than for a good play – and that importance in turn reflected the culture's fetishistic obsession with clothes as a mark of status and degree. And if for the theater the acquisition of clerical garments was a significant appropriation of symbolic power, why would the church part with that power? Because for the Anglican polemicists, as for a long tradition of moralists in the West, the theater signifies the unscrupulous manipulation for profit of popular faith; the cynical use of setting and props to generate unthinking consent; the external and trivialized staging of what should be deeply inward; the tawdry triumph of spectacle over reason; the evacuation of the divine presence from religious mystery, leaving only vivid but empty ceremonies; the transformation of faith into bad faith.[34] Hence selling Catholic vestments to the players was a form of symbolic aggression: a vivid, wry reminder that Catholicism, as Harsnett puts it, is "the Pope's playhouse."[35]

This blend of appropriation and aggression is similarly at work in the transfer of possession and exorcism from sacred to profane representation. *A Declaration of Egregious Popish Impostures* takes pains to identify exorcism not merely with "the theatrical" – a category that scarcely exists for Harsnett – but with the actual theater;

at issue is not so much a metaphorical concept as a functioning institution. For if Harsnett can drive exorcism into the theater – if he can show that the stately houses in which the rituals were performed were playhouses, that the sacred garments were what he calls a "lousy holy wardrobe" (78), that the terrifying writhings were simulations, that the uncanny signs and wonders were contemptible stage tricks, that the devils were the "cashiered wooden-beaten" Vices from medieval drama (115), and that the exorcists were "vagabond players, that coast from Town to Town" (149) – then the ceremony and everything for which it stands will, as far as he is concerned, be emptied out. And with this emptying out Harsnett will have driven exorcism from the center to the periphery – in the case of London quite literally to the periphery, where increasingly stringent urban regulation had already driven the public playhouses.

In this symbolically charged zone of pollution, disease, and licentious entertainment Harsnett seeks to situate the practice of exorcism.[36] What had once occurred in solemn glory at the very center of the city would now be staged alongside the culture's other vulgar spectacles and illusions. Indeed the sense of the theater's tawdriness, marginality, and emptiness – the sense that everything the players touch is rendered hollow – underlies Harsnett's analysis not only of exorcism but of the entire Catholic church. Demonic possession is a particularly attractive cornerstone for such an analysis, not only because of its histrionic intensity but because the theater itself is by its nature bound up with possession. Harsnett did not have to believe that the cult of Dionysus out of which the Greek drama evolved was a cult of possession; even the ordinary and familiar theater of his own time depended upon the apparent transformation of the actor into the voice, the actions, and the face of another.

ii

With his characteristic opportunism and artistic self-consciousness, Shakespeare in his first known play, *The Comedy of Errors* (1590), was already toying with the connection between theater, illusion, and spurious possession. Antipholus of Syracuse, accosted by his twin's mistress, imagines that he is encountering the devil: "Sathan, avoid. I charge thee tempt me not" (4.3.48). The Ephesian Antipholus's wife, Adriana, dismayed by the apparently mad behavior of her husband, imagines that the devil has possessed him, and she dutifully calls in an exorcist: "Good Doctor Pinch, you are a conjurer, / Establish him in his true sense again." Pinch begins the solemn ritual:

> I charge thee, Sathan, hous'd within this man,
> To yield possession to my holy prayers,
> And to thy state of darkness hie thee straight:
> I conjure thee by all the saints in heaven!
> (4.4.54–7)

But he is interrupted with a box on the ears from the outraged husband: "Peace, doting wizard, peace! I am not mad." For the exorcist, such denials only confirm the presence of an evil spirit: "the fiend is strong within him" (4.4.107). At the scene's end, Antipholus is dragged away to be "bound and laid in some dark room."

The false presumption of demonic possession in *The Comedy of Errors* is not the result of deception; it is an instance of what Shakespeare's source calls a

"suppose" – an attempt to make sense of a series of bizarre actions gleefully generated by the comedy's screwball coincidences. Exorcism is the straw people clutch
at when the world seems to have gone mad. In *Twelfth Night*, written some ten
years later, Shakespeare's view of exorcism, though still comic, has darkened. Possession now is not a mistaken "suppose" but a fraud, a malicious practical joke played
on Malvolio. "Pray God he be not bewitch'd!" (3.4.101) Maria piously exclaims at
the sight of the cross-gartered, leering gull, and when he is out of earshot, Fabian
laughs: "If this were play'd upon a stage now, I could condemn it as an improbable
fiction" (3.4.127–8).[37] The theatrical self-consciousness is intensified when Feste the
clown is brought in to conduct a mock exorcism: "I would I were the first that ever
dissembled in such a gown" (4.2.5–6), he remarks sententiously as he disguises
himself as Sir Topas the curate. If the jibe had a specific reference for the play's
original audience, it would be to the Puritan Darrel, who had only recently been
convicted of dissembling in the exorcism of Sommers. Now, the scene would suggest, the tables are being turned on the self-righteous fanatic. "Good Sir Topas,"
pleads Malvolio, "do not think I am mad; they have laid me here in hideous darkness." "Fie, thou dishonest Sathan!" Feste replies; "I call thee by the most modest
terms, for I am one of those gentle ones that will use the devil himself with courtesy"
(4.2.29–33).

By 1600, then, Shakespeare had clearly marked out possession and exorcism as
frauds, so much so that in *All's Well That Ends Well* a few years later he could
casually use the term *exorcist* as a synonym for illusion monger: "Is there no exorcist
/ Beguiles the truer office of mine eyes?" cries the King of France when Helena,
whom he thought dead, appears before him; "Is't real that I see?" (5.3.304–6). When
in 1603 Harsnett was whipping exorcism toward the theater, Shakespeare was already
at the entrance to the Globe to welcome it.

Given Harsnett's frequent expressions of the "antitheatrical prejudice," this welcome may seem strange, but in fact nothing in *A Declaration of Egregious Popish
Impostures* necessarily implies hostility to the theater as a professional institution. It
was Darrel, not Harsnett, who represented an implacable threat to the theater, for
where the Anglican polemicist saw the theatrical in the demonic, the Puritan polemicist saw the demonic in the theatrical: "The Devil," wrote Stephen Gosson, "is the
efficient cause of plays."[38] Harsnett's work attacks a form of theater that pretends it
is not entertainment but sober reality; his polemic virtually depends upon the existence of an officially designated commercial theater, marked off openly from all other
forms and ceremonies of public life precisely by virtue of its freely acknowledged
fictionality. Where there is no pretense to truth, there can be no *imposture:* this
argument permits so ontologically anxious a figure as Sir Philip Sidney to defend
poetry – "Now for the poet, he nothing affirms, and therefore never lieth."

In this spirit Puck playfully defends *A Midsummer Night's Dream:*

> If we shadows have offended,
> Think but this, and all is mended,
> That you have but slumb'red here
> While these visions did appear.
> And this weak and idle theme,
> No more yielding but a dream.
>
> (5.1.423–8)

With a similarly frank admission of illusion Shakespeare can open the theater to Harsnett's polemic. Indeed, as if Harsnett's momentum carried *him* into the theater along with the fraud he hotly pursues, Shakespeare in *King Lear* stages not only exorcism, but Harsnett *on* exorcism: "Five fiends have been in poor Tom at once: of lust, as Obidicut; Hobbididence, prince of dumbness; Mahu, of stealing; Modo, of murder; Flibbertigibbet, of mopping and mowing, who since possesses chambermaids and waiting-women" (4.1.58–63).[39]

Those in the audience who had read Harsnett's book or heard of the notorious Buckinghamshire exorcisms would recognize in Edgar's lines an odd joking allusion to the chambermaids, Sara and Friswood Williams, and the waiting woman, Ann Smith, principal actors in Father Edmunds's "devil Theater." The humor of the anachronism here is akin to that of the Fool's earlier quip, "This prophecy Merlin shall make, for I live before his time" (3.2.95–6); both sallies of wit show a cheeky self-consciousness that dares deliberately to violate the historical setting to remind the audience of the play's conspicuous doubleness, its simultaneous distance and contemporaneity.

A Declaration of Egregious Popish Impostures supplies Shakespeare not only with an uncanny anachronism but also with the model for Edgar's histrionic disguise. For it is not the *authenticity* of the demonology that the playwright finds in Harsnett – the usual reason for authorial recourse to a specialized source (as, for example, to a military or legal handbook) – but rather the inauthenticity of a theatrical role. Shakespeare appropriates for Edgar a documented fraud, complete with an impressive collection of what the *Declaration* calls "uncouth non-significant names" (46) that have been made to sound exotic and that carry with them a faint but ineradicable odor of spuriousness.

In Sidney's *Arcadia*, which provided the outline of the Gloucester subplot, the good son, having escaped his father's misguided attempt to kill him, becomes a soldier in another land and quickly distinguishes himself. Shakespeare insists not only on Edgar's perilous fall from his father's favor but upon his marginalization: Edgar becomes the possessed Poor Tom, the outcast with no possibility of working his way back toward the center. "My neighbors," writes John Bunyan in the 1660s, "were amazed at this my great conversion from prodigious profaneness to something like a moral life; and truly so well they might for this my conversion was as great as for a Tom of Bethlem to become a sober man."[40] Although Edgar is only a pretend Tom o'Bedlam and can return to the community when it is safe to do so, the force of Harsnett's argument makes mimed possession even more marginal and desperate than the real thing.

Indeed Edgar's desperation is bound up with the stress of "counterfeiting," a stress he has already noted in the presence of the mad and ruined Lear and now, in the lines I have just quoted, feels more intensely in the presence of his blinded and ruined father. He is struggling with the urge to stop playing or, as he puts it, with the feeling that he "cannot daub it further" (4.1.52). Why he does not simply reveal himself to Gloucester at this point is unclear. "And yet I must" is all he says of his continued disguise, as he recites the catalog of devils and leads his despairing father off to Dover Cliff.[41]

The subsequent episode – Gloucester's suicide attempt – deepens the play's brooding upon spurious exorcism. "It is a good *decorum* in a Comedy," writes Harsnett, "to give us empty names for things, and to tell us of strange Monsters within, where there be none" (142); so too the "Miracle-minter" Father Edmunds and his fellow exorcists manipulate their impressionable gulls: "The priests do report often in their patients hearing the dreadful forms, similitudes, and shapes, that the devils use to depart in out of those possessed bodies . . . : and this they tell with so grave a countenance, pathetical terms, and accommodate action, as it leaves a very deep impression in the memory, and fancy of their actors" (142–3). Thus by the power of theatrical suggestion the anxious subjects on whom the priests work their charms come to believe that they too have witnessed the devil depart in grotesque form from their own bodies, whereupon the priests turn their eyes heavenward and give thanks to the Blessed Virgin. In much the same manner Edgar persuades Gloucester that he stands on a high cliff, and then, after his credulous father has flung himself forward, Edgar switches roles and pretends that he is a bystander who has seen a demon depart from the old man:

> As I stood here below, methought his eyes
> Were two full moons; he had a thousand noses,
> Horns welk'd and waved like the enridged sea.
> It was some fiend; therefore, thou happy father,
> Think that the clearest gods, who make them honors
> Of men's impossibilities, have preserved thee.
>
> (4.6.69–74)

Edgar tries to create in Gloucester an experience of awe and wonder so intense that it can shatter his suicidal despair and restore his faith in the benevolence of the gods: "Thy life's a miracle" (4.6.55), he tells his father.[42] For Shakespeare as for Harsnett this miracle minting is the product of specifically histrionic manipulations; the scene at Dover is a disenchanted analysis of both religious and theatrical illusions. Walking about on a perfectly flat stage, Edgar does to Gloucester what the theater usually does to the audience: he persuades his father to discount the evidence of his senses – "Methinks the ground is even" – and to accept a palpable fiction: "Horrible steep" (4.6.3). But the audience at a play never absolutely accepts such fictions: we enjoy being brazenly lied to, we welcome for the sake of pleasure what we know to be untrue, but we withhold from the theater the simple assent we grant to everyday reality. And we enact this withholding when, depending on the staging, either we refuse to believe that Gloucester is on a cliff above Dover Beach or we realize that what we thought was a cliff (in the convention of theatrical representation) is in reality flat ground.

Hence in the midst of the apparent convergence of exorcism and theater, we return to the difference that enables *King Lear* to borrow comfortably from Harsnett: the theater elicits from us complicity rather than belief. Demonic possession is responsibly marked out for the audience as a theatrical fraud, designed to gull the unsuspecting: monsters such as the fiend with the thousand noses are illusions most easily imposed on the old, the blind, and the despairing; evil comes not from the mysterious otherworld of demons but from this world, the world of court and family intrigue. In *King Lear* there are no ghosts, as there are in *Richard III*, *Julius Caesar*, or *Hamlet*; no witches, as in *Macbeth*; no mysterious music of departing daemons, as in *Antony and Cleopatra*.

King Lear is haunted by a sense of rituals and beliefs that are no longer efficacious, that have been *emptied out*. The characters appeal again and again to the pagan gods, but the gods remain utterly silent.[43] Nothing answers to human questions but human voices; nothing breeds about the heart but human desires; nothing inspires awe or terror but human suffering and human depravity. For all the invocation of the gods in *King Lear*, it is clear that there are no devils.

Edgar is no more possessed than the sanest of us, and we can see for ourselves that there was no demon standing by Gloucester's side. Likewise Lear's madness has no supernatural origin; it is linked, as in Harsnett, to *hysterica passio*, exposure to the elements, and extreme anguish, and its cure comes at the hands not of an exorcist but of a doctor. His prescription involves neither religious rituals (as in Catholicism) nor fasting and prayer (as in Puritanism) but tranquilized sleep:

> Our foster-nurse of nature is repose,
> The which he lacks; that to provoke in him
> Are many simples operative, whose power
> Will close the eye of anguish.
>
> (4.4.12–15)[44]

King Lear's relation to Harsnett's book is one of reiteration then, a reiteration that signals a deeper and unexpressed institutional exchange. The official church dismantles and cedes to the players the powerful mechanisms of an unwanted and dangerous charisma; in return the players confirm the charge that those mechanisms are theatrical and hence illusory. The material structure of Elizabethan and Jacobean public theaters heightened this confirmation; unlike medieval drama, which was more fully integrated into society, Shakespeare's drama took place in carefully demarcated playgrounds. *King Lear* offers a double corroboration of Harsnett's arguments. Within the play, Edgar's possession is clearly designated as a fiction, and the play itself is bounded by the institutional signs of fictionality: the wooden walls of the play space, payment for admission, known actors playing the parts, applause, the dances that followed the performance.

The theatrical confirmation of the official position is neither superficial nor unstable. And yet, I want now to suggest, Harsnett's arguments are alienated from themselves when they make their appearance on the Shakespearean stage. This alienation may be set in the context of a more general observation: the closer Shakespeare seems to a source, the more faithfully he reproduces it on stage, the more devastating and decisive his transformation of it. Let us take, for a small initial instance, Shakespeare's borrowing from Harsnett of the unusual adjective *corky* – that is, sapless, dry, withered. The word appears in the *Declaration* in the course of a sardonic explanation of why, despite the canonist Mengus's rule that only old women are to be exorcised, Father Edmunds and his crew have a particular fondness for tying in a chair and exorcising young women. Along with more graphic sexual innuendos, Harsnett observes that the theatrical role of a demoniac requires "certain actions, motions, distortions, dislocations, writhings, tumblings, and turbulent passions . . . not to be performed but by suppleness of sinews. . . . It would (I fear me) pose all the cunning Exorcists, that are this day to be found, to teach an old corky woman to writhe, tumble, curvet, and fetch her morris gambols" (23).

Now Shakespeare's eye was caught by the word "corky," and he reproduces it in a reference to old Gloucester. But what had been a flourish of Harsnett's typically bullying comic style becomes part of the horror of an almost unendurable scene, a scene of torture that begins when Cornwall orders his servant to take the captive Gloucester and "Bind fast his corky arms" (3.7.29). The note of bullying humor is still present in the word, but it is present in the character of the torturer.

This one-word instance of repetition as transvaluation may suggest in the smallest compass what happens to Harsnett's work in the course of *Lear*. The *Declaration*'s arguments are loyally reiterated, but in a curiously divided form. The voice of skepticism is assimilated to Cornwall, to Goneril, and above all to Edmund, whose "naturalism" is exposed as the argument of the younger and illegitimate son bent on displacing his legitimate older brother and eventually on destroying his father. The fraudulent possession and exorcism are given to the legitimate Edgar, who is forced to such shifts by the nightmarish persecution directed against him. Edgar adopts the role of Poor Tom not out of a corrupt will to deceive but out of a commendable desire to survive. Modo, Mahu, and the rest are fakes, exactly as Harsnett said they were, but Edgar's impostures are the venial sins of a will to endure. And even "venial sins" is too strong: the clever inventions enable a decent and unjustly persecuted man to live. Similarly, there is no grotesque monster standing on the cliff with Gloucester – there is not even a cliff – but only Edgar, himself hunted down like an animal, trying desperately to save his father from suicidal despair.

All of this has an odd and unsettling resemblance to the situation of the Jesuits in England, if viewed from an unofficial perspective.[45] The resemblance does not necessarily resolve itself into an allegory in which Catholicism is revealed to be the persecuted legitimate elder brother forced to defend himself by means of theatrical illusions against the cold persecution of his skeptical bastard brother Protestantism. But the possibility of such a radical undermining of the orthodox position exists, and not merely in the cool light of our own historical distance. In 1610 a company of traveling players in Yorkshire included *King Lear* and *Pericles* in a repertoire that included a "St. Christopher Play" whose performance came to the attention of the Star Chamber. The plays were performed in the manor house of a recusant couple, Sir John and Lady Julyan Yorke, and the players themselves and their organizer, Sir Richard Cholmeley, were denounced for recusancy by their Puritan neighbor, Sir Posthumus Hoby.[46] It is difficult to resist the conclusion that someone in Stuart Yorkshire believed that *King Lear*, despite its apparent staging of a fraudulent possession, was not hostile, was strangely sympathetic even, to the situation of persecuted Catholics. At the very least, we may suggest, the current of sympathy is enough to undermine the intended effect of Harsnett's *Declaration*: an intensified adherence to the central system of official values. In Shakespeare, the realization that demonic possession is a theatrical imposture leads not to a clarification – the clear-eyed satisfaction of the man who refuses to be gulled – but to a deeper uncertainty, a loss of moorings, in the face of evil.

"Let them anatomize Regan," Lear raves, "see what breeds about her heart. Is there any cause in nature that make these hard hearts?" (3.6.76–8). We know that there is no cause *beyond* nature; the voices of evil in the play – "Thou, Nature, art my goddess"; "What need one?"; "Bind fast his corky arms" – do not well up from characters who are possessed. I have no wish to live in a culture where men believe in devils; I fully grasp that the torturers of this world are all too human. Yet Lear's anguished question insists on the pain this understanding brings, a pain that reaches beyond the king. Is it a relief to understand that the evil was not visited upon the characters by demonic agents but released from the structure of the family and the state by Lear himself?

Edgar's pretended demonic possession, by ironic contrast, is homiletic; the devil compels him to acts of self-punishment, the desperate masochism of the very poor, but not to acts of viciousness. Like the demoniacs who in Harsnett's contemptuous account praise the Mass and the Catholic church, Poor Tom gives a highly moral performance: "Take heed o' th' foul fiend. Obey thy parents, keep thy word's justice, swear not, commit not with man's sworn spouse, set not thy sweet heart on proud array. Tom's a-cold" (3.4.80–3). Is it a relief to know that Edgar only mimes this little sermon?

All attempts by the characters to explain or relieve their sufferings through the invocation of transcendent forces are baffled. Gloucester's belief in the influence of "these late eclipses in the sun and moon" (1.2.103) is dismissed decisively, even if the spokesman for the dismissal is the villainous Edmund. Lear appeals almost constantly to the gods:

> O Heavens!
> If you do love old men, if your sweet sway
> Allow obedience, if you yourselves are old,
> Make it your cause; send down, and take my part.
> (2.4.189–92)

But his appeals are left unanswered. The storm in the play seems to several characters to be of more than natural intensity, and Lear above all tries desperately to make it *mean* something (as a symbol of his daughters' ingratitude, a punishment for evil, a sign from the gods of the impending universal judgment), but the thunder refuses to speak. When Albany calls Goneril a "devil" and a "fiend" (4.2.59, 66), we know that he is not identifying her as a supernatural being – it is impossible, in this play, to witness the eruption of the denizens of hell into the human world – just as we know that Albany's prayer for "visible spirits" to be sent down by the heavens "to tame these vild offenses" (4.2.46–7) will be unanswered.

In *King Lear*, as Harsnett says of the Catholic church, "neither God, Angel, nor devil can be gotten to speak" (169). For Harsnett this silence betokens a liberation from lies; we have learned, as the last sentence of his tract puts it, "to loathe these despicable Impostures and return unto the truth" (*Declaration*, p. 171). But for Shakespeare the silence leads to the desolation of the play's close:

> Lend me a looking-glass,
> If that her breath will mist or stain the stone,
> Why then she lives.
> (5.3.262–4)

The lines voice a hope that has repeatedly tantalized the audience: a hope that Cordelia will not die, that the play will build toward a revelation powerful enough to justify Lear's atrocious suffering, that we are in the midst of what the Italians called a *tragedia di fin lieto*, that is, a play in which the villains absorb the tragic punishment while the good are wondrously restored.[47] Lear appeals, in effect, to the conventions of this genre. The close of a tragicomedy frequently requires the audience to will imaginatively a miraculous turn of events, often against the evidence of its senses (as when the audience persuades itself that the two actors playing Viola and Sebastian in *Twelfth Night* really *do* look identical, in spite of the ocular proof to the contrary, or when at the close of *The Winter's Tale* the audience accepts the fiction that Hermione is an unbreathing statue in order to experience the wonder of her resurrection). But the close of *King Lear* allows an appeal to such conventions only to reverse them with bitter irony: to believe Cordelia dead, the audience, insofar as it can actually see what is occurring onstage, must work against the evidence of its own senses. After all, the actor's breath would have misted the stone, and the feather held to Cordelia's mouth must have stirred. But we remain convinced that Cordelia is, as Lear first says, "dead as earth."

In the wake of Lear's first attempt to see some sign of life in Cordelia, Kent asks, "Is this the promis'd end?" Edgar echoes the question: "Or image of that horror?" And Albany says, "Fall, and cease!" By itself Kent's question has an oddly literary quality, as if he were remarking on the end of the play, either wondering what kind of ending this is or implicitly objecting to the disastrous turn of events. Edgar's response suggests that the "end" is the end of the world, the Last Judgment, here experienced not as a "promise" – the punishment of the wicked, the reward of the good – but as a "horror." But like Kent, Edgar is not certain about what he is seeing: his question suggests that he may be witnessing not the end itself but a possible "image" of it, while Albany's enigmatic "Fall, and cease!" empties even that image of significance. The theatrical means that might have produced a "counterfeit miracle" out of this moment are abjured; there will be no imposture, no histrionic revelation of the supernatural.

Lear repeats this miserable emptying out of the redemptive hope in his next lines:

> This feather stirs, she lives! If it be so,
> It is a chance which does redeem all sorrows
> That ever I have felt.
>
> (5.3.266–8)

Deeply moved by the sight of the mad king, a nameless gentleman had earlier remarked,

> Thou hast one daughter
> Who redeems nature from the general curse
> Which twain have brought her to.
>
> (4.6.205–7)

Now in Lear's words this vision of universal redemption through Cordelia is glimpsed again, intensified by the king's conscious investment in it.

What would it mean to "redeem" Lear's sorrows? To buy them back from the chaos and brute meaninglessness they now seem to signify? To reward the king with a gift so great that it outweighs the sum of misery in his entire long life? To reinterpret his pain as the necessary preparation – the price to be paid – for a consummate bliss? In the theater such reinterpretation would be represented by a spectacular turn in the plot – a surprise unmasking, a sudden reversal of fortunes, a resurrection – and this dramatic redemption, however secularized, would almost invariably recall the consummation devoutly wished by centuries of Christian believers. This consummation had in fact been represented again and again in medieval Resurrection plays, which offered the spectators ocular proof that Christ had risen.[48] Despite the pre-Christian setting of Shakespeare's play, Lear's craving for just such proof – "This feather stirs, she lives!"

– would seem to evoke precisely this theatrical and religious tradition, but only to reveal itself, in C. L. Barber's acute phrase, as "post-Christian."[49] *If it be so*: Lear's sorrows are not redeemed; nothing can turn them into joy, but the forlorn hope of an impossible redemption persists, drained of its institutional and doctrinal significance, empty and vain, cut off even from a theatrical realization, but like the dream of exorcism, ineradicable.

The close of *King Lear* in effect acknowledges that it can never satisfy this dream, but the acknowledgment must not obscure the play's having generated the craving for such satisfaction. That is, Shakespeare does not simply inherit and make use of an anthropological given; rather, at the moment when the official religious and secular institutions are, for their own reasons, abjuring the ritual they themselves once fostered, Shakespeare's theater moves to appropriate it. Onstage the ritual is effectively contained in the ways we have examined, but Shakespeare intensifies as a theatrical experience the need for exorcism, and his demystification of the practice is not identical in its interests to Harsnett's.

Harsnett's polemic is directed toward a bracing anger against the lying agents of the Catholic church and a loyal adherence to the true established Church of England. He writes as a representative of that true church, and this institutional identity is reinforced by the secular institutional imprimatur on the confessions that are appended to the *Declaration*. The joint religious and secular apparatus works to strip away imposture and discover the hidden reality that is, Harsnett says, the theater. Shakespeare's play dutifully reiterates this discovery: when Lear thinks he has found in Poor Tom "the thing itself," "unaccommodated man," he has in fact found a man playing a theatrical role. But if false religion is theater, and if the difference between true and false religion is the presence of theater, what happens when this difference is enacted in the theater?

What happens, as we have already begun to see, is that the official position is *emptied out*, even as it is loyally confirmed. This "emptying out" resembles Brecht's "alienation effect" and, even more, Althusser and Macheray's "internal distantiation." But the most fruitful terms for describing the felt difference between Shakespeare's art and the religious ideology to which it gives voice are to be found, I think, in the theological system to which Harsnett adhered. What is the status of the Law, asks Hooker, after the coming of Christ? Clearly the Savior effected the "evacuation of the Law of Moses." But did that abolition mean "that the very name of Altar, of Priest, of Sacrifice itself, should be banished out of the world"? No, replies Hooker; even after evacuation, "the words which were do continue: the only difference is, that whereas before they had a literal, they now have a metaphorical use, and are as so many notes of remembrance unto us, that what they did signify in the letter is accomplished in the truth."[50] Both exorcism and Harsnett's own attack on exorcism undergo a comparable process of evacuation and transformed reiteration in *King Lear*. Whereas before they had a literal, they now have a literary use and are as so many notes of remembrance unto us, that what they did signify in the letter is accomplished – with a drastic swerve from the sacred to the secular – in the theater.

Edgar's possession is a theatrical performance exactly in Harsnett's terms, but there is no saving institution, purged of theater, against which it may be set, nor is there a demonic institution that the performance may be shown to serve. On the contrary, Edgar mimes in response to a free-floating, contagious evil more terrible than anything Harsnett would allow. For Harsnett the wicked are corrupt individuals in the service of a corrupt church; in *King Lear* neither individuals nor institutions can adequately contain the released and enacted wickedness; the force of evil in the play is larger than any local habitation or name. In this sense, Shakespeare's tragedy reconstitutes as theater the demonic principle demystified by Harsnett. Edgar's fraudulent, histrionic performance is a response to this principle: evacuated rituals, drained of their original meaning, are preferable to no rituals at all.

Shakespeare does not counsel, in effect, that for the dream of a cure one accept the fraudulent institution as true – that is the argument of the Grand Inquisitor. He writes for the greater glory and profit of the theater, a fraudulent institution that never pretends to be anything but fraudulent, an institution that calls forth what is not, that signifies absence, that transforms the literal into the metaphorical, that evacuates everything it represents. By doing so the theater makes for itself the hollow round space within which it survives. The force of *King Lear* is to make us love the theater, to seek out its satisfactions, to serve its interests, to confer on it a place of its own, to grant it life by permitting it to reproduce itself over generations. Shakespeare's theater has outlived the institutions to which it paid homage, has lived to pay homage to other, competing, institutions that in turn it seems to represent and empty out. This complex, limited institutional independence, this marginal and impure autonomy, arises not out of an inherent, formal self-reflexiveness but out of the ideological matrix in which Shakespeare's theater is created and re-created.

Further institutional strategies lie beyond a love for the theater. In a move that Ben Jonson rather than Shakespeare seems to have anticipated, the theater itself comes to be emptied out in the interests of reading. In the argument made famous by Charles Lamb and Coleridge, and reiterated by Bradley, theatricality must be discarded to achieve absorption, and Shakespeare's imagination yields forth its sublime power not to a spectator but to one who, like Keats, sits down to reread *King Lear*. Where institutions like the King's Men had been thought to generate their texts, now texts like *King Lear* appear to generate their institutions. The commercial contingency of the theater gives way to the philosophical necessity of literature.

Why has our culture embraced *King Lear*'s massive display of mimed suffering and fraudulent exorcism? Because the judicial torture and expulsion of evil have for centuries been bound up with the display of power at the center of society. Because we no longer believe in the magical ceremonies through which devils were once made to speak and were driven out of the bodies of the possessed. Because the play recuperates and intensifies our need for these ceremonies, even though we do not believe in them, and performs them, carefully marked out for us as frauds, for our continued consumption. Because with our full complicity Shakespeare's company and scores of companies that followed have catered profitably to our desire for spectacular impostures.

And also, perhaps, because the Harsnetts of the world would free us from the oppression of false belief only to reclaim us more firmly for the official state church, and the "solution" – confirmed by the rechristening, as it were, of the devil as the pope – is hateful. Hence we embrace an alternative that seems to confirm the official line, and thereby to take its place in the central system of values, yet at the same time works to unsettle all official lines.[51] Shakespeare's theater empties out the center that it represents and in its cruelty – Edmund, Goneril, Regan, Cornwall, Gloucester,

Cordelia, Lear: all dead as earth – paradoxically creates in us the intimation of a fullness that we can savor only in the conviction of its irremediable loss:

> we that are young
> Shall never see so much, nor live so long.

Notes

1 Samuel Harsnett, *A Declaration of egregious Popish Impostures, to withdraw the harts of her Maiesties Subiects from their allegeance, and from the truth of Christian Religion professed in England, under the pretence of casting out deuils* (London: Iames Roberts, 1603). Harsnett's influence is noted in Lewis Theobald's edition of Shakespeare, first published in 1733. Shakespeare is likely to have known one of the principal exorcists, Robert Dibdale, the son of a Stratford Catholic family linked to the Hathaways.

On the clandestine exorcisms I am particularly indebted to D. P. Walker, *Unclean Spirits: Possession and Exorcism in France and England in the Late Sixteenth and Early Seventeenth Centuries* (Philadelphia: University of Pennsylvania Press, 1981).

2 A major exception, with conclusions different from my own, has recently been published: John L. Murphy, *Darkness and Devils: Exorcism and "King Lear"* (Athens: Ohio University Press, 1984). Murphy's study, which he kindly allowed me to read in galleys after hearing the present chapter delivered as a lecture, argues that exorcism is an aspect of clandestine political and religious resistance to Queen Elizabeth's rule. For thoughtful comments on Murphy's book by an expert on Harsnett, see F. W. Brownlow's review in *Philological Quarterly* 65 (1986): 131–3. See also, for interesting reflections, William Elton, *"King Lear" and the Gods* (San Marino, Calif.: Huntington Library, 1966). For useful accounts of Harsnett's relation to *Lear*, see *Narrative and Dramatic Sources of Shakespeare*, 8 vols., ed. Geoffrey Bullough (London: Routledge and Kegan Paul, 1958–75), 7:299–302; Kenneth Muir, "Samuel Harsnett and *King Lear*," *Review of English Studies* 2 (1951): 11–21, and Muir's edition of *Lear*, New Arden text (Cambridge, Mass.: Harvard University Press, 1952), pp. 253–6.

3 Michel de Montaigne, "Apology for Raymond Sebond," in *Complete Essays*, trans. Donald M. Frame (Stanford, Calif.: Stanford University Press, 1948), p. 331.

4 Edward Shils, *Center and Periphery: Essays in Macrosociology* (Chicago: University of Chicago Press, 1975), p. 257.

5 Peter Brown, *The Cult of the Saints: Its Rise and Function in Latin Christianity* (Chicago: University of Chicago Press, 1981), p. 107.

6 Sebastian Michaelis, *The Admirable Historie of the Possession and Conversion of a Penitent Woman*, trans. W. B. (London: William Aspley, 1613), p. 21. Mass exorcism was a particularly important phenomenon in sixteenth- and early seventeenth-century France. See Michel de Certeau, *La Possession de Loudun*, Collection Archive Series no. 37 (Paris: Gallimard, 1980); Robert Mandrou, *Magistrats et sorciers en France au XVIIe siècle* (Paris: Seuil, 1980); Robert Muchembled, *La Culture populaire et culture des élites* (Paris: Flammarion, 1977); Jonathan L. Pearl, "French Catholic Demonologists and Their Enemies in the Late Sixteenth and Early Seventeenth Centuries," *Church History* 52 (1983): 457–67; Henri Weber, "L'Exorcisme à la fin du seizième siècle, instrument de la Contre Réforme et spectacle baroque," *Nouvelle Revue du seizième siècle* 1 (1983): 79–101. For a comparison between exorcism in France and in England, see D. P. Walker, *Unclean Spirits*, and my own article, "Loudun and London," *Critical Inquiry* 12 (1986): 326–46. I have incorporated some pages from this article in the present chapter.

7 *A Booke Declaringe the Fearfull Vexasion of one Alexander Nyndge. Beynge moste Horriblye tormented wyth an euyll Spirit* (London: Thomas Colwell, 1573), p. Biiii^r.

8 Carlo Ginzburg, *I benandanti: Ricerche sulla stregoneria e sui culti agrari tra cinquecento e seicento* (Turin: Einaudi, 1966).

9 For Harsnett's comments on witchcraft, see *Declaration*, pp. 135–6. The relation between demonic possession and witchcraft is complex. John Darrel evidently had frequent recourse, in the midst of his exorcisms, to accusations of witchcraft whose evidence was precisely the demonic possessions; Harsnett remarks wryly that "of all the partes of the tragicall Comedie acted between him and *Somers*, there was no one Scene in it, wherein *M. Darrell* did with more courage and boldnes acte his part, then in this of the discouerie of witches" (*A Discovery of the Fraudulent Practises of J. Darrel ... concerning the pretended possession and dispossession of W. Somers, etc.* [1599], p. 142). There is a helpful discussion of possession and witchcraft, along with an important account of Harsnett and Darrel, in Keith Thomas, *Religion and the Decline of Magic* (London: Weidenfeld and Nicolson, 1971).

10 I borrow the phrase "central zone" from Edward Shils, for whom it is coterminous with society's central value system, a system constituted by the general standards of judgment and action and affirmed by the society's elite (*Center and Periphery*, p. 3). At the heart of the central value system is an affirmative attitude toward authority, which is endowed, however indirectly or remotely, with a measure of sacredness. "By their very possession of authority," Shils writes, elites "attribute to themselves an essential affinity with the sacred elements of their society, of which they regard themselves as the custodians" (5).

11 Brown, *Cult of the Saints*, pp. 109–11.

12 Thomas, *Religion and the Decline of Magic*, p. 485. "This effectively put an end to the practice," Thomas writes, "at least as far as conforming members of the Anglican Church were concerned."

13 S. M. Shirokogorov, *The Psycho-Mental Complex of the Tungus* (Peking: Routledge, 1935), p. 265.

14 Brown, *Cult of the Saints*, p. 110.

15 Michael MacDonald, *Mystical Bedlam* (Cambridge: Cambridge University Press, 1981). See also MacDonald's "Religion, Social Change, and Psychological Healing in England, 1600–1800," in *The Church and Healing*, ed. W. J. Shiels, Studies in Church History 19 (Oxford: Basil Blackwell, 1982); H. C. Erik Midelfort, "Madness and the Problems of Psychological History in the Sixteenth Century," *Sixteenth Century Journal* 12 (1981): 5–12.

16 *A Report Contayning a brief Narration of certain diuellish and wicked witcheries, practized by Olisse Barthram alias Doll Barthram in the Country of Suffolke*, bound with *The Triall of Maist. Dorrell, or A Collection of Defences against Allegations not yet suffered to receiue convenient answere* (1599), p. 94.

17 Iohn Swan, *A Trve and Briefe Report of Mary Glovers Vexation* (1603), p. 42.

18 *The Triall of Maist. Dorrell*, p. 29.

19 Quoted in [John Darrel,] *A Briefe Narration of the possession, dispossession, and repossession of William Sommers* (1598), pp. Diiv, Ciiiv.

20 *The Triall of Maist. Dorrell*, p. 8.

21 John Deacon and John Walker, *A Summarie Answere to al the material points in any of Master Darel his bookes* (London: George Bishop, 1601), pp. 237–8.

22 Harsnett sees this argument as a variant on the exorcists' general rule that "when the deuilles are cast out of man, they endeuoure by all the means they can, to perswade, that hee was neuer in them: that so the partie being vnthankefull to God for his deliuerance, they might the better reenter into him" (*Discovery*, p. 72). Harsnett cites the important exorcism manual by R. F. Hieronymus Mengus [Girolamo Menghi], *Flagellum Daemonum* (Bologna, 1582).

23 In 1524 Erasmus satirized exorcism by depicting it not simply as a fraud but as a play in five acts (*Exorcismus, sive spectrum*, in *The Colloquies of Erasmus*, trans. Craig R. Thompson [Chicago: University of Chicago Press, 1965], pp. 231–7). The play, in Erasmus's account, is an elaborate practical joke played on a character called Faunus, a gullible and pretentious parish priest who is cleverly induced to be an unwitting actor in an outlandish and grotesque theatrical performance. The representation of the demonic is spurious, but its effect on the victim of the joke is alarmingly real: "So thoroughly did this fancy obsess him that he dreamt of nothing but specters and evil spirits and talked of nothing else. His mental condition carried over into his very countenance, which became so pale, so drawn, so downcast that you would have said

he was a ghost, not a man" (237). A successful demon play can fashion the dreams of its victims, and illusions can inscribe themselves in the very bodies of those who believe in them.

The colloquy ostensibly celebrates the histrionic cunning of the jokers, but Erasmus makes it clear that there are larger institutional implications: a gifted director, an unscrupulous actor who has "perfect control of his expression," and a few props suffice not only to create an intense illusion of the demonic among large numbers of spectators but also to entice the gullible into participating in a play whose theatricality they cannot acknowledge. The defense against such impostures is a widespread public recognition of this theatricality and a consequent skepticism: "Up to this time I haven't, as a rule, had much faith in popular tales about apparitions," one of Erasmus's speakers concludes, "but hereafter I'll have even less" (237).

24 See Edmund Jorden, *A briefe discourse of a disease Called the Suffocation of the Mother* (London, 1603).

25 *A Report Contayning a brief Narration of certain diuellish and wicked witcheries*, pp. 99–100.

26 [Richard Baddeley,] *The Boy of Bilson, or A True Discovery of the Late Notorious Impostures of Certaine Romish Priests in their pretended Exorcisme, or expulsion of the Diuell out of a young Boy, named William Perry, sonne of Thomas Perry of Bilson* (London: F. K., 1622), p. 51. Baddeley is quoting from the Catholic account of the events, which, in order to dispute, he reprints: *A Faithfull Relation of the Proceedings of the Catholicke Gentlemen with the Boy of Bilson; shewing how they found him, on what termes they meddled with him, how farre they proceeded with him, and in what case, and for what cause they left to deale further with him* (in Baddeley, pp. 45–54).

27 In both England and France the reliability of the devil's testimony was debated extensively. "We ought not to beleeue the Diuell," writes the exorcist and inquisitor Sebastian Michaelis, "yet when hee is compelled to discourse and relate a truth, then wee should feare and tremble, for it is a token of the wrath of God" (*Admirable Historie of the Possession and Conversion of a Penitent Woman*, p. C7v). Michaelis's long account of his triumph over a devil named Verrine was published, the translator claims, to show "that the Popish Priests, in all Countries where men will beleeue them, are vniforme & like vnto themselues, since that which was done couertly in England, in the daies of Queene *Elizabeth*, by the Deuils of *Denham* in *Sara Williams* and her fellowes, is now publikely taken vp elsewhere by men of no small ranke" (A4r). This seems to me a disingenuous justification for publishing, without further annotation or qualification, over five hundred pages of Catholic apologetics, but obviously the Jacobean licensing authorities accepted the explanation.

28 [Darrel,] *A Briefe Narration of the possession, dispossession, and repossession of William Sommers*, p. Biiv.

29 "Let him be brought before some indifferent persons, let the depositions be read, and let him act the same in such maner, and forme as is deposed, by naturall, or artificiall power, then Mr. Dorrell will yeeld that he did conterfeit. If he cannot, (as vndoubtedlie he cannot,) then pleade no longer for the Deuill; but punish that imp of Satan as a wicked lier, and blasphemer of the mightie worke of God" (*Briefe Narration*, p. Biiv).

30 *Booke of Miracles*, quoted in Harsnett, *Declaration*, pp. 113–14.

31 In Haiti, for example, an individual possessed by a *loa*, or spirit, is led to the vestry of the sanctuary, where he chooses the costume appropriate to the particular spirit that has possessed him; dressed in this costume – for Baron Saturday, a black suit, starched cuffs, top hat, and white gloves; for the peasant god Zaka, a straw hat, pouch, and pipe; and so forth – he returns to the clearing and performs for the assembled crowd the appropriate mimes, monologues, and dances (Alfred Metraux, "Dramatic Elements in Ritual Possession," *Diogenes* 11 [1964]: 18–36). In Sri Lanka, exorcisms integrate feasting, the making of ritual offerings, dancing, the singing of sacred texts, drumming, masking, and the staging of improvised, frequently obscene, comedies. The comedies are at once explicitly theatrical and integral to the healing process.

In a major study of exorcism rituals performed in and near the town of Galle in southern Sri Lanka, Bruce Kapferer observes that demons in Sinhalese culture are understood to operate by means of illusions; the disorder and suffering that these illusions occasion are combated by spectacular demystifying counter-illusions. Hence exorcists "consider their healing rites to be elaborate tricks which they play on demons": to induce demons to treat the illusory as reality is to gain control over them (Bruce Kapferer, *A Celebration of Demons: Exorcism and the Aesthetics of Healing in Sri Lanka* [Bloomington: Indiana University Press, 1983], p. 112). Demonic possession has disturbed a hierarchical order that must be restored by humiliating the demons and returning them to their rightful subordinate position in the order of things. This restoration is achieved through ceremonies that "place major aesthetic forms into relation and locate them at points when particular transformations in meaning and experience are understood by exorcists to be occurring or are to be effected" (8). The ceremonies transform demonic identity into normal social identity; the individual is returned to himself and hence to his community whose solidarity is not only mirrored but constituted by the aesthetic experience. Exorcists then are "the masters of illusion" (113), and their histrionic skills do not arouse doubts about their authenticity but heighten confidence in their powers.

    For further reflections on demonic possession, see Ernst Arbman, *Ecstasy or Religious Trance* (Norstedts: Svenska Bokforlaget, 1963), 3 vols., esp. chapter 9; *Disguises of the Demonic: Contemporary Perspectives on the Power of Evil*, ed. Alan M. Olson (New York: Association Press, n.d.); I. M. Lewis, *Ecstatic Religion: An Anthropological Study of Spirit Possession and Shamanism* (Harmondsworth: Penguin, 1971).

32   Michel Leiris, *La Possession et ses aspects théâtraux chez les Ethiopiens de Gondar* (Paris: Plon, 1958).

33   This argument has the curious effect of identifying all exorcisms, including those conducted by nonconformist preachers, with the pope. On attacks on the Catholic church as a theater, see Jonas Barish, *The Antitheatrical Prejudice* (Berkeley: University of California Press, 1981), pp. 66–131 passim.

34   At least since Plato there has been a powerful tendency to identify the stage with unreality, debased imitation, and outright counterfeiting. Like the painter, says Socrates in the *Republic*, the tragic poet is an imitator of objects that are themselves imitations and hence "thrice removed from the king and from the truth" (597e). Though this position had its important Christian adherents, it is not, of course, the only intellectual current in the West; not only do medieval mystery plays depend upon a conviction that dramatic performance does not contradict religious truth, but the Mass itself appears to have been conceived by several important medieval thinkers as analogous to theatrical representation. For further discussion, see my "Loudun and London," pp. 328–9.

35   *Discovery*, p. A3r. As Catholic priests "have transformed the celebrating of the Sacrament of the *Lords supper* into a *Masse-game*, and all other partes of the *Ecclesiasticall service* into *theatricall sights*," writes another sixteenth-century Protestant polemicist, "so, in steede of *preaching the word*, they caused it to be played" (John Rainolds, cited in Barish, *The Antitheatrical Prejudice*, p. 163).

36   Harsnett was not alone, of course. See, for example, John Gee: "The Jesuits being or having Actors of such dexterity, I see no reason but that they should set up a company for themselves, which surely will put down The Fortune, Red-Bull, Cock-pit, and Globe" (John Gee, *New Shreds of the Old Snare* [London, 1624]). I owe this reference, along with powerful reflections on the significance of the public theater's physical marginality, to Steven Mullaney.

37   This sentiment could serve as the epigraph to both of Harsnett's books on exorcism; it is the root perception from which most of Harsnett's rhetoric grows.

38   Stephen Gosson, *Plays Confuted in Five Actions* (c. 1582), cited in E. K. Chambers, *The Elizabethan Stage*, 4 vols. (Oxford: Clarendon, 1923), 4:215.

39   These lines were included in the quarto but omitted from the folio. For the tangled textual history, see Michael J. Warren, "Quarto and Folio *King Lear*, and the Interpretation of Albany and Edgar," in *Shakespeare: Pattern of Excelling Nature*, ed. David Bevington and Jay L. Halio (Newark: University of Delaware Press, 1978), pp. 95–107; Steven Urkowitz, *Shakespeare's Revision of "King Lear"* (Princeton: Princeton University Press, 1980); and Gary Taylor, "The War in *King Lear*," *Shakespeare Survey* 33 (1980): 27–34. Presumably, by the time the folio appeared, the point of the allusion to Harsnett would have been lost, and the lines were dropped.

40   John Bunyan, *Grace Abounding to the Chief of Sinners*, ed. Roger Sharrock (London: Clarendon Press, 1966), p. 15.

41 Edgar's later explanation – that he feared for his father's ability to sustain the shock of an encounter – is, like so many explanations in *King Lear*, too little, too late. On this characteristic belatedness as an element of the play's greatness, see Stephen Booth, *"King Lear," "Macbeth," Indefinition, and Tragedy* (New Haven: Yale University Press, 1983).

42 On "counterfeit miracles" produced to arouse awe and wonder, see especially Harsnett, *Discovery*, Epistle to the Reader.

43 Words, signs, gestures that claim to be in touch with super-reality, with absolute goodness and absolute evil, are exposed as vacant – illusions manipulated by the clever and imposed on the gullible.

44 This is, in effect, Edmund Jorden's prescription for cases such as Lear's, in *A briefe discourse of a disease*.

45 "It is even possible," writes Peter Milward, S. J., "that the lot of such priests as Weston and Dibdale provided Shakespeare with a suggestion for his portrayal of Edgar in hiding" (*Shakespeare's Religious Background* [London: Sidgwick and Jackson, 1973], p. 54). But I cannot agree with Milward's view that Shakespeare continually "laments 'the plight of his poor country' since the day Henry VIII decided to break with Rome" (224).

46 On the Yorkshire performance, see John Murphy, *Darkness and Devils*, pp. 93–118.

47 In willing this disenchantment against the evidence of our senses, we pay tribute to the theater. Harsnett has been twisted around to make this tribute possible. Harsnett several times characterizes exorcism as a "tragicomedy" (*Discovery*, p. 142; *Declaration*, p. 150). On Harsnett's conception of tragicomedy, see Herbert Berry, "Italian Definitions of Tragedy and Comedy Arrive in England," *Studies in English Literature* 14 (1974):179–87.

48 O. B. Hardison, Jr., *Christian Rite and Christian Drama in the Middle Ages: Essays in the Origin and Early History of Modern Drama* (Baltimore: Johns Hopkins University Press, 1965), esp. pp. 220–52.

49 C. L. Barber, "The Family in Shakespeare's Development: Tragedy and Sacredness," in *Representing Shakespeare: New Psychoanalytic Essays*, ed. Murray M. Schwartz and Coppélia Kahn (Baltimore: Johns Hopkins University Press, 1980), p. 196.

50 Richard Hooker, *Laws of Ecclesiastical Polity*, 1:582–83. This truth, which is the triumph of the metaphorical over the literal, confers on the church the liberty to use certain names and rites, even though they have been abolished. The entire passage in Hooker is powerfully suggestive for understanding the negotiation between the domain of literature and the domain of religion:

> They which honour the Law as an image of the wisdom of God himself, are notwithstanding to know that the same had an end in Christ. But what? Was the Law so abolished with Christ, that after his ascension the office of Priests became immediately wicked, and the very name hateful, as importing the exercise of an ungodly function? No, as long as the glory of the Temple continued, and till the time of that final desolation was accomplished, the very Christian Jews did continue with their sacrifices and other parts of legal service. That very Law therefore which our Saviour was to abolish, did not *so soon* become unlawful to be observed as some imagine; nor was it afterwards unlawful *so far*, that the very name of Altar, of Priest, of Sacrifice itself, should be banished out of the world. For though God do now hate sacrifice, whether it be heathenish or Jewish, so that we cannot have the same things which they had but with impiety; yet unless there be some greater let than the only evacuation of the Law of Moses, the names themselves may (I hope) be retained without sin, in respect of that proportion which things established by our Saviour have unto them which by him are abrogated. And so throughout all the writings of the ancient Fathers we see that the words which were do continue; the only difference is, that whereas before they had a literal, they now have a metaphorical use, and are so many notes of remembrance unto us, that what they did signify in the letter is accomplished in the truth. And as no man can deprive the Church of this liberty, to use names whereunto the Law was accustomed, so neither are we generally forbidden the use of things which the Law hath; though it neither command us any particular rite, as it did the Jews a number and the weightiest which it did command them are unto us in the Gospel prohibited. (4.11.10)

For the reference to Hooker I am indebted to John Coolidge.

51 "Truth to tell," writes Barthes, "the best weapon against myth is perhaps to mythify it in its turn, and to produce an *artificial myth:* and this reconstituted myth will in fact be a mythology" (Roland Barthes, *Mythologies*, trans. Annette Lavers [New York: Hill and Wang, 1972], p. 135).

CHAPTER 8

Melville, Delany, and New World Slavery

Eric Sundquist

This selection from Eric Sundquist's *To Wake the Nations* (1993) is an example of the rethinking of the literary history of the American Renaissance that occurred in the wake of the Civil Rights movement. Sundquist links Melville's novella *Benito Cereno* to both its discursive context in the debates over slavery in the 1850s and its historical affiliations with the slave revolts in Haiti at the turn of the nineteenth century. Like the New Historicists, Sundquist is interested in how literature works to shape perceptions of the social world and to bring about changes in social institutions.

> *Bones. I saw bones. They were stacked all the way to the top of the ship. I looked around. The underside of the whole ark was nothin but a great bonehouse. I looked and saw crews of black men handlin in them bones. There was a crew of two or three under every cabin around that ark. Why, there must have been a million cabins. They were doing it very carefully, like they were holdin onto babies or something precious. Standin like a captain was the old man we had seen top deck...*
>
> *I comest to think about a Sermon I heard about Ezekiel in the valley of dry bones. The old man was lookin at me now. He look like he was sizin me up...*
>
> *"Son, you are in the house of generations. Every African who lives in America has a part of his soul in this ark."*
>
> Henry Dumas, "Ark of Bones"

When the sixty-three slaves aboard Benito Cereno's ship revolted, killing twenty-five men, some in the course of struggle, some out of simple vengeance, they especially determined to slay their master, Don Alexandro Aranda, "because they said they could not otherwise obtain their liberty." To Amasa Delano's original account of the revolt, Melville's fictionalized version of the slave revolt aboard the *San Dominick* adds that the death would serve as a warning to the other seamen: not only that, but a warning that takes the form of deliberate terror. Aranda's body, instead of being thrown overboard, as in reality it was, is seemingly cannibalized or otherwise stripped of its flesh and the skeleton then *"substituted for the ship's proper figurehead – the image of Cristobal Colon, the discoverer of the New World,"* from whose first contact with the New World in Hispaniola – that is, San Domingo, or Haiti – flowed both untold prosperity and human slavery on an extraordinary scale.[1] (Again, I have retained the problematic designation New World because for both the Europeans and the Africans, whose perspective is most the concern of Melville and Delany, the Americas were the "New World.") The thirty-nine men from the *Santa Maria* whom Columbus left on the north coast of Navidad on Hispaniola in 1494 were killed by the native people after quarreling over gold and Indian women; on his second voyage in 1494 Columbus himself took command, suppressed an Indian uprising, and authorized an enslavement of Indians to work in the gold fields, which was destined to destroy close to 1 million natives, by some estimates, within fifteen years. Responding to pleas of the Dominican priests, led by Bartholomew de Las Casas, that the Indian population would not survive slavery, Charles V, Holy Roman Emperor, in 1517 authorized the first official transport of African slaves to San Domingo: the New World slave trade, destined to carry some 15 million slaves across the Atlantic by 1865, had begun.[2]

The substitution of Africans for New World Indians was justified by Las Casas on the supposedly humanitarian grounds that the blacks, unlike the Indians, were hardy and suited to such labors in a tropical climate. "Like oranges," wrote Antonio de Herrera in 1601, "they found their proper soil in Hispaniola, and it seemed even more natural than Guinea." Just so, added the American author who quoted Herrera in 1836: "The one race was annihilated by slavery, while the other has ever since continued to thrive and fatten upon it." Only the master class or their sympathizers could make such an argument. Their antagonists, such as the black abolitionists David Walker and Henry Highland Garnett, especially stigmatized Charles V and his "evil genius" Las Casas: "Clouds of infamy will thicken around them as the world moves on toward God."[3]

Like Melville, and like Martin Delany in his neglected novel *Blake; or the Huts of America*, Garnett took a perspective on African American slavery that is of marked importance but has played a comparatively small role in literary and cultural studies – namely, the recognition that slavery was hemispheric and that its fullest literary representation as well as its fullest political critique required a view that embraced several cultures, several nations, much as Du Bois was later to recognize that the attack on American racial injustice and the reconstruction of African American cultural history had to be pursued in a diasporic Pan-African framework. In each case the contemporary racial crisis could be shown to derive from historical forces of great complexity and sweep: in Du Bois's case the intertwined histories of slavery in the Americas and colonial rule in Africa (and the Third World generally); in that of Melville and Delany the contest of European and American political and religious power played out in the rise of the slave economies of the southern United States and Latin America, principally the Caribbean.

Alongside the embracing paradoxical outcome of prosperity and destruction brought on by the Columbian encroachment and settlements, the compressed structure of monastic symbolism in Melville's tale is meant to evoke the role of the Catholic church, the Dominicans in particular, in the initiation of New World slavery at the same time that it anticipates resonant elements of the crisis over slavery in the ante-bellum period. The comparison of Benito Cereno to Charles V, who had become a virtual tool of the Dominicans by the end of his reign, and Delano's momentary vision of the *San Dominick* as a "whitewashed monastery" or a shipload of Dominican "Black Friars pacing the cloisters" are only a few of the ecclesiastical scenes and metaphors that animate the tale. The aura of ruin and decay that links Benito Cereno and his ship to Charles V and his empire points forward as well to the contemporary demise of

Spanish power in the New World and the role of slave unrest in its revolutionary decline. George Bancroft in particular remarked the racist hypocrisy implicit in the coincidence of Charles's military liberation of white Christian slaves in Tunis and his enslavement of Africans bound for the Americas, and emphasized the further coincidence, virtually commonplace by Melville's day, that "Hayti, the first spot in America that received African slaves, was the first to set the example of African liberty." It is this coincidence and its ironic origins that are illuminated by Babo's symbolic display of the skeleton of a modern slaveholder in place of the image of Columbus. Along with the chalked admonition "*Follow your leader*," the skeleton too appears to Delano at the climactic moment when the frightened Benito Cereno and the former slave Babo, his "countenance lividly vindictive," plunge into his boat and the "piratical revolt" is unveiled: "All this, with what preceded, and what followed, occurred with such involutions of rapidity, that past, present, and future seemed one."[4]

For Delano, however, the mask is torn away only from the story's action and from the ship's figurehead, not from the allegory of Melville's tale. The benevolent American, self-satisfied and of good conscience, appears oblivious to the end to the meaning of Babo's terror and to the murderous satire contained in Melville's symbolic gesture. The masquerade performed by Babo and Benito Cereno to beguile Delano tests both the American captain's posture of innocence and that of Melville's audience. All three of the tale's actors play parts defined by the climactic phase slavery in the Americas had entered when Melville composed his simultaneously explosive and paralytic tale during the winter and spring of 1854–5. Their stylized enactment of a rebellion contained within the illusion of mastery, as though in ritual pantomime, finely depicts the haltingly realized potential for slave revolution in the New World, then entering its last phase in the mid-nineteenth century. Through the display of Aranda's skeleton, the sacred bones of Columbus, rumored still in 1830 to have been lodged in the cathedral of Santo Domingo before being transferred to Havana upon the Treaty of Basel in 1795, were joined to those of the millions of slaves who had sailed to their deaths in dark cargo holds or, if they survived the middle passage, under a brutal regime of field labor in the New World. Of them is built Benito Cereno's decaying ship the *San Dominick* as it drifts into the harbor of the Chilean island of Santa Maria: "Her keel seemed laid, her ribs put together, and she launched, from Ezekiel's Valley of Dry Bones."[5]

The American Civil War reduced New World slavery to Cuba and Brazil; it brought to an end the threatened extension of slavery throughout new territories of the United States as well as Caribbean and Latin American countries coveted by the South. *Benito Cereno*'s general significance in the debates over slavery in the 1850s is readily apparent; in addition, Melville's exploitation of the theme of balked revolution through an elaborate pattern of suppressed mystery and ironic revelation has helped draw attention to the wealth of symbolic meanings the slave revolt in San Domingo in the 1790s would have had for an alert audience in the immediate antebellum years. Even so, it has been easy for readers since then to miss the full implications of Melville's invocation of Caribbean revolution or to misconstrue the historical dimensions of his masquerade of rebellion. Abraham Lincoln's diplomatic recognition of Haiti in 1862 ensured the island's harassment of Confederate privateers, and black rule was hardly an issue between the two governments once the South seceded. Moreover, the Caribbean and Latin America ceased for the moment to be of pressing national interest once the issue of slavery was resolved and a transcontinental railroad completed later in the decade. The disappearance from view of the region until conflicts fifty and a hundred years later brought it back into the public mind – first in the Spanish-American War and subsequent military actions, and later through Cuba's critical role in the cold war – has contributed to the general disregard of its centrality in *Benito Cereno*, *Blake*, and other works of the period. As the possibilities for renewed Caribbean revolution linked to civil conflict in the United States unfolded in the 1850s, however, they brought into special tropological focus the historical and contemporary role of both San Domingo and, in the case of Delany, Cuba in the struggle over American slavery.

Although he plausibly argues that Babo is the most heroic character in Melville's fiction and declares the tale a masterpiece, C. L. R. James nonetheless laments that *Benito Cereno* is in essence propaganda posing as literature, a sign that Melville had "lost his vision of the future," which would allow him to see "what will endure and what will pass." James's judgment on this score is incorrect, and his casting of his critique in terms of Melville's historical vision seems obtuse in the case of *Benito Cereno*, a work preoccupied with, and guided by, the superimposition of critical historical moments. Still, James offers an important clue to the tale's strategy of claustrophobic repression and its narrative entanglement in the ritual staging of authority. By reconfiguring the machinery of slavery as a masquerade, exposing its appeal to natural law as the utmost artifice, Melville suggested that there was *no future*, as it were, for the experiment of American democracy so long as the paralysis of inequality continued. What is more, he wrote in a culture in which every gesture toward slave subversion was itself open to countersubversion – if not by proslavery polemicists then by the forces of northern political and popular culture. Many years in advance of the similar fate of *Uncle Tom's Cabin*, for example, the *Amistad* mutiny and Nat Turner's revolt had been appropriated by stage minstrelsy and drained of their import in productions that obscured the deaths of whites while focusing on the comic punishment of the rebels. (In one case Turner's revolt was merged with Gabriel's conspiracy under a title that turned both in the direction of Stowe's melodrama: "Uncle Gabriel the Negro General.")[6] Minstrelsy also lay to some degree behind Melville's imaginative recapitulation of New World slave history, but to altogether different purpose, for it offered to him, as it would to Twain, a means to see history itself dress in costume. If Melville's tale presents no clear solution to the problems of racism and bondage, it nevertheless stands forth like Aranda's skeleton, a figurehead of revolution and slavery in stunning crisis.

Memory, Authority, and the Shadowy Tableau

...a little island set in a smiling and fury-lurked and incredible indigo sea, which was the halfway point between what we call the jungle and what we call civilization, halfway between the dark, inscrutable continent from which the black blood, the black bones and flesh and thinking and remembering and hopes and desires, was ravished by violence, and the cold known land to which it was doomed, the civilized land and people which had expelled some of its own blood and thinking and desires that had become too crass to be faced and borne longer, and set it homeless and desperate on the lonely ocean...

William Faulkner, *Absalom, Absalom!*

In changing the name of Benito Cereno's ship from the *Tryal* to the *San Dominick*, Melville gave to Babo's slave revolt a specific character that has often been identified. Haiti, known as San Domingo (Saint-Domingue) before declaring its final independence from France in 1804 and adopting a native name,* remained a strategic point of reference in debates over slavery in the United States. In altering the date of Amasa Delano's encounter with Benito Cereno from 1805 to 1799, moreover, Melville accentuated the fact that his tale belonged to the Age of Revolution, in particular the period of violent struggle leading to Haitian independence presided over by the heroic black general Toussaint L'Ouverture, which prompted Jefferson to remark in 1797 that "the revolutionary storm, now sweeping the globe," shall, if nothing prevents it, make us "the murderers of our own children." As I have already noted in connection with Nat Turner's revolt, the example of Haiti was appropriated by proslavery and antislavery forces alike. Although it strengthened resistance to the slave trade, San Domingo's revolution also provided a setback to abolitionists who seized upon its extension of the principles of the Age of Revolution. The large number of refugee planters from the island who came to the South in the wake of the revolution spread tales of terror that were reawakened with each newly discovered conspiracy or revolt – most notably, of course, those of Gabriel Prosser, Denmark Vesey, and Turner – and the history of Haiti and its revolution became deeply ingrained in southern history. As the epigraph just quoted suggests, Faulkner, a century later, would provide an impressive representation of the interlocked destinies of revolutionized Haiti and the slaveholding South when he derived Thomas Sutpen's destiny from the historical convulsions of the island, "a theater for violence and injustice and bloodshed and all the satanic lusts of human greed and cruelty... a soil manured with black blood from two hundred years of oppression and exploitation." San Domingo thus offered both a distilled symbolic representation of the legacy of the American and French Revolutions, a realization of the Rights of Man, and a fearful prophecy of black rebellion throughout the New World.[7]

After Napoleon's plans to retake San Domingo (in order to retrieve in the Gulf of Mexico glory he had lost in the Mediterranean) were undercut by the demise of General Charles Leclerc's army in 1802, he lost the main reason to retain and occupy Louisiana. "Without that island," Henry Adams wrote, the colonial system "had hands, feet, and even a head, but no body. Of what use was Louisiana, when France had clearly lost the main colony which Louisiana was meant to feed and fortify?" The economic ruin and seeming barbarism of the island, and the excessive expense and loss of lives it would require to retrieve and rebuild, made San Domingo a lost cause of large dimensions to France and at the same time the key to an extraordinary territorial expansion of the United States – an expansion that would soon make the Caribbean appear as vital to American slave interests as it had been to France and prepare the way for the crisis question of slavery's expansion into new territories. In making their country "the graveyard of Napoleon's magnificent army as well as his imperial ambitions in the New World," Eugene Genovese has written, the slaves of

---

* In English and American usage of the nineteenth century, the entire island at times, and even after the revolution the western half (a French possession since the seventeenth century), was often designated San Domingo or St Domingo. The Spanish, eastern half (the Dominican Republic after 1844) was usually designated Santo Domingo, as was the principal city founded by the Columbian expeditions and named in memory of Columbus's father, Dominick.

San Domingo thus cleared the way for a different expression of New World colonial power destined to have more decisive and lasting effect on the stage of world history.[8]

Even though contention over the Gulf of Mexico did not ultimately play a large role in the Civil War, it seemed a vital issue throughout the 1850s – all the more so because, like Melville's tale, it represented the shadow play, one might say, of America's own incomplete Revolution and its ensuing domestic turmoil. It is, indeed, the spectral presence of San Domingo within Melville's story that constitutes the most somber, suffusing "shadow of the Negro" that falls on Benito Cereno (and Melville's reader) at the story's end. The threat of black rebellion is historically latent in all contemporary allusions to San Domingo – and always barely repressed, by extension, in the slaveholding South's psyche – but it also provides a continual analogue and point of reference for antebellum debates about the expansion of slavery. From Melville's perspective in the early 1850s, the nature and extent of future American power inevitably remained a function of the unfolding pattern of anticolonial and slave revolutions in the Americas. Although slaves fought at different times on opposing sides, the national revolutions of South and Central America in the early part of the century helped undermine slavery throughout the region (in most cases slaves were not freed immediately upon independence, but legislation abolishing slavery was at least initiated – in Mexico, Uruguay, Chile, Argentina, and Bolivia in the 1820s; in Venezuela and Peru in the 1850s). The end of slavery in the British West Indies in 1833 and in the Dutch and French islands in 1848 left the United States more and more an anomaly, its own revolutionary drama absurdly immobilized. Expansion and revolution were often linked, but not so expansion and antislavery. Thus, when extremists of southern slavery in the 1850s sought to increase their hegemony by encompassing slaveholding interests in Cuba and by extending the peculiar institution through new revolutions in Latin America, they ignored the degeneration of colonial rule on the one hand and on the other the trepidations expressed by one of the best known of South American revolutionaries, Francisco Miranda, who wrote as early as 1798: "As much as I desire the liberty and independence of the New World, I fear the anarchy of a revolutionary system. God forbid that these beautiful countries become, as St. Domingue, a theatre of blood and of crime under the pretext of establishing liberty. Let them rather remain if necessary one century more under the barbarous and imbecile oppression of Spain." Miranda's plea expresses well the paradox of New World liberation and of the United States' continued, expanding enslavement of Africans and their American-born children between 1776 and 1860. Drawn by the territorial dreams opened by Louisiana, the post-revolutionary generations advocated expansion through a conscious policy of America's manifest destiny to revolutionize the continent – eventually the entire hemisphere – spreading Anglo-Saxon free institutions, as one writer put it, from the Atlantic to the Pacific and "from the icy wilderness of the North to . . . the smiling and prolific South."[9]

That dreams of a global millennium always exceeded reality is less relevant than the fact that the harsh conflict between dream and reality was anchored in the wrenching paradox that had come to define New World revolution itself: would it advance freedom or increase slavery? The question could better be put differently: would it advance the cause of *slave* revolution? Although the North resisted the expansion of the Union for fear of advancing the power of slavery, not because it hoped to promote slave insurrection, expansion appears to have had the effect of dissipating the demographic cohesion and concentration that might have made American slave revolts more numerous or threatening in scope.[10] It was hardly clear in the 1850s that the expansion of slavery was, paradoxically, a means of containing slave rebellion in the South. At the time of *Benito Cereno*'s publication, the elimination of slavery was frequently *not* an adjunct to "revolutionizing" the hemisphere – or if not the hemisphere, then the Caribbean, where the energy of manifest destiny had been redirected after its initial efforts had failed to bring "All Mexico," as a popular slogan had it, into the United States orbit. The region offered in miniature an emblem of the Americas in their historical revolutionary moment, with the remnants of Spain's great empire (Benito Cereno), free blacks who had revolutionized their own nation (Babo), and American expansionist interests (Delano) all in contention.

Benito Cereno does not prophesy a civil war but rather anticipates, just as plausibly, an explosive heightening of the conflict between American democracy, Old World despotism, and Caribbean New World revolution. Its pervasive aura of paralysis, its revolutionary gestures held in perilous suspension, replicates in narrative form a crisis in temporality in which past, present, and future, as in Delano's moment of lucid perception, seem one. It is a universe, in Richard Chase's words, "poised upon a present that continually merges with the opulent debris of a dying past and reaches into a vacant and terrifying future." Melville's ship is a perfect chronotrope (in Bakhtin's phrase) of his story's engagement in the historical moment.[*] Operating simultaneously within the historical and the narratological registers, Melville maintains this text, like the progress of New World slavery, poised in a barely suppressed revolutionary gesture, one that seems to duplicate the prior navigation, the prior history, of the doomed *San Dominick*, which, "like a man lost in the woods, more than once . . . had doubled upon her own track." In addition to its formal and temporal significance, the double course of Melville's story suggests the essential doubleness of the American ship of state: at once the ark of the covenant that authorized both liberty and slavery, leaving the national mission adrift, becalmed amidst incalculable danger; and therefore the "ark of bones," the charnel house of slavery whose long, haunted middle passage is evoked in the superb story by Henry Dumas, written more than a century after *Benito Cereno*, from which this chapter's epigraph is drawn. Incorporating the tension between liberty and slavery into its formal structure and its cunning manipulation of authority, Melville's narrative voice expresses, by both suggesting and containing, the rebellion that cannot be completed, implicating at once the potential spread of black revolution to the United States and the paralyzed realization of America's own revolutionary inheritance. Melville's containment of Delano's own consciousness at the point of explosive possibility brings the narrative by analogous form into closer and closer coincidence with the rebellion on board the ship and the imminent spread of New World revolt, creating in the reader, as in Delano, "a fatality not to be withstood." Like the dramatic presentations of the

---

[*] "In the literary artistic chronotrope, spatial and temporal indicators are fused into one carefully thought-out, concrete whole. Time, as it were, thickens, takes on flesh, becomes artistically visible; likewise, space becomes charged and responsive to the movements of time, plot, and history. This intersection of axes and fusion of indicators characterizes the artistic chronotrope." See M. M. Bakhtin, *The Dialogic Imagination*, trans. Caryl Emerson and Michael Holquist (Austin: University of Texas Press, 1981), p. 84.

chained Atufal, the striking at intervals of the ship's flawed bell, and the seemingly "coincidental" activities of the oakum pickers, the singing women, and the hatchet polishers, the narrative voice performs an act of ritual control, regulating and containing acts of near revolt in which the ceremonial may at any moment give way to the actual, in which roles threaten to be reversed, and the figurative revolt contained in the liminal realm of Delano's consciousness threatens to be forced into the realm of the literal.[11]

To enter the realm of the literal, for Delano as well as for most of Melville's contemporary audience, was to enter a catalogue of nightmares and racial chaos. Readers of *Benito Cereno* who take account at all of Melville's use of the San Domingo Revolution focus for the most part on its extension of the French Revolution and the heroism of Toussaint. Yet the island's continuing turmoil in subsequent years not only kept it alive in the southern imagination of racial violence, as we have seen, but also made it of strategic significance in counterarguments to Caribbean filibustering, thus accentuating the standoff between imperial powers. For example, an 1850 pamphlet by Benjamin C. Clark, though sympathetic to Haitian freedom, condemned the "condition worse than that of slavery" into which he thought the island had been plunged by Great Britain's political maneuvering in the Caribbean; Haiti's failure to develop its resources and its continued threat of revolution to Cuba and the Dominican Republic thus made it a barrier both to United States interests in the region and to the emancipation of American slaves. On a different note, an essay entitled "About Niggers," appearing in one of the same 1855 issues of *Putnam's Monthly* that carried the serialization of *Benito Cereno*, argued that Haiti, unlike the United States, demonstrated that liberty and slavery cannot coexist and that the "terrible capacity for revenge" unleashed in the San Domingo Revolution proves that the "nigger" is "a man, not a baboon." The sarcastic article, in line with the general antislavery tone of *Putnam's*, anticipated black colonizationists in voicing the novel hope that the black West Indies would one day develop "a rich sensuous civilization which will bring a new force into thin-blooded intellectualism, and save our noble animal nature from extreme emasculation and contempt."[12] Melville's tale, antislavery though it may be, contains no invocation of noble savagery and no such hope about the fruitful merging of cultures.

Were the noble and humane Toussaint the only representative figure of the Haitain revolution, fears of slave insurrection in the United States might not have taken on such a vicious coloring. But when white Americans contemplated what would happen if the black revolt in San Domingo were "reenacted in South Carolina and Louisiana" and African American slaves wiped out "their wrongs in the blood of their oppressors," as William Wells Brown wrote in *St. Domingo: Its Revolutions and Its Patriots* (1855), not Toussaint but his successor as general in chief, Jean-Jacques Dessalines, sprang to mind. Whatever ambivalent gratitude might have existed toward Haiti for its mediating role in the United States' acquisition of Louisiana was diluted by the final achievement of independence under Dessalines in 1804. His tactics of deceitful assurance of safety to white landowners, followed by outright butchery, were almost certainly justified as a response to the equal terror waged against blacks in the French attempt to restore slavery, but they nevertheless enhanced his own claim that his rule would be initiated by vengeance against the French "cannibals" who have "taken pleasure in bathing their hands in blood of the sons of Haiti."[13] A sympathetic writer could claim in 1869 that the independence of Haiti constituted "the first great shock to

this gigantic evil [slavery] in modern times," but what southerners in particular remembered were accounts of drownings, burnings, rapes, limbs chopped off, eyes
gouged out, disembowelments – the sort of gothic violence typified by an episode in
Mary Hassal's so-called *Secret History; or, The Horrors of St. Domingo* (1808), in which
a young white woman refuses the proposal of one of Dessalines's chiefs: "The monster
gave her to his guard, who hung her by the throat on an iron hook in the market place,
where the lovely, innocent, unfortunate victim slowly expired."[14] Although Hassal's
"history" in both form and substance resembles epistolary novels such as *Wieland*, its
account of the Haitian trauma is hardly more sensational than the standard histories
and polemics of the day. Antislavery forces for good reason hesitated to invoke Haiti as
a model of black rule; even those sympathetic to its revolution considered its subsequent history violent and ruinous. Melville therefore took an extraordinary risk in his
characterization of Babo and his revolt, pushing to the limit his readers' capacity to
discriminate between just political resistance and macabre terror – or rather, to see
their necessary fusion.

Contemporary representations of Haiti's revolution and subsequent history provided Melville not just the central trope of slavery and its subversion but also a set
of discourses interweaving Jacobinism and the Inquisition, the terror of liberation
and the terror of repression. *De Bow's Review*, the influential organ of southern
interests, carried an essay in 1854 typical in its critique of Haitian commerce and
government that displays such arguments in miniature. For over thirty years, the
essay claims, the "march of civilization" has been dead in Haiti, its social condition
one of sustained indolence and immorality: "From its discovery by Columbus to the
present reign of Solouque [*sic*], the olive branch has withered under its pestilential
breath; and when the atheistical philosophy of revolutionary France added fuel to the
volcano of hellish passions which raged in its bosom, the horrors of the island
became a narrative which frightened our childhood, and still curdles our blood to
read. The triumphant negroes refined upon the tortures of the Inquisition in their
treatment of prisoners taken in battle. They tore them with red-hot pincers – sawed
them asunder between planks – roasted them by a slow fire – or tore out their eyes
with red-hot corkscrews." Here, then, are the central ingredients that Melville's tale
adds to Delano's own *Narrative*. The conflation of Spanish and French rule, coupled
with the allusion to the Inquisition, yokes anti-Catholic and anti-Jacobin sentiment.
Fear of spreading (black) revolution and fear of Inquisitorial violence were one.
Indeed, the rhetoric of manifest destiny in the Caribbean was often a mix of the two,
though with the submerged irony – one Melville treats with complex care – that
northern critics of slavery's expansion liked as well to employ the analogies of European despotism and Catholic subversion in attacking the South. For the North,
national expansion would morally entail the eradication of slavery, not its extension.
It would illuminate the world in such a way, Lyman Beecher had already argued in
A Plea for the West (1835), that "nation after nation, cheered by our example, will
follow in our footsteps till the whole earth is free . . . delivered from feudal ignorance
and servitude." The only danger, according to Beecher's anti-Catholic tract, lay in
the Roman church's attempt to salvage its dying power by subversion of liberty in
the New World, notably in South America, Canada, and San Domingo, which were
"destined to feel the quickening powers of Europe, as the only means remaining to
them of combating the march of liberal institutions . . . and perpetuating for a season
her political and ecclesiastical dominion." The slave power of the South, said the

generation of Beecher's children, would behave precisely the same way in order to rescue and extend their dying institution.[15]

As Melville was quick to comprehend, however, antislavery sentiment was frequently bound to a different but not entirely oppositional imperial agenda, and the antislavery imagination, no less than the proslavery, tended to collapse history into timeless images of terror and damnation. Theodore Parker, for instance, comparing the strength of Anglo-Saxon free institutions to the decay of Spain and her colonies in "The Nebraska Question" (1854), had no trouble linking together the early butchery and plunder of Indians in Hispaniola and greater Latin America in the name of the Virgin Mary, and the contemporary confluence of slaveholding power and Catholicism. Spain "rolled the Inquisition as a sweet morsel under her tongue...butchered the Moors and banished the plundered Jews," Parker wrote. In San Domingo she "reinvented negro Slavery" six thousand years after it had vanished in Egypt and "therewith stained the soil of America." With what legacy? Spain's two resulting American empires, Haiti and Brazil, so Parker saw it, were "despotism throned on bayonets"; over Cuba, France and England "still hold up the feeble hands of Spain"; most of South and Central America takes the form of a republic "whose only permanent constitution is a Cartridge-box"; and Mexico goes swiftly back to despotism, a rotting carcass about which "every raven in the hungry flock of American politicians...wipes his greedy beak, prunes his wings, and screams 'Manifest Destiny.'" Parker attacked the North for conciliating slave interests time after time (most recently in the Compromise of 1850) and predicted the slaveholders' attempted acquisition of Cuba, the Mesilla Valley, Nebraska, Mexico, Puerto Rico, Haiti, Jamaica and other Caribbean islands, the Sandwich Islands, and so on. In his view despotic, Catholic tyranny was at work, which so far the Puritan, Anglo-Saxon spirit of liberty and religious freedom had been unable to contain. "I never knew a Catholic Priest who favored freedom in America," Parker admonished. "A Slave himself, the medieval theocracy eats the heart out from the celibate Monk."[16]

Benito Cereno, as he delivers his halting, incoherent narrative to Delano, seems to be "eating his own words, even as he ever seemed eating his own heart." This coincidence in phrasing need do no more than remind us that Don Benito, who resembles a monk or a "hypochondriac abbott" and in the end retires to a monastery to die, is made by Melville a symbol of American paranoia about Spanish, Catholic, slaveholding despotism. To the extent that he also represents the southern planter, the dissipated cavalier spiritually wasted by his own terrifying enslavement, Benito Cereno requires the reader to see the tale in Parker's imperial terms, ones that most later readers of Melville's tale have lost sight of but that is crucial to the paralyzing crisis over slavery in the 1850s: North and South, like Delano and Cereno as they are mediated by Babo, play the parts of Anglo-Saxon and Roman-European currently working out the destiny of colonial territories enriched by African slavery in the New World. Benito Cereno, at once a genteel courtier ("a sort of Castilian Rothschild") and an impotent master painfully supported by the constant "half embrace of his servant," virtually is the Spanish New World, undermined by slave and nationalist revolutions and adrift aboard a deteriorated ghost ship on the revolutionary waters of history, which are now "like waved lead that has cooled and set in the smelter's mold." For his part, Delano, like the nation he represents, vacillates between dark suspicion and paternalistic disdain of the Spaniard. The tale cannily keeps hidden what Benito Cereno, the enfeebled master, knows well: that it is Babo who stages the events Delano witnesses aboard the *San Dominick*, artistically fashioning his former master like "a Nubian sculptor finishing off a white statue-head."[17] Melville's scenario – driving between the example of *De Bow's Review*, which saw Haiti as a volcano of Jacobin horrors, and that of Theodore Parker, who saw New World slaveholding itself as a manifestation of Old World despotism and popish insurgency – makes the African slave the true subversive, the exponent of revolutionary vengeance and the mock inquisitor of his now debilitated master.

Delano, as Jean Fagan Yellin suggests, may portray the stock Yankee traveler in plantation fiction, delighted by the warm patriarchal bond between the loyal, minstrel-like slave and his languid master. He may even, like Thomas Gray in his relationship to Nat Turner, penetrate the violent center of that relationship and yet prefer to ignore or mystify its meaning in a narrative dedicated to regulating and containing the threat of black revolution. Delano constantly enacts the mechanics of repression, not simply in the sense that he puts down the revolt aboard the *San Dominick* and thereby restores the authority that has been overturned, but also in the sense that his refusal to understand the "shadow" that has descended upon Benito Cereno is itself a psychologically and politically repressive act that replicates the ideology of America's crisis over slavery.[18] The repressing "bright sun" and "blue sky" that have "forgotten it all," which Delano invokes at the tale's conclusion, echo Daniel Webster's praise of the Union and the founding fathers in the wake of the nearly insurrectionary struggle over the Compromise of 1850: "A long and violent convulsion of the elements has just passed away," Webster remarked, "and the heavens, the skies, smile upon us." Benito Cereno's reply? "Because they have no memory . . . because they are not human."[19] . . .

Melville borrowed the rudiments of Amasa Delano's trusting disposition and generosity directly from the captain's own self-serving account, which records that the "*generous captain Amasa Delano*" much aided Benito Cereno (only to be poorly treated in return when he tried to claim his just salvage rights) and was himself saved from certain slaughter by his own "kindness," "sympathy," and "unusually pleasant" temperament. A passage earlier in Delano's *Narrative* might also have caught Melville's eye: "A man, who finds it hard to conceive of real benevolence in the motives of his fellow creatures, gives no very favourable testimony to the public in regard to the state of his own heart, or the elevation of his moral sentiments."[20] The self-serving nature of Delano's remarks aside, what is notable is the manner in which Melville may be said to have rendered perversely ironic the virtue of "benevolence," the central sentiment of abolitionist rhetoric since the mid-eighteenth century. Delano's response to the blacks is not "philanthropic" but "genial," it is true – but genial in the way one responds to Newfoundland dogs, natural valets and hairdressers, and minstrels performing "to some pleasant tune." In this passage Melville eviscerated less the American captain than northern liberalism for its profound indulgence in racialist interpretations of black character. *Uncle Tom's Cabin* was the rhetorical masterpiece of northern racialism, but William Ellery Channing's statement in *Slavery* (1835) is succinct: "The African is so affectionate, imitative, and docile that in favorable circumstances he catches much that is good; and accordingly the influence of a wise and kind master will be seen in the very countenance of his slaves."[21]

Melville's depiction of Delano is a parody of such sentiments. Although it may have had no particular source, his conception of Delano's stereotyping could have been drawn from a *Putnam's* essay, "Negro Minstrelsy – Ancient and Modern," appearing in January 1855 (the time at which he was composing his tale). In the course of a complimentary portrait of black minstrelsy as an art form, the writer observed: "The lightness and prevailing good humor of the negro songs, have been remarked upon. A true southern melody is seldom sentimental, and never melancholy. And this results directly from the character and habits of the colored race. No hardships or troubles can destroy, even check their happiness and levity." Of course, such a view of African American levity and docility, stock ingredients of the romantic racialism willfully played upon by Babo, was also but a thin cover for apprehensions that something more dangerous lurked behind the facade.[22] Like Delano's consciousness, however, the racialist argument, which was nothing less than the fundamental ideology of minstrelsy that would rule white America's view of blacks long past the Civil War, bespoke a national mission in which political regulation and racial hierarchy were raised to such a pitch that calculated manipulation cannot be divorced from naiveté. That, it may be, was Melville's America.

Melville's distillation of Delano's racialism and his manic benevolence into tropes of minstrelsy empties him of moral authority. An example of the mind at work in the *Putnam's* essay, Delano's offensive stereotypes allow us to see that the trope of African American docility and gaiety was generated as much by sympathetic liberalism as by the harsh regime of slavery. Minstrelsy – in effect, the complete show of the tale's action staged for Delano – is a product, as it were, of his mind, of his willingness to accept Babo's Sambo-like performance. Melville in this way nearly collapses the distance between proslavery and antislavery, South and North, so as to display the combined stagecraft that preserved slavery. Paternalistic benevolence is coextensive with minstrelsy, on the plantation or on the stage....

It is Delano, not Benito Cereno, for whom the slave's disfiguration could signify a love quarrel, and in whom the grammar of sentiment and the rhetoric of minstrelsy are most clearly united. In his foolhardy but carefully calibrated benevolence, the character of Delano represents both the founding fathers, who sanctioned slavery even as they recognized its contradiction of the Rights of Man, and the contemporary northern accommodationists, who too much feared sectional strife and economic turmoil to bring to the surface of consciousness a full recognition of slavery's ugliness in fact and in principle. San Domingo, like Nat Turner, was a lesson in racial fears as often for the North as for the South, for antislavery as for proslavery. The fundamental relation of terror that underlies the artificial levity of Babo's ministrations to his master constitutes Melville's devastating critique of such widespread northern racialism, of which Delano is merely a representative. Delano's "old weakness for negroes," surging forth precisely at Melville's greatest moment of terrifying invention, the shaving scene, is the revolutionary mind at odds with itself, impassioned for freedom but fearful of continuing revolution, energized by the ideals of paternalistic humanitarianism but blind to the recriminating violence they hold tenuously in check....

The Law of Nature or the Hive of Subtlety

The counterpointed plots at work in the political context of America's Caribbean interests is matched by the counterpointed actual or imagined plots that circulate throughout *Benito Cereno*. In his construction of slave revolution, however, Melville gave no easy quarter to the rights of black freedom; rather, he measured pragmatically the likely operation of the law and of race politics in America. Moreover, his fascination with revolt and mutiny, as *White Jacket* and *Billy Budd* remind us, was tempered always by his equal fascination with the mechanics of repression. Captain Vere's combined paternalism and rigid justice refine qualities found in both the fictional and the actual Captain Delano. Even for the good captain, like the good master, benevolence may be no barrier either to rebellion or to its consequences. "I have a great horror of the crime of mutiny," wrote Delano in a discussion of the case of the *Bounty* in his *Narrative*, for it leads only to greater abuses against the mutineers. "Vengeance will not always sleep, but wakes to pursue and overtake them." A virtual reign of terror against blacks followed Turner's insurrection. Likewise, Delano had to prevent the Spanish crew and Benito Cereno himself from "cutting to pieces and killing" the blacks after the *Tryal* had been retaken. But legal retribution followed the same instinct. At Concepción, as graphically as in Melville's tale, five of the rebels were sentenced to hanging and decapitation, their heads then "fixed on a pole, in the square of the port of Talcahuano, and the corpses of all... burnt to ashes." Justice here echoes revolution: among more gruesome brutalities, both sides in the San Domingo Revolution displayed the severed heads of their opponents; similarly, the heads of defeated black insurrectionists in Charleston in 1739, New Orleans in 1811, and Tennessee in 1856 were fixed on poles or carried in parades, while in the wake of Nat Turner's revolt, the head of a black man was impaled on a stake outside Jerusalem at an intersection that henceforth became known as Blackhead Signpost. Babo's head, "that hive of subtlety," gazes across the plaza toward St. Bartholomew's Church, where the recovered bones of Aranda lie, and beyond that the monastery where Benito Cereno lies dying, soon to "follow his leader."[23]

The repressive mechanisms of justice – legally authorized or not – worked swiftly to contain slave insurrection in the United States when it occurred. But full-scale insurrection was only the most extreme form of slave resistance, which appeared in many guises. In the atmosphere of crisis in which Melville wrote, it is important to add, simple escape from slavery had come to seem a potential revolutionary act, with its suppression guaranteed by the Fugitive Slave Law. Melville's investigation of revolt in *Benito Cereno* extrapolates from the controversial decisions upholding the Fugitive Slave Law rendered by his father-in-law, Massachusetts Supreme Court Chief Justice Lemuel Shaw, to more difficult and germane instances of revolt at sea.[24] Despite the fact that he held antislavery views while adhering to what he took to be the overriding primacy of the rule of law, Shaw is no doubt burlesqued alongside Webster as a man blinded by the ideology of Union. Delano appears to have none of the conscience of Justice Shaw, but in any case his mind is rendered by Melville not as a moral repository but as a sieve for the cascading dialectic between racial psychology and political power. The most difficult decision to make about *Benito Cereno*, in fact, is whether there is in Delano any difference whatsoever between blind ignorance and a calculating assertion of hierarchical power that hides behind ostensible ignorance.

But this tautological conundrum also resonates with contemporary ideological significance. Aside from the revolt of Turner, the instances of slave uprising that most drew public attention in the late antebellum period took place aboard ships and involved international rights entailing long court disputes. Like the revolt aboard the *San Dominick*, however, they also set the questions surrounding slaves' "right of revolution" in a framework at once terribly ambiguous and crystal clear. The case of the slave revolt aboard the *Creole* was the subject, as we have seen, of Frederick Douglass's short story "The Heroic Slave," which played ironically on the name of the revolt's leader, Madison Washington, to highlight the shadowed vision of the founding fathers. Indeed, Douglass himself once anticipated the climactic scene of *Benito Cereno*, in which Delano, echoing the satyr of the ship's sternpiece – "holding his foot on the prostrate neck of a writhing figure" – grinds the black rebel beneath his own foot. Speaking to a Boston antislavery audience in 1848, Douglass proclaimed: "There are many Madison Washingtons and Nathaniel Turners in the South, who would assert their rights to liberty, if you would take your feet from their necks, and your sympathy and aid from their oppressors." But the more famous case of the *Amistad*, whose slaves revolted in 1839 and were eventually captured off Long Island after an abortive attempt to sail to Africa, is even more likely to have been on Melville's mind – not least because the enactment of the revolt resembled that aboard the *Tryal-San Dominick* and because the slave leader, Joseph Cinque, was viewed by a contemporary white writer as an intriguing combination of guile and humanity, a man whose "moral sentiments and intellectual faculties predominate considerably over his animal propensities," but who "killed the Captain and crew with his own hand. Cutting their throats."

Henry Highland Garnett, Douglass, and other abolitionists celebrated Cinque's heroism, even considered him an American patriot; and when John Quincy Adams won freedom for the slaves before the Supreme Court (much to the embarrassment of President Van Buren and the outrage of the Spanish authorities, who had demanded their return to Cuba), he appealed to "the law of Nature and Nature's God on which our fathers placed our own national existence."[25] What, though, was the "law of Nature," and what evidence was there that it was synonymous with the law of the fathers? The Supreme Court rulings in both the *Creole* and *Amistad* cases were fraught with ambiguity, and as Robert Cover points out, Adams's appeal in the *Amistad* case contained what was perhaps a deliberate double entendre, a kind of tautology: Adams "could be saying that nature's law applied because there was no other law or that there was no other valid law because nature's law applied." Justice Joseph Story's opinion in the slaves' favor rested on the first side of this razor-sharp distinction; that is, he ruled that the *Amistad* slaves, because they were shown to be *bozales* (not *ladinos*, as the Cuban ship masters had claimed in their false documentation), were never legally enslaved (rendering both Spanish law and treaty inapplicable) and therefore had the right to embrace the law of nature, rebel against their captors, and attempt to sail to Africa. In the absence of positive law, the purportedly eternal principles of justice prevailed. Abolitionist celebration of the victory and of Adams's eloquent brief lost sight of the fact that Story's decision had done nothing to dislodge the notion that "legal" slaves were property and that they had no rights under American law. In the similar 1843 case of the American slave ship *Creole*, the inspiration for Douglass's "Heroic Slave," the slaves revolted off the coast of Virginia, en route to New Orleans, and sailed to Nassau, where they were freed by British authorities, despite the fact that they had been legal American slaves when they left port, sailing under the American flag to an American destination. Daniel Webster among others had celebrated the *Amistad* decision but refused to recognize the same rights in American slaves aboard the *Creole*. The perceived threat of the spread of black rebellion in the Caribbean was one difference, enduring contention with England another. Arguments by Joshua Giddings and William Jay to the effect that natural law superseded American law on the high seas were ignored by the arbitrator, who later decided that the United States' claims of remuneration were justified, and Giddings was censured in Congress for encouraging slave revolt.[26]

For a theory of emancipation, neither the *Amistad* nor the *Creole* provided particular solace. In both instances the freedom won by the slaves was undermined by the fact that no "right of revolution" had been recognized; the technical definition of legal slavery and the ambiguity of legal rights on the high seas interfered with clear enunciations of African American rights. Both the law of slavery and the proslavery ideology on which it was founded (in the North as well as the South) were so permeated with notions of nature's hierarchy – the distribution of sentiments and powers according to an imagined set of "natural" or divine ordinances – that no other conclusion seemed possible. Recognizing just this fact, Melville had to demonstrate that the very notion of the law of nature was itself riddled with assumptions that could as easily authorize racism as contravene it. Although Babo acts according to the laws both of nature and of the revolutionary fathers, Delano cannot conceive of such action in black slaves. Like the "naked nature" of the slave mothers aboard the *San Dominick*, which turns out to conceal in them a rage for torture and brutality surpassing that of the men (a feminine brutality corroborated, it might be added, by accounts of the San Domingo rebellion), the "natural" relationship of master and slave defined by the fathers, despite their inclusive dream of freedom, remained a disguise and a delusion.[27] Like many such delusions, however, the racialized law of nature was one of considerable force. The elaborate minstrel charade of Babo, with its regulating torment and display of intellectual prowess, entirely shatters the paternalistic benevolence and the law of nature governing proslavery. The master, Benito Cereno, is stripped of his soul as Aranda was stripped of his flesh. But this does not prevent the restoration of a regime of benevolent rule by Amasa Delano, the American captain. Tautologically, the law of nature is itself a "knot": it both is and *is not*; its application, as the opposing decisions of the *Amistad* and the *Creole* indicate, hinged upon the applicable artifices of human power, not on an abstract moral principle. Like the court decision, Delano's actions and his restorative narrative tell us that the law of nature is the law of power.

Although some readers have dismissed the legal documents at the conclusion of the tale as an aesthetic miscalculation or an unnecessary flaw resulting from Melville's hasty composition or his attempt to stretch his commercial reward from *Putnam's*,[28] a majority have seen in those documents an approximation of the full moral burden of the story, a burden that Delano escapes and to which Benito Cereno succumbs in the muted finale. In them is embedded the final account of the law of slavery in *Benito Cereno*; in them the revelation that the law of nature is an artifice of expediency leads only to the conclusion that artifice and nature form a tautology. Returning the tale to the actual historical narrative from which it emerged, like a "shadowy tableau" from the deep, and at the same time reconstituting the social and political conventions threatened by the revolt aboard the *San Dominick* and held in suspension by the play engendered in Delano's consciousness by Babo's masquerade and Melville's cunning narrative form, the legal deposition acts retrospectively to explain and endorse, in stately legal phrases, the urgent suppression of the slaves' revolt. Insofar as the depositions define the historical character of *Benito Cereno*, they do so by the virtually silent dictation of indirect speech reproduced in documents "selected, from among many others, for partial translation," but about which the suspicion arises in the tribunal that the deponent "raved of some things that could never have happened."[29] The flawed and cold-blooded depositions recount the rebellion selectively and retrospectively, and in doing so they reenact and respond to an escalating pressure to cure the disease aboard the *San Dominick*, restore regulation and order, and suppress the rebellion by legally deposing the fallen black king Babo.

It is on the authority of these markedly fragile and questionable legal documents that we are asked to reconstruct, in imagined memory, the black revolution that they formally suppress, and to distinguish between the voice of the tale, which engages in a rebellious creation of fiction, and the voice of the deposition, which apparently recites and reproduces the historical texts of the actual trial of the actual Captain Delano's actual account. The "fictitious story" dictated by Babo to Don Benito that the deposition alludes to but fails to reproduce thus points toward and in retrospect allies itself with the fiction of the mystery story created by Melville, itself suppressed and overturned by the stately, ceremonial, and "literal" language of the court. As a "key" that "fit[s] into the lock of the complications which precede it," the deposition ironically reverses these significant symbols of lock and key earlier ironically attached to Benito Cereno's mock power; for while it explains the mystery, unlocks it, the deposition also publicly and legally locks up the significance of the revolt in details and sentences that are as immune to subversion and irony as Delano's consciousness.[30] In its extreme act of countersubversion, the deposition overthrows the suspended irony that momentarily makes master slave and slave master, undoes roles and scenes in which rebellious metaphors have come dangerously close to becoming literal, restores the good weather and smooth sailing of a racially hierarchical "natural" world, and retrospectively suppresses the revolt of Melville's fictional version of Delano's history. The law of slavery, Melville seems to say, is the law of history.

And yet the final conversation of the tag ending, deferred by Melville and presented retrospectively, suggests that the authority of the deposition, riddled with lapses and obscured by "translation," is not complete, that in fact the hull of the *San Dominick*, "as a vault whose door has been flung back," does not lie completely "open to-day," but rather, like the enchanted deep, takes back what it gave while leaving a shadow of meaning suspended between revolt and deposition, subversion and countersubversion. The black right of revolution left suspended outside the confining chains of legal language is not more "natural" than social or political, nor does Melville come close to granting its moral authority anything like beneficence. It is simply one form of power standing behind the mask of another, waiting in the shadows for its turn. The full character of *Benito Cereno*'s ironic suspense and draining silence about crucial matters thus comes into proper perspective only at the end – not just the end of the mystery tale, when in a "flash of revelation" the truth of the revolt is revealed to Delano and the skeletal figurehead of the *San Dominick* is exposed, but in the end of the entire tale, when the two captains, in the scene given "retrospectively, and irregularly," stand once again in confrontation and the narrator proceeds to describe the spiritual wastage and death of Don Benito, and the "voiceless end" of Babo, his severed "head, that hive of subtlety, fixed on a pole in the Plaza."[31] The silence that follows the last conversation of Delano and Cereno, echoing the moments of suspended or suppressed power that animate Melville's whole tale, leaves the American and the Spaniard poised once again in that posture of flawed communication and failed communion that defines their relationship throughout the story of the slave revolt aboard the *San Dominick*, divided yet merged by the shadow play of Babo's revolt, which holds the New World history they together summarize in a state of haunting crisis.

The suspension of authority that envelops the *San Dominick* and its tale is a form of mutual *abdication*, a silence or refusal to speak and act that both expresses and withholds authority by keeping it readied for possible implementation. The link between Babo as artist and Melville as narrator – both silently engaged in the scheming of plots and the dictating of roles to their captains – that is suggested in the shaving ritual is reinforced in the scene of Babo's execution by the fact that the narrator's exposition has been a "hive of subtlety" all along. In a tale whose concealed "plot" characteristically proceeds by "whispering" and the exchange of "silent signs," Melville's own authorial abdication, like that of his characters, serves to form a moral riddle that deepens even as it is solved by fully participating in it. Like the "dusky comment of silence" that accompanies Babo's razoring, cunningly inserted between the talking and listening of the two captains, the silence that pervades Melville's tale in its atmosphere of suppressed articulation and failed communication is itself a form of expression that makes the ground the reader treads in *Benito Cereno*, a ground "every inch" of which, to borrow one of Cereno's final remarks to Delano, has been "mined into honey-combs," as perilously brittle as the decaying ship's balustrade, which at one point gives in to Delano's weight "like charcoal." After the confrontation of Delano and Cereno that produces the "shadow of the Negro," there is "no more conversation."[32]

In between rebellion and suppression, or between the creation of authority and its exercise of mastery and decay into enslaving conventions, lies silence. Frozen in indecision, the law derived from the *Creole* and *Amistad* cases, like the logic of the Fugitive Slave Law, was silent on the only issue that mattered to Babo. His silence, in turn, is the most powerful articulation of those unrecognized rights, no matter that they in turn may lead to the creation of a new racial hierarchy grounded in naked power. Babo's aspect seems to say, "Since I cannot do deeds, I will not speak words," and, when Don Benito faints in his presence, he forces Babo's legal identity to rest on the testimony of the sailors. Melville's characterization of Babo recalls the "martyr-like serenity" attributed to Cinque; it also recalls Denmark Vesey's co-conspirator Peter Poyas in his admonition to his comrades, "Do not open your lips! Die silent, as you shall see me do," as well as the language that John Beard used, in his then authoritative 1853 account of Toussaint and the San Domingo Revolution, to describe the rebels' reaction to extreme torture: "On the countenance of those who were led to death shone an anticipation of the liberty which they felt was about to grow on a land watered with the blood of their caste. They had the same firmness, the same resignation, the same enthusiasm as distinguished the martyr of the Christian religion. On the gibbets, in the flames, in the midst of tortures scarcely was a sigh to be heard; even the child hardly shed tears."[33]

Babo's silence also gathers together the powerful instances of silence articulated in the narrative – his own "dusky comment of silence" during the shaving, the Spanish sailor's "silent signs," the "unknown syllable" communicated among the hatchet polishers, Cereno's "mute dictatorship," the contagion of silence that overtakes Delano as well, Don Benito's terror that is "past all speech," and so on[34] – compressing all of them into the overwhelming *abdication* of his own silent death, which renounces power while at the same time reserving its volcanic energies in a radical shadow play staged within the legal theater of his own execution. Like Nat Turner and Gabriel Prosser, who refused to plead guilty to crimes that were crimes only within the narrow rule of law, not within the realm governed by the "law of nature," Babo will not speak within the language of a law that does not apply to him. As the paradoxical *Creole* and *Amistad* cases suggested, the rebels might legally *be slaves* by rule of law according to the state code of chattelism that could be adduced in certain circumstance, but in truth they were, no matter, *not slaves*. The law of slavery, the law of "man" and "thing," was a pure tautology in which is and is *not*, mastery and bondage, were entangled in a spiraling dialectic. In such a world violence followed by silence was enough to count as freedom.

Notes

1 Amasa Delano, *Narrative of Voyages and Travels in the Northern and Southern Hemispheres* (Boston: E. G. House, 1817), p. 336; see also Harold H. Scudder, "Melville's *Benito Cereno* and Captain Delano's Voyages," *PMLA* 43 (1928), pp. 502–32; Herman Melville, *Benito Cereno: Great Short Works of Herman Melville*, ed. Warner Berhoff (New York: Harper and Row, 1969), p. 310.

2 John Edwin Fagg, *Cuba, Haiti, and the Dominican Republic* (Englewood Cliffs, NJ: Prentice Hall, 1965), pp. 114–15; Jonathan Brown, *The History and Present Condition of St. Domingo*, 2 vols (Philadelphia: William Marshall, 1836), I, pp. 22–33; Samuel Eliot Morison, *Admiral of the Ocean: A Life of Christopher Columbus* (Boston: Little, Brown, 1942), pp. 297–313, 423–38; Daniel P. Mannix and Malcolm Cowley, *Black Cargoes: A History of the Atlantic Slave Trade, 1518–1865* (1962; rpt New York: Viking, 1965), pp. viii, 1–5. On Melville's use of Columbus, see also Mary Y. Hallab, "Victims of 'Malign Machinations': Irving's *Christopher Columbus* and Melville's 'Benito Cereno,'" *Journal of Narrative Technique* 9 (1979), pp. 199–206.

3 Antonio de Herrera, quoted in Brown, *History and Present Condition of St. Domingo*, I, pp. 36–7; Henry Highland Garnett, *The Past and Present Condition and Destiny of the Colored Race* (1848; reprint Miami: Mnemosyne Publishing, 1969), pp. 12–13.

4 Melville, *Benito Cereno*, pp. 246, 240; H. Bruce Franklin, *The Wake of the Gods: Melville's Mythology* (Stanford, Calif.: Stanford University Press, 1963), pp. 136–50; David Brion Davis, *Slavery and Human Progress* (New York: Oxford University Press, 1984), p. 40; George Bancroft, *History of the United States of America*, 10 vols (New York: Appleton and Co., 1885), I, pp. 121–5; Melville, *Benito Cereno*, pp. 294–5.

5 Charles McKenzie, *Notes on Haiti, Made during a Residence in That Republic*, 2 vols (London: Colburn and Bentley, 1830), I, pp. 263–6; Melville, *Benito Cereno*, p. 241. On Melville's composition of *Benito Cereno*, see Leon Howard, *Herman Melville: A Biography* (Berkeley: University of California Press, 1951), pp. 218–22.

6 C. L. R. James, *Mariners, Renegades, and Castaways: The Story of Herman Melville and the World We Live In* (London: Allison and Busby, 1985), p. 119; Robert C. Toll, *Blacking Up: The Minstrel Show in Nineteenth-Century America* (New York: Oxford University Press, 1974), p. 83.

7 Jefferson, letter of 1797, quoted in Winthrop D. Jordan, *White over Black: American Attitudes toward the Negro, 1550–1812* (1968; reprint New York: Norton, 1977), p. 387; David Brion Davis, *The Problem of Slavery in the Age of Revolution 1770–1823* (Ithaca, NY: Cornell University Press, 1975), pp. 329–30; Alfred N. Hunt, *Haiti's Influence on Antebellum America: Slumbering Volcano in the Caribbean* (Baton Rouge: Louisiana State University Press, 1988), pp. 37–83; C. L. R. James, *The Black Jacobins: Toussaint L'Ouverture and the San Domingo Rebellion*, rev. edn (New York: Vintage Books, 1963), p. 127; Clement Eaton, *The Freedom-of-Thought Struggle in the Old South*, rev. edn (New York: Harper and Row, 1964), pp. 89–90; William Faulkner, *Absalom, Absalom!* (1936; reprint New York: Vintage, 1972), pp. 250–1; Eugene D. Genovese, *From Rebellion to Revolution: Afro-American Slave Revolts in the Making of the New World* (1979; reprint New York: Vintage Books, 1981), pp. 35–7, 94–6; Jordan, *White over Blacks*, pp. 375–402.

8   Ludwell Lee Montague, *Haiti and the United States, 1714–1938* (Durham, NC: Duke University Press, 1940), pp. 35–46; Rayford W. Logan, *The Diplomatic Relations of the United States with Haiti, 1776–1891* (Chapel Hill: University of North Carolina Press, 1941), pp. 112–51; Henry Adams, *History of the United States during the Administration of Jefferson and Madison*, quoted in Logan, *Diplomatic Relations*, p. 142; Genovese, *From Rebellion to Revolution*, p. 85.

9   Genovese, *From Rebellion to Revolution*, pp. 119–21; C. Duncan Rice, *The Rise and Fall of Black Slavery* (1975; reprint Baton Rouge: Louisiana State University Press, 1976), pp. 262–3; Miranda, quoted in Salvador de Madariaga, *The Fall of the Spanish American Empire* (London: Houis, Carter, 1947), pp. 322–3; Jama Bennett, quoted in Frederick Merk, *Manifest Destiny and American Mission in American History* (1963; reprint New York: Vintage Books, 1966), p. 46. See also Allan Moore Emery, " 'Benito Cereno' and Manifest Destiny," *Nineteenth-Century Fiction* 39 (June 1984), pp. 48–68.

10 Herbert Aptheker, *American Negro Slave Revolts* (New York: International Publishers, 1952), p. 33; Genovese, *From Rebellion to Revolution*, p. 15.

11 Richard Chase, *Herman Melville: A Critical Study* (New York: Macmillan, 1949), p. 156; Melville, *Benito Cereno*, pp. 156, 250, 292, 261.

12 Benjamin C. Clark, *A Geographical Sketch of St. Domingo, Cuba, and Nicaragua* (Boston: Eastburn's Press, 1850), p. 7; "About Niggers," *Putnam's Monthly* 6 (December 1855), pp. 608–12.

13 William Wells Brown, *St. Domingo: Its Revolutions and Its Patriots* (Boston: Bela Marsh, 1855), pp. 32–3; James, *Black Jacobins*, pp. 360–74; MacKenzie, *Notes on Haiti*, II, p. 61. See also Brown, *History and Present Condition of St. Domingo*, II, pp. 152–4, 147–8.

14 Mark B. Bird, *The Black Man; Or, Haytian Independence* (New York: American News Co., 1869), pp. 60–1; Mary Hassal, *Secret History; or, The Horrors of St. Domingo* (Philadelphia: Bradford and Innskeep, 1808), pp. 151–3.

15 "Hayti and the Haytiens," *De Bow's Review* 16 (January 1854), p. 35; David Brion Davis, *The Slave Power Conspiracy and the Paranoid Style* (Baton Rouge: Louisiana State University Press, 1969), pp. 72–8; Lyman Beecher, *A Plea for the West* (Cincinnati: Truman and Smith, 1835), pp. 37, 109, 144.

16 Theodore Parker, "The Nebraska Question," in *Additional Speeches, Addresses, and Occasional Sermons*, 2 vols (Boston: Little, Brown, 1855), I, pp. 301–3, 352, 367, 378.

17 Melville, *Benito Cereno*, pp. 276, 245, 250–1, 258, 241, 239, 283. Cf. Carolyn Karcher, *Shadow over the Promised Land: Slavery, Race, and Violence in Melville's America* (Baton Rouge: Louisiana State University Press, 1980), pp. 136–9.

18 Jean Fagan Yellin, *The Intricate Knot: Black Figures in American Literature, 1776–1863* (New York: New York University Press, 1977), pp. 215–27; Melville, *Benito Cereno*, pp. 283, 314. See also James H. Kavanagh, "That Hive of Subtlety: 'Benito Cereno' and the Liberal Hero," in Sacvan Bercovitch and Myra Jehlen, eds, *Ideology and Classic American Literature* (New York: Cambridge University Press, 1986), pp. 352–83.

19 Melville, *Benito Cereno*, pp. 279, 314; Daniel Webster, *The Writings and Speeches of Daniel Webster*, 18 vols (Boston: Little, Brown, 1903), XIII, pp. 405–7. Cf. Michael Paul Rogin, *Subversive Genealogy: The Politics and Art of Herman Melville* (New York: Alfred A. Knopf, 1983), pp. 142–6.

20 Delano, *Narrative of Voyages*, pp. 337, 323, 73. On Delano's claim of salvage rights and further court documents related to the revolt, see Sterling Stuckey and Joshua Leslie, "Aftermath: Captain Delano's Claim against Benito Cereno," *Modern Philology* 85 (February 1988), pp. 265–87.

21 David Brion Davis, *The Problem of Slavery in Western Culture* (Ithaca, NY: Cornell University Press, 1966), pp. 333–90; Melville, *Benito Cereno*, pp. 278–9; William Ellery Channing, *Slavery* (Boston: James Munroe, 1835), p. 103.

22 [Y. S. Nadhanson,] "Negro Minstrelsy – Ancient and Modern," *Putnam's Monthly* 5 (January 1855), p. 74. For other relevant perspectives on romantic racialism, see George Fredrickson, *The Black Image in the White Mind: The Debate on Afro-American Character and Destiny, 1817–1914* (New York: Harper and Row, 1971), pp. 97–129, and Allan Moore Emery, "The Topicality of Depravity in 'Benito Cereno,' " *American Literature* 55 (October 1983), pp. 316–31.

23 Delano, *Narrative of Voyages*, pp. 146–7, 347; Joshua Leslie and Sterling Stuckey, "Avoiding the Tragedy of Benito Cereno: The Official Response to Babo's Revolt," *Criminal Justice History* 3 (1982), pp. 125–32; Aptheker, *American Negro Slave Revolts*, pp. 300–10; James, *Black Jacobins*, pp. 95–6; Genovese, *From Rebellion to Revolution*, pp. 43, 106; Vincent Harding, *There Is a River: The Black Struggle for Freedom in America* (New York: Random House, 1981), pp. 34–5, 99; Melville, *Benito Cereno*, p. 315.

24 See Brook Thomas, *Cross-Examinations of Law and Literature: Cooper, Hawthorne, Stowe, and Melville* (New York: Cambridge University Press, 1987), pp. 94–105.

25 Melville, *Benito Cereno*, pp. 241, 295; Frederick Douglass, quoted in Jane H. Pease and William H. Pease, *They Who Would Be Free: Blacks Search for Freedom, 1830–1861* (New York: Atheneum, 1974), pp. 236–7; *New London Gazette*, August 26, 1839, quoted in John W. Barber, *A History of the Amistad Captives* (New Haven: E. L. and J. W. Barber, 1840), p. 4.

26 John Quincy Adams, *Argument in the Case of the United States vs Cinque* (1841; reprint New York: Arno Press, 1969), p. 9. See also Cable, *Black Odyssey*, pp. 76–108; Sidney Kaplan, "Herman Melville and the American National Sin," *Journal of Negro History* 41 (October 1956), pp. 311–38; Rogin, *Subversive Genealogy*, pp. 211–12; and Howard Jones, *Mutiny on the Amistad: The Saga of a Slave Revolt and Its Impact on American Abolition, Law, and Diplomacy* (New York: Oxford University Press, 1987), pp. 175–82.

27 Robert M. Cover, *Justice Accused: Antislavery and the Judicial Process* (New Haven: Yale University Press, 1975), pp. 111–16, quote at p. 111; Jones, *Mutiny on the Amistad*, pp. 130–1, 146–7, 189–93.

28 Melville, *Benito Cereno*, pp. 268, 310; Delano, *Narrative of Voyages*, p. 341; James, *Black Jacobins*, p. 117; Franklin, *Present State of Hayti*, p. 62. On the appeal to "nature" in the antebellum discourse of racism, see, for example, William R. Stanton, *The Leopard's Spots: Scientific Attitudes toward Race in America, 1815–59* (Chicago: University of Chicago Press, 1966), and Reginald Horsman, *Race and Manifest Destiny: The Origins of American Racial Anglo-Saxonism* (Cambridge, Mass.: Harvard University Press, 1981), pp. 116–57.

29 Newton Arvin echoes the misguided sentiments of some early readers and reviewers when he calls the tale an "artistic miscarriage" and notes that "the scene of the actual mutiny on the *San Dominick*, which might have been transformed into an episode of great and frightful power, Melville was too tired to rewrite at all, and except for a few trifling details, he leaves it all as he found it, in the drearily prosaic prose of a judicial deposition." See *Herman Melville* (New York: William Sloane, 1950), pp. 238–9.

30 Melville, *Benito Cereno*, pp. 299–300.

31 Ibid., pp. 307, 313.

32 Ibid., pp. 313, 315.

33 Ibid., pp. 260, 313, 269, 314.

34 Ibid., p. 315. Barber, *A History of the Amistad Captives*, p. 4; Robert. S. Starobin (ed.), *Denmark Vesey: The Slave Conspiracy of 1822* (Englewood Cliffs, NJ: Prentice Hall, 1970), p. 112; John R. Beard, *The Life of Toussaint L'Ouverture: The Negro Patriot of Hayti* (1853; reprint Westport, Conn.: Negro Universities Press, 1970), p. 256. Cf. James, *Black Jacobins*, pp. 361–2, and Genovese, *From Rebellion to Revolution*, p. 108.

PART SEVEN

Political Criticism: From Marxism to Cultural Materialism

CHAPTER 1

Introduction: Starting with Zero

Julie Rivkin and Michael Ryan

A debate emerged in literary studies in the past several decades around what many see as the importation of politics to an endeavor that should concern itself with purely literary issues. The argument against the importation of politics assumes, of course, that politics was not in literature in the first place and that literary criticism, even when limited to a concern for form, style, theme, and the like, is not implicitly shaped by political choices. That question becomes especially marked when one considers works such as Conrad's *Heart of Darkness*, a novella about the brutalities of economic colonialism, or Shakespeare's *Henry* plays, which depict a ruler who engages in an unprovoked invasion of another land that resulted in thousands of deaths. A purely "literary" examination of the works in terms of narrative irony or rhetorical eloquence would seem to ask a great deal of readers. They have to ignore the palpable political issues these works address in order for literary form to be the main topic of critical conversation.

The entry of politics into literary discussion, beginning in the 1970s, was not so much an entry as a re-entry. If one goes back far enough in the library, one will find works of criticism in the nineteenth century that deal with liberalism in English literature or the way political struggles are rendered in literature. But in the era after World War II, when the US and the Soviet Union were engaged in a "Cold War," it was difficult for literary critics to frame literature politically, especially if that framing meant drawing on the concepts and vocabulary of Marxism. Marxism was critical of capitalism, and during that era, the "West" defined itself in terms of the defense of capitalism against the egalitarian aspirations of Marxist socialism.

The end of colonialism in the 1960s and 1970s spurred a new interest in Marxism and in Left politics in the US and in England. It was the generation of scholars who entered the profession during these years – Richard Ohmann, Martha Vicinus, Paul Lauter, Terry Eagleton, Fredric Jameson, and others – who were responsible for the re-entry of politics into literary study. Among other things, they argued that the exclusive concern with form that the New Criticism fostered was itself political. The erasure of history from literature constituted a turning away from crucial matters of political substance without which literature would not be literature. One could, of course, choose to study John Donne's poetry exclusively in terms of the structure of paradox, but that would be to ignore the rather loud din of battle in the background, as the English Civil War slowly unfolded.

There are many modern varieties of political criticism, and it is not unusual for political critics to combine approaches – feminism, Marxism, Post-structuralism, post-coloniality, etc. One of the most enduring forms of political criticism is Marxism. Although ostensibly a doctrine concerned more with economics and politics than with culture and literature, Marxism has from its inception in the late nineteenth century given rise to statements about the nature of art, literature, and culture. In contrast to Formalist approaches, which isolate the literary work from its historical context, Marxism begins with the assumption that literature can only be understood if its full context – historical, economic, social, economic, cultural – is taken into account. Moreover, for Marxists, literature is an active agent in its social and cultural world. It can work to expose wrongs in a society, or it can paper over troubling fissures and make a class-divided society seem unified and content. One major assumption of Marxists is that culture, including literature, functions to reproduce the class structure of society. It does so by representing class differences in such a way that they seem legitimate and natural. But many writers, themselves at times influenced by Marxist ideas, take up the pen (or the word processor) as a weapon in "class struggle." When Upton Sinclair wrote in a realistic vein about the wrong-doings of the giant meat companies in the US in *The Jungle*, he hoped to change the world by influencing public opinion, and he succeeded.

Marxism derives from the work of Karl Marx, a German philosopher who lived in Paris and London in the middle of the nineteenth century, a time of severe industrialization that was creating a new class of industrial workers that he called the "proletariat." When Marx wrote his major works *The German Ideology* (1846), *The Manifesto of the Communist Party* (1848), and *Capital* (1867), the ideals of socialism (that wealth should be distributed more equitably, that class differences should be abolished, that society should be devoted to providing for everyone's basic needs, etc.) were emerging in counterpoint to the principles and realities of industrial capitalism – individual freedom in economic matters, an intractable inequality in the distribution of wealth, severe class differentiation, and brutal poverty for those without property. It was also a time of revolution. Across Europe in 1848, monarchies were overthrown by democratic uprisings, and nations long dominated by others struggled for independence. In 1870–1, workers seized power in Paris, and the Commune briefly established an egalitarian alternative to capitalism before it was defeated by reactionary armies and the participants executed. It was a time when "bourgeois" society itself, which was organized around the ideal of the private accumulation of wealth in an economy unhampered by state regulation, was being challenged for the first time. That Marx was deeply influenced by his historical context is itself a lesson in Marxist methodology. According to Marx, we are all situated historically and socially, and our social and historical contexts "determine" or shape our lives. This is as true of literature as it is of human beings: literature is not, according to Marxist criticism, the expression of universal or eternal ideas, as the New Critics claimed, nor is it, as the Russian Formalists claimed, an autonomous realm of aesthetic or formal devices and techniques that act independently of their material setting in society and history. Rather, literature is in the first instance a social phenomenon, and as such, it cannot be studied independently of the social relations, the economic forms, and the political realities of the time in which it was written.

Marxist literary criticism has traditionally been concerned with studying the embeddedness of a work within its historical, social, and economic contexts. Some Marxist criticism argues that literature reflects unproblematically the values and ideals of the class in dominance. In order to make it onto the stage at all, Shakespeare's plays had somehow to address (which is to say, accept and further) the values and ideals of monarchial English culture. Shakespeare's history plays all celebrate kingship not because he was a political conservative but because the material context of literary production places limits on what can and cannot be said or expressed at a particular historical moment. Shakespeare could not have expressed counter-monarchial ideas and still been "Shakespeare," that is, someone hired to produce plays for the king's court. All literature is in this respect "determined" by economics, by the translation into cultural limitations and imperatives of the sheer weight of how material life in a society is conducted. Those limitations range from the choosing of what will or will not be published to the implanted selection procedures that readers inherit from schooling within a culture and that shape what and how they read (whether or not they can even understand the language of a play like *Lear*, for example).

This "reflectionist" approach to literature has been supplanted by critical approaches that emphasize the complexity of the relationships between literature and its ambient context. While some contemporary Marxist critics continue to emphasize the role of literature and of culture in reproducing class society, others look for ways in which literature undermines or subverts the dominant ideologies of the culture. One function of literature is to offer those on the losing end images that assure them that their situation of relative deprivation is the natural result of fair play and fair rules, not of systematic dispossession that is a structural feature of the society. In Shakespeare's plays, for example, the lower-class characters, though likeable and comic for the most part, seem to deserve their lower-class status. Their speech and patterns of thought suggest less refined natures than those possessed by their "betters," who usually happen to be aristocrats. The plays legitimate class division.

But literature also displays signs of contradictions (between classes, between ideologies and realities) that threaten society from within and are put on display in literature. No matter how much it spuriously resolves contradictions in society between the rich and the poor or between an ideal of "freedom" and a reality of economic enslavement, literature must also show them forth for all to see. According to this approach, all attempts to naturalize social divisions reveal their artificiality, and all ideological resolutions put their "imaginary" quality on display. In Shakespeare's plays, for example, the nobility may consistently triumph, but the very necessity of depicting such triumph over adversaries suggests that there is trouble, rather than peace and universal contentment, in the society. In the effort to reassure the nobility, the plays draw attention both to divisions in society and to the need on the part of those in power to make those divisions seem easily resolvable. The very effort suggests that the class differences harbor potential dangers for the rule of the aristocracy.

British Marxism has evolved in two different directions. Influenced less by dialectical theory, it has developed in much more historicist directions. Raymond Williams, for many years the sole practitioner of Marxist literary studies on either side of the Atlantic, helped to foster a concern in British Marxist literary criticism with the evolution of literature in relation to social, political, and economic changes. Terry Eagleton has refined this historicist approach by linking literary form to social ideology. According to Eagleton, literary form is itself ideological and laden with political meanings. In his book, *Criticism and Ideology* (1977), Eagleton argued that as one moves from the nineteenth into the twentieth century, works of literature provide different and differently ideological pictures of the social universe both in their content and in the way they are written. The organic form of the Romantics suggested a virtuously cohesive society in which class difference is an accepted feature of life, while T. S. Eliot's fragmented Modernist poetic form embodies his reactionary sense that modern democratic life represents a falling away from a good cultural tradition based on conservative values.

Another school of British Marxism, called Cultural Materialism, draws on Post-Structuralist and feminist theory. Cultural Materialist scholars such as Alan Sinfield take issue with the idea that literature reflects and promotes social power or embodies in an unproblematic way the interests of a ruling class. All power structures are contingent; that is, they lack a logical ground or a natural foundation. As a result, they must rely on cultural narratives that assure their legitimacy. Such narratives strive for plausibility, but they must work against the contingency of the institutions they defend, a contingency that leaves them open to counter-narratives that suggest different social possibilities. Moreover, all class-divided societies project into culture the instabilities on which they are built. Those instabilities register in literary works as dissidence and as dissonance. The narratives of such works usually evoke social adversaries in order to quell them, as, for example, Edmund in *King Lear* is evoked as a pretender to power but ultimately killed by "true" nobles. He represents a dissident presence in the social world of the era, a new class of merchants, small businessmen, and industrialists who were struggling for power against the reigning nobility. His presence in the play, moreover, produces dissonance within the play's discourse. True, "virtue" (the ideological term the nobility used to anoint itself with the right to rule) triumphs in the end, but it can do so only by evoking vice and by giving it time on stage. Even as the play asserts the right of the nobility to rule, it evokes the reality that such rule was being contested at the time. By having the defeat of Edmund hang solely on an act of violence (Edgar, the true noble, defeats him in combat), the play also draws attention to the fact that the nobility's claim to legitimacy is tenuous.

CHAPTER 2

Dialectics

G. W. F. Hegel

Hegel's philosophical method (outlined in this selection from his *Science of Logic*, 1816) was more than a method for thinking about knowledge. It was also a theory of politics, law, art, and history. Hegel saw the same process at work in each of these realms. That process consists of growth from particulars to universals, so that the universals ultimately include all concrete particulars within them. Marx borrowed Hegel's method and focused it on economic history and on the analysis of the structure of a capitalist economy.

The exposition of what alone can be the true method of philosophical science falls within the treatment of logic itself; for the method is the consciousness of the form of the inner self-movement of the content of logic. In the *Phenomenology of Mind* I have expounded an example of this method in application to a more concrete object, namely to consciousness. Here, we are dealing with forms of consciousness each of which in realizing itself at the same time abolishes and transcends itself, has for its result its own negation – and so passes into a higher form....

It is a fresh concept but higher and richer than its predecessor; for it is richer by the negation or opposite of the latter, therefore contains it, but also something more, and is the unity of itself and its opposite....

It is in this dialectic as it is here understood, that is, in the grasping of opposites in their unity or of the positive in the negative, that speculative thought consists....

[Dialectic] usually takes the following more precise form. It is shown that there belongs to some subject matter or other, for example the world, motion, point, and so on, some determination or other, for example (taking the objects in the order named), finitude in space or time, presence in this place, absolute negation of space; but further, that with equal necessity the opposite determination also belongs to the subject matter, for example infinity in space and time, non-presence in this place, relation to space and so spatiality.... The conclusion drawn from dialectic of this kind is in general the contradiction and nullity of the assertions made....

Thus all the oppositions that are assumed as fixed, as for example finite and infinite, individual and universal, are not in contradiction through, say, an external connection; on the contrary, as an examination of their nature has shown, they are in and for themselves a transition; the synthesis and the subject in which they appear is the product of their concept's own activity of conceptual reflection. If a consideration that ignores the concept stops short at their external relationship, isolates them and leaves them as fixed presuppositions, it is the concept, on the contrary, that keeps them steadily in view, moves them as their spirit or mind and brings out their dialectic.

Now this is the very standpoint indicated above from which a universal first, considered in and for itself, shows itself to be the other of itself. Taken quite generally, this determination can be taken to mean that what is at first immediate now appears as mediated, related to an other, or that the universal appears as a particular. Hence the second term that has thereby come into being is the negative of the first, and if we anticipate the subsequent progress, the first negative. The immediate, from this negative side, has been extinguished in the other, but the other is essentially not the empty negative, the nothing, that is taken to be the usual result of dialectic; rather is it the other of the first, the negative of the immediate; it is therefore determined as the mediated – contains in general the determination of the first within itself. Consequently the first is essentially preserved and retained even in the other. To hold fast to the positive in its negative, in the content of the presupposition, in the result, this is the most important feature in rational cognition; at the same time only the simplest reflection is needed to convince one of the absolute truth and necessity of this requirement and so far as examples of the proof of this are concerned, the whole of logic consists of such. . . .

Now since the first also is contained in the second, and the latter is the truth of the former, this unity can be expressed as a proposition in which the immediate is put as subject, and the mediated as its predicate; for example, the finite is infinite, one is many, the individual is the universal. However, the inadequate form of such propositions is at once obvious. In treating of the judgement it has been shown that its form in general, and most of all the immediate form of the positive judgement, is incapable of holding within its grasp speculative determinations and truth. The direct supplement to it, the negative judgement, would at least have to be added as well. . . .

The second determination, the negative or mediated, is at the same time also the mediating determination. It may be taken in the first instance as a simple determination, but in its truth it is a relation or relationship; for it is the negative, but the negative of the positive, and includes the positive within itself. It is therefore the other, but not the other of something to which it is indifferent – in that case it would not be an other, nor a relation or relationship – rather it is the other in its own self, the other of an other; therefore it includes its own other within it and is consequently as contradiction, the posited dialectic of itself. Because the first or the immediate is implicitly the concept, and consequently is also only implicitly the negative, the dialectical moment with it consists in positing in it the difference that it implicitly contains. The second, on the contrary, is itself the determinate moment, the difference or relationship; therefore with it the dialectical moment consists in positing the unity that is contained in it. If then the negative, the determinate, relationship, judgement, and all the determinations falling under this second moment do not at once appear on their own account as contradiction and as dialectical, this is solely the fault of a thinking that does not bring its thoughts together. For the material, the opposed determinations in one relation, is already posited and at hand for thought. But formal thinking makes identity its law, and allows the contradictory content before it to sink into the sphere of ordinary conception, into space and time, in which the contradictories are held asunder in juxtaposition and temporal succession and so come before consciousness without reciprocal contact. On this point, formal thinking lays down for its principle that contradiction is unthinkable; but as a matter of fact the thinking of contradiction is the essential moment of the concept. Formal thinking does in fact think contradiction, only it at once looks away from it, and in saying that it is unthinkable it merely passes over from it into abstract negation.

Now the negativity just considered constitutes the turning point of the movement of the concept. It is the simple point of the negative relation to self, the innermost source of all activity, of all animate and spiritual self-movement, the dialectical spirit that everything true possesses and through which alone it is true; for on this subjectivity alone rests the abolishing and transcendence of the opposition between concept and reality, and the unity that is truth. The second negative, the negative of the negative, at which we have arrived, is this abolishing and transcending of the contradiction, but just as little as the contradiction is it an act of external reflection, but rather the innermost, most objective moment of life and spirit, through which a subject, a person, a free being, exists. The relation of the negative to itself is to be regarded as the second premiss of the whole syllogism....Just as the first premiss is the moment of universality and communication, so the second is deter-mined by individuality, which in its relation to its other is primarily exclusive, for itself, and different. The negative appears as the mediating element, since it includes within it itself and the immediate whose negation it is. So far as these two determinations are taken in some relationship or other as externally related, the negative is only the formal mediating element; but as absolute negativity the negative moment of absolute mediation is the unity which is subjectivity and mind.

In this turning point of the method, the course of cognition at the same time returns into itself. As self-transcending and self-preserving contradiction this negativity is the restoration of the first immediacy, of simple universality; for the other of the other, the negative of the negative, is immediately the positive, the identical, the universal. If one insists on counting, this second immediate is, in the course of the method as a whole, the third term to the first immediate and the mediated....

Now more precisely the third is the immediate, but the immediate resulting from the simultaneous abolition and preservation of mediation, the simple resulting from the abolition and preservation of difference, the positive resulting from the abolition and preservation of the negative, the concept that has realized itself by means of its otherness and by the abolition and preservation of this reality has become united with itself, and has restored its absolute reality, its simple relation to itself. This result is therefore the truth. It is equally immediacy and mediation; but such forms of judgement as: the third is immediacy and mediation, or: it is the unity of them, are not capable of grasping it; for it is not a quiescent third, but, precisely as this unity, is self-mediating movement and activity. As that with which we began was the universal, so the result is the individual, the concrete, the subject; what the former is in itself, the latter is now equally for itself, the universal is posited in the subject. The first two moments of the triplicity are abstract, untrue moments which for that very reason are dialectical, and through this their negativity make themselves into the subject. The concept itself is for us, in the first instance, alike the universal that is in itself, and the negative that is for itself, and also the third, that which is both in and for itself, the universal that runs through all the moments of the syllogism; but the third is the conclusion, in which the concept through its negativity is mediated with itself and thereby posited for itself as the universal and the identity of its moments.

CHAPTER 3

Grundrisse

Karl Marx

Marx's notebooks for his major work *Capital* (1864) were written in the late 1850s and early 1860s. This selection from the notebook for 1858 is a good example of Marx using Hegel's dialectical method to think through a problem in economics.

When we consider a given country from a politico-economic stand-point, we begin with its population, its subdivision into classes, location in city, country, or by the sea, occupation in different branches of production; then we study its exports and imports, annual production and consumption, prices of commodities, etc. It seems to be the correct procedure to commence with the real and the concrete, the actual prerequisite; in the case of political economy, to commence with population, which is the basis and the author of the entire productive activity of society. Yet on closer consideration it proves to be wrong. Population is an abstraction, if we leave out for example the classes of which it consists. These classes, again, are but an empty word unless we know what are the elements on which they are based, such as wage-labor, capital, etc. These imply, in their turn, exchange, division of labor, prices, etc. Capital, for example, does not mean anything without wage-labor, value, money, price, etc. If we start out, therefore, with population, we do so with a chaotic conception of the whole, and by closer analysis we will gradually arrive at simpler ideas; thus we shall proceed from the imaginary concrete to less and less complex abstractions, until we arrive at the simplest determinations. This once attained, we might start on our return journey until we finally came back to population, but this time not as a chaotic notion of an integral whole, but as a rich aggregate of many determinations and relations. The form is the one which political economy had adopted in the past as its inception. The economists of the seventeenth century, for example, always started out with the living aggregate: population, nation, state, several states, etc., but in the end they invariably arrived by means of analysis at certain leading abstract general principles such as division of labor, money, value, etc. As soon as these separate elements had been more or less established by abstract reasoning, there arose the systems of political economy which start from simple conceptions such as labor, division of labor, demand, exchange value, and conclude with state, international exchange, and world market. The latter is manifestly the scientifically correct method. The concrete is concrete because it is a combination of many determinations, i.e. a unity of diverse elements. In our thought it therefore appears as a process of synthesis, as a result, and not as a starting-point, although it is the real starting-point and, therefore, also the starting-point of observation and conception. By the former method the complete conception passes into an abstract definition; by the latter the abstract definitions lead to the reproduction of the concrete subject in the course of reasoning. Hegel fell into the error, therefore, of considering the real as the result of self-coordinating, self-absorbed, and spontaneously operating thought, while the method of advancing from the abstract to the concrete is but the way of thinking by which the concrete is grasped and is reproduced in our mind as concrete. It is by no means, however, the process which itself generates the concrete. The simplest economic category, say, exchange value, implies the existence of population, population that is engaged in production under certain conditions; it also implies the existence of certain types of family, clan, or state, etc. It can have no other existence except as an abstract one-sided relation given concrete and living aggregate.

As a category, however, exchange value leads an antediluvian existence. Thus the consciousness for which comprehending thought is what is most real in man, for which the world is only real when comprehended (and philosophical consciousness is of this nature), mistakes the movement of categories for the real act of production (which unfortunately receives only its impetus from outside), whose result is the world; that is true – here we have, however, again a tautology – in so far as the concrete aggregate, as a thought aggregate, the concrete subject of our thought, is in fact a product of thought of comprehension; not, however, in the sense of a product of a self-emanating conception which works outside of and stands above observation and imagination, but of a conceptual working-over of observation and imagination. The whole, as it appears in our heads as a thought-aggregate, is the product of a thinking mind which grasps the world in the only way open to it, a way which differs from the one employed by the artistic, religious, or practical mind. The concrete subject continues to lead an independent existence after it has been grasped, as it did before, outside the head, so long as the head contemplates it only speculatively, theoretically. So that in the employment of the theoretical method in political economy, the subject, society must constantly be kept in mind as the premiss from which we start. But have these simple categories no independent historical or natural existence antedating the more concrete ones? That depends. For instance, in his *Philosophy of Right* Hegel rightly starts out with possession, as the simplest legal relation of individuals. But there is no such thing as possession before the family or the relations of lord and serf, which relations are a great deal more concrete, have come into existence. On the other hand, one would be right in saying that there are families and clans which only *possess*, but do not own things. The simpler category thus appears as a relation of simple family and clan communities with respect to property. In society the category appears as a simple relation of a developed organization, but the concrete substratum from which the relation of possession springs is always implied. One can imagine an isolated savage in possession of things. But in that case possession is no legal relation. It is not true that the family came as the result of the historical evolution of possession. On the contrary, the latter always implies the existence of this "more concrete category of law." Yet this much may be said, that the simple categories are the expression of relations in which the less developed concrete entity may have been realized without entering into the manifold relations and bearings which are mentally expressed in the concrete category; but when the concrete entity attains fuller development it will retain the same category as a subordinate relation.

Money may exist and actually had existed in history before capital or banks or wage-labor came into existence. With that in mind, it may be said: that the more simple category can serve as an expression of the predominant relations of an undeveloped whole or of the subordinate relations of a more developed whole, relations which had historically existed before the whole developed in the direction expressed in the more concrete category. To this extent, the course of abstract reasoning, which ascends from the most simple to the complex, corresponds to the actual process of history.

CHAPTER 4
The German Ideology

Karl Marx

In this early work (1846), Marx retells the story of human history from the perspective of who owns and who works. In this selection, he argues against a group of mid-nineteenth-century German thinkers who saw the world as an embodiment of spiritual ideas. Marx believed that there was no such thing as spirit. All life consists of physical or material processes. And human consciousness is part of those physical processes.

Men can be distinguished from animals by consciousness, by religion, or anything else you like. They themselves begin to distinguish themselves from animals as soon as they begin to produce their means of subsistence, a step which is conditioned by their physical organization. By producing their means of subsistence men are indirectly producing their actual material life.

The way in which men produce their means of subsistence depends first of all on the nature of the actual means of subsistence they find in existence and have to reproduce. This mode of production must not be considered simply as being the reproduction of the physical existence of the individuals. Rather it is a definite form of activity of these individuals, a definite form of expressing their life, a definite *mode of life* on their part. As individuals express their life, so they are. What they are, therefore coincides with their production, both with *what* they produce and with *how* they produce. The nature of individuals thus depends on the material conditions determining their production.

This production only makes its appearance with the *increase of population*. In its turn this presupposes the *intercourse* [*Verkehr*] of individuals with one another. The form of this intercourse is again determined by production.

The relations of different nations among themselves depend upon the extent to which each has developed its productive forces, the division of labor and internal intercourse. This statement is generally recognized. But not only the relation of one nation to others, but also the whole interval structure of the nation itself depends on the stage of development reached by its production and its internal and external intercourse. How far the productive forces of a nation are developed is shown most manifestly by the degree to which the division of labor has been carried. Each new productive force, insofar as it is not merely a quantitative extension of productive forces already known (for instance the bringing into cultivation of fresh land), causes a further development of the division of labor.

The division of labor inside a nation leads at first to the separation of industrial and commercial from agricultural labor, and hence to the separation of *town* and *country* and to the conflict of their interests. Its further development leads to the separation of commercial from industrial labor. At the same time through the division of labor inside these various branches there develop various divisions among the individuals cooperating in definite kinds of labor. The relative position of these individual groups is determined by the methods employed in agriculture, industry, and commerce (patriarchalism, slavery, estates, classes). These same conditions are to be seen (given a more developed intercourse) in the relations of different nations to one another.

The various stages of development in the division of labor are just so many different forms of ownership, i.e., the existing stage in the division of labor determines also the relations of individuals to one another with reference to the material, instrument, and product of labor.

The first form of ownership is tribal [*Stammeigentum*] ownership. It corresponds to the undeveloped stage of production, at which a people lives by hunting and fishing, by the rearing of beasts, or, in the highest stage, agriculture. In the latter case it presupposes a great mass of uncultivated stretches of land. The division of labor is at this stage still very elementary and is confined to a further extension of the natural division of labor existing in the family. The social structure is, therefore, limited to an extension of the family; patriarchal family chieftains, below them the members of the tribe, finally slaves. The slavery latent in the family only develops gradually with the increase of populations, the growth of wants, and with the extension of external relations, both of war and of barter.

The second form is the ancient communal and State ownership which proceeds especially from the union of several tribes into a city by agreement or by conquest, and which is still accompanied by slavery. Beside communal ownership we already find movable, and later also immovable, private property developing, but as an abnormal form subordinate to communal ownership. The citizens hold power over their laboring slaves only in their community, and on this account alone, therefore, they are bound to the form of communal ownership. It is the communal private property which compels the active citizens to remain in this spontaneously derived form of association over against their slaves. For this reason the whole structure of society based on this communal ownership, and with it the power of the people, decays in the same measure as, in particular, immovable private property evolves. The division of labor is already more developed. We already find the antagonism of town and country; later the antagonism between those states which represent town interests and those which represent country interests, and inside the towns themselves the antagonism between industry and maritime commerce. The class relation between citizens and slaves is now completely developed. . . .

The third form of ownership is feudal or estate property. If antiquity started out from the town and its little territory, the Middle Ages started out from the *country*. This different starting-point was determined by the sparseness of the political at that time, which was scattered over a large area and which received no large increase from the conquerors. In contrast to Greece and Rome, feudal development at the outset, therefore, extends over a territory, prepared by the Roman conflicts and the spread of agriculture; at first associated with them. The last centuries of the declining Roman Empire and its conquest by the barbarians destroyed a number of productive forces; agriculture had declined, industry had decayed for want of a market, trade had died out or been violently suspended, the rural and urban population had decreased. From these conditions and the mode of organization of the conquest determined by them, feudal property developed under the influence of the Germanic military constitution. Like tribal and communal ownership, it is based again on a community; but the directly producing class standing over against it is not, as in the case of the ancient community, the slaves, but the enserfed small peasantry. As soon as feudalism is fully developed, there also arises antagonism to the towns. The hierarchical structure of landownership, and the armed bodies of retainers associated with it, gave the nobility power over the serfs. This feudal organization was, just as much as the ancient communal ownership, an association against a subjected producing class; but the form of association and the relation to the direct producers were different because of the different conditions of production.

This feudal system of landownership had its counterpart in the *towns* in the shape of corporative property, the feudal organization of trades. Here property consisted chiefly in the labor of each individual person. The necessity for association against the organized robber nobility, the need for communal covered markets in an age when the industrialist was at the same time a merchant, the growing competition of the escaped serfs swarming into the rising towns, the feudal structure of the whole country, these combined to bring about the *guilds*. The gradually accumulated small capital of individual craftsmen and their stable numbers, as against the growing population, evolved the relation of journeyman and apprentice, which brought into being in the towns a hierarchy similar to that in the country.

Thus the chief form of property during the feudal epoch consisted on the one hand of landed property with serf labor chained to it, and on the other of the labor of the individual with small capital commanding the labor of journeymen. The organization of both was determined by the restricted conditions of production – the small-scale and primitive cultivation of the land, and the craft type of industry. There was little division of labor in the heyday of feudalism. Each country bore in itself the antithesis of town and country; the division into estates was certainly strongly marked; but apart from the differentiation of princes, nobility, clergy and peasants in the country and masters, journeymen, apprentices and soon also the rabble of casual laborers in the towns, no division of importance took place. In agriculture it was rendered difficult by the strip-system beside which the cottage industry of the peasants themselves emerged. In industry there was no division of labor at all in the individual trades themselves, and very little between them. The separation of industry and commerce was found already in existence in older towns; in the newer it only developed later, when the towns entered into mutual relations.

The grouping of larger territories into feudal kingdoms was a necessity for the landed nobility as for the towns. The organization of the ruling class, the nobility, had, therefore, everywhere a monarch at its head.

The fact is, therefore, that definite individuals who are productively active in a definite way enter into these definite social and political relations. Empirical observation must in each separate instance bring out empirically, all without mystification and speculation, the connection of the social and political structure with production. The social structure and the State are continually evolving out of the life process of definite individuals, but of individuals, not as they may appear in their own or other people's imagination, but as they *really* are; i.e., as they operate, produce materially, and hence as they work under specific material limits, presuppositions and conditions independent of their will.

The production of ideas, of conceptions, of consciousness is at first directly interwoven with the material activities and the material intercourse of men, the language
of real life. Conceiving, thinking, the mental intercourse of men, appear at this stage
as the direct efflux of their material behavior. The same applies to mental production
as expressed in the language of politics, laws, morality, religion, metaphysics, etc., of
a people. Men are the producers of their conceptions, ideas, etc. – real active men, as
they are conditioned by a particular development of their productive forces and of
the intercourse corresponding to these, up to its furthest forms. Consciousness can
never be anything else than conscious existence, and the existence of men is their
actual life-process. If in all ideology men and their circumstances appear upside-
down as in a *camera obscura*, this phenomenon arises just as much from their historical life-process as the inversion of objects on the retina does from their physical
life-process.

In direct contrast to German philosophy which descends from heaven to earth,
here we ascend from earth to heaven. That is to say, we do not set out from what
men say, imagine, conceive, nor from men as narrated, thought of, imagined, conceived, in order to arrive at men in the flesh. We set out from real, active men, and
on the basis of their real life-process we demonstrate the development of the ideological reflexes and echoes of this life-process. The phantoms formed in the human
brain are also, necessarily, sublimates of their material life-process, which is empirically verifiable and bound to material premises. Morality, religion, metaphysics, all the
rest of ideology and their corresponding forms of consciousness, thus no longer
retain the semblance of independence. They have no history, no development; but
men, developing their material production and their material intercourse, alter, along
with this their real existence, their thinking and the products of their thinking. Life
is not determined by consciousness, but consciousness by life. In the first method of
approach the starting-point is consciousness taken as the living individual; in the
second method, which conforms to real life, it is the real living individuals themselves, and consciousness is considered solely as *their* consciousness. ....

The ideas of the ruling class are in every epoch the ruling ideas: i.e., the class
which is the ruling *material* force of society, is at the same time its ruling *intellectual*
force. The class which has the means of material production at its disposal has
control at the same time over the means of material production, so that thereby,
generally speaking, the ideas of those who lack the means of mental production are
subject to it. The ruling ideas are nothing more than the ideal expression of the
dominant material relationships, the dominant material relationships grasped as
ideas; hence of the relationships which make the one class the ruling one, therefore,
the ideas of its dominance. The individuals composing the ruling class possess among
other things consciousness, and therefore think. Insofar, therefore, as they rule as a
class and determine the extent and compass of an epoch, it is self-evident that they
do this in its whole range, hence among other things rule also as thinkers, as producers of ideas, and regulate the production and distribution of the ideas of their age:
thus their ideas are the ruling ideas of the epoch. For instance, in an age and in a
country where royal power, aristocracy, and bourgeoisie are contending for mastery
and where, therefore, mastery is shared, the doctrine of the separation of powers
proves to be the dominant idea and is expressed as an "eternal law."

The division of labor, which we have already seen above as one of the chief forces
of history up till now, manifests itself also in the ruling class as the division of mental

and material labor, so that inside this class one part appears as the thinkers of the class (its active, conceptive ideologists, who make the perfecting of the illusion of the class about itself their chief source of livelihood), while the others' attitude to these ideas and illusions is more passive and receptive, because they are in reality the active members of this class and have less time to make up illusions and ideas about themselves. Within this class this cleavage can even develop into a certain opposition and hostility between the two parts, which, however, in the case of a practical collision, in which the class itself is endangered, automatically comes to nothing, in which case there also vanishes the semblance that the ruling ideas were not the ideas of the ruling class and had a power distinct from the power of this class. The existence of revolutionary ideas in a particular period presupposes the existence of a revolutionary class; about the premises for the latter sufficient has already been said above.

If now in considering the course of history we detach the ideas of the ruling class from the ruling class itself and attribute to them an independent existence, if we confine ourselves to saying that these or those ideas were dominant at a given time, without bothering ourselves about the conditions of production and the producers of these ideas, if we thus ignore the individuals and world conditions which are the source of the ideas, we can say, for instance, that during the time that the aristocracy was dominant, the concepts honor, loyalty, etc., were dominant, during the dominance of the bourgeoisie the concepts freedom, equality, etc. The ruling class itself on the whole imagines this to be so. This conception of history, which is common to all historians, particularly since the eighteenth century, will necessarily come up against the phenomenon that increasingly abstract ideas hold sway, i.e., ideas which increasingly take on the form of universality. For each new class which puts itself in the place of one ruling before it, is compelled, merely in order to carry through its aim, to represent its interest as the common interest of all the members of society, that is, expressed an ideal form: it has to give its ideas the form of universality, and represent them as the only rational, universally valid ones. The class making a revolution appears from the very start, if only because it is opposed to a *class*, not as a class but as the representative of the whole of society; it appears as the whole mass of society confronting the one ruling class.[1] It can do this because, to start with, its interest really is more connected to the common interest of all other non-ruling classes, because under the pressure of hitherto existing conditions its interest has not yet been able to develop as the particular interest of a particular class. Its victory, therefore, benefits also many individuals of the other classes which are not winning a dominant position, but only insofar as it now puts these individuals in a position to raise themselves into the ruling class. When the French bourgeoisie overthrew the power of the aristocracy, it thereby made it possible for many proletarians to raise themselves above the proletariat, but only insofar as they became bourgeois. Every new class, therefore, achieves its hegemony only on a broader basis than that of the class ruling previously, whereas the opposition of the non-ruling class against the new ruling class develops all the more sharply and profoundly. Both these things determine the fact that the struggle to be waged against this new ruling class, in its turn, aims at a more decided and radical negation of the previous conditions of society than could all previous classes which sought to rule.

This whole semblance, that the rule of a certain class is only the rule of certain ideas, comes to a natural end, of course, as soon as class rule in general ceases to be the form in which society is organized, that is to say, as soon as it is no longer necessary to represent a particular interest as general or the "general interest" as ruling.

Note

1 Marginal note by Marx: "Universality corresponds to (1) the class versus the estate, (2) the competition, world-wide intercourse, etc., (3) the great numerical strength of the ruling class, (4) the illusion of the *common* interests (in the beginning this illusion is true), (5) the delusion of the ideologists and the division of labor."

CHAPTER 5

Wage Labor and Capital

Karl Marx

Where does wealth come from? According to classical political economists, it arises magically in the marketplace when goods are sold for more than they cost to make. But if that is the case, don't they have to be worth more than they cost to make? Marx's question led him to what is called the "labor theory of value." He argued that the extra or "surplus value" in goods that allows them to be sold for more than they cost to make comes from labor. Workers put more value into a commodity or good than they are paid for. That difference allows goods to be worth more than they cost to produce. The secret of wealth is that workers are systematically underpaid.

Now, therefore, for the first question: *What are wages? How are they determined?*

If workers were asked: "How much are your wages?" one would reply: "I get a mark a day from my employer"; another, "I get two marks," and so on. According to the different trades to which they belong, they would mention different sums of money which they receive from their respective employers for the performance of a particular piece of work, for example, weaving a yard of linen or typesetting a printed sheet. In spite of the variety of their statements, they would all agree on one point: wages are the sum of money paid by the capitalist for a particular labor time or for a particular output of labor.

The capitalist, it seems, therefore, *buys* their labor with money. They *sell* him their labor for money. But this is merely the appearance. In reality what they sell to the capitalist for money is their labor power. The capitalist buys this labor power for a day, a week, a month, etc. And after he has bought it, he uses it by having the workers work for the stipulated time. For the same sum with which the capitalist has bought their labor power, for example, two marks, he could have bought two pounds of sugar or a definite amount of any other commodity. The two marks, with which he bought two pounds of sugar, are the *price* of the two pounds of sugar. The two marks, with which he bought twelve hours' use of labor power, are the price of twelve hours' labor. Labor power, therefore, is a commodity, neither more nor less than sugar. The former is measured by the clock, the latter by the scales.

The workers exchange their commodity, labor power, for the commodity of the capitalist, for money, and this exchange takes place in a specific ratio. So much money for so long a use of labor power. For twelve hours' weaving, two marks. And do not the two marks represent all the other commodities which I can buy for two marks? In fact, therefore, the worker has exchanged his commodity, labor power, for other commodities of all kinds and that in a specific ratio. By giving him two marks, the capitalist has given him so much meat, so much clothing, so much fuel, light, etc., in exchange for his day's labor. Accordingly, the two marks express the ratio in which labor power is exchanged for other commodities, the *exchange value* of his labor power. The exchange value of a commodity, reckoned in *money*, is what is called its *price*. Wages are only a special name for the price of labor power, commonly called the *price of labor*, for the price of this peculiar commodity which has no other repository than human flesh and blood.

Let us take any worker, say, a weaver. The capitalist supplies him with the loom and yarn. The weaver sets to work and the yarn is converted into linen. The capitalist takes possession of the linen and sells it say, for twenty marks. Now are the wages of the weaver a *share* in the linen, in the twenty marks, in the product of his labor? By no means. Long before the linen is sold, perhaps long before its weaving is finished, the weaver has received his wages. The capitalist, therefore, does not pay these wages with the money which he will obtain from the linen, but with money already on reserve. Just as the loom and the yarn are not the product of the weaver to whom they are supplied by the employers, so likewise with the commodities which the weaver receives in exchange for his commodity, labor power. It was possible that his employer found no purchaser at all for his linen. It was possible that he did not get even the amount of the wages by its sale. It is possible that he sells it very profitably in comparison with the weaver's wages. All that has nothing to do with the weaver. The capitalist buys the labor power of the weaver with a part of his available wealth, of his capital, just as he has bought the raw material – the yarn – and the instrument of labor – the loom – with another part of his wealth. After he has made these purchases, and these purchases include the labor power necessary for the production of linens, he produces only with the *raw materials and instruments of labor belonging to him*. For the latter include now, true enough, our good weaver as well, who has as little share in the product or the price of the product as the loom has.

Wages are, therefore, not the worker's share in the commodity produced by him. Wages are the part of already existing commodities with which the capitalist buys for himself a specific amount of productive labor power.

Labor power is, therefore, a commodity which its possessor, the worker, sells to capital. Why does he sell it? In order to live.

But the exercise of labor power, labor, is the worker's own activity, the manifestation of his own life. And this *life-activity* he sells to another person in order to secure the necessary *means* of subsistence. Thus his life-activity is for him only a means to enable him to exist. He works in order to live. He does not even reckon labor as part of his life, it is rather a sacrifice of his life. It is a commodity which he has made over to another. Hence, also, the product of his activity is not the object of his activity. What he produces for himself is not the silk that he weaves, not the gold that he draws from the mine, not the palace that he builds. What he produces for himself is *wages*, and silk, gold, palace resolve themselves for him into a specific quantity of the means of subsistence, perhaps into a cotton jacket, some copper coins, and a lodging in a cellar. And the worker, who for twelve hours weaves, spins, drills, turns, builds, shovels, breaks stones, carries loads, etc. – does he consider this twelve hours' weaving, spinning, drilling, turning, building, shoveling, stone breaking as a manifestation of his life, as life? On the contrary, life begins for him where this activity ceases, at table, in the public house, in bed. The twelve hours' labor, on the other hand, has no meaning for him as weaving, spinning, drilling, etc., but as *earnings* which bring him to the table, to the public house, into bed. If the silk worm were to spin in order to continue its existence as a caterpillar, it would be a complete wage-worker. Labor power was not always a *commodity*. Labor was not always wage labor, that is, *free labor*. The *slave* did not sell his labor power to the slave owner, any more than the ox sells its services to the peasant. The slave, together with his labor power, is sold once and for all to his owner. He is a commodity which can pass from the land of one owner to that of another. He is *himself* a commodity, but the labor power is not *his* commodity. The serf sells only a part of his labor power. He does not receive a wage from the owner of the land; rather the owner of the land receives a tribute from him.

The serf belongs to the land and turns over to the owner of the land the fruits thereof. The *free laborer*, on the other hand, sells himself and, indeed, sells himself piecemeal. He sells at auction eight, ten, twelve, fifteen hours of his life, day after day, to the highest bidder, to the owner of the raw materials, instruments of labor and means of subsistence, that is, to the capitalist. The worker belongs neither to an owner nor to the land, but eight, ten, twelve, fifteen hours of his daily life belong to him who buys them. The worker leaves the capitalist to whom he hires himself whenever he likes, and the capitalist discharges him whenever he thinks fit, as soon as he no longer gets any profit out of him, or not the anticipated profit. But the worker, whose sole source of livelihood is the sale of his labor power, cannot leave the *whole class of purchasers, that is, the capitalist class*, without renouncing his existence. He belongs not to this or that capitalist but to the *capitalist class*, and, moreover, it is his business to dispose of himself, that is, to find a purchaser within this capitalist class....

Now, the same general laws that regulate the price of commodities in general of course also regulate *wages, the price of labor*.

Wages will rise and fall according to the relation of supply and demand, according to the turn taken by the competition between the buyers of labor power, the capitalists, and the sellers of labor power, the workers. The fluctuations in wages correspond in general to the fluctuations in prices of commodities. *Within these fluctuations, however, the price of labor will be determined by the cost of production, by the labor time necessary to produce this commodity – labor power.*

What, then, is the cost of production of labor power?

It is the cost required for maintaining the worker as a worker and of developing him into a worker.

The less the period of training, therefore, that any work requires, the smaller is the cost of production of the worker and the lower is the price of his labor, his wages. In those branches of industry in which hardly any period of apprenticeship is required and where the mere bodily existence of the worker suffices, the cost necessary for his production is almost confined to the commodities necessary for keeping him alive and capable of working. The *price* of his labor will, therefore, be determined by the *price of the necessary means of subsistence*.

Another consideration, however, also comes in. The manufacturer in calculating his cost of production and, accordingly, the price of the products, takes into account the wear and tear of the instruments of labor. If, for example, a machine costs him 1,000 marks and wears out in ten years, he adds 100 marks annually to the price of the commodities so as to be able to replace the worn-out machine by a new one at the end of ten years. In the same way, in calculating the cost of production of simple labor power there must be included the cost of reproduction, whereby the race of workers is enabled to multiply and to replace worn-out workers by new ones. Thus the depreciation of the worker is taken into account in the same way as the depreciation of the machine.

The cost of production of simple labor power, therefore, amounts to *the cost of existence and reproduction of the worker*. The price of this cost of existence and reproduction constitutes wages. Wages so determined are called the *wage minimum*. This wage minimum, like the determination of the price of commodities by the cost of production in general, does not hold good for the *single individual* but for the *species*. Individual workers, millions of workers, do not get enough to be able to exist and reproduce themselves; *but the wages of the whole working class* levels down, with their fluctuations to this minimum.

Now that we have arrived at an understanding of the most general laws which regulate wages like the price of any other commodity, we can go into our subject more specifically.

Capital consists of raw materials, instruments of labor and means of subsistence of all kinds, which are utilized in order to produce new raw materials, new instruments of labor, and new means of subsistence. All these component parts of capital are creations of labor, products of labor, *your accumulated labor*. Which serves as a means of new production is capital.

So say the economists.

What is a Negro slave? A man of the black race. The one explanation is as good as the other.

A Negro is a Negro. He only becomes a slave in certain relations. A cotton-spinning jenny is a machine for spinning cotton. It becomes my *capital* only in certain relations. Torn from these relationships it is no more capital than gold in itself is *money* or sugar the price of sugar.

In production, men not only act on nature but also on one another. They produce only by cooperating in a certain way and mutually exchanging their activities. In order to produce, they enter into specific, determinate connections and relations with one another and only within these social connections and relations does their action on nature, does production, take place.

These social relations into which the producers enter with one another, the conditions under which they exchange their activities and participate in the whole act of production, will naturally vary according to the character of the means of production. With the invention of a new instrument of warfare, firearms, the whole internal organization of the army necessarily changed; the relationships within which individuals can constitute an army and act as an army were transformed and the relations of different armies to one another also changed.

Thus the social relations within which individuals produce, *the social relations of production, change, are transformed, with the change and development of the material means of production, the productive forces. The relations of production in their totality constitute what are called the social relations, society, and, particularly, a society at a specific stage of historical development*, a society with a peculiar, distinctive character. *Ancient* society, *feudal* society, *bourgeois* society are such totalities of production relations, each of which at the same time denotes a particular stage of development in the history of mankind.

Capital, also, is a social relation of production. *It is a bourgeois production relation*, a production relation of bourgeois society. Are not the means of subsistence, the instruments of labor, the raw materials of which capital consists, produced and accumulated under given social conditions, in particular social relations? Are they not utilized for new production under given social conditions, as specific social relations? And is it not just this specifically social character which turns the products serving for new production into *capital*?

Capital consists not only of means of subsistence, instruments of labor, and raw materials, not only of material products; it consists just as much of *exchange values*! All the products of which it consists are *commodities*. Capital is, therefore, not only a sum of material products; it is a sum of commodities, of exchange values, of *social magnitudes*.

Capital remains the same, whether we put cotton in place of wool, rice in place of wheat, or steamships in place of railways, provided only that the cotton, the rice, the steamships – the body of capital – have the same exchange value, the same price as the wool, the wheat, the railways in which it was previously incorporated. The body of capital can change continually without the capital suffering the slightest alteration.

But while all capital is a sum of commodities, that is, of exchange values, not every sum of commodities, of exchange values, is capital.

Every sum of exchange values is an exchange value. Every separate exchange value is a sum of exchange values. For instance, a house that is worth 1,000 marks is an exchange value of 1,000 marks. A piece of paper worth a pfennig is a sum of exchange values of one-hundred hundredths of a pfennig. Products which are exchangeable for others are commodities. The particular ratio in which they are exchangeable constitutes their *exchange value* or, expressed in money, their *price*. The quantity of these products can change nothing in their quality of being *commodities* or representing an *exchange value* or having a definite price. Whether a tree is large or small it is a tree. Whether we exchange iron for other products in ounces or in hundred-weights, does this make any difference in its character as commodity, as exchange value? It is a commodity of greater or lesser value, of higher or lower price, depending upon the quantity.

How, then, does any amount of commodities, of exchange value, become capital?

By maintaining and multiplying itself as an independent social *power*, that is, as the *power of a portion of society*, by means of its *exchange for direct, living labor power*. The existence of a class which possesses nothing but its capacity to labor is a necessary prerequisite of capital.

It is only the domination of accumulated, past, materialized labor over direct, living labor that turns accumulated labor into capital.

Capital does not consist in accumulated labor serving living labor as a means for new production. It consists in living labor serving accumulated labor as a means of maintaining and multiplying the exchange value of the latter.

What takes place in the exchange between capitalist and wage-worker?

The worker receives means of subsistence in exchange for his labor power, but the capitalist receives in exchange for his means of subsistence labor, the productive activity of the worker, the creative power whereby the worker not only replaces what he consumes but *gives to the accumulated labor a greater value than it previously possessed*. The worker receives a part of the available means of subsistence from the capitalist. For what purpose do these means of subsistence serve him? For immediate consumption. As soon, however, as I consume the means of subsistence, they are irretrievably lost to me unless I use the time during which I am kept alive by them in order to purchase new means of subsistence, in order during consumption to create by my labor new values in place of the values which perish in being consumed. But it is just this noble reproductive power that the worker surrenders to the capitalist in exchange for means of subsistence received. He has, therefore, lost it for himself.

Let us take an example: a tenant farmer gives his day laborer five silver groschen a day. For these five silver groschen the laborer works all day on the farmer's field and thus secures him a return of ten silver groschen. The farmer not only gets the value replaced that he has to give the day laborer; he doubles it. He has therefore employed, consumed, the five silver groschen that he gave to the laborer in a fruitful, productive manner. He has bought with the five silver groschen just that labor and power of the laborer which produces agricultural products of double value and makes ten silver groschen out of five. The day laborer, on the other hand, receives in place of his productive power, the effect of which he has bargained away to the farmer's five silver groschen, which he exchanges for means of subsistence, and these he consumes with greater or less rapidity. The five silver groschen have, therefore, been consumed in a double way, *reproductively* for capital, for they have been exchanged for labor power which produced ten silver groschen, *unproductively* for the workers, for they have been exchanged for means of subsistence which have disappeared forever and the value of which he can only recover by repeating the same exchange with the farmer. *Thus capital presupposes wage labor; wage labor presupposes capital. They reciprocally condition the existence of each other; they reciprocally bring forth each other.*

Does a worker in a cotton factor produce merely cotton textiles? No, he produces capital. He produces values which serve afresh to command his labor and by means of it to create new values...

CHAPTER 6

Capital

Karl Marx

With the publication of the first volume of *Capital* in 1867, Marx put forth his most detailed critique of economic life. In it, he attempted to provide a scientific explanation of his contention that a capitalist economic system requires the appropriation from workers of more value than they are paid for. From a methodological point of view, the section of the "fetishism of commodities" has been important for political critics of literature and culture. In it, Marx argues that the way the reality of the economy appears to us is just the opposite of how it operates. We see the end products of labor on the marketplace in the form of commodities (or goods for sale) and mistakenly think they are the cause of wealth. We thus fetishize the objects that appeal most immediately to our senses, but in so doing, we ignore the invisible relations of production that give rise to those objects.

Commodities

The Two Factors of a Commodity: Use-Value and Value (The Substance of Value and the Magnitude of Value)

The wealth of those societies in which the capitalist mode of production prevails presents itself as "an immense accumulation of commodities," its unit being a single commodity. Our investigation must therefore begin with the analysis of a commodity.

A commodity is, in the first place, an object outside us, a thing that by its properties satisfies human wants of some sort or another. The nature of such wants, whether, for instance, they spring from the stomach or from fancy, makes no difference.[1] Neither are we here concerned to know how the object satisfies these wants whether directly as means of subsistence, or indirectly as means of production.

Every useful thing, as iron, paper, &c., may be looked at from the two points of view of quality and quantity. It is an assemblage of many properties, and may therefore be of use in various ways. To discover the various uses of things is the work of history.[2] So also is the establishment of socially recognized standards of measure for the quantities of these useful objects. The diversity of these measures has its origin partly in the diverse nature of the objects to be measured, partly in convention.

The utility of a thing makes it a use-value.[3] But this utility is not a thing of air. Being limited by the physical properties of the commodity, it has no existence apart from that commodity. A commodity, such as iron, corn, or a diamond, is therefore, so far as it is a material thing, a use-value, something useful. This property of a commodity is independent of the amount of labor required to appropriate its useful qualities. When treating of use-value, we always assume to be dealing with definite quantities, such as dozens of watches, yards of linen, or tons of iron. The use-values of commodities furnish the material for a special study, that of the commercial knowledge of commodities.[4] Use-values become a reality only by use or consumption: they also constitute the substance of all wealth, whatever may be the social form of that wealth. In the form of society we are about to consider, they are, in addition, the material depositories of exchange-value.

Exchange-value, at first sight, presents itself as a quantitative relation, as the proportion in which values in use of one sort are exchanged for those of another sort,[5] a relation constantly changing with time and place. Hence exchange-value appears to be something accidental and purely relative, and consequently an intrinsic value, i.e., an exchange-value that is inseparably connected with, inherent in commodities, seems a contradiction in terms.[6] Let us consider the matter a little more closely.

A given commodity, e.g., a quarter of wheat, is exchanged for x blacking, y silk, or z gold, &c. – in short, for other commodities in the most different proportions. Instead of one exchange-value, the wheat has, therefore, a great many. But since x blacking, y silk, or z gold, &c., each represent the exchange-value of one quarter of wheat, x blacking, y silk, z gold, &c., must, as exchange-values, be replaceable by each other, or equal to each other. Therefore, first: the valid exchange-values of a given commodity express something equal; secondly, exchange-value, generally, is only the mode of expression, the phenomenal form, of something contained in it, yet distinguishable from it.

Let us take two commodities, e.g., corn and iron. The proportions in which they are exchangeable, whatever those proportions may be, can always be represented by an equation in which a given quantity of corn is equated to some quantity of iron: e.g., 1 quarter corn $= x$ cwt. iron. What does this equation tell us? It tells us that in two different things – in 1 quarter of corn and x cwt. of iron – there exists in equal quantities something common to both. The two things must therefore be equal to a third, which in itself is neither the one nor the other. Each of them, so far as it is exchange-value, must therefore be reducible to this third.

A simple geometrical illustration will make this clear. In order to calculate and compare the areas of rectilinear figures, we decompose them into triangles. But the area of the triangle itself is expressed by something totally different from its visible figure, namely, by half the product of the base into the altitude. In the same way the exchange-values of commodities must be capable of being expressed in terms of something common to them all, of which thing they represent a greater or less quantity.

This common "something" cannot be either a geometrical, a chemical, or any other natural property of commodities. Such properties claim our attention only in so far as they affect the utility of those commodities, make them use-values. But the exchange of commodities is evidently an act characterized by a total abstraction from use-value. Then one use-value is just as good as another, provided only it be present in sufficient quantity. Or, as old Barbon says, "one sort of wares are as good as another, if the values be equal. There is no difference or distinction in things of equal value.... An hundred pounds' worth of lead or iron, is of as great value as one hundred pounds' worth of silver or gold." As use-values, commodities are, above all, of different qualities, but as exchange-values they are merely different quantities, and consequently do not contain an atom of use-value.

If then we leave out of consideration the use-value of commodities, they have only one common property left, that of being products of labor. But even the product of labor itself has undergone a change in our hands. If we make abstraction from its use-value, we make abstraction at the same time from the material elements and shapes that make the product a use-value; we see in it no longer a table, a house, yarn, or any other useful thing. Its existence as a material thing is put out of sight. Neither can it any longer be regarded as the product of the labor of the joiner, the mason, the spinner, or of any other definite kind of productive labor. Along with the useful qualities of the products themselves, we put out of sight both the useful character of the various kinds of labor embodied in them, and the concrete forms of that labor; there is nothing left but what is common to them all; all are reduced to one and the same sort of labor, human labor in the abstract.

Let us now consider the residue of each of these products; it consists of the same unsubstantial reality in each, a mere congelation of homogeneous human labor, of labor-power expended without regard to the mode of its expenditure. All that these things now tell us is, that human labor-power has been expended in their production, that human labor is embodied in them. When looked at as crystals of this social substance common to them all, they are – Values. . . .

The Fetishism of Commodities and the Secret Thereof

[F]rom the moment that men in any way work for one another, their labor assumes a social form.

Whence, then, arises the enigmatical character of the product of labor, so soon as it assumes the form of commodities? Clearly from this form itself. The equality of all sorts of human labor is expressed objectively by their products all being equally values; the measure of the expenditure of labor-power by the duration of that expenditure, takes the form of the quantity of value of the products of labor; and finally, the mutual relations of the producers, within which the social character of their labor affirms itself, take the form of a social relation between the products.

A commodity is therefore a mysterious thing, simply because in it the social character of men's labor appears to them as an objective character stamped upon the product of that labor; because the relation of the producers to the sum total of their own labor is presented to them as a social relation, existing not between themselves, but between the products of their labor. This is the reason why the products of labor become commodities, social things whose qualities are at the same time perceptible and imperceptible by the senses. In the same way the light from an object is perceived by us not as the subjective excitation of our optic nerve, but as the objective form of something outside the eye itself. But, in the act of seeing, there is at all events, an actual passage of light from one thing to another, from the external object to the eye. There is a physical relation between physical things. But it is different with commodities. There, the existence of the things *qua* commodities, and the value relation between the products of labor which stamps them as commodities, have absolutely no connection with their physical properties and with the material relations arising therefrom. There it is a definite social relation between men, that assumes, in their eyes, the fantastic form of a relation between things. In order, therefore, to find an analogy, we must have recourse to the mist-enveloped regions of the religious world. In that world the productions of the human brain appear as independent beings endowed with life, and entering into relation both with one another and the human race. So it is in the world of commodities with the products of men's hands. This I call the Fetishism which attaches itself to the products of labor, so soon as they are produced as commodities, and which is therefore inseparable from the production of commodities.

This Fetishism of commodities has its origin, as the foregoing analysis has already shown, in the peculiar social character of the labor that produces them.

As a general rule, articles of utility become commodities, only because they are products of the labor of private individuals or groups of individuals who carry on their work independently of each other. The sum total of the labor of all these private individuals forms the aggregate labor of society. Since the producers do not come into social contact with each other until they exchange their products, the specific social character of each producer's labor does not show itself except in the act of exchange. In other words, the labor of the individual asserts itself as a part of the labor of society, only by means of the relations which the act of exchange establishes directly between the products, and indirectly, through them, between the producers. To the latter, therefore, the relations connecting the labor of one individual with that of the rest appear, not as direct social relations between individuals at work, but as what they really are, material relations between persons and social relations between things. It is only by being exchanged that the products of labor acquire, as values, one uniform social status, distinct from their varied forms of existence as objects of utility. This division of a product into a useful thing and a value becomes practically important, only when exchange has acquired such an extension that useful articles are produced for the purpose of being exchanged, and their character as values has therefore to be taken into account, beforehand, during production. From this moment the labor of the individual producer acquires socially a twofold character. On the one hand, it must, as a definite useful kind of labor, satisfy a definite social want, and thus hold its place as part and parcel of the collective labor of all, as a branch of a social division of labor that has sprung up spontaneously. On the other hand, it can satisfy the manifold wants of the individual producer himself, only in so far as the mutual exchangeability of all kinds of useful private labor is an established social fact, and therefore the private useful labor of each producer ranks on an equality with that of all others. The equalization of the most different kinds of labor can be the result only of an abstraction from their inequalities, or of reducing them to their common denominator, viz., expenditure of human labor-power or human labor in the abstract. The twofold social character of the labor of the individual appears to him, when reflected in his brain, only under those forms which are impressed upon that labor in everyday practice by the exchange of products. In this way, the character that his own labor possesses of being socially useful takes the form of the condition, that the product must be not only useful, but useful for others, and the social character that his particular labor has of being the equal of all other particular kinds of labor, takes the form that all the physically different articles that are the products of labor, have one common quality, viz., that of having value.

Hence, when we bring the products of our labor into relation with each other as values, it is not because we see in these articles the material receptacles of homogeneous human labor. Quite the contrary: whenever, by an exchange, we equate as values our different products, by that very act, we also equate, as human labor, the different kinds of labor expended upon them. We are not aware of this, nevertheless we do it. Value, therefore, does not stalk about with a label describing what it is. It is value, rather, that converts every product into a social hieroglyphic. Later on, we try to decipher the hieroglyphic, to get behind the secret of our own social products; for to stamp an object of utility as a value, is just as much a social product as language. The recent scientific discovery, that the products of labor, so far as they are values, are but material expressions of the human labor spent in their production, marks, indeed, an epoch in the history of the development of the human race, but, by no means, dissipates the mist through which the social character of labor appears to us to be an objective character of the products themselves. The fact, that in the particular form of production with which we are dealing, viz., the production of commodities, the specific social character of private labor carried on independently consists in the equality of every kind of that labor, by virtue of its being human labor, which character, therefore, assumes in the product the form of value – this fact appears to the producers, notwithstanding the discovery above referred to, to be just as real and final, as the fact that, after the discovery by science of the component gases of air, the atmosphere itself remained unaltered.

What, first of all, practically concerns producers when they make an exchange, is the question, how much of some other product they get for their own? in what proportions the products are exchangeable? When these proportions have, by custom, attained a certain stability, they appear to result from the nature of the products, so that, for instance, one ton of iron and two ounces of gold appear as naturally to be of equal value as a pound of gold and a pound of iron in spite of their different physical and chemical qualities appear to be of equal weight. The character of having value, when once impressed upon products, obtains fixity only by reason of their acting and re-acting upon each other as quantities of value. These quantities vary continually, independently of the will, foresight, and action of the producers. To them, their own social action takes the form of the action of objects, which rule the producers instead of being ruled by them. It requires a fully developed production of commodities before, from accumulated experience alone, the scientific conviction springs up, that all the different kinds of private labor, which are carried on independently of each other, and yet as spontaneously developed branches of the social division of labor, are continually being reduced to the quantitative proportions in which society requires them. And why? Because, in the midst of all the accidental and ever fluctuating exchange-relations between the products, the labor-time socially necessary for their production forcibly asserts itself like an over-riding law of nature. The law of gravity thus asserts itself when a house falls about our ears.[7] The determination of the magnitude of value by labor-time is therefore a secret, hidden under the apparent fluctuations in the relative values of commodities. Its discovery, while removing all appearance of mere accidentality from the determination of the magnitude of the values of products, yet in no way alters the mode in which that determination takes place.

Man's reflections on the forms of social life, and consequently, also, his scientific analysis of those forms, take a course directly opposite to that of their actual historical development. He begins, post festum, with the results of the process of development ready to hand before him. The characters that stamp products as commodities, and whose establishment is a necessary preliminary to the circulation of commodities, have already acquired the stability of natural, self-understood forms of social life, before man seeks to decipher, not their historical character, for in his eyes they are immutable, but their meaning. Consequently it was the analysis of the prices of commodities that alone led to the determination of the magnitude of value, and it was the common expression of all commodities in money that alone led to the establishment of their characters as values. It is, however, just this ultimate money form of the world of commodities that actually conceals, instead of disclosing, the social character of private labor, and the social relations between the individual producers. When I state that coats or boots stand in a relation to linen, because it is the universal incarnation of abstract human labor, the absurdity of the statement is self-evident. Nevertheless, when the producers of coats and boots compare those articles with linen, or, what is the same thing, with gold or silver, as the universal equivalent, they express the relation between their own private labor and the collective labor of society in the same absurd form.

The categories of bourgeois economy consist of such like forms. They are forms of thought expressing with social validity the conditions and relations of a definite, historically determined mode of production, viz., the production of commodities. The whole mystery of commodities, all the magic and necromancy that surrounds the products of labor as long as they take the form of commodities, vanishes therefore, so soon as we come to other forms of production.

Since Robinson Crusoe's experiences are a favorite theme with political economists let us take a look at him on his island. Moderate though he be, yet some few wants he has to satisfy, and must therefore do a little useful work of various sorts, such as making tools and furniture, taming goats, fishing and hunting. Of his prayers and the like we take no account, since they are a source of pleasure to him, and he looks upon them as so much recreation. In spite of the variety of his work, he knows that his labor, whatever its form, is but the activity of one and the same Robinson, and consequently, that it consists of nothing but different modes of human labor. Necessity itself compels him to apportion his time accurately between his different kinds of work. Whether one kind occupies a greater space in his general activity than another, depends on the difficulties, greater or less as the case may be, to be overcome in attaining the useful effect aimed at. This our friend Robinson soon learns by experience, and having rescued a watch, ledger, and pen and ink from the wreck, commences, like a true-born Briton, to keep a set of books. His stock-book contains a list of the objects of utility that belong to him, of the operations necessary for their production, and lastly, of the labor-time that definite quantities of those objects have, on an average, cost him. All the relations between Robinson and the objects that form this wealth of his own creation, are here so simple and clear as to be intelligible without exertion, even to Mr Sedley Taylor. And yet those relations contain all that is essential to the determination of value.

Let us now transport ourselves from Robinson's island bathed in light to the European Middle Ages shrouded in darkness. Here, instead of the independent man, we find everyone dependent, serfs and lords, vassals and suzerains, laymen and clergy. Personal dependence here characterizes the social relations of production just as much as it does the other spheres of life organized on the basis of that production. But for the very reason that personal dependence forms the groundwork of society, there is no necessity for labor and its products to assume a fantastic form different from their reality. They take the shape, in the transactions of society, of services in kind and payments in kind. Here the particular and natural form of labor, and not, as in a society based on production of commodities, its general abstract form, is the immediate social form of labor. Compulsory labor is just as properly measured by time, as commodity-producing labor; but every serf knows that what he expends in the service of his lord, is a specific quantity of his own personal labor-power. The tithe to be rendered to the priest is more matter of fact than his blessing. No matter, then, what we may think of the parts played by the different classes of people themselves in this society, the social relations between individuals in the performance of their labor, appear at all events as their own mutual personal relations, and are not disguised under the shape of social relations between the products of labor.

For an example of labor in common or directly associated labor, we have no occasion to go back to that spontaneously developed form which we find on the threshold of the history of all civilized races.[8] We have one close at hand in the patriarchal industries of a peasant family, that produces corn, cattle, yarn, linen, and clothing for home use. These different articles are, as regards the family, so many products of its labor, but as between themselves, they are not commodities. The different kinds of labor, such as tillage, cattle, tending, spinning, weaving, and making clothes, which result in the various products, are in themselves, and such as they are, direct social functions, because functions of the family, which, just as much as a society based on the production of commodities, possesses a spontaneously developed system of division of labor. The distribution of the work within the family, and the regulation of the labor-time of the several members, depend as well upon differences of age and sex as upon natural conditions varying with the seasons. The labor-power of each individual, by its very nature, operates in this case merely as a definite portion of the whole labor-power of the family, and therefore, the measure of the expenditure of individual labor-power by its duration, appears here by its very nature as a social character of their labor.

Let us now picture to ourselves, by way of change, a community of free individuals, carrying on their work with the means of production in common, in which the labor-power of all the different individuals is consciously applied as the combined labor-power of the community. All the characteristics of Robinson's labor are here repeated, but with this difference, that they are social, instead of individual. Everything produced by him was exclusively the result of his own personal labor, and therefore simply an object of use for himself. The total product of our community is a social product. One portion serves as fresh means of production and remains social. But another portion is consumed by the members as means of subsistence. A distribution of this portion amongst them is consequently necessary. The mode of this distribution will vary with the productive organization of the community, and the degree of historical development attained by the producers. We will assume, but merely for the salve of a parallel with the production of commodities, that the share of each individual producer in the means of subsistence is determined by his labor-time. Labor-time would, in that case, play a double part. Its apportionment in accordance with a definite social plan maintains the proper proportion between the different kinds of work to be done and the various wants of the community. On the other hand, it also serves as a measure of the portion of the common labor borne by each individual, and of his share in the part of the total product destined for individual consumption. The social relations of the individual producers, with regard both to their labor and to its products, are in this case perfectly simple and intelligible, and that with regard not only to production but also to distribution.

Notes

1   "Desire implies want; it is the appetite of the mind, and as natural as hunger to the body. . . . The greatest number (of things) have their value from supplying the wants of the mind." Nicholas Barbon, "A Discourse Concerning Coining the New Money Lighter. In Answer to Mr. Locke's Considerations," &c. (London, 1696), p. 2.

2   "Things have an intrinsick vertue" (this is Barbon's special term for value in use) "which in all places have the same vertue; as the loadstone to attract iron" (1. c., p. 6). The property which the magnet possesses of attracting iron, became of use only after by means of that property the polarity of the magnet had been discovered.

3   "The natural worth of anything consists in its fitness to supply the necessities, or serve the conveniences of human life." (John Locke, "Some Considerations on the Consequences of the Lowering of Interest, 1691" in *Works*, Edit. (London, 1777), vol. II, p. 28.) In English writers of the seventeenth century we frequently find "worth" in the sense of value in use, and "value" in the sense of exchange-value. This is quite in accordance with the spirit of a language that likes to use a Teutonic word for the actual thing, and a Romance word for its reflexion. [Marx.]

4   In bourgeois societies the economic *fictio juris* prevails, that everyone, as a buyer, possesses an encyclopaedic knowledge of commodities.

5   "La valeur consiste dans le rapport d'échange qui se trouve entre telle chose et telle autre, entre telle mesure d'une production, et telle mesure d'une autre." (Le Trosne, "De l'Intérêt Social," *Physiocrates*, Ed. Daire (Paris, 1846), p. 889.) ["Value consists in the relationship of exchange between one thing and another, between one measure of production and another such measure."]

6   "Nothing can have an intrinsick value." (N. Barbon, 1. c., p. 6); or as Butler says – "The value of a thing is just as much as it will bring."

7   "What are we to think of a law that asserts itself only by periodical revolution? It is just nothing but a law of Nature, founded on the want of knowledge of those whose action is the subject of it." (Friedrich Engels, "Umrisse zu einer Kritik der Nationalökonomie," in the "Deutsch-französische Jahrbücher," edited by Arnold Ruge and Karl Marx (Paris, 1844).)

8   "A ridiculous presumption has latterly got abroad that common property in its primitive form is specifically a Slavonian, or even exclusively Russian, form. It is the primitive form that we can prove to have existed amongst Romans, Teutons, and Celts, and even to this day we find numerous examples, ruins though they be, in India. A more exhaustive study of Asiatic, and especially of Indian forms of common property, would show how from the different forms of primitive common property, different forms of its dissolution have been developed. Thus, for instance, the various original types of Roman and Teutonic private property are deducible from different forms of Indian common property." (Karl Marx, "Zur Kritik," &c., p. 10.)

CHAPTER 7

Hegemony

Antonio Gramsci

Antonio Gramsci was a leading socialist newspaper editor in Italy in the early part of the twentieth century. He was imprisoned by the Fascists, a right-wing group that came to power violently in 1924 and immediately began to suppress the socialist movement for economic equality. Gramsci was imprisoned in 1927, but he was permitted to keep notebooks. The notebooks had to be submitted to a censor, so Gramsci was careful to write them in a coded manner. In this selection (1930–2), he discusses his concept of social power or domination, which he calls "hegemony." Gramsci was innovative in his perception that power can be maintained without force if the consent of the dominated can be obtained through education and through other kinds of cultural labor on the part of such intellectuals as priests and journalists.

The relationship between the intellectuals and the world of production is not as direct as it is with the fundamental social groups but is, in varying degrees, "mediated" by the whole fabric of society and by the complex of superstructures, of which the intellectuals are, precisely, the "functionaries." It should be possible both to measure the "organic quality" [*organicità*] of the various intellectual strata and their degree of connection with a fundamental social group, and to establish a gradation of their functions and of the superstructures from the bottom to the top (from the structural base upwards). What we can do, for the moment, is to fix two major superstructural "levels": the one that can be called "civil society," that is, the ensemble of organisms called "private," that of "political society" or "the State." These two levels correspond on the one hand to the function of "hegemony" which the dominant group exercises throughout society and, on the other hand, to that of "direct domination" or command exercised through the State and "juridical" government. The functions in question are precisely organizational and connective. The intellectuals are the dominant group's "deputies" exercising the subaltern functions of social hegemony and political government.

These comprise:

1 The "spontaneous" consent given by the great masses of the population to the general direction imposed on social life by the dominant fundamental group; this consent is "historically" caused by the prestige (and consequent confidence) which the dominant group enjoys because of its position and function in the world of production.
2 The apparatus of state coercive power which "legally" enforces discipline on those groups who do not "consent" either actively or passively. This apparatus is, however, constituted for the whole of society in anticipation of moments of crisis of command and direction when spontaneous consent has failed.

CHAPTER 8

Discourse in the Novel

Mikhail Bakhtin

Mikhail Bakhtin was one of the most influential thinkers of the late twentieth century for literary and cultural studies. Bakhtin drew attention to the way literature weaves discourses together from disparate social sources. Bakhtin also helped reconceptualize literary language. According to the theory, all words exist in dialog with other words. The theory shifts emphasis away from individual literary works and toward the intertextual world in which individual literary works are set. This selection dates from 1934–5.

The novel can be defined as a diversity of social speech types, sometimes even diversity of languages and a diversity of individual voices, artistically organized. The internal stratification of any single national language into social dialects, characteristic group behavior, professional jargons, generic languages, languages of generations and age groups, tendentious languages, languages of the authorities, of various circles and of passing fashions, languages that serve the specific sociopolitical purposes of the day, even of the hour (each day has its own slogan, its own vocabulary, its own emphases) – this internal stratification present in every language of its historical existence is the indispensable prerequisite for the novel as a genre. The novel orchestrates all its themes, the totality of the world of objects and ideas depicted and expressed in it, by means of the social diversity of speech types [*raznorecie*] and by the differing individual voices that flourish under such conditions. Authorial speech, the speeches of narrators, inserted genres, the speech of characters are merely those fundamental compositional unities with whose help heteroglossia [*raznorecie*] can enter the novel; each of them permits a multiplicity of social voices and a wide variety of their links and interrelationships (always more or less dialogized). These distinctive links and interrelationships between utterances and languages, this movement of the theme through different languages and speech types, its dispersion into the rivulets and droplets of social heteroglossia, its dialogization – this is the basic distinguishing feature of the stylistics of the novel.

Such a combining of languages and styles into a higher unity is unknown to traditional stylistics; it has no method for approaching the distinctive social dialogue among languages that is present in the novel . . .

Language – like the living concrete environment in which the consciousness of the verbal artist lives – is never unitary. It is unitary only as an abstract grammatical system of normative forms, taken in isolation from the uninterrupted process of historical becoming that is characteristic of all living language. Actual social life and historical becoming create within an abstractly unitary national language a multitude of concrete worlds, a multitude of bounded verbal ideological and social belief systems;

within these various systems (identical in the abstract) are elements of language filled with various semantic and axiological content and each with its own different sound.

Literary language – both spoken and written – although it is unitary not only in its shared, abstract, linguistic markers but also in its forms for conceptualizing these abstract markers, is itself stratified and heteroglot in its aspect as an expressive system, that is, in the forms that carry its meanings.

This stratification is accomplished first of all by the specific organisms called *genres*. Certain features of language (lexicological, semantic, syntactic) will knit together with the intentional aim, and with the overall accentual system inherent in one or another genre: oratorical, publicistic, newspaper and journalistic genres, the genres of low literature (penny dreadfuls, for instance) or, finally, the various genres of high literature. Certain features of language take on the specific flavor of a given genre: they knit together with specific points of view, specific approaches, forms of thinking, nuances and accents characteristic of the given genre.

In addition, there is interwoven with this generic stratification of language a *professional* stratification of language, in the broad sense of the term "professional": the language of the lawyer, the doctor, the businessman, the politician, the public education teacher and so forth, and these sometimes coincide with, and sometimes depart from, the stratification into genres. It goes without saying that these languages differ from each other not only in their vocabularies; they involve specific forms for manifesting intentions, forms for making conceptualization and evaluation concrete. And even the very language of the writer (the poet or novelist) can be taken as a professional jargon on a par with professional jargons.

But the situation is far from exhausted by the generic and professional stratification of the common literary language. Although at its very core literary language is frequently socially homogeneous, as the oral and written language of a dominant social group, there is nevertheless always present, even here, a certain degree of social differentiation, a social stratification, that in other eras can become extremely acute. Social stratification may here and there coincide with generic and professional stratification, but in essence it is, of course, a thing completely autonomous and peculiar to itself.

Social stratification is also and primarily determined by differences between the forms used to convey meaning and between the expressive planes of various belief systems – that is, stratification expresses itself in typical differences in ways used to conceptualize and accentuate elements of language, and stratification may not violate the abstractly linguistic dialectological unity of the shared literary language.

What is more, all socially significant world views have the capacity to exploit the intentional possibilities of language through the medium of their specific concrete instancing. Various tendencies (artistic and otherwise), circles, journals, particular newspapers, even particular significant artistic works and individual persons are all capable of stratifying language, in proportion to their social significance; they are capable of attracting its words and forms into their orbit by means of their own characteristic intentions and accents, and in so doing to a certain extent alienating these words and forms from other tendencies, parties, artistic works and persons.

Every socially significant verbal performance has the ability – sometime for a long period of time, and for a wide circle of persons – to infect with its own intention certain aspects of language that had been affected by its semantic and expressive impulse, imposing on them specific semantic nuances and specific axiological overtones; thus, it can create slogan-words, curse-words, praise-words and so forth.

In any given historical moment of verbal-ideological life, each generation at each social level has its own language; moreover, every age group has as a matter of fact its own language, its own vocabulary, its own particular accentual system that, in their turn, vary depending on social level, academic institution (the language of the cadet, the high school student, the trade school student are all different languages) and other stratifying factors. All this is brought about by socially typifying languages, no matter how narrow the social circle in which they are spoken. It is even possible to have a family jargon define the societal limits of a language, as, for instance, the jargon of the Irtenevs in Tolstoy, with its special vocabulary and unique accentual system.

And finally, at any given moment, languages of various epochs and periods of socio-ideological life cohabit with one another. Even languages of the day exist: one could say that today's and yesterday's socio-ideological and political "day" do not, in a certain sense, share the same language; every day represents another socio-ideological semantic "state of affairs," another vocabulary, another accentual system, with its own slogans, its own ways of assigning blame and praise. Poetry depersonalizes "days" in language, while prose, as we shall see, often deliberately intensifies difference between them, gives them embodied representation and dialogically opposes them to one another in unresolvable dialogues.

Thus at any given moment of its historical existence, language is heteroglot from top to bottom: it represents the coexistence of socio-ideological contradictions between the present and the past, between differing epochs of the past, between different socio-ideological groups in the present, between tendencies, schools, circles and so forth, all given a bodily form. These "languages" of heteroglossia intersect each other in a variety of ways, forming new socially typifying "languages" . . .

In actual fact, however, there does exist a common plane that methodologically justifies our juxtaposing them: all languages of heteroglossia, whatever the principle underlying them and making each unique, are specific points of view on the world, forms for conceptualizing the world in words, specific world views, each characterized by its own objects, meanings and values. As such they may be juxtaposed to one another, mutually supplement one another, contradict one another and be interrelated dialogically. As such they encounter one another and coexist in the consciousness of real people – first and foremost, in the creative consciousness of people who write novels. As such, these languages live a real life, they struggle and evolve in an environment of social heteroglossia. Therefore they are all able to enter into the unitary plane of the novel, which can unite in itself parodic stylizations of generic languages, various forms of stylizations and illustrations of professional and period-bound languages, the languages of particular generations, of social dialects and others (as occurs, for example, in the English comic novel). They may all be drawn in by the novelists for the orchestration of his themes and for the refracted (indirect) expression of his intentions and values . . .

As a result of the work done by all these stratifying forces in language, there are not "neutral" words and forms – words and forms that can belong to "no one"; language has been completely taken over, shot through with intentions and accents. For any individual consciousness living in it, language is not an abstract system of normative forms but rather a concrete heteroglot conception of the world. All words have the "taste" of a profession, a genre, a tendency, a party, a particular work, a particular person, a generation, an age group, the day and hour. Each word tastes of the context and contexts in which it has lived its socially charged life; all words and forms are populated by intentions. Contextual overtones (generic, tendentious, individualistic) are inevitable in the word.

As a living, socio-ideological concrete thing, as heteroglot opinion, language, for the individual consciousness, lies on the borderline between oneself and the other. The word in language is half someone else's. It becomes "one's own" only when the speaker populates it with his own intention, his own accent, when he appropriates the word, adapting it to his own semantic and expressive intention. Prior to this moment of appropriation, the word does not exist in a neutral and impersonal language (it is not, after all, out of a dictionary that the speaker gets his words!), but rather it exists in other people's mouths, in other people's contexts, serving other people's intentions: it is from there that one must take the word, and make it one's own. And not all words for just anyone submit equally easily to this appropriation, to this seizure and transformation into private property; many words stubbornly resist, others remain alien, sound foreign in the mouth of the one who appropriated them and who now speaks them; they cannot be assimilated into his context and fall out of it; it is as if they put themselves in quotation marks against the will of the speaker. Language is not a neutral medium that passes freely and easily into the private property of the speaker's intentions; it is populated – overpopulated – with the intentions of others. Expropriating it, forcing it to submit to one's own intentions and accents, is a difficult and complicated process.

Concrete socio-ideological language consciousness, as it becomes creative – that is, as it becomes active as literature – discovers itself already surrounded by heteroglossia and not at all a singly, unitary language, inviolable and indisputable. The actively literary linguistic consciousness at all times and everywhere (that is, in all epochs of literature historically available to us) comes upon "languages," and not language. Consciousness finds itself inevitably facing the necessity of *having to choose a language*. With each literary-verbal performance, consciousness must actively orient itself amidst heteroglossia, it must move in and occupy a position for itself within it, it chooses, in other words, a "language." Only by remaining in a closed environment, one without writing or thought, completely off the maps of socio-ideological becoming, could a man fail to sense this activity of selecting a language and rest assured in the inviolability of his own language, the conviction that his language is redetermined.

Even such a man, however, deals not in fact with a single language, but with languages – except that the place occupied by each of these languages is fixed and indisputable, the movement from one to the other is predetermined and not a thought process; it is as if these languages were in different chambers. They do not collide with each other in his consciousness, there is no attempt to coordinate them, to look at one of these languages through the eyes of another language.

Thus an illiterate peasant, miles away from any urban center naively immersed in an unmoving and for him unshakeable everyday world, nevertheless lived in several language systems: he prayed to God in one language (Church Slavonic), sang songs in another, spoke to his family in a third and, when he began to dictate petitions to the local authorities through a scribe, he tried speaking yet a fourth language (the official-literate language, "paper language"). All these are *different languages*, even from the point of view of abstract socio-dialectological markers. But these languages were not dialogically coordinated in the linguistic consciousness of the peasant; he passed from one to the other without thinking, automatically: each was indisputably in its own place, and the place of each was indisputable. He was not yet able to regard one language (and the verbal world corresponding to it) through the eyes of another language (that is, the language of everyday life and the everyday world with the language of prayer or song, or vice versa).[1]

As soon as a critical interanimation of languages began to occur in the consciousness of our peasant, as soon as it became clear that these were not only various different languages but even internally variegated languages, that the ideological systems and approaches to the world that were indissolubly connected with these languages contradicted each other and in no way could live in peace and quiet with one another – then the inviolability and predetermined quality of these languages came to an end, and the necessity of actively choosing one's orientation among them began.

The language and world of prayer, the language and world of song, the language and world of labor and everyday life, the specific language and world of local authorities, the new language and world of the workers freshly immigrated to the city – all these languages and worlds sooner or later emerged from a state of peaceful and moribund equilibrium and revealed the speech diversity in each.

The prose writer as a novelist does not strip away the intentions of others from the heteroglot language of his works, he does not violate those socio-ideological cultural horizons (big and little worlds) that open up behind heteroglot languages – rather, he welcomes them into his work. The prose writer makes use of words that are already populated with the social intentions of others and compels them to serve his own new intentions, to serve a second master...

In the English comic novel we find a comic-parodic reprocessing of almost all the levels of literary language, both conversational and written, that were current at the time. Almost every... classic representative of this generic type is an encyclopedia of all strata and forms of literary language: depending on the subject being represented, the storyline parodically reproduces first the forms of parliamentary eloquence, then the eloquence of the court, or particular forms of parliamentary protocol, or court protocol, or forms used by reporters in newspaper articles, or the dry business language of the City, or the dealings of speculators, or the pedantic speech of scholars, or the high epic style, or Biblical style, or the style of the hypocritical moral sermon or finally the way one or another concrete and socially determined personality, the subject of the story, happens to speak.

This usually parodic stylization of generic, professional and other strata of language is sometimes interrupted by the direct authorial word (usually as an expression of pathos, of Sentimental or idyllic sensibility), which directly embodies (without any refracting) semantic and axiological intentions of the author. But the primary source of language usage in the comic novel is a highly specific treatment of "common language." This "common language" – usually the average norm of spoken and written language for a given social group – is taken by the author precisely as the *common view*, as the verbal approach to people and things normal for a given sphere of society, as the *going point of view* and the going *value*. To one degree or another, the author distances himself from this common language, he steps back and objectifies it, forcing his own intentions to refract and diffuse themselves through the medium of this common view that has become embodied in language (a view that is always superficial and frequently hypocritical)...

Against this same backdrop of the "common language," of the impersonal, going opinion, one can also isolate in the comic novel those parodic stylizations of generic, professional and other languages we have mentioned, as well as compact masses of direct authorial discourse – pathos-filled, moral-didactic, sentimental-elegiac or idyllic. In the comic novel the direct authorial word is thus realized in direct, un-qualified stylizations of poetic genres (idyllic, elegiac, etc.) or stylizations of rhetorical genres (the pathetic, the moral-didactic). Shifts from common language to parodying of generic and other languages and shifts to the direct authorial word may be gradual, or may be on the contrary quite abrupt. Thus does the system of language work in the comic novel.

We will pause for analysis on several examples from Dickens, from his novel *Little Dorrit*.

(1)

the conference was held at four or five o'clock in the afternoon, when all the region of Harley Street, Cavendish Square, was resonant of carriage-wheels and double-knocks. It had reached this point when Mr. Merdle came home *from his daily occupation of causing the British name to be more respected in all part of the civilized globe capable of appreciation of wholewide commercial enterprise and gigantic combinations of skill and capital*. For, though nobody knew with the least precision what Mr. Merdle's business was, except that it was to coin money, these were the terms in which everybody defined it on all ceremonious occasions, and which it was the last new polite reading of the parable of the camel and the needle's eye to accept without inquiry. (Book 1, ch. 33)

The italicized portion represents a parodic stylization of the language of ceremonial speeches (in parliaments and at banquets). The shift into this style is prepared for by the sentence's construction, which from the very beginning is kept within bounds by a somewhat ceremonious epic tone. Further on – and already in the language of the author (and consequently in a different style) – the parodic meaning of the ceremoni-ousness of Merdle's labors becomes apparent: such a characterization turns out to be "another's speech," to be taken only in quotation marks ("these were the terms in which everybody defined it on all ceremonious occasions").

Thus the speech of another is introduced into the author's discourse (the story) in *concealed form*, that is, without any of the *formal* markers usually accompanying such speech, whether direct or indirect. But this is not just another's speech in the same "language" – it is another's utterance in a language that is itself "other" to the author as well, in the archaicized language of oratorical genres associated with hypo-critical official celebration.

(2)

In a day or two it was announced to all the town, that Edmund Sparkler, Esquire, son-in-law of the eminent Mr. Merdle of worldwide renown, was made one of the Lords of the Circumlocution Office; and proclamation was issued, to all true believers, that this admirable *appointment was to be hailed as a graceful and gracious mark of homage, rendered by the graceful and gracious Decimus, to that commercial interest which must ever in a great commercial country – and all the rest of it with blast of trumpet*. So, bolstered by this mark of Government homage, the *wonderful* Bank and all the other *wonderful* undertakings went on and went up; and gapers came to Harley Street, Cavendish Square, only to look at the house where the golden wonder lived. (Book 2, ch. 12)

Here, in the italicized portion, another's speech in another's (official-ceremonial) language is openly introduced as indirect discourse. But it is surrounded by the hidden, diffused speech of another (in the same official-ceremonial language) that clears the way for the introduction of a form more easily perceived *as* another's speech and that can reverberate more fully as such. The clearing of the way comes with the word "Esquire," characteristic of official speech, added to Sparkler's name; the final confirmation that this is another's speech comes with the epithet "wonderful." This epithet does not of course belong to the author but to that same "general opinion" that had created the commotion around Merdle's inflated enterprises.

(3)

> It was a dinner to provoke an appetite, though he had not had one. The rarest dishes,
> sumptuously cooked and sumptuously served; the choicest fruits, the most exquisite
> wines; marvels of workmanship in gold and silver, china and glass; innumerable things
> delicious to the senses of taste, smell, and sight, were insinuated into its composition.
> *O, what a wonderful man this Merdle, what a great man, what a master man, how blessedly
> and enviably endowed* – in one word what a rich man! (Book 2, ch. 12)

The beginning is a parodic stylization of high epic style. What follows is an enthusiastic glorification of Merdle, a chorus of his admirers in the form of the concealed speech of another (the italicized portion). The whole point here is to expose the real basis for such glorification, which is to unmask the chorus's hypocrisy: "wonderful," "great," "master," "endowed" can all be replaced by the single word "rich." This act of authorial unmasking, which is openly accomplished within the boundaries of a single simple sentence, merges with the unmasking of another's speech. The ceremonial emphasis on glorification is complicated by a second emphasis that is indignant, ironic, and this is the one that ultimately predominates in the final unmasking words of the sentence.

We have before us a typical double-accented, double-styled *hybrid construction*.

What we are calling a hybrid construction is an utterance that belongs, by its grammatical (syntactic) and compositional markers, to a single speaker, but that actually contains mixed within it two utterances, two speech manners, two styles, two "languages," two semantic and axiological belief systems. We repeat, there is no formal – compositional and syntactic – boundary between these utterances, styles, languages, belief systems; the division of voices and languages takes place within the limits of a single syntactic whole, often within the limits of a simple sentence. It frequently happens that even one and the same word will belong simultaneously to two languages, two belief systems that intersect in a hybrid construction – and, consequently, the word has two contradictory meanings, two accents (examples below). As we shall see, hybrid constructions are of enormous significance in novel style.

(4)

> But Mr. Tite Barnacle was a buttoned-up man, and *consequently* a weighty one. (Book
> 2, ch. 12)

The above sentence is an example of *pseudo-objective motivation*, one of the forms for concealing another's speech – in this example, the speech of "current opinion." If judged by the formal markers above, the logic motivating the sentence seems to belong to the author, i.e., he is formally at one with it; but in actual fact, the motivation lies within the subjective belief system of his characters, or of general opinion.

Pseudo-objective motivation is generally characteristic of novel style,[2] since it is one of the manifold forms for concealing another's speech in hybrid constructions. Subordinate conjunctions and link words ("thus," "because," "for the reason that," "in spite of" and so forth), as well as words used to maintain a logical sequence ("therefore," "consequently," etc.) lose their direct authorial intention, take on the flavor of someone else's language, become refracted or even completely reified.

Such motivation is especially characteristic of comic style, in which someone else's speech is dominant (the speech of concrete persons, or, more often, a collective voice).[3]

(5)

> As a vast fire will fill the air to a great distance with its roar, so the sacred flame which the mighty Barnacles had fanned caused the air to resound more and more with the name of Merdle. It was deposited on every lip, and carried into every ear. There never was, there never had been, there never again should be, such a man as Mr. Merdle. Nobody, as aforesaid, knew what he had done, but *everybody knew him to be the greatest that had appeared.* (Book 2, ch. 13)

Here we have an epic, "Homeric" introduction (parodic, of course) into whose frame the crowd's glorification of Merdle has been inserted (concealed speech of another in another's language). We then get direct authorial discourse; however, the author gives an objective tone to this "aside" by suggesting that "everybody knew" (the italicized portion). It is as if even the author himself did not doubt the fact....

Heteroglossia, once incorporated into the novel (whatever the forms for its incorporation), *is another's speech in another's language*, serving to express authorial intentions but in a refracted way. Such speech constitutes a special type of *double-voiced discourse* ...

From this follows the decisive and distinctive importance of the novel as a genre: the human being in the novel is first, foremost and always a speaking human being; the novel requires speaking persons bringing with them their own unique ideological discourse, their own language.

The fundamental condition, that which makes a novel a novel, that which is responsible for its stylistic uniqueness, is the *speaking person and his discourse*.

The topic of a speaking person has enormous importance in everyday life. In real life we hear speech about speakers and their discourse at every step. We can go so far as to say that in real life people talk most of all about what others talk about – they transmit, recall, weigh and pass judgment on other people's words, opinions, assertions, information; people are upset by others' words or agree with them, contest them, refer to them and so forth. Were we to eavesdrop on snatches of raw dialogue in the street, in a crowd, in lines, in a foyer and so forth, we would hear how often the words "he says," "people say," "he said ..." are repeated, and in the conversational hurly-burly of people in a crowd, everything often fuses into one big "he says ... you say ... I say ..." Reflect how enormous is the weight of "everyone says" and "it is said" in public opinion, public rumor, gossip, slander and so forth. One must also consider the psychological importance in our lives of what others say about us, and the importance, for us, of understanding and interpreting these words of others ("living hermeneutics").

The importance of this motif is in no way diminished in the higher and better-organized areas of everyday communication. Every conversation is full of transmissions and interpretations of other people's words. At every step one meets a "quotation" or a "reference" to something that a particular person said, a reference to "people say" or "everyone says," to the words of the person one is talking with, or to one's own previous words, to a newspaper, an official decree, a document, a book and so forth. The majority of our information and opinions is usually not communicated in direct form as our own, but with reference to some indefinite and general source: "I heard," "It's generally held that...," "It is thought that..." and so forth. Take one of the most widespread occurrences in our everyday life, conversations about some official meeting: they are all constructed on the transmission, interpretation and evaluation of various kinds of verbal performance resolutions, the rejected and accepted corrections that are made to them and so forth. Thus talk goes on about speaking people and their words everywhere – this motif returns again and again; it either accompanies the development of the other topics in everyday life, or directly governs speech as its leading theme...

The topic of a speaking person takes on quite another significance in the ordinary ideological workings of our consciousness, in the process of assimilating our consciousness to the ideological world. The ideological becoming of a human being, in this view, is the process of selectively assimilating the words of others.

When verbal disciplines are taught in school, two basic modes are recognized for the appropriation and transmission – simultaneously – of another's words (a text, a rule, a model): "reciting by heart" and "retelling in one's own words." The latter mode poses on a small scale the task implicit in all prose stylistics: retelling a text in one's own words is to a certain extent a double-voiced narration of another's words, for indeed "one's own words" must not completely dilute the quality that makes another's words unique; a retelling in one's own words should have a mixed character, able when necessary to reproduce the style and expressions of the transmitted text. It is this second mode used in schools for transmitting another's discourse, "retelling in one's own words," that includes within it an entire series of forms for the appropriation while transmitting of another's words, depending upon the character of the text being appropriated and the pedagogical environment in which it is understood and evaluated.

The tendency to assimilate others' discourse takes on an even deeper and more basic significance in an individual's ideological becoming, in the most fundamental sense. Another's discourse performs here no longer as information, directions, rules, models and so forth – but strives rather to determine the very bases of our ideological interrelations with the world, the very basis of our behavior; it performs here as *authoritative discourse*, and an *internally persuasive discourse*.

Both the authority of discourse and its internal persuasiveness may be united in a single word – one that is *simultaneously* authoritative and internally persuasive – despite the profound differences between these two categories of alien discourse. But such unity is rarely a given – it happens more frequently that an individual's becoming, an ideological process, is characterized precisely by a sharp gap between these two categories: in one, the authoritative word (religious, political, moral; the

word of a father, of adults and of teachers, etc.) that does not know internal persuasiveness, in the other internally persuasive word that is denied all privilege, backed
up by no authority at all, and is frequently not even acknowledged in society (not
by public opinion, nor by scholarly norms, nor by criticism), not even in the legal
code. The struggle and dialogic interrelationship of these categories of ideological
discourse are what usually determine the history of an individual ideological
consciousness.

The authoritative word demands that we acknowledge it, that we make it our own;
it binds us, quite independent of any power it might have to persuade us internally;
we encounter it with its authority already fused to it. The authoritative word is
located in a distanced zone, organically connected with a past that is felt to be
hierarchically higher. It is, so to speak, the word of the fathers. Its authority was
already *acknowledged* in the past. It is a *prior* discourse. It is therefore not a question
of choosing it from among other possible discourses that are its equal. It is given (it
sounds) in lofty spheres, not those of familiar contact. Its language is a special (as it
were, hieratic) language. It can be profaned. It is akin to taboo, i.e., a name that must
not be taken in vain.

We cannot embark here on a survey of the many and varied types of authoritative
discourse (for example, the authority of religious dogma, or of acknowledged scientific truth or of a currently fashionable book), nor can we survey different degrees of
authoritativeness. For our purposes only formal features for the transmission and
representation of authoritative discourse are important, those common to all types
and degrees of such discourse.

The degree to which a word may be conjoined with authority – whether the
authority is recognized by us or not – is what determines its specific demarcation
and individuation in discourse; it requires a *distance vis-à-vis* itself (this distance may
be valorized as positive or as negative, just as our attitude toward it may be sympathetic or hostile). Authoritative discourse may organize around itself great masses of
other types of discourses (which interpret it, praise it, apply it in various ways), but
the authoritative discourse itself does not merge with these (by means of, say, gradual
transitions); it remains sharply demarcated, compact and inert: it demands, so to
speak, not only quotation marks but a demarcation even more magisterial, a special
script, for instance.[4] It is considerably more difficult to incorporate semantic changes
into such a discourse, even with the help of a framing context: its semantic structure
is static and dead, for it is fully complete, it has but a single meaning, the letter is
fully sufficient to the sense and calcifies it.

It is not a free appropriation and assimilation of the word itself that authoritative
discourse seeks to elicit from us; rather, it demands our unconditional allegiance.
Therefore authoritative discourse permits no play with the context framing it, no
play with its borders, no gradual and flexible transitions, no spontaneously creative
stylizing variants on it. It enters our verbal consciousness as a compact and indivisible mass; one must either totally affirm it, or totally reject it. It is indissolubly fused
with its authority – with political power, an institution, a person – and it stands and
falls together with that authority. One cannot divide it up – agree with one part,
accept but not completely another part, reject utterly a third part. Therefore the
distance we ourselves observe *vis-à-vis* this authoritative discourse remains unchanged in all its projections: a playing with distances, with fusion and dissolution,
with approach and retreat, is not here possible.

All these functions determine the uniqueness of authoritative discourse, both as a concrete means for formulating itself during transmission and as its distinctive means for being framed by contexts. The zone of the framing context must likewise be distanced – no familiar contact is possible here either. The one perceiving and under-standing this discourse is a distant descendant; there can be no arguing with him.

These factors also determine the potential role of authoritative discourse in prose. Authoritative discourse cannot be represented – it is only transmitted. Its inertia, its semantic finiteness and calcification, the degree to which it is hard-edged, a thing in its own right, the impermissibility of any free stylistic development in relation to it – all this renders the artistic representation of authoritative discourse impossible. Its role in the novel is insignificant. It is by its very nature incapable of being double-voiced; it cannot enter into hybrid constructions. If completely deprived of its au-thority it becomes simply an object, a *relic*, a *thing*. It enters the artistic context as an alien body, there is no space around it to play in, no contradictory emotions – it is not surrounded by an agitated and cacophonous dialogic life, and the context around it dies, words dry up. For this reason images of official-authoritative truth, images of virtue of any sort: monastic, spiritual, bureaucratic, moral, etc., have never been successful in the novel. It suffices to mention the hopeless attempts of Gogol and Dostoevsky in this regard. For this reason the authoritative text always remains, in the novel, a dead quotation, something that falls out of the artistic context (for example, the evangelical texts in Tolstoy at the end of *Resurrection*).[5]

Authoritative discourses may embody various contents: authority as such, or the authoritativeness of tradition, of generally acknowledged truths, of the official line and other similar authorities. These discourses may have a variety of zones (deter-mined by the degree to which they are distanced from the zone of contact) with a variety of relations to the presumed listener or interpreter (the apperceptive back-ground presumed by the discourse, the degree of reciprocation between the two and so forth).

In the history of literary language, there is a struggle constantly being waged to overcome the official line with its tendency to distance itself from the zone of contact, a struggle against various kinds and degrees of authority. In this process discourse gets drawn into the contact zone, which results in semantic and emotionally expressive (intonational) changes: there is a weakening and degradation of the cap-acity to generate metaphors, and discourse becomes more reified, more concrete, more filled with everyday elements and so forth. All of this has been studied by psychology, but not from the point of view of its verbal formulation in possible inner monologues of developing human beings, the monologue that lasts a whole life. What confronts us is the complex problem presented by forms capable of expressing such a (dialogized) monologue.

When someone else's ideological discourse is internally persuasive for us and acknowledged by us, entirely different possibilities open up. Such discourse is of decisive significance in the evolution of an individual consciousness: consciousness awakens to independent ideological life precisely in a world of alien discourses sur-rounding it, and from which it cannot initially separate itself; the process of distin-guishing between one's own and another's discourse, between one's own and another's thought, is activated rather late in development. When thought begins to work in an independent, experimenting and discriminating way, what first occurs is a separation between internally persuasive discourse and authoritarian enforced discourse, along with a rejection of those congeries of discourses that do not matter to us, that do not touch us.

Internally persuasive discourse – as opposed to one that is externally authoritative – is, as it is affirmed through assimilation, tightly interwoven with "one's own word."[6] In the everyday rounds of our consciousness, the internally persuasive word is half-ours and half-someone else's. Its creativity and productiveness consist precisely in the fact that such a word awakens new and independent words, that it organizes masses of our words from within, and does not remain in an isolated and static condition. It is not so much interpreted by us as it is further, that is, freely, developed, applied to new material, new conditions; it enters into interanimating relationships with new contexts. More than that, it enters into an intense interaction, a *struggle* with other internally persuasive discourses. Our ideological development is just such an intense struggle within us for hegemony among various available verbal and ideological points of view, approaches, directions and values. The semantic structure of an internally persuasive discourse is *not finite*, it is *open*; in each of the new contexts that dialogize it, this discourse is able to reveal ever newer *ways to mean*.

Notes

1 We are of course deliberately simplifying: the real-life peasant could and did do this to a certain extent.
2 Such a device is unthinkable in the epic.
3 Cf. the grotesque pseudo-objective motivations in Gogol.
4 Often the authoritative word is in fact a word spoken by another in a foreign language (cf. for example the phenomenon of foreign-language religious texts in most cultures).
5 When analyzing a concrete example of authoritative discourse in a novel, it is necessary to keep in mind the fact that purely authoritative discourse may, in another epoch, be internally persuasive; this is especially true where ethics are concerned.
6 One's own discourse is gradually and slowly wrought out of others' words that have been acknowledged and assimilated, and the boundaries between the two are at first scarcely perceptible.

CHAPTER 9

Rabelais and His World

Mikhail Bakhtin

Bakhtin's study of Rabelais (1965) transformed what might have been another obscure academic monograph regarding a writer more known for his scatological novels than for his philosophical significance into a philosophical meditation on the nature of social power and the cultural significance of rhetorical forms.

Carnival is the people's second life, organized on the basis of laughter. It is a festive life. Festivity is a peculiar quality of all comic rituals and spectacles of the Middle Ages.

All these forms of carnival were also linked externally to the feasts of the Church...

The official feasts of the Middle Ages, whether ecclesiastic, feudal, or sponsored by the state, did not lead the people out of the existing world order and created no second life. On the contrary, they sanctioned the existing pattern of things and reinforced it. The link with time became formal; changes and moments of crisis were relegated to the past. Actually, the official feast looked back at the past and used the past to consecrate the present. Unlike the earlier and purer feast, the official feast asserted all that was stable, unchanging, perennial: the existing hierarchy, the existing religious, political, and moral values, norms, and prohibitions. It was the triumph of a truth already established, the predominant truth that was put forward as eternal and indisputable. This is why the tone of the official feast was monolithically serious and why the element of laughter was alien to it. The true nature of human festivity was betrayed and distorted. But this true festive character was indestructible; it had to be tolerated and even legalized outside the official sphere and had to be turned over to the popular sphere of the marketplace.

As opposed to the official feast, one might say that carnival celebrated temporary liberation from the prevailing truth and from the established order; it marked the suspension of all hierarchical rank, privileges, norms, and prohibitions. Carnival was the true feast of time, the feast of becoming, change, and renewal. It was hostile to all that was immortalized and completed.

The suspension of all hierarchical precedence during carnival time was of particular significance. Rank was especially evident during official feasts; everyone was expected to appear in the full regalia of his calling, rank, and merits and to take the place corresponding to his position. It was a consecration of inequality. On the contrary, all were considered equal during carnival. Here, in the town square, a special form of free and familiar contact reigned among people who were usually divided by the barriers of caste, property, profession, and age. The hierarchical background and the extreme corporative and caste divisions of the medieval social order were exceptionally strong. Therefore such free, familiar contacts were deeply felt and formed an essential element of the carnival spirit. People were, so to speak, reborn for new, purely human relations. These truly human relations were not only a fruit of imagination or abstract thought; they were experienced. The utopian ideal and the realistic merged in this carnival experience, unique of its kind.

This temporary suspension, both ideal and real, of hierarchical rank created during carnival time a special type of communication impossible in everyday life. This led to the creation of special forms of marketplace speech and gesture, frank and free, permitting no distance between those who came in contact with each other and liberating from norms of etiquette and decency imposed at other times. A special carnivalesque, marketplace style of expression was formed which we find abundantly represented in Rabelais' novel [*Pantagruel*].

During the century-long development of the medieval carnival, prepared by thousands of years of ancient comic ritual, including the primitive Saturnalias, a special idiom of forms and symbols was evolved – an extremely rich idiom that expressed the unique yet complex carnival experience of the people. This experience, opposed to all that was ready-made and completed, to all pretense at immutability, sought a dynamic expression; it demanded ever changing, playful, undefined forms. All the symbols of the carnival idiom are filled with this pathos of change and renewal, with the sense of the gay relativity of prevailing truths and authorities. We find here a characteristic logic, the peculiar logic of the "inside out" (*à l'envers*), of the "turn-about," of a continual shifting from top to bottom, from front to rear, of numerous parodies and travesties, humiliations, profanations, comic crownings and uncrownings. A second life, a second world of folk culture is thus constructed; it is to a certain extent a parody of the extracarnival life, a "world inside out." We must stress, however, that the carnival is far distant from the negative and formal parody of modern times. Folk humor denies, but it revives and renews at the same time. Bare negation is completely alien to folk culture.

Our introduction has merely touched upon the exceptionally rich and original idiom of carnival forms and symbols. The principal aim of the present work is to understand this half-forgotten idiom, in so many ways obscure to us. For it is precisely this idiom which was used by Rabelais, and without it we would fail to understand Rabelais' system of images...

It is usually pointed out that in Rabelais' work the material bodily principle, that is, images of the human body with its food, drink, defecation, and sexual life, plays a predominant role. Images of the body are offered, moreover, in an extremely exaggerated form...

The images of the material bodily principle in the work of Rabelais (and of the other writers of the Renaissance) are the heritage, only somewhat modified by the Renaissance, of the culture of folk humor. They are the heritage of that peculiar type of imagery and, more broadly speaking, of that peculiar aesthetic concept which is characteristic of this folk culture and which differs sharply from the aesthetic concept of the following ages. We shall call it conditionally the concept of grotesque realism.

The material bodily principle in grotesque realism is offered in its all-popular festive and utopian aspect. The cosmic, social, and bodily elements are given here as an indivisible whole. And this whole is gay and gracious.

In grotesque realism, therefore, the bodily element is deeply positive. It is presented not in a private, egotistic form, severed from the other spheres of life, but as something universal, representing all the people. As such it is opposed to severance from the material and bodily roots of the world; it makes no pretense to renunciation of the earthy, or independence of the earth and the body. We repeat: the body and bodily life have here a cosmic and at the same time an all-people's character; this is not the body and its physiology in the modern sense of these words, because it is not individualized. The material bodily principle is contained not in the biological individual, not in the bourgeois ego, but in the people, a people who are continually growing and renewed. This is why all that is bodily becomes grandiose, exaggerated, immeasurable.

This exaggeration has a positive, assertive character. The leading themes of these images of bodily life are fertility, growth, and a brimming-over abundance. Manifestations of this life refer not to the isolated biological individual, not to the private, egotistic "economic man," but to the collective ancestral body of all the people. Abundance and the all-people's element also determine the gay and festive character of all images of bodily life; they do not reflect the drabness of everyday existence. The material bodily principle is a triumphant, festive principle, it is a "banquet for all the world."[1] This character is preserved to a considerable degree in Renaissance literature, and most fully, of course, in Rabelais.

The essential principle of grotesque realism is degradation, that is, the lowering of all that is high, spiritual, ideal, abstract; it is a transfer to the material level, to the sphere of earth and body in their indissoluble unity...

Not only parody in its narrow sense but all the other forms of grotesque realism degrade, bring down to earth, turn their subject into flesh. This is the peculiar trait of this genre which differentiates it from all the forms of medieval high art and literature. The people's laughter which characterized all the forms of grotesque realism from immemorial times was linked with the bodily lower stratum. Laughter degrades and materializes...

Degradation here means coming down to earth, the contact with earth as an element that swallows up and gives birth at the same time. To degrade is to bury, to sow, and to kill simultaneously, in order to bring forth something more and better. To degrade also means to concern oneself with the lower stratum of the body, the life of the belly and the reproductive organs; it therefore relates to acts of defecation and copulation, conception, pregnancy, and birth. Degradation digs a bodily grave for a new birth; it has not only a destructive, negative aspect, but also a regenerating one. To degrade an object does not imply merely hurling it into the void of non-existence, into absolute destruction, but to hurl it down to the reproductive lower stratum, the zone in which conception and a new birth take place. Grotesque realism knows no other lower level; it is the fruitful earth and the womb. It is always conceiving.

This is the reason why medieval parody is unique, quite unlike the purely formalist literary parody of modern times, which has a solely negative character and is deprived of regenerating ambivalence...

In the age of Rabelais abuses and curses still retained their full meaning in the popular language from which his novel sprang, and above all they retained their positive, regenerating pole. They were closely related to all the forms of degradation inherited from grotesque realism; they belonged to the popular-festive travesties of carnival, to the images of the diableries, of the underworld, of the *soties*. This is why abusive language played an important part in Rabelais' novel...

The marketplace of the Middle Ages and the Renaissance was a world in itself, a world which was one; all "performances" in this area, from loud cursing to the organized show, had something in common and were imbued with the same atmosphere of freedom, frankness, and familiarity. Such elements of familiar speech as profanities, oaths, and curses were fully legalized in the marketplace and were easily adopted by all the festive genres, even by Church drama. The marketplace was the center of all that is unofficial; it enjoyed a certain extraterritoriality in a world of official order and official ideology, it always remained "with the people."

This popular aspect was especially apparent on feast days...

In the marketplace a special kind of speech was heard, almost a language of its own, quite unlike the language of Church, palace, courts, and institutions. It was also unlike the tongue of official literature or of the ruling classes – the aristocracy, the nobles, the high-ranking clergy and the top burghers – though the elemental force of the folk idiom penetrated even these circles. On feast days, especially during the carnivals, this force broke through every sphere, and even through the Church, as in "the feast of fools." The festive marketplace combined many genres and forms, all filled with the same unofficial spirit.

In all world literature there is probably no other work reflecting so fully and deeply all aspects of the life of the marketplace as does Rabelais' novel...

Rabelais was familiar with the marketplace and fairs of his time. As we shall see, he made good use of his experience and projected it forcefully in his novel...

How is the prologue of *Pantagruel* constructed? It begins thus:

> O most illustrious and most valorous champions, gentlemen and all others who delight in honest entertainment and wit. I address this book to you. You have read and digested the *Mighty and Inestimable Chronicles of the Huge Giant Gargantua*. Like true believers you have taken them upon faith as you do the texts of the Holy Gospel. Indeed, having run out of gallant speeches, you have often spent hours at a time relating lengthy stories culled from these *Chronicles* to a rapt audience of noble dames and matrons of high degree. On this count, then, you deserve vast praise and sempiternal memory. (Book 2, Prologue)

Here we see combined the praise of the "Chronicles of Gargantua" and of the readers who enjoy this chapbook. The praise and glorification are composed in the advertising spirit of the barker at a show or the hawker of chapbooks, who praise not only their wondrous merchandise but also the "most illustrious" public. This is a typical example of the tone and style of the fair...

The prologue ends in a torrent of abuses and curses hurled at the author if there is a single lie in his book, as well as at those who do not believe him:

> However, before I conclude this prologue, I hereby deliver myself up body and soul, belly and bowels, to a hundred thousand basketfuls of raving demons, if I have lied so much as once throughout this book. By the same token, may St. Anthony sear you with his erysipelatous fire...may Mahomet's disease whirl you in epileptic jitters... may the festers, ulcers and chancres of every purulent pox infect, scathe, mangle and rend you, entering your bumgut as tenuously as mercuralized cow's hair...and may you vanish into an abyss of brimstone and fire, like Sodom and Gomorrah, if you do not believe implicitly what I am about to relate in the present *Chronicles*...(Book 2, Prologue)

These are typical Billingsgate abuses. The passing from excessive praise to excessive invective is characteristic, and the change from the one to the other is perfectly legitimate. Praise and abuse are, so to speak, the two sides of the same coin. If the right side is praise, the wrong side is abuse, and vice versa. The Billingsgate idiom is a two-faced Janus. The praise, as we have said, is ironic and ambivalent. It is on the brink of abuse; the one leads to the other, and it is impossible to draw the line between them. Though divided in form they belong to the same body, or to the two bodies in one, which abuses while praising and praises while abusing. This is why in familiar Billingsgate talk abusive words, especially indecent ones, are used in the affectionate and complimentary sense. (We shall further analyze many examples from Rabelais.) This grotesque language, particularly in its oldest form, was oriented toward the world and toward all the world's phenomena in their condition of unfinished metamorphosis: the passing from night to morning, from winter to spring, from the old to the new, from death to birth. Therefore, this talk showers both compliments and curses...

It is based on the conception of the world as eternally unfinished: a world dying and being born at the same time, possessing as it were two bodies. The dual image combining praise and abuse seeks to grasp the very moment of this change, the transfer from the old to the new, from death to life. Such an image crowns and uncrowns at the same moment. In the development of class society such a conception of the world can only be expressed in unofficial culture. There is no place for it in the culture of the ruling classes; here praise and abuse are clearly divided and static, for official culture is founded on the principle of an immovable and unchanging hierarchy in which the higher and the lower never merge...

Such is the structure of *Pantagruel*'s prologue. It is written from beginning to end in the style and tone of the marketplace. We hear the cry of the barker, the quack, the hawker of miracle drugs, and the bookseller; we hear the curses that alternate with ironic advertisements and ambiguous praise. The prologue is organized according to the popular verbal genres of hawkers. The words are actually a cry, that is, a loud interjection in the midst of a crowd, coming out of the crowd and addressed to it. The man who is speaking is one with the crowd; he does not present himself as its opponent, nor does he teach, accuse, or intimidate it. He *laughs* with it. There is not the slightest tone of morose seriousness in his oration, no fear, piety, or humility. This is an absolutely gay and fearless talk, free and frank, which echoes in the festive square beyond all verbal prohibitions, limitations, and conventions.

At the same time, however, this entire prologue is a parody and travesty of the ecclesiastical method of persuasion. Behind the "Chronicles" stands the Gospel; behind the offer of the "Chronicles" as the only book of salvation stands the exclusiveness of the Church's truth; behind the abuses and curses are the Church's intolerance, intimidation, and *autos-da-fé*. The ecclesiastical policy is translated into the language of ironical hawking. But the prologue is wider and deeper than the usual grotesque parody. It travesties the very foundations of medieval thought, the methods of establishing truth and conviction which are inseparable from fear, violence, morose and narrow-minded seriousness and intolerance. The prologue introduces us into a completely different atmosphere, the atmosphere of fearless, free, and gay truth...

This debasement of suffering and fear is an important element in the general system of degradation directed at medieval seriousness. Indeed all Rabelais' prologues are devoted to this theme. We saw that the prologue of *Pantagruel* is a travesty that transposes the medieval conception of the only salutary truth into the flippant language of advertising. The prologue of *Gargantua* debases the "hidden meaning," the "secret," the "terrifying mysteries" of religion, politics, and economics. Degradation is achieved by transforming these mysteries into festive scenes of eating and drinking. Laughter must liberate the gay truth of the world from the veils of gloomy lies spun by the seriousness of fear, suffering, and violence...

It would be a mistake to think that the Rabelaisian debasement of fear and suffering was prompted by coarse cynicism. We must not forget that the image of defecation, like all the images of the lower stratum, is ambivalent and that the element of reproductive force, birth, and renewal is alive in it. We have already sought to prove this, and we find here further substantiation. Speaking of the masochism of the gloomy slanderers, Rabelais also mentions sexual stimulus together with defecation.

At the end of the Fourth Book Panurge, who defecated from fear and was mocked by his companions, finally rids himself of his terror and regains his cheerfulness. He exclaims:

> Oh, ho, ho, ho, ho! What the devil is this? Do you call this ordure, ejection, excrement, evacuation, *dejecta*, fecal matter, *egesta, copros, scatos*, dung, crap, turds? Not at all, not at all: it is but the fruit of the shittim tree, 'Selah! Let us drink.' (Book 4, Chapter 67)

These are the last words of the Fourth Book, and actually the last sentence of the entire book that was written by Rabelais' own hand. Here we find twelve synonyms for excrement, from the most vulgar to the most scientific. At the end it is described as a tree, something rare and pleasant. And the tirade concludes with an invitation to drink, which in Rabelaisian imagery means to be in communion with truth.

Here we find the ambivalent image of excrement, its relation to regeneration and renewal and its special role in overcoming fear. Excrement is gay matter; in the ancient scatological images, as we have said, it is linked to the generating force and to fertility. On the other hand, excrement is conceived as something *intermediate between earth and body*, as something relating the one to the other. It is also an intermediate between the living body and dead disintegrating matter that is being transformed into earth, into manure. The living body returns to the earth its excrement, which fertilizes the earth as does the body of the dead. Rabelais was able to distinguish these nuances clearly. As we shall see further, they were not alien to his medical views. Moreover, as an artist and an heir to grotesque realism, he conceived excrement as both joyous and sobering matter, at the same time debasing and tender; it combined the grave and birth in their lightest, most comic, least terrifying form.

Therefore, there is nothing grossly cynical in Rabelais' scatological images, nor in the other images of grotesque realism: the slinging of dung, the drenching in urine, the volley of scatological abuse hurled at the old, dying, yet generating world. All these images represent the gay funeral of this old world; they are (in the dimension of laughter) like handfuls of sod gently dropped into the open grave, like seeds sown in the earth's bosom. If the image is applied to the gloomy, disincarnated medieval truth, it symbolizes bringing it "down to earth" through laughter.

All this should not be forgotten in the analysis of the scatological images that abound in Rabelais' novel.

Note

1 A popular Russian expression in old tales and epics to describe a great banquet, usually the happy ending of the story. [Trans.]

CHAPTER 10

Ideology and Ideological State Apparatuses

Louis Althusser

Louis Althusser was the leading Structuralist Marxist philosopher in France in the 1960s. His books included *For Marx* (1965) and *Lenin and Philosophy* (1971). In this his most famous essay, published in 1968, he describes ideology, which traditionally had been characterized as a species of "false consciousness," as a set of practices and institutions that sustain an individual's imaginary relationship to his or her material conditions of existence.

Ideology is a "Representation" of the Imaginary Relationship of Individuals to their Real Conditions of Existence

In order to approach my central thesis on the structure and functioning of ideology, I shall first present two theses, one negative, the other positive. The first concerns the object which is "represented" in the imaginary form of ideology, the second concerns the materiality of ideology.

THESIS 1: Ideology represents the imaginary relationship of individuals to their real conditions of existence.

We commonly call religious ideology, ethical ideology, legal ideology, political ideology, etc., so many "world outlooks." Of course, assuming that we do not live one of these ideologies as the truth (e.g. "believe" in God, Duty, Justice, etc. . . .), we admit that the ideology we are discussing from a critical point of view, examining it as the ethnologist examines the myths of a "primitive society," that these "world outlooks" are largely imaginary, i.e. do not "correspond to reality."

However, while admitting that they do not correspond to reality, i.e. that they constitute an illusion, we admit that they do make allusion to reality, and that they need only be "interpreted" to discover the reality of the world behind their imaginary representation of that world (ideology = *illusion/allusion*).

There are different types of interpretation, the most famous of which are the *mechanistic* type, current in the eighteenth century (God is the imaginary representation of the real King), and the *"hermeneutic"* interpretation, inaugurated by the earliest Church Fathers, and revived by Feuerbach and the theologico-philosophical school which descends from him, e.g. the theologian Barth (to Feuerbach, for example, God is the essence of real Man). The essential point is that on condition that we interpret the imaginary transposition (and inversion) of ideology we arrive at the conclusion that in ideology "men represent their real conditions of existence to themselves in an imaginary form."

Unfortunately, this interpretation leaves one small problem unsettled: why do men "need" this imaginary transposition of their real conditions of existence in order to "represent to themselves" their real conditions of existence?

The first answer (that of the eighteenth century) proposes a simple solution: Priests or Despots are responsible. They "forged" the Beautiful Lies so that, in the belief that they were obeying God, men would in fact obey the Priests and Despots, who are usually in alliance in their imposture, the Priests acting in the interests of the Despots or *vice versa*, according to the political positions of the "theoreticians" concerned. There is therefore a cause for the imaginary transposition of the real conditions of existence: that cause is the existence of a small number of cynical men who base their domination and exploitation of the "people" on a falsified representation of the world which they have imagined in order to enslave other minds by dominating their imaginations.

The second answer (that of Feuerbach, taken over word for word by Marx in his *Early Works*) is more "profound," i.e. just as false. It, too, seeks and finds a cause for the imaginary transposition and distortion of men's real conditions of existence, in short, for the alienation in the imaginary of the representation of men's conditions of existence. This cause is no longer Priests or Despots, nor their active imagination and the passive imagination of their victims. This cause is the material alienation which reigns in the conditions of existence of men themselves. This is how, in *The Jewish Question* and elsewhere, Marx defends the Feuerbachian idea that men make themselves an alienated (= imaginary) representation of their conditions of existence because these conditions of existence are themselves alienating (in the *1844 Manuscripts*: because these conditions are dominated by the essence of alienated society – "*alienated labor*").

All these interpretations thus take literally the thesis which they presuppose, and on which they depend, i.e. that what is reflected in the imaginary representation of the world found in an ideology is the conditions of existence of men, i.e. their real world.

Now I can return to a thesis which I have already advanced: it is not their real conditions of existence, their real world, that "men" "represent to themselves" in ideology, but above all it is their relation to those conditions of existence which is represented to them there. It is this relation which is at the center of every ideological, i.e. imaginary, representation of the real world. It is this relation that contains the "cause" which has to explain the imaginary distortion of the ideological representation of the real world. Or rather, to leave aside the language of causality, it is necessary to advance the thesis that it is the *imaginary nature of this relation* which underlies all the imaginary distortion that we can observe (if we do not live in its truth) in all ideology.

To speak in a Marxist language, if it is true that the representation of the real conditions of existence of the individuals occupying the posts of agents of production, exploitation, repression, ideologization and scientific practice, does in the last analysis arise from the relations of production, and from relations deriving from the relations of production, we can say the following: all ideology represents in its necessarily imaginary distortion not the existing relations of production (and the other relations that derive from them), but above all the (imaginary) relationship of individuals to the relations of production and the relations that derive from them. What is represented in ideology is therefore not the system of the real relations which govern the existence of individuals, but the imaginary relation of those individuals to the real relations in which they live.

If this is the case, the question of the "cause" of the imaginary distortion of the real relations in ideology disappears and must be replaced by a different question: why is the representation given to individuals of their (individual) relation to the social relations which govern their conditions of existence and their collective and individual life necessarily an imaginary relation? And what is the nature of this imaginariness? Posed in this way, the question explodes the solution by a "clique,"[1] by a group of individuals (Priests or Despots) who are the authors of the great ideological mystification, just as it explodes the solution by the alienated character of the real world. We shall see why later in my exposition. For the moment I shall go no further.

THESIS II: Ideology has a material existence.

I have already touched on this thesis by saying that the "ideas" or "representations," etc., which seem to make up ideology do not have an ideal (*idéale* or *idéelle*) or spiritual existence, but a material existence. I even suggested that the ideal (*idéale*, *idéelle*) and spiritual existence of "ideas" arises exclusively in an ideology of the "idea" and of ideology, and let me add, in an ideology of what seems to have "founded" this conception since the emergence of the sciences, i.e. what the practicians of the sciences represent to themselves in their spontaneous ideology as "ideas," true or false. Of course, presented in affirmative form, this thesis is unproven. I simply ask that the reader be favorably disposed towards it, say, in the name of materialism. A long series of arguments would be necessary to prove it.

This hypothetical thesis of the not spiritual but material existence of "ideas" or other "representations" is indeed necessary if we are to advance in our analysis of the nature of ideology. Or rather, it is merely useful to us in order the better to reveal what every at all serious analysis of any ideology will immediately and empirically show to every observer, however critical.

While discussing the ideological State apparatuses and their practices, I said that each of them was the realization of an ideology (the unity of these different regional ideologies – religious, ethical, legal, political, aesthetic, etc. being assured by their subjection to the ruling ideology). I now return to this thesis: an ideology always exists in an apparatus, and its practice, or practices. This existence is material.

Of course, the material existence of the ideology in an apparatus and its practices does not have the same modality as the material existence of a paving-stone or a rifle. But, at the risk of being taken for a Neo-Aristotelian (NB Marx had a very high regard for Aristotle), I shall say that "matter is discussed in many senses," or rather that it exists in different modalities, all rooted in the last instance in "physical" matter.

Having said this, let me move straight on and see what happens to the "individuals" who live in ideology, i.e. in a determinate (religious, ethical, etc.) representation of the world whose imaginary distortion depends on their imaginary relation to their conditions of existence, in other words, in the last instance, to the relations of production and to class relations (ideology = an imaginary relation to real relations). I shall say that this imaginary relation is itself endowed with a material existence.

Now I observe the following.

An individual believes in God, or Duty, or Justice, etc. This belief derives (for everyone, i.e. for all those who live in an ideological representation of ideology, which reduces ideology to ideas endowed by definition with a spiritual existence) from the ideas of the individual concerned, i.e. from him as a subject with a consciousness which contains the ideas of his belief. In this way, i.e. by means of the absolutely ideological "conceptual" device (*dispositif*) thus set up (a subject endowed with a consciousness in which he freely forms or freely recognizes ideas in which he believes), the (material) attitude of the subject concerned naturally follows.

The individual in question behaves in such and such a way, adopts such and such a practical attitude, and, what is more, participates in certain regular practices which are those of the ideological apparatus on which "depend" the ideas which he has in all consciousness freely chosen as a subject. If he believes in God, he goes to Church to attend Mass, kneels, prays, confesses, does penance (once it was material in the ordinary sense of the term) and naturally repents and so on. If he believes in Duty, he will have the corresponding attitudes, inscribed in ritual practices "according to the correct principles." If he believes in Justice, he will submit unconditionally to the rules of the Law, and may even protest when they are violated, sign petitions, take part in a demonstration, etc.

Throughout this schema we observe that the ideological representation of ideology is itself forced to recognize that every "subject" endowed with a "consciousness" and believing in the "ideas" that his "consciousness" inspires in him and freely accepts, must "*act* according to his ideas," must therefore inscribe his own ideas as a free subject in the actions of his material practice. If he does not do so, "that is wicked."

Indeed, if he does not do what he ought to do as a function of what he believes, it is because he does something else, which, still as a function of the same idealist scheme, implies that he has other ideas in his head as well as those he proclaims, and that he acts according to these other ideas, as a man who is either "inconsistent" ("no one is willingly evil") or cynical, or perverse.

In every case, the ideology of ideology thus recognizes, despite its imaginary distortion, that the "ideas" of a human subject exist in his actions, or ought to exist in his actions, and if that is not the case, it lends him other ideas corresponding to the actions (however perverse) that he does perform. This ideology talks of actions: I shall talk of actions inserted into *practices*. And I shall point out that these practices are governed by the *rituals* in which these practices are inscribed, within the *material existence of an ideological apparatus*, be it only a small part of that apparatus: a small mass in a small church, a funeral, a minor match at a sports club, a school day, a political party meeting, etc.

Besides, we are indebted to Pascal's defensive "dialectic" for the wonderful formula which will enable us to invert the order of the notional schema of ideology. Pascal says more or less: "Kneel down, move your lips in prayer, and you will believe." He thus scandalously inverts the order of things, bringing, like Christ, not peace but strife, and in addition something hardly Christian (for woe to him who brings scandal into the world!) – scandal itself. A fortunate scandal which makes him stick with Jansenist defiance to a language that directly names the reality.

I will be allowed to leave Pascal to the arguments of his ideological struggle with the religious ideological State apparatus of his day. And I shall be expected to use a more directly Marxist vocabulary, if that is possible, for we are advancing in still poorly explored domains.

I shall therefore say that, where only a single subject (such and such an individual) is concerned, the existence of the ideas of his belief is material in that *his ideas are his material actions inserted into material practices governed by material rituals which are themselves defined by the material ideological apparatus from which derive the ideas of that subject.* Naturally, the four inscriptions of the adjective "material" in my proposition must be affected by different modalities: the materialities of a displacement for going to mass, of kneeling down, of the gesture of the sign of the cross, or of the *mea culpa*, of a sentence, of a prayer, of an act of contrition, of a penitence, of a gaze, of a hand-shake, of an external verbal discourse or an "internal" verbal discourse (consciousness), are not one and the same materiality. I shall leave on one side the problem of a theory of the differences between the modalities of materiality.

It remains that in this inverted presentation of things, we are not dealing with an "inversion" at all, since it is clear that certain notions have purely and simply disappeared from our presentation, whereas others on the contrary survive, and new terms appear.

Disappeared: the term *ideas*.
Survive: the terms *subject, consciousness, belief, actions*.
Appear: the terms *practices, rituals, ideological apparatus*.

It is therefore not an inversion or overturning (except in the sense in which one might say a government or a glass is overturned), but a reshuffle (of a non-ministerial type), a rather strange reshuffle, since we obtain the following result.

Ideas have disappeared as such (insofar as they are endowed with an ideal or spiritual existence), to the precise extent that it has emerged that their existence is inscribed in the actions of practices governed by rituals defined in the last instance by an ideological apparatus. It therefore appears that the subject acts insofar as he is acted by the following system (set out in the order of its real determination): ideology existing in a material ideological apparatus, prescribing material practices governed by a material ritual, which practices exist in the material actions of a subject acting in all consciousness according to his belief.

But this very presentation reveals that we have retained the following notions: subject, consciousness, belief, actions. From this series I shall immediately extract the decisive central term on which everything else depends: the notion of the *subject*.

And I shall immediately set down two conjoint theses:

1 there is no practice except by and in an ideology;
2 there is no ideology except by the subject and for subjects.

I can now come to my central thesis.

Ideology Interpellates Individuals as Subjects

This thesis is simply a matter of making my last proposition explicit: there is no ideology except by the subject and for subjects. Meaning, there is no ideology except for concrete subjects, and this destination for ideology is only made possible by the subject: meaning, *by the category of the subject* and its functioning.

By this I mean that, even if it only appears under this name (the subject) with the rise of bourgeois ideology, above all with the rise of legal ideology,[2] the category of the subject (which may function under other names: e.g., as the soul in Plato, as God, etc.) is the constitutive category of all ideology, whatever its determination (regional or class) and whatever its historical date – since ideology has no history.

I say: the category of the subject is constitutive of all ideology, but at the same time and immediately I add that *the category of the subject is only constitutive of all ideology insofar as all ideology has the function (which defines it) of "constituting" concrete individuals as subjects.* In the interaction of this double constitution exists the functioning of all ideology, ideology being nothing but its functioning in the material forms of existence of that functioning.

In order to grasp what follows, it is essential to realize that both he who is writing these lines and the reader who reads them are themselves subjects, and therefore ideological subjects (a tautological proposition), i.e. that the author and the reader of these lines both live "spontaneously" or "naturally" in ideology in the sense in which I have said that "man is an ideological animal by nature."

That the author, insofar as he writes the lines of a discourse which claims to be scientific, is completely absent as a "subject" from "his" scientific discourse (for all scientific discourse is by definition a subject-less discourse, there is no "Subject of science" except in an ideology of science) is a different question which I shall leave on one side for the moment.

As St Paul admirably put it, it is in the "Logos," meaning in ideology, that we "live, move and have our being." It follows that, for you and for me, the category of the subject is a primary "obviousness" (obviousnesses are always primary): it is clear that you and I are subjects (free, ethical, etc. . . .). Like all obviousnesses, including those that make a word "name a thing" or "have a meaning" (therefore including the obviousness of the "transparency" of language), the "obviousness" that you and I are subjects – and that that does not cause any problems – is an ideological effect, the elementary ideological effect.[3] It is indeed a peculiarity of ideology that it imposes (without appearing to do so, since these are "obviousnesses") obviousnesses as obviousnesses, which we cannot *fail to recognize* and before which we have the inevitable and natural reaction of crying out (aloud or in the "still, small voice of conscience"): "That's obvious! That's right! That's true!"

At work in this reaction is the ideological function which is one of the two functions of ideology as such (its inverse being the function of *misrecognition – méconnaissance*).

To take a highly "concrete" example, we all have friends who, when they knock on our door and we ask, through the door, the question "Who's there?," answer (since "it's obvious") "It's me." And we recognize that "it is him," or "her." We open the door, and "it's true, it really was she who was there." To take another example, when we recognize somebody of our (previous) acquaintance ((*re*)- *connaissance*) in the street, we show him that we have recognized him (and have recognized that he has recognized us) by saying to him "Hello, my friend," and shaking his hand (a material ritual practice of ideological recognition in everyday life – in France, at least; elsewhere, there are other rituals).

In this preliminary remark and these concrete illustrations, I only wish to point out that you and I are *always already* subjects, and as such constantly practice the rituals of ideological recognition, which guarantee for us that we are indeed concrete, individual, distinguishable and (naturally) irreplaceable subjects. The writing I am currently executing and the reading you are currently[4] performing are also in this respect rituals of ideological recognition, including the "obviousness" with which the "truth" or "error" of my reflections may impose itself on you.

But to recognize that we are subjects and that we function in the practical rituals of the most elementary everyday life (the hand-shake, the fact of calling you by your name, the fact of knowing, even if I do not know what it is, that you "have" a name of your own, which means that you are recognized as a unique subject, etc.) – this recognition only gives us the "consciousness" of our incessant (eternal) practice of ideological recognition – its consciousness, i.e. its *recognition* – but in no sense does it give us the (scientific) *knowledge* of the mechanism of this recognition. Now it is this knowledge that we have to reach, if you will, while speaking in ideology, and from within ideology we have to outline a discourse which tries to break with ideology, in order to dare to be the beginning of a scientific (i.e. subjectless) discourse on ideology.

Thus in order to represent why the category of the "subject" is constitutive of ideology, which only exists by constituting concrete subjects as subjects, I shall employ a special mode of exposition: "concrete" enough to be recognized, but abstract enough to be thinkable and thought, giving rise to a knowledge.

As a first formulation I shall say: *all ideology hails or interpellates concrete individuals as concrete subjects*, by the functioning of the category of the subject.

This is a proposition which entails that we distinguish for the moment between concrete individuals on the one hand and concrete subjects on the other, although at this level concrete subjects only exist insofar as they are supported by a concrete individual.

I shall then suggest that ideology "acts" or "functions" in such a way that it "recruits" subjects among the individuals (it recruits them all), or "transforms" the individuals into subjects (it transforms them all) by that very precise operation which I have called *interpellation* or hailing, and which can be imagined along the lines of the most commonplace everyday police (or other) hailing: "Hey, you there!"[5]

Assuming that the theoretical scene I have imagined takes place in the street, the hailed individual will turn round. By this mere one-hundred-and-eighty-degree physical conversion, he becomes a *subject*. Why? Because he has recognized that the hail was "really" addressed to him, and that "it was *really him* who was hailed" (and not someone else). Experience shows that the practical telecommunication of hailings is such that they hardly ever miss their man: verbal call or whistle, the one hailed always recognizes that it is really him who is being hailed. And yet it is a strange phenomenon, and one which cannot be explained solely by "guilt feelings," despite the large numbers who "have something on their consciences."

Naturally for the convenience and clarity of my little theoretical theater I have had to present things in the form of a sequence, with a before and an after, and thus in the form of a temporal succession. There are individuals walking along. Somewhere (usually behind them) the hail rings out: "Hey, you there!" One individual (nine times out of ten it is the right one) turns round, believing/suspecting/knowing that it is for him, i.e. recognizing that "it really is he" who is meant by the hailing. But in reality these things happen without any succession. The existence of ideology and the hailing or interpellation of individuals as subjects are one and the same thing.

I might add: what thus seems to take place outside ideology (to be precise, in the street), in reality takes place in ideology. What really takes place in ideology seems therefore to take place outside it. That is why those who are in ideology believe themselves by definition outside ideology: one of the effects of ideology is the practical *denial* of the ideological character of ideology by ideology: ideology never says, "I am ideological." It is necessary to be outside ideology, i.e. in scientific knowledge, to be able to say: I am in ideology (a quite exceptional case) or (the general case): I was in ideology. As is well known, the accusation of being in ideology only applies to others, never to oneself (unless one is really a Spinozist or a Marxist, which, in this matter, is to be exactly the same thing). Which amounts to saying that ideology *has no outside* (for itself), but at the same time *that it is nothing but outside* (for science and reality).

Spinoza explained this completely two centuries before Marx, who practiced it but without explaining it in detail. But let us leave this point, although it is heavy with consequences, consequences which are not just theoretical, but also directly political, since, for example, the whole theory of criticism and self-criticism, the golden rule of the Marxist-Leninist practice of the class struggle, depends on it.

Thus ideology hails or interpellates individuals as subjects. As ideology is eternal, I must now suppress the temporal form in which I have presented the functioning of ideology, and say: ideology has always-already interpellated individuals as subjects; which amounts to making it clear that individuals are always-already interpellated by ideology as subjects, which necessarily leads us to one last proposition: *individuals are always-already subjects*. Hence individuals are "abstract" with respect to the subjects which they always-already are. This proposition might seem paradoxical.

That an individual is always-already a subject, even before he is born, is nevertheless the plain reality, accessible to everyone and not a paradox at all. Freud shows that individuals are always "abstract" with respect to the subjects they always-already are, simply noting the ideological ritual that surrounds the expectation of a "birth," that "happy event." Everyone knows how much and in what way an unborn child is expected. Which amounts to saying, very prosaically, if we agree to drop the "sentiments," i.e. the forms of family ideology (paternal/maternal/conjugal/fraternal) in which the unborn child is expected: it is certain in advance that it will bear its father's name, and will therefore have an identity and be irreplaceable. Before its birth, the child is therefore always-already a subject, appointed as a subject in and by the specific familial ideological configuration in which it is "expected" once it has been conceived. I hardly need add that this familial ideological configuration is, in its uniqueness, highly structured, and that it is in this implacable and more or less "pathological" (presupposing that any meaning can be assigned to that term) structure that the former subject-to-be will have to "find" "its" place, i.e., "become" the sexual subject (boy or girl) which it already is in advance. It is clear that this ideological constraint and pre-appointment, and all the rituals of rearing and then education in the family, have some relationship with what Freud studied in the forms of the pre-genital and genital "stages" of sexuality, i.e. in the "grip" of what Freud registered by its effects as being the unconscious. But let us leave this point, too, to one side. . . .

Let me summarize what we have discovered about ideology in general.
The duplicate mirror-structure of ideology ensures simultaneously:

1   the interpellation of "individuals" as subjects;
2   their subjection to the Subject;[6]
3   the mutual recognition of subjects and Subject, the subjects' recognition of each
    other, and finally the subject's recognition of himself;[7]
4   the absolute guarantee that everything really is so, and that on condition that the
    subjects recognize what they are and behave accordingly, everything will be all
    right: Amen – "*So be it.*"

Result: caught in this quadruple system of interpellation as subjects, of subjection to
the Subject, of universal recognition and of absolute guarantee, the subjects "work,"
they "work by themselves" in the vast majority of cases, with the exception of the
"bad subjects" who on occasion provoke the intervention of one of the detachments of
the (repressive) State apparatus. But the vast majority of (good) subjects work all right
"all by themselves," i.e. by ideology (whose concrete forms are realized in the Ideological State Apparatuses [ISAs]). They are inserted into practices governed by the
rituals of the ISAs. They "recognize" the existing state of affairs (*das Bestehende*), that
"it really is true that it is so and not otherwise," and that they must be obedient to
God, to their conscience, to the priest, to de Gaulle, to the boss, to the engineer, that
thou shalt "love thy neighbour as thyself," etc. Their concrete, material behavior is
simply the inscription in life of the admirable words of the prayer: "Amen – *So be it.*"

Yes, the subjects "work by themselves." The whole mystery of this effect lies in
the first two moments of the quadruple system I have just discussed, or, if you
prefer, in the ambiguity of the term *subject*. In the ordinary use of the term, subject
in fact means: (1) a free subjectivity, a center of initiatives, author of and responsible
for its actions; (2) a subjected being who submits to a higher authority, and is
therefore stripped of all freedom except that of freely accepting his submission. This
last note gives us the meaning of this ambiguity, which is merely a reflection of the
effect which produces it: the individual *is interpellated as a (free) subject in order that
he shall (freely) accept his subjection*, i.e. in order that he shall make the gestures and
actions of his subjection "all by himself." *There are no subjects except by and for their
subjection.* That is why they "work all by themselves."

"*So be it!*..." This phrase which registers the effect to be obtained proves that it
is not "naturally" so ("naturally": outside the prayer, i.e. outside the ideological
intervention). This phrase proves that it *has* to be so if things are to be what they
must be, and let us let the words slip: if the reproduction of the relations of production is to be assured, even in the processes of production and circulation, every day,
in the "consciousness," i.e. in the attitudes of the individual subjects occupying the
posts which the socio-technical division of labor assigns to them in production,
exploitation, repression, ideologization, scientific practice, etc. Indeed, what is really
in question in this mechanism of the mirror recognition of the Subject and of the
individuals interpellated as subjects, and of the guarantee given by the Subject to the
subjects if they freely accept their subjection to the Subject's "commandments"?
The reality in question in this mechanism, the reality which is necessarily *misrecognized* (*méconnue*) in the very forms of recognition (ideology = misrecognition/ignor-
ance) is indeed, in the last resort, the reproduction of the relations of production and
of the relations deriving from them.

Notes

1 I use this very modern term deliberately. For even in Communist circles, unfortunately, it is a commonplace to "explain" some political deviation (left or right opportunism) by the action of a "clique."

2 Which borrowed the legal category of "subject in law" to make an ideological notion: man is by nature a subject.

3 Linguists and those who appeal to linguistics for various purposes often run up against difficulties which arise because they ignore the action of the ideological effects in all discourses – including even scientific discourses.

4 NB: this double "currently" is one more proof of the fact that ideology is "eternal," since these two "currentlys" are separated by an indefinite interval; I am writing these lines on April 6, 1969, you may read them at any subsequent time.

5 Hailing as an everyday practice subject to a precise ritual takes a quite "special" form in the policeman's practice of "hailing," which concerns the hailing of "suspects."

6 By "Subject," Althusser means the deity. [Eds.]

7 Hegel is (unknowingly) an admirable "theoretician" of ideology insofar as he is a "theoretician" of Universal Recognition who unfortunately ends up in the ideology of Absolute Knowledge. Feuerbach is an astonishing "theoretician" of the mirror connexion, who unfortunately ends up in the ideology of the Human Essence. To find the material with which to construct a theory of the guarantee, we must turn to Spinoza.

CHAPTER 11

For a Theory of Literary Production

Pierre Macherey

Pierre Macherey's 1966 book, *For a Theory of Literary Production*, offered an innovative new way of approaching the study of literary works from a Marxist perspective. Marxists had traditionally considered history to be the external context to which a text referred. Macherey, relying on ideas from his teacher Louis Althusser, instead offered an intrinsic approach to the study of history in literary texts. In what amounts to a "textual unconscious," history appears in a work of literature as an absence that can nevertheless be deciphered through critical analysis. It is what the text does not want to say but still announces.

Implicit and Explicit

In order to ascertain their real opinions, I ought to take cognisance of what they practised rather than of what they said, not only because, in the corruption of our manners, there are few disposed to speak exactly as they believe, but also because very many are not aware of what it is that they really believe, for as the act of mind by which a thing is believed is different from that by which we know we believe it, the one act is often found without the other.

(Descartes, *Discourse on Method*, III)

For there to be a critical discourse which is more than a superficial and futile *reprise* of the work, the speech stored in the book must be incomplete; because it has not said everything, there remains the possibility of saying something else, *after another fashion*. The recognition of the area of shadow in or around the work is the initial moment of criticism. But we must examine the nature of this shadow: does it denote a true absence, or is it the extension of a half-presence? This can be reformulated in terms of a previous question: Will it be the pillar of an explanation or the pretext for an interpretation?

Initially, we will be inclined to say that criticism, in relation to its object, is its *explication*. What, then, is involved in making explicit? Explicit is to implicit as explication is to implication: these oppositions derive from the distinction between the manifest and the latent, the discovered and the concealed. That which is formally accounted for, expressed, and even concluded, is explicit: the 'explicit' at the end of a book echoes the 'incipit' at the beginning, and indicates that 'all is (has been) said'. To explicate comes from *explicare*: to display and unfold. 'Spread eagle', a heraldic term: one with wings outstretched. And thus the critic, opening the book – whether he intends to find buried treasure there, or whether he wants to see it flying with its own wings – means to give it a different status, or even a different appearance. It might be said that the aim of criticism is to *speak the truth*, a truth not unrelated to the book, but not as the content of its expression. In the book, then, not everything is said, and for everything to be said we must await the critical 'explicit', which may actually be interminable. Nevertheless, although the critical discourse is not spoken by the book, it is in some way the property of the book, constantly alluded to, though never announced openly. What is this silence – an accidental hesitation, or a statutory necessity? Whence the problem: are there books which say what they mean, without being critical books, that is to say, without *depending directly* on other books?

Here we recognise the classic problem of the interpretation of latent meaning. But, in this new instance, the problem tends to take a new form: in fact, the language of the book claims to be a language complete in itself, the source and measure of all 'diction'. The conclusion is inscribed even in its initial moments. Unwinding *within a closed circle*, this language reveals only . . . itself; it has only its *own* content and its *own* limits, and the 'explicit' is imprinted on each of these terms. Yet it is not perfect: under close scrutiny the speech inscribed by the book appears interminable; but it takes this absence of a conclusion as its ending. In the space in which the work unfolds, everything is to be said, and is therefore never said, but this does not suffer being altered by any other discourse, enclosed as it is within the definitive limits which constitute its imperfection. This seems to be the origin of criticism's inability to add anything to the discourse of the work: at most, it might extend the work – either in a reduction or in a pursuit of its discourse.

Yet it remains obvious that although the work is self-sufficient it does not contain or engender its own theory; it does not *know* itself. When the critic speaks he is not repeating, reproducing or remaking it; neither is he illuminating its dark corners, filling its margins with annotation, specifying that which was never specific. When the critical discourse begins from the hypothesis that the work speaks falteringly, it is not with the aim of *completing* it, reducing its deficiencies, as though the book were too small for the space it occupied. We have seen that a knowledge of the work is not elaborated within the work, but supposes a distance between knowledge and its object; to know what the writer is saying, it is not enough to *let him speak*, for his speech is hollow and can never be completed at its own level. Theoretical inquiry rejects the notion of the *space* or *site* of the work. Critical discourse does not attempt to complete the book, for theory begins from that incompleteness which is so radical that it cannot be located.

Thus, the silence of the book is not a lack to be remedied, an inadequacy to be made up for. It is not a temporary silence that could be finally abolished. We must distinguish the necessity of this silence. For example, it can be shown that it is the juxtaposition and conflict of several meanings which produces the radical otherness which shapes the work: this conflict is not resolved or absorbed, but simply *displayed*.

Thus the work cannot speak of the more or less complex opposition which structures it; though it is its expression and embodiment. In its every particle, the work *manifests*, uncovers, what it cannot say. This silence gives it life.

The Spoken and the Unspoken

The speech of the book comes from a certain silence, a matter which it endows with form, a ground on which it traces a figure. Thus, the book is not self-sufficient; it is necessarily accompanied by a *certain absence*, without which it would not exist. A knowledge of the book must include a consideration of this absence.

This is why it seems useful and legitimate to ask of every production what it tacitly implies, what it does not say. Either all around or in its wake the explicit requires the implicit: for in order to say anything, there are other things *which must not be said*. Freud relegated this *absence of certain words* to a new place which he was the first to explore, and which he paradoxically *named*: the unconscious. To reach utterance, all speech envelops itself in the unspoken. We must ask why it does not speak of this interdict: can it be identified before one might wish to acknowledge it? There is not even the slightest hint of the absence of what it does not, perhaps cannot, say: the disavowal (*dénégation*) extends even to the act that banished the forbidden term; its absence is unacknowledged.

This moment of absence founds the speech of the work. Silences shape all speech. Banality?

Can we say that this silence is hidden? What is it? A condition of existence – point of departure, methodical beginning – essential foundation – ideal culmination – absolute origin which lends meaning to the endeavour? Means or form of connection?

Can we make this silence speak? What is the unspoken saying? What does it mean? To what extent is dissimulation a way of speaking? Can something that has hidden *itself* be recalled to our presence? Silence as the source of expression. Is what I am really saying what I am not saying? Hence the main risk run by those who would say everything. After all, perhaps the work is not hiding what it does not say; this is simply *missing*.

Yet the unspoken has many other resources: it assigns speech to its exact position, designating its domain. By speech, silence becomes the centre and principle of expression, its vanishing point. Speech eventually has nothing more to tell us: we investigate the silence, for it is the silence that is doing the speaking.

Silence reveals speech – unless it is speech that reveals the silence.

These two methods of explanation by recourse to the latent or concealed are not equivalent: it is the second which allows least value to the latent, since there appears an absence of speech through the absent speech, that is to say, a certain presence which it is enough to extricate. There is agreement to relate speech to its contrary, figure and ground. But there is a reluctance to leave these terms in equilibrium, an urge to resolve them: figure or ground? Here, once again, we encounter all the ambiguities of the notions of origin and creation. The unacknowledged coexistence of the visible and the hidden: the visible is merely the hidden in a different guise. The problem is merely to *pass across* from the one to the other.

The first image is the more profound, in so far as it enables us to recuperate the form of the second without becoming trapped in a mechanical problematic of transition: in being a necessary medium of expression, this ground of silence does not lose its significance. It is not the sole meaning, but that which endows meaning with a meaning: it is this silence which tells us – not just anything, since it exists to say nothing – which informs us of the precise conditions for the appearance of an utterance, and thus its limits, giving its real significance, without, for all that, speaking in its place. The latent is an intermediate means: this does not amount to pushing it into the background; it simply means that the latent is not another meaning which ultimately and miraculously *dispels* the first (manifest) meaning. Thus, we can see that meaning is in the *relation* between the implicit and the explicit, not on one or the other side of that fence: for in the latter case, we should be obliged to choose, in other words, as ever, translation or commentary.

What is important in the work is what it does not say. This is not the same as the careless notation 'what it refuses to say', although that would in itself be interesting: a method might be built on it, with the task of *measuring silences*, whether acknowledged or unacknowledged. But rather than this, what the work *cannot say* is important, because there the elaboration of the utterance is acted out, in a sort of journey to silence.

The basic issue, then, is to know whether we can examine that absence of speech which is the prior condition of all speech.

> Insidious Questions: When we are confronted with any manifestation which someone has permitted us to see, we may ask: what is it meant to conceal? What is it meant to draw our attention from? What prejudice does it seek to raise? and again, how far does the subtlety of the dissimulation go? and in what respect is the man mistaken? (*The Dawn of Day*, section 523)

For Nietzsche, these are insidious questions, *Hinterfrage*, questions which come from behind, held in reserve, lying in wait, snares.

'It might be asked': thus Nietzsche inquires, and even before showing how to put questions, he points out the necessity of *asking* questions; for there are several. The object or target of these questions is 'all that a man allows to appear'. Everything: that is to say that the Nietzschean interrogation – which is the precise opposite of an examination, since, as we shall see, it reaches the point of calling itself into question – is of such theoretical generality that we may wonder if it is legitimate to apply it to the specific domain of literary production. What in fact 'becomes visible' is the work, all the works. We shall try to apply this general proposition to a specific domain.

'All that a man allows to appear': obviously the German words say more than the English. *Lassen*: this is both to do, to allow, and to oblige. This word, better than any other, designates the act of literary production. It reveals it – on condition that we do not search there for the shapes of some evocative magic: inspiration, visitation or creation. Production: to show and to reveal. The question 'What does he mean?' proves that it is not a matter of dispossession. Also 'to reveal' is an affirmation rather than a decision: the expression of an active force, which yet does not exclude a certain autonomous actualisation of the visible.

Interrogation penetrates certain actions: 'hiding', 'diverting attention', and, further on, 'cheating'. Obviously, linking all these, there is a single impulse: 'hiding' is to keep from sight; 'diverting attention' is to show without being seen, to prevent what is visible from being seen; which also expresses the image of 'dissimulation': to dissimulate requires action. Therefore everything happens as though the accent had been shifted: the work is revealed to itself and to others on two different levels: it makes visible, and it makes invisible. Not because something has to be hidden in order to show something else; but because attention is diverted from the very thing which is shown. This is the superposition of utterance and statement (*du parler et du dire*): if the author does not always say what he states, he does not necessarily state what he says.

In the text from Nietzsche, then, it is a question of a prejudice, a mystification, a deception. Not by virtue of this or that particular word, but because of speech itself, all speech. A prejudice is that which is not judged in language but before it, but which is nevertheless offered as a judgment. Prejudice, the pseudo-judgment, is the utterance which remains imperceptibly beyond language.

Yet this proposition has two meanings: speech evokes a prejudice as a judgment; but equally, by the *fact of evocation*, it holds it up as a prejudice. It creates an allegory of judgment. And speech exists because it wishes for this allegory whose appearance it prepares for. This is the portion of the visible and the invisible, the revealed and the concealed, of language and silence.

Then we arrive at the meaning of the last questions. '*And yet*': we move to a new level of the systematic order, in what is almost an inversion. It could be said that there is a question directed at the first questions. This question which completes the construction of the trap challenges the first question, setting off the structure of the work and the structure of the criticism of it.

$$\left. \begin{array}{l} \text{utterance} \\ \text{question 1} \end{array} \right\} \textit{question 2}$$

We can then ask to what extent the first question was based on an error: because this dissimulation applies to everything it must not be thought that it is total and unlimited. Since it is a relative silence which depends on an even more silent margin, it is impossible to dissemble the truth of language.

Naturally it is incorrect to see in this equivocation of speech its division into the spoken and the unspoken; a division which is only possible because it makes speech depend on a fundamental veracity, a plenitude of expression, a reflection of the Hegelian dialectic – that dialectic which Nietzsche (like Marx, an enemy of idols) could only contemplate in its inverted form. If it is insisted that we find references to these questions in poetic form, we would do better to take them from the work of Spinoza. The transition from dissimulation to error, with the essential moment of 'and yet', is also the movement to the third kind of knowledge. In a famous book, Spinoza has posed Nietzsche's questions, posed them concerning Scripture, which could once have seemed to be the model of all books.

So the real trap of language is its tacit positiveness which makes it into a truly active insistence: the error belongs as much with the one who reveals it as it does with the one who asks the first questions, the critic.

The ordinary critic (the one who stops at the first question) and the author are equally remote from a true appreciation of the work: but there is another kind of critic who asks the second question.

The labyrinth of the two questions – a labyrinth in reverse, because it leads to a way out – endlessly proposes a choice between a false and a true subtlety: the one views the author from the critic's point of view, as a critic; the other only judges him when it has taken up position in the expressive veracity of language, and his language. Torn from the false limits of its empirical presence, the work then begins to acquire a significance.

The Two Questions

Thus the critical task is not simple: it necessarily implies the superposition of two questions. To know the work, we must move outside it. Then, in the second moment, we question the work in its alleged plenitude; not from a different point of view, a different side – by translating it into a different language, or by applying a different standard – but not entirely from within, from what it says and asserts that it says. Conjecturally, the work has its *margins*, an area of incompleteness from which we can observe its birth and its production.

The critical problem will be in the conjunction of the two questions; not in a choice between them, but in the point from which they appear to become differentiated. The complexity of the critical problem will be the articulation between the two questions. To grasp this *articulation* is to accept a discontinuity, to establish a discontinuity: the questions are not spontaneously given in their specificity. Initially, the questions must be asked – asked simultaneously, in a way that amounts to allowing them an equal status.

The recognition of this simultaneity, which precludes any notion of priority, is fundamental because it makes possible – from the beginning – an exorcism of the ghosts of aesthetic legality: by the fact that the question which is supposed to inhabit the mind of the writer is not simple, but divided by its reference to another question, the problem to be explicitly resolved will not be merely the realisation of a project according to the rules of validity (beauty) and conformity (fidelity). Even the question of the formal limits imposed on expression will no longer form part of the problem: it will be completely eliminated as a distinct element of the problematic. In so far as a conscious intention to realise a project of writing begins inevitably by taking the form of an ideological imperative – something *to say* (not the acceptance of rules), in other words something that must not be said – it will have to adopt the conditions of the possibility of such an undertaking: the implements, the actual means of this practice; and the rules will play their part in so far as they are *directly* useful.

The real problem is not that of being restricted by rules – or the absence of such a restriction – but the necessity of inventing forms of expression, or merely finding them: not ideal forms, or forms derived from a principle which transcends the enterprise itself, but forms which can be used immediately as the means of expression for a determinate content; likewise, the question of the value of these forms cannot reach beyond this immediate issue. However, these forms do not exist just in the mode of an immediate presence: they can survive beyond the moment of their usefulness, and it will be seen that this poses a very serious problem; they can be revived, in which case they will have undergone a slight but crucial change in value which must be determined. In fact, these forms do not appear instantaneously but at the end of a long history – a history of the elaboration of ideological themes. The history of forms – which will subsequently be designated as *themes*, in the strict sense of the word – corresponds to the history of ideological themes; indeed, they are exactly parallel, as can easily be demonstrated with the history of any idea: that of Robinson Crusoe, for example. The form takes shape or changes in response to new imperatives of the idea: but it is also capable of independent transformations, or of an inertia, which bends the path of ideological history. But, whatever the mode of its realisation, there is always a correspondence, which could thus be considered automatic: refuting the conception of these two histories as the expression of a superficial question – which is not self-sufficient, because it is based on a parallelism – the question of the work. The level of interpretation determined by this parallelism will only acquire meaning from the elucidation of another level, with which it will have a determining relationship: the question of this question.

The investigation into the conditions of the possibility of the work is accomplished in the answer to an explicit question, but it will not be able to seek the conditions of those conditions, nor will it be able to see that this answer constitutes a question. Nevertheless, the second question will necessarily be posed within the first question, or even through it. It is this second question which, for us, defines the space of history: it reveals the work in so far as it entertains a specific but undisguised (which does not mean innocent) relation with history. We must show, through the study of an effort of expression, how it is possible to render visible the conditions of this effort – conditions of which it has no awareness, though this does not mean that it does not apprehend them: the work encounters the question of questions as an obstacle; it is only aware of the conditions which it adopts or utilises. We could account for this latent knowledge (which necessarily exists, since without it the work would be accomplished no further than if the explicit conditions were not realised) by recourse to *the unconscious of the work* (not of the author). But this unconscious does not perform as an understudy – on the contrary, it arises in the interior of the labour itself: there it is at work – nor as an extension of the explicit purpose, since it derives from a completely different principle. Neither is it a question of another consciousness: the consciousness of another or others, or the other consciousness of the same thing. There is no understudy creative-unconscious to the creative pseudo-consciousness: if there is an unconscious it cannot be creative, in so far as it precedes all production as its condition. It is a question of something other than consciousness: what we are seeking is analogous to that relationship which Marx acknowledges when he insists on seeing material relations as being derived from the social infrastructure behind all ideological phenomena, not in order to explain these phenomena as emanations from the infrastructure, which would amount to saying that the ideological is the economic in another form: whence the possibility of reducing the ideological to the economic.

For Marx and Engels, the study of an ideological phenomenon – that is to say, a conflict at the level of ideology – cannot be isolated from the movement at the economic level: not because it is a different conflict, a different form of the conflict, but because it is the conflict of this conflict. The composition of *an* ideology implies the relation of the ideological to the economic.

The problem of the work, if it exists, is now squarely posed in and by the work, but it is something altogether different from the awareness of a problem. This is why an authentic explanation must attend to several levels at once, though never failing to consider them separately, in their specificity:

1 The first question, properly interior to the work, in the sense of an intimacy, remains diffuse: indeed, it is there and not there, divided between several determinations which give it the status of a quasi-presence. Materially scattered, it must be reconstituted, recalled, recognised. But it would be incorrect to present this task as a deciphering: the secret is not hidden, and in any case *does not conceal itself*, does not resist this census which is a simple classification, changing at most its form; it loses nothing of its nature, its vividness, its mystery.

This first procedure is a question, if you will, of structures. But we have gone far beyond that formulation: to conclude with structures is merely to gather the scattered limbs. It would not be correct to believe that one had thus established a system. What system? In what relation to other systems? In what relation to that which is not part of the system?

2 Once the question has emerged from its half-light, we must find its meaning and its importance. It might be suggested: inscribe it in ideological history, the history which generates the succession of questions and the thread of problematics. But this inscription is not calculated by the simple situation of the question in relation to other questions, or by the presence of history outside this particular work, in so far as it gives it both its domain and its place. This history is not in a simple external relation to the work: it is present in the work, in so far as the emergence of the work required this history, which is its only principle of reality and also supplies its means of expression. This history, which is not merely the history of works of the same nature, entirely determines the work: gives the work its reality, but also that which it is not, and this is the most important. To anticipate an example which will subsequently be analysed, if Jules Verne chose to be the spokesman of a certain ideological condition, he could not choose to be what he in fact became. He chose to be the spokesman for a certain condition; he expressed that choice. These are two different operations, the conjuncture of which constitutes a specific enterprise: in this case, the production of a certain number of books. These are the two 'choices'; the gap between them measures the absence within the work, but they cannot be judged by the same standards, because they are not of the same nature.

It must then be possible to examine a work from an accurate description which respects the specificity of this work, but which is more than just a new exposition of its content, in the form of a systematisation, for example. For as we quickly come to realise, we can only describe, only remain within the work, if we also decide to go beyond it: to bring out, for example, what the work is *compelled* to say in order to say what it *wants* to say, because not only would the work have wanted not to say it (which is another question), but certainly the work did not want to say it. Thus, it is not a question of introducing a historical explanation which is stuck on to the work from the outside. On the contrary, we must show a sort of splitting within the work: this division is *its* unconscious, in so far as it possesses one – the unconscious which is history, the play of history beyond its edges, encroaching on those edges: this is why it is possible to trace the path which leads from the haunted work to that which haunts it. Once again it is not a question of redoubling the work with an unconscious, but a question of revealing in the very gestures of expression that which it is not. Then, the reverse side of what is written will be history itself.

Moreover, we shall be looking within the work itself for reasons for moving beyond it: from the explicit question, and from the reply which it actually elicits – the form of the question being legible in this answer – we shall certainly be able to put the question of the question, and not the one apart from the other. This endeavour is full of surprises: we realise that in seeking the meaning of the work – not the meaning that it gives itself but the meaning that seizes hold of it – we have at our disposal, in turning to the work itself, material that is already prepared, already invested by the question which we are going to ask. The real resistances are elsewhere, in the reader we might say: but they do not hinder this unforeseen inquiry, for the work – it is absurd to repeat this – does not say what it does not say. This is precisely the opposite of an interpretation or a commentary: an interpretation seeks *pretexts*, but the explanation proposed here finds its object wholly prepared and is content to give a true idea of it.

To take a specific example which will later be studied in detail: the 'problem' of Jules Verne breaks down into *two questions*. The important thing is that this dissociation itself remains *within* the problem, that the coherence of the problem should survive: we shall not, for example, be trying to find two Jules Vernes, or to establish a preference for a particular Jules Verne at the expense of all the other possible Jules Vernes. This problem, because it concerns a literary object, is crystallised in what we can call a theme, which is, in its abstract form, the conquest of nature; in the ideological realisation which gives it the form of a *motif*: the voyage, or Robinson Crusoe (a veritable ideological obsession with Verne, and present in all his books, even if only as an allusion). This theme can be studied at two different levels:

1   The utilisation of the theme: initially the adventures of its form, which moreover contain (even though the collocation of the words is casual) the form of the adventure. This raises the question of the writer at work.
2   The meaning of the theme: not a meaning which exists independently of the work, but the meaning that the theme actually acquires within the work.

First question: the work originates in a secret to be *explained*.

Second question: the work is realised in the revelation of its secret. The simultaneity of the two questions defines a minute rupture, minutely distinct from a continuity. It is this rupture which must be studied.

CHAPTER 12

The Sublime Object of Ideology

Slavoj Žižek

Slavoj Žižek is most often associated with Lacanian psychoanalysis. In *The Sublime Object of Ideology* (1989), he blends Lacan with Marx and, in this selection, makes a link between the psychoanalytic theory of fantasy and the Marxist theory of ideology.

Marx, Freud: The Analysis of Form

According to Lacan, it was none other than Karl Marx who invented the notion of symptom. Is this Lacanian thesis just a sally of wit, a vague analogy, or does it possess a pertinent theoretical foundation? If Marx really articulated the notion of the symptom as it is also at work in the Freudian field, then we must ask ourselves the Kantian question concerning the epistemological "conditions of possibility" of such an encounter: how was it possible for Marx, in his analysis of the world of commodities, to produce a notion which applies also to the analysis of dreams, hysterical phenomena, and so on?

The answer is that there is a fundamental homology between the interpretative procedure of Marx and Freud – more precisely, between their analysis of commodity and of dreams. In both cases the point is to avoid the properly fetishistic fascination of the "content" supposedly hidden behind the form: the "secret" to be unveiled through analysis is not the content hidden by the form (the form of commodities, the form of dreams) but, on the contrary, *the "secret" of this form itself*. The theoretical intelligence of the form of dreams does not consist in penetrating from the manifest content to its "hidden kernel," to the latent dream-thoughts; it consists in the answer to the question: why have the latent dream-thoughts assumed such a form, why were they transposed into the form of a dream? It is the same with commodities: the real problem is not to penetrate to the "hidden kernel" of the commodity – the determination of its value by the quantity of the work consumed in its production – but to explain why work assumed the form of the value of a commodity, why it can affirm its social character only in the commodity-form of its product. . . .

The structure is always triple; there are always *three* elements at work: the *manifest dream-text*, the *latent dream-content* or thought, and the *unconscious desire* articulated in a dream. This desire attaches itself to the dream, it intercalates itself in the interspace between the latent thought and the manifest text; it is therefore not "more concealed, deeper" in relation to the latent thought, it is decidedly more "on the surface," consisting entirely of the signifier's mechanisms, of the treatment to which the latent thought is submitted. In other words, its only place is in the *form* of the "dream": the real subject matter of the dream (the unconscious desire) articulates itself in the dream-work, in the elaboration of its "latent content.". . .

The crucial thing to note here is that we find exactly the same articulation in two stages with Marx, in his analysis of the "secret of the commodity-form."

First, we must break the appearance according to which the value of a commodity depends on pure hazard – on an accidental interplay between supply and demand, for example. We must accomplish the crucial step of conceiving the hidden "meaning" behind the commodity-form, the signification "expressed" by this form; we must penetrate the "secret" of the value of commodities:

> The determination of the magnitude of value by labor-time is therefore a secret, hidden under the apparent fluctuations in the relative values of commodities. Its discovery, while removing all appearance of mere accidentality from the determination of the magnitude of the values of products, yet in no way alters the mode in which that determination takes place.[1]

But as Marx points out, there is a certain "yet": the unmasking of the secret *is not sufficient*. Classical bourgeois political economy has already discovered the "secret" of the commodity-form; its limit is that it is not able to disengage itself from this fascination in the secret hidden behind the commodity-form – that its attention is captivated by labor as the true source of wealth. In other words, classical political economy is interested only in contents concealed behind the commodity-form, which is why it cannot explain the true secret, not the secret *behind* the form but *the secret of this form itself*. In spite of its quite correct explanation of the "secret of the magnitude of value," the commodity remains for classical political economy a mysterious, enigmatic thing. It is the same as with the dream: even after we have explained its hidden meaning, its latent thought, the dream remains an enigmatic phenomenon; what is not yet explained is simply its form, the process by means of which the hidden meaning disguised itself in such a form.

We must, then, accomplish another crucial step and analyze the genesis of the commodity-form itself. It is not sufficient to reduce the form to the essence, to the hidden kernel, we must also examine the process – homologous to the "dream-work" – by means of which the concealed content assumes such a form, because, as Marx points out: "Whence, then, arises the enigmatical character of the product of labor, as soon as it assumes the form of commodities? Clearly from this form itself."[2] It is this step towards the genesis of the form that classical political economy cannot accomplish, and this is its crucial weakness:

> Political economy has indeed analyzed value and its magnitude, however incompletely, and has uncovered the content concealed within these forms. But it has never once asked the question why this content has assumed that particular form, that is to say, why labor is expressed in value, and why the measurement of labor by its duration is expressed in the magnitude of the value of the product.[3]

The Unconscious of the Commodity-Form

Why did the Marxian analysis of the commodity-form – which, *prima facie*, concerns a purely economic question – exert such an influence in the general field of social

sciences; why has it fascinated generations of philosophers, sociologists, art historians, and others? Because it offers a kind of matrix enabling us to generate all other
forms of the "fetishistic inversion": it is as if the dialectics of the commodity-form
presents us with a pure – distilled, so to speak – version of a mechanism offering us a
key to the theoretical understanding of phenomena which, at first sight, have nothing
whatsoever to do with the field of political economy (law, religion, and so on). In the
commodity-form there is definitely more at stake than the commodity-form itself,
and it was precisely this "more" which exerted such a fascinating power of attraction. The theoretician who has gone furthest in unfolding the universal reach of the
commodity-form is indubitably Alfred Sohn-Rethel, one of the "fellow travelers" of
the Frankfurt School. His fundamental thesis was that

> the formal analysis of the commodity holds the key not only to the critique of political
> economy, but also to the historical explanation of the abstract conceptual mode of
> thinking and of the division of intellectual and manual labor which came into existence
> with it.[4]

In other words, in the structure of the commodity-form it is possible to find the
transcendental subject: the commodity-form articulates in advance the anatomy, the
skeleton of the Kantian transcendental subject – that is, the network of transcendental categories which constitute the *a priori* frame of "objective" scientific knowledge.
Herein lies the paradox of the commodity-form: it – this inner-worldly, "pathological" (in the Kantian meaning of the word) phenomenon – offers us a key to
solving the fundamental question of the theory of knowledge: objective knowledge
with universal validity – how is this possible?

After a series of detailed analyses, Sohn-Rethel came to the following conclusion:
the apparatus of categories presupposed, implied by the scientific procedure (that,
of course, of the Newtonian science of nature), the network of notions by means of
which it seizes nature, is already present in the social effectivity, already at work in
the act of commodity exchange. Before thought could arrive at pure *abstraction*,
the abstraction was already at work in the social effectivity of the market. The
exchange of commodities implies a double abstraction: the abstraction from
the changeable character of the commodity during the act of exchange and the
abstraction from the concrete, empirical, sensual, particular character of the commodity (in the act of exchange, the distinct, particular qualitative determination of a
commodity is not taken into account; a commodity is reduced to an abstract entity
which – irrespective of its particular nature, of its "use-value" – possesses "the same
value" as another commodity for which it is being exchanged).

Before thought could arrive at the idea of a purely *quantitative* determination, a
sine qua non of the modern science of nature, pure quantity was already at work in
money, that commodity which renders possible the commensurability of the value of
all other commodities notwithstanding their particular qualitative determination.
Before physics could articulate the notion of a purely abstract *movement* going on in a
geometric space, independently of all qualitative determinations of the moving
objects, the social act of exchange had already realized such a "pure," abstract
movement which leaves totally intact the concrete-sensual properties of the object
caught in movement: the transference of property. And Sohn-Rethel demonstrated
the same about the relationship of substance and its accidents, about the notion of

causality operative in Newtonian science – in short, about the whole network of categories of pure reason.

In this way, the transcendental subject, the support of the net of *a priori* categories, is confronted with the disquieting fact that it depends, in its very formal genesis, on some inner-worldly, "pathological" process – a scandal, a nonsensical impossibility from the transcendental point of view, in so far as the formal-transcendental *a priori* is by definition independent of all positive contents: a scandal corresponding perfectly to the "scandalous" character of the Freudian unconscious, which is also unbearable from the transcendental-philosophical perspective. That is to say, if we look closely at the ontological status of what Sohn-Rethel calls the "real abstraction" [*das reale Abstraktion*] (that is, the act of abstraction at work in the very *effective* process of the exchange of commodities), the homology between its status and that of the unconscious, this signifying chain which persists on "another Scene," is striking: *the "real abstraction" is the unconscious of the transcendental subject,* the support of objective-universal scientific knowledge. . . .

This does not mean, on the other hand, that everyday "practical" consciousness, as opposed to the philosophical-theoretical one – the consciousness of the individuals partaking in the act of exchange – is not also subjected to a complementary blindness. During the act of exchange, individuals proceed as "practical solipsists," they misrecognize the socio-synthetic function of exchange: that is the level of the "real abstraction" as the form of socialization of private production through the medium of the market: "What the commodity owners do in an exchange relation is practical solipsism – irrespective of what they think and say about it."[5] Such a misrecognition is the *sine qua non* of the effectuation of an act of exchange – if the participants were to take note of the dimension of "real abstraction," the "effective" act of exchange itself would no longer be possible:

> Thus, in speaking of the abstractness of exchange we must be careful not to apply the term to the consciousness of the exchange agents. They are supposed to be occupied with the use of the commodities they see, but occupied in their imagination only. It is the action of exchange, and the action alone, that is abstract . . . the abstractness of that action cannot be noted when it happens because the consciousness of its agents is taken up with their business and with the empirical appearance of things which pertain to their use. One could say that the abstractness of their action is beyond realization by the actors because their very consciousness stands in the way. Were the abstractness to catch their minds their action would cease to be exchange and the abstraction would not arise.[6]

This misrecognition brings about the fissure of the consciousness into "practical" and "theoretical": the proprietor partaking in the act of exchange proceeds as a "practical solipsist": he overlooks the universal, socio-synthetic dimension of his act, reducing it to a casual encounter of atomized individuals in the market. This "repressed" *social* dimension of his act emerges thereupon in the form of its contrary – as universal Reason turned towards the observation of nature (the network of categories of "pure reason" as the conceptual frame of natural sciences).

The crucial paradox of this relationship between the social effectivity of the commodity exchange and the "consciousness" of it is that – to use again a concise formulation by Sohn-Rethel – "this non-knowledge of the reality is part of its very essence": the social effectivity of the exchange process is a kind of reality which is possible only on condition that the individuals partaking in it are *not* aware of its proper logic; that is, a kind of reality *whose very ontological consistency implies a certain non-knowledge of its participants* – if we come to "know too much," to pierce the true functioning of social reality, this reality would dissolve itself.

This is probably the fundamental dimension of "ideology": ideology is not simply a "false consciousness," an illusory representation of reality, it is rather this reality itself which is already to be conceived as "ideological" – *"ideological" is a social reality whose very existence implies the non-knowledge of its participants as to its essence* – that is, the social effectivity, the very reproduction of which implies that the individuals "do not know what they are doing." *"Ideological" is not the "false consciousness" of a (social) being but this being itself in so far as it is supported by "false consciousness."* Thus we have finally reached the dimension of the symptom, because one of its possible definitions would also be "a formation whose very consistency implies a certain non-knowledge on the part of the subject": the subject can "enjoy his symptom" only in so far as its logic escapes him – the measure of the success of its interpretation is precisely its dissolution.

The Social Symptom

How, then, can we define the Marxian symptom? Marx "invented the symptom" (Lacan) by means of detecting a certain fissure, an asymmetry, a certain "pathological" imbalance which belies the universalism of the bourgeois "rights and duties." This imbalance, far from announcing the "imperfect realization" of these universal principles – that is, an insufficiency to be abolished by further development – functions as their constitutive moment: the "symptom" is, strictly speaking, a particular element which subverts its own universal foundation, a species subverting its own genus. In this sense, we can say that the elementary Marxian procedure of "criticism of ideology" is already "symptomatic": it consists in detecting a point of breakdown *heterogenous* to a given ideological field and at the same time *necessary* for that field to achieve its closure, its accomplished form.

This procedure thus implies a certain logic of exception: every ideological Universal – for example freedom, equality – is "false" in so far as it necessarily includes a specific case which breaks its unity, lays open its falsity. Freedom, for example: a universal notion comprising a number of species (freedom of speech and press, freedom of consciousness, freedom of commerce, political freedom, and so on) but also, by means of a structural necessity, a specific freedom (that of the worker to sell freely his own labor on the market) which subverts this universal notion. That is to say, this freedom is the very opposite of effective freedom: by selling his labor "freely," the worker loses his freedom – the real content of this free act of sale is the worker's enslavement to capital. The crucial point is, of course, that it is precisely this paradoxical freedom, the form of its opposite, which closes the circle of "bourgeois freedoms."

The same can also be shown for fair, equivalent exchange, this ideal of the market. When, in pre-capitalist society, the production of commodities has not yet attained universal character – that is, when it is still so-called "natural production" which predominates – the proprietors of the means of production are still themselves producers (as a rule, at least): it is artisan production; the proprietors themselves work and sell their products on the market. At this stage of development there is no exploitation (in principle, at least – that is, if we do not consider the exploitation of apprentices, and so on); the exchange on the market is equivalent, every commodity is paid its full value. But as soon as production for the market prevails in the economic edifice of a given society, this *generalization* is necessarily accompanied by the appearance of a new, paradoxical type of commodity: the labor force, the workers who are not them-selves proprietors of the means of production and who are consequently obliged to sell on the market their own labor instead of the products of their labor.

With this new commodity, the equivalent exchange becomes its own negation – the very form of exploitation, of appropriation of the surplus-value. The crucial point not to be missed here is that this negation is strictly *internal* to equivalent exchange, not its simple violation: the labor force is not "exploited" in the sense that its full value is not remunerated; in principle at least, the exchange between labor and capital is wholly equivalent and equitable. The catch is that the labor force is a peculiar commodity, the use of which – labor itself – produces a certain surplus-value, and it is this surplus over the value of the labor force itself which is appropri-ated by the capitalist.

We have here again a certain ideological Universal, that of equivalent and equit-able exchange, and a particular paradoxical exchange – that of the labor force for its wages – which, precisely as an equivalent, functions as the very form of exploitation. The "quantitative" development itself, the universalization of the production of commodities, brings about a new "quality," the emergence of a new commodity representing the internal negation of the universal principle of equivalent exchange of commodities; in other words, *it brings about a symptom*. And in the Marxian perspective, *utopian* socialism consists in the very belief that a society is possible in which the relations of exchange are universalized and production for the market predominates, but workers themselves none the less remain proprietors of their means of production and are therefore not exploited – in short, "utopian" conveys a belief in the possibility of *a universality without its symptom*, without the point of exception functioning as its internal negation.

This is also the logic of the Marxian critique of Hegel, of the Hegelian notion of society as a rational totality: as soon as we try to conceive the existing social order as a rational totality, we must include in it a paradoxical element which, without ceasing to be its internal constituent, functions as its symptom – subverts the very universal rational principle of this totality. For Marx, this "irrational" element of the existing society was, of course, the proletariat, "the unreason of reason itself" (Marx), the point at which the Reason embodied in the existing social order encounters its own unreason. . . .

Cynicism as a Form of Ideology

The most elementary definition of ideology is probably the well-known phrase from Marx's *Capital*: "Sie wissen das nicht, aber sie tun es" – "*they do not know it, but they are doing it*." The very concept of ideology implies a kind of basic, consti-tutive naiveté: the misrecognition of its own presuppositions, of its own effec-tive conditions, a distance, a divergence between so-called social reality and our distorted representation, our false consciousness of it. That is why such a "naive consciousness" can be submitted to a critical-ideological procedure. The aim of this procedure is to lead the naive ideological consciousness to a point at which it can recognize its own effective conditions, the social reality that it is distorting, and through this very act dissolve itself. In the more sophisticated versions of the critics of ideology – that developed by the Frankfurt School, for example – it is not just a question of seeing things (that is, social reality) as they "really are," of throwing away the distorting spectacles of ideology; the main point is to see how the reality itself cannot reproduce itself without this so-called ideological mystification. The mask is not simply hiding the real state of things; the ideological distortion is written into its very essence.

We find, then, the paradox of a being which can: reproduce itself only in so far as it is misrecognized and overlooked: the moment we see it "as it really is," this being dissolves itself into nothingness or, more precisely, it changes into another kind of reality. That is why we must avoid the simple metaphors of demasking, of throwing away the veils which are supposed to hide the naked reality. We can see why Lacan, in his *Seminar on the Ethics of Psychoanalysis*, distances himself from the liberating gesture of saying finally that "the emperor has no clothes." The point is, as Lacan puts it, that the emperor is naked only beneath his clothes, so if there is an unmasking gesture of psychoanalysis, it is closer to Alphonse Allais's well-known joke, quoted by Lacan: somebody points at a woman and utters a horrified cry, "Look at her, what a shame, under her clothes, she is totally naked."[7]

But all this is already well known: it is the classic concept of ideology as "false consciousness," misrecognition of the social reality which is part of this reality itself. Our question is: Does this concept of ideology as a naive consciousness still apply to today's world? Is it still operating today? In the *Critique of Cynical Reason* (1983), a great bestseller in Germany, Peter Sloterdijk puts forward the thesis that ideology's dominant mode of functioning is cynical, which renders impossible – or, more precisely, vain – the classic critical-ideological procedure. The cynical subject is quite aware of the distance between the ideological mask and the social reality, but he none the less still insists upon the mask. The formula, as proposed by Sloterdijk, would then be: "they know very well what they are doing, but still, they are doing it." Cynical reason is no longer naive, but is a paradox of an enlightened false consciousness: one knows the falsehood very well, one is well aware of a particular interest hidden behind an ideological universality, but still one does not renounce it.

We must distinguish this cynical position strictly from what Sloterdijk calls *kynicism*. Kynicism represents the popular, plebeian rejection of the official culture by means of irony and sarcasm: the classical kynical procedure is to confront the pathetic phrases of the ruling official ideology – its solemn, grave tonality – with everyday banality and to hold them up to ridicule, thus exposing behind the sublime noblesse of the ideological phrases the egotistical interests, the violence, the brutal claims to power. This procedure, then, is more pragmatic than argumentative: it subverts the official proposition by confronting it with the situation of its enunciation; it proceeds *ad hominem* (for example when a politician preaches the duty of patriotic sacrifice, kynicism exposes the personal gain he is making from the sacrifice of others).

Cynicism is the answer of the ruling culture to this kynical subversion: it recognizes, it takes into account, the particular interest behind the ideological universality, the distance between the ideological mask and the reality, but it still finds reasons to retain the mask. This cynicism is not a direct position of immorality, it is more like morality itself put in the service of immorality – the model of cynical wisdom is to conceive probity, integrity, as a supreme form of dishonesty, and morals as a supreme form of profligacy, the truth as the most effective form of a lie. This cynicism is therefore a kind of perverted "negation of the negation" of the official ideology confronted with illegal enrichment, with robbery, the cynical reaction consists in saying that legal enrichment is a lot more effective and, moreover, protected by the law. As Bertolt Brecht puts it in his *Threepenny Opera*: "what is the robbery of a bank compared to the founding of a new bank?"

It is clear, therefore, that confronted with such cynical reason, the traditional critique of ideology no longer works. We can no longer subject the ideological text to "symptomatic reading," confronting it with its blank spots, with what it must repress to organize itself, to preserve its consistency – cynical reason takes this distance into account in advance. Is then the only issue left to us to affirm that, with the reign of cynical reason, we find ourselves in the so-called post-ideological world? Even Adorno came to this conclusion, starting from the premiss that ideology is, strictly speaking, only a system which makes a claim to the truth – that is, which is not simply a lie but a lie experienced as truth, a lie which pretends to be taken seriously. Totalitarian ideology no longer has this pretension. It is no longer meant, even by its authors, to be taken seriously – its status is just that of a means of manipulation, purely external and instrumental; its rule is secured not by its truth-value but by simple extra-ideological violence and promise of gain.

It is here, at this point, that the distinction between *symptom* and *fantasy* must be introduced in order to show how the idea that we live in a post-ideological society proceeds a little too quickly: cynical reason, with all its ironic detachment, leaves untouched the fundamental level of ideological fantasy, the level on which ideology structures the social reality itself.

Ideological Fantasy

If we want to grasp this dimension of fantasy, we must return to the Marxian formula "they do not know it, but they are doing it," and pose ourselves a very simple question: Where is the place of ideological illusion, in the "knowing" or in the "doing" in the reality itself? At first sight, the answer seems obvious: ideological illusion lies in the "knowing." It is a matter of a discordance between what people are effectively doing and what they think they are doing – ideology consists in the very fact that the people "do not know what they are really doing," that they have a false representation of the social reality to which they belong (the distortion produced, of course, by the same reality). Let us take again the classic Marxian example of so-called commodity fetishism: money is in reality just an embodiment, a condensation, a materialization of a network of social relations – the fact that it functions as a universal equivalent of all commodities is conditioned by its position in the texture of social relations. But to the individuals themselves, this function of money – to be the embodiment of wealth – appears as an immediate, natural property of a thing called "money," as if money is already in itself, in its immediate material reality, the embodiment of wealth. Here, we have touched upon the classic Marxist motive of "reification": behind the things, the relation between things, we must detect the social relations, the relations between human subjects.

But such a reading of the Marxian formula leaves out an illusion, an error, a distortion which is already at work in the social reality itself, at the level of what the individuals are *doing*, and not only what they *think* or *know* they are doing. When individuals use money, they know very well that there is nothing magical about it – that money, in its materiality, is simply an expression of social relations. The every-day spontaneous ideology reduces money to a simple sign giving the individual possessing it a right to a certain part of the social product. So, on an everyday level, the individuals know very well that there are relations between people behind the relations between things. The problem is that in their social activity itself, in what they are *doing*, they are *acting* as if money, in its material reality, is the immediate embodiment of wealth as such. They are fetishists in practice, not in theory. What they "do not know," what they misrecognize, is the fact that in their social reality itself, in their social activity – in the act of commodity exchange – they are guided by the fetishistic illusion.

To make this clear, let us again take the classic Marxian motive of the speculative inversion of the relationship between the Universal and the Particular. The Universal is just a property of particular objects which really exist, but when we are victims of commodity fetishism it appears as if the concrete content of a commodity (its use-value) is an expression of its abstract universality (its exchange-value) – the abstract Universal, the Value, appears as a real Substance which successively incarnates itself in a series of concrete objects. That is the basic Marxian thesis: it is already the effective world of commodities which behaves like a Hegelian subject-substance, like a Universal going through a series of particular embodiments. Marx speaks about "commodity metaphysics," about the "religion of everyday life." The roots of philo-sophical speculative idealism are in the social reality of the world of commodities; it is this world which behaves "idealistically" – or, as Marx puts it in the first chapter of the first edition of *Capital*:

> This *inversion* through which what is sensible and concrete counts only as a phenomenal form of what is abstract and universal, contrary to the real state of things where the abstract and the universal count only as a property of the concrete – such an inversion is characteristic of the expression of value, and it is this inversion which, at the same time, makes the understanding of this expression so difficult. If I say: Roman law and German law are both laws, it is something which goes by itself. But if, on the contrary, I say: THE Law, this abstract thing, realizes itself in Roman law and in German law, i.e. in these concrete laws, the interconnection becomes mystical.[8]

The question to ask again is: Where is the illusion here? We must not forget that the bourgeois individual, in his everyday ideology, is definitely not a speculative Hegelian: he does not conceive the particular content as resulting from an autono-mous movement of the universal Idea. He is, on the contrary, a good Anglo-Saxon nominalist, thinking that the Universal is a property of the Particular – that is, of really existing things. Value in itself does not exist, there are just individual things which, among other properties, have value. The problem is that in his practice, in his real activity, he acts as if the particular things (the commodities) were just so many embodiments of universal Value. To rephrase Marx: *He knows very well that Roman law and German law are just two kinds of law, but in his practice, he acts as if the Law itself, this abstract entity, realizes itself in Roman law and in German law.*

So now we have made a decisive step forward; we have established a new way to read the Marxian formula "they do not know it, but they are doing it." The illusion is not on the side of knowledge, it is already on the side of reality itself, of what the people are doing. What they do not know is that their social reality itself, their activity, is guided by an illusion, by a fetishistic inversion. What they overlook, what they misrecognize, is not the reality but the illusion which is structuring their reality, their real social activity. They know very well how things really are, but still they are doing it as if they did not know. The illusion is therefore double: it consists in overlooking the illusion which is structuring our real, effective relationship to reality. And this overlooked, unconscious illusion is what may be called the ideological fantasy.

If our concept of ideology remains the classic one in which the illusion is located in knowledge, then today's society must appear post-ideological: the prevailing ideology is that of cynicism; people no longer believe in ideological truth; they do not take ideological propositions seriously. The fundamental level of ideology, however, is not of an illusion masking the real state of things but that of an (unconscious) fantasy structuring our social reality itself. And at this level, we are of course far from being post-ideological society. Cynical distance is just one way – one of many ways – to blind ourselves to the structuring power of ideological fantasy: even if we do not take things seriously, even if we keep an ironical distance, *we are still doing them*.

It is from this standpoint that we can account for the formula of cynical reason proposed by Sloterdijk: "they know very well what they are doing, but still, they are doing it." If the illusion were on the side of knowledge, then the cynical position would really be a post-ideological position, simply a position without illusions: "they know what they are doing, and they are doing it." But if the place of the illusion is in the reality of doing itself, then this formula can be read in quite another way: "they know that, in their activity, they are following an illusion, but still, they are doing it." For example, they know that their idea of Freedom is masking a particular form of exploitation, but they still continue to follow this idea of Freedom. . . .

Let us explain by starting from the fundamental Lacanian thesis that in the opposition between dream and reality, fantasy is on the side of reality; it is, as Lacan once said, the support that gives consistency to what we call "reality."

In his *Seminar on the Four Fundamental Concepts of Psychoanalysis*, Lacan develops this through an interpretation of the well-known dream about the "burning child":

> A father had been watching beside his child's sick-bed for days and nights on end. After the child had died, he went into the next room to lie down, but left the door open so that he could see from his bedroom into the room in which his child's body was laid out, with tall candles standing round it. An old man had been engaged to keep watch over it, and sat beside the body murmuring prayers. After a few hours' sleep, the father had a dream that his child was standing beside his bed, caught him by the arm and whispered to him reproachfully: "Father, don't you see I'm burning?" He woke up, noticed a bright glare of light from the next room, hurried into it and found the old watchman had dropped off to sleep and that the wrappings and one of the arms of his beloved child's dead body had been burned by a lighted candle that had fallen on them.[9]

The usual interpretation of this dream is based on a thesis that one of the functions of the dream is to enable the dreamer to prolong his sleep. The sleeper is suddenly exposed to an exterior irritation, a stimulus coming from reality (the ringing of an alarm clock, knocking on the door, or, in this case, the smell of smoke), and to prolong his sleep he quickly, on the spot, constructs a dream: a little scene, a small story, which includes this irritating element. However, the external irritation soon becomes too strong and the subject is awakened.

The Lacanian reading is directly opposed to this. The subject does not awake himself when the external irritation becomes too strong; the logic of his awakening is quite different. First he constructs a dream, a story which enables him to prolong his sleep, to avoid awakening into reality. But the thing that he encounters in the dream, the reality of his desire, the Lacanian Real – in our case, the reality of the child's reproach to his father, "Can't you see that I am burning?," implying the father's fundamental guilt – is more terrifying than so-called external reality itself, and that is why he awakens: to escape the Real of his desire, which announces itself in the terrifying dream. He escapes into so-called reality to be able to continue to sleep, to maintain his blindness, to elude awakening into the Real of his desire. We can rephrase here the old "hippy" motto of the 1960s: reality is for those who cannot support [tolerate] the dream. "Reality" is a fantasy-construction which enables us to mask the Real of our desire.[10]

It is exactly the same with ideology. Ideology is not a dreamlike illusion that we build to escape insupportable [intolerable] reality, in its basic dimension it is a fantasy-construction which serves as a support for our "reality" itself: an "illusion" which structures our effective, real social relations and thereby masks some insupportable, real, impossible kernel (conceptualized by Ernesto Laclau and Chantal Mouffe as "antagonism": a traumatic social division which cannot be symbolized). The function of ideology is not to offer us a point of escape from our reality but to offer us the social reality itself as an escape from some traumatic, real kernel. . . .

Fantasy as a Support of Reality

This problem must be approached from the Lacanian thesis that it is only in the dream that we come close to the real awakening – that is, to the Real of our desire. When Lacan says that the last support of what we call "reality" is a fantasy, this is definitely not to be understood in the sense of "life is just a dream," "what we call reality is just an illusion," and so forth. We find such a theme in many science-fiction stories: reality as a generalized dream or illusion. The story is usually told from the perspective of a hero who gradually makes the horrifying discovery that all the people around him are not really human beings but some kind of automatons, robots, who only look and act like real human beings; the final point of these stories is of course the hero's discovery that he himself is also such an automaton and not a real human being. Such a generalized illusion is impossible: we find the same paradox in a well-known drawing by Escher of two hands drawing each other.

The Lacanian thesis is, on the contrary, that there is always a hard kernel, a leftover which persists and cannot be reduced to a universal play of illusory mirroring. The difference between Lacan and "naive realism" is that for Lacan, *the only point at which we approach this hard kernel of the Real is indeed the dream*. When we awaken into reality after a dream, we usually say to ourselves "it was just a dream," thereby blinding ourselves to the fact that in our everyday, wakening reality we are *nothing but a consciousness of this dream*. It was only in the dream that we approached the fantasy-framework which determines our activity, our mode of acting in reality itself.

It is the same with the ideological dream, with the determination of ideology as a dreamlike construction hindering us from seeing the real state of things, reality as such. In vain do we try to break out of the ideological dream by "opening our eyes and trying to see reality as it is," by throwing away the ideological spectacles as the subjects of such a post-ideological, objective, sober look, free of so-called ideological prejudices, as the subjects of a look which views the facts as they are, we remain throughout "the consciousness of our ideological dream." The only way to break the power of our ideological dream is to confront the Real of our desire which announces itself in this dream.

Let us examine anti-Semitism. It is not enough to say that we must liberate ourselves of so-called "anti-Semitic prejudices" and learn to see Jews as they really are – in this way we will certainly remain victims of these so-called prejudices. We must confront ourselves with how the ideological figure of the "Jew" is invested with our unconscious desire, with how we have constructed this figure to escape a certain deadlock of our desire.

Let us suppose, for example, that an objective look would confirm – why not? – that Jews really do financially exploit the rest of the population, that they do sometimes seduce our young daughters, that some of them do not wash regularly. Is it not clear that this has nothing to do with the real roots of our anti-Semitism? Here, we have only to remember the Lacanian proposition concerning the pathologically jealous husband: even if all the facts he quotes in support of his jealousy are true, even if his wife really is sleeping around with other men, this does not change one bit the fact that his jealousy is a pathological, paranoid construction.

Let us ask ourselves a simple question: In the Germany of the late 1930s, what would be the result of such a non-ideological, objective approach? Probably something like: "The Nazis are condemning the Jews too hastily, without proper argument, so let us take a cool, sober look and see if they are really guilty or not, let us see if there is some truth in the accusations against them." Is it really necessary to add that such an approach would merely confirm our so-called "unconscious prejudices" with additional rationalizations? The proper answer to anti-Semitism is therefore not "Jews are really not like that" but "the anti-Semitic idea of Jew has nothing to do with Jews; the ideological figure of a Jew is a way to stitch up the inconsistency of our own ideological system."

That is why we are also unable to shake so-called ideological prejudices by taking into account the pre-ideological level of everyday experience. The basis of this argument is that the ideological construction always finds its limits in the field of everyday experience – that it is unable to reduce, to contain, to absorb, and annihilate this level. Let us again take a typical individual in Germany in the late 1930s. He is bombarded by anti-Semitic propaganda depicting a Jew as a monstrous incarnation of Evil, the great wire-puller, and so on. But when he returns home he encounters Mr Stern, his neighbor, a good man to chat with in the evenings, whose children play with his. Does not this everyday experience offer an irreducible resistance to the ideological construction?

The answer is, of course, no. If everyday experience offers such a resistance, then the anti-Semitic ideology has not yet really grasped us. An ideology is really "holding us" only when we do not feel any opposition between it and reality – that is, when the ideology succeeds in determining the mode of our everyday experience of reality itself. How then would our poor German, if he were a good anti-Semite, react to this gap between the ideological figure of the Jew (schemer, wire-puller, exploiting our brave men and so on) and the common everyday experience of his good neighbor, Mr Stern? His answer would be to turn this gap, this discrepancy itself, into an argument for anti-Semitism: "You see how dangerous they really are? It is difficult to recognize their real nature. They hide it behind the mask of everyday appearance – and it is exactly this hiding of one's real nature, this duplicity, that is a basic feature of the Jewish nature." An ideology really succeeds when even the facts which at first sight contradict it start to function as arguments in its favor.

Notes

1   Karl Marx, *Capital* (London, 1974), p. 74.
2   Ibid., p. 76.
3   Alfred Sohn-Rethel, *Intellectual and Manual Labor* (London, 1978), p. 31.
4   Ibid., p. 33.
5   Ibid., p. 42.
6   Ibid., pp. 26–7.
7   Jacques Lacan, *Le Séminaire VI – L'éthique de la psychanalyse* (Paris, 1986), p. 231.
8   Marx, *Capital*, p. 132.
9   Sigmund Freud, *The Interpretation of Dreams* (Harmondsworth, 1977), p. 652.
10   Jacques Lacan, *The Four Fundamental Concepts of Psychoanalysis* (Harmondsworth, 1979), chs 5 and 6.

CHAPTER 13

Difference and the Future

Antonio Negri

Antonio Negri, an Italian political philosopher, was one of the most innovative Marxist thinkers of the latter half of the twentieth century. His writings range from philosophical treatises to political pamphlets. As a result of his political activity, he was imprisoned for many years and was also obliged to live in exile in France. In this selection from his book on Spinoza, *The Savage Anomaly: Power and Potential in Baruch Spinoza* (1981), he argues for a new materialism that emphasizes the democratic potential of the mass of people to create a new world.

Negative Thought and Constitutive Thought

In the context of seventeenth-century philosophy Spinoza accomplishes a miracle by subordinating the crisis to the project. Only he, an anomalous and irreducible figure, assumes the crisis of the Renaissance utopia as the reality to be mastered. The theoretical mastery must have the very same potential of absoluteness as does the utopia that is in crisis. Spinoza's philosophical anomaly consists of this: of the irreducibility of his thought to the development of Modern rationalism and empiricism, which are philosophies subordinated to the crisis, philosophies that are always dualistic and irresolute, versed in transcendence as the exclusive territory of the ideal replication and the practical domination of the world – and, therefore, philosophies that function toward the definition of the bourgeoisie, toward its definitive self-recognition as the class of the crisis and of its mediation. Against Descartes, Spinoza reappropriates the crisis as an ontological element; against Hobbes, Spinoza functionalizes the crisis within the constructivism of ontology.[1]

Out of this substantial rupture the entire development of Spinozian philosophy unfolds. As we asked, then, at the beginning of this study: Are there two Spinozas? Certainly, there are. There is the Spinoza who pushes the Renaissance utopia up to the point of the crisis and who develops it in the paradox of the world, and there is the Spinoza who intervenes in this paradox and invests it with a strategy of ethical reconstruction. These two Spinozas are two phases of a unitary speculative project, two moments of the solution of the very same problem. We can describe it using contemporary terminology: negative thought moving toward constitutive thought. In effect, Spinoza carries out a destructive critique of the scheme of the homology of the absolute, moving from within the absolute and leading its organizational conditions into antinomies that are insoluble, given that the conditions of organization will not be revolutionized: This is the negative moment of the theory. Too often, on this limit of the investigation of the theoretical crisis, thought comes to a halt. The conditions of life of the critiqued theoretical organism seem in every way to represent the absolute conditions of doing philosophy. Negative thought concludes, then, on that limit, in a cynical conception of being, in a pure, projective pragmatism that is indifferent to every ontological content – and in this, it is formally hypostatizing the logical order of the system under critique.[2] After Wittgenstein comes Heidegger. Spinoza is an alternative to this philosophical course. He is the refoundation of the conditions of our ability to think the world. Not a philosophy of beginning, and not even a new beginning: Here to begin again is not to select, discriminate, and fix new points of support but to assume the entire dimension of being as the horizon of construction, of the rationally directed possibility of liberation. The space of the crisis is the ontological condition of a project of transformation; the limit inheres in the infinite as a condition of liberation. This grafting of constitutive thought onto critical and negative thought represents the solution to the theoretical enigmas that were posed by bourgeois philosophy as the basis of its specific mystification of the world, in other words, of its ideology and of the figure of its appropriative activity.

The points that Spinozian thought attacks, inasmuch as it is negative thought, are to a large extent those that determine the homology and finalism of multiplicity. A univocal conception of being is posed against every spatial homology, in favor of the plural versatility of being and, once again, against every temporal finalization of its development. The Spinozian mechanism denies any possibility of a conception of the world that is not represented as a singular, flat, and superficial emergence of being. God is the thing. God is multiplicity. The one and the multiple are equivalent and indistinguishable forces: On the terrain of the absolute the numerical sequence could not be given if not as an assumption of the totality of events. Each is absolute in itself.[3] The points on which constitutive thought is developed are those that result from the critical process: points, instances, events that (in the relationship of definitive metaphysical opening) are submitted once again to the tension, the power of the totality of being. The reconstruction of the world is thus the very process of the continual physical composition and recomposition of things – and, with absolute constitutive mechanisms of historical, practical, and ethico-political nature.

This process and these passages are not dialectical: The dialectic has no place in Spinoza, because the constitutive process of the ontology does not know negativity and emptiness if not in the form of the paradox and of the theoretical revolution.[4] The constitutive process accumulates being qualitatively and quantitatively; it always moves into new spaces, it constructs. Spinozian logic does not know the hypothesis, it knows only the trace, the symptom.[5] The versatility of being, which it accounts for, is within a woven fabric of material acts that, in diverse compositions and figures, experience a process of combination and self-formation. The ethics shows this dynamism fully unfolded. From Proposition 13 of part II of the *Ethics* through parts III and IV (the true heart of Spinoza's thought) the passage from physicality to ethicality is developed outside of any formalism, in terms that are instead axiomatic and phenomenological. In its global design and composition the *Ethics* is primarily a set of axioms for a phenomenology of constitutive praxis. The *Ethics* is a methodological work, not because its prolix geometrical method is a paradigm for research but, rather, because it is an open work, a definition of a first sketch of the human task of appropriating and constructing the world. A series of absolutely Modern conditions thus serves the function of the elementary goals of Spinoza's discourse: It is not only an inductive spirit that is developed to the point of realizing the pleasure of symptomatic knowledge but also a sure materialism and a secure collectivism that function as the presuppositions of the process of constitution. To the same degree that the philosophy of emanation (recomposed in Renaissance terms) and the theory of the attributes and that of parallelism diminish or fade under the pressure of negative thought, the world reappears in its material freshness, the society reemerges in its collective determination. Materialism and collectivism are fundamental aspects of constitutive thought. Ontological constitution can be given only as the appropriation and accumulation of material elements, both physical and social. Once again, here the dialectic has no place: Spinozian thought, just as it does not know the negative, does not know the verticality of the mechanisms of sublimation and supersession (or, better, it knows them as temptations from which to liberate itself). What is new and qualitatively different in Spinoza is marked by the complexity of the constitutive processes, in their dynamic (inertial) determination on the physical plane and in the determination that they impose, *appetitus* and *cupiditas*, on the ethical and historical plane. The physical and ethical constitutive dynamism concludes, then, this first, rigorously materialistic foundation of Modern thought.

The relationship between negative thought and constitutive thought that results from Spinoza's philosophy is decisive also on the terrain of the theory of science. In Spinoza science is recognized as constructiveness, freedom, and innovation. It is in no way teleologically or theologically conditioned. The scientific model that capitalism produces for its own development is implicated in the critique carried out by negative thought. If capitalism is a historically absolute force, which produces organization and hierarchy and which imposes production in the form of profit, its science cannot but be teleological. Here, negative thought's polemic rebels directly against it.[6] Certainly, science can be conceived only as a practical force, and therefore science is in every case connected to mechanisms of rule: But Modern science is a mapping or plan of absolute Power (*potestas*). Thus, since its means of existence are teleological, its absolute authority can be founded only on dualism, on the transcendental basis of profit and command. Where, then, can we situate the critique? Precisely in the intersection of science and Power, in the absoluteness that the scientific determination concedes to Power. As command, as hierarchy, as wealth. The essential difference that Spinozian thought poses in opposition to the development of Modern thought is founded on the critique of the attempt to homologize science and Power, presented in any way, structural or formal, Hobbesian or Cartesian. The presuppositions of this critique launch Spinozian thought onto the terrain of a philosophy of the future, of an anticipation that, in the radicality of its polemical impact, has already gained an adequate perspective to recognize the epochal crisis of science and the capitalist system.[7] In contrast to all this stands constitutive thought. And that is the necessity and the possibility of science being used as a machine of liberation. This is the fundamental point. The intersection between negative thought and constitutive thought determines a harmonic force at the point of resonance between the critiqued totality and the project of liberation. The vastness of the project of liberation integrates the radicality of the negative project of the critique. Thus, science is brought back to the ethico-political dimension, it is filled with hope. We have already noted this: The Dutch cultural climate of Spinoza's time, in its relative autonomy and as a historical anomaly, does not experience the dissolution of the civil context in which science is jointly and coherently developed. The academies of the absolute Power are not imposed, and the cultural unity persists, represented as the symbiosis of ethical and cognitive virtues. What the Spinozian conception of science proposes, then, is not an ancient project. It is, rather, an essential aspect of the operations of supersession and dislocation accomplished by the projective time of his philosophy, in opposition to the historical time of its existence: It is a moment of prefiguration, of creativity, of liberation. The constitutive project must therefore pose science as a nonfinalized essence, as an accumulation of liberatory acts. It must pose science not as nature but as second nature, not as knowledge but as appropriation, not as individual appropriation but as collective appropriation, not as Power (*potestas*) but as power (*potentia*). The "*Ethica ordine geometrico demonstrata*" is science itself – the science of an objective being that knows liberation as its own nature, as its own progressive tension.[8]

What is stunning, in this frame of reconstruction, is the enormousness of Spinoza's project. We ourselves would not know how to account for it historically except as the transfer of a religious and metaphysical foundation into a humanistic and revolutionary project. The historical elements of this transfer, however, have only a secondary importance; they have, rather, in their absoluteness, an internal, expansive rhythm, such that the critique transforms their origin, not because it cuts into and reduces the power of that origin but, rather, because it adjusts that power and reorganizes it. Spinoza accomplishes the synthesis of traditional philosophical components by means of breaking and shattering. It is useless to pursue the presuppositions of Spinozian philosophy if we do not look for them in the qualitative leap determined by his philosophy. The continuity of Spinozian thought with respect to the preceding course of the history of metaphysics consists of a radical discontinuity, one that exalts the utopia of consciousness and freedom (a patrimony of Western thought) in a project of liberation. The perspective of the world is not a utopia, the immanentism is not aesthetic, and the liberation is no longer artisanal, but all of this is presupposed, it is taken as a basis. Spinoza redefines the problem of Modern philosophy, which is the conquest of the world and the liberation of humanity, and destroys both its multiple antinomies and the continually resurgent separation (dualistic, transcendental, etc.) in the theory of knowledge and history, in the same way that criticism has always destroyed Zenonian sophism: moving forward, putting reality in motion. Spinoza's philosophy is born from the radicalization of the ontological paradox of being: in the recognition that the hypostasis, the only possible hypostasis, is that of the world and of the development of its necessity from physics to practice. It is a conception of the world that immediately produces, as if from its own basis, a completely modern conception of science and worldly knowledge, both technical and liberatory. It is a radically materialistic conception of being and of the world.

To us it seems that this difference, which Spinoza's thought constitutes in the history of Western metaphysics, represents an extremely high point of the theoretical development of modern thought. In other words, Spinoza's thought seems to us to represent a strategy for superseding the antinomies of bourgeois thought. But because bourgeois ideology is essentially based on antinomies, this supersession is a supersession *tout court* of the ideology. Spinoza gives us being in its immediateness. He destroys the homology between the mediations of articulations of being and the mediations and articulations of bourgeois Power. He presents us with the world as a territory of a joyous construction of immediate human needs.[9] The Spinozian difference gives philosophy a materialistic twist that perhaps gains a definitive meaning only at the level of the mature investigation of the crisis of late capitalism: Its strategy is contemporary, its seed has developed its potential. The history of materialist philosophy presents us with a path that is fundamentally subordinated and, at times, completely parasitic, at least in the realm of Modern and contemporary thought. Now, confronted by Spinozian thought and integrated by it, this tradition is powerfully renewed.[10] Its innovative spirit is picked up by the humanistic and practical foundation of Spinoza's constitutive thought.[11] Spinoza's thought is completely idealistic when it is presented as negative thought, when it develops the bourgeois utopia, living it in the extreme, abstract consequences of its spiritual idyll; it is, in contrast, completely materialistic as soon as it is reassembled in a constructive way, inverting the impossibility of an ideal world in the materialistic tension of its components and embracing these in a practical project, in a violent dynamism of worldly liberation. "*Benedictus maledictus*": never has a philosopher been more rightly hated by his times, a bourgeois and capitalist epoch. Never has a philosophy been felt to be more different. In effect, it attacked that which the ideology and common sentiment, guided by Power, then experienced as most substantial and most its own. Leo Strauss notes: "If it is true that every complete society necessarily recognizes something about which it is absolutely forbidden to laugh, we may say that the determination to transgress that prohibition, *sanza alcuno rispetto*, is of the essence of Machiavelli's intention."[12] And of Spinoza's intention, too. He breaks with the historical times of his philosophy in the most decisive way. He projects, in an adequate way, the rupture toward the future, toward the conditions of thought that permit the hegemony of the project of liberation.

And therefore we can see just how constructive this Spinozian difference is, just how constructive this negativity really is! The organic interweaving of these two motifs is fundamental in the history of European philosophy. Spinoza is the first to mold this logical mechanism that bourgeois philosophy would constantly and continually try to abrogate during its subsequent development. In Kantianism, as in classical idealism, Spinoza continually remains the object of opposition and polemic:[13] What is destroyed is precisely the intersection between the negation of the ideology and the construction of the world, the inherence of the limit, of the materiality, to the infinite. For all the idealistic traditions and positions, negative thought can exist only as *skepsis*, as *pars destruens* – woe to those who confuse it with the project! Idealistic thought wants the ingenuousness and the purity of the foundation: It cannot accept the powerful, complex, spurious territoriality and circulation and versatility of being that Spinoza's negative thought constructs. In idealism love for the truth is dissociated from passion for the real being. This operation undoubtedly has a mystifying effect. In Spinoza truth and being find an exclusivity of reciprocal effects that only constitutive, material, and collective practice can interpret, articulate, and produce: In Spinoza transcendental schematism is only practical and material. The world exalts its very own absoluteness only by recognizing itself in its very own givenness. It is absolute in its particularity. It is rational in the process of liberation. Finite and infinite produce the tension toward liberation. One cannot speak of the world other than in its absoluteness, and this absoluteness lives by that which is real. In Spinoza, at the origin of the Modern world, metaphysical theory and the theory of science are given in complete agreement for the first time. They represent the alternative to the entire subsequent path of metaphysics and of the bourgeois theory of science. Spinoza lives as an alternative: Today this alternative is real. The Spinozian analytic of full space and open time are becoming an ethics of liberation in all the dimensions that this discourse constructs and makes available.

The Ethics and Politics of the Disutopia

Spinoza's true politics is his metaphysics. Against the potentialities of this metaphysics, the polemic of bourgeois thought and all the mystificatory attempts that go under the emblem of "Spinozism" discharge their weapons. But Spinoza's metaphysics is articulated in his political discourse, and some of its potentialities are developed specifically in this field. Here we must try to identify them.

Spinoza's metaphysics presents us with being as productive force and ethics as need or, better, as a phenomenological articulation of productive needs. In this frame the problem of the production and appropriation of the world becomes fundamental. But this problem is not specific to Spinoza: The seventeenth century presents this very same problem and presents it as resolved according to a fundamental axis, that of the hypostasis of command, that of the hierarchy of order and the levels of appropriation. Following seventeenth-century philosophy we can recognize two fundamental ideological figures, understood as founding and representing, with the bourgeois order, the ideology of the *ancien régime*. On one side are the various reformulations of Neoplatonism, from Henry More to Christian spiritualism,[14] and on the other side, mechanistic thought.[15] Both of these theories serve the function of representing the new, decisive phenomenon on the scene: the market. Both explain its articulations of labor and value and the circulation of production for the accumulation of profit and the foundation of command. The Neoplatonic scheme introduces hierarchy into the fluid system of the market, and the mechanistic scheme exalts command as a dualistic tension called for, desired, demanded by the market. Between these two ideologies (the Neoplatonic is generally grouped in the post-Renaissance rather than in the seventeenth century proper) runs the great crisis of the first half of the century: Mechanism is the bourgeois philosophy of the crisis, the ideal form of the restructuring of the market and its ideology, the new technology of absolute Power.[16] In this context the utopia of productive force, which is the indestructible legacy of the humanistic revolution, is shattered and reproduced: shattered in the illusion (and it really was an illusion) of a social and collective continuity of a process of appropriation of nature and wealth; reproduced, at first, as the idea of command and, subsequently, as the hypothesis of an abundant and progressive appropriation in the form of profit. This is the idea of the market: a (mysterious and sublime) duplication of labor and value. Progressive optimism, rational direction, and faith in the results of optimization all extend across the relationship exploitation–profit.[17] The metaphysics of productive force, ruptured by the crisis, is reorganized by the market; seventeenth-century philosophy is its representation. This is the fundamental theory around which the baroque culture of the bourgeoisie is arranged: an interiorization of the material effects of the crisis and a utopian and nostalgic reproduction of the totality as a cover over the mechanisms of the market. We must pay close attention here: The hegemony of this finalizing frame, which functionally traverses almost all of the philosophies of the century, including Hobbes, Descartes, and Leibniz,[18] is so strong that it imposes, during that century itself and in its immediate surroundings, a homologous reading of Spinoza's thought – this is "Spinozism"! It is the forceful reduction of Spinoza's metaphysics to a Neoplatonized, emanationist ideology, to a reproduction of the late Renaissance image of the bourgeois social order. Is Spinoza baroque? No, but if we find, through this line of thinking, a spurious and worn-out figure that rejects the crisis, that repeats the utopia in its ingenuous Renaissance form, what we have found is merely Spinozism.[19] When classical idealism takes up Spinoza, in effect it only takes up (or invents?) Spinozism, a Renaissance philosophy of the bourgeois revolution of the capitalist market![20]

Spinoza's mature thought is a metaphysics of productive force that rejects the critical rupture of the market as an arcane and transcendental episode, that instead interprets (immediately) the relationship between appropriative tension and productive force as the fabric of liberation. Materialistic, social, and collective. Spinoza's rejection does not deny the reality of the critical rupture of the market; rather, it intervenes in its determinate, seventeenth-century solution. It assumes the crisis as an element of the development of the human essence, negates the utopia of the market, and affirms the disutopia of development. The collective character of appropriation is primary and immediate, and it immediately appears as struggle – not separation but, rather, constitution. In short, it is the determinate refusal of the bourgeois and capitalistic organization of the relationship between productive force and appropriation. But we will speak more of this, and more extensively, below. Here, instead, it is worth dwelling a bit on the depth of the Spinozian rupture, on the theoretical importance of the centrality of the disutopia, because this is the point around which a radical and seminal alternative to bourgeois thought is identified, an alternative between the discovery and theoretical exaltation of productive force and, in opposition, its bourgeois organization. The history of modern thought must be seen as a problematic of the new productive force. The ideologically hegemonic vein of thought is that which functions toward the development of the bourgeoisie. This vein yields to the ideology of the market, in the determinate form imposed by the new mode of production. The problem, as we have amply demonstrated, is the hypostasis of the dualism of the market within the metaphysical system: from Hobbes to Rousseau, from Kant to Hegel. This is, then, the central vein of modern philosophy: The mystification of the market becomes a utopia of development. In opposition, there is the Spinozian rupture – but, before it, there is already the one worked by Machiavelli, and after it, the one sanctioned by Marx. The disutopia of the market becomes, in this case, an affirmation of productive force as a terrain of liberation. We could never insist enough on this immanent and possible alternative in the history of Western thought. It is a sign of dignity, to the same extent that the other is an emblem of infamy. Spinoza's rupture grasps the heart of the mystification; it assumes the first real instance of the critical mechanism of the market as a symptom and as a demonstration of its infamy. The market is superstition, but superstition positioned to destroy human creativity, to create fear against productive force: an obstacle to block the path of constitution and liberation. The depth of Spinoza's rupture could not be larger and more significant.

Let us return, then, to the content of Spinoza's disutopia. It is a metaphysics of being presented as a physics of power (*potentia*) and an ethics of constitution. We have already seen the pains that Spinoza takes in developing this research hypothesis, in the process of arriving at its very definition. Now we must take up the political specificity of this development. Disutopia: or, rather, an interweaving of the constitutive tendency and the determinate, critical limit. This interweaving is seen by Spinoza on a horizon of absolute immanence. There is no superior, transcendent plane associated with the concept of constitution. Every articulation of the process is therefore uniquely and exclusively entrusted to its ethical projectivity. It lives in a progressive tension that runs, without resolution in continuity, from the physical dimension to the ethical. And this is a constructive tension of being. Being and nonbeing affirm each other and negate each other simply, discretely, immediately. There is no dialectic. Being is being, nonbeing is nothing. Nothing: phantasm, superstition, shadows. It is opposition. It is an obstacle of the constructive project. In contrast, the metaphysics of being passes directly over into ethics and politics. This, too, experiences the temptation and the danger of nothingness. But here the temptation is precisely to dominate it absolutely. In Spinoza's disutopia the centrality of politics is an affirmation of the absolute positivity of being. In contrast to a hegemonic political theory that wants to make politics into a realm of cunning and domination, Spinoza affirms politics as "moderated" Power, and that is as a determinate constitution of consensus and organization for collective freedom. In contrast to a political theory that tries to be an absolute theory of obligation, Spinoza poses every basis of normativity in the processes of the imagination. In contrast to an ideology that wants to make the organization of society a simulation of the market, Spinoza counterposes the constitution of society as a mapping of the development of the productive forces. In Spinoza, *potentia* and appropriation are the constitutive elements of human collectivity and the conditions of its progressive liberation. Against the possessive individualism that hegemonically characterizes seventeenth-century philosophy, Spinoza affirms the alternative of a constitutive process, not linear but actual, not teleological but determinate and effectual. Freedom that by developing itself constitutes being; being that by constituting itself determines freedom. Actuality that can only be prefigured in the measure of its effectuality; necessity that is posed as an effect and a measure of freedom.

Some have spoken of a liberal Spinoza, and others, of a democratic Spinoza. By the same standard one could also speak of an aristocratic Spinoza or a monarchical Spinoza – and it has been done. Perhaps also an anarchic Spinoza? No one has ever said that. And yet this field of attributing the various labels from the theory of the forms of government and the State to the form of Spinoza's politics is so inane that one might even say an "anarchic" Spinoza! On the other hand, is not this claim, of "atheism" and "anarchism," precisely the accusation that was directed at him during the centuries of the *ancien régime*? But this is senseless. The problem is not, in fact, the form of government but the form of liberation. Spinoza's political problem is that of giving to freedom and reason, to the immediateness of needs and their social and collective transcription, the absoluteness of the potentiality of being. Every definition of the forms of government must square accounts with the thematic of the power of being. But in this process itself, it dissolves. Politics is a primary function of experience and of knowledge in that it fixes a relationship between a tension toward liberation and a determinate limit. But this relationship is indefatigably surpassed, not by a system of negations, not by a series of commands, but by further, full, material projects of appropriation. The only accumulation that Spinoza knows is that of the collective labor of liberation.

Politics remains at the center of Spinozian metaphysics, and there it reveals its alternative proposal with respect to the course of modern Western thought. It illustrates this metaphysical alternative from the theoretical point of view. But more importantly, it makes the alternative explicit and demonstrates it from the practical point of view. Centuries of struggle by oppressed minorities, by the exploited proletariat, and centuries of the investigation of freedom (and the great social uprisings

intent on the destruction of the new system of domination imposed by the bourgeoisie, and the maturation and explosion of the antagonisms that the new mode of
production has unleashed) can all be traced back to Spinoza's thought as a highly
expressive summit. Spinozian politics, as a function of a metaphysical alternative, is a
real and true historical antithesis of the development of the capitalist mode of production. The fact that appropriation is here a constitutive key, and not the basis of
the legitimation of a norm of domination, demonstrates and prefigures the real
relationship that is constituted through the centuries of European history between
the theoretical experience of humanism and the concrete experience of liberation.
Philosophy is grand and beautiful, through the circuitous path of the destruction of
the misery of reality: Spinoza is a testimony to its virtues![21]

We should return, nonetheless, to the disutopia. It is not conceived as a residual
moment, or only something that is dialectically relevant, not even in opposition to the
hegemonic and dominant currents of modern and contemporary thought! Spinoza's
disutopia is a revolt, a rebellion, only to the extent that it is, first of all, wealth. The
tension between limit and tendency that constitute it, the metaphysically appropriative and constitutive thrust that form it – all of this is wealth; it is a liberation of
productive force. One could say, certainly straining the discourse but still developing
it in its own rationality, that the force of the disutopia is situated beyond the exposition itself of the ethics and the politics, that it is, in effect, a philosophy of transition
to a society completely, radically constituted on the basis of freedom! Are we discerning a utopian element in the disutopia? Many interpreters have thought it necessary
to bring out this consequence, in various different forms.[22] Reading Spinoza, the soul
is drawn, in effect, toward this conclusion. But the critical intelligence cannot accept
it. In part V of the *Ethics* itself it is always the constitutive tension that, in effect, has
the upper hand, even when the utopia rises up again in such a vigorous way. In fact,
the emancipatory thrust of the theory of the disutopia is never in any way situated on
the horizon of a hypostatizing mechanism. Emancipation is a transition not because it
intuits the future but because it permeates and animates the present. Emancipation is
a need, an ontological system of needs that is made actual and that determines a new
composition and a new present by means of reality, animating the present, constituting that paradoxical and effective point of coincidence between necessity and possibility that is the metaphysical mark of Spinozian being. *Potentia-appetitus-cupiditas-
mens*: A constitutive praxis forms the disutopia. The disutopia is the theoretical
recognition of determinateness, of phenomenology, of praxis. Disutopia as a determination, as a determinate actuality. Emancipation is the disutopia. In other words,
the abundance and the terrific productivity of being are presupposed by the emancipatory process, and the disutopia shows its power on this basis. Being is mature
enough for freedom. Freedom and happiness, therefore, are constructed as manifestations of being. Disutopia means pursuing the tracks of the power of being. But even
this definition runs the risk of being deceitful: Because, in Spinoza, the relationship
between expression and givenness, between tendency and limit, between creation and
the created, is always so strict and so closely connected to the concrete determinations of being, merely speaking of or referring to the power of being as such runs
the risk of reintroducing unacceptable dualisms or the semblances of a formal being.
No, the flatness and the integrity of being are what show its power; its givenness is
that which measures its actuality! Emancipation is therefore the weaving together of
plural, ethically motivated human activity with the power of being presented in its

givenness and determination. Emancipation is therefore the organization of the infinite, the declaration of human power as a determinate expression of the indefinite. The disutopia is the specific form of the organization of the infinite.

The anomaly of Spinoza's thought with respect to his times is made, therefore, a savage anomaly: savage because it is articulated on the density and the multiplicity of affirmations that rise up out of the unlimited affability of the infinite. In Spinoza we find the pleasure of the infinite being, the pleasure of the world. When the paradox of the world, and the open tension contained in it between the positive infinity and the infinity of determinations, is developed in activity and is recognized in the constitutive process, the pleasure of the world begins to become central, and the anomaly is made savage: savage because it is connected to the inexhaustible multiplicity of being, to its blossomings, which are as vast as they are agitated in flux. Spinoza's being is savage and restive and multiple in its expressions. It is versatile and savage. There is always something new in Spinozian ontology, not only in the historical ontology that is revealed through its development but above all in the essential ontology that emanates from the opening of being, from its depths. In the passage from physical power to moral *cupiditas* to *mens*. And then we see the savage anomaly as a quality of the organization of the infinite, as a principal characteristic of that tension between infinite and determination, between tendency and limit, that constitutes the mode of presentation of the power of the infinite. The savage anomaly is not, then, only a character of the historical situation of Spinoza's thought in his times and in the development of Western philosophy, and it is not only a definition of the richness of his thought and of its opening toward the future: It is also a fundamental moment and real mode of the expression of being. The Spinozian disutopia is the pleasure of the savage anomaly of being. And here, then, many of the threads that are woven into Spinoza's philosophy stand out again on the surface. They form, as historical components, his system only inasmuch as they are defined within the attraction of the savage complexity of the system. As do all the products of high technology, his thought contains the complexity of its apparatus within the power of productive force and, moreover, shows this complexity as an irreducible singularity. The disutopia is both a critique of what exists, of the components, and a positive, singular construction of the present. It is the complexity of the components and the simplicity of composition. It is the singularity of the expression of surfaces, to the point of becoming the pleasure and the sweetness of the world. This Spinozian conclusion is totally irreducible. In very elementary terms, perhaps a bit extreme but certainly intense, we could say that in Spinoza productive force is subjected to nothing but itself, and, in particular, domination is taken away from the relations of production: Instead, productive force seeks to dominate the relations of production from its own point of view, through its own power. It is this conception of productive force (with its material and ontological referent) that gives Spinoza's philosophy and its conception of being an inexhaustible richness, a savage determination.

Constitution and Production

Productive force and relations of production: The contradiction is not metaphysical but material, determinate. Spinoza's thought, in its universal meaning, can be reduced to this simple affirmation. Productive force emanates from the infinity of being, and its unique organization is given in the movement of the infinite. Every subordination and ordering of productive force that is not the autonomous movement of its own constitutive force is negativity, antagonism, emptiness. The expression of productive force is given materially, always balanced on the margin of being, where the constitution finds the support to project outward, like a power of the future. The expression of productive force is given cumulatively on the physical plane and collectively on the ethical plane, always as a result of the theoretical and practical process that, like the expression of productive force itself, is the very self-formation of the being that exists. Productive force is, therefore, immediately constitution, and constitution is the form in which productive force reveals being. Material production, political organization, ethical and cognitive liberation are all posed at the intersection between production force and the positive constitution of the world. The production-constitution relationship, then, is the key to the articulation of being, a unitary process that can be appreciated from various points of view but that remains, in its essence, unitary.

It is possible to consider it, then, in the context of thought and of the metaphysical dynamics as such, where we deal with being in its construction, between first and second nature, between physicality and ethicality: This is the terrain of the appropriation of nature and the constitution of the world. By antonomasia. Secondly, the production–constitution relationship can be appreciated on the political plane, where the fundamental nexus is expressed in the reduction of multiplicity to the unity of collectivity and in the constitutive definition of collectivity as practical power (*potentia*), as the civilizing and normalizing power in social, human relationships. Finally, the relationship can be considered on the ethical plane in the real sense or, rather, on the plane of the consciousness of liberation: Ontology and politics yield here to the desire for happiness; they are articulated in the individual and collective investigation of the expression of a plane of being, of a complete emancipation from the misery of life, of a happiness that would be the joy, the pleasure, the exaltation that being itself is.

Production as a constitutive ontology. Spinoza founds this possibility of philosophy, or rather of the destruction of philosophy, with absolute coherence. Constitutive ontology recognizes production within the structure of being. It is not possible to say being, except in terms of production. The critique of being is the critique of production. In its process of constitution, productive being advances along a path that, cumulatively (and that is according to a rigorously quantitative and mechanical logic), forms strata and levels of the world. Every singular event of a physical nature is a determinate condensation of the cumulative process of being. Spinozian metaphysics discovers a physics, which in turn it produces. Physics, or rather the specific negation of philosophy as a generic science of being, becomes the basis of the Spinozian system. It is a solid basis for a dynamic that has grown and articulated. From nature to second nature. Human activity extends the power of nature. The articulation of nature matures, and it is recycled in the activity of the mind. The relationship between nature and second nature, this fundamental node of constitutive ontology, is organized by human intelligence. Human intelligence is the articulation of nature. From nature it grasps and develops the constructive potentiality. Almost in the indistinctness, reason is born. The imagination is born, the power that is fundamental to the Spinozian system! This discrete and very powerful point, at the center of the problem of seventeenth-century philosophy and its dualistic ambiguity of psychological indistinctness (the principle of the baroque, seventeenth-century liquidation of the unity of nature, in the very moment when the theory of passions first comes into sight) – well, this is the turning point for the inversion of the seventeenth-century problematic: because, in effect, Spinoza presents precisely here, in the imagination, the fulcrum for the construction of the world. The imagination is physicality that achieves intelligence, the body that is constructed in the mind. The imagination is both a declaration that the theory of parallelism is incidental and a substitute for it: the mind comes to be formed in an orderly fashion – at least according to the constitutive order that the savage versatility of being determines. There are no discontinuities in Spinoza's thought but an infinite number of catastrophes, which reformulate the continuity of being along the line of the imagination, of a depth of productive attribution that, like the water in the earth and in bodies, circulates everywhere. Omnipresent. Like a motor that, in an orderly way, drives transmission belts in every direction and governs the perfection of other motors. The imagination is the heart of the constitutive ontology because it is at the center and is the emblem of its continuity, of the absolute univocality of the order of being. Because it is the dynamic motor of being. It shows being as production. Second nature is the human-made world. However, the Spinozian sense of the unity of being, of its dense, compact reality, is such that at times the human-made world seems to be pressed against metaphysical nature as if against a backdrop so bright that it cannot stand out. But this is pure and simple appearance. Actually, if it is true that Spinoza still sees the world of industry, at the dawn of capitalism, as relatively insignificant with respect to the world of natural production, this attitude is misleading. Because the concept of production in Spinoza is not only the foundation of the dynamic of being but also, more importantly, the key to its complexity, to its articulation, to its expansivity. Second nature is born of the collective imagination of humanity, because science is precisely this: the productive result of the appropriative spirit of nature that the human community possesses and develops. The process of civilization is an accumulation of productive capacity. It is the destruction of the necessity that is not liberated, and therefore the destruction of contingency, and therefore the destruction of nonbeing. Thus, we touch on the paradox of Spinozian thought and its humanism: There is no longer nature, in Spinoza, but only second nature; the world is not nature but production. The continuity of being is not formed in a process that leads from a principle to a result, from a cause to an effect (on this nexus and in this direction); rather, it is revealed as given, as a product, as a conclusion. The result is the principle. Produced, constituted being is the principle of production and constitution. Every articulation is led back to production as if to its own principle. But the principle is actuality, it is the actual richness of the movements of being. It is its constituted present. This inversion of production in the principle of a constitutive ontology is the symbol of the liberation of productive forces from the relations of production, no matter how they are given or how firm they are. It is the principle of revolution at the basis of Modern philosophy.

Constitutive ontology is made political. In Spinoza the passage to politics is absolutely necessary; the identification of the subjective articulation of the development of being must be political. Spinoza's political theory is a theory of the political composition of subjectivity. The passage from nature to second nature, from physics to human action, must be mediated by subjectivity. It would be completely abstract to ask ourselves about the influences on Spinoza's politics without, beforehand, having posed the problem of situating the politics in the Spinozian system and the need for recognizing its position as a theoretical node. Spinozian politics, then, is the theory of the "subjective" continuity of being. The subject is the product of the physical accumulation of movements. The collective subject can only be appreciated as a physics of collective behaviors. Subjectivity is a composition, first physical and then historical. The theory of the subject is a theory of composition. Well, then, we should follow this constitutive theory, in all its terrific productivity! Production and constitution are given here at a level of elaboration that has already produced a result: Production is always more efficient as constitution is more complex. The collective subject looks to politics for the rationale of its dynamism. And it is a dynamism that is both productive and constitutive. Even in this case the relations of production are subordinated to productive force: Power (*potestas*) is subordinated to power (*potentia*). Political constitution is always set in motion by the resistance to Power. It is a physics of resistance: No complexity of constitution is given that is not also a complexity of declarations of power, of expressions of production. Political constitution is a productive machine of second nature, of the transformative appropriation of nature, and therefore a machine for the attack and the destruction of Power. Power (*potestas*) is contingency. The process of being, the always-more-complex affirmation of subjective power, and the construction of the necessity of being all excavate the basis of Power, to demolish it. Power (*potestas*) is superstition, the organization of fear, nonbeing; power opposes it by constituting itself collectively. The appropriation of nature is completely inverted here: It deals now with the production of the conditions of power – once again, we find the paradox of the result, of actual power, of the fullness of being! In the composition of subjectivity there is always progressively more of that sociability and collective intelligence that raise power up against Power, that make Power an always more subordinated and transient form with respect to human, intersubjective productivity, with respect to the mature composition of subjectivity. It is in the critique of theology that Spinozian philosophy begins an investigation of the development of subjectivity as a power of being, as a progression of always-more-developed compositions. Theology is a theory of alienation that serves Power: dualism, as always, in service to Power, as a line of the legitimation of command, as a separation of the relations of production from productive force. The theological critique (and the critical exegesis of the religious tradition) dissolves its mystifying form and shows its contingency, its historical, residual character. Inasmuch as theology serves Power, it comes to be dissolved little by little. The development of subjective power, in the process of the destruction of theological illusion, gathers together all that has accumulated in being, all that being has produced, historically, by means of and against the mystification, toward a greater human sociability, and reappropriates it, redefines it. This process, however, does not come to an end until power can fully insist on itself, on its own absolute autonomy and productivity. The time of the appropriation of first and second nature has a real existence only as a form of the fullness of being. If there is a before, it leads to being; if there is an after, it is always commensurate with pure power and its tension, outside of any finalistic frame.

This unfolding of natural productivity, just like that of subjectivity, toward the perfection of composition leads to the final stratum of the Spinozian problematic: perfection, the ethics of liberation, its presuppositions, its power, its results. But here a contradiction seems to emerge: From the ontological and antifinalistic horizon, in effect, Spinozian philosophy casts this problematic toward the interiority and intensity of being. Why? Why does a philosophy that is completely open in its movement toward the totality of being, in its tension from the microcosm to the macrocosm, dictate its conclusion by subjective perfection? Even if this question is legitimate, still the response is clear, and excludes any contradiction. If there is a limit, it is more historical than theoretical. The subjectivity toward which Spinozian mediation develops is, in fact, the actual limit of the ethical and political disutopia. There is no intimism in this, nothing individual, nothing mystical. There is nothing in this to detract from the continuity and expansivity of being. The subject, in either its individual or collective figure, is the point on which the productive force of being is shown to be an identity with the constitution of the figures of being. The subject is the ontological site of the determination and, therefore, of emancipation. The entire metaphysical frame is completed in this intensity. Therefore, there is nothing immobile in this finale synthesis: There is, rather, the activity of liberation, which is made dense, heavy, and yet always open, always more perfect. We grasp the highest metaphysical perfection on the line of the accomplished subjectivity. We grasp it as the satisfaction of a production that sees the perfection of its own composition. In a chain of the woven being of infinite presents, the conclusion is, once again, the present, its joy, all of given being. We must insist on this: The limit, this determinate appearance of the subject, at this level of its composition, is the totality of given being. Perfection resides in this limit, not in any transcendence present in being. The tension and the supersession are needs, not ideals, just as perfection is ontological, not utopian. The utopia itself is closed within being, and its dignity is that of being materially composed in subjective desire. This is how Spinozian ethics comes to a close.

To be reopened in every moment of being. The Spinozian problematic of spatial being, as spatial constitution, of spatial production, coming to an end, is a proposal for the metaphysics of time. Not of time as becoming, as the most recent Modern philosophy would have it: because the Spinozian perspective excludes every philosophy of becoming outside of the determination of constitution. Rather, it is a proposal of metaphysics of time as constitution, the time of further constitution, the time that extends beyond the actuality of being, the being that constructs and selects its future. A philosophy of the future. If until now we have often insisted on the opening of Spinozian thought toward the future, as a correlate of its anomalous ideological power and historical situation, now the sign of temporality, in Spinozian thought, must be tracked down further in the depths, and that is, on the surfaces of the ontology. Here the inscription of power in being opens being toward the future. The essential tension wants existence. The cumulative process that constructs the world wants a further time, a future. The composition of the subject accumulates the past only to make it tend toward the future. Being is temporal tension. If difference founds the future, then here the future ontologically founds difference. This reciprocal relationship is the fabric of construction. And then, qualitatively, being is emancipation, that is, once again, the perfection of the tendency in future time. Infinitely extended toward infinite perfection. A continuous transition toward always greater perfection. Being produces itself. The relationship between being, production, and constitution is the dimension of the future. Knowledge is nothing but the continual analytic of this progression, of this weaving together, of this continual accumulation of being. Being is greater tension toward the future as its present density grows to a higher level. The future is not a procession of acts but a dislocation worked by the infinite mass of intensive being: a linear, spatial displacement. Time is being. Time is the being of the totality. Of transformation, of wealth, of freedom. But all this goes together. Being that is dislocated from one point to the next in space, in its infinity, in its totality, accomplishes a passage in order of perfection, that is, in its construction. Not in relation to any other, but only in relation to itself. Therefore, it is liberation, emancipation, transition. Time is ontology. Constitution internal to production, and also internal to freedom.

Spinoza's metaphysics of production defines on the theoretical terrain the conditions for the possibility of a phenomenology of collective praxis. Freeing itself from the relations of production and showing itself as immediately constitutive, productive force displays the possibility for the world to be unfolded and analyzed and transformed according to desire. The Spinozian paradox consists of the absolute material determination of this project. Collective praxis is determinate. Its figures are constituted. Their content is liberation. The form is material and collective. Desire is produced at the level of the composition of the subject. This subjective nexus of the objective complexity of being constitutes the most specific determination of Spinoza's thought, considered in its historical context – and considered as a metaphysical proposal. Now, in this sense, the production–constitution relationship represents the fulcrum of Spinozian projectivity. It is the surpassing of any possibility of logic, both classical and dialectical. And it is perhaps, still, the contemporary meaning of his thought. It is for this reason that, concluding this first exploration of Spinoza's thought, it is worth insisting with extreme clarity on this dimension that Spinozian thought offers for our consideration. Spinoza, pushing forward the identity of production and constitution, at the origins of capitalist civilization, destroys the possibility of a dialectic of Power (*potestas*) and opens the perspective of power (*potentia*). Scientifically, this rupture expresses the necessity for and shows the form of a phenomenology of collective praxis. Today, in an epoch characterized by the crisis of capitalism, this rupture between (capitalistic) relations of production and (proletarian) productive force has again reached a point of extreme tension. *Potestas* and *potentia* are presented as an absolute antagonism. The independence of productive force, then, can find in Spinoza an important source of reference, it can find in the development of his hypothesis a line on which to historically organize itself. Clearly, on the basis of a hypothesis: which is that of recognizing that the development of bourgeois culture has not completely disfigured the history of its origins. "Is it still possible to isolate from the process of the disaggregation of democratic society the elements that – linked to its origins and to its dream – do not deny a solidarity with a future society, with humanity itself? German scholars who have abandoned their country would not have saved much, and would have had little to lose, if the response to this question were not yes. The attempt to read it on the lips of history is not an academic attempt."[23]

Notes

1 On this topic allow me once again to refer to my *Descartes politico o della ragionevole ideologia* (Milan, 1970). In addition, see C. B. Macpherson's *The Political Theory of Possessive Individualism: Hobbes to Locke* (Oxford, 1975). The distance that separates Spinoza from Descartes and

Hobbes is testimony to the reality of the Spinozian anomaly in modern thought. It would be interesting to ask ourselves why this anomaly was not sufficiently emphasized (except in polemical and demonic terms) in the years after Spinoza's death. Here I want only to focus on the particularly strong political persecution waged against Spinozian thought and the ideological repression intent on mutilating and slandering it. This leads, once again, to a general observation: It is primarily on the political level, in the history of thought, that Spinozian philosophy is persecuted. It is important to emphasize this: His terrific metaphysical installation was quickly recognized as politics and presented itself immediately as revolutionary thought. This confirms my hypothesis: Spinoza's true politics is his metaphysics.

2   For some remarks on the crisis in negative thought and the definition of its theoretical limits, allow me to refer to my review of *Krisis* by Massimo Cacciari (Milan, 1976), published in *Aut-Aut*, no. 155–6 (1976). In the review, although I admire Cacciari's wonderful attempt to positively recuperate the efficacy of negative thought, I also note the limits that this and every other such attempt at recuperation will encounter if negative thought is not wedded with constitutive thought.

3   Obviously, here I am going back to G. Deleuze, *Spinoza et le problème de l'expression* (Paris, 1968), as I have often done above. The great merit of Deleuze's approach is the fact that he grasps the dimension of the singularity and the surface of Spinoza's thought, bringing the system all the way to the point that we have called "the paradox of the world." But this intuition and this demonstration can, in my view, be amplified and carried forward to construct not only the basis but also the elaboration of a "second" part: that in which thought of singularity and surface develops into constructive and constitutive thought. Deleuze almost arrives at this understanding when he insists on the "second Spinoza," the Spinoza of the Scholia, of the unfurled ethical arguments. However, he tends to situate this figure on the terrain of ethical science as such and in the field of grand moral rhetoric, rather than on the terrain of a new apprehension of being. In any case, I want to take this opportunity to say that without Deleuze's work, my work would have been impossible.

4   P. Macherey, in *Hegel ou Spinoza* (Paris, 1979), has better than any other interpreter emphasized the distance between Spinoza and dialectical thought. However, also in this case, his theoretical preoccupations do not press his intuition to the point of giving it the full explication it deserves. The strictly Althusserian foundation of Macherey's work obstructs his passage from the critical definition of dialectics and from the profound study of the analytical axes of Spinozian thought to a definition of the constitutive horizon that belongs to it.

5   See the article by C. Ginzburg in the collection *La crisi della ragione* (Turin, 1979). I do not think that, by including it in my vision of Spinoza, I strain the meaning that Ginzburg gives to "symptomatic knowledge" (*sapere indiziario*). I am not claiming that this is an identity but only that my Spinoza hints at that concrete synthesis of knowledge that symptomatic knowledge marks, a knowledge that is not "minor" but undoubtedly metaphysical.

6   On the development of modern science and on its perfectly functional character in the development of capitalism, or rather in theology, seen as an agent internal to science, see Paul Feyerabend, *Against Method: Outline of an Anarchist Theory of Knowledge* (London, 1975). It is obvious that when we attribute to Spinoza a speculative aspect that implies a polemic against modern science, we are making a second-level reflection on his thought. But this is important if one of the fundamental aims of a renewed historiography of modern thought is to shatter the univocality of its development, grasping the alternative possibilities internal to it. In this book, as in our *Descartes politico*, we have tried to put this idea in practice considering the development of modern political thought. It is equally necessary to attempt this operation on scientific thought as such. Feyerabend is very stimulating in this regard.

7   All of Modern thought, the thought of the origins of capitalism, should be reevaluated from the perspective of the crisis of capitalism. The identification of the specific synthesis that capitalist development imposes on its genetic components cannot be resolved in a pure functional scheme (as, for example, Borkenau attempts in his work, which is nonetheless extremely important, on the genesis of manufacturing thought). Today, the development is accomplished, the crisis of capitalism is mature: We are no longer wrapped up in its movements, but now, from a distance,

we can see its genetic components clearly. The possible alternative to this development, to the degree at least to which it is presented as revolutionary, should be linked with the theoretical consideration from the perspective of the crisis. I think that this has been accomplished by A. Sohn-Rethel in his *Intellectual and Manual Labor: A Critique of Epistemology* (Atlantic Highlands, NJ, 1977). It is a good model to keep in mind.

8 Allow me to here emphasize the importance that a similar model of philosophical thought has in the history of revolutionary thought, by referring to my *Marx beyond Marx* (South Hadley, Mass., 1984).

9 From different perspectives S. Zac and G. Deleuze, among others, refer explicitly to this idea of a philosophy of needs as the fabric of a (not insignificant) part of Spinozian thought. This thinking is directly in line with the work of A. Marcuse and A. Heller.

10 I am referring only to the old *Geschichte der Materialismus* by Lange, in the limits of its synthesis of positivism and Neokantianism. In fact, materialism has not been historicized! Perhaps it is precisely this point that reveals the way materialism has been twice subordinated in the Modern age: first to the development of the grand, sublime line of philosophy and second to the history of science. Although we now have great masterworks on the primary figures of ancient materialism (Democritus, Epicurus, etc.), we are still lacking such work on the Modern figures.

11 On the practical origin of humanism and the transformations it undergoes in Spinoza (and on the direction of those transformations) see M. Rubel, "Marx à la rencontre de Spinoza," in *Études de marxologie* (January–February 1978), pp. 239–65. But see also, on this topic, some clear intuitions by R. Mondolfo, "Il concetto marxistico della *umwälsende Praxis* e i suoi germi in Bruno e Spinoza," in *Festschrift für Carl Grinber* (Leipzig, 1932).

12 L. Strauss, *Thoughts on Machiavelli* (Glencoe, Ill., 1958), p. 40.

13 On the relationship between Spinoza and classical idealism see *Texte zur Entwicklung des Spinozismus*, ed. N. Altwicker (Darmstadt, 1971).

14 The literature on this extremely important passage in Modern philosophy is, to my knowledge, neither rich enough nor precise enough, despite the numerous works that various authors have produced. In effect, the entire historical significance of the Neoplatonic renewal has been investigated more profoundly in the realm of the philosophy of science (by Koyré, for example) than it has in political theory or economic sciences. Obviously, this lack should be filled as soon as possible. On More, his relations with Descartes and with Continental philosophy in general, see my *Descartes politico*. Naturally, the framework of any such work on Neoplatonism at the origins of industrial civilization should include the post-Cartesian philosophers, who had strong spiritualistic tendencies.

15 Mechanistic thought has been studied much more extensively. On the one hand, we have the very important work of Borkenau, and on the other, the work of Lenobke. Even though their points of departure and their methodologies are completely different, both of these authors reach singularly univocal conclusions.

16 On this topic see my article "Problemi dello Stato moderno," *Rivista critica de storia della filosofia* (1967). In this work I consider the fundamental theses on the absolutistic reorganization of the State and on its connection with the various forms of seventeenth-century philosophy.

17 On the idea of the market allow me once again to refer to Carlo Benetti's *Adamo Smith* (Milan, 1978). It is in this frame that one should try to understand the futile, spiritualistic attempts to reintroduce dualism into Spinoza's thought. The primary example of this approach is the work of F. Alquié, referred to several times above, on the theme *"idea"* – *"idea idearum,"* that is, on the spiritualistic and ideal, gnoseological and ontological, duplication of Spinoza's thought.

18 See Jon Elster, *Leibniz and the Development of Economic Rationalism* (Oslo, 1975).

19 Try to imagine, for example, what Descartes's attitude would have been with regard to Spinoza's philosophy. To my thinking there would have been a revival of those Renaissance conceptions that Spinoza continually argued against (see Gouhier). Probably, he would have flattened Spinoza's thought onto that of Lull or More. Such readings are very common in the history of Spinoza interpretations.

20   It is beyond doubt that Spinozism appears in Hegel as a utopian philosophy of capitalism. It is
     an objectivism of being and the beginnings of the dialectic of negation; in other words, Hegel
     identifies Spinoza as the philosopher of the utopia of production and the first author to
     identify the critical rhythm of the development of production. Hegel is prepared to philosoph-
     ically, absolutely complete this initial design. Spinozism is therefore reduced from the begin-
     ning to a philosophy of the relation between productive force and relations of production. But
     Spinoza's thought is something altogether different!

21   On this dimension of Spinoza's thought, on the dignity of the struggle for freedom that
     organically marks it and identifies it as great philosophy, allow me to refer to Leo Strauss,
     Persecution and the Art of Writing (Glencoe, Ill., 1952).

22   Such different authors as Zac, Corsi, and Alquié all arrive at this conclusion.

23   Walter Benjamin, *Gesammelte Schriften* B. III, t. 9 (Frankfurt, 1972), p. 526.

CHAPTER 14

Cultural Materialism, *Othello*, and the Politics of Plausibility

Alan Sinfield

Alan Sinfield's *Faultlines* (1992) is one of the best examples of Cultural Materialism at work. This chapter on Shakespeare's *Othello* is an especially forceful rendering of the Cultural Materialist argument that texts are not simple registers of social power. Rather, they must necessarily harbor dissident, fractious energies that undermine the sense of cohesive certainty that ruling elites seek to impose on a culture.

'Tis apt and of great credit

Cassio, in Shakespeare's *Othello*, is discovered in a drunken brawl. He laments: "Reputation, reputation, I ha' lost my reputation!" (2.3.254).[1] Iago replies, "You have lost no reputation at all, unless you repute yourself such a loser" (2.3.261–3), but this assertion is absurd (though attractive), since reputation is by definition a social construct, concerned entirely with one's standing in the eyes of others. In fact, language and reality are always interactive, dependent upon social recognition; reputation is only a specially explicit instance. Meaning, communication, language work only because they are shared. If you invent your own language, no one else will understand you; if you persist, you will be thought mad. Iago is telling Cassio to disregard the social basis of language, to make up his own meanings for words; it is the more perverse because Iago is the great manipulator of the prevailing stories of his society.

Stephen Greenblatt has remarked how Othello's identity depends upon a constant performance of his "story";[2] when in difficulty, his immediate move is to rehearse his nobility and service to the state. Actually, all the characters in *Othello* are telling stories, and to convince others even more than themselves. At the start, Iago and Roderigo are concocting a story – a sexist and racist story about how Desdemona is in "the gross clasps of a lascivious Moor" (1.1.126). Brabantio believes this story and repeats it to the Senate, but Othello contests it with his "tale":

> I will a round unvarnish'd tale deliver,
> Of my whole course of love.
>
> (1.3.90–1)

The tale is – that Othello told a story. Brabantio "Still question'd me the story of my life" (1.3.129), and this story attracted Desdemona. She asked to hear it through, observing,

> if I had a friend that lov'd her,
> I should but teach him how to tell my story,
> And that would woo her.
>
> (1.3.163–5)

So the action advances through a contest of stories, and the conditions of plausibility are therefore crucial – they determine which stories will be believed. Brabantio's case is that Othello must have enchanted Desdemona – anything else is implausible:

> She is abus'd, stol'n from me and corrupted,
> By spells and medicines, bought of mountebanks,
> For nature so preposterously to err,
> (Being not deficient, blind, or lame of sense,)
> Sans witchcraft could not.
>
> (1.3.60–4)

To Brabantio, for Desdemona to love Othello would be preposterous, an error of nature. To make this case, he depends on the plausibility, to the Senate, of the notion that Blacks are inferior outsiders. This, evidently, is a good move. Even characters who want to support Othello's story accept that he is superficially inappropriate as a husband for Desdemona. She says as much herself when she declares, "I saw Othello's visage in his mind" (1.3.252): this means, he may look like a black man but really he is very nice. And the Duke finally tells Brabantio: "Your son-in-law is far more fair than black" (1.3.290) – meaning, Othello doesn't have many of those unpleasant characteristics that we all know belong to Blacks, he is really quite like a white man.

With the conditions of plausibility so stacked against him, two main strategies are available to Othello, and he uses both. One is to appear very calm and responsible – as the Venetians imagine themselves to be. But also, and shrewdly, he uses the racist idea of himself as exotic: he says he has experienced "hair-breadth scapes," redemption from slavery, hills "whose heads touch heaven," cannibals, anthropophagi, "and men whose heads / Do grow beneath their shoulders" (1.3.129–45). These adventures are of course implausible – but not when attributed to an exotic. Othello has little credit by normal upper-class Venetian criteria, but when he plays on his strangeness, the Venetians tolerate him, for he is granting, in more benign form, part of Brabantio's case.

Partly, perhaps, because the senators need Othello to fight the Turks for them, they allow his story to prevail. However, this is not, of course, the end of the story. Iago repeats his racist and sexist tale to Othello, and persuades him of its credibility:

> I know our country disposition well . . .
> She did deceive her father, marrying you . . .
> Not to affect many proposed matches,
> Of her own clime, complexion, and degree,
> Whereto we see in all things nature tends . . .
>
> (3.3.205, 210, 233–5)

Othello is persuaded of his inferiority and of Desdemona's inconstancy, and he proceeds to act as if they were true. "Haply, for I am black," he muses (3.3.267), and begins to take the role of the "erring barbarian" (1.3.356–7) that he is alleged to be. As Ania Loomba puts it, "Othello moves from being a colonised subject existing on the terms of white Venetian society and trying to internalise its ideology, towards being marginalised, outcast and alienated from it in every way, until he occupies his 'true' position as its other."[3] It is very difficult not to be influenced by a story, even about yourself, when everyone else is insisting upon it. So in the last lines of the play, when he wants to reassert himself, Othello "recognizes" himself as what Venetian culture has really believed him to be: an ignorant, barbaric outsider – like, he says, the "base Indian" who threw away a pearl. Virtually, this is what Althusser means by "interpellation": Venice hails Othello as a barbarian, and he acknowledges that it is he they mean.[4]

Iago remarks that the notion that Desdemona loves Cassio is "apt and of great credit" (2.1.282); and that his advice to Cassio to press Desdemona for his reinstatement is "Probal to thinking" (2.3.329). Iago's stories work because they are plausible – to Roderigo, Brabantio, the Senate, even to Othello himself. As Peter Stallybrass has observed, Iago is convincing not because he is "superhumanly ingenious but, to the contrary, because his is the voice of 'common sense', the ceaseless repetition of the always-already 'known', the culturally 'given'."[5] The racism and sexism in the play should not be traced just to Iago's character, therefore, or to his arbitrary devilishness, but to the Venetian culture that sets the conditions of plausibility.

The Production of Ideology

I have spoken of stories because I want an inclusive term that will key in my theory to the continuous and familiar discourses of everyday life. But in effect I have been addressing the production of ideology. Societies need to produce materially to continue – they need food, shelter, warmth; goods to exchange with other societies; a transport and information infrastructure to carry those processes. Also, they have to produce ideologically (Althusser makes this argument at the start of his essay on ideological state apparatuses).[6] They need knowledges to keep material production going – diverse technical skills and wisdoms in agriculture, industry, science, medicine, economics, law, geography, languages, politics, and so on. And they need understandings, intuitive and explicit, of a system of social relationships within which the whole process can take place more or less evenly. Ideology produces, makes plausible, concepts and systems to explain who we are, who the others are, how the world works.

The strength of ideology derives from the way it gets to be common sense; it "goes without saying." For its production is not an external process, stories are not outside ourselves, something we just hear or read about. Ideology makes sense for us – of us – because it is already proceeding when we arrive in the world, and we come to consciousness in its terms. As the world shapes itself around and through us, certain interpretations of experience strike us as plausible: they fit with what we have experienced already, and are confirmed by others around us. So we complete what Colin Sumner calls a "circle of social reality": "understanding produces its own social reality at the same time as social reality produces its own understanding."[7] This is apparent when we observe how people in other cultures than our own make good sense of the world in ways that seem strange to us: their outlook is supported by their social context. For them, those frameworks of perception, maps of meaning, work.

The conditions of plausibility are therefore crucial. They govern our understandings of the world and how to live in it, thereby seeming to define the scope of feasible political change. Most societies retain their current shape, not because dissidents are penalized or incorporated, though they are, but because many people believe that things have to take more or less their present form – that improvement is not feasible, at least through the methods to hand. That is why one recognizes a dominant ideology: were there not such a powerful (plausible) discourse, people would not acquiesce in the injustice and humiliation that they experience. To insist on ideological construction is not to deny individual agency (though it makes individual agency less interesting). Rather, the same structure informs individuals and the society. Anthony Giddens compares the utterance of a grammatical sentence, which is governed by the lexicon and syntactical rules that constitute the language, but is individual and, through its utterance, may both confirm and slightly modify the language.[8]

Ideology is produced everywhere and all the time in the social order, but some institutions – by definition, those that usually corroborate the prevailing power arrangements – are vastly more powerful than others. The stories they endorse are more difficult to challenge, even to disbelieve. Such institutions, and the people in them, are also constituted in ideology; they are figures in its stories. At the same time, I would not want to lose a traditional sense of the power elite in the state exercising authority, through the ideological framework it both inhabits and maintains, over subordinate groups. This process may be observed in Shakespearean plays, where the most effective stories are given specific scope and direction by powerful men. They authorize scripts, we may say, that the other characters resist only with difficulty. Very often this does not require any remarkable intervention, or seems to involve only a "restoration of order," for the preferences of the ruling elite are already attuned to the system as it is already running. Conversely, scripting from below by lower-order characters immediately appears subversive; consider Shylock, Malvolio, Don John, Iago, Edmund, Macbeth, Caliban. Women may disturb the system (I return to this shortly), and in early comedies they are allowed to script, sometimes even in violation of parental wishes, but their scripts lead to the surrender of their power in the larger story of marriage. Elsewhere, women who script men are bad – Goneril and Regan, Lady Macbeth, the Queen in Cymbeline. Generally, the scripting of women by men is presented as good for them. Miranda's marriage in *The Tempest* seems to be all that Prospero has designed it to be. In *Measure for Measure*, Isabella is given by the Duke the script she ought to want – all the men in the play have conspired to draw her away from an independent life in the convent. To be sure, these are not the scripts of men only. As Stephen Orgel remarks, the plays must have appealed to the women in the audience as well: these were the fantasies of a whole culture.[9] But insofar as they show the powerful dominating the modes in which ideology is realized, these plays record an insight into ideology and power.

The state is the most powerful scriptor; it is best placed to enforce its story. In *Othello*, the Duke offers Brabantio, for use against Desdemona's alleged enchanter, "the bloody book of law" (1.3.67–70): the ruling elite have written this, and they decree who shall apply it. At the end of the play, Othello tries to control the story that will survive him – "When you shall these unlucky deeds relate, / Speak of them as they are" (5.2.342–3). However, the very last lines are spoken by Lodovico, the Venetian nobleman and representative of the Senate: "Myself will straight aboard, and to the state / This heavy act with heavy heart relate." The state and the ruling elite will tell Othello's story in the way they choose. They will try to control Iago's story as well, torturing him until he speaks what they want to hear: the state falls back on direct coercion when its domination of the conditions of plausibility falters. Through violence against Iago, the state means to make manifest his violence while legitimating its own.

The relation between violence and the ideological power of the state may be glimpsed in the way Othello justifies himself, in his last speech, as a good Venetian: he boasts of killing someone. Not Desdemona – that, he now agrees, was bad – but "a malignant and a turban'd Turk," who "Beat a Venetian, and traduc'd the state." Othello says he "took by the throat the circumcised dog, / And smote him thus" (5.2.352–7). And so, upon this recollection, Othello stabs himself, recognizing himself, for the last time, as an outsider, a discredit to the social order he has been persuaded to respect. Innumerable critics discuss Othello's suicide, but I haven't noticed them worrying about the murdered Turk. Being malignant, circumcised, and wearing a turban into the bargain, he seems not to require the sensitive attention of literary critics in Britain and North America. The character critic might take this reported murder as a last-minute revelation of Othello's long-standing propensity to desperate violence when people say things he doesn't like. But the violence here is not Othello's alone, any more than Venetian racism and sexism are particular to individuals. Othello's murder of the Turk is the kind of thing the Venetian state likes – or so we must assume, since Othello is in good standing in Venice as a state servant, and presents the story to enhance his credit. "He was great of heart," Cassio enthuses (5.2.362), pleased that he has found something to retrieve his respect for Othello. In respect of murdering state enemies, at least, he was a good citizen.

It is a definition of the state, almost, that it claims a monopoly of legitimate violence, and the exercise of that violence is justified through stories about the barbarity of those who are constituted as its demonized others. For the Venetians, as for the Elizabethans, the Turks were among the barbarians.[10] In actuality, in most states that we know of, the civilized and the barbaric are not very different from each other; that is why maintaining the distinction is such a constant ideological task. It is not altogether Othello's personal achievement, or his personal failure, therefore, when he kills himself declaring, with respect to the Turk, that he "smote him thus." Othello becomes a good subject once more by accepting within himself the state's distinction between civilized and barbaric. This "explains" how he has come to murder Desdemona: it was the barbarian beneath, or rather in, the skin. And when he kills himself it is even better, because he eradicates the intolerable confusion of finding both the citizen and the alien in the same body. Othello's particular circumstances bring into visibility, for those who want to see, the violence upon which the state and its civilization rest.

Structure and Individuals

My argument has reached the point where I have to address the scope for dissidence within ideological construction. "The class which is the ruling material force is, at the same time, its ruling intellectual force. The class which has the means of material

production at its disposal, has control at the same time over the means of mental production," Marx and Engels declare in *The German Ideology*.[11] The point is surely only
sensible: groups with material power will dominate the institutions that deal with
ideas. That is why people can be persuaded to believe things that are neither just,
humane, nor to their advantage. The issue is pressed harder in modern cultural theory.
In work deriving from Althusser and Foucault, distinct as those two sources are,
ideological constructedness, not just of our ideas but of our subjectivities, seems to
control the scope for dissident thought and expression. This is a key question: if we
come to consciousness within a language that is continuous with the power structures
that sustain the social order, how can we conceive, let alone organize, resistance?

The issue has been raised sharply by feminist critics, in particular Lynda E. Boose
and Carol Thomas Neely. They accuse both new historicism and cultural materialism
of theorizing power as an unbreakable system of containment, a system that positions
subordinate groups as effects of the dominant, so that female identity, for instance,
appears to be something fathered upon women by patriarchy.[12] How, it is asked, can
women produce a dissident perspective from such a complicit ideological base? And
so with other subordinated groups: if the conditions of plausibility persuade black or
gay people to assume subjectivities that suit the maintenance of the social order, how
is a radical black or gay consciousness to arise?

Kathleen McLuskie's argument that *Measure for Measure* and *King Lear* are organized from a male point of view has received particular attention. There is no way,
McLuskie says, to find feminist heroines in Regan and Goneril, the wicked women,
or in the good woman, Cordelia. Feminist criticism "is restricted to exposing its own
exclusion from the text."[13] The alternative feminist position, which we may term a
humanist or essentialist feminism, is stated by Carolyn Ruth Swift Lenz, Gayle
Greene, and Carol Thomas Neely in their groundbreaking collection of essays, *The
Woman's Part*. They believe feminist critics should, typically, be finding that Shakespeare's women characters are *not* male constructions – not "the saints, monsters, or
whores their critics have often perceived them to be." Rather, "like the male characters the women are complex and flawed, like them capable of passion and pain,
growth and decay."[14] This perspective is evidently at odds with the approach I am
presenting. In my view, when traditional critics perceive Shakespearean women characters in terms of stereotypes, they are often more or less right. Such critics recognize in the plays the ideological structures that our cultures have been producing.
My dispute with them begins when they admire the patterns they find and collaborate in rendering them plausible, instead of offering a critique of them. As McLuskie
says, we should attend to "the narrative, poetic and theatrical strategies which construct the plays' meanings and position the audience to understand their events from
a particular point of view."[15]

There are in fact two issues here. One is whether there is (for women or men) any
such fullness of personhood as Lenz, Greene, and Neely propose, or whether subjectivity is, as I have been arguing, an effect of cultural production. The other is the
authority of Shakespeare: can we reasonably assume that he anticipated a progressive
modern sexual politics? As McLuskie points out, he was working within "an entertainment industry which, as far as we know, had no women shareholders, actors,
writers, or stage hands" (p. 92). Ultimately these issues converge: the idea that
Shakespearean texts tune into an essential humanity, transcending cultural production, is aligned with the idea that individual characters do that. As Lynda Boose says,

the question is whether the human being is conceived as inscribing "at least something universal that transcends history, or as an entity completely produced by its historical culture." Boose credits McLuskie with "unblinkered honesty," but complains that one has "to renounce completely one's pleasure in Shakespeare and embrace instead the rigorous comforts of ideological correctness."[16] Maybe one does (try listening again to the words of most Christmas carols); but pleasure in Shakespeare is a complex phenomenon, and it may not be altogether incompatible with a critical attitude to ideology in the plays.

The essentialist-humanist approach to literature and sexual politics depends upon the belief that the individual is the probable, indeed necessary, source of truth and meaning. Literary significance and personal significance seem to derive from and speak to individual consciousnesses. But thinking of ourselves as essentially individual tends to efface processes of cultural production and, in the same movement, leads us to imagine ourselves to be autonomous, self-determining. It is not individuals but power structures that produce the system within which we live and think, and focusing upon the individual makes it hard to discern those structures; and if we discern them, hard to do much about them, since that would require collective action. To adopt the instance offered by Richard Ohmann in his book *English in America,* each of us buys an automobile because we need it to get around, and none of us, individually, does much damage to the environment or other people. But from that position it is hard to get to address, much less do anything about, whether we should be living in an automobile culture at all.[17]

I believe feminist anxiety about derogation of the individual in cultural materialism is misplaced, since personal subjectivity and agency are, anyway, unlikely sources of dissident identity and action. Political awareness does not arise out of an essential, individual, self-consciousness of class, race, nation, gender, or sexual orientation; but from involvement in a *milieu,* a *subculture.* "In acquiring one's conception of the world one belongs to a particular grouping which is that of all the social elements which share the same mode of thinking and acting," Gramsci observes.[18] It is through such sharing that one may learn to inhabit plausible oppositional preoccupations and forms – ways of relating to others – and hence develop a plausible oppositional selfhood. That is how successful movements have worked.

These issues have been most thoroughly considered by recent theorists of lesbian identity. Judith Butler argues against a universalist concept, "woman," not only on the ground that it effaces diversities of time and place, but also because it is oppressive: it necessarily involves "the exclusion of those who fail to conform to unspoken normative requirements of the subject."[19] Butler asks if "unity" is indeed necessary for effective political action, pointing out that "the articulation of an identity within available cultural terms instates a definition that forecloses in advance the emergence of new identity concepts in and through politically engaged actions" (p. 15). For agency to operate, Butler points out, a "doer" does not have to be in place first; rather, she or he is constructed through the deed. Identity develops, precisely, in the process of signification: "identity is always already signified, and yet continues to signify as it circulates within various interlocking discourses" (pp. 142–3). So "construction is not opposed to agency; it is the necessary scene of agency, the very terms in which agency is articulated and becomes culturally intelligible" (p. 147). Identity is not that which produces culture, nor even that which is produced as a static entity by culture: rather, the two are the same process.

If these arguments are correct, then it is not necessary to envisage, as Neely does, "some area of 'femaleness' that is part biological, part psychical, part experiential, part cultural and that is not utterly inscribed by and in thrall to patriarchal ideology and that makes possible female discourse."[20] "Female discourse" will be the discourse that women work out together at a historical conjuncture, and it will be rendered plausible by social interaction, especially among women. Desdemona gets closest to seeing what is going on when she talks with Emilia (what she needs is a refuge for battered wives); Othello gets it wrong because he has no reliable friends with whom to check out his perceptions. Subcultures constitute consciousness, in principle, in the same way that dominant ideologies do – but in partly dissident forms. In that bit of the world where the subculture runs, you can feel confident, as we used to say, that Black is beautiful, gay is good: there, those stories work, they build their own kinds of interactive plausibility. Validating the individual may seem attractive because it appears to empower him or her, but actually it undervalues potential resources of collective understanding and resistance.

Entrapment and Faultlines

While the ideology of individualism is associated mainly with traditional modes of literary criticism, the poststructuralist vein in recent cultural work, including new historicism, has also helped to obscure the importance of collectivities and social location. A principal theoretical task in such work has been to reassess the earlier Marxist base/superstructure model, whereby culture was seen as a one-way effect of economic organization. (In apparent ignorance of this work, much of which has been conducted in Europe, J. Hillis Miller supposes that people of "the so-called left" hold "an unexamined ideology of the material base.")[21] It was necessary to abandon that model, but in the process, as Peter Nicholls has pointed out, the tendency in new historicism has been "to replace a model of mechanical causality with one of structural homology." And this works to "displace the concepts of production and class which would initiate a thematics of historical change." Homology discovers synchronic structural connectedness without determination, sometimes without pressure or tension. Hence "the problem of ideology becomes a purely superstructural one."[22] The agency that has sunk from view, following Nicholls's argument, is that, not of individuals, but of classes, class fractions, and groups. Yet Marx was surely right to envisage such collectivities as the feasible agents of historical change.

New historicism has been drawn to what I call the "entrapment model" of ideology and power, whereby even, or especially, maneuvers that seem designed to challenge the system help to maintain it. Don E. Wayne says new historicism has often shown "how different kinds of discourse intersect, contradict, destabilize, cancel, or modify each other ... seek[ing] to demonstrate how a dominant ideology will give a certain rein to alternative discourses, ultimately appropriating their vitality and containing their oppositional force."[23] The issue informs the ambiguous title of *Renaissance Self-Fashioning*; Stephen Greenblatt's central figures aspired to fashion themselves, but he finds that their selves were fashioned for them. So Wyatt "cannot fashion himself in opposition to power and the conventions power deploys; on the contrary, those conventions are precisely what constitute Wyatt's self-fashioning."[24]

Hence Carolyn Porter's complaint that the subordinate seems a mere discursive effect of the dominant in new historicism.[25]

Of course, not all work generally dubbed "new historicist" takes such a line (not that of Louis Adrian Montrose). Nor is entrapment only here at issue – it arises generally in functionalism, structuralism, and Althusserian Marxism. Greenblatt has recently denied proposing that resistance is always coopted, and he is in my view right to say that his "Invisible Bullets" essay has often been misinterpreted.[26] I associate the entrapment model with new historicism nevertheless, because its treatment there has been distinctively subtle, powerful, and pressured, and because it is, of course, not by chance that this aspect of new historicism has been emphasized. The notion that dissidence is characteristically contained has caught the imagination of the profession. Therefore, even while acknowledging the diversity and specificity of actual writing, it is the aspect of new-historicist thought that has to be addressed.

An instance that confronts the entrapment model at its heart is the risk that the legally constituted ruler might not be able to control the military apparatus. Valuable new historicist analyses, considering the interaction of the monarch and the court, have tended to discover "power" moving in an apparently unbreakable circle – proceeding from and returning to the monarch. But although absolutist ideology represents the ruler as the necessary and sufficient source of national unity, the early modern state depended in the last analysis, like other states, upon military force. The obvious instance is the Earl of Essex's rebellion in 1601. With the queen aging and military success in Cadiz to his credit, it was easy for the charismatic earl to suppose that he should not remain subordinate. Ideological and military power threaten to split apart; it is a faultline in the political structure. Indeed, army coups against legitimate but militarily dependent political leaders still occur all the time. In the United States, during the Korean War, General Douglas MacArthur believed he could override the authority of President Harry S. Truman.

In *Macbeth*, Duncan has the legitimacy but Macbeth is the best fighter. Duncan cannot but delegate power to subordinates, who may turn it back upon him – the initial rebellion is that of the Thane of Cawdor, in whom Duncan says he "built / An absolute trust."[27] If the thought of revolt can enter the mind of Cawdor, then it will occur to Macbeth, and others; its source is not just personal (Macbeth's ambition). Of course, it is crucial to the ideology of absolutism to deny that the state suffers such a structural flaw. Hence the projection of the whole issue onto a supernatural backdrop of good and evil, and the implication that disruption must derive, or be crucially reinforced, from outside (by the Weird Sisters and the distinctively demonic Lady Macbeth). Macbeth's mistake, arguably, is that he falls for Duncan's ideology and loses his nerve. However, this does not mean that absolutist ideology was inevitably successful – when Charles I tried to insist upon it there was a revolution.

Henry V offers a magical resolution of this faultline by presenting the legitimate king as the triumphant war leader. The pressure of aspiration and anxiety around the matter may be gauged from the reference to Essex by the Chorus of Act 5. In the most specific contemporary allusion in any Shakespeare play, Henry V's return from France is compared first to Caesar's return as conqueror to Rome and then to Essex's anticipated return from Ireland:

> As, by a lower but by loving likelihood,
> Were now the general of our gracious empress,

> As in good time he may, from Ireland coming,
> Bringing rebellion broached on his sword,
> How many would the peaceful city quit
> To welcome him! much more, and much more cause,
> Did they this Harry.[28]

Notice the prudent qualification that this is "a lower … likelihood" insofar as Essex is but "the general of our gracious empress"; Harry would be welcomed "much more, and much more cause." The text strives to envisage a leader whose power, unlike that of the queen, would be uncontestable, but yet at the same time that of the queen. Promoting Elizabeth to empress (of Ireland) seems to give her a further edge over her commander. Even so the comparisons refuse to stabilize, for Henry V himself has just been likened to a caesar, and Julius Caesar threatened the government after his triumphal entry into Rome. And Elizabeth becomes empress only through Essex's military success, and that very success would enhance his potential for revolt. With the city specified as "peaceful," it seems only thoughtful to wonder whether it would remain so. However, faultlines are by definition resistant to the fantasies that would erase them. The epilogue to *Henry V* has to record that the absolutist pyramid collapsed with the accession of Henry VI, who, precisely, was not the strongest military leader. And Essex failed to mobilize sufficient support to bring Elizabeth within his power.

My argument is that dissident potential derives ultimately not from essential qualities in individuals (though they have qualities) but from conflict and contradiction that the social order inevitably produces within itself, even as it attempts to sustain itself. Despite their power, dominant ideological formations are always, in practice, under pressure, striving to substantiate their claim to superior plausibility in the face of diverse disturbances. Hence Raymond Williams's observation that ideology has always to be *produced*: "Social orders and cultural orders must be seen as being actively made: actively and continuously, or they may quite quickly break down."[29] Conflict and contradiction stem from the very strategies through which ideologies strive to contain the expectations that they need to generate. This is where failure – inability or refusal – to identify one's interests with the dominant may occur, and hence where dissidence may arise. In this argument the dominant and subordinate are structurally linked, but not in the way criticized by Carolyn Porter when she says that although "masterless men" (her instance) may ultimately have been controlled, "their subversive resistance cannot [therefore] be understood simply as the product of the dominant culture's power."[30] It was the Elizabethan social structure that produced unemployed laborers, and military leaders, but it could not then prevent such figures conceiving and enacting dissident practices, especially if they were able to constitute milieux within which dissidence might be rendered plausible.

Desdemona's Defiance

Another key point at which to confront the entrapment model concerns the scope of women. *Othello*, like many contemporary texts, betrays an obsessive concern with disorder; the ideology and power of the ruling elite are reasserted at the end of the play, but equilibrium is not, by any means, easily regained. The specific disruption stems from Desdemona's marital choice.[31] At her first entrance, her father asks her: "Do you perceive in all this noble company, / Where most you owe obedience?" She replies that she sees "a divided duty" – to her father and her husband: "I am hitherto your daughter: but here's my husband: / And so much duty as my mother show'd / To you, preferring you before her father, / So much I challenge, that I may profess, / Due to the Moor my Lord." (1.3.179–89). And to justify the latter allegiance, she declares: "I did love the Moor, to live with him" (1.2.248). This is a paradigm instance. For, in her use of the idea of a divided duty to justify elopement with an inappropriate man, Desdemona has not discovered a distinctive, radical insight (any more than Cordelia does when she uses it). She is offering a straightforward elaboration of official doctrine, which said that a woman should obey the male head of her family, who should be first her father (or failing that a brother or uncle), then her husband. Before marriage, the former; afterwards, the latter. Ideally, from the point of view of the social order, it would all be straightforward. The woman's transition from daughter to wife – from one set of duties to another – would be accomplished smoothly, with the agreement of all parties. But things could go wrong here; it was an insecure moment in patriarchy. The danger derived from a fundamental complication in the ideology of gender relations. Marriage was the institution through which property arrangements were made and inheritance secured, but it was supposed also to be a fulfilling personal relationship. It was held that the people being married should act in obedience to their parents, but also that they should love each other.[32] The "divided duty" was not especially Desdemona's problem, therefore; it is how the world was set up for her.

The Reformation intensified the issue by shifting both the status and the nature of marriage. The Catholic church held that the three reasons for matrimony were, first, to beget children; second, to avoid carnal sin; and third, for mutual help and comfort. Protestants stressed the third objective, often promoting it to first place; the homily "Of the State of Matrimony" says: "it is instituted of God, to the intent that man and woman should live lawfully in a perpetual friendly fellowship, to bring forth fruit, and to avoid fornication."[33] Thus protestants defined marriage more positively, as a mutual, fulfilling, reciprocal relationship. However, they were not prepared to abandon patriarchal authority; it was too important to the system. In *Arcadia*, Philip Sidney presents an ideal marriage of reciprocity and mutual love, that of Argalus and Parthenia: "A happy couple: he joying in her, she joying in herself, but in herself, because she enjoyed him: both increasing their riches by giving to each other; each making one life double, because they made a double life one." However, the passage concludes: "he ruling, because she would obey, or rather because she would obey, she therein ruling."[34] Does this mean that Parthenia was fulfilled in her subordinate role; or that by appearing submissive she managed to insinuate her own way? Neither seems ideal. In *The Anatomy of Melancholy*, Robert Burton displays a protestant enthusiasm: "You know marriage is honourable, a blessed calling, appointed by God himself in paradise; it breeds true peace, tranquillity, content and happiness." But the elaboration is tricky: "The husband rules her as head, but she again commands his heart, he is her servant, she his only joy and content." The alternation of head and heart sounds reciprocal but is not, for we know that the head should rule the heart. Then the strong phrasing of "servant" reverses altogether the initial priority, introducing language more appropriate to romantic love; and finally "only joy and content"[35] seems to privilege the wife but also places upon her an obligation to please. Coercion and liberty jostle together unresolved, and this is characteristic of protestant attitudes.

In fact, protestantism actually strengthened patriarchal authority. The removal of the mediatory priest threw upon the head of household responsibility for the spiritual life and devout conduct of the family. Also, there was a decline in the significance of great magnates who might stand between subject and monarch. From these developments, protestants devised a comprehensive doctrine of social control, with a double chain of authority running from God to the husband to the individual, and from God to the monarch to the subject. The homily "Against Disobedience and Wilful Rebellion" derives earthly rule from God and parallels the responsibilities of the monarch and the head of household. Indeed, the latter could be said to have the more important role. "A master in his family hath all the offices of Christ, for he must rule, and teach, and pray; rule like a king, and teach like a prophet, and pray like a priest," Henry Smith declared in "A Preparative to Marriage" (1591). This leaves little space for independence for offspring, or anyone else in the household.[36] Smith says parents must control marital choice because, after all, they have the property: "If children may not make other contracts without [parents'] good will, shall they contract marriage, which have nothing to maintain it after, unless they return to beg of them whom they scorned before?"[37] As with other business deals, it is wrong to enter into marriage unless you can sustain the costs. This was one extreme; at the other, only radicals like the Digger Gerrard Winstanley proposed that "every man and woman shall have the free liberty to marry whom they love."[38] In between, most commentators fudged the question, suggesting that children might exercise a right of refusal, or that even if they didn't like their spouses at first, they would learn to get on. "A couple is that whereby two persons standing in mutual relation to each other are combined together, as it were, into one. And of these two the one is always higher and beareth rule: the other is lower and yieldeth subjection," William Perkins declared.[39] The boundaries are plainly unclear, and conflict is therefore likely. Hence the awkward bullying and wheedling in the disagreements between Portia and Bassanio, Caesar and Portia, Othello and Desdemona, Macbeth and Lady Macbeth, Leontes and Hermione. Lawrence Stone says dutiful children experienced "an impossible conflict of role models. They had to try to reconcile the often incompatible demands for obedience to parental wishes on the one hand and expectations of affection in marriage on the other."[40] At this point, the dominant ideology had not quite got its act together.

Parental influence over marriage in early modern England is nowadays often regarded simply as an instance of the oppressiveness of patriarchy, but that is not quite all. The ambiguity of official doctrine afforded one distinct point at which a woman such as Desdemona could produce a crisis in the patriarchal story. "Despite the economic and social mechanisms that reinforced parental authority, it was in marriage that parents were most often defied," Dympna Callaghan observes.[41] All too often, such defiance provoked physical and mental violence; at the least it must have felt very unpleasant. That is how it is when you disturb the system – the tendency of ideology is, precisely, to produce good subjects who feel uncomfortable when they transgress. But contradictions in the ideology of marriage produced, nevertheless, an opportunity for dissidence, and even before the appearance of *Othello*, we are told, Desdemona was exploiting it – refusing "The wealthy curled darlings of our nation" (1.2.68). Her more extreme action – marrying without parental permission, outside the ruling oligarchy, and outside the race – is so disruptive that the chief (male) council of the state delays its business. "For if such actions may have passage free," Brabantio says, "Bond-slaves, and pagans, shall our statesmen be" (1.2.98). Desdemona throws the system into disarray – and just when the men are busy with one of their wars – killing people because of their honor and their property – proving their masculinity to each other.

To be sure, Desdemona was claiming only what Louis Montrose calls "the limited privilege of giving herself,"[42] and her moment of power ends once the men have accepted her marriage. But then dissident opportunities always are limited – otherwise we would not be living as we do. Revolutionary change is rare and usually dependent upon a prior buildup of small breaks; often there are great personal costs. The point of principle is that scope for dissident understanding and action occurs not because women characters, Shakespeare, and feminist readers have a privileged vantage point outside the dominant, but because the social order *cannot but produce* faultlines through which its own criteria of plausibility fall into contest and disarray. This has been theorized by Stuart Hall and his colleagues at the Centre for Contemporary Cultural Studies at the University of Birmingham:

> the dominant culture of a complex society is never a homogeneous structure. It is layered, reflecting different interests within the dominant class (e.g. an aristocratic versus a bourgeois outlook), containing different traces from the past (e.g. religious ideas within a largely secular culture), as well as emergent elements in the present. Subordinate cultures will not always be in open conflict with it. They may, for long periods, coexist with it, negotiate the spaces and gaps in it, make inroads into it, "warrening [*sic*] it from within.[43]

Observe that this account does not offer to decide whether or not dissidence will be contained; it may not even be actualized, but may lie dormant, becoming disruptive only at certain conjunctures. But if ideology is so intricately "layered," with so many potential modes of relation to it, it cannot but allow awareness of its own operations. In *Othello*, Emilia takes notable steps towards a dissident perception:

> But I do think it is their husbands' faults
> If wives do fall: say, that they slack their duties,
> And pour our treasures into foreign laps;
> Or else break out in peevish jealousies,
> Throwing restraint upon us; or say they strike us...
> (4.3.86–90)

Emilia has heard the doctrine of mutual fulfillment in marriage, and from the gap between it and her experience, she is well able to mount a critique of the double standard. At faultlines, such as I am proposing here, a dissident perspective may be discovered and articulated.

The crisis over marital choice illustrates how stories work in culture. It appears again and again – in *A Midsummer Night's Dream, The Merchant of Venice, The Taming of the Shrew, Romeo and Juliet, Measure for Measure, King Lear, The Winter's Tale, The Tempest.* Roughly speaking, in comedies parents are eventually reconciled to children's wishes; in tragedies (as in *Othello*), precipitate actions without parental authority lead to disaster. And in writing, on through the ensuing centuries until the late nineteenth century, the arranged versus the love-match is a recurring theme in literature. This is how culture elaborates itself. In these texts, through diverse genres and institutions, people were talking to each other about an aspect of their life that they found hard to handle. When a part of our worldview threatens disruption by manifestly failing to cohere with the rest, then we reorganize and retell its story, trying to get it into shape – back into the old shape if we are conservative-minded, or into a new shape if we are more adventurous. The question of the arranged versus the love-match died out in fiction in the late nineteenth century because then, for most people in Britain, it was resolved in favor of children's preferences, and therefore became uninteresting (but not, however, for British families deriving recently from Asia). The other great point at which the woman could disturb the system was by loving a man not her husband, and that is why adultery is such a prominent theme in literature. It upsets the husband's honor, his masculinity, and (through the bearing of illegitimate children) his property. Even the rumor of Desdemona's adultery is enough to send powerful men in the state into another anxiety.

This is why it is not unpromising to seek in literature our preoccupations with class, race, gender, and sexual orientation: it is likely that literary texts will address just such controversial aspects of our ideological formation. Those faultline stories are the ones that require most assiduous and continuous reworking; they address the awkward, unresolved issues, the ones in which the conditions of plausibility are in dispute. For authors and readers, after all, want writing to be interesting. The task for a political criticism, then, is to observe how stories negotiate the faultlines that distress the prevailing conditions of plausibility.

Reading Dissidence

The reason why textual analysis can so readily demonstrate dissidence being incorporated is that dissidence operates, necessarily, with reference to dominant structures. It has to invoke those structures to oppose them, and therefore can always, *ipso facto*, be discovered reinscribing that which it proposes to critique. "Power relations are always two-way; that is to say, however subordinate an actor may be in a social relationship, the very fact of involvement in that relationship gives him or her a certain amount of power over the other," Anthony Giddens observes.[44] The inter-involvement of resistance and control is systemic: it derives from the way language and culture get articulated. Any utterance is bounded by the other utterances that the language makes possible. Its shape is the correlative of theirs: as with the duck/rabbit drawing, when you see the duck the rabbit lurks round its edges, constituting an alternative that may spring into visibility. Any position supposes its intrinsic opposition. All stories comprise within themselves the ghosts of the alternative stories they are trying to exclude.

It does not follow, therefore, that the outcome of the inter-involvement of resistance and control must be the incorporation of the subordinate. Indeed, Foucault says the same, though he is often taken as the theorist of entrapment. In *The History of Sexuality: An Introduction*, he says there is no "great Refusal," but envisages "a plurality of resistances . . . spread over time and space at varying densities, at times mobilising groups or individuals in a definitive way." He *denies* that these must be "only a reaction or rebound, forming with respect to the basic domination an underside that is in the end always passive, doomed to perpetual defeat."[45] In fact, a dissident text may derive its leverage, its purchase, precisely from its partial implication with the dominant. It may embarrass the dominant by appropriating its concepts and imagery. For instance, it seems clear that nineteenth-century legal, medical, and sexological discourses on homosexuality made possible new forms of control; but, at the same time, they also made possible what Foucault terms "a 'reverse' discourse," whereby "homosexuality began to speak in its own behalf, to demand that its legitimacy or 'naturality' be acknowledged, often in the same vocabulary, using the same categories by which it was medically disqualified."[46] Deviancy returns from abjection by deploying just those terms that relegated it there in the first place. A dominant discourse cannot prevent "abuse" of its resources. Even a text that aspires to contain a subordinate perspective must first bring it into visibility; even to misrepresent, one must present. And once that has happened, there can be no guarantee that the subordinate will stay safely in its prescribed place. Readers do not have to respect closures – we do not, for instance, have to accept that the independent women characters in Shakespearean comedies find their proper destinies in the marriage deals at the ends of those plays. We can insist on our sense that the middle of such a text arouses expectations that exceed the closure.

Conversely, a text that aspires to dissidence cannot control meaning either. It is bound to slide into disabling nuances that it fails to anticipate, and it cannot prevent the drawing of reactionary inferences by readers who want to do that. (Among other things, this might serve as a case against ultra-leftism, by which I mean the complacency of finding everyone else to be ideologically suspect.) There can be no security in textuality: no scriptor can control the reading of his or her text. And when, in any instance, either incorporation or resistance turns out to be the more successful, that is not in the nature of things. It is because of their relative strengths in that situation. So it is not quite as Jonathan Goldberg has recently put it, turning the entrapment model inside out, that "dominant discourses allow their own subversion precisely because hegemonic control is an impossible dream, a self-deluding fantasy."[47] Either outcome depends on the specific balance of historical forces. Essex's rebellion failed because he could not muster adequate support on the day. It is the same with competence. Williams remarks that the development of writing reinforced cultural divisions, but also that "there was no way to teach a man to read the Bible ... which did not also enable him to read the radical press." Keith Thomas observes that "the uneven social distribution of literacy skills greatly widened the gulf between the classes"; but he illustrates also the fear that "if the poor learned to read and write they would become seditious, atheistical, and discontented with their humble position."[48] Both may occur, in varying degrees; it was, and is, all to play for.

It is to circumvent the entrapment model that I have generally used the term *dissident* rather than *subversive,* since the latter may seem to imply achievement that something *was subverted* – and hence (since mostly the government did not fall, patriarchy did not crumble) that containment must have occurred. "Dissidence" I take to imply refusal of an aspect of the dominant, without prejudging an outcome. This may sound like a weaker claim, but I believe it is actually stronger insofar as it posits a field necessarily open to continuing contest, in which at some conjunctures the dominant will lose ground while at others the subordinate will scarcely maintain its position. As Jonathan Dollimore has said, dissidence may provoke brutal repression, and that shows not that it was all a ruse of power to consolidate itself, but that "the challenge really *was* unsettling."[49]

The implications of these arguments for literary criticism are substantial, for it follows that formal textual analysis cannot determine whether a text is subversive or contained. The historical conditions in which it is being deployed are decisive. "Nothing can be intrinsically or essentially subversive in the sense that prior to the event subversiveness can be more than potential; in other words it cannot be guaranteed a priori, independent of articulation, context and reception," Dollimore observes.[50] Nor, independently of context, can anything be said to be safely contained. This prospect scandalizes literary criticism, because it means that meaning is not adequately deducible from the text-on-the-page. The text is always a site of cultural contest, but it is never a self-sufficient site.

It is a key proposition of cultural materialism that the specific historical conditions in which institutions and formations organize and are organized by textualities must be addressed. That is what Raymond Williams was showing us for thirty years. The entrapment model is suspiciously convenient for literary criticism, because it means that little would be gained by investigating the specific historical effectivity of texts. And, indeed, Don Wayne very shrewdly suggests that the success of prominent new historicists may derive in large part from their skills in close reading – admittedly of a far wider range of texts – which satisfy entirely traditional criteria of performativity in academic criticism.[51] Cultural materialism calls for modes of knowledge that literary criticism scarcely possesses, or even knows how to discover – modes, indeed, that hitherto have been cultivated distinctively within that alien other of essentialist humanism, Marxism. These knowledges are in part the provinces of history and other social sciences – and, of course, they bring in their train questions of historiography and epistemology that require theory more complex than the tidy poststructuralist formula that everything, after all, is a text (or that everything is theater). This prospect is valuable in direct proportion to its difficulty for, as Foucault maintains, the boundaries of disciplines effect a policing of discourses, and their erosion may, in itself, help to "detach the power of truth from the forms of hegemony (social, economic and cultural) within which it operates at the present time" in order to constitute "a new politics of truth."[52]

Shakespearean plays are themselves powerful stories. They contribute to the perpetual contest of stories that constitutes culture: its representations, and our critical accounts of them, reinforce or challenge prevailing notions of what the world is like, of how it might be. "The detailed and substantial *performance of a known model* of 'people like this, relations like this', is in fact the real achievement of most serious novels and plays," Raymond Williams observes; by appealing to the reader's sense of how the world is, the text affirms the validity of the model it invokes. Among other things, *Othello* invites *recognition* that this is how people are, how the world goes. That is why the criteria of plausibility are political. This effect is not countered, as essentialist-humanists have long supposed, by literary quality; the more persuasive the writing, the greater its potential for political intervention.

The quintessential traditional critical activity was always interpretive, getting the text to make sense. Hence the speculation about character motivation, image patterns, thematic integration, structure: the task always was *to help the text into coherence.* And the discovery of coherence was taken as the demonstration of quality. However, such practice may feed into a reactionary politics. The easiest way to make *Othello* plausible in Britain is to rely on the lurking racism, sexism, and superstition in British culture. Why does Othello, who has considerable experience of people, fall so conveniently for Iago's stories? We can make his gullibility plausible by suggesting that black people are generally of a rather simple disposition. To explain why Desdemona elopes with Othello and then becomes so submissive, we might appeal to a supposedly fundamental silliness and passivity of women. Baffled in the attempt to find motive for Iago's malignancy, we can resort to the devil, or the consequence of skepticism towards conventional morality, or homosexuality. Such interpretations might be plausible; might "work," as theater people say; but only because they activate regressive aspects of our cultural formation.

Actually, coherence is a chimera, as my earlier arguments should suggest. No story can contain all the possibilities it brings into play; coherence is always selection. And the range of feasible readings depends not only on the text but on the conceptual framework within which we address it. Literary criticism tells its own stories. It is, in effect, a subculture, asserting its own distinctive criteria of plausibility. Education has taken as its brief the socialization of students into these criteria, while masking this project as the achievement by talented individuals (for it is in the program that most should fail) of a just and true reading of texts that are just and true. A cultural materialist practice will review the institutions that retell the Shakespeare stories, and will attempt also a self-consciousness about its own situation within those institutions. We need not just to produce different readings but to shift the criteria of plausibility.

Notes

1 *Othello* is quoted from the New Arden edition, ed. M. R. Ridley (London: Methuen, 1962). An earlier version of parts of this paper, entitled "Othello and the Politics of Character," was published in Manuel Barbeito, ed., *In Mortal Shakespeare: Radical Readings* (Santiago: University de Santiago de Compostela, 1989).

2 Stephen Greenblatt, *Renaissance Self-Fashioning* (Chicago: University of Chicago Press, 1980), p. 245; and also pp. 234–9, and Greenblatt, "Psychoanalysis and Renaissance Culture," in Patricia Parker and David Quint, eds., *Literary Theory/Renaissance Texts* (Baltimore: Johns Hopkins University Press, 1986), p. 218. On stories in *Othello*, see further Jonathan Goldberg, "Shakespearean Inscriptions: The Voicing of Power," in Patricia Parker and Geoffrey Hartman, eds., *Shakespeare and the Question of Theory* (New York: Methuen, 1985), pp. 131–2.

3 Ania Loomba, *Gender, Race, Renaissance Drama* (Manchester University Press, 1989), p. 48. See also Doris Adler, "The Rhetoric of Black and White in Othello," *Shakespeare Quarterly* 25 (1974), pp. 248–57.

4 Louis Althusser, "Ideological State Apparatuses," in Althusser, *Lenin and Philosophy and Other Essays,* trans. Ben Brewster (London: New Left Books, 1971), pp. 160–5.

5 Peter Stallybrass, "Patriarchal Territories: The Body Enclosed," in Margaret W. Ferguson, Maureen Quilligan, and Nancy J. Vickers, eds., *Rewriting the Renaissance* (Chicago: University of Chicago Press, 1986), p. 139. Greenblatt makes a comparable point about Jews in Marlowe's *Jew of Malta,* though in *Othello* he stresses Iago's "ceaseless narrative invention": see *Renaissance Self-Fashioning,* pp. 208, 235. On Blacks in Shakespearean England, see Loomba, *Gender, Race, Renaissance Drama,* pp. 42–52; Ruth Cowhig, "Blacks in English Renaissance Drama and the Role of Shakespeare's *Othello,*" in David Dabydeen, ed., *The Black Presence in English Literature* (Manchester: Manchester University Press, 1985).

6 Althusser, *Lenin and Philosophy,* pp. 123–8. For further elaboration of the theory presented here, see Alan Sinfield, *Literature, Politics and Culture in Postwar Britain* (Oxford: Blackwell; Berkeley: University of California Press, 1989), ch. 3.

7 Colin Sumner, *Reading Ideologies* (London and New York: Academic Press, 1979), p. 288.

8 Anthony Giddens, *Central Problems in Social Theory* (London: Macmillan, 1979), pp. 69–71, 77–8. Giddens's development of *langue* and *parole* is anticipated in Michel Foucault, *The Order of Things* (London: Tavistock, 1970), p. 380.

9 Stephen Orgel, "Nobody's Perfect: Or Why Did the English Stage Take Boys for Women?" *South Atlantic Quarterly* 88 (1989), pp. 7–29, pp. 8–10. Jonathan Goldberg writes of the Duke's scripting in *Measure For Measure* in his *James I and the Politics of Literature* (Baltimore: Johns Hopkins University Press, 1983), pp. 230–9. See also Steven Mullaney, *The Place of the Stage* (Chicago: University of Chicago Press, 1988), pp. 107–10.

10 On attitudes to Turks, see Simon Shepherd, *Marlowe and the Politics of Elizabethan Theatre* (New York: St Martin's Press, 1986), pp. 142–9. The later part of Othello's career, in fact, has been devoted entirely to state violence – as Martin Orkin has suggested, he is sent to Cyprus to secure it for the colonial power: see Orkin, *Shakespeare Against Apartheid* (Craighall, South Africa: Ad. Donker, 1987), pp. 88–96.

11 Karl Marx and Friedrich Engels, *The German Ideology* (London: Lawrence and Wishart, 1965), p. 61. See further Althusser, *Lenin and Philosophy*, pp. 139–42; Pierre Bourdieu, "Cultural Reproduction and Social Reproduction," in Richard Brown, ed., *Knowledge, Education and Cultural Change* (London: Tavistock, 1973).

12 See Lynda Boose, "The Family in Shakespearean Studies; or – Studies in the Family of Shakespeareans; or – the Politics of Politics," *Renaissance Quarterly* 40 (1987), pp. 707–42; Carol Thomas Neely, "Constructing the Subject: Feminist Practice and the New Renaissance Discourses," *English Literary Renaissance* 18 (1988), pp. 5–18.

13 Kathleen McLuskie, "The Patriarchal Bard: Feminist Criticism and Shakespeare," in Jonathan Dollimore and Alan Sinfield, eds., *Political Shakespeare* (Manchester: Manchester University Press; Ithaca: Cornell University Press, 1985), p. 97. For a reply to her critics by Kathleen McLuskie, see her *Renaissance Dramatists* (Hemel Hempstead: Harvester Wheatsheaf, 1989), pp. 224–9; and for further comment, Jonathan Dollimore, "Shakespeare, Cultural Materialism, Feminism and Marxist Humanism," *New Literary History* 21 (1990), pp. 471–93.

14 Carol Ruth Swift Lenz, Gayle Greene, and Carol Thomas Neely, eds., *The Woman's Part* (Urbana: University of Illinois Press, 1980), p. 5.

15 McLuskie, "Patriarchal Bard," p. 92.

16 Boose, "Family," pp. 734, 726, 724. See also Ann Thompson, " 'The warrant of womanhood': Shakespeare and Feminist Criticism," in Graham Holderness, ed., *The Shakespeare Myth* (Manchester: Manchester University Press, 1988); Judith Newton, "History as Usual?: Feminism and the New Historicism," *Cultural Critique* 9 (1988), pp. 87–121.

17 Richard Ohmann, *English in America* (New York: Oxford University Press, 1976), p. 313. See V. N. Vološinov, *Marxism and the Philosophy of Language*, trans. Ladislav Matejka and I. R. Titunik (New York and London: Seminar Press, 1973), pp. 17–24, 83–98.

18 Antonio Gramsci, *Selections from the Prison Notebooks*, ed. and trans. Quintin Hoare and Geoffrey Nowell-Smith (London: Lawrence and Wishart, 1971), p. 324.

19 Judith Butler, *Gender Trouble* (London: Routledge, 1990), p. 6. See Celia Kitzinger, *The Social Construction of Lesbianism* (London: Sage, 1987). Diana Fuss asks: "Is politics based on identity, or is identity based on politics?" (*Essentially Speaking* [London: Routledge, 1989], p. 100).

20 Neely, "Constructing the Subject," p. 7.

21 J. Hillis Miller, "Presidential Address, 1986: The Triumph of Theory, and the Resistance of Reading, and the Question of the Material Base," *PMLA* 102 (1987), pp. 281–91, pp. 290–1. Cf., e.g., Raymond Williams, "Base and Superstructure in Marxist Cultural Theory," *New Left Review* 82 (1973), pp. 3–16; reprinted in Williams, *Problems in Materialism and Culture* (London: Verso, 1980; New York: Schocken Books, 1981). James Holstun, "Ranting at the New Historicism," *English Literary Renaissance* 19 (1989), pp. 189–225, makes more effort than most to address European/Marxist work.

22 Peter Nicholls, "State of the Art: Old Problems and the New Historicism," *Journal of American Studies* 23 (1989), pp. 423–34, pp. 428, 429.

23 Don. E. Wayne, "New Historicism," in Malcolm Kelsall, Martin Coyle, Peter Garside, and John Peck, eds., *Encyclopedia of Literature and Criticism* (London: Routledge, 1990), p. 795.

I am grateful to Professor Wayne for showing this essay to me in typescript. Further on this topic, see Jean E. Howard and Marion F. O'Connor, "Introduction," Don. E. Wayne, "Power, Politics and the Shakespearean Text: Recent Criticism in England and the United States," and Walter Cohen, "Political Criticism of Shakespeare," all in Jean E. Howard and Marion F. O'Connor, eds., *Shakespeare Reproduced* (London: Methuen, 1987); Louis Montrose, "Professing the Renaissance: The Poetics and Politics of Culture," in H. Aram Veeser, ed, *The New Historicism* (New York: Routledge, 1989), pp. 20–4; Alan Liu, "The Power of Formalism: The New Historicism," *English Literary History* 56 (1989), pp. 721–77.

24 Greenblatt, *Renaissance Self-Fashioning*, pp. 120, 209–14.

25 Carolyn Porter, "Are We Being Historical Yet?" *South Atlantic Quarterly* 87 (1988), pp. 743–86; see also Porter, "History and Literature: 'After the New Criticism,'" *New Literary History* 21 (1990), pp. 253–72.

26 Stephen Greenblatt, *Learning to Curse: Essays in Early Modern Culture* (London: Routledge, 1990), pp. 164–6.

27 William Shakespeare, *Macbeth*, ed. Kenneth Muir, 9th edn (London: Methuen, 1962), pp. 164–6.

28 William Shakespeare, *King Henry V*, ed. J. H. Walter (London: Methuen, 1954), Act 5, Chorus, 29–35.

29 Raymond Williams, *Culture* (Glasgow: Fontana, 1981), p. 201.

30 Porter, "Are We Being Historical Yet?" p. 774. For important recent discussions of the scope for movement in the early modern state, see Richard Cust and Ann Hughes, eds., *Conflict in Early Stuart England* (London: Longman, 1989), esp. Johann Sommerville, "Ideology, Property and the Constitution."

31 I am not happy that race and sexuality tend to feature in distinct parts of this chapter; in this respect, my wish to clarify certain theoretical arguments has produced some simplification. Of course, race and sexuality are intertwined, in *Othello* as elsewhere. See Loomba, *Gender, Race, Renaissance Drama*, pp. 48–62; Karen Newman, "'And wash the Ethiop white': Femininity and the Monstrous in Othello," in Howard and O'Connor, eds., *Shakespeare Reproduced*; Jonathan Dollimore, *Sexual Dissidence* (Oxford: Oxford University Press, 1991), part 4.

32 I set out this argument in Alan Sinfield, *Literature in Protestant England, 1560–1660* (London: Croom Helm, 1983), ch. 4. See also Juliet Dusinberre, *Shakespeare and the Nature of Women* (London: Macmillan, 1976); Simon Shepherd, *Amazons and Warrior Women* (Brighton: Harvester, 1981), pp. 53–6, 107–18; Catherine Belsey, *The Subject of Tragedy* (London: Methuen, 1985), ch. 7; Dympna Callaghan, *Woman and Gender in Renaissance Tragedy* (Atlantic Highlands, NJ: Humanities Press, 1989), ch. 2 *et passim*; McLuskie, *Renaissance Dramatists*, pp. 31–9, 50–5 *et passim*.

33 *Certain Sermons or Homilies* (London: Society for Promoting Religious Knowledge, 1899), p. 534.

34 Sir Philip Sidney, *Arcadia*, ed. Maurice Evans (Harmondsworth, Penguin Books, 1977), p. 501.

35 Robert Burton, *The Anatomy of Melancholy*, ed. Holbrook Jackson (London: Dent, 1932), 3, pp. 52–3.

36 *Certain Sermons*, p. 589.

37 Henry Smith, *Works*, with a memoir by Thomas Fuller (Edinburgh, 1886), 1, pp. 32, 19.

38 Gerrard Winstanley, *Works*, ed. G. H. Sabine (Ithaca, NY: Cornell University Press, 1941), p. 599.

39 William Perkins, *Christian Economy* (1609), in *The Work of William Perkins*, ed. Ian Breward (Abingdon: Sutton Courtenay Press, 1970), pp. 418.

40 Lawrence Stone, *The Family, Sex and Marriage* (London: Weidenfeld and Nicolson, 1977), p. 137. See also ibid., pp. 151–9, 178–91, 195–302; Charles and Katherine George, *The Protestant Mind of the English Reformation* (Princeton: Princeton University Press, 1961), pp. 257–94; Christopher Hill, *Society and Puritanism in Pre-Revolutionary England* (London: Panther, 1969), pp. 429–67; Louis Adrian Montrose, "'Shaping Fantasies': Figurations of Gender and Power in Elizabethan Culture," in Stephen Greenblatt, ed., *Representing the English Renaissance* (Berkeley: University of California Press, 1988), pp. 37–40; Lisa Jardine, *Still*

Harping on Daughters (Brighton: Harvester, 1983), ch. 3; Leonard Tennenhouse, *Power on Display* (London: Methuen, 1986), pp. 17–30, 147–54; Patrick Collinson, *The Birthpangs of Protestant England* (London: Macmillan, 1988), ch. 3.

41 Callaghan, *Woman and Gender*, p. 21; also pp. 19–22, 101–5. On women's scope for negotiation, see also Ann Rosalind Jones, *The Currency of Eros: Women's Love Lyric in Europe, 1540–1620* (Bloomington: Indiana University Press, 1990), pp. 1–10.

42 Montrose, "'Shaping Fantasies,'" p. 37. For the thought that the men in *Othello* are preoccupied with their masculinity but ineffectual, see Carol Thomas Neely, *Broken Nuptials in Shakespeare's Plays* (New Haven: Yale University Press, 1985), pp. 119–22.

43 John Clarke, Stuart Hall, Tony Jefferson, and Brian Roberts, "Subcultures, Cultures and Class," in Stuart Hall and Tony Jefferson, eds., *Resistance through Rituals* (London: Hutchinson; Birmingham: Centre for Contemporary Cultural Studies, 1976), p. 12. The final phrase is quoted from E. P. Thompson's essay "The Peculiarities of the English."

44 Giddens, *Central Problems*, p. 6. See further Raymond Williams, *Marxism and Literature* (Oxford: Oxford University Press, 1977), pp. 108–27; Fredric Jameson, "Reification and Utopia in Mass Culture," *Social Text* 1 (1979), pp. 144–8; Colin Gordon, "Afterword," in Michel Foucault, *Power/Knowledge* (Brighton: Harvester, 1980).

45 Michel Foucault, *The History of Sexuality: Volume 1*, trans. Robert Hurley (New York: Random House, Vintage Books, 1980), pp. 95–6. Also, as Jonathan Culler has remarked, Foucault's exposure of the ubiquity of regulatory practices may itself be experienced as liberatory: Culler, *Framing the Sign* (Oxford: Blackwell Publishers, 1988), pp. 66–7.

46 Foucault, *History of Sexuality*, p. 101. See Jonathan Dollimore and Alan Sinfield, "Culture and Textuality: Debating Cultural Materialism," *Textual Practice* 4, no.1 (Spring 1990), pp. 91–100, p. 95; and Jonathan Dollimore, "Sexuality, Subjectivity and Transgression: The Jacobean Connection," *Renaissance Drama*, NS 17 (1986), pp. 53–82.

47 Jonathan Goldberg, "Speculations: *Macbeth* and Source," in Howard and O'Connor, eds., *Shakespeare Reproduced*, pp. 244, 247. See also Jonathan Goldberg, *Wanting Matter: From the Hands of the English Renaissance* (Stanford, Calif.: Stanford University Press, 1990), esp. pp. 41–55.

48 Williams, *Culture*, pp. 94, 110; Keith Thomas, "The Meaning of Literacy in Early Modern England," in Gerd Baumann, ed., *The Written Word: Literacy in Transition* (Oxford: Clarendon Press, 1986), pp. 116, 118.

49 Dollimore, "Shakespeare, Cultural Materialism, Feminism and Marxist Humanism," p. 482. See also Holstun, "Ranting at the New Historicism."

50 Dollimore and Sinfield, *Political Shakespeare*, p. 13; discussed in Dollimore and Sinfield, "Culture and Textuality." See also Alan Liu's argument that we need to consider not only subjects and representation, but action: Liu, "Power of Formalism," pp. 734–5.

51 Wayne, "New Historicism," in Kelsall, Coyle, Garside, and Peck, eds., *Encyclopedia*, pp. 801–2. See also Culler, *Framing*, p. 37; Porter, "History and Literature," pp. 253–6.

52 "The Political Function of the Intellectual," trans. Colin Gordon, *Radical Philosophy* 17 (1977), pp. 12–15, p. 14; see Eve Tavor Bannet, *Structuralism and the Logic of Dissent* (London: Macmillan, 1989), pp. 170–8.

PART EIGHT

Feminism

CHAPTER 1

Introduction: Feminist Paradigms

Julie Rivkin and Michael Ryan

Contemporary feminist literary criticism begins as much in the women's movement of the late 1960s and early 1970s as it does in the academy. Its antecedents go back much further, of course, whether one takes Virginia Woolf's *A Room of One's Own* or an even earlier text as a point of departure (Maggie Humm cites *Inanna*, a text written 2,000 years before the Bible, which presents the fate of a goddess who questions sexual discourse). Feminist criticism's self-transformations over the past several decades as it engages with both critiques from within and encounters from without – encounters with psychoanalysis, Marxism, Post-Structuralisms, ethnic studies, post-colonial theory, and lesbian and gay studies – have produced a complex proliferation of work not easily subsumed to a single description. The title of a recent collection of essays – *Conflicts in Feminism*[1] – speaks to the situation of feminist criticism at the present: equality versus difference, cultural feminism versus Post-Structuralist feminism, essentialism versus social constructionism. Feminism *and* gender theory? Feminism *or* gender theory? Feminism with ethnic specificity or with other crossings? Feminism national or feminism international? If the student of literature in the early 1970s was moved to ask why is there not a *feminist* criticism, the student of literary theory in the late 1990s might well be moved to shift the emphasis and ask but why is there not *a* feminist criticism? The frustrations of proliferation can also be construed as the pains of progress, and if the tone of feminist criticism has lost the celebratory solidarity of its early days, it has gained a much needed complexity of analysis. An analysis of gender that "ignores" race, class, nationality, and sexuality is one that assumes a white, middle-class, heterosexual woman inclined toward motherhood as the subject of feminism; only by questioning the status of the subject of feminism – "woman" – does a feminist criticism avoid replicating the masculinist cultural error of taking the dominant for the universal.

For the women's movement of the 1960s and early 1970s the subject of feminism was women's experience under patriarchy, the long tradition of male rule in society which silenced women's voices, distorted their lives, and treated their concerns as peripheral. To be a woman under such conditions was in some respects not to exist at all. "When We Dead Awaken" seemed to Adrienne Rich a justified title for an address regarding women at the Modern Language Association in 1970.[2] With other noteworthy feminists of the 1960s and 1970s like Germaine Greer (*The Female Eunuch*) and Kate Millett (*Sexual Politics*), Rich inspired into life a school of feminist literary criticism that took the history of women's oppression and the silencing of their voices as twin beacons to guide its work. But how was that history to be interpreted, those voices to be read? Were they the voices of fellow beings who

shared a common biology or ontology? Or were history and social context so constitutive of all being that no thing called "woman" could be said to exist outside them?
Was "woman" something to be escaped from or into?

Early on, feminist scholars realized that the "canon" taught in schools was overwhelmingly male. To be a woman graduate student in the 1960s was to hear recog-
nizably male points of view, some of which were noticeably misogynist, declared to
be "universal." Were there no women writers, then, aside from George Eliot and
Jane Austen, Willa Cather or Emily Dickinson? And how were feminist scholars to
deal with the canon? Elaine Showalter set about reconstructing a history of women
writers (*A Literature of Their Own*). Judith Fetterley took up the question of how
women are represented in "great" American literature (*The Resisting Reader*). And
Sandra Gilbert and Susan Gubar examined the issue of what it meant for women
writers to seek entry to a tradition dominated by images that did such violence to
women (*The Madwoman in the Attic*).

The movement very quickly leapt across ethnic and gender boundaries (if indeed,
given Rich's work both on her own ethnicity and her own gender difference, it might
not be said to always have been across such boundaries). African American feminist
scholars like Mary Helen Washington, Barbara Smith, and bell hooks depicted a
history of African American women's experience along the twin axes of race and
gender that had a unique specificity. Lesbian feminist critics like Bonnie Zimmerman
and Susan Griffin reconstructed a hidden tradition of lesbian writing and explored
the experience of radical alterity within a heterosexist world. Feminist literary scholarship in the 1970s and early 1980s was a rich, sometimes vexed, sometimes conviv-
ial, world in which words like "sisterhood" had a certain currency.

This early period is sometimes described as having two stages, one concerned with
the critique of misogynist stereotypes in male literature, the other devoted to the
recovery of a lost tradition and to the long labor of historical reconstruction. Banished from education and from public life, women writers had found refuge in
literary forms despised by men, in diaries and letters and in sentimental fiction.
Feminist scholars began to notice how the seemingly disinterested aesthetic categories that imbued literary scholarship in the academy automatically disqualified such
writing from consideration for inclusion in the canon.

The mid-1980s are in retrospect a moment of great change in feminist criticism.
What is called "French feminism" – essentially the work of Julia Kristeva, Luce
Irigaray, and Hélène Cixous – began to have an impact on how feminist scholars
thought about their work and about the assumptions that inspired it. "Woman," that
unproblematic "character" of feminist stories about the world, suddenly became a
matter of interpretation. Gender, rather than be the sight line that allowed one to trace
woman's banishment from an androcentric culture, might instead be a construct of
culture, something written into the psyche by language. Liberal and radical feminists
had been in disagreement since the 1970s regarding the direction the women's movement should take – toward a deeper identification with a female "essence" or toward a
departure from the way women had been made to be by patriarchy, the very thing
radical feminists construed as essentially female. That difference now gained volatility
within feminist literary critical discussions, and two perspectives began to form, one
"constructionist" or accepting of the idea that gender is made by culture in history,
the other "essentialist," more inclined to the idea that gender reflects a natural difference between men and women that is as much psychological, even linguistic, as it is

biological. And there was no possible meeting of minds between the two, for each necessarily denied the other. Feminism was suddenly feminisms.

Each perspective derived support from different theoretical sources, and both, curiously enough, found support in French Post-Structuralism. The essentialists looked to the work of feminist psychoanalyst Nancy Chodorow (*The Reproduction of Mothering*), ethical philosopher Carol Gilligan (*In a Different Voice*), and French feminist philosopher Luce Irigaray (*Speculum of the Other Woman* and *This Sex Which Is Not One*) and argued that women's physical differences alone (birthing, lactation, menstruation, etc.) make them more connected with matter or with the physical world than men. Luce Irigaray distinguishes between blood and sham, between the direct link to material nature in women's bodies and the flight from such contact that is the driving force of male abstraction, its pretense to be above matter and outside of nature (in civilization). She notes how matter (which she links etymologically to maternity and to the matrix, the space that is the prop for male philosophical speculation or abstract thinking) is irreducible to male Western concep-tuality; outside and making possible, yet impossible to assimilate to male reason, matter is what makes women women, an identity and an experience of their own, forever apart from male power and male concepts.

Women, essentialists argued, are innately capable of offering a different ethics from men, one more attuned to preserving the earth from destruction by weapons devised by men. Men must abstract themselves from the material world as they separate from mothers in order to acquire a license to enter the patriarchate, and they consequently adopt a violent and aggressive posture toward the world left behind, which is now construed as an "object." The primary matter they must separate from is the mother, who for them represents the tie to nature that must be overcome by the cut into abstraction that inaugurates civilization as men understand it (a set of abstract rules for assigning identities, appropriate social roles and the like that favor male power over women). Women, on the other hand, are not required to separate from the mother as they acquire a gender identity; they simply identify with the closest person to them as they grow up, their own mother. No cut is required, no separation that launches a precarious journey toward a fragile "identity" predicated on separation that simply denies its links to the physical world. Essentialist feminists argued that men think in terms of rights when confronted with ethical issues, while women think in terms of responsibilities to others. Women are more caring because their psychological and physical ties to physical being remain unbroken.

While one strand of essentialist theory finds common ground with Post-Structuralism around the body (that which male-defined reason must transcend but which includes and exceeds it always), another finds in Post-Structuralism an argu-ment against all identity. What lies outside male reason is precisely everything such reason abhors – contradiction, nonidentity, fluidity, nonrationality, illogicality, mixing of genres, etc. Domination through categorical analysis (the violent cut of distinction) is impossible in the realm of matter where things flow into one another and are unamenable to philosophical opposition. Woman names this nonidentity, and her language, what the French feminists call *écriture féminine* or feminine writing, is exercised in a heterogeneous style that deliberately undermines all the hierarchical orders of male rationalist philosophy by breaking from the ideal of coherent meaning and good rational style. (It should be noted that for writers like Cixous, feminine writing also characterizes the work of male writers like Joyce.)

The constructivist position took inspiration from the Marxist theory of the social construction of individual subjectivity (Althusser) and from the Post-Structuralist idea that language writes rather than reflects identities. Gender identity is no less a construction of patriarchal culture than the idea that men are somehow superior to women; both are born at the same time and with the same stroke of the pen. The psychology or identity that feminist essentialists think is different from men's is merely the product of conditioning under patriarchy, a conditioning to be caring, relational, and maternal that may make women seem more ethical than men, but a conditioning nonetheless. The constructionists worried that the essentialists were taking an effect to be a cause, interpreting the subordination of women as women's nature. What must change, they contended, is not the way androcentric culture traps and stifles a woman's identity that should be liberated into separation, but rather the way all gender, both male and female, is fabricated. Marxist feminists especially noted that much of what the essentialists took to be signs of a good female nature were in fact attributes assigned women in capitalist culture to make them better domestic laborers, better angels in the house.

At its most radical, the constructivist counter-paradigm embraces such categories as performativity, masquerade, and imitation, which are seen as cultural processes that generate gender identities that only appear to possess a pre-existing natural or material substance. Of more importance than physical or biological difference might be psychological identity (across a range from "masculine" to "feminine," from aggressivity and self-assertiveness to emotional flexibility and psychological relationality). Women can be just as much "masculine" as men, and biological men might simply be "masculine" (or pretend to be such) only out of obedience to cultural codes. Feminist critics like Judith Butler began to argue in the mid-1980s that all gender is "performative," an imitation of a code that refers to no natural substance. Masculine means not feminine as much as it means anything natural. Susan Jeffords in *The Remasculinization of American Culture* notices, for example, that male masculinity in US culture after the Vietnam War is constructed through an expulsion of emotional traits associated with femininity.

The encounter with psychoanalysis has been crucial to the development of contemporary feminist thinking about literature and culture. Millett attacked Freud's most noteworthy mistakes regarding women, but later feminists have argued that the engagement with psychoanalysis should not be one entirely of rejection. Juliet Mitchell has argued that what is important about Freud is the theory of engendering. Gender is socially constructed, and although Freud's own account is patriarchal, other accounts are possible, as are other ways of constructing human subjectivity. While Freud favored the Oedipal drama of gender inscription, whereby the father's intervention between mother and son initiates the separation that preserves civilization, feminists have urged that greater attention be given the pre-Oedipal period, one shaped by the child's relationship with its mother (at least in traditional households in which men work and women do domestic labor). In the mother–child relationship might be found more of the constituents of identity (as object relations psychoanalytic theory claims) than are given during the later Oedipal stage. This shift in attention has the virtue of displacing a central theoretical premise of patriarchal culture – that fathers determine sexual identity – but it broaches the dangerous possibility of reducing a sociological postulate – mothering – to a biological destiny. Is "mothering" constructed within patriarchy as the other of "fathering" (understood as nondomestic labor), or is it a value, an ideal, and a human relationship that offers a way out of patriarchy, a different voice and perhaps even a different language?

Feminist literary criticism moves with time from the criticism of writing by men and the exploration of writing by women to a questioning of what it means at all to engage with or in language. If all language carries worlds within it, assumptions and values that lie embedded in the simplest of utterances, then how can women take up such language, the language of patriarchy, and hope to use it to forge a better world for women? Or is language neutral, an indifferent instrument that can be wielded in any number of socially constructive ways? And what does it mean here to speak of "a better world for women"? Is that not to nominate into an indifferent identity a splintered multiplicity of women's lives around the world and around any one community or society? And if feminism, in its inspiration, is about the painful particularities of any one person's experience, their right to be heard despite centuries of deafness and deliberate, systematic muting, then how can it especially name into silence voices that know no language with which to speak? Shouldn't women especially know what it means to need to speak and be denied a language with which to speak? Yet isn't to speak for "other" women, women outside the glow of the tent lights of highly literate literary culture, even if it is to take up their cause and stand in for them at the podium of history, to do what men have always done for women? How can language be given when it takes so much away? Yet a woman was stoned to death on March 30, 1997, for being in the company of someone not of her "kin." If silence is complicity, what form should speech take in such a situation? Should it adopt the language of rights, the one created by men? Or is there a different construction of the problem, one less abstract, made more angry by painful experience, that is more appropriately "feminist"?

At its outer boundary, the feminist literary criticism that arose in the 1960s and 1970s in the US and the Commonwealth countries discovers the conditions as well as the limits of its own possibility in language and in literacy. And by looking beyond the boundary it encounters its own origin in the pain of denied speech and the presumption of assigned speech. There as well, perhaps, from the achieved vantage of an international, transethnic, parasexual perspective, it discovers a field of work that takes it back beyond its own beginning in the emergence from silence into language – to undo the silence of those who still do not speak.

Notes

1 Marianne Hirsch and Evelyn Fox Keller, eds., *Conflicts in Feminism* (New York and London: Routledge, 1990).
2 Adrienne Rich, "When We Dead Awaken: Writing as Re-Vision," in *On Lies, Secrets Silence: Selected Prose 1966–1978* (New York: Norton, 1979).

CHAPTER 2

The Traffic in Women

Gayle Rubin

This 1975 essay by feminist anthropologist Gayle Rubin quickly became a key text of feminist argument in the 1970s. At that time, feminists were trying to find their place in relation to three of the dominant schools of thought on the academic Left – Freudian psychoanalysis, Structural anthropology, and Marxism. Rubin's essay notes the points of helpful contact for feminists with these schools as well as the moments of dissonance.

The literature on women – both feminist and anti-feminist – is a long rumination on the question of the nature and genesis of women's oppression and social subordination. The question is not a trivial one, since the answers given it determine our visions of the future, and our evaluation of whether or not it is realistic to hope for a sexually egalitarian society. More importantly, the analysis of the causes of women's oppression forms the basis for any assessment of just what would have to be changed in order to achieve a society without gender hierarchy. Thus, if innate male aggression and dominance are at the root of female oppression, then the feminist program would logically require either the extermination of the offending sex, or else a eugenics project to modify its character. If sexism is a by-product of capitalism's relentless appetite for profit, then sexism would wither away in the advent of a successful socialist revolution. If the world historical defeat of women occurred at the hands of an armed patriarchal revolt, then it is time for Amazon guerrillas to start training in the Adirondacks.

It lies outside the scope of this paper to conduct a sustained critique of some of the currently popular explanations of the genesis of sexual inequality – theories such as the popular evolution exemplified by *The Imperial Animal*, the alleged overthrow of prehistoric matriarchies, or the attempt to extract all of the phenomena of social subordination from the first volume of *Capital*. Instead, I want to sketch some elements of an alternate explanation of the problem.

Marx once asked: "What is a Negro slave? A man of the black race. The one explanation is as good as the other. A Negro is a Negro. He only becomes a slave in certain relations. A cotton spinning jenny is a machine for spinning cotton. It becomes capital only in certain relations. Torn from these relationships it is no more capital than gold in itself is money or sugar is the price of sugar."[1] One might paraphrase: What is a domesticated woman? A female of the species. The one explanation is as good as the other. A woman is a woman. She only becomes a domestic, a wife, a chattel, a playboy bunny, a prostitute, or a human dictaphone in certain relations. Torn from these relationships, she is no more the helpmate of man than gold in itself is money...etc. What then are these relationships by which a female becomes an oppressed woman? The place to begin to unravel the system of relation-ships by which women become the prey of men is in the overlapping works of Claude Lévi-Strauss and Sigmund Freud. The domestication of women, under other names, is discussed at length in both of their œuvre. In reading through these works, one begins to have a sense of a systematic social apparatus which takes up females as raw materials and fashions domesticated women as products. Neither Freud nor Lévi-Strauss sees his work in this light, and certainly neither turns a critical glance upon the processes he describes. Their analyses and descriptions must be read, therefore, in something like the way in which Marx read the classical political econo-mists who preceded him.[2] Freud and Lévi-Strauss are in some sense analogous to Ricardo and Smith: They see neither the implications of what they are saying, nor the implicit critique which their work can generate when subjected to a feminist eye. Nevertheless, they provide conceptual tools with which one can build descriptions of the part of social life which is the locus of the oppression of women, of sexual minorities, and of certain aspects of human personality within individuals. I call that part of social life the "sex/gender system," for lack of a more elegant term. As a preliminary definition, a "sex/gender system" is the set of arrangements by which a society transforms biological sexuality into products of human activity, and in which these transformed sexual needs are satisfied.

The purpose of this essay is to arrive at a more fully developed definition of the sex/gender system, by way of a somewhat idiosyncratic and exegetical reading of Lévi-Strauss and Freud. I use the word "exegetical" deliberately. The dictionary defines "exegesis" as a "critical explanation or analysis; especially, interpretation of the Scriptures." At times, my reading of Lévi-Strauss and Freud is freely interpret-ive, moving from the explicit content of a text to its presuppositions and implica-tions. My reading of certain psychoanalytic texts is filtered through a lens provided by Jacques Lacan, whose own interpretation of the Freudian scripture has been heavily influenced by Lévi-Strauss.[3]

I will return later to a refinement of the definition of a sex/gender system. First, however, I will try to demonstrate the need for such a concept by discussing the failure of classical Marxism to fully express or conceptualize sex oppression. This failure results from the fact that Marxism, as a theory of social life, is relatively unconcerned with sex. In Marx's map of the social world, human beings are workers, peasants, or capitalists; that they are also men and women is not seen as very significant. By contrast, in the maps of social reality drawn by Freud and Lévi-Strauss, there is a deep recognition of the place of sexuality in society, and of the profound differences between the social experience of men and women.

Marx

There is no theory which accounts for the oppression of women – in its endless variety and monotonous similarity, cross-culturally and throughout history – with anything like the explanatory power of the Marxist theory of class oppression. There-fore, it is not surprising that there have been numerous attempts to apply Marxist analysis to the question of women. There are many ways of doing this. It has been argued that women are a reserve labor force for capitalism, that women's generally lower wages provide extra surplus to a capitalist employer, that women serve the ends of capitalist consumerism in their roles as administrators of family consumption, and so forth.

However, a number of articles have tried to do something much more ambitious – to locate the oppression of women in the heart of the capitalist dynamic by pointing to the relationship between housework and the reproduction of labor. To do this is to place women squarely in the definition of capitalism, the process in which capital is produced by the extraction of surplus value from labor by capital.[4]

Briefly, Marx argued that capitalism is distinguished from all other modes of production by its unique aim: the creation and expansion of capital. Whereas other modes of production might find their purpose in making useful things to satisfy human needs, or in producing a surplus for a ruling nobility, or in producing to insure sufficient sacrifice for the edification of the gods, capitalism produces capital. Capitalism is a set of social relations – forms of property, and so forth – in which production takes the form of turning money, things, and people into capital. And capital is a quantity of goods or money which, when exchanged for labor, reproduces and augments itself by extracting unpaid labor, or surplus value, from labor and into itself.

> The result of the capitalist production process is neither a mere produce (use-value) nor a commodity, that is, a use-value which has exchange-value. Its result, its product, is the creation of surplus-value for capital, and consequently the actual transformation of money or commodity into capitals.[5]

The exchange between capital and labor which produces surplus value, and hence capital, is highly specific. The worker gets a wage; the capitalist gets the things the worker has made during his or her time of employment. If the total value of the things the worker has made exceeds the value of his or her wage, the aim of capitalism has been achieved. The capitalist gets back the cost of the wage, plus an increment – surplus value. This can occur because the wage is determined not by the value of what the laborer makes, but by the value of what it takes to keep him or her going – to reproduce him or her from day to day, and to reproduce the entire work force from one generation to the next. Thus, surplus value is the difference between what the laboring class produces as a whole, and the amount of that total which is recycled into maintaining the laboring class.

> The capital given in exchange for labor power is converted into necessaries, by the consumption of which the muscles, nerves, bones, and brains of existing laborers are reproduced, and new laborers are begotten... the individual consumption of the laborer, whether it proceed within the workshop or outside it, whether it be part of the process of production or not, forms therefore a factor of the production and reproduction of capital; just as cleaning machinery does.[6]

> Given the individual, the production of labor-power consists in his reproduction of himself or his maintenance. For his maintenance he requires a given quantity of the means of subsistence.... Labor-power sets itself in action only by working. But thereby a definite quantity of human muscle, brain, nerve, etc., is wasted, and these require to be restored.[7]

The amount of the difference between the reproduction of labor power and its products depends, therefore, on the determination of what it takes to reproduce that labor power. Marx tends to make that determination on the basis of the quantity of commodities – food, clothing, housing, fuel – which would be necessary to maintain the health, life, and strength of a worker. But these commodities must be consumed before they can be sustenance, and they are not immediately in consumable form when they are purchased by the wage. Additional labor must be performed upon these things before they can be turned into people. Food must be cooked, clothes cleaned, beds made, wood chopped, etc. Housework is therefore a key element in the process of the reproduction of the laborer from whom surplus value is taken. Since it is usually women who do housework, it has been observed that it is through the reproduction of labor power that women are articulated into the surplus value nexus which is the sine qua non of capitalism.[8] It can be further argued that since no wage is paid for housework, the labor of women in the home contributes to the ultimate quantity of surplus value realized.

Women are oppressed in societies which can by no stretch of the imagination be described as capitalist. In the Amazon valley and the New Guinea Highlands, women are frequently kept in their place by gang rape when the ordinary mechanisms of masculine intimidation prove insufficient. "We tame our women with the banana," said one Mundurucu man.[9] The ethnographic record is littered with practices whose effect is to keep women "in their place" – men's cults, secret initiations, arcane male knowledge, etc. And pre-capitalist, feudal Europe was hardly a society in which there was no sexism. Capitalism has taken over, and rewired notions of male and female which predate it by centuries. No analysis of the reproduction of labor power under capitalism can explain foot-binding, chastity belts, or any of the incredible array of Byzantine, fetishized indignities, let alone the more ordinary ones, which have been inflicted upon women in various times and places. The analysis of the reproduction of labor power does not even explain why it is usually women who do domestic work in the home, rather than men.

In this light it is interesting to return to Marx's discussion of the reproduction of labor. What is necessary to reproduce the worker is determined in part by the bio-logical needs of the human organism, in part by the physical conditions of the place in which it lives, and in part by cultural tradition. Marx observed that beer is necessary for the reproduction of the English working class, and wine necessary for the French.

> [T]he number and extent of his [the worker's] so-called necessary wants, as also the modes of satisfying them, are themselves the product of historical development, and depend therefore to a great extent on the degree of civilization of a country, more particularly on the conditions under which, and consequently on the habits and degree of comfort in which, the class of free laborers has been formed. In contradistinction therefore to the case of other commodities, there enters into the determination of the value of labor-power a historical and moral element.[10]

It is precisely this "historical and moral element" which determines that a "wife" is among the necessities of a worker, that women rather than men do housework, and that capitalism is heir to a long tradition in which women do not inherit, in which women do not lead, and in which women do not talk to god. It is this "historical and moral element" which presented capitalism with a cultural heritage of forms of masculinity and femininity. It is within this "historical and moral element" that the entire domain of sex, sexuality, and sex oppression is subsumed. And the briefness of

Marx's comment only serves to emphasize the vast area of social life which it covers and leaves unexamined. Only by subjecting this "historical and moral element" to analysis can the structure of sex oppression be delineated.

Engels

In *The Origin of the Family, Private Property, and the State*, Engels sees sex oppression as part of capitalism's heritage from prior social forms. Moreover, Engels integrates sex and sexuality into his theory of society. *Origin* is a frustrating book. Like the nineteenth-century tomes on the history of marriage and the family which it echoes, the state of the evidence in *Origin* renders it quaint to a reader familiar with more recent developments in anthropology. Nevertheless, it is a book whose considerable insight should not be overshadowed by its limitations. The idea that the "relations of sexuality" can and should be distinguished from the "relations of production" is not the least of Engels' intuitions:

> According to the materialistic conception, the determining factor in history is, in the final instance, the production and reproduction of immediate life. This again, is of a twofold character: on the one hand, the production of the means of existence, of food, clothing, and shelter and the tools necessary for that production; on the other side, the production of human beings themselves, the propagation of the species. The social organization under which the people of a particular historical epoch and a particular country live is determined by both kinds of production: by the stage of development of labor on the one hand, and of the family on the other.[11]

This passage indicates an important recognition – that a human group must do more than apply its activity to reshaping the natural world in order to clothe, feed, and warm itself. We usually call the system by which elements of the natural world are transformed into objects of human consumption the "economy." But the needs which are satisfied by economic activity even in the richest, Marxian sense, do not exhaust fundamental human requirements. A human group must also reproduce itself from generation to generation. The needs of sexuality and procreation must be satisfied as much as the need to eat, and one of the most obvious deductions which can be made from the data of anthropology is that these needs are hardly ever satisfied in any "natural" form, any more than are the needs for food. Hunger is hunger, but what counts as food is culturally determined and obtained. Every society has some form of organized economic activity. Sex is sex, but what counts as sex is equally culturally determined and obtained. Every society also has a sex gender system – a set of arrangements by which the biological raw material of human sex and procreation is shaped by human, social intervention and satisfied in a conventional manner, no matter how bizarre some of the conventions may be.[12]

The realm of human sex, gender, and procreation has been subjected to, and changed by, relentless social activity for millennia. Sex as we know it – gender identity, sexual desire and fantasy, concepts of childhood – is itself a social product. We need to understand the relations of its production, and forget, for a while, about food, clothing, automobiles, and transistor radios. In most Marxist tradition, and even in Engels' book, the concept of the "second aspect of material life" has tended to fade into the background, or to be incorporated into the usual notions of "material life." Engels' suggestion has never been followed up and subjected to the refinement which it needs. But he does indicate the existence and importance of the domain of social life which I want to call the sex/gender system.

Other names have been proposed for the sex/gender system. The most common alternatives are "mode of reproduction" and "patriarchy." It may be foolish to quibble about terms, but both of these can lead to confusion. All three proposals have been made in order to introduce a distinction between "economic" systems and "sexual" systems, and to indicate that sexual systems have a certain autonomy and cannot always be explained in terms of economic forces. "Mode of reproduction," for instance, has been proposed in opposition to the more familiar "mode of production." But this terminology links the "economy" to production, and the sexual system to "reproduction." It reduces the richness of either system, since "productions" and "reproductions" take place in both. Every mode of production involves reproduction – of tools, labor, and social relations. We cannot relegate all of the multi-faceted aspects of social reproduction to the sex system. Replacement of machinery is an example of reproduction in the economy. On the other hand, we cannot limit the sex system to "reproduction" in either the social or biological sense of the term. A sex/gender system is not simply the reproductive moment of a "mode of production." The formation of gender identity is an example of production in the realm of the sexual system. And a sex/gender system involves more than the "relations of procreation," reproduction in the biological sense.

The term "patriarchy" was introduced to distinguish the forces maintaining sexism from other social forces, such as capitalism. But the use of "patriarchy" obscures other distinctions. Its use is analogous to using capitalism to refer to all modes of production, whereas the usefulness of the term "capitalism" lies precisely in that it distinguishes between the different systems by which societies are provisioned and organized. Any society will have some system of "political economy." Such a system may be egalitarian or socialist. It may be class stratified, in which case the oppressed class may consist of serfs, peasants, or slaves. The oppressed class may consist of wage laborers, in which case the system is properly labeled "capitalist." The power of the term lies in its implication that, in fact, there are alternatives to capitalism.

Similarly, any society will have some systematic ways to deal with sex, gender, and babies. Such a system may be sexually egalitarian, at least in theory, or it may be "gender stratified," as seems to be the case for most or all of the known examples. But it is important – even in the face of a depressing history – to maintain a distinction between the human capacity and necessity to create a sexual world, and the empirically oppressive ways in which sexual worlds have been organized. Patriarchy subsumes both meanings into the same term. Sex/gender system, on the other hand, is a neutral term which refers to the domain and indicates that oppression is not inevitable in that domain, but is the product of the specific social relations which organize it.

Finally, there are gender-stratified systems which are not adequately described as patriarchal. Many New Guinea societies (Enga, Maring, Bena Bena, Huli, Melpa, Kuma, Gahuku Gama, Fore, Marind Anim, ad nauseam) are viciously oppressive to women. But the power of males in these groups is not founded on their roles as fathers or patriarchs, but on their collective adult maleness, embodied in secret cults, men's houses, warfare, exchange networks, ritual knowledge, and various initiation procedures. Patriarchy is a specific form of male dominance, and the use of the term ought to be confined to the Old Testament-type pastoral nomads from whom the term comes, or groups like them. Abraham was a Patriarch – one old man whose absolute power over wives, children, herds, and dependents was an aspect of the institution of fatherhood, as defined in the social group in which he lived.

Whichever term we use, what is important is to develop concepts to adequately describe the social organization of sexuality and the reproduction of the conventions of sex and gender. We need to pursue the project Engels abandoned when he located the subordination of women in a development within the mode of production.[13] To do this, we can imitate Engels in his method rather than in his results. Engels approached the task of analyzing the "second aspect of material life" by way of an examination of a theory of kinship systems. Kinship systems are and do many things. But they are made up of, and reproduce, concrete forms of socially organized sexuality. Kinship systems are observable and empirical forms of sex/gender systems.

Kinship

(On the part played by sexuality in the transition from ape to "man.")

To an anthropologist, a kinship system is not a list of biological relatives. It is a system of categories and statuses which often contradict actual genetic relationships. There are dozens of examples in which socially defined kinship statuses take precedence over biology. The Nuer custom of "woman marriage" is a case in point. The Nuer define the status of fatherhood as belonging to the person in whose name cattle bridewealth is given for the mother. Thus, a woman can be married to another woman, and be husband to the wife and father of her children, despite the fact that she is not the inseminator.[14]

In pre-state societies, kinship is the idiom of social interaction, organizing economic, political, and ceremonial, as well as sexual, activity. One's duties; responsibilities, and privileges *vis-à-vis* others are defined in terms of mutual kinship or lack thereof. The exchange of goods and services, production and distribution, hostility and solidarity, ritual and ceremony, all take place within the organizational structure of kinship. The ubiquity and adaptive effectiveness of kinship has led many anthropologists to consider its invention, along with the invention of language, to have been the developments which decisively marked the discontinuity between semi-human hominids and human beings.[15]

While the idea of the importance of kinship enjoys the status of a first principle in anthropology, the internal workings of kinship systems have long been a focus for intense controversy. Kinship systems vary wildly from one culture to the next. They contain all sorts of bewildering rules which govern whom one may or may not marry. Their internal complexity is dazzling. Kinship systems have for decades provoked the anthropological imagination into trying to explain incest taboos, cross-cousin marriage, terms of descent, relationships of avoidance or forced intimacy, clans and sections, taboos on names – the diverse array of items found in descriptions of actual kinship systems. In the nineteenth century, several thinkers attempted to write comprehensive accounts of the nature and history of human sexual systems.[16] One of these was *Ancient Society*, by Lewis Henry Morgan. It was this book which inspired

Engels to write *The Origin of the Family, Private Property, and the State*. Engels' theory is based upon Morgan's account of kinship and marriage.

In taking up Engels' project of extracting a theory of sex oppression from the study of kinship, we have the advantage of the maturation of ethnology since the nineteenth century. We also have the advantage of a peculiar and particularly appropriate book, Lévi-Strauss' *The Elementary Structures of Kinship*. This is the boldest twentieth-century version of the nineteenth-century project to understand human marriage. It is a book in which kinship is explicitly conceived of as an imposition of cultural organization upon the facts of biological procreation. It is permeated with an awareness of the importance of sexuality in human society. It is a description of society which does not assume an abstract, genderless human subject. On the contrary, the human subject in Lévi-Strauss' work is always either male or female, and the divergent social destinies of the two sexes can therefore be traced. Since Lévi-Strauss sees the essence of kinship systems to lie in an exchange of women between men, he constructs an implicit theory of sex oppression. Aptly, the book is dedicated to the memory of Lewis Henry Morgan.

> "Vile and precious merchandise"
>
> *Monique Wittig*

The Elementary Structures of Kinship is a grand statement on the origin and nature of human society. It is a treatise on the kinship systems of approximately one-third of the ethnographic globe. Most fundamentally, it is an attempt to discern the structural principles of kinship. Lévi-Strauss argues that the application of these principles (summarized in the last chapter of *Elementary Structures*) to kinship data reveals an intelligible logic to the taboos and marriage rules which have perplexed and mystified Western anthropologists. He constructs a chess game of such complexity that it cannot be recapitulated here. But two of his chess pieces are particularly relevant to women – the "gift" and the incest taboo, whose dual articulation adds up to his concept of the exchange of women.

Elementary Structures is in part a radical gloss on another famous theory of primitive social organization, Mauss' *Essay on the Gift*.[17] It was Mauss who first theorized as to the significance of one of the most striking features of primitive societies: the extent to which giving, receiving, and reciprocating gifts dominates social intercourse. In such societies, all sorts of things circulate in exchange – food, spells, rituals, words, names, ornaments, tools, and dowers.

> Your own mother, your own sister, your own pigs, your own yams that you have piled up, you may not eat. Other people's mothers, other people's sisters, other people's pigs, other people's yams that they have piled up, you may eat.[18]

In a typical gift transaction, neither party gains anything. In the Trobriand Islands, each household maintains a garden of yams and each household eats yams. But the yams a household grows and the yams it eats are not the same. At harvest time, a man sends the yams he has cultivated to the household of his sister; the household in which he lives is provisioned by his wife's brother.[19] Since such a procedure appears to be a useless one from the point of view of accumulation or trade, its logic has been sought elsewhere. Mauss proposed that the significance of gift giving is that it expresses, affirms, or creates a social link between the partners of an exchange. Gift giving confers upon its participants a special relationship of trust, solidarity, and mutual aid. One can solicit a friendly relationship in the offer of a gift; acceptance implies a willingness to return a gift and a confirmation of the relationship. Gift exchange may also be the idiom of competition and rivalry. There are many examples in which one person humiliates another by giving more than can be reciprocated. Some political systems, such as the Big Man systems of Highland New Guinea, are based on exchange which is unequal on the material plane. An aspiring Big Man wants to give away more goods than can be reciprocated. He gets his return in political prestige.

Although both Mauss and Lévi-Strauss emphasize the solidary aspects of gift exchange, the other purposes served by gift giving only strengthen the point that it is a ubiquitous means of social commerce. Mauss proposed that gifts were the threads of social discourse, the means by which such societies were held together in the absence of specialized governmental institutions. "The gift is the primitive way of achieving the peace that in civil society is secured by the state.... Composing society, the gift was the liberation of culture."[20]

Lévi-Strauss adds to the theory of primitive reciprocity the idea that marriages are a most basic form of gift exchange, in which it is women who are the most precious of gifts. He argues that the incest taboo should best be understood as a mechanism to insure that such exchanges take place between families and between groups. Since the existence of incest taboos is universal, but the content of their prohibitions variable, they cannot be explained as having the aim of preventing the occurrence of genetically close matings. Rather, the incest taboo imposes the social aim of exogamy and alliance upon the biological events of sex and procreation. The incest taboo divides the universe of sexual choice into categories of permitted and prohibited sexual partners. Specifically, by forbidding unions within a group it enjoins marital exchange between groups.

> The prohibition on the sexual use of a daughter or a sister compels them to be given in marriage to another man, and at the same time it establishes a right to the daughter or sister of this other man.... The woman whom one does not take is, for that very reason, offered up.[21]

> The prohibition of incest is less a rule prohibiting marriage with the mother, sister, or daughter, than a rule obliging the mother, sister, or daughter to be given to others. It is the supreme rule of the gift....[22]

The result of a gift of women is more profound than the result of other gift transactions, because the relationship thus established is not just one of reciprocity, but one of kinship. The exchange partners have become affines, and their descendants will be related by blood: "Two people may meet in friendship and exchange gifts and yet quarrel and fight in later times, but intermarriage connects them in a permanent manner."[23] As is the case with other gift giving, marriages are not always so simply activities to make peace. Marriages may be highly competitive, and there are plenty of affines who fight each other. Nevertheless, in a general sense the argument is that the taboo on incest results in a wide network of relations, a set of people whose connections with one another are a kinship structure. All other levels, amounts, and directions of exchange – including hostile ones – are ordered by this structure. The marriage ceremonies recorded in the ethnographic literature are moments in a ceaseless and ordered procession in which women, children, shells, words, cattle names, fish, ancestors, whales' teeth, pigs, yams, spells, dances, mats, etc., pass from hand to hand, leaving as their tracks the ties that bind. Kinship is organization, and organization gives power. But who is organized?

If it is women who are being transacted, then it is the men who give and take them who are linked, the women being a conduit of a relationship rather than a partner to it.[24] The exchange of women does not necessarily imply that women are objectified, in the modern sense, since objects in the primitive world are imbued with highly personal qualities. But it does imply a distinction between gift and giver. If women are the gifts, then it is men who are the exchange partners. And it is the partners, not the presents, upon whom reciprocal exchange confers its quasi-mystical power of social linkage. The relations of such a system are such that women are in no position to realize the benefits of their own circulation. As long as the relations specify that men exchange women, it is men who are the beneficiaries of the product of such exchanges – social organization.

> The total relationship of exchange which constitutes marriage is not established between a man and a woman, but between two groups of men, and the woman figures only as one of the objects in the exchange, not as one of the partners.... This remains true even when the girl's feelings are taken into consideration, as, moreover, is usually the case. In acquiescing to the proposed union, she precipitates or allows the exchange to take place, she cannot alter its nature.[25]

To enter into a gift exchange as a partner, one must have something to give. If women are for men to dispose of, they are in no position to give themselves away.

> "What woman," mused a young Northern Melpa man, "is ever strong enough to get up and say, 'Let us make *moka*, let us find wives and pigs, let us give our daughters to men, let us wage war, let us kill our enemies!' No indeed not!... they are little rubbish things who stay at home simply, don't you see?"[26]

What women indeed! The Melpa women of whom the young man spoke can't get wives, they *are* wives, and what they get are husbands, an entirely different matter. The Melpa women can't give their daughters to men, because they do not have the same rights in their daughters that their male kin have, rights of bestowal (although *not* of ownership).

The "exchange of women" is a seductive and powerful concept. It is attractive in that it places the oppression of women within social systems, rather than in biology. Moreover, it suggests that we look for the ultimate locus of women's oppression within the traffic in women, rather than within the traffic in merchandise. It is certainly not difficult to find ethnographic and historical examples of trafficking in women. Women are given in marriage, taken in battle, exchanged for favors, sent as tribute, traded, bought, and sold. Far from being confined to the "primitive" world, these practices seem only to become more pronounced and commercialized in more "civilized" societies. Men are of course also trafficked – but as slaves, hustlers, athletic stars, serfs, or as some other catastrophic social status, rather than as men.

Women are transacted as slaves, serfs, and prostitutes, but also simply as women. And if men have been sexual subjects – exchangers – and women sexual semi-objects – gifts – for much of human history, then many customs, clichés, and personality traits seem to make a great deal of sense (among others, the curious custom by which a father gives away the bride). . . .

The exchange of women is also a problematic concept. Since Lévi-Strauss argues that the incest taboo and the results of its application constitute the origin of culture, it can be deduced that the world historical defeat of women occurred with the origin of culture, and is a prerequisite of culture. If his analysis is adopted in its pure form, the feminist program must include a task even more onerous than the extermination of men; it must attempt to get rid of culture and substitute some entirely new phenomena on the face of the earth. However, it would be a dubious proposition at best to argue that if there were no exchange of women there would be no culture, if for no other reason than that culture is, by definition, inventive. It is even debatable that "exchange of women" adequately describes all of the empirical evidence of kinship systems. Some cultures, such as the Lele and the Kuma, exchange women explicitly and overtly. In other cultures, the exchange of women can be inferred. In some – particularly those hunters and gatherers excluded from Lévi-Strauss' sample – the efficacy of the concept becomes altogether questionable. What are we to make of a concept which seems so useful and yet so difficult?

The "exchange of women" is neither a definition of culture nor a system in and of itself. The concept is an acute, but condensed, apprehension of certain aspects of the social relations of sex and gender. A kinship system is an imposition of social ends upon a part of the natural world. It is therefore "production" in the most general sense of the term: a molding, a transformation of objects (in this case, people) to and by a subjective purpose. It has its own relations to production, distribution, and exchange, which include certain "property" forms in people. These forms are not exclusive private property rights, but rather different sorts of rights that various people have over other people. Marriage transactions – the gifts and material which circulate in the ceremonies marking a marriage – are a rich source of data for determining exactly who has which rights in whom. It is not difficult to deduce from such transactions that in most cases women's rights are considerably more residual than those of men.

Kinship systems do not merely exchange women. They exchange sexual access, genealogical statuses, lineage names and ancestors, rights and people – men, women, and children – in concrete systems of social relationships. These relationships always include certain rights for men, others for women. "Exchange of women" is a shorthand for expressing that the social relations of a kinship system specify that men have certain rights in their female kin, and that women do not have the same rights either to themselves or to their male kin. In this sense, the exchange of women is a profound perception of a system in which women do not have full rights to themselves. The exchange of women becomes an obfuscation if it is seen as a cultural necessity and when it is used as the single tool with which an analysis of a particular kinship system is approached.

If Lévi-Strauss is correct in seeing the exchange of women as a fundamental principle of kinship, the subordination of women can be seen as a product of the relationships by which sex and gender are organized and produced. The economic oppression of women is derivative and secondary. But there is an "economics" of sex and gender, and what we need is a political economy of sexual systems. We need to study each society to determine the exact mechanisms by which particular conventions of sexuality are produced and maintained. The "exchange of women" is an initial step toward building an arsenal of concepts with which sexual systems can be described.

Deeper into the Labyrinth

More concepts can be derived from an essay by Lévi-Strauss, "The Family," in which he introduces other considerations into his analysis of kinship. In *The Elementary Structures of Kinship*, he describes rules and systems of sexual combination. In "The Family," he raises the issue of the preconditions necessary for marriage systems to operate. He asks what sort of "people" are required by kinship systems, by way of an analysis of the sexual division of labor.

Although every society has some sort of division of tasks by sex, the assignment of any particular task to one sex or the other varies enormously. In some groups, agriculture is the work of women, in others, the work of men. Women carry the heavy burdens in some societies, men in others. There are even examples of female hunters and warriors, and of men performing child-care tasks. Lévi-Strauss concludes from a survey of the division of labor by sex that it is not a biological specialization, but must have some other purpose. This purpose, he argues, is to insure the union of men and women by making the smallest viable economic unit contain at least one man and one woman.

> The very fact that it [the sexual division of labor] varies endlessly according to the society selected for consideration shows that...it is the mere fact of its existence which is mysteriously required, the form under which it comes to exist being utterly irrelevant, at least from the point of view of any natural necessity...[T]he sexual division of labor is nothing else than a device to institute a reciprocal state of dependency between the sexes.[27]

The division of labor by sex can therefore be seen as a "taboo": a taboo against the sameness of men and women, a taboo dividing the sexes into two mutually exclusive categories, a taboo which exacerbates the biological differences between the sexes and thereby *creates* gender. The division of labor can also be seen as a taboo against sexual arrangements other than those containing at least one man and one woman, thereby enjoining heterosexual marriage.

The argument in "The Family" displays a radical questioning of all human sexual arrangements, in which no aspect of sexuality is taken for granted as "natural" (Hertz constructs a similar argument for a thoroughly cultural explanation of the denigration of left-handedness).[28] Rather, all manifest forms of sex and gender are seen as being constituted by the imperatives of social systems. From such a perspective, even *The Elementary Structures of Kinship* can be seen to assume certain preconditions. In purely logical terms, a rule forbidding some marriages and commanding others presupposes a rule enjoining marriage. And marriage presupposes individuals who are disposed to marry.

It is of interest to carry this kind of deductive enterprise even further than Lévi-Strauss does, and to explicate the logical structure which underlies his entire analysis of kinship. At the most general level, the social organization of sex rests upon gender, obligatory heterosexuality, and the constraint of female sexuality.

Gender is a socially imposed division of the sexes. It is a product of the social relations of sexuality. Kinship systems rest upon marriage. They therefore transform males and females into "men" and "women," each an incomplete half which can only find wholeness when united with the other. Men and women are, of course, different. But they are not as different as day and night, earth and sky, yin and yang, life and death. In fact, from the standpoint of nature, men and women are closer to each other than either is to anything else – for instance, mountains, kangaroos, or coconut palms. The idea that men and women are more different from one another than either is from anything else must come from somewhere other than nature. Furthermore, although there is an average difference between males and females on a variety of traits, the range of variation of those traits shows considerable overlap. There will always be some women who are taller than some men, for instance, even though men are on the average taller than women. But the idea that men and women are two mutually exclusive categories must arise out of something other than a nonexistent "natural" opposition.[29] Far from being an expression of natural differences, exclusive gender identity is the suppression of natural similarities. It requires repression: in men, of whatever is the local version of "feminine" traits; in women, of the local definition of "masculine" traits. The division of the sexes has the effect of repressing some of the personality characteristics of virtually everyone, men and women. The same social system which oppresses women in its relations of exchange, oppresses everyone in its insistence upon a rigid division of personality.

Furthermore, individuals are engendered in order that marriage be guaranteed. Lévi-Strauss comes dangerously close to saying that heterosexuality is an instituted process. If biological and hormonal imperatives were as overwhelming as popular mythology would have them, it would hardly be necessary to insure heterosexual unions by means of economic interdependency. Moreover, the incest taboo presupposes a prior, less articulate taboo on homosexuality. A prohibition against some heterosexual unions assumes a taboo against non-heterosexual unions. Gender is not only an identification with one sex; it also entails that sexual desire be directed toward the other sex. The sexual division of labor is implicated in both aspects of gender – male and female it creates them, and it creates them heterosexual. The suppression of the homosexual component of human sexuality, and by corollary, the oppression of homosexuals, is therefore a product of the same system whose rules and relations oppress women. . . .

In fact, the situation is not so simple, as is obvious when we move from the level of generalities to the analysis of specific sexual systems. Kinship systems do not merely encourage heterosexuality to the detriment of homosexuality. In the first place, specific forms of heterosexuality may be required. For instance, some marriage systems have a rule of obligatory cross-cousin marriage. A person in such a system is not only heterosexual, but "cross-cousin-sexual." If the rule of marriage further specifies matrilateral cross-cousin marriage, then a man will be "mother's-brother's-daughter-sexual" and a woman will be "father's-sister's-son-sexual."

On the other hand, the very complexities of a kinship system may result in particular forms of institutionalized homosexuality. In many New Guinea groups, men and women are considered to be so inimical to one another that the period spent by a male child *in utero* negates his maleness. Since male life force is thought to reside in semen, the boy can overcome the malevolent effects of his fetal history by obtaining and consuming semen. He does so through a homosexual partnership with an older male kinsman.[30]

In kinship systems where bridewealth determines the statuses of husband and wife, the simple prerequisites of marriage and gender may be overridden. Among the Azande, women are monopolized by older men. A young man of means may, however, take a boy as wife while he waits to come of age. He simply pays a bridewealth (in spears) for the boy, who is thereby turned into a wife.[31] In Dahomey, a women could turn herself into a husband if she possessed the necessary bridewealth.[32]

The institutionalized "transvesticism" of the Mohave permitted a person to change from one sex to the other. An anatomical man could become a woman by means of a special ceremony, and an anatomical woman could in the same way become a man. The transvestite then took a wife or husband of her/his own anatomical sex and opposite social sex. These marriages, which we would label homosexual, were heterosexual ones by Mohave standards, unions of opposite socially defined sexes. By comparison with our society, this whole arrangement permitted a great deal of freedom. However, a person was not permitted to be some of both genders – he/she could be either male or female, but not a little of each.[33]

In all of the above examples, the rules of gender division and obligatory heterosexuality are present even in their transformations. These two rules apply equally to the constraint of both male and female behavior and personality. Kinship systems dictate some sculpting of the sexuality of both sexes. But it can be deduced from *The Elementary Structures of Kinship* that more constraint is applied to females when they are pressed into the service of kinship than to males. If women are exchanged, in whatever sense we take the term, marital debts are reckoned in female flesh. A woman must become the sexual partner of some man to whom she is owed as return on a previous marriage. If a girl is promised in infancy, her refusal to participate as an adult would disrupt the flow of debts and promises. It would be in the interests of the smooth and continuous operation of such a system if the woman in question did not have too many ideas of her own about whom she might want to sleep with. From the standpoint of the system, the preferred female sexuality would be one which responded to the desire of others, rather than one which actively desired and sought a response.

This generality, like the ones about gender and heterosexuality, is also subject to considerable variation and free play in actual systems. The Lele and the Kuma provide two of the clearest ethnographic examples of the exchange of women. Men in both cultures are perpetually engaged in schemes which necessitate that they have full control over the sexual destinies of their female kinswomen. Much of the drama in both societies consists in female attempts to evade the sexual control of their kinsmen. Nevertheless, female resistance in both cases is severely circumscribed.[34]

One last generality could be predicted as a consequence of the exchange of women under a system in which rights to women are held by men. What would happen if our hypothetical woman not only refused the man to whom she was promised, but asked for a woman instead? If a single refusal were disruptive, a double refusal would be insurrectionary. If each woman is promised to some man, neither has a right to dispose of herself. If two women managed to extricate themselves from the debt nexus, two other women would have to be found to replace them. As long as men have rights in women which women do not have in themselves, it would be sensible to expect that homosexuality in women would be subject to more suppression than in men.

In summary, some basic generalities about the organization of human sexuality can be derived from an exegesis of Lévi-Strauss' theories of kinship. These are the incest taboo, obligatory heterosexuality, and an asymmetric division of the sexes. The asymmetry of gender – the difference between exchanger and exchanged – entails the constraint of female sexuality. Concrete kinship systems will have more specific conventions, and these conventions vary a great deal. While particular socio-sexual systems vary, each one is specific, and individuals within it will have to conform to a finite set of possibilities. Each new generation must learn and become its sexual destiny, each person must be encoded with its appropriate status within the system. It would be extraordinary for one of us to calmly assume that we would conventionally marry a mother's brother's daughter, or a father's sister's son. Yet there are groups in which such a marital future is taken for granted.

Anthropology, and descriptions of kinship systems, do not explain the mechanisms by which children are engraved with the conventions of sex and gender. Psychoanalysis, on the other hand, is a theory about the reproduction of kinship. Psychoanalysis describes the residue left within individuals by their confrontation with the rules and regulations of sexuality of the societies to which they are born.

Psychoanalysis and Its Discontents

The battle between psychoanalysis and the women's and gay movements has become legendary. In part, this confrontation between sexual revolutionaries and the clinical establishment has been due to the evolution of psychoanalysis in the United States, where clinical tradition has fetishized anatomy. The child is thought to travel through its organismic stages until it reaches its anatomical destiny and the missionary position. Clinical practice has often seen its mission as the repair of individuals who somehow have become derailed en route to their "biological" aim. Transforming moral law into scientific law, clinical practice has acted to enforce sexual convention upon unruly participants. In this sense, psychoanalysis has often become more than a theory of the mechanisms of the reproduction of sexual arrangements; it has been one of those mechanisms. Since the aim of the feminist and gay revolts is to dismantle the apparatus of sexual enforcement, a critique of psychoanalysis has been in order. . . .

The organization of sex and gender once had functions other than itself – it organized society. Now, it only organizes and reproduces itself. The kinds of relationships of sexuality established in the dim human past still dominate our sexual lives, our ideas about men and women, and the ways we raise our children. But they lack the functional load they once carried. One of the most conspicuous features of kinship is that it has been systematically stripped of its functions – political, economic, educational, and organizational. It has been reduced to its barest bones – *sex and gender*.

Human sexual life will always be subject to convention and human intervention. It will never be completely "natural," if only because our species is social, cultural, and articulate. The wild profusion of infantile sexuality will always be tamed. The confrontation between immature and helpless infants and the developed social life of their elders will probably always leave some residue of disturbance. But the mechanisms and aims of this process need not be largely independent of conscious choice. Cultural evolution provides us with the opportunity to seize control of the means of sexuality, reproduction, and socialization, and to make conscious decisions to liberate human sexual life from the archaic relationships which deform it. Ultimately, a thoroughgoing feminist revolution would liberate more than women. It would liberate forms of sexual expression, and it would liberate human personality from the straitjacket of gender.

"Daddy, daddy, you bastard, I'm through."

Sylvia Plath

In the course of this essay I have tried to construct a theory of women's oppression by borrowing concepts from anthropology and psychoanalysis. But Lévi-Strauss and Freud write within an intellectual tradition produced by a culture in which women are oppressed. The danger in my enterprise is that the sexism in the tradition of which they are a part tends to be dragged in with each borrowing. "We cannot utter a single destructive proposition which has not already slipped into the form, the logic, and the implicit postulations of precisely what it seeks to contest."[35] And what slips in is formidable. Both psychoanalysis and structural anthropology are, in one sense, the most sophisticated ideologies of sexism around.[36]

For instance, Lévi-Strauss sees women as being like words, which are misused when they are not "communicated" and exchanged. On the last page of a very long book, he observes that this creates something of a contradiction in women, since women are at the same time "speakers" and "spoken." His only comment on this contradiction is this:

> But woman could never become just a sign and nothing more, since even in a man's world she is still a person, and since insofar as she is defined as a sign she must be recognized as a generator of signs. In the matrimonial dialogue of men, woman is never purely what is spoken about; for if women in general represent a certain category of signs, destined to a certain kind of communication, each woman preserves a particular value arising from her talent, before and after marriage, for taking her part in a duet. In contrast to words, which have wholly become signs, woman has remained at once a sign and a value. *This explains why the relations between the sexes have preserved that affective richness, ardour and mystery which doubtless originally permeated the entire universe of human communications.*[37]

This is an extraordinary statement. Why is he not, at this point, denouncing what kinship systems do to women, instead of presenting one of the greatest rip-offs of all time as the root of romance?

A similar insensitivity is revealed within psychoanalysis by the inconsistency with which it assimilates the critical implications of its own theory. For instance, Freud did not hesitate to recognize that his findings posed a challenge to conventional morality:

> We cannot avoid observing with critical eyes, and we have found that it is impossible to give our support to conventional sexual morality or to approve highly of the means by which society attempts to arrange the practical problems of sexuality in life. We can

demonstrate with ease that what the world calls its code of morals demands more sacrifices than it is worth, and that its behavior is neither dictated by honesty nor instituted with wisdom.[38]

Nevertheless, when psychoanalysis demonstrates with equal facility that the ordinary components of feminine personality are masochism, self-hatred, and passivity,[39] a similar judgment is not made. Instead, a double standard of interpretation is employed. Masochism is bad for men, essential to women. Adequate narcissism is necessary for men, impossible for women. Passivity is tragic in man, while lack of passivity is tragic in a woman.

It is this double standard which enables clinicians to try to accommodate women to a role whose destructiveness is so lucidly detailed in their own theories. It is the same inconsistent attitude which permits therapists to consider lesbianism as a problem to be cured, rather than as the resistance to a bad situation that their own theory suggests.[40]

There are points within the analytic discussions of femininity where one might say, "This is oppression of women," or "We can demonstrate with ease that what the world calls femininity demands more sacrifices than it is worth." It is precisely at such points that the implications of the theory are ignored, and are replaced with formulations whose purpose is to keep those implications firmly lodged in the theoretical unconscious. It is at these points that all sorts of mysterious chemical substances, joys in pain, and biological aims are substituted for a critical assessment of the costs of femininity. These substitutions are the symptoms of theoretical repression, in that they are not consistent with the usual canons of psychoanalytic argument. The extent to which these rationalizations of femininity go against the grain of psychoanalytic logic is strong evidence for the extent of the need to suppress the radical and feminist implications of the theory of femininity (Deutsch's discussions are excellent examples of this process of substitution and repression).

The argument which must be woven in order to assimilate Lévi-Strauss and Freud into feminist theory is somewhat tortuous. I have engaged it for several reasons. First, while neither Lévi-Strauss nor Freud questions the undoubted sexism endemic to the systems they describe, the questions which ought to be posed are blindingly obvious. Secondly, their work enables us to isolate sex and gender from "mode of production," and to counter a certain tendency to explain sex oppression as a reflex of economic forces. Their work provides a framework in which the full weight of sexuality and marriage can be incorporated into an analysis of sex oppression. It suggests a conception of the women's movement as analogous to, rather than isomorphic with, the working-class movement, each addressing a different source of human discontent. In Marx's vision, the working-class movement would do more than throw off the burden of its own exploitation. It also had the potential to change society, to liberate humanity, to create a classless society. Perhaps the women's movement has the task of effecting the same kind of social change for a system of which Marx had only an imperfect apperception. Something of this sort is implicit in Wittig – the dictatorship of the Amazon *guerillères* is a temporary means for achieving a genderless society.

The sex/gender system is not immutably oppressive and has lost much of its traditional function. Nevertheless, it will not wither away in the absence of opposition. It still carries the social burden of sex and gender, of socializing the young, and of providing ultimate propositions about the nature of human beings themselves.

And it serves economic and political ends other than those it was originally designed to further.[41] The sex/gender system must be reorganized through political action.

Finally, the exegesis of Lévi-Strauss and Freud suggests a certain vision of feminist politics and the feminist utopia. It suggests that we should not aim for the elimination of men, but for the elimination of the social system which creates sexism and gender. I personally find a vision of an Amazon matriarchate, in which men are reduced to servitude or oblivion (depending on the possibilities for parthenogenetic reproduction), distasteful and inadequate. Such a vision maintains gender and the division of the sexes. It is a vision which simply inverts the arguments of those who base their case for inevitable male dominance on ineradicable and significant biological differences between the sexes. But we are not only oppressed as women, we are oppressed by having to be women, or men as the case may be. I personally feel that the feminist movement must dream of even more than the elimination of the oppression of women. It must dream of the elimination of obligatory sexualities and sex roles. The dream I find most compelling is one of an androgynous and genderless (though not sexless) society, in which one's sexual anatomy is irrelevant to who one is, what one does, and with whom one makes love.

The Political Economy of Sex

It would be nice to be able to conclude here with the implications for feminism and gay liberation of the overlap between Freud and Lévi-Strauss. But I must suggest, tentatively, a next step on the agenda: a Marxian analysis of sex/gender systems. Sex/gender systems are not ahistorical emanations of the human mind; they are products of historical human activity.

We need, for instance, an analysis of the evolution of sexual exchange along the lines of Marx's discussion in *Capital* of the evolution of money and commodities. There is an economics and a politics to sex/gender systems which is obscured by the concept of "exchange of women." For instance, a system in which women are exchangeable only for one another has different effects on women than one in which there is a commodity equivalent for women.

> That marriage in simple societies involves an "exchange" is a somewhat vague notion that has often confused the analysis of social systems. The extreme case is the exchange of "sisters," formerly practiced in parts of Australia and Africa. Here the term has the precise dictionary meaning of "to be received as an equivalent for," "to give and receive reciprocally." From quite a different standpoint the virtually universal incest prohibition means that marriage systems necessarily involve "exchanging" siblings for spouses, giving rise to a reciprocity that is purely notational. But in most societies marriage is mediated by a set of intermediary transactions. If we see these transactions as simply implying immediate or long-term reciprocity, then the analysis is likely to be blurred.... The analysis is further limited if one regards the passage of property simply as a symbol of the transfer of rights, for then the nature of the objects handed over ... is of little importance.... Neither of these approaches is wrong; both are inadequate.[42]

There are systems in which there is no equivalent for a woman. To get a wife, a man must have a daughter, a sister, or other female kinswoman in whom he has a right of bestowal. He must have control over some female flesh. The Lele and Kuma are cases in point. Lele men scheme constantly in order to stake claims in some as yet unborn girl, and scheme further to make good their claims.[43] A Kuma girl's marriage is determined by an intricate web of debts, and she has little say in choosing her husband. A girl is usually married against her will, and her groom shoots an arrow into her thigh to symbolically prevent her from running away. The young wives almost always do run away, only to be returned to their new husbands by an elaborate conspiracy enacted by their kin and affines.[44]

In other societies, there is an equivalent for women. A woman can be converted into bridewealth, and bridewealth can be in turn converted into a woman. The dynamics of such systems vary accordingly, as does the specific kind of pressure exerted upon women. The marriage of a Melpa woman is not a return for a previous debt. Each transaction is self-contained, in that the payment of a bridewealth in pigs and shells will cancel the debt. The Melpa woman therefore has more latitude in choosing her husband than does her Kuma counterpart. On the other hand, her destiny is linked to bridewealth. If her husband's kin are slow to pay, her kin may encourage her to leave him. On the other hand, if her consanguineal kin are satisfied with the balance of payments, they may refuse to back her in the event that she wants to leave her husband. Moreover, her male kinsmen use the bridewealth for their own purposes, in *moka* exchange and for their own marriages. If a woman leaves her husband, some or all of the bridewealth will have to be returned. If, as is usually the case, the pigs and shells have been distributed or promised, her kin will be reluctant to back her in the event of marital discord. And each time a woman divorces and remarries, her value in bridewealth tends to depreciate. On the whole, her male consanguines will lose in the event of a divorce, unless the groom has been delinquent in his payments. While the Melpa woman is freer as a new bride than a Kuma woman, the bridewealth system makes divorce difficult or impossible.[45]

In some societies, like the Nuer, bridewealth can only be converted into brides. In others, bridewealth can be converted into something else, like political prestige. In this case, a woman's marriage is implicated in a political system. In the Big Man systems of Highland New Guinea, the material which circulates for women also circulates in the exchanges on which political power is based. Within the political system, men are in constant need of valuables to disburse, and they are dependent upon input. They depend not only upon their immediate partners, but upon the partners of their partners, to several degrees of remove. If a man has to return some bridewealth he may not be able to give it to someone who planned to give it to someone else who intended to use it to give a feast upon which his status depends. Big Men are therefore concerned with the domestic affairs of others, whose relationship with them may be extremely indirect. There are cases in which headmen intervene in marital disputes involving indirect trading partners in order that *moka* exchanges not be disrupted.[46] The weight of this entire system may come to rest upon one woman kept in a miserable marriage.

In short, there are other questions to ask of a marriage system than whether or not it exchanges women. Is the woman traded for a woman, or is there an equivalent? Is this equivalent only for women, or can it be turned into something else? If it can be turned into something else, is it turned into political power or wealth? On the other hand, can bridewealth be obtained only in marital exchange, or can it be obtained from elsewhere? Can women be accumulated through amassing wealth? Can wealth be accumulated by disposing of women? Is a marriage system part of a system of stratification?[47]

These last questions point to another task for a political economy of sex. Kinship and marriage are always parts of total social systems, and are always tied into economic and political arrangements.

> Lévi-Strauss . . . rightly argues that the structural implications of a marriage can only be understood if we think of it as one item in a whole series of transactions between kin groups. So far, so good. But in none of the examples which he provides in his book does he carry this principle far enough. The reciprocities of kinship obligation are not merely symbols of alliance, they are also economic transactions, political transactions, charters to rights of domicile and land use. No useful picture of "how a kinship system works" can be provided unless these several aspects or implications of the kinship organization are considered simultaneously.[48]

Among the Kachin, the relationship of a tenant to a landlord is also a relationship between a son-in-law and a father-in-law. "The procedure for acquiring land rights of any kind is in almost all cases tantamount to marrying a woman from the lineage of the lord."[49] In the Kachin system, bridewealth moves from commoners to aristocrats, women moving in the opposite direction.

> From an economic aspect the effect of matrilateral cross-cousin marriage is that, on balance, the headman's lineage constantly pays wealth to the chief's lineage in the form of bridewealth. The payment can also, from an analytical point of view, be regarded as a rent paid to the senior landlord by the tenant. The most important part of this payment is in the form of consumer goods – namely cattle. The chief converts this perishable wealth into imperishable prestige through the medium of spectacular feasting. The ultimate consumers of the goods are in this way the original producers, namely, the commoners who attend the feast.[50]

In another example, it is traditional in the Trobriands for a man to send a harvest gift – *urigubu* – of yams to his sister's household. For the commoners, this amounts to a simple circulation of yams. But the chief is polygamous, and marries a woman from each subdistrict within his domain. Each of these subdistricts therefore sends *urigubu* to the chief, providing him with a bulging storehouse out of which he finances feasts, craft production, and *kula* expeditions. This "fund of power" underwrites the political system and forms the basis for chiefly power.[51]

In some systems, position in a political hierarchy and position in a marriage system are intimately linked. In traditional Tonga, women married up in rank. Thus, low-ranking lineages would send women to higher-ranking lineages. Women of the highest lineage were married into the "house of Fiji," a lineage defined as outside the political system. If the highest-ranking chief gave his sister to a lineage other than one which had no part in the ranking system, he would no longer be the highest-ranking chief. Rather, the lineage of his sister's son would outrank his own. In times of political rearrangement, the demotion of the previous high-ranking lineage was formalized when it gave a wife to a lineage which it had formerly outranked. In traditional Hawaii, the situation was the reverse. Women married down, and the dominant lineage gave wives to junior lines. A paramount would either marry a sister or obtain a wife from Tonga. When a junior lineage usurped rank, it formalized its position by giving a wife to its former senior line.

There is even some tantalizing data suggesting that marriage systems may be implicated in the evolution of social strata, and perhaps in the development of early states. The first round of the political consolidation which resulted in the formation of a state in Madagascar occurred when one chief obtained title to several autonomous districts through the vagaries of marriage and inheritance.[52] In Samoa, legends place the origin of the paramount title – the *Tafa'ifa* – as a result of intermarriage between ranking members of four major lineages. My thoughts are too speculative, my data too sketchy, to say much on this subject. But a search ought to be undertaken for data which might demonstrate how marriage systems intersect with large-scale political processes like state-making. Marriage systems might be implicated in a number of ways: in the accumulation of wealth and the maintenance of differential access to political and economic resources; in the building of alliances; in the consolidation of high-ranking persons into a single closed strata of endogamous kin.

These examples – like the Kachin and the Trobriand ones – indicate that sexual systems cannot, in the final analysis, be understood in complete isolation. A full-bodied analysis of women in a single society, or throughout history, must take *everything* into account: the evolution of commodity forms in women, systems of land tenure, political arrangements, subsistence technology, etc. Equally important, economic and political analyses are incomplete if they do not consider women, marriage, and sexuality. Traditional concerns of anthropology and social science – such as the evolution of social stratification and the origin of the state – must be reworked to include the implications of matrilateral cross-cousin marriage, surplus extracted in the form of daughters, the conversion of female labor into male wealth, the conversion of female lives into marriage alliances, the contribution of marriage to political power, and the transformations which all of these varied aspects of society have undergone in the course of time.

This sort of endeavor is, in the final analysis, exactly what Engels tried to do in his effort to weave a coherent analysis of so many of the diverse aspects of social life. He tried to relate men and women, town and country, kinship and state, forms of property, systems of land tenure, convertibility of wealth, forms of exchange, the technology of food production, and forms of trade, to name a few, into a systematic historical account. Eventually, someone will have to write a new version of *The Origin of the Family, Private Property, and the State*, recognizing the mutual interdependence of sexuality, economics, and politics without underestimating the full significance of each in human society.

Notes

Acknowledgments are an inadequate expression of how much this essay, like most, is the product of many minds. They are also necessary to free others of the responsibility for what is ultimately a personal vision of a collective conversation. I want to free and thank the following persons: Tom Anderson and Arlene Gorelick, with whom I co-authored the essay from which this one evolved; Rayna Reiter, Larry Shields, Ray Kelly, Peggy White, Norma Diamond, Randy Reiter, Frederick Wyatt, Anne Locksley, Juliet Mitchell, and Susan Harding, for countless conversations and ideas;

Marshall Sahlins, for the revelation of anthropology; Lynn Eden, for sardonic editing; the members of Women's Studies 340/004, for my initiation into teaching; Sally Brenner, for heroic typing; Susan Lowes, for incredible patience; and Emma Goldman, for the title.

1 Karl Marx, *Wage Labor and Capital* (New York: International Publishers, 1971), p. 28.

2 Louis Althusser and Etienne Balibar, *Reading Capital* (London: New Left Books, 1970), pp. 11–69.

3 Moving between Marxism, structuralism, and psychoanalysis produces a certain clash of epistemologies. In particular, structuralism is a can from which worms crawl out all over the epistemological map. Rather than trying to cope with this problem, I have more or less ignored the fact that Lacan and Lévi-Strauss are among the foremost living ancestors of the contemporary French intellectual revolution (see Michel Foucault, *The Order of Things* (New York, 1970)). It would be fun, interesting, and, if this were France, essential, to start my argument from the center of the structuralist maze and work my way out from there, along the lines of a "dialectical theory of signifying practices" (see Robert Hefner, "The *Tel Quel* Ideology: Material Practice Upon Material Practice," *Substance* 8 (1974), pp. 127–38).

4 Margaret Benston, "The Political Economy of Women's Liberation," *Monthly Review* 21, no. 4 (1969), pp. 13–27; Mariarosa Dalla Costa and Selma James, *The Power of Women and the Subversion of the Community* (Bristol: Falling Wall Press, 1972); Isabel Larguia and John Dumoulin, "Towards a Science of Women's Liberation," *NACLA Newsletter* 6, no. 10 (1972), pp. 3–20; Ira Gerstein, "Domestic Work and Capitalism," *Radical America* 7, nos 4 and 5 (1973), pp. 101–28; Lise Vogel, "The Earthly Family," *Radical America* 7, nos 4 and 5 (1973), pp. 9–50; Wally Secombe, "Housework Under Capitalism," *New Left Review* 83 (1973), pp. 3–24; Jean Gardiner, "Political Economy of Female Labor in Capitalist Society," unpublished manuscript; M. and J. Rowntree, "More on the Political Economy of Women's Liberation," *Monthly Review* 21, no. 8 (1970), pp. 26–32.

5 Karl Marx, *Theories of Surplus Value*, Part 1 (Moscow: Progress Publishers, 1969), p. 399.

6 Karl Marx, *Capital*, vol. 1 (New York: International Publishers, 1972), p. 572.

7 Ibid., p. 171.

8 A lot of the debate on women and housework has centered around the question of whether or not housework is "productive" labor. Strictly speaking, housework is not ordinarily "productive" in the technical sense of the term (I. Gough, "Marx and Productive Labor," *New Left Review* 76 (1972), pp. 47–72; Marx, *Theories of Surplus Value*, pp. 387–413). But this distinction is irrelevant to the main line of the argument. Housework may not be "productive," in the sense of directly producing surplus value and capital, and yet be a crucial element in the production of surplus value and capital by the capitalist. But to explain women's usefulness to capitalism is one thing. To argue that this usefulness explains the genesis of the oppression of women is quite another. It is precisely at this point that the analysis of capitalism ceases to explain very much about women and the oppression of women.

9 Robert Murphy, "Social Structure and Sex Antagonism," *Southwestern Journal of Anthropology* 15, no. 1 (1959), pp. 81–96.

10 Marx, *Capital*, p. 171.

11 Frederick Engels, *The Origin of the Family, Private Property, and the State* (New York: International Publishers, 1972), pp. 71–2.

12 That some of them are pretty bizarre, from our point of view, only demonstrates the point that sexuality is expressed through the intervention of culture. (See Clellan Ford and Frank Beach, *Patterns of Sexual Behavior* (New York: Harper, 1972).) Some examples may be chosen from among the exotica in which anthropologists delight.

    Among the Banaro, marriage involves several socially sanctioned sexual partnerships. When a woman is married, she is initiated into intercourse by the sib-friend of her groom's father. After bearing a child by this man, she begins to have intercourse with her husband. She also has an institutionalized partnership with the sib-friend of her husband. A man's partners include his wife, the wife of his sib-friend, and the wife of his sib-friend's son (See Richard Thurnwald, "Banaro Society," *Memoirs of the American Anthropological Association* 3, no. 4

(1916), pp. 251–391.) Multiple intercourse is a more pronounced custom among the Marind Anim. At the time of marriage the bride has intercourse with all of the members of the groom's clan, the groom coming last. Every major festival is accompanied by a practice known as otiv-bombari, in which semen is collected for ritual purposes. A few women have intercourse with many men, and the resulting semen is collected in coconut-shell buckets. A Marind male is subjected to multiple homosexual intercourse during initiation (J. Van Baal, *Dema* (The Hague: Nijhoff, 1966)). Among the Etoro, heterosexual intercourse is taboo for between 205 and 260 days a year (Raymond Kelly, "Witchcraft and Sexual Relations: An Exploration of the Social and Semantic Implications of the Structure of Belief," paper read at the 73rd Annual Meeting of the American Anthropological Association, Mexico City). In much of New Guinea, men fear copulation and think that it will kill them if they engage in it without magical precautions (R. M. Glasse, "The Mask of Venery," paper read at the 70th annual meeting of the American Anthropological Association, New York City, December 1971; M. J. Meggitt, "Male–Female Relationships in the Highlands of Australian New Guinea," *American Anthropologist* 66, no. 4, part 2 (1972), pp. 204–24). Usually, such ideas of feminine pollution express the subordination of women. But symbolic systems contain internal contradictions, whose logical extensions sometimes lead to inversions of the propositions on which a system is based. In New Britain, men's fear of sex is so extreme that rape appears to be feared by men rather than women. Women run after the men, who flee from them, women are the sexual aggressors, and it is bridegrooms who are reluctant (Jane C. Goodale and Ann Chowning, "The Contaminating Woman," paper read at the 70th annual meeting of the American Anthropological Association, 1971). Other interesting sexual variations can be found in Yalmon ("On the Purity of Women in the Castes of Ceylon and Malabar," *Journal of the Royal Anthropological Institute* 93, no. 1 (1963), pp. 25–58) and K. Gough ("The Nayars and the Definition of Marriage," *Journal of the Royal Anthropological Institute* 89 (1959), pp. 23–4).

13 Engels thought that men acquired wealth in the form of herds and, wanting to pass this wealth to their own children, overthrew "mother right" in favor of patrilineal inheritance. "The overthrow of mother right was the *world historical defeat of the female sex*. The man took command in the home also; the woman was degraded and reduced to servitude; she became the slave of his lust and a mere instrument for the production of children" (Engels, *Origin of the Family*, pp. 120–1; italics in original). As has been often pointed out, women do not necessarily have significant social authority in societies practicing matrilineal inheritance (David Schneider and Kathleen Gough (eds.), *Matrilineal Kinship* (Berkeley: University of California Press, 1961)).

14 E. E. Evans-Pritchard, *Kinship and Marriage Among the Nuer* (London: Oxford University Press, 1951), pp. 107–9.

15 Marshall Sahlins, "The Origin of Society," *Scientific American* 203, no. 3 (1960), pp. 76–86; Frank Livingstone, "Genetics, Ecology, and the Origins of Incest and Exogamy," *Current Anthropology* 10, no. 1 (1969), pp. 45–9; Claude Lévi-Strauss, *The Elementary Structures of Kinship* (Boston: Beacon Press, 1969).

16 See Elizabeth Fee, "The Sexual Politics of Victorian Social Anthropology," *Feminist Studies* (Winter/Spring 1973), pp. 23–9.

17 See Marshall Sahlins, *Stone Age Economics* (Chicago: Aldine Atherton, 1972), ch. 4.

18 Claude Lévi-Strauss, *The Elementary Structures of Kinship* (Boston: Beacon Press, 1969), p. 27.

19 Bronislaw Malinowski, *The Sexual Life of Savages* (London: Routledge, 1929).

20 Sahlins, *Stone Age Economics*, pp. 169, 175.

21 Lévi-Strauss, *Elementary Structures*, p. 51.

22 Ibid., p. 481.

23 Best, cited in Lévi-Strauss, *Elementary Structures*, p. 481.

24 "What, would you like to marry your sister? What is the matter with you? Don't you want a brother-in-law? Don't you realize that if you marry another man's sister and another man marries your sister, you will have at least two brothers-in-law, while if you marry your own sister you will have none? With whom will you hunt, with whom will you garden, whom will you go visit?" (Arapesh, cited in Lévi-Strauss, *Elementary Structures*, p. 485).

25 Lévi-Strauss, *Elementary Structures*, p. 161. This analysis of society as based on bonds between men by means of women makes the separatist responses of the women's movement thoroughly intelligible. Separatism can be seen as a mutation in social structure, as an attempt to form social groups based on unmediated bonds between women. It can also be seen as a radical denial of men's "rights" in women and as a claim by women of rights in themselves.

26 Marilyn Strathern, *Women In Between* (New York: Seminar, 1971), p. 161.

27 Claude Lévi-Strauss, "The Family," in H. Shapiro (ed.), *Man, Culture, and Society* (London: Oxford University Press, 1971), pp. 347–8.

28 Robert Hertz, *Death and the Right Hand* (Glencove, 1960).

29 "The woman shall not wear that which pertaineth unto a man neither shall a man put on a woman's garment: for all that do so *are* abomination unto the LORD they God" (Deuteronomy 22:5; emphasis not mine).

30 Kelly, "Witchcraft and Sexual Relations"; Van Baal, *Dema*; F. E. Williams, *Papuans of the Trans-Fly* (Oxford: Clarendon, 1936).

31 E. E. Evans-Pritchard, "Sexual Inversion Among the Azande," *American Anthropologist* 72 (1970), pp. 1428–34.

32 Melville Herskovitz, "A Note on 'Woman Marriage' in Dahomey," *Africa* 10, no. 3 (1937), pp. 335–41.

33 George Devereaux, "Institutionalized Homosexuality Among Mohave Indians," *Human Biology* 9 (1937), pp. 498–529; Douglas McMurtrie, "A Legend of Lesbian Love Among North American Indians," *Urologic and Cutaneous Review* (April, 1914), pp. 192–3; David Sonenschein, "Homosexuality as a Subject of Anthropological Investigation," *Anthropological Quarterly* 2 (1966), pp. 73–82.

34 Mary Douglas, *The Lele of Kasai* (London: Oxford University Press, 1963); Marie Reay, *The Kuma* (London: Cambridge University Press, 1959).

35 Jacques Derrida, "Structure, Sign, and Play," in R. Macksey and E. Donatio (eds.), *The Structuralist Controversy* (Baltimore: Johns Hopkins University Press, 1972), p. 250.

36 Parts of Wittig's *Les Guerillères* (New York: Avon, 1973) appear to be tirades against Lévi-Strauss and Lacan. For instance:

> Has he not indeed written, power and the possession of women leisure and the enjoyment of women? He writes that you are currency, an item of exchange. He writes, barter, barter, possession and acquisition of women and merchandise. Better for you to see your guts in the sun and utter the death rattle than to live a life that anyone can appropriate. What belongs to you on this earth? Only death. No power on earth can take that away from you. And – consider, explain, tell yourself – if happiness consists in the possession of something, then hold fast to this sovereign happiness – to die. (pp. 115–16; see also pp. 106–7; 113–14; 134)

The awareness of French feminists of Lévi-Strauss and Lacan is most clearly evident in a group called "Psychoanalyse et Politique," which defined its task as a feminist use and critique of Lacanian psychoanalysis.

37 Lévi-Strauss, *Elementary Structures*, p. 496; my italics.

38 Sigmund Freud, *A General Introduction to Psychoanalysis* (Garden City, NY: Garden City Publishing Company, 1943), pp. 376–7.

39 "Every woman adores a fascist" – Sylvia Plath.

40 One clinician, Charlotte Wolff (*Love Between Women* (London: Duckworth, 1971)) has taken the psychoanalytic theory of womanhood to its logical extreme and proposed that lesbianism is a healthy response to female socialization.

> Women who do not rebel against the status of object have declared themselves defeated as persons in their own right. (p. 65)

The lesbian girl is the one who, by all means at her disposal, will try to find a place of safety inside and outside the family, through her fight for equality with the male. She will not, like other women, play up to him: indeed, she despises the very idea of it. (p. 59)

The lesbian was and is unquestionably in the avant-garde of the fight for equality of the sexes, and for the psychical liberation of women. (p. 66)

It is revealing to compare Wolff's discussion with the articles on lesbianism in Marmor, *Sexual Inversion* (London: Basic Books, 1965).

41 John Finley Scott, "The Role of Collegiate Sororities in Maintaining Class and Ethnic Endogamy," *American Sociological Review* 30, no. 4 (1965), pp. 415–26.

42 Jack Goody and S. J. Tambiah, *Bridewealth and Dowry* (Cambridge: Cambridge University Press, 1973), p. 2.

43 Douglas, *The Lele of Kasai*.

44 Reay, *The Kuma*.

45 Strathern, *Women In Between*.

46 Ralph Bulmer, "Political Aspects of the Moka Ceremonial Exchange System Among the Kyaka People of the Western Highlands of New Guinea," *Oceania* 31, no. 1 (1969), pp. 1–13.

47 Another line of inquiry would compare bridewealth systems to dowry systems. Many of these questions are treated in Goody and Tambiah, *Bridewealth and Dowry*.

48 Edmund Leach, *Rethinking Anthropology* (New York: Humanities Press, 1971), p. 90.

49 Ibid., p. 88.

50 Ibid., p. 89.

51 Bronislaw Malinowski, "The Primitive Economics of the Trobriand Islanders," in T. Harding and B. Wallace, eds., *Cultures of the Pacific* (New York: Free Press, 1970).

52 Henry Wright, personal communication.

CHAPTER 3

The Power of Discourse and the Subordination of the Feminine

Luce Irigaray

French philosopher Luce Irigaray published two highly influential books in the 1970s – *Speculum of the Other Woman* (1975) and *This Sex Which Is Not One* (1977). The first was a meditation on the history of Western philosophy from the perspective of women. The second was a more polemical feminist text that advanced the ideas of separatism, the idea that women should withdraw from patriarchy entirely and constitute an alternative arena of their own. In this selection, Irigaray discusses the male philosophic tradition as one founded on a speculative separation from matter. What she calls "the feminine" – everything having to do with matter and the contact between material planes – has to be subordinated to a masculine idealizing tendency that uses the feminine as a mirror for its own narcissistic speculations.

Unless we limit ourselves naively – or perhaps strategically – to some kind of limited or marginal issue, it is indeed precisely philosophical discourse that we have to challenge, and disrupt, inasmuch as this discourse sets forth the law for all others, inasmuch as it constitutes the discourse on discourse.

Thus we have had to go back to it in order to try to find out what accounts for the power of its systematicity, the force of its cohesion, the resourcefulness of its strategies, the general applicability of its law and its value. That is, its *position of mastery*, and of potential reappropriation of the various productions of history....

How can we introduce ourselves into such a tightly woven systematicity?

There is, in an initial phase, perhaps only one "path," the one historically assigned to the feminine: that of mimicry. One must assume the feminine role deliberately. Which means already to convert a form of subordination into an affirmation, and thus to begin to thwart it. Whereas a direct feminine challenge to this condition means demanding to speak as a (masculine) "subject," that is, it means to postulate a relation to the intelligible that would maintain sexual difference.

To play with mimesis is thus, for a woman, to try to recover the place of her exploitation by discourse, without allowing herself to be simply reduced to it. It means to resubmit herself – inasmuch as she is on the side of the "perceptible," of "matter" – to "ideas," in particular to ideas about herself, that are elaborated in/by a masculine logic, but so as to make "visible," by an effect of playful repetition, what was supposed to remain invisible – the cover-up of a possible operation of the feminine in language. It also means "to unveil" the fact that, if women are such good mimics, it is because they are not simply absorbed in this function. *They also remain elsewhere*: another case of the persistence of "matter," but also of "sexual pleasure."

Elsewhere of "matter": if women can play with mimesis, it is because they are capable of bringing new nourishment to its operation. Because they have always nourished this operation?

Is not the "first" stake in mimesis that of re-producing (from) nature? Of giving it form in order to appropriate it for oneself. As guardians of "nature," are not women the ones who maintain, thus who make possible, the resource of mimesis for men? For the logos?

It is here, of course, that the hypothesis of a reversal – within the phallic order – is always possible. Re-semblance cannot do without red blood. Mother-matter-nature must go on forever nourishing speculation.[1] But this re-source is also rejected as the waste product of reflection, cast outside as what resists it: as madness. Besides the ambivalence that the nourishing phallic mother attracts to herself, this function leaves woman's sexual pleasure aside.

That *"elsewhere" of female pleasure* might rather be sought first in the place where it sustains ek-stasy in the transcendental. The place where it serves as security for a narcissism extrapolated into the "God" of men. It can play this role only at the price of its ultimate withdrawal from prospection, of its "virginity" unsuited for the representation of self. Feminine pleasure has to remain inarticulate in language, in its own language, if it is not to threaten the underpinnings of logical operations. And so what is most strictly forbidden to women today is that they should attempt to express their own pleasure.

That "elsewhere" of feminine pleasure can be found only at the price of *crossing back through the mirror that subtends all* [philosophical] *speculation*. For this pleasure is not simply situated in a process of reflection or mimesis, nor on one side of this process or the other: neither on the near side, the empirical realm that is opaque to all language, nor on the far side, the self-sufficient infinite of the God of men. Instead, it refers all these categories and ruptures back to the necessities of the self-representation of phallic desire in discourse. A playful crossing, and an unsettling one, which would allow woman to rediscover the place of her "self-affection." Of her "god," we might say. A god to which one can obviously not have recourse – unless its duality is granted – without leading the feminine right back into the phallocratic economy . . .

For to speak *of* or *about* woman may always boil down to, or be understood as, a recuperation of the feminine within a logic that maintains it in repression, censorship, nonrecognition.

In other words, the issue is not one of elaborating a new theory of which woman would be the *subject* or the *object*, but of jamming the theoretical machinery itself, of suspending its pretension to the production of a truth and of a meaning that are excessively univocal. Which presupposes that women do not aspire simply to be men's equals in knowledge. That they do not claim to be rivaling men in constructing a logic of the feminine that would still take onto-theo-logic as its model, but that they are rather attempting to wrest this question away from the economy of the logos. They should not put it, then, in the form "What is woman?" but rather, repeating/interpreting the way in which, within discourse, the feminine finds itself defined as lack, deficiency, or as imitation and negative image of the subject, they should signify that with respect to this logic a *disruptive excess* is possible on the feminine side.

An excess that exceeds common sense only on condition that the feminine not renounce its "style." Which, of course, is not a style at all, according to the traditional way of looking at things.

This "style," or "writing," of women tends to put the torch to fetish words, proper terms, well-constructed forms. This "style" does not privilege sight,[2] instead, it takes each figure back to its source, which is among other things *tactile*. It comes back in touch with itself in that origin without ever constituting in it, constituting itself in it, as some sort of unity. Simultaneity is its "proper" aspect – a proper(ty) that is never fixed in the possible identity-to-self of some form or other. It is always *fluid*, without neglecting the characteristics of fluids that are difficult to idealize: those rubbings between two infinitely near neighbors that create a dynamics. Its "style" resists and explodes every firmly established form, figure, idea or concept. Which does not mean that it lacks style, as we might be led to believe by a discursivity that cannot conceive of it. But its "style" cannot be upheld as a thesis, cannot be the object of a position.

And even the motifs of "self-touching," of "proximity," isolated as such or reduced to utterances could effectively pass for an attempt to appropriate the feminine to discourse. We would still have to ascertain whether "touching oneself," that (self) touching, the desire for the proximate rather than for (the) proper(ty), and so on, might not imply a mode of exchange irreducible to any *centering*, any *centerism*, given the way the "self-touching" of female "self-affection" comes into play as a rebounding from one to the other without any possibility of interruption and given that, in this interplay, proximity confounds any adequation, any appropriation.

But of course if these were only "motifs" without any work on and/or with language, the discursive economy could remain intact. How, then, are we to try to redefine this language work that would leave space for the feminine? Let us say that every dichotomizing – and at the same time redoubling – break, including the one between enunciation and utterance has to be disrupted. Nothing is ever to be *posited* that is not also reversed and caught up again *in the supplementarity of this reversal*. To put it another way: there would no longer be either a right side or a wrong side of discourse, or even of texts, but each passing from one to the other would make audible and comprehensible even what resists the recto–verso structure that shores up common sense. If this is to be practiced for every meaning posited – for every word, utterance, sentence, but also of course for every phoneme, every letter – we need to proceed in such a way that linear reading is no longer possible: that is, the retroactive impact of the end of each word, utterance, or sentence upon its beginning must be taken into consideration in order to undo the power of its teleological effect, including its deferred action. That would hold good also for the opposition between structures of horizontality and verticality that are at work in language.

What allows us to proceed in this way is that we interpret, at each "moment," the *specular make-up* of discourse, that is, the self-reflecting (stratifiable) organization of the subject in that discourse. An organization that maintains, among other things, the break between what is perceptible and what is intelligible, and thus maintains the submission, subordination, and exploitation of the "feminine."

This language work would thus attempt to thwart any manipulation of discourse that would also leave discourse intact. Not, necessarily, in the utterance, but in its *autological presupposition*. Its function would thus be to *cast phallocentrism, phallocratism*, loose from its moorings in order to return the masculine to its own language, leaving open the possibility of a different language. Which means that the masculine would no longer be "everything." That it could no longer, all by itself define, circumvene, circumscribe, the properties of any thing and everything. That the right to define every value – including the abusive privilege of appropriation – would no longer belong to it.

Notes

1 [Speculation is Irigaray's term for male philosophy inasmuch as it seeks the mirror of man (his specular image) in the matter of nature, which for Irigaray is connoted by the term red blood to suggest that speculation or abstract reasoning in meta-empirical concepts is a defensive turning away from the threat of the loss of male mastery that the formlessness of matter represents.]
2 Sight for Irigaray is associated with the male desire to see things clearly and logically and to master them theoretically. [Eds.]

CHAPTER 4

Women on the Market

Luce Irigaray

In this dense selection from *This Sex*, Irigaray refers to the ideas prevalent regarding women up to the 1970s. For anthropologist Claude Lévi-Strauss in his study of kinship, women were commodities whose exchange among tribes guaranteed peaceful coexistence by creating extended family structures among strangers. For Freud, women were normally heterosexual, and if they ventured into homosexuality or lesbianism, they were merely seeking a model of a man in their female partner. Irigaray points out that the exchange of women established relations between men; the old family system was essentially "homosexual" (although she is using the term metaphorically). Once again, she argues here for a separation of women from men, so that female "commodities" who are traded by men to establish homosocial bonds can have their own identities and their own lives among themselves.

The society we know, our own culture, is based upon the exchange of women. Without the exchange of women, we are told, we would fall back into the anarchy (?) of the natural world, the randomness (?) of the animal kingdom. The passage into the social order, into the symbolic order, into order as such, is assured by the fact that men, or groups of men, circulate women among themselves, according to a rule known as the incest taboo.

Whatever familial form this prohibition may take in a given state of society, its signification has a much broader impact. It assures the foundation of the economic, social, and cultural order that has been ours for centuries.

Why exchange women? Because they are "scarce [commodities]...essential to the life of the group," the anthropologist tells us.[1] Why this characteristic of scarcity, given the biological equilibrium between male and female births? Because the "deep polygamous tendency, which exists among all men, always makes the number of available women seem insufficient. Let us add that, even if there were as many women as men, these women would not all be equally desirable...and that, by definition..., the most desirable women must form a minority."[2]

Are men all equally desirable? Do women have no tendency toward polygamy? The good anthropologist does not raise such questions. *A fortiori*: why are men not objects of exchange among women? It is because women's bodies – through their use, consumption, and circulation – provide for the condition making social life and culture possible, although they remain an unknown "infrastructure" of the elaboration of that social life and culture. The exploitation of the matter that has been sexualized female is so integral a part of our sociocultural horizon that there is no way to interpret it except within this horizon.

In still other words: all the systems of exchange that organize patriarchal societies and all the modalities of productive work that are recognized, valued, and rewarded in these societies are men's business. The production of women, signs, and commodities is always referred back to men (when a man buys a girl, he "pays" the father or the brother, not the mother...), and they always pass from one man to another, from one group of men to another. The work force is thus always assumed to be masculine, and "products" are objects to be used, objects of transaction among men alone.

Which means that the possibility of our social life, of our culture, depends upon a ho(m)mo-sexual monopoly? The law that orders our society is the exclusive valorization of men's needs/desires, of exchanges among men. What the anthropologist calls the passage from nature to culture thus amounts to the institution of the reign of hom(m)o-sexuality. Not in an "immediate" practice, but in its "social" mediation. From this point on, patriarchal societies might be interpreted as societies functioning in the mode of "semblance." The value of symbolic and imaginary productions is superimposed upon, and even substituted for, the value of relations of material, natural, and corporal (re)production.

   In this new matrix of History, in which man begets man as his own likeness, wives, daughters, and sisters have value only in that they serve as the possibility of, and potential benefit in, relations among men. The use of and traffic in women subtend and uphold the reign of masculine hom(m)o-sexuality, even while they maintain that hom(m)o-sexuality in speculations, mirror games, identifications, and more or less rivalrous appropriations, which defer its real practice. Reigning everywhere, although prohibited in practice, hom(m)o-sexuality is played out through the bodies of women, matter, or sign, and heterosexuality has been up to now just an alibi for the smooth workings of man's relations with himself, of relations among men. Whose "sociocultural endogamy" excludes the participation of that other, so foreign to the social order: woman. Exogamy doubtless requires that one leave one's family, tribe, or clan, in order to make alliances. All the same, it does not tolerate marriage with populations that are too far away, too far removed from the prevailing cultural rules. A sociocultural endogamy would thus forbid commerce *with* women. Men make commerce *of* them, but they do not enter into any exchanges *with* them. Is this perhaps all the more true because exogamy is an economic issue, perhaps even subtends economy as such? The exchange of women as goods accompanies and stimulates exchanges of other "wealth" among groups of men. The economy – in both the narrow and the broad sense – that is in place in our societies thus requires that women lend themselves to alienation in consumption, and to exchanges in which they do not participate, and that men be exempt from being used and circulated like commodities.

Marx's analysis of commodities as the elementary form of capitalist wealth can thus be understood as an interpretation of the status of woman in so-called patriarchal societies. The organization of such societies, and the operation of the symbolic system on which this organization is based – a symbolic system whose instrument and representative is the proper name: the name of the father, the name of God – contain in a nuclear form the developments that Marx defines as characteristic of a capitalist regime: the submission of "nature" to a "labor" on the part of men who thus constitute "nature" as use value and exchange value; the division of labor among private producer-owners who exchange their women-commodities among themselves, but also among producers and exploiters or exploitees of the social order; the standardization of women according to proper names that determine their equivalences; a tendency to accumulate wealth, that is, a tendency for the representatives of the most "proper" names – the leaders – to capitalize more women than the others; a progression of the social work of the symbolic toward greater and greater abstraction; and so forth.

To be sure, the means of production have evolved, new techniques have been developed, but it does seem that as soon as the father-man was assured of his reproductive power and had marked his products with his name, that is, from the very origin of private property and the patriarchal family, social exploitation occurred. In other words, all the social regimes of "History" are based upon the exploitation of one "class" of producers, namely, women. Whose reproductive use value (reproductive of children and of the labor force) and whose constitution as exchange value underwrite the symbolic order as such, without any compensation in kind going to them for that "work." For such compensation would imply a double system of exchange, that is, a shattering of the monopolization of the proper name (and of what it signifies as appropriative power) by father-men.

Thus the social body would be redistributed into producer-subjects no longer functioning as commodities because they provided the standard of value for commodities, and into commodity-objects that ensured the circulation of exchange without participating in it as subjects.

Let us now reconsider a few points[3] in Marx's analysis of value that seem to describe the social status of women.

Wealth amounts to a subordination of the use of things to their accumulation. Then would *the way women are used matter less than their number?* The possession of a woman is certainly indispensable to man for the reproductive use value that she represents; but what he desires is to have them all. To "accumulate" them, to be able to count off his conquests, seductions, possessions, both sequentially and cumulatively, as measure or standard(s).

All but one? For if the series could be closed, value might well lie, as Marx says, in the relation among them rather than in the relation to a standard that remains external to them – whether gold or phallus.

The use made of women is thus of less value than their appropriation one by one. And their "usefulness" is not what counts the most. Woman's price is not determined by the "properties" of her body – although her body constitutes the *material* support of that price.

But when women are exchanged, woman's body must be treated as an *abstraction*. The exchange operation cannot take place in terms of some intrinsic, immanent value of the commodity. It can only come about when two objects – two women – are in a relation of equality with a third term that is neither the one nor the other. It is thus not as "women" that they are exchanged, but as women reduced to some common feature – their current price in gold, or phalluses – and of which they would represent a plus or minus quantity. Not a plus or a minus of feminine qualities, obviously.

Since these qualities are abandoned in the long run to the needs of the consumer, *woman has value on the market by virtue of one single quality: that of being a product of man's "labor."*

On this basis, each one looks exactly like every other. They all have the same phantom-like reality. Metamorphosed in identical *sublimations*, samples of the same indistinguishable work, all these objects now manifest just one thing, namely, that in their production a force of human labor has been expended, that labor has accumulated in them. In their role as crystals of that common social substance, they are deemed to have value.

As commodities, women are thus two things at once: utilitarian objects and bearers of value. "They manifest themselves therefore as commodities, or have the form of commodities, only in so far as they have two forms, a physical or natural form, and a value form" (p. 55).

But "the reality of the value of commodities differs in this respect from Dame Quickly, that we don't know 'where to have it' " (ibid.). *Woman, object of exchange, differs from woman, use value, in that one doesn't know how to take (hold of) her*, for since "the value of commodities is the very opposite of the coarse materiality of their substance, not an atom of matter enters into its composition. Turn and examine a single commodity, by itself, as we will. Yet in so far as it remains an object of value, it seems impossible to grasp it" (ibid.). The value of a woman always escapes: black continent, hole in the symbolic, breach in discourse... It is only in the operation of exchange among women that something of this – something enigmatic, to be sure – can be felt. *Woman thus has value only in that she can be exchanged.* In the passage from one to the other, something else finally exists beside the possible utility of the "coarseness" of her body. But this value is not found, is not recaptured, in her. It is only her measurement against a third term that remains external to her, and that makes it possible to compare her with another woman, that permits her to have a relation to another commodity in terms of an equivalence that remains foreign to both.

Women-as-commodities are thus subject to a schism that divides them into the categories of usefulness and exchange value; into matter-body and an envelope that is precious but impenetrable, ungraspable, and not susceptible to appropriation by women themselves; into private use and social use.

In order to have a *relative value*, a commodity has to be confronted with another commodity that serves as its equivalent. Its value is never found to lie within itself. And the fact that it is worth more or less is not its own doing but comes from that to which it may be equivalent. Its value is *transcendent* to itself, *super-natural, ek-static*.

In other words, for the commodity, there is no mirror that copies it so that it may be at once itself and its "own" reflection. One commodity cannot be mirrored in another, as man is mirrored in his fellow man. For when we are dealing with commodities the self-same, mirrored, is not "its" own likeness, contains nothing of its properties, its qualities, its "skin and hair." The likeness here is only a measure expressing the *fabricated* character of the commodity, its trans-formation by man's (social, symbolic) "labor." The mirror that envelops and paralyzes the commodity specularizes, speculates (on) man's "labor." *Commodities, women, are a mirror of value of and for man.* In order to serve as such, they give up their bodies to men as the supporting material of specularization, of speculation. They yield to him their natural and social value as a locus of imprints, marks, and mirage of his activity.

Commodities among themselves are thus not equal, nor alike, nor different. They only become so when they are compared by and for man. And *the prosopopoeia of the relation of commodities among themselves is a projection* through which producers-exchangers make them reenact before their eyes their operations of specula(riza)tion. Forgetting that in order to reflect (oneself), to speculate (oneself), it is necessary to be a "subject," and that matter can serve as a support for speculation but cannot itself speculate in any way.

Thus, starting with the simplest relation of equivalence between commodities, starting with the possible exchange of women, the entire enigma of the money form – of the phallic function – is implied. That is, the appropriation-disappropriation by man, for man, of nature and its productive forces, insofar as a certain mirror now divides and travesties both nature and labor. Man endows the commodities he produces with a narcissism that blurs the seriousness of utility, of use. Desire, as soon as there is exchange, "perverts" need. But that perversion will be attributed to commodities and to their alleged relations. Whereas they can have no relationships except from the perspective of speculating third parties.

The economy of exchange – of desire – is man's business. For two reasons: the exchange takes place between masculine subjects, and it requires a *plus-value* added to the body of the commodity, a supplement which gives it a valuable form. That supplement will be found, Marx writes, in another commodity, whose use value becomes, from that point on, a standard of value.

But that surplus-value enjoyed by one of the commodities might vary: "just as many a man strutting about in a gorgeous uniform counts for more than when in mufti" (p. 60). Or just as "*A*, for instance, cannot be 'your majesty' to *B*, unless at the same time majesty in *B*'s eyes assume the bodily form of *A*, and, what is more, with every new father of the people, changes its features, hair, and many other things besides" (ibid.). Commodities – "things" produced – would thus have the respect due the uniform, majesty, paternal authority. And even God. "The fact that it is value, is made manifest by its equality with the coat, just as the sheep's nature of a Christian is shown in his resemblance to the Lamb of God" (ibid.).

Commodities thus share in the cult of the father, and never stop striving to resemble, to copy, the one who is his representative. It is from that resemblance, from that imitation of what represents paternal authority, that commodities draw their value – for men. But it is upon commodities that the producers-exchangers bring to bear this power play. "We see, then, all that our analysis of the value of commodities has already told us, is told us by the linen itself, so soon as it comes into communication with another commodity, the coat. Only it betrays its thoughts in that language with which alone it is familiar, the language of commodities. In order to tell us that its own value is created by labour in its abstract character of human labour, it says that the coat, in so far as it is worth as much as the linen, and therefore is value, consists of the same labour as the linen. In order to inform us that its sublime reality as value is not the same as its buckram body, it says that value has the appearance of a coat, and consequently that so far as the linen is value, it and the coat are as like as two peas. We may here remark, that the language of commodities has, besides Hebrew, many other more or less correct dialects. The German 'werthsein,' to be worth, for instance, expresses in a less striking manner than the Romance verbs 'valere,' 'valer,' 'valoir,' that the equating of commodity B to commodity A, is commodity A's own mode of expressing its value. Paris vaut bien une messe" (pp. 60–1).

   So commodities speak. To be sure, mostly dialects and patois, languages hard for "subjects" to understand. The important thing is that they be preoccupied with their respective values, that their remarks confirm the exchangers' plans for them.

The body of a commodity thus becomes, for another such commodity, a mirror of its value. Contingent upon a bodily *supplement*. A supplement *opposed* to use value, a supplement representing the commodity's *super-natural* quality (an imprint that is purely social in nature), a supplement completely different from the body itself, and from its properties, a supplement that nevertheless exists only on condition that one commodity agrees to relate itself to another considered as equivalent: "For instance, one man is king only because other men stand in the relation of subjects to him" (p. 66, n. 1).

   This supplement of equivalency translates concrete work into abstract work. In other words, in order to be able to incorporate itself into a mirror of value, it is necessary that the work itself reflect only its property of human labor: that the body of a commodity be nothing more than the materialization of an abstract human labor. That is, that it have no more body, matter, nature, but that it be objectivization, a crystallization as visible object, of man's activity.

In order to become equivalent, a commodity changes bodies. A super-natural, metaphysical origin is substituted for its material origin. Thus its body becomes a transparent body, *pure phenomenality of value.* But this transparency constitutes a supplement to the material opacity of the commodity.

   Once again there is a schism between the two. Two sides, two poles, nature and society are divided, like the perceptible and the intelligible, matter and form, the empirical and the transcendental . . . The commodity, like the sign, suffers from metaphysical dichotomies. Its value, its truth, lies in the social element. But this social element is added on to its nature, to its matter, and the social subordinates it as a lesser value, indeed as nonvalue. Participation in society requires that the body submit itself to a specularization, a speculation, that transforms it into a value-bearing object, a standardized sign, an exchangeable signifier, a "likeness" with reference to an authoritative model. *A commodity – a woman – is divided into two irreconcilable "bodies":* her "natural" body and her socially valued, exchangeable body, which is a particularly mimetic expression of masculine values. No doubt these values also express "nature," that is, the expenditure of physical force. But this latter – essentially masculine, moreover – serves for the fabrication, the transformation, the technicization of natural productions. And it is this *super*-natural property that comes to constitute the value of the product. Analyzing value in this way, Marx exposes the meta-physical character of social operations.

The commodity is thus a dual entity as soon as its value comes to possess a phenomenal form of its own, distinct from its natural form: that of exchange value. And it never possesses this form if it is considered in isolation. A commodity has this phenomenal form added on to its nature only in relation to another commodity.

As among signs, value appears only when a relationship has been established. It remains the case that the establishment of relationships cannot be accomplished by the commodities themselves, but depends upon the operation of two exchangers. The exchange value of two signs, two commodities, two women, is a representation of the needs/desires of consumer-exchanger subjects: in no way is it the "property" of the signs/articles/women themselves. At the most, the commodities – or rather the relationships among them – are the material alibi for the desire for relations among men. To this end, the commodity is disinvested of its body and reclothed in a form that makes it suitable for exchange among men.

But, in this value-bearing form, the desire for that exchange, and the reflection of his own value and that of his fellow man that man seeks in it, are ek-stasized. In that suspension in the commodity of the relationship among men, producer-consumer-exchanger subjects are alienated. In order that they might "bear" and support that alienation, commodities for their part have always been dispossessed of their specific value. On this basis, one may affirm that the value of the commodity takes on *indifferently* any given form of use value. The price of the articles, in fact, no longer comes from *their* natural form, from *their* bodies, *their* language, but from the fact that they mirror the need/desire for exchanges among men. To do this, the commodity obviously cannot exist alone, but there is no such thing as a commodity, either, so long as there are not *at least two men* to make an exchange. In order for a product – a woman? – to have value, two men, at least, have to invest (in) her.

The general equivalent of a commodity no longer functions as a commodity itself. A pre-eminent mirror, transcending the world of merchandise, it guarantees the possibility of universal exchange among commodities. Each commodity may become equivalent to every other from the viewpoint of that sublime standard, but the fact that the judgment of their value depends upon some transcendental element renders them provisionally incapable of being directly exchanged for each other. They are exchanged by means of the general equivalent – as Christians love each other in God, to borrow a theological metaphor dear to Marx.

That ek-static reference separates them radically from each other. *An abstract and universal value preserves them from use and exchange among themselves.* They are, as it were, transformed into value-invested idealities. Their concrete forms, their specific qualities, and all the possibilities of "real" relations with them or among them are reduced to their common character as products of man's labor and desire.

We must emphasize also that *the general equivalent*, since it is no longer a commodity, *is no longer useful. The standard as such is exempt from use.*

Though a commodity may at first sight appear to be "a very trivial thing, and easily understood, . . . it is, in reality, a very queer thing, abounding in metaphysical subtleties and theological niceties" (p. 81). No doubt, "so far as it is a value in use, there is nothing mysterious about it. . . . But, so soon as [a wooden table, for example] steps forth as a commodity, it is changed into something transcendent. It not only stands with its feet on the ground, but, in relation to all other commodities, it stands on its head, and evolves out of its wooden brain grotesque ideas, far more wonderful than 'table-turning' ever was" (pp. 81–2).

"The mystical character of commodities does not originate, therefore, in their use value. Just as little does it proceed from the nature of the determining factors of value. For, in the first place, however varied the useful kinds of labour, or productive activities, may be, it is a physiological fact, that they are functions of the human organism" (p. 82), which, for Marx, does not seem to constitute a mystery in any way... The material contribution and support of bodies in societal operations pose no problems for him, except as production and expenditure of energy.

Where, then, does the enigmatic character of the product of labor come from, as soon as this product takes on the form of a commodity? It comes, obviously, from that form itself. *Then where does the enigmatic character of women come from?* Or even that of their supposed relations among themselves? Obviously, from the "form" of the needs/desires of man, needs/desires that women bring to light although men do not recognize them in that form. That form, those women, are always enveloped, veiled.

In any case, "the existence of things *qua* commodities, and the value relation between the products of labour which stamps them as commodities, have absolutely no connection with their physical properties and with the material relations arising therefrom. [With commodities] it is a definite social relation between men, that assumes, in their eyes, the fantastic form of a relation between things" (p. 83). *This phenomenon has no analogy except in the religious world.* "In that world the productions of the human brain appear as independent beings endowed with life, and entering into relation both with one another and the human race. So it is in the world of commodities with the products of men's hands" (ibid.). Hence the fetishism attached to these products of labor as soon as they present themselves as commodities.

Hence *women's role as fetish-objects*, inasmuch as, in exchanges, they are the manifestation and the circulation of a power of the Phallus, establishing relationships of men with each other?

Hence the following remarks:

On value.

It represents the equivalent of labor force, of an expenditure of energy, of toil. In order to be measured, these latter must be *abstracted* from all immediately natural qualities, from any concrete individual. A process of generalization and of universalization imposes itself in the operation of social exchanges. Hence the reduction of man to a "concept" – that of his labor force – and the reduction of his product to an "object," the visible, material correlative of that concept.

The characteristics of "sexual pleasure" corresponding to such a social state are thus the following: its productivity, but one that is necessarily laborious, even painful; its abstract form; its need/desire to crystallize in a transcendental element of wealth the standard of all value; its need for a material support where the relation of appropriation to and of that standard is measured; its exchange relationships – always rivalrous – among men alone, and so on.

Are not these modalities the ones that might define the economy of (so-called) *masculine sexuality?* And is libido not another name for the abstraction of "energy" in a productive power? For the work of nature? Another name for the desire to accumulate goods? Another name for the subordination of the specific qualities of bodies to a – neutral? – power that aims above all to transform them in order to possess them?

Does pleasure, for masculine sexuality, consist in anything other than the appropriation of nature, in the desire to make it (re)produce, and in exchanges of its/these products with other members of society? An essentially *economic* pleasure.

Thus the following question: *what needs/ desires of (so-called) masculine sexuality have presided over the evolution of a certain social order*, from its primitive form, private property, to its developed form, capital? But also: *to what extent are these needs/ desires the effect of a social mechanism*, in part autonomous, that produces them as such?

On the status of women in such a social order.

What makes such an order possible, what assures its foundation, is thus *the exchange of women*. The circulation of women among men is what establishes the operations of society, at least of patriarchal society. Whose presuppositions include the following: the appropriation of nature by man; the transformation of nature according to "human" criteria, defined by men alone; the submission of nature to labor and technology; the reduction of its material, corporeal, perceptible qualities to man's practical concrete activity; the equality of women among themselves, but in terms of laws of equivalence that remain external to them; the constitution of women as "objects" that emblematize the materialization of relations among men, and so on.

In such a social order, women thus represent a natural value and a social value. Their "development" lies in the passage from one to the other. But this passage never takes place simply.

As mother, woman remains on the side of (re)productive *nature* and, because of this, man can never fully transcend his relation to the "natural." His social existence, his economic structures and his sexuality are always tied to the work of nature: these structures thus always remain at the level of the earliest appropriation, that of the constitution of nature as landed property, and of the earliest labor, which is agricultural. But this relationship to productive nature, an insurmountable one, has to be denied so that relations among men may prevail. This means that mothers, reproductive instruments marked with the name of the father and enclosed in his house, must be private property, excluded from exchange. The *incest taboo* represents this refusal to allow productive nature to enter into exchanges among men. As both natural value and use value, mothers cannot circulate in the form of commodities without threatening the very existence of the social order. Mothers are essential to its (re)production (particularly inasmuch as they are [re]productive of children and of the labor force: through maternity, child-rearing, and domestic maintenance in general). Their responsibility is to maintain the social order without intervening so as to change it. Their products are legal tender in that order, moreover, only if they are marked with the name of the father, only if they are recognized within his law: that is, only insofar as they are appropriated by him. Society is the place where man engenders himself, where man produces himself as man, where man is born into "human," "super-natural" existence.

The virginal woman, on the other hand, is pure exchange value. She is nothing but the possibility, the place, the sign of relations among men. In and of herself, she does not exist: she is a simple envelope veiling what is really at stake in social exchange. In this sense, her natural body disappears into its representative function. *Red blood* remains on the mother's side, but it has no price, as such, in the social order; woman, for her part, as medium of exchange, is no longer anything but *semblance*. The ritualized passage from woman to mother is accomplished by the *violation of an envelope:* the hymen, which has taken on the value of *taboo*, the taboo of virginity. Once deflowered, woman is relegated to the status of use value, to her entrapment in private property; she is removed from exchange among men.

The *prostitute* remains to be considered. Explicitly condemned by the social order, she is implicitly tolerated. No doubt because the break between usage and exchange is, in her case, less clear-cut? In her case, the qualities of woman's body are "useful." However, these qualities have "value" only because they have already been appropriated by a man, and because they serve as the locus of relations – hidden ones – between men. Prostitution amounts to *usage that is exchanged*. Usage that is not merely potential: it has already been realized. The woman's body is valuable because it has already been used. In the extreme case, the more it has served, the more it is worth. Not because its natural assets have been put to use this way, but, on the contrary, because its nature has been "used up," and has become once again no more than a vehicle for relations among men.

Mother, virgin, prostitute: these are the social roles imposed on women. The characteristics of (so-called) feminine sexuality derive from them: the valorization of reproduction and nursing; faithfulness; modesty, ignorance of and even lack of interest in sexual pleasure; a passive acceptance of men's "activity"; seductiveness, in order to arouse the consumers' desire while offering herself as its material support without getting pleasure herself... *Neither as mother nor as virgin nor as prostitute has woman any right to her own pleasure.*

Of course the theoreticians of sexuality are sometimes astonished by women's frigidity. But, according to them, this frigidity is explained more by an impotence inherent to feminine "nature" than by the submission of that nature to a certain type of society. However, *what is required of a "normal" feminine sexuality is oddly evocative of the characteristics of the status of a commodity*. With references to and rejections of the "natural" – physiological and organic nature, and so on – that are equally ambiguous.
   And, in addition:

– just as nature has to be subjected to man in order to become a commodity, so, it appears, does "the development of a normal woman." A development that amounts, for the feminine, to subordination to the forms and laws of masculine activity. The rejection of the mother – imputed to woman – would find its "cause" here;

– just as, in commodities, natural utility is overridden by the exchange function, so the properties of a woman's body have to be suppressed and subordinated to the exigencies of its transformation into an object of circulation among men;

– just as a commodity has no mirror it can use to reflect itself, so woman serves as reflection, as image of and for man, but lacks specific qualities of her own. Her value-invested form amounts to what man inscribes in and on its matter: that is, her body;

– just as commodities cannot make exchanges among themselves without the intervention of a subject that measures them against a standard, so it is with women. Distinguished, divided, separated, classified as like and unlike, according to whether they have been judged exchangeable. In themselves, among themselves, they are amorphous and confused: natural body, maternal body, doubtless useful to the consumer, but without any possible identity or communicable value;

– just as commodities, despite their resistance, become more or less autonomous repositories for the value of human work, so, as mirrors of and for man, women more or less unwittingly come to represent the danger of a disappropriation of masculine power: the phallic mirage;

– just as a commodity finds the expression of its value in an equivalent – in the last analysis, a general one – that necessarily remains external to it, so woman derives her price from her relation to the male sex, constituted as a transcendental value: the phallus. And indeed the enigma of "value" lies in the most elementary relation among commodities. Among women. For, uprooted from their "nature," they no longer relate to each other except in terms of what they represent in men's desire, and according to the "forms" that this imposes upon them. Among themselves, they are separated by his speculations.

This means that the division of "labor" – sexual labor in particular – requires that woman maintain in her own body the material substratum of the object of desire, but that she herself never have access to desire. The economy of desire – of exchange – is man's business. And that economy subjects women to a schism that is necessary to symbolic operations: red blood/semblance; body/value-invested envelope; matter/medium of exchange; (re)productive nature/fabricated femininity ... That schism – characteristic of all speaking nature, someone will surely object – is experienced by women without any possible profit to them. And without any way for them to transcend it. They are not even "conscious" of it. The symbolic system that cuts them in two this way is in no way appropriate to them. In them, "semblance" remains external, foreign to "nature." *Socially*, they are "objects" for and among men and furthermore they cannot do anything but mimic a "language" that they have not produced; *naturally*, they remain amorphous, suffering from drives without any possible representatives or representations. For them, the transformation of the natural into the social does not take place, except to the extent that they function as components of private property, or as commodities.

Characteristics of this social order

This type of social system can be interpreted as *the practical realization of the metaphysical*. As the *practical destiny* of the metaphysical, it would also represent its *most fully realized form*. Operating in such a way, moreover, that subjects themselves, being implicated in it through and through, being produced in it as concepts, would lack the means to analyze it. Except in an after-the-fact way whose delays are yet to be fully measured . . .

This practical realization of the meta-physical has as its founding operation the appropriation of woman's body by the father or his substitutes. It is marked by women's submission to a system of general equivalents, the proper name representing the father's monopoly of power. It is from this standardization that women receive their value, as they pass from the state of nature to the status of social object. This trans-formation of women's bodies into use values and exchange values inaugurates the symbolic order. But that order depends upon a *nearly pure added value*. Women, animals endowed with speech like men, assure the possibility of the use and circulation of the symbolic without being recipients of it. Their nonaccess to the symbolic is what has established the social order. Putting men in touch with each other, in relations among themselves, women only fulfill this role by relinquishing their right to speech and even to animality. No longer in the natural order, not yet in the social order that they nonetheless maintain, women are the symptom of the exploitation of individuals by a society that remunerates them only partially, or even not at all, for their "work." Unless subordination to a system that utilizes you and oppresses you should be considered as sufficient compensation . . . ? Unless the fact that women are branded with the proper name – of the "father" – should be viewed as the symbolic payment awarded them for sustaining the social order with their bodies?

But by submitting women's bodies to a general equivalent, to a transcendent, supernatural value, men have drawn the social structure into an ever greater process of abstraction, to the point where they themselves are produced in it as pure concepts: having surmounted all their "perceptible" qualities and individual differences, they are finally reduced to the average productivity of their labor. The power of this practical economy of the meta-physical comes from the fact that "physiological" energy is transformed into abstract value without the mediation of an intelligible elaboration. No individual subject can be credited any longer with bringing about this transformation. It is only after the fact that the subject might possibly be able to analyze his determination as such by the social structure. And even then it is not certain that his love of gold would not make him give up everything else before he would renounce the cult of this fetish. "The saver thus sacrifices to this fetish all the penchants of his flesh. No one takes the gospel of renunciation more seriously than he."

Fortunately – if we may say so – women/commodities would remain, as simple "objects" of transaction among men. Their situation of specific exploitation in exchange operations – sexual exchange, and economic, social, and cultural exchanges in general – might lead them to offer a new critique of the political economy." *A critique that would no longer avoid that of discourse, and more generally of the symbolic system, in which it is realized*. Which would lead to interpreting in a different way the impact of symbolic social labor in the analysis of relations of production.

For, without the exploitation of women, what would become of the social order? What modifications would it undergo if women left behind their condition as commodities – subject to being produced, consumed, valorized, circulated, and so on, by men alone – and took part in elaborating and carrying out exchanges? Not by reproducing, by copying, the "phallocratic" models that have the force of law today, but by socializing in a different way the relation to nature, matter, the body, language, and desire.

Notes

This text was originally published as "Le marché des femmes," in *Sessualità e politica* (Milan: Feltrinelli, 1978).

1 Claude Lévi-Strauss, *The Elementary Structures of Kinship (Les Structures élémentaires de la Parenté*, 1949, rev. 1967), trans. James Harle Bell, John Richard von Sturmer, and Rodney Needham (Boston, 1969), p. 36.

2 Ibid., p. 38.

3 All the quotations in the remainder of this chapter are excerpted from Marx's *Capital*, section 1, chapter 1. (The page numbers given in the text refer to the Modern Library edition, trans. Samuel Moore and Edward Aveling, ed. Frederick Engels, rev. Ernest Untermann [New York, 1906].) Will it be objected that this interpretation is analogical by nature? I accept the question, on condition that it be addressed also, and in the first place, to Marx's analysis of commodities. Did not Aristotle, a "great thinker" according to Marx, determine the relation of form to matter by analogy with the relation between masculine and feminine? Returning to the question of the difference between the sexes would amount instead, then, to going back through analogism.

CHAPTER 5

The Madwoman in the Attic

Sandra Gilbert and Susan Gubar

Gilbert and Gubar's multi-volume history of women in literature began in 1980 with the publication of *The Madwoman in the Attic*. It was followed by *No Man's Land: The Place of Women Writers in the 20th Century* (1988). Gilbert and Gubar's books were the first to review in a complete way the place of women both as literary figures and as writers. Drawing on the work of Harold Bloom regarding poetic identity, they argued that women could not become writers and assume a writer's identity until they found appropriate models for themselves in the tradition. Given the way women were represented, that was a difficult task at best. Their argument in this selection is that even the positive images of women in literature express negative energies and desires on the part of male writers.

Before the woman writer can journey through the looking glass toward literary autonomy...she must come to terms with the images on the surface of the glass, with, that is, those mythic masks male artists have fastened over her human face both to lessen their dread of her "inconstancy" and by identifying her with the "eternal types" they have themselves invented to possess her more thoroughly. Specifically, as we will try to show here, a woman writer must examine, assimilate, and transcend the extreme images of "angel" and "monster" which male authors have generated for her. Before we women can write, declared Virginia Woolf, we must "kill" the "angel in the house."[1] In other words, women must kill the aesthetic ideal through which they themselves have been "killed" into art. And similarly, all women writers must kill the angel's necessary opposite and double, the "monster" in the house, whose Medusa-face also kills female creativity. For us as feminist critics, however, the Woolfian act of "killing" both angels and monsters must here begin with an understanding of the nature and origin of these images. At this point in our construction of a feminist poetics, then, we really must dissect in order to murder. And we must particularly do this in order to understand literature by women because, as we shall show, the images of "angel" and "monster" have been so ubiquitous throughout literature by men that they have also pervaded women's writing to such an extent that few women have definitively "killed" either figure. Rather, the female imagination has perceived itself, as it were, through a glass darkly: until quite recently the woman writer has had (if only unconsciously) to define herself as a mysterious creature who resides behind the angel or monster or angel/monster image that lives on what Mary Elizabeth Coleridge called "the crystal surface."...

For all literary artists, of course, self-definition necessarily precedes self-assertion: the creative "I AM" cannot be uttered if the "I" knows not what it is. But for the female artist the essential process of self-definition is complicated by all those patriarchal definitions that intervene between herself and herself. From Anne Finch's Ardelia, who struggles to escape the male designs in which she feels herself enmeshed, to Sylvia Plath's "Lady Lazarus," who tells "Herr Doktor...Herr Enemy" that "I am your opus,"/"I am your valuable," the woman writer acknowledges with pain, confusion, and anger that what she sees in the mirror is usually a male construct, the "pure gold baby" of male brains, a glittering and wholly artificial child. With Christina Rossetti, moreover, she realizes that the male artist often "feeds" upon his female subject's face "not as she is but as she fills his dreams." Finally, as "A Woman's Poem" of 1859 simply puts it, the woman writer insists that "You [men] make the worlds wherein you move.... Our world (alas you make that too!)" – and in its narrow confines, "shut in four blank walls...we act our parts."

Though the highly stylized women's roles to which this last poem alludes are all ultimately variations upon the roles of angel and monster, they seem on the surface quite varied, because so many masks, reflecting such an elaborate typology, have been invented for women. A crucial passage from Elizabeth Barrett Browning's *Aurora Leigh* suggests both the mystifying deathliness and the mysterious variety female artists perceive in male imagery of women. Contemplating a portrait of her mother which, significantly, was made after its subject was dead (so that it is a kind of death mask, an image of a woman metaphorically killed into art) the young Aurora broods on the work's iconography. Noting that her mother's chambermaid had insisted upon having her dead mistress painted in "the red stiff silk" of her court dress rather than in an "English-fashioned shroud," she remarks that the effect of this unlikely costume was "very strange." As the child stared at the painting, her mother's "swan-like supernatural white life" seemed to mingle with "whatever I last read, or heard, or dreamed," and thus in its charismatic beauty, her mother's image became

> by turns
> Ghost, fiend, and angel, fairy, witch, and sprite;
> A dauntless Muse who eyes a dreadful Fate;
> A loving Psyche who loses sight of Love;
> A still Medusa with mild milky brows.
> All curdled and all clothed upon with snakes
> Whose slime falls fast as sweat will; or anon
> Our Lady of the Passion, stabbed with swords
> Where the Babe sucked; or Lamia in her first
> Moonlighted pallor, ere she shrunk and blinked,
> And shuddering wriggled down to the unclean;
> Or my own mother, leaving her last smile
> In her last kiss upon the baby-mouth
> My father pushed down on the bed for that;
> Or my dead mother, without smile or kiss,
> Buried at Florence.

The female forms Aurora sees in her dead mother's picture are extreme, melodramatic, gothic – "Ghost, fiend, and angel, fairy, witch, and sprite" – specifically, as she tells us, because her reading merges with her seeing. What this implies, however, is not only that she herself is fated to inhabit male-defined masks and costumes, as her mother did, but that male-defined masks and costumes inevitably inhabit *her*, altering her vision. Aurora's self-development as a poet is the central concern of Barrett Browning's *Bildungsroman* in verse, but if she is to be a poet she must deconstruct the dead self that is a male "opus" and discover a living, "inconstant" self. She must, in other words, replace the "copy" with the "individuality," as Barrett Browning once said she thought she herself had done in her mature art. Significantly, however, the "copy" selves depicted in Aurora's mother's portrait ultimately represent, once again, the moral extremes of angel ("angel," "fairy," and perhaps "sprite") and monster ("ghost," "witch," "fiend").

In her brilliant and influential analysis of the question "Is Female to Male as Nature Is to Culture?" the anthropologist Sherry Ortner notes that in every society "the psychic mode associated with women seems to stand at both the bottom and the top of the scale of human modes of relating." Attempting to account for this "symbolic ambiguity," Ortner explains "both the subversive feminine symbols (witches, evil eye, menstrual pollution, castrating mothers) and the feminine symbols of transcendence (mother goddesses, merciful dispensers of salvation, female symbols of justice)" by pointing out that women "can appear from certain points of view to stand both under and over (but really simply outside of) the sphere of culture's hegemony."[2] That is, precisely because a woman is denied the autonomy – the subjectivity – that the pen represents, she is not only excluded from culture (whose emblem might well be the pen) but she also becomes herself an embodiment of just those extremes of mysterious and intransigent Otherness which culture confronts with worship or fear, love or loathing. As "Ghost, fiend, and angel, fairy, witch, and sprite," she mediates between the male artist and the Unknown, simultaneously teaching him purity and instructing him in degradation. . . .

In the Middle Ages, of course, mankind's great teacher of purity was the Virgin Mary, a mother goddess who perfectly fitted the female role Ortner defines as "merciful dispenser of salvation." For the more secular nineteenth century, however, the eternal type of female purity was represented not by a madonna in heaven but by an angel in the house. Nevertheless, there is a clear line of literary descent from divine Virgin to domestic angel, passing through (among many others) Dante, Milton, and Goethe.

Like most Renaissance neo-Platonists, Dante claimed to know God and His Virgin handmaid by knowing the Virgin's virgin attendant, Beatrice. Similarly, Milton, despite his undeniable misogyny (which we shall examine later), speaks of having been granted a vision of "my late espoused saint," who

> Came vested all in white, pure as her mind.
> Her face was veiled, yet to my fancied sight,
> Love, sweetness, goodness, in her person shined
> So clear, as in no face with more delight.

In death, in other words, Milton's human wife has taken on both the celestial brightness of Mary and (since she has been "washed from spot of childbed taint") the virginal purity of Beatrice. In fact, if she could be resurrected in the flesh she might now be an angel in the house, interpreting heaven's luminous mysteries to her wondering husband.

The famous vision of the "Eternal Feminine" (*Das Ewig-Weibliche*) with which Goethe's *Faust* concludes presents women from penitent prostitutes to angelic virgins in just this role of interpreters or intermediaries between the divine Father and his human sons. The German of *Faust*'s "Chorus Mysticus" is extraordinarily difficult to translate in verse, but Hans Eichner's English paraphrase easily suggests the way in which Goethe's image of female intercessors seems almost to be a revision of Milton's "late espoused saint": "All that is transitory is merely symbolical; here (that is to say, in the scene before you) the inaccessible is (symbolically) portrayed and the inexpressible is (symbolically) made manifest. The eternal feminine (i.e. the eternal principle symbolized by woman) draws us to higher spheres." Meditating on the exact nature of this eternal feminine, moreover, Eichner comments that for Goethe the "ideal of contemplative purity" is always feminine while "the ideal of significant action is masculine."[3] Once again, therefore, it is just because women are defined as wholly passive, completely void of generative power (like "Cyphers") that they become numinous to male artists. For in the metaphysical emptiness their "purity" signifies they are, of course, *self-less*, with all the moral and psychological implications that word suggests.

Elaborating further on Goethe's eternal feminine, Eichner gives an example of the culmination of Goethe's "chain of representatives of the 'noblest femininity'": Makarie, in the late novel *Wilhelm Meister's Travels*. His description of her usefully summarizes the philosophical background of the angel in the house:

> She...leads a life of almost pure contemplation.... in considerable isolation on a country estate...a life without external events – a life whose story cannot be told as there is no story. Her existence is not useless. On the contrary...she shines like a beacon in a dark world, like a motionless lighthouse by which others, the travellers whose lives do have a story, can set their course. When those involved in feeling and action turn to her in their need, they are never dismissed without advice and consolation. She is an ideal, a model of selflessness and of purity of heart.[4]

She has no story of her own but gives "advice and consolation" to others, listens, smiles, sympathizes: such characteristics show that Makarie is not only the descendant of Western culture's cloistered virgins but also the direct ancestress of Coventry Patmore's angel in the house, the eponymous heroine of what may have been the middle nineteenth century's most popular book of poems.

Dedicated to "the memory of her by whom and for whom I became a poet," Patmore's *The Angel in the House* is a verse-sequence which hymns the praises and narrates the courtship and marriage of Honoria, one of the three daughters of a country Dean, a girl whose unselfish grace, gentleness, simplicity, and nobility reveal that she is not only a pattern Victorian lady but almost literally an angel on earth. Certainly her spirituality interprets the divine for her poet husband, so that

> No happier post than this I ask,
> To live her laureate all my life.
> On wings of love uplifted free,
> And by her gentleness made great,
> I'll teach how noble man should be
> To match with such a lovely mate.[5]

Honoria's essential virtue, in other words, is that her virtue makes her *man* "great." In and of herself, she is neither great nor extraordinary. Indeed, Patmore adduces many details to stress the almost pathetic ordinariness of her life: she picks violets, loses her gloves, feeds her birds, waters her rose plot, and journeys to London on a train with her father the Dean, carrying in her lap a volume of Petrarch borrowed from her lover but entirely ignorant that the book is, as he tells us, "worth its weight in gold." In short, like Goethe's Makarie, Honoria has no story except a sort of anti-story of selfless innocence based on the notion that "Man must be pleased; but him to please / Is woman's pleasure."[6]

Significantly, when the young poet-lover first visits the Deanery where his Honoria awaits him like Sleeping Beauty or Snow White, one of her sisters asks him if, since leaving Cambridge, he has "outgrown" Kant and Goethe. But if his paean of praise to the *Ewig-Weibliche* in rural England suggests that he has not, at any rate, outgrown the latter of these, that is because for Victorian men of letters Goethe represented not collegiate immaturity but moral maturity. After all, the climactic words of *Sartor Resartus*, that most influential masterpiece of Victorian sagacity, were "Close thy *Byron*; open thy *Goethe*,"[7] and though Carlyle was not specifically thinking of what came to be called "the woman question," his canonization of Goethe meant, among other things, a new emphasis on the eternal feminine, the angel-woman Patmore describes in his verses, Aurora Leigh perceives in her mother's picture, and Virginia Woolf shudders to remember.

Of course, from the eighteenth century on, conduct books for ladies had proliferated, enjoining young girls to submissiveness, modesty, selflessness; reminding all women that they should be angelic. There is a long and crowded road from *The Booke of Curtesye* (1477) to the columns of "Dear Abby," but social historians have fully explored its part in the creation of those "eternal feminine" virtues of modesty, gracefulness, purity, delicacy, civility, compliancy, reticence, chastity, affability, politeness – all of which are modes of mannerliness that contributed to Honoria's angelic innocence. Ladies were assured by the writers of such conduct books that "There are Rules for all our Actions, even down to Sleeping with a good Grace," and they were told that this good Grace was a woman's duty to her husband because "if Woman owes her Being to the Comfort and Profit of man, 'tis highly reasonable that she should be careful and diligent to content and please him."[8]

The arts of pleasing men, in other words, are not only angelic characteristics; in more worldly terms, they are the proper acts of a lady. "What shall I do to gratify myself or to be admired?" is not the question a lady asks on arising, declared Mrs Sarah Ellis, Victorian England's foremost preceptress of female morals and manners, in 1844. No, because she is "the least engaged of any member of the household," a woman of right feeling should devote herself to the good of others.[9] And she should do this silently, without calling attention to her exertions because "all that would tend to draw away her thoughts from others and fix them on herself, ought to be avoided as an evil to her."[10] Similarly, John Ruskin affirmed in 1865 that the woman's "power is not for rule, not for battle, and her intellect is not for invention or creation, but for sweet orderings" of domesticity.[11] Plainly, both writers meant that, enshrined within her home, a Victorian angel-woman should become her husband's holy refuge from the blood and sweat that inevitably accompanies a "life of significant action," as well as, in her "contemplative purity," a living memento of the otherness of the divine.

At times, however, in the severity of her selflessness, as well as in the extremity of her alienation from ordinary fleshly life, this nineteenth-century angel-woman becomes not just a memento of otherness but actually a *memento mori* or, as Alexander Welsh has noted, an "Angel of Death." Discussing Dickens's heroines in particular and what he calls Victorian "angelology" in general, Welsh analyzes the ways in which a spiritualized heroine like Florence Dombey "assists in the translation of the dying to a future state," not only by officiating at the sickbed but also by maternally welcoming the sufferer "from the other side of death."[12] But if the angel-woman in some curious way simultaneously inhabits both this world and the next, then there is a sense in which, besides ministering to the dying, she is herself already dead. Welsh muses on "the apparent reversibility of the heroine's role, whereby the acts of dying and of saving someone from death seem confused," and he points out that Dickens actually describes Florence Dombey as having the unearthly serenity of one who is dead.[13] A spiritual messenger, an interpreter of mysteries to wondering and devoted men, the *Ewig-Weibliche* angel becomes, finally, a messenger of the mystical otherness of death.

As Ann Douglas has recently shown, the nineteenth-century cult of such death-angels as Harriet Beecher Stowe's little Eva or Dickens's little Nell resulted in a veritable "domestication of death," producing both a conventionalized iconography and a stylized hagiography of dying women and children.[14] Like Dickens's dead-alive Florence Dombey, for instance, Louisa May Alcott's dying Beth March is a household saint, and the deathbed at which she surrenders herself to heaven is the ultimate shrine of the angel-woman's mysteries. At the same time, moreover, the aesthetic cult of ladylike fragility and delicate beauty – no doubt associated with the moral cult of the angel-woman – obliged "genteel" women to "kill" themselves (as Lederer observed) into art objects: slim, pale, passive beings whose "charms" eerily recalled the snowy, porcelain immobility of the dead. Tight-lacing, fasting, vinegar-drinking, and similar cosmetic or dietary excesses were all parts of a physical regimen that helped women either to feign morbid weakness or actually to "decline" into real illness. Beth March's beautiful ladylike sister Amy is thus in her artful way, as pale and frail as her consumptive sibling, and together these two heroines constitute complementary halves of the emblematic "beautiful woman" whose death, thought Edgar Allan Poe, "is unquestionably the most poetical topic in the world."[15]

Whether she becomes an *objet d'art* or a saint, however, it is the surrender of her self – of her personal comfort, her personal desires, or both – that is the beautiful angel-woman's key act, while it is precisely this sacrifice which dooms her both to death and to heaven. For to be selfless is not only to be noble, it is to be dead. A life that has no story, like the life of Goethe's Makarie, is really a life of death, a death-in-life. The ideal of "contemplative purity" evokes, finally, both heaven and the grave. To return to Aurora Leigh's catalogue then – her vision of "Ghost, fiend, and angel, fairy, witch, and sprite" in her mother's portrait – there is a sense in which as a celestial "angel" Aurora's mother is also a somewhat sinister "ghost," because she wears the face of the spiritualized Victorian woman who, having died to her own desires, her own self, her own life, leads a posthumous existence in her own lifetime.

As Douglas reminds us too, though, the Victorian domestication of death represents not just an acquiescence in death by the selfless, but also a secret striving for power by the powerless. "The tombstone," she notes, "is the sacred emblem in the cult of the overlooked."[16] Exorcised from public life, denied the pleasures (though not the pains) of sensual existence, the Victorian angel in the house was allowed to hold sway over at least one realm beyond her own household: the kingdom of the dead. But if, as nurse and comforter, spirit-guide and mystical messenger, a woman ruled the dying and the dead, might not even her admirers sometimes fear that, besides dying or easing death, she could *bring* death? As Welsh puts it, "the power of an angel to save implies, even while it denies, the power of death." Speaking of angelic Agnes Wickfield (in *David Copperfield*), he adds a sinister but witty question: "Who, in the language of detective fiction, was the last person to see Dora Copperfield alive?"[17]

Neither Welsh nor Dickens does more than hint at the angel-woman's pernicious potential. But in this context a word to the wise is enough, for such a hint helps explain the fluid metamorphoses that the figure of Aurora's mother undergoes. Her images of "Ghost, fiend, and angel, fairy, witch and sprite," we begin to see, are inextricably linked, one to another, each to its opposite. Certainly, imprisoned in the coffinlike shape of a death angel, a woman might long demonically for escape. In addition, if as death angel the woman suggests a providentially selfless mother, delivering the male soul from one realm to another, the same woman's maternal power implies, too, the fearful bondage of mortality into which every mother delivers her children. Finally, the fact that the angel-woman manipulates her domestic/mystical sphere in order to ensure the well-being of those entrusted to her care reveals that she *can* manipulate; she can scheme; she can plot – stories as well as strategies.

The Victorian angel's scheming, her mortal fleshliness, and her repressed (but therefore all the more frightening) capacity for explosive rage are often subtly acknowledged, even in the most glowing texts of male "angelographers." Patmore's Honoria, for instance, proves to be considerably more duplicitous than at first she seemed. "To the sweet folly of the dove," her poet-lover admits, "She joins the cunning of the snake." To be sure, the speaker shows that her wiliness is exercised in a "good" cause: "to rivet and exalt his love." Nevertheless,

> Her mode of candour is deceit;
> And what she thinks from what she'll say
> (Although I'll never call her cheat)
> Lies far as Scotland from Cathay.[18]

Clearly, the poet is here acknowledging his beloved's potential for what Austen's Captain Harville called "inconstancy" – that is, her stubborn autonomy and unknowable subjectivity, meaning the ineradicable selfishness that underlies even her angelic renunciation of self.

Similarly, exploring analogous tensions between flesh and spirit in yet another version of the angel-woman, Dante Gabriel Rossetti places his "Blessed Damozel" behind "golden barriers" in heaven, but then observes that she is still humanly embodied. The bars she leans on are oddly warm; her voice, her hair, her tears are weirdly real and sensual, perhaps to emphasize the impossibility of complete spirituality for any woman. This "damozel's" life-in-death, at any rate, is still in some sense physical and therefore (paradoxically) emblematic of mortality. But though Rossetti wrote "The Blessed Damozel" in 1846, sixteen years before the suicide of his wife and model Elizabeth Siddal, the secret anxieties such imagery expressed came to the surface long after Lizzie's death. In 1869, to retrieve a poetry manuscript he had sentimentally buried with this beloved woman whose face "fill[ed] his dreams" – buried as if woman and artwork were necessarily inseparable – Rossetti had Lizzie's coffin exhumed, and literary London buzzed with rumors that her hair had "continued to grow after her death, to grow so long, so beautiful, so luxuriantly as to fill the coffin with its gold!"[19] As if symbolizing the indomitable earthliness that no woman, however angelic, could entirely renounce, Lizzie Siddal Rossetti's hair leaps like a metaphor for monstrous female sexual energies from the literal and figurative coffins in which her artist-husband enclosed her. To Rossetti, its assertive radiance made the dead Lizzie seem both terrifyingly physical and fiercely supernatural. "'Mid change the changeless night environeth, / Lies all that golden hair undimmed in death," he wrote.[20]

If we define a woman like Rossetti's dead wife as indomitably earthly yet somehow supernatural, we are defining her as a witch or monster, a magical creature of the lower world who is a kind of antithetical mirror image of an angel. As such, she still stands, in Sherry Ortner's words, "both under and over (but really simply outside of) the sphere of culture's hegemony." But now, as a representative of otherness, she incarnates the damning otherness of the flesh rather than the inspiring otherness of the spirit, expressing what – to use Anne Finch's words – men consider her own "presumptuous" desires rather than the angelic humility and "dullness" for which she was designed. Indeed, if we return to the literary definitions of "authority" with which we began this discussion, we will see that the monster-woman, threatening to replace her angelic sister, embodies intransigent female autonomy and thus represents both the author's power to allay "his" anxieties by calling their source bad names (witch, bitch, fiend, monster) and, simultaneously, the mysterious power of the character who refuses to stay in her textually ordained "place" and thus generates a story that "gets away" from its author.

Because, as Dorothy Dinnerstein has proposed, male anxieties about female autonomy probably go as deep as everyone's mother-dominated infancy, patriarchal texts have traditionally suggested that every angelically selfless Snow White must be hunted, if not haunted, by a wickedly assertive Stepmother: for every glowing portrait of submissive women enshrined in domesticity, there exists an equally important negative image that embodies the sacrilegious fiendishness of what William Blake called the "Female Will." Thus, while male writers traditionally praise the simplicity of the dove, they invariably castigate the cunning of the serpent – at least when that cunning is exercised in her own behalf. Similarly, assertiveness, aggressiveness – all characteristics of a male life of "significant action" – are "monstrous" in women precisely because "unfeminine" and therefore unsuited to a gentle life of "contemplative purity." Musing on "The Daughter of Eve," Patmore's poet-speaker remarks, significantly, that

> The woman's gentle mood o'erstept
> With hers my love, that lightly scans
> The rest, and does in her accept
> All her own faults, but none of man's.[21]

Luckily, his Honoria has no such vicious defects; her serpentine cunning, as we noted earlier, is concentrated entirely on pleasing her lover. But repeatedly, throughout most male literature, a sweet heroine inside the house (like Honoria) is opposed to a vicious bitch outside.

Behind Thackeray's angelically submissive Amelia Sedley, for instance – an Honoria whose career is traced in gloomier detail than that of Patmore's angel – lurks *Vanity Fair*'s stubbornly autonomous Becky Sharp, an independent "charmer" whom the novelist at one point actually describes as a monstrous and snaky sorceress:

> In describing this siren, singing and smiling, coaxing and cajoling, the author, with modest pride, asks his readers all around has he once forgotten the laws of politeness, and showed the monster's hideous tail above water? No! Those who like may peep down under waves that are pretty transparent, and see it writhing and twirling, diabolically hideous and slimy, flapping amongst bones, or curling around corpses; but above the water line, I ask, has not everything been proper, agreeable, and decorous.[22]

As this extraordinary passage suggests, the monster may not only be concealed *behind* the angel, she may actually turn out to reside *within* (or in the lower half of) the angel. Thus, Thackeray implies, every angel in the house – "proper, agreeable, and decorous," "coaxing and cajoling" hapless men – is really, perhaps, a monster, "diabolically hideous and slimy."

"A woman in the shape of a monster," Adrienne Rich observes in "Planetarium," "a monster in the shape of a woman / the skies are full of them."[23] Because the skies *are* full of them, even if we focus only on those female monsters who are directly related to Thackeray's serpentine siren, we will find that such monsters have long inhabited male texts. Emblems of filthy materiality, committed only to their own private ends, these women are accidents of nature, deformities meant to repel, but in their very freakishness they possess unhealthy energies, powerful and dangerous arts. Moreover, to the extent that they incarnate male dread of women and, specifically, male scorn of female creativity, such characters have drastically affected the self-images of women writers, negatively reinforcing those messages of submissiveness conveyed by their angelic sisters.

The first book of Spenser's *The Faerie Queene* introduces a female monster who serves as a prototype of the entire line. *Errour* is half woman, half serpent, "Most lothsom, filthie, foule, and full of vile disdaine" (I.1.126). She breeds in a dark den where her young suck on her poisonous dugs or creep back into her mouth at the sight of hated light, and in battle against the noble Red-crosse Knight, she spews out a flood of books and papers, frogs and toads. Symbolizing the dangerous effect of misdirected and undigested learning, her filthiness adumbrates that of two other powerful females in book I, Duessa and Lucifera. But because these other women can create false appearances to hide their vile natures, they are even more dangerous.

Like Errour, Duessa is deformed below the waist, as if to foreshadow *Lear*'s "But to the girdle do the Gods inherit, / Beneath is all the fiend's." When, like all witches, she must do penance at the time of the new moon by bathing with herbs traditionally used by such other witches as Scylla, Circe, and Medea, her "neather parts" are revealed as "misshapen, monstruous."[24] But significantly, Duessa deceives and ensnares men by assuming the shape of Una, the beautiful and angelic heroine who represents Christianity, charity, docility. Similarly, Lucifera lives in what seems to be a lovely mansion, a cunningly constructed House of Pride whose weak foundation and ruinous rear quarters are carefully concealed. Both women use their arts of deception to entrap and destroy men, and the secret, shameful ugliness of both is closely associated with their hidden genitals – that is, with their femaleness.

Descending from Patristic misogynists like Tertullian and St Augustine through Renaissance and Restoration literature – through Sidney's Cecropia, Shakespeare's Lady Macbeth and his Goneril and Regan, Milton's Sin (and even, as we shall see, his Eve) – the female monster populates the works of the satirists of the eighteenth century, a company of male artists whose virulent visions must have been particularly alarming to feminine readers in an age when women had just begun to "attempt the pen." These authors attacked literary women on two fronts. First, and most obviously, through the construction of cartoon figures like Sheridan's Mrs Malaprop and Fielding's Mrs Slipslop, and Smollett's Tabitha Bramble, they implied that language itself was almost literally alien to the female tongue. In the mouths of women, vocabulary loses meaning, sentences dissolve, literary messages are distorted or destroyed. At the same time, more subtly but perhaps for that reason even more significantly, such authors devised elaborate anti-romances to show that the female "angel" was really a female "fiend," the ladylike paragon really an unladylike monster. Thus while the "Bluestocking" Anne Finch would find herself directly caricatured (as she was by Pope and Gay) as a character afflicted with the "poetical Itch" like Phoebe Clinket in *Three Hours After Marriage*,[25] she might well feel herself to be indirectly but even more profoundly attacked by Johnson's famous observation that a woman preacher was like a dog standing on its hind legs, or by the suggestion – embedded in works by Swift, Pope, Gay, and others – that *all* women were inexorably and inescapably monstrous, in the flesh as well as in the spirit. Finally, in a comment like Horace Walpole's remark that Mary Wollstonecraft was "a hyena in petticoats," the two kinds of misogynistic attacks definitively merged.[26]

It is significant, then, that Jonathan Swift's disgust with the monstrous females who populate so many of his verses seems to have been caused specifically by the inexorable failure of female art. Like disgusted Gulliver, who returns to England only to prefer the stable to the parlor, his horses to his wife, Swift projects his horror of time, his dread of physicality, on to another stinking creature – the degenerate woman. Probably the most famous instance of this projection occurs in his so-called dirty poems. In these works, we peer behind the facade of the angel-woman to discover that, say, the idealized "Caelia, Caelia, Caelia, shits!" We discover that the seemingly unblemished Chloe must "either void or burst," and that the female "inner space" of the "Queen of Love" is like a foul chamber pot.[27] Though some critics have suggested that the misogyny implied by Swift's characterizations of these women is merely ironic, what emerges from his most furious poems in this vein is a horror of female flesh and a revulsion at the inability – the powerlessness – of female arts to redeem or to transform the flesh. Thus for Swift female sexuality is consistently equated with degeneration, disease, and death, while female arts are trivial attempts to forestall an inevitable end.

Significantly, as if defining the tradition of duplicity in which even Patmore's uxorious speaker placed his heroine, Swift devotes many poems to an examination of the role deception plays in the creation of a saving but inadequate fiction of femininity. In "A Beautiful Young Nymph," a battered prostitute removes her wig, her crystal eye, her teeth, and her padding at bedtime, so that the next morning she must employ all her "Arts" to reconstruct her "scatter'd Parts."[28] Such as they are, however, her arts only contribute to her own suffering or that of others, and the same thing is true of Diana in "The Progress of Beauty," who awakes as a mingled mass of dirt and sweat, with cracked lips, foul teeth, and gummy eyes, to spend four hours artfully reconstructing herself. Because she is inexorably rotting away, however, Swift declares that eventually all forms will fail, for "Art no longer can prevayl / When the Materialls all are gone."[29] The strategies of Chloe, Caelia, Corinna, and Diana – artists manqué – all have no success, Swift shows, except in temporarily staving off dissolution, for like Pope's "Sex of Queens," Swift's females are composed of what Pope called "Matter too soft," and their arts are thus always inadequate.[30] ...

For the most part, eighteenth-century satirists limited their depiction of the female monster to low mimetic equivalents like Phoebe Clinket or Swift's corroding coquettes. But there were several important avatars of the monster-woman who retained the allegorical anatomy of their more fantastic precursors. In *The Battle of the Books*, for instance, Swift's "Goddess Criticism" clearly symbolizes the demise of wit and learning. Devouring numberless volumes in a den as dark as Errour's, she is surrounded by relatives like Ignorance, Pride, Opinion, Noise, Impudence, and Pedantry, and she herself is as allegorically deformed as any of Spenser's females.

> The Goddess herself had claws like a Cat; her Head, and Ears, and Voice, resembled those of an Ass; Her Teeth fallen out before; Her Eyes turned inward, as if she lookt only upon Herself; Her diet was the overflowing of her own Gall: Her Spleen was so large, as to stand prominent like a Dug of the first Rate, nor wanted Excrescencies in forms of Teats, at which a Crew of ugly Monsters were greedily sucking; and what is wonderful to conceive, the bulk of Spleen increased faster than the Sucking could diminish it.[31]

Like Spenser's Errour and Milton's Sin, Criticism is linked by her processes of eternal breeding, eating, spewing, feeding, and redevouring to biological cycles all three poets view as destructive to transcendent, intellectual life. More, since all the creations of each monstrous mother are her excretions, and since all her excretions are both her food and her weaponry, each mother forms with her brood a self-enclosed system, cannibalistic and solipsistic: the creativity of the world made flesh is annihilating. At the same time, Swift's spleen-producing and splenetic Goddess cannot be far removed from the Goddess of Spleen in Pope's *The Rape of the Lock*, and – because she is a mother Goddess – she also has much in common with the Goddess of Dullness who appears in Pope's *Dunciad*. The parent of "Vapours and Female Wit," the "Hysteric or Poetic fit," the Queen of Spleen rules over all women between the ages of fifteen and fifty, and thus, as a sort of patroness of the female sexual cycle, she is associated with the same anti-creation that characterizes Errour, Sin, and Criticism.[32] Similarly, the Goddess of Dullness, a nursing mother worshipped by a society of dunces, symbolizes the failure of culture, the failure of art, and the death of the satirist. The huge daughter of Chaos and Night, she rocks the laureate in her ample lap while handing out rewards and intoxicating drinks to her dull sons. A Queen of Ooze, whose inertia comments on idealized Queens of Love, she nods and all of Nature falls asleep, its light destroyed by the stupor that spreads throughout the land in the milk of her "kindness."[33]

In all these incarnations – from Errour to Dullness, from Goneril and Regan to Chloe and Caelia – the female monster is a striking illustration of Simone de Beauvoir's thesis that woman has been made to represent all of man's ambivalent feelings about his own inability to control his own physical existence, his own birth and death. As the Other, woman comes to represent the contingency of life, life that is made to be destroyed. "It is the horror of his own carnal contingence," de Beauvoir notes, "which [man] projects upon [woman]."[34] In addition, as Karen Horney and Dorothy Dinnerstein have shown, male dread of women, and specifically the infantile dread of maternal autonomy, has historically objectified itself in vilification of women, while male ambivalence about female "charms" underlies the traditional images of such terrible sorceress-goddesses as the Sphinx, Medusa, Circe, Kali, Delilah, and Salome, all of whom possess duplicitous arts that allow them both to seduce and to steal male generative energy.[35]

The sexual nausea associated with all these monster-women helps explain why so many real women have for so long expressed loathing of (or at least anxiety about) their own, inexorably female bodies. The "killing" of oneself into an art object – the pruning and preening, the mirror madness, and concern with odors and aging, with hair which is invariably too curly or too lank, with bodies too thin or too thick – all this testifies to the efforts women have expended not just trying to be angels but trying *not* to become female monsters. More significantly for our purposes, however, the female freak is and has been a powerfully coercive and monitory image for women secretly desiring to attempt the pen, an image that helped enforce the injunctions to silence implicit also in the concept of the *Ewig-Weibliche*. If becoming an *author* meant mistaking one's "sex and way," if it meant becoming an "unsexed" or perversely sexed female, then it meant becoming a monster or freak, a vile Errour, a grotesque Lady Macbeth, a disgusting goddess of Dullness, or (to name a few later witches) a murderous Lamia, a sinister Geraldine. Perhaps, then, the "presumptuous" effort should not be made at all. Certainly the story of Lilith, one more monster-woman – indeed, according to Hebrew mythology, both the first woman *and* the first monster – specifically connects poetic presumption with madness, freakishness, monstrosity.

Created not from Adam's rib but, like him, from the dust, Lilith was Adam's first wife, according to apocryphal Jewish lore. Because she considered herself his equal, she objected to lying beneath him, so that when he tried to force her submission, she became enraged and, speaking the Ineffable Name, flew away to the edge of the Red Sea to reside with demons. Threatened by God's angelic emissaries, told that she must return or daily lose a hundred of her demon children to death, Lilith preferred punishment to patriarchal marriage, and she took her revenge against both God and Adam by injuring babies – especially male babies, who were traditionally thought to be more vulnerable to her attacks. What her history suggests is that in patriarchal culture, female speech and female "presumption" – that is, angry revolt against male domination – are inextricably linked and inevitably daemonic. Excluded from the human community, even from the semidivine communal chronicles of the Bible, the figure of Lilith represents the price women have been told they must pay for attempting to define themselves. And it is a terrible price: cursed both because she is a character who "got away" and because she dared to usurp the essentially literary authority implied by the act of naming, Lilith is locked into a vengeance (child-killing) which can only bring her more suffering (the killing of her own children). And even the nature of her one-woman revolution emphasizes her helplessness and her isolation, for her protest takes the form of a refusal and a departure, a flight of escape rather than an active rebellion like, say, Satan's. As a paradigm of both the "witch" and the "fiend" of Aurora Leigh's "Ghost, fiend, and angel, fairy, witch and sprite," Lilith reveals, then, just how difficult it is for women even to attempt the pen. And from George MacDonald, the Victorian fantasist who portrayed her in his astonishing *Lilith* as a paradigm of the self-tormenting assertive woman, to Laura Riding, who depicted her in "Eve's Side of It" as an archetypal woman Creator, the problem Lilith represents has been associated with the problems of female authorship and female authority.[36] Even if they had not studied her legend, literary women like Anne Finch, bemoaning the double bind in which the mutually dependent images of angel and monster had left them, must have gotten the message Lilith incarnates: a life of feminine submission, of "contemplative purity," is a life of silence, a life that has no pen and no story, while a life of female rebellion, of "significant action," is a life that must be silenced, a life whose monstrous pen tells a terrible story. Either way, the images on the surface of the looking glass, into which the female artist peers in search of her *self*, warn her that she is or must be a "Cypher," framed and framed up, indited and indicted.

. . . Yet, despite the obstacles presented by those twin images of angel and monster, despite the fears of sterility and the anxieties of authorship from which women have suffered, generations of texts *have* been possible for female writers. By the end of the eighteenth century – and here is the most important phenomenon we will see throughout this volume – women were not only writing, they were conceiving fictional worlds in which patriarchal images and conventions were severely, radically revised. And as self-conceiving women from Anne Finch and Anne Elliot to Emily Brontë and Emily Dickinson rose from the glass coffin of the male-authored text, as they exploded out of the Queen's looking glass, the old silent dance of death became a dance of triumph, a dance into speech, a dance of authority.

Notes

1 Virginia Woolf, "Professions for Women," *The Death of the Moth and Other Essays* (New York: Harcourt, Brace, 1942), pp. 236–8.

2 Sherry Ortner, "Is Female to Male as Nature Is to Culture?" in Michelle Zimbalist Rosaldo and Louise Lamphere (eds.), *Woman, Culture, and Society* (Stanford, Calif.: Stanford University Press, 1974), p. 8ff.

3 Hans Eichner, "The Eternal Feminine: An Aspect of Goethe's Ethics," in Johann Wolfgang von Goethe, *Faust*, Norton Critical Edition, trans. Walter Arnold, ed. Cyrus Hamlin (New York: Norton, 1976), pp. 616, 617. Significantly, even when talk (rather than silence) is considered specifically feminine, it is only talk and not action, as the motto *Fatti maschi, parole femine* implies: Deeds are masculine, words are feminine.

4 Ibid., p. 620. Obviously Makarie's virtues foreshadow (besides those of Patmore's Honoria), those of Virginia Woolf's Mrs Ramsay, in *To the Lighthouse*, for Mrs Ramsay is also a kind of "lighthouse" of sympathy and beauty.

5 Coventry Patmore, *The Angel in the House* (London: George Bell and Son, 1885), p. 17.

6 Ibid., p. 73.

7 Thomas Carlyle, "The Everlasting Yea," *Sartor Resartus*, Book 2, ch. 9.

8 Abbé d'Ancourt, *The Lady's Preceptor*, 3rd edn (London: J. Walts, 1745), p. 8.

9 Mrs Sarah Ellis, *The Women of England* (New York, 1844), pp. 9–10.

10 Mrs Ellis, *The Family Monitor and Domestic Guide* (New York: Henry G. Langley, 1844), p. 35.

11 John Ruskin, "Of Queens' Gardens," *Sesame and Lilies* (New York: Charles E. Merrill, 1899), p. 23.

12 Alexander Welsh, *The City of Dickens* (London: Oxford University Press, 1971), p. 184.

13 Ibid., pp. 187, 190.

14 Ann Douglas, "The Domestication of Death," in *The Feminization of American Culture* (New York: Knopf, 1977), pp. 200–6.

15 "The Philosophy of Composition," *The Complete Poems and Stories of Edgar Allan Poe, with Selections from his Critical Writings*, ed. A. H. Quinn (New York: Knopf, 1951), vol. 2, p. 982.

16 Douglas, *Feminization of American Culture*, p. 202.

17 Welsh, *City of Dickens*, pp. 182–3.

18 Patmore, *Angel in the House*, pp. 175–6.

19 Oswald Doughty, A *Victorian Romantic: Dante Gabriel Rossetti* (London: Frederick Muller, 1949), p. 417.

20 Quoted in ibid., p. 418. For a thorough examination, from another perspective, of the ambiguous beauty/terror of the dead woman, see Mario Praz, *The Romantic Agony* (London: Oxford, 1970), esp. "The Beauty of the Medusa," pp. 23–45.

21 Patmore, *Angel in the House*, p. 91.

22 William Makepeace Thackeray, *Vanity Fair*, ed. Geoffrey and Kathleen Tillotson (Boston: Houghton Mifflin, 1963), p. 617.

23 Adrienne Rich, *Poems, Selected and New, 1950–1974* (New York: Norton, 1975), p. 146.

24 *King Lear*, 4.4.142–3; *The Faerie Queene*, I.2.361.

25 John Gay, Alexander Pope, and John Arbuthnot, *Three Hours After Marriage*, ed. Richard Morton and William M. Peterson, Lake Erie College Studies, vol. I (Painesville, Ohio: Lake Erie College Press, 1961), p. 22.

26 Walpole to Hannah More, January 24, 1795.

27 *The Poems of Jonathan Swift*, ed. Harold Williams, 3 vols (Oxford: Clarendon Press, 1937), vol. 2, p. 383, ll. 67–8.

28 Swift, "A Beautiful Young Nymph," vol. 2, p. 583, ll. 67–8.

29 Swift, "The Progress of Beauty," vol. 1, pp. 228, ll. 77–8.

30 "Epistle II. To a Lady," *The Poems of Alexander Pope*, ed. John Butt (New Haven: Yale University Press, 1963), p. 560, 1.219, 1.3.

31 Jonathan Swift, *A Tale of a Tub, to Which is Added the Battle of the Books and the Mechanical Operations of the Spirit*, ed. A. C. Guthkelch and D. Nichol Smith (Oxford: Clarendon Press, 1920), p. 240.

32 Pope, *The Rape of the Lock*, canto 4, ll. 58–60, in *The Poems of Alexander Pope*, p. 234.

33 Pope, *The Dunciad in Four Books* (1743), canto 1, ll. 311–18, in *The Poems of Alexander Pope*, p. 734.

34 Simone de Beauvoir, *The Second Sex*, p. 138.

35 Karen Horney, "The Dread of Woman," in *Feminine Psychology* (New York: Norton, 1973), pp. 133–46; Dorothy Dinnerstein, *The Mermaid and the Minotaur*, pp. 124–54. For discussions of the "Medusa Complex" and its misogynistic messages see also Philip Slater, *The Glory of Hera* (Boston: Beacon, 1968) and R. D. Laing, *The Divided Self* (London: Penguin Books, 1965).

36 For discussions of Lilith see *A Dictionary of the Bible*, ed. James Hustings (Edinburgh, 1950); also Louis Ginzberg, *The Legends of the Jews* (Philadelphia: The Jewish Publication Society of America, 1961), pp. 65–6; and R. H. Gaster, *Orientalia* 11 (1942): 41–79. Also see George MacDonald, *Lilith*, and Laura Riding, "Eve's Side of It."

CHAPTER 6

The Hand That Rocks the Cradle

Coppélia Kahn

In this 1985 essay, Coppélia Kahn provides a summary of the gender theories that were having a powerful influence on especially American feminism in the decade of the 1980s, a time that witnessed a resurgence of interest in the pre-Oedipal period of childhood that is traditionally a period when children's lives are more likely to be shaped by the influence of mothers. Many feminists of that period explored the implications of a mother-centered psychoanalysis for the study of female writers.

The question is breathtakingly basic, yet so novel that it might seem to be no question at all: Why do women mother children as well as give birth to them? Why is it women who assume responsibility for children after they are born and weaned, who spend hours and years as their constant companions, nurturing them emotionally and physically, and making them fit for adult society? What authorizes this universal division of labor which makes women, no matter how much time they spend away from home, what other work they do, or how much "help" their husbands give them, the persons on whom we all depend not only for survival at first, but ultimately for the bedrock of existence, a sense of self? And what effect does this arrangement have on gender, the way in which we define and live our maleness and femaleness? Finally, how can understanding the phenomenon of mothering extend psychoanalytic theory, and how does it lead to the reinterpretation of texts, both psychoanalytic and literary?

These questions are suggested by the works of four well-known feminist writers: Jean Baker Miller, Adrienne Rich, Dorothy Dinnerstein, and Nancy Chodorow.[1] As a group, they argue that the institution of motherhood is the root cause of the oppression of women and the sexual malaise experienced by men and women. I mean "cause" in an atemporal sense, for of course we don't know whether mothering by women ever "began" at a certain point in history. Rather, motherhood (these authors suggest) is the "cause" of the oppression of women in the sense that it is necessary for that oppression, and the oppression of women is inevitable given the institution of motherhood. In this essay I intend to examine the ideas put forth by these four authors, and in order to suggest how they may sustain and expand the enterprise of feminist criticism, to interpret some texts by Freud in the light of those ideas.

Let me first state briefly what these authors have in common, without trying to do justice to the range and complexity of their respective arguments. To begin with, they all regard gender less as a biological fact than as a social product, an institution learned through and perpetuated by culture. And they see this gender system not as a mutually beneficial and equitable division of roles, but as a perniciously symbiotic polarity that denies full humanity to both sexes while meshing – and helping to create – their neuroses. Second, they describe the father-absent, mother-involved nuclear family as creating the gender identities that perpetuate patriarchy and the denigration of women. In Chodorow's account, women as mothers produce daughters with mothering capacities and the desire to mother which itself grows out of the mother–daughter relationship. They also produce sons whose nurturant capacities and needs have been systematically curtailed in order to prepare them for their future as fathers. Third (and most important), because a woman is the first significant other through whom both girls and boys realize subjectivity, women in general become charged with the ambivalence of fear and desire which is the inevitable by-product of that process. The child's love for the mother doesn't come under the sway of the reality principle, in that the child doesn't at first recognize that the mother exists or has interests apart from it. Selfhood at first consists largely of the hard-won recognition that such separateness does exist. Thus the mother, and all women perceived in her shadow, are tainted with the grandiose expectations and bitter disappointments of a necessarily alienated subjectivity. In contrast, the child tends to perceive its father from the beginning as a separate being, and thus love and hate for the father, including that of the Oedipus complex, *does* fit under the reality principle. The father stands outside the charmed preoedipal dyad while, "for children of both genders, mothers represent regression and the lack of autonomy."[2]

A focus on the primacy of the mother's role in ego formation is not in itself new. It follows upon the attempts of such theorists as Melanie Klein, Michael and Alice Balint, and John Bowlby to cast light on that dim psychic region that Freud likened to the Minoan civilization preceding the Greek, "grey with age, and shadowy and almost impossible to revivify."[3] But, as Susan Suleiman has noted, "it is as if, for psychoanalysis, the only self worth worrying about in the mother–child relationship were that of the child."[4] What distinguishes these recent accounts of the mother–child relationship from previous ones is their insistence on historical contingency rather than biological destiny. According to these authors, psychoanalytic theory makes several questionable assumptions about the role of gender and family in the formation of the ego. First, the assumption that the sexual division of labor, gender personality, and heterosexuality rest on a biological and instinctual basis. Second, that proper ego development requires a nuclear family with authority vested in the father and "an inevitable and necessary single mother–infant relationship."[5] Third, that (as Adrienne Rich says), "the two-person mother–child relationship is by nature regressive, circular, unproductive, and that all culture depends on the father–son relationship.... Through the resolution of the Oedipal complex, the boy makes his way into the male world ... of patriarchal law and order."[6]

In contrast, these four authors believe that the breast is an institution sustained by patriarchal powers, and that in turn it reinforces that power. They present, in effect, a collective vision of how maternal power in the nursery defines gender so as to foster patriarchal power in the public world. Chodorow's book offers an incisive critique and revision of psychoanalytic theories of gender development. You will recall that Freud locates the beginning of our perception of gender in anatomical difference; centers it, with sublime phallocentrism, on the possession or lack of a penis; and portrays the establishment of gender as the product of the Oedipus complex. Chodorow, taking an object relations approach that stresses social rather than instinctual factors, argues that children realize their gender well before the Oedipus complex, by about the age of three, mainly through the identification and social ascription that occurs first and crucially in their relationships with their mothers. A mother is of the same gender as her daughter, and of a different gender from her son; thus she treats them differently. Mothers of daughters, Chodorow says, tend to experience them as physical and mental extensions of themselves, creating a deeper identification and more prolonged symbiosis with them than with their sons. Clinical evidence, she asserts, shows that girls simply do not, as Freud claimed, abandon their mothers as love objects at the inception of the Oedipus complex, nor do they perceive themselves as castrated.

Rather, they remain deeply identified with their mothers through adolescence, gaining their sense of femaleness first from this identification and not, as Freud would have it, from turning to their fathers as heterosexual objects and wishing to have babies from them. Thus Chodorow distinguishes two coexistent levels of gender identity: one oriented homosexually toward the mother, one heterosexually toward the father. She also recasts penis envy, that bugaboo which has justifiably angered many feminists and regrettably alienated them from psychoanalysis. Like the boy, the girl begins life psychically merged with her mother, and when she begins to separate from her, she longs for that primal oneness but also fears it as annihilation of self. Because she is of the same sex as her mother and thus is more profoundly attached to her than the boy is, she desires a penis as a crucial sign of difference, to serve as a defense against the undertow of merger with the mother and, as a symbol of power, to establish herself against the woman she has known as all-powerful. She wants a penis, then, insofar as she wants to detach herself from her mother and become an autonomous person, not because she feels castrated without one.

Without seeking to do so, it seems, Chodorow reorients psychoanalytic theory with the feminist consciousness that has rejected the notion of woman as castrated man. She has discovered, in the mother–daughter relationship and in other relations among women, rich, various, and vital sources of feminine selfhood. She also provides "a context for understanding Freud's account of superego formation in women, without imposing the value judgments he insists on," by showing how it happens that women in general have a capacity for empathy built into themselves in a way that men do not.[7] Because of the lengthy identification with her mother, a girl's ego boundaries are less firmly, less defensively established than a boy's, and she experiences herself as less differentiated from, more continous with and related to the external object world than a boy. She tends, as Carol Gilligan has argued, to conceive ethical issues in particularized, relational ways rather than abstractly.[8] Chodorow's account of female development, then, gives Freud's famous description of the female superego a different context and tone. Indeed, it *is* "never so inexorable, so impersonal, so independent of its emotional origins as we require it to be in men."[9]

Chodorow's work is no less valuable for its account of masculine development than for its account of feminine development. If "the basic feminine sense of self is connected to the world, the basic masculine sense of self is separate," she holds.[10] This separateness arises because a boy must establish his gender identity in opposition to his mother's gender. To do so he must separate more firmly from his mother than does a girl, who can model her femaleness on her mother. Furthermore, mothers tend to treat their sons as objects separate from them, and to push them out of identification with themselves sooner and harder into an Oedipally toned relationship defined by gender difference. Very early, phallic-masculine self-definition becomes entwined with issues of object relations and separateness of self which have little connotation of gender for girls.[11] On the other hand, the boy's Oedipus complex is more decisively resolved than the girl's. Because his heterosexual Oedipal love for the mother is an extension of his infantile love, it is more intense and thus more strenuously repressed. His rivalry with the father for the mother also intensifies his love for her and strengthens its repression. Thus the masculine personality tends to be formed through denial of connection with femininity and all relationships stemming from the crucial first one with the mother. Certain activities must be defined as masculine and superior to the maternal world of childhood, and women's activities must, correspondingly, be denigrated. In this sense, it is the boy and not the girl, as in the Freudian account, who must make a difficult switch – not a switch in love object from mother to father, from homosexual to heterosexual, but a switch in major identification, from identifying with the mother to identifying with the father.

Rich, Miller, and Dinnerstein in effect continue into adulthood Chodorow's account of the en-gendering of women. They elucidate the new symbiosis between male and female adult personalities which replaces the earlier one of mother and child. Rich and Dinnerstein are particularly eloquent and convincing on the ways in which woman's body becomes "the carnal scapegoat" for our fears of the flesh and mortality, or the idol in which we try to recreate our lost union with mother-as-flesh. Since, whether we are men or women, our earliest carnal interaction takes place with a woman, the female body becomes the locale par excellence of fleshly bliss. Men tend either to exalt its charms or to revile its functions. Women are encouraged to behave narcissistically as sex objects or masochistically as mothers, either position being a defense against the female body's resonance with primitive fears and needs.

Rich shows how male fears of woman's childbearing powers, and by extension her "transformative power" over nature (in cooking, pottery, and weaving, for example), have imprisoned women in motherhood. Patriarchal mythology, she holds, has used the ideal of maternal altruism to deny the male fear and loathing of women's bodies. As mother and only as mother, woman is exonerated of Eve's crime. The mother's assumed capacity for unconditional love, uncontaminated by self-interest or anger, makes her sacred; her pain in childbirth, her self-sacrifice in childraising purify her sexuality. "Women who refuse to become mothers are dangerous," and men tend to perceive women either as mothers, purged of sexual taint, or antimothers, whores and witches. "Maternal altruism is the one quality universally approved and supported in women," Rich claims.[12]

What Rich describes as maternal altruism Miller elucidates as the principle on which the female ego, patterned by mothering, is built: selfhood achieved through serving others' needs and interests, as if women had none of their own. Women feel useful and worthy and function well, Miller explains, when they can regard their ambitious strivings as if they served others. Once a man has defined his masculinity by other than altruistic standards, he may choose to see himself as serving others, but women are not encouraged to satisfy their drives in a direct relation to reality as men are. Their egos, embedded in relationships, as Chodorow maintains, tend to mediate not their own drives but their drives in the service of another.

Miller poignantly describes the catch-22 quality of gender definition as both sexes experience it, a self-defeating complementarity of traits and frustrations. People of both sexes develop their selfhood by affiliation, by bonds with others, but women's sense of self tends to be founded on affiliation, while men direct themselves toward significant enterprise and starve inwardly for deeper affiliation. As infants, men enjoy affiliation with and through their mothers; but when they become men, they are encouraged to build their lives on self-aggrandizement, competition, and aggression. Rewarded for doing so, they must then struggle to redevelop the capacities for affiliation and nurturance they have previously denied. On the other hand, Miller says, women end up "doing good and feeling bad" when, after they altruistically pour their energies into the service of others, that service goes unrecognized and their own needs are frustrated.[13] For finally, despite the idealization of motherhood, it is men's work that really counts.

The work of Chodorow, Dinnerstein, Miller, and Rich provides a basis for reading Freud's theory of gender as itself a patriarchal text. As such, it is all the more useful to feminist critics, I think, in their efforts to decipher the psychodynamics of other patriarchal texts. In 1926 Karen Horney noted, in "The Flight from Womanhood," that men in analysis revealed a surprisingly intense envy of pregnancy, childbirth, motherhood, and suckling, and suggested that the attribution of penis envy to women might be a way of denying what looked like womb envy.[14] She also argued that Freud's conception of feminine development matches the ideas he attributes to the four-year-old Oedipal boy – that a girl once had a penis, was castrated, came to regard herself as inferior because of her loss, and was subject to lifelong envy of boys who had them.

The recent theory and research on which these four writers base their critiques of mothering as an exclusively feminine vocation enable us to find the subtext of Freud's account of femininity. These critiques suggest that it is only the penis that keeps a man from feeling like a woman, or being part of a woman as he once was. Men must insist on the superiority of the penis and their exclusive possession of it, or women will claim it, as they once claimed so much, for theirs. The impetus behind phallocentrism, then, is what Rich calls "matrophobia" – not the fear of one's mother or of motherhood, but of becoming like one's mother as in the original identification of the child with its mother, and thus losing one's gender identity as a male.[15]

In Freud, such matrophobia takes the form of a nearly lifelong reluctance to confront the child's, especially the male child's, early and close relationship to his mother. In the letters to Fliess in the 1890s, written as Freud stood on the brink of discovering his own Oedipus complex, he recounts a series of dreams that shadow forth his feelings about his experience of being mothered. Freud had, in effect, two mothers – his natural mother and the old Czech peasant woman who served as his nursemaid till he was two and a half. As Jim Swan shows, this circumstance encouraged Freud in maintaining a split between the internalized good and bad mothers that (psychoanalytic theory maintains) we all introject.[16] It helped him to preserve into his old age an idealized love for his natural mother, who died when he was seventy-four.[17]

According to Swan, in these early dreams the nursemaid appears ambivalently as both the young Freud's seductress and his punisher.[18] She is his "*Urheberin*" – in Swan's translation, the first to raise him up; that is, to give him an erection in the course of bathing or dressing him, to show him his maleness. But she is also the one who "scorns" or "shames" him for being clumsy and unable to do things for himself. When Freud recalls that this "Nannie" bathed him in reddish water in which she had previously washed herself, clearly an image of fusion with the mother, he strongly suggests – though without realizing it – that he identified himself with her. But his memory or fantasy that he stole coins and gave them to her is even more revealing. A few letters after recounting it, he tells Fliess that he was mistaken; he has learned that in fact it was the old woman who stole from him, and that she was arrested, convicted, and imprisoned for doing so. The mistake shows that he identified himself with her, and this time he seems to admit it: "I equals she," he writes to Fliess. But he thereby indicates transformation by the dreamwork, not the infant's deeper sense of "I *am* she" which survives in his unconscious. Swan argues that Freud fancied himself stealing and giving to his nurse because of this deeper kind of identification in which he does to her in reverse what he feels she has done to him: robbed him of that precious coin, his masculinity – the very masculinity she first gave him by arousing him, and then took away by shaming him.

Freud's early case histories reveal, Iza Erlich maintains, an "ironic discrepancy between his insistence on the importance of the mother in the oedipal love-hate triangle and the relatively pallid picture of the mother which he draws."[19] Looking at the stories of Dora (1905), Little Hans (1909), and the Rat Man (1909), she finds that Freud portrays the fathers in these family dramas as complex, interesting people and the mothers as drab, monochromatic creatures destined to play limited roles. I would add that in "Dora" he consistently swerves past clues that might lead toward Dora's relationship with her mother and pursues those that lead toward her father and Herr K.[20] His brilliant probing impels him to posit, behind her anger at her father, her disgust for Herr K., and her disillusionment with Frau K., that she is in some sense in love with each of them. But he never questions the feelings she expresses for her mother:

> I never made her mother's acquaintance. From the accounts given me by the girl and her father I was led to imagine her as an uncultivated woman and above all as a foolish one, who had concentrated all her interests upon domestic affairs, especially since her husband's illness and the estrangement to which it led. She presented the picture, in fact, of what might be called the "housewife's psychosis." She had no understanding for her children's more active interests, and was occupied all day long in cleaning the house with its furniture and utensils and keeping them clean – to such an extent as to make it almost impossible to use or enjoy them.... The relations between the girl and her mother had been unfriendly for years. The daughter looked down on her mother and used to criticize her mercilessly, and she had withdrawn completely from her influence.[21]

Freud finds no connection between this woman's obsessive cleanliness and the probability (which he mentions in a footnote) that her husband had infected her with venereal disease, which resulted in a vaginal discharge for which she sought treatment at a spa. Though he regards Dora's persistent cough as an upward displacement of her mother's illness, he links it to an identification with her father rather than with her mother. While he cleverly parallels Dora, the K.'s governess, and Frau K. because they have all served as mother substitutes for girl "children" and then betrayed them when their interest in a man required them to do so, he pursues the heterosexual connection to the exclusion of the homosexual, mother-identified dimension of these relationships. Finally, when Dora's second dream produces an association to the Sistine Madonna, before which she had once remained "rapt in silent admiration" for two hours, he links it to her identification with a certain young man rather than with her mother, the original madonna in everyone's life, boy or girl.[22] As Erlich comments, "It is as if Freud could not bring himself to look closely at the mother, the figure his theory proclaims to be so central."[23]

A comparison between Freud's two most extensive pieces of art criticism, "Leonardo da Vinci and a Memory of His Childhood" (1919) and "The Moses of Michelangelo" (1914), highlights his male-centered view of the mothering role and his preference for identifying with father figures. In these essays, written not long after the case histories discussed above, he addresses himself to two masterpieces powerfully resonant with traditional images of mothers and fathers. The Leonardo essay focuses on the riddle of the artist's career: the mysterious inhibition that caused him to forsake art for scientific investigation. In the course of answering the riddle, Freud elaborates on several topics that will become major psychoanalytic concerns: repression and sublimation in artistic creativity, the genesis of homosexuality, infantile theories of sexuality, and narcissism. The objects at the essay's center – Leonardo's brief description of a childhood memory and his paintings of the *Mona Lisa* and *St. Anne with the Madonna and Child* – are surrounded with a dense cloud of fascinating theory and speculation about that dim Minoan region of early mother–child relations. The *Moses* essay, in contrast, focuses on a single hard, clear object – the famous statue. Though Freud begins with a frank declaration of his own strong reactions to it, his approach is objective and empirical, involving detailed description of specific features and comparison of authorities. He spends only a paragraph on Michelangelo's life and the motives behind his portrayal of Moses, and confines himself to one specific question about the interpretation of the statue.

Broadly speaking, when Freud writes about Leonardo his language is often tender and impassioned. Though he doesn't allude to his own involvement in the subject, clearly it moves him. But when he writes about Michelangelo's *Moses*, even though he declares, "No piece of statuary has ever made a stronger impression on me than this," his dispassionate, objective stance serves to suppress that reaction. In the Leonardo essay he is moved by the maternal images he describes so vividly, but doesn't declare his feelings as his own; in the *Moses* essay he admits his feelings for the patriarchal image but then in effect denies them. The disparity is fully consonant with the ideas of mothers and fathers the two essays elaborate.

A conception of the mother as one who gives, then takes away; seduces, then shames, like the nurse of Freud's early memories, lies at the heart of the Leonardo essay. Making use of Leonardo's notebooks and of biographical data, Freud constructs a sentimental account of the artist's early development centered on his relationship to his mother, "Caterina, the poor peasant girl" who brought into the world an illegitimate son destined to become Leonardo, the great artist. Freud pictures Caterina as an unwed mother who compensates herself for the loss of a lover and her son for the absence of a father by taking her little boy in the place of a husband. Fondling and kissing him passionately, she robbed him, "by the too early maturing of his erotism," says Freud, "of a part of his masculinity" and set him on his course toward homosexuality.[24] But in the same paragraph he posits a notion of mothering which ultimately seems to encourage just this kind of robbery: "A mother's love for the infant she suckles and cares for is ... in the nature of a completely satisfying love-relation, which not only fulfills every mental wish but also every physical need."[25] Here Freud presents mothering from the woman's point of view as he imagines it. The child is everything to its mother, as no adult love partner could be. The mother gets total satisfaction from her child, and the child gets the same from its mother. Such merging of needs and desires Freud portrays as unambivalently benign for *both* mother and child.

When he examines mothering from the child's point of view, however, that child sees like a man, and it is a different story altogether. Turning to the *Mona Lisa*'s smile, Freud argues that Leonardo found the model for it in Caterina's countenance, which held "the promise of unbounded tenderness and at the same time sinister menace," presumably the menace of robbing him of his masculinity. Both he and the critics he quotes at some length indulge their strikingly ambivalent feelings toward mothers and women as mothers by mystifying them and projecting them onto Mona Lisa. They endow her with both "tenderness and coquetry," with "the charm of deceit, the kindness that conceals a cruel purpose," and with "instincts of conquest, of ferocity, all the heredity of the species, the will to seduce and ensnare."[26]

Freud finds a more benign duality in Leonardo's *St. Anne with the Madonna and Child*. The artist composed the picture so as to melt the two women into a single form, with the virgin seated on her mother's lap, reaching toward the Christ Child. Grandmother and mother are equally young and beautiful, and "endowed with the blissful smile of the joy of motherhood." Thus Leonardo, Freud says, has synthesized "the history of his childhood," merging his true mother, Caterina, from whom he was separated before he reached five, and his father's young wife, who became his stepmother when he entered the paternal household.[27] It is not only Leonardo's two mothers we can see here, but Freud's and everyman's. In the letters to Fliess, amid his several recollections of the old woman who bathed, scolded, and stole from him, Freud mentions his own mother, but formally, in Latin, as "*matrem...nudam*."[28] Like the men whose sexual problems he discusses in two important essays written during the same period as the Leonardo essay, "A Special Type of Object Choice Made by Men" (1910) and "A Prevalent Form of Degradation in Erotic Life" (1912), Freud has split her into two images: the chaste, distant madonna and the ugly, sexual nursemaid. In these two essays Freud connects such a duality to the Oedipus complex. But in the light of the gender theories I discussed earlier, it seems more likely to originate in male preoedipal experience, which produces men who feel their gender endangered by a mother's love, and who therefore in one breath idealize that love and in the next call it deceitful and seductive.

If we look into Freud's associations with the figure of Moses, the topic of the second essay, we encounter a quite different constellation of feelings, concerning the father. Let us begin where Freud begins, after some general opening remarks, to look at the statue of the patriarch:

> For no piece of statuary has ever made a stronger impression on me than this. How often have I mounted the steep steps of the unlovely Corso Cavour to the lonely place where the deserted church stands, and have essayed to support the angry scorn of the hero's glance! Sometimes I have crept cautiously out of the half-gloom of the interior as though I myself belonged to the mob upon whom his eye is turned – the mob which can hold fast no conviction, which has neither faith nor patience and which rejoices when it has regained its illusory idols.[29]

The statue stands in Rome, a city of special meaning to Freud. In the original edition of *The Interpretation of Dreams* (1900) he recounts a revealing series of dreams based on a longing to visit Rome, and remarks that the longing must remain such. Then, in 1909, when his work has gained recognition, he adds in a footnote, "I discovered long since that it only needs a little courage to fulfill wishes which till then have been regarded as unattainable."[30] For him, Moses, Rome, and unattainable wishes are interconnected.

Moses, like Oedipus, is one of Freud's heroic images of himself in *The Interpretation of Dreams*. Both are entrusted with leading an imperiled people to safety, and both in the course of doing so bring back forbidden knowledge from realms considered sacred. Freud thought of Rome in connection with his boyhood hero Hannibal, who as a Carthaginian had challenged Roman superiority, but without being able to conquer the city.[31] Hannibal was thus akin to a Jew challenging the Gentile establishment – another forbidden act, attractive to Freud, who felt and fought anti-Semitism all his life. In his own Oedipal dream, recounted piecemeal in the dream book, he feels ashamed of his father for not standing up for himself as a Jew when an anti-Semite humiliates him. That father shames him in a different way, however, by saying, "The boy will come to nothing," when Freud intrudes into his parents' bedroom and urinates on the floor.[32] Thus when Freud, surpassing Hannibal, enters Rome and ferrets out the meaning of a statue of the first Jewish patriarch, the act symbolizes his attainment of manhood in a way best described by Freud's reaction when he reached the Acropolis: "It seems as though the essence of success were to have gotten farther than one's father, and as though to excel one's father were forbidden."[33] In the passage from the Moses essay quoted above, Freud casts himself in the role of a Moses climbing the steep steps of lonely self-analysis and professional isolation toward a Sinai of divine secrets. The statue that bends an angry glance on him is his masculine ego ideal, and the childish, fickle mob that Moses found worshiping the golden calf when he descended from the mountain is the weak, "womanish" part of himself that Freud feared giving in to. The passage springs from memories of self-reproaches arising from his fear of not being man enough for the great task he had set himself.[34]

The question of interpretation on which the essay centers concerns what action is implied by the pose of the patriarch, who sits holding the tables of the law entrusted to him by God on the mountain. Does Michelangelo depict a historical Moses just descended from Sinai, now about to "let loose his rage upon his faithless people," or an eternal "character-type... embodying an inexhaustible inner force which tames the recalcitrant world?" In putting the question to his readers, Freud again interjects his own reactions:

> I can recollect my own disillusionment when, during my first visit to the church, I used to sit down in front of the statue in the expectation that I should now see how it would start up on its raised foot, hurl the Tables of the Law to the ground, and let fly its wrath. Nothing of the kind happened. Instead, the stone image became more and more transfixed, an almost oppressively solemn calm emanated from it, and I was obliged to realize that something was represented here that could stay without change: that this Moses would remain sitting like this in his wrath forever.[35]

I hear in this passage an echo of Freud's disappointment with the father who remained calm when a Gentile taunted him, and of his determination not to let a hostile world prevent him from reaching his promised land, the discovery of the unconscious.

But, not allowing personal feeling to interfere with the task at hand, Freud fixes his eyes on the statue and argues that, after all, the second view of a restrained and temperate Moses is the more nearly correct, given the evidence the statue offers. If Moses were to leap up in vindictive anger, the precious tables would slip from his grasp and shatter; the divine secret of the Law which God has given to his chosen people would be lost, and they would never reach the promised land. Rather, says Freud, the position of the leader's right hand and beard indicate that he has already felt but subdued a surge of wrath, precisely in order to keep the tables from harm, "so that the giant frame with its tremendous physical power becomes only a concrete expression of the highest mental achievement that is possible in a man, that of struggling successfully against an inward passion for the sake of a cause to which he has devoted himself."[36] "The highest mental achievement that is possible in a man" – that is, in a patriarch, the model for all men – is the opposite of the highest achievement, not exactly a mental one, he envisions for a woman: the "completely satisfying love-relationship which fulfills not only every mental wish but every physical need" – mothering a child. Men have causes and women have babies. Men repress their feelings and thereby perform great tasks of leadership; women indulge their feelings and thereby produce women who also indulge them, and men who repress them for fear of being like women.

Only in 1931 (interestingly, about a year after his own mother died) did Freud suggest, in "Female Sexuality," that the child *first* identifies with its mother – but with reference to a girl, not a boy. Long before that date he viewed a boy's identification with his mother as pathogenic; it could lead to homosexuality, an outcome of the negative resolution of the Oedipus complex in which a boy wants to be, like his mother, the passive object of his father's love. In fact, Freud characterizes identification in general as regressive (in "Mourning and Melancholia," 1917) and at the same time sex-types it; the passivity and loss of ego-boundaries identification it entails belong to a feminine mode and emanate from a time when all that an infant experienced came from a woman. As Jim Swan argues, for Freud

maturity (that is, *masculine* maturity) means being well defended against one's past, which amounts to the same thing as having a strong capacity for resisting identification. ...In effect, Freud's picture of maturity is of a man driven to outrun ...identification with the body of his mother, the original unity of mother and infant.[37]

In *The Interpretation of Dreams* Freud says, "There is at least one spot in every dream at which it is unplumbable – a navel, as it were, that is its point of contact with the unknown."[38] For the first psychoanalyst, the "navel" of psychic development is identification with the mother.[39] It is "unknown" to him not because it is unknowable but because he is a man, because manhood as patriarchal culture creates it depends on denying, in myriad ways, the powerful ambivalence that the mother inspires. Part of our task as feminist critics, I suggest, is to excavate that gray, shadowy region of identification, particularly male identification with the mother, and trace its influence on perceptions and depictions of women in patriarchal texts.

Notes

A portion of this essay, in an earlier version, appeared in "Excavating 'Those Dim Minoan Regions': Maternal Subtexts in Patriarchal Literature," *Diacritics*, 12 (Summer 1982), 32–41. Reprinted by permission of the publisher, The Johns Hopkins University Press.

1 Jean Baker Miller, *Toward A New Psychology of Women* (Boston: Beacon Press, 1976); Adrienne Rich, *Of Woman Born: Motherhood as Experience and Institution* (New York: Harper & Row, 1976); Nancy Chodorow, *The Reproduction of Mothering: Psychoanalysis and the Sociology of Gender* (Berkeley: University of California Press, 1979); Dorothy Dinnerstein, *The Mermaid and the Minotaur: Sexual Arrangements and Human Malaise* (New York: Harper & Row, 1976).

2 Chodorow, *Reproduction of Mothering*, 181.

3 Freud uses these words to describe the first attachment to the mother in "Female Sexuality" (1931), in *Standard Edition*, XXI, 225. For contributions to understanding of this phase, see Melanie Klein, "Love, Guilt, and Reparation," in *Love, Hate, and Reparation* by Melanie Klein and Joan Riviere (New York: Norton, 1964), 57–119; Alice Balint, *The Early Years of Life: A Psychoanalytic Study* (New York: Basic Books, 1954); Michael Balint (ed.), *Primary Love and Psychoanalytic Technique* (New York: Liveright, 1965); John Bowlby, *Attachment and Loss*, 2 vols. (New York, Basic Books, 1969).

4 Susan Rubin Suleiman, "Writing and Motherhood."

5 Chodorow, *Reproduction of Mothering*, 73.

6 Rich, *Of Woman Born*, 196.

7 Chodorow, *Reproduction of Mothering*, 169.

8 Carol Gilligan, *In a Different Voice* (Cambridge: Harvard University Press, 1982).

9 Sigmund Freud, "Some Psychical Consequences of the Anatomical Distinction between the Sexes" (1925), in *Standard Edition*, XIX, 243–60.

10 Chodorow, *Reproduction of Mothering*, 169.

11 See Robert J. Stoller, "Facts and Fancies: An Examination of Freud's Concept of Bisexuality," in *Women and Analysis: Dialogues on Psychoanalytic Views of Femininity*, ed. Jean Strouse (New York: Grossman, 1974), 343–64.

12 Rich, *Of Woman Born*, 164, 212.

13 Miller, *Toward a New Psychology*, 48–59.

14 Karen Horney, "The Flight from Womanhood," in *Feminine Psychology* (New York: Norton, 1967), 54–70.

15 Rich, *Of Woman Born*, 237; she takes the term from Lynn Sukenick.

16 Jim Swan, "*Mater* and Nannie: Freud's Two Mothers and the Discovery of the Oedipus Complex," *American Imago*, 31 (1974), 1–64. I am much indebted to this brilliant, wide-ranging article.

17 Freud, the eldest of seven surviving children, once remarked, "A man who has been the indisputable favorite of his mother keeps for life the feeling of a conqueror, that confidence of his success that often induces real success" (quoted by Lionel Trilling in his introduction to the abridged edition of *The Life and Works of Sigmund Freud*, by Ernest Jones [New York: Doubleday, 1963]). When his mother died, he wrote, "I was not allowed to die as long as she was alive, and now I may. Somehow the values of life have notably changed in the deeper layers" (Jones, 470).

18 See Freud to Wilhelm Fliess, October 3, 1897, in *Standard Edition*, I, 261–2; Swan comments on this letter in "*Mater* and Nannie," 16–18.

19 Iza S. Erlich, "What Happened to Jocasta?" *Bulletin of the Menninger Clinic*, 41 (May 1977), 280–4.

20 For other kinds of swerves, see Steven Marcus, "Freud and Dora: Story, History, Case History," *Partisan Review*, 41 (1974), 12–23, 89–108, and Maria Ramas, "Freud's Dora, Dora's Hysteria: The Negation of a Woman's Rebellion," *Feminist Studies*, 6 (1980), 472–510, for a cogent feminist interpretation of the Dora case. Marcus comments on Freud's lack of clarity about female sexual development on 96–8.

21 Freud, "Fragment of an Analysis of a Case of Hysteria," in *Standard Edition*, VII, 20.

22 Freud, "Fragment of an Analysis," 47–8, 96.

23 Erlich, "What Happened to Jocasta?" 284.

24 Freud, "Leonardo da Vinci and a Memory of His Childhood," *Standard Edition*, XI, 117. While it is the father's absence as well as the mother's excessive affection that, Freud maintains, is likely to fixate the son at a narcissistic stage of object relations and turn him toward homosexuality, throughout his essay he is much more concerned with the mother's role than with the father's. He does point out, however, that Leonardo's identification with his father had both negative and positive effects on his career.

25 Freud, "Leonardo da Vinci," 117.

26 Ibid., 109.

27 Ibid., 113.

28 Freud to Fliess, October 4, 1897, in *Standard Edition*, I, 262.

29 Freud, "The Moses of Michelangelo," in *Standard Edition*, XIII, 213.

30 Freud, *The Interpretation of Dreams*, in *Standard Edition*, IV, 194.

31 Ibid., 196–7.

32 Ibid., 216. For an interpretation of the Rome dreams in the context of Freud's political and cultural experience, see Carl E. Schorske, "Politics and Patricide in Freud's *Interpretation of Dreams*," in Schorske, *Fin-de-Siècle Vienna* (New York: Random House, 1980), 181–207. Schorske suggests that for Freud, Rome ambivalently represented both an oedipal mother to be possessed and an oedipal father to be overcome.

33 Freud, "A Disturbance of Memory on the Acropolis," in *Standard Edition*, XXII, 247.

34 With regard to similar anxieties about conflicting male and female capacities within Freud, as expressed in the Irma dream, Erik H. Erikson comments:

> To overcome mankind's resistance, the dreamer had to learn to become his own patient and subject of investigation: to deliver free associations to himself; to unveil horrible insights to himself; to identify himself with himself in the double roles of observer and observed.... This, in view of the strong maleness of scientific approach cultivated by the bearded savants of his day and age ... constituted an unfathomable division within the observer's self, a division of vague "feminine yielding" and persistent masculine precision: this, I feel, is one of the central meanings of the Irma dream. ["The Dream Specimen of Psychoanalysis," in *Psychoanalytic Psychiatry and Psychology: Clinical and Theoretical Papers*, Austen Riggs Center, vol. 1 (New York: International Universities Press, 1954), 164]

35 Freud, "Moses of Michelangelo," 220.

36 Ibid., 236.

37 Swan, "*Mater* and Nannie," 9–10.

38 Freud, *Interpretation of Dreams*, 111.

39 For a fascinating explication of the dream as maternal object and of interpretation as the oedipal act of penetrating the mother, see David Willbern, "Freud and the Inter-penetration of Dreams," *Diacritics*, 9 (Spring 1979), 98–110.

CHAPTER 7

Three Women's Texts and a Critique of Imperialism

Gayatri Chakravorty Spivak

Gayatri Chakravorty Spivak has written widely on post-colonialism, feminism, and Post-Structuralist literary theory. In this 1986 essay, she criticizes American feminists for ignoring the figure of Bertha Mason in Charlotte Brontë's *Jane Eyre*, and she offers an alternative to the dominant liberal individualism of US feminism that takes the historical reality of imperialism and colonialism into account.

It should not be possible to read nineteenth-century British literature without re-membering that imperialism, understood as England's social mission, was a crucial part of the cultural representation of England to the English. The role of literature in the production of cultural representation should not be ignored. These two obvious "facts" continue to be disregarded in the reading of nineteenth-century British litera-ture. This itself attests to the continuing success of the imperialist project, displaced and dispersed into more modern forms.

If these "facts" were remembered, not only in the study of British literature but in the study of the literatures of the European colonizing cultures of the great age of imperialism, we would produce a narrative, in literary history, of the "worlding" of what is now called "the Third World." To consider the Third World as distant cultures, exploited but with rich intact literary heritages waiting to be recovered, interpreted, and curricularized in English translation fosters the emergence of "the Third World" as a signifier that allows us to forget that "worlding," even as it expands the empire of the literary discipline.[1]

It seems particularly unfortunate when the emergent perspective of feminist criti-cism reproduces the axioms of imperialism. A basically isolationist admiration for the literature of the female subject in Europe and Anglo-America establishes the high feminist norm. It is supported and operated by an information-retrieval approach to "Third World" literature which often employs a deliberately "nontheoretical" meth-odology with self-conscious rectitude.

In this essay, I will attempt to examine the operation of the "worlding" of what is today "the Third World" by what has become a cult text of feminism: *Jane Eyre*.[2] I plot the novel's reach and grasp, and locate its structural motors. I read *Wide Sargasso Sea* as *Jane Eyre*'s reinscription and *Frankenstein* as an analysis – even a deconstruction – of a "worlding" such as *Jane Eyre*'s.[3]

I need hardly mention that the object of my investigation is the printed book, not its "author." To make such a distinction is, of course, to ignore the lessons of deconstruction. A deconstructive critical approach would loosen the binding of the book, undo the opposition between verbal text and the bio-graphy of the named subject "Charlotte Brontë," and see the two as each other's "scene of writing." In such a reading, the life that writes itself as "my life" is as much a production in psychosocial space (other names can be found) as the book that is written by the holder of that named life – a book that is then consigned to what *is* most often recognized as genuinely "social": the world of publication and distribution.[4] To touch Brontë's "life" in such a way, however, would be too risky here. We must rather strategically take shelter in an essentialism which, not wishing to lose the important advantages won by US mainstream feminism, will continue to honor the suspect binary oppositions – book and author, individual and history – and start with an assurance of the following sort: my readings here do not seek to undermine the excellence of the individual artist. If even minimally successful, the readings will incite a degree of rage against the imperialist narrativization of history, that it should produce so abject a script for her. I provide these assurances to allow myself some room to situate feminist individualism in its historical determination rather than simply to canonize it as feminism as such.

Sympathetic US feminists have remarked that I do not do justice to Jane Eyre's subjectivity. A word of explanation is perhaps in order. The broad strokes of my presuppositions are that what is at stake, for feminist individualism in the age of imperialism, is precisely the making of human beings, the constitution and "interpellation" of the subject not only as individual but as "individualist."[5] This stake is represented on two registers: childbearing and soul making. The first is domestic-society-through-sexual-reproduction cathected as "companionate love"; the second is the imperialist project cathected as civil-society-through-social-mission. As the female individualist, not-quite/not-male, articulates herself in shifting relationship to what is at stake, the "native female" as such (*within* discourse, *as* a signifier) is excluded from any share in this emerging norm.[6] If we read this account from an isolationist perspective in a "metropolitan" context, we see nothing there but the psychobiography of the militant female subject. In a reading such as mine, in contrast, the effort is to wrench oneself away from the mesmerizing focus of the "subject-constitution" of the female individualist.

To develop further the notion that my stance need not be an accusing one, I will refer to a passage from Roberto Fernández Retamar's "Caliban."[7] José Enrique Rodó had argued in 1900 that the model for the Latin American intellectual in relationship to Europe could be Shakespeare's Ariel.[8] In 1971 Retamar, denying the possibility of an identifiable "Latin American Culture," recast the model as Caliban. Not surprisingly, this powerful exchange still excludes any specific consideration of the civilizations of the Maya, the Aztecs, the Incas, or the smaller nations of what is now called Latin America. Let us note carefully that, at this stage of my argument, this "conversation" between Europe and Latin America (without a specific consideration of the political economy of the "worlding" of the "native") provides a sufficient thematic description of our attempt to confront the ethnocentric and reverse-ethnocentric benevolent double bind (that is, considering the "native" as object for enthusiastic information-retrieval and thus denying its own "worlding") that I sketched in my opening paragraphs.

In a moving passage in "Caliban," Retamar locates both Caliban and Ariel in the postcolonial intellectual:

> There is no real Ariel–Caliban polarity: both are slaves in the hands of Prospero, the foreign magician. But Caliban is the rude and unconquerable master of the island, while Ariel, a creature of the air, although also a child of the isle, is the intellectual.

> The deformed Caliban – enslaved, robbed of his island, and taught the language by Prospero – rebukes him thus: "You taught me language, and my profit on't / Is, I know how to curse." ["C," pp. 28, 11]

As we attempt to unlearn our so-called privilege as Ariel and "seek from [a certain] Caliban the honor of a place in his rebellious and glorious ranks," we do not ask that our students and colleagues should emulate us but that they should attend to us ("C," p. 72). If, however, we are driven by a nostalgia for lost origins, we too run the risk of effacing the "native" and stepping forth as "the real Caliban," of forgetting that he is a name in a play, an inaccessible blankness circumscribed by an interpretable text.[9] The stagings of Caliban work alongside the narrativization of history: claiming to *be* Caliban legitimizes the very individualism that we must persistently attempt to undermine from within.

Elizabeth Fox-Genovese, in an article on history and women's history, shows us how to define the historical moment of feminism in the West in terms of female access to individualism.[10] The battle for female individualism plays itself out within the larger theater of the establishment of meritocratic individualism, indexed in the aesthetic field by the ideology of "the creative imagination." Fox-Genovese's presupposition will guide us into the beautifully orchestrated opening of *Jane Eyre*.

It is a scene of the marginalization and privatization of the protagonist: "There was no possibility of taking a walk that day.... Out-door exercise was now out of the question. I was glad of it," Brontë writes (*JE*, p. 9). The movement continues as Jane breaks the rules of the appropriate topography of withdrawal. The family at the center withdraws into the sanctioned architectural space of the withdrawing room or drawing room; Jane inserts herself – "I slipped in" – into the margin – "A small breakfast-room *adjoined* the drawing room" (*JE*, p. 9; my emphasis).

The manipulation of the domestic inscription of space within the upwardly mobilizing currents of the eighteenth- and nineteenth-century bourgeoisie in England and France is well known. It seems fitting that the place to which Jane withdraws is not only not the withdrawing room but also not the dining room, the sanctioned place of family meals. Nor is it the library, the appropriate place for reading. The breakfast room "contained a book-case" (*JE*, p. 9). As Rudolph Ackerman wrote in his *Repository* (1823), one of the many manuals of taste in circulation in nineteenth-century England, these low bookcases and stands were designed to "contain all the books that may be desired for a sitting-room without reference to the library."[11] Even in this already triply off-center place, "having drawn the red moreen curtain nearly close, I [Jane] was shrined in double retirement" (*JE*, pp. 9–10).

Here in Jane's self-marginalized uniqueness, the reader becomes her accomplice: the reader and Jane are united – both are reading. Yet Jane still preserves her odd privilege, for she continues never quite doing the proper thing in its proper place. She cares little for reading what is *meant* to be read: the "letter-press." *She* reads the pictures. The power of this singular hermeneutics is precisely that it can make the outside inside. "At intervals, while turning over the leaves of my book, I studied the aspect of that winter afternoon." Under "the clear panes of glass," the rain no longer penetrates, "the drear November day" is rather a one-dimensional "aspect" to be "studied," not decoded like the "letter-press" but, like pictures, deciphered by the unique creative imagination of the marginal individualist (*JE*, p. 10).

Before following the track of this unique imagination, let us consider the suggestion that the progress of *Jane Eyre* can be charted through a sequential arrangement of the family/counter-family dyad. In the novel, we encounter, first, the Reeds as the legal family and Jane, the late Mr. Reed's sister's daughter, as the representative of a near incestuous counter-family; second, the Brocklehursts, who run the school Jane is sent to, as the legal family and Jane, Miss Temple, and Helen Burns as a counter-family that falls short because it is only a community of women; third, Rochester and the mad Mrs. Rochester as the legal family and Jane and Rochester as the illicit counter-family. Other items may be added to the thematic chain in this sequence: Rochester and Céline Varens as structurally functional counter-family; Rochester and Blanche Ingram as dissimulation of legality – and so on. It is during this sequence that Jane is moved from the counter-family to the family-in-law. In the next sequence, it is Jane who restores full family status to the as-yet-incomplete community of siblings, the Riverses. The final sequence of the book is a *community of families*, with Jane, Rochester, and their children at the center.

In terms of the narrative energy of the novel, how is Jane moved from the place of the counter-family to the family-in-law? It is the active ideology of imperialism that provides the discursive field.

(My working definition of "discursive field" must assume the existence of discrete "systems of signs" at hand in the socius, each based on a specific axiomatics. I am identifying these systems as discursive fields. "Imperialism as social mission" generates the possibility of one such axiomatics. How the individual artist taps the discursive field at hand with a sure touch, if not with transhistorical clairvoyance, in order to make the narrative structure move I hope to demonstrate through the following example. It is crucial that we extend our analysis of this example beyond the minimal diagnosis of "racism.")

Let us consider the figure of Bertha Mason, a figure produced by the axiomatics of imperialism. Through Bertha Mason, the white Jamaican Creole, Brontë renders the human/animal frontier as acceptably indeterminate, so that a good greater than the letter of the Law can be broached. Here is the celebrated passage, given in the voice of Jane:

> In the deep shade, at the further end of the room, a figure ran backwards and forwards. What it was, whether beast or human being, one could not...tell: it grovelled, seemingly, on all fours; it snatched and growled like some strange wild animal: but it was covered with clothing, and a quantity of dark, grizzled hair, wild as a mane, hid its head and face. [*JE*, p. 295]

In a matching passage, given in the voice of Rochester speaking *to* Jane, Brontë presents the imperative for a shift beyond the Law as divine injunction rather than human motive. In the terms of my essay, we might say that this is the register not of mere marriage or sexual reproduction but of Europe and its not-yet-human Other, of soul making. The field of imperial conquest is here inscribed as Hell:

"One night I had been awakened by her yells . . . it was a fiery West Indian night. . . . "

" 'This life,' said I at last, 'is hell! – this is the air – those are the sounds of the bottomless pit! *I have a right* to deliver myself from it if I can. . . . Let me break away, and go home to God!' . . .

"A wind fresh from Europe blew over the ocean and rushed through the open casement: the storm broke, streamed, thundered, blazed, and the air grew pure. . . . It was true Wisdom that consoled me in that hour, and showed me the right path. . . .

"The sweet wind from Europe was still whispering in the refreshed leaves, and the Atlantic was thundering in glorious liberty. . . .

" 'Go,' said Hope, 'and live again in Europe. . . . You have done all that God and Humanity require of you.' " [*JE*, pp. 310–11; my emphasis]

It is the unquestioned ideology of imperialist axiomatics, then, that conditions Jane's move from the counter-family set to the set of the family-in-law. Marxist critics such as Terry Eagleton have seen this only in terms of the ambiguous *class* position of the governess.[12] Sandra Gilbert and Susan Gubar, on the other hand, have seen Bertha Mason only in psychological terms, as Jane's dark double.[13]

I will not enter the critical debates that offer themselves here. Instead, I will develop the suggestion that nineteenth-century feminist individualism could conceive of a "greater" project than access to the closed circle of the nuclear family. This is the project of soul making beyond "mere" sexual reproduction. Here the native "subject" is not almost an animal but rather the object of what might be termed the terrorism of the categorical imperative.

I am using "Kant" in this essay as a metonym for the most flexible ethical moment in the European eighteenth century. Kant words the categorical imperative, conceived as the universal moral law given by pure reason, in this way: "In all creation every thing one chooses and over which one has any power, may be used *merely as means;* man alone, and with him every rational creature, is an *end in himself.*" It is thus a moving displacement of Christian ethics from religion to philosophy. As Kant writes: "With this agrees very well the possibility of such a command as: *Love God above everything, and thy neighbor as thyself.* For as a command it requires respect for a law which *commands love* and does not leave it to our own arbitrary choice to make this our principle."[14]

The "categorical" in Kant cannot be adequately represented in determinately grounded action. The dangerous transformative power of philosophy, however, is that its formal subtlety can be travestied in the service of the state. Such a travesty in the case of the categorical imperative can justify the imperialist project by producing the following formula: *make* the heathen into a human so that he can be treated as an end in himself.[15] This project is presented as a sort of tangent in *Jane Eyre*, a tangent that escapes the closed circle of the *narrative* conclusion. The tangent narrative is the story of St. John Rivers, who is granted the important task of concluding the *text*.

At the novel's end, the *allegorical* language of Christian psychobiography – rather than the textually constituted and seemingly *private* grammar of the creative imagination which we noted in the novel's opening – marks the inaccessibility of the imperialist project as such to the nascent "feminist" scenario. The concluding passage of *Jane Eyre* places St. John Rivers within the fold of *Pilgrim's Progress*. Eagleton pays no attention to this but accepts the novel's ideological lexicon, which establishes St. John Rivers' heroism by identifying a life in Calcutta with an unquestioning choice of death. Gilbert and Gubar, by calling *Jane Eyre* "Plain Jane's progress," see the novel as simply replacing the male protagonist with the female. They do not notice the distance between sexual reproduction and soul making, both actualized by the unquestioned idiom of imperialist presuppositions evident in the last part of *Jane Eyre*:

> Firm, faithful, and devoted, full of energy, and zeal, and truth, [St. John Rivers] labours for his race.... His is the sternness of the warrior Greatheart, who guards his pilgrim convoy from the onslaught of Apollyon.... His is the ambition of the high master-spirit[s] ... who stand without fault before the throne of God; who share the last mighty victories of the Lamb; who are called, and chosen, and faithful. [*JE*, p. 455]

Earlier in the novel, St. John Rivers himself justifies the project: "My vocation? My great work? ... My hopes of being numbered in the band who have merged all ambitions in the glorious one of bettering their race – of carrying knowledge into the realms of ignorance – of substituting peace for war – freedom for bondage – religion for superstition – the hope of heaven for the fear of hell?" (*JE*, p. 376). Imperialism and its territorial and subject-constituting project are a violent deconstruction of these oppositions.

When Jean Rhys, born on the Caribbean island of Dominica, read *Jane Eyre* as a child, she was moved by Bertha Mason: "I thought I'd try to write her a life."[16] *Wide Sargasso Sea*, the slim novel published in 1965, at the end of Rhys' long career, is that "life."

I have suggested that Bertha's function in *Jane Eyre* is to render indeterminate the boundary between human and animal and thereby to weaken her entitlement under the spirit if not the letter of the Law. When Rhys rewrites the scene in *Jane Eyre* where Jane hears "a snarling, snatching sound, almost like a dog quarrelling" and then encounters a bleeding Richard Mason (*JE*, p. 210), she keeps Bertha's humanity, indeed her sanity as critic of imperialism, intact. Grace Poole, another character originally in *Jane Eyre*, describes the incident to Bertha in *Wide Sargasso Sea*: "So you don't remember that you attacked this gentleman with a knife? ... I didn't hear all he said except 'I cannot interfere legally between yourself and your husband'. It was when he said 'legally' that you flew at him'" (*WSS*, p. 150). In Rhys' retelling, it is the dissimulation that Bertha discerns in the word "legally" – not an innate bestiality – that prompts her violent *re*action.

In the figure of Antoinette, whom in *Wide Sargasso Sea* Rochester violently renames Bertha, Rhys suggests that so intimate a thing as personal and human identity might be determined by the politics of imperialism. Antoinette, as a white Creole child growing up at the time of emancipation in Jamaica, is caught between the English imperialist and the black native. In recounting Antoinette's development, Rhys reinscribes some thematics of Narcissus.

There are, noticeably, many images of mirroring in the text. I will quote one from the first section. In this passage, Tia is the little black servant girl who is Antoinette's close companion: "We had eaten the same food, slept side by side, bathed in the same river. As I ran, I thought, I will live with Tia and I will be like her.... When I was close I saw the jagged stone in her hand but I did not see her throw it.... We stared at each other, blood on my face, tears on hers. It was as if I saw myself. Like in a looking glass" (*WSS*, p. 38).

A progressive sequence of dreams reinforces this mirror imagery. In its second occurrence, the dream is partially set in a *hortus conclusus*, or "enclosed garden" – Rhys uses the phrase (*WSS*, p. 50) – a Romance rewriting of the Narcissus topos as the place of encounter with Love.[17] In the enclosed garden, Antoinette encounters not Love but a strange threatening voice that says merely "in here," inviting her into a prison which masquerades as the legalization of love (*WSS*, p. 50).

In Ovid's *Metamorphoses*, Narcissus' madness is disclosed when he recognizes his Other as his self: "Iste ego sum."[18] Rhys makes Antoinette see her *self* as her Other, Brontë's Bertha. In the last section of *Wide Sargasso Sea*, Antoinette acts out *Jane Eyre*'s conclusion and recognizes herself as the so-called ghost in Thornfield Hall: "I went into the hall again with the tall candle in my hand. It was then that I saw her – the ghost. The woman with streaming hair. She was surrounded by a gilt frame but I knew her" (*WSS*, p. 154). The gilt frame encloses a mirror: as Narcissus' pool reflects the selfed Other, so this "pool" reflects the Othered self. Here the dream sequence ends, with an invocation of none other than Tia, the Other that could not be selfed, because the fracture of imperialism rather than the Ovidian pool intervened. (I will return to this difficult point.) "That was the third time I had my dream, and it ended....I called 'Tia' and jumped and woke" (*WSS*, p. 155). It is now, at the very end of the book, that Antoinette/Bertha can say: "Now at last I know why I was brought here and what I have to do" (*WSS*, pp. 155–6). We can read this as her having been brought into the England of Brontë's novel: "This cardboard house" – a book between cardboard covers – "where I walk at night is not England" (*WSS*, p. 148). In this fictive England, she must play out her role, act out the transformation of her "self" into that fictive Other, set fire to the house and kill herself, so that Jane Eyre can become the feminist individualist heroine of British fiction. I must read this as an allegory of the general epistemic violence of imperialism, the construction of a self-immolating colonial subject for the glorification of the social mission of the colonizer. At least Rhys sees to it that the woman from the colonies is not sacrificed as an insane animal for her sister's consolation.

Critics have remarked that *Wide Sargasso Sea* treats the Rochester character with understanding and sympathy.[19] Indeed, he narrates the entire middle section of the book. Rhys makes it clear that he is a victim of the patriarchal inheritance law of entailment rather than of a father's natural preference for the firstborn: in *Wide Sargasso Sea*, Rochester's situation is clearly that of a younger son dispatched to the colonies to buy an heiress. If in the case of Antoinette and her identity, Rhys utilizes the thematics of Narcissus, in the case of Rochester and his patrimony, she touches on the thematics of Oedipus. (In this she has her finger on our "historical moment." If, in the nineteenth century, subject-constitution is represented as childbearing and soul making, in the twentieth century psychoanalysis allows the West to plot the itinerary of the subject from Narcissus [the "imaginary"] to Oedipus [the "symbolic"]. This subject, however, is the normative male subject. In Rhys' reinscription of these themes, divided between the female and the male protagonist, feminism and a critique of imperialism become complicit.)

In place of the "wind from Europe" scene, Rhys substitutes the scenario of a suppressed letter to a father, a letter which would be the "correct" explanation of the tragedy of the book.[20] "I thought about the letter which should have been written to England a week ago. Dear Father..." (*WSS*, p. 57). This is the first instance: the letter not written. Shortly afterward:

Dear Father. The thirty thousand pounds have been paid to me without question or condition. No provision made for her (that must be seen to).... I will never be a disgrace to you or to my dear brother the son you love. No begging letters, no mean requests. None of the furtive shabby manoeuvres of a younger son. I have sold my soul or you have sold it, and after all is it such a bad bargain? The girl is thought to be beautiful, she is beautiful. And yet... [*WSS*, p. 59]

This is the second instance: the letter not sent. The formal letter is uninteresting; I will quote only a part of it:

Dear Father, we have arrived from Jamaica after an uncomfortable few days. This little estate in the Windward Islands is part of the family property and Antoinette is much attached to it.... All is well and has gone according to your plans and wishes. I dealt of course with Richard Mason.... He seemed to become attached to me and trusted me completely. This place is very beautiful but my illness has left me too exhausted to appreciate it fully. I will write again in a few days' time. [*WSS*, p. 63]

And so on.

Rhys' version of the Oedipal exchange is ironic, not a closed circle. We cannot know if the letter actually reaches its destination. "I wondered how they got their letters posted," the Rochester figure muses. "I folded mine and put it into a drawer of the desk.... There are blanks in my mind that cannot be filled up" (*WSS*, p. 64). It is as if the text presses us to note the analogy between letter and mind.

Rhys denies to Brontë's Rochester the one thing that is supposed to be secured in the Oedipal relay: the Name of the Father, or the patronymic. In *Wide Sargasso Sea*, the character corresponding to Rochester has no name. His writing of the final version of the letter to his father is supervised, in fact, by an image of the *loss* of the patronymic: "There was a crude bookshelf made of three shingles strung together over the desk and I looked at the books, Byron's poems, novels by Sir Walter Scott, *Confessions of an Opium Eater*... and on the last shelf, *Life and Letters of*... The rest was eaten away" (*WSS*, p. 63).

Wide Sargasso Sea marks with uncanny clarity the limits of its own discourse in Christophine, Antoinette's black nurse. We may perhaps surmise the distance between *Jane Eyre* and *Wide Sargasso Sea* by remarking that Christophine's unfinished story is the tangent to the latter narrative, as St. John Rivers' story is to the former. Christophine is not a native of Jamaica; she is from Martinique. Taxonomically, she belongs to the category of the good servant rather than that of the pure native. But within these borders, Rhys creates a powerfully suggestive figure.

Christophine is the first interpreter and named speaking subject in the text. "The Jamaican ladies had never approved of my mother, 'because she pretty like pretty self' Christophine said," we read in the book's opening paragraph (*WSS*, p. 15). I have taught this book five times, once in France, once to students who had worked on the book with the well-known Caribbean novelist Wilson Harris, and once at a prestigious institute where the majority of the students were faculty from other universities. It is part of the political argument I am making that all these students blithely stepped over this paragraph without asking or knowing what Christophine's patois, so-called incorrect English, might mean.

Christophine is, of course, a commodified person. "'She was your father's wedding present to me'" explains Antoinette's mother, "'one of his presents'" (*WSS*,

p. 18). Yet Rhys assigns her some crucial functions in the text. It is Christophine who judges that black ritual practices are culture-specific and cannot be used by whites as cheap remedies for social evils, such as Rochester's lack of love for Antoinette. Most important, it is Christophine alone whom Rhys allows to offer a hard analysis of Rochester's actions, to challenge him in a face-to-face encounter. The entire extended passage is worthy of comment. I quote a brief extract:

> "She is Creole girl, and she have the sun in her. Tell the truth now. She don't come to your house in this place England they tell me about, she don't come to your beautiful house to beg you to marry with her. No, it's you come all the long way to her house – it's you beg her to marry. And she love you and she give you all she have. Now you say you don't love her and you break her up. What you do with her money, eh?" [And then Rochester, the white man, comments silently to himself] Her voice was still quiet but with a hiss in it when she said "money." [*WSS*, p. 130]

Her analysis is powerful enough for the white man to be afraid: "I no longer felt dazed, tired, half hypnotized, but alert and wary, ready to defend myself" (*WSS*, p. 130).

Rhys does not, however, romanticize individual heroics on the part of the oppressed. When the Man refers to the forces of Law and Order, Christophine recognizes their power. This exposure of civil inequality is emphasized by the fact that, just before the Man's successful threat, Christophine had invoked the emancipation of slaves in Jamaica by proclaiming: "No chain gang, no tread machine, no dark jail either. This is free country and I am free woman" (*WSS*, p. 131).

As I mentioned above, Christophine is tangential to this narrative. She cannot be contained by a novel which rewrites a canonical English text within the European novelistic tradition in the interest of the white Creole rather than the native. No perspective *critical* of imperialism can turn the Other into a self, because the project of imperialism has always already historically refracted what might have been the absolutely Other into a domesticated Other that consolidates the imperialist self.[21] The Caliban of Retamar, caught between Europe and Latin America, reflects this predicament. We can read Rhys' reinscription of Narcissus as a thematization of the same problematic.

Of course, we cannot know Jean Rhys' feelings in the matter. We can, however, look at the scene of Christophine's inscription in the text. Immediately after the exchange between her and the Man, well before the conclusion, she is simply driven out of the story, with neither narrative nor characterological explanation or justice. "'Read and write I don't know. Other things I know.' She walked away without looking back" (*WSS*, p. 133).

Indeed, if Rhys rewrites the madwoman's attack on the Man by underlining of the misuse of "legality," she cannot deal with the passage that corresponds to St. John Rivers' own justification of his martyrdom, for it has been displaced into the current idiom of modernization and development. Attempts to construct the "Third World Woman" as a signifier remind us that the hegemonic definition of literature is itself caught within the history of imperialism. A full literary reinscription cannot easily flourish in the imperialist fracture or discontinuity, covered over by an alien legal system masquerading as Law as such, an alien ideology established as only Truth, and a set of human sciences busy establishing the "native" as self-consolidating Other.

In the Indian case at least, it would be difficult to find an ideological clue to the planned epistemic violence of imperialism merely by rearranging curricula or syllabi within existing norms of literary pedagogy. For a later period of imperialism – when the constituted colonial subject has firmly taken hold – straightforward experiments of comparison can be undertaken, say, between the functionally witless India of *Mrs. Dalloway*, on the one hand, and literary texts produced in India in the 1920s, on the other. But the first half of the nineteenth century resists questioning through literature or literary criticism in the narrow sense, because both are implicated in the project of producing Ariel. To reopen the fracture without succumbing to a nostalgia for lost origins, the literary critic must turn to the archives of imperial governance.

In conclusion, I shall look briefly at Mary Shelley's *Frankenstein*, a text of nascent feminism that remains cryptic, I think, simply because it does not speak the language of feminist individualism which we have come to hail as the language of high feminism within English literature. It is interesting that Barbara Johnson's brief study tries to rescue this recalcitrant text for the service of feminist autobiography.[22] Alternatively, George Levine reads *Frankenstein* in the context of the creative imagination and the nature of the hero. He sees the novel as a book about its own writing and about writing itself, a Romantic allegory of reading within which Jane Eyre as unselfconscious critic would fit quite nicely.[23]

I propose to take *Frankenstein* out of this arena and focus on it in terms of that sense of English cultural identity which I invoked at the opening of this essay. Within that focus we are obliged to admit that, although *Frankenstein* is ostensibly about the origin and evolution of man in society, it does not deploy the axiomatics of imperialism.

Let me say at once that there is plenty of incidental imperialist sentiment in *Frankenstein*. My point, within the argument of this essay, is that the discursive field of imperialism does not produce unquestioned ideological correlatives for the narrative structuring of the book. The discourse of imperialism surfaces in a curiously powerful way in Shelley's novel, and I will later discuss the moment at which it emerges.

Frankenstein is not a battleground of male and female individualism articulated in terms of sexual reproduction (family and female) and social subject-production (race and male). That binary opposition is undone in Victor Frankenstein's laboratory – an artificial womb where both projects are undertaken simultaneously, though the terms are never openly spelled out. Frankenstein's apparent antagonist is God himself as Maker of Man, but his real competitor is also woman as the maker of children. It is not just that his dream of the death of mother and bride and the actual death of his bride are associated with the visit of his monstrous homoerotic "son" to his bed. On a much more overt level, the monster is a bodied "corpse," unnatural because bereft of a determinable childhood: "No father had watched my infant days, no mother had blessed me with smiles and caresses; or if they had, all my past was now a blot, a blind vacancy in which I distinguished nothing" (*F*, pp. 57, 115). It is Frankenstein's own ambiguous and miscued understanding of the real motive for the monster's vengefulness that reveals his own competition with woman as maker:

I created a rational creature and was bound towards him to assure, as far as was in my power, his happiness and well-being. This was my duty, but there was another still paramount to that. My duties towards the beings of my own species had greater claims to my attention because they included a greater proportion of happiness or misery. Urged by this view, I refused, and I did right in refusing, to create a companion for the first creature. [*F*, p. 206]

It is impossible not to notice the accents of transgression inflecting Frankenstein's demolition of his experiment to create the future Eve. Even in the laboratory, the woman-in-the-making is not a bodied corpse but "a human being." The (il)logic of the metaphor bestows on her a prior existence which Frankenstein aborts, rather than an anterior death which he reembodies: "The remains of the half-finished creature, whom I had destroyed, lay scattered on the floor, and I almost felt as if I had mangled the living flesh of a human being" (*F*, p. 163).

In Shelley's view, man's hubris as soul maker both usurps the place of God and attempts – vainly – to sublate woman's physiological prerogative.[24] Indeed, indulging a Freudian fantasy here, I could urge that, if to give and withhold to/from the mother a phallus is *the* male fetish, then to give and withhold to/from the man a womb might be the female fetish.[25] The icon of the sublimated womb in man is surely his productive brain, the box in the head.

In the judgment of classical psychoanalysis, the phallic mother exists only by virtue of the castration-anxious son; in *Frankenstein*'s judgment, the hysteric father (Victor Frankenstein gifted with his laboratory – the womb of theoretical reason) cannot produce a daughter. Here the language of racism – the dark side of imperialism understood as social mission – combines with the hysteria of masculism into the idiom of (the withdrawal of) sexual reproduction rather than subject-constitution. The roles of masculine and feminine individualists are hence reversed and displaced. Frankenstein cannot produce a "daughter" because "she might become ten thousand times more malignant than her mate . . . [and because] one of the first results of those sympathies for which the demon thirsted would be children, and a race of devils would be propagated upon the earth who might make the very existence of the species of man a condition precarious and full of terror" (*F*, p. 158). This particular narrative strand also launches a thoroughgoing critique of the eighteenth-century European discourses on the origin of society through (Western Christian) man. Should I mention that, much like Jean-Jacques Rousseau's remark in his *Confessions*, Frankenstein declares himself to be "by birth a Genevese" (*F*, p. 31)?

In this overly didactic text, Shelley's point is that social engineering should not be based on pure, theoretical, or natural-scientific reason alone, which is her implicit critique of the utilitarian vision of an engineered society. To this end, she presents in the first part of her deliberately schematic story three characters, childhood friends, who seem to represent Kant's three-part conception of the human subject: Victor Frankenstein, the forces of theoretical reason or "natural philosophy"; Henry Clerval, the forces of practical reason or "the moral relations of things"; and Elizabeth Lavenza, that aesthetic judgment – "the aerial creation of the poets" – which, according to Kant, is "a suitable mediating link connecting the realm of the concept of nature and that of the concept of freedom . . . (which) promotes . . . *moral* feeling" (*F*, pp. 37, 36).[26]

This three-part subject does not operate harmoniously in *Frankenstein*. That Henry Clerval, associated as he is with practical reason, should have as his "design . . . to visit India, in the belief that he had in his knowledge of its various languages, and in the views he had taken of its society, the means of materially assisting the progress of European colonization and trade" is proof of this, as well as part of the incidental imperialist sentiment that I speak of above (*F*, pp. 151–2). I should perhaps point out that the language here is entrepreneurial rather than missionary:

> He came to the university with the design of making himself complete master of the Oriental languages, as thus he should open a field for the plan of life he had marked out for himself. Resolved to pursue no inglorious career, he turned his eyes towards the East as affording scope for his spirit of enterprise. The Persian, Arabic, and Sanskrit languages engaged his attention. [*F*, pp. 66–7]

But it is of course Victor Frankenstein, with his strange itinerary of obsession with natural philosophy, who offers the strongest demonstration that the multiple perspectives of the three-part Kantian subject cannot co-operate harmoniously. Frankenstein creates a putative human subject out of natural philosophy alone. According to his own miscued summation: "In a fit of enthusiastic madness I created a rational creature" (*F*, p. 206). It is not at all farfetched to say that Kant's categorical imperative can most easily be mistaken for the hypothetical imperative – a command to ground in cognitive comprehension what can be apprehended only by moral will – by putting natural philosophy in the place of practical reason.

I should hasten to add here that just as readings such as this one do not necessarily accuse Charlotte Brontë the named individual of harboring imperialist sentiments, so also they do not necessarily commend Mary Shelley the named individual for writing a successful Kantian allegory. The most I can say is that it is possible to read these texts, within the frame of imperialism and the Kantian ethical moment, in a politically useful way. Such an approach presupposes that a "disinterested" reading attempts to render transparent the interests of the hegemonic readership. (Other "political" readings – for instance, that the monster is the nascent working class – can also be advanced.)

Frankenstein is built in the established epistolary tradition of multiple frames. At the heart of the multiple frames, the narrative of the monster (as reported by Frankenstein to Robert Walton, who then recounts it in a letter to his sister) is of his almost learning, clandestinely, to be human. It is invariably noticed that the monster reads *Paradise Lost* as true history. What is not so often noticed is that he also reads Plutarch's *Lives*, "the histories of the first founders of the ancient republics," which he compares to "the patriarchal lives of my protectors" (*F*, pp. 123, 124). And his *education* comes through "Volney's *Ruins of Empires*," which purported to be a prefiguration of the French Revolution, published after the event and after the author had rounded off his theory with practice (*F*, p. 113). It is an attempt at an enlightened universal secular, rather than a Eurocentric Christian, history, written from the perspective of a narrator "from below," somewhat like the attempts of Eric Wolf or Peter Worsley in our own time.[27]

This Caliban's education in (universal secular) humanity takes place through the monster's eavesdropping on the instruction of an Ariel – Safie, the Christianized "Arabian" to whom "a residence in Turkey was abhorrent" (*F*, p. 121). In depicting Safie, Shelley uses some commonplaces of eighteenth-century liberalism that are shared by many today: Safie's Muslim father was a victim of (bad) Christian religious prejudice and yet was himself a wily and ungrateful man not as morally refined as her (good) Christian mother. Having tasted the emancipation of woman, Safie could not go home. The confusion between "Turk" and "Arab" has its counterpart in present-day confusion about Turkey and Iran as "Middle Eastern" but not "Arab."

Although we are a far cry here from the unexamined and covert axiomatics of imperialism in *Jane Eyre*, we will gain nothing by celebrating the time-bound pieties that Shelley, as the daughter of two antievangelicals, produces. It is more interesting for us that Shelley differentiates the Other, works at the Caliban/Ariel distinction, and *cannot* make the monster identical with the proper recipient of these lessons. Although he had "heard of the discovery of the American hemisphere and *wept with Safie* over the helpless fate of its original inhabitants," Safie cannot reciprocate his attachment. When she first catches sight of him, "Safie, unable to attend to her friend [Agatha], rushed out of the cottage" (*F*, pp. 114 [my emphasis], 129).

In the taxonomy of characters, the Muslim-Christian Safie belongs with Rhys' Antoinette/Bertha. And indeed, like Christophine the good servant, the subject created by the fiat of natural philosophy is the tangential unresolved moment in *Frankenstein*. The simple suggestion that the monster is human inside but monstrous outside and only provoked into vengefulness is clearly not enough to bear the burden of so great a historical dilemma.

At one moment, in fact, Shelley's Frankenstein does try to tame the monster, to humanize him by bringing him within the circuit of the Law. He "repair[s] to a criminal judge in the town and... relate[s his] history briefly but with firmness" – the first and disinterested version of the narrative of Frankenstein – "marking the dates with accuracy and never deviating into invective or exclamation.... When I had concluded my narration I said, 'This is the being whom I accuse and for whose seizure and punishment I call upon you to exert your whole power. It is your duty as a magistrate'" (*F*, pp. 189, 190). The sheer social reasonableness of the mundane voice of Shelley's "Genevan magistrate" reminds us that the absolutely Other cannot be selfed, that the monster has "properties" which will not be contained by "proper" measures:

> "I will exert myself [he says], and if it is in my power to seize the monster, be assured that he shall suffer punishment proportionate to his crimes. But I fear, from what you have yourself described to be his properties, that this will prove impracticable; and thus, while every proper measure is pursued, you should make up your mind to disappointment." [*F*, p. 190]

In the end, as is obvious to most readers, distinctions of human individuality themselves seem to fall away from the novel. Monster, Frankenstein, and Walton seem to become each other's relays. Frankenstein's story comes to an end in death; Walton concludes his own story within the frame of his function as letter writer. In the *narrative* conclusion, he is the natural philosopher who learns from Frankenstein's example. At the end of the *text*, the monster, having confessed his guilt toward his maker and ostensibly intending to immolate himself, is borne away on an ice raft. We do not see the conflagration of his funeral pile – the self-immolation is not consummated in the text: he too cannot be contained by the text. In terms of narrative logic, he is "lost in darkness and distance" (*F*, p. 211) – these are the last words of the novel – into an existential temporality that is coherent with neither the territorializing individual imagination (as in the opening of *Jane Eyre*) nor the authoritative scenario of Christian psychobiography (as at the end of Brontë's work). The very relationship between sexual reproduction and social subject-production – the dynamic nineteenth-century topos of feminism-in-imperialism – remains problematic within the limits of Shelley's text and, paradoxically, constitutes its strength.

Earlier, I offered a reading of woman as womb holder in *Frankenstein*. I would now suggest that there is a framing woman in the book who is neither tangential, nor encircled, nor yet encircling. "Mrs. Saville," "excellent Margaret," "beloved Sister" are her address and kinship inscriptions (*F*, pp. 15, 17, 22). She is the occasion, though not the protagonist, of the novel. She is the feminine *subject* rather than the female individualist: she is the irreducible *recipient*-function of the letters that constitute *Frankenstein*. I have commented on the singular appropriative hermeneutics of the reader reading with Jane in the opening pages of *Jane Eyre*. Here the reader must read with Margaret Saville in the crucial sense that she must *intercept* the recipient-function, read the letters *as* recipient, in order for the novel to exist.[28] Margaret Saville does not respond to close the text as frame. The frame is thus simultaneously not a frame, and the monster can step "beyond the text" and be "lost in darkness." Within the allegory of our reading, the place of both the English lady and the unnamable monster are left open by this great flawed text. It is satisfying for a postcolonial reader to consider this a noble resolution for a nineteenth-century English novel. This is all the more striking because, on the anecdotal level, Shelley herself abundantly "identifies" with Victor Frankenstein.[29]

I must myself close with an idea that I cannot establish within the limits of this essay. Earlier I contended that *Wide Sargasso Sea* is necessarily bound by the reach of the European novel. I suggested that, in contradistinction, to reopen the epistemic fracture of imperialism without succumbing to a nostalgia for lost origins, the critic must turn to the archives of imperialist governance. I have not turned to those archives in these pages. In my current work, by way of a modest and inexpert "reading" of "archives," I try to extend, outside of the reach of the European novelistic tradition, the most powerful suggestion in *Wide Sargasso Sea*: that *Jane Eyre* can be read as the orchestration and staging of the self-immolation of Bertha Mason as "good wife." The power of that suggestion remains unclear if we remain insufficiently knowledgeable about the history of the legal manipulation of widow-sacrifice in the entitlement of the British government in India. I would hope that an informed critique of imperialism, granted some attention from readers in the First World, will at least expand the frontiers of the politics of reading.

Notes

1   My notion of the "worlding of a world" upon what must be assumed to be uninscribed earth is a vulgarization of Martin Heidegger's idea; see "The Origin of the Work of Art," *Poetry, Language, Thought*, trans. Albert Hofstadter (New York, 1977), pp. 17–87.

2   See Charlotte Brontë, *Jane Eyre* (New York, 1960); all further references to this work, abbreviated *JE*, will be included in the text.

3   See Jean Rhys, *Wide Sargasso Sea* (Harmondsworth, 1966); all further references to this work, abbreviated *WSS*, will be included in the text. And see Mary Shelley, *Frankenstein; or, The Modern Prometheus* (New York, 1965); all further references to this work, abbreviated *F*, will be included in the text.

4 I have tried to do this in my essay "Unmaking and Making in *To the Lighthouse*," in *Women and Language in Literature and Society*, ed. Sally McConnell-Ginet, Ruth Borker, and Nelly Furman (New York, 1980), pp. 310–27.

5 As always, I take my formula from Louis Althusser, "Ideology an Ideological State Apparatuses (Notes towards an Investigation)," "*Lenin and Philosophy" and Other Essays*, trans. Ben Brewster (New York, 1971), pp. 127–86. For an acute differentiation between the individual and individualism, see V. N. Vološinov, *Marxism and the Philosophy of Language*, trans. Ladislav Matejka and I. R. Titunik, Studies in Language, vol. 1 (New York, 1973), pp. 93–4 and 152–3. For a "straight" analysis of the roots and ramifications of English "individualism," see C. B. MacPherson, *The Political Theory of Possessive Individualism: Hobbes to Locke* (Oxford, 1962). I am grateful to Jonathan Rée for bringing this book to my attention and for giving a careful reading of all but the very end of the present essay.

6 I am constructing an analogy with Homi Bhabha's powerful notion of "not-quite/not-white" in his "Of Mimicry and Man: The Ambiguity of Colonial Discourse," *October* 28 (Spring 1984): 132. I should also add that I use the word "native" here in reaction to the term "Third World Woman." It cannot, of course, apply with equal historical justice to both the West Indian and the Indian contexts nor to contexts of imperialism by transportation.

7 See Roberto Fernández Retamar, "Caliban: Notes towards a Discussion of Culture in Our America," trans. Lynn Garafola, David Arthur McMurray, and Robert Márquez, *Massachusetts Review* 15 (Winter–Spring 1974): 7–72; all further references to this work, abbreviated "C," will be included in the text.

8 See José Enrique Rodó, *Ariel*, ed. Gordon Brotherston (Cambridge, 1967).

9 For an elaboration of "an inaccessible blankness circumscribed by an interpretable text," see my "Can the Subaltern Speak?" *Marxism and the Interpretation of Culture*, ed. Cary Nelson (Urbana, Ill., 1988).

10 See Elizabeth Fox-Genovese, "Placing Women's History in History," *New Left Review* 133 (May–June 1982): 5–29.

11 Rudolph Ackerman, *The Repository of Arts, Literature, Commerce, Manufactures, Fashions, and Politics* (London, 1823), p. 310.

12 See Terry Eagleton, *Myths of Power: A Marxist Study of the Brontës* (London, 1975); this is one of the general presuppositions of his book.

13 See Sandra M. Gilbert and Susan Gubar, *The Madwoman in the Attic: The Woman Writer and the Nineteenth-Century Literary Imagination* (New Haven, Conn., 1979), pp. 360–2.

14 Immanuel Kant, *Critique of Practical Reason, the "Critique of Pure Reason," the "Critique of Practical Reason" and Other Ethical Treatises, the "Critique of Judgement,"* trans. J. M. D. Meiklejohn et al. (Chicago, 1952), pp. 328, 326.

15 I have tried to justify the reduction of sociohistorical problems to formulas or propositions in my essay "Can the Subaltern Speak?" The "travesty" I speak of does not befall the Kantian ethic in its purity as an accident but rather exists within its lineaments as a possible supplement. On the register of the human being as child rather than heathen, my formula can be found, for example, in "What Is Enlightenment?" in Kant, *"Foundations of the Metaphysics of Morals," "What Is Enlightenment?" and a Passage from "The Metaphysics of Morals,"* trans. and ed. Lewis White Beck (Chicago, 1950). I have profited from discussing Kant with Jonathan Rée.

16 Jean Rhys, in an interview with Elizabeth Vreeland, quoted in Nancy R. Harrison, *Jean Rhys and the Novel as Women's Text* (Chapel Hill, NC, 1988). This is an excellent, detailed study of Rhys.

17 See Louise Vinge, *The Narcissus Theme in Western European Literature Up to the Early Nineteenth Century*, trans. Robert Dewsnap et al. (Lund, 1967), ch. 5.

18 For a detailed study of this text, see John Brenkman, "Narcissus in the Text," *Georgia Review* 30 (Summer 1976): 293–327.

19 See, e.g., Thomas F. Staley, *Jean Rhys: A Critical Study* (Austin, Tex. 1979), pp. 108–16; it is interesting to note Staley's masculist discomfort with this and his consequent dissatisfaction with Rhys' novel.

20   I have tried to relate castration and suppressed letters in my "The Letter As Cutting Edge,"
     in *Literature and Psychoanalysis; The Question of Reading: Otherwise*, ed. Shoshana Felman
     (New Haven, Conn., 1981), pp. 208–26.

21   This is the main argument of my "Can the Subaltern Speak?"

22   See Barbara Johnson, "My Monster/My Self," *Diacritics* 12 (Summer 1982): 2–10.

23   See George Levine, *The Realistic Imagination: English Fiction from Frankenstein to Lady
     Chatterley* (Chicago, 1981), pp. 23–35.

24   Consult the publications of the Feminist International Network for the best overview of the
     current debate on reproductive technology.

25   For the male fetish, see Sigmund Freud, "Fetishism," *The Standard Edition of the Complete
     Psychological Works of Sigmund Freud*, ed. and trans. James Strachey et al., 24 vols. (London,
     1953–74), 21:152–7. For a more "serious" Freudian study of *Frankenstein*, see Mary Jacobus,
     "Is There a Woman in This Text?" *New Literary History* 14 (Autumn 1982): 117–41. My
     "fantasy" would of course be disproved by the "fact" that it is more difficult for a woman to
     assume the position of fetishist than for a man; see Mary Ann Doane, "Film and the Mas-
     querade: Theorising the Female Spectator," *Screen* 23 (Sept.–Oct. 1982): 74–87.

26   Kant, *Critique of Judgement*, trans. J. H. Bernard (New York, 1951), p. 39.

27   See [Constantin François Chasseboeuf de Volney], *The Ruins; or, Meditations on the Revolu-
     tions of Empires*, trans. pub. (London, 1811). Johannes Fabian has shown us the manipulation
     of time in "new" secular histories of a similar kind; see *Time and the Other: How Anthropology
     Makes Its Object* (New York, 1983). See also Eric R. Wolf, *Europe and the People without
     History* (Berkeley and Los Angeles, 1982), and Peter Worsley, *The Third World*, 2nd edn.
     (Chicago, 1973); I am grateful to Dennis Dworkin for bringing the latter book to my attention.
     The most striking ignoring of the monster's education through Volney is in Gilbert's other-
     wise brilliant "Horror's Twin: Mary Shelley's Monstrous Eve," *Feminist Studies* 4 (June
     1980): 48–73. Gilbert's essay reflects the absence of race-determinations in a certain sort of
     feminism. Her present work has most convincingly filled in this gap; see, e.g., her recent piece
     on H. Rider Haggard's *She* ("Rider Haggard's Heart of Darkness," *Partisan Review* 50, no. 3
     [1983]: 444–53).

28   "A letter is always and *a priori* intercepted, . . . the 'subjects' are neither the senders nor the
     receivers of messages. . . . The letter is constituted . . . by its interception" (Jacques Derrida,
     "Discussion," after Claude Rabant, "Il n'a aucune chance de l'entendre," in *Affranchissement:
     Du transfert et de la lettre*, ed. René Major [Paris, 1981], p. 106; my translation). Margaret
     Saville is not made to appropriate the reader's "subject" into the signature of her own
     "individuality."

29   The most striking "internal evidence" is the admission in the "Author's Introduction" that,
     after dreaming of the yet-unnamed Victor Frankenstein figure and being terrified (through,
     yet not quite through, him) by the monster in a scene she later reproduced in *Frankenstein's*
     story, Shelley began her tale "on the morrow . . . with the words 'It was on a dreary night of
     November'" (*F*, p. xi). Those are the opening words of chapter 5 of the finished book, where
     Frankenstein begins to recount the actual making of his monster (see *F*, p. 56).

CHAPTER 8

Age, Race, Class, and Sex: Women Redefining Difference

Audre Lorde

In this 1984 essay, African American poet Audre Lorde outlines some of the problems facing feminism in general and African American feminists in particular. She notes a number of differences that undermine feminist solidarity across ethnic, class, and sex-preference lines. She calls for a more ample kind of feminism, one that would be attentive to the double oppression faced by women of color.

Much of western European history conditions us to see human differences in simplistic opposition to each other: dominant/subordinate, good/bad, up/down, superior/inferior. In a society where the good is defined in terms of profit rather than in terms of human need, there must always be some group of people who, through systematized oppression, can be made to feel surplus, to occupy the place of the dehumanized inferior. Within this society, that group is made up of Black and Third World people, working-class people, older people, and women.

As a forty-nine-year-old Black lesbian feminist socialist mother of two, including one boy, and a member of an interracial couple, I usually find myself a part of some group defined as other, deviant, inferior, or just plain wrong. Traditionally, in american society, it is the members of oppressed, objectified groups who are expected to stretch out and bridge the gap between the actualities of our lives and the consciousness of our oppressor. For in order to survive, those of us for whom oppression is as american as apple pie have always had to be watchers, to become familiar with the language and manners of the oppressor, even sometimes adopting them for some illusion of protection. Whenever the need for some pretense of communication arises, those who profit from our oppression call upon us to share our knowledge with them. In other words, it is the responsibility of the oppressed to teach the oppressors their mistakes. I am responsible for educating teachers who dismiss my children's culture in school. Black and Third World people are expected to educate white people as to our humanity. Women are expected to educate men. Lesbians and gay men are expected to educate the heterosexual world. The oppressors maintain their position and evade responsibility for their own actions. There is a constant drain of energy which might be better used in redefining ourselves and devising realistic scenarios for altering the present and constructing the future.

Institutionalized rejection of difference is an absolute necessity in a profit economy which needs outsiders as surplus people. As members of such an economy, we have *all* been programmed to respond to the human differences between us with fear and loathing and to handle that difference in one of three ways: ignore it, and if that is not possible, copy it if we think it is dominant, or destroy it if we think it is subordinate. But we have no patterns for relating across our human differences as equals. As a result, those differences have been misnamed and misused in the service of separation and confusion.

Certainly there are very real differences between us of race, age, and sex. But it is not those differences between us that are separating us. It is rather our refusal to recognize those differences, and to examine the distortions which result from our misnaming them and their effects upon human behavior and expectation.

Racism, the belief in the inherent superiority of one race over all others and thereby the right to dominance. Sexism, the belief in the inherent superiority of one sex over the other and thereby the right to dominance. Ageism. Heterosexism. Elitism. Classism.

It is a lifetime pursuit for each one of us to extract these distortions from our living at the same time as we recognize, reclaim, and define those differences upon which they are imposed. For we have all been raised in a society where those distortions were endemic within our living. Too often, we pour the energy needed for recognizing and exploring difference into pretending those differences are insurmountable barriers, or that they do not exist at all. This results in a voluntary isolation, or false and treacherous connections. Either way, we do not develop tools for using human difference as a springboard for creative change. . . .

Somewhere, on the edge of consciousness, there is what I call a *mythical norm*, which each one of us within our hearts knows "that is not true." In America, this norm is usually defined as white, thin, male, young, heterosexual, christian, and financially secure. It is with this mythical norm that the trappings of power reside within this society. Those of us who stand outside that power often identify one way in which we are different, and we assume that to be the primary cause of all oppression, forgetting other distortions around difference, some of which we ourselves may be practicing. By and large within the women's movement today, white women focus upon their oppression as women and ignore differences of race, sexual preference, class, and age. There is a pretense to a homogeneity of experience covered by the word *sisterhood* that does not in fact exist.

Unacknowledged class differences rob women of each other's energy and creative insight. Recently a women's magazine collective made the decision for one issue to print only prose, saying poetry was a less "rigorous" or "serious" art form. Yet even the form our creativity takes is often a class issue. Of all the art forms, poetry is the most economical. It is the one which is the most secret, which requires the least physical labor, the least material, and the one which can be done between shifts, in the hospital pantry, on the subway, and on scraps of surplus paper. Over the last few years, writing a novel on tight finances, I came to appreciate the enormous differences in the material demands between poetry and prose. As we reclaim our literature, poetry has been the major voice of poor, working-class, and Colored women. A room of one's own may be a necessity for writing prose, but so are reams of paper, a typewriter, and plenty of time. The actual requirements to produce the visual arts also help determine, along class lines, whose art is whose. In this day of inflated prices for material, who are our sculptors, our painters, our photographers? When we speak of a broadly based women's culture, we need to be aware of the effect of class and economic differences on the supplies available for producing art.

As we move toward creating a society within which we can each flourish, ageism is another distortion of relationship which interferes without vision. By ignoring the past, we are encouraged to repeat its mistakes. The "generation gap" is an important social tool for any repressive society. If the younger members of a community view the older members as contemptible or suspect or excess, they will never be able to join hands and examine the living memories of the community, nor ask the all important question, "Why?" This gives rise to a historical amnesia that keeps us working to invent the wheel every time we have to go to the store for bread.

We find ourselves having to repeat and relearn the same old lessons over and over that our mothers did because we do not pass on what we have learned, or because we are unable to listen. For instance, how many times has this all been said before? For another, who would have believed that once again our daughters are allowing their bodies to be hampered and purgatoried by girdles and high heels and hobble skirts?

Ignoring the differences of race between women and the implications of those differences presents the most serious threat to the mobilization of women's joint power.

As white women ignore their built-in privilege of whiteness and define *woman* in terms of their own experience alone, then women of Color become "other," the outsider whose experience and tradition is too "alien" to comprehend. An example of this is the signal absence of the experience of women of Color as a resource for women's studies courses. The literature of women of Color is seldom included in women's literature courses and almost never in other literature courses, nor in women's studies as a whole. All too often, the excuse given is that the literatures of women of Color can only be taught by Colored women, or that they are too difficult to understand, or that classes cannot "get into" them because they come out of experiences that are "too different." I have heard this argument presented by white women of otherwise quite clear intelligence, women who seem to have no trouble at all teaching and reviewing work that comes out of the vastly different experiences of Shakespeare, Molière, Dostoyefsky, and Aristophanes. Surely there must be some other explanation.

This is a very complex question, but I believe one of the reasons white women have such difficulty reading Black women's work is because of their reluctance to see Black women as women and different from themselves. To examine Black women's literature effectively requires that we be seen as whole people in our actual complexities – as individuals, as women, as human – rather than as one of those problematic but familiar stereotypes provided in this society in place of genuine images of Black women. And I believe this holds true for the literatures of other women of Color who are not Black.

The literatures of all women of Color recreate the textures of our lives, and many white women are heavily invested in ignoring the real differences. For as long as any difference between us means one of us must be inferior, then the recognition of any difference must be fraught with guilt. To allow women of Color to step out of stereotypes is too guilt provoking, for it threatens the complacency of those women who view oppression only in terms of sex.

Refusing to recognize difference makes it impossible to see the different problems and pitfalls facing us as women.

Thus, in a patriarchal power system where whiteskin privilege is a major prop, the entrapments used to neutralize Black women and white women are not the same. For example, it is easy for Black women to be used by the power structure against Black men, not because they are men, but because they are Black. Therefore, for Black women, it is necessary at all times to separate the needs of the oppressor from our own legitimate conflicts within our communities. This same problem does not exist for white women. Black women and men have shared racist oppression and still share it, although in different ways. Out of that shared oppression we have developed joint defenses and joint vulnerabilities to each other that are not duplicated in the white community, with the exception of the relationship between Jewish women and Jewish men.

On the other hand, white women face the pitfall of being seduced into joining the oppressor under the pretense of sharing power. This possibility does not exist in the same way for women of Color. The tokenism that is sometimes extended to us is not an invitation to join power; our racial "otherness" is a visible reality that makes that quite clear. For white women there is a wider range of pretended choices and rewards for identifying with patriarchal power and its tools.

Today, with the defeat of ERA, the tightening economy, and increased conservatism, it is easier once again for white women to believe the dangerous fantasy that if you are good enough, pretty enough, sweet enough, quiet enough, teach the children to behave, hate the right people, and marry the right men, then you will be allowed to co-exist with patriarchy in relative peace, at least until a man needs your job or the neighborhood rapist happens along. And true, unless one lives and loves in the trenches it is difficult to remember that the war against dehumanization is ceaseless.

But Black women and our children know the fabric of our lives is stitched with violence and with hatred, that there is no rest. We do not deal with it only on the picket lines, or in dark midnight alleys, or in the places where we dare to verbalize our resistance. For us, increasingly, violence weaves through the daily tissues of our living – in the supermarket, in the classroom, in the elevator, in the clinic and the schoolyard, from the plumber, the baker, the saleswoman, the bus driver, the bank teller, the waitress who does not serve us.

Some problems we share as women, some we do not. You fear your children will grow up to join the patriarchy and testify against you, we fear our children will be dragged from a car and shot down in the street, and you will turn your backs upon the reasons they are dying.

The threat of difference has been no less blinding to people of Color. Those of us who are Black must see that the reality of our lives and our struggle does not make us immune to the errors of ignoring and misnaming difference. Within Black communities where racism is a living reality, differences among us often seem dangerous and suspect. The need for unity is often misnamed as a need for homogeneity, and a Black feminist vision mistaken for betrayal of our common interests as a people. Because of the continuous battle against racial erasure that Black women and Black men share, some Black women still refuse to recognize that we are also oppressed as women, and that sexual hostility against Black women is practiced not only by the white racist society, but implemented within our Black communities as well. It is a disease striking the heart of Black nationhood, and silence will not make it disappear. Exacerbated by racism and the pressures of powerlessness, violence against Black women and children often becomes a standard within our communities, one by which manliness can be measured. But these woman-hating acts are rarely discussed as crimes against Black women.

As a group, women of Color are the lowest-paid wage earners in america. We are the primary targets of abortion and sterilization abuse, here and abroad. In certain parts of Africa, small girls are still being sewed shut between their legs to keep them docile and for men's pleasure. This is known as female circumcision, and it is not a cultural affair as the late Jomo Kenyatta insisted, it is a crime against Black women.

Black women's literature is full of the pain of frequent assault, not only by a racist patriarchy, but also by Black men. Yet the necessity for and history of shared battle have made us, Black women, particularly vulnerable to the false accusation that antisexist is anti-Black. Meanwhile, woman-hating as a recourse of the powerless is sapping strength from Black communities, and our very lives. Rape is on the increase, reported and unreported, and rape is not aggressive sexuality, it is sexualized aggression. As Kalamuya Salaam, a Black male writer points out, "As long as male domination exists, rape will exist. Only women revolting and men made conscious of their responsibility to fight sexism can collectively stop rape."[1]

Differences between ourselves as Black women are also being misnamed and used to separate us from one another. As a Black lesbian feminist comfortable with the many different ingredients of my identity, and a woman committed to racial and sexual freedom from oppression, I find I am constantly being encouraged to pluck out some one aspect of myself and present this as the meaningful whole, eclipsing or denying the other parts of self. But this is a destructive and fragmenting way to live. My fullest concentration of energy is available to me only when I integrate all the parts of who I am, openly, allowing power from particular sources of my living to flow back and forth freely through all my different selves, without the restrictions of externally imposed definition. Only then can I bring myself and my energies as a whole to the service of those struggles which I embrace as part of my living.

A fear of lesbians, or of being accused of being a lesbian, has led many Black women into testifying against themselves. It has led some of us into destructive alliances, and others into despair and isolation. In the white women's communities, heterosexism is sometimes a result of identifying with the white patriarchy, a rejection of that interdependence between women-identified women which allows the self to be, rather than to be used in the service of men. Sometimes it reflects a die-hard belief in the protective coloration of heterosexual relationships, sometimes a self-hate which all women have to fight against, taught us from birth.

Although elements of these attitudes exist for all women, there are particular resonances of heterosexism and homophobia among Black women. Despite the fact that woman-bonding has a long and honorable history in the African and African American communities, and despite the knowledge and accomplishments of many strong and creative women-identified Black women in the political, social, and cultural fields, heterosexual Black women often tend to ignore or discount the existence and work of Black lesbians. Part of this attitude has come from an understandable terror of Black male attack within the close confines of Black society, where the punishment for any female self-assertion is still to be accused of being a lesbian and therefore unworthy of the attention or support of the scarce Black male. But part of this need to misname and ignore Black lesbians comes from a very real fear that openly women-identified Black women who are no longer dependent upon men for their self-definition may well reorder our whole concept of social relationships.

Black women who once insisted that lesbianism was a white woman's problem now insist that Black lesbians are a threat to Black nationhood, are consorting with the enemy, are basically un-Black. These accusations, coming from the very women to whom we look for deep and real understanding, have served to keep many Black lesbians in hiding, caught between the racism of white women and the homophobia of their sisters. Often, their work has been ignored, trivialized, or misnamed, as with the work of Angelina Grimke, Alice Dunbar-Nelson, Lorraine Hansberry. Yet women-bonded women have always been some part of the power of Black communities, from our unmarried aunts to the amazons of Dahomey.

And it is certainly not Black lesbians who are assaulting women and raping children and grandmothers on the streets of our communities.

Across this country, as in Boston during the spring of 1979 following the unsolved murders of twelve Black women, Black lesbians are spearheading movements against violence against Black women.

What are the particular details within each of our lives that can be scrutinized and altered to help bring about change? How do we redefine difference for all women? It is not our differences which separate women, but our reluctance to recognize those differences and to deal effectively with the distortions which have resulted from the ignoring and misnaming of those differences.

As a tool of social control, women have been encouraged to recognize only one area of human difference as legitimate, those differences which exist between women and men. And we have learned to deal across those differences with the urgency of all oppressed subordinates. All of us have had to learn to live or work or coexist with men, from our fathers on. We have recognized and negotiated these differences, even when this recognition only continued the old dominant/subordinate mode of human relationship, where the oppressed must recognize the masters' difference in order to survive.

But our future survival is predicated upon our ability to relate within equality. As women, we must root out internalized patterns of oppression within ourselves if we are to move beyond the most superficial aspects of social change. Now we must recognize differences among women who are our equals, neither inferior nor superior, and devise ways to use each other's difference to enrich our visions and our joint struggles.

The future of our earth may depend upon the ability of all women to identify and develop new definitions of power and new patterns of relating across difference. The old definitions have not served us, nor the earth that supports us. The old patterns, no matter how cleverly rearranged to imitate progress, still condemn us to cosmetically altered repetitions of the same old exchanges, the same old guilt, hatred, recrimination, lamentation, and suspicion.

For we have, built into all of us, old blueprints of expectation and response, old structures of oppression, and these must be altered at the same time as we alter the living conditions which are a result of those structures. For the master's tools will never dismantle the master's house.

As Paulo Freire shows so well in *The Pedagogy of the Oppressed*, the true focus of revolutionary change is never merely the oppressive situations which we seek to escape, but that piece of the oppressor which is planted deep within each of us, and which knows only the oppressors' tactics, the oppressors' relationships.

Change means growth, and growth can be painful. But we sharpen self-definition by exposing the self in work and struggle together with those whom we define as different from ourselves, although sharing the same goals. For Black and white, old and young, lesbian and heterosexual women alike, this can mean new paths to our survival.

We have chosen each other
and the edge of each others battles
the war is the same
if we lose someday
women's blood will congeal
upon a dead planet
if we win
there is no telling
we seek beyond history
for a new and more possible meeting.[2]

Notes

1 From "Rape: A Radical Analysis, An African-American Perspective," by Kalamuya Salaam, in *Black Books Bulletin*, vol. 6, no. 4 (1980).
2 Seabury Press, New York, 1970. From "Outlines," unpublished poem.

CHAPTER 9

"A Great Way to Fly": Nationalism, the State, and the Varieties of Third-World Feminism

Geraldine Heng

In this essay from the 1997 collection *Feminist Genealogies, Colonial Legacies, Democratic Futures*, edited by Jacqui Alexander and Chandra Talpade Mohanty, medievalist Geraldine Heng examines the conflict between traditional gender ideology and the movement for the liberation of women in Third World contexts.

Third-World feminism, by virtue of its vexed historical origins and complicated negotiations with contemporary state apparatuses, is necessarily a chimerical, hydra-headed creature, surviving in a plethora of lives and guises. In some countries, it may manifest itself as an organized national movement, complete with networks and regional chapters. In other countries, it may exist only as a kind of hit-and-run guerilla feminism: a feminism, perhaps, that arises spontaneously around issue-centered activity, that organizes itself in small, temporary neighborhood groupings which may eschew or refuse the name of feminism; or a feminism which piggybacks on that ubiquitous institution of the Third World, the nongovernmental organization (NGO). Third-World feminisms do not have the luxury of predictability; and a feminist theory that would be global in its compass, as in its intentions, must expect to be surprised by the strategies, appearance, and forms of feminism that emerge and are effective in Third-World contexts. As Third-World feminists themselves realize only too well, the difficulty of discussing Third-World feminism arises in the first instance as a difficulty of identifying the concretions and forms of effectivity in the Third World that can be grasped as feminist.

Whatever the particular shape of the local manifestations, however, all Third-World feminisms contend, in differing equations, with three principal factors that condition their emergence and survival. First, Third-World feminism is haunted by its historical origins, which continue to overshadow its character and future prospects. Historically, almost without exception, feminism has arisen in the Third World in tandem with nationalist movements – whether in the form of anticolonial/anti-imperialist struggles, national modernization and reform movements, or religious-nationalist cultural-nationalist revivalisms. Feminism has coexisted with these movements in a complicated relationship of sympathy and support, mutual use and mutual cooperation, and unacknowledged contestatory tension. As Kumari Jayawardena's

(1986) groundbreaking study of early feminisms in the Middle East, South, Southeast, and East Asia repeatedly attests, feminist movements in the Third World have almost always grown out of the same historical soil, and at a similar historical moment, as nationalism. However, because the contestatory nature of the relationship between feminism and nationalism remains underemphasized in scholarship on the subject, both at the historical origin of feminism and nationalism and today, the subtext of many an academic study on women and Third-World anti-imperialist struggle, national reform, or national liberation movements is also inadvertently the record of a triumphant nationalism that makes its gains and wins its accomplishments at the expense of a subordinated feminism.[1]

It is a truism that nationalist movements have historically supported women's issues as part of a process of social inclusion, in order to yoke the mass energy of as many community groups as possible to the nationalist cause (Anderson 1983). I would emphasize, however, that nationalist movements make common cause with women's issues and feminism equally because nationalism requires a certain self-representational vocabulary – a definitional apparatus to imagine and describe itself, to constitute itself ideologically, and to win an essential symbolic momentum. Throughout global history, with few exceptions, women, the feminine, and figures of gender, have traditionally anchored the nationalist imaginary – that undisclosed ideological matrix of nationalist culture. For example, at some point of their historical emergence, nations and nationalisms inevitably posit and naturalize a strategic set of relationships linking land, language, history, and people to produce a crucial nexus of pivotal terms – "motherland," "mother tongue," historical or traditional "mother culture," "founding fathers," etc. – that will hold together the affective conditions, the emotive core, of nationalist ideology and pull a collection of disparate peoples into a self-identified nation.[2] Women's issues do not only offer nationalist movements a vital social platform for the collective mobilization of multiple community groups. Female emancipation – a powerful political symbol describing at once a separation from the past, the aspirations of an activist present, and the utopia of an imagined national future – supplies a mechanism of self-description and self-projection of incalculably more than pragmatic value in the self-fashioning of nations and nationalisms.[3]

The manipulation of women's issues as an ideological and political resource in Third-World nationalist history commonly develops, in contemporary contexts, into the manipulation of women themselves as a socioeconomic resource in Third-World nation-states. While early Third-World feminism negotiated relations of mutual use and mutual contestation with early nationalism, contemporary Third-World feminism is forced to enter into and negotiate a more troubled, complex, and sometimes dangerous oppositional relationship to the contemporary Third-World state. The second factor, then, that impinges upon the character of feminism in the Third World is the presence, intervention, and role of the state itself. In contemporary Southeast Asia, the state, at its most benign, is a fiscal beneficiary of the exploitation of women, and, at its least benign, an active agent structuring the exploitation itself.

In Thailand and the Philippines, for instance, the state's GNP is bolstered substantially by prostitution, a growth industry that fuels the tourist trade, and sustains foreign exchange income. Thai NGOs estimate a growth figure of two million prostitutes by the year 2000, of which (with the intensifying fear of AIDS and the concomitant increased demand for virgins and children) as many as 800,000 would be children under fifteen years of age (Tan 1991). This spectacularly cynical form of female/child exploitation has perhaps been the most extensively studied of feminist issues: the critical nexus of state policy, foreign capital, banks, and the hotel-construction industry, that supports and encourages Thai prostitution, for example, has been cogently documented (Truong 1990). By contrast, the exportation of Filipino, Thai, Indonesian, Sri Lankan, and other female domestic workers to East Asian, Middle Eastern, and First-World destinations is only beginning to be studied. Yet, the Philippines exports 60,000 female domestic workers to Hong Kong alone, and reaps HK $1 billion annually from remittances these workers send back ("Filipino Senator Calls for Ban"); in Singapore, there were 65,000 foreign domestic workers in 1992 (Heyzer and Wee 1992). Host countries, like the countries of origin of the domestic workers, also profit from the expropriation of female domestic labor that is commonly left outside the purview of protective employment legislation. Singapore, for example, extracts a maid "levy" from the employers of domestic workers (since April 1991, S$300 per worker), a sum that is often greater than the wages the workers themselves earn. The Singapore government reaps S$234 million annually from the maid levy (Heyzer and Wee 1992), and a massive S$1.3 billion in 1992 from all foreign-worker levies ("Govt. Replies to MPs"). Malaysia expected to garner M$80 million from levies on foreign workers in 1992 ("Govt. Likely to Collect $48m"). More invisibly, but just as exploitatively, state-owned or state-affiliated airline industries throughout Southeast Asia (and South and East Asian countries) routinely sell the sexualized images and personal charm and services of their female flight attendants, in the highly competitive and highly profitable commercial air-travel market, through aggressive global marketing and media advertising, for the profit of the national coffers.

The forceful divergence of feminist and national interests in the Third World is further complicated by the looming and often interventionist role of the state as a regulatory, juridical, administrative, or military force in Third-World countries. Because governments in contemporary Southeast Asia exercise considerable control over public institutions and organizations within state boundaries, for instance, feminism often adapts by refusing to constitute feminist activity along formal lines. To evade state control, legislative interference, or other governmental regulatory activity, feminism in Southeast Asia has sometimes assumed the character of informal collectivities and local groups, existing humbly but usefully as small-scale feminisms.

A third factor mediating the adaptations and strategies of feminism in the Third World is the ambivalence of Third-World nations – and Third-World nationalism – to the advent of modernity. Perhaps because nationalism is itself of modern provenance or because the nation is a modern construct whose ideological bases must be continually renewed and secured, an attendant anxiety over modernity, particularly in the sociocultural register, is endemic in Third-World contexts. Even where a systemic transformation to modernity, in economic and social organization, is sought and implemented by nations and nationalisms in the Third World as a desideratum of development, a resistance to the totalizing implications of modernization is invariably sedimented at some juncture of the modernization process. Acceptance of modernity's incursions, then, comes to operate selectively: a division in the rhetoric of nationalist discourse appears, distinguishing between the technological and economic machinery of modernization (which can continue to be deemed useful, indeed, essential to the nation), and the cultural apparatus of modernization – the alarming detritus of modernity's social effects – which may be guarded against as contaminating, dangerous, and undesirable.[4] Correlatively, in countries where modernization or reform follows the nation's emergence from Western colonial subjection, or where a resurgent religious traditionalism is the dominant mode of nationalist culture, nationalist antipathy to modernity's social impact may be expressed as antipathy to the West and to Western cultural modalities. The ease with which, historically, the "modern" and the "Western" have been conflated and offered as synonymous, interchangeable counters in both nationalist and Orientalist discourse has meant that a nationalist accusation of modern and/or foreign – that is to say, Western – provenance or influence, when directed at a social movement, has been sufficient for the movement's delegitimization.

Given feminism's uneasy status in the Third World, its problematic relations with nationalism, and (like nationalism) its relatively brief genealogy, Third-World feminism has been especially liable to manipulation by nationalists for its symbolizing potential, as a capsule instance of the encroachment of modernity and/or Westernization. Just as women's issues, female emancipation, and feminism lend themselves to nationalist self-figuration at a given historical moment of nationalist formation, so do they lend themselves to the symptomatic figuration of nationalism's ambivalence to both modernity and the West. Antifeminist nationalists in Egypt and elsewhere in the Middle East, for instance, have historically represented feminism as the subversive figure, at once of a destabilizing modernity and of a presumptuous Western imperialism (Philipp 1978). Indeed, nationalism is so powerful a force in the Third World that to counter the charge of antinationalism – the assertion that feminism is of foreign origin and influence, and therefore implicitly or expressly antinational – the strategic response of a Third-World feminism under threat must be, and has sometimes been, to assume the nationalist mantle itself: seeking legitimation and ideological support in local cultural history, by finding feminist or protofeminist myths, laws, customs, characters, narratives, and origins in the national or communal past or in strategic interpretations of religious history or law. That is to say, through the glass of First-World feminisms, Third-World feminisms may appear to be willfully naïve, nativist, or essentialist in their ideological stakes: the requirement of an unexceptionable genealogy, history, or tradition for feminism must assume decisive priority.

In the section that follows, I track the vicissitudes and adaptations of feminism in one Southeast Asian country, focusing with particular, though not exclusive, emphasis on the postcolonial nation-state of Singapore.

A common denominator in the linked national histories of Singapore, Malaysia, and Indonesia is the appearance of feminism in dramatic concert with nationalism in anticolonial independence movements. Feminist women leaders arose who were also prominent nationalist political organizers; political parties on the left and the right articulated feminist goals in the anti-imperialist struggle, with the twin aims of mobilizing mass support and attaching to themselves a powerfully symbolic instrument of ideological self-description; women's groups were institutionalized that had formal affiliations to, or close informal ties with, national political parties; and, finally, all three countries witnessed the absorption of feminist leaders and feminist issues into political structures that dispersed and disengaged feminist interests in the postcolonial period.

In contrast to the history of feminism in Indonesia,[5] where the first institutional women's movements began as independent partners of nationalist organizations to which they were not initially subordinated, feminism in Singapore and Malaysia arose as a subset of nationalist politics, so that the hierarchical relationship of feminism to nationalism – an asymmetry of tension and use – was plainly visible from the outset. The two principal factions contesting for national political power in the wake of British colonial administration in Singapore – a Communist faction, later grouped as the Barisan Socialist, and social democrats organized as the People's Action Party, or PAP (which subsequently formed the postcolonial government that rules Singapore today) – both harnessed feminist issues to their national platforms. The first created a Singapore Women's Federation as a front organization for revolutionary activity, and the second sponsored a Women's League and women's subcommittees in 1956 under the direction of central PAP party leadership.[6]

By their own recorded account, the People's Action Party saw women's issues and feminist-activist women as a resource to be mined. A former Cabinet Minister notes in passing that "the Communists had recognized the potential of exploiting [the] injustice [suffered by women]" before the PAP had, "and were first in the field to organise women into their fold" (Ong 1979).[7] Significantly, the theme of female emancipation enabled the essentially reform-minded PAP, whose leadership was dominated by English-educated male elites, to present itself in powerfully revolutionary terms, the ideological resonance of which echoed and approximated the revolutionary discourse of their competitors, the Chinese-educated and China-backed Communists, whose own impetus and direction issued from the revolutionary politics of the People's Republic of China. In a section of the party's 1959 manifesto, *The Tasks Ahead: PAP's Five-Year Plan 1959–1964*, which originally appeared as a pre-election campaign speech by the most prominent woman feminist leader in the party, Chan Choy Siong, the theme of female emancipation is presented ringingly, in a reverberative vision of the imagined nation-to-be as a feminist-socialist utopia within a section entitled "Women in the New Singapore"[8]: "In a full socialist society, for which the P.A.P. will work for [*sic*], all people will have equal rights and opportunities, irrespective of sex, race or religion. There is no place in a socialist society for the exploitation of women."[9] The manifesto announces a feminist agenda in the declarative terms of social revolution:

We will encourage women to take an active part in politics. We will help them organise a unified women's movement to fight for women's rights. We will encourage women to play their proper part in Government administration. We will open up new avenues of employment for women. We will insist that the welfare of widows and orphans must be the responsibility of Government. We will insist that married women be given an opportunity to live a full life, including the right to work on level terms with others. Under the law maternity leave and allowances will be compulsory. The P.A.P. Government will establish more creches to look after children while mothers are at work. We will encourage factories employing large numbers of women to provide creches on factory sites. The present marriage laws which permit polygamy will be amended. The P.A.P. believes that a necessary condition for a stable home and family is monogamous marriage...it is essential that women and their families should be protected against unscrupulous husbands who treat their wives as chattels and abandon their children and families without any thought for their future. (*The Tasks Ahead*)[10]

PAP and Communist women worked to advance feminist and party goals without distinguishing between these interests, within the overarching frame and under the orders of their institutional organizations. A PAP-authorized history of the party, published in 1979, baldly chronicles the cooptation of women's energies for party purposes in the simple language of use: "The Women's League was active in rallying women members and supporters to campaign for the PAP.... They were especially effective in house to house canvassing, cooking food for Party workers, distributing leaflets, and providing speakers at rallies. The women worked as hard as the men and their contribution to the success of the Party was visible to all" (Ong 1979). After the PAP successfully wrested power and constituted a national government, Chan Choy Siong was sidelined in the Party. Unlike her male compatriots and peers, she was never destined to achieve Cabinet rank. In a parliament of eighty-one elected representatives in Singapore in 1993, among seventy-seven PAP Members of Parliament, two are women.[11] Once the PAP assumed national control, Communist women activists – more difficult to track because of their self-protective anonymity and their subsequent dispersal – were either forcibly deported to China and exiled or politically rehabilitated by the new national government; some went underground, slipping away to join the proscribed Malayan Communist Party (MCP), to wage guerilla warfare against the postcolonial governments of Singapore and Malaysia.[12]

In Malaysia, as in Singapore, the first women's political movement, Angkatan Wanita Sedar (AWAS, or the Movement of Conscious Women), would seem to have been created at the instigation of a nationalist political party. In 1945, Parti Kebangsaan Melayu Malaya (the PKMM, or Malay Nationalist Party) founded AWAS, as much because women were needed by the party as "to arouse in Malay women the consciousness of equal rights they have with men, to free them from old bonds of tradition and to socialize them'" (Dancz 1987). AWAS fell victim in the nationalist cause in 1948, proscribed by the British colonial administration.[13] Typically, AWAS's core leadership of politically active women – Malay women politicized by an early radical Islamic education in Indonesia in the 1930s, under Indonesian teachers active in the nationalist struggle against the Dutch colonial administration – were absorbed into women's sections of national political parties or the Communist underground (Dancz 1987; Karim 1983). Aishah Ghani, the first president of AWAS, became a member of the women's division of the United Malay Nationalist Organization (UMNO), the principal political party of the ruling National Front in postcolonial Malaysia, and eventually served as president of UMNO's second women's wing (Wanita UMNO) and Minister of Social Welfare in the Malaysian Cabinet. Sakinah Junid enlisted in the Pan-Malayan Islamic Party (PMIP) – now Parti Islam Se Malaya (PAS) – and later became president of Parti Islam's women's section, Dewan Muslimat; Samsiah Fakeh, the second president of AWAS, "continued her revolutionary struggles underground, working closely with the Malayan Communist Party" (Karim 1983).[14]

In Singapore, in 1961, the postindependence government formed by the People's Action Party passed legislation addressing the legal rights of women and children, in partial fulfillment of campaign pledges to feminist nationalists and female voters. This legislative document, known as the Women's Charter, synchronously enfranchised women and produced, effectually, a legal definition of feminine identity codified around marriage, divorce, and relationship to children, as much as it also ruled in other matters on women's status as individual citizens. The Charter, in effect, legislated a description of female identity by establishing legal responses to a wide-ranging set of presumptive questions (What is a woman? What does she need? What is the nature/what are the conditions of her sexuality? What is her place? What is the place of her relationships to others?). In thus specifying legal conditions pertaining specially to women and children – awarding, in that process, rights that were un-questionably vital, indeed, essential to women at the time – the Charter also enacted and codified a description of women as specially gendered subjects under the law, a sexualized codification directed specially to the state's female citizens.[15] No compar-able legislation exists that describes the configuration or borders of masculine iden-tity under the law.

Historically, the enactment of the Women's Charter was simultaneously an enfran-chising and a disenfranchising moment for feminists. After the establishment of the Charter, it was widely felt that there were "no more problems" confronting women,[16] because the most urgent and dramatic inequities had been addressed. Men and women alike felt that Singaporean women, unlike women in other Third-World nations, had no need of feminism or a feminist movement, and until the 1980s, women's groups in Singapore assumed the form of recreational, athletic, or cultural clubs, charity or professional associations, and social work and community service organizations – a voluntary or involuntary playing-out, at the community level, of the authorized identities established for women under the law.

The production and legitimation of particular feminine identities – commonly an implicit, more than an explicit, process – is of enduring importance to contemporary Third-World states. A dramatic example is the (re)donning of the *hijab* or veil by Muslim women in the Middle East, signalling the deployment of a traditional femi-nine identity as a powerfully symbolic icon of Islamic cultural nationalism.[17] In Singapore, in 1983, the very survival of the nation was presented as hingeing on the production of appropriate kinds of feminine identity when Prime Minister Lee Kuan Yew raised the specter of a dystopian national future that would unfold if well-educated women willfully continued to refuse to marry and reproduce children in numbers adequate to the maintenance of class and racial elites (Heng and Devan 1992). States also profit from the manipulation of women and feminine identity as an economic resource: the production of a sexualized femininity as a commodity for negotiation and trading in the profitable, if competitive, air-travel-services market in Asia underscores the necessarily oppositional relationship between feminist interests and state-sponsored descriptions of the national interest in the contemporary Third World.[18]

Singapore, in particular, has exploited a sexualized Asian femininity to sell the services of its national air carrier, Singapore Airlines (SIA), with incomparably spec-tacular commercial success.[19] So globally familiar is the airline's "Singapore Girl" – never a "woman," and certainly no mere "flight attendant," but "a great way to fly," as every male business traveler around the world knows – that Madame Tussaud's of London, when it "wanted to feature a figure from air travel" among its waxworks, "found the Singapore Girl to be the most recognizable air travel figure in the world today" (Lee 1993). That the image of the Singapore woman which the airline and the state sell on the air services market is a sexual one is readily attested to. Singapore law courts recently tried a rash of sexual-molestation cases, where male air passengers of varied descriptions, races, and national origins had apparently found it impossible to resist fondling or otherwise sexually handling stewardesses on SIA flights. Indeed, so successful at evocation is the soft-focus image of the "Singapore Girl" in her figure-hugging, Pierre Balmain-designed *sarong kebaya*, that a bar-cum-brothel in Thailand was reported to have clad its hostesses in copycat imitations of the SIA flight uniform (Tan 1991).[20]

Singapore is not, however, unique among Third-World states in touting and marketing the serviceability of its women and a fantasmatic Asian femininity. A recent multipart feature in the *Asia Magazine* (16–18 August 1991) admiringly reports how Thailand, Malaysia, the Philippines, and Indonesia all exploit, with varying degrees of success, a calculated image of their female citizens to promote national airline industries. Playing to a fantasy of what Asian women are putatively like, the countries describe the romantic sexuality, exoticism, beauty, youth, and charm of their female flight attendants, and the women's innate, instinctual desire to please and serve. The phenomenon of trading in feminine identity is commonplace in Asia; any cursory survey of the advertising of other Asian carriers will disclose the extent to which Third-World nations in the East casually sell the sexualized images and personal services of their female national subjects on the world market.[21]

That the legitimation of some feminine identities over others can be a matter of considerable national profit and national interest in the Third-World state is clear from this commercial equation. In Singapore, the proven and continuing success of the national carrier's advertising campaigns is propped upon an exploitation of the discourse of Orientalism, a Western discourse which the Eastern state rides in its flawless manipulation of a projected feminine image. In the course of that manipulation, an exemplary collusion is put in place between postcolonial state corporatism (SIA as a government-affiliated national carrier) and neocolonial Orientalist discourse on the serviceability and exoticism of the Asian woman: a collusion that produces, through the *techne* of transnational global advertising and marketing, a commercial enterprise generating substantial fiscal surpluses, and vindicated at the outset as nationalist. For the nationalist credentials of this particular project of antifeminist exploitation are never in doubt. Corporate and marketing executives of Singapore Airlines and the carrier's advertising agency, the Batey Group, when condescending to defend their marketing strategies to Singapore feminists, have instinctively tricked themselves out in nationalist drag.

More recently, the editor of the *Straits Times*, the country's principal English-language daily newspaper, insinuated a suggestion that attempts by Western nations to spread the values of liberal democracy, human rights, and civil liberties to developing nations may be driven, sinisterly, by a covert desire to weaken the economic competitiveness of the Third World. Festooning himself with the impeccable nationalist credentials of state-sponsored sexism, the editor smirked: "Younger Singaporeans should think hard before they lap up whatever is in vogue. . . . Is the Singapore Girl really a sexist symbol that ought to be replaced or would agitation on this issue erode Singapore Airlines' competitive edge? They would do well to remember that competition between nations can only hot up, and that losers will be left by the wayside." The accompanying cartoon illustrating the editor's contentions featured a set of posters on a barbed-wire fence representing the constitutive barrier of a Western checkpoint on the correctness of the political record of developing nations. One of the posters demands the presentation of a human-rights record; on another poster is emblazoned "Women's Rights Charter." Surreptitiously, the illustration and the newspaper columnist tap a reservoir of Third-World suspicion at the multifariousness of Western imperialisms, and clearly, feminism and human rights are here offered as imperialisms of the economically corrosive, objectionably vogueish kind.[22]

By contrast, Malaysian feminists note the more explicit and direct depiction of feminism by Islamic nationalists in Malaysia as a pernicious species of cultural infiltration – as a foreign, Western, and modern encroachment that symbolizes the many encroachments that have undermined Malay Muslim culture from the beginning of colonization:

> The massive recruitments of Malaysian women into [the *dakwa* Islamic movement] is perceived . . . to be part of a re-education or resocialization process, whereby women can be rescued from the throes of Westernization that have permeated Malay culture from the beginning of colonialism to the present . . . These community movements are a powerful instrumental force in projecting feminism as a component of Western liberalism which has no niche in Eastern cultures. (Karim 727)

One feminist response to the imputation by Malay Islamic nationalists that feminism is Western, antitraditional, or secular in its origins and nature, has been to cite contemporary feminist Islamic exegetes on the Qu'rän who offer rereadings of that sacred text as authorizing the equality of men and women.[23] Another feminist strategy in Southeast Asia has also been to suggest a local genealogy for feminism, by pointing to notable women figures in communal or national history and folklore. In the Philippines, for instance, there were "pre-Spanish priestesses or *katalonans* . . . heroines of the Spanish revolution, the women leaders of the Japanese occupation" (Shahani 1975); in Vietnam, there were the feminist Ho Xuan Huong and folkloric resistance fighters like the Trung sisters and Trieu Thi Trinh, or Doan Thi Diem, and Bui Thi Xuan[24] (Marr 1976); Singapore had the community-founding matriarch Yang Meleking (Wee 1987); and "the traditionally high status of women" in the Southeast Asian region's past, particularly before colonization, is frequently cited (Shahani 1975).[25]

However partial or interstitial such efforts, the fundamentally oppositional relations between the interests of the state and those of feminism in the contemporary Third World makes dangerous the total abandonment of nationalist discourse, of any variety, to the exclusive monopoly of the state. In Singapore, the state's successful combination of nationalist discourse – in particular, the discourse of national survival and of approved forms of political participation – together with a formidable array of instrumentalities and apparatuses of power at the state's disposal, has determined the very nature and horizon of possibility for feminist activism.

In May 1987, twenty-two persons were arrested by the Singapore government under the powers granted by the Internal Security Act, as part of a putative "Marxist conspiracy" ostensibly threatening the state and national interests. Among the political prisoners were two founder-members of the Association of Women for Action and Research (AWARE), a vigorous feminist organization then practicing critique and activism on a variety of fronts. A number of other founder-members were convinced that they had themselves either narrowly escaped detention, or were yet vulnerable to arbitrary seizure. The government immediately disseminated propaganda justifying the arrests and proceeded to ban or dismantle community activist groups it identified as Marxist- or left-oriented. Shocked, perhaps, into a sense of immediate vulnerability, or possibly convinced of a threat to its legitimacy and survival, AWARE was silent on the arrests, took no stand on the political prisoners, and issued no statements on its imprisoned founder-members. The two women, with the other prisoners, were detained without trial and subjected to physical and psychological abuse. One of them was subsequently rehabilitated, and released after a public confession and renunciation of politics; the other eventually fled to self-exile in the United Kingdom.[26]

The arrest of its founder-members proved to be a watershed in the self-defined role and activism of AWARE. Created in December 1985 by a group of feminist women whose political opinions ranged from ideological left to liberal center, AWARE, unlike other women's groups in Singapore, had a reputation for being confrontational and critical, its politics "vociferous." In recent years, however, AWARE's public profile has quietly altered, and the organization has come to emphasize community and welfare services to women, rather than critique. Its current commitments include a scheme for loans to women "to prevent women from falling into the hands of loan sharks" (Chau 1992), and a telephone "Helpline" that women can call for advice and counseling on a range of problems, including "marital difficulties," "issues such as male–female relationships," "family sexuality, mental health problems, violence against women, work-related issues and medical matters" (AWARE round-up 1993, 39). In 1992, its executive director was quoted as saying that "the association's main emphasis now is research" ("Winning by Persuasion" 1993), and AWARE's president in 1992–93 was quoted in a women's fashion magazine as saying that she preferred the term "woman centredness" to describe her commitment, rather than the term "feminism," because "feminism is a lonely cause. You are always met with disagreement and disfavour."[27]

Whatever the organization's self-definition today, the work that AWARE undertakes is excellent feminist work in the context of Singapore society. Many of the organization's projects are identifiably if quietly feminist: its Helpline is a version of a battered-women's emergency hotline; it organizes reading and discussion sessions for children on gender roles, workshops for women on a variety of subjects, support groups, free legal consultation sessions, and a reading circle and film nights to discuss women's issues. AWARE's research projects and publications target women in the workplace and childcare facilities, information-gathering on women and health, child education and gender socialization issues, and the generation of feminist literary and discursive materials. In reporting on the organization's current projects, AWARE's mailings to members disclose that the organization works for social change by appealing to, negotiating with, and petitioning various government bodies invisibly, behind the scenes.

That is to say: AWARE's varied activities share the common factor of emphasizing service, information, and support, while avoiding analysis and engagement of a directly and stringently political kind. In particular, the organization avoids engagement with subjects that would be deemed sensitive or suspect by the Singapore government. These would include all issues of race, class, ethnicity, and sexual preference; the identification of structural and systemic, rather than contingent, inequities in society; the analysis of state apparatuses of power in the lives of Singapore women; and, indeed, government policies and positions on controversial issues of national importance, including a national population policy thinly premised on a form of social eugenics (Heng and Devan 1992). In the voiding of controversy, then, AWARE in effect requires itself to practice a form of feminism that is ironically evacuated of political content. It is a feminism, moreover, that must of necessity disengage itself from all recognition of difference, all social fronts, beyond the single focal point of gender; a feminism that must look past race, class, ethnicity, and sexuality; ignore the operations of ideology, of transnational collusions, and of technologies and instrumentalities of power; and blind itself to the controlling and manipulative force of state institutions; a feminism that must, in short, bracket off and put aside the varied discursivities, categories of difference, and totalizing institutions that crisscross and intersect with gender in the real world.

Indeed, Article 23 (e) of the constitution of AWARE, in compliance with legislation governing the formation and activities of societies in Singapore, explicitly prohibits the organization from involvement in the political: "The Society shall not indulge in any political activity or allow its funds and/or premises to be used for political purposes."[28] Implicit in this formulation is the understanding that what constitutes "political activity," and what defines a purpose as "political," will, in the context of Singapore – given the history of the Singapore government's use of its powers for political detention – be decided upon contingently, from moment to moment, by the state as it sees fit.[29]

Despite the carefully noncritical face of feminism in Singapore, however, the PAP moved to establish a Women's Wing within its own party in 1989, ostensibly in order to "help raise public awareness about women's issues" – some fourteen years after the PAP's Women's Affairs Bureau had become defunct. The move, in effect, added the Party's presence to the extant women's groups in Singapore, a presence through which the Party apparently hoped to wrest the initiative and ground – as well as public attention – on women's issues. Sensing a potential risk in the divergence of feminist interests from state interests, even in the light of the peaceable activities among women's groups in Singapore, the government moved to co-opt organizational energies nationally, by constituting, as before, a feminist group of sorts under its own party banner.[30] Unlike the fiery manifesto of 1959, however, the PAP's public statement on the Wing details, in no uncertain terms, the subordination of the Wing's semifeminist interests to the party and party-defined national interests. "The Wing," the Party declared, rather than constituting "a women's lobby group" or "pressure group," would instead "help Singaporean women become better informed about national issues." Chief among its charges would be the duty of "familiarizing members with the PAP philosophy, the role of women in politics, the national budget, health and other issues" ("PAP's Women's Wing" 1992). The year after its inception, the Wing was assigned by the PAP leadership "the task of looking into a proposal to set up a family services centre to coordinate welfare programmes for the needy" ("Women's Wing to Study" 1990); in 1993, Prime Minister Goh Chok Tong, responding to a suggestion that a Women's Affairs Bureau be reestablished in the Party, remarked that such a bureau, if formed, "should not confine itself to tackling 'women's problems.' Instead, it would have to address family and social problems as well" ("Worrying Trends" 1993). The Party today continues to assign a rag-bag of duties and tasks to its Women's Wing, most of which, true to the received notions established by the Women's Charter, of what constitutes women's concerns and issues, concentrates on the provision of service to others, notably children, families, and the poor.

In June 1993, two books commissioned by the Women's Wing, addressing the status of women in Singapore, were publicly launched. The texts, one academic and the other popular, offer the most feminist of the Wing's articulated positions on women in Singapore, and perhaps express the extent of what might be hoped for from a government-authorized, state-managed, and party-directed "women's movement" in the Third World. A newspaper article, reporting on the books' contents, mistily notes: "Realities of gender differences are implicitly acknowledged, there is pride in past achievements, hope in looking ahead and a gentle prodding for more attention to be paid to the inequalities and challenges that remain" ("Story of the Singapore Woman" 1993). For all the misty hopefulness palpable in the equating of "inequalities" with "challenges," however, the launching of the books was used, with brutal irony, as an occasion for the current Prime Minister of Singapore to reiterate the accusations directed against women by his predecessor ten years before. Highly educated women, Prime Minister Goh noted pointedly, were still not reproducing babies at a rate adequate to the maintenance of class elites. This, he implied, was a women's issue of the utmost urgency.[31] Without any apparent consciousness of insult or irony, or even condescension, the Prime Minister went on to close the issue of gender inequalities in Singapore: "While some differences remained in the way men and women were treated, such as in the country's immigration laws, these were products of the largely patriarchal society here and would have to be accepted, he said" ("Worrying Trends" 1993).[32]

The PAP's attempt to coopt feminism to subserve the party's political purposes, state legislation prohibiting registered organizations from activity that might be construed as "political," even the arrest of individual feminists under the Internal Security Act in Singapore – all these events inscribe relatively dulcet moments in the history and fortunes of Third-World feminism. Saskia Wieringa, charting the history of the Indonesian left-feminist organization Gerakan Wanita Indonesia (or GERWANI), a movement whose membership in 1965 comprised 1.5 million people, records the starkest possible fate for institutional feminism in the Third World when she details the organization's destruction by the Indonesian military government, and the torture, brutalization, and demonization of GERWANI women. Indeed, the array of hazards confronting feminism in the Third World is instructive. Because of the vast instrumentalities that range from preventive or punitive legislation to military or police intervention – and because an institutionalized feminist movement draws attention to itself and appears to the state to possess a capacity, incipient or actual, for the exertion of pressure on national political culture – successful forms of feminism in the Third World have sometimes been informal, unobtrusive, small-scale feminisms.[33] Feminist scholars observe that some of the most effective feminist groups in Southeast Asia – effective in the constituencies of women they reach, their commitment to critical and transformative work, and their empowerment of women at the grassroots level – are often not even registered organizations as such (Heyzer 1986). Many are simply "small groups of women, made up frequently of trusted friends," though these groups may be "more or less aware of one another" and may "exist within networks" (128). Organizing women in poor communities, rural villages, plantations, or city squatter areas in Malaysia, the Philippines, and Thailand, these feminists work with local women in order ultimately to "phase themselves out of... leadership positions as the local women become more confident" (128). In a different locality of the Third World, Peruvian feminists have concluded that, as Saskia Wieringa notes, "it is not necessary to join in a large-scale movement... you can work in a much more fruitful way in small autonomous groups" (Wieringa 1988).

The relative safety or success of small-scale feminist activism in the Third World should not, however, be overemphasized. In Singapore, from 1982 to 1987, guerilla feminisms of precisely this nature existed: informal collectivities of women supported and aided domestic workers abused by employers, offered legal services in working-class districts to prostitutes and disenfranchised others, conducted social analysis and critique through community theater and drama, met to discuss, educate, critique and transform on a variety of fronts. In many ways, the organization which became AWARE was forged in that critical matrix of repeated, issue-specific, local interventions. Nevertheless, this feminist network of small groups was inexorably dismantled when the Singapore government banned a number of community networks in 1987, in the name of an alleged plot against the state.

No variety of feminism in the Third World, then, is secure from the intervention of the state, nor from the power of any who are able to wield the discourse of nationalism with unchallenged authority. The history of feminism in Singapore, as elsewhere, has been instructive. Rights historically granted to women by patriarchal authority in order to accomplish nationalist goals and agendas do not necessarily constitute acts of feminism, though as practices of power, the granting of such rights may function, both initially and today, to the very real advantage of women. In contrast, rights seized upon and practices initiated by women in the pursuit of their imagined collective interest, even if – like the work of AWARE and others – such practices and acts seem only uncomfortably or unfamiliarly to fit received descriptions of feminism, are indisputably feminist practices. For in Third-World states, ultimately, all feminisms are at risk; all must write their own scripts and plot their continuing survival from moment to moment. It is a profound tribute to feminist resourcefulness and tenacity that varieties of feminism continue to survive and proliferate in the multiple localities of the Third World today.[34]

Notes

This article could not have been completed without the help of Suporn Arriwong, a student of exemplary resourcefulness and a friend of remarkable generosity. Sarinah Terimo, Merilyn Ellorin, and Agnes Tan all lent useful research assistance. Shaan Heng-Devan provided the necessary impetus for the article's completion, and Janadas Devan, in his role as best and most helpful critic, offered a soberingly incisive, essential critique.

1   See, for instance, Marr (1975) on the history of nationalism and feminism in Vietnam; Croll (1978) on the historical record in the People's Republic of China; Vreede-de Stuers (1960) on Indonesian anticolonial history; and individual articles in the excellent collections by Beck and Keddie (1978) and Kandiyoti (1991), documenting women's movements and issues in the Middle East and the Islamic world. More recent scholarship has begun to correct the under-emphasis; see, for example, Chatterjee (1989), Halliday (1991), and Katrak (1992). Enloe (1989) offers an instance of an explicit discussion of the contest between feminism and nationalism not only in the Third World but equally in First-World national history (54).

2   As a meaningful narrative, nationalism attains much of its emotive power – and considerable oppositional force in independence struggles – by that specific invocation of imagined (and imaginary) relations between land, language, people, and history. The would-be nation is represented, perhaps, as a cherished "motherland" to be protected and renewed; an essential "mother tongue" is recovered and promulgated in the nationalist cause; or a selective configuration of womanhood,

or traditional "mother culture," is posited, then defended, by those who eventually become the "founding fathers" of the nation (which is subsequently "born"). Inevitably, the nationalist invocation of discriminate figures produces a disposition of use, and of power, that is gendered and sexualized – with the feminine being positioned as a crucial foundational term and a resource to be fought over for possession, definition, and control. By way of example, Marr notes that in Vietnam in 1926, the protonationalist author Trinh Dinh Ru urged Vietnamese children to "love our country in the same way as we love our mother," adding, "We are born in Vietnam, making Vietnam our Mother country. Those who keep on referring to France as the Mother Country are really wrong! Only French people can properly call France the Mother Country" (379).

3   In Vietnam, by 1945, Marr observes, "Equal rights for women, and the contributions of women to the new society, served as powerful – perhaps essential – weapons in the post-1945 Resistance War" (371).

4   Partha Chatterjee argues convincingly that modernity can be made "consistent with the nationalist project" also through the institution of a principle of selection that separates the "domain of culture into two spheres": a "material" sphere, or public life, where Westernization may be tolerated, and a "spiritual" sphere, constituted mainly as the private, domestic space inhabited and figured by women, where the encroachments of modernity must be warded off, to preserve a traditional national culture (237–9).

5   On the long and complex history of feminism and nationalism in Indonesia, too tortuous to rehearse here, see Vreede-de Stuers (1960), and Wieringa (1988).

6   Women's groups of other kinds, formed by a tiny minority of English-educated, middle- and upper-middle-class women, also existed in the 1950s. These included a professional association (the Professional Women's Association), a league of voters (the Singapore League of Women Voters), and the Singapore Council of Women (SCW), formed in 1952 by an Iranian woman, Shirin Fozdar. The SCW, under a "committee of fifteen middle-aged wives of wealthy men" (Lim 1984/85, 47) and the dynamic Shirin Fozdar, appealed without success to the British colonial administration and to local political figures for advocacy on issues such as polygamy, concubinage, and marital-status laws (Lim 1984/85, 46–51). None of these groups had the membership base, the mass appeal, or the capacity for mobilization demonstrated by the nationalist and revolutionary women's groups.

7   Ong, Pang Boon. 1979. "Problems of Part Organisation: The Pro-Communist Challenge from Within 1954–57." In *People's Action Party 1954–1979: Petir 25th Anniversary Issue*. Singapore: Central Executive Committee People's Action Party, pp. 44–59. Dennis Bloodworth, a British journalist domiciled in Singapore, chronicles his first encounter with the ranks of Communist women thus: "When I attended my first anti-colonial rally in Singapore in 1956, the rows of grim, bespectacled female faces beneath dead straight fringes that could have been chopped with shears had me swivelling nervously in my seat to check the exits" (1986, 100). It is, of course, a cliché of Hollywood and Western Orientalist discourse, that Communists and Chinese – unlike the strongly individualized Western hero – are uniformly homogeneous and undifferentiated people, an undiversified "yellow peril," as it were.

8   Chan Choy Siong instituted the Women's League in the PAP. In the 1959 General Elections, the PAP fielded Chan Choy Siong, Ho Puay Choo, Oh Su Chen, Fung Yin Ching, and Sahorah binte Ahmat, all of whom campaigned on women's issues and were successfully elected in their constituencies. All the Chinese women were Chinese-dialect or Mandarin speakers, able to appeal to the public at a grassroots level, and specifically to women in the majority Chinese-speaking population. Kwa Geok Choo, the wife of the man who became Singapore's first Prime Minister, Lee Kuan Yew, was deployed by the party to canvass English-speaking women voters, and made a single speech over Radio Singapore in 1959 on women's issues.

9   By contrast, Article 12 of the Constitution of the Republic of Singapore, in guaranteeing the rights of citizens, no longer makes mention of equality of gender: "There shall be no discrimination against citizens of Singapore on the ground only of religion, race, descent or place of birth in any law or in the appointment of any office or employment under a public authority or in the administration of any law relating to the acquisition, holding or carrying on of any trade, business, profession, vocation or employment." Discrimination in employment on the basis of

gender is thus constitutionally legal in Singapore, despite the express declaration of the PAP manifesto of 1959 that "The P.A.P. believes in the principle of equal pay for equal work" (17). A publication of the Singapore Association of Women Lawyers (SAWL) accordingly warns women that "it is not unlawful for a person to refuse to employ you merely on the ground that you are a woman (who may get married, or are already married and have a child or children). It is also not unlawful for a person to refuse to promote you or refuse to send you for training merely on the ground that you are a woman. Because the law is silent, you have no right to equal pay for equal work" (*Legal Status of Singapore Women*, 30). Special provisions in the Constitution also secure citizenship status for the children of male Singapore citizens, when the children are born outside Singapore, but not for the children of female citizens (*Legal Status of Singapore Women*, 20).

10 In contrast to this declaration of 1959, the Prime Minister of Singapore, Goh Chok Tong, was quoted in a 1993 newspaper report as saying that "it is neither possible nor wise to have complete equality of the sexes.... Some differences between the sexes were a product of the society here and would have to be accepted." The report continues: "The Prime Minister argued that minor areas where women were not treated in the same way as men should be expected in a largely patriarchal society.... Mr. Goh said that these differences should not be regarded as 'pockets of discrimination.'" Instead, they were "anthropological asymmetries" or products of the society's traditions. "In other words, these differences have to be accepted" ("Worrying Trends" 1993). Goh's predecessor, Prime Minister Lee Kuan Yew, in 1983, in an exhibition of distress over falling birth rates among highly-educated elites in Singapore, speculated thoughtfully on the possibility of reintroducing polygamy (i.e., polygyny) as a possible solution (see Heng and Devan 1992, 249).

11 One of the six Nominated Members of Parliament – nonconstituency and nonelected MPs who are formally "nominated" by a majority in Parliament to serve as MPs – is, however, a woman. Kanwaljit Soin, a former president of the Association of Women for Action and Research (AWARE) and a dedicated feminist, announced, on acceptance of her nomination, that she would make women her special constituency or electoral "ward." A newspaper columnist observes that from 1970 to 1984 there were no women MPs whatsoever in Parliament, a record that was breached only in 1984, when three women PAP MPs were elected (Henson 1993).

12 For his unauthorized history of Singapore, Dennis Bloodworth successfully interviewed a handful of former Communist women, whom he mentions by name and sobriquet: Linda Chen [Mock Hock], "Sweegor," "Sister Fong," and the "the Red Ballerina" (Goh Lay Kuan).

13 Wazir-jahan Karim, director of the KANITA Project, a women's studies program in Malaysia, considers AWAS a separate organization from PKMM, assigning the impetus for its creation not to "the Executive Committee of the MNP under its [male] president, Dr. Burhanuddin [Helmi]," but to AWAS's core women leaders, Aishah Ghani, Sakinah Junid, and Samsiah Fakeh, with "warm support and encouragement from members of the Malay National Party (PKMM)" [Karim 1983, 722]. Even by this alternative account of its origin, AWAS would seem to have been a strongly nationalist organization, one that saw feminist advocacy in the context of national responsibilities, as its second president, Samsiah Fakeh, made plain: "If the women have sufficient amount of grey matter to see and understand the problems of the country and possess the capacity to realize the significance of their responsibility; if men are born with equal rights; if the world is stepping toward a more stable and sound democratic regime; there is no justifiable excuse for the women being denied their rights in determining internal and external policies when the consequences of such decisions are to be shouldered by both" (Dancz 1987, 86, 87).

14 Karim has argued that the "phenomenal expansion of the political party system in the pre- and immediate post-independence period" in Malaysia co-opted feminist energies and directions after the demise of AWAS, channeling activist women into "formal structures of institutionalized political membership" (Karim 1983, 726) and "government-initiated women's movements like Wanita Umno and KEMAS" (the People's Progress Movement). Here they

play "supporting roles in male-dominated organizations and institutions" (729), but remain essentially "female functionaries" (722, 728). It is "within the women's division of the major political parties that feminist leaders attempt to draw attention to women's issues and rights, though problems relating to sexual discrimination in wages and employment or political under-representation are seldom highlighted or seriously discussed. They generally broach topics of women's welfare, morals and family needs which do not contravene socially acceptable norms and values" (726). The problem of government-sponsored "feminism" and women's groups is discussed below in the context of Singapore.

15 Indeed, much of the Charter extends over what might be called the territory of the sexual: conditions of legal marriage, separation, and divorce; rights and duties of spouses, the welfare of children, and wife and child maintenance; laws pertaining to prostitution, brothels, sexual offenses, intercourse with female minors, etc. Nonsexualized items in the Charter include the right to hold, inherit, and alienate property; to engage in a profession, trade, or social activity; to sue and be sued in one's own name; to enter into contracts on one's own, etc. Interestingly, in the configuration of feminine identity produced by the Charter, a woman has the legal right to retain her personal name and family name after marriage, but the Charter does not protect her right to assign her family name to her children, if she so chooses. The Registration of Births and Deaths Act, Chapter 267, Section 10, awards only fathers the right to transmit their surname to children born in legal marriage. The Charter's provisions do not apply, moreover, to Muslim women in Singapore. Marriage, divorce, and inheritance laws for Muslims fall under the purview of the *shariah* courts.

16 A newspaper report on the 1983 launching of two books commissioned by the PAP's Women's Wing, typically begins, "Singapore women have it good." It continues, "Everything changed after the 1961 Women's Charter.... In the wake of the adjustments following that legislation, women have enjoyed equal rights in nearly every area" ("Story of the Singapore Woman," 1993). While the Women's Charter was undeniably a remarkably progressive document for its time, its institution did not prevent the Singapore government itself from enacting inequities against women. Among these are: medical benefits for the children and spouse of male, but not female government employees; a quota for medical training at university level which only admits one woman for every two men; and altered admissions criteria to the National University of Singapore from 1983, when it was discovered that, because of superior academic performance, increased numbers of women were annually being admitted over men to the university.

17 It is worth repeating that all nationalisms seem to require, for their self-description and ideological imperatives, the production and manipulation of feminine identity. Islamic cultural nationalism is no exception: A recent *Newsweek* article ("The Trials of Muslim Europe") on Islamic cultural nationalism in Europe in the 1990s was typically accompanied by a powerfully symbolic photograph of veiled Muslim women in a street march, carrying a banner depicting a veiled woman cradling a peace dove in her hands, and a placard with the blazon, "Le 'Hijab' est notre honneur" prominently displayed. Beck and Keddie (1978, 13) note, in an excellent discussion, that the reproduction of neotraditionalist forms of feminine identity is mitigated where left movements are also active in nationalist struggles, an observation that is more fully developed in Molyneux's (1991) impressive study of legal reforms in socialist Yemen. That the donning of the veil does not, however, automatically signify a retrogressive resubordination of women has of course been argued repeatedly by Third-World feminists. For an instance of the veil's usefulness to Southeast Asian Muslim women – Malay factory workers in Malaysia negotiating complex new economic, sexual, and social identities – see Aihwa Ong (1987, 136 *et passim*).

18 National carriers in Southeast Asia are typically state-owned, state-managed, or government-linked institutions. PT Garuda Indonesia (slated to be privatized in late 1996 or in 1997, according to the Indonesian Transport Minister) is owned and managed by the state; Thai Airways International, Philippine Airlines, and Singapore Airlines are partly privatized, with the government as direct or indirect majority shareholder. Until January 1993, the commander-in-chief of the Thai air force was also chairman of Thai International's board of directors,

while the chairman of Singapore Airlines is the current Permanent Secretary of the Ministry of National Development in Singapore.

19 SIA's annual report for 1990–91, for instance, lamenting the slowdown of the global economy, especially in Australia, North America, and the United Kingdom, and the escalation of fuel prices as a result of the Gulf War, recorded the "significantly lower" profit before tax of $1.16 billion, "down 19.2% from 1989–90" (65). Air traffic to Europe, the Americas, and Australia contributed 64.5 percent of the airline's income in 1990–91 (69).

20 Reports in the *Straits Times* have described the molesters as Americans, Germans, British, Australians, Japanese, and Sri Lankans, holding such occupations as businessmen, oil riggers, metal workers, divers, supervisors, etc. The sexual fondling of the flight attendants by male passengers has become so notorious a problem that a *Straits Times* columnist was moved to wonder if it might be "the free flow of liquor" on SIA flights that is responsible for the harassment (Tan 1993).

21 Troung (1990, 179) quotes typical advertising copy for Thai Airways: "Smooth as silk is a beautifully prepared meal by a delicious hostess"; "Some say it's our beautiful wide-bodied DC-10s that cause so many heads to turn at airports throughout the world. We think our beautiful slim-bodied hostesses have a lot to do with it." A random sampling of print ads in Asian periodicals confirms the directional drift. An Asiana ad (featuring a nude woman wrapped in a transparent cape with the colours of the airline's logo) offers "the charms and softness of our Asiana girls . . . happily ironing out all the little wrinkles of business travel, just for you." A Pakistan International ad gushes: "Our air hostesses have an unfair advantage. They begin their training years ahead of others . . . in Pakistan, all girls are schooled at home in the art of hospitality." Indeed, not only airlines, but also hotels, vacation resorts, restaurants, etc., in Asia would seem to offer the charms of Asian women in advertising that sells seduction and service simultaneously to the potential consumer. By contrast, advertising for non-Asian airlines may be slightly more diverse in theme. A Qantas print ad features a map of Australia; a Lufthansa ad headlined "We spoil our passengers as much as we spoil our aircraft," depicts a uniformed male flight attendant amusing a little girl, with a glove puppet. Non-Asian airlines, of course, by no means forswear the exploitation of feminine identity and services, as United Airlines' historically infamous "Fly Me" advertising campaign in the US once attested. More recently, Lauda Air of Austria has been castigated by Thai NGOs for an advertisement in the airline's inflight magazine featuring child prostitution in Thailand as a selling point to tempt potential air passengers ("Thai Group Slams Lauda Air Ad" 1992).

22 That Western imperialisms are, in fact, multifarious and resourceful has historically complicated feminist projects and the critique of antifeminist nationalist rhetoric in the Third World. Fatima Mernissi, for instance, cites "the paternalistic defence of Muslim women's lot" by Western colonialists as responsible for alienating nationalist intellectuals "who had previously supported the liberation of Muslim women" (1987, 7). The work of Indian feminists, on the manipulation, by British colonialists, of the traditional Hindu practice of *Sati* or widow-immolation, to support the imperialist project in India and imperialist propaganda, is well-documented.

23 Articles in the Malaysian press have mentioned the revisionary work, for instance, of Amina Wadud-Muhsin, an African-American Koranic scholar formerly with the International Islamic University. While claiming to be an exegetical conservative, Wadud forcefully asserts that "the most sacred postulates" in Islam "are universal and non-sexist," and that it is male bias and "corrupt interpretations" in the exegetical tradition that have been responsible for apparent antifeminism in Islam (Ismail 1990; "A Woman's View"). Hers is a strategy, of course, in line with a time-honored history of similar claims by profeminist male nationalists in the Middle East such as Qasim Amin (see Philipp 1978, Jayawardena 1986, etc.). Malaysian feminists – as Norma Mohamed Sharif, a graduate student at the University of Texas at Austin, recently reminded me – might also counter the Islamic nationalist charge that feminism is foreign by pointing out that the exegetical tradition in Islam, grounded in the Middle East and Arabism, is itself foreign to Malaysia. By contrast, Norma observes, *adat*, or customary law governing Malay communal life in Malaysia, is incontestably local in its origins and traditions, and often affords Malay Muslim women more rights than *shariah* law. That is to say, in Malaysia, Malay

ethnic nationalism and pride and the historical continuity of Malay identity are at least potentially in conflict with Malay Islamic nationalism, and might constitute fertile ground for
feminists who would assert the local origins and rights of feminism.

24 Interestingly, perhaps inevitably, these heroines – particularly when they are figures from
contemporary history – are also often nationalist heroines, and figure in themselves and in
their historical status the competitive tension of feminism and nationalism. The strategy of
sifting the past for figures, values, and narratives that would serve to provide a legitimizing
genealogy for what is essentially a modern movement is, of course, a nationalist strategy as
much as a feminist one in the Third World. In the search for an authoritative (and authorizing) originary past, as in so many other projects, feminism and nationalism find themselves on
parallel trajectories.

25 "In the pre-colonial era, indigenous Malay women had a relatively high status, as is generally
the case in Southeast Asia. Malay mythology is replete with the legends of queens and
matriarchs, particularly in the pre-Islamic era" (Wee 1987, 5).

26 The arrests received worldwide attention from the international human-rights community,
from members of the US Congress, and from members of the European Parliament, in part
because it was widely believed, both within and outside Singapore, that the government had
applied the powers of the Internal Security Act (ISA) against individuals who were critical of
the government but who did not constitute a security threat to the state. The ISA, an
instrument bequeathed by the British colonial administration to its erstwhile colony, had been
periodically invoked by the government to detain individuals linked to the proscribed Malayan
Communist Party (MCP). Prior to the 1987 arrests, however, the government had been careful
to establish publicly, in each spate of arrests, the precise relation between the persons arrested
and the Communist underground in Singapore and Malaysia. Detainees were also typically
offered the option of release if they would agree to abjure, in writing, any commitment to
violence as a means of political change. By contrast, no mention was made of Communists or
the MCP in the 1987 arrests. The government only claimed, confusingly, that the community
activists, dramatists, lawyers, student unionists, and feminists they arrested were either
"Marxist" conspirators, the dupes of Marxist conspirators, or both simultaneously, and none
was offered release in exchange for abjuring the violent overthrow of an elected government.
The two founder-members of AWARE arrested were Teresa Lim Li Kok, then treasurer of
AWARE, and Tang Fong Har, who escaped rearrest in 1988 by her sojourn in Britain.
A number of the other women detainees (this round of political detentions were remarkable
also in that more women than men were arrested) were also members of AWARE.

27 "Claire finds the label 'feminist' frightens many people. 'People see feminists as unhappy,
ugly, and single. Feminism is a lonely cause. You are always met with disagreement and
disfavour. I prefer the term "woman centredness."' AWARE believes that men and women
should work in a shared partnership, not see themselves as battle opponents. Feminism is not
an anti-man stand." (Saini 1992, 102).

28 While registered societies in Singapore are required to restrict their activity to the nonpolitical,
individual women associated with these organizations have sometimes been able to articulate
multiple political concerns, especially in their personal capacity. Kanwaljit Soin and Constance
Singam, past presidents of AWARE and the Singapore Council of Women's Organizations
(SCWO), have written together to the national press on the issue of race; Vivienne Wee, a
former Honorary General Secretary of AWARE, has conducted research and analysis on
transnational migrant domestic labor in her academic work as an anthropologist; Anamah Tan,
president of the SCWO and a lawyer by profession, has written to the press petitioning the
government (unfortunately without success) to require standardized legal contracts for the
protection of foreign domestic workers in Singapore.

29 The Singapore government is not, of course, unique in thus arrogating to itself the powers of
arbitrary definition. A feminist scholar notes, for instance, "Any concern which is now voiced
[about the] difficult social and economic situation [of economically-disadvantaged women in
Indonesia, and] how this relates to women's subordination, is branded as political" (Wieringa
1988, 85). Nor is AWARE unique, as a feminist group, in its adaptation to the social condi-

tions in which it finds itself. A recent academic study observes that the Thai feminist NGO, Friends of Women, "[i]n past years...has tried to get rid of its image as a militant or radical women's group in order to gain general social support. It has tended to take a less active role in controversial issues such as prostitution and instead concentrates on such immediate action as helping rape victims" (Tantiwiramanond and Pandey 1991, 151).

30 Only AWARE has been distinctly identified, in the public mind, as a feminist group. Other organizations that have been active on women's issues include the Singapore Association of Women Lawyers (SAWL), founded in 1974, which offers free legal advocacy services to women and has directed efforts at educating women on their rights under the law; and the Singapore Council of Women's Organisations (SCWO), founded in 1940, and representing thirty-eight groups and societies, with a total of close to 100,000 members. Because the SCWO is an umbrella body for a diversity of interests, however – member organizations include religious groups, a travel club, business and professional associations, school-alumni groups, government-affiliated organizations, and a netball club – much of the SCWO's direction at any point of time is necessarily dependent upon its immediate leadership. In recent years, under presidents Constance Singam and Anamah Tan, the SCWO has had a palpably feminist cast.

31 Unlike his predecessor, former Prime Minister Lee, however, Goh nominally soft-pedals the eugenic equation. Although Goh tartly observed that "[w]omen with no formal schooling produced 2.5 times as many children as those with tertiary qualifications in 1970. The ratio went up to 2.8 in 1940 and 2.9 last year" ("Worrying Trends"), he nonetheless added as a concession, "Do not get me wrong. I am not saying that the less-educated women should have fewer children. It is a question of balance. If the ratio was one to one, or even one to two, it would not be a problem." The newspaper report went on to say that Goh "added that this imbalance was significant as talented people were needed to help create jobs for the less educated."

32 According to one of the two volumes produced by the PAP's Women's Wing, Singapore ranks forty-first among ninety-nine countries in a study on the status of women around the world conducted by the Population Crisis Committee in Washington, DC (Wong and Leong 1993, 10). This places Singapore after Hong Kong (thirty-second), Japan (thirty-fourth), and Taiwan (thirty-ninth) in the treatment of female citizens, but, as the editors take the trouble to note, before the other countries of the Association of Southeast Asian Nations (ASEAN), Pakistan and Bangladesh.

33 The Thai groups EMPOWER, Friends of Women (FOW), and the Women's Information Centre (WIC) of the Foundation for Women (FFW), for instance, are small-scale and dynamic, as scholars have noted. EMPOWER's work, in supporting and authorizing the most disenfranchised and alienated of women in Thai society – prostitutes, including children – through drama, education projects, self-help activities, and even a newsletter, is particularly impressive (Tantiwiramanond and Pandey 1991).

34 Since June 1993, a number of fine studies by Deniz Kandiyoti (1994), Rajeswari Mohan (1994), and others have appeared in print, theorizing Third-World feminism along trajectories similar to or divergent from the trajectory I outline above. I have learned much from this recent body of work, and from the lively, interrogative, and very diverse graduate students who participated in my 1995 seminar at the University of Texas on international feminisms.

Works Cited

"Abusive Bosses Will Be Barred from Hiring Maids: Move to Punish Errant Employers, Says Ministry," *Straits Times* (Singapore), August 7, 1990, p. 3.

Anderson, Benedict. 1983. *Imagined Communities: Reflections on the Origin and Spread of Nationalism.* London: Verso.

AWARE round-up. 1993. *Awareness: A Journal of the Association of Women for Action and Research* (Singapore) 1, no. 1 (May 1993): 38–42.

Beck, Lois, and Nikki Keddie (eds.). 1978. *Women in the Muslim World*. Cambridge, Mass. and London: Harvard University Press.

Bloodworth, Dennis. 1986. *The Tiger and the Trojan Horse*. Singapore: Times Books International.

Chatterjee, Partha. 1989. "The Nationalist Resolution of the Women's Question." In Kumkum Sangari and Sudesh Vaid (eds.), *Recasting Women: Essays in Colonial History*. New Delhi: Kali for Women, pp. 233–53.

Croll, Elisabeth. 1978. *Feminism and Socialism in China*. London: Routledge & Kegan Paul.

Dancz, Virginia H. 1987. *Women and Party Politics in Peninsular Malaysia*. Singapore: Oxford University Press.

Enloe, Cynthia. 1989. *Bananas, Beaches, & Bases: Making Feminist Sense of International Politics*. Berkeley/Los Angeles: University of California Press.

"Filipino Senator Calls for Ban on Maids Bound for HK: Rising Abuse and Exploitation, Says Head Senate Labour Panel." *Sunday Times* (Singapore), May 19, 1991, p. 12.

"Govt Likely to Collect $48m in Foreign Worker Levy: About 200,000 Expected to Register by the Middle of Next Year." *Straits Times* (Singapore), December 14, 1991, p. 19.

"Govt Replies to MPs on COE Premiums and Levies Collected." *Straits Times* (Singapore), August 7, 1992, p. 25.

Halliday, Fred. 1991. "Hidden from International Relations: Women and the International Arena." In Rebecca Grant and Kathleen Newland (eds.), *Gender and International Relations*. Bloomington/Indianapolis: Indiana University Press, pp. 158–69.

Heng, Geraldine, and Janadas Devan. 1992. "State Fatherhood: The Politics of Nationalism, Sexuality, and Race in Singapore." In Andrew Parker, Mary Russo, Doris Sommer, Patricia Yaeger (eds.), *Nationalisms and Sexualities*, New York and London: Routledge, pp. 243–64.

Henson, Bertha. 1993. "Double Burden of Home and Career Keeping Women from Politics." *Straits Times* (Singapore), News Extra Section, June 19, 1993, p. 11.

Heyzer, Noeleen. 1986. *Working Women in South-East Asia: Development, Subordination and Emancipation*. Philadelphia: Open University Press, 1986.

Heyzer, Noeleen, and Vivienne Wee. 1992. "Domestic Workers in Transient Overseas Employment: Who Benefits, Who Profits?" Paper presented to the Regional Policy Dialogue on Foreign Domestic Workers: International Migration, Employment and National Politics, Colombo, Sri Lanka, August 10–14, 1992.

Ismail, Rose. "Man, Woman and Erroneous Thoughts." *New Sunday Times*, 20 May 1990.

Jayawardena, Kumari. 1986. *Feminism and Nationalism in the Third World*. London: Zed Books, and New Delhi: Kali for Women.

Karim, Wazir-jahan. 1983. "Malay Women's Movements: Leadership and Processes of Change." *International Social Science Journal* 35, no. 4 (1983): 719–31.

Kandiyoti, Deniz (ed.). 1991. *Women, Islam and the State*. London: Macmillan.

——"Identity and Its Discontents: Women and the Nation." In *Colonial Discourse and Post-Colonial Theory: A Reader*. ed. Patrick Williams and Laura Chrisman. New York: Columbia University Press, 1994, pp. 376–91.

Katrak, Ketu H. 1992. "Indian Nationalism, Gandhian 'Satyagraha,' and Representations of Female Sexuality." In Andrew Parker, Mary Russo, Doris Sommer, and Patricia Yaeger (eds.), *Nationalisms and Sexualities*. New York/London: Routledge, pp. 395–406.

Lim, Seow Yoke. 1984/85. "Women in Singapore Politics 1945–1970." Unpublished Academic Exercise, Department of History, National University of Singapore.

"Maid Abuse Very Rare in S'pore, Say Agencies: Fewer than 1% of Maids They Handle Have Reported Ill-Treatment." *Straits Times* (Singapore), February 15, 1991, p. 16.

Marr, David. 1976. "The 1920s Women's Rights Debates in Vietnam." *Journal of Asian Studies* 35, no. 3 (1976): 371–89.

Mernissi, Fatima. 1987. *Beyond the Veil: Male-Female Dynamics in Modern Muslim Society*. Bloomington and Indianapolis: Indiana University Press.

Mohan, Rajeswari. "The Crisis of Femininity and Modernity in the Third World." *Genders* 19, (1994): 223–56.

Molyneux, Maxine. 1991. "The Law, the State and Socialist Policies with Regard to Women: The Case of the People's Democratic Republic of Yemen 1967–1990." In Deniz Kandiyoti (ed.), *Women, Islam and the State*. London: Macmillan, pp. 237–71.

Ong, Aihwa. 1987: *Spirits of Resistance and Capitalist Discipline*. Albany: State University of New York Press.

Ong, Pang Boon. 1979. "Problems of Party Organisation: The Pro-Communist Challenge from Within 1954–'57." In *People's Action Party 1954–1979: Petir 25th Anniversary Issue*. Singapore: Central Executive Committee People's Action Party, pp. 44–59.

"PAP's Women's Wing Will Inform, Not Lobby: Aline." *Straits Times* (Singapore), July 29, 1992, p. 18.

People's Action Party. 1959. "Women in the New Singapore." In *The Tasks Ahead: P.A.P's Five-year Plan 1959–1964*. Singapore: Petir, Organ of the People's Action Party, pp. 17–19.

Philipp, Thomas. 1978. "Feminism and Nationalist Politics in Egypt." In Lois Beck and Nikki Keddie (eds.), *Women in the Muslim World*. Cambridge, Mass. and London: Harvard University Press, pp. 277–94.

Saini, Rohaniah. 1992. "Women for Women." *Her World* (October 1992): 99–112.

Shahani, Leticia R. 1975. "Liberating the Filipino Woman." *Philippines Quarterly* 7, no. 4 (December 1975): 36–40.

Singapore Airlines Annual Report. 1990–91. Singapore: Singapore National Printers.

Singapore Association of Women Lawyers. 1986. *Legal Status of Singapore Women*. Singapore: Asiapac Books.

"Story of the Singapore Woman." *Straits Times* (Singapore), June 12, 1993, Life! section, p. 2.

Tan, Lian Choo. 1991. "Sex, Generals and Women Wronged in Thailand." *Straits Times* (Singapore), September 27, 1991, p. 34.

Tan, Sai Siong. 1993. "Molesting of S'pore Girls: Time SIA Stopped the Party." *Straits Times* (Singapore), May 8, 1993, p. 35.

Tantiwiramanond, Darunee, and Shashi Ranjan Pandey. 1991. *By Women, For Women: A Study of Women's Organizations in Thailand*. Singapore: Institute of Southeast Asian Studies, Social Issues in Southeast Asia Research, Notes and Discussions Paper No. 72.

"Thai Group Slams Lauda Air Ad: It Encourages Child Sex, Task Force Alleges." *Straits Times* (Singapore), August 11, 1992, p. 17.

"The Trials of Muslim Europe." *Newsweek* (January 27, 1992): 14–15.

Truong, Thanh-Dam. 1990. *Sex, Money and Morality: Prostitution and Tourism in Southeast Asia*. London and New Jersey: Zed Books.

Vargas, Virginia. 1988. "The Feminist Movement in Peru: Inventory and Perspectives." In Saskia Wieringa (ed.), *Women's Struggles and Strategies*. Aldershot: Gower, pp. 136–54.

"Veil Viewed as Symbol of Resistance in Gaza Strip." *Straits Times* (Singapore), August 23, 1991, p. 15.

Vreede-de Stuers, Cora. 1960. *The Indonesian Woman: Struggles and Achievements*. The Hague: Mouton.

Wee, Vivienne. "The Ups and Downs of Women's Status in Singapore: A Chronology of Some Landmark Events (1950–1987)." *Commentary: Journal of the National University of Singapore Society*. Vol. 7, nos. 2–3 (December 1987): 5–12.

Wieringa, Saskia. 1988. "Aborted Feminism in Indonesia: A History of Indonesian Socialist Feminism." In Saskia Wieringa (ed.), *Women's Struggles and Strategies*. Aldershot: Gower, pp. 69–89.

"Winning by Persuasion." *Straits Times* (Singapore), September 3, 1993, Life! Section, p. 2.

"A Woman's View." *Straits Times*, 17 August 1992.

"Women's Wing to Study Family Services Idea." *Straits Times* (Singapore), February 27, 1990, p. 25.

Wong, Aline K., and Leong Wai Kum (eds.). 1993. *Singapore Women: Three Decades of Change*. Singapore: Times Academic Press.

"Worrying Trends Threaten Family Life." *Straits Times* (Singapore), June 14, 1993, p. 1.

PART NINE

Gender Studies

CHAPTER 1

Introduction: Contingencies of Gender

Julie Rivkin and Michael Ryan

In 1968 a revolution occurred. It seemed small at first, but like many other small gestures of rebellion, it represented the first significant fissure in the crystalline edifice of a certain social order. Ultimately that fissure widened, and in spreading broke the system that defined what otherwise might have been a night's fun as a gesture of rebellion in the first place. In retrospect, the fact that a group of gays, lesbians, and transvestites should resist undergoing the by then routine procedure of being harassed and arrested by the New York police seems fairly happenstance. But something much bigger was at stake in the riot that occurred that night. That something was the regime of what Adrienne Rich calls "compulsory heterosexuality." That regime had as a major correlate (if not presupposition) the banishment of alternative sexual practices and the violation of bearers of non-heterosexual gender identities. If women were to be compelled to be child-productive wives by the dominant social group of heterosexual men, then women's friendships would be deemed suspicious, and lesbianism would be enjoined. If men were to behave in accordance with the dictates of compulsory heterosexuality and not engage in sexual practices that placed the reigning code of heterosexual masculinity in question, then their friendships too would be suspect, and male homosexuality would also be forbidden. Those guilty of daring to challenge this social and cultural regime – Oscar Wilde comes to mind – would be the objects of calumny, if not of overt violence. And all of this would be called "normality" while all of "that" would be stigmatized as "perversion." That science and medicine were complicit in this regime only says once again, in case it needs repeating, that science and medicine could do to rethink their founding rationalist criteria and their principles of social constitution, two things that always coexist but whose coexistence science always has trouble recognizing.

The emergence of a Gay and Lesbian Liberation Movement in the late 1960s and early 1970s intersected necessarily with the work of feminists who were concerned with issues of sexuality and of gender identity. For a time, the two movements seemed to share a common ground; women and gays were objects of oppression by a dominant male heterosexual group. But in other respects (and in hindsight), there were grounds for difference.

In the 1980s, feminism began to change direction. For some time, feminist theorists had been discussing the idea that there might be a difference within feminism proper between biological sexual identity (the physical difference that makes women women and men men) and gender identity. If biological sexual identity belonged to nature and could allow a general class of "women" to be identified as "not male," gender identity seemed more subject to the contingencies of culture and history, more something constructed in and variable across society and through history. It might not lend itself to an opposition such as that between "man" and "woman." The generality of the category "women" might in fact conceal and suppress differentiations between women in regard to choice of sexual object, sexual practices, and psychological identities, some of which might be "masculine." While a masculine woman would for Feminists of the 1970s be "male-identified," for the emerging Gender Studies and Gay/Lesbian Theories of the 1980s, such a person might simply be one of a variety of possible gender and sexual locations, an intersection of biology and culture, or physicality and psychology that is not easily identified (and certainly not easily vilified). The path-breaking work of anthropologists like Gayle Rubin and historians like Alan Bray and Michel Foucault bore out the point that gender is variable: in history and between societies, there is variation between different ways of practicing sex and being one gender or another. Sexual practices like anal intercourse, intercourse between women, fellatio, and cunnilingus are coded differently across different societies and throughout history. Anal intercourse and fellatio between men were common in fifth-century Greek society, and only later (in the late nineteenth century, according to Foucault) would they be "discovered" to be signs of an identifiable "perversion." Christianity stands between the two dates or sites and probably has a great deal to do with how non-reproductive sexual practices became stigmatized over time.

Gay and lesbian scholars during the 1970s and 1980s began to peel away the layers of prejudice that had made it almost impossible, before the Stonewall riot, to study the history of gay and lesbian writing or to analyze how gays and lesbian life and experience were distorted in cultural history. Some of this early work included Guy Hocquengham's examination of the psychology of homophobia, Jeffrey Weeks's history of "coming out," Richard Dyer's exploration of representations of gays and lesbians in film, Terry Castle's study of "things not fit to be mentioned" in eighteenth-century literature, Lillian Faderman's work on love between women in the Renaissance, the Combahee River Collective's manifesto for African American lesbians, Andrew Britton's rebuttal of normative homophobia on the intellectual Left, Adrienne Rich's celebrated statement against "compulsory heterosexuality," Sharon O'Brien's exploration of Willa Cather's problematic attitude toward her own lesbianism, John D'Emilio's history of how homosexuals were minoritized in US culture, and Jeffrey Escoffier's analysis of the need for a gay revolution equivalent to the socialist one against capitalism. One of the more attention-getting publications during this period was the translation of the first volume of Foucault's *History of Sexuality* (1978). Foucault's argument that "homosexuality" is a social, medical, and ontological category invented in the late nineteenth century and imposed on sexual practices that prior to that point had enjoyed an absence of such "scientific" scrutiny provided impetus to the idea that modern heterocentric gender culture founds itself on the anathemizing of non-reproductive sexual alternatives that are in fact everywhere present in human society.

In the mid to late 1970s and into the early 1980s, a new field of Gender Studies constituted itself in conjunction with Gay and Lesbian Studies. It turned its attention on all gender formations, both heterosexual and homosexual. Gender scholars found that heterosexuality can be understood as forming a continuum with homosexuality in that such ideals as heterosexual masculinity seem inseparable from a "panic" component, an apotropaic move or turn away from a certain homosexuality that helps construct heterosexuality. In *Between Men* (1985), Eve Sedgwick notices that male heterosexual desire is always modeled on another male's desire and always has a "homosocial" cast. The male bonding that sutures patriarchy is necessarily homophilic and forms a continuum with homosexuality.

More so than Gay Studies, Lesbian Studies has demonstrated a tendency towards separatism, perhaps because as women, lesbians suffer a double oppression. (If one factors in ethnic prejudice, as in the case of Gloria Anzaldua (*Borderlands/ La Frontera*), the sense of pain grows exponentially.) A separatist strand of Lesbian Studies was theorized by Monique Wittig ("The Straight Mind," 1980) and Luce Irigaray (in her *This Sex Which Is Not One* (1977; English translation, 1985)). Lesbian women, Irigaray argues, can only exist as such in a world of their own apart from patrocentric culture. The difference of Lesbian Studies from Feminism also began to be marked at this time. Judith Butler's *Gender Trouble* (1990) made the argument against enclosing Lesbian Studies within Feminism emphatic by deconstructing the very notion of an identity of "woman" and demonstrating that all gender identity is a performance, an apparent substance that is an effect of a prior act of imitation. That same year Eve Kosofsky Sedgwick published her celebrated theoretical analysis of "closeting" (*Epistemology of the Closet*). Building on her earlier work, Sedgwick contends that one cannot logically separate men-loving-men within patriarchy from homosexuality. Sedgwick's work demonstrates the significance of Post-Structuralist thinking for Gender Theory, since it underscores the contingency of all supposedly axiomatic oppositions as that between homosexuality and heterosexuality. Sexuality and gender are variable and indeterminate; they do not align with simple polarities and can take multiple, highly differentiated forms. In 1994, Lee Edelman's *Homographesis* brought deconstructive theory to bear on the question of gay identity and the issue of recognizability. The gay is a "homograph," someone who simulates the "normality" of masculinity or heterosexuality only to displace them as grounding ontological categories.

In the mid to late 1980s, Acquired Immune Deficiency Syndrome killed many people in the gay community. Queer Theory, which emerged around this time, is in some respects a response to the epidemic, both a way of providing gays and lesbians with a common term around which to unite and a more radical way of calling attention to the issues raised by them. Queer Theory adopted a term of stigmatization ("queer" being a derogatory name for a gay or lesbian person) and turned it against the perpetrator by transforming it into a token of pride. The shift in name also indicates a shift in analytic strategy, for now gay and lesbian theorists began to explore the "queerness" of supposedly "normal" sexual culture. The controversy over the photographs of Robert Mapplethorpe, some of which depict aspects of the gay sadomasochistic subculture, helped focus attention on the mendacity of a heterosexual sex gender system that condemned as "perversion" in others what it practiced on a routine basis in its own homes. The work of Michael Moon and Paul Morrison is especially compelling in this regard. Morrison suggests that one reason Mapplethorpe's pictures of men in leather bound with chains sitting in living rooms and looking very normal, almost like dinner guests awaiting their cue to head for the table, were so disturbing to the dominant heterosexual community is that they draw attention to the discipline and coercion operative in those living rooms. That discipline is normal, whereas the gay mimesis or enactment of such violence in the routines of sadism or masochism is stigmatized.[1] In a similar fashion, Moon uses Freud's notion of the "uncanny," the disturbing other within, to intimate that routine male heterosexual identity is premised on violent competition between men that has a sadistic component. Where we draw the lines between normal and nonnormal is, Moon suggests, entirely contingent.[2]

Gender Studies, Gay/Lesbian Studies, and Queer Theory have delineated three broad areas of work in literary and cultural theory. First, the examination of the history of the oppression of gays, lesbians, and practitioners of sexualities other than those deemed normal by the dominant heterosexual group. Second, the exploration of the countercultures of gay and lesbian writing that existed in parallel fashion with the dominant heterosexual culture. And third, the analysis of the instability and indeterminacy of all gender identity, such that even "normal" heterosexuality itself might be seen as a kind of panicked closure imposed on a variable, contingent, and multiple sexuality whose mobility and potentiality is signaled by the worlds of possibility opened up by gays and lesbians.

Notes

1 Paul Morrison, "Coffee Table Sex," *Genders*, no. 11 (Fall 1991), pp. 17–34.
2 Moon's essay is included in this anthology (see pp. 922–34).

CHAPTER 2

Sexual Transformations

Gayle Rubin

Published in 1984, this essay by Gayle Rubin combines history with anthropology. It provides an account of how the lives of gays and lesbians have changed over the past several centuries, as Western culture moved from intolerance to tolerance regarding homosexuality. Rubin notes that the rise of urban subcultures was crucial in the development of homosexuality.

Sexual Transformation

As defined by the ancient civil or canonical codes, sodomy was a category of forbidden acts; their perpetrator was nothing more than the juridical subject of them. The nineteenth-century homosexual became a personage, a past, a case history, and a childhood, in addition to being a type of life, a life form, and a morphology, with an indiscreet anatomy and possibly a mysterious physiology.... The sodomite had been a temporary aberration; the homosexual was now a species.[1]

In spite of many continuities with ancestral forms, modern sexual arrangements have a distinctive character which sets them apart from preexisting systems. In Western Europe and the United States, industrialization and urbanization reshaped the traditional rural and peasant populations into a new urban industrial and service workforce. It generated new forms of state apparatus, reorganized family relations, altered gender roles, made possible new forms of identity, produced new varieties of social inequality, and created new formats for political and ideological conflict. It also gave rise to a new sexual system characterized by distinct types of sexual persons, populations, stratification, and political conflict.

The writings of nineteenth-century sexology suggest the appearance of a kind of erotic speciation. However outlandish their explanations, the early sexologists were witnessing the emergence of new kinds of erotic individuals and their aggregation into rudimentary communities. The modern sexual system contains sets of these sexual populations, stratified by the operation of an ideological and social hierarchy. Differences in social value create friction among these groups, who engage in political contests to alter or maintain their place in the ranking. Contemporary sexual politics should be reconceptualized in terms of the emergence and on-going development of this system, its social relations, the ideologies which interpret it, and its characteristic modes of conflict.

Homosexuality is the best example of this process of erotic speciation. Homosexual behavior is always present among humans. But in different societies and epochs it may be rewarded or punished, required or forbidden, a temporary experience or a life-long vocation. In some New Guinea societies, for example, homosexual activities are obligatory for all males. Homosexual acts are considered utterly masculine, roles are based on age, and partners are determined by kinship status.[2] Although these men engage in extensive homosexual and pedophile behavior, they are neither homosexuals nor pederasts.

Nor was the sixteenth-century sodomite a homosexual. In 1631, Mervyn Touchet, Earl of Castlehaven, was tried and executed for sodomy. It is clear from the proceedings that the earl was not understood by himself or anyone else to be a particular kind of sexual individual. "While from the twentieth-century viewpoint Lord Castlehaven obviously suffered from psychosexual problems requiring the services of an analyst, from the seventeenth-century viewpoint he had deliberately broken the Law of God and the Laws of England, and required the simpler services of an executioner." The earl did not slip into his tightest doublet and waltz down to the nearest gay tavern to mingle with his fellow sodomists. He stayed in his manor house and buggered his servants. Gay self-awareness, gay pubs, the sense of group commonality, and even the term homosexual were not part of the earl's universe.

The New Guinea bachelor and the sodomite nobleman are only tangentially related to a modern gay man, who may migrate from rural Colorado to San Francisco in order to live in a gay neighborhood, work in a gay business, and participate in an elaborate experience that includes a self-conscious identity, group solidarity, a literature, a press, and a high level of political activity. In modern, Western, industrial societies, homosexuality has acquired much of the institutional structure of an ethnic group.[3]

The relocation of homoeroticism into these quasi-ethnic, nucleated, sexually constituted communities is to some extent a consequence of the transfers of population brought about by industrialization. As laborers migrated to work in cities, there were increased opportunities for voluntary communities to form. Homosexually inclined women and men, who would have been vulnerable and isolated in most pre-industrial villages, began to congregate in small corners of the big cities. Most large nineteenth-century cities in Western Europe and North America had areas where men could cruise for other men. Lesbian communities seem to have coalesced more slowly and on a smaller scale. Nevertheless, by the 1890s, there were several cafes in Paris near the Place Pigalle which catered to a lesbian clientele, and it is likely that there were similar places in the other major capitals of Western Europe.

Areas like these acquired bad reputations, which alerted other interested individuals of their existence and location. In the United States, lesbian and gay male territories were well established in New York, Chicago, San Francisco, and Los Angeles in the 1950s. Sexually motivated migration to places such as Greenwich Village had become a sizable sociological phenomenon. By the late 1970s, sexual migration was occurring on a scale so significant that it began to have a recognizable impact on urban politics in the United States, with San Francisco being the most notable and notorious example.[4]

Prostitution has undergone a similar metamorphosis. Prostitution began to change from a temporary job to a more permanent occupation as a result of nineteenth-century agitation, legal reform, and police persecution. Prostitutes, who had been part of the general working-class population, became increasingly isolated as members of an outcast group.[5] Prostitutes and other sex workers differ from homosexuals and other sexual minorities. Sex work is an occupation, while sexual deviation is an erotic preference. Nevertheless, they share some common features of social organization. Like homosexuals, prostitutes are a criminal sexual population stigmatized on the basis of sexual activity. Prostitutes and male homosexuals are the primary prey of vice police everywhere.[6] Like gay men, prostitutes occupy well-demarcated urban territories and battle with police to defend and maintain those territories. The legal persecution of both populations is justified by an elaborate ideology which classifies them as dangerous and inferior undesirables who are not entitled to be left in peace.

Besides organizing homosexuals and prostitutes into localized populations, the "modernization of sex" has generated a system of continual sexual ethnogenesis. Other populations of erotic dissidents – commonly known as the "perversions" or the "paraphilias" – also began to coalesce. Sexualities keep marching out of the *Diagnostic and Statistical Manual* and on to the pages of social history. At present, several other groups are trying to emulate the successes of homosexuals. Bisexuals, sadomasochists, individuals who prefer cross-generational encounters, transsexuals, and transvestites are all in various states of community formation and identity acquisition. The perversions are not proliferating as much as they are attempting to acquire social space, small businesses, political resources, and a measure of relief from the penalties for sexual heresy.

Notes

1 Michel Foucault, *The History of Sexuality* (New York: Pantheon, 1978).
2 Caroline Brigham, "Seventeenth-Century Attitudes Toward Deviant Sex," *Journal of Interdisciplinary Review of Modern Sociology* (Spring 1971), p. 465.
3 Stephen O. Murray, "The Institutional Elaboration of a Quasi-Ethnic Community," *International Review of Modern Sociology* (July–December 1979).
4 For a further elaboration of these processes, see Allan Bérubé, "Behind the Spectre of San Francisco," *Body Politic* (April 1981), "Marching to a Different Drummer," *Advocate* (October 15, 1981); John D'Emilio, "Gay Politics, Gay Community: San Francisco's Experience," *Socialist Review*, no. 55 (January–February 1981); Foucault, *History of Sexuality*; Bert Hansen, "The Historical Construction of Homosexuality," *Radical History Review*, no. 20 (Spring/Summer 1979); Jeffrey Weeks, *Coming Out: Homosexual Politics in Britain from the Nineteenth Century to the Present* (New York: Quartet, 1977); Jeffrey Weeks, *Sex, Politics, and Society: The Regulation of Sexuality Since 1800* (New York: Longman, 1981).
5 Judith R. Walkowitz, *Prostitution and Victorian Society* (Cambridge: Cambridge University Press, 1980).
6 Vice cops also harass all sex businesses, be these gay bars, gay baths, adult book stores, the producers and distributors of commercial erotica, or swing clubs.

CHAPTER 3

The History of Sexuality

Michel Foucault

The post-1969 emergence of a movement promoting equal rights for gays, lesbians, and transsexuals gained assistance from the French intellectual community in 1976 with the publication of the first volume of Michel Foucault's three-volume *History of Sexuality*. Foucault converted the sexological discourse that had made homosexuals into a prejudicial object of study into an object of study in its own right. He thereby reframed the debate over homosexuality in a new and quite liberatory way.

The Perverse Implantation

A possible objection: it would be a mistake to see in this proliferation of discourses [regarding sexuality in the eighteenth and nineteenth centuries] merely a quantitative phenomenon, something like a pure increase, as if what was said in them were immaterial, as if the fact of speaking about sex were of itself more important than the forms of imperatives that were imposed on it by speaking about it. For was this transformation of sex into discourse not governed by the endeavor to expel from reality the forms of sexuality that were not amenable to the strict economy of reproduction: to say no to unproductive activities, to banish casual pleasures, to reduce or exclude practices whose object was not procreation? Through the various discourses, legal sanctions against minor perversions were multiplied; sexual irregularity was annexed to mental illness; from childhood to old age, a norm of sexual development was defined and all the possible deviations were carefully described; pedagogical controls and medical treatments were organized; around the least fantasies, moralists, but especially doctors, brandished the whole emphatic vocabulary of abomination. Were these anything more than means employed to absorb, for the benefit of a genitally centered sexuality, all the fruitless pleasures? All this garrulous attention which has us in a stew over sexuality, is it not motivated by one basic concern: to ensure population, to reproduce labor capacity, to perpetuate the form of social relations: in short, to constitute a sexuality that is economically useful and politically conservative?

I still do not know whether this is the ultimate objective. But this much is certain: reduction has not been the means employed for trying to achieve it. The nineteenth century and our own have been rather the age of multiplication: a dispersion of sexualities, a strengthening of their disparate forms, a multiple implantation of "perversions." Our epoch has initiated sexual heterogeneities.

Up to the end of the eighteenth century, three major explicit codes – apart from the customary regularities and constraints of opinion – governed sexual practices:

canonical law, the Christian pastoral, and civil law. They determined, each in its own way, the division between licit and illicit. They were all centered on matrimonial relations: the marital obligation, the ability to fulfill it, the manner in which one complied with it, the requirements and violences that accompanied it, the useless or unwarranted caresses for which it was a pretext, its fecundity or the way one went about making it sterile, the moments when one demanded it (dangerous periods of pregnancy or breast-feeding, forbidden times of Lent or abstinence), its frequency or infrequency, and so on. It was this domain that was especially saturated with prescriptions. The sex of husband and wife was beset by rules and recommendations. The marriage relation was the most intense focus of constraints; it was spoken of more than anything else; more than any other relation, it was required to give a detailed accounting of itself. It was under constant surveillance: if it was found to be lacking, it had to come forward and plead its case before a witness. The "rest" remained a good deal more confused: one only has to think of the uncertain status of "sodomy," or the indifference regarding the sexuality of children.

Moreover, these different codes did not make a clear distinction between violations of the rules of marriage and deviations with respect to genitality. Breaking the rules of marriage or seeking strange pleasures brought an equal measure of condemnation. On the list of grave sins, and separated only by their relative importance, there appeared debauchery (extramarital relations), adultery, rape, spiritual or carnal incest, but also sodomy, or the mutual "caress." As to the courts, they could condemn homosexuality as well as infidelity, marriage without parental consent, or bestiality. What was taken into account in the civil and religious jurisdictions alike was a general unlawfulness. Doubtless acts "contrary to nature" were stamped as especially abominable, but they were perceived simply as an extreme form of acts "against the law"; they were infringements of decrees which were just as sacred as those of marriage, and which had been established for governing the order of things and the plan of beings. Prohibitions bearing on sex were essentially of a juridical nature. The "nature" on which they were based was still a kind of law. For a long time hermaphrodites were criminals, or crime's offspring, since their anatomical disposition, their very being, confounded the law that distinguished the sexes and prescribed their union.

The discursive explosion of the eighteenth and nineteenth centuries caused this system centered on legitimate alliance to undergo two modifications. First, a centrifugal movement with respect to heterosexual monogamy. Of course, the array of practices and pleasures continued to be referred to it as their internal standard; but it was spoken of less and less, or in any case with a growing moderation. Efforts to find out its secrets were abandoned; nothing further was demanded of it than to define itself from day to day. The legitimate couple, with its regular sexuality, had a right to more discretion. It tended to function as a norm, one that was stricter, perhaps, but quieter. On the other hand, what came under scrutiny was the sexuality of children, mad men and women, and criminals; the sensuality of those who did not like the opposite sex; reveries, obsessions, petty manias, or great transports of rage. It was time for all these figures, scarcely noticed in the past, to step forward and speak, to make the difficult confession of what they were. No doubt they were condemned all the same; but they were listened to; and if regular sexuality happened to be questioned once again, it was through a reflux movement, originating in these peripheral sexualities.

Whence the setting apart of the "unnatural" as a specific dimension in the field of sexuality. This kind of activity assumed an autonomy with regard to the other condemned forms such as adultery or rape (and the latter were condemned less and less): to marry a close relative or practice sodomy, to seduce a nun or engage in sadism, to deceive one's wife or violate cadavers, became things that were essentially different. The area covered by the Sixth Commandment began to fragment. Similarly, in the civil order, the confused category of "debauchery," which for more than a century had been one of the most frequent reasons for administrative confinement, came apart. From the debris, there appeared on the one hand infractions against the legislation (or morality) pertaining to marriage and the family, and on the other, offenses against the regularity of a natural function (offenses which, it must be added, the law was apt to punish). Here we have a likely reason, among others, for the prestige of Don Juan, which three centuries have not erased. Underneath the great violator of the rules of marriage – stealer of wives, seducer of virgins, the shame of families, and an insult to husbands and fathers – another personage can be glimpsed: the individual driven, in spite of himself, by the somber madness of sex. Underneath the libertine, the pervert. He deliberately breaks the law, but at the same time, something like a nature gone awry transports him far from all nature; his death is the moment when the supernatural return of the crime and its retribution thwarts the flight into counternature. There were two great systems conceived by the West for governing sex: the law of marriage and the order of desires – and the life of Don Juan overturned them both. We shall leave it to psychoanalysts to speculate whether he was homosexual, narcissistic, or impotent.

Although not without delay and equivocation, the natural laws of matrimony and the immanent rules of sexuality began to be recorded on two separate registers. There emerged a world of perversion which partook of that of legal or moral infraction, yet was not simply a variety of the latter. An entire sub-race was born, different – despite certain kinship ties – from the libertines of the past. From the end of the eighteenth century to our own, they circulated through the pores of society; they were always hounded, but not always by laws; were often locked up, but not always in prisons; were sick perhaps, but scandalous, dangerous victims, prey to a strange evil that also bore the name of vice and sometimes crime. They were children wise beyond their years, precocious little girls, ambiguous schoolboys, dubious servants and educators, cruel or maniacal husbands, solitary collectors, ramblers with bizarre impulses; they haunted the houses of correction, the penal colonies, the tribunals, and the asylums; they carried their infamy to the doctors and their sickness to the judges. This was the numberless family of perverts who were on friendly terms with delinquents and akin to madmen. In the course of the century they successively bore the stamp of "moral folly," "genital neurosis," "aberration of the genetic instinct," "degenerescence," or "physical imbalance."

What does the appearance of all these peripheral sexualities signify? Is the fact that they could appear in broad daylight a sign that the code had become more lax? Or does the fact that they were given so much attention testify to a stricter regime and to its concern to bring them under close supervision? In terms of repression, things are unclear. There was permissiveness, if one bears in mind that the severity of the codes relating to sexual offenses diminished considerably in the nineteenth century and that law itself often deferred to medicine. But an additional ruse of severity, if one thinks of all the agencies of control and all the mechanisms of surveillance that were put into operation by pedagogy or therapeutics. It may be the case that the intervention of the Church in conjugal sexuality and its rejection of "frauds" against procreation had lost much of their insistence over the previous two hundred years. But medicine made a forceful entry into the pleasures of the couple: it created an entire organic, functional, or mental pathology arising out of "incomplete" sexual practices; it carefully classified all forms of related pleasures; it incorporated them into the notions of "development" and instinctual "disturbances"; and it undertook to manage them.

Perhaps the point to consider is not the level of indulgence or the quantity of repression but the form of power that was exercised. When this whole thicket of disparate sexualities was labeled, as if to disentangle them from one another, was the object to exclude them from reality? It appears, in fact, that the function of the power exerted in this instance was not that of interdiction, and that it involved four operations quite different from simple prohibition.

1 Take the ancient prohibitions of consanguine marriages (as numerous and complex as they were) or the condemnation of adultery, with its inevitable frequency of occurrence; or on the other hand, the recent controls through which, since the nineteenth century, the sexuality of children has been subordinated and their "solitary habits" interfered with. It is clear that we are not dealing with one and the same power mechanism. Not only because in the one case it is a question of law and penality, and in the other, medicine and regimentation; but also because the tactics employed are not the same. On the surface, what appears in both cases is an effort at elimination that was always destined to fail and always constrained to begin again. But the prohibition of "incests" attempted to reach its objective through an asymptotic decrease in the thing it condemned, whereas the control of infantile sexuality hoped to reach it through a simultaneous propagation of its own power and of the object on which it was brought to bear. It proceeded in accordance with a twofold increase extended indefinitely. Educators and doctors combatted children's onanism like an epidemic that needed to be eradicated. What this actually entailed throughout this whole secular campaign that mobilized the adult world around the sex of children, was using these tenuous pleasures as a prop, constituting them as secrets (that is, forcing them into hiding so as to make possible their discovery), tracing them back to their source, tracking them from their origins to their effects, searching out everything that might cause them or simply enable them to exist. Wherever there was the chance they might appear, devices of surveillance were installed; traps were laid for compelling admissions; inexhaustible and corrective discourses were imposed, parents and teachers were alerted, and left with the suspicion that all children were guilty, and with the fear of being themselves at fault if their suspicions were not sufficiently strong; they were kept in readiness in the face of this recurrent danger; their conduct was prescribed and their pedagogy recodified; an entire medico-sexual regime took hold of the family milieu. The child's "vice" was not so much an enemy as a support; it may have been designated as the evil to be eliminated, but the extraordinary effort that went into the task that was bound to fail leads one to suspect that what was demanded of it was to persevere, to proliferate to the limits of the visible and the invisible, rather than to disappear for good. Always relying on this support, power advanced, multiplied its relays and its effects, while its target expanded, subdivided, and branched out, penetrating further into reality at the same pace. In appearance, we are dealing with a barrier system; but in fact, all around the child, indefinite *lines of penetration* were disposed.

2 This new persecution of the peripheral sexualities entailed an *incorporation of perversions* and a new *specification of individuals*. As defined by the ancient civil or canonical codes, sodomy was a category of forbidden acts; their perpetrator was nothing more than the juridical subject of them. The nineteenth-century homosexual became a personage, a past, a case history, and a childhood, in addition to being a type of life, a life form, and a morphology, with an indiscreet anatomy and possibly a mysterious physiology. Nothing that went into his total composition was unaffected by his sexuality. It was everywhere present in him: at the root of all his actions because it was their insidious and indefinitely active principle; written immodestly on his face and body because it was a secret that always gave itself away. It was consubstantial with him, less as a habitual sin than as a singular nature. We must not forget that the psychological, psychiatric, medical category of homosexuality was constituted from the moment it was characterized – Westphal's famous article of 1870 on "contrary sexual sensations" can stand as its date of birth[1] – less by a type of sexual relations than by a certain quality of sexual sensibility, a certain way of inverting the masculine and the feminine in oneself. Homosexuality appeared as one of the forms of sexuality when it was transposed from the practice of sodomy onto a kind of interior androgyny, a hermaphrodism of the soul. The sodomite had been a temporary aberration; the homosexual was now a species.

So too were all those minor perverts whom nineteenth-century psychiatrists ento-mologized by giving them strange baptismal names: there were Krafft-Ebing's zoo-philes and zooerasts, Rohleder's auto-monosexualists; and later, mixoscopophiles, gynecomasts, presbyophiles, sexoesthetic inverts, and dyspareunist women. These fine names for heresies referred to a nature that was overlooked by the law, but not so neglectful of itself that it did not go on producing more species, even where there was no order to fit them into. The machinery of power focused on this whole alien strain did not aim to suppress it, but rather to give it an analytical, visible, and permanent reality: it was implanted in bodies, slipped in beneath modes of conduct, made into a principle of classification and intelligibility, established as a *raison d'être* and a natural order of disorder. Not the exclusion of these thousand aberrant sexual-ities, but the specification, the regional solidification of each one of them. The strategy behind this dissemination was to strew reality with them and incorporate them into the individual.

3 More than the old taboos, this form of power demanded constant, attentive, and curious presences for its exercise; it presupposed proximities; it proceeded through examination and insistent observation; it required an exchange of discourses, through questions that extorted admissions, and confidences that went beyond the questions that were asked. It implied a physical proximity and an interplay of intense sensa-tions. The medicalization of the sexually peculiar was both the effect and the instru-ment of this. Imbedded in bodies, becoming deeply characteristic of individuals, the oddities of sex relied on a technology of health and pathology. And conversely, since sexuality was a medical and medicalizable object, one had to try and detect it – as a lesion, a dysfunction, or a symptom – in the depths of the organism, or on the surface of the skin, or among all the signs of behavior. The power which thus took charge of sexuality set about contacting bodies, caressing them with its eyes, intensi-fying areas, electrifying surfaces, dramatizing troubled moments. It wrapped the sexual body in its embrace. There was undoubtedly an increase in effectiveness and an extension of the domain controlled; but also a sensualization of power and a gain

of pleasure. This produced a twofold effect: an impetus was given to power through its very exercise; an emotion rewarded the overseeing control and carried it further; the intensity of the confession renewed the questioner's curiosity; the pleasure discovered fed back to the power that encircled it. But so many pressing questions singularized the pleasures felt by the one who had to reply. They were fixed by a gaze, isolated and animated by the attention they received. Power operated as a mechanism of attraction; it drew out those peculiarities over which it kept watch. Pleasure spread to the power that harried it; power anchored the pleasure it uncovered.

The medical examination, the psychiatric investigation, the pedagogical report, and family controls may have the overall and apparent objective of saying no to all wayward or unproductive sexualities, but the fact is that they function as mechanisms with a double impetus: pleasure and power. The pleasure that comes of exercising a power that questions, monitors, watches, spies, searches out, palpates, brings to light; and on the other hand, the pleasure that kindles at having to evade this power, flee from it, fool it, or travesty it. The power that lets itself be invaded by the pleasure it is pursuing; and opposite it, power asserting itself in the pleasure of showing off, scandalizing, or resisting. Capture and seduction, confrontation and mutual reinforcement: parents and children, adults and adolescents, educator and students, doctors and patients, the psychiatrist with his hysteric and his perverts, all have played this game continually since the nineteenth century. These attractions, these evasions, these circular incitements have traced around bodies and sexes, not boundaries not to be crossed, but *perpetual spirals of power and pleasure.*

4 Whence those *devices of sexual saturation* so characteristic of the space and the social rituals of the nineteenth century. People often say that modern society has attempted to reduce sexuality to the couple – the heterosexual and, insofar as possible, legitimate couple. There are equal grounds for saying that it has, if not created, at least outfitted and made to proliferate, groups with multiple elements and a circulating sexuality: a distribution of points of power, hierarchized and placed opposite to one another; "pursued" pleasures, that is, both sought after and searched out; compartmental sexualities that are tolerated or encouraged; proximities that serve as surveillance procedures, and function as mechanisms of intensification; contacts that operate as inductors. This is the way things worked in the case of the family, or rather the household, with parents, children, and in some instances, servants. Was the nineteenth-century family really a monogamic and conjugal cell? Perhaps to a certain extent. But it was also a network of pleasures and powers linked together at multiple points and according to transformable relationships. The separation of grown-ups and children, the polarity established between the parents' bedroom and that of the children (it became routine in the course of the century when working-class housing construction was undertaken), the relative segregation of boys and girls, the strict instructions as to the care of nursing infants (maternal breast-feeding, hygiene), the attention focused on infantile sexuality, the supposed dangers of masturbation, the importance attached to puberty, the methods of surveillance suggested to parents, the exhortations, secrets, and fears, the presence – both valued and feared – of servants: all this made the family, even when brought down to its smallest dimensions, a complicated network, saturated with multiple, fragmentary, and mobile sexualities. To reduce them to the conjugal relationship, and then to project the latter, in the form of a forbidden desire, onto the children, cannot account

for this apparatus which, in relation to these sexualities was less a principle of inhibition than an inciting and multiplying mechanism. Educational or psychiatric institutions, with their large populations, their hierarchies, their spatial arrangements, their surveillance systems, constituted, alongside the family, another way of distributing the interplay of powers and pleasures; but they too delineated areas of extreme sexual saturation, with privileged spaces or rituals such as the classroom, the dormitory, the visit, and the consultation. The forms of a nonconjugal, nonmonogamous sexuality were drawn there and established.

Nineteenth-century "bourgeois" society – and it is doubtless still with us – was a society of blatant and fragmented perversion. And this was not by way of hypocrisy, for nothing was more manifest and more prolix, or more manifestly taken over by discourses and institutions. Not because, having tried to erect too rigid or too general a barrier against sexuality, society succeeded only in giving rise to a whole perverse outbreak and a long pathology of the sexual instinct. At issue, rather, is the type of power it brought to bear on the body and on sex. In point of fact, this power had neither the form of the law, nor the effects of the taboo. On the contrary, it acted by multiplication of singular sexualities. It did not set boundaries for sexuality; it extended the various forms of sexuality, pursuing them according to lines of indefinite penetration. It did not exclude sexuality, but included it in the body as a mode of specification of individuals. It did not seek to avoid it; it attracted its varieties by means of spirals in which pleasure and power reinforced one another. It did not set up a barrier; it provided places of maximum saturation. It produced and determined the sexual mosaic. Modern society is perverse, not in spite of its puritanism or as if from a backlash provoked by its hypocrisy; it is in actual fact, and directly, perverse.

In actual fact, manifold sexualities – those which appear with the different ages (sexualities of the infant or the child), those which become fixated on particular tastes or practices (the sexuality of the invert, the gerontophile, the fetishist), those which, in a diffuse manner, invest relationships (the sexuality of doctor and patient, teacher and student, psychiatrist and mental patient), those which haunt spaces (the sexuality of the home, the school, the prison) – all form the correlate of exact procedures of power. We must not imagine these things that were formerly tolerated attracted notice and received a pejorative designation when the time came to give a regulative role to the one type of sexuality that was capable of reproducing labor power and the form of the family. These polymorphous conducts were actually extracted from people's bodies and from their pleasures; or rather, they were solidified in them; they were drawn out, revealed, isolated, intensified, incorporated, by multifarious power devices. The growth of perversions is not a moralizing theme that obsessed the scrupulous minds of the Victorians. It is the real product of the encroachment of a type of power on bodies and their pleasures. It is possible that the West has not been capable of inventing any new pleasures, and it has doubtless not discovered any original vices. But it has defined new rules for the game of powers and pleasures. The frozen countenance of the perversions is a fixture of this game.

Directly. This implantation of multiple perversions is not a mockery of sexuality taking revenge on a power that has thrust on it an excessively repressive law. Neither are we dealing with paradoxical forms of pleasure that turn back on power and invest it in the form of a "pleasure to be endured." The implantation of perversions is an instrument-effect: it is through the isolation, intensification, and consolidation of peripheral sexualities that the relations of power to sex and pleasure branched out and multiplied, measured the body, and penetrated modes of conduct. And accompanying this encroachment of powers, scattered sexualities rigidified, became stuck to an age, a place, a type of practice. A proliferation of sexualities through the extension of power, an optimization of the power to which each of these local sexualities gave a surface of intervention: this concatenation, particularly since the nineteenth century, has been ensured and relayed by the countless economic interests which, with the help of medicine, psychiatry, prostitution, and pornography, have tapped into both this analytical multiplication of pleasure and this optimization of the power that controls it. Pleasure and power do not cancel or turn back against one another; they seek out, overlap, and reinforce one another. They are linked together by complex mechanisms and devices of excitation and incitement.

We must therefore abandon the hypothesis that modern industrial societies ushered in an age of increased sexual repression. We have not only witnessed a visible explosion of unorthodox sexualities; but – and this is the important point – a deployment quite different from the law, even if it is locally dependent on procedures of prohibition, has ensured, through a network of interconnecting mechanisms, the proliferation of specific pleasures and the multiplication of disparate sexualities. It is said that no society has been more prudish; never have the agencies of power taken such care to feign ignorance of the thing they prohibited, as if they were determined to have nothing to do with it. But it is the opposite that has become apparent, at least after a general review of the facts: never have there existed more centers of power; never more attention manifested and verbalized; never more circular contacts and linkages; never more sites where the intensity of pleasures and the persistency of power catch hold, only to spread elsewhere.

Note

1 Carl Westphal, *Archiv für Neurologie*, 1870.

CHAPTER 4

Performative Acts and Gender Constitution

Judith Butler

Judith Butler's book *Gender Trouble: Feminism and the Subversion of Identity* (1990) helped to found contemporary Queer Theory. In this 1988 essay, she begins to develop her ideas regarding the relationship between performance and gender identity. For Butler, gender is entirely imitative. She quarrels with Freud, who contended that lesbians strive to imitate a masculine ideal. Lesbianism, in Freudian theory, has no secure ontological status as a gender; rather, it is a neurotic imitation, a desire on the part of women to be men. Butler argues that all gender can be understood, using Freud's own account of how identity is formed, as an imitation of an ideal or norm. One cannot therefore distinguish between the original and the imitation. All gender identity is performed or enacted.

Philosophers rarely think about acting in the theatrical sense, but they do have a discourse of "acts" that maintains associative semantic meanings with theories of performance and acting. For example, John Searle's "speech acts," those verbal assurance and promises which seem not only to refer to a speaking relationship, but to constitute a moral bond between speakers, illustrate one of the illocutionary gestures that constitutes the stage of the analytic philosophy of language. Further, "action theory," a domain of moral philosophy, seeks to understand what it is "to do" prior to any claim of what one *ought* to do. Finally, the phenomenological theory of "acts," espoused by Edmund Husserl, Maurice Merleau-Ponty, and George Herbert Mead, among others, seeks to explain the mundane way in which social agents *constitute* social reality through language, gesture, and all manner of symbolic social sign. Though phenomenology sometimes appears to assume the existence of a choosing and constituting agent prior to language (who poses as the sole source of its constituting acts), there is also a more radical use of the doctrine of constitution that takes the social agent as an *object* rather than the subject of constitutive acts.

When Simone de Beauvoir claims, "one is not born, but, rather, *becomes* a woman," she is appropriating and reinterpreting this doctrine of constituting acts from the phenomenological tradition.[1] In this sense, gender is in no way a stable identity or locus of agency from which various acts proceed; rather, it is an identity tenuously constituted in time – an identity instituted through a *stylized repetition of acts*. Further, gender is instituted through the stylization of the body and, hence, must be understood as the mundane way in which bodily gestures, movements, and enactments of various kinds constitute the illusion of an abiding gendered self. This formulation moves the conception of gender off the ground of a substantial model of identity to one that requires a conception of a constituted *social temporality*. Significantly, if gender is instituted through acts which are internally discontinuous, then the *appearance of substance* is precisely that, a constructed identity, a performative accomplishment which the mundane social audience, including the actors themselves, come to believe and to perform in the mode of belief. If the ground of gender identity is the stylized repetition of acts through time, and not a seemingly seamless identity, then the possibilities of gender transformation are to be found in the arbitrary relation between such acts, in the possibility of a different sort of repeating, in the breaking or subversive repetition of that style.

Through the conception of gender acts sketched above, I will try to show some ways in which reified and naturalized conceptions of gender might be understood as constituted and, hence, capable of being constituted differently. In opposition to theatrical or phenomenological models which take the gendered self to be prior to its acts, I will understand constituting acts not only as constituting the identity of the actor, but as constituting that identity as a compelling illusion, an object of *belief*. In the course of making my argument, I will draw from theatrical, anthropological, and philosophical discourses, but mainly phenomenology, to show that what is called gender identity is a performative accomplishment compelled by social sanction and taboo. In its very character as performative resides the possibility of contesting its reified status.

I Sex/gender: Feminist and Phenomenological Views

Feminist theory has often been critical of naturalistic explanations of sex and sexuality that assume that the meaning of women's social existence can be derived from some fact of their physiology. In distinguishing sex from gender, feminist theorists have disputed causal explanations that assume that sex dictates or necessitates certain social meanings for women's experience. Phenomenological theories of human embodiment have also been concerned to distinguish between the various physiological and biological causalities that structure bodily existence and the *meanings* that embodied existence assumes in the context of lived experience. In Merleau-Ponty's reflections in *The Phenomenology of Perception* on "the body in its sexual being," he takes issue with such accounts of bodily experience and claims that the body is "an historical idea" rather than "a natural species."[2] Significantly, it is this claim that Simone de Beauvoir cites in *The Second Sex* when she sets the stage for her claim that "woman," and by extension, any gender, is an historical situation rather than a natural fact.[3]

In both contexts, the existence and facticity of the material or natural dimensions of the body are not denied, but reconceived as distinct from the process by which the body comes to bear cultural meanings. For both Beauvoir and Merleau-Ponty, the body is understood to be an active process of embodying certain cultural and historical possibilities, a complicated process of appropriation which any phenomenological theory of embodiment needs to describe. In order to describe the gendered body, a phenomenological theory of constitution requires an expansion of the conventional view of acts to mean both that which constitutes meaning and that through which meaning is performed or enacted. In other words, the acts by which gender is constituted bear similarities to performative acts within theatrical contexts. My task, then, is to examine in what ways gender is constructed through specific corporeal acts, and what possibilities exist for the cultural transformation of gender through such acts.

Merleau-Ponty maintains not only that the body is an historical idea but a set of possibilities to be continually realized. In claiming that the body is an historical idea, Merleau-Ponty means that it gains its meaning through a concrete and historically mediated expression in the world. That the body is a set of possibilities signifies (a) that its appearance in the world, for perception, is not predetermined by some manner of interior essence, and (b) that its concrete expression in the world must be understood as the taking up and rendering specific of a set of historical possibilities. Hence, there is an agency which is understood as the process of rendering such possibilities determinate. These possibilities are necessarily constrained by available historical conventions. The body is not a self-identical or merely factic materiality; it is a materiality that bears meaning, if nothing else, and the manner of this bearing is fundamentally dramatic. By dramatic I mean only that the body is not merely matter but a continual and incessant *materializing* of possibilities. One is not simply a body, but, in some very key sense, one does one's body and, indeed, one does one's body differently from one's contemporaries and from one's embodied predecessors and successors as well.

It is, however, clearly unfortunate grammar to claim that there is a "we" or an "I" that does its body, as if a disembodied agency preceded and directed an embodied exterior. More appropriate, I suggest, would be a vocabulary that resists the substance metaphysics of subject–verb formations and relies instead on an ontology of present participles. The "I" that is its body is, of necessity, a mode of embodying, and the "what" that it embodies is possibilities. But here again the grammar of the formulation misleads, for the possibilities that are embodied are not fundamentally exterior or antecedent to the process of embodying itself. As an intentionally organized materiality, the body is always an embodying *of* possibilities both conditioned and circumscribed by historical convention. In other words, the body *is* a historical situation, as Beauvoir has claimed, and is a manner of doing, dramatizing, and *reproducing* a historical situation.

To do, to dramatize, to reproduce, these seem to be some of the elementary structures of embodiment. This doing of gender is not merely a way in which embodied agents are exterior, surfaced, open to the perception of others. Embodiment clearly manifests a set of strategies or what Sartre would perhaps have called a style of being or Foucault, "a stylistics of existence." This style is never fully self-styled, for living styles have a history, and that history conditions and limits possibilities. Consider gender, for instance, as *a corporeal style*, an "act," as it were, which is both intentional and performative, where "performative" itself carries the double-meaning of "dramatic" and "non-referential."

When Beauvoir claims that "woman" is a historical idea and not a natural fact, she clearly underscores the distinction between sex, as biological facticity, and gender, as the cultural interpretation or signification of that facticity. To be female is, according to that distinction, a facticity which has no meaning, but to be a woman is to have *become* a woman, to compel the body to conform to an historical idea of "woman," to induce the body to become a cultural sign, to materialize oneself in obedience to an historically delimited possibility, and to do this as a sustained and repeated corporeal project. The notion of a "project," however, suggests the originating force of a radical will, and because gender is a project which has cultural survival as its end, the term *"strategy"* better suggests the situation of duress under which gender performance always and variously occurs. Hence, as a strategy of survival, gender is a performance with clearly punitive consequences. Discrete genders are part of what "humanizes" individuals within contemporary culture; indeed, those who fail to do their gender right are regularly punished. Because there is neither an "essence" that gender expresses or externalizes nor an objective ideal to which gender aspires; because gender is not a fact, the various acts of gender create the idea of gender, and without those acts, there would be no gender at all. Gender is, thus, a construction that regularly conceals its genesis. The tacit collective agreement to perform, produce, and sustain discrete and polar genders as cultural fictions is obscured by the credibility of its own production. The authors of gender become entranced by their own fictions whereby the construction compels one's belief in its necessity and naturalness. The historical possibilities materialized through various corporeal styles are nothing other than those punitively regulated cultural fictions that are alternatively embodied and disguised under duress.

How useful is a phenomenological point of departure for a feminist description of gender? On the surface it appears that phenomenology shares with feminist analysis a commitment to grounding theory in lived experience, and in revealing the way in which the world is produced through the constituting acts of subjective experience. Clearly, not all feminist theory would privilege the point of view of the subject (Kristeva once objected to feminist theory as "too existentialist"),[4] and yet the feminist claim that the personal is political suggests, in part, that subjective experience is not only structured by existing political arrangements, but effects and structures those arrangements in turn. Feminist theory has sought to understand the way in which systemic or pervasive political and cultural structures are enacted and reproduced through individual acts and practices, and how the analysis of ostensibly personal situations is clarified through situating the issues in a broader and shared cultural context. Indeed, the feminist impulse, and I am sure there is more than one, has often emerged in the recognition that my pain or my silence or my anger or my perception is finally not mine alone, and that it delimits me in a shared cultural situation which in turn enables and empowers me in certain unanticipated ways. The personal is thus implicitly political inasmuch as it is conditioned by shared social structures, but the personal has also been immunized against political challenge to the extent that public/private distinctions endure. For feminist theory, then, the personal becomes an expansive category, one which accommodates, if only implicitly, political structures usually viewed as public. Indeed, the very meaning of the political expands as well. At its best, feminist theory involves a dialectical expansion of both of these categories. My situation does not cease to be mine just because it is the situation of someone else, and my acts, individual as they are, nevertheless reproduce the situation of my gender, and do that in various ways. In other words, there is, latent in the personal is political formulation of feminist theory, a supposition that the life-world of gender relations is constituted, at least partially, through the concrete and historically mediated *acts* of individuals. Considering that "the" body is invariably transformed into his body or her body, the body is only known through its gendered appearance. It would seem imperative to consider the way in which this gendering of the body occurs. My suggestion is that the body becomes its gender through a series of acts which are renewed, revised, and consolidated through time. From a feminist point of view, one might try to reconceive the gendered body as the legacy of sedimented acts rather than a predetermined or foreclosed structure, essence or fact, whether natural, cultural, or linguistic.

The feminist appropriation of the phenomenological theory of constitution might employ the notion of an *act* in a richly ambiguous sense. If the personal is a category which expands to include the wider political and social structures, then the *acts* of the gendered subject would be similarly expansive. Clearly, there are political acts which are deliberate and instrumental actions of political organizing, resistance collective intervention with the broad aim of instating a more just set of social and political relations. There are thus acts which are done in the name of women, and then there are acts in and of themselves, apart from any instrumental consequence, that challenge the category of women itself. Indeed, one ought to consider the futility of a political program which seeks radically to transform the social situation of women without first determining whether the category of woman is socially constructed in such a way that to be a woman is, by definition, to be in an oppressed situation. In an understandable desire to forge bonds of solidarity, feminist discourse has often relied upon the category of woman as a universal presupposition of cultural experience which, in its universal status, provides a false ontological promise of eventual political solidarity. In a culture in which the false universal of "man" has for the most part been presupposed as coextensive with humanness itself, feminist theory has sought with success to bring female specificity into visibility and to rewrite the history of culture in terms which acknowledge the presence, the influence, and the oppression of women. Yet, in this effort to combat the invisibility of women as a category feminists run the risk of rendering visible a category which may or may not be representative of the concrete lives of women. As feminists, we have been less eager, I think, to consider the status of the category itself and, indeed, to discern the conditions of oppression which issue from an unexamined reproduction of gender identities which sustain discrete and binary categories of man and woman.

When Beauvoir claims that woman is an "historical situation," she emphasizes that the body suffers a certain cultural construction, not only through conventions that sanction and proscribe how one acts one's body, the "act" or performance that one's body is, but also in the tacit conventions that structure the way the body is culturally perceived. Indeed, if gender is the cultural significance that the sexed body assumes, and if that significance is codetermined through various acts and their cultural perception, then it would appear that from within the terms of culture it is not possible to know sex as distinct from gender. The reproduction of the category of gender is enacted on a large political scale, as when women first enter a profession or gain certain rights, or are reconceived in legal or political discourse in significantly new ways. But the more mundane reproduction of gendered identity takes place through the various ways in which bodies are acted in relationship to the deeply entrenched or sedimented expectations of gendered existence. Consider that there is a sedimentation of gender norms that produces the peculiar phenomenon of a natural sex, or a real woman, or any number of prevalent and compelling social fictions, and that this is a sedimentation that over time has produced a set of corporeal styles which, in reified form, appear as the natural configuration of bodies into sexes which exist in a binary relation to one another.

II Binary Genders and the Heterosexual Contract

To guarantee the reproduction of a given culture, various requirements, well-established in the anthropological literature of kinship, have instated sexual reproduction within the confines of a heterosexually-based system of marriage which requires the reproduction of human beings in certain gendered modes which, in effect, guarantee the eventual reproduction of that kinship system. As Foucault and others have pointed out, the association of a natural sex with a discrete gender and with an ostensibly natural "attraction" to the opposing sex/gender is an unnatural conjunction of cultural constructs in the service of reproductive interests.[5] Feminist cultural anthropology and kinship studies have shown how cultures are governed by conventions that not only regulate and guarantee the production, exchange, and consumption of material goods, but also reproduce the bonds of kinship itself, which require taboos and a punitive regulation of reproduction to effect that end. Lévi-Strauss has shown how the incest taboo works to guarantee the channeling of sexuality into various modes of heterosexual marriage.[6] Gayle Rubin has argued convincingly that the incest taboo produces certain kinds of discrete gendered identities and sexualities.[7] My point is simply that one way in which this system of compulsory heterosexuality is reproduced and concealed is through the cultivation of bodies into discrete sexes with "natural" appearances and "natural" heterosexual dispositions. Although the enthnocentric conceit suggests a progression beyond the mandatory structures of kinship relations as described by Lévi-Strauss, I would suggest, along with Rubin, that contemporary gender identities are so many marks or "traces" of residual kinship. The contention that sex, gender, and heterosexuality are historical products which have become conjoined and reified as natural over time has received a good deal of critical attention not only from Michel Foucault, but Monique Wittig, gay historians, and various cultural anthropologists and social psychologists in recent years.[8] These theories, however, still lack the critical resources for thinking radically about the historical sedimentation of sexuality and sex-related constructs if they do not delimit and describe the mundane manner in which these constructs are produced, reproduced, and maintained within the field of bodies.

Can phenomenology assist a feminist reconstruction of the sedimented character of sex, gender, and sexuality at the level of the body? In the first place, the phenomenological focus on the various acts by which cultural identity is constituted and assumed provides a felicitous starting point for the feminist effort to understand the mundane manner in which bodies get crafted into genders. The formulation of the body as a mode of dramatizing or enacting possibilities offers a way to understand how a cultural convention is embodied and enacted. But it seems difficult, if not impossible, to imagine a way to conceptualize the scale and systemic character of women's oppression from a theoretical position which takes constituting acts to be its point of departure. Although individual acts do work to maintain and reproduce systems of oppression and, indeed, any theory of personal political responsibility presupposes such a view, it doesn't follow that oppression is a sole consequence of such acts. One might argue that without human beings whose various acts, largely construed, produce and maintain oppressive conditions, those conditions would fall away, but note that the relation between acts and conditions is neither unilateral nor unmediated. There are social contexts and conventions within which certain acts not only become possible but become conceivable as acts at all. The transformation of social relations becomes a matter, then, of transforming hegemonic social conditions rather than the individual acts that are spawned by those conditions. Indeed, one runs the risk of addressing the merely indirect, if not epiphenomenal, reflection of those conditions if one remains restricted to a politics of acts.

But the theatrical sense of an "act" forces a revision of the individualist assumptions underlying the more restricted view of constituting acts within phenomenological discourse. As a given temporal duration within the entire performance, "acts" are a shared experience and "collective action." Just as within feminist theory the very category of the personal is expanded to include political structures, so is there a theatrically-based and, indeed, less individually oriented view of acts that goes some of the way to defusing the criticism of act theory as "too existentialist." The act that gender is, the act that embodied agents *are* inasmuch as they dramatically and actively embody and, indeed, *wear* certain cultural significations, is clearly not one's act alone. Surely, there are nuanced and individual ways of *doing* one's gender, but *that* one does it, and that one does it *in accord with* certain sanctions and prescriptions, is clearly not a fully individual matter. Here again, I don't mean to minimize the effect of certain gender norms which originate within the family and are enforced through certain familial modes of punishment and reward and which, as a consequence might be construed as highly individual, for even there family relations recapitulate, individualize, and specify pre-existing cultural relations; they are rarely, if even radically original. The act that one does, the act that one performs, is, in a sense, an act that has been going on before one arrived on the scene. Hence, gender is an act which has been rehearsed, much as a script survives the particular actors who make use of it; but which requires individual actors in order to be actualized and reproduced as reality once again. The complex components that go into an act must be distinguished in order to understand the kind of acting in concert and acting in accord which acting one's gender invariably is.

In what senses, then, is gender an act? As anthropologist Victor Turner suggests in his studies of ritual social drama, social action requires a performance which is *repeated*. This repetition is at once a reenactment and reexperiencing of a set of meanings already socially established; it is the mundane and ritualized form of their legitimation.[9] When this conception of social performance is applied to gender, it is clear that although there are individual bodies that enact these significations by becoming stylized into gendered modes, this "action" is immediately public as well. There are temporal and collective dimensions to these actions, and their public nature is not inconsequential; indeed, the performance is effected with the strategic aim of maintaining gender within its binary frame. Understood in pedagogical terms, the performance renders social laws explicit.

As a public action and performative act, gender is not a radical choice or project that reflects a merely individual choice, but neither is it imposed or inscribed upon the individual, as some post-structuralist displacements of the subject would contend. The body is not passively scripted with cultural codes, as if it were a lifeless recipient of wholly pre-given cultural relations. But neither do embodied selves pre-exist the cultural conventions which essentially signify bodies. Actors are always already on the stage, within the terms of the performance. Just as a script may be enacted in various ways, and just as the play requires both text and interpretation, so the gendered body acts its part in a culturally restricted corporeal space and enacts interpretations within the confines of already existing directives.

Although the links between a theatrical and a social role are complex and the distinctions not easily drawn (Bruce Wilshire points out the limits of the comparison in *Role-Playing and Identity: The Limits of Theatre as Metaphor*[10]), it seems clear that, although theatrical performances can meet with political censorship and scathing criticism, gender performances in non-theatrical contexts are governed by more clearly punitive and regulatory social conventions. Indeed, the sight of a transvestite onstage can compel pleasure and applause while the sight of the same transvestite on the seat next to us on the bus can compel fear, rage, even violence. The conventions which mediate proximity and identification in these two instances are clearly quite different. I want to make two different kinds of claims, regarding this tentative distinction. In the theatre, one can say, "this is just an act," and de-realize the act, make acting into something quite distinct from what is real. Because of this distinction, one can maintain one's sense of reality in the face of this temporary challenge to our existing ontological assumptions about gender arrangements; the various conventions which announce that "this is only a play" allows strict lines to be drawn between the performance and life. On the street or in the bus, the act becomes dangerous, if it does, precisely because there are no theatrical conventions to delimit the purely imaginary character of the act, indeed, on the street or in the bus, there is no presumption that the act is distinct from a reality; the disquieting effect of the act is that there are no conventions that facilitate making this separation. Clearly, there is theatre which attempts to contest or, indeed, break down those conventions that demarcate the imaginary from the real (Richard Schechner brings this out quite clearly in *Between Theatre and Anthropology*[11]). Yet in those cases one confronts the same phenomenon, namely, that the act is not contrasted with the real, but *constitutes* a reality that is in some sense new, a modality of gender that cannot readily be assimilated into the pre-existing categories that regulate gender reality. From the point of view of those established categories, one may want to claim, but oh, this is *really* a girl or a woman, or this is *really* a boy or a man, and further that the *appearance* contradicts the *reality* of the gender, that the discrete and familiar reality must be there, nascent, temporarily unrealized, perhaps realized at other times or other places. The transvestite, however, can do more than simply express the distinction between sex and gender, but challenges, at least implicitly, the distinction between appearance and reality that structures a good deal of popular thinking about gender identity. If the "reality" of gender is constituted by the performance itself, then there is no recourse to an essential and unrealized "sex" or "gender" which gender performances ostensibly express. Indeed, the transvestite's gender is as fully real as anyone whose performance complies with social expectations.

Gender reality is performative which means, quite simply, that it is real only to the extent that it is performed. It seems fair to say that certain kinds of acts are usually interpreted as expressive of a gender core or identity, and that these acts either conform to an expected gender identity or contest that expectation in some way. That expectation, in turn, is based upon the perception of sex, where sex is understood to be the discrete and factic datum of primary sexual characteristics. This implicit and popular theory of acts and gestures as *expressive* of gender suggests that gender itself is something prior to the various acts, postures, and gestures by which it is dramatized and known; indeed, gender appears to the popular imagination as a substantial core which might well be understood as the spiritual or psychological correlate of biological sex.[12] If gender attributes, however, are not expressive but performative, then these attributes effectively constitute the identity they are said to express or reveal. The distinction between expression and performativeness is quite crucial, for if gender attributes and acts, the various ways in which a body shows or produces its cultural signification, are performative, then there is no preexisting identity by which an act or attribute might be measured; there would be no true or false, real or distorted acts of gender, and the postulation of a true gender identity would be revealed as a regulatory fiction. That gender reality is created through sustained social performances means that the very notions of an essential sex, a true or abiding masculinity or femininity, are also constituted as part of the strategy by which the performative aspect of gender is concealed.

As a consequence, gender cannot be understood as a *role* which either expresses or disguises an interior "self," whether that "self" is conceived as sexed or not. As performance which is performative, gender is an "act," broadly construed, which constructs the social fiction of its own psychological interiority. As opposed to a view such as Erving Goffman's which posits a self which assumes and exchanges various "roles" within the complex social expectations of the "game" of modern life,[13] I am suggesting that this self is not only irretrievably "outside," constituted in social discourse, but that the ascription of interiority is itself a publicly regulated and sanctioned form of essence fabrication. Genders, then, can be neither true nor false, neither real nor apparent. And yet, one is compelled to live in a world in which genders constitute univocal signifiers, in which gender is stabilized, polarized, rendered discrete and intractable. In effect, gender is made to comply with a model of truth and falsity which not only contradicts its own performative fluidity, but serves a social policy of gender regulation and control. Performing one's gender wrong initiates a set of punishments both obvious and indirect, and performing it well provides the reassurance that there is an essentialism of gender identity after all. That this reassurance is so easily displaced by anxiety, that culture so readily punishes or marginalizes those who fail to perform the illusion of gender essentialism should be sign enough that on some level there is social knowledge that the truth or falsity of gender is only socially compelled and in no sense ontologically necessitated.[14]

III Feminist Theory: Beyond an Expressive Model of Gender

This view of gender does not pose as a comprehensive theory about what gender is or the manner of its construction, and neither does it prescribe an explicit feminist political program. Indeed, I can imagine this view of gender being used for a number of discrepant political strategies. Some of my friends may fault me for this and insist that any theory of gender constitution has political presuppositions and implications, and that it is impossible to separate a theory of gender from a political philosophy of feminism. In fact, I would agree, and argue that it is primarily political interests which create the social phenomena of gender itself, and that without a radical critique of gender constitution feminist theory fails to take stock of the way in which oppression structures the ontological categories through which gender is conceived. Gayatri Spivak has argued that feminists need to rely on an operational essentialism, a false ontology of women as a universal in order to advance a feminist political program.[15] She knows that the category of "women" is not fully expressive, that the multiplicity and discontinuity of the referent mocks and rebels against the univocity of the sign, but suggests it could be used for strategic purposes. Kristeva suggests something similar, I think, when she prescribes that feminists use the category of women as a political tool without attributing ontological integrity to the term, and adds that, strictly speaking, women cannot be said to exist.[16] Feminists might well worry about the political implications of claiming that women do not exist, especially in light of the persuasive arguments advanced by Mary Anne Warren in her book, *Gendercide*.[17] She argues that social policies regarding population control and reproductive technology are designed to limit and, at times, eradicate the existence of women altogether. In light of such a claim, what good does it do to quarrel about the metaphysical status of the term, and perhaps, for clearly political reasons, feminists ought to silence the quarrel altogether.

But it is one thing to use the term and know its ontological insufficiency and quite another to articulate a normative vision for feminist theory which celebrates or emancipates an essence, a nature, or a shared cultural reality which cannot be found. The option I am defending is not to redescribe the world from the point of view of women. I don't know what that point of view is, but whatever it is, it is not singular, and not mine to espouse. It would only be half-right to claim that I am interested in how the phenomenon of a men's or women's point of view gets constituted, for while I do think that those points of view are, indeed, socially constituted, and that a reflexive genealogy of those points of view is important to do, it is not primarily the gender episteme that I am interested in exposing, deconstructing, or reconstructing. Indeed, it is the presupposition of the category of woman itself that requires a critical genealogy of the complex institutional and discursive means by which it is constituted. Although some feminist literary critics suggest that the presupposition of sexual difference is necessary for all discourse, that position reifies sexual difference as the founding moment of culture and precludes an analysis not only of how sexual difference is constituted to begin with but how it is continuously constituted, both by the masculine tradition that preempts the universal point of view, and by those feminist positions that construct the univocal category of "women" in the name of expressing or, indeed, liberating a subjected class. As Foucault claimed about those humanist efforts to liberate the criminalized subject, the subject that is freed is even more deeply shackled than originally thought.[18]

Clearly, though, I envision the critical genealogy of gender to rely on a phenomenological set of presuppositions, most important among them the expanded conception of an "act" which is both socially shared and historically constituted, and which is performative in the sense I previously described. But a critical genealogy needs to be supplemented by a politics of performative gender acts, one which both redescribes existing gender identities and offers a prescriptive view about the kind of gender reality there ought to be. The redescription needs to expose the reifications that tacitly serve as substantial gender cores or identities, and to elucidate both the act and the strategy of disavowal which at once constitute and conceal gender as we live it. The prescription is invariably more difficult, if only because we need to think a world in which acts, gestures, the visual body, the clothed body, the various physical attributes usually associated with gender, *express nothing*. In a sense, the prescription is not utopian, but consists in an imperative to acknowledge the existing complexity of gender which our vocabulary invariably disguises and to bring that complexity into a dramatic cultural interplay without punitive consequences.

Certainly, it remains politically important to represent women, but to do that in a way that does not distort and reify the very collectivity the theory is supposed to emancipate. Feminist theory which presupposes sexual difference as the necessary and invariant theoretical point of departure clearly improves upon those humanist discourses which conflate the universal with the masculine and appropriate all of culture as masculine property. Clearly, it is necessary to reread the texts of western philosophy from the various points of view that have been excluded, not only to reveal the particular perspective and set of interests informing those ostensibly transparent descriptions of the real, but to offer alternative descriptions and prescriptions; indeed, to establish philosophy as a cultural practice, and to criticize its tenets from marginalized cultural locations. I have no quarrel with this procedure, and have clearly benefited from those analyses. My only concern is that sexual difference not become a reification which unwittingly preserves a binary restriction on gender identity and an implicitly heterosexual framework for the description of gender, gender identity, and sexuality. There is, in my view, nothing about femaleness that is waiting to be expressed; there is, on the other hand, a good deal about the diverse experiences of women that is being expressed and still needs to be expressed, but caution is needed with respect to that theoretical language, for it does not simply report a pre-linguistic experience, but constructs that experience as well as the limits of its analysis. Regardless of the pervasive character of patriarchy and the prevalence of sexual difference as an operative cultural distinction, there is nothing about a binary gender system that is given. As a corporeal field of cultural play, gender is a basically innovative affair, although it is quite clear that there are strict punishments for contesting the script by performing out of turn or through unwarranted improvisations. Gender is not passively scripted on the body, and neither is it determined by nature, language, the symbolic, or the overwhelming history of patriarchy. Gender is what is put on, invariably, under constraint, daily and incessantly, with anxiety and pleasure, but if this continuous act is mistaken for a natural or linguistic given, power is relinquished to expand the cultural field bodily through subversive performances of various kinds.

Notes

1 For a further discussion of Beauvoir's feminist contribution to phenomenological theory, see my "Variations on Sex and Gender: Beauvoir's *The Second Sex*," *Yale French Studies* 172 (1986).

2 Maurice Merleau-Ponty, "The Body is its Sexual Being," in *The Phenomenology of Perception*, trans. Colin Smith (Boston: Routledge and Kegan Paul, 1962).

3 Simone de Beauvoir, *The Second Sex*, trans. H. M. Parshley (New York: Vintage, 1974), 38.

4 Julia Kristeva, *Histoire d'amour* (Paris: Editions Denoel, 1983), 242.

5 See Michel Foucault, *The History of Sexuality: An Introduction*, trans. Robert Hurley (New York: Random House, 1980), 154: "the notion of 'sex' made it possible to group together, in an artificial unity, anatomical elements, biological functions, conducts, sensations, and pleasures, and it enabled one to make use of this fictitious unity as a causal principle."

6 See Claude Lévi-Strauss, *The Elementary Structures of Kinship* (Boston: Beacon Press, 1965).

7 Gayle Rubin, "The Traffic in Women: Notes on the 'Political Economy' of Sex," in *Toward an Anthropology of Women*, ed. Rayna R. Reiter (New York: Monthly Review Press, 1975), 178–85.

8 See my "Variations on Sex and Gender: Beauvoir, Wittig, and Foucault," in *Feminism as Critique*, ed. Seyla Benhabib and Drucila Cornell (London: Basil Blackwell, 1987 [distributed by University of Minnesota Press]).

9 See Victor Turner, *Dramas, Fields, and Metaphors* (Ithaca, NY: Cornell University Press, 1974). Clifford Geertz suggests in "Blurred Genres: The Refiguration of Thought," in *Local Knowledge, Further Essays in Interpretive Anthropology* (New York: Basic Books, 1983), that the theatrical metaphor is used by recent social theory in two, often opposing, ways. Ritual theorists like Victor Turner focus on a notion of social drama of various kinds as a means for settling internal conflict within a culture and regenerating social cohesion. On the other hand, symbolic action approaches, influenced by figures as diverse as Emile Durkheim, Kenneth Burke, and Michel Foucault, focus on the way in which political authority and questions of legitimation are thematized and settled within the terms of performed meaning. Geertz himself suggests that the tension might be viewed dialectically; his study of political organization in Bali as a "theatre-state" is a case in point. In terms of an explicitly feminist account of gender as performative, it seems clear to me that an account of gender as ritualized, public performance must be combined with an analysis of the political sanctions and taboos under which that performance may and may not occur within the public sphere free of punitive consequence.

10 Bruce Wilshire, *Role-Playing and Identity: The Limits of Theatre as Metaphor* (Boston: Routledge and Kegan Paul, 1981).

11 Richard Schechner, *Between Theatre and Anthropology* (Philadelphia: University of Pennsylvania Press, 1985). See especially, "News, Sex, and Performance," 295–324.

12 In *Mother Camp* (Prentice Hall, 1974), anthropologist Esther Newton gives an urban ethnography of drag queens in which she suggests that all gender might be understood on the model of drag. In *Gender: An Ethnomethodological Approach* (Chicago: University of Chicago Press, 1978), Suzanne J. Kessler and Wendy McKenna argue that gender is an "accomplishment" which requires the skills of constructing the body into a socially legitimate artifice.

13 See Erving Goffman, *The Presentation of Self in Everyday Life* (Garden City, NY: Doubleday, 1959).

14 See Michel Foucault's edition of *Herculine Barbin: The Journals of a Nineteenth Century French Hermaphrodite*, trans. Richard McDougall (New York: Pantheon Books, 1984), for an interesting display of the horror evoked by intersexed bodies. Foucault's introduction makes clear that the medical delimitation of univocal sex is yet another wayward application of the discourse on truth-as-identity. See also the work of Robert Edgerton in *American Anthropologist* on the cross-cultural variations of response to hermaphroditic bodies.

15 Remarks at the Center for Humanities, Wesleyan University, Spring 1985.

16 Julia Kristeva, "Woman Can Never Be Defined," trans. Marilyn A. August, in *New French Feminisms*, ed. Elaine Marks and Isabelle de Courtivron (Totowa, NJ: Schocken, 1981).

17 Mary Anne Warren, *Gendercide: The Implications of Sex Selection* (Totowa, NJ: Rowman and Allanheld, 1985).

18 Ibid.; Michel Foucault, *Discipline and Punish: The Birth of the Prison*, trans. Alan Sheridan (New York: Vintage Books, 1978).

CHAPTER 5

Epistemology of the Closet

Eve Kosofsky Sedgwick

Eve Sedgwick's *Epistemology of the Closet* (1990) is part of the body of scholarship and theory that grew especially in the 1980s and 1990s around the issue of gay and lesbian representation in literature. Sedgwick's work is important for the way it conceives of that issue in terms of the question of knowledge and secrecy. Important in her work as well is the argument that sexuality and gender do not match up in any easily identifiable manner. As many gay theorists noted regarding the US Supreme Court's rulings against homosexuals, the very "unnatural" sexual practices that supposedly distinguish gays from straights are practiced by many heterosexual couples.

Historically, the framing of *Epistemology of the Closet* begins with a puzzle. It is a rather amazing fact that, of the very many dimensions along which the genital activity of one person can be differentiated from that of another (dimensions that include preference for certain acts, certain zones or sensations, certain physical types, a certain frequency, certain symbolic investments, certain relations of age or power, a certain species, a certain number of participants, etc. etc. etc.), precisely one, the gender of object choice, emerged from the turn of the century, and has remained, as *the* dimension denoted by the now ubiquitous category of "sexual orientation." This is not a development that would have been foreseen from the viewpoint of the fin de siècle itself, where a rich stew of male algolagnia, child-love, and autoeroticism, to mention no more of its components, seemed to have as indicative a relation as did homosexuality to the whole, obsessively entertained problematic of sexual "perversion" or, more broadly, "decadence." Foucault, for instance, mentions the hysterical woman and the masturbating child, along with "entomologized" sexological categories such as zoophiles, zooerasts, auto-monosexualists, and gynecomasts, as typifying the new sexual taxonomies, the *"specification of individuals"* that facilitated the modern freighting of sexual definition with epistemological and power relations.[1] True as his notation is, it suggests without beginning to answer the further question: why the category of "the masturbator," to choose only one example, should by now have entirely lost its diacritical potential for specifying a particular kind of person, an identity, at the same time as it continues to be true – becomes increasingly true – that, for a crucial strain of Western discourse, in Foucault's words "the homosexual was now a species."[2] So, as a result, is the heterosexual, and between *these* species the human species has come more and more to be divided. *Epistemology of the Closet* does not have an explanation to offer for this sudden, radical condensation of sexual categories; instead of speculating on its causes, the book explores its unpredictably varied and acute implications and consequences.

At the same time that this process of sexual specification or species-formation was going on, the book will argue, less stable and identity-bound understandings of sexual choice also persisted and developed, often among the same people or inter-woven in the same systems of thought. Again, the book will not suggest (nor do I believe there currently exists) any standpoint of thought from which the rival claims of these minoritizing and universalizing understandings of sexual definition could be decisively arbitrated as to their "truth." Instead, the performative effects of the self-contradictory discursive field of force created by their overlap will be my subject. And, of course, it makes every difference that these impactions of homo/heterosexual definition took place in a setting, not of spacious emotional or analytic impartiality, but rather of urgent homophobic pressure to devalue one of the two nominally symmetrical forms of choice.

As several of the formulations above would suggest, one main strand of argument in this book is deconstructive, in a fairly specific sense. The analytic move it makes is to demonstrate that categories presented in a culture as symmetrical binary oppos-itions – heterosexual/homosexual, in this case – actually subsist in a more unsettled and dynamic tacit relation according to which, first, term B is not symmetrical with but subordinated to term A; but, second, the ontologically valorized term A actually depends for its meaning on the simultaneous subsumption and exclusion of term B; hence, third, the question of priority between the supposed central and the supposed marginal category of each dyad is irresolvably unstable, an instability caused by the fact that term B is constituted as at once internal and external to term A. Harold Beaver, for instance, in an influential 1981 essay sketched the outlines of such a deconstructive strategy:

> The aim must be to reverse the rhetorical opposition of what is "transparent" or "natural" and what is "derivative" or "contrived" by demonstrating that the qualities predicated of "homosexuality" (as a dependent term) are in fact a condition of "hetero-sexuality"; that "heterosexuality," far from possessing a privileged status, must itself be treated as a dependent term.[3]

To understand these conceptual relations as irresolvably unstable is not, however, to understand them as inefficacious or innocuous. It is at least premature when Roland Barthes prophesies that "once the paradigm is blurred, utopia begins: mean-ing and sex become the objects of free play, at the heart of which the (polysemant) forms and the (sensual) practices, liberated from the binary prison, will achieve a state of infinite expansion."[4] To the contrary, a deconstructive understanding of these binarisms makes it possible to identify them as sites that are *peculiarly* densely charged with lasting potentials for powerful manipulation – through precisely the mechanisms of self-contradictory definition or, more succinctly, the double bind. Nor is a deconstructive analysis of such definitional knots, however necessary, at all sufficient to disable them. Quite the opposite: I would suggest that an understanding of their irresolvable instability has been continually available, and has continually lent discursive authority, to antigay as well as to gay cultural forces of this century. Beaver makes an optimistic prediction that "by disqualifying the autonomy of what was deemed spontaneously immanent, the whole sexual system is fundamentally decentred and exposed."[5] But there is reason to believe that the oppressive sexual system of the past hundred years was if anything born and bred (if I may rely on the pith of a fable whose value doesn't, I must hope, stand or fall with its history of racist uses) in the briar patch of the most notorious and repeated decenterings and exposures.

These deconstructive contestations can occur, moreover, only in the context of an entire cultural network of normative definitions, definitions themselves equally unstable but responding to different sets of contiguities and often at a different rate. The master terms of a particular historical moment will be those that are so situated as to entangle most inextricably and at the same time most differentially the filaments of other important definitional nexuses. In arguing that homo/heterosexual definition has been a presiding master term of the past century, one that has the same, primary importance for all modern Western identity and social organization (and not merely for homosexual identity and culture) as do the more traditionally visible cruxes of gender, class, and race, I'll argue that the now chronic modern crisis of homo/ heterosexual definition has affected our culture through its ineffaceable marking particularly of the categories secrecy/disclosure, knowledge/ignorance, private/ public, masculine/feminine, majority/minority, innocence/initiation, natural/artificial, new/old, discipline/terrorism, canonic/noncanonic, wholeness/decadence, urbane/provincial, domestic/foreign, health/illness, same/different, active/passive, in/out, cognition/paranoia, art/kitsch, utopia/apocalypse, sincerity/sentimentality, and voluntarity/addiction.[6] And rather than embrace an idealist faith in the necessarily, immanently self-corrosive efficacy of the contradictions inherent to these definitional binarisms, I will suggest instead that contests for discursive power can be specified as competitions for the material or rhetorical leverage required to set the terms of, and to profit in some way from, the operations of such an incoherence of definition.

Perhaps I should say something about the project of hypothesizing that certain binarisms that structure meaning in a culture may be "ineffaceably marked" by association with this one particular problematic – ineffaceably even when invisibly. Hypothesizing is easier than proving, but indeed I cannot imagine the protocol by which such hypotheses might be *tested*; they must be deepened and broadened – not the work of one book – and used, rather than proved or disproved by a few examples. The collecting of instances of each binarism that would appear to "common sense" to be unmarked by issues of homo/heterosexual definition, though an inexhaustibly stimulating heuristic, is not, I believe, a good test of such a hypothesis. After all, the particular kinds of skill that might be required to produce the most telling interpretations have hardly been a valued part of the "common sense" of this epistemologically cloven culture. If a painstaking process of accumulative reading and historical de- and recontextualization does not render these homologies resonant and productive, that is the only test they can directly fail, the only one they need to pass.

The structure of the present book has been markedly affected by this intuition – by a sense that the cultural interrogations it aims to make imperative will be trivialized or evacuated, at this early stage, to the degree that their procedures seem to partake of the a priori. I've wanted the book to be inviting (as well as imperative) but resolutely non-algorithmic. A point of the book is *not to know* how far its insights and projects are generalizable, not to be able to say in advance where the semantic specificity of these issues gives over to (or: itself structures?) the syntax of a "broader" or more abstractable critical project. In particular, the book aims to resist in every way it can the deadening pretended knowingness by which the chisel of modern homo/heterosexual definitional crisis tends, in public discourse, to be hammered most fatally home....

> *Axiom 2: The study of sexuality is not coextensive with the study of gender; correspondingly, antihomophobic inquiry is not coextensive with feminist inquiry. But we can't know in advance how they will be different.*

Sex, gender, sexuality: three terms whose usage relations and analytical relations are almost irremediably slippery. The charting of a space between something called "sex" and something called "gender" has been one of the most influential and successful undertakings of feminist thought. For the purposes of that undertaking, "sex" has had the meaning of a certain group of irreducible, biological differentiations between members of the species *Homo sapiens* who have XX and those who have XY chromosomes. These include (or are ordinarily thought to include) more or less marked dimorphisms of genital formation, hair growth (in populations that have body hair), fat distribution, hormonal function, and reproductive capacity. "Sex" in this sense – what I'll demarcate as "chromosomal sex" – is seen as the relatively minimal raw material on which is then based the social construction of *gender*. Gender, then, is the far more elaborated, more fully and rigidly dichotomized social production and reproduction of male and female identities and behaviors – of male and female *persons* – in a cultural system for which "male/female" functions as a primary and perhaps model binarism affecting the structure and meaning of many, many other binarisms whose apparent connection to chromosomal sex will often be exiguous or nonexistent. Compared to chromosomal sex, which is seen (by these definitions) as tending to be immutable, immanent in the individual, and biologically based, the meaning of gender is seen as culturally mutable and variable, highly relational (in the sense that each of the binarized genders is defined primarily by its relation to the other), and inextricable from a history of power differentials between genders. This feminist charting of what Gayle Rubin refers to as a "sex/gender system,"[7] the system by which chromosomal sex is turned into, and processed as, cultural gender, has tended to minimize the attribution of people's various behaviors and identities to chromosomal sex and to maximize their attribution to socialized gender constructs. The purpose of that strategy has been to gain analytic and critical leverage on the female-disadvantaging social arrangements that prevail at a given time in a given society, by throwing into question their legitimative ideological grounding in biologically based narratives of the "natural."

"Sex" is, however, a term that extends indefinitely beyond chromosomal sex. That its history of usage often overlaps with what might, now, more properly be called "gender" is only one problem. ("I can only love someone of my own sex." Shouldn't "sex" be "gender" in such a sentence? "M. saw that the person who approached was of the opposite sex." Genders – insofar as there are two and they are defined in contradistinction to one another – may be said to be opposite; but in what sense is XX the opposite of XY?) Beyond chromosomes, however, the association of "sex," precisely through the physical body, with reproduction and with genital activity and sensation keeps offering new challenges to the conceptual clarity or even possibility of sex/gender differentiation. There is a powerful argument to be made that a primary (or *the* primary) issue in gender differentiation and gender struggle is the question of who is to have control of women's (biologically) distinctive reproductive capability. Indeed, the intimacy of the association between several of the most signal forms of gender oppression and "the facts" of women's bodies and women's reproductive activity has led some radical feminists to question, more or less explicitly, the usefulness of insisting on a sex/gender distinction. For these reasons, even usages involving the "sex/gender system" within feminist theory are able to use "sex/gender" only to delineate a problematical *space* rather than a crisp distinction. My own loose usage in this book will be to denominate that problematized space of the sex/gender system, the whole package of physical and cultural distinctions between women and men, more simply under the rubric "gender." I do this in order to reduce the likelihood of confusion between "sex" in the sense of "the space of differences between male and female" (what I'll be grouping under "gender") and "sex" in the sense of sexuality.

For meanwhile the whole realm of what modern culture refers to as "sexuality" and *also* calls "sex" – the array of acts, expectations, narratives, pleasures, identity-formations, and knowledges, in both women and men, that tends to cluster most densely around certain genital sensations but is not adequately defined by them – that realm is virtually impossible to situate on a map delimited by the feminist-defined sex/gender distinction. To the degree that it has a center or starting point in certain physical sites, acts, and rhythms associated (however contingently) with procreation or the potential for it, "sexuality" in this sense may seem to be of a piece with "chromosomal sex": biologically necessary to species survival, tending toward the individually immanent, the socially immutable, the given. But to the extent that, as Freud argued and Foucault assumed, the distinctively sexual nature of human sexuality has to do precisely with its excess over or potential difference from the bare choreographies of procreation, "sexuality" might be the very opposite of what we originally referred to as (chromosomal-based) sex: it could occupy, instead, even more than "gender" the polar position of the relational, the social/symbolic, the constructed, the variable, the representational (see Figure 1). To note that, according to these different findings, *something* legitimately called sex or sexuality is all over the experiential and conceptual map is to record a problem less resolvable than a necessary choice of analytic paradigms or a determinate slippage of semantic meaning; it is rather, I would say, true to quite a range of contemporary worldviews and intuitions to find that sex/sexuality *does* tend to represent the full spectrum of positions between the most intimate and the most social, the most predetermined and the most aleatory, the most physically rooted and the most symbolically infused, the most innate and the most learned, the most autonomous and the most relational traits of being.

If all this is true of the definitional nexus between sex and sexuality, how much less simple, even, must be that between sexuality and gender. It will be an assumption of this study that there is always at least the potential for an analytic distance between gender and sexuality, even if particular manifestations or features of particular sexualities are among the things that plunge women and men most ineluctably into the discursive, institutional, and bodily enmeshments of gender definition, gender relation, and gender inequality. This, too, has been posed by Gayle Rubin:

> I want to challenge the assumption that feminism is or should be the privileged site of a theory of sexuality. Feminism is the theory of gender oppression. . . . Gender affects the operation of the sexual system, and the sexual system has had gender-specific manifestations. But although sex and gender are related, they are not the same thing.[8]

Biological	Cultural
Essential	Constructed
Individually immanent	Relatinal

Constructivist Feminist Analysis

chromosomal sex ——————————————————————————— gender
                                                        gender inequality

Radical Feminist Analysis

chromosomal sex
reproductive relations ————————————————————— reproductive relations
sexual inequality   sexual inequality

Foucault-influenced Analysis

chromosomal sex ————————————— reproduction ————————————— sexuality

Figure 1. Some Mappings of Sex, Gender, and Sexuality

This book will hypothesize, with Rubin, that the question of gender and the question of sexuality, inextricable from one another though they are in that each can be expressed only in the terms of the other, are nonetheless not the same question, that in twentieth-century Western culture gender and sexuality represent two analytic axes that may productively be imagined as being as distinct from one another as, say, gender and class, or class and race. Distinct, that is to say, no more than minimally, but nonetheless usefully.

Under this hypothesis, then, just as one has learned to assume that every issue of racial meaning must be embodied through the specificity of a particular class position – and every issue of class, for instance, through the specificity of a particular gender position – so every issue of gender would necessarily be embodied through the specificity of a particular sexuality, and vice versa; but nonetheless there could be use in keeping the analytic axes distinct.

An objection to this analogy might be that gender is *definitionally* built into determinations of sexuality, in a way that neither of them is definitionally intertwined with, for instance, determinations of class or race. It is certainly true that without a concept of gender there could be, quite simply, no concept of homo- or heterosexuality. But many other dimensions of sexual choice (auto- or alloerotic, within or between generations, species, etc.) have no such distinctive, explicit definitional connection with gender; indeed, some dimensions of sexuality might be tied, not to gender, but *instead* to differences or similarities of race or class. The definitional narrowing-down in this century of sexuality as a whole to a binarized calculus of *homo*- or *hetero*sexuality is a weighty fact but an entirely historical one. To use that fait accompli as a reason for analytically conflating sexuality per se with gender would obscure the degree to which the fact itself requires explanation. It would also, I think, risk obscuring yet again the extreme intimacy with which all these available analytic axes do after all mutually constitute one another: to assume the distinctiveness of the *intimacy* between sexuality and gender might well risk assuming too much about the definitional *separability* of either of them from determinations of, say, class or race.

It may be, as well, that a damaging bias toward heterosocial or heterosexist assumptions inheres unavoidably in the very concept of gender. This bias would be built into any gender-based analytic perspective to the extent that gender definition and gender identity are necessarily relational between genders – to the extent, that is, that in any gender system, female identity or definition is constructed by analogy, supplementarity, or contrast to male, or vice versa. Although many gender-based forms of analysis do involve accounts, sometimes fairly rich ones, of intragender behaviors and relations, the ultimate definitional appeal in any gender-based analysis must necessarily be to the diacritical frontier between different genders. This gives heterosocial and heterosexual relations a conceptual privilege of incalculable consequence. Undeniably, residues, markers, tracks, signs referring to that diacritical frontier between genders are everywhere, as well, internal to and determinative of the experience of each gender and its intragender relations; gender-based analysis can never be dispensed with in even the most purely intragender context. Nevertheless it seems predictable that the analytic bite of a purely gender-based account will grow less incisive and direct as the distance of its subject from a social interface between different genders increases. It is unrealistic to expect a close, textured analysis of same-sex relations through an optic calibrated in the first place to the coarser stigmata of gender difference.[9] The development of an alternative analytic axis – call it sexuality – might well be, therefore, a particularly urgent project for gay/lesbian and antihomophobic inquiry.

It would be a natural corollary to Axiom 2 to hypothesize, then, that gay/lesbian and antihomophobic inquiry still has a lot to learn from asking questions that feminist inquiry has learned to ask – but only so long as we don't demand to receive the same answers in both interlocutions. In a comparison of feminist and gay theory as they currently stand, the newness and consequent relative underdevelopment of gay theory are seen most clearly in two manifestations. First, we are by now very used to asking as feminists what we aren't yet used to asking as antihomophobic readers: how a variety of forms of oppression intertwine systemically with each other; and especially how the person who is disabled through one set of oppressions may *by the same positioning* be enabled through others. For instance, the understated demeanor of educated women in our society tends to mark both their deference to educated men and their expectation of deference from women and men of lower class. Again, a woman's use of a married name makes graphic at the same time her subordination as a woman and her privilege as a presumptive heterosexual. Or, again, the distinctive vulnerability to rape of women of all races has become in this country a powerful tool for the racist enforcement by which white people, including women, are privileged at the expense of Black people of both genders. That one is *either* oppressed *or* an oppressor, or that if one happens to be both, the two are not likely to have much to do with each other, still seems to be a common assumption, however, in at any rate male gay writing and activism,[10] as it hasn't for a long time been in careful feminist work.

Indeed, it was the long, painful realization, *not* that all oppressions are congruent, but that they are *differently* structured and so must intersect in complex embodiments that was the first great heuristic breakthrough of socialist-feminist thought and of the thought of women of color.[11] This realization has as its corollary that the comparison of different axes of oppression is a crucial task, not for any purpose of ranking oppressions, but to the contrary because each oppression is likely to be in a uniquely indicative relation to certain distinctive nodes of cultural organization. The *special* centrality of homophobic oppression in the twentieth century, I will be arguing, has resulted from its inextricability from the question of knowledge and the processes of knowing in modern Western culture at large.

The second and perhaps even greater heuristic leap of feminism has been the recognition that categories of gender and, hence, oppressions of gender can have a structuring force for nodes of thought, for axes of cultural discrimination, whose thematic subject isn't explicitly gendered at all. Through a series of developments structured by the deconstructive understandings and procedures sketched above, we have now learned as feminist readers that dichotomies in a given text of culture as opposed to nature, public as opposed to private, mind as opposed to body, activity as opposed to passivity, etc. etc., are, under particular pressures of culture and history, likely places to look for implicit allegories of the relations of men to women; more, that to fail to analyze such nominally ungendered constructs in gender terms can itself be a gravely tendentious move in the gender politics of reading. This has given us ways to ask the question of gender about texts even where the culturally "marked" gender (female) is not present as either author or thematic.

The dichotomy heterosexual/homosexual, as it has emerged through the last century of Western discourse, would seem to lend itself peculiarly neatly to a set of analytic moves learned from this deconstructive moment in feminist theory. In fact, the dichotomy heterosexual/homosexual fits the deconstructive template much more neatly than male/female itself does, and hence, importantly differently. The most dramatic difference between gender and sexual orientation – that virtually all people are publicly and unalterably assigned to one or the other gender, and from birth – seems if anything to mean that it is, rather, sexual orientation, with its far greater potential for rearrangement, ambiguity, and representational doubleness, that would offer the apter deconstructive object. An essentialism of sexual object-choice is far less easy to maintain, far more visibly incoherent, more visibly stressed and challenged at every point in the culture than any essentialism of gender. This is not an argument for any epistemological or ontological privileging of an axis of sexuality over an axis of gender; but it is a powerful argument for their potential distinctness one from the other.

Even given the imperative of constructing an account of sexuality irreducible to gender, however, it should already be clear that there are certain distortions necessarily built into the relation of gay/lesbian and antihomophobic theory to a larger project of conceiving a theory of sexuality as a whole. The two can after all scarcely be coextensive. And this is true not because "gay/lesbian and antihomophobic theory" would fail to cover heterosexual as well as same-sex object-choice (any more than "feminist theory" would fail to cover men as well as women), but rather because, as we have noted, sexuality extends along so many dimensions that aren't well described in terms of the gender of object-choice at all. Some of these dimensions are habitually condensed under the rubrics of object-choice, so that certain discriminations of (for instance) *act* or of (for another instance) *erotic localization* come into play, however implicitly and however incoherently, when categories of object-choice are mobilized. One used, for instance, to hear a lot about a high developmental stage called "heterosexual genitality," as though cross-gender object-choice automatically erased desires attaching to mouth, anus, breasts, feet, etc.; a certain anal-erotic salience of male homosexuality is if anything increasingly strong under the glare of heterosexist AIDS-phobia; and several different historical influences have led to the de-genitalization and bodily diffusion of many popular, and indeed many lesbian, understandings of lesbian sexuality. Other dimensions of sexuality, however, distinguish object-choice quite differently (e.g., human/animal, adult/child, singular/plural, autoerotic/alloerotic) or are not even about object choice (e.g., orgasmic/nonorgasmic, noncommercial/commercial, using bodies only/using manufactured objects, in private/in public, spontaneous/scripted).[12] Some of these other dimensions of sexuality have had high diacritical importance in different historical contexts (e.g., human/animal, autoerotic/alloerotic). Others, like adult/child object choice, visibly do have such importance today, but without being very fully subsumed under the hetero/homosexual binarism. Still others, including a host of them I haven't mentioned or couldn't think of, subsist in this culture as nondiacritical differences, differences that seem to make little difference beyond themselves – except that the hyperintensive structuring of sexuality in our culture sets several of them, for instance, at the exact border between legal and illegal. What I mean at any rate to emphasize is that the implicit condensation of "sexual theory" into "gay/lesbian and antihomophobic theory," which corresponds roughly to our by now unquestioned reading of the phrase "sexual orientation" to mean "gender of object-choice," is at the very least damagingly skewed by the specificity of its historical placement.

Notes

1 Michel Foucault, *History of Sexuality: An Introduction*, trans. Robert Hurley (New York: Random House, 1980), pp. 105, 43.
2 Ibid., p. 43.
3 Harold Beaver, "Homosexual Signs," *Critical Inquiry* 8 (Autumn 1981): 115.
4 *Roland Barthes by Roland Barthes*, trans. Richard Howard (New York: Hill and Wang, 1977), p. 133.
5 Beaver, "Homosexual Signs," pp. 115–16.
6 My casting of all these definitional nodes in the form of binarisms, I should make explicit, has to do not with a mystical faith in the number two but, rather, with the felt need to schematize in some consistent way the treatment of social vectors so exceedingly various. The kind of falsification necessarily performed on each by this reduction cannot, unfortunately, itself be consistent. But the scope of the kind of hypothesis I want to pose does seem to require a drastic reductiveness, at least in its initial formulations.
7 Gayle Rubin, "The Traffic in Women: Notes on the 'Political Economy' of Sex," in Rayna R. Reiter (ed.), *Toward an Anthropology of Women* (New York: Monthly Review Press, 1975), pp. 157–210.
8 Rubin, "Thinking Sex: Notes for a Radical Theory of the Politics of Sexuality." In Carole S. Vance, ed., *Pleasure and Danger: Exploring Female Sexuality* (Boston: Routledge, 1984), pp. 307–8.
9 For valuable related discussions, see Katie King, "The Situation of Lesbianism as Feminism's Magical Sign: Contests for Meaning and the US Women's Movement, 1968–1972," in *Communication* 9 (1986): 65–91. Special issue, "Feminist Critiques of Popular Culture," ed. Paula A. Treichler and Ellen Wartella, 9: 65–91; and Teresa de Lauretis, "Sexual Indifference and Lesbian Representation," *Theatre Journal* 40 (May 1988): 155–77.
10 Gay male–centered work that uses more complex models to investigate the intersection of different oppressions includes Gay Left Collective (eds.), *Homosexuality: Power and Politics*

(London: Allison & Busby, 1980); Paul Hoch, *White Hero Black Beast: Racism, Sexism, and the Mask of Masculinity* (London: Pluto, 1979); Guy Hocquenghem, *Homosexual Desire*, trans. Daniella Dangoor (London: Allison & Busby, 1978); Mario Mieli, *Homosexuality and Liberation: Elements of a Gay Critique*, trans. David Fernbach (London: Gay Men's Press, 1980); D. A. Miller, *The Novel and the Police* (Berkeley and Los Angeles: University of California Press, 1988); Michael Moon, "'The Gentle Boy from the Dangerous Classes': Pederasty, Domesticity, and Capitalism in Horatio Alger," *Representations*, no. 19 (Summer 1987): 87–110; Michael Moon, *Disseminating Whitman* (Cambridge, Mass.: Harvard University Press, 1990); and Jeffrey Weeks, *Sexuality and its Discontents: Meanings, Myths and Modern Sexualities* (London: Longman, 1980).

11   The influential socialist-feminist investigations have included Michèle Barrett, *Women's Oppression Today: Problems in Marxist Feminist Analysis* (London: Verso, 1980); Zillah Eisenstein (ed.), *Capitalist Patriarchy and the Case for Socialist Feminism* (New York: Monthly Review Press, 1979); and Juliet Mitchell, *Women's Estate* (New York: Vintage, 1973). On the intersections of racial with gender and sexual oppressions, see, for example, Elly Bulkin, Barbara Smith, and Minnie Bruce Pratt, *Yours in Struggle: Three Feminist Perspectives on Anti-Semitism and Racism* (New York: Long Haul Press, 1984); Bell Hooks [Gloria Watkins], *Feminist Theory: From Margin to Center* (Boston: South End Press, 1984); Katie King, "Audre Lorde's Lacquered Layerings: The Lesbian Bar as a Site of Literary Production," *Cultural Studies* 2, no. 3 (1988): 321–42; Audre Lorde, *Sister Outsider: Essays and Speeches* (Trumansburg, NY: The Crossing Press, 1984); Cherríe Moraga, *Loving in the War Years: Lo que nunca paso por sus labios* (Boston: South End Press, 1983); Cherríe Moraga and Gloria Anzaldua (eds.), *This Bridge Called My Back: Writings by Radical Women of Color* (Watertown: Persephone, 1981; rpt. edn., New York: Kitchen Table: Women of Color Press, 1984); and Barbara Smith (ed.), *Home Girls: A Black Feminist Anthology* (New York: Kitchen Table: Women of Color Press, 1983). Good overviews of several of these intersections as they relate to women and in particular to lesbians, can be found in Ann Snitow, Christine Stansell, and Sharon Thompson (eds.), *The Powers of Desire: The Politics of Sexuality* (New York: Monthly Review/New Feminist Library, 1983); Vance, *Pleasure and Danger*; and de Lauretis, "Sexual Indifference."

12   This list owes something to Rubin, "Thinking Sex," esp. pp. 281–2.

CHAPTER 6

A Small Boy and Others: Sexual Disorientation in Henry James, Kenneth Anger, and David Lynch

Michael Moon

In his 1991 book, *A Small Boy and Others*, Michael Moon explores the vexations of supposedly normal heterosexual identity and ranges widely into the realm of so-called perverse
sexual practices and orientations. In this selection, he wittily juxtaposes a short story of
man–boy love by Henry James, an underground art-house movie about gay bikers by
Kenneth Anger, and David Lynch's film about the weird cohabitation of middle-class sexual
normality and perverse sexuality.

In this essay I am concerned with a group of texts that have been produced over the
past century: chiefly, Henry James's "The Pupil" (1891), Kenneth Anger's film
Scorpio Rising (1964), and David Lynch's *Blue Velvet* (1986). I shall be analyzing the
ways in which each of these texts draws much of its considerable uncanny energies
from representing heavily ritualized performances of some substantial part of the
whole round of "perverse" desires and fantasies, autoerotic, homoerotic, voyeuristic,
exhibitionistic, incestuous, fetishistic, and sadomasochistic. Particularly striking are
the ways in which all these texts foreground the mimed and ventriloquized qualities
of the performances of ritual induction and initiation into "perverse circles" which
they represent, rather than attempting to de-emphasize the mimetic secondariness of
these representations, as realist texts and ordinary pornography both commonly do.
Since René Girard launched his influential critique of the object-theory of desire
twenty-five years ago, his argument that it is not the putative object of desire but
mimesis that is primary in the formation of desire has been usefully elaborated by a
number of theorists.[1] Of these, Mikkel Borch-Jacobsen's recent rereading of Girard's
hypothesis "against" some similarly fundamental hypotheses of Freud's has been
highly suggestive for my own current project. "[D]esire is mimetic before it is
anything else," Borch-Jacobsen writes.[2] Rather than focusing on simple triangula-
tions of desire among persons, as he criticizes Girard for doing, he attempts to
theorize the thoroughly disorienting effects mimesis has on desire ("[D]esire is not
oriented by pleasure, it is (dis)oriented by mimesis," p. 34).

In the texts I am looking at, I want to consider some of the ways in which
sexuality is not so much oriented by its object, by the perceived gender or age, race,
social class, body type, style of dress, etc., of its object, as it is *disoriented* by mimesis.
There are many more people who respond strongly (whether or not they recognize or

acknowledge any positive component to their response) to images of male–male sadomasochism, for example, than there are people who identify themselves as gay-male sadomasochists – this at least became clear in the aftermath of the controversy about the Corcoran Gallery's cancellation of its projected exhibition of Robert Mapplethorpe's photographs. The reason for this strong response is not simply because these images induce the viewer at least momentarily to violate (painfully and/or pleasurably, depending on one's point of view) the general interdiction of sadomasochistic object-choice among males in our society, for just such object-choices flourish in many institutional settings; relations of inflicting and receiving psychological and physical pain, with the sexual element of this interchange suppressed or not, are considered not shocking aberrations but ordinary and even necessary practice in the military, in prisons, in many corporate organizations, athletic teams, and schools of all levels. It is the domestication of many of these procedures into "discipline," the daily practice of institutional "law and order," with only those interchanges that are most flagrantly sexually enacted isolated and stigmatized as "sexual perversion," that conduces most of us to disavow our insiders' knowledge of sadomasochistic pleasures most of the time.

As with other kinds of largely disavowed knowledges, the knowledge of ostensibly minority pleasures like sadomasochism plays constantly around the margins of perception of the "normal" majority – that most audacious of theoretical fictions. If in an important sense *no* desire is our own – i.e., originates with us; if desire is indeed primarily induced by imitation, mimed and ventriloquized, then it is impossible to maintain our ordinary "orienting" notions of which desires we are at home with and which ones we are not. Powerful images of ostensibly perverse desires and fantasies disorient our currently prevailing assumptions – symmetrical and pluralistic – about our own and other people's sexual orientations by bringing home to us the shapes of desires and fantasies that we ordinarily disavow as our own. In forcing us to recognize at least liminally our own familiarity or "at-home-ness" with these desires, these images produce *unheimlich* – uncanny – effects. In the texts I am discussing, the process of inducing uncanny effects is inseparable from the related process of inducing effects of what I am calling sexual disorientation to denote the position of reader- or viewer-subjects at least temporarily dislocated from what they consider their "home" sexual orientation and "disorientingly" circulated through a number of different positions on the wheel of "perversions," positions which render moot or irrelevant our current basic "orienting" distinction, homo/heterosexual. I am interested in doing this not in order to try to efface this distinction, which on the gay side has been so murderously enforced over the past century, never more so than it is today, but, to the contrary, to extend our thinking about the dependence of both so-called high and popular culture during the same period on the sexually "perverse" for their energies and often for their representational programs.

Roy Orbison's 1963 song "In Dreams" figures importantly in *Blue Velvet*. It begins, "A candy-colored clown they call the sandman tiptoes to my room every night,/Just to sprinkle stardust and to whisper, 'Go to sleep, everything is all right.'" Orbison's "candy-colored clown they call the sandman" has commonly been taken to mean – as so much figurative writing in pop music of the sixties and after has been – simply "drugs," in this case "downs" or "sleepers." Without discounting this entirely, I want to press on the intertextual relation of the "sandman" of Orbison's and Lynch's texts with that of E. T. A. Hoffmann's 1816 story "The

Sandman" and Freud's 1919 essay "The Uncanny," which takes Hoffmann's story as its model literary text.

In Hoffmann's story, a young student named Nathanael believes that an old instrument-peddler who calls himself "Coppola" is the same man who, as the lawyer Coppelius, used to pay mysterious nocturnal visits to Nathanael's father, until the night the boy's father was killed by an explosion and fire in his study, from the scene of which Coppelius supposedly fled. During this time the child Nathanael had developed the fixed notion that old Coppelius was the nursery-fable figure "the Sandman" in the flesh – rather repellent flesh, little Nathanael thinks.

Freud interprets the story's uncanny effects as proceeding from castration anxieties, which it registers around the figure of Nathanael who displaces his fear of castration by his father onto his father's evil and uncanny double, Coppelius.[3] As is the case with so many of Freud's key formulations, we get only the "heterosexual plot" of the "sandman" narrative in his reading of it. Neither Freud nor any of the other readers who have published interpretations of the story has, to my knowledge, made anything of the narrative's continuous engagement with a thematics of male–male sadomasochism and pedophilia, as when Nathanael says that Coppelius had "mishandled" or "manhandled" him once when he caught the boy spying on him and his father, violently twisting his hands and feet and moving as if to pluck out his eyes.[4] Later in the story Nathanael claims Coppelius "had entered him and possessed him" at the time he caught him spying (p. 292). Nathanael's "madness" takes the form of a series of hysterical outbursts in which he keeps crying, "Whirl round, circle of fire! Merrily, merrily! Aha lovely wooden doll, whirl round!" (pp. 303, 308). It is possible to see how the hallucinatory contents of his delirium may derive from a premature and precocious induction into the "perverse" "circle of fire" he enters when as a child he spies on the mysterious nocturnal activities of his father with Coppelius. He keeps hysterically mistaking his relation to the "lovely wooden doll"; in the second half of the story he falls in love with the girl-automaton Olympia, a figure which is on one level of his confused thoughts an image of his physically invaded child self and on another an image of his infantile perception of the phallus of the father and/or Coppelius as a terrifying and powerful machine ("wooden doll, whirl round!"). Lacan speaks of one of the primary significations of the phallus as being its character as the visible sign of the sexual link, or what he calls the "*copula*,"[5] and Nathanael's belief that Coppelius renamed himself "Coppola" after his attack on him and his alleged murder of his father underscores Coppelius's position as phallic terrorist in Nathanael's story.

Part of the uncanny power of Hoffmann's "The Sandman" no doubt derives from the undecidable relation of this "perverse" narrative to the familiar Oedipal one about Nathanael's relation to his father and his female sweethearts which psychoanalytic theory has privileged. Hoffmann's text reveals with stunning force how thoroughly any given reader, including Freud and subsequent critics of "The Sandman," may be both "at home" and "not at home," simultaneously and in undecidable combination, with these powerful and "perverse" undercurrents. The film *Blue Velvet*, too, oscillates between a conventional, linear, Oedipal plot and a "perverse," circular, and ritualistic one. The trajectory of the Oedipal plot of *Blue Velvet* is also racist, sexist, ageist, and homophobic in the ways to which the Oedipal so readily lends itself: a young man must negotiate what is represented as being the treacherous path between an older, ostensibly exotic, sexually "perverse" woman and a younger, racially "whiter," sexually "normal" one, and he must at the same time and as part of the same process negotiate an even more perilous series of interactions with the older woman's violent and murderous criminal lover and the younger woman's protective police-detective father. This heterosexual plot resolves itself in classic Oedipal fashion: the young man, Jeffrey, destroys the demonic criminal "father" and rival, Frank; rescues the older woman, Dorothy, from Frank's sadistic clutches; and then relinquishes her to her fate and marries the perky young daughter of the good cop.[6]

But that is not the whole story of the film: there is an anarchic second plot that emerges intermittently but unmistakably in which subject positions and transferrals of identities and desires are highly volatile. Young Jeffrey arrives at the film's end at the object of his Oedipal destination, the high-school student Sandy (notice how the name of even this character, the only principal one in the film supposedly located well outside the "perverse" circuits it traverses, links her with Orbison's and Hoffmann's uncanny "sandmen"), but he is frequently swept off course from this Oedipal trajectory, not only by his attraction to and involvement with Dorothy, "the Blue Velvet Lady," but by his only marginally less intense "involvement" with her lover Frank and the other men who surround him. There are two moments in the film which I shall discuss at some length in which the supercharged valencies of male–male desire are represented with particular graphic power. In these scenes, characters enact a whole series of uncanny relationships between males of different ages, social classes, and supposed sexual orientations – orientations which get thoroughly disoriented when they get swept near the flame of "perverse" desire that flows around the figures of the chief sadomasochistic pair, Frank and Dorothy.

Anyone who watches *Blue Velvet* with "The Sandman" in mind may well be struck by how densely intertextual the film is with the story, not only in its repeated evocations of the figure of "the sandman," but also in its "perverse" plot: as in Hoffmann's "The Sandman," a young male gets unexpectedly initiated into a circle of sadomasochistic and fetishistic desires. Lynch's characters, like Hoffmann's, indulge in a round of spying and retributive and eroticized beating on each other, and of mimed and ventriloquized desire. Early in the film Jeffrey hides in Dorothy's closet and spies on her. When she catches him, she forces him to strip at knifepoint and subsequently introduces him to sadomasochistic sex, as both direct participant and voyeur. When on one occasion later in the film Frank catches Jeffrey leaving Dorothy's apartment, he forces both of them to come with him for what he calls a "joyride," the first stop of which is at Ben's, where Jeffrey is preliminarily punched a time or two (by Frank and Ben) and Ben, looking heavily made-up, lip-synchs Roy Orbison's song about "the candy-colored clown they call the sandman," until he is interrupted by a grimacing Frank, who manically orders everyone present to get on with the "joyride."

The initiation ritual to which Frank is subjecting Jeffrey at this point in the film is extremely ambiguous: the younger man is being intimidated and frightened away from Frank and his circle of perversions at the same time that he is being forced and welcomed into it. The contradictions do not stop at the figure of Jeffrey; they extend to everyone present at the scene of initiation: in Frank's obvious pleasure *and* pain during Ben's lip-synching; in Ben's "suave" behavior toward Frank, as Frank calls it, and Ben's sadistic behavior toward Jeffrey (he hits him in the stomach), as well as in Ben's being both male and "made up," i.e., wearing cosmetics; in Dorothy's being brought to Ben's both to be terrorized and punished and to be allowed to see her small child, who is being held hostage there; in the mixed atmosphere of Ben's place, which appears to be a whorehouse with a staff of mostly grandmotherly-looking whores, several of whom are sitting around a coffee-table, suburban-homestyle, chatting with Ben when Frank and his party arrive. Ben's lip-synching of "In Dreams" functions as both a kind of "tribute" to Frank and also as a kind of threat to Jeffrey that some uncanny figure called "the candy-colored clown" or "sandman" is going to "get him" – but, as one sees in the pain Frank registers in his face during the latter part of the lip-synch, this figure "gets" Frank, too; he seems almost on the verge of breaking down before he yanks the tape from the player and orders everyone to "hit the fuckin' road."

When Frank, Dorothy, Jeffrey, and the others make their next stop it is at a deserted spot far out in the country. Here Frank starts hyperventilating and playing sadistically with Dorothy's breasts. Unable to remain in the voyeuristic position in which he has been placed for the moment, Jeffrey first orders Frank to "leave [Dorothy] alone" and then leaps forward from the backseat of the car and punches Frank in the face. Frank orders Raymond and his other henchmen to pull the boy out of the car and to put the song "Candy-Colored Clown" ("In Dreams") on the car's tapeplayer. The action between Frank and Jeffrey becomes most densely ritualistic at this point. Frank smears lipstick on his mouth and kisses it onto Jeffrey's lips pleading with him to leave Dorothy alone (the same thing Jeffrey had ordered him to do a minute before), and threatening to send him "a love letter" if he does not, explaining to him that by "a love letter" he means "a bullet from a fuckin' gun." "If you get a love letter from me, you're fucked *forever*," Frank tells Jeffrey. He then starts speaking to Jeffrey the words of the song playing on the tapeplayer: "In dreams I walk with you, / In dreams I talk to you; / In dreams you're mine, all of the time, / We're together in dreams." Frank then wipes the lipstick from the boy's lips with a swatch of blue velvet, instructs the other men to "hold him tight for me," and, to the crescendo of the song's chorus ("It's too bad that these things / Can only happen in my dreams"), begins to beat Jeffrey mercilessly. As Jeffrey presumably loses consciousness, the music and the scene fade out.

When Lynch has Frank mouth the words of the song a second time, this time directly to a Jeffrey whom he has ritually prepared for a beating by "kissing" lipstick onto his mouth and wiping it off with a piece of blue velvet, it is as though Lynch is both daring the viewer to recognize the two men's desire for each other that the newly discovered sadomasochistic bond that unites them induces them to feel *and* at the same time to recognize the perhaps more fearful knowledge that what most of us consider our deepest and strongest desires are not our own, that our dreams and fantasies are only copies, audio- and videotapes, of the desires of others and our utterances of them lip-synchings of these circulating, endlessly reproduced and reproducible desires. Lip-synching is the ideal form of enunciation for the ritualized and serious game of "playing with fire" – i.e., with the game of inducing male homosexual panic and of recognizing, at least in flashes, the strong S-M component of male–male violence – that Frank, Ben, and Jeffrey play: lip-synching a pop song allows Ben to "come on" to Frank, and Frank in turn to "come on" to Jeffrey, singing about how "In Dreams" they possess the man to whom they're singing – without doing so in any way that "counts" for more than the phantasmatic and mimicked moments the two pairs of men share.

The lip-synch/lipstick initiation to which Frank subjects Jeffrey ritualistically enacts the rupture between the sayable and the unsayable about the intense sadomasochistic bond between them, both as they transact this bond through their shared involvement with Dorothy, and as it threatens, just at this point in the film, to bypass mediation through her – i.e., to become simply a male–male S-M relationship. It also marks the point of lack on the part of both men of an "original" voice or "original" utterance and the consequently ventriloquistic character of their – and our – desires. The fascination with other men's lips, with men kissing each other, especially in the context of a sadomasochistic relationship, and with the look of smeared lipstick on men's lips – all these bespeak the generally enforced misrecognition of many men most of the time of the relation between their own ostensibly "normal" male heterosexuality and their relation to the penetrable orifices of their own and other males' bodies; it is a sign of the "scandal" of the liminal gendering – one might say the minimal gendering – of the mouth and anus, the repression of which "scandal" so much energy and anxiety in straight-male relations are invested in concealing and revealing, as is evident in the most basic buzzwords of male–male abuse, "cock sucker" and "asshole" and "faggot," a set of terms and relationships of male–male power into which almost every small boy in our culture is interpellated as a crucial part of his elementary education. The "candy-colored clown they call the sandman" whom Ben and Frank mimic (the "made-up" and intensely flashlit look of both their faces as they lip-synch is a sign that they are "clowning") is a figure for the circulation through the men in these scenes of a mostly disavowed familiarity with, and in varying degrees, adeptness at, sadomasochistic desire and practices between males.

It would be a significant oversight to ignore the roles of the women in these scenes – Dorothy especially and the other woman who joins the "joyride" at Ben's – in the initiation ritual carried out on Jeffrey. Dorothy moves over to the driver's seat when Frank and the other men drag Jeffrey out of the car to beat him, but her real position remains abject: she shouts, "Frank, stop! Frank, stop!" – to no avail – then lays her arms and her head on the steering wheel and weeps, as Frank carries on with the ritual violence in which she is relegated to the position of a Stabat Mater who can't bear to look. The other woman who has joined the group is unphased, is perfectly "at home," with the scene of male–male sadomasochism she has been transported to witness: she climbs out of the car onto its roof, where she dances to the strains of "In Dreams," combined with the rhythmic sound (the "beat") of Frank's fists falling on Jeffrey's body, with the mechanical imperturbability of Olympia, Nathanael's automaton-sweetheart in Hoffmann's "The Sandman."

It is surely relevant to the way women in this scene are relegated to positions of either abjection or affectlessness to mention that, as Lynch had it in the original script for *Blue Velvet*, Frank was, at this point in the film, supposed to rape Jeffrey, to enact literally his telling Dorothy, in response to her fearful question when they leave Ben's, "Where are we going?," "We're takin' your neighbor [Jeffrey] out to the country to fuck."[7] Lynch's decision to film the scene "otherwise," to transmute Frank's violation of Jeffrey and his body from a literal rape to a symbolic ritual, raises questions about the way males and male bodies are privileged in this film and the way women – again, Dorothy especially – are abjected in it. It is important in this connection, for example, that the representational economy of nakedness in the film is initially presented as a gender-symmetrical one: Jeffrey spies on Dorothy undressing as he hides in her closet, and when Dorothy discovers him she forces him to undress while she watches. But there is no scene performed by a male that corresponds to the climactic one late in the film performed by Rossellini, when, as

Dorothy, she comes staggering, naked and incoherent, out into the street where Sandy's drunken ex-boyfriend and his buddies are picking a fight with Jeffrey. Dorothy's punctual arrival, nude, at a second scene of male–male violence has the effect of rescuing Jeffrey from a second beating; catching sight of her, the drunken ex-boyfriend first asks Jeffrey mockingly, "Is that your mother?" (thereby voicing for Jeffrey and the viewer the Oedipal anxieties the film frequently both engages and mocks), but even the drunken teenage boy seems to lose interest in baiting Jeffrey when he sees how badly off Dorothy really is. There is a dynamic relation between Jeffrey's being let off the hook – not only from the violence being immediately threatened at this point in the narrative but from any real threat of violence for the rest of the film – and Dorothy's being reduced at this climactic moment to a literal vision of staggering naked abjection. The excessive and appalling degree to which Dorothy and her body are exposed to the general gaze at this point serves the other characters and their director-author to underwrite the "happy ending" which subsumes Jeffrey and Sandy and, supposedly, Dorothy and her little son (her lover Frank and her captive husband both die in the violence at the end of the film). We should also recognize how it serves retroactively to underwrite Lynch's sublimation of male–male rape in the scene between Frank and Jeffrey into a beating that leaves sexual violation enacted only on a symbolic plane.

One of the most pervasive of the fantasies informing the "perverse" initiation rituals I'm discussing and the uncanny, sexually disorienting effects they produce is that of a person's being able to ravish and hold captive another person by the unaided agency of a powerful gaze, and the attendant danger of this gaze's making its director more rather than less highly susceptible to other people's gazes (in *Blue Velvet*, for example, Frank tries repeatedly to control Dorothy's and Jeffrey's gazing behavior toward him). The fantasy of the pupil of the eye as the focal point of visual and erotic capture is at the core of Henry James's tale "The Pupil," which treats of a series of visual and erotic captures and struggles to escape both into and away from a "perverse" circle constituted by a brilliant little boy, his loving and beloved tutor, and the boy's mother, who is attractive and socially ambitious but perpetually financially embarrassed. The precincts of James's fiction may seem remote from those of a recent and flagrantly "perverse" film like *Blue Velvet*, but they are not as far apart as they may at first appear. Despite James's own announced distaste for the project of some of his contemporaries of representing "perversion" relatively openly and sensationally – Wilde's *Dorian Gray*, for example – James's own literary explorations of the circulation of "perverse" desires are elaborate and searching, and remarkably unconstrained by contemporary standards of gentility and prudery. "The Pupil" was summarily rejected by the editor of the *Atlantic Monthly*, one of the very few times one of James's fictions was declined by the journals to which he regularly contributed. James professed to be unable to understand why, but it may well have been because it produced the same kinds of discomfort in the editor that an anonymous critic writing in the *Independent* expressed a few years later in response to *The Turn of the Screw*. "How Mr. James could...choose to make such a study of infernal human debauchery...is unaccountable," the reviewer writes, going on to say, "The study...affects the reader with a disgust that is not to be expressed. The feeling after perusal of the horrible story is that one has been assisting in an outrage upon...human innocence, and helping to debauch – at least by standing helplessly by – the pure and trusting nature of children. Human imagination can go no further into infamy, literary art could not be used with more refined subtlety of spiritual defilement."[8] In other words, James's work looked to some of his contemporaries – and may look to us, if we allow it to – the way *Blue Velvet* looks to us: shocking and disturbing. Or to put it another way, if James were writing today, his work would look more like *Blue Velvet* than it would like Merchant and Ivory's ponderously reverent period "recreations" of his novels.

One thing James's work registers continuously that Merchant and Ivory's betrays little feeling for is the investment of "sexiness" in the fetish-character of a given epoch's favored fashions in dress and styles of interior decoration. The Paris of the Second Empire was the most formative setting of Jame's childhood according to his own testimony, and it is a principal setting of "The Pupil." The bourgeois culture of this period may be said to have had its own intense velvet fetish. According to Walter Benjamin in his study of Baudelaire, bourgeois domestic interiors at the latter end of the period had become velvet- and plush-lined carapaces for a social class that seemed to want to insulate itself from the world from which it derived its wealth and power behind a grotesque barrier of such luxury fabrics – in clothing for ordinary and ceremonial occasions, in upholstery and wallcoverings, and, perhaps most significantly, in linings for instrument cases, jewelry boxes, and coffins.[9]

"Velvet" is everywhere in James, once one becomes aware of it, and it is there unsurprisingly, given the characteristic settings and concerns of his fiction – freedom and domination, glamor and stigma, during what he calls in the preface to "The Pupil" "the classic years of the great American–European legend." When the tutor Pemberton in "The Pupil" wonders resentfully how his penurious employers can manage to keep installing themselves in what the narrator calls the "velvety *entresols*" of the best hotels in Paris, "the most expensive city in Europe," "velvet" still bears the unambiguously positive charge it had carried forty years before in Thackeray's *Vanity Fair*, the repository of so many of James's basic props for signaling fine degrees of upward and downward social mobility, as when Becky Sharp finds herself at one of the peaks of her success being waited on by a "velvet-footed butler."[10] There is a striking detail in the opening lines of "The Pupil," however, that suggests the more ambiguous charge a luxury fabric could bear as sign late in the nineteenth century. When the characters of Pemberton the tutor and Mrs Moreen are first introduced, he is called simply "[t]he poor young man" and his new employer, Mrs Moreen, is "the large, affable lady who sat there drawing a pair of soiled *gants de Suède* through a fat, jewelled hand."[11] This description occurs in the second sentence of the story and it is easy enough for one to overlook it as a gratuitous "realistic" detail, but on reflection one can see in what rich detail these images signify "trouble ahead" for Pemberton and even the ambiguous nature of that "trouble." Mrs Moreen's gesture of drawing her soiled suede gloves through her "fat, jewelled hand" mimes an unspoken desire – not necessarily her own – for her son, who is both the only other person present at this conversation and the most mixed quantity in the story, the figure in it who is neither entirely innocent of the shabbiness or willful moral abjectness of the rest of the Moreen family, nor entirely guilty of it, but rather only tainted or "soiled" with it by unavoidable association. Pemberton squirms with discomfort during this initial (and initiatory) interview because Mrs Moreen is performing this curious mime of displaying a bit of her dirty laundry to him instead of settling the matter of his salary, which the narrator refers to as "the question of terms." What Pemberton does not see at the beginning of the story is that while his salary is not being discussed, his real compensation for his work – an invitation to desire Morgan – is being repeatedly issued in mime by Mrs Moreen. His intense but unnamed relationship to her little son – here is the real "question of terms" that is in contest in the story and beyond it – will partake of the mixed character of her "soiled" gloves. Rather than being something that sets them apart from the rest of the Moreen household, the "scandal" of the intimacy between tutor and pupil is perfectly "at home" with the more inclusive "scandal" of the kind of mixed clean-and-dirty surface Mrs Moreen and the rest of the family show to the world. I shall return to the detail of the soiled gloves a little later on.

When Morgan dies at the story's climax, his body doesn't end up simply in his tutor's arms, as it might if the story were just a pederastic idyll, as I would argue it is not, nor does his body end up in his mother's arms, in the kind of vignette that would anticipate the similar death of little Miles in the arms of his governess at the climax of *The Turn of the Screw*. Rather, the body of the dead boy ends up suspended between his tutor and his mother. When Pemberton sees that Morgan is dead, the narrator says, "[h]e pulled him half out of his mother's hands, and for a moment, while they held him together, they looked, in their dismay, into each other's eyes." The resemblance of this last image in the tale to its first one is striking: young Morgan's dead body occupies precisely the place of the dirty suede gloves, but this time instead of merely noticing them unreflectively while Mrs Moreen pulls them through her hands, Pemberton actively intervenes to draw Morgan's body "half out of [her] hands." Suspended between childhood and manhood (he has grown from age eleven to fifteen in the course of the story) and between mother and tutor, Morgan's body at the moment of death becomes a kind of uncanny puppet, a "soiled" handpuppet like a "soiled" glove. Although Pemberton and Mrs Moreen have repeatedly quarreled over which of them has made the greater "sacrifice" for Morgan, the boy himself ends up, perhaps not entirely unwillingly, the sacrificial victim of the rituals the three practice, leaving tutor and mother in the utterly abject position of members of a collapsed cult.

I want to consider a little further the possible significance of "soiled" suede as a figure for relations in "The Pupil." Like those of "velvet," the erotic and class associations of "suede" have shifted and mutated considerably over the past century and more. The possible erotic association that makes soiled "suede" rather than velvet the appropriate figure for whatever unnameable bond unites Mrs Moreen and her little son at the beginning of the story, a bond into which they admit, and with which they secure Pemberton, is primarily a verbal one: English-language guides to proper dress from mid-century forward inform the reader that the newly fashionable fabric "*Suede*" is "undressed kid." Those who would argue that "undressed kid" could not have meant, even subliminally, "undressed child" to James and his readers because "kid" did not then in that place and time commonly mean "child," need only look in the *OED* to see that it was precisely in the decade or two before "The Pupil" was written that "kid" as a term for "child" ceased to be "low slang" as it long had been and entered into common use among the English upper class as a term of familiar affection for a child or children of one's own: William Morris writes of the health of his "kid" in a personal letter of the 1860s, and Lord Shaftesbury makes a notation of several happy days spent with his "wife and kids" in a passage from his journal published in the 1880s. If my translations of the phrase "drawing a pair of soiled *gants de Suède* through a fat, jewelled hand" into "handling dirty undressed-kid gloves" and, possibly, into other permutations of that phrase, including "handling a dirty undressed kid," seem farfetched, it is only because the erotic wish encrypted, mimed but unspoken, in the text of "The Pupil" is precisely the kind of meaning that requires just such high-intensity translation or decoding – not only because James may have been to some degree unconscious of this meaning but also because of our own resistance to recognizing the access to "perverse" energies that his writing frequently affords us.

Rather than assenting to the notion that texts like "The Pupil" and *Blue Velvet* are historically, politically, and stylistically remote from each other and consequently not susceptible to the same modes of interpretation, I want to argue that the successful obfuscation of these kinds of connections by several successive generations of literary critics has done a deep disservice not only to James's writing, but also to the historical and political configuration in which it was produced and to the culture of our own day, which has, for all its differences, by no means resolved the kinds of political and sexual-political conflicts James anatomizes so unsparingly. To indulge an invidious comparison for a moment, I think James's practice in "The Pupil" is, if anything, more rather than less radical than Lynch's in *Blue Velvet*. The film's marginalization of Ben, the only character in the film explicitly marked as gay, is a sign of this. In effect quarantined from the rest of the film, his appearance is restricted to only one scene, although what he fleetingly represents – ties between men *not* mediated through a captive woman – is not. Lynch's raising the age of his boy-initiate Jeffrey into his early twenties is another significant normalizing gesture on his part; if *Blue Velvet* has been a controversial film, imagine how much more so it would have been if Lynch had followed James's practice in "The Pupil" of making his boy-initiate a boy – i.e., not over fifteen.[12] Discarding the "heterosexual plot" on which narratives of "perverse initiation," from Hoffmann's "The Sandman" to *Blue Velvet*, have traditionally depended, James in "The Pupil" produces his "perverse" plot almost undiluted by normalizing or heterosexualizing measures.

One must look beyond the example of Lynch to someone like Kenneth Anger, I think, to find work that explores the dynamics of "perverse" desire as uncompromisingly as James does. Anger is one of the figures who represents something closest to a "direct route" between figures like James and Lynch. In thirteen segments of complex montage, each set to a different pop tune of the two-or-three-year period before the film was made – the ancestors of today's ubiquitous rock videos – Anger's film shows the members of a motorcycle gang preparing for a race by tinkering with their bikes, dressing up in elaborate fetish gear, snorting cocaine, and performing a series of rituals including a mock orgy-and-torture session. These fetishistic and largely mock-sadomasochistic preparations culminate in a motorcycle rally in which the bikers race their 'cycles around a track to the tune of such pop songs as "Point of No Return" and "Wipe-Out" – terms that may well remind us of what the group of texts I've been discussing represent as the traumatic and irreversibly shattering qualities of precocious initiation into "perverse circles."

One way of reading *Blue Velvet* is as a text that Lynch unfolded out of the "Blue Velvet" segment of Anger's 1964 film *Scorpio Rising*. In this segment, as Bobby Vinton croons "She wore blue velvet," the film represents not a woman in blue velvet but a bike boy (three of them, in fact) in blue *denim* donning black leather and chains. While the song invites its auditor to fantasize a specularized and fetishized girl or woman – a figure like Lynch's Dorothy, "the Blue Velvet Lady" – Anger's film presents specularized and fetishized boys. Rather than the kind of undisrupted miming or lip-synching that characterizes male behavior and serves as a vehicle for a limited range of male–male desires in Lynch's film, Anger's film at moments like the one I am considering drives a wedge between the aural effects and the visual ones it is producing. By representing leather boys "dressing up" to the tune of the song "Blue Velvet," Anger produces the disorienting shock effect – quite successfully, judging from the outraged reception and censorship of the film during the early years of its reception – of placing males in the position of the specularized and fetishized "supposed-to-be female" figure of sexist – and heterosexist – representational regimes.

The kinds of erotic and erotically disorienting substitutions in which *Scorpio Rising* deals, of which the blue-velvet bike-boys episode is a chief example, are certainly an important aspect of the pleasures of Anger's text. Another aspect of this pleasure I would not overlook is the one common to this as well as to all of the other texts I have been discussing of representing the fetish – whether it be velvet or suede, denim or leather – as a primary focus of the various "perverse" desires that all these texts mime; in them, the fetish is an exemplarily disoriented marker of desire, not itself either the object of desire, nor simply the kind of substitute phallus it is in classical Freudian theory but something – at least as much a practice as it is an object – that locates itself undecidably between mimetic desire and the indefinitely wide range of objects on which that desire may fasten. *Scorpio Rising* literalizes more thoroughly than any other text of which I am aware not only the priority of mimetic desire over object-desire, but also the priority of the fetish over other "perverse" investments.

One further link from Anger back to James's milieu passes through the figure of Aleister Crowley, someone whose work and career have been perhaps even more important for Anger than those of the two gay film directors whose influence is most obvious in his work, Eisenstein and Cocteau. A generation younger than James and exactly the kind of cultivator of a "perverse" public image that James strenuously avoided associating himself with, Crowley began his career as a member, along with Yeats and others, of the occult society of the Order of the Golden Dawn. Crowley spent most of his career performing and writing about forms of ritual magic based on "perverse" sexual practices, and Anger has been an avowed disciple of his since boyhood. Anger's precocity was the first very notable fact of his own career; the story of its beginning reads like one of the tales of always-premature, "perverse" initiation I have been considering. Left on his own one weekend by his parents when he was seventeen, Anger, no doubt fulfilling many suburban parents' worst nightmare about their offspring, made a film – *Fireworks* – starring himself about a seventeen-year-old boy who is "picked up" by a gang of sailors and raped and disemboweled by them. That the atmosphere of the film is lyrical and witty rather than horrific suggests that Jean Genêt might have had little to teach this boy-filmmaker about "perverse" desires and their representation. As the narrator of "The Pupil" says of Pemberton the tutor's efforts to fathom the remarkable resourcefulness and resilience of his little charge, "When he tried to figure to himself the morning twilight of childhood, so as to deal with it safely, he perceived that it was never fixed, never arrested, that ignorance, at the instant one touched it, was already flushing faintly into knowledge, that there was nothing that at a given moment you could say a clever child didn't know. It seemed to him that *he* both knew too much to imagine Morgan's simplicity and too little to disembroil his tangle." Like little Morgan and his tutor and the other "small boys" and young men that figure in these texts, we all often find ourselves possessing what seems to be both more knowledge than we can use and less than we need when we try to think about such difficult issues as our own relations to children and young people, including our students, and our no less complicated relations to our own child selves. Those uncanny figures, as James writes, sometimes seemed to know their most painful lessons almost before they learned them. As I think the examples I have been discussing suggest, we have much to learn from these child-figures when they return to haunt us with their uncommon knowledge of the "perverse" energies that impel desire.

Notes

1   For Girard's major formulations of his theory, see "Triangular Desire," the first chapter of *Deceit, Desire, and the Novel: Self and Other in Literary Structure*, trans. Yvonne Freccero (Baltimore: Johns Hopkins University Press, 1965), pp. 1–52; "From Mimetic Desire to the Monstrous Double," in *Violence and the Sacred*, trans. Patrick Gregory (Baltimore: Johns Hopkins University Press, 1977), pp. 143–68; "Mimetic Desire," in *Things Hidden Since the Foundation of the World*, trans. Stephen Bann and Michael Metteer (Stanford, Calif.: Stanford University Press, 1987), pp. 283–347; and Walter Burkert, René Girard, and Jonathan Z. Smith, *Violent Origins: Ritual Killing and Cultural Formation*, ed. Roger G. Hamerton Kelly (Stanford, Calif.: Stanford University Press, 1987), esp. pp. 7–20 and 121–9. Eve Kosofsky Sedgwick's reformulation of Girard in the opening pages of *Between Men: English Literature and Male Homosocial Desire* (New York: Columbia University Press, 1985), esp. pp. 21–5, has had a formative effect on my thinking about the relation between gender and sexuality and the circuits of desire, in this project as in previous ones. I am very grateful to Eve for her generous and challenging conversation during the time I was planning this essay – as I am to Jonathan Goldberg for his characteristically unstinting attention to several early drafts of it. I also wish to thank Marcie Frank and Stephen Orgel for several extremely helpful suggestions for improving it.

2   Mikkel Borch-Jacobsen, *The Freudian Subject*, trans. Catherine Porter (Stanford, Calif.: Stanford University Press, 1988), p. 26. Hereafter cited in the text by page number.

3   "The 'Uncanny,'" in Philip Rieff, ed., *Studies in Parapsychology* (New York: Collier, 1963), pp. 19–60.

4   "The Sandman," in E. T. A. Hoffmann, *Tales of Hoffmann* (Harmondsworth: Penguin, 1982), p. 282. Hereafter cited in the text by page number.

5   Lacan equates the phallus with the "*copula*" in "The Signification of the Phallus," *Ecrits: A Selection*, trans. Alan Sheridan (New York: Norton, 1977), p. 287.

6   Kyle MacLachlan plays Jeffrey in *Blue Velvet*; Laura Dern, Sandy; Dennis Hopper, Frank; Isabella Rossellini, Dorothy; and Dean Stockwell, Ben.

7   Andy Warhol's diary entry for December 15, 1986, reads in part: "Dennis [Hopper] told me the other night that they cut the scene out of *Blue Velvet* where he rapes Dean Stockwell or Dean Stockwell rapes him and there's lipstick on somebody's ass" (*The Andy Warhol Diaries*, ed. Pat Hackett [New York: Warner, 1989], p. 784). Warhol's account of this is obviously somewhat garbled, but it does suggest that Lynch had planned (and he and his actors had perhaps filmed) a more literal male–male rape scene than the "symbolic" one that appears in the film.

8   The *Independent* (January 5, 1899), p. 73; reprinted in Robert Kimbrough (ed.), *Henry James: The Turn of the Screw* (New York: Norton, 1966), p. 175. Shoshana Felman discusses this review in *Writing and Madness: Literature/ Philosophy/ Psychoanalysis*, trans. Martha Noel Evans and the author with the assistance of Brian Massumi (Ithaca, NY: Cornell University Press, 1985), pp. 143–4.

9   Walter Benjamin, *Charles Baudelaire: A Lyric Poet in the Era of High Capitalism*, trans. Harry Zohn (London: Verso, 1983), pp. 46–7.
10 William Makepeace Thackeray, *Vanity Fair* (New York: New American Library, 1962), p. 257.
11 Citations to the text of "The Pupil" are to Leon Edel's edition of the tale in *The Complete Tales of Henry James*, vol. 7, 1888–91 (Philadelphia: Lippincott, 1963).
12 Joshua Wilner has urged me to consider that it may be more proper to think of the young man Pemberton as the initiate in James's story, rather than the boy Morgan. Yet even if one grants this, James's practice remains radical: if we take Pemberton to be James's initiate, and he is roughly as old as Lynch's Jeffrey (i.e., no longer a boy, definitely a young man), it is nevertheless true of James's two "initiators" (Morgan and his mother) that one of them is hardly more than a child. Frank and Dorothy, the primary initiators in Lynch's film, are by contrast represented as being emphatically no longer young, while Jeffrey's young girlfriend Sandy is conventionally represented as someone who is just outgrowing the role of being an innocent child.

CHAPTER 7

Female Masculinity

Judith Halberstam

Judith Halberstam has been in the forefront of the academic movement to draw attention to the cultural forms of gender multiplicity. In her 1998 book, *Female Masculinity*, she explores different gender possibilities and the manifold formulations gender performance can assume.

> *What's the use of being a little boy if you are going to grow up to be a man?*
> *Gertrude Stein*, Everybody's Autobiography *(1937)*

The Real Thing

What is "masculinity"? This has been probably the most common question that I have faced over the past five years while writing on the topic of female masculinity. If masculinity is not the social and cultural and indeed political expression of maleness, then what is it? I do not claim to have any definitive answer to this question, but I do have a few proposals about why masculinity must not and cannot and should not reduce down to the male body and its effects. I also venture to assert that although we seem to have a difficult time defining masculinity, as a society we have little trouble in recognizing it, and indeed we spend massive amounts of time and money ratifying and supporting the versions of masculinity that we enjoy and trust; many of these "heroic masculinities" depend absolutely on the subordination of alternative masculinities. I claim in this book that far from being an imitation of maleness, female masculinity actually affords us a glimpse of how masculinity is constructed as masculinity. In other words, female masculinities are framed as the rejected scraps of dominant masculinity in order that male masculinity may appear to be the real thing. But what we understand as heroic masculinity has been produced by and across both male and female bodies.

This opening chapter does not simply offer a conventional theoretical introduction to the enterprise of conceptualizing masculinity without men; rather, it attempts to compile the myths and fantasies about masculinity that have ensured that masculinity and maleness are profoundly difficult to pry apart. I then offer, by way of a preliminary attempt to reimagine masculinity, numerous examples of alternative masculinities in fiction, film, and lived experience. These examples are mostly queer and female, and they show clearly how important it is to recognize alternative masculinities when and where they emerge. Throughout this introduction, I detail the many ways in which female masculinity has been blatantly ignored both in the culture at large and within academic studies of masculinity. This widespread indifference to female masculinity, I suggest, has clearly ideological motivations and has sustained the complex social structures that wed masculinity to maleness and to power and domination. I firmly believe that a sustained examination of female masculinity can make crucial interventions within gender studies, cultural studies, queer studies, and mainstream discussions of gender in general.

Masculinity in this society inevitably conjures up notions of power and legitimacy and privilege; it often symbolically refers to the power of the state and to uneven distributions of wealth. Masculinity seems to extend outward into patriarchy and inward into the family; masculinity represents the power of inheritance, the consequences of the traffic in women, and the promise of social privilege. But, obviously, many other lines of identification traverse the terrain of masculinity, dividing its power into complicated differentials of class, race, sexuality, and gender. If what we call "dominant masculinity" appears to be a naturalized relation between maleness and power, then it makes little sense to examine men for the contours of that masculinity's social construction. Masculinity, this book will claim, becomes legible as masculinity where and when it leaves the white male middle-class body. Arguments about excessive masculinity tend to focus on black bodies (male and female), latino/a bodies, or working-class bodies, and insufficient masculinity is all too often figured by Asian bodies or upper-class bodies; these stereotypical constructions of variable masculinity mark the process by which masculinity becomes dominant in the sphere of white middle-class maleness. But all too many studies that currently attempt to account for the power of white masculinity recenter this white male body by concentrating all their analytical efforts on detailing the forms and expressions of white male dominance. Numerous studies of Elvis, white male youth, white male feminism, men and marriage, and domestications of maleness amass information about a subject whom we know intimately and ad nauseam. This study professes a degree of indifference to the whiteness of the male and the masculinity of the white male and the project of naming his power: male masculinity figures in my project as a hermeneutic, and as a counterexample to the kinds of masculinity that seem most informative about gender relations and most generative of social change. This book seeks Elvis only in the female Elvis impersonator Elvis Herselvis; it searches for the political contours of masculine privilege not in men but in the lives of aristocratic European cross-dressing women in the 1920s; it describes the details of masculine difference by comparing not men and women but butch lesbians and female-to-male transsexuals; it examines masculinity's iconicity not in the male matinee idol but in a history of butches in cinema; it finds, ultimately, that the shapes and forms of modern masculinity are best showcased within female masculinity.

How else to begin a book on female masculinity but by deposing one of the most persistent of male heroes: Bond, James Bond. To illustrate my point that modern masculinity is most easily recognized as female masculinity, consider the James Bond action film, in which male masculinity very often appears as only a shadow of a more powerful and convincing alternative masculinity. In *Goldeneye* (1995), for example, Bond battles the usual array of bad guys: Commies, Nazis, mercenaries, and a super-aggressive violent femme type. He puts on his usual performance of debonair action adventure hero, and he has his usual supply of gadgetry to aid him – a retractable belt, a bomb disguised as a pen, a laser weapon watch, and so on. But there's something curiously lacking in *Goldeneye*, namely, credible masculine power. Bond's boss, M, is a noticeably butch older woman who calls Bond a dinosaur and chastises him for being a misogynist and a sexist. His secretary, Miss Moneypenny, accuses him of sexual harassment, his male buddy betrays him and calls him a dupe, and ultimately women seem not to go for his charms – bad suits and lots of sexual innuendo – which seem as old and as ineffective as his gadgets.

Masculinity, in this rather actionless film, is primarily prosthetic and, in this and countless other action films, has little if anything to do with biological maleness and signifies more often as a technical special effect. In *Goldeneye* it is M who most convincingly performs masculinity, and she does so partly by exposing the sham of Bond's own performance. It is M who convinces us that sexism and misogyny are not necessarily part and parcel of masculinity, even though historically it has become difficult, if not impossible, to untangle masculinity from the oppression of women. The action adventure hero should embody an extreme version of normative masculinity, but instead we find that excessive masculinity turns into a parody or exposure of the norm. Because masculinity tends to manifest as natural gender itself, the action flick, with its emphases on prosthetic extension, actually undermines the heterosexuality of the hero even as it extends his masculinity. So, in *Goldeneye*, for example, Bond's masculinity is linked not only to a profoundly unnatural form of masculine embodiment but also to gay masculinities. In the scene in which Bond goes to pick up his newest set of gadgets, a campy and almost queeny science nerd gives Bond his brand-new accessories and demonstrates each one with great enthusiasm. It is no accident that the science nerd is called Agent Q. We might read Agent Q as a perfect model of the interpenetration of queer and dominant regimes – Q is precisely an agent, a queer subject who exposes the workings of dominant heterosexual masculinity. The gay masculinity of Agent Q and the female masculinity of M provide a remarkable representation of the absolute dependence of dominant masculinities on minority masculinities.

When you take his toys away, Bond has very little propping up his performance of masculinity. Without the slick suit, the half smile, the cigarette lighter that transforms into a laser gun, our James is a hero without the action or the adventure. The masculinity of the white male, what we might call "epic masculinity," depends absolutely, as any Bond flick demonstrates, on a vast subterranean network of secret government groups, well-funded scientists, the army, and an endless supply of both beautiful bad babes and beautiful good babes, and finally it relies heavily on an immediately recognizable "bad guy." The "bad guy" is a standard generic feature of epic masculinity narratives: think only of *Paradise Lost* and its eschatological separation between God and Devil; Satan, if you like, is the original bad guy. Which is not to say that the bad guy's masculinity bars him from the rewards of male privilege – on the contrary, bad guys may also look like winners, but they just tend to die more quickly. Indeed, there is currently a line of clothing called Bad Boy that revels in the particular power of the bad guy and reveals how quickly transgression adds up to nothing more than consumerism in the sphere of the white male. Another line of clothing that indulges in the consumer potential of male rebellion is No Fear gear. This label features advertisements with skydiving, surfing, car-racing men who show their manliness by wearing the No Fear logo and practicing death-defying stunts in their leisure time. To test how domesticated this label actually is, we have only to imagine what No Fear might mean for women. It might mean learning how to shoot a gun or working out or taking up a martial art, but it would hardly translate into skydiving. Obviously, then, No Fear is a luxury and can in no way be equated with any form of social rebellion.

There is also a long literary and cinematic history that celebrates the rebellion of the male. If James Stewart, Gregory Peck, and Fred Astaire represent a few faces of good-guy appeal, James Dean, Marlon Brando, and Robert De Niro represent the bad-guy appeal, and really it becomes quite hard to separate one group from the other. Obviously, bad-boy representations in the 1950s captured something of a white working-class rebellion against middle-class society and against particular forms of domestication, but today's rebel without a cause is tomorrow's investment banker, and male rebellion tends toward respectability as the rewards for conformity quickly come to outweigh the rewards for social rebellion. To paraphrase Gertrude Stein, what's the point of being a rebel boy if you are going to grow up to be a man? Obviously, where and when rebellion ceases to be white middle-class male rebellion (individualized and localized within the lone male or even generalized into the boy gang) and becomes class rebellion or race rebellion, a very different threat emerges.

Tomboys

What happens when boy rebellion is located not in the testosterone-induced pout of the hooligan but in the sneer of the tomboy? Tomboyism generally describes an extended childhood period of female masculinity. If we are to believe general ac- counts of childhood behavior, tomboyism is quite common for girls and does not generally give rise to parental fears. Because comparable cross-identification behav- iors in boys do often give rise to quite hysterical responses, we tend to believe that female gender deviance is much more tolerated than male gender deviance.[1] I am not sure that tolerance in such matters can be measured or at any rate that responses to childhood gender behaviors necessarily tell us anything concrete about the permitted parameters of adult male and female gender deviance. Tomboyism tends to be associ- ated with a "natural" desire for the greater freedoms and mobilities enjoyed by boys. Very often it is read as a sign of independence and self-motivation, and tomboyism may even be encouraged to the extent that it remains comfortably linked to a stable sense of a girl identity. Tomboyism is punished, however, when it appears to be the sign of extreme male identification (taking a boy's name or refusing girl clothing of any type) and when it threatens to extend beyond childhood and into adolescence.[2] Teenage tomboyism presents a problem and tends to be subject to the most severe efforts to reorient. We could say that tomboyism is tolerated as long as the child remains prepubescent; as soon as puberty begins, however, the full force of gender conformity descends on the girl. Gender conformity is pressed onto all girls, not just tomboys, and this is where it becomes hard to uphold the notion that male femininity presents a greater threat to social and familial stability than female masculinity. Female adolescence represents the crisis of coming of age as a girl in a male- dominated society. If adolescence for boys represents a rite of passage (much cele- brated in Western literature in the form of the *bildungsroman*), and an ascension to some version (however attenuated) of social power, for girls, adolescence is a lesson in restraint, punishment, and repression. It is in the context of female adolescence that the tomboy instincts of millions of girls are remodeled into compliant forms of femininity.

That any girls do emerge at the end of adolescence as masculine women is quite amazing. The growing visibility and indeed respectability of lesbian communities to some degree facilitate the emergence of masculine young women. But as even a cursory survey of popular cinema confirms, the image of the tomboy can be tolerated only within a narrative of blossoming womanhood; within such a narrative, tomboyism represents a resistance to adulthood itself rather than to adult femininity. In both the novel and film versions of the classic tomboy narrative *The Member of the Wedding*, by Carson McCullers, tomboy Frankie Addams fights a losing battle against womanhood, and the text locates womanhood or femininity as a crisis of representation that confronts the heroine with unacceptable life options. As her brother's wedding approaches, Frankie Addams pronounces herself mired in a realm of unbelonging, outside the symbolic partnership of the wedding but also alienated from belonging in almost every category that might describe her. McCullers writes: "It happened that green and crazy summer when Frankie was twelve years old. This was the summer when for a long time she had not been a member. She belonged to no club and was a member of nothing in the world. Frankie was an unjoined person who hung around in doorways, and she was afraid."[3] McCullers positions Frankie on the verge of adolescence ("when Frankie was twelve years old") and in the midst of an enduring state of being "unjoined": "She belonged to no club and was a member of nothing in the world." While childhood in general may qualify as a period of "unbelonging," for the boyish girl arriving on the doorstep of womanhood, her status as "unjoined" marks her out for all manner of social violence and opprobrium. As she dawdles in the last light of childhood, Frankie Addams has become a tomboy who "hung around in doorways, and she was afraid."

As a genre, the tomboy film suggests that the categories available to women for racial, gendered, and sexual identification are simply inadequate. In her novel, McCullers shows this inadequacy to be a direct result of the tyranny of language – a structure that fixes people and things in place artificially but securely. Frankie tries to change her identity by changing her name: "Why is it against the law to change your name?" she asks Berenice (107). Berenice answers: "Because things accumulate around your name," and she stresses that without names, confusion would reign and "the whole world would go crazy." But Berenice also acknowledges that the fixity conferred by names also traps people into many different identities, racial as well as gendered: "We all of us somehow caught. . . . And maybe we wants to widen and bust free. But no matter what we do we still caught" (113). Frankie thinks that naming represents the power of definition, and name changing confers the power to re-imagine identity, place, relation, and even gender. "I wonder if it is against the law to change your name," says Frankie, "Or add to it. . . . Well I don't care. . . . F. Jasmine Addams" (15).

Psychoanalysis posits a crucial relationship between language and desire such that language structures desire and expresses therefore both the fullness and the futility of human desire – full because we always desire, futile because we are never satisfied. Frankie in particular understands desire and sexuality to be the most regimented forms of social conformity – we are supposed to desire only certain people and only in certain ways, but her desire does not work that way, and she finds herself torn between longing and belonging. Because she does not desire in conventional ways, Frankie seeks to avoid desire altogether. Her struggle with language, her attempts to remake herself through naming and remake the world with a new order of being, are ultimately heroic, but unsuccessful. McCullers's pessimism has to do with a sense of the overwhelming "order of things," an order that cannot be affected by the individual, and works through things as basic as language, and forces nonmembers into memberships they cannot fulfill.

My book refuses the futility long associated with the tomboy narrative and instead seizes on the opportunity to recognize and ratify differently gendered bodies and subjectivities. Moving from the nineteenth century to the present and examining diaries, court cases, novels, letters, films, performances, events, critical essays, videos, news items, and testimonies, this book argues for the production of new taxonomies, what Eve K. Sedgwick humorously called "nonce taxonomies" in *Epistemology of the Closet*, classifications of desire, physicality, and subjectivity that attempt to intervene in hegemonic processes of naming and defining. Nonce taxonomies are categories that we use daily to make sense of our worlds but that work so well that we actually fail to recognize them. In this book, I attempt to bring some of the nonce taxonomies of female masculinity into view, and I detail the histories of the suppression of these categories. Here, and in the rest of the book, I am using the topic of female masculinity to explore a queer subject position that can successfully challenge hegemonic models of gender conformity. Female masculinity is a particularly fruitful site of investigation because it has been vilified by heterosexist and feminist/womanist programs alike; unlike male femininity, which fulfills a kind of ritual function in male homosocial cultures, female masculinity is generally received by hetero- and homonormative cultures as a pathological sign of misidentification and maladjustment, as a longing to be and to have a power that is always just out of reach. Within a lesbian context, female masculinity has been situated as the place where patriarchy goes to work on the female psyche and reproduces misogyny within femaleness. There have been to date remarkably few studies or theories about the inevitable effects of a fully articulated female masculinity on a seemingly fortified male masculinity. Sometimes female masculinity coincides with the excesses of male supremacy, and sometimes it codifies a unique form of social rebellion; often female masculinity is the sign of sexual alterity, but occasionally it marks heterosexual variation; sometimes female masculinity marks the place of pathology, and every now and then it represents the healthful alternative to what are considered the histrionics of conventional femininities.

I want to carefully produce a model of female masculinity that remarks on its multiple forms but also calls for new and self-conscious affirmations of different gender taxonomies. Such affirmations begin not by subverting masculine power or taking up a position against masculine power but by turning a blind eye to conventional masculinities and refusing to engage. Frankie Addams, for example, constitutes her rebellion not in opposition to the law but through indifference to the law: she recognizes that it may be against the law to change one's name or add to it, but she also has a simple response to such illegal activity: "Well, I don't care." I am not suggesting in this book that we follow the futile path of what Foucault calls "saying no to power," but I am asserting that power may inhere within different forms of refusal: "Well, I don't care."

Queer Methodologies

This book deploys numerous methodologies in order to pursue the multiple forms of gender variance presented within female masculinity. On account of the interdisciplinary nature of my project, I have had to craft a methodology out of available disciplinary methods. Deploying what I would call a "queer methodology," I have used some combination of textual criticism, ethnography, historical survey, archival research, and the production of taxonomies. I call this methodology "queer" because it attempts to remain supple enough to respond to the various locations of information on female masculinity and betrays a certain disloyalty to conventional disciplinary methods. Obviously, I could have produced methodological consistency by confining myself to literary texts, but the queer methodology used here, then, typifies just one of the forms of refusal that I discussed in my last section.

Although some of the most informative work on alternative sexual communities has come in the form of ethnography, and although autobiographies and narrative histories tend to be the material that we turn to for information on sexual identities, there is nonetheless some disagreement among queer scholars about how we should collect and interpret such information on sexual identity. Indeed, some of the most bitter and long-lasting disagreements within queer studies have been about disciplinarity and methodology. Whereas some cultural studies proponents have argued that social science methods of collecting, collating, and presenting sexual data through surveys and other methods of social research tend to rediscover the sexual systems they already know rather than finding out about those they do not, social science proponents argue that cultural studies scholars do not pay enough attention to the material realities of queer life. And while there has been plenty of discussion in the academy about the need for interdisciplinary work, there has been far less support for such work in the university at large. A project such as this one, therefore, risks drawing criticism from historians for not providing a proper history, from literary critics for not focusing on literary texts, and from social scientists for not deploying the traditional tools of social science research. While I take full responsibility for all the errors I may make in my attempts to produce readings and histories and ethnography, I also recognize that this book exemplifies the problem confronted by queer studies itself: How do we forge queer methodologies while as scholars we reside in traditional departments?

At least one method of sex research that I reject in creating a queer methodology is the traditional social science project of surveying people and expecting to squeeze truth from raw data. In a review essay in the *New York Review of Books* about a series of new sex surveys, R. C. Lewontin comments on the difficulty associated with this social science approach to sexuality: "Given the social circumstances of sexual activity, there seems no way to find out what people do 'in the bedroom' except to ask them. But the answers they give cannot be put to the test of incredulity."[4] Lewontin suggests that people tend not to be truthful when it comes to reporting on their own sexual behavior (men exaggerate and women downplay, for example), and there are no ways to make allowances for personal distortion within social science methods. Furthermore, social scientists seem not to be concerned with the high levels of untruth in relation to sexuality but spend all their energy on solving methodological problems. Ultimately, Lewontin claims – and I think he has a point – social science surveys are "demonstrations of what their planners already believed they knew to be true" (25). At a time when the humanities are under severe scrutiny and attack, it is important to point to the reliance of social science methods on strategies such as narrative analysis, interpretation, and speculation. As Lewontin says in his conclusion: "How then can there be a social science? The answer surely is to be less ambitious and stop trying to make sociology into a natural science although it is, indeed, the study of natural objects" (29). This is not to say, however, that traditional social science research methods such as questionnaires are never appropriate. Indeed, there are certain questions that can be answered only by survey methods in the realm of sexuality (i.e., how many lesbians are using dental dams? What age-groups or social classes do these lesbians belong to?), but all too often surveys are used to try to gather far less factual information, and all subtlety tends to be lost.[5]

There is some irony in the apparent impossibility of applying traditional social science methods to the study of sex because as queer sociologists are all too quick to point out, many of the theoretical systems that we use to talk about sex, such as social constructionism, come from sociology. In a recent "queer" issue of *Sociological Theory*, a group of sociologists attempted to account for the currently strained relations between sociological theory and queer theory. Steven Epstein pointed out that sociology asserted that sexuality was socially constructed and indeed that "without seeking to minimize the importance of other disciplines, I would suggest that neither queer theory nor lesbian and gay studies in general could be imagined in their present forms without the contributions of sociological theory."[6] Arlene Stein and Ken Plummer continue Epstein's line of inquiry and add a critique of the present state of queer theory:

> Queer theorists... appreciate the extent to which the texts of literature and mass culture shape sexuality, but their weakness is that they rarely, if ever, move beyond the text. There is a dangerous tendency for the new queer theorists to ignore "real" queer life as it is materially experienced across the world, while they play with the free-floating signifiers of texts.[7]

In an effort to restore sociology to its proper place within the study of sexuality, Stein and Plummer have reinvested here in a clear and verifiable difference between the real and the textual, and they designate textual analysis as a totally insular activity with no referent, no material consequences, and no intellectual gain. But as Lewontin's review suggested, it is precisely this belief in the real and the material as separate from the represented and the textual that creates the problems of survey analysis. To be fair, Stein and Plummer are clearly not suggesting merely a quantitative approach to the study of sexuality and queer subcultures, but they do, on some level, seem to have re-created some essential divide between the truth of sexual behavior and the fiction of textual analysis.

The answer to the problem of how to study sexuality, I am trying to suggest, must lie to some extent in an interdisciplinary approach that can combine information culled from people with information culled from texts. So, whereas Cindy Patton, for example, in "Tremble Hetero Swine," remarks with dismay on the dominance of "textually based forms of queer theory," we must question whether there is a form of queer theory or sexual theory that is not textually based.[8] Isn't a sexual ethnographer studying texts? And doesn't a social historian collate evidence from texts? Sometimes the texts are oral histories, sometimes they might be interview material, sometimes they might be fiction or autobiography, but given our basic formulation of sex as "private," something that happens when other people are not around, there is no way to objectively observe "in the bedroom." Conversely, readings of texts also require historical contexts and some relation to the lived experience of subjects. The text-based methodologies err on the side of abstraction, and the sociological studies err on the side of overly rationalizing sexual behavior. Finally, although some have criticized literary or cultural studies approaches to identity construction as apolitical or ahistorical, theories that tie the history of sexuality unproblematically to economics or the movement of capital tend to produce exactly the linear narratives of rational progress and modernization that sexuality seems to resist.

A queer methodology, in a way, is a scavenger methodology that uses different methods to collect and produce information on subjects who have been deliberately or accidentally excluded from traditional studies of human behavior. The queer methodology attempts to combine methods that are often cast as being at odds with each other, and it refuses the academic compulsion toward disciplinary coherence. Although this book will be immediately recognizable as a work of cultural studies, it will not shy away from the more empirical methods associated with ethnographic research.

Constructing Masculinities

Within cultural studies itself, masculinity has recently become a favorite topic. I want to try here to account for the growing popularity of a body of work on masculinity that evinces absolutely no interest in masculinity without men. I first noticed the unprecedented interest in masculinity in April 1994 when the DIA Center for the Performing Arts convened a group of important intellectuals to hold forth on the topic of masculinities. On the opening night of this event, one commentator wondered, "Why masculinity, why now?" Several others, male critics and scholars, gave eloquent papers about their memories of being young boys and about their relationships with their fathers. The one lesbian on the panel, a poet, read a moving poem about rape. At the end of the evening, only one panelist had commented on the limitations of a discussion of masculinity that interpreted "masculinity" as a synonym for men or maleness.[9] This lonely intervention highlighted the gap between mainstream discussions of masculinity and men and ongoing queer discussions about masculinity, which extend far beyond the male body. Indeed, in answer to the naive question that began the evening. "Why masculinities, why now?" one might state: Because masculinity in the 1990s has finally been recognized as, at least in part, a construction by female- as well as male-born people.[10]

The anthology that the conference produced provides more evidence of the thoroughgoing association that the editors have made between masculinity and maleness. The title page features a small photographic illustration of a store sign advertising clothing as "Fixings for Men." This illustration has been placed just below the title, *Constructing Masculinity*, and forces the reader to understand the construction of masculinity as the outfitting of males within culture. The introduction to the volume attempts to diversify this definition of masculinity by using Judith Butler's and Eve Sedgwick's contributions to suggest that the anthology recognizes the challenges made by gays, lesbians, and queers to the terms of gender normativity. The editors insist that masculinity is multiple and that "far from just being about men, the idea of masculinity engages, inflects, and shapes everyone."[11] The commitment to the representation of masculinity as multiple is certainly borne out in the first essay in the volume, by Eve Sedgwick, in which she proposes that masculinity may have little to do with men, and is somewhat extended by Butler's essay "Melancholy Gender." But Sedgwick also critiques the editors for having proposed a book and a conference on masculinity that remain committed to linking masculinity to maleness. Although the introduction suggests that the editors have heeded Sedgwick's call for gender diversity, the rest of the volume suggests otherwise. There are many fascinating essays in this anthology, but there are no essays specifically on female masculinity. Although gender-queer images by Loren Cameron and Cathy Opie adorn the pages of the book, the text contains no discussions of these images. The book circles around discussions of male icons such as Clint Eastwood and Steven Seagal; it addresses the complex relations between fathers and sons; it examines topics such as how science defines men and masculinity and the law. The volume concludes with an essay by Stanley Aronowitz titled "My Masculinity," an autobiographically inflected consideration of various forms of male power.

None of my analysis here is to say that this is an uninteresting anthology or that the essays are somehow wrong or misguided, but I am trying to point out that the editorial statement at the beginning of the volume is less a prologue to what follows and more of an epilogue that describes what a volume on masculinity *should* do as opposed to what the anthology does do. Even when the need for an analysis of female masculinity has been acknowledged, in other words, it seems remarkably difficult to follow through on. What is it then that, to paraphrase Eve Sedgwick's essay, makes it so difficult *not* to presume an essential relation between masculinity and men?[12]

By beginning with this examination of the *Constructing Masculinity* conference and anthology, I do not want to give the impression that the topic of female masculinities must always be related to some larger topic, some more general set of masculinities that has been, and continues to be, about men. Nor do I want to suggest that gender theory is the true origin of gender knowledges. Rather, this conference and book merely emphasize the lag between community knowledges and practices and academic discourses.[13] I believe it is both helpful and important to contextualize a discussion of female and lesbian masculinities in direct opposition to a more generalized discussion of masculinity within cultural studies that seems intent on insisting that masculinity remain the property of male bodies. The continued refusal in Western society to admit ambiguously gendered bodies into functional social relations (evidenced, for example, by our continued use of either/or bathrooms, either women or men) is, I will claim, sustained by a conservative and protectionist attitude by men in general toward masculinity. Such an attitude has been bolstered by a more general disbelief in female masculinity. I can only describe such disbelief in terms of a failure in a collective imagination: in other words, female-born people have been making convincing and powerful assaults on the coherence of male masculinity for well over a hundred years; what prevents these assaults from taking hold and accomplishing the diminution of the bonds between masculinity and men? Somehow, despite multiple images of strong women (such as bodybuilder Bev Francis or tennis player Martina Navratilova), of cross-identifying women (Radclyffe Hall or Ethel Smyth), of masculine-coded public figures (Janet Reno), of butch superstars (k. d. lang), of muscular and athletic women (Jackie Joyner-Kersee), of female-born transgendered people (Leslie Feinberg), there is still no general acceptance or even recognition of masculine women and boyish girls. This book addresses itself to this collective failure to imagine and ratify the masculinity produced by, for, and within women.

In case my concerns about the current discussions of masculinity in cultural studies sound too dismissive, I want to look in an extended way at what happens when academic discussions of male masculinity take place to the exclusion of discussions of more wide-ranging masculinities. While it may seem that I am giving an inordinate amount of attention to what is after all just one intervention into current discussions, I am using one book as representative of a whole slew of other studies of masculinity that replicate the intentions and the mistakes of this one. In an anthology called *Boys: Masculinities in Contemporary Culture*, edited by Paul Smith for a Cultural Studies series, Smith suggests that masculinity must always be thought of "in the plural" as masculinities "defined and cut through by differences and contradictions of all sorts."[14] The plurality of masculinities for Smith encompasses a dominant white masculinity that is crisscrossed by its others, gay, bisexual, black, Asian, and Latino masculinities. Although the recognition of a host of masculinities makes sense, Smith chooses to focus on dominant white masculinity to the exclusion of the other masculinities he has listed. Smith, predictably, warns the reader not to fall into the trap of simply critiquing dominant masculinity or simply celebrating minority masculinities, and then he makes the following foundational statement:

> And it may well be the case, as some influential voices often tell us, that masculinity or masculinities are in some real sense not the exclusive "property" of biologically male subjects – it's true that many female subjects lay claim to masculinity as their property. Yet in terms of cultural and political *power*, it still makes a difference when masculinity coincides with biological maleness. (4)

What is immediately noticeable to me here is the odd attribution of immense power to those "influential voices" who keep telling us that masculinity is not the property of men. There is no naming of these influential voices, and we are left supposing that "influence" has rendered the "female masculinity theorists" so powerful that names are irrelevant: these voices, one might suppose, are hegemonic. Smith goes on to plead with the reader, asking us to admit that the intersection of maleness and masculinity does "still" make a difference. His appeal here to common sense allows him to sound as if he is trying to reassert some kind of rationality to a debate that is spinning off into totally inconsequential discussions. Smith is really arguing that we must turn to dominant masculinity to begin deconstructing masculinity because it is the equation of maleness plus masculinity that adds up to social legitimacy. As I argued earlier in this chapter, however, precisely because white male masculinity has obscured all other masculinities, we have to turn away from its construction to bring other more mobile forms of masculinity to light. Smith's purpose in his reassertion of the difference that male masculinity makes is to uncover the "cultural and political *power*" of this union in order to direct our attention to the power of patriarchy. The second part of the paragraph makes this all too clear:

> Biological men – male-sexed beings – are after all, in varying degrees, the bearers of privilege and power within the systems against which women still struggle. The privilege and power are, of course, different for different men, endlessly diversified through the markers of class, nation, race, sexual preference and so on. But I'd deny that there are any men who are entirely outside of the ambit, let's say, of power and privilege *in relation to women*. In that sense it has to be useful to our thinking to recall that masculinities are not only a function of dominant notions of masculinity and not constituted solely in resistant

notions of "other" masculinities. In fact, masculinities exist inevitably in relation to what feminisms have construed as the system of patriarchy and patriarchal relations.[15]

The most noticeable feature of this paragraph is the remarkable stability of the terms "women" and "men." Smith advances here a slightly old-fashioned feminism that understands women as endlessly victimized within systems of male power. Woman, within such a model, is the name for those subjects within patriarchy who have no access to male power and who are regulated and confined by patriarchal structures. But what would Smith say to Monique Wittig's claim that lesbians are not women because they are not involved in the heterosexual matrix that produces sexual difference as a power relation? What can Smith add to Judith Butler's influential theory of "gender trouble," which suggests that "gender is a copy with no original" and that dominant sexualities and genders are in some sense imbued with a pathetic dependence on their others that puts them perpetually at risk? What would Smith say to Jacob Hale's claim that the genders we use as reference points in gender theory fall far behind community productions of alternative genderings?[16] Are butch dykes women? Are male transvestites men? How does gender variance disrupt the flow of powers presumed by patriarchy in relations between men and women? Smith, in other words, cannot take female masculinity into account because he sees it as inconsequential and secondary to much more important questions about male privilege. Again, this sounds more like a plaintive assertion that men *do* still access male power within patriarchy (don't they?), and it conveniently ignores the ways in which gender relations are scrambled where and when gender variance comes into play.

Smith's attempt to shore up male masculinity by dismissing the importance of other masculinities finds further expression in his attempt to take racialized masculinities into consideration. His introductory essay opens with a meditation on the complications of the O. J. Simpson case, and Smith wonders at the way popular discourse on the O. J. case sidesteps issues of masculinity and male domination in favor of race. When he hears a black male caller to a radio talk show link O. J.'s case to an ongoing conspiracy against black men in this country, Smith ponders: "His spluttering about the attempted genocide of black men reminded me, somehow, that another feature of the O. J. case was the way it had started with the prosecution trying to establish the relevance of O. J.'s record as a wife beater" (Smith, *Boys*, 1). Noting that the callers to the talk show did not have much to say about this leads Smith to wonder whether race can constitute a collective identity but masculinity cannot, and finally he suggests that although "it might be difficult to talk about race in this country, it is even more difficult to talk about masculinity" (1). If you are a white man, it is probably extremely difficult to talk about either race or masculinity let alone both at the same time. But, of course, race and masculinity, especially in the case of O. J., are not separable into tidy categories. Indeed, one might say that the caller's "spluttering" about conspiracies against black men constituted a far more credible race analysis in this case than Smith's articulation of the relations between race and masculinity. For Smith, masculinity in the case of O. J. constitutes a flow of domination that comes up against his blackness as a flow of subordination. There is no discussion here of the injustices of the legal system, the role of class and money in the trial, or the complicated history of relations between black men and white women. Smith uses O. J. as shorthand for a model that is supposed to suggest power and disempowerment in the same location.

I am taking so much time and effort to discount Smith's introduction to *Boys* because there is a casualness to his essay that both indicates his lack of any real investment in the project of alternative masculinities and suggests an unwillingness to think through the messy identifications that make up contemporary power relations around gender, race, and class. The book that Smith introduces also proves to have nothing much to offer to new discussions of masculinity, and we quickly find ourselves, from the opening essay on, in the familiar territory of men, boys, and their fathers. The first essay, for example, by Fred Pfeil, "A Buffalo, New York Story," tells a pitiful tale about father–son relations in the 1950s. In one memorable moment from the memoir, he (Fred) and Dad have cozied up on the couch to watch *Bonanza* while Mom and Sis are doing the dishes in the kitchen. Boy asks Dad "why bad guys were always so stupid," and Dad laughs and explains "because they were bad" (10). The story goes on to detail the innocent young boy's first brushes with his male relatives' racism and his own painful struggle with car sickness. Besides taking apart the dynamics of fathers and sons cozying up together to watch *Bonanza*, there most certainly are a multitude of important things to say about men and masculinity in patriarchy, but Smith and some of his contributors choose not to say them. We could be producing ethnographies on the aggressive and indeed protofascist masculinities produced by male sports fans.[17] Much work still remains to be done on the socialization (or lack thereof) of young men in high schools, on (particularly rich white male) domestic abusers, on the new sexism embodied by "sensitive men," on the men who participate in the traffic in mail-order brides and sex tourism (including a study of privileged white gay masculinity). But studies in male masculinity are predictably not so interested in taking apart the patriarchal bonds between white maleness and privilege; they are much more concerned to detail the fragilities of male socialization, the pains of manhood, and the fear of female empowerment.[18]

Because I have criticized Smith for his apparent lack of investment in the project of producing alternative masculinities, let me take a moment to make my own investments clear. Although I make my own masculinity the topic of my last chapter, it seems important to state that this book is an attempt to make my own female masculinity plausible, credible, and real. For a large part of my life, I have been stigmatized by a masculinity that marked me as ambiguous and illegible. Like many other tomboys, I was mistaken for a boy throughout my childhood, and like many other tomboy adolescents, I was forced into some semblance of femininity for my teenage years. When gender-ambiguous children are constantly challenged about their gender identity, the chain of misrecognitions can actually produce a new recognition: in other words, to be constantly mistaken for a boy, for many tomboys, can contribute to the production of a masculine identity. It was not until my midtwenties that I finally found a word for my particular gender configuration: butch. In my final chapter, "Raging Bull (Dyke)," I address the ways in which butches manage to affirm their masculinity despite the multiple sites in which that masculinity is challenged, denied, threatened, and violated.

The Bathroom Problem

If three decades of feminist theorizing about gender has thoroughly dislodged the notion that anatomy is destiny, that gender is natural, and that male and female are the only options, why do we still operate in a world that assumes that people who are not male are female, and people who are not female are male (and even that people who are not male are not people!). If gender has been so thoroughly defamiliarized, in other words, why do we not have multiple gender options, multiple gender categories, and real-life nonmale and nonfemale options for embodiment and identification? In a way, gender's very flexibility and seeming fluidity is precisely what allows dimorphic gender to hold sway. Because so few people actually match any given community standards for male or female, in other words, gender can be imprecise and therefore multiply relayed through a solidly binary system. At the same time, because the definitional boundaries of male and female are so elastic, there are very few people in any given public space who are completely unreadable in terms of their gender.

Ambiguous gender, when and where it does appear, is inevitably transformed into deviance, thirdness, or a blurred version of either male or female. As an example, in public bathrooms for women, various bathroom users tend to fail to measure up to expectations of femininity, and those of us who present in some ambiguous way are routinely questioned and challenged about our presence in the "wrong" bathroom. For example, recently, on my way to give a talk in Minneapolis, I was making a connection at Chicago's O'Hare airport. I strode purposefully into the women's bathroom. No sooner had I entered the stall than someone was knocking at the door: "Open up, security here!" I understood immediately what had happened. I had, once again, been mistaken for a man or a boy, and some woman had called security. As soon as I spoke, the two guards at the bathroom stall realized their error, mumbled apologies, and took off. On the way home from the same trip, in the Denver airport, the same sequence of events was repeated. Needless to say, the policing of gender within the bathroom is intensified in the space of the airport, where people are literally moving through space and time in ways that cause them to want to stabilize some boundaries (gender) even as they traverse others (national). However, having one's gender challenged in the women's rest room is a frequent occurrence in the lives of many androgynous or masculine women; indeed, it is so frequent that one wonders whether the category "woman," when used to designate public functions, is completely outmoded.[19]

It is no accident, then, that travel hubs become zones of intense scrutiny and observation. But gender policing within airport bathrooms is merely an intensified version of a larger "bathroom problem." For some gender-ambiguous women, it is relatively easy to "prove" their right to use the women's bathroom – they can reveal some decisive gender trait (a high voice, breasts), and the challenger will generally back off. For others (possibly low-voiced or hairy or breastless people), it is quite difficult to justify their presence in the women's bathroom, and these people may tend to use the men's bathroom, where scrutiny is far less intense. Obviously, in these bathroom confrontations, the gender-ambiguous person first appears as not-woman ("You are in the wrong bathroom!"), but then the person appears as something actually even more scary, not-man ("No, I am not," spoken in a voice recognized as not-male). Not-man and not-woman, the gender-ambiguous bathroom user is also not androgynous or in-between; this person is gender deviant.

For many gender deviants, the notion of passing is singularly unhelpful. Passing as a narrative assumes that there is a self that masquerades as another kind of self and does so successfully; at various moments, the successful pass may cohere into something akin to identity. At such a moment, the passer has *become*. What of a biological female who presents as butch, passes as male in some circumstances and reads as butch in others, and considers herself not to be a woman but maintains distance from the category "man"? For such a subject, identity might best be described as process with multiple sites for becoming and being. To understand such a process, we would need to do more than map psychic and physical journeys between male and female and within queer and straight space; we would need, in fact, to think in fractal terms and about gender geometries. Furthermore, I argue in chapter 4, in my discussion of the stone butch, when and where we discuss the sexualities at stake in certain gender definitions, very different identifications between sexuality, gender, and the body emerge. The stone butch, for example, in her self-definition as a non-feminine, sexually untouchable female, complicates the idea that lesbians share female sexual practices or women share female sexual desires or even that masculine women share a sense of what animates their particular masculinities.

I want to focus on what I am calling "the bathroom problem" because I believe it illustrates in remarkably clear ways the flourishing existence of gender binarism despite rumors of its demise. Furthermore, many normatively gendered women have no idea that a bathroom problem even exists and claim to be completely ignorant about the trials and tribulations that face the butch woman who needs to use a public bathroom. But queer literature is littered with references to the bathroom problem, and it would not be an exaggeration to call it a standard feature of the butch narrative. For example, Leslie Feinberg provides clear illustrations of the dimensions of the bathroom problem in *Stone Butch Blues*. In this narrative of the life of the he-she factory worker, Jess Goldberg, Jess recounts many occasions in which she has to make crucial decisions about whether she can afford to use the women's bathroom. On a shopping outing with some drag queens, Jess tells Peaches: "I gotta use the bathroom. God, I wish I could wait, but I can't." Jess takes a deep breath and enters the ladies' room:

> Two women were freshening their makeup in front of the mirror. One glanced at the other and finished applying her lipstick. "Is that a man or a woman?" she said to her friend as I passed them.
>
> The other woman turned to me. "This is the woman's bathroom," she informed me.
>
> I nodded. "I know."
>
> I locked the stall door behind me. Their laughter cut me to the bone. "You don't really know if that is a man or not," one woman said to the other. "We should call security to make sure."
>
> I flushed the toilet and fumbled with my zipper in fear. Maybe it was just an idle threat. Maybe they really would call security. I hurried out of the bathroom as soon as I heard both women leave.[20]

For Jess, the bathroom represents a limit to her ability to move around in the public sphere. Her body, with its needs and physical functions, imposes a limit on her attempts to function normally despite her variant gender presentation. The women in the rest room, furthermore, are depicted as spiteful, rather than fearful. They toy with Jess by calling into question her right to use the rest room and threatening to call the police. As Jess puts it: "They never would have made fun of a guy like that." In other words, if the women were truly anxious for their safety, they would not have toyed with the intruder, and they would not have hesitated to call the police.

Their casualness about calling security indicates that they know Jess is a woman but want to punish her for her inappropriate self-presentation.

Another chronicle of butch life, *Throw It to the River*, by Nice Rodriguez, a Filipina-Canadian writer, also tells of the bathroom encounter. In a story called "Every Full Moon," Rodriguez tells a romantic tale about a butch bus conductor called Remedios who falls in love with a former nun called Julianita. Remedios is "muscular around the arms and shoulders," and her "toughness allows her to bully anyone who will not pay the fare."[21] She aggressively flirts with Julianita until Julianita agrees to go to a movie with Remedios. To prepare for her date, Remedios dresses herself up, carefully flattening out her chest with Band-Aids over the nipples: "She bought a white shirt in Divisoria just for this date. Now she worries that the cloth may be too thin and transparent, and that Julianita will be turned off when her nipples protrude out like dice" (33). With her "well-ironed jeans," her smooth chest, and even a man's manicure, Remedios heads out for her date. However, once out with Julianita, Remedios, now dressed in her butch best, has to be careful about public spaces. After the movie, Julianita rushes off to the washroom, but Remedios waits outside for her:

> She has a strange fear of ladies' rooms. She wishes there was another washroom some-where between the men's and the ladies' for queers like her. Most of the time she holds her pee – sometimes as long as half a day – until she finds a washroom where the users are familiar with her. Strangers take to her unkindly, especially elder women who inspect her from head to toe. (40–1)

Another time, Remedios tells of being chased from a ladies' room and beaten by a bouncer. The bathroom problem for Remedios and for Jess severely limits their ability to circulate in public spaces and actually brings them into contact with phys-ical violence as a result of having violated a cardinal rule of gender: one must be readable at a glance. After Remedios is beaten for having entered a ladies' room, her father tells her to be more careful, and Rodriguez notes: "She realized that being cautious means swaying her hips and parading her boobs when she enters any ladies room" (30).

If we use the paradigm of the bathroom as a limit of gender identification, we can measure the distance between binary gender schema and lived multiple gendered experiences. The accusation "you're in the wrong bathroom" really says two differ-ent things. First, it announces that your gender seems at odds with your sex (your apparent masculinity or androgyny is at odds with your supposed femaleness); second, it suggests that single-gender bathrooms are only for those who fit clearly into one category (male) or the other (female). Either we need open-access bathrooms or multigendered bathrooms, or we need wider parameters for gender identification. The bathroom, as we know it, actually represents the crumbling edifice of gender in the twentieth century. The frequency with which gender-deviant "women" are mis-taken for men in public bathrooms suggests that a large number of feminine women spend a large amount of time and energy policing masculine women. Something very different happens, of course, in the men's public toilet, where the space is more likely to become a sexual cruising zone than a site for gender repression. Lee Edelman, in an essay about the interpenetration of nationalism and sexuality, argues that "the institutional men's room constitutes a site at which the zones of public and private cross with a distinctive psychic charge."[22] The men's room, in other words, constitutes both an architecture of surveillance and an incitement to desire, a space of homosocial interaction and of homoerotic interaction.

So, whereas men's rest rooms tend to operate as a highly charged sexual space in which sexual interactions are both encouraged and punished, women's rest rooms tend to operate as an arena for the enforcement of gender conformity. Sex-segregated bathrooms continue to be necessary to protect women from male predations but also produce and extend a rather outdated notion of a public–private split between male and female society. The bathroom is a domestic space beyond the home that comes to represent domestic order, or a parody of it, out in the world. The women's bathroom accordingly becomes a sanctuary of enhanced femininity, a "little girl's room" to which one retreats to powder one's nose or fix one's hair. The men's bathroom signifies as the extension of the public nature of masculinity – it is precisely not domestic even though the names given to the sexual function of the bathroom – such as cottage or tearoom – suggest it is a parody of the domestic. The codes that dominate within the women's bathroom are primarily gender codes; in the men's room, they are sexual codes. Public sex versus private gender, openly sexual versus discreetly repressive, bathrooms beyond the home take on the proportions of a gender factory.

Marjorie Garber comments on the liminality of the bathroom in *Vested Interests* in a chapter on the perils and privileges of cross-dressing. She discusses the very different modes of passing and cross-dressing for cross-identified genetic males and females, and she observes that the rest room is a "potential waterloo" for both female-to-male (FTM) and male-to-female (MTF) cross-dressers and transsexuals.[23] For the FTM, the men's room represents the most severe test of his ability to pass, and advice frequently circulates within FTM communities about how to go unnoticed in male-only spaces. Garber notes: "The cultural paranoia of being caught in the ultimately wrong place, which may be inseparable from the pleasure of 'passing' in that same place, depends in part on the same cultural binarism, the idea that gender categories are sufficiently uncomplicated to permit self-assortment into one of the two 'rooms' without deconstructive reading" (47). It is worth pointing out here (if only because Garber does not) that the perils for passing FTMS in the men's room are very different from the perils of passing MTFS in the women's room. On the one hand, the FTM in the men's room is likely to be less scrutinized because men are not quite as vigilant about intruders as women for obvious reasons. On the other hand, if caught, the FTM may face some version of gender panic from the man who discovers him, and it is quite reasonable to expect and fear violence in the wake of such a discovery. The MTF, by comparison, will be more scrutinized in the women's room but possibly less open to punishment if caught. Because the FTM ventures into male territory with the potential threat of violence hanging over his head, it is crucial to recognize that the bathroom problem is much more than a glitch in the machinery of gender segregation and is better described in terms of the violent enforcement of our current gender system.

Garber's reading of the perilous use of rest rooms by both FTMS and MTFS develops out of her introductory discussion of what Lacan calls "urinary segregation." Lacan used the term to describe the relations between identities and signifiers, and he ultimately used the simple diagram of the rest room signs "Ladies" and "Gentlemen" to show that within the production of sexual difference, primacy is granted to the signifier over that which it signifies; in more simple terms, naming confers, rather than reflects, meaning.[24] In the same way, the system of urinary segregation creates the very functionality of the categories "men" and "women." Although restroom signs seem to serve and ratify distinctions that already exist, in actual fact these markers produce identifications within these constructed categories. Garber latches on to the notion of "urinary segregation" because it helps her to describe the processes of cultural binarism within the production of gender; for Garber, transvestites and transsexuals challenge this system by resisting the literal translation of the signs "Ladies" and "Gentlemen." Garber uses the figures of the transvestite and the transsexual to show the obvious flaws and gaps in a binary gender system; the transvestite, as interloper, creates a third space of possibility within which all binaries become unstable. Unfortunately, as in all attempts to break a binary by producing a third term, Garber's third space tends to stabilize the other two. In "Tearooms and Sympathy," Lee Edelman also turns to Lacan's term "urinary segregation," but Edelman uses Lacan's diagram to mark heterosexual anxiety "about the potential inscriptions of homosexual desire and about the possibility of knowing or recognizing whatever might constitute 'homosexual difference'" (160). Whereas for Garber it is the transvestite who marks the instability of the markers "Ladies" and "Gentlemen," for Edelman it is not the passing transvestite but the passing homosexual.

Both Garber and Edelman, interestingly enough, seem to fix on the men's room as the site of these various destabilizing performances. As I am arguing here, however, focusing exclusively on the drama of the men's room avoids the much more complicated theater of the women's room. Garber writes of urinary segregation: "For transvestites and transsexuals, the 'men's room' problem is really a challenge to the way in which such cultural binarism is read" (14). She goes on to list some cinematic examples of the perils of urinary segregation and discusses scenes from *Tootsie* (1982), *Cabaret* (1972), and the *Female Impersonator Pageant* (1975). Garber's examples are odd illustrations of what she calls "the men's room problem" if only because at least one of her examples (*Tootsie*) demonstrates gender policing in the women's room. Also, Garber makes it sound as if vigorous gender policing happens in the men's room while the women's room is more of a benign zone for gender enforcement. She notes: "In fact, the urinal has appeared in a number of fairly recent films as a marker of the ultimate 'difference' – or studied indifference" (14). Obviously, Garber is drawing a parallel here between the conventions of gender attribution within which the penis marks the "ultimate difference"; however, by not moving beyond this remarkably predictable description of gender differentiation, Garber overlooks the main distinction between gender policing in the men's room and in the women's room. Namely, in the women's room, it is not only the MTF but *all* gender-ambiguous females who are scrutinized, whereas in the men's room, biological men are rarely deemed out of place. Garber's insistence that there is "a third space of possibility" occupied by the transvestite has closed down the possibility that there may be a fourth, fifth, sixth, or one hundredth space beyond the binary. The "women's room problem" (as opposed to the "men's room problem") indicates a multiplicity of gender displays even within the supposedly stable category of "woman."

So what gender are the hundreds of female-born people who are consistently not read as female in the women's room? And because so many women clearly fail the women's room test, why have we not begun to count and name the genders that are clearly emerging at this time? One could answer this question in two ways: On the one hand, we do not name and notice new genders because as a society we are committed to maintaining a binary gender system. On the other hand, we could also say that the failure of "male" and "female" to exhaust the field of gender variation actually ensures the continued dominance of these terms. Precisely because virtually nobody fits the definitions of male and female, the categories gain power and currency from their impossibility. In other words, the very flexibility and elasticity of the terms "man" and "woman" ensures their longevity. To test this proposition, look around any public space and notice how few people present formulaic versions of gender and yet how few are unreadable or totally ambiguous. The "It's Pat" character on a *Saturday Night Live* skit dramatized the ways in which people insist on attributing gender in terms of male or female on even the most undecidable characters. The "It's Pat" character produced laughs by consistently sidestepping gender fixity – Pat's partner had a neutral name, and everything Pat did or said was designed to be read either way. Of course, the enigma that Pat represented could have been solved very easily; Pat's coworkers could simply have asked Pat what gender s/he was or preferred. This project on female masculinity is designed to produce more than two answers to that question and even to argue for a concept of "gender preference" as opposed to compulsory gender binarism. The human potential for incredibly precise classifications has been demonstrated in multiple arenas; why then do we settle for a paucity of classifications when it comes to gender? A system of gender preferences would allow for gender neutrality until such a time when the child or young adult announces his or her or its gender. Even if we could not let go of a binary gender system, there are still ways to make gender optional – people could come out as a gender in the way they come out as a sexuality. The point here is that there are many ways to depathologize gender variance and to account for the multiple genders that we already produce and sustain. Finally, as I suggested in relation to Garber's arguments about transvestism, "thirdness" merely balances the binary system and, furthermore, tends to homogenize many different gender variations under the banner of "other."

It is remarkably easy in this society not to look like a woman. It is relatively difficult, by comparison, not to look like a man: the threats faced by men who do not gender conform are somewhat different than for women. Unless men are consciously trying to look like women, men are less likely than women to fail to pass in the rest room. So one question posed by the bathroom problem asks, what makes femininity so approximate and masculinity so precise? Or to pose the question with a different spin, why is femininity easily impersonated or performed while masculinity seems resilient to imitation? Of course, this formulation does not easily hold and indeed quickly collapses into the exact opposite: why is it, in the case of the masculine woman in the bathroom, for example, that one finds the limits of femininity so quickly, whereas the limits of masculinity in the men's room seem fairly expansive?

We might tackle these questions by thinking about the effects, social and cultural, of reversed gender typing. In other words, what are the implications of male femininity and female masculinity? One might imagine that even a hint of femininity sullies or lowers the social value of maleness while all masculine forms of femaleness should result in an elevation of status.[25] My bathroom example alone proves that this is far from true. Furthermore, if we think of popular examples of approved female masculinity like a buffed Linda Hamilton in *Terminator 2* (1991) or a lean and mean

Sigourney Weaver in *Aliens*, it is not hard to see that what renders these performances of female masculinity quite tame is their resolute heterosexuality. Indeed, in
Alien Resurrection (1997), Sigourney Weaver combines her hard body with some light
flirtation with co-star Winona Ryder and her masculinity immediately becomes far
more threatening and indeed "alien." In other words, when and where female masculinity conjoins with possibly queer identities, it is far less likely to meet with
approval. Because female masculinity seems to be at its most threatening when
coupled with lesbian desire, in this book I concentrate on queer female masculinity
almost to the exclusion of heterosexual female masculinity. I have no doubt that
heterosexual female masculinity menaces gender conformity in its own way, but all
too often it represents an acceptable degree of female masculinity as compared to the
excessive masculinity of the dyke. It is important when thinking about gender variations such as male femininity and female masculinity not simply to create another
binary in which masculinity always signifies power; in alternative models of gender
variation, female masculinity is not simply the opposite of female femininity, nor is it
a female version of male masculinity. Rather, as we shall see in some of the artwork
and gender performances to follow, very often the unholy union of femaleness and
masculinity can produce wildly unpredictable results.

Notes

1 For an extension of this discussion of tomboys see my article "Oh Bondage Up Yours: Female
   Masculinity and the Tomboy," in *Sissies and Tomboys: A CLAGS Reader* (New York: New
   York University Press, forthcoming).
2 For more on the punishment of tomboys see Phyllis Burke, *Gender Shock: Exploding the Myths
   of Male and Female* (New York: Anchor Books, 1996). Burke analyzes some recent case histories of so-called GID or Gender Identity Disorder, in which little girls are carefully conditioned
   out of male behavior and into exceedingly constrictive forms of femininity.
3 Carson McCullers, *The Member of the Wedding* (1946; reprint, New York: Bantam, 1973), 1.
4 R. C. Lewontin, "Sex, Lies, and Social Science," *New York Review of Books* 42, no. 7
   (20 April 1995): 24.
5 Thanks to Esther Newton for making this point and suggesting when and how survey
   methods are useful. For an example of the kinds of questions used in sex surveys see John
   Gagnon et al., *Sex in America* (Boston: Little Brown, 1994). This particular volume is remarkable because the explicit questions it asks about the kinds of sex people were having focus
   obsessively on the couple, and the study links certain activities definitively to certain identities.
   So, for example, questions about anal sex are directed only at male/female and male/male
   couples because anal sex is defined as "when a man's penis is inside his partner's anus or
   rectum" (260). There are no questions directed specifically at female/female couples and no
   questions about sex toys or use of dildos or hands in this section.
6 Steven Epstein, "A Queer Encounter: Sociology and the Study of Sexuality," *Sociological
   Theory* 12, no. 2 (July 1994): 189.
7 Arlene Stein and Ken Plummer, "I Can't Even Think Straight": Queer Theory and the
   Missing Revolution in Sociology," *Sociological Theory* 12, no. 2 (July 1994): 184.
8 Cindy Patton, "Tremble Hetero Swine," in *Fear of a Queer Planet: Queer Politics and Social
   Theory*, ed. Michael Warner (Minneapolis: University of Minnesota Press, 1993), 165.
9 The conference papers were collected in a volume called *Constructing Masculinity*, ed. Maurice
   Berger, Brian Wallis, and Simon Watson (New York: Routledge, 1996), and the one intervention on behalf of nonmale masculinities was made by Eve Kosofsky Sedgwick.

10 I am using the terms "female born" and "male born" to indicate a social practice of assigning one of two genders to babies at birth. My terminology suggests that these assignations may not hold for the lifetime of the individual, and it suggests from the outset that binary gender continues to dominate our cultural and scientific notions of gender but that individuals inevitably fail to find themselves in only one of two options.

11 Berger, Wallis, and Watson, introduction to *Constructing Masculinity*, 7.

12 More and more journals are putting together special issues on masculinity, but I have yet to locate a single special issue with a single essay about female masculinity. The latest journal announcement that found its way to me was from *The Velvet Light Trap: A Critical Journal of Film and Television*. They announced an issue on "New Masculinities" that featured essays titled "The 'New Masculinity' in *Tootsie*," "On Fathers and Sons, Sex and Death," "Male Melodrama and the Feeling Man," and so forth. This is not to say that such topics are not interesting, only that the "new masculinities" sound remarkably like the old ones. See *The Velvet Light Trap*, "New Masculinities," no. 38 (Fall 1996).

13 Berger, Wallis, and Watson, *Constructing Masculinity*.

14 Paul Smith, ed., *Boys: Masculinities in Contemporary Culture* (Boulder, Colo.: Westview Press, 1996), 3.

15 Paul Smith, introduction to *Boys: Masculinities in Contemporary Culture*, 4–5.

16 See Monique Wittig, "The Straight Mind," in *The Straight Mind and Other Essays* (Boston: Beacon Press, 1992); Judith Butler, "Imitation and Gender Insubordination," in *Inside/Out: Lesbian Theories, Gay Theories*, ed. Diana Fuss (New York: Routledge, 1991), 13–31; Jacob Hale, "Are Lesbians Women?" *Hypatia* 11, no. 2 (Spring 1996): 94–121.

17 Indeed, one such ethnography has been carried out, but significantly it took English soccer hooligans as its topic. See Bill Buford's remarkable *Among the Thugs* (New York: Norton, 1992). A similar work on American male fans would be extremely useful.

18 For verification of such topics of concern just check out the men's sections that are popping up in your local bookstores. More specifically see the work of Michael Kimmel and Victor Seidler: Michael Kimmel, *Manhood in America: A Cultural History* (New York: Free Press, 1996); Victor J. Seidler, *Unreasonable Men: Masculinity and Social Theory* (New York: Routledge, 1994).

19 The continued viability of the category "woman" has been challenged in a variety of academic locations already: Monique Wittig, most notably, argued that "lesbians are not women" in her essay "The Straight Mind," 121. Wittig claims that because lesbians are refusing primary relations to men, they cannot occupy the position "woman." In another philosophical challenge to the category "woman," transgender philosopher Jacob Hale uses Monique Wittig's radical claim to theorize the possibility of gendered embodiments that exceed male and female (see Jacob Hale, "Are Lesbians Women?" *Hypatia* 11, no. 2 [Spring 1996]). Elsewhere, Cheshire Calhoun suggests that the category "woman" may actually "operate as a lesbian closet" (see Cheshire Calhoun, "The Gender Closet: Lesbian Disappearance under the Sign 'Women,'" *Feminist Studies* 21, no. 1 [Spring 1995]: 7–34).

20 Leslie Feinberg, *Stone Butch Blues: A Novel* (Ithaca, NY: Firebrand, 1993), 59.

21 Nice Rodriguez, *Throw It to the River* (Toronto, Canada: Women's Press, 1993), 25–6.

22 Lee Edelman, "Tearooms and Sympathy, or The Epistemology of the Water Closet," in *Homographesis: Essays in Gay Literary and Cultural Theory* (New York: Routledge, 1994), 158.

23 Marjorie Garber, *Vested Interests: Cross-Dressing and Cultural Anxiety* (New York: Routledge, 1992), 47. Obviously Garber's use of the term "waterloo" makes a pun out of the drama of bathroom surveillance. Although the pun is clever and even amusing, it is also troubling to see how often Garber turns to punning in her analyses. The constant use of puns throughout the book has the overall effect of making gender crossing sound like a game or at least trivializes the often life-or-death processes involved in cross-identification. This is not to say gender can never be a "laughing matter" and must always be treated seriously but only to question the use of the pun here as a theoretical method.

24 See Jacques Lacan, "The Agency of the Letter in the Unconscious," in *Ecrits: A Selection*, trans. Alan Sheridan (New York: Norton, 1977), 151.

25 Susan Bordo argues this in "Reading the Male Body," *Michigan Quarterly Review* 32, no. 4 (Fall 1993). She writes: "When masculinity gets 'undone' in this culture, the deconstruction nearly always lands us in the territory of the degraded; when femininity gets symbolically undone, the result is an immense elevation of status" (721).

PART TEN

Ethnic Literary and Cultural Studies: Critical Race Theory

CHAPTER 1

Introduction: Situating Race

Julie Rivkin and Michael Ryan

Ethnicity and race emerged as an important new approach to literary study in the late 1960s and early 1970s in the US academy. Writers from a diverse range of ethnic minority perspectives – African American, Asian American, Hispanic American, Native American, etc. – had been actively engaged with the problem of representing the experiences and the lives of the Anglo-American majority's "others." Writers such as Langston Hughes, Frank Chin, John Joseph Mathews, and Américo Paredes reflected in prose and in fiction on the conditions of minority ethnic life in a society dominated by another ethnic group's cultural vision and social interests. But it was not until the 1970s that courses and programs began to appear that consolidated a sense of the importance of representing the literatures of minority populations in the academy.

African American literature was the first to achieve widespread representation in the academy. The Civil Rights movement and the Black Arts movement created a new cultural impetus that led to new courses and programs in African-American literature in the 1970s. Such courses and programs constituted in their mere presence a theoretical statement; as Henry Louis Gates observes, "Unlike almost every other literary tradition, the Afro-American literary tradition was generated as a response to eighteenth- and nineteenth-century allegations that persons of African descent did not, and could not, create literature" (*Figures in Black*, 25).

Among the first wave of African American literary scholars in the US were Charles Davis, Mary Helen Washington, Barbara Christian, Darwin Turner, and Alan Ramperstad. Their work was soon followed by the work of scholars trained in the new critical approaches and literary theories of the 1970s and 1980s, critics such as Henry Louis Gates, Hortense Spillers, Hazel Carby, Valerie Smith, and Houston Baker. These critics developed a widely ranging body of scholarship, with some of its projects of revision and cultural recovery paralleling the projects of feminist criticism. Some critics concentrated on historical African-American literary movements such as the Harlem Renaissance; others studied the interface of white racism and black literary and cultural response throughout American history; others blended analyses of African-American musical culture with literary study. In some sense their work on culture is inseparable from that of the African-American writers whose work extended the very literary tradition now receiving such attention. The emergence of writers such as Amiri Baraka, Ishmael Reed, Toni Morrison, Edgar Wideman, and Alice Walker helped to further the new school of African-American literary criticism.

The Civil Rights Movement resulted as well in the emergence of movements for equal rights and equal status by other ethnic groups, such as Native Americans and

Hispanic Americans, and academic departments or programs devoted to the cultures of these groups quickly took shape. By the 1980s, a recognizable body of scholarship on Asian-American writing had also developed. Each of these new approaches was aided by the emergence of important new writers within each of their fields of study – Gerald Vizenor, Leslie Silko, and Louise Erdrich in Native American, Rudolfo Anaya and Sandra Cisneros in Chicano, and Maxine Hong Kingston and Amy Tan in Asian American.

The emergence of Native American literary studies coincides roughly with the renaissance in Native American literature initiated in 1968 with the publication of M. Scott Momaday's *House Made of Dawn*. The American Indian Movement in the late 1960s and early 1970s also drew attention to long-suppressed issues relating to the Native American presence in the mainstream culture defined and shaped by Anglo-American needs and concerns. Much of the early critical work by Kimberley Blaeser and Paula Gunn Allen on indigenous literature was concerned with preserving the religious, mythic, and oral dimensions of Native culture. The success and popularity of Leslie Marmon Silko's work, especially her novel *Ceremony*, worked to maintain that folkloric focus. Scholars such as Arnold Krupat drew on contemporary critical models in studying Native literature, but it was not until the 1990s that younger scholars versed in newer critical approaches, such as Robert Dale Parker and Carlton Smith, began to frame an understanding of such literature in contemporary theoretical terms. Their efforts are aided by the fact that more recent writers, such as Louise Erdrich and Thomas King, are more concerned with realist depictions of contemporary indigenous American life or with Post-Modern filterings of Native experience. Gerald Vizenor has been especially instrumental in merging a sensitive appreciation for Native tradition with impressive meditations on the relevance of Post-Structuralist theories to an accurate description of the complex cultural mediations through which Native life must be seen. Indeed, it is fair to say that Vizenor, like his counterpart Gómez-Peña, is one of the most brilliant theoreticians of contemporary American culture.

Latino and Chicano critics have also moved beyond the early folkloric emphasis of critics such as Paredes, whose *With His Pistol in His Hand* (1958) was one of the first works of Chicano cultural studies, and they have come to incorporate into their work the most advanced critical theories. The work of Latino and Chicano scholarship has focused extensively on the concept of the border, given the locus of Chicano life along the vexed border between the US and Mexico. In its bilingualism, its invocation of a new geography, its attention to (im)migration, Chicano studies has its own particular contributions to ethnic studies. Post-Structuralist concepts of territoriality and hybridity were well suited to the work of Chicano theorists, and those concepts were incorporated into a critical vocabulary specific to Chicano studies. "Border theory," as it came to be called, drew on Post-Structuralist theories of contingency, hybridity, and territoriality in analyzing literary works by such writers as Helena Maria Viramontes and Ana Castillo. In addition, Chicana cultural theorists allied themselves very early on with African American feminists to create a practically hybrid cultural movement. The collection by Chicana feminists and African American writers and critics – *This Bridge Called My Back* (1981) – was one of the most famous early texts of the feminist movement. One of its participants – Gloria Anzaldua – went on to write an important text of border theory – *Borderlands/La Frontera* (1987), a multilingual account of growing up along the border. Contemporary Chicano critics and theorists include such names as Guillermo Bomez-Peña, Renato Rosaldo, Hector Calderón, Ramón Saldívar, José David Saldívar, Juan Bruce-Novoa, and Norma Alarcón.

The successful emergence of popular Asian-American writers such as Maxine Hong Kingston and Amy Tan in the 1980s was predicated in part on the efforts of the Combined Asian Resources Project in the 1970s and on the publication of *Aiiieeeee! An Anthology of Asian-American Writers* in 1974. What these efforts exposed was the tremendous multiplicity within the term "Asian-American," which encompasses Chinese (themselves a diverse group), Japanese, Korean, Pacific, South Asian, Vietnamese, and other Asian-Americans. This enormous diversity also drew attention to the fact that while the category of ethnic studies takes a domestic location in the US, its existence is a product of transnational processes like colonialism, slavery, and immigration that have produced ethnic and racial diversities. It is perhaps not surprising that questions of cultural pluralism and ethnic identity-within-difference often come to the foreground as important concerns of writers from these Asian ethnic traditions. A not uncommon title of a critical essay on Asian-American literature as a result is "The Ambivalent American." With the erosion of segregation in the US in the post-Civil Rights Movement era, more and more Asian-Americans have been assimilating into the Anglo-dominated cultural "mainstream." Indeed, many works of fiction such as, perhaps most famously, *The Joy Luck Club* (1976) make this change its principal focus. Perhaps because their own life experiences, like those of Chicanos and Native peoples, have been fissured by the recent experience of immigration, exclusion, linguistic difference, and the ongoing experience of living on the fault-line between an unself-consciously dominant ethnic culture and their own marginalized culture, many Asian-American critics find Post-Structuralist theories of hybridity, difference, and ambivalence to be helpful in their work. Critics such as Shirley Geok-Lin Lim have also challenged the ideal of ethnic homogeneity that the dominant Anglo group fosters in order to dilute and, ultimately, destroy singular and different ethnic cultures.

Critics like Geok-lin have not been content to affirm the necessity of identity-within-difference in an ethnically plural society. Many ethnic studies scholars have begun to question the implicit assumptions that allow a white-dominated ethnic culture to present "color-blindness" as a norm for non-whites. The norm of whiteness became an object of critical study by the 1990s. Historian Theodore Allen in *The Invention of the White Race* (1994) and sociologist David Roediger in *The Wages of Whiteness* (1999) argued that the cultural category of whiteness came into being as a response to the presence of feared ethnic others such as African Americans in the United States. The category allowed for both self-identification and communal collusion against the feared "others." These scholarly findings gave rise to a new body of literary and cultural scholarship on whiteness by such scholars as Dana Nelson and Ruth Frankenburg.

The last two decades have seen the rise of an explicitly theoretical body of writing on race. In the 1990s, scholars such as Anthony Appiah (in *In My Father's House* [1992]) drew attention to scientific evidence to the effect that biological genetic differences did not sort themselves out into evenly distinguishable "races." Race is more a cultural and social category than a natural, genetic, or biological one. Different external traits such as skin color are not indices of separate racial identities. They are more akin to differences in hair color. Nevertheless, race does, as Cornell West argued, "matter." African Americans are, according to Toni Morrison, the "pariahs" of US society. The dominant US white group's culture is marked by traces of those whose violation has been a precondition of that group's cohesiveness both economically and culturally. As a result, there is, as Morrison, argues, an "africanist" presence, unacknowledged but palpable, in American literature. Many in the reparations movement argued that the same is true of the US economy, which grew and expanded in the early nineteenth century as a result of the unpaid labor of African slaves.

Looking backward as well as forward, the new scholarship on race has also focused critical attention on some of the early theorists of race. Preeminent among them is W. E. B. DuBois, whose work on a "racial concept" constituted the first real critique of a scientific racism inherited from the nineteenth century. That is, until DuBois, race was understood as a biological category, and in keeping with a social Darwinist perspective, this biological and essentialist view was also a justification for white supremacy. DuBois's movement toward a cultural understanding of race coincided with his sense of the historical sources of racial domination, and his work would be extremely important for a number of contemporary theorists, most notably Appiah and Henry Louis Gates.

One strand of the critical work on race came not out of the field of literary study, but rather out of the field of law. Critical race theory, adopted now by cultural critics as well as legal theorists, was an outgrowth of the critical legal studies movement and an important contribution to the new thinking about race. The founders of the movement are Derrick Bell, Richard Delgado, and Alan Freeman, and their work, which dates back to the mid-seventies, has been followed by that of a number of other legal scholars, including Kimberle Crenshaw, Angela Harris, Charles Lawrence, Mari Matsuda, and Patricia Williams. Critical race theorists emphasize the ways in which racism is normalized in US culture, such that the principles of liberalism are not adequate to address its distortions. In particular, critical race theorists question the view that color-blind or "formal" conceptions of equality can actually remedy the effects of a pervasive and deeply rooted social racism. Critical race theorists extend the early work of DuBois on a social rather than biological concept of race. Among the theorists working on the cultural construction of race are the sociologists Michael Omi and Howard Winant, and their concept of racial formation shows how conceptions of race are invariably linked to political projects, political projects which change across time and which work to change racial formations. For example, the current discourse of color-blindness, which might seem to echo the civil rights language of Martin Luther King, is in fact used today to justify an anti-affirmative action conservative agenda. The concept of racial formation thus has a pragmatist dimension, linked as it is to the political effects of a particular discourse of race.

Ethnic literary scholars face tasks similar to those that faced feminists – the constitution of a history or tradition and the examination, using the best methodological tools available, of the works of writers operating within the cultural framework of an ethnic group whose existence is defined by internal exclusion. Not surprisingly, these critics tend to focus on questions of identity and of representation. What does it mean to hold national citizenship and to belong to an ethnic group whose features and whose culture exist to one side of a mainstream that seems blissfully unaware of its own hegemony? How can any one person represent "their" ethnic culture? What is the identity of a culture torn between traditional values and contemporary changes that could be represented? And for whom and for what reason does such representation, generally in the mainstream culture, occur? As the size of non-Anglo ethnic populations in the US grows and as the culture becomes less hegemonically white and Anglo, a different set of concerns will no doubt begin to emerge. That change is greatly aided by the work of the various ethnic scholars whose work we present in this section.

CHAPTER 2

The Social Construction of Race

Ian F. Haney López

Critical Race Theory (2000), edited by Richard and Jea Delgado, brings together important statements in the field of legal race studies. In this selection, Ian F. Haney López summarizes the thinking that has cast doubt on the idea that race is a biological reality.

Under the jurisprudence of slavery as it stood in 1806, one's status followed the maternal line. A person born to a slave woman was a slave, one born to a free woman was free. In that year, three generations of enslaved women sued for freedom in Virginia on the ground that they descended from a free maternal ancestor. Yet, on the all-important issue of their descent, their faces and bodies provided the only evidence they or the owner who resisted their claims could bring before the court.

> The appellees...asserted this right [to be free] as having been descended, in the maternal line, from a free Indian woman; but their genealogy was very imperfectly stated....[T]he youngest...[had] the characteristic features, the complexion, the hair and eyes...the same with those of whites....Hannah [the mother], had long black hair, was of the right Indian copper colour, and was generally called an Indian by the neighbours....[1]

Because the Wrights, grandmother, mother, and daughter, could not prove they had a free maternal ancestor, nor could their owner, Hudgins, show their descent from a female slave, the side charged with the burden of proof would lose. Allocating that burden required the court to assign the plaintiffs a race. Under Virginia law, Blacks were presumably slaves and thus bore the burden of proving a free ancestor; Whites and Indians were presumably free and thus the burden of proving their descent fell on those alleging slave status. In order to determine whether the Wrights were Black and presumptively slaves or Indian and presumptively free, the court, in the person of Judge Tucker, devised a racial test:

> Nature has stampt upon the African and his descendants two characteristic marks, besides the difference of complexion, which often remain visible long after the characteristic distinction of colour either disappears or becomes doubtful; a flat nose and woolly head of hair. The latter of these disappears the last of all; and so strong an ingredient in the African constitution is this latter character, that it predominates uniformly where the party is in equal degree descended from parents of different complexions, whether white or Indians....So pointed is this distinction between the natives of Africa and the aborigines of America, that a man might as easily mistake the glossy, jetty clothing of an American bear for the wool of a black sheep, as the hair of an

American Indian for that of an African, or the descendant of an African. Upon these distinctions as connected with our laws, the burden of proof depends.[2]

The fate of the women rode upon the complexion of their face, the texture of their hair, and the width of their nose. Each of these characteristics served to mark their race, and their race in the end determined whether they were free or enslaved. The court decided for freedom:

> [T]he witnesses concur in assigning to the hair of Hannah ... the long, straight, black hair of the native aborigines of this country....
>
> ...
>
> [Verdict] pronouncing the appellees absolutely free ...[3]

After unknown lives lost in slavery, Judge Tucker freed three generations of women because Hannah's hair was long and straight.

Introduction: The Confounding Problem of Race

I begin this chapter with *Hudgins v. Wright* in part to emphasize the power of race in our society. Human fate still rides upon ancestry and appearance. The characteristics of our hair, complexion, and facial features still influence whether we are figuratively free or enslaved. Race dominates our personal lives. It manifests itself in our speech, dance, neighbors, and friends – "our very ways of talking, walking, eating and dreaming are ineluctably shaped by notions of race."[4] Race determines our economic prospects. The race-conscious market screens and selects us for manual jobs and professional careers, red-lines financing for real estate, green-lines our access to insurance, and even raises the price of that car we need to buy.[5] Race permeates our politics. It alters electoral boundaries, shapes the disbursement of local, state, and federal funds, fuels the creation and collapse of political alliances, and twists the conduct of law enforcement.[6] In short, race mediates every aspect of our lives.

Hudgins v. Wright also enables me to emphasize the role of law in reifying racial identities. By embalming in the form of legal presumptions and evidentiary burdens the prejudices society attached to vestiges of African ancestry, *Hudgins* demonstrates that the law serves not only to reflect but to solidify social prejudice, making law a prime instrument in the construction and reinforcement of racial subordination. Judges and legislators, in their role as arbiters and violent creators of the social order, continue to concentrate and magnify the power of race. Race suffuses all bodies of law, not only obvious ones like civil rights, immigration law, and federal Indian law, but also property law,[7] contracts law,[8] criminal law,[9] federal courts,[10] family law,[11] and even "the purest of corporate law questions within the most unquestionably Anglo scholarly paradigm."[12] I assert that no body of law exists untainted by the powerful astringent of race in our society.

In largest part, however, I begin with *Hudgins v. Wright* because the case provides an empirical definition of race. *Hudgins* tells us one is Black if one has a single African antecedent, or if one has a "flat nose" or a "woolly head of hair." I begin here because in the last two centuries our conception of race has not progressed much beyond the primitive view advanced by Judge Tucker.

Despite the pervasive influence of race in our lives and in US law, a review of opinions and articles by judges and legal academics reveals a startling fact: Few seem to know what race is and is not. Today most judges and scholars accept the common wisdom concerning race, without pausing to examine the fallacies and fictions on which ideas of race depend. In US society, "a kind of 'racial etiquette' exists, a set of interpretive codes and racial meanings which operate in the interactions of daily life.... Race becomes 'common sense' – a way of comprehending, explaining and acting in the world."[13] This social etiquette of common ignorance is readily apparent in the legal discourse of race. Rehnquist-Court Justices take this approach, speaking disingenuously of the peril posed by racial remediation to "a society where race is irrelevant," while nevertheless failing to offer an account of race that would bear the weight of their cynical assertions.[14] Arguably, critical race theorists, those legal scholars whose work seems most closely bound together by their emphasis on the centrality of race, follow the same approach when they powerfully decry the permanence of racism and persuasively argue for race consciousness, yet do so without explicitly suggesting what race might be.[15] Race may be America's single most confounding problem, but the confounding problem of race is that few people seem to know what race is.

In this essay, I define a "race" as a vast group of people loosely bound together by historically contingent, socially significant elements of their morphology and/or ancestry. I argue that race must be understood as a sui generis social phenomenon in which contested systems of meaning serve as the connections between physical features, faces, and personal characteristics. In other words, social meanings connect our faces to our souls. Race is neither an essence nor an illusion, but rather an ongoing, contradictory, self-reinforcing, plastic process subject to the macro forces of social and political struggle and the micro effects of daily decisions. As used here, the referents of terms like Black and White are social groups, not genetically distinct branches of humankind.

Note that Whites exist as a race under this definition. It is not only people of color who find their identities mediated by race, or who are implicated in the building and maintenance of racial constructs. White identity is just as much a racial fabrication, and Whites are equally, or even more highly, implicated in preserving the racially constructed status quo. I therefore explicitly encourage Whites to critically attend to racial constructs. Whites belong among those most deeply dedicated to fathoming the intricacies of race.

In this context, let me situate the theory I advance in terms of the epistemological significance of my own race and biography. I write as a Latino. The arguments I present no doubt reflect the less pronounced role physical features and ancestry play for my community as opposed to Blacks, the group most often considered in the elaboration of racial theories. Perhaps more importantly, I write from a perspective influenced by a unique biography. My older brother, Garth, and I are the only children of a fourth-generation Irish father, Terrence Eugene Haney, and a Salvadoran immigrant mother, Maria Daisy López de Haney. Sharing a similar morphology, Garth and I both have light but not white skin, dark brown hair, and dark brown eyes. We were raised in Hawaii, far from either my father's roots in Spokane, Washington, or my mother's family in San Salvador, El Salvador. Interestingly, Garth and I conceive of ourselves in different racial terms. For the most part, he considers his race transparent, something of a non-issue in the way Whites do, and he relates most easily with the Anglo side of the family. I, on the other hand, consider myself Latino and am in greatest contact with my maternal family. Perhaps presciently, my parents gave

Garth my paternal grandfather's name, Mark, for a middle name, thus christening him Garth Mark Haney. They gave me my maternal father's name, Fidencio. Affiliating with the Latino side of the family, in my first year of graduate school I followed Latino custom by appending my mother's family name to my own, rendering my name Ian Fidencio Haney López. No doubt influencing the theories of race I outline and subscribe to, in my experience race reveals itself as plastic, inconstant, and to some extent volitional. That is the thesis of this chapter.

Biological Race

There are no genetic characteristics possessed by all Blacks but not by non-Blacks; similarly, there is no gene or cluster of genes common to all Whites but not to non-Whites.[16] One's race is not determined by a single gene or gene cluster, as is, for example, sickle-cell anemia. Nor are races marked by important differences in gene frequencies, the rates of appearance of certain gene types. The data compiled by various scientists demonstrate, contrary to popular opinion, that intra-group differences exceed inter-group differences. That is, greater genetic variation exists *within* the populations typically labeled Black and White than *between* these populations.[17] This finding refutes the supposition that racial divisions reflect fundamental genetic differences.

Rather, the notion that humankind can be divided along White, Black, and Yellow lines reveals the social rather than the scientific origin of race. The idea that there exist three races, and that these races are "Caucasoid," "Negroid," and "Mongoloid," is rooted in the European imagination of the Middle Ages, which encompassed only Europe, Africa, and the Near East. This view found its clearest modern expression in Count Arthur de Gobineau's *Essay on the Inequality of Races*, published in France in 1853–5.[18] The peoples of the American continents, the Indian subcontinent, East Asia, Southeast Asia, and Oceania – living outside the imagination of Europe and Count Gobineau – are excluded from the three major races for social and political reasons, not for scientific ones. Nevertheless, the history of science has long been the history of failed efforts to justify these social beliefs.[19] Along the way, various minds tried to fashion practical human typologies along the following physical axes: skin color, hair texture, facial angle, jaw size, cranial capacity, brain mass, frontal lobe mass, brain surface fissures and convolutions, and even body lice. As one scholar notes, "[t]he nineteenth century was a period of exhaustive and – as it turned out – futile search for criteria to define and describe race differences."[20]

To appreciate the difficulties of constructing races solely by reference to physical characteristics, consider the attempt to define race by skin color. On the basis of white skin, for example, one can define a race that includes most of the peoples of Western Europe. However, this grouping is threatened by the subtle gradations of skin color as one moves south or east, and becomes untenable when the fair-skinned peoples of Northern China and Japan are considered. In 1922, in *Ozawa v. United States*,[21] the Supreme Court nicely explained this point. When Japanese-born Takao Ozawa applied for citizenship he asserted, as required by the Naturalization Act, that he was a "white person." Counsel for Ozawa pointedly argued that to reject Ozawa's petition for naturalization would be "to exclude a Japanese who is 'white' in color." This argument did not persuade the Court: "Manifestly, the test [of race] afforded by the mere color of the skin of each individual is impracticable as that differs greatly among persons of the same race, even among Anglo-Saxons, ranging by impercept-ible gradations from the fair blond to the swarthy brunette, the latter being darker than many of the lighter hued persons of the brown or yellow races."[22] In rejecting Ozawa's petition for citizenship, the Court recognized that racial boundaries do not in fact follow skin color. If they did, some now secure in their White status would have to be excluded, and others firmly characterized as non-Whites would need to be included. As the *Ozawa* Court correctly tells us, "mere color of the skin" does not provide a means to racially divide people.

The rejection of race in science is now almost complete. In the end, we should embrace historian Barbara Fields's succinct conclusion with respect to the plausibility of biological races: "Anyone who continues to believe in race as a physical attribute of individuals, despite the now commonplace disclaimers of biologists and geneticists, might as well also believe that Santa Claus, the Easter Bunny and the tooth fairy are real, and that the earth stands still while the sun moves."[23]

Racial Illusions

Unfortunately, few in this society seem prepared to relinquish fully their subscription to notions of biological race. This includes Congress and the Supreme Court. Con-gress' anachronistic understanding of race is exemplified by a 1988 statute that ex-plains that "the term 'racial group' means a set of individuals whose identity as such is distinctive in terms of physical characteristics or biological descent."[24] The Supreme Court, although purporting to sever race from biology, also seems incapable of doing so. In *Saint Francis College v. Al-Khazraji*,[25] the Court determined that an Arab could recover damages for racial discrimination under 42 U.S.C. § 1981. Writing for the Court, Justice White appeared to abandon biological notions of race in favor of a socio-political conception, explaining: "Clear-cut categories do not exist. The particular traits which have generally been chosen to characterize races have been criticized as having little biological significance. It has been found that differences between individ-uals of the same race are often greater than the differences between the 'average' individuals of different races."[26] Despite this seeming rejection of biological race, Justice White continued: "The Court of Appeals was thus quite right in holding that § 1981, 'at a minimum,' reaches discrimination against an individual 'because he or she is genetically part of an ethnically and physiognomically distinctive subgrouping of *homo sapiens.*'"[27] By adopting the lower court's language of genetics and distinctive subgroupings, Justice White demonstrates the Court's continued reliance on blood as a metonym for race. During oral argument in *Metrobroadcasting v. FCC*, Justice Scalia again revealed the Court's understanding of race as a matter of blood. Scalia attacked the argument that granting minorities broadcasting licenses would enhance diversity by blasting "the policy as a matter of 'blood,'" at one point charging that the policy reduced to a question of 'blood . . . blood, not background and environment.'"[28]

Racial Formation

Race must be viewed as a social construction. That is, human interaction rather than natural differentiation must be seen as the source and continued basis for racial categorization. The process by which racial meanings arise has been labeled racial formation.[29] In this formulation, race is not a determinant or a residue of some other social phenomenon, but rather stands on its own as an amalgamation of competing societal forces. Racial formation includes both the rise of racial groups and their constant reification in social thought. I draw upon this theory, but use the term "racial fabrication" in order to highlight four important facets of the social construction of race. First, humans rather than abstract social forces produce races. Second, as human constructs, races constitute an integral part of a whole social fabric that includes gender and class relations. Third, the meaning-systems surrounding race change quickly rather than slowly. Finally, races are constructed relationally, against one another, rather than in isolation. Fabrication implies the workings of human hands, and suggests the possible intention to deceive. More than the industrial term "formation," which carries connotations of neutral constructions and processes indifferent to individual intervention, referring to the fabrication of races emphasizes the human element and evokes the plastic and inconstant character of race. An archaeological exploration of the racial identity of Mexicans will illustrate these four elements of race.

In the early 1800s, people in the United States ascribed to Latin Americans nationalities and, separate from these, races. Thus, a Mexican might also be White, Indian, Black, or Asian. By the 1840s and 1850s, however, US Anglos looked with distaste upon Mexicans in terms that conflated and stigmatized their race and nationality. This animus had its source in the Anglo-Mexican conflicts in the Southwest, particularly in Texas and California. In the newly independent Texas, war propaganda from the 1830s and 1840s purporting to chronicle Mexican "atrocities" relied on racial disparagements. Little time elapsed following the US annexation of Mexican territory in 1848 before laws began to reflect and reify Anglo racial prejudices. Social prejudices quickly became legal ones, highlighting the close ties between race and law. In 1855, for example, the California Legislature targeted Mexicans as a racial group with the so-called "Greaser Act." Ostensibly designed to discourage vagrancy, the law specifically applied to "all persons who are commonly known as 'Greasers' or the issue of Spanish and Indian blood . . . and who go armed and are not peaceable and quiet persons."[30]

> Typifying the arrogant belligerence of the times are the writings of T. J. Farnham: No one acquainted with the indolent, mixed race of California, will ever believe that they will populate, much less, for any length of time, govern the country. The law of Nature which curses the mulatto here with a constitution less robust than that of either race from which he sprang, lays a similar penalty upon the mingling of the Indian and white races in California and Mexico. They must fade away; while the mixing of different branches of the Caucasian family in the States will continue to produce a race of men, who will enlarge from period to period the field of their industry and civil domination, until not only the Northern States of Mexico, but the Californias also, will open their glebe to the pressure of its unconquered arm. The old Saxon blood must stride the continent, must command all its northern shores, must here press the grape and the olive, here eat the orange and the fig, and in their own unaided might, erect the altar of civil and religious freedom on the plains of the Californias.[31]

We can use Farnham's racist hubris to illustrate the four points enumerated earlier regarding racial fabrication.

First, the transformation of "Mexican" from a nationality to a race came about through the dynamic interplay of myriad social forces. As the various strains in this passage indicate, Farnham's racialization of Mexicans does not occur in a vacuum, but in the context of dominant ideology, perceived economic interests, and psychological necessity. In unabashedly proclaiming the virtue of raising industry and harnessing nature, Farnham trumpeted the dominant Lockean ideology of the time, an ideology which served to confirm the superiority of the industrialized Yankees and the inferiority of the pastoral Mexicans and Indians, and to justify the expropriation of their lands.[32] By lauding the commercial and economic interests of colonial expansion, Farnham also appealed to the freebooting capitalist spirit of America, recounting to his East Coast readers the riches which lay for their taking in a California populated only by mixed-breed Mexicans. Finally, Farnham's assertions regarding the racial character of these Mexicans filled the psychological need to justify conquest: the people already in California, Farnham assured his readers, would "fade away" under Nature's curse, and in any event, were as a race "unfit" to govern their own land. Racial fabrication cannot be explained in terms of a few causal factors, but must be viewed as a complex process subject to manifold social forces.

Second, because races are constructed, ideas about race form part of a wider social fabric into which other relations, not least gender and class, are also woven. Farnham's choice of martial and masculine imagery is not an accident but a reflection of the close symbiosis in the construction of racial and gender hierarchies during the nineteenth century.[33] This close symbiosis was reflected, for example, in distinct patterns of gender racialization during the era of frontier expansion – the native men of the Southwest were depicted as indolent, slothful, cruel, and cowardly Mexicans, while the women were described as fair, virtuous, and lonely Spanish maidens. Consider the following leaden verse:

> The Spanish maid, with eye of fire,
> At balmy evening turns her lyre
> And, looking to the Eastern sky,
> Awaits our Yankee chivalry
> Whose purer blood and valiant arms,
> Are fit to clasp her budding charms.
>
> The *man*, her mate, is sunk in sloth –
> To love, his senseless heart is loth:
> The pipe and glass and tinkling lute,
> A sofa, and a dish of fruit;
> A nap, some dozen times by day;
> Somber and sad, and never gay.[34]

This doggerel depicts the Mexican women as Spanish, linking their sexual desirability to European origins, while concurrently comparing the purportedly slothful Mexican man to the ostensibly chivalrous Yankee. Social renditions of masculinity and femininity often carry with them racial overtones, just as racial stereotypes invariably embody some elements of sexual identity. The archaeology of race soon becomes the excavation of gender and sexual identity.

Farnham's appeal to industry also reveals the close interconnection between racial and class structures. The observations of Arizona mine owner Sylvester Mowry reflect this linkage: "The question of [resident Mexican] labor is one which commends itself to the attention of the capitalist: cheap, and under proper management, efficient and permanent. They have been peons for generations. They will remain so, as it is their natural condition."[35] When Farnham wrote in 1840 before US expansion into the Southwest, Yankee industry stood in counterpoint to Mexican indolence. When Mowry wrote in 1863, after fifteen years of US regional control, Anglo capitalism stood in a fruitful managerial relationship to cheap, efficient Mexican labor. The nearly diametric change in the conception of Mexicans held by Anglos, from indolent to industrious, reflects the emergence of an Anglo economic elite in the Southwest and illustrates the close connection between class relations and ideas about race. The syncretic nature of racial, gender, and class constructs suggests that a global approach to oppression is not only desirable, it is *necessary* if the amelioration of these destructive social hierarchies is to be achieved.

Third, as evidenced through a comparison of the stereotypes of Mexicans propounded by Farnham and Mowry, racial systems of meaning can change at a relatively rapid rate. In 1821, when Mexico gained its independence, its residents were not generally considered a race. Twenty years later, as Farnham's writing shows, Mexicans were denigrated in explicitly racial terms as indolent cowards. About another two decades after that, Mowry lauds Mexicans as naturally industrious and faithful. The rapid emergence of Mexicans as a race, and the singularly quick transformations wrought in their perceived racial character, exemplify the plasticity of race. Accretions of racial meaning are not sedimentary products which once deposited remain solid and unchanged, or subject only to a slow process of abrasion, erosion, and buildup. Instead, the processes of racial fabrication continuously melt down, mold, shatter, and recast races: races are not rocks, they are plastics.

Fourth and finally, races are relationally constructed. Despite their conflicting views on the work ethic of Mexicans, the fundamental message delivered by Farnham and Mowry is the same: though war, conquest, and expansion separate their writings, both tie race and class together in the exposition of Mexican inferiority and Anglo superiority. The denigration of Mexicans and the celebration of Anglos are inseverable. The attempt to racially define the conquered, subjugated or enslaved is at the same time an attempt to racially define the conquered, the subjugator, or the enslaver.[36] Races are categories of difference which exist only in society: They are produced by myriad conflicting social forces; they overlap and inform other social categories; they are fluid rather than static and fixed; and they make sense only in relationship to other racial categories, having no meaning or independent existence. Race is socially constructed.

Conclusion

I close where I began, with *Hudgins v. Wright*. The women in the case lived in a liminal area between races, being neither and yet both Black and Indian. Biologically, they were neither. Any objective basis for racial divisions fell into disrepute a hundred years ago, when early ethnology proved incapable of delineating strict demarcations across human diversity. Despite Judge Tucker's beliefs and the efforts of innumerable scientists, the history of nineteenth-century anthropology convincingly demonstrates that morphological traits cannot be deployed as physical arbiters of race. More recently, genetic testing has made clear the close connection all humans share, as well as the futility of explaining the differences that do exist in terms of racially relevant gene codes. The categories of race previously considered objective, such as Caucasoid, Negroid, and Mongoloid, are now widely regarded as empty relics, persistent shadows of the social belief in races that permeated early scientific thought. Biological race is an illusion.

Social race, however, is not, and it is here that the Wrights' race should be measured. At different times, the Wrights were socially both Black and Indian. As slaves and in the mind of Hudgins, they were Black; as free women and in their argument for liberty, they were Indian. The particular racial options confronting the Wrights reflect the history of racial fabrication in the United States. Races are thus not biological groupings, but social constructions. Even though far from objective, race remains obvious. Walking down the street, we consistently rely on pervasive social mythologies to assign races to the other pedestrians. The absence of any physical basis to race does not entail the conclusion that race is wholly hallucination. Race has its genesis and maintains its vigorous strength in the realm of social beliefs.

For the Wrights, their race was not a phantasm but a contested fact on which their continued enslavement turned. Their struggle makes clear the importance of chance, context, and choice in the social mechanics of race. Aspects of human variation like dark skin or African ancestry are chance, not denotations of distinct branches of humankind. These elements stand in as markers widely interpreted to connote racial difference only in particular social contexts. The local setting in turn provides the field of struggle on which social actors make racially relevant choices. For the Wrights, freedom came because they chose to contest their race. Without their decision to argue that they were Indian and thus free, generations to come might have been reared into slavery.

This is the promise of choice at its brightest: By choosing to resist racial constructions, we may emancipate ourselves and our children. Unfortunately, uncoerced choice in the arena of US race relations is rare, perhaps nonexistent. Two facets of this case demonstrate the darkened potential of choice. First, the women's freedom ultimately turned on Hannah's long straight hair, not on their decision to resist. Without the legal presumptions that favored their features, presumptions that were in a sense the concrete embodiments of the social context, they would have remained slaves. Furthermore, these women challenged their race, not the status ascribed to it. By arguing that they were Indian and not Black, free rather than enslaved, the women lent unfortunate legitimacy to the legal and social presumptions in favor of Black slavery. The context and consequences of the Wrights' actions confirm that choices are made in a harsh racist social setting that may facilitate but more likely will forestall freedom; and that in our decisions to resist, we may shatter but more probably will inadvertently strengthen the racial structures around us. Nevertheless, race is not an inescapable physical fact. Rather, it is a social construction that, however perilously, remains subject to contestation at the hands of individuals and communities alike.

Notes

1 Hudgins v. Wright, 11 Va. 134 (1 Hen. & M.) (Sup. Ct. App. 1806).
2 Ibid. at 139–40.

3   Ibid. at 140–1.

4   Michael Omi and Howard Winant, *Racial Formation in the United States: From the 1960s to the 1980s* (1986), 63.

5   See Ian Ayres, Fair Driving: Gender and Race Discrimination in Retail Car Negotiations, 104 *Harvard Law Review* 817 (1991).

6   See, e.g., Developments in the Law–Race and the Criminal Process, *Harvard Law Review* 1472 (1988).

7   See, e.g., Frances Lee Ansley, Race and the Core Curriculum in Legal Education, 79 *California Law Review* 1511, 1521–6 (1991).

8   See, e.g., Patricia J. Williams, *The Alchemy of Race and Rights* (1991).

9   See, e.g., Randall Kennedy, McCleskey v. Kemp: Race, Capital Punishment, and the Supreme Court, 101 *Harvard Law Review* 1388 (1988); Developments in the Law, supra note 6.

10 See, e.g., Judith Resnick, Dependent Sovereigns: Indian Tribes, States and the Federal Courts, 56 *University of Chicago Law Review* 671 (1989).

11 See, e.g., Elizabeth Bartholet, Where Do Black Children Belong? The Politics of Race Matching in Adoption, 139 *University of Pennsylvania Law Review*. 1163 (1991); Two Perry, Race and Child Placement: The Best Interests Test and the Cost of Discretion, 29 *Journal of Family Law* 51 (1990–1).

12 Duncan Kennedy, A Cultural Pluralist Case for Affirmative Action in Legal Academia, 1990 *Duke Law Journal* 705, 729 (citing Mario L. Baeza, Telecommunications Reregulation and Deregulation: The Impact on Opportunities for Minorities, 2 *Harvard Black Letter Journal* 7 (1985)).

13 Omi & Winant, *supra* note 4, at 62. For an extended discussion of "common sense" in the construction of racial identities, see Stuart Alan Clat *Fear of a Black Planet: Race, Identity Politics, and Common Sense*, 21 *Social Review* No. 3–4, 37 (1991).

14 City of Richmond v. J. A. Croson Co., 488 U.S. 469, 505 (1989). For a critique of Justice O'Connor's decision in Croson, see Patricia J. Williams, *The Obliging Shell: An Informal Essay on Formal Equal Opportunity*, 87 *Michigan Law Review* 2128 (1989).

15 See, e.g., Derrick Bell, *Faces at the Bottom* of the Well: The Immanence of Racism (1992); Gary Peller, Race Consciousness, 1990 *Duke Law Journal*.

16 See generally Leon Kamin et al., *Not in Our Genes: Biology, Ideology, and Human Nature* (1984); Alan Almquist & John Cronin, Fact, Fable and Myth on Human Evolution, 29 *Current Anthropology* 520 (1988); B. Bower, Race Falls from Grace, 140 *Science News* 380 (1991).

17 See Richard C. Lewontin, The Apportionment of Human Diversity, *Evolutionary Biology* 381, 397 (1972). See generally L. L. Cavalli-Sforza, The Genetics of Human Populations, 231 *Scientific American* 80 (Sept. 1974).

18 Thomas F. Gossett, *Race: The History of an Idea in America* 342–7 (1975).

19 See generally Stephen Jay Gould, *The Mismeasure of Man* (1981); William Stanton, *The Leopard's Spots: Scientific Attitudes Toward Race in America* 1815–59 (1960); Nancy Stepan, *The Idea of Race in Science: Great Britain, 1800–1960* (1982).

20 Gossett, *supra* note 18, at 65–83. Charles Darwin proposed several of these axes, arguing at one point that "[w]ith civilized nations, the reduced size of the jaws from lessened use, the habitual play of different muscles serving to express different emotions, and the increased size of the brain from greater intellectual activity, have together produced a considerable effect on their general appearance in comparison with savages." Ibid. at 78 (quoted without attribution to a specific source). Darwin also supposed that the body lice of some races could not live on the bodies of members of other races, thus prompting him to suggest that "a racial scale might be worked out by exposing doubtful cases to different varieties of lice." Ibid. at 81. Leonardo da Vinci is another icon of intellectual greatness guilty of harboring ridiculous ideas regarding race. Da Vinci attributed racial differences to the environment in a novel manner, arguing that those who lived in hotter climates worked at night and so absorbed dark pigments, while those in cooler climates were active during the day and correspondingly absorbed light pigments. Ibid. at 16.

21 260 U.S. 178 (1922).

22 Ibid. at 197.

23 See Barbara Jeanne Fields, Slavery, Race and Ideology in the United States of America, 181 *New Left Review* 95–6 (1990).

24 Genocide Convention Implementation Act of 1987, 18 U.S.C. § 1093 (1988).

25 481 U.S. 604 (1987).

26 Ibid. at 610, n.4.

27 Ibid. at 613.

28 Neil Gotanda, A Critique of "Our Constitution Is Color-Blind," 44 *Stanford Law Review* 1, 32 (1991) (citing Ruth Marcus, FCC Defends Minority License Policies: Case Before High Court Could Shape Future of Affirmative Action, *Washington Post* Mar. 29, 1990, at A8).

29 Omi & Winant, *supra* note 4, at 61.

30 Cal. Stat. 175 (1855), excerpted in Robert F. Heizer & Alan J. Almquist, *The Other Californians: Prejudice and Discrimination Under Spain, Mexico, and the United States to 1920*, at 151 (1971). The recollections of "Dame Shirley," who resided in a California mining camp between 1851 and 1852, record efforts by the ascendant Anglos to racially denigrate Mexicans. "It is very common to hear vulgar Yankees say of the Spaniards, 'Oh, they are half-civilized black men!' These unjust expressions naturally irritate the latter, many of whom are highly educated gentlemen of the most refined and cultivated manner." L. A. K. S. Clappe, *The Shirley Letters from the California Mines, 1851–1852*, at 158 (1922), quoted in Heizer & Almquist, *supra*, at 141.

31 T. J. Farnham, *Life, Adventures, and Travel in California* 413 (1840), quoted in Heizer & Almquist, *supra* note 30, at 140.

32 See generally Robert A. Williams, The Algebra of Federal Indian Law: The Hard Trail of Decolonizing and Americanizing the White Man's Indian Jurisprudence, 1986 *Wisconsin Law Review* 219.

33 See Nancy Leys Stepan, Race and Gender: The Role of Analogy in science, in *Anatomy of Racism* 38 (David Theo Goldberg ed. 1990).

34 Reginald Horsman, *Race and Manifest Destiny: The Origin of American Racial Anglo-Saxonism* 233 (1981) (citation omitted).

35 Sylvester Mowry, *The Geography of Arizona and Sono* (1863), quoted in Ronald Takaki, *Iron Cages: Race and Class in Nineteenth Century America* 163 (1990).

36 *See* Kimberlé Williams Crenshaw, Race, Reform, and Retrenchment: Transformation and Legitimation in Antidiscrimination Law, 101 *Harvard Law Review* 1331, 1373 (1988).

CHAPTER 3

Interrogating "Whiteness"

Shelley Fisher Fishkin

Anyone growing up in the 1950s in the US or Great Britain knew that Elvis Presley's White rock and roll was copied from Black rhythm and blues. Shelley Fisher Fishkin notes in "Interrogating 'Whiteness'" (an excerpt from "Interrogating 'Whiteness', complicating 'Blackness': Remapping American Culture," 1996) that the borrowing and copying back and forth between White and Black culture in the United States has been manifold. She also provides an excellent review of the scholarship on and discussions around "whiteness."

February 1992. I hadn't spoken with him in years, but I knew David Bradley would share my excitement, so I dialed his number.[1] "This may sound crazy," I remember saying, "but I think I've figured out—and can prove—that black speakers and oral traditions played an absolutely central role in the genesis of *Huckleberry Finn*. Twain couldn't have *written* the book without them. And hey, if Hemingway's right about all modern American literature coming from *Huck Finn*, then all modern American literature comes from those black voices as well. And as Ralph Ellison said when I interviewed him last summer, it all comes full circle because *Huck Finn* helps spark so much work by black writers in the twentieth century."

I stopped to catch my breath. There was a pause on the other end of the line. Then a question:

"Shelley, tell me one thing. Do you have tenure?"

"Yes, but what does that have to do with anything?" I asked.

"Thank God." he said. "Look, this stuff has been sitting there for a hundred years but nobody noticed because it didn't fit the paradigm. Whether they wanted to expand the canon or not, they all agreed that canonical American literature was 'white.' And whether they wanted black studies in the curriculum or not, they all agreed that African-American literature was 'black.' Now they'll have to start all over. Think about it."

I did.

In 1993, a year after that conversation, when my book *Was Huck Black? Mark Twain and African-American Voices* came out, I was aware of two or three books published that same year in the U.S. that tilled adjacent fields. The kinds of deep-going changes for which Bradley had argued seemed to be starting to happen. I sensed that my work might be part of a growing trend. But how many isolated academic forays add up to a "trend?" Ten? Twenty? Thirty?

In this essay I will provide a brief overview of over a hundred books and articles from fields including literary criticism, history, cultural studies, anthropology, popular culture, communication studies, music history, art history, dance history, humor studies, philosophy, linguistics and folklore, all published between 1990 and 1995 or forthcoming shortly. Taken together I believe that they mark the early 1990s as a defining moment in the study of American culture.

In the early 1990s, our ideas of "whiteness" were interrogated, our ideas of "blackness" were complicated, and the terrain we call "American culture" began to be remapped.[2]

Interrogating "Whiteness"

If you white, you all right . . . But if you black, get back.
    —African–American folk saying, later incorporated into a song[3]

To be white in America is to be very black. If you don't know how black you are, you don't know how American you are.
                                                        —Robert Farris Thompson[4]

Combatants in the canon wars of the 1980s argued that writing by African Americans had been previously unjustly excluded from the curriculum. New courses proliferated. But, as Dean Flower observed in the *Hudson Review* in 1994,

> the definition of "American" literature did not change. In the college classroom American literature was, and still mainly is, defined by the so-called "classic" texts and "major figures" – as if black writers had really made no difference in our literary history until, say, *Native Son*. Look in any publisher's college catalogue. The canonized (white) writers, who represent "the American tradition," are listed in one place, the African Americans appear in another. Students take courses on "Afro-American" writers or "Black Studies," almost always taught by persons of color, and they take courses in American literature, almost always taught by white persons in departments of English. The segregation could not be more emphatic.[5]

A study published in January 1990 found that college courses with such titles as "The Modern Novel" or "Modern Poetry" continued to be dominated by "works almost exclusively by elite white men."[6] Nonetheless, calling attention to the "whiteness" of the curriculum was still considered bizarre and provocative behavior. A professor who called the standard American literature survey she taught "White Male Writers" was held up to ridicule by *Time* magazine.[7] Evidently the editors subscribed to the idea (as George Lipsitz recently put it) that "whiteness never has to speak its name, never has to acknowledge its role as an organizing principle in social and cultural relations."[8] *Time's* behavior reflected the widely held assumptions that American culture is obviously white culture, and that stating the obvious is superfluous, irritating and perverse.

While the idea of the social construction of "blackness" was increasingly discussed in the 1980s, the idea of "whiteness" as a construct did not receive widespread attention until the 1990s. In the 1990s, scholars asked with increased frequency how the imaginative construction of "whiteness" had shaped American literature and American history. Some of our culture's most familiar (and canonical) texts and artifacts turned out to be less "white" on closer look than we may have thought; and the "whiteness" that had previously been largely invisible in the stories we told about who we were suddenly took center stage as the site where power and privilege converged and conspired to sabotage ideals of justice, equality and democracy.

With the 1992 publication of her book *Playing in the Dark: Whiteness and the Literary Imagination*, Toni Morrison launched an eloquent and provocative challenge to the privileged, naturalized "whiteness" of American literature. Expanding on her earlier groundbreaking *Michigan Quarterly* article, Morrison rejected the assumption that "traditional, canonical American literature is free of, uninformed, and unshaped by the four-hundred-year-old presence of, first, Africans and then African-Americans in the United States."[9] She made explicit that which had been implicit in American literary study from the start. "There seems to be a more or less tacit agreement among literary scholars," Morrison wrote, that, because American literature has been clearly the preserve "of white male views, genius, and power, those views, genius and power are without relationship to and are removed from the overwhelming presence of black people in the United States."[10] "The contemplation of this black presence," Morrison argues, "is central to any understanding of our national literature and should not be permitted to hover at the margins of the literary imagination."[11] Analyzing works by Poe, Hawthorne, Melville, Twain, Cather, and Hemingway, among others, *Playing in the Dark* challenged scholars to examine whiteness as an imaginative, social, and literary construction, to explore the ways in which "embedded assumptions of racial (not racist) language work in the literary enterprise that hopes and sometimes claims to be 'humanistic.' "[12] *Playing in the Dark* put the construction of "whiteness" on the table to be investigated, analyzed, punctured and probed. Morrison's book offered a set of questions and an agenda for research that resonated with a number of projects already under way (including my own)[13] and that also helped spark myriad new publications – including the volume at hand, Henry Wonham's *Criticism and the Color Line*.

The importance of this approach, however, was far from universally recognized. As Eric J. Sundquist observed in 1993 in *To Wake the Nations: Race in the Making of American Literature*, "it remains difficult for many readers to overcome their fundamental conception of 'American' literature as solely Anglo-European in inspiration and authorship, to which may then be added an appropriate number of valuable 'ethnic' or 'minority' texts."[14] Morrison, Sundquist, and I were suggesting that these divisions failed to do justice to the complex roots of American culture.

This argument did not burst onto the scene full-blown in the 1990s. Indeed, as early as 1970 Ralph Ellison had commented on white Americans' absurd self-delusions "over the true interrelatedess of blackness and whiteness."[15] In 1987, as I have noted, Toni Morrison laid important groundwork in "Unspeakable Things Unspoken" and Sundquist prepared the way as well in the late 1980s both with his own publications on Twain and Faulkner, and the essay collection on Stowe that he edited.[16] In a 1986 essay (in Sundquist's Stowe anthology) entitled "Sharing the Thunder: The Literary Exchanges of Harriet Beecher Stowe, Henry Bibb, and Frederick Douglass," Robert Stepto demonstrated the importance of investigating the African-American roots of canonical American fiction, a move that scholars would soon make with increasing frequency.[17]

Two other American critics pursued some preliminary explorations of this territory in the late 1980s as well. In his final chapter of *The Unusable Past: Theory and the Study of American Literature* (1986), for example, Russell Reising asked how the American Renaissance would look if we posited Frederick Douglass as central to it. In his imaginative juxtaposition of analyses of passages from Douglass and Thoreau in which both writers explore "America's blindness to its own darker truths,"[18] Reising demonstrates affinities and intersections previously missing, for the most part, from discussions of either writer. Reising argues that Douglass's life, his works, the institution of slavery and "the struggle against slavery waged by black and white alike are the material, social, and political basis on which the works of other major writers of the American Renaissance are founded. The dynamics of slavery made [their works] possible."[19] Aldon Lynn Nielson's 1988 book, *Reading Race: White American Poets and Racial Discourse in the Twentieth Century*, was another early study that argued that ideas about race played an important role in shaping canonical American literature, and a vein mined as well by several of the contributors to the 1989 volume *Slavery and the Literary Imagination*, edited by Deborah E. McDowell and Arnold Rampersad.[20] But if the 1980s brought a handful of essays and books, the early 1990s positively exploded with literary studies in this mode.

In the early 1990s a number of critics in addition to myself took up Morrison's challenge to examine mainstream American "literature for the impact Afro-American presence has had on the structure of the work, the linguistic practice, and fictional enterprise in which it is engaged."[21] Dana Nelson's *The Word in Black and White: Reading "Race" in American Literature 1638–1867* (1992) examined the ways in which seventeenth-, eighteenth- and early nineteenth-century white writers constructed versions of their own identity (and of American identity) by defining themselves as unlike various racial and ethnic "others"; Nelson offered fresh insight into familiar writers such as Cotton Mather, James Fenimore Cooper, William Gilmore Simms, and Catharine Maria Sedgwick.[22] Sterling Stuckey in *Going Through the Storm: The Influence of African American Art in History* (1994), Eric Sundquist in *To Wake the Nations* (1993), and Viola Sachs in *L'Imaginaire Melville* (1992) demonstrated Herman Melville's deep interest in African customs, myth, languages and traditions, and pointed out the African influences on works such as *Moby-Dick* and the short story "Benito Cereno."[23] (Sachs, for example, has uncovered numerous references to the Yoruba god Lebga in *Moby-Dick*. Stuckey and Sundquist have examined the use of Ashanti drumming and treatment of the dead in "Benito Cereno," suggesting that the treatment of the corpse of the rich slaveholder Aranda in "Benito Cereno" was not a racist allusion to African savagery, as critics have argued, but rather, evidence of Melville's insight into Ashanti rituals and the shrewd political use his characters made of those traditions.) And in "*Moby-Dick* and American Slave Narrative" (1994), Michael Berthold argued for the centrality of African-American traditions to Melville's art.[24] While my own work explored the ways in which African-American voices and oral traditions shaped *Huckleberry Finn*, the 1990s brought essays on Twain by Werner Sollors and by Lawrence Howe which examined the influence of slave narratives on *Connecticut Yankee* and *Life on the Mississippi*.[25] And in *Black and White Strangers: Race and American Literary Realism* (1993) Kenneth W. Warren examined the way implicit assumptions about race illuminate the work of Henry James and William Dean Howells.[26]

Warren (like Nelson, Sundquist, Stuckey and Sachs) argued for the importance of investigating "the mutually constitutive construction of 'black' and 'white' texts in American literature."[27] "Concerns about 'race' may structure our American texts, even when those texts are not 'about' race in any substantive way," Warren maintains.

"For James," he observes, "the art of fiction is always a reflection on the social conditions necessary for sustaining fiction as high art."[28] Warren's book sheds new light on both the fiction of James and Howells and the society that shaped it and that it helped shape. Along the way he generates some intriguing insights into turn-of-the-century culture – such as the "inadvertent alliance between Northern realism and Southern romance in an assault on the political idealism of the New England tradition."[29]

In recent studies of canonical white twentieth-century figures, as well, unexpected links to African and African-American culture are being explored. While Robert Fleissner examined the influence of African myths on T. S. Eliot, David Chinitz demonstrated intriguing connections between Eliot's poetry and jazz.[30] The construction of whiteness on the part of Eliot as well as other canonical white writers in the twentieth century was examined by Michael North in *The Dialect of Modernism: Race, Language & Twentieth-Century Literature* (1994). North explores the role of "racial masquerade" and "linguistic imitation" in the works of modernists including Gertrude Stein, T. S. Eliot, Ezra Pound and William Carlos Williams.[31] The course of modernist writing in America, North demonstrates, was shaped indelibly by the linguistic racial impersonations in which these writers engaged. Probing, for example, Pound's and Eliot's excursions into what they thought of as black dialect (lifted from "the world of Uncle Remus"), North observes that "preemptive mimicry of blacks is a traditional American device allowing whites to rebel against English culture and simultaneously use it to solidify their domination at home."[32] North also addresses the dynamics of William Carlos Williams's complicated attraction to African-American language and literature, as does Aldon L. Nielsen, in *Writing Between the Lines: Race and Intertextuality* (1994).[33] And in a series of articles culled from a longer work on the discourse of race in poetry, Rachel Blau DuPlessis examines some related issues not only in the work of Eliot, Pound and Williams, but also in the poetry of Vachel Lindsay, Wallace Stevens, Marianne Moore, Mina Loy, and Gertrude Stein.[34]

While Nielson, North and DuPlessis explore the complex relationship that white modernist poets like Pound, Eliot and Williams had to race-inflected language, Laura Doyle's *Bordering on the Body: The Race Mother in Modern Fiction* (1994) explores the centrality for white modernist novelists on both sides of the Atlantic – including James Joyce, Virginia Woolf and William Faulkner – of what Doyle refers to as the concept of the "race mother."[35] Ideas of "racial patriarchy," according to Doyle, play a key role in shaping the cultural matrix of high modernism.... Discussions of white modernists can be enriched by examinations of the role played by ideas of blackness – on both the linguistic and thematic levels – in the genesis of their work.[36]

The whiteness of several forms of popular culture, as well as high culture, was similarly interrogated in the early 1990s, as familiar artifacts generally understood as white were shown to have roots more complicated than previously recognized. Joe Adamson and David Roediger, for example, explored the African roots of Bugs Bunny.[37] As Roediger puts it in a 1994 essay (building on Adamson's extended treatment of the subject in his 1990 book on Bugs Bunny),

> Bugs' heritage is anything but white. The verb "bugs" [as in] "annoys" or "vexes," helps name the cartoon hero. Its roots, like those of "hip," lie partly in Wolof speech.
>
> Moreover, the fantastic idea that a vulnerable and weak rabbit could be tough and tricky enough to menace those who menace him enters American culture, as the historian Franklin Rosemont observes, largely via Br'er Rabbit tales.

These stories were told among various ethnic groups in West Africa, and further developed by American slaves before being popularized and bastardized by white collectors like Joel Chandler Harris. They were available both as literature and folklore to the white Southerner Tex Avery whose genius so helped to give us Bugs.[38]

And Howard L. Sacks and Judith Rose Sacks argued convincingly that a nineteenth-century black family in Ohio wrote "Dixie," the song that became known as the anthem of the Confederacy. Building their case from family records, public documents, and oral histories, the Sacks' *Way Up North in Dixie: A Black Family's Claim to the Confederate Anthem* (1993), detailed the history of the Snowdens, a farming family who performed banjo and fiddle tunes and popular songs for black and white audiences throughout rural central Ohio from the 1850s through the turn-of-the-century. The song's reputed white composer, Dan Emmett, heard the Snowdens sing the song and appropriated it as part of his minstrel show repertoire, bringing it to a wide and receptive public.[39]

The complex blend of appreciation and appropriation of black culture that the minstrel show represented was the subject of Eric Lott's *Love and Theft: Blackface Minstrelsy and the American Working Class* (1994), in which the role of the minstrel show in the construction of working-class white identity in nineteenth-century America receives the attention it has long deserved. Lott takes as his starting point the conventional view of the minstrel show: "While it was organized around the quite explicit 'borrowing' of black cultural materials for white dissemination, a borrowing that ultimately depended on the material relations of slavery, the minstrel show obscured these relations by pretending that slavery was amusing, right, and natural."[40] But, he continues, "I am not so sure that this is the end of the story."[41] In addition to being all of the above, Lott explains, "blackface performance, the first public acknowledgment by whites of black culture," required "small but significant crimes against settled ideas of racial demarcation" that have been little noticed before. Lott's larger concern is "how precariously nineteenth-century white working people lived their whiteness."[42]

Lott's stimulating study resonates with work in the field of history by David Roediger, whose important books *The Wages of Whiteness: Race and the Making of the American Working Class* (1991) and *Towards the Abolition of Whiteness* (1994) helped foreground whiteness on historians' agendas in the 1990s.[43] As Roediger observes in the latter volume:

When residents of the US talk about race, they too often talk only about African Americans, Native Americans, Hispanic Americans, and Asian Americans. If whites come into the discussion, it is only because they have "attitudes" towards nonwhites. Whites are assumed not to "have race," though they might be racists.[44]

But "the whiteness of white workers," Roediger demonstrates, "far from being natural and unchallengeable, is highly conflicted, burdensome, and even inhuman."[45] Roediger offers these essays – which investigate the construction of whiteness at various points in American labor history – as "political, as well as historical, interventions" designed to explode, as he puts it, "the idea that it is desirable or unavoidable to be white."[46] Roediger believes that "making whiteness, rather than simply white racism, the focus of study has had the effect of throwing into sharp relief the impact that the dominant racial identity in the US has had not only on the treatment of racial 'others' but also on the ways that whites think of themselves, of power, of pleasure, and of gender."[47] ...

The move to recover and value the black influences on so-called white American culture was paralleled by a move to foreground the nature of white privilege and racism in American society. The early 1990s brought stimulating new work on this subject by scholars including Theodore Allen, Neil Foley, George Lipsitz, Jane Marcus, Vron Ware, Ruth Frankenberg, and bell hooks.

Theodore W. Allen, for example, in the first volume of *The Invention of the White Race* (1994), addressed the process by which the Irish "became white" in the United States and became enlisted as intermediaries in and supporters of the dominant culture's system of racial oppression and class privilege.[48] Neil Foley, in a study of the racial politics of the socialist organizers in central Texas in the early twentieth century, explored a chapter of Texas history in which Mexican-Americans found themselves constructed by Anglos as "almost white."[49]

George Lipsitz aptly observed in "The Possessive Investment in Whiteness: Racialized Social Democracy and the 'White' Problem in American Studies" (1995) that

> More than the product of private prejudices, whiteness emerged as a relevant category in American life largely because of realities created by slavery and segregation, by immigration restriction and Indian policy, by conquest and colonialism. A fictive identity of "whiteness" appeared in law as an abstraction, and it became actualized in everyday life in many ways. American economic and political life gave different racial groups unequal access to citizenship and property, while cultural practices including wild west shows, minstrel shows, racist images in advertising, and Hollywood films institutionalized racism by uniting ethnically diverse European-American audiences into an imagined community – one called into being through inscribed appeals to the solidarity of white supremacy.[50]

Lipsitz recognizes the crucial role cultural practices have often played "in prefiguring, presenting, and preserving political coalitions based on identification with the fiction of 'whiteness,'" helping "people who left Europe as Calabrians or Bohemians become something called 'whites' when they got to America, and how that designation made all the difference in the world."[51] But he cautions scholars against allowing a focus on "cultural stories" to mask the legal, social, political and economic "efforts from colonial times to the present to create a possessive investment in whiteness for European Americans."[52] Brilliantly synthetic and carefully researched, Lipsitz's ambitious exploration of the public policy that shaped the "racialization of experience, opportunities, and rewards in the U.S." offers scholars a challenging agenda for further research.

The early 1990s also brought several examinations of whiteness in a particularly gendered context, including two studies of the ways in which a series of upper-class and middle-class English women in the late 19th- and early 20th-centuries deconstructed and reshaped their sense of whiteness as a result of their contact with African Americans. Jane Marcus's engaging article, "Bonding and Bondage: Nancy Cunard and the Making of the *Negro Anthology*," raises these provocative questions:

> What does it mean when Nancy Cunard switches roles and performs "the white woman being lynched" when in reality black men were being lynched in the name of revenge

for white woman's lost honor? Can the figure of the "white woman hanged, bound, manacled, enslaved," ever disrupt in performance the racial fears of sexual mixing she wants to explode? Or is she unaware of the act she is putting on? ... can she enact the erotics of the white slave along with the politics of the protest against racism?[53]

And Vron Ware, in *Beyond the Pale: White Women, Racism and History*, explores the role that Ida B. Wells and her attention to racial violence in turn-of-the-century America played in English reformers' constructions of their own identities as white women.[54]

The cognitive and emotional dimensions of American women's constructions of whiteness are the subjects of Ruth Frankenberg's "Whiteness and Americanness: Explaining the Constructions of Race, Culture and Nation in White Women's Life Narratives" (1994), and of Frankenberg's *White Women, Race Matters: The Social Construction of Whiteness* (1993).[55] Frankenberg believes that

> the tasks of redefining and rehistoricizing "whiteness" are ... vital concomitants of politicocultural struggles around race, from curriculum and canon transformation to the defense and extension of civil rights and racial equality. In other words, I would argue that critical engagements with the racial order must deconstruct and rearticulate whiteness at the same time as recentering the "others" upon whose existence the notion of whiteness depends.

Probing "the complex formation of white women's constructions of racialized selves," Frankenberg tries to rehistoricize the categories of race and culture insisting on antiessentialist conceptions of race, ethnicity, and culture, while at the same time emphasizing that these categories are made materially 'real' within matrices of power relations."[56] "It is critical to think clearly and carefully about the parts white people play in the maintenance of the racial order," Frankenberg believes, "and to ask how our locations in it – and our complicity with it – are marked by other dimensions of our privilege and oppression, including class, gender, and sexuality."[57]

As bell hooks notes in *Black Looks: Race and Representation* (1992):

> Whether they are able to enact it as a lived practice or not, many white folks active in anti-racist struggle today are able to acknowledge that all whites (as well as everyone else within white supremacist culture) have learned to overvalue "whiteness" even as they simultaneously learn to devalue blackness. They understand the need, at least intellectually, to alter their thinking. Central to this process of unlearning white supremacist attitudes and values is the destruction of the category of "whiteness."[58]

Notes

1   As far as I have acknowledged elsewhere, I track my awareness of the kinds of questions that indelibly shaped my research to a talk Bradley gave on *Huck Finn* in Hartford in 1985 that he titled "The First 'Nigger' Novel," in which he credited Twain with having written a seminal work of African-American literature. See Shelley Fisher Fishkin, *Was Huck Black? Mark Twain and African-American Voices* (New York: Oxford University Press, 1993) vii, 137.

2   The push toward multicultural education in the 1980s and 1990s sparked increased awareness of the interactions and interpenetration of a number of cultural traditions in addition to African-American, Anglo-American, and Euro-American: Latino, Asian-American, and Native American,

to name a few. I would not want my decision to frame this essay in "black" and "white" terms to be interpreted as a denial of the importance of these other groups and traditions in our efforts to reformulate and reconfigure our cultural narratives; I am simply choosing to focus, at this time, on one particular aspect of a complex set of issues. Indeed, perhaps the most apt term for describing the new perspectives on American identity that current research requires is Gloria Anzaldúa's concept of "mestiza consciousness," an idea that came from Anzaldúa's efforts to describe an identity that blended Anglo, Spanish, Mexican and Indian cultures, languages and gene pools. See Gloria Anzaldúa, *Borderlands: La Frontera/ The New Mestiza* (San Francisco: Spinsters/Aunt Lute, 1987). My own thoughts about the construction of cultural narratives have been deeply influenced by Anzaldúa's work and by the numerous conversations we have had on the subject over the last six years. My first public presentation of the ideas contained in this essay was in a paper entitled "America's Fear of her *Mestisaje*" that I delivered at a faculty colloquium (in which Anzaldúa also participated) at the Universidad Nacional Autónoma de México in Mexico City, June, 1992. My talk addressed, in part, the differences between a society like that of the US that denied the "*mestisaje*" at its core, and a society like that of Mexico that made the idea of "*mestisaje*" central to its official cultural narratives.

3   LeRoi Jones (Amiri Baraka), *Blues People* (New York: William Morrow, 1963), 185.

4   Robert Farris Thompson, Lecture on "The Kongo Atlantic Tradition," University of Texas, Austin, 28 February 1992.

5   Dean Flower, "Desegregating the Syllabus," *Hudson Review* (Winter 1994): 683–4.

6   Lee Katterman, "In Search of an 'American' Literature: UM Scholar Argues that Emphasis on the British Tradition Creates Damaging Myths," *Research News* (University of Michigan) 41 (January–February 1990), 14–15. David Bradley described a similar phenomenon in "Black and American, 1982," *Esquire*, May 1982. Rpt. in William Vesterman (ed.), *Essays for the '80s* (New York: Random House, 1987), 397–413. Also of interest is the Modern Language Association survey released in December, 1994, "What's Being Taught in Survey Courses?: Findings from a 1990–1991 MLA Survey of English Departments," which generated widespread media attention for its finding that, as the *Los Angeles Times* put it, "Dead white men are alive and well and being widely taught in college English courses." (Amy Wallace, "Defenders of Shakespeare Do Protest Too Much, Study Finds," *Los Angeles Times*, 29 December 1994).

7   William A. Henry III, "Upside Down in the Groves of Academe," *Time* (1 April 1991): 66–9. The professor was Valerie Babb of Georgetown University.

8   George Lipsitz, "The Possessive Investment in Whiteness: Racialized Social Democracy and the 'White' Problem in American Studies," *American Quarterly* 47 (September 1995):1–2. As Richard Dyer observes, "white power secures its dominance by seeming not to be anything in particular" (quoted in Lipsitz, "The Possessive Investment in Whiteness," 7).

9   Toni Morrison, *Playing in the Dark: Whiteness and the Literary Imagination* (Cambridge: Harvard University Press, 1992), 4–5.

10 Ibid., 5.

11 Ibid.

12 Ibid., xii–xiii.

13 In December 1991, I presented some of my preliminary research on the role African-American voices had played in shaping Mark Twain's art at an English department colloquium at Princeton University, which Toni Morrison attended. It was the first time I had presented any of this material in public. Toni Morrison's strong encouragement – immediately after my talk, at the dinner which followed, and in subsequent correspondence and conversations – helped prompt me to shelve other projects and devote all of my time to this one. At dinner I remember her describing the ways in which my research resonated with arguments she made in her forthcoming book, *Playing in the Dark*. By the time *Playing in the Dark* came out in the spring of 1992, I had progressed sufficiently on my own research to have sent off the manuscript to Oxford. That summer I was able to insert references to relevant passages from *Playing in the Dark* into *Was Huck Black? Mark Twain and African-American Voices* before it went into production.

14 Eric Sundquist, *To Wake the Nations: Race in the Making of American Literature* (Cambridge: Harvard University Press, 1993), 7.

15 Ellison wrote, "The Negro looks at the white man and finds it difficult to believe that the 'grays' – a negro term for white people – can be so absurdly self-deluded over the true interrelatedness of blackness and whiteness." "Change the Joke and Slip the Yoke," *Partisan Review* 25 (Spring 1958): 212–22. Rpt. in Ralph Ellison, *Shadow and Act* (New York: Random House, 1964), 55. Another critic who attended to the "interrelatedness of blackness and whiteness" early in the game was French scholar Viola Sachs, who asked questions in this vein in works including *Le Blanc et le Noir chez Melville et Faulkner* (Paris and the Hague: Mouton, 1974); *La Contre-Bible de Melville: Moby-Dick déchiffré* (Paris and the Hague: Mouton, 1975), *The Game of Creation: The Primeval Unlettered Language of Moby-Dick; or The Whale* (Paris: Editions de la Maison des Sciences de l'Homme, 1982), and *The Myth of America: Essays in the Structures of Literary Imagination* (Paris and the Hague: Mouton, 1973). See also Sachs (ed.), *L'Imaginaire-Melville: A French Point of View* (Saint-Denis, France: University Press of Vincennes, 1992).

16 Toni Morrison, "Unspeakable Things Unspoken: The Afro-American Presence in American Literature," *Michigan Quarterly Review* 28 (Winter 1989): 1–34; Eric Sundquist, "Mark Twain and Homer Plessy," *Representations* 24 (Fall 1988). Rpt. in Susan Gillman and Forrest G. Robinson (eds.), *Mark Twain's 'Pudd'nhead Wilson'* (Durham, NC: Duke University Press, 1990), 46–72; Eric Sundquist, "Faulkner, Race, and the Forms of American Fiction," in *Faulkner and Race: Faulkner and Yoknapatawpha*, ed. Doreen Fowler and Ann J. Abadie (Jackson: University Press of Mississippi, 1987), 1–34; Eric Sundquist (ed.), *New Essays on "Uncle Tom's Cabin"* (Cambridge and New York: Cambridge University Press, 1986). Other early studies which reflect aspects of the kind of approach Morrison urges include Sterling Brown's *The Negro in American Fiction* (Port Washington, NY: Kennikat Press, 1937); Seymour Gross and John Edward Hardy (eds.), *Images of the Negro in American Literature* (Chicago: University of Chicago Press, 1966); Jean Fagan Yellin's *The Intricate Knot: Black Figures in American Literature, 1776–1863* (New York: New York University Press, 1972); Carolyn Karcher's *Shadow over the Promised Land: Slavery, Race, and Violence in Melville's America* (Baton Rouge: Louisiana State University Press, 1980); and Michael Rogin's *Subversive Genealogies: The Politics and Art of Herman Melville* (Berkeley: University of California Press, 1985). Werner Sollors's pioneering book *Beyond Ethnicity: Consent and Descent in American Culture* (New York: Oxford University Press, 1986), as well as his edited collection, *The Invention of Ethnicity* (New York: Oxford University Press, 1989) must also be credited with helping to place on the agenda of contemporary scholars an issue that implicitly informs the studies discussed throughout this essay: the "constructed" nature of race and identity.

17 Robert Stepto, "Sharing the Thunder: The Literary Exchanges of Harriet Beecher Stowe, Henry Bibb, and Frederick Douglass," in Eric Sundquist (ed.), *New Essays*, 135–54.

18 Russell Reising, *The Unusable Past: Theory and the Study of American Literature* (New York and London: Methuen, 1986), 267.

19 Ibid., 271.

20 Aldon Lynn Nielson, *Reading Race: White American Poets and Racial Discourse in the Twentieth Century* (Athens: University of Georgia Press, 1988); Deborah E. McDowell and Arnold Rampersad (eds.), *Slavery and the Literary Imagination* (Baltimore: Johns Hopkins University Press, 1989).

21 Toni Morrison, "Unspeakable Things Unspoken," 19.

22 Dana Nelson, *The Word in Black and White: Reading "Race" in American Literature, 1638–1867* (New York: Oxford University Press, 1992).

23 Sterling Stuckey, "'Follow Your Leader': The Theme of Cannibalism in Melville's Benito Cereno," (1992) in *Going Through the Storm: The Influence of African American Art in History* (New York: Oxford University Press, 1994), 171–84; Eric Sundquist, "Melville, Delany, and New World Slavery," in *To Wake the Nations*, 135–221 (see also pp. 621–40 in this volume); Sachs, *L'Imaginaire-Melville*. Also relevant is the unpublished paper Sachs presented in Paris at an international meeting sponsored by the Laboratoire de Recherche sur l'Imaginaire Américain in the spring of 1993; the paper focused particularly on Legba allusions in *Moby-Dick*.

Carolyn Karcher also offers some preliminary examinations of the role of issues of race in Melville's work in *Shadow over the Promised Land*, as does Michael Rogin in *Subversive Genealogies*.

24 Michael Berthold, *"Moby-Dick* and American Slave Narrative," *Massachusetts Review* (Spring 1994): 135–48.

25 Werner Sollors, "Ethnicity," in *Critical Terms for Literary Study*, ed. Frank Lentriccia and Thomas McLaughlin (Chicago: University of Chicago Press, 1990), 288–305; Lawrence Howe, "Transcending the Limits of Experience: Mark Twain's *Life on the Mississippi," American Literature* 63 (September 1991): 420–39.

26 Kenneth W. Warren, *Black and White Strangers: Race and American Literary Realism* (Chicago: University of Chicago Press, 1993).

27 Ibid., 9.

28 Ibid., 10, 31.

29 Ibid., 15.

30 See Robert F. Fleissner, *T. S. Eliot and the Heritage of Africa* (New York: Peter Lang, 1992), and David Chinitz, "T. S. Eliot and the Cultural Divide," *PMLA* 110 (March 1995): 236–47, particularly 244–6.

31 Michael North, *The Dialect of Modernism: Race, Language & Twentieth-Century Literature* (New York: Oxford University Press, 1994), 3.

32 Ibid., 81.

33 Aldon L. Nielson, *Writing Between the Lines: Race and Intertextuality* (Athens: University of Georgia Press, 1994).

34 For discussions of Vachel Lindsay, T. S. Eliot, and Wallace Stevens, see Rachel Blau DuPlessis, "'HOO, HOO, HOO': Some Episodes in the Construction of Modern Whiteness," *American Literature* 67 (December 1995). For discussions of Wallace Stevens, Marianne Moore, William Carlos Williams, Mina Loy, Gertrude Stein, and Ezra Pound, see DuPlessis, "'Darken Your Speech': Racialized Cultural Work in Stevens, Moore, Williams, Loy, Stein and Pound," in Aldon L. Nielsen (ed.), *An Area of Act: Race and American Poetries and Poetics* (Urbana: University of Illinois Press, 1995). See also Charles Bernstein, "Professing Stein/Stein Professing," *Poetics Journal* 9 (1991): 44–50.

35 Doyle also examines treatment of the "race mother" figure by black novelists including Jean Toomer, Ralph Ellison, and Toni Morrison. Laura Doyle, *Bordering on the Body: The Race Mother in Modern Fiction* (New York: Oxford University Press, 1994).

36 Carla Peterson, "The Remaking of Americans: Gertrude Stein and African-American Musical Traditions." In *Criticism and the Color Line: Desegregating American Literary Studies*, ed. H. B. Woahan (New Brunswick, NJ: Rutgers University Press, 1996).

37 Joe Adamson, *Bugs Bunny: Fifty Years and Only One Gray Hare*, prefaces by Friz Freleng and Chuck Jones (New York: Holt, 1990); David Roediger, "A Long Journey to the Hip Hop Nation," *St. Louis Post-Dispatch*, 18 March 1994.

38 Ibid.

39 Howard I. Sacks and Judith Rose Sacks, *Way up North in Dixie: A Black Family's Claim to the Confederate Anthem* (Washington, DC: Smithsonian Institution Press, 1993).

40 Eric Lott, *Love and Theft: Blackface Minstrelsy and the American Working Class* (New York: Oxford University Press, 1993), 3.

41 Ibid., 3–4.

42 Ibid., 4. Some similarly complex approaches to the minstrel show in American popular culture emerge in Saidiya Hartman's book, *Scenes of Subjection* (New York: Oxford University Press, 1997). Among the many interesting offshoots of Lott's central discussion is his suggestion that many chapters of "white" cultural history usually written without reference to race – such as the history of cultural styles among whites known generally as "bohemianism" – must take into account an ever-present racial subtext (Lott, *Love and Theft*, 50–1).

43 David R. Roediger, *The Wages of Whiteness: Race and the Making of the American Working Class* (London and New York: Verso, 1991); David R. Roediger, *Towards the Abolition of Whiteness* (London and New York: Verso, 1994).

44 Roediger, *Towards the Abolition of Whiteness*, 12.
45 Ibid.
46 Ibid.
47 Ibid., 75. Roediger provides a useful overview of labor historians' responses to the issue of race in chapter 6 of *Towards the Abolition of Whiteness*, "The Crisis in Labor History: Race, Gender and the Replotting of the Working Class Past in the United States," 69–81. Roediger notes that "the recent outpouring of work on African-American, Asian-American and Latino labor history further signals the possibility that a consideration of race will structure, and not just appear episodically in, new attempts at synthesis in US working class history" (75). Some of the works Roediger credits with moving the field in this direction that appeared in the early 1990s are: Rick Halpern, "Race, Ethnicity and the Union in the Chicago Stockyards, 1917–1922," *International Review of Social History* 37 (1992): 25–58; Iver Bernstein, *The New York City Draft Riots: Their Significance for American Society and Politics in the Age of the Civil War* (1990), Eric Arnesen, *Waterfront Workers of New Orleans, Race, Class, and Politics* (1990), Eric Arnesen, "Rethinking the Historical Relationship between Black Workers and the Labor Movement," *Radical History Review* (1993); Wayne Durrill, *War of Another Kind: A Southern Community in the Great Rebellion* (1990), Nancy Quann Wickham, "Who Controls the Hiring Hall? The Struggle for Job Control in the ILWU during World War II," and Bruce Nelson, "Class and Race in the Crescent City: The ILWU from San Francisco to New Orleans," both in Steven Russwurm (ed.), *The CIO's Left-Led Unions* (1992), 19–68; the essays in Robert Zieger (ed.), *Organized Labor in the Twentieth Century South* (1991); Earl Lewis, *In Their Own Interest: Race, Class, and Power in Twentieth-Century Norfolk, Virginia* (1991); Joe William Trotter, *Coal, Class and Color: Blacks in Southern West Virginia, 1915–32* (1990); Robin D. G. Kelley, *Hammer and Hoe: Alabama Communists during the Great Depression* (1990) and "'We Are Not What We Seem': Rethinking Black Working-Class Opposition in the Jim Crow South," *Journal of American History* 80 (June 1993): 75–113; Mario T. Garcia, "Border Proletarians: Mexican-Americans and the International Union of Mine, Mill and Smelter Workers, 1939–1946," in Robin Asher and Charles Stephenson (eds.), *Labor Divided: Race and Ethnicity in United States Labor Struggles* (1990), 83–104. (See Roediger, *Towards the Abolition of Whiteness*, 80–1.)
48 Theodore W. Allen, *The Invention of the White Race, Volume One. Racial Oppression and Social Control* (London and New York: Verso, 1994).
49 Neil Foley, "'Almost White': Mexican Tenant Farmers and the Politics of Race in Socialist Central Texas, 1911–1917" (unpublished paper presented at the Southern Historical Association, Louisville, Kentucky, 11 November 1994).
50 George Lipsitz, "The Possessive Investment in Whiteness," 370.
51 Ibid.
52 Ibid., 372.
53 Jane Marcus, "Bonding and Bondage: Nancy Cunard and the Making of the Negro Anthology," in *Border, Boundaries & Frames: Cultural Criticism and Cultural Studies*, ed. Mae Henderson (New York: Routledge, 1994), 44–5.
54 Vron Ware, *Beyond the Pale: White Women, Racism and History* (London and New York: Verso, 1994).
55 Ruth Frankenberg, "Whiteness and Americanness: Explaining Constructions of Race, Culture and Nation in White Women's Life Narratives," in Gregory and Sanjek, *Race*, 62–77. See also Ruth Frankenberg, *White Women, Race Matters: The Social Construction of Whiteness* (Minneapolis: University of Minnesota Press, 1993).
56 Frankenberg, "Whiteness and Americanness," 66, 74.
57 Ibid., 75.
58 bell hooks, *Black Looks*, 12.

CHAPTER 4

The Blackness of Blackness: A Critique on the Sign and the Signifying Monkey

Henry Louis Gates

One of the most important voices in African American Studies in the US, Henry Louis Gates in his book *The Signifying Monkey* (1988) outlined an indigenous theory of African American literature that located in African sources the dominant motifs of African American literary practice. The Monkey is a trickster who in many folk poems and tales dupes his friend the Lion. He represents the dominant rhetorical form of Black literature, which, for Gates, consists of a tradition of writers who "trope" on their antecedents.

> *Signification is the Nigger's occupation.*
>
> Traditional[1]

> *Be careful what you do,*
> *Or Mumbo-Jumbo, God of the Congo,*
> *And all of the other*
> *Gods of the Congo,*
> *Mumbo-Jumbo will hoo-doo you,*
> *Mumbo-Jumbo will hoo-doo you,*
> *Mumbo-Jumbo will hoo-doo you.*
>
> Vachel Lindsay, *The Congo*

I need not trace in these pages the history of the concept of signification. Since Ferdinand de Saussure at least, signification has become a crucial aspect of much of contemporary theory. It is curious to me that this neologism in the Western tradition cuts across a term in the black vernacular tradition that is approximately two centuries old. Tales of the Signifying Monkey had their origins in slavery. Hundreds of these have been recorded since the nineteenth century. In black music, Jazz Gillum, Count Basie, Oscar Peterson, Oscar Browne, Jr., Little Willie Dixon, Nat "King" Cole, Otis Redding, Wilson Picket, and Johnny Otis – at least – have recorded songs called either "The Signifying Monkey" or simply "Signifyin(g)." My theory of interpretation, arrived at from within the black cultural matrix, is a theory of formal revisionism, it is tropological, it is often characterized by pastiche, and, most crucially, it turns on repetition of formal structures and their differences. Signification is a theory of reading that arises from Afro-American culture; learning how to signify is often part of our adolescent education. That it has not been drawn upon before as a theory of criticism attests to its sheer familiarity in the idiom. I had to step outside my culture, to defamiliarize the concept by translating it into a new mode of discourse, before I could see its potential in critical theory. My work with signification has now led me to undertake the analysis of the principles of interpretation implicit in the decoding of the signs used in the *Ifa* oracle, still very much alive among the Yoruba in Nigeria, in a manner only roughly related to Harold Bloom's use of the Kabbalah.

Signifyin(g): Definitions

Perhaps only Tar Baby is as enigmatic and compelling a figure from Afro-American mythic discourse as is that oxymoron, the Signifying Monkey.[2] The ironic reversal of a received racist image in the Western imagination of the black as simianlike, the Signifying Monkey – he who dwells at the margins of discourse, ever punning, ever troping, ever embodying the ambiguities of language – is our trope for repetition and revision, indeed our trope of chiasmus itself, repeating and reversing simultaneously as he does in one deft discursive act. If Vico and Burke or Nietzsche, de Man, and Bloom, are correct in identifying four and six master tropes, then we might think of these as the master's tropes and of signifying as the slave's trope, the trope of tropes, as Bloom characterizes metalepsis, "a trope-reversing trope, a figure of a figure." Signifying is a trope in which are subsumed several other rhetorical tropes, including metaphor, metonymy, synecdoche, and irony (the master tropes), and also hyperbole and litotes, and metalepsis (Bloom's supplement to Burke). To this list we could easily add aporia, chiasmus, and catechresis, all of which are used in the ritual of signifying.

Signifying, it is clear, in black discourse means modes of figuration itself. When one signifies, as Kimberly W. Benston puns, one "tropes-a-dope." Indeed, the black tradition itself has its own subdivisions of signifying, which we could readily identify with the typology of figures received from classical and medieval rhetoric, as Bloom has done with his "map of misprision." The black rhetorical tropes, subsumed under signifying, would include marking, loud-talking, testifying, calling out (of one's name), sounding, rapping, playing the dozens, and so on.[3]

Let us consider received definitions of the act of signifying and of black mythology's archetypal signifier, the Signifying Monkey. The Signifying Monkey is a trickster figure, of the order of the trickster figure of Yoruba mythology (*Esu-Elegbara* in Nigeria and *Legba* among the *Fon* in Dahomey), whose New World figurations (*Exu* in Brazil, *Echu-Elegua* in Cuba, *Papa Legba* in the pantheon of the *loa of Vaudou* in Haiti, and *Papa La Bas* in the *loa* of *Hoodoo* in the United States) speak eloquently of the unbroken arc of metaphysical presupposition and patterns of figuration shared through space and time among black cultures in West Africa, South America, the Caribbean, and in the United States. These trickster figures, aspects of *Esu*, are primarily mediators: as tricksters they are mediators, and their mediations are tricks.[4]

The versions of *Esu* are all messengers of the gods: he who interprets the will of god to people, he who carries the desires of people to the gods. *Esu* is guardian of the crossroads, master of style and the stylus, phallic god of generation and fecundity, master of the mystical barrier that separates the divine from the profane worlds. He is known as the divine linguist, the keeper of *ase* (*logos*) with which Olodumare created the universe.

In Yoruba mythology, *Esu* always limps because his legs are of different lengths: one is anchored in the realm of the gods, and the other rests in this human world.

The closest Western relative of *Esu*, of course, is Hermes; and, just as Hermes' role as interpreter lent his name readily to "hermeneutics," our metaphor for the study of the process of interpretation, so too can the figure of *Esu* stand as our metaphor for the act of interpretation itself for the critic of comparative black literature. In African and Latin American mythology, *Esu* is said to have taught *Ifa* how to read the signs formed by the sixteen sacred palmnuts which, when manipulated, configure into what is known as the signature of an *Odu*, two hundred and fifty-six of which comprise the corpus of *Ifa Divination*. The *Opon Ifa*, the carved wooden divination tray used in the art of interpretation, is said to contain at the center of its upper perimeter a carved image of *Esu*, meant to signify his relation to the act of interpretation, which we can translate either as *itumo* ("to unite or unknot knowledge") or as *yipada* ("to turn around or translate"). That which we now call close reading, the Yoruba call *Oda fa* ("reading the signs"). Above all else, *Esu* is the Black Interpreter, the Yoruba god of indeterminacy or *ariyemuye* (that which no sooner is held than it slips through one's fingers).[5] As Hermes is to hermeneutics, *Esu* is to *Esu tufunaalo* (bringing out the interstices of the riddle).

The *Esu* figures, among the Yoruba systems of thought in Dahomey and Nigeria, in Brazil and Cuba, in Haiti and at New Orleans, are divine; they are gods who function in sacred myths, as do characters in a narrative. *Esu*'s functional equivalent in Afro-American profane discourse is the Signifying Monkey, a figure who would seem to be distinctly Afro-American, probably derived from Cuban mythology, which generally depicts *Echu-Elegua* with a monkey at his side,[6] and who, unlike his Pan-African *Esu* cousins, exists in the discourse of mythology not primarily as a character in a narrative but rather as a vehicle for narration itself. It is from this corpus of narratives that signifying derives. The Afro-American rhetorical strategy of signifying is a rhetorical act that is not engaged in the game of information giving. Signifying turns on the play and chain of signifiers, and not on some supposedly transcendent signified. Alan Dundes suggests that the origins of signifying could "lie in African rhetoric." As anthropologists demonstrate, the Signifying Monkey is often called the Signifier, he who wreaks havoc upon the Signified. One is signified upon by the signifier. He is indeed the "signifier as such," in Julia Kristeva's phrase, "a presence that precedes the signification of object or emotion."[7]

Scholars have for some time commented upon the peculiar use of the word "signifying" in black discourse. Though sharing some connotations with the standard English-language word, "signifying" has rather unique definitions in black discourse. Roger D. Abrahams defines it as follows:

> Signifying seems to be a Negro term, in use if not in origin. It can mean any of a number of things; in the case of the toast about the signifying monkey, it certainly refers to the trickster's ability to talk with great innuendo, to carp, cajole, needle, and lie. It can mean in other instances the propensity to talk around a subject, never quite coming to the point. It can mean making fun of a person or situation. Also it can denote speaking with the hands and eyes, and in this respect encompasses a whole complex of expressions and gestures. Thus it is signifying to stir up a fight between neighbors by telling stories; it is signifying to make fun of a policeman by parodying his motions behind his back; it is signifying to ask for a piece of cake by saying, "my brother needs a piece of cake."[8]

Essentially, Abrahams concludes, signifying is a "technique of indirect argument or persuasion," "a language of implication," "to imply, goad, beg, boast, by indirect verbal or gestural means." "The name 'signifying,'" he concludes, "shows the monkey to be a trickster, signifying being the language of trickery, that set of words or gestures achieving Hamlet's 'direction through indirection.'" The monkey, in short, is not only a master of technique, as Abrahams concludes; he is technique, or style, or the literariness of literary language; he is the great Signifier. In this sense, one does not signify something; rather, one signifies in some way.[9]

There are thousands of "toasts" of the Signifying Monkey, most of which commence with a variant of the following formulaic lines:

> Deep down in the jungle so they say
> There's a signifying monkey down the way
> There hadn't been no disturbin' in the jungle for quite a bit,
> For up jumped the monkey in the tree one day and laughed,
> "I guess I'll start some shit."[10]

Endings, too, tend toward the formulaic, as in the following:

> "Monkey," said the Lion,
> Beat to his unbooted knees,
> "You and your signifying children
> Better stay up in the trees."
> Which is why today
> Monkey does his signifying
> A-way-up out of the way.[11]

In the narrative poems, the Signifying Monkey invariably repeats to his friend, the Lion, some insult purportedly generated by their mutual friend, the Elephant. The Lion, indignant and outraged, demands an apology of the Elephant, who refuses and then trounces the Lion. The Lion, realizing that his mistake was to take the monkey literally, returns to trounce the monkey. Although anthropologists and sociolinguists have succeeded in establishing a fair sample of texts of the Signifying Monkey, they have been less successful at establishing a consensus of definitions of black signifying.

In addition to Abrahams's definitions, definitions of signifying by Zora Neale Hurston, Thomas Kochman, Claudia Mitchell-Kernan, Geneva Smitherman, and Ralph Ellison are of interest here for what they reveal about the nature of Afro-American narrative parody, which I shall attempt first to define and then to employ in a reading of Ishmael Reed's *Mumbo Jumbo* as a pastiche of the Afro-American narrative tradition itself. Kochman argues that signifying depends upon the signifier repeating what someone else has said about a third person, in order to reverse the status of a relationship heretofore harmonious; signifying can also be employed to reverse or undermine pretense or even one's opinion about one's own status.[12] This use of repetition and reversal (chiasmus) constitutes an implicit parody of a subject's own complicity in illusion. Claudia Mitchell-Kernan, in perhaps the most thorough study of the concept, compares the etymology of "signifying" in black usage with usages from standard English:

> What is unique in Black English usage is the way in which signifying is extended to cover a range of meanings and events which are not covered in its Standard English usage. In the Black community it is possible to say, "He is signifying" and "Stop signifying" – sentences which would be anomalous elsewhere.[13]

Mitchell-Kernan points to the ironic, or dialectic, relationship between identical terms in standard and black English, which have vastly different meanings:

> The Black concept of signifying incorporates essentially a folk notion that dictionary entries for words are not always sufficient for interpreting meanings or messages, or that meanings goes beyond such interpretations. Complimentary remarks may be delivered in a left-handed fashion. A particular utterance may be an insult in one context and not another. What pretends to be informative may intend to be persuasive. The hearer is thus constrained to attend to all potential meaning carrying symbolic systems in speech events – the total universe of discourse.[14]

This is an excellent instance of the nature of signifying itself. Mitchell-Kernan refines these definitions somewhat by suggesting that the Signifying Monkey is able to signify upon the Lion only because the Lion does not understand the nature of the monkey's discourse: "There seems something of symbolic relevance from the perspective of language in this poem. The monkey and the lion do not speak the same language; the lion is not able to interpret the monkey's use of language." The monkey speaks figuratively, in a symbolic code; the lion interprets or reads literally and suffers the consequences of his folly, which is a reversal of his status as King of the Jungle. The monkey rarely acts in these narrative poems; he simply speaks. As the Signifier, he determines the actions of the Signified, the hapless Lion and the puzzled Elephant.[15]

As Mitchell-Kernan and Zora Neale Hurston attest, signifying is a sexless rhetorical game, despite the frequent use in the "masculine" versions of expletives that connote intimate relations with one's mother. Hurston, in *Mules and Men*, and Mitchell-Kernan, in her perceptive "Signifying, Loud-Talking, and Marking," are the first scholars to record and explicate female signifying rituals.[16] Zora Neale Hurston is the first author of the tradition to represent signifying itself as a vehicle of liberation for an oppressed woman, and as a rhetorical strategy in the narration of fiction.

Hurston, whose definition of the term in *Mules and Men* (1935) is one of the earliest in the linguistic literature, has made *Their Eyes Were Watching God* into a paradigmatic signifying text, for this novel resolves that implicit tension between the literal and the figurative contained in standard English usages of the term "signifying." *Their Eyes* represents the black trope of signifying both as thematic matter and as a rhetorical strategy of the novel itself. Janie, the protagonist, gains her voice on the porch of her husband's store, not only by engaging with the assembled men in the ritual of signifying (which her husband had expressly forbidden her to do) but also by openly signifying upon her husband's impotency. His image wounded fatally, her husband soon dies of a displaced "kidney" failure. Janie "kills" her husband rhetorically. Moreover, Hurston's masterful use of the indirect discourse allows her to signify upon the tension between the two voices of Jean Toomer's *Cane* by adding to direct and indirect speech a strategy through which she can privilege the black oral tradition, which Toomer found to be problematical and dying. Hurston's is the "speakerly text."

The text of *Their Eyes*, moreover, is itself a signifying structure, a structure of intertextual revision, because it revises key tropes and rhetorical strategies received from precursory texts, such as W. E. B. Du Bois's *A Quest of the Silver Fleece* and

Jean Toomer's *Cane*. Afro-American literary history is characterized by tertiary formal revision: Hurston's text (1937) revises Du Bois's novel (1911), and Toni Morrison in several texts revises Ellison and Hurston; similarly, Ellison (1951) revises Wright (1940, 1945), and Ishmael Reed (1972), among others, revises both. It is clear that black writers read and critique other black texts as an act of rhetorical self-definition. Our literary tradition exists because of these precisely chartable formal literary relationships.

The key aspect of signifying for Mitchell-Kernan is "its indirect intent or metaphorical reference," a rhetorical indirection which she says is "almost purely stylistic." Its art characteristics remain foregrounded. By "indirection," Mitchell-Kernan means that the correct semantic (referential interpretation) or signification of the utterance cannot be arrived at by a consideration of the dictionary meaning of the lexical items involved and the syntactic rules for their combination alone. The apparent significance of the message differs from its real significance. The apparent meaning of the sentence signifies its actual meaning.[17]

This rhetorical naming by indirection is, of course, central to our notions of figuration, troping, and of the parody of forms, or pastiche, in evidence when one writer repeats another's structure by one of several means, including a fairly exact repetition of a given narrative or rhetorical structure, filled incongruously with a ludicrous or incongruent content. T. Thomas Fortune's "The Black Man's Burden" is an excellent example of this form of pastiche, signifying as it does upon Kipling's "White Man's Burden":

> What is the Black Man's Burden,
> Ye hypocrites and vile,
> Ye whited sepulchres
> From th' Amazon to the Nile?
> What is the Black Man's Burden,
> Ye Gentile parasites,
> Who crush and rob your brother
> Of his manhood and his rights?

Dante Gabriel Rossetti's "Uncle Ned," a dialect verse parody of Stowe's *Uncle Tom's Cabin*, is a second example:

> Him tale dribble on and on widout a break,
> Till you hab no eyes for to see;
> When I reach Chapter 4 I had got a headache;
> So I had to let Chapter 4 be.

Another example of formal parody is to suggest a given structure precisely by failing to coincide with it – that is, to suggest it by dissemblance. Repetition of a form and then inversion of the same through a process of variation is central to jazz. A stellar example is John Coltrane's rendition of "My Favorite Things" compared to Julie Andrews's vapid original. Resemblance, then, can be evoked cleverly by dissemblance. Aristophanes's *The Frogs*, which parodies the styles of both Aeschylus and Euripides; Cervantes's relationship to the fiction of knight-errantry; Henry Fielding's parody of the Richardsonian novel of sentiment in *Joseph Andrews*, and Lewis Carroll's double parody in *Hiawatha's Photographing* (which draws upon Longfellow's rhythms to parody the convention of the family photograph) all come readily to mind. Ralph

Ellison defines the parody aspect of signifying in several ways relevant to our discussion below of the formal parody strategies at work in Ishmael Reed's *Mumbo Jumbo*.

In his complex short story "And Hickman Arrives" (1960), Ellison's narrator defines signifying in this way:

> And the two men [Daddy Hickman and Deacon Wilhite] standing side by side, the one large and dark, the other slim and light brown, the other reverends rowed behind them, their faces staring grim with engrossed attention to the reading of the Word, like judges in their carved, high-backed chairs. And the two voices beginning their call and countercall as Daddy Hickman began spelling out the text which Deacon Wilhite read, playing variations on the verses just as he did with his trombone when he really felt like signifying on a tune the choir was singing.[18]

Following this introduction, the two ministers demonstrate the definition of signification, which in turn is a signification upon the antiphonal structure of the Afro-American sermon. This parody of form is of the same order as Richard Pryor's parody of both the same sermonic structure and Stevie Wonder's "Living for the City," which he effects by speaking the lyrics of Wonder's song in the form of and with the intonation peculiar to the Afro-American sermon in his "reading" of "The Book of Wonder." Pryor's parody is a signification of the second order, revealing simultaneously the received structure of the sermon (by its presence, demystified here by its incongruous content), the structure of Wonder's music (by the absence of his form and the presence of his lyrics), and the complex yet direct formal relationship between the black sermon and Wonder's music specifically, as well as that between black sacred and secular narrative forms generally.

Ellison defines signifying in other ways as well. In his essay on Charlie Parker, entitled "On Bird, Bird-Watching, and Jazz" (1962), Ellison defines the satirical aspect of signifying as one aspect of riffing in jazz:

> But what kind of bird was Parker? Back during the thirties members of the old Blue Devils Orchestra celebrated a certain robin by playing a lugubrious little tune called "They Picked Poor Robin." It was a jazz community joke, musically an extended signifying riff or melodic naming of a recurrent human situation, and was played to satirize some betrayal of faith or loss of love observed from the bandstand.[19]

Here again, the parody is twofold, involving a formal parody of the melody of "They Picked Poor Robin" as well as a ritual naming, and therefore a troping, of an action observed from the bandstand.

Ellison, of course, is our Great Signifier himself, naming things by indirection and troping throughout his works. In his well-known review of LeRoi Jones's *Blues People*, Ellison defines signifying in yet a third sense, then signifies upon Jones's reading of Afro-American cultural history, which he argues is misdirected and wrongheaded. "The tremendous burden of sociology which Jones would place upon this body of music," writes Ellison, "is enough to give even the blues the blues." Ellison writes that Lydia Maria Child's title, *An Appeal in Favor of That Class of Americans called Africans*,

> sounds like a fine bit of contemporary ironic signifying – "signifying" here meaning, in the unwritten dictionary of American Negro usage, "rhetorical understatements." It

tells us much of the thinking of her opposition, and it reminds us that as late as the 1890s, a time when Negro composers, singers, dancers and comedians dominated the American musical stage, popular Negro songs (including James Weldon Johnson's "Under the Bamboo Tree," now immortalized by T. S. Eliot) were commonly referred to as "Ethiopian Airs."[20]

Ellison's stress upon "the unwritten dictionary of American Negro usage" reminds us of the problem of definitions, of signification itself, when one is translating between two languages. The Signifying Monkey, perhaps appropriately, seems to dwell at this space between two linguistic domains. One wonders, incidentally, about this Afro-American figure and a possible French connection between *signe* ("sign") and *singe* ("monkey").

Ellison's definition of the relation his works bear to those of Richard Wright constitutes our definition of narrative signification, pastiche, or critical parody, although he employs none of these terms. His explanation of what we might call implicit formal criticism, however, comprises what we have sometimes called troping, after Geoffrey Hartman, and which we might take to be a profound definition of critical signification itself. Writes Ellison:

> I felt no need to attack what I considered the limitations of [Wright's] vision because I was quite impressed by what he had achieved. And in this, although I saw with the black vision of Ham, I was, I suppose, as pious as Shem and Japheth. Still I would write my own books and they would be in themselves, implicitly, criticisms of Wright's; just as all novels of a given historical moment form an argument over the nature of reality and are, to an extent, criticisms each of the other.[21]

Ellison in his fictions signifies upon Wright by parodying Wright's literary structures through repetition and difference. Although this is not the place for a close reading of this formal relationship, the complexities of the parodying can be readily suggested. The play of language, the signifying, starts with the titles. *Native Son* and *Black Boy* – both titles connoting race, self, and presence – Ellison tropes with *Invisible Man*, invisibility an ironic response of absence to the would-be presence of "blacks" and "natives," while "man" suggests a more mature, stronger status than either "sons" or "boy." Ellison signifies upon Wright's distinctive version of naturalism with a complex rendering of modernism; Wright's reacting protagonist, voiceless to the last, Ellison signifies upon with a nameless protagonist who is nothing but voice, since it is he who shapes, edits, and narrates his own tale, thereby combining action with the representation of action, thereby defining reality by its representation. This unity of presence and representation is perhaps Ellison's most subtle reversal of Wright's theory of the novel as exemplified in *Native Son*, since Bigger's voicelessness and powerlessness to act (as opposed to react) signify an absence, despite the metaphor of presence found in the novel's title; the reverse obtains in *Invisible Man*, where the absence implied by invisibility is undermined by the presence of the narrator as the narrator of his own text.

There are other aspects of critical parody at play here, too, one of the funniest being Jack's glass eye plopping into his water glass before him, which is functionally equivalent to the action of Wright's protagonist in "The Man Who Lived Underground," as he stumbles over the body of a dead baby, deep down in the sewer. It is precisely at this point in the narrative that we know Fred Daniels to be "dead, baby," in the heavy-handed way that Wright's naturalism was self-consciously symbolic. If Daniels's fate is signified by the objects over which he stumbles in the darkness of the sewer, Ellison signifies upon Wright's novella by repeating this underground scene of discovery but having his protagonist burn the bits of paper through which he has allowed himself to be defined by others. By explicitly repeating and reversing key figures of Wright's fictions, and by defining implicitly in the process of narration a sophisticated form more akin to Hurston's *Their Eyes Were Watching God*, Ellison exposes naturalism to be merely a hardened convention of representation of "the Negro problem" and perhaps part of the problem itself. I cannot emphasize enough the major import of this narrative gesture to the subsequent development of black narrative forms, since Ellison recorded a new way of seeing and defined both a new manner of representation and its relation to the concept of presence. The formal relation that Ellison bears to Wright, Ishmael Reed bears to both, but principally to Ellison. Once again, Ellison has formulated this complex and inherently polemical intertextual relationship of formal signifying, in a refutation of Irving Howe's critique of his work: "I agree with Howe that protest is an element of all art, though it does not necessarily take the form of speaking for a political or social program. It might appear in a novel as a *technical assault against the styles* which have gone before [emphasis added]."[22] This form of critical parody, of repetition and inversion, is what I define to be critical signification, or formal signifying, and is my metaphor for literary history.

This chapter is a reading of the tertiary relationship among Reed's "post-modern" *Mumbo Jumbo* as a signification upon Wright's "realism" and Ellison's "modernism." The set of intertextual relations that I chart through formal signification is related to what Mikhail Bakhtin labels double-voiced discourse, which he subdivides into parodic narration and the hidden, or internal, polemic. These two types of double-voiced discourse can merge together, as they do in *Mumbo Jumbo*. Although Bakhtin's discourse typology is familiar, let me cite his definition of hidden polemic. In hidden polemic,

> the other speech act remains outside the boundaries of the author's speech, but it is implied or alluded to in that speech. The other speech act is not reproduced with a new intention, but shapes the author's speech while remaining outside its boundaries. Such is the nature of the hidden polemic....
>
> In hidden polemic the author's discourse is oriented toward its referential object, as in any other discourse, but at the same time each assertion about that object is constructed in such a way that, besides its referential meaning, the author's discourse brings a polemical attack to bear against another speech act, another assertion, on the same topic. Here one utterance focused on its referential object clashes with another utterance on the grounds of the referent itself. That other utterance is not reproduced; it is understood only in its import.[23]

Ellison's definition of the formal relationship his works bear to Wright's is a salient example of the hidden polemic: his texts clash with Wright's "on the ground of the referent itself." "As a result," Bakhtin continues, "the latter begins to influence the author's speech from within." This relationship Bakhtin calls double-voiced, whereby one speech act determines the internal structure of another, the second effecting the voice of the first, by absence, by difference.

Much of the Afro-American literary tradition can be read as successive attempts to create a new narrative space for representation of the recurring referent of

Afro-American literature, the so-called black experience. Certainly, we read the relation of Sterling Brown's regionalism to Jean Toomer's lyricism in this way, Hurston's lyricism to Wright's naturalism in this way, and Ellison's modernism to Wright's naturalism in this way as well. We might represent this set of relationships in the following schematic way, which is intended in no sense other than to be suggestive:[24]

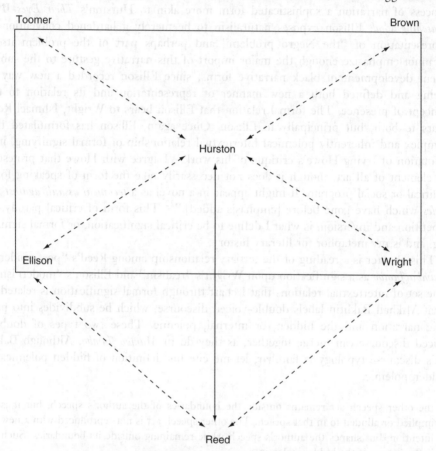

These relationships are reciprocal, because we are free to read in critical time machines, reading backwards, like Merlin moved through time. The direct relation most important to my own theory of reading is the solid black line that connects Reed with Hurston. Reed and Hurston seem to relish the play of the tradition, while Reed's work seems to be a magnificently conceived play on the tradition. Both Hurston and Reed write myths of Moses, both draw upon black sacred and secular myths discourse as metaphorical and metaphysical systems; both write self-reflexive texts which comment upon the nature of writing itself; both make use of the frame to bracket their narratives within narratives; and both are authors of fictions that I characterize as speakerly texts, texts that privilege the representation of the speaking black voice, of what the Formalists called *skaz*, and that Reed himself has defined as "an oral book, a talking book," a figure that occurs, remarkably enough, in four of the first five narratives in the black tradition in the eighteenth century.[25]

Reed's relation to these authors in the tradition is at all points double-voiced, since he seems to be especially concerned with employing satire to utilize literature in what

Northrop Frye calls "a special function of analysis, of breaking up the lumber of stereotypes, fossilized beliefs, superstitious terrors, crank theories, pedantic dogmatisms, oppressive fashions, and all other things that impede the free movement... of society."[26] Reed, of course, seems to be most concerned with the free movement of writing itself. In Reed's work, parody and hidden polemic overlap in a process Bakhtin describes thusly: "When parody becomes aware of substantial resistance, a certain forcefulness and profundity in the speech act it parodies, it takes on a new dimension of complexity via the tones of the hidden polemic.... A process of inner dialogization takes place within the parodic speech act."[27]

This internal dialogization can have curious implications, the most interesting of which perhaps is what Bakhtin describes as "the splitting of double-voice discourse into two speech acts, into the two entirely separate and autonomous voices." The clearest evidence that Reed in *Mumbo Jumbo* is signifying through parody as hidden polemic is his use of the two autonomous narrative voices, which he employs in the manner of, and renders through, foregrounding, to parody the two simultaneous stories of detective narration, that of the present and that of the past, in a narrative flow that moves hurriedly from cause to effect. In *Mumbo Jumbo*, however, the second narrative, that of the past, bears an ironic relation to the first narrative, that of the present, because it comments upon both the other narrative and the nature of its writing itself, in what Frye describes in another context as "the constant tendency to self-parody in satiric rhetoric which prevents even the process of writing itself from becoming an oversimplified convention or ideal." Reed's rhetorical strategy assumes the form of the relationship between the text and the criticism of that text, which serves as discourse upon that text.[28]

"Consult the Text"[29]

...A close reading of Reed's corpus of works suggests strongly that he seems to be concerned with the received form of the novel, with the precise rhetorical shape of the Afro-American literary tradition, and with the relation that the Afro-American tradition bears to the Western tradition. Reed's concerns, as exemplified in his narrative forms, would seem to be twofold: on the one hand with that relation his own art bears to his black literary precursors, whom we can identify to include Zora Neale Hurston, Richard Wright, James Baldwin, and Ralph Ellison, and on the other hand the process of willing into being a rhetorical structure, a literary language, replete with its own figures and tropes, but one that allows the black writer to posit a structure of feeling that simultaneously critiques both the metaphysical presuppositions inherent in Western ideas and forms of writing and the metaphorical system in which the blackness of the writer and his experience have been valorized as a "natural" absence. In the short term, that is, through six demanding novels,[30] Reed has apparently decided to criticize, through signification, what he seems to perceive to be the received and conventional structures of feeling that he has inherited from the Afro-American tradition itself, almost as if the sheer process of the analysis can clear a narrative space for his generation of writers as decidedly as Ellison's narrative response to Wright and naturalism cleared a space for Leon Forrest, Toni Morrison, Alice Walker, James Alan McPherson, and especially Reed himself.

By undertaking the difficult and subtle art of pastiche, Reed criticizes the Afro-American idealism of a transcendent black subject, integral and whole, self-sufficient and plentiful, the "always already" black signified, available for literary representation in received Western forms as would be the water ladled from a deep and dark well. Water can be poured into glasses or cups or canisters, but it remains water just the same. Put simply, Reed's fictions concern themselves with arguing that the so-called black experience cannot be thought of as a fluid content to be poured into received and static containers. For Reed, it is the signifier that both shapes and defines any discrete signified. And it is the signifiers of the Afro-American tradition with whom Reed is concerned.

This is not the place to read all of Reed's works against this thesis. Nevertheless, Reed's first novel lends credence to this sort of reading and also serves to create what we may call a set of generic expectations through which we read the rest of his works. His first novel, *The Free-Lance Pallbearers*, is, above all else, a parody of the confessional mode which is the fundamental, undergirding convention of Afro-American narrative, received, elaborated upon, and transmitted in a chartable heritage from Briton Hammon's captivity narrative of 1760 through the antebellum slave narratives to black autobiography into black fiction, especially the fictions of Hurston, Wright, Baldwin, and Ellison.[31] This narrative of Bukka Doopeyduk is a pastiche of the classic black narrative of the questing protagonist's "journey into the heart of whiteness"; but it parodies this narrative form by turning it inside out, exposing the character of the originals, and thereby defining their formulaic closures and disclosures. Doopeyduk's tale ends with his own crucifixion. As the narrator of his own story, therefore, Doopeyduk articulates literally from among the dead an irony implicit in all confessional and autobiographical modes, in which any author is forced by definition to imagine himself or herself to be dead. More specifically, Reed signifies upon *Black Boy* and *Go Tell It on the Mountain* in a foregrounded critique which can be read as an epigraph to the novel: "*read growing up in Soulsville first of three installments/ or what it means to be a backstage darkey.*" The "scat-singing voice" that introduces the novel, Reed foregrounds against the "other" voice of Doopeyduk, whose "second" voice narrates the novel's plot. Here, Reed parodies both Hurston's use of free indirect discourse in *Their Eyes Were Watching God* and Ellison's use of the foregrounded voice in the prologue and epilogue of *Invisible Man*, which frame his nameless protagonist's picaresque account of his own narrative. In *Yellow Back Radio Broke Down*, Reed more fully and successfully critiques both realism and modernism, as exemplified in a kind of writing that one character calls "those suffering books I wrote about my old neighborhood and how hard it was."[32]

Reed's third novel, *Mumbo Jumbo*, is about writing itself; not only in the figurative sense of the post-modern, self-reflexive text but also in a literal sense: "So Jes Grew is seeking its words. Its text. For what good is a liturgy without a text?" (*Mumbo Jumbo*, p. 6.) *Mumbo Jumbo* is both a book about texts and a book of texts, a composite narrative composed of subtexts, pretexts, post-texts, and narratives within narratives. It is both a definition of Afro-American culture and its deflation. "The Big Lie concerning Afro-American culture," *Mumbo Jumbo*'s dust jacket informs us, "is that it lacks a tradition." The big truth of the novel, on the other hand, is that this very tradition is as rife with hardened convention and presupposition as is the rest of the Western tradition. Even this cryptic riddle of Jes Grew and its text parodies Ellison: *Invisible Man*'s plot is set in motion with a riddle, while the theme of the relationship between words and texts echoes a key passage from Ellison's short story "And Hickman Arrives": "Good. Don't talk like I talk, talk like I say talk. Words are your business boy. Not just the word. Words are everything. The key to the Rock, the answer to the question."[33]

Let us examine the book's dust jacket. The signifying begins with the book's title. "*Mumbo Jumbo*" is the received and ethnocentric Western designation for both the rituals of black religions and all black languages themselves. A vulgarized Western translation of a Swahili phrase (*mambo, jambo*), *Mumbo Jumbo*, as *Webster's Third International Dictionary* defines it, connotes "language that is unnecessarily involved and difficult to understand: GIBBERISH." The Oxford English Dictionary cites its etymology as being "of unknown origin," implicitly serving here as the signified on which Reed's title signifies, recalling the myth of Topsy who "jes grew," with no antecedents, a phrase with which James Weldon Johnson characterizes the creative process of black sacred music. *Mumbo Jumbo*, then, signifies upon Western etymology, abusive Western practices of deflation through misnaming, as well as Johnson's specious designation of the anonymity of creation, which indeed is a major component of the Afro-American cultural tradition.

But there is more parody in this title. Whereas Ellison tropes the myth of presence in Wright's titles of *Native Son* and *Black Boy* through his title of *Invisible Man*, inverting the received would-be correlation between blackness and presence with a narrative strategy that correlates invisibility (ultimate sign of absence) with the presence of self-narration and therefore self-creation, Reed parodies all three titles by employing as his title the English-language parody of black language itself. Whereas the etymology of "*Mumbo Jumbo*" has been problematical for Western lexicographers, any Swahili speaker knows that the phrase derives from the common greeting *jambo* and its plural, *mambo*, which loosely translated means "What's happening?" Reed is also echoing Vachel Lindsay's ironic poem *The Congo*, cited as an epigraph to this essay, which proved to be so fatally influencing to the Harlem Renaissance poets, as Charles Davis has shown.[34] From its title on, the novel serves as a critique of black and Western literary forms and conventions, and complex relationships between the two.

Let us proceed with our examination of the book's cover. A repeated and reversed image of a crouching, sensuous Josephine Baker sits back to back, superimposed upon a rose. Counterposed to this image is a medallion containing a horse with two riders. These signs adumbrate the two central oppositions of the novel's complicated plot: the rose and the double image of Josephine Baker together form a cryptic *vé vé*. A *vé vé* is a key sign in Vaudou, a sign drawn on the ground with sand, cornmeal, flour, and coffee to represent the *loa*. The *loa* are the deities who comprise the pantheon of Vaudou's gods. The rose is a sign of Ezrulie, goddess of love, home, and purity, as are the images of Josephine Baker, who became the French goddess of love in the late 1920s, in their version of the Jazz Age. The doubled image, as if mirrored, is meant to suggest the divine crossroads, where human beings meet their fate, but also at the center of which presides the *loa*, Legba (*Esu*), guardian of the divine crossroads, messenger of the gods, the figure representing the interpreter and interpretation itself, the muse or loa of the critic. It is *Legba* who is master of that mystical barrier that separates the divine from the profane worlds. It is this complex yet cryptic *vé vé* that is meant both to placate *Legba* himself and to summon his attention and integrity in a double act of criticism and interpretation: that of Reed in the process of his representation of the tradition, to be found between the covers of the book, and that of the critic's interpretation of Reed's figured interpretation.

Located outside the *vé vé* as counterpoint, placed almost off the cover itself, is the sign of the Knights Templar, representing the heart of the Western tradition. The opposition represented here is between two distinct warring forces, two mutually exclusive modes of reading. Already, we are in the realm of doubles, but not the binary realm; rather, we are in the realm of doubled doubles. Not only are two distinct and conflicting metaphysical systems here represented and invoked, but Reed's cover also serves as an overture to the critique of dualism and binary opposition that serves as a major thrust to the text of *Mumbo Jumbo* itself. As we shall see, Reed also parodies this dualism (which Reed thinks is exemplified in Ellison's *Invisible Man*) in another text.

This critique of dualism is implicit in the novel's central speaking character, Papa La Bas. I emphasize speaking here because the novel's central character, of course, is Jes Grew itself, which never speaks and is never seen in its "abstract essence," only in discrete manifestations or "outbreaks." Jes Grew is the supraforce that sets the text of *Mumbo Jumbo* in motion, as it and Reed seek their texts, as all characters and events define themselves against this omnipresent, compelling force. Jes Grew, here, is a clever and subtle parody of similar forces invoked in the black novel of naturalism, most notably in Wright's *Native Son*.

Unlike Jes Grew, Papa La Bas does indeed speak. It is he who is the chief detective, in hard and fast pursuit of both Jes Grew and its text. This character's name is a conflation of two of the several names of *Esu*, the Pan-African trickster. Called Papa Legba, as his Haitian honorific, and invoked through the phrase "Eh La-Bas" in New Orleans jazz recordings of the twenties and thirties, Papa La Bas is the Afro-American trickster figure from black sacred tradition. His name, of course, is French for "over there," and his presence unites "over there" (Africa) with "right here." He is indeed the messenger of the gods, the divine Pan-African interpreter, pursuing, in the language of the text, "the Work"; which is not only Vaudou but also the very work (and play) of art itself. Papa La Bas is the figure of the critic in search of the text, decoding its tell-tale signs in the process. Even the four syllables of his name recall the text's play of doubles. Chief Sign Reader, La Bas is also, in a sense, a sign himself. Indeed, Papa La Bas's incessant and ingenious search for the text of Jes Grew, culminating as it does in his recitation and revision of the myth of Thoth's gift of writing to civilization, constitutes an argument against what Reed elsewhere terms "the so-called oral tradition" and in favor of the primacy and priority of the written text over the speaking voice. It is a brief for the permanence of the written text, for the need for criticism, for which La Bas's myth of origins also accounts. "Guides were initiated into the Book of Thoth, the 1st anthology written by the 1st choreographer" (*Mumbo Jumbo*, p. 167)....

Reed's signifying relation to Ellison is exemplified in his poem "Dualism: in Ralph Ellison's *Invisible Man*":

> i am outside of
> history. i wish
> i had some peanuts; it
> looks hungry there in
> its cage.

> i am inside of
> history. its hungrier than i
> thot.

The figure of history here is the Signifying Monkey; the poem signifies upon that repeated trope of dualism figured initially in black discourse in W. E. B. Du Bois's essay "Of Our Spiritual Strivings," which forms the first chapter of *The Souls of Black Folk*. The dualism parodied by Reed's poem is that represented in the epilogue of *Invisible Man*: "now I know men are different and that all life is divided and that only in division is there true health" (p. 499). For Reed, this belief in the reality of dualism spells death. Ellison here has refigured Du Bois's trope, which bears full citation:

> After the Egyptian and Indian, the Greek and Roman, the Teuton and Mongolian, the Negro is a sort of seventh son, born with a veil, and gifted with second-sight in this American world, – a world which yields him no true self-consciousness, but only lets him see himself through the revelation of the other world. It is a peculiar sensation, this double-consciousness, this sense of always looking at one's self through the eyes of others, measuring one's soul by the tape of a world that looks on in amused contempt and pity. One ever feels his twoness, – an American, a Negro; two souls, two thoughts, two unreconciled strivings; two warring ideals in one dark body, whose dogged strength alone keeps it from being torn asunder.
>
> The history of the American Negro is the history of this strife, – this longing to attain self-conscious manhood, to merge his double self into a better and truer self. In this merging he wishes neither of the older selves to be lost.[35]

Reed's poem parodies profoundly both the figure of the black as outsider and the figure of the divided self. For, he tells us, even these are only tropes, figures of speech, rhetorical constructs like "double-consciousness," and not some preordained reality or thing. To read these figures literally, Reed tells us, is to be duped by figuration, just like the Signified Lion. Reed has secured his place in the canon precisely by his critique of the received, repeated tropes peculiar to that very canon. His works are the grand works of critical signification.

Notes

1 Quoted in Roger D. Abrahams, *Deep Down in the Jungle: Negro Narrative Folklore from the Streets of Philadelphia* (Chicago: Aldine, 1970), p. 53.

2 On "Tar Baby," see Ralph Ellison, *Shadow and Act* (New York: Vintage Books, 1964), p. 147; and Toni Morrison, *Tar Baby* (New York: Alfred A. Knopf, 1981). On the black as quasi-simian, see Jean Bodin, *Method for the Easy Comprehension of History*, trans. Beatrice Reynolds (New York: Octagon Books, 1966), p. 105; Aristotle, *Historia Animalum*, trans. D'Arcy W. Thompson, in J. A. Smith and W. D. Ross (eds.), *The Works of Aristotle IV* (Oxford: Oxford University Press, 1910), 606b; Thomas Herbert, *Some Years Travels* (London: R. Everingham, 1677), pp. 16–17; John Locke, *An Essay Concerning Human Understanding* (London: A. Churchill and A. Manship, 1721), book III, chapter 6, section 23.

3 Geneva Smitherman defines these and other black tropes, then traces their use in several black texts. Smitherman's work, like that of Claudia Mitchell-Kernan and Roger Abrahams, is especially significant for literary theory. See Geneva Smitherman, *Talkin' and Testifyin': The Language of Black America* (Boston: Houghton Mifflin, 1977), pp. 101–67. See notes 12 and 13 below.

4   On versions of *Esu*, see Robert Parris Thompson, *Black Gods and Kings* (Bloomington: Indiana University Press, 1976), pp. 4/14/12, and Robert Farris Thompson, *Flash of the Spirit* (New York: Random House, 1983); Pierre Verger, *Notes sur le Culte des Orisa et Vodun* (Dakar: I.F.A.N., 1957); Joan Westcott, "The Sculpture and Myths of Eshu-Elegba," *Africa* XXXII, 4, pp. 336–53; Leo Frobenius, *The Voice of Africa* (London: Hutchinson, 1913); Melville J. and Frances Herskovits, *Dahomean Narrative* (Evanston, Ill.: Northwestern University Press, 1958); Wande Abimbola, *Sixteen Great Poems of Ifa* (New York: UNESCO, 1975); William R. Bascom, *Ifa Divination* (Bloomington: Indiana University Press, 1969); Ayodele Ogundipe, *Esu Elegbara: The Yoruba God of Chance and Uncertainty*, dissertation, Indiana University, 1978; E. Bolaji Idowu, *Olodiumare, God in Yoruba Belief* (London: Longman, 1962), pp. 80–5; Robert Pelton, *The Trickster in West Africa* (Los Angeles: University of California Press, 1980).

5   On *Esu* and indeterminacy, see Robert Plant Armstrong, *The Powers of Presence: Consciousness, Myth, and Affecting Presence* (Philadelphia: University of Pennsylvania Press, 1981), p. 4. See p. 43 for a drawing of *Opon Ifa*; and Thompson, *Black Gods and Kings*, ch. 5.

6   On *Esu* and the monkey, see Lydia Cabrerra, *El Monte: Notes sobre las religiones, la magía, las supersticiónes y el folklore de los negros criollos y el pueblo de Cuba* (Miami: Ediciones Universal, 1975), p. 84; and Alberto del Pozo, *Oricha* (Miami: Oricha, 1982), p. 1. On the Signifying Monkey, see Abrahams, *Deep Down in the Jungle*, pp. 51–3, 66, 113–19, 142–7, 153–6, and especially p. 264; Bruce Jackson, *"Get Your Ass in the Water and Swim Like Me": Narrative Poetry from Black Oral Tradition* (Cambridge, MA: Harvard University Press, 1974), pp. 161–80; Daryl Cumber Dance, *Shuckin' and Jivin': Folklore from Contemporary Black Americans* (Bloomington: Indiana University Press, 1978), pp. 197–9; Dennis Wepman, R. B. Newman, and M. B. Binderman, *The Life: The Lore and Folk Poetry of the Black Hustler* (Philadelphia: University of Pennsylvania Press, 1976), pp. 21–30; Lawrence W. Levine, *Black Culture and Black Consciousness: Afro-American Folk Thought from Slavery to Freedom* (New York: Oxford University Press, 1977), pp. 346, 378–80, 438; and Richard M. Dorson, *American Negro Folktales* (New York: Fawcett, 1967), pp. 98–9.

7   Julia Kristeva, *Desire in Language: A Semiotic Approach to Literature and Art* (New York: Columbia University Press, 1980), p. 31.

8   See Abrahams, *Deep Down in the Jungle*, pp. 51–3, 66, 113–19, 142–7, 153–6, and especially p. 264; Roger D. Abrahams, "Playing the Dozens," *Journal of American Folklore* 75 (1962), pp. 209–20; Roger D. Abrahams, "The Changing Concept of the Negro Hero," in Moody C. Boatright, Wilson M. Hudson, and Allen Maxwell (eds.), *The Golden Log* (Dallas: Texas Folklore Society, 1962), pp. 125 ff.; and Roger D. Abrahams, *Talking Black* (Rowley, Mass: Newbury House, 1976).

9   Abrahams, *Deep Down in the Jungle*, pp. 51–2, 66–7, p. 264. Abrahams's awareness of the need to define uniquely black significations is exemplary; as early as 1964, when he published the first edition of *Deep Down in the Jungle*, he saw fit to add a glossary as an appendix of "Unusual Terms and Expressions," a title that unfortunately suggests the social scientist's apologia. (Emphasis added.)

10 Quoted in Abrahams, *Deep Down in the Jungle*, p. 113. In the second line of the stanza, "motherfucker" is often substituted for "monkey."

11 "The Signifying Monkey," in Langston Hughes and Arna Bontemps (eds.), *Book of Negro Folklore* (New York: Dodd, Mead, 1958), pp. 365–6.

12 On signifying as a rhetorical trope, see Smitherman, *Talkin' and Testifyin'*, pp. 101–67; Thomas Kochman, *Rappin' and Stylin' Out: Communication in Urban Black America* (Urbana: University of Illinois Press, 1972); and Thomas Kochman, "'Rappin' in the Black Ghetto," *Trans-Action* 6, no. 4 (February 1969), p. 32; Alan Dundes, *Mother Wit from the Laughing Barrel* (Englewood Cliffs, NJ: Prentice-Hall, 1973), p. 310; Ethel M. Albert, "'Rhetoric,' 'Logic,' and 'Poetics' in Burund: Culture Patterning of Speech Behavior," in John J. Gumperz and Dell Hymes (eds.), *The Ethnography of Communication, American Anthropologist* 66, no. 6 (1964), pp. 35–54. One example of signifying can be gleaned from the following anecdote. While writing this essay, I asked a colleague, Dwight Andrews, if he had heard of the Signifying Monkey as a child. "Why, no" he replied intently. "I never heard of the Signifying

Monkey until I came to Yale and read about him in a book." I had been signified upon. If I had responded to Andrews, "I know what you mean; your Mama read to me from that same book the last time I was in Detroit," I would have signified upon him in return. See especially note 15 below.

13 Claudia Mitchell-Kernan, "Signifying," in Dundes, *Mother Wit*, p. 313; and Claudia Mitchell-Kernan, "Signifying, Loud-Talking, and Marking," in Kochman, *Rappin' and Stylin' Out*, pp. 315–36. For Zora Neale Hurston's definition of the term, see *Mules and Men: Negro Folktales and Voodoo Practices in the South* (New York: Harper and Row, 1970), p. 161.

14 Mitchell-Kernan, "Signifying," p. 314.

15 Ibid., pp. 323–5.

16 Mitchell-Kernan, "Signifying, Loud-Talking, and Marking," pp. 315–36.

17 Mitchell-Kernan, "Signifying," p. 325.

18 Ralph Ellison, "And Hickman Arrives," in Richard Barksdale and Keneth Kinnamon, eds., *Black Writers of America* (New York: Macmillan, 1972), p. 704.

19 Ralph Ellison, "On Bird, Bird-Watching, and Jazz," *Saturday Review*, July 20, 1962, reprinted in Ellison, *Shadow and Act*, p. 231.

20 Ralph Ellison, "Blues People," in Ellison, *Shadow and Act*, pp. 249, 250. The essay was first printed in *New York Review of Books*, February 6, 1964.

21 Ralph Ellison, "The World and the Jug," in Ellison, *Shadow and Act*, p. 117. The essay appeared first in *The New Leader*, December 9, 1963.

22 Ellison, *Shadow and Act*, p. 137.

23 Mikhail Bakhtin, "Discourse Typology in Prose," in Ladislas Matejka and Krytyna Pomorska, eds., *Readings in Russian Poetics: Formalist and Structuralist Views* (Cambridge, Mass.: MIT Press, 1971), pp. 176–99.

24 The use of interlocking triangles as a metaphor for the intertextual relationships of the tradition is not meant to suggest any form of concrete, inflexible reality. On the contrary, it is a systematic metaphor, as René Girard puts it, "systematically pursued." As Girard says (emphasis added): "The triangle is no Gestalt. The real structures are intersubjective. They cannot be localized anywhere; the triangle has no reality whatever; it is a systematic metaphor, systematically pursued. Because changes in size and shape do not destroy the identity of this figure, as we will see later, the diversity as well as the unity of the works can be simultaneously illustrated. The purpose and limitations of this structural geometry may become clearer through a reference to 'structural models.' The triangle is a model of a sort, or rather a whole family of models. But these models are not 'mechanical' like those of Claude Lévi-Strauss. They always allude to the mystery, transparent yet opaque, of human relations. All types of structural thinking assume that human reality is intelligible; it is a logos and, as such, it is an incipient logic, or it degrades itself into a logic.

"It can thus be systematized, at least up to a point, however unsystematic, irrational, and chaotic it may appear even to those, or rather especially to those who operate the system." (René Girard, *Deceit, Desire, and the Novel: Self and Other in Literary Structure* (Baltimore: Johns Hopkins University Press, 1965), pp. 2–3.)

25 For Ishmael Reed on "a talking book," see "Ishmael Reed: A Self Interview," *Black World*, June 1974, p. 25. For the slave narratives in which this figure appears, see James Albert Ukawsaw Gronniosaw, *A Narrative of the Most Remarkable Particulars of the Life of James Albert Ukawsaw Gronniosaw, An African Prince* (Bath, 1770); John Marrant, *Narrative of the Lord's Wonderful Dealings with John Marrant, A Black* (London: Gilbert and Plummer, 1785); Ottabah Cugoano, *Thoughts and Sentiments on the Evil and Wicked Traffic of the Slavery and Commerce of the Human Species* (London, 1787); and Olaudah Equiano, *The Interesting Narrative of the Life of Olaudah Equiano, or Gustavus Vassa, The African. Written by Himself* (London: printed for the author, 1789).

26 Northrop Frye, *Anatomy of Criticism* (Princeton: Princeton University Press, 1971), p. 233.

27 Bakhtin, "Discourse Typology," p. 190.

28 Frye, *Anatomy of Criticism*, p. 103.

29 Ellison, *Shadow and Act*, p. 140.

30 *The Free-Lance Pallbearers* (Garden City: Doubleday, 1967); *Yellow Back Radio Broke Down* (Garden City: Doubleday, 1969); *Mumbo Jumbo* (Garden City: Doubleday, 1972); *The Last Days of Louisiana Red* (New York: Random House, 1974); *Flight to Canada* (New York: Random House, 1976); *The Terrible Twos* (New York: St Martin's/Marek, 1982).

31 Neil Schmitz, "Neo-Hoodoo: The Experimental Fiction of Ishmael Reed," *20th Century Literature* 20, no. 2 (April 1974), pp. 126–8. Schmitz's splendid reading is, I believe, the first to discuss this salient aspect of Reed's rhetorical strategy.

32 For an excellent close reading of *Yellow Back Radio Broke Down*, see Michel Fabre, "Postmodern Rhetoric in Ishmael Reed's *Yellow Back Radio Broke Down*," in Peter Bruck and Wolfgang Karrer, eds., *The Afro-American Novel Since 1960* (Amsterdam: B. R. Gruner, 1982), pp. 167–88.

33 Ellison, "And Hickman Arrives," p. 701.

34 Charles T. Davis, *Black Is the Color of the Cosmos: Essays on Black Literature and Culture, 1942–1981*, ed. Henry Louis Gates, Jr (New York: Garland, 1982), pp. 167–233.

35 W. E. B. Du Bois, *The Souls of Black Folk* (New York: Fawcett, 1961), pp. 16–17.

CHAPTER 5

Playing in the Dark

Toni Morrison

Novelist Toni Morrison brought her intelligence to bear on questions of literary criticism in *Playing in the Dark* (1992), a series of lectures in which she took up the question of the place of African Americans in American literature. Drawing in this selection on the work of sociologist Orlando Patterson, who argues that the American concept of liberty depended for its definition on the existence of African slavery in America, she discusses the way the literature of the European-descended White population takes an "Africanist" presence for granted.

> *I am moved by fancies that are curled*
> *Around these images, and cling:*
> *The notion of some infinitely gentle*
> *Infinitely suffering thing.*
>
> T. S. Eliot, *"Preludes, IV"*

These chapters put forth an argument for extending the study of American literature into what I hope will be a wider landscape. I want to draw a map, so to speak, of a critical geography and use that map to open as much space for discovery, intellectual adventure, and close exploration as did the original charting of the New World – without the mandate for conquest. I intend to outline an attractive, fruitful, and provocative critical project, unencumbered by dreams of subversion or rallying gestures at fortress walls.

I would like it to be clear at the outset that I do not bring to these matters solely or even principally the tools of a literary critic. As a reader (before becoming a writer) I read as I had been taught to do. But books revealed themselves rather differently to me as a writer. In that capacity I have to place enormous trust in my ability to imagine others and my willingness to project consciously into the danger zones such others may represent for me. I am drawn to the ways all writers do this: the way Homer renders a heart-eating cyclops so that our hearts are wrenched with pity; the way Dostoevsky compels intimacy with Svidrigailov and Prince Myshkin. I am in awe of the authority of Faulkner's Benjy, James's Maisie, Flaubert's Emma, Melville's Pip, Mary Shelley's Frankenstein – each of us can extend the list.

I am interested in what prompts and makes possible this process of entering what one is estranged from – and in what disables the foray, for purposes of fiction, into corners of the consciousness held off and away from the reach of the writer's imagination. My work requires me to think about how free I can be as an African-American woman writer in my genderized, sexualized, wholly racialized world. To think about (and wrestle with) the full implications of my situation leads me to consider what happens when other writers work in a highly and historically racialized society. For them, as for me, imagining is not merely looking or looking at; nor is it taking oneself intact into the other. It is, for the purposes of the work, *becoming*.

My project rises from delight, not disappointment. It rises from what I know about the ways writers transform aspects of their social grounding into aspects of language, and the ways they tell other stories, fight secret wars, limn out all sorts of debates blanketed in their text. And rises from my certainty that writers always know, at some level, that they do this.

For some time now I have been thinking about the validity or vulnerability of a certain set of assumptions conventionally accepted among literary historians and critics and circulated as "knowledge." This knowledge holds that traditional, canonical American literature is free of, uninformed, and unshaped by the four-hundred-year-old presence of, first, Africans and then African-Americans in the United States. It assumes that this presence – which shaped the body politic, the Constitution, and the entire history of the culture – has had no significant place or consequence in the origin and development of that culture's literature. Moreover, such knowledge assumes that the characteristics of our national literature emanate from a particular "Americanness" that is separate from and unaccountable to this presence. There seems to be a more or less tacit agreement among literary scholars that, because American literature has been clearly the preserve of white male views, genius, and power, those views, genius, and power are without relationship to and removed from the overwhelming presence of black people in the United States. This agreement is made about a population that preceded every American writer of renown and was, I have come to believe, one of the most furtively radical impinging forces on the country's literature. The contemplation of this black presence is central to any understanding of our national literature and should not be permitted to hover at the margins of the literary imagination.

These speculations have led me to wonder whether the major and championed characteristics of our national literature – individualism, masculinity, social engagement versus historical isolation; acute and ambiguous moral problematics; the thematics of innocence coupled with an obsession with figurations of death and hell – are not in fact responses to a dark, abiding, signing Africanist presence. It has occurred to me that the very manner by which American literature distinguishes itself as a coherent entity exists because of this unsettled and unsettling population. Just as the formation of the nation necessitated coded language and purposeful restriction to deal with the racial disingenuousness and moral frailty at its heart, so too did the literature, whose founding characteristics extend into the twentieth century, reproduce the necessity for codes and restriction. Through significant and underscored omissions, startling contradictions, heavily nuanced conflicts, through the way writers peopled their work with the signs and bodies of this presence – one can see that a real or fabricated Africanist presence was crucial to their sense of Americanness. And it shows.

My curiosity about the origins and literary uses of this carefully observed, and carefully invented, Africanist presence has become an informal study of what I call American Africanism. It is an investigation into the ways in which a nonwhite, Africanlike (or Africanist) presence or persona was constructed in the United States, and the imaginative uses this fabricated presence served. I am using the term "Africanism" not to suggest the larger body of knowledge on Africa that the philosopher Valentine Mudimbe means by the term "Africanism," nor to suggest the varieties and complexities of African people and their descendants who have inhabited this country. Rather I use it as a term for the denotative and connotative blackness that African peoples have come to signify, as well as the entire range of views, assumptions, readings, and misreadings that accompany Eurocentric learning about these people. As a trope, little restraint has been attached to its uses. As a disabling virus within literary discourse, Africanism has become, in the Eurocentric tradition that American education favors, both a way of talking about and a way of policing matters of class, sexual license, and repression, formations and exercises of power, and meditations on ethics and accountability. Through the simple expedient of demonizing and reifying the range of color on a palette, American Africanism makes it possible to say and not say, to inscribe and erase, to escape and engage, to act out and act on, to historicize and render timeless. It provides a way of contemplating chaos and civilization, desire and fear, and a mechanism for testing the problems and blessings of freedom. The United States, of course, is not unique in the construction of Africanism. South America, England, France, Germany, Spain – the cultures of all these countries have participated in and contributed to some aspect of an "invented Africa." None has been able to persuade itself for long that criteria and knowledge could emerge outside the categories of domination. Among Europeans and the Europeanized, this shared process of exclusion – of assigning designation and value – has led to the popular and academic notion that racism is a "natural," if irritating, phenomenon. The literature of almost all these countries, however, is now subject to sustained critiques of its racialized discourse. The United States is a curious exception, even though it stands out as being the oldest democracy in which a black population accompanied (if one can use that word) and in many cases preceded the white settlers. Here in that nexus, with its particular formulations, and in the absence of real knowledge or open-minded inquiry about Africans and African-Americans, under the pressures of ideological and imperialistic rationales for subjugation, an American brand of Africanism emerged: strongly urged, thoroughly serviceable, companionably ego-reinforcing, and pervasive. For excellent reasons of state – because European sources of cultural hegemony were dispersed but not yet valorized in the new country – the process of organizing American coherence through a distancing Africanism became the operative mode of a new cultural hegemony.

These remarks should not be interpreted as simply an effort to move the gaze of African-American studies to a different site. I do not want to alter one hierarchy in order to institute another. It is true that I do not want to encourage those totalizing approaches to African-American scholarship which have no drive other than the exchange of dominations – dominant Eurocentric scholarship replaced by dominant Afrocentric scholarship. More interesting is what makes intellectual domination possible; how knowledge is transformed from invasion and conquest to revelation and choice; what ignites and informs the literary imagination, and what forces help establish the parameters of criticism.

Above all I am interested in how agendas in criticism have disguised themselves and, in so doing, impoverished the literature it studies. Criticism as a form of knowledge is capable of robbing literature not only of its own implicit and explicit ideology but of its ideas as well; it can dismiss the difficult, arduous work writers do to make an art that becomes and remains part of and significant within a human landscape. It is important to see how inextricable Africanism is or ought to be from the deliberations of literary criticism and the wanton, elaborate strategies undertaken to erase its presence from view.

What Africanism became for, and how it functioned in, the literary imagination is of paramount interest because it may be possible to discover, through a close look at literary "blackness," the nature – even the cause – of literary "whiteness." What is it *for*? What parts do the invention and development of whiteness play in the construction of what is loosely described as "American"? If such an inquiry ever comes to maturity, it may provide access to a deeper reading of American literature – a reading not completely available now, not least, I suspect, because of the studied indifference of most literary criticism to these matters.

One likely reason for the paucity of critical material on this large and compelling subject is that, in matters of race, silence and evasion have historically ruled literary discourse. Evasion has fostered another, substitute language in which the issues are encoded, foreclosing open debate. The situation is aggravated by the tremor that breaks into discourse on race. It is further complicated by the fact that the habit of ignoring race is understood to be a graceful, even generous, liberal gesture. To notice is to recognize an already discredited difference. To enforce its invisibility through silence is to allow the black body a shadowless participation in the dominant cultural body. According to this logic, every well-bred instinct argues *against noticing* and forecloses adult discourse. It is just this concept of literary and scholarly moeurs (which functions smoothly in literary criticism, but neither makes nor receives credible claims in other disciplines) that has terminated the shelf life of some once extremely well-regarded American authors and blocked access to remarkable insights in their works.

These moeurs are delicate things, however, which must be given some thought before they are abandoned. Not observing such niceties can lead to startling displays of scholarly lapses in objectivity. In 1936 an American scholar investigating the use of Negro so-called dialect in the works of Edgar Allan Poe (a short article clearly proud of its racial equanimity) opens this way: "Despite the fact that he grew up largely in the south and spent some of his most fruitful years in Richmond and Baltimore, Poe has little to say about the darky."[1]

Although I know this sentence represents the polite parlance of the day, that "darky" was understood to be a term more acceptable than "nigger," the grimace I made upon reading it was followed by an alarmed distrust of the scholar's abilities. If it seems unfair to reach back to the thirties for samples of the kind of lapse that can occur when certain manners of polite repression are waived, let me assure you equally egregious representations of the phenomenon are still common.

Another reason for this quite ornamental vacuum in literary discourse on the presence and influence of Africanist peoples in American criticism is the pattern of thinking about racialism in terms of its consequences on the victim – of always defining it assymetrically from the perspective of its impact on the object of racist policy and attitudes. A good deal of time and intelligence has been invested in the exposure of racism and the horrific results on its objects. There are constant, if erratic, liberalizing efforts to legislate these matters. There are also powerful and persuasive attempts to analyze the origin and fabrication of racism itself, contesting the assumption that it is an inevitable, permanent, and eternal part of all social landscapes. I do not wish to disparage these inquiries. It is precisely because of them that any progress at all has been accomplished in matters of racial discourse. But that well-established study should be joined with another, equally important one: the impact of racism on those who perpetuate it. It seems both poignant and striking how avoided and unanalyzed is the effect of racist inflection on the subject. What I propose here is to examine the impact of notions of racial hierarchy, racial exclusion, and racial vulnerability and availability on nonblacks who held, resisted, explored, or altered those notions. The scholarship that looks into the mind, imagination, and behavior of slaves is valuable. But equally valuable is a serious intellectual effort to see what racial ideology does to the mind, imagination, and behavior of masters.

Historians have approached these areas, as have social scientists, anthropologists, psychiatrists, and some students of comparative literature. Literary scholars have begun to pose these questions of various national literatures. Urgently needed is the same kind of attention paid to the literature of the western country that has one of the most resilient Africanist populations in the world – a population that has always had a curiously intimate and unhingingly separate existence within the dominant one. When matters of race are located and called attention to in American literature, critical response has tended to be on the order of a humanistic nostrum – or a dismissal mandated by the label "political." Excising the political from the life of the mind is a sacrifice that has proven costly. I think of this erasure as a kind of trembling hypochondria always curing itself with unnecessary surgery. A criticism that needs to insist that literature is not only "universal" but also "race-free" risks lobotomizing that literature, and diminishes both the art and the artist.

I am vulnerable to the inference here that my inquiry has vested interests; that because I am an African-American and a writer I stand to benefit in ways not limited to intellectual fulfillment from this line of questioning. I will have to risk the accusation because the point is too important: for both black and white American writers, in a wholly racialized society, there is no escape from racially inflected language, and the work writers do to unhobble the imagination from the demands of that language is complicated, interesting, and definitive.

Like thousands of avid but nonacademic readers, some powerful literary critics in the United States have never read, and are proud to say so, *any* African-American text. It seems to have done them no harm, presented them with no discernible limitations in the scope of their work or influence. I suspect, with much evidence to support the suspicion, that they will continue to flourish without any knowledge whatsoever of African-American literature. What is fascinating, however, is to observe how their lavish exploration of literature manages *not* to see meaning in the thunderous, theatrical presence of black surrogacy – an informing, stabilizing, and disturbing element – in the literature they do study. It is interesting, not surprising, that the arbiters of critical power in American literature seem to take pleasure in, indeed relish, their ignorance of African-American texts. What is surprising is that their refusal to read black texts – a refusal that makes no disturbance in their intellectual life – repeats itself when they reread the traditional, established works of literature worthy of their attention.

It is possible, for example, to read Henry James scholarship exhaustively and never arrive at a nodding mention, much less a satisfactory treatment, of the black woman who lubricates the turn of the plot and becomes the agency of moral choice and meaning in *What Maisie Knew*. Never are we invited to a reading of "The Beast in the Jungle" in which that figuration is followed to what seems to me its logical conclusion. It is hard to think of any aspect of Gertrude Stein's *Three Lives* that has not been covered, except the exploratory and explanatory uses to which she puts the black woman who holds center stage in that work. The urgency and anxiety in Willa Cather's rendering of black characters are liable to be missed entirely; no mention is made of the problem that race causes in the technique and the credibility of her last novel, *Sapphira and the Slave Girl*. These critics see no excitement or meaning in the tropes of darkness, sexuality, and desire in Ernest Hemingway or in his cast of black men. They see no connection between God's grace and Africanist "othering" in Flannery O'Connor. With few exceptions, Faulkner criticism collapses the major themes of that writer into discursive "mythologies" and treats the later works – whose focus is race and class – as minor, superficial, marked by decline.

An instructive parallel to this willed scholarly indifference is the centuries-long, hysterical blindness to feminist discourse and the way in which women and women's issues were read (or unread). Blatant sexist readings are on the decline, and where they still exist they have little effect because of the successful appropriation by women of their own discourse.

National literatures, like writers, get along the best way they can, and with what they can. Yet they do seem to end up describing and inscribing what is really on the national mind. For the most part, the literature of the United States has taken as its concern the architecture of a *new white man*. If I am disenchanted by the indifference of literary criticism toward examining the range of that concern, I do have a lasting resort: the writers themselves.

Writers are among the most sensitive, the most intellectually anarchic, most representative, most probing of artists. The ability of writers to imagine what is not the self, to familiarize the strange and mystify the familiar, is the test of their power. The languages they use and the social and historical context in which these languages signify are indirect and direct revelations of that power and its limitations. So it is to them, the creators of American literature, that I look for clarification about the invention and effect of Africanism in the United States.

My early assumptions as a reader were that black people signified little or nothing in the imagination of white American writers. Other than as objects of an occasional bout of jungle fever, other than to provide local color or to lend some touch of verisimilitude or to supply a needed moral gesture, humor, or bit of pathos, blacks made no appearance at all. This was a reflection, I thought, of the marginal impact that blacks had on the lives of the characters in the work as well as the creative imagination of the author. To imagine or write otherwise, to situate black people throughout the pages and scenes of a book like some government quota, would be ludicrous and dishonest.

But then I stopped reading as a reader and began to read as a writer. Living in a racially articulated and predicated world, I could not be alone in reacting to this aspect of the American cultural and historical condition. I began to see how the literature I revered, the literature I loathed, behaved in its encounter with racial ideology. American literature could not help being shaped by that encounter. Yes, I wanted to identify those moments when American literature was complicit in the fabrication of racism, but equally important, I still wanted to see when literature exploded and undermined it. Still, those were minor concerns. Much more important was to contemplate how Africanist personae, narrative, and idiom moved and enriched the text in self-conscious ways, to consider what the engagement meant for the work of the writer's imagination.

How does literary utterance arrange itself when it tries to imagine an Africanist other? What are the signs, the codes, the literary strategies designed to accommodate this encounter? What does the inclusion of Africans or African-Americans do to and for the "work." As a reader my assumption had always been that nothing "happens": Africans and their descendants were not in any sense that matters, *there*; and when they were there, they were decorative – displays of the agile writer's technical expertise. I assumed that since the author was not black, the appearance of Africanist characters or narrative or idiom in a work could never be *about* anything other than the "normal," unracialized, illusory white world that provided the fictional backdrop. Certainly no American text of the sort I am discussing was ever written *for* black people – no more than *Uncle Tom's Cabin* was written for Uncle Tom to read or be persuaded by. As a writer reading, I came to realize the obvious: the subject of the dream is the dreamer. The fabrication of an Africanist persona is reflexive; an extraordinary meditation on the self; a powerful exploration of the fears and desires that reside in the writerly conscious. It is an astonishing revelation of longing, of terror, of perplexity, of shame, of magnanimity. It requires hard work *not* to see this.

It is as if I had been looking at a fishbowl – the glide and flick of the golden scales, the green tip, the bolt of white careening back from the gills; the castles at the bottom, surrounded by pebbles and tiny, intricate fronds of green; the barely disturbed water, the flecks of waste and food, the tranquil bubbles traveling to the surface – and suddenly I saw the bowl, the structure that transparently (and invisibly) permits the ordered life it contains to exist in the large world. In other words, I began to rely on my knowledge of how books get written, how language arrives; my sense of how and why writers abandon or take on certain aspects of their project. I began to rely on my understanding of what the linguistic struggle requires of writers and what they make of the surprise that is the inevitable concomitant of the act of creation. What became transparent were the self-evident ways that Americans choose to talk about themselves through and within a sometimes allegorical, sometimes metaphorical, but always choked representation of an Africanist presence. I have made much here of a kind of willful critical blindness – a blindness that, if it had not existed, could have made these insights part of our routine literary heritage. Habit, manners, and political agenda have contributed to this refusal of critical insight. A case in point is Willa Cather's *Sapphira and the Slave Girl*, a text that has been virtually jettisoned from the body of American literature by critical consensus. References to this novel in much Cather scholarship are apologetic, dismissive, even cutting in their brief documentation of its flaws – of which there are a sufficient number. What remains less acknowledged is the source of its flaws and the conceptual problems that the book both poses and represents. Simply to assert the failure of Cather's gifts, the exhaustion of her perception, the narrowing of her canvas, evades the obligation to look carefully at what might have caused the book to fail – if "failure" is an intelligent term to apply to any fiction. (It is as if the realms of fiction and reality were divided by a line that, when maintained, offers the possibility of winning but, when crossed, signals the inevitability of losing.)

I suspect that the "problem" of *Sapphira and the Slave Girl* is not that it has a weaker vision or is the work of a weaker mind. The problem is trying to come to terms critically and artistically with the novel's concerns: the power and license of a white slave mistress over her female slaves. How can that *content* be subsumed by some other meaning? How can the story of a white mistress be severed from a consideration of race and the violence entailed in the story's premise? If *Sapphira and the Slave Girl* neither pleases nor engages us, it may be enlightening to discover why. It is as if this last book – this troublesome, quietly dismissed novel, very important to Cather – is not only about a fugitive but is itself a fugitive from its author's literary estate. It is also a book that describes and inscribes its narrative's own fugitive flight from itself. Our first hint of this flight appears in the title, *Sapphira and the Slave Girl*. The girl referred to is named Nancy. To have called the book "Sapphira and Nancy" would have lured Cather into dangerous deep water. Such a title would have clarified and drawn attention immediately to what the novel obscures even as it makes a valiant effort at honest engagement: the sycophancy of white identity. The story, briefly, is this.

Sapphira Colbert, an invalid confined to her chair and dependent on slaves for the most intimate services, has persuaded herself that her husband is having or aching to have a liaison with Nancy, the pubescent daughter of her most devoted female slave. It is clear from the beginning that Mistress Colbert is in error: Nancy is pure to the point of vapidity; Master Colbert is a man of modest habits, ambition, and imagination. Sapphira's suspicions, fed by her feverish imagination and by her leisure to have them, grow and luxuriate unbearably. She forms a plan. She will invite a malleable lecherous nephew, Martin, to visit and let his nature run its course: Nancy will be seduced. The purpose of arranging the rape of her young servant is to reclaim, for purposes not made clear, the full attentions of her husband.

Interference with these plans comes from Sapphira's daughter, Rachel, estranged from her mother primarily for her abolitionist views but also, we are led to believe, because Sapphira does not tolerate opposition. It is Rachel who manages to effect Nancy's escape to the north and freedom, with the timid help of her father, Mr. Colbert. A reconciliation of all of the white characters takes place when the daughter loses one of her children to diphtheria and is blessed with the recuperation of the other. The reconciliation of the two key black characters is rendered in a postscript in which many years later Nancy returns to see her aged mother and recount her post-flight adult narrative to the author, a child witnessing the return and the happiness that is the novel's dénouement. The novel was published in 1940, but has the shape and feel of a tale written or experienced much earlier.

This précis in no way does justice to the novel's complexities and its problems of execution. Both arise, I believe, not because Cather was failing in narrative power, but because of her struggle to address an almost completely buried subject: the interdependent working of power, race, and sexuality in a white woman's battle for coherence.

In some ways this novel is a classic fugitive slave narrative: a thrilling escape to freedom. But we learn almost nothing of the trials of the fugitive's journey because the emphasis is on Nancy's fugitive state within the house *before her escape*. And the real fugitive, the text asserts, is the slave mistress. Furthermore, the plot escapes the author's control and, as its own fugitive status becomes clear, is destined to point to the hopelessness of excising racial considerations from formulations of white identity.

Escape is the central focus of Nancy's existence on the Colbert farm. From the moment of her first appearance, she is forced to hide her emotions, her thoughts, and eventually her body from pursuers. Unable to please Sapphira, plagued by the jealousy of the darker-skinned slaves, she is also barred from help, instruction, or consolation from her own mother, Till. That condition could only prevail in a slave society where the mistress can count on (and an author can believe the reader does not object to) the complicity of a mother in the seduction and rape of her own daughter. Because Till's loyalty to and responsibility for her mistress is so primary, it never occurs and need not occur to Sapphira that Till might be hurt or alarmed by the violence planned for her only child. That assumption is based on another – that slave women are not mothers; they are "natally dead," with no obligations to their offspring or their own parents.

This breach startles the contemporary reader and renders Till an unbelievable and unsympathetic character. It is a problem that Cather herself seems hard put to address. She both acknowledges and banishes this wholly unanalyzed mother–daughter relationship by inserting a furtive exchange between Till and Rachel in chapter 10:

> . . . Till asked in a low, cautious murmur: "You ain't heard nothin', Miss Rachel?"
> "Not yet. When I do hear, I'll let you know. I saw her into good hands, Till. I don't doubt she's in Canada by this time, amongst English people."
> "Thank you, mam, Miss Rachel. I can't say no more. I don't want them niggers to see me cryin'. If she's up there with the English folks, she'll have some chance."[2]

The passage seems to come out of nowhere because there has been nothing in a hundred or so pages to prepare us for such maternal concern. "You ain't heard nothin'?" Till asks of Rachel. Just that – those four words – meaning: Is Nancy all right? Did she arrive safely? Is she alive? Is anybody after her? All of these questions lie in the one she does manage to ask. Surrounding this dialogue is the silence of four hundred years. It leaps out of the novel's void and out of the void of historical discourse on slave parent–child relationships and pain. The contemporary reader is relieved when Till finally finds the language and occasion to make this inquiry about the fate of her daughter. But nothing more is made of it. And the reader is asked to believe that the silence surrounding the inquiry as well as its delay are due to Till's greater concern about her status among dark-skinned "field" niggers. Clearly Cather was driven to create the exchange not to rehabilitate Till in our readerly eyes but because at some point the silence became an unbearable violence, even in a work full of violence and evasion. Consider the pressures exerted by the subject: the need to portray the faithful slave; the compelling attraction of exploring the possibilities of one woman's absolute power over the body of another woman; confrontation with an uncontested assumption of the sexual availability of black females; the need to make credible the bottomless devotion of the person on whom Sapphira was dependent. It is after all *hers*, this slave woman's body, in a way that her own invalid flesh is not. These fictional demands stretch to breaking all narrative coherence. It is no wonder that Nancy cannot think up her own escape and must be urged into taking the risk.

Nancy has to hide her interior life from hostile fellow slaves *and* her own mother. The absence of camaraderie between Nancy and the other slave women turns on the device of color fetish – the skin-color privilege that Nancy enjoys because she is lighter than the others and therefore enviable. The absence of mother love, always a troubling concern of Cather's, is connected to the assumption of a slave's natal isolation. These are bizarre and disturbing deformations of reality that normally lie mute in novels containing Africanist characters, but Cather does not repress them altogether. The character she creates is at once a fugitive within the household and a sign of the sterility of the fiction-making imagination when there is no available language to clarify or even name the source of unbelievability.

Interestingly, the other major cause of Nancy's constant state of flight is wholly credible: that she should be unarmed in the face of the nephew's sexual assault and that she alone is responsible for extracting herself from the crisis. We do not question her vulnerability. What becomes titillating in this wicked pursuit of innocence – what makes it something other than an American variant of *Clarissa* – is the racial component. The nephew is not even required to court or flatter Nancy. After an unsuccessful reach for her from the branches of a cherry tree, he can, and plans to, simply arrive wherever she is sleeping. And since Sapphira has ordered her to sleep in the hall on a pallet, Nancy is forced to sneak away in the dark to quarters where she may be, but is not certain to be, safe. Other than Rachel, the pro-abolitionist, Nancy has access to no one to whom she can complain, explain, object, or from whom she can seek protection. We must accept her total lack of initiative, for there are no exits. She has no recourse – except in miserable looks that arouse Rachel's curiosity.

Nor is there any law, if the nephew succeeds in the rape, to entertain her complaint. If she becomes pregnant as a result of the violence, the issue is a boon to the economy of the estate, not an injury to it. There is no father or, in this case, "stepfather" to voice a protest on Nancy's behalf, since honor was the first thing stripped from the man. He is a "capon," we are told, given to Till so that she will have no more children and can give her full attention and energy to Mistress Sapphira.

Rendered voiceless, a cipher, a perfect victim, Nancy runs the risk of losing the reader's interest. In a curious way, Sapphira's plotting, like Cather's plot, is without reference to the characters and exists solely for the ego-gratification of the slave mistress. This becomes obvious when we consider what would have been the consequences of a successful rape. Given the novel's own terms, there can be no grounds for Sapphira's thinking that Nancy can be "ruined" in the conventional sense. There is no question of marriage to Martin, to Colbert, to anybody. Then, too, why would such an assault move her slave girl outside her husband's interest? The probability is that it would secure it. If Mr Colbert is tempted by Nancy the chaste, is there anything in slavocracy to make him disdain Nancy the unchaste?

Such a breakdown in the logic and machinery of plot construction implies the powerful impact race has on narrative – and on narrative strategy. Nancy is not only the victim of Sapphira's evil, whimsical scheming. She becomes the unconsulted, appropriated ground of Cather's inquiry into what is of paramount importance to the author: the reckless, unabated power of a white woman gathering identity unto herself from the wholly available and serviceable lives of Africanist others. This seems to me to provide the coordinates of an immensely important moral debate.

This novel is not a story of a mean, vindictive mistress; it is the story of a desperate one. It concerns a troubled, disappointed woman confined to the prison of her defeated flesh, whose social pedestal rests on the sturdy spine of racial degradation; whose privileged gender has nothing that elevates it except color, and whose moral posture collapses without a whimper before the greater necessity of self-esteem, even though the source of that esteem is a delusion. For Sapphira too is a fugitive in this novel, committed to escape: from the possibility of developing her own adult personality and her own sensibilities, from her femaleness; from motherhood; from the community of women; from her body.

She escapes the necessity of inhabiting her own body by dwelling on the young, healthy, and sexually appetizing Nancy. She has transferred its care into the hands of others. In this way she escapes her illness, decay, confinement, anonymity, and physical powerlessness. In other words, she has the leisure and the instruments to construct a self; but the self she constructs must be – is conceivable only as – white. The surrogate black bodies become her hands and feet, her fantasies of sexual intimacy with her husband and not inconsiderably, her sole source of love.

If the Africanist characters and their condition are removed from the text of *Sapphira and the Slave Girl* we will not have a Miss Havisham immured or in flames. We have nothing: no process of deranged self-construction that can take for granted acquiescence in so awful an enterprise; no drama of limitless power. Sapphira can hide far more successfully than Nancy. She can, and does, remain outside the normal requirements of adult womanhood because of the infantilized Africanist population at her disposal.

The final fugitive in Cather's novel is the novel itself. The plot's own plotting to free the endangered slave girl (of no apparent interest, as we have seen, to the girl's mother or her slave associates) is designed for quite other purposes. It functions as a means for the author to meditate on the moral equivalence of free white women and enslaved black women. The fact that these equations are designed as mother–daughter pairings and relationships leads to the inescapable conclusion that Cather was dreaming and redreaming her problematic relationship with her own mother.

The imaginative strategy is a difficult one at best, an impossible one in the event – so impossible that Cather permits the novel to escape from the pages of fiction into nonfiction. For narrative credibility she substitutes her own determination to force the equation. It is an equation that must take place outside the narrative.

Sapphira and the Slave Girl turns at the end into a kind of memoir, the author's recollection of herself as a child witnessing the return, the reconciliation, and an imposed "all rightness" in untenable, outrageous circumstances. The silenced, acquiescent Africanist characters in the narrative are not less muzzled in the epilogue. The reunion – the drama of it, like its narrative function – is no more the slave characters' than their slave lives have been. The reunion is literally stage-managed for the author, now become a child. Till agrees to wait until little Willa is at the doorway before she permits herself the first sight she has had of her daughter in twenty-five years.

Only with Africanist characters is such a project thinkable: delayed gratification for the pleasure of a (white) child. When the embrace is over, Willa the white child accompanies the black mother and daughter into their narrative, listening to the dialogue but intervening in it at every turn. The shape and detail and substance of their lives are hers, not theirs. Just as Sapphira has employed these surrogate, serviceable black bodies for her own purposes of power without risk so the author employs them in behalf of her own desire for a *safe* participation in loss, in love, in chaos, in justice.

But things go awry. As often happens, characters make claims, impose demands of imaginative accountability over and above the author's will to contain them. Just as Rachel's intervention foils Sapphira's plot, so Cather's urgent need to know and understand this Africanist mother and daughter requires her to give them center stage. The child Cather listens to Till's stories, and the slave, silenced in the narrative, has the final words of the epilogue.

Yet even, or especially, here where the novel ends Cather feels obliged to gesture compassionately toward slavery. Through Till's agency the elevating benevolence of the institution is invoked. Serviceable to the last, this Africanist presence is permitted speech only to reinforce the slaveholders' ideology, in spite of the fact that it subverts the entire premise of the novel. Till's voluntary genuflection is as ecstatic as it is suspicious.

In returning to her childhood, at the end of her writing career, Cather returns to a very personal, indeed private experience. In her last novel she works out and toward the meaning of female betrayal as it faces the void of racism. She may not have arrived safely, like Nancy, but to her credit she did undertake the dangerous journey.

Notes

1 Killis Campbell, "Poe's Treatment of the Negro and of the Negro Dialect," *Studies in English* 16 (1936), p. 106.
2 Willa Cather, *Sapphira and the Slave Girl* (New York: Alfred A. Knopf, 1940), p. 49.

CHAPTER 6

Borderlands/La Frontera

Gloria Anzaldua

In her remarkable and celebrated book, *Borderlands/La Frontera* (1987) Chicana American writer Gloria Anzaldua explores the intermeshing of her personal experiences growing up along the border between the US and Mexico with the history of the land. That history included the forced expropriation by European Americans of land occupied by Hispanics. Anzaldua's discussion ranges from geography to language to sexuality.

Movimientos de rebeldía y las culturas que traicionan

Esos movimientos de rebeldía que tenemos en la sangre nosotros los mexicanos surgen como ríos desbocanados en mis venas. Y como mi raza que cada en cuando deja caer esa esclavitud de obedecer, de callarse y aceptar, en mi está la rebeldía encimita de mi carne. Debajo de mi humillada mirada está una cara insolente lista para explotar. Me costó muy caro mi rebeldía – acalambrada con desvelos y dudas, sintiendome inútil, estúpida, e impotente.

Me entra una rabia cuando alguien – sea mi mamá, la Iglesia, la cultura de los anglos – me dice haz esto, haz eso sin considerar mis deseos.

Repele. Hable pa' 'tras. Fui muy hocicona. Era indiferente a muchos valores de mi cultura. No me deje de los hombres. No fui buena ni obediente.

Pero he crecido. Ya no soló paso toda mi vida botando las costumbres y los valores de mi cultura que me traicionan. También recojo las costumbres que por el tiempo se han provado y las costumbres de respeto a las mujeres. But despite my growing tolerance, for this Chicana *la guerra de independencia* is a constant.

The Strength of My Rebellion

I have a vivid memory of an old photograph: I am six years old. I stand between my father and mother, head cocked to the right, the toes of my flat feet gripping the ground. I hold my mother's hand.

To this day I'm not sure where I found the strength to leave the source, the mother, disengage from my family, *mi tierra, mi gente*, and all that picture stood for. I had to leave home so I could find myself, find my own intrinsic nature buried under the personality that had been imposed on me.

I was the first in six generations to leave the Valley, the only one in my family to ever leave home. But I didn't leave all the parts of me: I kept the ground of my own being. On it I walked away, taking with me the land, the Valley, Texas. *Gané mi camino y me largué. Muy andariega mi hija.* Because I left of my own accord *me dicen,* "*¿Cómo te gusta la mala vida?*"

At a very early age I had a strong sense of who I was and what I was about and what was fair. I had a stubborn will. It tried constantly to mobilize my soul under my own regime, to live life on my own terms no matter how unsuitable to others they were. *Terca.* Even as a child I would not obey. I was "lazy." Instead of ironing my younger brothers' shirts or cleaning the cupboards, I would pass many hours studying, reading, painting, writing. Every bit of self-faith I'd painstakingly gathered took a beating daily. Nothing in my culture approved of me. *Había agarrado malos pasos.* Something was "wrong" with me. *Estaba mas alla de la tradición.*

There is a rebel in me – the Shadow-Beast. It is a part of me that refuses to take orders from outside authorities. It refuses to take orders from my conscious will, it threatens the sovereignty of my rulership. It is that part of me that hates constraints of any kind, even those self-imposed. At the least hint of limitations on my time or space by others, it kicks out with both feet. Bolts.

Cultural Tyranny

Culture forms our beliefs. We perceive the version of reality that it communicates. Dominant paradigms, predefined concepts that exist as unquestionable, unchallenge-able, are transmitted to us through the culture. Culture is made by those in power – men. Males make the rules and laws; women transmit them. How many times have I heard mothers and mothers-in-law tell their sons to beat their wives for not obeying them, for being *hociconas* (big mouths), for being *callajeras* (going to visit and gossip with neighbors), for expecting their husbands to help with the rearing of children and the housework, for wanting to be something other than housewives?

The culture expects women to show greater acceptance of, and commitment to, the value system than men. The culture and the Church insist that women are subservient to males. If a woman rebels she is a *mujer mala.* If a woman doesn't renounce herself in favor of the male, she is selfish. If a woman remains a *virgen* until she marries, she is a good woman. For a woman of my culture there used to be only three directions she could turn: to the Church as a nun, to the streets as a prostitute, or to the home as a mother. Today some of us have a fourth choice: entering the world by way of education and career and becoming self-autonomous persons. A very few of us. As a working-class people our chief activity is to put food in our mouths, a roof over our heads and clothes on our backs. Educating our children is out of reach for most of us. Educated or not, the onus is still on woman to be a wife/mother – only the nun can escape motherhood. Women are made to feel total failures if they don't marry and have children. "*¿Y cuándo te casas, Gloria? Se te va a pasar el tren.*" [Marriage will pass you by.] *Y yo les digo, "Pos si me caso, no va ser con un hombre." Se quedan calladitas. Sí, soy hija de la Chingada.* I've always been her daughter. *No 'tés chingando.*

Humans fear the supernatural, both the undivine (the animal impulses such as sexuality, the unconscious, the unknown, the alien) and the divine (the superhuman, the god in us). Culture and religion seek to protect us from these two forces. The female, by virtue of creating entities of flesh and blood in her stomach (she bleeds every month but does not die), by virtue of being in tune with nature's cycles, is feared. Because, according to Christianity and most other major religions, woman is carnal, animal, and closer to the undivine, she must be protected. Protected from herself. Woman is the stranger, the other. She is man's recognized nightmarish pieces, his Shadow-Beast. The sight of her sends him into a frenzy of anger and fear.

La gorra, el rebozo, la mantilla are symbols of my culture's "protection" of women. Culture (read males) professes to protect women. Actually it keeps women in rigidly defined roles. It keeps the girl child from other men – don't poach on my preserves, only I can touch my child's body. Our mothers taught us well, "*Los hombres nomás quieren una cosa*"; men aren't to be trusted, they are selfish and are like children. Mothers made sure we didn't walk into a room of brothers or fathers or uncles in nightgowns or shorts. We were never alone with men, not even those of our own family.

Through our mothers, the culture gave us mixed messages: *No voy a dejar que ningún pelado desgraciado maltrate a mis hijos.* And in the next breath it would say, *La mujer tiene que hacer lo que le diga el hombre.* Which was it to be – strong, or submissive, rebellious or conforming?

Tribal rights over those of the individual insured the survival of the tribe and were necessary then, and, as in the case of all indigenous peoples in the world who are still fighting off intentional, premeditated murder (genocide), they are still necessary.

Much of what the culture condemns focuses on kinship relationships. The welfare of the family, the community, and the tribe is more important than the welfare of the individual. The individual exists first as kin – as sister, as father, as *padrino* – and last as self.

In my culture, selfishness is condemned, especially in women; humility and self-lessness, the absence of selfishness, is considered a virtue. In the past, acting humble with members outside the family ensured that you would make no one *envidioso* (envious); therefore he or she would not use witchcraft against you. If you get above yourself, you're an *envidiosa*. If you don't behave like everyone else, *la gente* will say that you think you're better than others, *que te crees grande*. With ambition (condemned in the Mexican culture and valued in the Anglo) comes envy. *Respeto* carries with it a set of rules so that social categories and hierarchies will be kept in order: respect is reserved for *la abuela, papá, el patrón*, those with power in the community. Women are at the bottom of the ladder, one rung above the deviants. The Chicano, *mexicano*, and some Indian cultures have no tolerance for deviance. Deviance is whatever is condemned by the community. Most societies try to get rid of their deviants. Most cultures have burned and beaten their homosexuals and others who deviate from the sexual common.[1] The queer are the mirror reflecting the hererosexual tribe's fear: being different, being other and therefore lesser, therefore sub-human, inhuman, non-human.

Half and Half

There was a *muchacha* who lived near my house. *La gente del pueblo* talked about her being *una de las otras*, "of the Others." They said that for six months she was a woman who had a vagina that bled once a month, and that for the other six months she was a man, had a penis and she peed standing up. They called her half and half, *mita' y mita'*, neither one nor the other but a strange doubling, a deviation of nature that horrified, a work of nature inverted. But there is a magic aspect in abnormality and so-called deformity. Maimed, mad, and sexually different people were believed to possess supernatural powers by primal cultures' magico-religious thinking. For them, abnormality was the price a person had to pay for her or his inborn extraordinary gift.

There is something compelling about being both male and female, about having an entry into both worlds. Contrary to some psychiatric tenets, half and halfs are not suffering from a confusion of sexual identity, or even from a confusion of gender. What we are suffering from is an absolute despot duality that says we are able to be only one or the other. It claims that human nature is limited and cannot evolve into something better. But I, like other queer people, am two in one body, both male and female. I am the embodiment of the *hieros gamos:* the coming together of opposite qualities within.

Fear of Going Home: Homophobia

For the lesbian of color, the ultimate rebellion she can make against her native culture is through her sexual behavior. She goes against two moral prohibitions: sexuality and homosexuality. Being lesbian and raised Catholic, indoctrinated as straight, I *made the choice to be queer* (for some it is genetically inherent). It's an interesting path, one that continually slips in and out of the white, the Catholic, the Mexican, the indigenous, the instincts. In and out of my head. It makes for *loqueria*, the crazies. It is a path of knowledge – one of knowing (and of learning) the history of oppression of our *raza*. It is a way of balancing, of mitigating duality.

In a New England college where I taught, the presence of a few lesbians threw the more conservative heterosexual students and faculty into a panic. The two lesbian students and we two lesbian instructors met with them to discuss their fears. One of the students said, "I thought homophobia meant fear of going home after a residency."

And I thought, how apt. Fear of going home. And of not being taken in. We're afraid of being abandoned by the mother, the culture, *la Raza*, for being unacceptable, faulty, damaged. Most of us unconsciously believe that if we reveal this unacceptable aspect of the self our mother/culture/race will totally reject us. To avoid rejection, some of us conform to the values of the culture, push the unacceptable parts into the shadows. Which leaves only one fear – that we will be found out and that the Shadow-Beast will break out of its cage. Some of us take another route. We try to make ourselves conscious of the Shadow-Beast, stare at the sexual lust and lust for power and destruction we see on its face, discern among its features the undershadow that the reigning order of heterosexual males project on our Beast. Yet still others of us take it another step: we try to waken the Shadow-Beast inside us. Not many jump at the chance to confront the Shadow-Beast in the mirror without flinching at her lidless serpent eyes, her cold clammy moist hand dragging us underground, fangs bared and hissing. How does one put feathers on this particular serpent? But a few of us have been lucky – on the face of the Shadow-Beast we have seen not lust but tenderness; on its face we have uncovered the lie.

Intimate Terrorism: Life in the Borderlands

The world is not a safe place to live in. We shiver in separate cells in enclosed cities, shoulders hunched, barely keeping the panic below the surface of the skin, daily drinking shock along with our morning coffee, fearing the torches being set to our buildings, the attacks in the streets. Shutting down. Woman does not feel safe when her own culture, and white culture, are critical of her; when the males of all races hunt her as prey.

Alienated from her mother culture, "alien" in the dominant culture, the woman of color does not feel safe within the inner life of her Self. Petrified, she can't respond, her face caught berween *los intersticios*, the spaces between the different worlds she inhabits.

The ability to respond is what is meant by responsibility, yet our cultures take away our ability to act – shackle us in the name of protection. Blocked, immobilized, we can't move forward, can't move backwards. That writhing serpent movement, the very movement of life, swifter than lightning, frozen.

We do not engage fully. We do not make full use of our faculties. We abnegate. And there in front of us is the crossroads and choice: to feel a victim where someone else is in control and therefore responsible and to blame (being a victim and transferring the blame on culture, mother, father, ex-lover, friend, absolves me of responsibility), or to feel strong, and, for the most part, in control.

My Chicana identity is grounded in the Indian woman's history of resistance. The Aztec female rites of mourning were rites of defiance protesting the cultural changes which disrupted the equality and balance between female and male, and protesting their demotion to a lesser status, their denigration. Like *la Llorona*, the Indian woman's only means of protest was wailing.

So mamá, Raza, how wonderful, *no tener que rendir cuentas a nadie*. I feel perfectly free to rebel and to rail against my culture. I fear no betrayal on my part because, unlike Chicanas and other women of color who grew up white or who have only recently returned to their native cultural roots, I was totally immersed in mine. It wasn't until I went to high school that I "saw" whites. Until I worked on my master's degree I had not gotten within an arm's distance of them. I was totally immersed *en lo mexicano*, a rural, peasant, isolated, *mexicanismo*. To separate from my culture (as from my family) I had to feel competent enough on the outside and secure enough inside to live life on my own. Yet in leaving home I did not lose touch with my origins because *lo mexicano* is in my system. I am a turtle, wherever I go I carry "home" on my back.

Not me sold out my people but they me. So yes, though "home" permeates every sinew and cartilage in my body, I too am afraid of going home. Though I'll defend my race and culture when they are attacked by *non-mexicanos, conosco el malestar de me cultura*. I abhor some of my culture's ways, how it cripples its women, *como burras*, our strengths used against us, lowly *burras* bearing humility with dignity. The ability to serve, claim the males, is our highest virtue. I abhor how my culture makes *macho* caricatures of its men. No, I do not buy all the myths of the tribe into which I was born. I can understand why the more tinged with Anglo blood, the more adamantly my colored and colorless sisters glorify their colored culture's values – to offset the extreme devaluation of it by the white culture. It's a legitimate reaction. But I will not glorify those aspects of my culture which have injured me and which have injured me in the name of protecting me.

So, don't give me your tenets and your laws. Don't give me your lukewarm gods. What I want is an accounting with all three cultures – white, Mexican, Indian. I want the freedom to carve and chisel my own face, to staunch the bleeding with ashes, to fashion my own gods out of my entrails. And if going home is denied me then I will have to stand and claim my space, making a new culture – *una cultura mestiza* – with my own lumber, my own bricks and mortar and my own feminist architecture.

The Wounding of the *india*-Mestiza

Estas carnes indias que despreciamos nosotros los mexicanos asi como despreciamos y condenamos a nuestra madre, Malinali. Nos condenamos a nosotros mismos. Esta raza vencida, enemigo cuerpo.

Not me sold out my people but they me. *Malinali Tenepat* or *Malintzin*, has become known as *la Chingada* – the fucked one. She has become the bad word that passes a dozen times a day from the lips of Chicanos. Whore, prostitute, the woman who sold out her people to the Spaniards are epithets Chicanos spit out with contempt.

The worst kind of betrayal lies in making us believe that the Indian woman in us is the betrayer. We, *indias y mestizas*, police the Indian in us, brutalize and condemn her. Male culture has done a good job on us. *Son los costumbres que traicionan. La india en mí es la sombra: La Chingada, Tlazolteotl, Coatlicue. Son ellas que oyemos lamentando a sus hijas perdidas.*

Not me sold out my people but they me. Because of the color of my skin they betrayed me. The dark-skinned woman has been silenced, gagged, caged, bound into servitude with marriage, bludgeoned for 300 years, sterilized and castrated in the twentieth century. For 300 years she has been a slave, a force of cheap labor, colonized by the Spaniard, the Anglo, by her own people (and in Mesoamerica her lot under the Indian patriarchs was not free of wounding). For 300 years she was invisible, she was not heard. Many times she wished to speak, to act, to protest, to challenge. The odds were heavily against her. She hid her feelings; she hid her truths; she concealed her fire; but she kept stoking the inner flame. She remained faceless and voiceless, but a light shone through her veil of silence. And though she was unable to spread her limbs and though for her right now the sun has sunk under the earth and there is no moon, she continues to tend the flame. The spirit of the fire spurs her to fight for her own skin and a piece of ground to stand on, a ground from which to view the world – a perspective, a homeground where she can plumb the rich ancestral roots into her own ample *mestiza* heart. She waits till the waters are not so turbulent and the mountains not so slippery with sleet. Battered and bruised she waits, her bruises throwing her back upon herself and the rhythmic pulse of the feminine. *Coatlalopeuh* waits with her.

> *Aquí en la soledad prospera su rebeldía.*
> *En la soledad Ella prospera.*

How to Tame a Wild Tongue

"We're going to have to control your tongue," the dentist says, pulling out all the metal from my mouth. Silver bits plop and tinkle into the basin. My mouth is a motherlode.

The dentist is cleaning out my roots. I get a whiff of the stench when I gasp. "I can't cap that tooth yet, you're still draining," he says.

"We're going to have to do something about your tongue," I hear the anger rising in his voice. My tongue keeps pushing out the wads of cotton, pushing back the drills, the long thin needles. "I've never seen anything as strong or as stubborn," he says. And I think, how do you tame a wild tongue, train it to be quiet, how do you bridle and saddle it? How do you make it lie down?

> "Who is to say that robbing a people of
> its language is less violent than war?"
> Ray Gwyn Smith[2]

I remember being caught speaking Spanish at recess – that was good for three licks on the knuckles with a sharp ruler. I remember being sent to the corner of the classroom for "talking back" to the Anglo teacher when all I was trying to do was tell her how to pronounce my name. "If you want to be American, speak 'American.' If you don't like it, go back to Mexico where you belong."

"I want you to speak English. *Pa' hallar buen trabajo tiener que saber hablar el inglés bien. Qué vale toda tu educación si todavía hablas inglés con un* 'accent,'" my mother would say, mortified that I spoke English like a Mexican. At Pan American University, I, and all Chicano students were required to take two speech classes. Their purpose: to get rid of our accents.

Attacks on one's form of expression with the intent to censor are a violation of the First Amendment. *El Anglo con cara de inocente nos arrancó la lengua.* Wild tongues can't be tamed, they can only be cut out.

Overcoming the Tradition of Silence

Ahogadas, escupimos el oscuro
Peleando con nuestra propia sombra
el silencio nos sepulta

En boca cerrada no entran moscas. "Flies don't enter a closed mouth" is a saying I kept hearing when I was a child. *Ser habladora* was to be a gossip and a liar, to talk too much. *Muchachitas bien criadas*, well-bred girls don't answer back. *Es una falta de respeto* to talk back to one's mother or father. I remember one of the sins I'd recite to the priest in the confession box the few times I went to confession: talking back to my mother, *hablar pa' 'tras, repelar. Hocicona, repelona, chismosa*, having a big mouth, questioning, carrying tales are all signs of being *mal criada*. In my culture they are all words that are derogatory if applied to women – I've never heard them applied to men.

The first time I heard two women, a Puerto Rican and a Cuban, say the word "*nosotras*," I was shocked. I had not known the word existed. Chicanas use *nosotros* whether we're male or female. We are robbed of our female being by the masculine plural. Language is a male discourse.

> And our tongues have become
> dry the wilderness has

> dried out our tongues and
> we have forgotten speech.
> Irena Klepfisz[3]

Even our own people, other Spanish speakers *nos quieren poner candados en la boca.* They would hold us back with their bag of *reglas de academia.*

Oyé como ladra: el lenguaje de la frontera

Quien tiene boca se equivoca
Mexican saying

"*Pocho*, cultural traitor, you're speaking the oppressor's language by speaking English, you're ruining the Spanish language," I have been accused by various Latinos and Latinas. Chicano Spanish is considered by the purist and by most Latinos deficient, a mutilation of Spanish.

But Chicano Spanish is a border tongue which developed naturally. Change, *evolución, enriquecimiento de palabras nuevas por invención o adopción* have created variants of Chicano Spanish, un *nuevo lenguaje. Un lenguaje que corresponde a un modo de vivir.* Chicano Spanish is not incorrect, it is a living language.

For a people who are neither Spanish nor live in a country in which Spanish is the first language; for a people who live in a country in which English is the reigning tongue but who are not Anglo; for a people who cannot entirely identify with either standard (formal, Castilian) Spanish nor standard English, what recourse is left to them but to create their own language? A language which they can connect their identity to, one capable of communicating the realities and values true to themselves – a language with terms that are neither *español ni inglés*, but both. We speak a patois, a forked tongue, a variation of two languages.

Chicano Spanish sprang out of the Chicanos' need to identify ourselves as a distinct people. We needed a language with which we could communicate with ourselves, a secret language. For some of us, language is a homeland closer than the Southwest – for many Chicanos today live in the Midwest and the East. And because we are a complex, heterogeneous people, we speak many languages. Some of the languages we speak are:

1 Standard English
2 Working-class and slang English
3 Standard Spanish
4 Standard Mexican Spanish
5 North Mexican Spanish dialect
6 Chicano Spanish (Texas, New Mexico, Arizona and California have regional variations)
7 Tex-Mex
8 *Pachuco* (called *caló*)

My "home" tongues are the languages I speak with my sister and brothers, with my friends. They are the last five listed, with 6 and 7 being closest to my heart. From school, the media and job situations, I've picked up standard and working-class

English. From Mamagrande Locha and from reading Spanish and Mexican literature, I've picked up Standard Spanish and Standard Mexican Spanish. From *los recién llegados*, Mexican immigrants, and *braceros*, I learned the North Mexican dialect. With Mexicans I'll try to speak either Standard Mexican Spanish or the North Mexican dialect. From my parents and Chicanos living in the Valley, I picked up Chicano Texas Spanish, and I speak it with my mom, younger brother (who married a Mexican and who rarely mixes Spanish with English), aunts and older relatives.

With Chicanas from *Nuevo México* or *Arizona* I will speak Chicano Spanish a little, but often they don't understand what I'm saying. With most California Chicanas I speak entirely in English (unless I forget). When I first moved to San Francisco, I'd rattle off something in Spanish, unintentionally embarrassing them. Often it is only with another Chicana *tejana* that I can talk freely.

Words distorted by English are known as anglicisms or *pochismos*. The *pocho* is an anglicized Mexican or American of Mexican origin who speaks Spanish with an accent characteristic of North Americans and who distorts and reconstructs the language according to the influence of English. Tex-Mex, or Spanglish, comes most naturally to me. I may switch back and forth from English to Spanish in the same sentence or in the same word. With my sister and my brother Nune and with Chicano *tejano* contemporaries I speak in Tex-Mex.

From kids and people my own age I picked up *Pachuco*. *Pachuco* (the language of the zoot suiters) is a language of rebellion, both against Standard Spanish and Standard English. It is a secret language. Adults of the culture and outsiders cannot understand it. It is made up of slang words from both English and Spanish. *Ruca* means girl or woman, *vato* means guy or dude, *chale* means no, *simón* means yes, *churro* is sure, talk is *periquiar*, *pigionear* means petting, *que gacho* means how nerdy, *ponte águila* means watch out, death is called *la pelona*. Through lack of practice and not having others who can speak it, I've lost most of the *Pachuco* tongue.

Chicano Spanish

Chicanos, after 250 years of Spanish/Anglo colonization, have developed significant differences in the Spanish we speak. We collapse two adjacent vowels into a single syllable and sometimes shift the stress in certain words such as *maíz/maiz, cohete/cuete*. We leave out certain consonants when they appear between vowels: *lado/lao, mojado/mojao*. Chicanos from South Texas pronounce *f* as *j* as in *jue* (*fue*). Chicanos use "archaisms," words that are no longer in the Spanish language, words that have been evolved out. We say *semos, truje, haiga, ansina*, and *naiden*. We retain the "archaic" *j*, as in *jalar*, that derives from an earlier *h* (the French *halaror*, the Germanic *halon*, which was lost to standard Spanish in the sixteenth century), but which is still found in several regional dialects such as the one spoken in South Texas. (Due to geography, Chicanos from the Valley of South Texas were cut off linguistically from other Spanish speakers.) We tend to use words that the Spaniards brought over from Medieval Spain. The majority of the Spanish colonizers in Mexico and the Southwest came from Extremadura – Hernán Cortés was one of them – and Andalucía. Andalucians pronounce *ll* like a *y*, and their *d*'s tend to be absorbed by adjacent vowels: *tirado* becomes *tirao*. They brought *el lenguaje popular, dialectos y regionalismos*.[4]

Chicanos and other Spanish speakers also shift *ll* to *y* and *z* to *s*.[5] We leave out initial syllables, saying *tar* for *estar, toy* for *estoy, hora* for *ahora* (*cubanos* and *puertor-riqueños* also leave out initial letters of some words). We also leave out the final syllable such as *pa* for *para*. The intervocalic *y*, the *ll* as in *tortilla, ella, botella*, gets replaced by *tortia* or *tortiya, ea, botea*. We add an additional syllable at the beginning of certain words: *atocar* for *tocar, agastar* for *gastar*. Sometimes we say *lavaste las vacijas*, other times *lavates* (substituting the *ates* verb endings for the *aste*).

We use anglicisms, words borrowed from English: *bola* from ball, *carpeta* from carpet, *máchina de lavar* (instead of *lavadora*) from washing machine. Tex-Mex argot, created by adding a Spanish sound at the beginning or end of an English word such as *cookiar* for cook, *watchar* for watch, *parkiar for* park, and *rapiar* for rape, is the result of the pressures on Spanish speakers to adapt to English.

We don't use the word *vosotros/as* or its accompanying verb form. We don't say *claro* (to mean yes), *imagínate*, or *me emociona*, unless we picked up Spanish from Latinas, out of a book, or in a classroom. Other Spanish-speaking groups are going through the same, or similar, development in their Spanish.

Linguistic Terrorism

Deslenguadas. Somos los del español deficiente. We are your linguistic nightmare, your linguistic aberration, your linguistic *mestizaje*, the subject of your *burla*. Because we speak with tongues of fire we are culturally crucified. Racially, culturally and linguistically *somos huérfanos* – we speak an orphan tongue.

Chicanas who grew up speaking Chicano Spanish have internalized the belief that we speak poor Spanish. It is illegitimate, a bastard language. And because we internalize how our language has been used against us by the dominant culture, we use our language differences against each other.

Chicana feminists often skirt around each other with suspicion and hesitation. For the longest time I couldn't figure it out. Then it dawned on me. To be close to another Chicana is like looking into the mirror. We are afraid of what we'll see there. *Pena*. Shame. Low estimation of self. In childhood we are told that our language is wrong. Repeated attacks on our native tongue diminish our sense of self. The attacks continue throughout our lives.

Chicanas feel uncomfortable talking in Spanish to Latinas, afraid of their censure. Their language was not outlawed in their countries. They had a whole lifetime of being immersed in their native tongue; generations, centuries in which Spanish was a first language, taught in school, heard on radio and TV, and read in the newspaper.

If a person, Chicana or Latina, has a low estimation of my native tongue, she also has a low estimation of me. Often with *mexicanas y latinas* we'll speak English as a neutral language. Even among Chicanas we tend to speak English at parties or conferences. Yet, at the same time, we're afraid the other will think we're *agringadas* because we don't speak Chicano Spanish. We oppress each other trying to out-Chicano each other, vying to be the "real" Chicanas, to speak like Chicanos. There is no one Chicano language just as there is no one Chicano experience. A monolingual Chicana whose first language is English or Spanish is just as much a Chicana as one who speaks several variants of Spanish. A Chicana from Michigan or Chicago or

Detroit is just as much a Chicana as one from the Southwest. Chicano Spanish is as diverse linguistically as it is regionally.

By the end of this century, Spanish speakers will comprise the biggest minority group in the US, a country where students in high schools and colleges are encouraged to take French classes because French is considered more "cultured." But for a language to remain alive it must be used.[6] By the end of this century English, and not Spanish, will be the mother tongue of most Chicanos and Latinos.

So, if you want to really hurt me, talk badly about my language. Ethnic identity is twin skin to linguistic identity – I am my language. Until I can take pride in my language, I cannot take pride in myself. Until I can accept as legitimate Chicano Texas Spanish, Tex-Mex and all the other languages I speak, I cannot accept the legitimacy of myself. Until I am free to write bilingually and to switch codes without having always to translate, while I still have to speak English or Spanish when I would rather speak Spanglish, and as long as I have to accommodate the English speakers rather than having them accommodate me, my tongue will be illegitimate.

I will no longer be made to feel ashamed of existing. I will have my voice: Indian, Spanish, white. I will have my serpent's tongue – my woman's voice, my sexual voice, my poet's voice. I will overcome the tradition of silence.

> My fingers
> move sly against your palm
> Like women everywhere, we speak in code ...
> Melanie Kaye/Kantrowitz[7]

Vistas, corridos, y comida: My Native Tongue

In the 1960s, I read my first Chicano novel. It was *City of Night* by John Rechy, a gay Texan, son of a Scottish father and a Mexican mother. For days I walked around in stunned amazement that a Chicano could write and could get published. When I read *I Am Joaquín*[8] I was surprised to see a bilingual book by a Chicano in print. When I saw poetry written in Tex-Mex for the first time, a feeling of pure joy flashed through me. I felt like we really existed as a people. In 1971, when I started teaching High School English to Chicano students, I tried to supplement the required texts with works by Chicanos, only to be reprimanded and forbidden to do so by the principal. He claimed that I was supposed to teach "American" and English literature. At the risk of being fired, I swore my students to secrecy and slipped in Chicano short stories, poems, a play. In graduate school, while working toward a Ph.D., I had to "argue" with one advisor after the other, semester after semester, before I was allowed to make Chicano literature an area of focus.

Even before I read books by Chicanos or Mexicans, it was the Mexican movies I saw at the drive-in – the Thursday night special of $1.00 a carload – that gave me a sense of belonging. "*Vámonos a las vistas*," my mother would call out and we'd all – grandmother, brothers, sister and cousins – squeeze into the car. We'd wolf down cheese and bologna white bread sandwiches while watching Pedro Infante in melodramatic tearjerkers like *Nosotros los pobres*, the first "real" Mexican movie (that was not an imitation of European movies). I remember seeing *Cuando los hijos se van* and surmising that all Mexican movies played up the love a mother has for her children and what ungrateful sons and daughters suffer when they are not devoted to their mothers. I remember the singing-type "westerns" of Jorge Negrete and Miquel Aceves Mejia. When watching Mexican movies, I felt a sense of homecoming as well as alienation. People who were to amount to something didn't go to Mexican movies, or *bailes* or tune their radios to *bolero, rancherita*, and *corrido* music.

The whole time I was growing up, there was *norteño* music sometimes called North Mexican border music, or Tex-Mex music, or Chicano music, or *cantina* (bar) music. I grew up listening to *conjuntos*, three- or four-piece bands made up of folk musicians playing guitar, *bajo sexto*, drums and button accordion, which Chicanos had borrowed from the German immigrants who had come to Central Texas and Mexico to farm and build breweries. In the Rio Grande Valley, Steve Jordan and Little Joe Hernandez were popular, and Flaco Jiménez was the accordion king. The rhythms of Tex-Mex music are those of the polka, also adopted from the Germans, who in turn had borrowed the polka from the Czechs and Bohemians.

I remember the hot, sultry evenings when *corridos* – songs of love and death on the Texas–Mexican borderlands – reverberated out of cheap amplifiers from the local *cantinas* and wafted in through my bedroom window.

Corridos first became widely used along the South Texas/Mexican border during the early conflict between Chicanos and Anglos. The *corridos* are usually about Mexican heroes who do valiant deeds against the Anglo oppressors. Pancho Villa's song, "*La cucaracha*," is the most famous one. *Corridos* of John F. Kennedy and his death are still very popular in the Valley. Older Chicanos remember Lydia Mendoza, one of the great border *corrido* singers who was called *la Gloria de Tejas*. Her "*El tango negro*," sung during the Great Depression, made her a singer of the people. The ever-present *corridos* narrated one hundred years of border history, bringing news of events as well as entertaining. These folk musicians and folk songs are our chief cultural mythmakers, and they made our hard lives seem bearable.

I grew up feeling ambivalent about our music. Countrywestern and rock-and-roll had more status. In the 50s and 60s, for the slightly educated and *agringado* Chicanos, there existed a sense of shame at being caught listening to our music. Yet I couldn't stop my feet from thumping to the music, could not stop humming the words, nor hide from myself the exhilaration I felt when I heard it.

There are more subtle ways that we internalize identification, especially in the forms of images and emotions. For me food and certain smells are tied to my identity, to my homeland. Woodsmoke curling up to an immense blue sky; woodsmoke perfuming my grandmother's clothes, her skin. The stench of cow manure and the yellow patches on the ground; the crack of a .22 rifle and the reek of cordite. Homemade white cheese sizzling in a pan, melting inside a folded *tortilla*. My sister Hilda's hot, spicy menudo, *chile* colorado making it deep red, pieces of *panza* and hominy floating on top. My brother Carito barbequing fajitas in the backyard. Even now and 3,000 miles away, I can see my mother spicing the ground beef, pork and vension with *chile*. My mouth salivates at the thought of the hot steaming *tamales* I would be eating if I were home.

Si le preguntas a mi mamá, "¿Qué eres?"

"Identity is the essential core of who we are as individuals, the conscious experience of the self inside."

Kaufman[9]

Nosotros los Chicanos straddle the borderlands. On one side of us, we are constantly exposed to the Spanish of the Mexicans, on the other side we hear the Anglos' incessant clamoring so that we forget our language. Among ourselves we don't say *nosotros los americanos, o nosotros los españoles, o nosotros los hispanos.* We say *nosotros los mexicanos* (by *mexicanos* we do not mean citizens of Mexico; we do not mean a national identity but a racial one). We distinguish between *mexicanos del otro lado* and *mexicanos de este lado.* Deep in our hearts we believe that being Mexican has nothing to do with which country one lives in. Being Mexican is a state of soul – not one of mind, not one of citizenship. Neither eagle nor serpent, but both. And like the ocean, neither animal respects borders.

> *Dime con quien andas y te diré quien eres.*
> (Tell me who your friends are and I'll tell you who you are.)
> Mexican saying

Si le preguntas a mi mamá, "¿Qué eres?" te dira, "Soy mexicana." My brothers and sister say the same. I sometimes will answer "*soy mexicana*" and at others will say "*soy Chicana*" *o* "*soy tejana.*" But I identified as "*Raza*" before I ever identified as "*mexicana*" or "Chicana."

As a culture we call ourselves Spanish when referring to ourselves as a linguistic group and when copping out. It is then that we forget our predominant Indian genes. We are 70–80 percent Indian.[10] We call ourselves Hispanic[11] or Spanish-American or Latin American or Latin when linking ourselves to other Spanish-speaking peoples of the Western hemisphere and when copping out. We call ourselves Mexican-American[12] to signify we are neither Mexican nor American, but more the noun "American" than the adjective "Mexican" (and when copping out).

Chicanos and other people of color suffer economically for not acculturating. This voluntary (yet forced) alienation makes for psychological conflict, a kind of dual identity – we don't identify with the Anglo-American cultural values and we don't totally identify with the Mexican cultural values. We are a synergy of two cultures with various degrees of Mexicanness or Angloness. I have so internalized the border-land conflict that sometimes I feel like one cancels out the other and we are zero, nothing, no one. *A veces no soy nada ni nadie. Pero hasta cuando no lo soy, lo soy.*

When not copping out, when we know we are more than nothing, we call ourselves Mexican, referring to race and ancestry; *mestizo* when affirming both our Indian and Spanish (but we hardly ever own our Black ancestry); Chicano when referring to a politically aware people born and/or raised in the US; *Raza* when referring to Chicanos; *tejanos* when we are Chicanos from Texas.

Chicanos did not know we were a people until 1965 when Ceasar Chávez and the farmworkers united and *I Am Joaquín* was published and *la Raza Unida* party was formed in Texas. With that recognition, we became a distinct people. Something momentous happened to the Chicano soul – we became aware of our reality and acquired a name and a language (Chicano Spanish) that reflected that reality. Now that we had a name, some of the fragmented pieces began to fall together – who we were, what we were, how we had evolved. We began to get glimpses of what we might eventually become.

Yet the struggle of identities continues, the struggle of borders is our reality still. One day the inner struggle will cease and a true integration take place. In the meantime, *tenémos que hacer la lucha. ¿Quién está protegiendo los ranchos de migente? ¿Quién está tratando de cerrar la fisura entre la india y el blanco en nuestra sangre? El Chicano, si, el Chicano que anda como un ladrón en su propia casa.*

Los Chicanos, how patient we seem, how very patient. There is the quiet of the Indian about us.[13] We know how to survive. When other races have given up their tongue, we've kept ours. We know what it is to live under the hammer blow of the dominant *norteamericano* culture. But more than we count the blows, we count the days, the weeks, the years, the centuries, the eons until the white laws and commerce and customs will rot in the deserts they've created, lie bleached. *Humilides* yet proud, *quietos* yet wild, *nosotros los mexicanos–Chicanos* will walk by the crumbling ashes as we go about our business. Stubborn, persevering, impenetrable as stone, yet possessing a malleability that renders us unbreakable, we, the *mestizas* and *mestizos*, will remain.

Notes

1 Francisco Guerra, *The Pre-Columbian Mind: A Study into the Aberrant Nature of Sexual Drives, Drugs affecting Behavior, and the Attitude towards Life and Death, with a Survey of Psychotherapy in pre-Columbian America* (New York: Seminar Press, 1971).

2 Ray Gwyn Smith, *Moorland is Cold Country*, unpublished book.

3 Irena Klepfisz, "*Di rayze aheym*/The Journey Home," in Melanie Kaye/Kantrowitz and Irena Klepfisz, eds., *The Tribe of Dina: A Jewish Women's Anthology* (Montpelier, VT: Sinister Wisdom Books, 1986), p. 132.

4 Eduardo Hernandéz-Chávez, Andrew D. Cohen, and Anthony F. Beltramo, *El Lenguaje de los Chicanos: Regional and Social Characteristics of Language Used by Mexican Americans* (Arlington, Va.: Center for Applied Linguistics, 1975), p. 39.

5 Ibid., p. vxii.

6 Irena Klepfisz, "Secular Jewish Identity: Yidishkayt in America," in Kaye/Kantrowitz and Klepfisz, eds., *The Tribe of Dina*, p. 43.

7 Melanie Kaye/Kantrowitz, "Sign," in *We speak in Code: Poems and Other Writings* (Pittsburgh: Motheroot Publications, 1980), p. 85.

8 Rodolfo Gonzales, *I Am Joaquín/ Yo Soy Joaquín* (New York: Bantam Books, 1972). It was first published in 1967.

9 Gershen Kaufman, *Shame: The Power of Caring* (Cambridge, Mass.: Harvard University Press, 1980), p. 68.

10 John Chávez, *The Lost Land: The Chicano Images of the Southwest* (Albuquerque, N. Mex., 1984), pp. 88–90.

11 "Hispanic" is derived from *Hispanis* (*España*, a name given to the Iberian Peninsula in ancient times when it was a part of the Roman Empire) and is a term designated by the US government to make it easier to handle us on paper.

12 The Treaty of Guadalupe Hidalgo created the Mexican-American in 1848.

13 Anglos, in order to alleviate their guilt for dispossessing the Chicano, stressed the Spanish part of us and perpetrated the myth of the Spanish Southwest. We have accepted the fiction that we are Hispanic, that is Spanish, in order to accommodate ourselves to the dominant culture and its abhorrence of Indians. Chávez, *The Lost Land*, pp. 88–91.

CHAPTER 7

Heterogeneity, Hybridity, Multiplicity: Marking Asian American Differences

Lisa Lowe

In this 1991 essay that appeared in the first issue of the journal *Diaspora*, Lisa Lowe advances a nomadic or migratory paradigm for ethnic identity. Critical of the nativist discourse of ethnic identity, Lowe offers as an alternative an open, plural model of an interstitial ethnic being that adopts a strategic essentialism.

In a recent poem by Janice Mirikitani, a Japanese-American *nisei* woman describes her *sansei* daughter's rebellion.[1] The daughter's denial of Japanese-American culture and its particular notions of femininity reminds the *nisei* speaker that she, too, has denied her antecedents, rebelling against her own more traditional *issei* mother:

> I want to break tradition – unlock this room
> 　　where women dress in the dark.
> 　　Discover the lies my mother told me.
> 　　The lies that we are small and powerless
> 　　that our possibilities must be compressed
> 　　to the size of pearls, displayed only as
> 　　passive chokers, charms around our neck.
> Break Tradition.
> 　　I want to tell my daughter of this room
> 　　of myself
> 　　filled with tears of shakubatchi,
> 　　. . . . .
> 　　poems about madness,
> 　　sounds shaken from barbed wire and
> 　　goodbyes and miracles of survival.
> 　　This room of open window where daring ones escape.
> My daughter denies she is like me...
> 　　her pouting ruby lips, her skirts
> 　　swaying to salsa, teena marie and the stones,
> 　　her thighs displayed in carnivals of color.
> 　　I do not know the contents of her room.
> She mirrors my aging.
> She is breaking tradition. (9)

The *nisei* speaker repudiates the repressive confinements of her *issei* mother: the disciplining of the female body, the tedious practice of diminution, the silences of obedience. In turn, the crises that have shaped the *nisei* speaker – internment camps, sounds of threatening madness – are unknown to, and unheard by, her *sansei* teenage daughter. The three generations of Japanese immigrant women in this poem are separated by their different histories and by different conceptions of what it means to be female and Japanese. The poet who writes "I do not know the contents of her room" registers these separations as "breaking tradition."

In another poem, by Lydia Lowe, Chinese women workers are divided also by generation, but even more powerfully by class and language. The speaker is a young Chinese-American who supervises an older Chinese woman in a textile factory.

> The long bell blared,
> and then the *lo-ban*
> made me search all your bags
> before you could leave.
>
> Inside he sighed
> about slow work, fast hands,
> missing spools of thread –
> and I said nothing.
>
> I remember that day
> you came in to show me
> I added your tickets six zippers short.
> It was just a mistake.
>
> You squinted down
> at the check in your hands
> like an old village woman peers
> at some magician's trick.
>
> That afternoon
> when you thrust me your bags
> I couldn't look or raise my face.
> *Doi m-jyu.*
>
> Eyes on the ground,
> I could only see
> one shoe kicking against the other. (29)

This poem, too, invokes the breaking of tradition, although it thematizes another sort of stratification among Asian women: the structure of the factory places the English-speaking younger woman above the Cantonese-speaking older one. Economic relations in capitalist society force the young supervisor to discipline her elders, and she is acutely ashamed that her required behavior does not demonstrate the respect traditionally owed to parents and elders. Thus, both poems foreground commonly thematized *topoi* of diasporan cultures: the disruption and distortion of traditional cultural practices – like the practice of parental sacrifice and filial duty, or the practice of respecting hierarchies of age – not only as a consequence of immigration to the United States, but as a part of entering a society with different class stratifications and different constructions of gender roles. Some Asian American discussions cast the disruption of tradition as loss and represent the loss in terms of regret and shame, as in the latter poem. Alternatively, the traditional practices of family continuity and hierarchy may be figured as oppressively confining, as in Mirikitani's poem, in which the two generations of daughters contest the more restrictive female roles of the former generations. In either case, many Asian American discussions portray immigration and relocation to the United States in terms of a loss of the "original" culture in exchange for the new "American" culture.

In many Asian American novels, the question of the loss or transmission of the "original" culture is frequently represented in a family narrative, figured as generational conflict between the Chinese-born first generation and the American-born second generation.[2] Louis Chu's 1961 novel *Eat a Bowl of Tea*, for example, allegorizes in the conflicted relationship between father and son the differences between "native" Chinese values and the new "westernized" culture of Chinese-Americans. Other novels have taken up this generational theme; one way to read Maxine Hong Kingston's *The Woman Warrior* (1975) or Amy Tan's recent *The Joy Luck Club* (1989) is to understand them as versions of this generational model of culture, refigured in feminine terms, between mothers and daughters. However, I will argue that interpreting Asian American culture exclusively in terms of the master narratives of generational conflict and filial relation essentializes Asian American culture, obscuring the particularities and incommensurabilities of class, gender, and national diversities among Asians; the reduction of ethnic cultural politics to struggles between first and second generations displaces (and privatizes) inter-community differences into a familial opposition. To avoid this homogenizing of Asian Americans as exclusively hierarchical and familial, I would contextualize the "vertical" generational model of culture with the more "horizontal" relationship represented in Diana Chang's "The Oriental Contingent." In Chang's short story, two young women avoid the discussion of their Chinese backgrounds because each desperately fears that the other is "more Chinese," more "authentically" tied to the original culture. The narrator, Connie, is certain that her friend Lisa "never referred to her own background because it was more Chinese than Connie's, and therefore of a higher order. She was tact incarnate. All along, she had been going out of her way not to embarrass Connie. Yes, yes. Her assurance was definitely uppercrust (perhaps her father had been in the diplomatic service), and her offhand didacticness, her lack of self-doubt, was indeed characteristically Chinese-Chinese" (173). Connie feels ashamed because she assumes herself to be "a failed Chinese"; she fantasizes that Lisa was born in China, visits there frequently, and privately disdains Chinese-Americans. Her assumptions about Lisa prove to be quite wrong, however; Lisa is even more critical of herself for "not being genuine." For Lisa, as Connie eventually discovers, was born in Buffalo and was adopted by non-Chinese-American parents; lacking an immediate connection to Chinese culture, Lisa projects upon all Chinese the authority of being "more Chinese." Lisa confesses to Connie at the end of the story: "The only time I feel Chinese is when I'm embarrassed I'm not more Chinese – which is a totally Chinese reflex I'd give anything to be rid of!" (176). Chang's story portrays two women polarized by the degree to which they have each internalized a cultural definition of "Chineseness" as pure and fixed, in which any deviation is constructed as less, lower, and shameful. Rather than confirming the cultural model in which "ethnicity" is passed from generation to generation, Chang's story explores the "ethnic" relationship between women of the same generation. Lisa and Connie are ultimately able to reduce one another's guilt at not being "Chinese enough"; in one another they are able to find a common frame of reference. The story suggests that the making of Chinese-American culture – how ethnicity is imagined, practiced, continued – is worked out as much between ourselves and our communities as it is transmitted from one generation to another.

In this sense, Asian American discussions of ethnicity are far from uniform or consistent; rather, these discussions contain a wide spectrum of articulations that includes, at one end, the desire for an identity represented by a fixed profile of ethnic traits, and at another, challenges to the very notions of identity and singularity which celebrate ethnicity as a fluctuating composition of differences, intersections, and incommensurabilities. These latter efforts attempt to define ethnicity in a manner that accounts not only for cultural inheritance, but for active cultural construction, as well. In other words, they suggest that the making of Asian American culture may be a much "messier" process than unmediated vertical transmission from one generation to another, including practices that are partly inherited and partly modified, as well as partly invented.[3] As the narrator of *The Woman Warrior* suggests, perhaps one of the more important stories of Asian American experience is about the process of receiving, refiguring, and rewriting cultural traditions. She asks: "Chinese-Americans, when you try to understand what things in you are Chinese, how do you separate what is peculiar to childhood, to poverty, insanities, one family, your mother who marked your growing with stories, from what is Chinese? What is Chinese tradition and what is the movies?" (6). Or the dilemma of cultural syncretism might be posed in an interrogative version of the uncle's impromptu proverb in Wayne Wang's film *Dim Sum*: "You can take the girl out of Chinatown, but can you take the Chinatown out of the girl?" For rather than representing a fixed, discrete culture, "Chinatown" is itself the very emblem of fluctuating demographics, languages, and populations.[4]

I begin my article with these particular examples drawn from Asian American cultural texts in order to observe that what is referred to as "Asian America" is clearly a heterogeneous entity. From the perspective of the majority culture, Asian Americans may very well be constructed as different from, and other than, Euro-Americans. But from the perspectives of Asian Americans, we are perhaps even more different, more diverse, among ourselves: being men and women at different distances and generations from our "original" Asian cultures – cultures as different as Chinese, Japanese, Korean, Filipino, Indian, and Vietnamese – Asian Americans are born in the United States and born in Asia; of exclusively Asian parents and of mixed race; urban and rural; refugee and nonrefugee; communist-identified and anticommunist; fluent in English and non-English speaking; educated and working class. As with other diasporas in the United States, the Asian immigrant collectivity is unstable and changeable, with its cohesion complicated by intergenerationality, by various degrees of identification and relation to a "homeland," and by different extents of assimilation to and distinction from "majority culture" in the United States. Further, the historical contexts of particular waves of immigration within single groups contrast with one another; the Japanese-Americans who were interned during World War II encountered quite different social and economic barriers than those from Japan who arrive in southern California today. And the composition of different waves of immigrants differs in gender, class, and region. For example, the first groups of Chinese immigrants to the United States in 1850 were from four villages in Canton province, male by a ratio of 10 to 1, and largely of peasant backgrounds; the more recent Chinese immigrants are from Hong Kong, Taiwan, or the People's Republic (themselves quite heterogeneous and of discontinuous "origins"), or from the Chinese diaspora in other parts of Asia, such as Macao, Malaysia, or Singapore, and they are more often educated and middle-class men and women.[5] Further, once arriving in the United States, very few Asian immigrant cultures remain discrete, inpenetrable communities. The more recent groups mix, in varying degrees, with segments of the existing groups; Asian Americans may inter-marry with other ethnic groups, live in neighborhoods adjacent to them, or work in the same businesses and on the same factory assembly lines. The boundaries and definitions of Asian American culture are continually shifting and being contested from pressures both "inside" and "outside" the Asian origin community.

I stress heterogeneity, hybridity, and multiplicity in the characterization of Asian American culture as part of a twofold argument about cultural politics, the ultimate aim of that argument being to disrupt the current hegemonic relationship between "dominant" and "minority" positions. On the one hand, my observation that Asian Americans are heterogeneous is part of a strategy to destabilize the dominant discursive construction and determination of Asian Americans as a homogeneous group. Throughout the late nineteenth and early twentieth centuries, Asian immigration to the United States was managed by exclusion acts and quotes that relied upon racialist constructions of Asians as homogeneous;[6] the "model minority" myth and the informal quotas discriminating against Asians in university admissions policies are contemporary versions of this homogenization of Asians.[7] On the other hand, I underscore Asian American heterogeneities (particularly class, gender, and national differences among Asians) to contribute to a dialogue within Asian American discourse, to negotiate with those modes of argumentation that continue to uphold a politics based on ethnic "identity." In this sense, I argue for the Asian American necessity – politically, intellectually, and personally—to organize, resist, and theorize *as* Asian Americans, but at the same time I inscribe this necessity within a discussion of the risks of a cultural politics that relies upon the construction of sameness and the exclusion of differences.

1

The first reason to emphasize the dynamic fluctuation and heterogeneity of Asian American culture is to release our understandings of either the "dominant" or the emergent "minority" cultures as discrete, fixed, or homogeneous, and to arrive at a different conception of the general political terrain of culture in California, a useful focus for this examination since it has become commonplace to consider it an "ethnic state," embodying a new phenomenon of cultural adjacency and admixture.[8] For if minority immigrant cultures are perpetually changing – in their composition, config-uration, and signifying practices, as well as in their relations to one another – it follows that the "majority" or dominant culture, with which minority cultures are in continual relation, is also unstable and unclosed. The suggestion that the general social terrain of culture is open, plural, and dynamic reorients our understanding of what "cultural hegemony" is and how it works in contemporary California. It per-mits us to theorize about the roles that ethnic immigrant groups play in the making and unmaking of culture – and how these minority discourses challenge the existing structure of power, the existing hegemony.[9] We should remember that Antonio Gramsci writes about *hegemony* as not simply political or economic forms of rule but as the entire process of dissent and compromise through which a particular group is able to determine the political, cultural, and ideological character of a state (*Selections*). Hegemony does not refer exclusively to the process by which a dominant formation exercises its influence but refers equally to the process through which minority groups organize and contest any specific hegemony.[10] The reality of any specific hegemony is that, while it may be for the moment dominant, it is never absolute or conclusive. Hegemony, in Gramsci's thought, is a concept that describes both the social processes through which a particular dominance is maintained and those through which that dominance is challenged and new forces are articulated. When a hegemony representing the interests of a dominant group exists, it is always within the context of resistances from emerging "subaltern" groups.[11] We might say that hegemony is not only the political process by which a particular group constitutes itself as "the one" or "the majority" in relation to which "minorities" are defined and know themselves to be "other," but it is equally the process by which positions of otherness may ally and constitute a new majority, a "counterhegemony."[12]

The subaltern classes are, in Gramsci's definition, prehegemonic, not unified groups, whose histories are fragmented, episodic and identifiable only from a point of historical hindsight. They may go through different phases when they are subject to the activity of ruling groups, may articulate their demands through existing parties, and then may themselves produce new parties; in *The Prison Notebooks*, Gramsci describes a final phase at which the "formations [of the subaltern classes] assert integral autonomy" (52). The definition of the subaltern groups includes some noteworthy observations for our understanding of the roles of racial and ethnic immigrant groups in the United States. The assertion that the significant practices of the subaltern groups may not be understood as hegemonic until they are viewed with historical hindsight is interesting, for it suggests that some of the most powerful practices may not always be the explicitly oppositional ones, may not be understood by contemporaries, and may be less overt and recognizable than others. Provocative, too, is the idea that the subaltern classes are by definition "not unified"; that is, the subaltern is not a fixed, unified force of a single character. Rather, the assertion of "integral autonomy" by not unified classes suggests a coordination of distinct, yet allied, positions, practices, and movements – class-identified and not class-identified, in parties and not, ethnic-based and gender-based – each in its own not necessarily equivalent manner transforming and disrupting the apparatuses of a specific hegemony. The independent forms and locations of cultural challenge – ideological, as well as economic and political – constitute what Gramsci calls a "new historical bloc," a new set of relationships that together embody a different hegemony and a different balance of power. In this sense, we have in the growing and shifting ethnic minority populations in California an active example of this new historical bloc described by Gramsci; and in the negotiations between these ethnic groups and the existing majority over what interests precisely constitute the "majority," we have an illustration of the concept of hegemony, not in the more commonly accepted sense of "hegemony-maintenance," but in the often ignored sense of "hegemony-creation."[13] The observation that the Asian American community and other ethnic immigrant communities are heterogeneous lays the foundation for several political operations: first, by shifting, multiplying, and reconceiving the construction of society as composed of two numerically overdetermined camps called the majority and the minority, cultural politics is recast so as to account for a multiplicity of various, nonequivalent groups, one of which is Asian Americans. Second, the conception of ethnicity as heterogeneous provides a position for Asian Americans that is both ethnically specific, yet simultaneously uneven and unclosed; Asian Americans can articulate distinct group demands based on our particular histories of exclusion, but the redefined lack of closure – which reveals rather than conceals differences – opens political lines of affiliation with other groups (labor unions, other racial and ethnic groups, and gay, lesbian, and feminist groups) in the challenge to specific forms of domination insofar as they share common features.

2

In regard to the practice of "identity politics" within Asian American discourse, the articulation of an "Asian American identity" as an organizing tool has provided a concept of political unity that enables diverse Asian groups to understand our unequal circumstances and histories as being related; likewise, the building of "Asian American culture" is crucial, for it articulates and empowers our multicultural, multilingual Asian origin community vis-à-vis the institutions and apparatuses that exclude and marginalize us. But I want to suggest that essentializing Asian American identity and suppressing our differences – of national origin, generation, gender, party, class – risks particular dangers: not only does it underestimate the differences and hybridities among Asians, but it also inadvertently supports the racist discourse that constructs Asians as a homogeneous group, that implies we are "all alike" and conform to "types"; in this respect, a politics based exclusively on ethnic identity willingly accepts the terms of the dominant logic that organizes the heterogeneous picture of racial and ethnic diversity into a binary schema of "the one" and "the other." The essentializing of Asian American identity also reproduces oppositions that subsume other nondominant terms in the same way that Asians and other groups are disenfranchised by the dominant culture: to the degree that the discourse generalizes Asian American identity as male, women are rendered invisible; or to the extent that Chinese are presumed to be exemplary of all Asians, the importance of other Asian groups is ignored. In this sense, a politics based on ethnic identity facilitates the displacement of intercommunity differences – between men and women, or between workers and managers – into a false opposition of "nationalism" and "assimilation." We have an example of this in recent debates where Asian American feminists who challenge Asian American sexism are cast as "assimilationist," as betraying Asian American "nationalism."

To the extent that Asian American discourse articulates an identity in reaction to the dominant culture's stereotype, even to refute it, I believe the discourse may remain bound to, and overdetermined by, the logic of the dominant culture. In accepting the binary terms ("white" and "non-white," or "majority" and "minority") that structure institutional policies about ethnicity, we forget that these binary schemas are not neutral descriptions. Binary constructions of difference use a logic that prioritizes the first term and subordinates the second; whether the pair "difference" and "sameness" is figured as a binary synthesis that considers "difference" as always contained within the "same," or that conceives of the pair as an opposition in which "difference" structurally implies "sameness" as its complement, it is important to see each of these figurations as versions of the same binary logic. My argument for heterogeneity seeks to challenge the conception of difference as exclusively structured by a binary opposition between two terms by proposing instead another notion of difference that takes seriously the conditions of heterogeneity, multiplicity, and non-equivalence. I submit that the most exclusive construction of Asian American identity – which presumes masculinity, American birth, and speaking English – is at odds with the formation of important political alliances and affiliations with other groups across racial and ethnic, gender, sexuality, and class lines. An essentialized identity is an obstacle to Asian American women allying with other women of color, for example, and it can discourage laboring Asian Americans from joining unions with workers of other colors. It can short-circuit potential alliances against the dominant structures of power in the name of subordinating "divisive" issues to *the* national question.

Some of the limits of identity politics are discussed most pointedly by Frantz Fanon in his books about the Algerian resistance to French colonialism. Before ultimately turning to some Asian American cultural texts in order to trace the ways in which the dialogues about identity and difference are represented within the discourse, I would like to briefly consider one of Fanon's most important texts, *The Wretched of the Earth* (*Les damnés de la terre*, 1961). Although Fanon's treatise was cited in the 1960s as the manifesto for a nationalist politics of identity, rereading it now in the 1990s we find his text, ironically, to be the source of a serious critique of nationalism. Fanon argues that the challenge facing any movement dismantling colonialism (or a system in which one culture dominates another) is to provide for a new order that does not reproduce the social structure of the old system. This new order, he argues, must avoid the simple assimilation to the dominant culture's roles and positions by the emergent group, which would merely caricature the old colonialism, and it should be equally suspicious of an uncritical nativism, or racialism, appealing to essentialized notions of precolonial identity. Fanon suggests that another alternative is necessary, a new order, neither an assimilationist nor a nativist inversion, which breaks with the structures and practices of cultural domination and which continually and collectively criticizes the institutions of rule. One of the more remarkable turns in Fanon's argument occurs when he identifies both bourgeois assimilation and bourgeois nationalism as conforming to the same logic, as responses to colonialism that reproduce the same structure of cultural domination. It is in this sense that Fanon warns against the nationalism practiced by bourgeois neocolonial governments. Their nationalism, he argues, can be distorted easily into racism, territorialism, separatism, or ethnic dictatorships of one tribe or regional group over others; the national bourgeoisie replaces the colonizer, yet the social and economic structure remains the same.[14] Ironically, he points out, these separatisms, or "micro-nationalisms" (Mamadou Dia, qtd., in Fanon 158), are themselves legacies of colonialism. He writes: "By its very structure, colonialism is regionalist and separatist. Colonialism does not simply state the existence of tribes; it also reinforces and separates them" (94). That is, a politics of ethnic separatism is congruent with the divide-and-conquer logic of colonial domination. Fanon links the practices of the national bourgeoisie that has assimilated colonialist thought and practice with nativist practices that privilege one tribe or ethnicity over others; nativism and assimilationism are not opposites but similar logics both enunciating the old order.

Fanon's analysis implies that an essentialized bourgeois construction of "nation" is a classification that excludes other subaltern groups that could bring about substantive change in the social and economic relations, particularly those whose social marginalities are due to class: peasants, workers, transient populations. We can add to Fanon's criticism that the category of nation often erases a consideration of women and the fact of difference between men and women and the conditions under which they live and work in situations of cultural domination. This is why the concentration of women of color in domestic service or reproductive labor (childcare, homecare, nursing) in the contemporary United States is not adequately explained by a nation-based model of analysis (see Glenn). In light of feminist theory, which has gone the furthest in theorizing multiple inscription and the importance of positionalities, we can argue that it may be less meaningful to act exclusively in terms of a single valence or political interest – such as ethnicity or nation – than to acknowledge that social subjects are the sites of a variety of differences.[15] An Asian American subject is never purely and exclusively ethnic, for that subject is always of a particular class, gender, and sexual preference, and may therefore feel responsible to movements that are organized around these other designations. This is not to argue against the strategic importance of Asian American identity, nor against the building of Asian American culture. Rather, I am suggesting that acknowledging class and gender differences among Asian Americans does not weaken us as a group; to the contrary, these differences represent greater political opportunity to affiliate with other groups whose cohesions may be based on other valences of oppression.

3

As I have already suggested, within Asian American discourse there is a varied spectrum of discussion about the concepts of ethnic identity and culture. At one end, there are discussions in which ethnic identity is essentialized as the cornerstone of a nationalist liberation politics. In these discussions, the cultural positions of nationalism (or ethnicism, or nativism) and of assimilation are represented in polar opposition: nationalism affirming the separate purity of its ethnic culture is opposed to assimilation of the standards of dominant society. Stories about the loss of the "native" Asian culture tend to express some form of this opposition. At the same time, there are criticisms of this essentializing position, most often articulated by feminists who charge that Asian American nationalism prioritizes masculinity and does not account for women. At the other end, there are interventions that refuse static or binary conceptions of ethnicity, replacing notions of identity with multiplicity and shifting the emphasis for ethnic "essence" to cultural hybridity. Settling for neither nativism nor assimilation, these cultural texts expose the apparent opposition between the two as a constructed figure (as Fanon does when he observes that bourgeois assimilation and bourgeois nationalism often conform to the same colonialist logic). In tracing these different discussions about identity and ethnicity through Asian American cultural debates, literature, and film, I choose particular texts because they are accessible and commonly held. But I do not intend to limit *discourse* to

only these particular textual forms; by *discourse*, I intend a rather extended meaning –
a network that includes not only texts and cultural documents, but social practices,
formal and informal laws, policies of inclusion and exclusion, and institutional forms
of organization, for example, all of which constitute and regulate knowledge about
the object of that discourse, Asian America.

The terms of the debate about nationalism and assimilation become clearer if we
look first at the discussion of ethnic identity in certain debates about the representation
of culture. Readers of Asian American literature are familiar with attacks by Frank
Chin, Ben Tong, and others on Maxine Hong Kingston, attacks which have been cast
as nationalist criticisms of Kingston's "assimilationist" works. Her novel/autobiog-
raphy *The Woman Warrior* is the primary target of such criticism, since it is virtually
the only "canonized" piece of Asian American literature; its status can be measured by
the fact that the Modern Language Association is currently publishing *A Guide to
Teaching "The Woman Warrior"* in its series that includes guides to Cervantes's *Don
Quixote* and Dante's *Inferno*. A critique of how and why this text has become fetishized
as the exemplary representation of Asian American culture is necessary and important.
However, Chin's critique reveals other kinds of tensions in Asian American culture
that are worth noting. He does more than accuse Kingston of having exoticized Chinese-American culture; he argues that she has "feminized" Asian American literature
and undermined the power of Asian American men to combat the racist stereotypes of
the dominant white culture. Kingston and other women novelists such as Amy Tan,
he says, misrepresent Chinese history in order to exaggerate its patriarchal structure;
as a result, Chinese society is portrayed as being even more misogynistic than European society. While Chin and others have cast this conflict in terms of nationalism and
assimilationism, I think it may be more productive to see this debate, as Elaine Kim
does in a recent essay ("'Such Opposite'"), as a symptom of the tensions between
nationalist and feminist concerns in Asian American discourse. I would add to Kim's
analysis that the dialogue between nationalist and feminist concerns animates precisely
a debate about identity and difference, or identity and heterogeneity, rather than a
debate between nationalism and assimilationism; it is a debate in which Chin and
others stand at one end insisting upon a fixed masculinist identity, while Kingston,
Tan, or feminist literary critics like Shirley Lim and Amy Ling, with their representations of female differences and their critiques of sexism in Chinese culture, repeatedly
cast this notion of identity into question. Just as Fanon points out that some forms of
nationalism can obscure class, Asian American feminists point out that Asian American nationalism – or the construction of an essentialized, native Asian American subject – obscures gender. In other words, the struggle that is framed as a conflict
between the apparent opposites of nativism and assimilation can mask what is more
properly characterized as a struggle between the desire to essentialize ethnic identity
and the fundamental condition of heterogeneous differences against which such a
desire is spoken. The trope that opposes nativism and assimilationism can be itself a
colonialist figure used to displace the challenges of heterogeneity, or subalternity, by
casting them as assimilationist or anti-ethnic.

The trope that opposes nativism and assimilation not only organizes the cultural
debates of Asian American discourse but figures *in* Asian American literature, as
well. More often than not, however, this symbolic conflict between nativism and
assimilation is figured in the *topos* with which I began, that of generational conflict.
Although there are many versions of this *topos*, I will mention only a few in order to

elucidate some of the most relevant cultural tensions. In one model, a conflict between generations is cast in strictly masculinist terms, between father and son; in this model, mothers are absent or unimportant, and female figures exist only as peripheral objects to the side of the central drama of male conflict. Louis Chu's *Eat a Bowl of Tea* (1961) exemplifies this masculinist generational symbolism, in which a conflict between nativism and assimilation is allegorized in the relationship between the father Wah Gay and the son Ben Loy, in the period when the predominantly Cantonese New York Chinatown community changes from a "bachelor society" to a "family society."[16] Wah Gay wishes Ben Loy to follow Chinese tradition, and to submit to the father's authority, while the son balks at his father's "old ways" and wants to make his own choices. When Wah Gay arranges a marriage for Ben Loy, the son is forced to obey. Although the son had had no trouble leading an active sexual life before his marriage, once married, he finds himself to be impotent. In other words, Chu's novel figures the conflict of nativism and assimilation in terms of Ben Loy's sexuality: submitting to the father's authority, marrying the "nice Chinese girl" Mei Oi and having sons, is the so-called traditional Chinese male behavior. This path represents the nativist option, whereas Ben Loy's former behavior – carrying on with American prostitutes, gambling, etc. – represents the alleged path of assimilation. At the nativist Chinese extreme, Ben Loy is impotent and is denied access to erotic pleasure, and at the assimilationist American extreme, he has great access and sexual freedom. Allegorizing the choice between cultural options in the register of Ben Loy's sexuality, Chu's novel suggests that resolution lies at neither pole, but in a third "Chinese-American" alternative, in which Ben Loy is able to experience erotic pleasure with his Chinese wife. This occurs only when the couple moves away to another state, away from the father: Ben Loy's relocation to San Francisco's Chinatown and the priority of pleasure with Mei Oi over the begetting of a son (which, incidentally, they ultimately do have) both represent important breaks from his father's authority and from Chinese tradition. Following Fanon's observations about the affinities between nativism and assimilation, we can understand Chu's novel as an early masculinist rendering of culture as conflict between the apparent opposites of nativism and assimilation, with its Oedipal resolution in a Chinese-American male identity; perhaps only with hindsight can we propose that the opposition itself may be a construction that allegorizes the dialectic between an articulation of essentialized ethnic identity and the context of heterogeneous differences.

Amy Tan's much more recent *The Joy Luck Club* (1989) refigures this *topos* of generational conflict in a different social context, among first- and second-generation Mandarin Chinese in San Francisco, and more importantly, between women. Tan's *Joy Luck* displaces *Eat a Bowl* not only because it deviates from the figuration of Asian American identity in a masculine Oedipal dilemma by refiguring it in terms of mothers and daughters, but also because *Joy Luck* multiplies the sites of cultural conflict, positing a number of struggles – familial and extrafamilial – as well as resolutions, without privileging the singularity or centrality of one. In this way, *Joy Luck* ultimately thematizes and demystifies the central role of the mother–daughter relationship in Asian American culture.

Joy Luck represents the first-person narratives of four sets of Chinese-born mothers and their American-born daughters. The daughters attempt to come to terms with their mothers' demands, while the mothers simultaneously try to interpret their daughters' deeds, expressing a tension between the "Chinese" expectation of filial respect and the "American" inability to fulfill that expectation. By multiplying and subverting the model of generational discord with examples of generational concord, the novel calls attention to the heterogeneity of Chinese-American family relations. On the one hand, mothers like Ying-ying St. Clair complain about their daughters' Americanization:

> For all these years I kept my mouth closed so selfish desires would not fall out. And because I remained quiet for so long now my daughter does not hear me. She sits by her fancy swimming pool and hears only her Sony Walkman, her cordless phone, her big, important husband asking her why they have charcoal and no lighter fluid.
>
> ... because I moved so secretly now my daughter does not see me. She sees a list of things to buy, her checkbook out of balance, her ashtray sitting crooked on a straight table.
>
> And I want to tell her this: We are lost, she and I, unseen and not seeing, unheard and not hearing, unknown by others. (67)

The mother presents herself as having sacrificed everything for a daughter who has ignored these sacrifices. She sees her daughter as preoccupied with portable, mobile high-tech commodities which, characteristically, have no cords, no ties, emblematizing the mother's condemnation of a daughter who does not respect family bonds. The mother implies that the daughter recognizes that something is skewed and attempts to correct it – balancing her checkbook, straightening her house – but in the mother's eyes, she has no access to the real problems; being in America has taken this under-standing away. Her daughter, Lena, however, tends to view her mother as unreason-ably superstitious and domineering. Lena considers her mother's concern about her failing marriage as meddlesome; the daughter's interpretation of their antagonism emphasizes a cultural gap between the mother who considers her daughter's troubles her own, and the daughter who sees her mother's actions as intrusive, possessive, and worst of all, denying the daughter's own separate individuality.

On the other hand, in contrast to this and other examples of disjunction between the Chinese mothers and the Chinese-American daughters, *Joy Luck* also includes a relationship between mother and daughter in which there is an apparent coincidence of perspective; tellingly, in this example the mother has died, and it is left to the daughter to "eulogize" the mother by telling the mother's story. Jing-mei Woo makes a trip to China, to reunite with her recently deceased mother's two daughters by an earlier marriage, whom her mother had been forced to abandon almost 40 years before when fleeing China during the Japanese invasion. Jing-mei wants to fulfill her mother's last wish to see the long-lost daughters; she wishes to inscribe herself in her mother's place. Her narration of the reunion conveys her utopian belief in the possi-bility of recovering the past, of rendering herself coincident with her mother, narrat-ing her desire to become again "Chinese."

> My sisters and I stand, arms around each other, laughing and wiping the tears from each other's eyes. The flash of the Polaroid goes off and my father hands me the snapshot. My sisters and I watch quietly together, eager to see what develops.
>
> The gray-green surface changes to the bright colors of our three images, sharpening and deepening all at once. And although we don't speak, I know we all see it: Together we look like our mother. Her same eyes, her same mouth, open in surprise to see, at last, her long-cherished wish. (288)

Unlike Lena St. Clair, Jing-mei does not seek greater autonomy from her mother; she desires a lessening of the disparity between their positions that is accomplished through the narrative evocation of her mother after she has died. By contrasting different examples of mother–daughter discord and concord, *Joy Luck* allegorizes the heterogeneous culture in which the desire for identity and sameness (represented by Jing-mei's story) is inscribed within the context of Asian American differences and disjunctions (exemplified by the other three pairs of mothers and daughters). The novel formally illustrates that the articulation of one, the desire for identity, depends upon the existence of the others, or the fundamental horizon of differences.

Further, although *Joy Luck* has been heralded and marketed as a novel about mother–daughter relations in the Chinese-American family (one cover review characterizes it as a "story that shows us China, Chinese-American women and their families, and the mystery of the mother–daughter bond in ways that we have not experienced before"), I would suggest that the novel also represents antagonisms that are not exclusively generational but are due to different conceptions of class and gender among Chinese-Americans. Towards the end of the novel, Lindo and Waverly Jong reach a climax of misunderstanding, in a scene that takes place in a central site of American femininity: the beauty parlor. After telling the stylist to give her mother a "soft wave," Waverly asks her mother, Lindo, if she is in agreement. The mother narrates:

> I smile. I use my American face. That's the face Americans think is Chinese, the one they cannot undersand. But inside I am becoming ashamed. I am ashamed she is ashamed. Because she is my daughter and I am proud of her, and I am her mother but she is not proud of me. (265)

The American-born daughter believes she is treating her mother, rather magnanimously, to a day of pampering at a chic salon; the Chinese-born mother receives this gesture as an insult, clear evidence of a daughter ashamed of her mother's looks. The scene not only marks the separation of mother and daughter by generation but, perhaps less obviously, their separation by class and cultural differences that lead to different interpretations of how female identity is signified. On the one hand, the Chinese-born Lindo and American-born Waverly have different class values and opportunities; the daughter's belief in the pleasure of a visit to an expensive San Francisco beauty parlor seems senselessly extravagant to the mother whose rural family had escaped poverty only by marrying her to the son of a less humble family in their village. On the other hand, the mother and daughter also conflict over definitions of proper female behavior. Lindo assumes female identity is constituted in the practice of a daughter's deference to her elders, while for Waverly, it is determined by a woman's financial independence from her parents and her financial equality with men and by her ability to speak her desires, and it is cultivated and signified in the styles and shapes that represent middle-class feminine beauty. In this sense, I ultimately read *Joy Luck* not as a novel which exclusively depicts generational conflict among Chinese-American women, but rather as a text that thematizes the trope of the mother–daughter relationship in Asian American culture; that is, the novel comments upon the idealized construction of mother–daughter relationships (both in the majority culture's discourse about Asian Americans and in the Asian American discourse about ourselves), as well as upon the kinds of differences – of class and culturally specific definitions of gender – that are rendered invisible by the privileging of this trope.[17]

Before concluding, I want to turn to a final cultural text which not only restates the Asian American narrative that opposes nativism and assimilation but articulates a critique of that narrative, calling the nativist/assimilationist dyad into question. If *Joy Luck* poses an alternative to the dichotomy of nativism and assimilation by multiplying the generational conflict and demystifying the centrality of the mother–daughter relationship, then Peter Wang's film *A Great Wall* (1985) – both in its emplotment and in its very medium of representation – offers yet another version of this alternative. Wang's film unsettles both poles in the antinomy of nativist essentialism and assimilation by performing a continual geographical juxtaposition and exchange between a variety of cultural spaces. *A Great Wall* portrays the visit of Leo Fang's Chinese-American family to the People's Republic of China and their month-long stay with Leo's sister's family, the Chao family, in Beijing. The film concentrates on the primary contrast between the habits, customs, and assumptions of the Chinese in China and the Chinese-Americans in California by going back and forth between shots of Beijing and Northern California, in a type of continual filmic "migration" between the two, as if to thematize in its very form the travel between cultural spaces. From the first scene, however, the film foregrounds the idea that in the opposition between native and assimilated spaces, neither begins as a pure, un-contaminated site or origin; and as the camera eye shuttles back and forth between, both poles of the constructed opposition shift and change. (Indeed, the Great Wall of China, from which the film takes its title, is a monument to the historical condition that not even ancient China was "pure," but co-existed with "foreign barbarians" against which the Middle Kingdom erected such barriers.) In this regard, the film contains a number of emblematic images that call attention to the syncretic, composite quality of all cultural spaces: when the young Chinese Liu finishes the university entrance exam his scholar-father gives him a Coca-cola; children crowd around the single village television to watch a Chinese opera singer imitate Pavarotti singing Italian opera; the Chinese student learning English recites the Gettysburg Address. Although the film concentrates on both illustrating and dissolving the apparent opposition between Chinese Chinese and American Chinese, a number of other contrasts are likewise explored: the differences between generations both within the Chao and the Fang families (daughter Lili noisily drops her bike while her father practices tai chi; Paul kisses his Caucasian girlfriend and later tells his father that he believes all Chinese are racists when Leo suggests that he might date some nice Chinese girls); differences between men and women (accentuated by two scenes, one in which Grace Fang and Mrs. Chao talk about their husbands and children, the other in which Chao and Leo get drunk together); and, finally, the differences between capitalist and communist societies (highlighted in a scene in which the Chaos and Fangs talk about their different attitudes toward "work"). The representations of these other contrasts complicate and diversify the ostensible focus on cultural differences between Chinese and Chinese-Americans, as if to testify to the condition that there is never only one exclusive valence of difference, but rather cultural difference is always simultaneously bound up with gender, economics, age, and other distinctions. In other words, when Leo says to his wife that the Great Wall makes the city "just as difficult to leave as to get in," the wall at once signifies the construction of a variety of barriers – not only between Chinese and Americans, but between generations, men and women, capitalism and communism – as well as the impossibility of ever remaining bounded and inpenetrable, of resisting change, recomposition, and reinvention. We are reminded of this impossibility throughout the film, but it is perhaps best illustrated in the scene in which the Fang and Chao families play a rousing game of touch football on the ancient immovable Great Wall.

The film continues with a series of wonderful contrasts: the differences in the bodily comportments of the Chinese-American Paul and the Chinese Liu playing ping pong, between Leo's jogging and Mr. Chao's tai chi, between Grace Fang's and Mrs. Chao's ideas of what is fitting and fashionable for the female body. The two families have different senses of space and of the relation between family members. In one subplot, the Chinese-American cousin Paul is outraged to learn that Mrs. Chao reads her daughter Lili's mail; he asks Lili if she has ever heard of "privacy." This later results in a fight between Mrs. Chao and Lili in which Lili says she has learned from their American cousins that "it's not right to read other people's mail." Mrs. Chao retorts: "You're not 'other people,' you're my daughter. What is this thing, 'privacy'?" Lili explains to her that "privacy" can't be translated into Chinese. "Oh, so you're trying to hide things from your mother and use western words to trick her!" exclaims Mrs. Chao. Ultimately, just as the members of the Chao family are marked by the visit from their American relatives, the Fangs are altered by the time they return to California, each bringing back a memento or practice from their Chinese trip. In other words, rather than privileging either a nativist or assimilationist view, or even espousing a "Chinese-American" resolution of differences, *A Great Wall* performs a filmic "migration" by shuttling between the various cultural spaces; we are left, by the end of the film, with a sense of culture as dynamic and open, the result of a continual process of visiting and revisiting a plurality of cultural sites.

In keeping with the example of *A Great Wall*, we might consider as a possible model for the ongoing construction of ethnic identity the migratory process suggested by Wang's filming technique and emplotment: we might conceive of the making and practice of Asian American culture as nomadic, unsettled, taking place in the travel between cultural sites and in the multivocality of heterogeneous and conflicting positions. Taking seriously the heterogeneities among Asian Americans in California, we must conclude that the grouping "Asian American" is not a natural or static category; it is a socially constructed unity, a situationally specific position that we assume for political reasons. It is "strategic" in Gayatri Spivak's sense of a "strategic use of a positive essentialism in a scrupulously visible political interest" (206). The concept of "strategic essentialism" suggests that it is possible to utilize specific signifiers of ethnic identity, such as Asian American, for the purpose of contesting and disrupting the discourses that exclude Asian Americans, while simultaneously revealing the internal contradictions and slippages of Asian American so as to insure that such essentialisms will not be reproduced and proliferated by the very apparatuses we seek to disempower. I am not suggesting that we can or should do away with the notion of Asian American identity, for to stress only our differences would jeopardize the hard-earned unity that has been achieved in the last two decades of Asian American politics, the unity that is necessary if Asian Americans are to play a role in the new historical bloc of ethnic Californians. In fact, I would submit that the very freedom, in the 1990s, to explore the hybridities concealed beneath the desire of identity is permitted by the context of a strongly articulated essentialist politics. Just as the articulation of the desire for identity depends upon the existence of a fundamental horizon of differences, the articulation of differences dialectically depends upon a socially constructed and practiced notion of identity. I want simply to remark that in the 1990s, we can afford to rethink the notion of ethnic identity in terms of cultural, class, and gender differences, rather than pre-suming similarities and making the erasure of particularity the basis of unity. In the 1990s, we can diversify our political practices to include a more heterogeneous group and to enable crucial alliances with other groups – ethnicity-based, class-based, gender-based, and sexuality-based – in the ongoing work of transforming hegemony.

Notes

Many thanks to Elaine Kino for her thought-provoking questions, and for asking me to deliver portions of this essay as papers at the 1990 meetings of the Association of Asian American Studies and of the American Literature Association; to James Clifford, who also gave me the opportunity to deliver a version of this essay at a conference sponsored by the Center for Cultural Studies at UC Santa Cruz to the audience participants at all three conferences who asked stimulating questions which have helped me to rethink my original notions; and to Page duBois, Barbara Harlow, Susan Kirkpatrick, George Mariscal, Ellen Rooney, and Kathryn Shevelow, who read drafts and offered important comments and criticism.

1 *Nisei* refers to a second-generation Japanese-American, born to immigrant parents in the US; *Sansei*, a third-generation Japanese-American. *Issei* refers to a first-generation immigrant.
2 See Kim, *Asian*, for the most important book-length study of the literary representations of multi-generational Asian America.
3 Recent anthropological discussions of ethnic cultures as fluid and syncretic systems echo these concerns of Asian American writers. See, for example, Fischer; Clifford. For an anthropological study of Japanese-American culture that troubles the paradigmatic construction of kinship and filial relations as the central figure in culture, see Yanagisako.
4 We might think, for example, of the shifting of the Los Angeles "Chinatown" from its down-town location to the suburban community of Monterey Park. Since the 1970s, the former "Chinatown" has been superseded demographically and economically by Monterey Park, the home of many Chinese-Americans as well as newly arrived Chinese from Hong Kong and Taiwan. The Monterey Park community of 63,000 residents is currently over 50% Asian. On the social and political consequences of these changing demographics, see Fong.
5 Chan's history of the Chinese immigrant populations in California, *Bittersweet*, and her history of Asian Americans are extremely important in this regard. Numerous lectures by Ling-chi Wang at UC San Diego in 1987 and at UC Berkeley in 1988 have been very important to my understanding of the heterogeneity of waves of immigration across different Asian-origin groups.
6 The Chinese Exclusion Act of 1882 barred Chinese from entering the US, the National Origins Act prohibited the entry of Japanese in 1924, and the Tydings-McDuffie Act of 1934 limited Filipino immigrants to 50 people per year. Finally, the most tragic consequence of anti-Asian racism occurred during World War II when 120,000 Japanese-Americans (two-thirds of whom were American citizens by birth) were interned in camps. For a study of the anti-Japanese movement culminating in the immigration act of 1924, see Daniels. Takaki offers a general history of Asian origin immigrant groups in the United States.
7 The model minority myth constructs Asians as aggressively driven overachievers; it is a hom-ogenizing fiction which relies upon two strategies common in the subordinating construction of racial or ethnic otherness – the racial other as knowable, familiar ("like us"), and as incompre-hensible, threatening ("unlike us"); the model minority myth suggests both that Asians are over-achievers and "unlike us," and that they assimilate well, and are thus "like us." Asian Americans are continually pointing out that the model minority myth distorts the real gains, as well as the impediments, of Asian immigrants; by leveling and homogenizing all Asian groups, it erases the different rates of assimilation and the variety of class identities among various

Asian immigrant groups. Claiming that Asians are "overrepresented" on college campuses, the model minority myth is one of the justifications for the establishment of informal quotas in university admissions policies, similar to the university admission policies which discriminated against Jewish students from the 1930s to the 1950s.

8 In the last two decades, greatly diverse new groups have settled in California; demographers project that by the end of the century, the "majority" of the state will be comprised of ethnic "minority" groups. Due to recent immigrants, this influx of minorities is characterized also by greater diversity within individual groups: the group we call Asian Americans no longer denotes only Japanese, Chinese, Koreans, and Filipinos, but now includes Indian, Thai, Vietnamese, Cambodian, and Laotian groups; Latino communities in California are made up not only of Chicanos, but include Guatemalans, Salvadorans, and Colombians. It is not difficult to find Pakistani, Armenian, Lebanese, and Iranian enclaves in San Francisco, Los Angeles, or even San Diego. While California's "multi-culturalism" is often employed to support a notion of the "melting pot," to further an ideological assertion of equal opportunity for California's different immigrant groups, I am, in contrast, pursuing the ignored implications of this characterization of California as an ethnic state: that is, despite the increasing numbers of ethnic immigrants apparently racing to enjoy California's opportunities, for racial and ethnic immigrants there is no equality, but uneven development, nonequivalence, and cultural heterogeneities, not only between, but within, groups.

9 For an important elaboration of the concept of "minority discourse," see JanMohamed and Lloyd.

10 This notion of "the dominant" – defined by Williams in a chapter discussing the "Dominant, Residual, and Emergent" as "a cultural process . . . seized as a cultural system, with determinate dominant features: feudal culture or bourgeois culture or a transition from one to the other" – is often conflated in recent cultural theory with Gramsci's concept of hegemony. Indeed, Williams writes: "We have certainly still to speak of the 'dominant' and the 'effective,' and in these senses of the hegemonic" (121) as if the dominant and the hegemonic are synonymous.

11 See Gramsci, "History." Gramsci describes "subaltern" groups as by definition not unified, emergent, and always in relation to the dominant groups:

> The history of subaltern social groups is necessarily fragmented and episodic. There undoubtedly does exist a tendency to (at least provisional stages of) unification in the historical activity of these groups, but this tendency is continually interrupted by the activity of the ruling groups; it therefore can only be demonstrated when an historical cycle is completed and this cycle culminates in a success. Subaltern groups are always subject to the activity of ruling groups, even when they rebel and rise up: only 'permanent' victory breaks their subordination, and that not immediately. In reality, even when they appear triumphant, the subaltern groups are merely anxious to defend themselves (a truth which can be demonstrated by the history of the French Revolution at least up to 1830). Every trace of independent initiative on the part of subaltern groups should therefore be of incalculable value for the integral historian. (54–5)

12 "Hegemony" remains a suggestive construct in Gramsci, however, rather than an explicitly interpreted set of relations. Contemporary readers are left with the more specific task of distinguishing which particular forms of challenge to an existing hegemony are significantly transformative, and which forms may be neutralized or appropriated by the hegemony. Some cultural-critics contend that counterhegemonic forms and practices are tied by definition to the dominant culture and that the dominant culture simultaneously produces and limits its own forms of counter-culture. I am thinking here of some of the "new historicist" studies that use a particular notion of Foucault's discourse to confer authority to the "dominant," interpreting all forms of "subversion" as being ultimately "contained" by dominant ideology and institutions. Other cultural historians, such as Williams, suggest that because there is both identifiable variation in the social order over time, as well as variations in the forms of the counter-culture in different historical periods, we must conclude that some aspects of the oppositional forms are not reducible to the terms of the original hegemony. Still other theorists, such as Ernesto Leclau and Chantal Mouffe, have expanded Gramsci's notion of hegem-

ony to argue that in advanced capitalist society, the social field is not a totality consisting exclusively of the dominant and the counterdominant, but rather that "the social" is an open and uneven terrain of contesting articulations and signifying practices. Some of these articulations and practices are neutralized, while others can be linked to build important, pressures against an existing hegemony. See Laclau and Mouffe, especially pp. 134–45. They argue persuasively that no hegemonic logic can account for the totality of "the social" and that the open and incomplete character of the social field is the precondition of every hegemonic practice. For if the field of hegemony were conceived according to a "zero-sum" vision of possible positions and practices, then the very concept of hegemony, as plural and mutable formations and relations, would be rendered impossible. Elsewhere, in "Hegemony and New Political Subjects," Mouffe goes even further to elaborate the practical dimensions of the hegemonic principle in terms of contemporary social movements.

13 Adamson reads *The Prison Notebooks* as the postulation of Gramsci's activist and educationalist politics; in chapter 6, he discusses Gramsci's two concepts of hegemony: hegemony as the consensual basis of an existing political system in civil society, as opposed to violent oppression or domination, and hegemony as a historical phase of bourgeois development in which class is understood not only economically but also in terms of a common intellectual and moral awareness, an overcoming of the "economic-corporative" phase. Adamson associates the former (hegemony in its contrast to domination) with "hegemony-maintenance," and the latter (hegemony as a stage in the political moment) as "hegemony-creation." Sassoon provides an excellent discussion of Gramsci's key concepts; she both historicizes the concept of hegemony and discusses the implications of some of the ways in which hegemony has been interpreted. Sassoon emphasizes the degree to which hegemony is opposed to domination to evoke the way in which one social group influences other groups, making certain compromises with them in order to gain their consent for its leadership in society as a whole.

14 Amilcar Cabral, the Cape Verdean African nationalist leader and theorist, echoes some fundamental observations made by Fanon: that the national bourgeoisie will collaborate with the colonizers and that tribal fundamentalism must be overcome or it will defeat any efforts at unity. In 1969, Cabral wrote ironically in "Party Principles and Political Practice" of the dangers of tribalism and nativism: "No one should think that he is more African than another, even than some white man who defends the interests of Africa, merely because he is today more adept at eating with his hand, rolling rice into a ball and putting it into his mouth" (57).

15 I am thinking here especially of de Lauretis; Spivak; and Minh-ha. The latter explains the multiple inscription of women of color:

> [M]any women of color feel obliged [to choose] between ethnicity and womanhood: how can they? You never have/are one without the other. The idea of two illusorily separated identities, one ethnic, the other woman (or more precisely female), partakes in the Euro-American system of dualistic reasoning and its age-old divide-and-conquer tactics.... The pitting of anti-racist and anti-sexist struggles against one another allows some vocal fighters to dismiss blatantly the existence of either racism or sexism within their lines of action, as if oppression only comes in separate, monolithic forms. (105)

16 For a more extensive analysis of generational conflict in Chu's novel, see Gong. Gong asserts that "The father/son relationship represents the most critical juncture in the erosion of a traditional Chinese value system and the emergence of a Chinese American character. Change from Chinese to Chinese American begins here" (74–5).

17 There are many scenes that resonate with my suggestion that generational conflicts cannot be isolated from either class or the historicity of gender. In the third section of the novel, it is class difference in addition to generational strife that founds the antagonism between mother and daughter: Ying-ying St. Clair cannot understand why Lena and her husband, Harold, have spent an enormous amount of money to live in a barn in the posh neighborhood of Woodside. Lena says: "My mother knows, underneath all the fancy details that cost so much, this house is still a barn" (151). In the early relationship between Suyuan Woo and her daughter, Jing-mei, the mother pushes her daughter to become a success, to perform on the

piano; we can see that such desires are the reflection of the mother's former poverty, her lack of opportunity as both a poor refugee and a woman, but the daughter, trapped within a familial framework of explanation, sees her mother as punishing and invasive. Finally, the mother and daughter pair An-mei and Rose Hsu dramatize a conflict between the mother's belief that it is more honorable to keep personal problems within the Chinese family and the daughter's faith in western psychotherapy: the mother cannot understand why her daughter would pay a psychiatrist, a stranger, to talk about her divorce, instead of talking to her mother: the mother who was raised believing one must not show suffering to others because they, like magpies, would feed on your tears says of the daughter's psychiatrist, "really, he is just another bird drinking from your misery" (241).

Works Cited

Adamson, Walter. 1980. *Hegemony and Revolution: A Study of Antonio Gramsci's Political and Cultural Theory*. Berkeley: University of California Press.

Cabral, Amilcar. 1979. *Unity and Struggle: Speeches and Writings of Amilcar Cabral*, trans. Michael Wolfers. New York: Monthly Review.

Chan, Sucheng. 1991. *Asian Americans: An Interpretive History*. Boston: Twayne, 1991.

——1986. *This Bittersweet Soil: The Chinese in California Agriculture, 1860–1910*. Berkeley: University of California Press.

Chang, Diana. 1989. "The Oriental Contingent." *The Forbidden Stitch*, ed. Shirley Geok-Lin Lim, Mayumi Tsutakawa, and Margarita Donnelly. Corvallis: Calyx, 171–7.

Chu, Louis. 1961. *Eat a Bowl of Tea*. Seattle: University of Washington Press.

Clifford, James. 1988. *The Predicament of Culture: Twentieth Century Ethnography, Literature, and Art*. Cambridge, Mass.: Harvard University Press.

Daniels, Roger. 1962. *The Politics of Prejudice*. Berkeley: University of California Press.

de Lauretis, Teresa. 1987. *Technologies of Gender*. Bloomington: Indiana University Press.

Fanon, Frantz. 1961. *The Wretched of the Earth*, trans. Constance Farrington. New York: Grove.

Fischer, Michael M. J. 1986. "Ethnicity and the Post-modern Arts of Memory." *Writing Culture*, ed. James Clifford and George Marcus. Berkeley: University of California Press.

Fong, Timothy. "A Community Study of Monterey Park, California." Dissertation, University of California, Berkeley.

Glenn, Evelyn Nakano. 1981. "Occupational Ghettoization: Japanese-American Women and Domestic Service, 1905–1970." *Ethnicity* 8: 352–86.

Gong, Ted. 1980. "Approaching Cultural Change Through Literature: From Chinese to Chinese-American." *Amerasia* 7: 73–86.

Gramsci, Antonio. "History of the Subaltern Classes: Methodological Criteria." *Selections*, 52–60.

——1971. *Selections from the Prison Notebooks*, ed. and trans. Quinton Hoare and Geoffrey Nowell Smith. New York: International.

A Great Wall. 1985. Director Peter Wang. New Yorker Films.

JanMohamed, Abdul, and David Lloyd, eds., 1990. *The Nature and Context of Minority Discourse*. New York: Oxford University Press.

Kim, Elaine. 1982. *Asian American Literature: An Introduction to the Writings and Their Social Context*. Philadelphia: Temple University Press.

——1990. "'Such Opposite Creatures': Men and Women in Asian American Literature." *Michigan Quarterly Review*: 68–93.

Kingston, Maxine Hong. 1975. *The Woman Warrior*. New York: Randon House.

Laclau, Ernesto, and Chantal Mouffe. 1985. *Hegemony and Socialist Strategy*. London: Verso.

Lowe, Lydia. 1988. "Quitting Time." *Ikon 9, Without Ceremony: a special issue by Asian Women United*. Spec. issue of *Ikon* 9: 29.

Minh-ha, Trinh T. 1989. *Woman, Native, Other: Writing Postcoloniality and Feminism*. Bloomington: Indiana University Press.

Mirikitani, Janice. "Breaking Tradition." *Without Ceremony* 9.

Mouffe, Chantal. 1988. "Hegemony and New Political Subjects: Toward a New Concept of Democracy." *Marxism and the Interpretation of Culture*, ed. Cary Nelson and Lawrence Grossberg. Urbana: University of Illinois Press, 89–104.

Sassoon, Anne Showstack. 1982. "Hegemony, War of Position and Political Intervention." *Approaches to Gramsci*, ed. Anne Showstack Sassoon. London: Writers and Readers.

Spivak, Gayatri. 1987. *In Other Worlds*. London: Routledge.

Takaki, Ronald. 1989. *Strangers From a Different Shore: A History of Asian Americans*. Boston: Little, Brown.

Tan, Amy. 1989. *The Joy Luck Club*. New York: Putnam's.

Williams, Raymond. 1977. *Marxism and Literature*. Oxford: Oxford University Press.

Yanagisako, Sylvia. 1985. *Transforming the Past: Kinship and Tradition among Japanese Americans*. Stanford, Calif.: Stanford University Press.

CHAPTER 8

Tradition, Invention, and Aesthetics in Native American Literature

Robert Dale Parker

The work of Carlton Smith (*Coyote Kills John Wayne: Postmodernism and Contemporary Fictions of the Transcultural Frontier*, 2000) and Robert Dale Parker (*The Invention of Native American Literature*, 2003) is representative of a new wave of Native American scholarship that relies more on contemporary critical methods than on traditionalist assumptions about Native culture. In this selection from his book, Parker describes his attempt to resituate Native literature in the context of other literatures and to develop a non-essentialist concept of Native cultural identity.

This book proposes an interpretive history of the ways that Indian writers drew on Indian and literary traditions to invent a Native American literature. In the process, I distinguish two thresholds in Native American literary studies. The first is a threshold in the literature, which has now reached sufficient mass for critics to move beyond the worn generalizations about rediscovered identity, eloquent simplicity, nonlinearity, orality, and so on. The second is a threshold in the criticism, which has now succeeded (despite continuing difficulties) in establishing the texts and the field of Native American literary studies and is increasingly contributing to the theoretical debates raging across the international study of literature and the humanities.

Nevertheless, the bulk of the large, growing body of American Indian literature remains unknown to most critics and teachers of American literature. This book cannot give a complete picture; it cannot even accommodate all my own favorite works. Rather than writing a survey, therefore, I have pondered a selection of works as part of a broader effort to understand the growth of Indian literature historically and in formal terms. Like other peoples, American Indians have a long history of telling stories and taking aesthetic pleasure in language. Amid widespread confidence and pleasure in literature as an aesthetic category, and with widespread literacy, it makes sense that we see an ever-growing number of Indian writers, including writers of great skill and power. The same could be said of many other groups. Yet to many people the invention of Native American literature comes as a surprise, because it violates hardened stereotypes of Indians. Those stereotypes deflect attention from Indian intellectuality and literacy and often from Indian articulateness. Even for critics and teachers of Indian literature, or critics and teachers of American literature who have a passing acquaintance with Indian literature, the contemporary often shoulders aside the earlier history of Indian writing, especially the history before

N. Scott Momaday's 1968 *House Made of Dawn*, which ushered in what came to be called the Native American literary renaissance.[1]

This book takes the presence of Indian writing for granted, while recognizing that Indian writing has often had to confront the expectation that it doesn't exist or at least that it can't be very impressive artistically. The current tendency among some critics (though not so many as is often claimed) to set aside literary form and aesthetic taste has the accidental effect of allowing conservative readers to think that noncanonical works aren't terribly interesting as art. But the declining interest in literary aesthetics and the rising interest in understudied writing have partly separate histories. For some critics, an interest in literary form is contaminated by the history of the so-called new critics; many scholars came to identify the new critics' attention to literary form with their conservative politics. But an interest in form can come in many flavors; the conservatives don't own it. Even amid an array of competing or varying aesthetic tastes, there can be no brief for the noncontingent aesthetic taste that the new critics took for granted and that to much of the populace has come to seem like the only way to understand judgments of literary value. For such people, to make a claim for an art object is to make an absolute claim, but if art were absolute then we wouldn't need to think about it critically. As Barbara Herrnstein Smith has influentially argued, and as the prolific enthusiasms of popular culture testify, aesthetic taste has a thousand faces.

Meanwhile, the recent explosion of interest in understudied writing receives its impetus from urgent social motives, and for that reason some of its proponents have tried, with deliberation or obliviousness, to pry aesthetic questions away from criticism. But many of us who recognize the social imperatives driving us to read understudied writing also recognize aesthetic imperatives. We *like* this writing. We like the rhythms and resonances of its phrases, sentences, episodes, and ideas. The politics and the aesthetics of Indian writing (or any writing) are not the same, but they are not separable either. The new critics and their followers often masked their politics by posing their political judgments as aesthetic judgments and pretending to write politics out of criticism. They saw politics as the stuff of naive criticism, especially criticism from the left. By contrast, scholars and teachers devoted to noncanonical literature see no conflict in reading politically and reading aesthetically. We read for politics and aesthetics, and we read the rhythms and resonances of one as part of reading the rhythms and resonances of the other.

Much as I take the presence of Indian writing for granted, then, I also insist on the aesthetic value of Indian literature, together with its identity as *Indian*. There's nothing necessarily artistic in cultural identity, but in the act of expressing itself cultural identity takes on aesthetic form. It's not just that audiences will identify the expressions of Indians as Indian painting, writing, music, and so on, whether they are distinctively Indian or not, but also that what Indians do makes (and hence changes) what Indians are (Stuart Hall, "Cultural Identity"), often in defiance of or obliviousness to what audiences expect (even some Indian audiences).

To point these interests through a historical lens, then, takes us to a history of ways that Indian literary writing expressed itself as literary and as Indian. In the process, Indian writers invented a body of literature that we've come to call Native American literature, imagining an internal coherence we produce by our culturally driven need to imagine it. They laid the foundation for later Indian writers to connect to a tradition and to do something else – to break the paradigms that their predecessors labored so hard to establish, a process now well under way.[2]

In this context, *The Invention of Native American Literature* identifies a series of key issues in the emerging, imaginary coherence of Native American literature over roughly the last century. Specifically, I argue that the desire to invent a Native American literature returned Indian writing over and over to a set of topics partly chosen by and partly chosen for Indian writers. I identify four topics that in overlapping ways address gender, sexuality, stereotype, and the appropriation of Indian cultural and intellectual property. Those four topics are: young men's threatened masculinity, the oral, the poetic, and Indian cultures' aloof renegotiations of what the dominant culture understands as authority.

After beginning with a skeptical reconsideration of scholars' and writers' efforts to theorize an Indian aesthetic, I turn to a topic not addressed by earlier critics but made newly accessible by the revolution in feminist criticism and gender studies, namely, the preoccupation with a pattern of restless young men with nothing to do. At least, the restless young men suspect or feel pressured to believe that they have nothing to do. For they live amid the often misogynist cultural mythology that contact with Euro-Americans (even long after such contact is routine) has deprived Indian men of their traditional roles without a similar displacement of Indian women's roles. Moreover, their world has not managed to construct an Indian, unassimilating way to adapt masculine roles to the dominant, business-saturated culture's expectations of 9–5 breadwinning. I ask not whether such a mythology is accurate or inaccurate. Instead, I consider its effects on early Indian literature's efforts to reimagine Indian culture while inventing a specifically Indian literature, especially in a pair of landmark but understudied novels from the depression that much influenced later Indian writers.

Meanwhile, the accelerations of modernity, with the almost irresistible excitements and enticements of mass culture and the reconfigurations of what Walter Benjamin called "the work of art in the age of mechanical reproduction," contributed to an international modernist craving to preserve, recover, or memorialize a nostalgically imagined past. Amid the exploding growth of literacy and print culture, that past was often identified with orality – hence the growth and popularity of "folklore" and the vast project to transcribe and translate a supposedly disappearing American Indian oral culture. Many others have already noted the central role of oral storytelling in Indian culture and literature, and I do not wish to undermine their insights. Instead I reread those insights through the broader lenses of modernist nostalgia and its drive to construct the oral as a touchstone and core of Indian distinctiveness. That nostalgia helps open the door to the naive identification of orality with Indianness in a world of print literacy that condescends to orality, even as condescension is the tacit accomplice of romanticizing exaltation.

Jacques Derrida, in that vein, decries the western tendency to see oral and written cultures as radically different from each other. He critiques Claude Lévi-Strauss's "The Writing Lesson," a chapter in *Tristes Tropiques* that recounts introducing writing to Nambikwara Indians in Brazil (Lévi-Strauss, 294–300; *Of Grammatology*, 101–40). To be sure, for Lévi-Strauss and many others since, the desire to see the oral and written as separate takes the anticolonialist form of championing orality and sometimes of understanding orality as a special characteristic of Native peoples fading tragically before the colonialist onslaught. But Derrida casts that desire as ethnocentrism in the guise of anti-ethnocentrism; he sees it as ethnocentric for Lévi-Strauss (and others) to suppose that oral discourse lacks the intricacy of written discourse, a supposition typical even among those who, like Lévi-Strauss, romanticize oral culture.

Thus while the representation of orality and oral storytelling becomes a means for Indian writers to imagine an Indian literature, and for their characters – including the restless young men – to rethink their relation to the past, it also becomes a means for non-Indians to imagine escape from modernity, conflating Indians and Indian orality with a romantically recoverable past that can merge with the oral, often in the form of poetry. As poetry becomes the preferred form for representing traditional Indian oral narrative in print, the insistence on the poetic mystifies storytelling, orality, and poetry itself, and it displaces the actual poetry written by Indian writers. I write a new history of the aesthetics of Native American literature, therefore, through the linked preoccupations with restless young men, storytelling, orality, poetry, and Indian notions of authority as they come together in a series of precedent-setting novels, bodies of poetry, and bodies of theory about Indian oral storytelling as poetry.

In the central five chapters of this book, I identify a series of concerns or issues that American Indian writers have faced as they invented what eventually seemed to cohere as Native American literature. I use the word *invention* to suggest an air of the provisional, of ongoing process and construction, as opposed to a natural, inevitable effusion of Indian identity. To see Indian art as such an effusion is to suppose that Indian identity is ahistorical, static, and absolute rather than always being produced by Indians and, however cavalierly, by other people. After all, without non-Indians, no one could imagine Indians as a category. (The notion of invented here has more to do with Gerald Vizenor's view of Indianness and what he calls the "post-Indian" than with James Clifton's idea of "the invented Indian.")[3] I trust that other critics can identify issues beyond those addressed in this book. Still, I argue that these issues weave together to establish a Native American literature.

Chapters 2 and 3 read the preoccupation with restless young men with nothing to do in two Indian novels published during the depression, John Joseph Mathews's *Sundown* (1934) and D'Arcy McNickle's *The Surrounded* (1936), a preoccupation that continues with remarkable consistency through later Indian writing, including writing by women. The restless young men so absorb the wider culture's devaluing and emptying out of their roles that they can find nothing to do, or they so little value their doing that they misread it as nothing. Even sexually, they don't do much. They procrastinate, and what little they do, they do indifferently, hinting at but holding off a potential homosexuality or (more modestly) an interest in queerness. Their uncertain, passive masculinity offers a troubled medium for Indian modernity and gender relations, yet it also offers possibilities for rethinking gender, masculinity, sexuality, and an ethic of Indian work in ways these early novels find hard to imagine or follow through on. The depression proves provocative for such rethinking, because the great difficulty in finding paid work put pressure on the dominant culture's conflation of masculinity with business-oriented labor just when Indian writers were trying to reconcile their own relation to intersecting ideologies of labor, masculinity, business, and changing traditional cultures. While *Sundown* unwinds with little sense of any way out beyond an economic assimilation that it refuses, *The Surrounded* turns to traditional oral storytelling to construct Indian modernity and articulate it to an outside world. Meanwhile, that outside world seeks to temper the new age of mechanical reproduction by turning to a nostalgically recovered orality – often recovered, ironically, through the mechanical reproduction that prints Indian oral stories in written form as parts of novels and as Indian "poetry."

Picking up on that notion of orality, then, chapter 4 looks historically at the transcription of traditional Indian oral stories and the cultural translation of transcribed, translated stories into Indian "poetry," a new "Indian literature" that happens not to be written by Indians yet remains foundational to many non-Indians' imagination of what Indian writing might be. Here I critique a body of translation and transcription theory that has proved enormously influential in Indian studies and the wider study of oral literature and folklore. As McNickle's prose fiction captures the dominant culture's growing identification between orality and Indianness, the production of Indian oral stories as literary poetry merges that identification between the Indian and the oral with an identification of the Indian, the oral, and the poetical, which poses a problem for actual Indian poets.

Chapter 5, therefore, takes up the poetry of Ray A. Young Bear, whose lyrical poems scorn the non-Indian appropriation of Indian cultures and of the purportedly Indian poetical and oral, including the way that such appropriations can displace actual poetry actually written by Indians. But contrary to the dominant expectation of resistance, Young Bear and other Indian poets, such as Wendy Rose and Chrystos, don't counterpoise an authoritatively transcendent real Indianness to bulldoze over the faux-Indianness they find so preposterous. Simply to reverse who holds which position in the relation of dominator to dominated would lock in the structure of authority that Young Bear's poetry defies. By contrast, and in accord with traditional Meskwaki notions of authority, notions not incongruent with those of many other Indian peoples, Young Bear's epistemology is indifferent to the dominant presumption that culture and knowledge admit authoritative, stable readings. Young Bear's assumptions about authority cycle us back to the restless young men with nothing to do portrayed by Mathews, McNickle, and many later Indian writers, including Young Bear. For a lack of interest in authority won't translate into the Babbitt-ridden, business get-up-and-go of Euro-American masculinity that Mathews paints as descending onto the calmer, less hierarchical world of early twentieth-century Osage ways. The focalizing consciousness of Mathews's novel relies on regressive fantasies of a return to supposedly traditional ways imagined through an idealizing nostalgia, without the cultural repertoire to reenvision what the dominant ideology misreads as "nothing" and to translate it into cultural advocacy, into an epistemology of ordinary Indian living – something to do indeed. Young Bear provides an alternative of the sort that Mathews and McNickle sought and helped lay the groundwork for in their writing and their political activities but that, in an earlier, differently pressured age, they could not find the cultural vocabulary to envision.

With the achieved invention of Native American literature, we have that vocabulary now. In a culminating chapter, then, I follow how all these issues come together in two relatively recent novels about restless, passive, young or not-so-young men, Leslie Marmon Silko's now canonical *Ceremony* (1977) and Thomas King's less known but delightful *Medicine River* (1989). (King is better known for *Green Grass, Running Water*, 1993.) Both novels include oral storytelling, with *Ceremony* presenting oral stories in poetic form and *Medicine River* spoofing what non-Indians often don't get about storytelling while crafting its narrative structure on oral models and centrifugal assumptions about authority. Though I set this chapter up partly as a test of the larger argument, I don't approach it as an experiment so much as I set out to read the fate of these preoccupations as they all come together climactically in key novels of the Native American renaissance.

My final chapter continues to address Native American literature but this time as one among many American literatures. It poses more directly a question implicit in the rest of the book: when critics and teachers of literature broaden the range of materials that they study and teach, inciting what I call a "post-canon," how does that broadening change not just what we study and teach, but how we study and teach? Too often, critics and the general public address the movement to study texts from a wide range of social groups as if it were isolated from what we say about those texts, or assume that merely to widen the traditional range of texts is to reinvent what we say about literature and its representations. But the reinvention of literature offers more challenges than the writing about that reinvention usually supposes. This chapter brings together the active but still largely separate projects of retheorizing representation (how does a text represent or not represent a group of people whom the author does or does not belong to? – how does an Indian text represent or not represent Indian people?) and retheorizing canonicity (which texts and what range of texts should we write about and teach?). Each of these projects has gained its recent sophistications partly at the cost of ignoring the dialogues that are retheorizing the other. If a post-canon is to live up to its post-canonicity, it cannot reapply a discredited confidence about representation to a wider range of texts, assuming, for example, that a text by an African American writer bears a one-to-one relation to the representation of African Americans in general. Instead, a post-canon must think through the constraints of representation that impel us to a post-canon in the first place. Then our reading of Native American and other literatures can live up to the promises of post-canonicity by reinventing both the reading of representation and the representation of what we read.

My motives for studying Indian literature are aesthetic and literary. I cannot recall another critic of Indian literature who comes right out and says that, probably in part because it is difficult to say what we mean by aesthetic and literary pleasure. Many people who do not read much Indian writing never expect those of us who read it to seek it out and return to it for aesthetic reasons. But anyone who spends much time among critics of Indian literature will sense their excited pleasure in the writing.

What does it mean to say that I like what I read? It is easier to say what it doesn't mean. It doesn't mean that there is a universal standard of value, epitomized by such writers as Dante, Shakespeare, and Tolstoy and fulfilled again in Indian writing – or in any writing. It could mean that Indian writing offers a radically different set of standards and pleasures from canonical writing, so that if only readers would get a feel for those standards, then they would learn to love Indian writing as they or others love the writing of Dante, Shakespeare, Tolstoy, and their canonized cohorts. I hoped for that before starting to read Indian literature, and sometimes I found it, especially in some of the translated and transcribed oral stories of traditional storytellers, such as the violent tales from the northwest (see Jarold Ramsey, Siobhan Senier) or the trickster stories that Gerald Vizenor tries to embody in his extravagant fiction and theoretical writing. But for the most part, that's not what I found. Instead, I found the cadenced, resonant understatement of D'Arcy McNickle, Ray Young Bear's lyricism (whatever obstacles I also found in Young Bear's thicket of obscure references), Joy Harjo's common touch and lyrical anaphora, Louise Erdrich's lapidary metaphors, and Thomas King's wistful, amiable ironies. In other words, I found many of the same pleasures that I found in canonical writing, and plenty of other pleasures too, for Indian writers often write about different worlds from those of non-Indian writers. With modest exceptions – Mathews's and King's sense of plot, Young Bear's difficulty (or is that difficulty not so different from James Joyce's, Ezra Pound's, T. S. Eliot's, or Melvin Tolson's?) – I didn't need to come up with a noncanonical notion of aesthetics to appreciate Indian writing. Indian writing stands out (at least to me) not only for its differences from other writing, its profound differences of cultural reference and understanding, but also because so much of it is as good as the best other writing and good on pretty much the same terms as the other writing. Indeed, that matches a broader strain in the continuing history of contact between Indian and non-Indian cultures. Non-Indians – and Indians influenced by non-Indians (more precisely, Indians internalizing the dominant culture, which they are already influencing and part of) – often expect something exotic in Indians and Indian writing. But one of my goals in this book is to recover the extraordinary sense of ordinariness in Indian writing, an ordinariness that has profound aesthetic connotations through its pleasure in routine, in the beauty of continuity and daily life, in simply – as Young Bear and many others put it repeatedly – "being."

In that spirit, I am arguing that abstract descriptions of form (e.g., symmetrical, asymmetrical, linear, circular, lyrical, narrative) have no cultural specificity. This has everything to do with the arguments in chapters 4 and 6 about poetic form in oral narrative and in Silko's *Ceremony*, and in chapter 7 about the thickness of cultural description and study we need to see how a text uses form. In particular, I draw on the notion that communications theorists call the fallacy of technological determinism, namely, the fallacy that a given technology (the printing press, railroads, radio) necessarily produces a given cultural consequence. By contrast – the argument goes – the cultural consequence varies with how the technology gets used, despite our tendency to read a consequence back onto the technology itself. In the same way, a literary form, such as the novel, the autobiography, free indirect discourse, parallelism, repetition, and so on, doesn't inevitably carry a predictable cultural meaning or context (such as Indian or non-Indian), though we might read back onto it a cultural context that we have come to associate with it, as we might associate Navajo prayer with parallelism ("My feet restore for me, my legs restore for me, my body restore for me, my mind restore for me, my voice restore for me". Navajo prayer has much to do with parallelism, but parallelism doesn't inevitably lead to Navajo prayer. Any form that we might connect to Indian writing (or to the writing of any given Indian people) might also appear in other people's writing. If we deny that pliability of form, then we limit our chance to read what any particular tradition – such as Creek or Navajo, or a more broadly Indian tradition – does with that form.

It is therefore anything but a matter of discovering that Indian literature is worth reading because it abides by European or falsely universalized forms. On the contrary, my approach seeks to get at what Indian writing does with form. Such an approach has the effect of deprivileging and de-Europeanizing forms associated with literature written by whites and often glibly described as "complex," whereas the forms of "minority" literature are often described as "simple." But I don't suggest a deracializing or deculturalizing of form. Readers and writers will still culturalize form, and to the extent (debatable and variable) that we live in a race-saturated world, they will racialize form as well, with whatever mélange of cultural insight or oversimplification. The point is to identify the site of racialized and culturalized forms in the ways that we read instances of those forms, rather than in some essentializing way inherently in the forms themselves.

Yet, we might expect Indian writing to have a different aesthetic from non-Indian writing, and many critics claim that it does. For me to incline otherwise is to buck a growing trend. A novel like Silko's *Ceremony*, so the argument goes, is cyclical, rather than linear, fitting an Indian sense of nonlinear time. Paula Gunn Allen puts the argument famously in the title essay of her influential *The Sacred Hoop*, and the poet and critic Kimberly M. Blaeser has returned to it in an elegant article. Still, for readers of modernist and contemporary writers who defy linearity, from Woolf and Faulkner to Borges, Angela Carter, and many others, as well as earlier writers like Cervantes, Swift (e.g., *A Tale of a Tub*), or Sterne, Silko's commitment to nonlinear plot, however defining of *Ceremony* and her other writings, and however fascinating her version of nonlinearity, might not seem distinctive for its nonlinearity per se. As Sandra Adell says about efforts to construct a black aesthetic, "the more the black theorist writes in the interest of blackness, the greater his Eurocentrism." Adell's argument recalls Derrida's idea that Lévi-Strauss's anticolonialist desire to separate orality from literacy ends up as ethnocentrism in the guise of anti-ethnocentrism. In Indian studies, we might remind ourselves that Indian identity is unthinkable without contact and exchange between Indian and non-Indian cultures. Before that, there could be no concept of Indians. Hence the notion of an Indian aesthetic depends on non-Indians, just as the notion of non-Indian or "western" culture gathers its illusory coherence by depending on the worlds it seeks to expel. That does not necessarily mean there is no such thing as an Indian (or European) aesthetic, but it makes it recursively tricky to pin down what an Indian aesthetic might be. Thus, when Adell goes on to quote Lewis Nkosi writing that "the further back the African artist goes in exploring his tradition, the nearer he gets to the European avant-garde,"[4] we need to match Nkosi's insight by remembering that European, modernist avant-garde art depended on African and, broadly, on so-called non-western art.

I fear, then, that Blaeser's eloquent argument mostly comes down to platitude. "The works of Native American writers," she says, "both inadvertently and self-consciously embody literary processes and genres unlike those of the old canon. Many Indian authors have chosen purposefully to ignore standard rules and forms ill suited to Native storytelling. They strive to introduce different codes. Their works teach readers and critics new ways of reading and interacting with voices on the page" ("Like 'Reeds through the Ribs of a Basket,'" 266). All this sounds nice, but the same claims are often made for almost any group of writers. The romantic claim for newness and the structuralist claim for "codes" have their own histories apart from any connection to Indian writing. After some excellent readings of texts, Blaeser concludes with in effect a prose poem characterizing Indian writing and its aesthetic:

> Contemporary story told in a nonlinear fashion. The interweaving of the realities of this world and time with that of other worlds and other times. The transgressing of the boundaries of genre. The use of the circle as an aesthetic form instead of a straight line. The refusal to write an end to story because story always continues. The creating of characters whose beliefs and actions violate certain standards of morality or good taste.... Not explaining "logically" in cause and effect but believing in the chance of

life and the chance of a story.... Writing reality. Not writing literature. Writing revolution. Not writing literature. Writing life. (275)

These are common, almost platitudinous claims for many writers, Indian or not. More non-Native than Native writers practice the aesthetic (or collection of aesthetics) that Blaeser describes; nor is her aesthetic necessarily congenial to all Native writers. Native writers hold no privileged link to reality, revolution, or life; and not all Native writers stand ready to forswear genre, endings, characters who abide by morality or good taste, logic, literature, or even linearity.

To understand *Ceremony*, we need to ponder its nonlinear structure, but tying its structure to being Indian will not necessarily describe what other Indian literature is or prescribe what it should be. Duane Niatum, the poet and anthology editor, writes that he has "an arrow to chip" on this topic: "It is my opinion that there is not a Native American aesthetic that we can recognize as having separate principles from the standards of artists from Western European and American cultures. And anyone who claims there is encourages a conventional and prescriptive response from both Native Americans and those from other cultures. The result is that the reader's imagination is actually inhibited. Stereotypic expectations break down the free play between reader and writer" (554). In a similar if more politicized vein, Robert Allen Warrior says that "we do not have to wait to discover some essentially Indian form of writing.... However much these writers are performing an activity somehow continuous with that of storytellers and singers, they are also doing what poetry has done in its European forms and in other non-European contexts.... These poets have taken a European written form thousands of years old and transformed it ... to become a form of resistance against other European forms and systems" (117). Niatum goes on to draw connections between the Kiowa writer N. Scott Momaday or the Blackfeet and Gros Ventre writer James Welch and Joyce, Woolf, Faulkner, Hemingway, and Camus (557–61). But it's a tricky argument. He looks at a poem about a storm by Ted Hughes, the British poet (and later poet laureate), and finds features in it that sound Indian. "There is one exception, however," Niatum adds, going on to say – in intriguingly qualified language – that "a Blackfeet or a Navajo or a Swinomish writing about a similar experience – *if* well versed in the traditions of his or her ancestors *and* caring about the values enough to integrate them into his or her art – *might* respond to this storm, but far more humbly and openly (without Hughes's arrogance), having discovered from the people's songs, ancient sparks, that the way is to be with the turning earth, the blowing mist, the cycle of human as well as earthly changes" (557; emphasis added). According to Niatum, then, there is no Native American aesthetic, in the sense of a specifically Native form, but there are tendencies and topics (as Niatum hints wittily when he says that he has "an arrow to chip"), at least among Native writers who have the knowledge and desire to weave their writing into Native traditions. Niatum's inelegant exchange ("exception," "if," "might") seems to me exactly right and more trustworthy than any elegant formulation, any well-wrought urn we might craft to contain Indian aesthetics.

To critics of African American literature, the outlines of the debate might sound like a familiar echo after the Black Arts and Black Aesthetic movement of the 1960s, though the particulars and tones differ enormously. Niatum's inelegant exchange bears a likeness to the call of Henry Louis Gates Jr., arguing against the notion of a Black Aesthetic (*Figures in Black*, 38–46), for "a theory of criticism that is inscribed within the black vernacular tradition and that in turn informs the shape of the Afro-American literary tradition" (*Signifying Monkey*, xix). Niatum's playfully ironic "arrow to chip" and humble songs of "the blowing mist," with their nonlinear "cycle of human as well as earthly changes," aspire to such a vernacular for describing Indian writing. Whether that adds up to an Indian aesthetic, a specifically Indian form, might depend on the needs of the beholder, which can cycle and change from one setting to another.

Moreover, the classic statements from theorists of the Black Aesthetic often bear a good deal more nuance than their critics bequeathed to cultural memory. In "Towards a Black Aesthetic" (1968), Hoyt W. Fuller identified an array of black styles, but he began by lamenting the silly idea that black artistic expression is inevitably about blackness or suffering. He defined a black aesthetic as "a system of isolating and evaluating the artistic works of black people which reflect the special character and imperatives of black experience" (9). He never suggested that all artistic works by black people fill that function or that they do nothing else. Nor did he claim that all black writers whose work reflects black experience reflect it in the same way. Thus, Fuller advocated a black aesthetic without taking up the banner that scares off Niatum, the banner proclaiming that art without a black aesthetic isn't black, or that art without an Indian aesthetic isn't Indian. As Gates puts it:

> A descriptive formalism cannot bring a contrived unity to a tradition defined in the first instance by "ethnicity." Further, expectations that authors must be accountable spokespersons for their ethnic groups can well nigh be unbearable for an "ethnic" author. If black authors are primarily entrusted with producing the proverbial "text of blackness," they become vulnerable to the charge of betrayal if they shirk their "duty." . . . These burdens of representation can too often lead to demands for ideological "correctness" in an author's work, not to mention a prescriptive criticism that demands certain forms of allegiance and uniformity. (" 'Ethnic and Minority' Studies," 294)

Critics such as Allen or Blaeser (and I name only two of the best such critics as examples) end up implying, perhaps without meaning to, that to be an Indian writer you need to follow certain prescribed forms, such as non-linearity, and that without the prescribed forms, writing cannot be Indian.

By contrast, many of the most separatist Black Aesthetic theorists argued against defining a Black Aesthetic. Julian Mayfield wrote, "I cannot – will not – define my Black Aesthetic, nor will I allow it to be defined for me" (29). Even Don L. Lee wrote, "Finally, the Black Aesthetic cannot be defined in any definite way. To accurately and fully define a Black Aesthetic would automatically limit it" (246). Instead of describing the Black Aesthetic as typifying black writing, many Black Arts theorists rejected earlier black writing, unlike most Indian critics, who address their traditions with more deference. Instead of identifying with the past, many Black Arts and Black Aesthetic critics saw their ideas as a program for the future. "The Black Aesthetic, if it is anything," wrote Mayfield, "is the search for a new program, because all the old programs spawned out of the Judaeo-Christian spirit have failed us" (28). In Fuller's terms, the Black Aesthetic "is seeking new forms, new limits, new shapes" ("New Black Literature," 346). To Larry Neal, "the Black Arts Movement proposes a radical reordering of the western cultural aesthetic" (272). The differences between African American and Native American literary histories are at least as cautionary as the similarities may be instructive. But the outpouring of writing about a black aesthetic in the late 1960s and early 1970s offers a sounding board and stimulus for thinking about Native American aesthetics, even as the civil rights and black power movements helped inspire political change and assertiveness in Native America (and non-Anglo America in general).

Thomas King laments that "in our discussions of Native literature, we try to imagine that there is a racial denominator which full-bloods raised in cities, half-bloods raised on farms, quarter-bloods raised on reservations, Indians adopted and raised by white families, Indians who speak their tribal language, Indians who speak only English, traditionally educated Indians, university-trained Indians, Indians with little education, and the like all share. We know, of course, that there is not."[5] Underlining the inevitable unrepresentativeness and incompleteness of even a long list, King leaves off expected categories like full-bloods on reservations or quarter-bloods in cities. And we can multiply King's comments by the many groups of Indian people, racially quantified or not, that he doesn't mention.

I return then, circularly, to the representative example of nonlinearity as a potentially defining characteristic for a Native American aesthetic. Especially in narrative writing, which privileges – though it does not confine us to – reading from left to right (or in some languages from right to left), from top to bottom of the page, and from page to page in the same direction, nonlinearity is not an independent function. It never exists apart from linearity. Even when we see the circular or nonlinear as the negative of linearity, we still make linearity and nonlinearity partake of and define each other. The difference between them may apply more usefully to comparing Indian and non-Indian autobiography, as, historically, traditional autobiography depends on a linear, progressive model. But even a traditional autobiography begins where it ends, with the writing that the plot leads up to. In narrative theory, variations in linearity govern the defining formula of narrative, the *fabula* as opposed to the *sjuzet* (as the Russian formalists famously put it, in Russian);[6] the story as opposed to the plot (the Russian formalists, in English translation), to the narrative (Gérard Genette), to the discourse (Emile Benveniste, Seymour Chatman), or to the text (Shlomith Rimmon-Kenan); or, as I prefer to put it, the tale as opposed to the telling. The tale is the sequence of events as they happened, and the telling is the sequence of events as they are told – for example, told by a novel that narrates the tale. We can read the tale or the telling as linear or nonlinear, progressive or repetitive, but either way, the binary between tale and telling equally fits (and equally distorts) all narrative, Indian or not.

Hertha Dawn Wong points out that, while nonlinearity has been claimed as defining Indian autobiography, it has also been claimed as defining feminist autobiography (23). More broadly, nonlinearity plays a signal role in Hélène Cixous's controversial efforts, like those of Luce Irigaray, to define what Cixous has called *l'écriture féminine*, or feminine writing, efforts that have met at least as much scorn as acclaim, for many feminists fear that such terms clothe women's language in a dressed-up version of the same misogynist clichés about women's frivolous chatter that feminists set out to overturn. Even Cixous describes *l'écriture féminine* as a style of writing produced by male as well as female writers.

In the same vein, we might enjoy how Sherman Alexie's poem "One Stick Song" (*One Stick*, 35–40) plays riffs on the rhythms of a stick game song (a popular game in his part of Indian America), but in another context a non-Indian or an Indian writer might choose a similar form that would attract different associations. The form itself does not carry a cultural determinant apart from the context we read it through, even though that context makes his poem's form very Indian indeed (or very northwest Indian). Thus my approach differs from approaches that seek out transcendent formal characteristics, such as nonlinearity, as a means to define Indian writing. I read the Indian in Indian writing historically, rather than formally. I offer formalist readings but read form historically, not as a transhistorical vessel of essentialist identity.

"Scholars who write about an ethnic group to which they do not belong," notes bell hooks, "rarely discuss in the introductions to their work the ethical issues of their race privilege" (*Talking Back*, 44). I am white and lament that, as hooks notes, some people may unwittingly attribute greater authority to the work of white scholars. I would rather that people approached my work with extra skepticism. There is a great deal that some Native critics will understand that I would never anticipate. But just as my failures cannot reduce to my whiteness, so to reduce Native scholars' insights to their Nativeness would demean the work it took to reach those insights.

The community of scholars and critics has grown, in recent years, by increasingly recognizing the need to think through our perspectives and biases and by recognizing that we can never think them through entirely. I have my biases, and they range beyond color. I am – or try to be – a formalist and a politically poststructuralist, feminist, socio-historical critic on the left. I seek to write criticism that reads the social meanings and structures of literary forms and the formal structures and meanings of social representation, including gender. I lament the widespread tendency to read form and social representation as some kind of seesawing binary, as if when attention to one goes up then attention to the other must go down. On the contrary, I assume that form and social representation never separate, despite many readers' investment in imagining them separately, and even though no one kind of form (e.g., "Indian form," "western form," nonlinear form) can predict any particular kind of social representation.

But if we increasingly recognize the need to reflect on our perspectives and biases, we also fortify bias when we reduce it to essentialized racial categories, as we sometimes (and I put weight on the word *sometimes*) do when we say things like, as a white critic, I think such and such, or as an Indian critic, I think such and such, or as an Indian or white critic, someone else thinks such and such. I don't want to rule out those expressions, for their meaning varies with their context, and I think it's more useful to contemplate expressions like that and the need or pressure to use them than it is to rule them out or insist on them.[7]

In the meantime, some critics persist in misreading the project of writing about a people or its literature as writing for that people, in effect, as speaking for them.[8] Speaking for Indians is the furthest thing from my mind. Elizabeth Cook-Lynn denies, as well, that Indian poets can speak for their people, an idea that she calls "one of the great burdens of contemporary American Indian poets today, for it is widely believed that we 'speak for our tribes.' The frank truth is that I don't know very many poets who say, 'I speak for my people.' It is not only unwise; it is probably impossible, and it is very surely arrogant, for *We Are Self-Appointed*" ("You May Consider Speaking," 58). In an interview, Thomas King says that to

> speak for Native people...isn't a role I'm even interested in....There are enough people from the various tribes who speak both languages, who have very close ties, which I don't, to their tribe, who can do that for each one of the tribes. Everybody tries

to hit upon one particular Indian at any point in time to answer all the questions about Indian affairs in the whole of North America. Most Indians won't take that job, so people go looking for someone who will. Most times it's a non-Indian who thinks he knows all about Indians or a social guru like, say, Lynn Andrews. I get fairly appalled when that begins to happen. I don't really care if the person is Native or non-Native. But to put anybody into a role like that, particularly a non-Native, is maddening. (Interview with Hartmut Lutz, 109)

As Cook-Lynn and King indicate, plenty of Indians speak perfectly well for themselves, with no thanks needed to anyone else.[9] Their work has, among its least notable attributes, inspired this book and many others.

Happily, Indian literature offers much to choose from: this book could well address writings beyond those it concentrates on. Critics write about what moves them most and where they think they see ways to make a useful contribution, and in my case, that comes with fiction and poetry. As it happens, despite a proliferation of autobiography and the growth of Native theater,[10] poetry and fiction still rest at the center of what we see, ideologically, as "literature," thus playing a central role in the emerging imaginary coherence of Native American literature that this book sets out to describe.

My title, *The Invention of Native American Literature*, merges two different meanings of *invention*. One meaning describes the creation *of* Native literature: how it got started, historically. The other meaning describes the creation *by* Native literature: the ideas it invents. The second sense, less familiar in contemporary usage, comes from theories of rhetoric and refers to the act of imagining what to write about. In that context, I tend to concentrate on writers' early, formative work – McNickle's first novel, poems from Young Bear's first two books, Silko's and King's first novels. Warrior has spoken to the tendency of teaching and scholarship to focus on the first novels of Indian writers and neglect their later work. Many readers (including this one) were disappointed in the long-awaited second novels of Momaday (*The Ancient Child* [1989]) and Silko (*Almanac of the Dead* [1991]), but these novels have a following, and Momaday's and Silko's other writings have attracted much interest, especially *The Way to Rainy Mountain* (1969) and *Storyteller* (1981). I expect that Silko's *Gardens in the Dunes* (1999) will also attract much critical interest. The novels that Louise Erdrich published after her spectacular debut novel, *Love Medicine* (1983), have won a large audience, and Thomas King's second novel, *Green Grass, Running Water*, has received far more critical commentary than his first, promising that his continuing work (beginning with *Truth & Bright Water* [1999]) might attract considerable interest as well. But Warrior is right; first novels by most of the best-known Indian novelists (Momaday, Welch, Silko, Vizenor, and even Erdrich) have captured the bulk of critical and pedagogical attention, and I do little to change that. By concentrating on the formative works of writers who later go on in a multitude of additional directions, I bring those works together in their roles as bricks in a larger structure, the invention of Native American literature.

Close concentration on formative texts serves my nonessentialist approach, for essentialist assumptions have a tough time holding up under close study. Warrior notes that "a commitment to essentialized indigenous worldviews and consciousness, over the course of the decade [of the 1980s], became a pervasive and almost requisite feature of American Indian critical writing," but that the "dominating influence of essentialist understandings of Indian culture" has drawn increasing challenges (xvii).

He concludes that American Indian studies "continue[s] to be preoccupied with parochial questions of identity and authenticity. Essentialist categories still reign insofar as more of the focus of scholarship has been to reduce, constrain, and contain American Indian literature and thought and to establish why something or someone is 'Indian' than engage the myriad critical issues crucial to an Indian future" (xix). In line with Warrior, my attention goes not to why or whether someone or something is Indian, but to *how* they are Indian. In itself, anti-essentialism has become a critical commonplace (even while some people remain – as Warrior notes – oblivious to it). Still, it retains an edge in Indian studies that it may be losing in many other conversations, because, again as Warrior and Jace Weaver note, in Indian studies there remains so much pressure to essentialize.[11] Moreover, the nonessentialist approach of this book is not the point. If it were, this book would only rediscover a sometimes forgotten truism. Instead, the nonessentialist approach is an instrument, one among many, to readings of these texts' social and aesthetic energies and interests.

For literary criticism to seek the social apart from the aesthetic, as many readers expect, especially for criticism of literature written by people who are not white, is to reduce the critical project to what Gayatri Chakravorty Spivak aptly scorns as mere information retrieval ("Three Women's Texts," 243). Thus I return at the end of this introduction to where it began, with the writings that this book addresses as texts that offer their readers pleasure. The pleasure of these writings comes in the cultural, intellectual, and literary challenges they lay down, in turns of phrase, plot, imagination, and representation that invite us to pause and at the same time urge us to keep on reading, cycling on through Niatum's "human as well as earthly changes."

NOTES

1   The term comes from Kenneth Lincoln. A. LaVonne Brown Ruoff's foreword and other essays in the volume edited by Helen Jaskoski point out that earlier Indian writing has received less attention, and with Cheryl Walker and others they seek to remedy that imbalance. Craig S. Womack also argues for more attention to precontemporary Indian writing (2–4). Those beginning to study Indian writing would do well to start with two invaluable volumes: Paula Gunn Allen (ed.), *Studies in American Indian Literature*, and Ruoff, *American Indian Literatures*; Ruoff also provides the fullest bibliography.

2   Arnold Krupat provocatively begins to describe that process for 1990s Indian novelists (*Turn*, esp. 30–55), a discussion continued by Sidner Larson, 44–7.

3   For critiques of Clifton's volume, see Vine Deloria and the harsher account in Ward Churchill.

4   Adell, 131–2. I find Adell's challenging discussion of Houston Baker and Henry Louis Gates's efforts to establish a specifically African American criticism thought-provoking both in itself and for its potential analogies in Indian studies. See Adell, 118–37.

5   King, "Introduction," x–xi. For King's related comments in interviews, see "Interview with Thomas King" by Jeffrey Canton, 2, and interview by Hartmut Lutz, 108.

6   See Victor Shklovsky, Boris Eichenbaum, Boris Tomashevsky, and Victor Erlich, 239–46.

7   For thought-provoking examples of such contemplations, see bell hooks, *Talking Back*, 42–8, Diana Fuss, 113–19, hooks, *Teaching*, 77–92, and Judith Roof and Robyn Wiegman. For related discussions in Indian studies, see Devon A. Mihesuah (ed.), *Natives and Academics*.

8   On white critics writing about literature by nonwhites as speaking *for* nonwhites, when I would see them as speaking *about* nonwhites, or, still more narrowly, as speaking about literature by particular nonwhites, see Linda Alcoff, Elizabeth Abel, Margaret Homans, and Pamela L. Caughie.

9 Here I echo Gayatri Chakravorty Spivak's response (*Outside*, 60; *Critique*, 190–1) to Benita Parry regarding Parry's not-really-understanding critique of Spivak's famous essay "Can the Subaltern Speak?" ("Can the Subaltern Speak?" has appeared in two article versions, both listed in the Works Cited; the shorter version is more user-friendly. A third, long version appears in chap. 3 of Spivak's *Critique of Postcolonial Reason*, esp. 244–311.)

10 Book-length studies of Indian autobiography include Gretchen M. Bataille and Kathleen Mullen Sands, H. David Brumble III, Arnold Krupat, and Hertha Dawn Wong. On Native theater, see the *Native Playwrights Newsletter*.

11 Weaver, *That the People*, 22. For an effort to build a pro-essentialist argument, see Womack. Womack bases his portrayal of contemporary critical theory on ideas that had a brief vogue in the high deconstructionist moment of the late seventies and that virtually no one has advocated since then, although the rumor of their dominance has persisted, especially among right-wing pundits who would be anathema to Womack's anticapitalism. Just as I don't find Womack's arguments for essentialism convincing or well informed about the critical debates around essentialism, so I can't abide his implication that non-Native critics cannot contribute helpfully to the discussion of Native American literature. On the other hand, the often ugly history of white-produced writing about Indian peoples gives us reason to take Womack's point of view seriously. I also applaud his encouragement for the study of particular tribal literatures and the example he offers for a study of tribal literature that joins – as a work of writing – in the literature that it studies.

Works Cited

Abel, Elizabeth. 1993. "Black Writing, white Reading: Race and the Politics of Feminist Intepretation." *Critical Inquiry* 19: 470–98.

Adell, Sandra. 1994. *Double-Consciousness/Double-Bind: Theoretical Issues in Twentieth-Century Black Literature*. Urbana: University of Illinois Press.

Alcoff, Linda. 1991–2. "The Problem of Speaking for Others." *Cultural Critique* 20: 5–32.

Alexie, Sherman. 2000. *One Stick Song*. Brooklyn: Hanging Loose Press.

Allen Paula Gunn, ed. 1983. *Studies in American Indian Literature: Critical Essays and Course Designs*. New York: Modern Language Association.

Bataille, Gretchen M., and Kathleen Mullen Sands. 1984. *American Indian Women: Telling Their Lives*. Lincoln: University of Nebraska Press.

Benveniste, Emile. 1966. *Problems in General Linguistics*, trans. Mary Elizabeth Meek. Reprint 1971, Coral Gables: University of Miami Press.

Blaeser, Kimberly M. 1998. "Like Reeds through the Ribs of a Basket." In *Other Sisterhoods: Literary Theory and US Women of Color*, ed. Sandra Kumamotu Stanley. Urbana: University of Illinois Press, pp. 265–76. [Reprint of *American Indian Quarterly* 21 no. 4 (1997): 555–65.]

Brumble, H. David, III. 1988. *American Indian Autobiography*. Berkeley: University of California Press.

Caughie, Pamela L. 1999. *Passing and Pedagogy: The Dynamics of Responsibility*. Urbana: University of Illinois Press.

Chatman, Seymour. 1978. *Story and Discourse: Narrative Structure in Fiction and Film*. Ithaca, NY: Cornell University Press.

Churchill, Ward. 1992. "The New Racism: A Critique of James A. Clifton's *The Invented Indian*." In *Fantasies of the Master Race: Literature, Cinema, and the Colonization of American Indians*, ed. M. Annette Jaimes. Monroe, Maine: Common Courage, pp. 163–84.

Cixous, Hélène. 1976/1981. "The laugh of the Medusa," trans. Keith Cohen and Paula Cohen. In *New French Feminisms*, ed. Elaine Marks and Isabelle de Courtivron. New York: Schocken, pp. 245–64.

Cook-Lynn, Elizabeth. 1987. "You May Consider Speaking about Your Art..." In *I Tell You Now: Autobiographical Essays by Native American Writers*, ed. Brian Swann and Arnold Krupat. Lincoln: University of Nebraska Press, pp. 55–63.

Deloria, Vine, Jr. 1997. "Comfortable Fictions and the Struggle for Turf: An Essay Review of *The Invented Indian: Cultural Fictions and Government Policies*." In Devon A. Mihesuah, *American Indians: Stereotypes and Realities*. Atlanta: Clarity Press, pp. 65–83.

Derrida, Jacques. 1976. *Of Grammatology*, trans. Gayatri Chakravorty Spivak. Baltimore: Johns Hopkins University Press.

Fuller, Hoyt W. 1968/1971. "Towards a Black Aesthetic." Reprinted in *The Black Aesthetic*, ed. Addison Gayle Jr. Garden City, NY: Doubleday, pp. 3–17.

Fuss, Diana. 1989. *Essentially Speaking: Feminism, Nature, and Difference*. New York: Routledge.

Gates, Henry Louis, Jr. 1992. "'Ethnic and Minority' Studies." In *Introduction to Scholarship in Modern Languages and Literatures*, ed. Joseph Gibaldi. 2nd edn. New York: Modern Language Association, pp. 288–302.

—— 1987. *Figures in Black: Words, Signs, and the "Racial" Self*. New York: Oxford University Press.

—— 1988. *The Signifying Monkey: A Theory of Afro-American Literary Criticism*. New York: Oxford University Press.

Genette, Gérard. 1972/1980. *Narrative Discourse: An Essay in Method*, trans. Jane E. Lewin. Ithaca, NY: Cornell University Press.

Hall, Stuart. 1989. "Cultural Identity and Cinematic Representation." *Frameworks* 36: 68–81.

Homans, Margaret. 1994. "'Women of Color': Writers and Feminist Theory." *New Literary History* 25: 73–94.

hooks, bell. 1989. *Talking Back: Thinking Feminist, Thinking Black*. Boston: South End.

Jaskoski, Helen, ed. 1996. *Early Native American Writing: New Critical Essays*. Cambridge: Cambridge University Press.

King, Thomas. 1991. Interview by Hartmut Lutz. In Lutz, *Contemporary Challenges: Conversations with Canadian Native Authors*. Saskatoon: Fifth House, pp. 107–16.

—— 1990. "Interview with Thomas King." Interview by Constance Rooke. *World Literature Written in English* 30 no. 2: 62–76.

King, Thomas, ed. 1990. *All My Relations: An Anthology of Contemporary Canadian Native Fiction*. Toronto: McClelland and Stewart.

Krupat, Arnold. 1996. *The Turn to the Native: Studies in Criticism and Culture*. Lincoln: University of Nebraska Press.

Larson, Sidner. 2000. *Captured in the Middle: Tradition and Experience in Contemporary Native American Writing*. Seattle: University of Washington Press.

Lee, Don. L. 1971. "Toward a Definition: Black Poetry of the Sixties (After LeRoi Jones). In *The Black Aesthetic*, ed. Addison Gayle Jr. Garden City, NY: Doubleday, pp. 235–47.

Lévi-Strauss, Claude. 1974. *Tristes tropiques*, trans. John and Doreen Weightman. New York: Atheneum.

Mayfield, Julian. 1971. "You Touch My Black Aesthetic and I'll Touch Yours." In *The Black Aesthetic*, ed. Addison Gayle Jr. Garden City, NY: Doubleday, pp. 24–31.

Mihesuah, Devon A. 1997. *American Indians: Stereotypes and Realities*. Atlanta: Clarity Press.

Mihesuah, Devon A., ed. 1998. *Natives and Academics: Researching and Writing about American Indians*. Lincoln: University of Nebraska Press.

Neal, Larry. 1968/1971. "The Black Arts Movement." In *The Black Aesthetic*, ed. Addison Gayle Jr. Garden City, NY: Doubleday, pp. 272–90.

Niatum, Duane. 1978/1987. "On Stereotypes." In *Recovering the Word: Essays on Native American Literature*, ed. Brian Swann and Arnold Krupat. Berkeley: University of California Press, pp. 552–62.

Parry, Benita. 1987. "Problems in Current Theories of Colonial Discourse." *Oxford Literary Review* 9 nos. 1–2: 27–58.

Rimmon-Kenan, Shlomith. 1983. *Narrative Fiction: Contemporary Poetics*. London: Methuen.

Ruoff, A. LaVonne Brown. 1990. *American Indian Literatures: An Introduction, Bibliographic Review, and Selected Bibliography*. New York: Modern Language Association.

Spivak, Gayatri Chakravorty. 1999. *A Critique of Postcolonial Reason: Toward a History of the Vanishing Present*. Cambridge, Mass.: Harvard University Press.

——1993. *Outside in the Teaching Machine*. New York: Routledge.

——1985. "Three Women's Texts and a Critique of Imperialism." *Critical Inquiry* 12: 243–61.

Walker, Cheryl. 1998. *Indian Nation: Native American Literature and Nineteenth-Century Nationalisms*. Durham, NC: Duke University Press.

Warrior, Robert Allen. 1995. *Tribal Secrets: Recovering American Indian Intellectual Traditions*. Minneapolis: University of Minnesota Press.

Weaver, Jace. 1997. *That the People Might Live: Native American Literatures and Native American Community*. New York: Oxford University Press.

Womack, Craig S. 1999. *Red on Red: Native American Literary Separatism*. Minneapolis: University of Minnesota Press.

Wong, Hertha Dawn. 1992. *Sending My Heart Back Across the Years: Tradition and Innovation in Native American Autobiography*. New York: Oxford University Press.

PART ELEVEN

Colonial, Post–Colonial, and Transnational Studies

CHAPTER 1

Introduction: English Without Shadows: Literature on a World Scale

Julie Rivkin and Michael Ryan

"English," the name given the literary tradition of a body of work produced in the dialect of the southeastern region of an island off the west coast of Europe, supplanted the "Classics," the literature of two Mediterranean peninsulas dating back to over two thousand years ago, as the body of texts used in the cultural training of young professional men in Great Britain in the late nineteenth century. Instead of Homer, Aeschylus, Pindar, Seneca, and Cicero, men in training now read Shakespeare, Milton, Pope, Wordsworth, and Eliot. This change might have been inconsequential enough had Great Britain not been the center of a global empire. But because of that imperial status, "English" soon became a very powerful global cultural institution. Most of you reading this book will be doing so in the context of an "English Department" at an institution of higher learning. Those of you not doing so in such a context will probably be doing so for related reasons: either because you are in a literature department where the language in use is English even if the literature in question is not (is Australian or Canadian, say) or because the largest publishing market for literary discussions of any kind is in English even though your native language is something else.

While during the age of empire English the language was providing large parts of the world with a cultural, political, and economic *lingua franca* (as also French and Spanish) and English the cultural institution providing a supposedly universal set of ideals for proper living, people's lives were being changed and people's bodies moved in ways that made for painful and brutal contrasts to the benign values the English literary tradition supposedly fostered. The enslavement and displacement of large numbers of Africans to the Caribbean and North America is only the most powerful and violent example of such a counter-reality. The violence done by empire (with the US slave system being considered here a kind of internal imperialism) generated the negative energies that would eventually end empire and which have been the seeds out of which alternatives to "English" have grown.

That English the language and English the cultural institution are inseparable from the experience of empire does not mean that English is or was in itself an imperial undertaking. It was indeed used to help create a more "literate" and, one might argue, docile class of colonized subjects capable of co-administering empire, and English (the literary tradition and the conjoined academic institution) has for a long time and for reasons of empire occupied a central place in literature departments in many parts of the world. The cultural misconstrual of the local for the

universal could only endure for so long, however, and English's status for some time
has also been changing, as indigenous literatures, from Australia to Africa to North
America, have emerged to assume equal standing with or to displace entirely the
English tradition. Those changes are bound up with the end of official empire and
the transfer of political, if not always economic power, to formerly colonialized
peoples in the latter half of the twentieth century.

These historical developments wrought great changes in literature and in the
discussion and teaching of literature. Entire bodies of writing emerged out of the
imperial front, that line of contact between colonizer and colonized which is characterized as much by reciprocal envy and adulation as by reciprocal fear and resentment. On the one side of that front stand works like Forster's *Passage to India* or
Kipling's *Kim*, while on the other stand such works as Rhys's *Wide Sargasso Sea* or
Kincaid's *A Small Place*. Each colonized nation also produced its own body of
literature that dealt with the imperial experience or attempted to define a post-
imperial sense of national and cultural identity, with the works of African writers
such as Wole Soyinka and Ngugi wa Thiong'o being exemplary in this regard. In
places like the United States, the former slave population of displaced Africans has
given rise to a literary tradition of its own, many works of which, from the poetry of
Langston Hughes to the novels of Toni Morrison, seek to make sense of their history
and their continuing experience of racism. And throughout the world, peoples in
diasporic situations of dispersal sought to establish a sense of cultural and ethnic
identity within locales like England itself, where the majority ethnic group tended to
control the production of mainstream culture.

The 1960s are once again a time of enormous transformation. English in England
expanded to include the literature of the Commonwealth, while in the former colonies like the Caribbean it began to be displaced by indigenous traditions. In the US,
it came to embrace the long ignored tradition of African-American writing in the
form of Afro-American Programs. Such changes in institutional shape and disciplinary self-definition both fostered and were brought about by new developments in
literary criticism. Scholars emerged who were less interested in the European tradition and more interested in post-colonial writers like V. S. Naipaul or Nadine
Gordimer.

If English was losing some of its institutional power, it was also being cast in a
new light as a result of these developments. No longer could it present itself as a
repository of good values or of appropriate style if those values were connected,
albeit metonymically rather than metaphorically, to imperial violence or if that style
could be shown to be the result of a history of the forced displacement of other
linguistic forms which had the misfortune alone of being practiced by people with
smaller or no guns. Scholars began to take note of the fact that many great works of
English literature promoted beliefs and assumptions regarding other geographic
regions and other ethnic groups – from Shakespeare's Caliban to Brontë's Mrs
Rochester – that created the cultural preconditions for and no doubt enabled the
work of empire. The promotion of such beliefs and assumptions in literature,
Edward Said noted in his pathbreaking *Orientalism* (1978), was just one part of larger
processes of discursive construction in a variety of forms of writing, from novels to
scholarly treatises on geography and philology, that represented other peoples (in
Said's example, the people of "the Orient") as less civilized or less capable and as
needing western paternalist assistance. Any attention to processes of domination

usually spurs an interest in counter-processes of resistance, and as interest in colonial and post-colonial literature increased in the 1980s, attention turned, especially in the work of Homi Bhabha and in the collective volume *The Empire Writes Back* (1989), to the complex interface between colonizer and colonized, an interface that Bhabha found characterized as much by a subversive work of parody and mimicry as by straightforward domination. Later work along these lines, especially Paul Gilroy's *The Black Atlantic* (1993), has moved away from inter-national or inter-ethnic demarcations and toward an understanding of the para-national and trans-regional flows of culture. From the Caribbean to New York to London, black cultural influences and migrations tend not to heed traditional literary boundary lines, and these new realities demand new modes of non-national critical thinking.

Much of the early work in this rather large and diverse area of ethnic, post-colonial, and international studies was shaped by categories that have since been rethought by scholars in the field whose critical perspective is shaped by Structuralism, Feminism, and Post-Structuralism. While early anti-imperialist thinkers like DuBois and Fanon resorted to unproblematic notions of ethnic identity or to ideals of a traditional "people's culture," later thinkers have pointed out the isomorphism of racist and racialist ideologies as well as the mistake of assuming the unproblematic existence of such things as ethnic identities where fluctuation, change, and temporary blood-line settlements are more likely to be the case. Others have contended that recourse to a supposedly more authentic traditional culture as a counterpoint to imperial or neocolonial domination merely reduces the complex history of cultural change to an inaccurate folkloric myth and selectively privileges quaint "tribal" practices which are misconstrued as original and without history. Feminists have noted that there would be no ethnic identity without the forced containment and channeling of women's reproductive capacities along consanguine family and clan lines and that the privileging of ideals of ethnic or national cultural identity conceals internal fissures of gender and sexual domination. And Post-Structuralists in the field suggest that other concepts of identity, from the nation or the ethnic group to the national culture, are no longer relevant to a transnational, migratory, and diasporic world culture. What the experience of geographic displacement teaches is that all the supposedly stable equations of place, ethnos, and national political institution are imaginary constructs which displace displacement by substituting for the history of permanent migratory dislocation an ontologizing image of home or of a homeland, a proper place where a spuriously pure ethnos can authenticate itself.

The recent critical attention to such concepts as exile, home, and diaspora as much reflects the influence of Post-Structuralism's re-examination of taken-for-granted notions of identity as it does the experience of writers and theorists of African, Asian, or Caribbean descent who live in former imperial centers like Britain. DuBois first formulated the problematic nature of such experience when he spoke of "twoness," the twin experience of being both American and black, loyal to a nation while yet a victim of its prejudice against the minority ethnic group. For Fanon, the problem of twoness reappeared in a different guise, that of travelers to the imperial center from the colonized periphery who adopted the imperial culture as their own out of a sense of the inferiority of their own native culture. Since they wrote and since the emergence of new generations of people whose immigrant ethnic roots do not conflict with a sense of at-homeness in an imperial center like England, twoness gives way to a bilateral sense of parallel cultures and to a sense of multiple belongings, plural identities with no one more standard or normal or appropriate than another. And with that change of experience comes, of course, the possibility of multiple languages – not Creole or English, as Fanon noticed, but Creole and English.

What does all of this mean for English, for English as an academic institution that still in many places consists of the teaching of THE national tradition century by century? It has meant the creation of new slots for an African-American specialist or a Post-Colonial specialist. And it has meant the reconceptualization of at least twentieth-century English literature to include Commonwealth literature and the emergence of new ways of organizing the American literary canon so that it includes more African and other voices (the much praised Heath Anthology). But if one source of empire was the national parochialism embodied in the ideal of the teaching of one's national literature alone and one result of the new ethnic, post-colonial, and international criticism is a sense of how all national literatures, especially those with global connections or with apparently singular ethnic roots, always cast shadows and are therefore always shadowed by their others, from Caliban to Mrs Rochester to Beloved, then perhaps English itself should be reconsidered as a project of knowledge limited by national and linguistic boundaries. The national parochialism of empire continues as the national parochialism of "international competition," with each nation or ethnic group's imaginary sanctity and identity upheld by just the kind of national literary traditions and academic literary institutions that made English English. But by piercing its others and walking with its shadows, English also generated a migratory and cultural reciprocity that means that the future of English in England at least is necessarily multicultural and multiethnic (if not polylingual). It is also, Paul Gilroy would argue, transgeographical, a culture without national boundaries that thrives on lateral connections and syncretisms, a culture where in-betweenness replaces identity as the defining trope of cultural production. And such a new English is in some respects a model (shades of empire) for a new kind of Literature Department, one that would be at once national, international, and non-national or non-ethnic, one in which students might become as familiar with African as with English literature and learn thereby, not falsely universal values or accurately parochial national traditions, but the complex reality of difference.

CHAPTER 2

History

Dennis Walder

In this selection from his 1998 book, *Post-colonial Literatures in English: History, Language, Theory*, Dennis Walder provides an informative synopsis of some of the crucial issues raised by the colonial experience – violence, expropriation, conquest, slavery – and the way the colonizers tried to find ways to justify their activities.

> *The settler makes history; his life is an epoch, an Odyssey*
> Frantz Fanon, *The Wretched of the Earth* (1961), 1967

> *I met History once, but he ain't recognize me,*
> *A parchment Creole*
> Derek Walcott, '*The Schooner Flight*', 1979

> *But he shall also have*
> *cycles of history*
> *outnumbering the guns of supremacy*
> Arthur Nortje, '*Native's Letter*', 1973

This part is about the basic issues involved in studying post-colonial literatures. Getting to grips with these literatures involves getting to grips with three basic issues: history, language and theory. History has to do with context; language with medium; and theory, with approach. I will devote a chapter to each.

Making History

Let's start with history. There is a well-known rhyme which begins:

> In fourteen-hundred and ninety-two
> Columbus sailed the ocean blue

It was written by the American poetess, Winifred Sackville Stonier Jr, whose name has not survived as well as her little ditty. Generations of schoolchildren have learnt it to help them remember the date. And in 1992, publishers and the media world-wide set themselves up for what was meant to be the largest anniversary splash ever: the 500th anniversary of the arrival of Columbus in the New World. At least ten books came out in the UK alone, and a veritable flood of articles, television series, films, festivals and other celebrations emerged around the globe – including a World Expo event in Spain, whose monarchy funded the Genoese explorer, and a $40 million monument in the Dominican Republic, formerly part of Hispaniola, one of the first places he 'discovered'.

We all know Columbus arrived in the Americas when he did. But he wasn't the first European to arrive in the Americas – the Vikings got there before him; and some historians believe others preceded them. Furthermore, the indigenous peoples already knew about Turtle Island – they'd been there since 30,000 years BC, if not earlier. Nor had Columbus found what he was sent to find – a new route to Asia, displacing the Portuguese, whose recent voyages round the southern tip of Africa and across the Indian Ocean had already shown the way to get silks and spices and all the other things badly wanted in Europe. To his dying day Columbus insisted that the 'new' continent was India, a belief still commemorated in the name of the West Indies – original home of the Caribs and Arawaks, whose own place names he took to be mispronunciations of place names in the East. When Columbus landed in Guanahani in the Bahamas he thought he had arrived in India, and so, as the novelist V. S. Naipaul has put it, he called the people 'Indians, and Indians they remained, walking Indian file through the Indian corn'.[1]

For someone like Naipaul – the grandson of indentured labourers brought from India to replace freed African slaves on the sugar plantations in Trinidad – Columbus seems at least partially responsible for what he calls his 'improbable', his 'colonial' identity: an 'East Indian' from the West Indies. It is an identity created by others, by Europeans like Columbus. Like those who succeeded him, Columbus was following a European dream, a Christian vision of being the first man, Adam naming the world. On his third voyage, dedicated to the Holy Trinity, he imagined he saw three hills on a new island: he promptly named it Trinidad. As Naipaul reminded readers of *The Loss of El Dorado* (1969) Columbus dreamt also of gold. He believed he had found the mines of Solomon, the source of all the gold in the world. An indigenous Indian memory or legend added to the temptations for the Spaniards: of a chief who once a year was rolled in turpentine, covered in gold dust and who then dived into a lake – becoming el dorado, the gilded one. The dream of El Dorado, of a people and a place wealthy beyond anything previously experienced, always a step further on into the unknown, continues to grip the Western imagination, not least through its embodiment in Hollywood adventure films. What was being celebrated in 1992 was this complex mixture of imaginings, centred on the opening up of the world to European enterprise. And yet the impact of these imaginings upon those involved was far from imaginary.

Columbus's landfall at Guanahani and his further discoveries before returning triumphantly in 1493 to accept the prize for being first to see land (actually a member of his crew was first) led to a claim upon the peoples and territories of the New World by Europeans which was to end up with the death or enslavement of most of the original inhabitants, and the headlong exploitation of their resources. One in three of the indigenous population of Hispaniola were dead within two years of Columbus's arrival; in thirty years they had all been wiped out. What torture, disease and imprisonment did not achieve, mass suicide completed. Gaps in the local labour force were soon filled by slave labour from Africa; thereby initiating one of the worst aspects of European domination – the Atlantic slave trade.

The greed, violence and brutality of the conquest of Central America by the Spaniards offers another perspective upon the opening up of the world to the Europeans, a perspective which undermines the idea of an achievement deserving celebration. So it isn't too surprising to find that an 'anti-Columbus' campaign sprang up to coincide with the quinquennial celebrations in Europe and the Americas: to register not merely the inevitable disputes among historians about the details of Columbus's voyages and discoveries, but also the possibility of an alternative way of understanding what they mean at the end of the twentieth century. It's not easy to decide what Columbus's arrival in the New World means today: partly because we still live in a world shaped by the long colonial experience that arrival initiated; partly because, even if we understand that there is always more than one history, it is not so easy to enter into a new and unfamiliar one. And if we accept that an account of the colonization of the New World by the Spanish is not the same thing as an account of that process from the perspective of the colonized, there is also the point that it is different from later forms of European colonization in other parts of the world. Beyond dispute, however, is the fact of the spread of European power and culture, languages and literatures over the last five hundred years, and across the whole world; of which Columbus's voyages were the crucial early part.

This is not to ignore the immediately preceding Portuguese push around the Cape of Good Hope in search of spices and Christians on the Calicut coast. Rather, it is to identify the major factor in an unprecedented shift in global history, the results of which are still with us, even after decolonization. The spread of European power is one of the most astonishing features of modern world history – taking 'modern' to mean post-medieval. By 1800, some three hundred years after Columbus, European nations laid claim to more than half the world's land surface and, in varying degree, actually controlled about a third. Settler populations large enough to constitute new centres of civilization had developed in places as far apart as North America and South Africa; and almost everywhere else you could find European traders, merchants and missionaries. Only the interior of Africa was protected by disease and climate, although not for very long. It was during the hundred years after 1800 that Britain became the leading nation among those involved in this dramatic transformation of world relationships – a transformation based upon exploration, enterprise, government patronage and cultural (including technological) advantage.

Whose History?

The other side to this story as it develops from exploration to trade and conquest reflects not only the possession by Europeans – and, increasingly, the British – of powerful motives and overwhelming advantages leading to their domination over the peoples of America, Asia and Africa; it also reflects the limitations of these other civilizations. Yet the limitations were far from obvious at first. The year 1492 also marks the defeat of Islam in Spain, and the dispersal of a culture which, ironically enough, had first brought the astronomy and mathematics upon which European navigational supremacy was based. Like the Arabs, the Mayas, Aztecs and Incas of Central and South America all had mature and complex civilizations – the Aztec capital Tenochtitlan (later Mexico City) was five times larger than Madrid at the time of Spanish conquest. The trading ventures of Akbar, the great Mogul emperor of India, were on a much grander scale than those of his contemporary Elizabeth I of England, who granted a charter to what became known as the English East India Company on 31 December 1600. Indeed, not only was Akbar more powerful than any European monarch of the time; as soldier, politician, hunter, painter and book-lover, he was the complete 'renaissance man', his court more splendid than any in the West.

In Africa, a number of rich and ancient societies still flourished when Europeans began to arrive at the coasts; and although non-literate, these societies exhibited great confidence, coherence, moral and artistic vigour. Most of their towns lay beyond the observation of the West until the nineteenth century, when a different attitude towards African peoples prevailed – an attitude evident again in Conrad's *Heart of Darkness* (1899), which, for all its criticism of the Belgian exploitation of the Congo, shudders at every contact with indigenous people, depicted as demonic savages engaged in mysterious and peculiar rites. Yet the impressions of early Portuguese travellers to the Congo were of things strange and puzzling, rather than inviting contempt or any special sense of mystery:

> They ran into many surprising beliefs and superstitions, but few or none that seemed more disconcerting than others they could find at home. Victorious Congolese armies tended to see signs and ghostly symbols in the sky, yet there was nothing out of the way in that. The Portuguese themselves regularly saw angels, and so of course did other Europeans. More often than not they found it easy to accept the peoples of the Congo as natural equals and allies.[2]

The West African city of Benin, whose name belongs to some of the finest surviving sculptural artefacts in the world, was regarded by a Dutch visitor in 1602 as a great city, its dwellings, court and environment quite fairly compared with those of Amsterdam.[3] Viewing the early colonial past through the lens of later, predominantly Western, writings, obscures the existence of those civilizations and empires in South America, Asia, Africa and in the Arab world which flourished and often surpassed Europe in various ways until at least the sixteenth century and sometimes later.

Yet gradually, inevitably (with the inevitability of hindsight), it appears as if the inflexibility, weakness or ossification of these older feudal or slave-based empires, when brought into contact with the dynamic, emergent peoples of the new industrializing nation-states of north-west Europe, led to the spread of European, and especially British hegemony. 'Hegemony', rather than direct control: since, except in the Americas, where Spain and Portugal had established their rule from early on (and then lost it), it was not until the middle of the eighteenth century that European states or their representatives had the will or power to impose colonial rule over the rest of the world. Arab or Asian states continued to be their equals, even their superiors, in many respects, as some Europeans happily acknowledged – those mainly interested in exploiting existing trade links or collaborating with local suppliers, rather than, as happened during the nineteenth century, those who became part of that drive towards conquest and annexation, all too easily justified by contemporary evangelical and evolutionist notions of racial superiority. Even during the greatest spread of direct political control or administration, there was always also an important hinterland under semi-official or indirect European interference, where European manners and beliefs came to hold sway. This is especially important when considering the British Empire, which was always more of a cultural than a constitutional grouping.

The peak or climax of that Empire may be said to have occurred before its greatest extent in territorial terms. Jan (then James) Morris's brilliant if impressionistic three-volume account of the rise and fall of the British Empire (*Heaven's Command*, *Pax Britannica* and *Farewell the Trumpets*) situates the high-point at Queen Victoria's Diamond Jubilee of 1897, the celebration of which began when the Queen telegraphed this simple message from Buckingham Palace to almost every corner of the world: 'Thank my beloved people. May God bless them.' As Morris points out, the empire 'hitherto seen as a fairly haphazard accretion of possessions', now appeared to the British people to be settling into 'some gigantic pattern', distributing their power and values across the seas and continents, to the extent that 'they felt that their power was self-engendering, that they were riding a wave of destiny, sweeping them on to fulfilment'.[4] The new imperialism, as it is called, was a European phenomenon, the Western powers seeking expansion in the closing years of the nineteenth century to a degree previously unknown, leading to collisions and friction which were part of the slide towards the conflagration of 1914–18. But from the popular music-hall song which brought 'jingoism' into the English language, to the dum-dum bullet, from the Boy Scouts and cricket to sheep and steamships, courts and railways, the spread of British ways across the world seemed to themselves as to others, truly epic, and unique.

Equally unique, and characteristic, appeared to be the lack of uniformity amongst Britain's various possessions, dependencies, protectorates, Crown Colonies and dominions at the peak of Empire. At one end of the spectrum stood the great white self-governing colonies, semi-willingly released into semi-nationhood – Canada, the six Australian colonies, New Zealand, Cape Colony, Natal and Newfoundland. They were not fully independent, and Britain looked after security and foreign affairs. But they had their own parliaments, based on the British model, and could decide for themselves whether or not to go to war for Britain. Then came the Crown Colonies, like Gambia, Jamaica and Barbados, some ruled simply by a governor and his officials, others, with fully elected assemblies, although the governor could veto any legislation. Many territories were officially protectorates, run more or less like the Crown Colonies, but technically foreign countries, their citizens not British subjects. In three territories, including Rhodesia and Nigeria (and North Borneo), chartered companies were all-powerful, just as they had been earlier in by far the largest, and most sui generis of all, a kind of empire of its own: India.

The slow conquest of this, the largest and most important part of the British Empire, had begun as a matter of predatory and private exploitation, followed only gradually by moral and improving zeal, until the mixture of motives of the governing class were impossible to disentangle. D. K. Fieldhouse suggests that Britain's conquest of India changed the nature of the colonial enterprise, from 'the original self-governing settlement empire of America', to the 'polyglot and largely dependent empire of the nineteenth century'.[5] The American colonies were like Ireland, in that the settlers maintained a close and continuous connection with the metropolitan state, a relationship reproduced later by similar colonies in Canada, Australasia and South Africa; but by the nineteenth century the Empire was dominated by British involvement with territories with more resistant, independent or alien peoples than in the Americas. During the first (seventeenth- and eighteenth-century) phase of colonization, the empire included mainly English settlers, Amerindians and African slaves; once the American colonies had become independent, and British naval supremacy ensured the defeat of European competition, the move towards Asia and then Africa became irresistible. By the end of the nineteenth century most of the world belonged to a handful of great European powers, of which Britain was the greatest.

The 'Other' View

From early on, some Europeans recognized the value of what their civilization was destroying; and some questioned, even opposed, the colonizing process. One of these was the conquistador turned priest, Bartolomé de Las Casas (1484–1576), whose *Short Account of the Destruction of the Indies* (first published in 1552) represented the first of many struggles by Christian missionaries and enlightened Europeans against the behaviour of their compatriots abroad; although Las Casas (who preserved and edited Columbus's diaries) also saw the Spanish conquest as a great opportunity for Christian conversion, and his revelations were later used as much for the purposes of anti-Spanish propaganda as to undermine the achievements of Europe. Even today, in our post-holocaust times, Las Casas makes chilling reading. His task, as he saw it, was to bear witness to the manner in which a trading and evangelizing mission had been transformed into genocide, the predominantly peaceful and friendly indigenous peoples treated worse than wild dogs, in the headlong rush for precious metals, land and power. When Cortés and his men made their way to Tenochtitlan, they were greeted by the great king Montezuma himself on a gold litter, who made the Spaniards welcome, only 'or so I am reliably informed by a number of eye-witnesses' to be imprisoned 'by a trick', while Cortés left to deal with a troublesome inferior. The garrison decided to stage a show of strength in Cortés's absence, 'and thereby boost the fear they inspired in the people', who had meanwhile organized fiestas of traditional dancing throughout the city.

> These dances are called in the local language *mitotes* (those typical of the islands being known as *areitos*), and since these dances are the typical form of entertainment among the people, they deck themselves out in all their best finery. And the entertainments were organised with close attention to rank and station, the noblest of the citizens dancing nearest the building where their lord was being held. Close by this building, then, danced over two thousand youths of quality, the flower of the nobility of Montezuma's whole empire. Thither the Spanish captain made his way, accompanied by a platoon of his men, under pretence of wanting to watch the spectacle but in fact carrying orders to attack the revellers at a prearranged time, further platoons with identical orders having been dispatched to the other squares where entertainments were being staged. The nobles were totally absorbed in what they were doing and had no thought for their own safety when the soldiers drew their swords and shouting: 'For Saint James, and at 'em, men!' proceeded to slice open the lithe and naked bodies of the dancers and to spill their noble blood. Not one dancer was left alive, and the same story was repeated in the other squares throughout the city. This series of events caused horror, anguish and bitterness throughout the land; the whole nation was plunged into mourning and, until the end of time, or at least as long as a few of these people survive, they will not cease to tell and re-tell, in their *areitos* and dances, just as we do at home

in Spain with our ballads, this sad story of a massacre which wiped out their entire nobility, beloved and respected by them for generations and generations.[6]

Las Casas wrote to reverse the stereotyping assumption of the colonizers that the indigenous peoples were less than themselves, indeed less than human, and could therefore be maltreated with impunity. His suggestion was that the conquistadores, far from being the Christian heroes of ballad and romance who had defeated the 'Moorish barbarians', were themselves unchristian and barbaric in their relations to the American Indians, whom he characterizes in terms of innocence and purity. Unusually, the Montezuma massacre led to resistance (called 'defensive' and 'just' by Las Casas), and the dispersal of the Spaniards, who later regrouped and submitted the population to atrocities, rendering the province a near wasteland.

Las Casas' testimony is important not only as a record of a blot on European civilization in its expansive phase, but also as the first of many succeeding attempts to speak out on behalf of those who could not, because they had been murdered, silenced, or simply ignored. Sometimes those who spoke out came themselves from the invaded populations, even if they spoke the language of the invader. Inevitably, the voices of the colonizing, literate community have survived best, and yet it still requires a conscious refocusing of vision, to perceive the uncertainty and criticism which occasionally accompanied the quest for empire. Samuel Daniel's 'Epistle. To Prince Henry', written within a few years of the start of the British colonial enterprise in the Americas, has found space in a revisionist anthology of *Renaissance Verse* which reflects this shift in perspective: it asks the Prince – and, by implication, all his expansionist supporters – to

> Consider whither all the good that came
> From that new world to this, acquits the some
> Of th'ill events, which since hath by the same
> Accrewd to theis our parts of Christendome,
> Or wherein wee are bettred in our state
> By that accession, and the excessive vayne
> Of gould, which hath but here inhanc'd the rate
> Of things that doe, but as they did, conteyne;
> Or whither we, with what we had before
> Produc'd not fairer actions to behold
> Then since we have performd, and had not more
> Of men that time, when wee had less of gold.[7]

Unimpressive as verse, this does register reservations towards the militant colonialism of Drake, Spenser and Walter Raleigh, and the 'ill events' which accompanied their activities in 'that new world'.

More important, notice how it is, of course, *that* New World to the speaker of the poem, and those he addresses. As Tzvetan Todorov argues in *The Conquest of America*, the conquest, colonization, and destruction of the indigenous cultures of the Americas set the pattern for much of the history of Western colonialism thereafter. This was tied up with the creation of the 'Other': that is to say, the creation of the specific social groups who are not 'I' or 'we', in the writings or discourses about those 'other' people, in 'that' (therefore also 'other') place. As Todorov says, 'others' are also 'I's:

subjects just as I am, whom only my point of view – according to which all of them are *out there* and I alone am *in here* – separates and authentically distinguishes from myself. I can conceive of these others as an abstraction, as an instance of any individual's psychic configuration, as the Other – other in relation to myself, to *me*; or else as a specific social group to which *we* do not belong. This group in turn can be interior to society: women for men, the rich for the poor, the mad for the 'normal'; or it can be exterior to society, i.e., another society which will be near or far away, depending on the case: beings whom everything links to me on the cultural, moral, historical plane; or else unknown quantities, outsiders whose language and customs I do not understand, so foreign that in extreme instances I am reluctant to admit that they belong to the same species as my own.[8]

Todorov goes on to analyse numerous texts from the colonization of America, including Las Casas' writings, to demonstrate the way in which the indigenous Amerindians were viewed as 'other' to a greater or lesser degree; finally with the aim of ensuring that the story of a Mayan woman who was literally thrown to the dogs by the conquistadores is not forgotten.

The histories of the colonizing process (like all histories) have continually to be rewritten. But at the centre of that rewriting from the post-colonial perspective, is the reclamation of the voice(s) and experiences of the 'other'. Some perhaps can never be reclaimed. Some speak out through surprising channels – such as that of the Tory Dean of St Patrick's in Dublin, Jonathan Swift, mediated by his most well-known work, *Gulliver's Travels* (1746). Towards the end of Gulliver's adventures abroad, our hero hesitates to inform the government of his discoveries, and thereby

> enlarge his Majesty's dominions, because that enlargement typically involves a crew of pirates...driven by a storm they know not whither, at length a boy discovers land from the topmast, they go on shore to rob and plunder, they see an harmless people, are entertained with kindness, they give the country a new name, they take formal possession of it for the king, they set up a rotten plank or a stone for a memorial, they murder two or three dozen of the natives, bring away a couple more by force for a sample, return home, and get their pardon. Here commences a new dominion acquired with a title by *divine right*. Ships are sent with the first opportunity, the natives driven out or destroyed, their princes tortured to discover their gold, a free license given to all acts of inhumanity or lust, the earth reeking with the blood of its inhabitants: and this execrable crew of butchers employed in so pious an expedition, is a modern colony sent to convert and civilize an idolatrous and barbarous people.[9]

Swift seems to have the earlier history of the Americas in mind in this astonishing passage – astonishing because of the strength of its opposition to prevailing attitudes and assumptions, although perhaps not so surprising when one recalls his Irish origins. The first colonization of North America by English-speaking settlers in the early seventeenth century was contemporaneous with the far larger settlement of Ireland, mainly by Scottish Presbyterians, with the aim of 'reducing to civility' the indigenous, Gaelic-speaking Catholic people.[10]

Swift's version of the colonial enterprise suggests the later, Enlightenment willingness to admit the shared humanity of those civilizations outside Europe then coming under the sway of the British and the French – the dominant powers of the eighteenth century. On one level, what the representatives of these powers looked for

abroad was men that seemed to conform to European ideals: of high-minded, aristocratic scholarship; or later, of primitive virtue. 'Brahmin' and 'savage' became terms
of praise – for a time. And so Sanskrit, the learned language of the Indian subcontinent, was studied and admired, and its affinities with the classical languages of Europe
expounded by self-styled 'orientalists'; while a host of literary 'primitives', like black
Tarzans, turned up to question by their presence the supposed artificialities of European urban behaviour and belief. None of this halted the spread of colonization and
slavery, or the competition between European powers for trade and territory abroad,
most obviously in North America and the Indian subcontinent. None of it finally
undermined the presumption of 'otherness', as that most representative of Enlightenment figures, David Hume, revealed in 1753, when he argued that 'negroes and in
general all the other species of men' were 'naturally inferior to whites', on the
grounds that blacks in 'our colonies' and throughout Europe lacked the 'civilised'
arts, in particular, of writing.[11] The absence of writing was considered crucial,
and their possession of it (at least among the elites) was one reason why Hindu and
Muslim cultures were thought superior to slave or oral cultures in the Americas
and Africa.

Slavery and the 'Civilizing Mission'

This also meant, however, that: 'Wherever else the Briton went he felt and spoke as
representative of the power at whose feet crouched a hundred million Hindus.'[12] If,
by 1800, Britain had lost its American colonies, it had also taken a major stride
towards the conquest of its largest and most important colony, India, with Clive's
victory at Plassey (1757) and the establishment of East India Company rule over
Bengal. British power over the next hundred years radiated from there. Other territories were taken with the help of Indian troops, often at the expense of the Indian
tax-payer – in South Africa, for example. By 1900, the time had arrived of the
'sahib's war', in the words of the title of Kipling's Boer War story.

One of the causes of the South African War (1899–1902) was the longstanding
tension over slavery between the original, largely Dutch settlers, and the British (to
whom the Cape fell in 1806 as one of the prizes of the Napoleonic wars). Much of
the historiography of European expansion and American growth has, rightly, been
dominated by this subject.

There isn't room to go into it in any detail here. But a few points can be made. To
begin with, it was the lucrative prospect of providing the Spanish and Portuguese
colonies with African labour to replace the dwindling Amerindian (and 'poor white',
often Scots and Irish) supply which led Sir John Hawkins to transport the first
'cargo' of five hundred slaves from West Africa to the New World in 1562. Later, as
Britain established its own plantation colonies there, British interest in the slave trade
and slavery increased, until by the mid-eighteenth century, it had become the centre
of the Triangular Trade, and British ships carried manufactured goods to West
Africa, took slaves to the New World plantations, and brought back sugar, tobacco,
and cotton – thereby earning gigantic profits. Aboard ship, the Africans were treated
as an item of cargo, to be packed (or lost, or even thrown overboard, as in one
notorious incident of 1783, depicted by J. M. W. Turner's *Slave Ship*, 1840); on the
plantation, they were catalogued with livestock and treated as work-animals; while

back in Britain, where thousands of aristocratic or ex-planter households used slaves as domestic servants, they often wore padlocked collars, and were frequently mistreated. To justify all this, the usual arguments were advanced by churchmen, historians and philosophers (like Hume) to establish the inherent inferiority of the black race. And yet there was opposition, too; most notably from evangelicals such as John Newton (a converted slaver), which led Britain to abolish the trade in 1807, and finally slavery itself in 1834; this lead was followed by other European nations.

It is worth saying that there is no historical foundation for the notion that Europeans altogether imposed the slave trade on Africa, any more than there is for the idea that the institution of slavery was peculiar to Africa. Equally, however, Europeans dominated and then vastly enlarged the trade, turning it to their advantage and to Africa's loss, a loss countable in millions of dead; before at last the Europeans themselves, primarily the British, brought the appalling trade to an end. There has been slavery in one form or another before and since, in Africa and elsewhere; nevertheless, apart perhaps from disease, no single factor has been responsible for so much cruelty and misery at the time or later in the history of colonization. The Atlantic slave trade also brought about one of the largest migrations in history, involving during its peak in the eighteenth century, millions of people. Many slaves did not last long on the sugar and tobacco plantations for which they were first brought across the Atlantic, even supposing they survived the notorious 'middle passage'. But they became the main population of the Caribbean, and an important minority in the United States, maintaining fragments of their original customs, traditions and languages, in forms of folklore, music, religion, and speech.

According to the Trinidadian historian, C. L. R. James, in his classic study of *The Black Jacobins: Toussaint L'Ouverture and the San Domingo Revolution* (first published in 1938), one favourite slave song in the Caribbean, was about destroying the whites with all their possessions: the colonists knew it and tried to stamp it out, along with the voodoo cult with which it was associated; 'In vain. For over two hundred years the slaves sang it at their meetings, as the Jews sang of Zion, and the Bantu today sing in secret the national anthem of Africa.'[13] Ironically, the strength of ex-slave resistance to the plantation work was a major factor in one of the first large internal migrations of the British Empire, the hire and shipping of poor Indians and Chinese as indentured labourers to the West Indies – many of whom died on insanitary ships en route, and many more of whom remained when their contracts ran out, to add another strand to the social, racial and cultural mix of the Caribbean.

Behind the abolition of slavery lay the growing European conviction that there ought to be some goal beyond penetration and greed in their overseas expansion, a goal commonly expressed in the phrase 'civilizing mission'. Unfortunately this meant that whatever the whites did could be regarded in some way as 'civilized'; but it also meant accepting a sense of responsibility for what was done, whether as a missionary, civil servant, or 'Company officer'. The last word of Meadows Taylor's *Story of My Life* (1878), the autobiography of one type of British officer in India during the nineteenth century, was "duty"; his was the liberal, Christian view, in the best sense, according to which the Indians could not in the end be ruled by military or political, but only by moral power. And yet Taylor, who was in the service of a 'native prince' (the Nizam of Hyderabad), married the granddaughter of a begum of Oudh, spoke numerous Indian languages and was a master of the local dialect, and whose 'improving' activities are still remembered with respect and admiration among the people of the Deccan – Taylor himself could be heard echoing the racist ideology which became dominant with the Indian 'mutiny' or 'rising' of 1857, an event which transformed relations between ruler and ruled, ringing the death knell of 'progressive' attitudes towards Empire.

The 'New Imperialism' and Resistance

The 'new imperialism' was not new except for the increased pace and participation of European powers in Africa, the Far East and the Pacific from the 1880s onwards. Despite corruption and near-bankruptcy, Company rule in India continued long after state intervention became a necessity if the British were to keep this major market and source of raw materials. But after the events of 1857, the East India Company was abolished at last, and Queen Victoria was proclaimed Empress of India. Railways, and a more efficient administration were introduced; while the feudal princes who had supported the status quo during the rising became puppet rulers of 'independent' states – a development that became a hallmark of this phase of British imperialism, especially in tropical Africa where, as 'indirect rule', it allowed a handful of Britons to administer the lives of millions through their traditional chiefs. Lord Lugard, who introduced the system into Africa on the basis of his experience as a soldier in India, saw it as a way of bringing firm and impartial rule while respecting local customs and traditions. At its best, 'indirect rule' minimized the impact of colonial culture; but, as increasing numbers of Western-educated intellectuals later maintained, it also helped to preserve the conservative social order of the past with all its iniquities.

The Indian Mutiny or Rising – both terms are applicable depending on your point of view towards what began as discontent among the sepoy or 'native' soldiery, but then flared up because of wider discontents – this was one of a number of dramatic moments of resistance towards colonial rule from the 1780s onwards. Any history of Ireland will have at least half a dozen risings or rebellions in the index; but one of the most significant was that associated with Wolfe Tone and the United Irishmen, a group of radicals influenced by the American and French Revolutions in their demands, and whom Pitt put down with exceptional ferocity, sowing the seeds for more than a century of struggle between Irish 'patriots' and the British, not yet finally resolved, despite the arrival of the Irish Free State in 1922. Slaves in the Caribbean were among the first and most frequent to rise against their rulers, and in 1804, Haiti became the first independent black country as a result of the successful rebellion against the French led by the 'Black Jacobin', Toussaint L'Ouverture. A groundswell of rebellion continued throughout the region until, in 1865, Paul Bogle led a revolt of ex-slaves in Jamaica, which turned bloody in the face of white intransigence, led by Governor Eyre. Troops were sent in and more than 400 executed without proper trial. A commission of inquiry split public opinion at home, with Huxley, Spencer and J. S. Mill ranged against Dickens, Ruskin and Carlyle, who defended the governor against the 'nigger philanthropists' wanting him recalled (which he was). The South African War is often seen as a moment of resistance to imperial rule with a uniquely local twist: an almost exclusively white man's war; yet it took place within the context of a lengthy series of African risings, none of which, however, deflected the peace agreement by which the defeated Afrikaners became British citizens and their country another white dominion, with the rights of the black inhabitants set aside.

During the first three-quarters of the nineteenth century the British, unlike other European nations, such as the French, lacked any fixed or coherent colonial policy. In historian J. R. Seeley's memorable phrase, 'We seem, as it were, to have conquered and peopled half the world in a fit of absence of mind.'[14] In fact by then the British had conquered a quarter of the world. Yet there was truth in his remark. Until the 1880s, colonial expansion was largely undertaken by commercial companies rather than nation states, and the preceding hundred years had begun with a decrease in European (including British) control abroad, with the loss of the North and South American colonies. It was official British policy from the late eighteenth century onwards to resist further expansion, making an exception only for the acquisition of bases such as Shanghai and Singapore, or, in the 'white dominions' (Australia, New Zealand, Canada) and settler colonies such as the Cape and Natal, for immigration from distressed areas of the home country, on the assumption that these colonies would become self-supporting. An important distinction developed: between *settlement colonies*, established by Europeans who had left (or been sent from) their homes for religious, political or economic reasons; and *commercial colonies* (including military bases), used as sources of raw materials, whose first beneficiaries were private trading companies protected by the state. The discovery of diamonds in the 1860s and gold in the 1880s turned South Africa from the former to the latter, as one of the greatest colonial entrepreneurs of them all, Cecil Rhodes, was quick to realize.

Rhodes had a world outlook which chimed closely with that of a key figure who arrived at the Foreign Office in 1895 – Joseph Chamberlain. Already from the 1880s onwards there had arisen a kind of frenzy among all the major European powers for domination, so that by 1914 they controlled more than three-quarters of the world. The explanations for this 'new imperialism' are many, although one of the most influential remains that of the Liberal John A. Hobson, whose *Imperialism: A Study* (1902), based on a visit to South Africa, fed Lenin's conviction that imperialism was essentially and inevitably a creation of monopoly capitalism. The needs of the growing industrial–financial complex of the West, especially Britain, could only be satisfied through new investment in other parts of the world, with all the inequities and dependence that fostered.

Whatever the reasons for it – including the whole complex of motivating ideas associated with thinkers such as Charles Darwin, whose doctrine of natural selection was developed into a theory of racial superiority by Count de Gobineau (a hero of Hitler's) – the last two decades of the nineteenth century witnessed an unprecedented increase in the aggressive acquisition of territory, later nicknamed the 'scramble for Africa'. The advent of mass electorates and sensational journalism brought new audiences to cheer on the exploits of the 'pioneers' – farmers, missionaries, administrators and, as the popularity of Kipling's *Barrack-Room Ballads* (1890–2) proved, soldiers. This is not to deny the genuine appeal of the sense of duty inherent in Kipling's invocation to 'Take up the White Man's Burden' (in *The Times*, 1898); rather, it is to suggest the complex mingling of material and spiritual factors that underlay the often cruel and violent results, as Ashantis, Afghans, Dervishes, Matabele, Zulu and other indigenous peoples were subjugated.

From Empire to Commonwealth

The British Empire in its ascendancy before the First World War was a vast mosaic of colonies, states and territories, extending over a quarter of the globe (on which, as it was said, the sun did not set). Thinkers from Ruskin to Seeley saw it as the special genius of the Anglo-Saxon race to rule the world. The racial element in this dominant attitude helped ensure that white settlement colonies such as Australia or South Africa were moving towards forms of self-government, while 'native lands' or Crown Colonies in Africa, the East or the Caribbean remained under indirect, paternalistic rule. By the time Edward VII came to the throne, British prestige and self-confidence was at an all-time high, despite growing anti-imperialist feelings at home and abroad. The Empire stood by 'the mother country' and helped to win the war – India alone supplying 800,000 soldiers, of whom 65,000 died. Ireland, arguably the oldest colony, was split on the issue of whether to fight for the Empire (informally during the First World War, formally during the Second), although 200,000 Irishmen joined up, of whom 60,000 did not return.

By the mid-1960s, most British-held possessions were independent, the Empire had been dismantled, and in its place, the Commonwealth had come into being, with the Queen as its head. The fratricidal conflicts between the European powers had ensured both a dramatic decline in their ability to hold on to colonial empires, and their displacement by the superpowers. The transition from Empire to Commonwealth during the interwar years meant a continuation of white British hegemony, although nationalist feeling was growing apace, especially in India. The six white dominions (Australia, Canada, the Irish Free State, Newfoundland and New Zealand) had their status confirmed by the Statute of Westminster (1931) in terms which made them equal but autonomous, while united by their allegiance to the Crown. A key moment in the transition took place in April 1919, in the Jallianwallah Bagh at Amritsar in the Punjab, when General Dyer, a British officer in the Indian Army, ordered his soldiers to fire on a crowd of unarmed civilians, after an attack on an English woman, followed by protests in the city: nearly 400 were killed and over 1,000 wounded. The massacre, and the way in which Dyer's action was defended turned Gandhi (not long returned from two decades in South Africa representing Indian indentured labourers) against the British, and led to an upsurge in support for the Indian National Congress (founded 1885, and a model for the African National Congress of South Africa, founded 1912). Gandhi campaigned for an end to British rule; he also campaigned to improve the status of the untouchables, and women. He believed that peoples and nations should be self-sufficient, and he struggled in vain to overcome the growing gap between Hindu and Muslim which led to an explosion of violence coinciding with the granting of Independence in 1947, Partition, and his own assassination.

Indian independence marked the new, post-colonial era. Over the next fifteen years, forty countries with a population of eight hundred million won their independence from European colonizers. 'Never before in the whole of human history had so revolutionary a reversal occurred with such rapidity.'[15] The 1955 Bandung Conference of twenty-nine non-aligned African and Asian nations (often misleadingly called 'Third World') symbolized a new-found solidarity against the former imperialists. The failure of the British and French in their war against Egypt over the Suez

Canal the following year clarified the ending of the age of European colonial control. Among the English-speaking diaspora, a second Commonwealth came into existence, which by the 1960s was truly multiracial – a condition signalled most clearly by the departure from it of South Africa, under its white minority government. This was followed by the futile 'declaration of independence' by the settler regime in Rhodesia, which predictably led to a small but bloody guerrilla war, before the new, democratic state of Zimbabwe was declared in 1980 – an event which, equally predictably, did not bring the white minority regime further south to its senses, delaying the arrival of multiracial democracies in Namibia and South Africa until 1990 and 1994 respectively. The handing-over of Hong Kong to China in 1997 under a 'one country-two systems' agreement has seen another defining moment in world history, and a new version of the post-colonial moment.[16]

Summary

The impact of European (not only British) colonialism on the world was always a complex process, taking many forms. The damage to indigenous cultures, the suffering and loss of life, can never be measured; and the smouldering resentment of those formerly colonized for having been instilled with a sense of inferiority based on race is part of the price we all have to pay for the ascendancy enjoyed by the West since Columbus's first voyages. As Fanon described it, colonialism was a denial of all culture, history and value outside the colonizer's frame; in short, 'a systematic negation of the other person'.[17] On the other hand, the constructive, or at least modernizing effects of colonial rule are apparent too – from the introduction of railways to the breaking down of taboos; from the building of schools and hospitals, to the rediscovery and revitalization of cultures. Similarly profound and ambivalent has been the impact of colonization upon Europe, from the arrival of vast quantities of precious metals in the early years, to the effects of slavery and immigration more recently. In the post-colonial era, we cannot expect to agree about the weight or balance of these factors. Where we should be able to agree is that colonization is a process requiring analysis and interpretation. There is much about its histories that remains obscure, unknown, or open to debate.

Notes

1 V. S. Naipaul, 'East Indian' (1965), in V. S. Naipaul, *The Overcrowded Barracoon* (Penguin, 1976), p. 36.
2 Basil Davidson, *Black Mother: Africa and the Atlantic Slave Trade* (Pelican, 1980), p. 137.
3 Ibid., p. 232.
4 Jan (then James) Morris, *Pax Britannica* (Penguin, 1979), pp. 21–2. See also Denis Judd's chapter on the Diamond Jubilee in his *Empire: The British Imperial Experience from 1765 to the Present* (Fontana, 1997), pp. 130–53.
5 D. K. Fieldhouse, *The Colonial Empires: A Comparative Survey from the Eighteenth Century*, 2nd edn (Macmillan, 1982), pp. 72 ff.
6 Bartolomé de Las Casas, *A Short Account of the Destruction of the Indies*, ed. and trans. Nigel Griffin (Penguin, 1992), pp. 50–1.

7 *The Penguin Book of Renaissance Verse 1509–1659*, selection and introd. David Norbrook, ed. H. R. Woudhysen (Penguin, 1993), p. 434.

8 Tzvetan Todorov, *The Conquest of America: The Question of the Other*, first published 1982, trans. Richard Howard (HarperPerennial, 1992), p. 3.

9 Jonathan Swift, *Gulliver's Travels and Other Writings*, ed. Louis A. Landa (Oxford University Press, 1976), p. 237.

10 Lawrence James, *The Rise and Fall of the British Empire* (Abacus, 1995), p. 14.

11 David Hume, 'Of national characters' (1748), quoted by Henry Louis Gates Jr, *Figures in Black: Words, Signs and the 'Racial' Self* (Oxford University Press, 1989), p. 18.

12 Victor Kiernan, *The Lords of Human Kind: European Attitudes to the Outside World in the Imperial Age* (Pelican, 1972), pp. 25–6.

13 C. L. R. James, *The Black Jacobins* (Allison & Busby, 1991), p. 18.

14 J. R. Seeley, Lecture 1, *The Expansion of England* (1883).

15 Geoffrey Barraclough, *An Introduction to Contemporary History* (Pelican, 1967), p. 153.

16 See, for example, Martin Jacques, 'Sleeping giant wakes to claim the new century', *Observer* (15 June 1997), pp. 8–9.

17 Frantz Fanon, *The Wretched of the Earth* (Penguin 1967), p. 200.

CHAPTER 3

The Revival of the Imperial Spirit

C. C. Eldridge

C. C. Eldrige's brief work of history, *The Imperial Experience* (1996), is crammed with important quotations from British commentators on the subject of imperialism from Lord Curzon to Kipling. Eldridge traces the history of the "imperial idea" from its beginnings down to its decline in the middle of the twentieth century.

> England cannot afford to be little. She must be what she is, or nothing [....]
>
> Sir, England is the parent of many flourishing colonies – one of them is become an empire among the most powerful in the world. In every quarter of the globe we have planted the seeds of freedom, civilization and Christianity. To every quarter of the globe we have carried the language, the free institutions, the system of laws, which prevail in this country; – in every quarter they are fructifying and making progress; and if it be said by some selfish calculator, that we have done all this at the expense of sacrifices which we ought not to have made, my answer is, – in spite of these sacrifices, we are still the first and happiest people in the old world; and, whilst this is our lot, let us rejoice rather in that rich harvest of glory, which must belong to a nation that has laid the foundation of similar happiness and prosperity to other nations, kindred in blood, in habits, and in feelings to ourselves.
>
> William Huskisson, House of Commons,
2 May 1828, Speeches (1831), vol. 3, pp. 286–7

Such expressions of a sense of mission, of obligations incurred and responsibilities to be shouldered, as well as outright pride in British achievements overseas, were constantly made throughout the nineteenth century. In 1839, Thomas Carlyle asserted:

> To the English people in World History, there have been, shall I prophesy, two grand tasks assigned? Huge-looming through the dim tumult of the always incommensurable Present Time, outlines of two tasks disclose themselves: the grand industrial task of conquering some half or more of this Terraqueous Planet for the use of man; then secondly, the grand Constitutional task of sharing, in some pacific endurable manner, the fruit of said conquest, and showing how it might be done.
>
> T. Carlyle, Chartism (1839), chapter VIII, p. 214

The *Edinburgh Review* explained:

> It is a noble work to plant the foot of England and extend her sceptre by the banks of streams unnamed, and over regions yet unknown – and to conquer, not by the tyran-

nous subjugation of inferior races, but by the victories of mind over brute matter and blind mechanical obstacles. A yet nobler work it is to diffuse over a new created world the laws of Alfred, the language of Shakespeare, and the Christian religion, the last great heritage of man.

> *Edinburgh Review* (1850), vol. 41, p. 61

The custodians of empire in the early Victorian age emphasised the sense of duty, responsibility and self-sacrifice. Earl Grey, when defending his record as Colonial Secretary during the years 1846–52, stated:

> I conceive that, by the acquisition of its Colonial dominions, the Nation has incurred a responsibility of the highest kind, which it is not at liberty to throw off. The authority of the British Crown is at this moment the most powerful instrument, under Providence, of maintaining peace and order in many extensive regions of the earth, and thereby assists in diffusing amongst millions of the human race, the blessings of Christianity and civilization.

> Earl Grey, *The Colonial Policy of Lord John Russell's Administration* (1853), vol. 1, p. 14

Similar sentiments were repeated and emphasised by a later Colonial Secretary, the Earl of Carnarvon, when addressing the Philosophical Institution in Edinburgh in 1878:

> If we turn to that far larger empire over our native fellow-subjects of which I have spoken, the limits expand and the proportions rise till there forms itself a picture so vast and noble that the mind loses itself in the contemplation of what might be under the beneficent rule of Great Britain [....] There we have races struggling to emerge into civilization, to whom emancipation from servitude is but the foretaste of the far higher law of liberty and progress to which they may yet attain; and vast populations like those of India sitting like children in the shadow of doubt and poverty and sorrow, yet looking up to us for guidance and for help. To them it is our part to give wise laws, good government, and a well ordered finance, which is the foundation of good things in human communities; it is ours to supply them with a system where the humblest may enjoy freedom from oppression and wrong equally with the greatest; where the light of religion and morality can penetrate into the darkest dwelling places. This is the real fulfilment of our duties; this, again, I say, is the true strength and meaning of imperialism.

> Earl of Carnarvon, 'Imperial Administration',
> *Fortnightly Review* (December, 1878), vol. 24, pp. 763–4

The imperial idea was clearly present throughout the whole of the nineteenth century.

However, the atmosphere of the early and mid-Victorian years, before the full panoply of imperial ideology came into existence, was very different from that of the age of the New Imperialism. International economic and political conditions were entirely different and British attention focused on evangelical and humanitarian issues, the consolidation (rather than the extension) of the empire, on the colonies of British settlement rather than the tropics, and on the restructuring of the imperial relationship. Imperial ideology had yet to become embedded in British patriotism.

It is possible to trace the evolution of the imperial idea in Tennyson's political poems. For example, to the opening stanzas of 'Hail Briton':

> Hail Briton! in whatever zone
> Binds the broad earth beneath the blue,
> In ancient season or in new,
> No bolder front than thine is shown:
>
> Not for the wide sail-wandered tides
> That ever round thee come and go –
> The many ships of war that blow
> The battle from their oaken sides –
>
> Not for a power, that knows not check,
> To spread and float an ermined pall
> Of Empire, from the ruined wall
> Of royal Delhi to Quebec –
>
> Lord Tennyson, 'Hail Briton!' (1833), ll. 1–12

Tennyson later added:

> But that in righteousness thy power
> Doth stand, thine empire on thy word –
> In thee no traitor voice be heard
> Whatever danger threats the hour!
>
> God keep thee strong as thou art free,
> Free in the freedom of His law,
> And brave all wrong to overawe,
> Strong in the strength of unity!
>
> Symbol of loyal brotherhood!
> Lo, brother-hands shall raise the walls
> Of these their own Imperial Halls
> And toil within for brothers' good.
>
> God bless our work!
> God save our Empress-Queen!
>
> Harvard Manuscripts, Loose Paper 74 (1886),
> ll. 13–26, cited in *The Poems of Tennyson* (1987),
> edited by C. Ricks, vol. 1, p. 522

Tennyson's frequent revision of his political poems, adding a more explicit imperial dimension in the years post-1870, provides an interesting commentary on developing political attitudes towards empire during the early and mid-Victorian years.

It is also illuminating to trace the role of empire in the novels of the period. Too often has discussion been confined to the writings of a handful of late Victorians and Edwardians. Because tub-thumping jingoism was absent from the earlier years, it has frequently been assumed that little interest was shown in the growing empire. This is far from true. Its presence can be detected even in the serious domestic novels of the age. Sometimes, admittedly, it merely provided background colour or light relief, a convenient reason for the entry or exit of characters, a place for banishment or renewal, a utopia where even the unfortunate might prosper. In other novels, however, it plays a much more central role. Some writers contributed directly to discussions of the main imperial problems of the day.

India, for example, intrudes on the domestic novels of Jane Austen (*Sense and Sensibility*), Charlotte Brontë (*Jane Eyre*) and Elizabeth Gaskell (*Cranford*), as well as, more obviously, in the novels of William Makepeace Thackeray (*Vanity Fair, Pendennis, The Newcomes* and *The Tremendous Adventures of Major Gahagan*). The West Indian connection is also present in *Mansfield Park* and *Jane Eyre*. Australasia looms large in the writings of Dickens (*Great Expectations, David Copperfield* and 'The Convict's Return' in *Pickwick Papers*), Edward Bulwer-Lytton (*The Caxtons*), Trollope (*The Three Clerks, John Caldigate* and 'Harry Heathcote of Gangoil' in *The Graphic*, 1873), Henry Kingsley (*The Recollections of Geoffrey Hamlyn, The Hillyers and the Burtons*), Charles Reade (*It Is Never Too Late to Mend*), and Samuel Butler (*Erewhon*). In addition, Philip Meadows Taylor, the greatest Anglo-Indian writer before Kipling, wrote perceptively about thuggee (*Confessions of a Thug*) and the Indian Mutiny (*Seeta*). In fact, the Mutiny spawned a whole series of lesser novels: George Lawrence's *Maurice Dering*, James Grant's *First Love and Last Love: A Tale of the Indian Mutiny*, Henry Kingsley's *Stretton* and Sir George Chesney's *The Dilemma*. And when the names of Harriet Martineau (*Dawn Island*), R. M. Ballantyne and Captain Marryat are added to this list, and the contribution of Thomas Carlyle and the various publications of Anthony Trollope on the West Indies, Canada, Australia, New Zealand, South Africa and Ireland are recalled, it soon becomes apparent how omnipresent empire was in the literature of the early and mid-Victorian years. The absence of jingoism and belligerent expansionism, and the many discussions about the value and nature of the imperial relationship, were not the result of any general lack of belief in empire: they were more a product of the specific circumstances of the time.

The 'Little England' Era

The British empire suffered two blows in the late eighteenth century: the loss of the American colonies and Adam Smith's celebrated attack on the old colonial system in *An Inquiry into the Nature and Causes of the Wealth of Nations* (1776). The American Revolution led to a widespread assumption that the rest of the colonies of British settlement would inevitably leave the parental fold when they reached maturity. Mr Seagrave in Marryat's *Masterman Ready* acknowledged this when explaining to Master William why England and other nations were so anxious to have colonies:

> Because they tend so much to the prosperity of the mother country. In their infancy they generally are an expense to her, as they require her care; but as they advance, they are able to repay her by taking her manufactures, and returning for them their own produce; an exchange mutually advantageous, but more so to the mother country than to the colony, as the mother country, assuming to herself the right of supplying all the wants of the colony, has a market for the labour of her own people, without any competition. And here, my boy, you may observe what a parallel there is between a colony and the mother country and a child and its parents. In infancy, the mother country assists and supports the colony as an infant; as it advances and becomes vigorous, the colony returns the obligation: but the parallel does not end there. As soon as the colony has grown strong and powerful enough to take care of itself, it throws off the yoke of subjection, and declares itself independent; just as a son who has grown up to manhood, leaves his

father's house, and takes up a business to gain his own livelihood. This is as certain to be the case, as it is that a bird as soon as it can fly will leave its parent's nest.

Captain Marryat, *Masterman Ready* (1841), p. 116

Unfortunately, Seagrave's economic justification for colonies was rapidly losing its force. After Adam Smith's denunciation of the ramshackle and somewhat haphazardly applied series of commercial and navigation laws known as 'mercantilism', free-trade ideas gradually gained acceptance. As a result, the two main props of the eighteenth-century empire were demolished in the first half of the nineteenth century. Following two minor rebellions in the Canadas in 1837, autocratic government from Whitehall was swept aside as responsible government – the handing over of the control of internal affairs to locally elected assemblies – was introduced into most of the colonies of British settlement in British North America, Australia and New Zealand in the 1840s and 1850s. The same decades witnessed the triumph of the new economic doctrines of free trade.

Since there was no longer any obvious connection between commercial prosperity and the possession of empire, one school of thought (the so-called 'Manchester School') led by Cobden and Bright, viewed colonies as burdens on the British exchequer, especially where defence costs were concerned. Goldwin Smith, Regius Professor of Modern History at Oxford, put the matter squarely:

> The time was when the universal prevalence of commercial monopoly made it well worth our while to hold Colonies in dependence for the sake of commanding their trade. But that time is gone. Trade is everywhere free, or becoming free; and this expensive and perilous connection has entirely survived its sole legitimate cause. It is time that we should recognise the change that has come over the world.
>
> We have, in fact, long felt that the Colonies did nothing for us. We now are very naturally beginning to grumble at being put to the expense of doing anything for them. If they are to do nothing for us, and we are to do nothing for them, where is the use of continuing the connexion?
>
> G. Smith, *The Empire* (1863), p. 2

The book was a wholesale indictment of the imperial system.

Accordingly, calls for releasing the colonies of British settlement from the imperial yoke multiplied. In 1859, Anthony Trollope asserted that a state of dependency was not only humiliating, it retarded the growth of the colonies:

> We have a noble mission, but we are never content with it. It is not enough for us to beget nations, civilize countries, and instruct in truth and knowledge the dominant races of the coming ages. All this will not suffice unless also we can maintain a king over them! What is it to us, or even to them, who may be their king or ruler – or, to speak with a nearer approach to sense, from what source they may be governed – so long as they be happy, prosperous, and good? And yet there are men mad enough to regret the United States! Many men are mad enough to look forward with anything but composure to the inevitable, happily inevitable day, when Australia shall follow in the same path.
>
> A. Trollope, *The West Indies and the Spanish Main* (1859), p. 84

Similarly, in 1862, he declared:

A wish that British North America should ever be severed from England, or that the Australian colonies should ever be so severed, will be by many Englishmen deemed unpatriotic. But I think that such severance is to be wished if it be the case that the colonies standing alone would become more prosperous than they are under British rule. We have before us an example in the United States of the prosperity which has attended the rupture of such old ties [. . .] And if the States have so risen since they left their parent's apron string why should not British North America rise as high?

That the time has as yet come for such a rising I do not think: but that it will soon come I do most heartily hope.

A. Trollope, *North America* (1862), vol. 1, p. 29

Throughout the 1860s, 'separatist' ideas and the nature of the future relationship with the colonies of British settlement were subjects of vigorous discussion. In 1865 a dejected Matthew Arnold bewailed Britain's loss of vision and general decline:

> Yes, we arraign her! but she
> The weary Titan, with deaf
> Ears and labour-dimm'd eyes,
> Regarding neither to right
> Nor left, goes passively by,
> Staggering on to her goal;
> Bearing on shoulders immense,
> Atlantëan the load,
> Wellnigh not to be borne,
> Of the too vast orb of her fate.
>
> Matthew Arnold, 'Heine's Grave' (1865), ll. 87–96

However, after the controversy in 1869–70 surrounding the withdrawal of the last remaining imperial garrisons from Canada and New Zealand, a public outcry at home and in the colonies confirmed a more positive assessment of the imperial relationship. In the 1870s, the idea of an imperial federation gained popularity as British self-confidence faltered in the face of a deepening trade depression, the loss of British industrial and commercial supremacy in the world, and the growth of rival powers – principally the United States, the recently unified Germany, and an increasingly belligerent Russia. The international scene was thus set not only for a return to neo-mercantilist ideas but for the revival of an expansionist spirit in the 'Age of New Imperialism'.

Early and Mid-Victorian Attitudes Towards Empire

This somewhat gloomy picture, however, does not give an accurate impression of the role of empire, and attitudes towards it, in the early and mid-Victorian years. After 1783 the principle of imperial control was rapidly reasserted in Pitt's India Act (1784), the Canada Act (1791), and the Act of Union with Ireland (1801). No self-governing constitution was granted to any British dependency for 70 years after the surrender at Saratoga.

> Still shall thine empire's fabric stand,
> Admired and feared from land to land,

> Through every circling age renewed,
> Unchanged, unshaken, unsubdued;
> As rocks resist the wildest breeze,
> That sweeps thy tributary seas.
>
> Thomas Peacock, 'The Genius of the Thames'
> (1812), Part 2, XLV, ll. 9–14

The will to rule was not lost:

> [. . .] as for the colonies, we purpose through Heaven's blessing to retain them a while yet! Shame on us for unworthy sons of brave fathers if we do not. Brave fathers, by valiant blood and sweat, purchased for us, from the bounty of Heaven, rich possessions in all zones; and we, wretched imbeciles, cannot do the function of administering them? And because the accounts do not stand well in the ledger, our remedy is, not to take shame to ourselves, and repent in sackcloth and ashes, and amend our beggarly imbecilities and insincerities in that as in other departments of our business, but to fling the business overboard, and declare the business itself to be bad. We are a hopeful set of heirs to a big fortune!
>
> Bad state of the ledger will demonstrate that your way of dealing with your colonies is absurd, and urgently in want of reform; but to demonstrate that the Empire itself must be dismembered to bring the ledger straight? O never.
>
> T. Carlyle, *Latter-Day Pamphlets No. IV: The New Downing Street* (1850), p. 31

It was Great Britain's *duty* to rule:

> England will not readily admit that her own children are worth nothing but to be flung out of doors! England looking on her Colonies can say: 'Here are lands and seas, spice-lands, corn-lands, timber-lands, overarched by zodiacs and stars, clasped by many-sounding seas; wide spaces of the Maker's building, fit for the cradle yet of mighty Nations and their sciences and Heroisms. Fertile continents still inhabited by wild beasts are mine, into which all the distressed populations of Europe might pour themselves, and make at once an Old World and a New World human. By the eternal fiat of the gods, this must yet one day be; this, by all the Divine Silences that rule this Universe, silent to fools, eloquent and awful to the hearts of the wise, is incessantly at this moment, and at all moments, commanded to begin to be. Unspeakable deliverance, and new destiny of thousandfold expanded manfulness for all men, dawns out of the Future here. To me has fallen the godlike task of initiating all that: of me and of my Colonies, the abstruse Future asks, Are you wise enough for so sublime a destiny? Are you too foolish?'
>
> Ibid, pp. 31–2

A new justification for empire, replacing the older props of autocratic government and mercantilism, soon gained popularity: the idea of a great imperial destiny to plant British people and institutions overseas, based on the twin foundations of British emigration to, and investment in, colonies of British settlement. The empire could be used to remedy the social ills of the mother country.

The problem of population growth featured prominently in contemporary thinking after Thomas Malthus, in his *Essay on the Principle of Population* (1798), predicted wholesale starvation in the not too distant future. This preoccupation intensified in the years after the Napoleonic Wars when Great Britain experienced periods of trade depression, chronic unemployment and social unrest. The causes were held to be excess population and a glut of capital: commercial crises, business failures and widespread misery were caused by a fall in profits brought about by too much capital seeking investment. In 1812, Robert Southey wrote:

> We have Canada with all its territory, we have Surinam, the Cape Colony, Australasia [. . .] countries which are more than fifty-fold the area of the British isles, and which a thousand years of uninterrupted prosperity would scarcely suffice to people. It is time that Britain should become the hive of nations, and cast her swarms; and here are lands to receive them. What is required of government is to encourage emigration by founding settlements, and facilitating the means of transportation.
>
> R. Southey, 'On the State of the Poor, the Principle of
> Mr. Malthus's Essay on Population, and the
> Manufacturing System' (1812), in
> *Essays, Moral and Political* (1832), vol. 1, p. 154

In such circumstances, Wordsworth felt Great Britain had a 'special cause for joy':

> For, as the element of air affords
> An easy passage to the industrious bees
> Fraught with their burdens; and a way as smooth
> For those ordained to take their sounding flight
> From the thronged hive, and settle where they list
> In fresh abodes – their labour to renew;
> So the wide waters, open to the power,
> The will, the instincts, and appointed needs
> Of Britain, do invite her to cast off
> Her swarms, and in succession send them forth;
> Bound to establish new communities
> On every shore whose aspect favours hope
> Or bold adventure, promising to skill
> And perseverance their deserved reward.
>
> William Wordsworth, *The Excursion* (1814), Book 9, ll. 371–82

Samuel Coleridge agreed:

> Colonization is not only a manifest expedient for, but an imperative duty on, Great Britain. God seems to hold out his finger to us over the sea [. . . .] I think this country is now suffering grievously under an excessive accumulation of capital, which, having no field for profitable operation, is in a state of fierce civil war with itself.
>
> S. T. Coleridge, 4 May 1833, in T. Ashe (ed.),
> *The Table Talk and Omniana of
> Samuel Taylor Coleridge* (1884), p. 216

Carlyle adopted a similar stance in *Sartor Resartus* (1833–4) and *Chartism* (1839). Edward Gibbon Wakefield finally brought the various threads of the argument together in a scheme laid out in *A View of the Art of Colonization* (1849).

It was John Stuart Mill's conversion, however, which set the seal of approval on the new doctrines. In his *Principles of Political Economy* (1848), Mill concluded:

The exportation of labourers and capital from old to new countries, from a place where their productive power is less to a place where it is greater, increases by so much the aggregate produce of the labour and capital of the world. It adds to the joint wealth of the old and the new country, what amounts in a short period to many times the mere cost of effecting the transport. There needs be no hesitation in affirming that Colonization, in the present state of the world, is the best affair of business, in which the capital of an old and wealthy country can engage.

J. S. Mill, *Principles of Political Economy* (1848), p. 382

By the 1850s, the settlement colonies were depicted as lands of promise, of prosperity and happiness. In Edward Bulwer-Lytton's *The Caxtons*, Australia becomes a land not of transporation but of redemption. The politician, Trevanion, endorsing 'Sisty' Caxton's decision to emigrate, commends

sending out not only the paupers, the refuse of an over-populated state, but a large proportion of a better class – fellows full of pith and sap, and exuberant vitality, like yourself, blending [. . .] a certain portion of the aristocratic with the more democratic element; not turning a rabble loose upon a new soil, but planting in the foreign allotments all the rudiments of a harmonious state, analagous to that in the mother country – not only getting rid of hungry craving mouths, but furnishing vent for a waste surplus of intelligence and courage, which at home is really not needed, and more often comes to ill than to good – here only menaces our artificial embankments, but there, carried off in an aqueduct, might give life to a desert.

E. Bulwer-Lytton, *The Caxtons: A Family Picture* (1849), p. 380

There, Sisty's young companions experience social rehabilitation. Sisty concludes from his experiences:

There is something in this new soil – in the labour it calls forth, in the hope it inspires, in the sense of property, which I take to be the core of social morals – that expedites the work of redemption with marvellous rapidity. Take them altogether, whatever their origin, or whatever brought them hither, they are a fine, manly, frank-hearted race, these colonists now!

Ibid., p. 534

In *David Copperfield* (1849–50), New South Wales is the place where the Peggottys prosper and Mr Micawber becomes a colonial magistrate. Dickens also wrote many pro-emigration articles in his weekly periodical, *Household Words*, in the 1850s. When gold was discovered in Australia in 1851, an additional 'get-rich-quick' element was added to the story in Charles Reade's *It is Never Too Late to Mend* (1856), Henry Kingsley's *The Recollections of Geoffrey Hamlyn* (1859), Anthony Trollope's *The Three Clerks* (1858) and *John Caldigate* (1879). In *Australia and New Zealand* (1873), Trollope concluded:

The life of the artisan there is certainly a better life than he can find at home. He not only lives better, with more comfortable appurtenances around him, but he fills a higher position in reference to those around him, and has a greater consideration paid to him than would have fallen to his lot at home. He gets a better education for his children than he can in England, and may have a more assured hope of seeing them rise above himself, and has less cause to fear that they shall fall infinitely lower. Therefore I would say to any young man whose courage is high and whose intelligence is not below par, that he should not be satisfied to remain at home; but should come out [. . .] and try to win a higher lot and a better fortune than the old country can afford to give him.

A. Trollope, *Australia and New Zealand* (1873), vol. 1, p. 58

CHAPTER 4

Situating Colonial and Postcolonial Studies

Ania Loomba

Ania Loomba, in this selection from her 1998 book, *Colonialism–Postcolonialism* points out some problems with the terminology of colonialism and post-colonialism. Not all countries that are technically in "post-colonial" situations have the same experience of or relationship to the formerly colonizing countries. The meanings of the terms have to be seen as fluctuating according to context and situation.

Defining the Terms: Colonialism, Imperialism, Neo-colonialism, Postcolonialism

Colonialism and imperialism are often used interchangeably. The word colonialism, according to the *Oxford English Dictionary* (OED), comes from the Roman 'colonia' which meant 'farm' or 'settlement', and referred to Romans who settled in other lands but still retained their citizenship. Accordingly, the *OED* describes it as,

> a settlement in a new country . . . a body of people who settle in a new locality, forming a community subject to or connected with their parent state; the community so formed, consisting of the original settlers and their descendants and successors, as long as the connection with the parent state is kept up.

This definition, quite remarkably, avoids any reference to people other than the colonisers, people who might already have been living in those places where colonies were established. Hence it evacuates the word 'colonialism' of any implication of an encounter between peoples, or of conquest and domination. There is no hint that the 'new locality' may not be so 'new' and that the process of 'forming a community' might be somewhat unfair. Colonialism was not an identical process in different parts of the world but everywhere it locked the original inhabitants and the newcomers into the most complex and traumatic relationships in human history. In *The Tempest*, for example, Shakespeare's single major addition to the story he found in certain pamphlets about a shipwreck in the Bermudas was to make the island inhabited before Prospero's arrival (Hulme 1986b: 69). That single addition turned the adventure story into an allegory of the colonial encounter. The process of 'forming a community' in the new land necessarily meant *unforming* or re-forming the communities that existed there already, and involved a wide range of practices including trade, plunder, negotiation, warfare, genocide, enslavement and rebellions. Such practices produced and were produced through a variety of writings – public and private records, letters, trade documents, government papers, fiction and scientific literature. These practices and writings are an important part of all that contemporary studies of colonialism and postcolonialism try to make sense of.

So colonialism can be defined as the conquest and control of other people's land and goods. But colonialism in this sense is not merely the expansion of various European powers into Asia, Africa or the Americas from the sixteenth century onwards; it has been a recurrent and widespread feature of human history. At its height in the second century AD, the Roman Empire stretched from Armenia to the Atlantic. Under Genghis Khan in the thirteenth century, the Mongols conquered the Middle East as well as China. The Aztec Empire was established when, from the fourteenth to the sixteenth centuries, one of the various ethnic groups who settled in the valley of Mexico subjugated the others. Aztecs extracted tributes in services and goods from conquered regions, as did the Inca Empire which was the largest pre-industrial state in the Americas. In the fifteenth century too, various kingdoms in southern India came under the control of the Vijaynagara Empire, and the Ottoman Empire, which began as a minor Islamic principality in what is now western Turkey, extended itself over most of Asia Minor and the Balkans. At the beginning of the eighteenth century, it still extended from the Mediterranean to the Indian ocean, and the Chinese Empire was larger than anything Europe had seen. Modern European colonialism cannot be sealed off from these earlier histories of contact – the Crusades, or the Moorish invasion of Spain, the legendary exploits of Mongol rulers or the fabled wealth of the Incas or the Mughals were real or imagined fuel for the European journeys to different parts of the world. And yet, these newer European travels ushered in new and different kinds of colonial practices which altered the whole globe in a way that these other colonialisms did not.

How do we think about these differences? Was it that Europeans established empires far away from their own shores? Were they more violent or more ruthless? Were they better organised? Or a superior race? All of these explanations have in fact been offered to account for the global power and drastic effects of European colonialisms. Marxist thinking on the subject locates a crucial distinction between the two: whereas earlier colonialisms were pre-capitalist, modern colonialism was established alongside capitalism in Western Europe (see Bottomore 1983: 81–5). Modern colonialism did more than extract tribute, goods and wealth from the countries that it conquered – it restructured the economies of the latter, drawing them into a complex relationship with their own, so that there was a flow of human and natural resources between colonised and colonial countries. This flow worked in both directions – slaves and indentured labour as well as raw materials were transported to manufacture goods in the metropolis, or in other locations for metropolitan consumption, but the colonies also provided captive markets for European goods. Thus slaves were moved from Africa to the Americas, and in the West Indian plantations they produced sugar for consumption in Europe, and raw cotton was moved from India to be manufactured into cloth in England and then sold back to India whose own cloth production suffered as a result. In whichever direction human beings and materials travelled, the profits always flowed back into the so-called 'mother country'.

These flows of profits and people involved settlement and plantations as in the Americas, 'trade' as in India, and enormous global shifts of populations. Both the colonised and the colonisers moved: the former not only as slaves but also as indentured labourers, domestic servants, travellers and traders, and the colonial masters as administrators, soldiers, merchants, settlers, travellers, writers, domestic staff, missionaries, teachers and scientists. The essential point is that although European colonialisms involved a variety of techniques and patterns of domination, penetrating deep into some societies and involving a comparatively superficial contact with others, all of them produced the economic imbalance that was necessary for the growth of European capitalism and industry. Thus we could say that colonialism was the midwife that assisted at the birth of European capitalism, or that without colonial expansion the transition to capitalism could not have taken place in Europe.

The distinction between pre-capitalist and capitalist colonialisms is often made by referring to the latter as imperialism. This is somewhat misleading, because imperialism, like colonialism, stretches back to a pre-capitalist past. Imperial Russia, for example, was pre-capitalist, as was Imperial Spain. Some commentators place imperialism as *prior* to colonialism (Boehmer 1995: 3). Like 'colonialism', this concept too is best understood not by trying to pin it down to a single semantic meaning but by relating its shifting meanings to historical processes. Early in its usage in the English language it simply means 'command or superior power' (Williams 1976: 131). The *OED* defines 'imperial' as simply 'pertaining to empire', and 'imperialism' as the 'rule of an emperor, especially when despotic or arbitrary; the principle or spirit of empire; advocacy of what are held to be imperial interests'. As a matter of fact, the connection of *imperial* with *royal* authority is highly variable. While royalty were both financially and symbolically invested in early European colonisations, these ventures were in every case also the result of wider class and social interests. Thus although Ralegh named Virginia after his Queen, and trading privileges to the English in India or Turkey were sought and granted not simply in the name of the East India Company but to Englishmen as representatives of Elizabeth I or James I, it was a wider base of English merchants, traders, financiers as well as feudal lords that made English trade and colonialism possible. The same is true even of the Portuguese empire, where royal involvement was more spectacular.

In the early twentieth century, Lenin and Kautsky (among other writers) gave a new meaning to the word 'imperialism' by linking it to a particular stage of the development of capitalism. In *Imperialism, the Highest Stage of Capitalism* (1947), Lenin argued that the growth of 'finance-capitalism' and industry in the Western countries had created 'an enormous superabundance of capital'. This money could not be profitably invested at home where labour was limited. The colonies lacked capital but were abundant in labour and human resources. Therefore it needed to move out and subordinate non-industrialised countries to sustain its own growth. Lenin thus predicted that in due course the rest of the world would be absorbed by European finance capitalists. This global system was called 'imperialism' and constituted a particular stage of capitalist development – the 'highest' in Lenin's understanding because rivalry between the various imperial powers would catalyse their destruction and the demise of capitalism. It is this Leninist definition that allows some people to argue that capitalism is the distinguishing feature between colonialism and imperialism.

Direct colonial rule is not necessary for imperialism in this sense, because the economic (and social) relations of dependency and control ensure both captive labour as well as markets for European industry as well as goods. Sometimes the words 'neo-imperialism' or 'neo-colonialism' are used to describe these situations. In as much as the growth of European industry and finance-capital was achieved through colonial domination in the first place, we can also see that imperialism (in this sense) is the highest stage of colonialism. In the modern world then, we can distinguish between colonisation as the take over of territory, appropriation of material resources, exploitation of labour and interference with political and cultural structures of another territory or nation, and imperialism as a global system. However, there remains enormous ambiguity between the economic and political connotations of the word. If imperialism is defined as a political system in which an imperial centre governs colonised countries, then the granting of political independence signals the end of empire, the collapse of imperialism. However, if imperialism is primarily an economic system of penetration and control of markets, then political changes do not basically affect it, and may even redefine the term as in the case of 'American imperialism' which wields enormous military and economic power across the globe but without direct political control. The political sense was predominant however in the description of the relations between the former USSR and other Eastern European countries as 'Soviet imperialism'. As we will discuss in later sections, the tensions between economic and political connotations of imperialism also spill over into the understanding of racial oppression, and its relationship with class or other structures of oppression.

Thus, imperialism, colonialism and the differences between them are defined differently depending on their historical mutations. One useful way of distinguishing between them might be to not separate them in temporal but in spatial terms and to think of imperialism or neo-imperialism as the phenomenon that originates in the metropolis, the process which leads to domination and control. Its result, or what happens in the colonies as a consequence of imperial domination is colonialism or neo-colonialism. Thus the imperial country is the 'metropole' from which power flows, and the colony or neo-colony is the place which it penetrates and controls. Imperialism can function without formal colonies (as in United States imperialism today) but colonialism cannot.

These fluctuations also complicate the meanings of the term 'postcolonial', a term that is the subject of an ongoing debate, which we shall unravel slowly. It might seem that because the age of colonialism is over, and because the descendants of once-colonised peoples live everywhere, the whole world is postcolonial. And yet the term has been fiercely contested on many counts. To begin with, the prefix 'post' complicates matters because it implies an 'aftermath' in two senses – temporal, as in coming after, and ideological, as in supplanting. It is the second implication which critics of the term have found contestable: if the inequities of colonial rule have not been erased, it is perhaps premature to proclaim the demise of colonialism. A country may be both postcolonial (in the sense of being formally independent) and neo-colonial (in the sense of remaining economically and/or culturally dependent) at the same time. We cannot dismiss the importance of either formal decolonisation, or the fact that unequal relations of colonial rule are reinscribed in the contemporary imbalances between 'first' and 'third' world nations. The new global order does not depend upon direct rule. However, it does allow the economic, cultural and (to varying degrees) political penetration of some countries by others. This makes it debatable whether once-colonised countries can be seen as properly 'postcolonial' (see McClintock 1992).

Even in the temporal sense, the word postcolonial cannot be used in any single sense. Formal decolonisation has spanned three centuries, ranging from the eighteenth and nineteenth centuries in the Americas, Australia, New Zealand and South Africa, to the 1970s in the case of Angola and Mozambique. Pointing to this fact, Ella Shohat trenchantly asks, 'When exactly, then, does the "postcolonial" begin?' (1993: 103). This is not just a rhetorical question; Shohat's point is that these diverse beginnings indicate that colonialism was challenged from a variety of perspectives by people who were not all oppressed in the same way or to the same extent. Thus the politics of decolonisation in parts of Latin America or Australia or South Africa where white settlers formed their own independent nations is different from the dynamics of those societies where indigenous populations overthrew their European masters. The term is not only inadequate to the task of defining contemporary realities in the once-colonised countries, and vague in terms of indicating a specific period of history, but may also cloud the internal social and racial differences of many societies. Spanish colonies in Latin America, for example, became 'mixed' societies, in which local born whites (or 'creoles') and mestizos, or 'hybrids', dominated the native working population. Hybridity or mestizaje here included a complex internal hierarchy within various mixed peoples. As J. Jorge Klor de Alva explains, one's experience of colonial exploitation depended on one's position within this hierarchy:

> In most places, the original inhabitants, who logically grouped themselves into separate cultural units (i.e. ethnicities), all but disappeared after contact, wiped out physically by disease and abuse, and later, genetically and socially by miscegenation, and lastly, culturally, by the religious and political practices of the Europeans and their mixed progeny. Even in the regions where native peoples survived as corporate groups in their own greatly transformed communities, especially in the 'core' areas of Mesoamerica and the Andes, within two or three generations they were greatly reduced in number and politically and socially marginalized from the new centers of power. Thus, those who escaped the orbit of native communities but were still the most socially and economically proximate to these dispossessed peoples could be expected to distance themselves from them wherever possible.
>
> (1995: 243)

The term 'postcolonial' does not apply to those at the bottom end of this hierarchy, who are still 'at the far economic margins of the nation-state' so that nothing is 'post' about their colonisation. On the other hand, those elites who won the wars of independence from Spain, Alva argues, 'were never colonial subjects' and they 'established their own nation-states in the image of the motherland, tinged by the local color of some precontact practices and symbols, framed by many imperial period adaptations and suffused with European ideals, practices and material objects' (1995: 270). The elite creoles, writes another critic, Mary Louise Pratt, 'sought esthetic and ideological grounding as white Americans' and attempted to create 'an independent, decolonised American society and culture, while retaining European values and white supremacy' (1992: 175). The quarrels of these Americans with colonial powers were radically different from anti-colonial struggles in parts of Africa or Asia and so, Alva concludes, they cannot be considered 'postcolonial' in the same sense.

In Australia, New Zealand or Canada, 'hybridity' is less evident between descendants of white settlers and those of the original inhabitants. But because the former also feel estranged from Britain (or France) they want to be considered postcolonial subjects. However, we cannot explore in what ways they are postcolonial without also highlighting internal differences within these countries (Mishra and Hodge 1991: 413). White settlers were historically the agents of colonial rule, and their own subsequent development – cultural as well as economic – does not simply align them with other colonised peoples. No matter what their differences with the mother country, white populations here were not subject to the genocide, economic exploitation, cultural decimation and political exclusion felt by indigenous peoples or by other colonies. Although we cannot equate its history with those of these other settler-countries, the most bizarre instance of this may be South Africa, where nationalist Afrikaners 'continued to see themselves as victims of English colonisation and...the imagined continuation of this victimization was used to justify the maintenance of apartheid' (Jolly 1995: 22).

These internal fractures and divisions are important if 'postcolonialism' is to be anything more than a term signifying a technical transfer of governance. But at the same time, we cannot simply construct a global 'white' culture either. There are important differences of power and history between New Zealand or Canada and the European (or later United States) metropolis. Internal fractures also exist in countries whose postcolonial status is not usually contested, such as India. Here the ruptures have to do with class and ethnicity in a different sense. In a moving story, 'Shishu' (Children) the Bengali writer Mahasweta Devi describes how tribal peoples have been literally and figuratively crippled in post-independence India. National 'development' has no space for tribal cultures or beliefs, and the attitude of even the well-meaning government officer, Mr Singh, towards the tribals replicates colonialist views of non-Western peoples – to him, they are mysterious, superstitious, uncivilised, backward. In other words, they are like children who need to be brought in line with the rest of the country. The rebellious among them have literally been pushed into the forests and have been starving there for years. At the chilling climax of the tale, we are brought face to face with these 'children' who thrust their starved bodies towards Mr Singh, forcing the officer to recognise that they are not children at all but adult citizens of free India, and stunted by free India:

Fear – stark, unreasoning, naked fear – gripped him. Why this silent creeping forward? Why didn't they utter one word?...Why were they naked? And why such long hair? Children, he had always heard of children, but how come that one had white hair? Why did the women – no, no, girls – have dangling, withered breasts?...'We are not children. We are Agarias of the Village of Kuva....There are only fourteen of us left. Our bodies have shrunk without food. Our men are impotent, our women barren. That's why we steal the relief [the food Singh brings from the Government to distribute to the more docile among the tribals]. Don't you see we need food to grow to a human size again?'...

They cackled with savage and revengeful glee. Cackling, they ran around him. They rubbed their organs against him and told him they were adult citizens of India....

Singh's shadow covered their bodies. And the shadow brought the realization home to him.

They hated his height of five feet and nine inches.

They hated the normal growth of his body.

His normalcy was a crime they could not forgive.

Singh's cerebral cells tried to register the logical explanation but he failed to utter a single word. Why, why this revenge? He was just an ordinary Indian. He didn't have the stature of a healthy Russian, Canadian or American. He did not eat food that supplied enough calories for a human body. The World Health Organization said that it was a crime to deny the human body the right number of calories. . . .

(Mahasweta Devi 1993: 248–50)

Even as it is careful to demarcate between what is available to citizens of different nations, the story reminds us that anti-colonial movements have rarely represented the interests of all the peoples of a colonised country. After independence, these fissures can no longer be glossed over, which is why, like some of their Indian counterparts, African novelists since the 1960s can also be regarded as 'no longer committed to the nation' (Appiah 1996: 66). The newly independent nation-state makes available the fruits of liberation only selectively and unevenly: the dismantling of colonial rule did not automatically bring about changes for the better in the status of women, the working class or the peasantry in most colonised countries. 'Colonialism' is not just something that happens from outside a country or a people, not just something that operates with the collusion of forces inside, but a version of it can be duplicated from within. So that 'postcolonialism', far from being a term that can be indiscriminately applied, appears to be riddled with contradictions and qualifications.

It has been suggested that it is more helpful to think of postcolonialism not just as coming literally after colonialism and signifying its demise, but more flexibly as the contestation of colonial domination and the legacies of colonialism. Such a position would allow us to include people geographically displaced by colonialism such as African-Americans or people of Asian or Caribbean origin in Britain as 'postcolonial' subjects although they live within metropolitan cultures. It also allows us to incorporate the history of anti-colonial resistance with contemporary resistances to imperialism and to dominant Western culture. Jorge de Alva suggests that postcoloniality should 'signify not so much subjectivity "after" the colonial experience as a subjectivity of oppositionality to imperializing/colonizing (read: subordinating/subjectivizing) discourses and practices'. He justifies this by arguing that new approaches to history have discredited the idea of a single linear progression, focusing instead on 'a multiplicity of often conflicting and frequently parallel narratives'. Therefore, he suggests that we should 'remove postcoloniality from a dependence on an antecedent colonial condition' and 'tether the term to a post-structuralist stake that marks its appearance. That, I believe, is the way postcoloniality must be understood when applied to United States Latinos or Latin American hybrids' (Alva 1995: 245).

This statement is worth unpacking for it leads us into the heart of the controversy surrounding postcolonial studies today. Although we shall only discuss this controversy later in the book, we can take a quick look at the direction in which some current debates are moving. Alva wants to de-link the term postcoloniality from formal decolonisation because he thinks many people living in both once-colonised and once colonising countries are still subject to the oppressions put into place by colonialism. And he justifies this expansion of the term by referring to post-structuralist approaches to history which have suggested that the lives of various oppressed peoples can only be uncovered by insisting that there is no single history but a 'multiplicity of histories'. It was not only post-structuralists who discredited master narratives, feminists also insisted that such narratives had hidden women from history. Anti-colonial intellectuals also espoused a similar view. However, the idea has received its most sustained articulation within post-structuralist writing. Thus Alva suggests that postcoloniality is, and must be more firmly connected to, post-structuralist theories of history.

Recently, many critics of postcolonial theory have in fact blamed it for too much dependence upon post-structuralist or post-modern perspectives (which are often read as identical). They claim that the insistence on multiple histories and fragmentation within these perspectives has been detrimental to thinking about the global operation of capitalism today. The increasing fragmentation and mobility of communities and peoples needs to be contextualised in terms of the new ways in which global capitalism works. According to this argument, an accent on a multiplicity of histories serves to obfuscate the ways in which these histories are being connected anew by the international workings of multinational capital. Without this focus, the global imbalances of power are glossed over, and the world rendered 'seemingly shapeless' (Dirlik 1994: 355). A too-quick enlargement of the term postcolonial can indeed paradoxically flatten both past and contemporary situations. All 'subordinating' discourses and practices are not the same either over time or across the globe. Erstwhile colonial powers may be restructured by contemporary imperialism but they are not the same phenomena. Opposition to colonial rule was spearheaded by forms of nationalist struggle which cannot offer a blueprint for dealing with inequities of the contemporary world order. In fact, as the Mahasweta Devi story quoted above exemplifies, many struggles in the postcolonial world are sceptical about precisely those forces and discourses that were responsible for formal decolonisation.

And so, we might ask not only when does the postcolonial begin, but where is postcoloniality to be found? Although 'minority' peoples living in the West (and they may not in every place be literally a minority at all) and the peoples living in 'third world' countries share a history of colonial exploitation, may share cultural roots, and may also share an opposition to the legacy of colonial domination, their histories and present concerns cannot simply be merged. African-Americans and South African blacks, for example, may both be engaged in the reconstruction of their cultures, yet how can we forget that blacks in South Africa are the marginalised majority of the population or that African-Americans are citizens of the world's mightiest state although their own position within it might be marginal? These differences are highlighted by a production of Shakespeare's *Othello* by the South African actress Janet Suzman. Suzman had been living in Britain for many years when she returned home to mount the play for the Market Theatre in Johannesburg, in which she cast a black actor in the central role. In the context of a long history of *Othello* productions where the hero is played by a white man, or which simply gloss over the racial politics of the play in favour of the 'universal' themes of male jealousy, doomed love, and devoted female victims, and especially in the context of South Africa's laws against mixed marriages, this production was radical. And to place Othello in one of the cultures of 'his' origin is to allow us to rethink the entire history of the play. But at the same time, Shakespeare's drama is about a black man trying to live in a white society, assimilating yet maintaining his identity. His loneliness is an integral feature of the play – he is isolated from other black people, from his history and culture. To place Shakespeare's *Othello* in South Africa is to open up a powerful new reading of the play, but also to elide two different kinds of marginality: the one which arises out of displacement and another in which black people and cultures were victimised but not literally isolated from each other.

Othello's situation of course does not translate exactly into today's European context because so-called metropolitan societies are now literally changing their colours. Othello's successors are not so alone. And yet, British Asians face a different sort of pressure on their self-definition than people within India or Pakistan or Bangladesh. Further, by now there are as many differences between each of these groups as there are similarities. Similarly anti-colonial positions are embedded in specific histories, and cannot be collapsed into some pure oppositional essence. They also depended on the nature of colonial rule so that nationalist struggles in Algeria against the French were different from Indian resistance to the British, and neither can be equated to Vietnamese opposition to French and United States imperialism. As we will see, many writings on postcolonialism emphasise concepts like 'hybridity' and fragmentation and diversity, and yet they routinely claim to be describing 'the postcolonial condition', or 'the postcolonial subject' or 'the postcolonial woman'. At best, such terms are no more than a helpful shorthand, because they do not allow for differences between distinct kinds of colonial situations, or the workings of class, gender, location, race, caste or ideology among people whose lives have been restructured by colonial rule.

As mentioned earlier, by the 1930s colonialism had exercised its sway over 84.6 per cent of the land surface of the globe. This fact alone reminds us that it is impossible for European colonialism to have been a monolithic operation. Right from its earliest years it deployed diverse strategies and methods of control and of representation. European discourses about 'the other' are accordingly variable. But because they produced comparable (and sometimes uncannily similar) relations of inequity and domination the world over, it is sometimes overlooked that colonial methods and images varied hugely over time and place. Most contemporary commentators continue to generalise about colonialism from their specific knowledge of it in a particular place or time. Thus, for some critics such as Gayatri Spivak, nineteenth-century India, and particularly nineteenth-century Bengal, has become a privileged model for the colonised world. Laura Chrisman finds that 'an Oriental/Occidental binarism, in which continents and colonies which do not belong to this West/East axis are nonetheless absorbed into it' is detrimental to recovering the specificity of certain situations in Africa. Although such homogenising might partially have arisen from the desire to emphasise how colonial discourses themselves blur difference, its effect, as Chrisman points out, is to overlook how these discourses also deploy strategies of exaggerating and playing off differences among diverse others:

> It is just as important to observe differences between imperial practices – whether it be geographical/national (for example, the differences between the French imperialism of Baudelaire and the English imperialism of Kipling) or historical (say the differences between the early-nineteenth-century imperialism, prior to its formal codification, and late-nineteenth-century imperialism) – as it is to emphasize what all these formations have in common.
>
> (Chrisman 1994: 500)

The legacies of colonialism are thus varied and multiple even as they obviously share some important features.

If the term postcolonial is taken to signify an oppositional position or even desire, as Alva suggests, then it has the effect of collapsing various locations so that the specificities of all of them are blurred. Moreover, thought of as an oppositional stance, 'postcolonial' refers to specific groups of (oppressed or dissenting) people (or individuals within them) rather than to a location or a social order, which may include such people but is not limited to them. Postcolonial theory has been accused of precisely this: it shifts the focus from locations and institutions to individuals and their subjectivities. Postcoloniality becomes a vague condition of people anywhere and everywhere, and the specificities of locale do not matter. In part the dependence of postcolonial theory upon literary and cultural criticism, and upon post-structuralism is responsible for this shift. So we are back to the critique articulated earlier – that post-structuralism is responsible for current inadequacies in theorising postcoloniality. We will return to this issue when some of the terms in the debate have been further clarified. For now, we can see some of the problems with expanding the term postcolonial to signify a political position.

There is yet another issue at stake in the term, and this time the problem is not with 'post' but with 'colonial'. Analyses of 'postcolonial' societies too often work with the sense that colonialism is the only history of these societies. What came before colonial rule? What indigenous ideologies, practices and hierarchies existed alongside colonialism and interacted with it? Colonialism did not inscribe itself on a clean slate, and it cannot therefore account for everything that exists in 'postcolonial' societies. The food, or music, or languages, or arts of any culture that we think of as post-colonial evoke earlier histories or shades of culture that elude the term 'colonial'. Critics such as Gayatri Spivak have repeatedly cautioned against the idea that pre-colonial cultures are something that we can easily recover, warning that 'a nostalgia for lost origins can be detrimental to the exploration of social realities within the critique of imperialism' (1988: 271–313). Spivak is suggesting here that the pre-colonial is always reworked by the history of colonialism, and is not available to us in any pristine form that can be neatly separated from the history of colonialism. She is interested in emphasising the worlding (i.e. both the violation and the creation) of the 'third world' by colonial powers and therefore resists the romanticising of once-colonised societies 'as distant cultures, exploited but with rich intact heritages waiting to be recovered ...'. Other critics such as Kwame Anthony Appiah (1991) have also criticised the tendency to eulogise the pre-colonial past or romanticise native culture. Such 'nativism', they suggest, is espoused by both certain intellectuals within post-colonial societies and some First World academics. But while such caution is neces-sary, it can also lead to a reverse simplification, whereby the 'Third World' is seen as a world defined entirely by its relation to colonialism. Its histories are then flattened, and colonialism becomes their defining feature, whereas in several parts of the once-colonised world, historians are inclined to regard colonialism 'as a minor interruption' in a long, complex history (Vaughan 1993: 47).

Postcolonialism, then, is a word that is useful only if we use it with caution and qualifications. In this it can be compared to the concept of 'patriarchy' in feminist thought, which is applicable to the extent that it indicates male domination over women. But the ideology and practices of male domination are historically, geograph-ically and culturally variable. English patriarchal structures were different in the sixteenth century from what they are today, and they varied also between classes, then and now. All of these are further distinct from patriarchy in China, which is also variable over time and social groupings. But of course all of these also have something in common, so feminist theory has had to weave between analysing the universals and the particulars in the oppression of women. Patriarchy then becomes a useful shorthand for conveying a structure of inequity, which is, in practice, highly variable because it always works alongside other social structures. Similarly, the word 'postcolonial' is useful as a generalisation to the extent that 'it refers to a *process* of disengagement from the whole colonial syndrome, which takes many forms and is probably inescapable for all those whose worlds have been marked by that set of phenomena: "postcolonial" is (or should be) a descriptive not an evaluative term' (Hulme 1995: 120).

Postcolonial studies have shown that both the 'metropolis' and the 'colony' were deeply altered by the colonial process. *Both* of them are, accordingly, also restructured by decolonisation. This of course does not mean that both are postcolonial *in the same way*. Postcoloniality, like patriarchy, is articulated alongside other economic, social, cultural and historical factors, and therefore, in practice, it works quite differently in various parts of the world. Frankenburg and Mani (1993) and Hulme (1995) make this point by tracing some of the ways in which the meaning of the term shifts across different locations. Hulme argues that, contrary to Alva's suggestion, the American continent is postcolonial, even though its anti-colonial wars were not fought by the indigenous peoples. American postcoloniality, in Hulme's argument, is simply *different* from the one that operates in India, and it also includes enormous variety within itself (the USA is the world's leading imperialist power but it once was anti-colonial in a limited sense; the Caribbean and Latin America still struggle with the effects of colonial domination and neo-colonialism). To impose a single understanding of decolonisation would in fact erase the differences within that term. In this view, there is a productive tension between the temporal and the critical dimensions of the word postcolonial, but postcoloniality is not, Hulme points out, simply a 'merit badge' that can be worn at will. We can conclude, then, that the word 'postcolonial' is useful in indicating a general process with some shared features across the globe. But if it is uprooted from specific locations, 'postcoloniality' cannot be meaningfully investigated, and instead, the term begins to obscure the very relations of domination that it seeks to uncover.

Works Cited

Appiah, K. A. 1991. "Out of Africa: Topologies of Nativism." In *The Bounds of Race: Perspectives on Hegemony and Resistance*, ed. D. LaCapra. Ithaca, NY, and London: Cornell University Press, pp. 134–63.
—— 1996. "Is the Post in Postmodernism the Post in Postcolonialism?" In *Contemporary Postcolonial Theory: A Reader*, ed. P. Mongia. London: Edward Arnold.
Boehmer, E. 1995. *Colonial and Postcolonial Literature*. Oxford and New York: Oxford University Press.
Bottomore, T., ed. 1983. *A Dictionary of Marxist Thought*. Oxford: Blackwell.
Chrisman, L. 1994. "The Imperial Unconscious? Representations of Imperial Discourse." In *Colonial Discourse and Postcolonial Theory: A Reader*, ed. P. Williams and L. Chrisman. New York: Columbia University Press, pp. 498–516.
Dirlik, A. 1994. "The Postcolonial Aura: Third World Criticism in the Age of Global Capitalism." *Critical Inquiry* 20: 328–56.

Hulme, P. 1986. "Hurricane in the Caribbees: The Constitution of the Discourse of English Colonialism." In *Literature, Politics and Theory: Papers from the Essex Conference 1976–1984*, ed. F. Barker, P. Hulme, M. Iversen and D. Loxley. London: Methuen.

——1995. "Including America." *Ariel* 26: 117–23.

Jolly, R. 1995. "Contemporary Postcolonial Discourse and the New South Africa." *PMLA* 110: 17–29.

Klor de Alva, J. J. 1995. "The Postcolonization of the (Latin) American Experience: A Reconsideration of 'Colonialism,' 'Postcolonialism,' and 'Mestizaje.'" In *After Colonialism: Imperial Histories and Postcolonial Displacements*, ed. G. Prakash. Princeton, NJ: Princeton University Press, pp. 241–75.

Mani, L. 1992. "Cultural Theory, Colonial Texts: Reading Eyewitness Accounts of Widow Burning." In *Cultural Studies*, ed. L. Grossberg, C. Nelson and P. Treichler. New York and London: Routledge.

McClintock, A. 1992. "The Angel of Progress: Pitfalls of the Term 'Postcolonialism'." *Social Text* 31/32: 84–98. [See also pp. 185–96 in this volume.]

Mishra, V. and Hodge, B. 1991. "What is Postcolonialism?" *Textual Practice* 5: 399–415.

Pratt, M. L. 1992. *Imperial Eyes: Travel Writing and Transculturation*. London and New York: Routledge.

Shohat, E. 1993. "Notes on the 'Post-colonial'." *Social Text* 31/32: 99–113.

Spivak, G. C. 1988. "Can the Subaltern Speak?" In *Marxism and the Interpretation of Culture*, ed. C. Nelson and L. Grossberg. Basingstoke: Macmillan, pp. 271–313.

Vaughan, M. 1993. "Madness and Colonialism, Colonialism as Madness," *Paideuma* 39: 45–55.

Williams, R. 1976. *Keywords: A Vocabulary of Culture and Society*, New York: Oxford University Press.

CHAPTER 5

Jane Austen and Empire

Edward Said

Edward Said's *Orientalism* (1977) helped to create the new field of Colonial and Post-Colonial Studies. Said drew on the work of Structuralist historian Michel Foucault in his examination of how Western academic discourses described non-Western countries that were in the process of being colonized by Western Europe. The "Orient," as the East was called, was depicted in necessarily stereotypical ways in Western academic discourse, and that discourse often underwrote colonial policy and licensed further imperial undertakings. In his next major work, *Culture and Imperialism* (1993), from which this selection is taken, he examines the intertwining of literature with its imperial context.

We are on solid ground with V. G. Kiernan when he says that "empires must have a mould of ideas or conditioned reflexes to flow into, and youthful nations dream of a great place in the world as young men dream of fame and fortunes."[1] It is, as I have been saying throughout, too simple and reductive to argue that everything in European or American culture therefore prepares for or consolidates the grand idea of empire. It is also, however, historically inaccurate to ignore those tendencies – whether in narrative, political theory, or pictorial technique – that enabled, encouraged, and otherwise assured the West's readiness to assume and enjoy the experience of empire. If there was cultural resistance to the notion of an imperial mission, there was not much support for that resistance in the main departments of cultural thought. Liberal though he was, John Stuart Mill – as a telling case in point – could still say, "The sacred duties which civilized nations owe to the independence and nationality of each other, are not binding towards those to whom nationality and independence are certain evil, or at best a questionable good." Ideas like this were not original with Mill; they were already current in the English subjugation of Ireland during the sixteenth century and, as Nicholas Canny has persuasively demonstrated, were equally useful in the ideology of English colonization in the Americas.[2] Almost all colonial schemes begin with an assumption of native backwardness and general inadequacy to be independent, "equal," and fit.

Why that should be so, why sacred obligation on one front should not be binding on another, why rights accepted in one may be denied in another, are questions best understood in the terms of a culture well-grounded in moral, economic, and even metaphysical norms designed to approve a satisfying local, that is European, order and to permit the abrogation of the right to a similar order abroad. Such a statement may appear preposterous or extreme. In fact, it formulates the connection between Europe's wellbeing and cultural identity on the one hand and, on the other, the subjugation of imperial realms overseas rather too fastidiously and circumspectly.

Part of our difficulty today in accepting any connection at all is that we tend to reduce this complicated matter to an apparently simple causal one, which in turn produces a rhetoric of blame and defensiveness. I am *not* saying that the major factor in early European culture was that it *caused* late-nineteenth-century imperialism, and I am not implying that all the problems of the formerly colonial world should be blamed on Europe. I am saying, however, that European culture often, if not always, characterized itself in such a way as simultaneously to validate its own preferences while also advocating those preferences in conjunction with distant imperial rule. Mill certainly did: he always recommended that India *not* be given independence. When for various reasons imperial rule concerned Europe more intensely after 1880, this schizophrenic habit became useful.

The first thing to be done now is more or less to jettison simple causality in thinking through the relationship between Europe and the non-European world, and lessening the hold on our thought of the equally simple temporal sequence. We must not admit any notion, for instance, that proposes to show that Wordsworth, Austen, or Coleridge, because they wrote *before* 1857, actually caused the establishment of formal British governmental rule over India *after* 1857. We should try to discern instead a counterpoint between overt patterns in British writing about Britain and representations of the world beyond the British Isles. The inherent mode for this counterpoint is not temporal but spatial. How do writers in the period before the great age of explicit, programmatic colonial expansion – the "scramble for Africa," say – situate and see themselves and their work in the larger world? We shall find them using striking but careful strategies, many of them derived from expected sources – positive ideas of home, of a nation and its language, of proper order, good behavior, moral values.

But positive ideas of this sort do more than validate "our" world. They also tend to devalue other worlds and, perhaps more significantly from a retrospective point of view, they do not prevent or inhibit or give resistance to horrendously unattractive imperialist practices. No, cultural forms like the novel or the opera do not cause people to go out and imperialize – Carlyle did not drive Rhodes directly, and he certainly cannot be "blamed" for the problems in today's southern Africa – but it is genuinely troubling to see how little Britain's great humanistic ideas, institutions, and monuments, which we still celebrate as having the power ahistorically to command our approval, how little they stand in the way of the accelerating imperial process. We are entitled to ask how this body of humanistic ideas coexisted so comfortably with imperialism, and why – until the resistance to imperialism *in the imperial domain*, among Africans, Asians, Latin Americans, developed – there was little significant opposition or deterrence to empire at home. Perhaps the custom of distinguishing "our" home and order from "theirs" grew into a harsh political rule for accumulating more of "them" to rule, study, and subordinate. In the great, humane ideas and values promulgated by mainstream European culture, we have precisely that "mould of ideas or conditioned reflexes" of which Kiernan speaks, into which the whole business of empire later flowed.

The extent to which these ideas are actually invested in geographical distinctions between real places is the subject of Raymond Williams's richest book, *The Country and the City*. His argument concerning the interplay between rural and urban places in England admits of the most extraordinary transformations – from the pastoral populism of Langland, through Ben Jonson's country-house poems and the novels of Dickens's London, right up to visions of the metropolis in twentieth-century literature. Mainly, of course, the book is about how English culture has dealt with land, its possession, imagination, and organization. And while he does address the export of England to the colonies, Williams does so, as I suggested earlier, in a less focused way and less expansively than the practice actually warrants. Near the end of *The Country and the City* he volunteers that "from at least the mid–nineteenth century, and with important instances earlier, there was this larger context [the relationship between England and the colonies, whose effects on the English imagination "have gone deeper than can easily be traced"] within which every idea and every image was consciously and unconsciously affected." He goes on quickly to cite "the idea of emigration to the colonies" as one such image prevailing in various novels by Dickens, the Brontës, Gaskell, and rightly shows that "new rural societies," all of them colonial, enter the imaginative metropolitan economy of English literature via Kipling, early Orwell, Maugham. After 1880 there comes a "dramatic extension of landscape and social relations": this corresponds more or less exactly with the great age of empire.[3]

It is dangerous to disagree with Williams, yet I would venture to say that if one began to look for something like an imperial map of the world in English literature, it would turn up with amazing insistence and frequency well before the mid–nineteenth century. And turn up not only with the inert regularity suggesting something taken for granted, but – more interestingly – threaded through, forming a vital part of the texture of linguistic and cultural practice. There were established English offshore interests in Ireland, America, the Caribbean, and Asia from the sixteenth century on, and even a quick inventory reveals poets, philosophers, historians, dramatists, statesmen, novelists, travel writers, chroniclers, soldiers, and fabulists who prized, cared for, and traced these interests with continuing concern. (Much of this is well discussed by Peter Hulme in *Colonial Encounters*.)[4] Similar points may be made for France, Spain, and Portugal, not only as overseas powers in their own right, but as competitors with the British. How can we examine these interests at work in modern England before the age of empire, i.e., during the period between 1800 and 1870?

We would do well to follow Williams's lead, and look first at that period of crisis following upon England's wide-scale land enclosure at the end of the eighteenth century. The old organic rural communities were dissolved and new ones forged under the impulse of parliamentary activity, industrialization, and demographic dislocation, but there also occurred a new process of relocating England (and in France, France) within a much larger circle of the world map. During the first half of the eighteenth century, Anglo-French competition in North America and India was intense; in the second half there were numerous violent encounters between England and France in the Americas, the Caribbean, and the Levant, and of course in Europe itself. The major pre-Romantic literature in France and England contains a constant stream of references to the overseas dominions: one thinks not only of various Encyclopedists, the Abbé Raynal, de Brosses, and Volney, but also of Edmund Burke, Beckford, Gibbon, Johnson, and William Jones.

In 1902 J. A. Hobson described imperialism as the expansion of nationality, implying that the process was understandable mainly by considering *expansion* as the more important of the two terms, since "nationality" was a fully formed, fixed quantity,[5] whereas a century before it was still in the process of *being formed*, at home and abroad as well. In *Physics and Politics* (1887) Walter Bagehot speaks with extraordinary relevance of "nation-making." Between France and Britain in the late eighteenth century there were two contests: the battle for strategic gains abroad – in India, the Nile delta, the Western Hemisphere – and the battle for a triumphant nationality. Both battles contrast "Englishness" with "the French," and no matter how intimate and closeted the supposed English or French "essence" appears to be, it was almost always thought of as being (as opposed to already) made, and being fought out with the other great competitor. Thackeray's Becky Sharp, for example, is as much an upstart as she is because of her half-French heritage. Earlier in the century, the upright abolitionist posture of Wilberforce and his allies developed partly out of a desire to make life harder for French hegemony in the Antilles.[6]

These considerations suddenly provide a fascinatingly expanded dimension to *Mansfield Park* (1814), the most explicit in its ideological and moral affirmations of Austen's novels. Williams once again is in general dead right: Austen's novels express an "attainable quality of life," in money and property acquired, moral discriminations made, the right choices put in place, the correct "improvements" implemented, the finely nuanced language affirmed and classified. Yet, Williams continues,

> What [Cobbett] names, riding past on the road, are classes. Jane Austen, from inside the houses, can never see that, for all the intricacy of her social description. All her discrimination is, understandably, internal and exclusive. She is concerned with the conduct of people who, in the complications of improvement, are repeatedly trying to make themselves into a class. But where only one class is seen, no classes are seen.[7]

As a general description of how Austen manages to elevate certain "moral discriminations" into "an independent value," this is excellent. Where *Mansfield Park* is concerned, however, a good deal more needs to be said, giving greater explicitness and width to Williams's survey. Perhaps then Austen, and indeed, pre-imperialist novels generally, will appear to be more implicated in the rationale for imperialist expansion than at first sight they have been.

After Lukacs and Proust, we have become so accustomed to thinking of the novel's plot and structure as constituted mainly by temporality that we have overlooked the function of space, geography, and location. For it is not only the very young Stephen Dedalus, but every other young protagonist before him as well, who sees himself in a widening spiral at home, in Ireland, in the world. Like many other novels, *Mansfield Park* is very precisely about a series of both small and large dislocations and relocations in space that occur before, at the end of the novel, Fanny Price, the niece, becomes the spiritual mistress of Mansfield Park. And that place itself is located by Austen at the center of an arc of interests and concerns spanning the hemisphere, two major seas, and four continents.

As in Austen's other novels, the central group that finally emerges with marriage and property "ordained" is not based exclusively upon blood. Her novel enacts the disaffiliation (in the literal sense) of some members of a family, and the affiliation between others and one or two chosen and tested outsiders: in other words, blood relationships are not enough to assure continuity, hierarchy, authority, both domestic and international. Thus Fanny Price – the poor niece, the orphaned child from the outlying city of Portsmouth, the neglected, demure, and upright wallflower – gradually acquires a status commensurate with, even superior to, that of most of her more fortunate relatives. In this pattern of affiliation and in her assumption of authority, Fanny Price is relatively passive. She resists the misdemeanors and the importunings of others, and very occasionally she ventures actions on her own: all in all, though, one has the impression that Austen has designs for her that Fanny herself can scarcely comprehend, just as throughout the novel Fanny is thought of by everyone as "comfort" and "acquisition" despite herself. Like Kipling's Kim O'Hara, Fanny is both device and instrument in a larger pattern, as well as a fully fledged novelistic character.

Fanny, like Kim, requires direction, requires the patronage and outside authority that her own impoverished experience cannot provide. Her conscious connections are to some people and to some places, but the novel reveals other connections of which she has faint glimmerings that nevertheless demand her presence and service. She comes into a situation that opens with an intricate set of moves which, taken together, demand sorting out, adjustment, and rearrangement. Sir Thomas Bertram has been captivated by one Ward sister, the others have not done well, and "an absolute breach" opens up; their "circles were so distinct," the distances between them so great that they have been out of touch for eleven years;[8] fallen on hard times, the Prices seek out the Bertrams. Gradually, and even though she is not the eldest, Fanny becomes the focus of attention as she is sent to Mansfield Park, there to begin her new life. Similarly, the Bertrams have given up London (the result of Lady Bertram's "little ill health and a great deal of indolence") and come to reside entirely in the country.

What sustains this life materially is the Bertram estate in Antigua, which is not doing well. Austen takes pains to show us two apparently disparate but actually convergent processes: the growth of Fanny's importance to the Bertrams' economy, including Antigua, and Fanny's own steadfastness in the face of numerous challenges, threats, and surprises. In both, Austen's imagination works with a steel-like rigor through a mode that we might call geographical and spatial clarification. Fanny's ignorance when she arrives at Mansfield as a frightened ten-year-old is signified by her inability to "put the map of Europe together,"[9] and for much of the first half of the novel the action is concerned with a whole range of issues whose common denominator, misused or misunderstood, is space: not only is Sir Thomas in Antigua to make things better there and at home, but at Mansfield Park, Fanny, Edmund, and her aunt Norris negotiate where she is to live, read, and work, where fires are to be lit; the friends and cousins concern themselves with the improvement of estates, and the importance of chapels (i.e., religious authority) to domesticity is envisioned and debated. When, as a device for stirring things up, the Crawfords suggest a play (the tinge of France that hangs a little suspiciously over their background is significant), Fanny's discomfiture is polarizingly acute. She cannot participate, cannot easily accept that rooms for living are turned into theatrical space, although, with all its confusion of roles and purposes, the play, Kotzebue's *Lovers' Vows*, is prepared for anyway.

We are to surmise, I think, that while Sir Thomas is away tending his colonial garden, a number of inevitable mismeasurements (explicitly associated with feminine "lawlessness") will occur. These are apparent not only in innocent strolls by the three pairs of young friends through a park, in which people lose and catch sight of one another unexpectedly, but most clearly in the various flirtations and engagements between the young men and women left without true parental authority, Lady Bertram being indifferent, Mrs. Norris unsuitable. There is sparring, innuendo, perilous taking on of roles: all of this of course crystallizes in preparations for the play, in which something dangerously close to libertinage is about to be (but never is) enacted. Fanny, whose earlier sense of alienation, distance, and fear derives from her first uprooting, now becomes a sort of surrogate conscience about what is right and how far is too much. Yet she has no power to implement her uneasy awareness, and until Sir Thomas suddenly returns from "abroad," the rudderless drift continues.

When he does appear, preparations for the play are immediately stopped, and in a passage remarkable for its executive dispatch, Austen narrates the re-establishment of Sir Thomas's local rule:

> It was a busy morning with him. Conversation with any of them occupied but a small part of it. He had to reinstate himself in all the wonted concerns of his Mansfield life, to see his steward and his bailiff – to examine and compute – and, in the intervals of business, to walk into his stables and his gardens, and nearest plantations; but active and methodical, he had not only done all this before he resumed his seat as master of the house at dinner, he had also set the carpenter to work in pulling down what had been so lately put up in the billiard room, and given the scene painter his dismissal, long enough to justify the pleasing belief of his being then at least as far off as Northampton. The scene painter was gone, having spoilt only the floor of one room, ruined all the coachman's sponges, and made five of the under-servants idle and dissatisfied; and Sir Thomas was in hopes that another day or two would suffice to wipe away every outward memento of what had been, even to the destruction of every unbound copy of 'Lovers' Vows' in the house, for he was burning all that met his eye.[10]

The force of this paragraph is unmistakable. Not only is this a Crusoe setting things in order: it is also an early Protestant eliminating all traces of frivolous behavior. There is nothing in *Mansfield Park* that would contradict us, however, were we to assume that Sir Thomas does exactly the same things – on a larger scale – in his Antigua "plantations." Whatever was wrong there – and the internal evidence garnered by Warren Roberts suggests that economic depression, slavery, and competition with France were at issue[11] – Sir Thomas was able to fix, thereby maintaining his control over his colonial domain. More clearly than anywhere else in her fiction, Austen here synchronizes domestic with international authority, making it plain that the values associated with such higher things as ordination, law, and propriety must be grounded firmly in actual rule over and possession of territory. She sees clearly that to hold and rule Mansfield Park is to hold and rule an imperial estate in close, not to say inevitable association with it. What assures the domestic tranquillity and attractive harmony of one is the productivity and regulated discipline of the other.

Before both can be fully secured, however, Fanny must become more actively involved in the unfolding action. From frightened and often victimized poor relation she is gradually transformed into a directly participating member of the Bertram household at Mansfield Park. For this, I believe, Austen designed the second part of the book, which contains not only the failure of the Edmund–Mary Crawford romance as well as the disgraceful profligacy of Lydia and Henry Crawford, but Fanny Price's rediscovery and rejection of her Portsmouth home, the injury and incapacitation of Tom Bertram (the eldest son), and the launching of William Price's naval career. This entire ensemble of relationships and events is finally capped with Edmund's marriage to Fanny, whose place in Lady Bertram's household is taken by

Susan Price, her sister. It is no exaggeration to interpret the concluding sections of *Mansfield Park* as the coronation of an arguably unnatural (or at very least, illogical) principle at the heart of a desired English order. The audacity of Austen's vision is disguised a little by her voice, which despite its occasional archness is understated and notably modest. But we should not misconstrue the limited references to the outside world, her lightly stressed allusions to work, process, and class, her apparent ability to abstract (in Raymond Williams's phrase) "an everyday uncompromising morality which is in the end separable from its social basis." In fact Austen is far less diffident, far more severe.

The clues are to be found in Fanny, or rather in how rigorously we are able to consider her. True, her visit to her original Portsmouth home, where her immediate family still resides, upsets the aesthetic and emotional balance she has become accustomed to at Mansfield Park, and true she has begun to take its wonderful luxuries for granted, even as being essential. These are fairly routine and natural consequences of getting used to a new place. But Austen is talking about two other matters we must not mistake. One is Fanny's newly enlarged sense of what it means to be *at home*; when she takes stock of things after she gets to Portsmouth, this is not merely a matter of expanded space.

> Fanny was almost stunned. The smallness of the house, and thinness of the walls, brought every thing so close to her, that, added to the fatigue of her journey, and all her recent agitation, she hardly knew how to bear it. *Within* the room all was tranquil enough, for Susan having disappeared with the others, there were soon only her father and herself remaining; and he taking out a newspaper – the accustomary loan of a neighbour, applied himself to studying it, without seeming to recollect her existence. The solitary candle was held between himself and the paper, without any reference to her possible convenience; but she had nothing to do, and was glad to have the light screened from her aching head, as she sat in bewildered, broken, sorrowful contemplation.
> She was at home. But alas! it was not such a home, she had not such a welcome, as – she checked herself; she was unreasonable. . . . A day or two might shew the difference. *She* only was to blame. Yet she thought it would not have been so at Mansfield. No, in her uncle's house there would have been a consideration of times and seasons, a regulation of subject, a propriety, an attention towards every body which there was not here.[12]

In too small a space, you cannot see clearly, you cannot think clearly, you cannot have regulation or attention of the proper sort. The fineness of Austen's detail ("the solitary candle was held between himself and the paper, without any reference to her possible convenience") renders very precisely the dangers of unsociability, of lonely insularity, of diminished awareness that are rectified in larger and better administered spaces.

That such spaces are not available to Fanny by direct inheritance, legal title, by propinquity, contiguity, or adjacence (Mansfield Park and Portsmouth are separated by many hours' journey) is precisely Austen's point. To earn the right to Mansfield Park you must first leave home as a kind of indentured servant or, to put the case in extreme terms, as a kind of transported commodity – this, clearly, is the fate of Fanny and her brother William – but then you have the promise of future wealth. I think Austen sees what Fanny does as a domestic or small-scale movement in space that corresponds to the larger, more openly colonial movements of Sir Thomas, her mentor, the man whose estate she inherits. The two movements depend on each other.

The second more complex matter about which Austen speaks, albeit indirectly, raises an interesting theoretical issue. Austen's awareness of empire is obviously very different, alluded to very much more casually, than Conrad's or Kipling's. In her time the British were extremely active in the Caribbean and in South America, notably Brazil and Argentina. Austen seems only vaguely aware of the details of these activities, although the sense that extensive West Indian plantations were important was fairly widespread in metropolitan England. Antigua and Sir Thomas's trip there have a definitive function in *Mansfield Park*, which, I have been saying, is both incidental, referred to only in passing, and absolutely crucial to the action. How are we to assess Austen's few references to Antigua, and what are we to make of them interpretatively?

My contention is that by that very odd combination of casualness and stress, Austen reveals herself to be *assuming* (just as Fanny assumes, in both senses of the word) the importance of an empire to the situation at home. Let me go further. Since Austen refers to and uses Antigua as she does in *Mansfield Park*, there needs to be a commensurate effort on the part of her readers to understand concretely the historical valences in the reference; to put it differently, we should try to understand *what* she referred to, why she gave it the importance she did, and why indeed she made the choice, for she might have done something different to establish Sir Thomas's wealth. Let us now calibrate the signifying power of the references to Antigua in *Mansfield Park*; how do they occupy the place they do, what are they doing there?

According to Austen we are to conclude that no matter how isolated and insulated the English place (e.g., Mansfield Park), it requires overseas sustenance. Sir Thomas's property in the Caribbean would have had to be a sugar plantation maintained by slave labor (not abolished until the 1830s): these are not dead historical facts but, as Austen certainly knew, evident historical realities. Before the Anglo-French competition the major distinguishing characteristic of Western empires (Roman, Spanish, and Portuguese) was that the earlier empires were bent on loot, as Conrad puts it, on the transport of treasure from the colonies to Europe, with very little attention to development, organization, or system within the colonies themselves; Britain and, to a lesser degree, France both wanted to make their empires long-term, profitable, ongoing concerns, and they competed in this enterprise, nowhere more so than in the colonies of the Caribbean, where the transport of slaves, the functioning of large sugar plantations, and the development of sugar markets, which raised the issues of protectionism, monopolies, and price – all these were more or less constantly, competitively at issue.

Far from being nothing much "out there," British colonial possessions in the Antilles and Leeward Islands were during Jane Austen's time a crucial setting for Anglo-French colonial competition. Revolutionary ideas from France were being exported there, and there was a steady decline in British profits: the French sugar plantations were producing more sugar at less cost. However, slave rebellions in and out of Haiti were incapacitating France and spurring British interests to intervene more directly and to gain greater local power. Still, compared with its earlier prominence for the home market, British Caribbean sugar production in the nineteenth century had to compete with alternative sugar-cane supplies in Brazil and Mauritius, the emergence of a European beet-sugar industry, and the gradual dominance of free-trade ideology and practice.

In *Mansfield Park* – both in its formal characteristics and in its contents – a number of these currents converge. The most important is the avowedly complete subordination of colony to metropolis. Sir Thomas, absent from Mansfield Park, is never seen as *present* in Antigua, which elicits at most a half dozen references in the novel. There is a passage, a part of which I quoted earlier, from John Stuart Mill's *Principles of Political Economy* that catches the spirit of Austen's use of Antigua. I quote it here in full:

> These [outlying possessions of ours] are hardly to be looked upon as countries, carrying on an exchange of commodities with other countries, but more properly as outlying agricultural or manufacturing estates belonging to a larger community. Our West Indian colonies, for example, cannot be regarded as countries with a productive capital of their own . . . [but are rather] the place where England finds it convenient to carry on the production of sugar, coffee and a few other tropical commodities. All the capital employed is English capital; almost all the industry is carried on for English uses; there is little production of anything except for staple commodities, and these are sent to England, not to be exchanged for things exported to the colony and consumed by its inhabitants, but to be sold in England for the benefit of the proprietors there. The trade with the West Indies is hardly to be considered an external trade, but more resembles the traffic between town and country.[13]

To some extent Antigua is like London or Portsmouth, a less desirable setting than a country estate like Mansfield Park, but producing goods to be consumed by everyone (by the early nineteenth century every Britisher used sugar), although owned and maintained by a small group of aristocrats and gentry. The Bertrams and the other characters in *Mansfield Park* are a subgroup within the minority, and for them the island is wealth, which Austen regards as being converted to propriety, order, and, at the end of the novel, comfort, an added good. But why "added"? Because, Austen tells us pointedly in the final chapters, she wants to "restore every body, not greatly in fault themselves, to tolerable comfort, and to have done with all the rest."[14]

This can be interpreted to mean first that the novel has done enough in the way of destabilizing the lives of "every body" and must now set them at rest: actually Austen says this explicitly, in a bit of meta-fictional impatience, the novelist commenting on her own work as having gone on long enough and now needing to be brought to a close. Second, it can mean that "every body" may now be finally permitted to realize what it means to be properly at home, and at rest, without the need to wander about or to come and go. (This does not include young William, who, we assume, will continue to roam the seas in the British navy on whatever commercial and political missions may still be required. Such matters draw from Austen only a last brief gesture, a passing remark about William's "continuing good conduct and rising fame.") As for those finally resident in Mansfield Park itself, more in the way of domesticated advantages is given to these now fully acclimatized souls, and to none more than to Sir Thomas. He understands for the first time what has been missing in his education of his children, and he understands it in the terms paradoxically provided for him by unnamed outside forces, so to speak, the wealth of Antigua and the imported example of Fanny Price. Note here how the curious alternation of outside and inside follows the pattern identified by Mill of the outside *becoming* the inside by use and, to use Austen's word, "disposition":

Here [in his deficiency of training, of allowing Mrs. Norris too great a role, of letting his children dissemble and repress feeling] had been grievous mismanagement; but, bad as it was, he gradually grew to feel that it had not been the most direful mistake in his plan of education. Some thing must have been wanting *within*, or time would have worn away much of its ill effect. He feared that principle, active principle, had been wanting, that they had never been properly taught to govern their inclinations and tempers, by that sense of duty which can alone suffice. They had been instructed theoretically in their religion, but never required to bring it into daily practice. To be distinguished for elegance and accomplishments – the authorized object of their youth – could have had no useful influence that way, no moral effect on the mind. He had meant them to be good, but his cares had been directed to the understanding and manners, not the disposition; and of the necessity of self-denial and humility, he feared they had never heard from any lips that could profit them.[15]

What was wanting *within* was in fact supplied by the wealth derived from a West Indian plantation and a poor provincial relative, both brought in to Mansfield Park and set to work. Yet on their own, neither the one nor the other could have sufficed; they require each other and then, more important, they need executive disposition, which in turn helps to reform the rest of the Bertram circle. All this Austen leaves to her reader to supply in the way of literal explication.

And that is what reading her entails. But all these things having to do with the outside brought in seem unmistakably *there* in the suggestiveness of her allusive and abstract language. A principle "wanting *within*" is, I believe, intended to evoke for us memories of Sir Thomas's absences in Antigua, or the sentimental and near-whimsical vagary on the part of the three variously deficient Ward sisters by which a niece is displaced from one household to another. But that the Bertrams did become better if not altogether good, that some sense of duty was imparted to them, that they learned to govern their inclinations and tempers and brought religion into daily practice, that they "directed disposition": all of this did occur because outside (or rather outlying) factors were lodged properly inward, became native to Mansfield Park, with Fanny the niece its final spiritual mistress, and Edmund the second son its spiritual master.

An additional benefit is that Mrs. Norris is dislodged; this is described as "the great supplementary comfort of Sir Thomas's life."[16] Once the principles have been interiorized, the comforts follow: Fanny is settled for the time being at Thornton Lacey "with every attention to her comfort"; her home later becomes "the home of affection and comfort"; Susan is brought in "first as a comfort to Fanny, then as an auxiliary, and at last as her substitute"[17] when the new import takes Fanny's place by Lady Bertram's side. The pattern established at the outset of the novel clearly continues, only now it has what Austen intended to give it all along, an internalized and retrospectively guaranteed rationale. This is the rationale that Raymond Williams describes as "an everyday, uncompromising morality which is in the end separable from its social basis and which, in other hands, can be turned against it."

I have tried to show that the morality in fact is not separable from its social basis: right up to the last sentence, Austen affirms and repeats the geographical process of expansion involving trade, production, and consumption that predates, underlies, and guarantees the morality. And expansion, as Gallagher reminds us, whether "through colonial rule was liked or disliked, [its] desirability through one mode or another was generally accepted. So in the event there were few domestic constraints upon expansion."[18] Most critics have tended to forget or overlook that process, which has seemed less important to critics than Austen herself seemed to think. But interpreting Jane Austen depends on *who* does the interpreting, *when* it is done, and no less important, from *where* it is done. If with feminists, with great cultural critics sensitive to history and class like Williams, with cultural and stylistic interpreters, we have been sensitized to the issues their interests raise, we should now proceed to regard the geographical division of the world – after all significant to *Mansfield Park* – as not neutral (any more than class and gender are neutral) but as politically charged, beseeching the attention and elucidation its considerable proportions require. The question is thus not only how to understand and with what to connect Austen's morality and its social basis, but also *what* to read of it.

Take once again the casual references to Antigua, the ease with which Sir Thomas's needs in England are met by a Caribbean sojourn, the uninflected, unreflective citations of Antigua (or the Mediterranean, or India, which is where Lady Bertram, in a fit of distracted impatience, requires that William should go " 'that I may have a shawl. I think I will have two shawls.' ")[19] They stand for a significance "out there" that frames the genuinely important action *here*, but not for a great significance. Yet these signs of "abroad" include, even as they repress, a rich and complex history, which has since achieved a status that the Bertrams, the Prices, and Austen herself would not, could not recognize. To call this "the Third World" begins to deal with the realities but by no means exhausts the political or cultural history.

We must first take stock of *Mansfield Park*'s prefigurations of a later English history as registered in fiction. The Bertrams' usable colony in *Mansfield Park* can be read as pointing forward to Charles Gould's San Tomé mine in *Nostromo*, or to the Wilcoxes' Imperial and West African Rubber Company in Forster's *Howards End*, or to any of these distant but convenient treasure spots in *Great Expectations*, Jean Rhys's *Wide Sargasso Sea*, *Heart of Darkness* – resources to be visited, talked about, described, or appreciated for domestic reasons, for local metropolitan benefit. If we think ahead to these other novels, Sir Thomas's Antigua readily acquires a slightly greater density than the discrete, reticent appearances it makes in the pages of *Mansfield Park*. And already our reading of the novel begins to open up at those points where ironically Austen was most economical and her critics most (dare one say it?) negligent. Her "Antigua" is therefore not just a slight but a definite way of marking the outer limits of what Williams calls domestic improvements, or a quick allusion to the mercantile venturesomeness of acquiring overseas dominions as a source for local fortunes, or one reference among many attesting to a historical sensibility suffused not just with manners and courtesies but with contests of ideas, struggles with Napoleonic France, awareness of seismic economic and social change during a revolutionary period in world history.

Second, we must see "Antigua" held in a precise place in Austen's moral geography, and in her prose, by historical changes that her novel rides like a vessel on a mighty sea. The Bertrams could not have been possible without the slave trade, sugar, and the colonial planter class; as a social type Sir Thomas would have been familiar to eighteenth- and early-nineteenth-century readers who knew the powerful influence of the class through politics, plays (like Cumberland's *The West Indian*), and many other public activities (large houses, famous parties and social rituals, well-known commercial enterprises, celebrated marriages). As the old system of protected monopoly gradually disappeared and as a new class of settler-planters displaced the old absentee system, the West Indian interest lost dominance: cotton manufacture, an even more open system of trade, and abolition of the slave trade reduced the power and prestige of people like the Bertrams, whose frequency of sojourn in the Caribbean then decreased.

Thus Sir Thomas's infrequent trips to Antigua as an absentee plantation owner reflect the diminishment in his class's power, a reduction directly expressed in the title of Lowell Ragatz's classic *The Fall of the Planter Class in the British Caribbean, 1763–1833* (1928). But is what is hidden or allusive in Austen made sufficiently explicit more than one hundred years later in Ragatz? Does the aesthetic silence or discretion of a great novel in 1814 receive adequate explication in a major work of historical research a full century later? Can we assume that the process of interpretation is fulfilled, or will it continue as new material comes to light?

For all his learning Ragatz still finds it in himself to speak of "the Negro race" as having the following characteristics: "he stole, he lied, he was simple, suspicious, inefficient, irresponsible, lazy, superstitious, and loose in his sexual relations."[20] Such "history" as this therefore happily gave way to the revisionary work of Caribbean historians like Eric Williams and C. L. R. James, and more recently Robin Blackburn, in *The Overthrow of Colonial Slavery, 1776–1848*; in these works slavery and empire are shown to have fostered the rise and consolidation of capitalism well beyond the old plantation monopolies, as well as to have been a powerful ideological system whose original connection to specific economic interests may have gone, but whose effects continued for decades.

> The political and moral ideas of the age are to be examined in the very closest relation to the economic development....
>
> An outworn interest, whose bankruptcy smells to heaven in historical perspective, can exercise an obstructionist and disruptive effect which can only be explained by the powerful services it had previously rendered and the entrenchment previously gained....
> The ideas built on these interests continue long after the interests have been destroyed and work their old mischief, which is all the more mischievous because the interests to which they corresponded no longer exist.[21]

Thus Eric Williams in *Capitalism and Slavery* (1961). The question of interpretation, indeed of writing itself, is tied to the question of interests, which we have seen are at work in aesthetic as well as historical writing, then and now. We must not say that since *Mansfield Park* is a novel, its affiliations with a sordid history are irrelevant or transcended, not only because it is irresponsible to do so, but because we know too much to say so in good faith. Having read *Mansfield Park* as part of the structure of an expanding imperialist venture, one cannot simply restore it to the canon of "great literary masterpieces" – to which it most certainly belongs – and leave it at that. Rather, I think, the novel steadily, if unobtrusively, opens up a broad expanse of domestic imperialist culture without which Britain's subsequent acquisition of territory would not have been possible.

I have spent time on *Mansfield Park* to illustrate a type of analysis infrequently encountered in mainstream interpretations, or for that matter in readings rigorously based in one or another of the advanced theoretical schools. Yet only in the global perspective implied by Jane Austen and her characters can the novel's quite astonishing general position be made clear. I think of such a reading as completing or complementing others, not discounting or displacing them. And it bears stressing that because *Mansfield Park* connects the actualities of British power overseas to the domestic imbroglio within the Bertram estate, there is no way of doing such readings as mine, no way of understanding the "structure of attitude and reference" except by working through the novel. Without reading it in full, we would fail to understand the strength of that structure and the way it was activated and maintained in literature. But in reading it carefully, we can sense how ideas about dependent races and territories were held both by foreign-office executives, colonial bureaucrats, and military strategists and by intelligent novel-readers educating themselves in the fine points of moral evaluation, literary balance, and stylistic finish.

There is a paradox here in reading Jane Austen which I have been impressed by but can in no way resolve. All the evidence says that even the most routine aspects of holding slaves on a West Indian sugar plantation were cruel stuff. And everything we know about Austen and her values is at odds with the cruelty of slavery. Fanny Price reminds her cousin that after asking Sir Thomas about the slave trade, "There was such a dead silence"[22] as to suggest that one world could not be connected with the other since there simply is no common language for both. That is true. But what stimulates the extraordinary discrepancy into life is the rise, decline, and fall of the British empire itself and, in its aftermath, the emergence of a post-colonial consciousness. In order more accurately to read works like *Mansfield Park*, we have to see them in the main as resisting or avoiding that other setting, which their formal inclusiveness, historical honesty, and prophetic suggestiveness cannot completely hide. In time there would no longer be a dead silence when slavery was spoken of, and the subject became central to a new understanding of what Europe was.

It would be silly to expect Jane Austen to treat slavery with anything like the passion of an abolitionist or a newly liberated slave. Yet what I have called the rhetoric of blame, so often now employed by subaltern, minority, or disadvantaged voices, attacks her, and others like her, retrospectively, for being white, privileged, insensitive, complicit. Yes, Austen belonged to a slave-owning society, but do we therefore jettison her novels as so many trivial exercises in aesthetic frumpery? Not at all, I would argue, if we take seriously our intellectual and interpretative vocation to make connections, to deal with as much of the evidence as possible, fully and actually, to read what is there or not there, above all, to see complementarity and interdependence instead of isolated, venerated, or formalized experience that excludes and forbids the hybridizing intrusions of human history.

Mansfield Park is a rich work in that its aesthetic intellectual complexity requires that longer and slower analysis that is also required by its geographical problematic, a novel based in an England relying for the maintenance of its style on a Caribbean island. When Sir Thomas goes to and comes from Antigua, where he has property, that is not at all the same thing as coming to and going from Mansfield Park, where his presence, arrivals, and departures have very considerable consequences. But precisely because Austen is so summary in one context, so provocatively rich in the other, precisely because of that imbalance we are able to move in on the novel, reveal and accentuate the interdependence scarcely mentioned on its brilliant pages. A lesser work wears its historical affiliation more plainly; its worldliness is simple and direct, the way a jingoistic ditty during the Mahdist uprising or the 1857 Indian Rebellion connects directly to the situation and constituency that coined it. *Mansfield Park* encodes experiences and does not simply repeat them. From our later perspective we can interpret Sir Thomas's power to come and go in Antigua as stemming from the muted national experience of individual identity, behavior, and "ordination," enacted with such irony and taste at Mansfield Park. The task is to lose neither a true historical sense of the first, nor a full enjoyment or appreciation of the second, all the while seeing both together.

Notes

1   V. G. Kiernan, *Marxism and Imperialism* (New York: St. Martin's Press, 1974), p. 100.

2   John Stuart Mill, *Disquisitions and Discussions*, Vol. 3 (London: Longmans, Green, Reader & Dyer, 1875), pp. 167–8. For an earlier version of this see the discussion by Nicholas Canny, "The Ideology of English Colonization: From Ireland to America," *William and Mary Quarterly* 30 (1973), 575–98.

3   Raymond Williams, *The Country and the City* (London: Chatto & Windus, 1973), p. 281.

4   Peter Hulme, *Colonial Encounters: Europe and the Native Caribbean, 1492–1797* (London: Methuen, 1986). See also his anthology with Neil L. Whitehead, *Wild Majesty: Encounters with Caribs from Columbus to the Present Day* (Oxford: Clarendon Press, 1992).

5   Hobson, *Imperialism*, p. 6.

6   This is most memorably discussed in C. L. R. James's *The Black Jacobins: Toussaint L'Ouverture and the San Domingo Revolution* (1938; rprt. New York: Vintage, 1963), especially chapter 2, "The Owners." See also Robin Blackburn, *The Overthrow of Colonial Slavery, 1776–1848* (London: Verso, 1988), pp. 149–53.

7   Williams, *The Country and the City*, p. 117.

8   Jane Austen, *Mansfield Park*, ed. Tony Tanner (1814; rprt. Harmondsworth: Penguin, 1966), p. 42. The best account of the novel is in Tony Tanner's *Jane Austen* (Cambridge, Mass.: Harvard University Press, 1986).

9   Ibid., p. 54.

10 Ibid., p. 206.

11 Warren Roberts, *Jane Austen and the French Revolution* (London: Macmillan, 1979), pp. 97–8. See also Avrom Fleishman, *A Reading of* Mansfield Park: *An Essay in Critical Synthesis* (Minneapolis: University of Minnesota Press, 1967), pp. 36–9 and *passim*.

12 Austen, *Mansfield Park*, pp. 375–6.

13 John Stuart Mill, *Principles of Political Economy*, vol. 3, ed. J. M. Robson (Toronto: University of Toronto Press, 1965), p. 693. The passage is quoted in Sidney W. Mintz, *Sweetness and Power: The Place of Sugar in Modern History* (New York: Viking, 1985), p. 42.

14 Austen, *Mansfield Park*, p. 446.

15 Ibid., p. 448.

16 Ibid., p. 450.

17 Ibid., p. 456.

18 John Gallagher, *The Decline, Revival and Fall of the British Empire* (Cambridge: Cambridge University Press, 1982), p. 76.

19 Austen, *Mansfield Park*, p. 308.

20 Lowell Joseph Ragatz, *The Fall of the Planter Class in the British Caribbean, 1763–1833: A Study in Social and Economic History* (1928; rprt. New York: Octagon, 1963), p. 27.

21 Eric Williams, *Capitalism and Slavery* (New York: Russell & Russell, 1961), p. 211. See also his *From Columbus to Castro: The History of the Caribbean, 1492–1969* (London: Deutsch, 1970), pp. 177–254.

22 Austen, *Mansfield Park*, p. 213.

CHAPTER 6

Decolonising the Mind

Ngugi wa Thiong'o

Frantz Fanon distinguished in *The Wretched of the Earth* between writers who seek models for literature in the metropolitan countries and writers who seek models in the indigenous cultures of their own nations. While he warned of the danger of over-valuing native cultural forms, he also recognized their importance as means of resistance to colonial cultural domination. One such form of domination is language, and in *Black Skin, White Masks* Fanon also examines the pitfalls of allowing the colonial language to shape the identity of colonial subjects.

Kenyan writer Ngugi wa Thiong'o begins his book *Decolonising the Mind: The Politics of Language in African Literature* (1986) with the words: "This book...is my farewell to English as a vehicle for any of my writings. From now on it is Gikuyu and Kiswahili all the way." In the selections that follow from that book, he explains the reasoning behind that choice.

The Language of African Literature

I

The language of African literature cannot be discussed meaningfully outside the context of those social forces which have made it both an issue demanding our attention and a problem calling for a resolution.

On the one hand is imperialism in its colonial and neo-colonial phases continuously press-ganging the African hand to the plough to turn the soil over, and putting blinkers on him to make him view the path ahead only as determined for him by the master armed with the bible and the sword. In other words, imperialism continues to control the economy, politics, and cultures of Africa. But on the other, and pitted against it, are the ceaseless struggles of African people to liberate their economy, politics and culture from that Euro-American-based stranglehold to usher a new era of true communal self-regulation and self-determination. It is an ever-continuing struggle to seize back their creative initiative in history through a real control of all the means of communal self-definition in time and space. The choice of language and the use to which language is put is central to a people's definition of themselves in relation to their natural and social environment, indeed in relation to the entire universe. Hence language has always been at the heart of the two contending social forces in the Africa of the twentieth century.

The contention started a hundred years ago when in 1884 the capitalist powers of Europe sat in Berlin and carved an entire continent with a multiplicity of peoples, cultures, and languages into different colonies. It seems it is the fate of Africa to have her destiny always decided around conference tables in the metropolises of the western world: her submergence from self-governing communities into colonies was decided in Berlin; her more recent transition into neo-colonies along the same boundaries was negotiated around the same tables in London, Paris, Brussels and Lisbon. The Berlin-drawn division under which Africa is still living was obviously economic and political, despite the claims of bible-wielding diplomats, but it was also cultural. Berlin in 1884 saw the division of Africa into the different languages of the European powers. African countries, as colonies and even today as neo-colonies, came to be defined and to define themselves in terms of the languages of Europe: English-speaking, French-speaking or Portuguese-speaking African countries.[1]

Unfortunately writers who should have been mapping paths out of that linguistic encirclement of their continent also came to be defined and to define themselves in terms of the languages of imperialist imposition. Even at their most radical and pro-African position in their sentiments and articulation of problems they still took it as axiomatic that the renaissance of African cultures lay in the languages of Europe.

I should know!

II

In 1962 I was invited to that historic meeting of African writers at Makerere University College, Kampala, Uganda. The list of participants contained most of the names which have now become the subject of scholarly dissertations in universities all over the world. The title? 'A Conference of *African Writers of English Expression*'.[2]

I was then a student of *English* at Makerere, an overseas college of the University of London. The main attraction for me was the certain possibility of meeting Chinua Achebe. I had with me a rough typescript of a novel in progress, *Weep Not, Child*, and I wanted him to read it. In the previous year, 1961, I had completed *The River Between*, my first-ever attempt at a novel, and entered it for a writing competition organised by the East African Literature Bureau. I was keeping in step with the tradition of Peter Abrahams with his output of novels and autobiographies from *Path of Thunder* to *Tell Freedom* and followed by Chinua Achebe with his publication of *Things Fall Apart* in 1959. Or there were their counterparts in French colonies, the generation of Sédar Senghor and David Diop included in the 1947/48 Paris edition of *Anthologie de la nouvelle poésie nègre et malgache de langue française*. They all wrote in European languages as was the case with all the participants in that momentous encounter on Makerere hill in Kampala in 1962.

The title, 'A Conference of African Writers of English Expression', automatically excluded those who wrote in African languages. Now on looking back from the self-questioning heights of 1986, I can see this contained absurd anomalies. I, a student, could qualify for the meeting on the basis of only two published short stories, 'The Fig Tree (Mũgumo)' in a student journal, *Penpoint*, and 'The Return' in a new journal, *Transition*. But neither Shabaan Robert, then the greatest living East African poet with several works of poetry and prose to his credit in Kiswahili, nor Chief Fagunwa, the great Nigerian writer with several published titles in Yoruba, could possibly qualify.

The discussions on the novel, the short story, poetry, and drama were based on extracts from works in English and hence they excluded the main body of work in

Swahili, Zulu, Yoruba, Arabic, Amharic and other African languages. Yet, despite this exclusion of writers and literature in African languages, no sooner were the introductory preliminaries over than this Conference of 'African Writers of English Expression' sat down to the first item on the agenda: 'What is African Literature?'

The debate which followed was animated: Was it literature about Africa or about the African experience? Was it literature written by Africans? What about a non-African who wrote about Africa: did his work qualify as African literature? What if an African set his work in Greenland: did that qualify as African literature? Or were African languages the criteria? OK: what about Arabic, was it not foreign to Africa? What about French and English, which had become African languages? What if a European wrote about Europe in an African language? If...if...if...this or that, except the issue: the domination of our languages and cultures by those of imperialist Europe: in any case there was no Fagunwa or Shabaan Robert or any writer in African languages to bring the conference down from the realms of evasive abstractions. The question was never seriously asked: did what we wrote qualify as African literature? The whole area of literature and audience, and hence of language as a determinant of both the national and class audience, did not really figure: the debate was more about the subject matter and the racial origins and geographical habitation of the writer.

English, like French and Portuguese, was assumed to be the natural language of literary and even political mediation between African people in the same nation and between nations in Africa and other continents. In some instances these European languages were seen as having a capacity to unite African peoples against divisive tendencies inherent in the multiplicity of African languages within the same geographic state. Thus Ezekiel Mphahlele later could write, in a letter to *Transition* number 11, that English and French have become the common language with which to present a nationalist front against white oppressors, and even 'where the whiteman has already retreated, as in the independent states, these two languages are still a unifying force'.[3] In the literary sphere they were often seen as coming to save African languages against themselves. Writing a foreword to Birago Diop's book *Contes d'Amadou Koumba* Sédar Senghor commends him for using French to rescue the spirit and style of old African fables and tales. 'However while rendering them into French he renews them with an art which, while it respects the genius of the French language, that language of gentleness and honesty, preserves at the same time all the virtues of the negro-african languages.'[4] English, French and Portuguese had come to our rescue and we accepted the unsolicited gift with gratitude. Thus in 1964, Chinua Achebe, in a speech entitled 'The African Writer and the English Language', said:

> Is it right that a man should abandon his mother tongue for someone else's? It looks like a dreadful betrayal and produces a guilty feeling. But for me there is no other choice. I have been given the language and I intend to use it.[5]

See the paradox: the possibility of using mother-tongues provokes a tone of levity in phrases like 'a dreadful betrayal' and 'a guilty feeling'; but that of foreign languages produces a categorical positive embrace, what Achebe himself, ten years later, was to describe as this 'fatalistic logic of the unassailable position of English in our literature'.[6]

The fact is that all of us who opted for European languages – the conference participants and the generation that followed them – accepted that fatalistic logic to a greater or lesser degree. We were guided by it and the only question which preoccupied us was how best to make the borrowed tongues carry the weight of our African experience by, for instance, making them 'prey' on African proverbs and other pecularities of African speech and folklore. For this task, Achebe (*Things Fall Apart*; *Arrow of God*), Amos Tutuola (*The Palm-wine Drinkard*; *My Life in the Bush of Ghosts*), and Gabriel Okara (*The Voice*) were often held as providing the three alternative models. The lengths to which we were prepared to go in our mission of enriching foreign languages by injecting Senghorian 'black blood' into their rusty joints, is best exemplified by Gabriel Okara in an article reprinted in *Transition*:

> As a writer who believes in the utilization of African ideas, African philosophy and African folklore and imagery to the fullest extent possible, I am of the opinion the only way to use them effectively is to translate them almost literally from the African language native to the writer into whatever European language he is using as medium of expression. I have endeavoured in my words to keep as close as possible to the vernacular expressions. For, from a word, a group of words, a sentence and even a name in any African language, one can glean the social norms, attitudes and values of a people.
>
> In order to capture the vivid images of African speech, I had to eschew the habit of expressing my thoughts first in English. It was difficult at first, but I had to learn. I had to study each Ijaw expression I used and to discover the probable situation in which it was used in order to bring out the nearest meaning in English. I found it a fascinating exercise.[7]

Why, we may ask, should an African writer, or any writer, become so obsessed by taking from his mother-tongue to enrich other tongues? Why should he see it as his particular mission? We never asked ourselves: how can we enrich our languages? How can we 'prey' on the rich humanist and democratic heritage in the struggles of other peoples in other times and other places to enrich our own? Why not have Balzac, Tolstoy, Sholokov, Brecht, Lu Hsun, Pablo Neruda, H. C. Anderson, Kim Chi Ha, Marx, Lenin, Albert Einstein, Galileo, Aeschylus, Aristotle and Plato in African languages? And why not create literary monuments in our own languages? Why in other words should Okara not sweat it out to create in Ijaw, which he acknowledges to have depths of philosophy and a wide range of ideas and experiences? What was our responsibility to the struggles of African peoples? No, these questions were not asked. What seemed to worry us more was this: after all the literary gymnastics of preying on our languages to add life and vigour to English and other foreign languages, would the result be accepted as good English or good French? Will the owner of the language criticise our usage? Here we were more assertive of our rights! Chinua Achebe wrote:

> I feel that the English language will be able to carry the weight of my African experience. But it will have to be a new English, still in full communion with its ancestral home but altered to suit new African surroundings.[8]

Gabriel Okara's position on this was representative of our generation:

Some may regard this way of writing English as a desecration of the language. This is of course not true. Living languages grow like living things, and English is far from a dead language. There are American, West Indian, Australian, Canadian and New Zealand versions of English. All of them add life and vigour to the language while reflecting their own respective cultures. Why shouldn't there be a Nigerian or West African English which we can use to express our own ideas, thinking and philosophy in our own way?[9]

How did we arrive at this acceptance of 'the fatalistic logic of the unassailable position of English in our literature', in our culture and in our politics? What was the route from the Berlin of 1884 via the Makerere of 1962 to what is still the prevailing and dominant logic a hundred years later? How did we, as African writers, come to be so feeble towards the claims of our languages on us and so aggressive in our claims on other languages, particularly the languages of our colonization?

Berlin of 1884 was effected through the sword and the bullet. But the night of the sword and the bullet was followed by the morning of the chalk and the blackboard. The physical violence of the battlefield was followed by the psychological violence of the classroom. But where the former was visibly brutal, the latter was visibly gentle, a process best described in Cheikh Hamidou Kane's novel *Ambiguous Adventure* where he talks of the methods of the colonial phase of imperialism as consisting of knowing how to kill with efficiency and to heal with the same art.

> On the Black Continent, one began to understand that their real power resided not at all in the cannons of the first morning but in what followed the cannons. Therefore behind the cannons was the new school. The new school had the nature of both the cannon and the magnet. From the cannon it took the efficiency of a fighting weapon. But better than the cannon it made the conquest permanent. The cannon forces the body and the school fascinates the soul.[10]

In my view language was the most important vehicle through which that power fascinated and held the soul prisoner. The bullet was the means of the physical subjugation. Language was the means of the spiritual subjugation. Let me illustrate this by drawing upon experiences in my own education, particularly in language and literature.

III

I was born into a large peasant family: father, four wives and about twenty-eight children. I also belonged, as we all did in those days, to a wider extended family and to the community as a whole.

We spoke Gĩkũyũ as we worked in the fields. We spoke Gĩkũyũ in and outside the home. I can vividly recall those evenings of story telling around the fireside. It was mostly the grown-ups telling the children but everybody was interested and involved. We children would re-tell the stories the following day to other children who worked in the fields picking the pyrethrum flowers, tea-leaves or coffee beans of our European and African landlords.

The stories, with mostly animals as the main characters, were all told in Gĩkũyũ. Hare, being small, weak but full of innovative wit and cunning, was our hero. We identified with him as he struggled against the brutes of prey like lion, leopard, hyena. His victories were our victories and we learnt that the apparently weak can outwit the strong. We followed the animals in their struggle against hostile nature – drought, rain, sun, wind – a confrontation often forcing them to search for forms of co-operation. But we were also interested in their struggles amongst themselves, and particularly between the beasts and the victims of prey. These twin struggles, against nature and other animals, reflected real-life struggles in the human world.

Not that we neglected stories with human beings as the main characters. There were two types of characters in such human-centred narratives: the species of truly human beings with qualities of courage, kindness, mercy, hatred of evil, concern for others; and a man-eat-man two-mouthed species with qualities of greed, selfishness, individualism and hatred of what was good for the larger co-operative community. Co-operation as the ultimate good in a community was a constant theme. It could unite human beings with animals against ogres and beasts of prey, as in the story of how dove, after being fed with castor-oil seeds, was sent to fetch a smith working far away from home and whose pregnant wife was being threatened by these man-eating two-mouthed ogres.

There were good and bad story-tellers. A good one could tell the same story over and over again, and it would always be fresh to us, the listeners. He or she could tell a story told by someone else and make it more alive and dramatic. The differences really were in the use of words and images and the inflexion of voices to effect different tones.

We therefore learnt to value words for their meaning and nuances. Language was not a mere string of words. It had a suggestive power well beyond the immediate and lexical meaning. Our appreciation of the suggestive magical power of language was reinforced by the games we played with words through riddles, proverbs, transpositions of syllables, or through nonsensical but musically arranged words.[11] So we learnt the music of our language on top of the content. The language, through images and symbols, gave us a view of the world, but it had a beauty of its own. The home and the field were then our pre-primary school but what is important, for this discussion, is that the language of our evening teach-ins, and the language of our immediate and wider community, and the language of our work in the fields were one.

And then I went to school, a colonial school, and this harmony was broken. The language of my education was no longer the language of my culture. I first went to Kamaandura, missionary run, and then to another called Maanguuũ run by nationalists grouped around the Gĩkũyũ Independent and Karinga Schools Association. Our language of education was still Gĩkũyũ. The very first time I was ever given an ovation for my writing was over a composition in Gĩkũyũ. So for my first four years there was still harmony between the language of my formal education and that of the Limuru peasant community.

It was after the declaration of a state of emergency over Kenya in 1952 that all the schools run by patriotic nationalists were taken over by the colonial regime and were placed under District Education Boards chaired by Englishmen. English became the language of my formal education. In Kenya, English became more than a language: it was *the* language, and all the others had to bow before it in deference.

Thus one of the most humiliating experiences was to be caught speaking Gĩkũyũ in the vicinity of the school. The culprit was given corporal punishment – three to five strokes of the cane on bare buttocks – or was made to carry a metal plate around the neck with inscriptions such as I AM STUPID or I AM A DONKEY. Sometimes the culprits were fined money they could hardly afford. And how did the teachers catch the culprits? A button was initially given to one pupil who was supposed to hand it over to whoever was caught speaking his mother tongue. Whoever had the button at the end of the day would sing who had given it to him and the ensuing process would bring out all the culprits of the day. Thus children were turned into witch-hunters and in the process were being taught the lucrative value of being a traitor to one's immediate community.

The attitude to English was the exact opposite: any achievement in spoken or written English was highly rewarded; prizes, prestige, applause; the ticket to higher realms. English became the measure of intelligence and ability in the arts, the sciences, and all the other branches of learning. English became *the* main determinant of a child's progress up the ladder of formal education.

As you may know, the colonial system of education in addition to its apartheid racial demarcation had the structure of a pyramid: a broad primary base, a narrowing secondary middle, and an even narrower university apex. Selections from primary into secondary were through an examination, in my time called Kenya African Preliminary Examination, in which one had to pass six subjects ranging from Maths to Nature Study and Kiswahili. All the papers were written in English. Nobody could pass the exam who failed the English language paper no matter how brilliantly he had done in the other subjects. I remember one boy in my class of 1954 who had distinctions in all subjects except English, which he had failed. He was made to fail the entire exam. He went on to become a turn boy in a bus company. I who had only passes but a credit in English got a place at the Alliance High School, one of the most elitist institutions for Africans in colonial Kenya. The requirements for a place at the University, Makerere University College, were broadly the same: nobody could go on to wear the undergraduate red gown, no matter how brilliantly they had performed in all the other subjects unless they had a credit – not even a simple pass! – in English. Thus the most coveted place in the pyramid and in the system was only available to the holder of an English language credit card. English was the official vehicle and the magic formula to colonial elitedom.

Literary education was now determined by the dominant language while also reinforcing that dominance. Orature (oral literature) in Kenyan languages stopped. In primary school I now read simplified Dickens and Stevenson alongside Rider Haggard. Jim Hawkins, Oliver Twist, Tom Brown – not Hare, Leopard and Lion – were now my daily companions in the world of imagination. In secondary school, Scott and G. B. Shaw vied with more Rider Haggard, John Buchan, Alan Paton, Captain W. E. Johns. At Makerere I read English: from Chaucer to T. S. Eliot with a touch of Graham Greene.

Thus language and literature were taking us further and further from ourselves to other selves, from our world to other worlds.

What was the colonial system doing to us Kenyan children? What were the consequences of, on the one hand, this systematic suppression of our languages and the literature they carried, and on the other the elevation of English and the literature it carried? To answer those questions, let me first examine the relationship of language to human experience, human culture, and the human perception of reality.

IV

Language, any language, has a dual character: it is both a means of communication and a carrier of culture. Take English. It is spoken in Britain and in Sweden and in Denmark. But for Swedish and Danish people English is only a means of communication with non-Scandinavians. It is not a carrier of their culture. For the British, and particularly the English, it is additionally, and inseparably from its use as a tool of communication, a carrier of their culture and history. Or take Swahili in East and Central Africa. It is widely used as a means of communication across many nationalities. But it is not the carrier of a culture and history of many of those nationalities. However in parts of Kenya and Tanzania, and particularly in Zanzibar, Swahili is inseparably both a means of communication and a carrier of the culture of those people to whom it is a mother-tongue.

Language as communication has three aspects or elements. There is first what Karl Marx once called the language of real life,[12] the element basic to the whole notion of language, its origins and development: that is, the relations people enter into with one another in the labour process, the links they necessarily establish among themselves in the act of a people, a community of human beings, producing wealth or means of life like food, clothing, houses. A human community really starts its historical being as a community of co-operation in production through the division of labour; the simplest is between man, woman and child within a household; the more complex divisions are between branches of production such as those who are sole hunters, sole gatherers of fruits or sole workers in metal. Then there are the most complex divisions such as those in modern factories where a single product, say a shirt or a shoe, is the result of many hands and minds. Production is co-operation, is communication, is language, is expression of a relation between human beings and it is specifically human.

The second aspect of language as communication is speech and it imitates the language of real life, that is communication in production. The verbal signposts both reflect and aid communication or the relations established between human beings in the production of their means of life. Language as a system of verbal signposts makes that production possible. The spoken word is to relations between human beings what the hand is to the relations between human beings and nature. The hand through tools mediates between human beings and nature and forms the language of real life: spoken words mediate between human beings and form the language of speech.

The third aspect is the written signs. The written word imitates the spoken. Where the first two aspects of language as communication through the hand and the spoken word historically evolved more or less simultaneously, the written aspect is a much later historical development. Writing is representation of sounds with visual symbols, from the simplest knot among shepherds to tell the number in a herd or the hieroglyphics among the Agĩkũyũ gicaandi singers and poets of Kenya, to the most complicated and different letter and picture writing systems of the world today.

In most societies the written and the spoken languages are the same, in that they represent each other: what is on paper can be read to another person and be received as that language which the recipient has grown up speaking. In such a society there is broad harmony for a child between the three aspects of language as communication. His interaction with nature and with other men is expressed in written and spoken symbols or signs which are both a result of that double interaction and a reflection of it. The association of the child's sensibility is with the language of his experience of life.

But there is more to it: communication between human beings is also the basis and process of evolving culture. In doing similar kinds of things and actions over and over again under similar circumstances, similar even in their mutability, certain patterns, moves, rhythms, habits, attitudes, experiences and knowledge emerge. Those experiences are handed over to the next generation and become the inherited basis for their further actions on nature and on themselves. There is a gradual accumulation of values which in time become almost self-evident truths governing their conception of what is right and wrong, good and bad, beautiful and ugly, courageous and cowardly, generous and mean in their internal and external relations. Over a time this becomes a way of life distinguishable from other ways of life. They develop a distinctive culture and history. Culture embodies those moral, ethical and aesthetic values, the set of spiritual eyeglasses, through which they come to view themselves and their place in the universe. Values are the basis of a people's identity, their sense of particularity as members of the human race. All this is carried by language. Language as culture is the collective memory bank of a people's experience in history. Culture is almost indistinguishable from the language that makes possible its genesis, growth, banking, articulation and indeed its transmission from one generation to the next.

Language as culture also has three important aspects. Culture is a product of the history which it in turn reflects. Culture in other words is a product and a reflection of human beings communicating with one another in the very struggle to create wealth and to control it. But culture does not merely reflect that history, or rather it does so by actually forming images or pictures of the world of nature and nurture. Thus the second aspect of language as culture is as an image-forming agent in the mind of a child. Our whole conception of ourselves as a people, individually and collectively, is based on those pictures and images which may or may not correctly correspond to the actual reality of the struggles with nature and nurture which produced them in the first place. But our capacity to confront the world creatively is dependent on how those images correspond or not to that reality, how they distort or clarify the reality of our struggles. Language as culture is thus mediating between me and my own self; between my own self and other selves; between me and nature. Language is mediating in my very being. And this brings us to the third aspect of language as culture. Culture transmits or imparts those images of the world and reality through the spoken and the written language, that is through a specific language. In other words, the capacity to speak, the capacity to order sounds in a manner that makes for mutual comprehension between human beings is universal. This is the universality of language, a quality specific to human beings. It corresponds to the universality of the struggle against nature and that between human beings. But the particularity of the sounds, the words, the word order into phrases and sentences, and the specific manner, or laws, of their ordering is what distinguishes one language from another. Thus a specific culture is not transmitted through language in its universality but in its particularity as the language of a specific community with a specific history. Written literature and orature are the main means by which a particular language transmits the images of the world contained in the culture it carries.

Language as communication and as culture are then products of each other. Communication creates culture: culture is a means of communication. Language carries culture, and culture carries, particularly through orature and literature, the entire body of values by which we come to perceive ourselves and our place in the world. How people perceive themselves affects how they look at their culture, at their politics and at the social production of wealth, at their entire relationship to nature and to other beings. Language is thus inseparable from ourselves as a community of human beings with a specific form and character, a specific history, a specific relationship to the world.

V

So what was the colonialist imposition of a foreign language doing to us children?

The real aim of colonialism was to control the people's wealth: what they produced, how they produced it, and how it was distributed; to control, in other words, the entire realm of the language of real life. Colonialism imposed its control of the social production of wealth through military conquest and subsequent political dictatorship. But its most important area of domination was the mental universe of the colonised, the control, through culture, of how people perceived themselves and their relationship to the world. Economic and political control can never be complete or effective without mental control. To control a people's culture is to control their tools of self-definition in relationship to others.

For colonialism this involved two aspects of the same process: the destruction or the deliberate undervaluing of a people's culture, their art, dances, religions, history, geography, education, orature and literature, and the conscious elevation of the language of the coloniser. The domination of a people's language by the languages of the colonising nations was crucial to the domination of the mental universe of the colonised.

Take language as communication. Imposing a foreign language, and suppressing the native languages as spoken and written, were already breaking the harmony previously existing between the African child and the three aspects of language. Since the new language as a means of communication was a product of and was reflecting the 'real language of life' elsewhere, it could never as spoken or written properly reflect or imitate the real life of that community. This may in part explain why technology always appears to us as slightly external, *their* product and not *ours*. The word 'missile' used to hold an alien far-away sound until I recently learnt its equivalent in Gĩkũyũ, *ngurukuhĩ*, and it made me apprehend it differently. Learning, for a colonial child, became a cerebral activity and not an emotionally felt experience.

But since the new, imposed languages could never completely break the native languages as spoken, their most effective area of domination was the third aspect of language as communication, the written. The language of an African child's formal education was foreign. The language of the books he read was foreign. The language of his conceptualisation was foreign. Thought, in him, took the visible form of a foreign language. So the written language of a child's upbringing in the school (even his spoken language within the school compound) became divorced from his spoken language at home. There was often not the slightest relationship between the child's written world, which was also the language of his schooling, and the world of his immediate environment in the family and the community. For a colonial child, the harmony existing between the three aspects of language as communication was irrevocably broken. This resulted in the disassociation of the sensibility of that child from his natural and social environment, what we might call colonial alienation. The alienation became reinforced in the teaching of history, geography, music, where bourgeois Europe was always the centre of the universe.

This disassociation, divorce, or alienation from the immediate environment becomes clearer when you look at colonial language as a carrier of culture.

Since culture is a product of the history of a people which it in turn reflects, the child was now being exposed exclusively to a culture that was a product of a world external to himself. He was being made to stand outside himself to look at himself.

Catching Them Young is the title of a book on racism, class, sex, and politics in children's literature by Bob Dixon. 'Catching them young' as an aim was even more true of a colonial child. The images of this world and his place in it implanted in a child take years to eradicate, if they ever can be.

Since culture does not just reflect the world in images but actually, through those very images, conditions a child to see that world in a certain way, the colonial child was made to see the world and where he stands in it as seen and defined by or reflected in the culture of the language of imposition.

And since those images are mostly passed on through orature and literature it meant the child would now only see the world as seen in the literature of his language of adoption. From the point of view of alienation, that is of seeing oneself from outside oneself as if one was another self, it does not matter that the imported literature carried the great humanist tradition of the best in Shakespeare, Goethe, Balzac, Tolstoy, Gorky, Brecht, Sholokhov, Dickens. The location of this great mirror of imagination was necessarily Europe and its history and culture and the rest of the universe was seen from that centre.

But obviously it was worse when the colonial child was exposed to images of his world as mirrored in the written languages of his coloniser. Where his own native languages were associated in his impressionable mind with low status, humiliation, corporal punishment, slow-footed intelligence and ability or downright stupidity, non-intelligibility and barbarism, this was reinforced by the world he met in the works of such geniuses of racism as a Rider Haggard or a Nicholas Monsarrat; not to mention the pronouncement of some of the giants of western intellectual and political establishment, such as Hume ('... the negro is naturally inferior to the whites...'),[13] Thomas Jefferson ('... the blacks... are inferior to the whites on the endowments of both body and mind...'),[14] or Hegel with his Africa comparable to a land of child-hood still enveloped in the dark mantle of the night as far as the development of self-conscious history was concerned. Hegel's statement that there was nothing harmonious with humanity to be found in the African character is representative of the racist images of Africans and Africa such a colonial child was bound to encounter in the literature of the colonial languages.[15] The results could be disastrous.

In her paper read to the conference on the teaching of African literature in schools held in Nairobi in 1973, entitled 'Written Literature and Black Images',[16] the Kenyan writer and scholar Professor Mĩcere Mũgo related how a reading of the description of Gagool as an old African woman in Rider Haggard's *King Solomon's Mines* had for a long time made her feel mortal terror whenever she encountered old African women. In his autobiography *This Life* Sydney Poitier describes how, as a result of the literature he had read, he had come to associate Africa with snakes. So on arrival in Africa and being put up in a modern hotel in a modern city, he could not sleep because he kept on looking for snakes everywhere, even under the bed. These two have been able to pinpoint the origins of their fears. But for most others the negative image becomes internalised and it affects their cultural and even political choices in ordinary living.

Thus Léopold Sédar Senghor has said very clearly that although the colonial language had been forced upon him, if he had been given the choice he would still have opted for French. He becomes lyrical in his subservience to French:

We express ourselves in French since French has a universal vocation and since our message is also addressed to French people and others. In our languages [i.e. African languages] the halo that surrounds the words is by nature merely that of sap and blood; French words send out thousands of rays like diamonds.[17]

Senghor has now been rewarded by being anointed to an honoured place in the French Academy – that institution for safe-guarding the purity of the French language.

In Malawi, Banda has erected his own monument by way of an institution, the Kamuzu Academy, designed to aid the brightest pupils of Malawi in their mastery of English.

> It is a grammar school designed to produce boys and girls who will be sent to universities like Harvard, Chicago, Oxford, Cambridge and Edinburgh and be able to compete on equal terms with others elsewhere.
>
> The President has instructed that Latin should occupy a central place in the curriculum. All teachers must have had at least some Latin in their academic background. Dr Banda has often said that no one can fully master English without knowledge of languages such as Latin and French . . . [18]

For good measure no Malawian is allowed to teach at the academy – none is good enough – and all the teaching staff has been recruited from Britain. A Malawian might lower the standards, or rather, the purity of the English language. Can you get a more telling example of hatred of what is national, and a servile worship of what is foreign even though dead?

In history books and popular commentaries on Africa, too much has been made of the supposed differences in the policies of the various colonial powers, the British indirect rule (or the pragmatism of the British in their lack of a cultural programme!) and the French and Portuguese conscious programme of cultural assimilation. These are a matter of detail and emphasis. The final effect was the same: Senghor's embrace of French as this language with a universal vocation is not so different from Chinua Achebe's gratitude in 1964 to English – 'those of us who have inherited the English language may not be in a position to appreciate the value of the inheritance.'[19] The assumptions behind the practice of those of us who have abandoned our mother-tongues and adopted European ones as the creative vehicles of our imagination, are not different either.

Thus the 1962 conference of 'African Writers of English Expression' was only recognising, with approval and pride of course, what through all the years of selective education and rigorous tutelage, we had already been led to accept: the 'fatalistic logic of the unassailable position of English in our literature'. The logic was embodied deep in imperialism; and it was imperialism and its effects that we did not examine at Makerere. It is the final triumph of a system of domination when the dominated start singing its virtues. . . .

The Quest for Relevance

I

So far I have talked about language in creative literature generally and in theatre and fiction in particular. I should have gone on to talk about 'The language of African poetry' but the same arguments apply even more poignantly in the area of poetry.

The existence and the continuing growth of poetry in African languages, clearly and unequivocally so in orature (oral literature), make it manifestly absurd to talk of African poetry in English, French or Portuguese. Afro-European poetry, yes; but not to be confused with African poetry which is the poetry composed by Africans in African languages. For instance, written poetry in Swahili goes back to many centuries. While the poetic political compositions of the great anti-imperialist Somali fighter, Hassan, will be known by heart by every Somali-speaking herdsman, not a line by even the best of African poets in foreign languages will be known by any peasant anywhere in Africa. As for a discussion of the other language of poetry – where poetry, like theatre and fiction, is considered as a language in itself with its own structures of beats, metres, rhymes, half-rhymes, internal rhymes, lines and images – it calls for different resources including a knowledge of the particular African languages of its expression, which I cannot, at present, even pretend to possess.

Instead, I shall attempt to sum up what we have so far been discussing by looking at what immediately underlies the politics of language in African literature; that is the search for a liberating perspective within which to see ourselves clearly in relationship to ourselves and to other selves in the universe. I shall call this 'a quest for relevance' and I want to look at it as far as it relates, not to just the writing of literature, but to the teaching of that literature in schools and universities and to the critical approaches. In other words, given that there is literature in Africa and in the world, in what order should it be presented to the child and how? This involves two processes: the choice of material and the attitude to, or interpretation of, that material. These two processes will themselves affect and be affected by the national and the class bases of the choice and the attitude to the material chosen. Finally the national and even the class bases of our choice and perspective will affect and be affected by the philosophic base from which we look at reality, a matter over which there can never be any legislation. Already as you can see we are entangled in a kind of vicious circle with everything affecting and being affected by everything else. But let me explain the question of base.

How we see a thing – even with our eyes – is very much dependent on where we stand in relationship to it. For instance we are all in this lecture theatre. But what we see of the room and how much of it we see is dependent on where we are now sitting as we listen to this talk. For instance you all can see the wall behind me: and I can see the wall behind you. Some of you are seated in such places as physically allow you to see much more of this room than others. What is clear is that were we to leave this room and describe it, we would end up with as many descriptions of this room as there are people here tonight. Do you know the story of the seven blind men who went to see an elephant? They used to have so many conflicting speculations as to the physical make-up of an elephant. Now at last they had a chance to touch and feel it. But each touched a different part of the animal: leg, ear, tusk, tail, side, trunk, belly and so they went home even more divided as to the physical nature, shape and size of an elephant. They obviously stood in different positions or physical bases in their exploration of the elephant. Now, the base need not be physical but could also be philosophical, class or national.

In this book I have pointed out that how we view ourselves, our environment even, is very much dependent on where we stand in relationship to imperialism in its colonial and neo-colonial stages; that if we are to do anything about our individual and collective being today, then we have to coldly and consciously look at what imperialism has been doing to us and to our view of ourselves in the universe. Certainly the quest for relevance and for a correct perspective can only be understood and be meaningfully resolved within the context of the general struggle against imperialism.

It is not always easy to see this in literature. But precisely because of that, I want to use the example of the struggle over what is to be taught, and in what order, with what attitudes or critical approaches, to illustrate the anti-imperialist context of the quest for relevance in Africa today. I want to start with a brief description of what has been called 'the great Nairobi literature debate' on the teaching of literature in universities and schools.

II

The debate started innocuously when on 20 September 1968 the then head of the English Department, Dr James Stewart, presented proposals to the Arts Faculty Board on the development of the English Department. The proposals were in many ways pertinent. But they were all preceded by two crucial sentences:

> The English department has had a long history at this college and has built up a strong syllabus which *by its study of the historic continuity of a single culture throughout the period of emergence of the modern west* makes it an important companion to History and to Philosophy and Religious Studies. However, it is bound to become less *British*, more open to other writing in English (American, Caribbean, African, Commonwealth) and also to continental writing, for comparative purposes.[20]

A month later on 24 October 1968 three African lecturers and researchers at the University responded to Dr Stewart's proposals by calling for the abolition of the English Department as then constituted. They questioned the underlying assumption that the English tradition and the emergence of the modern west were the central root of Kenya's and Africa's consciousness and cultural heritage. They rejected the underlying notion that Africa was an extension of the West. Then followed the crucial rejoinder:

> Here then, is our main question: if there is a need for a 'study of the historic continuity of a single culture', why can't this be African? Why can't African literature be at the centre so that we can view other cultures in relationship to it?[21]

Hell was let loose. For the rest of 1968 and spilling over into 1969 the debate raged on, engulfing the entire faculty and the university. Thus within four sentences the stage was set for what has become the most crucial debate on the politics of literature and culture even in Kenya of today. What was interesting was that the details of the debate were the same: all sides were agreed on the need to include African, European and other literatures. But what would be the centre? And what would be the periphery, so to speak? How would the centre relate to the periphery? Thus the question of the base of the take-off, the whole question of perspective and relevance, altered the weight and relationship of the various parts and details to each other.

In order to see the significance of the debate and why it raised so much temper we have to put it in a historical context of the rise of English studies in Africa, of the kind of literature an African student was likely to encounter and of the role of culture in the imperialist domination of Africa.

III

English studies in schools and higher institutions of learning became systematised after the Second World War with the setting up of the overseas extensions of the University of London in Uganda, Nigeria, Ghana, Sierra Leone, Kenya and Tanzania; and with very few variations they offered what also obtained in London. The syllabus of the English Department for instance meant a study of the history of English literature from Shakespeare, Spenser and Milton to James Joyce and T. S. Eliot, I. A. Richards and the inevitable F. R. Leavis. Matthew Arnold's quest for the sweetness and light of a hellenized English middle class; T. S. Eliot's high culture of an Anglo-Catholic feudal tradition, suspiciously close to the culture of the 'high table' and to the racial doctrines of those born to rule; the Leavisite selected 'Great Tradition of English Literature' and his insistence on the moral significance of literature; these great three dominated our daily essays. How many seminars we spent on detecting this moral significance in every paragraph, in every word, even in Shakespeare's commas and fullstops? For some reason the two most outstanding critical minds that might have made my study of English Literature really meaningful even in a colonial setting – Arnold Kettle and Raymond Williams – were studied, if at all, only remotely and fleetingly even in the time from 1959 to 1964. But here I am not looking at which writer or critic was more suitable to our situation or even the difference in their world outlook. What was more important was that they all fell within English tradition except in the study of drama where names like those of Aeschylus, Sophocles and Aristotle or Ibsen, Chekhov, Strindberg and Synge would appear quaint and strange in their very unEnglishness. The centrality and the universality of the English tradition was summed up in the title of an inaugural lecture by Professor Warner of Makerere, *Shakespeare in Africa*, in which he grew almost ecstatic about the fact that some of his students had been able to recognise some characters of Jane Austen's novels in their own African villages. So, English literature was applicable to Africa too: the defence of English studies in an African situation was now complete. In schools the English language and English literature syllabuses were tailored to prepare the lucky few for an English degree at university. So the syllabuses had the same pattern. Shakespeare, Milton, Wordsworth, Shelley, Keats and Kipling were familiar names long before I knew I would even make it to Makerere.

In my book, *Writers in Politics* – particularly in the essay 'Literature and Society' – I have tried to sum up the kind of literature available to African children in the classrooms and libraries for their school and university education, by placing it into three broad categories.

First was the great humanist and democratic tradition of European literature: Aeschylus, Sophocles, Shakespeare, Balzac, Dickens, Dostoevsky, Tolstoy, Gorky and Brecht to mention just a few names. But their literature, even at its most humane and universal, necessarily reflected the European experience of history. The world of its setting and the world it evoked would be more familiar to a child brought up in the same landscape than to one brought up outside, no matter how the latter might try to see Jane Austen's characters in the gossiping women of his rural African setting. This was not helped by a critical tradition that often presented these writers, Shakespeare included, as if they were mindless geniuses whose only consist-ent quality was a sense of compassion. These writers, who had the sharpest and most penetrating observations on the European bourgeois culture, were often taught as if their only concern was with the universal themes of love, fear, birth and death. Sometimes their greatness was presented as one more English gift to the world alongside the bible and the needle. William Shakespeare and Jesus Christ had brought light to darkest Africa. There was a teacher in our school who used to say that Shakespeare and Jesus used very simple English, until someone pointed out that Jesus spoke Hebrew. The 'Great Tradition' of English literature was the great trad-ition of 'literature'!

Then there was the literature of liberal Europeans who often had Africa as the subject of their imaginative explorations. The best example is Alan Paton's *Cry the Beloved Country*. Here an African eschewing violence, despite the racist violence around him, is the perfect hero. The Reverend Stephen Kumalo is presented in such a way that all our sympathies are with him. He is the embodiment of the biblical man who offers the enemy the left cheek to strike, after the right cheek has already been bashed in by the same enemy. Kumalo is the earlier literary version in an African setting of those Americans in the sixties who thought they could stop the Vietnam war by blowing bubbles and offering flowers to club and gun wielding policemen. Joyce Cary in *Mister Johnson* had gone a stage further in his liberalism. In this novel he offered an idiotic African as the hero. Mister Johnson is the dancing, fun-loving African full of emotional vitality and the endearing human warmth of a child. In the novel he is condemned to death. What was his dearest wish? To be shot dead by the European District Officer. The District Officer grants him that wish. Don't we do the same for our horses and cats? The point is that in the novel the reader is supposed to admire both the District Officer and Mister Johnson: they have established a human contact – that of the rider and the horse, the master and his servant. Karen Blixen's book *Out of Africa* falls within the same liberal mould: to her Africans are a special species of human beings endowed with a great spirituality and a mystical apprehension of reality or else with the instinct and vitality of animals, qualities which 'we in Europe' have lost.

The third category was the downright racist literature of writers like Rider Haggard, Elspeth Huxley, Robert Ruark, and Nicholas Monsarrat. In such a litera-ture there were only two types of Africans: the good and the bad. The good African was the one who co-operated with the European coloniser; particularly the African who helped the European coloniser in the occupation and subjugation of his own people and country. Such a character was portrayed as possessing qualities of strength, intelligence and beauty. But it was the strength and the intelligence and the beauty of a sell-out. The bad African character was the one who offered resistance to the foreign conquest and occupation of his country. Such a character was portrayed as being ugly, weak, cowardly and scheming. The reader's sympathies are guided in such a way as to make him identify with Africans collaborating with colonialism and to make him distance himself from those offering political and military resistance to colonialism. One can see the same schema at work today in the portrayal of the various African regimes in the Western media. Those regimes, as in Kenya and Ivory Coast, which have virtually mortgaged the future of their countries to Euro-American imperialism, are portrayed as being pragmatic, realistic, stable, democratic and they are often shown as having achieved unparalleled economic growth for their countries. But other regimes like those of Nkrumah's Ghana or Nasser's Egypt which strove for a measure of national self-reliance are portrayed as being simplistic, unrealistic, doctrinaire, authoritarian and are often shown as having brought only economic chaos to their countries. Thus imaginative literature had created the necessary racist vocabulary and symbols long before the TV and the popular media had come to dominate the scene.

African children who encountered literature in colonial schools and universities were thus experiencing the world as defined and reflected in the European experience of history. Their entire way of looking at the world, even the world of the immediate environment, was Eurocentric. Europe was the centre of the universe. The earth moved around the European intellectual scholarly axis. The images children encountered in literature were reinforced by their study of geography and history, and science and technology where Europe was, once again, the centre. This in turn fitted well with the cultural imperatives of British imperialism. In this book I have in fact tried to show how the economic control of the African people was effected through politics and culture. Economic and political control of a people can never be complete without cultural control, and here literary scholarly practice, irrespective of any individual interpretation and handling of the practice, fitted well the aim and the logic of the system as a whole. After all, the universities and colleges set up in the colonies after the war were meant to produce a native elite which would later help prop up the Empire. The cool, level-headed servant of the Empire celebrated in Kipling's poem 'If'; the gentleman who could keep his head against the rising storms of resistance; the gentleman who would meet with triumph and disaster and treat those two imposters just the same; the gentleman who had not the slightest doubt about the rightness of colonialism despite the chorus of doubt around; this gentleman was now being given African robes in the post-war schools and universities of an ageing imperialism.

The structures of the literary studies evolved in the colonial schools and universities had continued well into independence era completely unaffected by any winds of cultural change. The irony of all this was that these departments were being run in countries where the oral tradition, the basis of all genres of written literature be it a poem, a play, or a story, was beating with life and energy, and yet they were unaffected by the surging creative storm all around them. The study of the historic continuity of a single culture throughout the period of emergence of the modern west was still the organising principle of literature teaching in schools and colleges.

Seen against this background, the rejection of that principle in 1968 was therefore more than a rejection of a principle in a literary academic debate. It was questioning the underlying assumptions behind the entire system that we had inherited and had continued to run without basic questions about national perspective and relevance. The question is this: from what base do we look at the world?

IV

Three lecturers, Owuor Anyumba, Taban Lo Liyong and myself, were emphatic in our rejection and affirmation: our statement said,

> We reject the primacy of English literature and cultures. The aim, in short, should be to orientate ourselves towards placing Kenya, East Africa and then Africa in the centre.

All other things are to be considered in their relevance to our situation and their contribution towards understanding ourselves... In suggesting this we are not rejecting other streams, especially the western stream. We are only clearly mapping out the directions and perspectives the study of culture and literature will inevitably take in an African university.[22]

We proposed a new organising principle which would mean a study of Kenyan and East African literature, African literature, third world literature and literature from the rest of the world. We concluded:

We want to establish the centrality of Africa in the department. This, we have argued, is justifiable on various grounds, the most important one being that education is a means of knowledge about ourselves. Therefore, after we have examined ourselves, we radiate outwards and discover peoples and worlds around us. With Africa at the centre of things, not existing as an appendix or a satellite of other countries and literatures, things must be seen from the African perspective.[23]

But our boldest call was for the placing, within the national perspective, of oral literature (orature) at the centre of the syllabus:

The oral tradition is rich and many-sided... the art did not end yesterday; it is a living tradition... familiarity with oral literature could suggest new structures and techniques; and could foster attitudes of mind characterized by the willingness to experiment with new forms... The study of the Oral Tradition would therefore supplement (not replace) courses in Modern African Literature. By discovering and proclaiming loyalty to indigenous values, the new literature would on the one hand be set in the stream of history to which it belongs and so be better appreciated; and on the other be better able to embrace and assimilate other thoughts without losing its roots.[24]

Orature has its roots in the lives of the peasantry. It is primarily their compositions, their songs, their art, which forms the basis of the national and resistance culture during the colonial and neo-colonial times. We three lecturers were therefore calling for the centrality of peasant and worker heritage in the study of literature and culture.

The new organising principle was accepted after a long debate which engulfed the entire University and which, at one time, also included all the participants at the 1969 Nairobi Conference of English and Literature Departments of the Universities of East and Central Africa. African Orature; literature by Africans from the Continent, the Caribbean, and Afro-America; literature of 'third' world peoples from Asia and Latin America; literature from the rest of the world including Europe and North America; roughly in that order of relevance, relationship and perspective, would form the basis of a new literature syllabus with English as the mediating language. The actual syllabus resulting from the 1968–9 debate was necessarily a compromise. For instance East African poetry was to be taught in *its European context*. It was not until 1973, when the majority of the staff in the department were Africans, that the syllabus was streamlined to reflect the new perspectives without a qualifying apologia.

The growth of the Literature Department at the University of Nairobi, a department which has produced students who can, by starting from their environment, freely link the rural and urban experiences of Kenyan and African literature to that of Garcia Marquez, Richard Wright, George Lamming, Balzac, Dickens, Shakespeare and Brecht is a far cry from those days in the fifties and sixties when they used to try and detect Jane Austen's characters in their villages.

V

But that was not the end of the Nairobi Literature Debate.[25] In September 1974 a crucial conference on 'The Teaching of African Literature in Kenyan Schools' was held at Nairobi School. The conference was jointly organised by the Department of Literature, University of Nairobi and the Inspectorate of English in the Ministry of Education. It was attended by two hundred secondary school teachers of literature and English; the staff of the departments of literature and of the faculties of education, University of Nairobi and Kenyatta University College; delegates from departments of literatures of Dar es Salaam, Makerere and Malawi Universities; representatives of the Inspectorate of English, Ministry of Education and of the Kenya Institute of Education; observers from the Ministry of Education in Tanzania and Uganda; representatives from the then East African Community; East Africa Examination Council; East Africa Literature Bureau; trade union delegates from the Kenya National Union of Teachers (KNUT); and four publishers: Jomo Kenyatta Foundation, East African Literature Bureau, East Africa Publishing House and Oxford University Press. As if to give it an even more truly international character, there were visiting delegates from the University of West Indies at Mona, Jamaica, the University of Ife, Nigeria and from Auckland University, New Zealand. This impressive gathering was the result of hard organisational efforts of the steering committee chaired by Eddah Gachukia and S. A. Akivaga.

The conference was clearly motivated by the same quest for relevance which earlier had led to the reconstitution of the Department of Literature. In the recommendations of a working committee elected by the conference, it is argued that:

> Prior to independence, education in Kenya was an instrument of colonial policy designed to educate the people of Kenya into acceptance of their role as the colonized. The education system at independence was therefore an inheritance of colonialism so that literature syllabuses were centred on the study of an English literary tradition taught by English teachers. Such a situation meant that Kenyan children were alienated from their own experience [and] identity in an independent African country.[26]

Addressing itself to questions of language and literature, a resolution passed at the end of the conference stated:

> The present language and literature syllabuses are inadequate and irrelevant to the needs of the country. They are so organised that a Kenyan child knows himself through London and New York. Both should therefore be completely overhauled at all levels of our education system and particularly in schools.[27]

The conference, which was charged with examining the role of literature in society and the nature of literature taught in secondary schools and its relevance to Kenya's present day needs, called for the centrality of oral literature as a take-off base to contemporary literature. They argued that a sound educational policy was one which enabled students to study the culture and the environment of their society first, then set it in relation to the culture and environment of other societies: 'African literature, literature of the African diaspora, and all other literatures of related experiences must be at the core of the syllabuses.'[28] A working committee set up by the conference with Dougal Blackburn as Chairman and R. Gacheche as the Secretary came up with detailed recommendations on policy and on syllabuses along the principles outlined in the conference resolution. The seventy-three page document was titled: *Teaching of Literature in Kenya Secondary Schools – Recommendations of the Working Committee* and was clearly the result of months of hard work and commitment.

Looking at the document ten years later, one is struck, not so much by their critique of the existing syllabuses or by their detailed proposals for change – though both are impressive and still relevant to the similar debates and issues today – but by the consciousness that guided the critique and the proposals.

The pan-African consciousness is strong. The authors see Africa as one and they reject the division of Africa into sub-Saharan (Black Africa; Real Africa) and Northern (Arabic; Foreign; Mediterranean Africa). They want a Kenyan child to be exposed to the literature from north, south, west and east Africa:

> The centuries old Arab civilization has exerted tremendous influence on the literature of modern North Africa and also many parts of the continent. To date their influence has been denied by our educators and the literature of North Africa and the Arab world has largely been ignored.[29]

The authors want to pursue the African connection to the four corners of the earth, so to speak, and they want Kenyan children to be exposed to those historical links of biology, culture and struggle, particularly in Afro-American and Caribbean literature:

> It is often asked, why study Caribbean and Afro-American literature? What is the connection between African and the West Indian and Afro-American?
> (a) We have the same bio-geographic roots: the people of the West Indies and Afro-America are Africans who, a few hundred years ago, were brutally uprooted from the African continent.
> (b) We have shared the same past of humiliation and exploitation under slavery, and colonialism: we have also shared the glorious past of struggle, and fight against the same force.
> (c) Equally important we have the same aspirations for the total liberation of all the black people, in the world.
> Their literature, like our literature embodies all the above aspects of *our struggle for a cultural identity*.
> Apart from that, African peoples of the Diaspora have contributed much to Africa's cultural and political growth. Blyden, C. L. R. James, George Padmore, W. E. Dubois, Marcus Garvey and many others were part and parcel of Africa's struggle for independence. The literary movements from the West Indies and from Afro-America have creatively interacted with those in Africa. Aimé Césaire, Frantz Fanon, Claude McKay, Langston Hughes, Léon Damas, René Dépestre, Paul Robeson – all these giants of culture and the arts have positively contributed to the growth of African Literature.
> Most of these comments would apply equally well to the literature of the third world especially that of Asia and Latin America.[30]

Africa; African connections; third world; indeed, the authors of the report are very conscious of the internationalist setting and context of the national experience. Like the university Literature Department, which was conscious of the immense value of world literature, they too refused to substitute national chauvinism for the British colonial chauvinism of the existing syllabuses. A Kenyan child would be exposed to world literature and the democratic tradition in world literature.

> In accordance with the principle of teaching beginning with the students' immediate environment and moving out towards the world, the teaching of non-African literature in schools should aim to introduce the Kenyan student to *the world context of the black experience*. Such study should therefore include European and American literature, with their historical and present influences on the societies and literatures of black peoples, and a study of literature from other parts of the third world such as Latin America and Asia. Criteria for selection should attempt to balance: literary excellence, social relevance, and narrative interest. *The aim is to instil in the student a critical love of literature, which will both encourage its pursuit in later years and ensure that such a pursuit is engaged in fruitfully*... Given the nature of Kenyan society, we recommend that attention be paid to literature expressing the experience of a changing society, and that it be ensured that the variety of experience of different classes in society be covered.[31]

Their recommendations for the teaching of world literature come face to face with the issue of language; and they have authors which include Tolstoy, Gogol, Gorky, Dostoevksy (Russian); Zola, Balzac, Flaubert (French); Ibsen (Norwegian); Faulkner, Arthur Miller, Upton Sinclair, Hemingway (American); Dickens, Shakespeare, Conrad, Yeats, Synge (British and Irish); Mann and Brecht (German). They see the necessity or inevitability of continued use of English, but they strongly call for Swahili to be made compulsory in all schools but particularly for those students of English and literature and drama:

> A clear programme of Swahili literature be introduced and be made compulsory in schools.
>
> *Every language has its own social and cultural basis, and these are instrumental in the formation of mental processes and value judgements.* Whereas it is accepted that we use English and will continue to do so for a long time to come, the strength and depth of our cultural grounding will ultimately depend on our ability to invoke the idiom of African Culture in a language that is closer to it. Swahili has a major and an increasing role to play in Kenya, and needs to be given greater emphasis than it has hitherto been accorded.
>
> An immediate step that should be taken to fulfill this aim is that adequate numbers of Swahili teachers should be trained.[32]

All in all, the report is shot through and through with a consciousness that literature is a powerful instrument in evolving the cultural ethos of a people. They see literature as part of the whole ideological mechanism for integrating a people into the values of a dominant class, race, or nation. Imperialism, particularly during colonialism, provides the best example of how literature as an element of culture was used in the domination of Africa. The report notes:

> That Africa as a continent has been a victim of forces of colonial exploitation, oppression and human degradation. In the field of culture she was taught to look on Europe as her

teacher and the centre of man's civilization, and herself as the pupil. In this event Western culture became the centre of Africa's process of learning, and Africa was relegated to the background. Africa uncritically imbibed values that were alien and had no immediate relevance to her people. Thus was the richness of Africa's cultural heritage degraded, and her people labelled as primitive and savage. The colonizer's values were placed in the limelight, and in the process, evolved a new African who denied his original image, and exhibited a considerable lack of confidence in his creative potential.[33]

The writers are therefore shocked that syllabuses designed to meet the needs of colonialism should continue well into the independence era.

It was noted with shock and concern that even ten years after Independence, in practically every school in the republic our students were still being *subjected to alien cultural values which are meaningless especially to our present needs*. Almost all books used in our schools are written by foreign authors; out of 57 texts of drama studied at EAACE level in our schools between 1968 and 1972 only one was African. It became obvious that very little is being done in schools to expose our students to their cultural and physical environment.[34]

They are therefore conscious of the fact that an actual literature syllabus, no matter how far reaching in its scope and composition of texts and authors, is limited unless literature is seen and taught as an ideological component of the continuing national liberation process. In one of their conclusions they write:

Three major principles that emerged from the conference have guided the discussions of the working committee and the preparation of this final report.
 (i) *A people's culture is an essential component in defining and revealing their world outlook. Through it, mental processes can be conditioned, as was the case with the formal education provided by the colonial governments in Africa.*
 (ii) A sound educational policy is one which enables students to *study the culture and environment of their own society first, then* in relation to the culture and environment of other societies.
 (iii) *For the education offered today to be positive and to have creative potential for Kenya's future it must be seen as an essential part of the continuing national liberation process.*[35]

The hell let loose by the conference and by its subsequent recommendations was almost a repeat of the 1968–9 University-based debate. But now the debate became national. Some newspapers opened their pages to the literature debate revealing in the process a wide range of views on the issue from extreme hostility to passionate commitment. Believe it or not, in the early seventies academics and teachers could hold such a debate and assert the primacy of the Kenyan people and their experience of the history of struggle without fear of being labelled Marxist, Communist or radical and being hauled into prisons and detention camps. Even so the proposals and the model syllabus worked out to reflect the new perspective of Kenya, East Africa, Africa, Third World and the rest of the world, were not readily accepted by the Ministry of Education. They became the subject of a continuing debate and struggle in the educational corridors of power. The proposals were strengthened and argued about in yet other follow-up conferences and in 1981 were still a matter of controversy. In 1982 a syllabus like that of the Literature Department was labelled by some political elements as Marxist. Kenya-centrism or Afrocentrism was now equated with Marxism.

I am not sure if today the proposals have been accepted or not. I think some elements, like the oral literature components, have been introduced in the school literature curriculum. But I expect the controversy continues. For the quest for relevance and the entire literature debate was not really about the admissibility of this or that text, this or that author, though it often expressed itself as such. It was really about the direction, the teaching of literature, as well as of history, politics, and all the other arts and social sciences, ought to take in Africa today. The debate, in other words, was about the inherited colonial education system and the consciousness it necessarily inculcated in the African mind. What directions should an education system take in an Africa wishing to break with neo-colonialism? What should be the philosophy guiding it? How does it want the 'New Africans' to view themselves and their universe? From what base: Afrocentric or Eurocentric? What then are the materials they should be exposed to: and in what order and perspective? Who should be interpreting that material to them: an African or non-African? If African, what kind of African? One who has internalized the colonial world outlook or one attempting to break free from the inherited slave consciousness? And what were the implications of such an education system for the political and economic set up or status quo? In a neo-colonialist context, would such an education system be possible? Would it not in fact come into conflict with political and economic neo-colonialism?

Whether recommendations in the quest for relevance are successful or not ultimately depends on the entire government policy towards culture, education and language, and on where and how it stands in the anti-imperialist process in Africa today.

Whatever the destiny of the 1974 proposals on literature in schools, the values, assumptions and the attitudes underlying the entire 'Nairobi Literature Debate' are today at the heart of the contending social forces in Kenya, in Africa and in the third world and they all boil down to the question of relevance, in philosophical, class and national terms.

Notes

1   'European languages became so important to the Africans that they defined their own identities partly by reference to those languages. Africans began to describe each other in terms of being either Francophone or English-speaking Africans. The continent itself was thought of in terms of French-speaking states, English-speaking states and Arabic-speaking states.'
Ali A. Mazrui, *Africa's International Relations*, London: 1977, p. 92.
    Arabic does not quite fall into that category. Instead of Arabic-speaking states as an example, Mazrui should have put Portuguese-speaking states. Arabic is now an African language unless we want to write off all the indigenous populations of North Africa, Egypt, Sudan as not being Africans.
    And as usual with Mazrui his often apt and insightful descriptions, observations, and comparisons of the contemporary African realities as affected by Europe are, unfortunately, often tinged with approval or a sense of irreversible inevitability.

2   The conference was organized by the anti-Communist Paris-based but American-inspired and financed Society for Cultural Freedom which was later discovered actually to have been financed by CIA. It shows how certain directions in our cultural, political, and economic choices can be masterminded from the metropolitan centres of imperialism.

3   This is an argument often espoused by colonial spokesmen. Compare Mphahlele's comment with that of Geoffrey Moorhouse in *Manchester Guardian Weekly*, 15 July 1964, as quoted by Ali A. Mazrui and Michael Tidy in their work *Nationalism and New States in Africa*, London: 1984.

'On both sides of Africa, moreover, in Ghana and Nigeria, in Uganda and in Kenya, the spread of education has led to an increased demand for English at primary level. *The remarkable thing is that English has not been rejected as a symbol of Colonialism; it has rather been adopted as a politically neutral language beyond the reproaches of tribalism.* It is also a more attractive proposition in Africa than in either India or Malaysia because comparatively few Africans are completely literate in the vernacular tongues and even in the languages of regional communication, Hausa and Swahili, which are spoken by millions, and only read and written by thousands.' (my italics)

Is Moorhouse telling us that the English language is politically neutral vis-à-vis Africa's confrontation with neo-colonialism? Is he telling us that by 1964 there were more Africans literate in European languages than in African languages? That Africans could not, even if that was the case, be literate in their own national languages or in the regional languages? Really is Mr Moorhouse tongue-tying the African?

4   The English title is *Tales of Amadou Koumba*, published by Oxford University Press. The translation of this particular passage from the *Présence Africaine*, Paris edition of the book was done for me by Dr Bachir Diagne in Bayreuth.

5   The paper is now in Achebe's collection of essays *Morning Yet on Creation Day*, London: 1975.

6   In the introduction to *Morning Yet on Creation Day* Achebe obviously takes a slightly more critical stance from his 1964 position. The phrase is apt for a whole generation of us African writers.

7   *Transition* no. 10, September 1963, reprinted from *Dialogue*, Paris.

8   Chinua Achebe 'The African Writer and the English Language', in *Morning Yet on Creation Day*.

9   Gabriel Okara, *Transition* no. 10, September 1963.

10   Cheikh Hamidou Kane *L'aventure ambiguë* (English translation: *Ambiguous Adventure*). This passage was translated for me by Bachir Diagne.

11   Example from a tongue twister: 'Kaana ka Nikoora koona koora koora: na ko koora koona kaana ka Nikoora koora koora.' I'm indebted to Wangui wa Goro for this example. 'Nichola's child saw a baby frog and ran away: and when the baby frog saw Nichola's child it also ran away.' A Gĩkũyũ speaking child has to get the correct tone and length of vowel and pauses to get it right. Otherwise it becomes a jumble of *k*'s and *r*'s and *na*'s.

12   'The production of ideas, of conceptions, of consciousness, is at first directly interwoven with the material activity and the material intercourse of men, the language of real life. Conceiving, thinking, the mental intercourse of men, appear at this stage as the direct efflux of their material behaviour. The same applies to mental production as expressed in the language of politics, laws, morality, religion, metaphysics, etc., of a people. Men are the producers of their conceptions, ideas etc. – real, active men, as they are conditioned by a definite development of their productive forces and of the intercourse corresponding to these, up to its furthest form.' Marx and Engels, German Ideology, the first part published under the title, *Feuerbach: Opposition of the Materialist and Idealist Outlooks*, London: 1973, p. 8.

13   Quoted in Eric Williams *A History of the People of Trinidad and Tobago*, London 1964, p. 32.

14   Eric Williams, ibid., p. 31.

15   In references to Africa in the introduction to his lectures in *The Philosophy of History*, Hegel gives historical, philosophical, rational expression and legitimacy to every conceivable European racist myth about Africa. Africa is even denied her own geography where it does not correspond to the myth. Thus Egypt is not part of Africa; and North Africa is part of Europe. Africa proper is the especial home of ravenous beasts, snakes of all kinds. The African is not part of humanity. Only slavery to Europe can raise him, possibly, to the lower ranks of humanity. Slavery is good for the African. 'Slavery is in and for itself *injustice*, for the essence of humanity is *freedom*; but for this man must be matured. The gradual abolition of slavery is therefore wiser and more equitable than its sudden removal.' (Hegel *The Philosophy of History*, Dover edition, New York: 1956, pp. 91–9.) Hegel clearly reveals himself as the nineteenth-century Hitler of the intellect.

16   The paper is now in Akivaga and Gachukiah's *The Teaching of African Literature in Schools*, published by Kenya Literature Bureau.

17   Senghor, Introduction to his poems, 'Éthiopiques, le 24 Septembre 1954', in answering the question: 'Pourquoi, dès lors, écrivez-vous en français?' Here is the whole passage in French. See how lyrical Senghor becomes as he talks of his encounter with French language and French literature.

> Mais on me posera la question: 'Pourquoi, dès lors, écrivez-vous en français?' parce que nous sommes des métis culturels, parce que, si nous sentons en nègres, nous nous exprimons en français, parce que le français est une langue à vocation universelle, que notre message s'adresse *aussi* aux Français de France et aux autres hommes, parce que le français est une langue 'de gentillesse et d'honnêteté'. Qui a dit que c'était une langue grise et atone d'ingénieurs et de diplomates? Bien sûr, moi aussi, je l'ai dit un jour, pour les besoins de ma thèse. On me le pardonnera. Car je sais ses ressources pour l'avoir goûté, mâché, enseigné, et qu'il est la langue des dieux. Écoutez donc Corneille, Lautréamont, Rimbaud, Péguy et Claudel. Écoutez le grand Hugo. Le français, ce sont les grandes orgues qui se prêtent à tous les timbres, à tous les effets, des douceurs les plus suaves aux fulgurances de l'orage. Il est, tour à tour ou en même temps, flûte, hautbois, trompette, tamtam et même canon. Et puis le français nous a fait don de ses mots abstraits – si rares dans nos langues maternelles –, où les larmes se font pierres précieuses. Chez nous, les mots sont naturellement nimbés d'un halo de sève et de sang; les mots du français rayonnent de mille feux, comme des diamants. Des fusées qui éclairent notre nuit.

See also Senghor's reply to a question on language in an interview by Armand Guiber and published in *Présence Africaine* 1962 under the title, Leópold Sédar Senghor:

> Il est vrai que le français n'est pas ma langue maternelle. J'ai commencé de l'apprendre à sept ans, par des mots comme 'confitures' et 'chocolat'. Aujourd'hui, je pense naturellement en Français, et je comprend le Français – faut-il en avoir honte? Mieux qu'aucune autre langue. C'est dire que le Français n'est plus pour moi un 'véhicule étranger' mais la forme d'expression naturelle de ma pensée.
>
> Ce qui m'est étrange dans le français, c'est peut-être son style:
> Son architecture classique. Je suis naturellement porté à gonfler d'image son cadre étroit, sans la poussée de la chaleur émotionelle.

18   *Zimbabwe Herald* August 1981.

19   Chinua Achebe 'The African Writer and the English Language' in *Morning Yet on Creation Day*, p. 59.

20   Ngũgĩ wa Thiong'o *Homecoming* (London, 1969), p. 145.

21   Ibid., p. 146.

22   Ibid., p. 146.

23   Ibid., p. 150.

24   Ibid., p. 148.

25   The debate and the conferences that followed have also been the subject of scholarly dissertations – see for instance, Anne Walmsley *Literature in Kenyan Education – Problems and Choices in Author as Producer Strategy*, MA dissertation, Sussex Unversity.

26   Recommendations of the Working Committee, p. 7.

27   Ibid., p. 8.

28   Ibid., p. 8.

29   Ibid., p. 59.

30   Ibid., pp. 61–2.

31   Ibid., pp. 70–1.

32   Ibid., p. 21.

33   Ibid., p. 7.

34   Ibid., pp. 7–8.

35   Ibid., pp. 19–20.

CHAPTER 7

English in the Caribbean

Edward Kamau Brathwaite

Caribbean poet Edward Kamau Brathwaite in this 1981 essay takes a very different approach from Ngugi wa Thiong'o. He argues that standard colonial English has been altered by the literary practices of Caribbean writers, who have appropriated it for the creation of a new "creolized" or mixed language.

> *You may excel*
> *in knowledge of their tongue*
> *and universal ties may bind you close to them;*
> *but what they say, and how they feel –*
> *the subtler details of their meaning,*
> *thinking, feeling, reaching –*
> *these are closed to you and me...*
> *as are, indeed, the interleaves of speech*
> *– our speech – which fall to them...*
>

dead leaves...

G. Adali-Morty, *"Belonging" from Messages*

> *The Negro in the West Indies becomes proportionately whiter – that is, he becomes closer to being a real human being – in direct ratio to his mastery of the language.*
> Frantz Fanon, *Peau noire, masque blanc*

> *Yurokon held the twine in his hands as if with a snap, a single fierce pull, he would break it* now *at last. Break the land. Break the sea. Break the savannah. Break the forest. Break the twig. Break the bough.*
> Wilson Harris, *Sleepers of Roraima*

What I am going to talk about is language from the Caribbean, the process of using English in a different way from the "norm." English in a sense as I prefer to call it. English in an ancient sense. English in a very traditional sense. And sometimes not English at all, but language.

I start my thoughts, taking up from the discussion developed after Dennis Brutus's excellent presentation. Without logic, and through instinct, the people who spoke with Dennis from the floor yesterday brought up the question of language. Actually, Dennis's presentation had nothing to do with language. He was speaking about the structural condition of South Africa. But instinctively people recognized that the structural condition described by Dennis had very much to do with language. He didn't concentrate on the language aspect of it because there wasn't enough time and because it was not his main concern. But it was interesting that your instincts, not your logic, moved you toward the question of the relationship between language and culture, language and structure. In his case, it was English, and English as spoken by Africans, and the native languages as spoken by Africans.

We in the Caribbean have a similar kind of plurality. We have English, which is the imposed language on much of the archipelago; it is an imperial language, as are French, Dutch, and Spanish. We also have what we call Creole English, which is a mixture of English and an adaptation that English took in the new environment of the Caribbean when it became mixed with the other imported languages. We have also what is called *nation language*, which is the kind of English spoken by the people who were brought to the Caribbean, not the official English now, but the language of slaves and laborers – the servants who were brought in by the conquistadors. Finally, we have the remnants of ancestral languages still persisting in the Caribbean. There is Amerindian, which is active in certain parts of Central America but not in the Caribbean because the Amerindians are a destroyed people, and their languages were practically destroyed. We have Hindi, spoken by some of the more traditional East Indians who live in the Caribbean, and there are also varieties of Chinese.[1] And, miraculously, there are survivals of African languages still persisting in the Caribbean. So we have that spectrum – that prism – of languages similar to the kind of structure that Dennis described for South Africa. Now, I have to give you some kind of background to the development of these languages, the historical development of this plurality, because I can't take it for granted that you know and understand the history of the Caribbean.

The Caribbean is a set of islands stretching out from Florida in a mighty curve. You must know of the Caribbean at least from television, at least now with hurricane David* coming right into it. The islands stretch out in an arc of some two thousand miles from Florida through the Atlantic to the South American coast, and they were originally inhabited by Amerindian people, Taino, Siboney, Carib, Arawak.

In 1492, Columbus "discovered" (as it is said) the Caribbean, and with that discovery came the intrusion of European culture and peoples and a fragmentation of the original Amerindian culture. We had Europe "nationalizing" itself, and there were Spanish, French, English, and Dutch conquerors so that people had to start speaking (and thinking in) four metropolitan languages rather than possibly a single native language. Then with the destruction of the Amerindians, which took place within thirty years of Columbus's discovery (one million dead a year), it was necessary for the Europeans to import new labor bodies into the Caribbean. And the most convenient form of labor was the labor on the very edge of the trade winds – the labor on the edge of the slave trade winds, the labor on the edge of the hurricane, the labor on the edge of West Africa. And so the peoples of Ashanti, Congo, Nigeria, from all that mighty coast of western Africa were imported into the Caribbean. And we had the arrival in that area of a new language structure. It consisted of many languages, but basically they had a common semantic and stylistic form.[2] What these languages had to do, however, was to submerge themselves, because officially the conquering peoples – the

---

* This talk was presented at Harvard late in August 1979. Hurricanes ravish the Caribbean and the southern coasts of the United States in the summer of every year.

Spaniards, the English, the French, and the Dutch – insisted that the language of public discourse and conversation, of obedience, command, and reception, should be English, French, Spanish, or Dutch. They did not wish to hear people speaking Ashanti or any of the Congolese languages. So there was a submergence of this imported language. Its status became one of inferiority. Similarly, its speakers were slaves. They were conceived of as inferiors – nonhuman, in fact. But this very submergence served an interesting intercultural purpose, because although people continued to speak English as it was spoken in Elizabethan times and on through the Romantic and Victorian ages, that English was, nonetheless, still being influenced by the underground language, the submerged language that the slaves had brought. And that underground language was itself constantly transforming itself into new forms. It was moving from a purely African form to a form that was African, but which was adapted to the new environment and adapted to the cultural imperative of the European languages. And it was influencing the way in which the French, Dutch, and Spanish spoke their own languages. So there was a very complex process taking place, which is now beginning to surface in our literature.

In the Caribbean, as in South Africa (and in any area of cultural imperialism for that matter), the educational system did not recognize the presence of these various languages. What our educational system did was to recognize and maintain the language of the conquistador – the language of the planter, the language of the official, the language of the Anglican preacher. It insisted that not only would English be spoken in the Anglophone Caribbean, but that the educational system would carry the contours of an English heritage. Hence, as Dennis said, Shakespeare, George Eliot, Jane Austen – British literature and literary forms, the models that were intimate to Europe, that were intimate to Great Britain, that had very little to do, really, with the environment and the reality of the Caribbean – were dominant in the Caribbean educational system. It was a very surprising situation. People were forced to learn things that had no relevance to themselves. Paradoxically, in the Caribbean (as in many other "cultural disaster" areas), the people educated in this system came to know more, even today, about English kings and queens than they do about our own national heroes, our own slave rebels – the people who helped to build and to destroy our society. We are more excited by English literary models, by the concept of, say, Sherwood Forest and Robin Hood, than we are by Nanny of the Maroons, a name some of us didn't even know until a few years ago.[3] And in terms of what we write, our perceptual models, we are more conscious (in terms of sensibility) of the falling of snow for instance – the models are all there for the falling of the snow – than of the force of the hurricanes that take place every year. In other words, we haven't got the syllables, the syllabic intelligence, to describe the hurricane, which is our own experience;[4] whereas we can describe the imported alien experience of the snowfall. It is that kind of situation that we are in.

Now the Creole adaptation to that is the little child who, instead of writing in an essay "The snow was falling on the fields of Shropshire" (which is what our children literally were writing until a few years ago, below drawings they made of white snow fields and the corn-haired people who inhabited such a landscape), wrote "The snow was falling on the cane fields."[5] The child had not yet reached the obvious statement that it wasn't snow at all, but rain that was probably falling on the cane fields. She was trying to have both cultures at the same time. But that is creolization.

What is even more important, as we develop this business of emergent language in the Caribbean, is the actual rhythm and the syllables, the very body work, in a way, of the language. What English has given us as a model for poetry, and to a lesser extent, prose (but poetry is the basic tool here), is the pentameter: "The cúrfew tólls the knéll of párting dáy." There have, of course, been attempts to break it. And there were other dominant forms like, for example, *Beowulf* (c. 750), *The Seafarer*, and what Langland (1322?–1400?) had produced:

> For trewthe telleth that love. is triacle of hevene;
> May no synne be on him sene. that useth that spise,
> And alle his werkes he wrougte. with love as him liste.

Or, from *Piers the Plowman* (which does not make it into *Palgrave's Golden Treasury*, but which we all had to "do" at school) the haunting prologue:

> In a somer seson. whan soft was the sonne
> I shope me into shroudes. as I a shepe were

which has recently inspired our own Derek Walcott with his first major nation language effort:

> In idle August, while the sea soft,
> and leaves of brown islands stick to the rim
> of this Caribbean, I blow out the light
> by the dreamless face of Maria Concepcion
> to ship as a seaman on the schooner *Flight*.[6]

But by the time we reach Chaucer (1345–1400), the pentameter prevails. Over in the New World, the Americans – Walt Whitman – tried to bridge or to break the pentameter through a cosmic movement, a large movement of sound. Cummings tried to fragment it. And Marianne Moore attacked it with syllabics. But basically the pentameter remained, and it carries with it a certain kind of experience, which is not the experience of a hurricane. The hurricane does not roar in pentameter. And that's the problem: how do you get a rhythm that approximates the natural experience, the environmental experience? We have been trying to break out of the entire pentametric model in the Caribbean and to move into a system that more closely and intimately approaches our own experience. So that is what we are talking about now.

It is nation language in the Caribbean that, in fact, largely ignores the pentameter. Nation language is the language that is influenced very strongly by the African model, the African aspect of our New World/Caribbean heritage. English it may be in terms of its lexicon, but it is not English in terms of its syntax. And English it certainly is not in terms of its rhythm and timbre, its own sound explosion. In its contours, it is not English, even though the words, as you hear them, would be English to a greater or lesser degree. And this brings us back to the question that some of you raised yesterday: can English be a revolutionary language? And the lovely answer that came back was: it is not English that is the agent. It is not language, but people, who make revolutions.

I think, however, that language does really have a role to play here, certainly in the Caribbean. But it is an English that is not the standard, imported, educated English, but that of the submerged, surrealist experience and sensibility, which has always been there and which is now increasingly coming to the surface and influencing the perception of contemporary Caribbean people. It is what I call, as I say, *nation language*. I use the term in contrast to *dialect*. The word dialect has been bandied about for a long time, and it carries very pejorative overtones. Dialect is thought of as bad English. Dialect is "inferior English." Dialect is the language when you want to make fun of someone. Caricature speaks in dialect. Dialect has a long history coming from the plantation where people's dignity is distorted through their language and the descriptions that the dialect gave to them. Nation language, on the other hand, is the submerged area of that dialect that is much more closely allied to the African aspect of experience in the Caribbean. It may be in English, but often it is in an English which is like a howl, or a shout, or a machine-gun, or the wind, or a wave. It is also like the blues. And sometimes it is English and African at the same time. I am going to give you some examples. But I should tell you that the reason I have to talk so much is that there has been very little written about our nation language. I bring you to the notion of nation language but I can refer you to very little literature, to very few resources. I cannot refer you to what you call an *establishment*. I cannot really refer you to authorities because there aren't any.[7] One of our urgent tasks now is to try to create our own authorities. But I will give you a few ideas of what people have tried to do.

The forerunner of all this was, of course, Dante Alighieri who, at the beginning of the fourteenth century, argued, in *De vulgari eloquentia* (1304), for the recognition of the (his own) Tuscan vernacular as the nation language to replace Latin as the most natural, complete, and accessible means of verbal expression. And the movement was, in fact, successful throughout Europe with the establishment of national languages and literatures. But these very successful national languages then proceeded to ignore local European colonial languages such as Basque and Gaelic, and to suppress overseas colonial languages wherever they were heard. And it was not until the appearance of Burns in the eighteenth century and Rothenberg, Trask, Vansina, Tedlock, Waley, Walton, Whallon, Jahn, Jones, Whitely, Beckwith, Herskovitz, and Ruth Finnegan, among many others in this century, that we have returned, at least to the notion of oral literature, although I don't need to remind you that oral literature is our oldest form of "auriture" and that it continues richly throughout the world today.[8]

In the Caribbean, our novelists have always been conscious of these native resources, but the critics and academics have, as is often the case, lagged far behind. Indeed, until 1970, there was a positive intellectual, almost social, hostility to the concept of dialect as language. But there were some significant studies in linguistics, such as Beryl Lofton Bailey's *Jamaican Creole Syntax: A Transformational Approach*; also: F. G. Cassidy, *Jamaica Talk*; Cassidy and R. B. LePage, *Dictionary of Jamaican English*; and, still to come, Richard Allsopp's mind-blowing *Dictionary of Caribbean English*. There are three glossaries from Frank Collymore in Barbados and A. J. Seymour and John R. Rickford of Guyana; and studies on the African presence in Caribbean language by Mervyn Alleyne, Beverley Hall, and Maureen Warner Lewis.[9] In addition, there has been work by Douglas Taylor and Cicely John, among others, on aspects of some of the Amerindian languages; and Dennis Craig, Laurence Carrington, Velma Pollard, and several others at the University of the West Indies' School of Education have done some work on the structure of nation language and its psychosomosis in and for the class-room.

Few of the writers mentioned, however, have gone into nation language as it affects literature. They have set out its grammar, syntax, transformation, structure, and all of those things. But they haven't really been able to make any contact between the nation language and its expression in our literature. Recently, a French poet and novelist from Martinique, Edouard Glissant, had a remarkable article in *Alcheringa*, a nation language journal published at Boston University. The article was called "Free and Forced Poetics," and in it, for the first time, I feel an effort to describe what nation language really means.[10] For the author of the article it is the language of enslaved persons. For him, nation language is a strategy: the slave is forced to use a certain kind of language in order to disguise himself, to disguise his personality, and to retain his culture. And he defines that language as "forced poet-ics" because it is a kind of prison language, if you want to call it that.

And then we have another nation language poet, Bruce St. John, from Barbados, who has written some informal introductions to his own work which describe the nature of the experiments that he is conducting and the kind of rules that he begins to perceive in the way that he uses his language.[11]

I myself have an article called "Jazz and the West Indian novel," which appeared in a journal called *Bim* in the early 1960s,[12] and there I attempt to show that the connection between native musical structures and the native language is very neces-sary to the understanding of nation language. That music is, in fact, the surest threshold to the language that comes out of it.[13]

So that is all we have to offer as authority, which isn't very much, really. But that is how it is. And in fact, one characteristic of nation language is its orality. It is from "the oral tradition." And therefore you wouldn't really expect that large, encyclo-pedic body of learned comment on it that you would expect for a written language and literature.

Now I'd like to describe for you some of the characteristics of our nation language. First of all it is from, as I've said, an oral tradition. The poetry, the culture itself, exists not in a dictionary but in the tradition of the spoken word. It is based as much on sound as it is on song. That is to say, the noise that it makes is part of the meaning, and if you ignore the noise (or what you would think of as noise, shall I say), then you lose part of the meaning. When it is written, you lose the sound or the noise, and therefore you lose part of the meaning. Which is, again, why I have to have a tape recorder for this presentation. I want you to get the sound of it, rather than the sight of it.

Now in order to break down the pentameter, we discovered an ancient form which was always there, the calypso.[14] This is a form that I think everyone knows about. It does not employ the iambic pentameter. It employs dactyls. It therefore mandates the use of the tongue in a certain way, the use of sound in a certain way. It is a model that we are moving naturally toward now.

(Iambic Pentameter)	To be or not to be, that is the question
(Kaiso)	The stone had skidded arc'd and bloomed into islands
	Cuba San Domingo
	Jamaica Puerto Rico

But not only is there a difference in syllabic or stress pattern, there is an important difference in shape of intonation. In the Shakespeare (above), the voice travels in a single forward plane toward the horizon of its end. In the kaiso, after the skimming movement of the first line, we have a distinct variation. The voice dips and deepens to describe an intervallic pattern. And then there are more ritual forms like *kumina*, like *shango*, the religious forms,[15] which I won't have time to go into here, but which begin to disclose the complexity that is possible with nation language. What I am attempting to do this morning is to give you a kind of vocabulary introduction to nation language, rather than an analysis of its more complex forms. But I want to make the point that the forms are capable of remarkable complexity, and if there were time I could take you through some of the more complex musical/literary forms as well.

The other thing about nation language is that it is part of what may be called *total expression*, a notion that is not unfamiliar to you because you are coming back to that kind of thing now. Reading is an isolated, individualistic expression. The oral tradition, on the other hand, makes demands not only on the poet but also on the audience to complete the community: the noise and sounds that the poet makes are responded to by the audience and are returned to him. Hence we have the creation of a continuum where the meaning truly resides. And this total expression comes about because people live in the open air, because people live in conditions of poverty, because people come from a historical experience where they had to rely on their own breath patterns rather than on paraphernalia like books and museums. They had to depend on *immanence*, the power within themselves, rather than the technology outside themselves.

Let me begin by playing for you, first of all, some West Indian poets who are writing in standard English, or if you like, in West Indian standard English. The first poet is Claude McKay, who some people think of as American. He appears in American anthologies, especially anthologies of black writing. (Until recently, American anthologies hardly ever contained black writers, except perhaps Phillis Wheatley.) But McKay (1889–1940) was born in Jamaica and was a policeman in the constabulary there for some years before emigrating to the States where he quickly became a leading figure in what has come to be known as the Harlem Renaissance. But although he is very much identified with the black movement, he was, except perhaps during the most productive years of his life, rather ambivalent about his negritude.[16] And in this recording made toward the end of his life in the forties, when he had moved from communism to catholicism, for instance, he is saying, in this lead-in to his most famous and militant poem, "If we must die," a banner poem if ever there was one (it is a counter-lynching poem), that he is a *poet*, not a *black* poet, and not, as he said in those days, a "coloured" poet. And he goes on to recount the story of how a copy of "If we must die" was found on the body of a dead (white) soldier during the First World War. The newspapers recorded the occasion and everyone started quoting the poem. But no one, McKay says, said – "perhaps they did not even know" – that he was black. Which was okay by him, he says, because it helped ensure his "universality." (Winston Churchill also quoted this poem – without attributing it to the author who, when he had gone to Bernard Shaw for encouragement in earlier days, had been advised by the Grand Old Man [after Shaw had taken a shrewd look at him] that he'd better try it as a boxer!)

Well, that's the first stage and story of our literature. We want to be universal, to be universally accepted. But it's the terrible terms meted out for universality that interest me. In order to be "universal" McKay forsook his nation language, forsook his early mode of poetry and went to the sonnet.[17] And his sonnet, "St Isaac's Church, Petrograd," is a poem that could have been written by a European, perhaps most intimately by a Russian in Petrograd. It certainly could have been written by any poet of the post-Victorian era. The only thing that retains its uniqueness here (in terms of my notion of nation language) is the tone of the poet's voice. But the form and the content are very closely connected to European models. This does not mean that it is a bad poem or that I am putting it down. I am merely saying that, aesthetically, there are no unique elements in this poem apart from the voice of the poet reciting his own poem. And I will have a musical model that will appear after you have listened to the poem, and you can tell me whether you think I am fair or not. [On tape: McKay reading his sonnet followed by the "Agnus Dei" from Fauré's *Requiem*.]

> Bow down my soul in worship very low
> And in the holy silences be lost
> Bow down before the marble Man of Woe,
> Bow down before the singing angel host . . . [18]

The only trouble is that McKay had "trouble" with his syllables, his Clarendon syllables are very "evident," and he didn't always say "the," but sometimes said "de," which is a form in nation language. And these elisions, the sound of them, subtly erode, somewhat, the classical pentametric of the sonnet. . . .

Our second poet is George Campbell, also of Jamaica. In 1945, Jamaica was, after a long history of struggle, granted by Britain the right to move toward self-government and independence with a new political constitution and the formation of the People's National Party. George Campbell was very moved by, and involved in, these events, and he wrote what I consider his finest poem:

> On this momentous night O God help us.
> With faith we now challenge our destiny.
> Tonight masses of men will shape, will hope,
> Will dream with us; so many years hang on
> Acceptance. Why is that knocking against
> The door? . . . . is it you
> Looking for a destiny, or is it
> Noise of the storm?[19]

Now you see here a man who is becoming conscious of his nationality. But when he comes to write his greatest poem, he is still writing a Miltonic ode; or perhaps it is because he's writing his greatest poem, that it must be given that kind of nobility.[20] And it is read by our Milton of the Caribbean, George Lamming, our great organ voice, a voice that Lamming himself, in his book *The Pleasures of Exile* (1960) recognizes as one of the finest in English orature. But the point is that from my perspective, George Campbell's ode, fittingly read by George Lamming, isn't giving us any unique element in terms of the Caribbean environment. But it is still a beautiful poem wonderfully read. [On tape: Lamming reading Campbell's poem. . . .]

Must the horse rule the rider or the man
The horse.
Wind where cometh the fine technique
Of rule passing through me? My hands wet with
The soil and I knowing my world

[The reading was followed by the opening of Beethoven's Fifth Symphony][21]

The models are important here, you see. The McKay can be matched with Fauré, Campbell/Lamming with Beethoven. What follows next on the tape, however, is equally important because our local Beethoven employs a completely different model. I'm not saying his model is equal to the Fifth Symphony, but it makes a similar statement, and it gets us into what I now consider the nation or native language. Big Yout's sound poem, "Salaman Agundy," begins with a scream (On tape: Big Yout's "Screamin' Target"/"Salaman Agundy" from the LP *Screamin' Target* [Kingston, *c*.1972]), followed by the bass-based reggae canter of downbeat on the first "syllable" of the first and second bars, followed by a syncopation on the third third, followed by full offbeat/downbeats in the fourth:

The other model that we have, and that we have always had in the Caribbean, is the calypso, and we are going to hear now the Mighty Sparrow singing a kaiso which came out in the early sixties. It marked, in fact, the first major change in consciousness that we all shared. And Sparrow made a criticism of all that I and Dennis have been saying about the educational system. In "Dan is the Man in the Van" he says that the education we get from England has really made us idiots because all of those things that we had to read about: Robin Hood, King Alfred and the Cakes, King Arthur and the Knights of the Round Table, all of these things really haven't given us anything but empty words. And he did it in the calypso form. And you should hear the rhyme scheme of this poem. He is rhyming on "n's" and "l's," and he is creating a cluster of syllables and a counterpoint between voice and orchestra, between individual and community, within the formal notion of "call and response," which becomes typical of our nation in the revolution.

(Solo) Acordin to de education you get   when you small
     You(ll) grow up wi(th) true ambition an respec for one an all
     But in MY days in school   they teach me like a fool
     THE THINGS THEY TEACH ME A SHOULDA BEEN A BLOCK-
        HEADED MULE
(Chorus) *Pussy has finish his work long ago*
     An now he restin an ting
     Solomon Agundy was born on a MunDEE
     DE ASS IN DE LION SKIN....[22]

I could bring you a book, *The Royal Reader*, or the one referred to by Sparrow, *Nelson's West Indian Reader* by J. O. Cutteridge, that we had to learn at school by heart. It contained phrases like: "the cow jumped over the moon," "ding dong bell, pussy in the well," and so on. I mean, that was our beginning of an understanding of literature. Literature started (startled, really) literally at that level, with that kind of model. The problem of transcending this is what I am talking about now.

A more complex form by Sparrow is this next poem, "Ten to One Is Murder." Now it's interesting how this goes, because Sparrow has been accused of shooting someone on the eve of Carnival, just before Lent. (Kaiso and Carnival are two of our great folk expressions.) Now Sparrow apparently shot someone, but because of the popular nature of the calypsonian, he was able to defend himself long before he got into court by creating the scenario for the reason why he shot the man. He shot the man, he says, because for no reason at all, ten irates suddenly appear one night, surround him, and started throwing stones. The one in front was a very good pelter, and Sparrow didn't know what to do. He couldn't even find shelter. So he ran and ran and ran until finally he remembered that he had a gun (a wedger) in his pocket. He was forced to take it out and shoot *pow pow pow* and the crowd start to scatter. As a result he had the community on his side before the trial even started. But even if he hadn't written the song, he would have had the community on his side because here you have a folk poet; and folk poets are the spokesmen whose whole concern is to express the experiences of the people rather than the experiences of the elite. But here is "Ten to One Is Murder." Each slash phrase is an impressionistic brush stroke:

> About ten in de night on de fifth of October
> *Ten to One is Murder!*
> Way down Henry Street, up by H. G. M. Walker
> *Ten to One is Murder!*
> Well, de leader of de gang was a lot like a pepperrr
> *Ten to One is Murder!*
> An every man in de gang had a white-handle razorrr
> *Ten to One is Murder!*
> They say ah push a gal from Grenada
> *Ten to One is Murder!*...[23]

Now that is dramatic monologue which, because of its call-and-response structure (in addition, of course, to its own intrinsic drama), is capable of extension on stage. There is in fact a tent form known as calypso drama, which calls upon Trinidadian nation forms like *grand charge, picong, robber talk*, and so on, which Sparrow is in fact consciously using in this calypso, and which some of the younger Trinidadian nation poets like Malik, Questel, and Christopher Laird, for example, are bringing into play in their poetry.

> Man a start to sweat. Man a soakin wet
> Mama so much threat: that's a night a can never forget
> *Ten to One is Murder!*...

Next we have the poet who has been writing nation all her life and who, because of that, has been ignored until recently: the poet Louise Bennett (Miss Lou) of Jamaica. Now this is very interesting because she is middle class, and "middle class" means brown, urban, respectable, and standard English, and "the snow was falling in the canefields."[24] It certainly doesn't mean an entrenched economic/political position, as in Europe. For instance, Miss Lou's mother's and Miss Lou's own upbringing was "rural St Mary," hence the honorable Louise's natural and rightful knowledge of the folk.[25] (It was not until the post-independence seventies that she was officially – as distinct from popularly – recognized and given the highest honors, including the right to the title of Honorable.) But one is supposed, as V. S. Naipaul once said at a memorable Writers Conference in Jamaica, to graduate out of these things;[26] therefore there is no reason why Louise should have persisted with Anancy and Auntie Roachie and *boonoonoonoos* an *parangles* an *ting*, when she could have opted for "And how are you today," the teeth and lips tight and closed around the mailed fist of a smile. But her instincts were that she should use the language of her people. The consequence was that for years (since 1936?) she performed her work in crowded village halls across the island, and until 1945 could get nothing accepted by the *Gleaner*, the island's largest, oldest (estab. 1854), and often only newspaper. (Claude McKay had been published in Kingston, including in the *Gleaner*, in 1912, but he had had an influential white sponsor, the Englishman Walter Jeckyll, compiler of *Jamaican Song and Story* [1907].)[27] And although by 1962 she had already published nine books,[28] Miss Lou does not appear among the poets in the *Independent Anthology of Jamaican Poetry*, but is at the back of the book, like an afterthought if not an embarrassment, under "Miscellaneous." She could not be accepted, even at the moment of political independence, as a poet. Though all this, as I say, is dramatically altered now with the Revolution of the late sixties, her consciousness of this unfortunate situation remains where it hurts most: "I have been set apart by other creative writers a long time ago because of the language I speak and work in . . . From the beginning nobody recognized me as a writer."[29] I couldn't satisfactorily reproduce in print Miss Lou's "Street Cries" played for the lecture from her long-playing album *Miss Lou's Views*.[30] Here instead are two examples of her more "formal" verse from the book collection *Jamaica Labrish*, recordings from which, Miss Lou informs me, should be available alongside the revised edition of *Labrish* quite soon.[31] First, "Pedestrian Crosses":

> If a cross yuh dah-cross,
> Beg yuh cross mek me pass.
> Dem yah crossin' is crosses yuh know!
> Koo de line! Yuh noh se
> Cyar an truck backa me?
> Hear dah hoganeer one deh dah-blow!
>
> Missis, walk fas' an cross!
> Pickney, cross mek me pass!
> Lady, galang an mine yuh business!
> Ole man mek up yuh mine
> Walk between dem white line!
> Wat a crosses dem crossin yah is!
>
> . . .
>
> De crossin a-stop we from pass mek dem cross,
> But nutten dah-stop dem from cross mek we pass,
> Dem yah crossin is crosses fe true![32]

And "Dutty Tough" begins:

> Sun a-shine but tings noh bright,

> Doah pot a-bwile, bickle noh nuff,
> River flood but water scarce yaw,
> Rain a-fall but dutty tuff!

And ends on this note of social commentary:

> De price o' bread gan up so high
> Dat we haffe agree,
> Fe cut we y'eye pon bread an all
> Tun dumplin refugee!
>
> An all dem mawga smaddy weh
> Dah-gwan like fat is sin,
> All dem deh weh dah-fas' wid me,
> Ah lef dem to dumplin!
>
> Sun a-shine an pot a-bwile, but
> Ting noh bright, bickle noh nuff!
> Rain a-fall, river dah-flood, but
> Wata scarce an dutty tuff!³³

Notes

1   No one, as far as I know, has yet made a study of the impact of Asiatic language structures on the contemporary languages of the Caribbean, and even the study of the African impact is still in its infancy. For development of Anglophone Caribbean culture, see Edward Kamau Brathwaite, *Contradictory Omens: Cultural Diversity and Integration in the Caribbean* (Mona, Jamaica: Savacou Publications, 1974).

2   See Alan Lomax, "Africanisms in New World Negro Music: A Cantometric Analysis," in *Research and Resources of Haiti*, ed. Richard P. Schaedel (New York: Research Institute for the Study of Man, 1969) and in *The Haitian Potential*, ed. Vera Rubin and Richard P. Schaedel (New York: Teachers College Press, 1975); Mervyn C. Alleyne, "The Linguistic Continuity of Africa in the Caribbean," *Black Academy Review* 1, no. 4 (Winter 1970): 3–16.

3   The Maroons were Africans and escaped slaves who, after running away or participating in successful rebellions, set up autonomous societies throughout plantation America in marginal and certainly inaccessible areas outside European influence. See Richard Price, ed., *Maroon Societies: Rebel Slave Communities in the Americas* (Garden City, New York: Anchor Books, 1973). Nanny of the Maroons, an ex-Ashanti (?) Queen Mother, is regarded as one of the greatest of the Jamaica freedom fighters. See Edward Kamau Brathwaite, *Wars of Respect: Nanny, Sam Sharpe, and the Struggle for People's Liberation* (Kingston, Jamaica: Agency for Public Information, 1977).

4   But see Anthony Hinkson's Barbados hurricane poem, "Janet," in his unpublished collection "Slavation" (Bridgetown, Barbados: unpublished, c.1976).

5   I am indebted to Ann Walmsley, editor of the anthology *The Sun's Eye: West Indian Writing for Young Readers* (London: Longmans, Green & Co. Ltd., 1968), for this example. For experiences of teachers trying to cope with West Indian English in Britain, see Chris Searle, *The Forsaken Lover: White Words and Black People* (London: Routledge & Kegan Paul, 1972) and *Okike* 15 (August 1979).

6   Derek Walcott, "The Schooner *Flight*," in *The Star-Apple Kingdom* (New York: Farrar, Straus and Giroux, 1979), p. 3. William Langland's prelude to *Piers the Plowman* is often softened into "In somer season, whan soft was the sonne/I shope me in shroudes as I shepe were," which places it closer to Walcott – and to the pentameter.

7   But see the paragraphs and notes that follow.

8   See, for example, Ruth Finnegan, *Oral Literature in Africa* (Oxford: Clarendon Press, 1970); idem, *Oral Poetry: Its Nature, Significance, and Social Context* (Cambridge: At the University Press, 1977); idem, ed., *Penguin Anthology of Oral Poetry* (Harmondsworth: Penguin, 1977); B. W. Andrzejewski and I. M. Lewis, *Somali Poetry: An Introduction* (Oxford: Clarendon Press, 1964); Jan Vansina, *Oral Tradition: A Study in Historical Methodology*, trans. H. M. Wright (London: Routledge & Kegan Paul, 1965); S. A. Babalola, *The Content and Form of Yoruba Ijala* (Oxford: Clarendon Press, 1966); Ulli Beier, ed., *Yoruba Poetry: An Anthology of Traditional Poems* (Cambridge: At the University Press, 1970); Marshall McLuhan, *The Gutenberg Galaxy: The Making of Typographic Man* (Toronto: University of Toronto Press, 1962); J. H. K. Nketia, *Funeral Dirges of the Akan People* (Achimota: n.p., 1955); I. and P. Opie, *The Lore and Language of Schoolchildren* (Oxford: Clarendon Press, 1967); B. A. Ogot, *History of the Southern Lue* (Nairobi: East African Publishing House, 1967); Jerome Rothenberg, ed., *Technicians of the Sacred: A Range of Poetries from Africa, America, Asia, and Oceania* (New York: Doubleday & Co., Inc., 1968); Dennis Tedlock, *Finding the Centre: Narrative Poetry of the Zuni Indians* (New York: Dial Press, 1972); R. Egudu and D. Nwoga, *Ibgo Traditional Verse* (London: Heinemann Educational Books Ltd., 1973); and the wonderfully rich literature on black culture in the Americas.

9   Frank Collymore, *Notes for a Glossary of Words and Phrases of Barbadian Dialect* (Bridgetown, Barbados: Advocate Co., 1955); A. J. Seymour, *Dictionary of Guyanese Folklore* (Georgetown, Guyana: National History and Arts Council, 1975); John R. Rickford, ed., *A Festival of Guyanese Words: Papers on Various Aspects of Guyanese Vocabulary* (Georgetown, Guyana: University of Guyana [mimeographed], 1978); Mervyn Alleyne, "The Cultural Matrix of Caribbean Dialects" (unpublished paper, University of the West Indies, Mona, West Indies, n.d.); "What is 'Jamaican' in Our Language?" a review of F. G. Cassidy and R. B. LePage's *Dictionary* in *Sunday Gleaner*, 9 July 1967. See also Maureen Warner Lewis (sometimes Warner), "African Feasts in Trinidad," *ASAWI Bulletin* 4 (1971); idem, "Africans in 19th-Century Trinidad," *ASAWI Bulletin* 5 (1972) and 6 (1973); idem, "Trinidad Yoruba – Notes on Survival," *Caribbean Quarterly* 17 (1971); idem, *The Nkuyu: Spirit Messengers of the Kumina* (Mona, West Indies: Savacou Publications, 1977), also in *Savacou* 13 (1977); idem, *Notes to Masks* [a study of Edward Kamau Brathwaite's poem] (Benin City, Nigeria: Ethiopia Press, 1977). See also Edward Kamau Brathwaite, "Brother Mais," [a study of Roger Mais's novel, *Brother Man*] *Tapia* (27 October 1974), which in an earlier version is the "Introduction" to Roger Mais, *Brother Man* (London: Heinemann Educational Books Ltd., 1974); idem, "Jazz and the West Indian Novel," *Bim* 44–6 (1967–68); idem, "The African Presence in Caribbean Literature," *Daedalus* (Spring 1974), reprinted in *Slavery, Colonialism, and Racism*, ed. Sidney Mintz (New York: W. W. Norton and Co., 1974), and trans. into Spanish in *Africa en America Latina*, ed. Manuel Moreno Fraginals (Paris: UNESCO, 1977); idem, "Kumina: The Spirit of African Survival in Jamaica," *Jamaica Journal* 42 (1978), and (in an earlier version) in *The African Dispersal* (Brookline, Mass.: Afro-American Studies Program, Boston University, 1979).

10 Edouard Glissant, "Free and Forced Poetics," *Alcheringa* 2 (1976).

11 See Bruce St. John's Introduction to his "Bumbatuk" poems, *Revista de Letras* (Mayaguez: University of Puerto Rico, 1972).

12 Brathwaite, "Jazz and the West Indian Novel."

13 Extended versions of this lecture attempt to demonstrate the link between music and language structures: e.g., Edward Kamau Brathwaite and *kaiso, aladura, sookee*, sermon, post-bop; Shake Keane and jazz, *cadence* and *anansesem*; Kwesi Johnson and Oku Onoura and reggae/dub; Michael Smith and ring-game and drum-beat; Malik and worksong; Paul Keens-Douglas and *conte*; Louise Bennett (Miss Lou) and folksay and street shout; Bruce St. John and litany. Recent developments in kaiso (Shadow/*Bass man*, Short Shirt/*Tourist Leggo*, Sparrow/*Music an Rhythm; How you Jammin So*) suggest even more complex sound/shape developments.

14 The calypso (kaiso) is well treated in historical and musicological perspective by J. D. Elder, *Evolution of the Traditional Calypso of Trinidad and Tobago: A Sociohistorical Analysis of Song-*

change (Ann Arbor, Mich.: University Microfilms, 1967), and by Errol Hill, *The Trinidad Carnival* (Austin: University of Texas Press, 1972). But it is Gordon Rohlehr, a critic and reader in English at the University of the West Indies, who, apart from a few comments by C. L. R. James and Derek Walcott, is almost the only major Caribbean writer to have dealt with the literary aspects of kaiso, and with the relationship between kaiso (and reggae) and literature. Among Rohlehr's articles are: "Sparrow and the Language of Calypso," *CAM Newsletter* 2 (1967), and *Savacou* 2 (1970); "Calypso and Morality," *Moko* (17 June 1969); "The Calypso as Rebellion," *S.A.G.* 3 (1970); "Sounds and Pressure: Jamaican Blues," *Cipriani Labour College Review* (Jan. 1970); "Calypso and Politics," *Moko* (29 Oct. 1971); "Forty Years of Calypso," *Tapia* (3 and 17 Sept. 1972 and 8 Oct. 1972); "Samuel Selvon and the Language of the People," in Edward Baugh, ed., *Critics on Caribbean Literature* (London: George Allen & Unwin, 1978), pp. 153–61; and "The Folk in Caribbean Literature," *Tapia* (17 Dec. 1972).

15 See G. E. Simpson, *Religious Cults of the Caribbean* (Rio Piedras, Puerto Rico: Institute of Caribbean Studies of the University of Puerto Rico, 1970); Honor Ford-Smith, "The Performance Aspect of Kumina Ritual," Seminar Paper, Department of English, University of the West Indies, Mona, Jamaica (1976); and works by Brathwaite and Warner Lewis, as cited in note 9 above.

16 See Wayne F. Cooper, *The Passion of Claude McKay: Selected Poetry and Prose, 1912–1948* (New York: Schocken Books, 1973).

17 Claude McKay's first two books of poetry (1912), written in Jamaica, are unique in that they are the first all-dialect collections from an Anglophone Caribbean poet. They are, however, *dialect* as distinct from *nation* because McKay allowed himself to be imprisoned in the pentameter; he did not let his language find its own parameters, though this raises the tricky question of *critical relativity*. Could McKay, in the Jamaica of 1912, have done it any different – with a Svengali like Walter Jekyll, for instance, plus his *Dan-is-the-man-in-the-van* schoolteacher brother? We can certainly note the results of his literary colonialism in the primordial (?) anglicanism of *Constab Ballads* (London: Watts, 1912) and *Songs of Jamaica* (Kingston, Jamaica: Aston W. Gardner, 1912):

> I've a longin' in me dept's of heart
> 	dat I can conquer not,
> 'Tis a wish dat I've been havin' from since
> 	I could form a t'o't,
> Just to view de homeland England, in de streets of London walk
> An' to see de famous sights dem
> 	'bouten which dere's so much talk . . .
>
> ("Old England," *Songs*, p. 63)

By the time we reach Louise Bennett in the forties there is much less of a problem. Although the restrictive forms are still there, there is a world of difference in the activity of the language, and one suspects that this very restriction (the formal meter) is used as an aid to memory in performance. Many less adventurous spirits in the fifties attempted dialect in their first editions but revised them upward in subsequent versions. We are fortunate to have for purposes of comparison, in N. R. Millington's *Lingering Thoughts* (Bridgetown, Barbados: privately published, 1954), two versions of "On Return from a Foreign Land" (the dialect is entirely absent from subsequent editions):

Oh, what a rare delight	"Who you and whay you come from?
To see you once again!	Yuh voice soun' Bajun
Your kindly, strong, familiar face	An' yuh face familiuh.
Comes easily to my remembrance.	Las' time I see yuh was 'pon Roebuck
Our last meeting was on Roebuck	Street
Street	Dat use' to be suh full o' holes
which used to be so rutty.	But now un hear dat all de roads been
The mule-drawn car is gone;	tar
Gone, too, the railway;	De tramcars gone, de train gone too

Running on the tarmac	An' buses runnin' everywhay
Are the fussy buses.	At any owuh o' de day.
Small estates are combining into	De little estates all shut down,
large ...	An' everybody rush to town ..."
(p. 40)	(p. 43)

Two more points are that Millington places the dialect version in quotes to signal (for him) its dramatic/conversational mode; and, at a reading of this poem by the author in 1979, he removed the awkward standard English "rutty" and imported from the dialect version the more natural "full of holes."

18   Claude McKay, "St Issac's Church, Petrograd," first published in *Survey Graphic* 53 (1925), and subsequently in *Selected Poems of Claude McKay* (New York: Bookman Associates, 1953), p. 84, and in Cooper, ed., *Passion of Claude McKay*, p. 127; it was also read and recorded by the author in Arna Bontemps (ed.), *Anthology of Negro Poets* (New York: Folkways Records, FL 9791, 1966).

19   George Campbell, "On this Night," in *First Poems* (Kingston, Jamaica: privately published, 1945), p. 67.

20   See the discussion of the issue of McKay and *critical relativity* in note 17, above.

21   The tape recordings used in this lecture were taken from a wide variety of sources: long-playing albums (LPs), field recordings, copies from radio broadcasts, interviews, etc. The Lamming recording is from one of our finest radio programs, *New World of the Caribbean*, a series sponsored by Bookers of Guyana and broadcast on Radio Guyana in 1955–6. It was conceived and written by Lamming and Wilson Harris and produced for radio by Rafiq Khan. The Lamming reading of Campbell's poem had as background the theme music of the entire series, Dvořák's *New World* Symphony.

22   The Mighty Sparrow (Slinger Francisco), "Dan is the man in the van," on an EP (extended play, 45 rpm) recording (Port of Spain, Trinidad: National Recording Co., 1958?). The fourth line of each quatrain, shouted by Sparrow on this recording, represents the "response" part of this form and is sometimes sung by chorus and/or audience. For the text of this kaiso, see *One Hundred and Twenty Calypsoes to Remember ... by the Mighty Sparrow* (Port of Spain, Trinidad: National Recording Co., 1963), p. 86.

23   The Mighty Sparrow, "Ten to One Is Murder" (EP recording) (Port of Spain, Trinidad, National Recording Co., 1960). For the text see *One Hundred and Twenty Calypsoes*, p. 37.

24   For the role of color in the Caribbean, see Fernando Henriques, *Family and Colour in Jamaica* (London: Eyre & Spottiswoode, 1953).

25   See the Ph.D. dissertation (in progress) by Mary Jane Hewitt (Department of English and History, University of the West Indies, Mona, Jamaica), on Louise Bennett and Zora Neale Hurston as "cultural conservators."

26   ACLALS (Association of Commonwealth Literature and Language Societies) Conference held at the University of the West Indies, Mona, Jamaica, in January 1971; see Edward Kamau Brathwaite, "The Love Axe/l: Developing a Caribbean Aesthetic," in *Reading Black: Essays in the Criticism of African, Caribbean, and Black American Literature*, ed. Houston A. Baker, Jr. (Ithaca, NY: Cornell University Press, 1976), pp. 20–36; also published in *Bim* 61–3 (1977–8).

27   McKay's relationship with Jekyll is recorded in McKay's autobiography, *My Green Hills of Jamaica* (Kingston, Jamaica: Heinemann Educational Books [Caribbean] Ltd., 1979), pp. 65–72, 76–9. For a useful note on Jekyll, see Cooper, *Passion of Claude McKay*, pp. 318–19.

28   Ms. Bennett's first book of poetry, *Dialect Verses*, was printed for the author in Kingston, Jamaica, by the Gleaner Co. in 1940 – five years before the editor of the *Gleaner* recognized her.

29   Louise Bennett, *Caribbean Quarterly* 4, nos. 1 and 2 (March–June 1968): 98.

30   Federal 204, Federal Records, Kingston, Jamaica, 1967.

31   Personal communication, Louise Bennett Coverley (25 Sept. 1978).

32   Louise Bennett, "Pedestrian Crosses," in *Jamaica Labrish* (Kingston, Jamaica: Sangster's Book Stores Jamaica, 1966), p. 74.

33   Louise Bennett, "Dutty tough," in *Jamaica Labrish*, pp. 120–1. The tyranny of the pentameter can be seen/heard quite clearly here, although Miss Lou erodes and transforms this with the sound of her language. Its "riddim" sets up a counterpoint *against* the pentameter: "River flood but water scarce/yaw; yuh noh se/Cyar an truck *backa me*." The Africanisms *koo de, galang, yah, yaw, noh nuff, deh dah-blow*, and *fe*, for example, carry this even further, crystallizing in brilliant roots images such as "like fat is sin" and "tun dumplin refugee," which not only has its English meaning, but its folk-speech underdrone of African sound words for food: *tun, tum, tuntum*, and *fungee*. A whole essay could (and should) be written on the phonemic structure of nation language and how this relates to syntax and prosody, in addition to the historical and critical/comparative approaches hinted at in note 17 of this study.

CHAPTER 8

Signs Taken for Wonders

Homi K. Bhabha

While many Colonial and Post-Colonial scholars have been concerned with developing accounts of the workings of imperial consciousness in literature and culture, others have noticed the instabilities and ambivalences inherent in any attempt to impose domination on another people. The term "resistance" has also been used to characterize the way colonized peoples react to the imposition on them of an alien language and culture. Homi K. Bhabha has taken the lead in articulating the dissonance at the heart of the colonial discursive enterprise. His concepts of ambivalence, mimicry, and hybridity have become central to many scholars' understanding of how colonialism both works and is unworked. In this essay from 1985, he introduces the concepts of ambivalence and hybridity.

> *A remarkable peculiarity is that they (the English) always write the personal pronoun I with a capital letter. May we not consider this Great I as an unintended proof how much an Englishman thinks of his own consequence?*
> – Robert Southey, *Letters from England*

There is a scene in the cultural writings of English colonialism which repeats so insistently after the early nineteenth century – and, through that repetition, so triumphantly *inaugurates* a literature of empire – that I am bound to repeat it once more. It is the scenario, played out in the wild and wordless wastes of colonial India, Africa, the Caribbean, of the sudden, fortuitous discovery of the English book. It is, like all myths of origin, memorable for its balance between epiphany and enunciation. The discovery of the book is, at once, a moment of originality and authority, as well as a process of displacement that, paradoxically, makes the presence of the book wondrous to the extent to which it is repeated, translated, misread, displaced. It is with the emblem of the English book – "signs taken for wonders" – as an insignia of colonial authority and a signifier of colonial desire and discipline, that I want to begin this essay.

In the first week of May 1817, Anund Messeh, one of the earliest Indian catechists, made a hurried and excited journey from his mission in Meerut to a grove of trees just outside Delhi.

> He found about 500 people, men, women and children, seated under the shade of the trees, and employed, as had been related to him, in reading and conversation. He went up to an elderly looking man, and accosted him, and the following conversation passed.
> 'Pray who are all these people? and whence come they?' 'We are poor and lowly, and

we read and love this book.' – 'What is that book?' 'The book of God!' – 'Let me look at it, if you please.' Anund, on opening the book, perceived it to be the Gospel of our Lord, translated into the Hindoostanee Tongue, many copies of which seemed to be in the possession of the party: some were PRINTED, others WRITTEN by themselves from the printed ones. Anund pointed to the name of Jesus, and asked, 'Who is that?' 'That is God! He gave us this book.' – 'Where did you obtain it?' 'An Angel from heaven gave it us, at Hurdwar fair.' – 'An Angel?' 'Yes, to us he was God's Angel: but he was a man, a learned Pundit.' (Doubtless these translated Gospels must have been the books distributed, five or six years ago, at Hurdwar by the Missionary.) 'The written copies we write ourselves, having no other means of obtaining more of this blessed word.' – 'These books,' said Anund, 'teach the religion of the European Sahibs. It is THEIR book; and they printed it in our language, for our use.' 'Ah! no,' replied the stranger, 'that cannot be, for they eat flesh.' – 'Jesus Christ,' said Anund, 'teaches that it does not signify what a man eats or drinks. EATING is nothing before God. *Not that which entereth into a man's mouth defileth him, but that which cometh out of the mouth, this defileth a man:* for vile things come forth from the heart. *Out of the heart proceed evil thoughts, murders, adulteries, fornications, thefts; and these are the things that defile.'*

'That is true; but how can it be the European Book, when we believe that it is God's gift to us? He sent it to us at Hurdwar.' 'God gave it long ago to the Sahibs, and THEY sent it to us.' ... The ignorance and simplicity of many are very striking, never having heard of a printed book before; and its very appearance was to them miraculous. A great stir was excited by the gradual increasing information hereby obtained, and all united to acknowledge the superiority of the doctrines of this Holy Book to every thing which they had hitherto heard or known. An indifference to the distinctions of Caste soon manifested itself; and the interference and tyrannical authority of the Brahmins became more offensive and contemptible. At last, it was determined to separate themselves from the rest of their Hindoo Brethren; and to establish a party of their own choosing, four or five, who could read the best, to be the public teachers from this newly-acquired Book. ... Anund asked them, 'Why are you all dressed in white?' 'The people of God should wear white raiment,' was the reply, 'as a sign that they are clean, and rid of their sins.' – Anund observed, 'You ought to be BAPTIZED, in the name of the Father, and of the Son, and of the Holy Ghost. Come to Meerut: there is a Christian Padre there; and he will shew you what you ought to do.' They answered, 'Now we must go home to the harvest; but, as we mean to meet once a year, perhaps the next year we may come to Meerut.' ... I explained to them the nature of the Sacrament and of Baptism; in answer to which, they replied, 'We are willing to be baptized, but we will never take the Sacrament. To all the other customs of Christians we are willing to conform, but not to the Sacrament, because the Europeans eat cow's flesh, and this will never do for us.' To this I answered, 'This WORD is of God, and not of men; and when HE makes your hearts to understand, then you will PROPERLY comprehend it.' They replied, 'If all our country will receive this Sacrament, then will we.' I then observed, 'The time is at hand, when all the countries will receive this WORD!' They replied, 'True!'[1]

Almost a hundred years later, in 1902, Joseph Conrad's Marlow, traveling in the Congo, in the night of the first ages, without a sign and no memories, cut off from the comprehension of his surroundings, desperately in need of a deliberate belief, comes upon Towson's (or Towser's) *Inquiry into some Points of Seamanship.*

Not a very enthralling book; but at the first glance you could see there a singleness of intention, an honest concern for the right way of going to work, which made these humble pages, thought out so many years ago, luminous with another than a professional light.... I assure you to leave off reading was like tearing myself away from the shelter of an old and solid friendship....

"It must be this miserable trader – this intruder," exclaimed the manager, looking back malevolently at the place we had left. "He must be English," I said.[2]

Half a century later, a young Trinidadian discovers that same volume of Towson's in that very passage from Conrad and draws from it a vision of literature and a lesson of history. "The scene," writes V. S. Naipaul,

> answered some of the political panic I was beginning to feel.
>   To be a colonial was to know a kind of security; it was to inhabit a fixed world. And I suppose that in my fantasy I had seen myself coming to England as to some purely literary region, where, untrammeled by the accidents of history or background, I could make a romantic career for myself as a writer. But in the new world I felt that ground move below me.... Conrad... had been everywhere before me. Not as a man with a cause, but a man offering... a vision of the world's half-made societies... where always "something inherent in the necessities of successful action... carried with it the moral degradation of the idea." Dismal but deeply felt: a kind of truth and half a consolation.[3]

Written as they are in the name of the father and the author, these texts of the civilizing mission immediately suggest the triumph of the colonialist moment in early English Evangelism and modern English literature. The discovery of the book installs the sign of appropriate representation: the word of God, truth, art creates the conditions for a beginning, a practice of history and narrative. But the institution of the Word in the wilds is also an *Entstellung*, a process of displacement, distortion, dislocation, repetition[4] – the dazzling light of literature sheds only areas of darkness. Still the idea of the English book is presented as universally adequate: like the "metaphoric writing of the West," it communicates "the immediate vision of the thing, freed from the discourse that accompanied it, or even encumbered it."[5]

Shortly before the discovery of the book, Marlow interrogates the odd, inappropriate, "colonial" transformation of a textile into an uncertain textual sign, possibly a fetish:

> Why? Where did he get it? Was it a badge – an ornament – a charm – a propitiatory act? Was there any idea at all connected with it? It looked startling round his black neck, this bit of white thread from beyond the seas.[6]

Such questions of the historical act of enunciation, which carry a political intent, are lost, a few pages later, in the myth of origins and discovery. The immediate vision of the book figures those ideological correlatives of the Western sign – empiricism, idealism, mimeticism, monoculturalism (to use Edward Said's term) – that sustain a tradition of English "national" authority. It is, significantly, a normalizing myth whose organics and revisionary narrative is also the history of that nationalist discipline of Commonwealth history and its equally expansionist epigone, Commonwealth literature. Their versions of traditional, academicist wisdom moralize the conflictual moment of colonialist intervention into that constitutive chain of exemplum and imitation, what Friedrich Nietzsche describes as the monumental history beloved of "gifted egoists and visionary scoundrels."[7] For despite first appearances, a repetition of the episodes of the book reveals that they represent important moments in the historical transformation and discursive transfiguration of the colonial text and context.

Anund Messeh's riposte to the natives who refuse the sacrament – "the time is at hand when all countries *will* receive this WORD" (my emphasis) – is both firmly and timely spoken in 1817. For it represents a shift away from the "orientalist" educational practice of, say, Warren Hastings and the much more interventionist and "interpellative" ambition of Charles Grant for a culturally and linguistically homogeneous English India. It was with Grant's election to the board of the East India Company in 1794 and to Parliament in 1802, and through his energetic espousal of the Evangelical ideals of the Clapham sect, that the East India Company reintroduced a "pious clause" into its charter for 1813. By 1817 the Church Missionary Society ran sixty-one schools, and in 1818 it commissioned the Burdwan Plan, a central plan of education for instruction in the English language. The aim of the plan anticipates, almost to the word, Thomas Macaulay's infamous 1835 "Minute on Education": "to form a body of well instructed labourers, competent in their proficiency in English to act as Teachers, Translators, and Compilers of useful works for the masses of the people."[8] Anund Messeh's lifeless repetition of chapter and verse, his artless technique of translation, participate in one of the most artful technologies of colonial power. In the same month that Anund Messeh discovered the miraculous effects of the book outside Delhi – May 1817 – a correspondent of the Church Missionary Society wrote to London describing the method of English education at Father John's mission in Tranquebar:

> The principal method of teaching them the English language would be by giving them English phrases and sentences, with a translation for them to commit to memory. These sentences might be so arranged as to teach them whatever sentiments the instructor should choose. They would become, in short, attached to the Mission; and though first put into the school from worldly motives alone, should any of them be converted, accustomed as they are to the language, manners and climate of the country, they might soon be prepared for a great usefulness in the cause of religion.... In this way the Heathens themselves might be made the instruments of pulling down their own religion, and of erecting in its ruins the standards of the Cross. [*MR*, May 1817, p. 187]

Marlow's ruminative closing statement, "He must be English," acknowledges at the heart of darkness, in Conrad's *fin de siècle* malaise which Ian Watt so thoroughly describes, the particular debt that both Marlow and Conrad owe to the ideals of English "liberty" and its liberal-conservative culture.[9] Caught as he is – between the madness of "prehistoric" Africa and the unconscious desire to repeat the traumatic intervention of modern colonialism within the compass of a seaman's yarn – Towson's manual provides Marlow with a singleness of intention. It is the book of work that turns delirium into the discourse of civil address. For the ethic of work, as Conrad was to exemplify in "Tradition" (1918), provides a sense of right conduct and honour achievable only through the acceptance of those "customary" norms which are the signs of culturally cohesive "civil" communities.[10] These aims of the civilizing mission, endorsed in the "idea" of British imperialism and enacted on the red sections of the map, speak with a peculiarly English authority based upon the *customary practice* on which both English common law and the English national language rely for their effectivity and appeal.[11] It is the ideal of English civil discourse that permits Conrad to entertain the ideological ambivalences that riddle his narratives. It is under its watchful eye that he allows the fraught text of late nineteenth-century imperialism to implode within the practices of early modernism. The devastating effects of such an encounter are not only contained in an (un)common yarn; they are concealed in the propriety of a civil "lie" told to the Intended (the complicity of the customary?): "The horror! The horror!" must not be repeated in the drawing-rooms of Europe.

It is to preserve the peculiar sensibility of what he understands as a tradition of civility that Naipaul "translates" Conrad, from Africa to the Caribbean, in order to transform the despair of postcolonial history into an appeal for the autonomy of art. The more fiercely he believes that "the wisdom of the heart ha[s] no concern with the erection or demolition of theories," the more convinced he becomes of the unmediated nature of the Western book – "the words it pronounces have the value of acts of integrity."[12] The values that such a perspective generates for his own work, and for the once colonized world it chooses to represent and evaluate, are visible in the hideous panorama that some of his titles provide: *The Loss of El Dorado*, *The Mimic Men*, *An Area of Darkness*, *A Wounded Civilization*, *The Overcrowded Barracoon*.

The discovery of the English book establishes both a measure of mimesis and a mode of civil authority and order. If these scenes, as I've narrated them, suggest the triumph of the writ of colonialist power, then it must be conceded that the wily letter of the law inscribes a much more ambivalent text of authority. For it is in between the edict of Englishness and the assault of the dark unruly spaces of the earth, through an act of repetition, that the colonial text emerges uncertainly. Anund Messeh disavows the natives' disturbing questions as he returns to repeat the now questionable "authority" of Evangelical dicta; Marlow turns away from the African jungle to recognize, in retrospect, the peculiarly "English" quality of the discovery of the book; Naipaul turns his back on the hybrid half-made colonial world to fix his eye on the universal domain of English literature. What we witness is neither an untroubled, innocent dream of England nor a "secondary revision" of the nightmare of India, Africa, the Caribbean. What is "English" in these discourses of colonial power cannot be represented as a plenitude or a "full" presence; it is determined by its belatedness. As a signifier of authority, the English book acquires its meaning *after* the traumatic scenario of colonial difference, cultural or racial, returns the eye of power to some prior, archaic image or identity. Paradoxically, however, such an image can neither be "original" – by virtue of the act of repetition that constructs it – nor "identical" – by virtue of the difference that defines it. Consequently, the colonial presence is always ambivalent, split between its appearance as original and authoritative and its articulation as repetition and difference.

It is this ambivalence that makes the boundaries of colonial "positionality" – the division of self/other – and the question of colonial power – the differentiation of colonizer/colonized – different from both the Hegelian master/slave dialectic or the phenomenological projection of Otherness. It is a *différance* produced within the act of enunciation as a specifically colonial articulation of those two disproportionate sites of colonial discourse and power: the colonial scene as the invention of historicity, mastery, mimesis or as the "other scene" of *Entstellung*, displacement, fantasy, psychic defence, and an "open" textuality. Such a dis-play of difference produces a mode of authority that is agonistic (rather than antagonistic). Its discriminatory effects are visible in those split subjects of the racist stereotype – the simian Negro, the effeminate Asiatic male – which ambivalently fix identity as the fantasy of difference.[13] To recognize the *différance* of the colonial presence is to realize that the colonial text occupies that space of double inscription, hallowed – no, hollowed – by Jacques Derrida:

> whenever any writing both marks and goes back over its mark with an undecidable stroke... [this] double mark escapes the pertinence or authority of truth: it does not overturn it but rather inscribes it within its play as one of its functions or parts. This displacement does not take place, has not taken place once as an *event*. It does not occupy a simple place. It does not take place *in* writing. This dis-location (is what) writes/is written. [*D*, p. 193]

How can the question of authority, the power and presence of the English, be posed in the interstices of a double inscription? I have no wish to replace an idealist myth – the metaphoric English book – with a historicist one – the colonialist project of English civility. Such a reductive reading would deny what is obvious, that the representation of colonial authority depends less on a universal symbol of English identity than on its productivity as a sign of difference. Yet in my use of "English" there is a "transparency" of reference that registers a certain obvious presence: the Bible translated into Hindi, propagated by Dutch or native catechists, is still the English book; a Polish émigré, deeply influenced by Gustave Flaubert, writing about Africa, produces an English classic. What is there about such a process of visibility and recognition that never fails to be an authoritative acknowledgement without ceasing to be a "spacing between desire and fulfillment, between perpetuation and its recollection... [a] medium [which] has nothing to do with a center" (*D*, p. 212)?

This question demands a departure from Derrida's objectives in "The Double Session"; a turning away from the vicissitudes of interpretation in the mimetic act of reading to the question of the effects of power, the inscription of strategies of individuation and domination in those "dividing practices" which construct the colonial space – a departure from Derrida which is also a return to those moments in his essay when he acknowledges the problematic of "presence" as a certain quality of discursive transparency which he describes as "the production of *mere* reality-effects" or "the effect of content" or as the problematic relation between the "medium of writing and the determination of each textual unit." In the rich ruses and rebukes with which he shows up the "false appearance of the present," Derrida fails to decipher the specific and determinate system of *address* (not referent) that is signified by the "effect of content" (see *D*, pp. 173–85). It is precisely such a strategy of address – the *immediate presence* of the English – that engages the questions of authority that I want to raise. When the ocular metaphors of presence refer to the process by which content is fixed as an "effect of the present," we encounter not plenitude but the structured gaze of power whose objective is authority, whose "subjects" are historical.

The reality effect constructs a mode of address in which a complementarity of meaning – not a correspondential notion of truth, as antirealists insist – produces the moment of discursive transparency. It is the moment when, "under the false appearance of the present," the semantic seems to prevail over the syntactic, the signified over the signifier. Contrary to current avant-garde orthodoxy, however, the transparent is neither simply the triumph of the "imaginary" capture of the subject in realist narrative nor the ultimate interpellation of the individual by ideology. It is not a proposal that you cannot positively refuse. It is better described, I suggest, as a form of the *disposal* of those discursive signs of presence/the present within the strategies that articulate the range of meanings from "dispose to disposition." Transparency is the action of the distribution and arrangement of differential spaces, positions, knowledges in relation to each other, relative to a differential, not inherent, sense of order. This effects a regulation of spaces and places that is authoritatively assigned; it puts the addressee into the proper frame or condition for some action or result. Such a mode of governance addresses itself to a form of conduct that is achieved through a reality effect that equivocates between the sense of disposal, as the bestowal of a frame of reference, and disposition, as mental inclination, a frame of mind. Such equivocation allows neither an equivalence of the two sites of disposal nor their division as self/other, subject/object. Transparency achieves an effect of authority in the present (and an authoritative presence) through a process similar to what Michel Foucault describes as "an effect of finalisation, relative to an objective," without its necessary attribution to a subject that makes a prohibitory law, thou shalt or thou shalt not.[14]

The place of difference and otherness, or the space of the adversarial, within such a system of "disposal" as I've proposed, is never entirely on the outside or implacably oppositional. It is a pressure, and a presence, that acts constantly, if unevenly, along the entire boundary of authorization, that is, on the surface between what I've called disposal-as-bestowal and disposition-as-inclination. The contour of difference is agonistic, shifting, splitting, rather like Freud's description of the system of consciousness which occupies a position in space lying on the borderline between outside and inside, a surface of protection, reception, and projection.[15] The power play of presence is lost if its transparency is treated naively as the nostalgia for plenitude that should be flung repeatedly into the abyss – *mise en abîme* – from which its desire is born. Such theoreticist anarchism cannot intervene in the agonistic space of authority where

> the true and the false are separated and specific effects of power [are] attached to the true, it being understood also that it is not a matter of a battle "on behalf" of the truth, but of a battle about the status of truth and the economic and political role it plays.[16]

It is precisely to intervene in such a battle for the *status* of the truth that it becomes crucial to examine the *presence* of the English book. For it is this *surface* that stabilizes the agonistic colonial space; it is its *appearance* that regulates the ambivalence between origin and *Entstellung*, discipline and desire, mimesis and repetition.

Despite appearances, the text of transparency inscribes a double vision: the field of the "true" emerges as a visible effect of knowledge/power only after the regulatory and displacing division of the true and the false. From this point of view, discursive "transparency" is best read in the photographic sense in which a transparency is also always a negative, processed into visibility through the technologies of reversal, enlargement, lighting, editing, projection, not a source but a re-source of light. Such a bringing to light is never a prevision; it is always a question of the provision of visibility as a capacity, a strategy, an agency but also in the sense in which the prefix pro(vision) might indicate an elision of sight, delegation, substitution, contiguity, in place of ... what?

This is the question that brings us to the ambivalence of the presence of authority, peculiarly visible in its colonial articulation. For if transparency signifies discursive closure – intention, image, author – it does so through a disclosure of its *rules of recognition* – those social texts of epistemic, ethnocentric, nationalist intelligibility which cohere in the address of authority as the "present," the voice of modernity. The acknowledgement of authority depends upon the immediate – unmediated – visibility of its rules of recognition as the unmistakable referent of historical necessity. In the doubly inscribed space of colonial representation where the presence of authority – the English book – is also a question of its repetition and displacement, where transparency is *technē*, the immediate visibility of such a régime of recognition is resisted. Resistance is not necessarily an oppositional act of political intention, nor is it the simple negation or exclusion of the "content" of an other culture, as a difference once perceived. It is the effect of an ambivalence produced within the rules of recognition of dominating discourses as they articulate the signs of cultural difference and reimplicate them within the deferential relations of colonial power – hierarchy, normalization, marginalization, and so forth. For domination is achieved through a process of disavowal that denies the *différance* of colonialist power – the chaos of its intervention as *Entstellung*, its dislocatory presence – in order to preserve the authority of its identity in the universalist narrative of nineteenth-century historical and political evolutionism.

The exercise of colonialist authority, however, requires the production of differentiations, individuations, identity effects through which discriminatory practices can map out subject populations that are tarred with the visible and transparent mark of power. Such a mode of subjection is distinct from what Foucault describes as "power through transparency": the reign of opinion, after the late eighteenth century, which could not tolerate areas of darkness and sought to exercise power through the mere fact of things being known and people seen in an immediate, collective gaze.[17] What radically differentiates the exercise of colonial power is the unsuitability of the Enlightenment assumption of collectivity and the eye that beholds it. For Jeremy Bentham (as Michel Perrot points out), the small group is representative of the whole society – the part is *already* the whole. Colonial authority requires modes of discrimination (cultural, racial, administrative...) that disallow a stable unitary assumption of collectivity. The "part" (which must be the colonialist foreign body) must be representative of the "whole" (conquered country), but the right of representation is based on its radical difference. Such doublethink is made viable only through the strategy of disavowal just described, which requires a theory of the "hybridization" of discourse and power that is ignored by Western post-structuralists who engage in the battle for "power" as the purists of difference.

The discriminatory effects of the discourse of cultural colonialism, for instance, do not simply or singly refer to a "person," or to a dialectical power struggle between self and Other, or to a discrimination between mother culture and alien cultures. Produced through the strategy of disavowal, the *reference* of discrimination is always to a process of splitting as the condition of subjection: a discrimination between the mother culture and its bastards, the self and its doubles, where the trace of what is disavowed is not repressed but repeated as something *different* – a mutation, a hybrid. It is such a partial and double force that is more than the mimetic but less than the symbolic, that disturbs the visibility of the colonial presence and makes the recognition of its authority problematic. To be authoritative, its rules of recognition must reflect consensual knowledge or opinion; to be powerful, these rules of recognition must be breached in order to represent the exorbitant objects of discrimination that lie beyond its purview. Consequently, if the unitary (and essentialist) reference to race, nation, or cultural tradition is essential to preserve the presence of authority as an immediate mimetic effect, such essentialism must be exceeded in the articulation of "differentiatory," discriminatory identities.

To demonstrate such an "excess" is not merely to celebrate the joyous power of the signifier. Hybridity is the sign of the productivity of colonial power, its shifting forces and fixities; it is the name for the strategic reversal of the process of domination through disavowal (that is, the production of discriminatory identities that secure the "pure" and original identity of authority). Hybridity is the revaluation of the assumption of colonial identity through the repetition of discriminatory identity effects. It displays the necessary deformation and displacement of all sites of discrimination and domination. It unsettles the mimetic or narcissistic demands of colonial power but reimplicates its identifications in strategies of subversion that turn the gaze of the discriminated back upon the eye of power. For the colonial hybrid is the articulation of the ambivalent space where the rite of power is enacted on the site of desire, making its objects at once disciplinary and disseminatory – or, in my mixed metaphor, a negative transparency. If discriminatory effects enable the authorities to keep an eye on them, their proliferating difference evades that eye, escapes that surveillance. Those discriminated against may be instantly recognized, but they also force a re-cognition of the immediacy and articulacy of authority – a disturbing effect that is familiar in the repeated hesitancy afflicting the colonialist discourse when it contemplates its discriminated subjects: the *inscrutability* of the Chinese, the *unspeakable* rites of the Indians, the *indescribable* habits of the Hottentots. It is not that the voice of authority is at a loss for words. It is, rather, that the colonial discourse has reached that point when, faced with the hybridity of its objects, the *presence* of power is revealed as something other than what its rules of recognition assert.

If the effect of colonial power is seen to be the *production* of hybridization rather than the noisy command of colonialist authority or the silent repression of native traditions, then an important change of perspective occurs. It reveals the ambivalence at the source of traditional discourses on authority and enables a form of subversion, founded on that uncertainty, that turns the discursive conditions of dominance into the grounds of intervention. It is traditional academic wisdom that the presence of authority is properly established through the nonexercise of private judgment and the exclusion of reasons, in conflict with the authoritative reason. The recognition of authority, however, requires a validation of its source that must be immediately, even intuitively, apparent – "You have that in your countenance which I would fain call master" – and held in common (rules of recognition). What is left unacknowledged is the paradox of such a demand for proof and the resulting ambivalence for positions of authority. If, as Steven Lukes rightly says, the acceptance of authority excludes any evaluation of the content of an utterance, and if its source, which must be acknowledged, disavows both conflicting reasons and personal judgment, then can the "signs" or "marks" of authority be anything more than "empty" presences of strategic devices?[18] Need they be any the less effective because of that? Not less effective but effective in a different form, would be our answer.

Tom Nairn reveals a basic ambivalence between the symbols of English imperialism which could not help "looking universal" and a "hollowness [that] sounds through the English imperialist mind in a thousand forms: in Rider Haggard's necrophilia, in Kipling's moments of gloomy doubt,... in the gloomy cosmic truth of Forster's Marabar caves."[19] Nairn explains this "imperial delirium" as the disproportion between the grandiose rhetoric of English imperialism and the *real* economic and political situation of late Victorian England. I would like to suggest that these crucial moments in English literature are not simply crises of England's own making. They are also the signs of a discontinuous history, an estrangement of the English book. They mark the disturbance of its authoritative representations by the uncanny forces of race, sexuality, violence, cultural and even climatic differences which emerge in the colonial discourse as the mixed and split texts of hybridity. If the appearance of the English book is read as a production of colonial hybridity, then it no longer simply commands authority. It gives rise to a series of *questions of authority* that, in my bastardized repetition, must sound strangely familiar:

> Was it a badge – an ornament – a charm – a propitiatory act? Was there any idea at all connected with it? It looked startling in this black neck of the woods, this bit of white writing from beyond the seas.

In repeating the scenario of the English book, I hope I have succeeded in representing a colonial difference: it is the effect of uncertainty that afflicts the discourse of power, an uncertainty that estranges the familiar symbol of English "national" authority and emerges from its colonial appropriation as the sign of its difference. Hybridity is the name of this displacement of value from symbol to sign that causes the dominant discourse to split along the axis of its power to be representative, authoritative. Hybridity represents that ambivalent "turn" of the discriminated subject into the terrifying, exorbitant object of paranoid classification – a disturbing questioning of the images and presences of authority. To grasp the ambivalence of hybridity, it must be distinguished from an inversion that would suggest that the originary is, really, only the "effect" of an *Entstellung*. Hybridity has no such perspective of depth or truth to provide: it is not a third term that resolves the tension between two cultures, or the two scenes of the book, in a dialectical play of "recognition." The displacement from symbol to sign creates a crisis for any concept of authority based on a system of recognition: colonial specularity, doubly inscribed, does not produce a mirror where the self apprehends itself; it is always the split screen of the self and its doubling, the hybrid.

These metaphors are very much to the point, because they suggest that colonial hybridity is not a *problem* of genealogy or identity between two *different* cultures which can then be resolved as an issue of cultural relativism. Hybridity is a *problematic* of colonial representation and individuation that reverses the effects of the colonialist disavowal, so that other "denied" knowledges enter upon the dominant discourse and estrange the basis of its authority – its rules of recognition. Again, it must be stressed, it is not simply the *content* of disavowed knowledges – be they forms of cultural Otherness or traditions of colonialist treachery – that return to be acknowledged as counterauthorities. For the resolution of conflicts between authorities, civil discourse always maintains an adjudicative procedure. What is irremediably estranging in the presence of the hybrid – in the revaluation of the symbol of national authority as the sign of colonial difference – is that the difference of cultures can no longer be identified or evaluated as objects of epistemological or moral contemplation: they are not simply *there* to be seen or appropriated.

Hybridity reverses the *formal* process of disavowal so that the violent dislocation, the *Entstellung* of the act of colonization, becomes the *conditionality* of colonial discourse. The presence of colonialist authority is no longer immediately visible; its discriminatory identifications no longer have their authoritative reference to this culture's cannibalism or that people's perfidy. As an articulation of displacement and dislocation, it is now possible to identify "the cultural" as a disposal of power, a negative transparency that comes to be agonistically constructed *on the boundary* between frame of reference/frame of mind. It is crucial to remember that the colonial construction of the cultural (the site of the civilizing mission) through the process of disavowal is authoritative to the extent to which it is structured around the ambivalence of splitting, denial, repetition – strategies of defence that mobilize culture as an open-textured, warlike strategy whose aim "is rather a continued agony than a total disappearance of the pre-existing culture."[20] To see the cultural not as the *source* of conflict – *different* cultures – but as the *effect* of discriminatory practices – the production of cultural *differentiation* as signs of authority – changes its value and its rules of recognition. What is preserved is the visible surfaces of its artefacts – the mere *visibility* of the symbol, as a fleeting immediacy. Hybridity intervenes in the exercise of authority not merely to indicate the impossibility of its identity but to represent the unpredictability of its presence. The book retains its presence, but it is no longer a representation of an essence; it is now a partial presence, a (strategic) device in a specific colonial engagement, an appurtenance of authority.

This partializing process of hybridity is best described as a metonymy of presence. It shares Sigmund Freud's valuable insight into the strategy of disavowal as the persistence of the narcissistic demand in the acknowledgement of difference.[21] This, however, exacts a price, for the existence of two contradictory knowledges (multiple beliefs) splits the ego (or the discourse) into two psychical attitudes, and forms of knowledge, toward the external world. The first of these takes reality into consideration while the second replaces it with a product of desire. What is remarkable is that these two contradictory objectives always represent a "partiality" in the construction of the fetish object, at once a substitute for the phallus and a mark of its absence. There is an important difference between fetishism and hybridity. The fetish reacts to the change in the value of the phallus by fixing on an object *prior to the perception of difference*, an object that can metaphorically substitute for its presence while registering the difference. So long as it fulfills the fetishistic ritual, the object can look like anything (or nothing!). The hybrid object, however, retains the actual semblance of the authoritative symbol but revalues its presence by resiting it as the signifier of *Entstellung – after the intervention of difference*. It is the power of this strange metonymy of presence to so disturb the systematic (and systemic) construction of discriminatory knowledges that the cultural, once recognized as the medium of authority, becomes virtually unrecognizable. Culture, as a colonial space of intervention and agonism, as the trace of the displacement of symbol to sign, can be transformed by the unpredictable and partial desire of hybridity. Deprived of their full presence, the knowledges of cultural authority may be articulated with forms of "native" knowledges or faced with those discriminated subjects that they must rule but can no longer represent. This may lead, as in the case of the natives outside Delhi, to questions of authority that the authorities – the Bible included – cannot answer.

Such a process is not the deconstruction of a cultural system from the margins of its own aporia nor, as in Derrida's "Double Session," the mime that haunts mimesis. The display of hybridity – its peculiar "replication" – terrorizes authority with the *ruse* of recognition, its mimicry, its mockery.

Such a reading of colonial authority profoundly unsettles the demand that figures at the centre of the originary myth of colonialist power. It is the demand that *the space it occupies be unbounded*, its reality *coincident* with the emergence of an imperialist narrative and history, its discourse *nondialogic*, its enunciation *unitary*, unmarked by the trace of difference – a demand that is recognizable in a range of justificatory Western "civil" discourses where the presence of the "colony" often alienates its own language of liberty and reveals its universalist concepts of labour and property as particular, post-Enlightenment ideological and technological practices. Consider, for example: Locke's notion of the wasteland of Carolina – "Thus in the beginning all the World was *America*"; Montesquieu's emblem of the wasteful and disorderly life and labour in despotic societies – "When the savages of Louisiana are desirous of fruit, they cut the tree to the root, and gather the fruit"; Grant's belief in the impossibility of law and history in Muslim and Hindu India – "where treasons and revolutions are continual; by which the insolent and abject frequently change places"; or the contemporary Zionist myth of the neglect of Palestine – "of a *whole* territory," Said writes, "essentially unused, unappreciated, misunderstood . . . *to be made* useful, appreciated, understandable."[22]

What renders this demand of colonial power impossible is precisely the point at which the question of authority emerges. For the unitary voice of command is interrupted by questions that arise from these heterogeneous sites and circuits of power which, though momentarily "fixed" in the authoritative alignment of subjects, must continually be re-presented in the production of terror or fear – the paranoid threat from the hybrid is finally uncontainable because it breaks down the symmetry and duality of self/Other, inside/outside. In the productivity of power, the boundaries of authority – its reality effects – are always besieged by "the other scene" of fixations and phantoms. We can now understand the link between the psychic and political that is suggested in Frantz Fanon's figure of speech: the colon is an exhibitionist, because his *preoccupation* with security makes him "remind the native out loud that there he alone is master."[23] The native, caught in the chains of colonialist command, achieves a "pseudopetrification" which further incites and excites him, thus making the settler-native boundary an anxious and ambivalent one. What then presents itself as the subject of authority in the discourse of colonial power is, in fact, a desire that so exceeds the original authority of the book and the immediate visibility of its metaphoric writing that we are bound to ask: What does colonial power want? My answer is only partially in agreement with Lacan's *vel* or Derrida's veil or hymen. For the desire of colonial discourse *is* a splitting of hybridity that is *less than one and double*; and if that sounds enigmatic, it is because its explanation has to wait upon the authority of those canny questions that the natives put, so insistently, to the English book.

The native questions quite literally turn the origin of the book into an enigma. First: *How can the word of God come from the flesh-eating mouths of the English?* – a question that faces the unitary and universalist assumption of authority with the cultural difference of its historical moment of enunciation. And later: *How can it be the* European *Book, when we believe that it is God's gift to us? He sent it to Hurdwar.*

This is not merely an illustration of what Foucault would call the capillary effects of the microtechnics of power. It reveals the penetrative power – *both* psychic and social – of the technology of the printed word in early nineteenth-century rural India. Imagine the scene: the Bible, perhaps translated into a North Indian dialect like Brigbhasha, handed out free or for one rupee within a culture where usually only caste Hindus would possess a copy of the Scriptures, and received in awe by the natives as both a novelty and a household deity. Contemporary missionary records reveal that, in Middle India alone, by 1815 we could have witnessed the spectacle of the Gospel "doing its own work," as the Evangelicals put it, in at least eight languages and dialects, with a first edition of between one thousand and ten thousand copies in each translation (see *MR*, May 1816, pp. 181–2). It is the force of these colonialist practices that produce that discursive tension between Anund Messeh, whose address *assumes* its authority, and the natives who question the English presence and seek a culturally differentiated, "colonial" authority *to* address.

The subversive character of the native questions will be realized only once we recognize the strategic disavowal of cultural/historical difference in Anund Messeh's Evangelical discourse. Having introduced the *presence* of the English and their *intercession* – "God gave [the Book] long ago to the Sahibs, and THEY sent it to us" – he then disavows that political/linguistic "imposition" by attributing the intervention of the Church to the power of God and the received authority of chapter and verse. What is being disavowed is not entirely visible in Anund Messeh's contradictory statements, at the level of the "enounced." What he, as well as the English Bible-in-disguise, must conceal are their particular enunciatory conditions – that is, the design of the Burdwan Plan to deploy "natives" to destroy native culture and religion. This is done through the repeated production of a teleological narrative of Evangelical witness: eager conversions, bereft Brahmins, and Christian gatherings. The descent from God to the English is both linear and circular: "This WORD is of God, and not of men; and when HE makes your hearts to understand, then you will PROPERLY comprehend." The historical "evidence" of Christianity is plain for all to see, Indian evangelists would have argued, with the help of William Paley's *Evidences of Christianity* (1791), the most important missionary manual throughout the nineteenth century. The miraculous authority of colonial Christianity, they would have held, lies precisely in its being both English and universal, empirical and uncanny, for "ought we not rather to expect that such a Being on occasions of peculiar importance, may interrupt the order which he had appointed?"[24] The Word, no less theocratic than logocentric, would have certainly borne absolute witness to the gospel of Hurdwar had it not been for the rather tasteless fact that most Hindus were vegetarian!

By taking their stand on the grounds of dietary law, the natives resist the miraculous equivalence of God and the English. They introduce the practice of colonial cultural differentiation *as* an indispensable *enunciative function* in the discourse of authority – a function Foucault describes as linked to "a 'referential' that ... forms the place, the condition, the field of emergence, the *authority to differentiate* between individuals or objects, states of things and relations that are brought into play by the statement itself; it defines the possibilities of appearance and delimitation."[25] Through the natives' strange questions, it is possible to see, with historical hindsight, what they resisted in questioning the presence of the English – as religious mediation and as a cultural and linguistic medium. What is the value of English in the offering of the Hindi Bible? It is the creation of a print technology calculated to produce a visual effect that will not "look like the work of foreigners"; it is the decision to produce simple, abridged tracts of the plainest narrative that may inculcate the habit of "private, solitary reading," as a missionary wrote in 1816, so that the natives may resist the Brahmin's "monopoly of knowledge" and lessen their dependence on their own religious and cultural traditions; it is the opinion of the Reverend Donald Corrie that "on learning English they acquire ideas quite new, and of the first importance, respecting God and his government" (*MR*, July 1816, p. 193; Nov. 1816, pp. 444–5; Mar. 1816, pp. 106–7). It is the shrewd view of an unknown native, in 1819:

> For instance, I take a book of yours and read it awhile and whether I become a Christian or not, I leave the book in my family: after my death, my son, conceiving that I would leave nothing useless or bad in my house, will look into the book, understand its contents, consider that his father left him that book, and become a Christian. [*MR*, Jan. 1819, p. 27]

When the natives demand an Indianized Gospel, they are using the powers of hybridity to resist baptism and to put the project of conversion in an impossible position. Any adaptation of the Bible was forbidden by the evidences of Christianity, for, as the bishop of Calcutta preached in his Christmas sermon in 1815: "I mean that it is a Historical Religion: the History of the whole dispensation is before us from the creation of the world to the present hour: and it is throughout consistent with itself and with the attributes of God" (*MR*, Jan. 1817, p. 31). Their stipulation that only mass conversion would persuade them to take the sacrament touches on a tension between missionary zeal and the East India Company Statutes for 1814 which strongly advised against such proselytizing. When they make these intercultural, hybrid demands, the natives are both challenging the boundaries of discourse and subtly changing its terms by setting up another specifically colonial space of power/knowledge. And they do this under the eye of authority, through the production of "partial" knowledges and positionalities in keeping with my earlier, more general explanation of hybridity. Such objects of knowledges make the signifiers of authority enigmatic in a way that is "less than one and double." They change their conditions of recognition while maintaining their visibility; they introduce a lack that is then represented as a doubling or mimicry. This mode of discursive disturbance is a sharp practice, rather like that of the perfidious barbers in the bazaars of Bombay who do not mug their customers with the blunt Lacanian *vel* "Your money or your life," leaving them with nothing. No, these wily oriental thieves, with far greater skill, pick their clients' pockets and cry out, "How the master's face shines!" and then, in a whisper, "But he's lost his mettle!"

And this traveler's tale, told by a native, is an emblem of that form of splitting – less than one and double – that I have suggested for the reading of the ambivalence of colonial cultural texts. In estranging the word of God from the English medium, the natives' questions dispense the logical order of the discourse of authority – "These books...teach the religion of the European Sahibs. It is THEIR Book; and they printed it in our language, for our use." The natives expel the copula, or middle term, of the Evangelical "power = knowledge" equation, which then disarticulates the structure of the God-Englishman equivalence. Such a crisis in the positionality and propositionality of colonialist authority destabilizes the sign of authority. For by alienating "English" as the middle term, the presence of authority is freed of a range of ideological correlates – for instance, intentionality, originality, authenticity, cultural normativity. The Bible is now ready for a specific colonial appropriation. On the one hand, its paradigmatic presence as the Word of God is assiduously preserved: it is only to the direct quotations from the Bible that the natives give their unquestioning approval – "True!" The expulsion of the copula, however, empties the presence of its syntagmatic supports – codes, connotations, and cultural associations that give it contiguity and continuity – that make its presence culturally and politically authoritative.

In this sense, then, it may be said that the *presence* of the book has acceded to the logic of the signifier and has been "separated," in Lacan's use of the term, from "itself." If, on one side, its authority, or some symbol or meaning of it, is maintained – willy-nilly, *less than one* – then, on the other, it fades. It is at the point of its fading that the signifier of presence gets caught up in an alienating strategy of doubling or repetition. Doubling repeats the fixed and empty presence of authority by articulating it syntagmatically with a range of differential knowledges and positionalities that both estrange its "identity" and produce new forms of knowledge, new modes of differentiation, new sites of power. In the case of the colonial discourse, these syntagmatic appropriations of presence confront it with those contradictory and threatening differences of its enunciative function that had been disavowed. In their repetition, these disavowed knowledges return to make the presence of authority uncertain. This may take the form of multiple or contradictory belief, as in some forms of native knowledges: "We are willing to be baptized, but we will never take the Sacrament." Or they may be forms of mythic explanation that refuse to acknowledge the agency of the Evangelicals: "An Angel from heaven gave it [the Bible] us at Hurdwar fair." Or they may be the fetishistic repetition of litany in the face of an unanswerable challenge to authority: for instance, Anund Messeh's "*Not that which entereth into a man's mouth defileth him, but that which cometh out of the mouth.*"

In each of these cases we see a colonial doubling which I've described as a strategic displacement of value through a process of the metonymy of presence. It is through this partial process, represented in its enigmatic, inappropriate signifiers – stereotypes, jokes, multiple and contradictory belief, the "native" Bible – that we begin to get a sense of a specific space of cultural colonial discourse. It is a "separate" space, a space of *separation* – less than one and double – which has been systematically denied by both colonialists and nationalists who have sought authority in the authenticity of "origins." It is precisely as a separation from origins and essences that this colonial space is constructed. It is separate, in the sense in which the French psychoanalyst Victor Smirnoff describes the separateness of the fetish as a "separateness that makes the fetish easily available, so that the subject can make use of it in his own way and establish it in an order of things that frees it from any subordination."[26]

The metonymic strategy produces the signifier of colonial *mimicry* as the affect of hybridity – at once a mode of appropriation and of resistance, from the disciplined to the desiring. As the discriminated object, the metonym of presence becomes the support of an authoritarian voyeurism, all the better to exhibit the eye of power. Then, as discrimination turns into the assertion of the hybrid, the insignia of authority becomes a mask, a mockery. After our experience of the native interrogation, it is difficult to agree entirely with Fanon that the psychic choice is to "turn white or disappear."[27] There is the more ambivalent, third choice: camouflage, mimicry, black skins/white masks. "Mimicry reveals something in so far as it is distinct from what might be called an *itself* that is behind. The effect of mimicry," writes Lacan, "is camouflage, in the strictly technical sense. It is not a question of harmonizing with the background but, against a mottled background, of being mottled – exactly like the technique of camouflage practised in human warfare."[28]

Read as a masque of mimicry, Anund Messeh's tale emerges as a *question* of colonial authority, an agonistic space. To the extent to which discourse is a form of defensive warfare, mimicry marks those moments of civil disobedience within the discipline of civility: signs of spectacular resistance. When the words of the master become the site of hybridity – the warlike sign of the native – then we may not only read between the lines but even seek to change the often coercive reality that they so lucidly contain. It is with the strange sense of a hybrid history that I want to end.

Despite Anund Messeh's miraculous evidence, "native Christians were never more than vain phantoms" as J. A. Dubois wrote in 1815, after twenty-five years in Madras. Their parlous partial state caused him particular anxiety,

> for in embracing the Christian religion they never entirely renounce their superstitions towards which they always keep a secret bent... there is no *unfeigned, undisguised* Christian among these Indians. [*MR*, Nov. 1816, p. 212]

And what of the native discourse? Who can tell?

The Reverend Mr. Corrie, the most eminent of the Indian evangelists, warned that

> till they came under the English Government, they have not been accustomed to assert the nose upon their face their own.... This temper prevails, more or less, in the converted. [*MR*, Mar. 1816, pp. 106–7]

Archdeacon Potts, in handing over charge to the Reverend J. P. Sperschneider in July 1818, was a good deal more worried:

> If you urge them with their gross and unworthy misconceptions of the nature and will of God or the monstrous follies of their fabulous theology, they will turn it off with a sly civility perhaps, or with a popular and careless proverb. [*MR*, Sept. 1818, p. 375]

Was it in the spirit of such sly civility that the native Christians parried so long with Anund Messeh and then, at the mention of baptism, politely excused themselves: "Now we must go home to the harvest.... perhaps the next year we may come to Meerut."

And what is the significance of the Bible? Who knows?

Three years before the native Christians received the Bible at Hurdwar, a schoolmaster named Sandappan wrote from southern India, asking for a Bible:

> Rev. Fr. Have mercy upon me. I am amongst so many craving beggars for the Holy Scriptures the chief craving beggar. The bounty of the bestowers of this treasure is so great I understand, that even this book is read in rice and salt-markets. [*MR*, June 1813, pp. 221–2]

But, in the same year – 1817 – as the miracle outside Delhi, a much-tried missionary wrote in some considerable rage:

> Still everyone would gladly receive a Bible. And why? That he may store it up as a curiosity; sell it for a few pice; or use it for waste paper.... Some have been bartered in the markets.... If these remarks are at all warranted then an indiscriminate distribution of the scriptures, to everyone who may say he wants a Bible, can be little less than a waste of time, a waste of money and a waste of expectations. For while the public are hearing of so many Bibles distributed, they expect to hear soon of a correspondent number of conversions. [*MR*, May 1817, p. 186]

Notes

I would like to thank Stephan Feuchtwang for his sustaining advice, Gayatri Spivak for suggesting that I should further develop my concept of colonial mimicry; Parveen Adams for her impeccable critique of the text; and Jacqueline Bhabha, whose political engagement with the discriminatory nature of British immigration and nationality law has convinced me of the modesty of the theoretical enterprise.

1 Missionary Register, Church Missionary Society, London, Jan. 1818, pp. 18–19; all further references to this work, abbreviated *MR*, will be included in the text, with dates and page numbers in parentheses.

2 Joseph Conrad, *Heart of Darkness*, ed. Paul O'Prey (Harmondsworth, 1983), pp. 71, 72.

3 V. S. Naipaul, "Conrad's Darkness," *The Return of Eva Perón* (New York, 1974), p. 233.

4 "Overall effect of the dream-work: the latent thoughts are transformed into a manifest formation in which they are not easily recognisable. They are not only transposed, as it were, into another key, but *they are also distorted in such a fashion that only an effort of interpretation can reconstitute them*" (J. Laplanche and J. B. Pontalis, *The Language of Psycho-Analysis*, trans. Donald Nicholson-Smith [London, 1980], p. 124; my emphasis). See also Samuel Weber's excellent chapter "Metapsychology Set Apart," *The Legend of Freud* (Minneapolis, 1982), pp. 32–60.

5 Jacques Derrida, *Dissemination*, trans. Barbara Johnson (Chicago, 1981), pp. 189–90; all further references to this work, abbreviated *D*, will be included in the text.

6 Conrad, *Heart of Darkness*, p. 45.

7 Friedrich Nietzsche, *Untimely Meditations*, trans. R. J. Hollingdale (Cambridge, 1983), p. 71.

8 Thomas Babington Macaulay, "Minute on Education," quoted in Elmer H. Cutts, "The Background of Macaulay's Minute," *American Historical Review* 58 (July 1953): 839.

9 See Ian Watt, *Conrad in the Nineteenth Century* (Berkeley and Los Angeles, 1979), chap. 4, pt. i.

10 See Conrad, "Tradition," *Notes on Life and Letters* (London, 1925), pp. 194–201.

11 See John Barrell's excellent chapter "The Language Properly So-called: The Authority of Common Usage," *English Literature in History, 1730–1780: An Equal Wide Survey* (New York, 1983), pp. 110–75.

12 Conrad, quoted in Naipaul, "Conrad's Darkness," p. 236.

13 See my "The Other Question – The Stereotype and Colonial Discourse," *Screen* 24 (Nov.–Dec. 1983): 18–36.

14 Michel Foucault, "The Confession of the Flesh," *Power/Knowledge: Selected Interviews and Other Writings, 1972–1977*, ed. Colin Gordon, trans. Gordon et al. (New York, 1980), p. 204.

15 See Sigmund Freud, *Beyond the Pleasure Principle*, trans. and ed. James Strachey (London, 1974), pp. 18–25.

16 Foucault, "Truth and Power," *Power/Knowledge*, p. 132.

17 Foucault, "The Eye of Power," *Power/Knowledge*, p. 154; and see pp. 152–6.

18 See Steven Lukes, "Power and Authority," in *A History of Sociological Analysis*, ed. Tom Bottomore and Robert Nisbet (New York, 1978), pp. 633–76.

19 Tom Nairn, *The Break-Up of Britain: Crisis and Neo-Nationalism* (London, 1981), p. 265.

20 Frantz Fanon, *Toward the African Revolution*, trans. Haakon Chevalier (Harmondsworth, 1967), p. 44.

21 See Freud, *An Outline of Psycho-Analysis*, trans. and ed. Strachey (London, 1973), pp. 59–61.

22 John Locke, "The Second Treatise of Government," *Two Treatises of Government* (New York, 1965), p. 343, par. 49; Baron de Montesquieu, *The Spirit of the Laws*, trans. Thomas Nugent (New York, 1949), p. 57; Charles Grant, "Observations on the State of Society among the Asiatic Subjects of Great Britain," *Sessional Papers of the East India Company* 10, no. 282 (1812–13): 70; Edward W. Said, *The Question of Palestine* (New York, 1979), p. 85.

23 Fanon, *The Wretched of the Earth*, trans. Constance Farrington (Harmondsworth, 1969), p. 42.

24 William Paley, quoted in D. L. LeMahieu, *The Mind of William Paley: A Philosopher and His Age* (Lincoln, Nebr., 1976), p. 97.

25 Foucault, *The Archaeology of Knowledge*, trans. A. M. Sheridan Smith (London, 1972), p. 91; my emphasis.

26 Victor N. Smirnoff, "The Fetishistic Transaction," in *Psychoanalysis in France*, ed. Serge Lebovici and Daniel Widlöcher (New York, 1980), p. 307.

27 See Fanon, "The Negro and Psychopathology," *Black Skin, White Masks*, trans. Charles Lam Markmann (New York, 1967).

28 Jacques Lacan, *The Four Fundamental Concepts of Psycho-analysis*, ed. Jacques-Alain Miller, trans. Alan Sheridan (New York, 1978), p. 99.

CHAPTER 9

The Angel of Progress: Pitfalls of the Term 'Post-colonialism'

Anne McClintock

In this 1992 essay from the journal *Social Text*, Anne McClintock argues against a narrative of progress in characterizing post-colonial nations. New forms of informal imperialism militate against simple economic measures of development, and secondary colonization constantly impedes "progress." She also notices the complexity and variety of "post-colonial" situations that undermine the ideal of a singular "post-colonial" condition that merits a single term. The essay is reprinted in shorter form in McClintock's important book, *Imperial Leather: Race, Gender, and Sexuality in the Imperial Contest* (1995).

> *His face is turned towards the past. . . . The angel would like to stay, awaken the dead, and make whole that which has been smashed. But a storm is blowing from Paradise; it has got caught in his wings with such violence that the angel can no longer close them. This storm irresistibly propels him into the future to which his back is turned, while the pile of debris before him grows skyward. This storm is what we call progress.*
>
> *Walter Benjamin*

To enter the Hybrid State exhibit on Broadway, you enter The Passage. Instead of a gallery, you find a dark antechamber, where one white word invites you forward: COLONIALISM. To enter colonial space, you stoop through a low door, only to be closeted in another black space – a curatorial reminder, however fleeting, of Fanon: 'The native is a being hemmed in'.[1] But the way out of colonialism, it seems, is forward. A second white word, POSTCOLONIALISM, invites you through a slightly larger door into the next stage of history, after which you emerge, fully erect, into the brightly lit and noisy HYBRID STATE.

I am fascinated less by the exhibit itself, than by the paradox between the idea of history that shapes 'The Passage', and the quite different idea of history that shapes the 'Hybrid State' exhibit itself. The exhibit celebrates 'parallel history':

> Parallel history points to the reality that there is no longer a mainstream view of American art culture, with several 'other', lesser important cultures surrounding it. Rather there exists a parallel history which is now changing our understanding of our transcultural understanding.[2]

Yet the exhibit's commitment to 'hybrid history' (multiple time) is contradicted by the linear logic of The Passage ('A Brief Route to Freedom'), which, as it turns out, rehearses one of the most tenacious tropes of colonialism. In colonial discourse, as in The Passage, space is time, and history is shaped around two, necessary movements: the 'progress' forward of humanity from slouching deprivation to erect, enlightened reason. The other movement presents the reverse: regression backwards from (white, male) adulthood to a primordial, black 'degeneracy' usually incarnated in women. The Passage rehearses this temporal logic: progress through the ascending doors, from primitive pre-history, bereft of language and light, through the epic stages of colonialism, post-colonialism and enlightened hybridity. Leaving the exhibit, history is traversed backwards. As in colonial discourse, the movement forward in space is backwards in time: from erect, verbal consciousness and hybrid freedom – signified by the (not very free) white rabbit called 'Free' which roams the exhibit – down through the historic stages of decreasing stature to the shambling, tongueless zone of the pre-colonial, from speech to silence, light to dark.

The paradox structuring the exhibit intrigues me, as it is a paradox, I suggest, that shapes the term 'post-colonialism'. I am doubly interested in the term, since the almost ritualistic ubiquity of 'post-' words in current culture (post-colonialism, post-modernism, post-structuralism, post-cold war, post-marxism, post-apartheid, post-Soviet, post-Ford, post-feminism, post-national, post-historic, even post-contemporary) signals, I believe, a widespread, epochal crisis in the idea of linear, historical 'progress'.

In 1855, the year of the first imperial Paris Exposition, Victor Hugo announced: 'Progress is the footsteps of God himself.' 'Post-colonial studies' has set itself against this imperial idea of linear time – the 'grand idea of Progress and Perfectability', as Baudelaire called it. Yet the *term* 'post-colonial', like the exhibit itself, is haunted by the very figure of linear 'development' that it sets out to dismantle. Metaphorically, the term 'post-colonialism' marks history as a series of stages along an epochal road from 'the pre-colonial', to 'the colonial', to 'the post-colonial' – an unbidden, if disavowed, commitment to linear time and the idea of 'development'. If a theoretical tendency to envisage 'Third World' literature as progressing from 'protest literature', to 'resistance literature', to 'national literature' has been criticized as rehearsing the Enlightenment trope of sequential, 'linear' progress, the term 'post-colonialism' is questionable for the same reason. Metaphorically poised on the border between old and new, end and beginning, the term heralds the end of a world era, but within the same trope of linear progress that animated that era.

If 'post-colonial' *theory* has sought to challenge the grand march of western historicism with its entourage of binaries (self–other, metropolis–colony, center–periphery, etc., the *term* 'post-colonialism' nonetheless re-orients the globe once more around a single, binary opposition: colonial/post-colonial. Moreover, theory is thereby shifted from the binary axis of *power* (colonizer/colonized – itself inadequately nuanced, as in the case of women) to the binary axis of *time*, an axis even less productive of political nuance since it does not distinguish between the beneficiaries of colonialism (the ex-colonizers) and the casualties of colonialism (the ex-colonized). The 'post-colonial scene' occurs in an entranced suspension of history, as if the definitive historical events have preceded us, and are not now in the making. If the theory promises a decentering of history in hybridity, syncreticism, multi-dimensional time, and so forth, the *singularity* of the term effects a re-centering of global history around the single rubric of European time. Colonialism returns at the moment of its disappearance.

The word 'post', moreover, reduces the cultures of peoples beyond colonialism to *prepositional* time. The term confers on colonialism the prestige of history proper; colonialism is the determining marker of history. Other cultures share only a chrono-logical, prepositional relation to a Euro-centered epoch that is over (post-), or not yet begun (pre-). In other words, the world's multitudinous cultures are marked, not positively by what distinguishes them, but by a subordinate, retrospective relation to linear, European time.

The term also signals a reluctance to surrender the privilege of seeing the world in terms of a singular and ahistorical abstraction. Rifling through the recent flurry of articles and books on 'post-colonialism', I am struck by how seldom the term is used to denote *multiplicity*. The following proliferate: '*the* post-colonial condition', '*the* post-colonial scene', '*the* post-colonial intellectual', '*the* emerging disciplinary space of post-colonialism', 'post-coloniality', '*the* post-colonial situation', 'post-colonial space', '*the* practice of postcoloniality', 'post-colonial discourse', and that most tedi-ous, generic hold-all: '*the* post-colonial Other'.

I am not convinced that one of the most important emerging areas of intellectual and political inquiry is best served by inscribing history as a single issue. Just as the singular category 'Woman' has been discredited as a bogus universal for feminism, incapable of distinguishing between the varied histories and imbalances in power among women, so the singular category 'post-colonial' may license too readily a panoptic tendency to view the globe within generic abstractions voided of political nuance. The arcing panorama of the horizon becomes thereby so expansive that international imbalances in power remain effectively blurred. Historically voided categories such as 'the other', 'the signifier', 'the signified', 'the subject', 'the phal-lus', 'the postcolonial', while having academic clout and professional marketability, run the risk of telescoping crucial geo-political distinctions into invisibility.

The authors of the recent book *The Empire Writes Back*, for example, defend the term 'post-colonial literature' on three grounds: it 'focuses on that relationship which has provided the most important creative and psychological impetus in the writing'; it expresses the 'rationale of the grouping in a common past' and it 'hints at the vision of a more liberated and positive future'.[3] Yet the inscription of history around a single 'continuity of preoccupations' and 'a common past' runs the risk of a fetish-istic disavowal of crucial international distinctions that are barely understood and inadequately theorized. Moreover, the authors decided, idiosyncratically to say the least, that the term 'post-colonialism' should not be understood as everything that has happened *since* European colonialism, but rather everything that has happened from the very *beginning* of colonialism, which means turning back the clocks and unrolling the maps of 'post-colonialism' to 1492, and earlier.[4] Whereupon, at a stroke, Henry James and Charles Brockden Brown, to name only two on their list, are awakened from their tête-à-tête with time, and ushered into 'the post-colonial scene' alongside more regular members like Ngũgĩ wa Thiong'o and Salman Rushdie.

Most problematically, the historical rupture suggested by the preposition 'post-' belies both the continuities and discontinuities of power that have shaped the legacies of the formal European and British colonial empires (not to mention the Islamic,

Japanese, Chinese, and other imperial powers). Political differences *between* cultures are thereby subordinated to their temporal distance *from* European colonialism. But 'post-colonialism' (like postmodernism) is unevenly developed globally. Argentina, formally independent of imperial Spain for over a century and a half, is not 'post-colonial' in the same way as Hong Kong (destined to be independent of Britain only in 1997). Nor is Brazil 'post-colonial' in the same way as Zimbabwe. Can most of the world's countries be said, in any meaningful or theoretically rigorous sense, to share a single 'common past', or a single common 'condition', called 'the post-colonial condition', or 'post-coloniality'? The histories of African colonization are certainly, in part, the histories of the collisions between European and Arab empires, and the myriad African lineage states and cultures. Can these countries now best be understood as shaped exclusively around the 'common' experience of European colonization? Indeed, many contemporary African, Latin American, Caribbean and Asian cultures, while profoundly affected by colonization, are not necessarily *primarily* preoccupied with their erstwhile contact with Europe.

On the other hand, the term 'post-colonialism' is, in many cases, prematurely celebratory. Ireland may, at a pinch, be 'post-colonial', but for the inhabitants of British-occupied Northern Ireland, not to mention the Palestinian inhabitants of the Israeli Occupied Territories and the West Bank, there may be nothing 'post' about colonialism at all. Is South Africa 'post-colonial'? East Timor? Australia? By what fiat of historical amnesia can the United States of America, in particular, qualify as 'post-colonial' – a term which can only be a monumental affront to the Native American peoples currently opposing the confetti triumphalism of 1992. One can also ask whether the emergence of Fortress Europe in 1992 may not signal the emergence of a new empire, as yet uncertain about the frontiers of its boundaries and global reach.

My misgivings, therefore, are not about the theoretical substance of 'post-colonial theory', much of which I greatly admire. Rather, I wish to question the orientation of the emerging discipline and its concomitant theories and curricular changes, around a singular, monolithic term, organized around a binary axis of time rather than power, and which, in its premature celebration of the pastness of colonialism, runs the risk of obscuring the continuities and discontinuities of colonial and imperial power. Nor do I want to banish the term to some chilly, verbal Gulag; there seems no reason why it should not be used judiciously in appropriate circumstances, in the context of other terms, if in a less grandiose and global role.

One might distinguish theoretically between a variety of forms of global domination. *Colonization* involves direct territorial appropriation of another geopolitical entity, combined with forthright exploitation of its resources and labor, and systematic interference in the capacity of the appropriated culture (itself not necessarily a homogeneous entity) to organize its dispensations of power. *Internal colonization* occurs where the dominant part of a country treats a group or region as it might a foreign colony. *Imperial colonization*, by extension, involves large-scale, territorial domination of the kind that gave late Victorian Britain and the European 'lords of humankind' control over 85% of the earth, and the USSR totalitarian rule over Hungary, Poland and Czechoslovakia in the twentieth century.

Colonization, however, may involve only one country. Currently, China keeps its colonial grip on Tibet's throat, as does Indonesia on East Timor, Israel on the Occupied Territories and the West Bank, and Britain on Northern Ireland. Since 1915,

South Africa has kept its colonial boot on Namibia's soil, first by League of Nations mandate, and then later in defiance of a UN General Assembly Resolution and a 1971 World Court Order. Only in 1990, having stripped Namibia of most of its diamond resources, was South Africa content to hand back the economically empty shell to the Namibians. Israel remains in partial occupation of Lebanon and Syria, as does Turkey of Cyprus. None of these countries can, with justice, be called 'post-colonial'.

Different forms of colonization have, moreover, given rise to different forms of de-colonization. Where *deep settler colonization* prevailed, as in Algeria, Kenya, Zimbabwe and Vietnam, colonial powers clung on with particular brutality.[5] Decolonization itself, moreover, has been unevenly won. In Zimbabwe, after a seven-year civil war of such ferocity that at the height of the war 500 people were killed every month and 40% of the country's budget was spent on the military, the Lancaster House Agreement choreographed by Britain in 1979 ensured that one-third of Zimbabwe's arable land (12 million hectares) was to remain in white hands, a minute fraction of the population.[6] In other words, while Zimbabwe gained formal political independence in 1980 (holding the chair of the 103-nation Non-Aligned Movement from 1986–1989) it has, economically, undergone only *partial decolonization*.

Break-away settler colonies can, moreover, be distinguished by their formal inde-pendence from the founding metropolitan country, along with continued control over the appropriated colony (thus displacing colonial control from the metropolis to the colony itself). The United States, South Africa, Australia, Canada and New Zealand remain, in my view, break-away settler colonies that have not undergone decoloniza-tion, nor, with the exception of South Africa, are they likely to in the near future.

Most importantly, orienting theory around the temporal axis colonial/post-colonial makes it easier *not* to see, and therefore harder to theorize, the continuities in inter-national imbalances in *imperial* power. Since the 1940s, the United States' imperial-ism-without-colonies has taken a number of distinct forms (military, political, economic and cultural), some concealed, some half-concealed. The power of US finance capital and huge multi-nationals to direct the flows of capital, commodities, armaments and media information around the world can have an impact as massive as any colonial regime. It is precisely the greater subtlety, innovation and variety of these forms of imperialism that makes the historical rupture implied by the term 'post-colonial' especially unwarranted.

'Post-colonial' Latin America has been invaded by the United States over a hun-dred times this century alone. Each time, the US has acted to install a dictatorship, prop up a puppet regime, or wreck a democracy. In the 1940s, when the climate for gunboat diplomacy chilled, United States' relations with Latin America were warmed by an economic imperial policy euphemistically dubbed 'Good Neighborliness', pri-marily designed to make Latin America a safer backyard for the US's virile agribusi-ness. The giant cold-storage ships of the United Fruit Company circled the world, taking bananas from poor agrarian countries dominated by monocultures and the marines to the tables of affluent US housewives.[7] And while Latin America hand-picked bananas for the United States, the United States hand-picked dictators for Latin America. In Chile, Allende's elected, socialist government was overthrown by a US-sponsored military coup. In Africa, more covert operations such as the CIA assassination of Patrice Lumumba in Zaire had consequences as far-reaching.

In the cold war climate of the 1980s, the US, still hampered by the Vietnam syndrome, fostered the more covert military policy of 'low intensity' conflicts (in El

Salvador and the Philippines), spawning death squads and proxy armies (Unita in Angola, and the Contras in Nicaragua) and training and aiding totalitarian military regimes in anti-democratic, 'counter-insurgency' tactics (El Salvador, Honduras, South Africa, Israel, and so forth). In Nicaragua in February 1990 the 'vote of fear' of continuing, covert war with the US brought down the Sandinistas.

The US's recent fits of thuggery in Libya, Grenada and Panama, and most calamitously in Iraq, have every characteristic of a renewed military imperialism, and a renewed determination to revamp military hegemony in a world in which it is rapidly losing economic hegemony. The attacks on Libya, Grenada and Panama (where victory was assured) were practice runs for the new imperialism, testing both the USSR's will to protest, and the US public's willingness to throw off the Vietnam syndrome, permitting thereby a more blatant era of intervening in Third World affairs. At the same time, having helped stoke the first Gulf War, the US had no intention of letting a new boy on the block assert colonial dominance in the region.

For three years before the second Gulf War, the US arms trade had been suffering a slump. After what one military industrialist gloatingly called the Gulf War's 'giant commercial-in-the-sky', US arms sales have soared. Nonetheless, if the US had the political muscle to resuscitate a nearly defunct Security Council and strong-arm a consensus through the UN, and the military capacity to make short shrift of 150,000 Iraqi soldiers and an estimated 200,000 civilians in one month, it did not have the economic means to pay for the war. Saddled with its own vast debts, the US has been massively paid off in reimbursements (an estimated $50 billion) by Saudi Arabia, Kuwait, Japan and Germany, so that it now appears in fact to have profited from the war to the tune of $4–5 billion. At the same time, most of the estimated $20 billion necessary to restore Kuwait will go to western, largely US, companies. The war has thus made ever more likely a global security system based on military muscle, not political cooperation, policed by the US's high-tech, mercenary army (and perhaps NATO), moving rapidly around the world, paid for by Germany and Japan, and designed to prevent regional, Third World consensuses from emerging. Far from heralding the end of imperial intervention, the second Gulf War simply marks a new kind of interventionism. Not only is the term 'post-colonial' inadequate to theorize these dynamics, it actively obscures the continuities and discontinuities of US power around the globe.

While some countries may be 'post-colonial' with respect to their erstwhile European masters, they may not be 'post-colonial' with respect to their new colonizing neighbours. Both Mozambique and East Timor, for example, became 'post-colonial' at much the same time, when the Portuguese empire decamped in the mid-seventies, and both remain cautionary tales against the utopian promise and global sweep of the preposition 'post'. In East Timor, the beds of the Portuguese were scarcely cold before the Indonesians invaded, in an especially violent colonial occupation that has lasted nearly two decades. The colonial travail of the East Timoreans has gone largely unprotested by the UN – the familiar plight of countries whose pockets aren't deep, and whose voices don't carry.

In Mozambique, on the other hand, after three centuries of colonial drubbing, the Portuguese were ousted in 1975 by Frelimo, Mozambique's socialist independence movement. But across the border, white Rhodesians, resentful of Mozambique's independence and socialist promise, spawned the Mozambique National Resistance (MNR), a bandit army bent only on sowing ruin. After Zimbabwe itself became politically independent of Britain in 1980, the MNR has continued to be sponsored by South Africa. A decade of the MNR's killing-raids and South Africa's predations has subjected the country to a fatal blood-letting and displaced nearly two million people, in a war so catastrophic that Frelimo has been forced to renounce Marxism and consider shaking hands with the bandits. Now Mozambique is in every sense a country on its knees. What might have been a 'post-colonial' showpiece has instead become the killing-fields of Southern Africa.

Yet neither the term 'post-colonial' nor 'neo-colonial' is truly adequate to account for the MNR. Neo-colonialism is not simply a repeat performance of colonialism, nor is it a slightly more complicated, Hegelian merging of 'tradition' and 'colonialism' into some new, historic hybrid. In recent years, the MNR has become inextricably shaped around local inter-ethnic rivalries, distinct religious beliefs, and notions of time and causality (especially ancestral intervention) which cannot be reduced to a western schema of linear time. More complex terms and analyses, of alternative times, histories and causalities, are required to deal with complexities that cannot be served under the single rubric 'post-colonialism'.

Singular universals such as 'the post-colonial intellectual' obscure international disparities in cultural power, electronic technology and media information. The role of 'Africa' in 'post-colonial theory' is different from the role of 'post-colonial theory' in Africa. In 1987, UNESCO calculated that Africa was spending only 0.3% of the world's $207 billion allocated to scientific research and development.[8] In 1975 the entire continent had only 180 daily newspapers, compared with 1,900 for the US, out of a world total of 7,970. By 1984, the number of African dailies dropped to 150, then staggered back to 180 in 1987 (the same figure as in 1955). In 1980, the annual production of films in the continent was 70. In contrast, the production of long films in Asia was 2,300 in 1965, and 2,100 in 1987.[9] The film industry in India remains the largest in the world, while Africa's share of TV receivers, radio transmitters and electronic hardware is minuscule.

The term 'post-colonialism' is prematurely celebratory and obfuscatory in more ways than one. The term becomes especially unstable with respect to women. In a world where women do two-thirds of the world's work, earn 10% of the world's income, and own less than 1% of the world's property, the promise of 'post-colonialism' has been a history of hopes postponed. It has generally gone unremarked that the national bourgeoisies and kleptocracies that stepped into the shoes of 'post-colonial' 'progress', and industrial 'modernisation' have been overwhelmingly and violently male. No 'post-colonial' state anywhere has granted women and men equal access to the rights and resources of the nation-state. Not only have the needs of 'post-colonial nations' been largely identified with male conflicts, male aspirations and male interests, but the very representation of 'national' power rests on prior constructions of gender power. Thus even for Fanon, who at other moments knew better, both 'colonizer' and 'colonized' are unthinkingly male: 'The look that the native turns on the settler is a look of lust... to sit at the settlers' table, to sleep in the settler's bed, with his wife, if possible. The colonized man is an envious man.'[10] Despite most anti-colonial nationalisms' investment in the rhetoric of popular unity, most have served more properly to institutionalize gender power. Marital laws, in particular, have served to ensure that for women citizenship in the nation-state is mediated by the marriage relation, so that a woman's *political* relation to the nation is submerged in, and subordinated to, her *social* relation to a man through marriage.

The global militarization of masculinity and the feminization of poverty have thus ensured that women and men do not live 'post-coloniality' in the same way, or share the same singular 'post-colonial condition'. In most countries, IMF and World Bank policy favoured cash-cropping and capital surplus in the systematic interests of men, and formed a predictable pattern where men were given the training, the inter-national aid, the machinery, the loans and cash. In Africa, women farmers produce 65%–80% of all agricultural produce, yet do not own the land they work, and are consistently by-passed by aid programs and 'development' projects.

The blame for women's continuing plight cannot be laid only at the door of colonialism, or footnoted and forgotten as a passing 'neo-colonial' dilemma. The continuing weight of male economic self-interest and the varied undertows of patri-archal Christianity, Confucianism and Islamic fundamentalism continue to legitimize women's barred access to the corridors of political and economic power, their persist-ent educational disadvantage, the bad infinity of the domestic double day, unequal child care, gendered malnutrition, sexual violence, genital mutilation and domestic battery. The histories of these male policies, while deeply implicated in colonialism, are not reducible to colonialism, and cannot be understood without distinct theories of gender power.

Finally, bogus universals such as 'the post-colonial woman' or 'the post-colonial other' obscure relations not only between men and women, but among women. Relations between a French tourist and the Haitian woman who washes her bed linen are not the same as the relations between their husbands. Films like *Out Of Africa*, clothing chains like Banana Republic and perfumes like 'Safari' all peddle neo-colonial nostalgia for an era when European women in brisk white shirts and safari green supposedly found freedom in empire: running coffee plantations, killing lions and zipping about the colonial skies in airplanes – an entirely misbegotten commercialization of white women's 'liberation' that has not made it any easier for women of color to form alliances with white women anywhere, let alone parry criti-cisms by male nationalists already hostile to feminism.

How, then, does one account for the curious ubiquity of the preposition 'post' in contemporary intellectual life, not only in the universities, but in newspaper columns and on the lips of media moguls? In the case of 'post-colonialism', at least, part of the reason is its academic marketability. While admittedly another p-c word, 'post-colonialism' is arguably more palatable and less foreign-sounding to sceptical deans than 'Third World Studies'. It also has a less accusatory ring than 'Studies in Neo-colonialism', say, or 'Fighting Two Colonialisms'. It is more global, and less fuddy-duddy, than 'Commonwealth Studies'. The term borrows, moreover, on the dazzling marketing success of the term 'post-modernism'. As the organizing rubric of an emerging field of disciplinary studies and an archive of knowledge, the term 'post-colonialism' makes possible the marketing of a whole new generation of panels, articles, books and courses.

The enthusiasm for 'post-' words, however, ramifies beyond the corridors of the university. The recurrent, almost ritualistic incantation of the preposition 'post' is a symptom, I believe, of a global crisis in ideologies of the future, particularly the ideology of 'progress'.

The first seismic shift in the idea of 'progress' came with the abrupt shift in US Third World policy in the 1980s. Emboldened in the 1950s by its economic 'great leap forward' (space, again, is time), the US was empowered to insist globally that other countries could 'progress' only if they followed the US road to mass-consumption prosperity. W. W. Rostow's 'Non-Communist Manifesto' envisaged the so-called 'developing' nations as passing through similar stages of development, out of tradition-bound poverty, through an industrialized modernization overseen by the US, the World Bank and the IMF, to mass-consumer prosperity. Nonetheless, except for the Japanese 'miracle' and the Four Tigers (Taiwan, Singapore, Hong Kong and South Korea), the vast majority of the world's populations have, since the 1940s, come to lag even further behind the consumer standards set by the west.[11]

Then, between 1979 (the second oil shock) and 1982 (the Mexican default), the world economy began to creak. Increasingly, it became clear that the US was no longer destined to be the only economic power of the future. Hobbled by its phenomenal debts, and increasingly diminished by the twin shadows of Japan and Germany, the US summarily abandoned the doctrine of global 'progress' and 'development'. During the Reagan era, the US instituted instead a bullying debt-servicing policy towards poorer countries, bolstered by aggressive competition with them on the market, and defended by sporadic fits of military gangsterism, as in Grenada and Panama. The cataclysmic war in the Gulf served only to underscore the point.

For many poorer countries, the shift in US policy meant abandoning overnight the fata morgana of capitalist 'progress', and settling for chronically stricken positions in the global hierarchy. Henceforth, they could aspire only to tighten their belts, service their debts, and maintain some credit. In 1974, Africa's debt–service ratio was a manageable 4.6%. Thirteen years later it had rocketed to 25%.[12] But the collapse of the US model of 'progress' has also meant the collapse, for many regimes, of the legitimacy of their national policies, in the panicky context of world-wide economic crisis, ecological calamity and spiralling popular desperation. Indeed, perhaps one reason, at least, for the burgeoning, populist appeal of Islamic fundamentalism is the failure of other models of capitalist or communist 'progress'. As a senior Libyan aide, Major Abdel-Salam Jalloud, has said of the destiny of the FIS in Algeria: 'It's impossible to turn back. The FIS has an appointment with history; it will not miss it.'[13]

A monotonously simple pattern has emerged. Despite the hauling down of colonial flags in the 1950s revamped economic imperialism has ensured that America and the former European colonial powers have become richer, while, with a tiny scattering of exceptions, their ex-colonies have become poorer.[14] In Africa before decolonization, World Bank projects were consistently supportive of the colonial economies. Since formal decolonization, contrary to the World Bank's vaunted technical 'neutrality' and myth of expertise, projects have aggressively favoured the refinement and streamlining of surplus extraction, cash crop exports, and large-scale projects going to the highest bidders, fostering thereby cartels and foreign operators, and ensuring that profits tumble into the coffers of the multinationals. During 1986, Africa lost $19 billion through collapsed export prices alone.[15] In 1988 and 1989, debt service payments from the Third World to the US were $100 billion.[16] At the same time, as Fanon predicted, Third World kleptocracies, military oligarchies and warlords have scrambled over each other to plunder the system. To protect these interests, the tiny, male elites of 'developing' countries have spent almost 2.4 trillion on the military between 1960 and 1987, almost twice the size of the entire Third World debt.[17] Now, after the 1980s' 'desperate decade' of debt, drought and destabilization, the majority of Third World countries are poorer than they were a decade ago.[18]

Twenty-eight million Africans face famine, and in countries like Mozambique, Ethiopia, Zaire and the Sudan the economies have simply collapsed.

The US's 'development' myth has had a grievous impact on global ecologies. By 1989, the World Bank had $225 billion in commitments to poorer countries, on condition that they, in turn, endure the purgatory of 'structural adjustment', export their way to 'progress', cut government spending on education and social services (with the axe falling most cruelly on women), devalue their currencies, remove trade barriers and raze their forests to pay their debts.[19] Under the financial spell of the US (and now Japan), and in the name of the fairy-tale of unlimited technological and capital 'growth', the World Bank engineered one ecological disaster after another: the Indonesian Transmigrasi programme, the Amazonian Grande Carajas iron-ore and strip-mining project, and Tucurui Dam deforestation project, and so on. The Polonordeste scheme in Brazil carved a paved highway through Amazonia, luring timber, mining and cattle ranching interests into the region with such calamitous impact that in May 1987 even the President of the World Bank, Mr Barber Conable, confessed he found the devastation 'sobering'.[20]

The Four 'miracle' Tigers have paid for progress with landscapes pitted with poisoned water, toxic soil, denuded mountains and dead coral seas. In 'miracle' Taiwan, an estimated 20% of the country's farmland is polluted by industrial waste, and 30% of the rice crops contain unsafe levels of heavy metals, mercury and cadmium.[21] A World Bank report in 1989 concluded gloomily that 'adjustment programs' carry the by-product that 'people below the poverty line will probably suffer irreparable damage in health, nutrition and education'.[22] Now Japan, insatiably hungry for timber and raw resources, is the major foreign aid donor, to the tune of $10 billion. In short, the World Bank and IMF 'road to progress' has proven a short road to what Susan George has called 'a fate worse than debt'.

To compound matters, the collapse of the US myth of 'progress' was swiftly followed by the collapse of the Soviet Union, which dragged down with it an entire master narrative of communist 'progress'. The zig-zag of Hegelian-Marxist 'progress', managed by a bureaucratic, command economy, had been destined to arrive ineluctably at its own utopian destination. The toppling of the Soviet Empire has meant, for many, the loss of a certain privileged relation to history as the epic unfolding of linear, if spasmodic, progress, and with it the promise that the bureaucratic, communist economy could one day outstrip the US in providing consumer abundance for all. As a result, there has also been some loss of political certitude in the inevitable role of the male (and, as it turns out, white) industrial working class as the privileged agent of history. If the bureaucracy of the Soviet Union fell, it was not under the weight of popular, industrial mobilization, but rather under the double weight of its economic corruption and manic military spending. The irony is not lost that the ascendant economies of Japan and Germany were historically denied the unsupportable burden of the arms race. Thus, despite the fact that men are slaughtering each other around the globe with increased dedication, there has been a certain loss of faith in masculine militarism as the inevitable guarantee of historical 'progress'. For the first time in history, moreover, the idea of industrial 'progress' impelled by technocratic 'development' is meeting the limits of the world's natural resources.

Ironically, the last zone on earth to embrace the ideology of capitalist 'development' may be the one now controlled by Mr Yeltsin and his allies. The world has watched awestruck as Yeltsin and his fellow-travellers swerved dizzyingly off the iron road of the centralized, communist, command economy, and lurched bumpily onto the capitalist road of decentralization, powered no longer by the dialectic as the motor and guarantee of 'progress', but by tear-away competition and mad marketeering. Never mind that this swerve is likely to unleash a disaster on a scale comparable to the famines that followed the original Bolshevik revolution, nor that the rough beast that slouches out of the chaos may, indeed, not be western capitalism at all, but a particularly grisly form of fascism.

For both communism and capitalism, 'progress' was both a journey forward and the beginning of a return; for as in all narratives of 'progress', to travel the 'road of progress' was to cover, once again, a road already travelled. The metaphor of the 'road' or 'railway' guaranteed that 'progress' was a fait accompli. The journey was possible because the road had already been made (by God, the Dialectic, the Weltgeist, the Cunning of History, the Law of the Market, Scientific Materialism). As Hegel decreed, 'progress' in the realm of history was possible because it has already been accomplished in the realm of 'truth'. But now, if the owl of Minerva has taken flight, there is widespread uncertainty whether it will return.

The collapse of both capitalist and communist teleologies of 'progress' has resulted in a doubled and overdetermined crisis in images of future time. The uncertain global situation has spawned a widespread sense of historic abandonment, of which the apocalyptic, time-stopped prevalence of 'post-' words is only one symptom. The storm of 'progress' had blown for both communism and capitalism alike. Now the wind is stilled, and the angel with hunched wings broods over the wreckage at its feet. In this calm at 'the end of history', the millennium has come too soon, and the air seems thick with omen.

Francis Fukuyama has declared history dead. Capitalism, he claims, has won the grand agon with communism, and is now 'post-historic'. Third World countries lag behind in the zone of the 'historic', where matters are decided by force.[23] Far from the 'end of history' and the triumph of US consumer capitalism, however, the new order of the day is most likely to be multi-polar competition between the four currently decisive regions of the world: Japan, the United States, Fortress Europe and the Middle East. The arms trade will continue, as the military-industrial wizards of Armageddon turn their attention from cold war scenarios to multiple, dispersed wars of attrition, fought by the US mercenary army and other proxies, and paid for by Japan and Germany. Within the US, with the vanishing of international communism as a rationale for militarism, new enemies will be found: the drug war, international 'terrorism', Japan, feminists, the PC hordes and 'tenured radicals', lesbians and gays, and any number of international 'ethnic' targets.

For this reason, there is some urgency in the need for innovative theories of history and popular memory, particularly mass-media memory. Asking what *single* term might adequately replace 'post-colonialism', for example, begs the question of rethinking the global situation as a *multiplicity* of powers and histories, which cannot be marshalled obediently under the flag of a single theoretical term, be that feminism, marxism or post-colonalism. Nor does intervening in history mean lifting, again, the mantle of 'progress' or the quill-pen of empiricism. 'For the native', as Fanon said, 'objectivity is always against him.' Rather, a *proliferation* of historically nuanced theories and strategies is called for, which may enable us to engage more effectively in the politics of affiliation, and the currently calamitous dispensations of power. Without a renewed will to intervene in the unacceptable, we face being becalmed in an historically empty space in which our sole direction is found by gazing back, spellbound, at the epoch behind us, in a perpetual present marked only as 'post'.

Notes

1   Frantz Fanon, *The Wretched of the Earth*. London: Penguin, 1963, p. 29.

2   Gallery Brochure, 'The Hybrid State Exhibit', Exit Art, 578 Broadway, New York (2 Nov.–14 Dec. 1991).

3   Bill Ashcroft, Gareth Griffiths and Helen Tiffin, *The Empire Writes Back: Theory and Practice in Post-colonial Literatures*. London: Routledge, 1989, p. 24.

4   'We use the term "post-colonial", however, to cover all the culture affected by the imperial process from the moment of colonization to the present day.' ibid., p. 2.

5   During the Algerian war of resistance, over a million Algerians died out of a total of about 9 million.

6   Andrew Meldrum, *The Guardian*, Thursday, 25 April 1991, p. 13.

7   Cynthia Enloe, *Bananas, Beaches and Bases: Making Feminist Sense of International Politics*. Berkeley, Calif.: University of Colorado Press 1989, ch. 6.

8   Davidson, *op. cit.*, p. 670.

9   Kinfe Abraham, 'The media crisis: Africa's exclusion zone', *SAPEM*, September 1990, pp. 47–9.

10   Fanon, *The Wretched of the Earth*, p. 30.

11   See Giovanni Arrighi, 'World income inequalities and the future of socialism', *New Left Review*, 189, September/October 1991, p. 40.

12   Davidson, p. 669.

13   *The Guardian*, Tuesday, 14 January 1992, p. 9.

14   The international monetary system set up at the Bretton Woods Conference in 1944 excluded Africa (still colonized) and most of what is now called the Third World, and was designed to achieve two explicit objectives: the reconstruction of Europe after World War II, and the expansion and maintenance (especially after decolonization) of international trade in the interests of the colonial powers and America. The president of the World Bank and the deputy managing director are always American, while by tradition the managing director is European. See Cheryl Payer, *The Debt Trap: The International Monetary Fund and the Third World*, Monthly Review Press: New York, 1974, and *idem*, *The World Bank: A Critical Analysis*. New York: Monthly Review Press, 1982.

15   Davidson, p. 669.

16   Robin Broad, John Cavanagh and Walden Bello, 'Sustainable development in the 1990s', in Chester Hartman and Pedro Vilanova (eds.), *Paradigms Lost: The Post Cold War Era*.

17   Ibid., p. 100. Calculations are based on figures in Ruth Leger Sivard, *World Military and Social Expenditures 1989*. Washington, DC: World Priorities, 1989, p. 6. A few African socialist states, like Angola and Mozambique, tried to dodge the IMF and WB's blandishments, until national economic mismanagement and South Africa's regional maulings forced them to bend the knee.

18   The World Bank has concluded that 'fifteen African countries were worse off in a number of economic categories after structural adjustment programs.... A World Bank study found that the debt-ridden developing countries under structural adjustment programs performed as well as non-recipients less than half the time.' Broad et al., 'Sustainable development', p. 96.

19   See Susan George, 'Managing the global house: redefining economics', in Jeremy Legger (ed.), *Global Warming: The Greenpeace Report*. Oxford and New York: Oxford University Press, 1990.

20   G. Hancock, *The Lords of Poverty*. London: Macmillan, 1989, p. 131, n. 14, citing Barber Conable's speech to the World Resources Institute, Washington, DC, 5 May 1987.

21   Broad et al., 'Sustainable development', p. 91.

22   Ibid., p. 95.

23   Francis Fukuyama, 'Forget Iraq – history is dead', *The Guardian*, 12 August 1990, p. 3.

CHAPTER 10

Casualties of Freedom

Chidi Okonkwo

In this selection from his 1999 book, *Decolonization Agonistics in Postcolonial Fiction*, scholar and playwright Chidi Okonkwo examines what he calls the sense of "disillusionment" that he finds in fiction by African and Caribbean writers. Such disillusionment springs from a combination of external and internal factors such as the continuing use of force by neocolonial countries to impose their will on weaker adversaries and the persistence of political corruption in the political elites of post-colonial countries.

The Internal Rot and the External Plot

Addressing the 1968 Uppsala conference on 'The Writer in Modern Africa', Wole Soyinka declared that 'the stage at which we find ourselves is the stage of disillusionment', a time for the writer to cease looking backwards 'to prospect in archaic fields for forgotten gems which would distract the present'.[1] With this, Soyinka summed up the new themes and mood that had quickly emerged in African decolonization literature so soon after the euphoria of independence in the preceding decade. Disillusionment was not peculiar to African writers and peoples, however. In the Caribbean, writers who had taken stock of their societies' performance following the end of direct rule by European colonizers were drawing similar conclusions. Among Polynesian writers, Albert Wendt began serious writing on a note of disillusionment,[2] like Nigeria's Wole Soyinka, but for the Maori novelists disillusionment did set in only after an initial period of hopes in the promise of biculturalism collided with the reality of Pakeha conceptions of biculturalism as assimilation of Maoris into Pakeha culture. Maori novels like Patricia Grace's *Mutuwhenua* and Witi Ihimaera's *Tangi*, which express some cautious optimism over biculturalism, have accordingly been followed by novels expressing disillusionment with Pakeha bad faith, such as Grace's *Potiki* (1986) and *Cousins* (1992) and Ihimaera's *The Matriarch* (1986). Interestingly, Wendt's novels of the 1990s, such as *Ola* (1991) and *Black Rainbow* (1992), have denounced New Zealand Pakeha racism in stronger terms than any of Grace's novels, so that it is safe to assert that there is a common Polynesian disenchantment with the Pakeha's performance.

Critiques of the societies cover a broad range of ills. In African, West Indian and Wendt's Samoan novels, society is perceived as having re-enslaved itself through self-violation and a frenzied pursuit of the material trappings of Western middle-class lifestyles, while governments are portrayed as having betrayed not only the nationalist ideals of the decolonization struggle but also the opportunities for self-reconstruction that independence has opened up. In their exploration of these failures, some novelists have begun with colonial society itself, probing the inchoate society on the eve of independence for clues to the post-independence miasma. The novelists recognize that the destruction of indigenous structures of order by colonialism leaves an ethical crisis when the colonial regime departs, as the normative structures or institutions of colonialism are incompatible with the needs of a sovereign people. Colonial institutions were created to facilitate the plunder rather than the development of colonial subjects. As Belgium's building of a nuclear power plant in Zaire after the Second World War shows, European colonial powers never seriously contemplated relinquishing power to the colonial subject at some future date until compelled to do so by a combination of the decolonization struggles of the mid-century, the exhaustion of the European powers themselves in the Second World War, and the rise of America and the Soviet Union as competing superpowers.

As they move into the independence era, many novelists have foregrounded the relationship between internal failures and global political-economic forces. A crucial issue until the late 1980s was the Cold War rivalry between the West and the Soviet Bloc frequently fought by proxy in the ex-colonial world. Treating their ex-colonies not as human beings nor independent states but as mere counters in their strategic manoeuvres, the West continued to interfere secretly or intervene openly in these states' affairs to overthrow governments that they considered ideologically unacceptable, murder leaders whose policies were considered hostile to Western interests, foment civil wars to destabilize some countries, or install puppet regimes. These states have thus had to contend with government by brigands, morons, lunatics, psychopaths and zombies in army uniform thrust upon them by America and her allies. The role of the West in Third World poverty and instability has been that of pirates who, having plundered and sunk a merchant ship, take up positions along the shore and shoot any survivors trying to swim to safety.

The career of Joseph Desiré Mobutu (alias Mobutu Sese Seko) in Zaire, the former 'Belgian' Congo now renamed Democratic Republic of Congo, is illustrative, but the Mobutu tragedy has been replayed on such other theatres as Nigeria, Uganda under Idi Amin, Angola and Mozambique whose farmlands have been sown with millions of landmines, and many parts of Asia and the Arab world. Now reviled in the Western press as one of history's most venal leaders of a postcolonial state, Mobutu was enthroned in Zaire by the Americans following the 1963 murder of Patrice Lumumba, the first post-Belgian prime minister of the country, whom the West considered a communist. Thrice in the following three decades, American and French governments employed ruthless military force to crush attempts by the Congolese people to overthrow the vainglorious and corrupt Western puppet.

This cynical policy was publicly acknowledged and defended by former American Assistant Secretary of State for Africa Mr Herman Cohen in a BBC Television interview in May 1997 – when, with the Soviet Union extinct, the West decided to discard Mobutu and enthrone the same man, Laurent Kabila, whose insurgency they had previously crushed. Mobutu's venality was therefore literally the venality of his masters. One finds here the full force of Robert Young's observation that 'European philosophy reduplicates Western foreign policy, where democracy at home is maintained through colonial or neocolonial oppression abroad'.[3] The spectacle of Kabila on television signing away immense chunks of Zairean mineral and forest resources to predatory American businessmen even before the exit of his used-up predecessor pointed to a replay of the Mobutu tragedy under Kabila, who was literally a hostage to his sponsors.

Given the West's total control of the production and dissemination of information, these destabilization programmes are easily hidden from the Western public, and the immense human tragedy attendant upon them has been attributed to some primordial savagery that supposedly lurks in the sub-conscious of black peoples. The West's removal of a leprous dictator it installed promptly triggers massive rewriting of history and dissemination of the new authorized version by the mass communications media, historians and academics, many of whom belong to the think-tanks that developed the policies in the first place. Accounts of the Congo/Zaire tragedy rarely mention the successive French presidents who regularly hunted with Mobutu, the Franco-American crushing of Congolese will, or the century-long unparalleled cannibalism practised on the Congolese by Belgium (with France and America biting off sizeable chunks too) which at the time of independence in 1963 left the huge country of over thirty million people with fewer than two dozen university graduates.

Decolonization novelists have accordingly initiated a counter-discourse which probes the undercurrents of history for forces that have contributed to the contemporary malaise of the ex-colonial states. While novelists like Chinua Achebe have adopted a broadly humanist approach, portraying post-independence failures in terms of the moral failures of the people and their leaders, and some like V. S. Naipaul have offered racial-ontological stereotypes, many others in Africa and the West Indies have interpreted post-independence failures as symptoms of a much deeper problem rooted in the colonial and neocolonial experiences of the societies. Debates between Europe and the Third World are also accompanied with debates among the novelists themselves about the origins, nature and processes of the ex-colonial states' predicament, and the solutions to which they are amenable. In the three sections below, the various responses are examined according to their broad affinities.

The Crossroads of History

Withdrawal of the occupying power leaves behind a mutilated society faced with the task of constructing a new self out of the ruins of precolonial culture in the face of new, countervailing forces unleashed by colonization. The crisis thus generated is one of the central themes of such novels as *No Longer at Ease*, *A Man of the People*, *Mimic Men*, *Mystic Masseur*, *Elvira* and *Sons for the Return Home*.

Achebe's *No Longer at Ease* (1960), set in the last years of direct British colonial rule, condenses the situation profoundly into its title, 'No Longer at Ease', derived from T. S. Eliot's 'Journey of the Magi', from which Achebe also takes his epigraph and controlling metaphor:

> We returned to our places, these Kingdoms
> But no longer at ease here, in the old dispensation,
> With an alien people clutching their gods
> I should be glad of another death.[4]

The 'alien people' met by Obi Okonkwo are, ironically, his own people. Obi Okonkwo, son of Nwoye (now called Isaac) of *Things Fall Apart*, returns after university studies in Britain to a Nigerian society in the lethal grips of that 'mere anarchy' loosed 'upon the world' in *Things Fall Apart*. In his own Igbo society, social values have become inverted and institutions fragmented. In Lagos, capital city of the emerging Nigerian state, ethnic loyalties and an amoral ethic of ravenous self-gratification have spawned a culture of corruption. Obi's nascent nationalism, with its vaguely formulated vision of a supra-ethnic Nigerian state, is inadequate to deal with the contradictions inherent in this situation, besides clashing with his Umuofia people's perception of themselves as a family competing with strangers in a territory which none of them identifies as 'home'. Achebe thus uncovers the crisis of building a modern nation state out of an agglomeration of ethnic states that have been indiscriminately amalgamated by colonialists to serve their own economic and strategic interests.

Umuofia epitomizes the numerous ethnic 'nations' in Obi's Nigeria. To each of these rival groupings, the new state is an ill-defined and alien territory presided over by an equally alien government. Spontaneous loyalty or patriotic attachment to such an entity is impossible. The narrator reveals that:

> The Umuofians...who leave their home town to find work in towns all over Nigeria regard themselves as sojourners...When they have saved up enough money they ask their relations at home to find them a wife, or they build a 'zinc' house on their family land. No matter where they are in Nigeria, they start a local branch of the Umuofia Progressive Union. (*NLAE* p. 4)

A little reflection reveals that this perception of the state is a direct consequence of the adversary relationship between the colonizer and the colonized. The colonial regime was 'other', an alien conqueror and immoral despoiler. Cheating or robbing the colonial regime was a repayment in kind for its own depredations. In *No Longer at Ease*, this relationship is linguistically embedded in the designation of the civil service as the 'whiteman's establishment' where the occupant of a 'European post' does the 'whiteman's work'. The state as mere territory rather than nation is thus conceptually polarized into 'home' and 'beyond'. 'Home' is the ethnic state, the human habitation, a moral universe regulated by clear concepts of right and wrong, while 'beyond' is the frontier, spirit land, the realm of chaos in which a quest hero/heroine pits his/her wits against rivals and monsters in a struggle for a boon which must be appropriated on behalf of the 'home'.[5] In effect, Umuofia perceptions of the new social formation are conditioned by attitudes to the colonial regime, Igbo traditions of representative government and models of human self-extension enshrined in myths, legends and folk tales.

This archetype is widespread in early African and Polynesian novels. In *Things Fall Apart*, Okonkwo whose fame has spread from Umuofia 'home' to Mbaino 'beyond' is mandated to lead Umuofia's delegation to Mbaino to demand reparations for the murder of an Umuofia woman. The Umuofia orator who addresses the assembly refers to Mbaino as 'those sons of wild beasts' (*TFA* p. 8). A similar attitude is expressed towards Okperi by Umuaro in *Arrow of God* (p. 20). Samoans in Wendt's *Sons for the Return Home* maintain that 'Samoa was the navel of the universe: the world ended within the visible horizons and reefs. Anything beyond that was [chaos]' (p. 179), and in *Banyan Tree* the cosmos is 'the familiar and secure world contained within the coral reef' (p. 8). Seclusion, intimacy and security are strongly emphasized in Grace's *Potiki*. Here, the cosmos consists of small Maori communities like the Tamihana family and the Te Ope. In both *Tangi* and *Whanau*, the cosmos is Waituhi, where the Whanau a Kai 'live close together, clustered around the meeting house, the painted Rongopai, which is the heart of the village' (*Whanau* p. 7). Even in Ngugi's novels, whose subject is the history of the entire Kenyan nation, the 'world' in the first three novels is represented by the small Gikuyu communities bounded by the ridges, first introduced in *The River Between*. 'The ridges were isolated', Ngugi writes. 'The people there led a life of their own, undisturbed by what happened outside or beyond' (*RB* p. 3).

To Umuofia in *No Longer at Ease*, therefore, Obi's journey to England (which the community sponsored at immense personal sacrifice) to acquire university education is indistinguishable from his journey to Lagos to acquire a well-paid civil service job. The community, in other words, attempts to interpret and control the present through an existing paradigm. 'In our folk stories', one of the elders congratulates Obi, 'a man gets to the land of spirits when he has passed seven rivers, seven forests and seven hills. Without doubt you have visited the land of spirits.' Obi is now 'a little child returned from wrestling in the spirit world' (p. 51). This is only a short step to his installation in the gallery of the clan's legendary heroes (p. 54), and his equation with his famous grandfather 'who faced the white man single-handed and died in the fight' (p. 53). By extension of the paradigm, too, the clansman 'hero' working in the 'beyond' is viewed as the community's champion, charged with fetching its share of the nation's wealth (*NLAE* p. 33). The incompatibility between the colonizer's and the colonized subjects' interests, the justification for nationalist agitation for decolonization, now militates against the healthy development of the new state.

It is in these terms that Achebe explores the story of Obi Okonkwo, who sets out to eradicate bribery, immorality and other causes of social chaos but ends up succumbing to them.[6] Arthur Ravenscroft's description of Obi's story as 'a paradigm of a man caught between the irreconcilable values of different ways of life [African and Western]'[7] merely betrays that skewed sense of morality by which the West regards its own gargantuan levels of corruption as mere aberrations while treating the same phenomena in other cultures as racial characteristics. Unequivocally deflating the colonial regime's claims to moral superiority, an Umuofia man observes that '[white people] eat bribe...more than black men nowadays' (*NLAE* p. 33). Colonialism itself is literally a form of armed robbery on a national scale, and Jamaica Kincaid has put the case more bluntly but with self-critical irony in *A Small Place*:

> Have you ever wondered to yourself why it is that all people like me seem to have learned from you is how to imprison and murder each other, how to govern badly, and how to take the wealth of our country and place it in Swiss bank accounts?...You came. You took things that were not yours, and you did not even, for appearances' sake, ask first...You murdered people. You imprisoned people. You robbed people. (pp. 34–5)

What E. N. Obiechina rightly identifies as polarization between rural and urban settings[8] is at the more fundamental level of historical development better explained in terms of contradictions between 'home' with clearly recognized norms and the pre-creation inchoateness of 'beyond'. In many African and Polynesian novels, the scheme is really not bi-polar but tri-polar, the home-versus-beyond polarity being complemented by the little enclave that ethnic migrants have tried to consecrate as home-away-from-home in the urban chaos, such as the Umuofia Progressive Union formed 'six years ago' in *No Longer at Ease*, and the Osa Descendants Union who in Soyinka's *The Interpreters* want their 'son' Egbo to leave his job in the Foreign Office and become their 'enlightened ruler' (*Interpreters* p. 10). Wendt's *Sons for the Return Home* unfolds through these three settings: Pakeha New Zealand as chaos, the Samoan world reincarnated in New Zealand by Samoans, and then the Samoan motherland which like Umuofia clings to its image of pristine purity. In *Cousins* which advocates Maori exploitation of all the opportunities of modernization offered by the society, there are distinctions nevertheless between the Maori home, the Pakeha-dominated capital city, and the Maori home-in-the-city which Maoris create for themselves in their quest to achieve modernization without succumbing to westernization and/or Pakeha assimilation programmes. Thus, Makareta who rebels against her clan in *Cousins* nevertheless serves them with her modern education and bilingualism, from the knowledge that 'it's not sticking to the old ways that's important' but 'us being us, using all the new knowledge our way. Everything new belongs to us too' (p. 235). The pattern also exists, though less elaborately, in such novels as Merle Collins' *Angel* and Grace Ogot's *The Graduate*.

The home-beyond polarity persists through Achebe's *A Man of the People* (1966) and *Anthills of the Savannah* (1987) and actually receives some validation in the latter from the national government's irresponsibility. In the former, the moral chaos of 'beyond' is gradually overwhelming the 'home' order. The people who ecstatically welcome the federal minister M. A. Nanga in the opening scene of *A Man of the People* know that he is corrupt, but naïvely accept this as part of the political culture of 'beyond' which has nothing to do with 'home' (p. 2). By contrast, the local shopkeeper Josiah's cheating of a blind man provokes instant ostracism (pp. 84–6). A character aphoristically sums up the ethical principle behind this: 'Josiah has taken away enough for the owner to notice' (p. 86). Odili's father amplifies: 'the owner was the village and the village had a mind; it could say no to sacrilege. But in the affairs of the nation there was no owner, the laws of the village became powerless' (p. 148). In the increasingly numerous intersections and overlaps of village and nation, this distinction becomes increasingly blurred.

Uncanny similarities exist between Obi Okonkwo and the unnamed hero of Wendt's *Sons for the Return Home*, who is only three years old when his family emigrates to New Zealand on a twenty-year sojourn to garner their own portion of the fabulous wealth reported by preceding sojourners. Both have similar personal and family backgrounds (Obi's father is a catechist, the boy's a deacon, their mothers are fanatical though inconsistent Christians), suffer estrangement from their indigenous cultures and new societies, and get entangled in calamitous romance with socially 'unacceptable' women which ends in pregnancy and abortion. Finally, both are vehicles through which others try to live their own dreams. Of equal importance is the two novelists' use of the love affairs to demonstrate that irrational dichotomies in human relationships are not constructed by white people alone. In Achebe's novel *Clara*, the Igbo woman involved with Obi is unacceptable because she belongs to the *osu* caste – a caste of ritual outsiders. For Wendt's Samoans, the problem is reverse-racism: the hero's mother does not want a white daughter-in-law and pressures her into aborting the baby.

Part I of *Sons* explores the background for this development. In Part II, the private world created by the lovers collides with public truths of race, and is irreparably fissured. Part III takes the story into the future by returning the sojourners to their Samoan past and origins, a society whose claims of pristine purity contrast sharply with its frantic pursuit of what Fanon aptly terms 'a kind of lactification'[9] (Chapters 15 and 16). The house built by the hero's father with his new wealth reveals a sick addiction to bourgeois papalagi culture, an absurdly over-furnished, under-utilized, worshipped possession within which the mother struts about preening her ill-fitting plumage and displaying all the ludicrous self-conceit of the Third World *parvenu*. In the national capital, Apia, 'money and the quality of a person's English were two of the town's peculiar ways of estimating status... Good English was proof that one was educated, sophisticated, civilised, totally removed from an "uneducated villager from the back"' (p. 195).

Traditional criticism has treated protagonists like Obi Okonkwo and Wendt's un-named hero as epitomes of a 'child of two worlds' crisis, enlightened individuals alienated from their societies by their acquired Western values. This is mistaken, for the cultures encountered by the returnees are not the original cultures they had left behind but new social formations spawned by the West as its own parody. Whatever conflict does take place between the two is therefore better understood as one between two progenies of the West. The 'gods' clutched by Obi Okonkwo's people and Wendt's Samoans – the sum total of their values – are not those of the original culture but those of the new Western parody. As a member of a local Christian family, Obi was estranged from Umuofia traditions even before his departure, while Wendt's hero left Samoa when he was too young to receive permanent imprints from Samoan culture. Even the latter's birth through a Caesarean operation performed by a European doctor in Samoa becomes, in retrospect, a pointer to his entanglement with European culture.

Such heroes are not Prometheans ruined by philistine society or any malevolent gods, but potential Prometheans who failed as a result of flaws in their own charac-ter. Obi acquires Western self-centredness that resents his kinsmen's 'interference' in his affairs, but the clan still comes to his aid in times of trouble. And although Albert Wendt has revealed that his hero's disillusionment mirrors his own at a correspond-ing age yet, by defining the hero's abdication of his communal role and going into exile through the myth of Maui's dastardly attempt to gain immortality by entering Hinenuite-Po's womb through her genitalia, Wendt critiques it as nihilistic (*Sons* p. 217).

Corruption assumes such endemic proportions in Armah's *The Beautyful Ones Are Not Yet Born* and *Fragments* and in Wole Soyinka's *The Interpreters*, that it is indi-viduals rather than communities that can form islands of morality. Both novelists interpret moral and political decay in terms of apostasy, the perversion of indigenous values in their mindless pursuit of the ephemeral Western culture which Armah represents as 'the gleam' in the first novel. Though indigenous systems were not perfect, they nevertheless rested on moral foundations that are absent from the system spawned by colonialism. Armah's *Fragments* thus explores the perversion of the Akan cosmic model of past-present-future (or the ancestors-the living-and unborn) relationships into a Melanesian cargo cult, described by the hero Baako as 'the expectancy, the waiting for bounty dropping from the sky through the benign intercession of dead ancestors' (p. 228).

According to J. H. Nketia in *Funeral Dirges of the Akan People*, mourners seeking to portray the indispensability of the deceased ask him to keep in touch with sur-vivors through exchange of gifts, this being a ritual codification of the normal exchanges, through 'someone who happened to be going in the desired direction', between friends or relations living far apart 'in the old Akan society, in which personal communication was neither easy nor quick'.[10] In the cultural chaos left by colonialism, this mentality stunts indigenous initiative and creativity while promoting vulgar consumerism and self-nullifying mimicry of the West.

As self-emasculating desire and the object of desire itself, 'the gleam' is incarnated in *The Beautyful Ones Are Not Yet Born* as the symbolically named Atlantic Caprice hotel owned by Europeans, and in *Fragments* as the Kalifonia Moonbeam Café (p. 23), representing in each the 'brothel of Europe' to which, in Fanon's theory of colonialism, the senile local elite reduce their newly independent state.[11] But neither Armah nor Soyinka exonerates the poor from culpability. 'The poor are rich in patience', Armah's hero sadly comments in *Fragments* (p. 39), becoming totally demoralized and apathetic when called upon 'to resent the powerful' (p. 152). In the last three chapters of the *Beautyful Ones*, it is 'the poor' – the hero himself, the corrupt minister Koomson's own surly boatman and the harbour watchman – who, for various personal reasons, aid Koomson's escape. As a social critic, Armah is averse to deferring the villain's punishment, and Koomson's escape route is none other than the hero's latrine, but the hero's creeping after the fugitive underscores his own complicity in the politician's evil. Consequently, Armah objectifies the hero's contradictions in the image of the chichidodo, the bird which 'hates excrement with all its soul' but thrives on lavatory maggots (p. 45). One of his strongest comments on the phenomenon of corruption appears in the memorable last scene of the novel, when soldiers who have just overthrown the rotten civilian government rob travellers at check-points while the bemused hero watches and a chichidodo alights on the roof of the school lavatory.

In Soyinka's *The Interpreters* it is the elite who frustrate the emergence of the 'beautyful ones', but it is the masses' complicity that pushes Sekoni, an Ogun–Prometheus fusion, into a nervous breakdown. A qualified electrical engineer, Sekoni returns to Nigeria with patriotic visions of helping to transform the backward country into a modern nation through his skills. His revolt against misuse of these talents in administrative jobs within the civil service incurs a punitive assignment to Ijioha (p. 26) where, as Prometheus, he builds an electricity-generating plant for the people. But his vision is thwarted by an alliance of local and foreign interests who have made enormous profits from the people's deprivation. A similar rot pervades the academic community, whose intellectual and moral bankruptcy is embodied in the 'petrified forest' imagery applied to the gaudy furnishings and synthetic flora of Professor Oguazor's sitting room (*Interpreters* pp. 141–2).

Soyinka's 'masses' are not morally different from the elite, except insofar as they lack the power to indulge in their own greed and viciousness. Primitive tribal and religious chauvinism, hypocrisy, fickle-mindedness and a capacity for unimaginable cruelty are just some of their characteristics. The blood-thirsty mob which tries to lynch a petty thief (*Interpreters* pp. 114–18) will 'reform tomorrow and cheer the larger thief returning from his twentieth Economic Mission and pluck his train from the mud, dog-wise, in their teeth' (p. 114). The aptly counterpoised funeral processions, one for the rich Sir Derinola and the other for an anonymous peasant (pp. 111–13), show that through their greed, reverence for wealth and awed obsequiousness before the rich, the poor do indeed psychologically aid and abet the rich men's criminality....

Leadership and the Meretricious Path to Power

Analyses of the role of the leadership in many of these novels reveal varying degrees of the influence of those two philosophers of Third World decolonization: Frantz Fanon and Walter Rodney. Fanon identifies two types of post-independent leader: the feudal overlord and the modern head of government. 'Having been upheld by the occupying power', the feudal leaders feel threatened by radical new ideas that challenge the basis of their power; 'Thus their enemy is not at all the occupying power with which they get along on the whole very well, but these people with modern ideas who mean to dislocate the aboriginal society.'[12] With a consciousness moulded by colonialism, the post-independence elite:

> organise the loot of whatever national resources exist [and] use today's national distress as a means of getting on through scheming and legal robbery, by import–export combines, limited liability companies gambling on the stock exchange, or unfair promotion ...As far as doctrine is concerned, they proclaim the pressing need of nationalising the robbery of the nation.[13]

Independence transforms the national leader from an embodiment of national aspirations into 'the general president of that company of profiteers...which constitute the national bourgeoisie'. The bourgeoisie itself, 'afflicted with precocious senility', strives to perpetuate the inequalities of colonial society, and therefore taking on 'the role of manager for Western enterprise...[sets] up its country as the brothel of Europe'.[14]

Going farther back than Fanon, Walter Rodney surveys the entire history of imperialism as an ideology and colonialism as the implementation of this ideology. The survey leads to three conclusions: first, that Europe's present wealth is founded upon the dispossession of (ex)colonized peoples; next, that to preserve this wealth, Europe employs all her resources, including overt and covert violence, to subvert the aspirations of the new states; and finally, that much of the Third World's chaos results either from a scramble for what the colonizers had not bothered to appropriate, or from direct instigation of sectional violence by Western governments and multinational corporations 'so as to keep the colonized from dealing with their principal contradictions with the European overlord'.[15] These forms of intervention noted by Rodney come in addition to the more direct forms involving overthrows of genuinely nationalist governments and replacing them with self-seeking traitors.

A major problem of leadership in the post-independence era, therefore, is what may be described as the meretricious path to power: the emergence of a leadership of political prostitutes, adventurers and opportunists who are bereft of nationalist consciousness or vision, and see themselves not as nation-builders but as heirs to the powers and privileges of the colonial regime. West Indian novelists like George Lamming (*In the Castle of My Skin*), Merle Collins (*Angel*) and V. S. Naipaul (*The Mystic Masseur*) all locate leadership failures partly in such circumstances, with the mid-century labour unrest in the Caribbean providing a ready pool of discontented workers who become malleable instruments in the hands of crafty, demagogic opportunists. In Wendt's *Pouliuli*, the morally and intellectually bankrupt Malaga Puta becomes Malaelua's parliamentary representative solely by virtue of his kinship with

Faleasa Osovae, the ruthless king-maker of Malaelua (p. 124). 'His Excellency Joseph Koomson, Minister Plenipotentiary, Member of the Presidential Commission, Hero of Socialist Labour' in Armah's *The Beautyful Ones Are Not Yet Born* rose from mediocrity to national eminence as a thieving minister in an ostensibly socialist regime committed to eradicating the legacy of colonialism while actually perpetuating those same legacies. In Achebe's *A Man of the People*, Nanga rises overnight from the parliamentary back benches to ministerial eminence through crude opportunism (*AMOP* pp. 3–7), and Odili Samalu follows suit in execution of a puerile scheme to revenge himself on Chief Nanga, who has seduced his woman (pp. 68–73).

Despite the ideological differences between Achebe and Naipaul, *A Man of the People* and *The Suffrage of Elvira* share a common perception of the meretricious rise to power. Naipaul's narrator's comment that the 1946 elections 'had taken nearly everyone by surprise', but this time around 'people began to see the possibilities' of commercializing them (pp. 13, 46) resonates in *A Man of the People* in Odili's account of Nanga's rise to political eminence: 'It was easy in those days – before we knew its cash price' (p. 3). Politicians who buy their way to power feel no obligations to the electorate, and in *Elvira* Harbans not only reneges on his promises but also becomes transformed from humble candidate to arrogant legislator (pp. 196–9).

Whether the leadership gains power through chicanery or through Western intervention, the consequence is the 'precocious senility' identified by Fanon, and explored as the 'Man Child' phenomenon in Armah's novels. The lament of the hero's friend in *The Beautyful Ones Are Not Yet Born* finds echoes in many ex-colonial states:

> How long will Africa be cursed with its leaders? There were men dying from loss of hope, and others finding gaudy ways to enjoy powers they did not have. We were ready for big and beautiful dreams, but what we had was our own black men hugging new paunches scrambling to ask the white man to welcome them onto our backs. (pp. 80–1)

In *Why Are We So Blest?*, the central question is posed by a maimed veteran of the African revolution: 'Who gained? . . . Who won?' (p. 24). 'The situation and the problems are real', Ngugi wa Thiong'o insists in a short note appended to his own *A Grain of Wheat*, 'sometimes too painfully real for the peasants who fought the British yet who now see all that they fought for being put on one side.' Armah graphically illuminates this debacle through analogy with the automotive internal combustion engine, especially through the pun on '*l'essence*, that which is essential; and *l'essence*, petrol' (p. 26). In a revolutionary war, the true militants 'are the essence.' But 'that also means they are the fuel for the revolution . . . Something pure, light, even spiritual, which consumes itself to push forward something heavier, more gross than itself' (p. 27). The crippled veteran (counterpart of the crippled Mau Mau guerrilla in Ngugi's *Petals of Blood*) sums up the tragedy. 'All the best ones died. And many of those left are cripples.'

For Ngugi, the real beneficiaries of the freedom struggle are wartime collaborators like Hawkins Kimeria and Ezekiel Waweru 'those who ran to the shelter of schools and universities and administration' (*POB* p. 60), and modern reprobates like Nderi wa Riera, Chui and Mzigo in *Petals of Blood*, Mwaura in *Devil on the Cross*, and John Boy in *Matigari*. In the blighted villages, peasants scratch out a wretched livelihood from exhausted soil. The landless who cannot get wage employment are reduced to hawking goods, begging, or prostitution if they are women. Women like Wanja (*Petals of Blood*) and Jacinta Warringa (*Devil on the Cross*) and Güthera (*Matigari*) symbolize life blighted by the neocolonialist socio-economic system. The history unfolding in these and many other novels of disillusionment has become a grim fulfilment of the bitter *bon mot* of the disgraced collaborator, Karanja, in Ngugi's *A Grain of Wheat*: 'the coming of black rule would not, could not mean, the end of white power' (p. 35).

George Lamming's *In the Castle of My Skin* (1953) was published nearly a decade and a half before Fanon's *The Wretched of the Earth* was published in English translation (1967), and explores the independence struggle of a backwater Barbadian village. But so prophetic is its presentation of the career of the leader who emerges from this struggle that the novel may rightly be regarded as the prototype of the novel of post-independence disillusionment. A school teacher bearing the ominous name of Mr Slime is dismissed from his job (or compelled to resign) for scandalous involvement with the Head Teacher's wife. He quickly repairs his fortune by opening a Friendly Society and Penny Bank which his unsuspecting followers happily patronize. He promptly converts economic into political power by inspiring the workers and the general populace with his fraudulent vision of a golden Jerusalem in which they own the land and receive fair wages for their labour. But the overthrow of the English landlord, Mr Creighton, merely ushers in the vicious cycle of betrayed hopes and false starts whose re-enactment all over the ex-colonial world has thrown into question the value and logic of independence.

Lamming powerfully prefigures this vicious cycle that will be unleashed with Mr Slime's emergence as leader. From the opening scene, the artist-hero, the boy G., through whose sensibility the experience will be unfolded, comments on weather phenomena and other foreboding of a pattern of change without progress, climaxing in a cloud epiphany of betrayal in Chapter 6. In the epiphany tableau, one half of the sky is an Edenic scene while the other portrays elemental turbulence. Yet in the Edenic half a white man and a black man are engaged in a violent altercation:

> The figures were still, and they looked across at each other hard and steady as if they were involved in a common chaos which neither could understand but greatly desired to redeem...And as they looked the clouds curving over and about their heads made an arc of words that read: ARE YOU NOT A BROTHER? The shapes sharpened in outline, the white one getting heavier and darker. (p. 111)

Two developments are fused in the morphing of white into black within the epiphany tableau: the white man's adoption of a black mask and the black man's assimilation of the white's essence. Here one finds the proxy and the clone rolled into one, and the question of brotherhood asserts the sameness of white ex-ruler and black clone even as it articulates the bewilderment of the black populace confronted with this monstrosity. This prefiguration materializes in the collusion between the new leader Mr Slime, the Head Teacher who had forced him to quit teaching, and the white ex-landlord Mr Creighton, within the syndicate that dispossesses the peasants. The Old Man, also called Pa, properly traces the pattern back to Africa's collaboration with Europeans in the transatlantic slave trade (pp. 210–11). It is now that one appreciates the full force of the novel's epigraph, taken from Walt Whitman's poem 'This Compost': 'Something startles me where I thought I was safest.'

This phenomenon of the leader as pimp and clone is aptly described by Kamau in Merle Collins' *Angel*: 'As long as we know dat even when we have black people in these parts, is really roast breadfruit we dealin wid. Is other people outside control dem. De profits not staying here. De blackness is only something de eye feel it see!' (*Angel* p. 157). One of the most memorable images of Leader's government is that of a bucket with a hole in the centre (p. 210).

White colonialism behind a black face, or the colonizer sneaking back through the backdoor, is illustrated clearly in Okri's mythical *The Famished Road* in the unexpected return of a murderous white man after five hundred years' supposed absence: 'His face and his nose and everything was exactly the same except that now he was a Yoruba man with fine marks on his face', and he follows the time-proven principle of neocolonialist infiltration, 'The only way to get out of Africa was to become an African' (*FR* p. 483). In Merle Collins' *Angel*, the people's misfortune begins with the emergence of a traitorous self-seeker as leader of the independence struggle. Leader, as he is fondly known by his followers, is able to exploit the working people's grievances against their predatory employers, and weld those followers into a force for nationalist resistance. But intelligent, unemotional observers like Doodsie, the heroine's mother, are able to penetrate the mask and the rhetoric. 'Dat man like a lotta flash', she warns her brother Regal (p. 13). The discovery that Leader's boss (against whom he has been leading a struggle) is his bestman at his wedding (p. 17) points to the emergence of a puppet government. By the time independence is granted, he has emerged as a clone of the colonial ruler and plantation owners, a rampaging tyrant and despoiler of his own people, until his career is terminated in a *coup d'état*.

Angel is one of the few novels that work Big Power aggression into the plot and story line, the historical event being the 1983 murder of the populist Prime Minister Maurice Bishop and overthrow of his populist government by a military cabal sponsored by the American government. Collins' treatment of this historical event provides a chilling demonstration of how ex-colonial states' attempts at self-development and genuine independence are violently thwarted by Western government and business interests. To the American government, Maurice Bishop's attempt to free Grenada from the stranglehold of American multinational corporations, by constructing an international airport with Cuban help, was equivalent to 'communism'. The number of Grenadans slaughtered in that heroic crusade against communism has been suppressed in the interest of 'national security'. The operation itself retrospectively illuminates a brief earlier incident, in which Angel's younger brother Rupert plays Jimmy Cliff's famous anti-Vietnam War music, 'Vietnam', without understanding either the words or the message ('Vietnam' sounds like 'The Egg Nog' to him) – another instance of the Western powers forcing war and unimaginable devastation upon a people in the name of securing the world for 'free enterprise'.

A variation on this is the colonial dictatorship's installation of a handpicked mediocre leadership to be its successor and implement its neocolonialist objectives. V. S. Naipaul explores the careers of two such 'leaders' in *The Mystic Masseur* and *Guerrillas*. Set in a Caribbean territory on the eve of independence, *The Mystic Masseur* explores the meretricious ascent of Ganesh Ramsumair from obscurity to political leadership. Like Odili in *A Man of the People*, Ganesh drifts into politics to settle a personal score (pp. 151–60), but is then taken over by others who want to use him to settle their own personal scores (pp. 144–51). The relationship between him and the colonial regime is again paradigmatic of the incompatibility between nationalist and colonialist aspirations. Ganesh's initial mask of populist nationalism earns him the Colonial Office's hypocritical derision as 'an irresponsible agitator with no following' (p. 214). But no sooner does he discard his pseudo-patriotic mask by branding striking workers as communists than he is adopted by the colonial regime, knighted, appointed to the Legislative Council when his people reject him, and sponsored on foreign missions as his masters' mouthpiece. By that strange irony which sometimes patterns life on art, Naipaul's own career was later to climax in a similar decoration.

Ganesh's denunciation of the workers as communists reveals the animal cunning of his kind, for this is just the cry that guarantees a knee-jerk reaction of support from the American government. In *Guerrillas*, the playboy Jimmy Ahmed's exhibition of some leadership quality recommends him to the metropolitan establishment by whom he is promptly 'taken up', 'programmed', 'made famous' and sent back to his people as a Trojan horse of leadership to blunt the edge of indigenous nationalism. The moment his 'revolutionaries' seem to be taking the role seriously, the American government sends in the bombers and fighter planes. 'The Americans shoot everybody', Harry de Tunja reports, and 'are not going to let anybody here stop them lifting the bauxite' (p. 194). The eerie shadows cast by American helicopters over the land (p. 193) and the attack submarines lurking like death in the besieged country's waters (p. 201) come to life in Grenada in 1983, grim reminders that in the crushing tragedy of poverty and instability in many ex-colonial states it is the Big Powers who play the role of malicious deities.

Notes

1 Wole Soyinka, 'The Writer in a Modern African State,' in Per Wastberg (ed.), *The Writer in Modern Africa* (Uppsala: Scandinavia Institute for African Studies, 1968), pp. 14–21 (16 and 17, *passim*).
2 Albert Wendt has revealed to Michael Neill that the hero's disillusionment in *Sons for the Return Home* 'was also my own as a young writer'. Alley and Williams, *In the Same Room*, p. 107.
3 Young, *White Mythologies*, p. 14.
4 See T. S. Eliot, 'Journey of the Magi', *Selected Poems* (London: Faber and Faber, 1961), pp. 97–8.
5 See also Chidi Okonkwo, 'Chinua Achebe: the Wrestler and the Challenge of Chaos', in Michael Parker and Roger Starkey (eds.), *Postcolonial Literatures: Achebe, Ngugi, Desai, Walcott* (London: Macmillan, 1995), pp. 83–100.
6 Cf. Okonkwo, 'Chinua Achebe'.
7 Arthur Ravenscroft, *Chinua Achebe* (London: Longman, 1969), p. 20.
8 Obiechina, *Culture, Tradition and Society*, pp. 136–7, 140–54, *passim*.
9 Frantz Fanon, *Black Skin, White Masks*, trans. Charles Lam Markmann (New York: Grove Press, 1967), p. 47.
10 Nketia, *Funeral Dirges of the Akan People*, pp. 47–8, *passim*.
11 Frantz Fanon, *The Wretched of the Earth*, trans. Constance Farrington (Harmondsworth: Penguin, 1967), p. 123.
12 Ibid., p. 42.
13 Ibid., pp. 37–8.
14 Ibid., p. 120–3, 123–41, *passim*.
15 Walter Rodney, *How Europe Underdeveloped Africa* (London: Bogle-L'Ouverture, 1972), p. 250.

CHAPTER 11

The Anxious Proximities of Settler (Post)colonial Relations[1]

Alan Lawson

In this innovative essay from a Commonwealth Studies collection entitled *Postcolonizing the Commonwealth* (2000), Alan Lawson, a specialist in "settler" literature, applies rhetorical theory to issues such as property ownership raised in settler cultures like Australia and Canada.

I want to investigate the way in which a particular type of culture – the ones we've got used to calling "settler" cultures – deal with their unfinished business. In particular, I want to find a useful way to talk about how certain kinds of business, especially narrative business and textual business, remain persistently unfinished; how certain kinds of stories keep being recirculated and just how readily they can be reactivated, recognized, and read.

As a way of concretizing my discussion of this discursive return, I begin by reading an obscure recent Australian "political" text. During and after the 1996 election in Australia, an extraordinarily uninformed populist politician called Pauline Hanson drew apparently substantial popular support for some ugly racist views. In 1997 she established a new political party, called "Pauline Hanson One Nation" and to mark its launch, her support movement published an oddly anonymous book called *The Truth*. The circulation of the book was largely restricted to party supporters but it was designed to be quoted by them.

> There are many documented examples of horrific acts committed by blacks against blacks. A former chairman of the Northern Lands Council described his ancestors to me as 'murderous nomads'. A famous singer proudly described how his grandfather led raids to massacre men from a neighbouring tribe. So why are our schoolchildren now taught a false history that depicts Aborigines as a peaceful, non-violent people living in harmony with nature until the arrival of the brutal Europeans?
>
> Why are schoolchildren not taught some aboriginal tribes killed mixed-race babies by placing them on ants' nests? Why are they not taught about contemporary racism resulting in extreme violence between the various tribes...? (131)

The book then presents a number of "sources, some of which include eyewitness accounts of Aboriginal cannibalism" (132); it concentrates especially on tales of Aborigines eating their own children. These sources, it says, "refute the view of the aborigines held by the new class.... [the aborigines] weren't romantic liberals" (137). And, it goes on,

> Another example of [real] genocide is the Maori occupation of New Zealand. The
> Maoris arrived in New Zealand around 1000 AD. The land was occupied by a people
> closely related to the Australian Aborigines. The Maori exterminated them.... The
> ancestors of the Amerindians, celebrated by liberals in films such as *Dances with Wolves*
> and *Pocahontas* genocided [sic] the original inhabitants to dominate their land. (138)

Not unexpectedly, it then cites the now discredited view that there were several
waves of Aboriginal immigration into Australia and that in this process the ancestors
of contemporary indigenous people had – violently, indeed genocidally – displaced
earlier, truly original first peoples. Three narratives are dependent upon this bad
history: the revisionist racist claim that our violent dispossession is a minor part of a
longer history of violent dispossession founded by indigenous peoples themselves; the
liberal nationalist view that the Aborigines are really like us (since they're said to be
descended from Dravidians expelled from India); and the assimilationist nationalist
view that the Aborigines are Australia's first immigrants (139).

Intriguingly, we do know how to read this. At crucial moments, we can predict
what the next narrative element will be. We may recognize some of these elements as
belonging to the form of urban myths, but others we recognize as reiterations of
colonialist tropes, familiar from texts of the colonial period. But how do they function; how, more importantly, do we to explain their persistence?[2] Even when discursive tropes do not "make sense" empirically (in relation to contemporary knowledge)
or in terms of new ideological understandings, they not only have a tendency to
endure, but their irruption into newer discursive frameworks would seem to signal
moments of cultural crisis.

What Provoked *this* Moment of Cultural Crisis?

Most obviously it was two native land claim cases in the High Court of Australia. In
1992, in the now-famous Mabo Case,[3] the High Court of Australia established (in
fact, *re*-established after about 100 years) a limited legal form of "Native Title" and
thereby seemed to open up the possibility of a vastly increased number of Aboriginal
Land Claims. Most spectacularly, the Mabo decision concluded that the doctrine of
Terra Nullius, which had been used for two centuries in British and Australian law to
deny native land claims, was itself untenable because the land was certainly not
empty at the moment of "settlement." *Terra Nullius* has been taken to mean Empty
Land – more precisely it means Nobody's Land. It had the discursive effect of
"evacuating" the country of its indigenous inhabitants. It is perfectly clear to the
present white inhabitants that Australia was neither Empty nor Nobody's in 1788
and the first settlers knew it equally well. So the doctrine of *Terra Nullius* represents,
inter alia, a cognitive dissonance, a gap between knowledge and belief, or, to put it
another way, a kind of repressed knowledge. It's also "bad history."

In the December 1996 Wik Case, the High Court ruled that Pastoral Leases might
not fully extinguish Native Title since they do not confer absolute title. This
reopened an interesting possibility of coexistence. It also occasioned some mass anxieties about boundaries; it "threw up" the nation's inability to read coexistence, to
understand the grammar of proximity. The anxiety signalled that some urgent cultural revision was needed to delegitimize the growing forces that were conspiring to

bring about Aboriginal–settler coexistence and it seemed that we would soon see the reinvocation of some of the old tropes of settler land-claiming: miscegenation, cannibalism, the dying race – tropes that viscerally register the anxiety, the horror, of proximity. In the same week as the Australian Cabinet finalized a Ten Point Plan to "disarm" the High Court's Wik decision, One Nation launched its infamous *The Truth* (from which I quoted above) that invoked (with obvious and explicit intent) the trope of Aboriginal cannibalism – the ultimate trope of the settler being swallowed.

Mabo to Wik: A Paradigm Shift in Four Years

It must be understood that the Mabo and Wik judgments are absolutely different. Mabo allowed for the separate existence of European and Aboriginal titles to land in quite separate locations and it firmly asserted two principles: that Aborigines had historical precedence, and that Europeans had legal precedence. These were principles that most "whitefella" Australians could fairly readily comprehend. It can be seen as a conservative judgment in that it asserted a notion of separateness, apartness. There was some land that, because Europeans had not yet done anything to it, might still have some residual Aboriginal claim as long as the appropriate aborigines had persisted in maintaining contact with it. This land might be said to have been "reserved." No ontological disputation is called up here, just a slightly inconvenient rearrangement of the real estate: there was European land and, somewhere else and mostly in undesirable spots, there was Aboriginal land. Missions, reserves, reservations, locations, and homelands: the colonized world is familiar with this sort of arrangement.

But three years later, in the Wik judgment, the same High Court revisited the history of the relationship of different forms of land title in a settler colony. It reinserts a notion of incomplete European occupation – specifically on Pastoral Leases – and it specifies those historical moments when the doctrine of *Terra Nullius* actually "gained ground" in Australia. It was not invented, as is often thought, at the beginning of European settlement in Australia in 1788 but some thirty to fifty years later when actual conflict over land-use began. As Henry Reynolds has pointed out, native title was accepted by many pioneer settlers and by the Colonial Office in Britain during the 1830s and 1840s (7). He cites several negotiations between pastoralists and traditional owners throughout the nineteenth century that "led to highly successful resolutions of the problem of providing for the mutual use of the same country" (8). The question of aboriginal rights became crucial after squatters (large landholders who gained title to land in certain areas merely by occupying it) gained security of tenure as a result of legislation in 1846. Earl Grey, the British Secretary of State, promptly instructed the Governor in Sydney "to take care they are not driven off all that country which is divided into grazing (stations)" (9).[4] Grey reiterated that pastoral leases granted merely rights to pasturage, and "that these leases are not intended to deprive the natives of their former right to hunt over these Districts, or to wander over them in search of subsistence, in the manner to which they have been heretofore accustomed, from the spontaneous produce of the soil."[5] Grey stipulated that Aboriginal access and use be "reserved" in *every* pastoral lease: by 1850, all leases in all of the Australian colonies contained such a reservation.

In effect, then, the High Court in 1996 rediscovered this ethical and legal notion of coexistence by finding that Native Title survives alongside pastoral title (although European Title still takes precedence when the two are in direct conflict). Wik, then, requires quite a shift. It requires not a notion of separation but one of simultaneity and proximity; it asserts that two laws – or, even more scandalously, two different systems of law – may apply to the one piece of land. That two laws might operate on the same site is a concept not unknown to British law: property law even now retains many kinds of residual natural entitlements to rights of way, fishing, hunting, etc. In China, during the period of British comprador activity before the annexation of Hong Kong, British law asserted the notion of extra-territoriality, which held that Western citizens acting in China were to be judged by British law; much the same is argued from time to time for Westerners "caught" in the clutches of Sharia law.

What we have after Wik, then, is a sign of the historical relationality from which neither the settler nor the indigene can be separated: the indigene cannot be relegated to something that is merely chronologically prior; the settler cannot merely come at the end of history, "the winning post." The phrase that Homi Bhabha (1998: 35) adapts from Derrida, "overlap without equivalence," might describe it. In this new conception of colonized space, the space of the colonizer and the colonized are not mutually exclusive: Wik requires a grammar of unequal proximity.

A Theory of Affect

It is clear that the appeal (more specifically, the address) of the passages I quoted from the Hanson book is not so much logical as affective. If we are to explain the persistence of certain narrative patterns in our cultures, we need both a Theory of Affect and a Theory of Effect to explain the joint appeals to what Aristotle called *pathos* and *logos*.

Perhaps the most useful place to start thinking about the affective functioning of repressed knowledge is Freud's 1919 essay on "The Uncanny." "The 'uncanny'," Freud writes, "is that class of the terrifying which leads back to something long known to us, once very familiar" (369–70). And he goes on to a crucial conclusion:

> if this is indeed the secret nature of the uncanny, we can understand why . . . speech has extended *das Heimliche* into its opposite *das Unheimliche*; for this uncanny is in reality nothing new or foreign, but something familiar and old-established in the mind that has been estranged only by the process of repression. (394)

He then shows how to draw this from the personal and psychoanalytical into a cultural frame in the following way:

> We – or our primitive forefathers – once believed in the possibility of these things . . . Nowadays we no longer believe in them, we have *surmounted* such ways of thought; but we do not feel quite sure of our new set of beliefs, and the old ones still exist within us ready to seize upon any confirmation. As soon as anything actually happens in our lives which seems to support the old, discarded beliefs we get a feeling of the "uncanny." (401–2)

These ideas are not new to the postcolonial field but I want to turn to how they might help us think about narrative persistence in "settler" cultures.

The Postcolonial Uncanny

Ken Gelder and Jane M. Jacobs have written most helpfully about this in an Australian context and it resonates readily for other settler cultures. Their reading of the postcolonial, post-Mabo, post-Wik, politics and pragmatics of land ownership in Australia is similar to – but more highly developed than – the one I have begun to outline above. They describe a

> postcolonial Australia, where, at the present moment, certain anxieties have arisen which have to do with how the nation seems suddenly to have become unfamiliar to itself. Are postcolonialism and anxiety always tied together?

they ask. I suggest that they probably are. "There is no doubt," they go on to say,

> that [Mabo] gave this coupling a certain intensification.... The rejection of *terra nullius* was certainly read by some as the moment when *all* (or at least, *too much*) of Australia might become available for Aboriginal reclamation. (150)

Now I think this is how Freud, after all this time, can be useful. What is crucial about Freud's uncanny is that it is not the unfamiliar which is the source of the anxiety: it is what Gelder and Jacobs call the sense "of being in place and 'out of place' *simultaneously*."

> in this moment of decolonisation, what is "ours" is also potentially, or even always already, "theirs": the one may also be the other. And because many land claims are either in the process of being dealt with or are yet to be made, a certain kind of un-settlement arises which is given expression by non-Aborigines and Aborigines alike – at the very moment when modern Australia happens to be talking about "reconciliation"....
> what is "ours" may also be "theirs," and vice versa... difference and "reconciliation" coexist uneasily together. In uncanny Australia, one place is always already another place because the issue of possession is never complete, never entirely settled. (151)

In this new (but also very old) conception of colonial relations, settlers and Aborigines thus "inhabit the same place, yet we seem to inhabit places which are *not* the same" (162). But that is not the end of the uncanny or of the cognitive dissonance that we have settled upon the land; Gelder and Jacobs make the valuable postcolonial point that:

> One of the problems... with aboriginal land claims in modern Australia is, precisely, that the claimant must establish familiarity with the land; one must behave, in other words, as if dispossession had never happened. There is no room in land claims for the articulation of what we might call an uncanny relationship to place, which would draw attention to the simultaneous experience of familiarity and unfamiliarity with the land. (165)

We can identify now some of the anxious tropes of proximity: of being consumed by indigeneity; of being lost in the space of the other; of the *unheimlichkeit* of home. They are not unfamiliar to those of us who have read the public and fictional discourses that have circulated in (and about) settler cultures. Before describing the particular functions of the tropes, I want to try to get at the question of how the tropes work in another way.

How did we get here?

When I began working in settler cultures in about 1986, one of the things that struck me was a sense of doubleness, duplicity, and ambivalence. At the time, the most familiar figuration of that doubleness had been "disjunction," even alienation. I myself had described Australian colonialism as characterized by "discrepancies between image and experience and discontinuities between culture and context" (Lawson, 1980: 135); W. H. New in *Among Worlds* talked about the "dualities that abound in Commonwealth literatures [that] express concretely this sense of incomplete options" (1). I also noted that some of those "second world" formations of doubleness were rhetorical: puns were pretty common and so was zeugma, but I was more interested in understanding the nature and mode of settler colonial relations and subjectivity as peculiarly doubled ones. At the time, I called settler cultures, "the Second World." It was, I said, meant to be a reading strategy rather than a cultural denominator, but the arithmetic of nations was always already hierarchical, as any number of critiques of Fredric Jameson's notorious "Third World Literature in an Era of Multinational Capitalism" have shown (for example, Ahmad, 1992).

Nevertheless, I took up Homi Bhabha's familiar observation that "the colonial text occupies that space of double inscription" (1985: 150) in a particular way: to highlight the endlessly problematic double inscription of authority and authenticity within settler cultures. The "double inscription of authority and authenticity" in cultures that are both colonizing and colonized produces always two kinds of authority and always two kinds of authenticity that the settler subject is consigned to desire and to disavow. The settler subject is signified, then, in a language of authority and in a language of resistance. The settler subject enunciates the authority that is in colonial discourse on behalf of the imperial enterprise, which he (and sometimes she) represents. The settler subject represents, but also mimics, the authentic imperial culture from which he (and more problematically, she) is separated. This is mimicry in Bhabha's special sense – that which is "*almost the same, but not quite*" (1984: 130) – since the authority is enunciated on behalf of, but never quite as, the Imperium.

Out of that mimicry emerges the menace of what Bhabha calls "the repetitious slippage of difference and desire" (131). In Western art, popular culture, history, fiction, and even in postcolonial theory, mimicry seems always to be found in the pathetic or scandalous performance of the colonized. But, in settler cultures, mimicry is a necessary and unavoidable part of the repertoire of the settler. This comes about because the "settler" subject exercises authority over the indigene and the land at the same time as translating desire for the indigene and the land into a desire for native authenticity. This can be read in numerous narratives of psychic encounter and indigenization. In reacting to that subordinacy, that incompleteness, that sign of something less, the settler mimics, appropriates, and desires (while simultaneously seeking to efface) the authority of the indigene. The typical settler narrative, then, has a doubled objective: the suppression or effacement of the indigene, and the concomitant indigenization of the settler. In becoming more like the indigene whom he mimics, the settler becomes less like the atavistic inhabitant of the cultural homeland whom he is also reduced to mimicking. The settler text is thus marked by counterfeitings of both emergence and origination.

The settler postcolonial subject, then, always speaks – wittingly or unwittingly – to both of its antecedent authorities and authenticities. In speaking back against the Imperium, in the interests of its own identity politics, the settler site of enunciation will always tend to reappropriate the position of all of those others *with and against whom* it has mediated that power. For any historicized, gendered, culturally specific site of enunciation, we need to identify the "prior" sites whose authorities either license the utterance or provoke the resistance. The settler, then, always addresses both the absent (and absentee) cultural authority of the Imperium and the unavailable (and effaced) cultural authority of the indigene. The settler is located at the point of negotiation between the contending authorities of Empire and Native, the place where the operations of colonial power as negotiation are made most intensely visible. To each of these First Worlds, the settler seems secondary, indeed supplementary.

But there is a problem in defining the authority of a cultural narrative by its endless secondariness to two primaries: the First World of the cultural origin (Europe) and the geo-legal-temporal First World of aboriginal peoples. Carrie Dawson's work on "imposture" in settler cultures showed the cul-de-sac of endless belatedness into which this argument might lead us. In response to that, I've been rethinking "secondariness to two primaries" as the form of a relation to two objects of (be)longing; to see it as signifying not belatedness but as a strong manifestation of the anxiety of proximity; not as imposture nor as weak mimesis, but capable of being read through one of the tropes of proximity as expressing a desire for and anxiety about a difficult (perhaps impossible), unequal, and incomplete relationality.

The settler, it increasingly seems to me, is above all a teller of tales, or more crucially a self-narrating subject. It is in narrative that settler subjectivity calls itself into being and it is in narratives that it can be located and its symptomatic utterances analyzed. That is to say, I'm drawn to an analysis whose object is not so much located in "culture" or consciousness but in texts, or more precisely in various forms of narrative (history, fiction, politics, public discourses by and large). I argue that settlers narrate themselves into subjectivity in the act of making particular narratives. Conflict in settler colonies therefore usually involves conflict over narrative or representation.

If "settler" is tendentious, what efficacious forms does it take? What kinds of stories does the settler tell? Is it possible to think of a cultural narratology, a cultural rhetoric? (See Bhabha, 1994, and Larsen, esp. 48–9.) How do we find a way of talking about the mode or manner in which these settler stories function? If we see these narratives as *strategies*, we can see them as having material effects, not simply systemic textual effects requiring explication. They constitute an invitation to notice the particular ways in which these settler narrative tropes rearrange the circumstances of our history and of our social relations; and how they foreclose on certain possibilities for social relations.

The process of "settlement" is always a project of both displacement and replacement. Prior owner-occupiers and prior figurations of space must be evacuated to make way for the settler and to conceal the actuality of violence. So settlers tell stories and devise images that emphasize the disappearance of native peoples: the last of his tribe (*The Last of the Mohicans*), the dying race, even tales of genocide: the

Tasmanian aborigines, the Newfoundland Beothuk. A related narrative tells of the disappearance of "pre-original" indigenes: the San ("Bushmen") of Southern Africa, the Moriori of New Zealand. This second narrative discredits the "originality" of the current indigenous population by depicting them as violent *arrivistes* who dispossessed the "true" (but now nonexistent) indigenes. Crucially, the political, legal, and psychological effects of the two narratives were similar: they erase the claim of indigenous peoples to "full" indigeneity and with it their rights to land ownership and cultural priority. These narratives were, and are, a powerful form of symbolic management. The occupation of land formerly owned by others always requires a cultural politics of representation.

The frequent "scientific" observation of the "dying race" in the nineteenth (and indeed the twentieth) century enabled a narrative of ethical indigenization in which the "settler" simply assumed the place of the disappearing indigene without the need for violence (or, of course, the designation "invader"). As Goldie rightly and usefully notices, these "last of his tribe" laments are crucial strategies in the replacement of the indigene by familiar forms of white indigeneity: pioneers, Mounties, cowboys, range-riders, Bushmen. Concurrently and consequently, white settlers referred to themselves and their culture as indigenous and in this way cemented their legitimacy, their own increasingly secure sense of moral, spiritual, and cultural belonging in the place they commonly (and revealingly) described as "new." A key function of this indigenizing narrative is to legitimize the settler, to put the settler in the cultural (moral) and discursive place of the indigene whose physical space has already been invaded. The indigenized settler is the figure who is ready to step in when the native "dies out." The native must *make way* for the settler because of the legal and moral prohibition of "invasion." But however strong the desire for disavowal, no disidentificatory gesture is fully available to the settler. In seeking to establish a nation, the settler must become native and write the epic of the nation's origin. But if the "Origin" is that which has no antecedent, the Ab-original presence is a serious impediment.

In the foundation of cultural nationalism itself, we can watch one vector of difference (the difference between colonizing subject and colonized subject: settler-indigene) being replaced by another (the difference between colonizing subject and Imperial centre: settler-imperium) in a strategic disavowal of the colonizing act. The national is what replaces the indigenous and in so doing it conceals its participation in colonization by nominating a new "colonized" subject – the colonizer or settler-invader. It was obvious even in that early work on settler subjectivity that the term "settler" itself was, and always had been, tendentious, polemic. The word "settler" was itself part of the process of invasion, a textual interpolation into history, but it also lays bare the slippage from invader to peaceful settler as a *strategy* within the project of imperialism.

The lands the settlers occupied were themselves given special discursive treatment. Wherever possible, the wildness, the vastness, the inhospitability (that is to say, the ungovernability) of the land was emphasized: its "emptiness" was of course strategic. Vast and empty lands, insistently recorded in both texts and visual images, cried out to the European imagination to be filled, and filled they were by people, crops, fences, and herds, but also by the maps, stories, and histories which, like the economically productive crops that legitimated the settlement, documented ownership. The management of the displacement of indigenous peoples moves from the physical domain (where it has been incomplete) to the symbolic domain. But delegitimization (or its cousin, exoticization) of the other as a strategy of identity formation – "we are not like them" – is not the only function of the settler tropes. I'm interested in how those tropes register "anxiety." The anxiety is to do with desire and identification on the one hand and projection and othering as cultural boundary marking on the other.

So, how do we rethink the settler paradigm as a mediatory relationship? My suggestion is zeugma – the figure of speech in which one word is placed in the same grammatical relation to two words but in quite different senses – as in Alexander Pope, "Or stain her honour, or her new brocade." Usually the doubled object contains one that is abstract and one that is concrete, or one that is literal and one that is metaphorical. Some classical rhetoricians distinguish between *syllepsis* in which the "yoking" is fully grammatical and *zeugma* in which it is not or not quite (e.g., Corbett, 1971). That zeugmatic lack of fit is quite useful. Zeugma, syllepsis, puns are all tropes of collocation, of awkward proximity: *they are about family trouble*, as Ross Chambers[6] has observed. They are about things that are *relatable but not commensurable* and that might be a way of rethinking the new postcolonial relations of land-ownership I mentioned earlier. This might be a way to read the coexistence of two incommensurable, politically unequal laws or epistemologies. It is also instructive that zeugma differs crucially from the model of the simple sentence – subject–verb–object – which has seductively offered a grammar for the outmoded transitive model of imperialism: A does X to B. And zeugma is also the paradigm of the continuous challenge to postcolonial intellectuals: how to be theorized and grounded at the same time; how to maintain that not quite grammatical relation.

What is a Trope?

For some time I have been troubled by the unreflective looseness with which so many of us use the word "trope" when we might mean "*topos*." In rhetoric, a trope is one of the figures of speech: metonymy, or say, zeugma. In Aristotle's *Rhetoric*, a *topos* is one of the "topics" of invention, that is, one of the suitable subjects for the orator. They are what is speakable. On one hand, it might be easy enough to explain how tropes work discursively – and synchronically – in any given textual moment. On the other hand, we might be able to explain how *topoi* work in narrative (and perhaps more broadly across culture). Whatever these things are, they hover uneasily between tropes and *topoi*, between rhetoric and narrative. I think we prefer to call them tropes (and treat them as rhetorical figures) because they *function* rhetorically, that is, they *turn* a history, a narrative; they function to persuade; they are strategic, polemical, and tendentious. Frank d'Angelo draws on the nineteenth-century rhetorician Theodore Hunt to describe a way in which "the topoi become displaced as inventional strategies and embedded in discourse as methods of organising ideas" (63). They naturalize particular kinds of relationships. But as we have noticed, they are remarkably persistent: how can they be reinvoked long past what might be thought to be their use-by date?

Affectively, I've tried to deal with this in terms of the "uncanny." For "effect," I turn to Fredric Jameson (whose three worlds theory I had personally repressed), this time the Jameson of *The Political Unconscious*. Here, Jameson talks of the "ideologeme, . . . a historically determinate conceptual or semic complex which can project itself variously in the form of a 'value system' or 'philosophical concept,' or in the form of a *protonarrative, a private or collective narrative fantasy*" (115; my italics) and he goes on importantly to insist that "the ideologeme itself [must be grasped] as a form of social praxis, that is, as a symbolic resolution to a concrete historical situation" (117).

Now here is how we might regain our groundedness, our ability to see what we've been calling tropes as "symbolic resolutions to concrete historical situations"; or, as I called then earlier, rearrangements of actual social and historical relations such as the genuinely difficult relation of races and places in the settler-colonial situation; in this sense they may be, or be part of, mediatory codes. Later, Jameson offers a model he calls "sedimentation" to explain how "the ideology of the form itself, thus sedimented, persists into later, more complex structures as a generic message which coexists – either as a contradiction or, on the other hand, as a mediatory or harmonising mechanism – with elements from later stages" (141).

> A specific narrative paradigm continues to emit its ideological signals long after its original content has become historically obsolete:...the most archaic layer of content continues to supply vitality and ideological legitimation to its later and quite different symbolic function. (186)

So what persists into contemporary narrative is sedimented ideologized narrative form. Predictably, Jameson also has an explanation of what it is we see when that sedimented narrative causes tension or fails. Briefly, the essential fact is that such a failure or deviation

> directs our attention to some of those determinate changes in the historical situation which block a full manifestation or replication of the structure on the discursive level. On the other hand, the failure of a particular generic structure, such as epic, to reproduce itself not only encourages a search for those substitute textual formations that appear in its wake, but more particularly alerts us to the historical ground, now no longer existent, in which the original structure was meaningful. (146)

Perhaps this allows us to think productively about the significance to us of Pauline Hanson's narrative of baby-eating Aborigines. Her narrative is a kind of failure in the sense that most of us find it difficult to read, so it directs us to reread the historical ground on which it was once meaningful and strategic.

Jameson's final lesson for me comes from his noting that the "ideologeme...exists nowhere as such:...it vanishes into the past...leaving only its traces – material signifiers, lexemes, enigmatic words and phrases – behind it" (201).

> ideologemes [are] free-floating narrative objects...which are never given directly in primary verbal form, but must always be re-constructed after the fact, as working hypothesis and subtext. (185)

Recurrent themes, then – what we've got used to calling tropes – such as the "lost child," the "half-breed," cannibalism, can only be understood as "so many allusions to *a more basic ideological 'sign'* which would have been grasped instinctively by any contemporary reader but from which we are culturally and historically distanced" (200).

What Are the Settler Narrative Tropes and What Are their Ideologemes?

The dying race

If the natives didn't die out quickly enough, their actual dying could be replaced by stories of their dying, by "the last of the tribe" poems and photographs. The Hanson narrative of Aborigines eating their own children is the ultimate disappearing race narrative.[7] Discursive space is in need of clearing as much as physical space.

And there's a temporality to all this too. There is the end of time (the last of his tribe, the dying race); there is also the moment before time starts, the frozen moment just before settlement/pacification (the pre-contact moment) figured as prehistory, golden age, essentialist past. In its more negative formation, this manifests as the "bad history" of *Terra Nullius* or as the persistent myth in all settler colonies of "the pre-aboriginal peoples who were here before the first nations," and functions as the corollary of the dying race: the indigenes weren't here at the beginning; they won't be here at the end.

Going native might mean any one of: "indigenization," that is, a tendentious settler identity claim; cultural loss or "contamination" for the settler; solidarity or "affiliation" with the other.

Incorporation

This is going native gone badly wrong. There are several complexly related versions of this trope in which the settler is consumed by the land: there is the lost child, the captivity narrative, shipwrecked sailor or vanished explorer, each of whom may be captive, foundling, or merely vanished. These are stories of incorporation in which the land is a metaphor for native, and they function as cautionary tales for women and children who might think of straying "out of place." Of course, incorporation also includes cannibalism and miscegenation.

But cannibalism is not simply like the others. Much of the modern literature on cannibalism is directed towards rehabilitating the accused from the taint of cannibalism because late twentieth-century anthropologists shared their ancestors' notion that cannibalism is the ultimate character flaw, the final boundary marker of civilized behavior, the line that no civilized white person would ever cross. Cannibalism is a very particular trope: it is about proximity *and* consumption.

The other trope that functions like this is miscegenation. It too contains the tension between anxiety and desire: for absorption, consumption, sameness. There is a complex chain of signification between desire for indigenized identity, spirituality, and land and the desire for indigenous women that needs to be explored (see Goldie 63–84).

Each of these tropes defines a moment when the desire for indigenization, the desire to stand in place of the native, has *gone too far*, they are then the metaphoric limit-cases for the going-native trope. They are sins of proximity, which remind us that settler desire must always be asymptotic.

Asymptosis

This is getting close, but never becoming the same. The "settler's" desire to "stand in" for the native produces ultimately and perhaps inevitably the unspeakable desire for miscegenation,[8] what in South Africa was once called the "taint." The insertion of the settler into the (physical and discursive) space of the indigene is simultaneously characterized by desire and disavowal. The movement into indigenous space must be asymptotic: indigeneity must be approached, even appropriated, certainly photographed, but never touched. This produces in the settler subject the anxiety of proximity. The self-indigenizing settler has to stop just short of going completely native and is, therefore, often represented as sexless.[9] The settler must stand just in front of, in the place of, but never in the body of, the indigene. The need, then, is to *dis*place rather than *re*place the other because the other must remain to signify the boundary of the self, to confirm the subjectivity of the settler. The "other," as a consequence of this "almost but not quite" move, is therefore always in some sense present, always "uncannily" ready for its return.

The other side of "settler" desire is to inherit "their" spiritual rites/rights to the land. This is figured in Fenimore Cooper's "Leatherstocking Tales" as well as numerous "settler" narratives in Canada, Australia, Southern Africa, and New Zealand. It is also expressed in the sentimentalization of the mixed-race figure who enacts a slippage between the white desire and the native right. All of these figure an unacknowledged recognition of native authority. I suggest that authenticity might turn out to be one of the settler tropes, too. It certainly is a device used by settlers to limit and regulate the speaking position of indigenes. Disciplining the authentic native was a form of regulation in apartheid South Africa, in treaty-negotiating Canada, in Australian social welfare arrangements that produced what is now known as "the Stolen Generation." It determines hierarchies of value and power. But authenticity has a tricky tendency to become authority: hence the anxiety in contemporary settler societies about indigenous authenticity. Now that the connection between native authenticity and authority is firmly, but not uncomplicatedly, established, it becomes necessary to regulate who may have access to it.

A Tropology

Having got from contemporary bad politics to Classical Rhetoric, I'd like to borrow an idea from Renaissance and later rhetoricians, who had schemes for classifying the tropes. The nineteenth-century rhetorician Theodore Hunt argued that figurative language followed laws of association that could be analyzed in three broad groups (d'Angelo 63):

> Figures of Resemblance (what we might call tropes of mimesis), which include simile, metaphor, allegory;
>> Figures of Contrast (or tropes of binarism), which include antithesis, epigram, irony;
>> Figures of Contiguity are the figures of association or (in my terms) tropes of proximity. They include metonymy, synecdoche, paronomasia and antanaclasis, syllepsis and zeugma.

This might provide a way of rereading, of remediating the narrative tropes we encounter. One could analyze the narrative tropes as expressing particular figures of speech and then read them into a classification of the tropes like Theodore Hunt's. To see the tropes functioning in this way as abstracted (re)iterations of ideologically determined, historically contingent narratives might enable us to reread them. As Ross Chambers has so usefully said, "What has been mediated can be re-mediated" (1). The tropes have been used to make colonial history/experience readable; they can therefore be used to make it re-readable. Just as the ghastly violence of colonial "settlement" was once forgotten, its relatively recent remembering has produced its own forgetting of historical instances of conscience and good faith: "as a result, the past has lost the authority it ought to have" (Atkinson 23). This is what rereading tropically might mean. We have become ostentatiously good at reading the past for its moral and ethical blindnesses: to do that is no longer a theoretical or a methodological challenge. What we need to be able to do next is to find a theorized methodology for rereading the past productively, not celebratively, not unreflectively, but with an eye to the contradictions that might enable us to learn our difficult relations better.

Notes

1   The present essay is primarily based on Lawson (2000); it also draws on material presented in Lawson (1991 and 1994) and Johnston and Lawson (2000).
2   Sara Mills (1995) forms the question this way: "How do we get past Foucault's argument in *The Order of Discourse*, that there are breaks between discursive domains and moments? How to deal with the permeability of discursive domains?" While, as Mills says, discursive histories are not at all simply continuous, neither are they marked by the kind of breaks that Foucault suggests.
3   For a useful concise discussion of the case see Borch.
4   Colonial Office, C.O. 201/382, cited in Reynolds, 9.
5   *Historical Records of Australia*, 1, v. 26. 225, cited in Reynolds.
6   Personal communication, Ross Chambers, 30 May 1997.
7   I am grateful to one of my graduate students, Paul Newman, for this observation.
8   I am grateful to J. M. Coetzee for some suggestive personal discussions on this point.
9   Like Natty Bumppo and other of James Fenimore Cooper's heroes.

References

Ahmad, Aijaz. 1987. "Jameson's Rhetoric of Otherness and the 'National Allegory'." *Social Text*, 17 (Fall): 3–25; reprinted in *In Theory: Classes, Nations, Literatures*. London: Verso, 1992, 95–122.
Atkinson, Alan. 1997. "The Unelected Conscience." *Quadrant*, June: 7–23.
Bhabha, Homi K. 1984. "Of Mimicry and Man: The Ambivalence of Colonial Discourse." *October*, 28: 125–33.
——1985. "Signs Taken for Wonders: Questions of Ambivalence and Authority under a Tree outside Delhi, May 1817." *Critical Inquiry* 12: 144–65. See also pp. 1167–84 in this book.
——1994. "DissemiNation: Time, Narrative and the Margins of the Modern Nation." In *The Location of Culture*. London: Routledge, 139–70.
——1998. "On the Irremovable Strangeness of Being Different." *PMLA* 113: 34–9.
Borch, Merete Falck. 1992. "Eddie Mabo and Others and the State of Queensland, 1992: The Significance of Court Recognition of Landrights in Australia." *Kunapipi*, 14.1: 1–12.

Chambers, Ross. 1994. "Fables of the Go-between." In *Literature and Opposition*, ed. Chris Worth, Pauline Nestor, and Marko Pavlyshyn. Clayton, Victoria: Monash Centre for Comparative Literature and Cultural Studies, 1–28.

Corbett, Edward P. J. 1971. *Classical Rhetoric for the Modern Student*. 2nd edn. New York: Oxford University Press.

D'Angelo, Frank. 1984. "The Evolution of the Analytic *Topoi*: A Speculative Enquiry." In *Essays on Classical Rhetoric and Modern Discourse*, ed. Robert J. Connors, Lisa S. Ede, and Andrea A. Lunsford. Carbondale: Southern Illinois University Press, 50–68.

Dawson, Carrie. 1998. "Never Cry Fraud: Remembering Grey Owl, Rethinking Imposture." *Essays on Canadian Writing*, 65: 120–40.

—— 2000 "Calling People Names: Reading Imposture, Confession and Testimony in *The English Patient*." *Studies in Canadian Literature*, 25.2: 50–73.

Freud, Sigmund. 1925 [1919]. "The Uncanny," trans. Alex Strachey. In *Collected Papers*, vol. 4, 368–407. London: International Psycho-Analytical Press.

Gelder, Ken, and Jane M. Jacobs. 1995. "Uncanny Australia." *UTS Review* 1.2: 150–69.

Goldie, Terry. 1989. *Fear and Temptation: The Image of the Indigene in Canadian, Australian, and New Zealand Literatures*. Kingston, Ontario: McGill-Queen's University Press.

[Hanson, Pauline] 1997. *The Truth: On Asian Immigration*, the *Aboriginal Question, the Gun Debate and the Future of Australia*. Ipswich, Queensland: [Pauline Hanson Support Movement], 109–55.

Jameson, Fredric. 1981. *The Political Unconscious: Narrative as a Socially Symbolic Act*. Ithaca, NY: Cornell University Press.

—— 1986. *Social Text*, 15 (Fall): 65–88; revised as "World Literature in an Era of Multinational Capitalism," in *The Current in Criticism*, ed. Clayton Koelb and Virgil Lokke. West Lafayette, Ind. : Purdue University Press 1987, 139–58.

Johnston, Anna, and Alan Lawson. 2000. "Settler Colonies: Australia, New Zealand, South Africa." Chapter 14 in *A Companion to Postcolonial Studies: A Historical Introduction*, ed. Henry Schwarz and Sangeeta Ray. Oxford: Blackwell, 370–6.

Larsen, Neil. 2000. "Imperialism, Colonialism, Postcolonialism." In *A Companion to Postcolonial Studies*, ed. Henry Schwarz and Sangeeta Ray. Oxford: Blackwell, 23–52.

Lawson, Alan. 1980. "Acknowledging Colonialism: Revisions of the Australian Tradition." In *Australia and Britain: Studies in a Changing Relationship*, ed. A. F. Madden and W. H. Morris-Jones. Sydney: Sydney University Press in association with the Institute of Commonwealth Studies, University of London; London: Frank Cass, 135–44.

—— 1991. "A Cultural Paradigm for the Second World." *Australian Canadian Studies* 9. 1–2: 67–78.

—— 1994. "Post-colonial Theory and the 'Settler' Subject." In *Testing the Limits: Post-colonial Theories and Canadian Literature*, ed. Diana Brydon. Special issue of *Essays on Canadian Writing*, 56 (Fall): 20–36.

—— 2000. "Proximities: From Asymptote to Zeugma." In *Postcolonizing the Commonwealth: Studies in Literature and Culture*, ed. Rowland Smith. Waterloo, Ontario: Wilfrid Laurier University Press, 19–37.

Mills, Sara. 1995. "The Discontinuity of Postcolonial Discourse." *ARIEL* 26.3: 73–88.

New, W. H. 1975. *Among Worlds: An Introduction to Modern Commonwealth and South African Fiction*. Erin, Ontario: Press Porcépic.

Reynolds, Henry. 1996. "Frontier History after Mabo." *Journal of Australian Studies*, 49: 4–11.

CHAPTER 12

A Small Place

Jamaica Kincaid

Jamaica Kincaid's *A Small Place* (1988) addresses the question of what might be called "secondary colonialism." Secondary colonialism occurs when inhabitants of wealthy, highly developed northern or western countries convert poorer, formerly colonial, usually southern and eastern countries into sites or objects of useful pleasure. Tourism is the most obvious example of such colonization, but it might also be said to assume more symbolic forms, as when the inhabitants of such poorer countries or the places themselves are converted into occasions for the creation of cultural meaning or the achievement of self-fulfillment by secondary colonists. E. M. Forster's *A Passage to India* is a clear example of such symbolic conversion.

If you go to Antigua as a tourist, this is what you will see. If you come by aeroplane you will land at the V. C. Bird International Airport. Vere Cornwall (V. C.) Bird is the Prime Minister of Antigua. You may be the sort of tourist who would wonder why a Prime Minister would want an airport named after him – why not a school, why not a hospital, why not some great public monument? You are a tourist and you have not yet seen a school in Antigua, you have not yet seen the hospital in Antigua, you have not yet seen a public monument in Antigua. As your plane descends to land, you might say, What a beautiful island Antigua is – more beautiful than any of the other islands you have seen, and they were very beautiful, in their way, but they were much too green, much too lush with vegetation, which indicated to you, the tourist, that they got quite a bit of rainfall, and rain is the very thing that you, just now, do not want, for you are thinking of the hard and cold and dark and long days you spent working in North America (or, worse, Europe), earning some money so that you could stay in this place (Antigua) where the sun always shines and where the climate is deliciously hot and dry for the four to ten days you are going to be staying there; and since you are on your holiday, since you are a tourist, the thought of what it might be like for someone who had to live day in day out in a place that suffers constantly from drought, and so has to watch carefully every drop of fresh water used (while at the same time surrounded by a sea and an ocean – the Caribbean Sea on one side, the Atlantic Ocean on the other), must never cross your mind.

You disembark from your plane. You go through customs. Since you are a tourist, a North American or European – to be frank, white and not an Antiguan black returning to Antigua from Europe or North America with cardboard boxes of much needed cheap clothes and food for relatives, you move through customs swiftly, you move through customs with ease. Your bags are not searched. You emerge from customs into the hot, clean air: immediately you feel cleansed, immediately you feel blessed (which is to say special); you feel free. You see a man, a taxi driver; you ask him to take you to your destination; he quotes you a price. You immediately think that the price is in the local currency, for you are a tourist and you are familiar with these things (rates of exchange) and you feel even more free, for things seem so cheap, but then your driver ends by saying, "In US currency." You may say, "Hmmmm, do you have a formal sheet that lists official prices and destinations?" Your driver obeys the law and shows you the sheet, and he apologizes for the incredible mistake he has made in quoting you a price off the top of his head which is so vastly different (favoring him) from the one listed. You are driven to your hotel by this taxi driver in his taxi, a brand-new Japanese-made vehicle. The road on which you are traveling is a very bad road, very much in need of repair. You are feeling wonderful, so you say, "Oh, what a marvelous change these bad roads are from the splendid highways I am used to in North America." (Or, worse, Europe.) Your driver is reckless; he is a dangerous man who drives in the middle of the road when he thinks no other cars are coming in the opposite direction, passes other cars on blind curves that run uphill, drives at sixty miles an hour on narrow, curving roads when the road sign, a rusting, beat-up thing left over from colonial days, says 40 MPH. This might frighten you (you are on your holiday; you are a tourist); this might excite you (you are on your holiday; you are a tourist), though if you are from New York and take taxis you are used to this style of driving: most of the taxi drivers in New York are from places in the world like this. You are looking out the window (because you want to get your money's worth); you notice that all the cars you see are brand-new, or almost brand-new, and that they are all Japanese made. There are no American cars in Antigua – no new ones, at any rate; none that were manufactured in the last ten years. You continue to look at the cars and you say to yourself, Why, they look brand-new, but they have an awful sound, like an old car – a very old, dilapidated car. How to account for that? Well, possibly it's because they use leaded gasoline in these brand-new cars whose engines were built to use non-leaded gasoline, but you musn't ask the person driving the car if this is so, because he or she has never heard of unleaded gasoline. You look closely at the car; you see that it's a model of a Japanese car that you might hesitate to buy; it's a model that's very expensive; it's a model that's quite impractical for a person who has to work as hard as you do and who watches every penny you earn so that you can afford this holiday you are on. How do they afford such a car? And do they live in a luxurious house to match such a car? Well, no. You will be surprised, then, to see that most likely the person driving this brand-new car filled with the wrong gas lives in a house that, in comparison, is far beneath the status of the car; and if you were to ask why you would be told that the banks are encouraged by the government to make loans available for cars, but loans for houses not so easily available; and if you ask again why, you will be told that the two main car dealerships in Antigua are owned in part or outright by ministers in government. Oh, but you are on holiday and the sight of these brand-new cars driven by people who may or may not have really passed their driving test (there was once a scandal about driving licenses for sale) would not really stir up these thoughts in you. You pass a building sitting in a sea of dust and you think, It's some latrines for people just passing by, but when you look again you see the building has written on it PIGOTT'S SCHOOL. You pass the hospital, the Holberton Hospital, and how wrong you are not to think about this, for though you are a tourist on your holiday, what if your heart should miss a few beats? What if a blood vessel in your neck should break? What if one of those people driving those brand-new cars filled with the wrong gas fails to pass safely while going uphill on a curve and you are in the car going in the opposite direction? Will you be comforted to know that the hospital is staffed with doctors that no actual Antiguan trusts; that Antiguans always say about the doctors, "I don't want them near me"; that Antiguans refer to them not as doctors but as "the three men" (there are three of them); that when the Minister of Health himself doesn't feel well he takes the first plane to New York to see a real doctor; that if any one of the ministers in government needs medical care he flies to New York to get it?

It's a good thing that you brought your own books with you, for you couldn't just go to the library and borrow some. Antigua used to have a splendid library but in The Earthquake (everyone talks about it that way – The Earthquake; we Antiguans, for I am one, have a great sense of things, and the more meaningful the thing, the more meaningless we make it) the library building was damaged. This was in 1974, and soon after that a sign was placed on the front of the building saying, THIS BUILDING WAS DAMAGED IN THE EARTHQUAKE OF 1974. REPAIRS ARE PENDING. The sign hangs there, and hangs there more than a decade later, with its unfulfilled promise of repair, and you might see this as a sort of quaintness on the part of these islanders, these people descended from slaves – what a strange, unusual perception of time they have. REPAIRS ARE PENDING, and here it is many years later, but perhaps in a world that is twelve miles long and nine miles wide (the size of Antigua) twelve years and twelve minutes and twelve days are all the same. The library is one of those splendid old buildings from colonial times, and the sign telling of the repairs is a splendid old sign from colonial times. Not very long after The Earthquake Antigua got its independence from Britain, making Antigua a state in its own right and Antiguans are so proud of this that each year, to mark the day, they go to church and thank God, a British God, for this. But you should not think of the confusion that must lie in all that and you must not think of the damaged library. You have brought your own books with you, and among them is one of those new books about economic history, one of those books explaining how the West (meaning Europe and North America after its conquest and settlement by Europeans) got rich: the West got nothing and then undervalued labor, for generations, of the people like me you see walking around you in Antigua but from the ingenuity of small shopkeepers in Sheffield and Yorkshire and Lancashire, or wherever; and what a great part the invention of the wristwatch played in it, for there was nothing noble-minded men could not do when they discovered they could slap time on their wrists just like that (isn't that the last straw; for not only did we have to suffer the unspeakableness of slavery, but the satisfaction to be had from "We made you bastards rich" is taken away, too), and so you needn't let that slightly funny feeling you have from time to time about exploitation, oppression, domination develop into full-fledged unease, discomfort; you could ruin your holiday. They are not responsible for what you have; you owe them nothing; in fact, you did them a big favor, and you can provide one hundred examples. For here you are now, passing by Government House. And here you are now, passing by the Prime Minister's Office and the Parliament Building, and overlooking these, with a splendid view of St John's Harbour, the American Embassy. If it were not for you, they would not have Government House, and Prime Minister's Office, and Parliament Building and embassy of powerful country. Now you are passing a mansion, an extraordinary house painted the color of old cow dung, with more aerials and antennas attached to it than you will see even at the American Embassy. The people who live in this house are a merchant family who came to Antigua from the Middle East less than twenty years ago. When this family first came to Antigua, they sold dry goods door to door from suitcases they carried on their backs. Now they own a lot of Antigua; they regularly lend money to the government, they build enormous (for Antigua), ugly (for Antigua), concrete buildings in Antigua's capital, St John's, which the government then rents for huge sums of money; a member of their family is the Antiguan Ambassador to Syria; Antiguans hate them. Not far from this mansion is another mansion, the home of a drug smuggler. Everybody knows he's a drug smuggler, and if just as you were driving by he stepped out of his door your driver might point him out to you as the notorious person that he is, for this drug smuggler is so rich people say he buys cars in tens – ten of this one, ten of that one and that he bought a house (another mansion) near Five Islands, contents included, with cash he carried in a suitcase: three hundred and fifty thousand American dollars, and, to the surprise of the seller of the house, lots of American dollars were left over. Overlooking the drug smuggler's mansion is yet another mansion, and leading up to it is the best paved road in all of Antigua – even better than the road that was paved for the Queen's visit in 1985 (when the Queen came, all the roads that she would travel on were paved anew, so that the Queen might have been left with the impression that riding in a car in Antigua was a pleasant experience). In this mansion lives a woman sophisticated people in Antigua call Evita. She is a notorious woman. She's young and beautiful and the girlfriend of somebody very high up in the government. Evita is notorious because her relationship with this high government official has made her the owner of boutiques and property and given her a say in cabinet meetings, and all sorts of other privileges such a relationship would bring a beautiful young woman.

Oh, but by now you are tired of all this looking, and you want to reach your destination – your hotel, your room. You long to refresh yourself; you long to eat some nice lobster, some nice local food. You take a bath, you brush your teeth. You get dressed again; as you get dressed, you look out the window. That water – have you ever seen anything like it? Far out, to the horizon, the color of the water is navy-blue; nearer, the water is the color of the North American sky. From there to the shore, the water is pale, silvery, clear, so clear that you can see its pinkish-white sand bottom. Oh, what beauty! Oh, what beauty! You have never seen anything like this. You are so excited. You breathe shallow. You breathe deep. You see a beautiful boy skimming the water, godlike, on a Windsurfer. You see an incredibly unattractive, fat, pastrylike-fleshed woman enjoying a walk on the beautiful sand with a man, an incredibly unattractive, fat, pastrylike-fleshed man; you see the pleasure they're taking in their surroundings. Still standing, looking out the window, you see yourself lying on the beach, enjoying the amazing sun (a sun so powerful and yet so beautiful, the way it is always overhead as if on permanent guard, ready to stamp out any cloud that dares to darken and so empty rain on you and ruin your holiday; a sun that is your personal friend). You see yourself taking a walk on that beach, you see yourself meeting new people (only they are new in a very limited way, for they are people just like you). You see yourself eating some delicious, locally grown food. You see yourself, yourself . . . You must not wonder what exactly happened to the contents of your lavatory when you flushed it. You must not wonder where your bath water went when you pulled out the stopper. You must not wonder what happened when you brushed your teeth. Oh, it might all end up in the water you are thinking of taking a swim in; the contents of your lavatory might, just might, graze gently against your ankle as you wade carefree in the water, for you see, in Antigua, there is no proper sewage-disposal system. But the Caribbean Sea is very big and the Atlantic Ocean is even bigger; it would amaze even you to know the number of black slaves this ocean has swallowed up. When you sit down to eat your delicious meal, it's better that you don't know that most of what you are eating came off a plane from Miami. And before it got on a plane in Miami, who knows where it came from? A good guess is that it came from a place like Antigua first, where it was grown dirt-cheap, went to Miami, and came back. There is a world of something in this, but I can't go into it right now.

The thing you have always suspected about yourself the minute you become a tourist is true: A tourist is an ugly human being. You are not an ugly person all the time; you are not an ugly person ordinarily; you are not an ugly person day to day. From day to day, you are a nice person. From day to day, all the people who are supposed to love you on the whole do. From day to day, as you walk down a busy street in the large and modern and prosperous city in which you work and live, dismayed, puzzled (a cliche, but only a cliche can explain you) at how alone you feel in this crowd, how awful it is to go unnoticed, how awful it is to go unloved, even as you are surrounded by more people than you could possibly get to know in a lifetime that lasted for millennia, and then out of the corner of your eye you see someone looking at you and absolute pleasure is written all over that person's face, and then you realize that you are not as revolting a presence as you think you are (for that look just told you so). And so, ordinarily, you are a nice person, an attractive person, a person capable of drawing to yourself the affection of other people (people just like you), a person at home in your own skin (sort of; I mean, in a way; I mean, your dismay and puzzlement are natural to you, because people like you just seem to be like that, and so many of the things people like you find admirable about yourselves – the things you think about, the things you think really define you – seem rooted in these feelings): a person at home in your own house (and all its nice house things), with its nice back yard (and its nice back-yard things), at home on your street, your church, in community activities, your job, at home with your family, your relatives, your friends – you are a whole person. But one day, when you are sitting somewhere, alone in that crowd, and that awful feeling of displacedness comes over you, and really, as an ordinary person you are not well equipped to look too far inward and set yourself aright, because being ordinary is already so taxing, and being ordinary takes all you have out of you, and though the words "I must get away" do not actually pass across your lips, you make a leap from being that nice blob just sitting like a boob in your amniotic sac of the modern experience to being a person visiting heaps of death and ruin and feeling alive and inspired at the sight of it; to being a person lying on some faraway beach, your stilled body stinking and glistening in the sand, looking like something first forgotten, then remembered, then not important enough to go back for; to being a person marveling at the harmony (ordinarily, what you would say is the backwardness) and the union these other people (and they are other people) have with nature. And you look at the things they can do with a piece of ordinary cloth, the things they fashion out of cheap, vulgarly colored (to you) twines, the way they squat down over a hole they have made in the ground, the hole itself is something to marvel at, and since you are being an ugly person this ugly but joyful thought will swell inside you: their ancestors were not clever in the way yours were and not ruthless in the way yours were, for then would it not be you who would be in harmony with nature and backwards in that charming way? An ugly thing, that is what you are when you become a tourist, an ugly, empty thing, a stupid thing, a piece of rubbish pausing here and there to gaze at this and taste that, and it will never occur to you that the people who inhabit the place in which you have just paused cannot stand you, that behind their closed doors they laugh at your strangeness (you do not look the way they look); the physical sight of you does not please them; you have bad manners (it is their custom to eat their food with their hands; you try eating their way, you look silly; you try eating the way you always eat, you look silly); they do not like the way you speak (you have an accent); they collapse helpless from laughter, mimicking the way they imagine you must look as you carry out some everyday bodily function. They do not like you. *They do not like me!* That thought never actually occurs to you. Still, you feel a little uneasy. Still you feel a little foolish. Still, you feel a little out of place. But the banality of your own life is very real to you; it drove you to this extreme, spending your days and your nights in the company of people who despise you, people you do not like really, people you would not want to have as your actual neighbor. And so you must devote yourself to puzzling out how much of what you are told is really, really true (Is ground-up bottle glass in peanut sauce really a delicacy around here, or will it do just what you think ground-up bottle glass will do? Is this rare, multicolored, snout-mouthed fish really an aphrodisiac, or will it cause you to fall asleep permanently?). Oh, the hard work all of this is, and is it any wonder, then, that on your return home you feel the need of a long rest, so that you can recover from your life as a tourist?

That the native does not like the tourist is not hard to explain. For every native of every place is a potential tourist, and every tourist is a native of somewhere. Every native everywhere lives a life of overwhelming and crushing banality and boredom and desperation and depression, and every deed, good and bad, is an attempt to forget this. Every native would like to find a way out, every native would like a rest, every native would like a tour. But some natives – most natives in the world – cannot go anywhere. They are too poor. They are too poor to go anywhere. They are too poor to escape the reality of their lives; and they are too poor to live properly in the place where they live, which is the very place you, the tourist, want to go – so when the natives see you, the tourist, they envy you, they envy your ability to leave your own banality and boredom, they envy your ability to turn their own banality and boredom into a source of pleasure for yourself.

PART TWELVE

Cultural Studies

CHAPTER 1

Introduction: The Politics of Culture

Julie Rivkin and Michael Ryan

The word "culture" acquired a new meaning in the 1960s and 1970s. Prior to that time, culture was associated with art, literature, and classical music. To have "culture" was to possess a certain taste for particular kinds of artistic endeavor. Anthropologists have always used the word "culture" in a much broader sense to mean forms of life and of social expression. The way people behave while eating, talking with each other, becoming sexual partners, interacting at work, engaging in ritualized social behavior such as family gatherings, and the like constitute a culture. This broad definition of the term includes language and the arts, but it also includes the regularities, procedures, and rituals of human life in communities.

Since the advent of Marxism in the nineteenth century, people have come to think of culture as being political. Culture is both a means of domination, of assuring the rule of one class or group over another, and a means of resistance to such domination, a way of articulating oppositional points of view to those in dominance. Theodor Adorno and Max Horkheimer, in their celebrated *Dialectic of Enlightenment*, argue that mass culture – the culture of television, radio, film, and cheap paperbacks – is a tool of domination, a way for capitalism to offer ephemeral gratification to people condemned to lives of work. In the 1960s in England, a rather different concept of culture emerged that was to prove the foundation of a new discipline called "Cultural Studies." Thinkers like Richard Hoggart, Raymond Williams, and E. P. Thompson came to see culture as a means of resistance to capitalism. If illiteracy was a way of keeping poor and working people away from intellectual instruments that might impel them to rebellion, literacy in the form of clandestine pamphlets and underground newspapers was a way of maintaining alternative perspectives to those demanded by the progress of industrial capitalism and the subsumption of the population to factory labor.

While in the US the study of culture was carried on in departments of Anthropology and Communications (where it assumed a fairly empiricist form as audience surveys and the like), in England in the late 1960s and 1970s, a unique confluence of disciplinary and intellectual currents occurred at the Centre for Contemporary Cultural Studies at Birmingham. Under the leadership of Stuart Hall, the workers at the Centre wove sociology, Marxist political theory, and Structuralist semiotics together to analyze such things as the way the media "policed" economic crises by portraying the world in a way favorable to those in power or how working-class youth resisted their assigned social roles through rituals of dress, dance, and music that offered a counterpoint to the work routines of modern economic life. One of the most celebrated works to come out of the Centre was Dick Hebdige's *Subculture: The Meaning of Style* (1979), which, among other things, examines the resistant quality of punk style in dress and music.

At the same time, Marxist critics like Fredric Jameson in the US developed a more refined version of the Frankfurt School model of domination and argued for the presence of detectable utopian impulses in mass culture. Working along these lines, Janice Radway examines such vilified popular forms as the romance novel and construed them as offering a way for women to resist the patriarchal structures imposed on their lives.

Television, advertising, and popular magazines became objects of analysis in the new field of cultural criticism. John Fiske develops a semiotic model for analyzing television programs in *Television Culture* (1987) that demonstrates the way representational codes and techniques shape our perceptions. And he argues that viewers or audiences regularly take away different meanings from those intended by the producers of television programs. Audiences can "decode" cultural messages in ways that allow them to think resistantly about their lives.

Culture, like capitalist society itself, is hierarchical. And French sociologist Pierre Bourdieu argues that culture is a way of distinguishing between positions in the social hierarchy. Those who are born into upper-class echelons will acquire dispositions that allow them to appreciate certain forms of culture (high art, for example), and such abilities will help them secure elevated positions in the class hierarchy. Working-class people, on the other hand, will acquire from their family contexts and the schools they attend cultural dispositions that prepare them for lives at the bottom of the class ladder. The social system thus tends to reproduce itself through culture and through schooling.

Cultural Studies can thus be approached from two quite incommensurable perspectives. One sees the media, television, film, and the like as instruments of economic, ethnic, and gender domination. Owned by large corporations and largely run by men, the media and the entertainment industry in general cannot help but assist the reproduction of the social system by allowing only certain kinds of imagery and ideas to gain access to mass audiences. Generated by those at the top of the social hierarchy, the media inevitably further attitudes and perceptions that assure its continuation. The other perspective sees culture from the bottom up and pays more attention to the way such forms as music, from African American spirituals to the blues to rock and roll, express energies and attitudes fundamentally at odds with the attitudes and assumptions (the deferment of gratification in order better to be able to work, for example) of the capitalist social order. Culture comes from below, and while it can be harnessed in profitable and ultimately socially conservative ways, it also represents the permanent possibility of eruption, of dissonance, and of an alternative imagination of reality.

CHAPTER 2

The Work of Art in the Age of Mechanical Reproduction

Walter Benjamin

In this 1935 essay German literary and cultural critic Walter Benjamin argues for a connection between changes in the technology of culture, such as the development of film and photography, and changes in consciousness. His concluding polemic is directed against the Futurists, a right-wing cultural group that thought war was an aesthetic experience.

In principle a work of art has always been reproducible. Man-made artifacts could always be imitated by men.... [P]rint is merely a special, though particularly important, case. During the Middle Ages engraving and etching were added to the woodcut; at the beginning of the nineteenth century lithography made its appearance. ...Just as lithography virtually implied the illustrated newspaper, so did photography foreshadow the sound film.... Around 1900 technical reproduction had reached a standard that not only permitted it to reproduce all transmitted works of art and thus to cause the most profound change in their impact upon the public; it also had captured a place of its own among the artistic processes. For the study of this standard nothing is more revealing than the nature of the repercussions that these two different manifestations – the reproduction of works of art and the art of the film – have had on art in its traditional form.

Even the most perfect reproduction of a work of art is lacking in one element: its presence in time and space, its unique existence at the place where it happens to be. This unique existence of the work of art determined the history to which it was subject throughout the time of its existence. This includes the changes which it may have suffered in physical condition over the years as well as the various changes in its ownerships.[1] The traces of the first can be revealed only by chemical or physical analyses which it is impossible to perform on a reproduction; changes of ownership are subject to a tradition which must be traced from the situation of the original.

The presence of the original is the prerequisite to the concept of authenticity. Chemical analyses of the patina of a bronze can help to establish this, as does the proof that a given manuscript of the Middle Ages stems from an archive of the fifteenth century. The whole sphere of authenticity is outside technical – and, of course, not only technical – reproducibility.[2] Confronted with its manual reproduction, which was usually branded as a forgery, the original preserved all its authority; not so *vis-à-vis* technical reproduction. The reason is twofold. First, process reproduction is more independent of the original than manual reproduction. For example, in photography, process reproduction can bring out those aspects of the original that are unattainable to the naked eye yet accessible to the lens, which is adjustable and chooses its angle at will. And photographic reproduction, with the aid of certain processes, such as enlargement or slow motion, can capture images which escape natural vision. Secondly, technical reproduction can put the copy of the original into situations which would be out of reach for the original itself.

Above all, it enables the original to meet the beholder halfway, be it in the form of a photograph or a phonograph record. The cathedral leaves its locale to be received in the studio of a lover of art; the choral production, performed in an auditorium or in the open air, resounds in the drawing room.

The situations into which the product of mechanical reproduction can be brought may not touch the actual work of art, yet the quality of its presence is always depreciated. This holds not only for the art work but also, for instance, for a landscape which passes in review before the spectator in a movie. In the case of the art object, a most sensitive nucleus – namely, its authenticity – is interfered with whereas no natural object is vulnerable on that score. The authenticity of a thing is the essence of all that is transmissible from its beginning, ranging from its substantive duration to its testimony to the history which it has experienced. Since the historical testimony rests on the authenticity, the former, too, is jeopardized by reproduction when substantive duration ceases to matter. And what is really jeopardized when the historical testimony is affected is the authority of the object.

One might subsume the eliminated element in the term "aura" and go on to say: that which withers in the age of mechanical reproduction is the aura of the work of art. This is a symptomatic process whose significance points beyond the realm of art. One might generalize by saying: the technique of reproduction detaches the reproduced object from the domain of tradition. By making many reproductions it substitutes a plurality of copies for a unique existence. And in permitting the reproduction to meet the beholder or listener in his own particular situation, it reactivates the object reproduced. These two processes lead to a tremendous shattering of tradition which is the obverse of the contemporary crisis and renewal of mankind. Both processes are intimately connected with the contemporary mass movements. Their most powerful agent is the film. Its social significance, particularly in its most positive form, is inconceivable without its destructive, cathartic aspect, that is, the liquidation of the traditional value of the cultural heritage. . . .

The uniqueness of a work of art is inseparable from its being imbedded in the fabric of tradition. This tradition itself is thoroughly alive and extremely changeable. An ancient statue of Venus, for example, stood in a different traditional context with the Greeks, who made it an object of veneration, than with the clerics of the Middle Ages, who viewed it as an ominous idol. Both of them, however, were equally confronted with its uniqueness, that is, its aura. Originally the contextual integration of art in tradition found its expression in the cult. We know that the earliest art works originated in the service of a ritual – first the magical, then the religious kind. It is significant that the existence of the work of art with reference to its aura is never entirely separated from its ritual function.[3] In other words, the unique value of the "authentic" work of art has its basis in ritual, the location of its original use value. This ritualistic basis, however remote, is still recognizable as secularized ritual even in the most profane forms of the cult of beauty.[4] The secular cult of beauty, developed during the Renaissance and prevailing for three centuries, clearly showed that ritualistic basis in its decline and the first deep crisis which befell it. With the advent of the first truly revolutionary means of reproduction, photography, simultaneously with the rise of socialism, art sensed the approaching crisis which has become evident a century later. At the time, art reacted with the doctrine of *l'art pour l'art*, that is, with a theology of art. This gave rise to what might be called a negative theology in the form of the idea of "pure" art, which not only denied any social function of art but also any categorizing by subject matter. (In poetry, Mallarmé was the first to take this position.)

An analysis of art in the age of mechanical reproduction must do justice to these relationships, for they lead us to an all-important insight: for the first time in world history, mechanical reproduction emancipates the work of art from its parasitical dependence on ritual. To an ever greater degree the work of art reproduced becomes the work of art designed for reproducibility.[5] From a photographic negative, for example, one can make any number of prints; to ask for the "authentic" print makes no sense. But the instant the criterion of authenticity ceases to be applicable to artistic production, the total function of art is reversed. Instead of being based on ritual, it begins to be based on another practice – politics....

With the emancipation of the various art practices from ritual go increasing opportunities for the exhibition of their products. It is easier to exhibit a portrait bust that can be sent here and there than to exhibit the statue of a divinity that has its fixed place in the interior of a temple. The same holds for the painting as against the mosaic or fresco that preceded it. And even though the public presentability of a mass originally may have been just as great as that of a symphony, the latter originated at the moment when its public presentability promised to surpass that of the mass.

With the different methods of technical reproduction of a work of art, its fitness for exhibition increased to such an extent that the quantitative shift between its two poles turned into a qualitative transformation of its nature. This is comparable to the situation of the work of art in prehistoric times when, by the absolute emphasis on its cult value, it was, first and foremost, an instrument of magic. Only later did it come to be recognized as a work of art. In the same way today, by the absolute emphasis on its exhibition value the work of art becomes a creation with entirely new functions, among which the one we are conscious of, the artistic function, later may be recognized as incidental.[6] This much is certain: today photography and the film are the most serviceable exemplifications of this new function....

Mechanical reproduction of art changes the reaction of the masses toward art. The reactionary attitude toward a Picasso painting changes into the progressive reaction toward a Chaplin movie. The progressive reaction is characterized by the direct, intimate fusion of visual and emotional enjoyment with the orientation of the expert. Such fusion is of great social significance. The greater the decrease in the social significance of an art form, the sharper the distinction between criticism and enjoyment by the public. The conventional is uncritically enjoyed, and the truly new is criticized with aversion. With regard to the screen, the critical and the receptive attitudes of the public coincide. The decisive reason for this is that individual reactions are predetermined by the mass audience response they are about to produce, and this is nowhere more pronounced than in the film. The moment these responses become manifest they control each other. Again, the comparison with painting is fruitful. A painting has always had an excellent chance to be viewed by one person or by a few. The simultaneous contemplation of paintings by a large public, such as developed in the nineteenth century, is an early symptom of the crisis of painting, a crisis which was by no means occasioned exclusively by photography but rather in a relatively independent manner by the appeal of art works to the masses.

Painting simply is in no position to present an object for simultaneous collective experience, as it was possible for architecture at all times, for the epic poem in the past, and for the movie today. Although this circumstance in itself should not lead one to conclusions about the social role of painting, it does constitute a serious threat as soon as painting, under special conditions and, as it were, against its nature, is confronted directly by the masses. In the churches and monasteries of the Middle Ages and at the princely courts up to the end of the eighteenth century, a collective reception of paintings did not occur simultaneously, but by graduated and hierarchized mediation. The change that has come about is an expression of the particular conflict in which painting was implicated by the mechanical reproducibility of paintings. Although paintings began to be publicly exhibited in galleries and salons, there was no way for the masses to organize and control themselves in their receptions. Thus the same public which responds in a progressive manner toward a grotesque film is bound to respond in a reactionary manner to surrealism.

The characteristics of the film lie not only in the manner in which man presents himself to mechanical equipment but also in the manner in which, by means of this apparatus, man can represent his environment. A glance at occupational psychology illustrates the testing capacity of the equipment. Psychoanalysis illustrates it in a different perspective. The film has enriched our field of perception with methods which can be illustrated by those of Freudian theory. Fifty years ago, a slip of the tongue passed more or less unnoticed. Only exceptionally may such a slip have revealed dimensions of depth in a conversation which had seemed to be taking its course on the surface. Since the *Psychopathology of Everyday Life* things have changed. This book isolated and made analyzable things which had heretofore floated along unnoticed in the broad stream of perception. For the entire spectrum of optical, and now also acoustical, perception the film has brought about a similar deepening of apperception. It is only an obverse of this fact that behavior items shown in a movie can be analyzed much more precisely and from more points of view than those presented on paintings or on the stage. As compared with painting, filmed behavior lends itself more readily to analysis because of its incomparably more precise statements of the situation. In comparison with the stage scene, the filmed behavior item lends itself more readily to analysis because it can be isolated more easily. This circumstance derives its chief importance from its tendency to promote the mutual penetration of art and science. Actually, of a screened behavior item which is neatly brought out in a certain situation, like a muscle of a body, it is difficult to say which is more fascinating, its artistic value or its value for science. To demonstrate the identity of the artistic and scientific uses of photography which heretofore usually were separated will be one of the revolutionary functions of the film.[7]

By close-ups of the things around us, by focusing on hidden details of familiar objects, by exploring commonplace milieus under the ingenious guidance of the camera, the film, on the one hand, extends our comprehension of the necessities which rule our lives; on the other hand, it manages to assure us of an immense and unexpected field of action. Our taverns and our metropolitan streets, our offices and furnished rooms, our railroad stations and our factories appeared to have us locked up hopelessly. Then came the film and burst this prison-world asunder by the dynamite of the tenth of a second, so that now, in the midst of its far-flung ruins and debris, we calmly and adventurously go traveling. With the close-up, space expands; with slow motion, movement is extended. The enlargement of a snapshot does not simply render more precise what in any case was visible, though unclear: it reveals entirely new structural formations of the subject. So, too, slow motion not only presents familiar qualities of movement but reveals in them entirely unknown ones "which, far from looking like retarded rapid movements, give the effect of singularly gliding, floating, supernatural motions."[8] Evidently a different nature opens itself to the camera than opens to the naked eye – if only because an unconsciously penetrated space is substituted for a space consciously explored by man. Even if one has a general knowledge of the way people walk, one knows nothing of a person's posture during the fractional second of a stride. The act of reaching for a lighter or a spoon is familiar routine, yet we hardly know what really goes on between hand and metal, not to mention how this fluctuates with our moods. Here the camera intervenes with the resources of its lowerings and liftings, its interruptions and isolations, its extensions and accelerations, its enlargements and reductions. The camera introduces us to unconscious optics as does psychoanalysis to unconscious impulses. . . .

The growing proletarianization of modern man and the increasing formation of masses are two aspects of the same process. Fascism attempts to organize the newly created proletarian masses without affecting the property structure which the masses strive to eliminate. Fascism sees its salvation in giving these masses not their right, but instead a chance to express themselves.[9] The masses have a right to change property relations; Fascism seeks to give them an expression while preserving property. The logical result of Fascism is the introduction of aesthetics into political life. The violation of the masses, whom Fascism, with its *Führer* cult, forces to their knees, has its counterpart in the violation of an apparatus which is pressed into the production of ritual values.

All efforts to render politics aesthetic culminate in one thing: war. War and war only can set a goal for mass movements on the largest scale while respecting the traditional property system. This is the political formula for the situation. The technological formula may be stated as follows: Only war makes it possible to mobilize all of today's technical resources while maintaining the property system. It goes without saying that the Fascist apotheosis of war does not employ such arguments. Still, Marinetti says in his manifesto on the Ethiopian colonial war:

> For twenty-seven years we Futurists have rebelled against the branding of war as antiaesthetic . . . Accordingly we state: . . . War is beautiful because it establishes man's dominion over the subjugated machinery by means of gas masks, terrifying megaphones, flame throwers, and small tanks. War is beautiful because it initiates the dreamt-of metalization of the human body. War is beautiful because it enriches a flowering meadow with the fiery orchids of machine guns. War is beautiful because it combines the gunfire, the cannonades, the cease-fire, the scents, and the stench of putrefaction into a symphony. War is beautiful because it creates new architecture, like that of the big tanks, the geometrical formation flights, the smoke spirals from burning villages, and many others . . . Poets and artists of Futurism! . . . remember these

principles of an aesthetics of war so that your struggle for a new literature and a new graphic art . . . may be illumined by them!

This manifesto has the virtue of clarity. Its formulations deserve to be accepted by dialecticians. To the latter, the aesthetics of today's war appears as follows: If the natural utilization of productive forces is impeded by the property system, the increase in technical devices, in speed, and in the sources of energy will press for an unnatural utilization, and this is found in war. The destructiveness of war furnishes proof that society has not been mature enough to incorporate technology as its organ, that technology has not been sufficiently developed to cope with the elemental forces of society. The horrible features of imperialistic warfare are attributable to the discrepancy between the tremendous means of production and their inadequate utilization in the process of production – in other words, to unemployment and the lack of markets. Imperialistic war is a rebellion of technology which collects, in the form of "human material," the claims to which society has denied its natural material. Instead of draining rivers, society directs a human stream into a bed of trenches; instead of dropping seeds from airplanes, it drops incendiary bombs over cities; and through gas warfare the aura is abolished in a new way.

"*Fiat ars – pereat mundus*," says Fascism, and, as Marinetti admits, expects war to supply the artistic gratification of a sense perception that has been changed by technology. This is evidently the consummation of "*l'art pour l'art*." Mankind, which in Homer's time was an object of contemplation for the Olympian gods, now is one for itself. Its self-alienation has reached such a degree that it can experience its own destruction as an aesthetic pleasure of the first order. This is the situation of politics which Fascism is rendering aesthetic. Communism responds by politicizing art.

Notes

1 Of course, the history of a work of art encompasses more than this. The history of the *Mona Lisa*, for instance, encompasses the kind and number of its copies made in the seventeenth, eighteenth, and nineteenth centuries.

2 Precisely because authenticity is not reproducible, the intensive penetration of certain (mechanical) processes of reproduction was instrumental in differentiating and grading authenticity. To develop such differentiations was an important function of the trade in works of art. The invention of the woodcut may be said to have struck at the root of the quality of authenticity even before its late flowering. To be sure, at the time of its origin a medieval picture of the Madonna could not yet be said to be "authentic." It became "authentic" only during the succeeding centuries and perhaps most strikingly so during the last one.

3 The definition of the aura as a "unique phenomenon of a distance however close it may be" represents nothing but the formulation of the cult value of the work of art in categories of space and time perception. Distance is the opposite of closeness. The essentially distant object is the unapproachable one. Unapproachability is indeed a major quality of the cult image. True to its nature, it remains "distant, however close it may be." The closeness which one may gain from its subject matter does not impair the distance which it retains in its appearance.

4 To the extent to which the cult value of the painting is secularized the ideas of its fundamental uniqueness lose distinctness. In the imagination of the beholder the uniqueness of the phenomena which hold sway in the cult image is more and more displaced by the empirical uniqueness of the creator or of his creative achievement. To be sure, never completely so; the concept of authenti-

city always transcends mere genuineness. (This is particularly apparent in the collector who always retains some traces of the fetishist and who, by owning the work of art, shares in its ritual power.) Nevertheless, the function of the concept of authenticity remains determinate in the evaluation of art; with the secularization of art authenticity displaces the cult value of the work.

5   In the case of films, mechanical reproduction is not as with literature and painting, an external condition for mass distribution. Mechanical reproduction is inherent in the very technique of film production. This technique not only permits in the most direct way but virtually causes mass distribution. It enforces distribution because the production of a film is so expensive that an individual who, for instance, might afford to buy a painting no longer can afford to buy a film. In 1927 it was calculated that a major film, in order to pay its way, had to reach an audience of nine million. With the sound film, to be sure, a setback in its international distribution occurred at first: audiences became limited by language barriers. This coincided with the Fascist emphasis on national interests. It is more important to focus on this connection with Fascism than on this setback, which was soon minimized by synchronization. The simultaneity of both phenomena is attributable to the depression. The same disturbances which, on a larger scale, led to an attempt to maintain the existing property structure by sheer force led the endangered film capital to speed up the development of the sound film. The introduction of the sound film brought about a temporary relief, not only because it again brought the masses into the theaters but also because it merged new capital from the electrical industry with that of the film industry. Thus, viewed from the outside, the sound film promoted national interests, but seen from the inside it helped to internationalize film production even more than previously.

6   Bertolt Brecht, on a different level, engaged in analogous reflections: "If the concept of 'work of art' can no longer be applied to the thing that emerges once the work is transformed into a commodity, we have to eliminate this concept with cautious care but without fear, lest we liquidate the function of the very thing as well. For it has to go through this phase without mental reservation, and not as noncommittal deviation from the straight path; rather, what happens here with the work of art will change it fundamentally and erase its past to such an extent that should the old concept be taken up again – and it will, why not? – it will no longer stir any memory of the thing it once designated."

7   Renaissance painting offers a revealing analogy to this situation. The incomparable development of this art and its significance rested not least on the integration of a number of new sciences, or at least of new scientific data. Renaissance painting made use of anatomy and perspective, of mathematics, meteorology, and chromatology. Valéry writes: "What could be further from us than the strange claim of a Leonardo to whom painting was a supreme goal and the ultimate demonstration of knowledge? Leonardo was convinced that painting demanded universal knowledge, and he did not even shrink from a theoretical analysis which to us is stunning because of its very depth and precision . . ." – Paul Valéry, *Pièces sur l'art*, "Autour de Corot" (Paris), p. 191.

8   Rudolf Arnheim, *Film als Kunst* (Berlin, 1931), p. 138.

9   One technical feature is significant here, especially with regard to newsreels, the propagandist importance of which can hardly be overestimated. Mass reproduction is aided especially by the reproduction of masses. In big parades and monster rallies, in sports events, and in war, all of which nowadays are captured by camera and sound recording, the masses are brought face to face with themselves. This process, whose significance need not be stressed, is intimately connected with the development of the techniques of reproduction and photography. Mass movements are usually discerned more clearly by a camera than by the naked eye. A bird's-eye view best captures gatherings of hundreds of thousands. And even though such a view may be as accessible to the human eye as it is to the camera, the image received by the eye cannot be enlarged the way a negative is enlarged. This means that mass movements, including war, constitute a form of human behavior which particularly favors mechanical equipment.

CHAPTER 3

The Culture Industry as Mass Deception

Max Horkheimer and Theodor Adorno

One of the few positive consequences of the displacement of European intellectuals during World War II was the arrival in Los Angeles of the German thinkers, Max Horkheimer and Theodor Adorno, who had worked together in the Institute for Social Research in Frankfurt before the war. In their 1944 book, *The Dialectic of Enlightenment*, they examine US popular culture, and their highly pessimistic conclusion was that it consists of routinized forms that diminish the complexity of human experience and serve the interests of powerful corporations.

The sociological theory that the loss of the support of objectively established religion, the dissolution of the last remnants of precapitalism, together with technological and social differentiation or specialization, have led to cultural chaos is disproved every day; for culture now impresses the same stamp on everything. Films, radio, and magazines make up a system which is uniform as a whole and in every part.... Under monopoly capitalism all mass culture is identical...

Interested parties explain the culture industry in technological terms. It is alleged that because millions participate in it, certain reproduction processes are necessary that inevitably require identical needs in innumerable places to be satisfied with identical goods. The technical contrast between the few production centers and the large number of widely dispersed consumption points is said to demand organization and planning by management. Furthermore, it is claimed that standards were based in the first place on consumers' needs, and for that reason were accepted with so little resistance. The result is the circle of manipulation and retroactive need in which the unity of the system grows ever stronger. No mention is made of the fact that the basis on which technology acquires power over society is the power of those whose economic hold over society is greatest. A technological rationale is the rationale of domination itself. It is the coercive nature of society alienated from itself. Automobiles, bombs, and movies keep the whole thing together until their leveling element shows its strength in the very wrong which it furthered. It has made the technology of the culture industry no more than the achievement of standardization and mass production, sacrificing whatever involved a distinction between the logic of the work and that of the social system. This is the result not of a law of movement in technology as such but of its function in today's economy. The need which might resist central control has already been suppressed by the control of the individual consciousness....

[A]ny trace of spontaneity from the public in official broadcasting is controlled and absorbed by talent scouts, studio competitions, and official programs of every kind selected by professionals. Talented performers belong to the industry long before it displays them; otherwise they would not be so eager to fit in. The attitude of the public, which ostensibly and actually favors the system of the culture industry, is a part of the system and not an excuse for it. If one branch of art follows the same formula as one with a very different medium and content; if the dramatic intrigue of broadcast soap operas becomes no more than useful material for showing how to master technical problems at both ends of the scale of musical experience – real jazz or a cheap imitation; or if a movement from a Beethoven symphony is crudely "adapted" for a film sound-track in the same way as a Tolstoy novel is garbled in a film script: then the claim that this is done to satisfy the spontaneous wishes of the public is no more than hot air. We are closer to the facts if we explain these phenomena as inherent in the technical and personnel apparatus which, down to its last cog, itself forms part of the economic mechanism of selection. In addition there is the agreement – or at least the determination – of all executive authorities not to produce or sanction anything that in any way differs from their own rules, their own ideas about consumers, or above all themselves.

In our age the objective social tendency is incarnate in the hidden subjective purposes of company directors, the foremost among whom are in the most powerful sectors of industry – steel, petroleum, electricity, and chemicals. Culture monopolies are weak and dependent in comparison. They cannot afford to neglect their appeasement of the real holders of power if their sphere of activity in mass society (a sphere producing a specific type of commodity which anyhow is still too closely bound up with easygoing liberalism and Jewish intellectuals) is not to undergo a series of purges. The dependence of the most powerful broadcasting company on the electrical industry, or of the motion picture industry on the banks, is characteristic of the whole sphere, whose individual branches are themselves economically interwoven. All are in such close contact that the extreme concentration of mental forces allows demarcation lines between different firms and technical branches to be ignored. The ruthless unity in the culture industry is evidence of what will happen in politics. Marked differentiations such as those of A and B films, or of stories in magazines in different price ranges, depend not so much on subject matter as on classifying, organizing, and labeling consumers. Something is provided for all so that none may escape; the distinctions are emphasized and extended. The public is catered to with a hierarchical range of mass-produced products of varying quality, thus advancing the rule of complete quantification. Everybody must behave (as if spontaneously) in accordance with his previously determined and indexed level, and choose the category of mass product turned out for his type. Consumers appear as statistics on research organization charts, and are divided by income groups into red, green, and blue areas; the technique is that used for any type of propaganda.

How formalized the procedure is can be seen when the mechanically differentiated products prove to be all alike in the end. That the difference between the Chrysler range and General Motors products is basically illusory strikes every child with a keen interest in varieties. What connoisseurs discuss as good or bad points serve only to perpetuate the semblance of competition and range of choice. The same applies to the Warner Brothers and Metro Goldwyn Mayer productions....

Not only are the hit songs, stars, and soap operas cyclically recurrent and rigidly invariable types, but the specific content of the entertainment itself is derived from them and only appears to change. The details are interchangeable. The short interval sequence which was effective in a hit song, the hero's momentary fall from grace (which he accepts as good sport), the rough treatment which the beloved gets from the male star, the latter's rugged defiance of the spoilt heiress, are, like all the other details, ready-made clichés to be slotted in anywhere; they never do anything more than fulfill the purpose allotted them in the overall plan. Their whole *raison d'être* is to confirm it by being its constituent parts. As soon as the film begins, it is quite clear how it will end, and who will be rewarded, punished, or forgotten. In light music, once the trained ear has heard the first notes of the hit song, it can guess what is coming and feel flattered when it does come. The average length of the short story has to be rigidly adhered to. Even gags, effects, and jokes are calculated like the setting in which they are placed. They are the responsibility of special experts and their narrow range makes it easy for them to be apportioned in the office. The development of the culture industry has led to the predominance of the effect, the obvious touch, and the technical detail over the work itself – which once expressed an idea, but was liquidated together with the idea. When the detail won its freedom, it became rebellious and, in the period from Romanticism to Expressionism, asserted itself as free expression, as a vehicle of protest against the organization. In music the single harmonic effect obliterated the awareness of form as a whole; in painting the individual color was stressed at the expense of pictorial composition; and in the novel psychology became more important than structure. The totality of the culture industry has put an end to this. Though concerned exclusively with effects, it crushes their insubordination and makes them subserve the formula, which replaces the work. The same fate is inflicted on whole and parts alike. The whole inevitably bears no relation to the details – just like the career of a successful man into which everything is made to fit as an illustration or a proof, whereas it is nothing more than the sum of all those idiotic events. The so-called dominant idea is like a file which ensures order but not coherence. The whole and the parts alike; there is no antithesis and no connection. Their prearranged harmony is a mockery of what had to be striven after in the great bourgeois works of art. In Germany the graveyard stillness of the dictatorship already hung over the gayest films of the democratic era. . . .

The stunting of the mass media consumer's powers of imagination and spontaneity does not have to be traced back to any psychological mechanisms; he must ascribe the loss of those attributes to the objective nature of the products themselves, especially to the most characteristic of them, the sound film. They are so designed that quickness, powers of observation, and experience are undeniably needed to apprehend them at all; yet sustained thought is out of the question if the spectator is not to miss the relentless rush of facts. Even though the effort required for his response is semi-automatic, no scope is left for the imagination. Those who are so absorbed by the world of the movie – by its images, gestures, and words – that they are unable to supply what really makes it a world, do not have to dwell on particular points of its mechanics during a screening. All the other films and products of the entertainment industry which they have seen have taught them what to expect; they react automatically. The might of industrial society is lodged in men's minds. The entertainments manufacturers know that their products will be consumed with alertness even when the customer is distraught, for each of them is a model of the huge economic machinery which has always sustained the masses, whether at work or at leisure – which is akin to work. From *every* sound film and every broadcast program the social effect can be inferred which is exclusive to none but is shared by all alike. The culture industry as a whole has molded men as a type unfailingly reproduced in every product. All the agents of this process, from the producer to the women's clubs, take good care that the simple reproduction of this mental state is not nuanced or extended in any way. . . .

Nevertheless, this caricature of style does not amount to something beyond the genuine style of the past. In the culture industry the notion of genuine style is seen to be the aesthetic equivalent of domination. Style considered as mere aesthetic regularity is a romantic dream of the past. The unity of style not only of the Christian Middle Ages but of the Renaissance expresses in each case the different structure of social power, and not the obscure experience of the oppressed in which the general was enclosed. The great artists were never those who embodied a wholly flawless and perfect style, but those who used style as a way of hardening themselves against the chaotic expression of suffering, as a negative truth. The style of their works gave what was expressed that force without which life flows away unheard. Those very art forms which are known as classical, such as Mozart's music, contain objective trends which represent something different to the style which they incarnate. As late as Schoenberg and Picasso, the great artists have retained a mistrust of style, and at crucial points have subordinated it to the logic of the matter. What Dadaists and Expressionists called the untruth of style as such triumphs today in the sung jargon of a crooner, in the carefully contrived elegance of a film star, and even in the admirable expertise of a photograph of a peasant's squalid hut. Style represents a promise in every work of art. That which is expressed is subsumed through style into the dominant forms of generality, into the language of music, painting, or words, in the hope that it will be reconciled thus with the idea of true generality. This promise held out by the work of art that it will create truth by lending new shape to the conventional social forms is as necessary as it is hypocritical. It unconditionally posits the real forms of life as it is by suggesting that fulfillment lies in their aesthetic derivatives. To this extent the claim of art is always ideology too. However, only in this confrontation with tradition of which style is the record can art express suffering. That factor in a work of art which enables it to transcend reality certainly cannot be detached from style; but it does not consist of the harmony actually realized, of any doubtful unity of form and content, within and without, of individual and society; it is to be found in those features in which discrepancy appears: in the necessary failure of the passionate striving for identity. Instead of exposing itself to this failure in which the style of the great work of art has always achieved self-negation, the inferior work has always relied on its similarity with others – on a surrogate identity.

In the culture industry this imitation finally becomes absolute. Having ceased to be anything but style, it reveals the latter's secret: obedience to the social hierarchy. Today aesthetic barbarity completes what has threatened the creations of the spirit since they were gathered together as culture and neutralized. To speak of culture was always contrary to culture. Culture as a common denominator already contains in embryo that schematization and process of cataloging and classification which bring culture within the sphere of administration. And it is precisely the industrialized, the consequent, subsumption which entirely accords with this notion of culture. By subordinating in the same way and to the same end all areas of intellectual creation, by occupying men's senses from the time they leave the factory in the evening to the time they clock in again the next morning with matter that bears the impress of the labor process they themselves have to sustain throughout the day, this subsumption mockingly satisfies the concept of a unified culture which the philosophers of personality contrasted with mass culture.

CHAPTER 4

The Practice of Everyday Life

Michel de Certeau

In his 1984 book, *The Practice of Everyday Life*, Michel de Certeau describes what might be called the "other side" of Bourdieu's highly deterministic model of the social and cultural universe. For Bourdieu, the structure supersedes and shapes all the individual or particular decisions that social agents might make or the actions that they might take. But social and cultural life, according to Certeau, is not entirely accounted for in this model of total determination. Human agency has some leeway to "err" or wander from the lines prescribed by the overarching structure of society. An important word for Certeau is "tactics," those discrete individuated actions and decisions that are not part of an overarching design or strategy. The tactical use of cultural forms can allow one to elude structural determination. Other theorists of culture will use a more explicitly political vocabulary of "resistance" to describe the ability of agents to undo the power of social determination. The creation of counter-hegemonic rituals and stylistic practices allows for an element of nonsense and play in an otherwise purely deterministic social universe.

In spite of measures taken to repress or conceal it, *la perruque* (or its equivalent [doing one's own work in one's employer's time]) is infiltrating itself everywhere and becoming more and more common. It is only one case among all the practices which introduce *artistic* tricks and competitions of *accomplices* into a system that reproduces and partitions through work or leisure. Sly as a fox and twice as quick: there are countless ways of "making do."

From this point of view, the dividing line no longer falls between work and leisure. These two areas of activity flow together. They repeat and reinforce each other. Cultural techniques that camouflage economic reproduction with fictions of surprise ("the event"), of truth ("information") or communication ("promotion") spread through the workplace. Reciprocally, cultural production offers an area of expansion for rational operations that permit work to be managed by dividing it (analysis), tabulating it (synthesis) and aggregating it (generalization). A distinction is required other than the one that distributes behaviors according to their *place* (of work or leisure) and qualifies them thus by the fact that they are located on one or another square of the social checkerboard – in the office, in the workshop, or at the movies. There are differences of another type. They refer to the *modalities* of action, to the *formalities* of practices. They traverse the frontiers dividing time, place, and type of action into one part assigned for work and another for leisure. For example, *la perruque* grafts itself onto the system of the industrial assembly line (its counterpoint, in the same place), as a variant of the activity which, outside the factory (in another place), takes the form of *bricolage*.

Although they remain dependent upon the possibilities offered by circumstances, these transverse *tactics* do not obey the law of the place, for they are not defined or identified by it. In this respect, they are not any more localizable than the technocratic (and scriptural) *strategies* that seek to create places in conformity with abstract models. But what distinguishes them at the same time concerns the *types of operations* and the role of spaces: strategies are able to produce, tabulate, and impose these spaces, when those operations take place, whereas tactics can only use, manipulate, and divert these spaces.

We must therefore specify the operational schemas. Just as in literature one differentiates "styles" or ways of writing, one can distinguish "ways of operating" – ways of walking, reading, producing, speaking, etc. These styles of action intervene in a field which regulates them at a first level (for example, at the level of the factory system), but they introduce into it a way of turning it to their advantage that obeys other rules and constitutes something like a second level interwoven into the first (for instance, *la perruque*). These "ways of operating" are similar to "instructions for use," and they create a certain play in the machine through a stratification of different and interfering kinds of functioning. Thus a North African living in Paris or Roubaix (France) insinuates *into* the system imposed on him by the construction of a low-income housing development or of the French language the ways of "dwelling" (in a house or a language) peculiar to his native Kabylia. He superimposes them and, by that combination, creates for himself a space in which he can find *ways of using* the constraining order of the place or of the language. Without leaving the place where he has no choice but to live and which lays down its law for him, he establishes within it a degree of *plurality* and creativity. By an art of being in between, he draws unexpected results from his situation.

These modes of use – or rather re-use – multiply with the extension of acculturation phenomena, that is, with the displacements that substitute manners or "methods" of transiting toward an identification of a person by the place in which he lives or works. That does not prevent them from corresponding to a very ancient art of "making do." I give them the name of uses, even though the word most often designates stereotyped procedures accepted and reproduced by a group, its "ways and customs." The problem lies in the ambiguity of the word, since it is precisely a matter of recognizing in these "uses" "actions" (in the military sense of the word) that have their own formality and inventiveness and that discreetly organize the multiform labor of consumption.

Use, or Consumption

In the wake of the many remarkable works that have analyzed "cultural products," the system of their production,[1] the geography of their distribution and the situation of consumers in that geography,[2] it seems possible to consider these products no longer merely as data on the basis of which statistical tabulations of their circulation can be drawn up or the economic functioning of their diffusion understood, but also as parts of the repertory with which users carry out operations of their own. Henceforth, these facts are no longer the data of our calculations, but rather the lexicon of users' practices. Thus, once the images broadcast by television and the time spent in front of the TV set have been analyzed, it remains to be asked what the consumer *makes* of these images and during these hours. The thousands of people who buy a health magazine, the customers in a supermarket, the practitioners of urban space, the consumers of newspaper stories and legends – what do they make of what they "absorb," receive, and pay for? What do they do with it?

The enigma of the consumer-sphinx. His products are scattered in the graphs of televised, urbanistic, and commercial production. They are all the less visible because the networks framing them are becoming more and more tightly woven, flexible, and totalitarian. They are thus protean in form, blending in with their surroundings, and liable to disappear into the colonizing organizations whose products leave no room where the consumers can mark their activity. The child still scrawls and daubs on his schoolbooks; even if he is punished for this crime, he has made a space for himself and signs his existence as an author on it. The television viewer cannot write anything on the screen of his set. He has been dislodged from the product; he plays no role in its apparition. He loses his author's rights and becomes, or so it seems, a pure receiver, the mirror of a multiform and narcissistic actor. Pushed to the limit, he would be the image of appliances that no longer need him in order to produce themselves, the reproduction of a "celibate machine."[3]

In reality, a rationalized, expansionist, centralized, spectacular and clamorous production is confronted by an entirely different kind of production, called "consumption" and characterized by its ruses, its fragmentation (the result of the circumstances), its poaching, its clandestine nature, its tireless but quiet activity, in short by its quasi-invisibility, since it shows itself not in its own products (where would it place them?) but in an art of using those imposed on it.

The cautious yet fundamental inversions brought about by consumption in other societies have long been studied. Thus the spectacular victory of Spanish colonization over the indigenous Indian cultures was diverted from its intended aims by the use made of it: even when they were subjected, indeed even when they accepted their subjection, the Indians often used the laws, practices, and representations that were imposed on them by force or by fascination to ends other than those of their conquerors; they made something else out of them; they subverted them from within – not by rejecting them or by transforming them (though that occurred as well), but by many different ways of using them in the service of rules, customs or convictions foreign to the colonization which they could not escape.[4] They metaphorized the dominant order: they made it function in another register. They remained other within the system which they assimilated and which assimilated them externally. They diverted it without leaving it. Procedures of consumption maintained their difference in the very space that the occupier was organizing.

Is this an extreme example? No, even if the resistance of the Indians was founded on a memory tattooed by oppression, a past inscribed on their body.[5] To a lesser degree, the same process can be found in the use made in "popular" milieus of the cultures diffused by the "elites" that produce language. The imposed knowledge and symbolisms become objects manipulated by practitioners who have not produced them. The language produced by a certain social category has the power to extend its conquests into vast areas surrounding it, "deserts" where nothing equally articulated seems to exist, but in doing so it is caught in the trap of its assimilation by a jungle of procedures rendered invisible to the conqueror by the very victories he seems to have won. However spectacular it may be, his privilege is likely to be only apparent if it merely serves as a framework for the stubborn, guileful, everyday practices that make use of it. What is called "popularization" or "degradation" of a culture is from this point of view a partial and caricatural aspect of the revenge that utilizing tactics take on the power that dominates production. In any case, the consumer cannot be identified or qualified by the newspapers or commercial products he assimilates: between the person (who uses them) and these products (indexes of the "order" which is imposed on him), there is a gap of varying proportions opened by the use that he makes of them.

Use must thus be analyzed in itself. There is no lack of models, especially so far as language is concerned; language is indeed the privileged terrain on which to discern the formal rules proper to such practices. Gilbert Ryle, borrowing Saussure's distinction between "*langue*" (a system) and "*parole*" (an act), compared the former to a fund of *capital* and the latter to the *operations* it makes possible: on the one hand, a stock of materials, on the other, transactions and uses.[6] In the case of consumption, one could almost say that production furnishes the capital and that users, like renters, acquire the right to operate on and with this fund without owning it. But the comparison is valid only for the relation between the knowledge of a language and "speech acts." From this alone can be derived a series of questions and categories which have permitted us, especially since Bar-Hillel's work, to open up within the study of language (*semiosis* or *semiotics*) a particular area (called *pragmatics*) devoted to use, notably to *indexical expressions*, that is, "words and sentences of which the reference cannot be determined without knowledge of the context of use."[7]

We shall return later to these inquiries which have illuminated a whole region of everyday practices (the use of language); at this point, it suffices to note that they are based on a problematics of enunciation.[8] By situating the act in relation to its circumstances, "contexts of use" draw attention to the traits that specify the act of speaking (or practice of language) and are its effects. Enunciation furnishes a model of these characteristics, but they can also be discovered in the relation that other practices (walking, residing, etc.) entertain with non-linguistic systems. Enunciation presupposes: (1) a *realization* of the linguistic system through a speech act that actualizes some of its potential (language is real only in the act of speaking); (2) an *appropriation* of language by the speaker who uses it; (3) the postulation of an interlocutor (real or fictive) and thus the constitution of a relational *contract* or allocution (one speaks to someone); (4) the establishment of a *present* through the act of the "I" who speaks, and conjointly, since "the present is properly the source of time," the organization of a temporality (the present creates a before and an after) and the existence of a "now" which is the presence to the world.[9]

These elements (realizing, appropriating, being inscribed in relations, being situated in time) make of enunciation, and secondarily of use, a nexus of circumstances, a nexus adherent to the "context" from which it can be distinguished only by abstraction. Indissociable from the present *instant*, from particular circumstances and from a *faire* (a peculiar way of doing things, of producing language and of modifying the dynamics of a relation), the speech act is at the same time a use *of* language and an operation performed *on* it. We can attempt to apply this model to many non-linguistic operations by taking as our hypothesis that all these uses concern consumption.

We must, however, clarify the nature of these operations from another angle, not on the basis of the relation they entertain with a system or an order, but insofar as *power relationships* define the networks in which they are inscribed and delimit the circumstances from which they can profit. In order to do so, we must pass from a linguistic frame of reference to a polemological one. We are concerned with battles or games between the strong and the weak, and with the "actions" which remain possible for the latter.

Strategies and Tactics

Unrecognized producers, poets of their own affairs, trailblazers in the jungles of functionalist rationality, consumers produce something resembling the "*lignes d'erre*" described by Deligny.[10] They trace "indeterminate trajectories"[11] that are apparently meaningless, since they do not cohere with the constructed, written, and prefabricated space through which they move. They are sentences that remain unpredictable within the space ordered by the organizing techniques of systems. Although they use as their *material* the *vocabularies* of established languages (those of television, newspapers, the supermarket or city planning), although they remain within the framework of prescribed *syntaxes* (the temporal modes of schedules, paradigmatic organizations of places, etc.), these "traverses" remain heterogeneous to the systems they infiltrate and in which they sketch out the guileful ruses of *different* interests and desires. They circulate, come and go, overflow and drift over an imposed terrain, like the snowy waves of the sea slipping in among the rocks and defiles of an established order.

Statistics can tell us virtually nothing about the currents in this sea theoretically governed by the institutional frameworks that it in fact gradually erodes and displaces. Indeed, it is less a matter of a liquid circulating in the interstices of a solid than of different *movements* making use of the elements of the terrain. Statistical study is satisfied with classifying, calculating and tabulating these elements – "lexical" units, advertising words, television images, manufactured products, constructed places, etc. – and they do it with categories and taxonomies that conform to those of industrial or administrative production. Hence such study can grasp only the material used by consumer practices – a material which is obviously that imposed on everyone by production – and not the *formality* proper to these practices, their surreptitious and guileful "movement," that is, the very activity of "making do." The strength of these computations lies in their ability to divide, but this analytical ability eliminates the possibility of representing the tactical trajectories which, according to their own criteria, select fragments taken from the vast ensembles of production in order to compose new stories with them.

What is counted is *what* is used, not the *ways* of using. Paradoxically, the latter become invisible in the universe of codification and generalized transparency. Only the effects (the quantity and locus of the consumed products) of these waves that flow in everywhere remain perceptible. They circulate without being seen, discernible only through the objects that they move about and erode. The practices of consumption are the ghosts of the society that carries their name. Like the "spirits" of former times, they constitute the multiform and occult postulate of productive activity.

In order to give an account of these practices, I have resorted to the category of "trajectory."[12] It was intended to suggest a temporal movement through space, that is, the unity of a diachronic *succession* of points through which it passes, and not the *figure* that these points form on a space that is supposed to be synchronic or chronic. Indeed, this "representation" is insufficient, precisely because a trajectory is drawn, and time and movement are thus reduced to a line that can be seized as a whole by the eye and read in a single moment, as one projects onto a map the path taken by someone walking through a city. However useful this "flattening out" may be, it transforms the *temporal* articulation of places into a *spatial* sequence of points. A graph takes the place of an operation. A reversible sign (one that can be read in both directions, once it is projected onto a map) is substituted for a practice indissociable from particular moments and "opportunities," and thus irreversible (one cannot go backward in time, or have another chance at missed opportunities). It is thus a mark *in place of* acts, a relic in place of performances: it is only their remainder, the sign of their erasure. Such a projection postulates that it is possible to take the one (the mark) for the other (operations articulated on occasions). This is a *quid pro quo* typical of the reductions which a functionalist administration of space must make in order to be effective.

A distinction between *strategies* and *tactics* appears to provide a more adequate initial schema. I call a *strategy* the calculation (or manipulation) of power relationships that becomes possible as soon as a subject with will and power (a business, an army, a city, a scientific institution) can be isolated. It postulates a *place* that can be delimited as its *own* and serve as the base from which relations with an *exteriority* composed of targets or threats (customers or competitors, enemies, the country surrounding the city, objectives and objects of research, etc.) can be managed. As in management, every "strategic" rationalization seeks first of all to distinguish its "own" place, that is, the place of its own power and will, from an "environment." A Cartesian attitude, if you wish: it is an effort to delimit one's own place in a world bewitched by the invisible powers of the Other. It is also the typical attitude of modern science, politics, and military strategy.

The establishment of a break between a place appropriated as one's own and its other is accompanied by important effects, some of which we must immediately note:

(1) The "proper" is *a triumph of place over time*. It allows one to capitalize acquired advantages, to prepare future expansions, and thus to give oneself a certain independence with respect to the variability of circumstances. It is a mastery of time through the foundation of an autonomous place.

(2) It is also a mastery of places through sight. The division of space makes possible a *panoptic practice* proceeding from a place whence the eye can transform foreign forces into objects that can be observed and measured, and thus control and "include" them within its scope of vision.[13] To be able to see (far into the distance) is also to be able to predict, to run ahead of time by reading a space.

(3) It would be legitimate to define the *power of knowledge* by this ability to transform the uncertainties of history into readable spaces. But it would be more correct to recognize in these "strategies" a specific type of knowledge, one sustained and determined by the power to provide oneself with one's own place. Thus military or scientific strategies have always been inaugurated through the constitution of their "own" areas (autonomous cities, "neutral" or "independent" institutions, laboratories pursuing "disinterested" research, etc.). In other words, *a certain power is the precondition of this knowledge* and not merely its effect or its attribute. It makes this knowledge possible and at the same time determines its characteristics. It produces itself in and through this knowledge.

By contrast with a strategy (whose successive shapes introduce a certain play into this formal schema and whose link with a particular historical configuration of rationality should also be clarified), a *tactic* is a calculated action determined by the absence of a proper locus. No delimitation of an exteriority, then, provides it with the condition necessary for autonomy. The space of a tactic is the space of the other. Thus it must play on and with a terrain imposed on it and organized by the law of a foreign power. It does not have the means to *keep to itself*, at a distance, in a position of withdrawal, foresight, and self-collection: it is a maneuver "within the enemy's field of vision," as von Bülow put it,[14] and within enemy territory. It does not, therefore, have the options of planning general strategy and viewing the adversary as a whole within a distinct, visible, and objectifiable space. It operates in isolated actions, blow by blow. It takes advantage of "opportunities" and depends on them, being without any base where it could stockpile its winnings, build up its own position, and plan raids. What it wins it cannot keep. This nowhere gives a tactic mobility, to be sure, but a mobility that must accept the chance offerings of the moment, and seize on the wing the possibilities that offer themselves at any given moment. It must vigilantly make use of the cracks that particular conjunctions open in the surveillance of the proprietary powers. It poaches in them. It creates surprises in them. It can be where it is least expected. It is a guileful ruse.

In short, a tactic is an art of the weak. Clausewitz noted this fact in discussing deception in his treatise *On War*. The more a power grows, the less it can allow itself to mobilize part of its means in the service of deception: it is dangerous to deploy large forces for the sake of appearances; this sort of "demonstration" is generally useless and "the gravity of bitter necessity makes direct action so urgent that it leaves no room for this sort of game." One deploys his forces, one does not take chances with feints. Power is bound by its very visibility. In contrast, trickery is possible for the weak, and often it is his only possibility, as a "last resort": "The weaker the forces at the disposition of the strategist, the more the strategist will be able to use deception."[15] I translate: the more the strategy is transformed into tactics.

Clausewitz also compares trickery to wit: "Just as wit involves a certain legerdemain relative to ideas and concepts, trickery is a sort of legerdemain relative to acts."[16] This indicates the mode in which a tactic, which is indeed a form of legerdemain, takes an order by surprise. The art of "pulling tricks" involves a sense of the opportunities afforded by a particular occasion. Through procedures that Freud makes explicit with reference to wit,[17] a tactic boldly juxtaposes diverse elements in order suddenly to produce a flash shedding a different light on the language of a place and to strike the hearer. Cross-cuts, fragments, cracks and lucky hits in the framework of a system, consumers' ways of operating are the practical equivalents of wit.

Lacking its own place, lacking a view of the whole, limited by the blindness (which may lead to perspicacity) resulting from combat at close quarters, limited by the possibilities of the moment, a tactic is determined by the *absence of power* just as a strategy is organized by the postulation of power. From this point of view, the dialectic of a tactic may be illuminated by the ancient art of sophistic. As the author of a great "strategic" system, Aristotle was already very interested in the procedures of this enemy which perverted, as he saw it, the order of truth. He quotes a formula of this protean, quick, and surprising adversary that, by making explicit the basis of sophistic, can also serve finally to define a tactic as I understand the term here: it is a matter, Corax said, of "making the worse argument seem the better."[18] In its paradoxical concision, this formula delineates the relationship of forces that is the starting point for an intellectual creativity as persistent as it is subtle, tireless, ready for every opportunity, scattered over the terrain of the dominant order and foreign to the rules laid down and imposed by a rationality founded on established rights and property.

In sum, strategies are actions which, thanks to the establishment of a place of power (the property of a proper), elaborate theoretical places (systems and totalizing discourses) capable of articulating an ensemble of physical places in which forces are distributed. They combine these three types of places and seek to master each by means of the others. They thus privilege spatial relationships. At the very least they attempt to reduce temporal relations to spatial ones through the analytical attribution of a proper place to each particular element and through the combinatory organization of the movements specific to units or groups of units. The model was military before it became "scientific." Tactics are procedures that gain validity in relation to the pertinence they lend to time – to the circumstances which the precise instant of an intervention transforms into a favorable situation, to the rapidity of the movements that change the organization of a space, to the relations among successive moments in an action, to the possible intersections of durations and heterogeneous rhythms, etc. In this respect, the difference corresponds to two historical options regarding action and security (options that moreover have more to do with constraints than with possibilities): strategies pin their hopes on the resistance that the *establishment of a place* offers to the erosion of time; tactics on a clever *utilization of time*, of the opportunities it presents and also of the play that it introduces into the foundations of power. Even if the methods practiced by the everyday art of war never present themselves in such a clear form, it nevertheless remains the case that the two ways of acting can be distinguished according to whether they bet on place or on time.

The Rhetorics of Practice, Ancient Ruses

Various theoretical comparisons will allow us better to characterize the tactics or the polemology of the "weak." The "figures" and "turns" analyzed by *rhetoric* are particularly illuminating in this regard. Freud already noticed this fact and used them in his studies on wit and on the forms taken by the return of the repressed within the field of an order: verbal economy and condensation, double meanings and misinterpretations, displacements and alliterations, multiple uses of the same material, etc.[19] There is nothing surprising about these homologies between practical ruses and rhetorical movements. In relation to the legalities of syntax and "proper" sense, that is, in relation to the general definition of a "proper" (as opposed to what is not "proper"), the good and bad tricks of rhetoric are played on the terrain that has been set aside in this way. They are manipulations of language relative to occasions and are intended to seduce, captivate, or invert the linguistic position of the addressee.[20] Whereas grammar watches over the "propriety" of terms, rhetorical alterations (metaphorical drifts, elliptical condensations, metonymic miniaturizations, etc.) point to the use of language by speakers in particular situations of ritual or actual linguistic combat. They are the indexes of consumption and of the interplay of forces. They depend on a problematics of enunciation. In addition, although (or because) they are excluded in principle from scientific discourse, these "ways of speaking" provide the analysis of "ways of operating" with a repertory of models and hypotheses. After all, they are merely variants within a general semiotics of tactics. To be sure, in order to work out that semiotics, it would be necessary to review arts of thinking and acting other than the one that the articulation of a certain rationality has founded on the delimitation of a proper: from the sixty-four hexagrams of the Chinese *I-Ching*[21] or the Greek *mētis*[22] to the Arabic *ḥīla*,[23] other "logics" can be discerned.

I am not concerned directly here with the constitution of such a semiotics, but rather with suggesting some ways of thinking about everyday practices of consumers, supposing from the start that they are of a tactical nature. Dwelling, moving about, speaking, reading, shopping, and cooking are activities that seem to correspond to the characteristics of tactical ruses and surprises: clever tricks of the "weak" within the order established by the "strong," an art of putting one over on the adversary on his own turf, hunter's tricks, maneuverable, polymorph mobilities, jubilant, poetic, and warlike discoveries.

Perhaps these practices correspond to an ageless art which has not only persisted through the institutions of successive political orders but goes back much farther than our histories and forms strange alliances preceding the frontiers of humanity. These practices present in fact a curious analogy, and a sort of immemorial link, to the simulations, tricks, and disguises that certain fishes or plants execute with extraordinary virtuosity. The procedures of this art can be found in the farthest reaches of the domain of the living, as if they managed to surmount not only the strategic distributions of historical institutions but also the break established by the very institution of consciousness. They maintain formal continuities and the permanence of a memory without language, from the depths of the oceans to the streets of our great cities.

In any event, on the scale of contemporary history, it also seems that the generalization and expansion of technocratic rationality have created, between the links of the system, a fragmentation and explosive growth of these practices which were formerly regulated by stable local units. Tactics are more and more frequently going off their tracks. Cut loose from the traditional communities that circumscribed their functioning, they have begun to wander everywhere in a space which is becoming at once more homogeneous and more extensive. Consumers are transformed into immigrants. The system in which they move about is too vast to be able to fix them in one place, but too constraining for them ever to be able to escape from it and go into exile elsewhere. There is no longer an elsewhere. Because of this, the "strategic" model is also transformed, as if defeated by its own success: it was by definition based on the definition of a "proper" distinct from everything else; but now that "proper" has become the whole. It could be that, little by little, it will exhaust its capacity to transform itself and constitute only the space (just as totalitarian as the cosmos of ancient times) in which a cybernetic society will arise, the scene of the Brownian movements of invisible and innumerable tactics. One would thus have a proliferation of aleatory and indeterminable manipulations within an immense framework of socioeconomic constraints and securities: myriads of almost invisible movements, playing on the more and more refined texture of a place that is even, continuous, and constitutes a proper place for all people. Is this already the present or the future of the great city?

Leaving aside the multimillennial archeology of ruses as well as the possibility of their anthill-like future, the study of a few current everyday tactics ought not to forget the horizon from which they proceed, nor, at the other extreme, the horizon towards which they are likely to go. The evocation of these perspectives on the distant past or future at least allows us to resist the effects of the fundamental but often exclusive and obsessive analysis that seeks to describe institutions and the mechanisms of *repression*. The privilege enjoyed by the problematics of repression in the field of research should not be surprising: scientific institutions belong to the system which they study, they conform to the well-known genre of the family story (an ideological criticism does not change its functioning in any way; the criticism merely creates the appearance of a distance for scientists who are members of the institution); they even add the disturbing charm of devils or bogey-men whose stories are told during long evenings around the family hearth. But this elucidation of the apparatus by itself has the disadvantage of *not seeing* practices which are heterogeneous to it and which it represses or thinks it represses. Nevertheless, they have every chance of surviving this apparatus *too*, and, in any case, they are *also* part of social life, and all the more resistant because they are more flexible and adjusted to perpetual mutation. When one examines this fleeting and permanent reality carefully, one has the impression of exploring the night-side of societies, a night longer than their day, a dark sea from which successive institutions emerge, a maritime immensity on which socioeconomic and political structures appear as ephemeral islands.

The imaginary landscape of an inquiry is not without value, even if it is without rigor. It restores what was earlier called "popular culture," but it does so in order to transform what was represented as a matrix-force of history into a mobile infinity of tactics. It thus keeps before our eyes the structure of a social imagination in which the problem constantly takes different forms and begins anew. It also wards off the effects of an analysis which necessarily grasps these practices only on the margins of a technical apparatus, at the point where they alter or defeat its instruments. It is the study itself which is marginal with respect to the phenomena studied. The landscape that represents these phenomena in an imaginary mode thus has an overall corrective and therapeutic value in resisting their reduction by a lateral examination. It at least assures their presence as ghosts. This return to another scene thus reminds us of the relation between the experience of these practices and what remains of them in an analysis. It is evidence, evidence which can only be fantastic and not scientific, of the disproportion between everyday tactics and a strategic elucidation. Of all the things everyone does, how much gets written down? Between the two, the image, the phantom of the expert but mute body, preserves the difference.

Notes

1 See in particular A. Huet et al., *La Marchandise culturelle* (Paris: CNRS, 1977), which is not satisfied merely with analyzing products (photos, records, prints), but also studies a system of commercial repetition and ideological reproduction.

2 See, for example, *Pratiques culturelles des Français* (Paris: Secrétariat d'Etat à la Culture – SER, 1974), 2 vols. Alvin Toffler, *The Culture Consumers* (Baltimore: Penguin, 1965), remains fundamental and pioneering, although it is not statistically based and is limited to mass culture.

3 On the premonitory theme of the "celibate machine" in the art (M. Duchamp et al.) or the literature (from Jules Verne to Raymond Roussel) of the early twentieth century, see J. Clair et al., *Les Machines célibataires* (Venice: Alfieri, 1975).

4 See, for example, on the subject of the Aymaras of Peru and Bolivia, J.-E. Monast, *On les croyait Chrétiens: les Aymaras* (Paris: Cerf, 1969).

5 See M. de Certeau, "La longue marche indienne," in *Le Réveil indien en Amérique latine*, ed. Yves Materne and DIAL (Paris: Cerf, 1976), 119–35.

6 G. Ryle, "Use, Usage and Meaning," in *The Theory of Meaning*, ed. G. H. R. Parkinson (Oxford: Oxford University Press, 1968), 109–16. A large part of the volume is devoted to use.

7   Richard Montague, "Pragmatics," in *La Philosophie contemporaine*, ed. Raymond Klibansky (Firenze: La Nuova Italia, 1968), I, 102–22. Y. Bar-Hillel thus adopts a term of C. S. Peirce, of which the equivalents are, in B. Russell, "ego-centric particulars"; in H. Reichenbach, "token-reflexive expressions"; in N. Goodman, "indicator words"; in W. V. Quine, "non-eternal sentences"; etc. A whole tradition is inscribed in this perspective. Wittgenstein belongs to it as well, the Wittgenstein whose slogan was "Don't ask for the meaning; ask for the use" in reference to normal use, regulated by the institution that is language.

8   See "The Proverbial Enunciation," p. 18, *The Practice of Everyday Life*.

9   See Emile Benveniste, *Problèmes de linguistique générale* (Paris: Gallimard, 1974), II, 79–88.

10 Fernand Deligny, *Les Vagabonds efficaces* (Paris: Maspero, 1970), uses this word to describe the trajectories of young autistic people with whom he lives, writings that move through forests, wanderings that can no longer make a path through the space of language.

11 See "Indeterminate," p. 199, *The Practice of Everyday Life*.

12 Ibid.

13 According to John von Neumann and Oskar Morgenstern, *Theory of Games and Economic Behaviour*, 3rd edn. (New York: John Wiley, 1964), "there is only strategy when the other's strategy is included."

14 "Strategy is the science of military movements outside of the enemy's field of vision; tactics, within it" (von Bülow).

15 Karl von Clausewitz, *Vom Kriege*; see *De la guerre* (Paris: Minuit, 1955), 212–13; *On War*, trans. M. Howard and P. Paret (Princeton: Princeton University Press, 1976). This analysis can be found moreover in many other theoreticians, ever since Machiavelli. See Y. Delahaye, "Simulation et dissimulation," *La Ruse* (*Cause Commune* 1977/1) (Paris: UGE 10/18, 1977), 55–74.

16 Clausewitz, *De la guerre*, 212.

17 Freud, *Jokes and their Relation to the Unconscious*, trans. J. Strachey (London: The Hogarth Press and the Institute of Psychoanalysis, 1960).

18 Aristotle, *Rhetoric*, II, 24, 1402a: "by making the worse argument seem the better"; trans. W. Rhys Roberts (New York: The Modern Library, 1954). The same "discovery" is attributed to Tisias by Plato (*Phaedrus*, 273b–c). See also W. K. C. Guthrie, *The Sophists* (Cambridge: Cambridge University Press, 1971), 178–9. On Corax's *technē* mentioned by Aristotle in relation to the "loci of apparent enthymemes," see Ch. Perelman and L. Ollbrechts-Tyteca, *Traité de l'argumentation* (Bruxelles: Université Libre, 1970), 607–9.

19 Freud, *Jokes and their Relation to the Unconscious*, on the techniques of wit.

20 See S. Toulmin, *The Uses of Argument* (Cambridge: Cambridge University Press, 1958); Perelman and Ollbrechts-Tyteca, *Traité de l'argumentation*; J. Dubois et al., *Rhétorique générale* (Paris: Larousse, 1970); etc.

21 See *I-Ching*, the *Book of Changes*, which represents all the possible situations of beings in the course of the universe's mutations by means of 64 hexagrams formed by 6 interrupted or full lines.

22 M. Détienne and J.-P. Vernant, *Les Ruses de l'intelligence. La Mètis des Grecs* (Paris: Flammarion, 1974).

23 See M. Rodinson, *Islam et capitalisme* (Paris: Seuil, 1972); *Islam and Capitalism*, trans. B. Pearce (New York: Pantheon, 1973).

CHAPTER 5

Subculture: The Meaning of Style

Dick Hebdige

Dick Hebdige's 1979 study of the punk subculture, *Subculture: The Meaning of Style*, is one of the most important books to emerge from the Birmingham Center for Contemporary Cultural Studies, which was supervised for many years by Stuart Hall, a leading figure in British cultural studies. Hebdige considers punk to be a form of resistant meaning-making, an anti-bourgeois style that in some respects resembles earlier versions of the literary avant-garde.

Introduction: Subculture and Style

I managed to get about twenty photographs, and with bits of chewed bread I pasted them on the back of the cardboard sheet of regulations that hangs on the wall. Some are pinned up with bits of brass wire which the foreman brings me and on which I have to string coloured glass beads. Using the same beads with which the prisoners next door make funeral wreaths, I have made star-shaped frames for the most purely criminal. In the evening, as you open your window to the street, I turn the back of the regulation sheet towards me. Smiles and sneers, alike inexorable, enter me by all the holes I offer... They watch over my little routines.

Jean Genêt

In the opening pages of *The Thief's Journal*, Jean Genêt describes how a tube of Vaseline, found in his possession, is confiscated by the Spanish police during a raid. This "dirty, wretched object," proclaiming his homosexuality to the world, becomes for Genêt a kind of guarantee "the sign of a secret grace which was soon to save me from contempt." The discovery of the Vaseline is greeted with laughter in the record–office of the station, and the police "smelling of garlic, sweat and oil, but... strong in their moral assurance" subject Genêt to a tirade of hostile innuendo. The author joins in the laughter too ("though painfully") but later, in his cell, "the image of the tube of vaseline never left me."

> I was sure that this puny and most humble object would hold its own against them; by its mere presence it would be able to exasperate all the police in the world; it would draw down upon itself contempt, hatred, white and dumb rages.[1]

I have chosen to begin with these extracts from Genêt because he more than most has explored in both his life and his art the subversive implications of style. I shall be returning again and again to Genêt's major themes: the status and meaning of revolt, the idea of style as a form of Refusal, the elevation of crime into art (even though, in our case, the "crimes" are only broken codes). Like Genêt, we are interested in subculture – in the expressive forms and rituals of those subordinate groups – the teddy boys and mods and rockers, the skinheads and the punks – who are alternately dismissed, denounced, and canonized; treated at different times as threats to public order and as harmless buffoons. Like Genêt also, we are intrigued by the most mundane objects – a safety pin, a pointed shoe, a motor cycle – which, none the less, like the tube of Vaseline, take on a symbolic dimension, becoming a form of stigmata, tokens of a self-imposed exile. Finally, like Genêt, we must seek to recreate the dialectic between action and reaction which renders these objects meaningful. For, just as the conflict between Genêt's "unnatural" sexuality and the policemen's "legitimate" outrage can be encapsulated in a single object, so the tensions between dominant and subordinate groups can be found reflected in the surfaces of subculture – in the styles made up of mundane objects which have a double meaning. On the one hand, they warn the "straight" world in advance of a sinister presence – the presence of difference – and draw down upon themselves vague suspicions, uneasy laughter, "white and dumb rages." On the other hand, for those who erect them into icons, who use them as words or as curses, these objects become signs of forbidden identity, sources of value. Recalling his humiliation at the hands of the police, Genêt finds consolation in the tube of Vaseline. It becomes a symbol of his "triumph" – "I would indeed rather have shed blood than repudiate that silly object."[2]

The meaning of subculture is, then, always in dispute, and style is the area in which the opposing definitions clash with most dramatic force. Much of the available space in this book will therefore be taken up with a description of the process whereby objects are made to mean and mean again as "style" in subculture. As in Genêt's novels, this process begins with a crime against the natural order, though in this case the deviation may seem slight indeed – the cultivation of a quiff, the acquisition of a scooter or a record or a certain type of suit. But it ends in the construction of a style, in a gesture of defiance or contempt, in a smile or a sneer. It signals a Refusal. I would like to think that this Refusal is worth making, that these gestures have a meaning, that the smiles and the sneers have some subversive value, even if, in the final analysis, they are, like Genêt's gangster pin-ups, just the darker side of sets of regulations, just so much graffiti on a prison wall.

Even so, graffiti can make fascinating reading. They draw attention to themselves. They are an expression both of impotence and a kind of power – the power to disfigure. (Norman Mailer calls graffiti "Your presence on their Presence . . . hanging your alias on their scene.")[3] In this book I shall attempt to decipher the graffiti, to tease out the meanings embedded in the various post-war youth styles. . . .

Revolting Style

Nothing was holy to us. Our movement was neither mystical, communistic nor anarchistic. All of these movements had some sort of programme, but ours was completely nihilistic. We spat on everything, including ourselves. Our symbol was nothingness, a vacuum, a void.

George Grosz on Dada

We're so pretty, oh so pretty . . . vac-unt.

The Sex Pistols

Although it was often directly offensive (T-shirts covered in swear words) and threatening (terrorist/guerrilla outfits), punk style was defined principally through the violence of its "cut ups." Like Duchamp's "ready mades" – manufactured objects which qualified as art because he chose to call them such – the most unremarkable and inappropriate items – a pin, a plastic clothes peg, a television component, a razor blade, a tampon – could be brought within the province of punk (un)fashion. Anything within or without reason could be turned into part of what Vivienne Westwood called "confrontation dressing" so long as the rupture between "natural" and constructed context was clearly visible (i.e. the rule would seem to be: if the cap doesn't fit, wear it).

Objects borrowed from the most sordid of contexts found a place in the punks' ensembles: lavatory chains were draped in graceful arcs across chests encased in plastic bin-liners. Safety pins were taken out of their domestic "utility" context and worn as gruesome ornaments through the cheek, ear or lip. "Cheap" trashy fabrics (PVC, plastic, lurex, etc.) in vulgar designs (e.g. mock leopard skin) and "nasty" colors, long discarded by the quality end of the fashion industry as obsolete kitsch, were salvaged by the punks and turned into garments (fly boy drainpipes, "common" miniskirts) which offered self-conscious commentaries on the notions of modernity and taste. Conventional ideas of prettiness were jettisoned along with the traditional feminine lore of cosmetics. Contrary to the advice of every woman's magazine, make-up for both boys and girls was worn to be seen. Faces became abstract portraits: sharply observed and meticulously executed studies in alienation. Hair was obviously dyed (hay yellow, jet black, or bright orange with tufts of green or bleached in question marks), and T-shirts and trousers told the story of their own construction with multiple zips and outside seams clearly displayed. Similarly, fragments of school uniform (white bri-nylon shirts, school ties) were symbolically defiled (the shirts covered in graffiti, or fake blood; the ties left undone) and juxtaposed against leather drains or shocking pink mohair tops. The perverse and the abnormal were valued intrinsically. In particular, the illicit iconography of sexual fetishism was used to predictable effect. Rapist masks and rubber wear, leather bodices and fishnet stockings, implausibly pointed stiletto heeled shoes, the whole paraphernalia of bondage – the belts, straps and chains – were exhumed from the boudoir, closet and the pornographic film and placed on the street where they retained their forbidden connotations. Some young punks even donned the dirty raincoat – that most prosaic symbol of sexual "kinkiness" – and hence expressed their deviance in suitably proletarian terms.

Of course, punk did more than upset the wardrobe. It undermined every relevant discourse. Thus dancing, usually an involving and expressive medium in British rock and mainstream pop cultures, was turned into a dumbshow of blank robotics. Punk dances bore absolutely no relation to the desultory frugs and clinches which Geoff Mungham describes as intrinsic to the respectable working-class ritual of Saturday night at the Top Rank or Mecca.[4] Indeed, overt displays of heterosexual interest were generally regarded with contempt and suspicion (who let the BOF/wimp[5] in?) and conventional courtship patterns found no place on the floor in dances like the pogo, the pose and the robot. Though the pose did allow for a minimum sociability (i.e. it could involve two people) the "couple" were generally of the same sex and physical contact was ruled out of court as the relationship depicted in the dance was a "professional" one. One participant would strike a suitable cliché fashion pose while the other would fall into a classic "Bailey" crouch to snap an imaginary picture. The pogo forbade even this much interaction, though admittedly there was always a good deal of masculine jostling in front of the stage. In fact the pogo was a caricature – a *reductio ad absurdum* of all the solo dance styles associated with rock music. It resembled the "anti-dancing" of the "Leapniks" which Melly describes in connection with the trad boom.[6] The same abbreviated gestures – leaping into the air, hands clenched to the sides, to head an imaginary ball – were repeated without variation in time to the strict mechanical rhythms of the music. In contrast to the hippies' languid, free-form dancing, and the "idiot dancing" of the heavy metal rockers, the pogo made improvisation redundant: the only variations were imposed by changes in the tempo of the music – fast numbers being "interpreted" with manic abandon in the form of frantic on-the-spots, while the slower ones were pogoed with a detachment bordering on the catatonic.

The robot, a refinement witnessed only at the most exclusive punk gatherings, was both more "expressive" and less "spontaneous" within the very narrow range such terms acquired in punk usage. It consisted of barely perceptible twitches of the head and hands or more extravagant lurches (Frankenstein's first steps?) which were abruptly halted at random points. The resulting pose was held for several moments, even minutes, and the whole sequence was as suddenly, as unaccountably, resumed and re-enacted. Some zealous punks carried things one step further and choreographed whole evenings, turning themselves for a matter of hours, like Gilbert and George,[7] into automata, living sculptures.

The music was similarly distinguished from mainstream rock and pop. It was uniformly basic and direct in its appeal, whether through intention or lack of expertise. If the latter, then the punks certainly made a virtue of necessity ("We want to be amateurs" – Johnny Rotten). Typically, a barrage of guitars with the volume and treble turned to maximum accompanied by the occasional saxophone would pursue relentless (un)melodic lines against a turbulent background of cacophonous drumming and screamed vocals. Johnny Rotten succinctly defined punk's position on harmonics: "We're into chaos not music."

The names of the groups (the Unwanted, the Rejects, the Sex Pistols, the Clash, the Worst, etc.) and the titles of the songs: "Belsen was a Gas," "If You Don't Want to Fuck Me, fuck off," "I Wanna be Sick on You," reflected the tendency towards willful desecration and the voluntary assumption of outcast status which characterized the whole punk movement. Such tactics were, to adapt Lévi-Strauss's famous phrase, "things to whiten mother's hair with." In the early days at least, these "garage bands" could dispense with musical pretensions and substitute, in the traditional romantic terminology, "passion" for "technique," the language of the common man for the arcane posturings of the existing elite, the now familiar armory of frontal attacks for the bourgeois notion of entertainment or the classical concept of "high art."

It was in the performance arena that punk groups posed the clearest threat to law and order. Certainly, they succeeded in subverting the conventions of concert and nightclub entertainment. Most significantly, they attempted both physically and in terms of lyrics and life-style to move closer to their audiences. This in itself is by no means unique: the boundary between artist and audience has often stood as a metaphor in revolutionary aesthetics (Brecht, the surrealists, Dada, Marcuse, etc.) for that larger and more intransigent barrier which separates art and the dream from reality and life under capitalism.[8] The stages of those venues secure enough to host "new wave" acts were regularly invaded by hordes of punks, and if the management refused to tolerate such blatant disregard for ballroom etiquette, then the groups and their followers could be drawn closer together in a communion of spittle and mutual abuse. At the Rainbow Theatre in May 1977 as the Clash played "White Riot," chairs were ripped out and thrown at the stage. Meanwhile, every performance, however apocalyptic, offered palpable evidence that things could change, indeed were changing: that performance itself was a possibility no authentic punk should discount. Examples abounded in the music press of "ordinary fans" (Siouxsie of Siouxsie and the Banshees, Sid Vicious of the Sex Pistols, Mark P of *Sniffin Glue*, Jordan of the Ants) who had made the symbolic crossing from the dance floor to the stage. Even the humbler positions in the rock hierarchy could provide an attractive alternative to the drudgery of manual labor, office work or a youth on the dole. The Finchley Boys, for instance, were reputedly taken off the football terraces by the Stranglers and employed as roadies.

If these "success stories" were, as we have seen, subject to a certain amount of "skewed" interpretation in the press, then there were innovations in other areas which made opposition to dominant definitions possible. Most notably, there was an attempt, the first by a predominantly working-class youth culture, to provide an alternative critical space within the subculture itself to counteract the hostile or at least ideologically inflected coverage which punk was receiving in the media. The existence of an alternative punk press demonstrated that it was not only clothes or music that could be immediately and cheaply produced from the limited resources at hand. The fanzines (*Sniffin Glue, Ripped and Torn*, etc.) were journals edited by an individual or a group, consisting of reviews, editorials and interviews with prominent punks, produced on a small scale as cheaply as possible, stapled together and distributed through a small number of sympathetic retail outlets.

The language in which the various manifestoes were framed was determinedly "working class" (i.e. it was liberally peppered with swear words) and typing errors and grammatical mistakes, misspellings and jumbled pagination were left uncorrected in the final proof. Those corrections and crossings out that were made before publication were left to be deciphered by the reader. The overwhelming impression was one of urgency and immediacy, of a paper produced in indecent haste, of memos from the front line.

This inevitably made for a strident buttonholing type of prose which, like the music it described, was difficult to "take in" in any quantity. Occasionally a wittier, more abstract item – what Harvey Garfinkel (the American ethnomethodologist) might call an "aid to sluggish imaginations" – might creep in. For instance, *Sniffin Glue*, the first fanzine and the one which achieved the highest circulation, contained perhaps the single most inspired item of propaganda produced by the subculture – the definitive statement of punk's do-it-yourself philosophy – a diagram showing three finger positions on the neck of a guitar over the caption: "Here's one chord, here's two more, now form your own band."

Even the graphics and typography used on record covers and fanzines were homologous with punk's subterranean and anarchic style. The two typographic models were graffiti which was translated into a flowing "spray can" script, and the ransom note in which individual letters cut up from a variety of sources (newspapers, etc.) in different typefaces were pasted together to form an anonymous message. The Sex Pistols' "God Save the Queen" sleeve (later turned into T-shirts, posters, etc.), for instance, incorporated both styles: the roughly assembled legend was pasted across the Queen's eyes and mouth which were further disfigured by those black bars used in pulp detective magazines' subculture to conceal identity (i.e. they connote crime or scandal). Finally, the process of ironic self-abasement which characterized the subculture was extended to the name "punk" itself which, with its derisory connotations of "mean and petty villainy," "rotten," "worthless," etc. was generally preferred by hardcore members of the subculture to the more neutral "new wave."[9]

Style as Homology

The punk subculture, then, signified chaos at every level, but this was only possible because the style itself was so thoroughly ordered. The chaos cohered as a meaningful whole. We can now attempt to solve this paradox by referring to another concept originally employed by Lévi-Strauss: homology.

Paul Willis[10] first applied the term "homology" to subculture in his study of hippies and motor-bike boys using it to describe the symbolic fit between the values and lifestyles of a group, its subjective experience and the musical forms it uses to express or reinforce its focal concerns. In *Profane Culture*, Willis shows how, contrary to the popular myth which presents subcultures as lawless forms, the internal structure of any particular subculture is characterized by an extreme orderliness: each part is organically related to other parts and it is through the fit between them that the subcultural member makes sense of the world. For instance, it was the homology between an alternative value system ("Tune in, turn on, drop out"), hallucinogenic drugs and acid rock which made the hippy culture cohere as a "whole way of life" for individual hippies. In *Resistance Through Ritual*, Hall et al. crossed the concepts of homology and *bricolage* to provide a systematic explanation of why a particular subcultural style should appeal to a particular group of people. The authors asked the question: "What specifically does a subcultural style signify to the members of the subculture themselves?"

The answer was that the appropriated objects reassembled in the distinctive subculture ensembles were made "to reflect, express and resonate ... aspects of group life."[11] The objects chosen were, either intrinsically or in their adapted forms, homologous with the focal concerns, activities, group structure and collective self-image of the subculture. They were "objects in which (the subcultural members) could see their central values held and reflected."

The skinheads were cited to exemplify this principle. The boots, braces and cropped hair were only considered appropriate and hence meaningful because they communicated the desired qualities: "hardness, masculinity and working-classness." In this way, "[t]he symbolic objects – dress, appearance, language, ritual occasions, styles of interaction, music – were made to form a *unity* with the group's relations, situation, experience."

The punks would certainly seem to bear out this thesis. The subculture was nothing if not consistent. There was a homological relation between the trashy cut-up clothes and spiky hair, the pogo and amphetamines, the spitting, the vomiting, the format of the fanzines, the insurrectionary poses and the "soulless," frantically driven music. The punks wore clothes which were the sartorial equivalent of swear words, and they swore as they dressed – with calculated effect, lacing obscenities into record notes and publicity releases, interviews and love songs. Clothed in chaos, they produced Noise in the calmly orchestrated Crisis of everyday life in the late 1970s – a noise which made (no) sense in exactly the same way and to exactly the same extent as a piece of avant-garde music. If we were to write an epitaph for the punk subculture, we could do no better than repeat Poly Styrene's famous dictum: "Oh Bondage, Up Yours!," or somewhat more concisely: the forbidden is permitted, but by the same token, nothing, not even these forbidden signifiers (bondage, safety pins, chains, hair-dye, etc.) is sacred and fixed.

This absence of permanently sacred signifiers (icons) creates problems for the semiotician. How can we discern any positive values reflected in objects which were chosen only to be discarded? For instance, we can say that the early punk ensembles gestured towards the signified's "modernity" and "working-classness." The safety pins and bin liners signified a relative material poverty which was either directly experienced and exaggerated or sympathetically assumed, and which in turn was made to stand for the spiritual paucity of everyday life. In other words, the safety pins, etc. "enacted" that transition from real to symbolic scarcity which Paul Piccone[12] has described as the movement from "empty stomachs" to "empty spirits – and therefore an empty life notwithstanding [the] chrome and the plastic... of the life style of bourgeois society."

We could go further and say that even if the poverty was being parodied, the wit was undeniably barbed; that beneath the clownish make-up there lurked the un-accepted and disfigured face of capitalism; that beyond the horror circus antics a divided and unequal society was being eloquently condemned. However, if we were to go further still and describe punk music as the "sound of the Westway," or the pogo as the "high-rise leap," or to talk of bondage as reflecting the narrow options of working-class youth, we would be treading on less certain ground. Such readings are both too literal and too conjectural. They are extrapolations from the subculture's own prodigious rhetoric, and rhetoric is not self-explanatory: it may say what it means but it does not necessarily "mean" what it "says." In other words, it is opaque: its categories are part of its publicity. To return once more to Mepham,[13] "The true text is reconstructed not by a process of piecemeal decoding, but by the identification of the generative sets of ideological categories and its replacement by a different set."

To reconstruct the true text of the punk subculture, to trace the source of its subversive practices, we must first isolate the "generative set" responsible for the subculture's exotic displays: Certain semiotic facts are undeniable. The punk subculture, like every other youth culture, was constituted in a series of spectacular trans-formations of a whole range of commodities, values, common-sense attitudes, etc. It was through these adapted forms that certain sections of predominantly working-class youth were able to restate their opposition to dominant values and institutions. However, when we attempt to close in on specific items, we immediately encounter problems. What, for instance, was the swastika being used to signify?

We can see how the symbol was made available to the punks (via Bowie and Lou Reed's "Berlin" phase). Moreover, it clearly reflected the punks' interest in a decadent and evil Germany – a Germany which had "no future." It evoked a period redolent with a powerful mythology. Conventionally, as far as the British were concerned, the swastika signified "enemy." None the less, in punk usage, the symbol lost its "natural" meaning – fascism. The punks were not generally sympathetic to the parties of the extreme right. On the contrary, as I have argued, the conflict with the resurrected teddy boys and the widespread support for the anti-fascist movement (e.g. the Rock against Racism campaign) seem to indicate that the punk subculture grew up partly as an antithetical response to the reemergence of racism in the mid-70s. We must resort, then, to the most obvious of explanations – that the swastika was worn because it was guaranteed to shock. (A punk asked by *Time Out* (December 17–23, 1977) why she wore a swastika, replied: "Punks just like to be hated.") This represented more than a simple inversion or inflection of the ordinary meanings attached to an object. The signifier (swastika) had been willfully detached from the concept (Nazism) it conventionally signified, and although it had been repositioned (as "Berlin") within an alternative subcultural context, its primary value and appeal derived precisely from its lack of meaning: from its potential for deceit. It was exploited as an empty effect. We are forced to the conclusion that the central value "held and reflected" in the swastika was the communicated absence of any such identifiable values. Ultimately, the symbol was as "dumb" as the rage it provoked. The key to punk style remains elusive. Instead of arriving at the point where we can begin to make sense of the style, we have reached the very place where meaning itself evaporates. . . .

We can now look more closely at the relationship between experience, expression and signification in subculture; at the whole question of style and our reading of style. To return to our example, we have seen how the punk style fitted together homologically precisely through its lack of fit (hole: tee-shirt: spitting: applause: bin-liner: garment: anarchy: order) – by its refusal to cohere around a readily identifiable set of central values. It cohered, instead, *elliptically* through a chain of conspicuous absences. It was characterized by its unlocatedness – its blankness – and in this it can be contrasted with the skinhead style.

Whereas the skinheads theorized and fetishized their class position, in order to effect a "magical" return to an imagined past, the punks dislocated themselves from the parent culture and were positioned instead on the outside: beyond the comprehension of the average (wo)man in the street in a science fiction future. They played up their Otherness, "happening" on the world as aliens, inscrutables. Though punk rituals, accents and objects were deliberately used to signify working-classness, the exact origins of individual punks were disguised or symbolically disfigured by the make-up, masks and aliases which seem to have been used, like Breton's art, as ploys "to escape the principle of identity."[14]

This working-classness therefore tended to retain, *even in practice, even in its concretized forms*, the dimensions of an idea. It was abstract, disembodied, decontextualized. Bereft of the necessary details – a name, a home, a history – it refused to make sense, to be grounded, "read back" to its origins. It stood in violent contradiction to that other great punk signifier – sexual "kinkiness." The two forms of deviance – social and sexual – were juxtaposed to give an impression of multiple warping which was guaranteed to disconcert the most liberal of observers, to challenge the glib assertions of sociologists no matter how radical. In this way, although the punks referred continually to the realities of school, work, family and class, these references only made sense at one remove: they were passed through the fractured circuitry of punk style and re-presented as "noise," disturbance, entropy.

In other words, although the punks self-consciously mirrored what Paul Piccone calls the "pre-categorical realities" of bourgeois society – inequality, powerlessness, alienation – this was only possible because punk style had made a decisive break not only with the parent culture but with its own *location in experience*. This break was both inscribed and reenacted in the signifying practices embodied in punk style. The punk ensembles, for instance, did not so much magically resolve experienced contradictions as *represent* the experience of contradiction itself in the form of visual puns (bondage, the ripped tee-shirt, etc.). Thus while it is true that the symbolic objects in punk style (the safety pins, the pogo, the ECT hairstyles) were "made to form a '*unity*' with the group's relations, situations, experience," this unity was at once "ruptural" and "expressive," or more precisely it expressed itself through rupture.

This is not to say, of course, that all punks were equally aware of the disjunction between experience and signification upon which the whole style was ultimately based. The style no doubt made sense for the first wave of self-conscious innovators at a level which remained inaccessible to those who became punks after the subculture had surfaced and been publicized. Punk is not unique in this: the distinction between originals and hangers-on is always a significant one in subculture. Indeed, it is frequently verbalized (plastic punks or safety-pin people, burrhead rastas or rasta bandwagon, weekend hippies, etc. versus the "authentic" people). For instance, the mods had an intricate system of classification whereby the "faces" and "stylists" who made up the original coterie were defined against the unimaginative majority – the pedestrian "kids" and "scooter boys" who were accused of trivializing and coarsening the precious mod style. What is more, different youths bring different degrees of commitment to a subculture. It can represent a major dimension in people's lives – an axis erected in the face of the family around which a secret and immaculate identity can be made to cohere – or it can be a slight distraction, a bit of light relief from the monotonous but none the less paramount realities of school, home and work. It can be used as a means of escape, of total detachment from the surrounding terrain, or as a way of fitting back in to it and settling down after a week-end or evening spent letting off steam. In most cases it is used, as Phil Cohen suggests, magically to achieve both ends. However, despite these individual differences, the members of a subculture must share a common language. And if a style is really to catch on, if it is to become genuinely popular, it must say the right things in the right way at the right time. It must anticipate or encapsulate a mood, a moment. It must embody a sensibility, and the sensibility which punk style embodied was essentially dislocated, ironic and self-aware.

Notes

1   Jean Genêt, *The Thief's Journal* (London: Penguin, 1967).
2   Ibid.
3   Norman Mailer, *Advertisements for Myself* (New York: Panther, 1968).
4   In his P.O. account of the Saturday night dance in an industrial town, Mungham shows how the constricted quality of working-class life is carried over into the ballroom in the form of courtship rituals, masculine paranoia and an atmosphere of sullenly repressed sexuality. He paints a gloomy picture of joyless evenings spent in the desperate pursuit of "booze and birds" (or "blokes and a romantic bus-ride home") in a controlled setting where "spontaneity is regarded by managers and their staff – principally the bouncers – as the potential hand-maiden of rebellion." (G. Mungham, "Youth in Pursuit of Itself," in G. Mungham and G. Pearson (eds.), *Working-Class Youth Culture* (Routledge and Kegan Paul, 1976).
5   BOF = Boring old Fart; Wimp = "wet."
6   G. Melly, *Revolt into Style* (London: Penguin, 1972).

7　Gilbert and George mounted their first exhibition in 1970 when, clad in identical conservative suits, with metallized hands and faces, a glove, a stick and a tape recorder, they won critical acclaim by performing a series of carefully controlled and endlessly repeated movements on a dais while miming to Flanagan and Allen's "Underneath the Arches." Other pieces with titles like "Lost Day" and "Normal Boredom" have since been performed at a variety of major art galleries throughout the world.

8　Of course, rock music had always threatened to dissolve these categories, and rock performances were popularly associated with all forms of riot and disorder – from the slashing of cinema seats by teddy boys through Beatlemania to the hippy happenings and festivals where freedom was expressed less aggressively in nudity, drug taking and general "spontaneity." However punk represented a new departure.

9　The word "punk," like the black American "funk" and "superbad," would seem to form part of that "special language of fantasy and alienation" which Charles Winick describes, "in which values are reversed and in which 'terrible' is a description of excellence." (Charles Winick, "The Uses of Drugs by Jazz Musicians," *Social Problems* 7, no. 3 (Winter 1959).

　　See also Wolfe (*The Pump-House Gang* (New York: Bantam, 1969)) where he describes the "cruising" scene in Los Angeles in the mid-60s – a subculture of custom-built cars, sweatshirts and "high-piled, perfect coiffure" where "rank" was a term of approval:

Rank! Rank is just the natural outgrowth of Rotten . . . Roth and Schorsch grew up in the Rotten Era of Los Angeles teenagers. The idea was to have a completely rotten attitude towards the adult world, meaning, in the long run, the whole established status structure, the whole system of people organizing their lives around a job, fitting into the social structure, embracing the whole community. The idea in Rotten was to drop out of conventional status competition into the smaller netherworld of Rotten Teenagers and start one's own league.

10　Paul Willis, *Profane Culture* (London: Routledge and Kegan Paul, 1978).

11　S. Hall et.al., *Resistance Through Rituals* (London: Hutchinson, 1976).

12　Paul Piccone, "From Youth Culture to Political Praxis," *Radical America* (November 15, 1969).

13　John Mepham, "The Theory of Ideology in *Capital*," *Working Papers in Cultural Studies* 6 (University of Birmingham, 1974).

14　"Who knows if we are not somehow preparing ourselves to escape the principle of indentity?" (A. Breton, Preface to the 1920 Exhibition of Max Ernst).

CHAPTER 6

Culture, Ideology, Interpellation

John Fiske

In this excerpt from his 1987 essay on television news, John Fiske examines the way television now exemplifies Louis Althusser's theory of ideology as a form of interpellation or "hailing." According to Althusser, we are given a sense of being individual subjects by being addressed in certain ways by our culture. The news "speaks" to us and in so doing positions us as viewers of the world who share the assumptions of the news.

The term *culture*, as used in the phrase "cultural studies," is neither aesthetic nor humanist in emphasis, but political. Culture is not conceived of as the aesthetic ideals of form and beauty found in great art, or in more humanist terms as the voice of the "human spirit" that transcends boundaries of time and nation to speak to a hypothetical universal man (the gender is deliberate – women play little or no role in this conception of culture). Culture is not, then, the aesthetic products of the human spirit acting as a bulwark against the tide of grubby industrial materialism and vulgarity, but rather a way of living within an industrial society that encompasses all the meanings of that social experience.

Cultural studies is concerned with the generation and circulation of meanings in industrial societies....

[T]hey start with the belief that meanings and the making of them (which together constitute culture) are indivisibly linked to social structure and can only be explained in terms of that structure and its history. Correlatively, the social structure is held in place by, among other forces, the meanings that culture produces; as Stuart Hall says, "A set of social relations obviously requires meanings and frameworks which underpin them and hold them in place."[1] These meanings are not only meanings of social experience, but also meanings of self, that is, constructions of social identity that enable people living in industrial capitalist societies to make sense of themselves and their social relations. Meanings of experience and meanings of the subject (or self) who has that experience are finally part of the same cultural process.

Also underlying this work is the assumption that capitalist societies are divided societies. The primary axis of division was originally thought to be class, though gender and race have now joined it as equally significant producers of social difference. Other axes of division are nation, age group, religion, occupation, education, political allegiance, and so on. Society, then, is not an organic whole but a complex network of groups, each with different interests and related to each other in terms of their power relationship with the dominant classes. Social relations are understood in terms of social power, in terms of a structure of domination and subordination that is never static but is always the site of contestation and struggle. Social power is the power to get one's class or group interest served by the social structure as a whole, and social struggle – or, in traditional Marxist terms, the class struggle – is the contestation of this power by the subordinate groups. In the domain of culture, this contestation takes the form of the struggle for meaning, in which the dominant classes attempt to "naturalize" the meanings that serve their interests into the "commonsense" of society as a whole, whereas subordinate classes resist this process in various ways and to varying degrees and try to make meanings that serve their own interests. Some feminist work provides a clear example of this cultural struggle and contestation. Angela McRobbie and Lisa Lewis, for instance, both show how young girls are able to contest the patriarchal ideology structured into such films as *Flashdance* or the pop stars Madonna and Cindy Lauper and produce feminine readings of them.[2]

The attempt of the dominant classes to naturalize their meanings rarely, if ever, results from the conscious intention of individual members of those classes (though resistance to it is often, though not always, both conscious and intentional). Rather, it must be understood as the work of an ideology inscribed in the cultural and social practices of a class and therefore of the members of that class. And this brings us to another basic assumption: culture is ideological.

The cultural studies tradition does not view ideology in its vulgar Marxist sense of "false consciousness," for that has built into it the assumption that a true consciousness is not only possible but will actually occur when history brings about a proletarian society. This sort of idealism seems inappropriate to the late twentieth century, which appears to have demonstrated not the inevitable self-destruction of capitalism but its unpredicted (by Marx) ability to reproduce itself and to incorporate into itself the forces of resistance and opposition. History casts doubt on the possibility of a society without ideology, in which people have a true consciousness of their social relations.

Structuralism, another important influence on British cultural studies, also denies the possibility of a true consciousness, for it argues that reality can only be comprehended through language or other cultural meaning systems. Thus the idea of an objective, empirical "truth" is untenable. Truth must always be understood in terms of how it is made, for whom, and at what time it is "true." Consciousness is never the product of truth or reality but rather of culture, society, and history.

Althusser and Gramsci were the theorists who offered a way of accommodating both structuralism (and, incidentally, Freudianism) and the history of capitalism in the twentieth century with Marxism. For Althusser, ideology is not a static set of ideas imposed upon the subordinate by the dominant classes but rather a dynamic process constantly reproduced and reconstituted in practice – that is, in the ways that people think, act, and understand themselves and their relationship to society.[3] He rejects the old idea that the economic base of society determines the entire cultural superstructure. He replaces this base/superstructure model with his theory of over-determination, which not only allows the superstructure to influence the base but also produces a model of the relationship between ideology and culture that is not determined solely by economic relations. At the heart of this theory is the notion of ideological state apparatuses (ISAs), by which he means social institutions such as the family, the educational system, language, the media, the political system, and so on. These institutions produce in people the tendency to behave and think in socially acceptable ways (as opposed to repressive state apparatuses such as the police force or the law, which coerce people into behaving according to the social norms). The social norms, or that which is socially acceptable, are of course neither neutral nor objective; they have developed in the interests of those with social power, and they work to maintain their sites of power by naturalizing them into the commonsense – the only – social positions for power. Social norms are ideologically slanted in favor of a particular class or group of classes but are accepted as natural by other classes, even when the interests of those other classes are directly opposed by the ideology reproduced by living life according to those norms.

Social norms are realized in the day-to-day workings of the ideological state apparatuses. Each one of these institutions is "relatively autonomous," according to Althusser, and there are no overt connections between it and any of the others – the legal system is not explicitly connected to the school system nor to the media, for example – yet they all perform similar ideological work. They are all patriarchal; they are all concerned with the getting and keeping of wealth and possessions; and they all endorse individualism and competition between individuals. But the most significant feature of ISAs is that they all present themselves as socially neutral, as not favoring one particular class over any other. Each presents itself as a principled institutionalization of equality: the law, the media, and education all claim, loudly and often, to treat all individuals equally and fairly. The fact that the norms used to define equality and fairness are those derived from the interests of the white, male, middle classes is more or less adequately disguised by these claims of principle, though feminists and those working for racial and class harmony may claim that this disguise can be torn off with relative ease.

Althusser's theory of overdetermination explains this congruence between the "relatively autonomous" institutions by looking not to their roots in a common, determining economic base but to an overdetermining network of ideological interrelationships among all of them. The institutions appear autonomous only at the official level of stated policy, though the belief in this "autonomy" is essential for their ideological work. At the unstated level of ideology, however, each institution is related to all the others by an unspoken web of ideological interconnections, so that the operation of any one of them is "overdetermined" by its complex, invisible network of interrelationships with all the others. Thus the educational system, for example, cannot tell a story about the nature of the individual different from those told by the legal system, the political system, the family, and so on.

Ideology is not, then, a static set of ideas through which we view the world but a dynamic social practice, constantly in process, constantly reproducing itself in the ordinary workings of these apparatuses. It also works at the micro-level of the individual. To understand this we need to replace the idea of the individual with that of the subject. The individual is produced by nature, the subject by culture. Theories of the individual concentrate on differences between people and explain these differences as natural. Theories of the subject, on the other hand, concentrate on people's common experiences in a society as being the most productive way of explaining who (we think) we are. Althusser believes that we are all constituted as subjects-in-ideology by the ISAs, that the ideological norms naturalized in their practices constitute not only the sense of the world for us, but also our sense of ourselves, our sense of identity, and our sense of our relations to other people and to society in general. Thus we are each of us constituted as a subject in, and subject to, ideology. The subject, therefore, is a social construction, not a natural one. A biological female can have a masculine subjectivity (that is, she can make sense of the world and of her self and her place in that world through patriarchal ideology). Similarly, a black person can have a white subjectivity and a member of the working classes a middle-class one.

The ideological theory of the subject differs in emphasis, though not fundamentally, from that developed in psychoanalysis by placing greater emphasis on social and historical conditions, particularly those of class. Althusser drew upon Freudian theory to develop his idea of the subject. As Ann Kaplan notes, feminists too have used psychoanalytic theory, though much more sophisticatedly, to theorize the gendered subject. This gendered subject is more rooted in psychological processes, the ideological subject of Althusser in historical and social ones.

But both theories stress the role played by the media and language in this constant construction of the subject, by which we mean the constant reproduction of ideology in people. Althusser uses the words *interpellation* and *hailing* to describe this work of the media. These terms derive from the idea that any language, whether it be verbal, visual, tactile, or whatever, is part of social relations and that in communicating with someone we are reproducing social relationships.

In communicating with people, our first job is to "hail" them, almost as if hailing a cab. To answer, they have to recognize that it is to them, and not to someone else, that we are talking. This recognition derives from signs, carried in our language, of whom we think they are. We will hail a child differently from an adult, a male differently from a female, someone whose status is lower than ours differently from someone in a higher social position. In responding to our hail, the addressees recognize the social position our language has constructed, and if their response is cooperative, they adopt this same position. Hailing is the process by which language identifies and constructs a social position for the addressee. Interpellation is the larger process whereby language constructs social relations for both parties in an act of communication and thus locates them in the broader map of social relations in general.

Hailing is obviously crucial at the start of a "conversation," though its ideological work continues throughout. Look, for instance, at the opening statements of the anchor and reporter on a US network news report in April 1991:

Anchor:	There is growing concern tonight about the possible economic impact that a nationwide railroad strike set for midnight tonight poses. The unions and the railroads remain deadlocked. Wyatt Andrews brings us up to date on what President Bush and Congress may do about it.
Reporter:	By morning 230,000 rail workers might not be working on the railroad and the strike threatens millions of Americans. Just as thousands of commuters may find no train leaving the station beginning tonight at midnight.

The word *strike* hails us as anti-union, for "striking" is constructed as a negative action by labor unions that "threatens" the nation. By ascribing responsibility to the unions, the word hides the fact that management plays some role, possibly even a greater one, in the dispute. The report opposes the unions not to management but to "the railroads" and thus excludes the unions from them. This exclusion of the unions from the railroads allows the unspoken management to become synonymous with them, and ideology continues its work by constructing the railroads not as an industry but as a national resource and so uses them as a metonym for the nation and, by extension, of "us." Recognizing ourselves in the national "us" interpellated here, we participate in the work of ideology by adopting the anti-union subject position proposed for us. This subject-as-ideology is developed as the item progresses:

Passenger A:	Gas, miles, time. The highways are going to be packed. Not much we can do, though.
Passenger B:	I'm going to stay home. I've got an office in my home and I'm going to just stay there and work.
Reporter:	But the commuter inconvenience is nothing compared to the impact on freight trains. Up to half a million industrial jobs may be at stake. Whether it's cars in the heartland or chemicals in Kansas City, the railroads still carry more freight than either trucks or airplanes, meaning that the strike would threaten the heart of industrial America in the heart of this recession.
Railroad Official:	If we don't get this strike settled quickly a lot more people are going to be out of work, a lot more product is not going to be shipped and this economy's recovery is going to be set back immensely.
Reporter:	Negotiations meanwhile seem to be at bedrock bottom, on wages, on health care, and the number of workers per train. Both sides even late today were on opposite tracks. The unions complain the railroads blocked raises and stonewalled the negotiations for three years. The railroads accuse the unions of protecting legions of workers who essentially do nothing.
Railroad Official:	The issue with our union is between who works and who watches. That's the issue of whether we have excess people in the cab who don't have anything to do.

The national "we" is constructed as hard-working producers at the personal level by the passengers and at the industrial level by the reporter. The repeated use of the "heart" metaphor not only makes "America" into a living, breathing body (like the one "we" inhabit), but it constructs the unions as a potentially lethal disease, if not a stiletto-wielding assassin! The railroad official continues to conflate "the railroads" (by which he means "the management") with the national subject of the hard-working producer.

So far, the dispute has been cast solely in terms of the bad effects the unions have upon this national "us," and only in the reporter's next segment do we receive a hint that there are causes of the dispute that may both justify it and implicate management in it. These hints are left floating, so we have no way of assessing the reasonableness of the wage claims, for instance. The generalized terms – "on wages, on health care, on the number of workers per train" – contrast with the concrete realities of 230,000 unionists not working and of the millions of Americans, thousands of commuters, and up to half a million jobs that are threatened. We might like to think about the ideological practice of not allowing the unions to speak for themselves "live," but of putting their case into the words of the reporter management "us." Unionists would not, for instance, describe their negotiating opponents as "the railroads," nor would they categorize their arguments as mere "complaints" while according management's the stronger status of "accusations."

The news item concludes by continuing the ideological practice that by now seems so natural and familiar:

Reporter: What exactly happens in the morning? If you are a commuter, check locally. Some Amtrak and commuter trains will be operating and some of the unions say they will strike only freight lines and not passenger trains. In Washington, watch Capitol Hill. Tomorrow President Bush is likely to ask Congress to impose a solution: the move, the unions say, plays right into the railroads' hands. The unions have all along warned the railroads would stall the negotiations and force tonight's strike all in the snug belief that Congress would bail them out.

As Mimi White points out . . . this view of ideology as a process constantly at work, constructing people as subjects in an ideology that always serves the interests of the dominant classes, found powerful theoretical support in Gramsci's theory of hegemony. Originally, *hegemony* referred to the way that one nation could exert ideological and social, rather than military or coercive, power over another. However, cultural theorists tend to use the term to describe the process by which a dominant class wins the willing consent of the subordinate classes to the system that ensures their subordination. This consent must be constantly won and rewon, for people's material social experience constantly reminds them of the disadvantages of subordination and thus poses a constant threat to the dominant class. Like Althusser's theory of ideology, hegemony does not denote a static power relationship but a constant process of struggle in which the big guns belong to the side of those with social power, but in which victory does not necessarily go to the big guns – or, at least, in which that victory is not necessarily total. Indeed, the theory of hegemony foregrounds the notion of ideological struggle much more than does Althusser's ideological theory, which at times tends to imply that the power of ideology and the ISAs to form the subject in ways that suit the interests of the dominant class is almost irresistible. Hegemony, on the other hand, posits a constant contradiction between ideology and the social experience of the subordinate that makes this interface into an inevitable site of ideological struggle. In hegemonic theory, ideology is constantly up against forces of resistance. Consequently it is engaged in a constant struggle not just to extend its power but to hold on to the territory it has already colonized.

Notes

1 Stuart Hall, "The Narrative Construction of Reality," *Southern Review* 17 (1984), pp. 1–17.
2 Angela McRobbie, "Dance and Social Fantasy," in Angela McRobbie and Mica Nava, eds., *Gender and Generation* (London: Macmillan, 1984), pp. 130–61; Lisa Lewis, *Gender Politics and MTV: Voicing the Difference* (Philadelphia: Temple University Press, 1990).
3 Louis Althusser, "Ideology and Ideological State Apparatuses," in *Lenin and Philosophy and Other Essays* (London: New Left Books, 1971), pp. 127–86.

CHAPTER 7

Television Culture

John Fiske

John Fiske's book, *Television Culture* (1990), studies the way television is constructed using codes of representation that are invisible to viewers but that shape everything they see. A code is a term from linguistics and semiology that roughly means a "dictionary of meanings or effects." Each element of television, according to Fiske, is governed and generated by codes that lend meaning to everything from the kinds of actors, to the clothes they wear, to the way they speak, to the kinds of camera shots used to depict them.

[T]elevision broadcasts programs that are replete with potential meanings, and . . . it attempts to control and focus this meaningfulness into a more singular preferred meaning that performs the work of the dominant ideology. We shall need to interrogate this notion later, but I propose to start with a traditional semiotic account of how television makes, or attempts to make, meanings that serve the dominant interests in society, and how it circulates these meanings amongst the wide variety of social groups that constitute its audiences. I shall do this by analyzing a short segment of two scenes from a typical, prime-time, long-running series, *Hart to Hart*, in order to demonstrate some basic critical methodology and to raise some more complex theoretical questions that will be addressed later on in the book.

The Harts are a wealthy, high-living husband and wife detective team. In this particular episode they are posing as passengers on a cruise ship on which there has been a jewel robbery. In scene 1 they are getting ready for a dance during which they plan to tempt the thief to rob them, and are discussing how the robbery may have been effected. In scene 2 we meet the villain and villainess, who have already noticed Jennifer Hart's ostentatiously displayed jewels.

Scene 1

HERO:	He knew what he was doing to get into this safe.
HEROINE:	Did you try the numbers that Granville gave you?
HERO:	Yeh. I tried those earlier. They worked perfectly.
HEROINE:	Well you said it was an inside job, maybe they had the combination all the time.
HERO:	Just trying to eliminate all the possibilities. Can you check this out for me? (*He gestures to his bow tie.*)
HEROINE:	Mm. Yes I can. (*He hugs her.*) Mm. Light fingers. Oh, Jonathan.
HERO:	Just trying to keep my touch in shape.
HEROINE:	What about the keys to the door?
HERO:	Those keys can't be duplicated because of the code numbers. You have to have the right machines.

HEROINE:	Well, that leaves the window.
HERO:	The porthole.
HEROINE:	Oh yes. The porthole. I know they are supposed to be charming, but they always remind me of a laundromat.
HERO:	I took a peek out of there a while ago. It's about all you can do. It's thirty feet up to the deck even if you could make it down to the window, porthole. You'd have to be the thin man to squeeze through.
HEROINE:	What do you think? (*She shows her jewelry*.) Enough honey to attract the bees?
HERO:	Who knows? They may not be able to see the honey for the flowers.
HEROINE:	Oh, that's the cutest thing you've ever said to me, sugar. Well, shall we? (*Gestures towards the door*.)

Scene 2

VILLAIN:	I suppose you noticed some of the icing on Chamberlain's cup cake. I didn't have my jeweler's glass, but that bracelet's got to be worth at least fifty thousand. Wholesale.
VILLAINESS:	Patrick, if you're thinking what I know you're thinking, forget it. We've made our quota one hit on each ship. We said we weren't going to get greedy, remember.
VILLAIN:	But darling, it's you I'm thinking of. And I don't like you taking all those chances. But if we could get enough maybe we wouldn't have to go back to the Riviera circuit for years.
VILLAINESS:	That's what you said when we were there.
VILLAIN:	Well maybe a few good investments and we can pitch the whole bloody business. But we are going to need a bit more for our retirement fund.

The Codes of Television

Figure 1 shows the main codes that television uses and their relationship. A code is a rule-governed system of signs, whose rules and conventions are shared amongst members of a culture, and which is used to generate and circulate meanings in and for that culture. Codes are links between producers, texts, and audiences, and are the agents of intertextuality through which texts interrelate in a network of meanings that constitutes our cultural world. These codes work in a complex hierarchical structure that figure 1 oversimplifies for the sake of clarity. In particular, the categories of codes are arbitrary and slippery, as is their classification into levels in the hierarchy; for instance, I have put speech as a social code, and dialogue (i.e. scripted speech) as a technical one, but in practice the two are almost indistinguishable: social psychologists such as Berne[1] have shown us how dialogue in "real life" is frequently scripted for us by the interactional conventions of our culture. Similarly, I have called casting a conventional representational code, and appearance a social one, but the two differ only in intentionality and explicitness. People's appearance in "real life" is already encoded: in so far as we make sense of people by their appearance we do so according to conventional codes in our culture. The casting director is merely using these codes more consciously and more conventionally, which means more stereotypically.

An event to be televised is already encoded
by *social codes* such as those of:

Level one:
"REALITY"

    appearance, dress, make-up, environment, behavior, speech,
gesture, expression, sound, etc.
these are encoded electronically by:
technical codes such as those of:

Level two:
REPRESENTATION

    camera, lighting, editing, music, sound
which transmit the
conventional representational codes, which shape the
representations of, for example:
narrative, conflict, character, dialogue, setting, casting, etc.

Level three:
IDEOLOGY

    which are organized into coherence and social acceptability
by the *ideological codes*, such as those of:
individualism, patriarchy, race, class, materialism, capitalism, etc.

Figure 1: The codes of television

The point is that "reality" is already encoded, or rather the only way we can perceive and make sense of reality is by the codes of our culture. There may be an objective, empiricist, reality out there. But there is no universal, objective way of perceiving and making sense of it. What passes for reality in any culture is the product of that culture's codes, so "reality" is always already encoded, it is never "raw." If this piece of encoded reality is televised, the technical codes and representational conventions of the medium are brought to bear upon it so as to make it (a) transmittable technologically and (b) an appropriate cultural text for its audiences.

Some of the social codes which constitute our reality are relatively precisely definable in terms of the medium through which they are expressed – skin color, dress, hair, facial expression, and so on.

Others, such as those that make up a landscape, for example, may be less easy to specify systematically, but they are still present and working hard. Different sorts of trees have different connotative meanings encoded into them, so do rocks and birds. So a tree reflected in a lake, for example, is fully encoded even before it is photographed and turned into the setting for a romantic narrative. . . .

For instance, the conventions that govern the representation of speech as "realistic dialogue" in scene 1 result in the heroine asking questions while the hero provides the answers. The representational convention by which women are shown to lack knowledge which men possess and give to them is an example of the ideological code of patriarchy. Similarly the conventional representation of crime as theft of personal property is an encoding of the ideology of capitalism. The "naturalness" with which the two fit together in the scene is evidence of how these ideological codes work to organize the other codes into producing a congruent and coherent set of meanings that constitute the common sense of a society.

The process of making sense involves a constant movement up and down through the levels of the diagram, for sense can only be produced when "reality," representations, and ideology merge into a coherent, seemingly natural unity. Semiotic or cultural criticism deconstructs this unity and exposes its "naturalness" as a highly ideological construct.

A semiotic analysis attempts to reveal how these layers of encoded meanings are structured into television programs, even in as small a segment as the one we are working with. The small size of the segment encourages us to perform a detailed analytical reading of it, but prevents us talking about larger-scale codes, such as those of the narrative. But it does provide a good starting point for our work.

Camera Work

The camera is used through angle and deep focus to give us a perfect view of the scene, and thus a complete understanding of it. Much of the pleasure of television realism comes from this sense of omniscience that it gives us.... Camera distance is used to swing our sympathies away from the villain and villainess, and towards the hero and heroine. The normal camera distance in television is mid-shot to close-up, which brings the viewer into an intimate, comfortable relationship with the characters on the screen. But the villain and villainess are also shown in extreme close-up (ECU). Throughout this whole episode of *Hart to Hart* there are only three scenes in which ECUs are used: they are used only to represent hero/ine and villain/ess, and of the twenty-one ECUs, eighteen are of the villain/ess and only three of the hero/ine. Extreme close-ups become a codified way for representing villainy.

This encoding convention is not confined to fictional television, where we might think that its work upon the alignment of our sympathies, and thus on our moral judgment, is justified. It is also used in news and current affairs programs which present themselves as bringing reality to us "objectively." The court action resulting from General Westmoreland's libel suit against the CBS in 1985 revealed these codes more questionably at work in television reporting. Alex Jones recounts their use in his report of the trial for the *New York Times*.

> Among the more controversial techniques is placing an interviewee in partial shadow in order to lend drama to what is being said. Also debated is the use of extreme close-ups that tend to emphasize the tension felt by a person being interviewed. Viewers may associate the appearance of tension with lying or guilt.
>
> The extreme close-up can be especially damaging when an interview is carefully scripted and a cameraman is instructed to focus tightly on the person's face at the point when the toughest question is to be asked. Some documentary makers will not use such close-ups at all in interviews because they can be so misleading.
>
> The CBS documentary contained both a shadowed interview of a friendly witness and "tight shots" of General Westmoreland. Such techniques have been used in documentaries by other networks as well....

There are two possible sources of the conventions that govern the meanings generated by this code of camera distance. One is the social code of interpersonal distance: in western cultures the space within about 24 inches (60 cm) of us is encoded as private. Anyone entering it is being either hostile, when the entry is unwelcome, or intimate, when it is invited. ECUs replicate this, and are used for moments of televisual intimacy or hostility, and which meanings they convey depends on the other social and technical codes by which they are contextualized, and by the ideological codes brought to bear upon them. Here, they are used to convey hostility. The other source lies in the technical codes which imply that seeing closely means seeing better – the viewer can see *into* the villain, see *through* his words, and thus gains power over him, the power and the pleasure of "dominant specularity." These technical and social codes manifest the ideological encoding of villainy. . . .

Editing

The heroes are given more time (72 secs) than the villains (49), and more shots (10 as against 7), though both have an average shot length of 7 seconds. It is remarkable how consistent this is across different modes of television: it has become a conventional rhythm of television common to news, drama, and sport.

Music

The music linking the two scenes started in a major key, and changed to minor as the scene changed to the villains.

Casting

This technical code requires a little more discussion. The actors and actresses who are cast to play hero/ines, villain/esses and supporting roles are real people whose appearance is already encoded by our social codes. But they are equally media people, who exist for the viewer intertextually, and whose meanings are also intertextual. They bring with them not only residues of the meanings of other roles that they have played, but also their meanings from other texts such as fan magazines, showbiz gossip columns, and television criticism. . . .

Characters on television are not just representations of individual people but are encodings of ideology, "embodiments of ideological values." Gerbner's work showed that viewers were clear about the different characteristics of television heroes and villains on two dimensions only: heroes were more attractive and more successful than villains. Their attractiveness, or lack of it, is partly the result of the way they are encoded in the technical and social codes – camera work, lighting, setting, casting, etc., but the ideological codes are also important, for it is these that make sense out of the relationship between the technical code of casting and the social code of appearance, and that also relate their televisual use to their broader use in the culture at large. In his analysis of violence on television, Gerbner found that heroes and villains are equally likely to use violence and to initiate it, but that heroes were successful in their violence, whereas villains finally were not. Gerbner worked out a killers-to-killed ratio according to different categories of age, sex, class, and race. The killers category included heroes and villains, but the killed category included villains only. He found that a character who was white, male, middle class (or classless) and in the prime of life was very likely, if not certain, to be alive at the end of the program. Conversely characters who deviated from these norms were likely to be killed during the program in proportion to the extent of their deviance. We may use Gerbner's findings to theorize that heroes are socially central persons who embody the dominant ideology, whereas villains and victims are members of deviant or subordinate subcultures who thus embody the dominant ideology less completely, and may, in the case of villains, embody ideologies that oppose it. The textual opposition between hero/ine and villain/ess, and the violence by which this opposition is commonly dramatized, become metaphors for power relationships in society and thus a material practice through which the dominant ideology works.... The villain in this segment has hints of non-Americanness; some viewers have classed his accent, manner, and speech as British, for others his appearance has seemed Hispanic. But the hero and heroine are both clearly middle-class, white Americans, at home among the WASPs (White Anglo-Saxon Protestants). The villainess is Aryan, blonde, pretty, and younger than the villain. Gerbner's work would lead us to predict that his chances of surviving the episode are slim, whereas hers are much better. The prediction is correct. She finally changes sides and helps the hero/ine, whereas he is killed; hints of this are contained in her condemnation of the villain's greed, which positions her more centrally in the ideological discourse of economics....

Setting and Costume

The hero/ine's cabin is larger than that of the villain/ess: it is humanized, made more attractive by drapes and flowers, whereas the other is all sharp angles and hard lines. The villain wears a uniform that places him as a servant or employee and the villainess's dress is less tasteful, less expensive than the heroine's. These physical differences in the social codes of setting and dress are also bearers of the ideological codes of class, of heroism and villainy, of morality, and of attractiveness. These abstract ideological codes are condensed into a set of material social ones, and the materiality of the differences of the social codes is used to guarantee the truth and naturalness of the ideological. We must note, too, how some ideological codes are more explicit than others: the codes of heroism, villainy, and attractiveness are working fairly openly and acceptably. But under them the codes of class, race, and morality are working less openly and more questionably: their ideological work is to naturalize the correlation of lower-class, non-American with the less attractive, less moral, and therefore villainous. Conversely, the middle-class and the white American is correlated with the more attractive, the more moral and the heroic. This displacement of morality onto class is a common feature of our popular culture: Dorfman and Mattelart have shown how Walt Disney cartoons consistently express villainy through characteristics of working-class appearance and manner; indeed, they argue that the only time the working class appear in the middle-class world of Ducksville it is as villains....

Make-up

The same merging of the ideological codes of morality, attractiveness, and heroism/villainy, and their condensation into a material social code, can be seen in something as apparently insignificant as lipstick. The villainess has a number of signs that contradict her villainy (she is blonde, white American, pretty, and more moral than the villain). These predict her eventual conversion to the side of the hero and heroine, but she cannot look too like them at this early stage of the narrative, so her lips are made up to be thinner and less sexually attractive than the fuller lips of the heroine. The ideology of lipstick may seem a stretched concept, but it is in the aggregate of apparently insignificant encodings that ideology works most effectively.

Action

There are a number of significant similarities and differences between the actions of the hero/ine and the villain/ess. In both cabins the women are prettying themselves, the men are planning. This naturalizes the man's executive role of instigating action and the woman's role as object of the male gaze – notice the mirror in each cabin which enables her to see herself as "bearer of her own image"; the fact that this is common to both hero/ine and villain/ess puts it beyond the realm of conflict in the narrative and into the realm of everyday common sense within which the narrative is enacted. The other action common to both is the getting and keeping of wealth as a motive for action, and as a motor for the narrative: this also is not part of the conflict-to-be-resolved, but part of the ideological framework through which that conflict is viewed and made sense of.

A difference between the two is that of cooperation and closeness. The hero and heroine cooperate and come physically closer together, the villain and villainess, on the other hand, disagree and pull apart physically. In a society that places a high value on a man and woman being a close couple this is another bearer of the dominant ideology.

Dialogue

The dialogue also is used to affect our sympathy. That of the villain and villainess is restricted to their nefarious plans and their mutual disagreement, whereas the hero and heroine are allowed a joke (window/porthole/laundromat), an extended metaphor (honey and the bees), and the narrative time to establish a warm, cooperative relationship. . . .

Ideological Codes

These codes and the televisual codes which bring them to the viewer are both deeply embedded in the ideological codes of which they are themselves the bearers. If we adopt the same ideological practice in the decoding as the encoding we are drawn into the position of a white, male, middle-class American (or westerner) of conventional morality. The reading position is the social point at which the mix of televisual, social, and ideological codes comes together to make coherent, unified sense: in making sense of the program in this way we are indulging in an ideological practice ourselves, we are maintaining and legitimating the dominant ideology, and our reward for this is the easy pleasure of the recognition of the familiar and of its adequacy. We have already become a "reading subject" constructed by the text, and, according to Althusser, the construction of subjects-in-ideology is the major ideological practice in capitalist societies.

This ideological practice is working at its hardest in three narrative devices in this segment. The first is the window/porthole/laundromat joke, which, as we have seen, is used to marshal the viewer's affective sympathy on the side of the hero/ine. But it does more than that. Freud tells us that jokes are used to relieve the anxiety caused by repressed, unwelcome, or taboo meanings. This joke revolves around the "feminine" (as defined by our dominant culture) inability to understand or use technical language, and the equally "feminine" tendency to make sense of everything through a domestic discourse. "Porthole" is technical discourse-masculine: "window-laundromat" is domestic-nurturing discourse-feminine. The anxiety that the joke relieves is that caused by the fact that the heroine is a detective, is involved in the catching of criminals – activities that are part of the technical world of men in patriarchy. The joke is used to recuperate contradictory signs back into the dominant system, and to smooth over any contradictions that might disrupt the ideological homogeneity of the narrative. The attractiveness of the heroine must not be put at risk by allowing her challenge to patriarchy to be too stark – for attractiveness is always ideological, never merely physical or natural.

The metaphor that expresses the sexual attractiveness of women for men in terms of the attraction of honey and flowers for the bees works in a similar way. It naturalizes this attraction, masking its ideological dimension, and then extends this naturalness to its explanation of the attractiveness of other people's jewelry for lower-class non-American villains! The metaphor is working to naturalize cultural constructions of gender, class, and race.

The third device is that of jewelry itself. As we have seen, the getting and keeping of wealth is the major motor of the narrative, and jewelry is its material signifier. Three ideological codes intersect in the use of jewelry in this narrative: they are the codes of economics, gender, and class.

In the code of economics, the villain and villainess stress the jewelry's investment/exchange function: it is "worth at least fifty thousand wholesale," it forms "a retirement fund." For the hero and heroine and for the class they represent this function is left unstated: jewelry, if it is an investment, is one to hold, not cash in. It is used rather as a sign of class, of wealth, and of aesthetic taste.

The aesthetic sense, or good taste, is typically used as a bearer and naturalizer of class differences. The heroine deliberately overdoes the jewelry, making it vulgar and tasteless in order to attract the lower-class villain and villainess. They, in their turn, show their debased taste, their aesthetic insensitivity, by likening it to the icing on a cupcake. As Bourdieu has shown us, the function of aesthetics in our society is to make class-based and culture-specific differences of taste appear universal and therefore natural. The taste of the dominant classes is universalized by aesthetic theory out of its class origin; the metaphor of "taste" works in a similar way by displacing class differences onto the physical, and therefore natural, senses of the body.

The meaning of jewelry in the code of gender is clear. Jewels are the coins by which the female-as-patriarchal-commodity is bought, and wearing them is the sign both of her possession by a man, and of his economic and social status. Interestingly, in the code of gender, there is no class difference between hero/ine and villain/ess: the economics of patriarchy are the same for all classes, thus making it appear universal and natural that man provides for his woman.

This analysis has not only revealed the complexity of meanings encoded in what is frequently taken to be shallow and superficial, but it also implies that this complexity and subtlety has a powerful effect upon the audience. It implies that the wide variety of codes all cohere to present a unified set of meanings that work to maintain, legitimate, and naturalize the dominant ideology of patriarchal capitalism. . . .

Analysis [also] has to pay less attention to the textual strategies of preference or closure and more to the gaps and spaces that open television up to meanings not preferred by the textual structure, but that result from the social experience of the reader. . . .

This means that reading is not a garnering of meanings from the text but is a dialogue between text and the socially situated reader. As Morley says:

> Thus the meaning of the text must be thought in terms of which set of discourses it encounters in any particular set of circumstances, and how this encounter may restructure both the meaning of the text and the discourses which it meets. The meaning of the text will be constructed differently according to the discourses (knowledges, prejudices, resistances, etc.) brought to bear on the text by the reader and the crucial factor in the encounter of audience/subject and text will be the range of discourses at the disposal of the audience.[2]

. . . Both the text and the subjectivity are discursive constructs and both contain similar competing or contradictory discourses. It is out of these contradictions that the polysemy of the text and the multiplicity of readings arise.

Hodge and Tripp[3] provide good examples of multiple or contradictory readings made by viewers. They . . . assume that children are engaged in a constant active struggle to make sense out of their social experience, and that television plays an important role in that struggle.

Market research had found that one of the most popular programs with Australian school children was *Prisoner*, a soap opera set in a women's prison, and screened in the USA under the title *Prisoner: Cell Block H*. This appeared, on the face of it, to be a surprising choice for junior high school students.

Hodge and Tripp discovered that many of the children found, at varying levels of consciousness, and were able to articulate with varying degrees of explicitness, usefully significant parallels between the prison and the school. They perceived the following main similarities between prisoners and school students:

1 pupils are shut in;
2 pupils are separated from their friends;
3 pupils would not be there if they were not made to be;
4 pupils only work because they are punished if they do not, and it is less boring than doing nothing at all;
5 pupils have no rights: they can do nothing about an unfair teacher;
6 some teachers victimize their pupils;

7 there are gangs and leaders amongst the pupils;

8 there are silly rules which everyone tries to break.[4]

In their discussions the children showed that they made meanings out of *Prisoner* that connected the program to their own social experience. A textual study revealed many parallels between prison and school. In both there were recognizable role types amongst staff and prisoners that formed recognizable and usable categories with which students could "think" their school experience – the hard-bitten old warden/ teacher, the soft new one, the one you can take advantage of, the one you can't, and so on. Similarly there were prisoners who resisted the institution and fought it in all ways, those who played along with it and were the goody goodies, those who played along with it on the surface, but opposed it underneath, and so on. There were also strategies of resistance that applied to both: prisoners used a secret language, some-times of special private words, but more often of nudges, winks, glances, and *doubles entendres* to communicate amongst themselves under the noses of and in resistance to the wardens/teachers. There was an oppositional subculture of the public areas of the prison, particularly the laundry where many of them worked, that paralleled the oppositional school subculture of the lavatories, the locker rooms, and special corners of the yard. And in both institutions there was a consistent attempt by the official culture to colonize and control these areas, which was resisted and resented by the inmates who struggled to keep them within their own cultural control. . . .

Turnbull has found that young girl fans of the program find in it meanings that they can use to produce a sense of subcultural identity and esteem for themselves. Images of strong, active women fighting the system, gaining minor victories (although finally succumbing to it), give them pleasure (in the resistance) and a means of articulating a discourse of resistance to the dominant ideology that paralleled the discourse (often called rebelliousness) that they used to make sense of their social existence. The contra-dictions and struggle between authority and resistance to it existed in both the program and their subjectivities, and the meanings that were activated and the pleasures that were gained were the ones that made social sense to the subordinate and the powerless. . . .

There is some evidence that finding a discourse in a text that makes sense of one's experience of social powerlessness in a positive way is the vital first step towards being able to do something to change that powerlessness.

Hodge and Tripp's study of the ways that Australian Aboriginal children made sense of television is of significance here. They found that the children constructed a cultural category that included American blacks, American Indians, and themselves. This cultural category, a tool to think with, conceptualized the political and narrative powerlessness of non-whites in white society, and was used in making sense both of television and of social experience. A particularly popular program among these children was *Different Strokes*, whose leading character, an American black child adopted by a white family, they saw as Aboriginal. One can imagine the sort of sense they made of his small size, his eternal childishness, and the consistency with which he is "misunderstood" and set right by his white "father" and "elder sister," par-ticularly when we remember that American Indians are part of the same cultural category.

What the Aboriginal readers were demonstrating was the ability of a subculture to make its own sense out of a text that clearly bears the dominant ideology. The discourses of powerlessness through which they lived their lives activated a set of meanings that resisted those preferred by the dominant ideology. When they supported and identified with American Indians in their fights against white cowboys, they knew both that their side was doomed to lose, and that they were being obtuse or awkward in reading a western in this way. Reading television in this way provided them with a means of articulating their experience of powerlessness in a white-dominated society and the ability to articulate one's experience is a necessary prerequisite for developing the will to change it.

Mattelart, in his studies of the Third World reception of Hollywood television, comes to a similar conclusion:

> The messages of mass culture can be neutralized by the dominated classes who can produce their own antidotes by creating the sometimes contradictory seeds of a new culture.

Notes

1 E. Berne, *Games People Play: The Psychology of Human Relationships* (Harmondsworth: Penguin, 1964).
2 David Morley, *The Nationwide Audience: Structure and Decoding* (London: British Film Institute, 1980).
3 R. Hodge and D. Tripp, *Children and Television* (Cambridge: Polity Press, 1986).
4 Ibid., p. 49.

CHAPTER 8

Rap Music and the Poetics of Identity

Adam Krims

In this selection from *Rap Music and the Poetics of Identity* (2000), Adam Krims explores the meanings of a rap song by Ice Cube – "The Nigga Ya Love To Hate." He explores issues of identity and community, and he examines the "musical poetics" of the song.

This chapter is an attempt to examine a song and theorize some ways in which it may project (and help form) notions of a certain community and an identity; it will make use of the notions of musical poetics developed so far, at the greatest level of detail of any chapter in the book. "Identity" here does not necessarily mean "resistant identity"; thus, while the project here may resemble in some respects those for which music may be validated as radical practice or resistance to domination, the only operative assumption is that *somehow* the identities being discussed are formed symbolically – not necessarily that they overturn the discursive structures lined up against them. Thus, what was earlier referred to, following Jody Berland (1998), as the "optimism of cultural studies" is here replaced by something that might even, at one point in intellectual history, have been deemed "semiotic," an attempt at a description of how signification works. A further judgment about political function, it seems to me, requires a closer look at how acts of discourse circulate, and their distant, sometimes surprisingly contorted future in the throes of capital and its own far-flung social effects.

The present discussion takes some of its cues from notions of culture developed by James Clifford (1988).[1] Clifford argues that there has been an increasing sense, in the twentieth century, that the older "culture concept" no longer applies to the (post-)modern world; instead, there is a widespread "feeling of lost authenticity, of 'modernity' ruining some essence or source" (p. 4). Although this sense is often presented as a nostalgia for earlier "purity," Clifford "does not see the world as populated by endangered authenticities – pure products always going crazy" (p. 5). Rather, the situation, as he sees it, prompts the question, "What are the essential elements and boundaries of a culture?" (p. 8). He concludes that contemporary cultural identity can be understood "not as an archaic survival but as an ongoing process, politically contested and historically unfinished . . . a form of personal and collective self-fashioning" (p. 9). Accordingly, "cultural identity" is not a tie with some pure and distant past, so much as it is a matter of continual appropriation, revision, and creation in the present, with an eye toward the future. This creation, in turn, is necessarily imbricated in the intersections among what used to be considered "cultures":

> Because discourse in global power systems is elaborated vis-à-vis, a sense of difference or distinctness can never be located solely in the continuity of a culture or tradition. (p. 11)[2]

Cultural identity, then, is dialogic, or polylogic; it brings to the fore a "need to stage authenticity *in opposition to* external, often dominating alternatives" (p. 12; emphasis Clifford's). In the process, "[T]he roots of tradition are cut and retied, collective symbols appropriated from external influences" (p. 15); thus, "[t]wentieth-century identities no longer presuppose continuous cultures or traditions" (p. 14). In the specific case of art, the consequences are enormous:

> If authenticity is relational, there can be no essence except as a political, cultural invention, a local tactic... A whole structure of expectations about authenticity in culture and in art is thrown in doubt. (pp. 12–14)

The analysis presented here will illustrate one such "local tactic," in the specific context of music. If "culture" is constructed in a series of local acts of definition, music may carry the significance that Martin Stokes elaborates in his admirable introduction to *Ethnicity, Identity, and Music* (1994). There, noting the role that music often plays in building "notions of difference and social boundaries" (Stokes, 1994: p. 3), he asserts that "[m]usic does not... simply provide a marker in a pre-structured social space, but the means by which this space can be transformed" (Stokes 1994, p. 4).

Music can play a special role in establishing cultural identity, according to Stokes, because of its alliance with the construction of pleasures in a society: "It is perhaps this that distinguishes [musical] ethnicity... from the 'everyday' practices of boundary construction and maintenance with which much social anthropological writing on ethnicity is concerned" (Stokes 1994, p. 13). Most important for present purposes, Stokes points out a musical practice that bears directly on rap contexts:

> Subcultures borrow from the dominant culture, inflecting and inverting its signs to create a bricolage in which the signs of the dominant culture are "there" and just recognizable as such, but constituting a quite different, subversive whole. (p. 19)

Here, Stokes's description approaches what has been widely remarked in rap music, namely the process of "signifyin'" that Gates (1988) identifies as a central aspect of black cultural production. It will be seen in the analysis that follows that borrowing, "inflecting and inverting" signs of the (Eurocentric) culture constitute much of the "signifyin'" with which Ice Cube establishes a specific ethnicity.

Such a scenario should immediately raise the question, "Establishes an identity for whom?" Here issues of persona arise, issues that can only be contextualized in broader questions of early "gangsta" rap, and which are further magnified in the case of Ice Cube, one of the original public rappers in the genre. For one of the principal authenticating strategies of early gangsta rap has precisely been the symbolic collapsing of the MC onto the artist – the projection that the MC himself (with the gender-specific pronoun purposefully unmodified) *is* the persona – a voice from the "streets," speaking from authentic experience. Ice Cube's entire early persona, straight down to the ubiquitous scowl, depends on the collapsing of the angry, aggressive, and politically charged figure onto the historical figure of O'Shea Jackson (Ice Cube's given name); thus, while the identity formed in the song "The Nigga Ya Love to Hate" is as virtual, in a sense, as that of any singing or rapping voice in a song, the production of that identity serves a dual purpose. "The Nigga Ya Love to

Hate" here is both persona and artist, the formation of the necessary collapse of the two which one may see as synonymous with "keeping it real." The effectiveness of the collapsing strategy, including the effectiveness of the present song, may be measured, if not in any other way, in the more recent reproaches of Ice Cube among rap fans as having lost his edge, as having "sold out," precisely because he no longer performs songs that project the same persona. In a sense, the identity formed in "The Nigga Ya Love to Hate" continues to haunt Ice Cube's career, defining, in popular imagination, a persona now remembered as simply "the real Ice Cube"; the collapsing of persona and artist was all too effective.

The song, from Ice Cube's (1990a) first solo album (*AmeriKKKa's Most Wanted*) since leaving Niggas With Attitudes (NWA), was, like the other songs on the album, produced by The Bomb Squad.[3] This is significant for two major reasons. First, The Bomb Squad were (and now again are) the producers for Public Enemy. Public Enemy's production style generated a new model of hardness, complexity, and authenticity in rap music and ended up widely imitated. Thus, by engaging The Bomb Squad, Ice Cube was availing himself of a then-new sound, and furthermore – and importantly – a sound associated with politically engaged rap music, radical in a way closely associated with black nationalism. Second, Public Enemy is a New York group, thus establishing themselves as a geographic rival to Los Angeles artists like Ice Cube; and while the notorious and widely-hyped "East Coast/West Coast" rivalry was then only nascent (and largely because of the commercial success of NWA), the geographic contrast was already highly significant, and in fact, there were fans at the time that criticized Ice Cube for "selling out" to East Coast dominance.

But the commercial success of the album – and its survival in popular memory as one of the great all-time rap albums – eventually overshadowed those criticisms, and Ice Cube's collaboration with The Bomb Squad is often imaged, in fan reception, as an apex of political engagement and responsibility from which he has gradually declined. Thus, even now, something like a full decade after the release of the album, it looms as a highly significant presence in rap music and hip-hop culture; hence its meriting a detailed discussion.

In light of Clifford's discussion, the present analysis will seek out how Ice Cube establishes, in the musical poetics of the song, a certain vision of black ethnicity. Or rather, I should say, a specific position *within* an ethnicity, for with this song, Ice Cube defines a political stance within his community, not only against the hegemonic culture, but also against fellow blacks that he sees as helping to perpetuate that culture's injustices. Therefore, "The Nigga Ya Love to Hate" fashions what I will call "black revolutionary identity," i.e., an identity constructed for revolutionary black politics. With it, Ice Cube stakes out, for himself and, equivalently, the rapping persona, not only a boundary of blackness, but also a boundary of the "five percent nation."[4]

Some detailed discussion will be needed to show how this works, and this is where the "close reading" comes in. Stokes, in common with the other authors mentioned above, provides an indication that some attention to aesthetic detail is needed for the discussion of ethnicity in music:

> [It] is important that music and dance...not just [be] seen as static symbolic objects which have to be understood in a context, but are themselves a patterned context within which other things happen...Complex aesthetic vocabularies, or single terms covering

a complex semantic terrain point to minute and shifting subtleties of rhythm and texture which make or break the event... Without these qualities, however they are conceived in a particular society, the ritual event is powerless to make the expected and desired connections and transformations. (Stokes 1994, p. 5)

What follows is an attempt to observe just such a "patterned context" in action, creating Ice Cube's black revolutionary identity. Some terminology will be presented in order to show how this works, since much of the methodology of traditional music theory would be inadequate to the music at hand. Thus, our discussion will become technical; the level of detail, however, will remain engaged in the task of examining the song as a cultural production.

Figure 1 gives the lyrics to Ice Cube's "The Nigga Ya Love to Hate," from the album *AmeriKKKa's Most Wanted*. Each line is set by one measure in time. The lines (and measures) are numbered for later reference. The beginning of each line corresponds either to the downbeat or the first rapped section after the downbeat, while the rest of the line falls within the four-beat measure following that downbeat.

Crucial here is the technique of layering. As a procedure, layering is basic to this and many other rap (and often more generally, hip-hop) songs. Its significance to the present song should not be at all surprising, given the then-novel complexity and ambitiousness of the Bomb Squad's production techniques. Indeed, as will become clear, it is largely the interactions of layering with Ice Cube's MCing that form notions of a black revolutionary identity in the song.

Figure 2 gives what I call a *layering graph*.[5] The graph runs in eighty-eight numbered columns, which represent the successive measures of time, eighty-eight of them in all. The top two rows in each column count the measures, the first by tens and the second by ones. The third row, labeled "configs," shows *configurations* – this is what I call combinations of tracks which remain more or less stable over an extended period of the song. A vertical line indicates the beginning of a new configuration, while solid horizontal lines indicate a continuation of the last-numbered configuration; each new one is numbered just to the right of the vertical line. If a horizontal line restarts with no vertical line, the last-numbered configuration is restarting. A diagonal slash ("/") indicates a half-measure continuation.

The fourth row shows *upbeats*, that is, one-measure combinations of tracks that directly precede points of formal articulation in the song (e.g., beginnings of verses, beginnings of refrains, and so on). They are all indicated by one-measure horizontal lines and numbered below the lines. The fifth row shows what I call *adjuncts*, which are one or more tracks superimposed either to configurations or to refrains. They, too, are indicated by horizontal lines and numbered below the lines. To preserve proportions, the two-digit labels for adjuncts 10 through 20 are written vertically. No vertical lines separate each from the next, since all but adjunct 20 last one measure; adjunct 20 lasts two measures. The sixth row shows *refrains*, of which there are two in the song; both are seven-measure events featuring the shout "Fuck you, Ice Cube" and various responses. Both are numbered below the lines. Each of the last four rows just described will be referred to as a *layer*; thus there is a configuration layer, an upbeat layer, an adjunct layer, and a refrain layer. At the bottom of Figure 2, the three verses are represented by the numbers 1, 2, and 3. Verse 1 extends from line 1 through line 24; verse 2 extends from line 33 through line 56; and verse 3 extends from line 65 through line 86.

The song divides easily into four-measure groups from the very beginning; the groups are marked by breaks (rhythmic and semantic) in the rapping, and often by new musical events as well. These musical events tend to begin either at the commencement of each four-measure group or on the last measure of a four-measure group. In the former case, the event is labeled either a refrain (if it involves "Fuck you, Ice Cube" and responses thereto) or a configuration; in the latter case, it is labeled as a refrain. One exception is configuration 2, which arrives at measure 33, in the middle of a four-measure group; this will be discussed shortly. Adjuncts may arrive anywhere in the song; they are always accompanied by a configuration or a refrain, except in the last two measures of the song.

Each event is represented on the graph by a solid, continuous line. Below the beginning of each such line is an ordinal number; this number simply counts the different patterns within each type. For example, the "1" in the configuration row, measure 1, indicates "configuration 1," while the "2" in the configuration row, measure 33, indicates "configuration 2," and so on. When a vertical line interrupts a horizontal line and is followed by a new ordinal, there is a change in the pattern. A repeated ordinal reflects a repeated pattern; thus, the music of configuration 1', extending over measures 65–9, is repeated in measures 73–6. As a generic term, all numbered patterns within each layer will be four cells in the upbeat layer, twenty cells in the adjunct layer, and two cells in the refrain layer.

All layers have only one cell present at any one time, with one exception: adjuncts 12 and 1 occur together in measure 80 (symbolized in the figure by the subposition of "1" to "12" in the adjunct layer). As the figure shows, there is sometimes only one cell occurring overall at a given time, sometimes more than one.

Figure 3 gives further information about the cells. Each cell labeled in Figure 2 is listed in the left-hand column of Figure 3; in the right-hand column, each one is cued to the relevant text being rapped (except adjuncts 19 and 20, which occur after the end of the rapping). The cells are listed in their order of occurrence within the song. In the left-hand column are rows indicating the instruments present.[6] The central columns of the figure number beat-classes (BCs) 1 through 4, 1 being the downbeat of each measure and 4 being the pickup.[7] Each beat is divided into four equal-length subparts, marked by the letters x, y, and z. Thus, the first quarter-beat of each measure extends from 1 to 1x, the second quarter-beat from 1x to 1y, the third from 1y to 1z, and the fourth from 1z to 2. And so forth, for each of the four higher-level beats. Thus, in total, sixteen BCs or subdivisions are being counted in each measure. Only one sound in the song is placed between these BCs: the cow-bell in configs 1 and 1' is attacked halfway between BCs 1z and 2.

Filled triangles on Figure 3 indicate attacks by non-pitched percussion. Note names that are not underlined indicate attacks of pitches; when underlined (as during the upbeat 2 cell), they indicate chords of which the notes are the roots. Dotted lines (as in the refrain 1 cell) indicate that the sound preceding them is being sustained. In some places, information about a sound is provided in parentheses after the name of the instrument, in which case the symbol marking its attack may be neither a note-name nor a filled-in triangle. For instance, in config 1, for synth(esizer) 3, the notes D♭, B♭, A♭, F are specified as a chord. The attack of that chord is then indicated on BC 1z by a circled x. The arrows modifying the 's in refrain 1 indicate slight upwards and downwards variations in pitch; a cedilla attached to a note-name (as in upbeat 1) indicates a slight and quick upwards-sweeping grace note. In config 1', the parenthesized 1's and 2's after the rock and bass guitar labels indicate that the following music occurs during each first and second iteration of the cell, respectively. And the As in adjunct 19 are in parentheses to indicate that those notes sound much more softly than the simultaneous Cs.

All of this having been explained, we may turn now to Figures 1 through 3 in order to begin observing how the song stakes out a certain black revolutionary identity for the MC as a persona, and thus for Ice Cube as a public figure. It is perhaps easiest to begin with semantic aspects of the text, using Figure 1 as a guide.

Figure 1:   *The lyrics of Ice Cube's "The Nigga Ya Love to Hate"*

I heard
1   Pay back the muthafuckin' nigga, that's
2   Why I'm sick of gettin' treated like a goddamn
3   Step-child, fuck a punk 'cause I ain't him
4   You gotta deal with a nine-double-m,
5   The damn scum that you all hate, just
6   Think, if niggas decide to retaliate
7   And try to keep you from runnin' up, I never
8   Tell you to get down, it's all about comin' up,
9   So why did you go and ban the AK? The
10 Shit wasn't registered any fuckin' way,
11 So you better duck away, run, and hide out
12 When I'm runnin' real slow and the light's out,
13 'Cause I'm about to fuck up the program,
14 Shootin' out the window of a drop-top Brougham,
15 Well, I'm shootin', let's see who drops, the
16 Police, the media, or suckas that went pop,
17 The muthafuckas that say they too black,
18 Put 'em overseas, they be beggin' to come back,
19 And sayin' peep about gangs and drugs, you
20 Wanna sweep a nigga like me up under the
21 Rug, kickin' shit called Street Knowledge,
22 Why are more niggas in the pen than in college?
23 Because of that line, I might be your
24 Cell-mate, from the nigga you love to hate!

25 [group, shouting:] Fuck you, Ice Cube! [Ice Cube, rapping:] Yeah! Ha, ha!
26 It's the nigga you love to hate!
27 [group, shouting:] Fuck you, Ice Cube! [sample:] Anyway, yo' mutha
28 Warned ya about me. [Ice Cube, rapping:] It's the nigga you love to hate!
29 [sample, black man:] Yo, you ain't doin' nuthin' positive, you ain't – you ain't doin'
30 Nuthin' positive about it! What you got to say for ya-
31 Self? [Ice Cube, rapping, voice heavily processed:] You don't like how I'm living? Muthafuck you!
32 [Ice Cube, rapping, voice as before:] Once again, it's

33 All in the muthafuckin' cycle: 'Ice
34 Cube you bitch killa, cop killa,'
35 Yo! Runnin' through the lies like bruthas, no
36 Pot to piss in, I blew my piston,
37 Now who do you love to hate?

38   'Cause I talk shit and down the eight-ball,
39   'Cause I don't break, you beg and I fall off,
40   You cross color, might as well cut them balls off,
41   You git'cha ass ready for the lynching,
42   Da Mob is droppin' common sense in
43   We'll take and up here we'll shake any
44   Tom, Dick, and Hank, and git'cha ass
45   Thinkin' not about how right and wrong ya live, but how
46   Long ya live, I ain't with the bullshit,
47   I meet mo' bitches, mo' hoes,
48   Don't wanna sleep, so I keep poppin No-Doz,
49   And tellin' young people what they gotta know,
50   'Cause I hate it when niggas gotta lay low and
51   If you're locked up, I gotta get my style in
52   From San Quentin to Riker's Island,
53   We got 'em afraid of the funky shit
54   I like to clown, so pump up the sound in your
55   Jeep, make the ol' ladies say, "Oh my
56   God, hey, it's the nigga you love to hate!"

57   [group, shouting:] Fuck you, Ice Cube! [Ice Cube, rapping:] Yeah, c'mon,
58   Fool! It's the nigga you love to hate!
59   [group, shouting:] Fuck you, Ice Cube! [Ice Cube, rapping:] Yeah, what up,
60   Punk? It's the nigga you love to hate!
61   [Woman, shouting:] Yo, what the fuck you think you are, callin' us bitches?
62   We ain't all that! That's all I hear, "bitch, bitch"!
63   I ain't nobody's bitch! [Ice Cube, rapping:] A bitch is a
64   [group shout:] HOE! [spoken voice:] train [Ice Cube, rapping:] Soul

65   Train done lost they soul, just
66   Call it "Train" 'cause the bitches look like hoes,
67   I see a lot of others, damn!
68   It all hurts, look like a Bandstand,
69   You ask me, do I like Arsenio?
70   About as much as the Bicentennial,
71   I don't give a fuck about dissin' these
72   Fools, 'cause they all scared of the Ice Cube,
73   And what I say, what I betray, and
74   All that, and they ain't even seen a gat,
75   I don't want to see no dancin', I'm
76   Sick of that shit – listen to the hit! 'Cause
77   Y'all ever look and see another brotha on the
78   Video, tryin' to outdance each other?
79   I'm-a tell T-Bone to pass the bottle,
80   And don't give me that shit about "role model"
81   It ain't wise to chastise and preach,
82   Just open the eyes of each, 'cause
83   Laws are made to be broken up, what
84   Niggas need to do is start lookin' up, and
85   Build, mold, and fold themselves into
86   Shape, of the nigga you love to hate!

[two measures of music follow]

The song stages, among other things, Ice Cube's role in political and cultural resistance to the dominant white culture. (Many of his songs, especially from his early career, address this to some extent.) Verses in which Ice Cube raps alternate with refrains, in which Ice Cube confronts verbal attacks and responds to them. The first two verses, lines 1–24 and 33–56, elaborate what Ice Cube regards as politically motivated attempts to silence him, and his success at communicating despite them. The final verse, lines 65–86, criticizes other blacks in the entertainment industry for reinforcing existing power structures. At the end of the final verse, Ice Cube instructs listeners to emulate him, despite (and because of) his failure to conform to traditional images of "role models" that he obviously rejects.

The description he gives of other black performers in the final verse is a good place to begin observing how a black revolutionary identity arises in the song. He first identifies *Soul Train* (the 1960s–70s television show) as having "lost they soul" (ll. 64–5)[8] stating that the "bitches look like hoes" (ll. 65–6). (The misogyny of this statement will be discussed later.) It is compared to *American Band Stand* (a 1950s–70s television show designed primarily for white audiences). Next Arsenio is mentioned negatively, though a reason is not given (except for his being "scared of the Ice Cube") (ll. 69–72). Ice Cube then registers a general objection: "I don't wanna see no dancin', I'm / sick of that shit" (ll. 75–6). Then this objection is visualized: "'Cause / Y'all ever look and see another brotha on the / video, tryin' to outdance each other" (ll. 76–8). Ice Cube juxtaposes himself to this defiantly: "I'm-a tell T-Bone to pass the bottle, / And don't give me that shit about 'role model'" (ll. 79–80).

In this way, a connection is made between dancing and Ice Cube's rejection of some other black performers. In fact, in much of Ice Cube's music, and in some of his interviews, he has made clear that his music is only secondarily for entertainment; he thinks of his role as primarily that of an educator about life in the ghetto.[9] The use of rap music for dancing is, to him, a betrayal of that purpose.[10] He makes this point early in the song, in fact, when he says "I never / tell you to get down, it's all about comin' up" (ll. 7–8).[11] It is no coincidence, then, that one of the targets of his metaphorical drive-by attack is the "suckas that went pop" (l. 16).[12] References to his self-designated role as an educator occur frequently in the song (as in ll. 7–8, 19–22, 38, 42, 45–6, 49–50, 71–3, and 81–8).

Thus, a central dichotomy between Ice Cube and other black performers in the song is that of education versus entertainment, respectively. This is quite well established on the semantic level; our task will now be to trace it on other levels. We will begin with a look at the cells.

Figure 2 – the layering graph – shows that at all times during the song except the last two measures, one can hear either a configuration or a refrain; the exceptions are the upbeats and the last two measures, which will be discussed later. Figure 2 also shows that configuration 1 is present during most of the first fifty-six measures in the song. It is interrupted only by upbeat 1 in measure 20; refrain 1 in measures 25–31; upbeat 2 in measure 32; configuration 2 in measures 33–4; and upbeat 3 in measure 35.

Figure 4 isolates and collates the configurations and refrains from Figure 3, placing them in order of their appearance. These two categories of cells merit particular attention, since they are the longest-lasting cells in the song and thus are implicated in long-range musical processes. Among many parameters that could be used to characterize these cells, we will here concern ourselves with two: textural

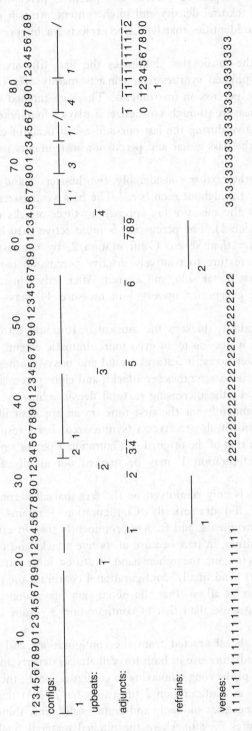

Figure 2: Layering graph of "The Nigga Ya Love to Hate"

density, and amount of pitched (versus non-pitched, percussive) material.[13] By following patterns of textural density and pitch content, we will provide some context for discussing the identities that Ice Cube projects for his persona (and thus, for himself).

Configuration 1, the music that dominates the first fifty-six measures, despite engaging three high-pitched synthesizers, consists mainly of a bass guitar, a bass synthesizer, and three percussion instruments. The high-pitched synthesizers attack only once each per measure (though synthesizer 3 plays a four-note chord). The bass synthesizer is only active during the last one-and-a-half beats of each measure, with three attacks. Thus, the bass guitar and percussion instruments provide most of the activity.

Refrain 1 thickens the texture considerably. Synthesizers 1 and 2 play loudly and are held continuously throughout each bar.[14] The bass synthesizer has eight attacks and plays throughout the measure (as opposed to three attacks at the end of the measure in configuration 1). The percussion is more active than in configuration 1, with ten attacks rather than seven. Configuration 2, by contrast – arriving after refrain 1 – thins the texture to relatively inactive percussion (seven attacks, as in configuration 1), a bass guitar solo, and a siren. After only two measures configuration 1 returns, and, except for upbeat 3 in measure 44, stays until the end of measure 56.

Refrain 2, like refrain 1, thickens the musical texture and introduces prominent pitched elements, but it does so to an even more dramatic extent. Instead of refrain 1's sustained synthesizer notes, it features a loud and busy (synthesized) brass ostinato (thirteen attacks), six bass synthesizer attacks, and eight percussion attacks.

With configuration 1', the increasing textural density climaxes. Not only does a rock guitar enter prominently for the first time (in an apparent illustration of *Soul Train* musical style), but it also receives a (synthesized) brass response, with a bass guitar part busier than that of the original configuration 1 (six or seven attacks, rather than five). Thus, configuration 1' may be marked out aurally as a highpoint of textural density.

Such an impression is only reinforced by the fact that after configuration 1', the texture thins quickly and dramatically. Configuration 3 retains only bass guitar among the pitched instruments, and far less prominently than in earlier cells (in part because of its low tessitura, in part because of its five attacks and only two different pitches). The percussion, on the other hand, features more attacks than in any previous cell (fourteen). And finally, configuration 4 continues the process by having no pitched instruments at all, so that the percussion plays alone. The percussion texture is actually less dense than that of configuration 3 – nine attacks instead of fourteen.

Some patterns may be abstracted from the configurations and refrains just described. There is a steady increase in both (overall attack) density and pitched material from the beginning of the song, climaxing in configuration 1'; the pitched material then drops off sharply at configuration 3 (measures 69–72). At this same time, the density of percussion increases suddenly and dramatically, only thinning slightly into configuration 4 (measures 77–80), where the pitched material finally drops out altogether. When configuration 1 returns at measure 81, the initial state of relatively low pitch and percussive density is restored.

Figure 3: Details of cells

config 1 — "Payback"

	1	x	y	z	2	x	y	z	3	x	y	z	4	x	y	z
synth 1 (cow bell)		C														
synth 2						F♯										
synth 3 (D♭/B♭/A♭/F)		⊗														
bass synth								Ç	B♭		G					
bass guitar	B♭				B♭				A♭		A♭		A♭			
synth whoosh	▲						▲									
snare				▲						▲						
bass drum	▲							▲		▲						

upbeat 1 — "Wanna sweep"

	1	x	y	z	2	x	y	z	3	x	y	z	4	x	y	z
bass synth								Ç	B♭		G					
synth whoosh	▲						▲									
snare				▲						▲						

adjunct 1 — "Cell-mate, from"

	1	x	y	z	2	x	y	z	3	x	y	z	4	x	y	z
high synth								Ç	B♭		C					

refrain 1 — "Fuck you, Ice Cube"

	1	x	y	z	2	x	y	z	3	x	y	z	4	x	y	z
synth 1	D	–	–	–	–	–	–	–	–	–	–	–	–	–	–	–
synth 2 (B,F,C?)	–	–	–	–	–	–	–	–	–	–	–	–	–	–	–	–
bass synth	Ḍ		Ḍ				Ḍ	Ḍ	Ḍ	Ḍ				Ḍ	Ḍ	
cymbals	▲						▲		▲				▲			
snare				▲						▲						
bass drum	▲				▲				▲	▲						

adjunct 2 — "You don't like"

	1	x	y	z	2	x	y	z	3	x	y	z	4	x	y	z
E♭ voice-press	▲	▲	▲	▲	▲		▲		▲		▲					

upbeat 2 — "Once again, it's"

	1	x	y	z	2	x	y	z	3	x	y	z	4	x	y	z
synth (high)	F	–	–	–	–	–	–	–	–	–	–	–	–	–	–	–
guitar – bar chords	B♭		B♭	B♭			D♭			E♭		F				
bass synth	B♭						D♭			E♭		F				
bass guitar	B♭						D♭			E♭		F				
cymbal	▲						▲			E♭	▲					
snare			▲	▲												
tambourine							▲	▲		▲	▲					
bass drum	▲						▲			▲						

config 2 — "all in the mutha-"

	1	x	y	z	2	x	y	z	3	x	y	z	4	x	y	z
siren					–	–	–	–	–							
bass guitar	E♭		E♭	B♭			D♭			D♭	E♭					
cymbal					▲											
snare					▲								▲			
bass drum						▲	▲		▲							

adjunct 3 — "Cube the bitch killa"

	1	x	y	z	2	x	y	z	3	x	y	z	4	x	y	z
electric scratching							▲	▲	▲	▲	▲	▲	▲	▲		

adjunct 4 — "Yo, runnin' through"

	1	x	y	z	2	x	y	z	3	x	y	z	4	x	y	z
bass guitar	E♭															

upbeat 3 — "Tom, Dick, and Hank"

	1	x	y	z	2	x	y	z	3	x	y	z	4	x	y	z
electric cymbal	▲		▲		▲	▲										
electric scratching									▲	▲	▲	▲				
bass guitar									Ç		B♭	G				

```
adjunct 5              1  x  y  z  2  x  y  z  3  x  y  z  4  x  y  z   "Thinkin' not about"
electric cymbal        ▲

adjunct 6              1  x  y  z  2  x  y  z  3  x  y  z  4  x  y  z   "Jeep, make the old"
synth (high)                             C - - -

refrain 2             1  x  y  z  2  x  y  z  3  x  y  z  4  x  y  z   "Fuck you, Ice Cube"
horns + bass guitar   G♭A♭   G♭C♭D♭G♭A♭   G♭C♭D♭G♭A♭   G♭
bass synth            A♭A♭              A♭A♭   A♭   A♭
snare                       ▲                    ▲
high hat              ▲    ▲          ▲    ▲
bass drum             ▲               ▲

adjunct 7             1  x  y  z  2  x  y  z  3  x  y  z  4  x  y  z   "Yo, what the fuck"
electric scratching          ▲
shout "Bitch!"                   !

adjunct 8             1  x  y  z  2  x  y  z  3  x  y  z  4  x  y  z   "We ain't all that!'
electric scratching     ▲    ▲    ▲
shout "Bitch!"                   !

adjunct 9             1  x  y  z  2  x  y  z  3  x  y  z  4  x  y  z   "I ain't nobody's"
stuttered "ah"           a  a     a  a  a  a

upbeat 4             1  x  y  z  2  x  y  z  3  x  y  z  4  x  y  z   "HO! (train)"
synth brass (vc 1)   E♭ - - - - - - - - - - - - - - - - - - - - - - - -
synth brass (vc 2)            A♭ - - - - - - - - - - - - - - - - - -
synth brass (vc 3)                     C - - - - - - - - - - - -
bass synth           A♭                    B♭

config 1'           1  x  y  z  2  x  y  z  3  x  y  z  4  x  y  z   "Train done lost"
rock guitar (1)      E♭   F       E♭   F       E♭   F
rock guitar (1)      C    D♭      C    D♭      C    D♭
rock guitar (2)      E♭   F       E♭   F
rock guitar (2)      C    D♭      C    D♭
synth brass                 B♭   A♭      B♭   A♭
synth (cow bell)          C
bass guitar (1)      B♭   B♭      A♭      C    C B♭ A♭
bass guitar (2)      B♭   B♭      A♭      A♭      A♭
high hat                  ▲               ▲
snare                     ▲               ▲
bass drum            ▲               ▲    ▲

config 3            1  x  y  z  2  x  y  z  3  x  y  z  4  x  y  z   "You ask me, do I"
bass guitar          B♭      B♭ B♭   A♭A♭
cymbal crash         ▲    ▲    ▲       ▲
snare                     ▲               ▲
bass drum            ▲    ▲       ▲ ▲    ▲    ▲ ▲ ▲

config 4            1  x  y  z  2  x  y  z  3  x  y  z  4  x  y  z   "Y'all ever look"
snare                     ▲
```

tom-tom		▲	
bass drum	▲ ▲ ▲▲ ▲ ▲ ▲		

adjunct 10	1 x y z 2 x y z 3 x y z 4 x y z	"Y'all ever look"	
cymbal	▲ ▲ ▲ ▲ ▲		

adjunct 11	1 x y z 2 x y z 3 x y z 4 x y z	"I'm-a tell T-Bone"	
wah-wah guitar	B♭		
	G		
phase-shifted drum	▲		
cymbal	▲ ▲ ▲ ▲ ▲ ▲		

adjunct 12(w/adj11)	1 x y z 2 x y z 3 x y z 4 x y z	"And don't give me"	
wah-wah guitar	B♭ B♭ B♭ B♭ B♭ B♭		
	G G G G G G		
phase-shifted drum	▲		

adjunct 13	1 x y z 2 x y z 3 x y z 4 x y z	"It ain't wise to"	
synth portamento	B♭ F D♭ E♭ D♭E♭ E♭ D♭E♭		
(imitating scratch,			
pitches approximate)			

adjunct 14	1 x y z 2 x y z 3 x y z 4 x y z	"Just open the minds"	
synth portamento	B♭ F D♭E♭ D♭E♭ D♭E♭		
(imitating scratch,			
pitches approximate)			

adjunct 15	1 x y z 2 x y z 3 x y z 4 x y z	" 'Cause laws are made"	
synth (becoming	D♭ E♭ ▲ ▲		
less pitched)			

adjunct 16	1 x y z 2 x y z 3 x y z 4 x y z	"Niggas got to do is"	
synth	▲ ▲ ▲ ▲▲▲▲▲		

adjunct 17	1 x y z 2 x y z 3 x y z 4 x y z	"Build, mold, and fold"	
synth	▲ ▲ ▲▲ ▲▲ ▲ ▲▲		

adjunct 18	1 x y z 2 x y z 3 x y z 4 x y z	"Shape of the nigga"	
synth	▲ - - - - - - - - - - - - ▲ ▲ ▲ ▲		

adjunct 19	1 x y z 2 x y z 3 x y z 4 x y z		
synth	C C		
	(A) (A)		
wah-wah guitar	C A		
cymbal	▲ ▲ ▲ ▲ ▲ ▲ ▲ ▲		

adjunct 20	1 x y z 2 x y z 3 x y z 4 x y z		
synth	▲		
wah-wah guitar	C A		
electric needle	▲		
scratch			
cymbal	▲ ▲ ▲		

Figure 4: Configurations and refrains in the song

```
config 1              1 x y z 2 x y z 3 x y z 4 x y z  "Payback"
synth 1 (cow bell)          C
synth 2                                 F#
synth 3 (D♭/B♭/A♭/F)    ⊗
bass synth                              Ç  B♭  G
bass guitar            B♭   B♭   A♭     A♭   A♭
synth whoosh           ▲         ▲
snare                       ▲         ▲
bass drum              ▲              ▲   ▲
```

```
refrain 1             1 x y z 2 x y z 3 x y z 4 x y z  "Fuck you, Ice Cube"
synth 1                D - - - - - - - - - - - - - - - - - - - - - - - - - -
synth 2 (B,F,C?)       - - - - - - - - - - - - - - - - - - - - - - - - - - -
bass synth             Ḍ  Ḋ        Ḋ Ḋ Ḍ  Ḋ       Ḋ Ḋ
cymbals                ▲         ▲   ▲       ▲
snare                       ▲         ▲
bass drum              ▲    ▲    ▲    ▲
```

```
config 2              1 x y z 2 x y z 3 x y z 4 x y z  "all in the mutha-"
siren                      - - - - - - - - - -
bass guitar            E♭   E♭ B♭  D♭      D♭ E♭
cymbal                      ▲
snare                       ▲
bass drum              ▲         ▲ ▲  ▲
```

```
refrain 2             1 x y z 2 x y z 3 x y z 4 x y z  "Fuck you, Ice Cube"
horns + bass guitar    G♭A♭  G♭C♭D♭G♭A♭  G♭C♭D♭G♭A♭  G♭
bass synth             A♭A♭         A♭A♭  A♭  A♭
snare                       ▲         ▲
high hat               ▲   ▲       ▲   ▲
bass drum              ▲         ▲
```

```
config 1'             1 x y z 2 x y z 3 x y z 4 x y z  "Train done lost"
rock guitar (1)        E♭   F    E♭   F    E♭   F
rock guitar (1)        C    D♭   C    D♭   C    D♭
rock guitar (2)        E♭   F    E♭   F
rock guitar (2)        C    D♭   C    D♭
synth brass                 B♭  A♭     B♭  A♭
synth (cow bell)            C
bass guitar (1)        B♭   B♭   A♭     C   C B♭ A♭
bass guitar (2)        B♭   B♭   A♭     A♭   A♭
high hat                    ▲         ▲
snare                       ▲         ▲
bass drum              ▲              ▲   ▲
```

```
config 3              1 x y z 2 x y z 3 x y z 4 x y z  "You ask me, do I"
bass guitar            B♭   B♭ B♭  A♭ A♭
cymbal crash           ▲   ▲   ▲       ▲
```

```
snare                              ▲                    ▲
bas drum        ▲      ▲       ▲▲       ▲     ▲▲▲
```
```
config 4        1 x y z 2 x y z 3 x y z 4 x y z   "Y'all ever look"
snare                              ▲
tom-tom                                        ▲
bass drum       ▲       ▲       ▲▲      ▲   ▲   ▲
```

Although relatively uncomplicated, the process just discussed leaves something out – configuration 2. Although only two measures long (measures 33–4), that configuration stands out because it does not fit into the process: it is less dense in attacks than configuration 1. Measures 33–4, then, are exceptional; we will shortly have reason to return to this point.

The process itself merits such detailed discussion because of the way it projects previously discussed semantic aspects of the lyrics. The initial density increase coincides with the bravado of the first two verses – detailing attempts to silence Ice Cube and how he overcomes them – and with the confrontations of the first two refrains. The process climaxes (measure 65) just as Ice Cube mentions the first of the black television entertainment media that he dislikes (*Soul Train*). The first quick decrease in density, focusing on percussion (measure 69), coincides with the second disdained black television program – Arsenio Hall's television show (at the time of the song's release among the most visible black presences on television, particularly for hip-hop fans and rap music listeners). And the final focus on percussion (measure 77) coincides with the final negative reference to black television entertainment (a more generalized image of blacks trying to "outdance each other").

Some might wish to ascribe these events to something akin to "word painting": configuration 1'''s rock guitar and brass may "paint" the 1960s and 1970s dance style of *Soul Train*; and the subsequent focus on percussion may "paint" the image of dancing. I have no problem with this interpretation, but it would not account for the specificity of the gestures (e.g., why just percussion for generalized reference to dancing, rather than, say, funk guitar?). Nor would it address larger developments in the song of which these late events form a part.

A return to the semantic register of the lyrics will help specify further. The dance aspect of music there is presented negatively, as are the people who sponsor their televised images. Thus, the isolation of a percussive dance beat is not a neutral illustration; rather, it is an ironic quotation. In this sense, the textural climax and the gradual isolation of percussion become an occasion for a two-sided projection of black musical identity. On the one hand, the musical elements gradually acquire rhythmic force and the percussion becomes prominent in the manner generally characteristic of break beats; this would normally be the occasion for an appreciation of the rhythmic drive that often helps propel rap music. But, on the other hand, this appreciation, and a common response – dance – are being stigmatized as contrary to the song's purpose. A pleasure is created at the same time as it is stigmatized.

This pleasure in rhythm is far from socially neutral in a society for which both pleasure and rhythm have historically been loaded with racialized discourses. The simple basic rhythms and complex counter-rhythms of rap music are closely related to (and often make explicit reference to) similar traits in other Afro-diasporic musics.[15] As such, the foregrounding of rhythm may invoke and reinforce old racist stereotypes about African-Americans. Thus, what is being stigmatized is not just a certain musical practice, but a whole complex of social representations of African-Americans, produced (for example, on television) for society as a whole.

The result of all this is what Gates (1988) would call a "motivated Signifyin'": an element of cultural production is quoted and troped for the purpose of critique. The consciousness that Ice Cube shows here about popular images of black people and black music would seem to indicate clear gestures toward establishing a counter-identity, for a certain aspect of hip-hop culture generally and for Ice Cube in particular.

Simultaneous with the intensification and isolation of rhythm, there is a more subtle process, but one that intersects some prominent gestures in the song. That process engages alternations and conflicts between duple and triple rhythms throughout the song. Figure 4 once again illustrates. Configuration 1 contains a combination of triple and duple rhythmic intervals. The percussion is steadily duple, with attacks always on the beat or on the "y" of some beat (with the exception of the final bass drum attack). The bass guitar, however, begins the measure with triplet intervals and then turns to duple intervals: its attacks occur at 1, 1z, 2y (thus so far in triplets), 3y, and 4y (these last two producing duple whole beats).[16] In this way, the bass guitar marks the first half of the measure in triplets and the second half in duplets.

The rhythmic dichotomy continues throughout the song in different contexts, sometimes between cells and sometimes within them. However, the conflict in rhythmic values builds slowly. Most of the cells in measures 1–65 have very few triplet rhythms and a great number of duple rhythms. There is one notable exception: in upbeat 3 (measure 45) an electric cymbal plays a triplet (attacks on 1, 1z, and 2y). Two factors underline this triplet: first, the cymbal is simultaneous with each of the rapped names in the line "Tom, Dick, and Hank"; second, it is the only instrumental sound at that point in the song. After this initial figure, the rest of the measure returns to a duple rhythm. We will return to this moment shortly.

The departure of configuration 1 at measure 57 discontinues the duple/triple rhythmic conflict temporarily. But the entry of configuration 1' in measure 65 re-introduces it, bringing the same superimposition of duple and triple values that had characterized configuration 1. The rock guitar, synthesized brass, and percussion all project duple rhythmic values; but the bass guitar again projects the initial triplets followed by the duplets that characterized configuration 1. (The bass guitar here also combines the bass guitar and bass synthesizer parts from configuration 1.)

After configuration 1', there are no significant triplets until adjunct 12; there, the wah-wah guitar attacks on 1, 1z, and 2y, after that reverting (like configurations 1 and 1') to duple rhythm. This instance is significant for two reasons. First, it is the first case of triplets in an adjunct; adjuncts, until this point, had reinforced duple rhythm. And second, it is the first of seven adjuncts which will now accompany every line remaining in the song; until this point, adjuncts had been distributed far more sparsely (as reference back to Figure 2 will show). Thus, these triplets commence a major mutation in the texture of the music and its rate of change.

The mutation has permanent effects: after adjunct 12, these triplets become common. They appear in adjunct 13's (measure 81) synthesizer part between BCs 1, 1z, and 2y; in adjunct 14's synthesizer part (perhaps trivially) between BCs 1 and 1z; in adjunct 15's synthesizer part between BCs 1, 1z, and 2y; in adjunct 16's synthesizer part between BCs 1, 1z, 2y, and 3x (thus extending one triplet farther than earlier cells); in adjunct 17's synthesizer part between BCs 1 and 1z and then 2y and 3x (with a duple value in between); in adjunct 19's wah–wah guitar and synthesizer parts between BCs 1 and 1z, and 3y and 4x, respectively (thus engaging those last two BCs for the first time as triplets); and in adjunct 20's wah–wah guitar part between BCs 1 and 1z. Thus, every adjunct after the twelfth engages triplets, except adjunct 18 (which, in fact, is very squarely duple).

It is important, also, that this concentration of triplets overlaps the end of configuration 4 and the final return of configuration 1. In that sense, it provides a link from one to the other. (This is especially notable, given the otherwise strong division between measures 80 and 81 by rhythm, rhyme scheme, configuration change, and break in syntax.) What, then, can be said about this linkage, given the concentration of rhythm already observed, and the associated semantics aspects of the lyrics?

Adjunct 17 (measure 85) may be a good place to begin an answer, because it stands out in a way analogous to upbeat 3. It will be recalled that upbeat 3 (measure 44) was a place where one instrument (an electric cymbal) played alone, where that instrument played a triplet, and where that triplet coincided with the rhythm of Ice Cube's rapping ("*Tom, Dick,* and *Hank*"). The relevant instrument in adjunct 17 is not isolated in the same way, since it sounds along with configuration 1. But the latter is a stable element, while the synthesizer is constantly changing; and the synthesizer is foregrounded in the mix. Adjunct 17's synthesizer, then, is foregrounded in a similar way to upbeat 3's electric cymbal. More important, it performs an analogous function: for here is the only other place where an instrumental part coincides with the rap's rhythm during four consecutive attacks. Specifically, the synthesizer's attacks on 1, 1z, 2x, and 2y coincide with the attacks of the words, "Build, mold, and fold."

Another relationship between upbeat 3 and adjunct 17 highlights their similarity. In measure 44, the syllables "Tom, Dick, and Hank" fall on BCs 1, 1z, 2x, and 2y, respectively; and upbeat 3's electric cymbal attacks on BCs 1, 1z, and 2y. One result is that the electric cymbal ends up reinforcing the proper nouns "Tom" "Dick" and "Hank" while leaving "and" unaccompanied; another result is that the electric cymbal, unlike the voice, ends up projecting two consecutive triplets. In measure 85, the words "Build, mold, and fold," like "Tom, Dick, and Hank," fall on BCs 1, 1z, 2x, and 2y, respectively. But adjunct 17's synthesizer attacks not only on BCs 1, 1z, and 2y, as had upbeat 3's electric cymbal; it also attacks on BC 2x.

So where upbeat 3 had failed to reinforce the word "and," adjunct 17 in fact does so. On the other hand, this extra attack interrupts the two consecutive triplets that had made upbeat 3 so distinctive. More informally, we might say that adjunct 17 supports the rapped words more fully, while upbeat 3 supports the rhythmic figure of a triplet more fully.

Semantically, adjunct 17 marks an important moment in the song. Its importance comes not only from setting the beginning of the final couplet; rather, the last six lines of the song are the most explicitly didactic: "It ain't wise to chastise and preach, / Just open the eyes of each, 'cause / Laws are made to be broken up, what / Niggas need to do is start lookin' up, and / Build, mold, and fold themselves into / Shape, of the nigga ya love to hate!" Not only does Ice Cube's political advocacy become most explicit here; the passage also recontextualizes the line "the nigga ya love to hate." Since that line is the refrain ending each section (and the title of the song), the recontextualization is dramatic. Although in earlier instances, the "nigga ya love to hate" is used sardonically – reflecting on those who think that way, rather than the "nigga" himself – the final couplet constitutes the only time that the phrase actually describes a desirable goal. Thus, when adjunct 17 presents the verbs "build, mold, and fold," it begins the transformation of one of the song's principal images: the "nigga ya love to hate" becomes an explicitly positive value.

Upbeat 3, on the other hand, supports different semantic value. "Tom, Dick, and Hank," in Ice Cube's music, refers metonymically to "white" people in general (appearing elsewhere on the album, as well). Since Eurocentric culture is painted in this song as an Other against which Ice Cube defines himself, "Tom, Dick, and Hank" is framed as a negative value.[17]

How, then, can we resolve the conflict between, on the one hand, the triplet figure's unfavorable semantic value in upbeat 3, and on the other hand, its favorable semantic value in adjunct 17? Perhaps it is an issue not so much of resolution as of mutation: the figure changes its value as the song progresses. This possibility allows us to reintroduce the general plethora of triplets already noted from measure 80 to the end of the song. It was noted above that from adjunct 12 (measure 80) to the end of the song, triplets appear in great numbers. This stretch of music coincides with the turn to didacticism (lines 80–6); the metaphors and exemplars of conflict and resistance that characterized most of the song fall away to explicit prescriptions for social change. The semantic transition would seem to indicate that Ice Cube involves triplets in his projection of a black revolutionary identity.

But this interpretation leaves two important loose ends. One is the projection of "Tom, Dick, and Hank" just discussed. The other is adjunct 18. That cell is a curious case, since it is the only one after adjunct 12 that does not present a triple rhythm. The anomaly is highlighted by the fact that adjunct 18 sets the final rapped lines of the song (line 86: "Shape, of the nigga ya love to hate").

We end up, then, with two symmetrical problems. On the one hand, one instance of triplets (an instance prominent for its isolation in an otherwise duple context) projects a "white" Other. On the other hand, one instance of exclusively duple meter (analogously prominent for its isolation in an otherwise triplet-heavy context) projects the black revolutionary figure being advocated. What these two instances have in common, however, is that each projects *a contested identity*.[18] In one case, the contest involves resistance to "Tom, Dick, and Hank"; in other words, Ice Cube uses this image to establish one term ("white" Eurocentric) of a binary value from which to differentiate himself – a solidly alien target of struggle. In the other case, "the nigga ya love to hate" emerges victoriously in the final rapped line: in the course of the song, Ice Cube has changed that phrase from a derogatory reference to a model of black resistance. In the latter context, it is significant that Ice Cube speaks of "build[ing], mold[ing], and fold[ing]" oneself into shape; the conscious effort to create an identity is explicit, as is its ongoing and dynamic nature.

Rhythmic variance from a local uniformity, then, appears to support a contest of identity. On this hearing, the saturation of triple rhythms in the final measures provides a context in which "the nigga ya love to hate" can itself emerge with an energetic resistance to the local rhythmic formations. It is perhaps not surprising that the final rapped line should be set apart in this way; for at the end of the song, the path for black resistance is made more explicit and the final (and summary) statement is made. This final statement invokes the same refrain that ends each verse (and which provides the title of the song). And it is precisely that phrase – "the nigga ya love to hate" – which is not only reiterated but also *recontextualized* in the course of the song. It begins, in the first verse, as an object of fear and animosity; in the second verse, the phrase is presented somewhat comically, as an utterance of the "ol' ladies," with Ice Cube encouraging his listeners to solicit the response; and in the third and final verse, the "nigga ya love to hate" is something to emulate as a strategy of political resistance.

If both "Tom, Dick, and Hank" and "the nigga ya love to hate" are projected by the strategy of local rhythmic anomaly, in another respect they are mirror images of each other. The former is a highly foregrounded triple rhythm in a duple context, while the latter is an isolated moment of duple rhythm. Thus, although the two are united in being contested identities, they are also opposed to each other in a binary configuration (as one might expect).

Once we have opened up this field of struggle and identity, many other aspects of the song can be seen in a similar light. We have already seen how Ice Cube identifies his particular strategy of political resistance late in the song with a decrease in pitched material and an increase in unpitched percussion. The identification was secured in the semantic field by his derogating "getting down" and images of blacks dancing on television. In the present context, it is crucial to notice that the negated images here are not "white," Eurocentric figures, but rather representations of other blacks. Thus, one of the broader musical and semantic processes in the song involves not the binary black/white, but rather a binary between a black identity that Ice Cube wishes to claim, and a different black identity that he wishes to reject. Importantly, this differentiation becomes most insistent and explicit, both semantically and musically, in the final verse (especially ll. 65–80), as Ice Cube prepares his closing prescription for black political action (ll. 81–6). And one of the technical aspects of this process – the gradual de-pitching of the synthesizer over adjuncts 13–20 – dovetails with the duple/triple rhythmic process in an interesting way: for it is precisely the now de-pitched synthesizer that in adjunct 17 supports the rhythm of "build, mold, and fold." Thus, although discussed separately, those two long-term productions of black identity intersect not only in the semantic field of the song, but also at a crucial moment in the musical development.

All this having been said, there is an issue that was mentioned earlier and whose discussion was promised: within the pattern of increasing, then decreasing, attack density that runs through the song, configuration 2 was noted as an anomaly. Although short-lived – lasting only two measures – it remains prominent, not only because it interrupts the broader pattern, but also because it marks the beginning of the second verse. Configuration 2 is also notable for supporting musically the most explicit reference so far to representation: "[Once again, it's/] All in the mutha-fuckin' cycle: Ice / Cube the bitch killa, cop killa." Although this "cycle" is not mentioned elsewhere in the song, it is clear what the cycle is perpetuating: a cultural image of Ice Cube as brutalizer and murderer of police and women (which is, of course, more broadly an image many have of rap musicians). Thus, this exceptional moment in the song highlights in its own way the issue of representation. This is especially so, since configuration 1 takes over from configuration 2 at just the point where discussion of representation (at least temporarily) ends, namely line 35.

Configuration 2 thus occupies an ironic position in the song. On the one hand, it interrupts a musical process involving representation – the gradual build in texture that culminates in configuration 1' and Ice Cube's assertion of a particular black identity; on the other hand, it introduces its own representation. The difference is, of course, that the image projected during configuration 2 is strictly one that Ice Cube is opposing, while configuration 1′ (and the other cells it surrounds) supports both opposed and favored representations. One could find a certain sense, then, in configuration 2's interrupting a larger process of constructing a positive representation; in itself, it projects a negative representation, a moment of slippage in a goal-oriented musical process.

But even that may be an oversimplification; because although configuration 2 is being painted here as exceptional, there is a sense in which its disruptive effects reach into other parts of the song. For contained within the lines it projects (ll. 33–4) are the ultimate objects of resistance in the song – not so much "white," Eurocentric culture per se, but rather the representations of black culture which the "nigga ya love to hate" both reinforces and challenges.

Further, there are senses in which cycles become more prominent at the same time that, ironically, Ice Cube's black revolutionary identity is being most strongly established (i.e., toward the end of the song). The first sense involves the length of the configurations; this can best be seen by reference back to Figure 2. In the first verse (ll. 1–24), there is no change in configuration (and furthermore, there are no adjuncts); there is no sense of transformation, much less cycle. In the second verse (measures 33–56), there is an odd proportion between the two configurations, 2 and 1; the former lasts two lines, while the latter lasts twenty-one lines (ll. 35–57, with upbeat 3 interrupting for one measure). Thus, although there is a change in the basic supporting music, there is no repeating proportional pattern. In the third verse, however, there is a pattern of 4:4:4:4:8 lines for configurations 1′, 3, 1′, 4, and 1, respectively.[19] In this sense, a cycle of four-line changes participates in Ice Cube's construction of a black revolutionary counter-identity (which is, after all, the project of the final verse). It may be heard as a counter-cycle: the explicitly mentioned "muthafuckin' cycle" of verse 2 (l. 33) is challenged and overturned by the musical cycle that ends the song.

The second sense in which cycles recur involves the use of adjuncts, also in the final verse. Again, reference back to Figure 2 will illustrate this. In the first three verses, adjuncts are scattered at irregular intervals: the first one occurs in line 24; the second one at line 31; the third and fourth ones at lines 34 and 35, respectively; the fifth one at line 45; the sixth one at line 55; and the seventh, eighth, and ninth ones at lines 61, 62, and 63, respectively. (These last three mentioned adjuncts will be discussed shortly.) In the third verse, however, the adjuncts take on an aspect of regularity. After an initial isolated adjunct 10 in line 77, the other adjuncts arrive, starting in line 79, at a rate of one per line. The pattern continues even beyond the rapped portion of the song, into the short instrumental postlude.

The third and final cycle engages a process discussed earlier. It will be recalled that in lines 7–8 and 75–80 Ice Cube stigmatizes the pleasures of rhythm and dancing. Adjuncts 14 through 18, however, gradually transform a constantly-present synthesizer from pitched to unpitched material. Thus, the concentration of rhythm makes a return, just after having been explicitly posed in opposition to Ice Cube's black revolutionary identity. The result is a more abstract "cycle" than the other two, but in a sense, a more important one. That "cycle" engages a process crucial to the song – the appropriation and transformation of a cultural seme. The focus on percussion in configuration 4 is marked as a negative value by the rapped text (ll. 75–81); but its return in the synthesizer then supports the final prescriptive statement of the song (ll. 81–6). Rather than simply being the return of a repressed value, the distillation of music into rhythmic activity involves a claim and a reinterpretation of a culturally loaded musical parameter.

Once this transformation is recognized, other aspects of the song can be seen in a similar light. The prominent descending minor thirds in the guitar during adjuncts 19 and 20, for example, are played with the same wah-wah timbre as the funk guitar in configuration 1′. But we could hardly accord them the same social value, after the activities of appropriation that separate them; the reclaiming of black music for Ice Cube's political purposes, starting with the explicit rejection of *Soul Train*, asserts that the wah-wah guitar cannot survive untouched in anything except an acoustic sense. (It is also worth noting, given the earlier discussion, that the notes here are triplets, unlike the wah-wah guitar notes in configuration 1′.)

The acts of adoption and revision just discussed lend perspective to the violent imagery of the song. The drive-by shootings of the "Police, the media, or suckas that went pop" (1. 16) are in fact revisions of their own constructions of black identity; the song itself accomplishes this. Likewise, Ice Cube advises the listener to "git'cha ass ready for the lynching" because "Da Mob [i.e., Da Lench Mob, Ice Cube's 'crew'] is droppin' common sense in" (ll. 41–2); if it had not already been clear from these lines alone that the lynching is metaphorical and involves education, then it should be abundantly clear by the end of the song.

The appropriations and revisions already discussed create a black revolutionary identity with no explicit gender. Still, some aspects of the imagery seem to implicate a male identity. And at one point, the song does integrate a gendered perspective to its identity, via a confrontation in one of its refrains.[20] Further, the confrontation is disturbing for its apparent misogyny. In lines 61–4, Ice Cube stages an encounter with a female critic.

She upbraids him for his referring to women as "bitches" (as indeed he does in quite a few songs), to which Ice Cube offers his response in line 63 with "A bitch is a..." Line 64 then brings a group shout (that is, with Ice Cube and some unidentified members of Da Lench Mob): "HOE!"[21] At that point, the response ("A bitch is a hoe!") seems redundant and therefore non-responsive. The failure to respond, in context, is abusive; the interrogating woman is treated as unworthy of substantive response, and one slur is reinforced by another.

But in the subsequent continuation, Ice Cube recontextualizes the event. This begins at the end of line 64, when, as the shout "HOE!" is still sustained, Ice Cube's voice is superimposed on BC 4, uttering only the syllable "train." That syllable is both rhythmically isolated from any other rapped material and less prominent in the mix; it therefore takes on the character of an aside, or a superimposition. Nevertheless, it provides an essential pivot to the next verse. The response to the interrogating woman is now, "A bitch is a HOE train." The utterance loses its ambiguity (even incomprehensibility) in the following verse, when Ice Cube says (ll. 65–6) "Soul Train done lost they soul, just / Call it 'Train,' 'cause the bitches look like hoes." It is this couplet that links the term "bitch" with the broader process of creating a black revolutionary identity. More specifically, the "bitches" ' looking like "hoes" is a feature of *Soul Train* that indicates that the latter has "lost its soul"; being a "hoe," then, as the verse goes on to make clear, involves succumbing to the "selling out" of black identity which *Soul Train* (or images of dancing blacks in general) represents for Ice Cube.

Is Ice Cube saying, then, that his use of the word "bitch" in his music refers exclusively to black women who have betrayed his notion of black identity, i.e., to "hoes"? Is his use of "bitch," then, less simply misogynist then one might otherwise assume? Unfortunately, such a conclusion would be overly hasty, and Ice Cube's use of the word "bitch" cannot be so easily rehabilitated. For one thing, a general survey of his music makes this interpretation difficult to sustain.[22] Also, his invocation of a word ("bitch") often used as a slur on women in general and inextricably tied into a history of misogyny cannot be considered entirely innocent. Then, too, if the "bitches look[ing] like hoes" is evidence that "Soul Train / Done lost they soul," then how could the term "bitch" be *equivalent* to the word "hoe"?

Perhaps here we have to recognize an ambivalence in the song toward its own misogyny. On the one hand, Ice Cube does create a female interrogator, and he does attempt to limit the term "bitch" only to certain kinds of women, based on their behavior (i.e., on their complicity with a black identity he wishes to reject). On the other hand, his own discourse, in this song and elsewhere, seems to reinscribe the misogyny.[23] If the project of "The Nigga Ya Love to Hate," as I have argued, is to create a black revolutionary identity, then that project must still be considered incomplete if it excludes or marginalizes half (or more) of the black population.

Two more items should be mentioned, here. First, the discussion here has focused largely on the "musical backdrop" for Ice Cube's rapping, as well as the interaction of that backdrop with semantic and social aspects of the words. Thus, the material aspects of his MCing – especially the rhythms, Ice Cube's "flow," placements within the overall mix – have been slighted at the expense of concentrating on other aspects of representation.[24] Second, the guitar triplets that appear in adjuncts 19 and 20 could hardly be ignored after the extended attention we have paid to the role of triple rhythms in the song. They appear after the end of the rapped section; they (along with the echo of the first one in adjunct 19) constitute the final rhythmically articulated events in the song (before the synthesizer fadeout); and they invoke not only the triple-rhythmic processes of the song, but also the particular and significant timbre of the wah-wah guitar. Since the wah-wah sound had previously been linked to the denigrated images of dancing blacks, its final and prominent appearance here is troubling. Does the synthesizer scratch that interrupts it and ends the song argue for a rap musical process (the scratch) as the elimination of an earlier (and problematized) musical style? Or is the wah-wah sound itself now transformed, after it has been embodied in the process of creating an alternative identity? In other words: is this yet another instance, like that of the triplets themselves, in which Ice Cube has appropriated and revised a musical/social meaning? It is tempting to hear this moment as a triumphant *Aufhebung*; but at the same time, we are constrained to recognize that, like the issue of misogyny, the revision of "blackness" in this song may be an open and unfinished process. There seems to me little doubt that this late musical event cannot remain unaffected by what has gone on before it; but at the same time, the return of the repressed – the images that Ice Cube is out to conquer – cannot simply be overcome by mastery, and Ice Cube's project here remains part of a much larger and more ambiguous social discourse.

It is to be hoped, however, that the foregoing has at least shown that "close reading" of musical processes may hold some promise for those of us who are interested in how rap may help to constitute imagined communities. Since the song examined here is formed within a very particular style and social-historical moment, among the many styles and moments of rap music and hip-hop culture, the above analysis could perhaps be taken metonymically, rather than as exemplifying a possible "central" practice of rap analysis. It could be taken to indicate that attention to "the music itself," rather than reinscribing the ideology of the art-work, may open itself onto larger, "extra-musical" social realities.

Notes

1 All further references to Clifford in this discussion refer to Clifford (1988) and will specify only the page number. At the same time, this analysis is not consistent with many of the critiques that Clifford poses for the issue of ethnographic authority (especially pp. 21–54). Instead, I would emphasize Clifford's recognition that "a purely dialogical authority [which he tends to favor] would repress the inescapable fact of textualization" (p. 43). Still, I would not pretend that this aspect of my analysis is consistent with Clifford's work. It is probably closer in spirit to Spivak (1988), in the sense that it considers the problem of subaltern self-representation.

2 This particular observation will be crucial, when it turns out that Ice Cube's fashioning of a black revolutionary identity is contingent on representations by the hegemonic culture he rejects.

3 Thus, an imperfection of the present discussion is my use of the phrase "Ice Cube" to describe a persona jointly formed by the efforts of Ice Cube and The Bomb Squad. While it could be argued that Ice Cube's oversight of the projects alone justifies discussing him as an active agent of the song, I would prefer to leave it that the phrase "Ice Cube" here is simply a relatively less awkward way to refer to what is, in reality, a collective agency (all of which is beside the greater question of music-industrial mediation).

4 "Five percent nation" refers to the idea, widespread in the Nation of Islam, that at any given time, only 5 percent of people in any population are politically aware enough to be influential. That 5 percent presumably determines the destiny of the other 95 percent of the population. It should not be confused with the Five Percent Nation religion, which takes its name from such an idea but has developed separately.

5 The use of layering graphs, rather than staff notation, is preferable here for several reasons. First, in textures such as those examined here, it can become difficult to project the separate activity of more than three or four sound sources at once, without an unwieldy number of staves; and the activity of separated layers will turn out to be crucial. Second, layering graphs allow easier and quicker reference to the exact metrical position of each event than traditional staff notation. Third, layering graphs arguably allow simpler projection of musical events and easier visual accessibility, without sacrificing information. Fourth, most of the events discussed here are either non-pitched (by traditional Western calibrations of pitch) or ambiguously pitched; thus, placement on staff lines designed primarily to represent pitch would be superfluous and potentially distracting, if not misleading. And finally, layering graphs do not rely to any substantial extent on musical "literacy"; thus, they remain accessible to some scholars who may otherwise be excluded from my discussion.

6 For the entirety of this chapter, all musical data, like the lyrics, is gathered according to my hearing of the song. Thus, I must accept responsibility for any misinterpretations.

7 Unlike in earlier chapters, I do not assign a BC 0. This is because the focus here will not be on modular rhythm. I have elected to use numbers that accord more closely with how musicians count the beats.

8 Henceforth, "l." or "ll." in parentheses followed by a number or numbers will refer to line numbers from Figure 1.

9 Ice Cube is explicit about this in hooks (1994) (pp. 129–30, 133–4). Ice Cube's claim of educational value is related both to the notion of "nation-conscious hip-hop" (i.e., rap music that helps to define a black political identity), and to the hip-hop cultural concept of "representin'." The latter is a complex term involving many strands of meaning, among which is the idea that

rap should clearly project its geographic and social contexts, if it is to remain "genuine." Krims explores some of the implications of the term.

10 In a duet that Ice Cube does with Scarface on the latter's album *The Diary* (1994), Scarface refers to rap as "our only way of communicatin' with our people."

11 Here, "get down" is used in the 1970s slang sense of enjoying the music in a visceral way – dancing, feeling the beat, and so on. "Comin' up" means growing up. Thus, Ice Cube is saying that he encourages his listeners to treat the music not as an occasion for dance, but rather as an occasion for learning.

12 That this image is metaphorical is obvious from the prospective targets: "the / police, the media, or suckas that went pop" (ll. 15–16). One could argue that the police may be the target of a literal drive-by shooting (despite the fact that in reality, it is other gangs that are normally targeted); but the addition of "the media" (a large, amorphous mass of individuals) and "suckas that went pop" (also a large number of people unlikely to be standing together somewhere) makes clear that it is not a literal drive-by that is being fantasized. Rather, Ice Cube's rapping and social instruction is the instrument of attack. The confusion of violent metaphors with the advocacy of literal violence is, in my view, one of the sources for much popular criticism of hard-core rap music, especially among those who are not familiar with it.

13 The isolation of these parameters should not, of course, be taken to imply that they are the only relevant ones. They are chosen here to illustrate our purposes, rather than to give a comprehensive analysis.

14 The synthesizers in each cell are numbered for reference only within that cell; so, for example, a "synth 1" in one cell may or may not be the same instrument as a "synth 1" in another cell.

15 Rose (1994) makes this point, pp. 64–74.

16 This is a fairly common rhythmic pattern for the bass in funk and dance styles. Walser (1995, p. 202) identifies it in a loop from a Public Enemy song, remarking that the pattern occurs often in African and Afro-diasporic musics.

17 It is possible to hear, in the "Dick," a suggestion of Dick Clark, host of *American Bandstand*. My thanks to David Lewin for pointing this out to me.

18 There is a vast literature dealing with ethnic identity as an object of public contest. The writings of Bakhtin are certainly seminal in this regard; Gardiner (1992) gives an excellent overview of Bakhtin's contributions to this issue. Said (1978) and Spivak (1987) demonstrate other approaches, specifically concerning marginalized ethnicities (and gender). Clifford (1988, pp. 177–246) provides an example of contested cultural identity in an unusual context.

19 The pattern is not perfect, however: this count includes the half-measure interruption of silence (1. 76) as part of the second configuration 1′. Interestingly, this gap itself supports the words "Listen to the hit!," thus engaging the construction of a revolutionary black identity, as discussed earlier.

20 Although this discussion has not focused on the refrains and their representations of conflict, they nevertheless hold a great deal of potential interest here, because they present the images Ice Cube is contesting not virtually (as in most of the song), but explicitly.

21 "Hoe" is a word from hip-hop slang. Although it stems from a pronunciation of "whore," it is often used as a derogatory term for all women, or large groups of women. In that sense, it is in some ways analogous to "bitch."

22 For example, "Don't Trust Em" (from Ice Cube 1992) projects an extremely unflattering and disturbing attitude toward women. On the other hand, Ice Cube has at times allowed for dialogue with black women, as in "It's a Man's World" (from Ice Cube 1990), a duet with Yo-Yo, a female MC whose career Ice Cube has been instrumental in promoting. Rose (1994, pp. 146–82) discusses dialogics between female and male rappers.

23 bell hooks's (1994) interview with Ice Cube underlines his ambiguous and often surprising attitudes toward his own apparent misogyny (pp. 125–43).

24 For example, the relationship of the rapped rhythm to the music seems to become increasingly skewed and complex as the song progresses. This, of course, could be linked, in an even more extended discussion, to the increasingly explicit resistance that Ice Cube musters to representations of black life. Walser (1995) observes a similar process in a song by Public Enemy.

References

Berland, Jody. 1998. "Locating, Listening: Technological Space, Popular Music, and Canadian Mediations." In Andrew Leyshon, David Matless, and George Revill, eds., *The Place of Music*. New York: Guilford, pp. 129–250.

Clifford, James. 1988. *The Predicament of Culture: Twentieth-century Ethnography, Literature, and Art*. Cambridge, Mass.: Harvard University Press.

Gardiner, Michael. 1992. *The Dialogics of Critique: M. M. Bakhtin and the Theory of Ideology*. London: Routledge.

Gates, Henry Louis Jr. 1988. *The Signifying Monkey: A Theory of African American Literary Criticism*. New York: Oxford University Press.

hooks, bell. 1994. *Outlaw Culture: Resisting Representations*. New York: Routledge.

Rose, Tricia. 1994. *Black Noise: Rap Music and Black Culture in Contemporary America*. Hanover, NH: University Press of New England.

Said, Edward. 1978. *Orientalism*. New York: Pantheon Books.

Spivak, Gayatri Chakravorty. 1987. *In Other Worlds: Essays in Cultural Politics*. New York: Methuen.

Stokes, Martin, ed. 1994. *Ethnicity, Identity, and Music: The Musical Construction of Place*. Oxford: Berg.

Walser, Robert. 1995. "Rhythm, Rhyme and Rhetoric in the Music of Public Enemy." *Ethnomusicology* 39, 193–218.

Index